Don't let anyone look down on you because you are young, but set an example for the believers in speech, in life, in love, in faith and in purity.

—1 Timothy 4:12

presented to

by

on

Thursday

Too Young?

Read 2 Chronicles 24:1 (page 518)

Some people think you have to be an adult in order to serve Jesus Christ. But I think being young opens up all kinds of doors for me to share my faith with other people. For example, most people make decisions about religion when they're young. And most of the people at my school would rather talk about faith with someone their own age. That means teenagers like me have a big responsibility to share our faith. This verse says that Joash was only 7 years old when he became king! It also tells us that he did what was right in God's sight.

It's easy to get discouraged and intimidated when we don't have all the answers. But we can be like Joash and stand up for God when we're young. God used this young king, not an adult, to show Israel how to live right. The world may not think we're qualified, but God does. He can, and will, use anyone who wants to serve him.

Ryan, age 14

What about You?

❶ When was the last time you got discouraged because of your age? What did you do about it?

❷ Brainstorm some ways you can serve God at your school or in your neighborhood. What are 2 things you can do that your parents or other adults can't? (go to youth group, skateboard, go on school class trips)

❸ Ask God to show you creative ways to serve him, no matter what your age.

Weekend

Which Way?

Read James 1:2–5 (page 1505)

Have you ever been lost? Maybe you got on the wrong trail on a youth group hike or maybe you just lost your mom in the store when you were little. You were stuck. You had no idea where to go.

Sometimes we face situations like that in other areas of life. Maybe you're trying to decide which parent to live with this year. Or you might be thinking about changing classes because you don't get along with your teacher. Or maybe a friend is begging you to do something you don't really want to do. Whatever the decision, you don't know which direction to go. And you're afraid that you might choose the wrong direction, so you don't choose anything at all.

On Tuesday, Noah reminded us in his devotion that God works things out for the best. Later in the week, Chris and Anna talked about trusting God to take care of us. Today James (in the Bible) tells us to do several things, including asking God to give us wisdom. He doesn't say that God will tell us *exactly* what to do; instead he says that God gives us the *wisdom* to decide.

When we face tough decisions about which direction to go, it's not always obvious to us which road to take. But we still have to make a decision, and trust that God will be with us whatever we decide. Guess what? That's exactly what God does! So if you're facing a decision with no obvious answer, don't choose the option of no decision at all. Ask God for wisdom, then make a choice and trust God for the best!

What about You?

❶ What decision are you struggling with right now?

❷ Write down the choices you have. List the good and bad points about each, then write a date by which you have to make a decision. Do what you can to make your decision by this date!

❸ Spend a few moments in prayer asking God for wisdom to help you make a good decision. Then thank him in advance for taking care of you regardless of your choice.

Contents

What's Up With This Bible?

What's in it, how to use it.

How do I know what's right and what's not? Should I hang out with those friends? Why do I need to go to church? What about sex?

Have you ever wondered about this kind of stuff? This Bible will help you figure out the answers. The *NIV Teen Devotional Bible* will teach you about God and how he wants you to live. This Bible is packed with fun stuff. Check out these features:

Fri**day**

Safe With God

Read Matthew 10:29–37

When I was about 6 or 7, I'd get really concerned about the wild animals near my house, especially during bad storms. It seemed like they had no one to take care of them. But this verse about the sparrows always helped me feel better, because it reminded me that God cares for them—and he cares for me even more.

God, the greatest Being in the universe, pays attention to little creatures like sparrows and 7-year-old girls. So no matter how stormy it gets outside or in my own life, I can take comfort in knowing God cares. Nothing is too big or scary for him.

Christina age 13

❶ Think of something that's very important to you. How do you take care of it? What are some similar ways God takes care of you?

❷ Walk around your house and notice all the things that keep you safe: locks on the doors, storm windows, maybe even a security system. How is God's protection even better than all of these things?

❸ Thank God for caring about you and protecting you.

Turn to page 1156 for your next devotion.

Daily Devotions

There's a devotion for every Monday through Friday of the year (260 of 'em). These devotions are written by teenagers. Get to know Christina, A.J., Katy, Mike, Jeff, and a bunch of other teenagers as they share with you what the Bible has to say about life as a teenager. The bottom of the page will tell you where to find the next day's devotion.

Weekend Devotions

There's a weekend devotion for every weekend of the year (52 of 'em). These devotions are written by youth leaders; they sum up or emphasize a key point in the previous week's devotions. Do 'em Saturday or Sunday—your choice.

Week**end.**

Dare to Ask

Read Luke 2:52 (page 1221)

In Thursday's devotion, Amy mentions how she tried to answer some questions her friends were asking her about Jesus. Do you ever have questions too? Do you ever wonder if this Christian stuff is worth it? Do you wonder if it's real?

It's OK to ask those questions. In fact (ready for this?), it's really good to ask those questions! This time of your life (junior high, middle school, young teen—whatever you want to call it) is all about change. Your body will change more during these years than at any other time other than when you were a little tiny baby. And that's not all: Your emotions are changing (have you noticed?); your brain is changing (you can think in new and different ways); and your faith is changing. Or, at least, your faith *should* be changing. Most Christian kids wander into their teen years with a faith (belief in God and God-stuff) that's pretty close to what their parents believe. But now you're beginning to form your own beliefs about everything, God included.

So go on, ask those tough questions. Ask your parents. Ask your youth leader. Ask your pastor. And definitely ask God. He, and his people, will help you understand and develop your own personal faith. That's a good thing!

❶ What are some of your biggest questions about God, the Bible and Christianity?

❷ Choose one question (you can choose more later) and talk about it with your parents, your youth leader or some other Christian adult.

❸ Ask God your question. Pray that he'll give you wisdom and understanding.

Turn to page 1209 for your next devotion.

Contributors
to the Teen Devotional Bible

Carla Barnhill & Mark Oestreicher, General Editors

Dr. Chap Clark
Associate Professor of Youth
and Family Ministries
Fuller Theological Seminary
Pasadena, CA

Gregg Farah
Youth Pastor
Antioch Bible Church
Bellevue, WA

Sam Fowler
Minister of Health and Recreation
Pasadena 1st Church of the Nazarene
Pasadena, CA

Curt Gibson
Junior High Pastor
Pasadena 1st Church of the Nazarene
Pasadena, CA

Rich Griffith
Junior High Pastor
Sugar Hill United Methodist Church
Sugar Hill, GA

Laura Gross
Junior High Ministry Volunteer
Lake Avenue Church
Pasadena, CA

Greg Lafferty
Teaching Pastor
Christ Community Church
St. Charles, IL

Tim McLaughlin
Product Director
Youth Specialties
El Cajon, CA

Mark Oestreicher
Vice President of Ministry Resources
Youth Specialties
El Cajon, CA

Darrell Pearson
Assistant Professor of Youth Ministries
Eastern College
St. Davids, PA

Dr. Marv Penner
Chair, Youth and Family Ministry
Department
Briercrest Schools
Caronport, SK (CANADA)

Kara Eckmann Powell
Assistant Pastor of Junior High Ministries
Lake Avenue Church
Pasadena, CA

Todd Temple
President
10 TO 20
Del Mar, CA

Eric Venable
Junior High Pastor
Emmanuel Faith Community Church
Escondido, CA

John Wilson
Junior High Pastor
Lake Avenue Church
Pasadena, CA

Mike Yaconelli
Owner
Youth Specialties
El Cajon, CA

Staff of *Campus Life* Magazine

Carla Barnhill	Chris Lutes
Martin Cockroft	Mark Moring
Elesha Hodge	Jennifer Ridenour
Doug Johnson	Marilyn Rowe

AND . . .
Other youth pastors/youth workers nation-
wide who worked with teens to provide the
devotions for this Bible. These devotions
came in from all over the nation—from
Alaska to Georgia, from Illinois to Colorado,
from Mississippi to Minnesota.

A special thanks to all the teens who wrote
the devotions in this Bible!

Book Introductions

There's a book introduction for every book of the Bible (66 of 'em). They each have 4 sections: the intro (it is what it is), the "cast of characters" (who's who), "Snapshots" (what's what—in bullet points) and "What's Up With That?" (something fun or interesting to think about from the book).

Huh?

There's a ton of these in your Bible (about 300 of 'em)! These commentaries are written by youth experts and will help you figure out some tough passages to understand. So when you're not sure what something means, look for one of these notes. They will give you some hints, tips—you know, help you get it.

Even When They Fell

Huh?

Numbers 14:19
The story of the Hebrews comes down to two things: their miserable failure and God's unending forgiveness. When God got them out of Egypt (remember that?), they *still* didn't want to trust him. They were acting stupid and selfish. But God is so great and so kind that he didn't zap them. He forgave them. (Yeah, they had to wander around for a few more years, but it could have been worse!) God does the same with us, you know.

Measuring Up

Genesis 6:14–16 If God showed up at your doorstep one day and said, "Yo, go build an ark," would you know what he was talking about? Neither did Noah. But while God didn't exactly drop a set of blueprints out of the sky to help Noah's big old shop project, God did give Noah some pretty specific instructions about what this "ark" thing was supposed to look like. Your Bible says the ark was 450 feet long—the length of 1½ football fields! There are all kinds of other measurements in the Bible, some of them in ancient terms like "cubits." (A cubit is about 18 inches. That means Goliath, who was 6 cubits and a span, was more than 9½ feet tall. Yikes!)

More Bible measurements:
- a "handbreadth" was about 3 inches (Exodus 25:25)
- a "span" was a little over 8½ inches (Exodus 28:16)
- a "step" or "pace" was about 3 feet (2 Samuel 6:13)
- a "finger" was about ¾ of an inch (Jeremiah 52:21)
- a "Sabbath day's walk" was about ¾ of a mile (Acts 1:12)

XtRas

Extras

There's a quarter of a ton of these in your Bible (about 70 of 'em). They tell you interesting, sometimes crazy tidbits about the Bible and its characters. Written by youth experts.

22 Full-color Pages

On one side, you'll see "Backstage Pass"—a behind-the-scenes look at what God thinks about issues that are most important to you. On the other side of the page you'll see "Extreme Faith"—actual questions by teens about faith and Christianity that are answered by youth experts like Dawson McAllister and Susie Shellenberger.

Subject Index

Do you want to read about a certain topic, like friends, forgiveness, loneliness or prayer? The subject index will tell you where to find a devotion that talks about this stuff in your Bible. The index starts on page 1577.

Plan of Salvation

Not sure how to share your faith with others? Or not sure about your own faith? Turn to page 1582 and read about Jesus and how to become a Christian.

Word of God

The most important part of this whole Bible is the Word of God. It is full of power. God has so much to say! The Bible is like a special letter from God to you. When you read it, you'll get to know God better. This Bible uses the New International Version (NIV) translation. Renowned by many of the world's leading Bible scholars and millions of satisfied Bible readers, the NIV is now the most widely read modern English translation in the world. It's written at an 8th grade reading level.

If you have any questions or remarks about this Bible, please write and tell us.

The Bible Editors
Zondervan Publishing House
5300 Patterson Avenue SE
Grand Rapids, MI 49530
www.zondervan.com

Genesis

START

As far as stories go, Genesis starts in a hurry. Act 1, Scene 1 opens with the lead character, God, making good things happen. (Hint: That's a recurring theme in the Bible.) Then the other 3 main characters enter the stage: first the humans, then Satan close on their heels. That's when the trouble starts, and it won't stop until the book of Revelation, some 1,500 pages later, when one of these characters makes a fiery exit. Guess which one.

But that's getting ahead of the story. Genesis gets things started: God invents a perfect world, Satan gets the first humans to mess it all up, and the first family and their descendants get scattered, drowned, kidnapped, enslaved and dragged through the desert on their various adventures. This book has it all: BIG stuff (creation), BAD stuff (the world's first sin), WET stuff (Noah's cruise), TALL stuff (the Babel Tower disaster), and a lot of really GOOD stuff about God. He never gives up trying to pull us humans back to him.

CAST OF Characters

God
The main character; also acts as creator and director of the entire Bible.

The First Family
Adam, Eve, their sons Cain and Abel, and a bunch of grandkids.

The Serpent
The original bad guy. He makes his short, sneaky appearance in chapter 3, then works his wickedness behind the scenes for the rest of the book—and for most of the Bible for that matter. His more common name is Satan.

Noah
The original skipper—he builds a big boat, saves his family and animals from ex-tremely wet weather conditions, and gives the world a fresh start after the serpent helps mess up the first one.

Abraham and Sarah
God sticks a "ha" in Abram's name, fiddles with his wife Sarai's name, then starts building an entire nation through this old-age couple's kid Isaac.

Jacob
Grandson of Abraham and Sarah, son of Isaac and the sneaky twin brother of Esau, Jacob (a.k.a. Israel) has a bunch of kids, including 12 sons who become the fathers of the 12 tribes of the Jewish nation.

Joseph
Jacob's favorite son. His brothers are lower than low. They sell him into slavery. Joseph gets carried off to Egypt, gets in good with the pharaoh and winds up saving his entire family—including his sorry bunch of brothers—from a famine (major food shortage).

Old
Testament

What's UP with That?

Maybe you've heard about the *patriarchs* (PAY-tree-arks) —the men God used to get the whole Jewish nation started. Here's the patriarchs' family tree—with some of the names missing. You'll find these names somewhere in the list of possibilities.

POSSIBILITY LIST

Arnold	Gideon
Asher	Isaac
Betsy	Jacob
Biff	Joseph
Dan	Judah
Ernesto	Moses
Fred	Noah
Gabriel	Oscar
Gertrude	Zippy

Abraham & Sarah

(see chapter 21)

_____ & Rebekah

(see chapter 25)

Esau   _____ & Rachel & Leah & Bilhah & Zilpah

(see chapter 30)

Reuben   Levi   _____   Gad   Issachar   _____

Simeon   _____   Naphtali   _____   Zebulun   Benjamin

answers in order: Isaac, Jacob, Judah, Dan, Asher, Joseph

Snap shots

- God creates a really cool world *(chapters 1—2)*

- The humans mess it up bad *(chapters 3—5)*

- High tide!—God uses Noah for a fresh start *(chapters 6—11)*

- Old folks Abraham and Sarah start a new nation *(chapters 12—25)*

- Grandson Jacob and his 12 tribe-starting sons *(chapters 25—36)*

- The adventures of Little Joseph *(chapters 37—50)*

The Beginning

1 In the beginning God created the heavens and the earth. ²Now the earth was*ᵃ* formless and empty, darkness was over the surface of the deep, and the Spirit of God was hovering over the waters.

³And God said, "Let there be light," and there was light. ⁴God saw that the light was good, and he separated the light from the darkness. ⁵God called the light "day," and the darkness he called "night." And there was evening, and there was morning—the first day.

⁶And God said, "Let there be an expanse between the waters to separate water from water." ⁷So God made the expanse and separated the water under the expanse from the water above it. And it was so. ⁸God called the expanse "sky." And there was evening, and there was morning—the second day.

⁹And God said, "Let the water under the sky be gathered to one place, and let dry ground appear." And it was so. ¹⁰God called the dry ground "land," and the gathered waters he called "seas." And God saw that it was good.

¹¹Then God said, "Let the land produce vegetation: seed-bearing plants and trees on the land that bear fruit with seed in it, according to their various kinds." And it was so. ¹²The land produced vegetation: plants bearing seed according to their kinds and trees bearing fruit with seed in it according to their kinds. And God saw that it was good. ¹³And there was evening, and there was morning—the third day.

¹⁴And God said, "Let there be lights in the expanse of the sky to separate the day from the night, and let them serve as signs to mark seasons and days and years, ¹⁵and let them be lights in the expanse of the sky to give light on the earth." And it was so. ¹⁶God made two great lights—the greater light to govern the day and the lesser light to govern the night. He also made the stars. ¹⁷God set them in the expanse of the sky to give light on the earth, ¹⁸to govern the day and the night, and to separate light from darkness. And God saw that it was good. ¹⁹And there was evening, and there was morning—the fourth day.

²⁰And God said, "Let the water teem with living creatures, and let birds fly above the earth across the expanse of the sky." ²¹So God created the great creatures of the sea and every living and moving thing with which the water teems, according to their kinds, and every winged bird according to its kind. And God saw that it was good. ²²God blessed them and said, "Be fruitful and increase in number and fill the water in the seas, and let the birds increase on the earth." ²³And there was evening, and there was morning—the fifth day.

²⁴And God said, "Let the land produce living creatures according to their kinds: livestock, creatures that move along the ground, and wild animals, each according to its kind." And it was so. ²⁵God made the wild animals according to their kinds, the livestock according to their kinds, and all the creatures that move along the ground according to their kinds. And God saw that it was good.

²⁶Then God said, "Let us make man in our image, in our likeness, and let them rule over the fish of the sea and the birds of the air, over the livestock, over all the earth,*ᵇ* and over all the creatures that move along the ground."

²⁷So God created man in his own image,
in the image of God he created him;
male and female he created them.

²⁸God blessed them and said to them, "Be fruitful and increase in number; fill the earth and subdue it. Rule over the fish of the sea and the birds of the air and over every living creature that moves on the ground." ²⁹Then God said, "I give you every seed-bearing plant on the face of the whole earth and every tree that has

---

ᵃ2 Or possibly *became*   *ᵇ26* Hebrew; Syriac *all the wild animals*

Preface

THE NEW INTERNATIONAL VERSION is a completely new translation of the Holy Bible made by over a hundred scholars working directly from the best available Hebrew, Aramaic and Greek texts. It had its beginning in 1965 when, after several years of exploratory study by committees from the Christian Reformed Church and the National Association of Evangelicals, a group of scholars met at Palos Heights, Illinois, and concurred in the need for a new translation of the Bible in contemporary English. This group, though not made up of official church representatives, was transdenominational. Its conclusion was endorsed by a large number of leaders from many denominations who met in Chicago in 1966.

Responsibility for the new version was delegated by the Palos Heights group to a self-governing body of fifteen, the Committee on Bible Translation, composed for the most part of biblical scholars from colleges, universities and seminaries. In 1967 the New York Bible Society (now the International Bible Society) generously undertook the financial sponsorship of the project—a sponsorship that made it possible to enlist the help of many distinguished scholars. The fact that participants from the United States, Great Britain, Canada, Australia and New Zealand worked together gave the project its international scope. That they were from many denominations—including Anglican, Assemblies of God, Baptist, Brethren, Christian Reformed, Church of Christ, Evangelical Free, Lutheran, Mennonite, Methodist, Nazarene, Presbyterian, Wesleyan and other churches—helped to safeguard the translation from sectarian bias.

How it was made helps to give the New International Version its distinctiveness. The translation of each book was assigned to a team of scholars. Next, one of the Intermediate Editorial Committees revised the initial translation, with constant reference to the Hebrew, Aramaic or Greek. Their work then went to one of the General Editorial Committees, which checked it in detail and made another thorough revision. This revision in turn was carefully reviewed by the Committee on Bible Translation, which made further changes and then released the final version for publication. In this way the entire Bible underwent three revisions, during each of which the translation was examined for its faithfulness to the original languages and for its English style.

All this involved many thousands of hours of research and discussion regarding the meaning of the texts and the precise way of putting them into English. It may well be that no other translation has been made by a more thorough process of review and revision from committee to committee than this one.

From the beginning of the project, the Committee on Bible Translation held to certain goals for the New International Version: that it would be an accurate translation and one that would have clarity and literary quality and so prove suitable for public and private reading, teaching, preaching, memorizing and liturgical use. The Committee also sought to preserve some measure of continuity with the long tradition of translating the Scriptures into English.

In working toward these goals, the translators were united in their commitment to the authority and infallibility of the Bible as God's Word in written form. They believe that it contains the divine answer to the deepest needs of humanity, that it sheds unique light on our path in a dark world, and that it sets forth the way to our eternal well-being.

The first concern of the translators has been the accuracy of the translation and its fidelity to the thought of the biblical writers. They have weighed the significance of the lexical and grammatical details of the Hebrew, Aramaic and Greek texts. At the same time, they have striven for more than a word-for-word translation. Because thought patterns and syntax differ from language to language, faithful communication of the meaning of the writers of the Bible demands frequent modifications in sentence structure and constant regard for the contextual meanings of words.

A sensitive feeling for style does not always accompany scholarship. Accordingly the Committee on Bible Translation submitted the developing version to a number of stylistic consultants. Two of them read every book of both Old and New Testaments twice—once before and once after the last major revision—and made invaluable suggestions. Samples of the translation were tested for clarity and ease of reading by various kinds of people—young and old, highly educated and less well educated, ministers and laymen.

Concern for clear and natural English—that the New International Version should be idiomatic but not idiosyncratic, contemporary but not dated—motivated the translators and consultants. At the same time, they tried to reflect the differing styles of the biblical writers. In view of the international use of English, the translators sought to avoid obvious Americanisms on the one hand and obvious Anglicisms on the other. A British edition reflects the comparatively few differences of significant idiom and of spelling.

As for the traditional pronouns "thou," "thee" and "thine" in reference to the Deity, the translators judged that to use these archaisms (along with the old verb forms such as "doest," "wouldest" and "hadst") would violate accuracy in translation. Neither Hebrew, Aramaic nor Greek uses special pronouns for the persons of the Godhead. A present-day translation is not enhanced by forms that in the time of the King James Version were used in everyday speech, whether referring to God or man.

For the Old Testament the standard Hebrew text, the Masoretic Text as published in the latest editions of *Biblia Hebraica*, was used throughout. The Dead Sea Scrolls contain material bearing on an earlier stage of the Hebrew text. They were consulted, as were the Samaritan Pentateuch and the ancient scribal traditions relating to textual changes. Sometimes a variant Hebrew reading in the margin of the Masoretic Text was followed instead of the text itself. Such instances, being variants within the Masoretic tradition, are not specified by footnotes. In rare cases, words in the consonantal text were divided differently from the way they appear in the Masoretic Text. Footnotes indicate this. The translators also consulted the more important early versions—the Septuagint; Aquila, Symmachus and Theodotion; the Vulgate; the Syriac Peshitta; the Targums; and for the Psalms the *Juxta Hebraica* of Jerome. Readings from these versions were occasionally followed where the Masoretic Text seemed doubtful and where accepted principles of textual criticism showed that one or more of these textual witnesses appeared to provide the correct reading. Such instances are footnoted. Sometimes vowel letters and vowel signs did not, in the judgment of the translators, represent the correct vowels for the original consonantal text. Accordingly some words were read with a different set of vowels. These instances are usually not indicated by footnotes.

The Greek text used in translating the New Testament was an eclectic one. No other piece of ancient literature has such an abundance of manuscript witnesses as does the New Testament. Where existing manuscripts differ, the translators made their choice of readings according to accepted principles of New Testament textual criticism. Footnotes call attention to places where there was uncertainty about what the original text was. The best current printed texts of the Greek New Testament were used.

There is a sense in which the work of translation is never wholly finished. This applies to all great literature and uniquely so to the Bible. In 1973 the New Testament in the New International Version was published. Since then, suggestions for corrections and revisions have been received from various sources. The Committee on Bible Translation carefully considered the suggestions and adopted a number of them. These were incorporated in the first printing of the entire Bible in 1978. Additional revisions were made by the Committee on Bible Translation in 1983 and appear in printings after that date.

As in other ancient documents, the precise meaning of the biblical texts is sometimes uncertain. This is more often the case with the Hebrew and Aramaic texts than with the Greek text. Although archaeological and linguistic discoveries in this century aid in understanding difficult passages, some uncertainties remain. The more significant of these have been called to the reader's attention in the footnotes.

In regard to the divine name *YHWH*, commonly referred to as the *Tetragrammaton*, the translators adopted the device used in most English versions of rendering that name as "Lord" in capital letters to distinguish it from *Adonai*, another Hebrew word rendered "Lord," for which small letters are used. Wherever the two names stand together in the Old Testament as a compound name of God, they are rendered "Sovereign Lord."

Because for most readers today the phrases "the Lord of hosts" and "God of hosts" have little meaning, this version renders them "the Lord Almighty" and "God Almighty." These renderings convey the sense of the Hebrew, namely, "he who is sovereign over all the 'hosts' (powers) in heaven and on earth, especially over the 'host' (armies) of Israel." For readers unacquainted with Hebrew this does not make clear the distinction between *Sabaoth* ("hosts" or "Almighty") and *Shaddai* (which can also be translated "Almighty"), but the latter occurs infrequently and is always footnoted. When *Adonai* and *YHWH Sabaoth* occur together, they are rendered "the Lord, the LORD Almighty."

As for other proper nouns, the familiar spellings of the King James Version are generally retained. Names traditionally spelled with "ch," except where it is final, are usually spelled in this translation with "k" or "c," since the biblical languages do not have the sound that "ch" frequently indicates in English—for example, in *chant*. For well-known names such as Zechariah, however, the traditional spelling has been retained. Variation in the spelling of names in the original languages has usually not been indicated. Where a person or place has two or more different names in the Hebrew, Aramaic or Greek texts, the more familiar one has generally been used, with footnotes where needed.

To achieve clarity the translators sometimes supplied words not in the original texts but required by the context. If there was uncertainty about such material, it is enclosed in brackets. Also for the sake of clarity or style, nouns, including some proper nouns, are sometimes substituted for pronouns, and vice versa. And though the Hebrew writers often shifted back and forth between first, second and third personal pronouns without change of antecedent, this translation often makes them uniform, in accordance with English style and without the use of footnotes.

Poetical passages are printed as poetry, that is, with indentation of lines and with separate stanzas. These are generally designed to reflect the structure of Hebrew poetry. This poetry is normally characterized by parallelism in balanced lines. Most of the poetry in the Bible is in the Old Testament, and scholars differ regarding the scansion of Hebrew lines. The translators determined the stanza divisions for the most part by analysis of the subject matter. The stanzas therefore serve as poetic paragraphs.

As an aid to the reader, italicized sectional headings are inserted in most of the books. They are not to be regarded as part of the NIV text, are not for oral reading, and are not intended to dictate the interpretation of the sections they head.

The footnotes in this version are of several kinds, most of which need no explanation. Those giving alternative translations begin with "Or" and generally introduce the alternative with the last word preceding it in the text, except when it is a single-word alternative; in poetry quoted in a footnote a slant mark indicates a line division. Footnotes introduced by "Or" do not have uniform significance. In some cases two possible translations were considered to have about equal validity. In other cases, though the translators were convinced that the translation in the text was correct, they judged that another interpretation was possible and of sufficient importance to be represented in a footnote.

In the New Testament, footnotes that refer to uncertainty regarding the original text are introduced by "Some manuscripts" or similar expressions. In the Old Testament, evidence for the reading chosen is given first and evidence for the alternative is added after a semicolon (for example: Septuagint; Hebrew *father*). In such notes the term "Hebrew" refers to the Masoretic Text.

It should be noted that minerals, flora and fauna, architectural details, articles of clothing and jewelry, musical instruments and other articles cannot always be identified with precision. Also measures of capacity in the biblical period are particularly uncertain (see the table of weights and measures following the text).

Like all translations of the Bible, made as they are by imperfect man, this one undoubtedly falls short of its goals. Yet we are grateful to God for the extent to which he has enabled us to realize these goals and for the strength he has given us and our colleagues to complete our task. We offer this version of the Bible to him in whose name and for whose glory it has been made. We pray that it will lead many into a better understanding of the Holy Scriptures and a fuller knowledge of Jesus Christ the incarnate Word, of whom the Scriptures so faithfully testify.

The Committee on Bible Translation
June 1978
(Revised August 1983)

Names of the translators and editors may be secured
from the International Bible Society
translation sponsors of the New International Version,
1820 Jet Stream Drive, Colorado Springs, Colorado
80921-3696 U.S.A.

fruit with seed in it. They will be yours for food. ³⁰And to all the beasts of the earth and all the birds of the air and all the creatures that move on the ground—everything that has the breath of life in it—I give every green plant for food." And it was so.

³¹God saw all that he had made, and it was very good. And there was evening, and there was morning—the sixth day.

2 Thus the heavens and the earth were completed in all their vast array.

²By the seventh day God had finished the work he had been doing; so on the seventh day he rested*ᵃ* from all his work. ³And God blessed the seventh day and made it holy, because on it he rested from all the work of creating that he had done.

Adam and Eve

⁴This is the account of the heavens and the earth when they were created.

When the LORD God made the earth and the heavens— ⁵and no shrub of the field had yet appeared on the earth*ᵇ* and no plant of the field had yet sprung up, for the LORD God had not sent rain on the earth*ᵇ* and there was no man to work the ground, ⁶but streams*ᶜ* came up from the earth and watered the whole surface of the ground— ⁷the LORD God formed the man*ᵈ* from the dust of the ground and breathed into his nostrils the breath of life, and the man became a living being.

⁸Now the LORD God had planted a garden in the east, in Eden; and there he put the man he had formed. ⁹And the LORD God made all kinds of trees grow out of the ground—trees that were pleasing to the eye and good for food. In the middle of the garden were the tree of life and the tree of the knowledge of good and evil.

ᵃ2 Or ceased; also in verse 3   ᵇ5 Or land; also in verse 6   ᶜ6 Or mist   ᵈ7 The Hebrew for man (adam) sounds like and may be related to the Hebrew for ground (adamah); it is also the name Adam (see Gen. 2:20).

Monday

Who Do You Look Like?

Read Genesis 1:27

There are lots of times when other people's opinions lead me to believe I'm somehow not important. When I get teased or picked on at school, it changes my image of myself. But when I read this verse, it brings things back into perspective. As long as I'm living the way God wants me to, it doesn't matter what people think about me. I am made in God's image, and I can feel good about who I am.

Being made in God's image doesn't mean God has the same hair I do or anything. It means that God made me exactly the way he wanted me to be. Knowing that God loves me so much helps me feel better about myself. That makes me want to learn more about him and let him shine through me so other people will see him in me.

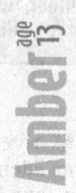
Amber age 13

What about You?

❶ Do you ever put yourself down for the way you look? What are you saying to God when you put down what he made?

❷ Create something that tells people something about you—a painting, a poem, a sculpture, a song. How do you feel about your creation? What do you want people to learn about you through your creation?

❸ Thank God for 1 or 2 things that make you who you are.

Turn to page 8 for your next devotion.

World's Biggest Mystery

Ever since anyone can remember, people have wondered about one thing: **Where did the world come from?** Genesis tells us. God *created* it. But that answer just opens up an even bigger question: Where did God come from?

And that question can't be answered. Because God didn't *come from* anywhere. He has no parents, no hometown, no birth certificate. The Bible explains it this way: "Before the mountains were born, or you brought forth the earth and the world, from everlasting to everlasting you are God" (Psalm 90:2, page 689).

God is *everlasting*—infinite, with no beginning and no end. But some people say, "*Everything* has a beginning. It's just *got* to." We even celebrate this fact through:

✗ Birthday parties (your own beginning)
✗ Wedding anniversaries
  (the beginning of a marriage)
✗ Christmas
  (beginning of Jesus' life on earth)
✗ New Year's Day
  (beginning of another year)

And for that matter, everything has to have an *end*, doesn't it? We make a big fuss about that too: finish lines and funerals and victory parties and graduation days. With all this attention to beginnings and endings, it's hard to imagine something (or someone) that has neither. We're only familiar with what is *finite*—infinity makes no sense at all.

Think about this: Everything in our world was started by something . . . or *someone*. You got your start from your *parents*. Your parents got their start from your *grandparents*. And those folks got their start from *their* parents, who got started by other parents, and so on. Chase that family tree all the way back to the very first humans, and you've still got to have someone there who started *them*.

Some people refuse to believe the Bible's story of creation. They claim that humans got their start through evolution, which got *its* start from a Big Bang. But that still doesn't solve the mystery: No matter who or what sits at the top of your "family tree"—Adam & Eve or Atom & Amoeba or Crash & Bang—*someone* made the very first move. *Someone* started it all.

Someone named God. And at that very moment, he invented something else: *Beginnings.* From that moment on, everything in the world would have one. So the next time someone asks you, *Where did God come from?*, you can say, "He didn't *come from* anywhere—he was already here when things started." And if that still doesn't make much sense, don't worry about it: You can ask God to explain it when you see him face to face.

---

¹⁰A river watering the garden flowed from Eden; from there it was separated into four headwaters. ¹¹The name of the first is the Pishon; it winds through the entire land of Havilah, where there is gold. ¹²(The gold of that land is good; aromatic resin*a* and onyx are also there.) ¹³The name of the second river is the Gihon; it winds through the entire land of Cush.*b* ¹⁴The name of the third river is the Tigris; it runs along the east side of Asshur. And the fourth river is the Euphrates.

¹⁵The LORD God took the man and put him in the Garden of Eden to work it and take care of it. ¹⁶And the LORD God com-

manded the man, "You are free to eat from any tree in the garden; ¹⁷but you must not eat from the tree of the knowledge of good and evil, for when you eat of it you will surely die."

¹⁸The LORD God said, "It is not good for the man to be alone. I will make a helper suitable for him."

¹⁹Now the LORD God had formed out of the ground all the beasts of the field and all the birds of the air. He brought them to the man to see what he would name them; and whatever the man called each

*a*12 Or *good; pearls* *b*13 Possibly southeast Mesopotamia living creature, that was its name. ²⁰So the man gave names to all the livestock, the birds of the air and all the beasts of the field.

But for Adam*ª* no suitable helper was found. ²¹So the LORD God caused the man to fall into a deep sleep; and while he was sleeping, he took one of the man's ribs*ᵇ* and closed up the place with flesh. ²²Then the LORD God made a woman from the rib*ᶜ* he had taken out of the man, and he brought her to the man.

²³The man said,

"This is now bone of my bones
  and flesh of my flesh;
she shall be called 'woman,'*ᵈ*
  for she was taken out of man."

²⁴For this reason a man will leave his father and mother and be united to his wife, and they will become one flesh.

²⁵The man and his wife were both naked, and they felt no shame.

The Fall of Man

3 Now the serpent was more crafty than any of the wild animals the LORD God had made. He said to the woman, "Did God really say, 'You must not eat from any tree in the garden'?"

²The woman said to the serpent, "We may eat fruit from the trees in the garden, ³but God did say, 'You must not eat fruit from the tree that is in the middle of the garden, and you must not touch it, or you will die.'"

⁴"You will not surely die," the serpent said to the woman. ⁵"For God knows that when you eat of it your eyes will be opened, and you will be like God, knowing good and evil."

Caught in the Act

Genesis 3:7

Have you ever been caught doing something you knew was wrong? That knot you felt in your stomach was your guilt. Adam and Eve were the first people to experience guilt after they ate the fruit from the wrong tree. They hid from God because they knew they were in trouble, and they felt ashamed. But there's good news for us—Jesus came and died so we can be forgiven. This means we don't have to hide from God when we feel guilty; we need to come to him and ask to be forgiven.

⁶When the woman saw that the fruit of the tree was good for food and pleasing to the eye, and also desirable for gaining wisdom, she took some and ate it. She also gave some to her husband, who was with her, and he ate it. ⁷Then the eyes of both of them were opened, and they realized they were naked; so they sewed fig leaves together and made coverings for themselves.

⁸Then the man and his wife heard the sound of the LORD God as he was walking in the garden in the cool of the day, and they hid from the LORD God among the trees of the garden. ⁹But the LORD God called to the man, "Where are you?"

¹⁰He answered, "I heard you in the garden, and I was afraid because I was naked; so I hid."

¹¹And he said, "Who told you that you were naked? Have you eaten from the tree that I commanded you not to eat from?"

¹²The man said, "The woman you put

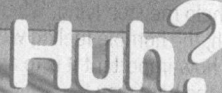

Much More Than Sex

Genesis 2:24

Adam was a lonely dude until (drum roll, please) God created the perfect companion: Eve. God designed marriage to be a permanent commitment of a man and a woman. Yeah, sex is part of this—and it's great to know this is part of God's perfect plan. But the "two becoming one" thing involves a lot more than sex. It's two lives becoming one—two stories becoming one.

ª20 Or the man ᵇ21 Or took part of the man's side
ᶜ22 Or part ᵈ23 The Hebrew for woman sounds like the Hebrew for man.

here with me—she gave me some fruit from the tree, and I ate it."

¹³Then the LORD God said to the woman, "What is this you have done?"

The woman said, "The serpent deceived me, and I ate."

¹⁴So the LORD God said to the serpent, "Because you have done this,

"Cursed are you above all the livestock
    and all the wild animals!
You will crawl on your belly
    and you will eat dust
    all the days of your life.
¹⁵And I will put enmity
    between you and the woman,
    and between your offspring^a and
        hers;
he will crush^b your head,
    and you will strike his heel."

¹⁶To the woman he said,

"I will greatly increase your pains in
        childbearing;

with pain you will give birth to
        children.
Your desire will be for your husband,
    and he will rule over you."

¹⁷To Adam he said, "Because you listened to your wife and ate from the tree about which I commanded you, 'You must not eat of it,'

"Cursed is the ground because of you;
    through painful toil you will eat
        of it
    all the days of your life.
¹⁸It will produce thorns and thistles for
        you,
    and you will eat the plants of the
        field.
¹⁹By the sweat of your brow
    you will eat your food
until you return to the ground,
    since from it you were taken;

^a15 Or seed ^b15 Or strike

Tuesday

A Real Guilt Trip

Read Genesis 3:1–13

I remember the first time I lied to my parents. I knew what "sin" meant before that, but it was the first time I really felt like I had sinned. It was horrible.

I hated feeling so guilty, and I told myself I'd never lie again. But then I told another lie. I felt bad, but not quite so bad as the first time. Before I knew it, I was lying all the time. It was like I couldn't stop.

Even though lying got easier and easier, the guilty feeling never totally went away. That's when I learned that guilt isn't always a bad thing. The bad feeling made me want to stop lying.

Finally, I asked God to forgive me and help me stop lying. When I apologized to my parents and told them the truth, the horrible feeling went away. I definitely learned a lesson about sin and how important it is to ask for forgiveness. I just wish I hadn't had to learn it the hard way.

Zach age 14

What about You?

❶ Think about when you've felt guilty and why.

❷ Are there any people you need to ask for forgiveness? Tell them you're sorry and ask for their forgiveness today.

❸ Identify a specific sin you've been struggling with and ask God to help you overcome it.

Turn to page 10 for your next devotion.

for dust you are
and to dust you will return."

[20]Adam[a] named his wife Eve,[b] because she would become the mother of all the living. [21]The LORD God made garments of skin for Adam and his wife and clothed them. [22]And the LORD God said, "The man has now become like one of us, knowing good and evil. He must not be allowed to reach out his hand and take also from the tree of life and eat, and live forever." [23]So the LORD God banished him from the Garden of Eden to work the ground from which he had been taken. [24]After he drove the man out, he placed on the east side[c] of the Garden of Eden cherubim and a flaming sword flashing back and forth to guard the way to the tree of life.

Cain and Abel

4 Adam[a] lay with his wife Eve, and she became pregnant and gave birth to Cain.[d] She said, "With the help of the LORD I have brought forth[e] a man." [2]Later she gave birth to his brother Abel.

Now Abel kept flocks, and Cain worked the soil. [3]In the course of time Cain brought some of the fruits of the soil as an offering to the LORD. [4]But Abel brought fat portions from some of the firstborn of his flock. The LORD looked with favor on Abel and his offering, [5]but on Cain and his offering he did not look with favor. So Cain was very angry, and his face was downcast.

[6]Then the LORD said to Cain, "Why are you angry? Why is your face downcast? [7]If you do what is right, will you not be accepted? But if you do not do what is right, sin is crouching at your door; it desires to have you, but you must master it."

[8]Now Cain said to his brother Abel, "Let's go out to the field."[f] And while they were in the field, Cain attacked his brother Abel and killed him.

[9]Then the LORD said to Cain, "Where is your brother Abel?"

"I don't know," he replied. "Am I my brother's keeper?"

[10]The LORD said, "What have you done? Listen! Your brother's blood cries out to me from the ground. [11]Now you are under a curse and driven from the ground,

---

Villains of Doom and Destruction

Genesis 3:1–15 Forget about Lex Luthor or Mr. Freeze. If you want to find the king of all villains, look no further than the Garden of Eden. That's where you'll find that smooth-talking, venomous serpent who conned Eve into big-time sin, and we all know what *that* led to. Of course, the evil snake was only the first in a long line of Biblical villains. Watch out for these baddies:

✗ **Pharaoh, King of Egypt**
Just call him "Pharaoh the Foul." This vile vermin made slaves of God's people and continually defied Moses' commands to "Let my people go!"
(Exodus 5:14–23)

✗ **Goliath, the Giant**
This big bully's presence alone made entire armies shake with fear.
(1 Samuel 17:4–7)

✗ **Queen Jezebel**
What a witch! She got a real kick out of killing off God's prophets. But, in the end, she was reduced to puppy chow.
(1 Kings 18:4; 2 Kings 9:22, 30–37)

✗ **Legion, the Army of Demons**
This demonic horde possessed a naked man and tormented (only temporarily!) a herd of stampeding pigs that ran over a cliff into the sea. Good thing they weren't strong swimmers.
(Luke 8:26–33)

---

which opened its mouth to receive your brother's blood from your hand. [12]When you work the ground, it will no longer yield its crops for you. You will be a restless wanderer on the earth."

[13]Cain said to the LORD, "My punishment is more than I can bear. [14]Today

---

[a]20,1 Or *The man*   [b]20 *Eve* probably means *living*.
[c]24 Or *placed in front*   [d]1 *Cain* sounds like the Hebrew for *brought forth* or *acquired*.   [e]1 Or *have acquired*   [f]8 Samaritan Pentateuch, Septuagint, Vulgate and Syriac; Masoretic Text does not have "Let's go out to the field."

you are driving me from the land, and I will be hidden from your presence; I will be a restless wanderer on the earth, and whoever finds me will kill me."

[15]But the LORD said to him, "Not so[a]; if anyone kills Cain, he will suffer vengeance seven times over." Then the LORD put a mark on Cain so that no one who found him would kill him. [16]So Cain went out from the LORD's presence and lived in the land of Nod,[b] east of Eden.

[17]Cain lay with his wife, and she became pregnant and gave birth to Enoch. Cain was then building a city, and he named it after his son Enoch. [18]To Enoch was born Irad, and Irad was the father of Mehujael, and Mehujael was the father of Methushael, and Methushael was the father of Lamech.

[19]Lamech married two women, one named Adah and the other Zillah. [20]Adah gave birth to Jabal; he was the father of those who live in tents and raise livestock. [21]His brother's name was Jubal; he was the father of all who play the harp and flute. [22]Zillah also had a son, Tubal-Cain, who forged all kinds of tools out of[c] bronze and iron. Tubal-Cain's sister was Naamah.

[23]Lamech said to his wives,

"Adah and Zillah, listen to me;
　　wives of Lamech, hear my words.
I have killed[d] a man for wounding me,
　　a young man for injuring me.
[24]If Cain is avenged seven times,
　　then Lamech seventy-seven times."

[25]Adam lay with his wife again, and she gave birth to a son and named him Seth,[e] saying, "God has granted me another child in place of Abel, since Cain killed him." [26]Seth also had a son, and he named him Enosh.

At that time men began to call on[f] the name of the LORD.

---

[a]15 Septuagint, Vulgate and Syriac; Hebrew *Very well*　[b]16 *Nod* means *wandering* (see verses 12 and 14).　[c]22 Or *who instructed all who work in*　[d]23 Or *I will kill*　[e]25 *Seth* probably means *granted*.　[f]26 Or *to proclaim*

Wednesday

Can Brothers and Sisters Be Friends?　　　Read Genesis 4:1–16

Since I'm the youngest of 5 kids, I know what it's like to fight with siblings. One of my sisters and I used to argue over the littlest things. And sometimes I wonder if I'll ever learn to love my brother. I don't know what it is about him, but some days I absolutely can't stand him!

But in the last few years, I've learned that fighting with my brothers and sisters is only one part of our relationship. Three of them have finished high school and moved away. When I think about them, I don't think about the arguments and the silly fights we had. I think about the fun we had together. I think about how much I miss them and love them.

When you get right down to it, brothers and sisters are some of the best friends you'll ever have. No matter how much you can't stand them sometimes, one day it'll hit you how important they are to you.

Heather age 13

What about You?

❶ What are 3 things you can do that will help you get along better with your brothers and sisters?

❷ Think of several ways you can show love to them. Do one of those things for them today.

❸ Ask God to help you all get along.

Turn to page 12 for your next devotion.

From Adam to Noah

5 This is the written account of Adam's line.

When God created man, he made him in the likeness of God. [2]He created them male and female and blessed them. And when they were created, he called them "man.a"

[3]When Adam had lived 130 years, he had a son in his own likeness, in his own image; and he named him Seth. [4]After Seth was born, Adam lived 800 years and had other sons and daughters. [5]Altogether, Adam lived 930 years, and then he died.

[6]When Seth had lived 105 years, he became the fatherb of Enosh. [7]And after he became the father of Enosh, Seth lived 807 years and had other sons and daughters. [8]Altogether, Seth lived 912 years, and then he died.

[9]When Enosh had lived 90 years, he became the father of Kenan. [10]And after he became the father of Kenan, Enosh lived 815 years and had other sons and daughters. [11]Altogether, Enosh lived 905 years, and then he died.

[12]When Kenan had lived 70 years, he became the father of Mahalalel. [13]And after he became the father of Mahalalel, Kenan lived 840 years and had other sons and daughters. [14]Altogether, Kenan lived 910 years, and then he died.

[15]When Mahalalel had lived 65 years, he became the father of Jared. [16]And after he became the father of Jared, Mahalalel lived 830 years and had other sons and daughters. [17]Altogether, Mahalalel lived 895 years, and then he died.

[18]When Jared had lived 162 years, he became the father of Enoch. [19]And after he became the father of Enoch, Jared lived 800 years and had other sons and daughters. [20]Altogether, Jared lived 962 years, and then he died.

[21]When Enoch had lived 65 years, he became the father of Methuselah. [22]And after he became the father of Methuselah, Enoch walked with God 300 years and had other sons and daughters. [23]Altogether, Enoch lived 365 years. [24]Enoch walked with God; then he was no more, because God took him away.

[25]When Methuselah had lived 187 years, he became the father of Lamech. [26]And after he became the father of Lamech, Methuselah lived 782 years and had other sons and daughters. [27]Altogether, Methuselah lived 969 years, and then he died.

[28]When Lamech had lived 182 years, he had a son. [29]He named him Noahc and said, "He will comfort us in the labor and painful toil of our hands caused by the ground the LORD has cursed." [30]After Noah was born, Lamech lived 595 years and had other sons and daughters. [31]Altogether, Lamech lived 777 years, and then he died.

[32]After Noah was 500 years old, he became the father of Shem, Ham and Japheth.

The Flood

6 When men began to increase in number on the earth and daughters were born to them, [2]the sons of God saw that the daughters of men were beautiful, and they married any of them they chose. [3]Then the LORD said, "My Spirit will not contend withd man forever, for he is mortale; his days will be a hundred and twenty years."

[4]The Nephilim were on the earth in those days—and also afterward—when the sons of God went to the daughters of men and had children by them. They were the heroes of old, men of renown.

[5]The LORD saw how great man's wickedness on the earth had become, and that every inclination of the thoughts of his heart was only evil all the time. [6]The LORD was grieved that he had made man on the earth, and his heart was filled with pain. [7]So the LORD said, "I will wipe mankind, whom I have created, from the face of the earth—men and animals, and creatures that move along the ground, and birds of the air—for I am grieved that I have made them." [8]But Noah found favor in the eyes of the LORD.

[9]This is the account of Noah.

Noah was a righteous man, blameless among the people of his time, and he

---

a2 Hebrew adam   b6 Father may mean ancestor; also in verses 7-26.   c29 Noah sounds like the Hebrew for comfort.   d3 Or My spirit will not remain in   e3 Or corrupt

walked with God. ¹⁰Noah had three sons: Shem, Ham and Japheth.

¹¹Now the earth was corrupt in God's sight and was full of violence. ¹²God saw how corrupt the earth had become, for all the people on earth had corrupted their ways. ¹³So God said to Noah, "I am going to put an end to all people, for the earth is filled with violence because of them. I am surely going to destroy both them and the earth. ¹⁴So make yourself an ark of cypress*ᵃ* wood; make rooms in it and coat it with pitch inside and out. ¹⁵This is how you are to build it: The ark is to be 450 feet long, 75 feet wide and 45 feet high.*ᵇ* ¹⁶Make a roof for it and finish*ᶜ* the ark to within 18 inches*ᵈ* of the top. Put a door in the side of the ark and make lower, middle and upper decks. ¹⁷I am going to bring floodwaters on the earth to destroy all life under the heavens, every creature that has the breath of life in it. Everything on earth will perish. ¹⁸But I will establish my covenant with you, and you will enter the ark—you and your sons and your wife and your sons' wives with you. ¹⁹You are to bring into the ark two of all living creatures, male and female, to keep them alive with you. ²⁰Two of every kind of bird, of every kind of animal and of every kind of creature that moves along the ground will come to you to be kept alive. ²¹You are to take every kind of food that is to be eaten and store it away as food for you and for them."

²²Noah did everything just as God commanded him.

7 The LORD then said to Noah, "Go into the ark, you and your whole family,

---

ᵃ14 The meaning of the Hebrew for this word is uncertain.   *ᵇ15* Hebrew *300 cubits long, 50 cubits wide and 30 cubits high* (about 140 meters long, 23 meters wide and 13.5 meters high)   *ᶜ16* Or *Make an opening for light by finishing*   *ᵈ16* Hebrew *a cubit* (about 0.5 meter)

Thursday

Taking a Stand
Read Genesis 6:9

My dad isn't a Christian, and he yells at me a lot. When I try to show him a Christian response by not yelling back, he calls me self-righteous and accuses me of having a stuck-up attitude. So here I am trying to take a stand for Jesus, and it seems like all it gets me is more trouble.

I'm glad I'm not the only one who's ever had this problem. Noah did too. He got criticized by everybody when he was building the ark. But he did what God asked him to do anyway, and he was blessed because of it. Noah and his family were the only people with a safe place to go when the flood came.

When I'm struggling to stand up for what's right, I can think about Noah and know that I'm doing the right thing. If I'm obedient, I know God will always provide a safe place for me too.

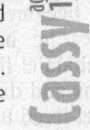
Cassy age 15

What about You?

❶ Think about a time someone made fun of you when you tried to do the right thing. What helped you stay strong?

❷ Write a letter of encouragement to someone who's been yelled at or put down (it could even be you). If you need ideas, check out Matthew 5:10–12, page 1146.

❸ Pray for the strength to take a stand for your faith even when it's not easy.

Turn to page 15 for your next devotion.

because I have found you righteous in this generation. [2]Take with you seven[a] of every kind of clean animal, a male and its mate, and two of every kind of unclean animal, a male and its mate, [3]and also seven of every kind of bird, male and female, to keep their various kinds alive throughout the earth. [4]Seven days from now I will send rain on the earth for forty days and forty nights, and I will wipe from the face of the earth every living creature I have made."

[5]And Noah did all that the LORD commanded him.

[6]Noah was six hundred years old when the floodwaters came on the earth. [7]And Noah and his sons and his wife and his sons' wives entered the ark to escape the waters of the flood. [8]Pairs of clean and unclean animals, of birds and of all creatures that move along the ground, [9]male and female, came to Noah and entered the ark, as God had commanded Noah. [10]And after the seven days the floodwaters came on the earth.

[11]In the six hundredth year of Noah's life, on the seventeenth day of the second month—on that day all the springs of the great deep burst forth, and the floodgates of the heavens were opened. [12]And rain fell on the earth forty days and forty nights.

[13]On that very day Noah and his sons, Shem, Ham and Japheth, together with his wife and the wives of his three sons, entered the ark. [14]They had with them every wild animal according to its kind, all livestock according to their kinds, every creature that moves along the ground according to its kind and every bird according to its kind, everything with wings. [15]Pairs of all creatures that have the breath of life in them came to Noah and entered the ark. [16]The animals going in were male and female of every living thing, as God had commanded Noah. Then the LORD shut him in.

[17]For forty days the flood kept coming on the earth, and as the waters increased they lifted the ark high above the earth. [18]The waters rose and increased greatly on the earth, and the ark floated on the surface of the water. [19]They rose greatly on the earth, and all the high mountains under the entire heavens were covered.

Measuring Up

Genesis 6:14–16 If God showed up at your doorstep one day and said, "Yo, go build an ark," would you know what he was talking about? Neither did Noah. But while God didn't exactly drop a set of blueprints out of the sky to help Noah's big old shop project, God did give Noah some pretty specific instructions about what this "ark" thing was supposed to look like. Your Bible says the ark was 450 feet long—the length of 1½ football fields! There are all kinds of other measurements in the Bible, some of them in ancient terms like "cubits." (A cubit is about 18 inches. That means Goliath, who was 6 cubits and a span, was more than 9½ feet tall. Yikes!)

More Bible measurements:
- ✗ a "handbreadth" was about 3 inches (Exodus 25:25)
- ✗ a "span" was a little over 8½ inches (Exodus 28:16)
- ✗ a "step" or "pace" was about 3 feet (2 Samuel 6:13)
- ✗ a "finger" was about ¾ of an inch (Jeremiah 52:21)
- ✗ a "Sabbath day's walk" was about ¾ of a mile (Acts 1:12)

[20]The waters rose and covered the mountains to a depth of more than twenty feet.[b] [21]Every living thing that moved on the earth perished—birds, livestock, wild animals, all the creatures that swarm over the earth, and all mankind. [22]Everything on dry land that had the breath of life in its nostrils died. [23]Every living thing on the face of the earth was wiped out; men and animals and the creatures that move along the ground and the birds of the air were wiped from

[a]2 Or seven pairs; also in verse 3   [b]20 Hebrew fifteen cubits (about 6.9 meters)   [c]20 Or rose more than twenty feet, and the mountains were covered

the earth. Only Noah was left, and those with him in the ark.

²⁴The waters flooded the earth for a hundred and fifty days.

8 But God remembered Noah and all the wild animals and the livestock that were with him in the ark, and he sent a wind over the earth, and the waters receded. ²Now the springs of the deep and the floodgates of the heavens had been closed, and the rain had stopped falling from the sky. ³The water receded steadily from the earth. At the end of the hundred and fifty days the water had gone down, ⁴and on the seventeenth day of the seventh month the ark came to rest on the mountains of Ararat. ⁵The waters continued to recede until the tenth month, and on the first day of the tenth month the tops of the mountains became visible.

⁶After forty days Noah opened the window he had made in the ark ⁷and sent out a raven, and it kept flying back and forth until the water had dried up from the earth. ⁸Then he sent out a dove to see if the water had receded from the surface of the ground. ⁹But the dove could find no place to set its feet because there was water over all the surface of the earth; so it returned to Noah in the ark. He reached out his hand and took the dove and brought it back to himself in the ark. ¹⁰He waited seven more days and again sent out the dove from the ark. ¹¹When the dove returned to him in the evening, there in its beak was a freshly plucked olive leaf! Then Noah knew that the water had receded from the earth. ¹²He waited seven more days and sent the dove out again, but this time it did not return to him.

¹³By the first day of the first month of Noah's six hundred and first year, the water had dried up from the earth. Noah then removed the covering from the ark and saw that the surface of the ground was dry. ¹⁴By the twenty-seventh day of the second month the earth was completely dry.

¹⁵Then God said to Noah, ¹⁶"Come out of the ark, you and your wife and your sons and their wives. ¹⁷Bring out every kind of living creature that is with you — the birds, the animals, and all the crea-

tures that move along the ground—so they can multiply on the earth and be fruitful and increase in number upon it."

¹⁸So Noah came out, together with his sons and his wife and his sons' wives. ¹⁹All the animals and all the creatures that move along the ground and all the birds—everything that moves on the earth—came out of the ark, one kind after another.

²⁰Then Noah built an altar to the LORD and, taking some of all the clean animals and clean birds, he sacrificed burnt offerings on it. ²¹The LORD smelled the

---

Give It Up

Huh?

Genesis 8:20
One way people show thanks to someone else is by giving him or her a gift. Noah gave God a thank-you gift. It's called a sacrifice because it means giving up something that's yours that you could use for yourself. Sometimes it's not easy to give things up, but it's a way to show God you appreciate him. Noah gave his best animals and birds to God as an expression of thanks. We can give to God also. We can give our money, time and talents as thank-you gifts to God.

---

pleasing aroma and said in his heart: "Never again will I curse the ground because of man, even though*a* every inclination of his heart is evil from childhood. And never again will I destroy all living creatures, as I have done.

²²"As long as the earth endures,
  seedtime and harvest,
  cold and heat,
  summer and winter,
  day and night
  will never cease."

God's Covenant With Noah

9 Then God blessed Noah and his sons, saying to them, "Be fruitful and increase in number and fill the earth.

---

20 Or man, for

²The fear and dread of you will fall upon all the beasts of the earth and all the birds of the air, upon every creature that moves along the ground, and upon all the fish of the sea; they are given into your hands. ³Everything that lives and moves will be food for you. Just as I gave you the green plants, I now give you everything.

⁴"But you must not eat meat that has its lifeblood still in it. ⁵And for your lifeblood I will surely demand an accounting. I will demand an accounting from every animal. And from each man, too, I will demand an accounting for the life of his fellow man.

⁶"Whoever sheds the blood of man,
   by man shall his blood be shed;
 for in the image of God
   has God made man.

⁷As for you, be fruitful and increase in number; multiply on the earth and increase upon it."

⁸Then God said to Noah and to his sons with him: ⁹"I now establish my covenant with you and with your descendants af-ter you ¹⁰and with every living creature that was with you—the birds, the livestock and all the wild animals, all those that came out of the ark with you—every living creature on earth. ¹¹I establish my covenant with you: Never again will all life be cut off by the waters of a flood; never again will there be a flood to destroy the earth."

¹²And God said, "This is the sign of the covenant I am making between me and you and every living creature with you, a covenant for all generations to come: ¹³I have set my rainbow in the clouds, and it will be the sign of the covenant between me and the earth. ¹⁴Whenever I bring clouds over the earth and the rainbow appears in the clouds, ¹⁵I will remember my covenant between me and you and all living creatures of every kind. Never again will the waters become a flood to destroy all life. ¹⁶Whenever the rainbow appears in the clouds, I will see it and remember the everlasting covenant between God and all living creatures of every kind on the earth."

¹⁷So God said to Noah, "This is the

Friday

Rainbow Reminder

Read Genesis 9:12-17

I've always known that God keeps his promises and listens when we pray. But these verses give me even more faith in God and his promises. Sometimes I need that extra faith, like when it feels like God isn't hearing my prayers, or when he answers them in a different way than I had hoped for.

Even though God is always listening to us and helping us out, we often can't see with our eyes exactly what he's doing. That's why a rainbow is so cool—it's something we can actually see that reminds us God is there. And because rainbows come after storms, they show us that God's there even when our situation looks bad. He's always there for us; no matter what happens, he'll keep his promises.

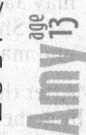

Amy, age 13

❶ What do you think of when you see a rainbow?

❷ Pull out a bunch of different colored clothes from your closet. Lay them on the floor in the shape of a rainbow. Think about God's faithfulness while you are making your rainbow.

❸ Thank God for being so faithful to you.

Turn to page 18 for your next devotion.

sign of the covenant I have established between me and all life on the earth."

The Sons of Noah

[18]The sons of Noah who came out of the ark were Shem, Ham and Japheth. (Ham was the father of Canaan.) [19]These were the three sons of Noah, and from them came the people who were scattered over the earth.

[20]Noah, a man of the soil, proceeded[a] to plant a vineyard. [21]When he drank some of its wine, he became drunk and lay uncovered inside his tent. [22]Ham, the father of Canaan, saw his father's nakedness and told his two brothers outside. [23]But Shem and Japheth took a garment and laid it across their shoulders; then they walked in backward and covered their father's nakedness. Their faces were turned the other way so that they would not see their father's nakedness.

[24]When Noah awoke from his wine and found out what his youngest son had done to him, [25]he said,

"Cursed be Canaan!
      The lowest of slaves
   will he be to his brothers."

[26]He also said,

"Blessed be the LORD, the God of
      Shem!
   May Canaan be the slave of Shem.[b]
[27]May God extend the territory of
      Japheth[c];
   may Japheth live in the tents of
      Shem,
   and may Canaan be his[d] slave."

[28]After the flood Noah lived 350 years. [29]Altogether, Noah lived 950 years, and then he died.

The Table of Nations

10 This is the account of Shem, Ham and Japheth, Noah's sons, who themselves had sons after the flood.

The Japhethites

[2]The sons[e] of Japheth:
   Gomer, Magog, Madai, Javan, Tubal, Meshech and Tiras.
[3]The sons of Gomer:
   Ashkenaz, Riphath and Togarmah.

[4]The sons of Javan:
   Elishah, Tarshish, the Kittim and the Rodanim.[f] [5](From these the maritime peoples spread out into their territories by their clans within their nations, each with its own language.)

The Hamites

[6]The sons of Ham:
   Cush, Mizraim,[g] Put and Canaan.
[7]The sons of Cush:
   Seba, Havilah, Sabtah, Raamah and Sabteca.
The sons of Raamah:
   Sheba and Dedan.

[8]Cush was the father[h] of Nimrod, who grew to be a mighty warrior on the earth. [9]He was a mighty hunter before the LORD; that is why it is said, "Like Nimrod, a mighty hunter before the LORD." [10]The first centers of his kingdom were Babylon, Erech, Akkad and Calneh, in[i] Shinar.[j] [11]From that land he went to Assyria, where he built Nineveh, Rehoboth Ir,[k] Calah [12]and Resen, which is between Nineveh and Calah; that is the great city.

[13]Mizraim was the father of
   the Ludites, Anamites, Lehabites, Naphtuhites, [14]Pathrusites, Casluhites (from whom the Philistines came) and Caphtorites.
[15]Canaan was the father of
   Sidon his firstborn,[l] and of the Hittites, [16]Jebusites, Amorites, Girgashites, [17]Hivites, Arkites, Sinites, [18]Arvadites, Zemarites and Hamathites.

Later the Canaanite clans scattered [19]and the borders of Canaan reached from Sidon toward Gerar as far as Gaza,

---

[a]20 Or *soil, was the first*   [b]26 Or *be his slave*
[c]27 *Japheth* sounds like the Hebrew for *extend.*
[d]27 Or *their*   [e]2 *Sons* may mean *descendants* or *successors* or *nations;* also in verses 3, 4, 6, 7, 20-23, 29 and 31.   [f]4 Some manuscripts of the Masoretic Text and Samaritan Pentateuch (see also Septuagint and 1 Chron. 1:7); most manuscripts of the Masoretic Text *Dodanim*   [g]6 That is, Egypt; also in verse 13   [h]8 *Father* may mean *ancestor* or *predecessor* or *founder;* also in verses 13, 15, 24 and 26.   [i]10 Or *Erech and Akkad—all of them in*   [j]10 That is, Babylonia   [k]11 Or *Nineveh with its city squares*   [l]15 Or *of the Sidonians, the foremost*

and then toward Sodom, Gomorrah, Admah and Zeboiim, as far as Lasha.

²⁰These are the sons of Ham by their clans and languages, in their territories and nations.

The Semites

²¹Sons were also born to Shem, whose older brother was*ᵃ* Japheth; Shem was the ancestor of all the sons of Eber.

²²The sons of Shem:
    Elam, Asshur, Arphaxad, Lud and Aram.
²³The sons of Aram:
    Uz, Hul, Gether and Meshech.*ᵇ*
²⁴Arphaxad was the father of*ᶜ* Shelah, and Shelah the father of Eber.
²⁵Two sons were born to Eber:
    One was named Peleg,*ᵈ* because in his time the earth was divided; his brother was named Joktan.
²⁶Joktan was the father of
    Almodad, Sheleph, Hazarmaveth, Jerah, ²⁷Hadoram, Uzal, Diklah, ²⁸Obal, Abimael, Sheba, ²⁹Ophir, Havilah and Jobab. All these were sons of Joktan.

³⁰The region where they lived stretched from Mesha toward Sephar, in the eastern hill country.

³¹These are the sons of Shem by their clans and languages, in their territories and nations.

³²These are the clans of Noah's sons, according to their lines of descent, within their nations. From these the nations spread out over the earth after the flood.

The Tower of Babel

11 Now the whole world had one language and a common speech. ²As men moved eastward,*ᵉ* they found a plain in Shinar*ᶠ* and settled there.

³They said to each other, "Come, let's make bricks and bake them thoroughly." They used brick instead of stone, and tar for mortar. ⁴Then they said, "Come, let us build ourselves a city, with a tower that reaches to the heavens, so that we may make a name for ourselves and not be scattered over the face of the whole earth."

⁵But the LORD came down to see the city and the tower that the men were building. ⁶The LORD said, "If as one people speaking the same language they have begun to do this, then nothing they plan to do will be impossible for them. ⁷Come, let us go down and confuse their language so they will not understand each other."

⁸So the LORD scattered them from there over all the earth, and they stopped building the city. ⁹That is why it was called Babel*ᵍ*—because there the LORD confused the language of the whole world. From there the LORD scattered them over the face of the whole earth.

Hello?

Huh?

Genesis 11:9

Hola, konnichi wa, ciao, aloha—there are hundreds of ways to say "hi" in our world. This is all the result of a bunch of folks way back when who thought they were way too cool. One moment they were all chattin', and the next moment nobody could understand a word the next guy was saying. God confused the language because the people weren't looking to him for direction but were relying on themselves instead.

From Shem to Abram

¹⁰This is the account of Shem.

Two years after the flood, when Shem was 100 years old, he became the father*ʰ* of Arphaxad. ¹¹And after he became the father of Arphaxad, Shem lived 500 years and had other sons and daughters.

¹²When Arphaxad had lived 35 years,

ᵃ21 Or Shem, the older brother of *ᵇ23 See Septuagint and 1 Chron. 1:17; Hebrew Mash* *ᶜ24 Hebrew; Septuagint father of Cainan, and Cainan was the father of* *ᵈ25 Peleg means division.* *ᵉ2 Or from the east; or in the east* *ᶠ2 That is, Babylonia* *ᵍ9 That is, Babylon; Babel sounds like the Hebrew for confused.* *ʰ10 Father may mean ancestor; also in verses 11-25.*

he became the father of Shelah. [13]And after he became the father of Shelah, Arphaxad lived 403 years and had other sons and daughters.[a]

[14]When Shelah had lived 30 years, he became the father of Eber. [15]And after he became the father of Eber, Shelah lived 403 years and had other sons and daughters.

[16]When Eber had lived 34 years, he became the father of Peleg. [17]And after he became the father of Peleg, Eber lived 430 years and had other sons and daughters.

[18]When Peleg had lived 30 years, he became the father of Reu. [19]And after he became the father of Reu, Peleg lived 209 years and had other sons and daughters.

[20]When Reu had lived 32 years, he became the father of Serug. [21]And after he became the father of Serug, Reu lived 207 years and had other sons and daughters.

[a] *12,13* Hebrew; Septuagint (see also Luke 3:35, 36 and note at Gen. 10:24) *35 years, he became the father of Cainan.* *13And after he became the father of Cainan, Arphaxad lived 430 years and had other sons and daughters, and then he died. When Cainan had lived 130 years, he became the father of Shelah. And after he became the father of Shelah, Cainan lived 330 years and had other sons and daughters*

Weekend.

Family Ties

Read Ephesians 5:1; 6:1-4 (page 1429)

This week's devotions from Genesis prove that even in Bible times people struggled to get along with their families. Hasn't changed much in a few thousand years, has it? And you thought you were the only one frustrated with your little brother.

It might seem hopeless in your house sometimes, but God gave us families so we could take care of each other. Heather struggled with her brothers and sisters—but realized later that she loved them. Zack lied to his parents and was afraid of their response—but found out just how much they cared about him.

Living in a family takes some giving on everyone's part, including yours. "Honor your father and mother . . ." Ephesians says. (It also says "Fathers, do not exasperate your children . . ."—bet your parents never bring that verse up!) "Honoring" can be tough, especially if your mom and dad aren't perfect, which of course they aren't. But neither are you. So, honor them anyway. Think of one thing that your parents need to be honored for. Do they work hard to put food on the table? Do they try their best to provide clothes for you? You might need to think about it for awhile, but parents deserve some honor and respect from you for something they're doing. Remember that the Bible tells us to do it—and gives us a nice promise for the future if we follow the instructions.

What about You?

❶ Think of the ways your parents show you they care.

❷ Think of one thing you can do this weekend to help your parents—then do it!

❸ Ask God to help you remember to see your family as friends who take care of each other. Thank him for giving you people to live with and care about.

Turn to page 20 for your next devotion.

²²When Serug had lived 30 years, he became the father of Nahor. ²³And after he became the father of Nahor, Serug lived 200 years and had other sons and daughters.

²⁴When Nahor had lived 29 years, he became the father of Terah. ²⁵And after he became the father of Terah, Nahor lived 119 years and had other sons and daughters.

²⁶After Terah had lived 70 years, he became the father of Abram, Nahor and Haran.

²⁷This is the account of Terah.

Terah became the father of Abram, Nahor and Haran. And Haran became the father of Lot. ²⁸While his father Terah was still alive, Haran died in Ur of the Chaldeans, in the land of his birth. ²⁹Abram and Nahor both married. The name of Abram's wife was Sarai, and the name of Nahor's wife was Milcah; she was the daughter of Haran, the father of both Milcah and Iscah. ³⁰Now Sarai was barren; she had no children.

³¹Terah took his son Abram, his grandson Lot son of Haran, and his daughter-in-law Sarai, the wife of his son Abram, and together they set out from Ur of the Chaldeans to go to Canaan. But when they came to Haran, they settled there.
³²Terah lived 205 years, and he died in Haran.

The Call of Abram

12 The LORD had said to Abram, "Leave your country, your people and your father's household and go to the land I will show you.

² "I will make you into a great nation
    and I will bless you;
  I will make your name great,
    and you will be a blessing.
³ I will bless those who bless you,
    and whoever curses you I will
      curse;
  and all peoples on earth
    will be blessed through you."

⁴So Abram left, as the LORD had told him; and Lot went with him. Abram was seventy-five years old when he set out from Haran. ⁵He took his wife Sarai, his nephew Lot, all the possessions they had accumulated and the people they had acquired in Haran, and they set out for the land of Canaan, and they arrived there.

⁶Abram traveled through the land as far as the site of the great tree of Moreh at Shechem. At that time the Canaanites were in the land. ⁷The LORD appeared to Abram and said, "To your offspring*ᵃ* I will give this land." So he built an altar there to the LORD, who had appeared to him.

⁸From there he went on toward the hills east of Bethel and pitched his tent, with Bethel on the west and Ai on the east. There he built an altar to the LORD and called on the name of the LORD. ⁹Then Abram set out and continued toward the Negev.

Abram in Egypt

¹⁰Now there was a famine in the land, and Abram went down to Egypt to live there for a while because the famine was severe. ¹¹As he was about to enter Egypt, he said to his wife Sarai, "I know what a beautiful woman you are. ¹²When the Egyptians see you, they will say, 'This is his wife.' Then they will kill me but will let you live. ¹³Say you are my sister, so that I will be treated well for your sake and my life will be spared because of you."

¹⁴When Abram came to Egypt, the Egyptians saw that she was a very beautiful woman. ¹⁵And when Pharaoh's officials saw her, they praised her to Pharaoh, and she was taken into his palace. ¹⁶He treated Abram well for her sake, and Abram acquired sheep and cattle, male and female donkeys, menservants and maidservants, and camels.

¹⁷But the LORD inflicted serious diseases on Pharaoh and his household because of Abram's wife Sarai. ¹⁸So Pharaoh summoned Abram. "What have you done to me?" he said. "Why didn't you tell me she was your wife? ¹⁹Why did you say, 'She is my sister,' so that I took her to be my wife? Now then, here is your wife. Take her and go!" ²⁰Then Pharaoh gave orders about Abram to his men, and they sent him on his way, with his wife and everything he had.

ᵃ7 Or *seed*

Abram and Lot Separate

13 So Abram went up from Egypt to the Negev, with his wife and everything he had, and Lot went with him. ²Abram had become very wealthy in livestock and in silver and gold.

³From the Negev he went from place to place until he came to Bethel, to the place between Bethel and Ai where his tent had been earlier ⁴and where he had first built an altar. There Abram called on the name of the LORD.

⁵Now Lot, who was moving about with Abram, also had flocks and herds and tents. ⁶But the land could not support them while they stayed together, for their possessions were so great that they were not able to stay together. ⁷And quarreling arose between Abram's herdsmen and the herdsmen of Lot. The Canaanites and Perizzites were also living in the land at that time.

⁸So Abram said to Lot, "Let's not have any quarreling between you and me, or between your herdsmen and mine, for we are brothers. ⁹Is not the whole land before you? Let's part company. If you go to the left, I'll go to the right; if you go to the right, I'll go to the left."

¹⁰Lot looked up and saw that the whole plain of the Jordan was well watered, like the garden of the LORD, like the land of Egypt, toward Zoar. (This was before the LORD destroyed Sodom and Gomorrah.) ¹¹So Lot chose for himself the whole plain of the Jordan and set out toward the east. The two men parted company: ¹²Abram lived in the land of Canaan, while Lot lived among the cities of the plain and pitched his tents near Sodom. ¹³Now the men of Sodom were wicked and were sinning greatly against the LORD.

¹⁴The LORD said to Abram after Lot had parted from him, "Lift up your eyes from where you are and look north and south, east and west. ¹⁵All the land that you see I will give to you and your offspring*ᵃ* forever. ¹⁶I will make your offspring like the dust of the earth, so that if anyone could count the dust, then your offspring could be counted. ¹⁷Go, walk through the

ᵃ15 Or seed; also in verse 16

Monday

The Right Move
Read Genesis 12:1-7

I was really having trouble with some other students at my school, so my parents moved me to a different school. I think God helped my parents make this decision, because changing schools has been one of the best things that's ever happened to me. For once in my life I feel like I belong somewhere, and I'm actually happy to go to school.

Change can be scary, but change can also be really good. We can find the courage to make big changes by knowing God will be with us wherever we go. That's how Abram had the courage to move his family miles and miles away from home. He loved God, and God loved him. Abram knew God only wanted the best for him. God wants the best for every one of us. When we know that, we can be brave enough to do anything.

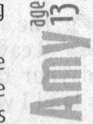
Amy age 13

What about You?

❶ What has been the biggest change in your life in the last year? How did God help you through it?

❷ Make a time line showing important changes in your life. When you finish, think about how God was with you through each change.

❸ Thank God for guiding you through life.

Turn to page 25 for your next devotion.

length and breadth of the land, for I am giving it to you."

[18]So Abram moved his tents and went to live near the great trees of Mamre at Hebron, where he built an altar to the LORD.

Abram Rescues Lot

14 At this time Amraphel king of Shinar,[a] Arioch king of Ellasar, Kedorlaomer king of Elam and Tidal king of Goiim [2]went to war against Bera king of Sodom, Birsha king of Gomorrah, Shinab king of Admah, Shemeber king of Zeboiim, and the king of Bela (that is, Zoar). [3]All these latter kings joined forces in the Valley of Siddim (the Salt Sea[b]). [4]For twelve years they had been subject to Kedorlaomer, but in the thirteenth year they rebelled.

[5]In the fourteenth year, Kedorlaomer and the kings allied with him went out and defeated the Rephaites in Ashteroth Karnaim, the Zuzites in Ham, the Emites in Shaveh Kiriathaim [6]and the Horites in the hill country of Seir, as far as El Paran near the desert. [7]Then they turned back and went to En Mishpat (that is, Kadesh), and they conquered the whole territory of the Amalekites, as well as the Amorites who were living in Hazazon Tamar.

[8]Then the king of Sodom, the king of Gomorrah, the king of Admah, the king of Zeboiim and the king of Bela (that is, Zoar) marched out and drew up their battle lines in the Valley of Siddim [9]against Kedorlaomer king of Elam, Tidal king of Goiim, Amraphel king of Shinar and Arioch king of Ellasar—four kings against five. [10]Now the Valley of Siddim was full of tar pits, and when the kings of Sodom and Gomorrah fled, some of the men fell into them and the rest fled to the hills. [11]The four kings seized all the goods of Sodom and Gomorrah and all their food; then they went away. [12]They also carried off Abram's nephew Lot and his possessions, since he was living in Sodom.

[13]One who had escaped came and reported this to Abram the Hebrew. Now Abram was living near the great trees of Mamre the Amorite, a brother[c] of Eshcol and Aner, all of whom were allied with Abram. [14]When Abram heard that his relative had been taken captive, he called out the 318 trained men born in his household and went in pursuit as far as Dan. [15]During the night Abram divided his men to attack them and he routed them, pursuing them as far as Hobah, north of Damascus. [16]He recovered all the goods and brought back his relative Lot and his possessions, together with the women and the other people.

[17]After Abram returned from defeating Kedorlaomer and the kings allied with him, the king of Sodom came out to meet him in the Valley of Shaveh (that is, the King's Valley).

[18]Then Melchizedek king of Salem[d] brought out bread and wine. He was priest of God Most High, [19]and he blessed Abram, saying,

"Blessed be Abram by God Most High,
   Creator[e] of heaven and earth.
[20]And blessed be[f] God Most High,
   who delivered your enemies into
      your hand."

Then Abram gave him a tenth of everything.

[21]The king of Sodom said to Abram, "Give me the people and keep the goods for yourself."

[22]But Abram said to the king of Sodom, "I have raised my hand to the LORD, God Most High, Creator of heaven and earth, and have taken an oath [23]that I will accept nothing belonging to you, not even a thread or the thong of a sandal, so that you will never be able to say, 'I made Abram rich.' [24]I will accept nothing but what my men have eaten and the share that belongs to the men who went with me—to Aner, Eshcol and Mamre. Let them have their share."

God's Covenant With Abram

15 After this, the word of the LORD came to Abram in a vision:

"Do not be afraid, Abram.
   I am your shield,[g]
   your very great reward.[h]"

---

[a]1 That is, Babylonia; also in verse 9   [b]3 That is, the Dead Sea   [c]13 Or *a relative*; or *an ally*   [d]18 That is, Jerusalem   [e]19 Or *Possessor*; also in verse 22   [f]20 Or *And praise be to*   [g]1 Or *sovereign*   [h]1 Or *shield; | your reward will be very great*

[2]But Abram said, "O Sovereign LORD, what can you give me since I remain childless and the one who will inherit[a] my estate is Eliezer of Damascus?" [3]And Abram said, "You have given me no children; so a servant in my household will be my heir."

[4]Then the word of the LORD came to him: "This man will not be your heir, but a son coming from your own body will be your heir." [5]He took him outside and said, "Look up at the heavens and count the stars—if indeed you can count them." Then he said to him, "So shall your offspring be."

[6]Abram believed the LORD, and he credited it to him as righteousness.

It's All Good

Huh?

Genesis 15:6

People often judge how good they are based on their actions. They add it up: *If I do more good than bad, then I am a good person.* But God doesn't look at it that way. With God it's not our actions that make us good; it's having a relationship with Jesus that counts. We shouldn't do good stuff to earn God's love or approval—we already have his approval if we accept Jesus' sacrifice. We are made right not by the good stuff we do but by having true faith in God. So doing good stuff is our way of saying a big thanks!

[7]He also said to him, "I am the LORD, who brought you out of Ur of the Chaldeans to give you this land to take possession of it."

[8]But Abram said, "O Sovereign LORD, how can I know that I will gain possession of it?"

[9]So the LORD said to him, "Bring me a heifer, a goat and a ram, each three years old, along with a dove and a young pigeon."

[10]Abram brought all these to him, cut them in two and arranged the halves opposite each other; the birds, however, he did not cut in half. [11]Then birds of prey

came down on the carcasses, but Abram drove them away.

[12]As the sun was setting, Abram fell into a deep sleep, and a thick and dreadful darkness came over him. [13]Then the LORD said to him, "Know for certain that your descendants will be strangers in a country not their own, and they will be enslaved and mistreated four hundred years. [14]But I will punish the nation they serve as slaves, and afterward they will come out with great possessions. [15]You, however, will go to your fathers in peace and be buried at a good old age. [16]In the fourth generation your descendants will come back here, for the sin of the Amorites has not yet reached its full measure."

[17]When the sun had set and darkness had fallen, a smoking firepot with a blazing torch appeared and passed between the pieces. [18]On that day the LORD made a covenant with Abram and said, "To your descendants I give this land, from the river[b] of Egypt to the great river, the Euphrates— [19]the land of the Kenites, Kenizzites, Kadmonites, [20]Hittites, Perizzites, Rephaites, [21]Amorites, Canaanites, Girgashites and Jebusites."

Hagar and Ishmael

16 Now Sarai, Abram's wife, had borne him no children. But she had an Egyptian maidservant named Hagar; [2]so she said to Abram, "The LORD has kept me from having children. Go, sleep with my maidservant; perhaps I can build a family through her."

Abram agreed to what Sarai said. [3]So after Abram had been living in Canaan ten years, Sarai his wife took her Egyptian maidservant Hagar and gave her to her husband to be his wife. [4]He slept with Hagar, and she conceived.

When she knew she was pregnant, she began to despise her mistress. [5]Then Sarai said to Abram, "You are responsible for the wrong I am suffering. I put my servant in your arms, and now that she knows she is pregnant, she despises me. May the LORD judge between you and me."

---

[a]2 The meaning of the Hebrew for this phrase is uncertain.   [b]18 Or *Wadi*

⁶"Your servant is in your hands," Abram said. "Do with her whatever you think best." Then Sarai mistreated Hagar; so she fled from her.

⁷The angel of the LORD found Hagar near a spring in the desert; it was the spring that is beside the road to Shur. ⁸And he said, "Hagar, servant of Sarai, where have you come from, and where are you going?"

"I'm running away from my mistress Sarai," she answered.

⁹Then the angel of the LORD told her, "Go back to your mistress and submit to her." ¹⁰The angel added, "I will so increase your descendants that they will be too numerous to count."

¹¹The angel of the LORD also said to her:

"You are now with child
    and you will have a son.
You shall name him Ishmael,ᵃ
    for the LORD has heard of your
        misery.
¹²He will be a wild donkey of a man;
    his hand will be against everyone
    and everyone's hand against him,
and he will live in hostility
    towardᵇ all his brothers."

¹³She gave this name to the LORD who spoke to her: "You are the God who sees me," for she said, "I have now seenᶜ the One who sees me." ¹⁴That is why the well was called Beer Lahai Roiᵈ; it is still there, between Kadesh and Bered.

¹⁵So Hagar bore Abram a son, and Abram gave the name Ishmael to the son she had borne. ¹⁶Abram was eighty-six years old when Hagar bore him Ishmael.

The Covenant of Circumcision

17 When Abram was ninety-nine years old, the LORD appeared to him and said, "I am God Almightyᵉ; walk before me and be blameless. ²I will confirm my covenant between me and you and will greatly increase your numbers."

³Abram fell facedown, and God said to him, ⁴"As for me, this is my covenant with you: You will be the father of many nations. ⁵No longer will you be called Abramᶠ; your name will be Abraham,ᵍ for I have made you a father of many na-

tions. ⁶I will make you very fruitful; I will make nations of you, and kings will come from you. ⁷I will establish my covenant as an everlasting covenant between me and you and your descendants after you for the generations to come, to be your God and the God of your descendants after you. ⁸The whole land of Canaan, where you are now an alien, I will give as an everlasting possession to you and your descendants after you; and I will be their God."

⁹Then God said to Abraham, "As for you, you must keep my covenant, you and your descendants after you for the generations to come. ¹⁰This is my covenant with you and your descendants after you, the covenant you are to keep: Every male among you shall be circumcised. ¹¹You are to undergo circumcision, and it will be the sign of the covenant between me and you. ¹²For the generations to come every male among you who is eight days old must be circumcised, including those born in your household or bought with money from a foreigner—those who are not your offspring. ¹³Whether born in your household or bought with your money, they must be circumcised. My covenant in your flesh is to be an everlasting covenant. ¹⁴Any uncircumcised male, who has not been circumcised in the flesh, will be cut off from his people; he has broken my covenant."

¹⁵God also said to Abraham, "As for Sarai your wife, you are no longer to call her Sarai; her name will be Sarah. ¹⁶I will bless her and will surely give you a son by her. I will bless her so that she will be the mother of nations; kings of peoples will come from her."

¹⁷Abraham fell facedown; he laughed and said to himself, "Will a son be born to a man a hundred years old? Will Sarah bear a child at the age of ninety?" ¹⁸And Abraham said to God, "If only Ishmael might live under your blessing!"

¹⁹Then God said, "Yes, but your wife Sarah will bear you a son, and you will

---

ᵃ11 *Ishmael* means *God hears.* ᵇ12 Or *live to the east / of* ᶜ13 Or *seen the back of* ᵈ14 *Beer Lahai Roi* means *well of the Living One who sees me.* ᵉ1 Hebrew *El-Shaddai* ᶠ5 *Abram* means *exalted father.* ᵍ5 *Abraham* means *father of many.*

call him Isaac.[a] I will establish my covenant with him as an everlasting covenant for his descendants after him. [20]And as for Ishmael, I have heard you: I will surely bless him; I will make him fruitful and will greatly increase his numbers. He will be the father of twelve rulers, and I will make him into a great nation. [21]But my covenant I will establish with Isaac, whom Sarah will bear to you by this time next year." [22]When he had finished speaking with Abraham, God went up from him.

[23]On that very day Abraham took his son Ishmael and all those born in his household or bought with his money, every male in his household, and circumcised them, as God told him. [24]Abraham was ninety-nine years old when he was circumcised, [25]and his son Ishmael was thirteen; [26]Abraham and his son Ishmael were both circumcised on that same day. [27]And every male in Abraham's household, including those born in his household or bought from a foreigner, was circumcised with him.

The Three Visitors

18 The LORD appeared to Abraham near the great trees of Mamre while he was sitting at the entrance to his tent in the heat of the day. [2]Abraham looked up and saw three men standing nearby. When he saw them, he hurried from the entrance of his tent to meet them and bowed low to the ground.

[3]He said, "If I have found favor in your eyes, my lord,[b] do not pass your servant by. [4]Let a little water be brought, and then you may all wash your feet and rest under this tree. [5]Let me get you something to eat, so you can be refreshed and then go on your way—now that you have come to your servant."

"Very well," they answered, "do as you say."

[6]So Abraham hurried into the tent to Sarah. "Quick," he said, "get three seahs[c] of fine flour and knead it and bake some bread."

[7]Then he ran to the herd and selected a choice, tender calf and gave it to a servant, who hurried to prepare it. [8]He then brought some curds and milk and the calf that had been prepared, and set these before them. While they ate, he stood near them under a tree.

[9]"Where is your wife Sarah?" they asked him.

"There, in the tent," he said.

[10]Then the LORD[d] said, "I will surely return to you about this time next year, and Sarah your wife will have a son."

Now Sarah was listening at the entrance to the tent, which was behind him. [11]Abraham and Sarah were already old and well advanced in years, and Sarah was past the age of childbearing. [12]So Sarah laughed to herself as she thought, "After I am worn out and my master[e] is old, will I now have this pleasure?"

[13]Then the LORD said to Abraham, "Why did Sarah laugh and say, 'Will I really have a child, now that I am old?' [14]Is anything too hard for the LORD? I will return to you at the appointed time next year and Sarah will have a son."

[15]Sarah was afraid, so she lied and said, "I did not laugh."

But he said, "Yes, you did laugh."

Abraham Pleads for Sodom

[16]When the men got up to leave, they looked down toward Sodom, and Abraham walked along with them to see them on their way. [17]Then the LORD said, "Shall I hide from Abraham what I am about to do? [18]Abraham will surely become a great and powerful nation, and all nations on earth will be blessed through him. [19]For I have chosen him, so that he will direct his children and his household after him to keep the way of the LORD by doing what is right and just, so that the LORD will bring about for Abraham what he has promised him."

[20]Then the LORD said, "The outcry against Sodom and Gomorrah is so great and their sin so grievous [21]that I will go down and see if what they have done is as bad as the outcry that has reached me. If not, I will know."

[22]The men turned away and went toward Sodom, but Abraham remained standing before the LORD.[f] [23]Then Abra-

---

[a] 19 Isaac means he laughs. [b] 3 Or O Lord [c] 6 That is, probably about 20 quarts (about 22 liters) [d] 10 Hebrew Then he [e] 12 Or husband [f] 22 Masoretic Text; an ancient Hebrew scribal tradition but the LORD remained standing before Abraham

ham approached him and said: "Will you sweep away the righteous with the wicked? [24]What if there are fifty righteous people in the city? Will you really sweep it away and not spare[a] the place for the sake of the fifty righteous people in it? [25]Far be it from you to do such a thing—to kill the righteous with the wicked, treating the righteous and the wicked alike. Far be it from you! Will not the Judge[b] of all the earth do right?"

[26]The LORD said, "If I find fifty righteous people in the city of Sodom, I will spare the whole place for their sake."

[27]Then Abraham spoke up again: "Now that I have been so bold as to speak to the Lord, though I am nothing but dust and ashes, [28]what if the number of the

righteous is five less than fifty? Will you destroy the whole city because of five people?"

"If I find forty-five there," he said, "I will not destroy it."

[29]Once again he spoke to him, "What if only forty are found there?"

He said, "For the sake of forty, I will not do it."

[30]Then he said, "May the Lord not be angry, but let me speak. What if only thirty can be found there?"

He answered, "I will not do it if I find thirty there."

[31]Abraham said, "Now that I have been so bold as to speak to the Lord, what if only twenty can be found there?"

[a]24 Or *forgive*; also in verse 26   [b]25 Or *Ruler*

Tuesday

His Word On It

Read Genesis 18:12-14

Sometimes it's easy to doubt that God is in control. When my little brother was born prematurely, he had a lot of health problems. One of the major problems was a hole in his heart. I didn't have much faith that God was really in control of the situation, because I was scared my brother might die. But God helped me see that nothing is out of his hands—not even a hole in the heart. Now my brother is 4 years old and doing fine.

I can understand why Sarah, Abraham's wife, doubted that she would have a child. After all, she was 90 years old! But God didn't think Sarah's old age was a problem, and he wasn't too happy with her unbelief. In verse 14, he asked Abraham, "Is anything too hard for the LORD?" Then God said he would come back in a year to visit Abraham and Sarah—and their new baby!

God wants us to trust him. When he makes a promise, he always keeps it. There are a ton of promises in the Bible that tell us God is in control of every situation. We know that's true, because we have his word on it.

❶ Even with all of God's promises in the Bible, why is it sometimes hard to trust God?

❷ On a piece of paper, write down something you're worried about right now. At the bottom of the page write, "God, I trust you to take care of this problem." Put the paper in your Bible or dresser drawer. When you feel God has helped you through this problem, take out the paper and write "THANK YOU!" across the center of the page.

❸ Thank God for taking care of the people and things you're concerned about.

Turn to page 30 for your next devotion.

He said, "For the sake of twenty, I will not destroy it."

³²Then he said, "May the Lord not be angry, but let me speak just once more. What if only ten can be found there?"

He answered, "For the sake of ten, I will not destroy it."

³³When the LORD had finished speaking with Abraham, he left, and Abraham returned home.

Sodom and Gomorrah Destroyed

19 The two angels arrived at Sodom in the evening, and Lot was sitting in the gateway of the city. When he saw them, he got up to meet them and bowed down with his face to the ground. ²"My lords," he said, "please turn aside to your servant's house. You can wash your feet and spend the night and then go on your way early in the morning."

"No," they answered, "we will spend the night in the square."

³But he insisted so strongly that they did go with him and entered his house. He prepared a meal for them, baking bread without yeast, and they ate. ⁴Before they had gone to bed, all the men from every part of the city of Sodom—both young and old—surrounded the house. ⁵They called to Lot, "Where are the men who came to you tonight? Bring them out to us so that we can have sex with them."

⁶Lot went outside to meet them and shut the door behind him ⁷and said, "No, my friends. Don't do this wicked thing. ⁸Look, I have two daughters who have never slept with a man. Let me bring them out to you, and you can do what you like with them. But don't do anything to these men, for they have come under the protection of my roof."

⁹"Get out of our way," they replied. And they said, "This fellow came here as an alien, and now he wants to play the judge! We'll treat you worse than them." They kept bringing pressure on Lot and moved forward to break down the door.

¹⁰But the men inside reached out and pulled Lot back into the house and shut the door. ¹¹Then they struck the men who were at the door of the house, young and old, with blindness so that they could not find the door.

¹²The two men said to Lot, "Do you have anyone else here—sons-in-law, sons or daughters, or anyone else in the city who belongs to you? Get them out of here, ¹³because we are going to destroy this place. The outcry to the LORD against its people is so great that he has sent us to destroy it."

¹⁴So Lot went out and spoke to his sons-in-law, who were pledged to marry*a* his daughters. He said, "Hurry and get out of this place, because the LORD is about to destroy the city!" But his sons-in-law thought he was joking.

¹⁵With the coming of dawn, the angels urged Lot, saying, "Hurry! Take your wife and your two daughters who are here, or you will be swept away when the city is punished."

¹⁶When he hesitated, the men grasped his hand and the hands of his wife and of his two daughters and led them safely out of the city, for the LORD was merciful to them. ¹⁷As soon as they had brought them out, one of them said, "Flee for your lives! Don't look back, and don't stop anywhere in the plain! Flee to the mountains or you will be swept away!"

¹⁸But Lot said to them, "No, my lords,*b* please! ¹⁹Your*c* servant has found favor in your*c* eyes, and you*c* have shown great kindness to me in sparing my life. But I can't flee to the mountains; this disaster will overtake me, and I'll die. ²⁰Look, here is a town near enough to run to, and it is small. Let me flee to it—it is very small, isn't it? Then my life will be spared."

²¹He said to him, "Very well, I will grant this request too; I will not overthrow the town you speak of. ²²But flee there quickly, because I cannot do anything until you reach it." (That is why the town was called Zoar.*d*)

²³By the time Lot reached Zoar, the sun had risen over the land. ²⁴Then the LORD rained down burning sulfur on Sodom and Gomorrah—from the LORD out of the heavens. ²⁵Thus he overthrew those cities

---

a 14 Or were married to   b 18 Or No, Lord; or No, my lord   c 19 The Hebrew is singular.   d 22 Zoar means small.

and the entire plain, including all those living in the cities—and also the vegetation in the land. ²⁶But Lot's wife looked back, and she became a pillar of salt.

²⁷Early the next morning Abraham got up and returned to the place where he had stood before the LORD. ²⁸He looked down toward Sodom and Gomorrah, toward all the land of the plain, and he saw dense smoke rising from the land, like smoke from a furnace.

²⁹So when God destroyed the cities of the plain, he remembered Abraham, and he brought Lot out of the catastrophe that overthrew the cities where Lot had lived.

Lot and His Daughters

³⁰Lot and his two daughters left Zoar and settled in the mountains, for he was afraid to stay in Zoar. He and his two daughters lived in a cave. ³¹One day the older daughter said to the younger, "Our father is old, and there is no man around here to lie with us, as is the custom all over the earth. ³²Let's get our father to drink wine and then lie with him and preserve our family line through our father."

³³That night they got their father to drink wine, and the older daughter went in and lay with him. He was not aware of it when she lay down or when she got up.

³⁴The next day the older daughter said to the younger, "Last night I lay with my father. Let's get him to drink wine again tonight, and you go in and lie with him so we can preserve our family line through our father." ³⁵So they got their father to drink wine that night also, and the younger daughter went and lay with him. Again he was not aware of it when she lay down or when she got up.

³⁶So both of Lot's daughters became pregnant by their father. ³⁷The older daughter had a son, and she named him Moab*a*; he is the father of the Moabites of today. ³⁸The younger daughter also had a son, and she named him Ben-Ammi*b*; he is the father of the Ammonites of today.

Abraham and Abimelech

20 Now Abraham moved on from there into the region of the Negev and lived between Kadesh and Shur. For a while he stayed in Gerar, ²and there Abraham said of his wife Sarah, "She is my sister." Then Abimelech king of Gerar sent for Sarah and took her.

³But God came to Abimelech in a dream one night and said to him, "You are as good as dead because of the woman you have taken; she is a married woman."

⁴Now Abimelech had not gone near her, so he said, "Lord, will you destroy an innocent nation? ⁵Did he not say to me, 'She is my sister,' and didn't she also say, 'He is my brother'? I have done this with a clear conscience and clean hands."

⁶Then God said to him in the dream, "Yes, I know you did this with a clear conscience, and so I have kept you from sinning against me. That is why I did not let you touch her. ⁷Now return the man's wife, for he is a prophet, and he will pray for you and you will live. But if you do not return her, you may be sure that you and all yours will die."

⁸Early the next morning Abimelech summoned all his officials, and when he told them all that had happened, they were very much afraid. ⁹Then Abimelech called Abraham in and said, "What have you done to us? How have I wronged you that you have brought such great guilt upon me and my kingdom? You have done things to me that should not be done." ¹⁰And Abimelech asked Abraham, "What was your reason for doing this?"

¹¹Abraham replied, "I said to myself, 'There is surely no fear of God in this place, and they will kill me because of my wife.' ¹²Besides, she really is my sister, the daughter of my father though not of my mother; and she became my wife. ¹³And when God had me wander from my father's household, I said to her, 'This is how you can show your love to me: Everywhere we go, say of me, "He is my brother." ' "

¹⁴Then Abimelech brought sheep and cattle and male and female slaves and gave them to Abraham, and he returned Sarah his wife to him. ¹⁵And Abimelech said, "My land is before you; live wherever you like."

---

a37 Moab sounds like the Hebrew for *from father.*
b38 Ben-Ammi means *son of my people.*

¹⁶To Sarah he said, "I am giving your brother a thousand shekels*ᵃ* of silver. This is to cover the offense against you before all who are with you; you are completely vindicated."

¹⁷Then Abraham prayed to God, and God healed Abimelech, his wife and his slave girls so they could have children again, ¹⁸for the LORD had closed up every womb in Abimelech's household because of Abraham's wife Sarah.

The Birth of Isaac

21 Now the LORD was gracious to Sarah as he had said, and the LORD did for Sarah what he had promised. ²Sarah became pregnant and bore a son to Abraham in his old age, at the very time God had promised him. ³Abraham gave the name Isaac*ᵇ* to the son Sarah bore him. ⁴When his son Isaac was eight days old, Abraham circumcised him, as God commanded him. ⁵Abraham was a hundred years old when his son Isaac was born to him.

⁶Sarah said, "God has brought me laughter, and everyone who hears about this will laugh with me." ⁷And she added, "Who would have said to Abraham that Sarah would nurse children? Yet I have borne him a son in his old age."

Hagar and Ishmael Sent Away

⁸The child grew and was weaned, and on the day Isaac was weaned Abraham held a great feast. ⁹But Sarah saw that the son whom Hagar the Egyptian had borne to Abraham was mocking, ¹⁰and she said to Abraham, "Get rid of that slave woman and her son, for that slave woman's son will never share in the inheritance with my son Isaac."

¹¹The matter distressed Abraham greatly because it concerned his son. ¹²But God said to him, "Do not be so distressed about the boy and your maidservant. Listen to whatever Sarah tells you, because it is through Isaac that your offspring*ᶜ* will be reckoned. ¹³I will make the son of the maidservant into a nation also, because he is your offspring."

¹⁴Early the next morning Abraham took some food and a skin of water and gave them to Hagar. He set them on her shoulders and then sent her off with the boy. She went on her way and wandered in the desert of Beersheba.

¹⁵When the water in the skin was gone, she put the boy under one of the bushes. ¹⁶Then she went off and sat down nearby, about a bowshot away, for she thought, "I cannot watch the boy die." And as she sat there nearby, she*ᵈ* began to sob.

¹⁷God heard the boy crying, and the angel of God called to Hagar from heaven and said to her, "What is the matter, Hagar? Do not be afraid; God has heard the boy crying as he lies there. ¹⁸Lift the boy up and take him by the hand, for I will make him into a great nation."

¹⁹Then God opened her eyes and she saw a well of water. So she went and filled the skin with water and gave the boy a drink.

²⁰God was with the boy as he grew up. He lived in the desert and became an archer. ²¹While he was living in the Desert of Paran, his mother got a wife for him from Egypt.

The Treaty at Beersheba

²²At that time Abimelech and Phicol the commander of his forces said to Abraham, "God is with you in everything you do. ²³Now swear to me here before God that you will not deal falsely with me or my children or my descendants. Show to me and the country where you are living as an alien the same kindness I have shown to you."

²⁴Abraham said, "I swear it."

²⁵Then Abraham complained to Abimelech about a well of water that Abimelech's servants had seized. ²⁶But Abimelech said, "I don't know who has done this. You did not tell me, and I heard about it only today."

²⁷So Abraham brought sheep and cattle and gave them to Abimelech, and the two men made a treaty. ²⁸Abraham set apart seven ewe lambs from the flock, ²⁹and Abimelech asked Abraham, "What is the meaning of these seven ewe lambs you have set apart by themselves?"

³⁰He replied, "Accept these seven lambs

ᵃ16 That is, about 25 pounds (about 11.5 kilograms)
ᵇ3 Isaac means *he laughs.*   *ᶜ12* Or *seed*
ᵈ16 Hebrew; Septuagint *the child*

from my hand as a witness that I dug this well."

³¹So that place was called Beersheba,ᵃ because the two men swore an oath there.

³²After the treaty had been made at Beersheba, Abimelech and Phicol the commander of his forces returned to the land of the Philistines. ³³Abraham planted a tamarisk tree in Beersheba, and there he called upon the name of the LORD, the Eternal God. ³⁴And Abraham stayed in the land of the Philistines for a long time.

Abraham Tested

22 Some time later God tested Abraham. He said to him, "Abraham!"

"Here I am," he replied.

²Then God said, "Take your son, your only son, Isaac, whom you love, and go to the region of Moriah. Sacrifice him there as a burnt offering on one of the mountains I will tell you about."

³Early the next morning Abraham got up and saddled his donkey. He took with him two of his servants and his son Isaac. When he had cut enough wood for the burnt offering, he set out for the place God had told him about. ⁴On the third day Abraham looked up and saw the place in the distance. ⁵He said to his servants, "Stay here with the donkey while I and the boy go over there. We will worship and then we will come back to you."

⁶Abraham took the wood for the burnt offering and placed it on his son Isaac, and he himself carried the fire and the knife. As the two of them went on together, ⁷Isaac spoke up and said to his father Abraham, "Father?"

"Yes, my son?" Abraham replied.

"The fire and wood are here," Isaac said, "but where is the lamb for the burnt offering?"

⁸Abraham answered, "God himself will provide the lamb for the burnt offering, my son." And the two of them went on together.

⁹When they reached the place God had told him about, Abraham built an altar there and arranged the wood on it. He bound his son Isaac and laid him on the altar, on top of the wood. ¹⁰Then he reached out his hand and took the knife

Finally a Substitute I Like

Huh?

Genesis 22:7, 13–14

In school when your teacher is absent you have a substitute. The sub takes the place of your teacher for the day (duh). The lamb was kind of like that for the people of Israel. The lamb's death was a substitute for the death the Israelites deserved because of sin. In the New Testament, Jesus is called the Lamb of God (John 1:19, 36, page 1267). He is our Lamb. Jesus' death on the cross was the substitute for us, taking the death we deserve.

to slay his son. ¹¹But the angel of the LORD called out to him from heaven, "Abraham! Abraham!"

"Here I am," he replied.

¹²"Do not lay a hand on the boy," he said. "Do not do anything to him. Now I know that you fear God, because you have not withheld from me your son, your only son."

¹³Abraham looked up and there in a thicket he saw a ramᵇ caught by its horns. He went over and took the ram and sacrificed it as a burnt offering instead of his son. ¹⁴So Abraham called that place The LORD Will Provide. And to this day it is said, "On the mountain of the LORD it will be provided."

¹⁵The angel of the LORD called to Abraham from heaven a second time ¹⁶and said, "I swear by myself, declares the LORD, that because you have done this and have not withheld your son, your only son, ¹⁷I will surely bless you and make your descendants as numerous as the stars in the sky and as the sand on the seashore. Your descendants will take possession of the cities of their enemies, ¹⁸and through your offspringᶜ all nations on earth will be blessed, because you have obeyed me."

ᵃ31 Beersheba can mean well of seven or well of the oath. ᵇ13 Many manuscripts of the Masoretic Text, Samaritan Pentateuch, Septuagint and Syriac; most manuscripts of the Masoretic Text a ram behind him. ᶜ18 Or seed

¹⁹Then Abraham returned to his servants, and they set off together for Beersheba. And Abraham stayed in Beersheba.

Nahor's Sons

²⁰Some time later Abraham was told, "Milcah is also a mother; she has borne sons to your brother Nahor: ²¹Uz the firstborn, Buz his brother, Kemuel (the father of Aram), ²²Kesed, Hazo, Pildash, Jidlaph and Bethuel." ²³Bethuel became the father of Rebekah. Milcah bore these eight sons to Abraham's brother Nahor. ²⁴His concubine, whose name was Reumah, also had sons: Tebah, Gaham, Tahash and Maacah.

The Death of Sarah

23 Sarah lived to be a hundred and twenty-seven years old. ²She died at Kiriath Arba (that is, Hebron) in the land of Canaan, and Abraham went to mourn for Sarah and to weep over her.

³Then Abraham rose from beside his dead wife and spoke to the Hittites.ᵃ He said, ⁴"I am an alien and a stranger among you. Sell me some property for a burial site here so I can bury my dead."

⁵The Hittites replied to Abraham, ⁶"Sir, listen to us. You are a mighty prince among us. Bury your dead in the choicest of our tombs. None of us will refuse you his tomb for burying your dead."

⁷Then Abraham rose and bowed down before the people of the land, the Hittites. ⁸He said to them, "If you are willing to let me bury my dead, then listen to me and intercede with Ephron son of Zohar on

ᵃ3 Or *the sons of Heth*; also in verses 5, 7, 10, 16, 18 and 20

Wednesday

The Hardest Test

Read Genesis 22:2

As a Christian, I need to be brave and obey God no matter what the risk might be. Maybe other kids will make fun of me. Maybe I won't understand what God wants me to do—he does work in mysterious ways sometimes. Maybe I'll have to give up what I want to do because God wants me to do something else. But if Abraham could trust God enough to obey his command about Isaac, I know I can too.

I do need to remember, though, that Abraham had known God a long time already when God tested him with Isaac. So even though Abraham might have thought God's command was crazy, he'd seen that God had been right so many times that he knew God couldn't be wrong this time. I don't know if I would have been brave enough to obey, but maybe that's because I don't know God as well as Abraham did. The more time I spend reading my Bible and praying, the more I learn to trust God and follow him. He really does want what's best for me.

 Lisa, age 13

 **What about You?**

❶ Think about a time when it was hard to trust in God, but you did it anyway. What did you learn from this experience?

❷ Memorize Psalm 118:6: "The LORD is with me; I will not be afraid. What can man do to me?" Use it to help you trust God when you are scared.

❸ Ask God for the strength to trust and obey him no matter what.

Turn to page 36 for your next devotion.

my behalf ⁹so he will sell me the cave of Machpelah, which belongs to him and is at the end of his field. Ask him to sell it to me for the full price as a burial site among you."

¹⁰Ephron the Hittite was sitting among his people and he replied to Abraham in the hearing of all the Hittites who had come to the gate of his city. ¹¹"No, my lord," he said. "Listen to me; I give*a* you the field, and I give*a* you the cave that is in it. I give*a* it to you in the presence of my people. Bury your dead."

¹²Again Abraham bowed down before the people of the land ¹³and he said to Ephron in their hearing, "Listen to me, if you will. I will pay the price of the field. Accept it from me so I can bury my dead there."

¹⁴Ephron answered Abraham, ¹⁵"Listen to me, my lord; the land is worth four hundred shekels*b* of silver, but what is that between me and you? Bury your dead."

¹⁶Abraham agreed to Ephron's terms and weighed out for him the price he had named in the hearing of the Hittites: four hundred shekels of silver, according to the weight current among the merchants.

¹⁷So Ephron's field in Machpelah near Mamre—both the field and the cave in it, and all the trees within the borders of the field—was deeded ¹⁸to Abraham as his property in the presence of all the Hittites who had come to the gate of the city. ¹⁹Afterward Abraham buried his wife Sarah in the cave in the field of Machpelah near Mamre (which is at Hebron) in the land of Canaan. ²⁰So the field and the cave in it were deeded to Abraham by the Hittites as a burial site.

Isaac and Rebekah

24 Abraham was now old and well advanced in years, and the LORD had blessed him in every way. ²He said to the chief*c* servant in his household, the one in charge of all that he had, "Put your hand under my thigh. ³I want you to swear by the LORD, the God of heaven and the God of earth, that you will not get a wife for my son from the daughters of the Canaanites, among whom I am living, ⁴but will go to my country and my

own relatives and get a wife for my son Isaac."

⁵The servant asked him, "What if the woman is unwilling to come back with me to this land? Shall I then take your son back to the country you came from?"

⁶"Make sure that you do not take my son back there," Abraham said. ⁷"The LORD, the God of heaven, who brought me out of my father's household and my native land and who spoke to me and promised me on oath, saying, 'To your offspring*d* I will give this land'—he will send his angel before you so that you can get a wife for my son from there. ⁸If the woman is unwilling to come back with you, then you will be released from this oath of mine. Only do not take my son back there." ⁹So the servant put his hand under the thigh of his master Abraham and swore an oath to him concerning this matter.

¹⁰Then the servant took ten of his master's camels and left, taking with him all kinds of good things from his master. He set out for Aram Naharaim*e* and made his way to the town of Nahor. ¹¹He had the camels kneel down near the well outside the town; it was toward evening, the time the women go out to draw water.

¹²Then he prayed, "O LORD, God of my master Abraham, give me success today, and show kindness to my master Abraham. ¹³See, I am standing beside this spring, and the daughters of the townspeople are coming out to draw water. ¹⁴May it be that when I say to a girl, 'Please let down your jar that I may have a drink,' and she says, 'Drink, and I'll water your camels too'—let her be the one you have chosen for your servant Isaac. By this I will know that you have shown kindness to my master."

¹⁵Before he had finished praying, Rebekah came out with her jar on her shoulder. She was the daughter of Bethuel son of Milcah, who was the wife of Abraham's brother Nahor. ¹⁶The girl was very beautiful, a virgin; no man had ever lain with her. She went down to the spring, filled her jar and came up again.

a11 Or sell   b15 That is, about 10 pounds (about 4.5 kilograms)   c2 Or oldest   d7 Or seed   e10 That is, Northwest Mesopotamia

[17]The servant hurried to meet her and said, "Please give me a little water from your jar."

[18]"Drink, my lord," she said, and quickly lowered the jar to her hands and gave him a drink.

[19]After she had given him a drink, she said, "I'll draw water for your camels too, until they have finished drinking." [20]So she quickly emptied her jar into the trough, ran back to the well to draw more water, and drew enough for all his camels. [21]Without saying a word, the man watched her closely to learn whether or not the LORD had made his journey successful.

[22]When the camels had finished drinking, the man took out a gold nose ring weighing a beka[a] and two gold bracelets weighing ten shekels.[b] [23]Then he asked, "Whose daughter are you? Please tell me, is there room in your father's house for us to spend the night?"

[24]She answered him, "I am the daughter of Bethuel, the son that Milcah bore to Nahor." [25]And she added, "We have plenty of straw and fodder, as well as room for you to spend the night."

[26]Then the man bowed down and worshiped the LORD, [27]saying, "Praise be to the LORD, the God of my master Abraham, who has not abandoned his kindness and faithfulness to my master. As for me, the LORD has led me on the journey to the house of my master's relatives."

[28]The girl ran and told her mother's household about these things. [29]Now Rebekah had a brother named Laban, and he hurried out to the man at the spring. [30]As soon as he had seen the nose ring, and the bracelets on his sister's arms, and had heard Rebekah tell what the man said to her, he went out to the man and found him standing by the camels near the spring. [31]"Come, you who are blessed by the LORD," he said. "Why are you standing out here? I have prepared the house and a place for the camels."

[32]So the man went to the house, and the camels were unloaded. Straw and fodder were brought for the camels, and water for him and his men to wash their feet. [33]Then food was set before him, but he said, "I will not eat until I have told you what I have to say."

"Then tell us," ˌLabanˌ said.

[34]So he said, "I am Abraham's servant. [35]The LORD has blessed my master abundantly, and he has become wealthy. He has given him sheep and cattle, silver and gold, menservants and maidservants, and camels and donkeys. [36]My master's wife Sarah has borne him a son in her[c] old age, and he has given him everything he owns. [37]And my master made me swear an oath, and said, 'You must not get a wife for my son from the daughters of the Canaanites, in whose land I live, [38]but go to my father's family and to my own clan, and get a wife for my son.'

[39]"Then I asked my master, 'What if the woman will not come back with me?'

[40]"He replied, 'The LORD, before whom I have walked, will send his angel with you and make your journey a success, so that you can get a wife for my son from my own clan and from my father's family. [41]Then, when you go to my clan, you will be released from my oath even if they refuse to give her to you—you will be released from my oath.'

[42]"When I came to the spring today, I said, 'O LORD, God of my master Abraham, if you will, please grant success to the journey on which I have come. [43]See, I am standing beside this spring; if a maiden comes out to draw water and I say to her, "Please let me drink a little water from your jar," [44]and if she says to me, "Drink, and I'll draw water for your camels too," let her be the one the LORD has chosen for my master's son.'

[45]"Before I finished praying in my heart, Rebekah came out, with her jar on her shoulder. She went down to the spring and drew water, and I said to her, 'Please give me a drink.'

[46]"She quickly lowered her jar from her shoulder and said, 'Drink, and I'll water your camels too.' So I drank, and she watered the camels also.

[47]"I asked her, 'Whose daughter are you?'

"She said, 'The daughter of Bethuel son of Nahor, whom Milcah bore to him.'

---

[a]22 That is, about 1/5 ounce (about 5.5 grams)
[b]22 That is, about 4 ounces (about 110 grams)
[c]36 Or his

"Then I put the ring in her nose and the bracelets on her arms, [48]and I bowed down and worshiped the LORD. I praised the LORD, the God of my master Abraham, who had led me on the right road to get the granddaughter of my master's brother for his son. [49]Now if you will show kindness and faithfulness to my master, tell me; and if not, tell me, so I may know which way to turn."

[50]Laban and Bethuel answered, "This is from the LORD; we can say nothing to you one way or the other. [51]Here is Rebekah; take her and go, and let her become the wife of your master's son, as the LORD has directed."

[52]When Abraham's servant heard what they said, he bowed down to the ground before the LORD. [53]Then the servant brought out gold and silver jewelry and articles of clothing and gave them to Rebekah; he also gave costly gifts to her brother and to her mother. [54]Then he and the men who were with him ate and drank and spent the night there.

When they got up the next morning, he said, "Send me on my way to my master."

[55]But her brother and her mother replied, "Let the girl remain with us ten days or so; then you[a] may go."

[56]But he said to them, "Do not detain me, now that the LORD has granted success to my journey. Send me on my way so I may go to my master."

[57]Then they said, "Let's call the girl and ask her about it." [58]So they called Rebekah and asked her, "Will you go with this man?"

"I will go," she said.

[59]So they sent their sister Rebekah on her way, along with her nurse and Abraham's servant and his men. [60]And they blessed Rebekah and said to her,

"Our sister, may you increase
   to thousands upon thousands;
may your offspring possess
   the gates of their enemies."

[61]Then Rebekah and her maids got ready and mounted their camels and went back with the man. So the servant took Rebekah and left.

[62]Now Isaac had come from Beer Lahai Roi, for he was living in the Negev. [63]He went out to the field one evening to meditate,[b] and as he looked up, he saw camels approaching. [64]Rebekah also looked up and saw Isaac. She got down from her camel [65]and asked the servant, "Who is that man in the field coming to meet us?"

"He is my master," the servant answered. So she took her veil and covered herself.

[66]Then the servant told Isaac all he had done. [67]Isaac brought her into the tent of his mother Sarah, and he married Rebekah. So she became his wife, and he loved her; and Isaac was comforted after his mother's death.

The Death of Abraham

25 Abraham took[c] another wife, whose name was Keturah. [2]She bore him Zimran, Jokshan, Medan, Midian, Ishbak and Shuah. [3]Jokshan was the father of Sheba and Dedan; the descendants of Dedan were the Asshurites, the Letushites and the Leummites. [4]The sons of Midian were Ephah, Epher, Hanoch, Abida and Eldaah. All these were descendants of Keturah.

[5]Abraham left everything he owned to Isaac. [6]But while he was still living, he gave gifts to the sons of his concubines and sent them away from his son Isaac to the land of the east.

[7]Altogether, Abraham lived a hundred and seventy-five years. [8]Then Abraham breathed his last and died at a good old age, an old man and full of years; and he was gathered to his people. [9]His sons Isaac and Ishmael buried him in the cave of Machpelah near Mamre, in the field of Ephron son of Zohar the Hittite, [10]the field Abraham had bought from the Hittites.[d] There Abraham was buried with his wife Sarah. [11]After Abraham's death, God blessed his son Isaac, who then lived near Beer Lahai Roi.

Ishmael's Sons

[12]This is the account of Abraham's son Ishmael, whom Sarah's maidservant, Hagar the Egyptian, bore to Abraham.

---

[a]55 Or *she*   [b]63 The meaning of the Hebrew for this word is uncertain.   [c]1 Or *had taken*   [d]10 Or *the sons of Heth*

[13]These are the names of the sons of Ishmael, listed in the order of their birth: Nebaioth the firstborn of Ishmael, Kedar, Adbeel, Mibsam, [14]Mishma, Dumah, Massa, [15]Hadad, Tema, Jetur, Naphish and Kedemah. [16]These were the sons of Ishmael, and these are the names of the twelve tribal rulers according to their settlements and camps. [17]Altogether, Ishmael lived a hundred and thirty-seven years. He breathed his last and died, and he was gathered to his people. [18]His descendants settled in the area from Havilah to Shur, near the border of Egypt, as you go toward Asshur. And they lived in hostility toward[a] all their brothers.

Jacob and Esau

[19]This is the account of Abraham's son Isaac.

Abraham became the father of Isaac, [20]and Isaac was forty years old when he married Rebekah daughter of Bethuel the Aramean from Paddan Aram[b] and sister of Laban the Aramean.

[21]Isaac prayed to the LORD on behalf of his wife, because she was barren. The LORD answered his prayer, and his wife Rebekah became pregnant. [22]The babies jostled each other within her, and she said, "Why is this happening to me?" So she went to inquire of the LORD.

[23]The LORD said to her,

"Two nations are in your womb,
   and two peoples from within you
      will be separated;
one people will be stronger than the
      other,
   and the older will serve the
      younger."

[24]When the time came for her to give birth, there were twin boys in her womb. [25]The first to come out was red, and his whole body was like a hairy garment; so they named him Esau.[c] [26]After this, his brother came out, with his hand grasping Esau's heel; so he was named Jacob.[d] Isaac was sixty years old when Rebekah gave birth to them.

[27]The boys grew up, and Esau became a skillful hunter, a man of the open country, while Jacob was a quiet man, staying among the tents. [28]Isaac, who had a taste for wild game, loved Esau, but Rebekah loved Jacob.

[29]Once when Jacob was cooking some stew, Esau came in from the open country, famished. [30]He said to Jacob, "Quick, let me have some of that red stew! I'm famished!" (That is why he was also called Edom.[e])

[31]Jacob replied, "First sell me your birthright."

[32]"Look, I am about to die," Esau said. "What good is the birthright to me?"

[33]But Jacob said, "Swear to me first." So he swore an oath to him, selling his birthright to Jacob.

[34]Then Jacob gave Esau some bread and some lentil stew. He ate and drank, and then got up and left.

So Esau despised his birthright.

Isaac and Abimelech

26 Now there was a famine in the land—besides the earlier famine of Abraham's time—and Isaac went to Abimelech king of the Philistines in Gerar. [2]The LORD appeared to Isaac and said, "Do not go down to Egypt; live in the land where I tell you to live. [3]Stay in this land for a while, and I will be with you and will bless you. For to you and your descendants I will give all these lands and will confirm the oath I swore to your father Abraham. [4]I will make your descendants as numerous as the stars in the sky and will give them all these lands, and through your offspring[f] all nations on earth will be blessed, [5]because Abraham obeyed me and kept my requirements, my commands, my decrees and my laws." [6]So Isaac stayed in Gerar.

[7]When the men of that place asked him about his wife, he said, "She is my sister," because he was afraid to say, "She is my wife." He thought, "The men of this place might kill me on account of Rebekah, because she is beautiful."

[8]When Isaac had been there a long time, Abimelech king of the Philistines looked down from a window and saw Isaac caressing his wife Rebekah. [9]So

---

[a]18 Or *lived to the east of*   [b]20 That is, Northwest Mesopotamia   [c]25 *Esau* may mean *hairy*; he was also called Edom, which means *red*.   [d]26 *Jacob* means *he grasps the heel* (figuratively, *he deceives*).   [e]30 *Edom* means red.   [f]4 Or *seed*

Abimelech summoned Isaac and said, "She is really your wife! Why did you say, 'She is my sister'?"

Isaac answered him, "Because I thought I might lose my life on account of her."

[10]Then Abimelech said, "What is this you have done to us? One of the men might well have slept with your wife, and you would have brought guilt upon us."

[11]So Abimelech gave orders to all the people: "Anyone who molests this man or his wife shall surely be put to death."

[12]Isaac planted crops in that land and the same year reaped a hundredfold, because the LORD blessed him. [13]The man became rich, and his wealth continued to grow until he became very wealthy. [14]He had so many flocks and herds and servants that the Philistines envied him. [15]So all the wells that his father's servants had dug in the time of his father Abraham, the Philistines stopped up, filling them with earth.

[16]Then Abimelech said to Isaac, "Move away from us; you have become too powerful for us."

[17]So Isaac moved away from there and encamped in the Valley of Gerar and settled there. [18]Isaac reopened the wells that had been dug in the time of his father Abraham, which the Philistines had stopped up after Abraham died, and he gave them the same names his father had given them.

[19]Isaac's servants dug in the valley and discovered a well of fresh water there. [20]But the herdsmen of Gerar quarreled with Isaac's herdsmen and said, "The water is ours!" So he named the well Esek,[a] because they disputed with him. [21]Then they dug another well, but they quarreled over that one also; so he named it Sitnah.[b] [22]He moved on from there and dug another well, and no one quarreled over it. He named it Rehoboth,[c] saying, "Now the LORD has given us room and we will flourish in the land."

[23]From there he went up to Beersheba. [24]That night the LORD appeared to him and said, "I am the God of your father Abraham. Do not be afraid, for I am with you; I will bless you and will increase the number of your descendants for the sake of my servant Abraham."

[25]Isaac built an altar there and called on the name of the LORD. There he pitched his tent, and there his servants dug a well.

[26]Meanwhile, Abimelech had come to him from Gerar, with Ahuzzath his personal adviser and Phicol the commander of his forces. [27]Isaac asked them, "Why have you come to me, since you were hostile to me and sent me away?"

[28]They answered, "We saw clearly that the LORD was with you; so we said, 'There ought to be a sworn agreement between us'—between us and you. Let us make a treaty with you [29]that you will do us no harm, just as we did not molest you but always treated you well and sent you away in peace. And now you are blessed by the LORD."

[30]Isaac then made a feast for them, and they ate and drank. [31]Early the next morning the men swore an oath to each other. Then Isaac sent them on their way, and they left him in peace.

[32]That day Isaac's servants came and told him about the well they had dug. They said, "We've found water!" [33]He called it Shibah,[d] and to this day the name of the town has been Beersheba.[e]

[34]When Esau was forty years old, he married Judith daughter of Beeri the Hittite, and also Basemath daughter of Elon the Hittite. [35]They were a source of grief to Isaac and Rebekah.

Jacob Gets Isaac's Blessing

27 When Isaac was old and his eyes were so weak that he could no longer see, he called for Esau his older son and said to him, "My son."

"Here I am," he answered.

[2]Isaac said, "I am now an old man and don't know the day of my death. [3]Now then, get your weapons—your quiver and bow—and go out to the open country to hunt some wild game for me. [4]Prepare me the kind of tasty food I like and bring it to me to eat, so that I may give you my blessing before I die."

[5]Now Rebekah was listening as Isaac

---

[a]20 *Esek* means *dispute.*   [b]21 *Sitnah* means *opposition.*   [c]22 *Rehoboth* means *room.*   [d]33 *Shibah* can mean *oath* or *seven.*   [e]33 *Beersheba* can mean *well of the oath* or *well of seven.*

spoke to his son Esau. When Esau left for the open country to hunt game and bring it back, [6]Rebekah said to her son Jacob, "Look, I overheard your father say to your brother Esau, [7]'Bring me some game and prepare me some tasty food to eat, so that I may give you my blessing in the presence of the LORD before I die.' [8]Now, my son, listen carefully and do what I tell you: [9]Go out to the flock and bring me two choice young goats, so I can prepare some tasty food for your father, just the way he likes it. [10]Then take it to your father to eat, so that he may give you his blessing before he dies."

[11]Jacob said to Rebekah his mother, "But my brother Esau is a hairy man, and I'm a man with smooth skin. [12]What if my father touches me? I would appear to be tricking him and would bring down a curse on myself rather than a blessing."

[13]His mother said to him, "My son, let the curse fall on me. Just do what I say; go and get them for me."

[14]So he went and got them and brought them to his mother, and she prepared some tasty food, just the way his father liked it. [15]Then Rebekah took the best clothes of Esau her older son, which she had in the house, and put them on her younger son Jacob. [16]She also covered his hands and the smooth part of his neck with the goatskins. [17]Then she handed to her son Jacob the tasty food and the bread she had made.

Thursday

Biting Off More Than You Can Chew

Read Genesis 27

My little brother isn't allowed to eat cookies, because he has this habit of sneaking them when he's not supposed to. I know it doesn't sound like a big deal, but he has a bad reaction to sugar whenever he eats too much of it. Well, one time he ate over half a package of Oreos. Talk about a sugar rush! When my parents asked him about it, he lied and told them he hadn't eaten the cookies. But finally he told them the truth. As punishment, my parents wouldn't let him eat any dessert for a week. I'm not sure what my brother learned, but I realized that it doesn't pay to deceive people.

In Genesis 27, Jacob pretended to be his older brother Esau so he could get the blessing from their father Isaac. And he did get the blessing! But Jacob lost his brother's trust. In fact, Esau swore he would kill Jacob, and Jacob had to flee the country.

That's the way lying is—it's easy to do, and sometimes you get what you want out of it. But in the end, you find yourself stuck in a bigger mess than you know how to get out of. You might turn people against you when they find out what you did. Worst of all, you make God unhappy. Lying won't get you anywhere.

Megan age 14

❶ When are you tempted to lie or cheat? What can you do to avoid giving in?

❷ Think of a recent lie you told. What were the consequences, if any? What would have been different if you'd told the truth?

❸ Ask God to help you be honest, even when it's hard. Thank him for his grace when you make mistakes.

Turn to page 45 for your next devotion.

¹⁸He went to his father and said, "My father."

"Yes, my son," he answered. "Who is it?"

¹⁹Jacob said to his father, "I am Esau your firstborn. I have done as you told me. Please sit up and eat some of my game so that you may give me your blessing."

²⁰Isaac asked his son, "How did you find it so quickly, my son?"

"The LORD your God gave me success," he replied.

²¹Then Isaac said to Jacob, "Come near so I can touch you, my son, to know whether you really are my son Esau or not."

²²Jacob went close to his father Isaac, who touched him and said, "The voice is the voice of Jacob, but the hands are the hands of Esau." ²³He did not recognize him, for his hands were hairy like those of his brother Esau; so he blessed him. ²⁴"Are you really my son Esau?" he asked.

"I am," he replied.

²⁵Then he said, "My son, bring me some of your game to eat, so that I may give you my blessing."

Jacob brought it to him and he ate; and he brought some wine and he drank. ²⁶Then his father Isaac said to him, "Come here, my son, and kiss me."

²⁷So he went to him and kissed him. When Isaac caught the smell of his clothes, he blessed him and said,

"Ah, the smell of my son
    is like the smell of a field
    that the LORD has blessed.
²⁸May God give you of heaven's dew
    and of earth's richness—
    an abundance of grain and new
      wine.
²⁹May nations serve you
    and peoples bow down to you.
Be lord over your brothers,
    and may the sons of your mother
      bow down to you.
May those who curse you be cursed
    and those who bless you be
      blessed."

³⁰After Isaac finished blessing him and Jacob had scarcely left his father's presence, his brother Esau came in from hunting. ³¹He too prepared some tasty food and brought it to his father. Then he said to him, "My father, sit up and eat some of my game, so that you may give me your blessing."

³²His father Isaac asked him, "Who are you?"

"I am your son," he answered, "your firstborn, Esau."

³³Isaac trembled violently and said, "Who was it, then, that hunted game and brought it to me? I ate it just before you came and I blessed him—and indeed he will be blessed!"

³⁴When Esau heard his father's words, he burst out with a loud and bitter cry and said to his father, "Bless me—me too, my father!"

³⁵But he said, "Your brother came deceitfully and took your blessing."

³⁶Esau said, "Isn't he rightly named Jacob[a]? He has deceived me these two times: He took my birthright, and now he's taken my blessing!" Then he asked, "Haven't you reserved any blessing for me?"

³⁷Isaac answered Esau, "I have made him lord over you and have made all his relatives his servants, and I have sustained him with grain and new wine. So what can I possibly do for you, my son?"

³⁸Esau said to his father, "Do you have only one blessing, my father? Bless me too, my father!" Then Esau wept aloud.

³⁹His father Isaac answered him,

"Your dwelling will be
    away from the earth's richness,
    away from the dew of heaven
      above.
⁴⁰You will live by the sword
    and you will serve your brother.
But when you grow restless,
    you will throw his yoke
      from off your neck."

Jacob Flees to Laban

⁴¹Esau held a grudge against Jacob because of the blessing his father had given him. He said to himself, "The days of mourning for my father are near; then I will kill my brother Jacob."

⁴²When Rebekah was told what her

---

a36 Jacob means *he grasps the heel* (figuratively, *he deceives*).

older son Esau had said, she sent for her younger son Jacob and said to him, "Your brother Esau is consoling himself with the thought of killing you. [43]Now then, my son, do what I say: Flee at once to my brother Laban in Haran. [44]Stay with him for a while until your brother's fury subsides. [45]When your brother is no longer angry with you and forgets what you did to him, I'll send word for you to come back from there. Why should I lose both of you in one day?"

[46]Then Rebekah said to Isaac, "I'm disgusted with living because of these Hittite women. If Jacob takes a wife from among the women of this land, from Hittite women like these, my life will not be worth living."

28 So Isaac called for Jacob and blessed[a] him and commanded him: "Do not marry a Canaanite woman. [2]Go at once to Paddan Aram,[b] to the house of your mother's father Bethuel. Take a wife for yourself there, from among the daughters of Laban, your mother's brother. [3]May God Almighty[c] bless you and make you fruitful and increase your numbers until you become a community of peoples. [4]May he give you and your descendants the blessing given to Abraham, so that you may take possession of the land where you now live as an alien, the land God gave to Abraham." [5]Then Isaac sent Jacob on his way, and he went to Paddan Aram, to Laban son of Bethuel the Aramean, the brother of Rebekah, who was the mother of Jacob and Esau.

[6]Now Esau learned that Isaac had blessed Jacob and had sent him to Paddan Aram to take a wife from there, and that when he blessed him he commanded him, "Do not marry a Canaanite woman," [7]and that Jacob had obeyed his father and mother and had gone to Paddan Aram. [8]Esau then realized how displeasing the Canaanite women were to his father Isaac; [9]so he went to Ishmael and married Mahalath, the sister of Nebaioth and daughter of Ishmael son of Abraham, in addition to the wives he already had.

Jacob's Dream at Bethel

[10]Jacob left Beersheba and set out for Haran. [11]When he reached a certain place,

he stopped for the night because the sun had set. Taking one of the stones there, he put it under his head and lay down to sleep. [12]He had a dream in which he saw a stairway[d] resting on the earth, with its top reaching to heaven, and the angels of God were ascending and descending on it. [13]There above it[e] stood the LORD, and he said: "I am the LORD, the God of your father Abraham and the God of Isaac. I will give you and your descendants the land on which you are lying. [14]Your descendants will be like the dust of the earth, and you will spread out to the west and to the east, to the north and to the south. All peoples on earth will be blessed through you and your offspring. [15]I am with you and will watch over you wherever you go, and I will bring you back to this land. I will not leave you until I have done what I have promised you."

[16]When Jacob awoke from his sleep, he thought, "Surely the LORD is in this place, and I was not aware of it." [17]He was afraid and said, "How awesome is this place! This is none other than the house of God; this is the gate of heaven."

[18]Early the next morning Jacob took the stone he had placed under his head and set it up as a pillar and poured oil on top of it. [19]He called that place Bethel,[f] though the city used to be called Luz. [20]Then Jacob made a vow, saying, "If God will be with me and will watch over me on this journey I am taking and will give me food to eat and clothes to wear [21]so that I return safely to my father's house, then the LORD[g] will be my God [22]and[h] this stone that I have set up as a pillar will be God's house, and of all that you give me I will give you a tenth."

Jacob Arrives in Paddan Aram

29 Then Jacob continued on his journey and came to the land of the eastern peoples. [2]There he saw a well in the field, with three flocks of sheep lying near it because the flocks were wa-

---

[a]1 Or greeted　[b]2 That is, Northwest Mesopotamia; also in verses 5, 6 and 7　[c]3 Hebrew El-Shaddai
[d]12 Or ladder　[e]13 Or There beside him　[f]19 Bethel means house of God.　[g]20,21 Or Since God . . . father's house, the LORD　[h]21,22 Or house, and the LORD will be my God, [22]then

tered from that well. The stone over the mouth of the well was large. ³When all the flocks were gathered there, the shepherds would roll the stone away from the well's mouth and water the sheep. Then they would return the stone to its place over the mouth of the well.

⁴Jacob asked the shepherds, "My brothers, where are you from?"

"We're from Haran," they replied.

⁵He said to them, "Do you know Laban, Nahor's grandson?"

"Yes, we know him," they answered.

⁶Then Jacob asked them, "Is he well?"

"Yes, he is," they said, "and here comes his daughter Rachel with the sheep."

⁷"Look," he said, "the sun is still high; it is not time for the flocks to be gathered. Water the sheep and take them back to pasture."

⁸"We can't," they replied, "until all the flocks are gathered and the stone has been rolled away from the mouth of the well. Then we will water the sheep."

⁹While he was still talking with them, Rachel came with her father's sheep, for she was a shepherdess. ¹⁰When Jacob saw Rachel daughter of Laban, his mother's brother, and Laban's sheep, he went over and rolled the stone away from the mouth of the well and watered his uncle's sheep. ¹¹Then Jacob kissed Rachel and began to weep aloud. ¹²He had told Rachel that he was a relative of her father and a son of Rebekah. So she ran and told her father.

¹³As soon as Laban heard the news about Jacob, his sister's son, he hurried to meet him. He embraced him and kissed him and brought him to his home, and there Jacob told him all these things. ¹⁴Then Laban said to him, "You are my own flesh and blood."

Jacob Marries Leah and Rachel

After Jacob had stayed with him for a whole month, ¹⁵Laban said to him, "Just because you are a relative of mine, should you work for me for nothing? Tell me what your wages should be."

¹⁶Now Laban had two daughters; the name of the older was Leah, and the name of the younger was Rachel. ¹⁷Leah had weak[a] eyes, but Rachel was lovely in form, and beautiful. ¹⁸Jacob was in love

with Rachel and said, "I'll work for you seven years in return for your younger daughter Rachel."

Love Struck

Genesis 29:16–30 Yeah, it's true. Sometimes love hurts. Take the major crush Jacob had on Rachel. When Jacob first saw Rachel, he told her dad, "I'll work for you for 7 years if you'll let me marry Rachel." Her dad agreed but then secretly "switched" brides on Jacob so he ended up marrying Rachel's sister instead. Jacob was ticked, but he agreed to work for seven *more* years to marry Rachel.

Jacob wasn't the only person in the Bible who was willing to do almost anything for love:

✗ Rebekah left her family and followed a stranger to a faraway land to marry Isaac, a man she'd never met (Genesis 24)

✗ Ruth slept at Boaz's feet all night to impress him (Ruth 3—4)

✗ Hosea followed God's command and married a prostitute named Gomer to demonstrate God's love (Hosea 1—3)

¹⁹Laban said, "It's better that I give her to you than to some other man. Stay here with me." ²⁰So Jacob served seven years to get Rachel, but they seemed like only a few days to him because of his love for her.

²¹Then Jacob said to Laban, "Give me my wife. My time is completed, and I want to lie with her."

²²So Laban brought together all the people of the place and gave a feast. ²³But when evening came, he took his daughter Leah and gave her to Jacob, and Jacob lay with her. ²⁴And Laban

---

ᵃ17 Or *delicate*

gave his servant girl Zilpah to his daughter as her maidservant.

²⁵When morning came, there was Leah! So Jacob said to Laban, "What is this you have done to me? I served you for Rachel, didn't I? Why have you deceived me?"

²⁶Laban replied, "It is not our custom here to give the younger daughter in marriage before the older one. ²⁷Finish this daughter's bridal week; then we will give you the younger one also, in return for another seven years of work."

²⁸And Jacob did so. He finished the week with Leah, and then Laban gave him his daughter Rachel to be his wife. ²⁹Laban gave his servant girl Bilhah to his daughter Rachel as her maidservant. ³⁰Jacob lay with Rachel also, and he loved Rachel more than Leah. And he worked for Laban another seven years.

Jacob's Children

³¹When the LORD saw that Leah was not loved, he opened her womb, but Rachel was barren. ³²Leah became pregnant and gave birth to a son. She named him Reuben,ᵃ for she said, "It is because the LORD has seen my misery. Surely my husband will love me now."

³³She conceived again, and when she gave birth to a son she said, "Because the LORD heard that I am not loved, he gave me this one too." So she named him Simeon.ᵇ

³⁴Again she conceived, and when she gave birth to a son she said, "Now at last my husband will become attached to me, because I have borne him three sons." So he was named Levi.ᶜ

³⁵She conceived again, and when she gave birth to a son she said, "This time I will praise the LORD." So she named him Judah.ᵈ Then she stopped having children.

ᵃ32 *Reuben* sounds like the Hebrew for *he has seen my misery*; the name means *see, a son.* ᵇ33 *Simeon* probably means *one who hears.* ᶜ34 *Levi* sounds like and may be derived from the Hebrew for *attached.* ᵈ35 *Judah* sounds like and may be derived from the Hebrew for *praise.*

Most Embarrassing Moments

Don't you just hate it when you get caught saying or doing something stupid? It happens to everyone—including some pretty famous people in the Old Testament.

What's that you say? God puts the ambitious builders of a certain tower in their place. One moment, they're conversing just fine. The next, no one can understand a word anyone else is saying. "I asked for a hammer, not a *ham sandwich!*" (see Genesis 11:1–9).

Surprise, Sweetie! Jacob is in love with Rachel. They decide to get married. Jacob wakes up the morning after the wedding, looks closely at the person beside him and screams. Turns out he *didn't* marry Rachel. He married Rachel's sister *Leah*. Oops (see Genesis 29:20–25).

You forgot something! Joseph's boss is pretty impressed with him and puts him in charge of the boss's house. The boss's wife likes Joe too . . . but in another way. She tries to seduce him by ripping off his clothes.

Joseph streaks out of the house leaving his coat behind (see Genesis 39:6–12).

Get off my back! When Balaam's donkey wisely makes a detour to avoid certain death, Balaam beats her. She tells him to knock it off. Balaam looks pretty silly talking to a donkey. And he looks absolutely stupid when it becomes clear that the donkey is smarter than he is (see Numbers 22:21–32, page 183).

What's the problem—is your god asleep? Elijah conducts a contest: Elijah and the real, living God versus a bunch of clueless prophets and their made-up god, Baal. First deity to show up wins. When Baal fails to make an appearance, Elijah taunts the Baal-worshipers, then asks God to show 'em his stuff (see 1 Kings 18:20–39, page 411).

30 When Rachel saw that she was not bearing Jacob any children, she became jealous of her sister. So she said to Jacob, "Give me children, or I'll die!"

²Jacob became angry with her and said, "Am I in the place of God, who has kept you from having children?"

³Then she said, "Here is Bilhah, my maidservant. Sleep with her so that she can bear children for me and that through her I too can build a family."

⁴So she gave him her servant Bilhah as a wife. Jacob slept with her, ⁵and she became pregnant and bore him a son. ⁶Then Rachel said, "God has vindicated me; he has listened to my plea and given me a son." Because of this she named him Dan.ᵃ

⁷Rachel's servant Bilhah conceived again and bore Jacob a second son. ⁸Then Rachel said, "I have had a great struggle with my sister, and I have won." So she named him Naphtali.ᵇ

⁹When Leah saw that she had stopped having children, she took her maidservant Zilpah and gave her to Jacob as a wife. ¹⁰Leah's servant Zilpah bore Jacob a son. ¹¹Then Leah said, "What good fortune!"ᶜ So she named him Gad.ᵈ

¹²Leah's servant Zilpah bore Jacob a second son. ¹³Then Leah said, "How happy I am! The women will call me happy." So she named him Asher.ᵉ

¹⁴During wheat harvest, Reuben went out into the fields and found some mandrake plants, which he brought to his mother Leah. Rachel said to Leah, "Please give me some of your son's mandrakes."

¹⁵But she said to her, "Wasn't it enough that you took away my husband? Will you take my son's mandrakes too?"

"Very well," Rachel said, "he can sleep with you tonight in return for your son's mandrakes."

¹⁶So when Jacob came in from the fields that evening, Leah went out to meet him. "You must sleep with me," she said. "I have hired you with my son's mandrakes." So he slept with her that night.

¹⁷God listened to Leah, and she became pregnant and bore Jacob a fifth son. ¹⁸Then Leah said, "God has rewarded me for giving my maidservant to my husband." So she named him Issachar.ᶠ

¹⁹Leah conceived again and bore Jacob a sixth son. ²⁰Then Leah said, "God has presented me with a precious gift. This time my husband will treat me with honor, because I have borne him six sons." So she named him Zebulun.ᵍ

²¹Some time later she gave birth to a daughter and named her Dinah.

²²Then God remembered Rachel; he listened to her and opened her womb. ²³She became pregnant and gave birth to a son and said, "God has taken away my disgrace." ²⁴She named him Joseph,ʰ and said, "May the LORD add to me another son."

Jacob's Flocks Increase

²⁵After Rachel gave birth to Joseph, Jacob said to Laban, "Send me on my way so I can go back to my own homeland. ²⁶Give me my wives and children, for whom I have served you, and I will be on my way. You know how much work I've done for you."

²⁷But Laban said to him, "If I have found favor in your eyes, please stay. I have learned by divination thatⁱ the LORD has blessed me because of you." ²⁸He added, "Name your wages, and I will pay them."

²⁹Jacob said to him, "You know how I have worked for you and how your livestock has fared under my care. ³⁰The little you had before I came has increased greatly, and the LORD has blessed you wherever I have been. But now, when may I do something for my own household?"

³¹"What shall I give you?" he asked.

"Don't give me anything," Jacob replied. "But if you will do this one thing for me, I will go on tending your flocks and watching over them: ³²Let me go through all your flocks today and remove from them every speckled or spotted sheep, every dark-colored lamb and every spotted or speckled goat. They will be my wages. ³³And my honesty will

---

ᵃ6 *Dan* here means *he has vindicated.* ᵇ8 *Naphtali* means *my struggle.* ᶜ11 Or *"A troop is coming!"* ᵈ11 *Gad* can mean *good fortune* or *a troop.* ᵉ13 *Asher* means *happy.* ᶠ18 *Issachar* sounds like the Hebrew for *reward.* ᵍ20 *Zebulun* probably means *honor.* ʰ24 *Joseph* means *may he add.* ⁱ27 Or possibly *have become rich and*

testify for me in the future, whenever you check on the wages you have paid me. Any goat in my possession that is not speckled or spotted, or any lamb that is not dark-colored, will be considered stolen."

³⁴"Agreed," said Laban. "Let it be as you have said." ³⁵That same day he removed all the male goats that were streaked or spotted, and all the speckled or spotted female goats (all that had white on them) and all the dark-colored lambs, and he placed them in the care of his sons. ³⁶Then he put a three-day journey between himself and Jacob, while Jacob continued to tend the rest of Laban's flocks.

³⁷Jacob, however, took fresh-cut branches from poplar, almond and plane trees and made white stripes on them by peeling the bark and exposing the white inner wood of the branches. ³⁸Then he placed the peeled branches in all the watering troughs, so that they would be directly in front of the flocks when they came to drink. When the flocks were in heat and came to drink, ³⁹they mated in front of the branches. And they bore young that were streaked or speckled or spotted. ⁴⁰Jacob set apart the young of the flock by themselves, but made the rest face the streaked and dark-colored animals that belonged to Laban. Thus he made separate flocks for himself and did not put them with Laban's animals. ⁴¹Whenever the stronger females were in heat, Jacob would place the branches in the troughs in front of the animals so they would mate near the branches, ⁴²but if the animals were weak, he would not place them there. So the weak animals went to Laban and the strong ones to Jacob. ⁴³In this way the man grew exceedingly prosperous and came to own large flocks, and maidservants and menservants, and camels and donkeys.

Jacob Flees From Laban

31 Jacob heard that Laban's sons were saying, "Jacob has taken everything our father owned and has gained all this wealth from what belonged to our father." ²And Jacob noticed that Laban's attitude toward him was not what it had been.

³Then the LORD said to Jacob, "Go back to the land of your fathers and to your relatives, and I will be with you."

⁴So Jacob sent word to Rachel and Leah to come out to the fields where his flocks were. ⁵He said to them, "I see that your father's attitude toward me is not what it was before, but the God of my father has been with me. ⁶You know that I've worked for your father with all my strength, ⁷yet your father has cheated me by changing my wages ten times. However, God has not allowed him to harm me. ⁸If he said, 'The speckled ones will be your wages,' then all the flocks gave birth to speckled young; and if he said, 'The streaked ones will be your wages,' then all the flocks bore streaked young. ⁹So God has taken away your father's livestock and has given them to me.

¹⁰"In breeding season I once had a dream in which I looked up and saw that the male goats mating with the flock were streaked, speckled or spotted. ¹¹The angel of God said to me in the dream, 'Jacob.' I answered, 'Here I am.' ¹²And he said, 'Look up and see that all the male goats mating with the flock are streaked, speckled or spotted, for I have seen all that Laban has been doing to you. ¹³I am the God of Bethel, where you anointed a pillar and where you made a vow to me. Now leave this land at once and go back to your native land.'"

¹⁴Then Rachel and Leah replied, "Do we still have any share in the inheritance of our father's estate? ¹⁵Does he not regard us as foreigners? Not only has he sold us, but he has used up what was paid for us. ¹⁶Surely all the wealth that God took away from our father belongs to us and our children. So do whatever God has told you."

¹⁷Then Jacob put his children and his wives on camels, ¹⁸and he drove all his livestock ahead of him, along with all the goods he had accumulated in Paddan Aram,ᵃ to go to his father Isaac in the land of Canaan.

¹⁹When Laban had gone to shear his sheep, Rachel stole her father's household gods. ²⁰Moreover, Jacob deceived Laban the Aramean by not telling him he

ᵃ18 That is, Northwest Mesopotamia

was running away. [21]So he fled with all he had, and crossing the River,[a] he headed for the hill country of Gilead.

Laban Pursues Jacob

[22]On the third day Laban was told that Jacob had fled. [23]Taking his relatives with him, he pursued Jacob for seven days and caught up with him in the hill country of Gilead. [24]Then God came to Laban the Aramean in a dream at night and said to him, "Be careful not to say anything to Jacob, either good or bad."

[25]Jacob had pitched his tent in the hill country of Gilead when Laban overtook him, and Laban and his relatives camped there too. [26]Then Laban said to Jacob, "What have you done? You've deceived me, and you've carried off my daughters like captives in war. [27]Why did you run off secretly and deceive me? Why didn't you tell me, so I could send you away with joy and singing to the music of tambourines and harps? [28]You didn't even let me kiss my grandchildren and my daughters good-by. You have done a foolish thing. [29]I have the power to harm you; but last night the God of your father said to me, 'Be careful not to say anything to Jacob, either good or bad.' [30]Now you have gone off because you longed to return to your father's house. But why did you steal my gods?"

[31]Jacob answered Laban, "I was afraid, because I thought you would take your daughters away from me by force. [32]But if you find anyone who has your gods, he shall not live. In the presence of our relatives, see for yourself whether there is anything of yours here with me; and if so, take it." Now Jacob did not know that Rachel had stolen the gods.

[33]So Laban went into Jacob's tent and into Leah's tent and into the tent of the two maidservants, but he found nothing. After he came out of Leah's tent, he entered Rachel's tent. [34]Now Rachel had taken the household gods and put them inside her camel's saddle and was sitting on them. Laban searched through everything in the tent but found nothing.

[35]Rachel said to her father, "Don't be angry, my lord, that I cannot stand up in your presence; I'm having my period."

So he searched but could not find the household gods.

[36]Jacob was angry and took Laban to task. "What is my crime?" he asked Laban. "What sin have I committed that you hunt me down? [37]Now that you have searched through all my goods, what have you found that belongs to your household? Put it here in front of your relatives and mine, and let them judge between the two of us.

[38]"I have been with you for twenty years now. Your sheep and goats have not miscarried, nor have I eaten rams from your flocks. [39]I did not bring you animals torn by wild beasts; I bore the loss myself. And you demanded payment from me for whatever was stolen by day or night. [40]This was my situation: The heat consumed me in the daytime and the cold at night, and sleep fled from my eyes. [41]It was like this for the twenty years I was in your household. I worked for you fourteen years for your two daughters and six years for your flocks, and you changed my wages ten times. [42]If the God of my father, the God of Abraham and the Fear of Isaac, had not been with me, you would surely have sent me away empty-handed. But God has seen my hardship and the toil of my hands, and last night he rebuked you."

[43]Laban answered Jacob, "The women are my daughters, the children are my children, and the flocks are my flocks. All you see is mine. Yet what can I do today about these daughters of mine, or about the children they have borne? [44]Come now, let's make a covenant, you and I, and let it serve as a witness between us."

[45]So Jacob took a stone and set it up as a pillar. [46]He said to his relatives, "Gather some stones." So they took stones and piled them in a heap, and they ate there by the heap. [47]Laban called it Jegar Sahadutha,[b] and Jacob called it Galeed.[c]

[48]Laban said, "This heap is a witness between you and me today." That is why it was called Galeed. [49]It was also called Mizpah,[d] because he said, "May the LORD

---

[a]21 That is, the Euphrates   [b]47 The Aramaic *Jegar Sahadutha* means *witness heap.*   [c]47 The Hebrew *Galeed* means *witness heap.*   [d]49 *Mizpah* means *watchtower.*

keep watch between you and me when we are away from each other. ⁵⁰If you mistreat my daughters or if you take any wives besides my daughters, even though no one is with us, remember that God is a witness between you and me."

⁵¹Laban also said to Jacob, "Here is this heap, and here is this pillar I have set up between you and me. ⁵²This heap is a witness, and this pillar is a witness, that I will not go past this heap to your side to harm you and that you will not go past this heap and pillar to my side to harm me. ⁵³May the God of Abraham and the God of Nahor, the God of their father, judge between us."

So Jacob took an oath in the name of the Fear of his father Isaac. ⁵⁴He offered a sacrifice there in the hill country and invited his relatives to a meal. After they had eaten, they spent the night there.

⁵⁵Early the next morning Laban kissed his grandchildren and his daughters and blessed them. Then he left and returned home.

Jacob Prepares to Meet Esau

32 Jacob also went on his way, and the angels of God met him. ²When Jacob saw them, he said, "This is the camp of God!" So he named that place Mahanaim.ᵃ

³Jacob sent messengers ahead of him to his brother Esau in the land of Seir, the country of Edom. ⁴He instructed them: "This is what you are to say to my master Esau: 'Your servant Jacob says, I have been staying with Laban and have remained there till now. ⁵I have cattle and donkeys, sheep and goats, menservants and maidservants. Now I am sending this message to my lord, that I may find favor in your eyes.'"

⁶When the messengers returned to Jacob, they said, "We went to your brother Esau, and now he is coming to meet you, and four hundred men are with him."

⁷In great fear and distress Jacob divided the people who were with him into two groups,ᵇ and the flocks and herds and camels as well. ⁸He thought, "If Esau comes and attacks one group,ᶜ the groupᶜ that is left may escape."

⁹Then Jacob prayed, "O God of my father Abraham, God of my father Isaac,

He's Down for the Count

Huh?

Genesis 32:24

What was Jacob thinking, getting into a wrestling match like this? Who in their right mind would want to take on God! Jacob wanted a blessing from God and was willing to go to the mat for it. Jacob received the blessing from God along with a new name, Israel, which means, "he struggles with God."

O LORD, who said to me, 'Go back to your country and your relatives, and I will make you prosper,' ¹⁰I am unworthy of all the kindness and faithfulness you have shown your servant. I had only my staff when I crossed this Jordan, but now I have become two groups. ¹¹Save me, I pray, from the hand of my brother Esau, for I am afraid he will come and attack me, and also the mothers with their children. ¹²But you have said, 'I will surely make you prosper and will make your descendants like the sand of the sea, which cannot be counted.'"

¹³He spent the night there, and from what he had with him he selected a gift for his brother Esau: ¹⁴two hundred female goats and twenty male goats, two hundred ewes and twenty rams, ¹⁵thirty female camels with their young, forty cows and ten bulls, and twenty female donkeys and ten male donkeys. ¹⁶He put them in the care of his servants, each herd by itself, and said to his servants, "Go ahead of me, and keep some space between the herds."

¹⁷He instructed the one in the lead: "When my brother Esau meets you and asks, 'To whom do you belong, and where are you going, and who owns all these animals in front of you?' ¹⁸then you are to say, 'They belong to your servant Jacob. They are a gift sent to my lord Esau, and he is coming behind us.'"

ᵃ2 Mahanaim means two camps.   ᵇ7 Or camps; also in verse 10   ᶜ8 Or camp

¹⁹He also instructed the second, the third and all the others who followed the herds: "You are to say the same thing to Esau when you meet him. ²⁰And be sure to say, 'Your servant Jacob is coming behind us.' " For he thought, "I will pacify him with these gifts I am sending on ahead; later, when I see him, perhaps he will receive me." ²¹So Jacob's gifts went on ahead of him, but he himself spent the night in the camp.

Jacob Wrestles With God

²²That night Jacob got up and took his two wives, his two maidservants and his eleven sons and crossed the ford of the Jabbok. ²³After he had sent them across the stream, he sent over all his possessions. ²⁴So Jacob was left alone, and a man wrestled with him till daybreak. ²⁵When the man saw that he could not overpower him, he touched the socket of Jacob's hip so that his hip was wrenched as he wrestled with the man. ²⁶Then the man said, "Let me go, for it is daybreak."

But Jacob replied, "I will not let you go unless you bless me."

²⁷The man asked him, "What is your name?"

"Jacob," he answered.

²⁸Then the man said, "Your name will no longer be Jacob, but Israel,ᵃ because you have struggled with God and with men and have overcome."

²⁹Jacob said, "Please tell me your name."

But he replied, "Why do you ask my name?" Then he blessed him there.

³⁰So Jacob called the place Peniel,ᵇ saying, "It is because I saw God face to face, and yet my life was spared."

ᵃ28 Israel means *he struggles with God.* ᵇ30 Peniel means *face of God.*

Friday

All-star Wrestling

Read Genesis 32:22–32

This past summer, I had a major pain in my left side. My mom thought it might be appendicitis, which would need to be operated on right away, so she rushed me to the doctor. In the car on the way, I was in a lot of pain and was really scared that I might need to have surgery. I kept asking God, "Why is this happening to me?" There was nothing I could do to feel better, and I was really frustrated with God for letting me be in all this pain.

But then I realized the best thing I could do was pray and ask God to help me. When I got to the doctor's office, they took some X rays that showed I didn't have appendicitis. They gave me some medicine for the pain and sent me home.

Even though I wanted to fix the situation, I couldn't. The only One who can completely control anything is God. Whenever I try to do things my own way, God usually shows me that I have to turn to him with my problems. Just like Jacob wrestled with God and realized God is always in control, it took some pain and fear for me to remember that God's in charge of everything.

Joel age 13

What about You?

❶ Have you ever felt like you were "wrestling" with God—trying to make him work things out your way? What happened?

❷ Grab a couple of friends and a tape recorder and record yourselves doing a play-by-play commentary on Jacob's wrestling match with God.

❸ Ask God to help you give him control of your life.

Turn to page 51 for your next devotion.

³¹The sun rose above him as he passed Peniel,ᵃ and he was limping because of his hip. ³²Therefore to this day the Israelites do not eat the tendon attached to the socket of the hip, because the socket of Jacob's hip was touched near the tendon.

Jacob Meets Esau

33 Jacob looked up and there was Esau, coming with his four hundred men; so he divided the children among Leah, Rachel and the two maidservants. ²He put the maidservants and their children in front, Leah and her children next, and Rachel and Joseph in the rear. ³He himself went on ahead and bowed down to the ground seven times as he approached his brother.

⁴But Esau ran to meet Jacob and embraced him; he threw his arms around his neck and kissed him. And they wept. ⁵Then Esau looked up and saw the women and children. "Who are these with you?" he asked.

Jacob answered, "They are the children God has graciously given your servant."

⁶Then the maidservants and their children approached and bowed down. ⁷Next, Leah and her children came and bowed down. Last of all came Joseph and Rachel, and they too bowed down.

⁸Esau asked, "What do you mean by all these droves I met?"

"To find favor in your eyes, my lord," he said.

⁹But Esau said, "I already have plenty, my brother. Keep what you have for yourself."

¹⁰"No, please!" said Jacob. "If I have found favor in your eyes, accept this gift from me. For to see your face is like seeing the face of God, now that you have received me favorably. ¹¹Please accept the present that was brought to you, for God has been gracious to me and I have all I need." And because Jacob insisted, Esau accepted it.

¹²Then Esau said, "Let us be on our way; I'll accompany you."

¹³But Jacob said to him, "My lord knows that the children are tender and that I must care for the ewes and cows that are nursing their young. If they are driven hard just one day, all the animals will die. ¹⁴So let my lord go on ahead of his servant, while I move along slowly at the pace of the droves before me and that of the children, until I come to my lord in Seir."

¹⁵Esau said, "Then let me leave some of my men with you."

"But why do that?" Jacob asked. "Just let me find favor in the eyes of my lord."

¹⁶So that day Esau started on his way back to Seir. ¹⁷Jacob, however, went to Succoth, where he built a place for himself and made shelters for his livestock. That is why the place is called Succoth.ᵇ

¹⁸After Jacob came from Paddan Aram,ᶜ he arrived safely at theᵈ city of Shechem in Canaan and camped within sight of the city. ¹⁹For a hundred pieces of silver,ᵉ he bought from the sons of Hamor, the father of Shechem, the plot of ground where he pitched his tent. ²⁰There he set up an altar and called it El Elohe Israel.ᶠ

Dinah and the Shechemites

34 Now Dinah, the daughter Leah had borne to Jacob, went out to visit the women of the land. ²When Shechem son of Hamor the Hivite, the ruler of that area, saw her, he took her and violated her. ³His heart was drawn to Dinah daughter of Jacob, and he loved the girl and spoke tenderly to her. ⁴And Shechem said to his father Hamor, "Get me this girl as my wife."

⁵When Jacob heard that his daughter Dinah had been defiled, his sons were in the fields with his livestock; so he kept quiet about it until they came home.

⁶Then Shechem's father Hamor went out to talk with Jacob. ⁷Now Jacob's sons had come in from the fields as soon as they heard what had happened. They were filled with grief and fury, because Shechem had done a disgraceful thing inᵍ Israel by lying with Jacob's daughter—a thing that should not be done.

⁸But Hamor said to them, "My son

ᵃ31 Hebrew *Penuel*, a variant of *Peniel*   ᵇ17 *Succoth* means *shelters*.   ᶜ18 That is, Northwest Mesopotamia   ᵈ18 Or *arrived at Shalem, a*   ᵉ19 Hebrew *hundred kesitahs*; a kesitah was a unit of money of unknown weight and value.   ᶠ20 *El Elohe Israel* can mean *God, the God of Israel* or *mighty is the God of Israel*.   ᵍ7 Or *against*

Shechem has his heart set on your daughter. Please give her to him as his wife. ⁹Intermarry with us; give us your daughters and take our daughters for yourselves. ¹⁰You can settle among us; the land is open to you. Live in it, trade*ᵃ* in it, and acquire property in it."

¹¹Then Shechem said to Dinah's father and brothers, "Let me find favor in your eyes, and I will give you whatever you ask. ¹²Make the price for the bride and the gift I am to bring as great as you like, and I'll pay whatever you ask me. Only give me the girl as my wife."

¹³Because their sister Dinah had been defiled, Jacob's sons replied deceitfully as they spoke to Shechem and his father Hamor. ¹⁴They said to them, "We can't do such a thing; we can't give our sister to a man who is not circumcised. That would be a disgrace to us. ¹⁵We will give our consent to you on one condition only: that you become like us by circumcising all your males. ¹⁶Then we will give you our daughters and take your daughters for ourselves. We'll settle among you and become one people with you. ¹⁷But if you will not agree to be circumcised, we'll take our sister*ᵇ* and go."

¹⁸Their proposal seemed good to Hamor and his son Shechem. ¹⁹The young man, who was the most honored of all his father's household, lost no time in doing what they said, because he was delighted with Jacob's daughter. ²⁰So Hamor and his son Shechem went to the gate of their city to speak to their fellow townsmen. ²¹"These men are friendly toward us," they said. "Let them live in our land and trade in it; the land has plenty of room for them. We can marry their daughters and they can marry ours. ²²But the men will consent to live with us as one people only on the condition that our males be circumcised, as they themselves are. ²³Won't their livestock, their property and all their other animals become ours? So let us give our consent to them, and they will settle among us."

²⁴All the men who went out of the city gate agreed with Hamor and his son Shechem, and every male in the city was circumcised.

²⁵Three days later, while all of them were still in pain, two of Jacob's sons, Simeon and Levi, Dinah's brothers, took their swords and attacked the unsuspecting city, killing every male. ²⁶They put Hamor and his son Shechem to the sword and took Dinah from Shechem's house and left. ²⁷The sons of Jacob came upon the dead bodies and looted the city where*ᶜ* their sister had been defiled. ²⁸They seized their flocks and herds and donkeys and everything else of theirs in the city and out in the fields. ²⁹They carried off all their wealth and all their women and children, taking as plunder everything in the houses.

³⁰Then Jacob said to Simeon and Levi, "You have brought trouble on me by making me a stench to the Canaanites and Perizzites, the people living in this land. We are few in number, and if they join forces against me and attack me, I and my household will be destroyed." ³¹But they replied, "Should he have treated our sister like a prostitute?"

Jacob Returns to Bethel

35 Then God said to Jacob, "Go up to Bethel and settle there, and build an altar there to God, who appeared to you when you were fleeing from your brother Esau."

²So Jacob said to his household and to all who were with him, "Get rid of the foreign gods you have with you, and purify yourselves and change your clothes. ³Then come, let us go up to Bethel, where I will build an altar to God, who answered me in the day of my distress and who has been with me wherever I have gone." ⁴So they gave Jacob all the foreign gods they had and the rings in their ears, and Jacob buried them under the oak at Shechem. ⁵Then they set out, and the terror of God fell upon the towns all around them so that no one pursued them.

⁶Jacob and all the people with him came to Luz (that is, Bethel) in the land of Canaan. ⁷There he built an altar, and he called the place El Bethel,*ᵈ* because it was there that God revealed himself to him when he was fleeing from his brother.

ᵃ10 Or *move about freely*; also in verse 21
ᵇ17 Hebrew *daughter*   *ᶜ27* Or *because*   *ᵈ7 El Bethel* means *God of Bethel*.

⁸Now Deborah, Rebekah's nurse, died and was buried under the oak below Bethel. So it was named Allon Bacuth.ᵃ

⁹After Jacob returned from Paddan Aram,ᵇ God appeared to him again and blessed him. ¹⁰God said to him, "Your name is Jacob,ᶜ but you will no longer be called Jacob; your name will be Israel.ᵈ" So he named him Israel.

¹¹And God said to him, "I am God Almightyᵉ; be fruitful and increase in number. A nation and a community of nations will come from you, and kings will come from your body. ¹²The land I gave to Abraham and Isaac I also give to you, and I will give this land to your descendants after you." ¹³Then God went up from him at the place where he had talked with him.

¹⁴Jacob set up a stone pillar at the place where God had talked with him, and he poured out a drink offering on it; he also poured oil on it. ¹⁵Jacob called the place where God had talked with him Bethel.ᶠ

The Deaths of Rachel and Isaac

¹⁶Then they moved on from Bethel. While they were still some distance from Ephrath, Rachel began to give birth and had great difficulty. ¹⁷And as she was having great difficulty in childbirth, the midwife said to her, "Don't be afraid, for you have another son." ¹⁸As she breathed her last—for she was dying—she named her son Ben-Oni.ᵍ But his father named him Benjamin.ʰ

¹⁹So Rachel died and was buried on the way to Ephrath (that is, Bethlehem). ²⁰Over her tomb Jacob set up a pillar, and to this day that pillar marks Rachel's tomb.

²¹Israel moved on again and pitched his tent beyond Migdal Eder. ²²While Israel was living in that region, Reuben went in and slept with his father's concubine Bilhah, and Israel heard of it.

Jacob had twelve sons:

²³The sons of Leah:

Reuben the firstborn of Jacob, Simeon, Levi, Judah, Issachar and Zebulun.

²⁴The sons of Rachel:

Joseph and Benjamin.

²⁵The sons of Rachel's maidservant Bilhah:

Dan and Naphtali.

²⁶The sons of Leah's maidservant Zilpah:

Gad and Asher.

These were the sons of Jacob, who were born to him in Paddan Aram.

²⁷Jacob came home to his father Isaac in Mamre, near Kiriath Arba (that is, Hebron), where Abraham and Isaac had stayed. ²⁸Isaac lived a hundred and eighty years. ²⁹Then he breathed his last and died and was gathered to his people, old and full of years. And his sons Esau and Jacob buried him.

Esau's Descendants

36 This is the account of Esau (that is, Edom).

²Esau took his wives from the women of Canaan: Adah daughter of Elon the Hittite, and Oholibamah daughter of Anah and granddaughter of Zibeon the Hivite— ³also Basemath daughter of Ishmael and sister of Nebaioth.

⁴Adah bore Eliphaz to Esau, Basemath bore Reuel, ⁵and Oholibamah bore Jeush, Jalam and Korah. These were the sons of Esau, who were born to him in Canaan.

⁶Esau took his wives and sons and daughters and all the members of his household, as well as his livestock and all his other animals and all the goods he had acquired in Canaan, and moved to a land some distance from his brother Jacob. ⁷Their possessions were too great for them to remain together; the land where they were staying could not support them both because of their livestock. ⁸So Esau (that is, Edom) settled in the hill country of Seir.

⁹This is the account of Esau the father of the Edomites in the hill country of Seir.

ᵃ8 *Allon Bacuth* means *oak of weeping.*   ᵇ9 That is, Northwest Mesopotamia; also in verse 26   ᶜ10 *Jacob* means *he grasps the heel* (figuratively, *he deceives*). ᵈ10 *Israel* means *he struggles with God.*   ᵉ11 Hebrew *El-Shaddai*   ᶠ15 *Bethel* means *house of God.* ᵍ18 *Ben-Oni* means *son of my trouble.* ʰ18 *Benjamin* means *son of my right hand.*

¹⁰These are the names of Esau's sons:
Eliphaz, the son of Esau's wife
Adah, and Reuel, the son of Esau's
wife Basemath.
¹¹The sons of Eliphaz:
Teman, Omar, Zepho, Gatam and
Kenaz.
¹²Esau's son Eliphaz also had a concubine named Timna, who bore
him Amalek. These were grandsons of Esau's wife Adah.
¹³The sons of Reuel:
Nahath, Zerah, Shammah and
Mizzah. These were grandsons of
Esau's wife Basemath.
¹⁴The sons of Esau's wife Oholibamah
daughter of Anah and granddaughter of Zibeon, whom she bore to Esau:
Jeush, Jalam and Korah.

¹⁵These were the chiefs among Esau's
descendants:
The sons of Eliphaz the firstborn of
Esau:
Chiefs Teman, Omar, Zepho,
Kenaz, ¹⁶Korah,ᵃ Gatam and Amalek. These were the chiefs descended from Eliphaz in Edom;
they were grandsons of Adah.
¹⁷The sons of Esau's son Reuel:
Chiefs Nahath, Zerah, Shammah
and Mizzah. These were the chiefs
descended from Reuel in Edom;
they were grandsons of Esau's
wife Basemath.
¹⁸The sons of Esau's wife Oholibamah:
Chiefs Jeush, Jalam and Korah.
These were the chiefs descended
from Esau's wife Oholibamah
daughter of Anah.
¹⁹These were the sons of Esau (that is,
Edom), and these were their chiefs.

²⁰These were the sons of Seir the Horite, who were living in the region:
Lotan, Shobal, Zibeon, Anah,
²¹Dishon, Ezer and Dishan. These
sons of Seir in Edom were Horite
chiefs.
²²The sons of Lotan:
Hori and Homam.ᵇ Timna was
Lotan's sister.
²³The sons of Shobal:
Alvan, Manahath, Ebal, Shepho
and Onam.

²⁴The sons of Zibeon:
Aiah and Anah. This is the Anah
who discovered the hot springsᶜ in
the desert while he was grazing
the donkeys of his father Zibeon.
²⁵The children of Anah:
Dishon and Oholibamah daughter
of Anah.
²⁶The sons of Dishonᵈ:
Hemdan, Eshban, Ithran and
Keran.
²⁷The sons of Ezer:
Bilhan, Zaavan and Akan.
²⁸The sons of Dishan:
Uz and Aran.
²⁹These were the Horite chiefs:
Lotan, Shobal, Zibeon, Anah,
³⁰Dishon, Ezer and Dishan. These
were the Horite chiefs, according
to their divisions, in the land of
Seir.

The Rulers of Edom

³¹These were the kings who reigned in
Edom before any Israelite king reignedᵉ:
³²Bela son of Beor became king of
Edom. His city was named Dinhabah.
³³When Bela died, Jobab son of Zerah
from Bozrah succeeded him as
king.
³⁴When Jobab died, Husham from the
land of the Temanites succeeded
him as king.
³⁵When Husham died, Hadad son of
Bedad, who defeated Midian in
the country of Moab, succeeded
him as king. His city was named
Avith.
³⁶When Hadad died, Samlah from
Masrekah succeeded him as king.
³⁷When Samlah died, Shaul from Rehoboth on the riverᶠ succeeded
him as king.
³⁸When Shaul died, Baal-Hanan son
of Acbor succeeded him as king.
³⁹When Baal-Hanan son of Acbor

ᵃ16 Masoretic Text; Samaritan Pentateuch (see also
Gen. 36:11 and 1 Chron. 1:36) does not have *Korah*.
ᵇ22 Hebrew *Hemam*, a variant of *Homam* (see
1 Chron. 1:39)   ᶜ24 Vulgate; Syriac *discovered
water;* the meaning of the Hebrew for this word is
uncertain.   ᵈ26 Hebrew *Dishan*, a variant of *Dishon*
ᵉ31 Or *before an Israelite king reigned over them*
ᶠ37 Possibly the Euphrates

died, Hadad[a] succeeded him as king. His city was named Pau, and his wife's name was Mehetabel daughter of Matred, the daughter of Me-Zahab.

[40]These were the chiefs descended from Esau, by name, according to their clans and regions:

Timna, Alvah, Jetheth, [41]Oholibamah, Elah, Pinon, [42]Kenaz, Teman, Mibzar, [43]Magdiel and Iram. These were the chiefs of Edom, according to their settlements in the land they occupied.

This was Esau the father of the Edomites.

Joseph's Dreams

37 Jacob lived in the land where his father had stayed, the land of Canaan.

[2]This is the account of Jacob.

Joseph, a young man of seventeen, was tending the flocks with his brothers, the sons of Bilhah and the sons of Zilpah, his father's wives, and he brought their father a bad report about them.

[3]Now Israel loved Joseph more than any of his other sons, because he had been born to him in his old age; and he made a richly ornamented[b] robe for him. [4]When his brothers saw that their father loved him more than any of them, they hated him and could not speak a kind word to him.

[5]Joseph had a dream, and when he told it to his brothers, they hated him all the more. [6]He said to them, "Listen to this dream I had: [7]We were binding sheaves of grain out in the field when suddenly my sheaf rose and stood upright, while your sheaves gathered around mine and bowed down to it."

[8]His brothers said to him, "Do you intend to reign over us? Will you actually rule us?" And they hated him all the more because of his dream and what he had said.

[9]Then he had another dream, and he told it to his brothers. "Listen," he said, "I had another dream, and this time the sun and moon and eleven stars were bowing down to me."

[10]When he told his father as well as his brothers, his father rebuked him and said, "What is this dream you had? Will your mother and I and your brothers actually come and bow down to the ground before you?" [11]His brothers were jealous of him, but his father kept the matter in mind.

Joseph Sold by His Brothers

[12]Now his brothers had gone to graze their father's flocks near Shechem, [13]and Israel said to Joseph, "As you know, your brothers are grazing the flocks near Shechem. Come, I am going to send you to them."

"Very well," he replied.

[14]So he said to him, "Go and see if all is well with your brothers and with the flocks, and bring word back to me." Then he sent him off from the Valley of Hebron.

When Joseph arrived at Shechem, [15]a man found him wandering around in the fields and asked him, "What are you looking for?"

[16]He replied, "I'm looking for my brothers. Can you tell me where they are grazing their flocks?"

[17]"They have moved on from here," the man answered. "I heard them say, 'Let's go to Dothan.' "

So Joseph went after his brothers and found them near Dothan. [18]But they saw him in the distance, and before he reached them, they plotted to kill him.

[19]"Here comes that dreamer!" they said to each other. [20]"Come now, let's kill him and throw him into one of these cisterns and say that a ferocious animal devoured him. Then we'll see what comes of his dreams."

[21]When Reuben heard this, he tried to rescue him from their hands. "Let's not take his life," he said. [22]"Don't shed any blood. Throw him into this cistern here in the desert, but don't lay a hand on him." Reuben said this to rescue him from them and take him back to his father.

[23]So when Joseph came to his brothers,

---

[a]39 Many manuscripts of the Masoretic Text, Samaritan Pentateuch and Syriac (see also 1 Chron. 1:50); most manuscripts of the Masoretic Text *Hadar*   [b]3 The meaning of the Hebrew for *richly ornamented* is uncertain; also in verses 23 and 32.

they stripped him of his robe—the richly ornamented robe he was wearing— ²⁴and they took him and threw him into the cistern. Now the cistern was empty; there was no water in it.

²⁵As they sat down to eat their meal, they looked up and saw a caravan of Ishmaelites coming from Gilead. Their camels were loaded with spices, balm and myrrh, and they were on their way to take them down to Egypt.

²⁶Judah said to his brothers, "What will we gain if we kill our brother and cover up his blood? ²⁷Come, let's sell him to the Ishmaelites and not lay our hands on him; after all, he is our brother, our own flesh and blood." His brothers agreed.

²⁸So when the Midianite merchants came by, his brothers pulled Joseph up out of the cistern and sold him for twenty shekels[a] of silver to the Ishmaelites, who took him to Egypt.

²⁹When Reuben returned to the cistern

---

a28 That is, about 8 ounces (about 0.2 kilogram)

Week end.

What a Relief   Read Matthew 18:21–35 (page 1167)

Have you ever been wandering around the mall and bumped into someone you treated poorly? You know, that former friend you ditched, only because your other friends thought she was a real loser? So to save face, you dropped the friend you really liked a lot. And now you can't avoid running straight into her (you think about ducking into the next store until you realize it's a maternity shop). Talk about uncomfortable. What can you say? What can you do?

On Thursday, Megan talked about the story of Jacob and Esau (remember, the stolen birthright brothers?). Did you know that Jacob later bumped into his brother Esau in the middle of nowhere? That big, tough, burly guy liked to go hunting and probably moonlighted as an ancient all-star wrestler! Jacob thought he was going to get the tar beat out of him, but instead Esau embraced him—it was forgive and forget. In that moment Jacob experienced the wonder of forgiveness.

In today's passage, Jesus' story of the unforgiving servant gives us some pointed words about forgiving other people. We're supposed to forgive other people over and over and over again. Has anyone ever forgiven you for something you did? Didn't it feel great?

Imagine how it would feel if that former friend in the mall looked at you with forgiveness in her eyes instead of revenge. It would feel good, wouldn't it? Now it's your turn.

❶ Who is one person you have been holding a grudge against for something they did to you or said about you? What would happen if you chose to forgive that person?

❷ Write down what you could do or say that would let this person know that you want to forgive them.

❸ Pray that God will help you forgive that person for the wrong they did to you.

Turn to page 53 for your next devotion.

and saw that Joseph was not there, he tore his clothes. ³⁰He went back to his brothers and said, "The boy isn't there! Where can I turn now?"

³¹Then they got Joseph's robe, slaughtered a goat and dipped the robe in the blood. ³²They took the ornamented robe back to their father and said, "We found this. Examine it to see whether it is your son's robe."

³³He recognized it and said, "It is my son's robe! Some ferocious animal has devoured him. Joseph has surely been torn to pieces."

³⁴Then Jacob tore his clothes, put on sackcloth and mourned for his son many days. ³⁵All his sons and daughters came to comfort him, but he refused to be comforted. "No," he said, "in mourning will I go down to the grave*a* to my son." So his father wept for him.

³⁶Meanwhile, the Midianites*b* sold Joseph in Egypt to Potiphar, one of Pharaoh's officials, the captain of the guard.

Judah and Tamar

38 At that time, Judah left his brothers and went down to stay with a man of Adullam named Hirah. ²There Judah met the daughter of a Canaanite man named Shua. He married her and lay with her; ³she became pregnant and gave birth to a son, who was named Er. ⁴She conceived again and gave birth to a son and named him Onan. ⁵She gave birth to still another son and named him Shelah. It was at Kezib that she gave birth to him.

⁶Judah got a wife for Er, his firstborn, and her name was Tamar. ⁷But Er, Judah's firstborn, was wicked in the Lord's sight; so the Lord put him to death.

⁸Then Judah said to Onan, "Lie with your brother's wife and fulfill your duty to her as a brother-in-law to produce offspring for your brother." ⁹But Onan knew that the offspring would not be his; so whenever he lay with his brother's wife, he spilled his semen on the ground to keep from producing offspring for his brother. ¹⁰What he did was wicked in the Lord's sight; so he put him to death also.

¹¹Judah then said to his daughter-in-law Tamar, "Live as a widow in your father's house until my son Shelah grows

up." For he thought, "He may die too, just like his brothers." So Tamar went to live in her father's house.

¹²After a long time Judah's wife, the daughter of Shua, died. When Judah had recovered from his grief, he went up to Timnah, to the men who were shearing his sheep, and his friend Hirah the Adullamite went with him.

¹³When Tamar was told, "Your father-in-law is on his way to Timnah to shear his sheep," ¹⁴she took off her widow's clothes, covered herself with a veil to disguise herself, and then sat down at the entrance to Enaim, which is on the road to Timnah. For she saw that, though Shelah had now grown up, she had not been given to him as his wife.

¹⁵When Judah saw her, he thought she was a prostitute, for she had covered her face. ¹⁶Not realizing that she was his daughter-in-law, he went over to her by the roadside and said, "Come now, let me sleep with you."

"And what will you give me to sleep with you?" she asked.

¹⁷"I'll send you a young goat from my flock," he said.

"Will you give me something as a pledge until you send it?" she asked.

¹⁸He said, "What pledge should I give you?"

"Your seal and its cord, and the staff in your hand," she answered. So he gave them to her and slept with her, and she became pregnant by him. ¹⁹After she left, she took off her veil and put on her widow's clothes again.

²⁰Meanwhile Judah sent the young goat by his friend the Adullamite in order to get his pledge back from the woman, but he did not find her. ²¹He asked the men who lived there, "Where is the shrine prostitute who was beside the road at Enaim?"

"There hasn't been any shrine prostitute here," they said.

²²So he went back to Judah and said, "I didn't find her. Besides, the men who lived there said, 'There hasn't been any shrine prostitute here.' "

*a35 Hebrew *Sheol* *b36 Samaritan Pentateuch, Septuagint, Vulgate and Syriac (see also verse 28); Masoretic Text *Medanites*

²³Then Judah said, "Let her keep what she has, or we will become a laughing-stock. After all, I did send her this young goat, but you didn't find her."

²⁴About three months later Judah was told, "Your daughter-in-law Tamar is guilty of prostitution, and as a result she is now pregnant."

Judah said, "Bring her out and have her burned to death!"

²⁵As she was being brought out, she sent a message to her father-in-law. "I am pregnant by the man who owns these," she said. And she added, "See if you recognize whose seal and cord and staff these are."

²⁶Judah recognized them and said, "She is more righteous than I, since I wouldn't give her to my son Shelah." And he did not sleep with her again.

²⁷When the time came for her to give birth, there were twin boys in her womb. ²⁸As she was giving birth, one of them put out his hand; so the midwife took a scarlet thread and tied it on his wrist and said, "This one came out first." ²⁹But when he drew back his hand, his brother came out, and she said, "So this is how you have broken out!" And he was named Perez.ᵃ ³⁰Then his brother, who had the scarlet thread on his wrist, came out and he was given the name Zerah.ᵇ

Joseph and Potiphar's Wife

39 Now Joseph had been taken down to Egypt. Potiphar, an Egyptian who was one of Pharaoh's officials, the captain of the guard, bought him from the Ishmaelites who had taken him there.

²The LORD was with Joseph and he prospered, and he lived in the house of his Egyptian master. ³When his master saw that the LORD was with him and that the LORD gave him success in everything he did, ⁴Joseph found favor in his eyes

---

ᵃ29 *Perez* means *breaking out.*   ᵇ30 *Zerah* can mean *scarlet* or *brightness.*

Monday

Run Away

Read Genesis 39

I'm really into skateboarding. One day I was out skating and I saw these older kids skating nearby. They were awesome skaters! So I went over and started talking to them. They seemed nice and said I could skate with them.

Then they pulled out some weed. It totally shocked me to see these kids smoking marijuana. They asked if I wanted any, and when I said no they started making fun of me and calling me a pansy. I just left.

When I read the story of Joseph running away from temptation, I can relate. Even though sometimes we'll be called names or made fun of for saying no to the stuff we know is wrong, God is going to be there for us and reward us for doing the right thing.

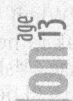
Jon age 13

❶ Imagine yourself saying no to something you know is wrong. What's the worst thing that could happen? What's the best thing?

❷ If you had a glass of kool-aid, and you left a piece of paper in it for a minute, what would happen to the paper? How is this an example of what happens when we give in to a "little" temptation?

❸ Read 1 Corinthians 10:13, page 1385. The next time you face temptation, stop, pray and ask God to show you a way to escape.

Turn to page 67 for your next devotion.

and became his attendant. Potiphar put him in charge of his household, and he entrusted to his care everything he owned. ⁵From the time he put him in charge of his household and of all that he owned, the LORD blessed the household of the Egyptian because of Joseph. The blessing of the LORD was on everything Potiphar had, both in the house and in the field. ⁶So he left in Joseph's care everything he had; with Joseph in charge, he did not concern himself with anything except the food he ate.

Now Joseph was well-built and handsome, ⁷and after a while his master's wife took notice of Joseph and said, "Come to bed with me!"

⁸But he refused. "With me in charge," he told her, "my master does not concern himself with anything in the house; everything he owns he has entrusted to my care. ⁹No one is greater in this house than I am. My master has withheld nothing from me except you, because you are his wife. How then could I do such a wicked thing and sin against God?" ¹⁰And though she spoke to Joseph day after day, he refused to go to bed with her or even be with her.

¹¹One day he went into the house to attend to his duties, and none of the household servants was inside. ¹²She caught him by his cloak and said, "Come to bed with me!" But he left his cloak in her hand and ran out of the house.

¹³When she saw that he had left his cloak in her hand and had run out of the house, ¹⁴she called her household servants. "Look," she said to them, "this Hebrew has been brought to us to make sport of us! He came in here to sleep with me, but I screamed. ¹⁵When he heard me scream for help, he left his cloak beside me and ran out of the house."

¹⁶She kept his cloak beside her until his master came home. ¹⁷Then she told him this story: "That Hebrew slave you brought us came to me to make sport of me. ¹⁸But as soon as I screamed for help, he left his cloak beside me and ran out of the house."

¹⁹When his master heard the story his wife told him, saying, "This is how your slave treated me," he burned with anger. ²⁰Joseph's master took him and put him in prison, the place where the king's prisoners were confined.

But while Joseph was there in the prison, ²¹the LORD was with him; he showed him kindness and granted him favor in the eyes of the prison warden. ²²So the warden put Joseph in charge of all those held in the prison, and he was made responsible for all that was done there. ²³The warden paid no attention to anything under Joseph's care, because the LORD was with Joseph and gave him success in whatever he did.

The Cupbearer and the Baker

40 Some time later, the cupbearer and the baker of the king of Egypt offended their master, the king of Egypt. ²Pharaoh was angry with his two officials, the chief cupbearer and the chief baker, ³and put them in custody in the house of the captain of the guard, in the same prison where Joseph was confined. ⁴The captain of the guard assigned them to Joseph, and he attended them.

After they had been in custody for some time, ⁵each of the two men—the cupbearer and the baker of the king of Egypt, who were being held in prison—had a dream the same night, and each dream had a meaning of its own.

⁶When Joseph came to them the next morning, he saw that they were dejected. ⁷So he asked Pharaoh's officials who were in custody with him in his master's house, "Why are your faces so sad today?"

⁸"We both had dreams," they answered, "but there is no one to interpret them."

Then Joseph said to them, "Do not interpretations belong to God? Tell me your dreams."

⁹So the chief cupbearer told Joseph his dream. He said to him, "In my dream I saw a vine in front of me, ¹⁰and on the vine were three branches. As soon as it budded, it blossomed, and its clusters ripened into grapes. ¹¹Pharaoh's cup was in my hand, and I took the grapes, squeezed them into Pharaoh's cup and put the cup in his hand."

¹²"This is what it means," Joseph said to him. "The three branches are three days. ¹³Within three days Pharaoh will lift up your head and restore you to your position, and you will put Pharaoh's cup

The Riddlers

Huh?

Genesis 40:8

You know how an answer sheet helps you "get" a riddle when you come up clueless? Joseph and Daniel were a couple of guys who were like riddle-meisters. People sometimes got messages from God in their dreams, and you know how dreams can be: pretty weird and confusing sometimes. So these guys would explain the dream and God's message to the people.

in his hand, just as you used to do when you were his cupbearer. ¹⁴But when all goes well with you, remember me and show me kindness; mention me to Pharaoh and get me out of this prison. ¹⁵For I was forcibly carried off from the land of the Hebrews, and even here I have done nothing to deserve being put in a dungeon."

¹⁶When the chief baker saw that Joseph had given a favorable interpretation, he said to Joseph, "I too had a dream: On my head were three baskets of bread.ᵃ ¹⁷In the top basket were all kinds of baked goods for Pharaoh, but the birds were eating them out of the basket on my head."

¹⁸"This is what it means," Joseph said. "The three baskets are three days. ¹⁹Within three days Pharaoh will lift off your head and hang you on a tree.ᵇ And the birds will eat away your flesh."

²⁰Now the third day was Pharaoh's birthday, and he gave a feast for all his officials. He lifted up the heads of the chief cupbearer and the chief baker in the presence of his officials: ²¹He restored the chief cupbearer to his position, so that he once again put the cup into Pharaoh's hand, ²²but he hangedᶜ the chief baker, just as Joseph had said to them in his interpretation.

²³The chief cupbearer, however, did not remember Joseph; he forgot him.

Pharaoh's Dreams

41 When two full years had passed, Pharaoh had a dream: He was standing by the Nile, ²when out of the river there came up seven cows, sleek and fat, and they grazed among the reeds. ³After them, seven other cows, ugly and gaunt, came up out of the Nile and stood beside those on the riverbank. ⁴And the cows that were ugly and gaunt ate up the seven sleek, fat cows. Then Pharaoh woke up.

⁵He fell asleep again and had a second dream: Seven heads of grain, healthy and good, were growing on a single stalk. ⁶After them, seven other heads of grain sprouted—thin and scorched by the east wind. ⁷The thin heads of grain swallowed up the seven healthy, full heads. Then Pharaoh woke up; it had been a dream.

⁸In the morning his mind was troubled, so he sent for all the magicians and wise men of Egypt. Pharaoh told them his dreams, but no one could interpret them for him.

⁹Then the chief cupbearer said to Pharaoh, "Today I am reminded of my shortcomings. ¹⁰Pharaoh was once angry with his servants, and he imprisoned me and the chief baker in the house of the captain of the guard. ¹¹Each of us had a dream the same night, and each dream had a meaning of its own. ¹²Now a young Hebrew was there with us, a servant of the captain of the guard. We told him our dreams, and he interpreted them for us, giving each man the interpretation of his dream. ¹³And things turned out exactly as he interpreted them to us: I was restored to my position, and the other man was hanged.ᶜ"

¹⁴So Pharaoh sent for Joseph, and he was quickly brought from the dungeon. When he had shaved and changed his clothes, he came before Pharaoh.

¹⁵Pharaoh said to Joseph, "I had a dream, and no one can interpret it. But I have heard it said of you that when you hear a dream you can interpret it."

¹⁶"I cannot do it," Joseph replied to Pharaoh, "but God will give Pharaoh the answer he desires."

¹⁷Then Pharaoh said to Joseph, "In my dream I was standing on the bank of the

ᵃ16 Or *three wicker baskets*   ᵇ19 Or *and impale you on a pole*   ᶜ22,13 Or *impaled*

Nile, [18]when out of the river there came up seven cows, fat and sleek, and they grazed among the reeds. [19]After them, seven other cows came up—scrawny and very ugly and lean. I had never seen such ugly cows in all the land of Egypt. [20]The lean, ugly cows ate up the seven fat cows that came up first. [21]But even after they ate them, no one could tell that they had done so; they looked just as ugly as before. Then I woke up.

[22]"In my dreams I also saw seven heads of grain, full and good, growing on a single stalk. [23]After them, seven other heads sprouted—withered and thin and scorched by the east wind. [24]The thin heads of grain swallowed up the seven good heads. I told this to the magicians, but none could explain it to me."

[25]Then Joseph said to Pharaoh, "The dreams of Pharaoh are one and the same. God has revealed to Pharaoh what he is about to do. [26]The seven good cows are seven years, and the seven good heads of grain are seven years; it is one and the same dream. [27]The seven lean, ugly cows that came up afterward are seven years, and so are the seven worthless heads of grain scorched by the east wind: They are seven years of famine.

[28]"It is just as I said to Pharaoh: God has shown Pharaoh what he is about to do. [29]Seven years of great abundance are coming throughout the land of Egypt, [30]but seven years of famine will follow them. Then all the abundance in Egypt will be forgotten, and the famine will ravage the land. [31]The abundance in the land will not be remembered, because the famine that follows it will be so severe. [32]The reason the dream was given to Pharaoh in two forms is that the matter has been firmly decided by God, and God will do it soon.

[33]"And now let Pharaoh look for a discerning and wise man and put him in charge of the land of Egypt. [34]Let Pharaoh appoint commissioners over the land to take a fifth of the harvest of Egypt during the seven years of abundance. [35]They should collect all the food of these good years that are coming and store up the grain under the authority of Pharaoh, to be kept in the cities for food. [36]This food should be held in reserve for the country, to be used during the seven years of famine that will come upon Egypt, so that the country may not be ruined by the famine."

[37]The plan seemed good to Pharaoh and to all his officials. [38]So Pharaoh asked them, "Can we find anyone like this man, one in whom is the spirit of God[a]?"

[39]Then Pharaoh said to Joseph, "Since God has made all this known to you, there is no one so discerning and wise as you. [40]You shall be in charge of my palace, and all my people are to submit to your orders. Only with respect to the throne will I be greater than you."

Joseph in Charge of Egypt

[41]So Pharaoh said to Joseph, "I hereby put you in charge of the whole land of Egypt." [42]Then Pharaoh took his signet ring from his finger and put it on Joseph's finger. He dressed him in robes of fine linen and put a gold chain around his neck. [43]He had him ride in a chariot as his second-in-command,[b] and men shouted before him, "Make way[c]!" Thus he put him in charge of the whole land of Egypt.

[44]Then Pharaoh said to Joseph, "I am Pharaoh, but without your word no one will lift hand or foot in all Egypt." [45]Pharaoh gave Joseph the name Zaphenath-Paneah and gave him Asenath daughter of Potiphera, priest of On,[d] to be his wife. And Joseph went throughout the land of Egypt.

[46]Joseph was thirty years old when he entered the service of Pharaoh king of Egypt. And Joseph went out from Pharaoh's presence and traveled throughout Egypt. [47]During the seven years of abundance the land produced plentifully. [48]Joseph collected all the food produced in those seven years of abundance in Egypt and stored it in the cities. In each city he put the food grown in the fields surrounding it. [49]Joseph stored up huge quantities of grain, like the sand of the sea; it was so much that he stopped keep-

---

[a]38 Or *of the gods*   [b]43 Or *in the chariot of his second-in-command*; or *in his second chariot*
[c]43 Or *Bow down*   [d]45 That is, Heliopolis; also in verse 50

ing records because it was beyond measure.

⁵⁰Before the years of famine came, two sons were born to Joseph by Asenath daughter of Potiphera, priest of On. ⁵¹Joseph named his firstborn Manasseh*a* and said, "It is because God has made me forget all my trouble and all my father's household." ⁵²The second son he named Ephraim*b* and said, "It is because God has made me fruitful in the land of my suffering."

⁵³The seven years of abundance in Egypt came to an end, ⁵⁴and the seven years of famine began, just as Joseph had said. There was famine in all the other lands, but in the whole land of Egypt there was food. ⁵⁵When all Egypt began to feel the famine, the people cried to Pharaoh for food. Then Pharaoh told all the Egyptians, "Go to Joseph and do what he tells you."

⁵⁶When the famine had spread over the whole country, Joseph opened the storehouses and sold grain to the Egyptians, for the famine was severe throughout Egypt. ⁵⁷And all the countries came to Egypt to buy grain from Joseph, because the famine was severe in all the world.

Joseph's Brothers Go to Egypt

42 When Jacob learned that there was grain in Egypt, he said to his sons, "Why do you just keep looking at each other?" ²He continued, "I have heard that there is grain in Egypt. Go down there and buy some for us, so that we may live and not die."

³Then ten of Joseph's brothers went down to buy grain from Egypt. ⁴But Jacob did not send Benjamin, Joseph's brother, with the others, because he was afraid that harm might come to him. ⁵So Israel's sons were among those who went to buy grain, for the famine was in the land of Canaan also.

⁶Now Joseph was the governor of the land, the one who sold grain to all its people. So when Joseph's brothers arrived, they bowed down to him with their faces to the ground. ⁷As soon as Joseph saw his brothers, he recognized them, but he pretended to be a stranger and spoke harshly to them. "Where do you come from?" he asked.

"From the land of Canaan," they replied, "to buy food."

⁸Although Joseph recognized his brothers, they did not recognize him. ⁹Then he remembered his dreams about them and said to them, "You are spies! You have come to see where our land is unprotected."

¹⁰"No, my lord," they answered. "Your servants have come to buy food. ¹¹We are all the sons of one man. Your servants are honest men, not spies."

¹²"No!" he said to them. "You have come to see where our land is unprotected."

¹³But they replied, "Your servants were twelve brothers, the sons of one man, who lives in the land of Canaan. The youngest is now with our father, and one is no more."

¹⁴Joseph said to them, "It is just as I told you: You are spies! ¹⁵And this is how you will be tested: As surely as Pharaoh lives, you will not leave this place unless your youngest brother comes here. ¹⁶Send one of your number to get your brother; the rest of you will be kept in prison, so that your words may be tested to see if you are telling the truth. If you are not, then as surely as Pharaoh lives, you are spies!" ¹⁷And he put them all in custody for three days.

¹⁸On the third day, Joseph said to them, "Do this and you will live, for I fear God: ¹⁹If you are honest men, let one of your brothers stay here in prison, while the rest of you go and take grain back for your starving households. ²⁰But you must bring your youngest brother to me, so that your words may be verified and that you may not die." This they proceeded to do.

²¹They said to one another, "Surely we are being punished because of our brother. We saw how distressed he was when he pleaded with us for his life, but we would not listen; that's why this distress has come upon us."

²²Reuben replied, "Didn't I tell you not to sin against the boy? But you wouldn't listen! Now we must give an accounting

---

a51 Manasseh sounds like and may be derived from the Hebrew for *forget*.   *b52 Ephraim* sounds like the Hebrew for *twice fruitful*.

for his blood." ²³They did not realize that Joseph could understand them, since he was using an interpreter.

²⁴He turned away from them and began to weep, but then turned back and spoke to them again. He had Simeon taken from them and bound before their eyes.

²⁵Joseph gave orders to fill their bags with grain, to put each man's silver back in his sack, and to give them provisions for their journey. After this was done for them, ²⁶they loaded their grain on their donkeys and left.

²⁷At the place where they stopped for the night one of them opened his sack to get feed for his donkey, and he saw his silver in the mouth of his sack. ²⁸"My silver has been returned," he said to his brothers. "Here it is in my sack."

Their hearts sank and they turned to each other trembling and said, "What is this that God has done to us?"

²⁹When they came to their father Jacob in the land of Canaan, they told him all that had happened to them. They said, ³⁰"The man who is lord over the land spoke harshly to us and treated us as though we were spying on the land. ³¹But we said to him, 'We are honest men; we are not spies. ³²We were twelve brothers, sons of one father. One is no more, and the youngest is now with our father in Canaan.'

³³"Then the man who is lord over the land said to us, 'This is how I will know whether you are honest men: Leave one of your brothers here with me, and take food for your starving households and go. ³⁴But bring your youngest brother to me so I will know that you are not spies but honest men. Then I will give your brother back to you, and you can trade*ᵃ* in the land.' "

³⁵As they were emptying their sacks, there in each man's sack was his pouch of silver! When they and their father saw the money pouches, they were frightened. ³⁶Their father Jacob said to them, "You have deprived me of my children. Joseph is no more and Simeon is no more, and now you want to take Benjamin. Everything is against me!"

³⁷Then Reuben said to his father, "You may put both of my sons to death if I do

not bring him back to you. Entrust him to my care, and I will bring him back."

³⁸But Jacob said, "My son will not go down there with you; his brother is dead and he is the only one left. If harm comes to him on the journey you are taking, you will bring my gray head down to the grave*ᵇ* in sorrow."

The Second Journey to Egypt

43 Now the famine was still severe in the land. ²So when they had eaten all the grain they had brought from Egypt, their father said to them, "Go back and buy us a little more food."

³But Judah said to him, "The man warned us solemnly, 'You will not see my face again unless your brother is with you.' ⁴If you will send our brother along with us, we will go down and buy food for you. ⁵But if you will not send him, we will not go down, because the man said to us, 'You will not see my face again unless your brother is with you.' "

⁶Israel asked, "Why did you bring this trouble on me by telling the man you had another brother?"

⁷They replied, "The man questioned us closely about ourselves and our family. 'Is your father still living?' he asked us. 'Do you have another brother?' We simply answered his questions. How were we to know he would say, 'Bring your brother down here'?"

⁸Then Judah said to Israel his father, "Send the boy along with me and we will go at once, so that we and you and our children may live and not die. ⁹I myself will guarantee his safety; you can hold me personally responsible for him. If I do not bring him back to you and set him here before you, I will bear the blame before you all my life. ¹⁰As it is, if we had not delayed, we could have gone and returned twice."

¹¹Then their father Israel said to them, "If it must be, then do this: Put some of the best products of the land in your bags and take them down to the man as a gift—a little balm and a little honey, some spices and myrrh, some pistachio nuts and almonds. ¹²Take double the amount of silver with you, for you must

ᵃ34 Or *move about freely*   *ᵇ38* Hebrew *Sheol*

return the silver that was put back into the mouths of your sacks. Perhaps it was a mistake. [13]Take your brother also and go back to the man at once. [14]And may God Almighty[a] grant you mercy before the man so that he will let your other brother and Benjamin come back with you. As for me, if I am bereaved, I am bereaved."

[15]So the men took the gifts and double the amount of silver, and Benjamin also. They hurried down to Egypt and presented themselves to Joseph. [16]When Joseph saw Benjamin with them, he said to the steward of his house, "Take these men to my house, slaughter an animal and prepare dinner; they are to eat with me at noon."

[17]The man did as Joseph told him and took the men to Joseph's house. [18]Now the men were frightened when they were taken to his house. They thought, "We were brought here because of the silver that was put back into our sacks the first time. He wants to attack us and overpower us and seize us as slaves and take our donkeys."

[19]So they went up to Joseph's steward and spoke to him at the entrance to the house. [20]"Please, sir," they said, "we came down here the first time to buy food. [21]But at the place where we stopped for the night we opened our sacks and each of us found his silver—the exact weight—in the mouth of his sack. So we have brought it back with us. [22]We have also brought additional silver with us to buy food. We don't know who put our silver in our sacks."

[23]"It's all right," he said. "Don't be afraid. Your God, the God of your father, has given you treasure in your sacks; I received your silver." Then he brought Simeon out to them.

[24]The steward took the men into Joseph's house, gave them water to wash their feet and provided fodder for their donkeys. [25]They prepared their gifts for Joseph's arrival at noon, because they had heard that they were to eat there.

[26]When Joseph came home, they presented to him the gifts they had brought into the house, and they bowed down before him to the ground. [27]He asked them how they were, and then he said, "How is

your aged father you told me about? Is he still living?"

[28]They replied, "Your servant our father is still alive and well." And they bowed low to pay him honor.

[29]As he looked about and saw his brother Benjamin, his own mother's son, he asked, "Is this your youngest brother, the one you told me about?" And he said, "God be gracious to you, my son." [30]Deeply moved at the sight of his brother, Joseph hurried out and looked for a place to weep. He went into his private room and wept there.

[31]After he had washed his face, he came out and, controlling himself, said, "Serve the food."

[32]They served him by himself, the brothers by themselves, and the Egyptians who ate with him by themselves, because Egyptians could not eat with Hebrews, for that is detestable to Egyptians. [33]The men had been seated before him in the order of their ages, from the firstborn to the youngest; and they looked at each other in astonishment. [34]When portions were served to them from Joseph's table, Benjamin's portion was five times as much as anyone else's. So they feasted and drank freely with him.

A Silver Cup in a Sack

44 Now Joseph gave these instructions to the steward of his house: "Fill the men's sacks with as much food as they can carry, and put each man's silver in the mouth of his sack. [2]Then put my cup, the silver one, in the mouth of the youngest one's sack, along with the silver for his grain." And he did as Joseph said.

[3]As morning dawned, the men were sent on their way with their donkeys. [4]They had not gone far from the city when Joseph said to his steward, "Go after those men at once, and when you catch up with them, say to them, 'Why have you repaid good with evil? [5]Isn't this the cup my master drinks from and also uses for divination? This is a wicked thing you have done.' "

[6]When he caught up with them, he repeated these words to them. [7]But they

[a]14 Hebrew *El-Shaddai*

said to him, "Why does my lord say such things? Far be it from your servants to do anything like that! ⁸We even brought back to you from the land of Canaan the silver we found inside the mouths of our sacks. So why would we steal silver or gold from your master's house? ⁹If any of your servants is found to have it, he will die; and the rest of us will become my lord's slaves."

¹⁰"Very well, then," he said, "let it be as you say. Whoever is found to have it will become my slave; the rest of you will be free from blame."

¹¹Each of them quickly lowered his sack to the ground and opened it. ¹²Then the steward proceeded to search, beginning with the oldest and ending with the youngest. And the cup was found in Benjamin's sack. ¹³At this, they tore their clothes. Then they all loaded their donkeys and returned to the city.

¹⁴Joseph was still in the house when Judah and his brothers came in, and they threw themselves to the ground before him. ¹⁵Joseph said to them, "What is this you have done? Don't you know that a man like me can find things out by divination?"

¹⁶"What can we say to my lord?" Judah replied. "What can we say? How can we prove our innocence? God has uncovered your servants' guilt. We are now my lord's slaves—we ourselves and the one who was found to have the cup."

¹⁷But Joseph said, "Far be it from me to do such a thing! Only the man who was found to have the cup will become my slave. The rest of you, go back to your father in peace."

¹⁸Then Judah went up to him and said: "Please, my lord, let your servant speak a word to my lord. Do not be angry with your servant, though you are equal to Pharaoh himself. ¹⁹My lord asked his servants, 'Do you have a father or a brother?' ²⁰And we answered, 'We have an aged father, and there is a young son born to him in his old age. His brother is dead, and he is the only one of his mother's sons left, and his father loves him.'

²¹"Then you said to your servants, 'Bring him down to me so I can see him for myself.' ²²And we said to my lord,

'The boy cannot leave his father; if he leaves him, his father will die.' ²³But you told your servants, 'Unless your youngest brother comes down with you, you will not see my face again.' ²⁴When we went back to your servant my father, we told him what my lord had said.

²⁵"Then our father said, 'Go back and buy a little more food.' ²⁶But we said, 'We cannot go down. Only if our youngest brother is with us will we go. We cannot see the man's face unless our youngest brother is with us.'

²⁷"Your servant my father said to us, 'You know that my wife bore me two sons. ²⁸One of them went away from me, and I said, "He has surely been torn to pieces." And I have not seen him since. ²⁹If you take this one from me too and harm comes to him, you will bring my gray head down to the grave[a] in misery.'

³⁰"So now, if the boy is not with us when I go back to your servant my father and if my father, whose life is closely bound up with the boy's life, ³¹sees that the boy isn't there, he will die. Your servants will bring the gray head of our father down to the grave in sorrow. ³²Your servant guaranteed the boy's safety to my father. I said, 'If I do not bring him back to you, I will bear the blame before you, my father, all my life!'

³³"Now then, please let your servant remain here as my lord's slave in place of the boy, and let the boy return with his brothers. ³⁴How can I go back to my father if the boy is not with me? No! Do not let me see the misery that would come upon my father."

Joseph Makes Himself Known

45 Then Joseph could no longer control himself before all his attendants, and he cried out, "Have everyone leave my presence!" So there was no one with Joseph when he made himself known to his brothers. ²And he wept so loudly that the Egyptians heard him, and Pharaoh's household heard about it.

³Joseph said to his brothers, "I am Joseph! Is my father still living?" But his brothers were not able to answer him,

---

[a]29 Hebrew *Sheol*; also in verse 31

because they were terrified at his presence.

[4]Then Joseph said to his brothers, "Come close to me." When they had done so, he said, "I am your brother Joseph, the one you sold into Egypt! [5]And now, do not be distressed and do not be angry with yourselves for selling me here, because it was to save lives that God sent me ahead of you. [6]For two years now there has been famine in the land, and for the next five years there will not be plowing and reaping. [7]But God sent me ahead of you to preserve for you a remnant on earth and to save your lives by a great deliverance.[a]

[8]"So then, it was not you who sent me here, but God. He made me father to Pharaoh, lord of his entire household and ruler of all Egypt. [9]Now hurry back to my father and say to him, 'This is what your son Joseph says: God has made me lord of all Egypt. Come down to me; don't delay. [10]You shall live in the region of Goshen and be near me—you, your children and grandchildren, your flocks and herds, and all you have. [11]I will provide for you there, because five years of famine are still to come. Otherwise you and your household and all who belong to you will become destitute.'

[12]"You can see for yourselves, and so can my brother Benjamin, that it is really I who am speaking to you. [13]Tell my father about all the honor accorded me in Egypt and about everything you have seen. And bring my father down here quickly."

[14]Then he threw his arms around his brother Benjamin and wept, and Benjamin embraced him, weeping. [15]And he kissed all his brothers and wept over them. Afterward his brothers talked with him.

[16]When the news reached Pharaoh's palace that Joseph's brothers had come, Pharaoh and all his officials were pleased. [17]Pharaoh said to Joseph, "Tell your brothers, 'Do this: Load your animals and return to the land of Canaan, [18]and bring your father and your families back to me. I will give you the best of the land of Egypt and you can enjoy the fat of the land.'

[19]"You are also directed to tell them, 'Do this: Take some carts from Egypt for your children and your wives, and get your father and come. [20]Never mind about your belongings, because the best of all Egypt will be yours.'"

[21]So the sons of Israel did this. Joseph gave them carts, as Pharaoh had commanded, and he also gave them provisions for their journey. [22]To each of them he gave new clothing, but to Benjamin he gave three hundred shekels[b] of silver and five sets of clothes. [23]And this is what he sent to his father: ten donkeys loaded with the best things of Egypt, and ten female donkeys loaded with grain and bread and other provisions for his journey. [24]Then he sent his brothers away, and as they were leaving he said to them, "Don't quarrel on the way!"

[25]So they went up out of Egypt and came to their father Jacob in the land of Canaan. [26]They told him, "Joseph is still alive! In fact, he is ruler of all Egypt." Jacob was stunned; he did not believe them. [27]But when they told him everything Joseph had said to them, and when he saw the carts Joseph had sent to carry him back, the spirit of their father Jacob revived. [28]And Israel said, "I'm convinced! My son Joseph is still alive. I will go and see him before I die."

Jacob Goes to Egypt

46 So Israel set out with all that was his, and when he reached Beersheba, he offered sacrifices to the God of his father Isaac.

[2]And God spoke to Israel in a vision at night and said, "Jacob! Jacob!"

"Here I am," he replied.

[3]"I am God, the God of your father," he said. "Do not be afraid to go down to Egypt, for I will make you into a great nation there. [4]I will go down to Egypt with you, and I will surely bring you back again. And Joseph's own hand will close your eyes."

[5]Then Jacob left Beersheba, and Israel's sons took their father Jacob and their children and their wives in the carts that Pharaoh had sent to transport him.

---

[a]7 Or *save you as a great band of survivors*
[b]22 That is, about 7 1/2 pounds (about 3.5 kilograms)

⁶They also took with them their livestock and the possessions they had acquired in Canaan, and Jacob and all his offspring went to Egypt. ⁷He took with him to Egypt his sons and grandsons and his daughters and granddaughters—all his offspring.

⁸These are the names of the sons of Israel (Jacob and his descendants) who went to Egypt:

Reuben the firstborn of Jacob.
⁹The sons of Reuben:
Hanoch, Pallu, Hezron and Carmi.
¹⁰The sons of Simeon:
Jemuel, Jamin, Ohad, Jakin, Zohar and Shaul the son of a Canaanite woman.
¹¹The sons of Levi:
Gershon, Kohath and Merari.
¹²The sons of Judah:
Er, Onan, Shelah, Perez and Zerah (but Er and Onan had died in the land of Canaan).
The sons of Perez:
Hezron and Hamul.
¹³The sons of Issachar:
Tola, Puah,ᵃ Jashubᵇ and Shimron.
¹⁴The sons of Zebulun:
Sered, Elon and Jahleel.
¹⁵These were the sons Leah bore to Jacob in Paddan Aram,ᶜ besides his daughter Dinah. These sons and daughters of his were thirty-three in all.

¹⁶The sons of Gad:
Zephon,ᵈ Haggi, Shuni, Ezbon, Eri, Arodi and Areli.
¹⁷The sons of Asher:
Imnah, Ishvah, Ishvi and Beriah.
Their sister was Serah.
The sons of Beriah:
Heber and Malkiel.
¹⁸These were the children born to Jacob by Zilpah, whom Laban had given to his daughter Leah—sixteen in all.

¹⁹The sons of Jacob's wife Rachel:
Joseph and Benjamin. ²⁰In Egypt, Manasseh and Ephraim were born to Joseph by Asenath daughter of Potiphera, priest of On.ᵉ
²¹The sons of Benjamin:
Bela, Beker, Ashbel, Gera, Naaman, Ehi, Rosh, Muppim, Huppim and Ard.

²²These were the sons of Rachel who were born to Jacob—fourteen in all.

²³The son of Dan:
Hushim.
²⁴The sons of Naphtali:
Jahziel, Guni, Jezer and Shillem.
²⁵These were the sons born to Jacob by Bilhah, whom Laban had given to his daughter Rachel—seven in all.

²⁶All those who went to Egypt with Jacob—those who were his direct descendants, not counting his sons' wives—numbered sixty-six persons. ²⁷With the two sonsᶠ who had been born to Joseph in Egypt, the members of Jacob's family, which went to Egypt, were seventyᵍ in all.

²⁸Now Jacob sent Judah ahead of him to Joseph to get directions to Goshen. When they arrived in the region of Goshen, ²⁹Joseph had his chariot made ready and went to Goshen to meet his father Israel. As soon as Joseph appeared before him, he threw his arms around his fatherʰ and wept for a long time.

³⁰Israel said to Joseph, "Now I am ready to die, since I have seen for myself that you are still alive."

³¹Then Joseph said to his brothers and to his father's household, "I will go up and speak to Pharaoh and will say to him, 'My brothers and my father's household, who were living in the land of Canaan, have come to me. ³²The men are shepherds; they tend livestock, and they have brought along their flocks and herds and everything they own.' ³³When Pharaoh calls you in and asks, 'What is your occupation?' ³⁴you should answer, 'Your servants have tended livestock from our boyhood on, just as our fathers did.' Then you will be allowed to settle in the region of Goshen, for all shepherds are detestable to the Egyptians."

ᵃ13 Samaritan Pentateuch and Syriac (see also 1 Chron. 7:1); Masoretic Text *Puvah*   ᵇ13 Samaritan Pentateuch and some Septuagint manuscripts (see also Num. 26:24 and 1 Chron. 7:1); Masoretic Text *Iob*   ᶜ15 That is, Northwest Mesopotamia   ᵈ16 Samaritan Pentateuch and Septuagint (see also Num. 26:15); Masoretic Text *Ziphion*   ᵉ20 That is, Heliopolis   ᶠ27 Hebrew; Septuagint *the nine children*   ᵍ27 Hebrew (see also Exodus 1:5 and footnote); Septuagint (see also Acts 7:14) *seventy-five*   ʰ29 Hebrew *around him*

47 Joseph went and told Pharaoh, "My father and brothers, with their flocks and herds and everything they own, have come from the land of Canaan and are now in Goshen." [2]He chose five of his brothers and presented them before Pharaoh.

[3]Pharaoh asked the brothers, "What is your occupation?"

"Your servants are shepherds," they replied to Pharaoh, "just as our fathers were." [4]They also said to him, "We have come to live here awhile, because the famine is severe in Canaan and your servants' flocks have no pasture. So now, please let your servants settle in Goshen."

[5]Pharaoh said to Joseph, "Your father and your brothers have come to you, [6]and the land of Egypt is before you; settle your father and your brothers in the best part of the land. Let them live in Goshen. And if you know of any among them with special ability, put them in charge of my own livestock."

[7]Then Joseph brought his father Jacob in and presented him before Pharaoh. After Jacob blessed[a] Pharaoh, [8]Pharaoh asked him, "How old are you?"

[9]And Jacob said to Pharaoh, "The years of my pilgrimage are a hundred and thirty. My years have been few and difficult, and they do not equal the years of the pilgrimage of my fathers." [10]Then Jacob blessed[b] Pharaoh and went out from his presence.

[11]So Joseph settled his father and his brothers in Egypt and gave them property in the best part of the land, the district of Rameses, as Pharaoh directed. [12]Joseph also provided his father and his brothers and all his father's household with food, according to the number of their children.

Joseph and the Famine

[13]There was no food, however, in the whole region because the famine was severe; both Egypt and Canaan wasted away because of the famine. [14]Joseph collected all the money that was to be found in Egypt and Canaan in payment for the grain they were buying, and he brought it to Pharaoh's palace. [15]When the money of the people of Egypt and Canaan was gone, all Egypt came to Joseph and said, "Give us food. Why should we die before your eyes? Our money is used up."

[16]"Then bring your livestock," said Joseph. "I will sell you food in exchange for your livestock, since your money is gone." [17]So they brought their livestock to Joseph, and he gave them food in exchange for their horses, their sheep and goats, their cattle and donkeys. And he brought them through that year with food in exchange for all their livestock.

[18]When that year was over, they came to him the following year and said, "We cannot hide from our lord the fact that since our money is gone and our livestock belongs to you, there is nothing left for our lord except our bodies and our land. [19]Why should we perish before your eyes—we and our land as well? Buy us and our land in exchange for food, and we with our land will be in bondage to Pharaoh. Give us seed so that we may live and not die, and that the land may not become desolate."

[20]So Joseph bought all the land in Egypt for Pharaoh. The Egyptians, one and all, sold their fields, because the famine was too severe for them. The land became Pharaoh's, [21]and Joseph reduced the people to servitude,[c] from one end of Egypt to the other. [22]However, he did not

---

AHHHH-CHUUUU!

Huh?

Genesis 47:10

"God bless you." Did you know that people used to think that when you sneezed you might die? So they would wish you good health (Gesundheit!) or God's blessing. When you "bless" someone, you're asking God to be good to that person. Kind of a cool thing to think about when you say "God bless you" to someone else. You're wishing them God's best.

---

[a]7 Or *greeted*   [b]10 Or *said farewell to*
[c]21 Samaritan Pentateuch and Septuagint (see also Vulgate); Masoretic Text *and he moved the people into the cities*

buy the land of the priests, because they received a regular allotment from Pharaoh and had food enough from the allotment Pharaoh gave them. That is why they did not sell their land.

²³Joseph said to the people, "Now that I have bought you and your land today for Pharaoh, here is seed for you so you can plant the ground. ²⁴But when the crop comes in, give a fifth of it to Pharaoh. The other four-fifths you may keep as seed for the fields and as food for yourselves and your households and your children."

²⁵"You have saved our lives," they said. "May we find favor in the eyes of our lord; we will be in bondage to Pharaoh."

²⁶So Joseph established it as a law concerning land in Egypt—still in force today—that a fifth of the produce belongs to Pharaoh. It was only the land of the priests that did not become Pharaoh's.

²⁷Now the Israelites settled in Egypt in the region of Goshen. They acquired property there and were fruitful and increased greatly in number.

²⁸Jacob lived in Egypt seventeen years, and the years of his life were a hundred and forty-seven. ²⁹When the time drew near for Israel to die, he called for his son Joseph and said to him, "If I have found favor in your eyes, put your hand under my thigh and promise that you will show me kindness and faithfulness. Do not bury me in Egypt, ³⁰but when I rest with my fathers, carry me out of Egypt and bury me where they are buried."

"I will do as you say," he said.

³¹"Swear to me," he said. Then Joseph swore to him, and Israel worshiped as he leaned on the top of his staff.ᵃ

Manasseh and Ephraim

48 Some time later Joseph was told, "Your father is ill." So he took his two sons Manasseh and Ephraim along with him. ²When Jacob was told, "Your son Joseph has come to you," Israel rallied his strength and sat up on the bed.

³Jacob said to Joseph, "God Almightyᵇ appeared to me at Luz in the land of Canaan, and there he blessed me ⁴and said to me, 'I am going to make you fruitful and will increase your numbers. I will make you a community of peoples, and I will give this land as an everlasting possession to your descendants after you.'

⁵"Now then, your two sons born to you in Egypt before I came to you here will be reckoned as mine; Ephraim and Manasseh will be mine, just as Reuben and Simeon are mine. ⁶Any children born to you after them will be yours; in the territory they inherit they will be reckoned under the names of their brothers. ⁷As I was returning from Paddan,ᶜ to my sorrow Rachel died in the land of Canaan while we were still on the way, a little distance from Ephrath. So I buried her there beside the road to Ephrath" (that is, Bethlehem).

⁸When Israel saw the sons of Joseph, he asked, "Who are these?"

⁹"They are the sons God has given me here," Joseph said to his father.

Then Israel said, "Bring them to me so I may bless them."

¹⁰Now Israel's eyes were failing because of old age, and he could hardly see. So Joseph brought his sons close to him, and his father kissed them and embraced them.

¹¹Israel said to Joseph, "I never expected to see your face again, and now God has allowed me to see your children too."

¹²Then Joseph removed them from Israel's knees and bowed down with his face to the ground. ¹³And Joseph took both of them, Ephraim on his right toward Israel's left hand and Manasseh on his left toward Israel's right hand, and brought them close to him. ¹⁴But Israel reached out his right hand and put it on Ephraim's head, though he was the younger, and crossing his arms, he put his left hand on Manasseh's head, even though Manasseh was the firstborn.

¹⁵Then he blessed Joseph and said,

"May the God before whom my
     fathers
   Abraham and Isaac walked,
the God who has been my shepherd
   all my life to this day,
¹⁶the Angel who has delivered me from
     all harm

ᵃ31 Or *Israel bowed down at the head of his bed*
ᵇ3 Hebrew *El-Shaddai*   ᶜ7 That is, Northwest
Mesopotamia

—may he bless these boys.
May they be called by my name
and the names of my fathers
Abraham and Isaac,
and may they increase greatly
upon the earth."

[17]When Joseph saw his father placing his right hand on Ephraim's head he was displeased; so he took hold of his father's hand to move it from Ephraim's head to Manasseh's head. [18]Joseph said to him, "No, my father, this one is the firstborn; put your right hand on his head."

[19]But his father refused and said, "I know, my son, I know. He too will become a people, and he too will become great. Nevertheless, his younger brother will be greater than he, and his descendants will become a group of nations." [20]He blessed them that day and said,

"In your[a] name will Israel pronounce
this blessing:
'May God make you like Ephraim
and Manasseh.'"

So he put Ephraim ahead of Manasseh.

[21]Then Israel said to Joseph, "I am about to die, but God will be with you[b] and take you[b] back to the land of your[b] fathers. [22]And to you, as one who is over your brothers, I give the ridge of land[c] I took from the Amorites with my sword and my bow."

Jacob Blesses His Sons

49 Then Jacob called for his sons and said: "Gather around so I can tell you what will happen to you in days to come.

[2]"Assemble and listen, sons of Jacob;
listen to your father Israel.

[3]"Reuben, you are my firstborn,
my might, the first sign of my
strength,
excelling in honor, excelling in
power.
[4]Turbulent as the waters, you will no
longer excel,
for you went up onto your father's
bed,
onto my couch and defiled it.

[5]"Simeon and Levi are brothers—

their swords[d] are weapons of
violence.
[6]Let me not enter their council,
let me not join their assembly,
for they have killed men in their
anger
and hamstrung oxen as they
pleased.
[7]Cursed be their anger, so fierce,
and their fury, so cruel!
I will scatter them in Jacob
and disperse them in Israel.

[8]"Judah,[e] your brothers will praise you;
your hand will be on the neck of
your enemies;
your father's sons will bow down to
you.
[9]You are a lion's cub, O Judah;
you return from the prey, my son.
Like a lion he crouches and lies down,
like a lioness—who dares to rouse
him?
[10]The scepter will not depart from
Judah,
nor the ruler's staff from between
his feet,
until he comes to whom it belongs[f]
and the obedience of the nations is
his.
[11]He will tether his donkey to a vine,
his colt to the choicest branch;
he will wash his garments in wine,
his robes in the blood of grapes.
[12]His eyes will be darker than wine,
his teeth whiter than milk.[g]

[13]"Zebulun will live by the seashore
and become a haven for ships;
his border will extend toward
Sidon.

[14]"Issachar is a rawboned[h] donkey
lying down between two
saddlebags.[i]
[15]When he sees how good is his resting
place
and how pleasant is his land,

---

[a]20 The Hebrew is singular.   [b]21 The Hebrew is plural.   [c]22 Or *And to you I give one portion more than to your brothers—the portion*   [d]5 The meaning of the Hebrew for this word is uncertain.   [e]8 *Judah* sounds like and may be derived from the Hebrew for *praise.*   [f]10 Or *until Shiloh comes;* or *until he comes to whom tribute belongs*   [g]12 Or *will be dull from wine, / his teeth white from milk*   [h]14 Or *strong*   [i]14 Or *campfires*

he will bend his shoulder to the
burden
and submit to forced labor.

¹⁶"Dan^a will provide justice for his
people
as one of the tribes of Israel.
¹⁷Dan will be a serpent by the
roadside,
a viper along the path,
that bites the horse's heels
so that its rider tumbles backward.

¹⁸"I look for your deliverance, O LORD.

¹⁹"Gad^b will be attacked by a band of
raiders,
but he will attack them at their
heels.

²⁰"Asher's food will be rich;
he will provide delicacies fit for a
king.

²¹"Naphtali is a doe set free
that bears beautiful fawns.^c

²²"Joseph is a fruitful vine,
a fruitful vine near a spring,
whose branches climb over a wall.^d
²³With bitterness archers attacked him;
they shot at him with hostility.
²⁴But his bow remained steady,
his strong arms stayed^e limber,
because of the hand of the Mighty
One of Jacob,
because of the Shepherd, the Rock
of Israel,
²⁵because of your father's God, who
helps you,
because of the Almighty,^f who
blesses you
with blessings of the heavens above,
blessings of the deep that lies
below,
blessings of the breast and womb.
²⁶Your father's blessings are greater
than the blessings of the ancient
mountains,
than^g the bounty of the age-old
hills.
Let all these rest on the head of
Joseph,
on the brow of the prince among^h
his brothers.

²⁷"Benjamin is a ravenous wolf;
in the morning he devours the prey,

in the evening he divides the
plunder."

²⁸All these are the twelve tribes of Israel, and this is what their father said to them when he blessed them, giving each the blessing appropriate to him.

The Death of Jacob

²⁹Then he gave them these instructions: "I am about to be gathered to my people. Bury me with my fathers in the cave in the field of Ephron the Hittite, ³⁰the cave in the field of Machpelah, near Mamre in Canaan, which Abraham bought as a burial place from Ephron the Hittite, along with the field. ³¹There Abraham and his wife Sarah were buried, there Isaac and his wife Rebekah were buried, and there I buried Leah. ³²The field and the cave in it were bought from the Hittites.ⁱ"

³³When Jacob had finished giving instructions to his sons, he drew his feet up into the bed, breathed his last and was gathered to his people.

50 Joseph threw himself upon his father and wept over him and kissed him. ²Then Joseph directed the physicians in his service to embalm his father Israel. So the physicians embalmed him, ³taking a full forty days, for that was the time required for embalming. And the Egyptians mourned for him seventy days.

⁴When the days of mourning had passed, Joseph said to Pharaoh's court, "If I have found favor in your eyes, speak to Pharaoh for me. Tell him, ⁵'My father made me swear an oath and said, "I am about to die; bury me in the tomb I dug for myself in the land of Canaan." Now let me go up and bury my father; then I will return.' "

⁶Pharaoh said, "Go up and bury your father, as he made you swear to do."

---

^a16 Dan here means he provides justice.   ^b19 Gad can mean attack and band of raiders.   ^c21 Or free; / he utters beautiful words   ^d22 Or Joseph is a wild colt, / a wild colt near a spring, / a wild donkey on a terraced hill   ^e23,24 Or archers will attack . . . will shoot . . . will remain . . . will stay   ^f25 Hebrew Shaddai   ^g26 Or of my progenitors, / as great as   ^h26 Or the one separated from   ⁱ32 Or the sons of Heth

⁷So Joseph went up to bury his father. All Pharaoh's officials accompanied him—the dignitaries of his court and all the dignitaries of Egypt— ⁸besides all the members of Joseph's household and his brothers and those belonging to his father's household. Only their children and their flocks and herds were left in Goshen. ⁹Chariots and horsemen[a] also went up with him. It was a very large company.

¹⁰When they reached the threshing floor of Atad, near the Jordan, they lamented loudly and bitterly; and there Joseph observed a seven-day period of mourning for his father. ¹¹When the Canaanites who lived there saw the mourning at the threshing floor of Atad, they said, "The Egyptians are holding a solemn ceremony of mourning." That is why that place near the Jordan is called Abel Mizraim.[b]

¹²So Jacob's sons did as he had commanded them: ¹³They carried him to the land of Canaan and buried him in the cave in the field of Machpelah, near Mamre, which Abraham had bought as a burial place from Ephron the Hittite, along with the field. ¹⁴After burying his father, Joseph returned to Egypt, together with his brothers and all the others who had gone with him to bury his father.

Joseph Reassures His Brothers

¹⁵When Joseph's brothers saw that their father was dead, they said, "What if

---

[a]9 Or *charioteers*   [b]11 *Abel Mizraim* means *mourning of the Egyptians.*

Tues day

Happy Endings

Read Genesis 50:19-21

When my grandpa died, I felt like the worst thing in the world had happened. I couldn't figure out why God would let someone I love die. But the more I thought about it, the more I realized God did something great for my grandpa: God ended Grandpa's pain and brought him to heaven. Even though I still miss my grandpa, I know he's happy spending eternity with God.

The story of Joseph is a great example of how God can take a bad situation and bring good out of it. Joseph lost everything—his family, his friends and his freedom. But God worked through Joseph to help the people of Egypt survive a drought and a famine. Joseph saved thousands of lives, something he probably couldn't have done if he'd stayed with his father and brothers. Joseph trusted God the whole time he was a slave. He never forgot that God loved him and was in control of everything.

God loves all of us, and he has a purpose for everything that happens.

Noah age 12

What about You?

❶ What was one time in your life that God turned something from bad to good?

❷ When you get your immunization shots, you're actually given a little tiny bit of the bacteria or virus that causes the illness! Talk with your health teacher or a nurse about why vaccinations work. Think about how bad things can strengthen your relationship with God.

❸ Ask God to help you trust him when life seems confusing.

Turn to page 73 for your next devotion.

Joseph holds a grudge against us and pays us back for all the wrongs we did to him?" [16]So they sent word to Joseph, saying, "Your father left these instructions before he died: [17]'This is what you are to say to Joseph: I ask you to forgive your brothers the sins and the wrongs they committed in treating you so badly.' Now please forgive the sins of the servants of the God of your father." When their message came to him, Joseph wept.

[18]His brothers then came and threw themselves down before him. "We are your slaves," they said.

[19]But Joseph said to them, "Don't be afraid. Am I in the place of God? [20]You intended to harm me, but God intended it for good to accomplish what is now being done, the saving of many lives. [21]So then, don't be afraid. I will provide for you and your children." And he reassured them and spoke kindly to them.

The Death of Joseph

[22]Joseph stayed in Egypt, along with all his father's family. He lived a hundred and ten years [23]and saw the third generation of Ephraim's children. Also the children of Makir son of Manasseh were placed at birth on Joseph's knees.[a]

[24]Then Joseph said to his brothers, "I am about to die. But God will surely come to your aid and take you up out of this land to the land he promised on oath to Abraham, Isaac and Jacob." [25]And Joseph made the sons of Israel swear an oath and said, "God will surely come to your aid, and then you must carry my bones up from this place."

[26]So Joseph died at the age of a hundred and ten. And after they embalmed him, he was placed in a coffin in Egypt.

[a]23 That is, were counted as his

Genesis Crossword Puzzle

Down

1. He gave us this so that we could see. (1:3)
2. A place east of Eden. (4:16)
3. Laban said to Jacob, "Please _____." (30:27)
4. As early as Genesis, the practice of _____ existed. (21:10)
5. These visitors were heavenly. (19:1)
6. God created us in his _____. (1:27)
7. God _____ everything. (1:1)
9. The first murder victim. (4:8)
11. _____ fell for 40 days and 40 nights. (7:12)
12. _____ shall be called "woman." (2:23)
14. The greater light. (1:16)
15. He made his first appearance to man in the Garden. He may be a snake, but his real name is _____. (3:1)
16. The ruler, or king, of the Egyptians, he was cursed because of Abram's lie. (12:15)
18. The very first man. (2:20)
19. The number of days it took God to create the earth, plus one. (2:2)
20. One of those evil cities. (19:24)
21. The serpent did this to Eve. (3:13)
22. Sodom and Gomorrah were destroyed by this. (19:24)
25. Jacob was a _____ with God. (32:24)
30. The _____ of God married daughters of men. (6:2)
31. Israel made Joseph a colorful one of these. (37:3)
32. Noah and his family survived this. (7:6)
34. Abram's nephew. (13:12)
35. Where Abram and Sarai went during a famine. (12:10)
36. How the animals went in the ark. (7:2)
40. The great tree of _____. (12:6)
41. Abraham's son. (22:2)
42. Isaac's wife. (24:67)
43. Esau liked to do this. (25:27)
44. This forced Abram into Egypt. (12:10)
48. Instead of Isaac, this was sacrificed. (22:13)

Across

1. Separated the waters. (1:10)
4. Abraham's wife. (17:15)
8. Their disobedience caused this to come into the world. (3:3)
10. Abram's new name was _____. (17:5)
12. Lot's wife was turned to this. (19:26)
13. God named these "seas." (1:10)
15. Another name for snake. (3:1)
17. Jacob grabbed this on Esau. (25:26)
18. Another name for "Creatures." (8:19)
20. Another name for "The Almighty." (1:1)
23. God created the _____. (1:1)
24. The flood wiped out ___ men. (6:5)
25. Eve was the first one. (2:23)
26. A place so evil, God destroyed it. (18:20)
27. Jared's son. (5:18)
29. How God spoke to Pharaoh. (41:1)
32. Not an apple, but a _____. (3:2)
33. Where Lot ran to escape. (19:22)
37. Jacob's favorite son. (37:3)
38. Hushim's father. (46:23)
39. What the Ark was made out of. (6:14)
41. Jacob's other name. (A Nation) (46:8)
43. One of Noah's sons. (6:10)
44. How long the rains lasted. (7:17)
45. Traded his inheritance for stew. (25:33–34)
46. Cain's occupation. (4:3)
47. Abraham was to do this to Isaac. (22:2)
49. Who built the Ark? 6:13–14
50. Traded stew for an inheritance. (25:33–34)
51. The 12 sons became the 12 _____ of Israel. (35:23–26)

Exodus

START

Cast OF Characters

Moses' Mom

This gutsy woman places her baby boy in a floating basket instead of drowning him in the Nile like Pharaoh ordered. And when Pharaoh's daughter needs someone to help raise the baby, she recruits Moses' mom for the job—without even knowing she's the real mom. Pretty cool.

Moses

(MOE-zus) Moses is the human hero in this book. He starts out as a miracle baby, grows to become a favorite of Pharaoh, then a murderer and finally leads God's people out of slavery. (He's also the author of this book.)

God

He makes lots of appearances in this book. God has a meeting with Moses at

By the end of the book of Genesis, the Israelites were just a big happy family, living as welcome guests in the land of Egypt. Exodus picks up the story a few hundred years later. How times have changed. Now the Jews are an exploding nation of slaves. The pharaoh (king) launches an extreme form of population control, ordering all baby boys to be thrown into the Nile River. Moses' mom obeys the order . . . but with one minor adjustment: She sticks him in a basket first!

Pharaoh's daughter finds the floating tot, adopts him, and soon Moses is in tight with the royal family, just as his ancestor Joseph had been before him. As an adult, Moses kills an Egyptian caught abusing an Israelite. He hides out in Midian to avoid the murder rap. That's when God introduces himself by way of the famous burning bush. Moses returns to Egypt on a mission from God—to free the Israelite slaves and lead them to the promised land.

Pharaoh gives in to Moses' demands only after God sends all sorts of terrible plagues. The Israelites pack up their stuff and head for the border. Pharaoh changes his mind just in time to get soaked (and croak) in the rapidly rising Red Sea.

Three months into the trip, the Israelites camp out at the foot of Mount Sinai. This is where God tells Moses the Ten Commandments and dozens of other laws to keep the people safe and sane. God also provides a blueprint for a portable tent-cathedral called the *tabernacle*. Exodus ends with God's glory taking up residence in the brand new tabernacle. It was easy to find that giant tent city: You just had to look for the cloud during the day and the fire at night. Anyhow . . . that's why the book's called "Exodus"—it's the story of the Israelites' *exit* from Egypt and slavery.

the burning bush and has lots of follow-up meetings with Moses through the rest of the book. God's first real appearance is on Mount Sinai, one-on-one with Moses.

Pharaoh (FAIR-oh)

That's what the Egyptians called their king. The pharaoh and Moses have it out big-time when Moses shows up demanding freedom for the Israelites.

Aaron (AIR-on)

He's Moses' brother and right hand man. Aaron goes with Moses to talk to the pharaoh and helps Moses get the Israelites outta town.

What's UP with That?

Pharaoh was a stubborn guy—

it took 10 awful plagues to convince him that God was serious about letting the Israelites go free. Fill in the correct plagues using the Plague Menu. Then choose the 3 plagues you think were the most awful.

Plague ❶ _____
Plague ❷ _____
Plague ❸ _____
Plague ❹ _____
Plague ❺ _____
Plague ❻ _____
Plague ❼ _____
Plague ❽ _____
Plague ❾ _____
Plague ❿ _____

Plague Menu

no TV for a week	man-eating hamsters
3 days of night	gnats not nice
hailin' like crazy	livestock becomes deadstock
Gross, yucky boils	grasshoppers-o-plenty
UFO invasion	uncontrollable drooling
death of first sons	river of blood
flies on us	
toilets backed up	
frogs, frogs, everywhere	

Snap Shots

- The river cruise, the murder, the fugitive *(chapters 1—2)*

- Brush fire! *(chapters 3—4)*

- Frogs, blood, gnats, darkness, yuck! *(chapters 5—11)*

- Run, Israel, run *(chapters 12—14)*

- Stop whining! *(chapters 15—18)*

- God shows up *(chapters 19—31)*

- The golden calf incident *(chapters 32—34)*

- Big tent revival *(chapters 35—40)*

answers: 1. Blood 2. frogs 3. Gnats 4. Flies 5. Livestock 6. Boils 7. Hail 8. Locusts 9. Darkness 10. Firstborn

The Israelites Oppressed

1 These are the names of the sons of Israel who went to Egypt with Jacob, each with his family: ²Reuben, Simeon, Levi and Judah; ³Issachar, Zebulun and Benjamin; ⁴Dan and Naphtali; Gad and Asher. ⁵The descendants of Jacob numbered seventy*ᵃ* in all; Joseph was already in Egypt.

⁶Now Joseph and all his brothers and all that generation died, ⁷but the Israelites were fruitful and multiplied greatly and became exceedingly numerous, so that the land was filled with them.

⁸Then a new king, who did not know about Joseph, came to power in Egypt. ⁹"Look," he said to his people, "the Israelites have become much too numerous for us. ¹⁰Come, we must deal shrewdly with them or they will become even more numerous and, if war breaks out, will join our enemies, fight against us and leave the country."

¹¹So they put slave masters over them to oppress them with forced labor, and they built Pithom and Rameses as store cities for Pharaoh. ¹²But the more they were oppressed, the more they multiplied and spread; so the Egyptians came to dread the Israelites ¹³and worked them ruthlessly. ¹⁴They made their lives bitter with hard labor in brick and mortar and with all kinds of work in the fields; in all their hard labor the Egyptians used them ruthlessly.

¹⁵The king of Egypt said to the Hebrew midwives, whose names were Shiphrah and Puah, ¹⁶"When you help the Hebrew women in childbirth and observe them on the delivery stool, if it is a boy, kill him; but if it is a girl, let her live." ¹⁷The midwives, however, feared God and did not do what the king of Egypt had told them to do; they let the boys live. ¹⁸Then the king of Egypt summoned the midwives and asked them, "Why have you done this? Why have you let the boys live?"

¹⁹The midwives answered Pharaoh, "Hebrew women are not like Egyptian women; they are vigorous and give birth before the midwives arrive."

²⁰So God was kind to the midwives and the people increased and became even more numerous. ²¹And because the midwives feared God, he gave them families of their own.

²²Then Pharaoh gave this order to all his people: "Every boy that is born*ᵇ* you must throw into the Nile, but let every girl live."

The Birth of Moses

2 Now a man of the house of Levi married a Levite woman, ²and she became pregnant and gave birth to a son. When she saw that he was a fine child, she hid him for three months. ³But when she could hide him no longer, she got a papyrus basket for him and coated it with tar and pitch. Then she placed the child in it and put it among the reeds along the bank of the Nile. ⁴His sister stood at a distance to see what would happen to him.

⁵Then Pharaoh's daughter went down to the Nile to bathe, and her attendants were walking along the river bank. She saw the basket among the reeds and sent her slave girl to get it. ⁶She opened it and saw the baby. He was crying, and she felt sorry for him. "This is one of the Hebrew babies," she said.

⁷Then his sister asked Pharaoh's daughter, "Shall I go and get one of the Hebrew women to nurse the baby for you?"

⁸"Yes, go," she answered. And the girl went and got the baby's mother. ⁹Pharaoh's daughter said to her, "Take this baby and nurse him for me, and I will pay you." So the woman took the baby and nursed him. ¹⁰When the child grew older, she took him to Pharaoh's daughter and he became her son. She named him Moses,*ᶜ* saying, "I drew him out of the water."

Moses Flees to Midian

¹¹One day, after Moses had grown up, he went out to where his own people were and watched them at their hard labor. He saw an Egyptian beating a He-

---

*ᵃ5 Masoretic Text (see also Gen. 46:27); Dead Sea Scrolls and Septuagint (see also Acts 7:14 and note at Gen. 46:27) seventy-five   *ᵇ22 Masoretic Text; Samaritan Pentateuch, Septuagint and Targums born to the Hebrews   *ᶜ10 Moses sounds like the Hebrew for draw out.

brew, one of his own people. [12]Glancing this way and that and seeing no one, he killed the Egyptian and hid him in the sand. [13]The next day he went out and saw two Hebrews fighting. He asked the one in the wrong, "Why are you hitting your fellow Hebrew?"

[14]The man said, "Who made you ruler and judge over us? Are you thinking of killing me as you killed the Egyptian?" Then Moses was afraid and thought, "What I did must have become known."

[15]When Pharaoh heard of this, he tried to kill Moses, but Moses fled from Pharaoh and went to live in Midian, where he sat down by a well. [16]Now a priest of Midian had seven daughters, and they came to draw water and fill the troughs to water their father's flock. [17]Some shepherds came along and drove them away, but Moses got up and came to their rescue and watered their flock.

[18]When the girls returned to Reuel their father, he asked them, "Why have you returned so early today?"

[19]They answered, "An Egyptian rescued us from the shepherds. He even drew water for us and watered the flock."

[20]"And where is he?" he asked his daughters. "Why did you leave him? Invite him to have something to eat."

[21]Moses agreed to stay with the man, who gave his daughter Zipporah to Moses in marriage. [22]Zipporah gave birth to a son, and Moses named him Gershom,[a] saying, "I have become an alien in a foreign land."

[a]22 *Gershom* sounds like the Hebrew for *an alien there.*

Wednesday

Never Fear! God's Here!

Read Exodus 1:22—2:4

One thing the story of Moses proves is that God is always there to help people through hard times. Moses' mother was scared that her baby would be killed, so she sent him down the river in a basket. She probably couldn't have done that if she didn't trust God to take care of her baby.

It's not easy to trust God when you're scared. And fear can make people do things that aren't very smart. When I was really little, my sisters played a trick on me. I was sitting on top of a table when my sisters turned off the lights and ran out of the room. I was so scared that I didn't know what to do. Finally, I decided to jump off the table. But instead of landing on the floor, I hit the door of our stereo cabinet, which was glass. I ended up needing stitches! I got hurt because I panicked. I would have been fine if I'd stayed calm and called for help.

I learned that getting all worked up when you're scared doesn't make things better. The best thing we can do is ask God for help and trust him to take care of us.

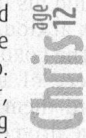
Chris age 12

What about You?

❶ What are some things you worry about? Why is it sometimes hard to trust God to take care of the difficult situations in our lives?

❷ Get some lint out of your pocket or find a little, short piece of thread. Now go into the bathroom and turn on the bathtub faucet. Send your little piece of whatever down the drain. As you watch it go away, think about how God takes your fears and worries and carries them away too.

❸ Ask God to help you trust him always—even in difficult times.

Turn to page 75 for your next devotion.

²³During that long period, the king of Egypt died. The Israelites groaned in their slavery and cried out, and their cry for help because of their slavery went up to God. ²⁴God heard their groaning and he remembered his covenant with Abraham, with Isaac and with Jacob. ²⁵So God looked on the Israelites and was concerned about them.

Moses and the Burning Bush

3 Now Moses was tending the flock of Jethro his father-in-law, the priest of Midian, and he led the flock to the far side of the desert and came to Horeb, the mountain of God. ²There the angel of the LORD appeared to him in flames of fire from within a bush. Moses saw that though the bush was on fire it did not burn up. ³So Moses thought, "I will go over and see this strange sight—why the bush does not burn up."

⁴When the LORD saw that he had gone over to look, God called to him from within the bush, "Moses! Moses!"

And Moses said, "Here I am."

⁵"Do not come any closer," God said. "Take off your sandals, for the place where you are standing is holy ground." ⁶Then he said, "I am the God of your father, the God of Abraham, the God of Isaac and the God of Jacob." At this, Moses hid his face, because he was afraid to look at God.

⁷The LORD said, "I have indeed seen the misery of my people in Egypt. I have heard them crying out because of their slave drivers, and I am concerned about their suffering. ⁸So I have come down to rescue them from the hand of the Egyptians and to bring them up out of that land into a good and spacious land, a land flowing with milk and honey—the home of the Canaanites, Hittites, Amorites, Perizzites, Hivites and Jebusites. ⁹And now the cry of the Israelites has reached me, and I have seen the way the Egyptians are oppressing them. ¹⁰So now, go. I am sending you to Pharaoh to bring my people the Israelites out of Egypt."

¹¹But Moses said to God, "Who am I, that I should go to Pharaoh and bring the Israelites out of Egypt?"

¹²And God said, "I will be with you. And this will be the sign to you that it is I who have sent you: When you have brought the people out of Egypt, you[a] will worship God on this mountain."

¹³Moses said to God, "Suppose I go to the Israelites and say to them, 'The God of your fathers has sent me to you,' and they ask me, 'What is his name?' Then what shall I tell them?"

¹⁴God said to Moses, "I AM WHO I AM.[b] This is what you are to say to the Israelites: 'I AM has sent me to you.' "

¹⁵God also said to Moses, "Say to the Israelites, 'The LORD,[c] the God of your fathers—the God of Abraham, the God of Isaac and the God of Jacob—has sent me to you.' This is my name forever, the name by which I am to be remembered from generation to generation.

¹⁶"Go, assemble the elders of Israel and say to them, 'The LORD, the God of your fathers—the God of Abraham, Isaac and Jacob—appeared to me and said: I have watched over you and have seen what has been done to you in Egypt. ¹⁷And I have promised to bring you up out of your misery in Egypt into the land of the Canaanites, Hittites, Amorites, Perizzites, Hivites and Jebusites—a land flowing with milk and honey.'

¹⁸"The elders of Israel will listen to you. Then you and the elders are to go to the king of Egypt and say to him, 'The LORD, the God of the Hebrews, has met with us. Let us take a three-day journey into the desert to offer sacrifices to the LORD our God.' ¹⁹But I know that the king of Egypt will not let you go unless a mighty hand compels him. ²⁰So I will stretch out my hand and strike the Egyptians with all the wonders that I will perform among them. After that, he will let you go.

²¹"And I will make the Egyptians favorably disposed toward this people, so that when you leave you will not go empty-handed. ²²Every woman is to ask her neighbor and any woman living in her house for articles of silver and gold and for clothing, which you will put on your sons and daughters. And so you will plunder the Egyptians."

---

a12 The Hebrew is plural.   *b14* Or *I WILL BE WHAT I WILL BE*   *c15* The Hebrew for LORD sounds like and may be derived from the Hebrew for *I AM* in verse 14.

Signs for Moses

4 Moses answered, "What if they do not believe me or listen to me and say, 'The LORD did not appear to you'?"

[2]Then the LORD said to him, "What is that in your hand?"

"A staff," he replied.

[3]The LORD said, "Throw it on the ground."

Moses threw it on the ground and it became a snake, and he ran from it. [4]Then the LORD said to him, "Reach out your hand and take it by the tail." So Moses reached out and took hold of the snake and it turned back into a staff in his hand. [5]"This," said the LORD, "is so that they may believe that the LORD, the God of their fathers—the God of Abraham, the God of Isaac and the God of Jacob—has appeared to you."

[6]Then the LORD said, "Put your hand inside your cloak." So Moses put his hand into his cloak, and when he took it out, it was leprous,[a] like snow.

[7]"Now put it back into your cloak," he said. So Moses put his hand back into his cloak, and when he took it out, it was restored, like the rest of his flesh.

[8]Then the LORD said, "If they do not believe you or pay attention to the first miraculous sign, they may believe the second. [9]But if they do not believe these two signs or listen to you, take some water from the Nile and pour it on the dry ground. The water you take from the river will become blood on the ground."

[10]Moses said to the LORD, "O Lord, I have never been eloquent, neither in the past nor since you have spoken to your servant. I am slow of speech and tongue."

[11]The LORD said to him, "Who gave man his mouth? Who makes him deaf or mute? Who gives him sight or makes him blind? Is it not I, the LORD? [12]Now go; I will help you speak and will teach you what to say."

[13]But Moses said, "O Lord, please send someone else to do it."

[14]Then the LORD's anger burned against

---

[a]6 The Hebrew word was used for various diseases affecting the skin—not necessarily leprosy.

Thursday

Following God

Read Exodus 4:11

When God asked Moses to lead the Israelites out of Egypt, Moses tried to get out of it by using a lame excuse. Moses said he wasn't a good enough speaker to lead God's people. God basically told him that he knew what Moses' mouth could do. After all, he was the One who created it!

God gives us the abilities that we need to obey him, and he'll always be there to help us out when things get tough. "I can't" doesn't cut it with God. He makes sure nobody has an excuse not to follow him.

God wants to use all of his children as witnesses for him. So even if I don't think I'm very good at talking with other people about my faith, God still wants me to give it a try. Obeying God might make me feel really uncomfortable sometimes, but I know it's what God wants from me.

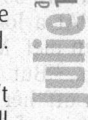

Julie, age 12

❶ Why is it sometimes hard to talk with other people about God?

❷ Make a list of some of your talents. How can you use these to be a witness for God?

❸ Tell God you're willing to follow him and trust him to give you everything you need to be a witness for him.

Turn to page 90 for your next devotion.

Moses and he said, "What about your brother, Aaron the Levite? I know he can speak well. He is already on his way to meet you, and his heart will be glad when he sees you. ¹⁵You shall speak to him and put words in his mouth; I will help both of you speak and will teach you what to do. ¹⁶He will speak to the people for you, and it will be as if he were your mouth and as if you were God to him. ¹⁷But take this staff in your hand so you can perform miraculous signs with it."

Moses Returns to Egypt

¹⁸Then Moses went back to Jethro his father-in-law and said to him, "Let me go back to my own people in Egypt to see if any of them are still alive."

Jethro said, "Go, and I wish you well."

¹⁹Now the LORD had said to Moses in Midian, "Go back to Egypt, for all the men who wanted to kill you are dead." ²⁰So Moses took his wife and sons, put them on a donkey and started back to Egypt. And he took the staff of God in his hand.

²¹The LORD said to Moses, "When you return to Egypt, see that you perform before Pharaoh all the wonders I have given you the power to do. But I will harden his heart so that he will not let the people go. ²²Then say to Pharaoh, 'This is what the LORD says: Israel is my firstborn son, ²³and I told you, "Let my son go, so he may worship me." But you refused to let him go; so I will kill your firstborn son.'"

²⁴At a lodging place on the way, the LORD met ₎Moses₎ᵃ and was about to kill him. ²⁵But Zipporah took a flint knife, cut off her son's foreskin and touched ₎Moses'₎ feet with it.ᵇ "Surely you are a bridegroom of blood to me," she said. ²⁶So the LORD let him alone. (At that time she said "bridegroom of blood," referring to circumcision.)

²⁷The LORD said to Aaron, "Go into the desert to meet Moses." So he met Moses at the mountain of God and kissed him. ²⁸Then Moses told Aaron everything the LORD had sent him to say, and also about all the miraculous signs he had commanded him to perform.

²⁹Moses and Aaron brought together all the elders of the Israelites, ³⁰and Aaron told them everything the LORD had said to Moses. He also performed the signs before the people, ³¹and they believed. And when they heard that the LORD was concerned about them and had seen their misery, they bowed down and worshiped.

Bricks Without Straw

5 Afterward Moses and Aaron went to Pharaoh and said, "This is what the LORD, the God of Israel, says: 'Let my people go, so that they may hold a festival to me in the desert.'"

²Pharaoh said, "Who is the LORD, that I should obey him and let Israel go? I do not know the LORD and I will not let Israel go."

³Then they said, "The God of the Hebrews has met with us. Now let us take a three-day journey into the desert to offer sacrifices to the LORD our God, or he may strike us with plagues or with the sword."

⁴But the king of Egypt said, "Moses and Aaron, why are you taking the people away from their labor? Get back to your work!" ⁵Then Pharaoh said, "Look, the people of the land are now numerous, and you are stopping them from working."

⁶That same day Pharaoh gave this order to the slave drivers and foremen in charge of the people: ⁷"You are no longer to supply the people with straw for making bricks; let them go and gather their own straw. ⁸But require them to make the same number of bricks as before; don't reduce the quota. They are lazy; that is why they are crying out, 'Let us go and sacrifice to our God.' ⁹Make the work harder for the men so that they keep working and pay no attention to lies."

¹⁰Then the slave drivers and the foremen went out and said to the people, "This is what Pharaoh says: 'I will not give you any more straw. ¹¹Go and get your own straw wherever you can find it, but your work will not be reduced at all.'" ¹²So the people scattered all over Egypt to gather stubble to use for straw. ¹³The slave drivers kept pressing them,

---

ᵃ24 Or ₎Moses' son₎; Hebrew him ᵇ25 Or and drew near ₎Moses'₎ feet saying, "Complete the work required of you for each day, just as when you had straw." ¹⁴The Israelite foremen appointed by Pharaoh's slave drivers were beaten and were asked, "Why didn't you meet your quota of bricks yesterday or today, as before?"

¹⁵Then the Israelite foremen went and appealed to Pharaoh: "Why have you treated your servants this way? ¹⁶Your servants are given no straw, yet we are told, 'Make bricks!' Your servants are being beaten, but the fault is with your own people."

¹⁷Pharaoh said, "Lazy, that's what you are—lazy! That is why you keep saying, 'Let us go and sacrifice to the LORD.' ¹⁸Now get to work. You will not be given any straw, yet you must produce your full quota of bricks."

¹⁹The Israelite foremen realized they were in trouble when they were told, "You are not to reduce the number of bricks required of you for each day." ²⁰When they left Pharaoh, they found Moses and Aaron waiting to meet them, ²¹and they said, "May the LORD look upon you and judge you! You have made us a stench to Pharaoh and his officials and have put a sword in their hand to kill us."

God Promises Deliverance

²²Moses returned to the LORD and said, "O Lord, why have you brought trouble upon this people? Is this why you sent me? ²³Ever since I went to Pharaoh to speak in your name, he has brought trouble upon this people, and you have not rescued your people at all."

6 Then the LORD said to Moses, "Now you will see what I will do to Pharaoh: Because of my mighty hand he will let them go; because of my mighty hand he will drive them out of his country."

²God also said to Moses, "I am the LORD. ³I appeared to Abraham, to Isaac and to Jacob as God Almighty,ᵃ but by my name the LORDᵇ I did not make myself known to them.ᶜ ⁴I also established my covenant with them to give them the land of Canaan, where they lived as aliens. ⁵Moreover, I have heard the groaning of the Israelites, whom the Egyptians are enslaving, and I have remembered my covenant.

⁶"Therefore, say to the Israelites: 'I am the LORD, and I will bring you out from under the yoke of the Egyptians. I will free you from being slaves to them, and I will redeem you with an outstretched arm and with mighty acts of judgment. ⁷I will take you as my own people, and I will be your God. Then you will know that I am the LORD your God, who brought you out from under the yoke of the Egyptians. ⁸And I will bring you to the land I swore with uplifted hand to give to Abraham, to Isaac and to Jacob. I will give it to you as a possession. I am the LORD.'"

⁹Moses reported this to the Israelites, but they did not listen to him because of their discouragement and cruel bondage.

¹⁰Then the LORD said to Moses, ¹¹"Go, tell Pharaoh king of Egypt to let the Israelites go out of his country."

¹²But Moses said to the LORD, "If the Israelites will not listen to me, why would Pharaoh listen to me, since I speak with faltering lipsᵈ?"

Family Record of Moses and Aaron

¹³Now the LORD spoke to Moses and Aaron about the Israelites and Pharaoh king of Egypt, and he commanded them to bring the Israelites out of Egypt.

The Name
Huh?

Exodus 6:2
Even God's name comforts his people. Think about what it represents: all-knowing, all-powerful, present everywhere. Trouble? God is there. Pain and suffering? God feels your pain. Fear? He comforts you. God's name gives you confidence that he is with you.

ᵃ3 Hebrew *El-Shaddai* ᵇ3 See note at Exodus 3:15. ᶜ3 Or *Almighty, and by my name the LORD did I not let myself be known to them?* ᵈ12 Hebrew *I am uncircumcised of lips*; also in verse 30

[14]These were the heads of their families[a]:

The sons of Reuben the firstborn son of Israel were Hanoch and Pallu, Hezron and Carmi. These were the clans of Reuben.

[15]The sons of Simeon were Jemuel, Jamin, Ohad, Jakin, Zohar and Shaul the son of a Canaanite woman. These were the clans of Simeon.

[16]These were the names of the sons of Levi according to their records: Gershon, Kohath and Merari. Levi lived 137 years.

[17]The sons of Gershon, by clans, were Libni and Shimei.

[18]The sons of Kohath were Amram, Izhar, Hebron and Uzziel. Kohath lived 133 years.

[19]The sons of Merari were Mahli and Mushi.

These were the clans of Levi according to their records.

[20]Amram married his father's sister Jochebed, who bore him Aaron and Moses. Amram lived 137 years.

[21]The sons of Izhar were Korah, Nepheg and Zicri.

[22]The sons of Uzziel were Mishael, Elzaphan and Sithri.

[23]Aaron married Elisheba, daughter of Amminadab and sister of Nahshon, and she bore him Nadab and Abihu, Eleazar and Ithamar.

[24]The sons of Korah were Assir, Elkanah and Abiasaph. These were the Korahite clans.

[25]Eleazar son of Aaron married one of the daughters of Putiel, and she bore him Phinehas.

These were the heads of the Levite families, clan by clan.

[26]It was this same Aaron and Moses to whom the LORD said, "Bring the Israelites out of Egypt by their divisions." [27]They were the ones who spoke to Pharaoh king of Egypt about bringing the Israelites out of Egypt. It was the same Moses and Aaron.

Aaron to Speak for Moses

[28]Now when the LORD spoke to Moses in Egypt, [29]he said to him, "I am the LORD. Tell Pharaoh king of Egypt everything I tell you."

[30]But Moses said to the LORD, "Since I speak with faltering lips, why would Pharaoh listen to me?"

7 Then the LORD said to Moses, "See, I have made you like God to Pharaoh, and your brother Aaron will be your prophet. [2]You are to say everything I command you, and your brother Aaron is to tell Pharaoh to let the Israelites go out of his country. [3]But I will harden Pharaoh's heart, and though I multiply my miraculous signs and wonders in Egypt, [4]he will not listen to you. Then I will lay my hand on Egypt and with mighty acts of judgment I will bring out my divisions, my people the Israelites. [5]And the Egyptians will know that I am the LORD when I stretch out my hand against Egypt and bring the Israelites out of it."

[6]Moses and Aaron did just as the LORD commanded them. [7]Moses was eighty years old and Aaron eighty-three when they spoke to Pharaoh.

Aaron's Staff Becomes a Snake

[8]The LORD said to Moses and Aaron, [9]"When Pharaoh says to you, 'Perform a miracle,' then say to Aaron, 'Take your staff and throw it down before Pharaoh,' and it will become a snake."

[10]So Moses and Aaron went to Pharaoh and did just as the LORD commanded. Aaron threw his staff down in front of Pharaoh and his officials, and it became a snake. [11]Pharaoh then summoned wise men and sorcerers, and the Egyptian magicians also did the same things by their secret arts: [12]Each one threw down his staff and it became a snake. But Aaron's staff swallowed up their staffs. [13]Yet Pharaoh's heart became hard and he would not listen to them, just as the LORD had said.

The Plague of Blood

[14]Then the LORD said to Moses, "Pharaoh's heart is unyielding; he refuses to let the people go. [15]Go to Pharaoh in the

---

[a]14 The Hebrew for *families* here and in verse 25 refers to units larger than clans.

morning as he goes out to the water. Wait on the bank of the Nile to meet him, and take in your hand the staff that was changed into a snake. ¹⁶Then say to him, 'The LORD, the God of the Hebrews, has sent me to say to you: Let my people go, so that they may worship me in the desert. But until now you have not listened. ¹⁷This is what the LORD says: By this you will know that I am the LORD: With the staff that is in my hand I will strike the water of the Nile, and it will be changed into blood. ¹⁸The fish in the Nile will die, and the river will stink; the Egyptians will not be able to drink its water.' "

¹⁹The LORD said to Moses, "Tell Aaron, 'Take your staff and stretch out your hand over the waters of Egypt—over the streams and canals, over the ponds and all the reservoirs'—and they will turn to blood. Blood will be everywhere in Egypt, even in the wooden buckets and stone jars."

²⁰Moses and Aaron did just as the LORD had commanded. He raised his staff in the presence of Pharaoh and his officials and struck the water of the Nile, and all the water was changed into blood. ²¹The fish in the Nile died, and the river smelled so bad that the Egyptians could not drink its water. Blood was everywhere in Egypt.

²²But the Egyptian magicians did the same things by their secret arts, and Pharaoh's heart became hard; he would not listen to Moses and Aaron, just as the LORD had said. ²³Instead, he turned and went into his palace, and did not take even this to heart. ²⁴And all the Egyptians dug along the Nile to get drinking water, because they could not drink the water of the river.

The Plague of Frogs

²⁵Seven days passed after the LORD struck the Nile. **8** ¹Then the LORD said to Moses, "Go to Pharaoh and say to him, 'This is what the LORD says: Let my people go, so that they may worship me. ²If you refuse to let them go, I will plague your whole country with frogs. ³The Nile will teem with frogs. They will come up into your palace and your bedroom and

---

Incredible Uses for Sticks

Exodus 7:8–13 In the Old Testament, sticks weren't only used to give Fido something to fetch. In Exodus 7, for example, Aaron tossed his stick (called a "staff") down in front of Pharaoh, and the stick turned into a snake. Not to be outdone, Pharaoh's magicians tossed their sticks down and they morphed into snakes too. No problem. Aaron's stick, er, snake, quickly gobbled up all of the magicians' snakes, er, sticks! But that's not all! Aaron and Moses used their incredible sticks to:

- ✗ turn a whole river into blood (7:17-21)
- ✗ create a major frog infestation (8:5-6)
- ✗ cause zillions of gnats to buzz into town (8:16-17)
- ✗ stir up a killer hailstorm (9:23-25)
- ✗ blow in a big-time locust invasion (10:13-15)
- ✗ make a dry road right down the middle of the sea (14:16)
- ✗ bring drinking water out of a dry old rock (17:6)

And you thought sticks were just for toasting s'mores!

---

onto your bed, into the houses of your officials and on your people, and into your ovens and kneading troughs. ⁴The frogs will go up on you and your people and all your officials.' "

⁵Then the LORD said to Moses, "Tell Aaron, 'Stretch out your hand with your staff over the streams and canals and ponds, and make frogs come up on the land of Egypt.' "

⁶So Aaron stretched out his hand over the waters of Egypt, and the frogs came up and covered the land. ⁷But the magicians did the same things by their secret

arts; they also made frogs come up on the land of Egypt.

[8]Pharaoh summoned Moses and Aaron and said, "Pray to the LORD to take the frogs away from me and my people, and I will let your people go to offer sacrifices to the LORD."

[9]Moses said to Pharaoh, "I leave to you the honor of setting the time for me to pray for you and your officials and your people that you and your houses may be rid of the frogs, except for those that remain in the Nile."

[10]"Tomorrow," Pharaoh said.

Moses replied, "It will be as you say, so that you may know there is no one like the LORD our God. [11]The frogs will leave you and your houses, your officials and your people; they will remain only in the Nile."

[12]After Moses and Aaron left Pharaoh, Moses cried out to the LORD about the frogs he had brought on Pharaoh. [13]And the LORD did what Moses asked. The frogs died in the houses, in the courtyards and in the fields. [14]They were piled into heaps, and the land reeked of them. [15]But when Pharaoh saw that there was relief, he hardened his heart and would not listen to Moses and Aaron, just as the LORD had said.

The Plague of Gnats

[16]Then the LORD said to Moses, "Tell Aaron, 'Stretch out your staff and strike the dust of the ground,' and throughout the land of Egypt the dust will become gnats." [17]They did this, and when Aaron stretched out his hand with the staff and struck the dust of the ground, gnats came upon men and animals. All the dust throughout the land of Egypt became gnats. [18]But when the magicians tried to produce gnats by their secret arts, they could not. And the gnats were on men and animals.

[19]The magicians said to Pharaoh, "This is the finger of God." But Pharaoh's heart was hard and he would not listen, just as the LORD had said.

The Plague of Flies

[20]Then the LORD said to Moses, "Get up early in the morning and confront Pharaoh as he goes to the water and say to

Get a Clue!

Huh?

Exodus 8:19

Frogs, gnats, flies, hail, boils . . . Is Pharaoh dense? When is he going to wake up and see that God's behind all of this? People often want to see it to believe it—especially when it comes to God. Pharaoh finally "got a clue." Should you too? Is God trying to get your attention?

him, 'This is what the LORD says: Let my people go, so that they may worship me. [21]If you do not let my people go, I will send swarms of flies on you and your officials, on your people and into your houses. The houses of the Egyptians will be full of flies, and even the ground where they are.

[22]" 'But on that day I will deal differently with the land of Goshen, where my people live; no swarms of flies will be there, so that you will know that I, the LORD, am in this land. [23]I will make a distinction[a] between my people and your people. This miraculous sign will occur tomorrow.' "

[24]And the LORD did this. Dense swarms of flies poured into Pharaoh's palace and into the houses of his officials, and throughout Egypt the land was ruined by the flies.

[25]Then Pharaoh summoned Moses and Aaron and said, "Go, sacrifice to your God here in the land."

[26]But Moses said, "That would not be right. The sacrifices we offer the LORD our God would be detestable to the Egyptians. And if we offer sacrifices that are detestable in their eyes, will they not stone us? [27]We must take a three-day journey into the desert to offer sacrifices to the LORD our God, as he commands us."

[28]Pharaoh said, "I will let you go to offer sacrifices to the LORD your God in the desert, but you must not go very far. Now pray for me."

[a]23 Septuagint and Vulgate; Hebrew *will put a deliverance*

[29]Moses answered, "As soon as I leave you, I will pray to the LORD, and tomorrow the flies will leave Pharaoh and his officials and his people. Only be sure that Pharaoh does not act deceitfully again by not letting the people go to offer sacrifices to the LORD."

[30]Then Moses left Pharaoh and prayed to the LORD, [31]and the LORD did what Moses asked: The flies left Pharaoh and his officials and his people; not a fly remained. [32]But this time also Pharaoh hardened his heart and would not let the people go.

The Plague on Livestock

9 Then the LORD said to Moses, "Go to Pharaoh and say to him, 'This is what the LORD, the God of the Hebrews, says: "Let my people go, so that they may worship me." [2]If you refuse to let them go and continue to hold them back, [3]the hand of the LORD will bring a terrible plague on your livestock in the field—on your horses and donkeys and camels and on your cattle and sheep and goats. [4]But the LORD will make a distinction between the livestock of Israel and that of Egypt, so that no animal belonging to the Israelites will die.' "

[5]The LORD set a time and said, "Tomorrow the LORD will do this in the land." [6]And the next day the LORD did it: All the livestock of the Egyptians died, but not one animal belonging to the Israelites died. [7]Pharaoh sent men to investigate and found that not even one of the animals of the Israelites had died. Yet his heart was unyielding and he would not let the people go.

The Plague of Boils

[8]Then the LORD said to Moses and Aaron, "Take handfuls of soot from a furnace and have Moses toss it into the air in the presence of Pharaoh. [9]It will become fine dust over the whole land of Egypt, and festering boils will break out on men and animals throughout the land."

[10]So they took soot from a furnace and stood before Pharaoh. Moses tossed it into the air, and festering boils broke out on men and animals. [11]The magicians could not stand before Moses because of the boils that were on them and on all the Egyptians. [12]But the LORD hardened Pharaoh's heart and he would not listen to Moses and Aaron, just as the LORD had said to Moses.

The Plague of Hail

[13]Then the LORD said to Moses, "Get up early in the morning, confront Pharaoh and say to him, 'This is what the LORD, the God of the Hebrews, says: Let my people go, so that they may worship me, [14]or this time I will send the full force of my plagues against you and against your officials and your people, so you may know that there is no one like me in all the earth. [15]For by now I could have stretched out my hand and struck you and your people with a plague that would have wiped you off the earth. [16]But I have raised you up[a] for this very purpose, that I might show you my power and that my name might be proclaimed in all the earth. [17]You still set yourself against my people and will not let them go. [18]Therefore, at this time tomorrow I will send the worst hailstorm that has ever fallen on Egypt, from the day it was founded till now. [19]Give an order now to bring your livestock and everything you have in the field to a place of shelter, because the hail will fall on every man and animal that has not been brought in and is still out in the field, and they will die.' "

[20]Those officials of Pharaoh who feared the word of the LORD hurried to bring their slaves and their livestock inside. [21]But those who ignored the word of the LORD left their slaves and livestock in the field.

[22]Then the LORD said to Moses, "Stretch out your hand toward the sky so that hail will fall all over Egypt—on men and animals and on everything growing in the fields of Egypt." [23]When Moses stretched out his staff toward the sky, the LORD sent thunder and hail, and lightning flashed down to the ground. So the LORD rained hail on the land of Egypt; [24]hail fell and lightning flashed back and forth. It was the worst storm in all the land of Egypt since it had become a nation.

[a]16 Or have spared you

²⁵Throughout Egypt hail struck everything in the fields—both men and animals; it beat down everything growing in the fields and stripped every tree. ²⁶The only place it did not hail was the land of Goshen, where the Israelites were.

²⁷Then Pharaoh summoned Moses and Aaron. "This time I have sinned," he said to them. "The LORD is in the right, and I and my people are in the wrong. ²⁸Pray to the LORD, for we have had enough thunder and hail. I will let you go; you don't have to stay any longer."

²⁹Moses replied, "When I have gone out of the city, I will spread out my hands in prayer to the LORD. The thunder will stop and there will be no more hail, so you may know that the earth is the LORD's. ³⁰But I know that you and your officials still do not fear the LORD God."

³¹(The flax and barley were destroyed, since the barley had headed and the flax was in bloom. ³²The wheat and spelt, however, were not destroyed, because they ripen later.)

³³Then Moses left Pharaoh and went out of the city. He spread out his hands toward the LORD; the thunder and hail stopped, and the rain no longer poured down on the land. ³⁴When Pharaoh saw that the rain and hail and thunder had stopped, he sinned again: He and his officials hardened their hearts. ³⁵So Pharaoh's heart was hard and he would not let the Israelites go, just as the LORD had said through Moses.

The Plague of Locusts

10 Then the LORD said to Moses, "Go to Pharaoh, for I have hardened his heart and the hearts of his officials so that I may perform these miraculous signs of mine among them ²that you may tell your children and grandchildren how I dealt harshly with the Egyptians and how I performed my signs among them, and that you may know that I am the LORD."

³So Moses and Aaron went to Pharaoh and said to him, "This is what the LORD, the God of the Hebrews, says: 'How long will you refuse to humble yourself before me? Let my people go, so that they may worship me. ⁴If you refuse to let them go, I will bring locusts into your country tomorrow. ⁵They will cover the face of the ground so that it cannot be seen. They will devour what little you have left after the hail, including every tree that is growing in your fields. ⁶They will fill your houses and those of all your officials and all the Egyptians—something neither your fathers nor your forefathers have ever seen from the day they settled in this land till now.' " Then Moses turned and left Pharaoh.

⁷Pharaoh's officials said to him, "How long will this man be a snare to us? Let the people go, so that they may worship the LORD their God. Do you not yet realize that Egypt is ruined?"

⁸Then Moses and Aaron were brought back to Pharaoh. "Go, worship the LORD your God," he said. "But just who will be going?"

⁹Moses answered, "We will go with our young and old, with our sons and daughters, and with our flocks and herds, because we are to celebrate a festival to the LORD."

¹⁰Pharaoh said, "The LORD be with you—if I let you go, along with your women and children! Clearly you are bent on evil.ᵃ ¹¹No! Have only the men go; and worship the LORD, since that's what you have been asking for." Then Moses and Aaron were driven out of Pharaoh's presence.

¹²And the LORD said to Moses, "Stretch out your hand over Egypt so that locusts will swarm over the land and devour everything growing in the fields, everything left by the hail."

¹³So Moses stretched out his staff over Egypt, and the LORD made an east wind blow across the land all that day and all that night. By morning the wind had brought the locusts; ¹⁴they invaded all Egypt and settled down in every area of the country in great numbers. Never before had there been such a plague of locusts, nor will there ever be again. ¹⁵They covered all the ground until it was black. They devoured all that was left after the hail—everything growing in the fields and the fruit on the trees. Nothing

ᵃ10 Or Be careful, trouble is in store for you!

green remained on tree or plant in all the land of Egypt. ¹⁶Pharaoh quickly summoned Moses and Aaron and said, "I have sinned against the LORD your God and against you. ¹⁷Now forgive my sin once more and pray to the LORD your God to take this deadly plague away from me."

¹⁸Moses then left Pharaoh and prayed to the LORD. ¹⁹And the LORD changed the wind to a very strong west wind, which caught up the locusts and carried them into the Red Sea.ᵃ Not a locust was left anywhere in Egypt. ²⁰But the LORD hardened Pharaoh's heart, and he would not let the Israelites go.

The Plague of Darkness

²¹Then the LORD said to Moses, "Stretch out your hand toward the sky so that darkness will spread over Egypt— darkness that can be felt." ²²So Moses stretched out his hand toward the sky, and total darkness covered all Egypt for three days. ²³No one could see anyone else or leave his place for three days. Yet all the Israelites had light in the places where they lived.

²⁴Then Pharaoh summoned Moses and said, "Go, worship the LORD. Even your women and children may go with you; only leave your flocks and herds behind."

²⁵But Moses said, "You must allow us to have sacrifices and burnt offerings to present to the LORD our God. ²⁶Our livestock too must go with us; not a hoof is to be left behind. We have to use some of them in worshiping the LORD our God, and until we get there we will not know what we are to use to worship the LORD."

²⁷But the LORD hardened Pharaoh's heart, and he was not willing to let them go. ²⁸Pharaoh said to Moses, "Get out of my sight! Make sure you do not appear before me again! The day you see my face you will die."

²⁹"Just as you say," Moses replied, "I will never appear before you again."

The Plague on the Firstborn

11 Now the LORD had said to Moses, "I will bring one more plague on Pharaoh and on Egypt. After that, he will let you go from here, and when he does,

he will drive you out completely. ²Tell the people that men and women alike are to ask their neighbors for articles of silver and gold." ³(The LORD made the Egyptians favorably disposed toward the people, and Moses himself was highly regarded in Egypt by Pharaoh's officials and by the people.)

⁴So Moses said, "This is what the LORD says: 'About midnight I will go throughout Egypt. ⁵Every firstborn son in Egypt will die, from the firstborn son of Pharaoh, who sits on the throne, to the firstborn son of the slave girl, who is at her hand mill, and all the firstborn of the cattle as well. ⁶There will be loud wailing throughout Egypt—worse than there has ever been or ever will be again. ⁷But among the Israelites not a dog will bark at any man or animal.' Then you will know that the LORD makes a distinction between Egypt and Israel. ⁸All these officials of yours will come to me, bowing down before me and saying, 'Go, you and all the people who follow you!' After that I will leave." Then Moses, hot with anger, left Pharaoh.

⁹The LORD had said to Moses, "Pharaoh will refuse to listen to you—so that my wonders may be multiplied in Egypt." ¹⁰Moses and Aaron performed all these wonders before Pharaoh, but the LORD hardened Pharaoh's heart, and he would not let the Israelites go out of his country.

The Passover

12 The LORD said to Moses and Aaron in Egypt, ²"This month is to be for you the first month, the first month of your year. ³Tell the whole community of Israel that on the tenth day of this month each man is to take a lambᵇ for his family, one for each household. ⁴If any household is too small for a whole lamb, they must share one with their nearest neighbor, having taken into account the number of people there are. You are to determine the amount of lamb needed in accordance with what each person will eat. ⁵The animals you choose must be year-old males without defect, and you

---

ᵃ19 Hebrew *Yam Suph*; that is, Sea of Reeds
ᵇ3 The Hebrew word can mean *lamb* or *kid*; also in verse 4.

may take them from the sheep or the goats. ⁶Take care of them until the fourteenth day of the month, when all the people of the community of Israel must slaughter them at twilight. ⁷Then they are to take some of the blood and put it on the sides and tops of the doorframes of the houses where they eat the lambs. ⁸That same night they are to eat the meat roasted over the fire, along with bitter herbs, and bread made without yeast. ⁹Do not eat the meat raw or cooked in water, but roast it over the fire—head, legs and inner parts. ¹⁰Do not leave any of it till morning; if some is left till morning, you must burn it. ¹¹This is how you are to eat it: with your cloak tucked into your belt, your sandals on your feet and your staff in your hand. Eat it in haste; it is the LORD's Passover.

¹²"On that same night I will pass through Egypt and strike down every firstborn—both men and animals—and I will bring judgment on all the gods of Egypt. I am the LORD. ¹³The blood will be a sign for you on the houses where you are; and when I see the blood, I will pass over you. No destructive plague will touch you when I strike Egypt.

¹⁴"This is a day you are to commemorate; for the generations to come you shall celebrate it as a festival to the LORD—a lasting ordinance. ¹⁵For seven days you are to eat bread made without yeast. On the first day remove the yeast from your houses, for whoever eats anything with yeast in it from the first day through the seventh must be cut off from Israel. ¹⁶On the first day hold a sacred assembly, and another one on the seventh day. Do no work at all on these days, except to prepare food for everyone to eat—that is all you may do.

¹⁷"Celebrate the Feast of Unleavened Bread, because it was on this very day that I brought your divisions out of Egypt. Celebrate this day as a lasting ordinance for the generations to come. ¹⁸In the first month you are to eat bread made without yeast, from the evening of the fourteenth day until the evening of the twenty-first day. ¹⁹For seven days no yeast is to be found in your houses. And whoever eats anything with yeast in it must be cut off from the community of Israel, whether he is an alien or native-born. ²⁰Eat nothing made with yeast. Wherever you live, you must eat unleavened bread."

²¹Then Moses summoned all the elders of Israel and said to them, "Go at once and select the animals for your families and slaughter the Passover lamb. ²²Take a bunch of hyssop, dip it into the blood in the basin and put some of the blood on the top and on both sides of the doorframe. Not one of you shall go out the door of his house until morning. ²³When the LORD goes through the land to strike down the Egyptians, he will see the blood on the top and sides of the doorframe and will pass over that doorway, and he will not permit the destroyer to enter your houses and strike you down.

²⁴"Obey these instructions as a lasting ordinance for you and your descendants. ²⁵When you enter the land that the LORD will give you as he promised, observe this ceremony. ²⁶And when your children ask you, 'What does this ceremony mean to you?' ²⁷then tell them, 'It is the Passover sacrifice to the LORD, who passed over the houses of the Israelites in Egypt and spared our homes when he struck down the Egyptians.'" Then the people bowed down and worshiped. ²⁸The Israelites did just what the LORD commanded Moses and Aaron.

²⁹At midnight the LORD struck down all the firstborn in Egypt, from the firstborn of Pharaoh, who sat on the throne, to the firstborn of the prisoner, who was in the dungeon, and the firstborn of all the livestock as well. ³⁰Pharaoh and all his officials and all the Egyptians got up during the night, and there was loud wailing in Egypt, for there was not a house without someone dead.

The Exodus

³¹During the night Pharaoh summoned Moses and Aaron and said, "Up! Leave my people, you and the Israelites! Go, worship the LORD as you have requested. ³²Take your flocks and herds, as you have said, and go. And also bless me."

³³The Egyptians urged the people to hurry and leave the country. "For otherwise," they said, "we will all die!" ³⁴So the people took their dough before the

yeast was added, and carried it on their shoulders in kneading troughs wrapped in clothing. ³⁵The Israelites did as Moses instructed and asked the Egyptians for articles of silver and gold and for clothing. ³⁶The LORD had made the Egyptians favorably disposed toward the people, and they gave them what they asked for; so they plundered the Egyptians.

³⁷The Israelites journeyed from Rameses to Succoth. There were about six hundred thousand men on foot, besides women and children. ³⁸Many other people went up with them, as well as large droves of livestock, both flocks and herds. ³⁹With the dough they had brought from Egypt, they baked cakes of unleavened bread. The dough was without yeast because they had been driven out of Egypt and did not have time to prepare food for themselves.

⁴⁰Now the length of time the Israelite people lived in Egypt[a] was 430 years. ⁴¹At the end of the 430 years, to the very day, all the LORD's divisions left Egypt. ⁴²Because the LORD kept vigil that night to bring them out of Egypt, on this night all the Israelites are to keep vigil to honor the LORD for the generations to come.

Passover Restrictions

⁴³The LORD said to Moses and Aaron, "These are the regulations for the Passover:

"No foreigner is to eat of it. ⁴⁴Any slave you have bought may eat of it after you have circumcised him, ⁴⁵but a temporary resident and a hired worker may not eat of it.

⁴⁶"It must be eaten inside one house; take none of the meat outside the house. Do not break any of the bones. ⁴⁷The whole community of Israel must celebrate it.

⁴⁸"An alien living among you who wants to celebrate the LORD's Passover must have all the males in his household circumcised; then he may take part like one born in the land. No uncircumcised male may eat of it. ⁴⁹The same law applies to the native-born and to the alien living among you."

⁵⁰All the Israelites did just what the LORD had commanded Moses and Aaron. ⁵¹And on that very day the LORD brought the Israelites out of Egypt by their divisions.

Consecration of the Firstborn

13 The LORD said to Moses, ²"Consecrate to me every firstborn male. The first offspring of every womb among the Israelites belongs to me, whether man or animal."

³Then Moses said to the people, "Commemorate this day, the day you came out of Egypt, out of the land of slavery, because the LORD brought you out of it with a mighty hand. Eat nothing containing yeast. ⁴Today, in the month of Abib, you are leaving. ⁵When the LORD brings you into the land of the Canaanites, Hittites, Amorites, Hivites and Jebusites—the land he swore to your forefathers to give you, a land flowing with milk and honey—you are to observe this ceremony in this month: ⁶For seven days eat bread made without yeast and on the seventh day hold a festival to the LORD. ⁷Eat unleavened bread during those seven days; nothing with yeast in it is to be seen among you, nor shall any yeast be seen anywhere within your borders. ⁸On that day tell your son, 'I do this because of what the LORD did for me when I came out of Egypt.' ⁹This observance will be for you like a sign on your hand and a reminder on your forehead that the law of the LORD is to be on your lips. For the LORD brought you out of Egypt with his mighty hand. ¹⁰You must keep this ordinance at the appointed time year after year.

¹¹"After the LORD brings you into the land of the Canaanites and gives it to you, as he promised on oath to you and your forefathers, ¹²you are to give over to the LORD the first offspring of every womb. All the firstborn males of your livestock belong to the LORD. ¹³Redeem with a lamb every firstborn donkey, but if you do not redeem it, break its neck. Redeem every firstborn among your sons.

[a]40 Masoretic Text; Samaritan Pentateuch and Septuagint *Egypt and Canaan*

You've Been Bought

Huh?

Exodus 13:13-15

In the days of slavery, some people bought slaves just so they could set them free. In the same way, the Israelites bought their firstborn sons back from God. The sacrifice of a lamb was the price that needed to be paid. Did you know God bought us too? We would be separated from him forever if he hadn't paid the price for us. He sacrificed his Son Jesus as a payment for us so we could have freedom and a relationship with him.

¹⁴"In days to come, when your son asks you, 'What does this mean?' say to him, 'With a mighty hand the LORD brought us out of Egypt, out of the land of slavery. ¹⁵When Pharaoh stubbornly refused to let us go, the LORD killed every firstborn in Egypt, both man and animal. This is why I sacrifice to the LORD the first male offspring of every womb and redeem each of my firstborn sons.' ¹⁶And it will be like a sign on your hand and a symbol on your forehead that the LORD brought us out of Egypt with his mighty hand."

Crossing the Sea

¹⁷When Pharaoh let the people go, God did not lead them on the road through the Philistine country, though that was shorter. For God said, "If they face war, they might change their minds and return to Egypt." ¹⁸So God led the people around by the desert road toward the Red Sea.[a] The Israelites went up out of Egypt armed for battle.

¹⁹Moses took the bones of Joseph with him because Joseph had made the sons of Israel swear an oath. He had said, "God will surely come to your aid, and then you must carry my bones up with you from this place."[b]

²⁰After leaving Succoth they camped at Etham on the edge of the desert. ²¹By day the LORD went ahead of them in a pillar of cloud to guide them on their way and by night in a pillar of fire to give them light, so that they could travel by day or night. ²²Neither the pillar of cloud by day nor the pillar of fire by night left its place in front of the people.

14 Then the LORD said to Moses, ²"Tell the Israelites to turn back and encamp near Pi Hahiroth, between Migdol and the sea. They are to encamp by the sea, directly opposite Baal Zephon. ³Pharaoh will think, 'The Israelites are wandering around the land in confusion, hemmed in by the desert.' ⁴And I will harden Pharaoh's heart, and he will pursue them. But I will gain glory for myself through Pharaoh and all his army, and the Egyptians will know that I am the LORD." So the Israelites did this.

⁵When the king of Egypt was told that the people had fled, Pharaoh and his officials changed their minds about them and said, "What have we done? We have let the Israelites go and have lost their services!" ⁶So he had his chariot made ready and took his army with him. ⁷He took six hundred of the best chariots, along with all the other chariots of Egypt, with officers over all of them. ⁸The LORD hardened the heart of Pharaoh king of Egypt, so that he pursued the Israelites, who were marching out boldly. ⁹The Egyptians—all Pharaoh's horses and chariots, horsemen[c] and troops—pursued the Israelites and overtook them as they camped by the sea near Pi Hahiroth, opposite Baal Zephon.

¹⁰As Pharaoh approached, the Israelites looked up, and there were the Egyptians, marching after them. They were terrified and cried out to the LORD. ¹¹They said to Moses, "Was it because there were no graves in Egypt that you brought us to the desert to die? What have you done to us by bringing us out of Egypt? ¹²Didn't we say to you in Egypt, 'Leave us alone; let us serve the Egyptians'? It would have been better for us to serve the Egyptians than to die in the desert!"

¹³Moses answered the people, "Do not be afraid. Stand firm and you will see the deliverance the LORD will bring you today. The Egyptians you see today you

---

[a]18 Hebrew *Yam Suph*; that is, Sea of Reeds
[b]19 See Gen. 50:25.   [c]9 Or *charioteers*; also in verses 17, 18, 23, 26 and 28

will never see again. [14]The LORD will fight for you; you need only to be still."

[15]Then the LORD said to Moses, "Why are you crying out to me? Tell the Israelites to move on. [16]Raise your staff and stretch out your hand over the sea to divide the water so that the Israelites can go through the sea on dry ground. [17]I will harden the hearts of the Egyptians so that they will go in after them. And I will gain glory through Pharaoh and all his army, through his chariots and his horsemen. [18]The Egyptians will know that I am the LORD when I gain glory through Pharaoh, his chariots and his horsemen."

[19]Then the angel of God, who had been traveling in front of Israel's army, withdrew and went behind them. The pillar of cloud also moved from in front and stood behind them, [20]coming between the armies of Egypt and Israel. Throughout the night the cloud brought darkness to the one side and light to the other side; so neither went near the other all night long.

[21]Then Moses stretched out his hand over the sea, and all that night the LORD drove the sea back with a strong east wind and turned it into dry land. The waters were divided, [22]and the Israelites went through the sea on dry ground, with a wall of water on their right and on their left.

[23]The Egyptians pursued them, and all Pharaoh's horses and chariots and horsemen followed them into the sea. [24]During the last watch of the night the LORD looked down from the pillar of fire and cloud at the Egyptian army and threw it into confusion. [25]He made the wheels of their chariots come off[a] so that they had difficulty driving. And the Egyptians said, "Let's get away from the Israelites! The LORD is fighting for them against Egypt."

[26]Then the LORD said to Moses, "Stretch out your hand over the sea so that the waters may flow back over the Egyptians and their chariots and horsemen." [27]Moses stretched out his hand over the sea, and at daybreak the sea went back to its place. The Egyptians were fleeing toward[b] it, and the LORD swept them into the sea. [28]The water flowed back and covered the chariots and horsemen—the entire army of Pharaoh that had followed the Israelites into the sea. Not one of them survived.

[29]But the Israelites went through the sea on dry ground, with a wall of water on their right and on their left. [30]That day the LORD saved Israel from the hands of the Egyptians, and Israel saw the Egyptians lying dead on the shore. [31]And when the Israelites saw the great power

Great Escapes

Exodus 14 It's amazing how God got his people out of some really big jams. Like in Exodus 14, when the Israelites were trying to get away from Pharaoh's army. They were backed up to the shore of the Red Sea with nowhere to run. It looked like the end of Israel. But Moses stuck out his staff and the sea split wide open, creating a dry escape route! The Israelites saw their chance and took it. When the Egyptian army came after them, the walls of water crashed down on Pharaoh's soldiers. And that was the end of that.

God was also the master of these great escapes:

✗ Jonah escaped drowning by being swallowed by an enormous fish. Before all that fishy stomach acid turned Jonah into fish food, God helped Jonah escape again with the help of a whale of a belch. (Jonah 1:15—2:10)

✗ Three buddies escaped becoming toast in a blazing furnace. Their death-defying feat had something to do with a mystery guest who joined them in the oven. (Daniel 3:19—27)

✗ Daniel escaped becoming lion food when an angel muzzled the ferocious felines. (Daniel 6:16—22)

---

[a]25 Or *He jammed the wheels of their chariots* (see Samaritan Pentateuch, Septuagint and Syriac)
[b]27 Or *from*

the LORD displayed against the Egyptians, the people feared the LORD and put their trust in him and in Moses his servant.

The Song of Moses and Miriam

15 Then Moses and the Israelites sang this song to the LORD:

"I will sing to the LORD,
  for he is highly exalted.
The horse and its rider
  he has hurled into the sea.
[2] The LORD is my strength and my song;
  he has become my salvation.
He is my God, and I will praise him,
  my father's God, and I will exalt
  him.
[3] The LORD is a warrior;
  the LORD is his name.
[4] Pharaoh's chariots and his army
  he has hurled into the sea.
The best of Pharaoh's officers
  are drowned in the Red Sea.[a]
[5] The deep waters have covered them;
  they sank to the depths like a stone.

[6] "Your right hand, O LORD,
  was majestic in power.
Your right hand, O LORD,
  shattered the enemy.
[7] In the greatness of your majesty
  you threw down those who opposed
  you.
You unleashed your burning anger;
  it consumed them like stubble.
[8] By the blast of your nostrils
  the waters piled up.
The surging waters stood firm like a
  wall;
  the deep waters congealed in the
  heart of the sea.

[9] "The enemy boasted,
  'I will pursue, I will overtake them.
I will divide the spoils;
  I will gorge myself on them.
I will draw my sword
  and my hand will destroy them.'
[10] But you blew with your breath,
  and the sea covered them.
They sank like lead
  in the mighty waters.

[11] "Who among the gods is like you,
  O LORD?
Who is like you—
  majestic in holiness,
  awesome in glory,
  working wonders?
[12] You stretched out your right hand
  and the earth swallowed them.

[13] "In your unfailing love you will lead
  the people you have redeemed.
In your strength you will guide them
  to your holy dwelling.
[14] The nations will hear and tremble;
  anguish will grip the people of
  Philistia.
[15] The chiefs of Edom will be terrified,
  the leaders of Moab will be seized
  with trembling,
the people[b] of Canaan will melt away;
[16]   terror and dread will fall upon
  them.
By the power of your arm
  they will be as still as a stone—
until your people pass by, O LORD,
  until the people you bought[c] pass
  by.
[17] You will bring them in and plant them
  on the mountain of your
  inheritance—
the place, O LORD, you made for your
  dwelling,
  the sanctuary, O Lord, your hands
  established.
[18] The LORD will reign
  for ever and ever."

[19] When Pharaoh's horses, chariots and horsemen[d] went into the sea, the LORD brought the waters of the sea back over them, but the Israelites walked through the sea on dry ground. [20] Then Miriam the prophetess, Aaron's sister, took a tambourine in her hand, and all the women followed her, with tambourines and dancing. [21] Miriam sang to them:

"Sing to the LORD,
  for he is highly exalted.
The horse and its rider
  he has hurled into the sea."

The Waters of Marah and Elim

[22] Then Moses led Israel from the Red Sea and they went into the Desert of Shur. For three days they traveled in the

---

[a]4 Hebrew *Yam Suph*; that is, Sea of Reeds; also in verse 22   [b]15 Or *rulers*   [c]16 Or *created*   [d]19 Or *charioteers*

desert without finding water. ²³When they came to Marah, they could not drink its water because it was bitter. (That is why the place is called Marah.ª) ²⁴So the people grumbled against Moses, saying, "What are we to drink?"

²⁵Then Moses cried out to the Lᴏʀᴅ, and the Lᴏʀᴅ showed him a piece of wood. He threw it into the water, and the water became sweet.

There the Lᴏʀᴅ made a decree and a law for them, and there he tested them. ²⁶He said, "If you listen carefully to the voice of the Lᴏʀᴅ your God and do what is right in his eyes, if you pay attention to his commands and keep all his decrees, I will not bring on you any of the diseases I brought on the Egyptians, for I am the Lᴏʀᴅ, who heals you."

²⁷Then they came to Elim, where there were twelve springs and seventy palm trees, and they camped there near the water.

Manna and Quail

16 The whole Israelite community set out from Elim and came to the Desert of Sin, which is between Elim and Sinai, on the fifteenth day of the second month after they had come out of Egypt. ²In the desert the whole community grumbled against Moses and Aaron. ³The Israelites said to them, "If only we had died by the Lᴏʀᴅ's hand in Egypt! There we sat around pots of meat and ate all the food we wanted, but you have brought us out into this desert to starve this entire assembly to death."

⁴Then the Lᴏʀᴅ said to Moses, "I will rain down bread from heaven for you. The people are to go out each day and gather enough for that day. In this way I will test them and see whether they will follow my instructions. ⁵On the sixth day they are to prepare what they bring in, and that is to be twice as much as they gather on the other days."

⁶So Moses and Aaron said to all the Israelites, "In the evening you will know that it was the Lᴏʀᴅ who brought you out of Egypt, ⁷and in the morning you will see the glory of the Lᴏʀᴅ, because he has heard your grumbling against him. Who are we, that you should grumble against us?" ⁸Moses also said, "You will know

that it was the Lᴏʀᴅ when he gives you meat to eat in the evening and all the bread you want in the morning, because he has heard your grumbling against him. Who are we? You are not grumbling against us, but against the Lᴏʀᴅ."

⁹Then Moses told Aaron, "Say to the entire Israelite community, 'Come before the Lᴏʀᴅ, for he has heard your grumbling.' "

¹⁰While Aaron was speaking to the whole Israelite community, they looked toward the desert, and there was the glory of the Lᴏʀᴅ appearing in the cloud.

¹¹The Lᴏʀᴅ said to Moses, ¹²"I have heard the grumbling of the Israelites. Tell them, 'At twilight you will eat meat, and in the morning you will be filled with bread. Then you will know that I am the Lᴏʀᴅ your God.' "

¹³That evening quail came and covered the camp, and in the morning there was a layer of dew around the camp. ¹⁴When the dew was gone, thin flakes like frost on the ground appeared on the desert floor. ¹⁵When the Israelites saw it, they said to each other, "What is it?" For they did not know what it was.

Moses said to them, "It is the bread the Lᴏʀᴅ has given you to eat. ¹⁶This is what the Lᴏʀᴅ has commanded: 'Each one is to gather as much as he needs. Take an omerᵇ for each person you have in your tent.' "

¹⁷The Israelites did as they were told; some gathered much, some little. ¹⁸And when they measured it by the omer, he who gathered much did not have too much, and he who gathered little did not have too little. Each one gathered as much as he needed.

¹⁹Then Moses said to them, "No one is to keep any of it until morning."

²⁰However, some of them paid no attention to Moses; they kept part of it until morning, but it was full of maggots and began to smell. So Moses was angry with them.

²¹Each morning everyone gathered as much as he needed, and when the sun grew hot, it melted away. ²²On the sixth

---

ª23 *Marah* means *bitter*. ᵇ16 That is, probably about 2 quarts (about 2 liters); also in verses 18, 32, 33 and 36 day, they gathered twice as much—two omers[a] for each person—and the leaders of the community came and reported this to Moses. [23]He said to them, "This is what the LORD commanded: 'Tomorrow is to be a day of rest, a holy Sabbath to the LORD. So bake what you want to bake and boil what you want to boil. Save whatever is left and keep it until morning.'"

[24]So they saved it until morning, as Moses commanded, and it did not stink or get maggots in it. [25]"Eat it today," Moses said, "because today is a Sabbath to the LORD. You will not find any of it on the ground today. [26]Six days you are to gather it, but on the seventh day, the Sabbath, there will not be any."

[27]Nevertheless, some of the people went out on the seventh day to gather it, but they found none. [28]Then the LORD said to Moses, "How long will you[b] refuse to keep my commands and my instruc-

tions? [29]Bear in mind that the LORD has given you the Sabbath; that is why on the sixth day he gives you bread for two days. Everyone is to stay where he is on the seventh day; no one is to go out." [30]So the people rested on the seventh day.

[31]The people of Israel called the bread manna.[c] It was white like coriander seed and tasted like wafers made with honey. [32]Moses said, "This is what the LORD has commanded: 'Take an omer of manna and keep it for the generations to come, so they can see the bread I gave you to eat in the desert when I brought you out of Egypt.'"

[33]So Moses said to Aaron, "Take a jar and put an omer of manna in it. Then

a22 That is, probably about 4 quarts (about 4.5 liters)   *b28* The Hebrew is plural.   *c31* Manna means *What is it?* (see verse 15).

Friday

No Worries

Read Exodus 16:1-12

A couple of years ago my dad almost lost his job. Instead of being laid off, his salary was cut big-time. Suddenly we couldn't buy a lot of the things we wanted, like nice clothes or a new car. But God provided everything we really needed, like food and shelter. It wasn't the most comfortable time for my family, but we never had to worry about the basics. God had them covered.

I knew God would provide for us because he always provides for his people. Even when the Israelites whined and complained and disobeyed God's rules about the manna in the desert, God never said, "Well, these people didn't do what I said, so now I'll just let them starve." He kept sending bread in the morning and meat at night.

God will always be there for me in hard times like he was with the Israelites. He'll be there for me in good times too. Just knowing how much he loves me makes me want to love him more.

Anna, age 17

❶ What are some ways people today act like the Israelites?

❷ Ask some Christian adults (possibly parents or grandparents) to tell you about a time they experienced serious money problems and what God taught them.

❸ Think of some ways God provides for his people. Send up a big "thank you!"

Turn to page 92 for your next devotion.

place it before the LORD to be kept for the generations to come."

³⁴As the LORD commanded Moses, Aaron put the manna in front of the Testimony, that it might be kept. ³⁵The Israelites ate manna forty years, until they came to a land that was settled; they ate manna until they reached the border of Canaan.

³⁶(An omer is one tenth of an ephah.)

Water From the Rock

17 The whole Israelite community set out from the Desert of Sin, traveling from place to place as the LORD commanded. They camped at Rephidim, but there was no water for the people to drink. ²So they quarreled with Moses and said, "Give us water to drink."

Moses replied, "Why do you quarrel with me? Why do you put the LORD to the test?"

³But the people were thirsty for water there, and they grumbled against Moses. They said, "Why did you bring us up out of Egypt to make us and our children and livestock die of thirst?"

⁴Then Moses cried out to the LORD, "What am I to do with these people? They are almost ready to stone me."

⁵The LORD answered Moses, "Walk on ahead of the people. Take with you some of the elders of Israel and take in your hand the staff with which you struck the Nile, and go. ⁶I will stand there before you by the rock at Horeb. Strike the rock, and water will come out of it for the people to drink." So Moses did this in the sight of the elders of Israel. ⁷And he called the place Massah*ᵃ* and Meribah*ᵇ* because the Israelites quarreled and because they tested the LORD saying, "Is the LORD among us or not?"

The Amalekites Defeated

⁸The Amalekites came and attacked the Israelites at Rephidim. ⁹Moses said to Joshua, "Choose some of our men and go out to fight the Amalekites. Tomorrow I will stand on top of the hill with the staff of God in my hands."

¹⁰So Joshua fought the Amalekites as Moses had ordered, and Moses, Aaron and Hur went to the top of the hill. ¹¹As long as Moses held up his hands, the Israelites were winning, but whenever he lowered his hands, the Amalekites were winning. ¹²When Moses' hands grew tired, they took a stone and put it under him and he sat on it. Aaron and Hur held his hands up—one on one side, one on the other—so that his hands remained steady till sunset. ¹³So Joshua overcame the Amalekite army with the sword.

¹⁴Then the LORD said to Moses, "Write this on a scroll as something to be remembered and make sure that Joshua hears it, because I will completely blot out the memory of Amalek from under heaven."

¹⁵Moses built an altar and called it The LORD is my Banner. ¹⁶He said, "For hands were lifted up to the throne of the LORD. The*ᶜ* LORD will be at war against the Amalekites from generation to generation."

Jethro Visits Moses

18 Now Jethro, the priest of Midian and father-in-law of Moses, heard of everything God had done for Moses and for his people Israel, and how the LORD had brought Israel out of Egypt.

²After Moses had sent away his wife Zipporah, his father-in-law Jethro received her ³and her two sons. One son was named Gershom,*ᵈ* for Moses said, "I have become an alien in a foreign land"; ⁴and the other was named Eliezer,*ᵉ* for he said, "My father's God was my helper; he saved me from the sword of Pharaoh."

⁵Jethro, Moses' father-in-law, together with Moses' sons and wife, came to him in the desert, where he was camped near the mountain of God. ⁶Jethro had sent word to him, "I, your father-in-law Jethro, am coming to you with your wife and her two sons."

⁷So Moses went out to meet his father-in-law and bowed down and kissed him. They greeted each other and then went into the tent. ⁸Moses told his father-in-law about everything the LORD had done to Pharaoh and the Egyptians for Israel's sake and about all the hardships they had

---

ᵃ7 Massah means *testing.* *ᵇ7 Meribah* means *quarreling.* *ᶜ16* Or *"Because a hand was against the throne of the LORD, the* *ᵈ3 Gershom* sounds like the Hebrew for *an alien there.* *ᵉ4 Eliezer* means *my God is helper.*

met along the way and how the LORD had saved them.

⁹Jethro was delighted to hear about all the good things the LORD had done for Israel in rescuing them from the hand of the Egyptians. ¹⁰He said, "Praise be to the LORD, who rescued you from the hand of the Egyptians and of Pharaoh, and who rescued the people from the hand of the Egyptians. ¹¹Now I know that the LORD is greater than all other gods, for he did this to those who had treated Israel arro-

gantly." ¹²Then Jethro, Moses' father-in-law, brought a burnt offering and other sacrifices to God, and Aaron came with all the elders of Israel to eat bread with Moses' father-in-law in the presence of God.

¹³The next day Moses took his seat to serve as judge for the people, and they stood around him from morning till evening. ¹⁴When his father-in-law saw all that Moses was doing for the people, he said, "What is this you are doing for the

---

Weekend.

Which Way?

Read James 1:2–5 (page 1505)

Have you ever been lost? Maybe you got on the wrong trail on a youth group hike or maybe you just lost your mom in the store when you were little. You were stuck. You had no idea where to go.

Sometimes we face situations like that in other areas of life. Maybe you're trying to decide which parent to live with this year. Or you might be thinking about changing classes because you don't get along with your teacher. Or maybe a friend is begging you to do something you don't really want to do. Whatever the decision, you don't know which direction to go. And you're afraid that you might choose the wrong direction, so you don't choose anything at all.

On Tuesday, Noah reminded us in his devotion that God works things out for the best. Later in the week, Chris and Anna talked about trusting God to take care of us. Today James (in the Bible) tells us to do several things, including asking God to give us wisdom. He doesn't say that God will tell us *exactly* what to do; instead he says that God gives us the *wisdom* to decide.

When we face tough decisions about which direction to go, it's not always obvious to us which road to take. But we still have to make a decision, and trust that God will be with us whatever we decide. Guess what? That's exactly what God does! So if you're facing a decision with no obvious answer, don't choose the option of no decision at all. Ask God for wisdom, then make a choice and trust God for the best!

❶ What decision are you struggling with right now?

❷ Write down the choices you have. List the good and bad points about each, then write a date by which you have to make a decision. Do what you can to make your decision by this date.

❸ Spend a few moments in prayer asking God for wisdom to help you make a good decision. Then thank him in advance for taking care of you regardless of your choice.

Turn to page 94 for your next devotion.

people? Why do you alone sit as judge, while all these people stand around you from morning till evening?"

¹⁵Moses answered him, "Because the people come to me to seek God's will. ¹⁶Whenever they have a dispute, it is brought to me, and I decide between the parties and inform them of God's decrees and laws."

¹⁷Moses' father-in-law replied, "What you are doing is not good. ¹⁸You and these people who come to you will only wear yourselves out. The work is too heavy for you; you cannot handle it alone. ¹⁹Listen now to me and I will give you some advice, and may God be with you. You must be the people's representative before God and bring their disputes to him. ²⁰Teach them the decrees and laws, and show them the way to live and the duties they are to perform. ²¹But select capable men from all the people—men who fear God, trustworthy men who hate dishonest gain—and appoint them as officials over thousands, hundreds, fifties and tens. ²²Have them serve as judges for the people at all times, but have them bring every difficult case to you; the simple cases they can decide themselves. That will make your load lighter, because they will share it with you. ²³If you do this and God so commands, you will be able to stand the strain, and all these people will go home satisfied."

²⁴Moses listened to his father-in-law and did everything he said. ²⁵He chose capable men from all Israel and made them leaders of the people, officials over thousands, hundreds, fifties and tens. ²⁶They served as judges for the people at all times. The difficult cases they brought to Moses, but the simple ones they decided themselves.

²⁷Then Moses sent his father-in-law on his way, and Jethro returned to his own country.

At Mount Sinai

19 In the third month after the Israelites left Egypt—on the very day—they came to the Desert of Sinai. ²After they set out from Rephidim, they entered the Desert of Sinai, and Israel camped there in the desert in front of the mountain.

³Then Moses went up to God, and the LORD called to him from the mountain and said, "This is what you are to say to the house of Jacob and what you are to tell the people of Israel: ⁴'You yourselves have seen what I did to Egypt, and how I carried you on eagles' wings and brought you to myself. ⁵Now if you obey me fully and keep my covenant, then out of all nations you will be my treasured possession. Although the whole earth is mine, ⁶youᵃ will be for me a kingdom of priests and a holy nation.' These are the words you are to speak to the Israelites."

⁷So Moses went back and summoned the elders of the people and set before them all the words the LORD had commanded him to speak. ⁸The people all responded together, "We will do everything the LORD has said." So Moses brought their answer back to the LORD.

⁹The LORD said to Moses, "I am going to come to you in a dense cloud, so that the people will hear me speaking with you and will always put their trust in you." Then Moses told the LORD what the people had said.

¹⁰And the LORD said to Moses, "Go to the people and consecrate them today and tomorrow. Have them wash their clothes ¹¹and be ready by the third day, because on that day the LORD will come down on Mount Sinai in the sight of all the people. ¹²Put limits for the people around the mountain and tell them, 'Be careful that you do not go up the mountain or touch the foot of it. Whoever touches the mountain shall surely be put to death. ¹³He shall surely be stoned or shot with arrows; not a hand is to be laid on him. Whether man or animal, he shall not be permitted to live.' Only when the ram's horn sounds a long blast may they go up to the mountain."

¹⁴After Moses had gone down the mountain to the people, he consecrated them, and they washed their clothes. ¹⁵Then he said to the people, "Prepare yourselves for the third day. Abstain from sexual relations."

¹⁶On the morning of the third day there was thunder and lightning, with a thick

---

ᵃ5,6 Or possession, for the whole earth is mine. ⁶You

cloud over the mountain, and a very loud trumpet blast. Everyone in the camp trembled. ¹⁷Then Moses led the people out of the camp to meet with God, and they stood at the foot of the mountain. ¹⁸Mount Sinai was covered with smoke, because the LORD descended on it in fire. The smoke billowed up from it like smoke from a furnace, the whole mountain*ᵃ* trembled violently, ¹⁹and the sound of the trumpet grew louder and louder. Then Moses spoke and the voice of God answered him.*ᵇ*

²⁰The LORD descended to the top of Mount Sinai and called Moses to the top of the mountain. So Moses went up ²¹and the LORD said to him, "Go down and warn the people so they do not force their way through to see the LORD and many of them perish. ²²Even the priests, who approach the LORD, must consecrate themselves, or the LORD will break out against them."

²³Moses said to the LORD, "The people cannot come up Mount Sinai, because you yourself warned us, 'Put limits around the mountain and set it apart as holy.'"

²⁴The LORD replied, "Go down and bring Aaron up with you. But the priests and the people must not force their way through to come up to the LORD, or he will break out against them."

²⁵So Moses went down to the people and told them.

The Ten Commandments

20 And God spoke all these words:

²"I am the LORD your God, who brought you out of Egypt, out of the land of slavery.

ᵃ18 Most Hebrew manuscripts; a few Hebrew manuscripts and Septuagint all the people   *ᵇ19 Or* and God answered him with thunder

---

Monday

God's Cool Rules   **Read Exodus 20:1-17**

By giving us the Ten Commandments, God lets us know that he isn't just some guy who sits back and says, "As long as you say you believe in me, you can do whatever you want." If we go against one of his absolute truths, it's definitely not OK with him.

What's really great about God's rules is that they make sense. We don't just have to follow them because he says so, even though that would be a good enough reason. Following the Ten Commandments makes our lives better too.

Like the one about honoring your parents. Life at home is a lot nicer when you obey Mom and Dad, isn't it? Or the commandment about coveting. Coveting just makes you want more and more until you're never satisfied. If you follow God's rules, you don't have to feel that way.

God really does know what's best for us. Obeying his commandments might seem frustrating sometimes, but it'll make us a lot happier in the end.

Kate age 12

What about You?

❶ Pick a commandment you have trouble keeping. What's happened when you've chosen not to obey this rule?

❷ Rewrite the Ten Commandments in your own words and tape up a copy where you'll see it every day.

❸ Ask God to help you be more obedient.

Turn to page 107 for your next devotion.

³ "You shall have no other gods before[a] me.

⁴ "You shall not make for yourself an idol in the form of anything in heaven above or on the earth beneath or in the waters below. ⁵You shall not bow down to them or worship them; for I, the LORD your God, am a jealous God, punishing the children for the sin of the fathers to the third and fourth generation of those who hate me, ⁶but showing love to a thousand generations of those who love me and keep my commandments.

⁷ "You shall not misuse the name of the LORD your God, for the LORD will not hold anyone guiltless who misuses his name.

⁸ "Remember the Sabbath day by keeping it holy. ⁹Six days you shall labor and do all your work, ¹⁰but the seventh day is a Sabbath to the LORD your God. On it you shall not do any work, neither you, nor your son or daughter, nor your manservant or maidservant, nor your animals, nor the alien within your gates. ¹¹For in six days the LORD made the heavens and the earth, the sea, and all that is in them, but he rested on the seventh day. Therefore the LORD blessed the Sabbath day and made it holy.

¹² "Honor your father and your mother, so that you may live long in the land the LORD your God is giving you.

¹³ "You shall not murder.

¹⁴ "You shall not commit adultery.

¹⁵ "You shall not steal.

¹⁶ "You shall not give false testimony against your neighbor.

¹⁷ "You shall not covet your neighbor's house. You shall not covet your neighbor's wife, or his manservant or maidservant, his ox or donkey, or anything that belongs to your neighbor."

¹⁸When the people saw the thunder and lightning and heard the trumpet and saw the mountain in smoke, they trembled with fear. They stayed at a distance ¹⁹and said to Moses, "Speak to us yourself and we will listen. But do not have God speak to us or we will die."

²⁰Moses said to the people, "Do not be afraid. God has come to test you, so that the fear of God will be with you to keep you from sinning."

²¹The people remained at a distance, while Moses approached the thick darkness where God was.

Idols and Altars

²²Then the LORD said to Moses, "Tell the Israelites this: 'You have seen for yourselves that I have spoken to you from heaven: ²³Do not make any gods to be alongside me; do not make for yourselves gods of silver or gods of gold.

²⁴ "Make an altar of earth for me and sacrifice on it your burnt offerings and fellowship offerings,[b] your sheep and goats and your cattle. Wherever I cause my name to be honored, I will come to you and bless you. ²⁵If you make an altar of stones for me, do not build it with dressed stones, for you will defile it if you use a tool on it. ²⁶And do not go up to my altar on steps, lest your nakedness be exposed on it.'

It's the Law

Huh?

Exodus 21:1

If people get caught breaking the law, they'll get punished and might even go to jail. Most societies have laws that are designed to protect people and help them live better lives. God's laws work the same way. God gave his laws to the Israelites, and to us, out of love.

21 "These are the laws you are to set before them:

---

[a]3 Or *besides* [b]24 Traditionally *peace offerings*

Hebrew Servants

2"If you buy a Hebrew servant, he is to serve you for six years. But in the seventh year, he shall go free, without paying anything. 3If he comes alone, he is to go free alone; but if he has a wife when he comes, she is to go with him. 4If his master gives him a wife and she bears him sons or daughters, the woman and her children shall belong to her master, and only the man shall go free.

5"But if the servant declares, 'I love my master and my wife and children and do not want to go free,' 6then his master must take him before the judges.a He shall take him to the door or the doorpost and pierce his ear with an awl. Then he will be his servant for life.

7"If a man sells his daughter as a servant, she is not to go free as menservants do. 8If she does not please the master who has selected her for himself,b he must let her be redeemed. He has no right to sell her to foreigners, because he has broken faith with her. 9If he selects her for his son, he must grant her the rights of a daughter. 10If he marries another woman, he must not deprive the first one of her food, clothing and marital rights. 11If he does not provide her with these three things, she is to go free, without any payment of money.

Personal Injuries

12"Anyone who strikes a man and kills him shall surely be put to death. 13However, if he does not do it intentionally, but God lets it happen, he is to flee to a place I will designate. 14But if a man schemes and kills another man deliberately, take him away from my altar and put him to death.

15"Anyone who attacksc his father or his mother must be put to death.

16"Anyone who kidnaps another and either sells him or still has him when he is caught must be put to death.

17"Anyone who curses his father or mother must be put to death.

18"If men quarrel and one hits the other with a stone or with his fistd and he does not die but is confined to bed, 19the one who struck the blow will not be held responsible if the other gets up and walks around outside with his staff; however, he must pay the injured man for the loss of his time and see that he is completely healed.

20"If a man beats his male or female slave with a rod and the slave dies as a direct result, he must be punished, 21but he is not to be punished if the slave gets up after a day or two, since the slave is his property.

22"If men who are fighting hit a pregnant woman and she gives birth prematurelye but there is no serious injury, the offender must be fined whatever the woman's husband demands and the court allows. 23But if there is serious injury, you are to take life for life, 24eye for eye, tooth for tooth, hand for hand, foot for foot, 25burn for burn, wound for wound, bruise for bruise.

26"If a man hits a manservant or maidservant in the eye and destroys it, he must let the servant go free to compensate for the eye. 27And if he knocks out the tooth of a manservant or maidservant, he must let the servant go free to compensate for the tooth.

28"If a bull gores a man or a woman to death, the bull must be stoned to death, and its meat must not be eaten. But the owner of the bull will not be held responsible. 29If, however, the bull has had the habit of goring and the owner has been warned but has not kept it penned up and it kills a man or woman, the bull must be stoned and the owner also must be put to death. 30However, if payment is demanded of him, he may redeem his life by paying whatever is demanded. 31This law also applies if the bull gores a son or daughter. 32If the bull gores a male or female slave, the owner must pay thirty shekelsf of silver to the master of the slave, and the bull must be stoned.

33"If a man uncovers a pit or digs one and fails to cover it and an ox or a donkey falls into it, 34the owner of the pit must pay for the loss; he must pay its owner, and the dead animal will be his.

35"If a man's bull injures the bull of another and it dies, they are to sell the live

---

a6 Or before God   b8 Or master so that he does not choose her   c15 Or kills   d18 Or with a tool   e22 Or she has a miscarriage   f32 That is, about 12 ounces (about 0.3 kilogram)

one and divide both the money and the dead animal equally. [36]However, if it was known that the bull had the habit of goring, yet the owner did not keep it penned up, the owner must pay, animal for animal, and the dead animal will be his.

Protection of Property

22 "If a man steals an ox or a sheep and slaughters it or sells it, he must pay back five head of cattle for the ox and four sheep for the sheep.

[2]"If a thief is caught breaking in and is struck so that he dies, the defender is not guilty of bloodshed; [3]but if it happens[a] after sunrise, he is guilty of bloodshed.

"A thief must certainly make restitution, but if he has nothing, he must be sold to pay for his theft.

[4]"If the stolen animal is found alive in his possession—whether ox or donkey or sheep—he must pay back double.

[5]"If a man grazes his livestock in a field or vineyard and lets them stray and they graze in another man's field, he must make restitution from the best of his own field or vineyard.

[6]"If a fire breaks out and spreads into thornbushes so that it burns shocks of grain or standing grain or the whole field, the one who started the fire must make restitution.

[7]"If a man gives his neighbor silver or goods for safekeeping and they are stolen from the neighbor's house, the thief, if he is caught, must pay back double. [8]But if the thief is not found, the owner of the house must appear before the judges[b] to determine whether he has laid his hands on the other man's property. [9]In all cases of illegal possession of an ox, a donkey, a sheep, a garment, or any other lost property about which somebody says, 'This is mine,' both parties are to bring their cases before the judges. The one whom the judges declare[c] guilty must pay back double to his neighbor.

[10]"If a man gives a donkey, an ox, a sheep or any other animal to his neighbor for safekeeping and it dies or is injured or is taken away while no one is looking, [11]the issue between them will be settled by the taking of an oath before the LORD that the neighbor did not lay hands on the other person's property. The

owner is to accept this, and no restitution is required. [12]But if the animal was stolen from the neighbor, he must make restitution to the owner. [13]If it was torn to pieces by a wild animal, he shall bring in the remains as evidence and he will not be required to pay for the torn animal.

[14]"If a man borrows an animal from his neighbor and it is injured or dies while the owner is not present, he must make restitution. [15]But if the owner is with the animal, the borrower will not have to pay. If the animal was hired, the money paid for the hire covers the loss.

Social Responsibility

[16]"If a man seduces a virgin who is not pledged to be married and sleeps with her, he must pay the bride-price, and she shall be his wife. [17]If her father absolutely refuses to give her to him, he must still pay the bride-price for virgins.

[18]"Do not allow a sorceress to live.

[19]"Anyone who has sexual relations with an animal must be put to death.

[20]"Whoever sacrifices to any god other than the LORD must be destroyed.[d]

[21]"Do not mistreat an alien or oppress him, for you were aliens in Egypt.

[22]"Do not take advantage of a widow or an orphan. [23]If you do and they cry out to me, I will certainly hear their cry. [24]My anger will be aroused, and I will kill you with the sword; your wives will become widows and your children fatherless.

[25]"If you lend money to one of my people among you who is needy, do not be like a moneylender; charge him no interest.[e] [26]If you take your neighbor's cloak as a pledge, return it to him by sunset, [27]because his cloak is the only covering he has for his body. What else will he sleep in? When he cries out to me, I will hear, for I am compassionate.

[28]"Do not blaspheme God[f] or curse the ruler of your people.

[29]"Do not hold back offerings from your granaries or your vats.[g]

---

[a]3 Or *if he strikes him*   [b]8 Or *before God*; also in verse 9   [c]9 Or *whom God declares*   [d]20 The Hebrew term refers to the irrevocable giving over of things or persons to the LORD, often by totally destroying them.   [e]25 Or *excessive interest*   [f]28 Or *Do not revile the judges*   [g]29 The meaning of the Hebrew for this phrase is uncertain.

"You must give me the firstborn of your sons. ³⁰Do the same with your cattle and your sheep. Let them stay with their mothers for seven days, but give them to me on the eighth day.

³¹"You are to be my holy people. So do not eat the meat of an animal torn by wild beasts; throw it to the dogs.

Laws of Justice and Mercy

23 "Do not spread false reports. Do not help a wicked man by being a malicious witness.

²"Do not follow the crowd in doing wrong. When you give testimony in a lawsuit, do not pervert justice by siding with the crowd, ³and do not show favoritism to a poor man in his lawsuit.

⁴"If you come across your enemy's ox or donkey wandering off, be sure to take it back to him. ⁵If you see the donkey of someone who hates you fallen down under its load, do not leave it there; be sure you help him with it.

⁶"Do not deny justice to your poor people in their lawsuits. ⁷Have nothing to do with a false charge and do not put an innocent or honest person to death, for I will not acquit the guilty.

⁸"Do not accept a bribe, for a bribe blinds those who see and twists the words of the righteous.

⁹"Do not oppress an alien; you yourselves know how it feels to be aliens, because you were aliens in Egypt.

Sabbath Laws

¹⁰"For six years you are to sow your fields and harvest the crops, ¹¹but during the seventh year let the land lie unplowed and unused. Then the poor among your people may get food from it, and the wild animals may eat what they leave. Do the same with your vineyard and your olive grove.

¹²"Six days do your work, but on the seventh day do not work, so that your ox and your donkey may rest and the slave born in your household, and the alien as well, may be refreshed.

¹³"Be careful to do everything I have said to you. Do not invoke the names of other gods; do not let them be heard on your lips.

The Three Annual Festivals

¹⁴"Three times a year you are to celebrate a festival to me.

¹⁵"Celebrate the Feast of Unleavened Bread; for seven days eat bread made without yeast, as I commanded you. Do this at the appointed time in the month of Abib, for in that month you came out of Egypt.

"No one is to appear before me empty-handed.

¹⁶"Celebrate the Feast of Harvest with the firstfruits of the crops you sow in your field.

"Celebrate the Feast of Ingathering at the end of the year, when you gather in your crops from the field.

¹⁷"Three times a year all the men are to appear before the Sovereign LORD.

¹⁸"Do not offer the blood of a sacrifice to me along with anything containing yeast.

"The fat of my festival offerings must not be kept until morning.

¹⁹"Bring the best of the firstfruits of your soil to the house of the LORD your God.

"Do not cook a young goat in its mother's milk.

God's Angel to Prepare the Way

²⁰"See, I am sending an angel ahead of you to guard you along the way and to bring you to the place I have prepared. ²¹Pay attention to him and listen to what he says. Do not rebel against him; he will not forgive your rebellion, since my Name is in him. ²²If you listen carefully to what he says and do all that I say, I will be an enemy to your enemies and will oppose those who oppose you. ²³My angel will go ahead of you and bring you into the land of the Amorites, Hittites, Perizzites, Canaanites, Hivites and Jebusites, and I will wipe them out. ²⁴Do not bow down before their gods or worship them or follow their practices. You must demolish them and break their sacred stones to pieces. ²⁵Worship the LORD your God, and his blessing will be on your food and water. I will take away sickness from among you, ²⁶and none will miscarry or be barren in your land. I will give you a full life span.

27"I will send my terror ahead of you and throw into confusion every nation you encounter. I will make all your enemies turn their backs and run. 28I will send the hornet ahead of you to drive the Hivites, Canaanites and Hittites out of your way. 29But I will not drive them out in a single year, because the land would become desolate and the wild animals too numerous for you. 30Little by little I will drive them out before you, until you have increased enough to take possession of the land.

31"I will establish your borders from the Red Sea[a] to the Sea of the Philistines,[b] and from the desert to the River.[c] I will hand over to you the people who live in the land and you will drive them out before you. 32Do not make a covenant with them or with their gods. 33Do not let them live in your land, or they will cause you to sin against me, because the worship of their gods will certainly be a snare to you."

The Covenant Confirmed

24 Then he said to Moses, "Come up to the LORD, you and Aaron, Nadab and Abihu, and seventy of the elders of Israel. You are to worship at a distance, 2but Moses alone is to approach the LORD; the others must not come near. And the people may not come up with him."

3When Moses went and told the people all the LORD's words and laws, they responded with one voice, "Everything the LORD has said we will do." 4Moses then wrote down everything the LORD had said.

He got up early the next morning and built an altar at the foot of the mountain and set up twelve stone pillars representing the twelve tribes of Israel. 5Then he sent young Israelite men, and they offered burnt offerings and sacrificed young bulls as fellowship offerings[d] to the LORD. 6Moses took half of the blood and put it in bowls, and the other half he sprinkled on the altar. 7Then he took the Book of the Covenant and read it to the people. They responded, "We will do everything the LORD has said; we will obey."

8Moses then took the blood, sprinkled it on the people and said, "This is the blood of the covenant that the LORD has made with you in accordance with all these words."

9Moses and Aaron, Nadab and Abihu, and the seventy elders of Israel went up 10and saw the God of Israel. Under his feet was something like a pavement made of sapphire,[e] clear as the sky itself. 11But God did not raise his hand against these leaders of the Israelites; they saw God, and they ate and drank.

12The LORD said to Moses, "Come up to me on the mountain and stay here, and I will give you the tablets of stone, with the law and commands I have written for their instruction."

13Then Moses set out with Joshua his aide, and Moses went up on the mountain of God. 14He said to the elders, "Wait here for us until we come back to you. Aaron and Hur are with you, and anyone involved in a dispute can go to them."

15When Moses went up on the mountain, the cloud covered it, 16and the glory of the LORD settled on Mount Sinai. For six days the cloud covered the mountain, and on the seventh day the LORD called to Moses from within the cloud. 17To the Israelites the glory of the LORD looked like a consuming fire on top of the mountain. 18Then Moses entered the cloud as he went on up the mountain. And he stayed on the mountain forty days and forty nights.

Offerings for the Tabernacle

25 The LORD said to Moses, 2"Tell the Israelites to bring me an offering. You are to receive the offering for me from each man whose heart prompts him to give. 3These are the offerings you are to receive from them: gold, silver and bronze; 4blue, purple and scarlet yarn and fine linen; goat hair; 5ram skins dyed red and hides of sea cows[f]; acacia wood; 6olive oil for the light; spices for the anointing oil and for the fragrant incense; 7and onyx stones and other gems to be mounted on the ephod and breastpiece.

a31 Hebrew Yam Suph; that is, Sea of Reeds   b31 That is, the Mediterranean   c31 That is, the Euphrates   d5 Traditionally peace offerings   e10 Or lapis lazuli   f5 That is, dugongs

⁸"Then have them make a sanctuary for me, and I will dwell among them. ⁹Make this tabernacle and all its furnishings exactly like the pattern I will show you.

The Ark

¹⁰"Have them make a chest of acacia wood—two and a half cubits long, a cubit and a half wide, and a cubit and a half high.ᵃ ¹¹Overlay it with pure gold, both inside and out, and make a gold molding around it. ¹²Cast four gold rings for it and fasten them to its four feet, with two rings on one side and two rings on the other. ¹³Then make poles of acacia wood and overlay them with gold. ¹⁴Insert the poles into the rings on the sides of the chest to carry it. ¹⁵The poles are to remain in the rings of this ark; they are not to be removed. ¹⁶Then put in the ark the Testimony, which I will give you.

¹⁷"Make an atonement coverᵇ of pure gold—two and a half cubits long and a cubit and a half wide.ᶜ ¹⁸And make two cherubim out of hammered gold at the ends of the cover. ¹⁹Make one cherub on one end and the second cherub on the other; make the cherubim of one piece with the cover, at the two ends. ²⁰The cherubim are to have their wings spread upward, overshadowing the cover with them. The cherubim are to face each other, looking toward the cover. ²¹Place the cover on top of the ark and put in the ark the Testimony, which I will give you. ²²There, above the cover between the two cherubim that are over the ark of the Testimony, I will meet with you and give you all my commands for the Israelites.

The Table

²³"Make a table of acacia wood—two cubits long, a cubit wide and a cubit and a half high.ᵈ ²⁴Overlay it with pure gold and make a gold molding around it. ²⁵Also make around it a rim a handbreadthᵉ wide and put a gold molding on the rim. ²⁶Make four gold rings for the table and fasten them to the four corners, where the four legs are. ²⁷The rings are to be close to the rim to hold the poles used in carrying the table. ²⁸Make the poles of acacia wood, overlay them with gold and carry the table with them. ²⁹And make its

plates and dishes of pure gold, as well as its pitchers and bowls for the pouring out of offerings. ³⁰Put the bread of the Presence on this table to be before me at all times.

The Lampstand

³¹"Make a lampstand of pure gold and hammer it out, base and shaft; its flower-like cups, buds and blossoms shall be of one piece with it. ³²Six branches are to extend from the sides of the lampstand—three on one side and three on the other. ³³Three cups shaped like almond flowers with buds and blossoms are to be on one branch, three on the next branch, and the same for all six branches extending from the lampstand. ³⁴And on the lampstand there are to be four cups shaped like almond flowers with buds and blossoms. ³⁵One bud shall be under the first pair of branches extending from the lampstand, a second bud under the second pair, and a third bud under the third pair—six branches in all. ³⁶The buds and branches shall all be of one piece with the lampstand, hammered out of pure gold.

³⁷"Then make its seven lamps and set them up on it so that they light the space in front of it. ³⁸Its wick trimmers and trays are to be of pure gold. ³⁹A talentᶠ of pure gold is to be used for the lampstand and all these accessories. ⁴⁰See that you make them according to the pattern shown you on the mountain.

The Tabernacle

26 "Make the tabernacle with ten curtains of finely twisted linen and blue, purple and scarlet yarn, with cherubim worked into them by a skilled craftsman. ²All the curtains are to be the same size—twenty-eight cubits long and four cubits wide.ᵍ ³Join five of the curtains together, and do the same with the

---

ᵃ10 That is, about 3 3/4 feet (about 1.1 meters) long and 2 1/4 feet (about 0.7 meter) wide and high
ᵇ17 Traditionally *a mercy seat*   ᶜ17 That is, about 3 3/4 feet (about 1.1 meters) long and 2 1/4 feet (about 0.7 meter) wide   ᵈ23 That is, about 3 feet (about 0.9 meter) long and 1 1/2 feet (about 0.5 meter) wide and 2 1/4 feet (about 0.7 meter) high
ᵉ25 That is, about 3 inches (about 8 centimeters)
ᶠ39 That is, about 75 pounds (about 34 kilograms)
ᵍ2 That is, about 42 feet (about 12.5 meters) long and 6 feet (about 1.8 meters) wide

other five. ⁴Make loops of blue material along the edge of the end curtain in one set, and do the same with the end curtain in the other set. ⁵Make fifty loops on one curtain and fifty loops on the end curtain of the other set, with the loops opposite each other. ⁶Then make fifty gold clasps and use them to fasten the curtains together so that the tabernacle is a unit.

⁷"Make curtains of goat hair for the tent over the tabernacle—eleven altogether. ⁸All eleven curtains are to be the same size—thirty cubits long and four cubits wide.*ᵃ* ⁹Join five of the curtains together into one set and the other six into another set. Fold the sixth curtain double at the front of the tent. ¹⁰Make fifty loops along the edge of the end curtain in one set and also along the edge of the end curtain in the other set. ¹¹Then make fifty bronze clasps and put them in the loops to fasten the tent together as a unit. ¹²As for the additional length of the tent curtains, the half curtain that is left over is to hang down at the rear of the tabernacle. ¹³The tent curtains will be a cubit*ᵇ* longer on both sides; what is left will hang over the sides of the tabernacle so as to cover it. ¹⁴Make for the tent a covering of ram skins dyed red, and over that a covering of hides of sea cows.*ᶜ*

¹⁵"Make upright frames of acacia wood for the tabernacle. ¹⁶Each frame is to be ten cubits long and a cubit and a half wide,*ᵈ* ¹⁷with two projections set parallel to each other. Make all the frames of the tabernacle in this way. ¹⁸Make twenty frames for the south side of the tabernacle ¹⁹and make forty silver bases to go under them—two bases for each frame, one under each projection. ²⁰For the other side, the north side of the tabernacle, make twenty frames ²¹and forty silver bases—two under each frame. ²²Make six frames for the far end, that is, the west end of the tabernacle, ²³and make two frames for the corners at the far end. ²⁴At these two corners they must be double from the bottom all the way to the top, and fitted into a single ring; both shall be like that. ²⁵So there will be eight frames and sixteen silver bases—two under each frame.

²⁶"Also make crossbars of acacia wood: five for the frames on one side of the tabernacle, ²⁷five for those on the other side, and five for the frames on the west, at the far end of the tabernacle. ²⁸The center crossbar is to extend from end to end at the middle of the frames. ²⁹Overlay the frames with gold and make gold rings to hold the crossbars. Also overlay the crossbars with gold.

³⁰"Set up the tabernacle according to the plan shown you on the mountain.

³¹"Make a curtain of blue, purple and scarlet yarn and finely twisted linen, with cherubim worked into it by a skilled craftsman. ³²Hang it with gold hooks on four posts of acacia wood overlaid with gold and standing on four silver bases. ³³Hang the curtain from the clasps and place the ark of the Testimony behind the curtain. The curtain will separate the Holy Place from the Most Holy Place. ³⁴Put the atonement cover on the ark of the Testimony in the Most Holy Place. ³⁵Place the table outside the curtain on the north side of the tabernacle and put the lampstand opposite it on the south side.

³⁶"For the entrance to the tent make a curtain of blue, purple and scarlet yarn and finely twisted linen—the work of an embroiderer. ³⁷Make gold hooks for this curtain and five posts of acacia wood overlaid with gold. And cast five bronze bases for them.

The Altar of Burnt Offering

27 "Build an altar of acacia wood, three cubits*ᵉ* high; it is to be square, five cubits long and five cubits wide.*ᶠ* ²Make a horn at each of the four corners, so that the horns and the altar are of one piece, and overlay the altar with bronze. ³Make all its utensils of bronze—its pots to remove the ashes, and its shovels, sprinkling bowls, meat forks and firepans. ⁴Make a grating for it, a bronze network, and make a bronze ring at each of the four corners of the network.

ᵃ8 That is, about 45 feet (about 13.5 meters) long and 6 feet (about 1.8 meters) wide   *ᵇ13* That is, about 1 1/2 feet (about 0.5 meter)   *ᶜ14* That is, dugongs   *ᵈ16* That is, about 15 feet (about 4.5 meters) long and 2 1/4 feet (about 0.7 meter) wide   *ᵉ1* That is, about 4 1/2 feet (about 1.3 meters)   *ᶠ1* That is, about 7 1/2 feet (about 2.3 meters) long and wide

⁵Put it under the ledge of the altar so that it is halfway up the altar. ⁶Make poles of acacia wood for the altar and overlay them with bronze. ⁷The poles are to be inserted into the rings so they will be on two sides of the altar when it is carried. ⁸Make the altar hollow, out of boards. It is to be made just as you were shown on the mountain.

The Courtyard

⁹"Make a courtyard for the tabernacle. The south side shall be a hundred cubits*a* long and is to have curtains of finely twisted linen, ¹⁰with twenty posts and twenty bronze bases and with silver hooks and bands on the posts. ¹¹The north side shall also be a hundred cubits long and is to have curtains, with twenty posts and twenty bronze bases and with silver hooks and bands on the posts.

¹²"The west end of the courtyard shall be fifty cubits*b* wide and have curtains, with ten posts and ten bases. ¹³On the east end, toward the sunrise, the courtyard shall also be fifty cubits wide. ¹⁴Curtains fifteen cubits*c* long are to be on one side of the entrance, with three posts and three bases, ¹⁵and curtains fifteen cubits long are to be on the other side, with three posts and three bases.

¹⁶"For the entrance to the courtyard, provide a curtain twenty cubits*d* long, of blue, purple and scarlet yarn and finely twisted linen—the work of an embroiderer—with four posts and four bases. ¹⁷All the posts around the courtyard are to have silver bands and hooks, and bronze bases. ¹⁸The courtyard shall be a hundred cubits long and fifty cubits wide,*e* with curtains of finely twisted linen five cubits*f* high, and with bronze bases. ¹⁹All the other articles used in the service of the tabernacle, whatever their function, including all the tent pegs for it and those for the courtyard, are to be of bronze.

Oil for the Lampstand

²⁰"Command the Israelites to bring you clear oil of pressed olives for the light so that the lamps may be kept burning. ²¹In the Tent of Meeting, outside the curtain that is in front of the Testimony, Aaron and his sons are to keep the lamps burn-ing before the LORD from evening till morning. This is to be a lasting ordinance among the Israelites for the generations to come.

The Priestly Garments

28 "Have Aaron your brother brought to you from among the Israelites, along with his sons Nadab and Abihu, Eleazar and Ithamar, so they may serve me as priests. ²Make sacred garments for your brother Aaron, to give him dignity and honor. ³Tell all the skilled men to whom I have given wisdom in such matters that they are to make garments for Aaron, for his consecration, so he may serve me as priest. ⁴These are the garments they are to make: a breastpiece, an ephod, a robe, a woven tunic, a turban and a sash. They are to make these sacred garments for your brother Aaron and his sons, so they may serve me as priests. ⁵Have them use gold, and blue, purple and scarlet yarn, and fine linen.

The Ephod

⁶"Make the ephod of gold, and of blue, purple and scarlet yarn, and of finely twisted linen—the work of a skilled craftsman. ⁷It is to have two shoulder pieces attached to two of its corners, so it can be fastened. ⁸Its skillfully woven waistband is to be like it—of one piece with the ephod and made with gold, and with blue, purple and scarlet yarn, and with finely twisted linen.

⁹"Take two onyx stones and engrave on them the names of the sons of Israel ¹⁰in the order of their birth—six names on one stone and the remaining six on the other. ¹¹Engrave the names of the sons of Israel on the two stones the way a gem cutter engraves a seal. Then mount the stones in gold filigree settings ¹²and fasten them on the shoulder pieces of the

---

a9 That is, about 150 feet (about 46 meters); also in verse 11   *b12* That is, about 75 feet (about 23 meters); also in verse 13   *c14* That is, about 22 1/2 feet (about 6.9 meters); also in verse 15   *d16* That is, about 30 feet (about 9 meters)   *e18* That is, about 150 feet (about 46 meters) long and 75 feet (about 23 meters) wide   *f18* That is, about 7 1/2 feet (about 2.3 meters)

ephod as memorial stones for the sons of Israel. Aaron is to bear the names on his shoulders as a memorial before the LORD. [13]Make gold filigree settings [14]and two braided chains of pure gold, like a rope, and attach the chains to the settings.

The Breastpiece

[15]"Fashion a breastpiece for making decisions—the work of a skilled craftsman. Make it like the ephod: of gold, and of blue, purple and scarlet yarn, and of finely twisted linen. [16]It is to be square—a span[a] long and a span wide—and folded double. [17]Then mount four rows of precious stones on it. In the first row there shall be a ruby, a topaz and a beryl; [18]in the second row a turquoise, a sapphire[b] and an emerald; [19]in the third row a jacinth, an agate and an amethyst; [20]in the fourth row a chrysolite, an onyx and a jasper.[c] Mount them in gold filigree settings. [21]There are to be twelve stones, one for each of the names of the sons of Israel, each engraved like a seal with the name of one of the twelve tribes.

[22]"For the breastpiece make braided chains of pure gold, like a rope. [23]Make two gold rings for it and fasten them to two corners of the breastpiece. [24]Fasten the two gold chains to the rings at the corners of the breastpiece, [25]and the other ends of the chains to the two settings, attaching them to the shoulder pieces of the ephod at the front. [26]Make two gold rings and attach them to the other two corners of the breastpiece on the inside edge next to the ephod. [27]Make two more gold rings and attach them to the bottom of the shoulder pieces on the front of the ephod, close to the seam just above the waistband of the ephod. [28]The rings of the breastpiece are to be tied to the rings of the ephod with blue cord, connecting it to the waistband, so that the breastpiece will not swing out from the ephod.

[29]"Whenever Aaron enters the Holy Place, he will bear the names of the sons of Israel over his heart on the breastpiece of decision as a continuing memorial before the LORD. [30]Also put the Urim and the Thummim in the breastpiece, so they may be over Aaron's heart whenever he enters the presence of the LORD. Thus Aaron will always bear the means of making decisions for the Israelites over his heart before the LORD.

Other Priestly Garments

[31]"Make the robe of the ephod entirely of blue cloth, [32]with an opening for the head in its center. There shall be a woven edge like a collar[d] around this opening, so that it will not tear. [33]Make pomegranates of blue, purple and scarlet yarn around the hem of the robe, with gold bells between them. [34]The gold bells and the pomegranates are to alternate around the hem of the robe. [35]Aaron must wear it when he ministers. The sound of the bells will be heard when he enters the Holy Place before the LORD and when he comes out, so that he will not die.

[36]"Make a plate of pure gold and engrave on it as on a seal: HOLY TO THE LORD. [37]Fasten a blue cord to it to attach it to the turban; it is to be on the front of the turban. [38]It will be on Aaron's forehead, and he will bear the guilt involved in the sacred gifts the Israelites consecrate, whatever their gifts may be. It will be on Aaron's forehead continually so that they will be acceptable to the LORD.

[39]"Weave the tunic of fine linen and make the turban of fine linen. The sash is to be the work of an embroiderer. [40]Make tunics, sashes and headbands for Aaron's sons, to give them dignity and honor. [41]After you put these clothes on your brother Aaron and his sons, anoint and ordain them. Consecrate them so they may serve me as priests.

[42]"Make linen undergarments as a covering for the body, reaching from the waist to the thigh. [43]Aaron and his sons must wear them whenever they enter the Tent of Meeting or approach the altar to minister in the Holy Place, so that they will not incur guilt and die.

"This is to be a lasting ordinance for Aaron and his descendants.

Consecration of the Priests

29 "This is what you are to do to consecrate them, so they may serve me as priests: Take a young bull

---

[a]16 That is, about 9 inches (about 22 centimeters) [b]18 Or *lapis lazuli* [c]20 The precise identification of some of these precious stones is uncertain. [d]32 The meaning of the Hebrew for this word is uncertain.

and two rams without defect. ²And from fine wheat flour, without yeast, make bread, and cakes mixed with oil, and wafers spread with oil. ³Put them in a basket and present them in it—along with the bull and the two rams. ⁴Then bring Aaron and his sons to the entrance to the Tent of Meeting and wash them with water. ⁵Take the garments and dress Aaron with the tunic, the robe of the ephod, the ephod itself and the breastpiece. Fasten the ephod on him by its skillfully woven waistband. ⁶Put the turban on his head and attach the sacred diadem to the turban. ⁷Take the anointing oil and anoint him by pouring it on his head. ⁸Bring his sons and dress them in tunics ⁹and put headbands on them. Then tie sashes on Aaron and his sons.ᵃ The priesthood is theirs by a lasting ordinance. In this way you shall ordain Aaron and his sons.

¹⁰"Bring the bull to the front of the Tent of Meeting, and Aaron and his sons shall lay their hands on its head. ¹¹Slaughter it in the LORD's presence at the entrance to the Tent of Meeting. ¹²Take some of the bull's blood and put it on the horns of the altar with your finger, and pour out the rest of it at the base of the altar. ¹³Then take all the fat around the inner parts, the covering of the liver, and both kidneys with the fat on them, and burn them on the altar. ¹⁴But burn the bull's flesh and its hide and its offal outside the camp. It is a sin offering.

¹⁵"Take one of the rams, and Aaron and his sons shall lay their hands on its head. ¹⁶Slaughter it and take the blood and sprinkle it against the altar on all sides. ¹⁷Cut the ram into pieces and wash the inner parts and the legs, putting them with the head and the other pieces. ¹⁸Then burn the entire ram on the altar. It is a burnt offering to the LORD, a pleasing aroma, an offering made to the LORD by fire.

¹⁹"Take the other ram, and Aaron and his sons shall lay their hands on its head. ²⁰Slaughter it, take some of its blood and put it on the lobes of the right ears of Aaron and his sons, on the thumbs of their right hands, and on the big toes of their right feet. Then sprinkle blood against the altar on all sides. ²¹And take some of the blood on the altar and some of the anointing oil and sprinkle it on Aaron and his garments and on his sons and their garments. Then he and his sons and their garments will be consecrated.

²²"Take from this ram the fat, the fat tail, the fat around the inner parts, the covering of the liver, both kidneys with the fat on them, and the right thigh. (This is the ram for the ordination.) ²³From the basket of bread made without yeast, which is before the LORD, take a loaf, and a cake made with oil, and a wafer. ²⁴Put all these in the hands of Aaron and his sons and wave them before the LORD as a wave offering. ²⁵Then take them from their hands and burn them on the altar along with the burnt offering for a pleasing aroma to the LORD, an offering made to the LORD by fire. ²⁶After you take the breast of the ram for Aaron's ordination, wave it before the LORD as a wave offering, and it will be your share.

²⁷"Consecrate those parts of the ordination ram that belong to Aaron and his sons: the breast that was waved and the thigh that was presented. ²⁸This is always to be the regular share from the Israelites for Aaron and his sons. It is the contribution the Israelites are to make to the LORD from their fellowship offerings.ᵇ

²⁹"Aaron's sacred garments will belong to his descendants so that they can be anointed and ordained in them. ³⁰The son who succeeds him as priest and comes to the Tent of Meeting to minister in the Holy Place is to wear them seven days.

³¹"Take the ram for the ordination and cook the meat in a sacred place. ³²At the entrance to the Tent of Meeting, Aaron and his sons are to eat the meat of the ram and the bread that is in the basket. ³³They are to eat these offerings by which atonement was made for their ordination and consecration. But no one else may eat them, because they are sacred. ³⁴And if any of the meat of the ordination ram or any bread is left over till morning, burn it up. It must not be eaten, because it is sacred.

³⁵"Do for Aaron and his sons everything I have commanded you, taking

ᵃ9 Hebrew; Septuagint *on them*   ᵇ28 Traditionally *peace offerings*

seven days to ordain them. ³⁶Sacrifice a bull each day as a sin offering to make atonement. Purify the altar by making atonement for it, and anoint it to consecrate it. ³⁷For seven days make atonement for the altar and consecrate it. Then the altar will be most holy, and whatever touches it will be holy.

³⁸"This is what you are to offer on the altar regularly each day: two lambs a year old. ³⁹Offer one in the morning and the other at twilight. ⁴⁰With the first lamb offer a tenth of an ephah*a* of fine flour mixed with a quarter of a hin*b* of oil from pressed olives, and a quarter of a hin of wine as a drink offering. ⁴¹Sacrifice the other lamb at twilight with the same grain offering and its drink offering as in the morning—a pleasing aroma, an offering made to the LORD by fire.

⁴²"For the generations to come this burnt offering is to be made regularly at the entrance to the Tent of Meeting before the LORD. There I will meet you and speak to you; ⁴³there also I will meet with the Israelites, and the place will be consecrated by my glory.

⁴⁴"So I will consecrate the Tent of Meeting and the altar and will consecrate Aaron and his sons to serve me as priests. ⁴⁵Then I will dwell among the Israelites and be their God. ⁴⁶They will know that I am the LORD their God, who brought them out of Egypt so that I might dwell among them. I am the LORD their God.

The Altar of Incense

30 "Make an altar of acacia wood for burning incense. ²It is to be square, a cubit long and a cubit wide, and two cubits high*c*—its horns of one piece with it. ³Overlay the top and all the sides and the horns with pure gold, and make a gold molding around it. ⁴Make two gold rings for the altar below the molding—two on opposite sides—to hold the poles used to carry it. ⁵Make the poles of acacia wood and overlay them with gold. ⁶Put the altar in front of the curtain that is before the ark of the Testimony—before the atonement cover that is over the Testimony—where I will meet with you.

⁷"Aaron must burn fragrant incense on the altar every morning when he tends the lamps. ⁸He must burn incense again when he lights the lamps at twilight so incense will burn regularly before the LORD for the generations to come. ⁹Do not offer on this altar any other incense or any burnt offering or grain offering, and do not pour a drink offering on it. ¹⁰Once a year Aaron shall make atonement on its horns. This annual atonement must be made with the blood of the atoning sin offering for the generations to come. It is most holy to the LORD."

Atonement Money

¹¹Then the LORD said to Moses, ¹²"When you take a census of the Israelites to count them, each one must pay the LORD a ransom for his life at the time he is counted. Then no plague will come on them when you number them. ¹³Each one who crosses over to those already counted is to give a half shekel,*d* according to the sanctuary shekel, which weighs twenty gerahs. This half shekel is an offering to the LORD. ¹⁴All who cross over, those twenty years old or more, are to give an offering to the LORD. ¹⁵The rich are not to give more than a half shekel and the poor are not to give less when you make the offering to the LORD to atone for your lives. ¹⁶Receive the atonement money from the Israelites and use it for the service of the Tent of Meeting. It will be a memorial for the Israelites before the LORD, making atonement for your lives."

Basin for Washing

¹⁷Then the LORD said to Moses, ¹⁸"Make a bronze basin, with its bronze stand, for washing. Place it between the Tent of Meeting and the altar, and put water in it. ¹⁹Aaron and his sons are to wash their hands and feet with water from it. ²⁰Whenever they enter the Tent of Meeting, they shall wash with water so that they will not die. Also, when they approach the altar to minister by presenting

---

a40 That is, probably about 2 quarts (about 2 liters)
b40 That is, probably about 1 quart (about 1 liter)
c2 That is, about 1 1/2 feet (about 0.5 meter) long and wide and about 3 feet (about 0.9 meter) high
d13 That is, about 1/5 ounce (about 6 grams); also in verse 15

an offering made to the LORD by fire, [21]they shall wash their hands and feet so that they will not die. This is to be a lasting ordinance for Aaron and his descendants for the generations to come."

Anointing Oil

[22]Then the LORD said to Moses, [23]"Take the following fine spices: 500 shekels[a] of liquid myrrh, half as much (that is, 250 shekels) of fragrant cinnamon, 250 shekels of fragrant cane, [24]500 shekels of cassia—all according to the sanctuary shekel—and a hin[b] of olive oil. [25]Make these into a sacred anointing oil, a fragrant blend, the work of a perfumer. It will be the sacred anointing oil. [26]Then use it to anoint the Tent of Meeting, the ark of the Testimony, [27]the table and all its articles, the lampstand and its accessories, the altar of incense, [28]the altar of burnt offering and all its utensils, and the basin with its stand. [29]You shall consecrate them so they will be most holy, and whatever touches them will be holy.

[30]"Anoint Aaron and his sons and consecrate them so they may serve me as priests. [31]Say to the Israelites, 'This is to be my sacred anointing oil for the generations to come. [32]Do not pour it on men's bodies and do not make any oil with the same formula. It is sacred, and you are to consider it sacred. [33]Whoever makes perfume like it and whoever puts it on anyone other than a priest must be cut off from his people.' "

Incense

[34]Then the LORD said to Moses, "Take fragrant spices—gum resin, onycha and galbanum—and pure frankincense, all in equal amounts, [35]and make a fragrant blend of incense, the work of a perfumer. It is to be salted and pure and sacred. [36]Grind some of it to powder and place it in front of the Testimony in the Tent of Meeting, where I will meet with you. It shall be most holy to you. [37]Do not make any incense with this formula for yourselves; consider it holy to the LORD. [38]Whoever makes any like it to enjoy its fragrance must be cut off from his people."

Bezalel and Oholiab

31 Then the LORD said to Moses, [2]"See, I have chosen Bezalel son of Uri, the son of Hur, of the tribe of Judah, [3]and I have filled him with the Spirit of God, with skill, ability and knowledge in all kinds of crafts— [4]to make artistic designs for work in gold, silver and bronze, [5]to cut and set stones, to work in wood, and to engage in all kinds of craftsmanship. [6]Moreover, I have appointed Oholiab son of Ahisamach, of the tribe of Dan, to help him. Also I have given skill to all the craftsmen to make everything I have commanded you: [7]the Tent of Meeting, the ark of the Testimony with the atonement cover on it, and all the other furnishings of the tent— [8]the table and its articles, the pure gold lampstand and all its accessories, the altar of incense, [9]the altar of burnt offering and all its utensils, the basin with its stand— [10]and also the woven garments, both the sacred garments for Aaron the priest and the garments for his sons when they serve as priests, [11]and the anointing oil and fragrant incense for the Holy Place. They are to make them just as I commanded you."

The Sabbath

[12]Then the LORD said to Moses, [13]"Say to the Israelites, 'You must observe my Sabbaths. This will be a sign between me and you for the generations to come, so you may know that I am the LORD, who makes you holy.[c]

[14]" 'Observe the Sabbath, because it is holy to you. Anyone who desecrates it must be put to death; whoever does any work on that day must be cut off from his people. [15]For six days, work is to be done, but the seventh day is a Sabbath of rest, holy to the LORD. Whoever does any work on the Sabbath day must be put to death. [16]The Israelites are to observe the Sabbath, celebrating it for the generations to come as a lasting covenant. [17]It will be a sign between me and the Israelites forever, for in six days the LORD

---

[a]23 That is, about 12 1/2 pounds (about 6 kilograms)
[b]24 That is, probably about 4 quarts (about 4 liters)
[c]13 Or who sanctifies you; or who sets you apart as holy

made the heavens and the earth, and on the seventh day he abstained from work and rested.' "

[18]When the LORD finished speaking to Moses on Mount Sinai, he gave him the two tablets of the Testimony, the tablets of stone inscribed by the finger of God.

The Golden Calf

32 When the people saw that Moses was so long in coming down from the mountain, they gathered around Aaron and said, "Come, make us gods[a] who will go before us. As for this fellow Moses who brought us up out of Egypt, we don't know what has happened to him." [2]Aaron answered them, "Take off the gold earrings that your wives, your sons and your daughters are wearing, and bring them to me." [3]So all the people took off their earrings and brought them to Aaron. [4]He took what they handed him and made it into an idol cast in the shape of a calf, fashioning it with a tool. Then they said, "These are your gods,[b] O Israel, who brought you up out of Egypt."

[5]When Aaron saw this, he built an altar in front of the calf and announced, "Tomorrow there will be a festival to the LORD." [6]So the next day the people rose early and sacrificed burnt offerings and presented fellowship offerings.[c] Afterward they sat down to eat and drink and got up to indulge in revelry.

[7]Then the LORD said to Moses, "Go down, because your people, whom you brought up out of Egypt, have become corrupt. [8]They have been quick to turn away from what I commanded them and have made themselves an idol cast in the shape of a calf. They have bowed down to it and sacrificed to it and have said, 'These are your gods, O Israel, who brought you up out of Egypt.'

[9]"I have seen these people," the LORD said to Moses, "and they are a stiff-necked people. [10]Now leave me alone so that my anger may burn against them

---

[a]1 Or *a god*; also in verses 23 and 31 [b]4 Or *This is your god*; also in verse 8 [c]6 Traditionally *peace offerings*

Tuesday

Get Back Here!

Read Exodus 32

It's so easy to turn away from God! Sometimes we get impatient, like the Israelites did when they were waiting for Moses to come down from the mountain. Sometimes we get frustrated because God does things his own way instead of the way we want him to. Sometimes we make idols too. Not golden cows! But we worship money, music, sports trophies and other "treasures."

God doesn't like it when we turn away from him. But he forgives us if we're sorry for our sins because he understands that we're not perfect. Sinning is part of human nature—even strong Christians can occasionally turn away from God. When we mess up we need to ask God for forgiveness and trust him to help us get back on track. And he will.

Jonathan14 age

What about You?

❶ List 5 reasons why you think people your age turn from God.

❷ Write a list of things you sometimes put ahead of God. Pray for strength to get rid of these "idols." Now throw the paper away as a sign you're "throwing away" the idols in your life.

❸ Ask God to strengthen your faith and help you not turn away from him.

Turn to page 111 for your next devotion.

and that I may destroy them. Then I will make you into a great nation."

¹¹But Moses sought the favor of the LORD his God. "O LORD," he said, "why should your anger burn against your people, whom you brought out of Egypt with great power and a mighty hand? ¹²Why should the Egyptians say, 'It was with evil intent that he brought them out, to kill them in the mountains and to wipe them off the face of the earth'? Turn from your fierce anger; relent and do not bring disaster on your people. ¹³Remember your servants Abraham, Isaac and Israel, to whom you swore by your own self: 'I will make your descendants as numerous as the stars in the sky and I will give your descendants all this land I promised them, and it will be their inheritance forever.' " ¹⁴Then the LORD relented and did not bring on his people the disaster he had threatened.

¹⁵Moses turned and went down the mountain with the two tablets of the Testimony in his hands. They were inscribed on both sides, front and back. ¹⁶The tablets were the work of God; the writing was the writing of God, engraved on the tablets.

¹⁷When Joshua heard the noise of the people shouting, he said to Moses, "There is the sound of war in the camp."

¹⁸Moses replied:

"It is not the sound of victory,
  it is not the sound of defeat;
  it is the sound of singing that I hear."

¹⁹When Moses approached the camp and saw the calf and the dancing, his anger burned and he threw the tablets out of his hands, breaking them to pieces at the foot of the mountain. ²⁰And he took the calf they had made and burned it in the fire; then he ground it to powder, scattered it on the water and made the Israelites drink it.

²¹He said to Aaron, "What did these people do to you, that you led them into such great sin?"

²²"Do not be angry, my lord," Aaron answered. "You know how prone these people are to evil. ²³They said to me, 'Make us gods who will go before us. As for this fellow Moses who brought us up out of Egypt, we don't know what has

happened to him.' ²⁴So I told them, 'Whoever has any gold jewelry, take it off.' Then they gave me the gold, and I threw it into the fire, and out came this calf!"

²⁵Moses saw that the people were running wild and that Aaron had let them get out of control and so become a laughingstock to their enemies. ²⁶So he stood at the entrance to the camp and said, "Whoever is for the LORD, come to me." And all the Levites rallied to him.

²⁷Then he said to them, "This is what the LORD, the God of Israel, says: 'Each man strap a sword to his side. Go back and forth through the camp from one end to the other, each killing his brother and friend and neighbor.' " ²⁸The Levites did as Moses commanded, and that day about three thousand of the people died. ²⁹Then Moses said, "You have been set apart to the LORD today, for you were against your own sons and brothers, and he has blessed you this day."

³⁰The next day Moses said to the people, "You have committed a great sin. But now I will go up to the LORD; perhaps I can make atonement for your sin."

Invisible Wall

Huh?

Exodus 32:30

When you act like a jerk to a friend, there's something between you—kind of like an invisible wall. But when you apologize, that wall can be removed, and your friendship can be OK again. *Atonement* (uh-TONE-ment) means getting rid of the wall between you and God. Israel used sacrifices as a way to remove the wall and make things right with God. When Jesus died for our sins, he removed the wall forever.

³¹So Moses went back to the LORD and said, "Oh, what a great sin these people have committed! They have made themselves gods of gold. ³²But now, please forgive their sin—but if not, then blot me out of the book you have written."

³³The LORD replied to Moses, "Whoever

has sinned against me I will blot out of my book. ³⁴Now go, lead the people to the place I spoke of, and my angel will go before you. However, when the time comes for me to punish, I will punish them for their sin."

³⁵And the LORD struck the people with a plague because of what they did with the calf Aaron had made.

33 Then the LORD said to Moses, "Leave this place, you and the people you brought up out of Egypt, and go up to the land I promised on oath to Abraham, Isaac and Jacob, saying, 'I will give it to your descendants.' ²I will send an angel before you and drive out the Canaanites, Amorites, Hittites, Perizzites, Hivites and Jebusites. ³Go up to the land flowing with milk and honey. But I will not go with you, because you are a stiff-necked people and I might destroy you on the way."

⁴When the people heard these distressing words, they began to mourn and no one put on any ornaments. ⁵For the LORD had said to Moses, "Tell the Israelites, 'You are a stiff-necked people. If I were to go with you even for a moment, I might destroy you. Now take off your ornaments and I will decide what to do with you.' " ⁶So the Israelites stripped off their ornaments at Mount Horeb.

The Tent of Meeting

⁷Now Moses used to take a tent and pitch it outside the camp some distance away, calling it the "tent of meeting." Anyone inquiring of the LORD would go to the tent of meeting outside the camp. ⁸And whenever Moses went out to the tent, all the people rose and stood at the entrances to their tents, watching Moses until he entered the tent. ⁹As Moses went into the tent, the pillar of cloud would come down and stay at the entrance, while the LORD spoke with Moses. ¹⁰Whenever the people saw the pillar of cloud standing at the entrance to the tent, they all stood and worshiped, each at the entrance to his tent. ¹¹The LORD would speak to Moses face to face, as a man speaks with his friend. Then Moses would return to the camp, but his young aide Joshua son of Nun did not leave the tent.

Moses and the Glory of the LORD

¹²Moses said to the LORD, "You have been telling me, 'Lead these people,' but you have not let me know whom you will send with me. You have said, 'I know you by name and you have found favor with me.' ¹³If you are pleased with me, teach me your ways so I may know you and continue to find favor with you. Remember that this nation is your people."

¹⁴The LORD replied, "My Presence will go with you, and I will give you rest."

¹⁵Then Moses said to him, "If your Presence does not go with us, do not send us up from here. ¹⁶How will anyone know that you are pleased with me and with your people unless you go with us? What else will distinguish me and your people from all the other people on the face of the earth?"

¹⁷And the LORD said to Moses, "I will do the very thing you have asked, because I am pleased with you and I know you by name."

¹⁸Then Moses said, "Now show me your glory."

¹⁹And the LORD said, "I will cause all my goodness to pass in front of you, and I will proclaim my name, the LORD, in your presence. I will have mercy on whom I will have mercy, and I will have compassion on whom I will have compassion. ²⁰But," he said, "you cannot see my face, for no one may see me and live."

²¹Then the LORD said, "There is a place near me where you may stand on a rock. ²²When my glory passes by, I will put you in a cleft in the rock and cover you with my hand until I have passed by. ²³Then I will remove my hand and you will see my back; but my face must not be seen."

The New Stone Tablets

34 The LORD said to Moses, "Chisel out two stone tablets like the first ones, and I will write on them the words that were on the first tablets, which you broke. ²Be ready in the morning, and then come up on Mount Sinai. Present yourself to me there on top of the mountain. ³No one is to come with you or be seen anywhere on the mountain; not even the flocks and herds may graze in front of the mountain."

⁴So Moses chiseled out two stone tablets like the first ones and went up Mount Sinai early in the morning, as the LORD had commanded him; and he carried the two stone tablets in his hands. ⁵Then the LORD came down in the cloud and stood there with him and proclaimed his name, the LORD. ⁶And he passed in front of Moses, proclaiming, "The LORD, the LORD, the compassionate and gracious God, slow to anger, abounding in love and faithfulness, ⁷maintaining love to thousands, and forgiving wickedness, rebellion and sin. Yet he does not leave the guilty unpunished; he punishes the children and their children for the sin of the fathers to the third and fourth generation."

⁸Moses bowed to the ground at once and worshiped. ⁹"O Lord, if I have found favor in your eyes," he said, "then let the Lord go with us. Although this is a stiff-necked people, forgive our wickedness and our sin, and take us as your inheritance."

¹⁰Then the LORD said: "I am making a covenant with you. Before all your people I will do wonders never before done in any nation in all the world. The people you live among will see how awesome is the work that I, the LORD, will do for you. ¹¹Obey what I command you today. I will drive out before you the Amorites, Canaanites, Hittites, Perizzites, Hivites and Jebusites. ¹²Be careful not to make a treaty with those who live in the land where you are going, or they will be a snare among you. ¹³Break down their altars, smash their sacred stones and cut down their Asherah poles.ᵃ ¹⁴Do not worship any other god, for the LORD, whose name is Jealous, is a jealous God.

¹⁵"Be careful not to make a treaty with those who live in the land; for when they prostitute themselves to their gods and sacrifice to them, they will invite you and you will eat their sacrifices. ¹⁶And when you choose some of their daughters as wives for your sons and those daughters prostitute themselves to their gods, they will lead your sons to do the same.

¹⁷"Do not make cast idols.

¹⁸"Celebrate the Feast of Unleavened Bread. For seven days eat bread made without yeast, as I commanded you. Do this at the appointed time in the month of Abib, for in that month you came out of Egypt.

¹⁹"The first offspring of every womb belongs to me, including all the firstborn males of your livestock, whether from herd or flock. ²⁰Redeem the firstborn donkey with a lamb, but if you do not redeem it, break its neck. Redeem all your firstborn sons.

"No one is to appear before me empty-handed.

²¹"Six days you shall labor, but on the seventh day you shall rest; even during the plowing season and harvest you must rest.

²²"Celebrate the Feast of Weeks with the firstfruits of the wheat harvest, and the Feast of Ingathering at the turn of the year.ᵇ ²³Three times a year all your men are to appear before the Sovereign LORD, the God of Israel. ²⁴I will drive out nations before you and enlarge your territory, and no one will covet your land when you go up three times each year to appear before the LORD your God.

²⁵"Do not offer the blood of a sacrifice to me along with anything containing yeast, and do not let any of the sacrifice from the Passover Feast remain until morning.

²⁶"Bring the best of the firstfruits of your soil to the house of the LORD your God.

"Do not cook a young goat in its mother's milk."

²⁷Then the LORD said to Moses, "Write down these words, for in accordance with these words I have made a covenant with you and with Israel." ²⁸Moses was there with the LORD forty days and forty nights without eating bread or drinking water. And he wrote on the tablets the words of the covenant—the Ten Commandments.

The Radiant Face of Moses

²⁹When Moses came down from Mount Sinai with the two tablets of the Testimony in his hands, he was not aware that his face was radiant because he had

---

ᵃ13 That is, symbols of the goddess Asherah
ᵇ22 That is, in the fall

spoken with the LORD. ³⁰When Aaron and all the Israelites saw Moses, his face was radiant, and they were afraid to come near him. ³¹But Moses called to them; so Aaron and all the leaders of the community came back to him, and he spoke to them. ³²Afterward all the Israelites came near him, and he gave them all the commands the LORD had given him on Mount Sinai.

³³When Moses finished speaking to them, he put a veil over his face. ³⁴But whenever he entered the LORD's presence to speak with him, he removed the veil until he came out. And when he came out and told the Israelites what he had been commanded, ³⁵they saw that his face was radiant. Then Moses would put the veil back over his face until he went in to speak with the LORD.

Sabbath Regulations

35 Moses assembled the whole Israelite community and said to them, "These are the things the LORD has commanded you to do: ²For six days, work is to be done, but the seventh day shall be your holy day, a Sabbath of rest to the LORD. Whoever does any work on it must be put to death. ³Do not light a fire in any of your dwellings on the Sabbath day."

Materials for the Tabernacle

⁴Moses said to the whole Israelite community, "This is what the LORD has commanded: ⁵From what you have, take an offering for the LORD. Everyone who is willing is to bring to the LORD an offering of gold, silver and bronze; ⁶blue, purple

---

Wednesday

Time to Shine

Read Exodus 34:29–35

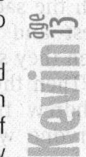

I saw a great example of what this passage is talking about during a short-term missions trip. Every morning, our group prayed and read the Bible. Throughout the long, hot days, we painted buildings, made picnic tables and witnessed to people. We could feel God's presence helping us to keep going. I think the time we spent with God each morning really showed.

Talking with God and spending time with him makes us feel radiant, kind of like how it made Moses radiant. People can see we're different when we've been spending time with God. We act different; we think different. If we really want to represent God to our friends, we need to spend quality time with God. I'm not always motivated to read my Bible, but these verses are a great reminder of how much I can change when I take time to really talk to God and listen to what he has to say to me.

❶ When was the last time you really spent time with God—not just a quick prayer, but real, quality time with God? How did you feel for the rest of that day?

❷ Take a good look at yourself in the mirror. What do you think other people see when they look at you? Do they see someone who's excited about life? Do they see someone who knows he or she is loved by God? Do they see someone they'd want to be like? What can you do to "radiate" God's love?

❸ Just for today, try to pray for a full 10 minutes. Concentrate on really having a conversation with God. Tell him what's going on in your life—what you're worried about, excited about, bored with, whatever.

Turn to page 138 for your next devotion.

and scarlet yarn and fine linen; goat hair; [7]ram skins dyed red and hides of sea cows[a]; acacia wood; [8]olive oil for the light; spices for the anointing oil and for the fragrant incense; [9]and onyx stones and other gems to be mounted on the ephod and breastpiece.

[10]"All who are skilled among you are to come and make everything the LORD has commanded: [11]the tabernacle with its tent and its covering, clasps, frames, crossbars, posts and bases; [12]the ark with its poles and the atonement cover and the curtain that shields it; [13]the table with its poles and all its articles and the bread of the Presence; [14]the lampstand that is for light with its accessories, lamps and oil for the light; [15]the altar of incense with its poles, the anointing oil and the fragrant incense; the curtain for the doorway at the entrance to the tabernacle; [16]the altar of burnt offering with its bronze grating, its poles and all its utensils; the bronze basin with its stand; [17]the curtains of the courtyard with its posts and bases, and the curtain for the entrance to the courtyard; [18]the tent pegs for the tabernacle and for the courtyard, and their ropes; [19]the woven garments worn for ministering in the sanctuary— both the sacred garments for Aaron the priest and the garments for his sons when they serve as priests."

[20]Then the whole Israelite community withdrew from Moses' presence, [21]and everyone who was willing and whose heart moved him came and brought an offering to the LORD for the work on the Tent of Meeting, for all its service, and for the sacred garments. [22]All who were willing, men and women alike, came and brought gold jewelry of all kinds: brooches, earrings, rings and ornaments. They all presented their gold as a wave offering to the LORD. [23]Everyone who had blue, purple or scarlet yarn or fine linen, or goat hair, ram skins dyed red or hides of sea cows brought them. [24]Those presenting an offering of silver or bronze brought it as an offering to the LORD, and everyone who had acacia wood for any part of the work brought it. [25]Every skilled woman spun with her hands and brought what she had spun—blue, purple or scarlet yarn or fine linen. [26]And all the women who were willing and had the skill spun the goat hair. [27]The leaders brought onyx stones and other gems to be mounted on the ephod and breastpiece. [28]They also brought spices and olive oil for the light and for the anointing oil and for the fragrant incense. [29]All the Israelite men and women who were willing brought to the LORD freewill offerings for all the work the LORD through Moses had commanded them to do.

Bezalel and Oholiab

[30]Then Moses said to the Israelites, "See, the LORD has chosen Bezalel son of Uri, the son of Hur, of the tribe of Judah, [31]and he has filled him with the Spirit of God, with skill, ability and knowledge in all kinds of crafts— [32]to make artistic designs for work in gold, silver and bronze, [33]to cut and set stones, to work in wood and to engage in all kinds of artistic craftsmanship. [34]And he has given both him and Oholiab son of Ahisamach, of the tribe of Dan, the ability to teach others. [35]He has filled them with skill to do all kinds of work as craftsmen, designers, embroiderers in blue, purple and scarlet yarn and fine linen, and weavers—all of them master craftsmen and designers.

36 [1]So Bezalel, Oholiab and every skilled person to whom the LORD has given skill and ability to know how to carry out all the work of constructing the sanctuary are to do the work just as the LORD has commanded."

[2]Then Moses summoned Bezalel and Oholiab and every skilled person to whom the LORD had given ability and who was willing to come and do the work. [3]They received from Moses all the offerings the Israelites had brought to carry out the work of constructing the sanctuary. And the people continued to bring freewill offerings morning after morning. [4]So all the skilled craftsmen who were doing all the work on the sanctuary left their work [5]and said to Moses, "The people are bringing more than enough for doing the work the LORD commanded to be done."

[6]Then Moses gave an order and they sent this word throughout the camp: "No

---

[a]7 That is, dugongs; also in verse 23

man or woman is to make anything else as an offering for the sanctuary." And so the people were restrained from bringing more, [7]because what they already had was more than enough to do all the work.

The Tabernacle

[8]All the skilled men among the workmen made the tabernacle with ten curtains of finely twisted linen and blue, purple and scarlet yarn, with cherubim worked into them by a skilled craftsman. [9]All the curtains were the same size—twenty-eight cubits long and four cubits wide.[a] [10]They joined five of the curtains together and did the same with the other five. [11]Then they made loops of blue material along the edge of the end curtain in one set, and the same was done with the end curtain in the other set. [12]They also made fifty loops on one curtain and fifty loops on the end curtain of the other set, with the loops opposite each other. [13]Then they made fifty gold clasps and used them to fasten the two sets of curtains together so that the tabernacle was a unit.

[14]They made curtains of goat hair for the tent over the tabernacle—eleven altogether. [15]All eleven curtains were the same size—thirty cubits long and four cubits wide.[b] [16]They joined five of the curtains into one set and the other six into another set. [17]Then they made fifty loops along the edge of the end curtain in one set and also along the edge of the end curtain in the other set. [18]They made fifty bronze clasps to fasten the tent together as a unit. [19]Then they made for the tent a covering of ram skins dyed red, and over that a covering of hides of sea cows.[c]

[20]They made upright frames of acacia wood for the tabernacle. [21]Each frame was ten cubits long and a cubit and a half wide,[d] [22]with two projections set parallel to each other. They made all the frames of the tabernacle in this way. [23]They made twenty frames for the south side of the tabernacle [24]and made forty silver bases to go under them—two bases for each frame, one under each projection. [25]For the other side, the north side of the tabernacle, they made twenty frames [26]and forty silver bases—two under each frame. [27]They made six frames for the far end, that is, the west end of the tabernacle, [28]and two frames were made for the corners of the tabernacle at the far end. [29]At these two corners the frames were double from the bottom all the way to the top and fitted into a single ring; both were made alike. [30]So there were eight frames and sixteen silver bases—two under each frame.

[31]They also made crossbars of acacia wood: five for the frames on one side of the tabernacle, [32]five for those on the other side, and five for the frames on the west, at the far end of the tabernacle. [33]They made the center crossbar so that it extended from end to end at the middle of the frames. [34]They overlaid the frames with gold and made gold rings to hold the crossbars. They also overlaid the crossbars with gold.

[35]They made the curtain of blue, purple and scarlet yarn and finely twisted linen, with cherubim worked into it by a skilled craftsman. [36]They made four posts of acacia wood for it and overlaid them with gold. They made gold hooks for them and cast their four silver bases. [37]For the entrance to the tent they made a curtain of blue, purple and scarlet yarn and finely twisted linen—the work of an embroiderer; [38]and they made five posts with hooks for them. They overlaid the tops of the posts and their bands with gold and made their five bases of bronze.

The Ark

37 Bezalel made the ark of acacia wood—two and a half cubits long, a cubit and a half wide, and a cubit and a half high.[e] [2]He overlaid it with pure gold, both inside and out, and made a gold molding around it. [3]He cast four gold rings for it and fastened them to its four feet, with two rings on one side and two rings on the other. [4]Then he made

---

[a]9 That is, about 42 feet (about 12.5 meters) long and 6 feet (about 1.8 meters) wide   [b]15 That is, about 45 feet (about 13.5 meters) long and 6 feet (about 1.8 meters) wide   [c]19 That is, dugongs   [d]21 That is, about 15 feet (about 4.5 meters) long and 2 1/4 feet (about 0.7 meter) wide   [e]1 That is, about 3 3/4 feet (about 1.1 meters) long and 2 1/4 feet (about 0.7 meter) wide and high

poles of acacia wood and overlaid them with gold. [5]And he inserted the poles into the rings on the sides of the ark to carry it.

[6]He made the atonement cover of pure gold—two and a half cubits long and a cubit and a half wide.[a] [7]Then he made two cherubim out of hammered gold at the ends of the cover. [8]He made one cherub on one end and the second cherub on the other; at the two ends he made them of one piece with the cover. [9]The cherubim had their wings spread upward, overshadowing the cover with them. The cherubim faced each other, looking toward the cover.

The Table

[10]They[b] made the table of acacia wood—two cubits long, a cubit wide, and a cubit and a half high.[c] [11]Then they overlaid it with pure gold and made a gold molding around it. [12]They also made around it a rim a handbreadth[d] wide and put a gold molding on the rim. [13]They cast four gold rings for the table and fastened them to the four corners, where the four legs were. [14]The rings were put close to the rim to hold the poles used in carrying the table. [15]The poles for carrying the table were made of acacia wood and were overlaid with gold. [16]And they made from pure gold the articles for the table—its plates and dishes and bowls and its pitchers for the pouring out of drink offerings.

The Lampstand

[17]They made the lampstand of pure gold and hammered it out, base and shaft; its flowerlike cups, buds and blossoms were of one piece with it. [18]Six branches extended from the sides of the lampstand—three on one side and three on the other. [19]Three cups shaped like almond flowers with buds and blossoms were on one branch, three on the next branch and the same for all six branches extending from the lampstand. [20]And on the lampstand were four cups shaped like almond flowers with buds and blossoms. [21]One bud was under the first pair of branches extending from the lampstand, a second bud under the second pair, and a third bud under the third pair—six

branches in all. [22]The buds and the branches were all of one piece with the lampstand, hammered out of pure gold. [23]They made its seven lamps, as well as its wick trimmers and trays, of pure gold. [24]They made the lampstand and all its accessories from one talent[e] of pure gold.

The Altar of Incense

[25]They made the altar of incense out of acacia wood. It was square, a cubit long and a cubit wide, and two cubits high[f]—its horns of one piece with it. [26]They overlaid the top and all the sides and the horns with pure gold, and made a gold molding around it. [27]They made two gold rings below the molding—two on opposite sides—to hold the poles used to carry it. [28]They made the poles of acacia wood and overlaid them with gold.

[29]They also made the sacred anointing oil and the pure, fragrant incense—the work of a perfumer.

The Altar of Burnt Offering

38 They[g] built the altar of burnt offering of acacia wood, three cubits[h] high; it was square, five cubits long and five cubits wide.[i] [2]They made a horn at each of the four corners, so that the horns and the altar were of one piece, and they overlaid the altar with bronze. [3]They made all its utensils of bronze—its pots, shovels, sprinkling bowls, meat forks and firepans. [4]They made a grating for the altar, a bronze network, to be under its ledge, halfway up the altar. [5]They cast bronze rings to hold the poles for the four corners of the bronze grating. [6]They made the poles of acacia wood and overlaid them with bronze. [7]They inserted the poles into the rings so they would be on the sides of the altar for carrying it. They made it hollow, out of boards.

---

[a]6 That is, about 3 3/4 feet (about 1.1 meters) long and 2 1/4 feet (about 0.7 meter) wide   [b]10 Or *He*; also in verses 11-29   [c]10 That is, about 3 feet (about 0.9 meter) long, 1 1/2 feet (about 0.5 meter) wide, and 2 1/4 feet (about 0.7 meter) high   [d]12 That is, about 3 inches (about 8 centimeters)   [e]24 That is, about 75 pounds (about 34 kilograms)   [f]25 That is, about 1 1/2 feet (about 0.5 meter) long and wide, and about 3 feet (about 0.9 meter) high   [g]1 Or *He*; also in verses 2-9   [h]1 That is, about 4 1/2 feet (about 1.3 meters)   [i]1 That is, about 7 1/2 feet (about 2.3 meters) long and wide

Basin for Washing

⁸They made the bronze basin and its bronze stand from the mirrors of the women who served at the entrance to the Tent of Meeting.

The Courtyard

⁹Next they made the courtyard. The south side was a hundred cubits*a* long and had curtains of finely twisted linen, ¹⁰with twenty posts and twenty bronze bases, and with silver hooks and bands on the posts. ¹¹The north side was also a hundred cubits long and had twenty posts and twenty bronze bases, with silver hooks and bands on the posts.

¹²The west end was fifty cubits*b* wide and had curtains, with ten posts and ten bases, with silver hooks and bands on the posts. ¹³The east end, toward the sunrise, was also fifty cubits wide. ¹⁴Curtains fifteen cubits*c* long were on one side of the entrance, with three posts and three bases, ¹⁵and curtains fifteen cubits long were on the other side of the entrance to the courtyard, with three posts and three bases. ¹⁶All the curtains around the courtyard were of finely twisted linen. ¹⁷The bases for the posts were bronze. The hooks and bands on the posts were silver, and their tops were overlaid with silver; so all the posts of the courtyard had silver bands.

¹⁸The curtain for the entrance to the courtyard was of blue, purple and scarlet yarn and finely twisted linen—the work of an embroiderer. It was twenty cubits*d* long and, like the curtains of the courtyard, five cubits*e* high, ¹⁹with four posts and four bronze bases. Their hooks and bands were silver, and their tops were overlaid with silver. ²⁰All the tent pegs of the tabernacle and of the surrounding courtyard were bronze.

The Materials Used

²¹These are the amounts of the materials used for the tabernacle, the tabernacle of the Testimony, which were recorded at Moses' command by the Levites under the direction of Ithamar son of Aaron, the priest. ²²(Bezalel son of Uri, the son of Hur, of the tribe of Judah, made everything the Lord commanded Moses; ²³with him was Oholiab son of Ahisamach, of the tribe of Dan—a craftsman and designer, and an embroiderer in blue, purple and scarlet yarn and fine linen.) ²⁴The total amount of the gold from the wave offering used for all the work on the sanctuary was 29 talents and 730 shekels,*f* according to the sanctuary shekel.

²⁵The silver obtained from those of the community who were counted in the census was 100 talents and 1,775 shekels,*g* according to the sanctuary shekel— ²⁶one beka per person, that is, half a shekel,*h* according to the sanctuary shekel, from everyone who had crossed over to those counted, twenty years old or more, a total of 603,550 men. ²⁷The 100 talents*i* of silver were used to cast the bases for the sanctuary and for the curtain—100 bases from the 100 talents, one talent for each base. ²⁸They used the 1,775 shekels*j* to make the hooks for the posts, to overlay the tops of the posts, and to make their bands.

²⁹The bronze from the wave offering was 70 talents and 2,400 shekels.*k* ³⁰They used it to make the bases for the entrance to the Tent of Meeting, the bronze altar with its bronze grating and all its utensils, ³¹the bases for the surrounding courtyard and those for its entrance and all the tent pegs for the tabernacle and those for the surrounding courtyard.

The Priestly Garments

39 From the blue, purple and scarlet yarn they made woven garments for ministering in the sanctuary. They also made sacred garments for Aaron, as the Lord commanded Moses.

---

a9 That is, about 150 feet (about 46 meters)
b12 That is, about 75 feet (about 23 meters)
c14 That is, about 22 1/2 feet (about 6.9 meters)
d18 That is, about 30 feet (about 9 meters) *e18* That is, about 7 1/2 feet (about 2.3 meters) *f24* The weight of the gold was a little over one ton (about 1 metric ton). *g25* The weight of the silver was a little over 3 3/4 tons (about 3.4 metric tons).
h26 That is, about 1/5 ounce (about 5.5 grams)
i27 That is, about 3 3/4 tons (about 3.4 metric tons)
j28 That is, about 45 pounds (about 20 kilograms)
k29 The weight of the bronze was about 2 1/2 tons (about 2.4 metric tons).

The Ephod

[2]They[a] made the ephod of gold, and of blue, purple and scarlet yarn, and of finely twisted linen. [3]They hammered out thin sheets of gold and cut strands to be worked into the blue, purple and scarlet yarn and fine linen—the work of a skilled craftsman. [4]They made shoulder pieces for the ephod, which were attached to two of its corners, so it could be fastened. [5]Its skillfully woven waistband was like it—of one piece with the ephod and made with gold, and with blue, purple and scarlet yarn, and with finely twisted linen, as the LORD commanded Moses.

[6]They mounted the onyx stones in gold filigree settings and engraved them like a seal with the names of the sons of Israel. [7]Then they fastened them on the shoulder pieces of the ephod as memorial stones for the sons of Israel, as the LORD commanded Moses.

The Breastpiece

[8]They fashioned the breastpiece—the work of a skilled craftsman. They made it like the ephod: of gold, and of blue, purple and scarlet yarn, and of finely twisted linen. [9]It was square—a span[b] long and a span wide—and folded double. [10]Then they mounted four rows of precious stones on it. In the first row there was a ruby, a topaz and a beryl; [11]in the second row a turquoise, a sapphire[c] and an emerald; [12]in the third row a jacinth, an agate and an amethyst; [13]in the fourth row a chrysolite, an onyx and a jasper.[d] They were mounted in gold filigree settings. [14]There were twelve stones, one for each of the names of the sons of Israel, each engraved like a seal with the name of one of the twelve tribes.

[15]For the breastpiece they made braided chains of pure gold, like a rope. [16]They made two gold filigree settings and two gold rings, and fastened the rings to two of the corners of the breastpiece. [17]They fastened the two gold chains to the rings at the corners of the breastpiece, [18]and the other ends of the chains to the two settings, attaching them to the shoulder pieces of the ephod at the front. [19]They made two gold rings and attached them to the other two corners of the breast-piece on the inside edge next to the ephod. [20]Then they made two more gold rings and attached them to the bottom of the shoulder pieces on the front of the ephod, close to the seam just above the waistband of the ephod. [21]They tied the rings of the breastpiece to the rings of the ephod with blue cord, connecting it to the waistband so that the breastpiece would not swing out from the ephod—as the LORD commanded Moses.

Other Priestly Garments

[22]They made the robe of the ephod entirely of blue cloth—the work of a weaver— [23]with an opening in the center of the robe like the opening of a collar,[e] and a band around this opening, so that it would not tear. [24]They made pomegranates of blue, purple and scarlet yarn and finely twisted linen around the hem of the robe. [25]And they made bells of pure gold and attached them around the hem between the pomegranates. [26]The bells and pomegranates alternated around the hem of the robe to be worn for ministering, as the LORD commanded Moses.

[27]For Aaron and his sons, they made tunics of fine linen—the work of a weaver— [28]and the turban of fine linen, the linen headbands and the undergarments of finely twisted linen. [29]The sash was of finely twisted linen and blue, purple and scarlet yarn—the work of an embroiderer—as the LORD commanded Moses.

[30]They made the plate, the sacred diadem, out of pure gold and engraved on it, like an inscription on a seal: HOLY TO THE LORD. [31]Then they fastened a blue cord to it to attach it to the turban, as the LORD commanded Moses.

Moses Inspects the Tabernacle

[32]So all the work on the tabernacle, the Tent of Meeting, was completed. The Israelites did everything just as the LORD commanded Moses. [33]Then they brought the tabernacle to Moses: the tent and all

[a]2 Or He; also in verses 7, 8 and 22   [b]9 That is, about 9 inches (about 22 centimeters)   [c]11 Or lapis lazuli   [d]13 The precise identification of some of these precious stones is uncertain.   [e]23 The meaning of the Hebrew for this word is uncertain.

Reasons to Believe

Back Stage Pass

If you ask 100 people, you'll probably find that more say they believe in God than say they do not. But it still seems like being a Christian isn't exactly a popular choice. Have you ever heard anybody say, "You don't *really* believe that stuff, do you?" or "What about all of those other religions that say they have the truth?" Every Christian needs to know why she believes what she believes. It's essential! Here are 5 reasons why Christians believe what we do about God and his Son, Jesus Christ:

God has proven he is real throughout time.

God is the one who made everything out of nothing (Genesis 1:1, page 4). By creating everything there is—the stars, oceans, plants, animals and people—God showed his incredible power to do something no human could ever do. The Bible tells us that this power is obvious to all people everywhere. And it says that everybody "knows" about God, deep in their hearts (Romans 1:20–21, page 1351). And God didn't stop creating when he finished the universe; he has been actively at work in people's lives (Exodus 14:21, page 87) in both "visible and invisible" dimensions—through stuff like love and music and beauty (Colossians 1:16, page 1443).

God came to earth to let us know what he's like.

Jesus Christ is not just some great religious guy who told us how to get to God. He is actually God who came to us (John 1:1–3, 14, page 1267; Philippians 1:5–11, page 1435). God knew we were lost without him because all people had been living like they didn't need him. But God loves us so much that he came down to earth as a baby to let us know what he's like and how much he cares. The true story of his incredible life—the things he did and said—have been passed on to us in the Bible.

Jesus came to earth to die.

It's clear from the life of Jesus that he came to earth "on a mission from God." He came to earth for one main reason—to die for you and me (John 3:16, page 1271). God had already set up the penalty for turning away from him—death. But Jesus took our place (Romans 5:8, page 1357). When you read about the last week of his life (Matthew 27, page 1183), it's clear that it was only because he was God that Jesus could have handled the pressure the way he did.

Jesus Christ is alive!

The biggest reason we can be confident that Christianity is real is because Jesus rose from the dead and is alive today (1 Corinthians 15:20, page 1393). Jesus' bones will never be discovered, because they aren't anywhere to be found! This is totally different from all other great and powerful leaders who have ever lived.

Followers of Jesus are changed people.

One other reason to believe in Jesus Christ is the fact that every disciple (other than Judas) believed in Jesus' resurrection until they died—they didn't change their minds! And today, millions of Christians would give their lives based on their belief that Christianity is true (Romans 8:11, page 1361). Could you?

eXtreme FAITH

"I'm a Christian, but sometimes I don't feel anything
when it comes to my faith.
Now I'm having doubts. How
can I be sure I'm saved?"

I'm going to answer your question by referring to the Bible; we'll always find the truth
in God's Word.

Romans 10:9 says, "If you confess with
your mouth, 'Jesus is Lord,' and believe in
your heart that God raised him from the
dead, you will be saved." It doesn't say,
"You *might* be saved"; it says, "You *will* be
saved."

What does it mean to believe in your heart?

Well, it's more than just
thinking about it. It's more than just saying
Jesus was a great teacher, or even saying
that Jesus was God's Son. To believe in your
heart means to trust him completely, to
love him completely, to be willing to follow
him for the rest of your life.

The verse also says we should "confess"
that Jesus is Lord. That simply means telling
others that you follow Jesus. Telling people
about Jesus doesn't make you a Christian,
but it is evidence that you are a Christian.

Another important verse is Ephesians 2:8,
that says, "It is by grace you have been
saved, through faith." You can't earn salvation. That's what "grace" means. You can't
earn God's love. It's not for sale. It's a gift
he wants to give you. And it's a gift you
accept through faith, and faith alone.

Now turn to Revelation 3:20 where Jesus
says, "I stand at the door and knock. If
anyone hears my voice and opens the
door, I will come in and eat with him, and
he with me." Ask yourself, "Have I opened
the door and invited Jesus into my life?" He
promises that if you invite him in, he will
come in. And if you've taken that step, you
can know that you're saved (see also
1 John 5:11–12, page 1534).

People sometimes get confused because they base their faith on their feelings.

I think "feel" is one of the
most dangerous words in Christianity. Our
feelings can be affected by a bad test
grade, the flu, a rainy day or the fight you
had with a friend. A lot of things can make
you feel bad, but these things have nothing to do with whether or not you are a
Christian. Even if you don't "feel" it, you
can be sure you're a Christian because of
the promises of Jesus and the words of
Scripture. Period.

Finally, look at John 10:27–29, where Jesus says no one can snatch us out of his hand.

That's the
punch line. We are in Jesus' grip of love and
faithfulness, and his grip is so strong, nothing can pull us out of it.

So keep believing. God keeps his promises.

*— Dawson McAllister, a popular youth speaker
and writer who hosts a live, nationally-syndicated radio call-in program for students
("Dawson McAllister Live") on Sunday nights.*

its furnishings, its clasps, frames, crossbars, posts and bases; ³⁴the covering of ram skins dyed red, the covering of hides of sea cows*ᵃ* and the shielding curtain; ³⁵the ark of the Testimony with its poles and the atonement cover; ³⁶the table with all its articles and the bread of the Presence; ³⁷the pure gold lampstand with its row of lamps and all its accessories, and the oil for the light; ³⁸the gold altar, the anointing oil, the fragrant incense, and the curtain for the entrance to the tent; ³⁹the bronze altar with its bronze grating, its poles and all its utensils; the basin with its stand; ⁴⁰the curtains of the courtyard with its posts and bases, and the curtain for the entrance to the courtyard; the ropes and tent pegs for the courtyard; all the furnishings for the tabernacle, the Tent of Meeting; ⁴¹and the woven garments worn for ministering in the sanctuary, both the sacred garments for Aaron the priest and the garments for his sons when serving as priests.

⁴²The Israelites had done all the work just as the LORD had commanded Moses. ⁴³Moses inspected the work and saw that they had done it just as the LORD had commanded. So Moses blessed them.

Setting Up the Tabernacle

40 Then the LORD said to Moses: ²"Set up the tabernacle, the Tent of Meeting, on the first day of the first month. ³Place the ark of the Testimony in it and shield the ark with the curtain. ⁴Bring in the table and set out what belongs on it. Then bring in the lampstand and set up its lamps. ⁵Place the gold altar of incense in front of the ark of the Testimony and put the curtain at the entrance to the tabernacle.

⁶"Place the altar of burnt offering in front of the entrance to the tabernacle, the Tent of Meeting; ⁷place the basin between the Tent of Meeting and the altar and put water in it. ⁸Set up the courtyard around it and put the curtain at the entrance to the courtyard.

⁹"Take the anointing oil and anoint the tabernacle and everything in it; consecrate it and all its furnishings, and it will be holy. ¹⁰Then anoint the altar of burnt offering and all its utensils; consecrate the altar, and it will be most holy.

¹¹Anoint the basin and its stand and consecrate them.

¹²"Bring Aaron and his sons to the entrance to the Tent of Meeting and wash them with water. ¹³Then dress Aaron in the sacred garments, anoint him and consecrate him so he may serve me as priest. ¹⁴Bring his sons and dress them in tunics. ¹⁵Anoint them just as you anointed their father, so they may serve me as priests. Their anointing will be to a priesthood that will continue for all generations to come." ¹⁶Moses did everything just as the LORD commanded him.

¹⁷So the tabernacle was set up on the first day of the first month in the second year. ¹⁸When Moses set up the tabernacle, he put the bases in place, erected the frames, inserted the crossbars and set up the posts. ¹⁹Then he spread the tent over the tabernacle and put the covering over the tent, as the LORD commanded him.

²⁰He took the Testimony and placed it in the ark, attached the poles to the ark and put the atonement cover over it. ²¹Then he brought the ark into the tabernacle and hung the shielding curtain and shielded the ark of the Testimony, as the LORD commanded him.

²²Moses placed the table in the Tent of Meeting on the north side of the tabernacle outside the curtain ²³and set out the bread on it before the LORD, as the LORD commanded him.

²⁴He placed the lampstand in the Tent

ᵃ34 That is, dugongs

of Meeting opposite the table on the south side of the tabernacle ²⁵and set up the lamps before the LORD, as the LORD commanded him.

²⁶Moses placed the gold altar in the Tent of Meeting in front of the curtain ²⁷and burned fragrant incense on it, as the LORD commanded him. ²⁸Then he put up the curtain at the entrance to the tabernacle.

²⁹He set the altar of burnt offering near the entrance to the tabernacle, the Tent of Meeting, and offered on it burnt offerings and grain offerings, as the LORD commanded him.

³⁰He placed the basin between the Tent of Meeting and the altar and put water in it for washing, ³¹and Moses and Aaron and his sons used it to wash their hands and feet. ³²They washed whenever they entered the Tent of Meeting or approached the altar, as the LORD commanded Moses.

³³Then Moses set up the courtyard around the tabernacle and altar and put up the curtain at the entrance to the courtyard. And so Moses finished the work.

The Glory of the LORD

³⁴Then the cloud covered the Tent of Meeting, and the glory of the LORD filled

the tabernacle. ³⁵Moses could not enter the Tent of Meeting because the cloud had settled upon it, and the glory of the LORD filled the tabernacle.

³⁶In all the travels of the Israelites, whenever the cloud lifted from above the tabernacle, they would set out; ³⁷but if the cloud did not lift, they did not set out—until the day it lifted. ³⁸So the cloud of the LORD was over the tabernacle by day, and fire was in the cloud by night, in the sight of all the house of Israel during all their travels.

Nothing Compares

Exodus 40:34

Have you ever been blown away by the beauty of a sunset? The best sunset you've ever seen, the best sunset anyone's ever seen, is *nothin'* compared to the beauty of God's glory. When God made himself known to the Israelites, he gave a personal introduction. For the Israelites, God's glory must have been wonderful and awesome and beautiful and scary and heart-stopping all at once!

Leviticus

START

CAST OF Characters

Levites (LEE-vites)
These are all the men whose family tree has Levi's name on it. The Levites are chosen by God to be priests, which gives them a bunch of special duties. But it's not something they get paid for. Instead, they get everything they need from the people they serve.

Moses (MOE-zus) and Aaron (AIR-on)
You know that Moses is the big leader and his brother Aaron is the assistant. But what you may not know is that they're Levites too. This makes sense since Moses himself wrote this book based on what God told him.

The Scapegoat
In one of the religious rituals explained in Leviticus, the priests chose a goat that

Leviticus is a strange name, but it simply means "about the Levites." The Levites were the descendants of Levi, one of Jacob's 12 sons. God told the Israelites that priests should be selected from Levi's tribe. So it makes sense that this book is really a manual for priests. It tells them how to conduct sacrifices, offerings and the other stuff that came with their job.

Remember, the book of Exodus ends right when the Israelites complete construction of their portable tent-cathedral, which they call the tabernacle. Now the priests need to know what to do with it. That's important, because God's glory lives inside! Leviticus explains their jobs.

After all the excitement in Exodus, the book of Leviticus just seems to sit there—no heavenly fireworks, no miraculous water tricks—just rules and procedures. And, in fact, it does just sit there, because that's what the Israelites are doing at the moment. They don't get to continue their journey to the promised land until the priest manual is complete.

When you read Leviticus, you get a glimpse of how *important* God is. He's very specific about his demands and expects them to be carried out exactly. You also get an idea of how much disobedience hurts him. When he lays out the recipe for a sacrifice, you know that sin is expensive—to God *and* sinner.

Through all the rules and regulations, you can see a God who's deeply concerned for his people. He has big plans for them, including making them a great nation and connecting his own Son with their family tree—he doesn't want them dying from food poisoning, lack of soapy baths or fighting in the streets. He's a strict yet loving Parent who wants his kids to survive in their new world.

will carry all the sins of the Israelite people, then send it into the desert, far from the people. Of course, the priests couldn't actually put the sins on it—God had to do that (which is exactly what he did when he placed our sins on Jesus, who carried them far away).

(NAY-dab)
Nadab and Abihu (a-BUY-hue)
Two of Aaron's sons who were training to be priests but didn't do what they were told . . . they got burned up.

(el-ee-AY-zar)
Eleazer and Ithamar (ITH-uh-mar)
Two more sons of Aaron. You guessed it—they were priests too. But they did things the right way . . . they didn't get burned up.

What's UP with That?

God knows how to throw some great parties. After all the sins were paid for, he told the people to celebrate! He even set aside special days throughout the year just for these parties. God called them feasts. See if you can match each feast (actually, only the 5 real ones) to its activity by connecting them with a line. (Hint: The answers are in chapter 23)

❶ Passover

❷ Feast of Firstfruits

❸ Feast of Weeks

❹ Feast of Trumpets

❺ The Day of Atonement

❻ Festival of Tabernacles

❼ Festival of Bob

Ⓐ Give up some fresh grain and a toddler lamb

Ⓑ Scapegoat up and runs off with the people's sins

Ⓒ Make leafy tents and camp out for a week

Ⓓ OK, OK, this one's not one

Ⓔ Recipe: 2 loaves, 2 rams, 1 bull, 1 lamb, a dash of crops, and throw in some drinks

Ⓕ Stop work and blow horns real loud

Ⓖ Eat bread that's not very fluffy

Snap Shots

- Lesson 1: How to offer a sacrifice *(chapters 1—7)*
- Lesson 2: How to become a priest *(chapters 8—9)*
- Lesson 3: How to get fired—or fried *(chapter 10)*
- Lesson 4: How to eat, stay clean and behave like you're supposed to *(chapters 11—22)*
- Lesson 5: How to throw a party *(chapter 23)*
- Lesson 6: How to do other important stuff *(chapters 24—27)*

answers: 1-g, 2-a, 3-e, 4-f, 5-b, 6-c, 7-d

The Burnt Offering

1 The LORD called to Moses and spoke to him from the Tent of Meeting. He said, [2]"Speak to the Israelites and say to them: 'When any of you brings an offering to the LORD, bring as your offering an animal from either the herd or the flock.

[3]" 'If the offering is a burnt offering from the herd, he is to offer a male without defect. He must present it at the entrance to the Tent of Meeting so that it[a] will be acceptable to the LORD. [4]He is to lay his hand on the head of the burnt offering, and it will be accepted on his behalf to make atonement for him. [5]He is to slaughter the young bull before the LORD, and then Aaron's sons the priests shall bring the blood and sprinkle it against the altar on all sides at the entrance to the Tent of Meeting. [6]He is to skin the burnt offering and cut it into pieces. [7]The sons of Aaron the priest are to put fire on the altar and arrange wood on the fire. [8]Then Aaron's sons the priests shall arrange the pieces, including the head and the fat, on the burning wood that is on the altar. [9]He is to wash the inner parts and the legs with water, and the priest is to burn all of it on the altar. It is a burnt offering, an offering made by fire, an aroma pleasing to the LORD.

[10]" 'If the offering is a burnt offering from the flock, from either the sheep or the goats, he is to offer a male without defect. [11]He is to slaughter it at the north side of the altar before the LORD, and Aaron's sons the priests shall sprinkle its blood against the altar on all sides. [12]He is to cut it into pieces, and the priest shall arrange them, including the head and the fat, on the burning wood that is on the altar. [13]He is to wash the inner parts and the legs with water, and the priest is to bring all of it and burn it on the altar. It is a burnt offering, an offering made by fire, an aroma pleasing to the LORD.

[14]" 'If the offering to the LORD is a burnt offering of birds, he is to offer a dove or a young pigeon. [15]The priest shall bring it to the altar, wring off the head and burn it on the altar; its blood shall be drained out on the side of the altar. [16]He is to remove the crop with its contents[b] and throw it to the east side of the altar, where the ashes are. [17]He shall tear it open by the wings, not severing it completely, and then the priest shall burn it on the wood that is on the fire on the altar. It is a burnt offering, an offering made by fire, an aroma pleasing to the LORD.

The Grain Offering

2 " 'When someone brings a grain offering to the LORD, his offering is to be of fine flour. He is to pour oil on it, put incense on it [2]and take it to Aaron's sons the priests. The priest shall take a handful of the fine flour and oil, together with all the incense, and burn this as a memorial portion on the altar, an offering made by fire, an aroma pleasing to the LORD. [3]The rest of the grain offering belongs to Aaron and his sons; it is a most holy part of the offerings made to the LORD by fire.

[4]" 'If you bring a grain offering baked in an oven, it is to consist of fine flour: cakes made without yeast and mixed with oil, or[c] wafers made without yeast and spread with oil. [5]If your grain offering is prepared on a griddle, it is to be made of fine flour mixed with oil, and without yeast. [6]Crumble it and pour oil on it; it is a grain offering. [7]If your grain offering is cooked in a pan, it is to be made of fine flour and oil. [8]Bring the grain offering made of these things to the LORD; present it to the priest, who shall take it to the altar. [9]He shall take out the memorial portion from the grain offering and burn it on the altar as an offering made by fire, an aroma pleasing to the LORD. [10]The rest of the grain offering belongs to Aaron and his sons; it is a most holy part of the offerings made to the LORD by fire.

[11]" 'Every grain offering you bring to the LORD must be made without yeast, for you are not to burn any yeast or honey in an offering made to the LORD by fire. [12]You may bring them to the LORD as an offering of the firstfruits, but they are not to be offered on the altar as a pleasing aroma. [13]Season all your grain offerings with salt. Do not leave the salt of the

---

[a]3 Or *he*   [b]16 Or *crop and the feathers*; the meaning of the Hebrew for this word is uncertain.   [c]4 Or *and*

covenant of your God out of your grain offerings; add salt to all your offerings.

¹⁴" 'If you bring a grain offering of firstfruits to the LORD, offer crushed heads of new grain roasted in the fire. ¹⁵Put oil and incense on it; it is a grain offering. ¹⁶The priest shall burn the memorial portion of the crushed grain and the oil, together with all the incense, as an offering made to the LORD by fire.

The Fellowship Offering

3 " 'If someone's offering is a fellowship offering,ᵃ and he offers an animal from the herd, whether male or female, he is to present before the LORD an animal without defect. ²He is to lay his hand on the head of his offering and slaughter it at the entrance to the Tent of Meeting. Then Aaron's sons the priests shall sprinkle the blood against the altar on all sides. ³From the fellowship offering he is to bring a sacrifice made to the LORD by fire: all the fat that covers the inner parts or is connected to them, ⁴both kidneys with the fat on them near the loins, and the covering of the liver, which he will remove with the kidneys. ⁵Then Aaron's sons are to burn it on the altar on top of the burnt offering that is on the burning wood, as an offering made by fire, an aroma pleasing to the LORD.

⁶" 'If he offers an animal from the flock as a fellowship offering to the LORD, he is to offer a male or female without defect. ⁷If he offers a lamb, he is to present it before the LORD. ⁸He is to lay his hand on the head of his offering and slaughter it in front of the Tent of Meeting. Then Aaron's sons shall sprinkle its blood against the altar on all sides. ⁹From the fellowship offering he is to bring a sacrifice made to the LORD by fire: its fat, the entire fat tail cut off close to the backbone, all the fat that covers the inner parts or is connected to them, ¹⁰both kidneys with the fat on them near the loins, and the covering of the liver, which he will remove with the kidneys. ¹¹The priest shall burn them on the altar as food, an offering made to the LORD by fire.

¹²" 'If his offering is a goat, he is to present it before the LORD. ¹³He is to lay his hand on its head and slaughter it in front of the Tent of Meeting. Then Aaron's sons shall sprinkle its blood against the altar on all sides. ¹⁴From what he offers he is to make this offering to the LORD by fire: all the fat that covers the inner parts or is connected to them, ¹⁵both kidneys with the fat on them near the loins, and the covering of the liver, which he will remove with the kidneys. ¹⁶The priest shall burn them on the altar as food, an offering made by fire, a pleasing aroma. All the fat is the LORD's.

¹⁷" 'This is a lasting ordinance for the generations to come, wherever you live: You must not eat any fat or any blood.' "

The Sin Offering

4 The LORD said to Moses, ²"Say to the Israelites: 'When anyone sins unintentionally and does what is forbidden in any of the LORD's commands—

³" 'If the anointed priest sins, bringing guilt on the people, he must bring to the LORD a young bull without defect as a sin offering for the sin he has committed. ⁴He is to present the bull at the entrance to the Tent of Meeting before the LORD. He is to lay his hand on its head and slaughter it before the LORD. ⁵Then the anointed priest shall take some of the bull's blood and carry it into the Tent of Meeting. ⁶He is to dip his finger into the blood and sprinkle some of it seven times before the LORD, in front of the curtain of the sanctuary. ⁷The priest shall then put some of the blood on the horns of the altar of fragrant incense that is before the LORD in the Tent of Meeting. The rest of the bull's blood he shall pour out at the base of the altar of burnt offering at the entrance to the Tent of Meeting. ⁸He shall remove all the fat from the bull of the sin offering—the fat that covers the inner parts or is connected to them, ⁹both kidneys with the fat on them near the loins, and the covering of the liver, which he will remove with the kidneys— ¹⁰just as the fat is removed from the oxᵇ sacrificed as a fellowship offering.ᶜ Then the priest

---

ᵃ1 Traditionally *peace offering*; also in verses 3, 6 and 9   ᵇ10 The Hebrew word can include both male and female.   ᶜ10 Traditionally *peace offering*; also in verses 26, 31 and 35

shall burn them on the altar of burnt offering. [11]But the hide of the bull and all its flesh, as well as the head and legs, the inner parts and offal— [12]that is, all the rest of the bull—he must take outside the camp to a place ceremonially clean, where the ashes are thrown, and burn it in a wood fire on the ash heap.

[13]" 'If the whole Israelite community sins unintentionally and does what is forbidden in any of the LORD's commands, even though the community is unaware of the matter, they are guilty. [14]When they become aware of the sin they committed, the assembly must bring a young bull as a sin offering and present it before the Tent of Meeting. [15]The elders of the community are to lay their hands on the bull's head before the LORD, and the bull shall be slaughtered before the LORD. [16]Then the anointed priest is to take some of the bull's blood into the Tent of Meeting. [17]He shall dip his finger into the blood and sprinkle it before the LORD seven times in front of the curtain. [18]He is to put some of the blood on the horns of the altar that is before the LORD in the Tent of Meeting. The rest of the blood he shall pour out at the base of the altar of burnt offering at the entrance to the Tent of Meeting. [19]He shall remove all the fat from it and burn it on the altar, [20]and do with this bull just as he did with the bull for the sin offering. In this way the priest will make atonement for them, and they will be forgiven. [21]Then he shall take the bull outside the camp and burn it as he burned the first bull. This is the sin offering for the community.

[22]" 'When a leader sins unintentionally and does what is forbidden in any of the commands of the LORD his God, he is guilty. [23]When he is made aware of the sin he committed, he must bring as his offering a male goat without defect. [24]He is to lay his hand on the goat's head and slaughter it at the place where the burnt offering is slaughtered before the LORD. It is a sin offering. [25]Then the priest shall take some of the blood of the sin offering with his finger and put it on the horns of the altar of burnt offering and pour out the rest of the blood at the base of the al-

tar. [26]He shall burn all the fat on the altar as he burned the fat of the fellowship offering. In this way the priest will make atonement for the man's sin, and he will be forgiven.

[27]" 'If a member of the community sins unintentionally and does what is forbidden in any of the LORD's commands, he is guilty. [28]When he is made aware of the sin he committed, he must bring as his offering for the sin he committed a female goat without defect. [29]He is to lay his hand on the head of the sin offering and slaughter it at the place of the burnt offering. [30]Then the priest is to take some of the blood with his finger and put it on the horns of the altar of burnt offering and pour out the rest of the blood at the base of the altar. [31]He shall remove all the fat, just as the fat is removed from the fellowship offering, and the priest shall burn it on the altar as an aroma pleasing to the LORD. In this way the priest will make atonement for him, and he will be forgiven.

[32]" 'If he brings a lamb as his sin offering, he is to bring a female without defect. [33]He is to lay his hand on its head and slaughter it for a sin offering at the place where the burnt offering is slaughtered. [34]Then the priest shall take some of the blood of the sin offering with his finger and put it on the horns of the altar of burnt offering and pour out the rest of the blood at the base of the altar. [35]He shall remove all the fat, just as the fat is removed from the lamb of the fellowship offering, and the priest shall burn it on the altar on top of the offerings made to the LORD by fire. In this way the priest will make atonement for him for the sin he has committed, and he will be forgiven.

5 " 'If a person sins because he does not speak up when he hears a public charge to testify regarding something he has seen or learned about, he will be held responsible.

[2]" 'Or if a person touches anything ceremonially unclean—whether the carcasses of unclean wild animals or of unclean livestock or of unclean creatures that move along the ground—even though he is unaware of it, he has become unclean and is guilty.

³“ 'Or if he touches human uncleanness—anything that would make him unclean—even though he is unaware of it, when he learns of it he will be guilty. ⁴“ 'Or if a person thoughtlessly takes an oath to do anything, whether good or evil—in any matter one might carelessly swear about—even though he is unaware of it, in any case when he learns of it he will be guilty.

⁵“ 'When anyone is guilty in any of these ways, he must confess in what way he has sinned ⁶and, as a penalty for the sin he has committed, he must bring to the LORD a female lamb or goat from the flock as a sin offering; and the priest shall make atonement for him for his sin.

⁷“ 'If he cannot afford a lamb, he is to bring two doves or two young pigeons to the LORD as a penalty for his sin—one for a sin offering and the other for a burnt offering. ⁸He is to bring them to the priest, who shall first offer the one for the sin offering. He is to wring its head from its neck, not severing it completely, ⁹and is to sprinkle some of the blood of the sin offering against the side of the altar; the rest of the blood must be drained out at the base of the altar. It is a sin offering. ¹⁰The priest shall then offer the other as a burnt offering in the prescribed way and make atonement for him for the sin he has committed, and he will be forgiven.

¹¹“ 'If, however, he cannot afford two doves or two young pigeons, he is to bring as an offering for his sin a tenth of an ephah*a* of fine flour for a sin offering. He must not put oil or incense on it, because it is a sin offering. ¹²He is to bring it to the priest, who shall take a handful of it as a memorial portion and burn it on the altar on top of the offerings made to the LORD by fire. It is a sin offering. ¹³In this way the priest will make atonement for him for any of these sins he has committed, and he will be forgiven. The rest of the offering will belong to the priest, as in the case of the grain offering.' "

The Guilt Offering

¹⁴The LORD said to Moses: ¹⁵“When a person commits a violation and sins unintentionally in regard to any of the LORD's holy things, he is to bring to the LORD as a penalty a ram from the flock, one without defect and of the proper value in silver, according to the sanctuary shekel.*b* It is a guilt offering. ¹⁶He must make restitution for what he has failed to do in regard to the holy things, add a fifth of the value to that and give it all to the priest, who will make atonement for him with the ram as a guilt offering, and he will be forgiven.

¹⁷“If a person sins and does what is forbidden in any of the LORD's commands, even though he does not know it, he is guilty and will be held responsible. ¹⁸He is to bring to the priest as a guilt offering a ram from the flock, one without defect and of the proper value. In this way the priest will make atonement for him for the wrong he has committed unintentionally, and he will be forgiven. ¹⁹It is a guilt offering; he has been guilty of*c* wrongdoing against the LORD."

6 The LORD said to Moses: ²“If anyone sins and is unfaithful to the LORD by deceiving his neighbor about something entrusted to him or left in his care or stolen, or if he cheats him, ³or if he finds lost property and lies about it, or if he swears falsely, or if he commits any such sin that people may do— ⁴when he thus sins and becomes guilty, he must return what he has stolen or taken by extortion, or what was entrusted to him, or the lost property he found, ⁵or whatever it was he swore falsely about. He must make restitution in full, add a fifth of the value to it and give it all to the owner on the day he presents his guilt offering. ⁶And as a penalty he must bring to the priest, that is, to the LORD, his guilt offering, a ram from the flock, one without defect and of the proper value. ⁷In this way the priest will make atonement for him before the LORD, and he will be forgiven for any of these things he did that made him guilty."

The Burnt Offering

⁸The LORD said to Moses: ⁹“Give Aaron and his sons this command: 'These are the regulations for the burnt offering:

---

a11 That is, probably about 2 quarts (about 2 liters)
b15 That is, about 2/5 ounce (about 11.5 grams)
c19 Or *has made full expiation for his*

The burnt offering is to remain on the altar hearth throughout the night, till morning, and the fire must be kept burning on the altar. [10]The priest shall then put on his linen clothes, with linen undergarments next to his body, and shall remove the ashes of the burnt offering that the fire has consumed on the altar and place them beside the altar. [11]Then he is to take off these clothes and put on others, and carry the ashes outside the camp to a place that is ceremonially clean. [12]The fire on the altar must be kept burning; it must not go out. Every morning the priest is to add firewood and arrange the burnt offering on the fire and burn the fat of the fellowship offerings[a] on it. [13]The fire must be kept burning on the altar continuously; it must not go out.

The Grain Offering

[14]" 'These are the regulations for the grain offering: Aaron's sons are to bring it before the LORD, in front of the altar. [15]The priest is to take a handful of fine flour and oil, together with all the incense on the grain offering, and burn the memorial portion on the altar as an aroma pleasing to the LORD. [16]Aaron and his sons shall eat the rest of it, but it is to be eaten without yeast in a holy place; they are to eat it in the courtyard of the Tent of Meeting. [17]It must not be baked with yeast; I have given it as their share of the offerings made to me by fire. Like the sin offering and the guilt offering, it is most holy. [18]Any male descendant of Aaron may eat it. It is his regular share of the offerings made to the LORD by fire for the generations to come. Whatever touches them will become holy.[b]' "

[19]The LORD also said to Moses, [20]"This is the offering Aaron and his sons are to bring to the LORD on the day he[c] is anointed: a tenth of an ephah[d] of fine flour as a regular grain offering, half of it in the morning and half in the evening. [21]Prepare it with oil on a griddle; bring it well-mixed and present the grain offering broken[e] in pieces as an aroma pleasing to the LORD. [22]The son who is to succeed him as anointed priest shall prepare it. It is the LORD's regular share and is to be burned completely. [23]Every grain offering of a priest shall be burned completely; it must not be eaten."

The Sin Offering

[24]The LORD said to Moses, [25]"Say to Aaron and his sons: 'These are the regulations for the sin offering: The sin offering is to be slaughtered before the LORD in the place the burnt offering is slaughtered; it is most holy. [26]The priest who offers it shall eat it; it is to be eaten in a holy place, in the courtyard of the Tent of Meeting. [27]Whatever touches any of the flesh will become holy, and if any of the blood is spattered on a garment, you must wash it in a holy place. [28]The clay pot the meat is cooked in must be broken; but if it is cooked in a bronze pot, the pot is to be scoured and rinsed with water. [29]Any male in a priest's family may eat it; it is most holy. [30]But any sin offering whose blood is brought into the Tent of Meeting to make atonement in the Holy Place must not be eaten; it must be burned.

The Guilt Offering

7 " 'These are the regulations for the guilt offering, which is most holy: [2]The guilt offering is to be slaughtered in the place where the burnt offering is slaughtered, and its blood is to be sprinkled against the altar on all sides. [3]All its fat shall be offered: the fat tail and the fat that covers the inner parts, [4]both kidneys with the fat on them near the loins, and the covering of the liver, which is to be removed with the kidneys. [5]The priest shall burn them on the altar as an offering made to the LORD by fire. It is a guilt offering. [6]Any male in a priest's family may eat it, but it must be eaten in a holy place; it is most holy.

[7]" 'The same law applies to both the sin offering and the guilt offering: They belong to the priest who makes atonement with them. [8]The priest who offers a burnt offering for anyone may keep its hide for himself. [9]Every grain offering baked in an oven or cooked in a pan or on a griddle belongs to the priest who

---

[a]12 Traditionally *peace offerings*   [b]18 Or *Whoever touches them must be holy*; similarly in verse 27   [c]20 Or *each*   [d]20 That is, probably about 2 quarts (about 2 liters)   [e]21 The meaning of the Hebrew for this word is uncertain.

offers it, [10]and every grain offering, whether mixed with oil or dry, belongs equally to all the sons of Aaron.

The Fellowship Offering

[11]" 'These are the regulations for the fellowship offering[a] a person may present to the LORD:

[12]" 'If he offers it as an expression of thankfulness, then along with this thank offering he is to offer cakes of bread made without yeast and mixed with oil, wafers made without yeast and spread with oil, and cakes of fine flour well-kneaded and mixed with oil. [13]Along with his fellowship offering of thanksgiving he is to present an offering with cakes of bread made with yeast. [14]He is to bring one of each kind as an offering, a contribution to the LORD; it belongs to the priest who sprinkles the blood of the fellowship offerings. [15]The meat of his fellowship offering of thanksgiving must be eaten on the day it is offered; he must leave none of it till morning.

[16]" 'If, however, his offering is the result of a vow or is a freewill offering, the sacrifice shall be eaten on the day he offers it, but anything left over may be eaten on the next day. [17]Any meat of the sacrifice left over till the third day must be burned up. [18]If any meat of the fellowship offering is eaten on the third day, it will not be accepted. It will not be credited to the one who offered it, for it is impure; the person who eats any of it will be held responsible.

[19]" 'Meat that touches anything ceremonially unclean must not be eaten; it must be burned up. As for other meat, anyone ceremonially clean may eat it. [20]But if anyone who is unclean eats any meat of the fellowship offering belonging to the LORD, that person must be cut off from his people. [21]If anyone touches something unclean—whether human uncleanness or an unclean animal or any unclean, detestable thing—and then eats any of the meat of the fellowship offering belonging to the LORD, that person must be cut off from his people.' "

Eating Fat and Blood Forbidden

[22]The LORD said to Moses, [23]"Say to the Israelites: 'Do not eat any of the fat of

cattle, sheep or goats. [24]The fat of an animal found dead or torn by wild animals may be used for any other purpose, but you must not eat it. [25]Anyone who eats the fat of an animal from which an offering by fire may be[b] made to the LORD must be cut off from his people. [26]And wherever you live, you must not eat the blood of any bird or animal. [27]If anyone eats blood, that person must be cut off from his people.' "

The Priests' Share

[28]The LORD said to Moses, [29]"Say to the Israelites: 'Anyone who brings a fellowship offering to the LORD is to bring part of it as his sacrifice to the LORD. [30]With his own hands he is to bring the offering made to the LORD by fire; he is to bring the fat, together with the breast, and wave the breast before the LORD as a wave offering. [31]The priest shall burn the fat on the altar, but the breast belongs to Aaron and his sons. [32]You are to give the right thigh of your fellowship offerings to the priest as a contribution. [33]The son of Aaron who offers the blood and the fat of the fellowship offering shall have the right thigh as his share. [34]From the fellowship offerings of the Israelites, I have taken the breast that is waved and the thigh that is presented and have given them to Aaron the priest and his sons as their regular share from the Israelites.' "

[35]This is the portion of the offerings made to the LORD by fire that were allotted to Aaron and his sons on the day they were presented to serve the LORD as priests. [36]On the day they were anointed, the LORD commanded that the Israelites give this to them as their regular share for the generations to come.

[37]These, then, are the regulations for the burnt offering, the grain offering, the sin offering, the guilt offering, the ordination offering and the fellowship offering, [38]which the LORD gave Moses on Mount Sinai on the day he commanded the Israelites to bring their offerings to the LORD, in the Desert of Sinai.

---

[a]11 Traditionally *peace offering*; also in verses 13-37
[b]25 Or *fire is*

The Ordination of Aaron and His Sons

8 The LORD said to Moses, ²“Bring Aaron and his sons, their garments, the anointing oil, the bull for the sin offering, the two rams and the basket containing bread made without yeast, ³and gather the entire assembly at the entrance to the Tent of Meeting.” ⁴Moses did as the LORD commanded him, and the assembly gathered at the entrance to the Tent of Meeting.

⁵Moses said to the assembly, “This is what the LORD has commanded to be done.” ⁶Then Moses brought Aaron and his sons forward and washed them with water. ⁷He put the tunic on Aaron, tied the sash around him, clothed him with the robe and put the ephod on him. He also tied the ephod to him by its skillfully woven waistband; so it was fastened on him. ⁸He placed the breastpiece on him and put the Urim and Thummim in the breastpiece. ⁹Then he placed the turban on Aaron's head and set the gold plate, the sacred diadem, on the front of it, as the LORD commanded Moses.

¹⁰Then Moses took the anointing oil and anointed the tabernacle and everything in it, and so consecrated them. ¹¹He sprinkled some of the oil on the altar seven times, anointing the altar and all its utensils and the basin with its stand, to consecrate them. ¹²He poured some of the anointing oil on Aaron's head and anointed him to consecrate him. ¹³Then he brought Aaron's sons forward, put tunics on them, tied sashes around them and put headbands on them, as the LORD commanded Moses.

¹⁴He then presented the bull for the sin offering, and Aaron and his sons laid their hands on its head. ¹⁵Moses slaughtered the bull and took some of the blood, and with his finger he put it on all the horns of the altar to purify the altar. He poured out the rest of the blood at the base of the altar. So he consecrated it to make atonement for it. ¹⁶Moses also took all the fat around the inner parts, the covering of the liver, and both kidneys and their fat, and burned it on the altar. ¹⁷But the bull with its hide and its flesh and its offal he burned up outside the camp, as the LORD commanded Moses.

¹⁸He then presented the ram for the burnt offering, and Aaron and his sons laid their hands on its head. ¹⁹Then Moses slaughtered the ram and sprinkled the blood against the altar on all sides. ²⁰He cut the ram into pieces and burned the head, the pieces and the fat. ²¹He washed the inner parts and the legs with water and burned the whole ram on the altar as a burnt offering, a pleasing aroma, an offering made to the LORD by fire, as the LORD commanded Moses.

²²He then presented the other ram, the ram for the ordination, and Aaron and his sons laid their hands on its head. ²³Moses slaughtered the ram and took some of its blood and put it on the lobe of Aaron's right ear, on the thumb of his right hand and on the big toe of his right foot. ²⁴Moses also brought Aaron's sons forward and put some of the blood on the lobes of their right ears, on the thumbs of their right hands and on the big toes of their right feet. Then he sprinkled blood against the altar on all sides. ²⁵He took the fat, the fat tail, all the fat around the inner parts, the covering of the liver, both kidneys and their fat and the right thigh. ²⁶Then from the basket of bread made without yeast, which was before the LORD, he took a cake of bread, and one made with oil, and a wafer; he put these on the fat portions and on the right thigh. ²⁷He put all these in the hands of Aaron and his sons and waved them before the LORD as a wave offering. ²⁸Then Moses took them from their hands and burned them on the altar on top of the burnt offering as an ordination offering, a pleasing aroma, an offering made to the LORD by fire. ²⁹He also took the breast—Moses' share of the ordination ram—and waved it before the LORD as a wave offering, as the LORD commanded Moses.

³⁰Then Moses took some of the anointing oil and some of the blood from the altar and sprinkled them on Aaron and his garments and on his sons and their garments. So he consecrated Aaron and his garments and his sons and their garments.

³¹Moses then said to Aaron and his sons, “Cook the meat at the entrance to the Tent of Meeting and eat it there with the bread from the basket of ordination

offerings, as I commanded, saying,[a] 'Aaron and his sons are to eat it.' [32]Then burn up the rest of the meat and the bread. [33]Do not leave the entrance to the Tent of Meeting for seven days, until the days of your ordination are completed, for your ordination will last seven days. [34]What has been done today was commanded by the LORD to make atonement for you. [35]You must stay at the entrance to the Tent of Meeting day and night for seven days and do what the LORD requires, so you will not die; for that is what I have been commanded." [36]So Aaron and his sons did everything the LORD commanded through Moses.

The Priests Begin Their Ministry

9 On the eighth day Moses summoned Aaron and his sons and the elders of Israel. [2]He said to Aaron, "Take a bull calf for your sin offering and a ram for your burnt offering, both without defect, and present them before the LORD. [3]Then say to the Israelites: 'Take a male goat for a sin offering, a calf and a lamb—both a year old and without defect—for a burnt offering, [4]and an ox[b] and a ram for a fellowship offering[c] to sacrifice before the LORD, together with a grain offering mixed with oil. For today the LORD will appear to you.' "

[5]They took the things Moses commanded to the front of the Tent of Meeting, and the entire assembly came near and stood before the LORD. [6]Then Moses said, "This is what the LORD has commanded you to do, so that the glory of the LORD may appear to you."

[7]Moses said to Aaron, "Come to the altar and sacrifice your sin offering and your burnt offering and make atonement for yourself and the people; sacrifice the offering that is for the people and make atonement for them, as the LORD has commanded."

[8]So Aaron came to the altar and slaughtered the calf as a sin offering for himself. [9]His sons brought the blood to him, and he dipped his finger into the blood and put it on the horns of the altar; the rest of the blood he poured out at the base of the altar. [10]On the altar he burned the fat, the kidneys and the covering of the liver from the sin offering, as the

LORD commanded Moses; [11]the flesh and the hide he burned up outside the camp.

[12]Then he slaughtered the burnt offering. His sons handed him the blood, and he sprinkled it against the altar on all sides. [13]They handed him the burnt offering piece by piece, including the head, and he burned them on the altar. [14]He washed the inner parts and the legs and burned them on top of the burnt offering on the altar.

[15]Aaron then brought the offering that was for the people. He took the goat for the people's sin offering and slaughtered it and offered it for a sin offering as he did with the first one.

[16]He brought the burnt offering and offered it in the prescribed way. [17]He also brought the grain offering, took a handful of it and burned it on the altar in addition to the morning's burnt offering.

[18]He slaughtered the ox and the ram as the fellowship offering for the people. His sons handed him the blood, and he sprinkled it against the altar on all sides. [19]But the fat portions of the ox and the ram—the fat tail, the layer of fat, the kidneys and the covering of the liver—[20]these they laid on the breasts, and then Aaron burned the fat on the altar. [21]Aaron waved the breasts and the right thigh before the LORD as a wave offering, as Moses commanded.

[22]Then Aaron lifted his hands toward the people and blessed them. And having sacrificed the sin offering, the burnt offering and the fellowship offering, he stepped down.

[23]Moses and Aaron then went into the Tent of Meeting. When they came out, they blessed the people; and the glory of the LORD appeared to all the people. [24]Fire came out from the presence of the LORD and consumed the burnt offering and the fat portions on the altar. And when all the people saw it, they shouted for joy and fell facedown.

The Death of Nadab and Abihu

10 Aaron's sons Nadab and Abihu took their censers, put fire in them

[a]31 Or I was commanded; [b]4 The Hebrew word can include both male and female; also in verses 18 and 19. [c]4 Traditionally peace offering; also in verses 18 and 22

and added incense; and they offered un-authorized fire before the LORD, contrary to his command. ²So fire came out from the presence of the LORD and consumed them, and they died before the LORD. ³Moses then said to Aaron, "This is what the LORD spoke of when he said:

" 'Among those who approach me
  I will show myself holy;
in the sight of all the people
  I will be honored.' "

Aaron remained silent.

⁴Moses summoned Mishael and Elza-phan, sons of Aaron's uncle Uzziel, and said to them, "Come here; carry your cousins outside the camp, away from the front of the sanctuary." ⁵So they came and carried them, still in their tunics, outside the camp, as Moses ordered.

⁶Then Moses said to Aaron and his sons Eleazar and Ithamar, "Do not let your hair become unkempt,ᵃ and do not tear your clothes, or you will die and the LORD will be angry with the whole com-munity. But your relatives, all the house of Israel, may mourn for those the LORD has destroyed by fire. ⁷Do not leave the entrance to the Tent of Meeting or you will die, because the LORD's anointing oil is on you." So they did as Moses said.

⁸Then the LORD said to Aaron, ⁹"You and your sons are not to drink wine or other fermented drink whenever you go into the Tent of Meeting, or you will die. This is a lasting ordinance for the gener-ations to come. ¹⁰You must distinguish between the holy and the common, be-tween the unclean and the clean, ¹¹and you must teach the Israelites all the de-crees the LORD has given them through Moses."

¹²Moses said to Aaron and his remain-ing sons, Eleazar and Ithamar, "Take the grain offering left over from the offer-ings made to the LORD by fire and eat it prepared without yeast beside the altar, for it is most holy. ¹³Eat it in a holy place, because it is your share and your sons' share of the offerings made to the LORD by fire; for so I have been commanded. ¹⁴But you and your sons and your daugh-ters may eat the breast that was waved and the thigh that was presented. Eat them in a ceremonially clean place; they

have been given to you and your chil-dren as your share of the Israelites' fel-lowship offerings.ᵇ ¹⁵The thigh that was presented and the breast that was waved must be brought with the fat portions of the offerings made by fire, to be waved before the LORD as a wave offering. This will be the regular share for you and your children, as the LORD has commanded."

¹⁶When Moses inquired about the goat of the sin offering and found that it had been burned up, he was angry with Elea-zar and Ithamar, Aaron's remaining sons, and asked, ¹⁷"Why didn't you eat the sin offering in the sanctuary area? It is most holy; it was given to you to take away the guilt of the community by making atonement for them before the LORD. ¹⁸Since its blood was not taken into the Holy Place, you should have eaten the goat in the sanctuary area, as I com-manded."

¹⁹Aaron replied to Moses, "Today they sacrificed their sin offering and their burnt offering before the LORD, but such things as this have happened to me. Would the LORD have been pleased if I had eaten the sin offering today?" ²⁰When Moses heard this, he was satisfied.

Clean and Unclean Food

11 The LORD said to Moses and Aaron, ²"Say to the Israelites: 'Of all the animals that live on land, these are the ones you may eat: ³You may eat any an-imal that has a split hoof completely di-vided and that chews the cud.

⁴" 'There are some that only chew the cud or only have a split hoof, but you must not eat them. The camel, though it chews the cud, does not have a split hoof; it is ceremonially unclean for you. ⁵The coney,ᶜ though it chews the cud, does not have a split hoof; it is unclean for you. ⁶The rabbit, though it chews the cud, does not have a split hoof; it is un-clean for you. ⁷And the pig, though it has a split hoof completely divided, does not chew the cud; it is unclean for you. ⁸You must not eat their meat or touch their carcasses; they are unclean for you.

⁹" 'Of all the creatures living in the

ᵃ6 Or *Do not uncover your heads*   ᵇ14 Traditionally *peace offerings*   ᶜ5 That is, the hyrax or rock badger

Old Rules

The Old Testament is filled with unusual rules and regulations. God didn't make them up just to frustrate people. He had very good reasons. Quite a few of them were given to protect his people from getting sick and dying. After all, he had a nation to build, and a Son to be born through that nation—so he could save the whole world. So God came up with some dietary rules, health regulations and even some dress codes:

Watch What You Eat! Back in the days before refrigerators and health inspectors, people often got sick and died from what they ate. God didn't want his people dying on him, so he gave them a strict set of dietary rules to keep them strong and healthy:

No Pork Chops! Pigs and certain other livestock carried diseases that made people sick. So no pork chops, bacon, rabbit stew or barbecued camel (Leviticus 11:3-7).

No Snacking on Certain Insects! It's hard to believe that God had to tell the people *not* to eat roaches, horseflies and daddy longleg spiders. But it's equally hard to believe that he told the people they *could* eat locusts, katydids and grasshoppers. Would you like yours with or without chocolate sprinkles? (Leviticus 11:20-23).

No Belly Draggers for Breakfast! That means don't get caught eating snakes, caterpillars and centipedes. God said that any creature that drags its belly along the ground, with or without legs, would make you dirty. When you were dirty on the inside, you had to go to the priest for cleansing. That was worse than being grounded (Leviticus 11:41-44).

Don't Touch! Believe it or not, humans have only recently discovered that many illnesses and diseases are spread through contact with things that are contaminated. God was way ahead of science on this fact:

Watch for Rashes! Skin diseases were rampant thousands of years ago. Some were merely rashes while others turned out to be leprosy. If you had a rash, you were taken to the priest and put in isolation for 7 days. If the rash spread, you were unclean, which meant another fun 7-day stay. If the sores faded, you were given a clean bill of health and sent home. If the rash never went away, you were separated from everyone for life (Leviticus 13:1-8).

Burn Your Dirty Laundry! People went so long without washing their clothes that all kinds of stuff began to grow on them. Mildew was especially bad. It could get to the point where it would spread through the clothes and make you sick as a dog. When that happened, you had to burn your clothes (Leviticus 13:47-52).

water of the seas and the streams, you may eat any that have fins and scales. ¹⁰But all creatures in the seas or streams that do not have fins and scales—whether among all the swarming things or among all the other living creatures in the water—you are to detest. ¹¹And since you are to detest them, you must not eat their meat and you must detest their carcasses. ¹²Anything living in the water that does not have fins and scales is to be detestable to you.

¹³" 'These are the birds you are to detest and not eat because they are detestable: the eagle, the vulture, the black vulture, ¹⁴the red kite, any kind of black kite, ¹⁵any kind of raven, ¹⁶the horned owl, the screech owl, the gull, any kind of hawk, ¹⁷the little owl, the cormorant, the great owl, ¹⁸the white owl, the desert owl, the osprey, ¹⁹the stork, any kind of heron, the hoopoe and the bat.[a]

²⁰" 'All flying insects that walk on all fours are to be detestable to you. ²¹There are, however, some winged creatures that walk on all fours that you may eat: those that have jointed legs for hopping on the ground. ²²Of these you may eat any kind of locust, katydid, cricket or grasshopper.

[a]19 The precise identification of some of the birds, insects and animals in this chapter is uncertain.

²³But all other winged creatures that have four legs you are to detest.

²⁴" 'You will make yourselves unclean by these; whoever touches their carcasses will be unclean till evening. ²⁵Whoever picks up one of their carcasses must wash his clothes, and he will be unclean till evening.

²⁶" 'Every animal that has a split hoof not completely divided or that does not chew the cud is unclean for you; whoever touches the carcass of any of them will be unclean. ²⁷Of all the animals that walk on all fours, those that walk on their paws are unclean for you; whoever touches their carcasses will be unclean till evening. ²⁸Anyone who picks up their carcasses must wash his clothes, and he will be unclean till evening. They are unclean for you.

²⁹" 'Of the animals that move about on the ground, these are unclean for you: the weasel, the rat, any kind of great lizard, ³⁰the gecko, the monitor lizard, the wall lizard, the skink and the chameleon. ³¹Of all those that move along the ground, these are unclean for you. Whoever touches them when they are dead will be unclean till evening. ³²When one of them dies and falls on something, that article, whatever its use, will be unclean, whether it is made of wood, cloth, hide or sackcloth. Put it in water; it will be unclean till evening, and then it will be clean. ³³If one of them falls into a clay pot, everything in it will be unclean, and you must break the pot. ³⁴Any food that could be eaten but has water on it from such a pot is unclean, and any liquid that could be drunk from it is unclean. ³⁵Anything that one of their carcasses falls on becomes unclean; an oven or cooking pot must be broken up. They are unclean, and you are to regard them as unclean. ³⁶A spring, however, or a cistern for collecting water remains clean, but anyone who touches one of these carcasses is unclean. ³⁷If a carcass falls on any seeds that are to be planted, they remain clean. ³⁸But if water has been put on the seed and a carcass falls on it, it is unclean for you.

³⁹" 'If an animal that you are allowed to eat dies, anyone who touches the carcass will be unclean till evening. ⁴⁰Any-

one who eats some of the carcass must wash his clothes, and he will be unclean till evening. Anyone who picks up the carcass must wash his clothes, and he will be unclean till evening.

⁴¹" 'Every creature that moves about on the ground is detestable; it is not to be eaten. ⁴²You are not to eat any creature that moves about on the ground, whether it moves on its belly or walks on all fours or on many feet; it is detestable. ⁴³Do not defile yourselves by any of these creatures. Do not make yourselves unclean by means of them or be made unclean by them. ⁴⁴I am the LORD your God; consecrate yourselves and be holy, because I am holy. Do not make yourselves unclean by any creature that moves about on the ground. ⁴⁵I am the LORD who brought you up out of Egypt to be your God; therefore be holy, because I am holy.

Holy

Leviticus 11:44–45

Leviticus means "concerning the Levites." The Levites were the religious leaders. This book gave them a bunch of rules about staying pure to please God. But the point of all these rules is *not* just to be religious but to be holy. Before Jesus came, the only way people could be around a holy God was to keep these rules. The Levites were to be holy just as God is holy; and holy means separate or set apart. But Jesus' death made us holy, so now we can come to God without all of those rules.

⁴⁶" 'These are the regulations concerning animals, birds, every living thing that moves in the water and every creature that moves about on the ground. ⁴⁷You must distinguish between the unclean and the clean, between living creatures that may be eaten and those that may not be eaten.' "

Purification After Childbirth

12 The LORD said to Moses, ²"Say to the Israelites: 'A woman who becomes pregnant and gives birth to a son will be ceremonially unclean for seven days, just as she is unclean during her monthly period. [3]On the eighth day the boy is to be circumcised. [4]Then the woman must wait thirty-three days to be purified from her bleeding. She must not touch anything sacred or go to the sanctuary until the days of her purification are over. [5]If she gives birth to a daughter, for two weeks the woman will be unclean, as during her period. Then she must wait sixty-six days to be purified from her bleeding.

[6]" 'When the days of her purification for a son or daughter are over, she is to bring to the priest at the entrance to the Tent of Meeting a year-old lamb for a burnt offering and a young pigeon or a dove for a sin offering. [7]He shall offer them before the LORD to make atonement for her, and then she will be ceremonially clean from her flow of blood.

" 'These are the regulations for the woman who gives birth to a boy or a girl. [8]If she cannot afford a lamb, she is to bring two doves or two young pigeons, one for a burnt offering and the other for a sin offering. In this way the priest will make atonement for her, and she will be clean.' "

Regulations About Infectious Skin Diseases

13 The LORD said to Moses and Aaron, [2]"When anyone has a swelling or a rash or a bright spot on his skin that may become an infectious skin disease,[a] he must be brought to Aaron the priest or to one of his sons[b] who is a priest. [3]The priest is to examine the sore on his skin, and if the hair in the sore has turned white and the sore appears to be more than skin deep,[c] it is an infectious skin disease. When the priest examines him, he shall pronounce him ceremonially unclean. [4]If the spot on his skin is white but does not appear to be more than skin deep and the hair in it has not turned white, the priest is to put the infected person in isolation for seven days. [5]On the seventh day the priest is to examine him, and if he sees that the sore is unchanged and has not spread in the skin, he is to keep him in isolation another seven days. [6]On the seventh day the priest is to examine him again, and if the

sore has faded and has not spread in the skin, the priest shall pronounce him clean; it is only a rash. The man must wash his clothes, and he will be clean. [7]But if the rash does spread in his skin after he has shown himself to the priest to be pronounced clean, he must appear before the priest again. [8]The priest is to examine him, and if the rash has spread in the skin, he shall pronounce him unclean; it is an infectious disease.

[9]"When anyone has an infectious skin disease, he must be brought to the priest. [10]The priest is to examine him, and if there is a white swelling in the skin that has turned the hair white and if there is raw flesh in the swelling, [11]it is a chronic skin disease and the priest shall pronounce him unclean. He is not to put him in isolation, because he is already unclean.

[12]"If the disease breaks out all over his skin and, so far as the priest can see, it covers all the skin of the infected person from head to foot, [13]the priest is to examine him, and if the disease has covered his whole body, he shall pronounce that person clean. Since it has all turned white, he is clean. [14]But whenever raw flesh appears on him, he will be unclean. [15]When the priest sees the raw flesh, he shall pronounce him unclean. The raw flesh is unclean; he has an infectious disease. [16]Should the raw flesh change and turn white, he must go to the priest. [17]The priest is to examine him, and if the sores have turned white, the priest shall pronounce the infected person clean; then he will be clean.

[18]"When someone has a boil on his skin and it heals, [19]and in the place where the boil was, a white swelling or reddish-white spot appears, he must present himself to the priest. [20]The priest is to examine it, and if it appears to be more than skin deep and the hair in it has turned white, the priest shall pronounce him unclean. It is an infectious skin disease that has broken out where the boil was. [21]But if, when the priest examines it,

---

[a]2 Traditionally *leprosy*; the Hebrew word was used for various diseases affecting the skin—not necessarily leprosy; also elsewhere in this chapter.
[b]2 Or *descendants* [c]3 Or *be lower than the rest of the skin*; also elsewhere in this chapter

there is no white hair in it and it is not more than skin deep and has faded, then the priest is to put him in isolation for seven days. ²²If it is spreading in the skin, the priest shall pronounce him unclean; it is infectious. ²³But if the spot is unchanged and has not spread, it is only a scar from the boil, and the priest shall pronounce him clean.

²⁴"When someone has a burn on his skin and a reddish-white or white spot appears in the raw flesh of the burn, ²⁵the priest is to examine the spot, and if the hair in it has turned white, and it appears to be more than skin deep, it is an infectious disease that has broken out in the burn. The priest shall pronounce him unclean; it is an infectious skin disease. ²⁶But if the priest examines it and there is no white hair in the spot and if it is not more than skin deep and has faded, then the priest is to put him in isolation for seven days. ²⁷On the seventh day the priest is to examine him, and if it is spreading in the skin, the priest shall pronounce him unclean; it is an infectious skin disease. ²⁸If, however, the spot is unchanged and has not spread in the skin but has faded, it is a swelling from the burn, and the priest shall pronounce him clean; it is only a scar from the burn.

²⁹"If a man or woman has a sore on the head or on the chin, ³⁰the priest is to examine the sore, and if it appears to be more than skin deep and the hair in it is yellow and thin, the priest shall pronounce that person unclean; it is an itch, an infectious disease of the head or chin. ³¹But if, when the priest examines this kind of sore, it does not seem to be more than skin deep and there is no black hair in it, then the priest is to put the infected person in isolation for seven days. ³²On the seventh day the priest is to examine the sore, and if the itch has not spread and there is no yellow hair in it and it does not appear to be more than skin deep, ³³he must be shaved except for the diseased area, and the priest is to keep him in isolation another seven days. ³⁴On the seventh day the priest is to examine the itch, and if it has not spread in the skin and appears to be no more than skin deep, the priest shall pronounce him clean. He must wash his clothes, and he

will be clean. ³⁵But if the itch does spread in the skin after he is pronounced clean, ³⁶the priest is to examine him, and if the itch has spread in the skin, the priest does not need to look for yellow hair; the person is unclean. ³⁷If, however, in his judgment it is unchanged and black hair has grown in it, the itch is healed. He is clean, and the priest shall pronounce him clean.

³⁸"When a man or woman has white spots on the skin, ³⁹the priest is to examine them, and if the spots are dull white, it is a harmless rash that has broken out on the skin; that person is clean.

⁴⁰"When a man has lost his hair and is bald, he is clean. ⁴¹If he has lost his hair from the front of his scalp and has a bald forehead, he is clean. ⁴²But if he has a reddish-white sore on his bald head or forehead, it is an infectious disease breaking out on his head or forehead. ⁴³The priest is to examine him, and if the swollen sore on his head or forehead is reddish-white like an infectious skin disease, ⁴⁴the man is diseased and is unclean. The priest shall pronounce him unclean because of the sore on his head.

⁴⁵"The person with such an infectious disease must wear torn clothes, let his hair be unkempt,ᵃ cover the lower part of his face and cry out, 'Unclean! Unclean!' ⁴⁶As long as he has the infection he remains unclean. He must live alone; he must live outside the camp.

Regulations About Mildew

⁴⁷"If any clothing is contaminated with mildew—any woolen or linen clothing, ⁴⁸any woven or knitted material of linen or wool, any leather or anything made of leather— ⁴⁹and if the contamination in the clothing, or leather, or woven or knitted material, or any leather article, is greenish or reddish, it is a spreading mildew and must be shown to the priest. ⁵⁰The priest is to examine the mildew and isolate the affected article for seven days. ⁵¹On the seventh day he is to examine it, and if the mildew has spread in the clothing, or the woven or knitted material, or the leather, whatever its use, it is a destructive mildew; the article is

---

ᵃ45 Or clothes, uncover his head

unclean. [52]He must burn up the clothing, or the woven or knitted material of wool or linen, or any leather article that has the contamination in it, because the mildew is destructive; the article must be burned up.

[53]"But if, when the priest examines it, the mildew has not spread in the clothing, or the woven or knitted material, or the leather article, [54]he shall order that the contaminated article be washed. Then he is to isolate it for another seven days. [55]After the affected article has been washed, the priest is to examine it, and if the mildew has not changed its appearance, even though it has not spread, it is unclean. Burn it with fire, whether the mildew has affected one side or the other. [56]If, when the priest examines it, the mildew has faded after the article has been washed, he is to tear the contaminated part out of the clothing, or the leather, or the woven or knitted material. [57]But if it reappears in the clothing, or in the woven or knitted material, or in the leather article, it is spreading, and whatever has the mildew must be burned with fire. [58]The clothing, or the woven or knitted material, or any leather article that has been washed and is rid of the mildew, must be washed again, and it will be clean."

[59]These are the regulations concerning contamination by mildew in woolen or linen clothing, woven or knitted material, or any leather article, for pronouncing them clean or unclean.

Cleansing From Infectious Skin Diseases

14 The LORD said to Moses, [2]"These are the regulations for the diseased person at the time of his ceremonial cleansing, when he is brought to the priest: [3]The priest is to go outside the camp and examine him. If the person has been healed of his infectious skin disease,[a] [4]the priest shall order that two live clean birds and some cedar wood, scarlet yarn and hyssop be brought for the one to be cleansed. [5]Then the priest shall order that one of the birds be killed over fresh water in a clay pot. [6]He is then to take the live bird and dip it, together with the cedar wood, the scarlet yarn and the hyssop, into the blood of the bird that

was killed over the fresh water. [7]Seven times he shall sprinkle the one to be cleansed of the infectious disease and pronounce him clean. Then he is to release the live bird in the open fields.

[8]"The person to be cleansed must wash his clothes, shave off all his hair and bathe with water; then he will be ceremonially clean. After this he may come into the camp, but he must stay outside his tent for seven days. [9]On the seventh day he must shave off all his hair; he must shave his head, his beard, his eyebrows and the rest of his hair. He must wash his clothes and bathe himself with water, and he will be clean.

[10]"On the eighth day he must bring two male lambs and one ewe lamb a year old, each without defect, along with three-tenths of an ephah[b] of fine flour mixed with oil for a grain offering, and one log[c] of oil. [11]The priest who pronounces him clean shall present both the one to be cleansed and his offerings before the LORD at the entrance to the Tent of Meeting.

[12]"Then the priest is to take one of the male lambs and offer it as a guilt offering, along with the log of oil; he shall wave them before the LORD as a wave offering. [13]He is to slaughter the lamb in the holy place where the sin offering and the burnt offering are slaughtered. Like the sin offering, the guilt offering belongs to the priest; it is most holy. [14]The priest is to take some of the blood of the guilt offering and put it on the lobe of the right ear of the one to be cleansed, on the thumb of his right hand and on the big toe of his right foot. [15]The priest shall then take some of the log of oil, pour it in the palm of his own left hand, [16]dip his right forefinger into the oil in his palm, and with his finger sprinkle some of it before the LORD seven times. [17]The priest is to put some of the oil remaining in his palm on the lobe of the right ear of the one to be cleansed, on the thumb of his right hand and on the big toe of his right

[a]3 Traditionally *leprosy*; the Hebrew word was used for various diseases affecting the skin—not necessarily leprosy; also elsewhere in this chapter.
[b]10 That is, probably about 6 quarts (about 6.5 liters)
[c]10 That is, probably about 2/3 pint (about 0.3 liter); also in verses 12, 15, 21 and 24

foot, on top of the blood of the guilt offering. [18]The rest of the oil in his palm the priest shall put on the head of the one to be cleansed and make atonement for him before the LORD.

[19]"Then the priest is to sacrifice the sin offering and make atonement for the one to be cleansed from his uncleanness. After that, the priest shall slaughter the burnt offering [20]and offer it on the altar, together with the grain offering, and make atonement for him, and he will be clean.

[21]"If, however, he is poor and cannot afford these, he must take one male lamb as a guilt offering to be waved to make atonement for him, together with a tenth of an ephah[a] of fine flour mixed with oil for a grain offering, a log of oil, [22]and two doves or two young pigeons, which he can afford, one for a sin offering and the other for a burnt offering.

[23]"On the eighth day he must bring them for his cleansing to the priest at the entrance to the Tent of Meeting, before the LORD. [24]The priest is to take the lamb for the guilt offering, together with the log of oil, and wave them before the LORD as a wave offering. [25]He shall slaughter the lamb for the guilt offering and take some of its blood and put it on the lobe of the right ear of the one to be cleansed, on the thumb of his right hand and on the big toe of his right foot. [26]The priest is to pour some of the oil into the palm of his own left hand, [27]and with his right forefinger sprinkle some of the oil from his palm seven times before the LORD. [28]Some of the oil in his palm he is to put on the same places he put the blood of the guilt offering—on the lobe of the right ear of the one to be cleansed, on the thumb of his right hand and on the big toe of his right foot. [29]The rest of the oil in his palm the priest shall put on the head of the one to be cleansed, to make atonement for him before the LORD. [30]Then he shall sacrifice the doves or the young pigeons, which the person can afford, [31]one[b] as a sin offering and the other as a burnt offering, together with the grain offering. In this way the priest will make atonement before the LORD on behalf of the one to be cleansed."

[32]These are the regulations for anyone who has an infectious skin disease and who cannot afford the regular offerings for his cleansing.

Cleansing From Mildew

[33]The LORD said to Moses and Aaron, [34]"When you enter the land of Canaan, which I am giving you as your possession, and I put a spreading mildew in a house in that land, [35]the owner of the house must go and tell the priest, 'I have seen something that looks like mildew in my house.' [36]The priest is to order the house to be emptied before he goes in to examine the mildew, so that nothing in the house will be pronounced unclean. After this the priest is to go in and inspect the house. [37]He is to examine the mildew on the walls, and if it has greenish or reddish depressions that appear to be deeper than the surface of the wall, [38]the priest shall go out the doorway of the house and close it up for seven days. [39]On the seventh day the priest shall return to inspect the house. If the mildew has spread on the walls, [40]he is to order that the contaminated stones be torn out and thrown into an unclean place outside the town. [41]He must have all the inside walls of the house scraped and the material that is scraped off dumped into an unclean place outside the town. [42]Then they are to take other stones to replace these and take new clay and plaster the house.

[43]"If the mildew reappears in the house after the stones have been torn out and the house scraped and plastered, [44]the priest is to go and examine it and, if the mildew has spread in the house, it is a destructive mildew; the house is unclean. [45]It must be torn down—its stones, timbers and all the plaster—and taken out of the town to an unclean place.

[46]"Anyone who goes into the house while it is closed up will be unclean till evening. [47]Anyone who sleeps or eats in the house must wash his clothes.

[48]"But if the priest comes to examine it and the mildew has not spread after the house has been plastered, he shall

[a]21 That is, probably about 2 quarts (about 2 liters)
[b]31 Septuagint and Syriac; Hebrew [31]such as the person can afford, one

pronounce the house clean, because the mildew is gone. ⁴⁹To purify the house he is to take two birds and some cedar wood, scarlet yarn and hyssop. ⁵⁰He shall kill one of the birds over fresh water in a clay pot. ⁵¹Then he is to take the cedar wood, the hyssop, the scarlet yarn and the live bird, dip them into the blood of the dead bird and the fresh water, and sprinkle the house seven times. ⁵²He shall purify the house with the bird's blood, the fresh water, the live bird, the cedar wood, the hyssop and the scarlet yarn. ⁵³Then he is to release the live bird in the open fields outside the town. In this way he will make atonement for the house, and it will be clean."

⁵⁴These are the regulations for any infectious skin disease, for an itch, ⁵⁵for mildew in clothing or in a house, ⁵⁶and for a swelling, a rash or a bright spot, ⁵⁷to determine when something is clean or unclean.

These are the regulations for infectious skin diseases and mildew.

Discharges Causing Uncleanness

15 The LORD said to Moses and Aaron, ²"Speak to the Israelites and say to them: 'When any man has a bodily discharge, the discharge is unclean. ³Whether it continues flowing from his body or is blocked, it will make him unclean. This is how his discharge will bring about uncleanness:

⁴" 'Any bed the man with a discharge lies on will be unclean, and anything he sits on will be unclean. ⁵Anyone who touches his bed must wash his clothes and bathe with water, and he will be unclean till evening. ⁶Whoever sits on anything that the man with a discharge sat on must wash his clothes and bathe with water, and he will be unclean till evening. ⁷" 'Whoever touches the man who has a discharge must wash his clothes and bathe with water, and he will be unclean till evening.

⁸" 'If the man with the discharge spits on someone who is clean, that person must wash his clothes and bathe with water, and he will be unclean till evening.

⁹" 'Everything the man sits on when riding will be unclean, ¹⁰and whoever touches any of the things that were under him will be unclean till evening; whoever picks up those things must wash his clothes and bathe with water, and he will be unclean till evening.

¹¹" 'Anyone the man with a discharge touches without rinsing his hands with water must wash his clothes and bathe with water, and he will be unclean till evening.

¹²" 'A clay pot that the man touches must be broken, and any wooden article is to be rinsed with water.

¹³" 'When a man is cleansed from his discharge, he is to count off seven days for his ceremonial cleansing; he must wash his clothes and bathe himself with fresh water, and he will be clean. ¹⁴On the eighth day he must take two doves or two young pigeons and come before the LORD to the entrance to the Tent of Meeting and give them to the priest. ¹⁵The priest is to sacrifice them, the one for a sin offering and the other for a burnt offering. In this way he will make atonement before the LORD for the man because of his discharge.

¹⁶" 'When a man has an emission of semen, he must bathe his whole body with water, and he will be unclean till evening. ¹⁷Any clothing or leather that has semen on it must be washed with water, and it will be unclean till evening. ¹⁸When a man lies with a woman and there is an emission of semen, both must bathe with water, and they will be unclean till evening.

¹⁹" 'When a woman has her regular flow of blood, the impurity of her monthly period will last seven days, and anyone who touches her will be unclean till evening.

²⁰" 'Anything she lies on during her period will be unclean, and anything she sits on will be unclean. ²¹Whoever touches her bed must wash his clothes and bathe with water, and he will be unclean till evening. ²²Whoever touches anything she sits on must wash his clothes and bathe with water, and he will be unclean till evening. ²³Whether it is the bed or anything she was sitting on, when anyone touches it, he will be unclean till evening.

²⁴" 'If a man lies with her and her monthly flow touches him, he will be unclean for seven days; any bed he lies on will be unclean.

²⁵" 'When a woman has a discharge of blood for many days at a time other than her monthly period or has a discharge that continues beyond her period, she will be unclean as long as she has the discharge, just as in the days of her period. ²⁶Any bed she lies on while her discharge continues will be unclean, as is her bed during her monthly period, and anything she sits on will be unclean, as during her period. ²⁷Whoever touches them will be unclean; he must wash his clothes and bathe with water, and he will be unclean till evening.

²⁸" 'When she is cleansed from her discharge, she must count off seven days, and after that she will be ceremonially clean. ²⁹On the eighth day she must take two doves or two young pigeons and bring them to the priest at the entrance to the Tent of Meeting. ³⁰The priest is to sacrifice one for a sin offering and the other for a burnt offering. In this way he will make atonement for her before the LORD for the uncleanness of her discharge.

³¹" 'You must keep the Israelites separate from things that make them unclean, so they will not die in their uncleanness for defiling my dwelling place,ᵃ which is among them.' "

³²These are the regulations for a man with a discharge, for anyone made unclean by an emission of semen, ³³for a woman in her monthly period, for a man or a woman with a discharge, and for a man who lies with a woman who is ceremonially unclean.

The Day of Atonement

16 The LORD spoke to Moses after the death of the two sons of Aaron who died when they approached the LORD. ²The LORD said to Moses: "Tell your brother Aaron not to come whenever he chooses into the Most Holy Place behind the curtain in front of the atonement cover on the ark, or else he will die, because I appear in the cloud over the atonement cover.

³"This is how Aaron is to enter the sanctuary area: with a young bull for a sin offering and a ram for a burnt offering. ⁴He is to put on the sacred linen tunic, with linen undergarments next to his body; he is to tie the linen sash around him and put on the linen turban. These are sacred garments; so he must bathe himself with water before he puts them on. ⁵From the Israelite community he is to take two male goats for a sin offering and a ram for a burnt offering.

⁶"Aaron is to offer the bull for his own sin offering to make atonement for himself and his household. ⁷Then he is to take the two goats and present them before the LORD at the entrance to the Tent of Meeting. ⁸He is to cast lots for the two goats—one lot for the LORD and the other for the scapegoat.ᵇ ⁹Aaron shall bring the goat whose lot falls to the LORD and sacrifice it for a sin offering. ¹⁰But the goat chosen by lot as the scapegoat shall be presented alive before the LORD to be used for making atonement by sending it into the desert as a scapegoat.

¹¹"Aaron shall bring the bull for his own sin offering to make atonement for himself and his household, and he is to slaughter the bull for his own sin offering. ¹²He is to take a censer full of burning coals from the altar before the LORD and two handfuls of finely ground fragrant incense and take them behind the curtain. ¹³He is to put the incense on the fire before the LORD, and the smoke of the incense will conceal the atonement cover above the Testimony, so that he will not die. ¹⁴He is to take some of the bull's blood and with his finger sprinkle it on the front of the atonement cover; then he shall sprinkle some of it with his finger seven times before the atonement cover.

¹⁵"He shall then slaughter the goat for the sin offering for the people and take its blood behind the curtain and do with it as he did with the bull's blood: He shall sprinkle it on the atonement cover and in front of it. ¹⁶In this way he will make atonement for the Most Holy Place because of the uncleanness and rebellion of the Israelites, whatever their sins have been. He is to do the same for the Tent of

---

ᵃ31 Or *my tabernacle*   ᵇ8 That is, the goat of removal; Hebrew *azazel*; also in verses 10 and 26

Meeting, which is among them in the midst of their uncleanness. [17]No one is to be in the Tent of Meeting from the time Aaron goes in to make atonement in the Most Holy Place until he comes out, having made atonement for himself, his household and the whole community of Israel.

[18]"Then he shall come out to the altar that is before the LORD and make atonement for it. He shall take some of the bull's blood and some of the goat's blood and put it on all the horns of the altar. [19]He shall sprinkle some of the blood on it with his finger seven times to cleanse it and to consecrate it from the uncleanness of the Israelites.

[20]"When Aaron has finished making atonement for the Most Holy Place, the Tent of Meeting and the altar, he shall bring forward the live goat. [21]He is to lay both hands on the head of the live goat and confess over it all the wickedness and rebellion of the Israelites—all their

sins—and put them on the goat's head. He shall send the goat away into the desert in the care of a man appointed for the task. [22]The goat will carry on itself all their sins to a solitary place; and the man shall release it in the desert.

[23]"Then Aaron is to go into the Tent of Meeting and take off the linen garments he put on before he entered the Most Holy Place, and he is to leave them there. [24]He shall bathe himself with water in a holy place and put on his regular garments. Then he shall come out and sacrifice the burnt offering for himself and the burnt offering for the people, to make atonement for himself and for the people. [25]He shall also burn the fat of the sin offering on the altar.

[26]"The man who releases the goat as a scapegoat must wash his clothes and bathe himself with water; afterward he may come into the camp. [27]The bull and the goat for the sin offerings, whose blood was brought into the Most Holy

---

Thursday

The Scapegoat

Read Leviticus 16

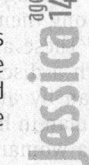

When my parents got divorced, I felt angry and bitter. I blamed all my hurt on everyone else. I hated the world, and I hated God. Because I didn't think anyone could understand my pain, I just kept it to myself.

In Leviticus 16, God tells Aaron to lay all the blame for the people's sins on one goat—the scapegoat—and let the other one go free. This passage helped me realize that if I had laid all my hurt on Jesus' shoulders instead of carrying it myself, I wouldn't have felt so alone. My heart would have healed a lot faster, and I could have forgiven my parents sooner.

We don't have to take everything on ourselves. We can give our burdens to Jesus, and, like the scapegoat, he carries them.

❶ Why do we try to hide our hurts? What good things can happen when we let others know we're hurting?

❷ On a small piece of paper, write down something that's really hurting you. Ask Jesus to take your hurt upon himself. Now tape the paper to a cross that you have. (If you don't have one, make one by putting popsicle sticks together with tape.) Remember that Jesus knows you and loves you. Thank him for caring about your needs.

❸ Tell God about other hurts in your life right now. Ask him to help you heal.

Turn to page 141 for your next devotion.

Place to make atonement, must be taken outside the camp; their hides, flesh and offal are to be burned up. [28]The man who burns them must wash his clothes and bathe himself with water; afterward he may come into the camp.

[29]"This is to be a lasting ordinance for you: On the tenth day of the seventh month you must deny yourselves[a] and not do any work—whether native-born or an alien living among you— [30]because on this day atonement will be made for you, to cleanse you. Then, before the LORD, you will be clean from all your sins. [31]It is a sabbath of rest, and you must deny yourselves; it is a lasting ordinance. [32]The priest who is anointed and ordained to succeed his father as high priest is to make atonement. He is to put on the sacred linen garments [33]and make atonement for the Most Holy Place, for the Tent of Meeting and the altar, and for the priests and all the people of the community. [34]"This is to be a lasting ordinance for you: Atonement is to be made once a year for all the sins of the Israelites."

And it was done, as the LORD commanded Moses.

Eating Blood Forbidden

17 The LORD said to Moses, [2]"Speak to Aaron and his sons and to all the Israelites and say to them: 'This is what the LORD has commanded: [3]Any Israelite who sacrifices an ox,[b] a lamb or a goat in the camp or outside of it [4]instead of bringing it to the entrance to the Tent of Meeting to present it as an offering to the LORD in front of the tabernacle of the LORD—that man shall be considered guilty of bloodshed; he has shed blood and must be cut off from his people. [5]This is so the Israelites will bring to the LORD the sacrifices they are now making in the open fields. They must bring them to the priest, that is, to the LORD, at the entrance to the Tent of Meeting and sacrifice them as fellowship offerings.[c] [6]The priest is to sprinkle the blood against the altar of the LORD at the entrance to the Tent of Meeting and burn the fat as an aroma pleasing to the LORD. [7]They must no longer offer any of their sacrifices to the goat idols[d] to whom they prostitute

themselves. This is to be a lasting ordinance for them and for the generations to come.'

[8]"Say to them: 'Any Israelite or any alien living among them who offers a burnt offering or sacrifice [9]and does not bring it to the entrance to the Tent of Meeting to sacrifice it to the LORD—that man must be cut off from his people.

[10]" 'Any Israelite or any alien living among them who eats any blood—I will set my face against that person who eats blood and will cut him off from his people. [11]For the life of a creature is in the blood, and I have given it to you to make atonement for yourselves on the altar; it is the blood that makes atonement for one's life. [12]Therefore I say to the Israelites, "None of you may eat blood, nor may an alien living among you eat blood."

[13]" 'Any Israelite or any alien living among you who hunts any animal or bird that may be eaten must drain out the blood and cover it with earth, [14]because the life of every creature is its blood. That is why I have said to the Israelites, "You must not eat the blood of any creature, because the life of every creature is its blood; anyone who eats it must be cut off."

[15]" 'Anyone, whether native-born or alien, who eats anything found dead or torn by wild animals must wash his clothes and bathe with water, and he will be ceremonially unclean till evening; then he will be clean. [16]But if he does not wash his clothes and bathe himself, he will be held responsible.' "

Unlawful Sexual Relations

18 The LORD said to Moses, [2]"Speak to the Israelites and say to them: 'I am the LORD your God. [3]You must not do as they do in Egypt, where you used to live, and you must not do as they do in the land of Canaan, where I am bringing you. Do not follow their practices. [4]You must obey my laws and be careful to follow my decrees. I am the LORD your God. [5]Keep my decrees and laws, for the man

---

[a]29 Or *must fast*; also in verse 31   [b]3 The Hebrew word can include both male and female.
[c]5 Traditionally *peace offerings*   [d]7 Or *demons*

Cool Rules

Huh?

Leviticus 18:3–5

Most people think that rules are a pain—sometimes they keep us from doing what we want to do. But God knows us better than we know ourselves. The cool thing about God is that if we pay attention to him, we get the most out of life. God's rules are cool rules!

who obeys them will live by them. I am the LORD.

⁶" 'No one is to approach any close relative to have sexual relations. I am the LORD.

⁷" 'Do not dishonor your father by having sexual relations with your mother. She is your mother; do not have relations with her.

⁸" 'Do not have sexual relations with your father's wife; that would dishonor your father.

⁹" 'Do not have sexual relations with your sister, either your father's daughter or your mother's daughter, whether she was born in the same home or elsewhere.

¹⁰" 'Do not have sexual relations with your son's daughter or your daughter's daughter; that would dishonor you.

¹¹" 'Do not have sexual relations with the daughter of your father's wife, born to your father; she is your sister.

¹²" 'Do not have sexual relations with your father's sister; she is your father's close relative.

¹³" 'Do not have sexual relations with your mother's sister, because she is your mother's close relative.

¹⁴" 'Do not dishonor your father's brother by approaching his wife to have sexual relations; she is your aunt.

¹⁵" 'Do not have sexual relations with your daughter-in-law. She is your son's wife; do not have relations with her.

¹⁶" 'Do not have sexual relations with your brother's wife; that would dishonor your brother.

¹⁷" 'Do not have sexual relations with both a woman and her daughter. Do not

have sexual relations with either her son's daughter or her daughter's daughter; they are her close relatives. That is wickedness.

¹⁸" 'Do not take your wife's sister as a rival wife and have sexual relations with her while your wife is living.

¹⁹" 'Do not approach a woman to have sexual relations during the uncleanness of her monthly period.

²⁰" 'Do not have sexual relations with your neighbor's wife and defile yourself with her.

²¹" 'Do not give any of your children to be sacrificed*a* to Molech, for you must not profane the name of your God. I am the LORD.

²²" 'Do not lie with a man as one lies with a woman; that is detestable.

²³" 'Do not have sexual relations with an animal and defile yourself with it. A woman must not present herself to an animal to have sexual relations with it; that is a perversion.

²⁴" 'Do not defile yourselves in any of these ways, because this is how the nations that I am going to drive out before you became defiled. ²⁵Even the land was defiled; so I punished it for its sin, and the land vomited out its inhabitants. ²⁶But you must keep my decrees and my laws. The native-born and the aliens living among you must not do any of these detestable things, ²⁷for all these things were done by the people who lived in the land before you, and the land became defiled. ²⁸And if you defile the land, it will vomit you out as it vomited out the nations that were before you.

²⁹" 'Everyone who does any of these detestable things—such persons must be cut off from their people. ³⁰Keep my requirements and do not follow any of the detestable customs that were practiced before you came and do not defile yourselves with them. I am the LORD your God.' "

Various Laws

19 The LORD said to Moses, ²"Speak to the entire assembly of Israel and say to them: 'Be holy because I, the LORD your God, am holy.

---

a21 Or to be passed through the fire

³" 'Each of you must respect his mother and father, and you must observe my Sabbaths. I am the LORD your God.

⁴" 'Do not turn to idols or make gods of cast metal for yourselves. I am the LORD your God.

⁵" 'When you sacrifice a fellowship offering*a* to the LORD, sacrifice it in such a way that it will be accepted on your behalf. ⁶It shall be eaten on the day you sacrifice it or on the next day; anything left over until the third day must be burned up. ⁷If any of it is eaten on the third day, it is impure and will not be accepted. ⁸Whoever eats it will be held responsible because he has desecrated what is holy to the LORD; that person must be cut off from his people.

⁹" 'When you reap the harvest of your land, do not reap to the very edges of your field or gather the gleanings of your harvest. ¹⁰Do not go over your vineyard a second time or pick up the grapes that

have fallen. Leave them for the poor and the alien. I am the LORD your God.

¹¹" 'Do not steal.

" 'Do not lie.

" 'Do not deceive one another.

¹²" 'Do not swear falsely by my name and so profane the name of your God. I am the LORD.

¹³" 'Do not defraud your neighbor or rob him.

" 'Do not hold back the wages of a hired man overnight.

¹⁴" 'Do not curse the deaf or put a stumbling block in front of the blind, but fear your God. I am the LORD.

¹⁵" 'Do not pervert justice; do not show partiality to the poor or favoritism to the great, but judge your neighbor fairly.

¹⁶" 'Do not go about spreading slander among your people.

" 'Do not do anything that endangers your neighbor's life. I am the LORD.

*a*5 Traditionally *peace offering*

Friday

A Little Respect

Read Leviticus 19:3

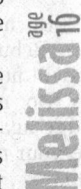

Everyone knows that God expects us to obey and honor our parents. But it's not always easy. When my mom and I fight, it's so tempting for me to yell at her. But whenever I do, I get in more trouble than if I would have shown her respect.

God put us in our families for a reason. Even when I'm having a hard time getting along with my mom, I have to remember that she is one of God's blessings to me. Yeah, sometimes it seems like my parents must be a "blessing in disguise," but the truth is, God knows what he's doing and can teach us a lot through our relationships with our parents. I think the most important thing I've learned is that obeying my mom is a lot like obeying God: It might not always be what I want, but it's what's best for me.

Melissa age 16

What about You?

❶ Think about some people in your life who deserve respect. What is one way you can show respect to others?

❷ Ask your parents how they feel when you show them respect. Now ask them how they feel when you're disrespectful. For the rest of the weekend, do your best to show them love and respect. And hey, keep it up!

❸ Thank God for your parents.

Turn to page 152 for your next devotion.

Fashion Taboos!

God wanted his people to be distinctive—that meant they were to look and act differently than the nations that surrounded them. Today we think of this as cultural diversity. Check out these fads:

No Mix and Match! You weren't allowed to mix your fabrics—no wool with linen. However, it seems that it was okay to wear stripes with plaids (Leviticus 19:19; Deuteronomy 22:11).

No Skinheads! Men weren't allowed to shave their heads or the sides of their beards. But curling those lovely locks was just fine (Leviticus 19:27).

No Body Piercing or Painting! It seems the common practice for mourning a lost loved one was cutting your body to demonstrate your pain. God didn't think this was such a hot idea. He called the body holy, and didn't want his kids to mark it up at all. That's right, tattoos were off limits too (Leviticus 19:28).

17" 'Do not hate your brother in your heart. Rebuke your neighbor frankly so you will not share in his guilt.

18" 'Do not seek revenge or bear a grudge against one of your people, but love your neighbor as yourself. I am the LORD.

19" 'Keep my decrees.

" 'Do not mate different kinds of animals.

" 'Do not plant your field with two kinds of seed.

" 'Do not wear clothing woven of two kinds of material.

20" 'If a man sleeps with a woman who is a slave girl promised to another man but who has not been ransomed or given her freedom, there must be due punishment. Yet they are not to be put to death, because she had not been freed. 21The man, however, must bring a ram to the entrance to the Tent of Meeting for a guilt offering to the LORD. 22With the ram of the guilt offering the priest is to make atonement for him before the LORD for the sin he has committed, and his sin will be forgiven.

23" 'When you enter the land and plant any kind of fruit tree, regard its fruit as forbidden.ᵃ For three years you are to consider it forbiddenᵃ; it must not be eaten. 24In the fourth year all its fruit will be holy, an offering of praise to the LORD. 25But in the fifth year you may eat its fruit. In this way your harvest will be increased. I am the LORD your God.

26" 'Do not eat any meat with the blood still in it.

" 'Do not practice divination or sorcery.

27" 'Do not cut the hair at the sides of your head or clip off the edges of your beard.

28" 'Do not cut your bodies for the dead or put tattoo marks on yourselves. I am the LORD.

29" 'Do not degrade your daughter by making her a prostitute, or the land will turn to prostitution and be filled with wickedness.

30" 'Observe my Sabbaths and have reverence for my sanctuary. I am the LORD.

31" 'Do not turn to mediums or seek out spiritists, for you will be defiled by them. I am the LORD your God.

32" 'Rise in the presence of the aged, show respect for the elderly and revere your God. I am the LORD.

33" 'When an alien lives with you in your land, do not mistreat him. 34The alien living with you must be treated as one of your native-born. Love him as yourself, for you were aliens in Egypt. I am the LORD your God.

35" 'Do not use dishonest standards when measuring length, weight or quantity. 36Use honest scales and honest weights, an honest ephahᵇ and an honest hin.ᶜ I am the LORD your God, who brought you out of Egypt.

37" 'Keep all my decrees and all my laws and follow them. I am the LORD.' "

ᵃ23 Hebrew *uncircumcised* ᵇ36 An ephah was a dry measure. ᶜ36 A hin was a liquid measure.

Punishments for Sin

20 The LORD said to Moses, ²"Say to the Israelites: 'Any Israelite or any alien living in Israel who gives*ª* any of his children to Molech must be put to death. The people of the community are to stone him. ³I will set my face against that man and I will cut him off from his people; for by giving his children to Molech, he has defiled my sanctuary and profaned my holy name. ⁴If the people of the community close their eyes when that man gives one of his children to Molech and they fail to put him to death, ⁵I will set my face against that man and his family and will cut off from their people both him and all who follow him in prostituting themselves to Molech.

⁶" 'I will set my face against the person who turns to mediums and spiritists to prostitute himself by following them, and I will cut him off from his people.

⁷" 'Consecrate yourselves and be holy, because I am the LORD your God. ⁸Keep my decrees and follow them. I am the LORD, who makes you holy.*ᵇ*

⁹" 'If anyone curses his father or mother, he must be put to death. He has cursed his father or his mother, and his blood will be on his own head.

¹⁰" 'If a man commits adultery with another man's wife—with the wife of his neighbor—both the adulterer and the adulteress must be put to death.

¹¹" 'If a man sleeps with his father's wife, he has dishonored his father. Both the man and the woman must be put to death; their blood will be on their own heads.

¹²" 'If a man sleeps with his daughter-in-law, both of them must be put to death. What they have done is a perversion; their blood will be on their own heads.

¹³" 'If a man lies with a man as one lies with a woman, both of them have done what is detestable. They must be put to death; their blood will be on their own heads.

¹⁴" 'If a man marries both a woman and her mother, it is wicked. Both he and they must be burned in the fire, so that no wickedness will be among you.

¹⁵" 'If a man has sexual relations with an animal, he must be put to death, and you must kill the animal.

¹⁶" 'If a woman approaches an animal to have sexual relations with it, kill both the woman and the animal. They must be put to death; their blood will be on their own heads.

¹⁷" 'If a man marries his sister, the daughter of either his father or his mother, and they have sexual relations, it is a disgrace. They must be cut off before the eyes of their people. He has dishonored his sister and will be held responsible.

¹⁸" 'If a man lies with a woman during her monthly period and has sexual relations with her, he has exposed the source of her flow, and she has also uncovered it. Both of them must be cut off from their people.

¹⁹" 'Do not have sexual relations with the sister of either your mother or your father, for that would dishonor a close relative; both of you would be held responsible.

²⁰" 'If a man sleeps with his aunt, he has dishonored his uncle. They will be held responsible; they will die childless.

²¹" 'If a man marries his brother's wife, it is an act of impurity; he has dishonored his brother. They will be childless.

²²" 'Keep all my decrees and laws and follow them, so that the land where I am bringing you to live may not vomit you out. ²³You must not live according to the customs of the nations I am going to drive out before you. Because they did all these things, I abhorred them. ²⁴But I said to you, "You will possess their land; I will give it to you as an inheritance, a land flowing with milk and honey." I am the LORD your God, who has set you apart from the nations.

²⁵" 'You must therefore make a distinction between clean and unclean animals and between unclean and clean birds. Do not defile yourselves by any animal or bird or anything that moves along the ground—those which I have set apart as unclean for you. ²⁶You are to be holy to me*ᶜ* because I, the LORD, am holy, and I have set you apart from the nations to be my own.

ª2 Or sacrifices; also in verses 3 and 4   ᵇ8 Or who sanctifies you; or who sets you apart as holy   ᶜ26 Or be my holy ones

27" 'A man or woman who is a medium or spiritist among you must be put to death. You are to stone them; their blood will be on their own heads.' "

Rules for Priests

21 The LORD said to Moses, "Speak to the priests, the sons of Aaron, and say to them: 'A priest must not make himself ceremonially unclean for any of his people who die, ²except for a close relative, such as his mother or father, his son or daughter, his brother, ³or an unmarried sister who is dependent on him since she has no husband—for her he may make himself unclean. ⁴He must not make himself unclean for people related to him by marriage,ᵃ and so defile himself.

⁵" 'Priests must not shave their heads or shave off the edges of their beards or cut their bodies. ⁶They must be holy to their God and must not profane the name of their God. Because they present the offerings made to the LORD by fire, the food of their God, they are to be holy.

⁷" 'They must not marry women defiled by prostitution or divorced from their husbands, because priests are holy to their God. ⁸Regard them as holy, because they offer up the food of your God. Consider them holy, because I the LORD am holy—I who make you holy.ᵇ

⁹" 'If a priest's daughter defiles herself by becoming a prostitute, she disgraces her father; she must be burned in the fire.

¹⁰" 'The high priest, the one among his brothers who has had the anointing oil poured on his head and who has been ordained to wear the priestly garments, must not let his hair become unkemptᶜ or tear his clothes. ¹¹He must not enter a place where there is a dead body. He must not make himself unclean, even for his father or mother, ¹²nor leave the sanctuary of his God or desecrate it, because he has been dedicated by the anointing oil of his God. I am the LORD.

¹³" 'The woman he marries must be a virgin. ¹⁴He must not marry a widow, a divorced woman, or a woman defiled by prostitution, but only a virgin from his own people, ¹⁵so he will not defile his offspring among his people. I am the LORD, who makes him holy.ᵈ' "

¹⁶The LORD said to Moses, ¹⁷"Say to Aaron: 'For the generations to come none of your descendants who has a defect may come near to offer the food of his God. ¹⁸No man who has any defect may come near: no man who is blind or lame, disfigured or deformed; ¹⁹no man with a crippled foot or hand, ²⁰or who is hunchbacked or dwarfed, or who has any eye defect, or who has festering or running sores or damaged testicles. ²¹No descendant of Aaron the priest who has any defect is to come near to present the offerings made to the LORD by fire. He has a defect; he must not come near to offer the food of his God. ²²He may eat the most holy food of his God, as well as the holy food; ²³yet because of his defect, he must not go near the curtain or approach the altar, and so desecrate my sanctuary. I am the LORD, who makes them holy.ᵉ' "

²⁴So Moses told this to Aaron and his sons and to all the Israelites.

22 The LORD said to Moses, ²"Tell Aaron and his sons to treat with respect the sacred offerings the Israelites consecrate to me, so they will not profane my holy name. I am the LORD.

³"Say to them: 'For the generations to come, if any of your descendants is ceremonially unclean and yet comes near the sacred offerings that the Israelites consecrate to the LORD, that person must be cut off from my presence. I am the LORD.

⁴" 'If a descendant of Aaron has an infectious skin diseaseᶠ or a bodily discharge, he may not eat the sacred offerings until he is cleansed. He will also be unclean if he touches something defiled by a corpse or by anyone who has an emission of semen, ⁵or if he touches any crawling thing that makes him unclean, or any person who makes him unclean, whatever the uncleanness may be. ⁶The one who touches any such thing

---

ᵃ4 Or *unclean as a leader among his people*   ᵇ8 Or *who sanctify you; or who set you apart as holy*   ᶜ10 Or *not uncover his head*   ᵈ15 Or *who sanctifies him; or who sets him apart as holy*   ᵉ23 Or *who sanctifies them; or who sets them apart as holy*   ᶠ4 Traditionally *leprosy*; the Hebrew word was used for various diseases affecting the skin—not necessarily leprosy.

will be unclean till evening. He must not eat any of the sacred offerings unless he has bathed himself with water. ⁷When the sun goes down, he will be clean, and after that he may eat the sacred offerings, for they are his food. ⁸He must not eat anything found dead or torn by wild animals, and so become unclean through it. I am the LORD.

⁹" 'The priests are to keep my requirements so that they do not become guilty and die for treating them with contempt. I am the LORD, who makes them holy.ᵃ

¹⁰" 'No one outside a priest's family may eat the sacred offering, nor may the guest of a priest or his hired worker eat it. ¹¹But if a priest buys a slave with money, or if a slave is born in his household, that slave may eat his food. ¹²If a priest's daughter marries anyone other than a priest, she may not eat any of the sacred contributions. ¹³But if a priest's daughter becomes a widow or is divorced, yet has no children, and she returns to live in her father's house as in her youth, she may eat of her father's food. No unauthorized person, however, may eat any of it.

¹⁴" 'If anyone eats a sacred offering by mistake, he must make restitution to the priest for the offering and add a fifth of the value to it. ¹⁵The priests must not desecrate the sacred offerings the Israelites present to the LORD ¹⁶by allowing them to eat the sacred offerings and so bring upon them guilt requiring payment. I am the LORD, who makes them holy.' "

Unacceptable Sacrifices

¹⁷The LORD said to Moses, ¹⁸"Speak to Aaron and his sons and to all the Israelites and say to them: 'If any of you—either an Israelite or an alien living in Israel—presents a gift for a burnt offering to the LORD, either to fulfill a vow or as a freewill offering, ¹⁹you must present a male without defect from the cattle, sheep or goats in order that it may be accepted on your behalf. ²⁰Do not bring anything with a defect, because it will not be accepted on your behalf. ²¹When anyone brings from the herd or flock a fellowship offeringᵇ to the LORD to fulfill a special vow or as a freewill offering, it must be without defect or blemish to be

acceptable. ²²Do not offer to the LORD the blind, the injured or the maimed, or anything with warts or festering or running sores. Do not place any of these on the altar as an offering made to the LORD by fire. ²³You may, however, present as a freewill offering an oxᶜ or a sheep that is deformed or stunted, but it will not be accepted in fulfillment of a vow. ²⁴You must not offer to the LORD an animal whose testicles are bruised, crushed, torn or cut. You must not do this in your own land, ²⁵and you must not accept such animals from the hand of a foreigner and offer them as the food of your God. They will not be accepted on your behalf, because they are deformed and have defects.' "

²⁶The LORD said to Moses, ²⁷"When a calf, a lamb or a goat is born, it is to remain with its mother for seven days. From the eighth day on, it will be acceptable as an offering made to the LORD by fire. ²⁸Do not slaughter a cow or a sheep and its young on the same day.

²⁹"When you sacrifice a thank offering to the LORD, sacrifice it in such a way that it will be accepted on your behalf. ³⁰It must be eaten that same day; leave none of it till morning. I am the LORD.

³¹"Keep my commands and follow them. I am the LORD. ³²Do not profane my holy name. I must be acknowledged as holy by the Israelites. I am the LORD, who makesᵈ you holyᵉ ³³and who brought you out of Egypt to be your God. I am the LORD."

23 The LORD said to Moses, ²"Speak to the Israelites and say to them: 'These are my appointed feasts, the appointed feasts of the LORD, which you are to proclaim as sacred assemblies.

The Sabbath

³" 'There are six days when you may work, but the seventh day is a Sabbath of rest, a day of sacred assembly. You are not to do any work; wherever you live, it is a Sabbath to the LORD.

ᵃ9 Or who sanctifies them; or who sets them apart as holy; also in verse 16   ᵇ21 Traditionally peace offering   ᶜ23 The Hebrew word can include both male and female.   ᵈ32 Or made   ᵉ32 Or who sanctifies you; or who sets you apart as holy

The Passover and Unleavened Bread

4" 'These are the LORD's appointed feasts, the sacred assemblies you are to proclaim at their appointed times: [5]The LORD's Passover begins at twilight on the fourteenth day of the first month. [6]On the fifteenth day of that month the LORD's Feast of Unleavened Bread begins; for seven days you must eat bread made without yeast. [7]On the first day hold a sacred assembly and do no regular work. [8]For seven days present an offering made to the LORD by fire. And on the seventh day hold a sacred assembly and do no regular work.' "

Firstfruits

[9]The LORD said to Moses, [10]"Speak to the Israelites and say to them: 'When you enter the land I am going to give you and you reap its harvest, bring to the priest a sheaf of the first grain you harvest. [11]He is to wave the sheaf before the LORD so it will be accepted on your behalf; the priest is to wave it on the day after the Sabbath. [12]On the day you wave the sheaf, you must sacrifice as a burnt offering to the LORD a lamb a year old without defect, [13]together with its grain offering of two-tenths of an ephah[a] of fine flour mixed with oil—an offering made to the LORD by fire, a pleasing aroma—and its drink offering of a quarter of a hin[b] of wine. [14]You must not eat any bread, or roasted or new grain, until the very day you bring this offering to your God. This is to be a lasting ordinance for the generations to come, wherever you live.

Feast of Weeks

[15]" 'From the day after the Sabbath, the day you brought the sheaf of the wave offering, count off seven full weeks. [16]Count off fifty days up to the day after the seventh Sabbath, and then present an offering of new grain to the LORD. [17]From wherever you live, bring two loaves made of two-tenths of an ephah of fine flour, baked with yeast, as a wave offering of firstfruits to the LORD. [18]Present with this bread seven male lambs, each a year old and without defect, one young bull and two rams. They will be a burnt offering to the LORD, together with their grain offerings and drink offerings—an offering made by fire, an aroma pleasing to the LORD. [19]Then sacrifice one male goat for a sin offering and two lambs, each a year old, for a fellowship offering.[c] [20]The priest is to wave the two lambs before the LORD as a wave offering, together with the bread of the firstfruits. They are a sacred offering to the LORD for the priest. [21]On that same day you are to proclaim a sacred assembly and do no regular work. This is to be a lasting ordinance for the generations to come, wherever you live.

[22]" 'When you reap the harvest of your land, do not reap to the very edges of your field or gather the gleanings of your harvest. Leave them for the poor and the alien. I am the LORD your God.' "

Feast of Trumpets

[23]The LORD said to Moses, [24]"Say to the Israelites: 'On the first day of the seventh month you are to have a day of rest, a sacred assembly commemorated with trumpet blasts. [25]Do no regular work, but present an offering made to the LORD by fire.' "

Day of Atonement

[26]The LORD said to Moses, [27]"The tenth day of this seventh month is the Day of Atonement. Hold a sacred assembly and deny yourselves,[d] and present an offering made to the LORD by fire. [28]Do no work on that day, because it is the Day of Atonement, when atonement is made for you before the LORD your God. [29]Anyone who does not deny himself on that day must be cut off from his people. [30]I will destroy from among his people anyone who does any work on that day. [31]You shall do no work at all. This is to be a lasting ordinance for the generations to come, wherever you live. [32]It is a sabbath of rest for you, and you must deny yourselves. From the evening of the ninth day of the month until the following evening you are to observe your sabbath."

---

[a]13 That is, probably about 4 quarts (about 4.5 liters); also in verse 17 [b]13 That is, probably about 1 quart (about 1 liter) [c]19 Traditionally *peace offering* [d]27 Or *and fast*; also in verses 29 and 32

Feast of Tabernacles

³³The LORD said to Moses, ³⁴"Say to the Israelites: 'On the fifteenth day of the seventh month the LORD's Feast of Tabernacles begins, and it lasts for seven days. ³⁵The first day is a sacred assembly; do no regular work. ³⁶For seven days present offerings made to the LORD by fire, and on the eighth day hold a sacred assembly and present an offering made to the LORD by fire. It is the closing assembly; do no regular work.

³⁷("'These are the LORD's appointed feasts, which you are to proclaim as sacred assemblies for bringing offerings made to the LORD by fire—the burnt offerings and grain offerings, sacrifices and drink offerings required for each day. ³⁸These offerings are in addition to those for the LORD's Sabbaths and[a] in addition to your gifts and whatever you have vowed and all the freewill offerings you give to the LORD.)

³⁹"'So beginning with the fifteenth day of the seventh month, after you have gathered the crops of the land, celebrate the festival to the LORD for seven days; the first day is a day of rest, and the eighth day also is a day of rest. ⁴⁰On the first day you are to take choice fruit from the trees, and palm fronds, leafy branches and poplars, and rejoice before the LORD your God for seven days. ⁴¹Celebrate this as a festival to the LORD for seven days each year. This is to be a lasting ordinance for the generations to come; celebrate it in the seventh month. ⁴²Live in booths for seven days: All native-born Israelites are to live in booths ⁴³so your descendants will know that I had the Israelites live in booths when I brought them out of Egypt. I am the LORD your God.'"

⁴⁴So Moses announced to the Israelites the appointed feasts of the LORD.

Oil and Bread Set Before the LORD

24 The LORD said to Moses, ²"Command the Israelites to bring you clear oil of pressed olives for the light so that the lamps may be kept burning continually. ³Outside the curtain of the Testimony in the Tent of Meeting, Aaron is to tend the lamps before the LORD from eve-

ning till morning, continually. This is to be a lasting ordinance for the generations to come. ⁴The lamps on the pure gold lampstand before the LORD must be tended continually.

⁵"Take fine flour and bake twelve loaves of bread, using two-tenths of an ephah[b] for each loaf. ⁶Set them in two rows, six in each row, on the table of pure gold before the LORD. ⁷Along each row put some pure incense as a memorial portion to represent the bread and to be an offering made to the LORD by fire. ⁸This bread is to be set out before the LORD regularly, Sabbath after Sabbath, on behalf of the Israelites, as a lasting covenant. ⁹It belongs to Aaron and his sons, who are to eat it in a holy place, because it is a most holy part of their regular share of the offerings made to the LORD by fire."

A Blasphemer Stoned

¹⁰Now the son of an Israelite mother and an Egyptian father went out among the Israelites, and a fight broke out in the camp between him and an Israelite. ¹¹The son of the Israelite woman blasphemed the Name with a curse; so they brought him to Moses. (His mother's name was Shelomith, the daughter of Dibri the Danite.) ¹²They put him in custody until the will of the LORD should be made clear to them.

¹³Then the LORD said to Moses: ¹⁴"Take the blasphemer outside the camp. All those who heard him are to lay their hands on his head, and the entire assembly is to stone him. ¹⁵Say to the Israelites: 'If anyone curses his God, he will be held responsible; ¹⁶anyone who blasphemes the name of the LORD must be put to death. The entire assembly must stone him. Whether an alien or native-born, when he blasphemes the Name, he must be put to death.

¹⁷"'If anyone takes the life of a human being, he must be put to death. ¹⁸Anyone who takes the life of someone's animal must make restitution—life for life. ¹⁹If anyone injures his neighbor, whatever he

---

[a]38 Or These feasts are in addition to the LORD's Sabbaths, and these offerings are *[b]5 That is, probably about 4 quarts (about 4.5 liters)*

has done must be done to him: ²⁰fracture for fracture, eye for eye, tooth for tooth. As he has injured the other, so he is to be injured. ²¹Whoever kills an animal must make restitution, but whoever kills a man must be put to death. ²²You are to have the same law for the alien and the native-born. I am the LORD your God.' "

²³Then Moses spoke to the Israelites, and they took the blasphemer outside the camp and stoned him. The Israelites did as the LORD commanded Moses.

The Sabbath Year

25 The LORD said to Moses on Mount Sinai, ²"Speak to the Israelites and say to them: 'When you enter the land I am going to give you, the land itself must observe a sabbath to the LORD. ³For six years sow your fields, and for six years prune your vineyards and gather their crops. ⁴But in the seventh year the land is to have a sabbath of rest, a sabbath to the LORD. Do not sow your fields or prune your vineyards. ⁵Do not reap what grows of itself or harvest the grapes of your untended vines. The land is to have a year of rest. ⁶Whatever the land yields during the sabbath year will be food for you—for yourself, your manservant and maidservant, and the hired worker and temporary resident who live among you, ⁷as well as for your livestock and the wild animals in your land. Whatever the land produces may be eaten.

The Year of Jubilee

⁸" 'Count off seven sabbaths of years—seven times seven years—so that the seven sabbaths of years amount to a period of forty-nine years. ⁹Then have the trumpet sounded everywhere on the tenth day of the seventh month; on the Day of Atonement sound the trumpet throughout your land. ¹⁰Consecrate the fiftieth year and proclaim liberty throughout the land to all its inhabitants. It shall be a jubilee for you; each one of you is to return to his family property and each to his own clan. ¹¹The fiftieth year shall be a jubilee for you; do not sow and do not reap what grows of itself or harvest the untended vines. ¹²For it is a jubilee and is to be holy for you; eat only what is taken directly from the fields.

¹³" 'In this Year of Jubilee everyone is to return to his own property.

¹⁴" 'If you sell land to one of your countrymen or buy any from him, do not take advantage of each other. ¹⁵You are to buy from your countryman on the basis of the number of years since the Jubilee. And he is to sell to you on the basis of the number of years left for harvesting crops. ¹⁶When the years are many, you are to increase the price, and when the years are few, you are to decrease the price, because what he is really selling you is the number of crops. ¹⁷Do not take advantage of each other, but fear your God. I am the LORD your God.

¹⁸" 'Follow my decrees and be careful to obey my laws, and you will live safely in the land. ¹⁹Then the land will yield its fruit, and you will eat your fill and live there in safety. ²⁰You may ask, "What will we eat in the seventh year if we do not plant or harvest our crops?" ²¹I will send you such a blessing in the sixth year that the land will yield enough for three years. ²²While you plant during the eighth year, you will eat from the old crop and will continue to eat from it until the harvest of the ninth year comes in.

²³" 'The land must not be sold permanently, because the land is mine and you are but aliens and my tenants. ²⁴Throughout the country that you hold as a possession, you must provide for the redemption of the land.

²⁵" 'If one of your countrymen becomes poor and sells some of his property, his nearest relative is to come and redeem what his countryman has sold. ²⁶If, however, a man has no one to redeem it for him but he himself prospers and acquires sufficient means to redeem it, ²⁷he is to determine the value for the years since he sold it and refund the balance to the man to whom he sold it; he can then go back to his own property. ²⁸But if he does not acquire the means to repay him, what he sold will remain in the possession of the buyer until the Year of Jubilee. It will be returned in the Jubilee, and he can then go back to his property.

²⁹" 'If a man sells a house in a walled

city, he retains the right of redemption a full year after its sale. During that time he may redeem it. ³⁰If it is not redeemed before a full year has passed, the house in the walled city shall belong permanently to the buyer and his descendants. It is not to be returned in the Jubilee. ³¹But houses in villages without walls around them are to be considered as open country. They can be redeemed, and they are to be returned in the Jubilee.

³²" 'The Levites always have the right to redeem their houses in the Levitical towns, which they possess. ³³So the property of the Levites is redeemable—that is, a house sold in any town they hold—and is to be returned in the Jubilee, because the houses in the towns of the Levites are their property among the Israelites. ³⁴But the pastureland belonging to their towns must not be sold; it is their permanent possession.

³⁵" 'If one of your countrymen becomes poor and is unable to support himself among you, help him as you would an alien or a temporary resident, so he can continue to live among you. ³⁶Do not take interest of any kind*ᵃ* from him, but fear your God, so that your countryman may continue to live among you. ³⁷You must not lend him money at interest or sell him food at a profit. ³⁸I am the LORD your God, who brought you out of Egypt to give you the land of Canaan and to be your God.

³⁹" 'If one of your countrymen becomes poor among you and sells himself to you, do not make him work as a slave. ⁴⁰He is to be treated as a hired worker or a temporary resident among you; he is to work for you until the Year of Jubilee. ⁴¹Then he and his children are to be released, and he will go back to his own clan and to the property of his forefathers. ⁴²Because the Israelites are my servants, whom I brought out of Egypt, they must not be sold as slaves. ⁴³Do not rule over them ruthlessly, but fear your God.

⁴⁴" 'Your male and female slaves are to come from the nations around you; from them you may buy slaves. ⁴⁵You may also buy some of the temporary residents living among you and members of their clans born in your country, and they will become your property. ⁴⁶You can will them to your children as inherited property and can make them slaves for life, but you must not rule over your fellow Israelites ruthlessly.

⁴⁷" 'If an alien or a temporary resident among you becomes rich and one of your countrymen becomes poor and sells himself to the alien living among you or to a member of the alien's clan, ⁴⁸he retains the right of redemption after he has sold himself. One of his relatives may redeem him: ⁴⁹An uncle or a cousin or any blood relative in his clan may redeem him. Or if he prospers, he may redeem himself. ⁵⁰He and his buyer are to count the time from the year he sold himself up to the Year of Jubilee. The price for his release is to be based on the rate paid to a hired man for that number of years. ⁵¹If many years remain, he must pay for his redemption a larger share of the price paid for him. ⁵²If only a few years remain until the Year of Jubilee, he is to compute that and pay for his redemption accordingly. ⁵³He is to be treated as a man hired from year to year; you must see to it that his owner does not rule over him ruthlessly.

⁵⁴" 'Even if he is not redeemed in any of these ways, he and his children are to be released in the Year of Jubilee, ⁵⁵for the Israelites belong to me as servants. They are my servants, whom I brought out of Egypt. I am the LORD your God.

Reward for Obedience

26 " 'Do not make idols or set up an image or a sacred stone for yourselves, and do not place a carved stone in your land to bow down before it. I am the LORD your God.

²" 'Observe my Sabbaths and have reverence for my sanctuary. I am the LORD.

³" 'If you follow my decrees and are careful to obey my commands, ⁴I will send you rain in its season, and the ground will yield its crops and the trees of the field their fruit. ⁵Your threshing will continue until grape harvest and the grape harvest will continue until planting, and you will eat all the food you want and live in safety in your land.

⁶" 'I will grant peace in the land, and

ᵃ36 Or take excessive interest; similarly in verse 37

you will lie down and no one will make you afraid. I will remove savage beasts from the land, and the sword will not pass through your country. [7]You will pursue your enemies, and they will fall by the sword before you. [8]Five of you will chase a hundred, and a hundred of you will chase ten thousand, and your enemies will fall by the sword before you.

[9]" 'I will look on you with favor and make you fruitful and increase your numbers, and I will keep my covenant with you. [10]You will still be eating last year's harvest when you will have to move it out to make room for the new. [11]I will put my dwelling place[a] among you, and I will not abhor you. [12]I will walk among you and be your God, and you will be my people. [13]I am the LORD your God, who brought you out of Egypt so that you would no longer be slaves to the Egyptians; I broke the bars of your yoke and enabled you to walk with heads held high.

Punishment for Disobedience

[14]" 'But if you will not listen to me and carry out all these commands, [15]and if

you reject my decrees and abhor my laws and fail to carry out all my commands and so violate my covenant, [16]then I will do this to you: I will bring upon you sudden terror, wasting diseases and fever that will destroy your sight and drain away your life. You will plant seed in vain, because your enemies will eat it. [17]I

will set my face against you so that you will be defeated by your enemies; those who hate you will rule over you, and you will flee even when no one is pursuing you.

[18]" 'If after all this you will not listen to me, I will punish you for your sins seven times over. [19]I will break down your stubborn pride and make the sky above you like iron and the ground beneath you like bronze. [20]Your strength will be spent in vain, because your soil will not yield its crops, nor will the trees of the land yield their fruit.

[21]" 'If you remain hostile toward me and refuse to listen to me, I will multiply your afflictions seven times over, as your sins deserve. [22]I will send wild animals against you, and they will rob you of your children, destroy your cattle and make you so few in number that your roads will be deserted.

[23]" 'If in spite of these things you do not accept my correction but continue to be hostile toward me, [24]I myself will be hostile toward you and will afflict you for your sins seven times over. [25]And I will bring the sword upon you to avenge the breaking of the covenant. When you withdraw into your cities, I will send a plague among you, and you will be given into enemy hands. [26]When I cut off your supply of bread, ten women will be able to bake your bread in one oven, and they will dole out the bread by weight. You will eat, but you will not be satisfied.

[27]" 'If in spite of this you still do not listen to me but continue to be hostile toward me, [28]then in my anger I will be hostile toward you, and I myself will punish you for your sins seven times over. [29]You will eat the flesh of your sons and the flesh of your daughters. [30]I will destroy your high places, cut down your incense altars and pile your dead bodies on the lifeless forms of your idols, and I will abhor you. [31]I will turn your cities into ruins and lay waste your sanctuaries, and I will take no delight in the pleasing aroma of your offerings. [32]I will lay waste the land, so that your enemies who live there will be appalled. [33]I will

God Means Business

Huh?

Leviticus 26:14–16

God loves us, but he also knows that, without him, we will get into big trouble. Some people think God gets mad and sends the trouble when we sin. But as we read the Bible, it is pretty clear that when we don't listen to him and don't obey him, our lives are a mess. That's why Jesus died—to pay the price for our sins.

[a] 11 Or *my tabernacle*

scatter you among the nations and will draw out my sword and pursue you. Your land will be laid waste, and your cities will lie in ruins. ³⁴Then the land will enjoy its sabbath years all the time that it lies desolate and you are in the country of your enemies; then the land will rest and enjoy its sabbaths. ³⁵All the time that it lies desolate, the land will have the rest it did not have during the sabbaths you lived in it.

³⁶" 'As for those of you who are left, I will make their hearts so fearful in the lands of their enemies that the sound of a windblown leaf will put them to flight. They will run as though fleeing from the sword, and they will fall, even though no one is pursuing them. ³⁷They will stumble over one another as though fleeing from the sword, even though no one is pursuing them. So you will not be able to stand before your enemies. ³⁸You will perish among the nations; the land of your enemies will devour you. ³⁹Those of you who are left will waste away in the lands of their enemies because of their sins; also because of their fathers' sins they will waste away.

⁴⁰" 'But if they will confess their sins and the sins of their fathers—their treachery against me and their hostility toward me, ⁴¹which made me hostile toward them so that I sent them into the land of their enemies—then when their uncircumcised hearts are humbled and they pay for their sin, ⁴²I will remember my covenant with Jacob and my covenant with Isaac and my covenant with Abraham, and I will remember the land. ⁴³For the land will be deserted by them and will enjoy its sabbaths while it lies desolate without them. They will pay for their sins because they rejected my laws and abhorred my decrees. ⁴⁴Yet in spite of this, when they are in the land of their enemies, I will not reject them or abhor them so as to destroy them completely, breaking my covenant with them. I am the LORD their God. ⁴⁵But for their sake I will remember the covenant with their ancestors whom I brought out of Egypt in the sight of the nations to be their God. I am the LORD.' "

⁴⁶These are the decrees, the laws and the regulations that the LORD established on Mount Sinai between himself and the Israelites through Moses.

Redeeming What Is the LORD's

27 The LORD said to Moses, ²"Speak to the Israelites and say to them: 'If anyone makes a special vow to dedicate persons to the LORD by giving equivalent values, ³set the value of a male between the ages of twenty and sixty at fifty shekels*ᵃ* of silver, according to the sanctuary shekel*ᵇ*; ⁴and if it is a female, set her value at thirty shekels.*ᶜ* ⁵If it is a person between the ages of five and twenty, set the value of a male at twenty shekels*ᵈ* and of a female at ten shekels.*ᵉ* ⁶If it is a person between one month and five years, set the value of a male at five shekels*ᶠ* of silver and that of a female at three shekels*ᵍ* of silver. ⁷If it is a person sixty years old or more, set the value of a male at fifteen shekels*ʰ* and of a female at ten shekels. ⁸If anyone making the vow is too poor to pay the specified amount, he is to present the person to the priest, who will set the value for him according to what the man making the vow can afford.

⁹" 'If what he vowed is an animal that is acceptable as an offering to the LORD, such an animal given to the LORD becomes holy. ¹⁰He must not exchange it or substitute a good one for a bad one, or a bad one for a good one; if he should substitute one animal for another, both it and the substitute become holy. ¹¹If what he vowed is a ceremonially unclean animal—one that is not acceptable as an offering to the LORD—the animal must be presented to the priest, ¹²who will judge its quality as good or bad. Whatever value the priest then sets, that is what it will be. ¹³If the owner wishes to redeem the animal, he must add a fifth to its value.

¹⁴" 'If a man dedicates his house as something holy to the LORD, the priest will judge its quality as good or bad.

ᵃ3 That is, about 1 1/4 pounds (about 0.6 kilogram); also in verse 16   *ᵇ3* That is, about 2/5 ounce (about 11.5 grams); also in verse 25   *ᶜ4* That is, about 12 ounces (about 0.3 kilogram)   *ᵈ5* That is, about 8 ounces (about 0.2 kilogram)   *ᵉ5* That is, about 4 ounces (about 110 grams); also in verse 7   *ᶠ6* That is, about 2 ounces (about 55 grams)   *ᵍ6* That is, about 1 1/4 ounces (about 35 grams)   *ʰ7* That is, about 6 ounces (about 170 grams)

Whatever value the priest then sets, so it will remain. ¹⁵If the man who dedicates his house redeems it, he must add a fifth to its value, and the house will again become his.

¹⁶" 'If a man dedicates to the LORD part of his family land, its value is to be set according to the amount of seed required for it—fifty shekels of silver to a homer*ᵃ* of barley seed. ¹⁷If he dedicates his field during the Year of Jubilee, the value that has been set remains. ¹⁸But if he dedicates his field after the Jubilee, the priest will determine the value according to the number of years that remain until the next Year of Jubilee, and its set value will be reduced. ¹⁹If the man who dedicates the field wishes to redeem it, he must add a fifth to its value, and the field will again become his. ²⁰If, however, he does not redeem the field, or if he has sold it to someone else, it can never be redeemed. ²¹When the field is released in the Jubilee, it will become holy, like a field devoted to the LORD; it will become the property of the priests.*ᵇ*

²²" 'If a man dedicates to the LORD a field he has bought, which is not part of his family land, ²³the priest will determine its value up to the Year of Jubilee, and the man must pay its value on that day as something holy to the LORD. ²⁴In the Year of Jubilee the field will revert to the person from whom he bought it, the one whose land it was. ²⁵Every value is to be set according to the sanctuary shekel, twenty gerahs to the shekel.

²⁶" 'No one, however, may dedicate the firstborn of an animal, since the firstborn already belongs to the LORD; whether an ox*ᶜ* or a sheep, it is the LORD's. ²⁷If it is

---

ᵃ16 That is, probably about 6 bushels (about 220 liters)   *ᵇ21* Or *priest*   *ᶜ26* The Hebrew word can include both male and female.

Week end.

Time for the Rules   Read Exodus 20:2–3 (page 94)

On Monday Kate wrote that "God's rules make sense" and went on to say that obeying God's commandments will "make us happier in the end." Kate is one sharp cookie! She understands a tough idea.

Most of us, at least sometimes, don't *feel* like God's laws and rules make sense. You know those times—when you know that lying will keep you out of trouble with your parents. Or when looking at the smartest kid's paper during a test will help you pass. Or when talking behind someone else's back is really fun. These are the times when it is easier, and sometimes more fun, to do the wrong thing.

Kate was right, when you think of life in terms of the long run. *Over time,* you'll be far happier and have better friendships if you trust the only true God to teach you how to live. When you say no to cheating or lying (even to your parents) or gossiping—you honor God. When you trust that God's advice is best in every situation, it's easier to do the right thing.

What about You?

❶ What is the hardest thing for you about trusting and obeying God's commandments?

❷ Which of the Ten Commandments is the toughest for you to follow? Talk to someone you trust and ask them to help you find some ways you can do better at obeying it.

❸ As you pray, ask God to help you obey that commandment.

Turn to page 172 for your next devotion.

one of the unclean animals, he may buy it back at its set value, adding a fifth of the value to it. If he does not redeem it, it is to be sold at its set value.

²⁸" 'But nothing that a man owns and devotes^a to the LORD—whether man or animal or family land—may be sold or redeemed; everything so devoted is most holy to the LORD.

²⁹" 'No person devoted to destruction^b may be ransomed; he must be put to death.

³⁰" 'A tithe of everything from the land, whether grain from the soil or fruit from the trees, belongs to the LORD; it is holy to the LORD. ³¹If a man redeems any of his tithe, he must add a fifth of the value to it. ³²The entire tithe of the herd and flock—every tenth animal that passes under the shepherd's rod—will be holy to the LORD. ³³He must not pick out the good from the bad or make any substitution. If he does make a substitution, both the animal and its substitute become holy and cannot be redeemed.' "

³⁴These are the commands the LORD gave Moses on Mount Sinai for the Israelites.

a28 The Hebrew term refers to the irrevocable giving over of things or persons to the LORD.   b29 The Hebrew term refers to the irrevocable giving over of things or persons to the LORD, often by totally destroying them.

Numbers

START

From the title you'd think this book was a math course. Really, it's not. The title refers to the numbers in a census that takes place in the beginning of the book. You see, the Israelites are still camped at the foot of Mount Sinai, right where they were at the end of the book of Exodus. And they didn't move a foot during the writing of that priest manual—the book of Leviticus.

In the book of Numbers, God tells Moses to make a head count of all adult males in the camp at the foot of Mount Sinai. The final figure comes to 603,550. That doesn't include women, children or Levite men. As priests, the Levites weren't allowed to fight, so the number gives Moses a count of available soldiers. So, in total, you get somewhere between 2 and 3 million Israelites. Big camp.

After celebrating their first annual Passover, the Israelites break camp and make for Kadesh Barnea. God tells Moses to send out a dozen spies to sneak into the promised land to get an idea of what they're up against. They return with a mixed report. The good news is it's a great place to live. The bad news is the people already living there may very well tear them to shreds. After hearing the news, the Israelites are ready to bag Moses and crawl back to Egypt. Bad move.

God had tested their faith, and they failed big-time. So instead of a short trip to the promised land, they sign themselves up for a 40-year detour through Nowheresville. The rest of the book covers the highs and lows of their wanderings—more pop quizzes from God, more flunking, trouble with the locals, a talking donkey and Moses' own major bad move. The book ends 39 years later when the Israelites are camped on the eastern side of the Jordan River, making plans to conquer the promised land.

Cast OF Characters

Moses (MOE-zus)
Yep, he's still with us—but he's getting to be kind of an old guy by now. Unfortunately, Mo makes a really bad move, hogs God's glory with a stupid water trick and finds out his ticket to the promised land has been revoked.

Caleb (CAY-lub) and Joshua
(JAH-shoo-wah)

Twelve spies went into the promised land to check out the enemy Israel would have to fight. Ten came back trembling in fear. Caleb and Josh alone said, "C'mon, we can *take* these guys!" (And of the 12, they alone return to the promised land later.)

Aaron (AIR-on)

Moses' brother and right-hand guy through thick and thin. In this book he gets a nice promotion to chief priest.

Balaam and Donkey (BAY-lum)

You've heard of knights in shining armor. Balaam wasn't one of those guys. He rode a donkey. And when he went to deliver a message, Balaam became so clueless that the donkey finally had to stop and talk some sense into him.

Balak (BAY-lack)

He was the king of Moab, one of Israel's enemies. He thought he was pretty powerful. Turns out he wasn't much of a king.

What's UP with That?

Remember good old Jacob? He's the one God nicknamed *Israel*, which is how the Israelites got the name of the nation: they were his descendants. He had 12 sons:

Reuben	Dan	Issachar
Simeon	Naphtali	Zebulun
Levi	Gad	Joseph
Judah	Asher	Benjamin

In Numbers chapters 32 and 34, Moses divides the land among 12 tribes—kind of like 12 states—of Israel. But now we've got a problem: On the map of ancient Israel, there are no states of *Levi* and *Joseph*. Instead, you find 2 other states: *Ephraim* and *Manasseh*. What's up with that?

It's simple. As priests, the Levites were supposed to be men of peace. They weren't allowed to fight or conquer the land. So instead of getting their own state, each tribe gave some of their land to the Levites. That way, the Israelites could be sure to have a priest nearby when they needed one. So, no state of *Levi*.

But we're still short one state. Moses took care of that too. To make up for the missing state of *Levi*, he divided Joseph's tribe into *two* half-tribes: *Ephraim* and *Manasseh*. These 2 guys were Joseph's sons, so everyone in Joseph's tribe was descended from one or the other. In the end, Israel wound up with 10 son-of-Jacob states, 2 son-of-Joseph states and priests scattered all over the country.

Snap Shots

- Roll call—Moses does a head count *(chapters 1—9)*

- Ready, march!—Israel hikes to Kadesh Barnea *(chapters 10—12)*

- Spy guys—the mission, the report *(chapter 13)*

- Wimps!—Israel chickens out, Moses goes for the glow, God says no *(chapters 14—20)*

- Detour—Israel spends 39 years learning to trust God *(chapters 20–21)*

- Almost there—just shy of the goal line, Israel prepares to conquer *(chapters 22—36)*

The Census

1 The LORD spoke to Moses in the Tent of Meeting in the Desert of Sinai on the first day of the second month of the second year after the Israelites came out of Egypt. He said: ²"Take a census of the whole Israelite community by their clans and families, listing every man by name, one by one. ³You and Aaron are to number by their divisions all the men in Israel twenty years old or more who are able to serve in the army. ⁴One man from each tribe, each the head of his family, is to help you. ⁵These are the names of the men who are to assist you:

from Reuben, Elizur son of Shedeur;
⁶ from Simeon, Shelumiel son of Zurishaddai;
⁷ from Judah, Nahshon son of Amminadab;
⁸ from Issachar, Nethanel son of Zuar;
⁹ from Zebulun, Eliab son of Helon;
¹⁰ from the sons of Joseph:
from Ephraim, Elishama son of Ammihud;
from Manasseh, Gamaliel son of Pedahzur;
¹¹ from Benjamin, Abidan son of Gideoni;
¹² from Dan, Ahiezer son of Ammishaddai;
¹³ from Asher, Pagiel son of Ocran;
¹⁴ from Gad, Eliasaph son of Deuel;
¹⁵ from Naphtali, Ahira son of Enan."

¹⁶These were the men appointed from the community, the leaders of their ancestral tribes. They were the heads of the clans of Israel. ¹⁷Moses and Aaron took these men whose names had been given, ¹⁸and they called the whole community together on the first day of the second month. The people indicated their ancestry by their clans and families, and the men twenty years old or more were listed by name, one by one, ¹⁹as the LORD commanded Moses. And so he counted them in the Desert of Sinai:

²⁰From the descendants of Reuben the firstborn son of Israel:
All the men twenty years old or more who were able to serve in the army were listed by name, one by one, according to the records of their clans and families. ²¹The number from the tribe of Reuben was 46,500.

²²From the descendants of Simeon:
All the men twenty years old or more who were able to serve in the army were counted and listed by name, one by one, according to the records of their clans and families. ²³The number from the tribe of Simeon was 59,300.

²⁴From the descendants of Gad:
All the men twenty years old or more who were able to serve in the army were listed by name, according to the records of their clans and families. ²⁵The number from the tribe of Gad was 45,650.

²⁶From the descendants of Judah:
All the men twenty years old or more who were able to serve in the army were listed by name, according to the records of their clans and families. ²⁷The number from the tribe of Judah was 74,600.

²⁸From the descendants of Issachar:
All the men twenty years old or more who were able to serve in the army were listed by name, according to the records of their clans and families. ²⁹The number from the tribe of Issachar was 54,400.

³⁰From the descendants of Zebulun:
All the men twenty years old or more who were able to serve in the army were listed by name, according to the records of their clans and families. ³¹The number from the tribe of Zebulun was 57,400.

³²From the sons of Joseph:
From the descendants of Ephraim:
All the men twenty years old or more who were able to serve in the army were listed by name, according to the records of their clans and families. ³³The number from the tribe of Ephraim was 40,500.

³⁴From the descendants of Manasseh:
All the men twenty years old or more who were able to serve in the army were listed by name, according to the records of their clans and families. ³⁵The number from the tribe of Manasseh was 32,200.

³⁶From the descendants of Benjamin:
All the men twenty years old or more who were able to serve in the army were listed by name, according to the records of their clans and families. ³⁷The number from the tribe of Benjamin was 35,400.

³⁸From the descendants of Dan:
All the men twenty years old or more who were able to serve in the army were listed by name, according to the records of their clans and families. ³⁹The number from the tribe of Dan was 62,700.

⁴⁰From the descendants of Asher:
All the men twenty years old or more who were able to serve in the army were listed by name, according to the records of their clans and families. ⁴¹The number from the tribe of Asher was 41,500.

⁴²From the descendants of Naphtali:
All the men twenty years old or more who were able to serve in the army were listed by name, according to the records of their clans and families. ⁴³The number from the tribe of Naphtali was 53,400.

⁴⁴These were the men counted by Moses and Aaron and the twelve leaders of Israel, each one representing his family. ⁴⁵All the Israelites twenty years old or more who were able to serve in Israel's army were counted according to their families. ⁴⁶The total number was 603,550.

⁴⁷The families of the tribe of Levi, however, were not counted along with the others. ⁴⁸The LORD had said to Moses: ⁴⁹"You must not count the tribe of Levi or include them in the census of the other Israelites. ⁵⁰Instead, appoint the Levites to be in charge of the tabernacle of the Testimony—over all its furnishings and everything belonging to it. They are to carry the tabernacle and all its furnishings; they are to take care of it and encamp around it. ⁵¹Whenever the tabernacle is to move, the Levites are to take it down, and whenever the tabernacle is to be set up, the Levites shall do it. Anyone else who goes near it shall be put to death. ⁵²The Israelites are to set up their tents by divisions, each man in his own camp under his own standard. ⁵³The Levites, however, are to set up their tents around the tabernacle of the Testimony so that wrath will not fall on the Israelite community. The Levites are to be responsible for the care of the tabernacle of the Testimony."

⁵⁴The Israelites did all this just as the LORD commanded Moses.

The Arrangement of the Tribal Camps

2 The LORD said to Moses and Aaron: ²"The Israelites are to camp around the Tent of Meeting some distance from it, each man under his standard with the banners of his family."

³On the east, toward the sunrise, the divisions of the camp of Judah are to encamp under their standard. The leader of the people of Judah is Nahshon son of Amminadab. ⁴His division numbers 74,600.

⁵The tribe of Issachar will camp next to them. The leader of the people of Issachar is Nethanel son of Zuar. ⁶His division numbers 54,400.

⁷The tribe of Zebulun will be next. The leader of the people of Zebulun is Eliab son of Helon. ⁸His division numbers 57,400.

⁹All the men assigned to the camp of Judah, according to their divisions, number 186,400. They will set out first.

¹⁰On the south will be the divisions of the camp of Reuben under their standard. The leader of the people of Reuben is Elizur son of Shedeur. ¹¹His division numbers 46,500.

¹²The tribe of Simeon will camp

next to them. The leader of the people of Simeon is Shelumiel son of Zurishaddai. [13]His division numbers 59,300.

[14]The tribe of Gad will be next. The leader of the people of Gad is Eliasaph son of Deuel.[a] [15]His division numbers 45,650.

[16]All the men assigned to the camp of Reuben, according to their divisions, number 151,450. They will set out second.

[17]Then the Tent of Meeting and the camp of the Levites will set out in the middle of the camps. They will set out in the same order as they encamp, each in his own place under his standard.

[18]On the west will be the divisions of the camp of Ephraim under their standard. The leader of the people of Ephraim is Elishama son of Ammihud. [19]His division numbers 40,500.

[20]The tribe of Manasseh will be next to them. The leader of the people of Manasseh is Gamaliel son of Pedahzur. [21]His division numbers 32,200.

[22]The tribe of Benjamin will be next. The leader of the people of Benjamin is Abidan son of Gideoni. [23]His division numbers 35,400.

[24]All the men assigned to the camp of Ephraim, according to their divisions, number 108,100. They will set out third.

[25]On the north will be the divisions of the camp of Dan, under their standard. The leader of the people of Dan is Ahiezer son of Ammishaddai. [26]His division numbers 62,700.

[27]The tribe of Asher will camp next to them. The leader of the people of Asher is Pagiel son of Ocran. [28]His division numbers 41,500.

[29]The tribe of Naphtali will be next. The leader of the people of Naphtali is Ahira son of Enan. [30]His division numbers 53,400.

[31]All the men assigned to the camp of Dan number 157,600. They

will set out last, under their standards.

[32]These are the Israelites, counted according to their families. All those in the camps, by their divisions, number 603,550. [33]The Levites, however, were not counted along with the other Israelites, as the LORD commanded Moses.

[34]So the Israelites did everything the LORD commanded Moses; that is the way they encamped under their standards, and that is the way they set out, each with his clan and family.

The Levites

3 This is the account of the family of Aaron and Moses at the time the LORD talked with Moses on Mount Sinai.

[2]The names of the sons of Aaron were Nadab the firstborn and Abihu, Eleazar and Ithamar. [3]Those were the names of Aaron's sons, the anointed priests, who were ordained to serve as priests. [4]Nadab and Abihu, however, fell dead before the LORD when they made an offering with unauthorized fire before him in the Desert of Sinai. They had no sons; so only Eleazar and Ithamar served as priests during the lifetime of their father Aaron.

[5]The LORD said to Moses, [6]"Bring the tribe of Levi and present them to Aaron the priest to assist him. [7]They are to perform duties for him and for the whole community at the Tent of Meeting by doing the work of the tabernacle. [8]They are to take care of all the furnishings of the Tent of Meeting, fulfilling the obligations of the Israelites by doing the work of the tabernacle. [9]Give the Levites to Aaron and his sons; they are the Israelites who are to be given wholly to him.[b] [10]Appoint Aaron and his sons to serve as priests; anyone else who approaches the sanctuary must be put to death."

[11]The LORD also said to Moses, [12]"I have

---

[a]14 Many manuscripts of the Masoretic Text, Samaritan Pentateuch and Vulgate (see also Num. 1:14); most manuscripts of the Masoretic Text *Reuel* [b]9 Most manuscripts of the Masoretic Text; some manuscripts of the Masoretic Text, Samaritan Pentateuch and Septuagint (see also Num. 8:16) *to me*

taken the Levites from among the Israelites in place of the first male offspring of every Israelite woman. The Levites are mine, [13]for all the firstborn are mine. When I struck down all the firstborn in Egypt, I set apart for myself every firstborn in Israel, whether man or animal. They are to be mine. I am the LORD."

[14]The LORD said to Moses in the Desert of Sinai, [15]"Count the Levites by their families and clans. Count every male a month old or more." [16]So Moses counted them, as he was commanded by the word of the LORD.

[17]These were the names of the sons of Levi:

Gershon, Kohath and Merari.

[18]These were the names of the Gershonite clans:

Libni and Shimei.

[19]The Kohathite clans:

Amram, Izhar, Hebron and Uzziel.

[20]The Merarite clans:

Mahli and Mushi.

These were the Levite clans, according to their families.

[21]To Gershon belonged the clans of the Libnites and Shimeites; these were the Gershonite clans. [22]The number of all the males a month old or more who were counted was 7,500. [23]The Gershonite clans were to camp on the west, behind the tabernacle. [24]The leader of the families of the Gershonites was Eliasaph son of Lael. [25]At the Tent of Meeting the Gershonites were responsible for the care of the tabernacle and tent, its coverings, the curtain at the entrance to the Tent of Meeting, [26]the curtains of the courtyard, the curtain at the entrance to the courtyard surrounding the tabernacle and altar, and the ropes—and everything related to their use.

[27]To Kohath belonged the clans of the Amramites, Izharites, Hebronites and Uzzielites; these were the Kohathite clans. [28]The number of all the males a month old or more was 8,600.[a] The Kohathites were responsible for the care of the sanctuary. [29]The Kohathite clans were to camp on the south side of the tabernacle. [30]The leader of the families of the Kohathite clans was Elizaphan son of Uzzi-

el. [31]They were responsible for the care of the ark, the table, the lampstand, the altars, the articles of the sanctuary used in ministering, the curtain, and everything related to their use. [32]The chief leader of the Levites was Eleazar son of Aaron, the priest. He was appointed over those who were responsible for the care of the sanctuary.

[33]To Merari belonged the clans of the Mahlites and the Mushites; these were the Merarite clans. [34]The number of all the males a month old or more who were counted was 6,200. [35]The leader of the families of the Merarite clans was Zuriel son of Abihail; they were to camp on the north side of the tabernacle. [36]The Merarites were appointed to take care of the frames of the tabernacle, its crossbars, posts, bases, all its equipment, and everything related to their use, [37]as well as the posts of the surrounding courtyard with their bases, tent pegs and ropes.

[38]Moses and Aaron and his sons were to camp to the east of the tabernacle, toward the sunrise, in front of the Tent of Meeting. They were responsible for the care of the sanctuary on behalf of the Israelites. Anyone else who approached the sanctuary was to be put to death.

[39]The total number of Levites counted at the LORD's command by Moses and Aaron according to their clans, including every male a month old or more, was 22,000.

[40]The LORD said to Moses, "Count all the firstborn Israelite males who are a month old or more and make a list of their names. [41]Take the Levites for me in place of all the firstborn of the Israelites, and the livestock of the Levites in place of all the firstborn of the livestock of the Israelites. I am the LORD."

[42]So Moses counted all the firstborn of the Israelites, as the LORD commanded him. [43]The total number of firstborn males a month old or more, listed by name, was 22,273.

[44]The LORD also said to Moses, [45]"Take

_____

[a]28 Hebrew; some Septuagint manuscripts *8,300*

the Levites in place of all the firstborn of Israel, and the livestock of the Levites in place of their livestock. The Levites are to be mine. I am the LORD. [46]To redeem the 273 firstborn Israelites who exceed the number of the Levites, [47]collect five shekels[a] for each one, according to the sanctuary shekel, which weighs twenty gerahs. [48]Give the money for the redemption of the additional Israelites to Aaron and his sons."

[49]So Moses collected the redemption money from those who exceeded the number redeemed by the Levites. [50]From the firstborn of the Israelites he collected silver weighing 1,365 shekels,[b] according to the sanctuary shekel. [51]Moses gave the redemption money to Aaron and his sons, as he was commanded by the word of the LORD.

The Kohathites

4 The LORD said to Moses and Aaron: [2]"Take a census of the Kohathite branch of the Levites by their clans and families. [3]Count all the men from thirty to fifty years of age who come to serve in the work in the Tent of Meeting.

[4]"This is the work of the Kohathites in the Tent of Meeting: the care of the most holy things. [5]When the camp is to move, Aaron and his sons are to go in and take down the shielding curtain and cover the ark of the Testimony with it. [6]Then they are to cover this with hides of sea cows,[c] spread a cloth of solid blue over that and put the poles in place.

[7]"Over the table of the Presence they are to spread a blue cloth and put on it the plates, dishes and bowls, and the jars for drink offerings; the bread that is continually there is to remain on it. [8]Over these they are to spread a scarlet cloth, cover that with hides of sea cows and put its poles in place.

[9]"They are to take a blue cloth and cover the lampstand that is for light, together with its lamps, its wick trimmers and trays, and all its jars for the oil used to supply it. [10]Then they are to wrap it and all its accessories in a covering of hides of sea cows and put it on a carrying frame.

[11]"Over the gold altar they are to spread a blue cloth and cover that with hides of sea cows and put its poles in place.

[12]"They are to take all the articles used for ministering in the sanctuary, wrap them in a blue cloth, cover that with hides of sea cows and put them on a carrying frame.

[13]"They are to remove the ashes from the bronze altar and spread a purple cloth over it. [14]Then they are to place on it all the utensils used for ministering at the altar, including the firepans, meat forks, shovels and sprinkling bowls. Over it they are to spread a covering of hides of sea cows and put its poles in place.

[15]"After Aaron and his sons have finished covering the holy furnishings and all the holy articles, and when the camp is ready to move, the Kohathites are to come to do the carrying. But they must not touch the holy things or they will die. The Kohathites are to carry those things that are in the Tent of Meeting.

[16]"Eleazar son of Aaron, the priest, is to have charge of the oil for the light, the fragrant incense, the regular grain offering and the anointing oil. He is to be in charge of the entire tabernacle and everything in it, including its holy furnishings and articles."

[17]The LORD said to Moses and Aaron, [18]"See that the Kohathite tribal clans are not cut off from the Levites. [19]So that they may live and not die when they come near the most holy things, do this for them: Aaron and his sons are to go into the sanctuary and assign to each man his work and what he is to carry. [20]But the Kohathites must not go in to look at the holy things, even for a moment, or they will die."

The Gershonites

[21]The LORD said to Moses, [22]"Take a census also of the Gershonites by their families and clans. [23]Count all the men from thirty to fifty years of age who come to serve in the work at the Tent of Meeting.

[24]"This is the service of the Gershonite clans as they work and carry burdens:

[a]47 That is, about 2 ounces (about 55 grams)
[b]50 That is, about 35 pounds (about 15.5 kilograms)
[c]6 That is, dugongs; also in verses 8, 10, 11, 12, 14 and 25

anything that comes from the grapevine, not even the seeds or skins.

5 " 'During the entire period of his vow of separation no razor may be used on his head. He must be holy until the period of his separation to the LORD is over; he must let the hair of his head grow long. 6Throughout the period of his separation to the LORD he must not go near a dead body. 7Even if his own father or mother or brother or sister dies, he must not make himself ceremonially unclean on account of them, because the symbol of his separation to God is on his head. 8Throughout the period of his separation he is consecrated to the LORD.

9 " 'If someone dies suddenly in his presence, thus defiling the hair he has dedicated, he must shave his head on the day of his cleansing—the seventh day. 10Then on the eighth day he must bring two doves or two young pigeons to the priest at the entrance to the Tent of Meeting. 11The priest is to offer one as a sin offering and the other as a burnt offering to make atonement for him because he sinned by being in the presence of the dead body. That same day he is to consecrate his head. 12He must dedicate himself to the LORD for the period of his separation and must bring a year-old male lamb as a guilt offering. The previous days do not count, because he became defiled during his separation.

13 " 'Now this is the law for the Nazirite when the period of his separation is over. He is to be brought to the entrance to the Tent of Meeting. 14There he is to present his offerings to the LORD: a year-old male lamb without defect for a burnt offering, a year-old ewe lamb without defect for a sin offering, a ram without defect for a fellowship offering,[a] 15together with their grain offerings and drink offerings, and a basket of bread made without yeast—cakes of fine flour mixed with oil, and wafers spread with oil.

16 " 'The priest is to present them before the LORD and make the sin offering and the burnt offering. 17He is to present the basket of unleavened bread and is to sacrifice the ram as a fellowship offering to the LORD, together with its grain offering and drink offering.

18 " 'Then at the entrance to the Tent of Meeting, the Nazirite must shave off the hair that he dedicated. He is to take the hair and put it in the fire that is under the sacrifice of the fellowship offering.

19 " 'After the Nazirite has shaved off the hair of his dedication, the priest is to place in his hands a boiled shoulder of the ram, and a cake and a wafer from the basket, both made without yeast. 20The priest shall then wave them before the LORD as a wave offering; they are holy and belong to the priest, together with the breast that was waved and the thigh that was presented. After that, the Nazirite may drink wine.

21 " 'This is the law of the Nazirite who vows his offering to the LORD in accordance with his separation, in addition to whatever else he can afford. He must fulfill the vow he has made, according to the law of the Nazirite.' "

The Priestly Blessing

22The LORD said to Moses, 23"Tell Aaron and his sons, 'This is how you are to bless the Israelites. Say to them:

24 " ' "The LORD bless you
          and keep you;
25 the LORD make his face shine upon
               you
          and be gracious to you;

Bless You!

Huh?

Numbers 6:22–27
The word *bless* means "to give a good word." This blessing is still used today as God's "good words" to us. God *is* doing those things for *you* right now. God is talking about you ("bless you") and is making sure you are being protected ("keep you"). God is even *shining* on you, and being cool ("gracious") to you. He's looking right at you, right now, and he's trying to give you a deep, inside calm. Wow! Do you feel his blessing?

---

[a]14 Traditionally *peace offering*; also in verses 17 and 18

²⁶the LORD turn his face toward you
and give you peace." '

²⁷"So they will put my name on the Israelites, and I will bless them."

Offerings at the Dedication of the Tabernacle

7 When Moses finished setting up the
tabernacle, he anointed it and consecrated it and all its furnishings. He also
anointed and consecrated the altar and
all its utensils. ²Then the leaders of Israel,
the heads of families who were the tribal
leaders in charge of those who were
counted, made offerings. ³They brought
as their gifts before the LORD six covered
carts and twelve oxen—an ox from each
leader and a cart from every two. These
they presented before the tabernacle.

⁴The LORD said to Moses, ⁵"Accept
these from them, that they may be used
in the work at the Tent of Meeting. Give
them to the Levites as each man's work
requires."

⁶So Moses took the carts and oxen and
gave them to the Levites. ⁷He gave two
carts and four oxen to the Gershonites,
as their work required, ⁸and he gave four
carts and eight oxen to the Merarites, as
their work required. They were all under
the direction of Ithamar son of Aaron,
the priest. ⁹But Moses did not give any to
the Kohathites, because they were to carry on their shoulders the holy things, for
which they were responsible.

¹⁰When the altar was anointed, the
leaders brought their offerings for its
dedication and presented them before the
altar. ¹¹For the LORD had said to Moses,
"Each day one leader is to bring his offering for the dedication of the altar."

¹²The one who brought his offering on
the first day was Nahshon son of Amminadab of the tribe of Judah.

¹³His offering was one silver plate
weighing a hundred and thirty shekels,ᵃ and one silver sprinkling bowl
weighing seventy shekels,ᵇ both according to the sanctuary shekel,
each filled with fine flour mixed
with oil as a grain offering; ¹⁴one
gold dish weighing ten shekels,ᶜ
filled with incense; ¹⁵one young
bull, one ram and one male lamb a
year old, for a burnt offering; ¹⁶one

male goat for a sin offering; ¹⁷and
two oxen, five rams, five male goats
and five male lambs a year old, to be
sacrificed as a fellowship offering.ᵈ
This was the offering of Nahshon
son of Amminadab.

¹⁸On the second day Nethanel son of
Zuar, the leader of Issachar, brought his
offering.

¹⁹The offering he brought was one
silver plate weighing a hundred and
thirty shekels, and one silver sprinkling bowl weighing seventy shekels, both according to the sanctuary
shekel, each filled with fine flour
mixed with oil as a grain offering;
²⁰one gold dish weighing ten shekels, filled with incense; ²¹one young
bull, one ram and one male lamb a
year old, for a burnt offering; ²²one
male goat for a sin offering; ²³and
two oxen, five rams, five male goats
and five male lambs a year old, to be
sacrificed as a fellowship offering.
This was the offering of Nethanel
son of Zuar.

²⁴On the third day, Eliab son of Helon,
the leader of the people of Zebulun,
brought his offering.

²⁵His offering was one silver plate
weighing a hundred and thirty shekels, and one silver sprinkling bowl
weighing seventy shekels, both according to the sanctuary shekel,
each filled with fine flour mixed
with oil as a grain offering; ²⁶one gold
dish weighing ten shekels, filled
with incense; ²⁷one young bull, one
ram and one male lamb a year old,
for a burnt offering; ²⁸one male goat
for a sin offering; ²⁹and two oxen,
five rams, five male goats and five
male lambs a year old, to be sacrificed as a fellowship offering. This
was the offering of Eliab son of
Helon.

ᵃ13 That is, about 3 1/4 pounds (about 1.5
kilograms); also elsewhere in this chapter   ᵇ13 That
is, about 1 3/4 pounds (about 0.8 kilogram); also
elsewhere in this chapter   ᶜ14 That is, about
4 ounces (about 110 grams); also elsewhere in this
chapter   ᵈ17 Traditionally *peace offering*; also
elsewhere in this chapter

[30]On the fourth day Elizur son of Shedeur, the leader of the people of Reuben, brought his offering.

[31]His offering was one silver plate weighing a hundred and thirty shekels, and one silver sprinkling bowl weighing seventy shekels, both according to the sanctuary shekel, each filled with fine flour mixed with oil as a grain offering; [32]one gold dish weighing ten shekels, filled with incense; [33]one young bull, one ram and one male lamb a year old, for a burnt offering; [34]one male goat for a sin offering; [35]and two oxen, five rams, five male goats and five male lambs a year old, to be sacrificed as a fellowship offering. This was the offering of Elizur son of Shedeur.

[36]On the fifth day Shelumiel son of Zurishaddai, the leader of the people of Simeon, brought his offering.

[37]His offering was one silver plate weighing a hundred and thirty shekels, and one silver sprinkling bowl weighing seventy shekels, both according to the sanctuary shekel, each filled with fine flour mixed with oil as a grain offering; [38]one gold dish weighing ten shekels, filled with incense; [39]one young bull, one ram and one male lamb a year old, for a burnt offering; [40]one male goat for a sin offering; [41]and two oxen, five rams, five male goats and five male lambs a year old, to be sacrificed as a fellowship offering. This was the offering of Shelumiel son of Zurishaddai.

[42]On the sixth day Eliasaph son of Deuel, the leader of the people of Gad, brought his offering.

[43]His offering was one silver plate weighing a hundred and thirty shekels, and one silver sprinkling bowl weighing seventy shekels, both according to the sanctuary shekel, each filled with fine flour mixed with oil as a grain offering; [44]one gold dish weighing ten shekels, filled with incense; [45]one young bull, one ram and one male lamb a year old, for a burnt offering; [46]one male goat

for a sin offering; [47]and two oxen, five rams, five male goats and five male lambs a year old, to be sacrificed as a fellowship offering. This was the offering of Eliasaph son of Deuel.

[48]On the seventh day Elishama son of Ammihud, the leader of the people of Ephraim, brought his offering.

[49]His offering was one silver plate weighing a hundred and thirty shekels, and one silver sprinkling bowl weighing seventy shekels, both according to the sanctuary shekel, each filled with fine flour mixed with oil as a grain offering; [50]one gold dish weighing ten shekels, filled with incense; [51]one young bull, one ram and one male lamb a year old, for a burnt offering; [52]one male goat for a sin offering; [53]and two oxen, five rams, five male goats and five male lambs a year old, to be sacrificed as a fellowship offering. This was the offering of Elishama son of Ammihud.

[54]On the eighth day Gamaliel son of Pedahzur, the leader of the people of Manasseh, brought his offering.

[55]His offering was one silver plate weighing a hundred and thirty shekels, and one silver sprinkling bowl weighing seventy shekels, both according to the sanctuary shekel, each filled with fine flour mixed with oil as a grain offering; [56]one gold dish weighing ten shekels, filled with incense; [57]one young bull, one ram and one male lamb a year old, for a burnt offering; [58]one male goat for a sin offering; [59]and two oxen, five rams, five male goats and five male lambs a year old, to be sacrificed as a fellowship offering. This was the offering of Gamaliel son of Pedahzur.

[60]On the ninth day Abidan son of Gideoni, the leader of the people of Benjamin, brought his offering.

[61]His offering was one silver plate weighing a hundred and thirty shekels, and one silver sprinkling bowl weighing seventy shekels, both

according to the sanctuary shekel, each filled with fine flour mixed with oil as a grain offering; [62]one gold dish weighing ten shekels, filled with incense; [63]one young bull, one ram and one male lamb a year old, for a burnt offering; [64]one male goat for a sin offering; [65]and two oxen, five rams, five male goats and five male lambs a year old, to be sacrificed as a fellowship offering. This was the offering of Abidan son of Gideoni.

[66]On the tenth day Ahiezer son of Ammishaddai, the leader of the people of Dan, brought his offering.

[67]His offering was one silver plate weighing a hundred and thirty shekels, and one silver sprinkling bowl weighing seventy shekels, both according to the sanctuary shekel, each filled with fine flour mixed with oil as a grain offering; [68]one gold dish weighing ten shekels, filled with incense; [69]one young bull, one ram and one male lamb a year old, for a burnt offering; [70]one male goat for a sin offering; [71]and two oxen, five rams, five male goats and five male lambs a year old, to be sacrificed as a fellowship offering. This was the offering of Ahiezer son of Ammishaddai.

[72]On the eleventh day Pagiel son of Ocran, the leader of the people of Asher, brought his offering.

[73]His offering was one silver plate weighing a hundred and thirty shekels, and one silver sprinkling bowl weighing seventy shekels, both according to the sanctuary shekel, each filled with fine flour mixed with oil as a grain offering; [74]one gold dish weighing ten shekels, filled with incense; [75]one young bull, one ram and one male lamb a year old, for a burnt offering; [76]one male goat for a sin offering; [77]and two oxen, five rams, five male goats and five male lambs a year old, to be sacrificed as a fellowship offering. This was the offering of Pagiel son of Ocran.

[78]On the twelfth day Ahira son of Enan, the leader of the people of Naphtali, brought his offering.

[79]His offering was one silver plate weighing a hundred and thirty shekels, and one silver sprinkling bowl weighing seventy shekels, both according to the sanctuary shekel, each filled with fine flour mixed with oil as a grain offering; [80]one gold dish weighing ten shekels, filled with incense; [81]one young bull, one ram and one male lamb a year old, for a burnt offering; [82]one male goat for a sin offering; [83]and two oxen, five rams, five male goats and five male lambs a year old, to be sacrificed as a fellowship offering. This was the offering of Ahira son of Enan.

[84]These were the offerings of the Israelite leaders for the dedication of the altar when it was anointed: twelve silver plates, twelve silver sprinkling bowls and twelve gold dishes. [85]Each silver plate weighed a hundred and thirty shekels, and each sprinkling bowl seventy shekels. Altogether, the silver dishes weighed two thousand four hundred shekels,[a] according to the sanctuary shekel. [86]The twelve gold dishes filled with incense weighed ten shekels each, according to the sanctuary shekel. Altogether, the gold dishes weighed a hundred and twenty shekels.[b] [87]The total number of animals for the burnt offering came to twelve young bulls, twelve rams and twelve male lambs a year old, together with their grain offering. Twelve male goats were used for the sin offering. [88]The total number of animals for the sacrifice of the fellowship offering came to twenty-four oxen, sixty rams, sixty male goats and sixty male lambs a year old. These were the offerings for the dedication of the altar after it was anointed.

[89]When Moses entered the Tent of Meeting to speak with the LORD, he heard the voice speaking to him from between the two cherubim above the atonement cover on the ark of the Testimony. And he spoke with him.

[a]85 That is, about 60 pounds (about 28 kilograms)
[b]86 That is, about 3 pounds (about 1.4 kilograms)

Setting Up the Lamps

8 The LORD said to Moses, ²"Speak to Aaron and say to him, 'When you set up the seven lamps, they are to light the area in front of the lampstand.' "

³Aaron did so; he set up the lamps so that they faced forward on the lampstand, just as the LORD commanded Moses. ⁴This is how the lampstand was made: It was made of hammered gold— from its base to its blossoms. The lampstand was made exactly like the pattern the LORD had shown Moses.

The Setting Apart of the Levites

⁵The LORD said to Moses: ⁶"Take the Levites from among the other Israelites and make them ceremonially clean. ⁷To purify them, do this: Sprinkle the water of cleansing on them; then have them shave their whole bodies and wash their clothes, and so purify themselves. ⁸Have them take a young bull with its grain offering of fine flour mixed with oil; then you are to take a second young bull for a sin offering. ⁹Bring the Levites to the front of the Tent of Meeting and assemble the whole Israelite community. ¹⁰You are to bring the Levites before the LORD, and the Israelites are to lay their hands on them. ¹¹Aaron is to present the Levites before the LORD as a wave offering from the Israelites, so that they may be ready to do the work of the LORD.

¹²"After the Levites lay their hands on the heads of the bulls, use the one for a sin offering to the LORD and the other for a burnt offering, to make atonement for the Levites. ¹³Have the Levites stand in front of Aaron and his sons and then present them as a wave offering to the LORD. ¹⁴In this way you are to set the Levites apart from the other Israelites, and the Levites will be mine.

¹⁵"After you have purified the Levites and presented them as a wave offering, they are to come to do their work at the Tent of Meeting. ¹⁶They are the Israelites who are to be given wholly to me. I have taken them as my own in place of the firstborn, the first male offspring from every Israelite woman. ¹⁷Every firstborn male in Israel, whether man or animal, is mine. When I struck down all the first-born in Egypt, I set them apart for myself. ¹⁸And I have taken the Levites in place of all the firstborn sons in Israel. ¹⁹Of all the Israelites, I have given the Levites as gifts to Aaron and his sons to do the work at the Tent of Meeting on behalf of the Israelites and to make atonement for them so that no plague will strike the Israelites when they go near the sanctuary."

²⁰Moses, Aaron and the whole Israelite community did with the Levites just as the LORD commanded Moses. ²¹The Levites purified themselves and washed their clothes. Then Aaron presented them as a wave offering before the LORD and made atonement for them to purify them. ²²After that, the Levites came to do their work at the Tent of Meeting under the supervision of Aaron and his sons. They did with the Levites just as the LORD commanded Moses.

²³The LORD said to Moses, ²⁴"This applies to the Levites: Men twenty-five years old or more shall come to take part in the work at the Tent of Meeting, ²⁵but at the age of fifty, they must retire from their regular service and work no longer. ²⁶They may assist their brothers in performing their duties at the Tent of Meeting, but they themselves must not do the work. This, then, is how you are to assign the responsibilities of the Levites."

The Passover

9 The LORD spoke to Moses in the Desert of Sinai in the first month of the second year after they came out of Egypt. He said, ²"Have the Israelites celebrate the Passover at the appointed time. ³Celebrate it at the appointed time, at twilight on the fourteenth day of this month, in accordance with all its rules and regulations."

⁴So Moses told the Israelites to celebrate the Passover, ⁵and they did so in the Desert of Sinai at twilight on the fourteenth day of the first month. The Israelites did everything just as the LORD commanded Moses.

⁶But some of them could not celebrate the Passover on that day because they were ceremonially unclean on account of a dead body. So they came to Moses and Aaron that same day ⁷and said to Moses,

"We have become unclean because of a dead body, but why should we be kept from presenting the LORD's offering with the other Israelites at the appointed time?"

⁸Moses answered them, "Wait until I find out what the LORD commands concerning you."

⁹Then the LORD said to Moses, ¹⁰"Tell the Israelites: 'When any of you or your descendants are unclean because of a dead body or are away on a journey, they may still celebrate the LORD's Passover. ¹¹They are to celebrate it on the fourteenth day of the second month at twilight. They are to eat the lamb, together with unleavened bread and bitter herbs. ¹²They must not leave any of it till morning or break any of its bones. When they celebrate the Passover, they must follow all the regulations. ¹³But if a man who is ceremonially clean and not on a journey fails to celebrate the Passover, that person must be cut off from his people because he did not present the LORD's offering at the appointed time. That man will bear the consequences of his sin.

¹⁴"'An alien living among you who wants to celebrate the LORD's Passover must do so in accordance with its rules and regulations. You must have the same regulations for the alien and the native-born.'"

The Cloud Above the Tabernacle

¹⁵On the day the tabernacle, the Tent of the Testimony, was set up, the cloud covered it. From evening till morning the cloud above the tabernacle looked like fire. ¹⁶That is how it continued to be; the cloud covered it, and at night it looked like fire. ¹⁷Whenever the cloud lifted from above the Tent, the Israelites set out; wherever the cloud settled, the Israelites encamped. ¹⁸At the LORD's command the Israelites set out, and at his command they encamped. As long as the cloud stayed over the tabernacle, they remained in camp. ¹⁹When the cloud remained over the tabernacle a long time, the Israelites obeyed the LORD's order and did not set out. ²⁰Sometimes the cloud was over the tabernacle only a few days; at the LORD's command they would encamp, and then at his command they

would set out. ²¹Sometimes the cloud stayed only from evening till morning, and when it lifted in the morning, they set out. Whether by day or by night, whenever the cloud lifted, they set out. ²²Whether the cloud stayed over the tabernacle for two days or a month or a year, the Israelites would remain in camp and not set out; but when it lifted, they would set out. ²³At the LORD's command they encamped, and at the LORD's command they set out. They obeyed the LORD's order, in accordance with his command through Moses.

The Silver Trumpets

10 The LORD said to Moses: ²"Make two trumpets of hammered silver, and use them for calling the community together and for having the camps set out. ³When both are sounded, the whole community is to assemble before you at the entrance to the Tent of Meeting. ⁴If only one is sounded, the leaders—the heads of the clans of Israel—are to assemble before you. ⁵When a trumpet blast is sounded, the tribes camping on the east are to set out. ⁶At the sounding of a second blast, the camps on the south are to set out. The blast will be the signal for setting out. ⁷To gather the assembly, blow the trumpets, but not with the same signal.

⁸"The sons of Aaron, the priests, are to blow the trumpets. This is to be a lasting ordinance for you and the generations to come. ⁹When you go into battle in your own land against an enemy who is oppressing you, sound a blast on the trumpets. Then you will be remembered by the LORD your God and rescued from your enemies. ¹⁰Also at your times of rejoicing—your appointed feasts and New Moon festivals—you are to sound the trumpets over your burnt offerings and fellowship offerings,ᵃ and they will be a memorial for you before your God. I am the LORD your God."

The Israelites Leave Sinai

¹¹On the twentieth day of the second month of the second year, the cloud lift-

ᵃ10 Traditionally *peace offerings*

ed from above the tabernacle of the Testimony. ¹²Then the Israelites set out from the Desert of Sinai and traveled from place to place until the cloud came to rest in the Desert of Paran. ¹³They set out, this first time, at the LORD's command through Moses.

¹⁴The divisions of the camp of Judah went first, under their standard. Nahshon son of Amminadab was in command. ¹⁵Nethanel son of Zuar was over the division of the tribe of Issachar, ¹⁶and Eliab son of Helon was over the division of the tribe of Zebulun. ¹⁷Then the tabernacle was taken down, and the Gershonites and Merarites, who carried it, set out.

¹⁸The divisions of the camp of Reuben went next, under their standard. Elizur son of Shedeur was in command. ¹⁹Shelumiel son of Zurishaddai was over the division of the tribe of Simeon, ²⁰and Eliasaph son of Deuel was over the division of the tribe of Gad. ²¹Then the Kohathites set out, carrying the holy things. The tabernacle was to be set up before they arrived.

²²The divisions of the camp of Ephraim went next, under their standard. Elishama son of Ammihud was in command. ²³Gamaliel son of Pedahzur was over the division of the tribe of Manasseh, ²⁴and Abidan son of Gideoni was over the division of the tribe of Benjamin.

²⁵Finally, as the rear guard for all the units, the divisions of the camp of Dan set out, under their standard. Ahiezer son of Ammishaddai was in command. ²⁶Pagiel son of Ocran was over the division of the tribe of Asher, ²⁷and Ahira son of Enan was over the division of the tribe of Naphtali. ²⁸This was the order of march for the Israelite divisions as they set out.

²⁹Now Moses said to Hobab son of Reuel the Midianite, Moses' father-in-law, "We are setting out for the place about which the LORD said, 'I will give it to you.' Come with us and we will treat you well, for the LORD has promised good things to Israel."

³⁰He answered, "No, I will not go; I am going back to my own land and my own people."

³¹But Moses said, "Please do not leave us. You know where we should camp in the desert, and you can be our eyes.

³²If you come with us, we will share with you whatever good things the LORD gives us."

³³So they set out from the mountain of the LORD and traveled for three days. The ark of the covenant of the LORD went before them during those three days to find them a place to rest. ³⁴The cloud of the LORD was over them by day when they set out from the camp.

³⁵Whenever the ark set out, Moses said,

"Rise up, O LORD!
    May your enemies be scattered;
    may your foes flee before you."

³⁶Whenever it came to rest, he said,

"Return, O LORD,
    to the countless thousands of
        Israel."

Fire From the LORD

11 Now the people complained about their hardships in the hearing of the LORD, and when he heard them his anger was aroused. Then fire from the LORD burned among them and consumed some of the outskirts of the camp. ²When the people cried out to Moses, he prayed to the LORD and the fire died down. ³So that place was called Taberah,ᵃ because fire from the LORD had burned among them.

Quail From the LORD

⁴The rabble with them began to crave other food, and again the Israelites started wailing and said, "If only we had meat to eat! ⁵We remember the fish we ate in Egypt at no cost—also the cucumbers, melons, leeks, onions and garlic. ⁶But now we have lost our appetite; we never see anything but this manna!"

⁷The manna was like coriander seed and looked like resin. ⁸The people went around gathering it, and then ground it in a handmill or crushed it in a mortar. They cooked it in a pot or made it into cakes. And it tasted like something made with olive oil. ⁹When the dew settled on the camp at night, the manna also came down.

ᵃ3 *Taberah* means *burning.*

[10]Moses heard the people of every family wailing, each at the entrance to his tent. The LORD became exceedingly angry, and Moses was troubled. [11]He asked the LORD, "Why have you brought this trouble on your servant? What have I done to displease you that you put the burden of all these people on me? [12]Did I conceive all these people? Did I give them birth? Why do you tell me to carry them in my arms, as a nurse carries an infant, to the land you promised on oath to their forefathers? [13]Where can I get meat for all these people? They keep wailing to me, 'Give us meat to eat!' [14]I cannot carry all these people by myself; the burden is too heavy for me. [15]If this is how you are going to treat me, put me to death right now—if I have found favor in your eyes—and do not let me face my own ruin."

[16]The LORD said to Moses: "Bring me seventy of Israel's elders who are known to you as leaders and officials among the people. Have them come to the Tent of Meeting, that they may stand there with you. [17]I will come down and speak with you there, and I will take of the Spirit that is on you and put the Spirit on them. They will help you carry the burden of the people so that you will not have to carry it alone.

[18]"Tell the people: 'Consecrate yourselves in preparation for tomorrow, when you will eat meat. The LORD heard you when you wailed, "If only we had meat to eat! We were better off in Egypt!" Now the LORD will give you meat, and you will eat it. [19]You will not eat it for just one day, or two days, or five, ten or twenty days, [20]but for a whole month—until it comes out of your nostrils and you loathe it—because you have rejected the LORD, who is among you, and have wailed before him, saying, "Why did we ever leave Egypt?" ' "

[21]But Moses said, "Here I am among six hundred thousand men on foot, and you say, 'I will give them meat to eat for a whole month!' [22]Would they have enough if flocks and herds were slaughtered for them? Would they have enough if all the fish in the sea were caught for them?"

[23]The LORD answered Moses, "Is the LORD's arm too short? You will now see whether or not what I say will come true for you."

[24]So Moses went out and told the people what the LORD had said. He brought together seventy of their elders and had them stand around the Tent. [25]Then the LORD came down in the cloud and spoke with him, and he took of the Spirit that was on him and put the Spirit on the seventy elders. When the Spirit rested on them, they prophesied, but they did not do so again.[a]

[26]However, two men, whose names were Eldad and Medad, had remained in the camp. They were listed among the elders, but did not go out to the Tent. Yet the Spirit also rested on them, and they prophesied in the camp. [27]A young man ran and told Moses, "Eldad and Medad are prophesying in the camp."

[28]Joshua son of Nun, who had been Moses' aide since youth, spoke up and said, "Moses, my lord, stop them!"

[29]But Moses replied, "Are you jealous for my sake? I wish that all the LORD's people were prophets and that the LORD would put his Spirit on them!" [30]Then Moses and the elders of Israel returned to the camp.

[31]Now a wind went out from the LORD and drove quail in from the sea. It brought them[b] down all around the camp to about three feet[c] above the ground, as far as a day's walk in any direction. [32]All that day and night and all the next day the people went out and gathered quail. No one gathered less than ten homers.[d] Then they spread them out all around the camp. [33]But while the meat was still between their teeth and before it could be consumed, the anger of the LORD burned against the people, and he struck them with a severe plague. [34]Therefore the place was named Kibroth Hattaavah,[e] because there they buried the people who had craved other food.

[35]From Kibroth Hattaavah the people traveled to Hazeroth and stayed there.

---

[a]25 Or *prophesied and continued to do so*   [b]31 Or *They flew*   [c]31 Hebrew *two cubits* (about 1 meter)   [d]32 That is, probably about 60 bushels (about 2.2 kiloliters)   [e]34 *Kibroth Hattaavah* means *graves of craving.*

Miriam and Aaron Oppose Moses

12 Miriam and Aaron began to talk against Moses because of his Cushite wife, for he had married a Cushite. ²"Has the LORD spoken only through Moses?" they asked. "Hasn't he also spoken through us?" And the LORD heard this.

³(Now Moses was a very humble man, more humble than anyone else on the face of the earth.)

⁴At once the LORD said to Moses, Aaron and Miriam, "Come out to the Tent of Meeting, all three of you." So the three of them came out. ⁵Then the LORD came down in a pillar of cloud; he stood at the entrance to the Tent and summoned Aaron and Miriam. When both of them stepped forward, ⁶he said, "Listen to my words:

"When a prophet of the LORD is
 among you,
I reveal myself to him in visions,
I speak to him in dreams.
⁷But this is not true of my servant
 Moses;
 he is faithful in all my house.
⁸With him I speak face to face,
 clearly and not in riddles;
 he sees the form of the LORD.
Why then were you not afraid
 to speak against my servant
 Moses?"

⁹The anger of the LORD burned against them, and he left them.

¹⁰When the cloud lifted from above the Tent, there stood Miriam—leprous,ᵃ like snow. Aaron turned toward her and saw that she had leprosy; ¹¹and he said to Moses, "Please, my lord, do not hold against us the sin we have so foolishly committed. ¹²Do not let her be like a stillborn infant coming from its mother's womb with its flesh half eaten away."

¹³So Moses cried out to the LORD, "O God, please heal her!"

¹⁴The LORD replied to Moses, "If her father had spit in her face, would she not have been in disgrace for seven days? Confine her outside the camp for seven days; after that she can be brought back." ¹⁵So Miriam was confined outside the camp for seven days, and the people did not move on till she was brought back.

¹⁶After that, the people left Hazeroth and encamped in the Desert of Paran.

Exploring Canaan

13 The LORD said to Moses, ²"Send some men to explore the land of Canaan, which I am giving to the Israelites. From each ancestral tribe send one of its leaders."

³So at the LORD's command Moses sent them out from the Desert of Paran. All of them were leaders of the Israelites. ⁴These are their names:

from the tribe of Reuben, Shammua
 son of Zaccur;
⁵from the tribe of Simeon, Shaphat
 son of Hori;
⁶from the tribe of Judah, Caleb son of
 Jephunneh;
⁷from the tribe of Issachar, Igal son
 of Joseph;
⁸from the tribe of Ephraim, Hoshea
 son of Nun;
⁹from the tribe of Benjamin, Palti son
 of Raphu;
¹⁰from the tribe of Zebulun, Gaddiel
 son of Sodi;
¹¹from the tribe of Manasseh (a tribe
 of Joseph), Gaddi son of Susi;
¹²from the tribe of Dan, Ammiel son
 of Gemalli;
¹³from the tribe of Asher, Sethur son
 of Michael;
¹⁴from the tribe of Naphtali, Nahbi
 son of Vophsi;
¹⁵from the tribe of Gad, Geuel son of
 Maki.

¹⁶These are the names of the men Moses sent to explore the land. (Moses gave Hoshea son of Nun the name Joshua.)

¹⁷When Moses sent them to explore Canaan, he said, "Go up through the Negev and on into the hill country. ¹⁸See what the land is like and whether the people who live there are strong or weak, few or many. ¹⁹What kind of land do they live in? Is it good or bad? What kind of towns do they live in? Are they unwalled or fortified? ²⁰How is the soil? Is it fertile

---

ᵃ10 The Hebrew word was used for various diseases affecting the skin—not necessarily leprosy.

or poor? Are there trees on it or not? Do your best to bring back some of the fruit of the land." (It was the season for the first ripe grapes.)

[21]So they went up and explored the land from the Desert of Zin as far as Rehob, toward Lebo[a] Hamath. [22]They went up through the Negev and came to Hebron, where Ahiman, Sheshai and Talmai, the descendants of Anak, lived. (Hebron had been built seven years before Zoan in Egypt.) [23]When they reached the Valley of Eshcol,[b] they cut off a branch bearing a single cluster of grapes. Two of them carried it on a pole between them, along with some pomegranates and figs. [24]That place was called the Valley of Eshcol because of the cluster of grapes the Israelites cut off there. [25]At the end of forty days they returned from exploring the land.

Report on the Exploration

[26]They came back to Moses and Aaron and the whole Israelite community at Kadesh in the Desert of Paran. There they reported to them and to the whole assembly and showed them the fruit of the land. [27]They gave Moses this account: "We went into the land to which you sent us, and it does flow with milk and honey! Here is its fruit. [28]But the people who live there are powerful, and the cities are fortified and very large. We even saw descendants of Anak there. [29]The Amalekites live in the Negev; the Hittites, Jebusites and Amorites live in the hill country; and the Canaanites live near the sea and along the Jordan."

[30]Then Caleb silenced the people be-

---

[a]21 Or *toward the entrance to*   [b]23 *Eshcol* means *cluster*; also in verse 24.

Monday

Whiner Warning

Read Numbers 14:1–4

Imagine that you're trying to plan a fun game for some little kids. But before the game even starts, the kids start complaining that it's taking too long and the game's going to be dumb anyway. Pretty soon nobody's having any fun at all. If the kids would have just trusted you to make the game fun, they could have had a great time. But their bad attitudes ruined the whole thing.

God had a plan for the Israelites too, but they ruined it with their whining and complaining. To punish them, God didn't let any of the complainers see the land he had promised them!

If we have the same bad attitude today, we can miss the good stuff God wants for us. Even when it seems like we have a lot to complain about, we need to trust that God will work everything out the best way possible. Then we can grow closer to him and set a good example for other people around us.

Karen age 12

❶ Why is complaining so easy? Why do you think God doesn't like it?

❷ Think of something you really don't like—cleaning your room, doing homework, baby-sitting your little brother, whatever. Then write down 5 *good* things about it.

❸ Ask God to help you resist complaining, even when you're unhappy about something.

Turn to page 184 for your next devotion.

fore Moses and said, "We should go up and take possession of the land, for we can certainly do it."

³¹But the men who had gone up with him said, "We can't attack those people; they are stronger than we are." ³²And they spread among the Israelites a bad report about the land they had explored. They said, "The land we explored devours those living in it. All the people we saw there are of great size. ³³We saw the Nephilim there (the descendants of Anak come from the Nephilim). We seemed like grasshoppers in our own eyes, and we looked the same to them."

The People Rebel

14 That night all the people of the community raised their voices and wept aloud. ²All the Israelites grumbled against Moses and Aaron, and the whole assembly said to them, "If only we had died in Egypt! Or in this desert! ³Why is the LORD bringing us to this land only to let us fall by the sword? Our wives and children will be taken as plunder. Wouldn't it be better for us to go back to Egypt?" ⁴And they said to each other, "We should choose a leader and go back to Egypt."

⁵Then Moses and Aaron fell facedown in front of the whole Israelite assembly gathered there. ⁶Joshua son of Nun and Caleb son of Jephunneh, who were among those who had explored the land, tore their clothes ⁷and said to the entire Israelite assembly, "The land we passed through and explored is exceedingly good. ⁸If the LORD is pleased with us, he will lead us into that land, a land flowing with milk and honey, and will give it to us. ⁹Only do not rebel against the LORD. And do not be afraid of the people of the land, because we will swallow them up. Their protection is gone, but the LORD is with us. Do not be afraid of them."

¹⁰But the whole assembly talked about stoning them. Then the glory of the LORD appeared at the Tent of Meeting to all the Israelites. ¹¹The LORD said to Moses, "How long will these people treat me with contempt? How long will they refuse to believe in me, in spite of all the miraculous signs I have performed among them? ¹²I will strike them down with a plague and destroy them, but I will make you into a nation greater and stronger than they."

¹³Moses said to the LORD, "Then the Egyptians will hear about it! By your power you brought these people up from among them. ¹⁴And they will tell the inhabitants of this land about it. They have already heard that you, O LORD, are with these people and that you, O LORD, have been seen face to face, that your cloud stays over them, and that you go before them in a pillar of cloud by day and a pillar of fire by night. ¹⁵If you put these people to death all at one time, the nations who have heard this report about you will say, ¹⁶'The LORD was not able to bring these people into the land he promised them on oath; so he slaughtered them in the desert.'

¹⁷"Now may the Lord's strength be displayed, just as you have declared: ¹⁸'The LORD is slow to anger, abounding in love and forgiving sin and rebellion. Yet he does not leave the guilty unpunished; he punishes the children for the sin of the fathers to the third and fourth generation.' ¹⁹In accordance with your great love, forgive the sin of these people, just as you have pardoned them from the time they left Egypt until now."

Even When They Fell

Huh?

Numbers 14:19
The story of the Hebrews comes down to two things: their miserable failure and God's unending forgiveness. When God got them out of Egypt (remember that?), they *still* didn't want to trust him. They were acting stupid and selfish. But God is so great and so kind that he didn't zap them. He forgave them. (Yeah, they had to wander around for a few more years, but it could have been worse!) God does the same with us, you know.

²⁰The LORD replied, "I have forgiven them, as you asked. ²¹Nevertheless, as surely as I live and as surely as the glory of the LORD fills the whole earth, ²²not

one of the men who saw my glory and the miraculous signs I performed in Egypt and in the desert but who disobeyed me and tested me ten times— [23]not one of them will ever see the land I promised on oath to their forefathers. No one who has treated me with contempt will ever see it. [24]But because my servant Caleb has a different spirit and follows me wholeheartedly, I will bring him into the land he went to, and his descendants will inherit it. [25]Since the Amalekites and Canaanites are living in the valleys, turn back tomorrow and set out toward the desert along the route to the Red Sea.[a]"

[26]The LORD said to Moses and Aaron: [27]"How long will this wicked community grumble against me? I have heard the complaints of these grumbling Israelites. [28]So tell them, 'As surely as I live, declares the LORD, I will do to you the very things I heard you say: [29]In this desert your bodies will fall—every one of you twenty years old or more who was counted in the census and who has grumbled against me. [30]Not one of you will enter the land I swore with uplifted hand to make your home, except Caleb son of Jephunneh and Joshua son of Nun. [31]As for your children that you said would be taken as plunder, I will bring them in to enjoy the land you have rejected. [32]But you—your bodies will fall in this desert. [33]Your children will be shepherds here for forty years, suffering for your unfaithfulness, until the last of your bodies lies in the desert. [34]For forty years—one year for each of the forty days you explored the land—you will suffer for your sins and know what it is like to have me against you.' [35]I, the LORD, have spoken, and I will surely do these things to this whole wicked community, which has banded together against me. They will meet their end in this desert; here they will die."

[36]So the men Moses had sent to explore the land, who returned and made the whole community grumble against him by spreading a bad report about it— [37]these men responsible for spreading the bad report about the land were struck down and died of a plague before the LORD. [38]Of the men who went to explore the land, only Joshua son of Nun and Caleb son of Jephunneh survived.

[39]When Moses reported this to all the Israelites, they mourned bitterly. [40]Early the next morning they went up toward the high hill country. "We have sinned," they said. "We will go up to the place the LORD promised."

[41]But Moses said, "Why are you disobeying the LORD's command? This will not succeed! [42]Do not go up, because the LORD is not with you. You will be defeated by your enemies, [43]for the Amalekites and Canaanites will face you there. Because you have turned away from the LORD, he will not be with you and you will fall by the sword."

[44]Nevertheless, in their presumption they went up toward the high hill country, though neither Moses nor the ark of the LORD's covenant moved from the camp. [45]Then the Amalekites and Canaanites who lived in that hill country came down and attacked them and beat them down all the way to Hormah.

Supplementary Offerings

15 The LORD said to Moses, [2]"Speak to the Israelites and say to them: 'After you enter the land I am giving you as a home [3]and you present to the LORD offerings made by fire, from the herd or the flock, as an aroma pleasing to the LORD— whether burnt offerings or sacrifices, for special vows or freewill offerings or festival offerings— [4]then the one who brings his offering shall present to the LORD a grain offering of a tenth of an ephah[b] of fine flour mixed with a quarter of a hin[c] of oil. [5]With each lamb for the burnt offering or the sacrifice, prepare a quarter of a hin of wine as a drink offering.

[6]" 'With a ram prepare a grain offering of two-tenths of an ephah[d] of fine flour mixed with a third of a hin[e] of oil, [7]and a third of a hin of wine as a drink offering. Offer it as an aroma pleasing to the LORD.

[8]" 'When you prepare a young bull as a burnt offering or sacrifice, for a special

---

[a]25 Hebrew *Yam Suph*; that is, Sea of Reeds
[b]4 That is, probably about 2 quarts (about 2 liters)
[c]4 That is, probably about 1 quart (about 1 liter); also in verse 5   [d]6 That is, probably about 4 quarts (about 4.5 liters)   [e]6 That is, probably about 1 1/4 quarts (about 1.2 liters); also in verse 7

vow or a fellowship offering[a] to the LORD, [9]bring with the bull a grain offering of three-tenths of an ephah[b] of fine flour mixed with half a hin[c] of oil. [10]Also bring half a hin of wine as a drink offering. It will be an offering made by fire, an aroma pleasing to the LORD. [11]Each bull or ram, each lamb or young goat, is to be prepared in this manner. [12]Do this for each one, for as many as you prepare.

[13] 'Everyone who is native-born must do these things in this way when he brings an offering made by fire as an aroma pleasing to the LORD. [14]For the generations to come, whenever an alien or anyone else living among you presents an offering made by fire as an aroma pleasing to the LORD, he must do exactly as you do. [15]The community is to have the same rules for you and for the alien living among you; this is a lasting ordinance for the generations to come. You and the alien shall be the same before the LORD: [16]The same laws and regulations will apply both to you and to the alien living among you.' "

[17]The LORD said to Moses, [18]"Speak to the Israelites and say to them: 'When you enter the land to which I am taking you [19]and you eat the food of the land, present a portion as an offering to the LORD. [20]Present a cake from the first of your ground meal and present it as an offering from the threshing floor. [21]Throughout the generations to come you are to give this offering to the LORD from the first of your ground meal.

Offerings for Unintentional Sins

[22] 'Now if you unintentionally fail to keep any of these commands the LORD gave Moses— [23]any of the LORD's commands to you through him, from the day the LORD gave them and continuing through the generations to come— [24]and if this is done unintentionally without the community being aware of it, then the whole community is to offer a young bull for a burnt offering as an aroma pleasing to the LORD, along with its prescribed grain offering and drink offering, and a male goat for a sin offering. [25]The priest is to make atonement for the whole Israelite community, and they will be forgiven, for it was not intentional and

they have brought to the LORD for their wrong an offering made by fire and a sin offering. [26]The whole Israelite community and the aliens living among them will be forgiven, because all the people were involved in the unintentional wrong.

[27] 'But if just one person sins unintentionally, he must bring a year-old female goat for a sin offering. [28]The priest is to make atonement before the LORD for the one who erred by sinning unintentionally, and when atonement has been made for him, he will be forgiven. [29]One and the same law applies to everyone who sins unintentionally, whether he is a native-born Israelite or an alien.

[30] 'But anyone who sins defiantly, whether native-born or alien, blasphemes the LORD, and that person must be cut off from his people. [31]Because he has despised the LORD's word and broken his commands, that person must surely be cut off; his guilt remains on him.' "

The Sabbath-Breaker Put to Death

[32]While the Israelites were in the desert, a man was found gathering wood on the Sabbath day. [33]Those who found him gathering wood brought him to Moses and Aaron and the whole assembly, [34]and they kept him in custody, because it was not clear what should be done to him. [35]Then the LORD said to Moses, "The man must die. The whole assembly must stone him outside the camp." [36]So the assembly took him outside the camp and stoned him to death, as the LORD commanded Moses.

Tassels on Garments

[37]The LORD said to Moses, [38]"Speak to the Israelites and say to them: 'Throughout the generations to come you are to make tassels on the corners of your garments, with a blue cord on each tassel. [39]You will have these tassels to look at and so you will remember all the commands of the LORD, that you may obey them and not prostitute yourselves by going after the lusts of your own hearts and eyes. [40]Then you will remember to

---

[a]8 Traditionally *peace offering* [b]9 That is, probably about 6 quarts (about 6.5 liters) [c]9 That is, probably about 2 quarts (about 2 liters); also in verse 10

obey all my commands and will be consecrated to your God. ⁴¹I am the LORD your God, who brought you out of Egypt to be your God. I am the LORD your God.' "

Korah, Dathan and Abiram

16 Korah son of Izhar, the son of Kohath, the son of Levi, and certain Reubenites—Dathan and Abiram, sons of Eliab, and On son of Peleth—became insolent[a] ²and rose up against Moses. With them were 250 Israelite men, well-known community leaders who had been appointed members of the council. ³They came as a group to oppose Moses and Aaron and said to them, "You have gone too far! The whole community is holy, every one of them, and the LORD is with them. Why then do you set yourselves above the LORD's assembly?"

⁴When Moses heard this, he fell facedown. ⁵Then he said to Korah and all his followers: "In the morning the LORD will show who belongs to him and who is holy, and he will have that person come near him. The man he chooses he will cause to come near him. ⁶You, Korah, and all your followers are to do this: Take censers ⁷and tomorrow put fire and incense in them before the LORD. The man the LORD chooses will be the one who is holy. You Levites have gone too far!"

⁸Moses also said to Korah, "Now listen, you Levites! ⁹Isn't it enough for you that the God of Israel has separated you from the rest of the Israelite community and brought you near himself to do the work at the LORD's tabernacle and to stand before the community and minister to them? ¹⁰He has brought you and all your fellow Levites near himself, but now you are trying to get the priesthood too. ¹¹It is against the LORD that you and all your followers have banded together. Who is Aaron that you should grumble against him?"

¹²Then Moses summoned Dathan and Abiram, the sons of Eliab. But they said, "We will not come! ¹³Isn't it enough that you have brought us up out of a land flowing with milk and honey to kill us in the desert? And now you also want to lord it over us? ¹⁴Moreover, you haven't

brought us into a land flowing with milk and honey or given us an inheritance of fields and vineyards. Will you gouge out the eyes of[b] these men? No, we will not come!"

¹⁵Then Moses became very angry and said to the LORD, "Do not accept their offering. I have not taken so much as a donkey from them, nor have I wronged any of them."

¹⁶Moses said to Korah, "You and all your followers are to appear before the LORD tomorrow—you and they and Aaron. ¹⁷Each man is to take his censer and put incense in it—250 censers in all—and present it before the LORD. You and Aaron are to present your censers also." ¹⁸So each man took his censer, put fire and incense in it, and stood with Moses and Aaron at the entrance to the Tent of Meeting. ¹⁹When Korah had gathered all his followers in opposition to them at the entrance to the Tent of Meeting, the glory of the LORD appeared to the entire assembly. ²⁰The LORD said to Moses and Aaron, ²¹"Separate yourselves from this assembly so I can put an end to them at once."

²²But Moses and Aaron fell facedown and cried out, "O God, God of the spirits of all mankind, will you be angry with the entire assembly when only one man sins?"

²³Then the LORD said to Moses, ²⁴"Say to the assembly, 'Move away from the tents of Korah, Dathan and Abiram.' "

²⁵Moses got up and went to Dathan and Abiram, and the elders of Israel followed him. ²⁶He warned the assembly, "Move back from the tents of these wicked men! Do not touch anything belonging to them, or you will be swept away because of all their sins." ²⁷So they moved away from the tents of Korah, Dathan and Abiram. Dathan and Abiram had come out and were standing with their wives, children and little ones at the entrances to their tents.

²⁸Then Moses said, "This is how you will know that the LORD has sent me to do all these things and that it was not my idea: ²⁹If these men die a natural death

---

[a] 1 Or *Peleth—took men*   [b] 14 Or *you make slaves of;* or *you deceive*

and experience only what usually happens to men, then the LORD has not sent me. ³⁰But if the LORD brings about something totally new, and the earth opens its mouth and swallows them, with everything that belongs to them, and they go down alive into the grave,ᵃ then you will know that these men have treated the LORD with contempt."

³¹As soon as he finished saying all this, the ground under them split apart ³²and the earth opened its mouth and swallowed them, with their households and all Korah's men and all their possessions. ³³They went down alive into the grave, with everything they owned; the earth closed over them, and they perished and were gone from the community. ³⁴At their cries, all the Israelites around them fled, shouting, "The earth is going to swallow us too!"

³⁵And fire came out from the LORD and consumed the 250 men who were offering the incense.

³⁶The LORD said to Moses, ³⁷"Tell Eleazar son of Aaron, the priest, to take the censers out of the smoldering remains and scatter the coals some distance away, for the censers are holy— ³⁸the censers of the men who sinned at the cost of their lives. Hammer the censers into sheets to overlay the altar, for they were presented before the LORD and have become holy. Let them be a sign to the Israelites."

³⁹So Eleazar the priest collected the bronze censers brought by those who had been burned up, and he had them hammered out to overlay the altar, ⁴⁰as the LORD directed him through Moses. This was to remind the Israelites that no one except a descendant of Aaron should come to burn incense before the LORD, or he would become like Korah and his followers.

⁴¹The next day the whole Israelite community grumbled against Moses and Aaron. "You have killed the LORD's people," they said.

⁴²But when the assembly gathered in opposition to Moses and Aaron and turned toward the Tent of Meeting, suddenly the cloud covered it and the glory of the LORD appeared. ⁴³Then Moses and Aaron went to the front of the Tent of Meeting, ⁴⁴and the LORD said to Moses, ⁴⁵"Get away from this assembly so I can put an end to them at once." And they fell facedown.

⁴⁶Then Moses said to Aaron, "Take your censer and put incense in it, along with fire from the altar, and hurry to the assembly to make atonement for them. Wrath has come out from the LORD; the plague has started." ⁴⁷So Aaron did as Moses said, and ran into the midst of the assembly. The plague had already started among the people, but Aaron offered the incense and made atonement for them. ⁴⁸He stood between the living and the dead, and the plague stopped. ⁴⁹But 14,700 people died from the plague, in addition to those who had died because of Korah. ⁵⁰Then Aaron returned to Moses at the entrance to the Tent of Meeting, for the plague had stopped.

The Budding of Aaron's Staff

17 The LORD said to Moses, ²"Speak to the Israelites and get twelve staffs from them, one from the leader of each of their ancestral tribes. Write the name of each man on his staff. ³On the staff of Levi write Aaron's name, for there must be one staff for the head of each ancestral tribe. ⁴Place them in the Tent of Meeting in front of the Testimony, where I meet with you. ⁵The staff belonging to the man I choose will sprout, and I will rid myself of this constant grumbling against you by the Israelites."

⁶So Moses spoke to the Israelites, and their leaders gave him twelve staffs, one for the leader of each of their ancestral tribes, and Aaron's staff was among them. ⁷Moses placed the staffs before the LORD in the Tent of the Testimony.

⁸The next day Moses entered the Tent of the Testimony and saw that Aaron's staff, which represented the house of Levi, had not only sprouted but had budded, blossomed and produced almonds. ⁹Then Moses brought out all the staffs from the LORD's presence to all the Israelites. They looked at them, and each man took his own staff.

¹⁰The LORD said to Moses, "Put back Aaron's staff in front of the Testimony, to

ᵃ30 Hebrew *Sheol*; also in verse 33

be kept as a sign to the rebellious. This will put an end to their grumbling against me, so that they will not die." [11]Moses did just as the LORD commanded him.

[12]The Israelites said to Moses, "We will die! We are lost, we are all lost! [13]Anyone who even comes near the tabernacle of the LORD will die. Are we all going to die?"

Duties of Priests and Levites

18 The LORD said to Aaron, "You, your sons and your father's family are to bear the responsibility for offenses against the sanctuary, and you and your sons alone are to bear the responsibility for offenses against the priesthood. [2]Bring your fellow Levites from your ancestral tribe to join you and assist you when you and your sons minister before the Tent of the Testimony. [3]They are to be responsible to you and are to perform all the duties of the Tent, but they must not go near the furnishings of the sanctuary or the altar, or both they and you will die. [4]They are to join you and be responsible for the care of the Tent of Meeting— all the work at the Tent—and no one else may come near where you are.

[5]"You are to be responsible for the care of the sanctuary and the altar, so that wrath will not fall on the Israelites again. [6]I myself have selected your fellow Levites from among the Israelites as a gift to you, dedicated to the LORD to do the work at the Tent of Meeting. [7]But only you and your sons may serve as priests in connection with everything at the altar and inside the curtain. I am giving you the service of the priesthood as a gift. Anyone else who comes near the sanctuary must be put to death."

Offerings for Priests and Levites

[8]Then the LORD said to Aaron, "I myself have put you in charge of the offerings presented to me; all the holy offerings the Israelites give me I give to you and your sons as your portion and regular share. [9]You are to have the part of the most holy offerings that is kept from the fire. From all the gifts they bring me as most holy offerings, whether grain or sin or guilt offerings, that part belongs to you and your sons. [10]Eat it as something most holy; every male shall eat it. You must regard it as holy.

[11]"This also is yours: whatever is set aside from the gifts of all the wave offerings of the Israelites. I give this to you and your sons and daughters as your regular share. Everyone in your household who is ceremonially clean may eat it.

[12]"I give you all the finest olive oil and all the finest new wine and grain they give the LORD as the firstfruits of their harvest. [13]All the land's firstfruits that they bring to the LORD will be yours. Everyone in your household who is ceremonially clean may eat it.

[14]"Everything in Israel that is devoted[a] to the LORD is yours. [15]The first offspring of every womb, both man and animal, that is offered to the LORD is yours. But you must redeem every firstborn son and every firstborn male of unclean animals. [16]When they are a month old, you must redeem them at the redemption price set at five shekels[b] of silver, according to the sanctuary shekel, which weighs twenty gerahs.

[17]"But you must not redeem the firstborn of an ox, a sheep or a goat; they are holy. Sprinkle their blood on the altar and burn their fat as an offering made by fire, an aroma pleasing to the LORD. [18]Their meat is to be yours, just as the breast of the wave offering and the right thigh are yours. [19]Whatever is set aside from the holy offerings the Israelites present to the LORD I give to you and your sons and daughters as your regular share. It is an everlasting covenant of salt before the LORD for both you and your offspring."

[20]The LORD said to Aaron, "You will have no inheritance in their land, nor will you have any share among them; I am your share and your inheritance among the Israelites.

[21]"I give to the Levites all the tithes in Israel as their inheritance in return for the work they do while serving at the Tent of Meeting. [22]From now on the Isra-

---

[a]14 The Hebrew term refers to the irrevocable giving over of things or persons to the LORD. [b]16 That is, about 2 ounces (about 55 grams)

elites must not go near the Tent of Meeting, or they will bear the consequences of their sin and will die. ²³It is the Levites who are to do the work at the Tent of Meeting and bear the responsibility for offenses against it. This is a lasting ordinance for the generations to come. They will receive no inheritance among the Israelites. ²⁴Instead, I give to the Levites as their inheritance the tithes that the Israelites present as an offering to the LORD. That is why I said concerning them: 'They will have no inheritance among the Israelites.' "

²⁵The LORD said to Moses, ²⁶"Speak to the Levites and say to them: 'When you receive from the Israelites the tithe I give you as your inheritance, you must present a tenth of that tithe as the LORD's offering. ²⁷Your offering will be reckoned to you as grain from the threshing floor or juice from the winepress. ²⁸In this way you also will present an offering to the LORD from all the tithes you receive from the Israelites. From these tithes you must give the LORD's portion to Aaron the priest. ²⁹You must present as the LORD's portion the best and holiest part of everything given to you.'

³⁰"Say to the Levites: 'When you present the best part, it will be reckoned to you as the product of the threshing floor or the winepress. ³¹You and your households may eat the rest of it anywhere, for it is your wages for your work at the Tent of Meeting. ³²By presenting the best part of it you will not be guilty in this matter; then you will not defile the holy offerings of the Israelites, and you will not die.' "

The Water of Cleansing

19 The LORD said to Moses and Aaron: ²"This is a requirement of the law that the LORD has commanded: Tell the Israelites to bring you a red heifer without defect or blemish and that has never been under a yoke. ³Give it to Eleazar the priest; it is to be taken outside the camp and slaughtered in his presence. ⁴Then Eleazar the priest is to take some of its blood on his finger and sprinkle it seven times toward the front of the Tent of Meeting. ⁵While he watches, the heifer is to be burned—its hide, flesh,

blood and offal. ⁶The priest is to take some cedar wood, hyssop and scarlet wool and throw them onto the burning heifer. ⁷After that, the priest must wash his clothes and bathe himself with water. He may then come into the camp, but he will be ceremonially unclean till evening. ⁸The man who burns it must also wash his clothes and bathe with water, and he too will be unclean till evening.

⁹"A man who is clean shall gather up the ashes of the heifer and put them in a ceremonially clean place outside the camp. They shall be kept by the Israelite community for use in the water of cleansing; it is for purification from sin. ¹⁰The man who gathers up the ashes of the heifer must also wash his clothes, and he too will be unclean till evening. This will be a lasting ordinance both for the Israelites and for the aliens living among them.

¹¹"Whoever touches the dead body of anyone will be unclean for seven days. ¹²He must purify himself with the water on the third day and on the seventh day; then he will be clean. But if he does not purify himself on the third and seventh days, he will not be clean. ¹³Whoever touches the dead body of anyone and fails to purify himself defiles the LORD's tabernacle. That person must be cut off from Israel. Because the water of cleansing has not been sprinkled on him, he is unclean; his uncleanness remains on him.

¹⁴"This is the law that applies when a person dies in a tent: Anyone who enters the tent and anyone who is in it will be unclean for seven days, ¹⁵and every open container without a lid fastened on it will be unclean.

¹⁶"Anyone out in the open who touches someone who has been killed with a sword or someone who has died a natural death, or anyone who touches a human bone or a grave, will be unclean for seven days.

¹⁷"For the unclean person, put some ashes from the burned purification offering into a jar and pour fresh water over them. ¹⁸Then a man who is ceremonially clean is to take some hyssop, dip it in the water and sprinkle the tent and all the furnishings and the people who were

there. He must also sprinkle anyone who has touched a human bone or a grave or someone who has been killed or someone who has died a natural death. ¹⁹The man who is clean is to sprinkle the unclean person on the third and seventh days, and on the seventh day he is to purify him. The person being cleansed must wash his clothes and bathe with water, and that evening he will be clean. ²⁰But if a person who is unclean does not purify himself, he must be cut off from the community, because he has defiled the sanctuary of the LORD. The water of cleansing has not been sprinkled on him, and he is unclean. ²¹This is a lasting ordinance for them.

"The man who sprinkles the water of cleansing must also wash his clothes, and anyone who touches the water of cleansing will be unclean till evening. ²²Anything that an unclean person touches becomes unclean, and anyone who touches it becomes unclean till evening."

Water From the Rock

20 In the first month the whole Israelite community arrived at the Desert of Zin, and they stayed at Kadesh. There Miriam died and was buried.

²Now there was no water for the community, and the people gathered in opposition to Moses and Aaron. ³They quarreled with Moses and said, "If only we had died when our brothers fell dead before the LORD! ⁴Why did you bring the LORD's community into this desert, that we and our livestock should die here? ⁵Why did you bring us up out of Egypt to this terrible place? It has no grain or figs, grapevines or pomegranates. And there is no water to drink!"

⁶Moses and Aaron went from the assembly to the entrance to the Tent of Meeting and fell facedown, and the glory of the LORD appeared to them. ⁷The LORD said to Moses, ⁸"Take the staff, and you and your brother Aaron gather the assembly together. Speak to that rock before their eyes and it will pour out its water. You will bring water out of the rock for the community so they and their livestock can drink."

⁹So Moses took the staff from the

LORD's presence, just as he commanded him. ¹⁰He and Aaron gathered the assembly together in front of the rock and Moses said to them, "Listen, you rebels, must we bring you water out of this rock?" ¹¹Then Moses raised his arm and struck the rock twice with his staff. Water gushed out, and the community and their livestock drank.

¹²But the LORD said to Moses and Aaron, "Because you did not trust in me enough to honor me as holy in the sight of the Israelites, you will not bring this community into the land I give them."

¹³These were the waters of Meribah,ᵃ where the Israelites quarreled with the LORD and where he showed himself holy among them.

Edom Denies Israel Passage

¹⁴Moses sent messengers from Kadesh to the king of Edom, saying:

"This is what your brother Israel says: You know about all the hardships that have come upon us. ¹⁵Our forefathers went down into Egypt, and we lived there many years. The Egyptians mistreated us and our fathers, ¹⁶but when we cried out to the LORD, he heard our cry and sent an angel and brought us out of Egypt.

"Now we are here at Kadesh, a town on the edge of your territory. ¹⁷Please let us pass through your country. We will not go through any field or vineyard, or drink water from any well. We will travel along the king's highway and not turn to the right or to the left until we have passed through your territory."

¹⁸But Edom answered:

"You may not pass through here; if you try, we will march out and attack you with the sword."

¹⁹The Israelites replied:

"We will go along the main road, and if we or our livestock drink any of your water, we will pay for it. We only want to pass through on foot—nothing else."

ᵃ13 Meribah means quarreling.

²⁰Again they answered:

"You may not pass through."

Then Edom came out against them with a large and powerful army. ²¹Since Edom refused to let them go through their territory, Israel turned away from them.

The Death of Aaron

²²The whole Israelite community set out from Kadesh and came to Mount Hor. ²³At Mount Hor, near the border of Edom, the LORD said to Moses and Aaron, ²⁴"Aaron will be gathered to his people. He will not enter the land I give the Israelites, because both of you rebelled against my command at the waters of Meribah. ²⁵Get Aaron and his son Eleazar and take them up Mount Hor. ²⁶Remove Aaron's garments and put them on his son Eleazar, for Aaron will be gathered to his people; he will die there."

²⁷Moses did as the LORD commanded: They went up Mount Hor in the sight of the whole community. ²⁸Moses removed Aaron's garments and put them on his son Eleazar. And Aaron died there on top of the mountain. Then Moses and Eleazar came down from the mountain, ²⁹and when the whole community learned that Aaron had died, the entire house of Israel mourned for him thirty days.

Arad Destroyed

21 When the Canaanite king of Arad, who lived in the Negev, heard that Israel was coming along the road to Atharim, he attacked the Israelites and captured some of them. ²Then Israel made this vow to the LORD: "If you will deliver these people into our hands, we will totally destroy[a] their cities." ³The LORD listened to Israel's plea and gave the Canaanites over to them. They completely destroyed them and their towns; so the place was named Hormah.[b]

The Bronze Snake

⁴They traveled from Mount Hor along the route to the Red Sea,[c] to go around Edom. But the people grew impatient on the way; ⁵they spoke against God and against Moses, and said, "Why have you brought us up out of Egypt to die in the desert? There is no bread! There is no water! And we detest this miserable food!"

⁶Then the LORD sent venomous snakes among them; they bit the people and many Israelites died. ⁷The people came to Moses and said, "We sinned when we spoke against the LORD and against you. Pray that the LORD will take the snakes away from us." So Moses prayed for the people.

⁸The LORD said to Moses, "Make a snake and put it up on a pole; anyone who is bitten can look at it and live." ⁹So Moses made a bronze snake and put it up on a pole. Then when anyone was bitten by a snake and looked at the bronze snake, he lived.

The Journey to Moab

¹⁰The Israelites moved on and camped at Oboth. ¹¹Then they set out from Oboth and camped in Iye Abarim, in the desert that faces Moab toward the sunrise. ¹²From there they moved on and camped in the Zered Valley. ¹³They set out from there and camped alongside the Arnon, which is in the desert extending into Amorite territory. The Arnon is the border of Moab, between Moab and the Amorites. ¹⁴That is why the Book of the Wars of the LORD says:

". . . Waheb in Suphah[d] and the
　　ravines,
　the Arnon ¹⁵and[e] the slopes of the
　　ravines
that lead to the site of Ar
and lie along the border of Moab."

¹⁶From there they continued on to Beer, the well where the LORD said to Moses, "Gather the people together and I will give them water."

¹⁷Then Israel sang this song:

"Spring up, O well!
　Sing about it,
¹⁸about the well that the princes dug,

---

[a]2 The Hebrew term refers to the irrevocable giving over of things or persons to the LORD, often by totally destroying them; also in verse 3.　[b]3 Hormah means destruction.　[c]4 Hebrew Yam Suph; that is, Sea of Reeds　[d]14 The meaning of the Hebrew for this phrase is uncertain.　[e]14,15 Or "I have been given from Suphah and the ravines / of the Arnon ¹⁵to

that the nobles of the people sank—
the nobles with scepters and staffs."

Then they went from the desert to Mattanah, [19]from Mattanah to Nahaliel, from
Nahaliel to Bamoth, [20]and from Bamoth
to the valley in Moab where the top of
Pisgah overlooks the wasteland.

Defeat of Sihon and Og

[21]Israel sent messengers to say to Sihon king of the Amorites:

[22]"Let us pass through your country. We will not turn aside into any
field or vineyard, or drink water
from any well. We will travel along
the king's highway until we have
passed through your territory."

[23]But Sihon would not let Israel pass
through his territory. He mustered his
entire army and marched out into the
desert against Israel. When he reached
Jahaz, he fought with Israel. [24]Israel,
however, put him to the sword and took
over his land from the Arnon to the Jabbok, but only as far as the Ammonites,
because their border was fortified. [25]Isra-
el captured all the cities of the Amorites
and occupied them, including Heshbon
and all its surrounding settlements.
[26]Heshbon was the city of Sihon king of
the Amorites, who had fought against
the former king of Moab and had taken
from him all his land as far as the Arnon.

[27]That is why the poets say:

"Come to Heshbon and let it be rebuilt;
    let Sihon's city be restored.

[28]"Fire went out from Heshbon,
    a blaze from the city of Sihon.
It consumed Ar of Moab,
    the citizens of Arnon's heights.
[29]Woe to you, O Moab!
    You are destroyed, O people of
        Chemosh!
He has given up his sons as fugitives
    and his daughters as captives
to Sihon king of the Amorites.

[30]"But we have overthrown them;
    Heshbon is destroyed all the way to
        Dibon.
We have demolished them as far as
        Nophah,
    which extends to Medeba."

[31]So Israel settled in the land of the
Amorites.

[32]After Moses had sent spies to Jazer,
the Israelites captured its surrounding
settlements and drove out the Amorites
who were there. [33]Then they turned and
went up along the road toward Bashan,
and Og king of Bashan and his whole
army marched out to meet them in battle
at Edrei.

[34]The LORD said to Moses, "Do not be
afraid of him, for I have handed him over
to you, with his whole army and his land.
Do to him what you did to Sihon king of
the Amorites, who reigned in Heshbon."

[35]So they struck him down, together
with his sons and his whole army, leaving them no survivors. And they took
possession of his land.

Balak Summons Balaam

22 Then the Israelites traveled to the
plains of Moab and camped along
the Jordan across from Jericho.[a]

[2]Now Balak son of Zippor saw all that
Israel had done to the Amorites, [3]and
Moab was terrified because there were so
many people. Indeed, Moab was filled
with dread because of the Israelites.

[4]The Moabites said to the elders of
Midian, "This horde is going to lick up
everything around us, as an ox licks up
the grass of the field."

So Balak son of Zippor, who was king
of Moab at that time, [5]sent messengers to
summon Balaam son of Beor, who was at
Pethor, near the River,[b] in his native land.
Balak said:

"A people has come out of Egypt;
they cover the face of the land and
have settled next to me. [6]Now come
and put a curse on these people, because they are too powerful for me.
Perhaps then I will be able to defeat
them and drive them out of the
country. For I know that those you
bless are blessed, and those you
curse are cursed."

[7]The elders of Moab and Midian left,
taking with them the fee for divination.

[a]1 Hebrew *Jordan of Jericho*; possibly an ancient
name for the Jordan River   [b]5 That is, the Euphrates

When they came to Balaam, they told him what Balak had said.

[8]"Spend the night here," Balaam said to them, "and I will bring you back the answer the LORD gives me." So the Moabite princes stayed with him.

[9]God came to Balaam and asked, "Who are these men with you?"

[10]Balaam said to God, "Balak son of Zippor, king of Moab, sent me this message: [11]'A people that has come out of Egypt covers the face of the land. Now come and put a curse on them for me. Perhaps then I will be able to fight them and drive them away.' "

[12]But God said to Balaam, "Do not go with them. You must not put a curse on those people, because they are blessed."

[13]The next morning Balaam got up and said to Balak's princes, "Go back to your own country, for the LORD has refused to let me go with you."

[14]So the Moabite princes returned to Balak and said, "Balaam refused to come with us."

[15]Then Balak sent other princes, more numerous and more distinguished than the first. [16]They came to Balaam and said:

> "This is what Balak son of Zippor says: Do not let anything keep you from coming to me, [17]because I will reward you handsomely and do whatever you say. Come and put a curse on these people for me."

[18]But Balaam answered them, "Even if Balak gave me his palace filled with silver and gold, I could not do anything great or small to go beyond the command of the LORD my God. [19]Now stay here tonight as the others did, and I will find out what else the LORD will tell me."

[20]That night God came to Balaam and said, "Since these men have come to summon you, go with them, but do only what I tell you."

Balaam's Donkey

[21]Balaam got up in the morning, saddled his donkey and went with the princes of Moab. [22]But God was very angry when he went, and the angel of the LORD stood in the road to oppose him. Balaam was riding on his donkey, and his two servants were with him. [23]When the donkey saw the angel of the LORD standing in the road with a drawn sword in his hand, she turned off the road into a field. Balaam beat her to get her back on the road.

[24]Then the angel of the LORD stood in a narrow path between two vineyards, with walls on both sides. [25]When the donkey saw the angel of the LORD, she pressed close to the wall, crushing Balaam's foot against it. So he beat her again.

[26]Then the angel of the LORD moved on ahead and stood in a narrow place where there was no room to turn, either to the right or to the left. [27]When the donkey saw the angel of the LORD, she lay down under Balaam, and he was angry and beat her with his staff. [28]Then the LORD opened the donkey's mouth, and she said to Balaam, "What have I done to you to make you beat me these three times?"

[29]Balaam answered the donkey, "You have made a fool of me! If I had a sword in my hand, I would kill you right now."

[30]The donkey said to Balaam, "Am I not your own donkey, which you have always ridden, to this day? Have I been in the habit of doing this to you?"

"No," he said.

[31]Then the LORD opened Balaam's eyes, and he saw the angel of the LORD standing in the road with his sword drawn. So he bowed low and fell facedown.

[32]The angel of the LORD asked him, "Why have you beaten your donkey these three times? I have come here to oppose you because your path is a reckless one before me.[a] [33]The donkey saw me and turned away from me these three times. If she had not turned away, I would certainly have killed you by now, but I would have spared her."

[34]Balaam said to the angel of the LORD, "I have sinned. I did not realize you were standing in the road to oppose me. Now if you are displeased, I will go back."

[35]The angel of the LORD said to Balaam, "Go with the men, but speak only what I tell you." So Balaam went with the princes of Balak.

---

[a]32 The meaning of the Hebrew for this clause is uncertain.

³⁶When Balak heard that Balaam was coming, he went out to meet him at the Moabite town on the Arnon border, at the edge of his territory. ³⁷Balak said to Balaam, "Did I not send you an urgent summons? Why didn't you come to me? Am I really not able to reward you?"

³⁸"Well, I have come to you now," Balaam replied. "But can I say just anything? I must speak only what God puts in my mouth."

³⁹Then Balaam went with Balak to Kiriath Huzoth. ⁴⁰Balak sacrificed cattle and sheep, and gave some to Balaam and the princes who were with him. ⁴¹The next morning Balak took Balaam up to Bamoth Baal, and from there he saw part of the people.

Balaam's First Oracle

23 Balaam said, "Build me seven altars here, and prepare seven bulls and seven rams for me." ²Balak did as Balaam said, and the two of them offered a bull and a ram on each altar.

³Then Balaam said to Balak, "Stay here beside your offering while I go aside. Perhaps the LORD will come to meet with me. Whatever he reveals to me I will tell you." Then he went off to a barren height.

⁴God met with him, and Balaam said, "I have prepared seven altars, and on each altar I have offered a bull and a ram."

⁵The LORD put a message in Balaam's mouth and said, "Go back to Balak and give him this message."

⁶So he went back to him and found him standing beside his offering, with all the princes of Moab. ⁷Then Balaam uttered his oracle:

"Balak brought me from Aram,
    the king of Moab from the eastern
        mountains.
'Come,' he said, 'curse Jacob for me;
    come, denounce Israel.'
⁸How can I curse
    those whom God has not cursed?

Tuesday

Keep Your Cool

Read Numbers 22:21–34

This passage reminds me of the time one of my teachers embarrassed me in front of the whole class. I misspelled a word on a test. When she handed back the test, she said, "Jeremiah, come here and spell this word correctly." Well, I got so angry, I just sat at my desk and wrote "I hate this teacher!" over and over again in my notebook. Instead of just calmly fixing my error, I let my embarrassment turn into anger and made a big deal out of nothing.

Balaam did the same thing. When his donkey wouldn't stay on the path, he got embarrassed and then angry. Instead of just staying calm, he hit his donkey and made a big fool of himself.

The next time I get embarrassed, I hope I can remember this story and stay calm. That's a whole lot better than acting foolish, like Balaam did.

Jeremiah, age 16

❶ How do you usually handle embarrassing situations? Does your reaction make the situation better or worse?

❷ Think back to the last time you were really embarrassed. What could you have done differently, and what would the result of that have been?

❸ Ask God to help you stay calm when you feel embarrassed.

Turn to page 206 for your next devotion.

How can I denounce
    those whom the LORD has not
      denounced?
⁹From the rocky peaks I see them,
    from the heights I view them.
I see a people who live apart
    and do not consider themselves one
      of the nations.
¹⁰Who can count the dust of Jacob
    or number the fourth part of Israel?
Let me die the death of the righteous,
    and may my end be like theirs!"

¹¹Balak said to Balaam, "What have you done to me? I brought you to curse my enemies, but you have done nothing but bless them!"

¹²He answered, "Must I not speak what the LORD puts in my mouth?"

Balaam's Second Oracle

¹³Then Balak said to him, "Come with me to another place where you can see them; you will see only a part but not all of them. And from there, curse them for me." ¹⁴So he took him to the field of Zophim on the top of Pisgah, and there he built seven altars and offered a bull and a ram on each altar.

¹⁵Balaam said to Balak, "Stay here beside your offering while I meet with him over there."

¹⁶The LORD met with Balaam and put a message in his mouth and said, "Go back to Balak and give him this message."

¹⁷So he went to him and found him standing beside his offering, with the princes of Moab. Balak asked him, "What did the LORD say?"

¹⁸Then he uttered his oracle:

"Arise, Balak, and listen;
    hear me, son of Zippor.
¹⁹God is not a man, that he should lie,
    nor a son of man, that he should
      change his mind.
Does he speak and then not act?
    Does he promise and not fulfill?
²⁰I have received a command to bless;
    he has blessed, and I cannot
      change it.

²¹"No misfortune is seen in Jacob,
    no misery observed in Israel.ᵃ
The LORD their God is with them;
    the shout of the King is among them.

²²God brought them out of Egypt;
    they have the strength of a wild ox.
²³There is no sorcery against Jacob,
    no divination against Israel.
It will now be said of Jacob
    and of Israel, 'See what God has
      done!'
²⁴The people rise like a lioness;
    they rouse themselves like a lion
that does not rest till he devours his
      prey
    and drinks the blood of his victims."

²⁵Then Balak said to Balaam, "Neither curse them at all nor bless them at all!"

²⁶Balaam answered, "Did I not tell you I must do whatever the LORD says?"

Balaam's Third Oracle

²⁷Then Balak said to Balaam, "Come, let me take you to another place. Perhaps it will please God to let you curse them for me from there." ²⁸And Balak took Balaam to the top of Peor, overlooking the wasteland.

²⁹Balaam said, "Build me seven altars here, and prepare seven bulls and seven rams for me." ³⁰Balak did as Balaam had said, and offered a bull and a ram on each altar.

24 Now when Balaam saw that it pleased the LORD to bless Israel, he did not resort to sorcery as at other times, but turned his face toward the desert. ²When Balaam looked out and saw Israel encamped tribe by tribe, the Spirit of God came upon him ³and he uttered his oracle:

"The oracle of Balaam son of Beor,
    the oracle of one whose eye sees
      clearly,
⁴the oracle of one who hears the words
    of God,
who sees a vision from the
    Almighty,ᵇ
who falls prostrate, and whose eyes
    are opened:

⁵"How beautiful are your tents,
    O Jacob,
    your dwelling places, O Israel!

ᵃ21 Or *He has not looked on Jacob's offenses / or on the wrongs found in Israel.*   ᵇ4 Hebrew *Shaddai*; also in verse 16

⁶"Like valleys they spread out,
    like gardens beside a river,
like aloes planted by the LORD,
    like cedars beside the waters.
⁷Water will flow from their buckets;
    their seed will have abundant water.

"Their king will be greater than Agag;
    their kingdom will be exalted.

⁸"God brought them out of Egypt;
    they have the strength of a wild ox.
They devour hostile nations
    and break their bones in pieces;
    with their arrows they pierce them.
⁹Like a lion they crouch and lie down,
    like a lioness—who dares to rouse
        them?

"May those who bless you be blessed
    and those who curse you be cursed!"

¹⁰Then Balak's anger burned against Balaam. He struck his hands together and said to him, "I summoned you to curse my enemies, but you have blessed them these three times. ¹¹Now leave at once and go home! I said I would reward you handsomely, but the LORD has kept you from being rewarded."

¹²Balaam answered Balak, "Did I not tell the messengers you sent me, ¹³'Even if Balak gave me his palace filled with silver and gold, I could not do anything of my own accord, good or bad, to go beyond the command of the LORD—and I must say only what the LORD says'? ¹⁴Now I am going back to my people, but come, let me warn you of what this people will do to your people in days to come."

Balaam's Fourth Oracle

¹⁵Then he uttered his oracle:

"The oracle of Balaam son of Beor,
    the oracle of one whose eye sees
        clearly,
¹⁶the oracle of one who hears the words
        of God,
    who has knowledge from the Most
        High,
    who sees a vision from the Almighty,
    who falls prostrate, and whose eyes
        are opened:

¹⁷"I see him, but not now;
    I behold him, but not near.

A star will come out of Jacob;
    a scepter will rise out of Israel.
He will crush the foreheads of Moab,
    the skulls*ᵃ* of*ᵇ* all the sons of Sheth.*ᶜ*
¹⁸Edom will be conquered;
    Seir, his enemy, will be conquered,
    but Israel will grow strong.
¹⁹A ruler will come out of Jacob
    and destroy the survivors of the
        city."

Balaam's Final Oracles

²⁰Then Balaam saw Amalek and uttered his oracle:

"Amalek was first among the nations,
    but he will come to ruin at last."

²¹Then he saw the Kenites and uttered his oracle:

"Your dwelling place is secure,
    your nest is set in a rock;
²²yet you Kenites will be destroyed
    when Asshur takes you captive."

²³Then he uttered his oracle:

"Ah, who can live when God does
        this?*ᵈ*
²⁴   Ships will come from the shores of
        Kittim;
they will subdue Asshur and Eber,
    but they too will come to ruin."

²⁵Then Balaam got up and returned home and Balak went his own way.

Moab Seduces Israel

25 While Israel was staying in Shittim, the men began to indulge in sexual immorality with Moabite women, ²who invited them to the sacrifices to their gods. The people ate and bowed down before these gods. ³So Israel joined in worshiping the Baal of Peor. And the LORD's anger burned against them.

⁴The LORD said to Moses, "Take all the leaders of these people, kill them and expose them in broad daylight before the LORD, so that the LORD's fierce anger may turn away from Israel."

ᵃ17 Samaritan Pentateuch (see also Jer. 48:45); the meaning of the word in the Masoretic Text is uncertain.   *ᵇ17* Or possibly *Moab, / batter*   *ᶜ17* Or *all the noisy boasters*   *ᵈ23* Masoretic Text; with a different word division of the Hebrew *A people will gather from the north.*

[5]So Moses said to Israel's judges, "Each of you must put to death those of your men who have joined in worshiping the Baal of Peor."

[6]Then an Israelite man brought to his family a Midianite woman right before the eyes of Moses and the whole assembly of Israel while they were weeping at the entrance to the Tent of Meeting. [7]When Phinehas son of Eleazar, the son of Aaron, the priest, saw this, he left the assembly, took a spear in his hand [8]and followed the Israelite into the tent. He drove the spear through both of them—through the Israelite and into the woman's body. Then the plague against the Israelites was stopped; [9]but those who died in the plague numbered 24,000.

[10]The LORD said to Moses, [11]"Phinehas son of Eleazar, the son of Aaron, the priest, has turned my anger away from the Israelites; for he was as zealous as I am for my honor among them, so that in my zeal I did not put an end to them. [12]Therefore tell him I am making my covenant of peace with him. [13]He and his descendants will have a covenant of a lasting priesthood, because he was zealous for the honor of his God and made atonement for the Israelites."

[14]The name of the Israelite who was killed with the Midianite woman was Zimri son of Salu, the leader of a Simeonite family. [15]And the name of the Midianite woman who was put to death was Cozbi daughter of Zur, a tribal chief of a Midianite family.

[16]The LORD said to Moses, [17]"Treat the Midianites as enemies and kill them, [18]because they treated you as enemies when they deceived you in the affair of Peor and their sister Cozbi, the daughter of a Midianite leader, the woman who was killed when the plague came as a result of Peor."

The Second Census

26 After the plague the LORD said to Moses and Eleazar son of Aaron, the priest, [2]"Take a census of the whole Israelite community by families—all those twenty years old or more who are able to serve in the army of Israel." [3]So on the plains of Moab by the Jordan across from Jericho,[a] Moses and Eleazar

the priest spoke with them and said, [4]"Take a census of the men twenty years old or more, as the LORD commanded Moses."

These were the Israelites who came out of Egypt:

[5]The descendants of Reuben, the firstborn son of Israel, were:

through Hanoch, the Hanochite clan;

through Pallu, the Palluite clan;

[6]through Hezron, the Hezronite clan;

through Carmi, the Carmite clan.

[7]These were the clans of Reuben; those numbered were 43,730.

[8]The son of Pallu was Eliab, [9]and the sons of Eliab were Nemuel, Dathan and Abiram. The same Dathan and Abiram were the community officials who rebelled against Moses and Aaron and were among Korah's followers when they rebelled against the LORD. [10]The earth opened its mouth and swallowed them along with Korah, whose followers died when the fire devoured the 250 men. And they served as a warning sign. [11]The line of Korah, however, did not die out.

[12]The descendants of Simeon by their clans were:

through Nemuel, the Nemuelite clan;

through Jamin, the Jaminite clan;

through Jakin, the Jakinite clan;

[13]through Zerah, the Zerahite clan;

through Shaul, the Shaulite clan.

[14]These were the clans of Simeon; there were 22,200 men.

[15]The descendants of Gad by their clans were:

through Zephon, the Zephonite clan;

through Haggi, the Haggite clan;

through Shuni, the Shunite clan;

[16]through Ozni, the Oznite clan;

through Eri, the Erite clan;

[17]through Arodi,[b] the Arodite clan;

through Areli, the Arelite clan.

[18]These were the clans of Gad; those numbered were 40,500.

---

[a]3 Hebrew *Jordan of Jericho*; possibly an ancient name for the Jordan River; also in verse 63
[b]17 Samaritan Pentateuch and Syriac (see also Gen. 46:16); Masoretic Text *Arod*

[19] Er and Onan were sons of Judah, but they died in Canaan.
[20] The descendants of Judah by their clans were:

through Shelah, the Shelanite clan;
through Perez, the Perezite clan;
through Zerah, the Zerahite clan.

[21] The descendants of Perez were:

through Hezron, the Hezronite clan;
through Hamul, the Hamulite clan.

[22] These were the clans of Judah; those numbered were 76,500.

[23] The descendants of Issachar by their clans were:

through Tola, the Tolaite clan;
through Puah, the Puite[a] clan;
[24] through Jashub, the Jashubite clan;
through Shimron, the Shimronite clan.

[25] These were the clans of Issachar; those numbered were 64,300.

[26] The descendants of Zebulun by their clans were:

through Sered, the Seredite clan;
through Elon, the Elonite clan;
through Jahleel, the Jahleelite clan.

[27] These were the clans of Zebulun; those numbered were 60,500.

[28] The descendants of Joseph by their clans through Manasseh and Ephraim were:

[29] The descendants of Manasseh:

through Makir, the Makirite clan (Makir was the father of Gilead);
through Gilead, the Gileadite clan.

[30] These were the descendants of Gilead:

through Iezer, the Iezerite clan;
through Helek, the Helekite clan;
[31] through Asriel, the Asrielite clan;
through Shechem, the Shechemite clan;
[32] through Shemida, the Shemidaite clan;
through Hepher, the Hepherite clan.

[33] (Zelophehad son of Hepher had no sons; he had only daughters, whose names were Mahlah, Noah, Hoglah, Milcah and Tirzah.)

[34] These were the clans of Manasseh; those numbered were 52,700.

[35] These were the descendants of Ephraim by their clans:

through Shuthelah, the Shuthelahite clan;
through Beker, the Bekerite clan;
through Tahan, the Tahanite clan.

[36] These were the descendants of Shuthelah:

through Eran, the Eranite clan.

[37] These were the clans of Ephraim; those numbered were 32,500.

These were the descendants of Joseph by their clans.

[38] The descendants of Benjamin by their clans were:

through Bela, the Belaite clan;
through Ashbel, the Ashbelite clan;
through Ahiram, the Ahiramite clan;
[39] through Shupham,[b] the Shuphamite clan;
through Hupham, the Huphamite clan.

[40] The descendants of Bela through Ard and Naaman were:

through Ard,[c] the Ardite clan;
through Naaman, the Naamite clan.

[41] These were the clans of Benjamin; those numbered were 45,600.

[42] These were the descendants of Dan by their clans:

through Shuham, the Shuhamite clan.

These were the clans of Dan: [43] All of them were Shuhamite clans; and those numbered were 64,400.

[44] The descendants of Asher by their clans were:

through Imnah, the Imnite clan;
through Ishvi, the Ishvite clan;
through Beriah, the Beriite clan;
[45] and through the descendants of Beriah:

through Heber, the Heberite clan;
through Malkiel, the Malkielite clan.

---

[a]23 Samaritan Pentateuch, Septuagint, Vulgate and Syriac (see also 1 Chron. 7:1); Masoretic Text *through Puvah, the Punite*   [b]39 A few manuscripts of the Masoretic Text, Samaritan Pentateuch, Vulgate and Syriac (see also Septuagint); most manuscripts of the Masoretic Text *Shephupham*   [c]40 Samaritan Pentateuch and Vulgate (see also Septuagint); Masoretic Text does not have *through Ard.*

⁴⁶(Asher had a daughter named Serah.)

⁴⁷These were the clans of Asher; those numbered were 53,400.

⁴⁸The descendants of Naphtali by their clans were:
> through Jahzeel, the Jahzeelite clan;
> through Guni, the Gunite clan;
⁴⁹ through Jezer, the Jezerite clan;
> through Shillem, the Shillemite clan.

⁵⁰These were the clans of Naphtali; those numbered were 45,400.

⁵¹The total number of the men of Israel was 601,730.

⁵²The LORD said to Moses, ⁵³"The land is to be allotted to them as an inheritance based on the number of names. ⁵⁴To a larger group give a larger inheritance, and to a smaller group a smaller one; each is to receive its inheritance according to the number of those listed. ⁵⁵Be sure that the land is distributed by lot. What each group inherits will be according to the names for its ancestral tribe. ⁵⁶Each inheritance is to be distributed by lot among the larger and smaller groups."

⁵⁷These were the Levites who were counted by their clans:
> through Gershon, the Gershonite clan;
> through Kohath, the Kohathite clan;
> through Merari, the Merarite clan.
⁵⁸ These also were Levite clans:
> the Libnite clan,
> the Hebronite clan,
> the Mahlite clan,
> the Mushite clan,
> the Korahite clan.

(Kohath was the forefather of Amram; ⁵⁹the name of Amram's wife was Jochebed, a descendant of Levi, who was born to the Levites[a] in Egypt. To Amram she bore Aaron, Moses and their sister Miriam. ⁶⁰Aaron was the father of Nadab and Abihu, Eleazar and Ithamar. ⁶¹But Nadab and Abihu died when they made an offering before the LORD with unauthorized fire.)

⁶²All the male Levites a month old or more numbered 23,000. They were not counted along with the other Israelites because they received no inheritance among them.

⁶³These are the ones counted by Moses and Eleazar the priest when they counted the Israelites on the plains of Moab by the Jordan across from Jericho. ⁶⁴Not one of them was among those counted by Moses and Aaron the priest when they counted the Israelites in the Desert of Sinai. ⁶⁵For the LORD had told those Israelites they would surely die in the desert, and not one of them was left except Caleb son of Jephunneh and Joshua son of Nun.

Zelophehad's Daughters

27 The daughters of Zelophehad son of Hepher, the son of Gilead, the son of Makir, the son of Manasseh, belonged to the clans of Manasseh son of Joseph. The names of the daughters were Mahlah, Noah, Hoglah, Milcah and Tirzah. They approached ²the entrance to the Tent of Meeting and stood before Moses, Eleazar the priest, the leaders and the whole assembly, and said, ³"Our father died in the desert. He was not among Korah's followers, who banded together against the LORD, but he died for his own sin and left no sons. ⁴Why should our father's name disappear from his clan because he had no son? Give us property among our father's relatives."

⁵So Moses brought their case before the LORD ⁶and the LORD said to him, ⁷"What Zelophehad's daughters are saying is right. You must certainly give them property as an inheritance among their father's relatives and turn their father's inheritance over to them.

⁸"Say to the Israelites, 'If a man dies and leaves no son, turn his inheritance over to his daughter. ⁹If he has no daughter, give his inheritance to his brothers. ¹⁰If he has no brothers, give his inheritance to his father's brothers. ¹¹If his father had no brothers, give his inheritance to the nearest relative in his clan, that he may possess it. This is to be a legal

---

[a]59 Or *Jochebed, a daughter of Levi, who was born to Levi*

requirement for the Israelites, as the LORD commanded Moses.' "

Joshua to Succeed Moses

[12]Then the LORD said to Moses, "Go up this mountain in the Abarim range and see the land I have given the Israelites. [13]After you have seen it, you too will be gathered to your people, as your brother Aaron was, [14]for when the community rebelled at the waters in the Desert of Zin, both of you disobeyed my command to honor me as holy before their eyes." (These were the waters of Meribah Kadesh, in the Desert of Zin.)

[15]Moses said to the LORD, [16]"May the LORD, the God of the spirits of all mankind, appoint a man over this community [17]to go out and come in before them, one who will lead them out and bring them in, so the LORD's people will not be like sheep without a shepherd." [18]So the LORD said to Moses, "Take Joshua son of Nun, a man in whom is the spirit,[a] and lay your hand on him. [19]Have him stand before Eleazar the priest and the entire assembly and commission him in their presence. [20]Give him some of your authority so the whole Israelite community will obey him. [21]He is to stand before Eleazar the priest, who will obtain decisions for him by inquiring of the Urim before the LORD. At his command he and the entire community of the Israelites will go out, and at his command they will come in." [22]Moses did as the LORD commanded him. He took Joshua and had him stand before Eleazar the priest and the whole assembly. [23]Then he laid his hands on him and commissioned him, as the LORD instructed through Moses.

Daily Offerings

28 The LORD said to Moses, [2]"Give this command to the Israelites and say to them: 'See that you present to me at the appointed time the food for my offerings made by fire, as an aroma pleasing to me.' [3]Say to them: 'This is the offering made by fire that you are to present to the LORD: two lambs a year old without defect, as a regular burnt offering each day. [4]Prepare one lamb in the morning and the other at twilight, [5]to-

gether with a grain offering of a tenth of an ephah[b] of fine flour mixed with a quarter of a hin[c] of oil from pressed olives. [6]This is the regular burnt offering instituted at Mount Sinai as a pleasing aroma, an offering made to the LORD by fire. [7]The accompanying drink offering is to be a quarter of a hin of fermented drink with each lamb. Pour out the drink offering to the LORD at the sanctuary. [8]Prepare the second lamb at twilight, along with the same kind of grain offering and drink offering that you prepare in the morning. This is an offering made by fire, an aroma pleasing to the LORD.

Sabbath Offerings

[9]" 'On the Sabbath day, make an offering of two lambs a year old without defect, together with its drink offering and a grain offering of two-tenths of an ephah[d] of fine flour mixed with oil. [10]This is the burnt offering for every Sabbath, in addition to the regular burnt offering and its drink offering.

Monthly Offerings

[11]" 'On the first of every month, present to the LORD a burnt offering of two young bulls, one ram and seven male lambs a year old, all without defect. [12]With each bull there is to be a grain offering of three-tenths of an ephah[e] of fine flour mixed with oil; with the ram, a grain offering of two-tenths of an ephah of fine flour mixed with oil; [13]and with each lamb, a grain offering of a tenth of an ephah of fine flour mixed with oil. This is for a burnt offering, a pleasing aroma, an offering made to the LORD by fire. [14]With each bull there is to be a drink offering of half a hin[f] of wine; with the ram, a third of a hin[g]; and with each lamb, a quarter of a hin. This is the monthly burnt offering to be made at each new moon during the year. [15]Besides the regular burnt offering with its

[a]18 Or Spirit   [b]5 That is, probably about 2 quarts (about 2 liters); also in verses 13, 21 and 29   [c]5 That is, probably about 1 quart (about 1 liter); also in verses 7 and 14   [d]9 That is, probably about 4 quarts (about 4.5 liters); also in verses 12, 20 and 28   [e]12 That is, probably about 6 quarts (about 6.5 liters); also in verses 20 and 28   [f]14 That is, probably about 2 quarts (about 2 liters)   [g]14 That is, probably about 1 1/4 quarts (about 1.2 liters)

drink offering, one male goat is to be presented to the LORD as a sin offering.

The Passover

[16] "'On the fourteenth day of the first month the LORD's Passover is to be held. [17]On the fifteenth day of this month there is to be a festival; for seven days eat bread made without yeast. [18]On the first day hold a sacred assembly and do no regular work. [19]Present to the LORD an offering made by fire, a burnt offering of two young bulls, one ram and seven male lambs a year old, all without defect. [20]With each bull prepare a grain offering of three-tenths of an ephah of fine flour mixed with oil; with the ram, two-tenths; [21]and with each of the seven lambs, one-tenth. [22]Include one male goat as a sin offering to make atonement for you. [23]Prepare these in addition to the regular morning burnt offering. [24]In this way prepare the food for the offering made by fire every day for seven days as an aroma pleasing to the LORD; it is to be prepared in addition to the regular burnt offering and its drink offering. [25]On the seventh day hold a sacred assembly and do no regular work.

Feast of Weeks

[26] "'On the day of firstfruits, when you present to the LORD an offering of new grain during the Feast of Weeks, hold a sacred assembly and do no regular work. [27]Present a burnt offering of two young bulls, one ram and seven male lambs a year old as an aroma pleasing to the LORD. [28]With each bull there is to be a grain offering of three-tenths of an ephah of fine flour mixed with oil; with the ram, two-tenths; [29]and with each of the seven lambs, one-tenth. [30]Include one male goat to make atonement for you. [31]Prepare these together with their drink offerings, in addition to the regular burnt offering and its grain offering. Be sure the animals are without defect.

Feast of Trumpets

29 "'On the first day of the seventh month hold a sacred assembly and do no regular work. It is a day for you to sound the trumpets. [2]As an aroma pleasing to the LORD, prepare a burnt of-

fering of one young bull, one ram and seven male lambs a year old, all without defect. [3]With the bull prepare a grain offering of three-tenths of an ephah[a] of fine flour mixed with oil; with the ram, two-tenths[b]; [4]and with each of the seven lambs, one-tenth.[c] [5]Include one male goat as a sin offering to make atonement for you. [6]These are in addition to the monthly and daily burnt offerings with their grain offerings and drink offerings as specified. They are offerings made to the LORD by fire—a pleasing aroma.

Day of Atonement

[7] "'On the tenth day of this seventh month hold a sacred assembly. You must deny yourselves[d] and do no work. [8]Present as an aroma pleasing to the LORD a burnt offering of one young bull, one ram and seven male lambs a year old, all without defect. [9]With the bull prepare a grain offering of three-tenths of an ephah of fine flour mixed with oil; with the ram, two-tenths; [10]and with each of the seven lambs, one-tenth. [11]Include one male goat as a sin offering, in addition to the sin offering for atonement and the regular burnt offering with its grain offering, and their drink offerings.

Feast of Tabernacles

[12] "'On the fifteenth day of the seventh month, hold a sacred assembly and do no regular work. Celebrate a festival to the LORD for seven days. [13]Present an offering made by fire as an aroma pleasing to the LORD, a burnt offering of thirteen young bulls, two rams and fourteen male lambs a year old, all without defect. [14]With each of the thirteen bulls prepare a grain offering of three-tenths of an ephah of fine flour mixed with oil; with each of the two rams, two-tenths; [15]and with each of the fourteen lambs, one-tenth. [16]Include one male goat as a sin offering, in addition to the regular burnt offering with its grain offering and drink offering.

[a]3 That is, probably about 6 quarts (about 6.5 liters); also in verses 9 and 14   [b]3 That is, probably about 4 quarts (about 4.5 liters); also in verses 9 and 14   [c]4 That is, probably about 2 quarts (about 2 liters); also in verses 10 and 15   [d]7 Or *must fast*

[17]" 'On the second day prepare twelve young bulls, two rams and fourteen male lambs a year old, all without defect. [18]With the bulls, rams and lambs, prepare their grain offerings and drink offerings according to the number specified. [19]Include one male goat as a sin offering, in addition to the regular burnt offering with its grain offering, and their drink offerings.

[20]" 'On the third day prepare eleven bulls, two rams and fourteen male lambs a year old, all without defect. [21]With the bulls, rams and lambs, prepare their grain offerings and drink offerings according to the number specified. [22]Include one male goat as a sin offering, in addition to the regular burnt offering with its grain offering and drink offering.

[23]" 'On the fourth day prepare ten bulls, two rams and fourteen male lambs a year old, all without defect. [24]With the bulls, rams and lambs, prepare their grain offerings and drink offerings according to the number specified. [25]Include one male goat as a sin offering, in addition to the regular burnt offering with its grain offering and drink offering.

[26]" 'On the fifth day prepare nine bulls, two rams and fourteen male lambs a year old, all without defect. [27]With the bulls, rams and lambs, prepare their grain offerings and drink offerings according to the number specified. [28]Include one male goat as a sin offering, in addition to the regular burnt offering with its grain offering and drink offering.

[29]" 'On the sixth day prepare eight bulls, two rams and fourteen male lambs a year old, all without defect. [30]With the bulls, rams and lambs, prepare their grain offerings and drink offerings according to the number specified. [31]Include one male goat as a sin offering, in addition to the regular burnt offering with its grain offering and drink offering.

[32]" 'On the seventh day prepare seven bulls, two rams and fourteen male lambs a year old, all without defect. [33]With the bulls, rams and lambs, prepare their grain offerings and drink offerings according to the number specified. [34]Include one male goat as a sin offering, in addition to the regular burnt offering with its grain offering and drink offering.

[35]" 'On the eighth day hold an assembly and do no regular work. [36]Present an offering made by fire as an aroma pleasing to the LORD, a burnt offering of one bull, one ram and seven male lambs a year old, all without defect. [37]With the bull, the ram and the lambs, prepare their grain offerings and drink offerings according to the number specified. [38]Include one male goat as a sin offering, in addition to the regular burnt offering with its grain offering and drink offering.

[39]" 'In addition to what you vow and your freewill offerings, prepare these for the LORD at your appointed feasts: your burnt offerings, grain offerings, drink offerings and fellowship offerings.[a]' "

[40]Moses told the Israelites all that the LORD commanded him.

Vows

30 Moses said to the heads of the tribes of Israel: "This is what the LORD commands: [2]When a man makes a vow to the LORD or takes an oath to obligate himself by a pledge, he must not break his word but must do everything he said.

[3]"When a young woman still living in her father's house makes a vow to the LORD or obligates herself by a pledge [4]and her father hears about her vow or pledge but says nothing to her, then all her vows and every pledge by which she obligated herself will stand. [5]But if her father forbids her when he hears about it, none of her vows or the pledges by which she obligated herself will stand; the LORD will release her because her father has forbidden her.

[6]"If she marries after she makes a vow or after her lips utter a rash promise by which she obligates herself [7]and her husband hears about it but says nothing to her, then her vows or the pledges by which she obligated herself will stand. [8]But if her husband forbids her when he hears about it, he nullifies the vow that

[a]39 Traditionally *peace offerings*

obligates her or the rash promise by which she obligates herself, and the LORD will release her.

⁹"Any vow or obligation taken by a widow or divorced woman will be binding on her.

¹⁰"If a woman living with her husband makes a vow or obligates herself by a pledge under oath ¹¹and her husband hears about it but says nothing to her and does not forbid her, then all her vows or the pledges by which she obligated herself will stand. ¹²But if her husband nullifies them when he hears about them, then none of the vows or pledges that came from her lips will stand. Her husband has nullified them, and the LORD will release her. ¹³Her husband may confirm or nullify any vow she makes or any sworn pledge to deny herself. ¹⁴But if her husband says nothing to her about it from day to day, then he confirms all her vows or the pledges binding on her. He confirms them by saying nothing to her when he hears about them. ¹⁵If, however, he nullifies them some time after he hears about them, then he is responsible for her guilt."

¹⁶These are the regulations the LORD gave Moses concerning relationships between a man and his wife, and between a father and his young daughter still living in his house.

Vengeance on the Midianites

31 The LORD said to Moses, ²"Take vengeance on the Midianites for the Israelites. After that, you will be gathered to your people."

³So Moses said to the people, "Arm some of your men to go to war against the Midianites and to carry out the LORD's vengeance on them. ⁴Send into battle a thousand men from each of the tribes of Israel." ⁵So twelve thousand men armed for battle, a thousand from each tribe, were supplied from the clans of Israel. ⁶Moses sent them into battle, a thousand from each tribe, along with Phinehas son of Eleazar, the priest, who took with him articles from the sanctuary and the trumpets for signaling.

⁷They fought against Midian, as the LORD commanded Moses, and killed every man. ⁸Among their victims were Evi, Rekem, Zur, Hur and Reba—the five kings of Midian. They also killed Balaam son of Beor with the sword. ⁹The Israelites captured the Midianite women and children and took all the Midianite herds, flocks and goods as plunder. ¹⁰They burned all the towns where the Midianites had settled, as well as all their camps. ¹¹They took all the plunder and spoils, including the people and animals, ¹²and brought the captives, spoils and plunder to Moses and Eleazar the priest and the Israelite assembly at their camp on the plains of Moab, by the Jordan across from Jericho.ᵃ

¹³Moses, Eleazar the priest and all the leaders of the community went to meet them outside the camp. ¹⁴Moses was angry with the officers of the army—the commanders of thousands and commanders of hundreds—who returned from the battle.

¹⁵"Have you allowed all the women to live?" he asked them. ¹⁶"They were the ones who followed Balaam's advice and were the means of turning the Israelites away from the LORD in what happened at Peor, so that a plague struck the LORD's people. ¹⁷Now kill all the boys. And kill every woman who has slept with a man, ¹⁸but save for yourselves every girl who has never slept with a man.

¹⁹"All of you who have killed anyone or touched anyone who was killed must stay outside the camp seven days. On the third and seventh days you must purify yourselves and your captives. ²⁰Purify every garment as well as everything made of leather, goat hair or wood."

²¹Then Eleazar the priest said to the soldiers who had gone into battle, "This is the requirement of the law that the LORD gave Moses: ²²Gold, silver, bronze, iron, tin, lead ²³and anything else that can withstand fire must be put through the fire, and then it will be clean. But it must also be purified with the water of cleansing. And whatever cannot withstand fire must be put through that water. ²⁴On the seventh day wash your clothes and you will be clean. Then you may come into the camp."

ᵃ12 Hebrew *Jordan of Jericho*; possibly an ancient name for the Jordan River

Dividing the Spoils

²⁵The LORD said to Moses, ²⁶"You and Eleazar the priest and the family heads of the community are to count all the people and animals that were captured. ²⁷Divide the spoils between the soldiers who took part in the battle and the rest of the community. ²⁸From the soldiers who fought in the battle, set apart as tribute for the LORD one out of every five hundred, whether persons, cattle, donkeys, sheep or goats. ²⁹Take this tribute from their half share and give it to Eleazar the priest as the LORD's part. ³⁰From the Israelites' half, select one out of every fifty, whether persons, cattle, donkeys, sheep, goats or other animals. Give them to the Levites, who are responsible for the care of the LORD's tabernacle." ³¹So Moses and Eleazar the priest did as the LORD commanded Moses.

³²The plunder remaining from the spoils that the soldiers took was 675,000 sheep, ³³72,000 cattle, ³⁴61,000 donkeys ³⁵and 32,000 women who had never slept with a man.

³⁶The half share of those who fought in the battle was:

337,500 sheep, ³⁷of which the tribute for the LORD was 675;
³⁸ 36,000 cattle, of which the tribute for the LORD was 72;
³⁹ 30,500 donkeys, of which the tribute for the LORD was 61;
⁴⁰ 16,000 people, of which the tribute for the LORD was 32.

⁴¹Moses gave the tribute to Eleazar the priest as the LORD's part, as the LORD commanded Moses.

⁴²The half belonging to the Israelites, which Moses set apart from that of the fighting men— ⁴³the community's half— was 337,500 sheep, ⁴⁴36,000 cattle, ⁴⁵30,500 donkeys ⁴⁶and 16,000 people. ⁴⁷From the Israelites' half, Moses selected one out of every fifty persons and animals, as the LORD commanded him, and gave them to the Levites, who were responsible for the care of the LORD's tabernacle.

⁴⁸Then the officers who were over the units of the army—the commanders of thousands and commanders of hun-

dreds—went to Moses ⁴⁹and said to him, "Your servants have counted the soldiers under our command, and not one is missing. ⁵⁰So we have brought as an offering to the LORD the gold articles each of us acquired—armlets, bracelets, signet rings, earrings and necklaces—to make atonement for ourselves before the LORD."

⁵¹Moses and Eleazar the priest accepted from them the gold—all the crafted articles. ⁵²All the gold from the commanders of thousands and commanders of hundreds that Moses and Eleazar presented as a gift to the LORD weighed 16,750 shekels.ᵃ ⁵³Each soldier had taken plunder for himself. ⁵⁴Moses and Eleazar the priest accepted the gold from the commanders of thousands and commanders of hundreds and brought it into the Tent of Meeting as a memorial for the Israelites before the LORD.

The Transjordan Tribes

32 The Reubenites and Gadites, who had very large herds and flocks, saw that the lands of Jazer and Gilead were suitable for livestock. ²So they came to Moses and Eleazar the priest and to the leaders of the community, and said, ³"Ataroth, Dibon, Jazer, Nimrah, Heshbon, Elealeh, Sebam, Nebo and Beon— ⁴the land the LORD subdued before the people of Israel—are suitable for livestock, and your servants have livestock. ⁵If we have found favor in your eyes," they said, "let this land be given to your servants as our possession. Do not make us cross the Jordan."

⁶Moses said to the Gadites and Reubenites, "Shall your countrymen go to war while you sit here? ⁷Why do you discourage the Israelites from going over into the land the LORD has given them? ⁸This is what your fathers did when I sent them from Kadesh Barnea to look over the land. ⁹After they went up to the Valley of Eshcol and viewed the land, they discouraged the Israelites from entering the land the LORD had given them. ¹⁰The LORD's anger was aroused that day and he swore this oath: ¹¹'Because they have not followed me wholeheartedly, not one

---

ᵃ52 That is, about 420 pounds (about 190 kilograms)

of the men twenty years old or more who came up out of Egypt will see the land I promised on oath to Abraham, Isaac and Jacob— ¹²not one except Caleb son of Jephunneh the Kenizzite and Joshua son of Nun, for they followed the LORD wholeheartedly.' ¹³The LORD's anger burned against Israel and he made them wander in the desert forty years, until the whole generation of those who had done evil in his sight was gone.

¹⁴"And here you are, a brood of sinners, standing in the place of your fathers and making the LORD even more angry with Israel. ¹⁵If you turn away from following him, he will again leave all this people in the desert, and you will be the cause of their destruction."

¹⁶Then they came up to him and said, "We would like to build pens here for our livestock and cities for our women and children. ¹⁷But we are ready to arm ourselves and go ahead of the Israelites until we have brought them to their place. Meanwhile our women and children will live in fortified cities, for protection from the inhabitants of the land. ¹⁸We will not return to our homes until every Israelite has received his inheritance. ¹⁹We will not receive any inheritance with them on the other side of the Jordan, because our inheritance has come to us on the east side of the Jordan."

²⁰Then Moses said to them, "If you will do this—if you will arm yourselves before the LORD for battle, ²¹and if all of you will go armed over the Jordan before the LORD until he has driven his enemies out before him— ²²then when the land is subdued before the LORD, you may return and be free from your obligation to the LORD and to Israel. And this land will be your possession before the LORD.

²³"But if you fail to do this, you will be sinning against the LORD; and you may be sure that your sin will find you out. ²⁴Build cities for your women and children, and pens for your flocks, but do what you have promised."

²⁵The Gadites and Reubenites said to Moses, "We your servants will do as our lord commands. ²⁶Our children and wives, our flocks and herds will remain here in the cities of Gilead. ²⁷But your servants, every man armed for battle, will cross over to fight before the LORD, just as our lord says."

²⁸Then Moses gave orders about them to Eleazar the priest and Joshua son of Nun and to the family heads of the Israelite tribes. ²⁹He said to them, "If the Gadites and Reubenites, every man armed for battle, cross over the Jordan with you before the LORD, then when the land is subdued before you, give them the land of Gilead as their possession. ³⁰But if they do not cross over with you armed, they must accept their possession with you in Canaan."

³¹The Gadites and Reubenites answered, "Your servants will do what the LORD has said. ³²We will cross over before the LORD into Canaan armed, but the property we inherit will be on this side of the Jordan."

³³Then Moses gave to the Gadites, the Reubenites and the half-tribe of Manasseh son of Joseph the kingdom of Sihon king of the Amorites and the kingdom of Og king of Bashan—the whole land with its cities and the territory around them.

³⁴The Gadites built up Dibon, Ataroth, Aroer, ³⁵Atroth Shophan, Jazer, Jogbehah, ³⁶Beth Nimrah and Beth Haran as fortified cities, and built pens for their flocks. ³⁷And the Reubenites rebuilt Heshbon, Elealeh and Kiriathaim, ³⁸as well as Nebo and Baal Meon (these names were changed) and Sibmah. They gave names to the cities they rebuilt.

³⁹The descendants of Makir son of Manasseh went to Gilead, captured it and drove out the Amorites who were there. ⁴⁰So Moses gave Gilead to the Makirites, the descendants of Manasseh, and they settled there. ⁴¹Jair, a descendant of Manasseh, captured their settlements and called them Havvoth Jair.ᵃ ⁴²And Nobah captured Kenath and its surrounding settlements and called it Nobah after himself.

Stages in Israel's Journey

33 Here are the stages in the journey of the Israelites when they came out of Egypt by divisions under the leadership of Moses and Aaron. ²At the LORD's command Moses recorded the

---

ᵃ41 Or them the settlements of Jair

stages in their journey. This is their journey by stages:

³The Israelites set out from Rameses on the fifteenth day of the first month, the day after the Passover. They marched out boldly in full view of all the Egyptians, ⁴who were burying all their firstborn, whom the LORD had struck down among them; for the LORD had brought judgment on their gods.

⁵The Israelites left Rameses and camped at Succoth.

⁶They left Succoth and camped at Etham, on the edge of the desert.

⁷They left Etham, turned back to Pi Hahiroth, to the east of Baal Zephon, and camped near Migdol.

⁸They left Pi Hahiroth[a] and passed through the sea into the desert, and when they had traveled for three days in the Desert of Etham, they camped at Marah.

⁹They left Marah and went to Elim, where there were twelve springs and seventy palm trees, and they camped there.

¹⁰They left Elim and camped by the Red Sea.[b]

¹¹They left the Red Sea and camped in the Desert of Sin.

¹²They left the Desert of Sin and camped at Dophkah.

¹³They left Dophkah and camped at Alush.

¹⁴They left Alush and camped at Rephidim, where there was no water for the people to drink.

¹⁵They left Rephidim and camped in the Desert of Sinai.

¹⁶They left the Desert of Sinai and camped at Kibroth Hattaavah.

¹⁷They left Kibroth Hattaavah and camped at Hazeroth.

¹⁸They left Hazeroth and camped at Rithmah.

¹⁹They left Rithmah and camped at Rimmon Perez.

²⁰They left Rimmon Perez and camped at Libnah.

²¹They left Libnah and camped at Rissah.

²²They left Rissah and camped at Kehelathah.

²³They left Kehelathah and camped at Mount Shepher.

²⁴They left Mount Shepher and camped at Haradah.

²⁵They left Haradah and camped at Makheloth.

²⁶They left Makheloth and camped at Tahath.

²⁷They left Tahath and camped at Terah.

²⁸They left Terah and camped at Mithcah.

²⁹They left Mithcah and camped at Hashmonah.

³⁰They left Hashmonah and camped at Moseroth.

³¹They left Moseroth and camped at Bene Jaakan.

³²They left Bene Jaakan and camped at Hor Haggidgad.

³³They left Hor Haggidgad and camped at Jotbathah.

³⁴They left Jotbathah and camped at Abronah.

³⁵They left Abronah and camped at Ezion Geber.

³⁶They left Ezion Geber and camped at Kadesh, in the Desert of Zin.

³⁷They left Kadesh and camped at Mount Hor, on the border of Edom.
³⁸At the LORD's command Aaron the priest went up Mount Hor, where he died on the first day of the fifth month of the fortieth year after the Israelites came out of Egypt. ³⁹Aaron was a hundred and twenty-three years old when he died on Mount Hor.

⁴⁰The Canaanite king of Arad, who lived in the Negev of Canaan, heard that the Israelites were coming.

⁴¹They left Mount Hor and camped at Zalmonah.

⁴²They left Zalmonah and camped at Punon.

⁴³They left Punon and camped at Oboth.

⁴⁴They left Oboth and camped at Iye Abarim, on the border of Moab.

---

[a]8 Many manuscripts of the Masoretic Text, Samaritan Pentateuch and Vulgate; most manuscripts of the Masoretic Text *left from before Hahiroth*   [b]10 Hebrew *Yam Suph*; that is, Sea of Reeds; also in verse 11

⁴⁵They left Iyim*ᵃ* and camped at Dibon Gad.

⁴⁶They left Dibon Gad and camped at Almon Diblathaim.

⁴⁷They left Almon Diblathaim and camped in the mountains of Abarim, near Nebo.

⁴⁸They left the mountains of Abarim and camped on the plains of Moab by the Jordan across from Jericho.*ᵇ* ⁴⁹There on the plains of Moab they camped along the Jordan from Beth Jeshimoth to Abel Shittim.

⁵⁰On the plains of Moab by the Jordan across from Jericho the LORD said to Moses, ⁵¹"Speak to the Israelites and say to them: 'When you cross the Jordan into Canaan, ⁵²drive out all the inhabitants of the land before you. Destroy all their carved images and their cast idols, and demolish all their high places. ⁵³Take possession of the land and settle in it, for I have given you the land to possess. ⁵⁴Distribute the land by lot, according to your clans. To a larger group give a larger inheritance, and to a smaller group a smaller one. Whatever falls to them by lot will be theirs. Distribute it according to your ancestral tribes.

⁵⁵" 'But if you do not drive out the inhabitants of the land, those you allow to remain will become barbs in your eyes and thorns in your sides. They will give you trouble in the land where you will live. ⁵⁶And then I will do to you what I plan to do to them.' "

Boundaries of Canaan

34 The LORD said to Moses, ²"Command the Israelites and say to them: 'When you enter Canaan, the land that will be allotted to you as an inheritance will have these boundaries:

³" 'Your southern side will include some of the Desert of Zin along the border of Edom. On the east, your southern boundary will start from the end of the Salt Sea,*ᶜ* ⁴cross south of Scorpion*ᵈ* Pass, continue on to Zin and go south of Kadesh Barnea. Then it will go to Hazar Addar and over to Azmon, ⁵where it will turn, join the Wadi of Egypt and end at the Sea.*ᵉ*

⁶" 'Your western boundary will be the coast of the Great Sea. This will be your boundary on the west.

⁷" 'For your northern boundary, run a line from the Great Sea to Mount Hor ⁸and from Mount Hor to Lebo*ᶠ* Hamath. Then the boundary will go to Zedad, ⁹continue to Ziphron and end at Hazar Enan. This will be your boundary on the north.

¹⁰" 'For your eastern boundary, run a line from Hazar Enan to Shepham. ¹¹The boundary will go down from Shepham to Riblah on the east side of Ain and continue along the slopes east of the Sea of Kinnereth.*ᵍ* ¹²Then the boundary will go down along the Jordan and end at the Salt Sea.

" 'This will be your land, with its boundaries on every side.' "

¹³Moses commanded the Israelites: "Assign this land by lot as an inheritance. The LORD has ordered that it be given to the nine and a half tribes, ¹⁴because the families of the tribe of Reuben, the tribe of Gad and the half-tribe of Manasseh have received their inheritance. ¹⁵These two and a half tribes have received their inheritance on the east side of the Jordan of Jericho,*ʰ* toward the sunrise."

¹⁶The LORD said to Moses, ¹⁷"These are the names of the men who are to assign the land for you as an inheritance: Eleazar the priest and Joshua son of Nun. ¹⁸And appoint one leader from each tribe to help assign the land. ¹⁹These are their names:

Caleb son of Jephunneh,
  from the tribe of Judah;
²⁰Shemuel son of Ammihud,
  from the tribe of Simeon;
²¹Elidad son of Kislon,
  from the tribe of Benjamin;
²²Bukki son of Jogli,
  the leader from the tribe of Dan;
²³Hanniel son of Ephod,

ᵃ45 That is, Iye Abarim   *ᵇ48* Hebrew *Jordan of Jericho;* possibly an ancient name for the Jordan River; also in verse 50   *ᶜ3* That is, the Dead Sea; also in verse 12   *ᵈ4* Hebrew *Akrabbim*   *ᵉ5* That is, the Mediterranean; also in verses 6 and 7   *ᶠ8* Or *to the entrance to*   *ᵍ11* That is, Galilee   *ʰ15* *Jordan of Jericho* was possibly an ancient name for the Jordan River.

the leader from the tribe of Manasseh son of Joseph;
²⁴Kemuel son of Shiphtan,
the leader from the tribe of Ephraim son of Joseph;
²⁵Elizaphan son of Parnach,
the leader from the tribe of Zebulun;
²⁶Paltiel son of Azzan,
the leader from the tribe of Issachar;
²⁷Ahihud son of Shelomi,
the leader from the tribe of Asher;
²⁸Pedahel son of Ammihud,
the leader from the tribe of Naphtali."

²⁹These are the men the LORD commanded to assign the inheritance to the Israelites in the land of Canaan.

Towns for the Levites

35 On the plains of Moab by the Jordan across from Jericho,ᵃ the LORD said to Moses, ²"Command the Israelites to give the Levites towns to live in from the inheritance the Israelites will possess. And give them pasturelands around the towns. ³Then they will have towns to live in and pasturelands for their cattle, flocks and all their other livestock.

⁴"The pasturelands around the towns that you give the Levites will extend out fifteen hundred feetᵇ from the town wall. ⁵Outside the town, measure three thousand feetᶜ on the east side, three thousand on the south side, three thousand on the west and three thousand on the north, with the town in the center. They will have this area as pastureland for the towns.

Cities of Refuge

⁶"Six of the towns you give the Levites will be cities of refuge, to which a person who has killed someone may flee. In addition, give them forty-two other towns. ⁷In all you must give the Levites forty-eight towns, together with their pasturelands. ⁸The towns you give the Levites from the land the Israelites possess are to be given in proportion to the inheritance of each tribe: Take many towns from a tribe that has many, but few from one that has few."

⁹Then the LORD said to Moses: ¹⁰"Speak to the Israelites and say to them: 'When you cross the Jordan into Canaan, ¹¹select some towns to be your cities of refuge, to which a person who has killed someone accidentally may flee. ¹²They will be places of refuge from the avenger, so that a person accused of murder may not die before he stands trial before the assembly. ¹³These six towns you give will be your cities of refuge. ¹⁴Give three on this side of the Jordan and three in Canaan as cities of refuge. ¹⁵These six towns will be a place of refuge for Israelites, aliens and any other people living among them, so that anyone who has killed another accidentally can flee there.

¹⁶" 'If a man strikes someone with an iron object so that he dies, he is a murderer; the murderer shall be put to death. ¹⁷Or if anyone has a stone in his hand that could kill, and he strikes someone so that he dies, he is a murderer; the murderer shall be put to death. ¹⁸Or if anyone has a wooden object in his hand that could kill, and he hits someone so that he dies, he is a murderer; the murderer shall be put to death. ¹⁹The avenger of blood shall put the murderer to death; when he meets him, he shall put him to death. ²⁰If anyone with malice aforethought shoves another or throws something at him intentionally so that he dies ²¹or if in hostility he hits him with his fist so that he dies, that person shall be put to death; he is a murderer. The avenger of blood shall put the murderer to death when he meets him.

²²" 'But if without hostility someone suddenly shoves another or throws something at him unintentionally ²³or, without seeing him, drops a stone on him that could kill him, and he dies, then since he was not his enemy and he did not intend to harm him, ²⁴the assembly must judge between him and the avenger of blood according to these regulations. ²⁵The assembly must protect the one accused of murder from the avenger of blood and send him back to the city of refuge to which he fled. He must stay

---

ᵃ1 Hebrew *Jordan of Jericho*; possibly an ancient name for the Jordan River   ᵇ4 Hebrew *a thousand cubits* (about 450 meters)   ᶜ5 Hebrew *two thousand cubits* (about 900 meters)

there until the death of the high priest, who was anointed with the holy oil.

²⁶" 'But if the accused ever goes outside the limits of the city of refuge to which he has fled ²⁷and the avenger of blood finds him outside the city, the avenger of blood may kill the accused without being guilty of murder. ²⁸The accused must stay in his city of refuge until the death of the high priest; only after the death of the high priest may he return to his own property.

²⁹" 'These are to be legal requirements for you throughout the generations to come, wherever you live.

³⁰" 'Anyone who kills a person is to be put to death as a murderer only on the testimony of witnesses. But no one is to be put to death on the testimony of only one witness.

³¹" 'Do not accept a ransom for the life of a murderer, who deserves to die. He must surely be put to death.

³²" 'Do not accept a ransom for anyone who has fled to a city of refuge and so allow him to go back and live on his own land before the death of the high priest.

³³" 'Do not pollute the land where you are. Bloodshed pollutes the land, and atonement cannot be made for the land on which blood has been shed, except by the blood of the one who shed it. ³⁴Do not defile the land where you live and where I dwell, for I, the LORD, dwell among the Israelites.' "

Inheritance of Zelophehad's Daughters

36 The family heads of the clan of Gilead son of Makir, the son of Manasseh, who were from the clans of the descendants of Joseph, came and spoke before Moses and the leaders, the heads of the Israelite families. ²They said, "When the LORD commanded my lord to give the land as an inheritance to the Israelites by lot, he ordered you to give the inheritance of our brother Zelophehad to his daughters. ³Now suppose they marry men from other Israelite tribes; then their inheritance will be taken from our ancestral inheritance and added to that of the tribe they marry into. And so part of the inheritance allotted to us will be taken away. ⁴When the Year of Jubilee for the Israelites comes, their inheritance will be added to that of the tribe into which they marry, and their property will be taken from the tribal inheritance of our forefathers."

⁵Then at the LORD's command Moses gave this order to the Israelites: "What the tribe of the descendants of Joseph is saying is right. ⁶This is what the LORD commands for Zelophehad's daughters: They may marry anyone they please as long as they marry within the tribal clan of their father. ⁷No inheritance in Israel is to pass from tribe to tribe, for every Israelite shall keep the tribal land inherited from his forefathers. ⁸Every daughter who inherits land in any Israelite tribe must marry someone in her father's tribal clan, so that every Israelite will possess the inheritance of his fathers. ⁹No inheritance may pass from tribe to tribe, for each Israelite tribe is to keep the land it inherits."

¹⁰So Zelophehad's daughters did as the LORD commanded Moses. ¹¹Zelophehad's daughters—Mahlah, Tirzah, Hoglah, Milcah and Noah—married their cousins on their father's side. ¹²They married within the clans of the descendants of Manasseh son of Joseph, and their inheritance remained in their father's clan and tribe.

¹³These are the commands and regulations the LORD gave through Moses to the Israelites on the plains of Moab by the Jordan across from Jericho.ᵃ

ᵃ13 Hebrew *Jordan of Jericho*; possibly an ancient name for the Jordan River

Deuteronomy

START

After wimping out at Kadesh Barnea, the Israelites have had 39 more years to get their lives in order and their priorities straight. They've done that by wandering around in the desert. By the time the wanderers reach the plains of Moab, just shy of the Jordan River goal line, most of the old folks have died off. In Deuteronomy, Moses calls a time-out and gives his final message to the *new* generation.

These kids are too young to remember crossing the Red Sea. They missed out on God's big entrance at Mount Sinai. To them, that whole thing with the Ten Commandments was like the 60s and 70s were to you: before their time. So old Moses gives them a history lesson. He reviews the stuff that got them out of Egypt, the covenant with God, and what happened when their parents and grandparents broke the deal.

Deuteronomy ends as Moses finishes his life's to-do list:

(a) Appoint Joshua as the new leader
(b) Write everything into a big fat book (*The Pentateuch*—the first 5 books of the Bible)
(c) Go up the mountain and see the promised land in the distance
(d) Die

Moses completes the list.

Cast OF Characters

Moses (MOE-zus)
Mo is now over 100 years old. He's led his people out of slavery in Egypt, through 40 years of trials and errors in the desert, and has set them right on the goal line, ready to conquer the promised land on the other side of the Jordan River.

Joshua
(JAH-shoo-wah)
Josh first showed up back in the book of Numbers. He and his buddy Caleb were the only two spies who looked at the promised land with excitement and courage instead of with fear and griping. Because of this, God blesses Joshua and makes him leader of the people after Moses dies.

Sihon of Heshbon and Og of Bashan
(SY-hahn of HESH-bahn)
(AHG of BAY-shahn)
These guys are kings of nations in the path of Israel's march to the promised land. They get snooty with Moses and God, and they pay the price: They get wiped off the map.

What's UP with That?

In most of this book, Moses describes the covenant God made with Israel. God promised to bless them with a bunch of really great things if they would live up to their end of the bargain. All they had to do was *obey God*. Here's a list of some of the things God promised. Look up the reference verses and cross out the items that *weren't* a part of the deal:

If you obey God, he will . . .

A Let you live long and prosper (6:2)

B Wipe out all diseases (6:41)

C Give you really fresh breath (6:57)

D Love you and bless you (7:13)

E Make your enemies go away (7:22)

F Give you a big-screen TV (7:30)

G Let you worship a golden cow in your spare time (9:16)

H Give you big farms and lots to eat (11:15)

answers: a, d, e, h

Snap shots

● "Let's review"—
Moses tells the young folks their history
(*chapters 1—3*)

● The Law, one more time—Moses reviews God's do's and don'ts
(*chapters 4—30*)

● The new guy—Joshua gets a promotion
(*chapter 31*)

● Moses says goodbye—a song, a glimpse at the goal, a hero dies
(*chapters 32—34*)

The Command to Leave Horeb

1 These are the words Moses spoke to all Israel in the desert east of the Jordan—that is, in the Arabah—opposite Suph, between Paran and Tophel, Laban, Hazeroth and Dizahab. ²(It takes eleven days to go from Horeb to Kadesh Barnea by the Mount Seir road.)

³In the fortieth year, on the first day of the eleventh month, Moses proclaimed to the Israelites all that the LORD had commanded him concerning them. ⁴This was after he had defeated Sihon king of the Amorites, who reigned in Heshbon, and at Edrei had defeated Og king of Bashan, who reigned in Ashtaroth.

⁵East of the Jordan in the territory of Moab, Moses began to expound this law, saying:

⁶The LORD our God said to us at Horeb, "You have stayed long enough at this mountain. ⁷Break camp and advance into the hill country of the Amorites; go to all the neighboring peoples in the Arabah, in the mountains, in the western foothills, in the Negev and along the coast, to the land of the Canaanites and to Lebanon, as far as the great river, the Euphrates. ⁸See, I have given you this land. Go in and take possession of the land that the LORD swore he would give to your fathers—to Abraham, Isaac and Jacob—and to their descendants after them."

The Appointment of Leaders

⁹At that time I said to you, "You are too heavy a burden for me to carry alone. ¹⁰The LORD your God has increased your numbers so that today you are as many as the stars in the sky. ¹¹May the LORD, the God of your fathers, increase you a thousand times and bless you as he has promised! ¹²But how can I bear your problems and your burdens and your disputes all by myself? ¹³Choose some wise, understanding and respected men from each of your tribes, and I will set them over you."

¹⁴You answered me, "What you propose to do is good."

¹⁵So I took the leading men of your tribes, wise and respected men, and appointed them to have authority over you—as commanders of thousands, of hundreds, of fifties and of tens and as tribal officials. ¹⁶And I charged your judges at that time: Hear the disputes between your brothers and judge fairly, whether the case is between brother Israelites or between one of them and an alien. ¹⁷Do not show partiality in judging; hear both small and great alike. Do not be afraid of any man, for judgment belongs to God. Bring me any case too hard for you, and I will hear it. ¹⁸And at that time I told you everything you were to do.

Spies Sent Out

¹⁹Then, as the LORD our God commanded us, we set out from Horeb and went toward the hill country of the Amorites through all that vast and dreadful desert that you have seen, and so we reached Kadesh Barnea. ²⁰Then I said to you, "You have reached the hill country of the Amorites, which the LORD our God is giving us. ²¹See, the LORD your God has given you the land. Go up and take possession of it as the LORD, the God of your fathers, told you. Do not be afraid; do not be discouraged."

²²Then all of you came to me and said, "Let us send men ahead to spy out the land for us and bring back a report about the route we are to take and the towns we will come to."

²³The idea seemed good to me; so I selected twelve of you, one man from each tribe. ²⁴They left and went up into the hill country, and came to the Valley of Eshcol and explored it. ²⁵Taking with them some of the fruit of the land, they brought it down to us and reported, "It is a good land that the LORD our God is giving us."

Rebellion Against the LORD

²⁶But you were unwilling to go up; you rebelled against the command of the LORD your God. ²⁷You grumbled in your tents and said, "The LORD hates us; so he brought us out of Egypt to deliver us into the hands of the Amorites to destroy us. ²⁸Where can we go? Our brothers have made us lose heart. They say, 'The people are stronger and taller than we are; the cities are large, with walls up to the sky. We even saw the Anakites there.' "

When God Says Go . . .

Huh?

Deuteronomy 1:26-28

God promised the Israelites a new land and a new life. He showed them the land and told them to go for it. But the people were afraid. They were more afraid of doing what God told them to do than they were afraid of God himself. That made God ticked. He *knew* what he was doing, but the people were too scared and stubborn to trust him.

²⁹Then I said to you, "Do not be terrified; do not be afraid of them. ³⁰The LORD your God, who is going before you, will fight for you, as he did for you in Egypt, before your very eyes, ³¹and in the desert. There you saw how the LORD your God carried you, as a father carries his son, all the way you went until you reached this place."

³²In spite of this, you did not trust in the LORD your God, ³³who went ahead of you on your journey, in fire by night and in a cloud by day, to search out places for you to camp and to show you the way you should go.

³⁴When the LORD heard what you said, he was angry and solemnly swore: ³⁵"Not a man of this evil generation shall see the good land I swore to give your forefathers, ³⁶except Caleb son of Jephunneh. He will see it, and I will give him and his descendants the land he set his feet on, because he followed the LORD whole-heartedly."

³⁷Because of you the LORD became angry with me also and said, "You shall not enter it, either. ³⁸But your assistant, Joshua son of Nun, will enter it. Encourage him, because he will lead Israel to inherit it. ³⁹And the little ones that you said would be taken captive, your children who do not yet know good from bad—they will enter the land. I will give it to them and they will take possession of it. ⁴⁰But as for you, turn around and set out toward the desert along the route to the Red Sea.ᵃ "

⁴¹Then you replied, "We have sinned against the LORD. We will go up and fight, as the LORD our God commanded us." So every one of you put on his weapons, thinking it easy to go up into the hill country.

⁴²But the LORD said to me, "Tell them, 'Do not go up and fight, because I will not be with you. You will be defeated by your enemies.' "

⁴³So I told you, but you would not listen. You rebelled against the LORD's command and in your arrogance you marched up into the hill country. ⁴⁴The Amorites who lived in those hills came out against you; they chased you like a swarm of bees and beat you down from Seir all the way to Hormah. ⁴⁵You came back and wept before the LORD, but he paid no attention to your weeping and turned a deaf ear to you. ⁴⁶And so you stayed in Kadesh many days—all the time you spent there.

Wanderings in the Desert

2 Then we turned back and set out toward the desert along the route to the Red Sea,ᵃ as the LORD had directed me. For a long time we made our way around the hill country of Seir.

²Then the LORD said to me, ³"You have made your way around this hill country long enough; now turn north. ⁴Give the people these orders: 'You are about to pass through the territory of your brothers the descendants of Esau, who live in Seir. They will be afraid of you, but be very careful. ⁵Do not provoke them to war, for I will not give you any of their land, not even enough to put your foot on. I have given Esau the hill country of Seir as his own. ⁶You are to pay them in silver for the food you eat and the water you drink.' "

⁷The LORD your God has blessed you in all the work of your hands. He has watched over your journey through this vast desert. These forty years the LORD your God has been with you, and you have not lacked anything.

⁸So we went on past our brothers the descendants of Esau, who live in Seir. We

ᵃ40,1 Hebrew *Yam Suph*; that is, Sea of Reeds

turned from the Arabah road, which comes up from Elath and Ezion Geber, and traveled along the desert road of Moab.

⁹Then the LORD said to me, "Do not harass the Moabites or provoke them to war, for I will not give you any part of their land. I have given Ar to the descendants of Lot as a possession."

¹⁰(The Emites used to live there—a people strong and numerous, and as tall as the Anakites. ¹¹Like the Anakites, they too were considered Rephaites, but the Moabites called them Emites. ¹²Horites used to live in Seir, but the descendants of Esau drove them out. They destroyed the Horites from before them and settled in their place, just as Israel did in the land the LORD gave them as their possession.)

¹³And the LORD said, "Now get up and cross the Zered Valley." So we crossed the valley.

¹⁴Thirty-eight years passed from the time we left Kadesh Barnea until we crossed the Zered Valley. By then, that entire generation of fighting men had perished from the camp, as the LORD had sworn to them. ¹⁵The LORD's hand was against them until he had completely eliminated them from the camp.

"My Achin' Feet!"

Huh?

Deuteronomy 2:14–15
The people told God, "Forget it—we're not going into that scary land!" (Even the toughest dudes were shaking in their boots!) So God said, "Fine! Whatever! I'll make you guys walk around for 40 years, and I'll wait until you guys croak; then I'll give your kids the choicest lots around." God could wait because he knows what he's doing . . . *always!*

¹⁶Now when the last of these fighting men among the people had died, ¹⁷the LORD said to me, ¹⁸"Today you are to pass by the region of Moab at Ar. ¹⁹When you come to the Ammonites, do not harass them or provoke them to war, for I will not give you possession of any land belonging to the Ammonites. I have given it as a possession to the descendants of Lot."

²⁰(That too was considered a land of the Rephaites, who used to live there; but the Ammonites called them Zamzummites. ²¹They were a people strong and numerous, and as tall as the Anakites. The LORD destroyed them from before the Ammonites, who drove them out and settled in their place. ²²The LORD had done the same for the descendants of Esau, who lived in Seir, when he destroyed the Horites from before them. They drove them out and have lived in their place to this day. ²³And as for the Avvites who lived in villages as far as Gaza, the Caphtorites coming out from Caphtorᵃ destroyed them and settled in their place.)

Defeat of Sihon King of Heshbon

²⁴"Set out now and cross the Arnon Gorge. See, I have given into your hand Sihon the Amorite, king of Heshbon, and his country. Begin to take possession of it and engage him in battle. ²⁵This very day I will begin to put the terror and fear of you on all the nations under heaven. They will hear reports of you and will tremble and be in anguish because of you."

²⁶From the desert of Kedemoth I sent messengers to Sihon king of Heshbon offering peace and saying, ²⁷"Let us pass through your country. We will stay on the main road; we will not turn aside to the right or to the left. ²⁸Sell us food to eat and water to drink for their price in silver. Only let us pass through on foot— ²⁹as the descendants of Esau, who live in Seir, and the Moabites, who live in Ar, did for us—until we cross the Jordan into the land the LORD our God is giving us." ³⁰But Sihon king of Heshbon refused to let us pass through. For the LORD your God had made his spirit stubborn and his heart obstinate in order to give him into your hands, as he has now done.

³¹The LORD said to me, "See, I have begun to deliver Sihon and his country

ᵃ23 That is, Crete

over to you. Now begin to conquer and possess his land."

32When Sihon and all his army came out to meet us in battle at Jahaz, 33the LORD our God delivered him over to us and we struck him down, together with his sons and his whole army. 34At that time we took all his towns and completely destroyed[a] them—men, women and children. We left no survivors. 35But the livestock and the plunder from the towns we had captured we carried off for ourselves. 36From Aroer on the rim of the Arnon Gorge, and from the town in the gorge, even as far as Gilead, not one town was too strong for us. The LORD our God gave us all of them. 37But in accordance with the command of the LORD our God, you did not encroach on any of the land of the Ammonites, neither the land along the course of the Jabbok nor that around the towns in the hills.

Defeat of Og King of Bashan

3 Next we turned and went up along the road toward Bashan, and Og king of Bashan with his whole army marched out to meet us in battle at Edrei. 2The LORD said to me, "Do not be afraid of him, for I have handed him over to you with his whole army and his land. Do to him what you did to Sihon king of the Amorites, who reigned in Heshbon." 3So the LORD our God also gave into our hands Og king of Bashan and all his army. We struck them down, leaving no survivors. 4At that time we took all his cities. There was not one of the sixty cities that we did not take from them—the whole region of Argob, Og's kingdom in Bashan. 5All these cities were fortified with high walls and with gates and bars, and there were also a great many unwalled villages. 6We completely destroyed[a] them, as we had done with Sihon king of Heshbon, destroying[a] every city—men, women and children. 7But all the livestock and the plunder from their cities we carried off for ourselves.

8So at that time we took from these two kings of the Amorites the territory east of the Jordan, from the Arnon Gorge as far as Mount Hermon. 9(Hermon is called Sirion by the Sidonians; the Amo-

rites call it Senir.) 10We took all the towns on the plateau, and all Gilead, and all Bashan as far as Salecah and Edrei, towns of Og's kingdom in Bashan. 11(Only Og king of Bashan was left of the remnant of the Rephaites. His bed[b] was made of iron and was more than thirteen feet long and six feet wide.[c] It is still in Rabbah of the Ammonites.)

Division of the Land

12Of the land that we took over at that time, I gave the Reubenites and the Gadites the territory north of Aroer by the Arnon Gorge, including half the hill country of Gilead, together with its towns. 13The rest of Gilead and also all of Bashan, the kingdom of Og, I gave to the half tribe of Manasseh. (The whole region of Argob in Bashan used to be known as a land of the Rephaites. 14Jair, a descendant of Manasseh, took the whole region of Argob as far as the border of the Geshurites and the Maacathites; it was named after him, so that to this day Bashan is called Havvoth Jair.[d]) 15And I gave Gilead to Makir. 16But to the Reubenites and the Gadites I gave the territory extending from Gilead down to the Arnon Gorge (the middle of the gorge being the border) and out to the Jabbok River, which is the border of the Ammonites. 17Its western border was the Jordan in the Arabah, from Kinnereth to the Sea of the Arabah (the Salt Sea[e]), below the slopes of Pisgah.

18I commanded you at that time: "The LORD your God has given you this land to take possession of it. But all your able-bodied men, armed for battle, must cross over ahead of your brother Israelites. 19However, your wives, your children and your livestock (I know you have much livestock) may stay in the towns I have given you, 20until the LORD gives rest to your brothers as he has to you, and they too have taken over the land that the LORD your God is giving them,

---

[a]34,6 The Hebrew term refers to the irrevocable giving over of things or persons to the LORD, often by totally destroying them.   [b]11 Or *sarcophagus*   [c]11 Hebrew *nine cubits long and four cubits wide* (about 4 meters long and 1.8 meters wide)   [d]14 Or *called the settlements of Jair*   [e]17 That is, the Dead Sea

across the Jordan. After that, each of you may go back to the possession I have given you."

Moses Forbidden to Cross the Jordan

²¹At that time I commanded Joshua: "You have seen with your own eyes all that the LORD your God has done to these two kings. The LORD will do the same to all the kingdoms over there where you are going. ²²Do not be afraid of them; the LORD your God himself will fight for you."

²³At that time I pleaded with the LORD: ²⁴"O Sovereign LORD, you have begun to show to your servant your greatness and your strong hand. For what god is there in heaven or on earth who can do the deeds and mighty works you do? ²⁵Let me go over and see the good land beyond the Jordan—that fine hill country and Lebanon."

²⁶But because of you the LORD was an-gry with me and would not listen to me. "That is enough," the LORD said. "Do not speak to me anymore about this matter. ²⁷Go up to the top of Pisgah and look west and north and south and east. Look at the land with your own eyes, since you are not going to cross this Jordan. ²⁸But commission Joshua, and encourage and strengthen him, for he will lead this people across and will cause them to in-herit the land that you will see." ²⁹So we stayed in the valley near Beth Peor.

Obedience Commanded

4 Hear now, O Israel, the decrees and laws I am about to teach you. Follow them so that you may live and may go in and take possession of the land that the LORD, the God of your fathers, is giving you. ²Do not add to what I command you and do not subtract from it, but keep the commands of the LORD your God that I give you.

Wednesday

Judgment? No Joke!
Read Deuteronomy 3:21–29

Wherever Moses and the Israelites went, they disobeyed God and suffered the consequences. Take Moses. He didn't even get to see the Promised Land. Things really haven't changed much since then. There's plenty of sin at my school. It's everywhere!

Lucky for me, I don't have to fight sin by myself. Only God can do that. What I can do is help people to know that Jesus will forgive their sins if they ask him to. People who learn about Jesus and become Christians don't have to think the end of the story is God's judgment. Sure, God doesn't like it when Christians mess up, and sometimes he lets them suffer the conse-quences for their choices, but he is always merciful if we ask his forgiveness.

People who live without faith in God have a lot to fear. People who live with faith in God have a lot to be thankful for. I know I'm thankful. Are you?

Wade age 13

What about You?

❶ Why do you think God is such a good judge?

❷ Think of some things, besides sin, that you can't fight by yourself. For each thing you think of, pick up something: a shoe, a stuffed animal, a pencil, whatever. When your hands are full, think of how hard it would be to try to carry all these things forever. Then drop everything, thank-ing God that he takes care of all your sins.

❸ Confess your sins to God and thank him for the forgiveness you have through Jesus.

Turn to page 210 for your next devotion.

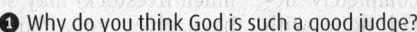

³You saw with your own eyes what the LORD did at Baal Peor. The LORD your God destroyed from among you everyone who followed the Baal of Peor, ⁴but all of you who held fast to the LORD your God are still alive today.

⁵See, I have taught you decrees and laws as the LORD my God commanded me, so that you may follow them in the land you are entering to take possession of it. ⁶Observe them carefully, for this will show your wisdom and understanding to the nations, who will hear about all these decrees and say, "Surely this great nation is a wise and understanding people." ⁷What other nation is so great as to have their gods near them the way the LORD our God is near us whenever we pray to him? ⁸And what other nation is so great as to have such righteous decrees and laws as this body of laws I am setting before you today?

⁹Only be careful, and watch yourselves closely so that you do not forget the things your eyes have seen or let them slip from your heart as long as you live. Teach them to your children and to their children after them. ¹⁰Remember the day you stood before the LORD your God at Horeb, when he said to me, "Assemble the people before me to hear my words so that they may learn to revere me as long as they live in the land and may teach them to their children." ¹¹You came near and stood at the foot of the mountain while it blazed with fire to the very heavens, with black clouds and deep darkness. ¹²Then the LORD spoke to you out of the fire. You heard the sound of words but saw no form; there was only a voice. ¹³He declared to you his covenant, the Ten Commandments, which he commanded you to follow and then wrote them on two stone tablets. ¹⁴And the LORD directed me at that time to teach you the decrees and laws you are to follow in the land that you are crossing the Jordan to possess.

Idolatry Forbidden

¹⁵You saw no form of any kind the day the LORD spoke to you at Horeb out of the fire. Therefore watch yourselves very carefully, ¹⁶so that you do not become corrupt and make for yourselves an idol, an image of any shape, whether formed like a man or a woman, ¹⁷or like any animal on earth or any bird that flies in the air, ¹⁸or like any creature that moves along the ground or any fish in the waters below. ¹⁹And when you look up to the sky and see the sun, the moon and the stars—all the heavenly array—do not be enticed into bowing down to them and worshiping things the LORD your God has apportioned to all the nations under heaven. ²⁰But as for you, the LORD took you and brought you out of the iron-smelting furnace, out of Egypt, to be the people of his inheritance, as you now are.

²¹The LORD was angry with me because of you, and he solemnly swore that I would not cross the Jordan and enter the good land the LORD your God is giving you as your inheritance. ²²I will die in this land; I will not cross the Jordan; but you are about to cross over and take possession of that good land. ²³Be careful not to forget the covenant of the LORD your God that he made with you; do not make for yourselves an idol in the form of anything the LORD your God has forbidden. ²⁴For the LORD your God is a consuming fire, a jealous God.

²⁵After you have had children and grandchildren and have lived in the land a long time—if you then become corrupt and make any kind of idol, doing evil in the eyes of the LORD your God and provoking him to anger, ²⁶I call heaven and earth as witnesses against you this day that you will quickly perish from the land that you are crossing the Jordan to possess. You will not live there long but will certainly be destroyed. ²⁷The LORD will scatter you among the peoples, and only a few of you will survive among the nations to which the LORD will drive you. ²⁸There you will worship man-made gods of wood and stone, which cannot see or hear or eat or smell. ²⁹But if from there you seek the LORD your God, you will find him if you look for him with all your heart and with all your soul. ³⁰When you are in distress and all these things have happened to you, then in later days you will return to the LORD your God and obey him. ³¹For the LORD your God is a merciful God; he will not abandon or

destroy you or forget the covenant with your forefathers, which he confirmed to them by oath.

The Lord Is God

[32] Ask now about the former days, long before your time, from the day God created man on the earth; ask from one end of the heavens to the other. Has anything so great as this ever happened, or has anything like it ever been heard of? [33] Has any other people heard the voice of God[a] speaking out of fire, as you have, and lived? [34] Has any god ever tried to take for himself one nation out of another nation, by testings, by miraculous signs and wonders, by war, by a mighty hand and an outstretched arm, or by great and awesome deeds, like all the things the Lord your God did for you in Egypt before your very eyes?

[35] You were shown these things so that you might know that the Lord is God; besides him there is no other. [36] From heaven he made you hear his voice to discipline you. On earth he showed you his great fire, and you heard his words from out of the fire. [37] Because he loved your forefathers and chose their descendants after them, he brought you out of Egypt by his Presence and his great strength, [38] to drive out before you nations greater and stronger than you and to bring you into their land to give it to you for your inheritance, as it is today.

[39] Acknowledge and take to heart this day that the Lord is God in heaven above and on the earth below. There is no other. [40] Keep his decrees and commands, which I am giving you today, so that it may go well with you and your children after you and that you may live long in the land the Lord your God gives you for all time.

Cities of Refuge

[41] Then Moses set aside three cities east of the Jordan, [42] to which anyone who had killed a person could flee if he had unintentionally killed his neighbor without malice aforethought. He could flee into one of these cities and save his life. [43] The cities were these: Bezer in the desert plateau, for the Reubenites; Ramoth in Gilead, for the Gadites; and Golan in Bashan, for the Manassites.

Introduction to the Law

[44] This is the law Moses set before the Israelites. [45] These are the stipulations, decrees and laws Moses gave them when they came out of Egypt [46] and were in the valley near Beth Peor east of the Jordan, in the land of Sihon king of the Amorites, who reigned in Heshbon and was defeated by Moses and the Israelites as they came out of Egypt. [47] They took possession of his land and the land of Og king of Bashan, the two Amorite kings east of the Jordan. [48] This land extended from Aroer on the rim of the Arnon Gorge to Mount Siyon[b] (that is, Hermon), [49] and included all the Arabah east of the Jordan, as far as the Sea of the Arabah,[c] below the slopes of Pisgah.

The Ten Commandments

5 Moses summoned all Israel and said:
Hear, O Israel, the decrees and laws I declare in your hearing today. Learn them and be sure to follow them. [2] The Lord our God made a covenant with us at Horeb. [3] It was not with our fathers that the Lord made this covenant, but with us, with all of us who are alive here today. [4] The Lord spoke to you face to face out of the fire on the mountain. [5] (At that time I stood between the Lord and you to declare to you the word of the Lord, because you were afraid of the fire and did not go up the mountain.) And he said:

[6] "I am the Lord your God, who brought you out of Egypt, out of the land of slavery.

[7] "You shall have no other gods before[d] me.

[8] "You shall not make for yourself an idol in the form of anything in heaven above or on the earth beneath or in the waters below. [9] You shall not bow down to them or worship them; for I, the Lord your God, am a jealous God, punishing the children for the sin of the fathers to the third and fourth generation of those who hate me, [10] but showing love to a thou-

---

[a]33 Or *of a god*   [b]48 Hebrew; Syriac (see also Deut. 3:9) *Sirion*   [c]49 That is, the Dead Sea   [d]7 Or *besides*

sand generations of those who love me and keep my commandments.

¹¹ "You shall not misuse the name of the LORD your God, for the LORD will not hold anyone guiltless who misuses his name.

¹² "Observe the Sabbath day by keeping it holy, as the LORD your God has commanded you. ¹³Six days you shall labor and do all your work, ¹⁴but the seventh day is a Sabbath to the LORD your God. On it you shall not do any work, neither you, nor your son or daughter, nor your manservant or maidservant, nor your ox, your donkey or any of your animals, nor the alien within your gates, so that your manservant and maidservant may rest, as you do. ¹⁵Remember that you were slaves in Egypt and that the LORD your God brought you out of there with a mighty hand and an outstretched arm. Therefore the LORD your God has commanded you to observe the Sabbath day.

¹⁶ "Honor your father and your mother, as the LORD your God has commanded you, so that you may live long and that it may go well with you in the land the LORD your God is giving you.

¹⁷ "You shall not murder.

¹⁸ "You shall not commit adultery.

¹⁹ "You shall not steal.

²⁰ "You shall not give false testimony against your neighbor.

²¹ "You shall not covet your neighbor's wife. You shall not set your desire on your neighbor's house or land, his manservant or maidservant, his ox or donkey, or anything that belongs to your neighbor."

²²These are the commandments the LORD proclaimed in a loud voice to your whole assembly there on the mountain from out of the fire, the cloud and the deep darkness; and he added nothing more. Then he wrote them on two stone tablets and gave them to me.

²³When you heard the voice out of the darkness, while the mountain was ablaze with fire, all the leading men of your tribes and your elders came to me. ²⁴And you said, "The LORD our God has shown us his glory and his majesty, and we have heard his voice from the fire. Today we have seen that a man can live even if God speaks with him. ²⁵But now, why should we die? This great fire will consume us, and we will die if we hear the voice of the LORD our God any longer. ²⁶For what mortal man has ever heard the voice of the living God speaking out of fire, as we have, and survived? ²⁷Go near and listen to all that the LORD our God says. Then tell us whatever the LORD our God tells you. We will listen and obey."

²⁸The LORD heard you when you spoke to me and the LORD said to me, "I have heard what this people said to you. Everything they said was good. ²⁹Oh, that their hearts would be inclined to fear me and keep all my commands always, so that it might go well with them and their children forever!

³⁰ "Go, tell them to return to their tents. ³¹But you stay here with me so that I may give you all the commands, decrees and laws you are to teach them to follow in the land I am giving them to possess."

³²So be careful to do what the LORD your God has commanded you; do not turn aside to the right or to the left. ³³Walk in all the way that the LORD your God has commanded you, so that you may live and prosper and prolong your days in the land that you will possess.

Love the LORD Your God

6 These are the commands, decrees and laws the LORD your God directed me to teach you to observe in the land that you are crossing the Jordan to possess, ²so that you, your children and their children after them may fear the LORD your God as long as you live by keeping all his decrees and commands that I give you, and so that you may enjoy long life. ³Hear, O Israel, and be careful to obey so that it may go well with you and that you may increase greatly in a land flowing with milk and honey, just as the LORD, the God of your fathers, promised you. ⁴Hear, O Israel: The LORD our God, the LORD is one.*ᵃ* ⁵Love the LORD your God with all your heart and with all your soul and with all your strength. ⁶These commandments that I give you today are to be upon your hearts. ⁷Impress them on your children. Talk about them when you sit at home and when you walk along the road, when you lie down and when you get up. ⁸Tie them as symbols on your hands and bind them on your foreheads. ⁹Write them on the doorframes of your houses and on your gates.

¹⁰When the LORD your God brings you into the land he swore to your fathers, to Abraham, Isaac and Jacob, to give you—a land with large, flourishing cities you did not build, ¹¹houses filled with all kinds of good things you did not provide, wells you did not dig, and vineyards and olive groves you did not plant—then when you eat and are satisfied, ¹²be careful that you do not forget the LORD, who brought you out of Egypt, out of the land of slavery.

¹³Fear the LORD your God, serve him only and take your oaths in his name. ¹⁴Do not follow other gods, the gods of the peoples around you; ¹⁵for the LORD your God, who is among you, is a jealous God and his anger will burn against you, and he will destroy you from the face of the land. ¹⁶Do not test the LORD your God as you did at Massah. ¹⁷Be sure to keep the commands of the LORD your God and the stipulations and decrees he has given you. ¹⁸Do what is right and good in the LORD's sight, so that it may go well with you and you may go in and take over the good land that the LORD promised on oath to your forefathers, ¹⁹thrusting out all your enemies before you, as the LORD said.

²⁰In the future, when your son asks you, "What is the meaning of the stipulations, decrees and laws the LORD our God

---

ᵃ4 Or The LORD our God is one LORD; or The LORD is our God, the LORD is one; or The LORD is our God, the LORD alone

---

Thursday

The Best Kind of Studying

Read Deuteronomy 6:4–9

If you're a Christian, it makes sense that you'd want to learn as much as you could about Jesus Christ and his Word. You can do that by talking about the Bible with your friends and family, writing down verses or memorizing them. You can also learn by going to church and listening to what your pastor or youth leader says.

Think about it—of all the things you learn in your life, what's the most important? It's not algebra or biology! Although studying these subjects is important and necessary, the most important thing is to know who God is and what he wants you to do in your life. And the more you learn about him, the more you feel secure and have strength for whatever challenges you have to face. Reading the Bible is the best kind of studying!

Kelli • age 13

What about You?

❶ Think of a time you really enjoyed reading the Bible. What made you so excited about it?

❷ Write down your favorite verse from the Bible. Then put it someplace where you'll see it every day.

❸ Thank God for giving us the Bible.

Turn to page 213 for your next devotion.

God—The BIG KAHUNA!

Huh?

Deuteronomy 6:13-15

The Old Testament is about one main thing: God is God, and we are not. That's it. He is the One who made it all, who knows best and who wants the greatest life for every person. *We* are the ones who keep messing up and hurting everything in sight. God has a *right* to be "jealous" because he is the One who made us, who owns us; he de- serves our trust.

has commanded you?" ²¹tell him: "We were slaves of Pharaoh in Egypt, but the LORD brought us out of Egypt with a mighty hand. ²²Before our eyes the LORD sent miraculous signs and wonders— great and terrible—upon Egypt and Phar- aoh and his whole household. ²³But he brought us out from there to bring us in and give us the land that he promised on oath to our forefathers. ²⁴The LORD com- manded us to obey all these decrees and to fear the LORD our God, so that we might always prosper and be kept alive, as is the case today. ²⁵And if we are care- ful to obey all this law before the LORD our God, as he has commanded us, that will be our righteousness."

Driving Out the Nations

7 When the LORD your God brings you into the land you are entering to possess and drives out before you many nations—the Hittites, Girgashites, Amo- rites, Canaanites, Perizzites, Hivites and Jebusites, seven nations larger and stronger than you— ²and when the LORD your God has delivered them over to you and you have defeated them, then you must destroy them totally.ᵃ Make no treaty with them, and show them no mercy. ³Do not intermarry with them. Do not give your daughters to their sons or take their daughters for your sons, ⁴for they will turn your sons away from fol- lowing me to serve other gods, and the LORD's anger will burn against you and will quickly destroy you. ⁵This is what

you are to do to them: Break down their altars, smash their sacred stones, cut down their Asherah polesᵇ and burn their idols in the fire. ⁶For you are a people holy to the LORD your God. The LORD your God has chosen you out of all the peoples on the face of the earth to be his people, his treasured possession.

⁷The LORD did not set his affection on you and choose you because you were more numerous than other peoples, for you were the fewest of all peoples. ⁸But it was because the LORD loved you and kept the oath he swore to your forefathers that he brought you out with a mighty hand and redeemed you from the land of slavery, from the power of Pharaoh king of Egypt. ⁹Know therefore that the LORD your God is God; he is the faithful God, keeping his covenant of love to a thou- sand generations of those who love him and keep his commands. ¹⁰But

> those who hate him he will repay to
> their face by destruction;
> he will not be slow to repay to their
> face those who hate him.

¹¹Therefore, take care to follow the com- mands, decrees and laws I give you to- day.

¹²If you pay attention to these laws and are careful to follow them, then the LORD your God will keep his covenant of love with you, as he swore to your fore- fathers. ¹³He will love you and bless you and increase your numbers. He will bless the fruit of your womb, the crops of your land—your grain, new wine and oil—the calves of your herds and the lambs of your flocks in the land that he swore to your forefathers to give you. ¹⁴You will be blessed more than any other people; none of your men or women will be childless, nor any of your livestock with- out young. ¹⁵The LORD will keep you free from every disease. He will not inflict on you the horrible diseases you knew in Egypt, but he will inflict them on all who hate you. ¹⁶You must destroy all the peoples the LORD your God gives over to

---

ᵃ2 The Hebrew term refers to the irrevocable giving over of things or persons to the LORD, often by totally destroying them; also in verse 26.   ᵇ5 That is, symbols of the goddess Asherah; here and elsewhere in Deuteronomy

you. Do not look on them with pity and do not serve their gods, for that will be a snare to you.

¹⁷You may say to yourselves, "These nations are stronger than we are. How can we drive them out?" ¹⁸But do not be afraid of them; remember well what the LORD your God did to Pharaoh and to all Egypt. ¹⁹You saw with your own eyes the great trials, the miraculous signs and wonders, the mighty hand and out- stretched arm, with which the LORD your God brought you out. The LORD your God will do the same to all the peoples you now fear. ²⁰Moreover, the LORD your God will send the hornet among them until even the survivors who hide from you have perished. ²¹Do not be terrified by them, for the LORD your God, who is among you, is a great and awesome God. ²²The LORD your God will drive out those nations before you, little by little. You will not be allowed to eliminate them all at once, or the wild animals will multiply around you. ²³But the LORD your God will deliver them over to you, throwing them into great confusion until they are de- stroyed. ²⁴He will give their kings into your hand, and you will wipe out their names from under heaven. No one will be able to stand up against you; you will destroy them. ²⁵The images of their gods you are to burn in the fire. Do not covet the silver and gold on them, and do not take it for yourselves, or you will be en- snared by it, for it is detestable to the LORD your God. ²⁶Do not bring a detest- able thing into your house or you, like it, will be set apart for destruction. Utterly abhor and detest it, for it is set apart for destruction.

Do Not Forget the LORD

8 Be careful to follow every command I am giving you today, so that you may live and increase and may enter and possess the land that the LORD promised on oath to your forefathers. ²Remember how the LORD your God led you all the way in the desert these forty years, to humble you and to test you in order to know what was in your heart, whether or not you would keep his commands. ³He humbled you, causing you to hunger and then feeding you with manna, which nei-

ther you nor your fathers had known, to teach you that man does not live on bread alone but on every word that comes from the mouth of the LORD. ⁴Your clothes did not wear out and your feet did not swell during these forty years. ⁵Know then in your heart that as a man disciplines his son, so the LORD your God disciplines you.

⁶Observe the commands of the LORD your God, walking in his ways and rever- ing him. ⁷For the LORD your God is bring- ing you into a good land—a land with streams and pools of water, with springs flowing in the valleys and hills; ⁸a land with wheat and barley, vines and fig trees, pomegranates, olive oil and honey; ⁹a land where bread will not be scarce and you will lack nothing; a land where the rocks are iron and you can dig copper out of the hills.

¹⁰When you have eaten and are satis- fied, praise the LORD your God for the good land he has given you. ¹¹Be careful that you do not forget the LORD your God, failing to observe his commands, his laws and his decrees that I am giving you this day. ¹²Otherwise, when you eat and are satisfied, when you build fine houses and settle down, ¹³and when your herds and flocks grow large and your sil- ver and gold increase and all you have is multiplied, ¹⁴then your heart will become proud and you will forget the LORD your God, who brought you out of Egypt, out of the land of slavery. ¹⁵He led you through the vast and dreadful desert, that thirsty and waterless land, with its venomous snakes and scorpions. He brought you water out of hard rock. ¹⁶He gave you manna to eat in the desert, something your fathers had never known, to humble and to test you so that in the end it might go well with you. ¹⁷You may say to yourself, "My power and the strength of my hands have pro- duced this wealth for me." ¹⁸But remem- ber the LORD your God, for it is he who gives you the ability to produce wealth, and so confirms his covenant, which he swore to your forefathers, as it is today.

¹⁹If you ever forget the LORD your God and follow other gods and worship and bow down to them, I testify against you today that you will surely be destroyed.

²⁰Like the nations the LORD destroyed before you, so you will be destroyed for not obeying the LORD your God.

Not Because of Israel's Righteousness

9 Hear, O Israel. You are now about to cross the Jordan to go in and dispossess nations greater and stronger than you, with large cities that have walls up to the sky. ²The people are strong and tall—Anakites! You know about them and have heard it said: "Who can stand up against the Anakites?" ³But be assured today that the LORD your God is the one who goes across ahead of you like a devouring fire. He will destroy them; he will subdue them before you. And you will drive them out and annihilate them quickly, as the LORD has promised you.

⁴After the LORD your God has driven them out before you, do not say to yourself, "The LORD has brought me here to take possession of this land because of my righteousness." No, it is on account of the wickedness of these nations that the LORD is going to drive them out before you. ⁵It is not because of your righteousness or your integrity that you are going in to take possession of their land; but on account of the wickedness of these nations, the LORD your God will drive them out before you, to accomplish what he swore to your fathers, to Abraham, Isaac and Jacob. ⁶Understand, then, that it is not because of your righteousness that the LORD your God is giving you this good land to possess, for you are a stiff-necked people.

The Golden Calf

⁷Remember this and never forget how you provoked the LORD your God to anger in the desert. From the day you left Egypt until you arrived here, you have been rebellious against the LORD. ⁸At Horeb you aroused the LORD's wrath so that he was angry enough to destroy you. ⁹When I went up on the mountain to receive the tablets of stone, the tablets of the covenant that the LORD had made with you, I stayed on the mountain forty days and forty nights; I ate no bread and drank no water. ¹⁰The LORD gave me two stone tablets inscribed by the finger of

---

Fri**day**

Thankfulness

Read Deuteronomy 8:10

What do you do when your mom comes home from the store with groceries? Look through the bags for your favorite snack? Maybe, if you're in the right mood, help her put things away? Do you ever stop to say "thank you"? I know I hardly ever do.

There must be days when my mom really doesn't want to go to the store. But she does it anyway—she gives up what she wants to help me out. And then I forget to even say thank you.

I don't do much better when it comes to thanking God. I mean, God's the One who gave me so many good things. By thanking God for everything he's done, I'll also get better at thanking other people, starting with my mom. She'll be so surprised!

Jennifer age 13

What about You?

❶ How do you feel when someone thanks you?

❷ Think of 3 people who help you a lot. Say "thank you" to them this week.

❸ Thank God for all the ways he helps you.

Turn to page 214 for your next devotion.

God. On them were all the commandments the LORD proclaimed to you on the mountain out of the fire, on the day of the assembly.

11At the end of the forty days and forty nights, the LORD gave me the two stone tablets, the tablets of the covenant. 12Then the LORD told me, "Go down from here at once, because your people whom you brought out of Egypt have become corrupt. They have turned away quickly from what I commanded them and have made a cast idol for themselves."

13And the LORD said to me, "I have seen this people, and they are a stiff-necked people indeed! 14Let me alone, so that I may destroy them and blot out their name from under heaven. And I will make you into a nation stronger and more numerous than they."

15So I turned and went down from the mountain while it was ablaze with fire. And the two tablets of the covenant were in my hands.*a* 16When I looked, I saw that you had sinned against the LORD your God; you had made for yourselves an idol cast in the shape of a calf. You had turned aside quickly from the way that the LORD had commanded you. 17So I

---

a15 Or And I had the two tablets of the covenant with me, one in each hand

---

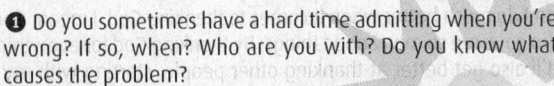

Week end.

About-face   Read Numbers 22:29–34 (page 183)

Jeremiah talked on Tuesday about how easy it is for embarrassment to turn into anger. He helped us see, from Balaam's story, that it's important to keep calm and ride out the storm when we get embarrassed.

But there is more to the story of Balaam. God wanted to make sure Balaam's motives were pure. And, because he knows everything, God knew that Balaam had a hidden agenda. And when Balaam saw God's angel, he "fell facedown."

Think about it: Why would Balaam fall down on his face? Do you think he just tripped? No, Balaam knew his own motives weren't pure, and he was afraid and ashamed and felt trapped. We don't know what he had in mind—money or power or something else. But whatever his motives, Balaam knew they would make God angry. When God reminded him, Balaam was truly sorry, and God sent him on his way once again.

When you act selfish or embarrassed or angry, God wants to get your attention. The key is to be willing to admit you're wrong when you blow it. Let God teach you how to live. He'll always help you when you sincerely ask him to.

What about You?

❶ Do you sometimes have a hard time admitting when you're wrong? If so, when? Who are you with? Do you know what causes the problem?

❷ See if you can think of one wrong thing you have done that you feel a little bit bad about. Do you need to ask for someone's forgiveness? Is there someone you can ask to help you make the wrong right?

❸ Ask God to bring to mind any wrong you have done that you haven't admitted, and then ask his forgiveness.

Turn to page 221 for your next devotion.

took the two tablets and threw them out of my hands, breaking them to pieces before your eyes.

[18]Then once again I fell prostrate before the LORD for forty days and forty nights; I ate no bread and drank no water, because of all the sin you had committed, doing what was evil in the LORD's sight and so provoking him to anger. [19]I feared the anger and wrath of the LORD, for he was angry enough with you to destroy you. But again the LORD listened to me. [20]And the LORD was angry enough with Aaron to destroy him, but at that time I prayed for Aaron too. [21]Also I took that sinful thing of yours, the calf you had made, and burned it in the fire. Then I crushed it and ground it to powder as fine as dust and threw the dust into a stream that flowed down the mountain.

[22]You also made the LORD angry at Taberah, at Massah and at Kibroth Hattaavah.

[23]And when the LORD sent you out from Kadesh Barnea, he said, "Go up and take possession of the land I have given you." But you rebelled against the command of the LORD your God. You did not trust him or obey him. [24]You have been rebellious against the LORD ever since I have known you.

[25]I lay prostrate before the LORD those forty days and forty nights because the LORD had said he would destroy you. [26]I prayed to the LORD and said, "O Sovereign LORD, do not destroy your people, your own inheritance that you redeemed by your great power and brought out of Egypt with a mighty hand. [27]Remember your servants Abraham, Isaac and Jacob. Overlook the stubbornness of this people, their wickedness and their sin. [28]Otherwise, the country from which you brought us will say, 'Because the LORD was not able to take them into the land he had promised them, and because he hated them, he brought them out to put them to death in the desert.' [29]But they are your people, your inheritance that you brought out by your great power and your outstretched arm."

Tablets Like the First Ones

10 At that time the LORD said to me, "Chisel out two stone tablets like

the first ones and come up to me on the mountain. Also make a wooden chest.[a] [2]I will write on the tablets the words that were on the first tablets, which you broke. Then you are to put them in the chest."

[3]So I made the ark out of acacia wood and chiseled out two stone tablets like the first ones, and I went up on the mountain with the two tablets in my hands. [4]The LORD wrote on these tablets what he had written before, the Ten Commandments he had proclaimed to you on the mountain, out of the fire, on the day of the assembly. And the LORD gave them to me. [5]Then I came back down the mountain and put the tablets in the ark I had made, as the LORD commanded me, and they are there now.

[6](The Israelites traveled from the wells of the Jaakanites to Moserah. There Aaron died and was buried, and Eleazar his son succeeded him as priest. [7]From there they traveled to Gudgodah and on to Jotbathah, a land with streams of water. [8]At that time the LORD set apart the tribe of Levi to carry the ark of the covenant of the LORD, to stand before the LORD to minister and to pronounce blessings in his name, as they still do today. [9]That is why the Levites have no share or inheritance among their brothers; the LORD is their inheritance, as the LORD your God told them.)

[10]Now I had stayed on the mountain forty days and nights, as I did the first time, and the LORD listened to me at this time also. It was not his will to destroy you. [11]"Go," the LORD said to me, "and lead the people on their way, so that they may enter and possess the land that I swore to their fathers to give them."

Fear the LORD

[12]And now, O Israel, what does the LORD your God ask of you but to fear the LORD your God, to walk in all his ways, to love him, to serve the LORD your God with all your heart and with all your soul, [13]and to observe the LORD's commands and decrees that I am giving you today for your own good?

[14]To the LORD your God belong the

---

[a]1 That is, an ark

heavens, even the highest heavens, the earth and everything in it. ¹⁵Yet the LORD set his affection on your forefathers and loved them, and he chose you, their descendants, above all the nations, as it is today. ¹⁶Circumcise your hearts, therefore, and do not be stiff-necked any longer. ¹⁷For the LORD your God is God of gods and Lord of lords, the great God, mighty and awesome, who shows no partiality and accepts no bribes. ¹⁸He defends the cause of the fatherless and the widow, and loves the alien, giving him food and clothing. ¹⁹And you are to love those who are aliens, for you yourselves were aliens in Egypt. ²⁰Fear the LORD your God and serve him. Hold fast to him and take your oaths in his name. ²¹He is your praise; he is your God, who performed for you those great and awesome wonders you saw with your own eyes. ²²Your forefathers who went down into Egypt were seventy in all, and now the LORD your God has made you as numerous as the stars in the sky.

Love and Obey the LORD

11 Love the LORD your God and keep his requirements, his decrees, his laws and his commands always. ²Remember today that your children were

"Obey"—That Dirty Word

Huh?

Deuteronomy 11:1

When you have to obey someone, doesn't it make your skin crawl? Maybe that's because we think obeying means we don't matter and don't have any say. It *feels* unfair and *seems* like a lousy way to teach people. But when God tells us to obey him, he means that he wants us to love him. The big part about loving God is trusting that he knows what he's doing. To obey God is cool, because his way of living is the best, most awesome and greatest way to live.

not the ones who saw and experienced the discipline of the LORD your God: his majesty, his mighty hand, his out-

stretched arm; ³the signs he performed and the things he did in the heart of Egypt, both to Pharaoh king of Egypt and to his whole country; ⁴what he did to the Egyptian army, to its horses and chariots, how he overwhelmed them with the waters of the Red Sea^a as they were pursuing you, and how the LORD brought lasting ruin on them. ⁵It was not your children who saw what he did for you in the desert until you arrived at this place, ⁶and what he did to Dathan and Abiram, sons of Eliab the Reubenite, when the earth opened its mouth right in the middle of all Israel and swallowed them up with their households, their tents and every living thing that belonged to them. ⁷But it was your own eyes that saw all these great things the LORD has done.

⁸Observe therefore all the commands I am giving you today, so that you may have the strength to go in and take over the land that you are crossing the Jordan to possess, ⁹and so that you may live long in the land that the LORD swore to your forefathers to give to them and their descendants, a land flowing with milk and honey. ¹⁰The land you are entering to take over is not like the land of Egypt, from which you have come, where you planted your seed and irrigated it by foot as in a vegetable garden. ¹¹But the land you are crossing the Jordan to take possession of is a land of mountains and valleys that drinks rain from heaven. ¹²It is a land the LORD your God cares for; the eyes of the LORD your God are continually on it from the beginning of the year to its end.

¹³So if you faithfully obey the commands I am giving you today—to love the LORD your God and to serve him with all your heart and with all your soul— ¹⁴then I will send rain on your land in its season, both autumn and spring rains, so that you may gather in your grain, new wine and oil. ¹⁵I will provide grass in the fields for your cattle, and you will eat and be satisfied.

¹⁶Be careful, or you will be enticed to turn away and worship other gods and bow down to them. ¹⁷Then the LORD's an-

^a4 Hebrew *Yam Suph*; that is, Sea of Reeds

ger will burn against you, and he will shut the heavens so that it will not rain and the ground will yield no produce, and you will soon perish from the good land the LORD is giving you. [18]Fix these words of mine in your hearts and minds; tie them as symbols on your hands and bind them on your foreheads. [19]Teach them to your children, talking about them when you sit at home and when you walk along the road, when you lie down and when you get up. [20]Write them on the doorframes of your houses and on your gates, [21]so that your days and the days of your children may be many in the land that the LORD swore to give your forefathers, as many as the days that the heavens are above the earth.

[22]If you carefully observe all these commands I am giving you to follow—to love the LORD your God, to walk in all his ways and to hold fast to him— [23]then the LORD will drive out all these nations before you, and you will dispossess nations larger and stronger than you. [24]Every place where you set your foot will be yours: Your territory will extend from the desert to Lebanon, and from the Euphrates River to the western sea.[a] [25]No man will be able to stand against you. The LORD your God, as he promised you, will put the terror and fear of you on the whole land, wherever you go.

[26]See, I am setting before you today a blessing and a curse— [27]the blessing if you obey the commands of the LORD your God that I am giving you today; [28]the curse if you disobey the commands of the LORD your God and turn from the way that I command you today by following other gods, which you have not known. [29]When the LORD your God has brought you into the land you are entering to possess, you are to proclaim on Mount Gerizim the blessings, and on Mount Ebal the curses. [30]As you know, these mountains are across the Jordan, west of the road,[b] toward the setting sun, near the great trees of Moreh, in the territory of those Canaanites living in the Arabah in the vicinity of Gilgal. [31]You are about to cross the Jordan to enter and take possession of the land the LORD your God is giving you. When you have taken it over and are living there, [32]be sure that

you obey all the decrees and laws I am setting before you today.

The One Place of Worship

12 These are the decrees and laws you must be careful to follow in the land that the LORD, the God of your fathers, has given you to possess—as long as you live in the land. [2]Destroy completely all the places on the high mountains and on the hills and under every spreading tree where the nations you are dispossessing worship their gods. [3]Break down their altars, smash their sacred stones and burn their Asherah poles in the fire; cut down the idols of their gods and wipe out their names from those places.

[4]You must not worship the LORD your God in their way. [5]But you are to seek the place the LORD your God will choose from among all your tribes to put his Name there for his dwelling. To that place you must go; [6]there bring your burnt offerings and sacrifices, your tithes and special gifts, what you have vowed to give and your freewill offerings, and the firstborn of your herds and flocks. [7]There, in the presence of the LORD your God, you and your families shall eat and shall rejoice in everything you have put your hand to, because the LORD your God has blessed you.

[8]You are not to do as we do here today, everyone as he sees fit, [9]since you have not yet reached the resting place and the inheritance the LORD your God is giving you. [10]But you will cross the Jordan and settle in the land the LORD your God is giving you as an inheritance, and he will give you rest from all your enemies around you so that you will live in safety. [11]Then to the place the LORD your God will choose as a dwelling for his Name— there you are to bring everything I command you: your burnt offerings and sacrifices, your tithes and special gifts, and all the choice possessions you have vowed to the LORD. [12]And there rejoice before the LORD your God, you, your sons and daughters, your menservants and maidservants, and the Levites from your

---

[a]24 That is, the Mediterranean   [b]30 Or *Jordan, westward*

towns, who have no allotment or inheritance of their own. ¹³Be careful not to sacrifice your burnt offerings anywhere you please. ¹⁴Offer them only at the place the LORD will choose in one of your tribes, and there observe everything I command you.

¹⁵Nevertheless, you may slaughter your animals in any of your towns and eat as much of the meat as you want, as if it were gazelle or deer, according to the blessing the LORD your God gives you. Both the ceremonially unclean and the clean may eat it. ¹⁶But you must not eat the blood; pour it out on the ground like water. ¹⁷You must not eat in your own towns the tithe of your grain and new wine and oil, or the firstborn of your herds and flocks, or whatever you have vowed to give, or your freewill offerings or special gifts. ¹⁸Instead, you are to eat them in the presence of the LORD your God at the place the LORD your God will choose—you, your sons and daughters, your menservants and maidservants, and the Levites from your towns—and you are to rejoice before the LORD your God in everything you put your hand to. ¹⁹Be careful not to neglect the Levites as long as you live in your land.

²⁰When the LORD your God has enlarged your territory as he promised you, and you crave meat and say, "I would like some meat," then you may eat as much of it as you want. ²¹If the place where the LORD your God chooses to put his Name is too far away from you, you may slaughter animals from the herds and flocks the LORD has given you, as I have commanded you, and in your own towns you may eat as much of them as you want. ²²Eat them as you would gazelle or deer. Both the ceremonially unclean and the clean may eat. ²³But be sure you do not eat the blood, because the blood is the life, and you must not eat the life with the meat. ²⁴You must not eat the blood; pour it out on the ground like water. ²⁵Do not eat it, so that it may go well with you and your children after you, because you will be doing what is right in the eyes of the LORD.

²⁶But take your consecrated things and whatever you have vowed to give, and go to the place the LORD will choose.

²⁷Present your burnt offerings on the altar of the LORD your God, both the meat and the blood. The blood of your sacrifices must be poured beside the altar of the LORD your God, but you may eat the meat. ²⁸Be careful to obey all these regulations I am giving you, so that it may always go well with you and your children after you, because you will be doing what is good and right in the eyes of the LORD your God.

²⁹The LORD your God will cut off before you the nations you are about to invade and dispossess. But when you have driven them out and settled in their land, ³⁰and after they have been destroyed before you, be careful not to be ensnared by inquiring about their gods, saying, "How do these nations serve their gods? We will do the same." ³¹You must not worship the LORD your God in their way, because in worshiping their gods, they do all kinds of detestable things the LORD hates. They even burn their sons and daughters in the fire as sacrifices to their gods.

³²See that you do all I command you; do not add to it or take away from it.

Worshiping Other Gods

13 If a prophet, or one who foretells by dreams, appears among you and announces to you a miraculous sign or wonder, ²and if the sign or wonder of which he has spoken takes place, and he says, "Let us follow other gods" (gods you have not known) "and let us worship them," ³you must not listen to the words of that prophet or dreamer. The LORD your God is testing you to find out whether you love him with all your heart and with all your soul. ⁴It is the LORD your God you must follow, and him you must revere. Keep his commands and obey him; serve him and hold fast to him. ⁵That prophet or dreamer must be put to death, because he preached rebellion against the LORD your God, who brought you out of Egypt and redeemed you from the land of slavery; he has tried to turn you from the way the LORD your God commanded you to follow. You must purge the evil from among you.

⁶If your very own brother, or your son or daughter, or the wife you love, or your

closest friend secretly entices you, saying, "Let us go and worship other gods" (gods that neither you nor your fathers have known, ⁷gods of the peoples around you, whether near or far, from one end of the land to the other), ⁸do not yield to him or listen to him. Show him no pity. Do not spare him or shield him. ⁹You must certainly put him to death. Your hand must be the first in putting him to death, and then the hands of all the people. ¹⁰Stone him to death, because he tried to turn you away from the LORD your God, who brought you out of Egypt, out of the land of slavery. ¹¹Then all Israel will hear and be afraid, and no one among you will do such an evil thing again.

¹²If you hear it said about one of the towns the LORD your God is giving you to live in ¹³that wicked men have arisen among you and have led the people of their town astray, saying, "Let us go and worship other gods" (gods you have not known), ¹⁴then you must inquire, probe and investigate it thoroughly. And if it is true and it has been proved that this detestable thing has been done among you, ¹⁵you must certainly put to the sword all who live in that town. Destroy it completely,ᵃ both its people and its livestock. ¹⁶Gather all the plunder of the town into the middle of the public square and completely burn the town and all its plunder as a whole burnt offering to the LORD your God. It is to remain a ruin forever, never to be rebuilt. ¹⁷None of those condemned thingsᵃ shall be found in your hands, so that the LORD will turn from his fierce anger; he will show you mercy, have compassion on you, and increase your numbers, as he promised on oath to your forefathers, ¹⁸because you obey the LORD your God, keeping all his commands that I am giving you today and doing what is right in his eyes.

Clean and Unclean Food

14 You are the children of the LORD your God. Do not cut yourselves or shave the front of your heads for the dead, ²for you are a people holy to the LORD your God. Out of all the peoples on the face of the earth, the LORD has chosen you to be his treasured possession.

³Do not eat any detestable thing. ⁴These are the animals you may eat: the ox, the sheep, the goat, ⁵the deer, the gazelle, the roe deer, the wild goat, the ibex, the antelope and the mountain sheep.ᵇ ⁶You may eat any animal that has a split hoof divided in two and that chews the cud. ⁷However, of those that chew the cud or that have a split hoof completely divided you may not eat the camel, the rabbit or the coney.ᶜ Although they chew the cud, they do not have a split hoof; they are ceremonially unclean for you. ⁸The pig is also unclean; although it has a split hoof, it does not chew the cud. You are not to eat their meat or touch their carcasses.

⁹Of all the creatures living in the water, you may eat any that has fins and scales. ¹⁰But anything that does not have fins and scales you may not eat; for you it is unclean.

¹¹You may eat any clean bird. ¹²But these you may not eat: the eagle, the vulture, the black vulture, ¹³the red kite, the black kite, any kind of falcon, ¹⁴any kind of raven, ¹⁵the horned owl, the screech owl, the gull, any kind of hawk, ¹⁶the little owl, the great owl, the white owl, ¹⁷the desert owl, the osprey, the cormorant, ¹⁸the stork, any kind of heron, the hoopoe and the bat.

¹⁹All flying insects that swarm are unclean to you; do not eat them. ²⁰But any winged creature that is clean you may eat.

²¹Do not eat anything you find already dead. You may give it to an alien living in any of your towns, and he may eat it, or you may sell it to a foreigner. But you are a people holy to the LORD your God.

Do not cook a young goat in its mother's milk.

Tithes

²²Be sure to set aside a tenth of all that your fields produce each year. ²³Eat the tithe of your grain, new wine and oil, and the firstborn of your herds and

---

ᵃ15,17 The Hebrew term refers to the irrevocable giving over of things or persons to the LORD, often by totally destroying them.   ᵇ5 The precise identification of some of the birds and animals in this chapter is uncertain.   ᶜ7 That is, the hyrax or rock badger

flocks in the presence of the LORD your God at the place he will choose as a dwelling for his Name, so that you may learn to revere the LORD your God always. ²⁴But if that place is too distant and you have been blessed by the LORD your God and cannot carry your tithe (because the place where the LORD will choose to put his Name is so far away), ²⁵then exchange your tithe for silver, and take the silver with you and go to the place the LORD your God will choose. ²⁶Use the silver to buy whatever you like: cattle, sheep, wine or other fermented drink, or anything you wish. Then you and your household shall eat there in the presence of the LORD your God and rejoice. ²⁷And do not neglect the Levites living in your towns, for they have no allotment or inheritance of their own.

²⁸At the end of every three years, bring all the tithes of that year's produce and store it in your towns, ²⁹so that the Levites (who have no allotment or inheritance of their own) and the aliens, the fatherless and the widows who live in your towns may come and eat and be satisfied, and so that the LORD your God may bless you in all the work of your hands.

The Year for Canceling Debts

15 At the end of every seven years you must cancel debts. ²This is how it is to be done: Every creditor shall cancel the loan he has made to his fellow Israelite. He shall not require payment from his fellow Israelite or brother, because the LORD's time for canceling debts has been proclaimed. ³You may require payment from a foreigner, but you must cancel any debt your brother owes you. ⁴However, there should be no poor among you, for in the land the LORD your God is giving you to possess as your inheritance, he will richly bless you, ⁵if only you fully obey the LORD your God and are careful to follow all these commands I am giving you today. ⁶For the LORD your God will bless you as he has promised, and you will lend to many nations but will borrow from none. You will rule over many nations but none will rule over you.

⁷If there is a poor man among your brothers in any of the towns of the land that the LORD your God is giving you, do not be hardhearted or tightfisted toward your poor brother. ⁸Rather be openhanded and freely lend him whatever he needs. ⁹Be careful not to harbor this wicked thought: "The seventh year, the year for canceling debts, is near," so that you do not show ill will toward your needy brother and give him nothing. He may then appeal to the LORD against you, and you will be found guilty of sin. ¹⁰Give generously to him and do so without a grudging heart; then because of this the LORD your God will bless you in all your work and in everything you put your hand to. ¹¹There will always be poor people in the land. Therefore I command you to be openhanded toward your brothers and toward the poor and needy in your land.

Freeing Servants

¹²If a fellow Hebrew, a man or a woman, sells himself to you and serves you six years, in the seventh year you must let him go free. ¹³And when you release him, do not send him away empty-handed. ¹⁴Supply him liberally from your flock, your threshing floor and your winepress. Give to him as the LORD your God has blessed you. ¹⁵Remember that you were slaves in Egypt and the LORD your God redeemed you. That is why I give you this command today.

¹⁶But if your servant says to you, "I do not want to leave you," because he loves you and your family and is well off with you, ¹⁷then take an awl and push it through his ear lobe into the door, and he will become your servant for life. Do the same for your maidservant.

¹⁸Do not consider it a hardship to set your servant free, because his service to you these six years has been worth twice as much as that of a hired hand. And the LORD your God will bless you in everything you do.

The Firstborn Animals

¹⁹Set apart for the LORD your God every firstborn male of your herds and flocks. Do not put the firstborn of your oxen to work, and do not shear the firstborn of your sheep. ²⁰Each year you and your

family are to eat them in the presence of the LORD your God at the place he will choose. ²¹If an animal has a defect, is lame or blind, or has any serious flaw, you must not sacrifice it to the LORD your God. ²²You are to eat it in your own towns. Both the ceremonially unclean and the clean may eat it, as if it were gazelle or deer. ²³But you must not eat the blood; pour it out on the ground like water.

Passover

16 Observe the month of Abib and celebrate the Passover of the LORD your God, because in the month of Abib he brought you out of Egypt by night. ²Sacrifice as the Passover to the LORD your God an animal from your flock or herd at the place the LORD will choose as a dwelling for his Name. ³Do not eat it with bread made with yeast, but for seven days eat unleavened bread, the bread of affliction, because you left Egypt in haste—so that all the days of your life

you may remember the time of your departure from Egypt. ⁴Let no yeast be found in your possession in all your land for seven days. Do not let any of the meat you sacrifice on the evening of the first day remain until morning.

⁵You must not sacrifice the Passover in any town the LORD your God gives you ⁶except in the place he will choose as a dwelling for his Name. There you must sacrifice the Passover in the evening, when the sun goes down, on the anniversary^a of your departure from Egypt. ⁷Roast it and eat it at the place the LORD your God will choose. Then in the morning return to your tents. ⁸For six days eat unleavened bread and on the seventh day hold an assembly to the LORD your God and do no work.

Feast of Weeks

⁹Count off seven weeks from the time you begin to put the sickle to the stand-

^a6 Or *down, at the time of day*

Mon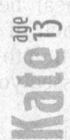day

A Major Celebration   **Read Deuteronomy 16:1–8**

If there's one thing we don't do enough of, it's celebrating. Think of all the things God has done for us: He provides us with food, a place to live, people who love us and, best of all, life with him forever. That's a lot to be excited about!

    God has given us so much, and he wants us to thank him for it. How? By celebrating! God wants us to enjoy his goodness and remember how much he's done for us. When we do, we will start to feel more happy about life. And when we think about all God has done for us, we'll want to start doing things for other people too.

    After all, who wants to celebrate alone?

❶ Think about some of the things God has done for you. Why is it so easy to take those things for granted? What would your life be like without God's many gifts?

❷ Make a top10 list of what you're thankful for, then party with some of God's wonderful gifts—yummy food, awesome music and great friends.

❸ Write a thank-you note to God, praising him for all he's given you.

Turn to page 226 for your next devotion.

ing grain. [10]Then celebrate the Feast of Weeks to the LORD your God by giving a freewill offering in proportion to the blessings the LORD your God has given you. [11]And rejoice before the LORD your God at the place he will choose as a dwelling for his Name—you, your sons and daughters, your menservants and maidservants, the Levites in your towns, and the aliens, the fatherless and the widows living among you. [12]Remember that you were slaves in Egypt, and follow carefully these decrees.

Feast of Tabernacles

[13]Celebrate the Feast of Tabernacles for seven days after you have gathered the produce of your threshing floor and your winepress. [14]Be joyful at your Feast—you, your sons and daughters, your menservants and maidservants, and the Levites, the aliens, the fatherless and the widows who live in your towns. [15]For seven days celebrate the Feast to the LORD your God at the place the LORD will choose. For the LORD your God will bless you in all your harvest and in all the work of your hands, and your joy will be complete.

[16]Three times a year all your men must appear before the LORD your God at the place he will choose: at the Feast of Unleavened Bread, the Feast of Weeks and the Feast of Tabernacles. No man should appear before the LORD empty-handed: [17]Each of you must bring a gift in proportion to the way the LORD your God has blessed you.

Judges

[18]Appoint judges and officials for each of your tribes in every town the LORD your God is giving you, and they shall judge the people fairly. [19]Do not pervert justice or show partiality. Do not accept a bribe, for a bribe blinds the eyes of the wise and twists the words of the righteous. [20]Follow justice and justice alone, so that you may live and possess the land the LORD your God is giving you.

Worshiping Other Gods

[21]Do not set up any wooden Asherah pole[a] beside the altar you build to the LORD your God, [22]and do not erect a sacred stone, for these the LORD your God hates.

17 Do not sacrifice to the LORD your God an ox or a sheep that has any defect or flaw in it, for that would be detestable to him.

[2]If a man or woman living among you in one of the towns the LORD gives you is found doing evil in the eyes of the LORD your God in violation of his covenant, [3]and contrary to my command has worshiped other gods, bowing down to them or to the sun or the moon or the stars of the sky, [4]and this has been brought to your attention, then you must investigate it thoroughly. If it is true and it has been proved that this detestable thing has been done in Israel, [5]take the man or woman who has done this evil deed to your city gate and stone that person to death. [6]On the testimony of two or three witnesses a man shall be put to death, but no one shall be put to death on the testimony of only one witness. [7]The hands of the witnesses must be the first in putting him to death, and then the hands of all the people. You must purge the evil from among you.

Law Courts

[8]If cases come before your courts that are too difficult for you to judge—whether bloodshed, lawsuits or assaults—take them to the place the LORD your God will choose. [9]Go to the priests, who are Levites, and to the judge who is in office at that time. Inquire of them and they will give you the verdict. [10]You must act according to the decisions they give you at the place the LORD will choose. Be careful to do everything they direct you to do. [11]Act according to the law they teach you and the decisions they give you. Do not turn aside from what they tell you, to the right or to the left. [12]The man who shows contempt for the judge or for the priest who stands ministering there to the LORD your God must be put to death. You must purge the evil from Israel. [13]All the people will hear and be afraid, and will not be contemptuous again.

[a]21 Or *Do not plant any tree dedicated to Asherah*

The King

[14]When you enter the land the LORD your God is giving you and have taken possession of it and settled in it, and you say, "Let us set a king over us like all the nations around us," [15]be sure to appoint over you the king the LORD your God chooses. He must be from among your own brothers. Do not place a foreigner over you, one who is not a brother Israelite. [16]The king, moreover, must not acquire great numbers of horses for himself or make the people return to Egypt to get more of them, for the LORD has told you, "You are not to go back that way again." [17]He must not take many wives, or his heart will be led astray. He must not accumulate large amounts of silver and gold.

[18]When he takes the throne of his kingdom, he is to write for himself on a scroll a copy of this law, taken from that of the priests, who are Levites. [19]It is to be with him, and he is to read it all the days of his life so that he may learn to revere the LORD his God and follow carefully all the words of this law and these decrees [20]and not consider himself better than his brothers and turn from the law to the right or to the left. Then he and his descendants will reign a long time over his kingdom in Israel.

Offerings for Priests and Levites

18 The priests, who are Levites—indeed the whole tribe of Levi—are to have no allotment or inheritance with Israel. They shall live on the offerings made to the LORD by fire, for that is their inheritance. [2]They shall have no inheritance among their brothers; the LORD is their inheritance, as he promised them.

[3]This is the share due the priests from the people who sacrifice a bull or a sheep: the shoulder, the jowls and the inner parts. [4]You are to give them the first-fruits of your grain, new wine and oil, and the first wool from the shearing of your sheep, [5]for the LORD your God has chosen them and their descendants out of all your tribes to stand and minister in the LORD's name always.

[6]If a Levite moves from one of your towns anywhere in Israel where he is living, and comes in all earnestness to the place the LORD will choose, [7]he may minister in the name of the LORD his God like all his fellow Levites who serve there in the presence of the LORD. [8]He is to share equally in their benefits, even though he has received money from the sale of family possessions.

Detestable Practices

[9]When you enter the land the LORD your God is giving you, do not learn to imitate the detestable ways of the nations there. [10]Let no one be found among you who sacrifices his son or daughter in[a] the fire, who practices divination or sorcery, interprets omens, engages in witchcraft, [11]or casts spells, or who is a medium or spiritist or who consults the dead. [12]Anyone who does these things is detestable to the LORD, and because of these detestable practices the LORD your God will drive out those nations before you. [13]You must be blameless before the LORD your God.

The Prophet

[14]The nations you will dispossess listen to those who practice sorcery or divination. But as for you, the LORD your God has not permitted you to do so. [15]The LORD your God will raise up for you a prophet like me from among your own brothers. You must listen to him. [16]For this is what you asked of the LORD your God at Horeb on the day of the assembly when you said, "Let us not hear the voice of the LORD our God nor see this great fire anymore, or we will die."

[17]The LORD said to me: "What they say is good. [18]I will raise up for them a prophet like you from among their brothers; I will put my words in his mouth, and he will tell them everything I command him. [19]If anyone does not listen to my words that the prophet speaks in my name, I myself will call him to account. [20]But a prophet who presumes to speak in my name anything I have not commanded him to say, or a prophet who speaks in the name of other gods, must be put to death."

---

[a]10 Or *who makes his son or daughter pass through*

So You Want to Lead?

Huh?

Deuteronomy 18:20

Some of God's people were supposed to speak on his behalf. They were called *prophets*, God's "mouth" to people. But if one of them said something that *wasn't* from God, God got pretty upset. Today people speak in God's name a lot, and we don't kill them when they're off base. But be careful. Make sure you listen to God and not someone who thinks he or she is God's direct messenger—that's why we have the Bible (duh!).

²¹You may say to yourselves, "How can we know when a message has not been spoken by the LORD?" ²²If what a prophet proclaims in the name of the LORD does not take place or come true, that is a message the LORD has not spoken. That prophet has spoken presumptuously. Do not be afraid of him.

Cities of Refuge

19 When the LORD your God has destroyed the nations whose land he is giving you, and when you have driven them out and settled in their towns and houses, ²then set aside for yourselves three cities centrally located in the land the LORD your God is giving you to possess. ³Build roads to them and divide into three parts the land the LORD your God is giving you as an inheritance, so that anyone who kills a man may flee there.

⁴This is the rule concerning the man who kills another and flees there to save his life—one who kills his neighbor unintentionally, without malice aforethought. ⁵For instance, a man may go into the forest with his neighbor to cut wood, and as he swings his ax to fell a tree, the head may fly off and hit his neighbor and kill him. That man may flee to one of these cities and save his life. ⁶Otherwise, the avenger of blood might pursue him in a rage, overtake him if the distance is too great, and kill him even though he is not deserving of death,

since he did it to his neighbor without malice aforethought. ⁷This is why I command you to set aside for yourselves three cities.

⁸If the LORD your God enlarges your territory, as he promised on oath to your forefathers, and gives you the whole land he promised them, ⁹because you carefully follow all these laws I command you today—to love the LORD your God and to walk always in his ways—then you are to set aside three more cities. ¹⁰Do this so that innocent blood will not be shed in your land, which the LORD your God is giving you as your inheritance, and so that you will not be guilty of bloodshed.

¹¹But if a man hates his neighbor and lies in wait for him, assaults and kills him, and then flees to one of these cities, ¹²the elders of his town shall send for him, bring him back from the city, and hand him over to the avenger of blood to die. ¹³Show him no pity. You must purge from Israel the guilt of shedding innocent blood, so that it may go well with you.

¹⁴Do not move your neighbor's boundary stone set up by your predecessors in the inheritance you receive in the land the LORD your God is giving you to possess.

Witnesses

¹⁵One witness is not enough to convict a man accused of any crime or offense he may have committed. A matter must be established by the testimony of two or three witnesses.

¹⁶If a malicious witness takes the stand to accuse a man of a crime, ¹⁷the two men involved in the dispute must stand in the presence of the LORD before the priests and the judges who are in office at the time. ¹⁸The judges must make a thorough investigation, and if the witness proves to be a liar, giving false testimony against his brother, ¹⁹then do to him as he intended to do to his brother. You must purge the evil from among you. ²⁰The rest of the people will hear of this and be afraid, and never again will such an evil thing be done among you. ²¹Show no pity: life for life, eye for eye, tooth for tooth, hand for hand, foot for foot.

Going to War

20 When you go to war against your enemies and see horses and chariots and an army greater than yours, do not be afraid of them, because the LORD your God, who brought you up out of Egypt, will be with you. ²When you are about to go into battle, the priest shall come forward and address the army. ³He shall say: "Hear, O Israel, today you are going into battle against your enemies. Do not be fainthearted or afraid; do not be terrified or give way to panic before them. ⁴For the LORD your God is the one who goes with you to fight for you against your enemies to give you victory."

⁵The officers shall say to the army: "Has anyone built a new house and not dedicated it? Let him go home, or he may die in battle and someone else may dedicate it. ⁶Has anyone planted a vineyard and not begun to enjoy it? Let him go home, or he may die in battle and someone else enjoy it. ⁷Has anyone become pledged to a woman and not married her? Let him go home, or he may die in battle and someone else marry her." ⁸Then the officers shall add, "Is any man afraid or fainthearted? Let him go home so that his brothers will not become disheartened too." ⁹When the officers have finished speaking to the army, they shall appoint commanders over it.

¹⁰When you march up to attack a city, make its people an offer of peace. ¹¹If they accept and open their gates, all the people in it shall be subject to forced labor and shall work for you. ¹²If they refuse to make peace and they engage you in battle, lay siege to that city. ¹³When the LORD your God delivers it into your hand, put to the sword all the men in it. ¹⁴As for the women, the children, the livestock and everything else in the city, you may take these as plunder for yourselves. And you may use the plunder the LORD your God gives you from your enemies. ¹⁵This is how you are to treat all the cities that are at a distance from you and do not belong to the nations nearby.

¹⁶However, in the cities of the nations the LORD your God is giving you as an inheritance, do not leave alive anything that breathes. ¹⁷Completely destroy*a* them—the Hittites, Amorites, Canaanites, Perizzites, Hivites and Jebusites—as the LORD your God has commanded you. ¹⁸Otherwise, they will teach you to follow all the detestable things they do in worshiping their gods, and you will sin against the LORD your God.

¹⁹When you lay siege to a city for a long time, fighting against it to capture it, do not destroy its trees by putting an ax to them, because you can eat their fruit. Do not cut them down. Are the trees of the field people, that you should besiege them?*b* ²⁰However, you may cut down trees that you know are not fruit trees and use them to build siege works until the city at war with you falls.

Atonement for an Unsolved Murder

21 If a man is found slain, lying in a field in the land the LORD your God is giving you to possess, and it is not known who killed him, ²your elders and judges shall go out and measure the distance from the body to the neighboring towns. ³Then the elders of the town nearest the body shall take a heifer that has never been worked and has never worn a yoke ⁴and lead her down to a valley that has not been plowed or planted and where there is a flowing stream. There in the valley they are to break the heifer's neck. ⁵The priests, the sons of Levi, shall step forward, for the LORD your God has chosen them to minister and to pronounce blessings in the name of the LORD and to decide all cases of dispute and assault. ⁶Then all the elders of the town nearest the body shall wash their hands over the heifer whose neck was broken in the valley, ⁷and they shall declare: "Our hands did not shed this blood, nor did our eyes see it done. ⁸Accept this atonement for your people Israel, whom you have redeemed, O LORD, and do not hold your people guilty of the blood of an innocent man." And the bloodshed will be atoned for. ⁹So you will purge from yourselves the guilt of shedding innocent

---

a17 The Hebrew term refers to the irrevocable giving over of things or persons to the LORD, often by totally destroying them.   *b19* Or *down to use in the siege, for the fruit trees are for the benefit of man.*

blood, since you have done what is right in the eyes of the LORD.

Marrying a Captive Woman

¹⁰When you go to war against your enemies and the LORD your God delivers them into your hands and you take captives, ¹¹if you notice among the captives a beautiful woman and are attracted to her, you may take her as your wife. ¹²Bring her into your home and have her shave her head, trim her nails ¹³and put aside the clothes she was wearing when captured. After she has lived in your house and mourned her father and mother for a full month, then you may go to her and be her husband and she shall be your wife. ¹⁴If you are not pleased with her, let her go wherever she wishes. You must not sell her or treat her as a slave, since you have dishonored her.

The Right of the Firstborn

¹⁵If a man has two wives, and he loves one but not the other, and both bear him sons but the firstborn is the son of the wife he does not love, ¹⁶when he wills his property to his sons, he must not give the rights of the firstborn to the son of the wife he loves in preference to his actual firstborn, the son of the wife he does not love. ¹⁷He must acknowledge the son of his unloved wife as the firstborn by giving him a double share of all he has. That son is the first sign of his father's strength. The right of the firstborn belongs to him.

A Rebellious Son

¹⁸If a man has a stubborn and rebellious son who does not obey his father and mother and will not listen to them when they discipline him, ¹⁹his father and mother shall take hold of him and bring him to the elders at the gate of his town. ²⁰They shall say to the elders, "This son of ours is stubborn and rebellious. He will not obey us. He is a profligate and a drunkard." ²¹Then all the men of his town shall stone him to death. You must purge

Tuesday

Rebel Child

Read Deuteronomy 21:18-21

Before I moved to California, I chose some wrong friends and did some things I knew I was not supposed to do. I tried drugs and alcohol, I hardly came home, and I was a D student. When my parents told me to do something, I would never do it.

These verses remind me that rebellion is a big deal in God's eyes. In Old Testament times, a rebellious child could be stoned to death by a whole town! I know that would never happen to me, but it sure makes me think twice about not obeying my parents.

Avoiding punishment is one reason why I obey my parents, but it's not the biggest one. Rebelling against my parents is sin—it's not what God wants me to do. Thinking about it that way helps. I want to obey my parents because I want to obey Jesus.

❶ Why do you think obeying your parents is so important to God?

❷ Try to see your parents' rules from their side. If you honestly don't get the reasons for some of them, ask your parents to help you understand.

❸ Thank God for your parents and ask him to help you obey them.

Turn to page 229 for your next devotion.

the evil from among you. All Israel will hear of it and be afraid.

Various Laws

[22]If a man guilty of a capital offense is put to death and his body is hung on a tree, [23]you must not leave his body on the tree overnight. Be sure to bury him that same day, because anyone who is hung on a tree is under God's curse. You must not desecrate the land the LORD your God is giving you as an inheritance.

22 If you see your brother's ox or sheep straying, do not ignore it but be sure to take it back to him. [2]If the brother does not live near you or if you do not know who he is, take it home with you and keep it until he comes looking for it. Then give it back to him. [3]Do the same if you find your brother's donkey or his cloak or anything he loses. Do not ignore it.

[4]If you see your brother's donkey or his ox fallen on the road, do not ignore it. Help him get it to its feet.

[5]A woman must not wear men's clothing, nor a man wear women's clothing, for the LORD your God detests anyone who does this.

[6]If you come across a bird's nest beside the road, either in a tree or on the ground, and the mother is sitting on the young or on the eggs, do not take the mother with the young. [7]You may take the young, but be sure to let the mother go, so that it may go well with you and you may have a long life.

[8]When you build a new house, make a parapet around your roof so that you may not bring the guilt of bloodshed on your house if someone falls from the roof.

[9]Do not plant two kinds of seed in your vineyard; if you do, not only the crops you plant but also the fruit of the vineyard will be defiled.[a]

[10]Do not plow with an ox and a donkey yoked together.

[11]Do not wear clothes of wool and linen woven together.

[12]Make tassels on the four corners of the cloak you wear.

Marriage Violations

[13]If a man takes a wife and, after lying with her, dislikes her [14]and slanders her

and gives her a bad name, saying, "I married this woman, but when I approached her, I did not find proof of her virginity," [15]then the girl's father and mother shall bring proof that she was a virgin to the town elders at the gate. [16]The girl's father will say to the elders, "I gave my daughter in marriage to this man, but he dislikes her. [17]Now he has slandered her and said, 'I did not find your daughter to be a virgin.' But here is the proof of my daughter's virginity." Then her parents shall display the cloth before the elders of the town, [18]and the elders shall take the man and punish him. [19]They shall fine him a hundred shekels of silver[b] and give them to the girl's father, because this man has given an Israelite virgin a bad name. She shall continue to be his wife; he must not divorce her as long as he lives.

[20]If, however, the charge is true and no proof of the girl's virginity can be found, [21]she shall be brought to the door of her father's house and there the men of her town shall stone her to death. She has done a disgraceful thing in Israel by being promiscuous while still in her father's house. You must purge the evil from among you.

[22]If a man is found sleeping with another man's wife, both the man who slept with her and the woman must die. You must purge the evil from Israel.

[23]If a man happens to meet in a town a virgin pledged to be married and he sleeps with her, [24]you shall take both of them to the gate of that town and stone them to death—the girl because she was in a town and did not scream for help, and the man because he violated another man's wife. You must purge the evil from among you.

[25]But if out in the country a man happens to meet a girl pledged to be married and rapes her, only the man who has done this shall die. [26]Do nothing to the girl; she has committed no sin deserving death. This case is like that of someone who attacks and murders his neighbor, [27]for the man found the girl out in the country, and though the betrothed girl

---

[a]9 Or *be forfeited to the sanctuary*   [b]19 That is, about 2 1/2 pounds (about 1 kilogram)

screamed, there was no one to rescue her.

²⁸If a man happens to meet a virgin who is not pledged to be married and rapes her and they are discovered, ²⁹he shall pay the girl's father fifty shekels of silver.[a] He must marry the girl, for he has violated her. He can never divorce her as long as he lives.

³⁰A man is not to marry his father's wife; he must not dishonor his father's bed.

Exclusion From the Assembly

23 No one who has been emasculated by crushing or cutting may enter the assembly of the LORD.

²No one born of a forbidden marriage[b] nor any of his descendants may enter the assembly of the LORD, even down to the tenth generation.

³No Ammonite or Moabite or any of his descendants may enter the assembly of the LORD, even down to the tenth generation. ⁴For they did not come to meet you with bread and water on your way when you came out of Egypt, and they hired Balaam son of Beor from Pethor in Aram Naharaim[c] to pronounce a curse on you. ⁵However, the LORD your God would not listen to Balaam but turned the curse into a blessing for you, because the LORD your God loves you. ⁶Do not seek a treaty of friendship with them as long as you live.

⁷Do not abhor an Edomite, for he is your brother. Do not abhor an Egyptian, because you lived as an alien in his country. ⁸The third generation of children born to them may enter the assembly of the LORD.

Uncleanness in the Camp

⁹When you are encamped against your enemies, keep away from everything impure. ¹⁰If one of your men is unclean because of a nocturnal emission, he is to go outside the camp and stay there. ¹¹But as evening approaches he is to wash himself, and at sunset he may return to the camp.

¹²Designate a place outside the camp where you can go to relieve yourself. ¹³As part of your equipment have something to dig with, and when you relieve yourself, dig a hole and cover up your excrement. ¹⁴For the LORD your God moves about in your camp to protect you and to deliver your enemies to you. Your camp must be holy, so that he will not see among you anything indecent and turn away from you.

Miscellaneous Laws

¹⁵If a slave has taken refuge with you, do not hand him over to his master. ¹⁶Let him live among you wherever he likes and in whatever town he chooses. Do not oppress him.

¹⁷No Israelite man or woman is to become a shrine prostitute. ¹⁸You must not bring the earnings of a female prostitute or of a male prostitute[d] into the house of the LORD your God to pay any vow, because the LORD your God detests them both.

¹⁹Do not charge your brother interest, whether on money or food or anything else that may earn interest. ²⁰You may charge a foreigner interest, but not a brother Israelite, so that the LORD your God may bless you in everything you put your hand to in the land you are entering to possess.

²¹If you make a vow to the LORD your God, do not be slow to pay it, for the LORD your God will certainly demand it of you and you will be guilty of sin. ²²But if you refrain from making a vow, you will not be guilty. ²³Whatever your lips utter you must be sure to do, because you made your vow freely to the LORD your God with your own mouth.

²⁴If you enter your neighbor's vineyard, you may eat all the grapes you want, but do not put any in your basket. ²⁵If you enter your neighbor's grainfield, you may pick kernels with your hands, but you must not put a sickle to his standing grain.

24 If a man marries a woman who becomes displeasing to him because he finds something indecent about her, and he writes her a certificate of divorce, gives it to her and sends her from his house, ²and if after she leaves his house she becomes the wife of another man, ³and her second husband dislikes

---

[a]29 That is, about 1 1/4 pounds (about 0.6 kilogram)   [b]2 Or *one of illegitimate birth*   [c]4 That is, Northwest Mesopotamia   [d]18 Hebrew *of a dog*

her and writes her a certificate of divorce, gives it to her and sends her from his house, or if he dies, ⁴then her first husband, who divorced her, is not allowed to marry her again after she has been defiled. That would be detestable in the eyes of the LORD. Do not bring sin upon the land the LORD your God is giving you as an inheritance.

⁵If a man has recently married, he must not be sent to war or have any other duty laid on him. For one year he is to be free to stay at home and bring happiness to the wife he has married.

⁶Do not take a pair of millstones—not even the upper one—as security for a debt, because that would be taking a man's livelihood as security.

⁷If a man is caught kidnapping one of his brother Israelites and treats him as a slave or sells him, the kidnapper must die. You must purge the evil from among you.

⁸In cases of leprous*a* diseases be very careful to do exactly as the priests, who are Levites, instruct you. You must follow carefully what I have commanded them. ⁹Remember what the LORD your God did to Miriam along the way after you came out of Egypt.

¹⁰When you make a loan of any kind to your neighbor, do not go into his house to get what he is offering as a pledge. ¹¹Stay outside and let the man to whom you are making the loan bring the pledge out to you. ¹²If the man is poor, do not go to sleep with his pledge in your possession. ¹³Return his cloak to him by sunset so that he may sleep in it. Then he will thank you, and it will be regarded as a righteous act in the sight of the LORD your God.

¹⁴Do not take advantage of a hired man who is poor and needy, whether he is a brother Israelite or an alien living in

---

a8 The Hebrew word was used for various diseases affecting the skin—not necessarily leprosy.

Wednesday

Care and Share

Read Deuteronomy 24:19–22

When I'm eating lunch in the cafeteria, sometimes I see that someone else has forgotten their lunch or forgotten to bring money to buy one. I should probably share some of my food with them. Often I think, *If I share my lunch, then I'll be hungry later.* But that's really no excuse. If I *don't* share my lunch, then the other kid will definitely be hungry later. I need to think about other people, because God cares for them as much as he cares for me. And if God cares, I should care too.

There are actually lots of good things that can come from sharing with other people. Once I start caring for people who have less than I do, I bet I'll want to do it more. And maybe other people will watch what I'm doing, and they'll want to do their part too. Next time I see someone who needs a hand, I'll try to help out.

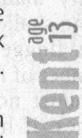

Kent age 13

❶ Why does God want us to help take care of people who are less fortunate than we are?

❷ Put an extra something in your lunch tomorrow—an orange, chips, even a candy bar. Look for a person you could give it to in the lunch room. Make their day!

❸ Ask God to help you be more generous.

Turn to page 245 for your next devotion.

one of your towns. [15]Pay him his wages each day before sunset, because he is poor and is counting on it. Otherwise he may cry to the LORD against you, and you will be guilty of sin.

[16]Fathers shall not be put to death for their children, nor children put to death for their fathers; each is to die for his own sin.

[17]Do not deprive the alien or the fatherless of justice, or take the cloak of the widow as a pledge. [18]Remember that you were slaves in Egypt and the LORD your God redeemed you from there. That is why I command you to do this.

[19]When you are harvesting in your field and you overlook a sheaf, do not go back to get it. Leave it for the alien, the fatherless and the widow, so that the LORD your God may bless you in all the work of your hands. [20]When you beat the olives from your trees, do not go over the branches a second time. Leave what remains for the alien, the fatherless and the widow. [21]When you harvest the grapes in your vineyard, do not go over the vines again. Leave what remains for the alien, the fatherless and the widow. [22]Remember that you were slaves in Egypt. That is why I command you to do this.

25 When men have a dispute, they are to take it to court and the judges will decide the case, acquitting the innocent and condemning the guilty. [2]If the guilty man deserves to be beaten, the judge shall make him lie down and have him flogged in his presence with the number of lashes his crime deserves, [3]but he must not give him more than forty lashes. If he is flogged more than that, your brother will be degraded in your eyes.

[4]Do not muzzle an ox while it is treading out the grain.

[5]If brothers are living together and one of them dies without a son, his widow must not marry outside the family. Her husband's brother shall take her and marry her and fulfill the duty of a brother-in-law to her. [6]The first son she bears shall carry on the name of the dead brother so that his name will not be blotted out from Israel.

[7]However, if a man does not want to marry his brother's wife, she shall go to the elders at the town gate and say, "My husband's brother refuses to carry on his brother's name in Israel. He will not fulfill the duty of a brother-in-law to me." [8]Then the elders of his town shall summon him and talk to him. If he persists in saying, "I do not want to marry her," [9]his brother's widow shall go up to him in the presence of the elders, take off one of his sandals, spit in his face and say, "This is what is done to the man who will not build up his brother's family line." [10]That man's line shall be known in Israel as The Family of the Unsandaled.

[11]If two men are fighting and the wife of one of them comes to rescue her husband from his assailant, and she reaches out and seizes him by his private parts, [12]you shall cut off her hand. Show her no pity.

[13]Do not have two differing weights in your bag—one heavy, one light. [14]Do not have two differing measures in your house—one large, one small. [15]You must have accurate and honest weights and measures, so that you may live long in the land the LORD your God is giving you. [16]For the LORD your God detests anyone who does these things, anyone who deals dishonestly.

[17]Remember what the Amalekites did to you along the way when you came out of Egypt. [18]When you were weary and worn out, they met you on your journey and cut off all who were lagging behind; they had no fear of God. [19]When the LORD your God gives you rest from all the enemies around you in the land he is giving you to possess as an inheritance, you shall blot out the memory of Amalek from under heaven. Do not forget!

Firstfruits and Tithes

26 When you have entered the land the LORD your God is giving you as an inheritance and have taken possession of it and settled in it, [2]take some of the firstfruits of all that you produce from the soil of the land the LORD your God is giving you and put them in a basket. Then go to the place the LORD your God will choose as a dwelling for his Name [3]and say to the priest in office at the time, "I declare today to the LORD your God that I have come to the land the LORD swore to our forefathers to give us." ⁴The priest shall take the basket from your hands and set it down in front of the altar of the LORD your God. ⁵Then you shall declare before the LORD your God: "My father was a wandering Aramean, and he went down into Egypt with a few people and lived there and became a great nation, powerful and numerous. ⁶But the Egyptians mistreated us and made us suffer, putting us to hard labor. ⁷Then we cried out to the LORD, the God of our fathers, and the LORD heard our voice and saw our misery, toil and oppression. ⁸So the LORD brought us out of Egypt with a mighty hand and an outstretched arm, with great terror and with miraculous signs and wonders. ⁹He brought us to this place and gave us this land, a land flowing with milk and honey; ¹⁰and now I bring the firstfruits of the soil that you, O LORD, have given me." Place the basket before the LORD your God and bow down before him. ¹¹And you and the Levites and the aliens among you shall rejoice in all the good things the LORD your God has given to you and your household.

¹²When you have finished setting aside a tenth of all your produce in the third year, the year of the tithe, you shall give it to the Levite, the alien, the fatherless and the widow, so that they may eat in your towns and be satisfied. ¹³Then say to the LORD your God: "I have removed from my house the sacred portion and have given it to the Levite, the alien, the fatherless and the widow, according to all you commanded. I have not turned aside from your commands nor have I forgotten any of them. ¹⁴I have not eaten any of the sacred portion while I was in mourning, nor have I removed any of it while I was unclean, nor have I offered any of it to the dead. I have obeyed the LORD my God; I have done everything you commanded me. ¹⁵Look down from heaven, your holy dwelling place, and bless your people Israel and the land you have given us as you promised on oath to our forefathers, a land flowing with milk and honey."

Follow the LORD's Commands

¹⁶The LORD your God commands you this day to follow these decrees and laws;

carefully observe them with all your heart and with all your soul. ¹⁷You have declared this day that the LORD is your God and that you will walk in his ways, that you will keep his decrees, commands and laws, and that you will obey him. ¹⁸And the LORD has declared this day that you are his people, his treasured possession as he promised, and that you are to keep all his commands. ¹⁹He has declared that he will set you in praise, fame and honor high above all the nations he has made and that you will be a people holy to the LORD your God, as he promised.

The Altar on Mount Ebal

27 Moses and the elders of Israel commanded the people: "Keep all these commands that I give you today. ²When you have crossed the Jordan into the land the LORD your God is giving you, set up some large stones and coat them with plaster. ³Write on them all the words of this law when you have crossed over to enter the land the LORD your God is giving you, a land flowing with milk and honey, just as the LORD, the God of your fathers, promised you. ⁴And when you have crossed the Jordan, set up these stones on Mount Ebal, as I command you today, and coat them with plaster. ⁵Build there an altar to the LORD your God, an altar of stones. Do not use any iron tool upon them. ⁶Build the altar of the LORD your God with fieldstones and offer burnt offerings on it to the LORD your God. ⁷Sacrifice fellowship offerings[a] there, eating them and rejoicing in the presence of the LORD your God. ⁸And you shall write very clearly all the words of this law on these stones you have set up."

Curses From Mount Ebal

⁹Then Moses and the priests, who are Levites, said to all Israel, "Be silent, O Israel, and listen! You have now become the people of the LORD your God. ¹⁰Obey the LORD your God and follow his commands and decrees that I give you today."

¹¹On the same day Moses commanded the people:

---

a7 Traditionally *peace offerings*

¹²When you have crossed the Jordan, these tribes shall stand on Mount Gerizim to bless the people: Simeon, Levi, Judah, Issachar, Joseph and Benjamin. ¹³And these tribes shall stand on Mount Ebal to pronounce curses: Reuben, Gad, Asher, Zebulun, Dan and Naphtali.

¹⁴The Levites shall recite to all the people of Israel in a loud voice:

¹⁵"Cursed is the man who carves an image or casts an idol—a thing detestable to the LORD, the work of the craftsman's hands—and sets it up in secret."

Then all the people shall say, "Amen!"

¹⁶"Cursed is the man who dishonors his father or his mother."

Then all the people shall say, "Amen!"

¹⁷"Cursed is the man who moves his neighbor's boundary stone."

Then all the people shall say, "Amen!"

¹⁸"Cursed is the man who leads the blind astray on the road."

Then all the people shall say, "Amen!"

¹⁹"Cursed is the man who withholds justice from the alien, the fatherless or the widow."

Then all the people shall say, "Amen!"

²⁰"Cursed is the man who sleeps with his father's wife, for he dishonors his father's bed."

Then all the people shall say, "Amen!"

²¹"Cursed is the man who has sexual relations with any animal."

Then all the people shall say, "Amen!"

²²"Cursed is the man who sleeps with his sister, the daughter of his father or the daughter of his mother."

Then all the people shall say, "Amen!"

²³"Cursed is the man who sleeps with his mother-in-law."

Then all the people shall say, "Amen!"

²⁴"Cursed is the man who kills his neighbor secretly."

Then all the people shall say, "Amen!"

²⁵"Cursed is the man who accepts a bribe to kill an innocent person."

Then all the people shall say, "Amen!"

²⁶"Cursed is the man who does not uphold the words of this law by carrying them out."

Then all the people shall say, "Amen!"

Blessings for Obedience

28 If you fully obey the LORD your God and carefully follow all his commands I give you today, the LORD your God will set you high above all the nations on earth. ²All these blessings will come upon you and accompany you if you obey the LORD your God:

³You will be blessed in the city and blessed in the country.

⁴The fruit of your womb will be blessed, and the crops of your land and the young of your livestock—the calves of your herds and the lambs of your flocks.

⁵Your basket and your kneading trough will be blessed.

⁶You will be blessed when you come in and blessed when you go out.

⁷The LORD will grant that the enemies who rise up against you will be defeated before you. They will come at you from one direction but flee from you in seven.

⁸The LORD will send a blessing on your barns and on everything you put your hand to. The LORD your God will bless you in the land he is giving you.

⁹The LORD will establish you as his holy people, as he promised you on oath, if you keep the commands of the LORD your God and walk in his ways. ¹⁰Then all the peoples on earth will see that you are called by the name of the LORD, and they will fear you. ¹¹The LORD will grant you abundant prosperity—in the fruit of your womb, the young of your livestock and the crops of your ground—in the land he swore to your forefathers to give you.

¹²The LORD will open the heavens, the storehouse of his bounty, to send rain on

your land in season and to bless all the work of your hands. You will lend to many nations but will borrow from none. ¹³The Lᴏʀᴅ will make you the head, not the tail. If you pay attention to the commands of the Lᴏʀᴅ your God that I give you this day and carefully follow them, you will always be at the top, never at the bottom. ¹⁴Do not turn aside from any of the commands I give you today, to the right or to the left, following other gods and serving them.

Curses for Disobedience

¹⁵However, if you do not obey the Lᴏʀᴅ your God and do not carefully follow all his commands and decrees I am giving you today, all these curses will come upon you and overtake you:

Bad Stuff

Huh?

Deuteronomy 28:15

When we don't obey God, all kinds of things get messed up. In fact, *everything* in life gets messed up. When you read the Old Testament, do you ever wonder why God gets so mad and expects so much of his followers? Well, it's because God loves us! Some people think God is uncool because bad stuff happens when we don't listen to him. But God is *way cool* because he gives us the freedom to make choices—even when he knows the results of our choices won't always be good.

¹⁶You will be cursed in the city and cursed in the country.

¹⁷Your basket and your kneading trough will be cursed.

¹⁸The fruit of your womb will be cursed, and the crops of your land, and the calves of your herds and the lambs of your flocks.

¹⁹You will be cursed when you come in and cursed when you go out.

²⁰The Lᴏʀᴅ will send on you curses, confusion and rebuke in everything you put your hand to, until you are destroyed

and come to sudden ruin because of the evil you have done in forsaking him.*a* ²¹The Lᴏʀᴅ will plague you with diseases until he has destroyed you from the land you are entering to possess. ²²The Lᴏʀᴅ will strike you with wasting disease, with fever and inflammation, with scorching heat and drought, with blight and mildew, which will plague you until you perish. ²³The sky over your head will be bronze, the ground beneath you iron. ²⁴The Lᴏʀᴅ will turn the rain of your country into dust and powder; it will come down from the skies until you are destroyed.

²⁵The Lᴏʀᴅ will cause you to be defeated before your enemies. You will come at them from one direction but flee from them in seven, and you will become a thing of horror to all the kingdoms on earth. ²⁶Your carcasses will be food for all the birds of the air and the beasts of the earth, and there will be no one to frighten them away. ²⁷The Lᴏʀᴅ will afflict you with the boils of Egypt and with tumors, festering sores and the itch, from which you cannot be cured. ²⁸The Lᴏʀᴅ will afflict you with madness, blindness and confusion of mind. ²⁹At midday you will grope about like a blind man in the dark. You will be unsuccessful in everything you do; day after day you will be oppressed and robbed, with no one to rescue you.

³⁰You will be pledged to be married to a woman, but another will take her and ravish her. You will build a house, but you will not live in it. You will plant a vineyard, but you will not even begin to enjoy its fruit. ³¹Your ox will be slaughtered before your eyes, but you will eat none of it. Your donkey will be forcibly taken from you and will not be returned. Your sheep will be given to your enemies, and no one will rescue them. ³²Your sons and daughters will be given to another nation, and you will wear out your eyes watching for them day after day, powerless to lift a hand. ³³A people that you do not know will eat what your land and labor produce, and you will have nothing but cruel oppression all your days. ³⁴The sights you see will drive you

a20 Hebrew me

mad. [35]The LORD will afflict your knees and legs with painful boils that cannot be cured, spreading from the soles of your feet to the top of your head.

[36]The LORD will drive you and the king you set over you to a nation unknown to you or your fathers. There you will worship other gods, gods of wood and stone. [37]You will become a thing of horror and an object of scorn and ridicule to all the nations where the LORD will drive you.

[38]You will sow much seed in the field but you will harvest little, because locusts will devour it. [39]You will plant vineyards and cultivate them but you will not drink the wine or gather the grapes, because worms will eat them. [40]You will have olive trees throughout your country but you will not use the oil, because the olives will drop off. [41]You will have sons and daughters but you will not keep them, because they will go into captivity. [42]Swarms of locusts will take over all your trees and the crops of your land.

[43]The alien who lives among you will rise above you higher and higher, but you will sink lower and lower. [44]He will lend to you, but you will not lend to him. He will be the head, but you will be the tail.

[45]All these curses will come upon you. They will pursue you and overtake you until you are destroyed, because you did not obey the LORD your God and observe the commands and decrees he gave you. [46]They will be a sign and a wonder to you and your descendants forever. [47]Because you did not serve the LORD your God joyfully and gladly in the time of prosperity, [48]therefore in hunger and thirst, in nakedness and dire poverty, you will serve the enemies the LORD sends against you. He will put an iron yoke on your neck until he has destroyed you.

[49]The LORD will bring a nation against you from far away, from the ends of the earth, like an eagle swooping down, a nation whose language you will not understand, [50]a fierce-looking nation without respect for the old or pity for the young. [51]They will devour the young of your livestock and the crops of your land until you are destroyed. They will leave you no grain, new wine or oil, nor any calves of your herds or lambs of your flocks until you are ruined. [52]They will lay siege to all the cities throughout your land until the high fortified walls in which you trust fall down. They will besiege all the cities throughout the land the LORD your God is giving you.

[53]Because of the suffering that your enemy will inflict on you during the siege, you will eat the fruit of the womb, the flesh of the sons and daughters the LORD your God has given you. [54]Even the most gentle and sensitive man among you will have no compassion on his own brother or the wife he loves or his surviving children, [55]and he will not give to one of them any of the flesh of his children that he is eating. It will be all he has left because of the suffering your enemy will inflict on you during the siege of all your cities. [56]The most gentle and sensitive woman among you—so sensitive and gentle that she would not venture to touch the ground with the sole of her foot—will begrudge the husband she loves and her own son or daughter [57]the afterbirth from her womb and the children she bears. For she intends to eat them secretly during the siege and in the distress that your enemy will inflict on you in your cities.

[58]If you do not carefully follow all the words of this law, which are written in this book, and do not revere this glorious and awesome name—the LORD your God— [59]the LORD will send fearful plagues on you and your descendants, harsh and prolonged disasters, and severe and lingering illnesses. [60]He will bring upon you all the diseases of Egypt that you dreaded, and they will cling to you. [61]The LORD will also bring on you every kind of sickness and disaster not recorded in this Book of the Law, until you are destroyed. [62]You who were as numerous as the stars in the sky will be left but few in number, because you did not obey the LORD your God. [63]Just as it pleased the LORD to make you prosper and increase in number, so it will please him to ruin and destroy you. You will be uprooted from the land you are entering to possess.

[64]Then the LORD will scatter you among all nations, from one end of the earth to the other. There you will worship other gods—gods of wood and stone,

which neither you nor your fathers have known. [65]Among those nations you will find no repose, no resting place for the sole of your foot. There the LORD will give you an anxious mind, eyes weary with longing, and a despairing heart. [66]You will live in constant suspense, filled with dread both night and day, never sure of your life. [67]In the morning you will say, "If only it were evening!" and in the evening, "If only it were morning!"—because of the terror that will fill your hearts and the sights that your eyes will see. [68]The LORD will send you back in ships to Egypt on a journey I said you should never make again. There you will offer yourselves for sale to your enemies as male and female slaves, but no one will buy you.

Renewal of the Covenant

29 These are the terms of the covenant the LORD commanded Moses to make with the Israelites in Moab, in addition to the covenant he had made with them at Horeb.

[2]Moses summoned all the Israelites and said to them:

Your eyes have seen all that the LORD did in Egypt to Pharaoh, to all his officials and to all his land. [3]With your own eyes you saw those great trials, those miraculous signs and great wonders. [4]But to this day the LORD has not given you a mind that understands or eyes that see or ears that hear. [5]During the forty years that I led you through the desert, your clothes did not wear out, nor did the sandals on your feet. [6]You ate no bread and drank no wine or other fermented drink. I did this so that you might know that I am the LORD your God.

[7]When you reached this place, Sihon king of Heshbon and Og king of Bashan came out to fight against us, but we defeated them. [8]We took their land and gave it as an inheritance to the Reubenites, the Gadites and the half-tribe of Manasseh.

[9]Carefully follow the terms of this covenant, so that you may prosper in everything you do. [10]All of you are standing today in the presence of the LORD your God—your leaders and chief men, your

elders and officials, and all the other men of Israel, [11]together with your children and your wives, and the aliens living in your camps who chop your wood and carry your water. [12]You are standing here in order to enter into a covenant with the LORD your God, a covenant the LORD is making with you this day and sealing with an oath, [13]to confirm you this day as his people, that he may be your God as he promised you and as he swore to your fathers, Abraham, Isaac and Jacob. [14]I am making this covenant, with its oath, not only with you [15]who are standing here with us today in the presence of the LORD our God but also with those who are not here today.

[16]You yourselves know how we lived in Egypt and how we passed through the countries on the way here. [17]You saw among them their detestable images and idols of wood and stone, of silver and gold. [18]Make sure there is no man or woman, clan or tribe among you today whose heart turns away from the LORD our God to go and worship the gods of those nations; make sure there is no root among you that produces such bitter poison.

[19]When such a person hears the words of this oath, he invokes a blessing on himself and therefore thinks, "I will be safe, even though I persist in going my own way." This will bring disaster on the watered land as well as the dry.[a] [20]The LORD will never be willing to forgive him; his wrath and zeal will burn against that man. All the curses written in this book will fall upon him, and the LORD will blot out his name from under heaven. [21]The LORD will single him out from all the tribes of Israel for disaster, according to all the curses of the covenant written in this Book of the Law.

[22]Your children who follow you in later generations and foreigners who come from distant lands will see the calamities that have fallen on the land and the diseases with which the LORD has afflicted it. [23]The whole land will be a burning waste of salt and sulfur—nothing planted, nothing sprouting, no vegetation growing on it. It will be like the destruc-

---

[a]19 Or *way, in order to add drunkenness to thirst."*

tion of Sodom and Gomorrah, Admah and Zeboiim, which the LORD overthrew in fierce anger. ²⁴All the nations will ask: "Why has the LORD done this to this land? Why this fierce, burning anger?"

²⁵And the answer will be: "It is because this people abandoned the covenant of the LORD, the God of their fathers, the covenant he made with them when he brought them out of Egypt. ²⁶They went off and worshiped other gods and bowed down to them, gods they did not know, gods he had not given them. ²⁷Therefore the LORD's anger burned against this land, so that he brought on it all the curses written in this book. ²⁸In furious anger and in great wrath the LORD uprooted them from their land and thrust them into another land, as it is now."

²⁹The secret things belong to the LORD our God, but the things revealed belong to us and to our children forever, that we may follow all the words of this law.

Prosperity After Turning to the LORD

30 When all these blessings and curses I have set before you come upon you and you take them to heart wherever the LORD your God disperses you among the nations, ²and when you and your children return to the LORD your God and obey him with all your heart and with all your soul according to everything I command you today, ³then the LORD your God will restore your fortunes[a] and have compassion on you and gather you again from all the nations where he scattered you. ⁴Even if you have been banished to the most distant land under the heavens, from there the LORD your God will gather you and bring you back. ⁵He will bring you to the land that belonged to your fathers, and you will take possession of it. He will make you more prosperous and numerous than your fathers. ⁶The LORD your God will circumcise your hearts and the hearts of your descendants, so that you may love him with all your heart and with all your soul, and live. ⁷The LORD your God will put all these curses on your enemies who hate and persecute you. ⁸You will again obey the LORD and follow all his commands I am giving you today. ⁹Then the LORD your God will

make you most prosperous in all the work of your hands and in the fruit of your womb, the young of your livestock and the crops of your land. The LORD will again delight in you and make you prosperous, just as he delighted in your fathers, ¹⁰if you obey the LORD your God and keep his commands and decrees that are written in this Book of the Law and turn to the LORD your God with all your heart and with all your soul.

The Offer of Life or Death

¹¹Now what I am commanding you today is not too difficult for you or beyond your reach. ¹²It is not up in heaven, so that you have to ask, "Who will ascend into heaven to get it and proclaim it to us so we may obey it?" ¹³Nor is it beyond the sea, so that you have to ask, "Who will cross the sea to get it and proclaim it to us so we may obey it?" ¹⁴No, the word is very near you; it is in your mouth and in your heart so you may obey it.

¹⁵See, I set before you today life and prosperity, death and destruction. ¹⁶For I command you today to love the LORD your God, to walk in his ways, and to keep his commands, decrees and laws; then you will live and increase, and the LORD your God will bless you in the land you are entering to possess.

¹⁷But if your heart turns away and you are not obedient, and if you are drawn away to bow down to other gods and worship them, ¹⁸I declare to you this day that you will certainly be destroyed. You will not live long in the land you are crossing the Jordan to enter and possess.

¹⁹This day I call heaven and earth as witnesses against you that I have set before you life and death, blessings and curses. Now choose life, so that you and your children may live ²⁰and that you may love the LORD your God, listen to his voice, and hold fast to him. For the LORD is your life, and he will give you many years in the land he swore to give to your fathers, Abraham, Isaac and Jacob.

Joshua to Succeed Moses

31 Then Moses went out and spoke these words to all Israel: ²"I am

---

a 3 Or will bring you back from captivity

now a hundred and twenty years old and I am no longer able to lead you. The LORD has said to me, 'You shall not cross the Jordan.' ³The LORD your God himself will cross over ahead of you. He will destroy these nations before you, and you will take possession of their land. Joshua also will cross over ahead of you, as the LORD said. ⁴And the LORD will do to them what he did to Sihon and Og, the kings of the Amorites, whom he destroyed along with their land. ⁵The LORD will deliver them to you, and you must do to them all that I have commanded you. ⁶Be strong and courageous. Do not be afraid or terrified because of them, for the LORD your God goes with you; he will never leave you nor forsake you."

⁷Then Moses summoned Joshua and said to him in the presence of all Israel, "Be strong and courageous, for you must go with this people into the land that the LORD swore to their forefathers to give them, and you must divide it among them as their inheritance. ⁸The LORD himself goes before you and will be with you; he will never leave you nor forsake you. Do not be afraid; do not be discouraged."

The Reading of the Law

⁹So Moses wrote down this law and gave it to the priests, the sons of Levi, who carried the ark of the covenant of the LORD, and to all the elders of Israel. ¹⁰Then Moses commanded them: "At the end of every seven years, in the year for canceling debts, during the Feast of Tabernacles, ¹¹when all Israel comes to appear before the LORD your God at the place he will choose, you shall read this law before them in their hearing. ¹²Assemble the people—men, women and children, and the aliens living in your towns—so they can listen and learn to fear the LORD your God and follow carefully all the words of this law. ¹³Their children, who do not know this law, must hear it and learn to fear the LORD your God as long as you live in the land you are crossing the Jordan to possess."

Israel's Rebellion Predicted

¹⁴The LORD said to Moses, "Now the day of your death is near. Call Joshua and present yourselves at the Tent of Meeting, where I will commission him." So Moses and Joshua came and presented themselves at the Tent of Meeting.

¹⁵Then the LORD appeared at the Tent in a pillar of cloud, and the cloud stood over the entrance to the Tent. ¹⁶And the LORD said to Moses: "You are going to rest with your fathers, and these people will soon prostitute themselves to the foreign gods of the land they are entering. They will forsake me and break the covenant I made with them. ¹⁷On that day I will become angry with them and forsake them; I will hide my face from them, and they will be destroyed. Many disasters and difficulties will come upon them, and on that day they will ask, 'Have not these disasters come upon us because our God is not with us?' ¹⁸And I will certainly hide my face on that day because of all their wickedness in turning to other gods.

¹⁹"Now write down for yourselves this song and teach it to the Israelites and have them sing it, so that it may be a witness for me against them. ²⁰When I have brought them into the land flowing with milk and honey, the land I promised on oath to their forefathers, and when they eat their fill and thrive, they will turn to other gods and worship them, rejecting me and breaking my covenant. ²¹And when many disasters and difficulties come upon them, this song will testify against them, because it will not be forgotten by their descendants. I know what they are disposed to do, even before I bring them into the land I promised them on oath." ²²So Moses wrote down this song that day and taught it to the Israelites.

²³The LORD gave this command to Joshua son of Nun: "Be strong and courageous, for you will bring the Israelites into the land I promised them on oath, and I myself will be with you."

²⁴After Moses finished writing in a book the words of this law from beginning to end, ²⁵he gave this command to the Levites who carried the ark of the covenant of the LORD: ²⁶"Take this Book of the Law and place it beside the ark of the covenant of the LORD your God. There it will remain as a witness against you.

²⁷For I know how rebellious and stiff-necked you are. If you have been rebellious against the LORD while I am still alive and with you, how much more will you rebel after I die! ²⁸Assemble before me all the elders of your tribes and all your officials, so that I can speak these words in their hearing and call heaven and earth to testify against them. ²⁹For I know that after my death you are sure to become utterly corrupt and to turn from the way I have commanded you. In days to come, disaster will fall upon you because you will do evil in the sight of the LORD and provoke him to anger by what your hands have made."

The Song of Moses

³⁰And Moses recited the words of this song from beginning to end in the hearing of the whole assembly of Israel:

Sing It, Moe!

Huh?

Deuteronomy 31:30—32:44

At the end of all the stuff Moses and his people went through—mostly because of how lame they were—Moses and the Israelites still sang the lead cut from their new CD: "My God is a *great* God." It is one of those tunes that is like a story in a song. Play some mellow music in the background as you read how God kept loving his people even when they blew him off!

32 Listen, O heavens, and I will speak;
    hear, O earth, the words of my mouth.
²Let my teaching fall like rain
    and my words descend like dew,
like showers on new grass,
    like abundant rain on tender plants.

³I will proclaim the name of the LORD.
    Oh, praise the greatness of our God!
⁴He is the Rock, his works are perfect,
    and all his ways are just.
A faithful God who does no wrong,
    upright and just is he.

⁵They have acted corruptly toward him;
    to their shame they are no longer his children,
    but a warped and crooked generation.ᵃ
⁶Is this the way you repay the LORD,
    O foolish and unwise people?
Is he not your Father, your Creator,ᵇ
    who made you and formed you?

⁷Remember the days of old;
    consider the generations long past.
Ask your father and he will tell you,
    your elders, and they will explain to you.
⁸When the Most High gave the nations their inheritance,
    when he divided all mankind,
he set up boundaries for the peoples
    according to the number of the sons of Israel.ᶜ
⁹For the LORD's portion is his people,
    Jacob his allotted inheritance.

¹⁰In a desert land he found him,
    in a barren and howling waste.
He shielded him and cared for him;
    he guarded him as the apple of his eye,
¹¹like an eagle that stirs up its nest
    and hovers over its young,
that spreads its wings to catch them
    and carries them on its pinions.
¹²The LORD alone led him;
    no foreign god was with him.

¹³He made him ride on the heights of the land
    and fed him with the fruit of the fields.
He nourished him with honey from the rock,
    and with oil from the flinty crag,
¹⁴with curds and milk from herd and flock
    and with fattened lambs and goats,
with choice rams of Bashan
    and the finest kernels of wheat.
You drank the foaming blood of the grape.

ᵃ5 Or *Corrupt are they and not his children, / a generation warped and twisted to their shame* ᵇ6 Or *Father, who bought you* ᶜ8 Masoretic Text; Dead Sea Scrolls (see also Septuagint) *sons of God*

¹⁵ Jeshurun[a] grew fat and kicked;
  filled with food, he became heavy
    and sleek.
He abandoned the God who made him
  and rejected the Rock his Savior.
¹⁶ They made him jealous with their
    foreign gods
  and angered him with their
    detestable idols.
¹⁷ They sacrificed to demons, which are
    not God—
  gods they had not known,
  gods that recently appeared,
  gods your fathers did not fear.
¹⁸ You deserted the Rock, who fathered
    you;
  you forgot the God who gave you
    birth.

¹⁹ The LORD saw this and rejected them
  because he was angered by his sons
    and daughters.
²⁰ "I will hide my face from them," he
    said,
  "and see what their end will be;
for they are a perverse generation,
  children who are unfaithful.
²¹ They made me jealous by what is no
    god
  and angered me with their
    worthless idols.
I will make them envious by those
  who are not a people;
  I will make them angry by a nation
    that has no understanding.
²² For a fire has been kindled by my
    wrath,
  one that burns to the realm of
    death[b] below.
It will devour the earth and its harvests
  and set afire the foundations of the
    mountains.

²³ "I will heap calamities upon them
  and spend my arrows against them.
²⁴ I will send wasting famine against
    them,
  consuming pestilence and deadly
    plague;
I will send against them the fangs of
    wild beasts,
  the venom of vipers that glide in
    the dust.
²⁵ In the street the sword will make them
    childless;
  in their homes terror will reign.

Young men and young women will
    perish,
  infants and gray-haired men.
²⁶ I said I would scatter them
  and blot out their memory from
    mankind,
²⁷ but I dreaded the taunt of the enemy,
  lest the adversary misunderstand
and say, 'Our hand has triumphed;
  the LORD has not done all this.' "

²⁸ They are a nation without sense,
  there is no discernment in them.
²⁹ If only they were wise and would
    understand this
  and discern what their end will be!
³⁰ How could one man chase a thousand,
  or two put ten thousand to flight,
unless their Rock had sold them,
  unless the LORD had given them up?
³¹ For their rock is not like our Rock,
  as even our enemies concede.
³² Their vine comes from the vine of
    Sodom
  and from the fields of Gomorrah.
Their grapes are filled with poison,
  and their clusters with bitterness.
³³ Their wine is the venom of serpents,
  the deadly poison of cobras.

³⁴ "Have I not kept this in reserve
  and sealed it in my vaults?
³⁵ It is mine to avenge; I will repay.
  In due time their foot will slip;
their day of disaster is near
  and their doom rushes upon them."

³⁶ The LORD will judge his people
  and have compassion on his
    servants
when he sees their strength is gone
  and no one is left, slave or free.
³⁷ He will say: "Now where are their
    gods,
  the rock they took refuge in,
³⁸ the gods who ate the fat of their
    sacrifices
  and drank the wine of their drink
    offerings?
Let them rise up to help you!
  Let them give you shelter!
³⁹ "See now that I myself am He!
  There is no god besides me.

---

[a] 15 *Jeshurun* means *the upright one*, that is, Israel.
[b] 22 Hebrew *to Sheol*

I put to death and I bring to life,
     I have wounded and I will heal,
     and no one can deliver out of my
          hand.
⁴⁰ I lift my hand to heaven and declare:
     As surely as I live forever,
⁴¹ when I sharpen my flashing sword
     and my hand grasps it in judgment,
     I will take vengeance on my
          adversaries
     and repay those who hate me.
⁴² I will make my arrows drunk with
          blood,
     while my sword devours flesh:
the blood of the slain and the captives,
     the heads of the enemy leaders."

⁴³ Rejoice, O nations, with his people,^{a,b}
     for he will avenge the blood of his
          servants;
     he will take vengeance on his enemies
     and make atonement for his land
          and people.

⁴⁴Moses came with Joshua^c son of Nun and spoke all the words of this song in the hearing of the people. ⁴⁵When Moses finished reciting all these words to all Israel, ⁴⁶he said to them, "Take to heart all the words I have solemnly declared to you this day, so that you may command your children to obey carefully all the words of this law. ⁴⁷They are not just idle words for you—they are your life. By them you will live long in the land you are crossing the Jordan to possess."

Moses to Die on Mount Nebo

⁴⁸On that same day the LORD told Moses, ⁴⁹"Go up into the Abarim Range to Mount Nebo in Moab, across from Jericho, and view Canaan, the land I am giving the Israelites as their own possession. ⁵⁰There on the mountain that you have climbed you will die and be gathered to your people, just as your brother Aaron died on Mount Hor and was gathered to his people. ⁵¹This is because both of you broke faith with me in the presence of the Israelites at the waters of Meribah Kadesh in the Desert of Zin and because you did not uphold my holiness among the Israelites. ⁵²Therefore, you will see the land only from a distance; you will not enter the land I am giving to the people of Israel."

Moses Blesses the Tribes

33 This is the blessing that Moses the man of God pronounced on the Israelites before his death. ²He said:

"The LORD came from Sinai
     and dawned over them from Seir;
     he shone forth from Mount Paran.
He came with^d myriads of holy ones
     from the south, from his mountain
          slopes.^e
³ Surely it is you who love the people;
     all the holy ones are in your hand.
At your feet they all bow down,
     and from you receive instruction,
⁴ the law that Moses gave us,
     the possession of the assembly of
          Jacob.
⁵ He was king over Jeshurun^f
     when the leaders of the people
          assembled,
     along with the tribes of Israel.

⁶ "Let Reuben live and not die,
     nor^g his men be few."

⁷And this he said about Judah:

"Hear, O LORD, the cry of Judah;
     bring him to his people.
With his own hands he defends his
          cause.
     Oh, be his help against his foes!"

⁸About Levi he said:

"Your Thummim and Urim belong
     to the man you favored.
You tested him at Massah;
     you contended with him at the
          waters of Meribah.
⁹ He said of his father and mother,
     'I have no regard for them.'
He did not recognize his brothers
     or acknowledge his own children,
but he watched over your word
     and guarded your covenant.
¹⁰ He teaches your precepts to Jacob
     and your law to Israel.
He offers incense before you

^a43 Or *Make his people rejoice, O nations*
^b43 Masoretic Text; Dead Sea Scrolls (see also Septuagint) *people, / and let all the angels worship him* / ^c44 Hebrew *Hoshea,* a variant of *Joshua*
^d2 Or *from*   ^e2 The meaning of the Hebrew for this phrase is uncertain.   ^f5 *Jeshurun* means *the upright one,* that is, Israel; also in verse 26.   ^g6 Or *but let*

and whole burnt offerings on your
  altar.
¹¹ Bless all his skills, O LORD,
  and be pleased with the work of his
    hands.
Smite the loins of those who rise up
    against him;
  strike his foes till they rise no
    more."

¹² About Benjamin he said:

"Let the beloved of the LORD rest
    secure in him,
  for he shields him all day long,
  and the one the LORD loves rests
    between his shoulders."

¹³ About Joseph he said:

"May the LORD bless his land
  with the precious dew from heaven
    above
  and with the deep waters that lie
    below;
¹⁴ with the best the sun brings forth
  and the finest the moon can yield;
¹⁵ with the choicest gifts of the ancient
    mountains
  and the fruitfulness of the
    everlasting hills;
¹⁶ with the best gifts of the earth and its
    fullness
  and the favor of him who dwelt in
    the burning bush.
Let all these rest on the head of
    Joseph,
  on the brow of the prince among*ᵃ*
    his brothers.
¹⁷ In majesty he is like a firstborn bull;
  his horns are the horns of a wild ox.
With them he will gore the nations,
  even those at the ends of the earth.
Such are the ten thousands of
    Ephraim;
  such are the thousands of
    Manasseh."

¹⁸ About Zebulun he said:

"Rejoice, Zebulun, in your going out,
  and you, Issachar, in your tents.
¹⁹ They will summon peoples to the
    mountain
  and there offer sacrifices of
    righteousness;
they will feast on the abundance of
    the seas,

on the treasures hidden in the
    sand."

²⁰ About Gad he said:

"Blessed is he who enlarges Gad's
    domain!
Gad lives there like a lion,
  tearing at arm or head.
²¹ He chose the best land for himself;
  the leader's portion was kept for
    him.
When the heads of the people
    assembled,
he carried out the LORD's righteous
    will,
  and his judgments concerning
    Israel."

²² About Dan he said:

"Dan is a lion's cub,
  springing out of Bashan."

²³ About Naphtali he said:

"Naphtali is abounding with the favor
    of the LORD
  and is full of his blessing;
he will inherit southward to the
    lake."

²⁴ About Asher he said:

"Most blessed of sons is Asher;
  let him be favored by his brothers,
  and let him bathe his feet in oil.
²⁵ The bolts of your gates will be iron
    and bronze,
  and your strength will equal your
    days.

²⁶ "There is no one like the God of
    Jeshurun,
  who rides on the heavens to help
    you
  and on the clouds in his majesty.
²⁷ The eternal God is your refuge,
  and underneath are the everlasting
    arms.
He will drive out your enemy before
    you,
  saying, 'Destroy him!'
²⁸ So Israel will live in safety alone;
  Jacob's spring is secure
in a land of grain and new wine,
  where the heavens drop dew.

ᵃ16 Or of the one separated from

²⁹Blessed are you, O Israel!
  Who is like you,
    a people saved by the LORD?
He is your shield and helper
    and your glorious sword.
Your enemies will cower before you,
    and you will trample down their
      high places.ᵃ"

The Death of Moses

34 Then Moses climbed Mount Nebo from the plains of Moab to the top of Pisgah, across from Jericho. There the LORD showed him the whole land—from Gilead to Dan, ²all of Naphtali, the territory of Ephraim and Manasseh, all the land of Judah as far as the western sea,ᵇ ³the Negev and the whole region from the Valley of Jericho, the City of Palms, as far as Zoar. ⁴Then the LORD said to him, "This is the land I promised on oath to Abraham, Isaac and Jacob when I said, 'I will give it to your descendants.' I have let you see it with your eyes, but you will not cross over into it."

⁵And Moses the servant of the LORD died there in Moab, as the LORD had said. ⁶He buried himᶜ in Moab, in the valley opposite Beth Peor, but to this day no one knows where his grave is. ⁷Moses was a hundred and twenty years old when he died, yet his eyes were not weak nor his strength gone. ⁸The Israelites grieved for Moses in the plains of Moab thirty days, until the time of weeping and mourning was over.

⁹Now Joshua son of Nun was filled with the spiritᵈ of wisdom because Moses had laid his hands on him. So the Israelites listened to him and did what the LORD had commanded Moses.

¹⁰Since then, no prophet has risen in Israel like Moses, whom the LORD knew face to face, ¹¹who did all those miraculous signs and wonders the LORD sent him to do in Egypt—to Pharaoh and to all his officials and to his whole land. ¹²For no one has ever shown the mighty power or performed the awesome deeds that Moses did in the sight of all Israel.

ᵃ29 Or *will tread upon their bodies*   ᵇ2 That is, the Mediterranean   ᶜ6 Or *He was buried*   ᵈ9 Or *Spirit*

Joshua

START

God's people had been circling in the desert for 40 years. Now God's about to give them clearance to land. The book of Joshua tells us about their arrival. This book begins where Deuteronomy left us—on the east side of the Jordan River. Joshua, who just got appointed as head honcho by Moses in the previous book, sends a pair of spies across the river to check out the city of Jericho, their first target. The 2 sneaky guys run into a prostitute named Rahab. She hides them when the cops come looking, then helps the spies escape so they can report back to the Israelites. Good thing, because if they hadn't returned, the Israelites might have chickened out *again*.

Joshua gets the good report from the spies and then leads Israel across the temporarily dry Jordan River in a scene much like the Red Sea crossing. Of course, Josh and his buddy Caleb are the only guys who appreciate the similarity because the rest of their generation had died in the desert.

Fresh and dry on the other side of the river, Joshua leads the people to Jericho, taking the city with a shout. Only Rahab and her family are saved in the massacre. The rest of the book describes what happens as the Israelites take over the promised land. Just like Deuteronomy, this book ends with the hero's death. Israel served God the whole time Joshua was in charge. Josh rocks.

Cast of Characters

Joshua (JAH-shoo-wah)
Josh was one of the 12 original spies back in Numbers. He and his buddy Caleb were the only 2 who didn't wimp out. Decades later, God remembers Joshua's courage: He becomes Israel's leader when Moses dies. He turns out to be an excellent choice.

Caleb (CAY-lub)
He's Joshua's faithful sidekick and fellow former spy. At 85, Caleb's still in the army—and loving it! When the war is over, God gives him a nice chunk of land as a retirement gift.

Rahab (RAY-hab)
She's a prostitute who lies to the cops to protect the spies sent to check out Jericho, then helps the spies escape. She and her family are the only ones who survive the destruction of the city. It's pretty cool that Israel's long, long journey from slavery in Egypt to freedom in their own land begins and ends with gutsy women who weren't afraid to stand up to authority and follow God instead. Moses' mom gets the whole thing started by putting her son in a basket. And at the end of the journey, Rahab saves the spies.

Achan (AKE-in)

This Israelite was either really bad or had a "low-wattage" problem (you know, he wasn't too bright). He knew the rules—"No plundering the enemy's stuff." But he stole stuff anyway and wound up losing everything—even his life.

The 12 Tribes

They're the descendants of the 12 sons of Jacob. Each tribe gets its own section of the promised land—kind of like states. The Levites (descendants of Jacob's son Levi) are priests, so they don't get their own state. Instead, they set up towns in *every* state. To make up for that missing 12th tribe, the descendants of Joseph break into two states: Manasseh and Ephraim.

What's UP with That?

Have you ever played a game of tag with a "safe zone"? It's a special place where you're safe from being tagged. Israel had their own "safe zones," called *cities of refuge*.

Here's how they worked:

Let's say a guy gets killed, and his brothers are convinced that you murdered him. The law says that murderers are to be put to death! But maybe it wasn't murder. Maybe it was an accident. You need time and a safe place to go until you can prove your innocence. If the dead guy's friends catch you, they might snuff you out before you have a chance to defend yourself. What do you do?

Run as fast as you can to a *city of refuge*. It's a safe zone . . . a place where the people will protect you until you can have a proper trial. If you're found innocent, you can't go home until the current chief priest dies (which shouldn't be long—these guys are pretty old). But if you're found guilty, you'll be the one doing the dying.

Snap shots

- God gives Joshua a job description *(chapter 1)*
- Sneaky stuff—Rahab, 2 spies and the news they bring *(chapter 2)*
- "Where have I seen this before?"—crossing the Jordan with dry feet *(chapters 3—4)*
- OK guys, it's time to circumcise *(chapter 5)*
- "Kaboom!"—Jericho falls down, can't get up *(chapter 6)*
- Achan's achin' to steal, gets caught, goodbye *(chapter 7)*
- Taking charge—Israel fights a bunch of battles *(chapters 8—12)*
- "It's settled"—tribes take their land, Joshua says farewell *(chapters 13—24)*

Friends

Oh no, *not again*, thought Sara. Standing right next to her were Natalie and Clara, talking about Clara's birthday party coming up on Saturday night. First Sara heard Marco and Matt talking about it during first period, then she overheard Stephanie and Dave talking about it at lunch; and now, right next to her very own locker, Natalie and Clara are bragging about the new outfits they bought for the party. *What should I do?* thought Sara. *Just pretend that I don't hear them making plans? Or walk away? Or ask if I can come too?* Before Sara had decided what to do, Natalie and Clara walked off to math class, leaving Sara alone. Way alone.

Everyone feels like Sara at times. It seems like everybody else has a best friend, a cool friend's party to go to or more e-mail messages than you do. If you've ever felt like Sara, you're not alone. Sure, maybe you feel alone, but you're actually surrounded by tons of others who feel just like you do.

The Bible has answers to every problem, including this one. Next time you feel lonely, try to remember some of what it says:

If you want to have good friends, you need to be a good friend. We're always waiting for other people to take the first step and call us or be nice to us. Guess what? They're waiting for us to make the first move. It's like a bunch of people watching a pizza get cold, all too scared to ask for the first piece. So why not make the first move? Make the first phone call. Be the one to say "I'm sorry" after you get in a fight with a friend (James 5:16, page 1511).

There's always someone else without a friend. It seems like everyone else is going to Clara's party, but remember that there are tons of other kids who aren't and who are probably feeling lonely just like you. Hook up with one of them (Ecclesiastes 4:9–12, page 777).

You always have one important friend. Make sure you add one name in capital letters to your list of friends. No, he's not flesh and blood, waiting at your locker. But that's part of what's so cool about him. JESUS is a friend who's with you all the time. Whether you end up going to Clara's party or just stay home and watch TV with your parents, Jesus is right there with you (Proverbs 18:24, page 753). He's with you as you read this. And he'll be with you when you put this down. The God of the universe is just waiting to spend time with you. Hey, have a blast hanging out with him today!

FAITH

"A Christian friend of mine was killed by a drunk driver. Why does God allow bad things to happen to his people?"

I can understand why you'd ask that question. But when tragic things happen, we make a mistake if we blame them on God.

The Bible clearly says that God does not create evil (see Genesis 1:31, page 5 and 1 Timothy 4:4, page 1466). Death came into the world when Adam and Eve sinned (see 1 Corinthians 15:21, page 1393), and it's going to be with us until Jesus comes back. There are a ton of evil forces in the world that cause us pain—including death. But God is hard at work fighting these forces. And one day, he's going to destroy death (see 1 Corinthians 15:26). In the meantime, God tells us that "in this world, you will have trouble. But take heart! I have overcome the world" (John 16:33).

A friend of mine, the chaplain of a college, was brokenhearted when he found out one of his brightest students, a Christian, had been hit by a bus and killed. One upset student asked my friend, "Why did Jesus kill Cliff?" My friend answered, "You're an intelligent person. You ought to be able to tell the difference between Jesus and a bus!"

While God doesn't make bad things happen, **the Bible promises us that in the midst of bad things, God works to bring good out of it all** (see Romans 8:28). There used to be a guy who had his own TV show. And one of the other guys on the show, José Melos, was a fantastic piano player. Sometimes the show host would walk over to the piano and slap his hands down on a bunch of keys. They made an awful sound, of course. Then he would say, "OK, José, let's see what you can make out of that mess!" José would then put his fingers on the exact keys the show host had played and build those sounds into a magnificent melody. Incredibly, the clashing sounds became a beautiful song.

God can do that with the messes in our lives. **God is able to take our tragedies, and the mistakes we make, and turn them into something beautiful.**

I'm a college professor. Sometimes I ask my students, "What is the most evil thing that ever happened in human history?" They always answer, "The crucifixion of Jesus!" Then I ask, "What is the most wonderful thing that ever happened in human history?" The same students say, "The crucifixion of Jesus!" This horrible event, which was the result of our sin, was taken by God and transformed into something that has blessed people everywhere.

God doesn't make bad things happen, but he is at work in the middle of all things, overcoming evil with good and turning tragedy into blessings. So, instead of asking, "Why does God allow bad things to happen?" we should be asking, "What can God do through this tragedy? How can I work with God to turn this into something good?"

— **Tony Campolo, sociology professor at Eastern College. Tony is a dynamic speaker and the author of several books for teens.**

The LORD Commands Joshua

1 After the death of Moses the servant of the LORD, the LORD said to Joshua son of Nun, Moses' aide: ²"Moses my servant is dead. Now then, you and all these people, get ready to cross the Jordan River into the land I am about to give to them—to the Israelites. ³I will give you every place where you set your foot, as I promised Moses. ⁴Your territory will extend from the desert to Lebanon, and from the great river, the Euphrates—all the Hittite country—to the Great Sea*a* on the west. ⁵No one will be able to stand up against you all the days of your life. As I was with Moses, so I will be with you; I will never leave you nor forsake you.

⁶"Be strong and courageous, because you will lead these people to inherit the land I swore to their forefathers to give them. ⁷Be strong and very courageous. Be careful to obey all the law my servant Moses gave you; do not turn from it to the right or to the left, that you may be successful wherever you go. ⁸Do not let this Book of the Law depart from your mouth; meditate on it day and night, so that you may be careful to do everything written in it. Then you will be prosperous

a4 That is, the Mediterranean

Mutter Mutter

Huh?

Joshua 1:8

When you need to memorize something, you say it over and over again with the idea it will stick in your brain. In Hebrew (the language this book was first written in), to *meditate* means "to mutter." We're supposed to mutter God's words to ourselves day and night. If we keep repeating the words of the Bible to ourselves, we will soon find them sticking where they matter most—in our hearts and minds. Mutter 'til it sticks!

Thursday

Strong on Faith

Read Joshua 1:7

I think a lot about my future. For instance, I really want to go to a good college. But to do that, I have to get great grades from now on. That means I have to work hard in school.

The problem is that I have a bad habit of watching too much TV. And when I watch TV, I don't get my homework done. If I don't get my homework done, I don't get good grades. See the problem?

God doesn't want me to be lazy or waste my brain. He wants me to do what's right, whether that's doing my best in school or following his commandments in other parts of my life.

God gave us the Ten Commandments so that we'd know how to live. He wants us to be strong in our faith and work hard at living by his commands.

Dan age 14

What about You?

❶ What are some things that hold you back from living your faith to the max?

❷ Ask your youth leader to help you make a plan for overcoming the things that hold you back.

❸ Ask God to help you be strong and courageous about your faith.

Turn to page 249 for your next devotion.

and successful. ⁹Have I not commanded you? Be strong and courageous. Do not be terrified; do not be discouraged, for the LORD your God will be with you wherever you go."

¹⁰So Joshua ordered the officers of the people: ¹¹"Go through the camp and tell the people, 'Get your supplies ready. Three days from now you will cross the Jordan here to go in and take possession of the land the LORD your God is giving you for your own.' "

¹²But to the Reubenites, the Gadites and the half-tribe of Manasseh, Joshua said, ¹³"Remember the command that Moses the servant of the LORD gave you: 'The LORD your God is giving you rest and has granted you this land.' ¹⁴Your wives, your children and your livestock may stay in the land that Moses gave you east of the Jordan, but all your fighting men, fully armed, must cross over ahead of your brothers. You are to help your brothers ¹⁵until the LORD gives them rest, as he has done for you, and until they too have taken possession of the land that the LORD your God is giving them. After that, you may go back and occupy your own land, which Moses the servant of the LORD gave you east of the Jordan toward the sunrise."

¹⁶Then they answered Joshua, "Whatever you have commanded us we will do, and wherever you send us we will go. ¹⁷Just as we fully obeyed Moses, so we will obey you. Only may the LORD your God be with you as he was with Moses. ¹⁸Whoever rebels against your word and does not obey your words, whatever you may command them, will be put to death. Only be strong and courageous!"

Rahab and the Spies

2 Then Joshua son of Nun secretly sent two spies from Shittim. "Go, look over the land," he said, "especially Jericho." So they went and entered the house of a prostitute[a] named Rahab and stayed there.

²The king of Jericho was told, "Look! Some of the Israelites have come here tonight to spy out the land." ³So the king of Jericho sent this message to Rahab: "Bring out the men who came to you and

entered your house, because they have come to spy out the whole land."

⁴But the woman had taken the two men and hidden them. She said, "Yes, the men came to me, but I did not know where they had come from. ⁵At dusk, when it was time to close the city gate, the men left. I don't know which way they went. Go after them quickly. You may catch up with them." ⁶(But she had taken them up to the roof and hidden them under the stalks of flax she had laid out on the roof.) ⁷So the men set out in pursuit of the spies on the road that leads to the fords of the Jordan, and as soon as the pursuers had gone out, the gate was shut.

⁸Before the spies lay down for the night, she went up on the roof ⁹and said to them, "I know that the LORD has given this land to you and that a great fear of you has fallen on us, so that all who live in this country are melting in fear because of you. ¹⁰We have heard how the LORD dried up the water of the Red Sea[b] for you when you came out of Egypt, and what you did to Sihon and Og, the two kings of the Amorites east of the Jordan, whom you completely destroyed.[c] ¹¹When we heard of it, our hearts melted and everyone's courage failed because of you, for the LORD your God is God in heaven above and on the earth below. ¹²Now then, please swear to me by the LORD that you will show kindness to my family, because I have shown kindness to you. Give me a sure sign ¹³that you will spare the lives of my father and mother, my brothers and sisters, and all who belong to them, and that you will save us from death."

¹⁴"Our lives for your lives!" the men assured her. "If you don't tell what we are doing, we will treat you kindly and faithfully when the LORD gives us the land."

¹⁵So she let them down by a rope through the window, for the house she lived in was part of the city wall. ¹⁶Now she had said to them, "Go to the hills so

---

[a]1 Or possibly *an innkeeper*　[b]10 Hebrew *Yam Suph*; that is, Sea of Reeds　[c]10 The Hebrew term refers to the irrevocable giving over of things or persons to the LORD, often by totally destroying them.

the pursuers will not find you. Hide yourselves there three days until they return, and then go on your way."

[17]The men said to her, "This oath you made us swear will not be binding on us [18]unless, when we enter the land, you have tied this scarlet cord in the window through which you let us down, and unless you have brought your father and mother, your brothers and all your family into your house. [19]If anyone goes outside your house into the street, his blood will be on his own head; we will not be responsible. As for anyone who is in the house with you, his blood will be on our head if a hand is laid on him. [20]But if you tell what we are doing, we will be released from the oath you made us swear."

[21]"Agreed," she replied. "Let it be as you say." So she sent them away and they departed. And she tied the scarlet cord in the window.

[22]When they left, they went into the hills and stayed there three days, until the pursuers had searched all along the road and returned without finding them. [23]Then the two men started back. They went down out of the hills, forded the river and came to Joshua son of Nun and told him everything that had happened to them. [24]They said to Joshua, "The LORD has surely given the whole land into our hands; all the people are melting in fear because of us."

Crossing the Jordan

3 Early in the morning Joshua and all the Israelites set out from Shittim and went to the Jordan, where they camped before crossing over. [2]After three days the officers went throughout the camp, [3]giving orders to the people: "When you see the ark of the covenant of the LORD your God, and the priests, who are Levites, carrying it, you are to move out from your positions and follow it. [4]Then you will know which way to go, since you have never been this way before. But keep a distance of about a thousand yards[a] between you and the ark; do not go near it."

[5]Joshua told the people, "Consecrate yourselves, for tomorrow the LORD will do amazing things among you."

[6]Joshua said to the priests, "Take up the ark of the covenant and pass on ahead of the people." So they took it up and went ahead of them.

[7]And the LORD said to Joshua, "Today I will begin to exalt you in the eyes of all Israel, so they may know that I am with you as I was with Moses. [8]Tell the priests who carry the ark of the covenant: 'When you reach the edge of the Jordan's waters, go and stand in the river.' "

[9]Joshua said to the Israelites, "Come here and listen to the words of the LORD your God. [10]This is how you will know that the living God is among you and that he will certainly drive out before you the Canaanites, Hittites, Hivites, Perizzites, Girgashites, Amorites and Jebusites. [11]See, the ark of the covenant of the Lord of all the earth will go into the Jordan ahead of you. [12]Now then, choose

[a]4 Hebrew *about two thousand cubits* (about 900 meters)

twelve men from the tribes of Israel, one from each tribe. ¹³And as soon as the priests who carry the ark of the LORD—the Lord of all the earth—set foot in the Jordan, its waters flowing downstream will be cut off and stand up in a heap."

¹⁴So when the people broke camp to cross the Jordan, the priests carrying the ark of the covenant went ahead of them. ¹⁵Now the Jordan is at flood stage all during harvest. Yet as soon as the priests who carried the ark reached the Jordan and their feet touched the water's edge, ¹⁶the water from upstream stopped flowing. It piled up in a heap a great distance away, at a town called Adam in the vicinity of Zarethan, while the water flowing down to the Sea of the Arabah (the Salt Sea*a*) was completely cut off. So the people crossed over opposite Jericho. ¹⁷The priests who carried the ark of the covenant of the LORD stood firm on dry ground in the middle of the Jordan, while all Israel passed by until the whole nation had completed the crossing on dry ground.

4 When the whole nation had finished crossing the Jordan, the LORD said to Joshua, ²"Choose twelve men from among the people, one from each tribe, ³and tell them to take up twelve stones from the middle of the Jordan from right where the priests stood and to carry them over with you and put them down at the place where you stay tonight."

⁴So Joshua called together the twelve men he had appointed from the Israelites, one from each tribe, ⁵and said to them, "Go over before the ark of the LORD your God into the middle of the Jordan. Each of you is to take up a stone on his shoulder, according to the number of the tribes of the Israelites, ⁶to serve as a sign among you. In the future, when your children ask you, 'What do these stones mean?' ⁷tell them that the flow of the Jordan was cut off before the ark of the covenant of the LORD. When it crossed the Jordan, the waters of the Jordan were cut off. These stones are to be a memorial to the people of Israel forever."

⁸So the Israelites did as Joshua commanded them. They took twelve stones from the middle of the Jordan, according to the number of the tribes of the Israel-

ites, as the LORD had told Joshua; and they carried them over with them to their camp, where they put them down. ⁹Joshua set up the twelve stones that had been*b* in the middle of the Jordan at the spot where the priests who carried the ark of the covenant had stood. And they are there to this day.

¹⁰Now the priests who carried the ark remained standing in the middle of the Jordan until everything the LORD had commanded Joshua was done by the people, just as Moses had directed Joshua. The people hurried over, ¹¹and as soon as all of them had crossed, the ark of the LORD and the priests came to the other side while the people watched. ¹²The men of Reuben, Gad and the half-tribe of Manasseh crossed over, armed, in front of the Israelites, as Moses had directed them. ¹³About forty thousand armed for battle crossed over before the LORD to the plains of Jericho for war.

¹⁴That day the LORD exalted Joshua in the sight of all Israel; and they revered him all the days of his life, just as they had revered Moses.

¹⁵Then the LORD said to Joshua, ¹⁶"Command the priests carrying the ark of the Testimony to come up out of the Jordan."

¹⁷So Joshua commanded the priests, "Come up out of the Jordan."

¹⁸And the priests came up out of the river carrying the ark of the covenant of the LORD. No sooner had they set their feet on the dry ground than the waters of the Jordan returned to their place and ran at flood stage as before.

¹⁹On the tenth day of the first month the people went up from the Jordan and camped at Gilgal on the eastern border of Jericho. ²⁰And Joshua set up at Gilgal the twelve stones they had taken out of the Jordan. ²¹He said to the Israelites, "In the future when your descendants ask their fathers, 'What do these stones mean?' ²²tell them, 'Israel crossed the Jordan on dry ground.' ²³For the LORD your God dried up the Jordan before you until you had crossed over. The LORD your God did to the Jordan just what he had done to

---

*a*16 That is, the Dead Sea   *b*9 Or *Joshua also set up twelve stones*

the Red Sea[a] when he dried it up before us until we had crossed over. [24]He did this so that all the peoples of the earth might know that the hand of the LORD is powerful and so that you might always fear the LORD your God."

Circumcision at Gilgal

5 Now when all the Amorite kings west of the Jordan and all the Canaanite kings along the coast heard how the LORD had dried up the Jordan before the Israelites until we had crossed over, their hearts melted and they no longer had the courage to face the Israelites.

[2]At that time the LORD said to Joshua, "Make flint knives and circumcise the Israelites again." [3]So Joshua made flint knives and circumcised the Israelites at Gibeath Haaraloth.[b]

[4]Now this is why he did so: All those who came out of Egypt—all the men of military age—died in the desert on the way after leaving Egypt. [5]All the people that came out had been circumcised, but all the people born in the desert during the journey from Egypt had not. [6]The Israelites had moved about in the desert forty years until all the men who were of military age when they left Egypt had died, since they had not obeyed the LORD. For the LORD had sworn to them that they would not see the land that he had solemnly promised their fathers to give us, a land flowing with milk and honey. [7]So he raised up their sons in their place, and these were the ones Joshua circumcised. They were still uncircumcised because they had not been circumcised on the way. [8]And after the whole nation had been circumcised, they remained where they were in camp until they were healed.

[9]Then the LORD said to Joshua, "Today I have rolled away the reproach of Egypt from you." So the place has been called Gilgal[c] to this day.

---

[a]23 Hebrew *Yam Suph*; that is, Sea of Reeds
[b]3 *Gibeath Haaraloth* means *hill of foreskins.*
[c]9 *Gilgal* sounds like the Hebrew for *roll.*

Friday

Nothing's Impossible

Read Joshua 4:4–9

Sometimes I'm afraid to talk to my friends about God. Some of them just seem like they're not interested at all. But these verses make one thing clear: If God can stop a raging river, he can definitely change a person's heart.

Joshua wanted his men to get stones from the Jordan River so they would remember God's power. The stones were a reminder of what God had done in the past . . . and a promise of what God could do in the future.

When something seems impossible, we only have to look at the "impossible" things God did throughout history to know that God can take care of anything.

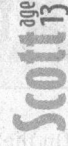
Scott age 13

What about You?

❶ Name something God did for you this week. Now take a little more time and think about what God has done for you in the past month and year.

❷ Now that you have those things in mind, write 'em down. Tuck that list into the book of Joshua. Think of it as your own personal history of God's faithfulness. Look at it every time something seems "impossible."

❸ Thank God for doing the impossible.

Turn to page 259 for your next devotion.

Wacky Weapons

Joshua 6:1–20 OK, you're a soldier guarding the city walls of Jericho. Say you look over the wall one day and see a bunch of guys marching around, making a lot of noise with their old beat-up horns. *Oooh, Scary!* you'd think to yourself while laughing at the horn-blowing hacks. But then something weird happens: The wall you are guarding starts to crumble, and you're face to face with a brassed-off horn player. Now who's laughing?

Trumpets aren't the only weird weapons you'll find in the Bible. Check out the following war stories:

✗ Samson used foxes and torches to scare away the Philistines (Judges 15:3–5)

✗ Gideon used trumpets, torches and jars to whup a huge army of Midianites (Judges 7:16–21)

✗ Jael used a glass of milk and a tent peg to take out the commander of the enemy army (Judges 4:18–21)

✗ Samson wielded a donkey's jawbone to kill a thousand men (Judges 15:15)

✗ Moses used his stick (and God's power!) to drown the Egyptians in the Red Sea (Exodus 14:19–31)

¹⁰On the evening of the fourteenth day of the month, while camped at Gilgal on the plains of Jericho, the Israelites celebrated the Passover. ¹¹The day after the Passover, that very day, they ate some of the produce of the land: unleavened bread and roasted grain. ¹²The manna stopped the day after*a* they ate this food from the land; there was no longer any manna for the Israelites, but that year they ate of the produce of Canaan.

The Fall of Jericho

¹³Now when Joshua was near Jericho, he looked up and saw a man standing in front of him with a drawn sword in his hand. Joshua went up to him and asked, "Are you for us or for our enemies?"

¹⁴"Neither," he replied, "but as commander of the army of the LORD I have now come." Then Joshua fell facedown to the ground in reverence, and asked him, "What message does my Lord*b* have for his servant?"

¹⁵The commander of the LORD's army replied, "Take off your sandals, for the place where you are standing is holy." And Joshua did so.

6 Now Jericho was tightly shut up because of the Israelites. No one went out and no one came in.

²Then the LORD said to Joshua, "See, I have delivered Jericho into your hands, along with its king and its fighting men. ³March around the city once with all the armed men. Do this for six days. ⁴Have seven priests carry trumpets of rams' horns in front of the ark. On the seventh day, march around the city seven times, with the priests blowing the trumpets. ⁵When you hear them sound a long blast on the trumpets, have all the people give a loud shout; then the wall of the city will collapse and the people will go up, every man straight in."

⁶So Joshua son of Nun called the priests and said to them, "Take up the ark of the covenant of the LORD and have seven priests carry trumpets in front of it." ⁷And he ordered the people, "Advance! March around the city, with the armed guard going ahead of the ark of the LORD."

⁸When Joshua had spoken to the people, the seven priests carrying the seven trumpets before the LORD went forward, blowing their trumpets, and the ark of the LORD's covenant followed them. ⁹The armed guard marched ahead of the priests who blew the trumpets, and the rear guard followed the ark. All this time the trumpets were sounding. ¹⁰But Joshua had commanded the people, "Do not give a war cry, do not raise your voices, do not say a word until the day I tell you to shout. Then shout!" ¹¹So he had the ark of the LORD carried around the city, circling it once. Then the people

a12 Or the day   b14 Or lord

returned to camp and spent the night there.

¹²Joshua got up early the next morning and the priests took up the ark of the LORD. ¹³The seven priests carrying the seven trumpets went forward, marching before the ark of the LORD and blowing the trumpets. The armed men went ahead of them and the rear guard followed the ark of the LORD, while the trumpets kept sounding. ¹⁴So on the second day they marched around the city once and returned to the camp. They did this for six days.

¹⁵On the seventh day, they got up at daybreak and marched around the city seven times in the same manner, except that on that day they circled the city seven times. ¹⁶The seventh time around, when the priests sounded the trumpet blast, Joshua commanded the people, "Shout! For the LORD has given you the city! ¹⁷The city and all that is in it are to be devoted[a] to the LORD. Only Rahab the prostitute[b] and all who are with her in her house shall be spared, because she hid the spies we sent. ¹⁸But keep away from the devoted things, so that you will not bring about your own destruction by taking any of them. Otherwise you will make the camp of Israel liable to destruction and bring trouble on it. ¹⁹All the silver and gold and the articles of bronze and iron are sacred to the LORD and must go into his treasury."

²⁰When the trumpets sounded, the people shouted, and at the sound of the trumpet, when the people gave a loud shout, the wall collapsed; so every man charged straight in, and they took the city. ²¹They devoted the city to the LORD and destroyed with the sword every living thing in it—men and women, young and old, cattle, sheep and donkeys.

²²Joshua said to the two men who had spied out the land, "Go into the prostitute's house and bring her out and all who belong to her, in accordance with your oath to her." ²³So the young men who had done the spying went in and brought out Rahab, her father and mother and brothers and all who belonged to her. They brought out her entire family and put them in a place outside the camp of Israel.

²⁴Then they burned the whole city and everything in it, but they put the silver and gold and the articles of bronze and iron into the treasury of the LORD's house. ²⁵But Joshua spared Rahab the prostitute, with her family and all who belonged to her, because she hid the men Joshua had sent as spies to Jericho—and she lives among the Israelites to this day.

²⁶At that time Joshua pronounced this solemn oath: "Cursed before the LORD is the man who undertakes to rebuild this city, Jericho:

"At the cost of his firstborn son
   will he lay its foundations;
at the cost of his youngest
   will he set up its gates."

²⁷So the LORD was with Joshua, and his fame spread throughout the land.

Achan's Sin

7 But the Israelites acted unfaithfully in regard to the devoted things[c]; Achan son of Carmi, the son of Zimri,[d] the son of Zerah, of the tribe of Judah, took some of them. So the LORD's anger burned against Israel.

²Now Joshua sent men from Jericho to Ai, which is near Beth Aven to the east of Bethel, and told them, "Go up and spy out the region." So the men went up and spied out Ai.

³When they returned to Joshua, they said, "Not all the people will have to go up against Ai. Send two or three thousand men to take it and do not weary all the people, for only a few men are there." ⁴So about three thousand men went up; but they were routed by the men of Ai, ⁵who killed about thirty-six of them. They chased the Israelites from the city gate as far as the stone quarries[e] and struck them down on the slopes. At this the hearts of the people melted and became like water.

a17 The Hebrew term refers to the irrevocable giving over of things or persons to the LORD, often by totally destroying them; also in verses 18 and 21.
b17 Or possibly *innkeeper*; also in verses 22 and 25
c1 The Hebrew term refers to the irrevocable giving over of things or persons to the LORD, often by totally destroying them; also in verses 11, 12, 13 and 15.   d1 See Septuagint and 1 Chron. 2:6; Hebrew *Zabdi*; also in verses 17 and 18.   e5 Or *as far as Shebarim*

⁶Then Joshua tore his clothes and fell facedown to the ground before the ark of the LORD, remaining there till evening. The elders of Israel did the same, and sprinkled dust on their heads. ⁷And

Ripped to Shreds

Huh?

Joshua 7:6

Joshua was in deep despair, wondering why God had brought the Israelites all this way only to have them destroyed by their enemies. Joshua felt so vulnerable, so unprotected that even his clothes seemed useless, and he ripped them in frustration. But he was wise and continued to look to God for help. And, of course, God came through.

Joshua said, "Ah, Sovereign LORD, why did you ever bring this people across the Jordan to deliver us into the hands of the Amorites to destroy us? If only we had been content to stay on the other side of the Jordan! ⁸O Lord, what can I say, now that Israel has been routed by its enemies? ⁹The Canaanites and the other people of the country will hear about this and they will surround us and wipe out our name from the earth. What then will you do for your own great name?"

¹⁰The LORD said to Joshua, "Stand up! What are you doing down on your face? ¹¹Israel has sinned; they have violated my covenant, which I commanded them to keep. They have taken some of the devoted things; they have stolen, they have lied, they have put them with their own possessions. ¹²That is why the Israelites cannot stand against their enemies; they turn their backs and run because they have been made liable to destruction. I will not be with you anymore unless you destroy whatever among you is devoted to destruction.

¹³"Go, consecrate the people. Tell them, 'Consecrate yourselves in preparation for tomorrow; for this is what the LORD, the God of Israel, says: That which is devoted is among you, O Israel. You cannot stand against your enemies until you remove it.

¹⁴"'In the morning, present yourselves tribe by tribe. The tribe that the LORD takes shall come forward clan by clan; the clan that the LORD takes shall come forward family by family; and the family that the LORD takes shall come forward man by man. ¹⁵He who is caught with the devoted things shall be destroyed by fire, along with all that belongs to him. He has violated the covenant of the LORD and has done a disgraceful thing in Israel!'"

¹⁶Early the next morning Joshua had Israel come forward by tribes, and Judah was taken. ¹⁷The clans of Judah came forward, and he took the Zerahites. He had the clan of the Zerahites come forward by families, and Zimri was taken. ¹⁸Joshua had his family come forward man by man, and Achan son of Carmi, the son of Zimri, the son of Zerah, of the tribe of Judah, was taken.

¹⁹Then Joshua said to Achan, "My son, give glory to the LORD,ᵃ the God of Israel, and give him the praise.ᵇ Tell me what you have done; do not hide it from me."

²⁰Achan replied, "It is true! I have sinned against the LORD, the God of Israel. This is what I have done: ²¹When I saw in the plunder a beautiful robe from Babylonia,ᶜ two hundred shekelsᵈ of silver and a wedge of gold weighing fifty shekels,ᵉ I coveted them and took them. They are hidden in the ground inside my tent, with the silver underneath."

²²So Joshua sent messengers, and they ran to the tent, and there it was, hidden in his tent, with the silver underneath. ²³They took the things from the tent, brought them to Joshua and all the Israelites and spread them out before the LORD.

²⁴Then Joshua, together with all Israel, took Achan son of Zerah, the silver, the robe, the gold wedge, his sons and daughters, his cattle, donkeys and sheep, his tent and all that he had, to the Valley of Achor. ²⁵Joshua said, "Why have you brought this trouble on us? The LORD will bring trouble on you today."

ᵃ19 A solemn charge to tell the truth   ᵇ19 Or and confess to him   ᶜ21 Hebrew Shinar   ᵈ21 That is, about 5 pounds (about 2.3 kilograms)   ᵉ21 That is, about 1 1/4 pounds (about 0.6 kilogram)

Ouch

Huh?

Joshua 7:25
Ever been hit by a rock? Hurts, huh? Stoning a person to death was a public punishment for lawbreaking sinners. In this case, Achan (ACHE-in) had disobeyed God and brought trouble on all the people of Israel. So he and all his stuff were pelted with stones until everything was destroyed and Achan was dead. Yeow!

Then all Israel stoned him, and after they had stoned the rest, they burned them. ²⁶Over Achan they heaped up a large pile of rocks, which remains to this day. Then the LORD turned from his fierce anger. Therefore that place has been called the Valley of Achor[a] ever since.

Ai Destroyed

8 Then the LORD said to Joshua, "Do not be afraid; do not be discouraged. Take the whole army with you, and go up and attack Ai. For I have delivered into your hands the king of Ai, his people, his city and his land. ²You shall do to Ai and its king as you did to Jericho and its king, except that you may carry off their plunder and livestock for yourselves. Set an ambush behind the city."

³So Joshua and the whole army moved out to attack Ai. He chose thirty thousand of his best fighting men and sent them out at night ⁴with these orders: "Listen carefully. You are to set an ambush behind the city. Don't go very far from it. All of you be on the alert. ⁵I and all those with me will advance on the city, and when the men come out against us, as they did before, we will flee from them. ⁶They will pursue us until we have lured them away from the city, for they will say, 'They are running away from us as they did before.' So when we flee from them, ⁷you are to rise up from ambush and take the city. The LORD your God will give it into your hand. ⁸When you have taken the city, set it on fire. Do what the

LORD has commanded. See to it; you have my orders."

⁹Then Joshua sent them off, and they went to the place of ambush and lay in wait between Bethel and Ai, to the west of Ai—but Joshua spent that night with the people.

¹⁰Early the next morning Joshua mustered his men, and he and the leaders of Israel marched before them to Ai. ¹¹The entire force that was with him marched up and approached the city and arrived in front of it. They set up camp north of Ai, with the valley between them and the city. ¹²Joshua had taken about five thousand men and set them in ambush between Bethel and Ai, to the west of the city. ¹³They had the soldiers take up their positions—all those in the camp to the north of the city and the ambush to the west of it. That night Joshua went into the valley.

¹⁴When the king of Ai saw this, he and all the men of the city hurried out early in the morning to meet Israel in battle at a certain place overlooking the Arabah. But he did not know that an ambush had been set against him behind the city. ¹⁵Joshua and all Israel let themselves be driven back before them, and they fled toward the desert. ¹⁶All the men of Ai were called to pursue them, and they pursued Joshua and were lured away from the city. ¹⁷Not a man remained in Ai or Bethel who did not go after Israel. They left the city open and went in pursuit of Israel.

¹⁸Then the LORD said to Joshua, "Hold out toward Ai the javelin that is in your hand, for into your hand I will deliver the city." So Joshua held out his javelin toward Ai. ¹⁹As soon as he did this, the men in the ambush rose quickly from their position and rushed forward. They entered the city and captured it and quickly set it on fire.

²⁰The men of Ai looked back and saw the smoke of the city rising against the sky, but they had no chance to escape in any direction, for the Israelites who had been fleeing toward the desert had turned back against their pursuers. ²¹For when Joshua and all Israel saw that the

ᵃ26 Achor means *trouble.*

ambush had taken the city and that smoke was going up from the city, they turned around and attacked the men of Ai. ²²The men of the ambush also came out of the city against them, so that they were caught in the middle, with Israelites on both sides. Israel cut them down, leaving them neither survivors nor fugitives. ²³But they took the king of Ai alive and brought him to Joshua.

²⁴When Israel had finished killing all the men of Ai in the fields and in the desert where they had chased them, and when every one of them had been put to the sword, all the Israelites returned to Ai and killed those who were in it. ²⁵Twelve thousand men and women fell that day—all the people of Ai. ²⁶For Joshua did not draw back the hand that held out his javelin until he had destroyed*a* all who lived in Ai. ²⁷But Israel did carry off for themselves the livestock and plunder of this city, as the LORD had instructed Joshua.

²⁸So Joshua burned Ai and made it a permanent heap of ruins, a desolate place to this day. ²⁹He hung the king of Ai on a tree and left him there until evening. At sunset, Joshua ordered them to take his body from the tree and throw it down at the entrance of the city gate. And they raised a large pile of rocks over it, which remains to this day.

The Covenant Renewed at Mount Ebal

³⁰Then Joshua built on Mount Ebal an altar to the LORD, the God of Israel, ³¹as Moses the servant of the LORD had commanded the Israelites. He built it according to what is written in the Book of the Law of Moses—an altar of uncut stones, on which no iron tool had been used. On it they offered to the LORD burnt offerings and sacrificed fellowship offerings.*b* ³²There, in the presence of the Israelites, Joshua copied on stones the law of Moses, which he had written. ³³All Israel, aliens and citizens alike, with their elders, officials and judges, were standing on both sides of the ark of the covenant of the LORD, facing those who carried it—the priests, who were Levites. Half of the people stood in front of Mount Gerizim and half of them in front of Mount Ebal, as Moses the servant of the

LORD had formerly commanded when he gave instructions to bless the people of Israel.

³⁴Afterward, Joshua read all the words of the law—the blessings and the curses—just as it is written in the Book of the Law. ³⁵There was not a word of all that Moses had commanded that Joshua did not read to the whole assembly of Israel, including the women and children, and the aliens who lived among them.

The Gibeonite Deception

9 Now when all the kings west of the Jordan heard about these things—those in the hill country, in the western foothills, and along the entire coast of the Great Sea*c* as far as Lebanon (the kings of the Hittites, Amorites, Canaanites, Perizzites, Hivites and Jebusites)—²they came together to make war against Joshua and Israel.

³However, when the people of Gibeon heard what Joshua had done to Jericho and Ai, ⁴they resorted to a ruse: They went as a delegation whose donkeys were loaded*d* with worn-out sacks and old wineskins, cracked and mended. ⁵The men put worn and patched sandals on their feet and wore old clothes. All the bread of their food supply was dry and moldy. ⁶Then they went to Joshua in the camp at Gilgal and said to him and the men of Israel, "We have come from a distant country; make a treaty with us."

⁷The men of Israel said to the Hivites, "But perhaps you live near us. How then can we make a treaty with you?"

⁸"We are your servants," they said to Joshua.

But Joshua asked, "Who are you and where do you come from?"

⁹They answered: "Your servants have come from a very distant country because of the fame of the LORD your God. For we have heard reports of him: all that he did in Egypt, ¹⁰and all that he did to the two kings of the Amorites east of

---

a26 The Hebrew term refers to the irrevocable giving over of things or persons to the LORD, often by totally destroying them.   *b31* Traditionally *peace offerings*   *c1* That is, the Mediterranean   *d4* Most Hebrew manuscripts; some Hebrew manuscripts, Vulgate and Syriac (see also Septuagint) *They prepared provisions and loaded their donkeys*

the Jordan—Sihon king of Heshbon, and Og king of Bashan, who reigned in Ashtaroth. [11]And our elders and all those living in our country said to us, 'Take provisions for your journey; go and meet them and say to them, "We are your servants; make a treaty with us." ' [12]This bread of ours was warm when we packed it at home on the day we left to come to you. But now see how dry and moldy it is. [13]And these wineskins that we filled were new, but see how cracked they are. And our clothes and sandals are worn out by the very long journey."

[14]The men of Israel sampled their provisions but did not inquire of the LORD. [15]Then Joshua made a treaty of peace with them to let them live, and the leaders of the assembly ratified it by oath.

[16]Three days after they made the treaty with the Gibeonites, the Israelites heard that they were neighbors, living near them. [17]So the Israelites set out and on the third day came to their cities: Gibeon, Kephirah, Beeroth and Kiriath Jearim. [18]But the Israelites did not attack them, because the leaders of the assembly had sworn an oath to them by the LORD, the God of Israel.

The whole assembly grumbled against the leaders, [19]but all the leaders answered, "We have given them our oath by the LORD, the God of Israel, and we cannot touch them now. [20]This is what we will do to them: We will let them live, so that wrath will not fall on us for breaking the oath we swore to them." [21]They continued, "Let them live, but let them be woodcutters and water carriers for the entire community." So the leaders' promise to them was kept.

[22]Then Joshua summoned the Gibeonites and said, "Why did you deceive us by saying, 'We live a long way from you,' while actually you live near us? [23]You are now under a curse: You will never cease to serve as woodcutters and water carriers for the house of my God." [24]They answered Joshua, "Your servants were clearly told how the LORD your God had commanded his servant Moses to give you the whole land and to wipe out all its inhabitants from before you. So we feared for our lives because of you, and that is why we did this. [25]We

are now in your hands. Do to us whatever seems good and right to you."

[26]So Joshua saved them from the Israelites, and they did not kill them. [27]That day he made the Gibeonites woodcutters and water carriers for the community and for the altar of the LORD at the place the LORD would choose. And that is what they are to this day.

The Sun Stands Still

10 Now Adoni-Zedek king of Jerusalem heard that Joshua had taken Ai and totally destroyed[a] it, doing to Ai and its king as he had done to Jericho and its king, and that the people of Gibeon had made a treaty of peace with Israel and were living near them. [2]He and his people were very much alarmed at this, because Gibeon was an important city, like one of the royal cities; it was larger than Ai, and all its men were good fighters. [3]So Adoni-Zedek king of Jerusalem appealed to Hoham king of Hebron, Piram king of Jarmuth, Japhia king of Lachish and Debir king of Eglon. [4]"Come up and help me attack Gibeon," he said, "because it has made peace with Joshua and the Israelites."

[5]Then the five kings of the Amorites—the kings of Jerusalem, Hebron, Jarmuth, Lachish and Eglon—joined forces. They moved up with all their troops and took up positions against Gibeon and attacked it.

[6]The Gibeonites then sent word to Joshua in the camp at Gilgal: "Do not abandon your servants. Come up to us quickly and save us! Help us, because all the Amorite kings from the hill country have joined forces against us."

[7]So Joshua marched up from Gilgal with his entire army, including all the best fighting men. [8]The LORD said to Joshua, "Do not be afraid of them; I have given them into your hand. Not one of them will be able to withstand you."

[9]After an all-night march from Gilgal, Joshua took them by surprise. [10]The LORD threw them into confusion before Israel, who defeated them in a great victory at

---

[a]*1 The Hebrew term refers to the irrevocable giving over of things or persons to the LORD, often by totally destroying them; also in verses 28, 35, 37, 39 and 40.*

Gibeon. Israel pursued them along the road going up to Beth Horon and cut them down all the way to Azekah and Makkedah. ¹¹As they fled before Israel on the road down from Beth Horon to Azekah, the LORD hurled large hailstones down on them from the sky, and more of them died from the hailstones than were killed by the swords of the Israelites.

¹²On the day the LORD gave the Amorites over to Israel, Joshua said to the LORD in the presence of Israel:

"O sun, stand still over Gibeon,
    O moon, over the Valley of Aijalon."
¹³So the sun stood still,
    and the moon stopped,
    till the nation avenged itself on*ᵃ* its
       enemies,

as it is written in the Book of Jashar.

The sun stopped in the middle of the sky and delayed going down about a full day. ¹⁴There has never been a day like it before or since, a day when the LORD listened to a man. Surely the LORD was fighting for Israel!

¹⁵Then Joshua returned with all Israel to the camp at Gilgal.

Five Amorite Kings Killed

¹⁶Now the five kings had fled and hidden in the cave at Makkedah. ¹⁷When Joshua was told that the five kings had been found hiding in the cave at Makkedah, ¹⁸he said, "Roll large rocks up to the mouth of the cave, and post some men there to guard it. ¹⁹But don't stop! Pursue your enemies, attack them from the rear and don't let them reach their cities, for the LORD your God has given them into your hand."

²⁰So Joshua and the Israelites destroyed them completely—almost to a man—but the few who were left reached their fortified cities. ²¹The whole army then returned safely to Joshua in the camp at Makkedah, and no one uttered a word against the Israelites.

²²Joshua said, "Open the mouth of the cave and bring those five kings out to me." ²³So they brought the five kings out of the cave—the kings of Jerusalem, Hebron, Jarmuth, Lachish and Eglon. ²⁴When they had brought these kings to Joshua, he summoned all the men of Is-

rael and said to the army commanders who had come with him, "Come here and put your feet on the necks of these kings." So they came forward and placed their feet on their necks.

²⁵Joshua said to them, "Do not be afraid; do not be discouraged. Be strong and courageous. This is what the LORD will do to all the enemies you are going to fight." ²⁶Then Joshua struck and killed the kings and hung them on five trees, and they were left hanging on the trees until evening.

²⁷At sunset Joshua gave the order and they took them down from the trees and threw them into the cave where they had been hiding. At the mouth of the cave they placed large rocks, which are there to this day.

²⁸That day Joshua took Makkedah. He put the city and its king to the sword and totally destroyed everyone in it. He left no survivors. And he did to the king of Makkedah as he had done to the king of Jericho.

Southern Cities Conquered

²⁹Then Joshua and all Israel with him moved on from Makkedah to Libnah and attacked it. ³⁰The LORD also gave that city and its king into Israel's hand. The city and everyone in it Joshua put to the sword. He left no survivors there. And he did to its king as he had done to the king of Jericho.

³¹Then Joshua and all Israel with him moved on from Libnah to Lachish; he took up positions against it and attacked it. ³²The LORD handed Lachish over to Israel, and Joshua took it on the second day. The city and everyone in it he put to the sword, just as he had done to Libnah. ³³Meanwhile, Horam king of Gezer had come up to help Lachish, but Joshua defeated him and his army—until no survivors were left.

³⁴Then Joshua and all Israel with him moved on from Lachish to Eglon; they took up positions against it and attacked it. ³⁵They captured it that same day and put it to the sword and totally destroyed everyone in it, just as they had done to Lachish.

ᵃ13 Or nation triumphed over

³⁶Then Joshua and all Israel with him went up from Eglon to Hebron and attacked it. ³⁷They took the city and put it to the sword, together with its king, its villages and everyone in it. They left no survivors. Just as at Eglon, they totally destroyed it and everyone in it.

³⁸Then Joshua and all Israel with him turned around and attacked Debir. ³⁹They took the city, its king and its villages, and put them to the sword. Everyone in it they totally destroyed. They left no survivors. They did to Debir and its king as they had done to Libnah and its king and to Hebron.

⁴⁰So Joshua subdued the whole region, including the hill country, the Negev, the western foothills and the mountain slopes, together with all their kings. He left no survivors. He totally destroyed all who breathed, just as the LORD, the God of Israel, had commanded. ⁴¹Joshua subdued them from Kadesh Barnea to Gaza and from the whole region of Goshen to Gibeon. ⁴²All these kings and their lands Joshua conquered in one campaign, because the LORD, the God of Israel, fought for Israel.

⁴³Then Joshua returned with all Israel to the camp at Gilgal.

Northern Kings Defeated

11 When Jabin king of Hazor heard of this, he sent word to Jobab king of Madon, to the kings of Shimron and Acshaph, ²and to the northern kings who were in the mountains, in the Arabah south of Kinnereth, in the western foothills and in Naphoth Dorᵃ on the west; ³to the Canaanites in the east and west; to the Amorites, Hittites, Perizzites and Jebusites in the hill country; and to the Hivites below Hermon in the region of Mizpah. ⁴They came out with all their troops and a large number of horses and chariots—a huge army, as numerous as the sand on the seashore. ⁵All these kings joined forces and made camp together at the Waters of Merom, to fight against Israel.

⁶The LORD said to Joshua, "Do not be afraid of them, because by this time tomorrow I will hand all of them over to Israel, slain. You are to hamstring their horses and burn their chariots."

⁷So Joshua and his whole army came against them suddenly at the Waters of Merom and attacked them, ⁸and the LORD gave them into the hand of Israel. They defeated them and pursued them all the way to Greater Sidon, to Misrephoth Maim, and to the Valley of Mizpah on the east, until no survivors were left. ⁹Joshua did to them as the LORD had directed: He hamstrung their horses and burned their chariots.

¹⁰At that time Joshua turned back and captured Hazor and put its king to the sword. (Hazor had been the head of all these kingdoms.) ¹¹Everyone in it they put to the sword. They totally destroyedᵇ them, not sparing anything that breathed, and he burned up Hazor itself.

¹²Joshua took all these royal cities and their kings and put them to the sword. He totally destroyed them, as Moses the servant of the LORD had commanded. ¹³Yet Israel did not burn any of the cities built on their mounds—except Hazor, which Joshua burned. ¹⁴The Israelites carried off for themselves all the plunder and livestock of these cities, but all the people they put to the sword until they completely destroyed them, not sparing anyone that breathed. ¹⁵As the LORD commanded his servant Moses, so Moses commanded Joshua, and Joshua did it; he left nothing undone of all that the LORD commanded Moses.

¹⁶So Joshua took this entire land: the hill country, all the Negev, the whole region of Goshen, the western foothills, the Arabah and the mountains of Israel with their foothills, ¹⁷from Mount Halak, which rises toward Seir, to Baal Gad in the Valley of Lebanon below Mount Hermon. He captured all their kings and struck them down, putting them to death. ¹⁸Joshua waged war against all these kings for a long time. ¹⁹Except for the Hivites living in Gibeon, not one city made a treaty of peace with the Israelites, who took them all in battle. ²⁰For it was the LORD himself who hardened their hearts to wage war against Israel, so that he might destroy them totally,

---

ᵃ2 Or *in the heights of Dor*   ᵇ11 The Hebrew term refers to the irrevocable giving over of things or persons to the LORD, often by totally destroying them; also in verses 12, 20 and 21.

exterminating them without mercy, as the LORD had commanded Moses.

²¹At that time Joshua went and destroyed the Anakites from the hill country: from Hebron, Debir and Anab, from all the hill country of Judah, and from all the hill country of Israel. Joshua totally destroyed them and their towns. ²²No Anakites were left in Israelite territory; only in Gaza, Gath and Ashdod did any survive. ²³So Joshua took the entire land, just as the LORD had directed Moses, and he gave it as an inheritance to Israel according to their tribal divisions.

Then the land had rest from war.

List of Defeated Kings

12 These are the kings of the land whom the Israelites had defeated and whose territory they took over east of the Jordan, from the Arnon Gorge to Mount Hermon, including all the eastern side of the Arabah:

²Sihon king of the Amorites,
who reigned in Heshbon. He ruled from Aroer on the rim of the Arnon Gorge—from the middle of the gorge—to the Jabbok River, which is the border of the Ammonites. This included half of Gilead. ³He also ruled over the eastern Arabah from the Sea of Kinnereth[a] to the Sea of the Arabah (the Salt Sea[b]), to Beth Jeshimoth, and then southward below the slopes of Pisgah.

⁴And the territory of Og king of Bashan, one of the last of the Rephaites, who reigned in Ashtaroth and Edrei. ⁵He ruled over Mount Hermon, Salecah, all of Bashan to the border of the people of Geshur and Maacah, and half of Gilead to the border of Sihon king of Heshbon.

⁶Moses, the servant of the LORD, and the Israelites conquered them. And Moses the servant of the LORD gave their land to the Reubenites, the Gadites and the half-tribe of Manasseh to be their possession.

⁷These are the kings of the land that Joshua and the Israelites conquered on the west side of the Jordan, from Baal Gad in the Valley of Lebanon to Mount Halak, which rises toward Seir (their lands Joshua gave as an inheritance to the tribes of Israel according to their tribal divisions— ⁸the hill country, the western foothills, the Arabah, the mountain slopes, the desert and the Negev—the lands of the Hittites, Amorites, Canaanites, Perizzites, Hivites and Jebusites):

⁹the king of Jericho	one
the king of Ai (near Bethel)	one
¹⁰the king of Jerusalem	one
the king of Hebron	one
¹¹the king of Jarmuth	one
the king of Lachish	one
¹²the king of Eglon	one
the king of Gezer	one
¹³the king of Debir	one
the king of Geder	one
¹⁴the king of Hormah	one
the king of Arad	one
¹⁵the king of Libnah	one
the king of Adullam	one
¹⁶the king of Makkedah	one
the king of Bethel	one
¹⁷the king of Tappuah	one
the king of Hepher	one
¹⁸the king of Aphek	one
the king of Lasharon	one
¹⁹the king of Madon	one
the king of Hazor	one
²⁰the king of Shimron Meron	one
the king of Acshaph	one
²¹the king of Taanach	one
the king of Megiddo	one
²²the king of Kedesh	one
the king of Jokneam in Carmel	one
²³the king of Dor (in Naphoth Dor[c])	one
the king of Goyim in Gilgal	one
²⁴the king of Tirzah	one

thirty-one kings in all.

Land Still to Be Taken

13 When Joshua was old and well advanced in years, the LORD said to him, "You are very old, and there are still very large areas of land to be taken over.

²"This is the land that remains: all the regions of the Philistines and Geshurites: ³from the Shihor River

---

[a]3 That is, Galilee   [b]3 That is, the Dead Sea   [c]23 Or *in the heights of Dor*

on the east of Egypt to the territory of Ekron on the north, all of it counted as Canaanite (the territory of the five Philistine rulers in Gaza, Ashdod, Ashkelon, Gath and Ekron— that of the Avvites); ⁴from the south, all the land of the Canaanites, from Arah of the Sidonians as far as Aphek, the region of the Amorites, ⁵the area of the Gebalites*ᵃ*; and all Lebanon to the east, from Baal Gad below Mount Hermon to Lebo*ᵇ* Hamath.

⁶"As for all the inhabitants of the mountain regions from Lebanon to Misrephoth Maim, that is, all the Sidonians, I myself will drive them out before the Israelites. Be sure to allocate this land to

Israel for an inheritance, as I have instructed you, ⁷and divide it as an inheritance among the nine tribes and half of the tribe of Manasseh."

Division of the Land East of the Jordan

⁸The other half of Manasseh,*ᶜ* the Reubenites and the Gadites had received the inheritance that Moses had given them east of the Jordan, as he, the servant of the LORD, had assigned it to them.

⁹It extended from Aroer on the rim of the Arnon Gorge, and from the

---

ᵃ5 That is, the area of Byblos   *ᵇ5* Or *to the entrance to*   *ᶜ8* Hebrew *With it* (that is, with the other half of Manasseh)

Week end.

Rules = Gifts?   **Read Deuteronomy 24:17-18 (page 230)**

This week we looked at celebrating life, honoring parents, giving to others, being strong in our faith and remembering that nothing is impossible with God.

Many people shy away from this part of the Bible because they get tired of all the rules, laws and commands God has given his people. But, as we read this week, God's laws are really all about celebrating, loving, honoring, caring and trusting him.

The verse above (stop and read it now, if you haven't already) reminds us that we have this little tendency to clobber each other whenever it suits us. But God wants us to know how much he cares, *especially* for those who are the most beaten-down and sad. Why? This passage tells us: "Remember that you were slaves in Egypt . . ." Just like God knew about the Israelites' trouble when they were in Egypt, he knows you sometimes feel down. God cares for you, and he knows your troubles.

So, when you think of the rules in the Bible, remember that they are a great gift. They're one of the ways God helps you to know that he really cares about you.

What about You?

❶ Is it hard for you to think of the rules and laws in the Bible as a gift? Why or why not?

❷ Can you remember a time when you were really sad or lonely or scared? How does it help to know God cares about you, especially when you are feeling like that?

❸ Pray for someone in your life who needs God's loving care right now.

Turn to page 271 for your next devotion.

town in the middle of the gorge, and included the whole plateau of Medeba as far as Dibon, [10]and all the towns of Sihon king of the Amorites, who ruled in Heshbon, out to the border of the Ammonites. [11]It also included Gilead, the territory of the people of Geshur and Maacah, all of Mount Hermon and all Bashan as far as Salecah— [12]that is, the whole kingdom of Og in Bashan, who had reigned in Ashtaroth and Edrei and had survived as one of the last of the Rephaites. Moses had defeated them and taken over their land. [13]But the Israelites did not drive out the people of Geshur and Maacah, so they continue to live among the Israelites to this day.

[14]But to the tribe of Levi he gave no inheritance, since the offerings made by fire to the LORD, the God of Israel, are their inheritance, as he promised them.

[15]This is what Moses had given to the tribe of Reuben, clan by clan:

[16]The territory from Aroer on the rim of the Arnon Gorge, and from the town in the middle of the gorge, and the whole plateau past Medeba [17]to Heshbon and all its towns on the plateau, including Dibon, Bamoth Baal, Beth Baal Meon, [18]Jahaz, Kedemoth, Mephaath, [19]Kiriathaim, Sibmah, Zereth Shahar on the hill in the valley, [20]Beth Peor, the slopes of Pisgah, and Beth Jeshimoth [21]—all the towns on the plateau and the entire realm of Sihon king of the Amorites, who ruled at Heshbon. Moses had defeated him and the Midianite chiefs, Evi, Rekem, Zur, Hur and Reba—princes allied with Sihon— who lived in that country. [22]In addition to those slain in battle, the Israelites had put to the sword Balaam son of Beor, who practiced divination. [23]The boundary of the Reubenites was the bank of the Jordan. These towns and their villages were the inheritance of the Reubenites, clan by clan.

[24]This is what Moses had given to the tribe of Gad, clan by clan:

[25]The territory of Jazer, all the towns of Gilead and half the Ammonite country as far as Aroer, near Rabbah; [26]and from Heshbon to Ramath Mizpah and Betonim, and from Mahanaim to the territory of Debir; [27]and in the valley, Beth Haram, Beth Nimrah, Succoth and Zaphon with the rest of the realm of Sihon king of Heshbon (the east side of the Jordan, the territory up to the end of the Sea of Kinnereth[a]). [28]These towns and their villages were the inheritance of the Gadites, clan by clan.

[29]This is what Moses had given to the half-tribe of Manasseh, that is, to half the family of the descendants of Manasseh, clan by clan:

[30]The territory extending from Mahanaim and including all of Bashan, the entire realm of Og king of Bashan—all the settlements of Jair in Bashan, sixty towns, [31]half of Gilead, and Ashtaroth and Edrei (the royal cities of Og in Bashan). This was for the descendants of Makir son of Manasseh—for half of the sons of Makir, clan by clan.

[32]This is the inheritance Moses had given when he was in the plains of Moab across the Jordan east of Jericho. [33]But to the tribe of Levi, Moses had given no inheritance; the LORD, the God of Israel, is their inheritance, as he promised them.

Division of the Land West of the Jordan

14 Now these are the areas the Israelites received as an inheritance in the land of Canaan, which Eleazar the priest, Joshua son of Nun and the heads of the tribal clans of Israel allotted to them. [2]Their inheritances were assigned by lot to the nine-and-a-half tribes, as the LORD had commanded through Moses. [3]Moses had granted the two-and-a-half tribes their inheritance east of the Jordan but had not granted the Levites an inheritance among the rest, [4]for the sons of Joseph had become two tribes— Manasseh and Ephraim. The Levites re-

[a]27 That is, Galilee

ceived no share of the land but only towns to live in, with pasturelands for their flocks and herds. ⁵So the Israelites divided the land, just as the LORD had commanded Moses.

Hebron Given to Caleb

⁶Now the men of Judah approached Joshua at Gilgal, and Caleb son of Jephunneh the Kenizzite said to him, "You know what the LORD said to Moses the man of God at Kadesh Barnea about you and me. ⁷I was forty years old when Moses the servant of the LORD sent me from Kadesh Barnea to explore the land. And I brought him back a report according to my convictions, ⁸but my brothers who went up with me made the hearts of the people melt with fear. I, however, followed the LORD my God wholeheartedly. ⁹So on that day Moses swore to me, 'The land on which your feet have walked will be your inheritance and that of your children forever, because you have followed the LORD my God wholeheartedly.'ᵃ

¹⁰"Now then, just as the LORD promised, he has kept me alive for forty-five years since the time he said this to Moses, while Israel moved about in the desert. So here I am today, eighty-five years old! ¹¹I am still as strong today as the day Moses sent me out; I'm just as vigorous to go out to battle now as I was then. ¹²Now give me this hill country that the LORD promised me that day. You yourself heard then that the Anakites were there and their cities were large and fortified, but, the LORD helping me, I will drive them out just as he said."

¹³Then Joshua blessed Caleb son of Jephunneh and gave him Hebron as his inheritance. ¹⁴So Hebron has belonged to Caleb son of Jephunneh the Kenizzite ever since, because he followed the LORD, the God of Israel, wholeheartedly. ¹⁵(Hebron used to be called Kiriath Arba after Arba, who was the greatest man among the Anakites.)

Then the land had rest from war.

Allotment for Judah

15 The allotment for the tribe of Judah, clan by clan, extended down to the territory of Edom, to the Desert of Zin in the extreme south.

²Their southern boundary started from the bay at the southern end of the Salt Sea,ᵇ ³crossed south of Scorpionᶜ Pass, continued on to Zin and went over to the south of Kadesh Barnea. Then it ran past Hezron up to Addar and curved around to Karka. ⁴It then passed along to Azmon and joined the Wadi of Egypt, ending at the sea. This is theirᵈ southern boundary.

⁵The eastern boundary is the Salt Sea as far as the mouth of the Jordan.

The northern boundary started from the bay of the sea at the mouth of the Jordan, ⁶went up to Beth Hoglah and continued north of Beth Arabah to the Stone of Bohan son of Reuben. ⁷The boundary then went up to Debir from the Valley of Achor and turned north to Gilgal, which faces the Pass of Adummim south of the gorge. It continued along to the waters of En Shemesh and came out at En Rogel. ⁸Then it ran up the Valley of Ben Hinnom along the southern slope of the Jebusite city (that is, Jerusalem). From there it climbed to the top of the hill west of the Hinnom Valley at the northern end of the Valley of Rephaim. ⁹From the hilltop the boundary headed toward the spring of the waters of Nephtoah, came out at the towns of Mount Ephron and went down toward Baalah (that is, Kiriath Jearim). ¹⁰Then it curved westward from Baalah to Mount Seir, ran along the northern slope of Mount Jearim (that is, Kesalon), continued down to Beth Shemesh and crossed to Timnah. ¹¹It went to the northern slope of Ekron, turned toward Shikkeron, passed along to Mount Baalah and reached Jabneel. The boundary ended at the sea.

¹²The western boundary is the coastline of the Great Sea.ᵉ

These are the boundaries around the people of Judah by their clans.

ᵃ9 Deut. 1:36   ᵇ2 That is, the Dead Sea; also in verse 5   ᶜ3 Hebrew *Akrabbim*   ᵈ4 Hebrew *your*
ᵉ12 That is, the Mediterranean; also in verse 47

[13]In accordance with the LORD's command to him, Joshua gave to Caleb son of Jephunneh a portion in Judah—Kiriath Arba, that is, Hebron. (Arba was the forefather of Anak.) [14]From Hebron Caleb drove out the three Anakites—Sheshai, Ahiman and Talmai—descendants of Anak. [15]From there he marched against the people living in Debir (formerly called Kiriath Sepher). [16]And Caleb said, "I will give my daughter Acsah in marriage to the man who attacks and captures Kiriath Sepher." [17]Othniel son of Kenaz, Caleb's brother, took it; so Caleb gave his daughter Acsah to him in marriage.

[18]One day when she came to Othniel, she urged him[a] to ask her father for a field. When she got off her donkey, Caleb asked her, "What can I do for you?"

[19]She replied, "Do me a special favor. Since you have given me land in the Negev, give me also springs of water." So Caleb gave her the upper and lower springs.

[20]This is the inheritance of the tribe of Judah, clan by clan:

[21]The southernmost towns of the tribe of Judah in the Negev toward the boundary of Edom were:

Kabzeel, Eder, Jagur, [22]Kinah, Dimonah, Adadah, [23]Kedesh, Hazor, Ithnan, [24]Ziph, Telem, Bealoth, [25]Hazor Hadattah, Kerioth Hezron (that is, Hazor), [26]Amam, Shema, Moladah, [27]Hazar Gaddah, Heshmon, Beth Pelet, [28]Hazar Shual, Beersheba, Biziothiah, [29]Baalah, Iim, Ezem, [30]Eltolad, Kesil, Hormah, [31]Ziklag, Madmannah, Sansannah, [32]Lebaoth, Shilhim, Ain and Rimmon—a total of twenty-nine towns and their villages.

[33]In the western foothills:

Eshtaol, Zorah, Ashnah, [34]Zanoah, En Gannim, Tappuah, Enam, [35]Jarmuth, Adullam, Socoh, Azekah, [36]Shaaraim, Adithaim and Gederah (or Gederothaim)[b]—fourteen towns and their villages.

[37]Zenan, Hadashah, Migdal Gad, [38]Dilean, Mizpah, Joktheel, [39]Lachish, Bozkath, Eglon, [40]Cabbon, Lahmas, Kitlish, [41]Gederoth, Beth Dagon, Naamah and Makkedah—sixteen towns and their villages.

[42]Libnah, Ether, Ashan, [43]Iphtah, Ashnah, Nezib, [44]Keilah, Aczib and Mareshah—nine towns and their villages.

[45]Ekron, with its surrounding settlements and villages; [46]west of Ekron, all that were in the vicinity of Ashdod, together with their villages; [47]Ashdod, its surrounding settlements and villages; and Gaza, its settlements and villages, as far as the Wadi of Egypt and the coastline of the Great Sea.

[48]In the hill country:

Shamir, Jattir, Socoh, [49]Dannah, Kiriath Sannah (that is, Debir), [50]Anab, Eshtemoh, Anim, [51]Goshen, Holon and Giloh—eleven towns and their villages.

[52]Arab, Dumah, Eshan, [53]Janim, Beth Tappuah, Aphekah, [54]Humtah, Kiriath Arba (that is, Hebron) and Zior—nine towns and their villages.

[55]Maon, Carmel, Ziph, Juttah, [56]Jezreel, Jokdeam, Zanoah, [57]Kain, Gibeah and Timnah—ten towns and their villages.

[58]Halhul, Beth Zur, Gedor, [59]Maarath, Beth Anoth and Eltekon—six towns and their villages.

[60]Kiriath Baal (that is, Kiriath Jearim) and Rabbah—two towns and their villages.

[61]In the desert:

Beth Arabah, Middin, Secacah, [62]Nibshan, the City of Salt and En Gedi—six towns and their villages.

[63]Judah could not dislodge the Jebusites, who were living in Jerusalem; to this day the Jebusites live there with the people of Judah.

Allotment for Ephraim and Manasseh

16 The allotment for Joseph began at the Jordan of Jericho,[c] east of the waters of Jericho, and

---

[a]18 Hebrew and some Septuagint manuscripts; other Septuagint manuscripts (see also note at Judges 1:14) Othniel, he urged her   [b]36 Or Gederah and Gederothaim   [c]1 Jordan of Jericho was possibly an ancient name for the Jordan River.

went up from there through the desert into the hill country of Bethel. ²It went on from Bethel (that is, Luz),ᵃ crossed over to the territory of the Arkites in Ataroth, ³descended westward to the territory of the Japhletites as far as the region of Lower Beth Horon and on to Gezer, ending at the sea. ⁴So Manasseh and Ephraim, the descendants of Joseph, received their inheritance.

⁵This was the territory of Ephraim, clan by clan:

The boundary of their inheritance went from Ataroth Addar in the east to Upper Beth Horon ⁶and continued to the sea. From Micmethath on the north it curved eastward to Taanath Shiloh, passing by it to Janoah on the east. ⁷Then it went down from Janoah to Ataroth and Naarah, touched Jericho and came out at the Jordan. ⁸From Tappuah the border went west to the Kanah Ravine and ended at the sea. This was the inheritance of the tribe of the Ephraimites, clan by clan. ⁹It also included all the towns and their villages that were set aside for the Ephraimites within the inheritance of the Manassites.

¹⁰They did not dislodge the Canaanites living in Gezer; to this day the Canaanites live among the people of Ephraim but are required to do forced labor.

17 This was the allotment for the tribe of Manasseh as Joseph's firstborn, that is, for Makir, Manasseh's firstborn. Makir was the ancestor of the Gileadites, who had received Gilead and Bashan because the Makirites were great soldiers. ²So this allotment was for the rest of the people of Manasseh—the clans of Abiezer, Helek, Asriel, Shechem, Hepher and Shemida. These are the other male descendants of Manasseh son of Joseph by their clans.

³Now Zelophehad son of Hepher, the son of Gilead, the son of Makir, the son of Manasseh, had no sons but only daughters, whose names were Mahlah, Noah, Hoglah, Milcah and Tirzah. ⁴They went to Eleazar the priest, Joshua son of Nun, and the leaders and said, "The LORD commanded Moses to give us an inheritance among our brothers." So Joshua gave them an inheritance along with the brothers of their father, according to the LORD's command. ⁵Manasseh's share consisted of ten tracts of land besides Gilead and Bashan east of the Jordan, ⁶because the daughters of the tribe of Manasseh received an inheritance among the sons. The land of Gilead belonged to the rest of the descendants of Manasseh.

⁷The territory of Manasseh extended from Asher to Micmethath east of Shechem. The boundary ran southward from there to include the people living at En Tappuah. ⁸(Manasseh had the land of Tappuah, but Tappuah itself, on the boundary of Manasseh, belonged to the Ephraimites.) ⁹Then the boundary continued south to the Kanah Ravine. There were towns belonging to Ephraim lying among the towns of Manasseh, but the boundary of Manasseh was the northern side of the ravine and ended at the sea. ¹⁰On the south the land belonged to Ephraim, on the north to Manasseh. The territory of Manasseh reached the sea and bordered Asher on the north and Issachar on the east. ¹¹Within Issachar and Asher, Manasseh also had Beth Shan, Ibleam and the people of Dor, Endor, Taanach and Megiddo, together with their surrounding settlements (the third in the list is Naphothᵇ). ¹²Yet the Manassites were not able to occupy these towns, for the Canaanites were determined to live in that region. ¹³However, when the Israelites grew stronger, they subjected the Canaanites to forced labor but did not drive them out completely.

¹⁴The people of Joseph said to Joshua, "Why have you given us only one allotment and one portion for an inheritance? We are a numerous people and the LORD has blessed us abundantly."

¹⁵"If you are so numerous," Joshua

ᵃ2 Septuagint; Hebrew *Bethel to Luz*   ᵇ11 That is, Naphoth Dor

answered, "and if the hill country of Ephraim is too small for you, go up into the forest and clear land for yourselves there in the land of the Perizzites and Rephaites."

¹⁶The people of Joseph replied, "The hill country is not enough for us, and all the Canaanites who live in the plain have iron chariots, both those in Beth Shan and its settlements and those in the Valley of Jezreel."

¹⁷But Joshua said to the house of Joseph—to Ephraim and Manasseh—"You are numerous and very powerful. You will have not only one allotment ¹⁸but the forested hill country as well. Clear it, and its farthest limits will be yours; though the Canaanites have iron chariots and though they are strong, you can drive them out."

Division of the Rest of the Land

18 The whole assembly of the Israelites gathered at Shiloh and set up the Tent of Meeting there. The country was brought under their control, ²but there were still seven Israelite tribes who had not yet received their inheritance.

³So Joshua said to the Israelites: "How long will you wait before you begin to take possession of the land that the LORD, the God of your fathers, has given you? ⁴Appoint three men from each tribe. I will send them out to make a survey of the land and to write a description of it, according to the inheritance of each. Then they will return to me. ⁵You are to divide the land into seven parts. Judah is to remain in its territory on the south and the house of Joseph in its territory on the north. ⁶After you have written descriptions of the seven parts of the land, bring them here to me and I will cast lots for you in the presence of the LORD our God. ⁷The Levites, however, do not get a portion among you, because the priestly service of the LORD is their inheritance. And Gad, Reuben and the half-tribe of Manasseh have already received their inheritance on the east side of the Jordan. Moses the servant of the LORD gave it to them."

⁸As the men started on their way to map out the land, Joshua instructed them, "Go and make a survey of the land

and write a description of it. Then return to me, and I will cast lots for you here at Shiloh in the presence of the LORD." ⁹So the men left and went through the land. They wrote its description on a scroll, town by town, in seven parts, and returned to Joshua in the camp at Shiloh. ¹⁰Joshua then cast lots for them in Shiloh in the presence of the LORD, and there he distributed the land to the Israelites according to their tribal divisions.

Allotment for Benjamin

¹¹The lot came up for the tribe of Benjamin, clan by clan. Their allotted territory lay between the tribes of Judah and Joseph:

¹²On the north side their boundary began at the Jordan, passed the northern slope of Jericho and headed west into the hill country, coming out at the desert of Beth Aven. ¹³From there it crossed to the south slope of Luz (that is, Bethel) and went down to Ataroth Addar on the hill south of Lower Beth Horon.

¹⁴From the hill facing Beth Horon on the south the boundary turned south along the western side and came out at Kiriath Baal (that is, Kiriath Jearim), a town of the people of Judah. This was the western side.

¹⁵The southern side began at the outskirts of Kiriath Jearim on the west, and the boundary came out at the spring of the waters of Nephtoah. ¹⁶The boundary went down to the foot of the hill facing the Valley of Ben Hinnom, north of the Valley of Rephaim. It continued down the Hinnom Valley along the southern slope of the Jebusite city and so to En Rogel. ¹⁷It then curved north, went to En Shemesh, continued to Geliloth, which faces the Pass of Adummim, and ran down to the Stone of Bohan son of Reuben. ¹⁸It continued to the northern slope of Beth Arabah[a] and on down into the Arabah. ¹⁹It then went to the northern slope of Beth Hoglah and came out at the northern bay of the Salt

---

[a] 18 Septuagint; Hebrew *slope facing the Arabah*

Sea,[a] at the mouth of the Jordan in the south. This was the southern boundary. [20]The Jordan formed the boundary on the eastern side.

These were the boundaries that marked out the inheritance of the clans of Benjamin on all sides.

[21]The tribe of Benjamin, clan by clan, had the following cities:

Jericho, Beth Hoglah, Emek Keziz, [22]Beth Arabah, Zemaraim, Bethel, [23]Avvim, Parah, Ophrah, [24]Kephar Ammoni, Ophni and Geba—twelve towns and their villages.

[25]Gibeon, Ramah, Beeroth, [26]Mizpah, Kephirah, Mozah, [27]Rekem, Irpeel, Taralah, [28]Zelah, Haeleph, the Jebusite city (that is, Jerusalem), Gibeah and Kiriath—fourteen towns and their villages.

This was the inheritance of Benjamin for its clans.

Allotment for Simeon

19 The second lot came out for the tribe of Simeon, clan by clan. Their inheritance lay within the territory of Judah. [2]It included:

Beersheba (or Sheba),[b] Moladah, [3]Hazar Shual, Balah, Ezem, [4]Eltolad, Bethul, Hormah, [5]Ziklag, Beth Marcaboth, Hazar Susah, [6]Beth Lebaoth and Sharuhen—thirteen towns and their villages;

[7]Ain, Rimmon, Ether and Ashan—four towns and their villages— [8]and all the villages around these towns as far as Baalath Beer (Ramah in the Negev).

This was the inheritance of the tribe of the Simeonites, clan by clan. [9]The inheritance of the Simeonites was taken from the share of Judah, because Judah's portion was more than they needed. So the Simeonites received their inheritance within the territory of Judah.

Allotment for Zebulun

[10]The third lot came up for Zebulun, clan by clan:

The boundary of their inheritance went as far as Sarid. [11]Going west it ran to Maralah, touched Dabbe-

sheth, and extended to the ravine near Jokneam. [12]It turned east from Sarid toward the sunrise to the territory of Kisloth Tabor and went on to Daberath and up to Japhia. [13]Then it continued eastward to Gath Hepher and Eth Kazin; it came out at Rimmon and turned toward Neah. [14]There the boundary went around on the north to Hannathon and ended at the Valley of Iphtah El. [15]Included were Kattath, Nahalal, Shimron, Idalah and Bethlehem. There were twelve towns and their villages.

[16]These towns and their villages were the inheritance of Zebulun, clan by clan.

Allotment for Issachar

[17]The fourth lot came out for Issachar, clan by clan. [18]Their territory included:

Jezreel, Kesulloth, Shunem, [19]Hapharaim, Shion, Anaharath, [20]Rabbith, Kishion, Ebez, [21]Remeth, En Gannim, En Haddah and Beth Pazzez. [22]The boundary touched Tabor, Shahazumah and Beth Shemesh, and ended at the Jordan. There were sixteen towns and their villages.

[23]These towns and their villages were the inheritance of the tribe of Issachar, clan by clan.

Allotment for Asher

[24]The fifth lot came out for the tribe of Asher, clan by clan. [25]Their territory included:

Helkath, Hali, Beten, Acshaph, [26]Allammelech, Amad and Mishal. On the west the boundary touched Carmel and Shihor Libnath. [27]It then turned east toward Beth Dagon, touched Zebulun and the Valley of Iphtah El, and went north to Beth Emek and Neiel, passing Cabul on the left. [28]It went to Abdon,[c] Rehob, Hammon and Kanah, as far as Greater Sidon. [29]The boundary then turned back toward Ramah and

---

[a]19 That is, the Dead Sea   [b]2 Or *Beersheba, Sheba*; 1 Chron. 4:28 does not have *Sheba*.   [c]28 Some Hebrew manuscripts (see also Joshua 21:30); most Hebrew manuscripts *Ebron*

went to the fortified city of Tyre, turned toward Hosah and came out at the sea in the region of Aczib, ³⁰Ummah, Aphek and Rehob. There were twenty-two towns and their villages.

³¹These towns and their villages were the inheritance of the tribe of Asher, clan by clan.

Allotment for Naphtali

³²The sixth lot came out for Naphtali, clan by clan:

³³Their boundary went from Heleph and the large tree in Zaanannim, passing Adami Nekeb and Jabneel to Lakkum and ending at the Jordan. ³⁴The boundary ran west through Aznoth Tabor and came out at Hukkok. It touched Zebulun on the south, Asher on the west and the Jordan*a* on the east. ³⁵The fortified cities were Ziddim, Zer, Hammath, Rakkath, Kinnereth, ³⁶Adamah, Ramah, Hazor, ³⁷Kedesh, Edrei, En Hazor, ³⁸Iron, Migdal El, Horem, Beth Anath and Beth Shemesh. There were nineteen towns and their villages.

³⁹These towns and their villages were the inheritance of the tribe of Naphtali, clan by clan.

Allotment for Dan

⁴⁰The seventh lot came out for the tribe of Dan, clan by clan. ⁴¹The territory of their inheritance included:

Zorah, Eshtaol, Ir Shemesh, ⁴²Shaalabbin, Aijalon, Ithlah, ⁴³Elon, Timnah, Ekron, ⁴⁴Eltekeh, Gibbethon, Baalath, ⁴⁵Jehud, Bene Berak, Gath Rimmon, ⁴⁶Me Jarkon and Rakkon, with the area facing Joppa.

⁴⁷(But the Danites had difficulty taking possession of their territory, so they went up and attacked Leshem, took it, put it to the sword and occupied it. They settled in Leshem and named it Dan after their forefather.)

⁴⁸These towns and their villages were the inheritance of the tribe of Dan, clan by clan.

Allotment for Joshua

⁴⁹When they had finished dividing the land into its allotted portions, the Israel-

ites gave Joshua son of Nun an inheritance among them, ⁵⁰as the Lord had commanded. They gave him the town he asked for—Timnath Serah*b* in the hill country of Ephraim. And he built up the town and settled there.

⁵¹These are the territories that Eleazar the priest, Joshua son of Nun and the heads of the tribal clans of Israel assigned by lot at Shiloh in the presence of the Lord at the entrance to the Tent of Meeting. And so they finished dividing the land.

Cities of Refuge

20 Then the Lord said to Joshua: ²"Tell the Israelites to designate the cities of refuge, as I instructed you through Moses, ³so that anyone who kills a person accidentally and unintentionally may flee there and find protection from the avenger of blood.

⁴"When he flees to one of these cities, he is to stand in the entrance of the city gate and state his case before the elders of that city. Then they are to admit him into their city and give him a place to live with them. ⁵If the avenger of blood pursues him, they must not surrender the one accused, because he killed his neighbor unintentionally and without malice aforethought. ⁶He is to stay in that city until he has stood trial before the assembly and until the death of the high priest who is serving at that time. Then he may go back to his own home in the town from which he fled."

⁷So they set apart Kedesh in Galilee in the hill country of Naphtali, Shechem in the hill country of Ephraim, and Kiriath Arba (that is, Hebron) in the hill country of Judah. ⁸On the east side of the Jordan of Jericho*c* they designated Bezer in the desert on the plateau in the tribe of Reuben, Ramoth in Gilead in the tribe of Gad, and Golan in Bashan in the tribe of Manasseh. ⁹Any of the Israelites or any alien living among them who killed someone accidentally could flee to these designated cities and not be killed by the

---

*a*34 Septuagint; Hebrew *west, and Judah, the Jordan;*   *b*50 Also known as *Timnath Heres* (see Judges 2:9)   *c*8 *Jordan of Jericho* was possibly an ancient name for the Jordan River.

avenger of blood prior to standing trial before the assembly.

Towns for the Levites

21 Now the family heads of the Levites approached Eleazar the priest, Joshua son of Nun, and the heads of the other tribal families of Israel ²at Shiloh in Canaan and said to them, "The LORD commanded through Moses that you give us towns to live in, with pasturelands for our livestock." ³So, as the LORD had commanded, the Israelites gave the Levites the following towns and pasturelands out of their own inheritance:

⁴The first lot came out for the Kohathites, clan by clan. The Levites who were descendants of Aaron the priest were allotted thirteen towns from the tribes of Judah, Simeon and Benjamin. ⁵The rest of Kohath's descendants were allotted ten towns from the clans of the tribes of Ephraim, Dan and half of Manasseh.

⁶The descendants of Gershon were allotted thirteen towns from the clans of the tribes of Issachar, Asher, Naphtali and the half-tribe of Manasseh in Bashan.

⁷The descendants of Merari, clan by clan, received twelve towns from the tribes of Reuben, Gad and Zebulun.

⁸So the Israelites allotted to the Levites these towns and their pasturelands, as the LORD had commanded through Moses.

⁹From the tribes of Judah and Simeon they allotted the following towns by name ¹⁰(these towns were assigned to the descendants of Aaron who were from the Kohathite clans of the Levites, because the first lot fell to them):

¹¹They gave them Kiriath Arba (that is, Hebron), with its surrounding pastureland, in the hill country of Judah. (Arba was the forefather of Anak.) ¹²But the fields and villages around the city they had given to Caleb son of Jephunneh as his possession.

¹³So to the descendants of Aaron the priest they gave Hebron (a city of refuge for one accused of murder), Libnah, ¹⁴Jattir, Eshtemoa, ¹⁵Holon, Debir, ¹⁶Ain, Juttah and Beth Shemesh, together with their pasturelands—nine towns from these two tribes.

¹⁷And from the tribe of Benjamin they gave them Gibeon, Geba, ¹⁸Anathoth and Almon, together with their pasturelands—four towns.

¹⁹All the towns for the priests, the descendants of Aaron, were thirteen, together with their pasturelands.

²⁰The rest of the Kohathite clans of the Levites were allotted towns from the tribe of Ephraim:

²¹In the hill country of Ephraim they were given Shechem (a city of refuge for one accused of murder) and Gezer, ²²Kibzaim and Beth Horon, together with their pasturelands—four towns.

²³Also from the tribe of Dan they received Eltekeh, Gibbethon, ²⁴Aijalon and Gath Rimmon, together with their pasturelands—four towns.

²⁵From half the tribe of Manasseh they received Taanach and Gath Rimmon, together with their pasturelands—two towns.

²⁶All these ten towns and their pasturelands were given to the rest of the Kohathite clans.

²⁷The Levite clans of the Gershonites were given:
from the half-tribe of Manasseh,
Golan in Bashan (a city of refuge for one accused of murder) and Be Eshtarah, together with their pasturelands—two towns;
²⁸from the tribe of Issachar,
Kishion, Daberath, ²⁹Jarmuth and En Gannim, together with their pasturelands—four towns;
³⁰from the tribe of Asher,
Mishal, Abdon, ³¹Helkath and Rehob, together with their pasturelands—four towns;
³²from the tribe of Naphtali,
Kedesh in Galilee (a city of refuge for one accused of murder), Hammoth Dor and Kartan, together with their pasturelands—three towns.
³³All the towns of the Gershonite clans were thirteen, together with their pasturelands.

³⁴The Merarite clans (the rest of the Levites) were given:

from the tribe of Zebulun,
Jokneam, Kartah, ³⁵Dimnah and Nahalal, together with their pasturelands—four towns;

³⁶from the tribe of Reuben,
Bezer, Jahaz, ³⁷Kedemoth and Mephaath, together with their pasturelands—four towns;

³⁸from the tribe of Gad,
Ramoth in Gilead (a city of refuge for one accused of murder), Mahanaim, ³⁹Heshbon and Jazer, together with their pasturelands—four towns in all.

⁴⁰All the towns allotted to the Merarite clans, who were the rest of the Levites, were twelve.

⁴¹The towns of the Levites in the territory held by the Israelites were forty-eight in all, together with their pasturelands. ⁴²Each of these towns had pasturelands surrounding it; this was true for all these towns.

⁴³So the LORD gave Israel all the land he had sworn to give their forefathers, and they took possession of it and settled there. ⁴⁴The LORD gave them rest on every side, just as he had sworn to their forefathers. Not one of their enemies withstood them; the LORD handed all their enemies over to them. ⁴⁵Not one of all the LORD's good promises to the house of Israel failed; every one was fulfilled.

Eastern Tribes Return Home

22 Then Joshua summoned the Reubenites, the Gadites and the half-tribe of Manasseh ²and said to them, "You have done all that Moses the servant of the LORD commanded, and you have obeyed me in everything I commanded. ³For a long time now—to this very day—you have not deserted your brothers but have carried out the mission the LORD your God gave you. ⁴Now that the LORD your God has given your brothers rest as he promised, return to your homes in the land that Moses the servant of the LORD gave you on the other side of the Jordan. ⁵But be very careful to keep the commandment and the law that Moses the servant of the LORD gave you: to love the LORD your God, to walk in all his ways, to obey his commands, to hold fast to him and to serve him with all your heart and all your soul."

⁶Then Joshua blessed them and sent them away, and they went to their homes. ⁷(To the half-tribe of Manasseh Moses had given land in Bashan, and to the other half of the tribe Joshua gave land on the west side of the Jordan with their brothers.) When Joshua sent them home, he blessed them, ⁸saying, "Return to your homes with your great wealth—with large herds of livestock, with silver, gold, bronze and iron, and a great quantity of clothing—and divide with your brothers the plunder from your enemies."

⁹So the Reubenites, the Gadites and the half-tribe of Manasseh left the Israelites at Shiloh in Canaan to return to Gilead, their own land, which they had acquired in accordance with the command of the LORD through Moses.

¹⁰When they came to Geliloth near the Jordan in the land of Canaan, the Reubenites, the Gadites and the half-tribe of Manasseh built an imposing altar there by the Jordan. ¹¹And when the Israelites heard that they had built the altar on the border of Canaan at Geliloth near the Jordan on the Israelite side, ¹²the whole assembly of Israel gathered at Shiloh to go to war against them.

¹³So the Israelites sent Phinehas son of Eleazar, the priest, to the land of Gilead—to Reuben, Gad and the half-tribe of Manasseh. ¹⁴With him they sent ten of the chief men, one for each of the tribes of Israel, each the head of a family division among the Israelite clans.

¹⁵When they went to Gilead—to Reuben, Gad and the half-tribe of Manasseh—they said to them: ¹⁶"The whole assembly of the LORD says: 'How could you break faith with the God of Israel like this? How could you turn away from the LORD and build yourselves an altar in rebellion against him now? ¹⁷Was not the sin of Peor enough for us? Up to this very day we have not cleansed ourselves from that sin, even though a plague fell on the community of the LORD! ¹⁸And are you now turning away from the LORD?

" 'If you rebel against the LORD today,

tomorrow he will be angry with the whole community of Israel. ¹⁹If the land you possess is defiled, come over to the LORD's land, where the LORD's tabernacle stands, and share the land with us. But do not rebel against the LORD or against us by building an altar for yourselves, other than the altar of the LORD our God. ²⁰When Achan son of Zerah acted unfaithfully regarding the devoted things,ᵃ did not wrath come upon the whole community of Israel? He was not the only one who died for his sin.' "

²¹Then Reuben, Gad and the half-tribe of Manasseh replied to the heads of the clans of Israel: ²²"The Mighty One, God, the LORD! The Mighty One, God, the LORD! He knows! And let Israel know! If this has been in rebellion or disobedience to the LORD, do not spare us this day. ²³If we have built our own altar to turn away from the LORD and to offer burnt offerings and grain offerings, or to sacrifice fellowship offeringsᵇ on it, may the LORD himself call us to account.

²⁴"No! We did it for fear that some day your descendants might say to ours, 'What do you have to do with the LORD, the God of Israel? ²⁵The LORD has made the Jordan a boundary between us and you—you Reubenites and Gadites! You have no share in the LORD.' So your descendants might cause ours to stop fearing the LORD.

²⁶"That is why we said, 'Let us get ready and build an altar—but not for burnt offerings or sacrifices.' ²⁷On the contrary, it is to be a witness between us and you and the generations that follow, that we will worship the LORD at his sanctuary with our burnt offerings, sacrifices and fellowship offerings. Then in the future your descendants will not be able to say to ours, 'You have no share in the LORD.'

²⁸"And we said, 'If they ever say this to us, or to our descendants, we will answer: Look at the replica of the LORD's altar, which our fathers built, not for burnt offerings and sacrifices, but as a witness between us and you.'

²⁹"Far be it from us to rebel against the LORD and turn away from him today by building an altar for burnt offerings, grain offerings and sacrifices, other than

the altar of the LORD our God that stands before his tabernacle."

³⁰When Phinehas the priest and the leaders of the community—the heads of the clans of the Israelites—heard what Reuben, Gad and Manasseh had to say, they were pleased. ³¹And Phinehas son of Eleazar, the priest, said to Reuben, Gad and Manasseh, "Today we know that the LORD is with us, because you have not acted unfaithfully toward the LORD in this matter. Now you have rescued the Israelites from the LORD's hand."

³²Then Phinehas son of Eleazar, the priest, and the leaders returned to Canaan from their meeting with the Reubenites and Gadites in Gilead and reported to the Israelites. ³³They were glad to hear the report and praised God. And they talked no more about going to war against them to devastate the country where the Reubenites and the Gadites lived.

³⁴And the Reubenites and the Gadites gave the altar this name: A Witness Between Us that the LORD is God.

Joshua's Farewell to the Leaders

23 After a long time had passed and the LORD had given Israel rest from all their enemies around them, Joshua, by then old and well advanced in years, ²summoned all Israel—their elders, leaders, judges and officials—and said to them: "I am old and well advanced in years. ³You yourselves have seen everything the LORD your God has done to all these nations for your sake; it was the LORD your God who fought for you. ⁴Remember how I have allotted as an inheritance for your tribes all the land of the nations that remain—the nations I conquered—between the Jordan and the Great Seaᶜ in the west. ⁵The LORD your God himself will drive them out of your way. He will push them out before you, and you will take possession of their land, as the LORD your God promised you.

⁶"Be very strong; be careful to obey all

ᵃ20 The Hebrew term refers to the irrevocable giving over of things or persons to the LORD, often by totally destroying them. ᵇ23 Traditionally *peace offerings*; also in verse 27 ᶜ4 That is, the Mediterranean

that is written in the Book of the Law of Moses, without turning aside to the right or to the left. ⁷Do not associate with these nations that remain among you; do not invoke the names of their gods or swear by them. You must not serve them or bow down to them. ⁸But you are to hold fast to the LORD your God, as you have until now.

⁹"The LORD has driven out before you great and powerful nations; to this day no one has been able to withstand you. ¹⁰One of you routs a thousand, because the LORD your God fights for you, just as he promised. ¹¹So be very careful to love the LORD your God.

¹²"But if you turn away and ally yourselves with the survivors of these nations that remain among you and if you intermarry with them and associate with them, ¹³then you may be sure that the LORD your God will no longer drive out these nations before you. Instead, they will become snares and traps for you, whips on your backs and thorns in your eyes, until you perish from this good land, which the LORD your God has given you.

¹⁴"Now I am about to go the way of all the earth. You know with all your heart and soul that not one of all the good promises the LORD your God gave you has failed. Every promise has been fulfilled; not one has failed. ¹⁵But just as every good promise of the LORD your God has come true, so the LORD will bring on you all the evil he has threatened, until he has destroyed you from this good land he has given you. ¹⁶If you violate the covenant of the LORD your God, which he commanded you, and go and serve other gods and bow down to them, the LORD's anger will burn against you, and you will quickly perish from the good land he has given you."

The Covenant Renewed at Shechem

24 Then Joshua assembled all the tribes of Israel at Shechem. He summoned the elders, leaders, judges and officials of Israel, and they presented themselves before God.

²Joshua said to all the people, "This is what the LORD, the God of Israel, says: 'Long ago your forefathers, including Te-rah the father of Abraham and Nahor, lived beyond the River[a] and worshiped other gods. ³But I took your father Abraham from the land beyond the River and led him throughout Canaan and gave him many descendants. I gave him Isaac, ⁴and to Isaac I gave Jacob and Esau. I assigned the hill country of Seir to Esau, but Jacob and his sons went down to Egypt.

⁵" 'Then I sent Moses and Aaron, and I afflicted the Egyptians by what I did there, and I brought you out. ⁶When I brought your fathers out of Egypt, you came to the sea, and the Egyptians pursued them with chariots and horsemen[b] as far as the Red Sea.[c] ⁷But they cried to the LORD for help, and he put darkness between you and the Egyptians; he brought the sea over them and covered them. You saw with your own eyes what I did to the Egyptians. Then you lived in the desert for a long time.

⁸" 'I brought you to the land of the Amorites who lived east of the Jordan. They fought against you, but I gave them into your hands. I destroyed them from before you, and you took possession of their land. ⁹When Balak son of Zippor, the king of Moab, prepared to fight against Israel, he sent for Balaam son of Beor to put a curse on you. ¹⁰But I would not listen to Balaam, so he blessed you again and again, and I delivered you out of his hand.

¹¹" 'Then you crossed the Jordan and came to Jericho. The citizens of Jericho fought against you, as did also the Amorites, Perizzites, Canaanites, Hittites, Girgashites, Hivites and Jebusites, but I gave them into your hands. ¹²I sent the hornet ahead of you, which drove them out before you—also the two Amorite kings. You did not do it with your own sword and bow. ¹³So I gave you a land on which you did not toil and cities you did not build; and you live in them and eat from vineyards and olive groves that you did not plant.'

¹⁴"Now fear the LORD and serve him with all faithfulness. Throw away the

---

[a]2 That is, the Euphrates; also in verses 3, 14 and 15   [b]6 Or charioteers   [c]6 Hebrew Yam Suph; that is, Sea of Reeds

gods your forefathers worshiped beyond the River and in Egypt, and serve the LORD. ¹⁵But if serving the LORD seems un-

desirable to you, then choose for yourselves this day whom you will serve,

whether the gods your forefathers served beyond the River, or the gods of the Amorites, in whose land you are living. But as for me and my household, we will serve the LORD."

¹⁶Then the people answered, "Far be it from us to forsake the LORD to serve other gods! ¹⁷It was the LORD our God himself who brought us and our fathers up out of Egypt, from that land of slavery, and performed those great signs before our eyes. He protected us on our entire journey and among all the nations through which we traveled. ¹⁸And the LORD drove out before us all the nations, including the Amorites, who lived in the land. We too will serve the LORD, because he is our God."

¹⁹Joshua said to the people, "You are not able to serve the LORD. He is a holy God; he is a jealous God. He will not forgive your rebellion and your sins. ²⁰If you forsake the LORD and serve foreign gods, he will turn and bring disaster on

---

Look Out for That Truck!

Huh?

Joshua 24:14

Fear protects us from stuff that may hurt us. You wouldn't stand in front of a speeding truck for fear you'd get hit and die. That's because you have a deep respect for the power of that massive truck against your breakable body. In a similar way, if you "fear" God (have a deep respect for who he is and for his power), you don't need to fear his judgment.

Monday

Who's Number One?   Read Joshua 24:14–15

Sometimes people get so obsessed with something they like—an object, a sport, a famous person or whatever—that they just don't leave time for God. For example, a guy in my small group at church told us he was so into skateboarding that his relationship with God was slipping. He realized he had to change some of his priorities. That got me thinking about my own favorite activities, and I realized I had to make some changes too.

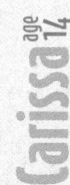

Just like people in Joshua's day, people today have a choice of who or what is number one in their lives. But there's only one right choice: God. If we seek God first, everything else will fall into place the way God wants it to. And while those other things come and go, God will never let us down.

God makes it very clear that we should live our lives for him, above anything or anyone else. Joshua put God first in his life. Have you?

What about You?

❶ Why do you think it's so tempting to live for something other than God?

❷ Draw a picture of a clock. For each hour of the day, write down one thing you can do to show God he's your top priority. Try to do those things for the rest of the day.

❸ Tell God you want to put him first, and ask him to help you do that.

Turn to page 279 for your next devotion.

you and make an end of you, after he has been good to you."

²¹But the people said to Joshua, "No! We will serve the LORD."

²²Then Joshua said, "You are witnesses against yourselves that you have chosen to serve the LORD."

"Yes, we are witnesses," they replied.

²³"Now then," said Joshua, "throw away the foreign gods that are among you and yield your hearts to the LORD, the God of Israel."

²⁴And the people said to Joshua, "We will serve the LORD our God and obey him."

²⁵On that day Joshua made a covenant for the people, and there at Shechem he drew up for them decrees and laws. ²⁶And Joshua recorded these things in the Book of the Law of God. Then he took a large stone and set it up there under the oak near the holy place of the LORD.

²⁷"See!" he said to all the people. "This stone will be a witness against us. It has heard all the words the LORD has said to us. It will be a witness against you if you are untrue to your God."

Buried in the Promised Land

²⁸Then Joshua sent the people away, each to his own inheritance.

²⁹After these things, Joshua son of Nun, the servant of the LORD, died at the age of a hundred and ten. ³⁰And they buried him in the land of his inheritance, at Timnath Serah[a] in the hill country of Ephraim, north of Mount Gaash.

³¹Israel served the LORD throughout the lifetime of Joshua and of the elders who outlived him and who had experienced everything the LORD had done for Israel.

³²And Joseph's bones, which the Israelites had brought up from Egypt, were buried at Shechem in the tract of land that Jacob bought for a hundred pieces of silver[b] from the sons of Hamor, the father of Shechem. This became the inheritance of Joseph's descendants.

³³And Eleazar son of Aaron died and was buried at Gibeah, which had been allotted to his son Phinehas in the hill country of Ephraim.

---

[a]30 Also known as *Timnath Heres* (see Judges 2:9)
[b]32 Hebrew *hundred kesitahs*; a kesitah was a unit of money of unknown weight and value.

Judges

START

The Israelites marched into the promised land with a roar. But by the time this book was written, it sounded more like a whimper. At the start, they follow God's instructions: Wipe out the local inhabitants—barbaric tribes of baby-killers, bogus-god worshipers and bullies. But when Israel's hero Joshua dies, they get lazy, stop fighting and start saying, "Well, the locals aren't really *that* bad." Wrong! God tells them to finish the job. Now the remaining troublemaker tribes are retaking their land, corrupting the Israelites with their sick religions and forcing them to work like slaves. Help!

God comes to the rescue (again!) by giving Israel *judges*—military and civil leaders to guide them to victory and faith in God. Not all the judges turn out so good, but several of them turn out to be smart, faithful heroes who help put Israel back on track. The book of Judges covers a 350-year roller coaster ride in Israel's history, but the ride ends on a bad turn: "In those days Israel had no king; everyone did as he saw fit."

Cast
OF
Characters

Othniel (OTH-nee-el)
Remember Caleb? He was Josh's buddy and one of the 12 spies back in the books of Numbers and Joshua. Well, Caleb has a little brother named Othniel who becomes the first judge. He puts the king of Mesopotamia in his place and keeps Israel on track for 40 years.

Gideon (GID-ee-on)
He's got 3 obvious traits: He's loyal to God, he's got *dozens* of kids and he's not real confident. Actually, he's kind of a wimp. God keeps after him to lead the people to victory against their enemies, and Gideon keeps refusing. Finally, God gives him a tiny army to fight the Midianites and shows him that victory is not a matter of whom you're fighting *against*, but whom you're fighting *for*. Gideon becomes a mighty warrior and a faithful judge to his people.

Ehud (EE-hud)
God picked Ehud to rescue the Israelites from the Moabites. He's shrewd, sneaky and good with a sword. Read his story and find out why his friends could have called him "Lefty."

Samson (SAM-son)
The superman of ancient Israel. He's a Nazirite—part of a special group of folks who don't drink, touch dead bodies or cut their hair. When he's right with God, Judge Samson is unstoppable against the Philistines. But when he gives in to sin—and to Delilah—he's wiped out by little more than a bad hair day.

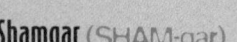

Shamgar (SHAM-gar)

We don't know much about this next judge except that he wipes out 600 Philistines with a big stick.

Abimelech
(uh-BIM-uh-leck)

One of Gideon's small army of sons. He murders all his brothers in his quest to be Israel's head guy. In the end, he does get crowned—by a woman on a roof, dropping a rock on his head. Ouch.

Deborah (DEB-uh-ruh)

Deb is a prophet who gets promoted to judge. She leads the troops to victory over the Canaanites, and Israel lives at peace for 40 years under her leadership.

Jephthah (JEFF-the)

His dad is Gilead, his mom is a prostitute and his half-brothers are really mean. But God helps him overcome all that and raises Judge Jephthah to master-warrior status against his enemy, the Ammonites.

What's UP with That?

When choosing his judges, God picked out some pretty colorful characters—**Deborah** the wonder-woman, **Gideon** the, uh . . . well . . . wimp, **Samson** the superhero. You've probably heard of them. But you may not know about **Ehud,** the James Bond of old Israel. Read about him in Judges 3:12–30, then see if you can select the right words to complete his sneaky story below:

Using his _____ *(left hand, right hand, teeth),* Ehud pulled out a doubled-edged sword strapped to his _____ *(left thigh, right thigh, camel)* and plunged it into King Eglon's _____ *(thick head, chubby cheek, fat belly).*

When the king's servants tried to get in, they found the doors _____ *(open, locked, blown off their hinges).* They weren't worried—they just figured the king was _____ *(napping, sitting on the toilet, on a conference call with Pharaoh).*

Finally, the servants got a key, went into the room and found the king _____ *(juggling, embarrassed, dead).* Meanwhile, Ehud sneaked away, then came back later with his _____ *(coroner, army, mom)* and beat the tar out of the _____ *(Moabites, stalactites, men in tights).* Then no one picked on Israel again for _____ *(5, 80, 1,000)* years.

Snap shots

- From war to whimper—Israel conquers most but not all of the land *(chapters 1—2)*
- Three great guys—Othniel, Ehud and Shamgar *(chapter 3)*
- And an awesome woman—the adventures of Deborah *(chapters 4—5)*
- Gideon finally gets the message *(chapters 6—8)*
- "Heads up!"—Abimelech's major headache *(chapter 9)*
- Jephthah's vivid victory and violent vow *(chapters 10—12)*
- Bad haircut—the rise and fall of Judge Samson *(chapters 13—16)*
- Sorry stories from the land without a king *(chapters 17—21)*

Israel Fights the Remaining Canaanites

1 After the death of Joshua, the Israelites asked the LORD, "Who will be the first to go up and fight for us against the Canaanites?"

[2]The LORD answered, "Judah is to go; I have given the land into their hands."

[3]Then the men of Judah said to the Simeonites their brothers, "Come up with us into the territory allotted to us, to fight against the Canaanites. We in turn will go with you into yours." So the Simeonites went with them.

[4]When Judah attacked, the LORD gave the Canaanites and Perizzites into their hands and they struck down ten thousand men at Bezek. [5]It was there that they found Adoni-Bezek and fought against him, putting to rout the Canaanites and Perizzites. [6]Adoni-Bezek fled, but they chased him and caught him, and cut off his thumbs and big toes.

[7]Then Adoni-Bezek said, "Seventy kings with their thumbs and big toes cut off have picked up scraps under my table. Now God has paid me back for what I did to them." They brought him to Jerusalem, and he died there.

[8]The men of Judah attacked Jerusalem also and took it. They put the city to the sword and set it on fire.

[9]After that, the men of Judah went down to fight against the Canaanites living in the hill country, the Negev and the western foothills. [10]They advanced against the Canaanites living in Hebron (formerly called Kiriath Arba) and defeated Sheshai, Ahiman and Talmai.

[11]From there they advanced against the people living in Debir (formerly called Kiriath Sepher). [12]And Caleb said, "I will give my daughter Acsah in marriage to the man who attacks and captures Kiriath Sepher." [13]Othniel son of Kenaz, Caleb's younger brother, took it; so Caleb gave his daughter Acsah to him in marriage.

[14]One day when she came to Othniel, she urged him[a] to ask her father for a field. When she got off her donkey, Caleb asked her, "What can I do for you?"

[15]She replied, "Do me a special favor. Since you have given me land in the Negev, give me also springs of water." Then Caleb gave her the upper and lower springs.

[16]The descendants of Moses' father-in-law, the Kenite, went up from the City of Palms[b] with the men of Judah to live among the people of the Desert of Judah in the Negev near Arad.

[17]Then the men of Judah went with the Simeonites their brothers and attacked the Canaanites living in Zephath, and they totally destroyed[c] the city. Therefore it was called Hormah.[d] [18]The men of Judah also took[e] Gaza, Ashkelon and Ekron—each city with its territory.

[19]The LORD was with the men of Judah. They took possession of the hill country, but they were unable to drive the people from the plains, because they had iron chariots. [20]As Moses had promised, Hebron was given to Caleb, who drove from it the three sons of Anak. [21]The Benjamites, however, failed to dislodge the Jebusites, who were living in Jerusalem; to this day the Jebusites live there with the Benjamites.

[22]Now the house of Joseph attacked Bethel, and the LORD was with them. [23]When they sent men to spy out Bethel (formerly called Luz), [24]the spies saw a man coming out of the city and they said to him, "Show us how to get into the city and we will see that you are treated well." [25]So he showed them, and they put the city to the sword but spared the man and his whole family. [26]He then went to the land of the Hittites, where he built a city and called it Luz, which is its name to this day.

[27]But Manasseh did not drive out the people of Beth Shan or Taanach or Dor or Ibleam or Megiddo and their surrounding settlements, for the Canaanites were determined to live in that land. [28]When Israel became strong, they pressed the Canaanites into forced labor but never drove them out completely. [29]Nor did Ephraim drive out the Canaanites living in Gezer, but the Canaanites continued to live there among them. [30]Neither did

---

[a]14 Hebrew; Septuagint and Vulgate *Othniel, he urged her* [b]16 That is, Jericho [c]17 The Hebrew term refers to the irrevocable giving over of things or persons to the LORD, often by totally destroying them. [d]17 *Hormah* means *destruction.* [e]18 Hebrew; Septuagint *Judah did not take*

Zebulun drive out the Canaanites living in Kitron or Nahalol, who remained among them; but they did subject them to forced labor. [31]Nor did Asher drive out those living in Acco or Sidon or Ahlab or Aczib or Helbah or Aphek or Rehob, [32]and because of this the people of Asher lived among the Canaanite inhabitants of the land. [33]Neither did Naphtali drive out those living in Beth Shemesh or Beth Anath; but the Naphtalites too lived among the Canaanite inhabitants of the land, and those living in Beth Shemesh and Beth Anath became forced laborers for them. [34]The Amorites confined the Danites to the hill country, not allowing them to come down into the plain. [35]And the Amorites were determined also to hold out in Mount Heres, Aijalon and Shaalbim, but when the power of the house of Joseph increased, they too were pressed into forced labor. [36]The boundary of the Amorites was from Scorpion[a] Pass to Sela and beyond.

The Angel of the LORD at Bokim

2 The angel of the LORD went up from Gilgal to Bokim and said, "I brought you up out of Egypt and led you into the land that I swore to give to your forefathers. I said, 'I will never break my covenant with you, [2]and you shall not make a covenant with the people of this land, but you shall break down their altars.' Yet you have disobeyed me. Why have you done this? [3]Now therefore I tell you that I will not drive them out before you; they will be thorns in your sides and their gods will be a snare to you."

[4]When the angel of the LORD had spoken these things to all the Israelites, the people wept aloud, [5]and they called that place Bokim.[b] There they offered sacrifices to the LORD.

Disobedience and Defeat

[6]After Joshua had dismissed the Israelites, they went to take possession of the land, each to his own inheritance. [7]The people served the LORD throughout the lifetime of Joshua and of the elders who outlived him and who had seen all the great things the LORD had done for Israel. [8]Joshua son of Nun, the servant of the

LORD, died at the age of a hundred and ten. [9]And they buried him in the land of his inheritance, at Timnath Heres[c] in the hill country of Ephraim, north of Mount Gaash.

[10]After that whole generation had been gathered to their fathers, another generation grew up, who knew neither the LORD nor what he had done for Israel. [11]Then the Israelites did evil in the eyes of the LORD and served the Baals. [12]They forsook the LORD, the God of their fathers, who had brought them out of Egypt. They followed and worshiped various gods of the peoples around them. They provoked the LORD to anger [13]because they forsook him and served Baal and the Ashtoreths. [14]In his anger against Israel the LORD handed them over to raiders who plundered them. He sold them to their enemies all around, whom they were no longer able to resist. [15]Whenever Israel went out to fight, the hand of the LORD was against them to defeat them, just as he had sworn to them. They were in great distress.

[16]Then the LORD raised up judges,[d] who saved them out of the hands of these raiders. [17]Yet they would not listen to their judges but prostituted themselves to other gods and worshiped them. Unlike their fathers, they quickly turned from the way in which their fathers had walked, the way of obedience to the LORD's commands. [18]Whenever the LORD raised up a judge for them, he was with the judge and saved them out of the hands of their enemies as long as the judge lived; for the LORD had compassion on them as they groaned under those who oppressed and afflicted them. [19]But when the judge died, the people returned to ways even more corrupt than those of their fathers, following other gods and serving and worshiping them. They refused to give up their evil practices and stubborn ways.

[20]Therefore the LORD was very angry with Israel and said, "Because this nation has violated the covenant that I laid down for their forefathers and has not

---

a36 Hebrew *Akrabbim*　*b5 Bokim* means *weepers.*
c9 Also known as *Timnath Serah* (see Joshua 19:50 and 24:30)　*d16* Or *leaders;* similarly in verses 17-19

listened to me, ²¹I will no longer drive out before them any of the nations Joshua left when he died. ²²I will use them to test Israel and see whether they will keep the way of the LORD and walk in it as their forefathers did." ²³The LORD had allowed those nations to remain; he did not drive them out at once by giving them into the hands of Joshua.

3 These are the nations the LORD left to test all those Israelites who had not experienced any of the wars in Canaan ²(he did this only to teach warfare to the descendants of the Israelites who had not had previous battle experience): ³the five rulers of the Philistines, all the Canaanites, the Sidonians, and the Hivites living in the Lebanon mountains from Mount Baal Hermon to Lebo*ᵃ* Hamath. ⁴They were left to test the Israelites to see whether they would obey the LORD's commands, which he had given their forefathers through Moses.

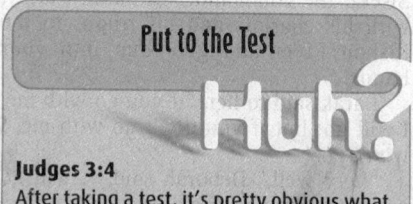

Put to the Test

Huh?

Judges 3:4

After taking a test, it's pretty obvious what you know and what you don't. When God tested the people of Israel (these weren't written tests, by the way), he was able to show them how much they still had to learn about faith and obedience.

⁵The Israelites lived among the Canaanites, Hittites, Amorites, Perizzites, Hivites and Jebusites. ⁶They took their daughters in marriage and gave their own daughters to their sons, and served their gods.

Othniel

⁷The Israelites did evil in the eyes of the LORD; they forgot the LORD their God and served the Baals and the Asherahs. ⁸The anger of the LORD burned against Israel so that he sold them into the hands of Cushan-Rishathaim king of Aram Naharaim,*ᵇ* to whom the Israelites were subject for eight years. ⁹But when they cried out to the LORD, he raised up for them a deliverer, Othniel son of Kenaz, Caleb's younger brother, who saved them. ¹⁰The Spirit of the LORD came upon him, so that he became Israel's judge*ᶜ* and went to war. The LORD gave Cushan-Rishathaim king of Aram into the hands of Othniel, who overpowered him. ¹¹So the land had peace for forty years, until Othniel son of Kenaz died.

Ehud

¹²Once again the Israelites did evil in the eyes of the LORD, and because they did this evil the LORD gave Eglon king of Moab power over Israel. ¹³Getting the Ammonites and Amalekites to join him, Eglon came and attacked Israel, and they took possession of the City of Palms.*ᵈ* ¹⁴The Israelites were subject to Eglon king of Moab for eighteen years.

¹⁵Again the Israelites cried out to the LORD, and he gave them a deliverer—Ehud, a left-handed man, the son of Gera the Benjamite. The Israelites sent him with tribute to Eglon king of Moab. ¹⁶Now Ehud had made a double-edged sword about a foot and a half*ᵉ* long, which he strapped to his right thigh under his clothing. ¹⁷He presented the tribute to Eglon king of Moab, who was a very fat man. ¹⁸After Ehud had presented the tribute, he sent on their way the men who had carried it. ¹⁹At the idols*ᶠ* near Gilgal he himself turned back and said, "I have a secret message for you, O king."

The king said, "Quiet!" And all his attendants left him.

²⁰Ehud then approached him while he was sitting alone in the upper room of his summer palace*ᵍ* and said, "I have a message from God for you." As the king rose from his seat, ²¹Ehud reached with his left hand, drew the sword from his right thigh and plunged it into the king's belly. ²²Even the handle sank in after the blade, which came out his back. Ehud did not pull the sword out, and the fat closed in over it. ²³Then Ehud went

---

ᵃ3 Or *to the entrance to*   *ᵇ8* That is, Northwest Mesopotamia   *ᶜ10* Or *leader*   *ᵈ13* That is, Jericho   *ᵉ16* Hebrew *a cubit* (about 0.5 meter)   *ᶠ19* Or *the stone quarries;* also in verse 26   *ᵍ20* The meaning of the Hebrew for this phrase is uncertain.

out to the porch*a*; he shut the doors of the upper room behind him and locked them.

²⁴After he had gone, the servants came and found the doors of the upper room locked. They said, "He must be relieving himself in the inner room of the house." ²⁵They waited to the point of embarrassment, but when he did not open the doors of the room, they took a key and unlocked them. There they saw their lord fallen to the floor, dead.

²⁶While they waited, Ehud got away. He passed by the idols and escaped to Seirah. ²⁷When he arrived there, he blew a trumpet in the hill country of Ephraim, and the Israelites went down with him from the hills, with him leading them.

²⁸"Follow me," he ordered, "for the LORD has given Moab, your enemy, into your hands." So they followed him down and, taking possession of the fords of the Jordan that led to Moab, they allowed no one to cross over. ²⁹At that time they struck down about ten thousand Moabites, all vigorous and strong; not a man escaped. ³⁰That day Moab was made subject to Israel, and the land had peace for eighty years.

Shamgar

³¹After Ehud came Shamgar son of Anath, who struck down six hundred Philistines with an oxgoad. He too saved Israel.

Tire Iron Warfare

Huh?

Judges 3:31

An oxgoad was a long stick with a small flat piece of iron on one end and a sharp point on the other. The sharp end was used to poke oxen so they'd keep moving when plowing fields. And the flat end was used to clean mud from the plow. Going after 600 men with one of these was like attacking an army with a tire iron. In other words, it was *crazy*! Shamgar must have been totally sure he had God on his side.

Deborah

4 After Ehud died, the Israelites once again did evil in the eyes of the LORD. ²So the LORD sold them into the hands of Jabin, a king of Canaan, who reigned in Hazor. The commander of his army was Sisera, who lived in Harosheth Haggoyim. ³Because he had nine hundred iron chariots and had cruelly oppressed the Israelites for twenty years, they cried to the LORD for help.

⁴Deborah, a prophetess, the wife of Lappidoth, was leading*b* Israel at that time. ⁵She held court under the Palm of Deborah between Ramah and Bethel in the hill country of Ephraim, and the Israelites came to her to have their disputes decided. ⁶She sent for Barak son of Abinoam from Kedesh in Naphtali and said to him, "The LORD, the God of Israel, commands you: 'Go, take with you ten thousand men of Naphtali and Zebulun and lead the way to Mount Tabor. ⁷I will lure Sisera, the commander of Jabin's army, with his chariots and his troops to the Kishon River and give him into your hands.'"

⁸Barak said to her, "If you go with me, I will go; but if you don't go with me, I won't go."

⁹"Very well," Deborah said, "I will go with you. But because of the way you are going about this,*c* the honor will not be yours, for the LORD will hand Sisera over to a woman." So Deborah went with Barak to Kedesh, ¹⁰where he summoned Zebulun and Naphtali. Ten thousand men followed him, and Deborah also went with him.

¹¹Now Heber the Kenite had left the other Kenites, the descendants of Hobab, Moses' brother-in-law,*d* and pitched his tent by the great tree in Zaanannim near Kedesh.

¹²When they told Sisera that Barak son of Abinoam had gone up to Mount Tabor, ¹³Sisera gathered together his nine hundred iron chariots and all the men with him, from Harosheth Haggoyim to the Kishon River.

*a*23 The meaning of the Hebrew for this word is uncertain. *b*4 Traditionally *judging* *c*9 Or *But on the expedition you are undertaking* *d*11 Or *father-in-law*

¹⁴Then Deborah said to Barak, "Go! This is the day the LORD has given Sisera into your hands. Has not the LORD gone ahead of you?" So Barak went down Mount Tabor, followed by ten thousand men. ¹⁵At Barak's advance, the LORD routed Sisera and all his chariots and army by the sword, and Sisera abandoned his chariot and fled on foot. ¹⁶But Barak pursued the chariots and army as far as Harosheth Haggoyim. All the troops of Sisera fell by the sword; not a man was left.

¹⁷Sisera, however, fled on foot to the tent of Jael, the wife of Heber the Kenite, because there were friendly relations between Jabin king of Hazor and the clan of Heber the Kenite.

¹⁸Jael went out to meet Sisera and said to him, "Come, my lord, come right in. Don't be afraid." So he entered her tent, and she put a covering over him.

¹⁹"I'm thirsty," he said. "Please give me some water." She opened a skin of milk, gave him a drink, and covered him up.

²⁰"Stand in the doorway of the tent," he told her. "If someone comes by and asks you, 'Is anyone here?' say 'No.' "

²¹But Jael, Heber's wife, picked up a tent peg and a hammer and went quietly to him while he lay fast asleep, exhausted. She drove the peg through his temple into the ground, and he died.

²²Barak came by in pursuit of Sisera, and Jael went out to meet him. "Come," she said, "I will show you the man you're looking for." So he went in with her, and there lay Sisera with the tent peg through his temple—dead.

²³On that day God subdued Jabin, the Canaanite king, before the Israelites. ²⁴And the hand of the Israelites grew

Tuesday

No Problem Is Too Big

Read Judges 4

There have been some times in my life when I thought a situation was totally hopeless. One time my dog ran away. Since we live in a big city, I thought I'd never see him again. I prayed about the situation, but I wasn't very hopeful.

A few days later, I heard a report on the radio that someone had found my dog. I couldn't believe it! Just when I was about to give up, God came through and brought him back.

OK, maybe that's nothing compared to the way God defeated Sisera's army in this chapter. And I know that even if my dog had never come back, God would still have been in control. But I think it's pretty clear that God can do anything. No barriers are too great for him to overcome, and no problems are too small for him to care about. Things don't always go the way we think they should. But God promises he always has a plan.

When I start to think something is impossible, or when I lose hope, I need to remember that God can handle any challenge, no matter how tough it is.

Jon · age 14

What about You?

❶ Name 2 or 3 situations when you've felt hopeless. How did God help you get through them?

❷ Write yourself a letter describing something that's challenging you right now. Next month at this time, open the letter and think about the ways God has helped you with your situation.

❸ Thank God for helping you deal with life's challenges.

Turn to page 282 for your next devotion.

stronger and stronger against Jabin, the Canaanite king, until they destroyed him.

The Song of Deborah

5 On that day Deborah and Barak son of Abinoam sang this song:

² "When the princes in Israel take the lead,
    when the people willingly offer themselves—
    praise the LORD!

³ "Hear this, you kings! Listen, you rulers!
    I will sing to*ᵃ* the LORD, I will sing;
    I will make music to*ᵇ* the LORD, the God of Israel.

⁴ "O LORD, when you went out from Seir,
    when you marched from the land of Edom,
  the earth shook, the heavens poured,
    the clouds poured down water.
⁵ The mountains quaked before the LORD, the One of Sinai,
    before the LORD, the God of Israel.

⁶ "In the days of Shamgar son of Anath,
    in the days of Jael, the roads were abandoned;
    travelers took to winding paths.
⁷ Village life*ᶜ* in Israel ceased,
    ceased until I,*ᵈ* Deborah, arose,
    arose a mother in Israel.
⁸ When they chose new gods,
    war came to the city gates,
  and not a shield or spear was seen
    among forty thousand in Israel.
⁹ My heart is with Israel's princes,
    with the willing volunteers among the people.
    Praise the LORD!

¹⁰ "You who ride on white donkeys,
    sitting on your saddle blankets,
  and you who walk along the road,
consider ¹¹the voice of the singers*ᵉ* at the watering places.
    They recite the righteous acts of the LORD,
    the righteous acts of his warriors*ᶠ* in Israel.

  "Then the people of the LORD
    went down to the city gates.

¹² "Wake up, wake up, Deborah!
    Wake up, wake up, break out in song!
  Arise, O Barak!
    Take captive your captives, O son of Abinoam.'

¹³ "Then the men who were left
    came down to the nobles;
  the people of the LORD
    came to me with the mighty.
¹⁴ Some came from Ephraim, whose roots were in Amalek;
    Benjamin was with the people who followed you.
  From Makir captains came down,
    from Zebulun those who bear a commander's staff.
¹⁵ The princes of Issachar were with Deborah;
    yes, Issachar was with Barak,
    rushing after him into the valley.
  In the districts of Reuben
    there was much searching of heart.
¹⁶ Why did you stay among the campfires*ᵍ*
    to hear the whistling for the flocks?
  In the districts of Reuben
    there was much searching of heart.
¹⁷ Gilead stayed beyond the Jordan.
    And Dan, why did he linger by the ships?
  Asher remained on the coast
    and stayed in his coves.
¹⁸ The people of Zebulun risked their very lives;
    so did Naphtali on the heights of the field.

¹⁹ "Kings came, they fought;
    the kings of Canaan fought
  at Taanach by the waters of Megiddo,
    but they carried off no silver, no plunder.
²⁰ From the heavens the stars fought,
    from their courses they fought against Sisera.
²¹ The river Kishon swept them away,
    the age-old river, the river Kishon.
  March on, my soul; be strong!

ᵃ3 Or of   *ᵇ3* Or / with song I will praise   *ᶜ7* Or Warriors   *ᵈ7* Or you   *ᵉ11* Or archers; the meaning of the Hebrew for this word is uncertain.   *ᶠ11* Or villagers   *ᵍ16* Or saddlebags

²²Then thundered the horses' hoofs—
  galloping, galloping go his mighty
      steeds.
²³'Curse Meroz,' said the angel of the
      LORD.
  'Curse its people bitterly,
because they did not come to help the
      LORD,
  to help the LORD against the
      mighty.'

²⁴"Most blessed of women be Jael,
  the wife of Heber the Kenite,
  most blessed of tent-dwelling
      women.
²⁵He asked for water, and she gave him
      milk;
  in a bowl fit for nobles she brought
      him curdled milk.
²⁶Her hand reached for the tent peg,
  her right hand for the workman's
      hammer.
She struck Sisera, she crushed his
      head,
  she shattered and pierced his
      temple.
²⁷At her feet he sank,
  he fell; there he lay.
At her feet he sank, he fell;
  where he sank, there he fell—dead.

²⁸"Through the window peered Sisera's
      mother;
  behind the lattice she cried out,
  'Why is his chariot so long in coming?
  Why is the clatter of his chariots
      delayed?'
²⁹The wisest of her ladies answer her;
  indeed, she keeps saying to herself,
³⁰'Are they not finding and dividing the
      spoils:
  a girl or two for each man,
  colorful garments as plunder for
      Sisera,
  colorful garments embroidered,
  highly embroidered garments for
      my neck—
all this as plunder?'

³¹"So may all your enemies perish,
      O LORD!
  But may they who love you be like
      the sun
  when it rises in its strength."

Then the land had peace forty years.

Gideon

6 Again the Israelites did evil in the
eyes of the LORD, and for seven years
he gave them into the hands of the Midianites. ²Because the power of Midian
was so oppressive, the Israelites prepared
shelters for themselves in mountain
clefts, caves and strongholds. ³Whenever
the Israelites planted their crops, the
Midianites, Amalekites and other eastern
peoples invaded the country. ⁴They
camped on the land and ruined the crops
all the way to Gaza and did not spare a
living thing for Israel, neither sheep nor
cattle nor donkeys. ⁵They came up with
their livestock and their tents like
swarms of locusts. It was impossible to
count the men and their camels; they invaded the land to ravage it. ⁶Midian so
impoverished the Israelites that they
cried out to the LORD for help.

⁷When the Israelites cried to the LORD
because of Midian, ⁸he sent them a
prophet, who said, "This is what the
LORD, the God of Israel, says: I brought
you up out of Egypt, out of the land of
slavery. ⁹I snatched you from the power
of Egypt and from the hand of all your
oppressors. I drove them from before you
and gave you their land. ¹⁰I said to you, 'I
am the LORD your God; do not worship
the gods of the Amorites, in whose land
you live.' But you have not listened
to me."

¹¹The angel of the LORD came and sat
down under the oak in Ophrah that belonged to Joash the Abiezrite, where his
son Gideon was threshing wheat in a
winepress to keep it from the Midianites.
¹²When the angel of the LORD appeared to
Gideon, he said, "The LORD is with you,
mighty warrior."

¹³"But sir," Gideon replied, "if the LORD
is with us, why has all this happened
to us? Where are all his wonders that
our fathers told us about when they
said, 'Did not the LORD bring us up out
of Egypt?' But now the LORD has abandoned us and put us into the hand of
Midian."

¹⁴The LORD turned to him and said, "Go
in the strength you have and save Israel
out of Midian's hand. Am I not sending
you?"

¹⁵"But Lord,ᵃ" Gideon asked, "how can I save Israel? My clan is the weakest in Manasseh, and I am the least in my family."

¹⁶The LORD answered, "I will be with you, and you will strike down all the Midianites together."

¹⁷Gideon replied, "If now I have found favor in your eyes, give me a sign that it is really you talking to me. ¹⁸Please do not go away until I come back and bring my offering and set it before you."

And the LORD said, "I will wait until you return."

¹⁹Gideon went in, prepared a young goat, and from an ephahᵇ of flour he made bread without yeast. Putting the meat in a basket and its broth in a pot, he brought them out and offered them to him under the oak.

²⁰The angel of God said to him, "Take the meat and the unleavened bread, place them on this rock, and pour out the broth." And Gideon did so. ²¹With the tip of the staff that was in his hand, the an-

gel of the LORD touched the meat and the unleavened bread. Fire flared from the rock, consuming the meat and the bread. And the angel of the LORD disappeared. ²²When Gideon realized that it was the angel of the LORD, he exclaimed, "Ah, Sovereign LORD! I have seen the angel of the LORD face to face!"

²³But the LORD said to him, "Peace! Do not be afraid. You are not going to die."

²⁴So Gideon built an altar to the LORD there and called it The LORD is Peace. To this day it stands in Ophrah of the Abiezrites.

²⁵That same night the LORD said to him, "Take the second bull from your father's herd, the one seven years old.ᶜ Tear down your father's altar to Baal and cut down the Asherah poleᵈ beside it. ²⁶Then build a proper kind ofᵉ altar to the LORD your

ᵃ15 Or sir   ᵇ19 That is, probably about 3/5 bushel (about 22 liters)   ᶜ25 Or *Take a full-grown, mature bull from your father's herd*   ᵈ25 That is, a symbol of the goddess Asherah; here and elsewhere in Judges   ᵉ26 Or *build with layers of stone an*

Wednesday

Who, Me?

Read Judges 6:11-16

When I started 7th grade last year, I felt that God was telling me to be a witness for him at my school. The thought of that scared me to death! After all, I was struggling with my own Christian life.

Even if we don't know what it is or how we can possibly do it, God has a job for each of us. Gideon thought of himself as the least important person in all of Israel, but God used him to lead his country to victory. It was difficult for Gideon to believe he could be used by God in such an awesome way, but God kept his word.

Sometimes I find it hard to believe that God can use me to spread the word about his love, but stories like Gideon's remind me that God can—and does—use all of us!

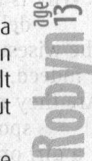
Robyn 13

What about You?

❶ Think of a time when God helped you accomplish something you didn't think you could do. Thank him for that experience.

❷ Do you have a friend who feels like he or she is failing at something? Encourage your friend to look to God for help.

❸ Remember the story of Gideon, and tell God you're willing to go wherever he leads you.

Turn to page 295 for your next devotion.

God on the top of this height. Using the wood of the Asherah pole that you cut down, offer the second[a] bull as a burnt offering."

²⁷So Gideon took ten of his servants and did as the LORD told him. But because he was afraid of his family and the men of the town, he did it at night rather than in the daytime.

²⁸In the morning when the men of the town got up, there was Baal's altar, demolished, with the Asherah pole beside it cut down and the second bull sacrificed on the newly built altar!

²⁹They asked each other, "Who did this?"

When they carefully investigated, they were told, "Gideon son of Joash did it."

³⁰The men of the town demanded of Joash, "Bring out your son. He must die, because he has broken down Baal's altar and cut down the Asherah pole beside it."

³¹But Joash replied to the hostile crowd around him, "Are you going to plead Baal's cause? Are you trying to save him? Whoever fights for him shall be put to death by morning! If Baal really is a god, he can defend himself when someone breaks down his altar." ³²So that day they called Gideon "Jerub-Baal,[b]" saying, "Let Baal contend with him," because he broke down Baal's altar.

³³Now all the Midianites, Amalekites and other eastern peoples joined forces and crossed over the Jordan and camped in the Valley of Jezreel. ³⁴Then the Spirit of the LORD came upon Gideon, and he blew a trumpet, summoning the Abiezrites to follow him. ³⁵He sent messengers throughout Manasseh, calling them to arms, and also into Asher, Zebulun and Naphtali, so that they too went up to meet them.

³⁶Gideon said to God, "If you will save Israel by my hand as you have promised— ³⁷look, I will place a wool fleece on the threshing floor. If there is dew only on the fleece and all the ground is dry, then I will know that you will save Israel by my hand, as you said." ³⁸And that is what happened. Gideon rose early the next day; he squeezed the fleece and wrung out the dew—a bowlful of water. ³⁹Then Gideon said to God, "Do not be

angry with me. Let me make just one more request. Allow me one more test with the fleece. This time make the fleece dry and the ground covered with dew." ⁴⁰That night God did so. Only the fleece was dry; all the ground was covered with dew.

Gideon Defeats the Midianites

7 Early in the morning, Jerub-Baal (that is, Gideon) and all his men camped at the spring of Harod. The camp of Midian was north of them in the valley near the hill of Moreh. ²The LORD said to Gideon, "You have too many men for me to deliver Midian into their hands. In order that Israel may not boast against me that her own strength has saved her, ³announce now to the people, 'Anyone who trembles with fear may turn back and leave Mount Gilead.' " So twenty-two thousand men left, while ten thousand remained.

⁴But the LORD said to Gideon, "There are still too many men. Take them down to the water, and I will sift them for you there. If I say, 'This one shall go with you,' he shall go; but if I say, 'This one shall not go with you,' he shall not go."

⁵So Gideon took the men down to the water. There the LORD told him, "Separate those who lap the water with their tongues like a dog from those who kneel down to drink." ⁶Three hundred men lapped with their hands to their mouths. All the rest got down on their knees to drink.

⁷The LORD said to Gideon, "With the three hundred men that lapped I will save you and give the Midianites into your hands. Let all the other men go, each to his own place." ⁸So Gideon sent the rest of the Israelites to their tents but kept the three hundred, who took over the provisions and trumpets of the others.

Now the camp of Midian lay below him in the valley. ⁹During that night the LORD said to Gideon, "Get up, go down against the camp, because I am going to give it into your hands. ¹⁰If you are afraid to attack, go down to the camp with your servant Purah ¹¹and listen to

---

[a]26 Or full-grown; also in verse 28   [b]32 Jerub-Baal means let Baal contend.

what they are saying. Afterward, you will be encouraged to attack the camp." So he and Purah his servant went down to the outposts of the camp. [12]The Midianites, the Amalekites and all the other eastern peoples had settled in the valley, thick as locusts. Their camels could no more be counted than the sand on the seashore.

[13]Gideon arrived just as a man was telling a friend his dream. "I had a dream," he was saying. "A round loaf of barley bread came tumbling into the Midianite camp. It struck the tent with such force that the tent overturned and collapsed."

[14]His friend responded, "This can be nothing other than the sword of Gideon son of Joash, the Israelite. God has given the Midianites and the whole camp into his hands."

[15]When Gideon heard the dream and its interpretation, he worshiped God. He returned to the camp of Israel and called out, "Get up! The LORD has given the Midianite camp into your hands." [16]Dividing the three hundred men into three companies, he placed trumpets and empty jars in the hands of all of them, with torches inside.

[17]"Watch me," he told them. "Follow my lead. When I get to the edge of the camp, do exactly as I do. [18]When I and all who are with me blow our trumpets, then from all around the camp blow yours and shout, 'For the LORD and for Gideon.' "

[19]Gideon and the hundred men with him reached the edge of the camp at the beginning of the middle watch, just after they had changed the guard. They blew their trumpets and broke the jars that were in their hands. [20]The three companies blew the trumpets and smashed the jars. Grasping the torches in their left hands and holding in their right hands the trumpets they were to blow, they shouted, "A sword for the LORD and for Gideon!" [21]While each man held his position around the camp, all the Midianites ran, crying out as they fled.

[22]When the three hundred trumpets sounded, the LORD caused the men throughout the camp to turn on each other with their swords. The army fled to Beth Shittah toward Zererah as far as the border of Abel Meholah near Tabbath. [23]Israelites from Naphtali, Asher and all Manasseh were called out, and they pursued the Midianites. [24]Gideon sent messengers throughout the hill country of Ephraim, saying, "Come down against the Midianites and seize the waters of the Jordan ahead of them as far as Beth Barah."

So all the men of Ephraim were called out and they took the waters of the Jordan as far as Beth Barah. [25]They also captured two of the Midianite leaders, Oreb and Zeeb. They killed Oreb at the rock of Oreb, and Zeeb at the winepress of Zeeb. They pursued the Midianites and brought the heads of Oreb and Zeeb to Gideon, who was by the Jordan.

Zebah and Zalmunna

8 Now the Ephraimites asked Gideon, "Why have you treated us like this? Why didn't you call us when you went to fight Midian?" And they criticized him sharply.

[2]But he answered them, "What have I accomplished compared to you? Aren't the gleanings of Ephraim's grapes better than the full grape harvest of Abiezer? [3]God gave Oreb and Zeeb, the Midianite leaders, into your hands. What was I able to do compared to you?" At this, their resentment against him subsided.

[4]Gideon and his three hundred men, exhausted yet keeping up the pursuit, came to the Jordan and crossed it. [5]He said to the men of Succoth, "Give my troops some bread; they are worn out, and I am still pursuing Zebah and Zalmunna, the kings of Midian."

[6]But the officials of Succoth said, "Do you already have the hands of Zebah and Zalmunna in your possession? Why should we give bread to your troops?"

[7]Then Gideon replied, "Just for that, when the LORD has given Zebah and Zalmunna into my hand, I will tear your flesh with desert thorns and briers."

[8]From there he went up to Peniel[a] and made the same request of them, but they answered as the men of Succoth had. [9]So he said to the men of Peniel, "When I re-

---

[a] 8 Hebrew *Penuel*, a variant of *Peniel*; also in verses 9 and 17

turn in triumph, I will tear down this tower."

¹⁰Now Zebah and Zalmunna were in Karkor with a force of about fifteen thousand men, all that were left of the armies of the eastern peoples; a hundred and twenty thousand swordsmen had fallen. ¹¹Gideon went up by the route of the nomads east of Nobah and Jogbehah and fell upon the unsuspecting army. ¹²Zebah and Zalmunna, the two kings of Midian, fled, but he pursued them and captured them, routing their entire army.

¹³Gideon son of Joash then returned from the battle by the Pass of Heres. ¹⁴He caught a young man of Succoth and questioned him, and the young man wrote down for him the names of the seventy-seven officials of Succoth, the elders of the town. ¹⁵Then Gideon came and said to the men of Succoth, "Here are Zebah and Zalmunna, about whom you taunted me by saying, 'Do you already have the hands of Zebah and Zalmunna in your possession? Why should we give bread to your exhausted men?' " ¹⁶He took the elders of the town and taught the men of Succoth a lesson by punishing them with desert thorns and briers. ¹⁷He also pulled down the tower of Peniel and killed the men of the town.

¹⁸Then he asked Zebah and Zalmunna, "What kind of men did you kill at Tabor?"

"Men like you," they answered, "each one with the bearing of a prince."

¹⁹Gideon replied, "Those were my brothers, the sons of my own mother. As surely as the LORD lives, if you had spared their lives, I would not kill you." ²⁰Turning to Jether, his oldest son, he said, "Kill them!" But Jether did not draw his sword, because he was only a boy and was afraid.

²¹Zebah and Zalmunna said, "Come, do it yourself. 'As is the man, so is his strength.' " So Gideon stepped forward and killed them, and took the ornaments off their camels' necks.

Gideon's Ephod

²²The Israelites said to Gideon, "Rule over us—you, your son and your grandson—because you have saved us out of the hand of Midian."

²³But Gideon told them, "I will not rule over you, nor will my son rule over you. The LORD will rule over you." ²⁴And he said, "I do have one request, that each of you give me an earring from your share of the plunder." (It was the custom of the Ishmaelites to wear gold earrings.)

²⁵They answered, "We'll be glad to give them." So they spread out a garment, and each man threw a ring from his plunder onto it. ²⁶The weight of the gold rings he asked for came to seventeen hundred shekels,ᵃ not counting the ornaments, the pendants and the purple garments worn by the kings of Midian or the chains that were on their camels' necks. ²⁷Gideon made the gold into an ephod, which he placed in Ophrah, his town. All Israel prostituted themselves by worshiping it there, and it became a snare to Gideon and his family.

Fashion Statement

Huh?

Judges 8:27

An ephod was an article of clothing, kind of like a robe, worn mostly by the high priests of Israel. It was usually made of linen, but, in this case, Gideon had made an ephod out of gold. Instead of drawing people to God, the ephod itself became an idol. The people of Israel were so distracted by the robe's beauty that they began to worship it—duh!

Gideon's Death

²⁸Thus Midian was subdued before the Israelites and did not raise its head again. During Gideon's lifetime, the land enjoyed peace forty years.

²⁹Jerub-Baal son of Joash went back home to live. ³⁰He had seventy sons of his own, for he had many wives. ³¹His concubine, who lived in Shechem, also bore him a son, whom he named Abimelech. ³²Gideon son of Joash died at a good old age and was buried in the tomb of his father Joash in Ophrah of the Abiezrites.

ᵃ26 That is, about 43 pounds (about 19.5 kilograms)

³³No sooner had Gideon died than the Israelites again prostituted themselves to the Baals. They set up Baal-Berith as their god and ³⁴did not remember the LORD their God, who had rescued them from the hands of all their enemies on every side. ³⁵They also failed to show kindness to the family of Jerub-Baal (that is, Gideon) for all the good things he had done for them.

Abimelech

9 Abimelech son of Jerub-Baal went to his mother's brothers in Shechem and said to them and to all his mother's clan, ²"Ask all the citizens of Shechem, 'Which is better for you: to have all seventy of Jerub-Baal's sons rule over you, or just one man?' Remember, I am your flesh and blood."

³When the brothers repeated all this to the citizens of Shechem, they were inclined to follow Abimelech, for they said, "He is our brother." ⁴They gave him seventy shekels^a of silver from the temple of Baal-Berith, and Abimelech used it to hire reckless adventurers, who became his followers. ⁵He went to his father's home in Ophrah and on one stone murdered his seventy brothers, the sons of Jerub-Baal. But Jotham, the youngest son of Jerub-Baal, escaped by hiding. ⁶Then all the citizens of Shechem and Beth Millo gathered beside the great tree at the pillar in Shechem to crown Abimelech king.

⁷When Jotham was told about this, he climbed up on the top of Mount Gerizim and shouted to them, "Listen to me, citizens of Shechem, so that God may listen to you. ⁸One day the trees went out to anoint a king for themselves. They said to the olive tree, 'Be our king.'

⁹"But the olive tree answered, 'Should I give up my oil, by which both gods and men are honored, to hold sway over the trees?'

¹⁰"Next, the trees said to the fig tree, 'Come and be our king.'

¹¹"But the fig tree replied, 'Should I give up my fruit, so good and sweet, to hold sway over the trees?'

¹²"Then the trees said to the vine, 'Come and be our king.'

¹³"But the vine answered, 'Should I give up my wine, which cheers both gods and men, to hold sway over the trees?'

¹⁴"Finally all the trees said to the thornbush, 'Come and be our king.'

¹⁵"The thornbush said to the trees, 'If you really want to anoint me king over you, come and take refuge in my shade; but if not, then let fire come out of the thornbush and consume the cedars of Lebanon!'

¹⁶"Now if you have acted honorably and in good faith when you made Abimelech king, and if you have been fair to Jerub-Baal and his family, and if you have treated him as he deserves— ¹⁷and to think that my father fought for you, risked his life to rescue you from the hand of Midian ¹⁸(but today you have revolted against my father's family, murdered his seventy sons on a single stone, and made Abimelech, the son of his slave girl, king over the citizens of Shechem because he is your brother)— ¹⁹if then you have acted honorably and in good faith toward Jerub-Baal and his family today, may Abimelech be your joy, and may you be his, too! ²⁰But if you have not, let fire come out from Abimelech and consume you, citizens of Shechem and Beth Millo, and let fire come out from you, citizens of Shechem and Beth Millo, and consume Abimelech!"

²¹Then Jotham fled, escaping to Beer, and he lived there because he was afraid of his brother Abimelech.

²²After Abimelech had governed Israel three years, ²³God sent an evil spirit between Abimelech and the citizens of Shechem, who acted treacherously against Abimelech. ²⁴God did this in order that the crime against Jerub-Baal's seventy sons, the shedding of their blood, might be avenged on their brother Abimelech and on the citizens of Shechem, who had helped him murder his brothers. ²⁵In opposition to him these citizens of Shechem set men on the hilltops to ambush and rob everyone who passed by, and this was reported to Abimelech.

²⁶Now Gaal son of Ebed moved with his brothers into Shechem, and its citizens put their confidence in him. ²⁷After

---

^a4 That is, about 1 3/4 pounds (about 0.8 kilogram)

they had gone out into the fields and gathered the grapes and trodden them, they held a festival in the temple of their god. While they were eating and drinking, they cursed Abimelech. ²⁸Then Gaal son of Ebed said, "Who is Abimelech, and who is Shechem, that we should be subject to him? Isn't he Jerub-Baal's son, and isn't Zebul his deputy? Serve the men of Hamor, Shechem's father! Why should we serve Abimelech? ²⁹If only this people were under my command! Then I would get rid of him. I would say to Abimelech, 'Call out your whole army!' "ᵃ

³⁰When Zebul the governor of the city heard what Gaal son of Ebed said, he was very angry. ³¹Under cover he sent messengers to Abimelech, saying, "Gaal son of Ebed and his brothers have come to Shechem and are stirring up the city against you. ³²Now then, during the night you and your men should come and lie in wait in the fields. ³³In the morning at sunrise, advance against the city. When Gaal and his men come out against you, do whatever your hand finds to do."

³⁴So Abimelech and all his troops set out by night and took up concealed positions near Shechem in four companies. ³⁵Now Gaal son of Ebed had gone out and was standing at the entrance to the city gate just as Abimelech and his soldiers came out from their hiding place.

³⁶When Gaal saw them, he said to Zebul, "Look, people are coming down from the tops of the mountains!"

Zebul replied, "You mistake the shadows of the mountains for men."

³⁷But Gaal spoke up again: "Look, people are coming down from the center of the land, and a company is coming from the direction of the soothsayers' tree."

³⁸Then Zebul said to him, "Where is your big talk now, you who said, 'Who is Abimelech that we should be subject to him?' Aren't these the men you ridiculed? Go out and fight them!"

³⁹So Gaal led outᵇ the citizens of Shechem and fought Abimelech. ⁴⁰Abimelech chased him, and many fell wounded in the flight—all the way to the entrance to the gate. ⁴¹Abimelech stayed in Aru-mah, and Zebul drove Gaal and his brothers out of Shechem.

⁴²The next day the people of Shechem went out to the fields, and this was reported to Abimelech. ⁴³So he took his men, divided them into three companies and set an ambush in the fields. When he saw the people coming out of the city, he rose to attack them. ⁴⁴Abimelech and the companies with him rushed forward to a position at the entrance to the city gate. Then two companies rushed upon those in the fields and struck them down. ⁴⁵All that day Abimelech pressed his attack against the city until he had captured it and killed its people. Then he destroyed the city and scattered salt over it.

⁴⁶On hearing this, the citizens in the tower of Shechem went into the stronghold of the temple of El-Berith. ⁴⁷When Abimelech heard that they had assembled there, ⁴⁸he and all his men went up Mount Zalmon. He took an ax and cut off some branches, which he lifted to his shoulders. He ordered the men with him, "Quick! Do what you have seen me do!" ⁴⁹So all the men cut branches and followed Abimelech. They piled them against the stronghold and set it on fire over the people inside. So all the people in the tower of Shechem, about a thousand men and women, also died.

⁵⁰Next Abimelech went to Thebez and besieged it and captured it. ⁵¹Inside the city, however, was a strong tower, to which all the men and women—all the people of the city—fled. They locked themselves in and climbed up on the tower roof. ⁵²Abimelech went to the tower and stormed it. But as he approached the entrance to the tower to set it on fire, ⁵³a woman dropped an upper millstone on his head and cracked his skull.

⁵⁴Hurriedly he called to his armor-bearer, "Draw your sword and kill me, so that they can't say, 'A woman killed him.' " So his servant ran him through, and he died. ⁵⁵When the Israelites saw that Abimelech was dead, they went home.

⁵⁶Thus God repaid the wickedness that

ᵃ29 Septuagint; Hebrew *him.*" *Then he said to Abimelech,* "Call out your whole army!"   ᵇ39 Or *Gaal went out in the sight of*

Abimelech had done to his father by murdering his seventy brothers. ⁵⁷God also made the men of Shechem pay for all their wickedness. The curse of Jotham son of Jerub-Baal came on them.

Tola

10 After the time of Abimelech a man of Issachar, Tola son of Puah, the son of Dodo, rose to save Israel. He lived in Shamir, in the hill country of Ephraim. ²He led*ᵃ* Israel twenty-three years; then he died, and was buried in Shamir.

Jair

³He was followed by Jair of Gilead, who led Israel twenty-two years. ⁴He had thirty sons, who rode thirty donkeys. They controlled thirty towns in Gilead, which to this day are called Havvoth Jair.*ᵇ* ⁵When Jair died, he was buried in Kamon.

Jephthah

⁶Again the Israelites did evil in the eyes of the LORD. They served the Baals and the Ashtoreths, and the gods of Aram, the gods of Sidon, the gods of Moab, the gods of the Ammonites and the gods of the Philistines. And because the Israelites forsook the LORD and no longer served him, ⁷he became angry with them. He sold them into the hands of the Philistines and the Ammonites, ⁸who that year shattered and crushed them. For eighteen years they oppressed all the Israelites on the east side of the Jordan in Gilead, the land of the Amorites. ⁹The Ammonites also crossed the Jordan to fight against Judah, Benjamin and the house of Ephraim; and Israel was in great distress. ¹⁰Then the Israelites cried out to the LORD, "We have sinned against you, forsaking our God and serving the Baals."

¹¹The LORD replied, "When the Egyptians, the Amorites, the Ammonites, the Philistines, ¹²the Sidonians, the Amalekites and the Maonites*ᶜ* oppressed you and you cried to me for help, did I not save you from their hands? ¹³But you have forsaken me and served other gods, so I will no longer save you. ¹⁴Go and cry out to the gods you have chosen. Let them save you when you are in trouble!"

¹⁵But the Israelites said to the LORD, "We have sinned. Do with us whatever you think best, but please rescue us now." ¹⁶Then they got rid of the foreign gods among them and served the LORD. And he could bear Israel's misery no longer.

¹⁷When the Ammonites were called to arms and camped in Gilead, the Israelites assembled and camped at Mizpah. ¹⁸The leaders of the people of Gilead said to each other, "Whoever will launch the attack against the Ammonites will be the head of all those living in Gilead."

11 Jephthah the Gileadite was a mighty warrior. His father was Gilead; his mother was a prostitute. ²Gilead's wife also bore him sons, and when they were grown up, they drove Jephthah away. "You are not going to get any inheritance in our family," they said, "because you are the son of another woman." ³So Jephthah fled from his brothers and settled in the land of Tob, where a group of adventurers gathered around him and followed him.

⁴Some time later, when the Ammonites made war on Israel, ⁵the elders of Gilead went to get Jephthah from the land of Tob. ⁶"Come," they said, "be our commander, so we can fight the Ammonites."

⁷Jephthah said to them, "Didn't you hate me and drive me from my father's house? Why do you come to me now, when you're in trouble?"

⁸The elders of Gilead said to him, "Nevertheless, we are turning to you now; come with us to fight the Ammonites, and you will be our head over all who live in Gilead."

⁹Jephthah answered, "Suppose you take me back to fight the Ammonites and the LORD gives them to me—will I really be your head?"

¹⁰The elders of Gilead replied, "The LORD is our witness; we will certainly do as you say." ¹¹So Jephthah went with the elders of Gilead, and the people made him head and commander over them. And he repeated all his words before the LORD in Mizpah.

ᵃ2 Traditionally *judged*; also in verse 3   *ᵇ4* Or *called the settlements of Jair*   *ᶜ12* Hebrew; some Septuagint manuscripts *Midianites*

¹²Then Jephthah sent messengers to the Ammonite king with the question: "What do you have against us that you have attacked our country?"

¹³The king of the Ammonites answered Jephthah's messengers, "When Israel came up out of Egypt, they took away my land from the Arnon to the Jabbok, all the way to the Jordan. Now give it back peaceably."

¹⁴Jephthah sent back messengers to the Ammonite king, ¹⁵saying:

"This is what Jephthah says: Israel did not take the land of Moab or the land of the Ammonites. ¹⁶But when they came up out of Egypt, Israel went through the desert to the Red Sea[a] and on to Kadesh. ¹⁷Then Israel sent messengers to the king of Edom, saying, 'Give us permission to go through your country,' but the king of Edom would not listen. They sent also to the king of Moab, and he refused. So Israel stayed at Kadesh.

¹⁸"Next they traveled through the desert, skirted the lands of Edom and Moab, passed along the eastern side of the country of Moab, and camped on the other side of the Arnon. They did not enter the territory of Moab, for the Arnon was its border.

¹⁹"Then Israel sent messengers to Sihon king of the Amorites, who ruled in Heshbon, and said to him, 'Let us pass through your country to our own place.' ²⁰Sihon, however, did not trust Israel[b] to pass through his territory. He mustered all his men and encamped at Jahaz and fought with Israel.

²¹"Then the LORD, the God of Israel, gave Sihon and all his men into Israel's hands, and they defeated them. Israel took over all the land of the Amorites who lived in that country, ²²capturing all of it from the Arnon to the Jabbok and from the desert to the Jordan.

²³"Now since the LORD, the God of Israel, has driven the Amorites out before his people Israel, what right have you to take it over? ²⁴Will you not take what your god Chemosh gives you? Likewise, whatever the LORD our God has given us, we will possess. ²⁵Are you better than Balak son of Zippor, king of Moab? Did he ever quarrel with Israel or fight with them? ²⁶For three hundred years Israel occupied Heshbon, Aroer, the surrounding settlements and all the towns along the Arnon. Why didn't you retake them during that time? ²⁷I have not wronged you, but you are doing me wrong by waging war against me. Let the LORD, the Judge,[c] decide the dispute this day between the Israelites and the Ammonites."

²⁸The king of Ammon, however, paid no attention to the message Jephthah sent him.

²⁹Then the Spirit of the LORD came upon Jephthah. He crossed Gilead and Manasseh, passed through Mizpah of Gilead, and from there he advanced against the Ammonites. ³⁰And Jephthah made a vow to the LORD: "If you give the Ammonites into my hands, ³¹whatever comes out of the door of my house to meet me when I return in triumph from the Ammonites will be the LORD's, and I will sacrifice it as a burnt offering."

³²Then Jephthah went over to fight the Ammonites, and the LORD gave them into his hands. ³³He devastated twenty towns from Aroer to the vicinity of Minnith, as far as Abel Keramim. Thus Israel subdued Ammon.

³⁴When Jephthah returned to his home in Mizpah, who should come out to meet him but his daughter, dancing to the sound of tambourines! She was an only child. Except for her he had neither son nor daughter. ³⁵When he saw her, he tore his clothes and cried, "Oh! My daughter! You have made me miserable and wretched, because I have made a vow to the LORD that I cannot break."

³⁶"My father," she replied, "you have given your word to the LORD. Do to me just as you promised, now that the LORD has avenged you of your enemies, the Ammonites. ³⁷But grant me this one request," she said. "Give me two months to

---

[a]16 Hebrew *Yam Suph*; that is, Sea of Reeds   [b]20 Or *however, would not make an agreement for Israel*   [c]27 Or *Ruler*

roam the hills and weep with my friends, because I will never marry."

³⁸"You may go," he said. And he let her go for two months. She and the girls went into the hills and wept because she would never marry. ³⁹After the two months, she returned to her father and he did to her as he had vowed. And she was a virgin.

From this comes the Israelite custom ⁴⁰that each year the young women of Israel go out for four days to commemorate the daughter of Jephthah the Gileadite.

Jephthah and Ephraim

12 The men of Ephraim called out their forces, crossed over to Za-phon and said to Jephthah, "Why did you go to fight the Ammonites without calling us to go with you? We're going to burn down your house over your head."

²Jephthah answered, "I and my people were engaged in a great struggle with the Ammonites, and although I called, you didn't save me out of their hands. ³When I saw that you wouldn't help, I took my life in my hands and crossed over to fight the Ammonites, and the LORD gave me the victory over them. Now why have you come up today to fight me?"

⁴Jephthah then called together the men of Gilead and fought against Ephraim. The Gileadites struck them down because the Ephraimites had said, "You Gileadites are renegades from Ephraim and Manas-

---

Eat Your Words!

Bold people say bold things . . . and often live just long enough to regret them. The lesson here is, don't make a promise you can't keep because God just might make you eat your words.

SAY IT

"Sure, you can go!" Pharaoh tells Moses to get out of town: "Up! Leave my people, you and the Israelites!" (Exodus 12:31).

"First one out the door dies!" Judge Jephthah makes a vow: " . . . whatever comes out of the door of my house to meet me when I return in triumph from the Ammonites will be the LORD's, and I will sacrifice it as a burnt offering" (Judges 11:30–31).

"You're dead meat!" Goliath laughs when Israel sends little Dave up to fight him: "Come here, and I'll give your flesh to the birds of the air and the beasts of the field" (1 Samuel 17:44).

"I've got it made!" A rich man makes his retirement plans: "Take life easy; eat, drink and be merry" (Luke 12:19).

"I'm there for you!" Peter promises Jesus: "Lord, I am ready to go with you to prison and to death" (Luke 22:33).

EAT IT!

Pharaoh changes his mind, chases after the Israelites and pays big consequences. His army drowns in the Red Sea (Exodus 14:5–28).

Jephthah annihilates the Ammonites . . . but his own daughter is first out the front door. She dies (Judges 11:32–40).

Goliath gets a swift rock to the head. Now he's dead (1 Samuel 17:48–50).

God changes plan: "You fool! This very night your life will be demanded from you. Then who will get what you have prepared for yourself?" (Luke 12:20).

Peter breaks his promise 3 times, just as Jesus said he would (Luke 22:54-62).

seh." ⁵The Gileadites captured the fords of the Jordan leading to Ephraim, and whenever a survivor of Ephraim said, "Let me cross over," the men of Gilead asked him, "Are you an Ephraimite?" If he replied, "No," ⁶they said, "All right, say 'Shibboleth.' " If he said, "Sibboleth," because he could not pronounce the word correctly, they seized him and killed him at the fords of the Jordan. Forty-two thousand Ephraimites were killed at that time.

⁷Jephthah led[a] Israel six years. Then Jephthah the Gileadite died, and was buried in a town in Gilead.

Ibzan, Elon and Abdon

⁸After him, Ibzan of Bethlehem led Israel. ⁹He had thirty sons and thirty daughters. He gave his daughters away in marriage to those outside his clan, and for his sons he brought in thirty young women as wives from outside his clan. Ibzan led Israel seven years. ¹⁰Then Ibzan died, and was buried in Bethlehem.

¹¹After him, Elon the Zebulunite led Israel ten years. ¹²Then Elon died, and was buried in Aijalon in the land of Zebulun.

¹³After him, Abdon son of Hillel, from Pirathon, led Israel. ¹⁴He had forty sons and thirty grandsons, who rode on seventy donkeys. He led Israel eight years. ¹⁵Then Abdon son of Hillel died, and was buried at Pirathon in Ephraim, in the hill country of the Amalekites.

The Birth of Samson

13 Again the Israelites did evil in the eyes of the LORD, so the LORD delivered them into the hands of the Philistines for forty years.

²A certain man of Zorah, named Manoah, from the clan of the Danites, had a wife who was sterile and remained childless. ³The angel of the LORD appeared to her and said, "You are sterile and childless, but you are going to conceive and have a son. ⁴Now see to it that you drink no wine or other fermented drink and that you do not eat anything unclean, ⁵because you will conceive and give birth to a son. No razor may be used on his head, because the boy is to be a Nazirite, set apart to God from birth, and he will begin the deliverance of

Israel from the hands of the Philistines."

⁶Then the woman went to her husband and told him, "A man of God came to me. He looked like an angel of God, very awesome. I didn't ask him where he came from, and he didn't tell me his name. ⁷But he said to me, 'You will conceive and give birth to a son. Now then, drink no wine or other fermented drink and do not eat anything unclean, because the boy will be a Nazirite of God from birth until the day of his death.' "

⁸Then Manoah prayed to the LORD: "O Lord, I beg you, let the man of God you sent to us come again to teach us how to bring up the boy who is to be born."

⁹God heard Manoah, and the angel of God came again to the woman while she was out in the field; but her husband Manoah was not with her. ¹⁰The woman hurried to tell her husband, "He's here! The man who appeared to me the other day!"

¹¹Manoah got up and followed his wife. When he came to the man, he said, "Are you the one who talked to my wife?"

"I am," he said.

¹²So Manoah asked him, "When your words are fulfilled, what is to be the rule for the boy's life and work?"

¹³The angel of the LORD answered, "Your wife must do all that I have told her. ¹⁴She must not eat anything that comes from the grapevine, nor drink any wine or other fermented drink nor eat anything unclean. She must do everything I have commanded her."

¹⁵Manoah said to the angel of the LORD, "We would like you to stay until we prepare a young goat for you."

¹⁶The angel of the LORD replied, "Even though you detain me, I will not eat any of your food. But if you prepare a burnt offering, offer it to the LORD." (Manoah did not realize that it was the angel of the LORD.)

¹⁷Then Manoah inquired of the angel of the LORD, "What is your name, so that we may honor you when your word comes true?"

¹⁸He replied, "Why do you ask my name? It is beyond understanding.[b]"

---

a7 Traditionally *judged*; also in verses 8-14
b18 Or *is wonderful*

¹⁹Then Manoah took a young goat, together with the grain offering, and sacrificed it on a rock to the LORD. And the LORD did an amazing thing while Manoah and his wife watched: ²⁰As the flame blazed up from the altar toward heaven, the angel of the LORD ascended in the flame. Seeing this, Manoah and his wife fell with their faces to the ground. ²¹When the angel of the LORD did not show himself again to Manoah and his wife, Manoah realized that it was the angel of the LORD.

²²"We are doomed to die!" he said to his wife. "We have seen God!"

²³But his wife answered, "If the LORD had meant to kill us, he would not have accepted a burnt offering and grain offering from our hands, nor shown us all these things or now told us this."

²⁴The woman gave birth to a boy and named him Samson. He grew and the LORD blessed him, ²⁵and the Spirit of the LORD began to stir him while he was in Mahaneh Dan, between Zorah and Eshtaol.

Samson's Marriage

14 Samson went down to Timnah and saw there a young Philistine woman. ²When he returned, he said to his father and mother, "I have seen a Philistine woman in Timnah; now get her for me as my wife."

³His father and mother replied, "Isn't there an acceptable woman among your relatives or among all our people? Must you go to the uncircumcised Philistines to get a wife?"

But Samson said to his father, "Get her for me. She's the right one for me." ⁴(His parents did not know that this was from the LORD, who was seeking an occasion to confront the Philistines; for at that time they were ruling over Israel.) ⁵Samson went down to Timnah together with his father and mother. As they approached the vineyards of Timnah, suddenly a young lion came roaring toward him. ⁶The Spirit of the LORD came upon him in power so that he tore the lion apart with his bare hands as he might have torn a young goat. But he told neither his father nor his mother what he had done. ⁷Then he went down and talked with the woman, and he liked her.

⁸Some time later, when he went back to marry her, he turned aside to look at the lion's carcass. In it was a swarm of bees and some honey, ⁹which he scooped out with his hands and ate as he went along. When he rejoined his parents, he gave them some, and they too ate it. But he did not tell them that he had taken the honey from the lion's carcass.

¹⁰Now his father went down to see the woman. And Samson made a feast there, as was customary for bridegrooms. ¹¹When he appeared, he was given thirty companions.

¹²"Let me tell you a riddle," Samson said to them. "If you can give me the answer within the seven days of the feast, I will give you thirty linen garments and thirty sets of clothes. ¹³If you can't tell me the answer, you must give me thirty linen garments and thirty sets of clothes."

"Tell us your riddle," they said. "Let's hear it."

¹⁴He replied,

"Out of the eater, something to eat;
    out of the strong, something sweet."

For three days they could not give the answer.

¹⁵On the fourth*a* day, they said to Samson's wife, "Coax your husband into explaining the riddle for us, or we will burn you and your father's household to death. Did you invite us here to rob us?"

¹⁶Then Samson's wife threw herself on him, sobbing, "You hate me! You don't really love me. You've given my people a riddle, but you haven't told me the answer."

"I haven't even explained it to my father or mother," he replied, "so why should I explain it to you?" ¹⁷She cried the whole seven days of the feast. So on the seventh day he finally told her, because she continued to press him. She in turn explained the riddle to her people.

¹⁸Before sunset on the seventh day the men of the town said to him,

"What is sweeter than honey?
    What is stronger than a lion?"

a15 Some Septuagint manuscripts and Syriac; Hebrew seventh

Samson said to them,

> "If you had not plowed with my heifer,
>   you would not have solved my
>   riddle."

¹⁹Then the Spirit of the LORD came upon him in power. He went down to Ashkelon, struck down thirty of their men, stripped them of their belongings and gave their clothes to those who had explained the riddle. Burning with anger, he went up to his father's house. ²⁰And Samson's wife was given to the friend who had attended him at his wedding.

Samson's Vengeance on the Philistines

15 Later on, at the time of wheat harvest, Samson took a young goat and went to visit his wife. He said, "I'm going to my wife's room." But her father would not let him go in.

²"I was so sure you thoroughly hated her," he said, "that I gave her to your friend. Isn't her younger sister more attractive? Take her instead."

³Samson said to them, "This time I have a right to get even with the Philistines; I will really harm them." ⁴So he went out and caught three hundred foxes and tied them tail to tail in pairs. He then fastened a torch to every pair of tails, ⁵lit the torches and let the foxes loose in the standing grain of the Philistines. He burned up the shocks and standing grain, together with the vineyards and olive groves.

⁶When the Philistines asked, "Who did this?" they were told, "Samson, the Timnite's son-in-law, because his wife was given to his friend."

So the Philistines went up and burned her and her father to death. ⁷Samson said to them, "Since you've acted like this, I won't stop until I get my revenge on you." ⁸He attacked them viciously and slaughtered many of them. Then he went down and stayed in a cave in the rock of Etam.

⁹The Philistines went up and camped in Judah, spreading out near Lehi. ¹⁰The men of Judah asked, "Why have you come to fight us?"

"We have come to take Samson prisoner," they answered, "to do to him as he did to us."

¹¹Then three thousand men from Judah went down to the cave in the rock of Etam and said to Samson, "Don't you realize that the Philistines are rulers over us? What have you done to us?"

He answered, "I merely did to them what they did to me."

¹²They said to him, "We've come to tie you up and hand you over to the Philistines."

Samson said, "Swear to me that you won't kill me yourselves."

¹³"Agreed," they answered. "We will only tie you up and hand you over to them. We will not kill you." So they bound him with two new ropes and led him up from the rock. ¹⁴As he approached Lehi, the Philistines came toward him shouting. The Spirit of the LORD came upon him in power. The ropes on his arms became like charred flax, and the bindings dropped from his hands. ¹⁵Finding a fresh jawbone of a donkey, he grabbed it and struck down a thousand men.

¹⁶Then Samson said,

> "With a donkey's jawbone
>   I have made donkeys of them.ᵃ
> With a donkey's jawbone
>   I have killed a thousand men."

¹⁷When he finished speaking, he threw away the jawbone; and the place was called Ramath Lehi.ᵇ

¹⁸Because he was very thirsty, he cried out to the LORD, "You have given your servant this great victory. Must I now die of thirst and fall into the hands of the uncircumcised?" ¹⁹Then God opened up the hollow place in Lehi, and water came out of it. When Samson drank, his strength returned and he revived. So the spring was called En Hakkore,ᶜ and it is still there in Lehi.

²⁰Samson ledᵈ Israel for twenty years in the days of the Philistines.

Samson and Delilah

16 One day Samson went to Gaza, where he saw a prostitute. He went in to spend the night with her. ²The

---

ᵃ16 Or made a heap or two; the Hebrew for donkey sounds like the Hebrew for heap.   ᵇ17 Ramath Lehi means jawbone hill.   ᶜ19 En Hakkore means caller's spring.   ᵈ20 Traditionally judged

people of Gaza were told, "Samson is here!" So they surrounded the place and lay in wait for him all night at the city gate. They made no move during the night, saying, "At dawn we'll kill him."

³But Samson lay there only until the middle of the night. Then he got up and took hold of the doors of the city gate, together with the two posts, and tore them loose, bar and all. He lifted them to his shoulders and carried them to the top of the hill that faces Hebron.

⁴Some time later, he fell in love with a woman in the Valley of Sorek whose name was Delilah. ⁵The rulers of the Philistines went to her and said, "See if you can lure him into showing you the secret of his great strength and how we can overpower him so we may tie him up and subdue him. Each one of us will give you eleven hundred shekels*ᵃ* of silver."

⁶So Delilah said to Samson, "Tell me the secret of your great strength and how you can be tied up and subdued."

⁷Samson answered her, "If anyone ties me with seven fresh thongs*ᵇ* that have not been dried, I'll become as weak as any other man."

⁸Then the rulers of the Philistines brought her seven fresh thongs that had not been dried, and she tied him with them. ⁹With men hidden in the room, she called to him, "Samson, the Philistines are upon you!" But he snapped the thongs as easily as a piece of string snaps when it comes close to a flame. So the secret of his strength was not discovered.

¹⁰Then Delilah said to Samson, "You have made a fool of me; you lied to me. Come now, tell me how you can be tied."

¹¹He said, "If anyone ties me securely with new ropes that have never been used, I'll become as weak as any other man."

¹²So Delilah took new ropes and tied him with them. Then, with men hidden in the room, she called to him, "Samson, the Philistines are upon you!" But he snapped the ropes off his arms as if they were threads.

¹³Delilah then said to Samson, "Until now, you have been making a fool of me and lying to me. Tell me how you can be tied."

He replied, "If you weave the seven braids of my head into the fabric on the loom, and tighten it with the pin, I'll become as weak as any other man." So while he was sleeping, Delilah took the seven braids of his head, wove them into the fabric ¹⁴and*ᶜ* tightened it with the pin.

Again she called to him, "Samson, the Philistines are upon you!" He awoke from his sleep and pulled up the pin and the loom, with the fabric.

¹⁵Then she said to him, "How can you say, 'I love you,' when you won't confide in me? This is the third time you have made a fool of me and haven't told me the secret of your great strength." ¹⁶With such nagging she prodded him day after day until he was tired to death.

¹⁷So he told her everything. "No razor has ever been used on my head," he said, "because I have been a Nazirite set apart to God since birth. If my head were shaved, my strength would leave me, and I would become as weak as any other man."

Groovy Hair, Man

Huh?

Judges 16:17
The Nazirites were a group of people who had made a vow (a promise) to separate themselves from the world they lived in—to give themselves completely to God. Samson's vow included an "I'll never ever cut my hair" clause. Breaking this vow would make God, the center of Samson's attention, well, no longer the center of Samson's attention. Whether we break or keep promises always says something about what we really value.

¹⁸When Delilah saw that he had told her everything, she sent word to the rulers of the Philistines, "Come back once more; he has told me everything." So the

ᵃ5 That is, about 28 pounds (about 13 kilograms)
ᵇ7 Or *bowstrings*; also in verses 8 and 9
ᶜ13,14 Some Septuagint manuscripts; Hebrew " *I can, if you weave the seven braids of my head into the fabric on the loom.*" ¹⁴*So she*

rulers of the Philistines returned with the silver in their hands. ¹⁹Having put him to sleep on her lap, she called a man to shave off the seven braids of his hair, and so began to subdue him.ᵃ And his strength left him.

²⁰Then she called, "Samson, the Philistines are upon you!"

He awoke from his sleep and thought, "I'll go out as before and shake myself free." But he did not know that the LORD had left him.

²¹Then the Philistines seized him, gouged out his eyes and took him down to Gaza. Binding him with bronze shackles, they set him to grinding in the prison. ²²But the hair on his head began to grow again after it had been shaved.

The Death of Samson

²³Now the rulers of the Philistines assembled to offer a great sacrifice to Dagon their god and to celebrate, saying,

"Our god has delivered Samson, our enemy, into our hands."

²⁴When the people saw him, they praised their god, saying,

"Our god has delivered our enemy
    into our hands,
the one who laid waste our land
    and multiplied our slain."

²⁵While they were in high spirits, they shouted, "Bring out Samson to entertain us." So they called Samson out of the prison, and he performed for them.

When they stood him among the pillars, ²⁶Samson said to the servant who held his hand, "Put me where I can feel the pillars that support the temple, so that I may lean against them." ²⁷Now the temple was crowded with men and women; all the rulers of the Philistines were

ᵃ19 Hebrew; some Septuagint manuscripts *and he began to weaken*

Thursday

God Is #1
Read Judges 16:4–22

When I read the story of Samson and Delilah, I get frustrated with Samson. It's like he doesn't realize how great his gift of strength really is. He doesn't realize God's given him something special, and he needs to protect it. He puts his own desires in front of God's plans for him. And you can see where that gets him—weak, blind and eventually dead!

The really frustrating part is that I do kind of the same thing. I put some of my own desires in front of God's. One of my biggest struggles is with my possessions. Sometimes they become more important to me than God. But when I think of them as gifts from him, it's a lot easier for me to put God first.

God and Samson had a special bond, even though Samson messed that up when he told Delilah the secret of his strength. I know God has a special bond with me too, and with all of his people. When I make God first in my life, that bond stays strong.

Dan age 14

❶ Think about a time when you've made something else more important than God. What happened? How did you feel?

❷ Make a list of things that are important to you. What can you do to make sure God is always first on your list?

❸ Pray that God will help you make him the most important part of your life.

Turn to page 304 for your next devotion.

there, and on the roof were about three thousand men and women watching Samson perform. [28]Then Samson prayed to the LORD, "O Sovereign LORD, remember me. O God, please strengthen me just once more, and let me with one blow get revenge on the Philistines for my two eyes." [29]Then Samson reached toward the two central pillars on which the temple stood. Bracing himself against them, his right hand on the one and his left hand on the other, [30]Samson said, "Let me die with the Philistines!" Then he pushed with all his might, and down came the temple on the rulers and all the people in it. Thus he killed many more when he died than while he lived.

[31]Then his brothers and his father's whole family went down to get him. They brought him back and buried him between Zorah and Eshtaol in the tomb of Manoah his father. He had led[a] Israel twenty years.

Micah's Idols

17 Now a man named Micah from the hill country of Ephraim [2]said to his mother, "The eleven hundred shekels[b] of silver that were taken from you and about which I heard you utter a curse—I have that silver with me; I took it."

Then his mother said, "The LORD bless you, my son!"

[3]When he returned the eleven hundred shekels of silver to his mother, she said, "I solemnly consecrate my silver to the LORD for my son to make a carved image and a cast idol. I will give it back to you."

[4]So he returned the silver to his mother, and she took two hundred shekels[c] of silver and gave them to a silversmith, who made them into the image and the idol. And they were put in Micah's house.

[5]Now this man Micah had a shrine, and he made an ephod and some idols and installed one of his sons as his priest. [6]In those days Israel had no king; everyone did as he saw fit.

[7]A young Levite from Bethlehem in Judah, who had been living within the clan of Judah, [8]left that town in search of some other place to stay. On his way[d] he came to Micah's house in the hill country of Ephraim.

[9]Micah asked him, "Where are you from?"

"I'm a Levite from Bethlehem in Judah," he said, "and I'm looking for a place to stay."

[10]Then Micah said to him, "Live with me and be my father and priest, and I'll give you ten shekels[e] of silver a year, your clothes and your food." [11]So the Levite agreed to live with him, and the young man was to him like one of his sons. [12]Then Micah installed the Levite, and the young man became his priest and lived in his house. [13]And Micah said, "Now I know that the LORD will be good to me, since this Levite has become my priest."

Danites Settle in Laish

18 In those days Israel[ ] had no king.

And in those days the tribe of the Danites was seeking a place of their own where they might settle, because they had not yet come into an inheritance among the tribes of Israel. [2]So the Danites sent five warriors from Zorah and Eshtaol to spy out the land and explore it. These men represented all their clans. They told them, "Go, explore the land."

The men entered the hill country of Ephraim and came to the house of Micah, where they spent the night. [3]When they were near Micah's house, they recognized the voice of the young Levite; so they turned in there and asked him, "Who brought you here? What are you doing in this place? Why are you here?"

[4]He told them what Micah had done for him, and said, "He has hired me and I am his priest."

[5]Then they said to him, "Please inquire of God to learn whether our journey will be successful."

[6]The priest answered them, "Go in peace. Your journey has the LORD's approval."

[7]So the five men left and came to Laish, where they saw that the people were living in safety, like the Sidonians, un-

---

[a]31 Traditionally *judged*   [b]2 That is, about 28 pounds (about 13 kilograms)   [c]4 That is, about 5 pounds (about 2.3 kilograms)   [d]8 Or *To carry on his profession*   [e]10 That is, about 4 ounces (about 110 grams)

suspecting and secure. And since their land lacked nothing, they were prosperous.[a] Also, they lived a long way from the Sidonians and had no relationship with anyone else.[b]

[8]When they returned to Zorah and Eshtaol, their brothers asked them, "How did you find things?"

[9]They answered, "Come on, let's attack them! We have seen that the land is very good. Aren't you going to do something? Don't hesitate to go there and take it over. [10]When you get there, you will find an unsuspecting people and a spacious land that God has put into your hands, a land that lacks nothing whatever."

[11]Then six hundred men from the clan of the Danites, armed for battle, set out from Zorah and Eshtaol. [12]On their way they set up camp near Kiriath Jearim in Judah. This is why the place west of Kiriath Jearim is called Mahaneh Dan[c] to this day. [13]From there they went on to the hill country of Ephraim and came to Micah's house.

[14]Then the five men who had spied out the land of Laish said to their brothers, "Do you know that one of these houses has an ephod, other household gods, a carved image and a cast idol? Now you know what to do." [15]So they turned in there and went to the house of the young Levite at Micah's place and greeted him. [16]The six hundred Danites, armed for battle, stood at the entrance to the gate. [17]The five men who had spied out the land went inside and took the carved image, the ephod, the other household gods and the cast idol while the priest and the six hundred armed men stood at the entrance to the gate.

[18]When these men went into Micah's house and took the carved image, the ephod, the other household gods and the cast idol, the priest said to them, "What are you doing?"

[19]They answered him, "Be quiet! Don't say a word. Come with us, and be our father and priest. Isn't it better that you serve a tribe and clan in Israel as priest rather than just one man's household?" [20]Then the priest was glad. He took the ephod, the other household gods and the carved image and went along with the people. [21]Putting their little children,

their livestock and their possessions in front of them, they turned away and left.

[22]When they had gone some distance from Micah's house, the men who lived near Micah were called together and overtook the Danites. [23]As they shouted after them, the Danites turned and said to Micah, "What's the matter with you that you called out your men to fight?"

[24]He replied, "You took the gods I made, and my priest, and went away. What else do I have? How can you ask, 'What's the matter with you?' "

[25]The Danites answered, "Don't argue with us, or some hot-tempered men will attack you, and you and your family will lose your lives." [26]So the Danites went their way, and Micah, seeing that they were too strong for him, turned around and went back home.

[27]Then they took what Micah had made, and his priest, and went on to Laish, against a peaceful and unsuspecting people. They attacked them with the sword and burned down their city. [28]There was no one to rescue them because they lived a long way from Sidon and had no relationship with anyone else. The city was in a valley near Beth Rehob.

The Danites rebuilt the city and settled there. [29]They named it Dan after their forefather Dan, who was born to Israel—though the city used to be called Laish. [30]There the Danites set up for themselves the idols, and Jonathan son of Gershom, the son of Moses,[d] and his sons were priests for the tribe of Dan until the time of the captivity of the land. [31]They continued to use the idols Micah had made, all the time the house of God was in Shiloh.

A Levite and His Concubine

19 In those days Israel had no king.

Now a Levite who lived in a remote area in the hill country of Ephraim took a concubine from Bethlehem in Judah.

---

[a]7 The meaning of the Hebrew for this clause is uncertain.   [b]7 Hebrew; some Septuagint manuscripts *with the Arameans*   [c]12 *Mahaneh Dan* means *Dan's camp.*   [d]30 An ancient Hebrew scribal tradition, some Septuagint manuscripts and Vulgate; Masoretic Text *Manasseh*

²But she was unfaithful to him. She left him and went back to her father's house in Bethlehem, Judah. After she had been there four months, ³her husband went to her to persuade her to return. He had with him his servant and two donkeys. She took him into her father's house, and when her father saw him, he gladly welcomed him. ⁴His father-in-law, the girl's father, prevailed upon him to stay; so he remained with him three days, eating and drinking, and sleeping there.

⁵On the fourth day they got up early and he prepared to leave, but the girl's father said to his son-in-law, "Refresh yourself with something to eat; then you can go." ⁶So the two of them sat down to eat and drink together. Afterward the girl's father said, "Please stay tonight and enjoy yourself." ⁷And when the man got up to go, his father-in-law persuaded him, so he stayed there that night. ⁸On the morning of the fifth day, when he rose to go, the girl's father said, "Refresh yourself. Wait till afternoon!" So the two of them ate together.

⁹Then when the man, with his concubine and his servant, got up to leave, his father-in-law, the girl's father, said, "Now look, it's almost evening. Spend the night here; the day is nearly over. Stay and enjoy yourself. Early tomorrow morning you can get up and be on your way home." ¹⁰But, unwilling to stay another night, the man left and went toward Jebus (that is, Jerusalem), with his two saddled donkeys and his concubine.

¹¹When they were near Jebus and the day was almost gone, the servant said to his master, "Come, let's stop at this city of the Jebusites and spend the night." ¹²His master replied, "No. We won't go into an alien city, whose people are not Israelites. We will go on to Gibeah." ¹³He added, "Come, let's try to reach Gibeah or Ramah and spend the night in one of those places." ¹⁴So they went on, and the sun set as they neared Gibeah in Benjamin. ¹⁵There they stopped to spend the night. They went and sat in the city square, but no one took them into his home for the night.

¹⁶That evening an old man from the hill country of Ephraim, who was living in Gibeah (the men of the place were Benjamites), came in from his work in the fields. ¹⁷When he looked and saw the traveler in the city square, the old man asked, "Where are you going? Where did you come from?"

¹⁸He answered, "We are on our way from Bethlehem in Judah to a remote area in the hill country of Ephraim where I live. I have been to Bethlehem in Judah and now I am going to the house of the LORD. No one has taken me into his house. ¹⁹We have both straw and fodder for our donkeys and bread and wine for ourselves your servants—me, your maidservant, and the young man with us. We don't need anything."

²⁰"You are welcome at my house," the old man said. "Let me supply whatever you need. Only don't spend the night in the square." ²¹So he took him into his house and fed his donkeys. After they had washed their feet, they had something to eat and drink.

²²While they were enjoying themselves, some of the wicked men of the city surrounded the house. Pounding on the door, they shouted to the old man who owned the house, "Bring out the man who came to your house so we can have sex with him."

²³The owner of the house went outside and said to them, "No, my friends, don't be so vile. Since this man is my guest, don't do this disgraceful thing. ²⁴Look, here is my virgin daughter, and his concubine. I will bring them out to you now, and you can use them and do to them whatever you wish. But to this man, don't do such a disgraceful thing."

²⁵But the men would not listen to him. So the man took his concubine and sent her outside to them, and they raped her and abused her throughout the night, and at dawn they let her go. ²⁶At daybreak the woman went back to the house where her master was staying, fell down at the door and lay there until daylight.

²⁷When her master got up in the morning and opened the door of the house and stepped out to continue on his way, there lay his concubine, fallen in the doorway of the house, with her hands on the threshold. ²⁸He said to her, "Get up; let's go." But there was no answer. Then the

man put her on his donkey and set out for home.

²⁹When he reached home, he took a knife and cut up his concubine, limb by limb, into twelve parts and sent them into all the areas of Israel. ³⁰Everyone who saw it said, "Such a thing has never been seen or done, not since the day the Israelites came up out of Egypt. Think about it! Consider it! Tell us what to do!"

Israelites Fight the Benjamites

20 Then all the Israelites from Dan to Beersheba and from the land of Gilead came out as one man and assembled before the LORD in Mizpah. ²The leaders of all the people of the tribes of Israel took their places in the assembly of the people of God, four hundred thousand soldiers armed with swords. ³(The Benjamites heard that the Israelites had gone up to Mizpah.) Then the Israelites said, "Tell us how this awful thing happened."

⁴So the Levite, the husband of the murdered woman, said, "I and my concubine came to Gibeah in Benjamin to spend the night. ⁵During the night the men of Gibeah came after me and surrounded the house, intending to kill me. They raped my concubine, and she died. ⁶I took my concubine, cut her into pieces and sent one piece to each region of Israel's inheritance, because they committed this lewd and disgraceful act in Israel. ⁷Now, all you Israelites, speak up and give your verdict."

⁸All the people rose as one man, saying, "None of us will go home. No, not one of us will return to his house. ⁹But now this is what we'll do to Gibeah: We'll go up against it as the lot directs. ¹⁰We'll take ten men out of every hundred from all the tribes of Israel, and a hundred from a thousand, and a thousand from ten thousand, to get provisions for the army. Then, when the army arrives at Gibeahᵃ in Benjamin, it can give them what they deserve for all this vileness done in Israel." ¹¹So all the men of Israel got together and united as one man against the city.

¹²The tribes of Israel sent men throughout the tribe of Benjamin, saying, "What about this awful crime that was committed among you? ¹³Now surrender those wicked men of Gibeah so that we may put them to death and purge the evil from Israel."

But the Benjamites would not listen to their fellow Israelites. ¹⁴From their towns they came together at Gibeah to fight against the Israelites. ¹⁵At once the Benjamites mobilized twenty-six thousand swordsmen from their towns, in addition to seven hundred chosen men from those living in Gibeah. ¹⁶Among all these soldiers there were seven hundred chosen men who were left-handed, each of whom could sling a stone at a hair and not miss.

¹⁷Israel, apart from Benjamin, mustered four hundred thousand swordsmen, all of them fighting men.

¹⁸The Israelites went up to Bethelᵇ and inquired of God. They said, "Who of us shall go first to fight against the Benjamites?"

The LORD replied, "Judah shall go first."

¹⁹The next morning the Israelites got up and pitched camp near Gibeah. ²⁰The men of Israel went out to fight the Benjamites and took up battle positions against them at Gibeah. ²¹The Benjamites came out of Gibeah and cut down twenty-two thousand Israelites on the battlefield that day. ²²But the men of Israel encouraged one another and again took up their positions where they had stationed themselves the first day. ²³The Israelites went up and wept before the LORD until evening, and they inquired of the LORD. They said, "Shall we go up again to battle against the Benjamites, our brothers?"

The LORD answered, "Go up against them."

²⁴Then the Israelites drew near to Benjamin the second day. ²⁵This time, when the Benjamites came out from Gibeah to oppose them, they cut down another eighteen thousand Israelites, all of them armed with swords.

²⁶Then the Israelites, all the people, went up to Bethel, and there they sat

---

ᵃ10 One Hebrew manuscript; most Hebrew manuscripts *Geba*, a variant of *Gibeah*   ᵇ18 Or *to the house of God*; also in verse 26 weeping before the LORD. They fasted that day until evening and presented burnt offerings and fellowship offerings[a] to the LORD. ²⁷And the Israelites inquired of the LORD. (In those days the ark of the covenant of God was there, ²⁸with Phinehas son of Eleazar, the son of Aaron, ministering before it.) They asked, "Shall we go up again to battle with Benjamin our brother, or not?"

The LORD responded, "Go, for tomorrow I will give them into your hands."

²⁹Then Israel set an ambush around Gibeah. ³⁰They went up against the Benjamites on the third day and took up positions against Gibeah as they had done before. ³¹The Benjamites came out to meet them and were drawn away from the city. They began to inflict casualties on the Israelites as before, so that about thirty men fell in the open field and on the roads—the one leading to Bethel and the other to Gibeah.

³²While the Benjamites were saying, "We are defeating them as before," the Israelites were saying, "Let's retreat and draw them away from the city to the roads."

³³All the men of Israel moved from their places and took up positions at Baal Tamar, and the Israelite ambush charged out of its place on the west[b] of Gibeah.[c] ³⁴Then ten thousand of Israel's finest men made a frontal attack on Gibeah. The fighting was so heavy that the Benjamites did not realize how near disaster was. ³⁵The LORD defeated Benjamin before Israel, and on that day the Israelites struck down 25,100 Benjamites, all armed with swords. ³⁶Then the Benjamites saw that they were beaten.

Now the men of Israel had given way before Benjamin, because they relied on the ambush they had set near Gibeah. ³⁷The men who had been in ambush made a sudden dash into Gibeah, spread out and put the whole city to the sword. ³⁸The men of Israel had arranged with the ambush that they should send up a great cloud of smoke from the city, ³⁹and then the men of Israel would turn in the battle.

The Benjamites had begun to inflict casualties on the men of Israel (about thirty), and they said, "We are defeat-

ing them as in the first battle." ⁴⁰But when the column of smoke began to rise from the city, the Benjamites turned and saw the smoke of the whole city going up into the sky. ⁴¹Then the men of Israel turned on them, and the men of Benjamin were terrified, because they realized that disaster had come upon them. ⁴²So they fled before the Israelites in the direction of the desert, but they could not escape the battle. And the men of Israel who came out of the towns cut them down there. ⁴³They surrounded the Benjamites, chased them and easily[d] overran them in the vicinity of Gibeah on the east. ⁴⁴Eighteen thousand Benjamites fell, all of them valiant fighters. ⁴⁵As they turned and fled toward the desert to the rock of Rimmon, the Israelites cut down five thousand men along the roads. They kept pressing after the Benjamites as far as Gidom and struck down two thousand more.

⁴⁶On that day twenty-five thousand Benjamite swordsmen fell, all of them valiant fighters. ⁴⁷But six hundred men turned and fled into the desert to the rock of Rimmon, where they stayed four months. ⁴⁸The men of Israel went back to Benjamin and put all the towns to the sword, including the animals and everything else they found. All the towns they came across they set on fire.

Wives for the Benjamites

21 The men of Israel had taken an oath at Mizpah: "Not one of us will give his daughter in marriage to a Benjamite."

²The people went to Bethel,[e] where they sat before God until evening, raising their voices and weeping bitterly. ³"O LORD, the God of Israel," they cried, "why has this happened to Israel? Why should one tribe be missing from Israel today?"

⁴Early the next day the people built an altar and presented burnt offerings and fellowship offerings.[f]

---

a26 Traditionally *peace offerings* *b33* Some Septuagint manuscripts and Vulgate; the meaning of the Hebrew for this word is uncertain. *c33* Hebrew *Geba,* a variant of *Gibeah* *d43* The meaning of the Hebrew for this word is uncertain. *e2* Or *to the house of God* *f4* Traditionally *peace offerings*

⁵Then the Israelites asked, "Who from all the tribes of Israel has failed to assemble before the LORD?" For they had taken a solemn oath that anyone who failed to assemble before the LORD at Mizpah should certainly be put to death.

⁶Now the Israelites grieved for their brothers, the Benjamites. "Today one tribe is cut off from Israel," they said. ⁷"How can we provide wives for those who are left, since we have taken an oath by the LORD not to give them any of our daughters in marriage?" ⁸Then they asked, "Which one of the tribes of Israel failed to assemble before the LORD at Mizpah?" They discovered that no one from Jabesh Gilead had come to the camp for the assembly. ⁹For when they counted the people, they found that none of the people of Jabesh Gilead were there.

¹⁰So the assembly sent twelve thousand fighting men with instructions to go to Jabesh Gilead and put to the sword those living there, including the women and children. ¹¹"This is what you are to do," they said. "Kill every male and every woman who is not a virgin." ¹²They found among the people living in Jabesh Gilead four hundred young women who had never slept with a man, and they took them to the camp at Shiloh in Canaan.

¹³Then the whole assembly sent an offer of peace to the Benjamites at the rock of Rimmon. ¹⁴So the Benjamites returned at that time and were given the women of Jabesh Gilead who had been spared. But there were not enough for all of them.

¹⁵The people grieved for Benjamin, because the LORD had made a gap in the tribes of Israel. ¹⁶And the elders of the assembly said, "With the women of Benjamin destroyed, how shall we provide wives for the men who are left? ¹⁷The Benjamite survivors must have heirs," they said, "so that a tribe of Israel will not be wiped out. ¹⁸We can't give them our daughters as wives, since we Israelites have taken this oath: 'Cursed be anyone who gives a wife to a Benjamite.' ¹⁹But look, there is the annual festival of the LORD in Shiloh, to the north of Bethel, and east of the road that goes from Bethel to Shechem, and to the south of Lebonah."

²⁰So they instructed the Benjamites, saying, "Go and hide in the vineyards ²¹and watch. When the girls of Shiloh come out to join in the dancing, then rush from the vineyards and each of you seize a wife from the girls of Shiloh and go to the land of Benjamin. ²²When their fathers or brothers complain to us, we will say to them, 'Do us a kindness by helping them, because we did not get wives for them during the war, and you are innocent, since you did not give your daughters to them.' "

²³So that is what the Benjamites did. While the girls were dancing, each man caught one and carried her off to be his wife. Then they returned to their inheritance and rebuilt the towns and settled in them.

²⁴At that time the Israelites left that place and went home to their tribes and clans, each to his own inheritance.

²⁵In those days Israel had no king; everyone did as he saw fit.

Ruth

START

The history books in the Old Testament overflow with blood and war and bad people doing bad things. But the book of Ruth isn't like that. It tells a great story of love, faith and family. And it's short!

Ruth isn't an Israelite. She's from Moab, a country next door to Israel. That's where she and her Israelite husband live, until the guy up and dies, leaving her a widow. Instead of moving back home or finding another Moabite husband, Ruth takes a bold step and moves to Bethlehem, Israel, to live with her Israelite mother-in-law Naomi (who, by the way, was also just widowed). That's where Ruth falls in love with a local guy named Boaz. They get married and have a son named Obed.

Here's the best part: Obed grows up and has a kid named Jesse. Ruth's grandson Jesse grows up and has a kid named—are you ready for this?—David. That's right, good old Ruth is the great-grandmother of Israel's all-time favorite king. And her family continues all the way on to—guess who?—Jesus!

CAST OF Characters

Ruth (ROOTH)
She didn't write this book, but she's the star character. She's not an Israelite, but she marries someone who is. Ruthy's a great woman.

Naomi (nay-OH-mee)
Ruth's Israelite mother-in-law and another great woman. When her husband and sons die (including Ruth's husband), she invites Ruth to come back to Bethlehem, Naomi's hometown. She becomes a matchmaker for Ruth and Boaz.

Boaz (BOE-az)
A good man related to Naomi's dead husband. In Jewish law, if a guy died, his relatives had the opportunity to marry his widow so that the land, property and wealth could stay in the family. That's what Boaz did for Naomi by marrying her daughter-in-law Ruth. (By the way, they call someone who does that a *kinsman-redeemer* because he redeems the future of his kinsman.)

Obed (OH-bed)
Ruth and Boaz's first kid. Obed grows up to become King David's granddad.

What's UP with That?

When Ruth married Boaz, she became a member of his tribe—Judah. It was a pretty popular tribe. Eventually it became the name of the whole country and rubbed off on the names of the region (Judea), religion (Judaism) and the people themselves (Jews).

Judah also became the *royal* tribe. Starting with Ruth's great-grandson David, most of the nation's kings came from this bloodline. Many centuries after David died, when the kingless Jews were being bullied by the Romans, they were hoping and praying for someone to rescue them like David did. They were looking for a king. To them, that meant someone from the tribe of Judah. They were looking for a descendant of David.

And that's exactly where King Jesus came from! Jesus' mom was married to Joseph, a great-great-great-... (you get the point) grandson of King David himself. And just to make sure no one missed the significance of this fact, God made sure that Jesus was born right when Joseph and Mary just happened to be visiting Bethlehem, the city of David, the capital of the good old tribe of Judah, right where Ruth and Boaz fell in love. Pretty amazing, isn't it? You can check out this family tree for yourself—it's listed in Matthew, chapter 1, page 1140.

PRETTY AMAZING!

Snap shots

- Wipeout... almost— Naomi and Ruth lose their husbands but stick together (*chapter 1*)

- Ruth gets a job— moves to Bethlehem, gets Boaz for a boss (*chapter 2*)

- Matchmaking—Naomi sets up the couple (*chapter 3*)

- Mr. & Mrs. Boaz—boss becomes husband, and baby makes 3 (*chapter 4*)

Naomi and Ruth

1 In the days when the judges ruled,[a] there was a famine in the land, and a man from Bethlehem in Judah, together with his wife and two sons, went to live for a while in the country of Moab. ²The man's name was Elimelech, his wife's name Naomi, and the names of his two sons were Mahlon and Kilion. They were Ephrathites from Bethlehem, Judah. And they went to Moab and lived there.

³Now Elimelech, Naomi's husband, died, and she was left with her two sons. ⁴They married Moabite women, one named Orpah and the other Ruth. After they had lived there about ten years, ⁵both Mahlon and Kilion also died, and Naomi was left without her two sons and her husband.

⁶When she heard in Moab that the LORD had come to the aid of his people by providing food for them, Naomi and her daughters-in-law prepared to return home from there. ⁷With her two daughters-in-law she left the place where she had been living and set out on the road that would take them back to the land of Judah.

⁸Then Naomi said to her two daughters-in-law, "Go back, each of you, to your mother's home. May the LORD show kindness to you, as you have shown to your dead and to me. ⁹May the LORD grant that each of you will find rest in the home of another husband."

Then she kissed them and they wept aloud ¹⁰and said to her, "We will go back with you to your people."

¹¹But Naomi said, "Return home, my daughters. Why would you come with me? Am I going to have any more sons, who could become your husbands?

a 1 Traditionally judged

Friday

I'm Going Too

Read Ruth 1:16-18

In this passage, Ruth is explaining to Naomi that she loves her and will stick with her through thick and thin. Now that's a great friend!

Not long ago, I heard a rumor about a friend of mine. People said she was talking about me behind my back. That really upset me and made me mad. I guess I believed the rumor about my friend without even stopping to think it might not be true. I should have remembered what a faithful friend she was. She had always stuck with me and been nice to me. There was no reason for me to doubt her friendship, except for this false rumor.

A real friend is a friend forever, not just for a summer or until you get out of the class you have together. And a real friend is loyal and faithful. God is that kind of friend. He never leaves us. Ruth understood this kind of faithfulness. I think that's why she wanted to do for Naomi what God had done for her.

Stacey age 13

What about You?

❶ Think about 2 of your closest friends. What do you like about them? What do you think they like about you?

❷ Call or e-mail your best bud and share how much you appreciate him or her.

❸ Thank God for faithful friends.

Turn to page 307 for your next devotion.

¹²Return home, my daughters; I am too old to have another husband. Even if I thought there was still hope for me—even if I had a husband tonight and then gave birth to sons— ¹³would you wait until they grew up? Would you remain unmarried for them? No, my daughters. It is more bitter for me than for you, because the LORD's hand has gone out against me!"

¹⁴At this they wept again. Then Orpah kissed her mother-in-law good-by, but Ruth clung to her.

¹⁵"Look," said Naomi, "your sister-in-law is going back to her people and her gods. Go back with her."

¹⁶But Ruth replied, "Don't urge me to leave you or to turn back from you. Where you go I will go, and where you stay I will stay. Your people will be my people and your God my God. ¹⁷Where you die I will die, and there I will be buried. May the LORD deal with me, be it ever so severely, if anything but death separates you and me." ¹⁸When Naomi realized that Ruth was determined to go with her, she stopped urging her.

¹⁹So the two women went on until they came to Bethlehem. When they arrived in Bethlehem, the whole town was stirred because of them, and the women exclaimed, "Can this be Naomi?"

²⁰"Don't call me Naomi,[a]" she told them. "Call me Mara,[b] because the Almighty[c] has made my life very bitter. ²¹I went away full, but the LORD has brought me back empty. Why call me Naomi? The LORD has afflicted[d] me; the Almighty has brought misfortune upon me."

²²So Naomi returned from Moab accompanied by Ruth the Moabitess, her daughter-in-law, arriving in Bethlehem as the barley harvest was beginning.

Ruth Meets Boaz

2 Now Naomi had a relative on her husband's side, from the clan of Elimelech, a man of standing, whose name was Boaz.

²And Ruth the Moabitess said to Naomi, "Let me go to the fields and pick up the leftover grain behind anyone in whose eyes I find favor."

Naomi said to her, "Go ahead, my daughter." ³So she went out and began to glean in the fields behind the harvesters. As it turned out, she found herself working in a field belonging to Boaz, who was from the clan of Elimelech.

⁴Just then Boaz arrived from Bethlehem and greeted the harvesters, "The LORD be with you!"

"The LORD bless you!" they called back.

⁵Boaz asked the foreman of his harvesters, "Whose young woman is that?"

⁶The foreman replied, "She is the Moabitess who came back from Moab with Naomi. ⁷She said, 'Please let me glean and gather among the sheaves behind the harvesters.' She went into the field and has worked steadily from morning till now, except for a short rest in the shelter."

Glean to the Right, Glean to the Left

Huh?

Ruth 2:6–7

Gleaning is the process of looking for good stuff left behind. This is what homeless people do when they look through a dumpster—they're hoping to find some food that's "good enough" to eat that someone left behind. For Ruth, gleaning meant walking behind the harvesters in a field, sorting through the remains of picked-over stalks and grain plants and looking for little bits of good food or grain. It was hard work for very little return.

⁸So Boaz said to Ruth, "My daughter, listen to me. Don't go and glean in another field and don't go away from here. Stay here with my servant girls. ⁹Watch the field where the men are harvesting, and follow along after the girls. I have told the men not to touch you. And whenever you are thirsty, go and get a drink from the water jars the men have filled."

¹⁰At this, she bowed down with her

---

[a]20 Naomi means pleasant; also in verse 21.
[b]20 Mara means bitter.   [c]20 Hebrew Shaddai; also in verse 21   [d]21 Or has testified against

face to the ground. She exclaimed, "Why have I found such favor in your eyes that you notice me—a foreigner?"

[11]Boaz replied, "I've been told all about what you have done for your mother-in-law since the death of your husband—how you left your father and mother and your homeland and came to live with a people you did not know before. [12]May the LORD repay you for what you have done. May you be richly rewarded by the LORD, the God of Israel, under whose wings you have come to take refuge."

[13]"May I continue to find favor in your eyes, my lord," she said. "You have given me comfort and have spoken kindly to your servant—though I do not have the standing of one of your servant girls."

[14]At mealtime Boaz said to her, "Come over here. Have some bread and dip it in the wine vinegar."

When she sat down with the harvesters, he offered her some roasted grain. She ate all she wanted and had some left over. [15]As she got up to glean, Boaz gave orders to his men, "Even if she gathers among the sheaves, don't embarrass her. [16]Rather, pull out some stalks for her from the bundles and leave them for her to pick up, and don't rebuke her."

[17]So Ruth gleaned in the field until evening. Then she threshed the barley she had gathered, and it amounted to about an ephah.[a] [18]She carried it back to town, and her mother-in-law saw how much she had gathered. Ruth also brought out and gave her what she had left over after she had eaten enough.

[19]Her mother-in-law asked her, "Where did you glean today? Where did you work? Blessed be the man who took notice of you!"

Then Ruth told her mother-in-law about the one at whose place she had been working. "The name of the man I worked with today is Boaz," she said.

[20]"The LORD bless him!" Naomi said to her daughter-in-law. "He has not stopped showing his kindness to the living and the dead." She added, "That man is our close relative; he is one of our kinsman-redeemers."

[21]Then Ruth the Moabitess said, "He even said to me, 'Stay with my workers until they finish harvesting all my grain.' "

[22]Naomi said to Ruth her daughter-in-law, "It will be good for you, my daughter, to go with his girls, because in someone else's field you might be harmed."

[23]So Ruth stayed close to the servant girls of Boaz to glean until the barley and wheat harvests were finished. And she lived with her mother-in-law.

Ruth and Boaz at the Threshing Floor

3 One day Naomi her mother-in-law said to her, "My daughter, should I not try to find a home[b] for you, where you will be well provided for? [2]Is not Boaz, with whose servant girls you have been, a kinsman of ours? Tonight he will be winnowing barley on the threshing floor. [3]Wash and perfume yourself, and put on your best clothes. Then go down to the threshing floor, but don't let him know you are there until he has finished eating and drinking. [4]When he lies down, note the place where he is lying. Then go and uncover his feet and lie down. He will tell you what to do."

[5]"I will do whatever you say," Ruth answered. [6]So she went down to the threshing floor and did everything her mother-in-law told her to do.

[7]When Boaz had finished eating and drinking and was in good spirits, he went over to lie down at the far end of the grain pile. Ruth approached quietly, uncovered his feet and lay down. [8]In the middle of the night something startled the man, and he turned and discovered a woman lying at his feet.

[9]"Who are you?" he asked.

"I am your servant Ruth," she said. "Spread the corner of your garment over me, since you are a kinsman-redeemer."

[10]"The LORD bless you, my daughter," he replied. "This kindness is greater than that which you showed earlier: You have not run after the younger men, whether rich or poor. [11]And now, my daughter, don't be afraid. I will do for you all you ask. All my fellow townsmen know that you are a woman of noble character.

---

[a]17 That is, probably about 3/5 bushel (about 22 liters)   [b]1 Hebrew *find rest* (see Ruth 1:9)

¹²Although it is true that I am near of kin, there is a kinsman-redeemer nearer than I. ¹³Stay here for the night, and in the morning if he wants to redeem, good; let him redeem. But if he is not willing, as surely as the LORD lives I will do it. Lie here until morning."

¹⁴So she lay at his feet until morning, but got up before anyone could be recognized; and he said, "Don't let it be known that a woman came to the threshing floor."

¹⁵He also said, "Bring me the shawl you are wearing and hold it out." When she did so, he poured into it six measures of barley and put it on her. Then he[a] went back to town.

¹⁶When Ruth came to her mother-in-law, Naomi asked, "How did it go, my daughter?"

Then she told her everything Boaz had done for her ¹⁷and added, "He gave me these six measures of barley, saying, 'Don't go back to your mother-in-law empty-handed.'"

¹⁸Then Naomi said, "Wait, my daughter, until you find out what happens. For

---

*a*15 Most Hebrew manuscripts; many Hebrew manuscripts, Vulgate and Syriac *she*

Week end.

"Whatever You Say . . ."

Read Ruth 3:1–6

One theme this week was trusting and obeying God. On Monday, Carissa said that "we should live our lives for him," and Robyn (Wednesday) reminded us that "God has a job for each of us." But obeying someone else is hard. The older you get, the more you want to make your own decisions, your own friends and your own plans. Sometimes your parents or step-parents ask you to do things that seem unreasonable, and the hardest thing in the world is to obey them. How *frustrating!*

But look at Ruth. She left home and married into a family in a new land. Her husband died. Then her brother-in-law, the last man in the family (really, really important in those days), kicked the bucket too. Even her sister-in-law ended up leaving. So Ruth was left with Naomi, her mother-in-law.

The quality that has made Ruth such a well-known and deeply loved heroine of the Bible was her willingness to listen to and obey Naomi, the person God had given Ruth to be her protector. If Ruth hadn't listened to Naomi, she would never have met Boaz, her future husband! (who was a totally cool guy, by the way). Naomi knew what was best for Ruth, and Ruth trusted her enough to obey her.

Sometimes the best way to obey God is to obey your parents (ouch).

❶ How hard is it for you to obey your parents (or guardian)? Are you more concerned with getting your own way than you are about listening to and learning from them?

❷ Make a commitment to try total obedience (no arguing or grumbling) for one week! Just try it!

❸ Pray for your parents (or guardian), and ask God to give you the ability to listen to them and to do what they say.

Turn to page 313 for your next devotion.

the man will not rest until the matter is settled today."

Boaz Marries Ruth

4 Meanwhile Boaz went up to the town gate and sat there. When the kinsman-redeemer he had mentioned came along, Boaz said, "Come over here, my friend, and sit down." So he went over and sat down.

²Boaz took ten of the elders of the town and said, "Sit here," and they did so. ³Then he said to the kinsman-redeemer, "Naomi, who has come back from Moab, is selling the piece of land that belonged to our brother Elimelech. ⁴I thought I should bring the matter to your attention and suggest that you buy it in the presence of these seated here and in the presence of the elders of my people. If you will redeem it, do so. But if you*ᵃ* will not, tell me, so I will know. For no one has the right to do it except you, and I am next in line."

"I will redeem it," he said.

⁵Then Boaz said, "On the day you buy the land from Naomi and from Ruth the Moabitess, you acquire*ᵇ* the dead man's widow, in order to maintain the name of the dead with his property."

⁶At this, the kinsman-redeemer said, "Then I cannot redeem it because I might endanger my own estate. You redeem it yourself. I cannot do it."

⁷(Now in earlier times in Israel, for the redemption and transfer of property to become final, one party took off his sandal and gave it to the other. This was the method of legalizing transactions in Israel.)

⁸So the kinsman-redeemer said to Boaz, "Buy it yourself." And he removed his sandal.

⁹Then Boaz announced to the elders and all the people, "Today you are witnesses that I have bought from Naomi all the property of Elimelech, Kilion and Mahlon. ¹⁰I have also acquired Ruth the Moabitess, Mahlon's widow, as my wife, in order to maintain the name of the dead with his property, so that his name will not disappear from among his family or from the town records. Today you are witnesses!"

¹¹Then the elders and all those at the gate said, "We are witnesses. May the LORD make the woman who is coming into your home like Rachel and Leah, who together built up the house of Israel. May you have standing in Ephrathah and be famous in Bethlehem. ¹²Through the

The "Kinsman-redeemer"

Huh?

Ruth 4:9–11

Kinsman is a family member, and a *redeemer* is somebody that "buys back" or "restores" something. In Ruth's day when a man died, a family member had to buy his land and stuff from the guy's mom and also marry the guy's wife, to keep it in the family (that's why he was called a kinsman-redeemer). Boaz was Ruth's kinsman-redeemer. Major bonus: They totally loved each other.

offspring the LORD gives you by this young woman, may your family be like that of Perez, whom Tamar bore to Judah."

The Genealogy of David

¹³So Boaz took Ruth and she became his wife. Then he went to her, and the LORD enabled her to conceive, and she gave birth to a son. ¹⁴The women said to Naomi: "Praise be to the LORD, who this day has not left you without a kinsman-redeemer. May he become famous throughout Israel! ¹⁵He will renew your life and sustain you in your old age. For your daughter-in-law, who loves you and who is better to you than seven sons, has given him birth."

¹⁶Then Naomi took the child, laid him in her lap and cared for him. ¹⁷The women living there said, "Naomi has a son." And they named him Obed. He was the father of Jesse, the father of David.

¹⁸This, then, is the family line of Perez:

ᵃ4 Many Hebrew manuscripts, Septuagint, Vulgate and Syriac; most Hebrew manuscripts *he*
ᵇ5 Hebrew; Vulgate and Syriac *Naomi, you acquire Ruth the Moabitess,*

Perez was the father of Hezron,
¹⁹Hezron the father of Ram,
  Ram the father of Amminadab,
²⁰Amminadab the father of Nahshon,
  Nahshon the father of Salmon,ᵃ
²¹Salmon the father of Boaz,
  Boaz the father of Obed,

²²Obed the father of Jesse,
  and Jesse the father of David.

ᵃ20 A few Hebrew manuscripts, some Septuagint manuscripts and Vulgate (see also verse 21 and Septuagint of 1 Chron. 2:11); most Hebrew manuscripts *Salma*

Women Who Changed History

Let's face it: The Bible mentions more men than women. The table of contents is your first clue. Just 2 books are named after women: Ruth and Esther. The guys get their names on 37 books, plus 2 books of Kings (not Queens). But that doesn't mean the women aren't important. Here are some of these world-changing women:

Moses' Mom gives birth to a baby boy. When Pharaoh commands all the Israelite moms to toss their baby boys into the Nile, this great woman obeys the rule . . . with one minor adjustment. She sticks her baby in a basket first. He floats, gets found, gets named and eventually leads the Israelites to freedom (Exodus 2:1–10, page 72).

Rahab is a prostitute in Jericho, a city that's the first stop on the Israelites' journey to conquer the promised land. She hides the Israelite spies who sneak into the city, lies to the cops about it and then helps the spies escape. If she had refused to help them, the Israelites waiting for the spies' report might have chickened out and spent another 40 years wandering in the desert (Joshua 2:1–16, page 246).

Ruth is a Moabite. When her Jewish husband dies, Ruth leaves her country to live with her mother-in-law in Israel. She marries again, has a kid named Obed, a grandkid named Jesse and a great-grandkid named David, who grows up to be a king. By the way, one of her very distant grandkids turns out to be Jesus (book of Ruth).

Hannah wants to have kids, but her pregnancy tests keep coming back negative. So she makes a deal with God: Let me have a kid, and I'll give the kid back to you. God keeps his part, Hannah keeps her part, and baby Samuel grows up in the home of Eli the priest. A couple of books in the Old Testament are written about Samuel's life and how he shook Israel back to its spiritual roots (1 Samuel 1:9–28, page 312).

Mary is a teenager, a virgin and engaged to a carpenter. Along comes an angel telling her she's about to become pregnant . . . with *God's Son!* She doesn't freak out about what her fiancé Joseph will say or what their families will do when they find out she's pregnant. Mary just accepts the job of being Jesus' mom, and she becomes the most loved woman the world has ever known (Luke 1:26–38, page 1218).

1 Samuel

START

CAST
OF
Characters

Samuel is the miracle baby of a childless woman named Hannah. She makes a promise to God that if he grants her a child, she'll give the tot back to him in thanks. God gives Hannah her wish and along comes Samuel. To hold up her end of the bargain, Hannah asks Eli, a priest, to raise her son in the temple and teach him how to follow God. While still a kid, Samuel gets the chance of a lifetime—God talks to him! How totally cool. God tells Samuel some ear-tingling news about his plans for the future.

As an adult, Samuel helps the people of Israel come to their senses, and they get down on their knees to God. Unfortunately, in all their excitement they start begging for a king. "You've got a King," says Samuel (that would be God). But they insist on the earthly king, so Samuel appoints Saul . . . a sorry choice, as it turns out.

This book covers these and lots of other big events that span a century of Israel's history, including King Saul's foolish bouts with evil, and the many adventures of David on his winding way to the throne.

Samuel

Remember all those judges in the book of Judges? Sam's the last one. After him, Israel does the king thing. Samuel is a great leader, a big-time prayer warrior. At the start of the book, he's a baby. By the end, he's an old man. He rocks for God through it all.

Hannah

Hannah wants to have a baby, but she can't get pregnant. Hannah makes a promise to God: "Give me a baby, and I'll give it back."

Jonathan

When King Saul gets it in his messed-up mind to kill young David, the king's son Jonathan saves David—they're buds. As it turns out, David becomes king—a job Prince Jon could have claimed for himself. But God

chose David instead, and Jon supported Dave all the way.

David

After a sorry start with Saul, Israel gets a new and better king. David's the youngest of his brothers (there were at least 8 of 'em); he's a shepherd and part-time harp player for the king he eventually replaces. He's not perfect, but he's gutsy, patient and totally loves God.

Eli

He's Priest #1—but not so good in the parenting department . . . at least not the first time around. His real sons are a total disgrace, sleeping with prostitutes and snacking on sacrifices. But Eli gets a second chance at raising a child when Samuel comes on the scene.

Saul

Israel's first king. Saul starts out humble, then gets

wigged-out on wickedness later. God and Samuel give Saul lots of chances to get straight, but he eventually stops listening to them and dies a miserable man.

Abigail

She's married to a loud-mouth named Nabal. When Loudmouth's mocking of the king is about to get him killed, Abigail's smooth words and sweet gifts to King David save the day. Then Loudmouth gets drunk, has a stroke and dies. David sends Abigail his condolences . . . and a marriage proposal. She says thank you . . . and yes.

What's UP with That?

One day King Saul thinks David's an OK guy, the next he's trying to shish-ka-bob David on a spear. David has plenty of chances to kill Saul, but he doesn't dare strike the king—especially one appointed by God. Finally, David decides to drop by the palace and make peace with Saul. But what if the king's in one of his murderous moods? How will Dave know "the coast is clear" to come inside? Jonathan and David are best buds. They figure out a plan. First, Jon will get a reading on his dad's feelings about David. Then he'll go outside and send a signal to Dave, who will be hiding in the field next door. Read 1 Samuel 20:18–22, then answer these questions:

❶ What is Jonathan going to shoot in the field?
   a. the messenger   c. a spear
   b. arrows   d. an elephant gun

❷ Who is Jonathan going to send to retrieve what he shot?
   a. a boy   c. a golden retriever
   b. a search party   d. David

❸ What is Jonathan going to shout if the king is in a good mood and the coast is clear?
   a. "The coast is clear"   c. "One if by land, two if by sea"
   b. "The eagle has landed" d. "Bring them here"

❹ But if the king is in a rotten mood, ready to kill David on sight, what will Jonathan shout?
   a. "Houston, we have a problem"
   b. "The arrows are beyond you"
   c. "There's a bee in a certain someone's bonnet"
   d. "The moose is loose"

Bonus Question: When it came time to send the signal to David, what did Jonathan actually shout?
   a. "The arrow fell short"
   b. "The arrow is still ahead of you"
   c. "Be a good little boy and hand over the bow"
   d. "Call an ambulance—I think I just shot my friend"

Snap shots

- Hannah prays, God delivers . . . Samuel! (chapters 1—2)

- The final judge—Samuel gets a call from God (chapter 3)

- Philistine follies—trouble with the enemy, something stolen and returned (chapters 4—7)

- "King, please"—Israel requests a royal ruler (chapter 8)

- Good start—Saul takes the throne, Samuel says goodbye (chapters 9—12)

- Sorry Saul—king messes up, tries to do better (chapters 13—15)

- "Go Dave!"—while future king conquers, Saul sinks his own kingship (chapters 16—31)

The Birth of Samuel

1 There was a certain man from Ramathaim, a Zuphite[a] from the hill country of Ephraim, whose name was Elkanah son of Jeroham, the son of Elihu, the son of Tohu, the son of Zuph, an Ephraimite. [2]He had two wives; one was called Hannah and the other Peninnah. Peninnah had children, but Hannah had none.

[3]Year after year this man went up from his town to worship and sacrifice to the LORD Almighty at Shiloh, where Hophni and Phinehas, the two sons of Eli, were priests of the LORD. [4]Whenever the day came for Elkanah to sacrifice, he would give portions of the meat to his wife Peninnah and to all her sons and daughters. [5]But to Hannah he gave a double portion because he loved her, and the LORD had closed her womb. [6]And because the LORD had closed her womb, her rival kept provoking her in order to irritate her. [7]This went on year after year. Whenever Hannah went up to the house of the LORD, her rival provoked her till she wept and would not eat. [8]Elkanah her husband would say to her, "Hannah, why are you weeping? Why don't you eat? Why are you downhearted? Don't I mean more to you than ten sons?"

[9]Once when they had finished eating and drinking in Shiloh, Hannah stood up. Now Eli the priest was sitting on a chair by the doorpost of the LORD's temple.[b] [10]In bitterness of soul Hannah wept much and prayed to the LORD. [11]And she made a vow, saying, "O LORD Almighty, if you will only look upon your servant's misery and remember me, and not forget your servant but give her a son, then I will give him to the LORD for all the days of his life, and no razor will ever be used on his head."

[12]As she kept on praying to the LORD, Eli observed her mouth. [13]Hannah was praying in her heart, and her lips were moving but her voice was not heard. Eli thought she was drunk [14]and said to her, "How long will you keep on getting drunk? Get rid of your wine."

[15]"Not so, my lord," Hannah replied, "I am a woman who is deeply troubled. I have not been drinking wine or beer; I was pouring out my soul to the LORD. [16]Do not take your servant for a wicked woman; I have been praying here out of my great anguish and grief."

[17]Eli answered, "Go in peace, and may the God of Israel grant you what you have asked of him."

[18]She said, "May your servant find favor in your eyes." Then she went her way and ate something, and her face was no longer downcast.

[19]Early the next morning they arose and worshiped before the LORD and then went back to their home at Ramah. Elkanah lay with Hannah his wife, and the LORD remembered her. [20]So in the course of time Hannah conceived and gave birth to a son. She named him Samuel,[c] saying, "Because I asked the LORD for him."

Hannah Dedicates Samuel

[21]When the man Elkanah went up with all his family to offer the annual sacrifice to the LORD and to fulfill his vow, [22]Hannah did not go. She said to her husband, "After the boy is weaned, I will take him and present him before the LORD, and he will live there always."

[23]"Do what seems best to you," Elkanah her husband told her. "Stay here until you have weaned him; only may the LORD make good his[d] word." So the woman stayed at home and nursed her son until she had weaned him. [24]After he was weaned, she took the boy with her, young as he was, along with a three-year-old bull,[e] an ephah[f] of flour and a skin of wine, and brought him to the house of the LORD at Shiloh. [25]When they had slaughtered the bull, they brought the boy to Eli, [26]and she said to him, "As surely as you live, my lord, I am the woman who stood here beside you praying to the LORD. [27]I prayed for this child, and the LORD has granted me what I asked of him. [28]So now I give him to the LORD. For his whole life he will be given over to the LORD." And he worshiped the LORD there.

---

[a]1 Or from Ramathaim Zuphim   [b]9 That is, tabernacle   [c]20 Samuel sounds like the Hebrew for heard of God.   [d]23 Masoretic Text; Dead Sea Scrolls, Septuagint and Syriac your   [e]24 Dead Sea Scrolls, Septuagint and Syriac; Masoretic Text with three bulls   [f]24 That is, probably about 3/5 bushel (about 22 liters)

Hannah's Prayer

2 Then Hannah prayed and said:

"My heart rejoices in the LORD;
   in the LORD my horn*a* is lifted high.
My mouth boasts over my enemies,
   for I delight in your deliverance.

[2] "There is no one holy*b* like the LORD;
   there is no one besides you;
   there is no Rock like our God.

[3] "Do not keep talking so proudly
   or let your mouth speak such
      arrogance,
for the LORD is a God who knows,
   and by him deeds are weighed.

[4] "The bows of the warriors are broken,
   but those who stumbled are armed
      with strength.

[5] Those who were full hire themselves
      out for food,
   but those who were hungry hunger
      no more.
She who was barren has borne seven
      children,
   but she who has had many sons
      pines away.

[6] "The LORD brings death and makes
      alive;
   he brings down to the grave*c* and
      raises up.

[7] The LORD sends poverty and wealth;
   he humbles and he exalts.

[8] He raises the poor from the dust
   and lifts the needy from the ash
      heap;

---

a1 Horn here symbolizes strength; also in verse 10.
b2 Or *no Holy One*   *c6* Hebrew *Sheol*

Monday

Someone Who Really Listens

Read 1 Samuel 1

A few months ago, I was praying for my friend Annie. She had a serious back problem called scoliosis, and she was scared she might have to have surgery. So in my prayers, I asked God to heal Annie's back.

Well, a few weeks later, Annie's back started to get better. We were at camp and people were praying for her. The pain she'd felt for months started to go away. It was a complete miracle! Now she doesn't have to have surgery, and she feels so much better.

That whole experience proved to me that God really does answer prayers. We're not talking to a brick wall when we pray—we're talking to Someone who really listens. That doesn't mean God will answer our prayers right away or give us everything we ask for. But even if Annie had needed surgery, I know God still would have answered our prayers by keeping her safe.

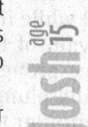 Josh age 15

 What about You?

❶ In this chapter, Hannah tells God she's sad and angry. When was the last time you were completely honest with God? Why do you think we are sometimes afraid to ask God for what we really want?

❷ For the next few days write down the things you pray about. Keep those notes handy. Whenever you feel like God has answered one of your prayers—and the answer might be no—write that down on the same list. (Remember, you might not be able to check everything off your list—God works in his time, not ours.)

❸ Think of your prayers as a chance to be really honest with God about what you want out of life. Then trust God to give you his best.

Turn to page 319 for your next devotion.

he seats them with princes
   and has them inherit a throne of
     honor.

"For the foundations of the earth are
   the LORD's;
   upon them he has set the world.
⁹He will guard the feet of his saints,
   but the wicked will be silenced in
     darkness.

"It is not by strength that one
   prevails;
10   those who oppose the LORD will be
     shattered.
He will thunder against them from
    heaven;
   the LORD will judge the ends of the
    earth.

"He will give strength to his king
   and exalt the horn of his anointed."

¹¹Then Elkanah went home to Ramah, but the boy ministered before the LORD under Eli the priest.

Eli's Wicked Sons

¹²Eli's sons were wicked men; they had no regard for the LORD. ¹³Now it was the practice of the priests with the people that whenever anyone offered a sacrifice and while the meat was being boiled, the servant of the priest would come with a three-pronged fork in his hand. ¹⁴He would plunge it into the pan or kettle or caldron or pot, and the priest would take for himself whatever the fork brought up. This is how they treated all the Israelites who came to Shiloh. ¹⁵But even before the fat was burned, the servant of the priest would come and say to the man who was sacrificing, "Give the priest some meat to roast; he won't accept boiled meat from you, but only raw."

¹⁶If the man said to him, "Let the fat be burned up first, and then take whatever you want," the servant would then answer, "No, hand it over now; if you don't, I'll take it by force."

¹⁷This sin of the young men was very great in the LORD's sight, for they[a] were treating the LORD's offering with contempt.

¹⁸But Samuel was ministering before the LORD—a boy wearing a linen ephod. ¹⁹Each year his mother made him a little robe and took it to him when she went up with her husband to offer the annual sacrifice. ²⁰Eli would bless Elkanah and his wife, saying, "May the LORD give you children by this woman to take the place of the one she prayed for and gave to the LORD." Then they would go home. ²¹And the LORD was gracious to Hannah; she conceived and gave birth to three sons and two daughters. Meanwhile, the boy Samuel grew up in the presence of the LORD.

²²Now Eli, who was very old, heard about everything his sons were doing to all Israel and how they slept with the women who served at the entrance to the Tent of Meeting. ²³So he said to them, "Why do you do such things? I hear from all the people about these wicked deeds of yours. ²⁴No, my sons; it is not a good report that I hear spreading among the LORD's people. ²⁵If a man sins against another man, God[b] may mediate for him; but if a man sins against the LORD, who will intercede for him?" His sons, however, did not listen to their father's rebuke, for it was the LORD's will to put them to death.

²⁶And the boy Samuel continued to grow in stature and in favor with the LORD and with men.

Prophecy Against the House of Eli

²⁷Now a man of God came to Eli and said to him, "This is what the LORD says: 'Did I not clearly reveal myself to your father's house when they were in Egypt under Pharaoh? ²⁸I chose your father out of all the tribes of Israel to be my priest, to go up to my altar, to burn incense, and to wear an ephod in my presence. I also gave your father's house all the offerings made with fire by the Israelites. ²⁹Why do you[c] scorn my sacrifice and offering that I prescribed for my dwelling? Why do you honor your sons more than me by fattening yourselves on the choice parts of every offering made by my people Israel?'

³⁰"Therefore the LORD, the God of Israel, declares: 'I promised that your house and your father's house would minister

---

a 17 Or *men*   *b 25* Or *the judges*   *c 29* The Hebrew is plural.

before me forever.' But now the LORD declares: 'Far be it from me! Those who honor me I will honor, but those who despise me will be disdained. ³¹The time is coming when I will cut short your strength and the strength of your father's house, so that there will not be an old man in your family line ³²and you will see distress in my dwelling. Although good will be done to Israel, in your family line there will never be an old man. ³³Every one of you that I do not cut off from my altar will be spared only to blind your eyes with tears and to grieve your heart, and all your descendants will die in the prime of life.

³⁴" 'And what happens to your two sons, Hophni and Phinehas, will be a sign to you—they will both die on the same day. ³⁵I will raise up for myself a faithful priest, who will do according to what is in my heart and mind. I will firmly establish his house, and he will minister before my anointed one always. ³⁶Then everyone left in your family line will come and bow down before him for a piece of silver and a crust of bread and plead, "Appoint me to some priestly office so I can have food to eat." ' "

The LORD Calls Samuel

3 The boy Samuel ministered before the LORD under Eli. In those days the word of the LORD was rare; there were not many visions.

²One night Eli, whose eyes were becoming so weak that he could barely see, was lying down in his usual place. ³The lamp of God had not yet gone out, and Samuel was lying down in the temple[a] of the LORD, where the ark of God was. ⁴Then the LORD called Samuel.

Samuel answered, "Here I am." ⁵And he ran to Eli and said, "Here I am; you called me."

But Eli said, "I did not call; go back and lie down." So he went and lay down.

⁶Again the LORD called, "Samuel!" And Samuel got up and went to Eli and said, "Here I am; you called me."

"My son," Eli said, "I did not call; go back and lie down."

⁷Now Samuel did not yet know the LORD: The word of the LORD had not yet been revealed to him.

⁸The LORD called Samuel a third time, and Samuel got up and went to Eli and said, "Here I am; you called me."

Then Eli realized that the LORD was calling the boy. ⁹So Eli told Samuel, "Go and lie down, and if he calls you, say, 'Speak, LORD, for your servant is listening.' " So Samuel went and lay down in his place.

¹⁰The LORD came and stood there, calling as at the other times, "Samuel! Samuel!"

Hello, This Is God

Huh?

1 Samuel 3:10

Would you recognize God's voice if he spoke to you? Do you expect the telephone to ring, or to receive an e-mail? Or maybe you check to see what's going on at www.God.com? Look at verses 4 through 10 and see how God called Samuel. It's comforting to see that even Samuel didn't know God's voice.

Then Samuel said, "Speak, for your servant is listening."

¹¹And the LORD said to Samuel: "See, I am about to do something in Israel that will make the ears of everyone who hears of it tingle. ¹²At that time I will carry out against Eli everything I spoke against his family—from beginning to end. ¹³For I told him that I would judge his family forever because of the sin he knew about; his sons made themselves contemptible,[b] and he failed to restrain them. ¹⁴Therefore, I swore to the house of Eli, 'The guilt of Eli's house will never be atoned for by sacrifice or offering.' "

¹⁵Samuel lay down until morning and then opened the doors of the house of the LORD. He was afraid to tell Eli the vision, ¹⁶but Eli called him and said, "Samuel, my son."

Samuel answered, "Here I am."

---

[a]3 That is, tabernacle   [b]13 Masoretic Text; an ancient Hebrew scribal tradition and Septuagint sons blasphemed God

[17] "What was it he said to you?" Eli asked. "Do not hide it from me. May God deal with you, be it ever so severely, if you hide from me anything he told you." [18] So Samuel told him everything, hiding nothing from him. Then Eli said, "He is the LORD; let him do what is good in his eyes."

[19] The LORD was with Samuel as he grew up, and he let none of his words fall to the ground. [20] And all Israel from Dan to Beersheba recognized that Samuel was attested as a prophet of the LORD. [21] The LORD continued to appear at Shiloh, and there he revealed himself to Samuel through his word.

[4] And Samuel's word came to all Israel.

The Philistines Capture the Ark

Now the Israelites went out to fight against the Philistines. The Israelites camped at Ebenezer, and the Philistines at Aphek. [2] The Philistines deployed their forces to meet Israel, and as the battle spread, Israel was defeated by the Philistines, who killed about four thousand of them on the battlefield. [3] When the soldiers returned to camp, the elders of Israel asked, "Why did the LORD bring defeat upon us today before the Philistines? Let us bring the ark of the LORD's covenant from Shiloh, so that it[a] may go with us and save us from the hand of our enemies."

[4] So the people sent men to Shiloh, and they brought back the ark of the covenant of the LORD Almighty, who is enthroned between the cherubim. And Eli's two sons, Hophni and Phinehas, were there with the ark of the covenant of God.

[5] When the ark of the LORD's covenant came into the camp, all Israel raised such a great shout that the ground shook. [6] Hearing the uproar, the Philistines asked, "What's all this shouting in the Hebrew camp?"

When they learned that the ark of the LORD had come into the camp, [7] the Philistines were afraid. "A god has come into the camp," they said. "We're in trouble! Nothing like this has happened before. [8] Woe to us! Who will deliver us from the hand of these mighty gods? They are the gods who struck the Egyptians with all kinds of plagues in the desert. [9] Be strong, Philistines! Be men, or you will be subject to the Hebrews, as they have been to you. Be men, and fight!"

[10] So the Philistines fought, and the Israelites were defeated and every man fled to his tent. The slaughter was very great; Israel lost thirty thousand foot soldiers. [11] The ark of God was captured, and Eli's two sons, Hophni and Phinehas, died.

Death of Eli

[12] That same day a Benjamite ran from the battle line and went to Shiloh, his clothes torn and dust on his head. [13] When he arrived, there was Eli sitting on his chair by the side of the road, watching, because his heart feared for the ark of God. When the man entered the town and told what had happened, the whole town sent up a cry. [14] Eli heard the outcry and asked, "What is the meaning of this uproar?"

The man hurried over to Eli, [15] who was ninety-eight years old and whose eyes were set so that he could not see. [16] He told Eli, "I have just come from the battle line; I fled from it this very day."

Eli asked, "What happened, my son?"

[17] The man who brought the news replied, "Israel fled before the Philistines, and the army has suffered heavy losses. Also your two sons, Hophni and Phinehas, are dead, and the ark of God has been captured."

[18] When he mentioned the ark of God, Eli fell backward off his chair by the side of the gate. His neck was broken and he died, for he was an old man and heavy. He had led[b] Israel forty years.

[19] His daughter-in-law, the wife of Phinehas, was pregnant and near the time of delivery. When she heard the news that the ark of God had been captured and that her father-in-law and her husband were dead, she went into labor and gave birth, but was overcome by her labor pains. [20] As she was dying, the women attending her said, "Don't despair; you have given birth to a son." But she did not respond or pay any attention.

a 3 Or he   b 18 Traditionally judged

²¹She named the boy Ichabod,ᵃ saying, "The glory has departed from Israel"—because of the capture of the ark of God and the deaths of her father-in-law and her husband. ²²She said, "The glory has departed from Israel, for the ark of God has been captured."

The Ark in Ashdod and Ekron

5 After the Philistines had captured the ark of God, they took it from Ebenezer to Ashdod. ²Then they carried the ark into Dagon's temple and set it beside Dagon. ³When the people of Ashdod rose early the next day, there was Dagon, fallen on his face on the ground before the ark of the LORD! They took Dagon and put him back in his place. ⁴But the following morning when they rose, there was Dagon, fallen on his face on the ground before the ark of the LORD! His head and hands had been broken off and were lying on the threshold; only his body remained. ⁵That is why to this day neither the priests of Dagon nor any others who enter Dagon's temple at Ashdod step on the threshold.

⁶The LORD's hand was heavy upon the people of Ashdod and its vicinity; he brought devastation upon them and afflicted them with tumors.ᵇ ⁷When the men of Ashdod saw what was happening, they said, "The ark of the god of Israel must not stay here with us, because his hand is heavy upon us and upon Dagon our god." ⁸So they called together all the rulers of the Philistines and asked them, "What shall we do with the ark of the god of Israel?"

They answered, "Have the ark of the god of Israel moved to Gath." So they moved the ark of the God of Israel.

⁹But after they had moved it, the LORD's hand was against that city, throwing it into a great panic. He afflicted the people of the city, both young and old, with an outbreak of tumors.ᶜ ¹⁰So they sent the ark of God to Ekron.

As the ark of God was entering Ekron, the people of Ekron cried out, "They have brought the ark of the god of Israel around to us to kill us and our people." ¹¹So they called together all the rulers of the Philistines and said, "Send the ark of the god of Israel away; let it go back to its own place, or itᵈ will kill us and our people." For death had filled the city with panic; God's hand was very heavy upon it. ¹²Those who did not die were afflicted with tumors, and the outcry of the city went up to heaven.

The Ark Returned to Israel

6 When the ark of the LORD had been in Philistine territory seven months, ²the Philistines called for the priests and the diviners and said, "What shall we do with the ark of the LORD? Tell us how we should send it back to its place."

³They answered, "If you return the ark of the god of Israel, do not send it away empty, but by all means send a guilt offering to him. Then you will be healed, and you will know why his hand has not been lifted from you."

⁴The Philistines asked, "What guilt offering should we send to him?"

They replied, "Five gold tumors and five gold rats, according to the number of the Philistine rulers, because the same plague has struck both you and your rulers. ⁵Make models of the tumors and of the rats that are destroying the country, and pay honor to Israel's god. Perhaps he will lift his hand from you and your gods and your land. ⁶Why do you harden your hearts as the Egyptians and Pharaoh did? When heᵉ treated them harshly, did they not send the Israelites out so they could go on their way?

⁷"Now then, get a new cart ready, with two cows that have calved and have never been yoked. Hitch the cows to the cart, but take their calves away and pen them up. ⁸Take the ark of the LORD and put it on the cart, and in a chest beside it put the gold objects you are sending back to him as a guilt offering. Send it on its way, ⁹but keep watching it. If it goes up to its own territory, toward Beth Shemesh, then the LORD has brought this great disaster on us. But if it does not, then we will know that it was not his hand that struck us and that it happened to us by chance."

ᵃ21 *Ichabod* means *no glory.*   ᵇ6 Hebrew; Septuagint and Vulgate *tumors. And rats appeared in their land, and death and destruction were throughout the city*   ᶜ9 Or *with tumors in the groin* (see Septuagint)   ᵈ11 Or *he*   ᵉ6 That is, God

[10]So they did this. They took two such cows and hitched them to the cart and penned up their calves. [11]They placed the ark of the LORD on the cart and along with it the chest containing the gold rats and the models of the tumors. [12]Then the cows went straight up toward Beth Shemesh, keeping on the road and lowing all the way; they did not turn to the right or to the left. The rulers of the Philistines followed them as far as the border of Beth Shemesh.

[13]Now the people of Beth Shemesh were harvesting their wheat in the valley, and when they looked up and saw the ark, they rejoiced at the sight. [14]The cart came to the field of Joshua of Beth Shemesh, and there it stopped beside a large rock. The people chopped up the wood of the cart and sacrificed the cows as a burnt offering to the LORD. [15]The Levites took down the ark of the LORD, together with the chest containing the gold objects, and placed them on the large rock. On that day the people of Beth Shemesh offered burnt offerings and made sacrifices to the LORD. [16]The five rulers of the Philistines saw all this and then returned that same day to Ekron.

[17]These are the gold tumors the Philistines sent as a guilt offering to the LORD—one each for Ashdod, Gaza, Ashkelon, Gath and Ekron. [18]And the number of the gold rats was according to the number of Philistine towns belonging to the five rulers—the fortified towns with their country villages. The large rock, on which[a] they set the ark of the LORD, is a witness to this day in the field of Joshua of Beth Shemesh.

[19]But God struck down some of the men of Beth Shemesh, putting seventy[b] of them to death because they had looked into the ark of the LORD. The people mourned because of the heavy blow the LORD had dealt them, [20]and the men of Beth Shemesh asked, "Who can stand in the presence of the LORD, this holy God? To whom will the ark go up from here?"

[21]Then they sent messengers to the people of Kiriath Jearim, saying, "The Philistines have returned the ark of the LORD. Come down and take it up to your place." [1]So the men of Kiriath Jearim came and took up the ark of the

7

LORD. They took it to Abinadab's house on the hill and consecrated Eleazar his son to guard the ark of the LORD.

Samuel Subdues the Philistines at Mizpah

[2]It was a long time, twenty years in all, that the ark remained at Kiriath Jearim, and all the people of Israel mourned and sought after the LORD. [3]And Samuel said to the whole house of Israel, "If you are returning to the LORD with all your hearts, then rid yourselves of the foreign gods and the Ashtoreths and commit yourselves to the LORD and serve him only, and he will deliver you out of the hand of the Philistines." [4]So the Israelites put away their Baals and Ashtoreths, and served the LORD only.

[5]Then Samuel said, "Assemble all Israel at Mizpah and I will intercede with the LORD for you." [6]When they had assembled at Mizpah, they drew water and poured it out before the LORD. On that day they fasted and there they confessed, "We have sinned against the LORD." And Samuel was leader[c] of Israel at Mizpah.

[7]When the Philistines heard that Israel had assembled at Mizpah, the rulers of the Philistines came up to attack them. And when the Israelites heard of it, they were afraid because of the Philistines. [8]They said to Samuel, "Do not stop crying out to the LORD our God for us, that he may rescue us from the hand of the Philistines." [9]Then Samuel took a suckling lamb and offered it up as a whole burnt offering to the LORD. He cried out to the LORD on Israel's behalf, and the LORD answered him.

[10]While Samuel was sacrificing the burnt offering, the Philistines drew near to engage Israel in battle. But that day the LORD thundered with loud thunder against the Philistines and threw them into such a panic that they were routed before the Israelites. [11]The men of Israel rushed out of Mizpah and pursued the Philistines, slaughtering them along the way to a point below Beth Car.

[12]Then Samuel took a stone and set it

---

[a]18 A few Hebrew manuscripts (see also Septuagint); most Hebrew manuscripts *villages as far as Greater Abel, where*　[b]19 A few Hebrew manuscripts; most Hebrew manuscripts and Septuagint *50,070*　[c]6 Traditionally *judge*

up between Mizpah and Shen. He named it Ebenezer,ᵃ saying, "Thus far has the LORD helped us." ¹³So the Philistines were subdued and did not invade Israelite territory again.

Throughout Samuel's lifetime, the hand of the LORD was against the Philistines. ¹⁴The towns from Ekron to Gath that the Philistines had captured from Israel were restored to her, and Israel delivered the neighboring territory from the power of the Philistines. And there was peace between Israel and the Amorites.

¹⁵Samuel continued as judge over Israel all the days of his life. ¹⁶From year to year he went on a circuit from Bethel to Gilgal to Mizpah, judging Israel in all those places. ¹⁷But he always went back to Ramah, where his home was, and there he also judged Israel. And he built an altar there to the LORD.

Israel Asks for a King

8 When Samuel grew old, he appointed his sons as judges for Israel. ²The name of his firstborn was Joel and the name of his second was Abijah, and they served at Beersheba. ³But his sons did not walk in his ways. They turned aside after dishonest gain and accepted bribes and perverted justice.

⁴So all the elders of Israel gathered together and came to Samuel at Ramah. ⁵They said to him, "You are old, and your sons do not walk in your ways; now appoint a king to leadᵇ us, such as all the other nations have."

⁶But when they said, "Give us a king to lead us," this displeased Samuel; so he prayed to the LORD. ⁷And the LORD told him: "Listen to all that the people are saying to you; it is not you they have rejected, but they have rejected me as their king. ⁸As they have done from the day I brought them up out of Egypt until this day, forsaking me and serving other gods, so they are doing to you. ⁹Now listen to them; but warn them solemnly and

ᵃ12 Ebenezer means stone of help.   ᵇ5 Traditionally judge; also in verses 6 and 20

Tuesday

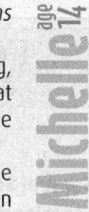

Believe It or Not

Read 1 Samuel 8:4–9

About a year ago, I had doubts about my faith. I would always be asking myself, *Is God really real? And if he is, why doesn't he ever show me signs of him being here?*

The Israelites felt sort of the same way. They wanted an earthly king, just like the other nations. They didn't have enough faith to believe that God was the best ruler for them. God quickly reminded them that he is the ultimate King, the only ruler Israel needed.

I think that all of us wonder where God is sometimes. We want someone we can see. But God wants us to trust him and have faith in him, even when we can't see him.

Michelle age 14

❶ Have you ever felt like God wasn't around? How did God eventually let you know that wasn't the case?

❷ For the next week, watch the weather. Think about how God is like the moon; some days he's easy to see, some days he's not, but no matter what, he's always there.

❸ Ask God to help you see him working in your life.

Turn to page 329 for your next devotion.

let them know what the king who will reign over them will do."

¹⁰Samuel told all the words of the LORD to the people who were asking him for a king. ¹¹He said, "This is what the king who will reign over you will do: He will take your sons and make them serve with his chariots and horses, and they will run in front of his chariots. ¹²Some he will assign to be commanders of thousands and commanders of fifties, and others to plow his ground and reap his harvest, and still others to make weapons of war and equipment for his chariots. ¹³He will take your daughters to be perfumers and cooks and bakers. ¹⁴He will take the best of your fields and vineyards and olive groves and give them to his attendants. ¹⁵He will take a tenth of your grain and of your vintage and give it to his officials and attendants. ¹⁶Your menservants and maidservants and the best of your cattle[a] and donkeys he will take for his own use. ¹⁷He will take a tenth of your flocks, and you yourselves will become his slaves. ¹⁸When that day comes, you will cry out for relief from the king you have chosen, and the LORD will not answer you in that day."

¹⁹But the people refused to listen to Samuel. "No!" they said. "We want a king over us. ²⁰Then we will be like all the other nations, with a king to lead us and to go out before us and fight our battles."

Everybody Else Has One

1 Samuel 8:20

Up to this point, God acted as Israel's King through the prophet Samuel. But the Israelites wanted to be like everyone else. They wanted a human king—you know, the crown, the velvet robe, the whole works. They just didn't realize they already had *the* King of kings.

---

²¹When Samuel heard all that the people said, he repeated it before the LORD. ²²The LORD answered, "Listen to them and give them a king."

Then Samuel said to the men of Israel, "Everyone go back to his town."

Samuel Anoints Saul

9 There was a Benjamite, a man of standing, whose name was Kish son of Abiel, the son of Zeror, the son of Becorath, the son of Aphiah of Benjamin. ²He had a son named Saul, an impressive young man without equal among the Israelites—a head taller than any of the others.

³Now the donkeys belonging to Saul's father Kish were lost, and Kish said to his son Saul, "Take one of the servants with you and go and look for the donkeys." ⁴So he passed through the hill country of Ephraim and through the area around Shalisha, but they did not find them. They went on into the district of Shaalim, but the donkeys were not there. Then he passed through the territory of Benjamin, but they did not find them.

⁵When they reached the district of Zuph, Saul said to the servant who was with him, "Come, let's go back, or my father will stop thinking about the donkeys and start worrying about us."

⁶But the servant replied, "Look, in this town there is a man of God; he is highly respected, and everything he says comes true. Let's go there now. Perhaps he will tell us what way to take."

⁷Saul said to his servant, "If we go, what can we give the man? The food in our sacks is gone. We have no gift to take to the man of God. What do we have?"

⁸The servant answered him again. "Look," he said, "I have a quarter of a shekel[b] of silver. I will give it to the man of God so that he will tell us what way to take." ⁹(Formerly in Israel, if a man went to inquire of God, he would say, "Come, let us go to the seer," because the prophet of today used to be called a seer.)

¹⁰"Good," Saul said to his servant. "Come, let's go." So they set out for the town where the man of God was.

¹¹As they were going up the hill to the town, they met some girls coming out to draw water, and they asked them, "Is the seer here?"

---

[a]16 Septuagint; Hebrew *young men*   [b]8 That is, about 1/10 ounce (about 3 grams)

¹²"He is," they answered. "He's ahead of you. Hurry now; he has just come to our town today, for the people have a sacrifice at the high place. ¹³As soon as you enter the town, you will find him before he goes up to the high place to eat. The people will not begin eating until he comes, because he must bless the sacrifice; afterward, those who are invited will eat. Go up now; you should find him about this time."

¹⁴They went up to the town, and as they were entering it, there was Samuel, coming toward them on his way up to the high place.

¹⁵Now the day before Saul came, the LORD had revealed this to Samuel: ¹⁶"About this time tomorrow I will send you a man from the land of Benjamin. Anoint him leader over my people Israel; he will deliver my people from the hand of the Philistines. I have looked upon my people, for their cry has reached me."

¹⁷When Samuel caught sight of Saul, the LORD said to him, "This is the man I spoke to you about; he will govern my people."

¹⁸Saul approached Samuel in the gateway and asked, "Would you please tell me where the seer's house is?"

¹⁹"I am the seer," Samuel replied. "Go up ahead of me to the high place, for today you are to eat with me, and in the morning I will let you go and will tell you all that is in your heart. ²⁰As for the donkeys you lost three days ago, do not worry about them; they have been found. And to whom is all the desire of Israel turned, if not to you and all your father's family?"

²¹Saul answered, "But am I not a Benjamite, from the smallest tribe of Israel, and is not my clan the least of all the clans of the tribe of Benjamin? Why do you say such a thing to me?"

²²Then Samuel brought Saul and his servant into the hall and seated them at the head of those who were invited—about thirty in number. ²³Samuel said to the cook, "Bring the piece of meat I gave you, the one I told you to lay aside."

²⁴So the cook took up the leg with what was on it and set it in front of Saul. Samuel said, "Here is what has been kept for you. Eat, because it was set aside for you for this occasion, from the time I said, 'I have invited guests.'" And Saul dined with Samuel that day.

²⁵After they came down from the high place to the town, Samuel talked with Saul on the roof of his house. ²⁶They rose about daybreak and Samuel called to Saul on the roof, "Get ready, and I will send you on your way." When Saul got ready, he and Samuel went outside together. ²⁷As they were going down to the edge of the town, Samuel said to Saul, "Tell the servant to go on ahead of us"—and the servant did so—"but you stay here awhile, so that I may give you a message from God."

10 Then Samuel took a flask of oil and poured it on Saul's head and kissed him, saying, "Has not the LORD anointed you leader over his inheritance?ᵃ ²When you leave me today, you will meet two men near Rachel's tomb, at Zelzah on the border of Benjamin. They will say to you, 'The donkeys you set out to look for have been found. And now your father has stopped thinking about them and is worried about you. He is asking, "What shall I do about my son?"'

³"Then you will go on from there until you reach the great tree of Tabor. Three men going up to God at Bethel will meet you there. One will be carrying three young goats, another three loaves of bread, and another a skin of wine. ⁴They will greet you and offer you two loaves of bread, which you will accept from them.

⁵"After that you will go to Gibeah of God, where there is a Philistine outpost. As you approach the town, you will meet a procession of prophets coming down from the high place with lyres, tambourines, flutes and harps being played before them, and they will be prophesying. ⁶The Spirit of the LORD will come upon you in power, and you will prophesy with them; and you will be changed into a different person. ⁷Once these signs are fulfilled, do whatever your hand finds to do, for God is with you.

ᵃ*1 Hebrew; Septuagint and Vulgate over his people Israel? You will reign over the LORD's people and save them from the power of their enemies round about. And this will be a sign to you that the LORD has anointed you leader over his inheritance:*

[8]"Go down ahead of me to Gilgal. I will surely come down to you to sacrifice burnt offerings and fellowship offerings,[a] but you must wait seven days until I come to you and tell you what you are to do."

Saul Made King

[9]As Saul turned to leave Samuel, God changed Saul's heart, and all these signs were fulfilled that day. [10]When they arrived at Gibeah, a procession of prophets met him; the Spirit of God came upon him in power, and he joined in their prophesying. [11]When all those who had formerly known him saw him prophesying with the prophets, they asked each other, "What is this that has happened to the son of Kish? Is Saul also among the prophets?"

[12]A man who lived there answered, "And who is their father?" So it became a saying: "Is Saul also among the prophets?" [13]After Saul stopped prophesying, he went to the high place.

[14]Now Saul's uncle asked him and his servant, "Where have you been?"

"Looking for the donkeys," he said. "But when we saw they were not to be found, we went to Samuel."

[15]Saul's uncle said, "Tell me what Samuel said to you."

[16]Saul replied, "He assured us that the donkeys had been found." But he did not tell his uncle what Samuel had said about the kingship.

[17]Samuel summoned the people of Israel to the LORD at Mizpah [18]and said to them, "This is what the LORD, the God of Israel, says: 'I brought Israel up out of Egypt, and I delivered you from the power of Egypt and all the kingdoms that oppressed you.' [19]But you have now rejected your God, who saves you out of all your calamities and distresses. And you have said, 'No, set a king over us.' So now present yourselves before the LORD by your tribes and clans."

[20]When Samuel brought all the tribes of Israel near, the tribe of Benjamin was chosen. [21]Then he brought forward the tribe of Benjamin, clan by clan, and Matri's clan was chosen. Finally Saul son of Kish was chosen. But when they looked for him, he was not to be found.

[22]So they inquired further of the LORD, "Has the man come here yet?"

And the LORD said, "Yes, he has hidden himself among the baggage."

[23]They ran and brought him out, and as he stood among the people he was a head taller than any of the others. [24]Samuel said to all the people, "Do you see the man the LORD has chosen? There is no one like him among all the people."

Then the people shouted, "Long live the king!"

[25]Samuel explained to the people the regulations of the kingship. He wrote them down on a scroll and deposited it before the LORD. Then Samuel dismissed the people, each to his own home.

[26]Saul also went to his home in Gibeah, accompanied by valiant men whose hearts God had touched. [27]But some troublemakers said, "How can this fellow save us?" They despised him and brought him no gifts. But Saul kept silent.

Saul Rescues the City of Jabesh

11 Nahash the Ammonite went up and besieged Jabesh Gilead. And all the men of Jabesh said to him, "Make a treaty with us, and we will be subject to you."

[2]But Nahash the Ammonite replied, "I will make a treaty with you only on the condition that I gouge out the right eye of every one of you and so bring disgrace on all Israel."

[3]The elders of Jabesh said to him, "Give us seven days so we can send messengers throughout Israel; if no one comes to rescue us, we will surrender to you."

[4]When the messengers came to Gibeah of Saul and reported these terms to the people, they all wept aloud. [5]Just then Saul was returning from the fields, behind his oxen, and he asked, "What is wrong with the people? Why are they weeping?" Then they repeated to him what the men of Jabesh had said.

[6]When Saul heard their words, the Spirit of God came upon him in power, and he burned with anger. [7]He took a pair of oxen, cut them into pieces, and sent the pieces by messengers through-

---

[a]8 Traditionally *peace offerings*

out Israel, proclaiming, "This is what will be done to the oxen of anyone who does not follow Saul and Samuel." Then the terror of the LORD fell on the people, and they turned out as one man. [8]When Saul mustered them at Bezek, the men of Israel numbered three hundred thousand and the men of Judah thirty thousand.

[9]They told the messengers who had come, "Say to the men of Jabesh Gilead, 'By the time the sun is hot tomorrow, you will be delivered.'" When the messengers went and reported this to the men of Jabesh, they were elated. [10]They said to the Ammonites, "Tomorrow we will surrender to you, and you can do to us whatever seems good to you."

[11]The next day Saul separated his men into three divisions; during the last watch of the night they broke into the camp of the Ammonites and slaughtered them until the heat of the day. Those who survived were scattered, so that no two of them were left together.

Saul Confirmed as King

[12]The people then said to Samuel, "Who was it that asked, 'Shall Saul reign over us?' Bring these men to us and we will put them to death."

[13]But Saul said, "No one shall be put to death today, for this day the LORD has rescued Israel."

[14]Then Samuel said to the people, "Come, let us go to Gilgal and there reaffirm the kingship." [15]So all the people went to Gilgal and confirmed Saul as king in the presence of the LORD. There they sacrificed fellowship offerings[a] before the LORD, and Saul and all the Israelites held a great celebration.

Samuel's Farewell Speech

12 Samuel said to all Israel, "I have listened to everything you said to me and have set a king over you. [2]Now you have a king as your leader. As for me, I am old and gray, and my sons are here with you. I have been your leader from my youth until this day. [3]Here I stand. Testify against me in the presence of the LORD and his anointed. Whose ox have I taken? Whose donkey have I taken? Whom have I cheated? Whom have I oppressed? From whose hand

have I accepted a bribe to make me shut my eyes? If I have done any of these, I will make it right."

[4]"You have not cheated or oppressed us," they replied. "You have not taken anything from anyone's hand."

[5]Samuel said to them, "The LORD is witness against you, and also his anointed is witness this day, that you have not found anything in my hand."

"He is witness," they said.

[6]Then Samuel said to the people, "It is the LORD who appointed Moses and Aaron and brought your forefathers up out of Egypt. [7]Now then, stand here, because I am going to confront you with evidence before the LORD as to all the righteous acts performed by the LORD for you and your fathers.

[8]"After Jacob entered Egypt, they cried to the LORD for help, and the LORD sent Moses and Aaron, who brought your forefathers out of Egypt and settled them in this place.

[9]"But they forgot the LORD their God; so he sold them into the hand of Sisera, the commander of the army of Hazor, and into the hands of the Philistines and the king of Moab, who fought against them. [10]They cried out to the LORD and said, 'We have sinned; we have forsaken the LORD and served the Baals and the Ashtoreths. But now deliver us from the hands of our enemies, and we will serve you.' [11]Then the LORD sent Jerub-Baal,[b] Barak,[c] Jephthah and Samuel,[d] and he delivered you from the hands of your enemies on every side, so that you lived securely.

[12]"But when you saw that Nahash king of the Ammonites was moving against you, you said to me, 'No, we want a king to rule over us'—even though the LORD your God was your king. [13]Now here is the king you have chosen, the one you asked for; see, the LORD has set a king over you. [14]If you fear the LORD and serve and obey him and do not rebel against his commands, and if both you and the king who reigns over you follow

---

[a]15 Traditionally *peace offerings*   [b]11 Also called *Gideon*   [c]11 Some Septuagint manuscripts and Syriac; Hebrew *Bedan*   [d]11 Hebrew; some Septuagint manuscripts and Syriac *Samson*

LORD your God—good! [15]But if you do not obey the LORD, and if you rebel against his commands, his hand will be against you, as it was against your fathers.

[16]"Now then, stand still and see this great thing the LORD is about to do before your eyes! [17]Is it not wheat harvest now? I will call upon the LORD to send thunder and rain. And you will realize what an evil thing you did in the eyes of the LORD when you asked for a king."

[18]Then Samuel called upon the LORD, and that same day the LORD sent thunder and rain. So all the people stood in awe of the LORD and of Samuel.

[19]The people all said to Samuel, "Pray to the LORD your God for your servants so that we will not die, for we have added to all our other sins the evil of asking for a king."

[20]"Do not be afraid," Samuel replied. "You have done all this evil; yet do not turn away from the LORD, but serve the LORD with all your heart. [21]Do not turn away after useless idols. They can do you no good, nor can they rescue you, because they are useless. [22]For the sake of his great name the LORD will not reject his people, because the LORD was pleased to make you his own. [23]As for me, far be it from me that I should sin against the LORD by failing to pray for you. And I will teach you the way that is good and right. [24]But be sure to fear the LORD and serve him faithfully with all your heart; consider what great things he has done for you. [25]Yet if you persist in doing evil, both you and your king will be swept away."

Samuel Rebukes Saul

13 Saul was ‚thirty[a] years old when he became king, and he reigned over Israel ‚forty-‚[b] two years.

[2]Saul[c] chose three thousand men from Israel; two thousand were with him at Micmash and in the hill country of Bethel, and a thousand were with Jonathan at Gibeah in Benjamin. The rest of the men he sent back to their homes.

[3]Jonathan attacked the Philistine outpost at Geba, and the Philistines heard about it. Then Saul had the trumpet blown throughout the land and said, "Let the Hebrews hear!" [4]So all Israel heard the news: "Saul has attacked the Philistine outpost, and now Israel has become a stench to the Philistines." And the people were summoned to join Saul at Gilgal.

[5]The Philistines assembled to fight Israel, with three thousand[d] chariots, six thousand charioteers, and soldiers as numerous as the sand on the seashore. They went up and camped at Micmash, east of Beth Aven. [6]When the men of Israel saw that their situation was critical and that their army was hard pressed, they hid in caves and thickets, among the rocks, and in pits and cisterns. [7]Some Hebrews even crossed the Jordan to the land of Gad and Gilead.

Saul remained at Gilgal, and all the troops with him were quaking with fear. [8]He waited seven days, the time set by Samuel; but Samuel did not come to Gilgal, and Saul's men began to scatter. [9]So he said, "Bring me the burnt offering and the fellowship offerings.[e]" And Saul offered up the burnt offering. [10]Just as he finished making the offering, Samuel arrived, and Saul went out to greet him.

[11]"What have you done?" asked Samuel.

Saul replied, "When I saw that the men were scattering, and that you did not come at the set time, and that the Philistines were assembling at Micmash, [12]I thought, 'Now the Philistines will come down against me at Gilgal, and I have not sought the LORD's favor.' So I felt compelled to offer the burnt offering."

[13]"You acted foolishly," Samuel said. "You have not kept the command the LORD your God gave you; if you had, he would have established your kingdom over Israel for all time. [14]But now your kingdom will not endure; the LORD has sought out a man after his own heart and appointed him leader of his people, because you have not kept the LORD's command."

---

a 1 A few late manuscripts of the Septuagint; Hebrew does not have *thirty.*   *b 1* See the round number in Acts 13:21; Hebrew does not have *forty-.*   *c 1,2* Or *and when he had reigned over Israel two years,* [2]*he*   *d 5* Some Septuagint manuscripts and Syriac; Hebrew *thirty thousand*   *e 9* Traditionally *peace offerings*

¹⁵Then Samuel left Gilgal[a] and went up to Gibeah in Benjamin, and Saul counted the men who were with him. They numbered about six hundred.

Israel Without Weapons

¹⁶Saul and his son Jonathan and the men with them were staying in Gibeah[b] in Benjamin, while the Philistines camped at Micmash. ¹⁷Raiding parties went out from the Philistine camp in three detachments. One turned toward Ophrah in the vicinity of Shual, ¹⁸another toward Beth Horon, and the third toward the borderland overlooking the Valley of Zeboim facing the desert.

¹⁹Not a blacksmith could be found in the whole land of Israel, because the Philistines had said, "Otherwise the Hebrews will make swords or spears!" ²⁰So all Israel went down to the Philistines to have their plowshares, mattocks, axes and sickles[c] sharpened. ²¹The price was two thirds of a shekel[d] for sharpening plowshares and mattocks, and a third of a shekel[e] for sharpening forks and axes and for repointing goads.

²²So on the day of the battle not a soldier with Saul and Jonathan had a sword or spear in his hand; only Saul and his son Jonathan had them.

Jonathan Attacks the Philistines

²³Now a detachment of Philistines had gone out to the pass at Micmash.

14 ¹One day Jonathan son of Saul said to the young man bearing his armor, "Come, let's go over to the Philistine outpost on the other side." But he did not tell his father.

²Saul was staying on the outskirts of Gibeah under a pomegranate tree in Migron. With him were about six hundred men, ³among whom was Ahijah, who was wearing an ephod. He was a son of Ichabod's brother Ahitub son of Phinehas, the son of Eli, the LORD's priest in Shiloh. No one was aware that Jonathan had left.

⁴On each side of the pass that Jonathan intended to cross to reach the Philistine outpost was a cliff; one was called Bozez, and the other Seneh. ⁵One cliff stood to the north toward Micmash, the other to the south toward Geba.

⁶Jonathan said to his young armor-bearer, "Come, let's go over to the outpost of those uncircumcised fellows. Perhaps the LORD will act in our behalf. Nothing can hinder the LORD from saving, whether by many or by few."

⁷"Do all that you have in mind," his armor-bearer said. "Go ahead; I am with you heart and soul."

⁸Jonathan said, "Come, then; we will cross over toward the men and let them see us. ⁹If they say to us, 'Wait there until we come to you,' we will stay where we are and not go up to them. ¹⁰But if they say, 'Come up to us,' we will climb up, because that will be our sign that the LORD has given them into our hands."

¹¹So both of them showed themselves to the Philistine outpost. "Look!" said the Philistines. "The Hebrews are crawling out of the holes they were hiding in." ¹²The men of the outpost shouted to Jonathan and his armor-bearer, "Come up to us and we'll teach you a lesson."

So Jonathan said to his armor-bearer, "Climb up after me; the LORD has given them into the hand of Israel."

¹³Jonathan climbed up, using his hands and feet, with his armor-bearer right behind him. The Philistines fell before Jonathan, and his armor-bearer followed and killed behind him. ¹⁴In that first attack Jonathan and his armor-bearer killed some twenty men in an area of about half an acre.[f]

Israel Routs the Philistines

¹⁵Then panic struck the whole army—those in the camp and field, and those in the outposts and raiding parties—and the ground shook. It was a panic sent by God.[g]

¹⁶Saul's lookouts at Gibeah in Benjamin saw the army melting away in all directions. ¹⁷Then Saul said to the men who were with him, "Muster the forces and see who has left us." When they did, it

was Jonathan and his armor-bearer who were not there.

[18] Saul said to Ahijah, "Bring the ark of God." (At that time it was with the Israelites.)[a] [19] While Saul was talking to the priest, the tumult in the Philistine camp increased more and more. So Saul said to the priest, "Withdraw your hand."

[20] Then Saul and all his men assembled and went to the battle. They found the Philistines in total confusion, striking each other with their swords. [21] Those Hebrews who had previously been with the Philistines and had gone up with them to their camp went over to the Israelites who were with Saul and Jonathan. [22] When all the Israelites who had hidden in the hill country of Ephraim heard that the Philistines were on the run, they joined the battle in hot pursuit. [23] So the LORD rescued Israel that day, and the battle moved on beyond Beth Aven.

Jonathan Eats Honey

[24] Now the men of Israel were in distress that day, because Saul had bound the people under an oath, saying, "Cursed be any man who eats food before evening comes, before I have avenged myself on my enemies!" So none of the troops tasted food.

[25] The entire army entered the woods, and there was honey on the ground. [26] When they went into the woods, they saw the honey oozing out, yet no one put his hand to his mouth, because they feared the oath. [27] But Jonathan had not heard that his father had bound the people with the oath, so he reached out the end of the staff that was in his hand and dipped it into the honeycomb. He raised his hand to his mouth, and his eyes brightened.[c] [28] Then one of the soldiers told him, "Your father bound the army under a strict oath, saying, 'Cursed be any man who eats food today!' That is why the men are faint.

[29] Jonathan said, "My father has made trouble for the country. See how my eyes brightened[d] when I tasted a little of this honey. [30] How much better it would have been if the men had eaten today some of the plunder they took from their enemies. Would not the slaughter of the Philistines have been even greater?"

[31] That day, after the Israelites had struck down the Philistines from Micmash to Aijalon, they were exhausted. [32] They pounced on the plunder and, taking sheep, cattle and calves, they butchered them on the ground and ate them, together with the blood. [33] Then someone said to Saul, "Look, the men are sinning against the LORD by eating meat that has blood in it."

"You have broken faith," he said. "Roll a large stone over here at once." [34] Then he said, "Go out among the men and tell them, 'Each of you bring me your cattle and sheep, and slaughter them here and eat them. Do not sin against the LORD by eating meat with blood still in it.' "

So everyone brought his ox that night and slaughtered it there. [35] Then Saul built an altar to the LORD; it was the first time he had done this.

[36] Saul said, "Let us go down after the Philistines by night and plunder them till dawn, and let us not leave one of them alive."

"Do whatever seems best to you," they replied.

But the priest said, "Let us inquire of God here."

[37] So Saul asked God, "Shall I go down after the Philistines? Will you give them into Israel's hand?" But God did not answer him that day.

[38] Saul therefore said, "Come here, all you who are leaders of the army, and let us find out what sin has been committed today. [39] As surely as the LORD who rescues Israel lives, even if it lies with my son Jonathan, he must die." But not one of the men said a word.

[40] Saul then said to all the Israelites, "You stand over there; I and Jonathan my son will stand over here."

"Do what seems best to you," the men replied.

[41] Then Saul prayed to the LORD, the God of Israel, "Give me the right answer."[e] And Jonathan and Saul were taken by

---

[a] 18 Hebrew; Septuagint "Bring the ephod." (At that time he wore the ephod before the Israelites.) [b] 25 Or Now all the people of the land [c] 27 Or his strength was renewed [d] 29 Or my strength was renewed [e] 41 Hebrew; Septuagint "Why have you not answered your servant today? If the fault is in me or my son Jonathan, respond with Urim, but if the men of Israel are at fault, respond with Thummim."

lot, and the men were cleared. ⁴²Saul said, "Cast the lot between me and Jonathan my son." And Jonathan was taken.

⁴³Then Saul said to Jonathan, "Tell me what you have done."

So Jonathan told him, "I merely tasted a little honey with the end of my staff. And now must I die?"

⁴⁴Saul said, "May God deal with me, be it ever so severely, if you do not die, Jonathan."

⁴⁵But the men said to Saul, "Should Jonathan die—he who has brought about this great deliverance in Israel? Never! As surely as the LORD lives, not a hair of his head will fall to the ground, for he did this today with God's help." So the men rescued Jonathan, and he was not put to death.

⁴⁶Then Saul stopped pursuing the Philistines, and they withdrew to their own land.

⁴⁷After Saul had assumed rule over Israel, he fought against their enemies on every side: Moab, the Ammonites, Edom, the kings*ᵃ* of Zobah, and the Philistines. Wherever he turned, he inflicted punishment on them.*ᵇ* ⁴⁸He fought valiantly and defeated the Amalekites, delivering Israel from the hands of those who had plundered them.

Saul's Family

⁴⁹Saul's sons were Jonathan, Ishvi and Malki-Shua. The name of his older daughter was Merab, and that of the younger was Michal. ⁵⁰His wife's name was Ahinoam daughter of Ahimaaz. The name of the commander of Saul's army was Abner son of Ner, and Ner was Saul's uncle. ⁵¹Saul's father Kish and Abner's father Ner were sons of Abiel.

⁵²All the days of Saul there was bitter war with the Philistines, and whenever Saul saw a mighty or brave man, he took him into his service.

The LORD Rejects Saul as King

15 Samuel said to Saul, "I am the one the LORD sent to anoint you king over his people Israel; so listen now to the message from the LORD. ²This is what the LORD Almighty says: 'I will punish the Amalekites for what they did to Israel when they waylaid them as they came up

from Egypt. ³Now go, attack the Amalekites and totally destroy*ᶜ* everything that belongs to them. Do not spare them; put to death men and women, children and infants, cattle and sheep, camels and donkeys.' "

⁴So Saul summoned the men and mustered them at Telaim—two hundred thousand foot soldiers and ten thousand men from Judah. ⁵Saul went to the city of Amalek and set an ambush in the ravine. ⁶Then he said to the Kenites, "Go away, leave the Amalekites so that I do not destroy you along with them; for you showed kindness to all the Israelites when they came up out of Egypt." So the Kenites moved away from the Amalekites.

⁷Then Saul attacked the Amalekites all the way from Havilah to Shur, to the east of Egypt. ⁸He took Agag king of the Amalekites alive, and all his people he totally destroyed with the sword. ⁹But Saul and the army spared Agag and the best of the sheep and cattle, the fat calves*ᵈ* and lambs—everything that was good. These they were unwilling to destroy completely, but everything that was despised and weak they totally destroyed.

¹⁰Then the word of the LORD came to Samuel: ¹¹"I am grieved that I have made Saul king, because he has turned away from me and has not carried out my instructions." Samuel was troubled, and he cried out to the LORD all that night.

¹²Early in the morning Samuel got up and went to meet Saul, but he was told, "Saul has gone to Carmel. There he has set up a monument in his own honor and has turned and gone on down to Gilgal."

¹³When Samuel reached him, Saul said, "The LORD bless you! I have carried out the LORD's instructions."

¹⁴But Samuel said, "What then is this bleating of sheep in my ears? What is this lowing of cattle that I hear?"

¹⁵Saul answered, "The soldiers brought

ᵃ47 Masoretic Text; Dead Sea Scrolls and Septuagint *king* *ᵇ47* Hebrew; Septuagint *he was victorious* *ᶜ3* The Hebrew term refers to the irrevocable giving over of things or persons to the LORD, often by totally destroying them; also in verses 8, 9, 15, 18, 20 and 21. *ᵈ9* Or *the grown bulls*; the meaning of the Hebrew for this phrase is uncertain.

Caught Cheating

Huh?

1 Samuel 15:13–14

Samuel's instructions were simple—destroy *all* the Amalekites and every single thing they own. The Amalekites were a group of raiders who attacked Moses unprovoked. God had declared that they were to be wiped out (see Exodus 17:8–16, page 91 and Deuteronomy 25:17–19, page 230), but Saul spared their king and the best of their livestock. Now Samuel confronts Saul about cheating on God's instructions.

them from the Amalekites; they spared the best of the sheep and cattle to sacrifice to the LORD your God, but we totally destroyed the rest."

¹⁶"Stop!" Samuel said to Saul. "Let me tell you what the LORD said to me last night."

"Tell me," Saul replied.

¹⁷Samuel said, "Although you were once small in your own eyes, did you not become the head of the tribes of Israel? The LORD anointed you king over Israel. ¹⁸And he sent you on a mission, saying, 'Go and completely destroy those wicked people, the Amalekites; make war on them until you have wiped them out.' ¹⁹Why did you not obey the LORD? Why did you pounce on the plunder and do evil in the eyes of the LORD?"

²⁰"But I did obey the LORD," Saul said. "I went on the mission the LORD assigned me. I completely destroyed the Amalekites and brought back Agag their king. ²¹The soldiers took sheep and cattle from the plunder, the best of what was devoted to God, in order to sacrifice them to the LORD your God at Gilgal."

²²But Samuel replied:

"Does the LORD delight in burnt offerings and sacrifices
    as much as in obeying the voice of the LORD?
To obey is better than sacrifice,
    and to heed is better than the fat of rams.

²³For rebellion is like the sin of divination,
    and arrogance like the evil of idolatry.
Because you have rejected the word of the LORD,
    he has rejected you as king."

²⁴Then Saul said to Samuel, "I have sinned. I violated the LORD's command and your instructions. I was afraid of the people and so I gave in to them. ²⁵Now I beg you, forgive my sin and come back with me, so that I may worship the LORD."

²⁶But Samuel said to him, "I will not go back with you. You have rejected the word of the LORD, and the LORD has rejected you as king over Israel!"

²⁷As Samuel turned to leave, Saul caught hold of the hem of his robe, and it tore. ²⁸Samuel said to him, "The LORD has torn the kingdom of Israel from you today and has given it to one of your neighbors—to one better than you. ²⁹He who is the Glory of Israel does not lie or change his mind; for he is not a man, that he should change his mind."

³⁰Saul replied, "I have sinned. But please honor me before the elders of my people and before Israel; come back with me, so that I may worship the LORD your God." ³¹So Samuel went back with Saul, and Saul worshiped the LORD.

³²Then Samuel said, "Bring me Agag king of the Amalekites."

Agag came to him confidently,ᵃ thinking, "Surely the bitterness of death is past."

³³But Samuel said,

"As your sword has made women childless,
    so will your mother be childless among women."

And Samuel put Agag to death before the LORD at Gilgal.

³⁴Then Samuel left for Ramah, but Saul went up to his home in Gibeah of Saul. ³⁵Until the day Samuel died, he did not go to see Saul again, though Samuel mourned for him. And the LORD was grieved that he had made Saul king over Israel.

ᵃ32 Or *him trembling, yet*

Samuel Anoints David

16 The LORD said to Samuel, "How long will you mourn for Saul, since I have rejected him as king over Israel? Fill your horn with oil and be on your way; I am sending you to Jesse of Bethlehem. I have chosen one of his sons to be king."

²But Samuel said, "How can I go? Saul will hear about it and kill me."

The LORD said, "Take a heifer with you and say, 'I have come to sacrifice to the LORD.' ³Invite Jesse to the sacrifice, and I will show you what to do. You are to anoint for me the one I indicate."

⁴Samuel did what the LORD said. When he arrived at Bethlehem, the elders of the town trembled when they met him. They asked, "Do you come in peace?"

⁵Samuel replied, "Yes, in peace; I have come to sacrifice to the LORD. Consecrate yourselves and come to the sacrifice with me." Then he consecrated Jesse and his sons and invited them to the sacrifice.

⁶When they arrived, Samuel saw Eliab and thought, "Surely the LORD's anointed stands here before the LORD."

⁷But the LORD said to Samuel, "Do not consider his appearance or his height, for I have rejected him. The LORD does not look at the things man looks at. Man looks at the outward appearance, but the LORD looks at the heart."

⁸Then Jesse called Abinadab and had him pass in front of Samuel. But Samuel said, "The LORD has not chosen this one either." ⁹Jesse then had Shammah pass by, but Samuel said, "Nor has the LORD chosen this one." ¹⁰Jesse had seven of his sons pass before Samuel, but Samuel said to him, "The LORD has not chosen these." ¹¹So he asked Jesse, "Are these all the sons you have?"

"There is still the youngest," Jesse answered, "but he is tending the sheep."

Samuel said, "Send for him; we will not sit down*a* until he arrives."

¹²So he sent and had him brought in.

a 11 Some Septuagint manuscripts; Hebrew not gather around

Wednesday

Looks Don't Count

Read 1 Samuel 16:7

A new kid came to our school last year, and he was a little on the heavy side. No one gave him a chance to show what kind of person he was; instead, everyone judged him by his weight. Unfortunately, I did too. Later in the year, many of us got to know him better, and he turned out to be really cool. I felt so guilty about the way we acted earlier, and I wish we hadn't judged him because of his appearance.

I'm sure everybody has treated someone unfairly at one time or another. And most of us can be kind of shallow and sometimes judge people by how they look. But God is never shallow. He cares about all of us—not because of what we look like, but because of who we are.

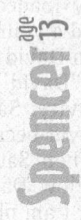

Spencer age 13

What about You?

❶ Try to remember a time you judged someone unfairly because of the way they looked. How did you feel about it later?

❷ Flip through your school yearbook. Pay special attention to all the different kinds of people you see. Why do you think God made each person unique?

❸ Thank God for the unique way he's made you. Thank him for the way he's made other people too.

Turn to page 333 for your next devotion.

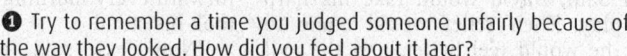

He was ruddy, with a fine appearance and handsome features.

Then the LORD said, "Rise and anoint him; he is the one."

¹³So Samuel took the horn of oil and anointed him in the presence of his brothers, and from that day on the Spirit of the LORD came upon David in power. Samuel then went to Ramah.

David in Saul's Service

¹⁴Now the Spirit of the LORD had departed from Saul, and an evil[a] spirit from the LORD tormented him.

¹⁵Saul's attendants said to him, "See, an evil spirit from God is tormenting you. ¹⁶Let our lord command his servants here to search for someone who can play the harp. He will play when the evil spirit from God comes upon you, and you will feel better."

¹⁷So Saul said to his attendants, "Find someone who plays well and bring him to me."

¹⁸One of the servants answered, "I have seen a son of Jesse of Bethlehem who knows how to play the harp. He is a brave man and a warrior. He speaks well and is a fine-looking man. And the LORD is with him."

¹⁹Then Saul sent messengers to Jesse and said, "Send me your son David, who is with the sheep." ²⁰So Jesse took a donkey loaded with bread, a skin of wine and a young goat and sent them with his son David to Saul.

²¹David came to Saul and entered his service. Saul liked him very much, and David became one of his armor-bearers. ²²Then Saul sent word to Jesse, saying, "Allow David to remain in my service, for I am pleased with him."

²³Whenever the spirit from God came upon Saul, David would take his harp and play. Then relief would come to Saul; he would feel better, and the evil spirit would leave him.

David and Goliath

17 Now the Philistines gathered their forces for war and assembled at Socoh in Judah. They pitched camp at Ephes Dammim, between Socoh and Azekah. ²Saul and the Israelites assembled and camped in the Valley of Elah and drew up their battle line to meet the Philistines. ³The Philistines occupied one hill and the Israelites another, with the valley between them.

⁴A champion named Goliath, who was from Gath, came out of the Philistine camp. He was over nine feet[b] tall. ⁵He had a bronze helmet on his head and wore a coat of scale armor of bronze weighing five thousand shekels[c]; ⁶on his legs he wore bronze greaves, and a bronze javelin was slung on his back. ⁷His spear shaft was like a weaver's rod, and its iron point weighed six hundred shekels.[d] His shield bearer went ahead of him.

⁸Goliath stood and shouted to the ranks of Israel, "Why do you come out and line up for battle? Am I not a Philistine, and are you not the servants of Saul? Choose a man and have him come down to me. ⁹If he is able to fight and kill me, we will become your subjects; but if I overcome him and kill him, you will become our subjects and serve us." ¹⁰Then the Philistine said, "This day I defy the ranks of Israel! Give me a man and let us fight each other." ¹¹On hearing the Philistine's words, Saul and all the Israelites were dismayed and terrified.

¹²Now David was the son of an Ephrathite named Jesse, who was from Bethlehem in Judah. Jesse had eight sons, and in Saul's time he was old and well advanced in years. ¹³Jesse's three oldest sons had followed Saul to the war: The firstborn was Eliab; the second, Abinadab; and the third, Shammah. ¹⁴David was the youngest. The three oldest followed Saul, ¹⁵but David went back and forth from Saul to tend his father's sheep at Bethlehem.

¹⁶For forty days the Philistine came forward every morning and evening and took his stand.

¹⁷Now Jesse said to his son David, "Take this ephah[e] of roasted grain and these ten loaves of bread for your brothers and hurry to their camp. ¹⁸Take along

---

a 14 Or *injurious;* also in verses 15, 16 and 23
b 4 Hebrew *was six cubits and a span* (about 3 meters)　*c 5* That is, about 125 pounds (about 57 kilograms)　*d 7* That is, about 15 pounds (about 7 kilograms)　*e 17* That is, probably about 3/5 bushel (about 22 liters)

these ten cheeses to the commander of their unit.*a* See how your brothers are and bring back some assurance*b* from them. ¹⁹They are with Saul and all the men of Israel in the Valley of Elah, fighting against the Philistines."

²⁰Early in the morning David left the flock with a shepherd, loaded up and set out, as Jesse had directed. He reached the camp as the army was going out to its battle positions, shouting the war cry. ²¹Israel and the Philistines were drawing up their lines facing each other. ²²David left his things with the keeper of supplies, ran to the battle lines and greeted his brothers. ²³As he was talking with them, Goliath, the Philistine champion from Gath, stepped out from his lines and shouted his usual defiance, and David heard it. ²⁴When the Israelites saw the man, they all ran from him in great fear.

²⁵Now the Israelites had been saying, "Do you see how this man keeps coming out? He comes out to defy Israel. The king will give great wealth to the man who kills him. He will also give him his daughter in marriage and will exempt his father's family from taxes in Israel."

²⁶David asked the men standing near him, "What will be done for the man who kills this Philistine and removes this disgrace from Israel? Who is this uncircumcised Philistine that he should defy the armies of the living God?"

²⁷They repeated to him what they had been saying and told him, "This is what will be done for the man who kills him."

²⁸When Eliab, David's oldest brother, heard him speaking with the men, he burned with anger at him and asked, "Why have you come down here? And with whom did you leave those few sheep in the desert? I know how conceited you are and how wicked your heart is; you came down only to watch the battle."

²⁹"Now what have I done?" said David. "Can't I even speak?" ³⁰He then turned away to someone else and brought up the same matter, and the men answered him as before. ³¹What David said was overheard and reported to Saul, and Saul sent for him.

³²David said to Saul, "Let no one lose heart on account of this Philistine; your servant will go and fight him."

³³Saul replied, "You are not able to go out against this Philistine and fight him; you are only a boy, and he has been a fighting man from his youth."

³⁴But David said to Saul, "Your servant has been keeping his father's sheep. When a lion or a bear came and carried off a sheep from the flock, ³⁵I went after it, struck it and rescued the sheep from its mouth. When it turned on me, I seized it by its hair, struck it and killed it. ³⁶Your servant has killed both the lion and the bear; this uncircumcised Philistine will be like one of them, because he has defied the armies of the living God. ³⁷The LORD who delivered me from the paw of the lion and the paw of the bear will deliver me from the hand of this Philistine."

Saul said to David, "Go, and the LORD be with you."

³⁸Then Saul dressed David in his own tunic. He put a coat of armor on him and a bronze helmet on his head. ³⁹David fastened on his sword over the tunic and tried walking around, because he was not used to them.

"I cannot go in these," he said to Saul, "because I am not used to them." So he took them off. ⁴⁰Then he took his staff in his hand, chose five smooth stones from the stream, put them in the pouch of his shepherd's bag and, with his sling in his hand, approached the Philistine.

The Underdog

Huh?

1 Samuel 17:40

This popular story helps us see that when it looks like the odds are against you, everything can change if God is on your side. As you see in verse 49, all it took was one stone to drop the giant.

---

a18 Hebrew *thousand*   *b18* Or *some token; or some pledge of spoils*

⁴¹Meanwhile, the Philistine, with his shield bearer in front of him, kept coming closer to David. ⁴²He looked David over and saw that he was only a boy, ruddy and handsome, and he despised him. ⁴³He said to David, "Am I a dog, that you come at me with sticks?" And the Philistine cursed David by his gods. ⁴⁴"Come here," he said, "and I'll give your flesh to the birds of the air and the beasts of the field!"

⁴⁵David said to the Philistine, "You come against me with sword and spear and javelin, but I come against you in the name of the LORD Almighty, the God of the armies of Israel, whom you have defied. ⁴⁶This day the LORD will hand you over to me, and I'll strike you down and cut off your head. Today I will give the carcasses of the Philistine army to the birds of the air and the beasts of the earth, and the whole world will know that there is a God in Israel. ⁴⁷All those gathered here will know that it is not by sword or spear that the LORD saves; for the battle is the LORD's, and he will give all of you into our hands."

⁴⁸As the Philistine moved closer to attack him, David ran quickly toward the battle line to meet him. ⁴⁹Reaching into his bag and taking out a stone, he slung it and struck the Philistine on the forehead. The stone sank into his forehead, and he fell facedown on the ground.

⁵⁰So David triumphed over the Philistine with a sling and a stone; without a sword in his hand he struck down the Philistine and killed him.

⁵¹David ran and stood over him. He took hold of the Philistine's sword and drew it from the scabbard. After he killed him, he cut off his head with the sword.

When the Philistines saw that their hero was dead, they turned and ran. ⁵²Then the men of Israel and Judah surged forward with a shout and pursued the Philistines to the entrance of Gathᵃ and to the gates of Ekron. Their dead were strewn along the Shaaraim road to Gath and Ekron. ⁵³When the Israelites returned from chasing the Philistines, they plundered their camp. ⁵⁴David took the Philistine's head and brought it to Jerusalem, and he put the Philistine's weapons in his own tent.

⁵⁵As Saul watched David going out to meet the Philistine, he said to Abner, commander of the army, "Abner, whose son is that young man?"

Abner replied, "As surely as you live, O king, I don't know."

⁵⁶The king said, "Find out whose son this young man is."

⁵⁷As soon as David returned from killing the Philistine, Abner took him and brought him before Saul, with David still holding the Philistine's head.

⁵⁸"Whose son are you, young man?" Saul asked him.

David said, "I am the son of your servant Jesse of Bethlehem."

Saul's Jealousy of David

18 After David had finished talking with Saul, Jonathan became one in spirit with David, and he loved him as himself. ²From that day Saul kept David with him and did not let him return to his father's house. ³And Jonathan made a covenant with David because he loved him as himself. ⁴Jonathan took off the robe he was wearing and gave it to David, along with his tunic, and even his sword, his bow and his belt.

⁵Whatever Saul sent him to do, David did it so successfullyᵇ that Saul gave him a high rank in the army. This pleased all the people, and Saul's officers as well.

⁶When the men were returning home after David had killed the Philistine, the women came out from all the towns of Israel to meet King Saul with singing and dancing, with joyful songs and with tambourines and lutes. ⁷As they danced, they sang:

"Saul has slain his thousands,
    and David his tens of thousands."

⁸Saul was very angry; this refrain galled him. "They have credited David with tens of thousands," he thought, "but me with only thousands. What more can he get but the kingdom?" ⁹And from that time on Saul kept a jealous eye on David.

¹⁰The next day an evilᶜ spirit from God came forcefully upon Saul. He was prophesying in his house, while David

ᵃ52 Some Septuagint manuscripts; Hebrew *a valley*   ᵇ5 Or *wisely*   ᶜ10 Or *injurious*

was playing the harp, as he usually did. Saul had a spear in his hand ¹¹and he hurled it, saying to himself, "I'll pin David to the wall." But David eluded him twice.

¹²Saul was afraid of David, because the LORD was with David but had left Saul. ¹³So he sent David away from him and gave him command over a thousand men, and David led the troops in their campaigns. ¹⁴In everything he did he had great success,ᵃ because the LORD was with him. ¹⁵When Saul saw how successfulᵇ he was, he was afraid of him. ¹⁶But all Israel and Judah loved David, because he led them in their campaigns.

¹⁷Saul said to David, "Here is my older daughter Merab. I will give her to you in marriage; only serve me bravely and fight the battles of the LORD." For Saul said to himself, "I will not raise a hand against him. Let the Philistines do that!"

¹⁸But David said to Saul, "Who am I, and what is my family or my father's clan in Israel, that I should become the king's son-in-law?" ¹⁹Soᶜ when the time came for Merab, Saul's daughter, to be given to David, she was given in marriage to Adriel of Meholah.

²⁰Now Saul's daughter Michal was in love with David, and when they told Saul about it, he was pleased. ²¹"I will give her to him," he thought, "so that she may be a snare to him and so that the hand of the Philistines may be against him." So Saul said to David, "Now you have a second opportunity to become my son-in-law."

²²Then Saul ordered his attendants: "Speak to David privately and say, 'Look, the king is pleased with you, and his at-

---

ᵃ14 Or *he was very wise* ᵇ15 Or *wise*
ᶜ19 Or *However,*

Thursday

Friends Forever

Read 1 Samuel 18:1-4

David and Jonathan had a great friendship that lasted because they truly loved God and each other. They went through some hard times together, but their friendship stayed strong.

My best friend and I have a relationship based on the Lord too. I'd do anything for her, and she feels the same about me. I know she'll warn me if I'm doing something I shouldn't. I know she'll help me grow in my faith. And I know she'll always tell me the truth about myself, even when I don't want to hear it.

Because she's such a good friend to me, I want to be a good friend to her. Being a good friend means being there for her. It means treating her with love and respect. It means not letting jealousy or little arguments come between us. Being a friend means loving my friend as much as I love myself. Sure, we have fights and don't always agree on everything. But because we both love God, we know we need to love each other too. That helps our friendship grow, even through difficult times.

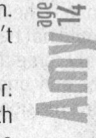
Amy, age 14

What about You?

❶ Think of some hard times you've been through with your friends. How did you get through them?

❷ Is there someone you know who needs a good friend? What is one thing you can do to reach out to that person?

❸ Ask God to help you be more loving, patient and caring toward your friends.

Turn to page 340 for your next devotion.

tendants all like you; now become his son-in-law.' "

²³They repeated these words to David. But David said, "Do you think it is a small matter to become the king's son-in-law? I'm only a poor man and little known."

²⁴When Saul's servants told him what David had said, ²⁵Saul replied, "Say to David, 'The king wants no other price for the bride than a hundred Philistine foreskins, to take revenge on his enemies.' " Saul's plan was to have David fall by the hands of the Philistines.

²⁶When the attendants told David these things, he was pleased to become the king's son-in-law. So before the allotted time elapsed, ²⁷David and his men went out and killed two hundred Philistines. He brought their foreskins and presented the full number to the king so that he might become the king's son-in-law. Then Saul gave him his daughter Michal in marriage.

David Collects "Scalps"

Huh?

1 Samuel 18:27

David wants to prove he is not exaggerating. Collecting foreskins would be like collecting scalps in cowboy-and-Indian days so that the number of kills from a battle could not be exaggerated. Foreskins could only come from non-Jews, since Jews were the only ones in the area that practiced circumcision.

²⁸When Saul realized that the LORD was with David and that his daughter Michal loved David, ²⁹Saul became still more afraid of him, and he remained his enemy the rest of his days.

³⁰The Philistine commanders continued to go out to battle, and as often as they did, David met with more success[a] than the rest of Saul's officers, and his name became well known.

Saul Tries to Kill David

19 Saul told his son Jonathan and all the attendants to kill David. But Jonathan was very fond of David ²and warned him, "My father Saul is looking for a chance to kill you. Be on your guard tomorrow morning; go into hiding and stay there. ³I will go out and stand with my father in the field where you are. I'll speak to him about you and will tell you what I find out."

⁴Jonathan spoke well of David to Saul his father and said to him, "Let not the king do wrong to his servant David; he has not wronged you, and what he has done has benefited you greatly. ⁵He took his life in his hands when he killed the Philistine. The LORD won a great victory for all Israel, and you saw it and were glad. Why then would you do wrong to an innocent man like David by killing him for no reason?"

⁶Saul listened to Jonathan and took this oath: "As surely as the LORD lives, David will not be put to death."

⁷So Jonathan called David and told him the whole conversation. He brought him to Saul, and David was with Saul as before.

⁸Once more war broke out, and David went out and fought the Philistines. He struck them with such force that they fled before him.

⁹But an evil[b] spirit from the LORD came upon Saul as he was sitting in his house with his spear in his hand. While David was playing the harp, ¹⁰Saul tried to pin him to the wall with his spear, but David eluded him as Saul drove the spear into the wall. That night David made good his escape.

¹¹Saul sent men to David's house to watch it and to kill him in the morning. But Michal, David's wife, warned him, "If you don't run for your life tonight, tomorrow you'll be killed." ¹²So Michal let David down through a window, and he fled and escaped. ¹³Then Michal took an idol[c] and laid it on the bed, covering it with a garment and putting some goats' hair at the head.

¹⁴When Saul sent the men to capture David, Michal said, "He is ill."

¹⁵Then Saul sent the men back to see David and told them, "Bring him up to

---

[a]30 Or *David acted more wisely* [b]9 Or *injurious*
[c]13 Hebrew *teraphim*; also in verse 16

me in his bed so that I may kill him."
¹⁶But when the men entered, there was
the idol in the bed, and at the head was
some goats' hair.

¹⁷Saul said to Michal, "Why did you
deceive me like this and send my enemy
away so that he escaped?"

Michal told him, "He said to me, 'Let
me get away. Why should I kill you?' "

¹⁸When David had fled and made his
escape, he went to Samuel at Ramah and
told him all that Saul had done to him.
Then he and Samuel went to Naioth and
stayed there. ¹⁹Word came to Saul: "David is in Naioth at Ramah"; ²⁰so he sent
men to capture him. But when they saw a
group of prophets prophesying, with
Samuel standing there as their leader, the
Spirit of God came upon Saul's men and
they also prophesied. ²¹Saul was told
about it, and he sent more men, and they
prophesied too. Saul sent men a third
time, and they also prophesied. ²²Finally,
he himself left for Ramah and went to
the great cistern at Secu. And he asked,
"Where are Samuel and David?"

"Over in Naioth at Ramah," they said.

²³So Saul went to Naioth at Ramah.
But the Spirit of God came even upon
him, and he walked along prophesying
until he came to Naioth. ²⁴He stripped off
his robes and also prophesied in
Samuel's presence. He lay that way all
that day and night. This is why people
say, "Is Saul also among the prophets?"

David and Jonathan

20 Then David fled from Naioth at
Ramah and went to Jonathan and
asked, "What have I done? What is my
crime? How have I wronged your father,
that he is trying to take my life?"

²"Never!" Jonathan replied. "You are
not going to die! Look, my father doesn't
do anything, great or small, without con-
fiding in me. Why would he hide this
from me? It's not so!"

³But David took an oath and said,
"Your father knows very well that I have
found favor in your eyes, and he has said
to himself, 'Jonathan must not know this
or he will be grieved.' Yet as surely as the
LORD lives and as you live, there is only a
step between me and death."

⁴Jonathan said to David, "Whatever

you want me to do, I'll do for you."

⁵So David said, "Look, tomorrow is the
New Moon festival, and I am supposed to
dine with the king; but let me go and
hide in the field until the evening of the
day after tomorrow. ⁶If your father
misses me at all, tell him, 'David earnestly asked my permission to hurry to Bethlehem, his hometown, because an annual
sacrifice is being made there for his
whole clan.' ⁷If he says, 'Very well,' then
your servant is safe. But if he loses his
temper, you can be sure that he is determined to harm me. ⁸As for you, show
kindness to your servant, for you have
brought him into a covenant with you
before the LORD. If I am guilty, then kill
me yourself! Why hand me over to your
father?"

⁹"Never!" Jonathan said. "If I had the
least inkling that my father was determined to harm you, wouldn't I tell you?"

¹⁰David asked, "Who will tell me if
your father answers you harshly?"

¹¹"Come," Jonathan said, "let's go out
into the field." So they went there together.

¹²Then Jonathan said to David: "By the
LORD, the God of Israel, I will surely
sound out my father by this time the day
after tomorrow! If he is favorably disposed toward you, will I not send you
word and let you know? ¹³But if my father is inclined to harm you, may the
LORD deal with me, be it ever so severely,
if I do not let you know and send you
away safely. May the LORD be with you as
he has been with my father. ¹⁴But show
me unfailing kindness like that of the
LORD as long as I live, so that I may not
be killed, ¹⁵and do not ever cut off your
kindness from my family—not even when
the LORD has cut off every one of David's
enemies from the face of the earth."

¹⁶So Jonathan made a covenant with
the house of David, saying, "May the
LORD call David's enemies to account."
¹⁷And Jonathan had David reaffirm his
oath out of love for him, because he
loved him as he loved himself.

¹⁸Then Jonathan said to David: "Tomorrow is the New Moon festival. You
will be missed, because your seat will be
empty. ¹⁹The day after tomorrow, toward
evening, go to the place where you hid

when this trouble began, and wait by the stone Ezel. ²⁰I will shoot three arrows to the side of it, as though I were shooting at a target. ²¹Then I will send a boy and say, 'Go, find the arrows.' If I say to him, 'Look, the arrows are on this side of you; bring them here,' then come, because, as surely as the LORD lives, you are safe; there is no danger. ²²But if I say to the boy, 'Look, the arrows are beyond you,' then you must go, because the LORD has sent you away. ²³And about the matter you and I discussed—remember, the LORD is witness between you and me forever."

²⁴So David hid in the field, and when the New Moon festival came, the king sat down to eat. ²⁵He sat in his customary place by the wall, opposite Jonathan,ᵃ and Abner sat next to Saul, but David's place was empty. ²⁶Saul said nothing that day, for he thought, "Something must have happened to David to make him ceremonially unclean—surely he is unclean." ²⁷But the next day, the second day of the month, David's place was empty again. Then Saul said to his son Jonathan, "Why hasn't the son of Jesse come to the meal, either yesterday or today?"

²⁸Jonathan answered, "David earnestly asked me for permission to go to Bethlehem. ²⁹He said, 'Let me go, because our family is observing a sacrifice in the town and my brother has ordered me to be there. If I have found favor in your eyes, let me get away to see my brothers.' That is why he has not come to the king's table."

³⁰Saul's anger flared up at Jonathan and he said to him, "You son of a perverse and rebellious woman! Don't I know that you have sided with the son of Jesse to your own shame and to the shame of the mother who bore you? ³¹As long as the son of Jesse lives on this earth, neither you nor your kingdom will be established. Now send and bring him to me, for he must die!"

³²"Why should he be put to death? What has he done?" Jonathan asked his father. ³³But Saul hurled his spear at him to kill him. Then Jonathan knew that his father intended to kill David.

³⁴Jonathan got up from the table in fierce anger; on that second day of the month he did not eat, because he was grieved at his father's shameful treatment of David.

³⁵In the morning Jonathan went out to the field for his meeting with David. He had a small boy with him, ³⁶and he said to the boy, "Run and find the arrows I shoot." As the boy ran, he shot an arrow beyond him. ³⁷When the boy came to the place where Jonathan's arrow had fallen, Jonathan called out after him, "Isn't the arrow beyond you?" ³⁸Then he shouted, "Hurry! Go quickly! Don't stop!" The boy picked up the arrow and returned to his master. ³⁹(The boy knew nothing of all this; only Jonathan and David knew.) ⁴⁰Then Jonathan gave his weapons to the boy and said, "Go, carry them back to town."

⁴¹After the boy had gone, David got up from the south side of the stone and bowed down before Jonathan three times, with his face to the ground. Then they kissed each other and wept together—but David wept the most.

⁴²Jonathan said to David, "Go in peace, for we have sworn friendship with each other in the name of the LORD, saying, 'The LORD is witness between you and me, and between your descendants and my descendants forever.'" Then David left, and Jonathan went back to the town.

David at Nob

21 David went to Nob, to Ahimelech the priest. Ahimelech trembled when he met him, and asked, "Why are you alone? Why is no one with you?"

²David answered Ahimelech the priest, "The king charged me with a certain matter and said to me, 'No one is to know anything about your mission and your instructions.' As for my men, I have told them to meet me at a certain place. ³Now then, what do you have on hand? Give me five loaves of bread, or whatever you can find."

⁴But the priest answered David, "I don't have any ordinary bread on hand; however, there is some consecrated bread here—provided the men have kept themselves from women."

ᵃ25 Septuagint; Hebrew wall. Jonathan arose

Quoted 1000 Years Later

Huh?

1 Samuel 21:4

What in the world is consecrated bread? Consecrated bread was supposed to be eaten only by priests, but David was desperate. So he and his companions ate the bread, and as a punishment, Saul slaughters 85 priests. Jesus referred to this time of David's struggle in Matthew 12:3–4 1000 years later (page 1158). Jesus is explaining that being holy means much more than keeping rituals.

[5]David replied, "Indeed women have been kept from us, as usual whenever[a] I set out. The men's things[b] are holy even on missions that are not holy. How much more so today!" [6]So the priest gave him the consecrated bread, since there was no bread there except the bread of the Presence that had been removed from before the LORD and replaced by hot bread on the day it was taken away.

[7]Now one of Saul's servants was there that day, detained before the LORD; he was Doeg the Edomite, Saul's head shepherd.

[8]David asked Ahimelech, "Don't you have a spear or a sword here? I haven't brought my sword or any other weapon, because the king's business was urgent."

[9]The priest replied, "The sword of Goliath the Philistine, whom you killed in the Valley of Elah, is here; it is wrapped in a cloth behind the ephod. If you want it, take it; there is no sword here but that one."

David said, "There is none like it; give it to me."

David at Gath

[10]That day David fled from Saul and went to Achish king of Gath. [11]But the servants of Achish said to him, "Isn't this David, the king of the land? Isn't he the one they sing about in their dances:

" 'Saul has slain his thousands,
    and David his tens of thousands'?"

[12]David took these words to heart and was very much afraid of Achish king of Gath. [13]So he pretended to be insane in their presence; and while he was in their hands he acted like a madman, making marks on the doors of the gate and letting saliva run down his beard.

[14]Achish said to his servants, "Look at the man! He is insane! Why bring him to me? [15]Am I so short of madmen that you have to bring this fellow here to carry on like this in front of me? Must this man come into my house?"

David at Adullam and Mizpah

22 David left Gath and escaped to the cave of Adullam. When his brothers and his father's household heard about it, they went down to him there. [2]All those who were in distress or in debt or discontented gathered around him, and he became their leader. About four hundred men were with him.

[3]From there David went to Mizpah in Moab and said to the king of Moab, "Would you let my father and mother come and stay with you until I learn what God will do for me?" [4]So he left them with the king of Moab, and they stayed with him as long as David was in the stronghold.

[5]But the prophet Gad said to David, "Do not stay in the stronghold. Go into the land of Judah." So David left and went to the forest of Hereth.

Saul Kills the Priests of Nob

[6]Now Saul heard that David and his men had been discovered. And Saul, spear in hand, was seated under the tamarisk tree on the hill at Gibeah, with all his officials standing around him. [7]Saul said to them, "Listen, men of Benjamin! Will the son of Jesse give all of you fields and vineyards? Will he make all of you commanders of thousands and commanders of hundreds? [8]Is that why you have all conspired against me? No one tells me when my son makes a covenant with the son of Jesse. None of you is concerned about me or tells me that my

---

[a]5 Or *from us in the past few days since*   [b]5 Or *bodies*

son has incited my servant to lie in wait for me, as he does today."

⁹But Doeg the Edomite, who was standing with Saul's officials, said, "I saw the son of Jesse come to Ahimelech son of Ahitub at Nob. ¹⁰Ahimelech inquired of the LORD for him; he also gave him provisions and the sword of Goliath the Philistine."

¹¹Then the king sent for the priest Ahimelech son of Ahitub and his father's whole family, who were the priests at Nob, and they all came to the king. ¹²Saul said, "Listen now, son of Ahitub."

"Yes, my lord," he answered.

¹³Saul said to him, "Why have you conspired against me, you and the son of Jesse, giving him bread and a sword and inquiring of God for him, so that he has rebelled against me and lies in wait for me, as he does today?"

¹⁴Ahimelech answered the king, "Who of all your servants is as loyal as David, the king's son-in-law, captain of your bodyguard and highly respected in your household? ¹⁵Was that day the first time I inquired of God for him? Of course not! Let not the king accuse your servant or any of his father's family, for your servant knows nothing at all about this whole affair."

¹⁶But the king said, "You will surely die, Ahimelech, you and your father's whole family."

¹⁷Then the king ordered the guards at his side: "Turn and kill the priests of the LORD, because they too have sided with David. They knew he was fleeing, yet they did not tell me."

But the king's officials were not willing to raise a hand to strike the priests of the LORD.

¹⁸The king then ordered Doeg, "You turn and strike down the priests." So Doeg the Edomite turned and struck them down. That day he killed eighty-five men who wore the linen ephod. ¹⁹He also put to the sword Nob, the town of the priests, with its men and women, its children and infants, and its cattle, donkeys and sheep.

²⁰But Abiathar, a son of Ahimelech son of Ahitub, escaped and fled to join David. ²¹He told David that Saul had killed the priests of the LORD. ²²Then David said to

Abiathar: "That day, when Doeg the Edomite was there, I knew he would be sure to tell Saul. I am responsible for the death of your father's whole family. ²³Stay with me; don't be afraid; the man who is seeking your life is seeking mine also. You will be safe with me."

David Saves Keilah

23 When David was told, "Look, the Philistines are fighting against Keilah and are looting the threshing floors," ²he inquired of the LORD, saying, "Shall I go and attack these Philistines?"

The LORD answered him, "Go, attack the Philistines and save Keilah."

³But David's men said to him, "Here in Judah we are afraid. How much more, then, if we go to Keilah against the Philistine forces!"

⁴Once again David inquired of the LORD, and the LORD answered him, "Go down to Keilah, for I am going to give the Philistines into your hand." ⁵So David and his men went to Keilah, fought the Philistines and carried off their livestock. He inflicted heavy losses on the Philistines and saved the people of Keilah. ⁶(Now Abiathar son of Ahimelech had brought the ephod down with him when he fled to David at Keilah.)

Saul Pursues David

⁷Saul was told that David had gone to Keilah, and he said, "God has handed him over to me, for David has imprisoned himself by entering a town with gates and bars." ⁸And Saul called up all his forces for battle, to go down to Keilah to besiege David and his men.

⁹When David learned that Saul was plotting against him, he said to Abiathar the priest, "Bring the ephod." ¹⁰David said, "O LORD, God of Israel, your servant has heard definitely that Saul plans to come to Keilah and destroy the town on account of me. ¹¹Will the citizens of Keilah surrender me to him? Will Saul come down, as your servant has heard? O LORD, God of Israel, tell your servant."

And the LORD said, "He will."

¹²Again David asked, "Will the citizens of Keilah surrender me and my men to Saul?"

And the LORD said, "They will."

¹³So David and his men, about six hundred in number, left Keilah and kept moving from place to place. When Saul was told that David had escaped from Keilah, he did not go there.

¹⁴David stayed in the desert strongholds and in the hills of the Desert of Ziph. Day after day Saul searched for him, but God did not give David into his hands.

¹⁵While David was at Horesh in the Desert of Ziph, he learned that Saul had come out to take his life. ¹⁶And Saul's son Jonathan went to David at Horesh and helped him find strength in God. ¹⁷"Don't be afraid," he said. "My father Saul will not lay a hand on you. You will be king over Israel, and I will be second to you. Even my father Saul knows this." ¹⁸The two of them made a covenant before the LORD. Then Jonathan went home, but David remained at Horesh.

¹⁹The Ziphites went up to Saul at Gibeah and said, "Is not David hiding among us in the strongholds at Horesh, on the hill of Hakilah, south of Jeshimon? ²⁰Now, O king, come down whenever it pleases you to do so, and we will be responsible for handing him over to the king."

²¹Saul replied, "The LORD bless you for your concern for me. ²²Go and make further preparation. Find out where David usually goes and who has seen him there. They tell me he is very crafty. ²³Find out about all the hiding places he uses and come back to me with definite information.ᵃ Then I will go with you; if he is in the area, I will track him down among all the clans of Judah."

²⁴So they set out and went to Ziph ahead of Saul. Now David and his men were in the Desert of Maon, in the Arabah south of Jeshimon. ²⁵Saul and his men began the search, and when David was told about it, he went down to the rock and stayed in the Desert of Maon. When Saul heard this, he went into the Desert of Maon in pursuit of David.

²⁶Saul was going along one side of the mountain, and David and his men were on the other side, hurrying to get away from Saul. As Saul and his forces were closing in on David and his men to capture them, ²⁷a messenger came to Saul, saying, "Come quickly! The Philistines are raiding the land." ²⁸Then Saul broke off his pursuit of David and went to meet the Philistines. That is why they call this place Sela Hammahlekoth.ᵇ ²⁹And David went up from there and lived in the strongholds of En Gedi.

David Spares Saul's Life

24 After Saul returned from pursuing the Philistines, he was told, "David is in the Desert of En Gedi." ²So Saul took three thousand chosen men from all Israel and set out to look for David and his men near the Crags of the Wild Goats.

³He came to the sheep pens along the way; a cave was there, and Saul went in to relieve himself. David and his men were far back in the cave. ⁴The men said, "This is the day the LORD spoke of when he saidᶜ to you, 'I will give your enemy into your hands for you to deal with as you wish.' " Then David crept up unnoticed and cut off a corner of Saul's robe.

⁵Afterward, David was conscience-stricken for having cut off a corner of his robe. ⁶He said to his men, "The LORD forbid that I should do such a thing to my master, the LORD's anointed, or lift my hand against him; for he is the anointed of the LORD." ⁷With these words David rebuked his men and did not allow them to attack Saul. And Saul left the cave and went his way.

⁸Then David went out of the cave and called out to Saul, "My lord the king!" When Saul looked behind him, David bowed down and prostrated himself with his face to the ground. ⁹He said to Saul, "Why do you listen when men say, 'David is bent on harming you'? ¹⁰This day you have seen with your own eyes how the LORD delivered you into my hands in the cave. Some urged me to kill you, but I spared you; I said, 'I will not lift my hand against my master, because he is the LORD's anointed.' ¹¹See, my father, look at this piece of your robe in my hand! I cut off the corner of your robe but did not kill you. Now understand and recognize that I am not guilty of wrongdoing or rebellion. I have not

---

ᵃ23 Or me at Nacon   ᵇ28 Sela Hammahlekoth means
rock of parting.   ᶜ4 Or "Today the LORD is saying

wronged you, but you are hunting me down to take my life. ¹²May the LORD judge between you and me. And may the LORD avenge the wrongs you have done to me, but my hand will not touch you. ¹³As the old saying goes, 'From evildoers come evil deeds,' so my hand will not touch you.

¹⁴"Against whom has the king of Israel come out? Whom are you pursuing? A dead dog? A flea? ¹⁵May the LORD be our judge and decide between us. May he consider my cause and uphold it; may he vindicate me by delivering me from your hand."

¹⁶When David finished saying this, Saul asked, "Is that your voice, David my son?" And he wept aloud. ¹⁷"You are more righteous than I," he said. "You have treated me well, but I have treated you badly. ¹⁸You have just now told me of the good you did to me; the LORD delivered me into your hands, but you did not kill me. ¹⁹When a man finds his enemy, does he let him get away unharmed? May the LORD reward you well for the way you treated me today. ²⁰I know that you will surely be king and that the kingdom of Israel will be established in your hands. ²¹Now swear to me by the LORD that you will not cut off my descendants or wipe out my name from my father's family."

²²So David gave his oath to Saul. Then Saul returned home, but David and his men went up to the stronghold.

David, Nabal and Abigail

25 Now Samuel died, and all Israel assembled and mourned for him; and they buried him at his home in Ramah.

Then David moved down into the Desert of Maon.ᵃ ²A certain man in

ᵃ1 Some Septuagint manuscripts; Hebrew *Paran*

Friday

Don't Fight Back

Read 1 Samuel 24:1–13

Chip, age 16

When some guys from school smashed my car window and stole my guitar, CD player and all my CDs, fighting back was exactly what I wanted to do. My friends even told me to find those guys and beat them up. It sure seemed like they deserved it!

In the passage for today, I know David must have been tempted to get Saul back for his evil deeds. After all, Saul had gathered 3,000 men to hunt David down—and this wasn't the first time he had tried to kill David. But David knew God wanted him to forgive Saul, and that's exactly what David did.

I was really angry when those guys at school trashed my car and took my things. But I didn't try to beat them up. And since they didn't hurt me, I decided not to press charges as long as they returned my stuff. It was up to God, not me, to do what he wanted with those guys. My job was to forgive.

What about You?

❶ When was the last time someone did something really mean to you? How did you respond? How should you have responded?

❷ Is there someone you need to forgive? Even if that person hasn't apologized to you, make a point of offering him or her your forgiveness as soon as you can.

❸ Ask God to help you forgive people who hurt you.

Turn to page 346 for your next devotion.

water jug that are near his head, and
let's go."

¹²So David took the spear and water
jug near Saul's head, and they left. No
one saw or knew about it, nor did anyone
wake up. They were all sleeping, because
the LORD had put them into a deep sleep.

¹³Then David crossed over to the other
side and stood on top of the hill some
distance away; there was a wide space
between them. ¹⁴He called out to the
army and to Abner son of Ner, "Aren't
you going to answer me, Abner?"

Abner replied, "Who are you who calls
to the king?"

¹⁵David said, "You're a man, aren't
you? And who is like you in Israel? Why
didn't you guard your lord the king?
Someone came to destroy your lord the
king. ¹⁶What you have done is not good.
As surely as the LORD lives, you and your
men deserve to die, because you did not
guard your master, the LORD's anointed.
Look around you. Where are the king's
spear and water jug that were near his
head?"

¹⁷Saul recognized David's voice and
said, "Is that your voice, David my son?"

David replied, "Yes it is, my lord the
king." ¹⁸And he added, "Why is my lord
pursuing his servant? What have I done,
and what wrong am I guilty of? ¹⁹Now
let my lord the king listen to his servant's
words. If the LORD has incited you
against me, then may he accept an offering. If, however, men have done it, may
they be cursed before the LORD! They
have now driven me from my share in
the LORD's inheritance and have said,
'Go, serve other gods.' ²⁰Now do not let
my blood fall to the ground far from the
presence of the LORD. The king of Israel
has come out to look for a flea—as one
hunts a partridge in the mountains."

²¹Then Saul said, "I have sinned. Come
back, David my son. Because you considered my life precious today, I will not try
to harm you again. Surely I have acted
like a fool and have erred greatly."

²²"Here is the king's spear," David answered. "Let one of your young men
come over and get it. ²³The LORD rewards
every man for his righteousness and
faithfulness. The LORD delivered you into
my hands today, but I would not lay a
hand on the LORD's anointed. ²⁴As surely
as I valued your life today, so may the
LORD value my life and deliver me from
all trouble."

²⁵Then Saul said to David, "May you be
blessed, my son David; you will do great
things and surely triumph."

So David went on his way, and Saul
returned home.

David Among the Philistines

27 But David thought to himself,
"One of these days I will be destroyed by the hand of Saul. The best
thing I can do is to escape to the land of
the Philistines. Then Saul will give up
searching for me anywhere in Israel, and
I will slip out of his hand."

²So David and the six hundred men
with him left and went over to Achish
son of Maoch king of Gath. ³David and
his men settled in Gath with Achish.
Each man had his family with him, and
David had his two wives: Ahinoam of
Jezreel and Abigail of Carmel, the widow
of Nabal. ⁴When Saul was told that David
had fled to Gath, he no longer searched
for him.

⁵Then David said to Achish, "If I have
found favor in your eyes, let a place be assigned to me in one of the country towns,
that I may live there. Why should your
servant live in the royal city with you?"

⁶So on that day Achish gave him Ziklag, and it has belonged to the kings of
Judah ever since. ⁷David lived in Philistine territory a year and four months.

⁸Now David and his men went up and
raided the Geshurites, the Girzites and
the Amalekites. (From ancient times
these peoples had lived in the land extending to Shur and Egypt.) ⁹Whenever
David attacked an area, he did not leave
a man or woman alive, but took sheep
and cattle, donkeys and camels, and
clothes. Then he returned to Achish.

¹⁰When Achish asked, "Where did you
go raiding today?" David would say,
"Against the Negev of Judah" or "Against
the Negev of Jerahmeel" or "Against the
Negev of the Kenites." ¹¹He did not leave
a man or woman alive to be brought to
Gath, for he thought, "They might inform
on us and say, 'This is what David did.' "
And such was his practice as long as he

Who Was That Masked Man?

1 Samuel 28 King Saul did some dumb things, but this was the dumbest: He called the Psychic Network! Saul was a little embarrassed about it, so he put on a disguise so nobody would recognize him. But the psychic (also known as the Witch of Endor) figured it out anyway and, boy, was she ticked! Others who pretended to be someone else:

× **Sarah** pretended to be her husband's sister (Genesis 12:10–20)

× **Jacob** pretended to be his brother Esau to steal a blessing (Genesis 27:1–40)

× **Leah** pretended to be her sister Rachel on Rachel's wedding night (Genesis 29:15–30)

× **David** pretended to be insane to escape the evil King Achish (1 Samuel 21:12—22:1)

lived in Philistine territory. ¹²Achish trusted David and said to himself, "He has become so odious to his people, the Israelites, that he will be my servant forever."

Saul and the Witch of Endor

28 In those days the Philistines gathered their forces to fight against Israel. Achish said to David, "You must understand that you and your men will accompany me in the army."

²David said, "Then you will see for yourself what your servant can do."

Achish replied, "Very well, I will make you my bodyguard for life."

³Now Samuel was dead, and all Israel had mourned for him and buried him in his own town of Ramah. Saul had expelled the mediums and spiritists from the land.

⁴The Philistines assembled and came and set up camp at Shunem, while Saul gathered all the Israelites and set up camp at Gilboa. ⁵When Saul saw the Philistine army, he was afraid; terror filled his heart. ⁶He inquired of the LORD, but the LORD did not answer him by dreams or Urim or prophets. ⁷Saul then said to his attendants, "Find me a woman who is a medium, so I may go and inquire of her."

"There is one in Endor," they said.

⁸So Saul disguised himself, putting on other clothes, and at night he and two men went to the woman. "Consult a spirit for me," he said, "and bring up for me the one I name."

⁹But the woman said to him, "Surely you know what Saul has done. He has cut off the mediums and spiritists from the land. Why have you set a trap for my life to bring about my death?"

¹⁰Saul swore to her by the LORD, "As surely as the LORD lives, you will not be punished for this."

¹¹Then the woman asked, "Whom shall I bring up for you?"

"Bring up Samuel," he said.

¹²When the woman saw Samuel, she cried out at the top of her voice and said to Saul, "Why have you deceived me? You are Saul!"

¹³The king said to her, "Don't be afraid. What do you see?"

The woman said, "I see a spirit*a* coming up out of the ground."

¹⁴"What does he look like?" he asked.

"An old man wearing a robe is coming up," she said.

Then Saul knew it was Samuel, and he bowed down and prostrated himself with his face to the ground.

¹⁵Samuel said to Saul, "Why have you disturbed me by bringing me up?"

"I am in great distress," Saul said. "The Philistines are fighting against me, and God has turned away from me. He no longer answers me, either by prophets or by dreams. So I have called on you to tell me what to do."

¹⁶Samuel said, "Why do you consult me, now that the LORD has turned away from you and become your enemy? ¹⁷The LORD has done what he predicted through me. The LORD has torn the kingdom out of your hands and given it to one of your

a 13 Or see spirits; or see gods

neighbors—to David. [18]Because you did not obey the LORD or carry out his fierce wrath against the Amalekites, the LORD has done this to you today. [19]The LORD will hand over both Israel and you to the Philistines, and tomorrow you and your sons will be with me. The LORD will also hand over the army of Israel to the Philistines."

[20]Immediately Saul fell full length on the ground, filled with fear because of Samuel's words. His strength was gone, for he had eaten nothing all that day and night.

[21]When the woman came to Saul and saw that he was greatly shaken, she said, "Look, your maidservant has obeyed you. I took my life in my hands and did what you told me to do. [22]Now please listen to your servant and let me give you some food so you may eat and have the strength to go on your way."

[23]He refused and said, "I will not eat."

But his men joined the woman in urging him, and he listened to them. He got up from the ground and sat on the couch.

[24]The woman had a fattened calf at the house, which she butchered at once. She took some flour, kneaded it and baked bread without yeast. [25]Then she set it before Saul and his men, and they ate. That same night they got up and left.

Achish Sends David Back to Ziklag

29 The Philistines gathered all their forces at Aphek, and Israel camped by the spring in Jezreel. [2]As the Philistine rulers marched with their units of hundreds and thousands, David and his men were marching at the rear with Achish. [3]The commanders of the Philistines asked, "What about these Hebrews?"

Achish replied, "Is this not David, who was an officer of Saul king of Israel? He has already been with me for over a year, and from the day he left Saul until now, I have found no fault in him."

[4]But the Philistine commanders were angry with him and said, "Send the man back, that he may return to the place you assigned him. He must not go with us into battle, or he will turn against us during the fighting. How better could he regain his master's favor than by taking the heads of our own men? [5]Isn't this the David they sang about in their dances:

" 'Saul has slain his thousands,
    and David his tens of thousands'?"

[6]So Achish called David and said to him, "As surely as the LORD lives, you have been reliable, and I would be pleased to have you serve with me in the army. From the day you came to me until now, I have found no fault in you, but the rulers don't approve of you. [7]Turn back and go in peace; do nothing to displease the Philistine rulers."

[8]"But what have I done?" asked David. "What have you found against your servant from the day I came to you until now? Why can't I go and fight against the enemies of my lord the king?"

[9]Achish answered, "I know that you have been as pleasing in my eyes as an angel of God; nevertheless, the Philistine commanders have said, 'He must not go up with us into battle.' [10]Now get up early, along with your master's servants who have come with you, and leave in the morning as soon as it is light."

[11]So David and his men got up early in the morning to go back to the land of the Philistines, and the Philistines went up to Jezreel.

David Destroys the Amalekites

30 David and his men reached Ziklag on the third day. Now the Amalekites had raided the Negev and Ziklag. They had attacked Ziklag and burned it, [2]and had taken captive the women and all who were in it, both young and old. They killed none of them, but carried them off as they went on their way.

[3]When David and his men came to Ziklag, they found it destroyed by fire and their wives and sons and daughters taken captive. [4]So David and his men wept aloud until they had no strength left to weep. [5]David's two wives had been captured—Ahinoam of Jezreel and Abigail, the widow of Nabal of Carmel. [6]David was greatly distressed because the men were talking of stoning him; each one was bitter in spirit because of his sons and daughters. But David found strength in the LORD his God.

[7]Then David said to Abiathar the

priest, the son of Ahimelech, "Bring me the ephod." Abiathar brought it to him, ⁸and David inquired of the LORD, "Shall I pursue this raiding party? Will I overtake them?"

"Pursue them," he answered. "You will certainly overtake them and succeed in the rescue."

⁹David and the six hundred men with him came to the Besor Ravine, where some stayed behind, ¹⁰for two hundred men were too exhausted to cross the ravine. But David and four hundred men continued the pursuit.

¹¹They found an Egyptian in a field and brought him to David. They gave him water to drink and food to eat— ¹²part of a cake of pressed figs and two cakes of raisins. He ate and was revived, for he had not eaten any food or drunk any water for three days and three nights.

¹³David asked him, "To whom do you belong, and where do you come from?"

He said, "I am an Egyptian, the slave of an Amalekite. My master abandoned me when I became ill three days ago. ¹⁴We raided the Negev of the Kerethites and the territory belonging to Judah and the Negev of Caleb. And we burned Ziklag."

Weekend.

Best Buds

Read 1 Samuel 20:4 (page 335)

This week you read about the incredible friendship between David and Jonathan. Jonathan's dad, Saul, hated David. Saul was jealous of David's looks, popularity and the way people treated him. So Jonathan was torn between his dad and his best friend. When push came to shove, Jonathan proved to be a really committed friend and even helped David by trying to talk Dad out of murder.

On Thursday Amy talked about her friend. She said, "Because she's such a good friend to me, I want to be a good friend to her." That's really the kind of relationship David and Jonathan had—they would do anything for each other.

Life is tough, and there are so many "enemies" around (enemies like loneliness, fear, distrust, to name a few) that we all need a good friend. The Bible gives us a great picture of what a friend is—not just someone to help *you* out, but someone you can help. Sometimes your friends need you a lot more than you need them (in today's passage David sure needed Jonathan more than Jonathan needed David!). And that's OK, because we all go through times when we need somebody to come through for us and don't have much to give back.

Let David and Jonathan teach you what it means to be a great friend.

What about You?

❶ What are the top 5 things you want and need in a friend? Do you have a friend who comes through on all 5? Now ask yourself whether you are that kind of friend to others.

❷ Get together with one good friend and share your list of the top 5 friendship qualities. Talk with your friend about how *you're* both doing with the items on the list.

❸ Pray for your friends, asking God to help you be better friends to each other.

Turn to page 361 for your next devotion.

¹⁵David asked him, "Can you lead me down to this raiding party?"

He answered, "Swear to me before God that you will not kill me or hand me over to my master, and I will take you down to them."

¹⁶He led David down, and there they were, scattered over the countryside, eating, drinking and reveling because of the great amount of plunder they had taken from the land of the Philistines and from Judah. ¹⁷David fought them from dusk until the evening of the next day, and none of them got away, except four hundred young men who rode off on camels and fled. ¹⁸David recovered everything the Amalekites had taken, including his two wives. ¹⁹Nothing was missing: young or old, boy or girl, plunder or anything else they had taken. David brought everything back. ²⁰He took all the flocks and herds, and his men drove them ahead of the other livestock, saying, "This is David's plunder."

²¹Then David came to the two hundred men who had been too exhausted to follow him and who were left behind at the Besor Ravine. They came out to meet David and the people with him. As David and his men approached, he greeted them. ²²But all the evil men and troublemakers among David's followers said, "Because they did not go out with us, we will not share with them the plunder we recovered. However, each man may take his wife and children and go."

²³David replied, "No, my brothers, you must not do that with what the LORD has given us. He has protected us and handed over to us the forces that came against us. ²⁴Who will listen to what you say? The share of the man who stayed with the supplies is to be the same as that of him who went down to the battle. All will share alike." ²⁵David made this a statute and ordinance for Israel from that day to this.

²⁶When David arrived in Ziklag, he sent some of the plunder to the elders of Judah, who were his friends, saying, "Here is a present for you from the plunder of the LORD's enemies."

²⁷He sent it to those who were in Bethel, Ramoth Negev and Jattir; ²⁸to those in Aroer, Siphmoth, Eshtemoa ²⁹and Racal; to those in the towns of the Jerahmeelites and the Kenites; ³⁰to those in Hormah, Bor Ashan, Athach ³¹and Hebron; and to those in all the other places where David and his men had roamed.

Saul Takes His Life

31 Now the Philistines fought against Israel; the Israelites fled before them, and many fell slain on Mount Gilboa. ²The Philistines pressed hard after Saul and his sons, and they killed his sons Jonathan, Abinadab and Malki-Shua. ³The fighting grew fierce around Saul, and when the archers overtook him, they wounded him critically.

⁴Saul said to his armor-bearer, "Draw your sword and run me through, or these uncircumcised fellows will come and run me through and abuse me."

But his armor-bearer was terrified and would not do it; so Saul took his own sword and fell on it. ⁵When the armor-bearer saw that Saul was dead, he too fell on his sword and died with him. ⁶So Saul and his three sons and his armor-bearer and all his men died together that same day.

⁷When the Israelites along the valley and those across the Jordan saw that the Israelite army had fled and that Saul and his sons had died, they abandoned their towns and fled. And the Philistines came and occupied them.

⁸The next day, when the Philistines came to strip the dead, they found Saul and his three sons fallen on Mount Gilboa. ⁹They cut off his head and stripped off his armor, and they sent messengers throughout the land of the Philistines to proclaim the news in the temple of their idols and among their people. ¹⁰They put his armor in the temple of the Ashtoreths and fastened his body to the wall of Beth Shan.

¹¹When the people of Jabesh Gilead heard of what the Philistines had done to Saul, ¹²all their valiant men journeyed through the night to Beth Shan. They took down the bodies of Saul and his sons from the wall of Beth Shan and went to Jabesh, where they burned them. ¹³Then they took their bones and buried them under a tamarisk tree at Jabesh, and they fasted seven days.

2 Samuel

START

Cast of Characters

David

He's a great warrior, big fan of God and Israel's greatest king. But he's far from perfect. In the end, he gets straight with God.

Joab (JOE-ab) and Abner (AB-nur)

Joab is David's top military man—the 2 fought together all those years when King Saul was trying to kill David. Abner was *Saul's* top general. Abner kills Joab's brother, and Joab gets revenge. The fight turns into a civil war.

(Yoo-RIGH-uh)
Uriah and Bathsheba (bath-SHE-bah)

They're married. The husband is a good soldier in David's army. The wife is a beautiful woman who takes a bath on her roof next door to David's house. David invites her over, and, to make a long story short, Bathsheba gets pregnant. After David's first plan fails, he has Uriah killed in battle. Dead men tell no tales. Now widowed, Bathsheba marries the king.

The *first* book of Samuel covers the rise and fall of Saul, Israel's first king. It also introduces David, the guy who's about to become the next king. That great moment happens in *this* book. David mourns Saul's death, then takes the throne—good news for the friends of God, but bad news for the enemies of God.

King David completes the work Joshua started long ago: He chases out the barbaric locals living off the land God gave to Israel. Things go great until David has a mid-life crisis. He stays home from the war, has an affair and then commits murder in an attempt to cover his sinful tracks. His friend Nathan the prophet isn't fooled; he slams David for his sins.

David and Bathsheba get married, but it isn't happily ever after. The baby conceived from the affair dies. And David's other kids get involved in stuff like rape, murder and civil war. But one of his kids—Solomon—turns out pretty good. He figures big in the next book and more besides. David restores his reign, but it's not as fun as it used to be.

In a fit of independence and against wise counsel, David orders a count of available soldiers—apparently to comfort himself with his battle strength. But think about it. God led Joshua to victory with a shout, and God gave Gideon just 300 men to take a nation. So he isn't too thrilled with David's order. The nation is hit with a 3-day plague as a consequence. David gets the hint and gets right with God.

Nathan (NAY-thun)
Nate's a prophet of God. He blows the whistle on David's adultery-murder caper. Good prophet!

Solomon (SAHL-uh-mun)
Bathsheba's second son by King David. More on him in the next book.

(AM-non, TAY-mar)
Amnon, Tamar and (AB-suh-lum) **Absalom**
Try to follow this: David's son Amnon rapes his own half sister Tamar. Absalom, Tamar's full brother, avenges his sister by killing their rapist half brother. Absalom escapes for a few years, then returns as an opposition leader, recruiting the people to war against his own father. Not a happy family.

What's Up with That?

Revenge

was pretty popular back in Bible times. It's *still* popular. When someone does something bad to you, you want to do it right back (God hates revenge—but lots of people do it anyway. Not good). When Abner killed Joab's brother, Joab killed Abner. When Amnon raped Tamar, Absalom killed Amnon. That's the way life was back then. Sadly, revenge is a way of life for many people today.

David, Israel's mightiest warrior-king, shows us that love is more powerful than revenge and hate.

☞ Saul was David's enemy and tried to kill him many times. David *could* have killed Saul. But he didn't. He left that decision to God.

☞ Saul's grandson Mephibosheth (ma-FIB-oh-sheth) was the only living heir to Saul's throne. Common sense says that David *should* have killed him, just to make sure he didn't try to claim that throne. David didn't. Instead he treated Mephibosheth like his own son—free to dine at his table!

☞ Absalom rebelled against his own dad and led an army to take over the country. David *could* have killed him. He didn't. Instead he did everything possible to save his son.

God sent us another king from Bethlehem to prove that love is the law. King Jesus shows us that love is more powerful than *anything*.

Snap shots

- Dave takes the throne . . . kind of *(chapter 1)*

- "Stop your bickering!"—a civil war keeps the tribes from uniting *(chapters 2—4)*

- David rules the whole nation, goes after the enemies of God *(chapters 5—10)*

- Sex and murder *(chapter 11)*

- The big turnaround— David sees his sin *(chapter 12)*

- Family sins—incest, rape, murder, mutiny *(chapters 13—19)*

- Sheba's revolt *(chapter 20)*

- The ups and downs of David's final days *(chapters 21—24)*

David Hears of Saul's Death

1 After the death of Saul, David returned from defeating the Amalekites and stayed in Ziklag two days. ²On the third day a man arrived from Saul's camp, with his clothes torn and with dust on his head. When he came to David, he fell to the ground to pay him honor.

³"Where have you come from?" David asked him.

He answered, "I have escaped from the Israelite camp."

⁴"What happened?" David asked. "Tell me."

He said, "The men fled from the battle. Many of them fell and died. And Saul and his son Jonathan are dead."

⁵Then David said to the young man who brought him the report, "How do you know that Saul and his son Jonathan are dead?"

⁶"I happened to be on Mount Gilboa," the young man said, "and there was Saul, leaning on his spear, with the chariots and riders almost upon him. ⁷When he turned around and saw me, he called out to me, and I said, 'What can I do?'

⁸"He asked me, 'Who are you?'

" 'An Amalekite,' I answered.

⁹"Then he said to me, 'Stand over me and kill me! I am in the throes of death, but I'm still alive.'

¹⁰"So I stood over him and killed him, because I knew that after he had fallen he could not survive. And I took the crown that was on his head and the band on his arm and have brought them here to my lord."

¹¹Then David and all the men with him took hold of their clothes and tore them. ¹²They mourned and wept and fasted till evening for Saul and his son Jonathan, and for the army of the LORD and the house of Israel, because they had fallen by the sword.

¹³David said to the young man who brought him the report, "Where are you from?"

"I am the son of an alien, an Amalekite," he answered.

¹⁴David asked him, "Why were you not afraid to lift your hand to destroy the LORD's anointed?"

¹⁵Then David called one of his men and said, "Go, strike him down!" So he struck him down, and he died. ¹⁶For David had said to him, "Your blood be on your own head. Your own mouth testified against you when you said, 'I killed the LORD's anointed.' "

David's Lament for Saul and Jonathan

¹⁷David took up this lament concerning Saul and his son Jonathan, ¹⁸and ordered that the men of Judah be taught this lament of the bow (it is written in the Book of Jashar):

¹⁹"Your glory, O Israel, lies slain on
    your heights.
  How the mighty have fallen!

²⁰"Tell it not in Gath,
    proclaim it not in the streets of
      Ashkelon,
  lest the daughters of the Philistines be
    glad,
    lest the daughters of the
      uncircumcised rejoice.

²¹"O mountains of Gilboa,
    may you have neither dew nor rain,
    nor fields that yield offerings of
      grain.
  For there the shield of the mighty was
    defiled,
    the shield of Saul—no longer rubbed
      with oil.

²²From the blood of the slain,
    from the flesh of the mighty,
  the bow of Jonathan did not turn
    back,
    the sword of Saul did not return
      unsatisfied.

²³"Saul and Jonathan—
    in life they were loved and
      gracious,
    and in death they were not parted.
  They were swifter than eagles,
    they were stronger than lions.

²⁴"O daughters of Israel,
    weep for Saul,
  who clothed you in scarlet and finery,
    who adorned your garments with
      ornaments of gold.

²⁵"How the mighty have fallen in battle!
    Jonathan lies slain on your heights.
²⁶I grieve for you, Jonathan my brother;
    you were very dear to me.

> Your love for me was wonderful,
> more wonderful than that of
> women.

²⁷"How the mighty have fallen!
The weapons of war have perished!"

David Anointed King Over Judah

2 In the course of time, David inquired of the LORD. "Shall I go up to one of the towns of Judah?" he asked.

The LORD said, "Go up."

David asked, "Where shall I go?"

"To Hebron," the LORD answered.

²So David went up there with his two wives, Ahinoam of Jezreel and Abigail, the widow of Nabal of Carmel. ³David also took the men who were with him, each with his family, and they settled in Hebron and its towns. ⁴Then the men of Judah came to Hebron and there they anointed David king over the house of Judah.

When David was told that it was the men of Jabesh Gilead who had buried Saul, ⁵he sent messengers to the men of Jabesh Gilead to say to them, "The LORD bless you for showing this kindness to Saul your master by burying him. ⁶May the LORD now show you kindness and faithfulness, and I too will show you the same favor because you have done this. ⁷Now then, be strong and brave, for Saul your master is dead, and the house of Judah has anointed me king over them."

War Between the Houses of David and Saul

⁸Meanwhile, Abner son of Ner, the commander of Saul's army, had taken Ish-Bosheth son of Saul and brought him over to Mahanaim. ⁹He made him king over Gilead, Ashuri[a] and Jezreel, and also over Ephraim, Benjamin and all Israel.

¹⁰Ish-Bosheth son of Saul was forty years old when he became king over Israel, and he reigned two years. The house of Judah, however, followed David. ¹¹The length of time David was king in Hebron over the house of Judah was seven years and six months.

¹²Abner son of Ner, together with the men of Ish-Bosheth son of Saul, left Mahanaim and went to Gibeon. ¹³Joab son of Zeruiah and David's men went out and met them at the pool of Gibeon. One group sat down on one side of the pool and one group on the other side.

¹⁴Then Abner said to Joab, "Let's have some of the young men get up and fight hand to hand in front of us."

"All right, let them do it," Joab said.

¹⁵So they stood up and were counted off—twelve men for Benjamin and Ish-Bosheth son of Saul, and twelve for David. ¹⁶Then each man grabbed his opponent by the head and thrust his dagger into his opponent's side, and they fell down together. So that place in Gibeon was called Helkath Hazzurim.[b]

¹⁷The battle that day was very fierce, and Abner and the men of Israel were defeated by David's men.

¹⁸The three sons of Zeruiah were there: Joab, Abishai and Asahel. Now Asahel was as fleet-footed as a wild gazelle. ¹⁹He chased Abner, turning neither to the right nor to the left as he pursued him. ²⁰Abner looked behind him and asked, "Is that you, Asahel?"

"It is," he answered.

²¹Then Abner said to him, "Turn aside to the right or to the left; take on one of the young men and strip him of his weapons." But Asahel would not stop chasing him.

²²Again Abner warned Asahel, "Stop chasing me! Why should I strike you down? How could I look your brother Joab in the face?"

²³But Asahel refused to give up the pursuit; so Abner thrust the butt of his spear into Asahel's stomach, and the spear came out through his back. He fell there and died on the spot. And every man stopped when he came to the place where Asahel had fallen and died.

²⁴But Joab and Abishai pursued Abner, and as the sun was setting, they came to the hill of Ammah, near Giah on the way to the wasteland of Gibeon. ²⁵Then the men of Benjamin rallied behind Abner. They formed themselves into a group and took their stand on top of a hill.

²⁶Abner called out to Joab, "Must the sword devour forever? Don't you realize

---

[a]9 Or *Asher* [b]16 *Helkath Hazzurim* means *field of daggers* or *field of hostilities.*

that this will end in bitterness? How long before you order your men to stop pursuing their brothers?"

²⁷Joab answered, "As surely as God lives, if you had not spoken, the men would have continued the pursuit of their brothers until morning.ᵃ"

²⁸So Joab blew the trumpet, and all the men came to a halt; they no longer pursued Israel, nor did they fight anymore.

²⁹All that night Abner and his men marched through the Arabah. They crossed the Jordan, continued through the whole Bithronᵇ and came to Mahanaim.

³⁰Then Joab returned from pursuing Abner and assembled all his men. Besides Asahel, nineteen of David's men were found missing. ³¹But David's men had killed three hundred and sixty Benjamites who were with Abner. ³²They took Asahel and buried him in his father's tomb at Bethlehem. Then Joab and his men marched all night and arrived at Hebron by daybreak.

3 The war between the house of Saul and the house of David lasted a long time. David grew stronger and stronger, while the house of Saul grew weaker and weaker.

²Sons were born to David in Hebron:
His firstborn was Amnon the son of Ahinoam of Jezreel;
³his second, Kileab the son of Abigail the widow of Nabal of Carmel;
the third, Absalom the son of Maacah daughter of Talmai king of Geshur;
⁴the fourth, Adonijah the son of Haggith;
the fifth, Shephatiah the son of Abital;
⁵and the sixth, Ithream the son of David's wife Eglah.
These were born to David in Hebron.

Abner Goes Over to David

⁶During the war between the house of Saul and the house of David, Abner had been strengthening his own position in the house of Saul. ⁷Now Saul had had a concubine named Rizpah daughter of Aiah. And Ish-Bosheth said to Abner,

"Why did you sleep with my father's concubine?"

⁸Abner was very angry because of what Ish-Bosheth said and he answered, "Am I a dog's head—on Judah's side? This very day I am loyal to the house of your father Saul and to his family and friends. I haven't handed you over to David. Yet now you accuse me of an offense involving this woman! ⁹May God deal with Abner, be it ever so severely, if I do not do for David what the LORD promised him on oath ¹⁰and transfer the kingdom from the house of Saul and establish David's throne over Israel and Judah from Dan to Beersheba." ¹¹Ish-Bosheth did not dare to say another word to Abner, because he was afraid of him.

¹²Then Abner sent messengers on his behalf to say to David, "Whose land is it? Make an agreement with me, and I will help you bring all Israel over to you."

¹³"Good," said David. "I will make an agreement with you. But I demand one thing of you: Do not come into my presence unless you bring Michal daughter of Saul when you come to see me." ¹⁴Then David sent messengers to Ish-Bosheth son of Saul, demanding, "Give me my wife Michal, whom I betrothed to myself for the price of a hundred Philistine foreskins."

¹⁵So Ish-Bosheth gave orders and had her taken away from her husband Paltiel son of Laish. ¹⁶Her husband, however, went with her, weeping behind her all the way to Bahurim. Then Abner said to him, "Go back home!" So he went back.

¹⁷Abner conferred with the elders of Israel and said, "For some time you have wanted to make David your king. ¹⁸Now do it! For the LORD promised David, 'By my servant David I will rescue my people Israel from the hand of the Philistines and from the hand of all their enemies.' "

¹⁹Abner also spoke to the Benjamites in person. Then he went to Hebron to tell David everything that Israel and the whole house of Benjamin wanted to do.

ᵃ27 Or *spoken this morning, the men would not have taken up the pursuit of their brothers*; or *spoken, the men would have given up the pursuit of their brothers by morning*　ᵇ29 Or *morning*; or *ravine*; the meaning of the Hebrew for this word is uncertain.

²⁰When Abner, who had twenty men with him, came to David at Hebron, David prepared a feast for him and his men. ²¹Then Abner said to David, "Let me go at once and assemble all Israel for my lord the king, so that they may make a compact with you, and that you may rule over all that your heart desires." So David sent Abner away, and he went in peace.

Joab Murders Abner

²²Just then David's men and Joab returned from a raid and brought with them a great deal of plunder. But Abner was no longer with David in Hebron, because David had sent him away, and he had gone in peace. ²³When Joab and all the soldiers with him arrived, he was told that Abner son of Ner had come to the king and that the king had sent him away and that he had gone in peace. ²⁴So Joab went to the king and said, "What have you done? Look, Abner came to you. Why did you let him go? Now he is gone! ²⁵You know Abner son of Ner; he came to deceive you and observe your movements and find out everything you are doing."

²⁶Joab then left David and sent messengers after Abner, and they brought him back from the well of Sirah. But David did not know it. ²⁷Now when Abner returned to Hebron, Joab took him aside into the gateway, as though to speak with him privately. And there, to avenge the blood of his brother Asahel, Joab stabbed him in the stomach, and he died.

²⁸Later, when David heard about this, he said, "I and my kingdom are forever innocent before the LORD concerning the blood of Abner son of Ner. ²⁹May his blood fall upon the head of Joab and upon all his father's house! May Joab's house never be without someone who has a running sore or leprosy *ᵃ* or who leans on a crutch or who falls by the sword or who lacks food."

³⁰(Joab and his brother Abishai murdered Abner because he had killed their brother Asahel in the battle at Gibeon.)

³¹Then David said to Joab and all the people with him, "Tear your clothes and put on sackcloth and walk in mourning in front of Abner." King David himself walked behind the bier. ³²They buried Abner in Hebron, and the king wept aloud at Abner's tomb. All the people wept also.

³³The king sang this lament for Abner:

"Should Abner have died as the
　　lawless die?
³⁴　Your hands were not bound,
　　your feet were not fettered.
You fell as one falls before wicked
　　men."

And all the people wept over him again. ³⁵Then they all came and urged David to eat something while it was still day; but David took an oath, saying, "May God deal with me, be it ever so severely, if I taste bread or anything else before the sun sets!"

³⁶All the people took note and were pleased; indeed, everything the king did pleased them. ³⁷So on that day all the people and all Israel knew that the king had no part in the murder of Abner son of Ner.

³⁸Then the king said to his men, "Do you not realize that a prince and a great man has fallen in Israel this day? ³⁹And today, though I am the anointed king, I am weak, and these sons of Zeruiah are too strong for me. May the LORD repay the evildoer according to his evil deeds!"

Ish-Bosheth Murdered

4 When Ish-Bosheth son of Saul heard that Abner had died in Hebron, he lost courage, and all Israel became alarmed. ²Now Saul's son had two men who were leaders of raiding bands. One was named Baanah and the other Recab; they were sons of Rimmon the Beerothite from the tribe of Benjamin—Beeroth is considered part of Benjamin, ³because the people of Beeroth fled to Gittaim and have lived there as aliens to this day.

⁴(Jonathan son of Saul had a son who was lame in both feet. He was five years old when the news about Saul and Jonathan came from Jezreel. His nurse picked him up and fled, but as she hurried to

ᵃ29 The Hebrew word was used for various diseases affecting the skin—not necessarily leprosy.

leave, he fell and became crippled. His name was Mephibosheth.)

[5]Now Recab and Baanah, the sons of Rimmon the Beerothite, set out for the house of Ish-Bosheth, and they arrived there in the heat of the day while he was taking his noonday rest. [6]They went into the inner part of the house as if to get some wheat, and they stabbed him in the stomach. Then Recab and his brother Baanah slipped away.

[7]They had gone into the house while he was lying on the bed in his bedroom. After they stabbed and killed him, they cut off his head. Taking it with them, they traveled all night by way of the Arabah. [8]They brought the head of Ish-Bosheth to David at Hebron and said to the king, "Here is the head of Ish-Bosheth son of Saul, your enemy, who tried to take your life. This day the LORD has avenged my lord the king against Saul and his offspring."

[9]David answered Recab and his brother Baanah, the sons of Rimmon the Beerothite, "As surely as the LORD lives, who has delivered me out of all trouble, [10]when a man told me, 'Saul is dead,' and thought he was bringing good news, I seized him and put him to death in Ziklag. That was the reward I gave him for his news! [11]How much more—when wicked men have killed an innocent man in his own house and on his own bed—should I not now demand his blood from your hand and rid the earth of you!"

[12]So David gave an order to his men, and they killed them. They cut off their hands and feet and hung the bodies by the pool in Hebron. But they took the head of Ish-Bosheth and buried it in Abner's tomb at Hebron.

David Becomes King Over Israel

5 All the tribes of Israel came to David at Hebron and said, "We are your own flesh and blood. [2]In the past, while Saul was king over us, you were the one who led Israel on their military campaigns. And the LORD said to you, 'You will shepherd my people Israel, and you will become their ruler.' "

[3]When all the elders of Israel had come to King David at Hebron, the king made a compact with them at Hebron before the

LORD, and they anointed David king over Israel.

[4]David was thirty years old when he became king, and he reigned forty years. [5]In Hebron he reigned over Judah seven years and six months, and in Jerusalem he reigned over all Israel and Judah thirty-three years.

David Conquers Jerusalem

[6]The king and his men marched to Jerusalem to attack the Jebusites, who lived there. The Jebusites said to David, "You will not get in here; even the blind and the lame can ward you off." They thought, "David cannot get in here." [7]Nevertheless, David captured the fortress of Zion, the City of David.

[8]On that day, David said, "Anyone who conquers the Jebusites will have to use the water shaft[a] to reach those 'lame and blind' who are David's enemies.[b]" That is why they say, "The 'blind and lame' will not enter the palace."

[9]David then took up residence in the fortress and called it the City of David. He built up the area around it, from the supporting terraces[c] inward. [10]And he became more and more powerful, because the LORD God Almighty was with him.

[11]Now Hiram king of Tyre sent messengers to David, along with cedar logs and carpenters and stonemasons, and they built a palace for David. [12]And David knew that the LORD had established him as king over Israel and had exalted his kingdom for the sake of his people Israel.

[13]After he left Hebron, David took more concubines and wives in Jerusalem, and more sons and daughters were born to him. [14]These are the names of the children born to him there: Shammua, Shobab, Nathan, Solomon, [15]Ibhar, Elishua, Nepheg, Japhia, [16]Elishama, Eliada and Eliphelet.

David Defeats the Philistines

[17]When the Philistines heard that David had been anointed king over Israel, they went up in full force to search for him, but David heard about it and went down to the stronghold. [18]Now the Phi-

---

[a]8 Or *use scaling hooks*   [b]8 Or *are hated by David*
[c]9 Or *the Millo*

listines had come and spread out in the Valley of Rephaim; ¹⁹so David inquired of the LORD, "Shall I go and attack the Philistines? Will you hand them over to me?"

The LORD answered him, "Go, for I will surely hand the Philistines over to you."

²⁰So David went to Baal Perazim, and there he defeated them. He said, "As waters break out, the LORD has broken out against my enemies before me." So that place was called Baal Perazim.ᵃ ²¹The Philistines abandoned their idols there, and David and his men carried them off.

²²Once more the Philistines came up and spread out in the Valley of Rephaim; ²³so David inquired of the LORD, and he answered, "Do not go straight up, but circle around behind them and attack them in front of the balsam trees. ²⁴As soon as you hear the sound of marching in the tops of the balsam trees, move quickly, because that will mean the LORD has gone out in front of you to strike the Philistine army." ²⁵So David did as the LORD commanded him, and he struck down the Philistines all the way from Gibeonᵇ to Gezer.

The Ark Brought to Jerusalem

6 David again brought together out of Israel chosen men, thirty thousand in all. ²He and all his men set out from Baalah of Judahᶜ to bring up from there the ark of God, which is called by the Name,ᵈ the name of the LORD Almighty, who is enthroned between the cherubim that are on the ark. ³They set the ark of God on a new cart and brought it from the house of Abinadab, which was on the hill. Uzzah and Ahio, sons of Abinadab, were guiding the new cart ⁴with the ark of God on it,ᵉ and Ahio was walking in front of it. ⁵David and the whole house of Israel were celebrating with all their might before the LORD, with songsᶠ and with harps, lyres, tambourines, sistrums and cymbals.

⁶When they came to the threshing floor of Nacon, Uzzah reached out and took hold of the ark of God, because the oxen stumbled. ⁷The LORD's anger burned against Uzzah because of his irreverent act; therefore God struck him down and he died there beside the ark of God.

Ark On the Move

Huh?

2 Samuel 6:6–7
Here's what happens when David doesn't follow God's instructions. You see, David wasn't supposed to be moving the ark with a cart to begin with. It's really David's fault that Uzzah died. Numbers 7:9 says that the ark is to be carried on the shoulders of the Kohathites, and there are specific instructions in Leviticus on how the ark is to be moved. Only a Levite was allowed to touch it. David learned that things must be done God's way.

⁸Then David was angry because the LORD's wrath had broken out against Uzzah, and to this day that place is called Perez Uzzah.ᵍ

⁹David was afraid of the LORD that day and said, "How can the ark of the LORD ever come to me?" ¹⁰He was not willing to take the ark of the LORD to be with him in the City of David. Instead, he took it aside to the house of Obed-Edom the Gittite. ¹¹The ark of the LORD remained in the house of Obed-Edom the Gittite for three months, and the LORD blessed him and his entire household.

¹²Now King David was told, "The LORD has blessed the household of Obed-Edom and everything he has, because of the ark of God." So David went down and brought up the ark of God from the house of Obed-Edom to the City of David with rejoicing. ¹³When those who were carrying the ark of the LORD had taken six steps, he sacrificed a bull and a fattened calf. ¹⁴David, wearing a linen

---

ᵃ20 *Baal Perazim* means *the lord who breaks out.*
ᵇ25 Septuagint (see also 1 Chron. 14:16); Hebrew *Geba*   ᶜ2 That is, Kiriath Jearim; Hebrew *Baale Judah,* a variant of *Baalah of Judah*   ᵈ2 Hebrew; Septuagint and Vulgate do not have *the Name.*
ᵉ3,4 Dead Sea Scrolls and some Septuagint manuscripts; Masoretic Text *cart ᵈand they brought it with the ark of God from the house of Abinadab, which was on the hill*   ᶠ5 See Dead Sea Scrolls, Septuagint and 1 Chronicles 13:8; Masoretic Text *celebrating before the LORD with all kinds of instruments made of pine.*   ᵍ8 *Perez Uzzah* means *outbreak against Uzzah.*

ephod, danced before the LORD with all his might, [15]while he and the entire house of Israel brought up the ark of the LORD with shouts and the sound of trumpets.

[16]As the ark of the LORD was entering the City of David, Michal daughter of Saul watched from a window. And when she saw King David leaping and dancing before the LORD, she despised him in her heart.

[17]They brought the ark of the LORD and set it in its place inside the tent that David had pitched for it, and David sacrificed burnt offerings and fellowship offerings[a] before the LORD. [18]After he had finished sacrificing the burnt offerings and fellowship offerings, he blessed the people in the name of the LORD Almighty. [19]Then he gave a loaf of bread, a cake of dates and a cake of raisins to each person in the whole crowd of Israelites, both men and women. And all the people went to their homes.

[20]When David returned home to bless his household, Michal daughter of Saul came out to meet him and said, "How the king of Israel has distinguished himself today, disrobing in the sight of the slave girls of his servants as any vulgar fellow would!"

[21]David said to Michal, "It was before the LORD, who chose me rather than your father or anyone from his house when he appointed me ruler over the LORD's people Israel—I will celebrate before the LORD. [22]I will become even more undignified than this, and I will be humiliated in my own eyes. But by these slave girls you spoke of, I will be held in honor."

[23]And Michal daughter of Saul had no children to the day of her death.

God's Promise to David

7 After the king was settled in his palace and the LORD had given him rest from all his enemies around him, [2]he said to Nathan the prophet, "Here I am, living in a palace of cedar, while the ark of God remains in a tent."

[3]Nathan replied to the king, "Whatever you have in mind, go ahead and do it, for the LORD is with you."

[4]That night the word of the LORD came to Nathan, saying:

[5]"Go and tell my servant David, 'This is what the LORD says: Are you the one to build me a house to dwell in? [6]I have not dwelt in a house from the day I brought the Israelites up out of Egypt to this day. I have been moving from place to place with a tent as my dwelling. [7]Wherever I have moved with all the Israelites, did I ever say to any of their rulers whom I commanded to shepherd my people Israel, "Why have you not built me a house of cedar?" '

[8]"Now then, tell my servant David, 'This is what the LORD Almighty says: I took you from the pasture and from following the flock to be ruler over my people Israel. [9]I have been with you wherever you have gone, and I have cut off all your enemies from before you. Now I will make your name great, like the names of the greatest men of the earth. [10]And I will provide a place for my people Israel and will plant them so that they can have a home of their own and no longer be disturbed. Wicked people will not oppress them anymore, as they did at the beginning [11]and have done ever since the time I appointed leaders[b] over my people Israel. I will also give you rest from all your enemies.

" 'The LORD declares to you that the LORD himself will establish a house for you: [12]When your days are over and you rest with your fathers, I will raise up your offspring to succeed you, who will come from your own body, and I will establish his kingdom. [13]He is the one who will build a house for my Name, and I will establish the throne of his kingdom forever. [14]I will be his father, and he will be my son. When he does wrong, I will punish him with the rod of men, with floggings inflicted by men. [15]But my love will never be taken away from him, as I took it away from Saul, whom I removed from before you. [16]Your house and your kingdom will endure

---

[a]17 Traditionally *peace offerings*; also in verse 18   [b]11 Traditionally *judges*

forever before me[a]; your throne will be established forever.' "

[17]Nathan reported to David all the words of this entire revelation.

David's Prayer

[18]Then King David went in and sat before the LORD, and he said:

"Who am I, O Sovereign LORD, and what is my family, that you have brought me this far? [19]And as if this were not enough in your sight, O Sovereign LORD, you have also spoken about the future of the house of your servant. Is this your usual way of dealing with man, O Sovereign LORD?

[20]"What more can David say to you? For you know your servant, O Sovereign LORD. [21]For the sake of your word and according to your will, you have done this great thing and made it known to your servant.

[22]"How great you are, O Sovereign LORD! There is no one like you, and there is no God but you, as we have heard with our own ears. [23]And who is like your people Israel—the one nation on earth that God went out to redeem as a people for himself, and to make a name for himself, and to perform great and awesome wonders by driving out nations and their gods from before your people, whom you redeemed from Egypt?[b] [24]You have established your people Israel as your very own forever, and you, O LORD, have become their God.

[25]"And now, LORD God, keep forever the promise you have made concerning your servant and his house. Do as you promised, [26]so that your name will be great forever. Then men will say, 'The LORD Almighty is God over Israel!' And the house of your servant David will be established before you.

[27]"O LORD Almighty, God of Israel, you have revealed this to your servant, saying, 'I will build a house for you.' So your servant has found courage to offer you this prayer. [28]O Sovereign LORD, you are God! Your words are trustworthy, and you have promised these good things to your servant. [29]Now be pleased to bless the house of your servant, that it may continue forever in your sight; for you, O Sovereign LORD, have spoken, and with your blessing the house of your servant will be blessed forever."

David's Victories

8 In the course of time, David defeated the Philistines and subdued them, and he took Metheg Ammah from the control of the Philistines.

[2]David also defeated the Moabites. He made them lie down on the ground and measured them off with a length of cord. Every two lengths of them were put to death, and the third length was allowed to live. So the Moabites became subject to David and brought tribute.

[3]Moreover, David fought Hadadezer son of Rehob, king of Zobah, when he went to restore his control along the Euphrates River. [4]David captured a thousand of his chariots, seven thousand charioteers[c] and twenty thousand foot soldiers. He hamstrung all but a hundred of the chariot horses.

[5]When the Arameans of Damascus came to help Hadadezer king of Zobah, David struck down twenty-two thousand of them. [6]He put garrisons in the Aramean kingdom of Damascus, and the Arameans became subject to him and brought tribute. The LORD gave David victory wherever he went.

[7]David took the gold shields that belonged to the officers of Hadadezer and brought them to Jerusalem. [8]From Tebah[d] and Berothai, towns that belonged to Hadadezer, King David took a great quantity of bronze.

[9]When Tou[e] king of Hamath heard that David had defeated the entire army of

---

[a]16 Some Hebrew manuscripts and Septuagint; most Hebrew manuscripts *you*   [b]23 See Septuagint and 1 Chron. 17:21; Hebrew *wonders for your land and before your people, whom you redeemed from Egypt, from the nations and their gods.*   [c]4 Septuagint (see also Dead Sea Scrolls and 1 Chron. 18:4); Masoretic Text *captured seventeen hundred of his charioteers*   [d]8 See some Septuagint manuscripts (see also 1 Chron. 18:8); Hebrew *Betah.*   [e]9 Hebrew *Toi*, a variant of *Tou*; also in verse 10

Hadadezer, [10]he sent his son Joram[a] to King David to greet him and congratulate him on his victory in battle over Hadadezer, who had been at war with Tou. Joram brought with him articles of silver and gold and bronze.

[11]King David dedicated these articles to the LORD, as he had done with the silver and gold from all the nations he had subdued: [12]Edom[b] and Moab, the Ammonites and the Philistines, and Amalek. He also dedicated the plunder taken from Hadadezer son of Rehob, king of Zobah.

[13]And David became famous after he returned from striking down eighteen thousand Edomites[c] in the Valley of Salt.

[14]He put garrisons throughout Edom, and all the Edomites became subject to David. The LORD gave David victory wherever he went.

David's Officials

[15]David reigned over all Israel, doing what was just and right for all his people. [16]Joab son of Zeruiah was over the army; Jehoshaphat son of Ahilud was recorder; [17]Zadok son of Ahitub and Ahimelech son of Abiathar were priests; Seraiah was secretary; [18]Benaiah son of Jehoiada was over the Kerethites and Pelethites; and David's sons were royal advisers.[d]

David and Mephibosheth

9 David asked, "Is there anyone still left of the house of Saul to whom I can show kindness for Jonathan's sake?"

[2]Now there was a servant of Saul's household named Ziba. They called him to appear before David, and the king said to him, "Are you Ziba?"

"Your servant," he replied.

[3]The king asked, "Is there no one still left of the house of Saul to whom I can show God's kindness?"

Ziba answered the king, "There is still a son of Jonathan; he is crippled in both feet."

[4]"Where is he?" the king asked.

Ziba answered, "He is at the house of Makir son of Ammiel in Lo Debar."

[5]So King David had him brought from Lo Debar, from the house of Makir son of Ammiel.

[6]When Mephibosheth son of Jonathan,

the son of Saul, came to David, he bowed down to pay him honor.

David said, "Mephibosheth!"

"Your servant," he replied.

[7]"Don't be afraid," David said to him, "for I will surely show you kindness for the sake of your father Jonathan. I will restore to you all the land that belonged to your grandfather Saul, and you will always eat at my table."

[8]Mephibosheth bowed down and said, "What is your servant, that you should notice a dead dog like me?"

[9]Then the king summoned Ziba, Saul's servant, and said to him, "I have given your master's grandson everything that belonged to Saul and his family. [10]You and your sons and your servants are to farm the land for him and bring in the crops, so that your master's grandson may be provided for. And Mephibosheth, grandson of your master, will always eat at my table." (Now Ziba had fifteen sons and twenty servants.)

[11]Then Ziba said to the king, "Your servant will do whatever my lord the king commands his servant to do." So Mephibosheth ate at David's[e] table like one of the king's sons.

[12]Mephibosheth had a young son named Mica, and all the members of Ziba's household were servants of Mephibosheth. [13]And Mephibosheth lived in Jerusalem, because he always ate at the king's table, and he was crippled in both feet.

David Defeats the Ammonites

10 In the course of time, the king of the Ammonites died, and his son Hanun succeeded him as king. [2]David thought, "I will show kindness to Hanun son of Nahash, just as his father showed kindness to me." So David sent a delegation to express his sympathy to Hanun concerning his father.

When David's men came to the land of the Ammonites, [3]the Ammonite nobles

---

[a]10 A variant of *Hadoram*   [b]12 Some Hebrew manuscripts, Septuagint and Syriac (see also 1 Chron. 18:11); most Hebrew manuscripts *Aram*   [c]13 A few Hebrew manuscripts, Septuagint and Syriac (see also 1 Chron. 18:12); most Hebrew manuscripts *Aram* (that is, Arameans)   [d]18 Or *were priests*   [e]11 Septuagint; Hebrew *my*

said to Hanun their lord, "Do you think David is honoring your father by sending men to you to express sympathy? Hasn't David sent them to you to explore the city and spy it out and overthrow it?" [4]So Hanun seized David's men, shaved off half of each man's beard, cut off their garments in the middle at the buttocks, and sent them away.

[5]When David was told about this, he sent messengers to meet the men, for they were greatly humiliated. The king said, "Stay at Jericho till your beards have grown, and then come back."

[6]When the Ammonites realized that they had become a stench in David's nostrils, they hired twenty thousand Aramean foot soldiers from Beth Rehob and Zobah, as well as the king of Maacah with a thousand men, and also twelve thousand men from Tob.

[7]On hearing this, David sent Joab out with the entire army of fighting men. [8]The Ammonites came out and drew up in battle formation at the entrance to their city gate, while the Arameans of Zobah and Rehob and the men of Tob and Maacah were by themselves in the open country.

[9]Joab saw that there were battle lines in front of him and behind him; so he selected some of the best troops in Israel and deployed them against the Arameans. [10]He put the rest of the men under the command of Abishai his brother and deployed them against the Ammonites. [11]Joab said, "If the Arameans are too strong for me, then you are to come to my rescue; but if the Ammonites are too strong for you, then I will come to rescue you. [12]Be strong and let us fight bravely for our people and the cities of our God. The LORD will do what is good in his sight."

[13]Then Joab and the troops with him advanced to fight the Arameans, and they fled before him. [14]When the Ammonites saw that the Arameans were fleeing, they fled before Abishai and went inside the city. So Joab returned from fighting the Ammonites and came to Jerusalem.

[15]After the Arameans saw that they had been routed by Israel, they regrouped. [16]Hadadezer had Arameans brought from beyond the River[a]; they went to Helam, with Shobach the commander of Hadadezer's army leading them.

[17]When David was told of this, he gathered all Israel, crossed the Jordan and went to Helam. The Arameans formed their battle lines to meet David and fought against him. [18]But they fled before Israel, and David killed seven hundred of their charioteers and forty thousand of their foot soldiers.[b] He also struck down Shobach the commander of their army, and he died there. [19]When all the kings who were vassals of Hadadezer saw that they had been defeated by Israel, they made peace with the Israelites and became subject to them.

So the Arameans were afraid to help the Ammonites anymore.

David and Bathsheba

11 In the spring, at the time when kings go off to war, David sent Joab out with the king's men and the whole Israelite army. They destroyed the Ammonites and besieged Rabbah. But David remained in Jerusalem.

[2]One evening David got up from his bed and walked around on the roof of the palace. From the roof he saw a woman bathing. The woman was very beautiful,

What You Don't Do

Huh?

2 Samuel 11:1–2
You've probably heard of David's "big sin" with Bathsheba—the snowball rolling out-of-control down a hill that resulted in not only adultery but also murder. But the part of David's sin you might not have heard about is that he shouldn't have been home in the first place. He should have been off to war with his army. Sometimes sinning includes what we *don't* do, not just what we do.

*a*16 That is, the Euphrates   *b*18 Some Septuagint manuscripts (see also 1 Chron. 19:18); Hebrew *horsemen*

³and David sent someone to find out about her. The man said, "Isn't this Bathsheba, the daughter of Eliam and the wife of Uriah the Hittite?" ⁴Then David sent messengers to get her. She came to him, and he slept with her. (She had purified herself from her uncleanness.) Then*a* she went back home. ⁵The woman conceived and sent word to David, saying, "I am pregnant."

⁶So David sent this word to Joab: "Send me Uriah the Hittite." And Joab sent him to David. ⁷When Uriah came to him, David asked him how Joab was, how the soldiers were and how the war was going. ⁸Then David said to Uriah, "Go down to your house and wash your feet." So Uriah left the palace, and a gift from the king was sent after him. ⁹But Uriah slept at the entrance to the palace with all his master's servants and did not go down to his house.

¹⁰When David was told, "Uriah did not go home," he asked him, "Haven't you just come from a distance? Why didn't you go home?"

¹¹Uriah said to David, "The ark and Israel and Judah are staying in tents, and my master Joab and my lord's men are camped in the open fields. How could I go to my house to eat and drink and lie with my wife? As surely as you live, I will not do such a thing!"

¹²Then David said to him, "Stay here one more day, and tomorrow I will send you back." So Uriah remained in Jerusalem that day and the next. ¹³At David's invitation, he ate and drank with him, and David made him drunk. But in the evening Uriah went out to sleep on his mat among his master's servants; he did not go home.

¹⁴In the morning David wrote a letter to Joab and sent it with Uriah. ¹⁵In it he wrote, "Put Uriah in the front line where the fighting is fiercest. Then withdraw from him so he will be struck down and die."

¹⁶So while Joab had the city under siege, he put Uriah at a place where he knew the strongest defenders were. ¹⁷When the men of the city came out and fought against Joab, some of the men in David's army fell; moreover, Uriah the Hittite died.

¹⁸Joab sent David a full account of the battle. ¹⁹He instructed the messenger: "When you have finished giving the king this account of the battle, ²⁰the king's anger may flare up, and he may ask you, 'Why did you get so close to the city to fight? Didn't you know they would shoot arrows from the wall? ²¹Who killed Abimelech son of Jerub-Besheth*b*? Didn't a woman throw an upper millstone on him from the wall, so that he died in Thebez? Why did you get so close to the wall?' If he asks you this, then say to him, 'Also, your servant Uriah the Hittite is dead.' "

²²The messenger set out, and when he arrived he told David everything Joab had sent him to say. ²³The messenger said to David, "The men overpowered us and came out against us in the open, but we drove them back to the entrance to the city gate. ²⁴Then the archers shot arrows at your servants from the wall, and some of the king's men died. Moreover, your servant Uriah the Hittite is dead."

²⁵David told the messenger, "Say this to Joab: 'Don't let this upset you; the sword devours one as well as another. Press the attack against the city and destroy it.' Say this to encourage Joab."

²⁶When Uriah's wife heard that her husband was dead, she mourned for him. ²⁷After the time of mourning was over, David had her brought to his house, and she became his wife and bore him a son. But the thing David had done displeased the LORD.

Nathan Rebukes David

12 The LORD sent Nathan to David. When he came to him, he said, "There were two men in a certain town, one rich and the other poor. ²The rich man had a very large number of sheep and cattle, ³but the poor man had nothing except one little ewe lamb he had bought. He raised it, and it grew up with him and his children. It shared his food, drank from his cup and even slept in his arms. It was like a daughter to him.

⁴"Now a traveler came to the rich man,

---

a4 Or *with her. When she purified herself from her uncleanness,* *b21* Also known as *Jerub-Baal* (that is, Gideon) but the rich man refrained from taking one of his own sheep or cattle to prepare a meal for the traveler who had come to him. Instead, he took the ewe lamb that belonged to the poor man and prepared it for the one who had come to him."

[5]David burned with anger against the man and said to Nathan, "As surely as the LORD lives, the man who did this deserves to die! [6]He must pay for that lamb four times over, because he did such a thing and had no pity."

[7]Then Nathan said to David, "You are the man! This is what the LORD, the God of Israel, says: 'I anointed you king over Israel, and I delivered you from the hand of Saul. [8]I gave your master's house to you, and your master's wives into your arms. I gave you the house of Israel and Judah. And if all this had been too little, I would have given you even more. [9]Why did you despise the word of the LORD by doing what is evil in his eyes? You struck down Uriah the Hittite with the sword and took his wife to be your own. You killed him with the sword of the Ammonites. [10]Now, therefore, the sword will never depart from your house, because you despised me and took the wife of Uriah the Hittite to be your own.'

[11]"This is what the LORD says: 'Out of your own household I am going to bring calamity upon you. Before your very eyes I will take your wives and give them to one who is close to you, and he will lie with your wives in broad daylight. [12]You did it in secret, but I will do this thing in broad daylight before all Israel.' "

[13]Then David said to Nathan, "I have sinned against the LORD."

Nathan replied, "The LORD has taken away your sin. You are not going to die.

Monday

Sin's Baggage

Read 2 Samuel 12:1–14

A few weeks ago, a family friend committed suicide. As I sat at the funeral, I saw this person's family crying in the front row of the church. The pain they felt was incredible, and they'll have it for the rest of their lives. His family has to live with the consequences of what he did.

King David's story is about living with sin's consequences. He slept with another man's wife, got her pregnant, then had her husband killed. David repented and was forgiven, but he still had to live with the results of his sin. And those results were awfully painful.

Sometimes people think sin is no big deal. They figure they can do what they want, ask for forgiveness and be off the hook with God. But every sin has consequences. Sin can make us feel guilty, hurt other people or even change our lives.

The story of David makes me think about my own decisions. If I do something I shouldn't, I know God will forgive me if I ask him to. But I also know I'll have to live with the consequences, no matter how painful they might be.

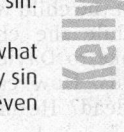
Kelly age 15

What about You?

❶ Think about some of the sinful things you've done. What were some of the consequences?

❷ Is there someone you've hurt in the past? What can you do to help heal your relationship?

❸ Are there some sins you need to be forgiven for? Tell God you're sorry for these sins and ask for his forgiveness.

Turn to page 371 for your next devotion.

'Fess Up!

Huh?

2 Samuel 12:13

Nathan told the king a parable that caught him completely off guard. When David responded in anger, Nathan charged him with committing the sin he had just condemned. Immediately David admits his sin—he doesn't for a second blame it on his circumstances or anyone else. He owns his sin-choice. Maybe that's part of why 1 Samuel 13:14 refers to David as "a man after [God's] own heart."

¹⁴But because by doing this you have made the enemies of the LORD show utter contempt,ᵃ the son born to you will die."

¹⁵After Nathan had gone home, the LORD struck the child that Uriah's wife had borne to David, and he became ill. ¹⁶David pleaded with God for the child. He fasted and went into his house and spent the nights lying on the ground. ¹⁷The elders of his household stood beside him to get him up from the ground, but he refused, and he would not eat any food with them.

¹⁸On the seventh day the child died. David's servants were afraid to tell him that the child was dead, for they thought, "While the child was still living, we spoke to David but he would not listen to us. How can we tell him the child is dead? He may do something desperate."

¹⁹David noticed that his servants were whispering among themselves and he realized the child was dead. "Is the child dead?" he asked.

"Yes," they replied, "he is dead."

²⁰Then David got up from the ground. After he had washed, put on lotions and changed his clothes, he went into the house of the LORD and worshiped. Then he went to his own house, and at his request they served him food, and he ate.

²¹His servants asked him, "Why are you acting this way? While the child was alive, you fasted and wept, but now that the child is dead, you get up and eat!"

²²He answered, "While the child was still alive, I fasted and wept. I thought, 'Who knows? The LORD may be gracious to me and let the child live.' ²³But now that he is dead, why should I fast? Can I bring him back again? I will go to him, but he will not return to me."

²⁴Then David comforted his wife Bathsheba, and he went to her and lay with her. She gave birth to a son, and they named him Solomon. The LORD loved him; ²⁵and because the LORD loved him, he sent word through Nathan the prophet to name him Jedidiah.ᵇ

²⁶Meanwhile Joab fought against Rabbah of the Ammonites and captured the royal citadel. ²⁷Joab then sent messengers to David, saying, "I have fought against Rabbah and taken its water supply. ²⁸Now muster the rest of the troops and besiege the city and capture it. Otherwise I will take the city, and it will be named after me."

²⁹So David mustered the entire army and went to Rabbah, and attacked and captured it. ³⁰He took the crown from the head of their kingᶜ—its weight was a talentᵈ of gold, and it was set with precious stones—and it was placed on David's head. He took a great quantity of plunder from the city ³¹and brought out the people who were there, consigning them to labor with saws and with iron picks and axes, and he made them work at brickmaking.ᵉ He did this to all the Ammonite towns. Then David and his entire army returned to Jerusalem.

Amnon and Tamar

13 In the course of time, Amnon son of David fell in love with Tamar, the beautiful sister of Absalom son of David.

²Amnon became frustrated to the point of illness on account of his sister Tamar, for she was a virgin, and it seemed impossible for him to do anything to her.

ᵃ14 Masoretic Text; an ancient Hebrew scribal tradition *this you have shown utter contempt for the LORD*   ᵇ25 *Jedidiah* means *loved by the LORD.*   ᶜ30 Or *of Milcom* (that is, Molech)   ᵈ30 That is, about 75 pounds (about 34 kilograms)   ᵉ31 The meaning of the Hebrew for this clause is uncertain.

³Now Amnon had a friend named Jonadab son of Shimeah, David's brother. Jonadab was a very shrewd man. ⁴He asked Amnon, "Why do you, the king's son, look so haggard morning after morning? Won't you tell me?"

Amnon said to him, "I'm in love with Tamar, my brother Absalom's sister."

⁵"Go to bed and pretend to be ill," Jonadab said. "When your father comes to see you, say to him, 'I would like my sister Tamar to come and give me something to eat. Let her prepare the food in my sight so I may watch her and then eat it from her hand.'"

⁶So Amnon lay down and pretended to be ill. When the king came to see him, Amnon said to him, "I would like my sister Tamar to come and make some special bread in my sight, so I may eat from her hand."

⁷David sent word to Tamar at the palace: "Go to the house of your brother Amnon and prepare some food for him." ⁸So Tamar went to the house of her brother Amnon, who was lying down. She took some dough, kneaded it, made the bread in his sight and baked it. ⁹Then she took the pan and served him the bread, but he refused to eat.

"Send everyone out of here," Amnon said. So everyone left him. ¹⁰Then Amnon said to Tamar, "Bring the food here into my bedroom so I may eat from your hand." And Tamar took the bread she had prepared and brought it to her brother Amnon in his bedroom. ¹¹But when she took it to him to eat, he grabbed her and said, "Come to bed with me, my sister."

¹²"Don't, my brother!" she said to him. "Don't force me. Such a thing should not be done in Israel! Don't do this wicked thing. ¹³What about me? Where could I get rid of my disgrace? And what about you? You would be like one of the wicked fools in Israel. Please speak to the king; he will not keep me from being married to you." ¹⁴But he refused to listen to her, and since he was stronger than she, he raped her.

¹⁵Then Amnon hated her with intense hatred. In fact, he hated her more than he had loved her. Amnon said to her, "Get up and get out!"

¹⁶"No!" she said to him. "Sending me away would be a greater wrong than what you have already done to me."

But he refused to listen to her. ¹⁷He called his personal servant and said, "Get this woman out of here and bolt the door after her." ¹⁸So his servant put her out and bolted the door after her. She was wearing a richly ornamented[a] robe, for this was the kind of garment the virgin daughters of the king wore. ¹⁹Tamar put ashes on her head and tore the ornamented[b] robe she was wearing. She put her hand on her head and went away, weeping aloud as she went.

²⁰Her brother Absalom said to her, "Has that Amnon, your brother, been with you? Be quiet now, my sister; he is your brother. Don't take this thing to heart." And Tamar lived in her brother Absalom's house, a desolate woman.

²¹When King David heard all this, he was furious. ²²Absalom never said a word to Amnon, either good or bad; he hated Amnon because he had disgraced his sister Tamar.

Absalom Kills Amnon

²³Two years later, when Absalom's sheepshearers were at Baal Hazor near the border of Ephraim, he invited all the king's sons to come there. ²⁴Absalom went to the king and said, "Your servant has had shearers come. Will the king and his officials please join me?"

²⁵"No, my son," the king replied. "All of us should not go; we would only be a burden to you." Although Absalom urged him, he still refused to go, but gave him his blessing.

²⁶Then Absalom said, "If not, please let my brother Amnon come with us."

The king asked him, "Why should he go with you?" ²⁷But Absalom urged him, so he sent with him Amnon and the rest of the king's sons.

²⁸Absalom ordered his men, "Listen! When Amnon is in high spirits from drinking wine and I say to you, 'Strike Amnon down,' then kill him. Don't be afraid. Have not I given you this order? Be strong and brave." ²⁹So Absalom's

---

ᵃ18 The meaning of the Hebrew for this phrase is uncertain.   ᵇ19 The meaning of the Hebrew for this word is uncertain.

men did to Amnon what Absalom had ordered. Then all the king's sons got up, mounted their mules and fled.

³⁰While they were on their way, the report came to David: "Absalom has struck down all the king's sons; not one of them is left." ³¹The king stood up, tore his clothes and lay down on the ground; and all his servants stood by with their clothes torn.

³²But Jonadab son of Shimeah, David's brother, said, "My lord should not think that they killed all the princes; only Amnon is dead. This has been Absalom's expressed intention ever since the day Amnon raped his sister Tamar. ³³My lord the king should not be concerned about the report that all the king's sons are dead. Only Amnon is dead."

³⁴Meanwhile, Absalom had fled.

Now the man standing watch looked up and saw many people on the road west of him, coming down the side of the hill. The watchman went and told the king, "I see men in the direction of Horonaim, on the side of the hill."[a]

³⁵Jonadab said to the king, "See, the king's sons are here; it has happened just as your servant said."

³⁶As he finished speaking, the king's sons came in, wailing loudly. The king, too, and all his servants wept very bitterly.

³⁷Absalom fled and went to Talmai son of Ammihud, the king of Geshur. But King David mourned for his son every day.

³⁸After Absalom fled and went to Geshur, he stayed there three years. ³⁹And the spirit of the king[b] longed to go to Absalom, for he was consoled concerning Amnon's death.

Absalom Returns to Jerusalem

14 Joab son of Zeruiah knew that the king's heart longed for Absalom. ²So Joab sent someone to Tekoa and had a wise woman brought from there. He said to her, "Pretend you are in mourning. Dress in mourning clothes, and don't use any cosmetic lotions. Act like a woman who has spent many days grieving for the dead. ³Then go to the king and speak these words to him." And Joab put the words in her mouth.

⁴When the woman from Tekoa went[c] to the king, she fell with her face to the ground to pay him honor, and she said, "Help me, O king!"

⁵The king asked her, "What is troubling you?"

She said, "I am indeed a widow; my husband is dead. ⁶I your servant had two sons. They got into a fight with each other in the field, and no one was there to separate them. One struck the other and killed him. ⁷Now the whole clan has risen up against your servant; they say, 'Hand over the one who struck his brother down, so that we may put him to death for the life of his brother whom he killed; then we will get rid of the heir as well.' They would put out the only burning coal I have left, leaving my husband neither name nor descendant on the face of the earth."

⁸The king said to the woman, "Go home, and I will issue an order in your behalf."

⁹But the woman from Tekoa said to him, "My lord the king, let the blame rest on me and on my father's family, and let the king and his throne be without guilt."

¹⁰The king replied, "If anyone says anything to you, bring him to me, and he will not bother you again."

¹¹She said, "Then let the king invoke the Lord his God to prevent the avenger of blood from adding to the destruction, so that my son will not be destroyed."

"As surely as the Lord lives," he said, "not one hair of your son's head will fall to the ground."

¹²Then the woman said, "Let your servant speak a word to my lord the king."

"Speak," he replied.

¹³The woman said, "Why then have you devised a thing like this against the people of God? When the king says this, does he not convict himself, for the king has not brought back his banished son? ¹⁴Like water spilled on the ground, which cannot be recovered, so we must die. But God does not take away life; instead, he

---

a34 Septuagint; Hebrew does not have this sentence.   *b39* Dead Sea Scrolls and some Septuagint manuscripts; Masoretic Text *But the spirit of David the king*   *c4* Many Hebrew manuscripts, Septuagint, Vulgate and Syriac; most Hebrew manuscripts *spoke*

devises ways so that a banished person may not remain estranged from him.

[15]"And now I have come to say this to my lord the king because the people have made me afraid. Your servant thought, 'I will speak to the king; perhaps he will do what his servant asks. [16]Perhaps the king will agree to deliver his servant from the hand of the man who is trying to cut off both me and my son from the inheritance God gave us.'

[17]"And now your servant says, 'May the word of my lord the king bring me rest, for my lord the king is like an angel of God in discerning good and evil. May the LORD your God be with you.' "

[18]Then the king said to the woman, "Do not keep from me the answer to what I am going to ask you."

"Let my lord the king speak," the woman said.

[19]The king asked, "Isn't the hand of Joab with you in all this?"

The woman answered, "As surely as you live, my lord the king, no one can turn to the right or to the left from anything my lord the king says. Yes, it was your servant Joab who instructed me to do this and who put all these words into the mouth of your servant. [20]Your servant Joab did this to change the present situation. My lord has wisdom like that of an angel of God—he knows everything that happens in the land."

[21]The king said to Joab, "Very well, I will do it. Go, bring back the young man Absalom."

[22]Joab fell with his face to the ground to pay him honor, and he blessed the king. Joab said, "Today your servant knows that he has found favor in your eyes, my lord the king, because the king has granted his servant's request."

[23]Then Joab went to Geshur and brought Absalom back to Jerusalem. [24]But the king said, "He must go to his own house; he must not see my face." So Absalom went to his own house and did not see the face of the king.

[25]In all Israel there was not a man so highly praised for his handsome appearance as Absalom. From the top of his head to the sole of his foot there was no blemish in him. [26]Whenever he cut the hair of his head—he used to cut his hair

from time to time when it became too heavy for him—he would weigh it, and its weight was two hundred shekels[a] by the royal standard.

[27]Three sons and a daughter were born to Absalom. The daughter's name was Tamar, and she became a beautiful woman.

[28]Absalom lived two years in Jerusalem without seeing the king's face. [29]Then Absalom sent for Joab in order to send him to the king, but Joab refused to come to him. So he sent a second time, but he refused to come. [30]Then he said to his servants, "Look, Joab's field is next to mine, and he has barley there. Go and set it on fire." So Absalom's servants set the field on fire.

[31]Then Joab did go to Absalom's house and he said to him, "Why have your servants set my field on fire?"

[32]Absalom said to Joab, "Look, I sent word to you and said, 'Come here so I can send you to the king to ask, "Why have I come from Geshur? It would be better for me if I were still there!" ' Now then, I want to see the king's face, and if I am guilty of anything, let him put me to death."

[33]So Joab went to the king and told him this. Then the king summoned Absalom, and he came in and bowed down with his face to the ground before the king. And the king kissed Absalom.

Absalom's Conspiracy

15 In the course of time, Absalom provided himself with a chariot and horses and with fifty men to run ahead of him. [2]He would get up early and stand by the side of the road leading to the city gate. Whenever anyone came with a complaint to be placed before the king for a decision, Absalom would call out to him, "What town are you from?" He would answer, "Your servant is from one of the tribes of Israel." [3]Then Absalom would say to him, "Look, your claims are valid and proper, but there is no representative of the king to hear you." [4]And Absalom would add, "If only I were appointed judge in the land! Then everyone who has a complaint or case

---

[a]26 That is, about 5 pounds (about 2.3 kilograms)

could come to me and I would see that he gets justice."

⁵Also, whenever anyone approached him to bow down before him, Absalom would reach out his hand, take hold of him and kiss him. ⁶Absalom behaved in this way toward all the Israelites who came to the king asking for justice, and so he stole the hearts of the men of Israel.

⁷At the end of four*a* years, Absalom said to the king, "Let me go to Hebron and fulfill a vow I made to the Lord. ⁸While your servant was living at Geshur in Aram, I made this vow: 'If the Lord takes me back to Jerusalem, I will worship the Lord in Hebron.*b*' "

⁹The king said to him, "Go in peace." So he went to Hebron.

¹⁰Then Absalom sent secret messengers throughout the tribes of Israel to say, "As soon as you hear the sound of the trumpets, then say, 'Absalom is king in Hebron.' " ¹¹Two hundred men from Jerusalem had accompanied Absalom. They had been invited as guests and went quite innocently, knowing nothing about the matter. ¹²While Absalom was offering sacrifices, he also sent for Ahithophel the Gilonite, David's counselor, to come from Giloh, his hometown. And so the conspiracy gained strength, and Absalom's following kept on increasing.

David Flees

¹³A messenger came and told David, "The hearts of the men of Israel are with Absalom."

¹⁴Then David said to all his officials who were with him in Jerusalem, "Come! We must flee, or none of us will escape from Absalom. We must leave immediately, or he will move quickly to overtake us and bring ruin upon us and put the city to the sword."

¹⁵The king's officials answered him, "Your servants are ready to do whatever our lord the king chooses."

¹⁶The king set out, with his entire household following him; but he left ten concubines to take care of the palace. ¹⁷So the king set out, with all the people following him, and they halted at a place some distance away. ¹⁸All his men marched past him, along with all the Kerethites and Pelethites; and all the six hundred Gittites who had accompanied him from Gath marched before the king.

¹⁹The king said to Ittai the Gittite, "Why should you come along with us? Go back and stay with King Absalom. You are a foreigner, an exile from your homeland. ²⁰You came only yesterday. And today shall I make you wander about with us, when I do not know where I am going? Go back, and take your countrymen. May kindness and faithfulness be with you."

²¹But Ittai replied to the king, "As surely as the Lord lives, and as my lord the king lives, wherever my lord the king may be, whether it means life or death, there will your servant be."

²²David said to Ittai, "Go ahead, march on." So Ittai the Gittite marched on with all his men and the families that were with him.

²³The whole countryside wept aloud as all the people passed by. The king also crossed the Kidron Valley, and all the people moved on toward the desert.

²⁴Zadok was there, too, and all the Levites who were with him were carrying the ark of the covenant of God. They set down the ark of God, and Abiathar offered sacrifices*c* until all the people had finished leaving the city.

²⁵Then the king said to Zadok, "Take the ark of God back into the city. If I find favor in the Lord's eyes, he will bring me back and let me see it and his dwelling place again. ²⁶But if he says, 'I am not pleased with you,' then I am ready; let him do to me whatever seems good to him."

²⁷The king also said to Zadok the priest, "Aren't you a seer? Go back to the city in peace, with your son Ahimaaz and Jonathan son of Abiathar. You and Abiathar take your two sons with you. ²⁸I will wait at the fords in the desert until word comes from you to inform me." ²⁹So Zadok and Abiathar took the ark of God back to Jerusalem and stayed there.

³⁰But David continued up the Mount of Olives, weeping as he went; his head was

---

*a*7 Some Septuagint manuscripts, Syriac and Josephus; Hebrew *forty* *b*8 Some Septuagint manuscripts; Hebrew does not have *in Hebron.* *c*24 Or *Abiathar went up*

covered and he was barefoot. All the people with him covered their heads too and were weeping as they went up. ³¹Now David had been told, "Ahithophel is among the conspirators with Absalom." So David prayed, "O LORD, turn Ahithophel's counsel into foolishness."

³²When David arrived at the summit, where people used to worship God, Hushai the Arkite was there to meet him, his robe torn and dust on his head. ³³David said to him, "If you go with me, you will be a burden to me. ³⁴But if you return to the city and say to Absalom, 'I will be your servant, O king; I was your father's servant in the past, but now I will be your servant,' then you can help me by frustrating Ahithophel's advice. ³⁵Won't the priests Zadok and Abiathar be there with you? Tell them anything you hear in the king's palace. ³⁶Their two sons, Ahimaaz son of Zadok and Jonathan son of Abiathar, are there with them. Send them to me with anything you hear."

³⁷So David's friend Hushai arrived at Jerusalem as Absalom was entering the city.

David and Ziba

16 When David had gone a short distance beyond the summit, there was Ziba, the steward of Mephibosheth, waiting to meet him. He had a string of donkeys saddled and loaded with two hundred loaves of bread, a hundred cakes of raisins, a hundred cakes of figs and a skin of wine.

²The king asked Ziba, "Why have you brought these?"

Ziba answered, "The donkeys are for the king's household to ride on, the bread and fruit are for the men to eat, and the wine is to refresh those who become exhausted in the desert."

³The king then asked, "Where is your master's grandson?"

Ziba said to him, "He is staying in Jerusalem, because he thinks, 'Today the house of Israel will give me back my grandfather's kingdom.' "

⁴Then the king said to Ziba, "All that belonged to Mephibosheth is now yours."

"I humbly bow," Ziba said. "May I find favor in your eyes, my lord the king."

Shimei Curses David

⁵As King David approached Bahurim, a man from the same clan as Saul's family came out from there. His name was Shimei son of Gera, and he cursed as he came out. ⁶He pelted David and all the king's officials with stones, though all the troops and the special guard were on David's right and left. ⁷As he cursed, Shimei said, "Get out, get out, you man of blood, you scoundrel! ⁸The LORD has repaid you for all the blood you shed in the household of Saul, in whose place you have reigned. The LORD has handed the kingdom over to your son Absalom. You have come to ruin because you are a man of blood!"

⁹Then Abishai son of Zeruiah said to the king, "Why should this dead dog curse my lord the king? Let me go over and cut off his head."

¹⁰But the king said, "What do you and I have in common, you sons of Zeruiah? If he is cursing because the LORD said to him, 'Curse David,' who can ask, 'Why do you do this?' "

¹¹David then said to Abishai and all his officials, "My son, who is of my own flesh, is trying to take my life. How much more, then, this Benjamite! Leave him alone; let him curse, for the LORD has told him to. ¹²It may be that the LORD will see my distress and repay me with good for the cursing I am receiving today."

¹³So David and his men continued along the road while Shimei was going along the hillside opposite him, cursing as he went and throwing stones at him and showering him with dirt. ¹⁴The king and all the people with him arrived at their destination exhausted. And there he refreshed himself.

The Advice of Hushai and Ahithophel

¹⁵Meanwhile, Absalom and all the men of Israel came to Jerusalem, and Ahithophel was with him. ¹⁶Then Hushai the Arkite, David's friend, went to Absalom and said to him, "Long live the king! Long live the king!"

¹⁷Absalom asked Hushai, "Is this the love you show your friend? Why didn't you go with your friend?"

¹⁸Hushai said to Absalom, "No, the one

chosen by the LORD, by these people, and by all the men of Israel—his I will be, and I will remain with him. ¹⁹Furthermore, whom should I serve? Should I not serve the son? Just as I served your father, so I will serve you."

²⁰Absalom said to Ahithophel, "Give us your advice. What should we do?"

²¹Ahithophel answered, "Lie with your father's concubines whom he left to take care of the palace. Then all Israel will hear that you have made yourself a stench in your father's nostrils, and the hands of everyone with you will be strengthened." ²²So they pitched a tent for Absalom on the roof, and he lay with his father's concubines in the sight of all Israel.

²³Now in those days the advice Ahithophel gave was like that of one who inquires of God. That was how both David and Absalom regarded all of Ahithophel's advice.

17 Ahithophel said to Absalom, "I would[a] choose twelve thousand men and set out tonight in pursuit of David. ²I would[b] attack him while he is weary and weak. I would[b] strike him with terror, and then all the people with him will flee. I would[b] strike down only the king ³and bring all the people back to you. The death of the man you seek will mean the return of all; all the people will be unharmed." ⁴This plan seemed good to Absalom and to all the elders of Israel.

⁵But Absalom said, "Summon also Hushai the Arkite, so we can hear what he has to say." ⁶When Hushai came to him, Absalom said, "Ahithophel has given this advice. Should we do what he says? If not, give us your opinion."

⁷Hushai replied to Absalom, "The advice Ahithophel has given is not good this time. ⁸You know your father and his men; they are fighters, and as fierce as a wild bear robbed of her cubs. Besides, your father is an experienced fighter; he will not spend the night with the troops. ⁹Even now, he is hidden in a cave or some other place. If he should attack your troops first,[c] whoever hears about it will say, 'There has been a slaughter among the troops who follow Absalom.' ¹⁰Then even the bravest soldier, whose heart is like the heart of a lion, will melt with fear, for all Israel knows that your father is a fighter and that those with him are brave.

¹¹"So I advise you: Let all Israel, from Dan to Beersheba—as numerous as the sand on the seashore—be gathered to you, with you yourself leading them into battle. ¹²Then we will attack him wherever he may be found, and we will fall on him as dew settles on the ground. Neither he nor any of his men will be left alive. ¹³If he withdraws into a city, then all Israel will bring ropes to that city, and we will drag it down to the valley until not even a piece of it can be found."

¹⁴Absalom and all the men of Israel said, "The advice of Hushai the Arkite is better than that of Ahithophel." For the LORD had determined to frustrate the good advice of Ahithophel in order to bring disaster on Absalom.

¹⁵Hushai told Zadok and Abiathar, the priests, "Ahithophel has advised Absalom and the elders of Israel to do such and such, but I have advised them to do so and so. ¹⁶Now send a message immediately and tell David, 'Do not spend the night at the fords in the desert; cross over without fail, or the king and all the people with him will be swallowed up.' "

¹⁷Jonathan and Ahimaaz were staying at En Rogel. A servant girl was to go and inform them, and they were to go and tell King David, for they could not risk being seen entering the city. ¹⁸But a young man saw them and told Absalom. So the two of them left quickly and went to the house of a man in Bahurim. He had a well in his courtyard, and they climbed down into it. ¹⁹His wife took a covering and spread it out over the opening of the well and scattered grain over it. No one knew anything about it.

²⁰When Absalom's men came to the woman at the house, they asked, "Where are Ahimaaz and Jonathan?"

The woman answered them, "They crossed over the brook."[d] The men searched but found no one, so they returned to Jerusalem.

²¹After the men had gone, the two

---

[a]1 Or Let me　[b]2 Or will　[c]9 Or When some of the men fall at the first attack　[d]20 Or "They passed by the sheep pen toward the water."

climbed out of the well and went to inform King David. They said to him, "Set out and cross the river at once; Ahithophel has advised such and such against you." ²²So David and all the people with him set out and crossed the Jordan. By daybreak, no one was left who had not crossed the Jordan.

²³When Ahithophel saw that his advice had not been followed, he saddled his donkey and set out for his house in his hometown. He put his house in order and then hanged himself. So he died and was buried in his father's tomb.

²⁴David went to Mahanaim, and Absalom crossed the Jordan with all the men of Israel. ²⁵Absalom had appointed Amasa over the army in place of Joab. Amasa was the son of a man named Jether,ᵃ an Israeliteᵇ who had married Abigail,ᶜ the daughter of Nahash and sister of Zeruiah the mother of Joab. ²⁶The Israelites and Absalom camped in the land of Gilead.

²⁷When David came to Mahanaim, Shobi son of Nahash from Rabbah of the Ammonites, and Makir son of Ammiel from Lo Debar, and Barzillai the Gileadite from Rogelim ²⁸brought bedding and bowls and articles of pottery. They also brought wheat and barley, flour and roasted grain, beans and lentils,ᵈ ²⁹honey and curds, sheep, and cheese from cows' milk for David and his people to eat. For they said, "The people have become hungry and tired and thirsty in the desert."

Absalom's Death

18 David mustered the men who were with him and appointed over them commanders of thousands and commanders of hundreds. ²David sent the troops out—a third under the command of Joab, a third under Joab's brother Abishai son of Zeruiah, and a third under Ittai the Gittite. The king told the troops, "I myself will surely march out with you."

³But the men said, "You must not go out; if we are forced to flee, they won't care about us. Even if half of us die, they won't care; but you are worth ten thousand of us.ᵉ It would be better now for you to give us support from the city."

⁴The king answered, "I will do whatever seems best to you."

So the king stood beside the gate while all the men marched out in units of hundreds and of thousands. ⁵The king commanded Joab, Abishai and Ittai, "Be gentle with the young man Absalom for my sake." And all the troops heard the king giving orders concerning Absalom to each of the commanders.

⁶The army marched into the field to fight Israel, and the battle took place in the forest of Ephraim. ⁷There the army of Israel was defeated by David's men, and the casualties that day were great— twenty thousand men. ⁸The battle spread out over the whole countryside, and the forest claimed more lives that day than the sword.

⁹Now Absalom happened to meet David's men. He was riding his mule, and as the mule went under the thick branches of a large oak, Absalom's head got caught in the tree. He was left hanging in midair, while the mule he was riding kept on going.

¹⁰When one of the men saw this, he told Joab, "I just saw Absalom hanging in an oak tree."

¹¹Joab said to the man who had told him this, "What! You saw him? Why didn't you strike him to the ground right there? Then I would have had to give you ten shekelsᶠ of silver and a warrior's belt."

¹²But the man replied, "Even if a thousand shekelsᵍ were weighed out into my hands, I would not lift my hand against the king's son. In our hearing the king commanded you and Abishai and Ittai, 'Protect the young man Absalom for my sake.'ʰ ¹³And if I had put my life in jeopardyⁱ—and nothing is hidden from

---

ᵃ25 Hebrew *Ithra*, a variant of *Jether*   ᵇ25 Hebrew and some Septuagint manuscripts; other Septuagint manuscripts (see also 1 Chron. 2:17) *Ishmaelite* or *Jezreelite*   ᶜ25 Hebrew *Abigal*, a variant of *Abigail*   ᵈ28 Most Septuagint manuscripts and Syriac; Hebrew *lentils, and roasted grain*   ᵉ3 Two Hebrew manuscripts, some Septuagint manuscripts and Vulgate; most Hebrew manuscripts *care; for now there are ten thousand like us*   ᶠ11 That is, about 4 ounces (about 115 grams)   ᵍ12 That is, about 25 pounds (about 11 kilograms)   ʰ12 A few Hebrew manuscripts, Septuagint, Vulgate and Syriac; most Hebrew manuscripts may be translated *Absalom, whoever you may be.*   ⁱ13 Or *Otherwise, if I had acted treacherously toward him*

Bad Hair Days

2 Samuel 18:9–15 Talk about a bummer! Absalom was riding his mule one day when his hair got caught in a tree. The mule kept walking, leaving Absalom dangling from the branches. Joab, the leader of King David's army, heard Absalom was hanging around and went to check it out—then he put 3 javelins into Absalom's heart. Don't you hate it when that happens? Other bad hair days:

✗ Who can forget Samson's run in with Delilah? (Judges 16:17–21)

✗ Elijah was very hairy (2 Kings 1:8), and Elisha was totally bald (2 Kings 2:23)

✗ Ezra reacted to the people's sins by pulling out his hair and his beard (Ezra 9:1–3), while Nehemiah pulled out the hair of people who sinned (Nehemiah 13:25)

the king—you would have kept your distance from me."

¹⁴Joab said, "I'm not going to wait like this for you." So he took three javelins in his hand and plunged them into Absalom's heart while Absalom was still alive in the oak tree. ¹⁵And ten of Joab's armor-bearers surrounded Absalom, struck him and killed him.

¹⁶Then Joab sounded the trumpet, and the troops stopped pursuing Israel, for Joab halted them. ¹⁷They took Absalom, threw him into a big pit in the forest and piled up a large heap of rocks over him. Meanwhile, all the Israelites fled to their homes.

¹⁸During his lifetime Absalom had taken a pillar and erected it in the King's Valley as a monument to himself, for he thought, "I have no son to carry on the memory of my name." He named the pillar after himself, and it is called Absalom's Monument to this day.

David Mourns

¹⁹Now Ahimaaz son of Zadok said, "Let me run and take the news to the king that the LORD has delivered him from the hand of his enemies."

²⁰"You are not the one to take the news today," Joab told him. "You may take the news another time, but you must not do so today, because the king's son is dead."

²¹Then Joab said to a Cushite, "Go, tell the king what you have seen." The Cushite bowed down before Joab and ran off.

²²Ahimaaz son of Zadok again said to Joab, "Come what may, please let me run behind the Cushite."

But Joab replied, "My son, why do you want to go? You don't have any news that will bring you a reward."

²³He said, "Come what may, I want to run."

So Joab said, "Run!" Then Ahimaaz ran by way of the plain*a* and outran the Cushite.

²⁴While David was sitting between the inner and outer gates, the watchman went up to the roof of the gateway by the wall. As he looked out, he saw a man running alone. ²⁵The watchman called out to the king and reported it.

The king said, "If he is alone, he must have good news." And the man came closer and closer.

²⁶Then the watchman saw another man running, and he called down to the gatekeeper, "Look, another man running alone!"

The king said, "He must be bringing good news, too."

²⁷The watchman said, "It seems to me that the first one runs like Ahimaaz son of Zadok."

"He's a good man," the king said. "He comes with good news."

²⁸Then Ahimaaz called out to the king, "All is well!" He bowed down before the king with his face to the ground and said, "Praise be to the LORD your God! He has delivered up the men who lifted their hands against my lord the king."

²⁹The king asked, "Is the young man Absalom safe?"

a23 That is, the plain of the Jordan

Ahimaaz answered, "I saw great confusion just as Joab was about to send the king's servant and me, your servant, but I don't know what it was."

³⁰The king said, "Stand aside and wait here." So he stepped aside and stood there.

³¹Then the Cushite arrived and said, "My lord the king, hear the good news! The LORD has delivered you today from all who rose up against you."

³²The king asked the Cushite, "Is the young man Absalom safe?"

The Cushite replied, "May the enemies of my lord the king and all who rise up to harm you be like that young man."

³³The king was shaken. He went up to the room over the gateway and wept. As he went, he said: "O my son Absalom! My son, my son Absalom! If only I had died instead of you—O Absalom, my son, my son!"

19 Joab was told, "The king is weeping and mourning for Absalom." ²And for the whole army the victory that day was turned into mourning, because on that day the troops heard it said, "The king is grieving for his son." ³The men stole into the city that day as men steal in who are ashamed when they flee from battle. ⁴The king covered his face and cried aloud, "O my son Absalom! O Absalom, my son, my son!"

⁵Then Joab went into the house to the king and said, "Today you have humiliated all your men, who have just saved your life and the lives of your sons and daughters and the lives of your wives and concubines. ⁶You love those who hate you and hate those who love you. You have made it clear today that the commanders and their men mean nothing to you. I see that you would be pleased if Absalom were alive today and

Tuesday

Too Stuck-up
Read 2 Samuel 18:9–18

I remember when we were playing another school in basketball for the second time in one season. The first time we'd played them, I had a great game and scored somewhere between 15 and 20 points. But when it was time for the second game, I was full of pride and played cocky. I ended up with 4 or 6 points, and we lost by about 25.

Absalom had a different problem: He was stuck up about his appearance, and especially his hair. He must have been growing it out for a long time if he had enough of it to get caught in a tree. He probably thought he looked all handsome until he was hanging in midair. Then I bet he looked pretty stupid.

No matter what it is you're overly proud about, that attitude's going to hurt you eventually. Besides, pride is totally opposite from what God wants us to be like. He wants us to be humble and not draw attention or glory to ourselves. Instead, we should glorify him.

What about You?

❶ What are some things you're tempted to be too proud about? How can you use those things to glorify God instead of yourself?

❷ Make a small sign that says *God's Gifts* and stick it on your mirror. Remember that everything you see in the mirror is a gift from God and should be used to glorify him.

❸ Ask God to help you get rid of any pride in your heart.

Turn to page 378 for your next devotion.

all of us were dead. [7]Now go out and encourage your men. I swear by the LORD that if you don't go out, not a man will be left with you by nightfall. This will be worse for you than all the calamities that have come upon you from your youth till now."

[8]So the king got up and took his seat in the gateway. When the men were told, "The king is sitting in the gateway," they all came before him.

David Returns to Jerusalem

Meanwhile, the Israelites had fled to their homes. [9]Throughout the tribes of Israel, the people were all arguing with each other, saying, "The king delivered us from the hand of our enemies; he is the one who rescued us from the hand of the Philistines. But now he has fled the country because of Absalom; [10]and Absalom, whom we anointed to rule over us, has died in battle. So why do you say nothing about bringing the king back?"

[11]King David sent this message to Zadok and Abiathar, the priests: "Ask the elders of Judah, 'Why should you be the last to bring the king back to his palace, since what is being said throughout Israel has reached the king at his quarters? [12]You are my brothers, my own flesh and blood. So why should you be the last to bring back the king?' [13]And say to Amasa, 'Are you not my own flesh and blood? May God deal with me, be it ever so severely, if from now on you are not the commander of my army in place of Joab.'"

[14]He won over the hearts of all the men of Judah as though they were one man. They sent word to the king, "Return, you and all your men." [15]Then the king returned and went as far as the Jordan.

Now the men of Judah had come to Gilgal to go out and meet the king and bring him across the Jordan. [16]Shimei son of Gera, the Benjamite from Bahurim, hurried down with the men of Judah to meet King David. [17]With him were a thousand Benjamites, along with Ziba, the steward of Saul's household, and his fifteen sons and twenty servants. They rushed to the Jordan, where the king was. [18]They crossed at the ford to take the king's household over and to do whatever he wished.

When Shimei son of Gera crossed the Jordan, he fell prostrate before the king [19]and said to him, "May my lord not hold me guilty. Do not remember how your servant did wrong on the day my lord the king left Jerusalem. May the king put it out of his mind. [20]For I your servant know that I have sinned, but today I have come here as the first of the whole house of Joseph to come down and meet my lord the king."

[21]Then Abishai son of Zeruiah said, "Shouldn't Shimei be put to death for this? He cursed the LORD's anointed."

[22]David replied, "What do you and I have in common, you sons of Zeruiah? This day you have become my adversaries! Should anyone be put to death in Israel today? Do I not know that today I am king over Israel?" [23]So the king said to Shimei, "You shall not die." And the king promised him on oath.

[24]Mephibosheth, Saul's grandson, also went down to meet the king. He had not taken care of his feet or trimmed his mustache or washed his clothes from the day the king left until the day he returned safely. [25]When he came from Jerusalem to meet the king, the king asked him, "Why didn't you go with me, Mephibosheth?"

[26]He said, "My lord the king, since I your servant am lame, I said, 'I will have my donkey saddled and will ride on it, so I can go with the king.' But Ziba my servant betrayed me. [27]And he has slandered your servant to my lord the king. My lord the king is like an angel of God; so do whatever pleases you. [28]All my grandfather's descendants deserved nothing but death from my lord the king, but you gave your servant a place among those who eat at your table. So what right do I have to make any more appeals to the king?"

[29]The king said to him, "Why say more? I order you and Ziba to divide the fields."

[30]Mephibosheth said to the king, "Let him take everything, now that my lord the king has arrived home safely."

[31]Barzillai the Gileadite also came down from Rogelim to cross the Jordan

Back Stage Pass

"Come over here. Right now."

These words would sound scary coming from that big bully at school, but keep reading.

"Come over here. Right now. Because I love you. All I want to do is help you. I will take care of you."

Sounds different now, doesn't it? That's because it's really God saying those words to you, not some tough guy at school. God wants you to come near to him, not because he's mean but because he loves you. And he wants you to get to know him right now.

But how do you get close to him? It's pretty easy, really. It's through God's grace. Try thinking of grace like God's hand reaching out to you to pull you close to him. That doesn't mean that God's big arm is a tractor-beam that's going to pull you into the sky and fly you to heaven right this second. What it does mean is that he's asking you to become like a little kid, crawling up into his big, soft lap, giving every part of your life to him.

Sometimes you might not want to give God every part of your life, but when you do give him all of yourself life gets really good! He's so smart and good that he will take better care of you than anyone else—including you.

The closer you get to God, the more you experience the cool stuff that comes with having him as your perfect Father and best friend. Paul writes about some of this cool stuff in Galatians 5:22–23, page 1421:

Joy. Even if your bike gets stolen, you can still be grateful for the other stuff that you have (Philippians 4:4, page 1439).

Peace. When your best friend is getting ready to move to another state, you won't freak out (Philippians 4:6–7).

Gentleness. If everyone else in your class is making fun of the girl with the big teeth who sits in front of you, you make an extra effort to be kind to her (Philippians 4:5).

Self-control. When you are tempted to check out the websites and chat rooms you know you shouldn't, you shut down your computer and phone a friend instead (2 Timothy 1:7, page 1472).

Can you feel God's hand reaching out to you? Ask him to draw you close. Today.

eXtreme FAITH

"If all my sins are forgiven, why do I still need to ask for forgiveness?"

We have God's promise that "if we confess our sins, he is faithful and just and will forgive us our sins and purify us from all unrighteousness" (1 John 1:9, page 1529). We can depend on this promise because God made it to us, and he never lies.

We also need to look at this promise as it fits in with the verses around it. In this first chapter, the apostle John is trying to help us understand a bigger idea. He reminds us that "God is light; in him there is no darkness at all" (1 John 1:5). This means God is perfect; there's not even a tiny bit of sin in him. When we come to God, we come into his light, where we can see things more clearly. It's like looking at your face in a big mirror under bright lights. You suddenly see things you didn't see before.

This is what happens when we really start to know God. We become aware of our sins. And if we are obedient, we confess them to God, and he forgives us. But we also become aware of God's righteousness and how different it is from the darkness in our lives. We realize we have sins we didn't know about before we came to him. This helps us be more humble and less proud about how "good" we are.

Then we realize we've been confessing only those obvious sins we can see with our human eyes. And we realize there are things about us that we can't see, but we know that God sees. So we confess not just our sins but our "sinfulness"—which includes our attitudes, our motives and the sin of not doing the right thing when we have the chance. This process is what John calls "walking in the light" (1 John 1:7).

John encourages us to always walk near God so we can be in his light and see our sins. And as we see our sins, we should always ask God to forgive us so we can have a good relationship with him and with one another. That's why Jesus told us to pray, "Forgive us our debts, as we also have forgiven our debtors" (Matthew 6:12, page 1148).

When we get a sense of how much God forgives us, we're less likely be proud or criticize others. And because God forgives us, he expects us to be forgiving too. If God can forgive the sins of other people, so can we. That's what it really means to "walk in his light"—to practice forgiveness all around.

— Jay Kesler, president of Taylor University and a former contributing editor to Campus Life magazine. Jay has also written several books for teens.

with the king and to send him on his way from there. ³²Now Barzillai was a very old man, eighty years of age. He had provided for the king during his stay in Mahanaim, for he was a very wealthy man. ³³The king said to Barzillai, "Cross over with me and stay with me in Jerusalem, and I will provide for you."

³⁴But Barzillai answered the king, "How many more years will I live, that I should go up to Jerusalem with the king? ³⁵I am now eighty years old. Can I tell the difference between what is good and what is not? Can your servant taste what he eats and drinks? Can I still hear the voices of men and women singers? Why should your servant be an added burden to my lord the king? ³⁶Your servant will cross over the Jordan with the king for a short distance, but why should the king reward me in this way? ³⁷Let your servant return, that I may die in my own town near the tomb of my father and mother. But here is your servant Kimham. Let him cross over with my lord the king. Do for him whatever pleases you."

³⁸The king said, "Kimham shall cross over with me, and I will do for him whatever pleases you. And anything you desire from me I will do for you."

³⁹So all the people crossed the Jordan, and then the king crossed over. The king kissed Barzillai and gave him his blessing, and Barzillai returned to his home.

⁴⁰When the king crossed over to Gilgal, Kimham crossed with him. All the troops of Judah and half the troops of Israel had taken the king over.

⁴¹Soon all the men of Israel were coming to the king and saying to him, "Why did our brothers, the men of Judah, steal the king away and bring him and his household across the Jordan, together with all his men?"

⁴²All the men of Judah answered the men of Israel, "We did this because the king is closely related to us. Why are you angry about it? Have we eaten any of the king's provisions? Have we taken anything for ourselves?"

⁴³Then the men of Israel answered the men of Judah, "We have ten shares in the king; and besides, we have a greater claim on David than you have. So why do you treat us with contempt? Were we

not the first to speak of bringing back our king?"

But the men of Judah responded even more harshly than the men of Israel.

Sheba Rebels Against David

20 Now a troublemaker named Sheba son of Bicri, a Benjamite, happened to be there. He sounded the trumpet and shouted,

"We have no share in David,
    no part in Jesse's son!
Every man to his tent, O Israel!"

²So all the men of Israel deserted David to follow Sheba son of Bicri. But the men of Judah stayed by their king all the way from the Jordan to Jerusalem.

³When David returned to his palace in Jerusalem, he took the ten concubines he had left to take care of the palace and put them in a house under guard. He provided for them, but did not lie with them. They were kept in confinement till the day of their death, living as widows.

⁴Then the king said to Amasa, "Summon the men of Judah to come to me within three days, and be here yourself." ⁵But when Amasa went to summon Judah, he took longer than the time the king had set for him.

⁶David said to Abishai, "Now Sheba son of Bicri will do us more harm than Absalom did. Take your master's men and pursue him, or he will find fortified cities and escape from us." ⁷So Joab's men and the Kerethites and Pelethites and all the mighty warriors went out under the command of Abishai. They marched out from Jerusalem to pursue Sheba son of Bicri.

⁸While they were at the great rock in Gibeon, Amasa came to meet them. Joab was wearing his military tunic, and strapped over it at his waist was a belt with a dagger in its sheath. As he stepped forward, it dropped out of its sheath.

⁹Joab said to Amasa, "How are you, my brother?" Then Joab took Amasa by the beard with his right hand to kiss him. ¹⁰Amasa was not on his guard against the dagger in Joab's hand, and Joab plunged it into his belly, and his intestines spilled out on the ground. Without being stabbed again, Amasa died. Then Joab

and his brother Abishai pursued Sheba son of Bicri.

¹¹One of Joab's men stood beside Amasa and said, "Whoever favors Joab, and whoever is for David, let him follow Joab!" ¹²Amasa lay wallowing in his blood in the middle of the road, and the man saw that all the troops came to a halt there. When he realized that everyone who came up to Amasa stopped, he dragged him from the road into a field and threw a garment over him. ¹³After Amasa had been removed from the road, all the men went on with Joab to pursue Sheba son of Bicri.

¹⁴Sheba passed through all the tribes of Israel to Abel Beth Maacah*a* and through the entire region of the Berites, who gathered together and followed him. ¹⁵All the troops with Joab came and besieged Sheba in Abel Beth Maacah. They built a siege ramp up to the city, and it stood against the outer fortifications. While they were battering the wall to bring it down, ¹⁶a wise woman called from the city, "Listen! Listen! Tell Joab to come here so I can speak to him." ¹⁷He went toward her, and she asked, "Are you Joab?"

"I am," he answered.

She said, "Listen to what your servant has to say."

"I'm listening," he said.

¹⁸She continued, "Long ago they used to say, 'Get your answer at Abel,' and that settled it. ¹⁹We are the peaceful and faithful in Israel. You are trying to destroy a city that is a mother in Israel. Why do you want to swallow up the LORD's inheritance?"

²⁰"Far be it from me!" Joab replied, "Far be it from me to swallow up or destroy! ²¹That is not the case. A man named Sheba son of Bicri, from the hill country of Ephraim, has lifted up his hand against the king, against David. Hand over this one man, and I'll withdraw from the city."

The woman said to Joab, "His head will be thrown to you from the wall."

²²Then the woman went to all the people with her wise advice, and they cut off the head of Sheba son of Bicri and threw it to Joab. So he sounded the trumpet, and his men dispersed from the city, each returning to his home. And Joab went back to the king in Jerusalem.

²³Joab was over Israel's entire army; Benaiah son of Jehoiada was over the Kerethites and Pelethites; ²⁴Adoniram*b* was in charge of forced labor; Jehoshaphat son of Ahilud was recorder; ²⁵Sheva was secretary; Zadok and Abiathar were priests; ²⁶and Ira the Jairite was David's priest.

The Gibeonites Avenged

21 During the reign of David, there was a famine for three successive years; so David sought the face of the LORD. The LORD said, "It is on account of Saul and his blood-stained house; it is because he put the Gibeonites to death."

²The king summoned the Gibeonites and spoke to them. (Now the Gibeonites were not a part of Israel but were survivors of the Amorites; the Israelites had sworn to spare them, but Saul in his zeal for Israel and Judah had tried to annihilate them.) ³David asked the Gibeonites, "What shall I do for you? How shall I make amends so that you will bless the LORD's inheritance?"

⁴The Gibeonites answered him, "We have no right to demand silver or gold from Saul or his family, nor do we have the right to put anyone in Israel to death."

"What do you want me to do for you?" David asked.

⁵They answered the king, "As for the man who destroyed us and plotted against us so that we have been decimated and have no place anywhere in Israel, ⁶let seven of his male descendants be given to us to be killed and exposed before the LORD at Gibeah of Saul—the LORD's chosen one."

So the king said, "I will give them to you."

⁷The king spared Mephibosheth son of Jonathan, the son of Saul, because of the oath before the LORD between David and Jonathan son of Saul. ⁸But the king took Armoni and Mephibosheth, the two sons of Aiah's daughter Rizpah, whom she

---

a14 Or Abel, even Beth Maacah; also in verse 15
*b24 Some Septuagint manuscripts (see also 1 Kings 4:6 and 5:14); Hebrew *Adoram*

had borne to Saul, together with the five sons of Saul's daughter Merab,[a] whom she had borne to Adriel son of Barzillai the Meholathite. [9]He handed them over to the Gibeonites, who killed and exposed them on a hill before the LORD. All seven of them fell together; they were put to death during the first days of the harvest, just as the barley harvest was beginning.

[10]Rizpah daughter of Aiah took sackcloth and spread it out for herself on a rock. From the beginning of the harvest till the rain poured down from the heavens on the bodies, she did not let the birds of the air touch them by day or the wild animals by night. [11]When David was told what Aiah's daughter Rizpah, Saul's concubine, had done, [12]he went and took the bones of Saul and his son Jonathan from the citizens of Jabesh Gilead. (They had taken them secretly from the public square at Beth Shan, where the Philistines had hung them after they struck Saul down on Gilboa.) [13]David brought the bones of Saul and his son Jonathan from there, and the bones of those who had been killed and exposed were gathered up.

[14]They buried the bones of Saul and his son Jonathan in the tomb of Saul's father Kish, at Zela in Benjamin, and did everything the king commanded. After that, God answered prayer in behalf of the land.

Wars Against the Philistines

[15]Once again there was a battle between the Philistines and Israel. David went down with his men to fight against the Philistines, and he became exhausted. [16]And Ishbi-Benob, one of the descendants of Rapha, whose bronze spearhead weighed three hundred shekels[b] and who was armed with a new sword, said he would kill David. [17]But Abishai son of Zeruiah came to David's rescue; he struck the Philistine down and killed him. Then David's men swore to him, saying, "Never again will you go out with us to battle, so that the lamp of Israel will not be extinguished."

[18]In the course of time, there was another battle with the Philistines, at Gob. At that time Sibbecai the Hushathite killed Saph, one of the descendants of Rapha.

[19]In another battle with the Philistines at Gob, Elhanan son of Jaare-Oregim[c] the Bethlehemite killed Goliath[d] the Gittite, who had a spear with a shaft like a weaver's rod.

[20]In still another battle, which took place at Gath, there was a huge man with six fingers on each hand and six toes on each foot—twenty-four in all. He also was descended from Rapha. [21]When he taunted Israel, Jonathan son of Shimeah, David's brother, killed him.

[22]These four were descendants of Rapha in Gath, and they fell at the hands of David and his men.

David's Song of Praise

22 David sang to the LORD the words of this song when the LORD delivered him from the hand of all his enemies and from the hand of Saul. [2]He said:

"The LORD is my rock, my fortress and
            my deliverer;
[3]   my God is my rock, in whom I take
            refuge,
   my shield and the horn[e] of my
            salvation.
He is my stronghold, my refuge and
            my savior—
   from violent men you save me.
[4]I call to the LORD, who is worthy of
            praise,
   and I am saved from my enemies.

[5]"The waves of death swirled about
            me;
   the torrents of destruction
            overwhelmed me.
[6]The cords of the grave[f] coiled around
            me;
   the snares of death confronted me.
[7]In my distress I called to the LORD;
   I called out to my God.
From his temple he heard my voice;
   my cry came to his ears.

---

[a]8 Two Hebrew manuscripts, some Septuagint manuscripts and Syriac (see also 1 Samuel 18:19); most Hebrew and Septuagint manuscripts *Michal*   [b]16 That is, about 7 1/2 pounds (about 3.5 kilograms)   [c]19 Or *son of Jair the weaver*   [d]19 Hebrew and Septuagint; 1 Chron. 20:5 *son of Jair killed Lahmi the brother of Goliath*   [e]3 *Horn* here symbolizes strength.   [f]6 Hebrew *Sheol*

8 "The earth trembled and quaked,
   the foundations of the heavens[a]
      shook;
   they trembled because he was
      angry.
9 Smoke rose from his nostrils;
   consuming fire came from his
      mouth,
   burning coals blazed out of it.
10 He parted the heavens and came
      down;
   dark clouds were under his feet.
11 He mounted the cherubim and flew;
   he soared[b] on the wings of the
      wind.
12 He made darkness his canopy around
      him—
   the dark[c] rain clouds of the sky.
13 Out of the brightness of his presence
   bolts of lightning blazed forth.
14 The LORD thundered from heaven;
   the voice of the Most High
      resounded.
15 He shot arrows and scattered the
      enemies,
   bolts of lightning and routed them.
16 The valleys of the sea were exposed
   and the foundations of the earth
      laid bare
   at the rebuke of the LORD,
      at the blast of breath from his
         nostrils.

17 "He reached down from on high and
      took hold of me;
   he drew me out of deep waters.
18 He rescued me from my powerful
      enemy,
   from my foes, who were too strong
      for me.
19 They confronted me in the day of my
      disaster,
   but the LORD was my support.
20 He brought me out into a spacious
      place;
   he rescued me because he delighted
      in me.

21 "The LORD has dealt with me
      according to my righteousness;
   according to the cleanness of my
      hands he has rewarded me.
22 For I have kept the ways of the LORD;
   I have not done evil by turning
      from my God.
23 All his laws are before me;

   I have not turned away from his
      decrees.
24 I have been blameless before him
   and have kept myself from sin.
25 The LORD has rewarded me according
      to my righteousness,
   according to my cleanness[d] in his
      sight.

26 "To the faithful you show yourself
      faithful,
   to the blameless you show yourself
      blameless,
27 to the pure you show yourself pure,
   but to the crooked you show
      yourself shrewd.
28 You save the humble,
   but your eyes are on the haughty to
      bring them low.
29 You are my lamp, O LORD;
   the LORD turns my darkness into
      light.
30 With your help I can advance against
      a troop[e];
   with my God I can scale a wall.

31 "As for God, his way is perfect;
   the word of the LORD is flawless.
   He is a shield
      for all who take refuge in him.
32 For who is God besides the LORD?
   And who is the Rock except our
      God?
33 It is God who arms me with strength[f]
   and makes my way perfect.
34 He makes my feet like the feet of a
      deer;
   he enables me to stand on the
      heights.
35 He trains my hands for battle;
   my arms can bend a bow of bronze.
36 You give me your shield of victory;
   you stoop down to make me great.
37 You broaden the path beneath me,
   so that my ankles do not turn.

38 "I pursued my enemies and crushed
      them;

a8 Hebrew; Vulgate and Syriac (see also Psalm 18:7)
mountains   *b11* Many Hebrew manuscripts (see also
Psalm 18:10); most Hebrew manuscripts *appeared*
c12 Septuagint and Vulgate (see also Psalm 18:11);
Hebrew *massed*   *d25* Hebrew; Septuagint and
Vulgate (see also Psalm 18:24) *to the cleanness of
my hands*   *e30* Or *can run through a barricade*
f33 Dead Sea Scrolls, some Septuagint manuscripts,
Vulgate and Syriac (see also Psalm 18:32); Masoretic
Text *who is my strong refuge*

I did not turn back till they were
destroyed.
³⁹I crushed them completely, and they
could not rise;
they fell beneath my feet.
⁴⁰You armed me with strength for
battle;
you made my adversaries bow at
my feet.
⁴¹You made my enemies turn their
backs in flight,
and I destroyed my foes.
⁴²They cried for help, but there was no
one to save them—
to the LORD, but he did not answer.
⁴³I beat them as fine as the dust of the
earth;
I pounded and trampled them like
mud in the streets.

⁴⁴"You have delivered me from the
attacks of my people;
you have preserved me as the head
of nations.
People I did not know are subject to
me,
⁴⁵   and foreigners come cringing to me;
as soon as they hear me, they obey
me.
⁴⁶They all lose heart;
they come trembling*ᵃ* from their
strongholds.

⁴⁷"The LORD lives! Praise be to my Rock!
Exalted be God, the Rock, my
Savior!
⁴⁸He is the God who avenges me,
who puts the nations under me,
⁴⁹   who sets me free from my enemies.
You exalted me above my foes;
from violent men you rescued me.
⁵⁰Therefore I will praise you, O LORD,
among the nations;
I will sing praises to your name.
⁵¹He gives his king great victories;
he shows unfailing kindness to his
anointed,
to David and his descendants
forever."

The Last Words of David

23 These are the last words of David:

"The oracle of David son of Jesse,
the oracle of the man exalted by the
Most High,

the man anointed by the God of
Jacob,
Israel's singer of songs*ᵇ*:

²"The Spirit of the LORD spoke through
me;
his word was on my tongue.
³The God of Israel spoke,
the Rock of Israel said to me:
'When one rules over men in righteousness,
when he rules in the fear of God,
⁴he is like the light of morning at
sunrise
on a cloudless morning,
like the brightness after rain
that brings the grass from the earth.'

⁵"Is not my house right with God?
Has he not made with me an
everlasting covenant,
arranged and secured in every part?
Will he not bring to fruition my
salvation
and grant me my every desire?
⁶But evil men are all to be cast aside
like thorns,
which are not gathered with the
hand.
⁷Whoever touches thorns
uses a tool of iron or the shaft of a
spear;
they are burned up where they lie."

David's Mighty Men

⁸These are the names of David's
mighty men:

Josheb-Basshebeth,*ᶜ* a Tahkemonite,*ᵈ*
was chief of the Three; he raised his
spear against eight hundred men, whom
he killed*ᵉ* in one encounter.
⁹Next to him was Eleazar son of Dodai
the Ahohite. As one of the three mighty
men, he was with David when they
taunted the Philistines gathered at Pas
Dammim*ᶠ* for battle. Then the men of

ᵃ46 Some Septuagint manuscripts and Vulgate
(see also Psalm 18:45); Masoretic Text *they arm
themselves.*   *ᵇ1* Or *Israel's beloved singer*
ᶜ8 Hebrew; some Septuagint manuscripts suggest
Ish-Bosheth, that is, *Esh-Baal* (see also 1 Chron.
11:11 *Jashobeam*).   *ᵈ8* Probably a variant of
Hacmonite (see 1 Chron. 11:11)   *ᵉ8* Some Septuagint
manuscripts (see also 1 Chron. 11:11); Hebrew and
other Septuagint manuscripts *Three; it was Adino
the Eznite who killed eight hundred men*   *ᶠ9* See
1 Chron. 11:13; Hebrew *gathered there.*

Israel retreated, [10]but he stood his ground and struck down the Philistines till his hand grew tired and froze to the sword. The LORD brought about a great victory that day. The troops returned to Eleazar, but only to strip the dead.

[11]Next to him was Shammah son of Agee the Hararite. When the Philistines banded together at a place where there was a field full of lentils, Israel's troops fled from them. [12]But Shammah took his stand in the middle of the field. He defended it and struck the Philistines down, and the LORD brought about a great victory.

[13]During harvest time, three of the thirty chief men came down to David at the cave of Adullam, while a band of Philistines was encamped in the Valley of Rephaim. [14]At that time David was in the stronghold, and the Philistine garrison was at Bethlehem. [15]David longed for water and said, "Oh, that someone would get me a drink of water from the well near the gate of Bethlehem!" [16]So the three mighty men broke through the Philistine lines, drew water from the well near the gate of Bethlehem and carried it back to David. But he refused to drink it; instead, he poured it out before the LORD. [17]"Far be it from me, O LORD, to do this!" he said. "Is it not the blood of men who went at the risk of their lives?" And David would not drink it.

Such were the exploits of the three mighty men.

[18]Abishai the brother of Joab son of Zeruiah was chief of the Three.[a] He raised his spear against three hundred men, whom he killed, and so he became as famous as the Three. [19]Was he not held in greater honor than the Three? He became their commander, even though he was not included among them.

[20]Benaiah son of Jehoiada was a valiant fighter from Kabzeel, who performed great exploits. He struck down

---

[a]18 Most Hebrew manuscripts (see also 1 Chron. 11:20); two Hebrew manuscripts and Syriac *Thirty*

Wednesday

The A-team

Read 2 Samuel 23:8–23

I wish I had read this passage last year when I was cut from the basketball team. I was crushed then, but now I know that God can use me even if I'm not the best at everything—even when I feel like the biggest loser, and I'm sure I'm not skilled at anything. Even then he can use me.

Just look at David's mighty men. They did all kinds of great deeds and became famous. But I doubt that they were always that way. I bet some of them even got cut from their high school, uhh, warrior team. But it didn't keep them down.

My name, Laura, means "victorious." And that's the way God sees me. I may never be a star basketball player, but I'll always have a place in his lineup.

❶ You probably aren't great at everything (no one is), but you're probably good at 1 or 2 things. What is something you do well?

❷ What does your name mean? Look it up in *What's in a Name* or another book. Why is your name important? Remember, God knows you by name, and he has a plan just for you.

❸ Ask God to help you discover and develop your talents.

Turn to page 387 for your next devotion.

two of Moab's best men. He also went down into a pit on a snowy day and killed a lion. [21]And he struck down a huge Egyptian. Although the Egyptian had a spear in his hand, Benaiah went against him with a club. He snatched the spear from the Egyptian's hand and killed him with his own spear. [22]Such were the exploits of Benaiah son of Jehoiada; he too was as famous as the three mighty men. [23]He was held in greater honor than any of the Thirty, but he was not included among the Three. And David put him in charge of his bodyguard.

[24]Among the Thirty were:
Asahel the brother of Joab,
Elhanan son of Dodo from Bethlehem,
[25]Shammah the Harodite,
Elika the Harodite,
[26]Helez the Paltite,
Ira son of Ikkesh from Tekoa,
[27]Abiezer from Anathoth,
Mebunnai[a] the Hushathite,
[28]Zalmon the Ahohite,
Maharai the Netophathite,
[29]Heled[b] son of Baanah the Netophathite,
Ithai son of Ribai from Gibeah in Benjamin,
[30]Benaiah the Pirathonite,
Hiddai[c] from the ravines of Gaash,
[31]Abi-Albon the Arbathite,
Azmaveth the Barhumite,
[32]Eliahba the Shaalbonite,
the sons of Jashen,
Jonathan [33]son of[d] Shammah the Hararite,
Ahiam son of Sharar[e] the Hararite,
[34]Eliphelet son of Ahasbai the Maacathite,
Eliam son of Ahithophel the Gilonite,
[35]Hezro the Carmelite,
Paarai the Arbite,
[36]Igal son of Nathan from Zobah,
the son of Hagri,[f]
[37]Zelek the Ammonite,
Naharai the Beerothite, the armorbearer of Joab son of Zeruiah,
[38]Ira the Ithrite,
Gareb the Ithrite

[39]and Uriah the Hittite.
There were thirty-seven in all.

David Counts the Fighting Men

24 Again the anger of the LORD burned against Israel, and he incited David against them, saying, "Go and take a census of Israel and Judah."

[2]So the king said to Joab and the army commanders[g] with him, "Go throughout the tribes of Israel from Dan to Beersheba and enroll the fighting men, so that I may know how many there are."

[3]But Joab replied to the king, "May the LORD your God multiply the troops a hundred times over, and may the eyes of my lord the king see it. But why does my lord the king want to do such a thing?"

[4]The king's word, however, overruled Joab and the army commanders; so they left the presence of the king to enroll the fighting men of Israel.

[5]After crossing the Jordan, they camped near Aroer, south of the town in the gorge, and then went through Gad and on to Jazer. [6]They went to Gilead and the region of Tahtim Hodshi, and on to Dan Jaan and around toward Sidon. [7]Then they went toward the fortress of Tyre and all the towns of the Hivites and Canaanites. Finally, they went on to Beersheba in the Negev of Judah.

[8]After they had gone through the entire land, they came back to Jerusalem at the end of nine months and twenty days.

[9]Joab reported the number of the fighting men to the king: In Israel there were eight hundred thousand able-bodied men who could handle a sword, and in Judah five hundred thousand.

[10]David was conscience-stricken after he had counted the fighting men, and he

a27 Hebrew; some Septuagint manuscripts (see also 1 Chron. 11:29) *Sibbecai* *b29* Some Hebrew manuscripts and Vulgate (see also 1 Chron. 11:30); most Hebrew manuscripts *Heleb* *c30* Hebrew; some Septuagint manuscripts (see also 1 Chron. 11:32) *Hurai* *d33* Some Septuagint manuscripts (see also 1 Chron. 11:34); Hebrew does not have *son of.* *e33* Hebrew; some Septuagint manuscripts (see also 1 Chron. 11:35) *Sacar* *f36* Some Septuagint manuscripts (see also 1 Chron. 11:38); Hebrew *Haggadi* *g2* Septuagint (see also verse 4 and 1 Chron. 21:2); Hebrew *Joab the army commander*

said to the LORD, "I have sinned greatly in what I have done. Now, O LORD, I beg you, take away the guilt of your servant. I have done a very foolish thing."

[11]Before David got up the next morning, the word of the LORD had come to Gad the prophet, David's seer: [12]"Go and tell David, 'This is what the LORD says: I am giving you three options. Choose one of them for me to carry out against you.' "

[13]So Gad went to David and said to him, "Shall there come upon you three[a] years of famine in your land? Or three months of fleeing from your enemies while they pursue you? Or three days of plague in your land? Now then, think it over and decide how I should answer the one who sent me."

[14]David said to Gad, "I am in deep distress. Let us fall into the hands of the LORD, for his mercy is great; but do not let me fall into the hands of men."

[15]So the LORD sent a plague on Israel from that morning until the end of the time designated, and seventy thousand of the people from Dan to Beersheba died. [16]When the angel stretched out his hand to destroy Jerusalem, the LORD was grieved because of the calamity and said to the angel who was afflicting the people, "Enough! Withdraw your hand." The angel of the LORD was then at the threshing floor of Araunah the Jebusite.

[17]When David saw the angel who was striking down the people, he said to the LORD, "I am the one who has sinned and done wrong. These are but sheep. What have they done? Let your hand fall upon me and my family."

David Builds an Altar

[18]On that day Gad went to David and said to him, "Go up and build an altar to the LORD on the threshing floor of Araunah the Jebusite." [19]So David went up, as the LORD had commanded through Gad. [20]When Araunah looked and saw the king and his men coming toward him, he went out and bowed down before the king with his face to the ground.

[21]Araunah said, "Why has my lord the king come to his servant?"

"To buy your threshing floor," David answered, "so I can build an altar to the LORD, that the plague on the people may be stopped."

[22]Araunah said to David, "Let my lord the king take whatever pleases him and offer it up. Here are oxen for the burnt offering, and here are threshing sledges and ox yokes for the wood. [23]O king, Araunah gives all this to the king." Araunah also said to him, "May the LORD your God accept you."

[24]But the king replied to Araunah, "No, I insist on paying you for it. I will not sacrifice to the LORD my God burnt offerings that cost me nothing."

So David bought the threshing floor and the oxen and paid fifty shekels[b] of silver for them. [25]David built an altar to the LORD there and sacrificed burnt offerings and fellowship offerings.[c] Then the LORD answered prayer in behalf of the land, and the plague on Israel was stopped.

---

[a]13 Septuagint (see also 1 Chron. 21:12); Hebrew *seven*   [b]24 That is, about 1 1/4 pounds (about 0.6 kilogram)   [c]25 Traditionally *peace offerings*

1 Kings

START

This book covers the first batch of kings, except for the first 2. Saul, Israel's first king, gets his story told in 1 Samuel. David is king #2, and he's the star of 2 Samuel. King Dave also gets some coverage in this new book, just long enough to appoint king #3—Bathsheba's young son Solomon.

Solomon slept through his greatest moment. In a dream, the young king asks God for wisdom. God is so pleased that he grants the request and throws in wealth and honor besides. Solomon immediately invests his gifts to build a strong national government, good relationships with foreign countries and a permanent temple in downtown Jerusalem. God allowed polygamy (being married to more than one wife), but Solomon takes this idea to the extreme: He had 300 wives! Not to mention 700 concubines—a polite word for someone who's somewhere between a wife and servant. Solomon's bunch of foreign women and their wacky religions become his downfall.

After Solomon's death, his son Rehoboam ascends to the throne. His first royal move is a royal flop: He tells everyone he's going to raise the taxes. The country's 10 northern states, or tribes, drop out of the union and make Jeroboam their king. Since that's most of the country, they get to keep the name *Israel*. That leaves Rehoboam with just the two southern tribe-states: Judah and Benjamin. *Judah* is the bigger one, so that's what they call the whole country. The rest of the book takes us on back-and-forth visits to each of the former partners as it spirals down through a line of kings, most of them rotten. In the contest of who can spiral down further, Israel wins, but Judah is close behind. God is still in the picture, but neither country seems to look for him very often.

Cast of Characters

Solomon
(SAHL-uh-mun)
He's Israel's third king and the son of David and Bathsheba. He is into prayer and wants to follow God's plan. He has his weaknesses, but he winds up becoming the wisest and richest man that ever lived.

Rehoboam
(ree-ha-BOW-um)
He's Solomon's son and the first in line for the throne after Dad. Rehoboam tries to raise taxes and winds up splitting his kingdom in 2.

Jeroboam
(jer-ah-BOW-um)
He's Solomon's military official. When the new king's tax plan flops, Jeroboam takes the 10

northern tribe-states and the country's name with him. He's the first new king of Israel, and, like pretty much every king that followed, he's rotten.

Elijah (ee-LIE-jah)

The new Israel has awful kings, but it has a great prophet. Elijah never dies! But you'll have to wait until the next book to see that.

Elisha (ee-LIE-shah)

Another great prophet. He's Elijah's protégé (apprentice, student). He's just getting started in this book. More on him in the next.

What's UP with That?

Who Am I?

Now that you've got an idea of who's who in 1 Kings, figure out which character on the right should be matched up with each statement on the left. We've even given you some hints, so try those before you check out the answers which are printed upside down at the bottom of this page.

1. I'm a wise guy who kept a baby from being cut in two. (3:16-28)
2. I'm a spicy girl who arrived in a camel caravan to Solomon. (10:1-5)
3. My hand got shriveled up when I stretched out my hand from the altar. (13:4-5)
4. I may be blind, but I can still recognize the wife of a king. (14:4-6)
5. I got my food delivered by "air mail." (17:1-6)
6. I built some new pillars and basins for God's house. (7:13-40)
7. I did what my friends told me instead of what some older guys recommended; it almost cost me my life. (12:8-18)
8. I told a woman that God would keep her flour and oil going and going. (17:13-16)
9. I built a fleet of boats to hunt down some gold, but God stopped my plan before the boats even left the bay. (22:41-50)
10. I got the reputation of being the baddest king around and eventually became a starving lion's dinner. (16:29-33; 20:36)

A. Jehoshaphat
B. Ahab
C. Solomon
D. Elijah
E. Jeroboam
F. Huram
G. Elijah (yes, again)
H. Rehoboam
I. Queen of Sheba
J. Ahijah

Snap Shots

- David passes the torch to Solomon (chapters 1—2)
- King Solomon asks for wisdom and gets the works (chapters 3—4)
- Construction zone— big temple, giant palace (chapters 5—8)
- Solomon rises, Solomon sets—he does great things, stupid things, then dies (chapters 9—11)
- Tax hike splits the country; Jeroboam takes northern crown (chapters 12—14)
- Bad and worse— 2 countries, lots of kings, mostly bad (chapters 15—16)
- The good guys—Elijah and his prophetic protégé Elisha (chapters 17—19)
- 2 A's and a J—Ahab, Ahaziah and Jehoshaphat; bad, bad, good (chapters 20–22)

Adonijah Sets Himself Up as King

1 When King David was old and well advanced in years, he could not keep warm even when they put covers over him. ²So his servants said to him, "Let us look for a young virgin to attend the king and take care of him. She can lie beside him so that our lord the king may keep warm."

³Then they searched throughout Israel for a beautiful girl and found Abishag, a Shunammite, and brought her to the king. ⁴The girl was very beautiful; she took care of the king and waited on him, but the king had no intimate relations with her.

⁵Now Adonijah, whose mother was Haggith, put himself forward and said, "I will be king." So he got chariots and horses[a] ready, with fifty men to run ahead of him. ⁶(His father had never interfered with him by asking, "Why do you behave as you do?" He was also very handsome and was born next after Absalom.)

⁷Adonijah conferred with Joab son of Zeruiah and with Abiathar the priest, and they gave him their support. ⁸But Zadok the priest, Benaiah son of Jehoiada, Nathan the prophet, Shimei and Rei[b] and David's special guard did not join Adonijah.

⁹Adonijah then sacrificed sheep, cattle and fattened calves at the Stone of Zoheleth near En Rogel. He invited all his brothers, the king's sons, and all the men of Judah who were royal officials, ¹⁰but he did not invite Nathan the prophet or Benaiah or the special guard or his brother Solomon.

¹¹Then Nathan asked Bathsheba, Solomon's mother, "Have you not heard that Adonijah, the son of Haggith, has become king without our lord David's knowing it? ¹²Now then, let me advise you how you can save your own life and the life of your son Solomon. ¹³Go in to King David and say to him, 'My lord the king, did you not swear to me your servant: "Surely Solomon your son shall be king after me, and he will sit on my throne"? Why then has Adonijah become king?' ¹⁴While you are still there talking to the king, I will come in and confirm what you have said."

¹⁵So Bathsheba went to see the aged king in his room, where Abishag the Shunammite was attending him. ¹⁶Bathsheba bowed low and knelt before the king.

"What is it you want?" the king asked.

¹⁷She said to him, "My lord, you yourself swore to me your servant by the LORD your God: 'Solomon your son shall be king after me, and he will sit on my throne.' ¹⁸But now Adonijah has become king, and you, my lord the king, do not know about it. ¹⁹He has sacrificed great numbers of cattle, fattened calves, and sheep, and has invited all the king's sons, Abiathar the priest and Joab the commander of the army, but he has not invited Solomon your servant. ²⁰My lord the king, the eyes of all Israel are on you, to learn from you who will sit on the throne of my lord the king after him. ²¹Otherwise, as soon as my lord the king is laid to rest with his fathers, I and my son Solomon will be treated as criminals."

²²While she was still speaking with the king, Nathan the prophet arrived. ²³And they told the king, "Nathan the prophet is here." So he went before the king and bowed with his face to the ground.

²⁴Nathan said, "Have you, my lord the king, declared that Adonijah shall be king after you, and that he will sit on your throne? ²⁵Today he has gone down and sacrificed great numbers of cattle, fattened calves, and sheep. He has invited all the king's sons, the commanders of the army and Abiathar the priest. Right now they are eating and drinking with him and saying, 'Long live King Adonijah!' ²⁶But me your servant, and Zadok the priest, and Benaiah son of Jehoiada, and your servant Solomon he did not invite. ²⁷Is this something my lord the king has done without letting his servants know who should sit on the throne of my lord the king after him?"

David Makes Solomon King

²⁸Then King David said, "Call in Bathsheba." So she came into the king's presence and stood before him.

²⁹The king then took an oath: "As

---

a5 Or *charioteers*   *b8* Or *and his friends*

surely as the LORD lives, who has delivered me out of every trouble, ³⁰I will surely carry out today what I swore to you by the LORD, the God of Israel: Solomon your son shall be king after me, and he will sit on my throne in my place."

³¹Then Bathsheba bowed low with her face to the ground and, kneeling before the king, said, "May my lord King David live forever!"

³²King David said, "Call in Zadok the priest, Nathan the prophet and Benaiah son of Jehoiada." When they came before the king, ³³he said to them: "Take your lord's servants with you and set Solomon my son on my own mule and take him down to Gihon. ³⁴There have Zadok the priest and Nathan the prophet anoint him king over Israel. Blow the trumpet and shout, 'Long live King Solomon!' ³⁵Then you are to go up with him, and he is to come and sit on my throne and reign in my place. I have appointed him ruler over Israel and Judah."

³⁶Benaiah son of Jehoiada answered the king, "Amen! May the LORD, the God of my lord the king, so declare it. ³⁷As the LORD was with my lord the king, so may he be with Solomon to make his throne even greater than the throne of my lord King David!"

³⁸So Zadok the priest, Nathan the prophet, Benaiah son of Jehoiada, the Kerethites and the Pelethites went down and put Solomon on King David's mule and escorted him to Gihon. ³⁹Zadok the priest took the horn of oil from the sacred tent and anointed Solomon. Then they sounded the trumpet and all the people shouted, "Long live King Solomon!" ⁴⁰And all the people went up after him, playing flutes and rejoicing greatly, so that the ground shook with the sound.

⁴¹Adonijah and all the guests who were with him heard it as they were finishing their feast. On hearing the sound of the trumpet, Joab asked, "What's the meaning of all the noise in the city?"

⁴²Even as he was speaking, Jonathan son of Abiathar the priest arrived. Adonijah said, "Come in. A worthy man like you must be bringing good news."

⁴³"Not at all!" Jonathan answered. "Our lord King David has made Solomon king. ⁴⁴The king has sent with him Zadok the priest, Nathan the prophet, Benaiah son of Jehoiada, the Kerethites and the Pelethites, and they have put him on the king's mule, ⁴⁵and Zadok the priest and Nathan the prophet have anointed him king at Gihon. From there they have gone up cheering, and the city resounds with it. That's the noise you hear. ⁴⁶Moreover, Solomon has taken his seat on the royal throne. ⁴⁷Also, the royal officials have come to congratulate our lord King David, saying, 'May your God make Solomon's name more famous than yours and his throne greater than yours!' And the king bowed in worship on his bed ⁴⁸and said, 'Praise be to the LORD, the God of Israel, who has allowed my eyes to see a successor on my throne today.' "

⁴⁹At this, all Adonijah's guests rose in alarm and dispersed. ⁵⁰But Adonijah, in fear of Solomon, went and took hold of the horns of the altar. ⁵¹Then Solomon was told, "Adonijah is afraid of King Solomon and is clinging to the horns of the altar. He says, 'Let King Solomon swear to me today that he will not put his servant to death with the sword.' "

⁵²Solomon replied, "If he shows himself to be a worthy man, not a hair of his head will fall to the ground; but if evil is found in him, he will die." ⁵³Then King Solomon sent men, and they brought him down from the altar. And Adonijah came and bowed down to King Solomon, and Solomon said, "Go to your home."

David's Charge to Solomon

2 When the time drew near for David to die, he gave a charge to Solomon his son.

²"I am about to go the way of all the earth," he said. "So be strong, show yourself a man, ³and observe what the LORD your God requires: Walk in his ways, and keep his decrees and commands, his laws and requirements, as written in the Law of Moses, so that you may prosper in all you do and wherever you go, ⁴and that the LORD may keep his promise to me: 'If your descendants watch how they live, and if they walk faithfully before me with all their heart and soul, you will never fail to have a man on the throne of Israel.'

⁵"Now you yourself know what Joab

son of Zeruiah did to me—what he did to the two commanders of Israel's armies, Abner son of Ner and Amasa son of Jether. He killed them, shedding their blood in peacetime as if in battle, and with that blood stained the belt around his waist and the sandals on his feet. ⁶Deal with him according to your wisdom, but do not let his gray head go down to the grave* in peace.

⁷"But show kindness to the sons of Barzillai of Gilead and let them be among those who eat at your table. They stood by me when I fled from your brother Absalom.

⁸"And remember, you have with you Shimei son of Gera, the Benjamite from Bahurim, who called down bitter curses on me the day I went to Mahanaim. When he came down to meet me at the Jordan, I swore to him by the LORD: 'I will not put you to death by the sword.' ⁹But now, do not consider him innocent. You are a man of wisdom; you will know what to do to him. Bring his gray head down to the grave in blood."

¹⁰Then David rested with his fathers and was buried in the City of David. ¹¹He had reigned forty years over Israel—seven years in Hebron and thirty-three in Jerusalem. ¹²So Solomon sat on the throne of his father David, and his rule was firmly established.

Solomon's Throne Established

¹³Now Adonijah, the son of Haggith, went to Bathsheba, Solomon's mother. Bathsheba asked him, "Do you come peacefully?"

He answered, "Yes, peacefully." ¹⁴Then he added, "I have something to say to you."

"You may say it," she replied.

¹⁵"As you know," he said, "the kingdom was mine. All Israel looked to me as their king. But things changed, and the kingdom has gone to my brother; for it has come to him from the LORD. ¹⁶Now I have one request to make of you. Do not refuse me."

"You may make it," she said.

¹⁷So he continued, "Please ask King Solomon—he will not refuse you—to give me Abishag the Shunammite as my wife."

¹⁸"Very well," Bathsheba replied, "I will speak to the king for you."

Attempted Weaseling

Huh?

1 Kings 2:13–18
Just before King David died, he named Solomon to be king. Solomon's brother, Adonijah, was jealous because he wanted to be king. This part of the Bible may sound weird, but what Adonijah wanted when he asked to marry "Abishag the Shunammite" (nice name, huh?) was a way to weasel his way into grabbing the throne from Solomon. During this time in history, the king of Israel had to be a guy who was honest and fair, but tough. Adonijah certainly wasn't!

¹⁹When Bathsheba went to King Solomon to speak to him for Adonijah, the king stood up to meet her, bowed down to her and sat down on his throne. He had a throne brought for the king's mother, and she sat down at his right hand.

²⁰"I have one small request to make of you," she said. "Do not refuse me."

The king replied, "Make it, my mother; I will not refuse you."

²¹So she said, "Let Abishag the Shunammite be given in marriage to your brother Adonijah."

²²King Solomon answered his mother, "Why do you request Abishag the Shunammite for Adonijah? You might as well request the kingdom for him—after all, he is my older brother—yes, for him and for Abiathar the priest and Joab son of Zeruiah!"

²³Then King Solomon swore by the LORD: "May God deal with me, be it ever so severely, if Adonijah does not pay with his life for this request! ²⁴And now, as surely as the LORD lives—he who has established me securely on the throne of my father David and has founded a dynasty for me as he promised—Adonijah shall be put to death today!" ²⁵So King

*⁶ Hebrew *Sheol*; also in verse 9

Solomon gave orders to Benaiah son of Jehoiada, and he struck down Adonijah and he died.

²⁶To Abiathar the priest the king said, "Go back to your fields in Anathoth. You deserve to die, but I will not put you to death now, because you carried the ark of the Sovereign LORD before my father David and shared all my father's hardships." ²⁷So Solomon removed Abiathar from the priesthood of the LORD, fulfilling the word the LORD had spoken at Shiloh about the house of Eli.

²⁸When the news reached Joab, who had conspired with Adonijah though not with Absalom, he fled to the tent of the LORD and took hold of the horns of the altar. ²⁹King Solomon was told that Joab had fled to the tent of the LORD and was beside the altar. Then Solomon ordered Benaiah son of Jehoiada, "Go, strike him down!"

³⁰So Benaiah entered the tent of the LORD and said to Joab, "The king says, 'Come out!'."

But he answered, "No, I will die here." Benaiah reported to the king, "This is how Joab answered me."

³¹Then the king commanded Benaiah, "Do as he says. Strike him down and bury him, and so clear me and my father's house of the guilt of the innocent blood that Joab shed. ³²The LORD will repay him for the blood he shed, because without the knowledge of my father David he attacked two men and killed them with the sword. Both of them—Abner son of Ner, commander of Israel's army, and Amasa son of Jether, commander of Judah's army—were better men and more upright than he. ³³May the guilt of their blood rest on the head of Joab and his descendants forever. But on David and his descendants, his house and his throne, may there be the LORD's peace forever."

³⁴So Benaiah son of Jehoiada went up and struck down Joab and killed him, and he was buried on his own land*a* in the desert. ³⁵The king put Benaiah son of Jehoiada over the army in Joab's position and replaced Abiathar with Zadok the priest.

³⁶Then the king sent for Shimei and said to him, "Build yourself a house in Jerusalem and live there, but do not go anywhere else. ³⁷The day you leave and cross the Kidron Valley, you can be sure you will die; your blood will be on your own head."

³⁸Shimei answered the king, "What you say is good. Your servant will do as my lord the king has said." And Shimei stayed in Jerusalem for a long time.

³⁹But three years later, two of Shimei's slaves ran off to Achish son of Maacah, king of Gath, and Shimei was told, "Your slaves are in Gath." ⁴⁰At this, he saddled his donkey and went to Achish at Gath in search of his slaves. So Shimei went away and brought the slaves back from Gath.

⁴¹When Solomon was told that Shimei had gone from Jerusalem to Gath and had returned, ⁴²the king summoned Shimei and said to him, "Did I not make you swear by the LORD and warn you, 'On the day you leave to go anywhere else, you can be sure you will die'? At that time you said to me, 'What you say is good. I will obey.' ⁴³Why then did you not keep your oath to the LORD and obey the command I gave you?"

⁴⁴The king also said to Shimei, "You know in your heart all the wrong you did to my father David. Now the LORD will repay you for your wrongdoing. ⁴⁵But King Solomon will be blessed, and David's throne will remain secure before the LORD forever."

⁴⁶Then the king gave the order to Benaiah son of Jehoiada, and he went out and struck Shimei down and killed him.

The kingdom was now firmly established in Solomon's hands.

Solomon Asks for Wisdom

3 Solomon made an alliance with Pharaoh king of Egypt and married his daughter. He brought her to the City of David until he finished building his palace and the temple of the LORD, and the wall around Jerusalem. ²The people, however, were still sacrificing at the high places, because a temple had not yet been built for the Name of the LORD. ³Solomon showed his love for the LORD by walking according to the statutes of

a34 Or buried in his tomb

his father David, except that he offered sacrifices and burned incense on the high places.

⁴The king went to Gibeon to offer sacrifices, for that was the most important high place, and Solomon offered a thousand burnt offerings on that altar. ⁵At Gibeon the LORD appeared to Solomon during the night in a dream, and God said, "Ask for whatever you want me to give you."

⁶Solomon answered, "You have shown great kindness to your servant, my father David, because he was faithful to you and righteous and upright in heart. You have continued this great kindness to him and have given him a son to sit on his throne this very day.

⁷"Now, O LORD my God, you have made your servant king in place of my father David. But I am only a little child and do not know how to carry out my duties. ⁸Your servant is here among the people you have chosen, a great people, too numerous to count or number. ⁹So give your servant a discerning heart to govern your people and to distinguish between right and wrong. For who is able to govern this great people of yours?"

¹⁰The Lord was pleased that Solomon had asked for this. ¹¹So God said to him, "Since you have asked for this and not for long life or wealth for yourself, nor have asked for the death of your enemies but for discernment in administering justice, ¹²I will do what you have asked. I will give you a wise and discerning

---

Thursday

Wise Guy

Read 1 Kings 3:5–15

If God ever came to me and said I could have anything I wanted, I sure hope I'd ask for wisdom like Solomon did. I mean, think about what Solomon did here. He could have had *anything*—all the money and fame in the world, power over all his enemies—anything at all. And what did he choose? Wisdom.

Of all the things Solomon might have wanted, the thing he wanted most was the wisdom to do God's will. He wanted to be a good king who would follow God and make good decisions. God gave Solomon just what he asked for and a lot more: God made Solomon the wisest man who ever lived, plus one of the richest and most honored.

All of us could use a little more wisdom. Most people have a hard time making good decisions, and a lot of Christians struggle to follow God. God doesn't always give us what we ask for, but he gives us what we need. When we ask God to help us grow closer to him and live for him, he'll give us exactly what we need to do it.

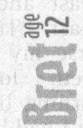
Bret age 12

What about You?

❶ Be honest. If you could ask God for anything, what would you want? How would getting that thing help you follow God?

❷ When you have trouble making a decision, create a "Pro and Con" list. Under "Pro" list all the good things that could happen if you went through with your decision. Under "Con" list all the bad things that could happen if you went through with your decision. By studying both lists, you'll probably have a good idea of what to do.

❸ Ask God to help you be a wise decision maker.

Turn to page 396 for your next devotion.

heart, so that there will never have been anyone like you, nor will there ever be. ¹³Moreover, I will give you what you have not asked for—both riches and honor—so that in your lifetime you will have no equal among kings. ¹⁴And if you walk in my ways and obey my statutes and commands as David your father did, I will give you a long life." ¹⁵Then Solomon awoke—and he realized it had been a dream.

He returned to Jerusalem, stood before the ark of the Lord's covenant and sacrificed burnt offerings and fellowship offerings.^a Then he gave a feast for all his court.

A Wise Ruling

¹⁶Now two prostitutes came to the king and stood before him. ¹⁷One of them said, "My lord, this woman and I live in the same house. I had a baby while she was there with me. ¹⁸The third day after my child was born, this woman also had a baby. We were alone; there was no one in the house but the two of us.

¹⁹"During the night this woman's son died because she lay on him. ²⁰So she got up in the middle of the night and took my son from my side while I your servant was asleep. She put him by her breast and put her dead son by my breast. ²¹The next morning, I got up to nurse my son—and he was dead! But when I looked at him closely in the morning light, I saw that it wasn't the son I had borne."

²²The other woman said, "No! The living one is my son; the dead one is yours."

But the first one insisted, "No! The dead one is yours; the living one is mine." And so they argued before the king.

²³The king said, "This one says, 'My son is alive and your son is dead,' while that one says, 'No! Your son is dead and mine is alive.'"

²⁴Then the king said, "Bring me a sword." So they brought a sword for the king. ²⁵He then gave an order: "Cut the living child in two and give half to one and half to the other."

²⁶The woman whose son was alive was filled with compassion for her son and said to the king, "Please, my lord, give her the living baby! Don't kill him!"

But the other said, "Neither I nor you shall have him. Cut him in two!"

²⁷Then the king gave his ruling: "Give the living baby to the first woman. Do not kill him; she is his mother."

²⁸When all Israel heard the verdict the king had given, they held the king in awe, because they saw that he had wisdom from God to administer justice.

Solomon's Officials and Governors

4 So King Solomon ruled over all Israel. ²And these were his chief officials:

Azariah son of Zadok—the priest;
³Elihoreph and Ahijah, sons of Shisha—secretaries;
Jehoshaphat son of Ahilud—recorder;
⁴Benaiah son of Jehoiada—commander in chief;
Zadok and Abiathar—priests;
⁵Azariah son of Nathan—in charge of the district officers;
Zabud son of Nathan—a priest and personal adviser to the king;
⁶Ahishar—in charge of the palace;
Adoniram son of Abda—in charge of forced labor.

⁷Solomon also had twelve district governors over all Israel, who supplied provisions for the king and the royal household. Each one had to provide supplies for one month in the year. ⁸These are their names:

Ben-Hur—in the hill country of Ephraim;
⁹Ben-Deker—in Makaz, Shaalbim, Beth Shemesh and Elon Bethhanan;
¹⁰Ben-Hesed—in Arubboth (Socoh and all the land of Hepher were his);
¹¹Ben-Abinadab—in Naphoth Dor^b (he was married to Taphath daughter of Solomon);
¹²Baana son of Ahilud—in Taanach and Megiddo, and in all of Beth Shan next to Zarethan below

---

^a15 Traditionally *peace offerings*   ^b11 Or *in the heights of Dor*

Baby Stories

Everyone on this earth starts out as a drooling, little kid in diapers, including some very important people in the Bible. Here are some famous Bible babies:

Isaac is Sarai's real son. She has him when she's 90 years old, which explains why God gives the new mother a new name—Sarah, for "princess"—and why she and her husband name the baby Isaac, which means "laughter." Their kid goes through a traumatic childhood experience when God tells his dad to sacrifice him. Abraham (formerly known as Abram) agrees to do it. God gives Abe an "A" on his faith test, and little Isaac lives to have kids of his own, including Jacob, who starts the Jewish nation (Genesis 17–18, 21, page 23).

Jacob & Esau are the twin sons of Isaac and Rebekah. Esau comes out first—he's the hairy one. When Jacob comes out, he's gripping Esau's heel. Since Esau is "older" (even by a minute), he's first in line for the inheritance. He loses his place in line when Jacob tricks their dad into giving the inheritance to him. Jacob becomes the father of the Jewish nation. Esau's descendants become the Edomites (Genesis 25:21–26, page 34).

Joseph is the long-awaited son of Jacob and Rachel. Long-awaited, because Jacob first marries Rachel's sister, Leah, by accident. Well not really accident—Leah's dad plans it that way. Jacob works for 14 years to "earn" both wives: the first 7 for Leah; the last 7 for Rachel.

The trio doesn't work too well, for Rachel particularly, because she can't get pregnant—at least not at first. By the time Joseph comes along, he has 10 other brothers by Leah. They think Joe's pretty strange. They're mostly jealous because Jacob loves Joseph and makes him a colorful robe. His brothers stuff him down a dry well, then sell him. But this big adventure ends with a joyful family reunion many years later (Genesis 30:22–24; Genesis 37, 40—46, page 41).

Moses almost doesn't make it to his first birthday. His folks are part of the exploding population of Jewish slaves in Egypt. Pharaoh figures the best way to control the population is to kill all the baby boys. He tells the Jewish moms to throw their babies into the Nile River. Mo's mom obeys the rule, but makes a minor adjustment: She sticks her baby in a floating basket first! She sees him again when Pharaoh's daughter needs someone to nurse the baby that the princess found floating in the river (Exodus 2:1–10, page 72).

Samuel's birth is a big deal to his mom, Hannah, because up to this point she couldn't have kids. To make matters worse, her husband's other wife has lots of them. Hannah asks God for a baby and tells him that he can have him back when the boy is old enough. So after he is weaned, Samuel joins the priesthood. God speaks audibly to Samuel, and he listens to every word. Those conversations pay off when he grows up and teaches kings like Saul and David to listen to what God says (1 and 2 Samuel, page 312).

Solomon is the second child of King David and Bathsheba. God blesses Solomon because he is loved by the Lord (that's what his name means). Sol asks God for wisdom, which makes God so happy that he gives him wealth and directions to build a big temple (2 Samuel 12:24–25, page 362; 1 Kings 3:3–13, page 386).

John the Baptist is named for the career he takes up as an adult. He is born just a few months before Jesus. His mom and dad are Elizabeth and Zechariah. Zech is in the temple being a priest when he gets the news from an angel that his wife is going to have a baby. He doubts it, because he and Elizabeth are pretty old. That isn't a big deal to God. To prove this to Zech, God takes away his voice as a sign that this baby will be born. Elizabeth gets a sign too when her relative, Mary, who happens to be pregnant with Jesus, comes to visit, and the two of them swap excited-mother stories (Luke 1, page 1217).

Jesus has a human mom, Mary, and a heavenly Dad, God. He's born 9 months after the angel Gabriel visits Mary and tells her that she will have a baby without having sex, which has never happened before. Mary is surprisingly calm about this, considering it would probably put her engagement to Joseph in jeopardy. God takes care of that problem, and Mary takes good care of raising the God baby. The best part of this birth announcement is that Jesus shows up in a manger, next to goats and sheep and other animals. His humble entry surprises everyone (Luke 1—2, page 1217).

Jezreel, from Beth Shan to Abel Meholah across to Jokmeam;

[13] Ben-Geber—in Ramoth Gilead (the settlements of Jair son of Manasseh in Gilead were his, as well as the district of Argob in Bashan and its sixty large walled cities with bronze gate bars);

[14] Ahinadab son of Iddo—in Mahanaim;

[15] Ahimaaz—in Naphtali (he had married Basemath daughter of Solomon);

[16] Baana son of Hushai—in Asher and in Aloth;

[17] Jehoshaphat son of Paruah—in Issachar;

[18] Shimei son of Ela—in Benjamin;

[19] Geber son of Uri—in Gilead (the country of Sihon king of the Amorites and the country of Og king of Bashan). He was the only governor over the district.

Solomon's Daily Provisions

[20] The people of Judah and Israel were as numerous as the sand on the seashore; they ate, they drank and they were happy. [21] And Solomon ruled over all the kingdoms from the River[a] to the land of the Philistines, as far as the border of Egypt. These countries brought tribute and were Solomon's subjects all his life.

[22] Solomon's daily provisions were thirty cors[b] of fine flour and sixty cors[c] of meal, [23] ten head of stall-fed cattle, twenty of pasture-fed cattle and a hundred sheep and goats, as well as deer, gazelles, roebucks and choice fowl. [24] For he ruled over all the kingdoms west of the River, from Tiphsah to Gaza, and had peace on all sides. [25] During Solomon's lifetime Judah and Israel, from Dan to Beersheba, lived in safety, each man under his own vine and fig tree.

[26] Solomon had four[d] thousand stalls for chariot horses, and twelve thousand horses.[e]

[27] The district officers, each in his month, supplied provisions for King Solomon and all who came to the king's table. They saw to it that nothing was lacking. [28] They also brought to the proper place their quotas of barley and straw for the chariot horses and the other horses.

Solomon's Wisdom

[29] God gave Solomon wisdom and very great insight, and a breadth of understanding as measureless as the sand on the seashore. [30] Solomon's wisdom was greater than the wisdom of all the men of the East, and greater than all the wisdom of Egypt. [31] He was wiser than any other man, including Ethan the Ezrahite—wiser than Heman, Calcol and Darda, the sons of Mahol. And his fame spread to all the surrounding nations. [32] He spoke three thousand proverbs and his songs numbered a thousand and five. [33] He described plant life, from the cedar of Lebanon to the hyssop that grows out of walls. He also taught about animals and birds, reptiles and fish. [34] Men of all nations came to listen to Solomon's wisdom, sent by all the kings of the world, who had heard of his wisdom.

Preparations for Building the Temple

5 When Hiram king of Tyre heard that Solomon had been anointed king to succeed his father David, he sent his envoys to Solomon, because he had always been on friendly terms with David. [2] Solomon sent back this message to Hiram:

[3] "You know that because of the wars waged against my father David from all sides, he could not build a temple for the Name of the LORD his God until the LORD put his enemies under his feet. [4] But now the LORD my God has given me rest on every side, and there is no adversary or disaster. [5] I intend, therefore, to build a temple for the Name of the LORD my God, as the LORD told my father David, when he said, 'Your son whom I will put on the throne in your place will build the temple for my Name.'

[6] "So give orders that cedars of

---

[a]21 That is, the Euphrates; also in verse 24
[b]22 That is, probably about 185 bushels (about 6.6 kiloliters)　[c]22 That is, probably about 375 bushels (about 13.2 kiloliters)　[d]26 Some Septuagint manuscripts (see also 2 Chron. 9:25); Hebrew forty　[e]26 Or charioteers

Lebanon be cut for me. My men will work with yours, and I will pay you for your men whatever wages you set. You know that we have no one so skilled in felling timber as the Sidonians."

[7]When Hiram heard Solomon's message, he was greatly pleased and said, "Praise be to the LORD today, for he has given David a wise son to rule over this great nation."

[8]So Hiram sent word to Solomon:

"I have received the message you sent me and will do all you want in providing the cedar and pine logs. [9]My men will haul them down from Lebanon to the sea, and I will float them in rafts by sea to the place you specify. There I will separate them and you can take them away. And you are to grant my wish by providing food for my royal household."

[10]In this way Hiram kept Solomon supplied with all the cedar and pine logs he wanted, [11]and Solomon gave Hiram twenty thousand cors[a] of wheat as food for his household, in addition to twenty thousand baths[b,c] of pressed olive oil. Solomon continued to do this for Hiram year after year. [12]The LORD gave Solomon wisdom, just as he had promised him. There were peaceful relations between Hiram and Solomon, and the two of them made a treaty.

[13]King Solomon conscripted laborers from all Israel—thirty thousand men. [14]He sent them off to Lebanon in shifts of ten thousand a month, so that they spent one month in Lebanon and two months at home. Adoniram was in charge of the forced labor. [15]Solomon had seventy thousand carriers and eighty thousand stonecutters in the hills, [16]as well as thirty-three hundred[d] foremen who supervised the project and directed the workmen. [17]At the king's command they removed from the quarry large blocks of quality stone to provide a foundation of dressed stone for the temple. [18]The craftsmen of Solomon and Hiram and the men of Gebal[e] cut and prepared the timber and stone for the building of the temple.

Solomon Builds the Temple

6 In the four hundred and eightieth[f] year after the Israelites had come out of Egypt, in the fourth year of Solomon's reign over Israel, in the month of Ziv, the second month, he began to build the temple of the LORD.

[2]The temple that King Solomon built for the LORD was sixty cubits long, twenty wide and thirty high.[g] [3]The portico at the front of the main hall of the temple extended the width of the temple, that is twenty cubits,[h] and projected ten cubits[i] from the front of the temple. [4]He made narrow clerestory windows in the temple. [5]Against the walls of the main hall and inner sanctuary he built a structure around the building, in which there were side rooms. [6]The lowest floor was five cubits[j] wide, the middle floor six cubits[k] and the third floor seven.[l] He made offset ledges around the outside of the temple so that nothing would be inserted into the temple walls.

[7]In building the temple, only blocks dressed at the quarry were used, and no hammer, chisel or any other iron tool was heard at the temple site while it was being built.

[8]The entrance to the lowest[m] floor was on the south side of the temple; a stairway led up to the middle level and from there to the third. [9]So he built the temple and completed it, roofing it with beams and cedar planks. [10]And he built the side rooms all along the temple. The height of each was five cubits, and they were attached to the temple by beams of cedar.

[11]The word of the LORD came to Solomon: [12]"As for this temple you are

---

[a]11 That is, probably about 125,000 bushels (about 4,400 kiloliters) [b]11 Septuagint (see also 2 Chron. 2:10); Hebrew *twenty cors* [c]11 That is, about 115,000 gallons (about 440 kiloliters) [d]16 Hebrew; some Septuagint manuscripts (see also 2 Chron. 2:2, 18) *thirty-six hundred* [e]18 That is, Byblos [f]1 Hebrew; Septuagint *four hundred and fortieth* [g]2 That is, about 90 feet (about 27 meters) long and 30 feet (about 9 meters) wide and 45 feet (about 13.5 meters) high [h]3 That is, about 30 feet (about 9 meters) [i]3 That is, about 15 feet (about 4.5 meters) [j]6 That is, about 7 1/2 feet (about 2.3 meters); also in verses 10 and 24 [k]6 That is, about 9 feet (about 2.7 meters) [l]6 That is, about 10 1/2 feet (about 3.1 meters) [m]8 Septuagint; Hebrew *middle*

building, if you follow my decrees, carry out my regulations and keep all my commands and obey them, I will fulfill through you the promise I gave to David your father. [13]And I will live among the Israelites and will not abandon my people Israel."

[14]So Solomon built the temple and completed it. [15]He lined its interior walls with cedar boards, paneling them from the floor of the temple to the ceiling, and covered the floor of the temple with planks of pine. [16]He partitioned off twenty cubits[a] at the rear of the temple with cedar boards from floor to ceiling to form within the temple an inner sanctuary, the Most Holy Place. [17]The main hall in front of this room was forty cubits[b] long. [18]The inside of the temple was cedar, carved with gourds and open flowers. Everything was cedar; no stone was to be seen.

[19]He prepared the inner sanctuary within the temple to set the ark of the covenant of the LORD there. [20]The inner sanctuary was twenty cubits long, twenty wide and twenty high.[c] He overlaid the inside with pure gold, and he also overlaid the altar of cedar. [21]Solomon covered the inside of the temple with pure gold, and he extended gold chains across the front of the inner sanctuary, which was overlaid with gold. [22]So he overlaid the whole interior with gold. He also overlaid with gold the altar that belonged to the inner sanctuary.

[23]In the inner sanctuary he made a pair of cherubim of olive wood, each ten cubits[d] high. [24]One wing of the first cherub was five cubits long, and the other wing five cubits—ten cubits from wing tip to wing tip. [25]The second cherub also measured ten cubits, for the two cherubim were identical in size and shape. [26]The height of each cherub was ten cubits. [27]He placed the cherubim inside the innermost room of the temple, with their wings spread out. The wing of one cherub touched one wall, while the wing of the other touched the other wall, and their wings touched each other in the middle of the room. [28]He overlaid the cherubim with gold.

[29]On the walls all around the temple, in both the inner and outer rooms, he carved cherubim, palm trees and open flowers. [30]He also covered the floors of both the inner and outer rooms of the temple with gold.

[31]For the entrance of the inner sanctuary he made doors of olive wood with five-sided jambs. [32]And on the two olive wood doors he carved cherubim, palm trees and open flowers, and overlaid the cherubim and palm trees with beaten gold. [33]In the same way he made four-sided jambs of olive wood for the entrance to the main hall. [34]He also made two pine doors, each having two leaves that turned in sockets. [35]He carved cherubim, palm trees and open flowers on them and overlaid them with gold hammered evenly over the carvings.

[36]And he built the inner courtyard of three courses of dressed stone and one course of trimmed cedar beams.

[37]The foundation of the temple of the LORD was laid in the fourth year, in the month of Ziv. [38]In the eleventh year in the month of Bul, the eighth month, the temple was finished in all its details according to its specifications. He had spent seven years building it.

God's Digs

Huh?

1 Kings 6:1–38
The temple was the one place on earth where God "lived." Of course, God doesn't really *live* anywhere. But because of people's sin and the way the world had blown off God, God needed to make sure that he was seen as separate from people. The temple was the one place God wanted people to come to him. When Jesus died, the temple became our hearts (see 1 Corinthians 3:16, page 1378 and 2 Corinthians 6:16, page 1404).

[a]16 That is, about 30 feet (about 9 meters)
[b]17 That is, about 60 feet (about 18 meters)
[c]20 That is, about 30 feet (about 9 meters) long, wide and high   [d]23 That is, about 15 feet (about 4.5 meters)

Solomon Builds His Palace

7 It took Solomon thirteen years, however, to complete the construction of
his palace. 2He built the Palace of the
Forest of Lebanon a hundred cubits long,
fifty wide and thirty high,[a] with four
rows of cedar columns supporting
trimmed cedar beams. 3It was roofed
with cedar above the beams that rested
on the columns—forty-five beams, fifteen to a row. 4Its windows were placed
high in sets of three, facing each other.
5All the doorways had rectangular
frames; they were in the front part in sets
of three, facing each other.[b]
6He made a colonnade fifty cubits long
and thirty wide.[c] In front of it was a portico, and in front of that were pillars and
an overhanging roof.
7He built the throne hall, the Hall of
Justice, where he was to judge, and he
covered it with cedar from floor to
ceiling.[d] 8And the palace in which he was
to live, set farther back, was similar in
design. Solomon also made a palace like
this hall for Pharaoh's daughter, whom
he had married.
9All these structures, from the outside
to the great courtyard and from foundation to eaves, were made of blocks of
high-grade stone cut to size and trimmed
with a saw on their inner and outer faces.
10The foundations were laid with large
stones of good quality, some measuring
ten cubits[e] and some eight.[f] 11Above were
high-grade stones, cut to size, and cedar
beams. 12The great courtyard was surrounded by a wall of three courses of
dressed stone and one course of trimmed
cedar beams, as was the inner courtyard of the temple of the LORD with its
portico.

The Temple's Furnishings

13King Solomon sent to Tyre and
brought Huram,[g] 14whose mother was a
widow from the tribe of Naphtali and
whose father was a man of Tyre and a
craftsman in bronze. Huram was highly
skilled and experienced in all kinds of
bronze work. He came to King Solomon
and did all the work assigned to him.
15He cast two bronze pillars, each eighteen cubits high and twelve cubits
around,[h] by line. 16He also made two
capitals of cast bronze to set on the tops
of the pillars; each capital was five
cubits[i] high. 17A network of interwoven
chains festooned the capitals on top of
the pillars, seven for each capital. 18He
made pomegranates in two rows[j] encircling each network to decorate the capitals on top of the pillars.[k] He did the
same for each capital. 19The capitals on
top of the pillars in the portico were in
the shape of lilies, four cubits[l] high. 20On
the capitals of both pillars, above the
bowl-shaped part next to the network,
were the two hundred pomegranates in
rows all around. 21He erected the pillars
at the portico of the temple. The pillar to
the south he named Jakin[m] and the one
to the north Boaz.[n] 22The capitals on top
were in the shape of lilies. And so the
work on the pillars was completed.
23He made the Sea of cast metal, circular in shape, measuring ten cubits[o] from
rim to rim and five cubits high. It took a
line of thirty cubits[p] to measure around
it. 24Below the rim, gourds encircled it—
ten to a cubit. The gourds were cast in
two rows in one piece with the Sea.
25The Sea stood on twelve bulls, three
facing north, three facing west, three
facing south and three facing east. The
Sea rested on top of them, and their
hindquarters were toward the center.
26It was a handbreadth[q] in thickness, and
its rim was like the rim of a cup, like a

[a]*2* That is, about 150 feet (about 46 meters) long, 75 feet (about 23 meters) wide and 45 feet (about 13.5 meters) high [b]*5* The meaning of the Hebrew for this verse is uncertain. [c]*6* That is, about 75 feet (about 23 meters) long and 45 feet (about 13.5 meters) wide [d]*7* Vulgate and Syriac; Hebrew *floor* [e]*10* That is, about 12 feet (about 3.6 meters) [f]*10* That is, about 15 feet (about 4.5 meters) [g]*13* Hebrew *Hiram*, a variant of *Huram*; also in verses 40 and 45 [h]*15* That is, about 27 feet (about 8.1 meters) high and 18 feet (about 5.4 meters) around [i]*16* That is, about 7 1/2 feet (about 2.3 meters); also in verse 23 [j]*18* Two Hebrew manuscripts and Septuagint; most Hebrew manuscripts *made the pillars, and there were two rows* [k]*18* Many Hebrew manuscripts and Syriac; most Hebrew manuscripts *pomegranates* [l]*19* That is, about 6 feet (about 1.8 meters); also in verse 38 [m]*21* *Jakin* probably means *he establishes.* [n]*21* *Boaz* probably means *in him is strength.* [o]*23* That is, about 15 feet (about 4.5 meters) [p]*23* That is, about 45 feet (about 13.5 meters) [q]*26* That is, about 3 inches (about 8 centimeters)

lily blossom. It held two thousand baths.*

²⁷He also made ten movable stands of bronze; each was four cubits long, four wide and three high.* ²⁸This is how the stands were made: They had side panels attached to uprights. ²⁹On the panels between the uprights were lions, bulls and cherubim—and on the uprights as well. Above and below the lions and bulls were wreaths of hammered work. ³⁰Each stand had four bronze wheels with bronze axles, and each had a basin resting on four supports, cast with wreaths on each side. ³¹On the inside of the stand there was an opening that had a circular frame one cubit* deep. This opening was round, and with its basework it measured a cubit and a half.* Around its opening there was engraving. The panels of the stands were square, not round. ³²The four wheels were under the panels, and the axles of the wheels were attached to the stand. The diameter of each wheel was a cubit and a half. ³³The wheels were made like chariot wheels; the axles, rims, spokes and hubs were all of cast metal.

³⁴Each stand had four handles, one on each corner, projecting from the stand. ³⁵At the top of the stand there was a circular band half a cubit* deep. The supports and panels were attached to the top of the stand. ³⁶He engraved cherubim, lions and palm trees on the surfaces of the supports and on the panels, in every available space, with wreaths all around. ³⁷This is the way he made the ten stands. They were all cast in the same molds and were identical in size and shape.

³⁸He then made ten bronze basins, each holding forty baths* and measuring four cubits across, one basin to go on each of the ten stands. ³⁹He placed five of the stands on the south side of the temple and five on the north. He placed the Sea on the south side, at the southeast corner of the temple. ⁴⁰He also made the basins and shovels and sprinkling bowls.

So Huram finished all the work he had undertaken for King Solomon in the temple of the LORD:

⁴¹the two pillars;
  the two bowl-shaped capitals on top of the pillars;
  the two sets of network decorating

the two bowl-shaped capitals on top of the pillars;
⁴²the four hundred pomegranates for the two sets of network (two rows of pomegranates for each network, decorating the bowl-shaped capitals on top of the pillars);
⁴³the ten stands with their ten basins;
⁴⁴the Sea and the twelve bulls under it;
⁴⁵the pots, shovels and sprinkling bowls.

All these objects that Huram made for King Solomon for the temple of the LORD were of burnished bronze. ⁴⁶The king had them cast in clay molds in the plain of the Jordan between Succoth and Zarethan. ⁴⁷Solomon left all these things unweighed, because there were so many; the weight of the bronze was not determined.

⁴⁸Solomon also made all the furnishings that were in the LORD's temple:

the golden altar;
the golden table on which was the bread of the Presence;
⁴⁹the lampstands of pure gold (five on the right and five on the left, in front of the inner sanctuary);
the gold floral work and lamps and tongs;
⁵⁰the pure gold basins, wick trimmers, sprinkling bowls, dishes and censers;
and the gold sockets for the doors of the innermost room, the Most Holy Place, and also for the doors of the main hall of the temple.

⁵¹When all the work King Solomon had done for the temple of the LORD was finished, he brought in the things his father David had dedicated—the silver and gold and the furnishings—and he placed them in the treasuries of the LORD's temple.

*26 That is, probably about 11,500 gallons (about 44 kiloliters); the Septuagint does not have this sentence.   *27 That is, about 6 feet (about 1.8 meters) long and wide and about 4 1/2 feet (about 1.3 meters) high   *31 That is, about 1 1/2 feet (about 0.5 meter)   *31 That is, about 2 1/4 feet (about 0.7 meter); also in verse 32   *35 That is, about 3/4 foot (about 0.2 meter)   *38 That is, about 230 gallons (about 880 liters)

The Ark Brought to the Temple

8 Then King Solomon summoned into his presence at Jerusalem the elders of Israel, all the heads of the tribes and the chiefs of the Israelite families, to bring up the ark of the LORD's covenant from Zion, the City of David. ²All the men of Israel came together to King Solomon at the time of the festival in the month of Ethanim, the seventh month.

³When all the elders of Israel had arrived, the priests took up the ark, ⁴and they brought up the ark of the LORD and the Tent of Meeting and all the sacred furnishings in it. The priests and Levites carried them up, ⁵and King Solomon and the entire assembly of Israel that had gathered about him were before the ark, sacrificing so many sheep and cattle that they could not be recorded or counted.

⁶The priests then brought the ark of the LORD's covenant to its place in the inner sanctuary of the temple, the Most Holy Place, and put it beneath the wings of the cherubim. ⁷The cherubim spread their wings over the place of the ark and overshadowed the ark and its carrying poles. ⁸These poles were so long that their ends could be seen from the Holy Place in front of the inner sanctuary, but not from outside the Holy Place; and they are still there today. ⁹There was nothing in the ark except the two stone tablets that Moses had placed in it at Horeb, where the LORD made a covenant with the Israelites after they came out of Egypt.

¹⁰When the priests withdrew from the Holy Place, the cloud filled the temple of the LORD. ¹¹And the priests could not perform their service because of the cloud, for the glory of the LORD filled his temple.

¹²Then Solomon said, "The LORD has said that he would dwell in a dark cloud; ¹³I have indeed built a magnificent temple for you, a place for you to dwell forever."

¹⁴While the whole assembly of Israel was standing there, the king turned around and blessed them. ¹⁵Then he said:

"Praise be to the LORD, the God of Israel, who with his own hand has fulfilled what he promised with his own mouth to my father David. For

he said, ¹⁶'Since the day I brought my people Israel out of Egypt, I have not chosen a city in any tribe of Israel to have a temple built for my Name to be there, but I have chosen David to rule my people Israel.'

¹⁷"My father David had it in his heart to build a temple for the Name of the LORD, the God of Israel. ¹⁸But the LORD said to my father David, 'Because it was in your heart to build a temple for my Name, you did well to have this in your heart. ¹⁹Nevertheless, you are not the one to build the temple, but your son, who is your own flesh and blood—he is the one who will build the temple for my Name.'

²⁰"The LORD has kept the promise he made: I have succeeded David my father and now I sit on the throne of Israel, just as the LORD promised, and I have built the temple for the Name of the LORD, the God of Israel. ²¹I have provided a place there for the ark, in which is the covenant of the LORD that he made with our fathers when he brought them out of Egypt."

Solomon's Prayer of Dedication

²²Then Solomon stood before the altar of the LORD in front of the whole assembly of Israel, spread out his hands toward heaven ²³and said:

"O LORD, God of Israel, there is no God like you in heaven above or on earth below—you who keep your covenant of love with your servants who continue wholeheartedly in your way. ²⁴You have kept your promise to your servant David my father; with your mouth you have promised and with your hand you have fulfilled it—as it is today.

²⁵"Now LORD, God of Israel, keep for your servant David my father the promises you made to him when you said, 'You shall never fail to have a man to sit before me on the throne of Israel, if only your sons are careful in all they do to walk before me as you have done.' ²⁶And now, O God of Israel, let your word that you

promised your servant David my father come true.

²⁷"But will God really dwell on earth? The heavens, even the highest heaven, cannot contain you. How much less this temple I have built! ²⁸Yet give attention to your servant's prayer and his plea for mercy, O LORD my God. Hear the cry and the prayer that your servant is praying in your presence this day. ²⁹May your eyes be open toward this temple night and day, this place of which you said, 'My Name shall be there,' so that you will hear the prayer your servant prays toward this place. ³⁰Hear the supplication of your servant and of your people Israel when they pray toward this place. Hear from heaven, your dwelling place, and when you hear, forgive.

³¹"When a man wrongs his neighbor and is required to take an oath and he comes and swears the oath before your altar in this temple, ³²then hear from heaven and act. Judge between your servants, condemning the guilty and bringing down on his own head what he has done. Declare the innocent not guilty, and so establish his innocence.

³³"When your people Israel have been defeated by an enemy because they have sinned against you, and when they turn back to you and confess your name, praying and making supplication to you in this temple, ³⁴then hear from heaven and forgive the sin of your people Israel and bring them back to the land you gave to their fathers.

³⁵"When the heavens are shut up and there is no rain because your people have sinned against you, and

---

Friday

Everywhere You Go

Read 1 Kings 8:27–28

During the Christmas season my youth group went downtown to watch the Christmas play, *The Nutcracker*. We wore our nicest clothes and goofiest slippers. (The play is all about dreaming, right?) While waiting in line outside the theater, we sang Christmas carols. Lots of people noticed us, and some of them even joined in. It felt great to witness to them about the birth of Jesus through our songs—and we were nowhere near a church building!

God is everywhere, and we need to tell people about him wherever we go. Church is still important, but most of our witnessing will be in other places—at school, on a sports team, even on a sidewalk outside a theater.

You never know what opportunities you'll have. But you can be sure that whatever and wherever they are, God wants you to use these moments to tell others about him.

Carissa, age 14

What about You?

❶ Of all the places you spend time, think of 2 where you can be a witness for God.

❷ Ask some Christian adults (like your parents or youth leaders) about unusual witnessing opportunities they've had.

❸ Pray and tell God you're willing to be his witness wherever he wants you to go. Be specific about your willingness to be a witness in the places listed in the first question.

Turn to page 403 for your next devotion.

when they pray toward this place and confess your name and turn from their sin because you have afflicted them, ³⁶then hear from heaven and forgive the sin of your servants, your people Israel. Teach them the right way to live, and send rain on the land you gave your people for an inheritance.

³⁷"When famine or plague comes to the land, or blight or mildew, locusts or grasshoppers, or when an enemy besieges them in any of their cities, whatever disaster or disease may come, ³⁸and when a prayer or plea is made by any of your people Israel—each one aware of the afflictions of his own heart, and spreading out his hands toward this temple— ³⁹then hear from heaven, your dwelling place. Forgive and act; deal with each man according to all he does, since you know his heart (for you alone know the hearts of all men), ⁴⁰so that they will fear you all the time they live in the land you gave our fathers.

⁴¹"As for the foreigner who does not belong to your people Israel but has come from a distant land because of your name— ⁴²for men will hear of your great name and your mighty hand and your outstretched arm—when he comes and prays toward this temple, ⁴³then hear from heaven, your dwelling place, and do whatever the foreigner asks of you, so that all the peoples of the earth may know your name and fear you, as do your own people Israel, and may know that this house I have built bears your Name.

⁴⁴"When your people go to war against their enemies, wherever you send them, and when they pray to the LORD toward the city you have chosen and the temple I have built for your Name, ⁴⁵then hear from heaven their prayer and their plea, and uphold their cause.

⁴⁶"When they sin against you—for there is no one who does not sin— and you become angry with them and give them over to the enemy, who takes them captive to his own land, far away or near; ⁴⁷and if they have a change of heart in the land where they are held captive, and repent and plead with you in the land of their conquerors and say, 'We have sinned, we have done wrong, we have acted wickedly'; ⁴⁸and if they turn back to you with all their heart and soul in the land of their enemies who took them captive, and pray to you toward the land you gave their fathers, toward the city you have chosen and the temple I have built for your Name; ⁴⁹then from heaven, your dwelling place, hear their prayer and their plea, and uphold their cause. ⁵⁰And forgive your people, who have sinned against you; forgive all the offenses they have committed against you, and cause their conquerors to show them mercy; ⁵¹for they are your people and your inheritance, whom you brought out of Egypt, out of that iron-smelting furnace.

⁵²"May your eyes be open to your servant's plea and to the plea of your people Israel, and may you listen to them whenever they cry out to you. ⁵³For you singled them out from all the nations of the world to be your own inheritance, just as you declared through your servant Moses when you, O Sovereign LORD, brought our fathers out of Egypt."

⁵⁴When Solomon had finished all these prayers and supplications to the LORD, he rose from before the altar of the LORD, where he had been kneeling with his hands spread out toward heaven. ⁵⁵He stood and blessed the whole assembly of Israel in a loud voice, saying:

⁵⁶"Praise be to the LORD, who has given rest to his people Israel just as he promised. Not one word has failed of all the good promises he gave through his servant Moses. ⁵⁷May the LORD our God be with us as he was with our fathers; may he never leave us nor forsake us. ⁵⁸May he turn our hearts to him, to walk in all his ways and to keep the commands, decrees and regulations he gave our fathers. ⁵⁹And may these

words of mine, which I have prayed before the LORD, be near to the LORD our God day and night, that he may uphold the cause of his servant and the cause of his people Israel according to each day's need, ⁶⁰so that all the peoples of the earth may know that the LORD is God and that there is no other. ⁶¹But your hearts must be fully committed to the LORD our God, to live by his decrees and obey his commands, as at this time."

The Dedication of the Temple

⁶²Then the king and all Israel with him offered sacrifices before the LORD. ⁶³Solomon offered a sacrifice of fellowship offerings^a to the LORD: twenty-two thousand cattle and a hundred and twenty thousand sheep and goats. So the king and all the Israelites dedicated the temple of the LORD.

⁶⁴On that same day the king consecrated the middle part of the courtyard in front of the temple of the LORD, and there he offered burnt offerings, grain offerings and the fat of the fellowship offerings, because the bronze altar before the LORD was too small to hold the burnt offerings, the grain offerings and the fat of the fellowship offerings.

⁶⁵So Solomon observed the festival at that time, and all Israel with him—a vast assembly, people from Lebo^b Hamath to the Wadi of Egypt. They celebrated it before the LORD our God for seven days and seven days more, fourteen days in all. ⁶⁶On the following day he sent the people away. They blessed the king and then went home, joyful and glad in heart for all the good things the LORD had done for his servant David and his people Israel.

The LORD Appears to Solomon

9 When Solomon had finished building the temple of the LORD and the royal palace, and had achieved all he had desired to do, ²the LORD appeared to him a second time, as he had appeared to him at Gibeon. ³The LORD said to him:

"I have heard the prayer and plea you have made before me; I have consecrated this temple, which you have built, by putting my Name

there forever. My eyes and my heart will always be there.

⁴"As for you, if you walk before me in integrity of heart and uprightness, as David your father did, and do all I command and observe my decrees and laws, ⁵I will establish your royal throne over Israel forever, as I promised David your father when I said, 'You shall never fail to have a man on the throne of Israel.'

⁶"But if you^c or your sons turn away from me and do not observe the commands and decrees I have given you^c and go off to serve other gods and worship them, ⁷then I will cut off Israel from the land I have given them and will reject this temple I have consecrated for my Name. Israel will then become a byword and an object of ridicule among all peoples. ⁸And though this temple is now imposing, all who pass by will be appalled and will scoff and say, 'Why has the LORD done such a thing to this land and to this temple?' ⁹People will answer, 'Because they have forsaken the LORD their God, who brought their fathers out of Egypt, and have embraced other gods, worshiping and serving them—that is why the LORD brought all this disaster on them.'"

Solomon's Other Activities

¹⁰At the end of twenty years, during which Solomon built these two buildings—the temple of the LORD and the royal palace— ¹¹King Solomon gave twenty towns in Galilee to Hiram king of Tyre, because Hiram had supplied him with all the cedar and pine and gold he wanted. ¹²But when Hiram went from Tyre to see the towns that Solomon had given him, he was not pleased with them. ¹³"What kind of towns are these you have given me, my brother?" he asked. And he called them the Land of Cabul,^d a name they have to this day. ¹⁴Now Hiram had sent to the king 120 talents^e of gold.

---

^a63 Traditionally *peace offerings*; also in verse 64
^b65 Or *from the entrance to*   ^c6 The Hebrew is plural.   ^d13 *Cabul* sounds like the Hebrew for *good-for-nothing.*   ^e14 That is, about 4 1/2 tons (about 4 metric tons)

[15]Here is the account of the forced labor King Solomon conscripted to build the LORD's temple, his own palace, the supporting terraces,[a] the wall of Jerusalem, and Hazor, Megiddo and Gezer. [16](Pharaoh king of Egypt had attacked and captured Gezer. He had set it on fire. He killed its Canaanite inhabitants and then gave it as a wedding gift to his daughter, Solomon's wife. [17]And Solomon rebuilt Gezer.) He built up Lower Beth Horon, [18]Baalath, and Tadmor[b] in the desert, within his land, [19]as well as all his store cities and the towns for his chariots and for his horses[c]—whatever he desired to build in Jerusalem, in Lebanon and throughout all the territory he ruled.

[20]All the people left from the Amorites, Hittites, Perizzites, Hivites and Jebusites (these peoples were not Israelites), [21]that is, their descendants remaining in the land, whom the Israelites could not exterminate[d]—these Solomon conscripted for his slave labor force, as it is to this day. [22]But Solomon did not make slaves of any of the Israelites; they were his fighting men, his government officials, his officers, his captains, and the commanders of his chariots and charioteers. [23]They were also the chief officials in charge of Solomon's projects—550 officials supervising the men who did the work.

[24]After Pharaoh's daughter had come up from the City of David to the palace Solomon had built for her, he constructed the supporting terraces.

[25]Three times a year Solomon sacrificed burnt offerings and fellowship offerings[e] on the altar he had built for the LORD, burning incense before the LORD along with them, and so fulfilled the temple obligations.

[26]King Solomon also built ships at Ezion Geber, which is near Elath in Edom, on the shore of the Red Sea.[f] [27]And Hiram sent his men—sailors who knew the sea—to serve in the fleet with Solomon's men. [28]They sailed to Ophir and brought back 420 talents[g] of gold, which they delivered to King Solomon.

The Queen of Sheba Visits Solomon

10 When the queen of Sheba heard about the fame of Solomon and his relation to the name of the LORD, she came to test him with hard questions. [2]Arriving at Jerusalem with a very great caravan—with camels carrying spices, large quantities of gold, and precious stones—she came to Solomon and talked with him about all that she had on her mind. [3]Solomon answered all her questions; nothing was too hard for the king to explain to her. [4]When the queen of Sheba saw all the wisdom of Solomon and the palace he had built, [5]the food on his table, the seating of his officials, the attending servants in their robes, his cupbearers, and the burnt offerings he made at[h] the temple of the LORD, she was overwhelmed.

[6]She said to the king, "The report I heard in my own country about your achievements and your wisdom is true. [7]But I did not believe these things until I came and saw with my own eyes. Indeed, not even half was told me; in wisdom and wealth you have far exceeded the report I heard. [8]How happy your men must be! How happy your officials, who continually stand before you and hear your wisdom! [9]Praise be to the LORD your God, who has delighted in you and placed you on the throne of Israel. Because of the LORD's eternal love for Israel, he has made you king, to maintain justice and righteousness."

[10]And she gave the king 120 talents[i] of gold, large quantities of spices, and precious stones. Never again were so many spices brought in as those the queen of Sheba gave to King Solomon.

[11](Hiram's ships brought gold from Ophir; and from there they brought great cargoes of almugwood[j] and precious stones. [12]The king used the almugwood to make supports for the temple of the LORD and for the royal palace, and to make harps and lyres for the musicians.

---

[a]15 Or the Millo; also in verse 24   [b]18 The Hebrew may also be read Tamar.   [c]19 Or charioteers   [d]21 The Hebrew term refers to the irrevocable giving over of things or persons to the LORD, often by totally destroying them.   [e]25 Traditionally peace offerings   [f]26 Hebrew Yam Suph; that is, Sea of Reeds   [g]28 That is, about 16 tons (about 14.5 metric tons)   [h]5 Or the ascent by which he went up to   [i]10 That is, about 4 1/2 tons (about 4 metric tons)   [j]11 Probably a variant of algumwood; also in verse 12

So much almugwood has never been imported or seen since that day.) ¹³King Solomon gave the queen of Sheba all she desired and asked for, besides what he had given her out of his royal bounty. Then she left and returned with her retinue to her own country.

Solomon's Splendor

¹⁴The weight of the gold that Solomon received yearly was 666 talents,[a] ¹⁵not including the revenues from merchants and traders and from all the Arabian kings and the governors of the land.

¹⁶King Solomon made two hundred large shields of hammered gold; six hundred bekas[b] of gold went into each shield. ¹⁷He also made three hundred small shields of hammered gold, with three minas[c] of gold in each shield. The king put them in the Palace of the Forest of Lebanon.

¹⁸Then the king made a great throne inlaid with ivory and overlaid with fine gold. ¹⁹The throne had six steps, and its back had a rounded top. On both sides of the seat were armrests, with a lion standing beside each of them. ²⁰Twelve lions stood on the six steps, one at either end of each step. Nothing like it had ever been made for any other kingdom. ²¹All King Solomon's goblets were gold, and all the household articles in the Palace of the Forest of Lebanon were pure gold. Nothing was made of silver, because silver was considered of little value in Solomon's days. ²²The king had a fleet of trading ships[d] at sea along with the ships of Hiram. Once every three years it returned, carrying gold, silver and ivory, and apes and baboons.

²³King Solomon was greater in riches and wisdom than all the other kings of the earth. ²⁴The whole world sought audience with Solomon to hear the wisdom God had put in his heart. ²⁵Year after year, everyone who came brought a gift—articles of silver and gold, robes, weapons and spices, and horses and mules.

²⁶Solomon accumulated chariots and horses; he had fourteen hundred chariots and twelve thousand horses,[e] which he kept in the chariot cities and also with him in Jerusalem. ²⁷The king made silver as common in Jerusalem as stones, and cedar as plentiful as sycamore-fig trees in the foothills. ²⁸Solomon's horses were imported from Egypt[f] and from Kue[g]—the royal merchants purchased them from Kue. ²⁹They imported a chariot from Egypt for six hundred shekels[h] of silver, and a horse for a hundred and fifty.[i] They also exported them to all the kings of the Hittites and of the Arameans.

Solomon's Wives

11 King Solomon, however, loved many foreign women besides Pharaoh's daughter—Moabites, Ammonites, Edomites, Sidonians and Hittites. ²They were from nations about which the LORD had told the Israelites, "You must not intermarry with them, because they will surely turn your hearts after their gods." Nevertheless, Solomon held fast to them in love. ³He had seven hundred wives of royal birth and three hundred concubines, and his wives led him astray. ⁴As Solomon grew old, his wives turned his heart after other gods, and his heart was not fully devoted to the LORD his God, as the heart of David his father had been. ⁵He followed Ashtoreth the goddess of the Sidonians, and Molech[j] the detestable god of the Ammonites. ⁶So Solomon did evil in the eyes of the LORD; he did not follow the LORD completely, as David his father had done.

⁷On a hill east of Jerusalem, Solomon built a high place for Chemosh the detestable god of Moab, and for Molech the detestable god of the Ammonites. ⁸He did the same for all his foreign wives, who burned incense and offered sacrifices to their gods.

⁹The LORD became angry with Solomon because his heart had turned away from the LORD, the God of Israel, who had appeared to him twice. ¹⁰Although he had forbidden Solomon to follow other gods, Solomon did not keep the LORD's com-

---

[a] 14 That is, about 25 tons (about 23 metric tons)
[b] 16 That is, about 7 1/2 pounds (about 3.5 kilograms) [c] 17 That is, about 3 3/4 pounds (about 1.7 kilograms) [d] 22 Hebrew of ships of Tarshish
[e] 26 Or charioteers [f] 28 Or possibly Muzur, a region in Cilicia; also in verse 29 [g] 28 Probably Cilicia
[h] 29 That is, about 15 pounds (about 7 kilograms)
[i] 29 That is, about 3 3/4 pounds (about 1.7 kilograms) [j] 5 Hebrew Milcom; also in verse 33

mand. ¹¹So the LORD said to Solomon, "Since this is your attitude and you have not kept my covenant and my decrees, which I commanded you, I will most certainly tear the kingdom away from you and give it to one of your subordinates. ¹²Nevertheless, for the sake of David your father, I will not do it during your lifetime. I will tear it out of the hand of your son. ¹³Yet I will not tear the whole kingdom from him, but will give him one tribe for the sake of David my servant and for the sake of Jerusalem, which I have chosen."

Solomon's Dating Service

Huh?

1 Kings 11:1–13
Solomon was a really smart guy, to be sure, but he had a few problems as God's king. A biggie was his love of women—700 wives and 300 "almost wives." Solomon was so into power and being a big-shot that he left God behind. God was sad, mad and knew that Solomon was leading the whole nation down the drain with him. Bummer!

Solomon's Adversaries

¹⁴Then the LORD raised up against Solomon an adversary, Hadad the Edomite, from the royal line of Edom. ¹⁵Earlier when David was fighting with Edom, Joab the commander of the army, who had gone up to bury the dead, had struck down all the men in Edom. ¹⁶Joab and all the Israelites stayed there for six months, until they had destroyed all the men in Edom. ¹⁷But Hadad, still only a boy, fled to Egypt with some Edomite officials who had served his father. ¹⁸They set out from Midian and went to Paran. Then taking men from Paran with them, they went to Egypt, to Pharaoh king of Egypt, who gave Hadad a house and land and provided him with food.

¹⁹Pharaoh was so pleased with Hadad that he gave him a sister of his own wife, Queen Tahpenes, in marriage. ²⁰The sister of Tahpenes bore him a son named Genubath, whom Tahpenes brought up in the royal palace. There Genubath lived with Pharaoh's own children.

²¹While he was in Egypt, Hadad heard that David rested with his fathers and that Joab the commander of the army was also dead. Then Hadad said to Pharaoh, "Let me go, that I may return to my own country."

²²"What have you lacked here that you want to go back to your own country?" Pharaoh asked.

"Nothing," Hadad replied, "but do let me go!"

²³And God raised up against Solomon another adversary, Rezon son of Eliada, who had fled from his master, Hadadezer king of Zobah. ²⁴He gathered men around him and became the leader of a band of rebels when David destroyed the forces*a* of Zobah; the rebels went to Damascus, where they settled and took control. ²⁵Rezon was Israel's adversary as long as Solomon lived, adding to the trouble caused by Hadad. So Rezon ruled in Aram and was hostile toward Israel.

Jeroboam Rebels Against Solomon

²⁶Also, Jeroboam son of Nebat rebelled against the king. He was one of Solomon's officials, an Ephraimite from Zeredah, and his mother was a widow named Zeruah.

²⁷Here is the account of how he rebelled against the king: Solomon had built the supporting terraces*b* and had filled in the gap in the wall of the city of David his father. ²⁸Now Jeroboam was a man of standing, and when Solomon saw how well the young man did his work, he put him in charge of the whole labor force of the house of Joseph.

²⁹About that time Jeroboam was going out of Jerusalem, and Ahijah the prophet of Shiloh met him on the way, wearing a new cloak. The two of them were alone out in the country, ³⁰and Ahijah took hold of the new cloak he was wearing and tore it into twelve pieces. ³¹Then he said to Jeroboam, "Take ten pieces for yourself, for this is what the LORD, the God of Israel, says: 'See, I am going to tear the kingdom out of Solomon's hand and give you ten tribes. ³²But for the sake

a24 Hebrew destroyed them   b27 Or the Millo

of my servant David and the city of Jerusalem, which I have chosen out of all the tribes of Israel, he will have one tribe. ³³I will do this because they have[a] forsaken me and worshiped Ashtoreth the goddess of the Sidonians, Chemosh the god of the Moabites, and Molech the god of the Ammonites, and have not walked in my ways, nor done what is right in my eyes, nor kept my statutes and laws as David, Solomon's father, did.

³⁴" 'But I will not take the whole kingdom out of Solomon's hand; I have made him ruler all the days of his life for the sake of David my servant, whom I chose and who observed my commands and statutes. ³⁵I will take the kingdom from his son's hands and give you ten tribes. ³⁶I will give one tribe to his son so that David my servant may always have a lamp before me in Jerusalem, the city where I chose to put my Name. ³⁷However, as for you, I will take you, and you will rule over all that your heart desires; you will be king over Israel. ³⁸If you do whatever I command you and walk in my ways and do what is right in my eyes by keeping my statutes and commands, as David my servant did, I will be with you. I will build you a dynasty as enduring as the one I built for David and will give Israel to you. ³⁹I will humble David's descendants because of this, but not forever.' "

⁴⁰Solomon tried to kill Jeroboam, but Jeroboam fled to Egypt, to Shishak the king, and stayed there until Solomon's death.

Solomon's Death

⁴¹As for the other events of Solomon's reign—all he did and the wisdom he displayed—are they not written in the book of the annals of Solomon? ⁴²Solomon reigned in Jerusalem over all Israel forty years. ⁴³Then he rested with his fathers and was buried in the city of David his father. And Rehoboam his son succeeded him as king.

Israel Rebels Against Rehoboam

12 Rehoboam went to Shechem, for all the Israelites had gone there to make him king. ²When Jeroboam son of Nebat heard this (he was still in Egypt, where he had fled from King Solomon), he returned from[b] Egypt. ³So they sent for Jeroboam, and he and the whole assembly of Israel went to Rehoboam and said to him: ⁴"Your father put a heavy yoke on us, but now lighten the harsh labor and the heavy yoke he put on us, and we will serve you."

⁵Rehoboam answered, "Go away for three days and then come back to me." So the people went away.

⁶Then King Rehoboam consulted the elders who had served his father Solomon during his lifetime. "How would you advise me to answer these people?" he asked.

⁷They replied, "If today you will be a servant to these people and serve them and give them a favorable answer, they will always be your servants."

⁸But Rehoboam rejected the advice the elders gave him and consulted the young men who had grown up with him and were serving him. ⁹He asked them, "What is your advice? How should we answer these people who say to me, 'Lighten the yoke your father put on us'?"

¹⁰The young men who had grown up with him replied, "Tell these people who have said to you, 'Your father put a heavy yoke on us, but make our yoke lighter'—tell them, 'My little finger is thicker than my father's waist. ¹¹My father laid on you a heavy yoke; I will make it even heavier. My father scourged you with whips; I will scourge you with scorpions.' "

¹²Three days later Jeroboam and all the people returned to Rehoboam, as the king had said, "Come back to me in three days." ¹³The king answered the people harshly. Rejecting the advice given him by the elders, ¹⁴he followed the advice of the young men and said, "My father made your yoke heavy; I will make it even heavier. My father scourged you with whips; I will scourge you with scorpions." ¹⁵So the king did not listen to the people, for this turn of events was from the LORD, to fulfill the word the LORD had spoken to Jeroboam son of Nebat through Ahijah the Shilonite.

---

a33 Hebrew; Septuagint, Vulgate and Syriac *because he has*   *b2* Or *he remained in*

¹⁶When all Israel saw that the king refused to listen to them, they answered the king:

"What share do we have in David,
  what part in Jesse's son?
To your tents, O Israel!

Look after your own house,
  O David!"

So the Israelites went home. ¹⁷But as for the Israelites who were living in the towns of Judah, Rehoboam still ruled over them.

Weekend.

One Thing After Another
Read 2 Samuel 11:2–5 (page 359)

Kelly began this week's devotionals with a story about a friend's suicide and how much pain this one action caused. Every time someone commits suicide, this one act of despair brings ripples of pain, confusion, fear and deep sadness to an entire community. But the point of Kelly's story was not the suicide itself but the tragic path that choices sometimes travel.

Take King David, for example. Even in these few verses (c'mon, read 'em), it's clear that David didn't start off deciding to have a son with a married woman and kill her husband in the process. Nope, he was just like the rest of us, moving ahead one little step at a time. He saw Bathsheba, thought she was cute and let his mind start asking, *What if nobody finds out?* . . . *What if it's just one time?* . . . *What if we're really careful?* . . . The king was at first attracted, then lustful and finally had to *"have"* Bathsheba. He didn't plan any of the next steps—pregnancy, murder and pain. He just let events happen, and one complication followed another.

Sin has a way of doing that. You make one little choice (a bad one) and try to cover it up or even ignore it, and you end up getting caught in a *bigger* sin than the first one. So many times this cycle continues. How would David's life have been different if, after the first sin (sex with Bathsheba—well, OK, technically *lusting* after Bathsheba and *planning* the sex was the *first* sin, and the sex was the *second*) he had confessed his sin and accepted the consequences? He probably wouldn't have been known as a murderer, would he?

This may sound harsh, but it's true: Stop the cycle of sin in your life. It can become a habit.

❶ Think of a time when you started out with one sin—a lie, stealing something, whatever—and it turned into a far worse problem for you. Think about what you could have done differently after the *first* sin. What might have happened?

❷ Decide whether or not you want to live differently from King David and not let one sin turn into several. If so, write out 1 John 1:9 on a note card and put it in your Bible, reading it every day this week: "If we confess our sins, he is faithful and just and will forgive us our sins and purify us from all unrighteousness."

❸ Pray that God will give you the courage to admit your wrongs right away, instead of trying to cover them up.

Turn to page 412 for your next devotion.

[18]King Rehoboam sent out Adoniram,[a] who was in charge of forced labor, but all Israel stoned him to death. King Rehoboam, however, managed to get into his chariot and escape to Jerusalem. [19]So Israel has been in rebellion against the house of David to this day.

[20]When all the Israelites heard that Jeroboam had returned, they sent and called him to the assembly and made him king over all Israel. Only the tribe of Judah remained loyal to the house of David.

[21]When Rehoboam arrived in Jerusalem, he mustered the whole house of Judah and the tribe of Benjamin—a hundred and eighty thousand fighting men—to make war against the house of Israel and to regain the kingdom for Rehoboam son of Solomon.

[22]But this word of God came to Shemaiah the man of God: [23]"Say to Rehoboam son of Solomon king of Judah, to the whole house of Judah and Benjamin, and to the rest of the people, [24]'This is what the LORD says: Do not go up to fight against your brothers, the Israelites. Go home, every one of you, for this is my doing.' " So they obeyed the word of the LORD and went home again, as the LORD had ordered.

Golden Calves at Bethel and Dan

[25]Then Jeroboam fortified Shechem in the hill country of Ephraim and lived there. From there he went out and built up Peniel.[b]

[26]Jeroboam thought to himself, "The kingdom will now likely revert to the house of David. [27]If these people go up to offer sacrifices at the temple of the LORD in Jerusalem, they will again give their allegiance to their lord, Rehoboam king of Judah. They will kill me and return to King Rehoboam."

[28]After seeking advice, the king made two golden calves. He said to the people, "It is too much for you to go up to Jerusalem. Here are your gods, O Israel, who brought you up out of Egypt." [29]One he set up in Bethel, and the other in Dan. [30]And this thing became a sin; the people went even as far as Dan to worship the one there.

[31]Jeroboam built shrines on high places and appointed priests from all sorts of people, even though they were not Levites. [32]He instituted a festival on the fifteenth day of the eighth month, like the festival held in Judah, and offered sacrifices on the altar. This he did in Bethel, sacrificing to the calves he had made. And at Bethel he also installed priests at the high places he had made. [33]On the fifteenth day of the eighth month, a month of his own choosing, he offered sacrifices on the altar he had built at Bethel. So he instituted the festival for the Israelites and went up to the altar to make offerings.

The Man of God From Judah

13 By the word of the LORD a man of God came from Judah to Bethel, as Jeroboam was standing by the altar to make an offering. [2]He cried out against the altar by the word of the LORD: "O altar, altar! This is what the LORD says: 'A son named Josiah will be born to the house of David. On you he will sacrifice the priests of the high places who now make offerings here, and human bones will be burned on you.' " [3]That same day the man of God gave a sign: "This is the sign the LORD has declared: The altar will be split apart and the ashes on it will be poured out."

[4]When King Jeroboam heard what the man of God cried out against the altar at Bethel, he stretched out his hand from the altar and said, "Seize him!" But the hand he stretched out toward the man shriveled up, so that he could not pull it back. [5]Also, the altar was split apart and its ashes poured out according to the sign given by the man of God by the word of the LORD.

[6]Then the king said to the man of God, "Intercede with the LORD your God and pray for me that my hand may be restored." So the man of God interceded with the LORD, and the king's hand was restored and became as it was before.

[7]The king said to the man of God, "Come home with me and have something to eat, and I will give you a gift."

---

[a]18 Some Septuagint manuscripts and Syriac (see also 1 Kings 4:6 and 5:14); Hebrew *Adoram*
[b]25 Hebrew *Penuel*, a variant of *Peniel*

⁸But the man of God answered the king, "Even if you were to give me half your possessions, I would not go with you, nor would I eat bread or drink water here. ⁹For I was commanded by the word of the LORD: 'You must not eat bread or drink water or return by the way you came.' " ¹⁰So he took another road and did not return by the way he had come to Bethel.

¹¹Now there was a certain old prophet living in Bethel, whose sons came and told him all that the man of God had done there that day. They also told their father what he had said to the king. ¹²Their father asked them, "Which way did he go?" And his sons showed him which road the man of God from Judah had taken. ¹³So he said to his sons, "Saddle the donkey for me." And when they had saddled the donkey for him, he mounted it ¹⁴and rode after the man of God. He found him sitting under an oak tree and asked, "Are you the man of God who came from Judah?"

"I am," he replied.

¹⁵So the prophet said to him, "Come home with me and eat."

¹⁶The man of God said, "I cannot turn back and go with you, nor can I eat bread or drink water with you in this place. ¹⁷I have been told by the word of the LORD: 'You must not eat bread or drink water there or return by the way you came.' "

¹⁸The old prophet answered, "I too am a prophet, as you are. And an angel said to me by the word of the LORD: 'Bring him back with you to your house so that he may eat bread and drink water.' " (But he was lying to him.) ¹⁹So the man of God returned with him and ate and drank in his house.

²⁰While they were sitting at the table, the word of the LORD came to the old prophet who had brought him back. ²¹He cried out to the man of God who had come from Judah, "This is what the LORD says: 'You have defied the word of the LORD and have not kept the command the LORD your God gave you. ²²You came back and ate bread and drank water in the place where he told you not to eat or drink. Therefore your body will not be buried in the tomb of your fathers.' "

²³When the man of God had finished eating and drinking, the prophet who had brought him back saddled his donkey for him. ²⁴As he went on his way, a lion met him on the road and killed him, and his body was thrown down on the road, with both the donkey and the lion standing beside it. ²⁵Some people who passed by saw the body thrown down there, with the lion standing beside the body, and they went and reported it in the city where the old prophet lived.

²⁶When the prophet who had brought him back from his journey heard of it, he said, "It is the man of God who defied the word of the LORD. The LORD has given him over to the lion, which has mauled him and killed him, as the word of the LORD had warned him."

²⁷The prophet said to his sons, "Saddle the donkey for me," and they did so. ²⁸Then he went out and found the body thrown down on the road, with the donkey and the lion standing beside it. The lion had neither eaten the body nor mauled the donkey. ²⁹So the prophet picked up the body of the man of God, laid it on the donkey, and brought it back to his own city to mourn for him and bury him. ³⁰Then he laid the body in his own tomb, and they mourned over him and said, "Oh, my brother!"

³¹After burying him, he said to his sons, "When I die, bury me in the grave where the man of God is buried; lay my bones beside his bones. ³²For the message he declared by the word of the LORD against the altar in Bethel and against all the shrines on the high places in the towns of Samaria will certainly come true."

³³Even after this, Jeroboam did not change his evil ways, but once more appointed priests for the high places from all sorts of people. Anyone who wanted to become a priest he consecrated for the high places. ³⁴This was the sin of the house of Jeroboam that led to its downfall and to its destruction from the face of the earth.

Ahijah's Prophecy Against Jeroboam

14 At that time Abijah son of Jeroboam became ill, ²and Jeroboam said to his wife, "Go, disguise yourself, so you won't be recognized as the wife of

Jeroboam. Then go to Shiloh. Ahijah the prophet is there—the one who told me I would be king over this people. ³Take ten loaves of bread with you, some cakes and a jar of honey, and go to him. He will tell you what will happen to the boy." ⁴So Jeroboam's wife did what he said and went to Ahijah's house in Shiloh.

Now Ahijah could not see; his sight was gone because of his age. ⁵But the LORD had told Ahijah, "Jeroboam's wife is coming to ask you about her son, for he is ill, and you are to give her such and such an answer. When she arrives, she will pretend to be someone else."

⁶So when Ahijah heard the sound of her footsteps at the door, he said, "Come in, wife of Jeroboam. Why this pretense? I have been sent to you with bad news. ⁷Go, tell Jeroboam that this is what the LORD, the God of Israel, says: 'I raised you up from among the people and made you a leader over my people Israel. ⁸I tore the kingdom away from the house of David and gave it to you, but you have not been like my servant David, who kept my commands and followed me with all his heart, doing only what was right in my eyes. ⁹You have done more evil than all who lived before you. You have made for yourself other gods, idols made of metal; you have provoked me to anger and thrust me behind your back.

¹⁰" 'Because of this, I am going to bring disaster on the house of Jeroboam. I will cut off from Jeroboam every last male in Israel—slave or free. I will burn up the house of Jeroboam as one burns dung, until it is all gone. ¹¹Dogs will eat those belonging to Jeroboam who die in the city, and the birds of the air will feed on those who die in the country. The LORD has spoken!'

¹²"As for you, go back home. When you set foot in your city, the boy will die. ¹³All Israel will mourn for him and bury him. He is the only one belonging to Jeroboam who will be buried, because he is the only one in the house of Jeroboam in whom the LORD, the God of Israel, has found anything good.

¹⁴"The LORD will raise up for himself a king over Israel who will cut off the family of Jeroboam. This is the day! What? Yes, even now.ᵃ ¹⁵And the LORD will strike Israel, so that it will be like a reed swaying in the water. He will uproot Israel from this good land that he gave to their forefathers and scatter them beyond the River,ᵇ because they provoked the LORD to anger by making Asherah poles.ᶜ ¹⁶And he will give Israel up because of the sins Jeroboam has committed and has caused Israel to commit."

¹⁷Then Jeroboam's wife got up and left and went to Tirzah. As soon as she stepped over the threshold of the house, the boy died. ¹⁸They buried him, and all Israel mourned for him, as the LORD had said through his servant the prophet Ahijah.

¹⁹The other events of Jeroboam's reign, his wars and how he ruled, are written in the book of the annals of the kings of Israel. ²⁰He reigned for twenty-two years and then rested with his fathers. And Nadab his son succeeded him as king.

Rehoboam King of Judah

²¹Rehoboam son of Solomon was king in Judah. He was forty-one years old when he became king, and he reigned seventeen years in Jerusalem, the city the LORD had chosen out of all the tribes of Israel in which to put his Name. His mother's name was Naamah; she was an Ammonite.

²²Judah did evil in the eyes of the LORD. By the sins they committed they stirred up his jealous anger more than their fathers had done. ²³They also set up for themselves high places, sacred stones and Asherah poles on every high hill and under every spreading tree. ²⁴There were even male shrine prostitutes in the land; the people engaged in all the detestable practices of the nations the LORD had driven out before the Israelites.

²⁵In the fifth year of King Rehoboam, Shishak king of Egypt attacked Jerusalem. ²⁶He carried off the treasures of the temple of the LORD and the treasures of the royal palace. He took everything, including all the gold shields Solomon had made. ²⁷So King Rehoboam made bronze

---

ᵃ14 The meaning of the Hebrew for this sentence is uncertain.　ᵇ15 That is, the Euphrates　ᶜ15 That is, symbols of the goddess Asherah; here and elsewhere in 1 Kings

shields to replace them and assigned these to the commanders of the guard on duty at the entrance to the royal palace. ²⁸Whenever the king went to the LORD's temple, the guards bore the shields, and afterward they returned them to the guardroom.

²⁹As for the other events of Rehoboam's reign, and all he did, are they not written in the book of the annals of the kings of Judah? ³⁰There was continual warfare between Rehoboam and Jeroboam. ³¹And Rehoboam rested with his fathers and was buried with them in the City of David. His mother's name was Naamah; she was an Ammonite. And Abijah*ᵃ* his son succeeded him as king.

Abijah King of Judah

15 In the eighteenth year of the reign of Jeroboam son of Nebat, Abijah*ᵇ* became king of Judah, ²and he reigned in Jerusalem three years. His mother's name was Maacah daughter of Abishalom.*ᶜ*

³He committed all the sins his father had done before him; his heart was not fully devoted to the LORD his God, as the heart of David his forefather had been. ⁴Nevertheless, for David's sake the LORD his God gave him a lamp in Jerusalem by raising up a son to succeed him and by making Jerusalem strong. ⁵For David had done what was right in the eyes of the LORD and had not failed to keep any of the LORD's commands all the days of his life—except in the case of Uriah the Hittite.

⁶There was war between Rehoboam*ᵈ* and Jeroboam throughout Abijah's lifetime. ⁷As for the other events of Abijah's reign, and all he did, are they not written in the book of the annals of the kings of Judah? There was war between Abijah and Jeroboam. ⁸And Abijah rested with his fathers and was buried in the City of David. And Asa his son succeeded him as king.

Asa King of Judah

⁹In the twentieth year of Jeroboam king of Israel, Asa became king of Judah, ¹⁰and he reigned in Jerusalem forty-one years. His grandmother's name was Maacah daughter of Abishalom.

¹¹Asa did what was right in the eyes of

Enough Scums Already

Huh?

1 Kings 15:11

After Solomon turned his back on God, the Lord let the Israelite kings continue their evil ways. King after king denied God and ignored the truth. But one guy finally came along who wanted to be a good king—Asa. Asa cared about what God wanted for the people. Even though the Israelites were God's chosen people, almost every king during this time was pretty scummy. Only Asa hung in there with God.

the LORD, as his father David had done. ¹²He expelled the male shrine prostitutes from the land and got rid of all the idols his fathers had made. ¹³He even deposed his grandmother Maacah from her position as queen mother, because she had made a repulsive Asherah pole. Asa cut the pole down and burned it in the Kidron Valley. ¹⁴Although he did not remove the high places, Asa's heart was fully committed to the LORD all his life. ¹⁵He brought into the temple of the LORD the silver and gold and the articles that he and his father had dedicated.

¹⁶There was war between Asa and Baasha king of Israel throughout their reigns. ¹⁷Baasha king of Israel went up against Judah and fortified Ramah to prevent anyone from leaving or entering the territory of Asa king of Judah.

¹⁸Asa then took all the silver and gold that was left in the treasuries of the LORD's temple and of his own palace. He entrusted it to his officials and sent them to Ben-Hadad son of Tabrimmon, the son of Hezion, the king of Aram, who was ruling in Damascus. ¹⁹"Let there be a treaty between me and you," he said, "as

---

ᵃ31 Some Hebrew manuscripts and Septuagint (see also 2 Chron. 12:16); most Hebrew manuscripts *Abijam*   *ᵇ1* Some Hebrew manuscripts and Septuagint (see also 2 Chron. 12:16); most Hebrew manuscripts *Abijam*; also in verses 7 and 8   *ᶜ2* A variant of *Absalom*; also in verse 10   *ᵈ6* Most Hebrew manuscripts; some Hebrew manuscripts and Syriac *Abijam* (that is, Abijah)

there was between my father and your father. See, I am sending you a gift of silver and gold. Now break your treaty with Baasha king of Israel so he will withdraw from me."

²⁰Ben-Hadad agreed with King Asa and sent the commanders of his forces against the towns of Israel. He conquered Ijon, Dan, Abel Beth Maacah and all Kinnereth in addition to Naphtali. ²¹When Baasha heard this, he stopped building Ramah and withdrew to Tirzah. ²²Then King Asa issued an order to all Judah—no one was exempt—and they carried away from Ramah the stones and timber Baasha had been using there. With them King Asa built up Geba in Benjamin, and also Mizpah.

²³As for all the other events of Asa's reign, all his achievements, all he did and the cities he built, are they not written in the book of the annals of the kings of Judah? In his old age, however, his feet became diseased. ²⁴Then Asa rested with his fathers and was buried with them in the city of his father David. And Jehoshaphat his son succeeded him as king.

Nadab King of Israel

²⁵Nadab son of Jeroboam became king of Israel in the second year of Asa king of Judah, and he reigned over Israel two years. ²⁶He did evil in the eyes of the LORD, walking in the ways of his father and in his sin, which he had caused Israel to commit.

²⁷Baasha son of Ahijah of the house of Issachar plotted against him, and he struck him down at Gibbethon, a Philistine town, while Nadab and all Israel were besieging it. ²⁸Baasha killed Nadab in the third year of Asa king of Judah and succeeded him as king.

²⁹As soon as he began to reign, he killed Jeroboam's whole family. He did not leave Jeroboam anyone that breathed, but destroyed them all, according to the word of the LORD given through his servant Ahijah the Shilonite— ³⁰because of the sins Jeroboam had committed and had caused Israel to commit, and because he provoked the LORD, the God of Israel, to anger.

³¹As for the other events of Nadab's reign, and all he did, are they not written

in the book of the annals of the kings of Israel? ³²There was war between Asa and Baasha king of Israel throughout their reigns.

Baasha King of Israel

³³In the third year of Asa king of Judah, Baasha son of Ahijah became king of all Israel in Tirzah, and he reigned twenty-four years. ³⁴He did evil in the eyes of the LORD, walking in the ways of Jeroboam and in his sin, which he had caused Israel to commit.

16 Then the word of the LORD came to Jehu son of Hanani against Baasha: ²"I lifted you up from the dust and made you leader of my people Israel, but you walked in the ways of Jeroboam and caused my people Israel to sin and to provoke me to anger by their sins. ³So I am about to consume Baasha and his house, and I will make your house like that of Jeroboam son of Nebat. ⁴Dogs will eat those belonging to Baasha who die in the city, and the birds of the air will feed on those who die in the country."

⁵As for the other events of Baasha's reign, what he did and his achievements, are they not written in the book of the annals of the kings of Israel? ⁶Baasha rested with his fathers and was buried in Tirzah. And Elah his son succeeded him as king.

⁷Moreover, the word of the LORD came through the prophet Jehu son of Hanani to Baasha and his house, because of all the evil he had done in the eyes of the LORD, provoking him to anger by the things he did, and becoming like the house of Jeroboam—and also because he destroyed it.

Elah King of Israel

⁸In the twenty-sixth year of Asa king of Judah, Elah son of Baasha became king of Israel, and he reigned in Tirzah two years.

⁹Zimri, one of his officials, who had command of half his chariots, plotted against him. Elah was in Tirzah at the time, getting drunk in the home of Arza, the man in charge of the palace at Tirzah. ¹⁰Zimri came in, struck him down and killed him in the twenty-seventh year of

Asa king of Judah. Then he succeeded him as king.

[11]As soon as he began to reign and was seated on the throne, he killed off Baasha's whole family. He did not spare a single male, whether relative or friend. [12]So Zimri destroyed the whole family of Baasha, in accordance with the word of the LORD spoken against Baasha through the prophet Jehu— [13]because of all the sins Baasha and his son Elah had committed and had caused Israel to commit, so that they provoked the LORD, the God of Israel, to anger by their worthless idols.

[14]As for the other events of Elah's reign, and all he did, are they not written in the book of the annals of the kings of Israel?

Zimri King of Israel

[15]In the twenty-seventh year of Asa king of Judah, Zimri reigned in Tirzah seven days. The army was encamped near Gibbethon, a Philistine town. [16]When the Israelites in the camp heard that Zimri had plotted against the king and murdered him, they proclaimed Omri, the commander of the army, king over Israel that very day there in the camp. [17]Then Omri and all the Israelites with him withdrew from Gibbethon and laid siege to Tirzah. [18]When Zimri saw that the city was taken, he went into the citadel of the royal palace and set the palace on fire around him. So he died, [19]because of the sins he had committed, doing evil in the eyes of the LORD and walking in the ways of Jeroboam and in the sin he had committed and had caused Israel to commit.

[20]As for the other events of Zimri's reign, and the rebellion he carried out, are they not written in the book of the annals of the kings of Israel?

Omri King of Israel

[21]Then the people of Israel were split into two factions; half supported Tibni son of Ginath for king, and the other half supported Omri. [22]But Omri's followers proved stronger than those of Tibni son of Ginath. So Tibni died and Omri became king.

[23]In the thirty-first year of Asa king of Judah, Omri became king of Israel, and he reigned twelve years, six of them in Tirzah. [24]He bought the hill of Samaria from Shemer for two talents[a] of silver and built a city on the hill, calling it Samaria, after Shemer, the name of the former owner of the hill.

[25]But Omri did evil in the eyes of the LORD and sinned more than all those before him. [26]He walked in all the ways of Jeroboam son of Nebat and in his sin, which he had caused Israel to commit, so that they provoked the LORD, the God of Israel, to anger by their worthless idols.

[27]As for the other events of Omri's reign, what he did and the things he achieved, are they not written in the book of the annals of the kings of Israel? [28]Omri rested with his fathers and was buried in Samaria. And Ahab his son succeeded him as king.

Ahab Becomes King of Israel

[29]In the thirty-eighth year of Asa king of Judah, Ahab son of Omri became king of Israel, and he reigned in Samaria over Israel twenty-two years. [30]Ahab son of Omri did more evil in the eyes of the LORD than any of those before him. [31]He not only considered it trivial to commit the sins of Jeroboam son of Nebat, but he also married Jezebel daughter of Ethbaal king of the Sidonians, and began to serve Baal and worship him. [32]He set up an altar for Baal in the temple of Baal that he built in Samaria. [33]Ahab also made an Asherah pole and did more to provoke the LORD, the God of Israel, to anger than did all the kings of Israel before him.

[34]In Ahab's time, Hiel of Bethel rebuilt Jericho. He laid its foundations at the cost of his firstborn son Abiram, and he set up its gates at the cost of his youngest son Segub, in accordance with the word of the LORD spoken by Joshua son of Nun.

Elijah Fed by Ravens

17 Now Elijah the Tishbite, from Tishbe[b] in Gilead, said to Ahab,

---

[a]24 That is, about 150 pounds (about 70 kilograms)
[b]1 Or *Tishbite, of the settlers*

Bird Food ... and Other Odd Treats

1 Kings 17:2–6 Elijah was out in the middle of nowhere—no grocery stores, no fast food drive-thrus, no munchies anywhere. But no problem: A bunch of birds brought him his food—bread and meat—twice a day for breakfast and dinner. Check out these other weird menus:

✗ Samson ate some honey found in a lion's dead body! (Judges 14:5–9)

✗ Ezekiel and John ate books! (Ezekiel 3:1–3; Revelation 10:9–10)

✗ John the Baptist ate big bugs! (Matthew 3:4)

"As the LORD, the God of Israel, lives, whom I serve, there will be neither dew nor rain in the next few years except at my word."

²Then the word of the LORD came to Elijah: ³"Leave here, turn eastward and hide in the Kerith Ravine, east of the Jordan. ⁴You will drink from the brook, and I have ordered the ravens to feed you there."

⁵So he did what the LORD had told him. He went to the Kerith Ravine, east of the Jordan, and stayed there. ⁶The ravens brought him bread and meat in the morning and bread and meat in the evening, and he drank from the brook.

The Widow at Zarephath

⁷Some time later the brook dried up because there had been no rain in the land. ⁸Then the word of the LORD came to him: ⁹"Go at once to Zarephath of Sidon and stay there. I have commanded a widow in that place to supply you with food." ¹⁰So he went to Zarephath. When he came to the town gate, a widow was there gathering sticks. He called to her and asked, "Would you bring me a little water in a jar so I may have a drink?" ¹¹As she was going to get it, he called, "And bring me, please, a piece of bread."

¹²"As surely as the LORD your God lives," she replied, "I don't have any bread—only a handful of flour in a jar and a little oil in a jug. I am gathering a few sticks to take home and make a meal for myself and my son, that we may eat it—and die."

¹³Elijah said to her, "Don't be afraid. Go home and do as you have said. But first make a small cake of bread for me from what you have and bring it to me, and then make something for yourself and your son. ¹⁴For this is what the LORD, the God of Israel, says: 'The jar of flour will not be used up and the jug of oil will not run dry until the day the LORD gives rain on the land.' "

¹⁵She went away and did as Elijah had told her. So there was food every day for Elijah and for the woman and her family. ¹⁶For the jar of flour was not used up and the jug of oil did not run dry, in keeping with the word of the LORD spoken by Elijah.

¹⁷Some time later the son of the woman who owned the house became ill. He grew worse and worse, and finally stopped breathing. ¹⁸She said to Elijah, "What do you have against me, man of God? Did you come to remind me of my sin and kill my son?"

¹⁹"Give me your son," Elijah replied. He took him from her arms, carried him to the upper room where he was staying, and laid him on his bed. ²⁰Then he cried out to the LORD, "O LORD my God, have you brought tragedy also upon this widow I am staying with, by causing her son to die?" ²¹Then he stretched himself out on the boy three times and cried to the LORD, "O LORD my God, let this boy's life return to him!"

²²The LORD heard Elijah's cry, and the boy's life returned to him, and he lived. ²³Elijah picked up the child and carried him down from the room into the house. He gave him to his mother and said, "Look, your son is alive!"

²⁴Then the woman said to Elijah, "Now I know that you are a man of God and that the word of the LORD from your mouth is the truth."

Elijah and Obadiah

18 After a long time, in the third year, the word of the LORD came to Elijah: "Go and present yourself to Ahab, and I will send rain on the land." ²So Elijah went to present himself to Ahab.

Now the famine was severe in Samaria, ³and Ahab had summoned Obadiah, who was in charge of his palace. (Obadiah was a devout believer in the LORD. ⁴While Jezebel was killing off the LORD's prophets, Obadiah had taken a hundred prophets and hidden them in two caves, fifty in each, and had supplied them with food and water.) ⁵Ahab had said to Obadiah, "Go through the land to all the springs and valleys. Maybe we can find some grass to keep the horses and mules alive so we will not have to kill any of our animals." ⁶So they divided the land they were to cover, Ahab going in one direction and Obadiah in another.

⁷As Obadiah was walking along, Elijah met him. Obadiah recognized him, bowed down to the ground, and said, "Is it really you, my lord Elijah?"

⁸"Yes," he replied. "Go tell your master, 'Elijah is here.' "

⁹"What have I done wrong," asked Obadiah, "that you are handing your servant over to Ahab to be put to death? ¹⁰As surely as the LORD your God lives, there is not a nation or kingdom where my master has not sent someone to look for you. And whenever a nation or kingdom claimed you were not there, he made them swear they could not find you. ¹¹But now you tell me to go to my master and say, 'Elijah is here.' ¹²I don't know where the Spirit of the LORD may carry you when I leave you. If I go and tell Ahab and he doesn't find you, he will kill me. Yet I your servant have worshiped the LORD since my youth. ¹³Haven't you heard, my lord, what I did while Jezebel was killing the prophets of the LORD? I hid a hundred of the LORD's prophets in two caves, fifty in each, and supplied them with food and water. ¹⁴And now you tell me to go to my master and say, 'Elijah is here.' He will kill me!"

¹⁵Elijah said, "As the LORD Almighty lives, whom I serve, I will surely present myself to Ahab today."

Elijah on Mount Carmel

¹⁶So Obadiah went to meet Ahab and told him, and Ahab went to meet Elijah. ¹⁷When he saw Elijah, he said to him, "Is that you, you troubler of Israel?"

¹⁸"I have not made trouble for Israel," Elijah replied. "But you and your father's family have. You have abandoned the LORD's commands and have followed the Baals. ¹⁹Now summon the people from all over Israel to meet me on Mount Carmel. And bring the four hundred and fifty prophets of Baal and the four hundred prophets of Asherah, who eat at Jezebel's table."

²⁰So Ahab sent word throughout all Israel and assembled the prophets on Mount Carmel. ²¹Elijah went before the people and said, "How long will you waver between two opinions? If the LORD is God, follow him; but if Baal is God, follow him."

But the people said nothing.

²²Then Elijah said to them, "I am the only one of the LORD's prophets left, but Baal has four hundred and fifty prophets. ²³Get two bulls for us. Let them choose one for themselves, and let them cut it into pieces and put it on the wood but not set fire to it. I will prepare the other bull and put it on the wood but not set fire to it. ²⁴Then you call on the name of your god, and I will call on the name of the LORD. The god who answers by fire—he is God."

Then all the people said, "What you say is good."

²⁵Elijah said to the prophets of Baal, "Choose one of the bulls and prepare it first, since there are so many of you. Call on the name of your god, but do not light the fire." ²⁶So they took the bull given them and prepared it.

Then they called on the name of Baal from morning till noon. "O Baal, answer us!" they shouted. But there was no response; no one answered. And they danced around the altar they had made.

²⁷At noon Elijah began to taunt them. "Shout louder!" he said. "Surely he is a god! Perhaps he is deep in thought, or busy, or traveling. Maybe he is sleeping and must be awakened." ²⁸So they shouted louder and slashed themselves with

swords and spears, as was their custom, until their blood flowed. ²⁹Midday passed, and they continued their frantic prophesying until the time for the evening sacrifice. But there was no response, no one answered, no one paid attention.

³⁰Then Elijah said to all the people, "Come here to me." They came to him, and he repaired the altar of the LORD, which was in ruins. ³¹Elijah took twelve stones, one for each of the tribes descended from Jacob, to whom the word of the LORD had come, saying, "Your name shall be Israel." ³²With the stones he built an altar in the name of the LORD, and he dug a trench around it large enough to hold two seahs*a* of seed. ³³He arranged the wood, cut the bull into pieces and laid it on the wood. Then he said to them, "Fill four large jars with water and pour it on the offering and on the wood."

³⁴"Do it again," he said, and they did it again.

"Do it a third time," he ordered, and they did it the third time. ³⁵The water ran down around the altar and even filled the trench.

³⁶At the time of sacrifice, the prophet Elijah stepped forward and prayed: "O LORD, God of Abraham, Isaac and Israel, let it be known today that you are God in Israel and that I am your servant and have done all these things at your command. ³⁷Answer me, O LORD, answer me, so these people will know that you, O LORD, are God, and that you are turning their hearts back again."

³⁸Then the fire of the LORD fell and burned up the sacrifice, the wood, the stones and the soil, and also licked up the water in the trench.

a32 That is, probably about 13 quarts (about 15 liters)

Mon**day**

What Matters Most?

Read 1 Kings 18:10-15

A lot of people whine about their lives. They complain, "Why me?" or "It's not fair." I admit, sometimes I'm like that too.

I play tennis, and you have to be really aggressive and competitive to play well. I was playing in a doubles match recently when the other team cheated to try to win. I got so frustrated with them calling fair balls "out." They were beating us so badly that I felt like giving up. It just didn't seem right. But my partner and I got over our frustration and decided to play even harder. And we knew it was better to lose honestly than cheat. In the end, we won the match!

That time, our decision to follow God's rules and be honest was rewarded right away. But sometimes life isn't like that. Sometimes you do everything you're supposed to and still don't win. That's just the way life is. What matters is obeying God and doing your best.

NIKKI • age 15

What about You?

❶ What are 2 reasons why we sometimes lose confidence in God?

❷ Look out the window toward the place where the sun rose today, yesterday and the day before. How can you be confident that it will come up again tomorrow? Can you have confidence in God for some of the same reasons?

❸ Ask God to help you trust him.

Turn to page 414 for your next devotion.

Fired Up!

1 Kings 18:38

The people of Israel were without leaders who loved God; they were drifting away, following other gods. Elijah came along and helped them remember just how strong the true God is. In fact, the battle here wasn't really God's way of showing that he was more powerful than other "gods." It was his way of showing that he is the *only* God!

³⁹When all the people saw this, they fell prostrate and cried, "The LORD—he is God! The LORD—he is God!"

⁴⁰Then Elijah commanded them, "Seize the prophets of Baal. Don't let anyone get away!" They seized them, and Elijah had them brought down to the Kishon Valley and slaughtered there.

⁴¹And Elijah said to Ahab, "Go, eat and drink, for there is the sound of a heavy rain." ⁴²So Ahab went off to eat and drink, but Elijah climbed to the top of Carmel, bent down to the ground and put his face between his knees.

⁴³"Go and look toward the sea," he told his servant. And he went up and looked.

"There is nothing there," he said.

Seven times Elijah said, "Go back."

⁴⁴The seventh time the servant reported, "A cloud as small as a man's hand is rising from the sea."

So Elijah said, "Go and tell Ahab, 'Hitch up your chariot and go down before the rain stops you.' "

⁴⁵Meanwhile, the sky grew black with clouds, the wind rose, a heavy rain came on and Ahab rode off to Jezreel. ⁴⁶The power of the LORD came upon Elijah and, tucking his cloak into his belt, he ran ahead of Ahab all the way to Jezreel.

Elijah Flees to Horeb

19 Now Ahab told Jezebel everything Elijah had done and how he had killed all the prophets with the sword. ²So Jezebel sent a messenger to Elijah to say, "May the gods deal with me, be it ever so severely, if by this time tomorrow I do not make your life like that of one of them."

³Elijah was afraid[a] and ran for his life. When he came to Beersheba in Judah, he left his servant there, ⁴while he himself went a day's journey into the desert. He came to a broom tree, sat down under it and prayed that he might die. "I have had enough, LORD," he said. "Take my life; I am no better than my ancestors." ⁵Then he lay down under the tree and fell asleep.

All at once an angel touched him and said, "Get up and eat." ⁶He looked around, and there by his head was a cake of bread baked over hot coals, and a jar of water. He ate and drank and then lay down again.

⁷The angel of the LORD came back a second time and touched him and said, "Get up and eat, for the journey is too much for you." ⁸So he got up and ate and drank. Strengthened by that food, he traveled forty days and forty nights until he reached Horeb, the mountain of God. ⁹There he went into a cave and spent the night.

The LORD Appears to Elijah

And the word of the LORD came to him: "What are you doing here, Elijah?"

¹⁰He replied, "I have been very zealous for the LORD God Almighty. The Israelites have rejected your covenant, broken down your altars, and put your prophets to death with the sword. I am the only one left, and now they are trying to kill me too."

¹¹The LORD said, "Go out and stand on the mountain in the presence of the LORD, for the LORD is about to pass by."

Then a great and powerful wind tore the mountains apart and shattered the rocks before the LORD, but the LORD was not in the wind. After the wind there was an earthquake, but the LORD was not in the earthquake. ¹²After the earthquake came a fire, but the LORD was not in the fire. And after the fire came a gentle whisper. ¹³When Elijah heard it, he pulled his cloak over his face and went out and stood at the mouth of the cave.

Then a voice said to him, "What are you doing here, Elijah?"

---

a3 Or Elijah saw

¹⁴He replied, "I have been very zealous for the LORD God Almighty. The Israelites have rejected your covenant, broken down your altars, and put your prophets to death with the sword. I am the only one left, and now they are trying to kill me too."

¹⁵The LORD said to him, "Go back the way you came, and go to the Desert of Damascus. When you get there, anoint Hazael king over Aram. ¹⁶Also, anoint Jehu son of Nimshi king over Israel, and anoint Elisha son of Shaphat from Abel Meholah to succeed you as prophet. ¹⁷Jehu will put to death any who escape the sword of Hazael, and Elisha will put to death any who escape the sword of Jehu. ¹⁸Yet I reserve seven thousand in Israel—all whose knees have not bowed down to Baal and all whose mouths have not kissed him."

The Call of Elisha

¹⁹So Elijah went from there and found Elisha son of Shaphat. He was plowing with twelve yoke of oxen, and he himself was driving the twelfth pair. Elijah went up to him and threw his cloak around him. ²⁰Elisha then left his oxen and ran after Elijah. "Let me kiss my father and mother good-by," he said, "and then I will come with you."

"Go back," Elijah replied. "What have I done to you?"

²¹So Elisha left him and went back. He took his yoke of oxen and slaughtered them. He burned the plowing equipment to cook the meat and gave it to the people, and they ate. Then he set out to follow Elijah and became his attendant.

Ben-Hadad Attacks Samaria

20 Now Ben-Hadad king of Aram mustered his entire army. Accompanied by thirty-two kings with their horses and chariots, he went up and besieged Samaria and attacked it. ²He sent messengers into the city to Ahab king of Israel, saying, "This is what Ben-Hadad says: ³'Your silver and gold are mine, and the best of your wives and children are mine.'"

Tuesday

Listening for Him

Read 1 Kings 19:9–13

When we pray to God, we don't really know how he'll answer us. We might be waiting for a big voice to say, "Do this!" Or we might look in all the wrong places, expecting to find a big billboard sign with the answer on it. Most of the time we have to wait patiently to find out what God says.

While we're waiting, it's really important to listen. Even though God is super-powerful, he can speak in a very quiet voice. Sometimes the answer to your prayer is just a little whisper in your heart. God can also "speak" through Bible reading, the pastor's sermon or even the advice of a friend.

It may take a while for you to figure out what God wants you to do. And when you do get an answer, it might not be the one you were hoping for. But God knows what he's doing, and we can know it too, if we listen.

Kate age 12

What about You?

❶ What are some different ways God answers our prayers?

❷ Ask some Christian adults, like your parents or your youth leaders, about the different ways God has answered their prayers.

❸ Take 2 minutes of prayer time just to listen to God. Thank him for all the ways he guides you.

Turn to page 426 for your next devotion.

⁴The king of Israel answered, "Just as you say, my lord the king. I and all I have are yours."

⁵The messengers came again and said, "This is what Ben-Hadad says: 'I sent to demand your silver and gold, your wives and your children. ⁶But about this time tomorrow I am going to send my officials to search your palace and the houses of your officials. They will seize everything you value and carry it away.' "

⁷The king of Israel summoned all the elders of the land and said to them, "See how this man is looking for trouble! When he sent for my wives and my children, my silver and my gold, I did not refuse him."

⁸The elders and the people all answered, "Don't listen to him or agree to his demands."

⁹So he replied to Ben-Hadad's messengers, "Tell my lord the king, 'Your servant will do all you demanded the first time, but this demand I cannot meet.' " They left and took the answer back to Ben-Hadad.

¹⁰Then Ben-Hadad sent another message to Ahab: "May the gods deal with me, be it ever so severely, if enough dust remains in Samaria to give each of my men a handful."

¹¹The king of Israel answered, "Tell him: 'One who puts on his armor should not boast like one who takes it off.' "

¹²Ben-Hadad heard this message while he and the kings were drinking in their tents,ᵃ and he ordered his men: "Prepare to attack." So they prepared to attack the city.

Ahab Defeats Ben-Hadad

¹³Meanwhile a prophet came to Ahab king of Israel and announced, "This is what the LORD says: 'Do you see this vast army? I will give it into your hand today, and then you will know that I am the LORD.' "

¹⁴"But who will do this?" asked Ahab.

The prophet replied, "This is what the LORD says: 'The young officers of the provincial commanders will do it.' "

"And who will start the battle?" he asked.

The prophet answered, "You will."

¹⁵So Ahab summoned the young offi-

cers of the provincial commanders, 232 men. Then he assembled the rest of the Israelites, 7,000 in all. ¹⁶They set out at noon while Ben-Hadad and the 32 kings allied with him were in their tents getting drunk. ¹⁷The young officers of the provincial commanders went out first.

Now Ben-Hadad had dispatched scouts, who reported, "Men are advancing from Samaria."

¹⁸He said, "If they have come out for peace, take them alive; if they have come out for war, take them alive."

¹⁹The young officers of the provincial commanders marched out of the city with the army behind them ²⁰and each one struck down his opponent. At that, the Arameans fled, with the Israelites in pursuit. But Ben-Hadad king of Aram escaped on horseback with some of his horsemen. ²¹The king of Israel advanced and overpowered the horses and chariots and inflicted heavy losses on the Arameans.

²²Afterward, the prophet came to the king of Israel and said, "Strengthen your position and see what must be done, because next spring the king of Aram will attack you again."

²³Meanwhile, the officials of the king of Aram advised him, "Their gods are gods of the hills. That is why they were too strong for us. But if we fight them on the plains, surely we will be stronger than they. ²⁴Do this: Remove all the kings from their commands and replace them with other officers. ²⁵You must also raise an army like the one you lost—horse for horse and chariot for chariot—so we can fight Israel on the plains. Then surely we will be stronger than they." He agreed with them and acted accordingly.

²⁶The next spring Ben-Hadad mustered the Arameans and went up to Aphek to fight against Israel. ²⁷When the Israelites were also mustered and given provisions, they marched out to meet them. The Israelites camped opposite them like two small flocks of goats, while the Arameans covered the countryside.

²⁸The man of God came up and told the king of Israel, "This is what the LORD says: 'Because the Arameans think the

---

ᵃ12 Or *in Succoth*; also in verse 16

LORD is a god of the hills and not a god of the valleys, I will deliver this vast army into your hands, and you will know that I am the LORD.' "

²⁹For seven days they camped opposite each other, and on the seventh day the battle was joined. The Israelites inflicted a hundred thousand casualties on the Aramean foot soldiers in one day. ³⁰The rest of them escaped to the city of Aphek, where the wall collapsed on twenty-seven thousand of them. And Ben-Hadad fled to the city and hid in an inner room.

³¹His officials said to him, "Look, we have heard that the kings of the house of Israel are merciful. Let us go to the king of Israel with sackcloth around our waists and ropes around our heads. Perhaps he will spare your life."

³²Wearing sackcloth around their waists and ropes around their heads, they went to the king of Israel and said, "Your servant Ben-Hadad says: 'Please let me live.' "

The king answered, "Is he still alive? He is my brother."

³³The men took this as a good sign and were quick to pick up his word. "Yes, your brother Ben-Hadad!" they said.

"Go and get him," the king said. When Ben-Hadad came out, Ahab had him come up into his chariot.

³⁴"I will return the cities my father took from your father," Ben-Hadad offered. "You may set up your own market areas in Damascus, as my father did in Samaria."

Ahab said, "On the basis of a treaty I will set you free." So he made a treaty with him, and let him go.

A Prophet Condemns Ahab

³⁵By the word of the LORD one of the sons of the prophets said to his companion, "Strike me with your weapon," but the man refused.

³⁶So the prophet said, "Because you have not obeyed the LORD, as soon as you leave me a lion will kill you." And after the man went away, a lion found him and killed him.

³⁷The prophet found another man and said, "Strike me, please." So the man struck him and wounded him. ³⁸Then the prophet went and stood by the road wait-ing for the king. He disguised himself with his headband down over his eyes. ³⁹As the king passed by, the prophet called out to him, "Your servant went into the thick of the battle, and someone came to me with a captive and said, 'Guard this man. If he is missing, it will be your life for his life, or you must pay a talent* of silver.' ⁴⁰While your servant was busy here and there, the man disappeared."

"That is your sentence," the king of Israel said. "You have pronounced it yourself."

⁴¹Then the prophet quickly removed the headband from his eyes, and the king of Israel recognized him as one of the prophets. ⁴²He said to the king, "This is what the LORD says: 'You have set free a man I had determined should die.ᵇ Therefore it is your life for his life, your people for his people.' " ⁴³Sullen and angry, the king of Israel went to his palace in Samaria.

Naboth's Vineyard

21 Some time later there was an incident involving a vineyard belonging to Naboth the Jezreelite. The vineyard was in Jezreel, close to the palace of Ahab king of Samaria. ²Ahab said to Naboth, "Let me have your vineyard to use for a vegetable garden, since it is close to my palace. In exchange I will give you a better vineyard or, if you prefer, I will pay you whatever it is worth."

³But Naboth replied, "The LORD forbid that I should give you the inheritance of my fathers."

⁴So Ahab went home, sullen and angry because Naboth the Jezreelite had said, "I will not give you the inheritance of my fathers." He lay on his bed sulking and refused to eat.

⁵His wife Jezebel came in and asked him, "Why are you so sullen? Why won't you eat?"

⁶He answered her, "Because I said to Naboth the Jezreelite, 'Sell me your vineyard; or if you prefer, I will give you an-

---

*39 That is, about 75 pounds (about 34 kilograms)
ᵇ42 The Hebrew term refers to the irrevocable giving over of things or persons to the LORD, often by totally destroying them.

other vineyard in its place.' But he said, 'I will not give you my vineyard.' "

⁷Jezebel his wife said, "Is this how you act as king over Israel? Get up and eat! Cheer up. I'll get you the vineyard of Naboth the Jezreelite."

⁸So she wrote letters in Ahab's name, placed his seal on them, and sent them to the elders and nobles who lived in Naboth's city with him. ⁹In those letters she wrote:

> "Proclaim a day of fasting and seat Naboth in a prominent place among the people. ¹⁰But seat two scoundrels opposite him and have them testify that he has cursed both God and the king. Then take him out and stone him to death."

¹¹So the elders and nobles who lived in Naboth's city did as Jezebel directed in the letters she had written to them. ¹²They proclaimed a fast and seated Naboth in a prominent place among the people. ¹³Then two scoundrels came and sat opposite him and brought charges against Naboth before the people, saying, "Naboth has cursed both God and the king." So they took him outside the city and stoned him to death. ¹⁴Then they sent word to Jezebel: "Naboth has been stoned and is dead."

¹⁵As soon as Jezebel heard that Naboth had been stoned to death, she said to Ahab, "Get up and take possession of the vineyard of Naboth the Jezreelite that he refused to sell you. He is no longer alive, but dead." ¹⁶When Ahab heard that Naboth was dead, he got up and went down to take possession of Naboth's vineyard.

¹⁷Then the word of the LORD came to Elijah the Tishbite: ¹⁸"Go down to meet Ahab king of Israel, who rules in Samaria. He is now in Naboth's vineyard, where he has gone to take possession of it. ¹⁹Say to him, 'This is what the LORD says: Have you not murdered a man and seized his property?' Then say to him, 'This is what the LORD says: In the place where dogs licked up Naboth's blood, dogs will lick up your blood—yes, yours!' "

²⁰Ahab said to Elijah, "So you have found me, my enemy!"

"I have found you," he answered, "because you have sold yourself to do evil in the eyes of the LORD. ²¹'I am going to bring disaster on you. I will consume your descendants and cut off from Ahab every last male in Israel—slave or free. ²²I will make your house like that of Jeroboam son of Nebat and that of Baasha son of Ahijah, because you have provoked me to anger and have caused Israel to sin.'

²³"And also concerning Jezebel the LORD says: 'Dogs will devour Jezebel by the wall of*ᵃ* Jezreel.'

²⁴"Dogs will eat those belonging to Ahab who die in the city, and the birds of the air will feed on those who die in the country."

²⁵(There was never a man like Ahab, who sold himself to do evil in the eyes of the LORD, urged on by Jezebel his wife. ²⁶He behaved in the vilest manner by going after idols, like the Amorites the LORD drove out before Israel.)

²⁷When Ahab heard these words, he tore his clothes, put on sackcloth and fasted. He lay in sackcloth and went around meekly.

²⁸Then the word of the LORD came to Elijah the Tishbite: ²⁹"Have you noticed how Ahab has humbled himself before me? Because he has humbled himself, I will not bring this disaster in his day, but I will bring it on his house in the days of his son."

Micaiah Prophesies Against Ahab

22 For three years there was no war between Aram and Israel. ²But in the third year Jehoshaphat king of Judah went down to see the king of Israel. ³The king of Israel had said to his officials, "Don't you know that Ramoth Gilead belongs to us and yet we are doing nothing to retake it from the king of Aram?"

⁴So he asked Jehoshaphat, "Will you go with me to fight against Ramoth Gilead?"

Jehoshaphat replied to the king of Israel, "I am as you are, my people as your people, my horses as your horses." ⁵But

---

ᵃ23 Most Hebrew manuscripts; a few Hebrew manuscripts, Vulgate and Syriac (see also 2 Kings 9:26) *the plot of ground at*

Jehoshaphat also said to the king of Israel, "First seek the counsel of the LORD."

⁶So the king of Israel brought together the prophets—about four hundred men—and asked them, "Shall I go to war against Ramoth Gilead, or shall I refrain?"

"Go," they answered, "for the Lord will give it into the king's hand."

⁷But Jehoshaphat asked, "Is there not a prophet of the LORD here whom we can inquire of?"

⁸The king of Israel answered Jehoshaphat, "There is still one man through whom we can inquire of the LORD, but I hate him because he never prophesies anything good about me, but always bad. He is Micaiah son of Imlah."

"The king should not say that," Jehoshaphat replied.

⁹So the king of Israel called one of his officials and said, "Bring Micaiah son of Imlah at once."

¹⁰Dressed in their royal robes, the king of Israel and Jehoshaphat king of Judah were sitting on their thrones at the threshing floor by the entrance of the gate of Samaria, with all the prophets prophesying before them. ¹¹Now Zedekiah son of Kenaanah had made iron horns and he declared, "This is what the LORD says: 'With these you will gore the Arameans until they are destroyed.'"

¹²All the other prophets were prophesying the same thing. "Attack Ramoth Gilead and be victorious," they said, "for the LORD will give it into the king's hand."

¹³The messenger who had gone to summon Micaiah said to him, "Look, as one man the other prophets are predicting success for the king. Let your word agree with theirs, and speak favorably."

¹⁴But Micaiah said, "As surely as the LORD lives, I can tell him only what the LORD tells me."

¹⁵When he arrived, the king asked him, "Micaiah, shall we go to war against Ramoth Gilead, or shall I refrain?"

"Attack and be victorious," he answered, "for the LORD will give it into the king's hand."

¹⁶The king said to him, "How many times must I make you swear to tell me nothing but the truth in the name of the LORD?"

¹⁷Then Micaiah answered, "I saw all Israel scattered on the hills like sheep without a shepherd, and the LORD said, 'These people have no master. Let each one go home in peace.'"

¹⁸The king of Israel said to Jehoshaphat, "Didn't I tell you that he never prophesies anything good about me, but only bad?"

¹⁹Micaiah continued, "Therefore hear the word of the LORD: I saw the LORD sitting on his throne with all the host of heaven standing around him on his right and on his left. ²⁰And the LORD said, 'Who will entice Ahab into attacking Ramoth Gilead and going to his death there?'

"One suggested this, and another that. ²¹Finally, a spirit came forward, stood before the LORD and said, 'I will entice him.'

²²"'By what means?' the LORD asked.

"'I will go out and be a lying spirit in the mouths of all his prophets,' he said.

"'You will succeed in enticing him,' said the LORD. 'Go and do it.'

²³"So now the LORD has put a lying spirit in the mouths of all these prophets of yours. The LORD has decreed disaster for you."

²⁴Then Zedekiah son of Kenaanah went up and slapped Micaiah in the face. "Which way did the spirit from*ᵃ* the LORD go when he went from me to speak to you?" he asked.

²⁵Micaiah replied, "You will find out on the day you go to hide in an inner room."

²⁶The king of Israel then ordered, "Take Micaiah and send him back to Amon the ruler of the city and to Joash the king's son ²⁷and say, 'This is what the king says: Put this fellow in prison and give him nothing but bread and water until I return safely.'"

²⁸Micaiah declared, "If you ever return safely, the LORD has not spoken through me." Then he added, "Mark my words, all you people!"

Ahab Killed at Ramoth Gilead

²⁹So the king of Israel and Jehoshaphat king of Judah went up to Ramoth Gilead. ³⁰The king of Israel said to Jehoshaphat,

ᵃ24 Or Spirit of

"I will enter the battle in disguise, but you wear your royal robes." So the king of Israel disguised himself and went into battle.

³¹Now the king of Aram had ordered his thirty-two chariot commanders, "Do not fight with anyone, small or great, except the king of Israel." ³²When the chariot commanders saw Jehoshaphat, they thought, "Surely this is the king of Israel." So they turned to attack him, but when Jehoshaphat cried out, ³³the chariot commanders saw that he was not the king of Israel and stopped pursuing him.

³⁴But someone drew his bow at random and hit the king of Israel between the sections of his armor. The king told his chariot driver, "Wheel around and get me out of the fighting. I've been wounded." ³⁵All day long the battle raged, and the king was propped up in his chariot facing the Arameans. The blood from his wound ran onto the floor of the chariot, and that evening he died. ³⁶As the sun was setting, a cry spread through the army: "Every man to his town; everyone to his land!"

³⁷So the king died and was brought to Samaria, and they buried him there. ³⁸They washed the chariot at a pool in Samaria (where the prostitutes bathed),ᵃ and the dogs licked up his blood, as the word of the LORD had declared.

³⁹As for the other events of Ahab's reign, including all he did, the palace he built and inlaid with ivory, and the cities he fortified, are they not written in the book of the annals of the kings of Israel? ⁴⁰Ahab rested with his fathers. And Ahaziah his son succeeded him as king.

Jehoshaphat King of Judah

⁴¹Jehoshaphat son of Asa became king of Judah in the fourth year of Ahab king of Israel. ⁴²Jehoshaphat was thirty-five years old when he became king, and he reigned in Jerusalem twenty-five years. His mother's name was Azubah daughter of Shilhi. ⁴³In everything he walked in the ways of his father Asa and did not stray from them; he did what was right in the eyes of the LORD. The high places, however, were not removed, and the people continued to offer sacrifices and burn incense there. ⁴⁴Jehoshaphat was also at peace with the king of Israel.

⁴⁵As for the other events of Jehoshaphat's reign, the things he achieved and his military exploits, are they not written in the book of the annals of the kings of Judah? ⁴⁶He rid the land of the rest of the male shrine prostitutes who remained there even after the reign of his father Asa. ⁴⁷There was then no king in Edom; a deputy ruled.

⁴⁸Now Jehoshaphat built a fleet of trading shipsᵇ to go to Ophir for gold, but they never set sail—they were wrecked at Ezion Geber. ⁴⁹At that time Ahaziah son of Ahab said to Jehoshaphat, "Let my men sail with your men," but Jehoshaphat refused.

⁵⁰Then Jehoshaphat rested with his fathers and was buried with them in the city of David his father. And Jehoram his son succeeded him.

Ahaziah King of Israel

⁵¹Ahaziah son of Ahab became king of Israel in Samaria in the seventeenth year of Jehoshaphat king of Judah, and he reigned over Israel two years. ⁵²He did evil in the eyes of the LORD, because he walked in the ways of his father and mother and in the ways of Jeroboam son of Nebat, who caused Israel to sin. ⁵³He served and worshiped Baal and provoked the LORD, the God of Israel, to anger, just as his father had done.

ᵃ38 Or *Samaria and cleaned the weapons*
ᵇ48 Hebrew *of ships of Tarshish*

2 Kings

This book continues the history of Israelite kings where 1 Kings left off. In the middle of the first book, the country splits in 2. The 10 tribe-states in the north keep the name *Israel*, but they blow off their God. The 2 southern tribe-states call themselves Judah, and they do a tiny bit better when it comes to God. But most of the kings in both countries turn out awful, and both countries get the stuffing beat out of them in the end.

Israel's rotten kings lead it straight into slavery under the unstoppable Assyrians. Judah manages to hold out longer thanks to an occasional godly king. But it eventually follows in the footsteps of its northern kin when the big bad Babylonians come to town. The citizens of Judah get hauled off to Babylon, and their captors knock down the wonderful temple King Solomon built. It's a sorry situation. After all these years, the Israelites are back where they started way back when they were wandering in the desert with Moses: on the wrong side of the Jordan River, hoping for a chance to try again.

Cast OF Characters

Elijah (ee-LIE-juh)

He's a fine old prophet—the guy who never dies! God lets him skip that chapter, sending a chariot from heaven to pick him up instead. What a ride!

Elisha (ee-LIE-shuh)

Elijah's student. Elisha asks God for a double helping of the spirit that fired up his teacher Elijah. And sure enough, God gives it to him.

Woman of Shunem
(SHOO-nem)

She helps Elisha. He repays her by prophesying that she'll have the son she's always wanted but couldn't have. God delivers, but her boy gets sick and dies. Elisha works a miracle and brings the boy back to life.

Naaman
(NAY-man)

A great warrior for the king of Aram. He's got a bad case of leprosy. Elisha gives him a strange prescription, and he almost doesn't take it. When he does as he's told, he's healed.

Gehazi (gih-HAY-zigh)

Elisha's servant and a pretty cool guy . . . till he gets greedy. When Elisha refuses to accept a payment gift from the former-leper Naaman (the healing was God's, not the prophet's), Gehazi keeps the gift for himself. Bad move. In addition to the gift, Gehazi walks away with the former leper's *leprosy*—and shares it with his family.

Kings of Israel

Bad, all bad. But as you'll find out, some are worse than others.

Kings of Judah

Mostly bad, a few good. The bad ones outnumber the good ones in the end, which spells the end of Judah—for a while anyway. The citizens go to detention in Babylon till God brings them back home again.

What's UP with That?

From the moment the Israelites stepped foot on the promised land, they got suckered into the goofy and disgusting religious practices of the locals: worshiping idols, praying to bogus gods, sleeping with prostitutes—even burning their own babies in sacrifices. That's why God had told them to totally destroy these wicked people and their disgusting religions.

But the Israelites didn't obey. Now, hundreds of years later, these sick religions rage like a cancer through the people. Occasionally, a good king would come along and destroy the evil shrines. That meant tearing down . . .

high places (shrines on hilltops used for sacrifices to various gods)

Asherah poles (statues to Asherah, a weird goddess)

Baal temples (shrines to the god Baal— a "godchild" of Asherah)

Unfortunately, most of the good kings (and there weren't many of them) left the cult shrines alone, so these awful religions didn't go away. In the end, God let the people have their way. They found out too late that their goofy gods couldn't save them. Only the one true God could do that, and they had forgotten all about him.

Snap shots

- Chariot of fire!—Elijah retires, takes express lane to heaven *(chapters 1—2)*

- Elisha graduates— teacher's blessing, great prayer, big miracles *(chapters 2—8)*

- Royal spiral—a bunch of kings, mostly sick and twisted *(chapters 8—16)*

- Israel bites the dust— Assyrians wipe northern kingdom off the map *(chapter 17)*

- "See what happens?"—Judah learns from Israel's mistakes . . . kind of *(chapters 18—24)*

- Judah bites the dust—Babylonians crush Jerusalem, take captives *(chapters 24—25)*

The Lord's Judgment on Ahaziah

1 After Ahab's death, Moab rebelled against Israel. ²Now Ahaziah had fallen through the lattice of his upper room in Samaria and injured himself. So he sent messengers, saying to them, "Go and consult Baal-Zebub, the god of Ekron, to see if I will recover from this injury."

³But the angel of the LORD said to Elijah the Tishbite, "Go up and meet the messengers of the king of Samaria and ask them, 'Is it because there is no God in Israel that you are going off to consult Baal-Zebub, the god of Ekron?' ⁴Therefore this is what the LORD says: 'You will not leave the bed you are lying on. You will certainly die!' " So Elijah went.

⁵When the messengers returned to the king, he asked them, "Why have you come back?"

⁶"A man came to meet us," they replied. "And he said to us, 'Go back to the king who sent you and tell him, "This is what the LORD says: Is it because there is no God in Israel that you are sending men to consult Baal-Zebub, the god of Ekron? Therefore you will not leave the bed you are lying on. You will certainly die!" ' "

⁷The king asked them, "What kind of man was it who came to meet you and told you this?"

⁸They replied, "He was a man with a garment of hair and with a leather belt around his waist."

The king said, "That was Elijah the Tishbite."

⁹Then he sent to Elijah a captain with his company of fifty men. The captain went up to Elijah, who was sitting on the top of a hill, and said to him, "Man of God, the king says, 'Come down!' "

¹⁰Elijah answered the captain, "If I am a man of God, may fire come down from heaven and consume you and your fifty men!" Then fire fell from heaven and consumed the captain and his men.

¹¹At this the king sent to Elijah another captain with his fifty men. The captain said to him, "Man of God, this is what the king says, 'Come down at once!' "

¹²"If I am a man of God," Elijah replied, "may fire come down from heaven and consume you and your fifty men!" Then the fire of God fell from heaven and consumed him and his fifty men.

¹³So the king sent a third captain with his fifty men. This third captain went up and fell on his knees before Elijah. "Man of God," he begged, "please have respect for my life and the lives of these fifty men, your servants! ¹⁴See, fire has fallen from heaven and consumed the first two captains and all their men. But now have respect for my life!"

¹⁵The angel of the LORD said to Elijah, "Go down with him; do not be afraid of him." So Elijah got up and went down with him to the king.

¹⁶He told the king, "This is what the LORD says: Is it because there is no God in Israel for you to consult that you have sent messengers to consult Baal-Zebub, the god of Ekron? Because you have done this, you will never leave the bed you are lying on. You will certainly die!" ¹⁷So he died, according to the word of the LORD that Elijah had spoken.

Because Ahaziah had no son, Joram*a* succeeded him as king in the second year of Jehoram son of Jehoshaphat king of Judah. ¹⁸As for all the other events of Ahaziah's reign, and what he did, are they not written in the book of the annals of the kings of Israel?

Elijah Taken Up to Heaven

2 When the LORD was about to take Elijah up to heaven in a whirlwind, Elijah and Elisha were on their way from Gilgal. ²Elijah said to Elisha, "Stay here; the LORD has sent me to Bethel."

But Elisha said, "As surely as the LORD lives and as you live, I will not leave you." So they went down to Bethel.

³The company of the prophets at Bethel came out to Elisha and asked, "Do you know that the LORD is going to take your master from you today?"

"Yes, I know," Elisha replied, "but do not speak of it."

⁴Then Elijah said to him, "Stay here, Elisha; the LORD has sent me to Jericho."

And he replied, "As surely as the LORD lives and as you live, I will not leave you." So they went to Jericho.

a17 Hebrew Jehoram, a variant of Joram

The Record Book

The Bible describes the stories of several world record holders—people whose accomplishments have yet to be beaten:

Sweetest Death: Enoch and Elijah tie for first place in this category—they never died! God lets them skip their death scenes and go straight to heaven (Genesis 5:24, page 11; 2 Kings 2:11).

Oldest Human: Methuselah lives to the ripe old age of 969. Imagine the wrinkles (Genesis 5:27, page 11).

Wisest Human: His advice is sought by all the world leaders of his time. He memorizes 3,000 proverbs and writes over 1,000 songs. He knows more about plants and animals than anyone, so he teaches biology in his spare time. Not Superman, but Solomon (1 Kings 3; 4:29–34).

Fastest Human: In a race between Elijah the sprinting prophet and a horse-drawn chariot, Elijah wins (1 Kings 18:46).

And now for some records about the Bible itself:

Shortest Verse: John 11:35, page 1287 (2 words)
Longest Verse: Esther 8:9, page 577 (72 words)
Shortest Chapter: Psalm 117, page 707 (2 verses)
Longest Chapter: Psalm 119, page 708 (176 verses)
Shortest Book: 3 John, page 1542 (15 verses)
Longest Book: Psalms (150 chapters)

⁵The company of the prophets at Jericho went up to Elisha and asked him, "Do you know that the LORD is going to take your master from you today?"

"Yes, I know," he replied, "but do not speak of it."

⁶Then Elijah said to him, "Stay here; the LORD has sent me to the Jordan."

And he replied, "As surely as the LORD lives and as you live, I will not leave you." So the two of them walked on.

⁷Fifty men of the company of the prophets went and stood at a distance, facing the place where Elijah and Elisha had stopped at the Jordan. ⁸Elijah took his cloak, rolled it up and struck the water with it. The water divided to the right and to the left, and the two of them crossed over on dry ground.

⁹When they had crossed, Elijah said to Elisha, "Tell me, what can I do for you before I am taken from you?"

"Let me inherit a double portion of your spirit," Elisha replied.

¹⁰"You have asked a difficult thing," Elijah said, "yet if you see me when I am taken from you, it will be yours—otherwise not."

¹¹As they were walking along and talking together, suddenly a chariot of fire and horses of fire appeared and separated the two of them, and Elijah went up to heaven in a whirlwind. ¹²Elisha saw this and cried out, "My father! My father! The chariots and horsemen of Israel!" And Elisha saw him no more. Then he took hold of his own clothes and tore them apart.

¹³He picked up the cloak that had fallen from Elijah and went back and stood on the bank of the Jordan. ¹⁴Then he took the cloak that had fallen from him and struck the water with it. "Where now is the LORD, the God of Elijah?" he asked. When he struck the water, it divided to the right and to the left, and he crossed over.

¹⁵The company of the prophets from Jericho, who were watching, said, "The spirit of Elijah is resting on Elisha." And they went to meet him and bowed to the ground before him. ¹⁶"Look," they said,

"we your servants have fifty able men. Let them go and look for your master. Perhaps the Spirit of the LORD has picked him up and set him down on some mountain or in some valley."

"No," Elisha replied, "do not send them."

[17]But they persisted until he was too ashamed to refuse. So he said, "Send them." And they sent fifty men, who searched for three days but did not find him. [18]When they returned to Elisha, who was staying in Jericho, he said to them, "Didn't I tell you not to go?"

Healing of the Water

[19]The men of the city said to Elisha, "Look, our lord, this town is well situated, as you can see, but the water is bad and the land is unproductive."

[20]"Bring me a new bowl," he said, "and put salt in it." So they brought it to him.

[21]Then he went out to the spring and threw the salt into it, saying, "This is what the LORD says: 'I have healed this water. Never again will it cause death or make the land unproductive.' " [22]And the water has remained wholesome to this day, according to the word Elisha had spoken.

Elisha Is Jeered

[23]From there Elisha went up to Bethel. As he was walking along the road, some youths came out of the town and jeered at him. "Go on up, you baldhead!" they said. "Go on up, you baldhead!" [24]He turned around, looked at them and called down a curse on them in the name of the LORD. Then two bears came out of the woods and mauled forty-two of the youths. [25]And he went on to Mount Carmel and from there returned to Samaria.

Moab Revolts

3 Joram[a] son of Ahab became king of Israel in Samaria in the eighteenth year of Jehoshaphat king of Judah, and he reigned twelve years. [2]He did evil in the eyes of the LORD, but not as his father and mother had done. He got rid of the sacred stone of Baal that his father had made. [3]Nevertheless he clung to the sins of Jeroboam son of Nebat, which he had caused Israel to commit; he did not turn away from them.

[4]Now Mesha king of Moab raised sheep, and he had to supply the king of Israel with a hundred thousand lambs and with the wool of a hundred thousand rams. [5]But after Ahab died, the king of Moab rebelled against the king of Israel. [6]So at that time King Joram set out from Samaria and mobilized all Israel. [7]He also sent this message to Jehoshaphat king of Judah: "The king of Moab has rebelled against me. Will you go with me to fight against Moab?"

"I will go with you," he replied. "I am as you are, my people as your people, my horses as your horses."

[8]"By what route shall we attack?" he asked.

"Through the Desert of Edom," he answered.

[9]So the king of Israel set out with the king of Judah and the king of Edom. After a roundabout march of seven days, the army had no more water for themselves or for the animals with them.

[10]"What!" exclaimed the king of Israel. "Has the LORD called us three kings together only to hand us over to Moab?"

[11]But Jehoshaphat asked, "Is there no prophet of the LORD here, that we may inquire of the LORD through him?"

An officer of the king of Israel answered, "Elisha son of Shaphat is here. He used to pour water on the hands of Elijah.[b]"

[12]Jehoshaphat said, "The word of the LORD is with him." So the king of Israel and Jehoshaphat and the king of Edom went down to him.

[13]Elisha said to the king of Israel, "What do we have to do with each other? Go to the prophets of your father and the prophets of your mother."

"No," the king of Israel answered, "because it was the LORD who called us three kings together to hand us over to Moab."

[14]Elisha said, "As surely as the LORD Almighty lives, whom I serve, if I did not have respect for the presence of Jehoshaphat king of Judah, I would not look at you or even notice you. [15]But now bring me a harpist."

---

[a]1 Hebrew *Jehoram*, a variant of *Joram*; also in verse 6   [b]11 That is, he was Elijah's personal servant.

While the harpist was playing, the hand of the LORD came upon Elisha [16]and he said, "This is what the LORD says: Make this valley full of ditches. [17]For this is what the LORD says: You will see neither wind nor rain, yet this valley will be filled with water, and you, your cattle and your other animals will drink. [18]This is an easy thing in the eyes of the LORD; he will also hand Moab over to you. [19]You will overthrow every fortified city and every major town. You will cut down every good tree, stop up all the springs, and ruin every good field with stones."

[20]The next morning, about the time for offering the sacrifice, there it was—water flowing from the direction of Edom! And the land was filled with water.

[21]Now all the Moabites had heard that the kings had come to fight against them; so every man, young and old, who could bear arms was called up and stationed on the border. [22]When they got up early in the morning, the sun was shining on the water. To the Moabites across the way, the water looked red—like blood. [23]"That's blood!" they said. "Those kings must have fought and slaughtered each other. Now to the plunder, Moab!"

[24]But when the Moabites came to the camp of Israel, the Israelites rose up and fought them until they fled. And the Israelites invaded the land and slaughtered the Moabites. [25]They destroyed the towns, and each man threw a stone on every good field until it was covered. They stopped up all the springs and cut down every good tree. Only Kir Hareseth was left with its stones in place, but men armed with slings surrounded it and attacked it as well.

[26]When the king of Moab saw that the battle had gone against him, he took with him seven hundred swordsmen to break through to the king of Edom, but they failed. [27]Then he took his firstborn son, who was to succeed him as king, and offered him as a sacrifice on the city wall. The fury against Israel was great; they withdrew and returned to their own land.

The Widow's Oil

4 The wife of a man from the company of the prophets cried out to Elisha, "Your servant my husband is dead, and you know that he revered the LORD. But now his creditor is coming to take my two boys as his slaves."

[2]Elisha replied to her, "How can I help you? Tell me, what do you have in your house?"

"Your servant has nothing there at all," she said, "except a little oil."

[3]Elisha said, "Go around and ask all your neighbors for empty jars. Don't ask for just a few. [4]Then go inside and shut the door behind you and your sons. Pour oil into all the jars, and as each is filled, put it to one side."

[5]She left him and afterward shut the door behind her and her sons. They brought the jars to her and she kept pouring. [6]When all the jars were full, she said to her son, "Bring me another one."

But he replied, "There is not a jar left." Then the oil stopped flowing.

[7]She went and told the man of God, and he said, "Go, sell the oil and pay your debts. You and your sons can live on what is left."

The Shunammite's Son Restored to Life

[8]One day Elisha went to Shunem. And a well-to-do woman was there, who urged him to stay for a meal. So whenever he came by, he stopped there to eat. [9]She said to her husband, "I know that this man who often comes our way is a holy man of God. [10]Let's make a small room on the roof and put in it a bed and a table, a chair and a lamp for him. Then he can stay there whenever he comes to us."

[11]One day when Elisha came, he went up to his room and lay down there. [12]He said to his servant Gehazi, "Call the Shunammite." So he called her, and she stood before him. [13]Elisha said to him, "Tell her, 'You have gone to all this trouble for us. Now what can be done for you? Can we speak on your behalf to the king or the commander of the army?' "

She replied, "I have a home among my own people."

[14]"What can be done for her?" Elisha asked.

Gehazi said, "Well, she has no son and her husband is old."

[15]Then Elisha said, "Call her." So he

called her, and she stood in the doorway. [16]"About this time next year," Elisha said, "you will hold a son in your arms."

"No, my lord," she objected. "Don't mislead your servant, O man of God!"

[17]But the woman became pregnant, and the next year about that same time she gave birth to a son, just as Elisha had told her.

[18]The child grew, and one day he went out to his father, who was with the reapers. [19]"My head! My head!" he said to his father.

His father told a servant, "Carry him to his mother." [20]After the servant had lifted him up and carried him to his mother, the boy sat on her lap until noon, and then he died. [21]She went up and laid him on the bed of the man of God, then shut the door and went out.

[22]She called her husband and said, "Please send me one of the servants and a donkey so I can go to the man of God quickly and return."

[23]"Why go to him today?" he asked. "It's not the New Moon or the Sabbath."

"It's all right," she said.

[24]She saddled the donkey and said to her servant, "Lead on; don't slow down for me unless I tell you." [25]So she set out and came to the man of God at Mount Carmel.

When he saw her in the distance, the man of God said to his servant Gehazi, "Look! There's the Shunammite! [26]Run to meet her and ask her, 'Are you all right? Is your husband all right? Is your child all right?' "

"Everything is all right," she said.

[27]When she reached the man of God at the mountain, she took hold of his feet. Gehazi came over to push her away, but

Wednesday

Part of His Plan

Read 2 Kings 4:8–37

My aunt recently died of cancer, and at first I couldn't understand why God would take away someone I loved. It all seemed like a big mistake.

Don't you think the Shunammite woman in this story felt the same way when her son died? She had waited almost her whole life to have a baby, but when she finally had one, he didn't even live very long. Why would God let that happen?

What the Shunammite woman learned was that God has a purpose for everything—even her son's death. It brought her closer to God because it gave her the chance to see a miracle. She learned a lot about God's power and goodness.

My aunt's death must be part of God's master plan too, even though I'm not sure how it all fits together. I know my aunt is happier in heaven, and I know I'm learning to trust God more. He doesn't make mistakes, and he never wants to hurt me. It's my mistake when I forget that.

Amanda age 12

What about You?

❶ Have you ever asked God why he allowed something bad to happen in your life? Looking back, what did you learn from that "bad" experience?

❷ Imagine you're the Shunammite woman. Write a letter to God describing how you felt when your son died, and then write another one about how you felt when he came back to life.

❸ Ask God to give you patience when you don't understand his plan.

Turn to page 452 for your next devotion.

the man of God said, "Leave her alone! She is in bitter distress, but the LORD has hidden it from me and has not told me why."

²⁸"Did I ask you for a son, my lord?" she said. "Didn't I tell you, 'Don't raise my hopes'?"

²⁹Elisha said to Gehazi, "Tuck your cloak into your belt, take my staff in your hand and run. If you meet anyone, do not greet him, and if anyone greets you, do not answer. Lay my staff on the boy's face."

³⁰But the child's mother said, "As surely as the LORD lives and as you live, I will not leave you." So he got up and followed her.

³¹Gehazi went on ahead and laid the staff on the boy's face, but there was no sound or response. So Gehazi went back to meet Elisha and told him, "The boy has not awakened."

³²When Elisha reached the house, there was the boy lying dead on his couch. ³³He went in, shut the door on the two of them and prayed to the LORD. ³⁴Then he got on the bed and lay upon the boy, mouth to mouth, eyes to eyes, hands to hands. As he stretched himself out upon him, the boy's body grew warm. ³⁵Elisha turned away and walked back and forth in the room and then got on the bed and stretched out upon him once more. The boy sneezed seven times and opened his eyes.

³⁶Elisha summoned Gehazi and said, "Call the Shunammite." And he did. When she came, he said, "Take your son." ³⁷She came in, fell at his feet and bowed to the ground. Then she took her son and went out.

Death in the Pot

³⁸Elisha returned to Gilgal and there was a famine in that region. While the company of the prophets was meeting with him, he said to his servant, "Put on the large pot and cook some stew for these men."

³⁹One of them went out into the fields to gather herbs and found a wild vine. He gathered some of its gourds and filled the fold of his cloak. When he returned, he cut them up into the pot of stew, though no one knew what they were. ⁴⁰The stew was poured out for the men, but as they began to eat it, they cried out, "O man of God, there is death in the pot!" And they could not eat it.

⁴¹Elisha said, "Get some flour." He put it into the pot and said, "Serve it to the people to eat." And there was nothing harmful in the pot.

Feeding of a Hundred

⁴²A man came from Baal Shalishah, bringing the man of God twenty loaves of barley bread baked from the first ripe grain, along with some heads of new grain. "Give it to the people to eat," Elisha said.

⁴³"How can I set this before a hundred men?" his servant asked.

But Elisha answered, "Give it to the people to eat. For this is what the LORD says: 'They will eat and have some left over.'" ⁴⁴Then he set it before them, and they ate and had some left over, according to the word of the LORD.

Naaman Healed of Leprosy

5 Now Naaman was commander of the army of the king of Aram. He was a great man in the sight of his master and highly regarded, because through him the LORD had given victory to Aram. He was a valiant soldier, but he had leprosy.ᵃ

²Now bands from Aram had gone out and had taken captive a young girl from Israel, and she served Naaman's wife. ³She said to her mistress, "If only my master would see the prophet who is in Samaria! He would cure him of his leprosy."

⁴Naaman went to his master and told him what the girl from Israel had said. ⁵"By all means, go," the king of Aram replied. "I will send a letter to the king of Israel." So Naaman left, taking with him ten talentsᵇ of silver, six thousand shekelsᶜ of gold and ten sets of clothing. ⁶The letter that he took to the king of Israel read: "With this letter I am sending my servant Naaman to you so that you may cure him of his leprosy."

ᵃ1 The Hebrew word was used for various diseases affecting the skin—not necessarily leprosy; also in verses 3, 6, 7, 11 and 27.   ᵇ5 That is, about 750 pounds (about 340 kilograms)   ᶜ5 That is, about 150 pounds (about 70 kilograms)

⁷As soon as the king of Israel read the letter, he tore his robes and said, "Am I God? Can I kill and bring back to life? Why does this fellow send someone to me to be cured of his leprosy? See how he is trying to pick a quarrel with me!"

⁸When Elisha the man of God heard that the king of Israel had torn his robes, he sent him this message: "Why have you torn your robes? Have the man come to me and he will know that there is a prophet in Israel." ⁹So Naaman went with his horses and chariots and stopped at the door of Elisha's house. ¹⁰Elisha sent a messenger to say to him, "Go, wash yourself seven times in the Jordan, and your flesh will be restored and you will be cleansed."

¹¹But Naaman went away angry and said, "I thought that he would surely come out to me and stand and call on the name of the LORD his God, wave his hand over the spot and cure me of my leprosy. ¹²Are not Abana and Pharpar, the rivers of Damascus, better than any of the waters of Israel? Couldn't I wash in them and be cleansed?" So he turned and went off in a rage.

¹³Naaman's servants went to him and said, "My father, if the prophet had told you to do some great thing, would you not have done it? How much more, then, when he tells you, 'Wash and be cleansed'!" ¹⁴So he went down and dipped himself in the Jordan seven times, as the man of God had told him, and his flesh was restored and became clean like that of a young boy.

¹⁵Then Naaman and all his attendants went back to the man of God. He stood before him and said, "Now I know that there is no God in all the world except in Israel. Please accept now a gift from your servant."

¹⁶The prophet answered, "As surely as the LORD lives, whom I serve, I will not accept a thing." And even though Naaman urged him, he refused.

¹⁷"If you will not," said Naaman, "please let me, your servant, be given as much earth as a pair of mules can carry, for your servant will never again make burnt offerings and sacrifices to any other god but the LORD. ¹⁸But may the LORD

forgive your servant for this one thing: When my master enters the temple of Rimmon to bow down and he is leaning on my arm and I bow there also— when I bow down in the temple of Rimmon, may the LORD forgive your servant for this."

¹⁹"Go in peace," Elisha said.

After Naaman had traveled some distance, ²⁰Gehazi, the servant of Elisha the man of God, said to himself, "My master was too easy on Naaman, this Aramean, by not accepting from him what he brought. As surely as the LORD lives, I will run after him and get something from him."

²¹So Gehazi hurried after Naaman. When Naaman saw him running toward him, he got down from the chariot to meet him. "Is everything all right?" he asked.

²²"Everything is all right," Gehazi answered. "My master sent me to say, 'Two young men from the company of the prophets have just come to me from the hill country of Ephraim. Please give them a talent*a* of silver and two sets of clothing.' "

²³"By all means, take two talents," said Naaman. He urged Gehazi to accept them, and then tied up the two talents of silver in two bags, with two sets of clothing. He gave them to two of his servants, and they carried them ahead of Gehazi. ²⁴When Gehazi came to the hill, he took the things from the servants and put them away in the house. He sent the men away and they left. ²⁵Then he went in and stood before his master Elisha.

"Where have you been, Gehazi?" Elisha asked.

"Your servant didn't go anywhere," Gehazi answered.

²⁶But Elisha said to him, "Was not my spirit with you when the man got down from his chariot to meet you? Is this the time to take money, or to accept clothes, olive groves, vineyards, flocks, herds, or menservants and maidservants? ²⁷Naaman's leprosy will cling to you and to your descendants forever." Then Gehazi went from Elisha's presence and he was leprous, as white as snow.

a22 That is, about 75 pounds (about 34 kilograms)

An Axhead Floats

6 The company of the prophets said to Elisha, "Look, the place where we meet with you is too small for us. ²Let us go to the Jordan, where each of us can get a pole; and let us build a place there for us to live."

And he said, "Go."

³Then one of them said, "Won't you please come with your servants?"

"I will," Elisha replied. ⁴And he went with them.

They went to the Jordan and began to cut down trees. ⁵As one of them was cutting down a tree, the iron axhead fell into the water. "Oh, my lord," he cried out, "it was borrowed!"

⁶The man of God asked, "Where did it fall?" When he showed him the place, Elisha cut a stick and threw it there, and made the iron float. ⁷"Lift it out," he said. Then the man reached out his hand and took it.

Elisha Traps Blinded Arameans

⁸Now the king of Aram was at war with Israel. After conferring with his officers, he said, "I will set up my camp in such and such a place."

⁹The man of God sent word to the king of Israel: "Beware of passing that place, because the Arameans are going down there." ¹⁰So the king of Israel checked on the place indicated by the man of God. Time and again Elisha warned the king, so that he was on his guard in such places.

¹¹This enraged the king of Aram. He summoned his officers and demanded of them, "Will you not tell me which of us is on the side of the king of Israel?"

¹²"None of us, my lord the king," said one of his officers, "but Elisha, the prophet who is in Israel, tells the king of Israel the very words you speak in your bedroom."

¹³"Go, find out where he is," the king ordered, "so I can send men and capture him." The report came back: "He is in Dothan." ¹⁴Then he sent horses and chariots and a strong force there. They went by night and surrounded the city.

¹⁵When the servant of the man of God got up and went out early the next morning, an army with horses and chariots had surrounded the city. "Oh, my lord, what shall we do?" the servant asked.

¹⁶"Don't be afraid," the prophet answered. "Those who are with us are more than those who are with them."

¹⁷And Elisha prayed, "O LORD, open his eyes so he may see." Then the LORD opened the servant's eyes, and he looked and saw the hills full of horses and chariots of fire all around Elisha.

Big-time Trust

Huh?

2 Kings 6:17–18

This part of the Bible tells about one of the greatest heroes in the Old Testament—Elisha. He really believes in God's power. In this passage, Elisha sees an army of angels that will protect him and his servant. Then he asks God to blind the attackers. Elisha really trusted in God's awesome power.

¹⁸As the enemy came down toward him, Elisha prayed to the LORD, "Strike these people with blindness." So he struck them with blindness, as Elisha had asked.

¹⁹Elisha told them, "This is not the road and this is not the city. Follow me, and I will lead you to the man you are looking for." And he led them to Samaria.

²⁰After they entered the city, Elisha said, "LORD, open the eyes of these men so they can see." Then the LORD opened their eyes and they looked, and there they were, inside Samaria.

²¹When the king of Israel saw them, he asked Elisha, "Shall I kill them, my father? Shall I kill them?"

²²"Do not kill them," he answered. "Would you kill men you have captured with your own sword or bow? Set food and water before them so that they may eat and drink and then go back to their master." ²³So he prepared a great feast for them, and after they had finished eating and drinking, he sent them away, and they returned to their master. So the

bands from Aram stopped raiding Israel's territory.

Famine in Besieged Samaria

²⁴Some time later, Ben-Hadad king of Aram mobilized his entire army and marched up and laid siege to Samaria. ²⁵There was a great famine in the city; the siege lasted so long that a donkey's head sold for eighty shekels[a] of silver, and a quarter of a cab[b] of seed pods[c] for five shekels.[d]

²⁶As the king of Israel was passing by on the wall, a woman cried to him, "Help me, my lord the king!"

²⁷The king replied, "If the LORD does not help you, where can I get help for you? From the threshing floor? From the winepress?" ²⁸Then he asked her, "What's the matter?"

She answered, "This woman said to me, 'Give up your son so we may eat him today, and tomorrow we'll eat my son.' ²⁹So we cooked my son and ate him. The next day I said to her, 'Give up your son so we may eat him,' but she had hidden him."

³⁰When the king heard the woman's words, he tore his robes. As he went along the wall, the people looked, and there, underneath, he had sackcloth on his body. ³¹He said, "May God deal with me, be it ever so severely, if the head of Elisha son of Shaphat remains on his shoulders today!"

³²Now Elisha was sitting in his house, and the elders were sitting with him. The king sent a messenger ahead, but before he arrived, Elisha said to the elders, "Don't you see how this murderer is sending someone to cut off my head? Look, when the messenger comes, shut the door and hold it shut against him. Is not the sound of his master's footsteps behind him?"

³³While he was still talking to them, the messenger came down to him. And the king said, "This disaster is from the LORD. Why should I wait for the LORD any longer?"

7 Elisha said, "Hear the word of the LORD. This is what the LORD says: About this time tomorrow, a seah[e] of flour will sell for a shekel[f] and two seahs[g] of barley for a shekel at the gate of Samaria."

²The officer on whose arm the king was leaning said to the man of God, "Look, even if the LORD should open the floodgates of the heavens, could this happen?"

"You will see it with your own eyes," answered Elisha, "but you will not eat any of it!"

The Siege Lifted

³Now there were four men with leprosy[h] at the entrance of the city gate. They said to each other, "Why stay here until we die? ⁴If we say, 'We'll go into the city'—the famine is there, and we will die. And if we stay here, we will die. So let's go over to the camp of the Arameans and surrender. If they spare us, we live; if they kill us, then we die."

⁵At dusk they got up and went to the camp of the Arameans. When they reached the edge of the camp, not a man was there, ⁶for the Lord had caused the Arameans to hear the sound of chariots and horses and a great army, so that they said to one another, "Look, the king of Israel has hired the Hittite and Egyptian kings to attack us!" ⁷So they got up and fled in the dusk and abandoned their tents and their horses and donkeys. They left the camp as it was and ran for their lives.

⁸The men who had leprosy reached the edge of the camp and entered one of the tents. They ate and drank, and carried away silver, gold and clothes, and went off and hid them. They returned and entered another tent and took some things from it and hid them also.

⁹Then they said to each other, "We're not doing right. This is a day of good news and we are keeping it to ourselves. If we wait until daylight, punishment will overtake us. Let's go at once and report this to the royal palace."

a25 That is, about 2 pounds (about 1 kilogram)
b25 That is, probably about 1/2 pint (about 0.3 liter)　*c25* Or *of doves' dung*　*d25* That is, about 2 ounces (about 55 grams)　*e1* That is, probably about 7 quarts (about 7.3 liters); also in verses 16 and 18　*f1* That is, about 2/5 ounce (about 11 grams); also in verses 16 and 18　*g1* That is, probably about 13 quarts (about 15 liters); also in verses 16 and 18　*h3* The Hebrew word is used for various diseases affecting the skin—not necessarily leprosy; also in verse 8.

¹⁰So they went and called out to the city gatekeepers and told them, "We went into the Aramean camp and not a man was there—not a sound of anyone—only tethered horses and donkeys, and the tents left just as they were." ¹¹The gatekeepers shouted the news, and it was reported within the palace.

¹²The king got up in the night and said to his officers, "I will tell you what the Arameans have done to us. They know we are starving; so they have left the camp to hide in the countryside, thinking, 'They will surely come out, and then we will take them alive and get into the city.' "

¹³One of his officers answered, "Have some men take five of the horses that are left in the city. Their plight will be like that of all the Israelites left here—yes, they will only be like all these Israelites who are doomed. So let us send them to find out what happened."

¹⁴So they selected two chariots with their horses, and the king sent them after the Aramean army. He commanded the drivers, "Go and find out what has happened." ¹⁵They followed them as far as the Jordan, and they found the whole road strewn with the clothing and equipment the Arameans had thrown away in their headlong flight. So the messengers returned and reported to the king. ¹⁶Then the people went out and plundered the camp of the Arameans. So a seah of flour sold for a shekel, and two seahs of barley sold for a shekel, as the LORD had said.

¹⁷Now the king had put the officer on whose arm he leaned in charge of the gate, and the people trampled him in the gateway, and he died, just as the man of God had foretold when the king came down to his house. ¹⁸It happened as the man of God had said to the king: "About this time tomorrow, a seah of flour will sell for a shekel and two seahs of barley for a shekel at the gate of Samaria."

¹⁹The officer had said to the man of God, "Look, even if the LORD should open the floodgates of the heavens, could this happen?" The man of God had replied, "You will see it with your own eyes, but you will not eat any of it!" ²⁰And that is exactly what happened to him, for the people trampled him in the gateway, and he died.

The Shunammite's Land Restored

8 Now Elisha had said to the woman whose son he had restored to life, "Go away with your family and stay for a while wherever you can, because the LORD has decreed a famine in the land that will last seven years." ²The woman proceeded to do as the man of God said. She and her family went away and stayed in the land of the Philistines seven years.

³At the end of the seven years she came back from the land of the Philistines and went to the king to beg for her house and land. ⁴The king was talking to Gehazi, the servant of the man of God, and had said, "Tell me about all the great things Elisha has done." ⁵Just as Gehazi was telling the king how Elisha had restored the dead to life, the woman whose son Elisha had brought back to life came to beg the king for her house and land.

Gehazi said, "This is the woman, my lord the king, and this is her son whom Elisha restored to life." ⁶The king asked the woman about it, and she told him.

Then he assigned an official to her case and said to him, "Give back everything that belonged to her, including all the income from her land from the day she left the country until now."

Hazael Murders Ben-Hadad

⁷Elisha went to Damascus, and Ben-Hadad king of Aram was ill. When the king was told, "The man of God has come all the way up here," ⁸he said to Hazael, "Take a gift with you and go to meet the man of God. Consult the LORD through him; ask him, 'Will I recover from this illness?' "

⁹Hazael went to meet Elisha, taking with him as a gift forty camel-loads of all the finest wares of Damascus. He went in and stood before him, and said, "Your son Ben-Hadad king of Aram has sent me to ask, 'Will I recover from this illness?' "

¹⁰Elisha answered, "Go and say to him, 'You will certainly recover'; but*ᵃ* the LORD has revealed to me that he will in fact die." ¹¹He stared at him with a fixed

---

ᵃ10 The Hebrew may also be read Go and say, 'You will certainly not recover,' for.

gaze until Hazael felt ashamed. Then the man of God began to weep.

[12]"Why is my lord weeping?" asked Hazael.

"Because I know the harm you will do to the Israelites," he answered. "You will set fire to their fortified places, kill their young men with the sword, dash their little children to the ground, and rip open their pregnant women."

[13]Hazael said, "How could your servant, a mere dog, accomplish such a feat?"

"The LORD has shown me that you will become king of Aram," answered Elisha.

[14]Then Hazael left Elisha and returned to his master. When Ben-Hadad asked, "What did Elisha say to you?" Hazael replied, "He told me that you would certainly recover." [15]But the next day he took a thick cloth, soaked it in water and spread it over the king's face, so that he died. Then Hazael succeeded him as king.

Jehoram King of Judah

[16]In the fifth year of Joram son of Ahab king of Israel, when Jehoshaphat was king of Judah, Jehoram son of Jehoshaphat began his reign as king of Judah. [17]He was thirty-two years old when he became king, and he reigned in Jerusalem eight years. [18]He walked in the ways of the kings of Israel, as the house of Ahab had done, for he married a daughter of Ahab. He did evil in the eyes of the LORD. [19]Nevertheless, for the sake of his servant David, the LORD was not willing to destroy Judah. He had promised to maintain a lamp for David and his descendants forever.

[20]In the time of Jehoram, Edom rebelled against Judah and set up its own king. [21]So Jehoram[a] went to Zair with all his chariots. The Edomites surrounded him and his chariot commanders, but he rose up and broke through by night; his army, however, fled back home. [22]To this day Edom has been in rebellion against Judah. Libnah revolted at the same time.

[23]As for the other events of Jehoram's reign, and all he did, are they not written in the book of the annals of the kings of Judah? [24]Jehoram rested with his fathers and was buried with them in the City of David. And Ahaziah his son succeeded him as king.

Ahaziah King of Judah

[25]In the twelfth year of Joram son of Ahab king of Israel, Ahaziah son of Jehoram king of Judah began to reign. [26]Ahaziah was twenty-two years old when he became king, and he reigned in Jerusalem one year. His mother's name was Athaliah, a granddaughter of Omri king of Israel. [27]He walked in the ways of the house of Ahab and did evil in the eyes of the LORD, as the house of Ahab had done, for he was related by marriage to Ahab's family.

[28]Ahaziah went with Joram son of Ahab to war against Hazael king of Aram at Ramoth Gilead. The Arameans wounded Joram; [29]so King Joram returned to Jezreel to recover from the wounds the Arameans had inflicted on him at Ramoth[b] in his battle with Hazael king of Aram.

Then Ahaziah son of Jehoram king of Judah went down to Jezreel to see Joram son of Ahab, because he had been wounded.

Jehu Anointed King of Israel

9 The prophet Elisha summoned a man from the company of the prophets and said to him, "Tuck your cloak into your belt, take this flask of oil with you and go to Ramoth Gilead. [2]When you get there, look for Jehu son of Jehoshaphat, the son of Nimshi. Go to him, get him away from his companions and take him into an inner room. [3]Then take the flask and pour the oil on his head and declare, 'This is what the LORD says: I anoint you king over Israel.' Then open the door and run; don't delay!"

[4]So the young man, the prophet, went to Ramoth Gilead. [5]When he arrived, he found the army officers sitting together. "I have a message for you, commander," he said.

"For which of us?" asked Jehu.

"For you, commander," he replied.

[6]Jehu got up and went into the house.

---

[a]21 Hebrew *Joram,* a variant of *Jehoram*; also in verses 23 and 24　　[b]29 Hebrew *Ramah,* a variant of *Ramoth*

Then the prophet poured the oil on Jehu's head and declared, "This is what the LORD, the God of Israel, says: 'I anoint you king over the LORD's people Israel. ⁷You are to destroy the house of Ahab your master, and I will avenge the blood of my servants the prophets and the blood of all the LORD's servants shed by Jezebel. ⁸The whole house of Ahab will perish. I will cut off from Ahab every last male in Israel—slave or free. ⁹I will make the house of Ahab like the house of Jeroboam son of Nebat and like the house of Baasha son of Ahijah. ¹⁰As for Jezebel, dogs will devour her on the plot of ground at Jezreel, and no one will bury her.' " Then he opened the door and ran.

¹¹When Jehu went out to his fellow officers, one of them asked him, "Is everything all right? Why did this madman come to you?"

"You know the man and the sort of things he says," Jehu replied.

¹²"That's not true!" they said. "Tell us." Jehu said, "Here is what he told me: 'This is what the LORD says: I anoint you king over Israel.' "

¹³They hurried and took their cloaks and spread them under him on the bare steps. Then they blew the trumpet and shouted, "Jehu is king!"

Jehu Kills Joram and Ahaziah

¹⁴So Jehu son of Jehoshaphat, the son of Nimshi, conspired against Joram. (Now Joram and all Israel had been defending Ramoth Gilead against Hazael king of Aram, ¹⁵but King Joram[a] had returned to Jezreel to recover from the wounds the Arameans had inflicted on him in the battle with Hazael king of Aram.) Jehu said, "If this is the way you feel, don't let anyone slip out of the city to go and tell the news in Jezreel." ¹⁶Then he got into his chariot and rode to Jezreel, because Joram was resting there and Ahaziah king of Judah had gone down to see him.

¹⁷When the lookout standing on the tower in Jezreel saw Jehu's troops approaching, he called out, "I see some troops coming."

"Get a horseman," Joram ordered. "Send him to meet them and ask, 'Do you come in peace?' "

¹⁸The horseman rode off to meet Jehu and said, "This is what the king says: 'Do you come in peace?' "

"What do you have to do with peace?" Jehu replied. "Fall in behind me."

The lookout reported, "The messenger has reached them, but he isn't coming back."

¹⁹So the king sent out a second horseman. When he came to them he said, "This is what the king says: 'Do you come in peace?' "

Jehu replied, "What do you have to do with peace? Fall in behind me."

²⁰The lookout reported, "He has reached them, but he isn't coming back either. The driving is like that of Jehu son of Nimshi—he drives like a madman."

²¹"Hitch up my chariot," Joram ordered. And when it was hitched up, Joram king of Israel and Ahaziah king of Judah rode out, each in his own chariot, to meet Jehu. They met him at the plot of ground that had belonged to Naboth the Jezreelite. ²²When Joram saw Jehu he asked, "Have you come in peace, Jehu?"

"How can there be peace," Jehu replied, "as long as all the idolatry and witchcraft of your mother Jezebel abound?"

²³Joram turned about and fled, calling out to Ahaziah, "Treachery, Ahaziah!"

²⁴Then Jehu drew his bow and shot Joram between the shoulders. The arrow pierced his heart and he slumped down in his chariot. ²⁵Jehu said to Bidkar, his chariot officer, "Pick him up and throw him on the field that belonged to Naboth the Jezreelite. Remember how you and I were riding together in chariots behind Ahab his father when the LORD made this prophecy about him: ²⁶'Yesterday I saw the blood of Naboth and the blood of his sons, declares the LORD, and I will surely make you pay for it on this plot of ground, declares the LORD.'[b] Now then, pick him up and throw him on that plot, in accordance with the word of the LORD."

²⁷When Ahaziah king of Judah saw what had happened, he fled up the road

---

[a]15 Hebrew *Jehoram*, a variant of *Joram*; also in verses 17 and 21-24   [b]26 See 1 Kings 21:19.

to Beth Haggan.ᵃ Jehu chased him, shouting, "Kill him too!" They wounded him in his chariot on the way up to Gur near Ibleam, but he escaped to Megiddo and died there. ²⁸His servants took him by chariot to Jerusalem and buried him with his fathers in his tomb in the City of David. ²⁹(In the eleventh year of Joram son of Ahab, Ahaziah had become king of Judah.)

Jezebel Killed

³⁰Then Jehu went to Jezreel. When Jezebel heard about it, she painted her eyes, arranged her hair and looked out of a window. ³¹As Jehu entered the gate, she asked, "Have you come in peace, Zimri, you murderer of your master?"ᵇ

³²He looked up at the window and called out, "Who is on my side? Who?" Two or three eunuchs looked down at him. ³³"Throw her down!" Jehu said. So they threw her down, and some of her blood spattered the wall and the horses as they trampled her underfoot.

³⁴Jehu went in and ate and drank. "Take care of that cursed woman," he said, "and bury her, for she was a king's daughter." ³⁵But when they went out to bury her, they found nothing except her skull, her feet and her hands. ³⁶They went back and told Jehu, who said, "This is the word of the LORD that he spoke through his servant Elijah the Tishbite: On the plot of ground at Jezreel dogs will devour Jezebel's flesh.ᶜ ³⁷Jezebel's body will be like refuse on the ground in the plot at Jezreel, so that no one will be able to say, 'This is Jezebel.' "

Ahab's Family Killed

10 Now there were in Samaria seventy sons of the house of Ahab. So Jehu wrote letters and sent them to Samaria: to the officials of Jezreel,ᵈ to the elders and to the guardians of Ahab's children. He said, ²"As soon as this letter reaches you, since your master's sons are with you and you have chariots and horses, a fortified city and weapons, ³choose the best and most worthy of your master's sons and set him on his father's throne. Then fight for your master's house."

⁴But they were terrified and said, "If two kings could not resist him, how can we?"

⁵So the palace administrator, the city governor, the elders and the guardians sent this message to Jehu: "We are your servants and we will do anything you say. We will not appoint anyone as king; you do whatever you think best."

⁶Then Jehu wrote them a second letter, saying, "If you are on my side and will obey me, take the heads of your master's sons and come to me in Jezreel by this time tomorrow."

Now the royal princes, seventy of them, were with the leading men of the city, who were rearing them. ⁷When the letter arrived, these men took the princes and slaughtered all seventy of them. They put their heads in baskets and sent them to Jehu in Jezreel. ⁸When the messenger arrived, he told Jehu, "They have brought the heads of the princes."

Then Jehu ordered, "Put them in two piles at the entrance of the city gate until morning."

⁹The next morning Jehu went out. He stood before all the people and said, "You are innocent. It was I who conspired against my master and killed him, but who killed all these? ¹⁰Know then, that not a word the LORD has spoken against the house of Ahab will fail. The LORD has done what he promised through his servant Elijah." ¹¹So Jehu killed everyone in Jezreel who remained of the house of Ahab, as well as all his chief men, his close friends and his priests, leaving him no survivor.

¹²Jehu then set out and went toward Samaria. At Beth Eked of the Shepherds, ¹³he met some relatives of Ahaziah king of Judah and asked, "Who are you?"

They said, "We are relatives of Ahaziah, and we have come down to greet the families of the king and of the queen mother."

¹⁴"Take them alive!" he ordered. So they took them alive and slaughtered them by the well of Beth Eked—forty-two men. He left no survivor.

ᵃ27 Or *fled by way of the garden house*   ᵇ31 Or *"Did Zimri have peace, who murdered his master?"*   ᶜ36 See 1 Kings 21:23.   ᵈ1 Hebrew; some Septuagint manuscripts and Vulgate *of the city*

[15]After he left there, he came upon Jehonadab son of Recab, who was on his way to meet him. Jehu greeted him and said, "Are you in accord with me, as I am with you?"

"I am," Jehonadab answered.

"If so," said Jehu, "give me your hand." So he did, and Jehu helped him up into the chariot. [16]Jehu said, "Come with me and see my zeal for the LORD." Then he had him ride along in his chariot.

[17]When Jehu came to Samaria, he killed all who were left there of Ahab's family; he destroyed them, according to the word of the LORD spoken to Elijah.

Ministers of Baal Killed

[18]Then Jehu brought all the people together and said to them, "Ahab served Baal a little; Jehu will serve him much. [19]Now summon all the prophets of Baal, all his ministers and all his priests. See that no one is missing, because I am going to hold a great sacrifice for Baal. Anyone who fails to come will no longer live." But Jehu was acting deceptively in order to destroy the ministers of Baal.

[20]Jehu said, "Call an assembly in honor of Baal." So they proclaimed it. [21]Then he sent word throughout Israel, and all the ministers of Baal came; not one stayed away. They crowded into the temple of Baal until it was full from one end to the other. [22]And Jehu said to the keeper of the wardrobe, "Bring robes for all the ministers of Baal." So he brought out robes for them.

[23]Then Jehu and Jehonadab son of Recab went into the temple of Baal. Jehu said to the ministers of Baal, "Look around and see that no servants of the LORD are here with you—only ministers of Baal." [24]So they went in to make sacrifices and burnt offerings. Now Jehu had posted eighty men outside with this warning: "If one of you lets any of the men I am placing in your hands escape, it will be your life for his life."

[25]As soon as Jehu had finished making the burnt offering, he ordered the guards and officers: "Go in and kill them; let no one escape." So they cut them down with the sword. The guards and officers threw the bodies out and then entered the inner shrine of the temple of Baal. [26]They brought the sacred stone out of the temple of Baal and burned it. [27]They demolished the sacred stone of Baal and tore down the temple of Baal, and people have used it for a latrine to this day.

[28]So Jehu destroyed Baal worship in Israel. [29]However, he did not turn away from the sins of Jeroboam son of Nebat, which he had caused Israel to commit—the worship of the golden calves at Bethel and Dan.

[30]The LORD said to Jehu, "Because you have done well in accomplishing what is right in my eyes and have done to the house of Ahab all I had in mind to do, your descendants will sit on the throne of Israel to the fourth generation." [31]Yet Jehu was not careful to keep the law of the LORD, the God of Israel, with all his heart. He did not turn away from the sins of Jeroboam, which he had caused Israel to commit.

[32]In those days the LORD began to reduce the size of Israel. Hazael overpowered the Israelites throughout their territory [33]east of the Jordan in all the land of Gilead (the region of Gad, Reuben and Manasseh), from Aroer by the Arnon Gorge through Gilead to Bashan.

[34]As for the other events of Jehu's reign, all he did, and all his achievements, are they not written in the book of the annals of the kings of Israel?

[35]Jehu rested with his fathers and was buried in Samaria. And Jehoahaz his son succeeded him as king. [36]The time that Jehu reigned over Israel in Samaria was twenty-eight years.

Athaliah and Joash

11 When Athaliah the mother of Ahaziah saw that her son was dead, she proceeded to destroy the whole royal family. [2]But Jehosheba, the daughter of King Jehoram[a] and sister of Ahaziah, took Joash son of Ahaziah and stole him away from among the royal princes, who were about to be murdered. She put him and his nurse in a bedroom to hide him from Athaliah; so he was not killed. [3]He remained hidden with his nurse at the temple of the LORD for six years while Athaliah ruled the land.

---

[a]2 Hebrew *Joram*, a variant of *Jehoram*

⁴In the seventh year Jehoiada sent for the commanders of units of a hundred, the Carites and the guards and had them brought to him at the temple of the LORD. He made a covenant with them and put them under oath at the temple of the LORD. Then he showed them the king's son. ⁵He commanded them, saying, "This is what you are to do: You who are in the three companies that are going on duty on the Sabbath—a third of you guarding the royal palace, ⁶a third at the Sur Gate, and a third at the gate behind the guard, who take turns guarding the temple—⁷and you who are in the other two companies that normally go off Sabbath duty are all to guard the temple for the king. ⁸Station yourselves around the king, each man with his weapon in his hand. Anyone who approaches your ranks[a] must be put to death. Stay close to the king wherever he goes."

⁹The commanders of units of a hundred did just as Jehoiada the priest ordered. Each one took his men—those who were going on duty on the Sabbath and those who were going off duty—and came to Jehoiada the priest. ¹⁰Then he gave the commanders the spears and shields that had belonged to King David and that were in the temple of the LORD. ¹¹The guards, each with his weapon in his hand, stationed themselves around the king—near the altar and the temple, from the south side to the north side of the temple.

¹²Jehoiada brought out the king's son and put the crown on him; he presented him with a copy of the covenant and proclaimed him king. They anointed him, and the people clapped their hands and shouted, "Long live the king!"

¹³When Athaliah heard the noise made by the guards and the people, she went to the people at the temple of the LORD. ¹⁴She looked and there was the king, standing by the pillar, as the custom was. The officers and the trumpeters were beside the king, and all the people of the land were rejoicing and blowing trumpets. Then Athaliah tore her robes and called out, "Treason! Treason!"

¹⁵Jehoiada the priest ordered the commanders of units of a hundred, who were in charge of the troops: "Bring her out between the ranks[b] and put to the sword anyone who follows her." For the priest had said, "She must not be put to death in the temple of the LORD." ¹⁶So they seized her as she reached the place where the horses enter the palace grounds, and there she was put to death.

¹⁷Jehoiada then made a covenant between the LORD and the king and people that they would be the LORD's people. He also made a covenant between the king and the people. ¹⁸All the people of the land went to the temple of Baal and tore it down. They smashed the altars and idols to pieces and killed Mattan the priest of Baal in front of the altars.

Then Jehoiada the priest posted guards at the temple of the LORD. ¹⁹He took with him the commanders of hundreds, the Carites, the guards and all the people of the land, and together they brought the king down from the temple of the LORD and went into the palace, entering by way of the gate of the guards. The king then took his place on the royal throne, ²⁰and all the people of the land rejoiced. And the city was quiet, because Athaliah had been slain with the sword at the palace.

²¹Joash[c] was seven years old when he began to reign.

Joash Repairs the Temple

12 In the seventh year of Jehu, Joash[d] became king, and he reigned in Jerusalem forty years. His mother's name was Zibiah; she was from Beersheba. ²Joash did what was right in the eyes of the LORD all the years Jehoiada the priest instructed him. ³The high places, however, were not removed; the people continued to offer sacrifices and burn incense there.

⁴Joash said to the priests, "Collect all the money that is brought as sacred offerings to the temple of the LORD—the money collected in the census, the money received from personal vows and the money brought voluntarily to the temple. ⁵Let every priest receive the money from one of the treasurers, and let it be used to

---

[a]8 Or *approaches the precincts*   [b]15 Or *out from the precincts*   [c]21 Hebrew *Jehoash,* a variant of *Joash*
[d]1 Hebrew *Jehoash,* a variant of *Joash*; also in verses 2, 4, 6, 7 and 18

repair whatever damage is found in the temple."

⁶But by the twenty-third year of King Joash the priests still had not repaired the temple. ⁷Therefore King Joash summoned Jehoiada the priest and the other priests and asked them, "Why aren't you repairing the damage done to the temple? Take no more money from your treasurers, but hand it over for repairing the temple." ⁸The priests agreed that they would not collect any more money from the people and that they would not repair the temple themselves.

⁹Jehoiada the priest took a chest and bored a hole in its lid. He placed it beside the altar, on the right side as one enters the temple of the LORD. The priests who guarded the entrance put into the chest all the money that was brought to the temple of the LORD. ¹⁰Whenever they saw that there was a large amount of money in the chest, the royal secretary and the high priest came, counted the money that had been brought into the temple of the LORD and put it into bags. ¹¹When the amount had been determined, they gave the money to the men appointed to supervise the work on the temple. With it they paid those who worked on the temple of the LORD—the carpenters and builders, ¹²the masons and stonecutters. They purchased timber and dressed stone for the repair of the temple of the LORD, and met all the other expenses of restoring the temple.

¹³The money brought into the temple was not spent for making silver basins, wick trimmers, sprinkling bowls, trumpets or any other articles of gold or silver for the temple of the LORD; ¹⁴it was paid to the workmen, who used it to repair the temple. ¹⁵They did not require an accounting from those to whom they gave the money to pay the workers, because they acted with complete honesty. ¹⁶The money from the guilt offerings and sin offerings was not brought into the temple of the LORD; it belonged to the priests.

¹⁷About this time Hazael king of Aram went up and attacked Gath and captured it. Then he turned to attack Jerusalem. ¹⁸But Joash king of Judah took all the sacred objects dedicated by his fathers—Jehoshaphat, Jehoram and Ahaziah, the kings of Judah—and the gifts he himself had dedicated and all the gold found in the treasuries of the temple of the LORD and of the royal palace, and he sent them to Hazael king of Aram, who then withdrew from Jerusalem.

¹⁹As for the other events of the reign of Joash, and all he did, are they not written in the book of the annals of the kings of Judah? ²⁰His officials conspired against him and assassinated him at Beth Millo, on the road down to Silla. ²¹The officials who murdered him were Jozabad son of Shimeath and Jehozabad son of Shomer. He died and was buried with his fathers in the City of David. And Amaziah his son succeeded him as king.

Jehoahaz King of Israel

13 In the twenty-third year of Joash son of Ahaziah king of Judah, Jehoahaz son of Jehu became king of Israel in Samaria, and he reigned seventeen years. ²He did evil in the eyes of the LORD by following the sins of Jeroboam son of Nebat, which he had caused Israel to commit, and he did not turn away from them. ³So the LORD's anger burned against Israel, and for a long time he kept them under the power of Hazael king of Aram and Ben-Hadad his son.

⁴Then Jehoahaz sought the LORD's favor, and the LORD listened to him, for he saw how severely the king of Aram was oppressing Israel. ⁵The LORD provided a deliverer for Israel, and they escaped from the power of Aram. So the Israelites lived in their own homes as they had before. ⁶But they did not turn away from the sins of the house of Jeroboam, which he had caused Israel to commit; they continued in them. Also, the Asherah pole*a* remained standing in Samaria.

⁷Nothing had been left of the army of Jehoahaz except fifty horsemen, ten chariots and ten thousand foot soldiers, for the king of Aram had destroyed the rest and made them like the dust at threshing time.

⁸As for the other events of the reign of Jehoahaz, all he did and his achievements, are they not written in the book

*a6 That is, a symbol of the goddess Asherah; here and elsewhere in 2 Kings

of the annals of the kings of Israel? [9]Je-
hoahaz rested with his fathers and was
buried in Samaria. And Jehoash[a] his son
succeeded him as king.

Jehoash King of Israel

[10]In the thirty-seventh year of Joash
king of Judah, Jehoash son of Jehoahaz
became king of Israel in Samaria, and he
reigned sixteen years. [11]He did evil in the
eyes of the LORD and did not turn away
from any of the sins of Jeroboam son of
Nebat, which he had caused Israel to
commit; he continued in them.

[12]As for the other events of the reign of
Jehoash, all he did and his achievements,
including his war against Amaziah king
of Judah, are they not written in the
book of the annals of the kings of Israel?
[13]Jehoash rested with his fathers, and
Jeroboam succeeded him on the throne.
Jehoash was buried in Samaria with the
kings of Israel.

[14]Now Elisha was suffering from the
illness from which he died. Jehoash king
of Israel went down to see him and wept
over him. "My father! My father!" he
cried. "The chariots and horsemen of Israel!"

[15]Elisha said, "Get a bow and some arrows," and he did so. [16]"Take the bow in
your hands," he said to the king of Israel.
When he had taken it, Elisha put his
hands on the king's hands.

[17]"Open the east window," he said, and
he opened it. "Shoot!" Elisha said, and he
shot. "The LORD's arrow of victory, the
arrow of victory over Aram!" Elisha declared. "You will completely destroy the
Arameans at Aphek."

[18]Then he said, "Take the arrows," and
the king took them. Elisha told him,
"Strike the ground." He struck it three
times and stopped. [19]The man of God was
angry with him and said, "You should
have struck the ground five or six times;
then you would have defeated Aram and
completely destroyed it. But now you
will defeat it only three times."

[20]Elisha died and was buried.

Now Moabite raiders used to enter the
country every spring. [21]Once while some
Israelites were burying a man, suddenly
they saw a band of raiders; so they threw
the man's body into Elisha's tomb. When

the body touched Elisha's bones, the man
came to life and stood up on his feet.

[22]Hazael king of Aram oppressed Israel
throughout the reign of Jehoahaz. [23]But
the LORD was gracious to them and had
compassion and showed concern for
them because of his covenant with Abraham, Isaac and Jacob. To this day he has
been unwilling to destroy them or banish
them from his presence.

[24]Hazael king of Aram died, and Ben-
Hadad his son succeeded him as king.
[25]Then Jehoash son of Jehoahaz recap-
tured from Ben-Hadad son of Hazael the
towns he had taken in battle from his father Jehoahaz. Three times Jehoash defeated him, and so he recovered the
Israelite towns.

Amaziah King of Judah

14 In the second year of Jehoash[b] son
of Jehoahaz king of Israel, Amaziah son of Joash king of Judah began to
reign. [2]He was twenty-five years old
when he became king, and he reigned
in Jerusalem twenty-nine years. His
mother's name was Jehoaddin; she was
from Jerusalem. [3]He did what was right
in the eyes of the LORD, but not as his father David had done. In everything he
followed the example of his father Joash.
[4]The high places, however, were not removed; the people continued to offer
sacrifices and burn incense there.

[5]After the kingdom was firmly in his
grasp, he executed the officials who had
murdered his father the king. [6]Yet he did
not put the sons of the assassins to death,
in accordance with what is written in the
Book of the Law of Moses where the LORD
commanded: "Fathers shall not be put to
death for their children, nor children put
to death for their fathers; each is to die
for his own sins."[c]

[7]He was the one who defeated ten
thousand Edomites in the Valley of Salt
and captured Sela in battle, calling it
Joktheel, the name it has to this day.

[8]Then Amaziah sent messengers to Jehoash son of Jehoahaz, the son of Jehu,

---

[a]9 Hebrew *Joash*, a variant of *Jehoash*; also in verses
12-14 and 25   [b]1 Hebrew *Joash*, a variant of
Jehoash; also in verses 13, 23 and 27
[c]6 Deut. 24:16

king of Israel, with the challenge: "Come, meet me face to face."

⁹But Jehoash king of Israel replied to Amaziah king of Judah: "A thistle in Lebanon sent a message to a cedar in Lebanon, 'Give your daughter to my son in marriage.' Then a wild beast in Lebanon came along and trampled the thistle underfoot. ¹⁰You have indeed defeated Edom and now you are arrogant. Glory in your victory, but stay at home! Why ask for trouble and cause your own downfall and that of Judah also?"

¹¹Amaziah, however, would not listen, so Jehoash king of Israel attacked. He and Amaziah king of Judah faced each other at Beth Shemesh in Judah. ¹²Judah was routed by Israel, and every man fled to his home. ¹³Jehoash king of Israel captured Amaziah king of Judah, the son of Joash, the son of Ahaziah, at Beth Shemesh. Then Jehoash went to Jerusalem and broke down the wall of Jerusalem from the Ephraim Gate to the Corner Gate—a section about six hundred feet long.ᵃ ¹⁴He took all the gold and silver and all the articles found in the temple of the LORD and in the treasuries of the royal palace. He also took hostages and returned to Samaria.

¹⁵As for the other events of the reign of Jehoash, what he did and his achievements, including his war against Amaziah king of Judah, are they not written in the book of the annals of the kings of Israel? ¹⁶Jehoash rested with his fathers and was buried in Samaria with the kings of Israel. And Jeroboam his son succeeded him as king.

¹⁷Amaziah son of Joash king of Judah lived for fifteen years after the death of Jehoash son of Jehoahaz king of Israel. ¹⁸As for the other events of Amaziah's reign, are they not written in the book of the annals of the kings of Judah?

¹⁹They conspired against him in Jerusalem, and he fled to Lachish, but they sent men after him to Lachish and killed him there. ²⁰He was brought back by horse and was buried in Jerusalem with his fathers, in the City of David.

²¹Then all the people of Judah took Azariah,ᵇ who was sixteen years old, and made him king in place of his father Amaziah. ²²He was the one who rebuilt Elath and restored it to Judah after Amaziah rested with his fathers.

Jeroboam II King of Israel

²³In the fifteenth year of Amaziah son of Joash king of Judah, Jeroboam son of Jehoash king of Israel became king in Samaria, and he reigned forty-one years. ²⁴He did evil in the eyes of the LORD and did not turn away from any of the sins of Jeroboam son of Nebat, which he had caused Israel to commit. ²⁵He was the one who restored the boundaries of Israel from Leboᶜ Hamath to the Sea of the Arabah,ᵈ in accordance with the word of the LORD, the God of Israel, spoken through his servant Jonah son of Amittai, the prophet from Gath Hepher.

²⁶The LORD had seen how bitterly everyone in Israel, whether slave or free, was suffering; there was no one to help them. ²⁷And since the LORD had not said he would blot out the name of Israel from under heaven, he saved them by the hand of Jeroboam son of Jehoash.

²⁸As for the other events of Jeroboam's reign, all he did, and his military achievements, including how he recovered for Israel both Damascus and Hamath, which had belonged to Yaudi,ᵉ are they not written in the book of the annals of the kings of Israel? ²⁹Jeroboam rested with his fathers, the kings of Israel. And Zechariah his son succeeded him as king.

Azariah King of Judah

15 In the twenty-seventh year of Jeroboam king of Israel, Azariah son of Amaziah king of Judah began to reign. ²He was sixteen years old when he became king, and he reigned in Jerusalem fifty-two years. His mother's name was Jecoliah; she was from Jerusalem. ³He did what was right in the eyes of the LORD, just as his father Amaziah had done. ⁴The high places, however, were not removed; the people continued to offer sacrifices and burn incense there.

⁵The LORD afflicted the king with

ᵃ13 Hebrew *four hundred cubits* (about 180 meters) ᵇ21 Also called *Uzziah* ᶜ25 Or *from the entrance to* ᵈ25 That is, the Dead Sea ᵉ28 Or *Judah*

leprosy[a] until the day he died, and he lived in a separate house.[b] Jotham the king's son had charge of the palace and governed the people of the land.

[6]As for the other events of Azariah's reign, and all he did, are they not written in the book of the annals of the kings of Judah? [7]Azariah rested with his fathers and was buried near them in the City of David. And Jotham his son succeeded him as king.

Zechariah King of Israel

[8]In the thirty-eighth year of Azariah king of Judah, Zechariah son of Jeroboam became king of Israel in Samaria, and he reigned six months. [9]He did evil in the eyes of the LORD, as his fathers had done. He did not turn away from the sins of Jeroboam son of Nebat, which he had caused Israel to commit.

[10]Shallum son of Jabesh conspired against Zechariah. He attacked him in front of the people,[c] assassinated him and succeeded him as king. [11]The other events of Zechariah's reign are written in the book of the annals of the kings of Israel. [12]So the word of the LORD spoken to Jehu was fulfilled: "Your descendants will sit on the throne of Israel to the fourth generation."[d]

Shallum King of Israel

[13]Shallum son of Jabesh became king in the thirty-ninth year of Uzziah king of Judah, and he reigned in Samaria one month. [14]Then Menahem son of Gadi went from Tirzah up to Samaria. He attacked Shallum son of Jabesh in Samaria, assassinated him and succeeded him as king.

[15]The other events of Shallum's reign, and the conspiracy he led, are written in the book of the annals of the kings of Israel.

[16]At that time Menahem, starting out from Tirzah, attacked Tiphsah and everyone in the city and its vicinity, because they refused to open their gates. He sacked Tiphsah and ripped open all the pregnant women.

Menahem King of Israel

[17]In the thirty-ninth year of Azariah king of Judah, Menahem son of Gadi became king of Israel, and he reigned in Samaria ten years. [18]He did evil in the eyes of the LORD. During his entire reign he did not turn away from the sins of Jeroboam son of Nebat, which he had caused Israel to commit.

[19]Then Pul[e] king of Assyria invaded the land, and Menahem gave him a thousand talents[f] of silver to gain his support and strengthen his own hold on the kingdom. [20]Menahem exacted this money from Israel. Every wealthy man had to contribute fifty shekels[g] of silver to be given to the king of Assyria. So the king of Assyria withdrew and stayed in the land no longer.

[21]As for the other events of Menahem's reign, and all he did, are they not written in the book of the annals of the kings of Israel? [22]Menahem rested with his fathers. And Pekahiah his son succeeded him as king.

Pekahiah King of Israel

[23]In the fiftieth year of Azariah king of Judah, Pekahiah son of Menahem became king of Israel in Samaria, and he reigned two years. [24]Pekahiah did evil in the eyes of the LORD. He did not turn away from the sins of Jeroboam son of Nebat, which he had caused Israel to commit. [25]One of his chief officers, Pekah son of Remaliah, conspired against him. Taking fifty men of Gilead with him, he assassinated Pekahiah, along with Argob and Arieh, in the citadel of the royal palace at Samaria. So Pekah killed Pekahiah and succeeded him as king.

[26]The other events of Pekahiah's reign, and all he did, are written in the book of the annals of the kings of Israel.

Pekah King of Israel

[27]In the fifty-second year of Azariah king of Judah, Pekah son of Remaliah became king of Israel in Samaria, and he reigned twenty years. [28]He did evil in the eyes of the LORD. He did not turn away

---

[a]5 The Hebrew word was used for various diseases affecting the skin—not necessarily leprosy.   [b]5 Or *in a house where he was relieved of responsibility*   [c]10 Hebrew; some Septuagint manuscripts *in Ibleam*   [d]12 2 Kings 10:30   [e]19 Also called *Tiglath-Pileser*   [f]19 That is, about 37 tons (about 34 metric tons)   [g]20 That is, about 1 1/4 pounds (about 0.6 kilogram)

from the sins of Jeroboam son of Nebat, which he had caused Israel to commit.

²⁹In the time of Pekah king of Israel, Tiglath-Pileser king of Assyria came and took Ijon, Abel Beth Maacah, Janoah, Kedesh and Hazor. He took Gilead and Galilee, including all the land of Naphtali, and deported the people to Assyria. ³⁰Then Hoshea son of Elah conspired against Pekah son of Remaliah. He attacked and assassinated him, and then succeeded him as king in the twentieth year of Jotham son of Uzziah.

³¹As for the other events of Pekah's reign, and all he did, are they not written in the book of the annals of the kings of Israel?

Jotham King of Judah

³²In the second year of Pekah son of Remaliah king of Israel, Jotham son of Uzziah king of Judah began to reign. ³³He was twenty-five years old when he became king, and he reigned in Jerusalem sixteen years. His mother's name was Jerusha daughter of Zadok. ³⁴He did what was right in the eyes of the LORD, just as his father Uzziah had done. ³⁵The high places, however, were not removed; the people continued to offer sacrifices and burn incense there. Jotham rebuilt the Upper Gate of the temple of the LORD.

³⁶As for the other events of Jotham's reign, and what he did, are they not written in the book of the annals of the kings of Judah? ³⁷(In those days the LORD began to send Rezin king of Aram and Pekah son of Remaliah against Judah.) ³⁸Jotham rested with his fathers and was buried with them in the City of David, the city of his father. And Ahaz his son succeeded him as king.

Ahaz King of Judah

16 In the seventeenth year of Pekah son of Remaliah, Ahaz son of Jotham king of Judah began to reign. ²Ahaz was twenty years old when he became king, and he reigned in Jerusalem sixteen years. Unlike David his father, he did not do what was right in the eyes of the LORD his God. ³He walked in the ways of the kings of Israel and even sacrificed his son in*a* the fire, following the detestable ways of the nations the LORD had driven out before the Israelites. ⁴He offered sacrifices and burned incense at the high places, on the hilltops and under every spreading tree.

⁵Then Rezin king of Aram and Pekah son of Remaliah king of Israel marched up to fight against Jerusalem and besieged Ahaz, but they could not overpower him. ⁶At that time, Rezin king of Aram recovered Elath for Aram by driving out the men of Judah. Edomites then moved into Elath and have lived there to this day.

⁷Ahaz sent messengers to say to Tiglath-Pileser king of Assyria, "I am your servant and vassal. Come up and save me out of the hand of the king of Aram and of the king of Israel, who are attacking me." ⁸And Ahaz took the silver and gold found in the temple of the LORD and in the treasuries of the royal palace and sent it as a gift to the king of Assyria. ⁹The king of Assyria complied by attacking Damascus and capturing it. He deported its inhabitants to Kir and put Rezin to death.

¹⁰Then King Ahaz went to Damascus to meet Tiglath-Pileser king of Assyria. He saw an altar in Damascus and sent to Uriah the priest a sketch of the altar, with detailed plans for its construction. ¹¹So Uriah the priest built an altar in accordance with all the plans that King Ahaz had sent from Damascus and finished it before King Ahaz returned. ¹²When the king came back from Damascus and saw the altar, he approached it and presented offerings*b* on it. ¹³He offered up his burnt offering and grain offering, poured out his drink offering, and sprinkled the blood of his fellowship offerings*c* on the altar. ¹⁴The bronze altar that stood before the LORD he brought from the front of the temple—from between the new altar and the temple of the LORD—and put it on the north side of the new altar.

¹⁵King Ahaz then gave these orders to Uriah the priest: "On the large new altar, offer the morning burnt offering and the evening grain offering, the king's burnt offering and his grain offering, and the burnt offering of all the people of the

---

a3 Or *even made his son pass through* *b12* Or *and went up* *c13* Traditionally *peace offerings*

Short Circuit

2 Kings 17:4 Uh, er, so . . . No, you're not mumbling. Just rattling off a few names. Check out the shortest names in the Bible:

✗ Uz and his brother Buz! (Genesis 22:21)

✗ Er (Genesis 38:2–3)

✗ Og (Deuteronomy 3:1)

✗ So (2 Kings 17:4)

✗ Ir (1 Chronicles 7:12)

The longest Bible name?
✗ Maher-Shalal-Hash-Baz (Isaiah 8:1)

land, and their grain offering and their drink offering. Sprinkle on the altar all the blood of the burnt offerings and sacrifices. But I will use the bronze altar for seeking guidance." ¹⁶And Uriah the priest did just as King Ahaz had ordered.

¹⁷King Ahaz took away the side panels and removed the basins from the movable stands. He removed the Sea from the bronze bulls that supported it and set it on a stone base. ¹⁸He took away the Sabbath canopy* that had been built at the temple and removed the royal entryway outside the temple of the LORD, in deference to the king of Assyria.

¹⁹As for the other events of the reign of Ahaz, and what he did, are they not written in the book of the annals of the kings of Judah? ²⁰Ahaz rested with his fathers and was buried with them in the City of David. And Hezekiah his son succeeded him as king.

Hoshea Last King of Israel

17 In the twelfth year of Ahaz king of Judah, Hoshea son of Elah became king of Israel in Samaria, and he reigned nine years. ²He did evil in the eyes of the LORD, but not like the kings of Israel who preceded him.

³Shalmaneser king of Assyria came up to attack Hoshea, who had been Shalmaneser's vassal and had paid him tribute. ⁴But the king of Assyria discovered that Hoshea was a traitor, for he had sent envoys to So*ᵇ* king of Egypt, and he no longer paid tribute to the king of Assyria, as he had done year by year. Therefore Shalmaneser seized him and put him in prison. ⁵The king of Assyria invaded the entire land, marched against Samaria and laid siege to it for three years. ⁶In the ninth year of Hoshea, the king of Assyria captured Samaria and deported the Israelites to Assyria. He settled them in Halah, in Gozan on the Habor River and in the towns of the Medes.

Israel Exiled Because of Sin

⁷All this took place because the Israelites had sinned against the LORD their God, who had brought them up out of Egypt from under the power of Pharaoh king of Egypt. They worshiped other gods ⁸and followed the practices of the nations the LORD had driven out before them, as well as the practices that the kings of Israel had introduced. ⁹The Israelites secretly did things against the LORD their God that were not right. From watchtower to fortified city they built themselves high places in all their towns. ¹⁰They set up sacred stones and Asherah poles on every high hill and under every spreading tree. ¹¹At every high place they burned incense, as the nations whom the LORD had driven out before them had done. They did wicked things that provoked the LORD to anger. ¹²They worshiped idols, though the LORD had said, "You shall not do this."*ᶜ* ¹³The LORD warned Israel and Judah through all his prophets and seers: "Turn from your evil ways. Observe my commands and decrees, in accordance with the entire Law that I commanded your fathers to obey and that I delivered to you through my servants the prophets."

¹⁴But they would not listen and were as stiff-necked as their fathers, who did not trust in the LORD their God. ¹⁵They re-

ª18 Or *the dais of his throne* (see Septuagint)
ᵇ4 Or *to Sais, to the; So* is possibly an abbreviation for *Osorkon.*   *ᶜ12* Exodus 20:4, 5

jected his decrees and the covenant he had made with their fathers and the warnings he had given them. They followed worthless idols and themselves became worthless. They imitated the nations around them although the LORD had ordered them, "Do not do as they do," and they did the things the LORD had forbidden them to do.

¹⁶They forsook all the commands of the LORD their God and made for themselves two idols cast in the shape of calves, and an Asherah pole. They bowed down to all the starry hosts, and they worshiped Baal. ¹⁷They sacrificed their sons and daughters in*ª* the fire. They practiced divination and sorcery and sold themselves to do evil in the eyes of the LORD, provoking him to anger.

¹⁸So the LORD was very angry with Israel and removed them from his presence. Only the tribe of Judah was left, ¹⁹and even Judah did not keep the commands of the LORD their God. They followed the practices Israel had introduced. ²⁰Therefore the LORD rejected all the people of Israel; he afflicted them and gave them into the hands of plunderers, until he thrust them from his presence.

²¹When he tore Israel away from the house of David, they made Jeroboam son of Nebat their king. Jeroboam enticed Israel away from following the LORD and caused them to commit a great sin. ²²The Israelites persisted in all the sins of Jeroboam and did not turn away from them ²³until the LORD removed them from his presence, as he had warned through all his servants the prophets. So the people of Israel were taken from their homeland into exile in Assyria, and they are still there.

Samaria Resettled

²⁴The king of Assyria brought people from Babylon, Cuthah, Avva, Hamath and Sepharvaim and settled them in the towns of Samaria to replace the Israelites. They took over Samaria and lived in its towns. ²⁵When they first lived there, they did not worship the LORD; so he sent lions among them and they killed some of the people. ²⁶It was reported to the king of Assyria: "The people you deported and resettled in the towns of Samaria do not know what the god of that country requires. He has sent lions among them, which are killing them off, because the people do not know what he requires."

²⁷Then the king of Assyria gave this order: "Have one of the priests you took captive from Samaria go back to live there and teach the people what the god of the land requires." ²⁸So one of the priests who had been exiled from Samaria came to live in Bethel and taught them how to worship the LORD.

²⁹Nevertheless, each national group made its own gods in the several towns where they settled, and set them up in the shrines the people of Samaria had made at the high places. ³⁰The men from Babylon made Succoth Benoth, the men from Cuthah made Nergal, and the men from Hamath made Ashima; ³¹the Avvites made Nibhaz and Tartak, and the Sepharvites burned their children in the fire as sacrifices to Adrammelech and Anammelech, the gods of Sepharvaim. ³²They worshiped the LORD, but they also appointed all sorts of their own people to officiate for them as priests in the shrines at the high places. ³³They worshiped the LORD, but they also served their own gods in accordance with the customs of the nations from which they had been brought.

³⁴To this day they persist in their former practices. They neither worship the LORD nor adhere to the decrees and ordinances, the laws and commands that the LORD gave the descendants of Jacob, whom he named Israel. ³⁵When the LORD made a covenant with the Israelites, he commanded them: "Do not worship any other gods or bow down to them, serve them or sacrifice to them. ³⁶But the LORD, who brought you up out of Egypt with mighty power and outstretched arm, is the one you must worship. To him you shall bow down and to him offer sacrifices. ³⁷You must always be careful to keep the decrees and ordinances, the laws and commands he wrote for you. Do not worship other gods. ³⁸Do not forget

ª17 Or They made their sons and daughters pass through

the covenant I have made with you, and do not worship other gods. [39]Rather, worship the LORD your God; it is he who will deliver you from the hand of all your enemies."

[40]They would not listen, however, but persisted in their former practices. [41]Even while these people were worshiping the LORD, they were serving their idols. To this day their children and grandchildren continue to do as their fathers did.

Hezekiah King of Judah

18 In the third year of Hoshea son of Elah king of Israel, Hezekiah son of Ahaz king of Judah began to reign. [2]He was twenty-five years old when he became king, and he reigned in Jerusalem twenty-nine years. His mother's name was Abijah[a] daughter of Zechariah. [3]He did what was right in the eyes of the LORD, just as his father David had done. [4]He removed the high places, smashed the sacred stones and cut down the Asherah poles. He broke into pieces the bronze snake Moses had made, for up to that time the Israelites had been burning incense to it. (It was called[b] Nehushtan.[c])

[5]Hezekiah trusted in the LORD, the God of Israel. There was no one like him among all the kings of Judah, either before him or after him. [6]He held fast to the LORD and did not cease to follow him; he kept the commands the LORD had given Moses. [7]And the LORD was with him; he was successful in whatever he undertook. He rebelled against the king of Assyria and did not serve him. [8]From watchtower to fortified city, he defeated the Philistines, as far as Gaza and its territory.

[9]In King Hezekiah's fourth year, which was the seventh year of Hoshea son of Elah king of Israel, Shalmaneser king of Assyria marched against Samaria and laid siege to it. [10]At the end of three years the Assyrians took it. So Samaria was captured in Hezekiah's sixth year, which was the ninth year of Hoshea king of Israel. [11]The king of Assyria deported Israel to Assyria and settled them in Halah, in Gozan on the Habor River and in towns of the Medes. [12]This happened because they had not obeyed the LORD their God, but had violated his covenant—all that Moses the servant of the LORD commanded. They neither listened to the commands nor carried them out.

[13]In the fourteenth year of King Hezekiah's reign, Sennacherib king of Assyria attacked all the fortified cities of Judah and captured them. [14]So Hezekiah king of Judah sent this message to the king of Assyria at Lachish: "I have done wrong. Withdraw from me, and I will pay whatever you demand of me." The king of Assyria exacted from Hezekiah king of Judah three hundred talents[d] of silver and thirty talents[e] of gold. [15]So Hezekiah gave him all the silver that was found in the temple of the LORD and in the treasuries of the royal palace.

[16]At this time Hezekiah king of Judah stripped off the gold with which he had covered the doors and doorposts of the temple of the LORD, and gave it to the king of Assyria.

Sennacherib Threatens Jerusalem

[17]The king of Assyria sent his supreme commander, his chief officer and his field commander with a large army, from Lachish to King Hezekiah at Jerusalem. They came up to Jerusalem and stopped at the aqueduct of the Upper Pool, on the

No Such Book, but . . .

Huh?

2 Kings 18:5–7

An old trick for pastors and youth workers is to say, "turn to Hezekiah 12." The problem is, there *is* no book of Hezekiah. All we have are a few pages about him, but he was one of the greatest kings in Israel's history. He followed God with his whole heart. He took great risks to honor God in his kingdom, even though it made some people mad. Hezekiah may not be famous or have a book of the Bible named after him, but he was a *real* believer in God.

---

[a]2 Hebrew *Abi*, a variant of *Abijah*   [b]4 Or *He called it*   [c]4 *Nehushtan* sounds like the Hebrew for *bronze* and *snake* and *unclean thing.*   [d]14 That is, about 11 tons (about 10 metric tons)   [e]14 That is, about 1 ton (about 1 metric ton)

road to the Washerman's Field. [18]They called for the king; and Eliakim son of Hilkiah the palace administrator, Shebna the secretary, and Joah son of Asaph the recorder went out to them.

[19]The field commander said to them, "Tell Hezekiah:

" 'This is what the great king, the king of Assyria, says: On what are you basing this confidence of yours? [20]You say you have strategy and military strength—but you speak only empty words. On whom are you depending, that you rebel against me? [21]Look now, you are depending on Egypt, that splintered reed of a staff, which pierces a man's hand and wounds him if he leans on it! Such is Pharaoh king of Egypt to all who depend on him. [22]And if you say to me, "We are depending on the LORD our God"—isn't he the one whose high places and altars Hezekiah removed, saying to Judah and Jerusalem, "You must worship before this altar in Jerusalem"?

[23]" 'Come now, make a bargain with my master, the king of Assyria: I will give you two thousand horses—if you can put riders on them! [24]How can you repulse one officer of the least of my master's officials, even though you are depending on Egypt for chariots and horsemen[a]? [25]Furthermore, have I come to attack and destroy this place without word from the LORD? The LORD himself told me to march against this country and destroy it.' "

[26]Then Eliakim son of Hilkiah, and Shebna and Joah said to the field commander, "Please speak to your servants in Aramaic, since we understand it. Don't speak to us in Hebrew in the hearing of the people on the wall."

[27]But the commander replied, "Was it only to your master and you that my master sent me to say these things, and not to the men sitting on the wall—who, like you, will have to eat their own filth and drink their own urine?"

[28]Then the commander stood and called out in Hebrew: "Hear the word of

the great king, the king of Assyria! [29]This is what the king says: Do not let Hezekiah deceive you. He cannot deliver you from my hand. [30]Do not let Hezekiah persuade you to trust in the LORD when he says, 'The LORD will surely deliver us; this city will not be given into the hand of the king of Assyria.'

[31]"Do not listen to Hezekiah. This is what the king of Assyria says: Make peace with me and come out to me. Then every one of you will eat from his own vine and fig tree and drink water from his own cistern, [32]until I come and take you to a land like your own, a land of grain and new wine, a land of bread and vineyards, a land of olive trees and honey. Choose life and not death!

"Do not listen to Hezekiah, for he is misleading you when he says, 'The LORD will deliver us.' [33]Has the god of any nation ever delivered his land from the hand of the king of Assyria? [34]Where are the gods of Hamath and Arpad? Where are the gods of Sepharvaim, Hena and Ivvah? Have they rescued Samaria from my hand? [35]Who of all the gods of these countries has been able to save his land from me? How then can the LORD deliver Jerusalem from my hand?"

[36]But the people remained silent and said nothing in reply, because the king had commanded, "Do not answer him."

[37]Then Eliakim son of Hilkiah the palace administrator, Shebna the secretary and Joah son of Asaph the recorder went to Hezekiah, with their clothes torn, and told him what the field commander had said.

Jerusalem's Deliverance Foretold

19 When King Hezekiah heard this, he tore his clothes and put on sackcloth and went into the temple of the LORD. [2]He sent Eliakim the palace administrator, Shebna the secretary and the leading priests, all wearing sackcloth, to the prophet Isaiah son of Amoz. [3]They told him, "This is what Hezekiah says: This day is a day of distress and rebuke and disgrace, as when children come to the point of birth and there is no strength to deliver them. [4]It may be that the LORD

[a]24 Or charioteers

your God will hear all the words of the field commander, whom his master, the king of Assyria, has sent to ridicule the living God, and that he will rebuke him for the words the LORD your God has heard. Therefore pray for the remnant that still survives.'"

⁵When King Hezekiah's officials came to Isaiah, ⁶Isaiah said to them, "Tell your master, 'This is what the LORD says: Do not be afraid of what you have heard—those words with which the underlings of the king of Assyria have blasphemed me. ⁷Listen! I am going to put such a spirit in him that when he hears a certain report, he will return to his own country, and there I will have him cut down with the sword.'"

⁸When the field commander heard that the king of Assyria had left Lachish, he withdrew and found the king fighting against Libnah.

⁹Now Sennacherib received a report that Tirhakah, the Cushite[a] king of Egypt, was marching out to fight against him. So he again sent messengers to Hezekiah with this word: ¹⁰"Say to Hezekiah king of Judah: Do not let the god you depend on deceive you when he says, 'Jerusalem will not be handed over to the king of Assyria.' ¹¹Surely you have heard what the kings of Assyria have done to all the countries, destroying them completely. And will you be delivered? ¹²Did the gods of the nations that were destroyed by my forefathers deliver them: the gods of Gozan, Haran, Rezeph and the people of Eden who were in Tel Assar? ¹³Where is the king of Hamath, the king of Arpad, the king of the city of Sepharvaim, or of Hena or Ivvah?"

Hezekiah's Prayer

¹⁴Hezekiah received the letter from the messengers and read it. Then he went up to the temple of the LORD and spread it out before the LORD. ¹⁵And Hezekiah prayed to the LORD: "O LORD, God of Israel, enthroned between the cherubim, you alone are God over all the kingdoms of the earth. You have made heaven and earth. ¹⁶Give ear, O LORD, and hear; open your eyes, O LORD, and see; listen to the words Sennacherib has sent to insult the living God.

¹⁷"It is true, O LORD, that the Assyrian kings have laid waste these nations and their lands. ¹⁸They have thrown their gods into the fire and destroyed them, for they were not gods but only wood and stone, fashioned by men's hands. ¹⁹Now, O LORD our God, deliver us from his hand, so that all kingdoms on earth may know that you alone, O LORD, are God."

Isaiah Prophesies Sennacherib's Fall

²⁰Then Isaiah son of Amoz sent a message to Hezekiah: "This is what the LORD, the God of Israel, says: I have heard your prayer concerning Sennacherib king of Assyria. ²¹This is the word that the LORD has spoken against him:

" 'The Virgin Daughter of Zion
    despises you and mocks you.
The Daughter of Jerusalem
    tosses her head as you flee.
²²Who is it you have insulted and
    blasphemed?
    Against whom have you raised your
      voice
and lifted your eyes in pride?
    Against the Holy One of Israel!
²³By your messengers
    you have heaped insults on the
      Lord.
And you have said,
    "With my many chariots
I have ascended the heights of the
      mountains,
    the utmost heights of Lebanon.
I have cut down its tallest cedars,
    the choicest of its pines.
I have reached its remotest parts,
    the finest of its forests.
²⁴I have dug wells in foreign lands
and drunk the water there.
With the soles of my feet
    I have dried up all the streams of
      Egypt."
²⁵" 'Have you not heard?
    Long ago I ordained it.
In days of old I planned it;
    now I have brought it to pass,
that you have turned fortified cities
    into piles of stone.
²⁶Their people, drained of power,
    are dismayed and put to shame.

---

[a] 9 That is, from the upper Nile region

They are like plants in the field,
　　like tender green shoots,
like grass sprouting on the roof,
　　scorched before it grows up.

²⁷ " 'But I know where you stay
　　and when you come and go
　　and how you rage against me.
²⁸ Because you rage against me
　　and your insolence has reached my
　　　　ears,
I will put my hook in your nose
　　and my bit in your mouth,
and I will make you return
　　by the way you came.'

²⁹"This will be the sign for you,
O Hezekiah:

"This year you will eat what grows by
　　itself,
　　and the second year what springs
　　　　from that.
But in the third year sow and reap,
　　plant vineyards and eat their fruit.
³⁰Once more a remnant of the house of
　　Judah
　　will take root below and bear fruit
　　　　above.
³¹For out of Jerusalem will come a
　　remnant,
　　and out of Mount Zion a band of
　　　　survivors.

The zeal of the LORD Almighty will accomplish this.

³²"Therefore this is what the LORD says
concerning the king of Assyria:

"He will not enter this city
　　or shoot an arrow here.
He will not come before it with shield
　　or build a siege ramp against it.
³³By the way that he came he will
　　　　return;
　　he will not enter this city,
　　　　declares the LORD.
³⁴I will defend this city and save it,
　　for my sake and for the sake of
　　　　David my servant."

³⁵That night the angel of the LORD went
out and put to death a hundred and
eighty-five thousand men in the Assyrian camp. When the people got up the
next morning—there were all the dead
bodies! ³⁶So Sennacherib king of Assyria

broke camp and withdrew. He returned to
Nineveh and stayed there.

³⁷One day, while he was worshiping in
the temple of his god Nisroch, his sons
Adrammelech and Sharezer cut him
down with the sword, and they escaped
to the land of Ararat. And Esarhaddon
his son succeeded him as king.

Hezekiah's Illness

20 In those days Hezekiah became ill
and was at the point of death. The
prophet Isaiah son of Amoz went to him
and said, "This is what the LORD says: Put
your house in order, because you are going to die; you will not recover."

²Hezekiah turned his face to the wall
and prayed to the LORD, ³"Remember,
O LORD, how I have walked before
you faithfully and with wholehearted
devotion and have done what is good
in your eyes." And Hezekiah wept bitterly.

⁴Before Isaiah had left the middle
court, the word of the LORD came to him:
⁵"Go back and tell Hezekiah, the leader
of my people, 'This is what the LORD, the
God of your father David, says: I have
heard your prayer and seen your tears; I
will heal you. On the third day from now
you will go up to the temple of the LORD.
⁶I will add fifteen years to your life. And
I will deliver you and this city from the
hand of the king of Assyria. I will defend
this city for my sake and for the sake of
my servant David.' "

⁷Then Isaiah said, "Prepare a poultice
of figs." They did so and applied it to the
boil, and he recovered.

⁸Hezekiah had asked Isaiah, "What will
be the sign that the LORD will heal me
and that I will go up to the temple of the
LORD on the third day from now?"

⁹Isaiah answered, "This is the LORD's
sign to you that the LORD will do what he
has promised: Shall the shadow go forward ten steps, or shall it go back ten
steps?"

¹⁰"It is a simple matter for the shadow
to go forward ten steps," said Hezekiah.
"Rather, have it go back ten steps."

¹¹Then the prophet Isaiah called upon
the LORD, and the LORD made the shadow
go back the ten steps it had gone down
on the stairway of Ahaz.

Envoys From Babylon

¹²At that time Merodach-Baladan son of Baladan king of Babylon sent Hezekiah letters and a gift, because he had heard of Hezekiah's illness. ¹³Hezekiah received the messengers and showed them all that was in his storehouses—the silver, the gold, the spices and the fine oil—his armory and everything found among his treasures. There was nothing in his palace or in all his kingdom that Hezekiah did not show them.

¹⁴Then Isaiah the prophet went to King Hezekiah and asked, "What did those men say, and where did they come from?"

"From a distant land," Hezekiah replied. "They came from Babylon."

¹⁵The prophet asked, "What did they see in your palace?"

"They saw everything in my palace," Hezekiah said. "There is nothing among my treasures that I did not show them."

¹⁶Then Isaiah said to Hezekiah, "Hear the word of the LORD: ¹⁷The time will surely come when everything in your palace, and all that your fathers have stored up until this day, will be carried off to Babylon. Nothing will be left, says the LORD. ¹⁸And some of your descendants, your own flesh and blood, that will be born to you, will be taken away, and they will become eunuchs in the palace of the king of Babylon."

¹⁹"The word of the LORD you have spoken is good," Hezekiah replied. For he thought, "Will there not be peace and security in my lifetime?"

²⁰As for the other events of Hezekiah's reign, all his achievements and how he made the pool and the tunnel by which he brought water into the city, are they not written in the book of the annals of the kings of Judah? ²¹Hezekiah rested with his fathers. And Manasseh his son succeeded him as king.

Manasseh King of Judah

21 Manasseh was twelve years old when he became king, and he reigned in Jerusalem fifty-five years. His mother's name was Hephzibah. ²He did evil in the eyes of the LORD, following the detestable practices of the nations the LORD had driven out before the Israelites. ³He rebuilt the high places his father Hezekiah had destroyed; he also erected altars to Baal and made an Asherah pole, as Ahab king of Israel had done. He bowed down to all the starry hosts and worshiped them. ⁴He built altars in the temple of the LORD, of which the LORD had said, "In Jerusalem I will put my Name." ⁵In both courts of the temple of the LORD, he built altars to all the starry hosts. ⁶He sacrificed his own son in*ᵃ* the fire, practiced sorcery and divination, and consulted mediums and spiritists. He did much evil in the eyes of the LORD, provoking him to anger.

⁷He took the carved Asherah pole he had made and put it in the temple, of which the LORD had said to David and to his son Solomon, "In this temple and in Jerusalem, which I have chosen out of all the tribes of Israel, I will put my Name forever. ⁸I will not again make the feet of the Israelites wander from the land I gave their forefathers, if only they will be careful to do everything I commanded them and will keep the whole Law that my servant Moses gave them." ⁹But the people did not listen. Manasseh led them astray, so that they did more evil than the nations the LORD had destroyed before the Israelites.

¹⁰The LORD said through his servants the prophets: ¹¹"Manasseh king of Judah has committed these detestable sins. He has done more evil than the Amorites who preceded him and has led Judah into sin with his idols. ¹²Therefore this is what the LORD, the God of Israel, says: I am going to bring such disaster on Jerusalem and Judah that the ears of everyone who hears of it will tingle. ¹³I will stretch out over Jerusalem the measuring line used against Samaria and the plumb line used against the house of Ahab. I will wipe out Jerusalem as one wipes a dish, wiping it and turning it upside down. ¹⁴I will forsake the remnant of my inheritance and hand them over to their enemies. They will be looted and plundered by all their foes, ¹⁵because they have done evil in my eyes and have provoked me to anger from the day their fore-

---

ᵃ6 Or He made his own son pass through

fathers came out of Egypt until this day."

¹⁶Moreover, Manasseh also shed so much innocent blood that he filled Jerusalem from end to end—besides the sin that he had caused Judah to commit, so that they did evil in the eyes of the LORD.

¹⁷As for the other events of Manasseh's reign, and all he did, including the sin he committed, are they not written in the book of the annals of the kings of Judah? ¹⁸Manasseh rested with his fathers and was buried in his palace garden, the garden of Uzza. And Amon his son succeeded him as king.

Amon King of Judah

¹⁹Amon was twenty-two years old when he became king, and he reigned in Jerusalem two years. His mother's name was Meshullemeth daughter of Haruz; she was from Jotbah. ²⁰He did evil in the eyes of the LORD, as his father Manasseh had done. ²¹He walked in all the ways of his father; he worshiped the idols his father had worshiped, and bowed down to them. ²²He forsook the LORD, the God of his fathers, and did not walk in the way of the LORD.

²³Amon's officials conspired against him and assassinated the king in his palace. ²⁴Then the people of the land killed all who had plotted against King Amon, and they made Josiah his son king in his place.

²⁵As for the other events of Amon's reign, and what he did, are they not written in the book of the annals of the kings of Judah? ²⁶He was buried in his grave in the garden of Uzza. And Josiah his son succeeded him as king.

The Book of the Law Found

22 Josiah was eight years old when he became king, and he reigned in Jerusalem thirty-one years. His mother's name was Jedidah daughter of Adaiah; she was from Bozkath. ²He did what was right in the eyes of the LORD and walked in all the ways of his father David, not turning aside to the right or to the left.

³In the eighteenth year of his reign, King Josiah sent the secretary, Shaphan son of Azaliah, the son of Meshullam, to the temple of the LORD. He said: ⁴"Go up to Hilkiah the high priest and have him get ready the money that has been brought into the temple of the LORD, which the doorkeepers have collected from the people. ⁵Have them entrust it to the men appointed to supervise the work on the temple. And have these men pay the workers who repair the temple of the LORD— ⁶the carpenters, the builders and the masons. Also have them purchase timber and dressed stone to repair the temple. ⁷But they need not account for the money entrusted to them, because they are acting faithfully."

⁸Hilkiah the high priest said to Shaphan the secretary, "I have found the Book of the Law in the temple of the LORD." He gave it to Shaphan, who read it. ⁹Then Shaphan the secretary went to the king and reported to him: "Your officials have paid out the money that was in the temple of the LORD and have entrusted it to the workers and supervisors at the temple." ¹⁰Then Shaphan the secretary informed the king, "Hilkiah the priest has given me a book." And Shaphan read from it in the presence of the king.

¹¹When the king heard the words of the Book of the Law, he tore his robes. ¹²He gave these orders to Hilkiah the priest, Ahikam son of Shaphan, Acbor son of Micaiah, Shaphan the secretary and Asaiah the king's attendant: ¹³"Go and inquire of the LORD for me and for the people and for all Judah about what is written in this book that has been found. Great is the LORD's anger that burns against us because our fathers have not obeyed the words of this book; they have not acted in accordance with all that is written there concerning us."

¹⁴Hilkiah the priest, Ahikam, Acbor, Shaphan and Asaiah went to speak to the prophetess Huldah, who was the wife of Shallum son of Tikvah, the son of Harhas, keeper of the wardrobe. She lived in Jerusalem, in the Second District.

¹⁵She said to them, "This is what the LORD, the God of Israel, says: Tell the man who sent you to me, ¹⁶'This is what the LORD says: I am going to bring disaster on this place and its people, according to everything written in the book the king of Judah has read. ¹⁷Because they have forsaken me and burned incense to

other gods and provoked me to anger by all the idols their hands have made,[a] my anger will burn against this place and will not be quenched.' ¹⁸Tell the king of Judah, who sent you to inquire of the LORD, 'This is what the LORD, the God of Israel, says concerning the words you heard: ¹⁹Because your heart was responsive and you humbled yourself before the LORD when you heard what I have spoken against this place and its people, that they would become accursed and laid waste, and because you tore your robes and wept in my presence, I have heard you, declares the LORD. ²⁰Therefore I will gather you to your fathers, and you will be buried in peace. Your eyes will not see all the disaster I am going to bring on this place.' "

So they took her answer back to the king.

Josiah Renews the Covenant

23 Then the king called together all the elders of Judah and Jerusalem. ²He went up to the temple of the LORD with the men of Judah, the people of Jerusalem, the priests and the prophets—all the people from the least to the greatest. He read in their hearing all the words of the Book of the Covenant, which had been found in the temple of the LORD. ³The king stood by the pillar and renewed the covenant in the presence of the LORD—to follow the LORD and keep his commands, regulations and decrees with all his heart and all his soul, thus confirming the words of the covenant written in this book. Then all the people pledged themselves to the covenant.

⁴The king ordered Hilkiah the high priest, the priests next in rank and the doorkeepers to remove from the temple of the LORD all the articles made for Baal and Asherah and all the starry hosts. He burned them outside Jerusalem in the fields of the Kidron Valley and took the ashes to Bethel. ⁵He did away with the pagan priests appointed by the kings of Judah to burn incense on the high places of the towns of Judah and on those around Jerusalem—those who burned incense to Baal, to the sun and moon, to the constellations and to all the starry hosts. ⁶He took the Asherah pole from

the temple of the LORD to the Kidron Valley outside Jerusalem and burned it there. He ground it to powder and scattered the dust over the graves of the common people. ⁷He also tore down the quarters of the male shrine prostitutes, which were in the temple of the LORD and where women did weaving for Asherah.

⁸Josiah brought all the priests from the towns of Judah and desecrated the high places, from Geba to Beersheba, where the priests had burned incense. He broke down the shrines[b] at the gates—at the entrance to the Gate of Joshua, the city governor, which is on the left of the city gate. ⁹Although the priests of the high places did not serve at the altar of the LORD in Jerusalem, they ate unleavened bread with their fellow priests.

¹⁰He desecrated Topheth, which was in the Valley of Ben Hinnom, so no one could use it to sacrifice his son or daughter in[c] the fire to Molech. ¹¹He removed from the entrance to the temple of the LORD the horses that the kings of Judah had dedicated to the sun. They were in the court near the room of an official named Nathan-Melech. Josiah then burned the chariots dedicated to the sun.

¹²He pulled down the altars the kings of Judah had erected on the roof near the upper room of Ahaz, and the altars Manasseh had built in the two courts of the temple of the LORD. He removed them from there, smashed them to pieces and threw the rubble into the Kidron Valley. ¹³The king also desecrated the high places that were east of Jerusalem on the south of the Hill of Corruption—the ones Solomon king of Israel had built for Ashtoreth the vile goddess of the Sidonians, for Chemosh the vile god of Moab, and for Molech[d] the detestable god of the people of Ammon. ¹⁴Josiah smashed the sacred stones and cut down the Asherah poles and covered the sites with human bones.

¹⁵Even the altar at Bethel, the high place made by Jeroboam son of Nebat, who had caused Israel to sin—even that altar and high place he demolished. He

---

[a]17 Or *by everything they have done*   [b]8 Or *high places*   [c]10 Or *to make his son or daughter pass through*   [d]13 Hebrew *Milcom*

burned the high place and ground it to powder, and burned the Asherah pole also. [16]Then Josiah looked around, and when he saw the tombs that were there on the hillside, he had the bones removed from them and burned on the altar to defile it, in accordance with the word of the LORD proclaimed by the man of God who foretold these things.

[17]The king asked, "What is that tombstone I see?"

The men of the city said, "It marks the tomb of the man of God who came from Judah and pronounced against the altar of Bethel the very things you have done to it."

[18]"Leave it alone," he said. "Don't let anyone disturb his bones." So they spared his bones and those of the prophet who had come from Samaria.

[19]Just as he had done at Bethel, Josiah removed and defiled all the shrines at the high places that the kings of Israel had built in the towns of Samaria that had provoked the LORD to anger. [20]Josiah slaughtered all the priests of those high places on the altars and burned human bones on them. Then he went back to Jerusalem.

[21]The king gave this order to all the people: "Celebrate the Passover to the LORD your God, as it is written in this Book of the Covenant." [22]Not since the days of the judges who led Israel, nor throughout the days of the kings of Israel and the kings of Judah, had any such Passover been observed. [23]But in the eighteenth year of King Josiah, this Passover was celebrated to the LORD in Jerusalem.

[24]Furthermore, Josiah got rid of the mediums and spiritists, the household gods, the idols and all the other detestable things seen in Judah and Jerusalem. This he did to fulfill the requirements of the law written in the book that Hilkiah the priest had discovered in the temple of the LORD. [25]Neither before nor after Josiah was there a king like him who turned to the LORD as he did—with all his heart and with all his soul and with all his strength, in accordance with all the Law of Moses.

[26]Nevertheless, the LORD did not turn away from the heat of his fierce anger, which burned against Judah because of all that Manasseh had done to provoke him to anger. [27]So the LORD said, "I will remove Judah also from my presence as I removed Israel, and I will reject Jerusalem, the city I chose, and this temple, about which I said, 'There shall my Name be.'[a]

[28]As for the other events of Josiah's reign, and all he did, are they not written in the book of the annals of the kings of Judah?

[29]While Josiah was king, Pharaoh Neco king of Egypt went up to the Euphrates River to help the king of Assyria. King Josiah marched out to meet him in battle, but Neco faced him and killed him at Megiddo. [30]Josiah's servants brought his body in a chariot from Megiddo to Jerusalem and buried him in his own tomb. And the people of the land took Jehoahaz son of Josiah and anointed him and made him king in place of his father.

Jehoahaz King of Judah

[31]Jehoahaz was twenty-three years old when he became king, and he reigned in Jerusalem three months. His mother's name was Hamutal daughter of Jeremiah; she was from Libnah. [32]He did evil in the eyes of the LORD, just as his fathers had done. [33]Pharaoh Neco put him in chains at Riblah in the land of Hamath[b] so that he might not reign in Jerusalem, and he imposed on Judah a levy of a hundred talents[c] of silver and a talent[d] of gold. [34]Pharaoh Neco made Eliakim son of Josiah king in place of his father Josiah and changed Eliakim's name to Jehoiakim. But he took Jehoahaz and carried him off to Egypt, and there he died. [35]Jehoiakim paid Pharaoh Neco the silver and gold he demanded. In order to do so, he taxed the land and exacted the silver and gold from the people of the land according to their assessments.

Jehoiakim King of Judah

[36]Jehoiakim was twenty-five years old when he became king, and he reigned in

---

[a]27 1 Kings 8:29   [b]33 Hebrew; Septuagint (see also 2 Chron. 36:3) *Neco at Riblah in Hamath removed him*   [c]33 That is, about 3 3/4 tons (about 3.4 metric tons)   [d]33 That is, about 75 pounds (about 34 kilograms)

Jerusalem eleven years. His mother's name was Zebidah daughter of Pedaiah; she was from Rumah. ³⁷And he did evil in the eyes of the LORD, just as his fathers had done.

24 During Jehoiakim's reign, Nebuchadnezzar king of Babylon invaded the land, and Jehoiakim became his vassal for three years. But then he changed his mind and rebelled against Nebuchadnezzar. ²The LORD sent Babylonian,ᵃ Aramean, Moabite and Ammonite raiders against him. He sent them to destroy Judah, in accordance with the word of the LORD proclaimed by his servants the prophets. ³Surely these things happened to Judah according to the LORD's command, in order to remove them from his presence because of the sins of Manasseh and all he had done, ⁴including the shedding of innocent blood. For he had filled Jerusalem with innocent blood, and the LORD was not willing to forgive.

⁵As for the other events of Jehoiakim's reign, and all he did, are they not written in the book of the annals of the kings of Judah? ⁶Jehoiakim rested with his fa-

thers. And Jehoiachin his son succeeded him as king.

⁷The king of Egypt did not march out from his own country again, because the king of Babylon had taken all his territory, from the Wadi of Egypt to the Euphrates River.

Jehoiachin King of Judah

⁸Jehoiachin was eighteen years old when he became king, and he reigned in Jerusalem three months. His mother's name was Nehushta daughter of Elnathan; she was from Jerusalem. ⁹He did evil in the eyes of the LORD, just as his father had done.

¹⁰At that time the officers of Nebuchadnezzar king of Babylon advanced on Jerusalem and laid siege to it, ¹¹and Nebuchadnezzar himself came up to the city while his officers were besieging it. ¹²Jehoiachin king of Judah, his mother, his attendants, his nobles and his officials all surrendered to him.

In the eighth year of the reign of the king of Babylon, he took Jehoiachin

ᵃ2 Or *Chaldean*

Thursday

Give 100 %

Read 2 Kings 23:25

Loving God the way King Josiah did isn't easy. Josiah had to take on the evil things that were happening in his whole country. I don't have a whole country to look after, thank goodness, but even changing my own life takes a lot of effort. Every day I see more ways I need to be obedient to God.

But however hard it is for me to get close to God, nothing I do could be harder than what he's already done for me. After all, he sent Jesus to die for me. When I think about it that way, I really want to love God with all my heart and soul and strength. That's the best way I know how to give back a little of the amazing love he's given me.

Karen age 12

What about You?

❶ What does it mean to be committed to God?

❷ Write down one way you need to be more obedient to God, and leave some space on the piece of paper. For the next week, give yourself a grade in that area every day.

❸ Praise God for the way you are growing in this area of your life.

Turn to page 464 for your next devotion.

prisoner. [13]As the LORD had declared, Nebuchadnezzar removed all the treasures from the temple of the LORD and from the royal palace, and took away all the gold articles that Solomon king of Israel had made for the temple of the LORD. [14]He carried into exile all Jerusalem: all the officers and fighting men, and all the craftsmen and artisans—a total of ten thousand. Only the poorest people of the land were left.

[15]Nebuchadnezzar took Jehoiachin captive to Babylon. He also took from Jerusalem to Babylon the king's mother, his wives, his officials and the leading men of the land. [16]The king of Babylon also deported to Babylon the entire force of seven thousand fighting men, strong and fit for war, and a thousand craftsmen and artisans. [17]He made Mattaniah, Jehoiachin's uncle, king in his place and changed his name to Zedekiah.

Zedekiah King of Judah

[18]Zedekiah was twenty-one years old when he became king, and he reigned in Jerusalem eleven years. His mother's name was Hamutal daughter of Jeremiah; she was from Libnah. [19]He did evil in the eyes of the LORD, just as Jehoiakim had done. [20]It was because of the LORD's anger that all this happened to Jerusalem and Judah, and in the end he thrust them from his presence.

The Fall of Jerusalem

Now Zedekiah rebelled against the king of Babylon.

25 So in the ninth year of Zedekiah's reign, on the tenth day of the tenth month, Nebuchadnezzar king of Babylon marched against Jerusalem with his whole army. He encamped outside the city and built siege works all around it. [2]The city was kept under siege until the eleventh year of King Zedekiah. [3]By the ninth day of the fourth[a] month the famine in the city had become so severe that there was no food for the people to eat. [4]Then the city wall was broken through, and the whole army fled at night through the gate between the two walls near the king's garden, though the Babylonians[b] were surrounding the city. They fled toward the Arabah,[c] [5]but the Babylonian[d]

army pursued the king and overtook him in the plains of Jericho. All his soldiers were separated from him and scattered, [6]and he was captured. He was taken to the king of Babylon at Riblah, where sentence was pronounced on him. [7]They killed the sons of Zedekiah before his eyes. Then they put out his eyes, bound him with bronze shackles and took him to Babylon.

[8]On the seventh day of the fifth month, in the nineteenth year of Nebuchadnezzar king of Babylon, Nebuzaradan commander of the imperial guard, an official of the king of Babylon, came to Jerusalem. [9]He set fire to the temple of the LORD, the royal palace and all the houses of Jerusalem. Every important building he burned down. [10]The whole Babylonian army, under the commander of the imperial guard, broke down the walls around Jerusalem. [11]Nebuzaradan the commander of the guard carried into exile the people who remained in the city, along with the rest of the populace and those who had gone over to the king of Babylon. [12]But the commander left behind some of the poorest people of the land to work the vineyards and fields.

[13]The Babylonians broke up the bronze pillars, the movable stands and the bronze Sea that were at the temple of the LORD and they carried the bronze to Babylon. [14]They also took away the pots, shovels, wick trimmers, dishes and all the bronze articles used in the temple service. [15]The commander of the imperial guard took away the censers and sprinkling bowls—all that were made of pure gold or silver.

[16]The bronze from the two pillars, the Sea and the movable stands, which Solomon had made for the temple of the LORD, was more than could be weighed. [17]Each pillar was twenty-seven feet[e] high. The bronze capital on top of one pillar was four and a half feet[f] high and was decorated with a network and pomegranates of bronze all around. The other pillar, with its network, was similar.

---

[a]3 See Jer. 52:6.   [b]4 Or *Chaldeans*; also in verses 13, 25 and 26   [c]4 Or *the Jordan Valley*   [d]5 Or *Chaldean*; also in verses 10 and 24   [e]17 Hebrew *eighteen cubits* (about 8.1 meters)   [f]17 Hebrew *three cubits* (about 1.3 meters)

¹⁸The commander of the guard took as prisoners Seraiah the chief priest, Zephaniah the priest next in rank and the three doorkeepers. ¹⁹Of those still in the city, he took the officer in charge of the fighting men and five royal advisers. He also took the secretary who was chief officer in charge of conscripting the people of the land and sixty of his men who were found in the city. ²⁰Nebuzaradan the commander took them all and brought them to the king of Babylon at Riblah. ²¹There at Riblah, in the land of Hamath, the king had them executed.

So Judah went into captivity, away from her land.

²²Nebuchadnezzar king of Babylon appointed Gedaliah son of Ahikam, the son of Shaphan, to be over the people he had left behind in Judah. ²³When all the army officers and their men heard that the king of Babylon had appointed Gedaliah as governor, they came to Gedaliah at Mizpah–Ishmael son of Nethaniah, Johanan son of Kareah, Seraiah son of Tanhumeth the Netophathite, Jaazaniah the son of the Maacathite, and their men. ²⁴Gedaliah took an oath to reassure them and their men. "Do not be afraid of the Babylonian officials," he said. "Settle

down in the land and serve the king of Babylon, and it will go well with you."

²⁵In the seventh month, however, Ishmael son of Nethaniah, the son of Elishama, who was of royal blood, came with ten men and assassinated Gedaliah and also the men of Judah and the Babylonians who were with him at Mizpah. ²⁶At this, all the people from the least to the greatest, together with the army officers, fled to Egypt for fear of the Babylonians.

Jehoiachin Released

²⁷In the thirty-seventh year of the exile of Jehoiachin king of Judah, in the year Evil-Merodach[a] became king of Babylon, he released Jehoiachin from prison on the twenty-seventh day of the twelfth month. ²⁸He spoke kindly to him and gave him a seat of honor higher than those of the other kings who were with him in Babylon. ²⁹So Jehoiachin put aside his prison clothes and for the rest of his life ate regularly at the king's table. ³⁰Day by day the king gave Jehoiachin a regular allowance as long as he lived.

ᵃ 27 Also called Amel-Marduk

1 Chronicles

START

CAST OF Characters

The Family
It's a big one! This book mentions most of the key fathers and sons from Adam to Solomon.

Saul (sawl)
Israel's first king. Not a very good one, but Ezra speaks kindly of him in this book and leaves out all the nasty stuff he did. (If you want the full story, check out 1 Samuel.)

David
He's the star of this book, Israel's second king, and the best one they ever had. He did some dumb stuff in his lifetime, but you won't read about most of it here. Ezra wants us to remember the *good* things David did. There's a lot to choose from.

David's Mighty Men
David rode with a posse of amazing fighting men. Together they took on Israel's worst enemies and whupped them good.

Solomon
(SAHL-uh-mun)
Israel's third king, David's son—a really smart guy. Professor Ezra teaches us more about Solomon in the second semester (2 Chronicles).

Here's the situation: The Jews are in big trouble because of their awful sins against God. Their country is splitting into 2 countries: Israel and Judah. But then the northern kingdom, Israel, gets wiped off the map by the Assyrians. That leaves just one country—until the Babylonians take over Judah and drag all the citizens off to Babylon. Now the surviving Jews are in detention for 70 years, waiting for a chance to go home and rebuild their country.

Ezra is one of those Jews living in Babylon. He's a good guy, and he wants to keep Jewish history and culture alive while he and his people are away from home. Most of all, he wants to remind them of their great God and all the things he's done for them. Maybe, just maybe, God will give them one more chance to build a Jewish nation dedicated to God.

Got the situation? Good. Because now you can understand what 1 and 2 Chronicles are about. These 2 books are Professor Ezra's history course for the Jews stuck in Babylon. From start to finish, Professor Ezra makes one thing clear: Israel has a *great* God. If they obey him like the heroes of their past did, they might just get a chance to rebuild their nation into something worth saving.

What's UP with That?

One of David's great accomplishments was bringing the ark of God to Jerusalem. He and the people made a big deal out of this occasion—it must have been something special. See if you can answer these ark questions. (For help, you might need to look up the passages listed in the "hints.")

1 The ark of God is . . .
a. a sacred boat Israel used to cross the Jordan River
b. a sacred chest
c. a scale model of Noah's ark
d. a small aardvark
(hint: Exodus 25:10)

2 The ark originally contained 3 things (pick 3):
a. the stone tablets containing the Ten Commandments (Testimony)
b. Elijah's bones
c. a jar of very old food
d. scale models of Noah's animals
e. paddles and life vests
f. Aaron's staff
(hints: Exodus 16:32–34; Numbers 17:8–11; Deuteronomy 10:4–5)

3 When the oxen pulling the ark cart stumble, Uzzah reaches out to steady the load. Then what happens?
a. Uzzah oozes into a big puddle
b. Uzzah sees Moses in a cloud
c. Uzzah gets a reward from David
d. Uzzah dies
(hint: 1 Chronicles 13:9–10)

4 When David brings the ark into Jerusalem, he's celebrating big-time. His wife Michal can see him from the window. She . . .
a. yells, "Honey, don't forget to stop at the store for some milk!"
b. throws a bucket of water on him
c. gets filled with hatred
d. takes a photo for the family album
(hint: 1 Chronicles 15:29)

Bonus Question: Centuries after David brought the ark to Jerusalem, it disappeared when the Babylonians destroyed the temple. Where is it now?
a. In a museum in Israel.
b. In a synagogue in Jerusalem.
c. At the bottom of the ocean in the Titanic.
d. No one knows.

Snap shots

- A bunch of sons—Israel's family tree from first human to first king *(chapters 1—9)*

- King #2—David takes the throne after Saul dies *(chapters 10—11)*

- David's posse—the mighty fighting men *(chapters 11—12)*

- Dance-o-rama—David delivers the ark. . .with singing and dancing *(chapters 13—17)*

- Big fights—the king's wartime adventures *(chapters 18—20)*

- Senseless census—Dave counts heads, then loses a few *(chapter 21)*

- Shape up—the king organizes the government in smart ways *(chapters 22—27)*

- Passing the torch—King #2 hands the country to his son Solomon *(chapters 28—29)*

correct answers: 1-b; 2-a, c, f; 3-d; 4-c; BQ-d

Historical Records From Adam to Abraham

To Noah's Sons

1 Adam, Seth, Enosh, [2]Kenan, Mahalalel, Jared, [3]Enoch, Methuselah, Lamech, Noah.

Israel's Who's Who

1 Chronicles 1:1

1 Chronicles (and 2 Chronicles too) represents a *snapshot* of history, but not a *videotape* of history. The lists in this first book were important to the Israelites because they helped people understand things about the temple and where their kings came from. They were not trying to talk about everything and everybody, just the most important stuff. Through these lists God shows that he *remembers the past*, and his work is connected to *people* from the past. God has *always* been active in the world, and he is active *now!*

[4]The sons of Noah:[a]
    Shem, Ham and Japheth.

The Japhethites

[5]The sons[b] of Japheth:
    Gomer, Magog, Madai, Javan, Tubal, Meshech and Tiras.
[6]The sons of Gomer:
    Ashkenaz, Riphath[c] and Togarmah.
[7]The sons of Javan:
    Elishah, Tarshish, the Kittim and the Rodanim.

The Hamites

[8]The sons of Ham:
    Cush, Mizraim,[d] Put and Canaan.
[9]The sons of Cush:
    Seba, Havilah, Sabta, Raamah and Sabteca.
    The sons of Raamah:
    Sheba and Dedan.
[10]Cush was the father[e] of
    Nimrod, who grew to be a mighty warrior on earth.
[11]Mizraim was the father of

the Ludites, Anamites, Lehabites, Naphtuhites, [12]Pathrusites, Casluhites (from whom the Philistines came) and Caphtorites.
[13]Canaan was the father of
    Sidon his firstborn,[f] and of the Hittites, [14]Jebusites, Amorites, Girgashites, [15]Hivites, Arkites, Sinites, [16]Arvadites, Zemarites and Hamathites.

The Semites

[17]The sons of Shem:
    Elam, Asshur, Arphaxad, Lud and Aram.
    The sons of Aram[g]:
    Uz, Hul, Gether and Meshech.
[18]Arphaxad was the father of Shelah, and Shelah the father of Eber.
[19]Two sons were born to Eber:
    One was named Peleg,[h] because in his time the earth was divided; his brother was named Joktan.
[20]Joktan was the father of
    Almodad, Sheleph, Hazarmaveth, Jerah, [21]Hadoram, Uzal, Diklah, [22]Obal,[i] Abimael, Sheba, [23]Ophir, Havilah and Jobab. All these were sons of Joktan.

[24]Shem, Arphaxad,[j] Shelah,
[25]Eber, Peleg, Reu,
[26]Serug, Nahor, Terah
[27]and Abram (that is, Abraham).

The Family of Abraham

[28]The sons of Abraham:
    Isaac and Ishmael.

Descendants of Hagar

[29]These were their descendants:
    Nebaioth the firstborn of Ishmael,

[a]4 Septuagint; Hebrew does not have *The sons of Noah:*   [b]5 *Sons* may mean *descendants* or *successors* or *nations*; also in verses 6-10, 17 and 20.   [c]6 Many Hebrew manuscripts and Vulgate (see also Septuagint and Gen. 10:3); most Hebrew manuscripts *Diphath*   [d]8 That is, Egypt; also in verse 11   [e]10 *Father* may mean *ancestor* or *predecessor* or *founder*; also in verses 11, 13, 18 and 20.   [f]13 Or *of the Sidonians, the foremost*   [g]17 One Hebrew manuscript and some Septuagint manuscripts (see also Gen. 10:23); most Hebrew manuscripts do not have this line.   [h]19 *Peleg* means *division.*   [i]22 Some Hebrew manuscripts and Syriac (see also Gen. 10:28); most Hebrew manuscripts *Ebal*   [j]24 Hebrew; some Septuagint manuscripts *Arphaxad, Cainan* (see also note at Gen. 11:10)

Kedar, Adbeel, Mibsam, ³⁰Mishma, Dumah, Massa, Hadad, Tema, ³¹Jetur, Naphish and Kedemah. These were the sons of Ishmael.

Descendants of Keturah

³²The sons born to Keturah, Abraham's concubine:
Zimran, Jokshan, Medan, Midian, Ishbak and Shuah.
The sons of Jokshan:
Sheba and Dedan.
³³The sons of Midian:
Ephah, Epher, Hanoch, Abida and Eldaah.
All these were descendants of Keturah.

Descendants of Sarah

³⁴Abraham was the father of Isaac.
The sons of Isaac:
Esau and Israel.

Esau's Sons

³⁵The sons of Esau:
Eliphaz, Reuel, Jeush, Jalam and Korah.
³⁶The sons of Eliphaz:
Teman, Omar, Zepho,ᵃ Gatam and Kenaz;
by Timna: Amalek.ᵇ
³⁷The sons of Reuel:
Nahath, Zerah, Shammah and Mizzah.

The People of Seir in Edom

³⁸The sons of Seir:
Lotan, Shobal, Zibeon, Anah, Dishon, Ezer and Dishan.
³⁹The sons of Lotan:
Hori and Homam. Timna was Lotan's sister.
⁴⁰The sons of Shobal:
Alvan,ᶜ Manahath, Ebal, Shepho and Onam.
The sons of Zibeon:
Aiah and Anah.
⁴¹The son of Anah:
Dishon.
The sons of Dishon:
Hemdan,ᵈ Eshban, Ithran and Keran.
⁴²The sons of Ezer:
Bilhan, Zaavan and Akan.ᵉ

The sons of Dishanᶠ:
Uz and Aran.

The Rulers of Edom

⁴³These were the kings who reigned in Edom before any Israelite king reignedᵍ:
Bela son of Beor, whose city was named Dinhabah.
⁴⁴When Bela died, Jobab son of Zerah from Bozrah succeeded him as king.
⁴⁵When Jobab died, Husham from the land of the Temanites succeeded him as king.
⁴⁶When Husham died, Hadad son of Bedad, who defeated Midian in the country of Moab, succeeded him as king. His city was named Avith.
⁴⁷When Hadad died, Samlah from Masrekah succeeded him as king.
⁴⁸When Samlah died, Shaul from Rehoboth on the riverʰ succeeded him as king.
⁴⁹When Shaul died, Baal-Hanan son of Acbor succeeded him as king.
⁵⁰When Baal-Hanan died, Hadad succeeded him as king. His city was named Pau,ⁱ and his wife's name was Mehetabel daughter of Matred, the daughter of Me-Zahab.
⁵¹Hadad also died.

The chiefs of Edom were:
Timna, Alvah, Jetheth, ⁵²Oholibamah, Elah, Pinon, ⁵³Kenaz, Teman, Mibzar, ⁵⁴Magdiel and Iram. These were the chiefs of Edom.

ᵃ36 Many Hebrew manuscripts, some Septuagint manuscripts and Syriac (see also Gen. 36:11); most Hebrew manuscripts *Zephi*   ᵇ36 Some Septuagint manuscripts (see also Gen. 36:12); Hebrew *Gatam, Kenaz, Timna and Amalek*   ᶜ40 Many Hebrew manuscripts and some Septuagint manuscripts (see also Gen. 36:23); most Hebrew manuscripts *Alian*   ᵈ41 Many Hebrew manuscripts and some Septuagint manuscripts (see also Gen. 36:26); most Hebrew manuscripts *Hamran*   ᵉ42 Many Hebrew and Septuagint manuscripts (see also Gen. 36:27); most Hebrew manuscripts *Zaavan, Jaakan*   ᶠ42 Hebrew *Dishon*, a variant of *Dishan*   ᵍ43 Or *before an Israelite king reigned over them*   ʰ48 Possibly the Euphrates   ⁱ50 Many Hebrew manuscripts, some Septuagint manuscripts, Vulgate and Syriac (see also Gen. 36:39); most Hebrew manuscripts *Pai*

Israel's Sons

2 These were the sons of Israel:
Reuben, Simeon, Levi, Judah,
Issachar, Zebulun, ²Dan, Joseph,
Benjamin, Naphtali, Gad and
Asher.

Judah

To Hezron's Sons

³The sons of Judah:
Er, Onan and Shelah. These three
were born to him by a Canaanite
woman, the daughter of Shua. Er,
Judah's firstborn, was wicked in
the LORD's sight; so the LORD put
him to death. ⁴Tamar, Judah's
daughter-in-law, bore him Perez
and Zerah. Judah had five sons in
all.

⁵The sons of Perez:
Hezron and Hamul.
⁶The sons of Zerah:
Zimri, Ethan, Heman, Calcol and
Darda*ᵃ*—five in all.
⁷The son of Carmi:
Achar,*ᵇ* who brought trouble on
Israel by violating the ban on tak-
ing devoted things.*ᶜ*
⁸The son of Ethan:
Azariah.
⁹The sons born to Hezron were:
Jerahmeel, Ram and Caleb.*ᵈ*

From Ram Son of Hezron

¹⁰Ram was the father of
Amminadab, and Amminadab the
father of Nahshon, the leader of
the people of Judah. ¹¹Nahshon
was the father of Salmon,*ᵉ* Salmon
the father of Boaz, ¹²Boaz the father of Obed and Obed the father
of Jesse.
¹³Jesse was the father of
Eliab his firstborn; the second son
was Abinadab, the third Shimea,
¹⁴the fourth Nethanel, the fifth
Raddai, ¹⁵the sixth Ozem and the
seventh David. ¹⁶Their sisters were
Zeruiah and Abigail. Zeruiah's
three sons were Abishai, Joab and
Asahel. ¹⁷Abigail was the mother
of Amasa, whose father was Jether the Ishmaelite.

Caleb Son of Hezron

¹⁸Caleb son of Hezron had children by
his wife Azubah (and by Jerioth).
These were her sons: Jesher, Shobab and Ardon. ¹⁹When Azubah
died, Caleb married Ephrath, who
bore him Hur. ²⁰Hur was the father
of Uri, and Uri the father of Bezalel.
²¹Later, Hezron lay with the daughter
of Makir the father of Gilead (he
had married her when he was
sixty years old), and she bore
him Segub. ²²Segub was the father
of Jair, who controlled twenty-
three towns in Gilead. ²³(But
Geshur and Aram captured Havvoth Jair,*ᶠ* as well as Kenath with
its surrounding settlements—sixty
towns.) All these were descendants of Makir the father of Gilead.
²⁴After Hezron died in Caleb Ephrathah, Abijah the wife of Hezron
bore him Ashhur the father*ᵍ* of Tekoa.

Jerahmeel Son of Hezron

²⁵The sons of Jerahmeel the firstborn
of Hezron:
Ram his firstborn, Bunah, Oren,
Ozem and*ʰ* Ahijah. ²⁶Jerahmeel
had another wife, whose name
was Atarah; she was the mother
of Onam.
²⁷The sons of Ram the firstborn of Jerahmeel:
Maaz, Jamin and Eker.
²⁸The sons of Onam:
Shammai and Jada.
The sons of Shammai:
Nadab and Abishur.
²⁹Abishur's wife was named Abihail,

*ᵃ6 Many Hebrew manuscripts, some Septuagint
manuscripts and Syriac (see also 1 Kings 4:31); most
Hebrew manuscripts Dara   ᵇ7 Achar means trouble;
Achar is called Achan in Joshua.   ᶜ7 The Hebrew
term refers to the irrevocable giving over of things
or persons to the LORD, often by totally destroying
them.   ᵈ9 Hebrew Kelubai, a variant of Caleb
ᵉ11 Septuagint (see also Ruth 4:21); Hebrew Salma
ᶠ23 Or captured the settlements of Jair   ᵍ24 Father
may mean civic leader or military leader; also in
verses 42, 45, 49-52 and possibly elsewhere.
ʰ25 Or Oren and Ozem, by*

who bore him Ahban and Molid.
30 The sons of Nadab:
Seled and Appaim. Seled died
without children.
31 The son of Appaim:
Ishi, who was the father of Sheshan.
Sheshan was the father of Ahlai.
32 The sons of Jada, Shammai's brother:
Jether and Jonathan. Jether died
without children.
33 The sons of Jonathan:
Peleth and Zaza.

These were the descendants of Jerahmeel.
34 Sheshan had no sons—only daughters.
He had an Egyptian servant
named Jarha. 35 Sheshan gave his
daughter in marriage to his servant
Jarha, and she bore him Attai.
36 Attai was the father of Nathan,
Nathan the father of Zabad,
37 Zabad the father of Ephlal,
Ephlal the father of Obed,
38 Obed the father of Jehu,
Jehu the father of Azariah,
39 Azariah the father of Helez,
Helez the father of Eleasah,
40 Eleasah the father of Sismai,
Sismai the father of Shallum,
41 Shallum the father of Jekamiah,
and Jekamiah the father of Elishama.

The Clans of Caleb

42 The sons of Caleb the brother of Jerahmeel:
Mesha his firstborn, who was the
father of Ziph, and his son Mareshah,[a] who was the father of Hebron.
43 The sons of Hebron:
Korah, Tappuah, Rekem and Shema. 44 Shema was the father of Raham, and Raham the father of
Jorkeam. Rekem was the father of
Shammai. 45 The son of Shammai
was Maon, and Maon was the father of Beth Zur.
46 Caleb's concubine Ephah was the
mother of Haran, Moza and
Gazez. Haran was the father of
Gazez.

47 The sons of Jahdai:
Regem, Jotham, Geshan, Pelet,
Ephah and Shaaph.
48 Caleb's concubine Maacah was the
mother of Sheber and Tirhanah.
49 She also gave birth to Shaaph
the father of Madmannah and to
Sheva the father of Macbenah and
Gibea. Caleb's daughter was Acsah. 50 These were the descendants
of Caleb.

The sons of Hur the firstborn of
Ephrathah:
Shobal the father of Kiriath Jearim, 51 Salma the father of Bethlehem, and Hareph the father of
Beth Gader.
52 The descendants of Shobal the father of Kiriath Jearim were:
Haroeh, half the Manahathites,
53 and the clans of Kiriath Jearim:
the Ithrites, Puthites, Shumathites
and Mishraites. From these descended the Zorathites and Eshta-
olites.
54 The descendants of Salma:
Bethlehem, the Netophathites, At-
roth Beth Joab, half the Manahathites, the Zorites, 55 and the
clans of scribes[b] who lived at Jabez: the Tirathites, Shimeathites
and Sucathites. These are the Kenites who came from Hammath,
the father of the house of Recab.[c]

The Sons of David

3 These were the sons of David born to
him in Hebron:
The firstborn was Amnon the son
of Ahinoam of Jezreel;
the second, Daniel the son of Abigail of Carmel;
2 the third, Absalom the son of Maacah daughter of Talmai king of
Geshur;
the fourth, Adonijah the son of
Haggith;
3 the fifth, Shephatiah the son of
Abital;
and the sixth, Ithream, by his wife
Eglah.

---

[a]42 The meaning of the Hebrew for this phrase is
uncertain. [b]55 Or of the Sopherites [c]55 Or father
of Beth Recab

⁴These six were born to David in Hebron, where he reigned seven years and six months.

David reigned in Jerusalem thirty-three years, ⁵and these were the children born to him there:

Shammua,ᵃ Shobab, Nathan and Solomon. These four were by Bathshebaᵇ daughter of Ammiel. ⁶There were also Ibhar, Elishua,ᶜ Eliphelet, ⁷Nogah, Nepheg, Japhia, ⁸Elishama, Eliada and Eliphelet—nine in all. ⁹All these were the sons of David, besides his sons by his concubines. And Tamar was their sister.

The Kings of Judah

¹⁰Solomon's son was Rehoboam,
Abijah his son,
Asa his son,
Jehoshaphat his son,
¹¹Jehoramᵈ his son,
Ahaziah his son,
Joash his son,
¹²Amaziah his son,
Azariah his son,
Jotham his son,
¹³Ahaz his son,
Hezekiah his son,
Manasseh his son,
¹⁴Amon his son,
Josiah his son.
¹⁵The sons of Josiah:
Johanan the firstborn,
Jehoiakim the second son,
Zedekiah the third,
Shallum the fourth.
¹⁶The successors of Jehoiakim:
Jehoiachinᵉ his son,
and Zedekiah.

The Royal Line After the Exile

¹⁷The descendants of Jehoiachin the captive:
Shealtiel his son, ¹⁸Malkiram, Pedaiah, Shenazzar, Jekamiah, Hoshama and Nedabiah.
¹⁹The sons of Pedaiah:
Zerubbabel and Shimei.
The sons of Zerubbabel:
Meshullam and Hananiah.
Shelomith was their sister.
²⁰There were also five others:
Hashubah, Ohel, Berekiah, Hasa-

diah and Jushab-Hesed.
²¹The descendants of Hananiah:
Pelatiah and Jeshaiah, and the sons of Rephaiah, of Arnan, of Obadiah and of Shecaniah.
²²The descendants of Shecaniah:
Shemaiah and his sons:
Hattush, Igal, Bariah, Neariah and Shaphat—six in all.
²³The sons of Neariah:
Elioenai, Hizkiah and Azrikam—three in all.
²⁴The sons of Elioenai:
Hodaviah, Eliashib, Pelaiah, Akkub, Johanan, Delaiah and Anani—seven in all.

Other Clans of Judah

4 The descendants of Judah:
Perez, Hezron, Carmi, Hur and Shobal.
²Reaiah son of Shobal was the father of Jahath, and Jahath the father of Ahumai and Lahad. These were the clans of the Zorathites.
³These were the sonsᶠ of Etam:
Jezreel, Ishma and Idbash. Their sister was named Hazzelelponi. ⁴Penuel was the father of Gedor, and Ezer the father of Hushah.
These were the descendants of Hur, the firstborn of Ephrathah and fatherᵍ of Bethlehem.
⁵Ashhur the father of Tekoa had two wives, Helah and Naarah.
⁶Naarah bore him Ahuzzam, Hepher, Temeni and Haahashtari. These were the descendants of Naarah.
⁷The sons of Helah:
Zereth, Zohar, Ethnan, ⁸and Koz, who was the father of Anub and Hazzobebah and of the clans of Aharhel son of Harum.

⁹Jabez was more honorable than his brothers. His mother had named him

ᵃ5 Hebrew *Shimea,* a variant of *Shammua* ᵇ5 One Hebrew manuscript and Vulgate (see also Septuagint and 2 Samuel 11:3); most Hebrew manuscripts *Bathshua* ᶜ6 Two Hebrew manuscripts (see also 2 Samuel 5:15 and 1 Chron. 14:5); most Hebrew manuscripts *Elishama* ᵈ11 Hebrew *Joram,* a variant of *Jehoram* ᵉ16 Hebrew *Jeconiah,* a variant of *Jehoiachin;* also in verse 17 ᶠ3 Some Septuagint manuscripts (see also Vulgate); Hebrew *father* ᵍ4 *Father* may mean *civic leader* or *military leader;* also in verses 12, 14, 17, 18 and possibly elsewhere.

What's in a Name?

Most folks in the Bible don't have last names. Their first name is their only name, so it's got to say a lot. Oftentimes a person's name described something significant—a character trait, a physical distinction or a hope his or her parents had. And some names were better than others:

Esau means "hairy." He's furrier than his twin brother Jacob, so it was easy to remember who was who: Harry is the hairy one. That's not a big deal till his nearly-blind dad Isaac gives the inheritance to Esau's smooth-skinned brother Jacob, who just happens to be wearing a hairy costume (Genesis 25:25, page 34).

Delilah probably means "weak, delicate." It's another good name gone bad. After Delilah gives Samson a haircut, he probably wanted to call her something else—because "Ms. Weak & Delicate" helps to defeat Israel's original tough guy (Judges 16, page 293).

Mahlon and Kilion mean "weakling" and "weary." These are the names of Naomi's 2 sons. The 2 kids grow up, get married and then die. By the way, Weakling's widow is Ruth; she does better with her next husband (Ruth 1:5).

Absalom means "father of peace." A good name, but this particular Absalom never quite lives up to it: He kills his half brother, tries to steal Israel from his dad King David, and dies unhappily in an oak tree (2 Samuel 13—18, page 362).

Jabez means "pain." His mom gives him that name because it's the sensation she most remembers from the childbirth. It's a tough name to live down. Jabez prays that God would not give him pain—God grants his request (1 Chronicles 4:9–10).

Maher-Shalal-Hash-Baz means "quick to the plunder, swift to the spoil." God tells the prophet Isaiah to give his son that name. The kid becomes a kind of political alarm clock, because God says that before he can say "Ma ma" and "Da da," Assyria will plunder Israel (Isaiah 8:1–4, page 807).

Jabez,[a] saying, "I gave birth to him in pain." [10]Jabez cried out to the God of Israel, "Oh, that you would bless me and enlarge my territory! Let your hand be with me, and keep me from harm so that I will be free from pain." And God granted his request.

[11]Kelub, Shuhah's brother, was the father of Mehir, who was the father of Eshton. [12]Eshton was the father of Beth Rapha, Paseah and Tehinnah the father of Ir Nahash.[b] These were the men of Recah.

[13]The sons of Kenaz:
Othniel and Seraiah.
The sons of Othniel:
Hathath and Meonothai.[c] [14]Meonothai was the father of Ophrah.
Seraiah was the father of Joab, the father of Ge Harashim.[d] It was called this because its people were craftsmen.

[15]The sons of Caleb son of Jephunneh:
Iru, Elah and Naam.
The son of Elah:
Kenaz.
[16]The sons of Jehallelel:
Ziph, Ziphah, Tiria and Asarel.
[17]The sons of Ezrah:
Jether, Mered, Epher and Jalon. One of Mered's wives gave birth to Miriam, Shammai and Ishbah the father of Eshtemoa. [18](His Judean wife gave birth to Jered the father of Gedor, Heber the father of Soco, and Jekuthiel the father of Zanoah.) These were the children of Pharaoh's daughter Bithiah, whom Mered had married.

[a]9 Jabez sounds like the Hebrew for pain. [b]12 Or of the city of Nahash [c]13 Some Septuagint manuscripts and Vulgate; Hebrew does not have and Meonothai. [d]14 Ge Harashim means valley of craftsmen.

¹⁹The sons of Hodiah's wife, the sister of Naham:
> the father of Keilah the Garmite, and Eshtemoa the Maacathite.

²⁰The sons of Shimon:
> Amnon, Rinnah, Ben-Hanan and Tilon.

The descendants of Ishi:
> Zoheth and Ben-Zoheth.

²¹The sons of Shelah son of Judah:
> Er the father of Lecah, Laadah the father of Mareshah and the clans of the linen workers at Beth Ashbea, ²²Jokim, the men of Cozeba, and Joash and Saraph, who ruled in Moab and Jashubi Lehem. (These records are from ancient times.) ²³They were the potters who lived at Netaim and Gederah; they stayed there and worked for the king.

Simeon

²⁴The descendants of Simeon:
> Nemuel, Jamin, Jarib, Zerah and Shaul;
²⁵Shallum was Shaul's son, Mibsam his son and Mishma his son.
²⁶The descendants of Mishma:
> Hammuel his son, Zaccur his son and Shimei his son.

²⁷Shimei had sixteen sons and six daughters, but his brothers did not have many children; so their entire clan did not become as numerous as the people of Judah. ²⁸They lived in Beersheba, Moladah, Hazar Shual, ²⁹Bilhah, Ezem, Tolad, ³⁰Bethuel, Hormah, Ziklag, ³¹Beth Marcaboth, Hazar Susim, Beth Biri and Shaaraim. These were their towns until the reign of David. ³²Their surrounding villages were Etam, Ain, Rimmon, Token and Ashan—five towns— ³³and all the villages around these towns as far as Baalath.ᵃ These were their settlements. And they kept a genealogical record.

³⁴Meshobab, Jamlech, Joshah son of Amaziah, ³⁵Joel, Jehu son of Joshibiah, the son of Seraiah, the son of Asiel, ³⁶also Elioenai, Jaakobah, Jeshohaiah, Asaiah, Adiel, Jesimiel, Benaiah, ³⁷and Ziza son of Shiphi, the son of Allon, the son of Jedaiah, the son of Shimri, the son of Shemaiah.

³⁸The men listed above by name were leaders of their clans. Their families increased greatly, ³⁹and they went to the outskirts of Gedor to the east of the valley in search of pasture for their flocks. ⁴⁰They found rich, good pasture, and the land was spacious, peaceful and quiet. Some Hamites had lived there formerly.

⁴¹The men whose names were listed came in the days of Hezekiah king of Judah. They attacked the Hamites in their dwellings and also the Meunites who were there and completely destroyedᵇ them, as is evident to this day. Then they settled in their place, because there was pasture for their flocks. ⁴²And five hundred of these Simeonites, led by Pelatiah, Neariah, Rephaiah and Uzziel, the sons of Ishi, invaded the hill country of Seir. ⁴³They killed the remaining Amalekites who had escaped, and they have lived there to this day.

Reuben

5 The sons of Reuben the firstborn of Israel (he was the firstborn, but when he defiled his father's marriage bed, his rights as firstborn were given to the sons of Joseph son of Israel; so he could not be listed in the genealogical record in accordance with his birthright, ²and though Judah was the strongest of his brothers and a ruler came from him, the rights of the firstborn belonged to Joseph)— ³the sons of Reuben the firstborn of Israel:
> Hanoch, Pallu, Hezron and Carmi.

⁴The descendants of Joel:
> Shemaiah his son, Gog his son, Shimei his son, ⁵Micah his son, Reaiah his son, Baal his son, ⁶and Beerah his son, whom Tiglath-Pileserᶜ king of Assyria took into exile. Beerah was a leader of the Reubenites.

⁷Their relatives by clans, listed

ᵃ33 Some Septuagint manuscripts (see also Joshua 19:8); Hebrew *Baal*   ᵇ41 The Hebrew term refers to the irrevocable giving over of things or persons to the LORD, often by totally destroying them.
ᶜ6 Hebrew *Tilgath-Pilneser*, a variant of *Tiglath-Pileser*; also in verse 26

according to their genealogical records:

Jeiel the chief, Zechariah, ⁸and Bela son of Azaz, the son of Shema, the son of Joel. They settled in the area from Aroer to Nebo and Baal Meon. ⁹To the east they occupied the land up to the edge of the desert that extends to the Euphrates River, because their livestock had increased in Gilead.

¹⁰During Saul's reign they waged war against the Hagrites, who were defeated at their hands; they occupied the dwellings of the Hagrites throughout the entire region east of Gilead.

Gad

¹¹The Gadites lived next to them in Bashan, as far as Salecah:

¹²Joel was the chief, Shapham the second, then Janai and Shaphat, in Bashan.

¹³Their relatives, by families, were:

Michael, Meshullam, Sheba, Jorai, Jacan, Zia and Eber—seven in all.

¹⁴These were the sons of Abihail son of Huri, the son of Jaroah, the son of Gilead, the son of Michael, the son of Jeshishai, the son of Jahdo, the son of Buz.

¹⁵Ahi son of Abdiel, the son of Guni, was head of their family.

¹⁶The Gadites lived in Gilead, in Bashan and its outlying villages, and on all the pasturelands of Sharon as far as they extended.

¹⁷All these were entered in the genealogical records during the reigns of Jotham king of Judah and Jeroboam king of Israel.

Fri day

Looking Inside Out

Read 1 Chronicles 5:24–25

I couldn't believe it. I turned on the TV and found out my favorite actor was dead. I'd always thought this guy had everything going for him. He seemed so cool, so fun, like he didn't have any problems. But when he died, all the news stories and interviews with his friends made it clear that he was a pretty unhappy, messed-up guy. And I never would have guessed it.

Just because someone *looks* like they've got a great life, it doesn't mean they do. And just because somebody makes it big on the social scene, it doesn't mean they've got it all together. That doesn't just apply to celebrities. Sometimes I get worried about what people think of me. I want them to like me, to think I'm cool. So I get caught up in how I look from the outside. But that really doesn't matter as much as what's going on inside me. If I don't have a strong relationship with God, it doesn't matter if other people think I'm cool or popular. The only thing that matters is staying true to God and living my life for him.

Lauren age 15

What about You?

❶ Think about some of the people the world considers successful. What do you really know about these people? How have they earned success?

❷ Think of people who have personal qualities you admire. How can you develop those traits in yourself?

❸ Ask God to help you see people as they really are. Ask him to bring positive role models into your life.

Turn to page 471 for your next devotion.

¹⁸The Reubenites, the Gadites and the half-tribe of Manasseh had 44,760 men ready for military service—able-bodied men who could handle shield and sword, who could use a bow, and who were trained for battle. ¹⁹They waged war against the Hagrites, Jetur, Naphish and Nodab. ²⁰They were helped in fighting them, and God handed the Hagrites and all their allies over to them, because they cried out to him during the battle. He answered their prayers, because they trusted in him. ²¹They seized the livestock of the Hagrites—fifty thousand camels, two hundred fifty thousand sheep and two thousand donkeys. They also took one hundred thousand people captive, ²²and many others fell slain, because the battle was God's. And they occupied the land until the exile.

The Half-Tribe of Manasseh

²³The people of the half-tribe of Manasseh were numerous; they settled in the land from Bashan to Baal Hermon, that is, to Senir (Mount Hermon).

²⁴These were the heads of their families: Epher, Ishi, Eliel, Azriel, Jeremiah, Hodaviah and Jahdiel. They were brave warriors, famous men, and heads of their families. ²⁵But they were unfaithful to the God of their fathers and prostituted themselves to the gods of the peoples of the land, whom God had destroyed before them. ²⁶So the God of Israel stirred up the spirit of Pul king of Assyria (that is, Tiglath-Pileser king of Assyria), who took the Reubenites, the Gadites and the half-tribe of Manasseh into exile. He took them to Halah, Habor, Hara and the river of Gozan, where they are to this day.

Levi

6 The sons of Levi:
Gershon, Kohath and Merari.
²The sons of Kohath:
Amram, Izhar, Hebron and Uzziel.
³The children of Amram:
Aaron, Moses and Miriam.
The sons of Aaron:
Nadab, Abihu, Eleazar and Ithamar.
⁴Eleazar was the father of Phinehas,

Phinehas the father of Abishua,
⁵Abishua the father of Bukki,
Bukki the father of Uzzi,
⁶Uzzi the father of Zerahiah,
Zerahiah the father of Meraioth,
⁷Meraioth the father of Amariah,
Amariah the father of Ahitub,
⁸Ahitub the father of Zadok,
Zadok the father of Ahimaaz,
⁹Ahimaaz the father of Azariah,
Azariah the father of Johanan,
¹⁰Johanan the father of Azariah (it was he who served as priest in the temple Solomon built in Jerusalem),
¹¹Azariah the father of Amariah,
Amariah the father of Ahitub,
¹²Ahitub the father of Zadok,
Zadok the father of Shallum,
¹³Shallum the father of Hilkiah,
Hilkiah the father of Azariah,
¹⁴Azariah the father of Seraiah,
and Seraiah the father of Jehozadak.
¹⁵Jehozadak was deported when the LORD sent Judah and Jerusalem into exile by the hand of Nebuchadnezzar.

¹⁶The sons of Levi:
Gershon,ᵃ Kohath and Merari.
¹⁷These are the names of the sons of Gershon:
Libni and Shimei.
¹⁸The sons of Kohath:
Amram, Izhar, Hebron and Uzziel.
¹⁹The sons of Merari:
Mahli and Mushi.
These are the clans of the Levites listed according to their fathers:
²⁰Of Gershon:
Libni his son, Jehath his son,
Zimmah his son, ²¹Joah his son,
Iddo his son, Zerah his son
and Jeatherai his son.
²²The descendants of Kohath:
Amminadab his son, Korah his son,
Assir his son, ²³Elkanah his son,
Ebiasaph his son, Assir his son,
²⁴Tahath his son, Uriel his son,
Uzziah his son and Shaul his son.

ᵃ16 Hebrew *Gershom,* a variant of *Gershon*; also in verses 17, 20, 43, 62 and 71

25 The descendants of Elkanah:
   Amasai, Ahimoth,
26 Elkanah his son,[a] Zophai his son,
   Nahath his son, 27 Eliab his son,
   Jeroham his son, Elkanah his son
   and Samuel his son.[b]
28 The sons of Samuel:
   Joel[c] the firstborn
   and Abijah the second son.
29 The descendants of Merari:
   Mahli, Libni his son,
   Shimei his son, Uzzah his son,
30 Shimea his son, Haggiah his son
   and Asaiah his son.

The Temple Musicians

31 These are the men David put in
charge of the music in the house of the
LORD after the ark came to rest there.
32 They ministered with music before the
tabernacle, the Tent of Meeting, until
Solomon built the temple of the LORD in
Jerusalem. They performed their duties
according to the regulations laid down
for them.
33 Here are the men who served, together with their sons:
   From the Kohathites:
   Heman, the musician,
      the son of Joel, the son of Samuel,
34 the son of Elkanah, the son of Jeroham,
      the son of Eliel, the son of Toah,
35 the son of Zuph, the son of Elkanah,
      the son of Mahath, the son of
      Amasai,
36 the son of Elkanah, the son of
   Joel,
      the son of Azariah, the son of
      Zephaniah,
37 the son of Tahath, the son of Assir,
      the son of Ebiasaph, the son of
      Korah,
38 the son of Izhar, the son of Kohath,
      the son of Levi, the son of Israel;
39 and Heman's associate Asaph, who
   served at his right hand:
   Asaph son of Berekiah, the son of
   Shimea,
40 the son of Michael, the son of
   Baaseiah,[d]
      the son of Malkijah, 41 the son of

Ethni,
   the son of Zerah, the son of Adaiah,
42 the son of Ethan, the son of Zimmah,
   the son of Shimei, 43 the son of Jahath,
   the son of Gershon, the son of
   Levi;
44 and from their associates, the Merarites, at his left hand:
   Ethan son of Kishi, the son of
   Abdi,
   the son of Malluch, 45 the son of
   Hashabiah,
   the son of Amaziah, the son of
   Hilkiah,
46 the son of Amzi, the son of Bani,
   the son of Shemer, 47 the son of
   Mahli,
   the son of Mushi, the son of Merari,
   the son of Levi.

48 Their fellow Levites were assigned to
all the other duties of the tabernacle, the
house of God. 49 But Aaron and his descendants were the ones who presented
offerings on the altar of burnt offering
and on the altar of incense in connection
with all that was done in the Most Holy
Place, making atonement for Israel, in
accordance with all that Moses the servant of God had commanded.

50 These were the descendants of Aaron:
   Eleazar his son, Phinehas his son,
   Abishua his son, 51 Bukki his son,
   Uzzi his son, Zerahiah his son,
52 Meraioth his son, Amariah his
   son,
   Ahitub his son, 53 Zadok his son
   and Ahimaaz his son.

54 These were the locations of their
settlements allotted as their territory

---

a 26 Some Hebrew manuscripts, Septuagint and
Syriac; most Hebrew manuscripts *Ahimoth* 26 *and
Elkanah. The sons of Elkanah:*   b 27 Some
Septuagint manuscripts (see also 1 Samuel 1:19,20
and 1 Chron. 6:33,34); Hebrew does not have *and
Samuel his son.*   c 28 Some Septuagint manuscripts
and Syriac (see also 1 Samuel 8:2 and 1 Chron.
6:33); Hebrew does not have *Joel.*   d 40 Most
Hebrew manuscripts; some Hebrew manuscripts,
one Septuagint manuscript and Syriac *Maaseiah*

(they were assigned to the descendants of Aaron who were from the Kohathite clan, because the first lot was for them):

⁵⁵They were given Hebron in Judah with its surrounding pasturelands. ⁵⁶But the fields and villages around the city were given to Caleb son of Jephunneh.

⁵⁷So the descendants of Aaron were given Hebron (a city of refuge), and Libnah,ᵃ Jattir, Eshtemoa, ⁵⁸Hilen, Debir, ⁵⁹Ashan, Juttahᵇ and Beth Shemesh, together with their pasturelands. ⁶⁰And from the tribe of Benjamin they were given Gibeon,ᶜ Geba, Alemeth and Anathoth, together with their pasturelands.

These towns, which were distributed among the Kohathite clans, were thirteen in all.

⁶¹The rest of Kohath's descendants were allotted ten towns from the clans of half the tribe of Manasseh.

⁶²The descendants of Gershon, clan by clan, were allotted thirteen towns from the tribes of Issachar, Asher and Naphtali, and from the part of the tribe of Manasseh that is in Bashan.

⁶³The descendants of Merari, clan by clan, were allotted twelve towns from the tribes of Reuben, Gad and Zebulun.

⁶⁴So the Israelites gave the Levites these towns and their pasturelands. ⁶⁵From the tribes of Judah, Simeon and Benjamin they allotted the previously named towns.

⁶⁶Some of the Kohathite clans were given as their territory towns from the tribe of Ephraim.

⁶⁷In the hill country of Ephraim they were given Shechem (a city of refuge), and Gezer,ᵈ ⁶⁸Jokmeam, Beth Horon, ⁶⁹Aijalon and Gath Rimmon, together with their pasturelands.

⁷⁰And from half the tribe of Manasseh the Israelites gave Aner and Bileam, together with their pasturelands, to the rest of the Kohathite clans.

⁷¹The Gershonites received the following:

From the clan of the half-tribe of Manasseh

they received Golan in Bashan and also Ashtaroth, together with their pasturelands;

⁷²from the tribe of Issachar they received Kedesh, Daberath, ⁷³Ramoth and Anem, together with their pasturelands;

⁷⁴from the tribe of Asher they received Mashal, Abdon, ⁷⁵Hukok and Rehob, together with their pasturelands;

⁷⁶and from the tribe of Naphtali they received Kedesh in Galilee, Hammon and Kiriathaim, together with their pasturelands.

⁷⁷The Merarites (the rest of the Levites) received the following:

From the tribe of Zebulun they received Jokneam, Kartah,ᵉ Rimmono and Tabor, together with their pasturelands;

⁷⁸from the tribe of Reuben across the Jordan east of Jericho they received Bezer in the desert, Jahzah, ⁷⁹Kedemoth and Mephaath, together with their pasturelands;

⁸⁰and from the tribe of Gad they received Ramoth in Gilead, Mahanaim, ⁸¹Heshbon and Jazer, together with their pasturelands.

Issachar

7 The sons of Issachar:
Tola, Puah, Jashub and Shimron—four in all.

²The sons of Tola:
Uzzi, Rephaiah, Jeriel, Jahmai, Ibsam and Samuel—heads of their families. During the reign of David, the descendants of Tola listed as fighting men in their genealogy numbered 22,600.

³The son of Uzzi:
Izrahiah.

The sons of Izrahiah:
Michael, Obadiah, Joel and Isshiah.

ᵃ57 See Joshua 21:13; Hebrew *given the cities of refuge: Hebron, Libnah.*   ᵇ59 Syriac (see also Septuagint and Joshua 21:16); Hebrew does not have *Juttah.*   ᶜ60 See Joshua 21:17; Hebrew does not have *Gibeon.*   ᵈ67 See Joshua 21:21; Hebrew *given the cities of refuge: Shechem, Gezer.*   ᵉ77 See Septuagint and Joshua 21:34; Hebrew does not have *Jokneam, Kartah.*

All five of them were chiefs. ⁴According to their family genealogy, they had 36,000 men ready for battle, for they had many wives and children.

⁵The relatives who were fighting men belonging to all the clans of Issachar, as listed in their genealogy, were 87,000 in all.

Benjamin

⁶Three sons of Benjamin:
Bela, Beker and Jediael.

⁷The sons of Bela:
Ezbon, Uzzi, Uzziel, Jerimoth and Iri, heads of families—five in all. Their genealogical record listed 22,034 fighting men.

⁸The sons of Beker:
Zemirah, Joash, Eliezer, Elioenai, Omri, Jeremoth, Abijah, Anathoth and Alemeth. All these were the sons of Beker. ⁹Their genealogical record listed the heads of families and 20,200 fighting men.

¹⁰The son of Jediael:
Bilhan.

The sons of Bilhan:
Jeush, Benjamin, Ehud, Kenaanah, Zethan, Tarshish and Ahishahar. ¹¹All these sons of Jediael were heads of families. There were 17,200 fighting men ready to go out to war.

¹²The Shuppites and Huppites were the descendants of Ir, and the Hushites the descendants of Aher.

Naphtali

¹³The sons of Naphtali:
Jahziel, Guni, Jezer and Shillemᵃ—the descendants of Bilhah.

Manasseh

¹⁴The descendants of Manasseh:
Asriel was his descendant through his Aramean concubine. She gave birth to Makir the father of Gilead. ¹⁵Makir took a wife from among the Huppites and Shuppites. His sister's name was Maacah.

Another descendant was named Zelophehad, who had only daughters.

¹⁶Makir's wife Maacah gave birth to a son and named him Peresh. His brother was named Sheresh, and his sons were Ulam and Rakem.

¹⁷The son of Ulam:
Bedan.

These were the sons of Gilead son of Makir, the son of Manasseh. ¹⁸His sister Hammoleketh gave birth to Ishhod, Abiezer and Mahlah.

¹⁹The sons of Shemida were:
Ahian, Shechem, Likhi and Aniam.

Ephraim

²⁰The descendants of Ephraim:
Shuthelah, Bered his son,
Tahath his son, Eleadah his son,
Tahath his son, ²¹Zabad his son
and Shuthelah his son.

Ezer and Elead were killed by the native-born men of Gath, when they went down to seize their livestock. ²²Their father Ephraim mourned for them many days, and his relatives came to comfort him. ²³Then he lay with his wife again, and she became pregnant and gave birth to a son. He named him Beriah,ᵇ because there had been misfortune in his family. ²⁴His daughter was Sheerah, who built Lower and Upper Beth Horon as well as Uzzen Sheerah.

²⁵Rephah was his son, Resheph his son,ᶜ
Telah his son, Tahan his son,
²⁶Ladan his son, Ammihud his son,
Elishama his son, ²⁷Nun his son
and Joshua his son.

²⁸Their lands and settlements included Bethel and its surrounding villages, Naaran to the east, Gezer and its villages to the west, and Shechem and its villages all the way to Ayyah and its villages. ²⁹Along the borders of Manasseh were Beth Shan, Taanach, Megiddo and Dor, together with their villages. The descendants of Joseph son of Israel lived in these towns.

ᵃ13 Some Hebrew and Septuagint manuscripts (see also Gen. 46:24 and Num. 26:49); most Hebrew manuscripts *Shallum*   ᵇ23 *Beriah* sounds like the Hebrew for *misfortune.*   ᶜ25 Some Septuagint manuscripts; Hebrew does not have *his son.*

Asher

30 The sons of Asher:

Imnah, Ishvah, Ishvi and Beriah.
Their sister was Serah.

31 The sons of Beriah:

Heber and Malkiel, who was the
father of Birzaith.

32 Heber was the father of Japhlet,
Shomer and Hotham and of their
sister Shua.

33 The sons of Japhlet:

Pasach, Bimhal and Ashvath.
These were Japhlet's sons.

34 The sons of Shomer:

Ahi, Rohgah,[a] Hubbah and Aram.

35 The sons of his brother Helem:

Zophah, Imna, Shelesh and Amal.

36 The sons of Zophah:

Suah, Harnepher, Shual, Beri, Im-
rah, 37 Bezer, Hod, Shamma, Shil-
shah, Ithran[b] and Beera.

38 The sons of Jether:

Jephunneh, Pispah and Ara.

39 The sons of Ulla:

Arah, Hanniel and Rizia.

40 All these were descendants of Asher—heads of families, choice men, brave
warriors and outstanding leaders. The
number of men ready for battle, as listed
in their genealogy, was 26,000.

The Genealogy of Saul the Benjamite

8 Benjamin was the father of Bela his
firstborn,

Ashbel the second son, Aharah
the third,

2 Nohah the fourth and Rapha the
fifth.

3 The sons of Bela were:

Addar, Gera, Abihud,[c] 4 Abishua,
Naaman, Ahoah, 5 Gera, Shephu-
phan and Huram.

6 These were the descendants of Ehud,
who were heads of families of
those living in Geba and were deported to Manahath:

7 Naaman, Ahijah, and Gera, who
deported them and who was the
father of Uzza and Ahihud.

8 Sons were born to Shaharaim in
Moab after he had divorced his
wives Hushim and Baara. 9 By his
wife Hodesh he had Jobab, Zibia,
Mesha, Malcam, 10 Jeuz, Sakia and
Mirmah. These were his sons,
heads of families. 11 By Hushim he
had Abitub and Elpaal.

12 The sons of Elpaal:

Eber, Misham, Shemed (who built
Ono and Lod with its surrounding
villages), 13 and Beriah and Shema,
who were heads of families of
those living in Aijalon and who
drove out the inhabitants of Gath.

14 Ahio, Shashak, Jeremoth, 15 Zebadiah, Arad, Eder, 16 Michael, Ish-
pah and Joha were the sons of
Beriah.

17 Zebadiah, Meshullam, Hizki, Heber,
18 Ishmerai, Izliah and Jobab were
the sons of Elpaal.

19 Jakim, Zicri, Zabdi, 20 Elienai, Zillethai, Eliel, 21 Adaiah, Beraiah and
Shimrath were the sons of Shimei.

22 Ishpan, Eber, Eliel, 23 Abdon, Zicri,
Hanan, 24 Hananiah, Elam, Antho-
thijah, 25 Iphdeiah and Penuel were
the sons of Shashak.

26 Shamsherai, Shehariah, Athaliah,
27 Jaareshiah, Elijah and Zicri were
the sons of Jeroham.

28 All these were heads of families,
chiefs as listed in their genealogy, and
they lived in Jerusalem.

29 Jeiel[d] the father[e] of Gibeon lived in
Gibeon.

His wife's name was Maacah,
30 and his firstborn son was Abdon, followed by Zur, Kish, Baal,
Ner,[f] Nadab, 31 Gedor, Ahio, Zeker
32 and Mikloth, who was the father
of Shimeah. They too lived near
their relatives in Jerusalem.

33 Ner was the father of Kish, Kish the
father of Saul, and Saul the father
of Jonathan, Malki-Shua, Abinadab and Esh-Baal.[g]

34 The son of Jonathan:

Merib-Baal,[h] who was the father
of Micah.

35 The sons of Micah:

---

a 34 Or *of his brother Shomer: Rohgah*   b 37 Possibly
a variant of *Jether*   c 3 Or *Gera the father of Ehud*
d 29 Some Septuagint manuscripts (see also 1 Chron.
9:35); Hebrew does not have *Jeiel.*   e 29 *Father* may
mean *civic leader* or *military leader.*   f 30 Some
Septuagint manuscripts (see also 1 Chron. 9:36);
Hebrew does not have *Ner.*   g 33 Also known as *Ish-
Bosheth*   h 34 Also known as *Mephibosheth*

Pithon, Melech, Tarea and Ahaz.
³⁶Ahaz was the father of Jehoaddah, Jehoaddah was the father of Alemeth, Azmaveth and Zimri, and Zimri was the father of Moza. ³⁷Moza was the father of Binea; Raphah was his son, Eleasah his son and Azel his son.
³⁸Azel had six sons, and these were their names:
Azrikam, Bokeru, Ishmael, Sheariah, Obadiah and Hanan. All these were the sons of Azel.
³⁹The sons of his brother Eshek:
Ulam his firstborn, Jeush the second son and Eliphelet the third. ⁴⁰The sons of Ulam were brave warriors who could handle the bow. They had many sons and grandsons—150 in all.
All these were the descendants of Benjamin.

9 All Israel was listed in the genealogies recorded in the book of the kings of Israel.

The People in Jerusalem

The people of Judah were taken captive to Babylon because of their unfaithfulness. ²Now the first to resettle on their own property in their own towns were some Israelites, priests, Levites and temple servants.

³Those from Judah, from Benjamin, and from Ephraim and Manasseh who lived in Jerusalem were:
⁴Uthai son of Ammihud, the son of Omri, the son of Imri, the son of Bani, a descendant of Perez son of Judah.
⁵Of the Shilonites:
Asaiah the firstborn and his sons.
⁶Of the Zerahites:
Jeuel.
The people from Judah numbered 690.
⁷Of the Benjamites:
Sallu son of Meshullam, the son of Hodaviah, the son of Hassenuah;
⁸Ibneiah son of Jeroham; Elah son of Uzzi, the son of Micri; and Meshullam son of Shephatiah, the son of Reuel, the son of Ibnijah.
⁹The people from Benjamin, as list-

ed in their genealogy, numbered 956. All these men were heads of their families.
¹⁰Of the priests:
Jedaiah; Jehoiarib; Jakin;
¹¹Azariah son of Hilkiah, the son of Meshullam, the son of Zadok, the son of Meraioth, the son of Ahitub, the official in charge of the house of God;
¹²Adaiah son of Jeroham, the son of Pashhur, the son of Malkijah; and Maasai son of Adiel, the son of Jahzerah, the son of Meshullam, the son of Meshillemith, the son of Immer.
¹³The priests, who were heads of families, numbered 1,760. They were able men, responsible for ministering in the house of God.
¹⁴Of the Levites:
Shemaiah son of Hasshub, the son of Azrikam, the son of Hashabiah, a Merarite; ¹⁵Bakbakkar, Heresh, Galal and Mattaniah son of Mica, the son of Zicri, the son of Asaph; ¹⁶Obadiah son of Shemaiah, the son of Galal, the son of Jeduthun; and Berekiah son of Asa, the son of Elkanah, who lived in the villages of the Netophathites.
¹⁷The gatekeepers:
Shallum, Akkub, Talmon, Ahiman and their brothers, Shallum their chief ¹⁸being stationed at the King's Gate on the east, up to the present time. These were the gatekeepers belonging to the camp of the Levites. ¹⁹Shallum son of Kore, the son of Ebiasaph, the son of Korah, and his fellow gatekeepers from his family (the Korahites) were responsible for guarding the thresholds of the Tent*ª* just as their fathers had been responsible for guarding the entrance to the dwelling of the LORD. ²⁰In earlier times Phinehas son of Eleazar was in charge of the gatekeepers, and the LORD was with him. ²¹Zechariah son of Meshelemiah was the gatekeeper at the entrance to the Tent of Meeting.

ª19 That is, the temple; also in verses 21 and 23

²²Altogether, those chosen to be gatekeepers at the thresholds numbered 212. They were registered by genealogy in their villages. The gatekeepers had been assigned to their positions of trust by David and Samuel the seer. ²³They and their descendants were in charge of guarding the gates of the house of the LORD—the house called the Tent. ²⁴The gatekeepers were on the four sides: east, west, north and south. ²⁵Their brothers in their villages had to come from time to time and share their duties for seven-day periods. ²⁶But the four principal gatekeepers, who were Levites, were entrusted with the responsibility for the rooms and treasuries in the house of God. ²⁷They would spend the night

---

Week end.

Be a Gatekeeper

Read 1 Chronicles 9:22–27

Many of this week's devotions talked about listening to God and loving him with boldness. In the passage you read today, you see that there were some people who had the job of being a "gatekeeper" in the temple. This job took a special kind of person, someone who really loved God and had a lot of confidence in him. A "gatekeeper" is someone who stands at a gate or doorway and decides who will enter and who will not. Gatekeepers had to be people who could be trusted to make sure that only those people who would honor God and his house could get inside the house of the Lord. They also held the key for opening the house of God, to allow those who wanted to worship God to enter.

As a follower of Jesus, you're a gatekeeper too. Your actions are a big key to what people think about Christians, the church and even Jesus himself. As a gatekeeper, you have the privilege both of serving God and helping people find the door to a relationship with him. How you treat others, how you live your life and show your faith in God will make a big difference in the way people see God.

The gatekeepers in Israel's day were treated with respect and honor; they were looked up to and trusted by everyone. In the same way, God wants to use you to bring people into his kingdom. As the apostle Paul wrote to his "son in the faith," Timothy: "Don't let anyone look down on you because you are young, but set an example for the believers in speech, in life, in love, in faith and in purity" (1 Timothy 4:12).

❶ How do you feel about being a "gatekeeper" for Jesus? Does it scare you to carry such a big responsibility? (Remember that God hasn't left you alone as a gatekeeper. He's promised to be with you, giving you the power and love to be an incredible gatekeeper!)

❷ Think of one person—in your school, neighborhood or family—who needs to see God. What's one way you can help that one person by living as a "gatekeeper"?

❸ Try to pray every day for a whole week for that one person, and see what God does.

Turn to page 483 for your next devotion.

stationed around the house of God, because they had to guard it; and they had charge of the key for opening it each morning.

28Some of them were in charge of the articles used in the temple service; they counted them when they were brought in and when they were taken out. 29Others were assigned to take care of the furnishings and all the other articles of the sanctuary, as well as the flour and wine, and the oil, incense and spices. 30But some of the priests took care of mixing the spices. 31A Levite named Mattithiah, the firstborn son of Shallum the Korahite, was entrusted with the responsibility for baking the offering bread. 32Some of their Kohathite brothers were in charge of preparing for every Sabbath the bread set out on the table.

33Those who were musicians, heads of Levite families, stayed in the rooms of the temple and were exempt from other duties because they were responsible for the work day and night.

34All these were heads of Levite families, chiefs as listed in their genealogy, and they lived in Jerusalem.

The Genealogy of Saul

35Jeiel the father[a] of Gibeon lived in Gibeon.

His wife's name was Maacah, 36and his firstborn son was Abdon, followed by Zur, Kish, Baal, Ner, Nadab, 37Gedor, Ahio, Zechariah and Mikloth. 38Mikloth was the father of Shimeam. They too lived near their relatives in Jerusalem.

39Ner was the father of Kish, Kish the father of Saul, and Saul the father of Jonathan, Malki-Shua, Abinadab and Esh-Baal.[b]

40The son of Jonathan:

Merib-Baal,[c] who was the father of Micah.

41The sons of Micah:

Pithon, Melech, Tahrea and Ahaz.[d]

42Ahaz was the father of Jadah, Jadah[e] was the father of Alemeth, Azmaveth and Zimri, and Zimri was the father of Moza. 43Moza was the father of Binea; Rephaiah was his son, Eleasah his son and

Azel his son.

44Azel had six sons, and these were their names:

Azrikam, Bokeru, Ishmael, Sheariah, Obadiah and Hanan. These were the sons of Azel.

Saul Takes His Life

10 Now the Philistines fought against Israel; the Israelites fled before them, and many fell slain on Mount Gilboa. 2The Philistines pressed hard after Saul and his sons, and they killed his sons Jonathan, Abinadab and Malki-Shua. 3The fighting grew fierce around Saul, and when the archers overtook him, they wounded him.

4Saul said to his armor-bearer, "Draw your sword and run me through, or these uncircumcised fellows will come and abuse me."

But his armor-bearer was terrified and would not do it; so Saul took his own sword and fell on it. 5When the armor-bearer saw that Saul was dead, he too fell on his sword and died. 6So Saul and his three sons died, and all his house died together.

7When all the Israelites in the valley saw that the army had fled and that Saul and his sons had died, they abandoned their towns and fled. And the Philistines came and occupied them.

8The next day, when the Philistines came to strip the dead, they found Saul and his sons fallen on Mount Gilboa. 9They stripped him and took his head and his armor, and sent messengers throughout the land of the Philistines to proclaim the news among their idols and their people. 10They put his armor in the temple of their gods and hung up his head in the temple of Dagon.

11When all the inhabitants of Jabesh Gilead heard of everything the Philistines had done to Saul, 12all their valiant men went and took the bodies of Saul and his sons and brought them to Jabesh.

---

[a]35 Father may mean civic leader or military leader. [b]39 Also known as Ish-Bosheth [c]40 Also known as Mephibosheth [d]41 Vulgate and Syriac (see also Septuagint and 1 Chron. 8:35); Hebrew does not have and Ahaz. [e]42 Some Hebrew manuscripts and Septuagint (see also 1 Chron. 8:36); most Hebrew manuscripts Jarah, Jarah

Then they buried their bones under the great tree in Jabesh, and they fasted seven days.

¹³Saul died because he was unfaithful to the LORD; he did not keep the word of the LORD and even consulted a medium for guidance, ¹⁴and did not inquire of the LORD. So the LORD put him to death and turned the kingdom over to David son of Jesse.

David Becomes King Over Israel

11 All Israel came together to David at Hebron and said, "We are your own flesh and blood. ²In the past, even while Saul was king, you were the one who led Israel on their military campaigns. And the LORD your God said to you, 'You will shepherd my people Israel, and you will become their ruler.' "

³When all the elders of Israel had come to King David at Hebron, he made a compact with them at Hebron before the LORD, and they anointed David king over Israel, as the LORD had promised through Samuel.

David Conquers Jerusalem

⁴David and all the Israelites marched to Jerusalem (that is, Jebus). The Jebusites who lived there ⁵said to David, "You will not get in here." Nevertheless, David captured the fortress of Zion, the City of David.

⁶David had said, "Whoever leads the attack on the Jebusites will become commander-in-chief." Joab son of Zeruiah went up first, and so he received the command.

⁷David then took up residence in the fortress, and so it was called the City of David. ⁸He built up the city around it, from the supporting terraces*ᵃ* to the surrounding wall, while Joab restored the rest of the city. ⁹And David became more and more powerful, because the LORD Almighty was with him.

David's Mighty Men

¹⁰These were the chiefs of David's mighty men—they, together with all Israel, gave his kingship strong support to extend it over the whole land, as the LORD had promised— ¹¹this is the list of David's mighty men:

Jashobeam,*ᵇ* a Hacmonite, was chief of the officers*ᶜ*; he raised his spear against three hundred men, whom he killed in one encounter.

¹²Next to him was Eleazar son of Dodai the Ahohite, one of the three mighty men. ¹³He was with David at Pas Dammim when the Philistines gathered there for battle. At a place where there was a field full of barley, the troops fled from the Philistines. ¹⁴But they took their stand in the middle of the field. They defended it and struck the Philistines down, and the LORD brought about a great victory.

¹⁵Three of the thirty chiefs came down to David to the rock at the cave of Adullam, while a band of Philistines was encamped in the Valley of Rephaim. ¹⁶At that time David was in the stronghold, and the Philistine garrison was at Bethlehem. ¹⁷David longed for water and said, "Oh, that someone would get me a drink of water from the well near the gate of Bethlehem!" ¹⁸So the Three broke through the Philistine lines, drew water from the well near the gate of Bethlehem and carried it back to David. But he refused to drink it; instead, he poured it out before the LORD. ¹⁹"God forbid that I should do this!" he said. "Should I drink the blood of these men who went at the risk of their lives?" Because they risked their lives to bring it back, David would not drink it.

Such were the exploits of the three mighty men.

²⁰Abishai the brother of Joab was chief of the Three. He raised his spear against three hundred men, whom he killed, and so he became as famous as the Three. ²¹He was doubly honored above the Three and became their commander, even though he was not included among them.

²²Benaiah son of Jehoiada was a valiant fighter from Kabzeel, who performed great exploits. He struck down two of Moab's best men. He also went down into a pit on a snowy day and killed a lion. ²³And he struck down an

---

ᵃ8 Or *the Millo*   *ᵇ11* Possibly a variant of *Jashob-Baal*   *ᶜ11* Or *Thirty*; some Septuagint manuscripts *Three* (see also 2 Samuel 23:8)

Egyptian who was seven and a half feet*
tall. Although the Egyptian had a spear
like a weaver's rod in his hand, Benaiah
went against him with a club. He
snatched the spear from the Egyptian's
hand and killed him with his own spear.
²⁴Such were the exploits of Benaiah son
of Jehoiada; he too was as famous as the
three mighty men. ²⁵He was held in
greater honor than any of the Thirty, but
he was not included among the Three.
And David put him in charge of his
bodyguard.

²⁶The mighty men were:

Asahel the brother of Joab,
Elhanan son of Dodo from Bethlehem,
²⁷Shammoth the Harorite,
Helez the Pelonite,
²⁸Ira son of Ikkesh from Tekoa,
Abiezer from Anathoth,
²⁹Sibbecai the Hushathite,
Ilai the Ahohite,
³⁰Maharai the Netophathite,
Heled son of Baanah the Netophathite,
³¹Ithai son of Ribai from Gibeah in
Benjamin,
Benaiah the Pirathonite,
³²Hurai from the ravines of Gaash,
Abiel the Arbathite,
³³Azmaveth the Baharumite,
Eliahba the Shaalbonite,
³⁴the sons of Hashem the Gizonite,
Jonathan son of Shagee the Hararite,
³⁵Ahiam son of Sacar the Hararite,
Eliphal son of Ur,
³⁶Hepher the Mekerathite,
Ahijah the Pelonite,
³⁷Hezro the Carmelite,
Naarai son of Ezbai,
³⁸Joel the brother of Nathan,
Mibhar son of Hagri,
³⁹Zelek the Ammonite,
Naharai the Berothite, the armor-
bearer of Joab son of Zeruiah,
⁴⁰Ira the Ithrite,
Gareb the Ithrite,
⁴¹Uriah the Hittite,
Zabad son of Ahlai,
⁴²Adina son of Shiza the Reubenite,
who was chief of the Reubenites,
and the thirty with him,

⁴³Hanan son of Maacah,
Joshaphat the Mithnite,
⁴⁴Uzzia the Ashterathite,
Shama and Jeiel the sons of Hotham the Aroerite,
⁴⁵Jediael son of Shimri,
his brother Joha the Tizite,
⁴⁶Eliel the Mahavite,
Jeribai and Joshaviah the sons of
Elnaam,
Ithmah the Moabite,
⁴⁷Eliel, Obed and Jaasiel the Mezo-
baite.

Warriors Join David

12 These were the men who came to
David at Ziklag, while he was banished from the presence of Saul son of
Kish (they were among the warriors who
helped him in battle; ²they were armed
with bows and were able to shoot arrows
or to sling stones right-handed or left-
handed; they were kinsmen of Saul from
the tribe of Benjamin):

³Ahiezer their chief and Joash the
sons of Shemaah the Gibeathite; Je-
ziel and Pelet the sons of Azmaveth;
Beracah, Jehu the Anathothite, ⁴and
Ishmaiah the Gibeonite, a mighty
man among the Thirty, who was a
leader of the Thirty; Jeremiah, Jahaziel, Johanan, Jozabad the Gedera-
thite, ⁵Eluzai, Jerimoth, Bealiah,
Shemariah and Shephatiah the Ha-
ruphite; ⁶Elkanah, Isshiah, Azarel,
Joezer and Jashobeam the Korahites; ⁷and Joelah and Zebadiah the
sons of Jeroham from Gedor.

⁸Some Gadites defected to David at his
stronghold in the desert. They were brave
warriors, ready for battle and able to
handle the shield and spear. Their faces
were the faces of lions, and they were as
swift as gazelles in the mountains.

⁹Ezer was the chief,
Obadiah the second in command,
Eliab the third,
¹⁰Mishmannah the fourth, Jeremiah
the fifth,
¹¹Attai the sixth, Eliel the seventh,
¹²Johanan the eighth, Elzabad the
ninth,

*²³ Hebrew *five cubits* (about 2.3 meters)

[13] Jeremiah the tenth and Macbannai the eleventh.

[14] These Gadites were army commanders; the least was a match for a hundred, and the greatest for a thousand. [15] It was they who crossed the Jordan in the first month when it was overflowing all its banks, and they put to flight everyone living in the valleys, to the east and to the west.

[16] Other Benjamites and some men from Judah also came to David in his stronghold. [17] David went out to meet them and said to them, "If you have come to me in peace, to help me, I am ready to have you unite with me. But if you have come to betray me to my enemies when my hands are free from violence, may the God of our fathers see it and judge you." [18] Then the Spirit came upon Amasai, chief of the Thirty, and he said:

"We are yours, O David!
  We are with you, O son of Jesse!
Success, success to you,
  and success to those who help you,
  for your God will help you."

So David received them and made them leaders of his raiding bands.

[19] Some of the men of Manasseh defected to David when he went with the Philistines to fight against Saul. (He and his men did not help the Philistines because, after consultation, their rulers sent him away. They said, "It will cost us our heads if he deserts to his master Saul.") [20] When David went to Ziklag, these were the men of Manasseh who defected to him: Adnah, Jozabad, Jediael, Michael, Jozabad, Elihu and Zillethai, leaders of units of a thousand in Manasseh. [21] They helped David against raiding bands, for all of them were brave warriors, and they were commanders in his army. [22] Day after day men came to help David, until he had a great army, like the army of God.[a]

Others Join David at Hebron

[23] These are the numbers of the men armed for battle who came to David at Hebron to turn Saul's kingdom over to him, as the LORD had said:

[24] men of Judah, carrying shield and spear—6,800 armed for battle;

[25] men of Simeon, warriors ready for battle—7,100;

[26] men of Levi—4,600, [27] including Jehoiada, leader of the family of Aaron, with 3,700 men, [28] and Zadok, a brave young warrior, with 22 officers from his family;

[29] men of Benjamin, Saul's kinsmen—3,000, most of whom had remained loyal to Saul's house until then;

[30] men of Ephraim, brave warriors, famous in their own clans—20,800;

[31] men of half the tribe of Manasseh, designated by name to come and make David king—18,000;

[32] men of Issachar, who understood the times and knew what Israel should do—200 chiefs, with all their relatives under their command;

[33] men of Zebulun, experienced soldiers prepared for battle with every type of weapon, to help David with undivided loyalty—50,000;

[34] men of Naphtali—1,000 officers, together with 37,000 men carrying shields and spears;

[35] men of Dan, ready for battle—28,600;

[36] men of Asher, experienced soldiers prepared for battle—40,000;

[37] and from east of the Jordan, men of Reuben, Gad and the half-tribe of Manasseh, armed with every type of weapon—120,000.

[38] All these were fighting men who volunteered to serve in the ranks. They came to Hebron fully determined to make David king over all Israel. All the rest of the Israelites were also of one mind to make David king. [39] The men spent three days there with David, eating and drinking, for their families had supplied provisions for them. [40] Also, their neighbors from as far away as Issachar, Zebulun and Naphtali came bringing food on donkeys, camels, mules and oxen. There were plentiful supplies of flour, fig cakes, raisin cakes, wine, oil, cattle and sheep, for there was joy in Israel.

a22 Or a great and mighty army

Bringing Back the Ark

13 David conferred with each of his officers, the commanders of thousands and commanders of hundreds. ²He then said to the whole assembly of Israel, "If it seems good to you and if it is the will of the LORD our God, let us send word far and wide to the rest of our brothers throughout the territories of Israel, and also to the priests and Levites who are with them in their towns and pasturelands, to come and join us. ³Let us bring the ark of our God back to us, for we did not inquire of[a] it[b] during the reign of Saul." ⁴The whole assembly agreed to do this, because it seemed right to all the people.

⁵So David assembled all the Israelites, from the Shihor River in Egypt to Lebo[c] Hamath, to bring the ark of God from Kiriath Jearim. ⁶David and all the Israelites with him went to Baalah of Judah (Kiriath Jearim) to bring up from there the ark of God the LORD, who is enthroned between the cherubim—the ark that is called by the Name.

⁷They moved the ark of God from Abinadab's house on a new cart, with Uzzah and Ahio guiding it. ⁸David and all the Israelites were celebrating with all their might before God, with songs and with harps, lyres, tambourines, cymbals and trumpets.

⁹When they came to the threshing floor of Kidon, Uzzah reached out his hand to steady the ark, because the oxen stumbled. ¹⁰The LORD's anger burned against Uzzah, and he struck him down because he had put his hand on the ark. So he died there before God.

¹¹Then David was angry because the LORD's wrath had broken out against Uzzah, and to this day that place is called Perez Uzzah.[d]

¹²David was afraid of God that day and asked, "How can I ever bring the ark of God to me?" ¹³He did not take the ark to be with him in the City of David. Instead, he took it aside to the house of Obed-Edom the Gittite. ¹⁴The ark of God remained with the family of Obed-Edom in his house for three months, and the LORD blessed his household and everything he had.

Did the Ark Have Power?

Huh?

1 Chronicles 13
Even though the movies show it as magical, the ark was nothing but a fancy box. But what it *represented* was God's holy presence on earth. People were supposed to respect God, not the box. When Uzzah was struck dead for touching the ark, it was God's reminder that he demands and deserves respect.

David's House and Family

14 Now Hiram king of Tyre sent messengers to David, along with cedar logs, stonemasons and carpenters to build a palace for him. ²And David knew that the LORD had established him as king over Israel and that his kingdom had been highly exalted for the sake of his people Israel.

³In Jerusalem David took more wives and became the father of more sons and daughters. ⁴These are the names of the children born to him there: Shammua, Shobab, Nathan, Solomon, ⁵Ibhar, Elishua, Elpelet, ⁶Nogah, Nepheg, Japhia, ⁷Elishama, Beeliada[c] and Eliphelet.

David Defeats the Philistines

⁸When the Philistines heard that David had been ʼanointed king over all Israel, they went up in full force to search for him, but David heard about it and went out to meet them. ⁹Now the Philistines had come and raided the Valley of Rephaim; ¹⁰so David inquired of God: "Shall I go and attack the Philistines? Will you hand them over to me?"

The LORD answered him, "Go, I will hand them over to you."

¹¹So David and his men went up to Baal Perazim, and there he defeated them. He said, "As waters break out, God has broken out against my enemies by

---

a 3 Or we neglected   b 3 Or him   c 5 Or to the entrance to   d 11 Perez Uzzah means outbreak against Uzzah.   c 7 A variant of Eliada

my hand." So that place was called Baal Perazim.[a] [12]The Philistines had abandoned their gods there, and David gave orders to burn them in the fire.

[13]Once more the Philistines raided the valley; [14]so David inquired of God again, and God answered him, "Do not go straight up, but circle around them and attack them in front of the balsam trees. [15]As soon as you hear the sound of marching in the tops of the balsam trees, move out to battle, because that will mean God has gone out in front of you to strike the Philistine army." [16]So David did as God commanded him, and they struck down the Philistine army, all the way from Gibeon to Gezer.

[17]So David's fame spread throughout every land, and the LORD made all the nations fear him.

The Ark Brought to Jerusalem

15 After David had constructed buildings for himself in the City of David, he prepared a place for the ark of God and pitched a tent for it. [2]Then David said, "No one but the Levites may carry the ark of God, because the LORD chose them to carry the ark of the LORD and to minister before him forever."

[3]David assembled all Israel in Jerusalem to bring up the ark of the LORD to the place he had prepared for it. [4]He called together the descendants of Aaron and the Levites:

[5]From the descendants of Kohath,
   Uriel the leader and 120 relatives;
[6]from the descendants of Merari,
   Asaiah the leader and 220 relatives;
[7]from the descendants of Gershon,[b]
   Joel the leader and 130 relatives;
[8]from the descendants of Elizaphan,
   Shemaiah the leader and 200 relatives;
[9]from the descendants of Hebron,
   Eliel the leader and 80 relatives;
[10]from the descendants of Uzziel,
   Amminadab the leader and 112 relatives.

[11]Then David summoned Zadok and Abiathar the priests, and Uriel, Asaiah, Joel, Shemaiah, Eliel and Amminadab the Levites. [12]He said to them, "You are the heads of the Levitical families; you and your fellow Levites are to consecrate yourselves and bring up the ark of the LORD, the God of Israel, to the place I have prepared for it. [13]It was because you, the Levites, did not bring it up the first time that the LORD our God broke out in anger against us. We did not inquire of him about how to do it in the prescribed way." [14]So the priests and Levites consecrated themselves in order to bring up the ark of the LORD, the God of Israel. [15]And the Levites carried the ark of God with the poles on their shoulders, as Moses had commanded in accordance with the word of the LORD.

[16]David told the leaders of the Levites to appoint their brothers as singers to sing joyful songs, accompanied by musical instruments: lyres, harps and cymbals.

[17]So the Levites appointed Heman son of Joel; from his brothers, Asaph son of Berekiah; and from their brothers the Merarites, Ethan son of Kushaiah; [18]and with them their brothers next in rank: Zechariah,[c] Jaaziel, Shemiramoth, Jehiel, Unni, Eliab, Benaiah, Maaseiah, Mattithiah, Eliphelehu, Mikneiah, Obed-Edom and Jeiel,[d] the gatekeepers.

[19]The musicians Heman, Asaph and Ethan were to sound the bronze cymbals; [20]Zechariah, Aziel, Shemiramoth, Jehiel, Unni, Eliab, Maaseiah and Benaiah were to play the lyres according to alamoth,[e] [21]and Mattithiah, Eliphelehu, Mikneiah, Obed-Edom, Jeiel and Azaziah were to play the harps, directing according to sheminith.[e] [22]Kenaniah the head Levite was in charge of the singing; that was his responsibility because he was skillful at it.

[23]Berekiah and Elkanah were to be doorkeepers for the ark. [24]Shebaniah, Joshaphat, Nethanel, Amasai, Zechariah, Benaiah and Eliezer the priests were to blow trumpets before the ark of God. Obed-Edom and Jehiah were also to be doorkeepers for the ark.

---

[a]11 Baal Perazim means the lord who breaks out.
[b]7 Hebrew Gershom, a variant of Gershon
[c]18 Three Hebrew manuscripts and most Septuagint manuscripts (see also verse 20 and 1 Chron. 16:5); most Hebrew manuscripts Zechariah son and or Zechariah, Ben and   [d]18 Hebrew; Septuagint (see also verse 21) Jeiel and Azaziah   [e]20,21 Probably a musical term

²⁵So David and the elders of Israel and the commanders of units of a thousand went to bring up the ark of the covenant of the LORD from the house of Obed-Edom, with rejoicing. ²⁶Because God had helped the Levites who were carrying the ark of the covenant of the LORD, seven bulls and seven rams were sacrificed. ²⁷Now David was clothed in a robe of fine linen, as were all the Levites who were carrying the ark, and as were the singers, and Kenaniah, who was in charge of the singing of the choirs. David also wore a linen ephod. ²⁸So all Israel brought up the ark of the covenant of the LORD with shouts, with the sounding of rams' horns and trumpets, and of cymbals, and the playing of lyres and harps.

²⁹As the ark of the covenant of the LORD was entering the City of David, Michal daughter of Saul watched from a window. And when she saw King David dancing and celebrating, she despised him in her heart.

16 They brought the ark of God and set it inside the tent that David had pitched for it, and they presented burnt offerings and fellowship offerings[a] before God. ²After David had finished sacrificing the burnt offerings and fellowship offerings, he blessed the people in the name of the LORD. ³Then he gave a loaf of bread, a cake of dates and a cake of raisins to each Israelite man and woman.

⁴He appointed some of the Levites to minister before the ark of the LORD, to make petition, to give thanks, and to praise the LORD, the God of Israel: ⁵Asaph was the chief, Zechariah second, then Jeiel, Shemiramoth, Jehiel, Mattithiah, Eliab, Benaiah, Obed-Edom and Jeiel. They were to play the lyres and harps, Asaph was to sound the cymbals, ⁶and Benaiah and Jahaziel the priests were to blow the trumpets regularly before the ark of the covenant of God.

David's Psalm of Thanks

⁷That day David first committed to Asaph and his associates this psalm of thanks to the LORD:

⁸Give thanks to the LORD, call on his name;

make known among the nations what he has done.
⁹Sing to him, sing praise to him;
tell of all his wonderful acts.
¹⁰Glory in his holy name;
let the hearts of those who seek the LORD rejoice.
¹¹Look to the LORD and his strength;
seek his face always.
¹²Remember the wonders he has done,
his miracles, and the judgments he pronounced,
¹³O descendants of Israel his servant,
O sons of Jacob, his chosen ones.

¹⁴He is the LORD our God;
his judgments are in all the earth.
¹⁵He remembers[b] his covenant forever,
the word he commanded, for a thousand generations,
¹⁶the covenant he made with Abraham,
the oath he swore to Isaac.
¹⁷He confirmed it to Jacob as a decree,
to Israel as an everlasting covenant:
¹⁸"To you I will give the land of Canaan
as the portion you will inherit."

¹⁹When they were but few in number,
few indeed, and strangers in it,
²⁰they[c] wandered from nation to nation,
from one kingdom to another.
²¹He allowed no man to oppress them;
for their sake he rebuked kings:
²²"Do not touch my anointed ones;
do my prophets no harm."

²³Sing to the LORD, all the earth;
proclaim his salvation day after day.
²⁴Declare his glory among the nations,
his marvelous deeds among all peoples.
²⁵For great is the LORD and most worthy of praise;
he is to be feared above all gods.
²⁶For all the gods of the nations are idols,
but the LORD made the heavens.
²⁷Splendor and majesty are before him;

---

[a]1 Traditionally *peace offerings*; also in verse 2
[b]15 Some Septuagint manuscripts (see also Psalm 105:8); Hebrew *Remember*   [c]18-20 One Hebrew manuscript, Septuagint and Vulgate (see also Psalm 105:12); most Hebrew manuscripts *inherit,* / ¹⁹*though you are but few in number,* / *few indeed, / and strangers in it."* / ²⁰*They*

strength and joy in his dwelling
place.
²⁸ Ascribe to the LORD, O families of
nations,
ascribe to the LORD glory and
strength,
²⁹ ascribe to the LORD the glory due his
name.
Bring an offering and come before
him;
worship the LORD in the splendor of
his^a holiness.
³⁰ Tremble before him, all the earth!
The world is firmly established; it
cannot be moved.
³¹ Let the heavens rejoice, let the earth
be glad;
let them say among the nations,
"The LORD reigns!"
³² Let the sea resound, and all that is in
it;
let the fields be jubilant, and
everything in them!
³³ Then the trees of the forest will sing,
they will sing for joy before the
LORD,
for he comes to judge the earth.

³⁴ Give thanks to the LORD, for he is
good;
his love endures forever.
³⁵ Cry out, "Save us, O God our Savior;
gather us and deliver us from the
nations,
that we may give thanks to your holy
name,
that we may glory in your praise."
³⁶ Praise be to the LORD, the God of
Israel,
from everlasting to everlasting.

Then all the people said "Amen" and
"Praise the LORD."

³⁷David left Asaph and his associates
before the ark of the covenant of the
LORD to minister there regularly, according to each day's requirements. ³⁸He also
left Obed-Edom and his sixty-eight associates to minister with them. Obed-Edom
son of Jeduthun, and also Hosah, were
gatekeepers.

³⁹David left Zadok the priest and his
fellow priests before the tabernacle of the
LORD at the high place in Gibeon ⁴⁰to
present burnt offerings to the LORD on

the altar of burnt offering regularly,
morning and evening, in accordance
with everything written in the Law of the
LORD, which he had given Israel. ⁴¹With
them were Heman and Jeduthun and the
rest of those chosen and designated by
name to give thanks to the LORD, "for his
love endures forever." ⁴²Heman and Jeduthun were responsible for the sounding of the trumpets and cymbals and for
the playing of the other instruments for
sacred song. The sons of Jeduthun were
stationed at the gate.

⁴³Then all the people left, each for his
own home, and David returned home to
bless his family.

God's Promise to David

17 After David was settled in his palace, he said to Nathan the prophet,
"Here I am, living in a palace of cedar,
while the ark of the covenant of the LORD
is under a tent."

²Nathan replied to David, "Whatever
you have in mind, do it, for God is with
you."

³That night the word of God came to
Nathan, saying:

⁴"Go and tell my servant David,
'This is what the LORD says: You are
not the one to build me a house to
dwell in. ⁵I have not dwelt in a
house from the day I brought Israel
up out of Egypt to this day. I have
moved from one tent site to another,
from one dwelling place to another.
⁶Wherever I have moved with all the
Israelites, did I ever say to any of
their leaders^b whom I commanded to
shepherd my people, "Why have you
not built me a house of cedar?" '

⁷"Now then, tell my servant David, 'This is what the LORD Almighty
says: I took you from the pasture
and from following the flock, to be
ruler over my people Israel. ⁸I have
been with you wherever you have
gone, and I have cut off all your enemies from before you. Now I will
make your name like the names of
the greatest men of the earth. ⁹And I

---

^a29 Or LORD with the splendor of   ^b6 Traditionally
judges; also in verse 10

will provide a place for my people Israel and will plant them so that they can have a home of their own and no longer be disturbed. Wicked people will not oppress them anymore, as they did at the beginning [10]and have done ever since the time I appointed leaders over my people Israel. I will also subdue all your enemies.

" 'I declare to you that the LORD will build a house for you: [11]When your days are over and you go to be with your fathers, I will raise up your offspring to succeed you, one of your own sons, and I will establish his kingdom. [12]He is the one who will build a house for me, and I will establish his throne forever. [13]I will be his father, and he will be my son. I will never take my love away from him, as I took it away from your predecessor. [14]I will set him over my house and my kingdom forever; his throne will be established forever.' "

[15]Nathan reported to David all the words of this entire revelation.

David's Prayer

[16]Then King David went in and sat before the LORD, and he said:

"Who am I, O LORD God, and what is my family, that you have brought me this far? [17]And as if this were not enough in your sight, O God, you have spoken about the future of the house of your servant. You have looked on me as though I were the most exalted of men, O LORD God.

[18]"What more can David say to you for honoring your servant? For you know your servant, [19]O LORD. For the sake of your servant and according to your will, you have done this great thing and made known all these great promises.

[20]"There is no one like you, O LORD, and there is no God but you, as we have heard with our own ears. [21]And who is like your people Israel—the one nation on earth whose God went out to redeem a people for himself, and to make a name for yourself, and to perform great and awesome wonders by driving out nations from before your people, whom you redeemed from Egypt? [22]You made your people Israel your very own forever, and you, O LORD, have become their God.

[23]"And now, LORD, let the promise you have made concerning your servant and his house be established forever. Do as you promised, [24]so that it will be established and that your name will be great forever. Then men will say, 'The LORD Almighty, the God over Israel, is Israel's God!' And the house of your servant David will be established before you.

[25]"You, my God, have revealed to your servant that you will build a house for him. So your servant has found courage to pray to you. [26]O LORD, you are God! You have promised these good things to your servant. [27]Now you have been pleased to bless the house of your servant, that it may continue forever in your sight; for you, O LORD, have blessed it, and it will be blessed forever."

Loved by God

Huh?

1 Chronicles 17:16–27

King David was great—the greatest leader in Israel's history. He was strong, smart, powerful, and people loved him. He had every reason to get stuck-up and full of himself, thinking he was Mr. Cool. But the *reason* why David was loved by God was that he knew who he was—an ordinary guy who had been lifted up by an extraordinary God.

David's Victories

18 In the course of time, David defeated the Philistines and subdued them, and he took Gath and its surrounding villages from the control of the Philistines.

²David also defeated the Moabites, and they became subject to him and brought tribute.

³Moreover, David fought Hadadezer king of Zobah, as far as Hamath, when he went to establish his control along the Euphrates River. ⁴David captured a thousand of his chariots, seven thousand charioteers and twenty thousand foot soldiers. He hamstrung all but a hundred of the chariot horses.

⁵When the Arameans of Damascus came to help Hadadezer king of Zobah, David struck down twenty-two thousand of them. ⁶He put garrisons in the Aramean kingdom of Damascus, and the Arameans became subject to him and brought tribute. The LORD gave David victory everywhere he went.

⁷David took the gold shields carried by the officers of Hadadezer and brought them to Jerusalem. ⁸From Tebah*a* and Cun, towns that belonged to Hadadezer, David took a great quantity of bronze, which Solomon used to make the bronze Sea, the pillars and various bronze articles.

⁹When Tou king of Hamath heard that David had defeated the entire army of Hadadezer king of Zobah, ¹⁰he sent his son Hadoram to King David to greet him and congratulate him on his victory in battle over Hadadezer, who had been at war with Tou. Hadoram brought all kinds of articles of gold and silver and bronze.

¹¹King David dedicated these articles to the LORD, as he had done with the silver and gold he had taken from all these nations: Edom and Moab, the Ammonites and the Philistines, and Amalek.

¹²Abishai son of Zeruiah struck down eighteen thousand Edomites in the Valley of Salt. ¹³He put garrisons in Edom, and all the Edomites became subject to David. The LORD gave David victory everywhere he went.

David's Officials

¹⁴David reigned over all Israel, doing what was just and right for all his people. ¹⁵Joab son of Zeruiah was over the army; Jehoshaphat son of Ahilud was recorder; ¹⁶Zadok son of Ahitub and Ahimelech*b* son of Abiathar were priests; Shavsha was secretary; ¹⁷Benaiah son of Jehoiada was over the Kerethites and Pelethites; and David's sons were chief officials at the king's side.

The Battle Against the Ammonites

19 In the course of time, Nahash king of the Ammonites died, and his son succeeded him as king. ²David thought, "I will show kindness to Hanun son of Nahash, because his father showed kindness to me." So David sent a delegation to express his sympathy to Hanun concerning his father.

When David's men came to Hanun in the land of the Ammonites to express sympathy to him, ³the Ammonite nobles said to Hanun, "Do you think David is honoring your father by sending men to you to express sympathy? Haven't his men come to you to explore and spy out the country and overthrow it?" ⁴So Hanun seized David's men, shaved them, cut off their garments in the middle at the buttocks, and sent them away.

⁵When someone came and told David about the men, he sent messengers to meet them, for they were greatly humiliated. The king said, "Stay at Jericho till your beards have grown, and then come back."

⁶When the Ammonites realized that they had become a stench in David's nostrils, Hanun and the Ammonites sent a thousand talents*c* of silver to hire chariots and charioteers from Aram Naharaim,*d* Aram Maacah and Zobah. ⁷They hired thirty-two thousand chariots and charioteers, as well as the king of Maacah with his troops, who came and camped near Medeba, while the Ammonites were mustered from their towns and moved out for battle.

⁸On hearing this, David sent Joab out with the entire army of fighting men. ⁹The Ammonites came out and drew up in battle formation at the entrance to their city, while the kings who had come were by themselves in the open country.

¹⁰Joab saw that there were battle lines in front of him and behind him; so he

---

a8 Hebrew *Tibhath,* a variant of *Tebah*   *b16* Some Hebrew manuscripts, Vulgate and Syriac (see also 2 Samuel 8:17); most Hebrew manuscripts *Abimelech*   *c6* That is, about 37 tons (about 34 metric tons)   *d6* That is, Northwest Mesopotamia

selected some of the best troops in Israel and deployed them against the Arameans. ¹¹He put the rest of the men under the command of Abishai his brother, and they were deployed against the Ammonites. ¹²Joab said, "If the Arameans are too strong for me, then you are to rescue me; but if the Ammonites are too strong for you, then I will rescue you. ¹³Be strong and let us fight bravely for our people and the cities of our God. The LORD will do what is good in his sight."

¹⁴Then Joab and the troops with him advanced to fight the Arameans, and they fled before him. ¹⁵When the Ammonites saw that the Arameans were fleeing, they too fled before his brother Abishai and went inside the city. So Joab went back to Jerusalem.

¹⁶After the Arameans saw that they had been routed by Israel, they sent messengers and had Arameans brought from beyond the River,ᵃ with Shophach the commander of Hadadezer's army leading them.

¹⁷When David was told of this, he gathered all Israel and crossed the Jordan; he advanced against them and formed his battle lines opposite them. David formed his lines to meet the Arameans in battle, and they fought against him. ¹⁸But they fled before Israel, and David killed seven thousand of their charioteers and forty thousand of their foot soldiers. He also killed Shophach the commander of their army.

¹⁹When the vassals of Hadadezer saw that they had been defeated by Israel, they made peace with David and became subject to him.

So the Arameans were not willing to help the Ammonites anymore.

The Capture of Rabbah

20 In the spring, at the time when kings go off to war, Joab led out the armed forces. He laid waste the land of the Ammonites and went to Rabbah and besieged it, but David remained in Jerusalem. Joab attacked Rabbah and left it in ruins. ²David took the crown from the head of their kingᵇ—its weight was found to be a talentᶜ of gold, and it was set with precious stones—and it was placed on David's head. He took a great

quantity of plunder from the city ³and brought out the people who were there, consigning them to labor with saws and with iron picks and axes. David did this to all the Ammonite towns. Then David and his entire army returned to Jerusalem.

War With the Philistines

⁴In the course of time, war broke out with the Philistines, at Gezer. At that time Sibbecai the Hushathite killed Sippai, one of the descendants of the Rephaites, and the Philistines were subjugated.

⁵In another battle with the Philistines, Elhanan son of Jair killed Lahmi the brother of Goliath the Gittite, who had a spear with a shaft like a weaver's rod.

⁶In still another battle, which took place at Gath, there was a huge man with six fingers on each hand and six toes on each foot—twenty-four in all. He also was descended from Rapha. ⁷When he taunted Israel, Jonathan son of Shimea, David's brother, killed him.

⁸These were descendants of Rapha in Gath, and they fell at the hands of David and his men.

David Numbers the Fighting Men

21 Satan rose up against Israel and incited David to take a census of Israel. ²So David said to Joab and the commanders of the troops, "Go and count the Israelites from Beersheba to Dan. Then report back to me so that I may know how many there are."

³But Joab replied, "May the LORD multiply his troops a hundred times over. My lord the king, are they not all my lord's subjects? Why does my lord want to do this? Why should he bring guilt on Israel?"

⁴The king's word, however, overruled Joab; so Joab left and went throughout Israel and then came back to Jerusalem. ⁵Joab reported the number of the fighting men to David: In all Israel there were one million one hundred thousand men who could handle a sword, including

---

ᵃ16 That is, the Euphrates   ᵇ2 Or of Milcom, that is, Molech   ᶜ2 That is, about 75 pounds (about 34 kilograms)

four hundred and seventy thousand in Judah.

⁶But Joab did not include Levi and Benjamin in the numbering, because the king's command was repulsive to him. ⁷This command was also evil in the sight of God; so he punished Israel.

⁸Then David said to God, "I have sinned greatly by doing this. Now, I beg you, take away the guilt of your servant. I have done a very foolish thing."

⁹The LORD said to Gad, David's seer, ¹⁰"Go and tell David, 'This is what the LORD says: I am giving you three options. Choose one of them for me to carry out against you.'"

¹¹So Gad went to David and said to him, "This is what the LORD says: 'Take

your choice: ¹²three years of famine, three months of being swept away*a* before your enemies, with their swords overtaking you, or three days of the sword of the LORD—days of plague in the land, with the angel of the LORD ravaging every part of Israel.' Now then, decide how I should answer the one who sent me."

¹³David said to Gad, "I am in deep distress. Let me fall into the hands of the LORD, for his mercy is very great; but do not let me fall into the hands of men."

¹⁴So the LORD sent a plague on Israel, and seventy thousand men of Israel fell

---

a 12 Hebrew; Septuagint and Vulgate (see also 2 Samuel 24:13) *of fleeing*

Monday

A Big Head?

Read 1 Chronicles 21:1–8

I really want to be a rapper. One Sunday morning I performed at my church. After the service, nearly everyone I knew told me I did a great job. Even people I had never seen congratulated me and told me it was awesome. I appreciated all the compliments, and I almost let their praise go to my head. But I tried to shake off the temptation of pride by acknowledging the truth: God has given me a talent, and all I can do is thank him for it. God hates selfish pride. He has given us everything. Without God we have nothing; we're completely helpless.

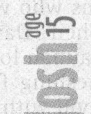
Josh age 15

King David was a powerful guy, and he let it go to his head. He thought he could use his own power to do things. But once he remembered that God is in control of everything, David was like, "Whoa, what was I thinking?" He had let pride get the best of him.

Whenever I'm tempted to be proud and think I'm really talented, I need to remember that it's only because of God that I have any talent at all. He deserves all the credit for everything I do.

What about You?

❶ What are some of the talents God has given you? How can you give him credit when you do something well?

❷ Think up a little prayer, a gesture, a song, whatever, that you can use to give thanks to God when you are successful at something. When you pass a test, get the part in a play or score the winning run, acknowledge God's gift to you by using your private symbol of thanks. If anyone asks what you're doing, tell 'em!

❸ Thank God for the talents he's given you and ask him to help you use them to show his love to others.

Turn to page 493 for your next devotion.

dead. ¹⁵And God sent an angel to destroy Jerusalem. But as the angel was doing so, the LORD saw it and was grieved because of the calamity and said to the angel who was destroying the people, "Enough! Withdraw your hand." The angel of the LORD was then standing at the threshing floor of Araunah[a] the Jebusite.

¹⁶David looked up and saw the angel of the LORD standing between heaven and earth, with a drawn sword in his hand extended over Jerusalem. Then David and the elders, clothed in sackcloth, fell facedown.

¹⁷David said to God, "Was it not I who ordered the fighting men to be counted? I am the one who has sinned and done wrong. These are but sheep. What have they done? O LORD my God, let your hand fall upon me and my family, but do not let this plague remain on your people."

¹⁸Then the angel of the LORD ordered Gad to tell David to go up and build an altar to the LORD on the threshing floor of Araunah the Jebusite. ¹⁹So David went up in obedience to the word that Gad had spoken in the name of the LORD.

²⁰While Araunah was threshing wheat, he turned and saw the angel; his four sons who were with him hid themselves. ²¹Then David approached, and when Araunah looked and saw him, he left the threshing floor and bowed down before David with his face to the ground.

²²David said to him, "Let me have the site of your threshing floor so I can build an altar to the LORD, that the plague on the people may be stopped. Sell it to me at the full price."

²³Araunah said to David, "Take it! Let my lord the king do whatever pleases him. Look, I will give the oxen for the burnt offerings, the threshing sledges for the wood, and the wheat for the grain offering. I will give all this."

²⁴But King David replied to Araunah, "No, I insist on paying the full price. I will not take for the LORD what is yours, or sacrifice a burnt offering that costs me nothing."

²⁵So David paid Araunah six hundred shekels[b] of gold for the site. ²⁶David built an altar to the LORD there and sacrificed burnt offerings and fellowship offerings.[c]

He called on the LORD, and the LORD answered him with fire from heaven on the altar of burnt offering.

²⁷Then the LORD spoke to the angel, and he put his sword back into its sheath. ²⁸At that time, when David saw that the LORD had answered him on the threshing floor of Araunah the Jebusite, he offered sacrifices there. ²⁹The tabernacle of the LORD, which Moses had made in the desert, and the altar of burnt offering were at that time on the high place at Gibeon. ³⁰But David could not go before it to inquire of God, because he was afraid of the sword of the angel of the LORD.

22 Then David said, "The house of the LORD God is to be here, and also the altar of burnt offering for Israel."

Preparations for the Temple

²So David gave orders to assemble the aliens living in Israel, and from among them he appointed stonecutters to prepare dressed stone for building the house of God. ³He provided a large amount of iron to make nails for the doors of the gateways and for the fittings, and more bronze than could be weighed. ⁴He also provided more cedar logs than could be counted, for the Sidonians and Tyrians had brought large numbers of them to David.

⁵David said, "My son Solomon is young and inexperienced, and the house to be built for the LORD should be of great magnificence and fame and splendor in the sight of all the nations. Therefore I will make preparations for it." So David made extensive preparations before his death.

⁶Then he called for his son Solomon and charged him to build a house for the LORD, the God of Israel. ⁷David said to Solomon: "My son, I had it in my heart to build a house for the Name of the LORD my God. ⁸But this word of the LORD came to me: 'You have shed much blood and have fought many wars. You are not to build a house for my Name, because you have shed much blood on the earth in my sight. ⁹But you will have a son who will

---

[a]15 Hebrew *Ornan*, a variant of *Araunah*; also in verses 18-28   [b]25 That is, about 15 pounds (about 7 kilograms)   [c]26 Traditionally *peace offerings*

be a man of peace and rest, and I will give him rest from all his enemies on every side. His name will be Solomon,[a] and I will grant Israel peace and quiet during his reign. [10]He is the one who will build a house for my Name. He will be my son, and I will be his father. And I will establish the throne of his kingdom over Israel forever."

Temple of Peace

Huh?

1 Chronicles 22:6–10

The temple was the place where God lived with the people (OK, he didn't *live* there, but it was where his holiness was available to them). David wanted to build an awesome temple, or "House of God." Although David was a great king loved by God, God didn't want him building it because David was a warrior-king and, during his time, lots of people were killed. So God chose a peaceful king—Solomon, David's son—to build it. That's why it's called "Solomon's temple."

[11]"Now, my son, the LORD be with you, and may you have success and build the house of the LORD your God, as he said you would. [12]May the LORD give you discretion and understanding when he puts you in command over Israel, so that you may keep the law of the LORD your God. [13]Then you will have success if you are careful to observe the decrees and laws that the LORD gave Moses for Israel. Be strong and courageous. Do not be afraid or discouraged.

[14]"I have taken great pains to provide for the temple of the LORD a hundred thousand talents[b] of gold, a million talents[c] of silver, quantities of bronze and iron too great to be weighed, and wood and stone. And you may add to them. [15]You have many workmen: stonecutters, masons and carpenters, as well as men skilled in every kind of work [16]in gold and silver, bronze and iron—craftsmen beyond number. Now begin the work, and the LORD be with you."

[17]Then David ordered all the leaders of Israel to help his son Solomon. [18]He said to them, "Is not the LORD your God with you? And has he not granted you rest on every side? For he has handed the inhabitants of the land over to me, and the land is subject to the LORD and to his people. [19]Now devote your heart and soul to seeking the LORD your God. Begin to build the sanctuary of the LORD God, so that you may bring the ark of the covenant of the LORD and the sacred articles belonging to God into the temple that will be built for the Name of the LORD."

The Levites

23 When David was old and full of years, he made his son Solomon king over Israel.

[2]He also gathered together all the leaders of Israel, as well as the priests and Levites. [3]The Levites thirty years old or more were counted, and the total number of men was thirty-eight thousand. [4]David said, "Of these, twenty-four thousand are to supervise the work of the temple of the LORD and six thousand are to be officials and judges. [5]Four thousand are to be gatekeepers and four thousand are to praise the LORD with the musical instruments I have provided for that purpose."

[6]David divided the Levites into groups corresponding to the sons of Levi: Gershon, Kohath and Merari.

Gershonites

[7]Belonging to the Gershonites:
Ladan and Shimei.

[8]The sons of Ladan:
Jehiel the first, Zetham and Joel—three in all.

[9]The sons of Shimei:
Shelomoth, Haziel and Haran—three in all.
These were the heads of the families of Ladan.

[10]And the sons of Shimei:
Jahath, Ziza,[d] Jeush and Beriah.

---

[a]9 Solomon sounds like and may be derived from the Hebrew for peace.   [b]14 That is, about 3,750 tons (about 3,450 metric tons)   [c]14 That is, about 37,500 tons (about 34,500 metric tons)   [d]10 One Hebrew manuscript, Septuagint and Vulgate (see also verse 11); most Hebrew manuscripts Zina

These were the sons of Shimei—
four in all.

¹¹ Jahath was the first and Ziza the
second, but Jeush and Beriah did
not have many sons; so they were
counted as one family with one
assignment.

Kohathites

¹² The sons of Kohath:

Amram, Izhar, Hebron and Uzziel—four in all.

¹³ The sons of Amram:

Aaron and Moses.

Aaron was set apart, he and his
descendants forever, to consecrate
the most holy things, to offer sacrifices before the LORD, to minister
before him and to pronounce
blessings in his name forever.
¹⁴ The sons of Moses the man of
God were counted as part of the
tribe of Levi.

¹⁵ The sons of Moses:

Gershom and Eliezer.

¹⁶ The descendants of Gershom:

Shubael was the first.

¹⁷ The descendants of Eliezer:

Rehabiah was the first.

Eliezer had no other sons, but the
sons of Rehabiah were very numerous.

¹⁸ The sons of Izhar:

Shelomith was the first.

¹⁹ The sons of Hebron:

Jeriah the first, Amariah the second, Jahaziel the third and Jekameam the fourth.

²⁰ The sons of Uzziel:

Micah the first and Isshiah the
second.

Merarites

²¹ The sons of Merari:

Mahli and Mushi.

The sons of Mahli:

Eleazar and Kish.

²² Eleazar died without having sons:
he had only daughters. Their
cousins, the sons of Kish, married
them.

²³ The sons of Mushi:

Mahli, Eder and Jerimoth—three
in all.

²⁴ These were the descendants of Levi
by their families—the heads of families as
they were registered under their names
and counted individually, that is, the
workers twenty years old or more who
served in the temple of the LORD. ²⁵ For
David had said, "Since the LORD, the God
of Israel, has granted rest to his people
and has come to dwell in Jerusalem forever, ²⁶ the Levites no longer need to carry the tabernacle or any of the articles
used in its service." ²⁷ According to the
last instructions of David, the Levites
were counted from those twenty years
old or more.

²⁸ The duty of the Levites was to help
Aaron's descendants in the service of the
temple of the LORD: to be in charge of the
courtyards, the side rooms, the purification of all sacred things and the perfor-
mance of other duties at the house of
God. ²⁹ They were in charge of the bread
set out on the table, the flour for the
grain offerings, the unleavened wafers,
the baking and the mixing, and all measurements of quantity and size. ³⁰ They
were also to stand every morning to
thank and praise the LORD. They were to
do the same in the evening ³¹ and whenever burnt offerings were presented to
the LORD on Sabbaths and at New Moon
festivals and at appointed feasts. They
were to serve before the LORD regularly
in the proper number and in the way prescribed for them.

³² And so the Levites carried out their
responsibilities for the Tent of Meeting,
for the Holy Place and, under their
brothers the descendants of Aaron, for
the service of the temple of the LORD.

The Divisions of Priests

24 These were the divisions of the
sons of Aaron:

The sons of Aaron were Nadab, Abihu,
Eleazar and Ithamar. ²But Nadab and
Abihu died before their father did, and
they had no sons; so Eleazar and Ithamar
served as the priests. ³With the help of
Zadok a descendant of Eleazar and
Ahimelech a descendant of Ithamar, David separated them into divisions for
their appointed order of ministering. ⁴A
larger number of leaders were found
among Eleazar's descendants than

among Ithamar's, and they were divided accordingly: sixteen heads of families from Eleazar's descendants and eight heads of families from Ithamar's descendants. [5]They divided them impartially by drawing lots, for there were officials of the sanctuary and officials of God among the descendants of both Eleazar and Ithamar.

[6]The scribe Shemaiah son of Nethanel, a Levite, recorded their names in the presence of the king and of the officials: Zadok the priest, Ahimelech son of Abiathar and the heads of families of the priests and of the Levites—one family being taken from Eleazar and then one from Ithamar.

[7]The first lot fell to Jehoiarib,
  the second to Jedaiah,
[8]the third to Harim,
  the fourth to Seorim,
[9]the fifth to Malkijah,
  the sixth to Mijamin,
[10]the seventh to Hakkoz,
  the eighth to Abijah,
[11]the ninth to Jeshua,
  the tenth to Shecaniah,
[12]the eleventh to Eliashib,
  the twelfth to Jakim,
[13]the thirteenth to Huppah,
  the fourteenth to Jeshebeab,
[14]the fifteenth to Bilgah,
  the sixteenth to Immer,
[15]the seventeenth to Hezir,
  the eighteenth to Happizzez,
[16]the nineteenth to Pethahiah,
  the twentieth to Jehezkel,
[17]the twenty-first to Jakin,
  the twenty-second to Gamul,
[18]the twenty-third to Delaiah
  and the twenty-fourth to Maaziah.

[19]This was their appointed order of ministering when they entered the temple of the LORD, according to the regulations prescribed for them by their forefather Aaron, as the LORD, the God of Israel, had commanded him.

The Rest of the Levites

[20]As for the rest of the descendants of Levi:
  from the sons of Amram: Shubael;
  from the sons of Shubael: Jehdeiah.

[21]As for Rehabiah, from his sons:
  Isshiah was the first.
[22]From the Izharites: Shelomoth;
  from the sons of Shelomoth: Jahath.
[23]The sons of Hebron: Jeriah the first,[a] Amariah the second, Jahaziel the third and Jekameam the fourth.
[24]The son of Uzziel: Micah;
  from the sons of Micah: Shamir.
[25]The brother of Micah: Isshiah;
  from the sons of Isshiah: Zechariah.
[26]The sons of Merari: Mahli and Mushi.
  The son of Jaaziah: Beno.
[27]The sons of Merari:
  from Jaaziah: Beno, Shoham, Zaccur and Ibri.
[28]From Mahli: Eleazar, who had no sons.
[29]From Kish: the son of Kish: Jerahmeel.
[30]And the sons of Mushi: Mahli, Eder and Jerimoth.

These were the Levites, according to their families. [31]They also cast lots, just as their brothers the descendants of Aaron did, in the presence of King David and of Zadok, Ahimelech, and the heads of families of the priests and of the Levites. The families of the oldest brother were treated the same as those of the youngest.

The Singers

25 David, together with the commanders of the army, set apart some of the sons of Asaph, Heman and Jeduthun for the ministry of prophesying, accompanied by harps, lyres and cymbals. Here is the list of the men who performed this service:

[2]From the sons of Asaph:
  Zaccur, Joseph, Nethaniah and Asarelah. The sons of Asaph were under the supervision of Asaph, who prophesied under the king's supervision.
[3]As for Jeduthun, from his sons:

---

[a]23 Two Hebrew manuscripts and some Septuagint manuscripts (see also 1 Chron. 23:19); most Hebrew manuscripts *The sons of Jeriah:*

Gedaliah, Zeri, Jeshaiah, Shimei,[a] Hashabiah and Mattithiah, six in all, under the supervision of their father Jeduthun, who prophesied, using the harp in thanking and praising the LORD.

4As for Heman, from his sons:
Bukkiah, Mattaniah, Uzziel, Shubael and Jerimoth; Hananiah, Hanani, Eliathah, Giddalti and Romamti-Ezer; Joshbekashah, Mallothi, Hothir and Mahazioth. 5All these were sons of Heman the king's seer. They were given him through the promises of God to exalt him.[b] God gave Heman fourteen sons and three daughters.

6All these men were under the supervision of their fathers for the music of the temple of the LORD, with cymbals, lyres and harps, for the ministry at the house of God. Asaph, Jeduthun and Heman were under the supervision of the king. 7Along with their relatives—all of them trained and skilled in music for the LORD—they numbered 288. 8Young and old alike, teacher as well as student, cast lots for their duties.

9The first lot, which was for Asaph, fell to Joseph,
　his sons and relatives,[c]　12[d]
the second to Gedaliah,
　he and his relatives and sons,　12
10the third to Zaccur,
　his sons and relatives,　12
11the fourth to Izri,[e]
　his sons and relatives,　12
12the fifth to Nethaniah,
　his sons and relatives,　12
13the sixth to Bukkiah,
　his sons and relatives,　12
14the seventh to Jesarelah,[f]
　his sons and relatives,　12
15the eighth to Jeshaiah,
　his sons and relatives,　12
16the ninth to Mattaniah,
　his sons and relatives,　12
17the tenth to Shimei,
　his sons and relatives,　12
18the eleventh to Azarel,[g]
　his sons and relatives,　12
19the twelfth to Hashabiah,
　his sons and relatives,　12
20the thirteenth to Shubael,

　his sons and relatives,　12
21the fourteenth to Mattithiah,
　his sons and relatives,　12
22the fifteenth to Jerimoth,
　his sons and relatives,　12
23the sixteenth to Hananiah,
　his sons and relatives,　12
24the seventeenth to Joshbeka-shah,
　his sons and relatives,　12
25the eighteenth to Hanani,
　his sons and relatives,　12
26the nineteenth to Mallothi,
　his sons and relatives,　12
27the twentieth to Eliathah,
　his sons and relatives,　12
28the twenty-first to Hothir,
　his sons and relatives,　12
29the twenty-second to Giddalti,
　his sons and relatives,　12
30the twenty-third to Mahazi-oth,
　his sons and relatives,　12
31the twenty-fourth to Romamti-Ezer,
　his sons and relatives,　12

The Gatekeepers

26 The divisions of the gatekeepers:

From the Korahites: Meshelemiah son of Kore, one of the sons of Asaph.

2Meshelemiah had sons:
Zechariah the firstborn,
Jediael the second,
Zebadiah the third,
Jathniel the fourth,
3Elam the fifth,
Jehohanan the sixth
and Eliehoenai the seventh.
4Obed-Edom also had sons:
Shemaiah the firstborn,
Jehozabad the second,
Joah the third,
Sacar the fourth,
Nethanel the fifth,
5Ammiel the sixth,
Issachar the seventh

---

a3 One Hebrew manuscript and some Septuagint manuscripts (see also verse 17); most Hebrew manuscripts do not have Shimei.　b5 Hebrew exalt the horn　c9 See Septuagint; Hebrew does not have his sons and relatives.　d9 See the total in verse 7; Hebrew does not have twelve.　e11 A variant of Zeri　f14 A variant of Asarelah　g18 A variant of Uzziel

and Peullethai the eighth.
(For God had blessed Obed-Edom.)

[6] His son Shemaiah also had sons, who were leaders in their father's family because they were very capable men. [7] The sons of Shemaiah: Othni, Rephael, Obed and Elzabad; his relatives Elihu and Semakiah were also able men. [8] All these were descendants of Obed-Edom; they and their sons and their relatives were capable men with the strength to do the work—descendants of Obed-Edom, 62 in all.

[9] Meshelemiah had sons and relatives, who were able men—18 in all.

[10] Hosah the Merarite had sons: Shimri the first (although he was not the firstborn, his father had appointed him the first), [11] Hilkiah the second, Tabaliah the third and Zechariah the fourth. The sons and relatives of Hosah were 13 in all.

[12] These divisions of the gatekeepers, through their chief men, had duties for ministering in the temple of the LORD, just as their relatives had. [13] Lots were cast for each gate, according to their families, young and old alike.

[14] The lot for the East Gate fell to Shelemiah.[a] Then lots were cast for his son Zechariah, a wise counselor, and the lot for the North Gate fell to him. [15] The lot for the South Gate fell to Obed-Edom, and the lot for the storehouse fell to his sons. [16] The lots for the West Gate and the Shalleketh Gate on the upper road fell to Shuppim and Hosah.

Guard was alongside of guard: [17] There were six Levites a day on the east, four a day on the north, four a day on the south and two at a time at the storehouse. [18] As for the court to the west, there were four at the road and two at the court itself.

[19] These were the divisions of the gatekeepers who were descendants of Korah and Merari.

The Treasurers and Other Officials

[20] Their fellow Levites were[b] in charge of the treasuries of the house of God and the treasuries for the dedicated things.

[21] The descendants of Ladan, who were Gershonites through Ladan and who were heads of families belonging to Ladan the Gershonite, were Jehieli, [22] the sons of Jehieli, Zetham and his brother Joel. They were in charge of the treasuries of the temple of the LORD.

[23] From the Amramites, the Izharites, the Hebronites and the Uzzielites:

[24] Shubael, a descendant of Gershom son of Moses, was the officer in charge of the treasuries. [25] His relatives through Eliezer: Rehabiah his son, Jeshaiah his son, Joram his son, Zicri his son and Shelomith his son. [26] Shelomith and his relatives were in charge of all the treasuries for the things dedicated by King David, by the heads of families who were the commanders of thousands and commanders of hundreds, and by the other army commanders. [27] Some of the plunder taken in battle they dedicated for the repair of the temple of the LORD. [28] And everything dedicated by Samuel the seer and by Saul son of Kish, Abner son of Ner and Joab son of Zeruiah, and all the other dedicated things were in the care of Shelomith and his relatives.

[29] From the Izharites: Kenaniah and his sons were assigned duties away from the temple, as officials and judges over Israel.

[30] From the Hebronites: Hashabiah and his relatives—seventeen hundred able men—were responsible in Israel west of the Jordan for all the work of the LORD and for the king's service. [31] As for the Hebronites, Jeriah was their chief according to the genealogical records of their families. In the fortieth year of David's reign a search was made in the records, and capable men among the Hebronites were found at Jazer in Gilead. [32] Jeriah had twenty-seven hundred relatives, who

---

a14 A variant of *Meshelemiah*   *b20* Septuagint; Hebrew *As for the Levites, Ahijah was*

were able men and heads of families, and King David put them in charge of the Reubenites, the Gadites and the half-tribe of Manasseh for every matter pertaining to God and for the affairs of the king.

Army Divisions

27 This is the list of the Israelites—heads of families, commanders of thousands and commanders of hundreds, and their officers, who served the king in all that concerned the army divisions that were on duty month by month throughout the year. Each division consisted of 24,000 men.

²In charge of the first division, for the first month, was Jashobeam son of Zabdiel. There were 24,000 men in his division. ³He was a descendant of Perez and chief of all the army officers for the first month. ⁴In charge of the division for the second month was Dodai the Ahohite; Mikloth was the leader of his division. There were 24,000 men in his division. ⁵The third army commander, for the third month, was Benaiah son of Jehoiada the priest. He was chief and there were 24,000 men in his division. ⁶This was the Benaiah who was a mighty man among the Thirty and was over the Thirty. His son Ammizabad was in charge of his division. ⁷The fourth, for the fourth month, was Asahel the brother of Joab; his son Zebadiah was his successor. There were 24,000 men in his division. ⁸The fifth, for the fifth month, was the commander Shamhuth the Izrahite. There were 24,000 men in his division. ⁹The sixth, for the sixth month, was Ira the son of Ikkesh the Tekoite. There were 24,000 men in his division. ¹⁰The seventh, for the seventh month, was Helez the Pelonite, an Ephraimite. There were 24,000 men in his division. ¹¹The eighth, for the eighth month, was Sibbecai the Hushathite, a Zerahite.

There were 24,000 men in his division. ¹²The ninth, for the ninth month, was Abiezer the Anathothite, a Benjamite. There were 24,000 men in his division. ¹³The tenth, for the tenth month, was Maharai the Netophathite, a Zerahite. There were 24,000 men in his division. ¹⁴The eleventh, for the eleventh month, was Benaiah the Pirathonite, an Ephraimite. There were 24,000 men in his division. ¹⁵The twelfth, for the twelfth month, was Heldai the Netophathite, from the family of Othniel. There were 24,000 men in his division.

Officers of the Tribes

¹⁶The officers over the tribes of Israel:

over the Reubenites: Eliezer son of Zicri;

over the Simeonites: Shephatiah son of Maacah;

¹⁷over Levi: Hashabiah son of Kemuel;

over Aaron: Zadok;

¹⁸over Judah: Elihu, a brother of David;

over Issachar: Omri son of Michael;

¹⁹over Zebulun: Ishmaiah son of Obadiah;

over Naphtali: Jerimoth son of Azriel;

²⁰over the Ephraimites: Hoshea son of Azaziah;

over half the tribe of Manasseh: Joel son of Pedaiah;

²¹over the half-tribe of Manasseh in Gilead: Iddo son of Zechariah;

over Benjamin: Jaasiel son of Abner;

²²over Dan: Azarel son of Jeroham.

These were the officers over the tribes of Israel.

²³David did not take the number of the men twenty years old or less, because the LORD had promised to make Israel as numerous as the stars in the sky. ²⁴Joab son of Zeruiah began to count the men but did not finish. Wrath came on Israel on account of this numbering, and the num-

ber was not entered in the book[a] of the annals of King David.

The King's Overseers

²⁵Azmaveth son of Adiel was in charge of the royal storehouses.

Jonathan son of Uzziah was in charge of the storehouses in the outlying districts, in the towns, the villages and the watchtowers.

²⁶Ezri son of Kelub was in charge of the field workers who farmed the land.

²⁷Shimei the Ramathite was in charge of the vineyards.

Zabdi the Shiphmite was in charge of the produce of the vineyards for the wine vats.

²⁸Baal-Hanan the Gederite was in charge of the olive and sycamore-fig trees in the western foothills.

Joash was in charge of the supplies of olive oil.

²⁹Shitrai the Sharonite was in charge of the herds grazing in Sharon.

Shaphat son of Adlai was in charge of the herds in the valleys.

³⁰Obil the Ishmaelite was in charge of the camels.

Jehdeiah the Meronothite was in charge of the donkeys.

³¹Jaziz the Hagrite was in charge of the flocks.

All these were the officials in charge of King David's property.

³²Jonathan, David's uncle, was a counselor, a man of insight and a scribe. Jehiel son of Hacmoni took care of the king's sons.

³³Ahithophel was the king's counselor. Hushai the Arkite was the king's friend. ³⁴Ahithophel was succeeded by Jehoiada son of Benaiah and by Abiathar.

Joab was the commander of the royal army.

David's Plans for the Temple

28 David summoned all the officials of Israel to assemble at Jerusalem: the officers over the tribes, the commanders of the divisions in the service of the king, the commanders of thousands and commanders of hundreds, and the officials in charge of all the property and livestock belonging to the king and his sons, together with the palace officials, the mighty men and all the brave warriors.

²King David rose to his feet and said: "Listen to me, my brothers and my people. I had it in my heart to build a house as a place of rest for the ark of the covenant of the LORD, for the footstool of our God, and I made plans to build it. ³But God said to me, 'You are not to build a house for my Name, because you are a warrior and have shed blood.'

⁴"Yet the LORD, the God of Israel, chose me from my whole family to be king over Israel forever. He chose Judah as leader, and from the house of Judah he chose my family, and from my father's sons he was pleased to make me king over all Israel. ⁵Of all my sons—and the LORD has given me many—he has chosen my son Solomon to sit on the throne of the kingdom of the LORD over Israel. ⁶He said to me: 'Solomon your son is the one who will build my house and my courts, for I have chosen him to be my son, and I will be his father. ⁷I will establish his kingdom forever if he is unswerving in carrying out my commands and laws, as is being done at this time.'

⁸"So now I charge you in the sight of all Israel and of the assembly of the LORD, and in the hearing of our God: Be careful to follow all the commands of the LORD your God, that you may possess this good land and pass it on as an inheritance to your descendants forever.

⁹"And you, my son Solomon, acknowledge the God of your father, and serve him with wholehearted devotion and with a willing mind, for the LORD searches every heart and understands every motive behind the thoughts. If you seek him, he will be found by you; but if you forsake him, he will reject you forever. ¹⁰Consider now, for the LORD has chosen you to build a temple as a sanctuary. Be strong and do the work."

¹¹Then David gave his son Solomon the plans for the portico of the temple, its buildings, its storerooms, its upper parts, its inner rooms and the place of atonement. ¹²He gave him the plans of all

*24 Septuagint; Hebrew *number.*

that the Spirit had put in his mind for the courts of the temple of the LORD and all the surrounding rooms, for the treasuries of the temple of God and for the treasuries for the dedicated things. [13]He gave him instructions for the divisions of the priests and Levites, and for all the work of serving in the temple of the LORD, as well as for all the articles to be used in its service. [14]He designated the weight of gold for all the gold articles to be used in various kinds of service, and the weight of silver for all the silver articles to be used in various kinds of service: [15]the weight of gold for the gold lampstands and their lamps, with the weight for each lampstand and its lamps; and the weight of silver for each silver lampstand and its lamps, according to the use of each lampstand; [16]the weight of gold for each table for consecrated bread; the weight of silver for the silver tables; [17]the weight of pure gold for the forks, sprinkling bowls and pitchers; the weight of gold for each gold dish; the weight of silver for each silver dish; [18]and the weight of the refined gold for the altar of incense. He also gave him the plan for the chariot, that is, the cherubim of gold that spread their wings and shelter the ark of the covenant of the LORD.

[19]"All this," David said, "I have in writing from the hand of the LORD upon me, and he gave me understanding in all the details of the plan."

[20]David also said to Solomon his son, "Be strong and courageous, and do the work. Do not be afraid or discouraged, for the LORD God, my God, is with you. He will not fail you or forsake you until all the work for the service of the temple of the LORD is finished. [21]The divisions of the priests and Levites are ready for all the work on the temple of God, and every willing man skilled in any craft will help you in all the work. The officials and all the people will obey your every command."

Gifts for Building the Temple

29 Then King David said to the whole assembly: "My son Solomon, the one whom God has chosen, is young and inexperienced. The task is great, because this palatial structure is not for man but for the LORD God. [2]With all my resources I have provided for the temple of my God—gold for the gold work, silver for the silver, bronze for the bronze, iron for the iron and wood for the wood, as well as onyx for the settings, turquoise,[a] stones of various colors, and all kinds of fine stone and marble—all of these in large quantities. [3]Besides, in my devotion to the temple of my God I now give my personal treasures of gold and silver for the temple of my God, over and above everything I have provided for this holy temple: [4]three thousand talents[b] of gold (gold of Ophir) and seven thousand talents[c] of refined silver, for the overlaying of the walls of the buildings, [5]for the gold work and the silver work, and for all the work to be done by the craftsmen. Now, who is willing to consecrate himself today to the LORD?"

[6]Then the leaders of families, the officers of the tribes of Israel, the commanders of thousands and commanders of hundreds, and the officials in charge of the king's work gave willingly. [7]They gave toward the work on the temple of God five thousand talents[d] and ten thousand darics[e] of gold, ten thousand talents[f] of silver, eighteen thousand talents[g] of bronze and a hundred thousand talents[h] of iron. [8]Any who had precious stones gave them to the treasury of the temple of the LORD in the custody of Jehiel the Gershonite. [9]The people rejoiced at the willing response of their leaders, for they had given freely and wholeheartedly to the LORD. David the king also rejoiced greatly.

David's Prayer

[10]David praised the LORD in the presence of the whole assembly, saying,

"Praise be to you, O LORD,
    God of our father Israel,

---

[a]2 The meaning of the Hebrew for this word is uncertain. [b]4 That is, about 110 tons (about 100 metric tons) [c]4 That is, about 260 tons (about 240 metric tons) [d]7 That is, about 190 tons (about 170 metric tons) [e]7 That is, about 185 pounds (about 84 kilograms) [f]7 That is, about 375 tons (about 345 metric tons) [g]7 That is, about 675 tons (about 610 metric tons) [h]7 That is, about 3,750 tons (about 3,450 metric tons)

from everlasting to everlasting.
¹¹ Yours, O LORD, is the greatness and
the power
and the glory and the majesty and
the splendor,
for everything in heaven and earth
is yours.
Yours, O LORD, is the kingdom;
you are exalted as head over all.
¹² Wealth and honor come from you;
you are the ruler of all things.
In your hands are strength and power
to exalt and give strength to all.
¹³ Now, our God, we give you thanks,
and praise your glorious name.

¹⁴"But who am I, and who are my
people, that we should be able to give as
generously as this? Everything comes
from you, and we have given you only
what comes from your hand. ¹⁵We are
aliens and strangers in your sight, as
were all our forefathers. Our days on

earth are like a shadow, without hope.
¹⁶O LORD our God, as for all this abun-
dance that we have provided for building
you a temple for your Holy Name, it
comes from your hand, and all of it belongs to you. ¹⁷I know, my God, that you
test the heart and are pleased with integrity. All these things have I given willingly and with honest intent. And now I
have seen with joy how willingly your
people who are here have given to you.
¹⁸O LORD, God of our fathers Abraham,
Isaac and Israel, keep this desire in the
hearts of your people forever, and keep
their hearts loyal to you. ¹⁹And give my
son Solomon the wholehearted devotion
to keep your commands, requirements
and decrees and to do everything to build
the palatial structure for which I have
provided."

²⁰Then David said to the whole assem-
bly, "Praise the LORD your God." So they
all praised the LORD, the God of their fa-

Tuesday

Liar, Liar

Read 1 Chronicles 29:17

God knows who's telling the truth and who's not. But sometimes it's tough
for *us* to figure it out. When I was in 6th grade, there was this girl who no
one trusted. It was impossible to tell whether she was being honest or lying.
I'd say that's a terrible reputation to have. I definitely don't want to be that
kind of person!

We should take David's example and follow God's rules for living,
because God never lacks integrity. When we do that, God will help us to be
"real" Christians—people who listen to God's Word and try to live out what
we believe.

David was a man after God's own heart. I want to be a girl after God's
own heart. If I'm that kind of person, I won't have to worry about my reputation, and I won't be a dishonest person.

Kate age 13

❶ Why is it tempting to stretch, hide or twist the truth? Think of the last
time you did this. How did you feel? How do you think God felt?

❷ Take a piece of plastic wrap, stretch and twist it, then try to get it
back to its original shape. That's like the reputation of someone who
warps the truth—you might be able to get it close to the original, but the
damage has been done.

❸ Ask God to help you be a person of integrity.

Turn to page 501 for your next devotion.

thers; they bowed low and fell prostrate before the LORD and the king.

Solomon Acknowledged as King

²¹The next day they made sacrifices to the LORD and presented burnt offerings to him: a thousand bulls, a thousand rams and a thousand male lambs, together with their drink offerings, and other sacrifices in abundance for all Israel. ²²They ate and drank with great joy in the presence of the LORD that day.

Then they acknowledged Solomon son of David as king a second time, anointing him before the LORD to be ruler and Zadok to be priest. ²³So Solomon sat on the throne of the LORD as king in place of his father David. He prospered and all Israel obeyed him. ²⁴All the officers and mighty men, as well as all of King David's sons, pledged their submission to King Solomon.

²⁵The LORD highly exalted Solomon in the sight of all Israel and bestowed on him royal splendor such as no king over Israel ever had before.

The Death of David

²⁶David son of Jesse was king over all Israel. ²⁷He ruled over Israel forty years—seven in Hebron and thirty-three in Jerusalem. ²⁸He died at a good old age, having enjoyed long life, wealth and honor. His son Solomon succeeded him as king.

²⁹As for the events of King David's reign, from beginning to end, they are written in the records of Samuel the seer, the records of Nathan the prophet and the records of Gad the seer, ³⁰together with the details of his reign and power, and the circumstances that surrounded him and Israel and the kingdoms of all the other lands.

2 Chronicles

START

Cast
OF
Characters

Solomon
(SAHL-uh-mun)
Israel's third king, son of David and Bathsheba. He has great gobs of everything—money, friends, wisdom and women. He builds Israel's first temple.

Rehoboam
(ree-ha-BOW-um)
Israel's fourth king, son of Solomon. Rehoboam proposes a tax hike, which splits the country in two. The 10 northern tribe-states keep the name *Israel* and form their own country. He winds up being king of just the two southern tribe-states, which form a new country called *Judah*.

Jeroboam
(Jerah-BOW-um)
King Solomon's top general. When Reho makes the dumb tax move, Jer becomes king of the new and smaller Israel. He's the first of a bunch of bad kings who eventually get Israel wiped off the map.

Kings of Judah
There's a bunch of them. Most aren't so good, but there are a few refreshing exceptions. The bad kings eventually get the country into big trouble with Babylon, and everyone gets sent away.

If you read 1 Chronicles, you know Ezra is one of the Jews who gets captured by the Babylonians when they destroy Jerusalem. His new job in Babylon is to teach his fellow Jews their history. That's important because the people are hoping God will give them another chance to build a nation that honors him. They blew it the first time. That's why they're stuck in Babylon.

The book of 2 Chronicles is the second semester of professor Ezra's history course. In the first semester (1 Chronicles), Ezra covered Jewish history from the first human (Adam) to Israel's first really great king (David). This book starts with the story of David's son Solomon and continues all the way to the fall of the nation of Judah.

Solomon, the builder of God's temple, gets lots of coverage in the first part of the book. Ezra would like to see the people build a nation and temple like Solomon's when they get resettled in their homeland. The rest of the book covers the subsequent kings, going light on their sins and heavy on their successes.

The book ends with the best news the Jews have had in a century: The king of Persia (who's now boss of the Babylonians too) gives the Jews permission to return to Jerusalem to live and rebuild God's house—you know, the temple.

Nebuchadnezzar
(neb-yoo-kad-NEZZ-ur)

He's king of Babylon. After Judah follows the evil ways of a long line of mostly bad kings, God lets King Nebby stomp all over Jerusalem. The surviving citizens get dragged off to Babylon.

Cyrus (SIGH-rus)

Cyrus is king of Persia, and one of the first things he does when he captures Babylon is to let the Jews go back to Judah. That's good news!

What's UP with That?

King Jehoshaphat is one of those rare, good kings of Judah. One of the best things he did was to lead his people to victory against their enemies. It was a very strange battle. Read about it in 2 Chronicles 20:20–30, then see if you can complete this story:

❶ On the morning of the battle, King Jehoshaphat got up early and . . .
   a. served his army breakfast
   b. gave his men a godly pep talk
   c. ran through the camp with a bugle to wake everyone up
   d. went for a swim

❷ Then the army went out to the battlefield. But instead of fighting, they . . .
   a. took one look at the enemy and ran for cover
   b. did their morning aerobic workout
   c. surrendered
   d. began to sing

❸ When the enemy troops saw this, they . . .
   a. died laughing
   b. died, but they weren't laughing
   c. captured Jehoshaphat
   d. surrendered

❹ Afterward, the good king's troops went out to the battlefield to collect the war spoils. It took them 3 days to gather it all. On the 4th day, they . . .
   a. slept in and ate pancakes
   b. melted all the enemy's jewelry into a giant, golden calf
   c. fought another battle
   d. praised God

answers: 1-b, 2-d, 3-b, 4-d

Snap shots

- Solomon gets it all!—fortune, fame and a fabulous brain *(chapters 1—2)*

- How to build a temple—blueprints for God's house *(chapters 3—7)*

- How to run a country—Solomon's grand government style *(chapters 8—10)*

- "Bad idea!"—Rehoboam's son splits the states *(chapters 10—12)*

- A & A—Kings Abijah and Asa and a couple of wars *(chapters 13—16)*

- King sings—Jehoshaphat serenades startled soldiers into submission *(chapters 17—20)*

- Mostly downhill—a bunch of kings, the good ones are rare *(chapters 21—35)*

- Babylon steals Judah, Persia gives it back *(chapter 36)*

Solomon Asks for Wisdom

1 Solomon son of David established himself firmly over his kingdom, for the LORD his God was with him and made him exceedingly great.

²Then Solomon spoke to all Israel—to the commanders of thousands and commanders of hundreds, to the judges and to all the leaders in Israel, the heads of families— ³and Solomon and the whole assembly went to the high place at Gibeon, for God's Tent of Meeting was there, which Moses the LORD's servant had made in the desert. ⁴Now David had brought up the ark of God from Kiriath Jearim to the place he had prepared for it, because he had pitched a tent for it in Jerusalem. ⁵But the bronze altar that Bezalel son of Uri, the son of Hur, had made was in Gibeon in front of the tabernacle of the LORD; so Solomon and the assembly inquired of him there. ⁶Solomon went up to the bronze altar before the LORD in the Tent of Meeting and offered a thousand burnt offerings on it.

⁷That night God appeared to Solomon and said to him, "Ask for whatever you want me to give you."

⁸Solomon answered God, "You have shown great kindness to David my father and have made me king in his place. ⁹Now, LORD God, let your promise to my father David be confirmed, for you have made me king over a people who are as numerous as the dust of the earth. ¹⁰Give me wisdom and knowledge, that I may lead this people, for who is able to govern this great people of yours?"

¹¹God said to Solomon, "Since this is your heart's desire and you have not asked for wealth, riches or honor, nor for the death of your enemies, and since you have not asked for a long life but for wisdom and knowledge to govern my people over whom I have made you king, ¹²therefore wisdom and knowledge will be given you. And I will also give you wealth, riches and honor, such as no king who was before you ever had and none after you will have."

¹³Then Solomon went to Jerusalem from the high place at Gibeon, from before the Tent of Meeting. And he reigned over Israel.

¹⁴Solomon accumulated chariots and horses; he had fourteen hundred chariots and twelve thousand horses,ᵃ which he kept in the chariot cities and also with him in Jerusalem. ¹⁵The king made silver and gold as common in Jerusalem as stones, and cedar as plentiful as sycamore-fig trees in the foothills. ¹⁶Solomon's horses were imported from Egyptᵇ and from Kueᶜ—the royal merchants purchased them from Kue. ¹⁷They imported a chariot from Egypt for six hundred shekelsᵈ of silver, and a horse for a hundred and fifty.ᵉ They also exported them to all the kings of the Hittites and of the Arameans.

Preparations for Building the Temple

2 Solomon gave orders to build a temple for the Name of the LORD and a royal palace for himself. ²He conscripted seventy thousand men as carriers and eighty thousand as stonecutters in the hills and thirty-six hundred as foremen over them.

³Solomon sent this message to Hiramᶠ king of Tyre:

"Send me cedar logs as you did for my father David when you sent him cedar to build a palace to live in. ⁴Now I am about to build a temple for the Name of the LORD my God and to dedicate it to him for burning fragrant incense before him, for setting out the consecrated bread regularly, and for making burnt offerings every morning and evening and on Sabbaths and New Moons and at the appointed feasts of the LORD our God. This is a lasting ordinance for Israel.

⁵"The temple I am going to build will be great, because our God is greater than all other gods. ⁶But who is able to build a temple for him, since the heavens, even the highest heavens, cannot contain him? Who then am I to build a temple for him,

---

ᵃ14 Or *charioteers*   ᵇ16 Or possibly *Muzur,* a region in Cilicia; also in verse 17   ᶜ16 Probably Cilicia   ᵈ17 That is, about 15 pounds (about 7 kilograms)   ᵉ17 That is, about 3 3/4 pounds (about 1.7 kilograms)   ᶠ3 Hebrew *Huram,* a variant of *Hiram;* also in verses 11 and 12

except as a place to burn sacrifices before him?

⁷"Send me, therefore, a man skilled to work in gold and silver, bronze and iron, and in purple, crimson and blue yarn, and experienced in the art of engraving, to work in Judah and Jerusalem with my skilled craftsmen, whom my father David provided.

⁸"Send me also cedar, pine and algum*ᵃ* logs from Lebanon, for I know that your men are skilled in cutting timber there. My men will work with yours ⁹to provide me with plenty of lumber, because the temple I build must be large and magnificent. ¹⁰I will give your servants, the woodsmen who cut the timber, twenty thousand cors*ᵇ* of ground wheat, twenty thousand cors of barley, twenty thousand baths*ᶜ* of wine and twenty thousand baths of olive oil."

¹¹Hiram king of Tyre replied by letter to Solomon:

"Because the LORD loves his people, he has made you their king."

¹²And Hiram added:

"Praise be to the LORD, the God of Israel, who made heaven and earth! He has given King David a wise son, endowed with intelligence and discernment, who will build a temple for the LORD and a palace for himself. ¹³"I am sending you Huram-Abi, a man of great skill, ¹⁴whose mother was from Dan and whose father was from Tyre. He is trained to work in gold and silver, bronze and iron, stone and wood, and with purple and blue and crimson yarn and fine linen. He is experienced in all kinds of engraving and can execute any design given to him. He will work with your craftsmen and with those of my lord, David your father.

¹⁵"Now let my lord send his servants the wheat and barley and the olive oil and wine he promised, ¹⁶and we will cut all the logs from Lebanon that you need and will float them in rafts by sea down to Joppa. You can then take them up to Jerusalem."

¹⁷Solomon took a census of all the aliens who were in Israel, after the census his father David had taken; and they were found to be 153,600. ¹⁸He assigned 70,000 of them to be carriers and 80,000 to be stonecutters in the hills, with 3,600 foremen over them to keep the people working.

Solomon Builds the Temple

3 Then Solomon began to build the temple of the LORD in Jerusalem on Mount Moriah, where the LORD had appeared to his father David. It was on the threshing floor of Araunah*ᵈ* the Jebusite, the place provided by David. ²He began building on the second day of the second month in the fourth year of his reign.

³The foundation Solomon laid for building the temple of God was sixty cubits long and twenty cubits wide*ᵉ* (using the cubit of the old standard). ⁴The portico at the front of the temple was twenty cubits*ᶠ* long across the width of the building and twenty cubits*ᵍ* high.

He overlaid the inside with pure gold. ⁵He paneled the main hall with pine and covered it with fine gold and decorated it with palm tree and chain designs. ⁶He adorned the temple with precious stones. And the gold he used was gold of Parvaim. ⁷He overlaid the ceiling beams, doorframes, walls and doors of the temple with gold, and he carved cherubim on the walls.

⁸He built the Most Holy Place, its length corresponding to the width of the temple—twenty cubits long and twenty cubits wide. He overlaid the inside with six hundred talents*ʰ* of fine gold. ⁹The gold nails weighed fifty shekels.*ⁱ* He also overlaid the upper parts with gold.

---

*ᵃ*8 Probably a variant of *almug*; possibly juniper *ᵇ*10 That is, probably about 125,000 bushels (about 4,400 kiloliters) *ᶜ*10 That is, probably about 115,000 gallons (about 440 kiloliters) *ᵈ*1 Hebrew *Ornan*, a variant of *Araunah* *ᵉ*3 That is, about 90 feet (about 27 meters) long and 30 feet (about 9 meters) wide *ᶠ*4 That is, about 30 feet (about 9 meters); also in verses 8, 11 and 13 *ᵍ*4 Some Septuagint and Syriac manuscripts; Hebrew *and a hundred and twenty* *ʰ*8 That is, about 23 tons (about 21 metric tons) *ⁱ*9 That is, about 1 1/4 pounds (about 0.6 kilogram)

[10] In the Most Holy Place he made a pair of sculptured cherubim and overlaid them with gold. [11] The total wingspan of the cherubim was twenty cubits. One wing of the first cherub was five cubits[a] long and touched the temple wall, while its other wing, also five cubits long, touched the wing of the other cherub. [12] Similarly one wing of the second cherub was five cubits long and touched the other temple wall, and its other wing, also five cubits long, touched the wing of the first cherub. [13] The wings of these cherubim extended twenty cubits. They stood on their feet, facing the main hall.[b]

[14] He made the curtain of blue, purple and crimson yarn and fine linen, with cherubim worked into it.

[15] In the front of the temple he made two pillars, which together were thirty-five cubits[c] long, each with a capital on top measuring five cubits. [16] He made interwoven chains[d] and put them on top of the pillars. He also made a hundred pomegranates and attached them to the chains. [17] He erected the pillars in the front of the temple, one to the south and one to the north. The one to the south he named Jakin[e] and the one to the north Boaz.[f]

The Ultimate House
Huh?

2 Chronicles 3:1-17

Solomon's temple was incredible—gold and expensive jewels everywhere, huge pillars, 3-D carvings and statues of little angels all over the place. You could make big bucks just charging admission. (But they didn't; they wanted people to come and worship God.) It was one of the world's most impressive buildings. But the best thing about it?—God was present there.

The Temple's Furnishings

4 He made a bronze altar twenty cubits long, twenty cubits wide and ten cubits high.[g] [2] He made the Sea of cast metal, circular in shape, measuring ten cubits from rim to rim and five cubits[h]

high. It took a line of thirty cubits[i] to measure around it. [3] Below the rim, figures of bulls encircled it—ten to a cubit.[j] The bulls were cast in two rows in one piece with the Sea.

[4] The Sea stood on twelve bulls, three facing north, three facing west, three facing south and three facing east. The Sea rested on top of them, and their hindquarters were toward the center. [5] It was a handbreadth[k] in thickness, and its rim was like the rim of a cup, like a lily blossom. It held three thousand baths.[l]

[6] He then made ten basins for washing and placed five on the south side and five on the north. In them the things to be used for the burnt offerings were rinsed, but the Sea was to be used by the priests for washing.

[7] He made ten gold lampstands according to the specifications for them and placed them in the temple, five on the south side and five on the north.

[8] He made ten tables and placed them in the temple, five on the south side and five on the north. He also made a hundred gold sprinkling bowls.

[9] He made the courtyard of the priests, and the large court and the doors for the court, and overlaid the doors with bronze. [10] He placed the Sea on the south side, at the southeast corner.

[11] He also made the pots and shovels and sprinkling bowls.

So Huram finished the work he had undertaken for King Solomon in the temple of God:

[12] the two pillars;
the two bowl-shaped capitals on top of the pillars;
the two sets of network decorating

---

[a] 11 That is, about 7 1/2 feet (about 2.3 meters); also in verse 15 [b] 13 Or facing inward [c] 15 That is, about 52 feet (about 16 meters) [d] 16 Or possibly made chains in the inner sanctuary; the meaning of the Hebrew for this phrase is uncertain. [e] 17 Jakin probably means he establishes. [f] 17 Boaz probably means in him is strength. [g] 1 That is, about 30 feet (about 9 meters) long and wide, and about 15 feet (about 4.5 meters) high [h] 2 That is, about 7 1/2 feet (about 2.3 meters) [i] 2 That is, about 45 feet (about 13.5 meters) [j] 3 That is, about 1 1/2 feet (about 0.5 meter) [k] 5 That is, about 3 inches (about 8 centimeters) [l] 5 That is, about 17,500 gallons (about 66 kiloliters)

the two bowl-shaped capitals on top of the pillars;
¹³the four hundred pomegranates for the two sets of network (two rows of pomegranates for each network, decorating the bowl-shaped capitals on top of the pillars);
¹⁴the stands with their basins;
¹⁵the Sea and the twelve bulls under it;
¹⁶the pots, shovels, meat forks and all related articles.

All the objects that Huram-Abi made for King Solomon for the temple of the LORD were of polished bronze. ¹⁷The king had them cast in clay molds in the plain of the Jordan between Succoth and Zarethan.ᵃ ¹⁸All these things that Solomon made amounted to so much that the weight of the bronze was not determined.

¹⁹Solomon also made all the furnishings that were in God's temple:

the golden altar;
the tables on which was the bread of the Presence;
²⁰the lampstands of pure gold with their lamps, to burn in front of the inner sanctuary as prescribed;
²¹the gold floral work and lamps and tongs (they were solid gold);
²²the pure gold wick trimmers, sprinkling bowls, dishes and censers; and the gold doors of the temple: the inner doors to the Most Holy Place and the doors of the main hall.

5 When all the work Solomon had done for the temple of the LORD was finished, he brought in the things his father David had dedicated—the silver and gold and all the furnishings—and placed them in the treasuries of God's temple.

The Ark Brought to the Temple

²Then Solomon summoned to Jerusalem the elders of Israel, all the heads of the tribes and the chiefs of the Israelite families, to bring up the ark of the LORD's covenant from Zion, the City of David. ³And all the men of Israel came together to the king at the time of the festival in the seventh month.

⁴When all the elders of Israel had arrived, the Levites took up the ark, ⁵and they brought up the ark and the Tent of Meeting and all the sacred furnishings in it. The priests, who were Levites, carried them up; ⁶and King Solomon and the entire assembly of Israel that had gathered about him were before the ark, sacrificing so many sheep and cattle that they could not be recorded or counted.

⁷The priests then brought the ark of the LORD's covenant to its place in the inner sanctuary of the temple, the Most Holy Place, and put it beneath the wings of the cherubim. ⁸The cherubim spread their wings over the place of the ark and covered the ark and its carrying poles. ⁹These poles were so long that their ends, extending from the ark, could be seen from in front of the inner sanctuary, but not from outside the Holy Place; and they are still there today. ¹⁰There was nothing in the ark except the two tablets that Moses had placed in it at Horeb, where the LORD made a covenant with the Israelites after they came out of Egypt.

¹¹The priests then withdrew from the Holy Place. All the priests who were there had consecrated themselves, regardless of their divisions. ¹²All the Levites who were musicians—Asaph, Heman, Jeduthun and their sons and relatives—stood on the east side of the altar, dressed in fine linen and playing cymbals, harps and lyres. They were accompanied by 120 priests sounding trumpets. ¹³The trumpeters and singers joined in unison, as with one voice, to give praise and thanks to the LORD. Accompanied by trumpets, cymbals and other instruments, they raised their voices in praise to the LORD and sang:

"He is good;
    his love endures forever."

Then the temple of the LORD was filled with a cloud, ¹⁴and the priests could not perform their service because of the cloud, for the glory of the LORD filled the temple of God.

6 Then Solomon said, "The LORD has said that he would dwell in a dark

ᵃ17 Hebrew Zeredatha, a variant of Zarethan

Back Stage Pass

If you had to tell someone what you think of your parents, what would you say? "They're awesome!" "I like my mom, but my dad is hard to get along with" or "My dad is so cool, but my mom . . ." or even, "I can't wait until I'm 18 and can leave!" And then there's the question of brothers and sisters! Whew!

Maybe you're one of those lucky few who thinks your family is the greatest. But most people have mixed feelings about their families. No matter where you are in this, God knows what you need in a family. Here's a bonus for Christians: God has given you 2 families.

THE GIFT OF A HUMAN FAMILY.

Your family, and each person in it, is a gift from God to you. He wants you to know that, besides himself, these are the best people for you to receive love from and give love to. And he wants you to know how to live with your family in a way that is loving, kind and best for everybody. Here's how:

God's design is for your parents and other family to teach you about God. Most kids don't really want their parents to teach them about God. It can seem so awkward and stiff. But, if your parents are Christians, ask them to tell you about their faith (Deuteronomy 6:7, page 210; 2 Timothy 1:5, page 1472). If your parents aren't Christians, God will work in other ways to teach you. Either way, when the time comes for you to have a family of your own, don't forget that God wants you to teach your kids about his love and power.

God wants you to respect and obey your parents. This is one of the BIGGIES in the Bible (found in the Ten Commandments). God always knows and asks us to do what's best for us—so this "obeying your parents" stuff must have good results. To honor and respect your parents means to listen to them, to take them seriously and treat them as people you really care about (Exodus 20:12, page 95; Matthew 15:4, page 1163).

Love is the key to having a great family. Don't wait for others to love you. Loving your family members is a good place for love to begin (Psalm 133:1, page 717; 1 Peter 3:8, page 1517).

THE GIFT OF BEING IN GOD'S FAMILY.

In Matthew 12:50, Jesus tells the crowds: "Whoever does the will of my Father in heaven is my brother and sister and mother." And throughout the Bible God tells us that, if we follow Jesus, we are God's children (Deuteronomy 14:1, page 219; Mark 10:14, page 1202). Because all of us Christians are God's kids, God wants us to live up to our family name (1 John 3, page 1531). When we know, love and follow Jesus, the Bible calls us "children of light" (Ephesians 5:8, page 1429). Being part of God's family means that we live our lives the way he wants us to.

(If something that's happening in your family seems far from loving, especially things like getting hit or being touched in sexual ways, you must talk to someone you trust at church or school—right away!)

> **"I'm confused about the Trinity. How can God be 3 people at once? And what role does each of the 3 play?"**

The Trinity—it's one of the most confusing and mysterious ideas in Christianity. The Bible is clear that God is 3-in-one: God the Father, God the Son, and God the Holy Spirit (see Matthew 28:18–20, page 1185). The 3 parts are separate personalities, each of them fully God. And yet together, they form one being: God. That means when you're talking about Jesus or the Holy Spirit, you're talking about God.

Yes, it's hard to understand—so hard that words don't really do the job. In the early days of the Old Testament, the Jewish people had no word for God at all. Even today, there are no words to fully describe God. That's why it's so difficult to "define" the Trinity. Still, words are all we have. And despite the limitations of our words, I'll do my best to answer your question about the roles of the Trinity.

First, there's God as "Father." That word suggests that God is in charge of the world as Creator, Controller and Provider. When we call God "Father," we refer to God's creative power, his work throughout history and his care for the universe. All things originate with God the Father; he sent both the Son (see John 3:16–17, page 1271) and the Holy Spirit (see John 14:26, page 1293) into the world.

Second, there's God as "Son," who is Jesus. When we refer to God as "Son," we describe the mystery and miracle of God becoming human. When God did this, in the person of Jesus, people saw him differently than just as Creator and Provider. But God remained God, even as he became a man. God the Son's role is to pay for our sins with his blood, which he did on the cross (see Romans 5:9, page 1357), and to act as a "mediator" between us and God (see 1 Timothy 2:5, page 1464).

Third, there's God as "Holy Spirit," which refers to God's presence in our lives today. The Holy Spirit has many roles. He helps us pray (Romans 8:26–27, page 1361), gives us new life (John 3:3–6, page 1270), comforts us (John 14:26–27), convicts us of sin (John 16:7–11), helps us to live holy lives (Romans 15:16), and lives inside us (Romans 8:11).

The Trinity is a tough idea for our human brains to understand. So when you find yourself wondering about this amazing mystery, let it be a reminder of God's awesome power and love.

—Buster Soaries, a popular youth speaker and the pastor of First Baptist Church of Lincoln Gardens in Somerset, New Jersey. He is also the host of the popular "Straight Up!" video series, which tackles the issues teens deal with every day.

cloud; ²I have built a magnificent temple for you, a place for you to dwell forever."

³While the whole assembly of Israel was standing there, the king turned around and blessed them. ⁴Then he said:

"Praise be to the LORD, the God of Israel, who with his hands has fulfilled what he promised with his mouth to my father David. For he said, ⁵'Since the day I brought my people out of Egypt, I have not chosen a city in any tribe of Israel to have a temple built for my Name to be there, nor have I chosen anyone to be the leader over my people Israel. ⁶But now I have chosen Jerusalem for my Name to be there, and I have chosen David to rule my people Israel.'

⁷"My father David had it in his heart to build a temple for the Name of the LORD, the God of Israel. ⁸But the LORD said to my father David, 'Because it was in your heart to build a temple for my Name, you did well to have this in your heart. ⁹Nevertheless, you are not the one to build the temple, but your son, who is your own flesh and blood—he is the one who will build the temple for my Name.'

¹⁰"The LORD has kept the promise he made. I have succeeded David my father and now I sit on the throne of Israel, just as the LORD promised, and I have built the temple for the Name of the LORD, the God of Israel. ¹¹There I have placed the ark, in which is the covenant of the LORD that he made with the people of Israel."

Solomon's Prayer of Dedication

¹²Then Solomon stood before the altar of the LORD in front of the whole assembly of Israel and spread out his hands. ¹³Now he had made a bronze platform, five cubits*a* long, five cubits wide and

---

a13 That is, about 7 1/2 feet (about 2.3 meters)

Wednesday

Sing It!

Read 2 Chronicles 5:12–13

I used to wonder why singing during youth group was such a big deal. So what if I kept talking to my friends when the leader was trying to lead songs? I thought singing was just something to do between games and the devotional—basically, a waste of time.

I can't remember what changed my mind, but I finally realized that the songs were part of our worship. Singing wasn't supposed to entertain me. It was supposed to help me get closer to God.

Now I'm one of the song leaders for my youth group, and I watch some of the other students goofing off like I used to. I just keep reminding them, "You're not singing for yourself—you're singing for the Lord. It doesn't even matter if you have a good voice. If you're singing with your heart, you sound great to him!"

Brian age 14

What about You?

❶ God didn't have to give us music. But why do you think he did?

❷ If you sing or play an instrument, think about getting involved in music at your church. Why not tell the song leaders at your church or youth group they're doing a great job?

❸ Sing your favorite praise song as a prayer to God.

Turn to page 518 for your next devotion.

three cubits[a] high, and had placed it in the center of the outer court. He stood on the platform and then knelt down before the whole assembly of Israel and spread out his hands toward heaven. [14]He said:

"O LORD, God of Israel, there is no God like you in heaven or on earth—you who keep your covenant of love with your servants who continue wholeheartedly in your way. [15]You have kept your promise to your servant David my father; with your mouth you have promised and with your hand you have fulfilled it—as it is today.

[16]"Now LORD, God of Israel, keep for your servant David my father the promises you made to him when you said, 'You shall never fail to have a man to sit before me on the throne of Israel, if only your sons are careful in all they do to walk before me according to my law, as you have done.' [17]And now, O LORD, God of Israel, let your word that you promised your servant David come true.

[18]"But will God really dwell on earth with men? The heavens, even the highest heavens, cannot contain you. How much less this temple I have built! [19]Yet give attention to your servant's prayer and his plea for mercy, O LORD my God. Hear the cry and the prayer that your servant is praying in your presence. [20]May your eyes be open toward this temple day and night, this place of which you said you would put your Name there. May you hear the prayer your servant prays toward this place. [21]Hear the supplications of your servant and of your people Israel when they pray toward this place. Hear from heaven, your dwelling place; and when you hear, forgive.

[22]"When a man wrongs his neighbor and is required to take an oath and he comes and swears the oath before your altar in this temple, [23]then hear from heaven and act. Judge between your servants, repaying the guilty by bringing down on his own head what he has done. De-clare the innocent not guilty and so establish his innocence.

[24]"When your people Israel have been defeated by an enemy because they have sinned against you and when they turn back and confess your name, praying and making supplication before you in this temple, [25]then hear from heaven and forgive the sin of your people Israel and bring them back to the land you gave to them and their fathers.

[26]"When the heavens are shut up and there is no rain because your people have sinned against you, and when they pray toward this place and confess your name and turn from their sin because you have afflicted them, [27]then hear from heaven and forgive the sin of your servants, your people Israel. Teach them the right way to live, and send rain on the land you gave your people for an inheritance.

[28]"When famine or plague comes to the land, or blight or mildew, locusts or grasshoppers, or when enemies besiege them in any of their cities, whatever disaster or disease may come, [29]and when a prayer or plea is made by any of your people Israel—each one aware of his afflictions and pains, and spreading out his hands toward this temple—[30]then hear from heaven, your dwelling place. Forgive, and deal with each man according to all he does, since you know his heart (for you alone know the hearts of men), [31]so that they will fear you and walk in your ways all the time they live in the land you gave our fathers.

[32]"As for the foreigner who does not belong to your people Israel but has come from a distant land because of your great name and your mighty hand and your outstretched arm—when he comes and prays toward this temple, [33]then hear from heaven, your dwelling place, and do whatever the foreigner asks of you, so that all the peoples of the earth may know your name and fear you,

as do your own people Israel, and may know that this house I have built bears your Name.

³⁴"When your people go to war against their enemies, wherever you send them, and when they pray to you toward this city you have chosen and the temple I have built for your Name, ³⁵then hear from heaven their prayer and their plea, and uphold their cause.

³⁶"When they sin against you—for there is no one who does not sin—and you become angry with them and give them over to the enemy, who takes them captive to a land far away or near; ³⁷and if they have a change of heart in the land where they are held captive, and repent and plead with you in the land of their captivity and say, 'We have sinned, we have done wrong and acted wickedly'; ³⁸and if they turn back to you with all their heart and soul in the land of their captivity where they were taken, and pray toward the land you gave their fathers, toward the city you have chosen and toward the temple I have built for your Name; ³⁹then from heaven, your dwelling place, hear their prayer and their pleas, and uphold their cause. And forgive your people, who have sinned against you.

⁴⁰"Now, my God, may your eyes be open and your ears attentive to the prayers offered in this place.

⁴¹"Now arise, O LORD God, and
    come to your resting place,
    you and the ark of your might.
May your priests, O LORD God, be
    clothed with salvation,
    may your saints rejoice in your
       goodness.
⁴²O LORD God, do not reject your
    anointed one.
    Remember the great love promised
       to David your servant."

The Dedication of the Temple

7 When Solomon finished praying, fire came down from heaven and consumed the burnt offering and the sacrifices, and the glory of the LORD filled the temple. ²The priests could not enter the temple of the LORD because the glory of the LORD filled it. ³When all the Israelites saw the fire coming down and the glory of the LORD above the temple, they knelt on the pavement with their faces to the ground, and they worshiped and gave thanks to the LORD, saying,

"He is good;
    his love endures forever."

⁴Then the king and all the people offered sacrifices before the LORD. ⁵And King Solomon offered a sacrifice of twenty-two thousand head of cattle and a hundred and twenty thousand sheep and goats. So the king and all the people dedicated the temple of God. ⁶The priests took their positions, as did the Levites with the LORD's musical instruments, which King David had made for praising the LORD and which were used when he gave thanks, saying, "His love endures forever." Opposite the Levites, the priests blew their trumpets, and all the Israelites were standing.

⁷Solomon consecrated the middle part of the courtyard in front of the temple of the LORD, and there he offered burnt offerings and the fat of the fellowship offerings,ᵃ because the bronze altar he had made could not hold the burnt offerings, the grain offerings and the fat portions.

⁸So Solomon observed the festival at that time for seven days, and all Israel with him—a vast assembly, people from Leboᵇ Hamath to the Wadi of Egypt. ⁹On the eighth day they held an assembly, for they had celebrated the dedication of the altar for seven days and the festival for seven days more. ¹⁰On the twenty-third day of the seventh month he sent the people to their homes, joyful and glad in heart for the good things the LORD had done for David and Solomon and for his people Israel.

The LORD Appears to Solomon

¹¹When Solomon had finished the temple of the LORD and the royal palace,

---

ᵃ7 Traditionally *peace offerings*   ᵇ8 Or *from the entrance to*

and had succeeded in carrying out all he had in mind to do in the temple of the LORD and in his own palace, [12]the LORD appeared to him at night and said:

"I have heard your prayer and have chosen this place for myself as a temple for sacrifices.

[13]"When I shut up the heavens so that there is no rain, or command locusts to devour the land or send a plague among my people, [14]if my people, who are called by my name, will humble themselves and pray and seek my face and turn from their wicked ways, then will I hear from heaven and will forgive their sin and will heal their land. [15]Now my eyes will be open and my ears attentive to the prayers offered in this place. [16]I have chosen and consecrated this temple so that my Name may be there forever. My eyes and my heart will always be there.

[17]"As for you, if you walk before me as David your father did, and do all I command, and observe my decrees and laws, [18]I will establish your royal throne, as I covenanted with David your father when I said, 'You shall never fail to have a man to rule over Israel.'

[19]"But if you[a] turn away and forsake the decrees and commands I have given you[a] and go off to serve other gods and worship them, [20]then I will uproot Israel from my land, which I have given them, and will reject this temple I have consecrated for my Name. I will make it a byword and an object of ridicule among all peoples. [21]And though this temple is now so imposing, all who pass by will be appalled and say, 'Why has the LORD done such a thing to this land and to this temple?' [22]People will answer, 'Because they have forsaken the LORD, the God of their fathers, who brought them out of Egypt, and have embraced other gods, worshiping and serving them—that is why he brought all this disaster on them.' "

Solomon's Other Activities

8 At the end of twenty years, during which Solomon built the temple of the LORD and his own palace, [2]Solomon rebuilt the villages that Hiram[b] had given him, and settled Israelites in them. [3]Solomon then went to Hamath Zobah and captured it. [4]He also built up Tadmor in the desert and all the store cities he had built in Hamath. [5]He rebuilt Upper Beth Horon and Lower Beth Horon as fortified cities, with walls and with gates and bars, [6]as well as Baalath and all his store cities, and all the cities for his chariots and for his horses[c]—whatever he desired to build in Jerusalem, in Lebanon and throughout all the territory he ruled.

[7]All the people left from the Hittites, Amorites, Perizzites, Hivites and Jebusites (these peoples were not Israelites), [8]that is, their descendants remaining in the land, whom the Israelites had not destroyed—these Solomon conscripted for his slave labor force, as it is to this day. [9]But Solomon did not make slaves of the Israelites for his work; they were his fighting men, commanders of his captains, and commanders of his chariots and charioteers. [10]They were also King Solomon's chief officials—two hundred and fifty officials supervising the men.

[11]Solomon brought Pharaoh's daughter up from the City of David to the palace he had built for her, for he said, "My wife must not live in the palace of David king of Israel, because the places the ark of the LORD has entered are holy."

[12]On the altar of the LORD that he had built in front of the portico, Solomon sacrificed burnt offerings to the LORD, [13]according to the daily requirement for offerings commanded by Moses for Sabbaths, New Moons and the three annual feasts—the Feast of Unleavened Bread, the Feast of Weeks and the Feast of Tabernacles. [14]In keeping with the ordinance of his father David, he appointed the divisions of the priests for their duties, and the Levites to lead the praise and to assist the priests according to each day's requirement. He also appointed the gate-

[a]19 The Hebrew is plural.   [b]2 Hebrew *Huram,* a variant of *Hiram*; also in verse 18   [c]6 Or *charioteers*

keepers by divisions for the various gates, because this was what David the man of God had ordered. ¹⁵They did not deviate from the king's commands to the priests or to the Levites in any matter, including that of the treasuries.

¹⁶All Solomon's work was carried out, from the day the foundation of the temple of the Lord was laid until its completion. So the temple of the Lord was finished.

¹⁷Then Solomon went to Ezion Geber and Elath on the coast of Edom. ¹⁸And Hiram sent him ships commanded by his own officers, men who knew the sea. These, with Solomon's men, sailed to Ophir and brought back four hundred and fifty talents[a] of gold, which they delivered to King Solomon.

The Queen of Sheba Visits Solomon

9 When the queen of Sheba heard of Solomon's fame, she came to Jerusalem to test him with hard questions. Arriving with a very great caravan—with camels carrying spices, large quantities of gold, and precious stones—she came to Solomon and talked with him about all she had on her mind. ²Solomon answered all her questions; nothing was too hard for him to explain to her. ³When the queen of Sheba saw the wisdom of Solomon, as well as the palace he had built, ⁴the food on his table, the seating of his officials, the attending servants in their robes, the cupbearers in their robes and the burnt offerings he made at[b] the temple of the Lord, she was overwhelmed.

⁵She said to the king, "The report I heard in my own country about your achievements and your wisdom is true. ⁶But I did not believe what they said until I came and saw with my own eyes. Indeed, not even half the greatness of your wisdom was told me; you have far exceeded the report I heard. ⁷How happy your men must be! How happy your officials, who continually stand before you and hear your wisdom! ⁸Praise be to the Lord your God, who has delighted in you and placed you on his throne as king to rule for the Lord your God. Because of the love of your God for Israel and his desire to uphold them forever, he has made you king over them, to maintain justice and righteousness."

⁹Then she gave the king 120 talents[c] of gold, large quantities of spices, and precious stones. There had never been such spices as those the queen of Sheba gave to King Solomon.

¹⁰(The men of Hiram and the men of Solomon brought gold from Ophir; they also brought algumwood[d] and precious stones. ¹¹The king used the algumwood to make steps for the temple of the Lord and for the royal palace, and to make harps and lyres for the musicians. Nothing like them had ever been seen in Judah.)

¹²King Solomon gave the queen of Sheba all she desired and asked for; he gave her more than she had brought to him. Then she left and returned with her retinue to her own country.

Solomon's Splendor

¹³The weight of the gold that Solomon received yearly was 666 talents,[e] ¹⁴not including the revenues brought in by merchants and traders. Also all the kings of Arabia and the governors of the land brought gold and silver to Solomon.

¹⁵King Solomon made two hundred large shields of hammered gold; six hundred bekas[f] of hammered gold went into each shield. ¹⁶He also made three hundred small shields of hammered gold, with three hundred bekas[g] of gold in each shield. The king put them in the Palace of the Forest of Lebanon.

¹⁷Then the king made a great throne inlaid with ivory and overlaid with pure gold. ¹⁸The throne had six steps, and a footstool of gold was attached to it. On both sides of the seat were armrests, with a lion standing beside each of them. ¹⁹Twelve lions stood on the six steps, one at either end of each step. Nothing like it had ever been made for any other kingdom. ²⁰All King Solomon's goblets were

---

[a] *18 That is, about 17 tons (about 16 metric tons)
[b] *4 Or *the ascent by which he went up to*   [c] *9 That is, about 4 1/2 tons (about 4 metric tons)
[d] *10 Probably a variant of *almugwood*   [e] *13 That is, about 25 tons (about 23 metric tons)   [f] *15 That is, about 7 1/2 pounds (about 3.5 kilograms)
[g] *16 That is, about 3 3/4 pounds (about 1.7 kilograms)

gold, and all the household articles in the Palace of the Forest of Lebanon were pure gold. Nothing was made of silver, because silver was considered of little value in Solomon's day. ²¹The king had a fleet of trading ships^a manned by Hiram's^b men. Once every three years it returned, carrying gold, silver and ivory, and apes and baboons.

²²King Solomon was greater in riches and wisdom than all the other kings of the earth. ²³All the kings of the earth sought audience with Solomon to hear the wisdom God had put in his heart.

World's Wisest King

Huh?

2 Chronicles 9:22–23

God gave King Solomon a great gift—he made him the wisest and richest guy in the world. In 2 Chronicles, Solomon not only sounds like he's wise and rich, but he also sounds as if he's a good guy too. But don't forget that 1 and 2 Chronicles is not interested in showing the kings' weaknesses, only their strengths. Look at 1 Kings 11 (page 400) if you want to read about Solomon's *dark* side.

²⁴Year after year, everyone who came brought a gift—articles of silver and gold, and robes, weapons and spices, and horses and mules.

²⁵Solomon had four thousand stalls for horses and chariots, and twelve thousand horses,^c which he kept in the chariot cities and also with him in Jerusalem. ²⁶He ruled over all the kings from the River^d to the land of the Philistines, as far as the border of Egypt. ²⁷The king made silver as common in Jerusalem as stones, and cedar as plentiful as sycamore-fig trees in the foothills. ²⁸Solomon's horses were imported from Egypt^e and from all other countries.

Solomon's Death

²⁹As for the other events of Solomon's reign, from beginning to end, are they not written in the records of Nathan the prophet, in the prophecy of Ahijah the Shilonite and in the visions of Iddo the seer concerning Jeroboam son of Nebat? ³⁰Solomon reigned in Jerusalem over all Israel forty years. ³¹Then he rested with his fathers and was buried in the city of David his father. And Rehoboam his son succeeded him as king.

Israel Rebels Against Rehoboam

10 Rehoboam went to Shechem, for all the Israelites had gone there to make him king. ²When Jeroboam son of Nebat heard this (he was in Egypt, where he had fled from King Solomon), he returned from Egypt. ³So they sent for Jeroboam, and he and all Israel went to Rehoboam and said to him: ⁴"Your father put a heavy yoke on us, but now lighten the harsh labor and the heavy yoke he put on us, and we will serve you."

⁵Rehoboam answered, "Come back to me in three days." So the people went away.

⁶Then King Rehoboam consulted the elders who had served his father Solomon during his lifetime. "How would you advise me to answer these people?" he asked.

⁷They replied, "If you will be kind to these people and please them and give them a favorable answer, they will always be your servants."

⁸But Rehoboam rejected the advice the elders gave him and consulted the young men who had grown up with him and were serving him. ⁹He asked them, "What is your advice? How should we answer these people who say to me, 'Lighten the yoke your father put on us'?"

¹⁰The young men who had grown up with him replied, "Tell the people who have said to you, 'Your father put a heavy yoke on us, but make our yoke lighter'—tell them, 'My little finger is thicker than my father's waist. ¹¹My father laid on you a heavy yoke; I will make it even heavier. My father scourged you with whips; I will scourge you with scorpions.' "

^a21 Hebrew *of ships that could go to Tarshish*
^b21 Hebrew *Huram*, a variant of *Hiram*   ^c25 Or *charioteers*   ^d26 That is, the Euphrates
^e28 Or possibly *Muzur*, a region in Cilicia

¹²Three days later Jeroboam and all the people returned to Rehoboam, as the king had said, "Come back to me in three days." ¹³The king answered them harshly. Rejecting the advice of the elders, ¹⁴he followed the advice of the young men and said, "My father made your yoke heavy; I will make it even heavier. My father scourged you with whips; I will scourge you with scorpions." ¹⁵So the king did not listen to the people, for this turn of events was from God, to fulfill the word the LORD had spoken to Jeroboam son of Nebat through Ahijah the Shilonite.

¹⁶When all Israel saw that the king refused to listen to them, they answered the king:

"What share do we have in David,
    what part in Jesse's son?
To your tents, O Israel!
    Look after your own house,
        O David!"

So all the Israelites went home. ¹⁷But as for the Israelites who were living in the towns of Judah, Rehoboam still ruled over them.

¹⁸King Rehoboam sent out Adoniram,ᵃ who was in charge of forced labor, but the Israelites stoned him to death. King Rehoboam, however, managed to get into his chariot and escape to Jerusalem. ¹⁹So Israel has been in rebellion against the house of David to this day.

11 When Rehoboam arrived in Jerusalem, he mustered the house of Judah and Benjamin—a hundred and eighty thousand fighting men—to make war against Israel and to regain the kingdom for Rehoboam.

²But this word of the LORD came to Shemaiah the man of God: ³"Say to Rehoboam son of Solomon king of Judah and to all the Israelites in Judah and Benjamin, ⁴'This is what the LORD says: Do not go up to fight against your brothers. Go home, every one of you, for this is my doing.' " So they obeyed the words of the LORD and turned back from marching against Jeroboam.

Rehoboam Fortifies Judah

⁵Rehoboam lived in Jerusalem and built up towns for defense in Judah:

⁶Bethlehem, Etam, Tekoa, ⁷Beth Zur, Soco, Adullam, ⁸Gath, Mareshah, Ziph, ⁹Adoraim, Lachish, Azekah, ¹⁰Zorah, Aijalon and Hebron. These were fortified cities in Judah and Benjamin. ¹¹He strengthened their defenses and put commanders in them, with supplies of food, olive oil and wine. ¹²He put shields and spears in all the cities, and made them very strong. So Judah and Benjamin were his.

¹³The priests and Levites from all their districts throughout Israel sided with him. ¹⁴The Levites even abandoned their pasturelands and property, and came to Judah and Jerusalem because Jeroboam and his sons had rejected them as priests of the LORD. ¹⁵And he appointed his own priests for the high places and for the goat and calf idols he had made. ¹⁶Those from every tribe of Israel who set their hearts on seeking the LORD, the God of Israel, followed the Levites to Jerusalem to offer sacrifices to the LORD, the God of their fathers. ¹⁷They strengthened the kingdom of Judah and supported Rehoboam son of Solomon three years, walking in the ways of David and Solomon during this time.

Rehoboam's Family

¹⁸Rehoboam married Mahalath, who was the daughter of David's son Jerimoth and of Abihail, the daughter of Jesse's son Eliab. ¹⁹She bore him sons: Jeush, Shemariah and Zaham. ²⁰Then he married Maacah daughter of Absalom, who bore him Abijah, Attai, Ziza and Shelomith. ²¹Rehoboam loved Maacah daughter of Absalom more than any of his other wives and concubines. In all, he had eighteen wives and sixty concubines, twenty-eight sons and sixty daughters.

²²Rehoboam appointed Abijah son of Maacah to be the chief prince among his brothers, in order to make him king. ²³He acted wisely, dispersing some of his sons throughout the districts of Judah and Benjamin, and to all the fortified cities. He gave them abundant provisions and took many wives for them.

ᵃ18 Hebrew *Hadoram*, a variant of *Adoniram*

Shishak Attacks Jerusalem

12 After Rehoboam's position as king was established and he had become strong, he and all Israel*a* with him abandoned the law of the LORD. ²Because they had been unfaithful to the LORD, Shishak king of Egypt attacked Jerusalem in the fifth year of King Rehoboam. ³With twelve hundred chariots and sixty thousand horsemen and the innumerable troops of Libyans, Sukkites and Cushites*b* that came with him from Egypt, ⁴he captured the fortified cities of Judah and came as far as Jerusalem.

⁵Then the prophet Shemaiah came to Rehoboam and to the leaders of Judah who had assembled in Jerusalem for fear of Shishak, and he said to them, "This is what the LORD says, 'You have abandoned me; therefore, I now abandon you to Shishak.'"

⁶The leaders of Israel and the king humbled themselves and said, "The LORD is just."

⁷When the LORD saw that they humbled themselves, this word of the LORD came to Shemaiah: "Since they have humbled themselves, I will not destroy them but will soon give them deliverance. My wrath will not be poured out on Jerusalem through Shishak. ⁸They will, however, become subject to him, so that they may learn the difference between serving me and serving the kings of other lands."

⁹When Shishak king of Egypt attacked Jerusalem, he carried off the treasures of the temple of the LORD and the treasures of the royal palace. He took everything, including the gold shields Solomon had made. ¹⁰So King Rehoboam made bronze shields to replace them and assigned these to the commanders of the guard on duty at the entrance to the royal palace. ¹¹Whenever the king went to the LORD's temple, the guards went with him, bearing the shields, and afterward they returned them to the guardroom.

¹²Because Rehoboam humbled himself, the LORD's anger turned from him, and he was not totally destroyed. Indeed, there was some good in Judah.

¹³King Rehoboam established himself firmly in Jerusalem and continued as king. He was forty-one years old when he became king, and he reigned seventeen years in Jerusalem, the city the LORD had chosen out of all the tribes of Israel in which to put his Name. His mother's name was Naamah; she was an Ammonite. ¹⁴He did evil because he had not set his heart on seeking the LORD.

¹⁵As for the events of Rehoboam's reign, from beginning to end, are they not written in the records of Shemaiah the prophet and of Iddo the seer that deal with genealogies? There was continual warfare between Rehoboam and Jeroboam. ¹⁶Rehoboam rested with his fathers and was buried in the City of David. And Abijah his son succeeded him as king.

Abijah King of Judah

13 In the eighteenth year of the reign of Jeroboam, Abijah became king of Judah, ²and he reigned in Jerusalem three years. His mother's name was Maacah,*c* a daughter*d* of Uriel of Gibeah.

There was war between Abijah and Jeroboam. ³Abijah went into battle with a force of four hundred thousand able fighting men, and Jeroboam drew up a battle line against him with eight hundred thousand able troops.

⁴Abijah stood on Mount Zemaraim, in the hill country of Ephraim, and said, "Jeroboam and all Israel, listen to me! ⁵Don't you know that the LORD, the God of Israel, has given the kingship of Israel to David and his descendants forever by a covenant of salt? ⁶Yet Jeroboam son of Nebat, an official of Solomon son of David, rebelled against his master. ⁷Some worthless scoundrels gathered around him and opposed Rehoboam son of Solomon when he was young and indecisive and not strong enough to resist them.

⁸"And now you plan to resist the kingdom of the LORD, which is in the hands of David's descendants. You are indeed a vast army and have with you the golden calves that Jeroboam made to be your gods. ⁹But didn't you drive out the priests of the LORD, the sons of Aaron, and the

---

a 1 That is, Judah, as frequently in 2 Chronicles
b 3 That is, people from the upper Nile region
c 2 Most Septuagint manuscripts and Syriac (see also 2 Chron. 11:20 and 1 Kings 15:2); Hebrew *Micaiah*
d 2 Or *granddaughter*

Levites, and make priests of your own as the peoples of other lands do? Whoever comes to consecrate himself with a young bull and seven rams may become a priest of what are not gods.

¹⁰"As for us, the LORD is our God, and we have not forsaken him. The priests who serve the LORD are sons of Aaron, and the Levites assist them. ¹¹Every morning and evening they present burnt offerings and fragrant incense to the LORD. They set out the bread on the ceremonially clean table and light the lamps on the gold lampstand every evening. We are observing the requirements of the LORD our God. But you have forsaken him. ¹²God is with us; he is our leader. His priests with their trumpets will sound the battle cry against you. Men of Israel, do not fight against the LORD, the God of your fathers, for you will not succeed."

¹³Now Jeroboam had sent troops around to the rear, so that while he was in front of Judah the ambush was behind them. ¹⁴Judah turned and saw that they were being attacked at both front and rear. Then they cried out to the LORD. The priests blew their trumpets ¹⁵and the men of Judah raised the battle cry. At the sound of their battle cry, God routed Jeroboam and all Israel before Abijah and Judah. ¹⁶The Israelites fled before Judah, and God delivered them into their hands. ¹⁷Abijah and his men inflicted heavy losses on them, so that there were five hundred thousand casualties among Israel's able men. ¹⁸The men of Israel were subdued on that occasion, and the men of Judah were victorious because they relied on the LORD, the God of their fathers.

¹⁹Abijah pursued Jeroboam and took from him the towns of Bethel, Jeshanah and Ephron, with their surrounding villages. ²⁰Jeroboam did not regain power during the time of Abijah. And the LORD struck him down and he died.

²¹But Abijah grew in strength. He married fourteen wives and had twenty-two sons and sixteen daughters.

²²The other events of Abijah's reign, what he did and what he said, are written in the annotations of the prophet Iddo.

14 And Abijah rested with his fathers and was buried in the City of David. Asa his son succeeded him as king, and in his days the country was at peace for ten years.

Asa King of Judah

²Asa did what was good and right in the eyes of the LORD his God. ³He removed the foreign altars and the high places, smashed the sacred stones and cut down the Asherah poles.ᵃ ⁴He commanded Judah to seek the LORD, the God of their fathers, and to obey his laws and commands. ⁵He removed the high places and incense altars in every town in Judah, and the kingdom was at peace under him. ⁶He built up the fortified cities of Judah, since the land was at peace. No one was at war with him during those years, for the LORD gave him rest.

⁷"Let us build up these towns," he said to Judah, "and put walls around them, with towers, gates and bars. The land is still ours, because we have sought the LORD our God; we sought him and he has given us rest on every side." So they built and prospered.

⁸Asa had an army of three hundred thousand men from Judah, equipped with large shields and with spears, and two hundred and eighty thousand from Benjamin, armed with small shields and with bows. All these were brave fighting men.

⁹Zerah the Cushite marched out against them with a vast armyᵇ and three hundred chariots, and came as far as Mareshah. ¹⁰Asa went out to meet him, and they took up battle positions in the Valley of Zephathah near Mareshah.

¹¹Then Asa called to the LORD his God and said, "LORD, there is no one like you to help the powerless against the mighty. Help us, O LORD our God, for we rely on you, and in your name we have come against this vast army. O LORD, you are our God; do not let man prevail against you."

¹²The LORD struck down the Cushites before Asa and Judah. The Cushites fled, ¹³and Asa and his army pursued them as far as Gerar. Such a great number of

---

ᵃ3 That is, symbols of the goddess Asherah; here and elsewhere in 2 Chronicles ᵇ9 Hebrew *with an army of a thousand thousands* or *with an army of thousands upon thousands*

Cushites fell that they could not recover; they were crushed before the LORD and his forces. The men of Judah carried off a large amount of plunder. ¹⁴They destroyed all the villages around Gerar, for the terror of the LORD had fallen upon them. They plundered all these villages, since there was much booty there. ¹⁵They also attacked the camps of the herdsmen and carried off droves of sheep and goats and camels. Then they returned to Jerusalem.

Asa's Reform

15 The Spirit of God came upon Azariah son of Oded. ²He went out to meet Asa and said to him, "Listen to me, Asa and all Judah and Benjamin. The LORD is with you when you are with him. If you seek him, he will be found by you, but if you forsake him, he will forsake you. ³For a long time Israel was without the true God, without a priest to teach and without the law. ⁴But in their distress they turned to the LORD, the God of Israel, and sought him, and he was found by them. ⁵In those days it was not safe to travel about, for all the inhabitants of the lands were in great turmoil. ⁶One nation was being crushed by another and one city by another, because God was troubling them with every kind of distress. ⁷But as for you, be strong and do not give up, for your work will be rewarded."

⁸When Asa heard these words and the prophecy of Azariah son of[a] Oded the prophet, he took courage. He removed the detestable idols from the whole land of Judah and Benjamin and from the towns he had captured in the hills of Ephraim. He repaired the altar of the LORD that was in front of the portico of the LORD's temple.

⁹Then he assembled all Judah and Benjamin and the people from Ephraim, Manasseh and Simeon who had settled among them, for large numbers had come over to him from Israel when they saw that the LORD his God was with him. ¹⁰They assembled at Jerusalem in the third month of the fifteenth year of Asa's reign. ¹¹At that time they sacrificed to the LORD seven hundred head of cattle and seven thousand sheep and goats from the plunder they had brought back. ¹²They

entered into a covenant to seek the LORD, the God of their fathers, with all their heart and soul. ¹³All who would not seek the LORD, the God of Israel, were to be put to death, whether small or great, man or woman. ¹⁴They took an oath to the LORD with loud acclamation, with shouting and with trumpets and horns. ¹⁵All Judah rejoiced about the oath because they had sworn it wholeheartedly. They sought God eagerly, and he was found by them. So the LORD gave them rest on every side.

¹⁶King Asa also deposed his grandmother Maacah from her position as queen mother, because she had made a repulsive Asherah pole. Asa cut the pole down, broke it up and burned it in the Kidron Valley. ¹⁷Although he did not remove the high places from Israel, Asa's heart was fully committed to the LORD all his life. ¹⁸He brought into the temple of God the silver and gold and the articles that he and his father had dedicated.

¹⁹There was no more war until the thirty-fifth year of Asa's reign.

Asa's Last Years

16 In the thirty-sixth year of Asa's reign Baasha king of Israel went up against Judah and fortified Ramah to prevent anyone from leaving or entering the territory of Asa king of Judah.

²Asa then took the silver and gold out of the treasuries of the LORD's temple and of his own palace and sent it to Ben-Hadad king of Aram, who was ruling in Damascus. ³"Let there be a treaty between me and you," he said, "as there was between my father and your father. See, I am sending you silver and gold. Now break your treaty with Baasha king of Israel so he will withdraw from me."

⁴Ben-Hadad agreed with King Asa and sent the commanders of his forces against the towns of Israel. They conquered Ijon, Dan, Abel Maim[b] and all the store cities of Naphtali. ⁵When Baasha heard this, he stopped building Ramah and abandoned his work. ⁶Then King Asa brought all the men of Judah, and they

---

[a]8 Vulgate and Syriac (see also Septuagint and verse 1); Hebrew does not have *Azariah son of*.
[b]4 Also known as *Abel Beth Maacah*

carried away from Ramah the stones and timber Baasha had been using. With them he built up Geba and Mizpah.

⁷At that time Hanani the seer came to Asa king of Judah and said to him: "Because you relied on the king of Aram and not on the LORD your God, the army of the king of Aram has escaped from your hand. ⁸Were not the Cushites*ᵃ* and Libyans a mighty army with great numbers of chariots and horsemen*ᵇ*? Yet when you relied on the LORD, he delivered them into your hand. ⁹For the eyes of the LORD range throughout the earth to strengthen those whose hearts are fully committed to him. You have done a foolish thing, and from now on you will be at war."

¹⁰Asa was angry with the seer because of this; he was so enraged that he put him in prison. At the same time Asa brutally oppressed some of the people.

¹¹The events of Asa's reign, from beginning to end, are written in the book of the kings of Judah and Israel. ¹²In the thirty-ninth year of his reign Asa was afflicted with a disease in his feet. Though his disease was severe, even in his illness he did not seek help from the LORD, but only from the physicians. ¹³Then in the forty-first year of his reign Asa died and rested with his fathers. ¹⁴They buried him in the tomb that he had cut out for himself in the City of David. They laid him on a bier covered with spices and various blended perfumes, and they made a huge fire in his honor.

Jehoshaphat King of Judah

17 Jehoshaphat his son succeeded him as king and strengthened himself against Israel. ²He stationed troops in all the fortified cities of Judah and put garrisons in Judah and in the towns of Ephraim that his father Asa had captured.

³The LORD was with Jehoshaphat because in his early years he walked in the ways his father David had followed. He did not consult the Baals ⁴but sought the God of his father and followed his commands rather than the practices of Israel. ⁵The LORD established the kingdom under his control; and all Judah brought gifts to Jehoshaphat, so that he had great wealth and honor. ⁶His heart was devoted

to the ways of the LORD; furthermore, he removed the high places and the Asherah poles from Judah.

⁷In the third year of his reign he sent his officials Ben-Hail, Obadiah, Zechariah, Nethanel and Micaiah to teach in the towns of Judah. ⁸With them were certain Levites—Shemaiah, Nethaniah, Zebadiah, Asahel, Shemiramoth, Jehonathan, Adonijah, Tobijah and Tob-Adonijah—and the priests Elishama and Jehoram. ⁹They taught throughout Judah, taking with them the Book of the Law of the LORD; they went around to all the towns of Judah and taught the people.

¹⁰The fear of the LORD fell on all the kingdoms of the lands surrounding Judah, so that they did not make war with Jehoshaphat. ¹¹Some Philistines brought Jehoshaphat gifts and silver as tribute, and the Arabs brought him flocks: seven thousand seven hundred rams and seven thousand seven hundred goats.

¹²Jehoshaphat became more and more powerful; he built forts and store cities in Judah ¹³and had large supplies in the towns of Judah. He also kept experienced fighting men in Jerusalem. ¹⁴Their enrollment by families was as follows:

From Judah, commanders of units of 1,000:
Adnah the commander, with 300,000 fighting men;
¹⁵next, Jehohanan the commander, with 280,000;
¹⁶next, Amasiah son of Zicri, who volunteered himself for the service of the LORD, with 200,000.
¹⁷From Benjamin:
Eliada, a valiant soldier, with 200,000 men armed with bows and shields;
¹⁸next, Jehozabad, with 180,000 men armed for battle.

¹⁹These were the men who served the king, besides those he stationed in the fortified cities throughout Judah.

Micaiah Prophesies Against Ahab

18 Now Jehoshaphat had great wealth and honor, and he allied

ᵃ8 That is, people from the upper Nile region
ᵇ8 Or *charioteers*

himself with Ahab by marriage. ²Some years later he went down to visit Ahab in Samaria. Ahab slaughtered many sheep and cattle for him and the people with him and urged him to attack Ramoth Gilead. ³Ahab king of Israel asked Jehoshaphat king of Judah, "Will you go with me against Ramoth Gilead?"

Jehoshaphat replied, "I am as you are, and my people as your people; we will join you in the war." ⁴But Jehoshaphat also said to the king of Israel, "First seek the counsel of the LORD."

⁵So the king of Israel brought together the prophets—four hundred men—and asked them, "Shall we go to war against Ramoth Gilead, or shall I refrain?"

"Go," they answered, "for God will give it into the king's hand."

⁶But Jehoshaphat asked, "Is there not a prophet of the LORD here whom we can inquire of?"

⁷The king of Israel answered Jehoshaphat, "There is still one man through whom we can inquire of the LORD, but I hate him because he never prophesies anything good about me, but always bad. He is Micaiah son of Imlah."

"The king should not say that," Jehoshaphat replied.

⁸So the king of Israel called one of his officials and said, "Bring Micaiah son of Imlah at once."

⁹Dressed in their royal robes, the king of Israel and Jehoshaphat king of Judah were sitting on their thrones at the threshing floor by the entrance to the gate of Samaria, with all the prophets prophesying before them. ¹⁰Now Zedekiah son of Kenaanah had made iron horns, and he declared, "This is what the LORD says: 'With these you will gore the Arameans until they are destroyed.'"

¹¹All the other prophets were prophesying the same thing. "Attack Ramoth Gilead and be victorious," they said, "for the LORD will give it into the king's hand."

¹²The messenger who had gone to summon Micaiah said to him, "Look, as one man the other prophets are predicting success for the king. Let your word agree with theirs, and speak favorably."

¹³But Micaiah said, "As surely as the LORD lives, I can tell him only what my God says."

¹⁴When he arrived, the king asked him, "Micaiah, shall we go to war against Ramoth Gilead, or shall I refrain?"

"Attack and be victorious," he answered, "for they will be given into your hand."

¹⁵The king said to him, "How many times must I make you swear to tell me nothing but the truth in the name of the LORD?"

¹⁶Then Micaiah answered, "I saw all Israel scattered on the hills like sheep without a shepherd, and the LORD said, 'These people have no master. Let each one go home in peace.'"

¹⁷The king of Israel said to Jehoshaphat, "Didn't I tell you that he never prophesies anything good about me, but only bad?"

¹⁸Micaiah continued, "Therefore hear the word of the LORD: I saw the LORD sitting on his throne with all the host of heaven standing on his right and on his left. ¹⁹And the LORD said, 'Who will entice Ahab king of Israel into attacking Ramoth Gilead and going to his death there?'

"One suggested this, and another that. ²⁰Finally, a spirit came forward, stood before the LORD and said, 'I will entice him.'

"'By what means?' the LORD asked.

²¹"'I will go and be a lying spirit in the mouths of all his prophets,' he said.

"'You will succeed in enticing him,' said the LORD. 'Go and do it.'

²²"So now the LORD has put a lying spirit in the mouths of these prophets of yours. The LORD has decreed disaster for you."

²³Then Zedekiah son of Kenaanah went up and slapped Micaiah in the face. "Which way did the spirit from*a* the LORD go when he went from me to speak to you?" he asked.

²⁴Micaiah replied, "You will find out on the day you go to hide in an inner room."

²⁵The king of Israel then ordered, "Take Micaiah and send him back to Amon the ruler of the city and to Joash the king's son, ²⁶and say, 'This is what the king says: Put this fellow in prison and give

ᵃ23 Or *Spirit of*

him nothing but bread and water until I return safely.' "

²⁷Micaiah declared, "If you ever return safely, the LORD has not spoken through me." Then he added, "Mark my words, all you people!"

Ahab Killed at Ramoth Gilead

²⁸So the king of Israel and Jehoshaphat king of Judah went up to Ramoth Gilead. ²⁹The king of Israel said to Jehoshaphat, "I will enter the battle in disguise, but you wear your royal robes." So the king of Israel disguised himself and went into battle.

³⁰Now the king of Aram had ordered his chariot commanders, "Do not fight with anyone, small or great, except the king of Israel." ³¹When the chariot commanders saw Jehoshaphat, they thought, "This is the king of Israel." So they turned to attack him, but Jehoshaphat cried out, and the LORD helped him. God drew them away from him, ³²for when the chariot commanders saw that he was not the king of Israel, they stopped pursuing him.

³³But someone drew his bow at random and hit the king of Israel between the sections of his armor. The king told the chariot driver, "Wheel around and get me out of the fighting. I've been wounded." ³⁴All day long the battle raged, and the king of Israel propped himself up in his chariot facing the Arameans until evening. Then at sunset he died.

19 When Jehoshaphat king of Judah returned safely to his palace in Jerusalem, ²Jehu the seer, the son of Hanani, went out to meet him and said to the king, "Should you help the wicked and love*ᵃ* those who hate the LORD? Because of this, the wrath of the LORD is upon you. ³There is, however, some good in you, for you have rid the land of the Asherah poles and have set your heart on seeking God."

Jehoshaphat Appoints Judges

⁴Jehoshaphat lived in Jerusalem, and he went out again among the people from Beersheba to the hill country of Ephraim and turned them back to the LORD, the God of their fathers. ⁵He ap-

pointed judges in the land, in each of the fortified cities of Judah. ⁶He told them, "Consider carefully what you do, because you are not judging for man but for the LORD, who is with you whenever you give a verdict. ⁷Now let the fear of the LORD be upon you. Judge carefully, for with the LORD our God there is no injustice or partiality or bribery."

⁸In Jerusalem also, Jehoshaphat appointed some of the Levites, priests and heads of Israelite families to administer the law of the LORD and to settle disputes. And they lived in Jerusalem. ⁹He gave them these orders: "You must serve faithfully and wholeheartedly in the fear of the LORD. ¹⁰In every case that comes before you from your fellow countrymen who live in the cities—whether bloodshed or other concerns of the law, commands, decrees or ordinances—you are to warn them not to sin against the LORD; otherwise his wrath will come on you and your brothers. Do this, and you will not sin.

¹¹"Amariah the chief priest will be over you in any matter concerning the LORD, and Zebadiah son of Ishmael, the leader of the tribe of Judah, will be over you in any matter concerning the king, and the Levites will serve as officials before you. Act with courage, and may the LORD be with those who do well."

Jehoshaphat Defeats Moab and Ammon

20 After this, the Moabites and Ammonites with some of the Meunites*ᵇ* came to make war on Jehoshaphat.

²Some men came and told Jehoshaphat, "A vast army is coming against you from Edom,*ᶜ* from the other side of the Sea.*ᵈ* It is already in Hazazon Tamar" (that is, En Gedi). ³Alarmed, Jehoshaphat resolved to inquire of the LORD, and he proclaimed a fast for all Judah. ⁴The people of Judah came together to seek help from the LORD; indeed, they came from every town in Judah to seek him.

⁵Then Jehoshaphat stood up in the

ᵃ2 Or *and make alliances with*   *ᵇ1* Some Septuagint manuscripts; Hebrew *Ammonites*   *ᶜ2* One Hebrew manuscript; most Hebrew manuscripts, Septuagint and Vulgate *Aram*   *ᵈ2* That is, the Dead Sea

assembly of Judah and Jerusalem at the temple of the LORD in the front of the new courtyard ⁶and said:

"O LORD, God of our fathers, are you not the God who is in heaven? You rule over all the kingdoms of the nations. Power and might are in your hand, and no one can withstand you. ⁷O our God, did you not drive out the inhabitants of this land before your people Israel and give it forever to the descendants of Abraham your friend? ⁸They have lived in it and have built in it a sanctuary for your Name, saying, ⁹'If calamity comes upon us, whether the sword of judgment, or plague or famine, we will stand in your presence before this temple that bears your Name and will cry out to you in our distress, and you will hear us and save us.'

¹⁰"But now here are men from Ammon, Moab and Mount Seir, whose territory you would not allow Israel to invade when they came from Egypt; so they turned away from them and did not destroy them. ¹¹See how they are repaying us by coming to drive us out of the possession you gave us as an inheritance. ¹²O our God, will you not judge them? For we have no power to face this vast army that is attacking us. We do not know what to do, but our eyes are upon you."

¹³All the men of Judah, with their wives and children and little ones, stood there before the LORD.

¹⁴Then the Spirit of the LORD came upon Jahaziel son of Zechariah, the son of Benaiah, the son of Jeiel, the son of Mattaniah, a Levite and descendant of Asaph, as he stood in the assembly.

¹⁵He said: "Listen, King Jehoshaphat and all who live in Judah and Jerusalem! This is what the LORD says to you: 'Do not be afraid or discouraged because of this vast army. For the battle is not yours, but God's. ¹⁶Tomorrow march down against them. They will be climbing up by the Pass of Ziz, and you will find them at the end of the gorge in the Desert of Jeruel. ¹⁷You will not have to fight this battle. Take up your positions; stand firm and see the deliverance the LORD will give you, O Judah and Jerusalem. Do not be afraid; do not be discouraged. Go out to face them tomorrow, and the LORD will be with you.' "

¹⁸Jehoshaphat bowed with his face to the ground, and all the people of Judah and Jerusalem fell down in worship before the LORD. ¹⁹Then some Levites from the Kohathites and Korahites stood up and praised the LORD, the God of Israel, with very loud voice.

²⁰Early in the morning they left for the Desert of Tekoa. As they set out, Jehoshaphat stood and said, "Listen to me, Judah and people of Jerusalem! Have faith in the LORD your God and you will be upheld; have faith in his prophets and you will be successful." ²¹After consulting the people, Jehoshaphat appointed men to sing to the LORD and to praise him for the splendor of his[a] holiness as they went out at the head of the army, saying:

"Give thanks to the LORD,
    for his love endures forever."

²²As they began to sing and praise, the LORD set ambushes against the men of Ammon and Moab and Mount Seir who were invading Judah, and they were defeated. ²³The men of Ammon and Moab rose up against the men from Mount Seir to destroy and annihilate them. After they finished slaughtering the men from Seir, they helped to destroy one another.

²⁴When the men of Judah came to the place that overlooks the desert and looked toward the vast army, they saw only dead bodies lying on the ground; no one had escaped. ²⁵So Jehoshaphat and his men went to carry off their plunder, and they found among them a great amount of equipment and clothing[b] and also articles of value—more than they could take away. There was so much plunder that it took three days to collect it. ²⁶On the fourth day they assembled in the Valley of Beracah, where they praised the LORD. This is why it is called the Valley of Beracah[c] to this day.

ᵃ21 Or him with the splendor of   ᵇ25 Some Hebrew manuscripts and Vulgate; most Hebrew manuscripts corpses   ᶜ26 Beracah means praise.

²⁷Then, led by Jehoshaphat, all the men of Judah and Jerusalem returned joyfully to Jerusalem, for the LORD had given them cause to rejoice over their enemies. ²⁸They entered Jerusalem and went to the temple of the LORD with harps and lutes and trumpets.

²⁹The fear of God came upon all the kingdoms of the countries when they heard how the LORD had fought against the enemies of Israel. ³⁰And the kingdom of Jehoshaphat was at peace, for his God had given him rest on every side.

The End of Jehoshaphat's Reign

³¹So Jehoshaphat reigned over Judah. He was thirty-five years old when he became king of Judah, and he reigned in Jerusalem twenty-five years. His mother's name was Azubah daughter of Shilhi. ³²He walked in the ways of his father Asa and did not stray from them; he did what was right in the eyes of the LORD. ³³The high places, however, were not removed, and the people still had not set their hearts on the God of their fathers.

³⁴The other events of Jehoshaphat's reign, from beginning to end, are written in the annals of Jehu son of Hanani, which are recorded in the book of the kings of Israel.

³⁵Later, Jehoshaphat king of Judah made an alliance with Ahaziah king of Israel, who was guilty of wickedness. ³⁶He agreed with him to construct a fleet of trading ships.ᵃ After these were built at Ezion Geber, ³⁷Eliezer son of Dodavahu of Mareshah prophesied against Jehoshaphat, saying, "Because you have made an alliance with Ahaziah, the LORD will destroy what you have made." The ships were wrecked and were not able to set sail to trade.ᵇ

21 Then Jehoshaphat rested with his fathers and was buried with them in the City of David. And Jehoram his son succeeded him as king. ²Jehoram's brothers, the sons of Jehoshaphat, were Azariah, Jehiel, Zechariah, Azariahu, Michael and Shephatiah. All these were sons of Jehoshaphat king of Israel.ᶜ ³Their father had given them many gifts of silver and gold and articles of value, as well as fortified cities in Judah, but he

had given the kingdom to Jehoram because he was his firstborn son.

Jehoram King of Judah

⁴When Jehoram established himself firmly over his father's kingdom, he put all his brothers to the sword along with some of the princes of Israel. ⁵Jehoram was thirty-two years old when he became king, and he reigned in Jerusalem eight years. ⁶He walked in the ways of the kings of Israel, as the house of Ahab had done, for he married a daughter of Ahab. He did evil in the eyes of the LORD. ⁷Nevertheless, because of the covenant the LORD had made with David, the LORD was not willing to destroy the house of David. He had promised to maintain a lamp for him and his descendants forever.

⁸In the time of Jehoram, Edom rebelled against Judah and set up its own king. ⁹So Jehoram went there with his officers and all his chariots. The Edomites surrounded him and his chariot commanders, but he rose up and broke through by night. ¹⁰To this day Edom has been in rebellion against Judah.

Libnah revolted at the same time, because Jehoram had forsaken the LORD, the God of his fathers. ¹¹He had also built high places on the hills of Judah and had caused the people of Jerusalem to prostitute themselves and had led Judah astray.

¹²Jehoram received a letter from Elijah the prophet, which said:

"This is what the LORD, the God of your father David, says: 'You have not walked in the ways of your father Jehoshaphat or of Asa king of Judah. ¹³But you have walked in the ways of the kings of Israel, and you have led Judah and the people of Jerusalem to prostitute themselves, just as the house of Ahab did. You have also murdered your own brothers, members of your father's house, men who were better than you. ¹⁴So now the LORD is about to strike your people, your sons, your wives and

---

ᵃ36 Hebrew *of ships that could go to Tarshish*
ᵇ37 Hebrew *sail for Tarshish*   ᶜ2 That is, Judah, as frequently in 2 Chronicles

everything that is yours, with a heavy blow. ¹⁵You yourself will be very ill with a lingering disease of the bowels, until the disease causes your bowels to come out.' "

¹⁶The LORD aroused against Jehoram the hostility of the Philistines and of the Arabs who lived near the Cushites. ¹⁷They attacked Judah, invaded it and carried off all the goods found in the king's palace, together with his sons and wives. Not a son was left to him except Ahaziah,ᵃ the youngest.

¹⁸After all this, the LORD afflicted Jehoram with an incurable disease of the bowels. ¹⁹In the course of time, at the end of the second year, his bowels came out because of the disease, and he died in great pain. His people made no fire in his honor, as they had for his fathers.

²⁰Jehoram was thirty-two years old when he became king, and he reigned in Jerusalem eight years. He passed away, to no one's regret, and was buried in the City of David, but not in the tombs of the kings.

Ahaziah King of Judah

22 The people of Jerusalem made Ahaziah, Jehoram's youngest son, king in his place, since the raiders, who came with the Arabs into the camp, had killed all the older sons. So Ahaziah son of Jehoram king of Judah began to reign.

²Ahaziah was twenty-twoᵇ years old when he became king, and he reigned in Jerusalem one year. His mother's name was Athaliah, a granddaughter of Omri.

³He too walked in the ways of the house of Ahab, for his mother encouraged him in doing wrong. ⁴He did evil in the eyes of the LORD, as the house of Ahab had done, for after his father's death they became his advisers, to his undoing. ⁵He also followed their counsel when he went with Joramᶜ son of Ahab king of Israel to war against Hazael king of Aram at Ramoth Gilead. The Arameans wounded Joram; ⁶so he returned to Jezreel to recover from the wounds they had inflicted on him at Ramothᵈ in his battle with Hazael king of Aram.

Then Ahaziahᵉ son of Jehoram king of Judah went down to Jezreel to see Joram son of Ahab because he had been wounded.

⁷Through Ahaziah's visit to Joram, God brought about Ahaziah's downfall. When Ahaziah arrived, he went out with Joram to meet Jehu son of Nimshi, whom the LORD had anointed to destroy the house of Ahab. ⁸While Jehu was executing judgment on the house of Ahab, he found the princes of Judah and the sons of Ahaziah's relatives, who had been attending Ahaziah, and he killed them. ⁹He then went in search of Ahaziah, and his men captured him while he was hiding in Samaria. He was brought to Jehu and put to death. They buried him, for they said, "He was a son of Jehoshaphat, who sought the LORD with all his heart." So there was no one in the house of Ahaziah powerful enough to retain the kingdom.

Athaliah and Joash

¹⁰When Athaliah the mother of Ahaziah saw that her son was dead, she proceeded to destroy the whole royal family of the house of Judah. ¹¹But Jehosheba,ᶠ the daughter of King Jehoram, took Joash son of Ahaziah and stole him away from among the royal princes who were about to be murdered and put him and his nurse in a bedroom. Because Jehosheba,ᶠ the daughter of King Jehoram and wife of the priest Jehoiada, was Ahaziah's sister, she hid the child from Athaliah so she could not kill him. ¹²He remained hidden with them at the temple of God for six years while Athaliah ruled the land.

23 In the seventh year Jehoiada showed his strength. He made a covenant with the commanders of units of a hundred: Azariah son of Jeroham, Ishmael son of Jehohanan, Azariah son of Obed, Maaseiah son of Adaiah, and Elishaphat son of Zicri. ²They went throughout Judah and gathered the Levites and the heads of Israelite families

---

ᵃ *17* Hebrew *Jehoahaz*, a variant of *Ahaziah*
ᵇ *2* Some Septuagint manuscripts and Syriac (see also 2 Kings 8:26); Hebrew *forty-two* ᶜ *5* Hebrew *Jehoram*, a variant of *Joram*; also in verses 6 and 7 ᵈ *6* Hebrew *Ramah*, a variant of *Ramoth* ᵉ *6* Some Hebrew manuscripts, Septuagint, Vulgate and Syriac (see also 2 Kings 8:29); most Hebrew manuscripts *Azariah* ᶠ *11* Hebrew *Jehoshabeath*, a variant of *Jehosheba*

from all the towns. When they came to Jerusalem, ³the whole assembly made a covenant with the king at the temple of God.

Jehoiada said to them, "The king's son shall reign, as the LORD promised concerning the descendants of David. ⁴Now this is what you are to do: A third of you priests and Levites who are going on duty on the Sabbath are to keep watch at the doors, ⁵a third of you at the royal palace and a third at the Foundation Gate, and all the other men are to be in the courtyards of the temple of the LORD. ⁶No one is to enter the temple of the LORD except the priests and Levites on duty; they may enter because they are consecrated, but all the other men are to guard what the LORD has assigned to them.ᵃ ⁷The Levites are to station themselves around the king, each man with his weapons in his hand. Anyone who enters the temple must be put to death. Stay close to the king wherever he goes."

⁸The Levites and all the men of Judah did just as Jehoiada the priest ordered. Each one took his men—those who were going on duty on the Sabbath and those who were going off duty—for Jehoiada the priest had not released any of the divisions. ⁹Then he gave the commanders of units of a hundred the spears and the large and small shields that had belonged to King David and that were in the temple of God. ¹⁰He stationed all the men, each with his weapon in his hand, around the king—near the altar and the temple, from the south side to the north side of the temple.

¹¹Jehoiada and his sons brought out the king's son and put the crown on him; they presented him with a copy of the covenant and proclaimed him king. They anointed him and shouted, "Long live the king!"

¹²When Athaliah heard the noise of the people running and cheering the king, she went to them at the temple of the LORD. ¹³She looked, and there was the king, standing by his pillar at the entrance. The officers and the trumpeters were beside the king, and all the people of the land were rejoicing and blowing trumpets, and singers with musical instruments were leading the praises. Then

Athaliah tore her robes and shouted, "Treason! Treason!"

¹⁴Jehoiada the priest sent out the commanders of units of a hundred, who were in charge of the troops, and said to them: "Bring her out between the ranksᵇ and put to the sword anyone who follows her." For the priest had said, "Do not put her to death at the temple of the LORD." ¹⁵So they seized her as she reached the entrance of the Horse Gate on the palace grounds, and there they put her to death.

¹⁶Jehoiada then made a covenant that he and the people and the kingᶜ would be the LORD's people. ¹⁷All the people went to the temple of Baal and tore it down. They smashed the altars and idols and killed Mattan the priest of Baal in front of the altars.

¹⁸Then Jehoiada placed the oversight of the temple of the LORD in the hands of the priests, who were Levites, to whom David had made assignments in the temple, to present the burnt offerings of the LORD as written in the Law of Moses, with rejoicing and singing, as David had ordered. ¹⁹He also stationed doorkeepers at the gates of the LORD's temple so that no one who was in any way unclean might enter.

²⁰He took with him the commanders of hundreds, the nobles, the rulers of the people and all the people of the land and brought the king down from the temple of the LORD. They went into the palace through the Upper Gate and seated the king on the royal throne, ²¹and all the people of the land rejoiced. And the city was quiet, because Athaliah had been slain with the sword.

Joash Repairs the Temple

24 Joash was seven years old when he became king, and he reigned in Jerusalem forty years. His mother's name was Zibiah; she was from Beersheba. ²Joash did what was right in the eyes of the LORD all the years of Jehoiada the priest. ³Jehoiada chose two wives for him, and he had sons and daughters.

ᵃ6 Or to observe the LORD's command not to enter
ᵇ14 Or out from the precincts   ᶜ16 Or covenant between the LORD, and the people and the king that they (see 2 Kings 11:17)

Kiddie King

Huh?

2 Chronicles 24:1–2

How would *you* have liked to become king when you were 7 years old? It might be fun for awhile, but that's a truckload of responsibility for such a young kid. Joash was a good king at first (as long as the priest Jehoiada was alive), but later he turned bad. Maybe he never had the chance to *learn* right from wrong growing up. Maybe he was forced to act too old too soon.

⁴Some time later Joash decided to restore the temple of the LORD. ⁵He called together the priests and Levites and said to them, "Go to the towns of Judah and collect the money due annually from all Israel, to repair the temple of your God. Do it now." But the Levites did not act at once.

⁶Therefore the king summoned Jehoiada the chief priest and said to him, "Why haven't you required the Levites to bring in from Judah and Jerusalem the tax imposed by Moses the servant of the LORD and by the assembly of Israel for the Tent of the Testimony?"

⁷Now the sons of that wicked woman Athaliah had broken into the temple of God and had used even its sacred objects for the Baals.

⁸At the king's command, a chest was made and placed outside, at the gate of the temple of the LORD. ⁹A proclamation was then issued in Judah and Jerusalem that they should bring to the LORD the tax that Moses the servant of God had required of Israel in the desert. ¹⁰All the officials and all the people brought their

Thursday

Too Young?
Read 2 Chronicles 24:1

Some people think you have to be an adult in order to serve Jesus Christ. But I think being young opens up all kinds of doors for me to share my faith with other people. For example, most people make decisions about religion when they're young. And most of the people at my school would rather talk about faith with someone their own age. That means teenagers like me have a big responsibility to share our faith. This verse says that Joash was only 7 years old when he became king! It also tells us that he did what was right in God's sight.

It's easy to get discouraged and intimidated when we don't have all the answers. But we can be like Joash and stand up for God when we're young. God used this young king, not an adult, to show Israel how to live right. The world may not think we're qualified, but God does. He can, and will, use anyone who wants to serve him.

Ryan, age 14

❶ When was the last time you got discouraged because of your age? What did you do about it?

❷ Brainstorm some ways you can serve God at your school or in your neighborhood. What are 2 things you can do that your parents or other adults can't? (go to youth group, skateboard, go on school class trips)

❸ Ask God to show you creative ways to serve him, no matter what your age.

Turn to page 522 for your next devotion.

contributions gladly, dropping them into the chest until it was full. ¹¹Whenever the chest was brought in by the Levites to the king's officials and they saw that there was a large amount of money, the royal secretary and the officer of the chief priest would come and empty the chest and carry it back to its place. They did this regularly and collected a great amount of money. ¹²The king and Jehoiada gave it to the men who carried out the work required for the temple of the LORD. They hired masons and carpenters to restore the LORD's temple, and also workers in iron and bronze to repair the temple.

¹³The men in charge of the work were diligent, and the repairs progressed under them. They rebuilt the temple of God according to its original design and reinforced it. ¹⁴When they had finished, they brought the rest of the money to the king and Jehoiada, and with it were made articles for the LORD's temple: articles for the service and for the burnt offerings, and also dishes and other objects of gold and silver. As long as Jehoiada lived, burnt offerings were presented continually in the temple of the LORD.

¹⁵Now Jehoiada was old and full of years, and he died at the age of a hundred and thirty. ¹⁶He was buried with the kings in the City of David, because of the good he had done in Israel for God and his temple.

The Wickedness of Joash

¹⁷After the death of Jehoiada, the officials of Judah came and paid homage to the king, and he listened to them. ¹⁸They abandoned the temple of the LORD, the God of their fathers, and worshiped Asherah poles and idols. Because of their guilt, God's anger came upon Judah and Jerusalem. ¹⁹Although the LORD sent prophets to the people to bring them back to him, and though they testified against them, they would not listen.

²⁰Then the Spirit of God came upon Zechariah son of Jehoiada the priest. He stood before the people and said, "This is what God says: 'Why do you disobey the LORD's commands? You will not prosper. Because you have forsaken the LORD, he has forsaken you.'"

²¹But they plotted against him, and by order of the king they stoned him to death in the courtyard of the LORD's temple. ²²King Joash did not remember the kindness Zechariah's father Jehoiada had shown him but killed his son, who said as he lay dying, "May the LORD see this and call you to account."

²³At the turn of the year,ᵃ the army of Aram marched against Joash; it invaded Judah and Jerusalem and killed all the leaders of the people. They sent all the plunder to their king in Damascus. ²⁴Although the Aramean army had come with only a few men, the LORD delivered into their hands a much larger army. Because Judah had forsaken the LORD, the God of their fathers, judgment was executed on Joash. ²⁵When the Arameans withdrew, they left Joash severely wounded. His officials conspired against him for murdering the son of Jehoiada the priest, and they killed him in his bed. So he died and was buried in the City of David, but not in the tombs of the kings.

²⁶Those who conspired against him were Zabad,ᵇ son of Shimeath an Ammonite woman, and Jehozabad, son of Shimrithᶜ a Moabite woman. ²⁷The account of his sons, the many prophecies about him, and the record of the restoration of the temple of God are written in the annotations on the book of the kings. And Amaziah his son succeeded him as king.

Amaziah King of Judah

25 Amaziah was twenty-five years old when he became king, and he reigned in Jerusalem twenty-nine years. His mother's name was Jehoaddinᵈ; she was from Jerusalem. ²He did what was right in the eyes of the LORD, but not wholeheartedly. ³After the kingdom was firmly in his control, he executed the officials who had murdered his father the king. ⁴Yet he did not put their sons to death, but acted in accordance with what is written in the Law, in the Book of Moses, where the LORD commanded: "Fathers shall not be put to death for their children, nor children put to death for

---

ᵃ23 Probably in the spring   ᵇ26 A variant of *Jozabad*   ᶜ26 A variant of *Shomer*
ᵈ1 Hebrew *Jehoaddan*, a variant of *Jehoaddin*

their fathers; each is to die for his own sins."[a]

[5]Amaziah called the people of Judah together and assigned them according to their families to commanders of thousands and commanders of hundreds for all Judah and Benjamin. He then mustered those twenty years old or more and found that there were three hundred thousand men ready for military service, able to handle the spear and shield. [6]He also hired a hundred thousand fighting men from Israel for a hundred talents[b] of silver.

[7]But a man of God came to him and said, "O king, these troops from Israel must not march with you, for the LORD is not with Israel—not with any of the people of Ephraim. [8]Even if you go and fight courageously in battle, God will overthrow you before the enemy, for God has the power to help or to overthrow."

[9]Amaziah asked the man of God, "But what about the hundred talents I paid for these Israelite troops?"

The man of God replied, "The LORD can give you much more than that."

[10]So Amaziah dismissed the troops who had come to him from Ephraim and sent them home. They were furious with Judah and left for home in a great rage.

[11]Amaziah then marshaled his strength and led his army to the Valley of Salt, where he killed ten thousand men of Seir. [12]The army of Judah also captured ten thousand men alive, took them to the top of a cliff and threw them down so that all were dashed to pieces.

[13]Meanwhile the troops that Amaziah had sent back and had not allowed to take part in the war raided Judean towns from Samaria to Beth Horon. They killed three thousand people and carried off great quantities of plunder.

[14]When Amaziah returned from slaughtering the Edomites, he brought back the gods of the people of Seir. He set them up as his own gods, bowed down to them and burned sacrifices to them. [15]The anger of the LORD burned against Amaziah, and he sent a prophet to him, who said, "Why do you consult this people's gods, which could not save their own people from your hand?"

[16]While he was still speaking, the king said to him, "Have we appointed you an adviser to the king? Stop! Why be struck down?"

So the prophet stopped but said, "I know that God has determined to destroy you, because you have done this and have not listened to my counsel."

[17]After Amaziah king of Judah consulted his advisers, he sent this challenge to Jehoash[c] son of Jehoahaz, the son of Jehu, king of Israel: "Come, meet me face to face."

[18]But Jehoash king of Israel replied to Amaziah king of Judah: "A thistle in Lebanon sent a message to a cedar in Lebanon, 'Give your daughter to my son in marriage.' Then a wild beast in Lebanon came along and trampled the thistle underfoot. [19]You say to yourself that you have defeated Edom, and now you are arrogant and proud. But stay at home! Why ask for trouble and cause your own downfall and that of Judah also?"

[20]Amaziah, however, would not listen, for God so worked that he might hand them over to Jehoash, because they sought the gods of Edom. [21]So Jehoash king of Israel attacked. He and Amaziah king of Judah faced each other at Beth Shemesh in Judah. [22]Judah was routed by Israel, and every man fled to his home. [23]Jehoash king of Israel captured Amaziah king of Judah, the son of Joash, the son of Ahaziah,[d] at Beth Shemesh. Then Jehoash brought him to Jerusalem and broke down the wall of Jerusalem from the Ephraim Gate to the Corner Gate—a section about six hundred feet[e] long. [24]He took all the gold and silver and all the articles found in the temple of God that had been in the care of Obed-Edom, together with the palace treasures and the hostages, and returned to Samaria.

[25]Amaziah son of Joash king of Judah lived for fifteen years after the death of Jehoash son of Jehoahaz king of Israel. [26]As for the other events of Amaziah's reign, from beginning to end, are they not written in the book of the kings of

---

[a]4 Deut. 24:16 [b]6 That is, about 3 3/4 tons (about 3.4 metric tons); also in verse 9 [c]17 Hebrew *Joash*, a variant of *Jehoash*; also in verses 18, 21, 23 and 25 [d]23 Hebrew *Jehoahaz*, a variant of *Ahaziah* [e]23 Hebrew *four hundred cubits* (about 180 meters)

Judah and Israel? [27]From the time that Amaziah turned away from following the LORD, they conspired against him in Jerusalem and he fled to Lachish, but they sent men after him to Lachish and killed him there. [28]He was brought back by horse and was buried with his fathers in the City of Judah.

Uzziah King of Judah

26 Then all the people of Judah took Uzziah,[a] who was sixteen years old, and made him king in place of his father Amaziah. [2]He was the one who rebuilt Elath and restored it to Judah after Amaziah rested with his fathers.

[3]Uzziah was sixteen years old when he became king, and he reigned in Jerusalem fifty-two years. His mother's name was Jecoliah; she was from Jerusalem. [4]He did what was right in the eyes of the LORD, just as his father Amaziah had done. [5]He sought God during the days of Zechariah, who instructed him in the fear[b] of God. As long as he sought the LORD, God gave him success.

[6]He went to war against the Philistines and broke down the walls of Gath, Jabneh and Ashdod. He then rebuilt towns near Ashdod and elsewhere among the Philistines. [7]God helped him against the Philistines and against the Arabs who lived in Gur Baal and against the Meunites. [8]The Ammonites brought tribute to Uzziah, and his fame spread as far as the border of Egypt, because he had become very powerful.

[9]Uzziah built towers in Jerusalem at the Corner Gate, at the Valley Gate and at the angle of the wall, and he fortified them. [10]He also built towers in the desert and dug many cisterns, because he had much livestock in the foothills and in the plain. He had people working his fields and vineyards in the hills and in the fertile lands, for he loved the soil.

[11]Uzziah had a well-trained army, ready to go out by divisions according to their numbers as mustered by Jeiel the secretary and Maaseiah the officer under the direction of Hananiah, one of the royal officials. [12]The total number of family leaders over the fighting men was 2,600. [13]Under their command was an army of 307,500 men trained for war,

a powerful force to support the king against his enemies. [14]Uzziah provided shields, spears, helmets, coats of armor, bows and slingstones for the entire army. [15]In Jerusalem he made machines designed by skillful men for use on the towers and on the corner defenses to shoot arrows and hurl large stones. His fame spread far and wide, for he was greatly helped until he became powerful.

[16]But after Uzziah became powerful, his pride led to his downfall. He was unfaithful to the LORD his God, and entered the temple of the LORD to burn incense on the altar of incense. [17]Azariah the priest with eighty other courageous priests of the LORD followed him in. [18]They confronted him and said, "It is not right for you, Uzziah, to burn incense to the LORD. That is for the priests, the descendants of Aaron, who have been consecrated to burn incense. Leave the sanctuary, for you have been unfaithful; and you will not be honored by the LORD God."

[19]Uzziah, who had a censer in his hand ready to burn incense, became angry. While he was raging at the priests in their presence before the incense altar in the LORD's temple, leprosy[c] broke out on his forehead. [20]When Azariah the chief priest and all the other priests looked at him, they saw that he had leprosy on his forehead, so they hurried him out. Indeed, he himself was eager to leave, because the LORD had afflicted him.

[21]King Uzziah had leprosy until the day he died. He lived in a separate house[d]—leprous, and excluded from the temple of the LORD. Jotham his son had charge of the palace and governed the people of the land.

[22]The other events of Uzziah's reign, from beginning to end, are recorded by the prophet Isaiah son of Amoz. [23]Uzziah rested with his fathers and was buried near them in a field for burial that

belonged to the kings, for people said, "He had leprosy." And Jotham his son succeeded him as king.

Jotham King of Judah

27 Jotham was twenty-five years old when he became king, and he reigned in Jerusalem sixteen years. His mother's name was Jerusha daughter of Zadok. ²He did what was right in the eyes of the LORD, just as his father Uzziah had done, but unlike him he did not enter the temple of the LORD. The people, however, continued their corrupt practices. ³Jotham rebuilt the Upper Gate of the temple of the LORD and did extensive work on the wall at the hill of Ophel. ⁴He built towns in the Judean hills and forts and towers in the wooded areas.

⁵Jotham made war on the king of the Ammonites and conquered them. That year the Ammonites paid him a hundred talents[a] of silver, ten thousand cors[b] of wheat and ten thousand cors of barley. The Ammonites brought him the same amount also in the second and third years.

⁶Jotham grew powerful because he walked steadfastly before the LORD his God.

⁷The other events in Jotham's reign, including all his wars and the other things he did, are written in the book of the kings of Israel and Judah. ⁸He was twenty-five years old when he became king, and he reigned in Jerusalem sixteen years. ⁹Jotham rested with his fathers and was buried in the City of David. And Ahaz his son succeeded him as king.

---

[a]5 That is, about 3 3/4 tons (about 3.4 metric tons)
[b]5 That is, probably about 62,000 bushels (about 2,200 kiloliters)

Friday

Tough on Sin   Read 2 Chronicles 26:16–23

God didn't go easy on King Uzziah. The king had gotten so proud that he thought he could break God's rules. But when Uzziah crossed the line, God punished him. God showed that even though he's patient and forgiving, he has his limits and will draw the line when it comes to punishment.

This story reminds me that God gets tough on sin, but it also tells me that, even when God punishes, he's still merciful. Now, it might not seem very merciful that Uzziah was struck with leprosy for the rest of his life. But at the end of the story, Uzziah got to be buried in the royal cemetery with all the other kings. Uzziah definitely paid for his pride, but his punishment didn't last forever. God forgave even him.

Sometimes I forget that mercy doesn't mean that God makes everything perfect again after I sin. I might have to pay some serious consequences. That's why it's so great to know that Jesus has already paid the most serious consequence—the death that I deserve. God's mercy will always be bigger than my sin.

❶ How would your idea of God be different if he didn't punish sin? How would your life be different?

❷ If someone has hurt you by their sin, what can you do to show them forgiveness?

❸ Thank God for his rules and for his mercy.

Turn to page 523 for your next devotion.

Ahaz King of Judah

28 Ahaz was twenty years old when he became king, and he reigned in Jerusalem sixteen years. Unlike David his father, he did not do what was right in the eyes of the LORD. ²He walked in the ways of the kings of Israel and also made cast idols for worshiping the Baals. ³He burned sacrifices in the Valley of Ben Hinnom and sacrificed his sons in the fire, following the detestable ways of the nations the LORD had driven out before the Israelites. ⁴He offered sacrifices and burned incense at the high places, on the hilltops and under every spreading tree. ⁵Therefore the LORD his God handed

him over to the king of Aram. The Arameans defeated him and took many of his people as prisoners and brought them to Damascus.

He was also given into the hands of the king of Israel, who inflicted heavy casualties on him. ⁶In one day Pekah son of Remaliah killed a hundred and twenty thousand soldiers in Judah—because Judah had forsaken the LORD, the God of their fathers. ⁷Zicri, an Ephraimite warrior, killed Maaseiah the king's son, Azrikam the officer in charge of the palace, and Elkanah, second to the king. ⁸The Israelites took captive from their kinsmen two hundred thousand wives,

---

Weekend.

Is Your Belief Yours?

Read 2 Chronicles 28:1–5

On Tuesday Kate talked about trying "to live out what we believe." Sometimes it's hard to know what you believe. It's pretty normal for teenagers to still be figuring this out (and that's OK!).

What do you love to do? Do you love sports or music or drama or school or reading? When you get to be a parent, you probably will be like most parents—you'll want your kids to love what you love.

Now, what's one thing your mom or dad enjoys that you really don't like very much? Maybe a certain sports team (Broncos versus the Chiefs), or a kind of food (pickled bologna or broccoli) or even music ("elevator music" versus your favorite band)?

King Jotham was a hero of Israel who "did what was right in the eyes of the LORD" (2 Chronicles 27:2). But his son, Ahaz, "did not do what was right in the eyes of the LORD" (2 Chronicles 28:1). Just because your mom or dad loves Jesus, or doesn't love Jesus, doesn't necessarily mean that you'll follow in their footsteps. Everyone has to choose for themselves who (or what) they're going to believe.

So, when you're trying to live out what you believe, whose belief is it? Yours?

❶ Do you see your faith as something you have "inherited" from your parents? Or is it your own faith? How do you know?

❷ Talk with your parents and ask them about their faith. Then talk to them about *your* faith.

❸ Decide what is true about *your* faith, and tell God what *you* want in your faith. Then be quiet and let him comfort you as his own special child, apart from your family, friends and church.

Turn to page 544 for your next devotion.

sons and daughters. They also took a great deal of plunder, which they carried back to Samaria.

⁹But a prophet of the LORD named Oded was there, and he went out to meet the army when it returned to Samaria. He said to them, "Because the LORD, the God of your fathers, was angry with Judah, he gave them into your hand. But you have slaughtered them in a rage that reaches to heaven. ¹⁰And now you intend to make the men and women of Judah and Jerusalem your slaves. But aren't you also guilty of sins against the LORD your God? ¹¹Now listen to me! Send back your fellow countrymen you have taken as prisoners, for the LORD's fierce anger rests on you."

¹²Then some of the leaders in Ephraim—Azariah son of Jehohanan, Berekiah son of Meshillemoth, Jehizkiah son of Shallum, and Amasa son of Hadlai—confronted those who were arriving from the war. ¹³"You must not bring those prisoners here," they said, "or we will be guilty before the LORD. Do you intend to add to our sin and guilt? For our guilt is already great, and his fierce anger rests on Israel."

¹⁴So the soldiers gave up the prisoners and plunder in the presence of the officials and all the assembly. ¹⁵The men designated by name took the prisoners, and from the plunder they clothed all who were naked. They provided them with clothes and sandals, food and drink, and healing balm. All those who were weak they put on donkeys. So they took them back to their fellow countrymen at Jericho, the City of Palms, and returned to Samaria.

¹⁶At that time King Ahaz sent to the king[a] of Assyria for help. ¹⁷The Edomites had again come and attacked Judah and carried away prisoners, ¹⁸while the Philistines had raided towns in the foothills and in the Negev of Judah. They captured and occupied Beth Shemesh, Aijalon and Gederoth, as well as Soco, Timnah and Gimzo, with their surrounding villages. ¹⁹The LORD had humbled Judah because of Ahaz king of Israel,[b] for he had promoted wickedness in Judah and had been most unfaithful to the LORD. ²⁰Tiglath-Pileser[c] king of Assyria

came to him, but he gave him trouble instead of help. ²¹Ahaz took some of the things from the temple of the LORD and from the royal palace and from the princes and presented them to the king of Assyria, but that did not help him.

²²In his time of trouble King Ahaz became even more unfaithful to the LORD. ²³He offered sacrifices to the gods of Damascus, who had defeated him; for he thought, "Since the gods of the kings of Aram have helped them, I will sacrifice to them so they will help me." But they were his downfall and the downfall of all Israel.

²⁴Ahaz gathered together the furnishings from the temple of God and took them away.[d] He shut the doors of the LORD's temple and set up altars at every street corner in Jerusalem. ²⁵In every town in Judah he built high places to burn sacrifices to other gods and provoked the LORD, the God of his fathers, to anger.

²⁶The other events of his reign and all his ways, from beginning to end, are written in the book of the kings of Judah and Israel. ²⁷Ahaz rested with his fathers and was buried in the city of Jerusalem, but he was not placed in the tombs of the kings of Israel. And Hezekiah his son succeeded him as king.

Hezekiah Purifies the Temple

29 Hezekiah was twenty-five years old when he became king, and he reigned in Jerusalem twenty-nine years. His mother's name was Abijah daughter of Zechariah. ²He did what was right in the eyes of the LORD, just as his father David had done.

³In the first month of the first year of his reign, he opened the doors of the temple of the LORD and repaired them. ⁴He brought in the priests and the Levites, assembled them in the square on the east side ⁵and said: "Listen to me, Levites! Consecrate yourselves now and consecrate the temple of the LORD, the God of your fathers. Remove all defile-

---

[a]16 One Hebrew manuscript, Septuagint and Vulgate (see also 2 Kings 16:7); most Hebrew manuscripts *kings*   [b]19 That is, Judah, as frequently in 2 Chronicles   [c]20 Hebrew *Tilgath-Pilneser*, a variant of *Tiglath-Pileser*   [d]24 Or *and cut them up*

ment from the sanctuary. ⁶Our fathers were unfaithful; they did evil in the eyes of the LORD our God and forsook him. They turned their faces away from the LORD's dwelling place and turned their backs on him. ⁷They also shut the doors of the portico and put out the lamps. They did not burn incense or present any burnt offerings at the sanctuary to the God of Israel. ⁸Therefore, the anger of the LORD has fallen on Judah and Jerusalem; he has made them an object of dread and horror and scorn, as you can see with your own eyes. ⁹This is why our fathers have fallen by the sword and why our sons and daughters and our wives are in captivity. ¹⁰Now I intend to make a covenant with the LORD, the God of Israel, so that his fierce anger will turn away from us. ¹¹My sons, do not be negligent now, for the LORD has chosen you to stand before him and serve him, to minister before him and to burn incense."

¹²Then these Levites set to work:

from the Kohathites,
> Mahath son of Amasai and Joel son of Azariah;

from the Merarites,
> Kish son of Abdi and Azariah son of Jehallelel;

from the Gershonites,
> Joah son of Zimmah and Eden son of Joah;

¹³from the descendants of Elizaphan,
> Shimri and Jeiel;

from the descendants of Asaph,
> Zechariah and Mattaniah;

¹⁴from the descendants of Heman,
> Jehiel and Shimei;

from the descendants of Jeduthun,
> Shemaiah and Uzziel.

¹⁵When they had assembled their brothers and consecrated themselves, they went in to purify the temple of the LORD, as the king had ordered, following the word of the LORD. ¹⁶The priests went into the sanctuary of the LORD to purify it. They brought out to the courtyard of the LORD's temple everything unclean that they found in the temple of the LORD. The Levites took it and carried it out to the Kidron Valley. ¹⁷They began the consecration on the first day of the first month, and by the eighth day of the month they reached the portico of the LORD. For eight more days they consecrated the temple of the LORD itself, finishing on the sixteenth day of the first month.

¹⁸Then they went in to King Hezekiah and reported: "We have purified the entire temple of the LORD, the altar of burnt offering with all its utensils, and the table for setting out the consecrated bread, with all its articles. ¹⁹We have prepared and consecrated all the articles that King Ahaz removed in his unfaithfulness while he was king. They are now in front of the LORD's altar."

²⁰Early the next morning King Hezekiah gathered the city officials together and went up to the temple of the LORD. ²¹They brought seven bulls, seven rams, seven male lambs and seven male goats as a sin offering for the kingdom, for the sanctuary and for Judah. The king commanded the priests, the descendants of Aaron, to offer these on the altar of the LORD. ²²So they slaughtered the bulls, and the priests took the blood and sprinkled it on the altar; next they slaughtered the rams and sprinkled their blood on the altar; then they slaughtered the lambs and sprinkled their blood on the altar. ²³The goats for the sin offering were brought before the king and the assembly, and they laid their hands on them. ²⁴The priests then slaughtered the goats and presented their blood on the altar for a sin offering to atone for all Israel, because the king had ordered the burnt offering and the sin offering for all Israel.

²⁵He stationed the Levites in the temple of the LORD with cymbals, harps and lyres in the way prescribed by David and Gad the king's seer and Nathan the prophet; this was commanded by the LORD through his prophets. ²⁶So the Levites stood ready with David's instruments, and the priests with their trumpets.

²⁷Hezekiah gave the order to sacrifice the burnt offering on the altar. As the offering began, singing to the LORD began also, accompanied by trumpets and the instruments of David king of Israel. ²⁸The whole assembly bowed in worship, while the singers sang and the trumpeters played. All this continued until the sacrifice of the burnt offering was completed.

²⁹When the offerings were finished, the king and everyone present with him knelt down and worshiped. ³⁰King Hezekiah and his officials ordered the Levites to praise the LORD with the words of David and of Asaph the seer. So they sang praises with gladness and bowed their heads and worshiped.

³¹Then Hezekiah said, "You have now dedicated yourselves to the LORD. Come and bring sacrifices and thank offerings to the temple of the LORD." So the assembly brought sacrifices and thank offerings, and all whose hearts were willing brought burnt offerings.

³²The number of burnt offerings the assembly brought was seventy bulls, a hundred rams and two hundred male lambs—all of them for burnt offerings to the LORD. ³³The animals consecrated as sacrifices amounted to six hundred bulls and three thousand sheep and goats. ³⁴The priests, however, were too few to skin all the burnt offerings; so their kinsmen the Levites helped them until the task was finished and until other priests had been consecrated, for the Levites had been more conscientious in consecrating themselves than the priests had been. ³⁵There were burnt offerings in abundance, together with the fat of the fellowship offerings[a] and the drink offerings that accompanied the burnt offerings.

So the service of the temple of the LORD was reestablished. ³⁶Hezekiah and all the people rejoiced at what God had brought about for his people, because it was done so quickly.

Hezekiah Celebrates the Passover

30 Hezekiah sent word to all Israel and Judah and also wrote letters to Ephraim and Manasseh, inviting them to come to the temple of the LORD in Jerusalem and celebrate the Passover to the LORD, the God of Israel. ²The king and his officials and the whole assembly in Jerusalem decided to celebrate the Passover in the second month. ³They had not been able to celebrate it at the regular time because not enough priests had consecrated themselves and the people had not assembled in Jerusalem. ⁴The plan seemed right both to the king and to

the whole assembly. ⁵They decided to send a proclamation throughout Israel, from Beersheba to Dan, calling the people to come to Jerusalem and celebrate the Passover to the LORD, the God of Israel. It had not been celebrated in large numbers according to what was written.

⁶At the king's command, couriers went throughout Israel and Judah with letters from the king and from his officials, which read:

"People of Israel, return to the LORD, the God of Abraham, Isaac and Israel, that he may return to you who are left, who have escaped from the hand of the kings of Assyria. ⁷Do not be like your fathers and brothers, who were unfaithful to the LORD, the God of their fathers, so that he made them an object of horror, as you see. ⁸Do not be stiff-necked, as your fathers were; submit to the LORD. Come to the sanctuary, which he has consecrated forever. Serve the LORD your God, so that his fierce anger will turn away from you. ⁹If you return to the LORD, then your brothers and your children will be shown compassion by their captors and will come back to this land, for the LORD your God is gracious and compassionate. He will not turn his face from you if you return to him."

¹⁰The couriers went from town to town in Ephraim and Manasseh, as far as Zebulun, but the people scorned and ridiculed them. ¹¹Nevertheless, some men of Asher, Manasseh and Zebulun humbled themselves and went to Jerusalem. ¹²Also in Judah the hand of God was on the people to give them unity of mind to carry out what the king and his officials had ordered, following the word of the LORD.

¹³A very large crowd of people assembled in Jerusalem to celebrate the Feast of Unleavened Bread in the second month. ¹⁴They removed the altars in Jerusalem and cleared away the incense altars and threw them into the Kidron Valley.

¹⁵They slaughtered the Passover lamb on the fourteenth day of the second

---

a 35 Traditionally peace offerings

month. The priests and the Levites were ashamed and consecrated themselves and brought burnt offerings to the temple of the LORD. ¹⁶Then they took up their regular positions as prescribed in the Law of Moses the man of God. The priests sprinkled the blood handed to them by the Levites. ¹⁷Since many in the crowd had not consecrated themselves, the Levites had to kill the Passover lambs for all those who were not ceremonially clean and could not consecrate their lambs to the LORD. ¹⁸Although most of the many people who came from Ephraim, Manasseh, Issachar and Zebulun had not purified themselves, yet they ate the Passover, contrary to what was written. But Hezekiah prayed for them, saying, "May the LORD, who is good, pardon everyone ¹⁹who sets his heart on seeking God—the LORD, the God of his fathers—even if he is not clean according to the rules of the sanctuary." ²⁰And the LORD heard Hezekiah and healed the people.

²¹The Israelites who were present in Jerusalem celebrated the Feast of Unleavened Bread for seven days with great rejoicing, while the Levites and priests sang to the LORD every day, accompanied by the LORD's instruments of praise.[a]

²²Hezekiah spoke encouragingly to all the Levites, who showed good understanding of the service of the LORD. For the seven days they ate their assigned portion and offered fellowship offerings[b] and praised the LORD, the God of their fathers.

²³The whole assembly then agreed to celebrate the festival seven more days; so for another seven days they celebrated joyfully. ²⁴Hezekiah king of Judah provided a thousand bulls and seven thousand sheep and goats for the assembly, and the officials provided them with a thousand bulls and ten thousand sheep and goats. A great number of priests consecrated themselves. ²⁵The entire assembly of Judah rejoiced, along with the priests and Levites and all who had assembled from Israel, including the aliens who had come from Israel and those who lived in Judah. ²⁶There was great joy in Jerusalem, for since the days of Solomon son of David king of Israel there had been nothing like this in Jerusalem. ²⁷The

priests and the Levites stood to bless the people, and God heard them, for their prayer reached heaven, his holy dwelling place.

31 When all this had ended, the Israelites who were there went out to the towns of Judah, smashed the sacred stones and cut down the Asherah poles. They destroyed the high places and the altars throughout Judah and Benjamin and in Ephraim and Manasseh. After they had destroyed all of them, the Israelites returned to their own towns and to their own property.

Contributions for Worship

²Hezekiah assigned the priests and Levites to divisions—each of them according to their duties as priests or Levites—to offer burnt offerings and fellowship offerings,[b] to minister, to give thanks and to sing praises at the gates of the LORD's dwelling. ³The king contributed from his own possessions for the morning and evening burnt offerings and for the burnt offerings on the Sabbaths, New Moons and appointed feasts as written in the Law of the LORD. ⁴He ordered the people living in Jerusalem to give the portion due the priests and Levites so they could devote themselves to the Law of the LORD. ⁵As soon as the order went out, the Israelites generously gave the firstfruits of their grain, new wine, oil and honey and all that the fields produced. They brought a great amount, a tithe of everything. ⁶The men of Israel and Judah who lived in the towns of Judah also brought a tithe of their herds and flocks and a tithe of the holy things dedicated to the LORD their God, and they piled them in heaps. ⁷They began doing this in the third month and finished in the seventh month. ⁸When Hezekiah and his officials came and saw the heaps, they praised the LORD and blessed his people Israel.

⁹Hezekiah asked the priests and Levites about the heaps; ¹⁰and Azariah the chief priest, from the family of Zadok, answered, "Since the people began to bring

---

[a]21 Or *priests praised the LORD every day with resounding instruments belonging to the LORD*
[b]22,2 Traditionally *peace offerings*

their contributions to the temple of the LORD, we have had enough to eat and plenty to spare, because the LORD has blessed his people, and this great amount is left over."

[11]Hezekiah gave orders to prepare storerooms in the temple of the LORD, and this was done. [12]Then they faithfully brought in the contributions, tithes and dedicated gifts. Conaniah, a Levite, was in charge of these things, and his brother Shimei was next in rank. [13]Jehiel, Azaziah, Nahath, Asahel, Jerimoth, Jozabad, Eliel, Ismakiah, Mahath and Benaiah were supervisors under Conaniah and Shimei his brother, by appointment of King Hezekiah and Azariah the official in charge of the temple of God.

[14]Kore son of Imnah the Levite, keeper of the East Gate, was in charge of the freewill offerings given to God, distributing the contributions made to the LORD and also the consecrated gifts. [15]Eden, Miniamin, Jeshua, Shemaiah, Amariah and Shecaniah assisted him faithfully in the towns of the priests, distributing to their fellow priests according to their divisions, old and young alike.

[16]In addition, they distributed to the males three years old or more whose names were in the genealogical records— all who would enter the temple of the LORD to perform the daily duties of their various tasks, according to their responsibilities and their divisions. [17]And they distributed to the priests enrolled by their families in the genealogical records and likewise to the Levites twenty years old or more, according to their responsibilities and their divisions. [18]They included all the little ones, the wives, and the sons and daughters of the whole community listed in these genealogical records. For they were faithful in consecrating themselves.

[19]As for the priests, the descendants of Aaron, who lived on the farm lands around their towns or in any other towns, men were designated by name to distribute portions to every male among them and to all who were recorded in the genealogies of the Levites.

[20]This is what Hezekiah did throughout Judah, doing what was good and right and faithful before the LORD his God. [21]In everything that he undertook in the service of God's temple and in obedience to the law and the commands, he sought his God and worked wholeheartedly. And so he prospered.

Sennacherib Threatens Jerusalem

32 After all that Hezekiah had so faithfully done, Sennacherib king of Assyria came and invaded Judah. He laid siege to the fortified cities, thinking to conquer them for himself. [2]When Hezekiah saw that Sennacherib had come and that he intended to make war on Jerusalem, [3]he consulted with his officials and military staff about blocking off the water from the springs outside the city, and they helped him. [4]A large force of men assembled, and they blocked all the springs and the stream that flowed through the land. "Why should the kings[a] of Assyria come and find plenty of water?" they said. [5]Then he worked hard repairing all the broken sections of the wall and building towers on it. He built another wall outside that one and reinforced the supporting terraces[b] of the City of David. He also made large numbers of weapons and shields.

[6]He appointed military officers over the people and assembled them before him in the square at the city gate and encouraged them with these words: [7]"Be strong and courageous. Do not be afraid or discouraged because of the king of Assyria and the vast army with him, for there is a greater power with us than with him. [8]With him is only the arm of flesh, but with us is the LORD our God to help us and to fight our battles." And the people gained confidence from what Hezekiah the king of Judah said.

[9]Later, when Sennacherib king of Assyria and all his forces were laying siege to Lachish, he sent his officers to Jerusalem with this message for Hezekiah king of Judah and for all the people of Judah who were there:

[10]"This is what Sennacherib king of Assyria says: On what are you basing your confidence, that you remain in Jerusalem under siege?

[a]4 Hebrew; Septuagint and Syriac *king* [b]5 Or *the Millo*

11When Hezekiah says, 'The LORD our God will save us from the hand of the king of Assyria,' he is misleading you, to let you die of hunger and thirst. 12Did not Hezekiah himself remove this god's high places and altars, saying to Judah and Jerusalem, 'You must worship before one altar and burn sacrifices on it'?

13"Do you not know what I and my fathers have done to all the peoples of the other lands? Were the gods of those nations ever able to deliver their land from my hand? 14Who of all the gods of these nations that my fathers destroyed has been able to save his people from me? How then can your god deliver you from my hand? 15Now do not let Hezekiah deceive you and mislead you like this. Do not believe him, for no god of any nation or kingdom has been able to deliver his people from my hand or the hand of my fathers. How much less will your god deliver you from my hand!"

16Sennacherib's officers spoke further against the LORD God and against his servant Hezekiah. 17The king also wrote letters insulting the LORD, the God of Israel, and saying this against him: "Just as the gods of the peoples of the other lands did not rescue their people from my hand, so the god of Hezekiah will not rescue his people from my hand." 18Then they called out in Hebrew to the people of Jerusalem who were on the wall, to terrify them and make them afraid in order to capture the city. 19They spoke about the God of Jerusalem as they did about the gods of the other peoples of the world— the work of men's hands.

20King Hezekiah and the prophet Isaiah *son of Amoz* cried out in prayer to heaven about this. 21And the LORD sent an angel, who annihilated all the fighting men and the leaders and officers in the camp of the Assyrian king. So he withdrew to his own land in disgrace. And when he went into the temple of his god, some of his sons cut him down with the sword.

22So the LORD saved Hezekiah and the people of Jerusalem from the hand of

---

God *Always* Wins!

Huh?

2 Chronicles 32:20–23

If you have read the Bible this far, you probably have seen an idea come up, over and over again. It's one of the basic things God wants all of us to remember: Our God is stronger than anything or anybody else in the world. We can trust him, for he will *always* take care of his people if we would only ask.

Sennacherib king of Assyria and from the hand of all others. He took care of them[a] on every side. 23Many brought offerings to Jerusalem for the LORD and valuable gifts for Hezekiah king of Judah. From then on he was highly regarded by all the nations.

Hezekiah's Pride, Success and Death

24In those days Hezekiah became ill and was at the point of death. He prayed to the LORD, who answered him and gave him a miraculous sign. 25But Hezekiah's heart was proud and he did not respond to the kindness shown him; therefore the LORD's wrath was on him and on Judah and Jerusalem. 26Then Hezekiah repented of the pride of his heart, as did the people of Jerusalem; therefore the LORD's wrath did not come upon them during the days of Hezekiah.

27Hezekiah had very great riches and honor, and he made treasuries for his silver and gold and for his precious stones, spices, shields and all kinds of valuables. 28He also made buildings to store the harvest of grain, new wine and oil; and he made stalls for various kinds of cattle, and pens for the flocks. 29He built villages and acquired great numbers of flocks and herds, for God had given him very great riches.

30It was Hezekiah who blocked the upper outlet of the Gihon spring and channeled the water down to the west side of the City of David. He succeeded in every-

---

a22 Hebrew; Septuagint and Vulgate He gave them rest

thing he undertook. ³¹But when envoys were sent by the rulers of Babylon to ask him about the miraculous sign that had occurred in the land, God left him to test him and to know everything that was in his heart.

³²The other events of Hezekiah's reign and his acts of devotion are written in the vision of the prophet Isaiah son of Amoz in the book of the kings of Judah and Israel. ³³Hezekiah rested with his fathers and was buried on the hill where the tombs of David's descendants are. All Judah and the people of Jerusalem honored him when he died. And Manasseh his son succeeded him as king.

Manasseh King of Judah

33 Manasseh was twelve years old when he became king, and he reigned in Jerusalem fifty-five years. ²He did evil in the eyes of the LORD, following the detestable practices of the nations the LORD had driven out before the Israelites. ³He rebuilt the high places his father Hezekiah had demolished; he also erected altars to the Baals and made Asherah poles. He bowed down to all the starry hosts and worshiped them. ⁴He built altars in the temple of the LORD, of which the LORD had said, "My Name will remain in Jerusalem forever." ⁵In both courts of the temple of the LORD, he built altars to all the starry hosts. ⁶He sacrificed his sons inᵃ the fire in the Valley of Ben Hinnom, practiced sorcery, divination and witchcraft, and consulted mediums and spiritists. He did much evil in the eyes of the LORD, provoking him to anger.

⁷He took the carved image he had made and put it in God's temple, of which God had said to David and to his son Solomon, "In this temple and in Jerusalem, which I have chosen out of all the tribes of Israel, I will put my Name forever. ⁸I will not again make the feet of the Israelites leave the land I assigned to your forefathers, if only they will be careful to do everything I commanded them concerning all the laws, decrees and ordinances given through Moses." ⁹But Manasseh led Judah and the people of Jerusalem astray, so that they did more evil than the nations the LORD had destroyed before the Israelites.

¹⁰The LORD spoke to Manasseh and his people, but they paid no attention. ¹¹So the LORD brought against them the army commanders of the king of Assyria, who took Manasseh prisoner, put a hook in his nose, bound him with bronze shackles and took him to Babylon. ¹²In his distress he sought the favor of the LORD his God and humbled himself greatly before the God of his fathers. ¹³And when he prayed to him, the LORD was moved by his entreaty and listened to his plea; so he brought him back to Jerusalem and to his kingdom. Then Manasseh knew that the LORD is God.

¹⁴Afterward he rebuilt the outer wall of the City of David, west of the Gihon spring in the valley, as far as the entrance of the Fish Gate and encircling the hill of Ophel; he also made it much higher. He stationed military commanders in all the fortified cities in Judah.

¹⁵He got rid of the foreign gods and removed the image from the temple of the LORD, as well as all the altars he had built on the temple hill and in Jerusalem; and he threw them out of the city. ¹⁶Then he restored the altar of the LORD and sacrificed fellowship offeringsᵇ and thank offerings on it, and told Judah to serve the LORD, the God of Israel. ¹⁷The people, however, continued to sacrifice at the high places, but only to the LORD their God.

¹⁸The other events of Manasseh's reign, including his prayer to his God and the words the seers spoke to him in the name of the LORD, the God of Israel, are written in the annals of the kings of Israel.ᶜ ¹⁹His prayer and how God was moved by his entreaty, as well as all his sins and unfaithfulness, and the sites where he built high places and set up Asherah poles and idols before he humbled himself—all are written in the records of the seers.ᵈ ²⁰Manasseh rested with his fathers and was buried in his palace. And Amon his son succeeded him as king.

ᵃ6 Or He made his sons pass through   ᵇ16 Traditionally peace offerings   ᶜ18 That is, Judah, as frequently in 2 Chronicles   ᵈ19 One Hebrew manuscript and Septuagint; most Hebrew manuscripts of Hozai

Amon King of Judah

²¹Amon was twenty-two years old when he became king, and he reigned in Jerusalem two years. ²²He did evil in the eyes of the LORD, as his father Manasseh had done. Amon worshiped and offered sacrifices to all the idols Manasseh had made. ²³But unlike his father Manasseh, he did not humble himself before the LORD; Amon increased his guilt.

²⁴Amon's officials conspired against him and assassinated him in his palace. ²⁵Then the people of the land killed all who had plotted against King Amon, and they made Josiah his son king in his place.

Josiah's Reforms

34 Josiah was eight years old when he became king, and he reigned in Jerusalem thirty-one years. ²He did what was right in the eyes of the LORD and walked in the ways of his father David, not turning aside to the right or to the left.

³In the eighth year of his reign, while he was still young, he began to seek the God of his father David. In his twelfth year he began to purge Judah and Jerusalem of high places, Asherah poles, carved idols and cast images. ⁴Under his direction the altars of the Baals were torn down; he cut to pieces the incense altars that were above them, and smashed the Asherah poles, the idols and the images. These he broke to pieces and scattered over the graves of those who had sacrificed to them. ⁵He burned the bones of the priests on their altars, and so he purged Judah and Jerusalem. ⁶In the towns of Manasseh, Ephraim and Simeon, as far as Naphtali, and in the ruins around them, ⁷he tore down the altars and the Asherah poles and crushed the idols to powder and cut to pieces all the incense altars throughout Israel. Then he went back to Jerusalem.

⁸In the eighteenth year of Josiah's reign, to purify the land and the temple, he sent Shaphan son of Azaliah and Maaseiah the ruler of the city, with Joah son of Joahaz, the recorder, to repair the temple of the LORD his God.

⁹They went to Hilkiah the high priest and gave him the money that had been brought into the temple of God, which the Levites who were the doorkeepers had collected from the people of Manasseh, Ephraim and the entire remnant of Israel and from all the people of Judah and Benjamin and the inhabitants of Jerusalem. ¹⁰Then they entrusted it to the men appointed to supervise the work on the LORD's temple. These men paid the workers who repaired and restored the temple. ¹¹They also gave money to the carpenters and builders to purchase dressed stone, and timber for joists and beams for the buildings that the kings of Judah had allowed to fall into ruin.

¹²The men did the work faithfully. Over them to direct them were Jahath and Obadiah, Levites descended from Merari, and Zechariah and Meshullam, descended from Kohath. The Levites—all who were skilled in playing musical instruments— ¹³had charge of the laborers and supervised all the workers from job to job. Some of the Levites were secretaries, scribes and doorkeepers.

The Book of the Law Found

¹⁴While they were bringing out the money that had been taken into the temple of the LORD, Hilkiah the priest found the Book of the Law of the LORD that had been given through Moses. ¹⁵Hilkiah said to Shaphan the secretary, "I have found the Book of the Law in the temple of the LORD." He gave it to Shaphan.

¹⁶Then Shaphan took the book to the king and reported to him: "Your officials are doing everything that has been committed to them. ¹⁷They have paid out the money that was in the temple of the LORD and have entrusted it to the supervisors and workers." ¹⁸Then Shaphan the secretary informed the king, "Hilkiah the priest has given me a book." And Shaphan read from it in the presence of the king.

¹⁹When the king heard the words of the Law, he tore his robes. ²⁰He gave these orders to Hilkiah, Ahikam son of Shaphan, Abdon son of Micah,ᵃ Shaphan the secretary and Asaiah the king's attendant: ²¹"Go and inquire of the LORD

ᵃ20 Also called *Acbor son of Micaiah*

for me and for the remnant in Israel and Judah about what is written in this book that has been found. Great is the LORD's anger that is poured out on us because our fathers have not kept the word of the LORD; they have not acted in accordance with all that is written in this book."

²²Hilkiah and those the king had sent with him*ª* went to speak to the prophetess Huldah, who was the wife of Shallum son of Tokhath,*ᵇ* the son of Hasrah,*ᶜ* keeper of the wardrobe. She lived in Jerusalem, in the Second District.

²³She said to them, "This is what the LORD, the God of Israel, says: Tell the man who sent you to me, ²⁴'This is what the LORD says: I am going to bring disaster on this place and its people—all the curses written in the book that has been read in the presence of the king of Judah. ²⁵Because they have forsaken me and burned incense to other gods and provoked me to anger by all that their hands have made,*ᵈ* my anger will be poured out on this place and will not be quenched.' ²⁶Tell the king of Judah, who sent you to inquire of the LORD, 'This is what the LORD, the God of Israel, says concerning the words you heard: ²⁷Because your heart was responsive and you humbled yourself before God when you heard what he spoke against this place and its people, and because you humbled yourself before me and tore your robes and wept in my presence, I have heard you, declares the LORD. ²⁸Now I will gather you to your fathers, and you will be buried in peace. Your eyes will not see all the disaster I am going to bring on this place and on those who live here.' "

So they took her answer back to the king.

²⁹Then the king called together all the elders of Judah and Jerusalem. ³⁰He went up to the temple of the LORD with the men of Judah, the people of Jerusalem, the priests and the Levites—all the people from the least to the greatest. He read in their hearing all the words of the Book of the Covenant, which had been found in the temple of the LORD. ³¹The king stood by his pillar and renewed the covenant in the presence of the LORD—to follow the LORD and keep his commands, regulations and decrees with all his heart and

all his soul, and to obey the words of the covenant written in this book.

³²Then he had everyone in Jerusalem and Benjamin pledge themselves to it; the people of Jerusalem did this in accordance with the covenant of God, the God of their fathers.

³³Josiah removed all the detestable idols from all the territory belonging to the Israelites, and he had all who were present in Israel serve the LORD their God. As long as he lived, they did not fail to follow the LORD, the God of their fathers.

Josiah Celebrates the Passover

35 Josiah celebrated the Passover to the LORD in Jerusalem, and the Passover lamb was slaughtered on the fourteenth day of the first month. ²He appointed the priests to their duties and encouraged them in the service of the LORD's temple. ³He said to the Levites, who instructed all Israel and who had been consecrated to the LORD: "Put the sacred ark in the temple that Solomon son of David king of Israel built. It is not to be carried about on your shoulders. Now serve the LORD your God and his people Israel. ⁴Prepare yourselves by families in your divisions, according to the directions written by David king of Israel and by his son Solomon.

⁵"Stand in the holy place with a group of Levites for each subdivision of the families of your fellow countrymen, the lay people. ⁶Slaughter the Passover lambs, consecrate yourselves and prepare the lambs for your fellow countrymen, doing what the LORD commanded through Moses."

⁷Josiah provided for all the lay people who were there a total of thirty thousand sheep and goats for the Passover offerings, and also three thousand cattle—all from the king's own possessions.

⁸His officials also contributed voluntarily to the people and the priests and Levites. Hilkiah, Zechariah and Jehiel, the administrators of God's temple, gave

---

ª22 One Hebrew manuscript, Vulgate and Syriac; most Hebrew manuscripts do not have had sent with him.   ᵇ22 Also called Tikvah   ᶜ22 Also called Harhas   ᵈ25 Or by everything they have done

the priests twenty-six hundred Passover offerings and three hundred cattle. ⁹Also Conaniah along with Shemaiah and Nethanel, his brothers, and Hashabiah, Jeiel and Jozabad, the leaders of the Levites, provided five thousand Passover offerings and five hundred head of cattle for the Levites.

¹⁰The service was arranged and the priests stood in their places with the Levites in their divisions as the king had ordered. ¹¹The Passover lambs were slaughtered, and the priests sprinkled the blood handed to them, while the Levites skinned the animals. ¹²They set aside the burnt offerings to give them to the subdivisions of the families of the people to offer to the LORD, as is written in the Book of Moses. They did the same with the cattle. ¹³They roasted the Passover animals over the fire as prescribed, and boiled the holy offerings in pots, caldrons and pans and served them quickly to all the people. ¹⁴After this, they made preparations for themselves and for the priests, because the priests, the descendants of Aaron, were sacrificing the burnt offerings and the fat portions until nightfall. So the Levites made preparations for themselves and for the Aaronic priests.

¹⁵The musicians, the descendants of Asaph, were in the places prescribed by David, Asaph, Heman and Jeduthun the king's seer. The gatekeepers at each gate did not need to leave their posts, because their fellow Levites made the preparations for them.

¹⁶So at that time the entire service of the LORD was carried out for the celebration of the Passover and the offering of burnt offerings on the altar of the LORD, as King Josiah had ordered. ¹⁷The Israelites who were present celebrated the Passover at that time and observed the Feast of Unleavened Bread for seven days. ¹⁸The Passover had not been observed like this in Israel since the days of the prophet Samuel; and none of the kings of Israel had ever celebrated such a Passover as did Josiah, with the priests, the Levites and all Judah and Israel who were there with the people of Jerusalem. ¹⁹This Passover was celebrated in the eighteenth year of Josiah's reign.

The Death of Josiah

²⁰After all this, when Josiah had set the temple in order, Neco king of Egypt went up to fight at Carchemish on the Euphrates, and Josiah marched out to meet him in battle. ²¹But Neco sent messengers to him, saying, "What quarrel is there between you and me, O king of Judah? It is not you I am attacking at this time, but the house with which I am at war. God has told me to hurry; so stop opposing God, who is with me, or he will destroy you."

²²Josiah, however, would not turn away from him, but disguised himself to engage him in battle. He would not listen to what Neco had said at God's command but went to fight him on the plain of Megiddo.

²³Archers shot King Josiah, and he told his officers, "Take me away; I am badly wounded." ²⁴So they took him out of his chariot, put him in the other chariot he had and brought him to Jerusalem, where he died. He was buried in the tombs of his fathers, and all Judah and Jerusalem mourned for him.

²⁵Jeremiah composed laments for Josiah, and to this day all the men and women singers commemorate Josiah in the laments. These became a tradition in Israel and are written in the Laments.

²⁶The other events of Josiah's reign and his acts of devotion, according to what is written in the Law of the LORD— ²⁷all the events, from beginning to end, are written in the book of the kings of

36 Israel and Judah. ¹And the people of the land took Jehoahaz son of Josiah and made him king in Jerusalem in place of his father.

Jehoahaz King of Judah

²Jehoahaz[a] was twenty-three years old when he became king, and he reigned in Jerusalem three months. ³The king of Egypt dethroned him in Jerusalem and imposed on Judah a levy of a hundred talents[b] of silver and a talent[c] of gold. ⁴The king of Egypt made Eliakim, a

---

[a]2 Hebrew *Joahaz*, a variant of *Jehoahaz*; also in verse 4   [b]3 That is, about 3 3/4 tons (about 3.4 metric tons)   [c]3 That is, about 75 pounds (about 34 kilograms)

brother of Jehoahaz, king over Judah and Jerusalem and changed Eliakim's name to Jehoiakim. But Neco took Eliakim's brother Jehoahaz and carried him off to Egypt.

Jehoiakim King of Judah

[5]Jehoiakim was twenty-five years old when he became king, and he reigned in Jerusalem eleven years. He did evil in the eyes of the LORD his God. [6]Nebuchadnezzar king of Babylon attacked him and bound him with bronze shackles to take him to Babylon. [7]Nebuchadnezzar also took to Babylon articles from the temple of the LORD and put them in his temple[a] there.

[8]The other events of Jehoiakim's reign, the detestable things he did and all that was found against him, are written in the book of the kings of Israel and Judah. And Jehoiachin his son succeeded him as king.

Jehoiachin King of Judah

[9]Jehoiachin was eighteen[b] years old when he became king, and he reigned in Jerusalem three months and ten days. He did evil in the eyes of the LORD. [10]In the spring, King Nebuchadnezzar sent for him and brought him to Babylon, together with articles of value from the temple of the LORD, and he made Jehoiachin's uncle,[c] Zedekiah, king over Judah and Jerusalem.

Zedekiah King of Judah

[11]Zedekiah was twenty-one years old when he became king, and he reigned in Jerusalem eleven years. [12]He did evil in the eyes of the LORD his God and did not humble himself before Jeremiah the prophet, who spoke the word of the LORD. [13]He also rebelled against King Nebuchadnezzar, who had made him take an oath in God's name. He became stiff-necked and hardened his heart and would not turn to the LORD, the God of Israel. [14]Furthermore, all the leaders of the priests and the people became more and more unfaithful, following all the detestable practices of the nations and defiling the temple of the LORD, which he had consecrated in Jerusalem.

The Fall of Jerusalem

[15]The LORD, the God of their fathers, sent word to them through his messengers again and again, because he had pity on his people and on his dwelling place. [16]But they mocked God's messengers, despised his words and scoffed at his prophets until the wrath of the LORD was aroused against his people and there was no remedy. [17]He brought up against them the king of the Babylonians,[d] who killed their young men with the sword in the sanctuary, and spared neither young man nor young woman, old man or aged. God handed all of them over to Nebuchadnezzar. [18]He carried to Babylon all the articles from the temple of God, both large and small, and the treasures of the LORD's temple and the treasures of the king and his officials. [19]They set fire to God's temple and broke down the wall of Jerusalem; they burned all the palaces and destroyed everything of value there.

[20]He carried into exile to Babylon the remnant, who escaped from the sword, and they became servants to him and his sons until the kingdom of Persia came to power. [21]The land enjoyed its sabbath rests; all the time of its desolation it rested, until the seventy years were completed in fulfillment of the word of the LORD spoken by Jeremiah.

[22]In the first year of Cyrus king of Persia, in order to fulfill the word of the LORD spoken by Jeremiah, the LORD moved the heart of Cyrus king of Persia to make a proclamation throughout his realm and to put it in writing:

[23]"This is what Cyrus king of Persia says:

" 'The LORD, the God of heaven, has given me all the kingdoms of the earth and he has appointed me to build a temple for him at Jerusalem in Judah. Anyone of his people among you—may the LORD his God be with him, and let him go up.' "

[a]7 Or *palace*   [b]9 One Hebrew manuscript, some Septuagint manuscripts and Syriac (see also 2 Kings 24:8); most Hebrew manuscripts *eight*
[c]10 Hebrew *brother*, that is, relative (see 2 Kings 24:17)   [d]17 Or *Chaldeans*

Ezra

START

Cast OF Characters

Ezra (EZZ-ruh)
He's a Jewish teacher, writer and priest. He gives the exiled Jews a great history lesson (1 and 2 Chronicles), and then uses *this* book to describe what happens when his people finally get their chance to go home. In the end, he gets to go home too—and rallies Jerusalem to revival.

Zerubbabel
(zuh-RUB-uh-bull)
His grandad was a wicked king of old Judah. He plays tour guide and leads the first batch of 50,000 Jews back to Jerusalem to get started on the temple reconstruction project.

Cyrus (SIGH-rus)
He's the new king of Persia—which means he's also

Professor Ezra and his fellow Jews are living in Babylon because their wicked kings made God so mad he let the Babylonians conquer their country. Now they're dreaming of the day when God might allow them to return home and try again. To help the Jews keep their dream alive, Ezra writes the two previous books (1 and 2 Chronicles) as a history course because, if they ever get a chance to go home, the Jews will need to repeat the good things in their history and avoid all the bad stuff.

Good news! The dream comes true! Babylon gets conquered by the Persians and the new king of Persia tells the Jews they can go home. Now they can rebuild their temple, their faith and their nation of Judah. Here's the story:

Zerubbabel leads about 50,000 Jews back to their homeland to get started on the temple reconstruction effort. After the foundation is laid, the project gets mixed reviews: The young folks are thrilled. But the old folks remember the bigger and better temple that Solomon built, so they weep in disappointment.

The project gets bogged down in political fighting. Then Darius, the new king of Persia, cuts through all the red tape, sends in some tax money and helps the Jews complete God's house. All this stuff happens while Ezra is still back in Persian Babylon. In the end, he gets to go home too. When Ezra arrives in Jerusalem, he rocks the city into revival. For the Jews, things are looking up again.

boss of the Babylonians he just conquered. King Cyrus gives the first batch of Jews permission to go home. He even sends them house-

warming gifts—some of the cool stuff that King Nebuchadnezzar had stolen from the temple when the Babylonians destroyed it.

Darius (DARE-ee-us)
Another Persian king. When Judah's neighbors try to trash the temple reconstruction project, good old Darius tells them to knock it off. He even gives some of the neighbors' taxes to the Jews to help them finish the project.

Artaxerxes
(ar-tuh-ZERK-seez)
One more king of Persia. He gives Professor Ezra permission to lead another batch of Jews back to Jerusalem. (Arty's stepmom was most likely Queen Esther, a great Jewish woman whose story is told in her own book—the book of Esther—up ahead about 50 pages or so.)

What's UP with That?

God has very strict rules for Israel. One of those rules is to stay away from its godless neighbors. That means don't marry their daughters and don't dabble in their pagan religions. But the Jews disobeyed that rule and turned their country into a religious circus. So God put a stop to their bad behavior by allowing Babylon to wipe them out.

Professor Ezra knows God's rules better than anyone. He knows exactly what happened when the Jews broke the rules. He doesn't want to see that happen again. When he finally gets to go back home to Jerusalem, he sees a sorry situation: Many of the Jews have married foreign women and allowed their goofy gods to move in too.

There's only one solution, and it's pretty painful. The professor gives it to them in chapter 10:10–12.

❶ Ezra's solution was . . .
    a. just live with it. God will give you a break
    b. teach your wives to speak with a Jewish accent
    c. send your foreign wives back where they came from
    d. kill all the rule-breakers

❷ When the people heard Ezra's solution, they . . .
    a. told him to be quiet
    b. figured he was just a crazy old man so they didn't have to do it
    c. packed up and moved back to Babylon
    d. agreed to do it

Can you imagine how tough that was on families? Ezra was telling them to put God first in their lives, *no matter how painful*. Could you do that? Is there something in *your* life that's so important you wouldn't even give it up for God? If there is, that thing is your god. The real God won't stand for being put in second place. Give him first place in your life. All the other stuff—no matter how good—is just. . . well, *other stuff*.

Snap shots

- Go home!—Cyrus sends the first batch of Jews back to Jerusalem (*chapters 1—2*)

- Get started!—Zerubbabel begins the temple reconstruction project (*chapter 3*)

- Red tape!—neighbors get jealous, cause trouble, work stops (*chapter 4*)

- Break's over!—the work continues, King Darius quiets the neighbors (*chapter 5*)

- All done!—the grand reopening of God's great house (*chapter 6*)

- Praise God!—Ezra returns, whips up a revival (*chapters 7—10*)

Cyrus Helps the Exiles to Return

1 In the first year of Cyrus king of Persia, in order to fulfill the word of the LORD spoken by Jeremiah, the LORD moved the heart of Cyrus king of Persia to make a proclamation throughout his realm and to put it in writing:

[2] "This is what Cyrus king of Persia says:

" 'The LORD, the God of heaven, has given me all the kingdoms of the earth and he has appointed me to build a temple for him at Jerusalem in Judah. [3] Anyone of his people among you—may his God be with him, and let him go up to Jerusalem in Judah and build the temple of the LORD, the God of Israel, the God who is in Jerusalem. [4] And the people of any place where survivors may now be living are to provide him with silver and gold, with goods and livestock, and with freewill offerings for the temple of God in Jerusalem.' "

[5] Then the family heads of Judah and Benjamin, and the priests and Levites—everyone whose heart God had moved—prepared to go up and build the house of the LORD in Jerusalem. [6] All their neighbors assisted them with articles of silver and gold, with goods and livestock, and with valuable gifts, in addition to all the freewill offerings. [7] Moreover, King Cyrus brought out the articles belonging to the temple of the LORD, which Nebuchadnezzar had carried away from Jerusalem and had placed in the temple of his god.[a] [8] Cyrus king of Persia had them brought by Mithredath the treasurer, who counted them out to Sheshbazzar the prince of Judah.

[9] This was the inventory:

gold dishes	30
silver dishes	1,000
silver pans[b]	29
[10] gold bowls	30
matching silver bowls	410
other articles	1,000

[11] In all, there were 5,400 articles of gold and of silver. Sheshbazzar brought all these along when the exiles came up from Babylon to Jerusalem.

The List of the Exiles Who Returned

2 Now these are the people of the province who came up from the captivity of the exiles, whom Nebuchadnezzar king of Babylon had taken captive to Babylon (they returned to Jerusalem and Judah, each to his own town, [2] in company with Zerubbabel, Jeshua, Nehemiah, Seraiah, Reelaiah, Mordecai, Bilshan, Mispar, Bigvai, Rehum and Baanah):

The list of the men of the people of Israel:

[3] the descendants of Parosh	2,172
[4] of Shephatiah	372
[5] of Arah	775
[6] of Pahath-Moab (through the line of Jeshua and Joab)	2,812
[7] of Elam	1,254
[8] of Zattu	945
[9] of Zaccai	760
[10] of Bani	642
[11] of Bebai	623
[12] of Azgad	1,222
[13] of Adonikam	666
[14] of Bigvai	2,056
[15] of Adin	454
[16] of Ater (through Hezekiah)	98
[17] of Bezai	323
[18] of Jorah	112
[19] of Hashum	223
[20] of Gibbar	95
[21] the men of Bethlehem	123
[22] of Netophah	56
[23] of Anathoth	128
[24] of Azmaveth	42
[25] of Kiriath Jearim,[c] Kephirah and Beeroth	743
[26] of Ramah and Geba	621
[27] of Micmash	122
[28] of Bethel and Ai	223
[29] of Nebo	52
[30] of Magbish	156
[31] of the other Elam	1,254
[32] of Harim	320
[33] of Lod, Hadid and Ono	725
[34] of Jericho	345
[35] of Senaah	3,630

[36] The priests:

---

[a] 7 Or *gods*　　[b] 9 The meaning of the Hebrew for this word is uncertain.　　[c] 25 See Septuagint (see also Neh. 7:29); Hebrew *Kiriath Arim*.

the descendants of Jedaiah
(through the family of
Jeshua)   973
[37] of Immer   1,052
[38] of Pashhur   1,247
[39] of Harim   1,017

[40] The Levites:

the descendants of Jeshua and
Kadmiel (through the line of
Hodaviah)   74

[41] The singers:

the descendants of Asaph   128

[42] The gatekeepers of the temple:

the descendants of
Shallum, Ater, Talmon,
Akkub, Hatita and Shobai   139

[43] The temple servants:

the descendants of
Ziha, Hasupha, Tabbaoth,
[44] Keros, Siaha, Padon,
[45] Lebanah, Hagabah, Akkub,
[46] Hagab, Shalmai, Hanan,
[47] Giddel, Gahar, Reaiah,
[48] Rezin, Nekoda, Gazzam,
[49] Uzza, Paseah, Besai,
[50] Asnah, Meunim, Nephussim,
[51] Bakbuk, Hakupha, Harhur,
[52] Bazluth, Mehida, Harsha,
[53] Barkos, Sisera, Temah,
[54] Neziah and Hatipha

[55] The descendants of the servants of
Solomon:

the descendants of
Sotai, Hassophereth, Peruda,
[56] Jaala, Darkon, Giddel,
[57] Shephatiah, Hattil,
Pokereth-Hazzebaim and Ami

[58] The temple servants and the
descendants of the servants of
Solomon   392

[59] The following came up from the
towns of Tel Melah, Tel Harsha, Ke-
rub, Addon and Immer, but they
could not show that their families
were descended from Israel:

[60] The descendants of
Delaiah, Tobiah and
Nekoda   652

[61] And from among the priests:

The descendants of
Hobaiah, Hakkoz and Barzillai
(a man who had married a
daughter of Barzillai the Gileadite
and was called by that name).
[62] These searched for their family
records, but they could not find
them and so were excluded from the
priesthood as unclean. [63] The governor ordered them not to eat any of
the most sacred food until there was
a priest ministering with the Urim
and Thummim.

No Roots, No Robes

Ezra 2:62–63

God set apart—or "made holy"—the Levites
to serve as priests in the temple. If anyone
else tried to be a priest, God would break
the entire nation's relationship with him. So
each priest had to trace his roots back to the
founding father, Levi. The rule was simple:
No roots, no robes. By the way, this explains
why there are so many name lists, or
genealogies, in the Bible. Everyone had to
prove he was legitimate. Even Jesus. That's
why the books of Matthew and Luke trace
his line back through King David, to prove
that he is the Messiah, our Savior and King.

[64] The whole company numbered
42,360, [65] besides their 7,337 menservants and maidservants; and they
also had 200 men and women singers. [66] They had 736 horses, 245
mules, [67] 435 camels and 6,720 donkeys.

[68] When they arrived at the house of
the LORD in Jerusalem, some of the heads
of the families gave freewill offerings toward the rebuilding of the house of God
on its site. [69] According to their ability
they gave to the treasury for this work
61,000 drachmas[a] of gold, 5,000 minas[b]
of silver and 100 priestly garments.

---

[a]69 That is, about 1,100 pounds (about 500 kilograms)
[b]69 That is, about 3 tons (about 2.9 metric tons)

⁷⁰The priests, the Levites, the singers, the gatekeepers and the temple servants settled in their own towns, along with some of the other people, and the rest of the Israelites settled in their towns.

Rebuilding the Altar

3 When the seventh month came and the Israelites had settled in their towns, the people assembled as one man in Jerusalem. ²Then Jeshua son of Jozadak and his fellow priests and Zerubbabel son of Shealtiel and his associates began to build the altar of the God of Israel to sacrifice burnt offerings on it, in accordance with what is written in the Law of Moses the man of God. ³Despite their fear of the peoples around them, they built the altar on its foundation and sacrificed burnt offerings on it to the LORD, both the morning and evening sacrifices. ⁴Then in accordance with what is written, they celebrated the Feast of Tabernacles with the required number of burnt offerings prescribed for each day. ⁵After that, they presented the regular burnt offerings, the New Moon sacrifices and the sacrifices for all the appointed sacred feasts of the LORD, as well as those brought as freewill offerings to the LORD. ⁶On the first day of the seventh month they began to offer burnt offerings to the LORD, though the foundation of the LORD's temple had not yet been laid.

Rebuilding the Temple

⁷Then they gave money to the masons and carpenters, and gave food and drink and oil to the people of Sidon and Tyre, so that they would bring cedar logs by sea from Lebanon to Joppa, as authorized by Cyrus king of Persia.

⁸In the second month of the second year after their arrival at the house of God in Jerusalem, Zerubbabel son of Shealtiel, Jeshua son of Jozadak and the rest of their brothers (the priests and the Levites and all who had returned from the captivity to Jerusalem) began the work, appointing Levites twenty years of age and older to supervise the building of the house of the LORD. ⁹Jeshua and his sons and brothers and Kadmiel and his sons (descendants of Hodaviah^a) and the sons of Henadad and their sons and brothers—all Levites—joined together in supervising those working on the house of God.

¹⁰When the builders laid the foundation of the temple of the LORD, the priests in their vestments and with trumpets, and the Levites (the sons of Asaph) with cymbals, took their places to praise the LORD, as prescribed by David king of Israel. ¹¹With praise and thanksgiving they sang to the LORD:

"He is good;
    his love to Israel endures forever."

And all the people gave a great shout of praise to the LORD, because the foundation of the house of the LORD was laid. ¹²But many of the older priests and Levites and family heads, who had seen the former temple, wept aloud when they saw the foundation of this temple being laid, while many others shouted for joy.

The Good Ol' Days

Huh?

Ezra 3:12

Ever hear your parents talk about "the good ol' days"? You know, how good life was "back then"? Parents often think stuff was better when they were kids. That's what's happening here. The older folks who remembered the previous temple (destroyed 50 years earlier) are sad that the new one doesn't seem to be as great.

¹³No one could distinguish the sound of the shouts of joy from the sound of weeping, because the people made so much noise. And the sound was heard far away.

Opposition to the Rebuilding

4 When the enemies of Judah and Benjamin heard that the exiles were building a temple for the LORD, the God of Israel, ²they came to Zerubbabel and to the heads of the families and said, "Let us help you build because, like you, we

---

^a9 Hebrew *Yehudah*, probably a variant of *Hodaviah*

seek your God and have been sacrificing to him since the time of Esarhaddon king of Assyria, who brought us here." [3]But Zerubbabel, Jeshua and the rest of the heads of the families of Israel answered, "You have no part with us in building a temple to our God. We alone will build it for the LORD, the God of Israel, as King Cyrus, the king of Persia, commanded us."

[4]Then the peoples around them set out to discourage the people of Judah and make them afraid to go on building.[a] [5]They hired counselors to work against them and frustrate their plans during the entire reign of Cyrus king of Persia and down to the reign of Darius king of Persia.

Later Opposition Under Xerxes and Artaxerxes

[6]At the beginning of the reign of Xerxes,[b] they lodged an accusation against the people of Judah and Jerusalem.

[7]And in the days of Artaxerxes king of Persia, Bishlam, Mithredath, Tabeel and the rest of his associates wrote a letter to Artaxerxes. The letter was written in Aramaic script and in the Aramaic language.[c,d]

[8]Rehum the commanding officer and Shimshai the secretary wrote a letter against Jerusalem to Artaxerxes the king as follows:

[9]Rehum the commanding officer and Shimshai the secretary, together with the rest of their associates—the judges and officials over the men from Tripolis, Persia,[e] Erech and Babylon, the Elamites of Susa, [10]and the other people whom the great and honorable Ashurbanipal[f] deported and settled in the city of Samaria and elsewhere in Trans-Euphrates.

[11](This is a copy of the letter they sent him.)

To King Artaxerxes,

From your servants, the men of Trans-Euphrates:

[12]The king should know that the Jews who came up to us from you have gone to Jerusalem and are re-building that rebellious and wicked city. They are restoring the walls and repairing the foundations.

[13]Furthermore, the king should know that if this city is built and its walls are restored, no more taxes, tribute or duty will be paid, and the royal revenues will suffer. [14]Now since we are under obligation to the palace and it is not proper for us to see the king dishonored, we are sending this message to inform the king, [15]so that a search may be made in the archives of your predecessors. In these records you will find that this city is a rebellious city, troublesome to kings and provinces, a place of rebellion from ancient times. That is why this city was destroyed. [16]We inform the king that if this city is built and its walls are restored, you will be left with nothing in Trans-Euphrates.

[17]The king sent this reply:

To Rehum the commanding officer, Shimshai the secretary and the rest of their associates living in Samaria and elsewhere in Trans-Euphrates:

Greetings.

[18]The letter you sent us has been read and translated in my presence. [19]I issued an order and a search was made, and it was found that this city has a long history of revolt against kings and has been a place of rebellion and sedition. [20]Jerusalem has had powerful kings ruling over the whole of Trans-Euphrates, and taxes, tribute and duty were paid to them. [21]Now issue an order to these men to stop work, so that this city will not be rebuilt until I so order. [22]Be careful not to neglect this matter. Why let this threat grow, to the detriment of the royal interests?

---

[a]4 Or *and troubled them as they built* [b]6 Hebrew *Ahasuerus*, a variant of Xerxes' Persian name [c]7 Or *written in Aramaic and translated* [d]7 The text of Ezra 4:8–6:18 is in Aramaic. [e]9 Or *officials, magistrates and governors over the men from* [f]10 Aramaic *Osnappar*, a variant of *Ashurbanipal*

²³As soon as the copy of the letter of King Artaxerxes was read to Rehum and Shimshai the secretary and their associates, they went immediately to the Jews in Jerusalem and compelled them by force to stop.

²⁴Thus the work on the house of God in Jerusalem came to a standstill until the second year of the reign of Darius king of Persia.

Tattenai's Letter to Darius

5 Now Haggai the prophet and Zechariah the prophet, a descendant of Iddo, prophesied to the Jews in Judah and Jerusalem in the name of the God of Israel, who was over them. ²Then Zerubbabel son of Shealtiel and Jeshua son of Jozadak set to work to rebuild the house of God in Jerusalem. And the prophets of God were with them, helping them.

³At that time Tattenai, governor of Trans-Euphrates, and Shethar-Bozenai and their associates went to them and asked, "Who authorized you to rebuild this temple and restore this structure?" ⁴They also asked, "What are the names of the men constructing this building?"ᵃ ⁵But the eye of their God was watching over the elders of the Jews, and they were not stopped until a report could go to Darius and his written reply be received.

⁶This is a copy of the letter that Tattenai, governor of Trans-Euphrates, and Shethar-Bozenai and their associates, the officials of Trans-Euphrates, sent to King Darius. ⁷The report they sent him read as follows:

To King Darius:

Cordial greetings.

⁸The king should know that we went to the district of Judah, to the temple of the great God. The people are building it with large stones and placing the timbers in the walls. The work is being carried on with diligence and is making rapid progress under their direction.

⁹We questioned the elders and asked them, "Who authorized you to rebuild this temple and restore this structure?" ¹⁰We also asked them their names, so that we could write down the names of their leaders for your information.

¹¹This is the answer they gave us:

"We are the servants of the God of heaven and earth, and we are rebuilding the temple that was built many years ago, one that a great king of Israel built and finished. ¹²But because our fathers angered the God of heaven, he handed them over to Nebuchadnezzar the Chaldean, king of Babylon, who destroyed this temple and deported the people to Babylon.

¹³"However, in the first year of Cyrus king of Babylon, King Cyrus issued a decree to rebuild this house of God. ¹⁴He even removed from the templeᵇ of Babylon the gold and silver articles of the house of God, which Nebuchadnezzar had taken from the temple in Jerusalem and brought to the templeᵇ in Babylon.

"Then King Cyrus gave them to a man named Sheshbazzar, whom he had appointed governor, ¹⁵and he told him, 'Take these articles and go and deposit them in the temple in Jerusalem. And rebuild the house of God on its site.' ¹⁶So this Sheshbazzar came and laid the foundations of the house of God in Jerusalem. From that day to the present it has been under construction but is not yet finished."

¹⁷Now if it pleases the king, let a search be made in the royal archives of Babylon to see if King Cyrus did in fact issue a decree to rebuild this house of God in Jerusalem. Then let the king send us his decision in this matter.

The Decree of Darius

6 King Darius then issued an order, and they searched in the archives stored in the treasury at Babylon. ²A scroll was found in the citadel of

---

ᵃ4 See Septuagint; Aramaic ⁴*We told them the names of the men constructing this building.* ᵇ14 Or *palace*

Ecbatana in the province of Media, and this was written on it:

Memorandum:

³In the first year of King Cyrus, the king issued a decree concerning the temple of God in Jerusalem:

Let the temple be rebuilt as a place to present sacrifices, and let its foundations be laid. It is to be ninety feet*a* high and ninety feet wide, ⁴with three courses of large stones and one of timbers. The costs are to be paid by the royal treasury. ⁵Also, the gold and silver articles of the house of God, which Nebuchadnezzar took from the temple in Jerusalem and brought to Babylon, are to be returned to their places in the temple in Jerusalem; they are to be deposited in the house of God.

⁶Now then, Tattenai, governor of Trans-Euphrates, and Shethar-Bozenai and you, their fellow officials of that province, stay away from there. ⁷Do not interfere with the work on this temple of God. Let the governor of the Jews and the Jewish elders rebuild this house of God on its site.

⁸Moreover, I hereby decree what you are to do for these elders of the Jews in the construction of this house of God:

The expenses of these men are to be fully paid out of the royal treasury, from the revenues of Trans-Euphrates, so that the work will not stop. ⁹Whatever is needed—young bulls, rams, male lambs for burnt offerings to the God of heaven, and wheat, salt, wine and oil, as requested by the priests in Jerusalem—must be given them daily without fail, ¹⁰so that they may offer sacrifices pleasing to the God of heaven and pray for the well-being of the king and his sons.

¹¹Furthermore, I decree that if anyone changes this edict, a beam is to be pulled from his house and he is to be lifted up and impaled on it. And for this crime his house is to be made a pile of rubble. ¹²May God, who has caused his Name to dwell there, overthrow any king or people who lifts a hand to change this decree or to destroy this temple in Jerusalem.

I Darius have decreed it. Let it be carried out with diligence.

Completion and Dedication of the Temple

¹³Then, because of the decree King Darius had sent, Tattenai, governor of Trans-Euphrates, and Shethar-Bozenai and their associates carried it out with diligence. ¹⁴So the elders of the Jews continued to build and prosper under the preaching of Haggai the prophet and Zechariah, a descendant of Iddo. They finished building the temple according to the command of the God of Israel and the decrees of Cyrus, Darius and Artaxerxes, kings of Persia. ¹⁵The temple was completed on the third day of the month Adar, in the sixth year of the reign of King Darius.

¹⁶Then the people of Israel—the priests, the Levites and the rest of the exiles—celebrated the dedication of the house of God with joy. ¹⁷For the dedication of this house of God they offered a hundred bulls, two hundred rams, four hundred male lambs and, as a sin offering for all Israel, twelve male goats, one for each of the tribes of Israel. ¹⁸And they installed the priests in their divisions and the Levites in their groups for the service of God at Jerusalem, according to what is written in the Book of Moses.

The Passover

¹⁹On the fourteenth day of the first month, the exiles celebrated the Passover. ²⁰The priests and Levites had purified themselves and were all ceremonially clean. The Levites slaughtered the Passover lamb for all the exiles, for their brothers the priests and for themselves. ²¹So the Israelites who had returned from the exile ate it, together with all who had separated themselves from the unclean practices of their Gentile neighbors in order to seek the LORD, the God of Israel. ²²For seven days they celebrated with joy

---

a3 Aramaic *sixty cubits* (about 27 meters)

the Feast of Unleavened Bread, because the LORD had filled them with joy by changing the attitude of the king of Assyria, so that he assisted them in the work on the house of God, the God of Israel.

Ezra Comes to Jerusalem

7 After these things, during the reign of Artaxerxes king of Persia, Ezra son of Seraiah, the son of Azariah, the son of Hilkiah, ²the son of Shallum, the son of Zadok, the son of Ahitub, ³the son of Amariah, the son of Azariah, the son of Meraioth, ⁴the son of Zerahiah, the son of Uzzi, the son of Bukki, ⁵the son of Abishua, the son of Phinehas, the son of Eleazar, the son of Aaron the chief priest— ⁶this Ezra came up from Babylon. He was a teacher well versed in the Law of Moses, which the LORD, the God of Israel, had given. The king had granted him everything he asked, for the hand of the LORD his God was on him. ⁷Some of the Israelites, including priests, Levites, singers, gatekeepers and temple servants, also came up to Jerusalem in the seventh year of King Artaxerxes.

⁸Ezra arrived in Jerusalem in the fifth month of the seventh year of the king. ⁹He had begun his journey from Babylon on the first day of the first month, and he arrived in Jerusalem on the first day of the fifth month, for the gracious hand of his God was on him. ¹⁰For Ezra had devoted himself to the study and observance of the Law of the LORD, and to teaching its decrees and laws in Israel.

King Artaxerxes' Letter to Ezra

¹¹This is a copy of the letter King Artaxerxes had given to Ezra the priest and teacher, a man learned in matters concerning the commands and decrees of the LORD for Israel:

¹²ᵃArtaxerxes, king of kings,

To Ezra the priest, a teacher of the Law of the God of heaven:

Greetings.

¹³Now I decree that any of the Israelites in my kingdom, including priests and Levites, who wish to go to Jerusalem with you, may go. ¹⁴You are sent by the king and his seven advisers to inquire about Judah and Jerusalem with regard to the Law of your God, which is in your hand. ¹⁵Moreover, you are to take with you the silver and gold that the king and his advisers have freely given to the God of Israel, whose dwelling is in Jerusalem, ¹⁶together with all the silver and gold you may obtain from the province of Babylon, as well as the freewill offerings of the people and priests for the temple of their God in Jerusalem. ¹⁷With this money be sure to buy bulls, rams and male lambs, together with their grain offerings and drink offerings, and sacrifice them on the altar of the temple of your God in Jerusalem.

¹⁸You and your brother Jews may then do whatever seems best with the rest of the silver and gold, in accordance with the will of your God. ¹⁹Deliver to the God of Jerusalem all the articles entrusted to you for worship in the temple of your God. ²⁰And anything else needed for the temple of your God that you may have occasion to supply, you may provide from the royal treasury.

²¹Now I, King Artaxerxes, order all the treasurers of Trans-Euphrates to provide with diligence whatever Ezra the priest, a teacher of the Law of the God of heaven, may ask of you— ²²up to a hundred talents[b] of silver, a hundred cors[c] of wheat, a hundred baths[d] of wine, a hundred baths[d] of olive oil, and salt without limit. ²³Whatever the God of heaven has prescribed, let it be done with diligence for the temple of the God of heaven. Why should there be wrath against the realm of the king and of his sons? ²⁴You are also to know that you have no authority to impose taxes, tribute or duty on

---

ᵃ12 The text of Ezra 7:12-26 is in Aramaic.
ᵇ22 That is, about 3 3/4 tons (about 3.4 metric tons)
ᶜ22 That is, probably about 600 bushels (about 22 kiloliters)   ᵈ22 That is, probably about 600 gallons (about 2.2 kiloliters)

any of the priests, Levites, singers, gatekeepers, temple servants or other workers at this house of God.

²⁵And you, Ezra, in accordance with the wisdom of your God, which you possess, appoint magistrates and judges to administer justice to all the people of Trans-Euphrates—all who know the laws of your God. And you are to teach any who do not know them. ²⁶Whoever does not obey the law of your God and the law of the king must surely be punished by death, banishment, confiscation of property, or imprisonment.

²⁷Praise be to the LORD, the God of our fathers, who has put it into the king's heart to bring honor to the house of the LORD in Jerusalem in this way ²⁸and who has extended his good favor to me before the king and his advisers and all the king's powerful officials. Because the hand of the LORD my God was on me, I took courage and gathered leading men from Israel to go up with me.

List of the Family Heads Returning With Ezra

8 These are the family heads and those registered with them who came up with me from Babylon during the reign of King Artaxerxes:

Monday

Being a Better Witness

Read Ezra 7:8–10

I really could have used this passage a few years ago. I had some friends who weren't Christians, but I had no idea how to witness to them. I hadn't really studied the Bible, and I didn't understand how important it was for me to show my faith through my life.

Those old friends are really lost. They are caught up in swearing, sex, drugs and whatever else they can find to fill the emptiness of not having Jesus in their lives. I know it's not my fault that they're doing these things, but if I had known the Bible better a few years ago, at least I could have tried to help them know Jesus.

During the time the book of Ezra was written, the Israelites were coming back from Babylon after living as captives. Their children no longer knew God's law. Ezra felt called to help get Israel back on track, but instead of just teaching others about God's law, he spent time studying it himself. He made sure *he* understood it before trying to tell others about it. God blessed Ezra for his faithfulness and hard work.

We can all learn a lot from Ezra's example. It's really important that we take time to study God's Word and know it. Then we can be better witnesses to our friends.

What about You?

❶ If someone asked you a tough question about the Bible, would you know how to find the answer? How can you be better prepared to talk with your non-Christian friends about Jesus?

❷ Think of some of the questions non-Christians might have about God. Over the next few days, look through your Bible and talk with your parents or youth pastor to find some answers. Then really study what the Bible has to say about those things. Also, check out the Plan of Salvation on page 1582.

❸ Ask God to help you live out the things you learn as you read your Bible.

Turn to page 555 for your next devotion.

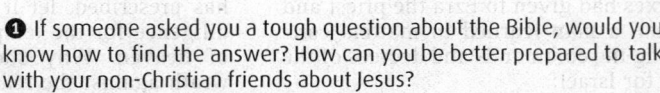

²of the descendants of Phinehas, Gershom;

of the descendants of Ithamar, Daniel;

of the descendants of David, Hattush ³of the descendants of Shecaniah;

of the descendants of Parosh, Zechariah, and with him were registered 150 men;

⁴of the descendants of Pahath-Moab, Eliehoenai son of Zerahiah, and with him 200 men;

⁵of the descendants of Zattu,ᵃ Shecaniah son of Jahaziel, and with him 300 men;

⁶of the descendants of Adin, Ebed son of Jonathan, and with him 50 men;

⁷of the descendants of Elam, Jeshaiah son of Athaliah, and with him 70 men;

⁸of the descendants of Shephatiah, Zebadiah son of Michael, and with him 80 men;

⁹of the descendants of Joab, Obadiah son of Jehiel, and with him 218 men;

¹⁰of the descendants of Bani,ᵇ Shelomith son of Josiphiah, and with him 160 men;

¹¹of the descendants of Bebai, Zechariah son of Bebai, and with him 28 men;

¹²of the descendants of Azgad, Johanan son of Hakkatan, and with him 110 men;

¹³of the descendants of Adonikam, the last ones, whose names were Eliphelet, Jeuel and Shemaiah, and with them 60 men;

¹⁴of the descendants of Bigvai, Uthai and Zaccur, and with them 70 men.

The Return to Jerusalem

¹⁵I assembled them at the canal that flows toward Ahava, and we camped there three days. When I checked among the people and the priests, I found no Levites there. ¹⁶So I summoned Eliezer, Ariel, Shemaiah, Elnathan, Jarib, Elnathan, Nathan, Zechariah and Meshullam, who were leaders, and Joiarib and Elnathan, who were men of learning, ¹⁷and I sent them to Iddo, the leader in Casiphia. I told them what to say to Iddo and his kinsmen, the temple servants in Casiphia, so that they might bring attendants to us for the house of our God. ¹⁸Because the gracious hand of our God was on us, they brought us Sherebiah, a capable man, from the descendants of Mahli son of Levi, the son of Israel, and Sherebiah's sons and brothers, 18 men; ¹⁹and Hashabiah, together with Jeshaiah from the descendants of Merari, and his brothers and nephews, 20 men. ²⁰They also brought 220 of the temple servants—a body that David and the officials had established to assist the Levites. All were registered by name.

²¹There, by the Ahava Canal, I proclaimed a fast, so that we might humble ourselves before our God and ask him for a safe journey for us and our children, with all our possessions. ²²I was ashamed to ask the king for soldiers and horsemen to protect us from enemies on the road, because we had told the king, "The gracious hand of our God is on everyone who looks to him, but his great anger is against all who forsake him." ²³So we fasted and petitioned our God about this, and he answered our prayer.

²⁴Then I set apart twelve of the leading priests, together with Sherebiah, Hashabiah and ten of their brothers, ²⁵and I weighed out to them the offering of silver and gold and the articles that the king, his advisers, his officials and all Israel present there had donated for the house of our God. ²⁶I weighed out to them 650 talentsᶜ of silver, silver articles weighing 100 talents,ᵈ 100 talentsᵈ of gold, ²⁷20 bowls of gold valued at 1,000 darics,ᵉ and two fine articles of polished bronze, as precious as gold.

²⁸I said to them, "You as well as these articles are consecrated to the LORD. The silver and gold are a freewill offering to the LORD, the God of your fathers. ²⁹Guard them carefully until you weigh them out in the chambers of the house of

---

ᵃ5 Some Septuagint manuscripts (also 1 Esdras 8:32); Hebrew does not have Zattu.   ᵇ10 Some Septuagint manuscripts (also 1 Esdras 8:36); Hebrew does not have Bani.   ᶜ26 That is, about 25 tons (about 22 metric tons)   ᵈ26 That is, about 3 3/4 tons (about 3.4 metric tons)   ᵉ27 That is, about 19 pounds (about 8.5 kilograms)

the LORD in Jerusalem before the leading priests and the Levites and the family heads of Israel." ³⁰Then the priests and Levites received the silver and gold and sacred articles that had been weighed out to be taken to the house of our God in Jerusalem.

³¹On the twelfth day of the first month we set out from the Ahava Canal to go to Jerusalem. The hand of our God was on us, and he protected us from enemies and bandits along the way. ³²So we arrived in Jerusalem, where we rested three days.

³³On the fourth day, in the house of our God, we weighed out the silver and gold and the sacred articles into the hands of Meremoth son of Uriah, the priest. Eleazar son of Phinehas was with him, and so were the Levites Jozabad son of Jeshua and Noadiah son of Binnui. ³⁴Everything was accounted for by number and weight, and the entire weight was recorded at that time.

³⁵Then the exiles who had returned from captivity sacrificed burnt offerings to the God of Israel: twelve bulls for all Israel, ninety-six rams, seventy-seven male lambs and, as a sin offering, twelve male goats. All this was a burnt offering to the LORD. ³⁶They also delivered the king's orders to the royal satraps and to the governors of Trans-Euphrates, who then gave assistance to the people and to the house of God.

Ezra's Prayer About Intermarriage

9 After these things had been done, the leaders came to me and said, "The people of Israel, including the priests and the Levites, have not kept themselves separate from the neighboring peoples with their detestable practices, like those of the Canaanites, Hittites, Perizzites, Jebusites, Ammonites, Moabites, Egyptians and Amorites. ²They have taken some of their daughters as wives for themselves and their sons, and have mingled the holy race with the peoples around them. And the leaders and officials have led the way in this unfaithfulness."

³When I heard this, I tore my tunic and cloak, pulled hair from my head and beard and sat down appalled. ⁴Then everyone who trembled at the words of the God of Israel gathered around me because of this unfaithfulness of the exiles. And I sat there appalled until the evening sacrifice.

⁵Then, at the evening sacrifice, I rose from my self-abasement, with my tunic and cloak torn, and fell on my knees with my hands spread out to the LORD my God ⁶and prayed:

"O my God, I am too ashamed and disgraced to lift up my face to you, my God, because our sins are higher than our heads and our guilt has reached to the heavens. ⁷From the days of our forefathers until now, our guilt has been great. Because of our sins, we and our kings and our priests have been subjected to the sword and captivity, to pillage and humiliation at the hand of foreign kings, as it is today.

⁸"But now, for a brief moment, the LORD our God has been gracious in leaving us a remnant and giving us a firm place in his sanctuary, and so our God gives light to our eyes and a little relief in our bondage. ⁹Though

Just a Few Huh?

Ezra 9:8
Ever been to an "Old Timer's" game? Retired baseball players come back for a day and play a couple of innings in their old-time uniforms. It's fun to watch, not to mention being a great history lesson on former players. That's kind of like the remnant Ezra describes. They were a group of Israelites who survived being captured by the nation of Babylon. They made it back to Israel and would continue to do whatever God wanted. Play ball!

we are slaves, our God has not deserted us in our bondage. He has shown us kindness in the sight of the kings of Persia: He has granted us new life to rebuild the house of our God and repair its ruins, and he has given us a wall of protection in Judah and Jerusalem.

¹⁰"But now, O our God, what can we say after this? For we have disregarded the commands ¹¹you gave through your servants the prophets when you said: 'The land you are entering to possess is a land polluted by the corruption of its peoples. By their detestable practices they have filled it with their impurity from one end to the other. ¹²Therefore, do not give your daughters in marriage to their sons or take their daughters for your sons. Do not seek a treaty of friendship with them at any time, that you may be strong and eat the good things of the land and leave it to your children as an everlasting inheritance.'

¹³"What has happened to us is a result of our evil deeds and our great guilt, and yet, our God, you have punished us less than our sins have deserved and have given us a remnant like this. ¹⁴Shall we again break your commands and intermarry with the peoples who commit such detestable practices? Would you not be angry enough with us to destroy us, leaving us no remnant or survivor? ¹⁵O LORD, God of Israel, you are righteous! We are left this day as a remnant. Here we are before you in our guilt, though because of it not one of us can stand in your presence."

The People's Confession of Sin

10 While Ezra was praying and confessing, weeping and throwing himself down before the house of God, a large crowd of Israelites—men, women and children—gathered around him. They too wept bitterly. ²Then Shecaniah son of Jehiel, one of the descendants of Elam, said to Ezra, "We have been unfaithful to our God by marrying foreign women from the peoples around us. But in spite of this, there is still hope for Israel. ³Now let us make a covenant before our God to send away all these women and their children, in accordance with the counsel of my lord and of those who fear the commands of our God. Let it be done ac-

cording to the Law. ⁴Rise up; this matter is in your hands. We will support you, so take courage and do it."

⁵So Ezra rose up and put the leading priests and Levites and all Israel under oath to do what had been suggested. And they took the oath. ⁶Then Ezra withdrew from before the house of God and went to the room of Jehohanan son of Eliashib. While he was there, he ate no food and drank no water, because he continued to mourn over the unfaithfulness of the exiles.

⁷A proclamation was then issued throughout Judah and Jerusalem for all the exiles to assemble in Jerusalem. ⁸Anyone who failed to appear within three days would forfeit all his property, in accordance with the decision of the officials and elders, and would himself be expelled from the assembly of the exiles.

⁹Within the three days, all the men of Judah and Benjamin had gathered in Jerusalem. And on the twentieth day of the ninth month, all the people were sitting in the square before the house of God, greatly distressed by the occasion and because of the rain. ¹⁰Then Ezra the priest stood up and said to them, "You have been unfaithful; you have married foreign women, adding to Israel's guilt. ¹¹Now make confession to the LORD, the God of your fathers, and do his will. Separate yourselves from the peoples around you and from your foreign wives."

Velcro Sin

Huh?

Ezra 10:11
Velcro's the best. It's a quick and easy way to stick 2 things together. (Tearing it apart lots of times in a quiet room is a great way to annoy people!) But it doesn't work when it's separated from itself—it won't stick to anything. Ezra thinks the Israelites are acting like Velcro because they stick to anything sinful. Ezra tells them to "separate themselves" from whatever causes them to sin so they'll be less likely to get stuck in sin's trap.

¹²The whole assembly responded with a loud voice: "You are right! We must do as you say. ¹³But there are many people here and it is the rainy season; so we cannot stand outside. Besides, this matter cannot be taken care of in a day or two, because we have sinned greatly in this thing. ¹⁴Let our officials act for the whole assembly. Then let everyone in our towns who has married a foreign woman come at a set time, along with the elders and judges of each town, until the fierce anger of our God in this matter is turned away from us." ¹⁵Only Jonathan son of Asahel and Jahzeiah son of Tikvah, supported by Meshullam and Shabbethai the Levite, opposed this.

¹⁶So the exiles did as was proposed. Ezra the priest selected men who were family heads, one from each family division, and all of them designated by name. On the first day of the tenth month they sat down to investigate the cases, ¹⁷and by the first day of the first month they finished dealing with all the men who had married foreign women.

Those Guilty of Intermarriage

¹⁸Among the descendants of the priests, the following had married foreign women:

From the descendants of Jeshua son of Jozadak, and his brothers: Maaseiah, Eliezer, Jarib and Gedaliah. ¹⁹(They all gave their hands in pledge to put away their wives, and for their guilt they each presented a ram from the flock as a guilt offering.)

²⁰From the descendants of Immer:
Hanani and Zebadiah.

²¹From the descendants of Harim:
Maaseiah, Elijah, Shemaiah, Jehiel and Uzziah.

²²From the descendants of Pashhur:
Elioenai, Maaseiah, Ishmael, Nethanel, Jozabad and Elasah.

²³Among the Levites:

Jozabad, Shimei, Kelaiah (that is, Kelita), Pethahiah, Judah and Eliezer.

²⁴From the singers:
Eliashib.

From the gatekeepers:
Shallum, Telem and Uri.

²⁵And among the other Israelites:

From the descendants of Parosh:
Ramiah, Izziah, Malkijah, Mijamin, Eleazar, Malkijah and Benaiah.

²⁶From the descendants of Elam:
Mattaniah, Zechariah, Jehiel, Abdi, Jeremoth and Elijah.

²⁷From the descendants of Zattu:
Elioenai, Eliashib, Mattaniah, Jeremoth, Zabad and Aziza.

²⁸From the descendants of Bebai:
Jehohanan, Hananiah, Zabbai and Athlai.

²⁹From the descendants of Bani:
Meshullam, Malluch, Adaiah, Jashub, Sheal and Jeremoth.

³⁰From the descendants of Pahath-Moab:
Adna, Kelal, Benaiah, Maaseiah, Mattaniah, Bezalel, Binnui and Manasseh.

³¹From the descendants of Harim:
Eliezer, Ishijah, Malkijah, Shemaiah, Shimeon, ³²Benjamin, Malluch and Shemariah.

³³From the descendants of Hashum:
Mattenai, Mattattah, Zabad, Eliphelet, Jeremai, Manasseh and Shimei.

³⁴From the descendants of Bani:
Maadai, Amram, Uel, ³⁵Benaiah, Bedeiah, Keluhi, ³⁶Vaniah, Meremoth, Eliashib, ³⁷Mattaniah, Mattenai and Jaasu.

³⁸From the descendants of Binnui:[a]
Shimei, ³⁹Shelemiah, Nathan, Adaiah, ⁴⁰Macnadebai, Shashai, Sharai, ⁴¹Azarel, Shelemiah, Shemariah, ⁴²Shallum, Amariah and Joseph.

⁴³From the descendants of Nebo:
Jeiel, Mattithiah, Zabad, Zebina, Jaddai, Joel and Benaiah.

⁴⁴All these had married foreign women, and some of them had children by these wives.[b]

---

[a]37,38 See Septuagint (also 1 Esdras 9:34); Hebrew Jaasu ³⁸and Bani and Binnui,　[b]44 Or and they sent them away with their children

Nehemiah

START

Cast OF Characters

Nehemiah
(nee-uh-MY-uh)

A great leader! Starts out on poison patrol for King Artaxerxes of Persia, then becomes foreman of the Walls of Jerusalem Restoration Project. When that's done, he becomes governor of Judah.

Artaxerxes
(ar-tuh-ZERK-seez)

As king of Persia, Arty gives Nehemiah permission to go to Jerusalem to rebuild the city walls.

The 3 Bullies: Sanballat, (san-BAL-et)
Tobiah (toe-BYE-uh)
and Geshem (GESH-um)

These leaders of 3 troublesome tribes don't like the Jews, and they hate the idea of Jerusalem getting its wall rebuilt. They gripe and threaten and spread lies—anything to foul up the construction project. But they can't stop God's work—no one can.

Ezra (EZZ-ruh)

He's a teacher, a priest and the writer of 1 and 2 Chronicles and Ezra. When the wall is finished, Professor Ezra opens God's Word and reads it to the people. Then he and Nehemiah fire up a big party to celebrate all the good stuff God has done.

Here's a recap: The Jews have abandoned the real God and chased after false gods. The Lord lets them do it, and when the Babylonians come to town with their big guns blazing (uh, they didn't have guns then, but you get the point), God doesn't stop them. The Jews get hauled off to Babylon and have plenty of time to figure out what they did wrong. Then a cool thing happens: Big bad Babylon gets pushed over by the Persians. The new Persian king lets a bunch of the Jews go home to Judah to rebuild the temple Babylon trashed. But some of the Jews stay where they are, working for Persia. That's where this story starts.

Nehemiah works for the Persian king Artaxerxes. He protects the king from assassination attempts by sampling the wine at each meal. If the wine is poisoned, the king is safe. And as long as it's not poisoned, Nehemiah is safe! One day Nehemiah hears that the people of Jerusalem are stressed out because they haven't had time or money to rebuild the city's security wall.

The news breaks Nehemiah's heart. The king gives him permission to go to Jerusalem to rebuild the wall. When Nehemiah gets into town, he puts on his hard hat and gets right to work. The giant project is finished in 52 days! He and Ezra invite the people to celebrate God's great blessing. Then Nehemiah takes off his hard hat, puts on a governor's uniform, and leads the Jews into new and better days.

What's UP with That?

Have you ever had one of those days when everything seems to get in your way? Nehemiah has weeks and weeks of those days. But he never gives up. See if you can pick his solutions to the problems he faces:

Problem ❶ Jerusalem's walls are gone, leaving the city unprotected. Nehemiah is stuck far away, working for the Persian king.

Solution:
- a. Forget about it. There's nothing he can do
- b. Whine and complain. Maybe somebody will do something
- c. Sneak out of town and try to fix it on his own
- d. Pray

Problem ❷ God leads Nehemiah to ask for permission to go to Jerusalem. He gets it. But what can Nehemiah do by himself? He'll need building materials, workers and cooperation from the Jews' troublesome neighbors.

Solution:
- a. Give up. The task is too big
- b. Just go to Jerusalem and figure it out later
- c. Get help from the king while he's got the chance
- d. Steal some workers and materials on his way out of town

Problem ❸ Nehemiah inspects the walls. They're in bad shape. It's a giant project to rebuild them. He'll need an army of workers. They'll fight, get in each other's way and need constant supervision.

Solution:
- a. Give up. It was a nice idea, but impossible
- b. Divide the task into sections and let each building team do their part
- c. Tell everyone to just start building. They'll figure it out
- d. Build a shorter wall—looks nice, less work

Problem ❹ The work is going well. In fact, it's going *too* well. Now the troublesome neighbors are trying to stop it by threatening to kill the workers. The crew may quit to stay alive.

Solution:
- a. Give up. What's the point of a walled city if there's no one left to live in it?
- b. Send money to the troublemakers to buy their peace
- c. Ignore the problem. A few murders is no big deal
- d. Provide security for the crew. Post guards at all times

Nehemiah faces many more problems. And for every problem, he comes up with a solution. When the situation seems hopeless, Nehemiah prays. When his workers have a problem, it becomes *his* problem. He figures out a solution to help *them* first. And that solves his problem too. The next time you're facing a problem that looks pretty bleak, do what Nehemiah does: Pray, then figure out the way!

Snap shots

- News from home—Nehemiah weeps, prays, asks to go to Jerusalem *(chapter 1)*

- You can go!—the foreman inspects the sorry site *(chapter 2)*

- Hard hats—the wall-building begins *(chapter 3)*

- Not so fast!—bullies befuddle builders, Nehemiah nixes nonsense *(chapters 4—6)*

- Big walls, small city—project complete, but the city's awfully sparse *(chapters 6—7)*

- The Word, the vow—the people renew their contract with God *(chapters 8—10)*

- Go Gov!—Nehemiah sets up the state for success *(chapters 11—13)*

answers: 1-d, 2-c, 3-b, 4-d

Nehemiah's Prayer

1 The words of Nehemiah son of Hacaliah:

In the month of Kislev in the twentieth year, while I was in the citadel of Susa, ²Hanani, one of my brothers, came from Judah with some other men, and I questioned them about the Jewish remnant that survived the exile, and also about Jerusalem.

³They said to me, "Those who survived the exile and are back in the province are in great trouble and disgrace. The wall of Jerusalem is broken down, and its gates have been burned with fire."

⁴When I heard these things, I sat down and wept. For some days I mourned and fasted and prayed before the God of heaven. ⁵Then I said:

"O LORD, God of heaven, the great and awesome God, who keeps his covenant of love with those who love him and obey his commands, ⁶let your ear be attentive and your eyes open to hear the prayer your servant is praying before you day and night for your servants, the people of Israel. I confess the sins we Israelites, including myself and my father's house, have committed against you. ⁷We have acted very wickedly toward you. We have not obeyed the commands, decrees and laws you gave your servant Moses.

⁸"Remember the instruction you gave your servant Moses, saying, 'If you are unfaithful, I will scatter you among the nations, ⁹but if you return to me and obey my commands, then even if your exiled people are at the farthest horizon, I will gather them from there and bring them to the place I have chosen as a dwelling for my Name.'

¹⁰"They are your servants and your people, whom you redeemed by your great strength and your mighty hand. ¹¹O Lord, let your ear be attentive to the prayer of this your servant and to the prayer of your servants who delight in revering your name. Give your servant

success today by granting him favor in the presence of this man."

I was cupbearer to the king.

Artaxerxes Sends Nehemiah to Jerusalem

2 In the month of Nisan in the twentieth year of King Artaxerxes, when wine was brought for him, I took the wine and gave it to the king. I had not been sad in his presence before; ²so the king asked me, "Why does your face look so sad when you are not ill? This can be nothing but sadness of heart."

I was very much afraid, ³but I said to the king, "May the king live forever! Why should my face not look sad when the city where my fathers are buried lies in ruins, and its gates have been destroyed by fire?"

No Sad Moods Allowed

Huh?

Nehemiah 2:1–3
As cupbearer, Nehemiah tasted the king's drinks before the king. That way, if someone spiked it with poison, Nehemiah would keel over first. So every workday had the potential of being a real bummer. And to make things worse, showing up sad to serve the king of Persia was punishable by death. But in this case, Nehemiah couldn't hide his sorrow over burned-out Jerusalem. Fortunately, God was with him. Not only was Nehemiah's life spared, but the king helped him lead the way in rebuilding Israel's holy city.

⁴The king said to me, "What is it you want?"

Then I prayed to the God of heaven, ⁵and I answered the king, "If it pleases the king and if your servant has found favor in his sight, let him send me to the city in Judah where my fathers are buried so that I can rebuild it."

⁶Then the king, with the queen sitting beside him, asked me, "How long will your journey take, and when will you get back?" It pleased the king to send me; so I set a time.

[7]I also said to him, "If it pleases the king, may I have letters to the governors of Trans-Euphrates, so that they will provide me safe-conduct until I arrive in Judah? [8]And may I have a letter to Asaph, keeper of the king's forest, so he will give me timber to make beams for the gates of the citadel by the temple and for the city wall and for the residence I will occupy?" And because the gracious hand of my God was upon me, the king granted my requests. [9]So I went to the governors of Trans-Euphrates and gave them the king's letters. The king had also sent army officers and cavalry with me.

[10]When Sanballat the Horonite and Tobiah the Ammonite official heard about this, they were very much disturbed that someone had come to promote the welfare of the Israelites.

Nehemiah Inspects Jerusalem's Walls

[11]I went to Jerusalem, and after staying there three days [12]I set out during the night with a few men. I had not told anyone what my God had put in my heart to do for Jerusalem. There were no mounts with me except the one I was riding on. [13]By night I went out through the Valley Gate toward the Jackal[a] Well and the Dung Gate, examining the walls of Jerusalem, which had been broken down, and its gates, which had been destroyed by fire. [14]Then I moved on toward the Fountain Gate and the King's Pool, but there was not enough room for my mount to get through; [15]so I went up the valley by night, examining the wall. Finally, I turned back and reentered through the Valley Gate. [16]The officials did not know where I had gone or what I was doing, because as yet I had said nothing to the Jews or the priests or nobles or officials or any others who would be doing the work.

[17]Then I said to them, "You see the trouble we are in: Jerusalem lies in ruins, and its gates have been burned with fire. Come, let us rebuild the wall of Jerusalem, and we will no longer be in disgrace." [18]I also told them about the gracious hand of my God upon me and what the king had said to me.

They replied, "Let us start rebuilding." So they began this good work.

[19]But when Sanballat the Horonite, Tobiah the Ammonite official and Geshem the Arab heard about it, they mocked and ridiculed us. "What is this you are doing?" they asked. "Are you rebelling against the king?"

[20]I answered them by saying, "The God of heaven will give us success. We his servants will start rebuilding, but as for you, you have no share in Jerusalem or any claim or historic right to it."

Builders of the Wall

3 Eliashib the high priest and his fellow priests went to work and rebuilt the Sheep Gate. They dedicated it and set its doors in place, building as far as the Tower of the Hundred, which they dedicated, and as far as the Tower of Hananel. [2]The men of Jericho built the adjoining section, and Zaccur son of Imri built next to them.

[3]The Fish Gate was rebuilt by the sons of Hassenaah. They laid its beams and put its doors and bolts and bars in place. [4]Meremoth son of Uriah, the son of Hakkoz, repaired the next section. Next to him Meshullam son of Berekiah, the son of Meshezabel, made repairs, and next to him Zadok son of Baana also made repairs. [5]The next section was repaired by the men of Tekoa, but their nobles would not put their shoulders to the work under their supervisors.[b]

[6]The Jeshanah[c] Gate was repaired by Joiada son of Paseah and Meshullam son of Besodeiah. They laid its beams and put its doors and bolts and bars in place. [7]Next to them, repairs were made by men from Gibeon and Mizpah—Melatiah of Gibeon and Jadon of Meronoth—places under the authority of the governor of Trans-Euphrates. [8]Uzziel son of Harhaiah, one of the goldsmiths, repaired the next section; and Hananiah, one of the perfume-makers, made repairs next to that. They restored[d] Jerusalem as far as the Broad Wall. [9]Rephaiah son of Hur, ruler of a half-district of Jerusalem, repaired the next section. [10]Adjoining this, Jedaiah son of Harumaph made repairs

---

[a]13 Or *Serpent* or *Fig*   [b]5 Or *their Lord* or *the governor*   [c]6 Or *Old*   [d]8 Or *They left out part of*

opposite his house, and Hattush son of Hashabneiah made repairs next to him. [11]Malkijah son of Harim and Hasshub son of Pahath-Moab repaired another section and the Tower of the Ovens. [12]Shallum son of Hallohesh, ruler of a half-district of Jerusalem, repaired the next section with the help of his daughters.

[13]The Valley Gate was repaired by Hanun and the residents of Zanoah. They rebuilt it and put its doors and bolts and bars in place. They also repaired five hundred yards[a] of the wall as far as the Dung Gate.

[14]The Dung Gate was repaired by Malkijah son of Recab, ruler of the district of Beth Hakkerem. He rebuilt it and put its doors and bolts and bars in place.

[15]The Fountain Gate was repaired by Shallun son of Col-Hozeh, ruler of the district of Mizpah. He rebuilt it, roofing it over and putting its doors and bolts and bars in place. He also repaired the wall of the Pool of Siloam,[b] by the King's Garden, as far as the steps going down from the City of David. [16]Beyond him, Nehemiah son of Azbuk, ruler of a half-district of Beth Zur, made repairs up to a point opposite the tombs[c] of David, as far as the artificial pool and the House of the Heroes.

[17]Next to him, the repairs were made by the Levites under Rehum son of Bani. Beside him, Hashabiah, ruler of half the district of Keilah, carried out repairs for his district. [18]Next to him, the repairs were made by their countrymen under Binnui[d] son of Henadad, ruler of the other half-district of Keilah. [19]Next to him, Ezer son of Jeshua, ruler of Mizpah, repaired another section, from a point facing the ascent to the armory as far as the angle. [20]Next to him, Baruch son of Zabbai zealously repaired another section, from the angle to the entrance of the house of Eliashib the high priest. [21]Next to him, Meremoth son of Uriah, the son of Hakkoz, repaired another section, from the entrance of Eliashib's house to the end of it.

[22]The repairs next to him were made by the priests from the surrounding region. [23]Beyond them, Benjamin and Has-shub made repairs in front of their house; and next to them, Azariah son of Maaseiah, the son of Ananiah, made repairs beside his house. [24]Next to him, Binnui son of Henadad repaired another section, from Azariah's house to the angle and the corner, [25]and Palal son of Uzai worked opposite the angle and the tower projecting from the upper palace near the court of the guard. Next to him, Pedaiah son of Parosh [26]and the temple servants living on the hill of Ophel made repairs up to a point opposite the Water Gate toward the east and the projecting tower. [27]Next to them, the men of Tekoa repaired another section, from the great projecting tower to the wall of Ophel.

[28]Above the Horse Gate, the priests made repairs, each in front of his own house. [29]Next to them, Zadok son of Immer made repairs opposite his house. Next to him, Shemaiah son of Shecaniah, the guard at the East Gate, made repairs. [30]Next to him, Hananiah son of Shelemiah, and Hanun, the sixth son of Zalaph, repaired another section. Next to them, Meshullam son of Berekiah made repairs opposite his living quarters. [31]Next to him, Malkijah, one of the goldsmiths, made repairs as far as the house of the temple servants and the merchants, opposite the Inspection Gate, and as far as the room above the corner; [32]and between the room above the corner and the Sheep Gate the goldsmiths and merchants made repairs.

Opposition to the Rebuilding

4 When Sanballat heard that we were rebuilding the wall, he became angry and was greatly incensed. He ridiculed the Jews, [2]and in the presence of his associates and the army of Samaria, he said, "What are those feeble Jews doing? Will they restore their wall? Will they offer sacrifices? Will they finish in a day? Can they bring the stones back to life from those heaps of rubble—burned as they are?"

---

[a]13 Hebrew *a thousand cubits* (about 450 meters)   [b]15 Hebrew *Shelah,* a variant of *Shiloah,* that is, Siloam   [c]16 Hebrew; Septuagint, some Vulgate manuscripts and Syriac *tomb*   [d]18 Two Hebrew manuscripts and Syriac (see also Septuagint and verse 24); most Hebrew manuscripts *Bavvai*

³Tobiah the Ammonite, who was at his side, said, "What they are building—if even a fox climbed up on it, he would break down their wall of stones!"

⁴Hear us, O our God, for we are despised. Turn their insults back on their own heads. Give them over as plunder in a land of captivity. ⁵Do not cover up their guilt or blot out their sins from your sight, for they have thrown insults in the face of*ª* the builders.

Bonk 'Em, God

Huh?

Nehemiah 4:4–5
Wow! Do you see what Nehemiah prayed? Pretty tough stuff. Is that allowed? Actually, it's right on. Nehemiah simply asks God to follow through on his promise to protect Israel. And instead of asking God for permission to take matters into his own hands, Nehemiah asks God to get the job done. Got a problem with someone? Talk to God about it and let him deal with the situation.

⁶So we rebuilt the wall till all of it reached half its height, for the people worked with all their heart.

⁷But when Sanballat, Tobiah, the Arabs, the Ammonites and the men of Ashdod heard that the repairs to Jerusalem's walls had gone ahead and that the gaps were being closed, they were very angry. ⁸They all plotted together to come and fight against Jerusalem and stir up trouble against it. ⁹But we prayed to our God and posted a guard day and night to meet this threat.

¹⁰Meanwhile, the people in Judah said, "The strength of the laborers is giving out, and there is so much rubble that we cannot rebuild the wall."

¹¹Also our enemies said, "Before they know it or see us, we will be right there among them and will kill them and put an end to the work."

¹²Then the Jews who lived near them came and told us ten times over, "Wherever you turn, they will attack us."

¹³Therefore I stationed some of the people behind the lowest points of the wall at the exposed places, posting them by families, with their swords, spears and bows. ¹⁴After I looked things over, I stood up and said to the nobles, the officials and the rest of the people, "Don't be afraid of them. Remember the Lord, who is great and awesome, and fight for your brothers, your sons and your daughters, your wives and your homes."

¹⁵When our enemies heard that we were aware of their plot and that God had frustrated it, we all returned to the wall, each to his own work.

¹⁶From that day on, half of my men did the work, while the other half were equipped with spears, shields, bows and armor. The officers posted themselves behind all the people of Judah ¹⁷who were building the wall. Those who carried materials did their work with one hand and held a weapon in the other, ¹⁸and each of the builders wore his sword at his side as he worked. But the man who sounded the trumpet stayed with me.

¹⁹Then I said to the nobles, the officials and the rest of the people, "The work is extensive and spread out, and we are widely separated from each other along the wall. ²⁰Wherever you hear the sound of the trumpet, join us there. Our God will fight for us!"

²¹So we continued the work with half the men holding spears, from the first light of dawn till the stars came out. ²²At that time I also said to the people, "Have every man and his helper stay inside Jerusalem at night, so they can serve us as guards by night and workmen by day." ²³Neither I nor my brothers nor my men nor the guards with me took off our clothes; each had his weapon, even when he went for water.*ᵇ*

Nehemiah Helps the Poor

5 Now the men and their wives raised a great outcry against their Jewish brothers. ²Some were saying, "We and our sons and daughters are numerous; in order for us to eat and stay alive, we must get grain."

ª5 Or have provoked you to anger before ᵇ23 The meaning of the Hebrew for this clause is uncertain.

³Others were saying, "We are mortgaging our fields, our vineyards and our homes to get grain during the famine."

⁴Still others were saying, "We have had to borrow money to pay the king's tax on our fields and vineyards. ⁵Although we are of the same flesh and blood as our countrymen and though our sons are as good as theirs, yet we have to subject our sons and daughters to slavery. Some of our daughters have already been enslaved, but we are powerless, because our fields and our vineyards belong to others."

⁶When I heard their outcry and these charges, I was very angry. ⁷I pondered them in my mind and then accused the nobles and officials. I told them, "You are exacting usury from your own countrymen!" So I called together a large meeting to deal with them ⁸and said: "As far as possible, we have bought back our Jewish brothers who were sold to the Gentiles. Now you are selling your brothers, only for them to be sold back to us!" They kept quiet, because they could find nothing to say.

⁹So I continued, "What you are doing is not right. Shouldn't you walk in the fear of our God to avoid the reproach of our Gentile enemies? ¹⁰I and my brothers and my men are also lending the people money and grain. But let the exacting of usury stop! ¹¹Give back to them immediately their fields, vineyards, olive groves and houses, and also the usury you are charging them—the hundredth part of the money, grain, new wine and oil."

¹²"We will give it back," they said.

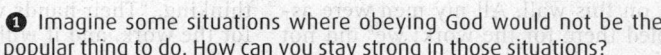

Tuesday

Better Than Popularity

Read Nehemiah 4:1–3

Some people make it pretty obvious that they think Christianity is foolish. Many TV characters and other famous people take strong stands against Christians and their beliefs. These criticisms might seem like a new problem, but they're really not. Reading these verses in Nehemiah reminds me that God's children were criticized for doing what was right even thousands of years ago!

Doing what God wants isn't always popular. But it's a mistake to think that being popular and cool is the most important goal in life. In fact, what my peers think of me is one of the worst ways to determine my self-worth. Being criticized by them isn't nearly as bad as disappointing God.

Whether we like it or not, God desires and expects us to take a stand for him every day of our lives. Sometimes this might be really hard, but we don't have to do it alone. God helped the Jews keep working on the wall when everybody was making fun of them for it. I know he'll help me obey him too, no matter what other people say.

Emile age 14

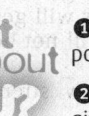
What about You?

❶ Imagine some situations where obeying God would not be the popular thing to do. How can you stay strong in those situations?

❷ Put a rock in a place where you can see it every day. When people give you a hard time about doing what's right, think about how God can help your faith be as solid as a "rock."

❸ Ask God to help you bless the people who criticize you (see Luke 6:27–28, page 1228).

Turn to page 560 for your next devotion.

No Strings Attached

Huh?

Nehemiah 5:7–11

Imagine giving a homeless man $5 for food, and then expecting him to give it back *plus interest* the next day! Seems crazy, but that was happening in Israel, and it's called "usury." Nehemiah was upset because officials were loaning money to those in need and then demanding they pay it back with interest. God wanted the officials to help those in need with no strings attached.

"And we will not demand anything more from them. We will do as you say."

Then I summoned the priests and made the nobles and officials take an oath to do what they had promised. [13]I also shook out the folds of my robe and said, "In this way may God shake out of his house and possessions every man who does not keep this promise. So may such a man be shaken out and emptied!"

At this the whole assembly said, "Amen," and praised the LORD. And the people did as they had promised.

[14]Moreover, from the twentieth year of King Artaxerxes, when I was appointed to be their governor in the land of Judah, until his thirty-second year—twelve years—neither I nor my brothers ate the food allotted to the governor. [15]But the earlier governors—those preceding me—placed a heavy burden on the people and took forty shekels[a] of silver from them in addition to food and wine. Their assistants also lorded it over the people. But out of reverence for God I did not act like that. [16]Instead, I devoted myself to the work on this wall. All my men were assembled there for the work; we[b] did not acquire any land.

[17]Furthermore, a hundred and fifty Jews and officials ate at my table, as well as those who came to us from the surrounding nations. [18]Each day one ox, six choice sheep and some poultry were prepared for me, and every ten days an abundant supply of wine of all kinds. In spite of all this, I never demanded the food allotted to the governor, because the demands were heavy on these people.

[19]Remember me with favor, O my God, for all I have done for these people.

Further Opposition to the Rebuilding

6 When word came to Sanballat, Tobiah, Geshem the Arab and the rest of our enemies that I had rebuilt the wall and not a gap was left in it—though up to that time I had not set the doors in the gates— [2]Sanballat and Geshem sent me this message: "Come, let us meet together in one of the villages[c] on the plain of Ono."

But they were scheming to harm me; [3]so I sent messengers to them with this reply: "I am carrying on a great project and cannot go down. Why should the work stop while I leave it and go down to you?" [4]Four times they sent me the same message, and each time I gave them the same answer.

[5]Then, the fifth time, Sanballat sent his aide to me with the same message, and in his hand was an unsealed letter [6]in which was written:

"It is reported among the nations—and Geshem[d] says it is true—that you and the Jews are plotting to revolt, and therefore you are building the wall. Moreover, according to these reports you are about to become their king [7]and have even appointed prophets to make this proclamation about you in Jerusalem: 'There is a king in Judah!' Now this report will get back to the king; so come, let us confer together."

[8]I sent him this reply: "Nothing like what you are saying is happening; you are just making it up out of your head."

[9]They were all trying to frighten us, thinking, "Their hands will get too weak for the work, and it will not be completed."

But I prayed, "Now strengthen my hands."

[10]One day I went to the house of She-

---

[a]15 That is, about 1 pound (about 0.5 kilogram)
[b]16 Most Hebrew manuscripts; some Hebrew manuscripts, Septuagint, Vulgate and Syriac *I*
[c]2 Or *in Kephirim*   [d]6 Hebrew *Gashmu*, a variant of *Geshem*

maiah son of Delaiah, the son of Mehetabel, who was shut in at his home. He said, "Let us meet in the house of God, inside the temple, and let us close the temple doors, because men are coming to kill you—by night they are coming to kill you."

[11]But I said, "Should a man like me run away? Or should one like me go into the temple to save his life? I will not go!" [12]I realized that God had not sent him, but that he had prophesied against me because Tobiah and Sanballat had hired him. [13]He had been hired to intimidate me so that I would commit a sin by doing this, and then they would give me a bad name to discredit me.

[14]Remember Tobiah and Sanballat, O my God, because of what they have done; remember also the prophetess Noadiah and the rest of the prophets who have been trying to intimidate me.

The Completion of the Wall

[15]So the wall was completed on the twenty-fifth of Elul, in fifty-two days. [16]When all our enemies heard about this, all the surrounding nations were afraid and lost their self-confidence, because they realized that this work had been done with the help of our God.

[17]Also, in those days the nobles of Judah were sending many letters to Tobiah, and replies from Tobiah kept coming to them. [18]For many in Judah were under oath to him, since he was son-in-law to Shecaniah son of Arah, and his son Jehohanan had married the daughter of Meshullam son of Berekiah. [19]Moreover, they kept reporting to me his good deeds and then telling him what I said. And Tobiah sent letters to intimidate me.

7 After the wall had been rebuilt and I had set the doors in place, the gatekeepers and the singers and the Levites were appointed. [2]I put in charge of Jerusalem my brother Hanani, along with[a] Hananiah the commander of the citadel, because he was a man of integrity and feared God more than most men do. [3]I said to them, "The gates of Jerusalem are not to be opened until the sun is hot. While the gatekeepers are still on duty, have them shut the doors and bar them. Also appoint residents of Jerusalem as guards, some at their posts and some near their own houses."

The List of the Exiles Who Returned

[4]Now the city was large and spacious, but there were few people in it, and the houses had not yet been rebuilt. [5]So my God put it into my heart to assemble the nobles, the officials and the common people for registration by families. I found the genealogical record of those who had been the first to return. This is what I found written there:

[6]These are the people of the province who came up from the captivity of the exiles whom Nebuchadnezzar king of Babylon had taken captive (they returned to Jerusalem and Judah, each to his own town, [7]in company with Zerubbabel, Jeshua, Nehemiah, Azariah, Raamiah, Nahamani, Mordecai, Bilshan, Mispereth, Bigvai, Nehum and Baanah):

The list of the men of Israel:

[8]the descendants of Parosh	2,172
[9]of Shephatiah	372
[10]of Arah	652
[11]of Pahath-Moab (through the line of Jeshua and Joab)	2,818
[12]of Elam	1,254
[13]of Zattu	845
[14]of Zaccai	760
[15]of Binnui	648
[16]of Bebai	628
[17]of Azgad	2,322
[18]of Adonikam	667
[19]of Bigvai	2,067
[20]of Adin	655
[21]of Ater (through Hezekiah)	98
[22]of Hashum	328
[23]of Bezai	324
[24]of Hariph	112
[25]of Gibeon	95
[26]the men of Bethlehem and Netophah	188
[27]of Anathoth	128
[28]of Beth Azmaveth	42
[29]of Kiriath Jearim, Kephirah and Beeroth	743
[30]of Ramah and Geba	621

[a]2 Or *Hanani, that is,*

[31] of Micmash   122
[32] of Bethel and Ai   123
[33] of the other Nebo   52
[34] of the other Elam   1,254
[35] of Harim   320
[36] of Jericho   345
[37] of Lod, Hadid and Ono   721
[38] of Senaah   3,930

[39] The priests:

the descendants of Jedaiah
(through the family of
Jeshua)   973
[40] of Immer   1,052
[41] of Pashhur   1,247
[42] of Harim   1,017

[43] The Levites:

the descendants of Jeshua
(through Kadmiel through
the line of Hodaviah)   74

[44] The singers:

the descendants of Asaph   148

[45] The gatekeepers:

the descendants of
Shallum, Ater, Talmon,
Akkub, Hatita and Shobai   138

[46] The temple servants:

the descendants of
Ziha, Hasupha, Tabbaoth,
[47] Keros, Sia, Padon,
[48] Lebana, Hagaba, Shalmai,
[49] Hanan, Giddel, Gahar,
[50] Reaiah, Rezin, Nekoda,
[51] Gazzam, Uzza, Paseah,
[52] Besai, Meunim, Nephussim,
[53] Bakbuk, Hakupha, Harhur,
[54] Bazluth, Mehida, Harsha,
[55] Barkos, Sisera, Temah,
[56] Neziah and Hatipha

[57] The descendants of the servants of
Solomon:

the descendants of
Sotai, Sophereth, Perida,
[58] Jaala, Darkon, Giddel,
[59] Shephatiah, Hattil,
Pokereth-Hazzebaim and Amon

[60] The temple servants and the
descendants of the servants
of Solomon   392

[61] The following came up from the
towns of Tel Melah, Tel Harsha, Ke-
rub, Addon and Immer, but they
could not show that their families
were descended from Israel:

[62] the descendants of
Delaiah, Tobiah and Nekoda   642

[63] And from among the priests:

the descendants of
Hobaiah, Hakkoz and Barzillai (a
man who had married a daughter of Barzillai the Gileadite and
was called by that name).
[64] These searched for their family
records, but they could not find
them and so were excluded from the
priesthood as unclean. [65] The governor, therefore, ordered them not to
eat any of the most sacred food until
there should be a priest ministering
with the Urim and Thummim.

[66] The whole company numbered
42,360, [67] besides their 7,337 menservants and maidservants; and they
also had 245 men and women singers. [68] There were 736 horses, 245
mules,[a] [69] 435 camels and 6,720 donkeys.

[70] Some of the heads of the families contributed to the work. The
governor gave to the treasury 1,000
drachmas[b] of gold, 50 bowls and
530 garments for priests. [71] Some of
the heads of the families gave to the
treasury for the work 20,000 drachmas[c] of gold and 2,200 minas[d] of
silver. [72] The total given by the rest
of the people was 20,000 drachmas
of gold, 2,000 minas[e] of silver and
67 garments for priests.

[73] The priests, the Levites, the gatekeepers, the singers and the temple
servants, along with certain of the
people and the rest of the Israelites,
settled in their own towns.

[a]68 Some Hebrew manuscripts (see also Ezra 2:66);
most Hebrew manuscripts do not have this verse.
[b]70 That is, about 19 pounds (about 8.5 kilograms)
[c]71 That is, about 375 pounds (about 170 kilograms);
also in verse 72   [d]71 That is, about 1 1/3 tons
(about 1.2 metric tons)   [e]72 That is, about 1 1/4
tons (about 1.1 metric tons)

Ezra Reads the Law

8 When the seventh month came and the Israelites had settled in their towns, [1]all the people assembled as one man in the square before the Water Gate. They told Ezra the scribe to bring out the Book of the Law of Moses, which the LORD had commanded for Israel.

[2]So on the first day of the seventh month Ezra the priest brought the Law before the assembly, which was made up of men and women and all who were able to understand. [3]He read it aloud from daybreak till noon as he faced the square before the Water Gate in the presence of the men, women and others who could understand. And all the people listened attentively to the Book of the Law.

[4]Ezra the scribe stood on a high wooden platform built for the occasion. Beside him on his right stood Mattithiah, Shema, Anaiah, Uriah, Hilkiah and Maaseiah; and on his left were Pedaiah, Mishael, Malkijah, Hashum, Hashbaddanah, Zechariah and Meshullam.

[5]Ezra opened the book. All the people could see him because he was standing above them; and as he opened it, the people all stood up. [6]Ezra praised the LORD, the great God; and all the people lifted their hands and responded, "Amen! Amen!" Then they bowed down and worshiped the LORD with their faces to the ground.

[7]The Levites—Jeshua, Bani, Sherebiah, Jamin, Akkub, Shabbethai, Hodiah, Maaseiah, Kelita, Azariah, Jozabad, Hanan and Pelaiah—instructed the people in the Law while the people were standing there. [8]They read from the Book of the Law of God, making it clear[a] and giving the meaning so that the people could understand what was being read.

[9]Then Nehemiah the governor, Ezra the priest and scribe, and the Levites who were instructing the people said to them all, "This day is sacred to the LORD your God. Do not mourn or weep." For all the people had been weeping as they listened to the words of the Law.

[10]Nehemiah said, "Go and enjoy choice food and sweet drinks, and send some to those who have nothing prepared. This day is sacred to our Lord. Do not grieve, for the joy of the LORD is your strength."

[11]The Levites calmed all the people, saying, "Be still, for this is a sacred day. Do not grieve."

[12]Then all the people went away to eat and drink, to send portions of food and to celebrate with great joy, because they now understood the words that had been made known to them.

[13]On the second day of the month, the heads of all the families, along with the priests and the Levites, gathered around Ezra the scribe to give attention to the words of the Law. [14]They found written in the Law, which the LORD had commanded through Moses, that the Israelites were to live in booths during the feast of the seventh month [15]and that they should proclaim this word and spread it throughout their towns and in Jerusalem: "Go out into the hill country and bring back branches from olive and wild olive trees, and from myrtles, palms and shade trees, to make booths"—as it is written.[b]

[16]So the people went out and brought back branches and built themselves booths on their own roofs, in their courtyards, in the courts of the house of God and in the square by the Water Gate and the one by the Gate of Ephraim. [17]The whole company that had returned from exile built booths and lived in them. From the days of Joshua son of Nun until

---

Attention!

Huh?

Nehemiah 8:5–6

Did you notice how the people responded when God's Word was read? First they stood up. A new game? Nope. The people stood to show respect, kind of like sitting up straight when the principal comes into your classroom. Then they bowed down with their faces to the ground! Were they looking for their contacts? No—they were so thankful for the Word of God that they bowed to thank and praise him. Are you grateful to have God's Word?

---

[a]8 Or God, translating it   [b]15 See Lev. 23:37-40.

that day, the Israelites had not celebrated it like this. And their joy was very great.

¹⁸Day after day, from the first day to the last, Ezra read from the Book of the Law of God. They celebrated the feast for seven days, and on the eighth day, in accordance with the regulation, there was an assembly.

The Israelites Confess Their Sins

9 On the twenty-fourth day of the same month, the Israelites gathered together, fasting and wearing sackcloth and having dust on their heads. ²Those of Israelite descent had separated themselves from all foreigners. They stood in their places and confessed their sins and the wickedness of their fathers. ³They stood where they were and read from the Book of the Law of the LORD their God for a quarter of the day, and spent another quarter in confession and in worshiping the LORD their God. ⁴Standing on the

stairs were the Levites—Jeshua, Bani, Kadmiel, Shebaniah, Bunni, Sherebiah, Bani and Kenani—who called with loud

Fashion Nugget

Huh?

Nehemiah 9:1
Clothing styles change as fast as the weather, but could sackcloth and ashes be the latest fashion statement here? What's that all about? People wore sackcloth (kind of like a giant garbage bag but made from goat hair) and sprinkled ashes on their head during times of sadness or as a way to protest. It might have been neater to just carry a sign (and less painful for the goat!), but this was a visible way of showing others how they felt.

Wednesday

Party On!

Read Nehemiah 8:10

I've been to parties that made me feel really horrible and low because everybody there was just putting on a show, getting all worried about how they looked and who paid attention to them. I've also been to parties that made me feel really happy because people were just being themselves and having a ton of fun. Most of the fun parties were youth group parties—but when I tell my other friends how much fun I had, they don't believe me!

Some of my friends think of God as a head honcho who sits on a big throne and orders people to "be good." I used to think of God that way too. But youth group activities, and verses like this one in Nehemiah, show me that God wants us to have fun too. He created a beautiful world for us, and I guess you could say he created fun. It's all part of the great life he wants us to have.

When I find my joy in God, my friends will see it. And maybe they'll want that joy too.

Carissa age 14

What about You?

❶ If you could plan the ultimate youth group activity, what would it be?

❷ Get a group of Christian friends together and throw a party—movies, a picnic, cookie-baking or whatever sounds fun to you. And be sure to invite your non-Christian friends!

❸ Thank God for fun!

Turn to page 574 for your next devotion.

voices to the LORD their God. ⁵And the Levites—Jeshua, Kadmiel, Bani, Hashabneiah, Sherebiah, Hodiah, Shebaniah and Pethahiah—said: "Stand up and praise the LORD your God, who is from everlasting to everlasting.ᵃ"

"Blessed be your glorious name, and may it be exalted above all blessing and praise. ⁶You alone are the LORD. You made the heavens, even the highest heavens, and all their starry host, the earth and all that is on it, the seas and all that is in them. You give life to everything, and the multitudes of heaven worship you.

⁷"You are the LORD God, who chose Abram and brought him out of Ur of the Chaldeans and named him Abraham. ⁸You found his heart faithful to you, and you made a covenant with him to give to his descendants the land of the Canaanites, Hittites, Amorites, Perizzites, Jebusites and Girgashites. You have kept your promise because you are righteous.

⁹"You saw the suffering of our forefathers in Egypt; you heard their cry at the Red Sea.ᵇ ¹⁰You sent miraculous signs and wonders against Pharaoh, against all his officials and all the people of his land, for you knew how arrogantly the Egyptians treated them. You made a name for yourself, which remains to this day. ¹¹You divided the sea before them, so that they passed through it on dry ground, but you hurled their pursuers into the depths, like a stone into mighty waters. ¹²By day you led them with a pillar of cloud, and by night with a pillar of fire to give them light on the way they were to take.

¹³"You came down on Mount Sinai; you spoke to them from heaven. You gave them regulations and laws that are just and right, and decrees and commands that are good. ¹⁴You made known to them your holy Sabbath and gave them commands, decrees and laws through your servant Moses. ¹⁵In their hunger you gave

them bread from heaven and in their thirst you brought them water from the rock; you told them to go in and take possession of the land you had sworn with uplifted hand to give them.

¹⁶"But they, our forefathers, became arrogant and stiff-necked, and did not obey your commands. ¹⁷They refused to listen and failed to remember the miracles you performed among them. They became stiff-necked and in their rebellion appointed a leader in order to return to their slavery. But you are a forgiving God, gracious and compassionate, slow to anger and abounding in love. Therefore you did not desert them, ¹⁸even when they cast for themselves an image of a calf and said, 'This is your god, who brought you up out of Egypt,' or when they committed awful blasphemies.

¹⁹"Because of your great compassion you did not abandon them in the desert. By day the pillar of cloud did not cease to guide them on their path, nor the pillar of fire by night to shine on the way they were to take. ²⁰You gave your good Spirit to instruct them. You did not withhold your manna from their mouths, and you gave them water for their thirst. ²¹For forty years you sustained them in the desert; they lacked nothing, their clothes did not wear out nor did their feet become swollen.

²²"You gave them kingdoms and nations, allotting to them even the remotest frontiers. They took over the country of Sihonᶜ king of Heshbon and the country of Og king of Bashan. ²³You made their sons as numerous as the stars in the sky, and you brought them into the land that you told their fathers to enter and possess. ²⁴Their sons went in and took possession of the land. You subdued before them the Canaanites, who lived in the land; you

---

ᵃ5 Or *God for ever and ever*   ᵇ9 Hebrew *Yam Suph*; that is, Sea of Reeds   ᶜ22 One Hebrew manuscript and Septuagint; most Hebrew manuscripts *Sihon, that is, the country of the*

handed the Canaanites over to them, along with their kings and the peoples of the land, to deal with them as they pleased. ²⁵They captured fortified cities and fertile land; they took possession of houses filled with all kinds of good things, wells already dug, vineyards, olive groves and fruit trees in abundance. They ate to the full and were well-nourished; they reveled in your great goodness.

²⁶"But they were disobedient and rebelled against you; they put your law behind their backs. They killed your prophets, who had admonished them in order to turn them back to you; they committed awful blasphemies. ²⁷So you handed them over to their enemies, who oppressed them. But when they were oppressed they cried out to you. From heaven you heard them, and in your great compassion you gave them deliverers, who rescued them from the hand of their enemies.

²⁸"But as soon as they were at rest, they again did what was evil in your sight. Then you abandoned them to the hand of their enemies so that they ruled over them. And when they cried out to you again, you heard from heaven, and in your compassion you delivered them time after time.

²⁹"You warned them to return to your law, but they became arrogant and disobeyed your commands. They sinned against your ordinances, by which a man will live if he obeys them. Stubbornly they turned their backs on you, became stiff-necked and refused to listen. ³⁰For many years you were patient with them. By your Spirit you admonished them through your prophets. Yet they paid no attention, so you handed them over to the neighboring peoples. ³¹But in your great mercy you did not put an end to them or abandon them, for you are a gracious and merciful God.

³²"Now therefore, O our God, the great, mighty and awesome God, who keeps his covenant of love, do not let all this hardship seem trifling in your eyes—the hardship that has come upon us, upon our kings and leaders, upon our priests and prophets, upon our fathers and all your people, from the days of the kings of Assyria until today. ³³In all that has happened to us, you have been just; you have acted faithfully, while we did wrong. ³⁴Our kings, our leaders, our priests and our fathers did not follow your law; they did not pay attention to your commands or the warnings you gave them. ³⁵Even while they were in their kingdom, enjoying your great goodness to them in the spacious and fertile land you gave them, they did not serve you or turn from their evil ways.

³⁶"But see, we are slaves today, slaves in the land you gave our forefathers so they could eat its fruit and the other good things it produces. ³⁷Because of our sins, its abundant harvest goes to the kings you have placed over us. They rule over our bodies and our cattle as they please. We are in great distress.

The Agreement of the People

³⁸"In view of all this, we are making a binding agreement, putting it in writing, and our leaders, our Levites and our priests are affixing their seals to it."

10 Those who sealed it were:

Nehemiah the governor, the son of Hacaliah.

Zedekiah, ²Seraiah, Azariah, Jeremiah,
³Pashhur, Amariah, Malkijah,
⁴Hattush, Shebaniah, Malluch,
⁵Harim, Meremoth, Obadiah,
⁶Daniel, Ginnethon, Baruch,
⁷Meshullam, Abijah, Mijamin,
⁸Maaziah, Bilgai and Shemaiah.
These were the priests.

⁹The Levites:

Jeshua son of Azaniah, Binnui of the sons of Henadad, Kadmiel,
¹⁰and their associates: Shebaniah, Hodiah, Kelita, Pelaiah, Hanan,
¹¹Mica, Rehob, Hashabiah,
¹²Zaccur, Sherebiah, Shebaniah,
¹³Hodiah, Bani and Beninu.

¹⁴The leaders of the people:

> Parosh, Pahath-Moab, Elam, Zattu, Bani,
> ¹⁵Bunni, Azgad, Bebai,
> ¹⁶Adonijah, Bigvai, Adin,
> ¹⁷Ater, Hezekiah, Azzur,
> ¹⁸Hodiah, Hashum, Bezai,
> ¹⁹Hariph, Anathoth, Nebai,
> ²⁰Magpiash, Meshullam, Hezir,
> ²¹Meshezabel, Zadok, Jaddua,
> ²²Pelatiah, Hanan, Anaiah,
> ²³Hoshea, Hananiah, Hasshub,
> ²⁴Hallohesh, Pilha, Shobek,
> ²⁵Rehum, Hashabnah, Maaseiah,
> ²⁶Ahiah, Hanan, Anan,
> ²⁷Malluch, Harim and Baanah.

²⁸"The rest of the people—priests, Levites, gatekeepers, singers, temple servants and all who separated themselves from the neighboring peoples for the sake of the Law of God, together with their wives and all their sons and daughters who are able to understand— ²⁹all these now join their brothers the nobles, and bind themselves with a curse and an oath to follow the Law of God given through Moses the servant of God and to obey carefully all the commands, regulations and decrees of the LORD our Lord.

³⁰"We promise not to give our daughters in marriage to the peoples around us or take their daughters for our sons.

³¹"When the neighboring peoples bring merchandise or grain to sell on the Sabbath, we will not buy from them on the Sabbath or on any holy day. Every seventh year we will forgo working the land and will cancel all debts.

³²"We assume the responsibility for carrying out the commands to give a third of a shekel*a* each year for the service of the house of our God: ³³for the bread set out on the table; for the regular grain offerings and burnt offerings; for the offerings on the Sabbaths, New Moon festivals and appointed feasts; for the holy offerings; for sin offerings to make atonement for Israel; and

for all the duties of the house of our God.

³⁴"We—the priests, the Levites and the people—have cast lots to determine when each of our families is to bring to the house of our God at set times each year a contribution of wood to burn on the altar of the LORD our God, as it is written in the Law.

³⁵"We also assume responsibility for bringing to the house of the LORD each year the firstfruits of our crops and of every fruit tree.

³⁶"As it is also written in the Law, we will bring the firstborn of our sons and of our cattle, of our herds and of our flocks to the house of our God, to the priests ministering there.

³⁷"Moreover, we will bring to the storerooms of the house of our God, to the priests, the first of our ground meal, of our ⌞grain⌟ offerings, of the fruit of all our trees and of our new wine and oil. And we will bring a tithe of our crops to the Levites, for it is the Levites who collect the tithes in all the towns where we work. ³⁸A priest descended from Aaron is to accompany the Levites when they receive the tithes, and the Levites are to bring a tenth of the tithes up to the house of our God, to the storerooms of the treasury. ³⁹The people of Israel, including the Levites, are to bring their contributions of grain, new wine and oil to the storerooms where the articles for the sanctuary are kept and where the ministering priests, the gatekeepers and the singers stay.

"We will not neglect the house of our God."

The New Residents of Jerusalem

11 Now the leaders of the people settled in Jerusalem, and the rest of the people cast lots to bring one out of every ten to live in Jerusalem, the holy city, while the remaining nine were to stay in their own towns. ²The people commended all the men who volunteered to live in Jerusalem.

a32 That is, about 1/8 ounce (about 4 grams)

³These are the provincial leaders who settled in Jerusalem (now some Israelites, priests, Levites, temple servants and descendants of Solomon's servants lived in the towns of Judah, each on his own property in the various towns, ⁴while other people from both Judah and Benjamin lived in Jerusalem):

From the descendants of Judah:

Athaiah son of Uzziah, the son of Zechariah, the son of Amariah, the son of Shephatiah, the son of Mahalaliel, a descendant of Perez; ⁵and Maaseiah son of Baruch, the son of Col-Hozeh, the son of Hazaiah, the son of Adaiah, the son of Joiarib, the son of Zechariah, a descendant of Shelah. ⁶The descendants of Perez who lived in Jerusalem totaled 468 able men.

⁷From the descendants of Benjamin:

Sallu son of Meshullam, the son of Joed, the son of Pedaiah, the son of Kolaiah, the son of Maaseiah, the son of Ithiel, the son of Jeshaiah, ⁸and his followers, Gabbai and Sallai—928 men. ⁹Joel son of Zicri was their chief officer, and Judah son of Hassenuah was over the Second District of the city.

¹⁰From the priests:

Jedaiah; the son of Joiarib; Jakin; ¹¹Seraiah son of Hilkiah, the son of Meshullam, the son of Zadok, the son of Meraioth, the son of Ahitub, supervisor in the house of God, ¹²and their associates, who carried on work for the temple—822 men; Adaiah son of Jeroham, the son of Pelaliah, the son of Amzi, the son of Zechariah, the son of Pashhur, the son of Malkijah, ¹³and his associates, who were heads of families—242 men; Amashsai son of Azarel, the son of Ahzai, the son of Meshillemoth, the son of Immer, ¹⁴and his*a* associates, who were able men—128. Their chief officer was Zabdiel son of Haggedolim.

¹⁵From the Levites:

Shemaiah son of Hasshub, the son of Azrikam, the son of Hashabiah, the son of Bunni; ¹⁶Shabbethai and Jozabad, two of the heads of the Levites, who had charge of the outside work of the house of God; ¹⁷Mattaniah son of Mica, the son of Zabdi, the son of Asaph, the director who led in thanksgiving and prayer; Bakbukiah, second among his associates; and Abda son of Shammua, the son of Galal, the son of Jeduthun. ¹⁸The Levites in the holy city totaled 284.

¹⁹The gatekeepers:

Akkub, Talmon and their associates, who kept watch at the gates—172 men.

²⁰The rest of the Israelites, with the priests and Levites, were in all the towns of Judah, each on his ancestral property. ²¹The temple servants lived on the hill of Ophel, and Ziha and Gishpa were in charge of them.

²²The chief officer of the Levites in Jerusalem was Uzzi son of Bani, the son of Hashabiah, the son of Mattaniah, the son of Mica. Uzzi was one of Asaph's descendants, who were the singers responsible for the service of the house of God. ²³The singers were under the king's orders, which regulated their daily activity.

²⁴Pethahiah son of Meshezabel, one of the descendants of Zerah son of Judah, was the king's agent in all affairs relating to the people.

²⁵As for the villages with their fields, some of the people of Judah lived in Kiriath Arba and its surrounding settlements, in Dibon and its settlements, in Jekabzeel and its villages, ²⁶in Jeshua, in Moladah, in Beth Pelet, ²⁷in Hazar Shual, in Beersheba and its settlements, ²⁸in Ziklag, in Meconah and its settlements, ²⁹in En Rimmon, in Zorah, in Jarmuth, ³⁰Zanoah, Adullam and their villages, in Lachish and its fields, and in Azekah and its settlements. So they were living all the way from Beersheba to the Valley of Hinnom.

³¹The descendants of the Benjamites from Geba lived in Micmash, Aija, Bethel

a14 Most Septuagint manuscripts; Hebrew their

and its settlements, ³²in Anathoth, Nob and Ananiah, ³³in Hazor, Ramah and Gittaim, ³⁴in Hadid, Zeboim and Neballat, ³⁵in Lod and Ono, and in the Valley of the Craftsmen.

³⁶Some of the divisions of the Levites of Judah settled in Benjamin.

Priests and Levites

12 These were the priests and Levites who returned with Zerubbabel son of Shealtiel and with Jeshua:

Seraiah, Jeremiah, Ezra,
²Amariah, Malluch, Hattush,
³Shecaniah, Rehum, Meremoth,
⁴Iddo, Ginnethon,ᵃ Abijah,
⁵Mijamin,ᵇ Moadiah, Bilgah,
⁶Shemaiah, Joiarib, Jedaiah,
⁷Sallu, Amok, Hilkiah and Jedaiah.

These were the leaders of the priests and their associates in the days of Jeshua.

⁸The Levites were Jeshua, Binnui, Kadmiel, Sherebiah, Judah, and also Mattaniah, who, together with his associates, was in charge of the songs of thanksgiving. ⁹Bakbukiah and Unni, their associates, stood opposite them in the services.

¹⁰Jeshua was the father of Joiakim, Joiakim the father of Eliashib, Eliashib the father of Joiada, ¹¹Joiada the father of Jonathan, and Jonathan the father of Jaddua.

¹²In the days of Joiakim, these were the heads of the priestly families:

of Seraiah's family, Meraiah;
of Jeremiah's, Hananiah;
¹³of Ezra's, Meshullam;
of Amariah's, Jehohanan;
¹⁴of Malluch's, Jonathan;
of Shecaniah's,ᶜ Joseph;
¹⁵of Harim's, Adna;
of Meremoth's,ᵈ Helkai;
¹⁶of Iddo's, Zechariah;
of Ginnethon's, Meshullam;
¹⁷of Abijah's, Zicri;
of Miniamin's and of Moadiah's, Piltai;
¹⁸of Bilgah's, Shammua;
of Shemaiah's, Jehonathan;
¹⁹of Joiarib's, Mattenai;
of Jedaiah's, Uzzi;
²⁰of Sallu's, Kallai;
of Amok's, Eber;
²¹of Hilkiah's, Hashabiah;
of Jedaiah's, Nethanel.

²²The family heads of the Levites in the days of Eliashib, Joiada, Johanan and Jaddua, as well as those of the priests, were recorded in the reign of Darius the Persian. ²³The family heads among the descendants of Levi up to the time of Johanan son of Eliashib were recorded in the book of the annals. ²⁴And the leaders of the Levites were Hashabiah, Sherebiah, Jeshua son of Kadmiel, and their associates, who stood opposite them to give praise and thanksgiving, one section responding to the other, as prescribed by David the man of God.

²⁵Mattaniah, Bakbukiah, Obadiah, Meshullam, Talmon and Akkub were gatekeepers who guarded the storerooms at the gates. ²⁶They served in the days of Joiakim son of Jeshua, the son of Jozadak, and in the days of Nehemiah the governor and of Ezra the priest and scribe.

Dedication of the Wall of Jerusalem

²⁷At the dedication of the wall of Jerusalem, the Levites were sought out from where they lived and were brought to Jerusalem to celebrate joyfully the dedication with songs of thanksgiving and with the music of cymbals, harps and lyres. ²⁸The singers also were brought together from the region around Jerusalem—from the villages of the Netophathites, ²⁹from Beth Gilgal, and from the area of Geba and Azmaveth, for the singers had built villages for themselves around Jerusalem. ³⁰When the priests and Levites had purified themselves ceremonially, they purified the people, the gates and the wall.

³¹I had the leaders of Judah go up on topᵉ of the wall. I also assigned two large choirs to give thanks. One was to proceed on topᶠ of the wall to the right, toward the Dung Gate. ³²Hoshaiah and half the leaders of Judah followed them, ³³along

---

ᵃ4 Many Hebrew manuscripts and Vulgate (see also Neh. 12:16); most Hebrew manuscripts *Ginnethoi*
ᵇ5 A variant of *Miniamin*   ᶜ14 Very many Hebrew manuscripts, some Septuagint manuscripts and Syriac (see also Neh. 12:3); most Hebrew manuscripts *Shebaniah's*   ᵈ15 Some Septuagint manuscripts (see also Neh. 12:3); Hebrew *Meraioth's*
ᵉ31 Or *go alongside*   ᶠ31 Or *proceed alongside*

with Azariah, Ezra, Meshullam, ³⁴Judah, Benjamin, Shemaiah, Jeremiah, ³⁵as well as some priests with trumpets, and also Zechariah son of Jonathan, the son of Shemaiah, the son of Mattaniah, the son of Micaiah, the son of Zaccur, the son of Asaph, ³⁶and his associates—Shemaiah, Azarel, Milalai, Gilalai, Maai, Nethanel, Judah and Hanani—with musical instruments prescribed by David the man of God. Ezra the scribe led the procession. ³⁷At the Fountain Gate they continued directly up the steps of the City of David on the ascent to the wall and passed above the house of David to the Water Gate on the east.

³⁸The second choir proceeded in the opposite direction. I followed them on top*a* of the wall, together with half the people—past the Tower of the Ovens to the Broad Wall, ³⁹over the Gate of Ephraim, the Jeshanah*b* Gate, the Fish Gate, the Tower of Hananel and the Tower of the Hundred, as far as the Sheep Gate. At the Gate of the Guard they stopped.

⁴⁰The two choirs that gave thanks then took their places in the house of God; so did I, together with half the officials, ⁴¹as well as the priests—Eliakim, Maaseiah, Miniamin, Micaiah, Elioenai, Zechariah and Hananiah with their trumpets— ⁴²and also Maaseiah, Shemaiah, Eleazar, Uzzi, Jehohanan, Malkijah, Elam and Ezer. The choirs sang under the direction of Jezrahiah. ⁴³And on that day they offered great sacrifices, rejoicing because God had given them great joy. The women and children also rejoiced. The sound of rejoicing in Jerusalem could be heard far away.

⁴⁴At that time men were appointed to be in charge of the storerooms for the contributions, firstfruits and tithes. From the fields around the towns they were to bring into the storerooms the portions required by the Law for the priests and the Levites, for Judah was pleased with the ministering priests and Levites. ⁴⁵They performed the service of their God and the service of purification, as did also the singers and gatekeepers, according to the commands of David and his son Solomon. ⁴⁶For long ago, in the days of David and Asaph, there had been directors for the singers and for the songs of praise and thanksgiving to God. ⁴⁷So in the days of Zerubbabel and of Nehemiah, all Israel contributed the daily portions for the singers and gatekeepers. They also set aside the portion for the other Levites, and the Levites set aside the portion for the descendants of Aaron.

Nehemiah's Final Reforms

13 On that day the Book of Moses was read aloud in the hearing of the people and there it was found written that no Ammonite or Moabite should ever be admitted into the assembly of God, ²because they had not met the Israelites with food and water but had hired Balaam to call a curse down on them. (Our God, however, turned the curse into a blessing.) ³When the people heard this law, they excluded from Israel all who were of foreign descent.

⁴Before this, Eliashib the priest had been put in charge of the storerooms of the house of our God. He was closely associated with Tobiah, ⁵and he had provided him with a large room formerly used to store the grain offerings and incense and temple articles, and also the tithes of grain, new wine and oil prescribed for the Levites, singers and gatekeepers, as well as the contributions for the priests.

⁶But while all this was going on, I was not in Jerusalem, for in the thirty-second year of Artaxerxes king of Babylon I had returned to the king. Some time later I asked his permission ⁷and came back to Jerusalem. Here I learned about the evil thing Eliashib had done in providing Tobiah a room in the courts of the house of God. ⁸I was greatly displeased and threw all Tobiah's household goods out of the room. ⁹I gave orders to purify the rooms, and then I put back into them the equipment of the house of God, with the grain offerings and the incense.

¹⁰I also learned that the portions assigned to the Levites had not been given to them, and that all the Levites and singers responsible for the service had gone back to their own fields. ¹¹So I rebuked the officials and asked them,

a38 Or them alongside   b39 Or Old

"Why is the house of God neglected?" Then I called them together and stationed them at their posts.

[12]All Judah brought the tithes of grain, new wine and oil into the storerooms. [13]I put Shelemiah the priest, Zadok the scribe, and a Levite named Pedaiah in charge of the storerooms and made Hanan son of Zaccur, the son of Mattaniah, their assistant, because these men were considered trustworthy. They were made responsible for distributing the supplies to their brothers.

[14]Remember me for this, O my God, and do not blot out what I have so faithfully done for the house of my God and its services.

[15]In those days I saw men in Judah treading winepresses on the Sabbath and bringing in grain and loading it on donkeys, together with wine, grapes, figs and all other kinds of loads. And they were bringing all this into Jerusalem on the Sabbath. Therefore I warned them against selling food on that day. [16]Men from Tyre who lived in Jerusalem were bringing in fish and all kinds of merchandise and selling them in Jerusalem on the Sabbath to the people of Judah. [17]I rebuked the nobles of Judah and said to them, "What is this wicked thing you are doing—desecrating the Sabbath day? [18]Didn't your forefathers do the same things, so that our God brought all this calamity upon us and upon this city? Now you are stirring up more wrath against Israel by desecrating the Sabbath."

[19]When evening shadows fell on the gates of Jerusalem before the Sabbath, I ordered the doors to be shut and not opened until the Sabbath was over. I stationed some of my own men at the gates so that no load could be brought in on the Sabbath day. [20]Once or twice the merchants and sellers of all kinds of goods spent the night outside Jerusalem. [21]But I warned them and said, "Why do you spend the night by the wall? If you do this again, I will lay hands on you." From that time on they no longer came on the Sabbath. [22]Then I commanded the Levites to purify themselves and go and guard the gates in order to keep the Sabbath day holy.

Remember me for this also, O my God, and show mercy to me according to your great love.

[23]Moreover, in those days I saw men of Judah who had married women from Ashdod, Ammon and Moab. [24]Half of their children spoke the language of Ashdod or the language of one of the other peoples, and did not know how to speak the language of Judah. [25]I rebuked them and called curses down on them. I beat some of the men and pulled out their hair. I made them take an oath in God's name and said: "You are not to give your daughters in marriage to their sons, nor are you to take their daughters in marriage for your sons or for yourselves. [26]Was it not because of

Nehemiah & the Numbskulls

Huh?

Nehemiah 13:25

People shouldn't solve problems with violence. But in this case, Nehemiah had little choice. The sin of marrying idol worshipers had caused the fall of the entire nation before, and now it was happening again. So Nehemiah cracked some heads. He figured it was better to beat the sin out of the godly than to let the godly get beaten by sin.

marriages like these that Solomon king of Israel sinned? Among the many nations there was no king like him. He was loved by his God, and God made him king over all Israel, but even he was led into sin by foreign women. [27]Must we hear now that you too are doing all this terrible wickedness and are being unfaithful to our God by marrying foreign women?"

[28]One of the sons of Joiada son of Eliashib the high priest was son-in-law to Sanballat the Horonite. And I drove him away from me.

²⁹Remember them, O my God, because they defiled the priestly office and the covenant of the priesthood and of the Levites.

³⁰So I purified the priests and the Levites of everything foreign, and assigned them duties, each to his own task. ³¹I also made provision for contributions of wood at designated times, and for the firstfruits.

Remember me with favor, O my God.

Esther

START

The Jews give up on God, so God lets their country of Judah get sacked by the Babylonians. The prisoners get marched off to Babylon and spend many years hoping God will give them another chance. He does! The Babylonians get stomped by the Persians, who let some of the Jews go home to rebuild Jerusalem. But some stay in Persia a while longer. Including the star of this book.

Esther is the wife of the Persian king Xerxes. She gets this plush job after her cousin Mordecai enters her in the king's personal beauty pageant. Esther takes first prize—she gets to marry the king and wear the best beauty pageant crown ever.

When Mordecai gets wind of a plot to kill all the Jews in Persia, he asks his cousin to use her queenly influence to stop it. At first Esther doesn't do anything. Maybe she doesn't want to tick off her husband. After all, the king's ex-wife lost her crown simply by refusing to come when Xerxes called her! But Mordecai keeps bugging Esther. After all, she's Jewish, so if the bad guys start killing Jews, she'll get snuffed out too. Esther gets the message and begs the king to stop the plot. She risks her marriage, and her very own life, to help God's people.

Cast OF Characters

Xerxes (ZERK-seez)
He's king of Persia. He gets rid of his first wife, then marries Esther. All in all, he's a pretty good guy. (He's also Artaxerxes' dad. Arty becomes the next king in Persia, which means he's Nehemiah's boss.)

Vashti (VASH-tee)
The bold ex-wife of King Xerxes. When the king wants to show her off to his party guests, she refuses to come. Then the king kicks her out of the palace.

Esther (ESS-ter)
She's a Jewish orphan, raised by her cousin in Persia. Esther wins a beauty pageant and gets to marry the king. When her big moment comes to save the Jews, her wisdom and bravery win out.

Mordecai
(MORE-deh-kie)
He's the other hero in the story. When Esther's folks die, Mordecai brings her up. After his cousin becomes queen, he helps her use her influence with the king to save the Jews from being killed.

Haman (HEY-mun)
The bad guy. Haman talks the king into an awful scheme to kill the Jews. But when the king changes his mind, it's Haman who gets killed.

What's UP with That?

Did you know that Esther is the only book in the Bible that doesn't mention God?

Yep, it's true: 10 chapters and not one of them mentions the Almighty! But if you read between the lines, you find him on every page.

Take a look: The king's right-hand man comes up with a plot to slaughter the Jews. The king agrees. Who could possibly change his mind? It would have to be someone even closer than the king's own adviser. Like a wife, for instance. But the king already has a wife named Vashti, and she probably doesn't give a rip about the Jews. Oops—scratch that. The king kicked *that* queen out of the house. Now he's got a new queen. A Jewish queen!

Does Queen Esther care about the Jews? Yep—in fact, she is one. Not only that, but her cousin Mordecai is asking for her help. Esther decides to confront the king, even if it means losing her own life. The king squashes the mass-murder plot. The Jews are saved.

A string of luck? A great gob of coincidences? Hardly. In each of these moments, you can see God at work behind the scenes. Nope, the people aren't *talking* about him. But they're *doing* what God planned. Cool!

Snap shots

- Xerxes' ex—Vashti says "No!"; king says "Go!" *(chapter 1)*

- Beauty Queen—Esther wins the pageant . . . and the king *(chapter 2)*

- Haman's plan— a plot to kill the Jews *(chapter 3)*

- "Do something, cousin!"—Mordecai exposes the plot *(chapter 4)*

- Esther's date with destiny—and the king *(chapter 5)*

- Hanging Haman—the bad guy goes bye-bye *(chapters 6—7)*

- Happy days—and a new Jewish holiday *(chapters 8—10)*

10 chapters and NOT ONE of them mentions the ALMIGHTY!

Queen Vashti Deposed

1 This is what happened during the time of Xerxes,[a] the Xerxes who ruled over 127 provinces stretching from India to Cush[b]: ²At that time King Xerxes reigned from his royal throne in the citadel of Susa, ³and in the third year of his reign he gave a banquet for all his nobles and officials. The military leaders of Persia and Media, the princes, and the nobles of the provinces were present.

⁴For a full 180 days he displayed the vast wealth of his kingdom and the splendor and glory of his majesty. ⁵When these days were over, the king gave a banquet, lasting seven days, in the enclosed garden of the king's palace, for all the people from the least to the greatest, who were in the citadel of Susa. ⁶The garden had hangings of white and blue linen, fastened with cords of white linen and purple material to silver rings on marble pillars. There were couches of gold and silver on a mosaic pavement of porphyry, marble, mother-of-pearl and other costly stones. ⁷Wine was served in goblets of gold, each one different from the other, and the royal wine was abundant, in keeping with the king's liberality. ⁸By the king's command each guest was allowed to drink in his own way, for the king instructed all the wine stewards to serve each man what he wished.

⁹Queen Vashti also gave a banquet for the women in the royal palace of King Xerxes.

¹⁰On the seventh day, when King Xerxes was in high spirits from wine, he commanded the seven eunuchs who served him—Mehuman, Biztha, Harbona, Bigtha, Abagtha, Zethar and Carcas— ¹¹to bring before him Queen Vashti, wearing her royal crown, in order to display her beauty to the people and nobles, for she was lovely to look at. ¹²But when the attendants delivered the king's command, Queen Vashti refused to come. Then the king became furious and burned with anger.

¹³Since it was customary for the king to consult experts in matters of law and justice, he spoke with the wise men who understood the times ¹⁴and were closest to the king—Carshena, Shethar, Admatha, Tarshish, Meres, Marsena and Memucan, the seven nobles of Persia and Media who had special access to the king and were highest in the kingdom.

¹⁵"According to law, what must be done to Queen Vashti?" he asked. "She has not obeyed the command of King Xerxes that the eunuchs have taken to her."

¹⁶Then Memucan replied in the presence of the king and the nobles, "Queen Vashti has done wrong, not only against the king but also against all the nobles and the peoples of all the provinces of King Xerxes. ¹⁷For the queen's conduct will become known to all the women, and so they will despise their husbands and say, 'King Xerxes commanded Queen Vashti to be brought before him, but she would not come.' ¹⁸This very day the Persian and Median women of the nobility who have heard about the queen's conduct will respond to all the king's nobles in the same way. There will be no end of disrespect and discord.

¹⁹"Therefore, if it pleases the king, let him issue a royal decree and let it be written in the laws of Persia and Media, which cannot be repealed, that Vashti is never again to enter the presence of King Xerxes. Also let the king give her royal position to someone else who is better than she. ²⁰Then when the king's edict is proclaimed throughout all his vast realm, all the women will respect their husbands, from the least to the greatest."

²¹The king and his nobles were pleased with this advice, so the king did as Memucan proposed. ²²He sent dispatches to all parts of the kingdom, to each province in its own script and to each people in its own language, proclaiming in each people's tongue that every man should be ruler over his own household.

Esther Made Queen

2 Later when the anger of King Xerxes had subsided, he remembered Vashti and what she had done and what he had decreed about her. ²Then the king's personal attendants proposed, "Let a search

---

[a]1 Hebrew *Ahasuerus*, a variant of Xerxes' Persian name; here and throughout Esther   [b]1 That is, the upper Nile region

be made for beautiful young virgins for the king. ³Let the king appoint commissioners in every province of his realm to bring all these beautiful girls into the harem at the citadel of Susa. Let them be placed under the care of Hegai, the king's eunuch, who is in charge of the women; and let beauty treatments be given to them. ⁴Then let the girl who pleases the king be queen instead of Vashti." This advice appealed to the king, and he followed it.

⁵Now there was in the citadel of Susa a Jew of the tribe of Benjamin, named Mordecai son of Jair, the son of Shimei, the son of Kish, ⁶who had been carried into exile from Jerusalem by Nebuchadnezzar king of Babylon, among those taken captive with Jehoiachinᵃ king of Judah. ⁷Mordecai had a cousin named Hadassah, whom he had brought up because she had neither father nor mother. This girl, who was also known as Esther, was lovely in form and features, and Mordecai had taken her as his own daughter when her father and mother died.

⁸When the king's order and edict had been proclaimed, many girls were brought to the citadel of Susa and put under the care of Hegai. Esther also was taken to the king's palace and entrusted to Hegai, who had charge of the harem. ⁹The girl pleased him and won his favor. Immediately he provided her with her beauty treatments and special food. He assigned to her seven maids selected from the king's palace and moved her and her maids into the best place in the harem.

¹⁰Esther had not revealed her nationality and family background, because Mordecai had forbidden her to do so. ¹¹Every day he walked back and forth near the courtyard of the harem to find out how Esther was and what was happening to her.

¹²Before a girl's turn came to go in to King Xerxes, she had to complete twelve months of beauty treatments prescribed for the women, six months with oil of myrrh and six with perfumes and cosmetics. ¹³And this is how she would go to the king: Anything she wanted was given her to take with her from the harem to the king's palace. ¹⁴In the evening she would go there and in the morning return to another part of the harem to the care of Shaashgaz, the king's eunuch who was in charge of the concubines. She would not return to the king unless he was pleased with her and summoned her by name.

¹⁵When the turn came for Esther (the girl Mordecai had adopted, the daughter of his uncle Abihail) to go to the king, she asked for nothing other than what Hegai, the king's eunuch who was in charge of the harem, suggested. And Esther won the favor of everyone who saw her. ¹⁶She was taken to King Xerxes in the royal residence in the tenth month, the month of Tebeth, in the seventh year of his reign.

¹⁷Now the king was attracted to Esther more than to any of the other women, and she won his favor and approval more than any of the other virgins. So he set a royal crown on her head and made her queen instead of Vashti. ¹⁸And the king gave a great banquet, Esther's banquet, for all his nobles and officials. He proclaimed a holiday throughout the provinces and distributed gifts with royal liberality.

Mordecai Uncovers a Conspiracy

¹⁹When the virgins were assembled a second time, Mordecai was sitting at the king's gate. ²⁰But Esther had kept secret her family background and nationality just as Mordecai had told her to do, for she continued to follow Mordecai's instructions as she had done when he was bringing her up.

²¹During the time Mordecai was sitting at the king's gate, Bigthanaᵇ and Teresh, two of the king's officers who guarded the doorway, became angry and conspired to assassinate King Xerxes. ²²But Mordecai found out about the plot and told Queen Esther, who in turn reported it to the king, giving credit to Mordecai. ²³And when the report was investigated and found to be true, the two officials were hanged on a gallows.ᶜ All this was

ᵃ6 Hebrew *Jeconiah*, a variant of *Jehoiachin*
ᵇ21 Hebrew *Bigthan*, a variant of *Bigthana*   ᶜ23 Or *were hung* (or *impaled*) *on poles*; similarly elsewhere in Esther

recorded in the book of the annals in the presence of the king.

Haman's Plot to Destroy the Jews

3 After these events, King Xerxes honored Haman son of Hammedatha, the Agagite, elevating him and giving him a seat of honor higher than that of all the other nobles. ²All the royal officials at the king's gate knelt down and paid honor to Haman, for the king had commanded this concerning him. But Mordecai would not kneel down or pay him honor.

³Then the royal officials at the king's gate asked Mordecai, "Why do you disobey the king's command?" ⁴Day after day they spoke to him but he refused to comply. Therefore they told Haman about it to see whether Mordecai's behavior would be tolerated, for he had told them he was a Jew.

⁵When Haman saw that Mordecai would not kneel down or pay him honor, he was enraged. ⁶Yet having learned who Mordecai's people were, he scorned the idea of killing only Mordecai. Instead Haman looked for a way to destroy all Mordecai's people, the Jews, throughout the whole kingdom of Xerxes.

⁷In the twelfth year of King Xerxes, in the first month, the month of Nisan, they cast the *pur* (that is, the lot) in the presence of Haman to select a day and month. And the lot fell on* the twelfth month, the month of Adar.

⁸Then Haman said to King Xerxes, "There is a certain people dispersed and scattered among the peoples in all the provinces of your kingdom whose customs are different from those of all other people and who do not obey the king's laws; it is not in the king's best interest to tolerate them. ⁹If it pleases the king, let a decree be issued to destroy them, and I will put ten thousand talents* of silver into the royal treasury for the men who carry out this business."

¹⁰So the king took his signet ring from his finger and gave it to Haman son of Hammedatha, the Agagite, the enemy of the Jews. ¹¹"Keep the money," the king said to Haman, "and do with the people as you please."

¹²Then on the thirteenth day of the first month the royal secretaries were summoned. They wrote out in the script of each province and in the language of each people all Haman's orders to the king's satraps, the governors of the various provinces and the nobles of the various peoples. These were written in the name of King Xerxes himself and sealed with his own ring. ¹³Dispatches were sent by couriers to all the king's provinces with the order to destroy, kill and annihilate all the Jews—young and old, women and little children—on a single day, the thirteenth day of the twelfth month, the month of Adar, and to plunder their goods. ¹⁴A copy of the text of the edict was to be issued as law in every province and made known to the people of every nationality so they would be ready for that day.

¹⁵Spurred on by the king's command, the couriers went out, and the edict was issued in the citadel of Susa. The king and Haman sat down to drink, but the city of Susa was bewildered.

Mordecai Persuades Esther to Help

4 When Mordecai learned of all that had been done, he tore his clothes, put on sackcloth and ashes, and went out into the city, wailing loudly and bitterly. ²But he went only as far as the king's gate, because no one clothed in sackcloth was allowed to enter it. ³In every province to which the edict and order of the king came, there was great mourning among the Jews, with fasting, weeping and wailing. Many lay in sackcloth and ashes.

⁴When Esther's maids and eunuchs came and told her about Mordecai, she was in great distress. She sent clothes for him to put on instead of his sackcloth, but he would not accept them. ⁵Then Esther summoned Hathach, one of the king's eunuchs assigned to attend her, and ordered him to find out what was troubling Mordecai and why.

⁶So Hathach went out to Mordecai in the open square of the city in front of the king's gate. ⁷Mordecai told him

---

a 7 Septuagint; Hebrew does not have *And the lot fell on.*   *b 9* That is, about 375 tons (about 345 metric tons)

everything that had happened to him, including the exact amount of money Haman had promised to pay into the royal treasury for the destruction of the Jews. [8]He also gave him a copy of the text of the edict for their annihilation, which had been published in Susa, to show to Esther and explain it to her, and he told him to urge her to go into the king's presence to beg for mercy and plead with him for her people.

[9]Hathach went back and reported to Esther what Mordecai had said. [10]Then she instructed him to say to Mordecai, [11]"All the king's officials and the people of the royal provinces know that for any man or woman who approaches the king in the inner court without being summoned the king has but one law: that he be put to death. The only exception to this is for the king to extend the gold scepter to him and spare his life. But thirty days have passed since I was called to go to the king."

[12]When Esther's words were reported to Mordecai, [13]he sent back this answer: "Do not think that because you are in the king's house you alone of all the Jews will escape. [14]For if you remain silent at this time, relief and deliverance for the Jews will arise from another place, but you and your father's family will perish. And who knows but that you have come to royal position for such a time as this?"

[15]Then Esther sent this reply to Mordecai: [16]"Go, gather together all the Jews who are in Susa, and fast for me. Do not eat or drink for three days, night or day. I and my maids will fast as you do. When this is done, I will go to the king, even

---

Thursday

When the Going Gets Tough

Read Esther 4:14–16

When my best friend moved away, I couldn't understand why God allowed it to happen. I mean, I know God has a plan and wants the best for us, but it seemed like he wanted to mess up my life. I doubted that anything good could come of the situation.

Thousands of years ago, Esther and her cousin Mordecai were in a bad situation too—way worse than mine. The Jews' lives were in danger, and it would have been easy for them to complain and get discouraged. But Mordecai reminded Esther that God does have a purpose, even when everything seems to be falling apart.

When I read these verses, I realized that, since God has come this far with me, he'll stay with me and guide me no matter what happens. This is especially true in difficult times when we can't figure out what God's up to. All of us are here on earth for a reason—not just to live and die. We can trust God's purpose for us.

Christina age 13

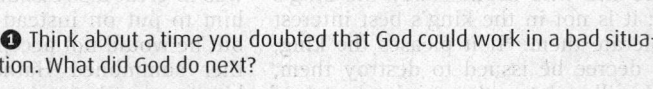
What about You?

❶ Think about a time you doubted that God could work in a bad situation. What did God do next?

❷ The next time it looks like everything is falling apart, take a walk in a park. Observe the life around you—birds, squirrels, trees and so on. Look at the ways God takes care of his creation. How does he take care of you?

❸ Tell God about anything that's discouraging you. Ask him to remind you of his presence in your life.

Turn to page 583 for your next devotion.

though it is against the law. And if I perish, I perish."

¹⁷So Mordecai went away and carried out all of Esther's instructions.

Esther's Request to the King

5 On the third day Esther put on her royal robes and stood in the inner court of the palace, in front of the king's hall. The king was sitting on his royal throne in the hall, facing the entrance. ²When he saw Queen Esther standing in the court, he was pleased with her and held out to her the gold scepter that was in his hand. So Esther approached and touched the tip of the scepter.

³Then the king asked, "What is it, Queen Esther? What is your request? Even up to half the kingdom, it will be given you."

⁴"If it pleases the king," replied Esther, "let the king, together with Haman, come today to a banquet I have prepared for him."

⁵"Bring Haman at once," the king said, "so that we may do what Esther asks."

So the king and Haman went to the banquet Esther had prepared. ⁶As they were drinking wine, the king again asked Esther, "Now what is your petition? It will be given you. And what is your request? Even up to half the kingdom, it will be granted."

⁷Esther replied, "My petition and my request is this: ⁸If the king regards me with favor and if it pleases the king to grant my petition and fulfill my request, let the king and Haman come tomorrow to the banquet I will prepare for them. Then I will answer the king's question."

Haman's Rage Against Mordecai

⁹Haman went out that day happy and in high spirits. But when he saw Mordecai at the king's gate and observed that he neither rose nor showed fear in his presence, he was filled with rage against Mordecai. ¹⁰Nevertheless, Haman restrained himself and went home.

Calling together his friends and Zeresh, his wife, ¹¹Haman boasted to them about his vast wealth, his many sons, and all the ways the king had honored him and how he had elevated him above the other nobles and officials. ¹²"And

that's not all," Haman added. "I'm the only person Queen Esther invited to accompany the king to the banquet she gave. And she has invited me along with the king tomorrow. ¹³But all this gives me no satisfaction as long as I see that Jew Mordecai sitting at the king's gate."

¹⁴His wife Zeresh and all his friends said to him, "Have a gallows built, seventy-five feet[a] high, and ask the king in the morning to have Mordecai hanged on it. Then go with the king to the dinner and be happy." This suggestion delighted Haman, and he had the gallows built.

Mordecai Honored

6 That night the king could not sleep; so he ordered the book of the chronicles, the record of his reign, to be brought in and read to him. ²It was found recorded there that Mordecai had exposed Bigthana and Teresh, two of the king's officers who guarded the doorway, who had conspired to assassinate King Xerxes.

³"What honor and recognition has Mordecai received for this?" the king asked.

"Nothing has been done for him," his attendants answered.

⁴The king said, "Who is in the court?" Now Haman had just entered the outer court of the palace to speak to the king about hanging Mordecai on the gallows he had erected for him.

⁵His attendants answered, "Haman is standing in the court."

"Bring him in," the king ordered.

⁶When Haman entered, the king asked him, "What should be done for the man the king delights to honor?"

Now Haman thought to himself, "Who is there that the king would rather honor than me?" ⁷So he answered the king, "For the man the king delights to honor, ⁸have them bring a royal robe the king has worn and a horse the king has ridden, one with a royal crest placed on its head. ⁹Then let the robe and horse be entrusted to one of the king's most noble princes. Let them robe the man the king delights to honor, and lead him on the horse through the city streets, proclaiming

a14 Hebrew *fifty cubits* (about 23 meters)

before him, 'This is what is done for the man the king delights to honor!' "

¹⁰"Go at once," the king commanded Haman. "Get the robe and the horse and do just as you have suggested for Mordecai the Jew, who sits at the king's gate. Do not neglect anything you have recommended."

¹¹So Haman got the robe and the horse. He robed Mordecai, and led him on horseback through the city streets, proclaiming before him, "This is what is done for the man the king delights to honor!"

¹²Afterward Mordecai returned to the king's gate. But Haman rushed home, with his head covered in grief, ¹³and told Zeresh his wife and all his friends everything that had happened to him.

His advisers and his wife Zeresh said to him, "Since Mordecai, before whom your downfall has started, is of Jewish origin, you cannot stand against him—you will surely come to ruin!" ¹⁴While they were still talking with him, the king's eunuchs arrived and hurried Haman away to the banquet Esther had prepared.

Haman Hanged

7 So the king and Haman went to dine with Queen Esther, ²and as they were drinking wine on that second day, the king again asked, "Queen Esther, what is your petition? It will be given you. What is your request? Even up to half the kingdom, it will be granted."

³Then Queen Esther answered, "If I have found favor with you, O king, and if it pleases your majesty, grant me my life—this is my petition. And spare my people—this is my request. ⁴For I and my people have been sold for destruction and slaughter and annihilation. If we had merely been sold as male and female slaves, I would have kept quiet, because no such distress would justify disturbing the king.ᵃ"

⁵King Xerxes asked Queen Esther, "Who is he? Where is the man who has dared to do such a thing?"

⁶Esther said, "The adversary and enemy is this vile Haman."

Then Haman was terrified before the king and queen. ⁷The king got up in a rage,

left his wine and went out into the palace garden. But Haman, realizing that the king had already decided his fate, stayed behind to beg Queen Esther for his life.

⁸Just as the king returned from the palace garden to the banquet hall, Haman was falling on the couch where Esther was reclining.

The king exclaimed, "Will he even molest the queen while she is with me in the house?"

As soon as the word left the king's mouth, they covered Haman's face. ⁹Then Harbona, one of the eunuchs attending the king, said, "A gallows seventy-five feetᵇ high stands by Haman's house. He had it made for Mordecai, who spoke up to help the king."

The king said, "Hang him on it!" ¹⁰So they hanged Haman on the gallows he had prepared for Mordecai. Then the king's fury subsided.

The King's Edict in Behalf of the Jews

8 That same day King Xerxes gave Queen Esther the estate of Haman, the enemy of the Jews. And Mordecai came into the presence of the king, for Esther had told how he was related to her. ²The king took off his signet ring, which he had reclaimed from Haman, and presented it to Mordecai. And Esther appointed him over Haman's estate.

³Esther again pleaded with the king, falling at his feet and weeping. She begged him to put an end to the evil plan of Haman the Agagite, which he had devised against the Jews. ⁴Then the king extended the gold scepter to Esther and she arose and stood before him.

⁵"If it pleases the king," she said, "and if he regards me with favor and thinks it the right thing to do, and if he is pleased with me, let an order be written overruling the dispatches that Haman son of Hammedatha, the Agagite, devised and wrote to destroy the Jews in all the king's provinces. ⁶For how can I bear to see disaster fall on my people? How can I bear to see the destruction of my family?"

ᵃ4 Or *quiet, but the compensation our adversary offers cannot be compared with the loss the king would suffer*   ᵇ9 Hebrew *fifty cubits* (about 23 meters)

⸍ ⁷King Xerxes replied to Queen Esther and to Mordecai the Jew, "Because Haman attacked the Jews, I have given his estate to Esther, and they have hanged him on the gallows. ⁸Now write another decree in the king's name in behalf of the Jews as seems best to you, and seal it with the king's signet ring—for no document written in the king's name and sealed with his ring can be revoked."

⁹At once the royal secretaries were summoned—on the twenty-third day of the third month, the month of Sivan. They wrote out all Mordecai's orders to the Jews, and to the satraps, governors and nobles of the 127 provinces stretching from India to Cush.ᵃ These orders were written in the script of each province and the language of each people and also to the Jews in their own script and language. ¹⁰Mordecai wrote in the name of King Xerxes, sealed the dispatches with the king's signet ring, and sent them by mounted couriers, who rode fast horses especially bred for the king.

¹¹The king's edict granted the Jews in every city the right to assemble and protect themselves; to destroy, kill and annihilate any armed force of any nationality or province that might attack them and their women and children; and to plunder the property of their enemies. ¹²The day appointed for the Jews to do this in all the provinces of King Xerxes was the thirteenth day of the twelfth month, the month of Adar. ¹³A copy of the text of the edict was to be issued as law in every province and made known to the people of every nationality so that the Jews would be ready on that day to avenge themselves on their enemies.

¹⁴The couriers, riding the royal horses, raced out, spurred on by the king's command. And the edict was also issued in the citadel of Susa.

¹⁵Mordecai left the king's presence wearing royal garments of blue and white, a large crown of gold and a purple robe of fine linen. And the city of Susa held a joyous celebration. ¹⁶For the Jews it was a time of happiness and joy, gladness and honor. ¹⁷In every province and in every city, wherever the edict of the king went, there was joy and gladness among the Jews, with feasting and celebrating. And many people of other nationalities became Jews because fear of the Jews had seized them.

Triumph of the Jews

9 On the thirteenth day of the twelfth month, the month of Adar, the edict commanded by the king was to be carried out. On this day the enemies of the Jews had hoped to overpower them, but now the tables were turned and the Jews got the upper hand over those who hated them. ²The Jews assembled in their cities in all the provinces of King Xerxes to attack those seeking their destruction. No one could stand against them, because the people of all the other nationalities were afraid of them. ³And all the nobles of the provinces, the satraps, the governors and the king's administrators helped the Jews, because fear of Mordecai had seized them. ⁴Mordecai was prominent in the palace; his reputation spread throughout the provinces, and he became more and more powerful.

⁵The Jews struck down all their enemies with the sword, killing and destroying them, and they did what they pleased to those who hated them. ⁶In the citadel of Susa, the Jews killed and destroyed five hundred men. ⁷They also killed Parshandatha, Dalphon, Aspatha, ⁸Poratha, Adalia, Aridatha, ⁹Parmashta, Arisai, Aridai and Vaizatha, ¹⁰the ten sons of Haman son of Hammedatha, the enemy of the Jews. But they did not lay their hands on the plunder.

¹¹The number of those slain in the citadel of Susa was reported to the king that same day. ¹²The king said to Queen Esther, "The Jews have killed and destroyed five hundred men and the ten sons of Haman in the citadel of Susa. What have they done in the rest of the king's provinces? Now what is your petition? It will be given you. What is your request? It will also be granted."

¹³"If it pleases the king," Esther answered, "give the Jews in Susa permission to carry out this day's edict tomorrow also, and let Haman's ten sons be hanged on gallows."

¹⁴So the king commanded that this be

ᵃ9 That is, the upper Nile region

done. An edict was issued in Susa, and they hanged the ten sons of Haman. [15]The Jews in Susa came together on the fourteenth day of the month of Adar, and they put to death in Susa three hundred men, but they did not lay their hands on the plunder.

[16]Meanwhile, the remainder of the Jews who were in the king's provinces also assembled to protect themselves and get relief from their enemies. They killed seventy-five thousand of them but did not lay their hands on the plunder. [17]This happened on the thirteenth day of the month of Adar, and on the fourteenth they rested and made it a day of feasting and joy.

Purim Celebrated

[18]The Jews in Susa, however, had assembled on the thirteenth and fourteenth, and then on the fifteenth they rested and made it a day of feasting and joy.

[19]That is why rural Jews—those living in villages—observe the fourteenth of the month of Adar as a day of joy and feasting, a day for giving presents to each other.

[20]Mordecai recorded these events, and he sent letters to all the Jews throughout the provinces of King Xerxes, near and far, [21]to have them celebrate annually the fourteenth and fifteenth days of the month of Adar [22]as the time when the Jews got relief from their enemies, and as the month when their sorrow was turned into joy and their mourning into a day of celebration. He wrote them to observe the days as days of feasting and joy and giving presents of food to one another and gifts to the poor.

[23]So the Jews agreed to continue the celebration they had begun, doing what Mordecai had written to them. [24]For Haman son of Hammedatha, the Agagite, the enemy of all the Jews, had plotted against the Jews to destroy them and had cast the *pur* (that is, the lot) for their ruin and destruction. [25]But when the plot came to the king's attention,[a] he issued written orders that the evil scheme Haman had devised against the Jews should come back onto his own head, and that he and his sons should be hanged on the

gallows. [26](Therefore these days were called Purim, from the word *pur*.) Because of everything written in this letter and because of what they had seen and what had happened to them, [27]the Jews took it upon themselves to establish the custom that they and their descendants and all who join them should without fail observe these two days every year, in the way prescribed and at the time appointed. [28]These days should be remembered and observed in every generation by every family, and in every province and in every city. And these days of Purim should never cease to be celebrated by the Jews, nor should the memory of them die out among their descendants.

[29]So Queen Esther, daughter of Abihail, along with Mordecai the Jew, wrote with full authority to confirm this second letter concerning Purim. [30]And Mordecai sent letters to all the Jews in the 127 provinces of the kingdom of Xerxes—words of goodwill and assurance—[31]to establish these days of Purim at their designated times, as Mordecai the Jew and Queen Esther had decreed for them, and as they had established for themselves and their descendants in regard to their times of fasting and lamentation. [32]Esther's decree confirmed these regulations about Purim, and it was written down in the records.

[a]25 Or *when Esther came before the king*

A Special Holiday Huh?

Esther 9:24–26

Jewish people today still celebrate a holiday called Purim. Back in chapter 3 we read about a guy named Haman who made plans to destroy the Jews and cast the "pur" (or lot) to wipe them out forever. But God worked through Esther to foil Haman's plans. Every year in the middle of February or March, Jews throw a big party with a bunch of presents to celebrate the way God delivered them from Haman.

The Greatness of Mordecai

10 King Xerxes imposed tribute throughout the empire, to its distant shores. ²And all his acts of power and might, together with a full account of the greatness of Mordecai to which the king had raised him, are they not written in the book of the annals of the kings of Media and Persia? ³Mordecai the Jew was second in rank to King Xerxes, preeminent among the Jews, and held in high esteem by his many fellow Jews, because he worked for the good of his people and spoke up for the welfare of all the Jews.

Job

START

Imagine having everything you've ever wanted: tons of cool clothes, the best video games and computer stuff, more CDs than you could ever listen to, a bedroom to die for. Add to that an awesome family and a healthy body.

Now imagine all that stuff being zapped. All of it—gone!

That's what happened to Job. He had land-o-plenty, tons of cows and other animals, a bunch of really swell kids, and felt like a hundred bucks. And God allowed Satan to take it all away.

In the middle of all this, Job learns a great lesson about God: Even when it doesn't feel like it, God is in control.

CAST OF Characters

Job (Jobe)
This guy had it all; then this guy had nothing. Job is one of the wealthiest men of his time—and he wants to live for God too! Even when all his stuff is taken away from him, Job still holds onto his faith (although he does throw a temper tantrum with God, which probably isn't a very good idea).

Eliphaz (ELL-ih-faz)
One of Job's buddies. Eliphaz is a fountain of lousy advice.

Bildad (Bill-dad)
Another bud. Just like Eliphaz, he should've just kept his mouth shut.

Zophar (ZO-far)
The third friend. His ideas are just as unhelpful as those of the other 2 friends.

God
The Creator and Supreme Ruler of the universe. God listens to all of Job's complaining and all the ridiculous suggestions of Job's friends. Then he makes a big-time appearance near the end of the book when he asks Job a bunch of questions and sets the record straight.

What's UP with That?

In chapters 38—41, God asks Job a whole gob of questions. God's point is this: "Look, Job, I know everything there is to know—including you, Job. I'm in charge of everything. So trust me!"

Which of the following questions does God ask Job?
(answers are upside down at the bottom)

A Who decided the outline of the oceans?

B Who decided to give you two nose holes?

C Have you ever given strength to a horse?

D Can you put a rope through the nose of a sea creature?

E Have you ever wrestled a hamster?

F When was the last time you ate waffles?

G If you know everything about the earth, tell me about it!

H Job, c'mon and tell me; have you ever tied up an elephant or roped a giant squid?

I Do you make baby eagles drink blood?

J Can you tell me about sea monkeys?

answers: a (38:8), c (39:19), d (41:2), g (38:18), i (39:30)

Snap shots

- Job says "Adios" to his goodies *(chapter 1)*

- Ouch! *(chapter 2)*

- Job whines like a baby (who wouldn't!) *(chapters 3, 6—7, 9—10)*

- Job gets some bad advice *(chapters 4—5, 8, 11)*

- Job asks, "Why me?" *(chapters 12—14, 16—17, 19, 21, 23—24, 26—31*

- Job get some more bad advice *(chapters 15, 18, 20, 22, 25, 32—37)*

- God asks Job, "Can you spin the world on your finger?" *(chapters 38—41)*

- Job says, "You're in charge, God" *(chapter 42)*

Prologue

1 In the land of Uz there lived a man whose name was Job. This man was blameless and upright; he feared God and shunned evil. ²He had seven sons and three daughters, ³and he owned seven thousand sheep, three thousand camels, five hundred yoke of oxen and five hundred donkeys, and had a large number of servants. He was the greatest man among all the people of the East.

⁴His sons used to take turns holding feasts in their homes, and they would invite their three sisters to eat and drink with them. ⁵When a period of feasting had run its course, Job would send and have them purified. Early in the morning he would sacrifice a burnt offering for each of them, thinking, "Perhaps my children have sinned and cursed God in their hearts." This was Job's regular custom.

Job's First Test

⁶One day the angels*ᵃ* came to present themselves before the LORD, and Satan*ᵇ* also came with them. ⁷The LORD said to Satan, "Where have you come from?"

Satan answered the LORD, "From roaming through the earth and going back and forth in it."

⁸Then the LORD said to Satan, "Have you considered my servant Job? There is no one on earth like him; he is blameless and upright, a man who fears God and shuns evil."

⁹"Does Job fear God for nothing?" Satan replied. ¹⁰"Have you not put a hedge around him and his household and everything he has? You have blessed the work of his hands, so that his flocks and herds are spread throughout the land. ¹¹But stretch out your hand and strike everything he has, and he will surely curse you to your face."

¹²The LORD said to Satan, "Very well, then, everything he has is in your hands, but on the man himself do not lay a finger."

Then Satan went out from the presence of the LORD.

¹³One day when Job's sons and daughters were feasting and drinking wine at the oldest brother's house, ¹⁴a messenger came to Job and said, "The oxen were plowing and the donkeys were grazing nearby, ¹⁵and the Sabeans attacked and carried them off. They put the servants to the sword, and I am the only one who has escaped to tell you!"

¹⁶While he was still speaking, another messenger came and said, "The fire of God fell from the sky and burned up the sheep and the servants, and I am the only one who has escaped to tell you!"

¹⁷While he was still speaking, another messenger came and said, "The Chaldeans formed three raiding parties and swept down on your camels and carried them off. They put the servants to the sword, and I am the only one who has escaped to tell you!"

¹⁸While he was still speaking, yet another messenger came and said, "Your sons and daughters were feasting and drinking wine at the oldest brother's house, ¹⁹when suddenly a mighty wind swept in from the desert and struck the four corners of the house. It collapsed on them and they are dead, and I am the only one who has escaped to tell you!"

²⁰At this, Job got up and tore his robe and shaved his head. Then he fell to the ground in worship ²¹and said:

> "Naked I came from my mother's
> womb,
> and naked I will depart.*ᶜ*

It's All About Respect

Job 1:1, 8–9

Maybe you can play hoops, but imagine going one-on-one against pro basketball's best player. Would you be afraid? Opposing players and coaches fear this great player; but it's not a "BOO!" kind of fear. It's all about respect. They know what he can do, so they fear his abilities. Job is described as a man who "feared God." He knew God and loved God. And because of his respect for him, Job loved to obey God.

ᵃ6 Hebrew the sons of God   ᵇ6 Satan means accuser.
ᶜ21 Or will return there

The LORD gave and the LORD has taken
away;
may the name of the LORD be
praised."

²²In all this, Job did not sin by charging God with wrongdoing.

Job's Second Test

2 On another day the angels[a] came to
present themselves before the LORD,
and Satan also came with them to
present himself before him. ²And the
LORD said to Satan, "Where have you
come from?"

Satan answered the LORD, "From
roaming through the earth and going
back and forth in it."

³Then the LORD said to Satan, "Have
you considered my servant Job? There is
no one on earth like him; he is blameless
and upright, a man who fears God and
shuns evil. And he still maintains his integrity, though you incited me against
him to ruin him without any reason."

⁴"Skin for skin!" Satan replied. "A man
will give all he has for his own life. ⁵But
stretch out your hand and strike his flesh
and bones, and he will surely curse you
to your face."

⁶The LORD said to Satan, "Very well,
then, he is in your hands; but you must
spare his life."

⁷So Satan went out from the presence
of the LORD and afflicted Job with painful sores from the soles of his feet to the
top of his head. ⁸Then Job took a piece of
broken pottery and scraped himself with
it as he sat among the ashes.

⁹His wife said to him, "Are you still
holding on to your integrity? Curse God
and die!"

¹⁰He replied, "You are talking like a
foolish[b] woman. Shall we accept good
from God, and not trouble?"

In all this, Job did not sin in what he
said.

---

[a]1 Hebrew *the sons of God*   [b]10 The Hebrew word
rendered *foolish* denotes moral deficiency.

Fri day

Be Quiet!

Read Job 2:13

Often when I'm mad about something, I want to get my feelings out by
talking things over with friends or even talking out loud to myself. Actually, now that I think about it, I never like to be quiet, no matter what mood
I'm in. I guess it's just easier to make noise than to be silent.

When all kinds of terrible things happened to Job, he couldn't find any
words to say for a whole week. Even his friends kept quiet. From these verses
I can see that there are times when it's best for me just not to talk, that I
should just listen instead. And I shouldn't only listen during the bad times!
God wants me to know I can come to him anytime. I need to learn to listen to
him, and that often means keeping my mouth shut—at least for awhile.

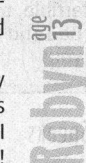

Robyn age 13

What about You?

❶ Sometimes talking about how we feel is a good thing. But think
about how being quiet can help you sort out your feelings.

❷ Take 5 minutes each day this week to simply sit and think about
God. To give your mind a jump-start, pretend that you are interviewing
him. Ask who, what, where, why, when questions. At the end of the
week, jot down what you learned about God.

❸ Ask God to help you listen as he speaks to your heart.

Turn to page 593 for your next devotion.

Job's Three Friends

¹¹When Job's three friends, Eliphaz the Temanite, Bildad the Shuhite and Zophar the Naamathite, heard about all the troubles that had come upon him, they set out from their homes and met together by agreement to go and sympathize with him and comfort him. ¹²When they saw him from a distance, they could hardly recognize him; they began to weep aloud, and they tore their robes and sprinkled dust on their heads. ¹³Then they sat on the ground with him for seven days and seven nights. No one said a word to him, because they saw how great his suffering was.

Birthday Blues

Huh?

Job 3:1

You know those terrible, horrible, no good, very bad days, when you wish you could hit rewind and get a do-over? Job definitely had one of those! Because of that he "cursed the day of his birth." No, Job didn't need his mouth washed out with soap. Instead, he wished he had never been born. He was getting so much bad news that he wanted to give up. But he didn't—and God got him through the tough stuff! When you have a terrible, no good, very bad day, hold on to God and know that he is holding on to you!

Job Speaks

3 After this, Job opened his mouth and cursed the day of his birth. ²He said:

³ "May the day of my birth perish,
     and the night it was said, 'A boy is
        born!'
⁴ That day—may it turn to darkness;
     may God above not care about it;
     may no light shine upon it.
⁵ May darkness and deep shadow*ᵃ* claim
       it once more;
     may a cloud settle over it;
     may blackness overwhelm its light.
⁶ That night—may thick darkness seize
       it;

     may it not be included among the
        days of the year
     nor be entered in any of the
        months.
⁷ May that night be barren;
     may no shout of joy be heard in it.
⁸ May those who curse days*ᵇ* curse that
       day,
     those who are ready to rouse
        Leviathan.
⁹ May its morning stars become dark;
     may it wait for daylight in vain
     and not see the first rays of dawn,
¹⁰ for it did not shut the doors of the
       womb on me
     to hide trouble from my eyes.

¹¹ "Why did I not perish at birth,
     and die as I came from the womb?
¹² Why were there knees to receive me
     and breasts that I might be nursed?
¹³ For now I would be lying down in
       peace;
     I would be asleep and at rest
¹⁴ with kings and counselors of the
       earth,
     who built for themselves places now
       lying in ruins,
¹⁵ with rulers who had gold,
     who filled their houses with silver.
¹⁶ Or why was I not hidden in the
       ground like a stillborn child,
     like an infant who never saw the
       light of day?
¹⁷ There the wicked cease from turmoil,
     and there the weary are at rest.
¹⁸ Captives also enjoy their ease;
     they no longer hear the slave
       driver's shout.
¹⁹ The small and the great are there,
     and the slave is freed from his
       master.

²⁰ "Why is light given to those in misery,
     and life to the bitter of soul,
²¹ to those who long for death that does
       not come,
     who search for it more than for
       hidden treasure,
²² who are filled with gladness
     and rejoice when they reach the
       grave?
²³ Why is life given to a man
     whose way is hidden,

ᵃ5 Or and the shadow of death   *ᵇ8 Or the sea*

whom God has hedged in?
²⁴For sighing comes to me instead of
food;
my groans pour out like water.
²⁵What I feared has come upon me;
what I dreaded has happened to me.
²⁶I have no peace, no quietness;
I have no rest, but only turmoil."

Eliphaz

4 Then Eliphaz the Temanite replied:

²"If someone ventures a word with
you, will you be impatient?
But who can keep from speaking?
³Think how you have instructed many,
how you have strengthened feeble
hands.
⁴Your words have supported those who
stumbled;
you have strengthened faltering
knees.
⁵But now trouble comes to you, and
you are discouraged;
it strikes you, and you are
dismayed.
⁶Should not your piety be your
confidence
and your blameless ways your hope?

⁷"Consider now: Who, being innocent,
has ever perished?
Where were the upright ever
destroyed?
⁸As I have observed, those who plow
evil
and those who sow trouble reap it.
⁹At the breath of God they are
destroyed;
at the blast of his anger they perish.
¹⁰The lions may roar and growl,
yet the teeth of the great lions are
broken.
¹¹The lion perishes for lack of prey,
and the cubs of the lioness are
scattered.

¹²"A word was secretly brought to me,
my ears caught a whisper of it.
¹³Amid disquieting dreams in the night,
when deep sleep falls on men,
¹⁴fear and trembling seized me
and made all my bones shake.
¹⁵A spirit glided past my face,
and the hair on my body stood on
end.

¹⁶It stopped,
but I could not tell what it was.
A form stood before my eyes,
and I heard a hushed voice:
¹⁷'Can a mortal be more righteous than
God?
Can a man be more pure than his
Maker?
¹⁸If God places no trust in his servants,
if he charges his angels with error,
¹⁹how much more those who live in
houses of clay,
whose foundations are in the dust,
who are crushed more readily than
a moth!
²⁰Between dawn and dusk they are
broken to pieces;
unnoticed, they perish forever.
²¹Are not the cords of their tent pulled
up,
so that they die without wisdom?'ᵃ

5 "Call if you will, but who will
answer you?
To which of the holy ones will you
turn?
²Resentment kills a fool,
and envy slays the simple.
³I myself have seen a fool taking root,
but suddenly his house was cursed.
⁴His children are far from safety,
crushed in court without a defender.
⁵The hungry consume his harvest,
taking it even from among thorns,
and the thirsty pant after his
wealth.
⁶For hardship does not spring from the
soil,
nor does trouble sprout from the
ground.
⁷Yet man is born to trouble
as surely as sparks fly upward.

⁸"But if it were I, I would appeal to
God;
I would lay my cause before him.
⁹He performs wonders that cannot be
fathomed,
miracles that cannot be counted.
¹⁰He bestows rain on the earth;
he sends water upon the
countryside.
¹¹The lowly he sets on high,

ᵃ21 Some interpreters end the quotation after
verse 17.

and those who mourn are lifted to
  safety.
¹²He thwarts the plans of the crafty,
  so that their hands achieve no
    success.
¹³He catches the wise in their
    craftiness,
  and the schemes of the wily are
    swept away.
¹⁴Darkness comes upon them in the
    daytime;
  at noon they grope as in the night.
¹⁵He saves the needy from the sword in
    their mouth;
  he saves them from the clutches of
    the powerful.
¹⁶So the poor have hope,
  and injustice shuts its mouth.

¹⁷"Blessed is the man whom God
    corrects;
  so do not despise the discipline of
    the Almighty.ᵃ
¹⁸For he wounds, but he also binds up;
  he injures, but his hands also heal.
¹⁹From six calamities he will rescue
    you;
  in seven no harm will befall you.
²⁰In famine he will ransom you from
    death,
  and in battle from the stroke of the
    sword.
²¹You will be protected from the lash of
    the tongue,
  and need not fear when destruction
    comes.
²²You will laugh at destruction and
    famine,
  and need not fear the beasts of the
    earth.
²³For you will have a covenant with the
    stones of the field,
  and the wild animals will be at
    peace with you.
²⁴You will know that your tent is
    secure;
  you will take stock of your property
    and find nothing missing.
²⁵You will know that your children will
    be many,
  and your descendants like the grass
    of the earth.
²⁶You will come to the grave in full
    vigor,
  like sheaves gathered in season.

²⁷"We have examined this, and it is
    true.
  So hear it and apply it to yourself."

Job 6

Then Job replied:

²"If only my anguish could be weighed
  and all my misery be placed on the
    scales!
³It would surely outweigh the sand of
    the seas—
  no wonder my words have been
    impetuous.
⁴The arrows of the Almighty are in me,
  my spirit drinks in their poison;
  God's terrors are marshaled against
    me.
⁵Does a wild donkey bray when it has
    grass,
  or an ox bellow when it has fodder?
⁶Is tasteless food eaten without salt,
  or is there flavor in the white of an
    eggᵇ?
⁷I refuse to touch it;
  such food makes me ill.

⁸"Oh, that I might have my request,
  that God would grant what I hope
    for,
⁹that God would be willing to crush me,
  to let loose his hand and cut me off!
¹⁰Then I would still have this
    consolation—
  my joy in unrelenting pain—
  that I had not denied the words of
    the Holy One.

¹¹"What strength do I have, that I
    should still hope?
  What prospects, that I should be
    patient?
¹²Do I have the strength of stone?
  Is my flesh bronze?
¹³Do I have any power to help myself,
  now that success has been driven
    from me?

¹⁴"A despairing man should have the
    devotion of his friends,
  even though he forsakes the fear of
    the Almighty.

ᵃ17 Hebrew *Shaddai*; here and throughout Job
ᵇ6 The meaning of the Hebrew for this phrase is
uncertain.

¹⁵But my brothers are as undependable
    as intermittent streams,
    as the streams that overflow
¹⁶when darkened by thawing ice
    and swollen with melting snow,
¹⁷but that cease to flow in the dry season,
    and in the heat vanish from their
    channels.

Told You So

Huh?

Job 6:14–17

It really hurts when you make a mistake and a friend says, "I told you so." During tough times you need friends who will help you, not turn against you. Well, Job was hurtin' big-time and needed some encouragement. Even though he didn't do anything wrong, his friends were sure he did. Job needed friends who would love him. They could've helped Job much more if they had prayed with him, stayed with him—you know, just listened and been there with him.

¹⁸Caravans turn aside from their routes;
    they go up into the wasteland and
    perish.
¹⁹The caravans of Tema look for water,
    the traveling merchants of Sheba
    look in hope.
²⁰They are distressed, because they had
    been confident;
    they arrive there, only to be
    disappointed.
²¹Now you too have proved to be of no
    help;
    you see something dreadful and are
    afraid.
²²Have I ever said, 'Give something on
    my behalf,
    pay a ransom for me from your
    wealth,
²³deliver me from the hand of the enemy,
    ransom me from the clutches of the
    ruthless'?
²⁴"Teach me, and I will be quiet;
    show me where I have been wrong.
²⁵How painful are honest words!

    But what do your arguments prove?
²⁶Do you mean to correct what I say,
    and treat the words of a despairing
    man as wind?
²⁷You would even cast lots for the
    fatherless
    and barter away your friend.

²⁸"But now be so kind as to look at me.
    Would I lie to your face?
²⁹Relent, do not be unjust;
    reconsider, for my integrity is at
    stake.^a
³⁰Is there any wickedness on my lips?
    Can my mouth not discern malice?

7 "Does not man have hard service on
    earth?
    Are not his days like those of a
    hired man?
²Like a slave longing for the evening
    shadows,
    or a hired man waiting eagerly for
    his wages,
³so I have been allotted months of
    futility,
    and nights of misery have been
    assigned to me.
⁴When I lie down I think, 'How long
    before I get up?'
    The night drags on, and I toss till
    dawn.
⁵My body is clothed with worms and
    scabs,
    my skin is broken and festering.

⁶"My days are swifter than a weaver's
    shuttle,
    and they come to an end without
    hope.
⁷Remember, O God, that my life is but
    a breath;
    my eyes will never see happiness
    again.
⁸The eye that now sees me will see me
    no longer;
    you will look for me, but I will be
    no more.
⁹As a cloud vanishes and is gone,
    so he who goes down to the grave^b
    does not return.
¹⁰He will never come to his house
    again;
    his place will know him no more.

^a29 Or *my righteousness still stands*   ^b9 Hebrew
Sheol

11 "Therefore I will not keep silent;
I will speak out in the anguish of
my spirit,
I will complain in the bitterness of
my soul.
12 Am I the sea, or the monster of the
deep,
that you put me under guard?
13 When I think my bed will comfort me
and my couch will ease my
complaint,
14 even then you frighten me with dreams
and terrify me with visions,
15 so that I prefer strangling and death,
rather than this body of mine.
16 I despise my life; I would not live
forever.
Let me alone; my days have no
meaning.

17 "What is man that you make so much
of him,
that you give him so much
attention,
18 that you examine him every morning
and test him every moment?
19 Will you never look away from me,
or let me alone even for an instant?
20 If I have sinned, what have I done to
you,
O watcher of men?
Why have you made me your target?
Have I become a burden to you?[a]
21 Why do you not pardon my offenses
and forgive my sins?
For I will soon lie down in the dust;
you will search for me, but I will be
no more."

That Hurts

Job 7:20–21
What do you say when a friend goes
through really tough times? "Uh, well, gee,
sorry." It's tough, huh? Sometimes all you
can do is be there and remind your friends
that God is still with them. In this passage
Job is asking God when his suffering will
end. He's hurting. All he can do is keep
trusting God. But that's enough. It'll get
Job through.

Bildad

8 Then Bildad the Shuhite replied:

2 "How long will you say such things?
Your words are a blustering wind.
3 Does God pervert justice?
Does the Almighty pervert what is
right?
4 When your children sinned against
him,
he gave them over to the penalty of
their sin.
5 But if you will look to God
and plead with the Almighty,
6 if you are pure and upright,
even now he will rouse himself on
your behalf
and restore you to your rightful
place.
7 Your beginnings will seem humble,
so prosperous will your future be.

8 "Ask the former generations
and find out what their fathers
learned,
9 for we were born only yesterday and
know nothing,
and our days on earth are but a
shadow.
10 Will they not instruct you and tell
you?
Will they not bring forth words
from their understanding?
11 Can papyrus grow tall where there is
no marsh?
Can reeds thrive without water?
12 While still growing and uncut,
they wither more quickly than
grass.
13 Such is the destiny of all who forget
God;
so perishes the hope of the godless.
14 What he trusts in is fragile[b];
what he relies on is a spider's web.
15 He leans on his web, but it gives
way;
he clings to it, but it does not
hold.
16 He is like a well-watered plant in the
sunshine,

[a]20 A few manuscripts of the Masoretic Text, an
ancient Hebrew scribal tradition and Septuagint;
most manuscripts of the Masoretic Text *I have
become a burden to myself.*   [b]14 The meaning of the
Hebrew for this word is uncertain.

spreading its shoots over the garden;
[17] it entwines its roots around a pile of rocks
and looks for a place among the stones.
[18] But when it is torn from its spot,
that place disowns it and says,
'I never saw you.'
[19] Surely its life withers away,
and[a] from the soil other plants grow.

[20] "Surely God does not reject a blameless man
or strengthen the hands of evildoers.
[21] He will yet fill your mouth with laughter
and your lips with shouts of joy.
[22] Your enemies will be clothed in shame,
and the tents of the wicked will be no more."

Job

9

Then Job replied:

[2] "Indeed, I know that this is true.
But how can a mortal be righteous before God?
[3] Though one wished to dispute with him,
he could not answer him one time out of a thousand.
[4] His wisdom is profound, his power is vast.
Who has resisted him and come out unscathed?
[5] He moves mountains without their knowing it
and overturns them in his anger.
[6] He shakes the earth from its place
and makes its pillars tremble.
[7] He speaks to the sun and it does not shine;
he seals off the light of the stars.
[8] He alone stretches out the heavens
and treads on the waves of the sea.
[9] He is the Maker of the Bear and Orion,
the Pleiades and the constellations of the south.
[10] He performs wonders that cannot be fathomed,
miracles that cannot be counted.
[11] When he passes me, I cannot see him;

when he goes by, I cannot perceive him.
[12] If he snatches away, who can stop him?
Who can say to him, 'What are you doing?'
[13] God does not restrain his anger;
even the cohorts of Rahab cowered at his feet.

[14] "How then can I dispute with him?
How can I find words to argue with him?
[15] Though I were innocent, I could not answer him;
I could only plead with my Judge for mercy.
[16] Even if I summoned him and he responded,
I do not believe he would give me a hearing.
[17] He would crush me with a storm
and multiply my wounds for no reason.
[18] He would not let me regain my breath
but would overwhelm me with misery.
[19] If it is a matter of strength, he is mighty!
And if it is a matter of justice, who will summon him[b]?
[20] Even if I were innocent, my mouth would condemn me;
if I were blameless, it would pronounce me guilty.

[21] "Although I am blameless,
I have no concern for myself;
I despise my own life.
[22] It is all the same; that is why I say,
'He destroys both the blameless and the wicked.'
[23] When a scourge brings sudden death,
he mocks the despair of the innocent.
[24] When a land falls into the hands of the wicked,
he blindfolds its judges.
If it is not he, then who is it?

[25] "My days are swifter than a runner;
they fly away without a glimpse of joy.

---

[a] 19 Or Surely all the joy it has / is that
[b] 19 See Septuagint; Hebrew me.

²⁶ They skim past like boats of papyrus,
  like eagles swooping down on their
    prey.
²⁷ If I say, 'I will forget my complaint,
  I will change my expression, and
    smile,'
²⁸ I still dread all my sufferings,
  for I know you will not hold me
    innocent.
²⁹ Since I am already found guilty,
  why should I struggle in vain?
³⁰ Even if I washed myself with soap*ᵃ*
  and my hands with washing soda,
³¹ you would plunge me into a slime pit
  so that even my clothes would
    detest me.

³² "He is not a man like me that I might
    answer him,
  that we might confront each other
    in court.
³³ If only there were someone to
    arbitrate between us,
  to lay his hand upon us both,
³⁴ someone to remove God's rod from me,
  so that his terror would frighten me
    no more.
³⁵ Then I would speak up without fear of
    him,
  but as it now stands with me, I
    cannot.

10 "I loathe my very life;
  therefore I will give free rein to
    my complaint
  and speak out in the bitterness of
    my soul.
² I will say to God: Do not condemn me,
  but tell me what charges you have
    against me.
³ Does it please you to oppress me,
  to spurn the work of your hands,
  while you smile on the schemes of
    the wicked?
⁴ Do you have eyes of flesh?
  Do you see as a mortal sees?
⁵ Are your days like those of a mortal
  or your years like those of a man,
⁶ that you must search out my faults
  and probe after my sin—
⁷ though you know that I am not guilty
  and that no one can rescue me from
    your hand?

⁸ "Your hands shaped me and made me.
  Will you now turn and destroy me?
⁹ Remember that you molded me like
    clay.
  Will you now turn me to dust
    again?
¹⁰ Did you not pour me out like milk
  and curdle me like cheese,
¹¹ clothe me with skin and flesh
  and knit me together with bones
    and sinews?
¹² You gave me life and showed me
    kindness,
  and in your providence watched
    over my spirit.

¹³ "But this is what you concealed in
    your heart,
  and I know that this was in your
    mind:
¹⁴ If I sinned, you would be watching
    me
  and would not let my offense go
    unpunished.
¹⁵ If I am guilty—woe to me!
  Even if I am innocent, I cannot lift
    my head,
  for I am full of shame
  and drowned inᵇ my affliction.
¹⁶ If I hold my head high, you stalk me
    like a lion
  and again display your awesome
    power against me.
¹⁷ You bring new witnesses against me
  and increase your anger toward me;
  your forces come against me wave
    upon wave.

¹⁸ "Why then did you bring me out of
    the womb?
  I wish I had died before any eye
    saw me.
¹⁹ If only I had never come into being,
  or had been carried straight from
    the womb to the grave!
²⁰ Are not my few days almost over?
  Turn away from me so I can have a
    moment's joy
²¹ before I go to the place of no return,
  to the land of gloom and deep
    shadow,ᶜ
²² to the land of deepest night,
  of deep shadow and disorder,
  where even the light is like
    darkness."

ᵃ30 Or *snow*   ᵇ15 Or *and aware of*   ᶜ21 Or *and the*
shadow of death; also in verse 22

Zophar

11 Then Zophar the Naamathite replied:

² "Are all these words to go unanswered?
  Is this talker to be vindicated?
³ Will your idle talk reduce men to
    silence?
  Will no one rebuke you when you
    mock?
⁴ You say to God, 'My beliefs are
    flawless
  and I am pure in your sight.'
⁵ Oh, how I wish that God would speak,
  that he would open his lips against
    you
⁶ and disclose to you the secrets of
    wisdom,
    for true wisdom has two sides.
  Know this: God has even forgotten
    some of your sin.

⁷ "Can you fathom the mysteries of
    God?
  Can you probe the limits of the
    Almighty?
⁸ They are higher than the heavens—
    what can you do?
  They are deeper than the depths of
    the grave*ᵃ*—what can you
    know?
⁹ Their measure is longer than the earth
  and wider than the sea.

¹⁰ "If he comes along and confines you
    in prison
  and convenes a court, who can
    oppose him?
¹¹ Surely he recognizes deceitful men;
  and when he sees evil, does he not
    take note?
¹² But a witless man can no more
    become wise
  than a wild donkey's colt can be
    born a man.*ᵇ*

¹³ "Yet if you devote your heart to him
  and stretch out your hands to him,
¹⁴ if you put away the sin that is in your
    hand
  and allow no evil to dwell in your
    tent,
¹⁵ then you will lift up your face without
    shame;
  you will stand firm and without
    fear.

¹⁶ You will surely forget your trouble,
  recalling it only as waters gone by.
¹⁷ Life will be brighter than noonday,
  and darkness will become like
    morning.
¹⁸ You will be secure, because there is
    hope;
  you will look about you and take
    your rest in safety.
¹⁹ You will lie down, with no one to
    make you afraid,
  and many will court your favor.
²⁰ But the eyes of the wicked will fail,
  and escape will elude them;
    their hope will become a dying
    gasp."

Job

12 Then Job replied:

² "Doubtless you are the people,
  and wisdom will die with you!
³ But I have a mind as well as you;
  I am not inferior to you.
  Who does not know all these
    things?

⁴ "I have become a laughingstock to my
    friends,
  though I called upon God and he
    answered—
  a mere laughingstock, though
    righteous and blameless!
⁵ Men at ease have contempt for
    misfortune
  as the fate of those whose feet are
    slipping.
⁶ The tents of marauders are
    undisturbed,
  and those who provoke God are
    secure—
  those who carry their god in their
    hands.*ᶜ*

⁷ "But ask the animals, and they will
    teach you,
  or the birds of the air, and they will
    tell you;
⁸ or speak to the earth, and it will teach
    you,
  or let the fish of the sea inform you.
⁹ Which of all these does not know

---

*ᵃ8 Hebrew than Sheol   *ᵇ12 Or wild donkey can be
born tame   *ᶜ6 Or secure / in what God's hand
brings them

that the hand of the LORD has done this?
¹⁰ In his hand is the life of every creature
and the breath of all mankind.
¹¹ Does not the ear test words
as the tongue tastes food?
¹² Is not wisdom found among the aged?
Does not long life bring understanding?

¹³ "To God belong wisdom and power;
counsel and understanding are his.
¹⁴ What he tears down cannot be rebuilt;
the man he imprisons cannot be released.
¹⁵ If he holds back the waters, there is drought;
if he lets them loose, they devastate the land.
¹⁶ To him belong strength and victory;
both deceived and deceiver are his.
¹⁷ He leads counselors away stripped
and makes fools of judges.
¹⁸ He takes off the shackles put on by kings
and ties a loinclothᵃ around their waist.
¹⁹ He leads priests away stripped
and overthrows men long established.
²⁰ He silences the lips of trusted advisers
and takes away the discernment of elders.
²¹ He pours contempt on nobles
and disarms the mighty.
²² He reveals the deep things of darkness
and brings deep shadows into the light.
²³ He makes nations great, and destroys them;
he enlarges nations, and disperses them.
²⁴ He deprives the leaders of the earth of their reason;
he sends them wandering through a trackless waste.
²⁵ They grope in darkness with no light;
he makes them stagger like drunkards.

13 "My eyes have seen all this,
my ears have heard and understood it.
² What you know, I also know;
I am not inferior to you.

³ But I desire to speak to the Almighty
and to argue my case with God.
⁴ You, however, smear me with lies;
you are worthless physicians, all of you!
⁵ If only you would be altogether silent!
For you, that would be wisdom.
⁶ Hear now my argument;
listen to the plea of my lips.
⁷ Will you speak wickedly on God's behalf?
Will you speak deceitfully for him?
⁸ Will you show him partiality?
Will you argue the case for God?
⁹ Would it turn out well if he examined you?
Could you deceive him as you might deceive men?
¹⁰ He would surely rebuke you
if you secretly showed partiality.
¹¹ Would not his splendor terrify you?
Would not the dread of him fall on you?
¹² Your maxims are proverbs of ashes;
your defenses are defenses of clay.

¹³ "Keep silent and let me speak;
then let come to me what may.
¹⁴ Why do I put myself in jeopardy
and take my life in my hands?
¹⁵ Though he slay me, yet will I hope in him;
I will surelyᵇ defend my ways to his face.
¹⁶ Indeed, this will turn out for my deliverance,
for no godless man would dare come before him!
¹⁷ Listen carefully to my words;
let your ears take in what I say.
¹⁸ Now that I have prepared my case,
I know I will be vindicated.
¹⁹ Can anyone bring charges against me?
If so, I will be silent and die.

²⁰ "Only grant me these two things, O God,
and then I will not hide from you:
²¹ Withdraw your hand far from me,
and stop frightening me with your terrors.
²² Then summon me and I will answer,
or let me speak, and you reply.

ᵃ 18 Or *shackles of kings / and ties a belt*   ᵇ 15 Or *He will surely slay me; I have no hope — / yet I will*

²³How many wrongs and sins have I
       committed?
   Show me my offense and my sin.
²⁴Why do you hide your face
   and consider me your enemy?
²⁵Will you torment a windblown leaf?
   Will you chase after dry chaff?
²⁶For you write down bitter things
       against me
   and make me inherit the sins of my
       youth.
²⁷You fasten my feet in shackles;
   you keep close watch on all my
       paths

by putting marks on the soles of my
   feet.
²⁸"So man wastes away like something
       rotten,
   like a garment eaten by moths.

14 "Man born of woman
   is of few days and full of
       trouble.
²He springs up like a flower and
       withers away;
   like a fleeting shadow, he does not
       endure.
³Do you fix your eye on such a one?

Weekend.

That's Just the Way It Is

Read John 16:33 (page 1296)

In the last week you've been reading all about problems: Tim's friends making poor decisions; Emile's lessons in handling criticism; Christina's best friend moving away. Like the Bible characters they wrote about—Ezra, Nehemiah, Esther and Job—these students are finding that life doesn't always come easy.

You're bound to discover this too. Did you know that Jesus actually promised you problems? Well, he did, and his promises always come true. So when trouble hits, don't be surprised. And don't automatically assume that it's your fault. God does discipline his kids when they veer off course. But sometimes problems come not because you've done something bad, but because you've done something good.

Think about it. If Ezra didn't want to teach God's Word . . . if Nehemiah didn't want to rebuild Jerusalem . . . if Esther didn't want to save her people . . . if Job hadn't been so squeaky-clean, *their lives would have been much easier!* Things got messy because they followed God fully. That's just the way it is, so take a lesson.

You're going to have problems one way or another. You can rebel and bring them on yourself, or you can obey and wait for trouble to find you. Do your best to live a life of obedience to God. And remember Jesus' promise: "Take heart! I have overcome the world!"

❶ What are your biggest problems right now? Do you think you brought them on yourself or have they come from another source?

❷ What is one good choice God is calling you to make that could result in trouble coming your way? (Like witnessing to a friend or standing up for what you believe in.)

❸ Ask God to give you the courage to be completely devoted to him, so you can take the heat for being his disciple.

Turn to page 598 for your next devotion.

Will you bring him[a] before you for judgment?

⁴Who can bring what is pure from the impure?
No one!

⁵Man's days are determined;
you have decreed the number of his months
and have set limits he cannot exceed.

⁶So look away from him and let him alone,
till he has put in his time like a hired man.

⁷"At least there is hope for a tree:
If it is cut down, it will sprout again,
and its new shoots will not fail.

⁸Its roots may grow old in the ground
and its stump die in the soil,

⁹yet at the scent of water it will bud
and put forth shoots like a plant.

¹⁰But man dies and is laid low;
he breathes his last and is no more.

¹¹As water disappears from the sea
or a riverbed becomes parched and dry,

¹²so man lies down and does not rise;
till the heavens are no more, men will not awake
or be roused from their sleep.

¹³"If only you would hide me in the grave[b]
and conceal me till your anger has passed!
If only you would set me a time
and then remember me!

¹⁴If a man dies, will he live again?
All the days of my hard service
I will wait for my renewal[c] to come.

¹⁵You will call and I will answer you;
you will long for the creature your hands have made.

¹⁶Surely then you will count my steps
but not keep track of my sin.

¹⁷My offenses will be sealed up in a bag;
you will cover over my sin.

¹⁸"But as a mountain erodes and crumbles
and as a rock is moved from its place,

¹⁹as water wears away stones
and torrents wash away the soil,
so you destroy man's hope.

²⁰You overpower him once for all, and he is gone;
you change his countenance and send him away.

²¹If his sons are honored, he does not know it;
if they are brought low, he does not see it.

²²He feels but the pain of his own body
and mourns only for himself."

Eliphaz

15 Then Eliphaz the Temanite replied:

²"Would a wise man answer with empty notions
or fill his belly with the hot east wind?

³Would he argue with useless words,
with speeches that have no value?

⁴But you even undermine piety
and hinder devotion to God.

⁵Your sin prompts your mouth;
you adopt the tongue of the crafty.

⁶Your own mouth condemns you, not mine;
your own lips testify against you.

⁷"Are you the first man ever born?
Were you brought forth before the hills?

⁸Do you listen in on God's council?
Do you limit wisdom to yourself?

⁹What do you know that we do not know?
What insights do you have that we do not have?

¹⁰The gray-haired and the aged are on our side,
men even older than your father.

¹¹Are God's consolations not enough for you,
words spoken gently to you?

¹²Why has your heart carried you away,
and why do your eyes flash,

¹³so that you vent your rage against God
and pour out such words from your mouth?

¹⁴"What is man, that he could be pure,
or one born of woman, that he could be righteous?

---

[a] 3 Septuagint, Vulgate and Syriac; Hebrew me
[b] 13 Hebrew Sheol   [c] 14 Or release

15 If God places no trust in his holy
    ones,
    if even the heavens are not pure in
       his eyes,
16 how much less man, who is vile and
    corrupt,
    who drinks up evil like water!

17 "Listen to me and I will explain to
    you;
    let me tell you what I have seen,
18 what wise men have declared,
    hiding nothing received from their
      fathers
19 (to whom alone the land was given
    when no alien passed among them):
20 All his days the wicked man suffers
    torment,
    the ruthless through all the years
      stored up for him.
21 Terrifying sounds fill his ears;
    when all seems well, marauders
      attack him.
22 He despairs of escaping the darkness;
    he is marked for the sword.
23 He wanders about—food for vultures[a];
    he knows the day of darkness is at
      hand.
24 Distress and anguish fill him with
    terror;
    they overwhelm him, like a king
      poised to attack,
25 because he shakes his fist at God
    and vaunts himself against the
      Almighty,
26 defiantly charging against him
    with a thick, strong shield.

27 "Though his face is covered with fat
    and his waist bulges with flesh,
28 he will inhabit ruined towns
    and houses where no one lives,
    houses crumbling to rubble.
29 He will no longer be rich and his
    wealth will not endure,
    nor will his possessions spread over
      the land.
30 He will not escape the darkness;
    a flame will wither his shoots,
    and the breath of God's mouth will
      carry him away.
31 Let him not deceive himself by
    trusting what is worthless,
    for he will get nothing in return.
32 Before his time he will be paid in full,
    and his branches will not flourish.

33 He will be like a vine stripped of its
    unripe grapes,
    like an olive tree shedding its
      blossoms.
34 For the company of the godless will
    be barren,
    and fire will consume the tents of
      those who love bribes.
35 They conceive trouble and give birth
    to evil;
    their womb fashions deceit."

Job

16

    Then Job replied:

2 "I have heard many things like these;
    miserable comforters are you all!
3 Will your long-winded speeches never
    end?
    What ails you that you keep on
      arguing?
4 I also could speak like you,
    if you were in my place;
   I could make fine speeches against
      you
    and shake my head at you.
5 But my mouth would encourage you;
    comfort from my lips would bring
      you relief.

6 "Yet if I speak, my pain is not
    relieved;
    and if I refrain, it does not go away.
7 Surely, O God, you have worn me out;
    you have devastated my entire
      household.
8 You have bound me—and it has
    become a witness;
    my gauntness rises up and testifies
      against me.
9 God assails me and tears me in his
    anger
    and gnashes his teeth at me;
    my opponent fastens on me his
      piercing eyes.
10 Men open their mouths to jeer at me;
    they strike my cheek in scorn
    and unite together against me.
11 God has turned me over to evil men
    and thrown me into the clutches of
      the wicked.
12 All was well with me, but he shattered
    me;

[a]23 Or *about, looking for food*

yet[a] in[b] my flesh I will see God;
²⁷ I myself will see him
with my own eyes--I, and not another.
How my heart yearns within me!

²⁸ "If you say, 'How we will hound him,
since the root of the trouble lies in
him,'[c]
²⁹ you should fear the sword yourselves;
for wrath will bring punishment by
the sword,
and then you will know that there
is judgment.[d]"

Zophar

20 Then Zophar the Naamathite replied:

² "My troubled thoughts prompt me to
answer
because I am greatly disturbed.
³ I hear a rebuke that dishonors me,
and my understanding inspires me
to reply.

⁴ "Surely you know how it has been
from of old,

ever since man[e] was placed on the
earth,
⁵ that the mirth of the wicked is brief,
the joy of the godless lasts but a
moment.
⁶ Though his pride reaches to the
heavens
and his head touches the clouds,
⁷ he will perish forever, like his own
dung;
those who have seen him will say,
'Where is he?'
⁸ Like a dream he flies away, no more
to be found,
banished like a vision of the night.
⁹ The eye that saw him will not see him
again;
his place will look on him no more.
¹⁰ His children must make amends to the
poor;

---

[a]26 Or *And after I awake, / though this body has
been destroyed, / then* ‎ [b]26 Or */ apart from*
[c]28 Many Hebrew manuscripts, Septuagint and
Vulgate; most Hebrew manuscripts *me* ‎ [d]29 Or /
that you may come to know the Almighty
[e]4 Or *Adam*

Monday

Filling in the Gaps

Read Job 19:25-27

After my dad died, a huge part of my life died with him. The pain was
almost too much to handle. But God helped me. Through my dad's death,
I learned that, no matter what happens, God will always be there for me.
I could lose everything I think is important, but I won't ever lose God—not as
long as I'm a Christian. I'm not afraid of losing my possessions or of surviving life's hard times, because I know God will fill in the gaps like he has
in the past.

No matter where we go, no matter what we do, God is with us. He loves
us and cares about us and will never leave our side. We can lose everything
else, but we just can't lose God.

What about You?

❶ Why is it hard to have faith when things aren't going well? Where do
you find encouragement in the hard times?

❷ Start a journal of the ways God has helped you through some rough
spots. Next time you're struggling, read through your journal to help
you remember how God has been with you in the past.

❸ Thank God for helping you deal with difficult times.

Turn to page 607 for your next devotion.

his own hands must give back his
  wealth.
¹¹ The youthful vigor that fills his bones
  will lie with him in the dust.

¹² "Though evil is sweet in his mouth
  and he hides it under his tongue,
¹³ though he cannot bear to let it go
  and keeps it in his mouth,
¹⁴ yet his food will turn sour in his
      stomach;
  it will become the venom of
      serpents within him.
¹⁵ He will spit out the riches he
      swallowed;
  God will make his stomach vomit
      them up.
¹⁶ He will suck the poison of serpents;
  the fangs of an adder will kill him.
¹⁷ He will not enjoy the streams,
  the rivers flowing with honey and
      cream.
¹⁸ What he toiled for he must give back
      uneaten;
  he will not enjoy the profit from his
      trading.
¹⁹ For he has oppressed the poor and left
      them destitute;
  he has seized houses he did not
      build.

²⁰ "Surely he will have no respite from
      his craving;
  he cannot save himself by his
      treasure.
²¹ Nothing is left for him to devour;
  his prosperity will not endure.
²² In the midst of his plenty, distress will
      overtake him;
  the full force of misery will come
      upon him.
²³ When he has filled his belly,
  God will vent his burning anger
      against him
  and rain down his blows upon him.
²⁴ Though he flees from an iron weapon,
  a bronze-tipped arrow pierces him.
²⁵ He pulls it out of his back,
  the gleaming point out of his liver.
  Terrors will come over him;
²⁶   total darkness lies in wait for his
      treasures.
  A fire unfanned will consume him
  and devour what is left in his tent.
²⁷ The heavens will expose his guilt;
  the earth will rise up against him.

²⁸ A flood will carry off his house,
  rushing waters*a* on the day of God's
      wrath.
²⁹ Such is the fate God allots the wicked,
  the heritage appointed for them by
      God."

21 Then Job replied:

² "Listen carefully to my words;
  let this be the consolation you give
      me.
³ Bear with me while I speak,
  and after I have spoken, mock on.

⁴ "Is my complaint directed to man?
  Why should I not be impatient?
⁵ Look at me and be astonished;
  clap your hand over your mouth.
⁶ When I think about this, I am
      terrified;
  trembling seizes my body.
⁷ Why do the wicked live on,
  growing old and increasing in
      power?
⁸ They see their children established
      around them,
  their offspring before their eyes.
⁹ Their homes are safe and free from
      fear;
  the rod of God is not upon them.
¹⁰ Their bulls never fail to breed;
  their cows calve and do not
      miscarry.
¹¹ They send forth their children as a
      flock;
  their little ones dance about.
¹² They sing to the music of tambourine
      and harp;
  they make merry to the sound of
      the flute.
¹³ They spend their years in prosperity
  and go down to the grave*b* in
      peace.*c*
¹⁴ Yet they say to God, 'Leave us alone!
  We have no desire to know your
      ways.
¹⁵ Who is the Almighty, that we should
      serve him?
  What would we gain by praying to
      him?'

---

a28 Or *The possessions in his house will be carried
off, / washed away*   *b13* Hebrew *Sheol*   *c13* Or *in
an instant*

¹⁶But their prosperity is not in their
  own hands,
    so I stand aloof from the counsel of
    the wicked.

¹⁷"Yet how often is the lamp of the
  wicked snuffed out?
    How often does calamity come
    upon them,
      the fate God allots in his anger?
¹⁸How often are they like straw before
  the wind,
    like chaff swept away by a gale?
¹⁹It is said, 'God stores up a man's
  punishment for his sons.'
    Let him repay the man himself, so
    that he will know it!
²⁰Let his own eyes see his destruction;
    let him drink of the wrath of the
    Almighty.ᵃ
²¹For what does he care about the
  family he leaves behind
    when his allotted months come to
    an end?

²²"Can anyone teach knowledge to God,
    since he judges even the highest?
²³One man dies in full vigor,
    completely secure and at ease,
²⁴his bodyᵇ well nourished,
    his bones rich with marrow.
²⁵Another man dies in bitterness of
  soul,
    never having enjoyed anything
    good.
²⁶Side by side they lie in the dust,
    and worms cover them both.

²⁷"I know full well what you are
  thinking,
    the schemes by which you would
    wrong me.
²⁸You say, 'Where now is the great
  man's house,
    the tents where wicked men
    lived?'
²⁹Have you never questioned those who
  travel?
    Have you paid no regard to their
    accounts—
³⁰that the evil man is spared from the
  day of calamity,
    that he is delivered fromᶜ the day of
    wrath?
³¹Who denounces his conduct to his
  face?

Who repays him for what he has
  done?
³²He is carried to the grave,
    and watch is kept over his tomb.
³³The soil in the valley is sweet to him;
    all men follow after him,
      and a countless throng goesᵈ before
      him.

³⁴"So how can you console me with
  your nonsense?
    Nothing is left of your answers but
    falsehood!"

Eliphaz

22 Then Eliphaz the Temanite replied:

²"Can a man be of benefit to God?
    Can even a wise man benefit him?
³What pleasure would it give the
  Almighty if you were
  righteous?
    What would he gain if your ways
    were blameless?
⁴"Is it for your piety that he rebukes
  you
    and brings charges against you?
⁵Is not your wickedness great?
    Are not your sins endless?
⁶You demanded security from your
  brothers for no reason;
    you stripped men of their clothing,
    leaving them naked.
⁷You gave no water to the weary
    and you withheld food from the
    hungry,
⁸though you were a powerful man,
  owning land—
    an honored man, living on it.
⁹And you sent widows away
  empty-handed
    and broke the strength of the
    fatherless.
¹⁰That is why snares are all around
  you,
    why sudden peril terrifies you,
¹¹why it is so dark you cannot see,
    and why a flood of water covers
    you.

ᵃ17-20 Verses 17 and 18 may be taken as
exclamations and 19 and 20 as declarations.
ᵇ24 The meaning of the Hebrew for this word is
uncertain.   ᶜ30 Or man is reserved for the day
of calamity, / that he is brought forth to
ᵈ33 Or / as a countless throng went

¹²"Is not God in the heights of heaven?
  And see how lofty are the highest
    stars!
¹³Yet you say, 'What does God know?
  Does he judge through such
    darkness?
¹⁴Thick clouds veil him, so he does not
    see us
  as he goes about in the vaulted
    heavens.'
¹⁵Will you keep to the old path
  that evil men have trod?
¹⁶They were carried off before their time,
  their foundations washed away by a
    flood.
¹⁷They said to God, 'Leave us alone!
  What can the Almighty do to us?'
¹⁸Yet it was he who filled their houses
    with good things,
  so I stand aloof from the counsel of
    the wicked.

¹⁹"The righteous see their ruin and
    rejoice;
  the innocent mock them, saying,
²⁰'Surely our foes are destroyed,
  and fire devours their wealth.'

²¹"Submit to God and be at peace with
    him;
  in this way prosperity will come to
    you.
²²Accept instruction from his mouth
  and lay up his words in your heart.
²³If you return to the Almighty, you will
    be restored:
  If you remove wickedness far from
    your tent
²⁴and assign your nuggets to the dust,
  your gold of Ophir to the rocks in
    the ravines,
²⁵then the Almighty will be your gold,
  the choicest silver for you.
²⁶Surely then you will find delight in
    the Almighty
  and will lift up your face to God.
²⁷You will pray to him, and he will hear
    you,
  and you will fulfill your vows.
²⁸What you decide on will be done,
  and light will shine on your ways.
²⁹When men are brought low and you
    say, 'Lift them up!'
  then he will save the downcast.
³⁰He will deliver even one who is not
    innocent,

who will be delivered through the
  cleanness of your hands."

Job

23

Then Job replied:

²"Even today my complaint is bitter;
  his hand^a is heavy in spite of^b my
    groaning.
³If only I knew where to find him;
  if only I could go to his dwelling!
⁴I would state my case before him
  and fill my mouth with arguments.
⁵I would find out what he would
    answer me,
  and consider what he would say.
⁶Would he oppose me with great
    power?
  No, he would not press charges
    against me.
⁷There an upright man could present
    his case before him,
  and I would be delivered forever
    from my judge.

⁸"But if I go to the east, he is not there;
  if I go to the west, I do not find
    him.
⁹When he is at work in the north, I do
    not see him;
  when he turns to the south, I catch
    no glimpse of him.
¹⁰But he knows the way that I take;
  when he has tested me, I will come
    forth as gold.
¹¹My feet have closely followed his
    steps;
  I have kept to his way without
    turning aside.
¹²I have not departed from the
    commands of his lips;
  I have treasured the words of his
    mouth more than my daily
    bread.

¹³"But he stands alone, and who can
    oppose him?
  He does whatever he pleases.
¹⁴He carries out his decree against me,
  and many such plans he still has in
    store.
¹⁵That is why I am terrified before him;
  when I think of all this, I fear him.

^{a}2 Septuagint and Syriac; Hebrew / *the hand on me*
^{b}2 Or *heavy on me in*

[16]God has made my heart faint;
  the Almighty has terrified me.
[17]Yet I am not silenced by the
    darkness,
  by the thick darkness that covers
    my face.

24

  "Why does the Almighty not set
    times for judgment?
Why must those who know him
    look in vain for such days?
[2]Men move boundary stones;
  they pasture flocks they have
    stolen.
[3]They drive away the orphan's donkey
  and take the widow's ox in pledge.
[4]They thrust the needy from the path
  and force all the poor of the land
    into hiding.
[5]Like wild donkeys in the desert,
  the poor go about their labor of
    foraging food;
  the wasteland provides food for
    their children.
[6]They gather fodder in the fields
  and glean in the vineyards of the
    wicked.
[7]Lacking clothes, they spend the night
    naked;
  they have nothing to cover
    themselves in the cold.
[8]They are drenched by mountain rains
  and hug the rocks for lack of
    shelter.
[9]The fatherless child is snatched from
    the breast;
  the infant of the poor is seized for a
    debt.
[10]Lacking clothes, they go about naked;
  they carry the sheaves, but still go
    hungry.
[11]They crush olives among the
    terraces[a];
  they tread the winepresses, yet
    suffer thirst.
[12]The groans of the dying rise from the
    city,
  and the souls of the wounded cry
    out for help.
  But God charges no one with
    wrongdoing.
[13]"There are those who rebel against the
    light,
  who do not know its ways
  or stay in its paths.

[14]When daylight is gone, the murderer
    rises up
  and kills the poor and needy;
  in the night he steals forth like a
    thief.
[15]The eye of the adulterer watches for
    dusk;
  he thinks, 'No eye will see me,'
  and he keeps his face concealed.
[16]In the dark, men break into houses,
  but by day they shut themselves in;
  they want nothing to do with the
    light.
[17]For all of them, deep darkness is their
    morning[b];
  they make friends with the terrors
    of darkness.[c]
[18]"Yet they are foam on the surface of
    the water;
  their portion of the land is cursed,
  so that no one goes to the
    vineyards.
[19]As heat and drought snatch away the
    melted snow,
  so the grave[d] snatches away those
    who have sinned.
[20]The womb forgets them,
  the worm feasts on them;
evil men are no longer remembered
  but are broken like a tree.
[21]They prey on the barren and childless
    woman,
  and to the widow show no
    kindness.
[22]But God drags away the mighty by his
    power;
  though they become established,
    they have no assurance of life.
[23]He may let them rest in a feeling of
    security,
  but his eyes are on their ways.
[24]For a little while they are exalted, and
    then they are gone;
  they are brought low and gathered
    up like all others;
  they are cut off like heads of grain.

[25]"If this is not so, who can prove me
    false
  and reduce my words to nothing?"

---

[a]11 Or *olives between the millstones*; the meaning of
the Hebrew for this word is uncertain. [b]17 Or *them,
their morning is like the shadow of death* [c]17 Or *of
the shadow of death* [d]19 Hebrew *Sheol*

Bildad

25 Then Bildad the Shuhite replied:

² "Dominion and awe belong to God;
  he establishes order in the heights
    of heaven.
³ Can his forces be numbered?
  Upon whom does his light not rise?
⁴ How then can a man be righteous
    before God?
  How can one born of woman be
    pure?
⁵ If even the moon is not bright
  and the stars are not pure in his eyes,
⁶ how much less man, who is but a
    maggot—
  a son of man, who is only a worm!"

Job

26 Then Job replied:

² "How you have helped the powerless!
  How you have saved the arm that is
    feeble!
³ What advice you have offered to one
    without wisdom!
  And what great insight you have
    displayed!
⁴ Who has helped you utter these
    words?
  And whose spirit spoke from your
    mouth?

⁵ "The dead are in deep anguish,
  those beneath the waters and all
    that live in them.
⁶ Death*a* is naked before God;
  Destruction*b* lies uncovered.
⁷ He spreads out the northern skies
    over empty space;
  he suspends the earth over nothing.
⁸ He wraps up the waters in his clouds,
  yet the clouds do not burst under
    their weight.
⁹ He covers the face of the full moon,
  spreading his clouds over it.
¹⁰ He marks out the horizon on the face
    of the waters
  for a boundary between light and
    darkness.
¹¹ The pillars of the heavens quake,
  aghast at his rebuke.
¹² By his power he churned up the sea;
  by his wisdom he cut Rahab to
    pieces.

¹³ By his breath the skies became fair;
  his hand pierced the gliding serpent.
¹⁴ And these are but the outer fringe of
    his works;
  how faint the whisper we hear of
    him!
  Who then can understand the
    thunder of his power?"

27 And Job continued his discourse:

² "As surely as God lives, who has
    denied me justice,
  the Almighty, who has made me
    taste bitterness of soul,
³ as long as I have life within me,
  the breath of God in my nostrils,
⁴ my lips will not speak wickedness,
  and my tongue will utter no deceit.
⁵ I will never admit you are in the
    right;
  till I die, I will not deny my
    integrity.
⁶ I will maintain my righteousness and
    never let go of it;
  my conscience will not reproach me
    as long as I live.

⁷ "May my enemies be like the wicked,
  my adversaries like the unjust!
⁸ For what hope has the godless when
    he is cut off,
  when God takes away his life?
⁹ Does God listen to his cry
  when distress comes upon him?
¹⁰ Will he find delight in the Almighty?
  Will he call upon God at all times?

¹¹ "I will teach you about the power of
    God;
  the ways of the Almighty I will not
    conceal.
¹² You have all seen this yourselves.
  Why then this meaningless talk?

¹³ "Here is the fate God allots to the
    wicked,
  the heritage a ruthless man receives
    from the Almighty:
¹⁴ However many his children, their fate
    is the sword;
  his offspring will never have
    enough to eat.
¹⁵ The plague will bury those who
    survive him,

*a*6 Hebrew *Sheol*   *b*6 Hebrew *Abaddon*

and their widows will not weep for
them.
¹⁶Though he heaps up silver like dust
and clothes like piles of clay,
¹⁷what he lays up the righteous will
wear,
and the innocent will divide his
silver.
¹⁸The house he builds is like a moth's
cocoon,
like a hut made by a watchman.
¹⁹He lies down wealthy, but will do so
no more;
when he opens his eyes, all is gone.
²⁰Terrors overtake him like a flood;
a tempest snatches him away in the
night.
²¹The east wind carries him off, and he
is gone;
it sweeps him out of his place.
²²It hurls itself against him without
mercy
as he flees headlong from its
power.
²³It claps its hands in derision
and hisses him out of his place.

28

"There is a mine for silver
and a place where gold is
refined.
²Iron is taken from the earth,
and copper is smelted from ore.
³Man puts an end to the darkness;
he searches the farthest recesses
for ore in the blackest darkness.
⁴Far from where people dwell he cuts a
shaft,
in places forgotten by the foot of
man;
far from men he dangles and sways.
⁵The earth, from which food comes,
is transformed below as by fire;
⁶sapphires*a* come from its rocks,
and its dust contains nuggets of
gold.
⁷No bird of prey knows that hidden
path,
no falcon's eye has seen it.
⁸Proud beasts do not set foot on it,
and no lion prowls there.
⁹Man's hand assaults the flinty rock
and lays bare the roots of the
mountains.
¹⁰He tunnels through the rock;
his eyes see all its treasures.

¹¹He searches*b* the sources of the rivers
and brings hidden things to light.

¹²"But where can wisdom be found?
Where does understanding dwell?
¹³Man does not comprehend its worth;
it cannot be found in the land of
the living.
¹⁴The deep says, 'It is not in me';
the sea says, 'It is not with me.'
¹⁵It cannot be bought with the finest
gold,
nor can its price be weighed in
silver.
¹⁶It cannot be bought with the gold of
Ophir,
with precious onyx or sapphires.
¹⁷Neither gold nor crystal can compare
with it,
nor can it be had for jewels of
gold.
¹⁸Coral and jasper are not worthy of
mention;
the price of wisdom is beyond
rubies.
¹⁹The topaz of Cush cannot compare
with it;
it cannot be bought with pure gold.

²⁰"Where then does wisdom come from?
Where does understanding dwell?
²¹It is hidden from the eyes of every
living thing,
concealed even from the birds of
the air.
²²Destruction*c* and Death say,
'Only a rumor of it has reached our
ears.'
²³God understands the way to it
and he alone knows where it dwells,
²⁴for he views the ends of the earth
and sees everything under the
heavens.
²⁵When he established the force of the
wind
and measured out the waters,
²⁶when he made a decree for the rain
and a path for the thunderstorm,
²⁷then he looked at wisdom and
appraised it;
he confirmed it and tested it.
²⁸And he said to man,

*a6 Or lapis lazuli; also in verse 16   b11 Septuagint,
Aquila and Vulgate; Hebrew He dams up
c22 Hebrew Abaddon*

'The fear of the Lord—that is
wisdom,
and to shun evil is understanding.' "

29

Job continued his discourse:

2 "How I long for the months gone by,
for the days when God watched
over me,
3 when his lamp shone upon my head
and by his light I walked through
darkness!
4 Oh, for the days when I was in my
prime,
when God's intimate friendship
blessed my house,
5 when the Almighty was still with me
and my children were around me,
6 when my path was drenched with
cream
and the rock poured out for me
streams of olive oil.

7 "When I went to the gate of the city
and took my seat in the public
square,
8 the young men saw me and stepped
aside
and the old men rose to their feet;
9 the chief men refrained from speaking
and covered their mouths with their
hands;
10 the voices of the nobles were hushed,
and their tongues stuck to the roof
of their mouths.
11 Whoever heard me spoke well of me,
and those who saw me commended
me,
12 because I rescued the poor who cried
for help,
and the fatherless who had none to
assist him.
13 The man who was dying blessed me;
I made the widow's heart sing.
14 I put on righteousness as my clothing;
justice was my robe and my turban.
15 I was eyes to the blind
and feet to the lame.
16 I was a father to the needy;
I took up the case of the stranger.
17 I broke the fangs of the wicked
and snatched the victims from their
teeth.

18 "I thought, 'I will die in my own
house,
my days as numerous as the grains
of sand.
19 My roots will reach to the water,
and the dew will lie all night on my
branches.
20 My glory will remain fresh in me,
the bow ever new in my hand.'

21 "Men listened to me expectantly,
waiting in silence for my counsel.
22 After I had spoken, they spoke no
more;
my words fell gently on their ears.
23 They waited for me as for showers
and drank in my words as the
spring rain.
24 When I smiled at them, they scarcely
believed it;
the light of my face was precious to
them.[a]
25 I chose the way for them and sat as
their chief;
I dwelt as a king among his troops;
I was like one who comforts
mourners.

30

"But now they mock me,
men younger than I,
whose fathers I would have disdained
to put with my sheep dogs.
2 Of what use was the strength of their
hands to me,
since their vigor had gone from
them?
3 Haggard from want and hunger,
they roamed[b] the parched land
in desolate wastelands at night.
4 In the brush they gathered salt herbs,
and their food[c] was the root of the
broom tree.
5 They were banished from their fellow
men,
shouted at as if they were thieves.
6 They were forced to live in the dry
stream beds,
among the rocks and in holes in the
ground.
7 They brayed among the bushes
and huddled in the undergrowth.
8 A base and nameless brood,
they were driven out of the land.

9 "And now their sons mock me in
song;

---

*a*24 The meaning of the Hebrew for this clause is
uncertain.   *b*3 Or *gnawed*   *c*4 Or *fuel*

I have become a byword among
them.
[10]They detest me and keep their
distance;
they do not hesitate to spit in my
face.
[11]Now that God has unstrung my bow
and afflicted me,
they throw off restraint in my
presence.
[12]On my right the tribe[a] attacks;
they lay snares for my feet,
they build their siege ramps against
me.
[13]They break up my road;
they succeed in destroying me—
without anyone's helping them.[b]
[14]They advance as through a gaping
breach;
amid the ruins they come rolling in.
[15]Terrors overwhelm me;
my dignity is driven away as by the
wind,
my safety vanishes like a cloud.

[16]"And now my life ebbs away;
days of suffering grip me.
[17]Night pierces my bones;
my gnawing pains never rest.
[18]In his great power God becomes like
clothing to me[c];
he binds me like the neck of my
garment.
[19]He throws me into the mud,
and I am reduced to dust and ashes.

[20]"I cry out to you, O God, but you do
not answer;
I stand up, but you merely look at
me.
[21]You turn on me ruthlessly;
with the might of your hand you
attack me.
[22]You snatch me up and drive me before
the wind;
you toss me about in the storm.
[23]I know you will bring me down to
death,
to the place appointed for all the
living.

[24]"Surely no one lays a hand on a
broken man
when he cries for help in his
distress.
[25]Have I not wept for those in trouble?

Has not my soul grieved for the
poor?
[26]Yet when I hoped for good, evil came;
when I looked for light, then came
darkness.
[27]The churning inside me never stops;
days of suffering confront me.
[28]I go about blackened, but not by the
sun;
I stand up in the assembly and cry
for help.
[29]I have become a brother of jackals,
a companion of owls.
[30]My skin grows black and peels;
my body burns with fever.
[31]My harp is tuned to mourning,
and my flute to the sound of wailing.

31 "I made a covenant with my eyes
not to look lustfully at a girl.
[2]For what is man's lot from God above,
his heritage from the Almighty on
high?
[3]Is it not ruin for the wicked,
disaster for those who do wrong?
[4]Does he not see my ways
and count my every step?

[5]"If I have walked in falsehood
or my foot has hurried after deceit—
[6]let God weigh me in honest scales
and he will know that I am
blameless—
[7]if my steps have turned from the path,
if my heart has been led by my
eyes,
or if my hands have been defiled,
[8]then may others eat what I have
sown,
and may my crops be uprooted.

[9]"If my heart has been enticed by a
woman,
or if I have lurked at my neighbor's
door,
[10]then may my wife grind another
man's grain,
and may other men sleep with her.
[11]For that would have been shameful,
a sin to be judged.
[12]It is a fire that burns to Destruction[d];
it would have uprooted my harvest.

a 12 The meaning of the Hebrew for this word is
uncertain.   *b 13* Or *me. / 'No one can help him,'
they say.*   *c 18* Hebrew; Septuagint *God grasps my
clothing*   *d 12* Hebrew *Abaddon*

¹³ "If I have denied justice to my
menservants and maidservants
when they had a grievance against
me,

¹⁴ what will I do when God confronts
me?
What will I answer when called to
account?

¹⁵ Did not he who made me in the womb
make them?
Did not the same one form us both
within our mothers?

¹⁶ "If I have denied the desires of the
poor
or let the eyes of the widow grow
weary,

¹⁷ if I have kept my bread to myself,
not sharing it with the fatherless—

¹⁸ but from my youth I reared him as
would a father,

and from my birth I guided the
widow—

¹⁹ if I have seen anyone perishing for
lack of clothing,
or a needy man without a garment,

²⁰ and his heart did not bless me
for warming him with the fleece
from my sheep,

²¹ if I have raised my hand against the
fatherless,
knowing that I had influence in
court,

²² then let my arm fall from the shoulder,
let it be broken off at the joint.

²³ For I dreaded destruction from God,
and for fear of his splendor I could
not do such things.

²⁴ "If I have put my trust in gold
or said to pure gold, 'You are my
security,'

Tuesday

Hormones in Check

Read Job 31:1–4

Sometimes it seems like I'm surrounded by beautiful girls. They're on TV, in movies, even in my school. And since I'm a teenage guy, it would only be normal for me to drool over them, right? Well, sort of.

As a Christian, I have to remember that God told guys not to lust after girls, no matter how beautiful they are. And even though it's not always easy to follow that commandment, I know that's what God wants me to do.

I think that's why Job made a "covenant with [his] eyes." It's not enough to say to myself, *I won't look* when my friends pass around a pornographic magazine or want me to check out a pretty girl. I also have to promise myself to stay away from the kind of stuff that might tempt me. And I have to make sure my friends know where I stand.

I also need to remember, like Job did, that God is paying attention to what I do. If I lust after a girl, God knows it. I can't hide from him or pretend it didn't happen. Life is full of temptations. But God wants us to follow him, not our hormones.

❶ What does it mean to make a "covenant" with yourself? How can you keep the promises you make to yourself?

❷ List 3 ways you can show respect to a guy (if you're a girl) or a girl (if you're a guy).

❸ Ask God to help you resist sexual temptation.

Turn to page 617 for your next devotion.

²⁵ if I have rejoiced over my great
    wealth,
    the fortune my hands had gained,
²⁶ if I have regarded the sun in its
    radiance
    or the moon moving in splendor,
²⁷ so that my heart was secretly enticed
    and my hand offered them a kiss of
    homage,
²⁸ then these also would be sins to be
    judged,
    for I would have been unfaithful to
    God on high.

²⁹ "If I have rejoiced at my enemy's
    misfortune
    or gloated over the trouble that
    came to him—
³⁰ I have not allowed my mouth to sin
    by invoking a curse against his
    life—
³¹ if the men of my household have
    never said,
    'Who has not had his fill of Job's
    meat?'—
³² but no stranger had to spend the night
    in the street,
    for my door was always open to the
    traveler—
³³ if I have concealed my sin as men do,[a]
    by hiding my guilt in my heart
³⁴ because I so feared the crowd
    and so dreaded the contempt of the
    clans
    that I kept silent and would not go
    outside

³⁵ ("Oh, that I had someone to hear me!
    I sign now my defense—let the
    Almighty answer me;
    let my accuser put his indictment in
    writing.
³⁶ Surely I would wear it on my
    shoulder,
    I would put it on like a crown.
³⁷ I would give him an account of my
    every step;
    like a prince I would approach
    him.)—

³⁸ "if my land cries out against me
    and all its furrows are wet with
    tears,
³⁹ if I have devoured its yield without
    payment
    or broken the spirit of its tenants,

⁴⁰ then let briers come up instead of wheat
    and weeds instead of barley."

The words of Job are ended.

Elihu

32 So these three men stopped answering Job, because he was righteous in his own eyes. ²But Elihu son of Barakel the Buzite, of the family of Ram, became very angry with Job for justifying himself rather than God. ³He was also angry with the three friends, because they had found no way to refute Job, and yet had condemned him.[b] ⁴Now Elihu had waited before speaking to Job because they were older than he. ⁵But when he saw that the three men had nothing more to say, his anger was aroused.

⁶So Elihu son of Barakel the Buzite said:

"I am young in years,
    and you are old;
that is why I was fearful,
    not daring to tell you what I know.
⁷ I thought, 'Age should speak;
    advanced years should teach
    wisdom.'
⁸ But it is the spirit[c] in a man,
    the breath of the Almighty, that
    gives him understanding.
⁹ It is not only the old[d] who are wise,
    not only the aged who understand
    what is right.

¹⁰ "Therefore I say: Listen to me;
    I too will tell you what I know.
¹¹ I waited while you spoke,
    I listened to your reasoning;
    while you were searching for words,
¹²   I gave you my full attention.
But not one of you has proved Job
    wrong;
    none of you has answered his
    arguments.
¹³ Do not say, 'We have found wisdom;
    let God refute him, not man.'
¹⁴ But Job has not marshaled his words
    against me,
    and I will not answer him with your
    arguments.

---

[a]33 Or as Adam did   [b]3 Masoretic Text; an ancient Hebrew scribal tradition Job, and so had condemned God   [c]8 Or Spirit; also in verse 18   [d]9 Or many; or great

¹⁵"They are dismayed and have no more
        to say;
    words have failed them.
¹⁶Must I wait, now that they are silent,
        now that they stand there with no
        reply?
¹⁷I too will have my say;
    I too will tell what I know.
¹⁸For I am full of words,
    and the spirit within me compels
        me;
¹⁹inside I am like bottled-up wine,
    like new wineskins ready to burst.
²⁰I must speak and find relief;
    I must open my lips and reply.
²¹I will show partiality to no one,
    nor will I flatter any man;
²²for if I were skilled in flattery,
    my Maker would soon take me
        away.

33 "But now, Job, listen to my
        words;
    pay attention to everything I say.
²I am about to open my mouth;
    my words are on the tip of my
        tongue.
³My words come from an upright
        heart;
    my lips sincerely speak what I
        know.
⁴The Spirit of God has made me;
    the breath of the Almighty gives me
        life.
⁵Answer me then, if you can;
    prepare yourself and confront me.
⁶I am just like you before God;
    I too have been taken from clay.
⁷No fear of me should alarm you,
    nor should my hand be heavy upon
        you.

⁸"But you have said in my hearing—
    I heard the very words—
⁹'I am pure and without sin;
    I am clean and free from guilt.
¹⁰Yet God has found fault with me;
    he considers me his enemy.
¹¹He fastens my feet in shackles;
    he keeps close watch on all my
        paths.'
¹²"But I tell you, in this you are not
        right,
    for God is greater than man.
¹³Why do you complain to him

that he answers none of man's
        words*a*?
¹⁴For God does speak—now one way,
        now another—
    though man may not perceive it.
¹⁵In a dream, in a vision of the night,
    when deep sleep falls on men
        as they slumber in their beds,
¹⁶he may speak in their ears
    and terrify them with warnings,
¹⁷to turn man from wrongdoing
    and keep him from pride,
¹⁸to preserve his soul from the pit,*b*
    his life from perishing by the
        sword.*c*
¹⁹Or a man may be chastened on a bed
        of pain
    with constant distress in his bones,
²⁰so that his very being finds food
        repulsive
    and his soul loathes the choicest
        meal.
²¹His flesh wastes away to nothing,
    and his bones, once hidden, now
        stick out.
²²His soul draws near to the pit,*d*
    and his life to the messengers of
        death.*e*
²³"Yet if there is an angel on his side
    as a mediator, one out of a
        thousand,
    to tell a man what is right for him,
²⁴to be gracious to him and say,
    'Spare him from going down to the
        pit*f*;
    I have found a ransom for him'—
²⁵then his flesh is renewed like a
        child's;
    it is restored as in the days of his
        youth.
²⁶He prays to God and finds favor with
        him,
    he sees God's face and shouts for
        joy;
    he is restored by God to his
        righteous state.
²⁷Then he comes to men and says,
    'I sinned, and perverted what was
        right,
    but I did not get what I deserved.

a13 Or *that he does not answer for any of his
actions*   *b18* Or *preserve him from the grave*   *c18* Or
from crossing the River   *d22* Or *He draws near to
the grave*   *e22* Or *to the dead*   *f24* Or *grave*

28 He redeemed my soul from going
        down to the pit,[a]
    and I will live to enjoy the light.'

29 "God does all these things to a man—
        twice, even three times—
30 to turn back his soul from the pit,[b]
    that the light of life may shine on
        him.

31 "Pay attention, Job, and listen to me;
    be silent, and I will speak.
32 If you have anything to say, answer
        me;
    speak up, for I want you to be
        cleared.
33 But if not, then listen to me;
    be silent, and I will teach you
        wisdom."

34 Then Elihu said:

2 "Hear my words, you wise men;
    listen to me, you men of learning.
3 For the ear tests words
    as the tongue tastes food.
4 Let us discern for ourselves what is
        right;
    let us learn together what is good.

5 "Job says, 'I am innocent,
    but God denies me justice.
6 Although I am right,
    I am considered a liar;
    although I am guiltless,
    his arrow inflicts an incurable
        wound.'
7 What man is like Job,
    who drinks scorn like water?
8 He keeps company with evildoers;
    he associates with wicked men.
9 For he says, 'It profits a man nothing
    when he tries to please God.'

10 "So listen to me, you men of
        understanding.
    Far be it from God to do evil,
    from the Almighty to do wrong.
11 He repays a man for what he has
        done;
    he brings upon him what his
        conduct deserves.
12 It is unthinkable that God would do
        wrong,
    that the Almighty would pervert
        justice.
13 Who appointed him over the earth?

Who put him in charge of the whole
        world?
14 If it were his intention
    and he withdrew his spirit[c] and
        breath,
15 all mankind would perish together
    and man would return to the dust.

16 "If you have understanding, hear this;
    listen to what I say.
17 Can he who hates justice govern?
    Will you condemn the just and
        mighty One?
18 Is he not the One who says to kings,
        'You are worthless,'
    and to nobles, 'You are wicked,'
19 who shows no partiality to princes
    and does not favor the rich over the
        poor,
    for they are all the work of his
        hands?
20 They die in an instant, in the middle
        of the night;
    the people are shaken and they pass
        away;
    the mighty are removed without
        human hand.

21 "His eyes are on the ways of men;
    he sees their every step.
22 There is no dark place, no deep
        shadow,
    where evildoers can hide.
23 God has no need to examine men
        further,
    that they should come before him
        for judgment.
24 Without inquiry he shatters the
        mighty
    and sets up others in their place.
25 Because he takes note of their deeds,
    he overthrows them in the night
    and they are crushed.
26 He punishes them for their wickedness
    where everyone can see them,
27 because they turned from following
        him
    and had no regard for any of his
        ways.
28 They caused the cry of the poor to
        come before him,
    so that he heard the cry of the
        needy.

a28 Or *redeemed me from going down to the grave*
b30 Or *turn him back from the grave*   c14 Or *Spirit*

²⁹But if he remains silent, who can
    condemn him?
  If he hides his face, who can see
    him?
  Yet he is over man and nation alike,
³⁰ to keep a godless man from ruling,
    from laying snares for the people.

³¹"Suppose a man says to God,
    'I am guilty but will offend no more.'
³²Teach me what I cannot see;
  if I have done wrong, I will not do
    so again.'
³³Should God then reward you on your
    terms,
  when you refuse to repent?
  You must decide, not I;
    so tell me what you know.

³⁴"Men of understanding declare,
  wise men who hear me say to me,
³⁵'Job speaks without knowledge;
  his words lack insight.'
³⁶Oh, that Job might be tested to the
    utmost
  for answering like a wicked man!
³⁷To his sin he adds rebellion;
  scornfully he claps his hands
    among us
  and multiplies his words against
    God."

35   Then Elihu said:

²"Do you think this is just?
  You say, 'I will be cleared by God.'ᵃ
³Yet you ask him, 'What profit is it to
    me,ᵇ
  and what do I gain by not sinning?'

⁴"I would like to reply to you
  and to your friends with you.
⁵Look up at the heavens and see;
  gaze at the clouds so high above
    you.
⁶If you sin, how does that affect him?
  If your sins are many, what does
    that do to him?
⁷If you are righteous, what do you give
    to him,
  or what does he receive from your
    hand?
⁸Your wickedness affects only a man
    like yourself,
  and your righteousness only the
    sons of men.

⁹"Men cry out under a load of
    oppression;
  they plead for relief from the arm of
    the powerful.
¹⁰But no one says, 'Where is God my
    Maker,
  who gives songs in the night,
¹¹who teaches more to us than toᶜ the
    beasts of the earth
  and makes us wiser thanᵈ the birds
    of the air?'
¹²He does not answer when men cry out
  because of the arrogance of the
    wicked.
¹³Indeed, God does not listen to their
    empty plea;
  the Almighty pays no attention to
    it.
¹⁴How much less, then, will he listen
  when you say that you do not see
    him,
  that your case is before him
  and you must wait for him,
¹⁵and further, that his anger never
    punishes
  and he does not take the least
    notice of wickedness.ᵉ
¹⁶So Job opens his mouth with empty
    talk;
  without knowledge he multiplies
    words."

36   Elihu continued:

²"Bear with me a little longer and I will
    show you
  that there is more to be said in
    God's behalf.
³I get my knowledge from afar;
  I will ascribe justice to my Maker.
⁴Be assured that my words are not
    false;
  one perfect in knowledge is with
    you.

⁵"God is mighty, but does not despise
    men;
  he is mighty, and firm in his
    purpose.
⁶He does not keep the wicked alive
  but gives the afflicted their rights.

ᵃ2 Or *My righteousness is more than God's*   ᵇ3 Or
you   ᶜ11 Or *teaches us by*   ᵈ11 Or *us wise by*
ᵉ15 Symmachus, Theodotion and Vulgate; the
meaning of the Hebrew for this word is uncertain.

⁷He does not take his eyes off the
righteous;
he enthrones them with kings
and exalts them forever.
⁸But if men are bound in chains,
held fast by cords of affliction,
⁹he tells them what they have
done—
that they have sinned arrogantly.
¹⁰He makes them listen to correction
and commands them to repent of
their evil.
¹¹If they obey and serve him,
they will spend the rest of their
days in prosperity
and their years in contentment.
¹²But if they do not listen,
they will perish by the sword^a
and die without knowledge.

¹³"The godless in heart harbor
resentment;
even when he fetters them, they do
not cry for help.
¹⁴They die in their youth,
among male prostitutes of the
shrines.
¹⁵But those who suffer he delivers in
their suffering;
he speaks to them in their
affliction.

¹⁶"He is wooing you from the jaws of
distress
to a spacious place free from
restriction,
to the comfort of your table laden
with choice food.
¹⁷But now you are laden with the
judgment due the wicked;
judgment and justice have taken
hold of you.
¹⁸Be careful that no one entices you by
riches;
do not let a large bribe turn you
aside.
¹⁹Would your wealth
or even all your mighty efforts
sustain you so you would not be in
distress?
²⁰Do not long for the night,
to drag people away from their
homes.^b
²¹Beware of turning to evil,
which you seem to prefer to
affliction.

²²"God is exalted in his power.
Who is a teacher like him?
²³Who has prescribed his ways for him,
or said to him, 'You have done
wrong'?
²⁴Remember to extol his work,
which men have praised in song.
²⁵All mankind has seen it;
men gaze on it from afar.
²⁶How great is God—beyond our
understanding!
The number of his years is past
finding out.

²⁷"He draws up the drops of water,
which distill as rain to the streams^c;
²⁸the clouds pour down their moisture
and abundant showers fall on
mankind.
²⁹Who can understand how he spreads
out the clouds,
how he thunders from his pavilion?
³⁰See how he scatters his lightning
about him,
bathing the depths of the sea.
³¹This is the way he governs^d the
nations
and provides food in abundance.
³²He fills his hands with lightning
and commands it to strike its mark.
³³His thunder announces the coming
storm;
even the cattle make known its
approach.^e

37 "At this my heart pounds
and leaps from its place.
²Listen! Listen to the roar of his voice,
to the rumbling that comes from his
mouth.
³He unleashes his lightning beneath
the whole heaven
and sends it to the ends of the
earth.
⁴After that comes the sound of his
roar;
he thunders with his majestic voice.
When his voice resounds,
he holds nothing back.
⁵God's voice thunders in marvelous
ways;

---

^a12 Or *will cross the River*   ^b20 The meaning of
the Hebrew for verses 18-20 is uncertain.   ^c27 Or
distill from the mist as rain   ^d31 Or *nourishes*
^e33 Or *announces his coming— / the One zealous
against evil*

he does great things beyond our
understanding.
⁶He says to the snow, 'Fall on the
earth,'
and to the rain shower, 'Be a
mighty downpour.'
⁷So that all men he has made may
know his work,
he stops every man from his labor.ᵃ
⁸The animals take cover;
they remain in their dens.
⁹The tempest comes out from its
chamber,
the cold from the driving winds.
¹⁰The breath of God produces ice,
and the broad waters become
frozen.
¹¹He loads the clouds with moisture;
he scatters his lightning through
them.
¹²At his direction they swirl around
over the face of the whole earth
to do whatever he commands them.
¹³He brings the clouds to punish men,
or to water his earthᵇ and show his
love.

¹⁴"Listen to this, Job;
stop and consider God's wonders.
¹⁵Do you know how God controls the
clouds
and makes his lightning flash?
¹⁶Do you know how the clouds hang
poised,
those wonders of him who is perfect
in knowledge?
¹⁷You who swelter in your clothes
when the land lies hushed under the
south wind,
¹⁸can you join him in spreading out the
skies,
hard as a mirror of cast bronze?

¹⁹"Tell us what we should say to him;
we cannot draw up our case
because of our darkness.
²⁰Should he be told that I want to
speak?
Would any man ask to be
swallowed up?
²¹Now no one can look at the sun,
bright as it is in the skies
after the wind has swept them
clean.
²²Out of the north he comes in golden
splendor;

God comes in awesome majesty.
²³The Almighty is beyond our reach and
exalted in power;
in his justice and great
righteousness, he does not
oppress.
²⁴Therefore, men revere him,
for does he not have regard for all
the wise in heart?ᶜ"

The Lᴏʀᴅ Speaks

38 Then the Lᴏʀᴅ answered Job out
of the storm. He said:

²"Who is this that darkens my counsel
with words without knowledge?
³Brace yourself like a man;
I will question you,
and you shall answer me.

⁴"Where were you when I laid the
earth's foundation?
Tell me, if you understand.

Tough Guy

Huh?

Job 38:1–4
Big, tough bullies are pretty funny to watch when they're confronted with someone bigger and tougher than they are. They get quiet real quick! Job wasn't a big bully, but he had been acting fairly tough up to this point. He's looking for answers and wants God to speak up. Well, God speaks up and probably freaks Job out! Job gets quiet real quick and listens to God's monster truckload of questions. Job learns a lesson: God has all the answers and can be trusted.

⁵Who marked off its dimensions?
Surely you know!
Who stretched a measuring line
across it?
⁶On what were its footings set,
or who laid its cornerstone—
⁷while the morning stars sang together
and all the angelsᵈ shouted for joy?

ᵃ7 Or | he fills all men with fear by his power
ᵇ13 Or to favor them   ᶜ24 Or for he does not have
regard for any who think they are wise.   ᵈ7 Hebrew
the sons of God

⁸"Who shut up the sea behind doors
    when it burst forth from the womb,
⁹when I made the clouds its garment
    and wrapped it in thick darkness,
¹⁰when I fixed limits for it
    and set its doors and bars in place,
¹¹when I said, 'This far you may come
        and no farther;
    here is where your proud waves
        halt'?

¹²"Have you ever given orders to the
        morning,
    or shown the dawn its place,
¹³that it might take the earth by the
        edges
    and shake the wicked out of it?
¹⁴The earth takes shape like clay under
        a seal;
    its features stand out like those of a
        garment.
¹⁵The wicked are denied their light,
    and their upraised arm is broken.

¹⁶"Have you journeyed to the springs of
        the sea
    or walked in the recesses of the
        deep?
¹⁷Have the gates of death been shown
        to you?
    Have you seen the gates of the
        shadow of death*ᵃ*?
¹⁸Have you comprehended the vast
        expanses of the earth?
    Tell me, if you know all this.

¹⁹"What is the way to the abode of
        light?
    And where does darkness reside?
²⁰Can you take them to their places?
    Do you know the paths to their
        dwellings?
²¹Surely you know, for you were
        already born!
    You have lived so many years!

²²"Have you entered the storehouses of
        the snow
    or seen the storehouses of the hail,
²³which I reserve for times of trouble,
    for days of war and battle?
²⁴What is the way to the place where
        the lightning is dispersed,
    or the place where the east winds
        are scattered over the earth?
²⁵Who cuts a channel for the torrents of
        rain,

and a path for the thunderstorm,
²⁶to water a land where no man lives,
    a desert with no one in it,
²⁷to satisfy a desolate wasteland
    and make it sprout with grass?
²⁸Does the rain have a father?
    Who fathers the drops of dew?
²⁹From whose womb comes the ice?
    Who gives birth to the frost from
        the heavens
³⁰when the waters become hard as
        stone,
    when the surface of the deep is
        frozen?

³¹"Can you bind the beautiful*ᵇ* Pleiades?
    Can you loose the cords of Orion?
³²Can you bring forth the constellations
        in their seasons*ᶜ*
    or lead out the Bear*ᵈ* with its cubs?
³³Do you know the laws of the
        heavens?
    Can you set up ⌊God's*ᵉ*⌋ dominion
        over the earth?

³⁴"Can you raise your voice to the
        clouds
    and cover yourself with a flood of
        water?
³⁵Do you send the lightning bolts on
        their way?
    Do they report to you, 'Here we
        are'?
³⁶Who endowed the heart*ᶠ* with wisdom
    or gave understanding to the
        mind*ᶠ*?
³⁷Who has the wisdom to count the
        clouds?
    Who can tip over the water jars of
        the heavens
³⁸when the dust becomes hard
    and the clods of earth stick
        together?

³⁹"Do you hunt the prey for the lioness
    and satisfy the hunger of the lions
⁴⁰when they crouch in their dens
    or lie in wait in a thicket?
⁴¹Who provides food for the raven
    when its young cry out to God
    and wander about for lack of food?

---

*ᵃ*17 Or *gates of deep shadows*   *ᵇ*31 Or *the twinkling;*
or *the chains of the*   *ᶜ*32 Or *the morning star in its*
season   *ᵈ*32 Or *out Leo*   *ᵉ*33 Or *his;* or *their*
*ᶠ*36 The meaning of the Hebrew for this word is
uncertain.

39 "Do you know when the
mountain goats give birth?
Do you watch when the doe bears
her fawn?
[2] Do you count the months till they
bear?
Do you know the time they give
birth?
[3] They crouch down and bring forth
their young;
their labor pains are ended.
[4] Their young thrive and grow strong in
the wilds;
they leave and do not return.

[5] "Who let the wild donkey go free?
Who untied his ropes?
[6] I gave him the wasteland as his home,
the salt flats as his habitat.
[7] He laughs at the commotion in the
town;
he does not hear a driver's shout.
[8] He ranges the hills for his pasture
and searches for any green thing.

[9] "Will the wild ox consent to serve you?
Will he stay by your manger at
night?
[10] Can you hold him to the furrow with
a harness?
Will he till the valleys behind you?
[11] Will you rely on him for his great
strength?
Will you leave your heavy work to
him?
[12] Can you trust him to bring in your
grain
and gather it to your threshing
floor?

[13] "The wings of the ostrich flap joyfully,
but they cannot compare with the
pinions and feathers of the
stork.
[14] She lays her eggs on the ground
and lets them warm in the sand,
[15] unmindful that a foot may crush
them,
that some wild animal may trample
them.
[16] She treats her young harshly, as if
they were not hers;
she cares not that her labor was in
vain,
[17] for God did not endow her with
wisdom

or give her a share of good sense.
[18] Yet when she spreads her feathers to
run,
she laughs at horse and rider.

[19] "Do you give the horse his strength
or clothe his neck with a flowing
mane?
[20] Do you make him leap like a locust,
striking terror with his proud
snorting?
[21] He paws fiercely, rejoicing in his
strength,
and charges into the fray.
[22] He laughs at fear, afraid of nothing;
he does not shy away from the
sword.
[23] The quiver rattles against his side,
along with the flashing spear and
lance.
[24] In frenzied excitement he eats up the
ground;
he cannot stand still when the
trumpet sounds.
[25] At the blast of the trumpet he snorts,
'Aha!'
He catches the scent of battle from
afar,
the shout of commanders and the
battle cry.

[26] "Does the hawk take flight by your
wisdom
and spread his wings toward the
south?
[27] Does the eagle soar at your command
and build his nest on high?
[28] He dwells on a cliff and stays there at
night;
a rocky crag is his stronghold.
[29] From there he seeks out his food;
his eyes detect it from afar.
[30] His young ones feast on blood,
and where the slain are, there is
he."

40 The LORD said to Job:

[2] "Will the one who contends with the
Almighty correct him?
Let him who accuses God answer
him!"

[3] Then Job answered the LORD:

[4] "I am unworthy—how can I reply to
you?

I put my hand over my mouth.
⁵I spoke once, but I have no answer—
  twice, but I will say no more."

⁶Then the LORD spoke to Job out of the storm:

⁷"Brace yourself like a man;
  I will question you,
  and you shall answer me.

⁸"Would you discredit my justice?
  Would you condemn me to justify
    yourself?
⁹Do you have an arm like God's,
  and can your voice thunder like
    his?
¹⁰Then adorn yourself with glory and
    splendor,
  and clothe yourself in honor and
    majesty.
¹¹Unleash the fury of your wrath,
  look at every proud man and bring
    him low,
¹²look at every proud man and humble
    him,
  crush the wicked where they stand.
¹³Bury them all in the dust together;
  shroud their faces in the grave.
¹⁴Then I myself will admit to you
  that your own right hand can save
    you.

¹⁵"Look at the behemoth,[a]
  which I made along with you
  and which feeds on grass like an ox.
¹⁶What strength he has in his loins,
  what power in the muscles of his
    belly!
¹⁷His tail[b] sways like a cedar;
  the sinews of his thighs are
    close-knit.
¹⁸His bones are tubes of bronze,
  his limbs like rods of iron.
¹⁹He ranks first among the works of God,
  yet his Maker can approach him
    with his sword.
²⁰The hills bring him their produce,
  and all the wild animals play
    nearby.
²¹Under the lotus plants he lies,
  hidden among the reeds in the
    marsh.
²²The lotuses conceal him in their
    shadow;
  the poplars by the stream surround
    him.

²³When the river rages, he is not
    alarmed;
  he is secure, though the Jordan
    should surge against his
    mouth.
²⁴Can anyone capture him by the eyes,[c]
  or trap him and pierce his nose?

41 "Can you pull in the leviathan[d]
    with a fishhook
  or tie down his tongue with a rope?
²Can you put a cord through his nose
  or pierce his jaw with a hook?
³Will he keep begging you for mercy?
  Will he speak to you with gentle
    words?
⁴Will he make an agreement with you
  for you to take him as your slave
    for life?
⁵Can you make a pet of him like a bird
  or put him on a leash for your
    girls?
⁶Will traders barter for him?
  Will they divide him up among the
    merchants?
⁷Can you fill his hide with harpoons
  or his head with fishing spears?
⁸If you lay a hand on him,
  you will remember the struggle and
    never do it again!
⁹Any hope of subduing him is false;
  the mere sight of him is
    overpowering.
¹⁰No one is fierce enough to rouse him.
  Who then is able to stand against
    me?
¹¹Who has a claim against me that I
    must pay?
  Everything under heaven belongs to
    me.

¹²"I will not fail to speak of his limbs,
  his strength and his graceful form.
¹³Who can strip off his outer coat?
  Who would approach him with a
    bridle?
¹⁴Who dares open the doors of his
    mouth,
  ringed about with his fearsome
    teeth?
¹⁵His back has[e] rows of shields
  tightly sealed together;

---

[a]15 Possibly the hippopotamus or the elephant
[b]17 Possibly trunk   [c]24 Or *by a water hole*
[d]1 Possibly the crocodile   [e]15 Or *His pride is his*

¹⁶each is so close to the next
that no air can pass between.
¹⁷They are joined fast to one another;
they cling together and cannot be
parted.
¹⁸His snorting throws out flashes of
light;
his eyes are like the rays of dawn.
¹⁹Firebrands stream from his mouth;
sparks of fire shoot out.
²⁰Smoke pours from his nostrils
as from a boiling pot over a fire of
reeds.
²¹His breath sets coals ablaze,
and flames dart from his mouth.
²²Strength resides in his neck;
dismay goes before him.
²³The folds of his flesh are tightly
joined;
they are firm and immovable.
²⁴His chest is hard as rock,
hard as a lower millstone.
²⁵When he rises up, the mighty are
terrified;

they retreat before his thrashing.
²⁶The sword that reaches him has no
effect,
nor does the spear or the dart or the
javelin.
²⁷Iron he treats like straw
and bronze like rotten wood.
²⁸Arrows do not make him flee;
slingstones are like chaff to him.
²⁹A club seems to him but a piece of
straw;
he laughs at the rattling of the
lance.
³⁰His undersides are jagged potsherds,
leaving a trail in the mud like a
threshing sledge.
³¹He makes the depths churn like a
boiling caldron
and stirs up the sea like a pot of
ointment.
³²Behind him he leaves a glistening
wake;
one would think the deep had white
hair.

Wednesday

Who Do You Think You Are?

Read Job 41—42

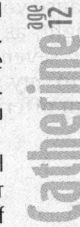

Do you ever have a hard time trusting God? I do. I sometimes think I can handle life all by myself, like I'm the only one who really knows what I need. I forget that God is the One who's really got things under control. In these chapters, God goes into detail about all the things he can do. He reminds Job that everything that happens in the world is in God's control. It's almost like God's asking Job, "Hey, who's the boss here, buddy—you or me?"

I hope I never have to suffer like Job did. But even if I do, I hope I'll remember that God will always help me through my problems in one way or another. I can trust God with everything, because he is ultimately in control of the whole universe.

❶ Why is it sometimes hard to trust that God is in control?

❷ For the next half hour, go someplace where you can be alone and try to live as though you own nothing but the clothes on your back. Don't talk to your family or friends, don't use any of your possessions, don't even pet your dog. If your life were like this all the time, how would you feel about God? When the time is up, re-read these chapters.

❸ Thank God for being in control of your life and everything around you.

Turn to page 621 for your next devotion.

³³ Nothing on earth is his equal—
     a creature without fear.
³⁴ He looks down on all that are
        haughty;
     he is king over all that are proud."

Job

42   Then Job replied to the LORD:

² "I know that you can do all things;
     no plan of yours can be thwarted.
³ You asked, 'Who is this that obscures
        my counsel without
        knowledge?'
    Surely I spoke of things I did not
        understand,
    things too wonderful for me to
        know.

⁴ "You said, 'Listen now, and I will
        speak;
    I will question you,
     and you shall answer me.'
⁵ My ears had heard of you
     but now my eyes have seen you.
⁶ Therefore I despise myself
     and repent in dust and ashes."

Epilogue

⁷ After the LORD had said these things to Job, he said to Eliphaz the Temanite, "I am angry with you and your two friends, because you have not spoken of me what is right, as my servant Job has. ⁸ So now take seven bulls and seven rams and go to my servant Job and sacrifice a burnt offering for yourselves. My servant Job will pray for you, and I will accept his prayer and not deal with you according to your folly. You have not spoken of me what is right, as my servant Job has." ⁹ So Eliphaz the Temanite, Bildad the Shuhite and Zophar the Naamathite did what the LORD told them; and the LORD accepted Job's prayer.

¹⁰ After Job had prayed for his friends, the LORD made him prosperous again and gave him twice as much as he had before. ¹¹ All his brothers and sisters and everyone who had known him before came and ate with him in his house. They comforted and consoled him over all the trouble the LORD had brought upon him, and each one gave him a piece of silver^a and a gold ring.

¹² The LORD blessed the latter part of Job's life more than the first. He had fourteen thousand sheep, six thousand camels, a thousand yoke of oxen and a thousand donkeys. ¹³ And he also had seven sons and three daughters. ¹⁴ The first daughter he named Jemimah, the second Keziah and the third Keren-Happuch. ¹⁵ Nowhere in all the land were there found women as beautiful as Job's daughters, and their father granted them an inheritance along with their brothers.

¹⁶ After this, Job lived a hundred and forty years; he saw his children and their children to the fourth generation. ¹⁷ And so he died, old and full of years.

^a 11 Hebrew *him a kesitah*; a kesitah was a unit of money of unknown weight and value.

Psalms

START

Let's get 2 things straight: 1.) A psalm is a song. Psalm. Song. Same thing. Poetry put to music. The book of Psalms is simply a collection of old, Jewish songs. Songs Jews sang—still sing—during worship, holy days and festivals. Christians have been singing these ancient songs too—though often put to contemporary music instead of harps and organs.

2.) Songs can be pretty boring when they're just read, because songs are meant to be sung. Just reading the lyrics can be as boring as just reading the script of a play. To feel the range of passions in these psalms— the joy, sadness, anger, peace—they've really got to be sung.

The book started as a diary of the prayers and emotions of King David and others (yes, the same David who, as a young man, tossed a rock at and cut the head off of the Philistine champion Goliath). Here are some songs he wrote and prayed to God—"When I feel lonely" (Psalm 22), "When I'm caught in the web of sin" (Psalm 51), "When so-called friends lie about me behind my back" (Psalms 62 and 64), "When I need forgiveness" (Psalm 69), "When I get ticked off at my enemies" (Psalms 109 and 137).

Other songwriters contributed their songs to King David's, and pretty soon this songbook became the Hebrew national songbook—a hymnal for 3,000 years of Jewish worship and a source for lots of newer Christian songs too.

Cast of Characters

David
His wild rise to power— from kid brother to national hero to man-on-the-run— was followed by a kingly rule and his awesome military campaigns that broadened Israel's borders. But it was also full of conflict from within David's own family resulting in a civil war and the messy, premature deaths of some of his children. Through it all, you get the feeling that David and God loved each other tons.

Asaph (AY-saff)
A songwriter. Probably something like a worship leader or song leader (in synagogues today, they're called cantors). Not including David, he wrote the most songs that can be traced to an individual writer.

Sons of Korah (KOH-rah)
Full-time songwriters on Jerusalem's Music Row.

Plain Folks Like Us
As they walked from all over Israel to Jerusalem for big festivals and holidays, they sang what were called "songs of ascent." (Because Jerusalem sat on a hill, all roads to it were uphill.) (Psalms 120—134)

What's UP with That?

Alphabet Songs

In this collection of 150 songs, several of them are acrostic poems. It'd be like a guy named Buzz writing this mini-psalm:

Always God watches me (I'm Buzz).

Before the world was, God was.

Creation is his gift, for free.

Darkness does not frighten me.

. . . and so on. Besides the goofy rhyme, you can see how each line begins with the next letter of the alphabet. If you think for a moment, you can see the purpose behind writing songs like this . . . yes, they're easier to memorize! You can see acrostic songs in Psalms 25, 34, 37, 111, 112, 119 and 145. But, uh, you might not recognize the alphabet—since it's the Hebrew alphabet!

Psalm 119 is *really* different. This chapter has the most verses of any chapter in the Bible, and every verse is about the Word of God. Those funny headings that start each group of 8 verses are actually the names of Hebrew alphabet letters. That's right. Instead of Hebrew children chanting, "Ay, bee, cee, dee, ee, eff, gee . . . " they say "aleph, beth, gimel, daleth, he . . . " So in Psalm 119, the first 8 verses all begin, in Hebrew, with the letter *aleph*. The next 8 verses (9–16) all begin with the Hebrew letter *beth*, and so on.

Try this: Choose any 4 consecutive letters of the alphabet, and write a mini-psalm/song of your own to God in this space. It doesn't have to rhyme, but it can if you want it to; you just have to start each line with the next letter in the alphabet.

_____

_____

_____

_____

Snap shots

- Mostly songs that David probably wrote, with a few from the Sons of Korah *(chapters 1—72)*

- Worship songs mostly by Asaph and by the Sons of Korah *(chapters 73—89)*

- Worship songs celebrating God's reign over all the earth, mostly by unknown authors *(chapters 90—106)*

- Worship songs celebrating God's revelation through his great works and his powerful Word, mostly by unknown authors *(chapters 107—150)*

BOOK I
Psalms 1–41

Psalm 1

¹Blessed is the man
who does not walk in the counsel of
the wicked
or stand in the way of sinners
or sit in the seat of mockers.
²But his delight is in the law of the LORD,
and on his law he meditates day
and night.
³He is like a tree planted by streams of
water,
which yields its fruit in season
and whose leaf does not wither.
Whatever he does prospers.

⁴Not so the wicked!
They are like chaff
that the wind blows away.
⁵Therefore the wicked will not stand in
the judgment,
nor sinners in the assembly of the
righteous.

⁶For the LORD watches over the way of
the righteous,
but the way of the wicked will
perish.

Psalm 2

¹Why do the nations conspire[a]
and the peoples plot in vain?

a1 Hebrew; Septuagint rage

Thursday

Warning Signs

Read Psalm 1

It would be easy to jump into the wrong crowd at school and get into all kinds of bad stuff. But Psalm 1 reminds me that the way of the wicked is a road to destruction.

Of course, that road might *look* really good. When I think about it, I imagine wet cement. Usually you can't tell that cement is wet unless there are signs to warn you. If you don't see the signs, you might just walk right onto the stuff, thinking that it's a safe place to stand. In reality, it's a terrible place that's super hard to get out of.

As Christians, we need to look at the "warning signs" God gives to help us avoid the way of the wicked—like the ones found in Psalm 1. We should watch out for people who don't take God seriously and make sure we don't join in their sinful activities. Instead, we should be sure our words and actions are pleasing to God.

This passage tells us that those who meditate on God's laws will experience God's blessing on what they say and what they do. Now that's something you know you can stand on!

Aaron age 14

What about You?

❶ Think about a time you did something you knew was wrong. Was it worth it? How do you think God helps you choose the right way?

❷ For the next few days, be on the lookout for warning signs—road signs, computer warnings, anything you can find. If you could post these kinds of warning signs on the road of life, where would you put them and what would they say?

❸ Ask God to help you do what is right.

Turn to page 625 for your next devotion.

[2] The kings of the earth take their stand
  and the rulers gather together
 against the LORD
  and against his Anointed One.[a]
[3] "Let us break their chains," they say,
  "and throw off their fetters."

[4] The One enthroned in heaven laughs;
  the Lord scoffs at them.
[5] Then he rebukes them in his anger
  and terrifies them in his wrath,
   saying,
[6] "I have installed my King[b]
  on Zion, my holy hill."

[7] I will proclaim the decree of the LORD:

He said to me, "You are my Son[c];
  today I have become your Father.[d]
[8] Ask of me,
  and I will make the nations your
   inheritance,
  the ends of the earth your
   possession.
[9] You will rule them with an iron
   scepter[e];
  you will dash them to pieces like
   pottery."

[10] Therefore, you kings, be wise;
  be warned, you rulers of the earth.
[11] Serve the LORD with fear
  and rejoice with trembling.
[12] Kiss the Son, lest he be angry
  and you be destroyed in your way,
 for his wrath can flare up in a
   moment.
  Blessed are all who take refuge in
   him.

Psalm 3

A psalm of David. When he fled
from his son Absalom.

[1] O LORD, how many are my foes!
  How many rise up against me!
[2] Many are saying of me,
  "God will not deliver him."   Selah[f]
[3] But you are a shield around me,
   O LORD;
  you bestow glory on me and lift[g] up
   my head.
[4] To the LORD I cry aloud,
  and he answers me from his holy
   hill.   Selah

[5] I lie down and sleep;
  I wake again, because the LORD
   sustains me.
[6] I will not fear the tens of thousands
  drawn up against me on every side.

[7] Arise, O LORD!
  Deliver me, O my God!
 Strike all my enemies on the jaw;
  break the teeth of the wicked.

Tell Me How You Really Feel

Huh?

Psalm 3:7

"Break the teeth of the wicked"—this is not exactly the nicest prayer you've ever heard, but it's a good one for 2 reasons. First, it reminds us that we can be (and should be) honest with God. He doesn't want to hear sugarcoated words if we have super frustrated hearts. Tell him the truth. Second, it teaches us that praying for the defeat of evil is good, especially if our desire is to see God's goodness win. Scholars call such prayers "imprecatory psalms." (Use the term, impress your pastor!)

[8] From the LORD comes deliverance.
  May your blessing be on your
   people.   Selah

Psalm 4

For the director of music. With stringed instruments.
A psalm of David.

[1] Answer me when I call to you,
   O my righteous God.
 Give me relief from my distress;
  be merciful to me and hear my
   prayer.

[2] How long, O men, will you turn my
   glory into shame[h]?

---

[a]2 Or *anointed one* [b]6 Or *king* [c]7 Or *son*; also in
verse 12 [d]7 Or *have begotten you* [e]9 Or *will break
them with a rod of iron* [f]2 A word of uncertain
meaning, occurring frequently in the Psalms;
possibly a musical term [g]3 Or LORD, / *my Glorious
One, who lifts* [h]2 Or *you dishonor my Glorious One*

How long will you love delusions
  and seek false gods*a*?   *Selah*
[3] Know that the LORD has set apart the
  godly for himself;
  the LORD will hear when I call to him.

[4] In your anger do not sin;
  when you are on your beds,
  search your hearts and be silent.
                                    Selah

[5] Offer right sacrifices
  and trust in the LORD.

[6] Many are asking, "Who can show us
  any good?"
  Let the light of your face shine
  upon us, O LORD.
[7] You have filled my heart with greater
  joy
  than when their grain and new wine
  abound.
[8] I will lie down and sleep in peace,
  for you alone, O LORD,
  make me dwell in safety.

Psalm 5

For the director of music. For flutes.
A psalm of David.

[1] Give ear to my words, O LORD,
  consider my sighing.
[2] Listen to my cry for help,
  my King and my God,
  for to you I pray.
[3] In the morning, O LORD, you hear my
  voice;
  in the morning I lay my requests
  before you
  and wait in expectation.

[4] You are not a God who takes pleasure
  in evil;
  with you the wicked cannot dwell.
[5] The arrogant cannot stand in your
  presence;
  you hate all who do wrong.
[6] You destroy those who tell lies;
  bloodthirsty and deceitful men
  the LORD abhors.

[7] But I, by your great mercy,
  will come into your house;
  in reverence will I bow down
  toward your holy temple.
[8] Lead me, O LORD, in your
  righteousness

because of my enemies—
  make straight your way before me.

[9] Not a word from their mouth can be
  trusted;
  their heart is filled with destruction.
  Their throat is an open grave;
  with their tongue they speak deceit.
[10] Declare them guilty, O God!
  Let their intrigues be their downfall.
  Banish them for their many sins,
  for they have rebelled against you.

[11] But let all who take refuge in you be
  glad;
  let them ever sing for joy.
  Spread your protection over them,
  that those who love your name may
  rejoice in you.
[12] For surely, O LORD, you bless the
  righteous;
  you surround them with your favor
  as with a shield.

Psalm 6

For the director of music. With stringed instruments.
According to sheminith.b
A psalm of David.

[1] O LORD, do not rebuke me in your
  anger
  or discipline me in your wrath.
[2] Be merciful to me, LORD, for I am
  faint;
  O LORD, heal me, for my bones are
  in agony.
[3] My soul is in anguish.
  How long, O LORD, how long?

[4] Turn, O LORD, and deliver me;
  save me because of your unfailing
  love.
[5] No one remembers you when he is
  dead.
  Who praises you from the gravec?

[6] I am worn out from groaning;
  all night long I flood my bed with
  weeping
  and drench my couch with tears.
[7] My eyes grow weak with sorrow;
  they fail because of all my foes.

[8] Away from me, all you who do evil,

a2 Or seek lies   bTitle: Probably a musical term
c5 Hebrew Sheol

Hang On!

Huh?

Psalm 6:3

"How long, O LORD" is a regularly repeated phrase in Psalms. It expresses the impatience people feel in tough times. They want so badly for God to fix things, but God often waits. Not that he likes to watch people suffer; he just loves to see them grow. Nothing builds our faith and endurance muscles like problems. So when we cry out, "What are you waiting for?" God often replies, "I am waiting for you to grow. Hang on! I am with you; I love you, and I will not let this last forever."

    for the LORD has heard my weeping.
⁹The LORD has heard my cry for
     mercy;
    the LORD accepts my prayer.
¹⁰All my enemies will be ashamed and
     dismayed;
    they will turn back in sudden
     disgrace.

Psalm 7

A *shiggaion*ᵃ of David, which he sang to the LORD
concerning Cush, a Benjamite.

¹O LORD my God, I take refuge in you;
    save and deliver me from all who
     pursue me,
²or they will tear me like a lion
    and rip me to pieces with no one to
     rescue me.

³O LORD my God, if I have done this
    and there is guilt on my hands—
⁴if I have done evil to him who is at
     peace with me
    or without cause have robbed my
     foe—
⁵then let my enemy pursue and
     overtake me;
    let him trample my life to the
     ground
    and make me sleep in the dust.
                    Selah

⁶Arise, O LORD, in your anger;

rise up against the rage of my
     enemies.
    Awake, my God; decree justice.
⁷Let the assembled peoples gather
     around you.
    Rule over them from on high;
⁸   let the LORD judge the peoples.
  Judge me, O LORD, according to my
     righteousness,
    according to my integrity, O Most
     High.
⁹O righteous God,
    who searches minds and hearts,
  bring to an end the violence of the
     wicked
    and make the righteous secure.

¹⁰My shieldᵇ is God Most High,
    who saves the upright in heart.
¹¹God is a righteous judge,
    a God who expresses his wrath
     every day.
¹²If he does not relent,
    heᶜ will sharpen his sword;
    he will bend and string his bow.
¹³He has prepared his deadly weapons;
    he makes ready his flaming
     arrows.

¹⁴He who is pregnant with evil
    and conceives trouble gives birth to
     disillusionment.
¹⁵He who digs a hole and scoops it out
    falls into the pit he has made.
¹⁶The trouble he causes recoils on
     himself;
    his violence comes down on his
     own head.

¹⁷I will give thanks to the LORD because
    of his righteousness
    and will sing praise to the name of
     the LORD Most High.

Psalm 8

For the director of music. According to *gittith*.ᵈ
A psalm of David.

¹O LORD, our Lord,
    how majestic is your name in all
     the earth!

ᵃTitle: Probably a literary or musical term   ᵇ10 Or
sovereign   ᶜ12 Or *If a man does not repent, / God*
ᵈTitle: Probably a musical term

You have set your glory
  above the heavens.
² From the lips of children and infants
  you have ordained praise*ᵃ*
because of your enemies,
  to silence the foe and the avenger.

³ When I consider your heavens,
  the work of your fingers,
the moon and the stars,
  which you have set in place,
⁴ what is man that you are mindful of
    him,
  the son of man that you care for
    him?
⁵ You made him a little lower than the
    heavenly beings*ᵇ*
  and crowned him with glory and
    honor.

⁶ You made him ruler over the works of
    your hands;
  you put everything under his feet:
⁷ all flocks and herds,
  and the beasts of the field,

⁸ the birds of the air,
  and the fish of the sea,
  all that swim the paths of the seas.

⁹ O LORD, our Lord,
  how majestic is your name in all
    the earth!

Psalm 9*ᶜ*

For the director of music. To the tune of
"The Death of the Son." A psalm of David.

¹ I will praise you, O LORD, with all my
    heart;
  I will tell of all your wonders.
² I will be glad and rejoice in you;
  I will sing praise to your name,
    O Most High.

ᵃ2 Or *strength* *ᵇ5* Or *than God* *ᶜ*Psalms 9 and 10
may have been originally a single acrostic poem,
the stanzas of which begin with the successive
letters of the Hebrew alphabet. In the Septuagint
they constitute one psalm.

Friday

All My Heart!

Read Psalm 9:1–2, 7–11

I'm a member of the boys' choir at my church, and we're supposed to praise God with our songs. The problem is, some of the boys don't even sing. They just act like they're singing. Or they talk and goof around the whole time, which is even worse. Some of the ones who do sing probably just come for the candy we get after choir practice is over.

Sure, there are times when my mind wanders and I don't think about what I'm singing. But God wants my whole attention—and not just when I'm singing. I should praise him with "all my heart" when I'm reading my Bible, sitting in church or wherever I am.

One of my favorite songs is "Our God Is an Awesome God." God is awesome! We should let him know that we really believe it.

Malachi age 12

What about You?

❶ Why do we worship? How can we make sure we're really worshiping God when we sing in church? Besides singing, what are other ways we worship?

❷ Write your own praise song to God. You don't have to show anybody, and you don't even have to sing it. Just sit down with a piece of paper and tell God what he means to you. Then read, sing or pray the song to God.

❸ Ask God to help you give him your full attention.

Turn to page 628 for your next devotion.

[3] My enemies turn back;
　　they stumble and perish before you.
[4] For you have upheld my right and my
　　　cause;
　　you have sat on your throne,
　　　judging righteously.
[5] You have rebuked the nations and
　　　destroyed the wicked;
　　you have blotted out their name for
　　　ever and ever.
[6] Endless ruin has overtaken the enemy,
　　you have uprooted their cities;
　　even the memory of them has
　　　perished.

[7] The LORD reigns forever;
　　he has established his throne for
　　　judgment.
[8] He will judge the world in
　　　righteousness;
　　he will govern the peoples with
　　　justice.
[9] The LORD is a refuge for the oppressed,
　　a stronghold in times of trouble.
[10] Those who know your name will trust
　　　in you,
　　for you, LORD, have never forsaken
　　　those who seek you.

[11] Sing praises to the LORD, enthroned in
　　　Zion;
　　proclaim among the nations what
　　　he has done.
[12] For he who avenges blood remembers;
　　he does not ignore the cry of the
　　　afflicted.

[13] O LORD, see how my enemies persecute
　　　me!
　　Have mercy and lift me up from the
　　　gates of death,
[14] that I may declare your praises
　　in the gates of the Daughter of Zion
　　and there rejoice in your salvation.
[15] The nations have fallen into the pit
　　　they have dug;
　　their feet are caught in the net they
　　　have hidden.
[16] The LORD is known by his justice;
　　the wicked are ensnared by the
　　　work of their hands.
　　　　　　　　　　Higgaion.[a] *Selah*
[17] The wicked return to the grave,[b]
　　all the nations that forget God.
[18] But the needy will not always be
　　　forgotten,

nor the hope of the afflicted ever
　　perish.

[19] Arise, O LORD, let not man triumph;
　　let the nations be judged in your
　　　presence.
[20] Strike them with terror, O LORD;
　　let the nations know they are but
　　　men.　　　　　　　　　　*Selah*

Psalm 10[c]

[1] Why, O LORD, do you stand far off?
　　Why do you hide yourself in times
　　　of trouble?

[2] In his arrogance the wicked man
　　　hunts down the weak,
　　who are caught in the schemes he
　　　devises.
[3] He boasts of the cravings of his heart;
　　he blesses the greedy and reviles the
　　　LORD.
[4] In his pride the wicked does not seek
　　　him;
　　in all his thoughts there is no room
　　　for God.
[5] His ways are always prosperous;
　　he is haughty and your laws are far
　　　from him;
　　he sneers at all his enemies.
[6] He says to himself, "Nothing will
　　　shake me;
　　I'll always be happy and never have
　　　trouble."
[7] His mouth is full of curses and lies
　　　and threats;
　　trouble and evil are under his
　　　tongue.
[8] He lies in wait near the villages;
　　from ambush he murders the
　　　innocent,
　　watching in secret for his victims.
[9] He lies in wait like a lion in cover;
　　he lies in wait to catch the helpless;
　　he catches the helpless and drags
　　　them off in his net.
[10] His victims are crushed, they collapse;
　　they fall under his strength.

[a] 16 Or *Meditation*; possibly a musical notation
[b] 17 Hebrew *Sheol*　　[c] Psalms 9 and 10 may have been
originally a single acrostic poem, the stanzas of
which begin with the successive letters of the
Hebrew alphabet. In the Septuagint they constitute
one psalm.

[11] He says to himself, "God has
          forgotten;
   he covers his face and never sees."

[12] Arise, LORD! Lift up your hand, O God.
   Do not forget the helpless.
[13] Why does the wicked man revile God?
   Why does he say to himself,
      "He won't call me to account"?
[14] But you, O God, do see trouble and
          grief;
   you consider it to take it in hand.
   The victim commits himself to you;
      you are the helper of the fatherless.
[15] Break the arm of the wicked and evil
          man;
   call him to account for his
          wickedness
      that would not be found out.

[16] The LORD is King for ever and ever;
   the nations will perish from his
          land.
[17] You hear, O LORD, the desire of the
          afflicted;
   you encourage them, and you listen
          to their cry,
[18] defending the fatherless and the
          oppressed,
   in order that man, who is of the
          earth, may terrify no more.

Psalm 11

For the director of music. Of David.

[1] In the LORD I take refuge.
   How then can you say to me:
      "Flee like a bird to your mountain.
[2] For look, the wicked bend their bows;
   they set their arrows against the
          strings
   to shoot from the shadows
      at the upright in heart.
[3] When the foundations are being
          destroyed,
   what can the righteous do[a]?"

[4] The LORD is in his holy temple;
   the LORD is on his heavenly throne.
   He observes the sons of men;
      his eyes examine them.
[5] The LORD examines the righteous,
   but the wicked[b] and those who love
          violence
      his soul hates.

God Hates Sin

Psalm 11:5
Think about your parents or someone else who loves you. Because they love you very much, they hate things like drugs and bad language and not trying in school. They can't stand anything that is against your best. God is the same way. He loves us all, but he hates our sinful behavior. Although he is patient and does not always punish sin right away, God will not put up with it forever.

[6] On the wicked he will rain
   fiery coals and burning sulfur;
      a scorching wind will be their lot.

[7] For the LORD is righteous,
   he loves justice;
      upright men will see his face.

Psalm 12

For the director of music. According to *sheminith*.[c]
A psalm of David.

[1] Help, LORD, for the godly are no more;
   the faithful have vanished from
          among men.
[2] Everyone lies to his neighbor;
   their flattering lips speak with
          deception.

[3] May the LORD cut off all flattering
          lips
   and every boastful tongue
[4] that says, "We will triumph with our
          tongues;
   we own our lips[d]—who is our
          master?"

[5] "Because of the oppression of the weak
          and the groaning of the needy,
   I will now arise," says the LORD.
      "I will protect them from those who
          malign them."

---

[a]3 Or *what is the Righteous One doing*   [b]5 Or *The*
LORD, the Righteous One, examines the wicked, /
[c]Title: Probably a musical term   [d]4 Or */ our lips are*
our plowshares

⁶ And the words of the LORD are
     flawless,
     like silver refined in a furnace of
     clay,
     purified seven times.

⁷ O LORD, you will keep us safe
     and protect us from such people
     forever.
⁸ The wicked freely strut about

when what is vile is honored
     among men.

Psalm 13

For the director of music.
A psalm of David.

¹ How long, O LORD? Will you forget me
     forever?

Week end.

What Happens When We Worship?   Read 2 Chronicles 20:1–30 (page 513)

On Friday Malachi reminded us to worship with all our hearts, which makes good sense. After all, it would be weird to go to a roller rink and not skate. Or to go to a game and not cheer. Or to go to church and not sing. We've got to get into it, heart and soul.

But why is it so important? What happens when we worship? Here are four great things:

First, **God** feels good. He loves nothing better than to hear his kids belt out his praises. Your worship brings a huge smile to his face.

Second, **believers** grow through worship. They get in touch with God; they sing words that strengthen their faith; they learn to express themselves without worrying what others think. In other words, singing is good for you—and hey, it's better than eating lima beans.

Third, **outsiders** are drawn to God when we worship. They see our love and start wondering, "What's up with these people? They actually believe God is here!" That's the first step in reaching them. It's like Jesus said: "But I, when I am lifted up from the earth, will draw all men to myself"(John 12:32).

Fourth, **enemies** are defeated. That's the point of the story in 2 Chronicles 20. When God's people faced a huge army, they marched to the battle lines singing. They knew they couldn't win by swinging swords, so they launched worship warheads—and it worked. Check out verse 22. As they began to sing, the Lord ambushed the invaders and they were defeated! So worship hard this weekend—who knows what may happen as a result!

❶ What's your biggest hang-up when it comes to worship? Do you dislike your singing voice? Do you worry about looking like a geek in front of all your friends? What holds you back?

❷ Take a big risk the next time you're at church—worship God with your whole heart. Pretend no one else is there. If you usually don't sing, then sing. If you sing but don't clap, then clap. Try doing something new to really get into worshiping God.

❸ Ask God to make himself real to you as you worship—and to do all 4 of the things above as a result.

Turn to page 630 for your next devotion.

Self-image

Back Stage Pass

Jessica had so much fun in 4th and 5th grade. She had lots of friends and was happy most of the time. She was really good at softball and played shortstop on a local team. When she sang in her church's children's choir, she sang loudly and proudly! But now Jessica is in 7th grade, and things are different. She's still good at softball and singing, but you'd never know it—because she dropped out of both. And she's not happy very often either. Jessica's convinced she's a loser. She's sure that she's not good enough, smart enough, pretty enough, cool enough.

Do you ever feel like Jessica? You know what? That's totally and completely normal! Your body's changing like a Transformer. Your brain is upgrading like an old computer becoming a more current model. Your emotions sometimes feel like a never-ending roller coaster. Your relationship with your parents is probably mutating and twisting and straining and stressing. And your faith, your beliefs about God and Christianity, probably feels like it's been tossed into a microwave—getting zapped and cooked and bombarded with things you don't understand—on it's way to being a little different from the set of beliefs you had as a little kid.

Sometimes all this change, all this topsy-turvy confusion, can make you ask questions about yourself. Lots of teens (like Jessica) really struggle with their self-image (how you think and feel about yourself). Here are some things God wants you to understand:

You are a perfect and special creation of God. God made lots and lots of stuff. But he tells you in the Bible that you are his best work and the most favorite thing he created (Genesis 1:27 and 31, page 4; Ephesians 2:10, page 1425).

God knows everything about you and loves you exactly the way you are. The Bible says that God knew you even before you were born (Jeremiah 1:5, page 877). And it says that God knows absolutely everything there is to know about you—even more than you know about yourself (Psalm 139, page 721). Best of all, the Bible says God loves you the way you are, even with all the changes you're going through!

You are a child of God! That's right: If you've started a relationship with God, he says you are his kid! Knowing that you're a child of the God of the universe should help your self-image a bit, don't you think?!

FAITH

"God doesn't really need us, so why did he create us?"

Great question, and you're not the first to ask it. King David asked pretty much the same thing in Psalm 8:4: "What is man that you are mindful of him, the son of man that you care for him?" Why did God make us? To answer that, we need to know 3 things:

First, and you mentioned this in your question, it wasn't because he needed us. Acts 17:25 says, "[God] . . . is not served by human hands, as if he needed anything."

And he didn't make us because he was lonely. Long before we were here, God the Father already had "company" with his Son and the Holy Spirit, referred to in Genesis 1:26: "Let us make man in our image." All of God's needs for companionship are met within the Trinity. He also didn't make us because he needed people to tell him how great he is. God is totally secure in who he is—and he always has been.

Second, despite not needing us, God chose to create us anyway, out of his great love. Yes, God loved us before he even created us. This concept is bigger than our tiny brains, but it's true; that's what "everlasting" love means. God is love (see 1 John 4:8, page 1532), and because of that love and his wonderful creativity, he made us so we can enjoy all that he is and all that he's done.

Third, God created us to fulfill his eternal plan. I could write pages and pages about this, but let me simply say that God, in his infinite wisdom, chose to make us a part of his eternal plan. What part do we play in this plan? Well, the Bible is full of instructions for how we should live our lives. But here are a few key verses to remember:

"**Love** the LORD your God with all your heart and with all your soul and with all your strength" (Deuteronomy 6:5).

"**Love** your neighbor as yourself" (Matthew 22:39).

"**We are God's workmanship,** created in Christ Jesus to do good works, which God prepared in advance for us to do" (Ephesians 2:10).

Perhaps the most important part we play in God's eternal plan is to point people to eternal life with God—through his Son Jesus Christ.

But it's also important to note that we have a choice in all of this. We're not God's toy soldiers. God gives us freedom of choice. Bottom line: God may not need us, but we certainly need him. I hope you've made the choice to put your trust completely in him—and play an exciting part in his loving, eternal plan.

— Dawson McAllister, a popular youth speaker and writer who hosts a live, nationally-syndicated radio call-in program for students ("Dawson McAllister Live") on Sunday nights.

How long will you hide your face
  from me?
[2] How long must I wrestle with my
  thoughts
  and every day have sorrow in my
  heart?
How long will my enemy triumph
  over me?

[3] Look on me and answer, O LORD my
  God.
  Give light to my eyes, or I will sleep
  in death;
[4] my enemy will say, "I have overcome
  him,"
  and my foes will rejoice when I fall.

[5] But I trust in your unfailing love;
  my heart rejoices in your salvation.
[6] I will sing to the LORD,
  for he has been good to me.

Psalm 14

For the director of music. Of David.

[1] The fool[a] says in his heart,
  "There is no God."
They are corrupt, their deeds are vile;
  there is no one who does good.

[2] The LORD looks down from heaven
  on the sons of men
to see if there are any who understand,
  any who seek God.
[3] All have turned aside,
  they have together become corrupt;
there is no one who does good,
  not even one.

[4] Will evildoers never learn—
  those who devour my people as
    men eat bread
  and who do not call on the LORD?
[5] There they are, overwhelmed with
  dread,
  for God is present in the company
    of the righteous.
[6] You evildoers frustrate the plans of
  the poor,
  but the LORD is their refuge.

[7] Oh, that salvation for Israel would
  come out of Zion!
When the LORD restores the fortunes
  of his people,
  let Jacob rejoice and Israel be glad!

Psalm 15

A psalm of David.

[1] LORD, who may dwell in your
  sanctuary?
  Who may live on your holy hill?

[2] He whose walk is blameless
  and who does what is righteous,
who speaks the truth from his heart
[3]   and has no slander on his tongue,
who does his neighbor no wrong
  and casts no slur on his fellowman,
[4] who despises a vile man
  but honors those who fear the LORD,
who keeps his oath
  even when it hurts,
[5] who lends his money without usury
  and does not accept a bribe against
    the innocent.

He who does these things
  will never be shaken.

Psalm 16

A *miktam*[b] of David.

[1] Keep me safe, O God,
  for in you I take refuge.

[2] I said to the LORD, "You are my Lord;

Perfect Portion

Psalm 16:5
Portion size is an important factor in restaurants. Some places have great food but small portions. Others have bad food and lots of it. The trick is finding great food and a portion size to match. In this verse, David talks about his portion. It's huge and tasty, because it is God himself. God is the portion—the food, the life, the pleasure—of every believer. Other people go for big houses, big cars, big money. Christians go for God; he satisfies our every need.

[a] 1 The Hebrew words rendered *fool* in Psalms denote one who is morally deficient.   [b] Title: Probably a literary or musical term

apart from you I have no good
  thing."
³ As for the saints who are in the
  land,
  they are the glorious ones in whom
  is all my delight.ᵃ
⁴ The sorrows of those will increase
  who run after other gods.
 I will not pour out their libations of
  blood
  or take up their names on my lips.

⁵ LORD, you have assigned me my
  portion and my cup;
  you have made my lot secure.
⁶ The boundary lines have fallen for me
  in pleasant places;
  surely I have a delightful
  inheritance.

⁷ I will praise the LORD, who counsels
  me;
  even at night my heart instructs me.

⁸ I have set the LORD always before
  me.
  Because he is at my right hand,
  I will not be shaken.

⁹ Therefore my heart is glad and my
  tongue rejoices;
  my body also will rest secure,
¹⁰ because you will not abandon me to
  the grave,ᵇ
  nor will you let your Holy Oneᶜ see
  decay.
¹¹ You have madeᵈ known to me the path
  of life;
  you will fill me with joy in your
  presence,
  with eternal pleasures at your right
  hand.

ᵃ3 Or As for the pagan priests who are in the land /
and the nobles in whom all delight, I said:
ᵇ10 Hebrew Sheol   ᶜ10 Or your faithful one   ᵈ11 Or
You will make

Monday

Cross Your Heart?

Read Psalm 15:1–4

Once I promised a friend I wouldn't tell her secret, but then I broke my promise and told it anyway. My friend got so mad at me! And I really can't blame her. I would have been mad too if someone blabbed my secrets all over the place.

My only excuse for telling the secret was that this other friend of mine was really begging me to tell her. At first I said no, but eventually I gave in. So basically I had a choice: I could have one friend upset with me for telling, or I could have the other one upset with me for not telling. I made the wrong choice. I should have kept my promise.

Psalm 15:4 shows us that God likes it when we keep our word—even when that's hard for us to do. God isn't interested in our excuses. He wants our obedience.

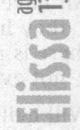

Elissa age 13

❶ Think of a time when it was hard to keep a promise. Did you make the right choice or the wrong choice? How might you handle the situation differently if it came up again?

❷ Write a note to yourself reminding you of one promise you want to keep. Post it on a mirror, the refrigerator, or someplace where you'll see it every day. Keep it there until you follow through on your promise.

❸ Ask God to help you be a trustworthy person.

Turn to page 634 for your next devotion.

Psalm 17

A prayer of David.

[1] Hear, O LORD, my righteous plea;
    listen to my cry.
Give ear to my prayer—
    it does not rise from deceitful lips.
[2] May my vindication come from you;
    may your eyes see what is right.

[3] Though you probe my heart and
        examine me at night,
    though you test me, you will find
        nothing;
    I have resolved that my mouth will
        not sin.
[4] As for the deeds of men—
    by the word of your lips
    I have kept myself
    from the ways of the violent.
[5] My steps have held to your paths;
    my feet have not slipped.

[6] I call on you, O God, for you will
        answer me;
    give ear to me and hear my prayer.
[7] Show the wonder of your great love,
    you who save by your right hand
    those who take refuge in you from
        their foes.
[8] Keep me as the apple of your eye;
    hide me in the shadow of your wings
[9] from the wicked who assail me,
    from my mortal enemies who
        surround me.

[10] They close up their callous hearts,
    and their mouths speak with
        arrogance.
[11] They have tracked me down, they now
        surround me,
    with eyes alert, to throw me to the
        ground.
[12] They are like a lion hungry for prey,
    like a great lion crouching in cover.

[13] Rise up, O LORD, confront them, bring
        them down;
    rescue me from the wicked by your
        sword.
[14] O LORD, by your hand save me from
        such men,
    from men of this world whose
        reward is in this life.

You still the hunger of those you
        cherish;

    their sons have plenty,
    and they store up wealth for their
        children.
[15] And I—in righteousness I will see your
        face;
    when I awake, I will be satisfied
        with seeing your likeness.

Psalm 18

For the director of music. Of David the servant
of the LORD. He sang to the LORD the words of
this song when the LORD delivered him
from the hand of all his enemies and
from the hand of Saul. He said:

[1] I love you, O LORD, my strength.

[2] The LORD is my rock, my fortress and
        my deliverer;
    my God is my rock, in whom I take
        refuge.
    He is my shield and the horn[a] of my
        salvation, my stronghold.
[3] I call to the LORD, who is worthy of
        praise,
    and I am saved from my enemies.

[4] The cords of death entangled me;
    the torrents of destruction
        overwhelmed me.
[5] The cords of the grave[b] coiled around
        me;
    the snares of death confronted me.
[6] In my distress I called to the LORD;
    I cried to my God for help.
From his temple he heard my voice;
    my cry came before him, into his
        ears.

[7] The earth trembled and quaked,
    and the foundations of the
        mountains shook;
    they trembled because he was
        angry.
[8] Smoke rose from his nostrils;
    consuming fire came from his
        mouth,
    burning coals blazed out of it.
[9] He parted the heavens and came
        down;
    dark clouds were under his feet.
[10] He mounted the cherubim and flew;
    he soared on the wings of the wind.

---

a2 Horn here symbolizes strength.   *b5* Hebrew *Sheol*

¹¹ He made darkness his covering, his
canopy around him—
the dark rain clouds of the sky.
¹² Out of the brightness of his presence
clouds advanced,
with hailstones and bolts of
lightning.
¹³ The LORD thundered from heaven;
the voice of the Most High
resounded.ᵃ
¹⁴ He shot his arrows and scattered the
enemies,
great bolts of lightning and routed
them.
¹⁵ The valleys of the sea were exposed
and the foundations of the earth
laid bare
at your rebuke, O LORD,
at the blast of breath from your
nostrils.

¹⁶ He reached down from on high and
took hold of me;
he drew me out of deep waters.
¹⁷ He rescued me from my powerful
enemy,
from my foes, who were too strong
for me.
¹⁸ They confronted me in the day of my
disaster,
but the LORD was my support.
¹⁹ He brought me out into a spacious
place;
he rescued me because he delighted
in me.

²⁰ The LORD has dealt with me according
to my righteousness;
according to the cleanness of my
hands he has rewarded me.
²¹ For I have kept the ways of the
LORD;
I have not done evil by turning
from my God.
²² All his laws are before me;
I have not turned away from his
decrees.
²³ I have been blameless before him
and have kept myself from sin.
²⁴ The LORD has rewarded me according
to my righteousness,
according to the cleanness of my
hands in his sight.

²⁵ To the faithful you show yourself
faithful,
to the blameless you show yourself
blameless,
²⁶ to the pure you show yourself pure,
but to the crooked you show
yourself shrewd.
²⁷ You save the humble
but bring low those whose eyes are
haughty.
²⁸ You, O LORD, keep my lamp burning;
my God turns my darkness into
light.
²⁹ With your help I can advance against
a troopᵇ;
with my God I can scale a wall.

³⁰ As for God, his way is perfect;
the word of the LORD is flawless.
He is a shield
for all who take refuge in him.
³¹ For who is God besides the LORD?
And who is the Rock except our
God?
³² It is God who arms me with strength
and makes my way perfect.
³³ He makes my feet like the feet of a
deer;
he enables me to stand on the
heights.
³⁴ He trains my hands for battle;
my arms can bend a bow of bronze.
³⁵ You give me your shield of victory,
and your right hand sustains me;
you stoop down to make me great.
³⁶ You broaden the path beneath me,
so that my ankles do not turn.

³⁷ I pursued my enemies and overtook
them;
I did not turn back till they were
destroyed.
³⁸ I crushed them so that they could not
rise;
they fell beneath my feet.
³⁹ You armed me with strength for
battle;
you made my adversaries bow at
my feet.
⁴⁰ You made my enemies turn their
backs in flight,
and I destroyed my foes.
⁴¹ They cried for help, but there was no
one to save them—

ᵃ13 Some Hebrew manuscripts and Septuagint (see
also 2 Samuel 22:14); most Hebrew manuscripts
resounded, / amid hailstones and bolts of lightning
ᵇ29 Or *can run through a barricade*

to the LORD, but he did not answer.
⁴² I beat them as fine as dust borne on
the wind;
I poured them out like mud in the
streets.

⁴³ You have delivered me from the
attacks of the people;
you have made me the head of
nations;
people I did not know are subject to
me.
⁴⁴ As soon as they hear me, they obey
me;
foreigners cringe before me.
⁴⁵ They all lose heart;
they come trembling from their
strongholds.

⁴⁶ The LORD lives! Praise be to my
Rock!
Exalted be God my Savior!
⁴⁷ He is the God who avenges me,
who subdues nations under me,
⁴⁸ who saves me from my enemies.
You exalted me above my foes;
from violent men you rescued me.
⁴⁹ Therefore I will praise you among the
nations, O LORD;
I will sing praises to your name.
⁵⁰ He gives his king great victories;
he shows unfailing kindness to his
anointed,
to David and his descendants
forever.

Psalm 19

For the director of music.
A psalm of David.

¹ The heavens declare the glory of God;
the skies proclaim the work of his
hands.
² Day after day they pour forth speech;
night after night they display
knowledge.
³ There is no speech or language
where their voice is not heard.[a]
⁴ Their voice[b] goes out into all the
earth,
their words to the ends of the
world.

In the heavens he has pitched a tent
for the sun,

God's Sky Writing

Huh?

Psalm 19:1–2
A painting in a museum says something
about the artist. The universe around us
says something about the Creator. Outer
space tells us about God's size. The sun tells
us about God's power. Flowers tell us about
God's beauty. Anybody with half a byte of
brain power can see there is a God. Scholars
call this "general revelation."

⁵ which is like a bridegroom coming
forth from his pavilion,
like a champion rejoicing to run his
course.
⁶ It rises at one end of the heavens
and makes its circuit to the other;
nothing is hidden from its heat.

⁷ The law of the LORD is perfect,
reviving the soul.
The statutes of the LORD are
trustworthy,
making wise the simple.
⁸ The precepts of the LORD are right,
giving joy to the heart.
The commands of the LORD are
radiant,
giving light to the eyes.
⁹ The fear of the LORD is pure,
enduring forever.
The ordinances of the LORD are sure
and altogether righteous.
¹⁰ They are more precious than gold,
than much pure gold;
they are sweeter than honey,
than honey from the comb.
¹¹ By them is your servant warned;
in keeping them there is great
reward.

¹² Who can discern his errors?
Forgive my hidden faults.
¹³ Keep your servant also from willful
sins;
may they not rule over me.

---

*a3 Or They have no speech, there are no words; / no
sound is heard from them*   *b4 Septuagint, Jerome
and Syriac; Hebrew line*

Then will I be blameless,
    innocent of great transgression.

14 May the words of my mouth and the
    meditation of my heart
be pleasing in your sight,
    O LORD, my Rock and my Redeemer.

Psalm 20

For the director of music.
A psalm of David.

1 May the LORD answer you when you
    are in distress;
may the name of the God of Jacob
    protect you.
2 May he send you help from the
    sanctuary
and grant you support from Zion.
3 May he remember all your sacrifices
    and accept your burnt offerings.
                           Selah

4 May he give you the desire of your
    heart
and make all your plans succeed.
5 We will shout for joy when you are
    victorious
and will lift up our banners in the
    name of our God.
May the LORD grant all your
    requests.

6 Now I know that the LORD saves his
    anointed;
he answers him from his holy
    heaven
with the saving power of his right
    hand.
7 Some trust in chariots and some in
    horses,
but we trust in the name of the
    LORD our God.
8 They are brought to their knees and
    fall,
but we rise up and stand firm.

Tuesday

Look Around!

Read Psalm 19:1–6

If I'm ever tempted to think that maybe there's no God at all, all I have to do is look around and see the beauty of nature everywhere. Just by looking at people, trees, the sun and everything else in the world, I know there is a God.

God doesn't try to hide from people. He wants us to "see" him in his creation. And he wants Christians to remind nonbelievers that there is a God. God has shown himself to everyone—but some people just don't (or won't) notice until someone tells them where to look.

It's incredible that God created everything—even me! The world God made shows me so much about him: that he's creative, that he's beautiful and that he cares about everything he's made. Most of all, God's creation helps me see that he's real.

Becky age 13

❶ What do the things in your bedroom say about you? Besides the things Becky says in the last paragraph above, what does God's world say about him?

❷ Take a shoe box outdoors and fill it with beautiful things: a leaf, a rock, a flower—whatever you can find. Thank God for every item.

❸ Praise God for his power and majesty.

Turn to page 636 for your next devotion.

9 O LORD, save the king!
  Answer[a] us when we call!

Psalm 21

*For the director of music.
A psalm of David.*

1 O LORD, the king rejoices in your
    strength.
  How great is his joy in the victories
    you give!
2 You have granted him the desire of
    his heart
  and have not withheld the request
    of his lips.   *Selah*
3 You welcomed him with rich blessings
  and placed a crown of pure gold on
    his head.
4 He asked you for life, and you gave it
    to him—
  length of days, for ever and ever.
5 Through the victories you gave, his
    glory is great;
  you have bestowed on him splendor
    and majesty.
6 Surely you have granted him eternal
    blessings
  and made him glad with the joy of
    your presence.
7 For the king trusts in the LORD;
  through the unfailing love of the
    Most High
  he will not be shaken.

8 Your hand will lay hold on all your
    enemies;
  your right hand will seize your foes.
9 At the time of your appearing
  you will make them like a fiery
    furnace.
  In his wrath the LORD will swallow
    them up,
  and his fire will consume them.
10 You will destroy their descendants
    from the earth,
  their posterity from mankind.
11 Though they plot evil against you
  and devise wicked schemes, they
    cannot succeed;
12 for you will make them turn their
    backs
  when you aim at them with drawn
    bow.
13 Be exalted, O LORD, in your strength;

Hey, Didn't Jesus Say That?

Huh?

Psalm 22:1

David wrote these words, but Jesus quoted
them while he was hanging on the cross.
Psalm 22, like many other psalms, is known
as a "Messianic psalm." It tells about
David's life, but it also foretells about Jesus
the Messiah's life. God had a cool way of
taking Old Testament events and using
them like fingers pointing us to Christ. In
literature we call it "foreshadowing." In the
Bible we just call it prophecy. Did you know
there are over 300 prophecies about Jesus
in the Old Testament? That's a lot of "fingers" pointing to Jesus!

we will sing and praise your
  might.

Psalm 22

*For the director of music. To the tune of
"The Doe of the Morning." A psalm of David.*

1 My God, my God, why have you
    forsaken me?
  Why are you so far from saving me,
  so far from the words of my
    groaning?
2 O my God, I cry out by day, but you
    do not answer,
  by night, and am not silent.

3 Yet you are enthroned as the Holy
    One;
  you are the praise of Israel.[b]
4 In you our fathers put their trust;
  they trusted and you delivered
    them.
5 They cried to you and were saved;
  in you they trusted and were not
    disappointed.

6 But I am a worm and not a man,
  scorned by men and despised by the
    people.

*a9 Or save! / O King, answer   b3 Or Yet you are
holy, / enthroned on the praises of Israel*

7 All who see me mock me;
  they hurl insults, shaking their
    heads:
8 "He trusts in the LORD;
  let the LORD rescue him.
 Let him deliver him,
  since he delights in him."

9 Yet you brought me out of the womb;
  you made me trust in you
  even at my mother's breast.
10 From birth I was cast upon you;
  from my mother's womb you have
    been my God.
11 Do not be far from me,
  for trouble is near
  and there is no one to help.

12 Many bulls surround me;
  strong bulls of Bashan encircle me.
13 Roaring lions tearing their prey
  open their mouths wide against me.
14 I am poured out like water,
  and all my bones are out of joint.
 My heart has turned to wax;
  it has melted away within me.
15 My strength is dried up like a
    potsherd,

and my tongue sticks to the roof of
  my mouth;
you lay me*a* in the dust of death.
16 Dogs have surrounded me;
  a band of evil men has encircled
    me,
  they have pierced*b* my hands and
    my feet.
17 I can count all my bones;
  people stare and gloat over me.
18 They divide my garments among
    them
  and cast lots for my clothing.

19 But you, O LORD, be not far off;
  O my Strength, come quickly to
    help me.
20 Deliver my life from the sword,
  my precious life from the power of
    the dogs.
21 Rescue me from the mouth of the
    lions;
  save*c* me from the horns of the wild
    oxen.

*a15 Or / I am laid b16 Some Hebrew manuscripts,
Septuagint and Syriac; most Hebrew manuscripts /
like the lion, c21 Or / you have heard*

Wednesday

Holding On

Read Psalm 22

I was in a musical based on the Psalms, and I sang a song called "My God, My God" based on the first few verses of Psalm 22. It was a pretty intense (and almost depressing) song with lots of questions and complaints to God. David was in bad shape when he wrote Psalm 22. And I can understand why Jesus quoted from this psalm when he was at his lowest point—dying on the cross.

But that's not the end of the psalm, or the end of the story. The ultimate message of the psalm is that God never leaves us—even when other people say he has, or when it seems like we're totally alone. He never abandoned David. He never abandoned Jesus. And he'll never abandon you or me.

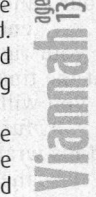

Viannah age 13

❶ What was the loneliest time in your life? How did God help you get through it?

❷ Write down some similarities between David's psalm and Jesus' death. (You can read about the crucifixion in Matthew 27:32–56, page 1183.)

❸ Thank God for always hearing your cries for help.

Turn to page 641 for your next devotion.

22 I will declare your name to my

brothers;

in the congregation I will praise
you.
23 You who fear the LORD, praise him!
All you descendants of Jacob, honor
him!
Revere him, all you descendants of
Israel!
24 For he has not despised or disdained
the suffering of the afflicted one;
he has not hidden his face from him
but has listened to his cry for help.

25 From you comes the theme of my
praise in the great assembly;
before those who fear you[a] will I
fulfill my vows.
26 The poor will eat and be satisfied;
they who seek the LORD will praise
him--
may your hearts live forever!
27 All the ends of the earth
will remember and turn to the LORD,
and all the families of the nations
will bow down before him,
28 for dominion belongs to the LORD
and he rules over the nations.

29 All the rich of the earth will feast and
worship;
all who go down to the dust will
kneel before him—
those who cannot keep themselves
alive.
30 Posterity will serve him;
future generations will be told
about the Lord.
31 They will proclaim his righteousness
to a people yet unborn—
for he has done it.

Psalm 23

A psalm of David.

1 The LORD is my shepherd, I shall not
be in want.
2 He makes me lie down in green
pastures,
he leads me beside quiet waters,
3 he restores my soul.
He guides me in paths of
righteousness
for his name's sake.
4 Even though I walk

through the valley of the shadow of

death,[b]

I will fear no evil,
for you are with me;
your rod and your staff,
they comfort me.

5 You prepare a table before me
in the presence of my enemies.
You anoint my head with oil;
my cup overflows.
6 Surely goodness and love will follow
me
all the days of my life,
and I will dwell in the house of the
LORD
forever.

Psalm 24

Of David. A psalm.

1 The earth is the LORD's, and
everything in it,
the world, and all who live in it;
2 for he founded it upon the seas
and established it upon the waters.

3 Who may ascend the hill of the LORD?
Who may stand in his holy place?
4 He who has clean hands and a pure
heart,
who does not lift up his soul to an
idol
or swear by what is false.[c]
5 He will receive blessing from the LORD
and vindication from God his savior.
6 Such is the generation of those who
seek him,
who seek your face, O God of
Jacob.[d]   *Selah*

7 Lift up your heads, O you gates;
be lifted up, you ancient doors,
that the King of glory may come in.
8 Who is this King of glory?
The LORD strong and mighty,
the LORD mighty in battle.
9 Lift up your heads, O you gates;
lift them up, you ancient doors,
that the King of glory may come in.
10 Who is he, this King of glory?

---

*a25 Hebrew him b4 Or through the darkest valley
c4 Or swear falsely d6 Two Hebrew manuscripts
and Syriac (see also Septuagint); most Hebrew
manuscripts face, Jacob*

Your Own Words

Sometimes the best way to understand a Scripture passage is to put it in your own words. When Psalm 23 was written, most people had a pretty good idea what it was like to be a shepherd. Shepherds were everywhere. They watched out for their sheep and kept them safe. Use your own words to make this psalm come to life for you.

1 The LORD is my shepherd, I shall not be in want. _____

_____

_____

_____

2 He makes me lie down in green pastures, he leads me beside quiet waters, _____

_____

_____

3 he restores my soul. He guides me in paths of righteousness for his name's sake. _____

_____

_____

4 Even though I walk through the valley of the shadow of death, I will fear no evil, for

you are with me; your rod and your staff, they comfort me. _____

_____

_____

_____

5 You prepare a table before me in the presence of my enemies. You anoint my head with oil; my cup overflows. _____

_____

_____

_____

6 Surely goodness and love will follow me all the days of my life, and I will dwell in the house of the LORD forever. _____

_____

_____

_____

The LORD Almighty—
he is the King of glory.   *Selah*

Psalm 25[a]

Of David.

[1] To you, O LORD, I lift up my soul;
[2]   in you I trust, O my God.
Do not let me be put to shame,
  nor let my enemies triumph over me.
[3] No one whose hope is in you
  will ever be put to shame,
but they will be put to shame
  who are treacherous without excuse.

[4] Show me your ways, O LORD,
  teach me your paths;
[5] guide me in your truth and teach me,

for you are God my Savior,
  and my hope is in you all day long.
[6] Remember, O LORD, your great mercy
  and love,
  for they are from of old.
[7] Remember not the sins of my youth
  and my rebellious ways;
according to your love remember me,
  for you are good, O LORD.

[8] Good and upright is the LORD;
  therefore he instructs sinners in his ways.
[9] He guides the humble in what is right
  and teaches them his way.
[10] All the ways of the LORD are loving
  and faithful

[a] This psalm is an acrostic poem, the verses of which begin with the successive letters of the Hebrew alphabet.

for those who keep the demands of
his covenant.
[11] For the sake of your name, O LORD,
forgive my iniquity, though it is
great.
[12] Who, then, is the man that fears the
LORD?
He will instruct him in the way
chosen for him.
[13] He will spend his days in prosperity,
and his descendants will inherit the
land.
[14] The LORD confides in those who fear
him;
he makes his covenant known to
them.
[15] My eyes are ever on the LORD,
for only he will release my feet
from the snare.

[16] Turn to me and be gracious to me,
for I am lonely and afflicted.
[17] The troubles of my heart have
multiplied;
free me from my anguish.
[18] Look upon my affliction and my
distress
and take away all my sins.
[19] See how my enemies have increased
and how fiercely they hate me!
[20] Guard my life and rescue me;
let me not be put to shame,
for I take refuge in you.
[21] May integrity and uprightness protect
me,
because my hope is in you.

[22] Redeem Israel, O God,
from all their troubles!

Psalm 26

Of David.

[1] Vindicate me, O LORD,
for I have led a blameless life;
I have trusted in the LORD
without wavering.
[2] Test me, O LORD, and try me,
examine my heart and my mind;
[3] for your love is ever before me,
and I walk continually in your truth.
[4] I do not sit with deceitful men,
nor do I consort with
hypocrites;
[5] I abhor the assembly of evildoers

and refuse to sit with the wicked.
[6] I wash my hands in innocence,
and go about your altar, O LORD,
[7] proclaiming aloud your praise
and telling of all your wonderful
deeds.
[8] I love the house where you live,
O LORD,
the place where your glory dwells.

[9] Do not take away my soul along with
sinners,
my life with bloodthirsty men,
[10] in whose hands are wicked schemes,
whose right hands are full of bribes.
[11] But I lead a blameless life;
redeem me and be merciful to me.
[12] My feet stand on level ground;
in the great assembly I will praise
the LORD.

Psalm 27

Of David.

[1] The LORD is my light and my
salvation—
whom shall I fear?
The LORD is the stronghold of my life—
of whom shall I be afraid?
[2] When evil men advance against me
to devour my flesh,[a]
when my enemies and my foes attack
me,
they will stumble and fall.
[3] Though an army besiege me,
my heart will not fear;
though war break out against me,
even then will I be confident.

[4] One thing I ask of the LORD,
this is what I seek:
that I may dwell in the house of the
LORD
all the days of my life,
to gaze upon the beauty of the LORD
and to seek him in his temple.
[5] For in the day of trouble
he will keep me safe in his
dwelling;
he will hide me in the shelter of his
tabernacle
and set me high upon a rock.
[6] Then my head will be exalted

---

[a] *2 Or to slander me*

above the enemies who surround me;
at his tabernacle will I sacrifice with
        shouts of joy;
    I will sing and make music to the
        LORD.

[7] Hear my voice when I call, O LORD;
    be merciful to me and answer me.
[8] My heart says of you, "Seek his[a]
        face!"
    Your face, LORD, I will seek.
[9] Do not hide your face from me,
    do not turn your servant away in
        anger;
    you have been my helper.
Do not reject me or forsake me,
    O God my Savior.
[10] Though my father and mother forsake
        me,
    the LORD will receive me.
[11] Teach me your way, O LORD;
    lead me in a straight path
        because of my oppressors.
[12] Do not turn me over to the desire of
        my foes,
    for false witnesses rise up against me,
        breathing out violence.

[13] I am still confident of this:
    I will see the goodness of the LORD
        in the land of the living.
[14] Wait for the LORD;
    be strong and take heart
        and wait for the LORD.

Psalm 28

Of David.

[1] To you I call, O LORD my Rock;
    do not turn a deaf ear to me.
For if you remain silent,
    I will be like those who have gone
        down to the pit.
[2] Hear my cry for mercy
    as I call to you for help,
as I lift up my hands
    toward your Most Holy Place.

[3] Do not drag me away with the wicked,
    with those who do evil,
who speak cordially with their
        neighbors
    but harbor malice in their hearts.
[4] Repay them for their deeds
    and for their evil work;

repay them for what their hands have
        done
    and bring back upon them what
        they deserve.
[5] Since they show no regard for the
        works of the LORD
    and what his hands have done,
he will tear them down
    and never build them up again.

[6] Praise be to the LORD,
    for he has heard my cry for mercy.
[7] The LORD is my strength and my
        shield;
    my heart trusts in him, and I am
        helped.
My heart leaps for joy
    and I will give thanks to him in song.

[8] The LORD is the strength of his people,
    a fortress of salvation for his
        anointed one.
[9] Save your people and bless your
        inheritance;
    be their shepherd and carry them
        forever.

Psalm 29

A psalm of David.

[1] Ascribe to the LORD, O mighty ones,
    ascribe to the LORD glory and
        strength.
[2] Ascribe to the LORD the glory due his
        name;
    worship the LORD in the splendor of
        his[b] holiness.

[3] The voice of the LORD is over the waters;
    the God of glory thunders,
    the LORD thunders over the mighty
        waters.
[4] The voice of the LORD is powerful;
    the voice of the LORD is majestic.
[5] The voice of the LORD breaks the
        cedars;
    the LORD breaks in pieces the cedars
        of Lebanon.
[6] He makes Lebanon skip like a calf,
    Sirion[c] like a young wild ox.
[7] The voice of the LORD strikes
    with flashes of lightning.

---

[a]8 Or *To you, O my heart, he has said, "Seek my*
[b]2 Or *LORD with the splendor of* [c]6 That is, Mount
Hermon

⁸The voice of the LORD shakes the
desert;
the LORD shakes the Desert of
Kadesh.
⁹The voice of the LORD twists the oaks*a*
and strips the forests bare.
And in his temple all cry, "Glory!"

¹⁰The LORD sits*b* enthroned over the
flood;
the LORD is enthroned as King
forever.
¹¹The LORD gives strength to his people;
the LORD blesses his people with
peace.

Psalm 30

*A psalm. A song. For the dedication
of the temple.*c *Of David.*

¹I will exalt you, O LORD,
for you lifted me out of the depths
and did not let my enemies gloat
over me.
²O LORD my God, I called to you for
help
and you healed me.

³O LORD, you brought me up from the
grave*d*;
you spared me from going down
into the pit.

⁴Sing to the LORD, you saints of his;
praise his holy name.
⁵For his anger lasts only a moment,
but his favor lasts a lifetime;
weeping may remain for a night,
but rejoicing comes in the morning.

⁶When I felt secure, I said,
"I will never be shaken."
⁷O LORD, when you favored me,
you made my mountain*e* stand firm;
but when you hid your face,
I was dismayed.

⁸To you, O LORD, I called;
to the Lord I cried for mercy:
⁹"What gain is there in my
destruction,*f*
in my going down into the pit?
Will the dust praise you?
Will it proclaim your faithfulness?

*a9 Or LORD makes the deer give birth   b10 Or sat
cTitle: Or palace   d3 Hebrew Sheol   e7 Or hill
country   f9 Or there if I am silenced*

Thursday

Get a Grip

Read Psalm 29:11

I don't handle stress well. When I was in 7th grade, I got behind on my schoolwork. I got super worried about missing due dates and turning reports in late. I was too stressed out to concentrate, so the work just piled up. I couldn't sleep very well, I felt sort of sick all the time, and I even got into fights with my friends.

I finally figured out I needed God's help to deal with all my stress. And sure enough, God helped me calm down and get a grip on my life again.

No matter how stressful my life gets, I know I can handle it with God's help.

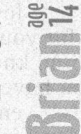

❶ What causes stress in your life? How do you handle stress?

❷ When you feel stressed out, make a list of what's on your mind. Then write down what you can do about those things. Take care of the stuff you can control, and don't worry about the stuff you can't.

❸ Ask God to bring you a sense of peace when you start to lose it.

Turn to page 644 for your next devotion.

¹⁰Hear, O LORD, and be merciful to me;
O LORD, be my help."

¹¹You turned my wailing into dancing;
you removed my sackcloth and
clothed me with joy,
¹²that my heart may sing to you and
not be silent.
O LORD my God, I will give you
thanks forever.

Psalm 31

For the director of music.
A psalm of David.

¹In you, O LORD, I have taken refuge;
let me never be put to shame;
deliver me in your righteousness.
²Turn your ear to me,
come quickly to my rescue;
be my rock of refuge,
a strong fortress to save me.
³Since you are my rock and my
fortress,
for the sake of your name lead and
guide me.
⁴Free me from the trap that is set for
me,
for you are my refuge.
⁵Into your hands I commit my spirit;
redeem me, O LORD, the God of
truth.

⁶I hate those who cling to worthless
idols;
I trust in the LORD.
⁷I will be glad and rejoice in your
love,
for you saw my affliction
and knew the anguish of my soul.
⁸You have not handed me over to the
enemy
but have set my feet in a spacious
place.

⁹Be merciful to me, O LORD, for I am in
distress;
my eyes grow weak with sorrow,
my soul and my body with grief.
¹⁰My life is consumed by anguish
and my years by groaning;
my strength fails because of my
affliction,ᵃ
and my bones grow weak.
¹¹Because of all my enemies,

I am the utter contempt of my
neighbors;
I am a dread to my friends—
those who see me on the street flee
from me.
¹²I am forgotten by them as though I
were dead;
I have become like broken pottery.
¹³For I hear the slander of many;
there is terror on every side;
they conspire against me
and plot to take my life.

¹⁴But I trust in you, O LORD;
I say, "You are my God."
¹⁵My times are in your hands;
deliver me from my enemies
and from those who pursue me.
¹⁶Let your face shine on your servant;
save me in your unfailing love.
¹⁷Let me not be put to shame, O LORD,
for I have cried out to you;
but let the wicked be put to shame
and lie silent in the grave.ᵇ
¹⁸Let their lying lips be silenced,
for with pride and contempt
they speak arrogantly against the
righteous.

¹⁹How great is your goodness,
which you have stored up for those
who fear you,
which you bestow in the sight of
men
on those who take refuge in you.
²⁰In the shelter of your presence you
hide them
from the intrigues of men;
in your dwelling you keep them safe
from accusing tongues.

²¹Praise be to the LORD,
for he showed his wonderful love to
me
when I was in a besieged city.
²²In my alarm I said,
"I am cut off from your sight!"
Yet you heard my cry for mercy
when I called to you for help.

²³Love the LORD, all his saints!
The LORD preserves the faithful,
but the proud he pays back in full.
²⁴Be strong and take heart,
all you who hope in the LORD.

ᵃ10 Or guilt   ᵇ17 Hebrew Sheol

Psalm 32

Of David. A *maskil.*[a]

[1] Blessed is he
  whose transgressions are forgiven,
  whose sins are covered.
[2] Blessed is the man
  whose sin the LORD does not count
    against him
  and in whose spirit is no deceit.

[3] When I kept silent,
  my bones wasted away
  through my groaning all day long.
[4] For day and night
  your hand was heavy upon me;
  my strength was sapped
    as in the heat of summer.   *Selah*

Sin Is a Leech

Huh?

Psalm 32:3–4
Like a bunch of nasty blood-sucking worms,
sin will sap the life right out of you. David
found this out after his sexual sin with
Bathsheba. When he tried to hide what
he'd done, it almost killed him. It cut off
the spiritual strength David drew from his
relationship with God, and he felt the
effects physically. Only through open,
honest confession could the leech of
David's sin be pulled from his soul.

[5] Then I acknowledged my sin to you
  and did not cover up my iniquity.
I said, "I will confess
  my transgressions to the LORD"—
and you forgave
  the guilt of my sin.   *Selah*

[6] Therefore let everyone who is godly
    pray to you
  while you may be found;
surely when the mighty waters rise,
  they will not reach him.
[7] You are my hiding place;
  you will protect me from trouble
  and surround me with songs of
    deliverance.   *Selah*

[8] I will instruct you and teach you in
    the way you should go;
  I will counsel you and watch over
    you.
[9] Do not be like the horse or the mule,
  which have no understanding
but must be controlled by bit and
    bridle
  or they will not come to you.
[10] Many are the woes of the wicked,
  but the LORD's unfailing love
  surrounds the man who trusts in
    him.
[11] Rejoice in the LORD and be glad, you
    righteous;
  sing, all you who are upright in
    heart!

Psalm 33

[1] Sing joyfully to the LORD, you
    righteous;
  it is fitting for the upright to praise
    him.
[2] Praise the LORD with the harp;
  make music to him on the
    ten-stringed lyre.
[3] Sing to him a new song;
  play skillfully, and shout for joy.

[4] For the word of the LORD is right and
    true;
  he is faithful in all he does.
[5] The LORD loves righteousness and
    justice;
  the earth is full of his unfailing love.

[6] By the word of the LORD were the
    heavens made,
  their starry host by the breath of his
    mouth.
[7] He gathers the waters of the sea into
    jars[b];
  he puts the deep into storehouses.
[8] Let all the earth fear the LORD;
  let all the people of the world revere
    him.
[9] For he spoke, and it came to be;
  he commanded, and it stood firm.
[10] The LORD foils the plans of the
    nations;
  he thwarts the purposes of the
    peoples.

[a]Title: Probably a literary or musical term   [b]7 Or *sea
as into a heap*

¹¹But the plans of the LORD stand firm
    forever,
  the purposes of his heart through all
    generations.

¹²Blessed is the nation whose God is the
    LORD,
  the people he chose for his
    inheritance.
¹³From heaven the LORD looks down
  and sees all mankind;
¹⁴from his dwelling place he watches
  all who live on earth—
¹⁵he who forms the hearts of all,
  who considers everything they do.
¹⁶No king is saved by the size of his
    army;
  no warrior escapes by his great
    strength.
¹⁷A horse is a vain hope for
    deliverance;
  despite all its great strength it
    cannot save.
¹⁸But the eyes of the LORD are on those
  who fear him,
  on those whose hope is in his
    unfailing love,
¹⁹to deliver them from death
  and keep them alive in famine.

²⁰We wait in hope for the LORD;
  he is our help and our shield.
²¹In him our hearts rejoice,
  for we trust in his holy name.
²²May your unfailing love rest upon us,
    O LORD,
  even as we put our hope in you.

Psalm 34ᵃ

*Of David. When he pretended to be insane
before Abimelech, who drove
him away, and he left.*

¹I will extol the LORD at all times;
  his praise will always be on my
    lips.
²My soul will boast in the LORD;
  let the afflicted hear and rejoice.
³Glorify the LORD with me;
  let us exalt his name together.

⁴I sought the LORD, and he answered
    me;
  he delivered me from all my fears.
⁵Those who look to him are radiant;

ᵃThis psalm is an acrostic poem, the verses of which
begin with the successive letters of the Hebrew
alphabet.

Friday

Music to His Ears

Read Psalm 33:1–5

You know how hearing your favorite song always makes you smile, even if you're having a bad day? Or how certain situations remind you of different songs? When my dog died, a song from church kept running through my mind. As I hummed it, I started to feel better. Sometimes music's rhythm and joyful notes make me feel so much better.

    Well, when God hears us singing praises to him, it's like he's hearing his song. So if music is the way you like to praise God, that's great with him. Keep on singing!

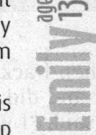

❶ What's your favorite church song? How does it make you feel to sing it?

❷ This week as you go to worship, look closely at the words to the songs you sing. What do they tell you about God? What do they tell you about being a Christian? Sing them as prayers to God.

❸ Thank God for the gift of music.

Turn to page 646 for your next devotion.

their faces are never covered with
shame.
⁶This poor man called, and the LORD
heard him;
he saved him out of all his troubles.
⁷The angel of the LORD encamps
around those who fear him,
and he delivers them.

⁸Taste and see that the LORD is good;
blessed is the man who takes refuge
in him.
⁹Fear the LORD, you his saints,
for those who fear him lack
nothing.
¹⁰The lions may grow weak and hungry,
but those who seek the LORD lack no
good thing.

¹¹Come, my children, listen to me;
I will teach you the fear of the LORD.
¹²Whoever of you loves life
and desires to see many good days,
¹³keep your tongue from evil
and your lips from speaking lies.
¹⁴Turn from evil and do good;
seek peace and pursue it.

¹⁵The eyes of the LORD are on the
righteous
and his ears are attentive to their
cry;
¹⁶the face of the LORD is against those
who do evil,
to cut off the memory of them from
the earth.

¹⁷The righteous cry out, and the LORD
hears them;
he delivers them from all their
troubles.
¹⁸The LORD is close to the brokenhearted
and saves those who are crushed in
spirit.

¹⁹A righteous man may have many
troubles,
but the LORD delivers him from
them all;
²⁰he protects all his bones,
not one of them will be broken.

²¹Evil will slay the wicked;
the foes of the righteous will be
condemned.
²²The LORD redeems his servants;
no one will be condemned who
takes refuge in him.

Psalm 35

Of David.

¹Contend, O LORD, with those who
contend with me;
fight against those who fight
against me.
²Take up shield and buckler;
arise and come to my aid.
³Brandish spear and javelinᵃ
against those who pursue me.
Say to my soul,
"I am your salvation."

⁴May those who seek my life
be disgraced and put to shame;
may those who plot my ruin
be turned back in dismay.
⁵May they be like chaff before the
wind,
with the angel of the LORD driving
them away;
⁶may their path be dark and slippery,
with the angel of the LORD pursuing
them.
⁷Since they hid their net for me
without cause
and without cause dug a pit for me,
⁸may ruin overtake them by surprise—
may the net they hid entangle them,
may they fall into the pit, to their
ruin.
⁹Then my soul will rejoice in the LORD
and delight in his salvation.
¹⁰My whole being will exclaim,
"Who is like you, O LORD?
You rescue the poor from those too
strong for them,
the poor and needy from those who
rob them."

¹¹Ruthless witnesses come forward;
they question me on things I know
nothing about.
¹²They repay me evil for good
and leave my soul forlorn.
¹³Yet when they were ill, I put on
sackcloth
and humbled myself with fasting.
When my prayers returned to me
unanswered,
¹⁴ I went about mourning
as though for my friend or brother.

ᵃ3 Or *and block the way*

I bowed my head in grief
  as though weeping for my mother.
¹⁵But when I stumbled, they gathered in
    glee;
  attackers gathered against me when
    I was unaware.
  They slandered me without ceasing.
¹⁶Like the ungodly they maliciously
    mocked*;*
  they gnashed their teeth at me.

¹⁷O Lord, how long will you look on?
  Rescue my life from their ravages,
  my precious life from these lions.
¹⁸I will give you thanks in the great
    assembly;
  among throngs of people I will
    praise you.

a 16 Septuagint; Hebrew may mean ungodly circle of mockers.

Weekend.

All the Time You Need

Read Psalm 90:12 (page 689)

We each have 1,440 minutes in each day—time to waste or time to use wisely. Brian was really honest last Thursday when he admitted that time often seems too short. It seems like there are too many places to go, people to see and homework assignments to finish in those 1,440 minutes. And that creates stress.

Here's an old story that may help. A teacher once brought a one-gallon can into his classroom and set it before his students. He placed 5 large rocks in the can, filling it to the brim. Showing the can to his students, he asked, "Is this can full?"

They all nodded yes.

"No it's not," the teacher said, "the can is barely half-filled." Then he took out a bag of gravel and poured it into the space around the rocks. Next he produced a bag of sand and poured it into the nooks and crannies around the gravel. Finally, he pulled out a bottle of water and slowly poured it in the can until it reached the top.

"Now the can is full," the teacher said. "But here's the real question: What does this teach you about your busy schedule?"

The students thought for a moment. Then one girl said, "It shows you that no matter how full your schedule, there's always room for more."

"That's not quite it," the teacher responded. "It should teach you that unless you put in the big rocks first, they'll never fit."

If you're like most kids today, you have a ton to do. So ask God to give you a heart of wisdom so you can use your time well. And make sure the "big rocks"—priorities like quiet time, youth group and homework—get into your schedule first. Otherwise, they'll never fit.

❶ What would you say are the 5 most important things God wants you to do with your time next week?

❷ Get your activity calendar and make sure these fit in first. Even obvious things like quiet time and sleep ought to be *written down.*

❸ Pray Psalm 90:12 every day for the next week. Ask God (and your parents) to help you put the "big rocks" where they should be.

Turn to page 648 for your next devotion.

¹⁹Let not those gloat over me
　who are my enemies without cause;
　let not those who hate me without
　　reason
　maliciously wink the eye.
²⁰They do not speak peaceably,
　but devise false accusations
　against those who live quietly in
　　the land.
²¹They gape at me and say, "Aha! Aha!
　With our own eyes we have seen it."

²²O LORD, you have seen this; be not
　　silent.
　Do not be far from me, O Lord.
²³Awake, and rise to my defense!
　Contend for me, my God and Lord.
²⁴Vindicate me in your righteousness,
　　O LORD my God;
　do not let them gloat over me.
²⁵Do not let them think, "Aha, just what
　　we wanted!"
　or say, "We have swallowed him up."

²⁶May all who gloat over my distress
　be put to shame and confusion;
　may all who exalt themselves over me
　be clothed with shame and disgrace.
²⁷May those who delight in my
　　vindication
　shout for joy and gladness;
　may they always say, "The LORD be
　　exalted,
　who delights in the well-being of
　　his servant."
²⁸My tongue will speak of your
　　righteousness
　and of your praises all day long.

Psalm 36

For the director of music.
Of David the servant of the LORD.

¹An oracle is within my heart
　concerning the sinfulness of the
　　wicked:ᵃ
There is no fear of God
　before his eyes.
²For in his own eyes he flatters himself
　too much to detect or hate his sin.
³The words of his mouth are wicked
　and deceitful;
　he has ceased to be wise and to do
　　good.
⁴Even on his bed he plots evil;

he commits himself to a sinful
　　course
　and does not reject what is wrong.

⁵Your love, O LORD, reaches to the
　　heavens,
　your faithfulness to the skies.
⁶Your righteousness is like the mighty
　　mountains,
　your justice like the great deep.
　O LORD, you preserve both man and
　　beast.
⁷　How priceless is your unfailing
　　love!
　Both high and low among men
　findᵇ refuge in the shadow of your
　　wings.
⁸They feast on the abundance of your
　　house;
　you give them drink from your river
　　of delights.
⁹For with you is the fountain of life;
　in your light we see light.

¹⁰Continue your love to those who
　　know you,
　your righteousness to the upright in
　　heart.
¹¹May the foot of the proud not come
　　against me,
　nor the hand of the wicked drive me
　　away.
¹²See how the evildoers lie fallen—
　thrown down, not able to rise!

Psalm 37ᶜ

Of David.

¹Do not fret because of evil men
　or be envious of those who do
　　wrong;
²for like the grass they will soon
　　wither,
　like green plants they will soon die
　　away.

³Trust in the LORD and do good;
　dwell in the land and enjoy safe
　　pasture.
⁴Delight yourself in the LORD

ᵃ1 Or heart: / Sin proceeds from the wicked.
ᵇ7 Or love, O God! / Men find; or love! / Both
heavenly beings and men / find   ᶜThis psalm is an
acrostic poem, the stanzas of which begin with the
successive letters of the Hebrew alphabet.

and he will give you the desires of
    your heart.

⁵ Commit your way to the L<small>ORD</small>;
    trust in him and he will do this:
⁶ He will make your righteousness shine
    like the dawn,
    the justice of your cause like the
      noonday sun.

⁷ Be still before the L<small>ORD</small> and wait
    patiently for him;
    do not fret when men succeed in
      their ways,
    when they carry out their wicked
      schemes.

⁸ Refrain from anger and turn from
    wrath;
    do not fret—it leads only to evil.
⁹ For evil men will be cut off,
    but those who hope in the L<small>ORD</small> will
      inherit the land.

¹⁰ A little while, and the wicked will be
    no more;

though you look for them, they will
    not be found.
¹¹ But the meek will inherit the land
    and enjoy great peace.

¹² The wicked plot against the
    righteous
    and gnash their teeth at them;
¹³ but the Lord laughs at the wicked,
    for he knows their day is coming.

¹⁴ The wicked draw the sword
    and bend the bow
    to bring down the poor and needy,
    to slay those whose ways are
      upright.
¹⁵ But their swords will pierce their own
    hearts,
    and their bows will be broken.

¹⁶ Better the little that the righteous
    have
    than the wealth of many wicked;
¹⁷ for the power of the wicked will be
    broken,
    but the L<small>ORD</small> upholds the righteous.

Monday

No Fair!

Psalm 37:1–4

Sometimes life just doesn't seem fair! My little brother goofs up a lot, and whenever he gets in trouble, it seems like I get punished too. I think my mom likes to cover all the bases. But it makes me mad, because I haven't done anything wrong.

    I need to remember that God sees everything. Even when life seems unfair, God's going to make everything work out in the end. And if I keep my mind on all that God's done for me, maybe I won't get so upset when my life doesn't go how I think it should. I can still "trust in the L<small>ORD</small> and do good," knowing God's got it all under control. It's never fun when we're treated unfairly, but it helps to know we're not alone.

Jeff age 13

❶ Think about a time you were treated unfairly. How did you react? How might you have reacted differently?

❷ The next time you play a game with some friends, try this: Play fair and don't complain about anything! Even if you feel cheated, don't complain. How did your "little experiment" affect your friends? How did it affect you?

❸ Ask God to help you trust him when life doesn't seem fair.

Turn to page 650 for your next devotion.

¹⁸The days of the blameless are known
     to the LORD,
  and their inheritance will endure
     forever.
¹⁹In times of disaster they will not
     wither;
  in days of famine they will enjoy
     plenty.

²⁰But the wicked will perish:
  The LORD's enemies will be like the
     beauty of the fields,
  they will vanish—vanish like smoke.

²¹The wicked borrow and do not repay,
  but the righteous give generously;
²²those the LORD blesses will inherit the
     land,
  but those he curses will be cut off.

²³If the LORD delights in a man's way,
  he makes his steps firm;
²⁴though he stumble, he will not fall,
  for the LORD upholds him with his
     hand.

²⁵I was young and now I am old,
  yet I have never seen the righteous
     forsaken
  or their children begging bread.
²⁶They are always generous and lend
     freely;
  their children will be blessed.

²⁷Turn from evil and do good;
  then you will dwell in the land
     forever.
²⁸For the LORD loves the just
  and will not forsake his faithful ones.

  They will be protected forever,
  but the offspring of the wicked will
     be cut off;
²⁹the righteous will inherit the land
  and dwell in it forever.

³⁰The mouth of the righteous man utters
     wisdom,
  and his tongue speaks what is just.
³¹The law of his God is in his heart;
  his feet do not slip.

³²The wicked lie in wait for the
     righteous,
  seeking their very lives;
³³but the LORD will not leave them in
     their power
  or let them be condemned when
     brought to trial.

³⁴Wait for the LORD
  and keep his way.
  He will exalt you to inherit the land;
  when the wicked are cut off, you
     will see it.

³⁵I have seen a wicked and ruthless man
  flourishing like a green tree in its
     native soil,
³⁶but he soon passed away and was no
     more;
  though I looked for him, he could
     not be found.

³⁷Consider the blameless, observe the
     upright;
  there is a future*a* for the man of
     peace.
³⁸But all sinners will be destroyed;
  the future*b* of the wicked will be cut
     off.

³⁹The salvation of the righteous comes
     from the LORD;
  he is their stronghold in time of
     trouble.
⁴⁰The LORD helps them and delivers
     them;
  he delivers them from the wicked
     and saves them,
  because they take refuge in him.

Psalm 38

A psalm of David. A petition.

¹O LORD, do not rebuke me in your
     anger
  or discipline me in your wrath.
²For your arrows have pierced me,
  and your hand has come down
     upon me.
³Because of your wrath there is no
     health in my body;
  my bones have no soundness
     because of my sin.
⁴My guilt has overwhelmed me
  like a burden too heavy to bear.

⁵My wounds fester and are loathsome
  because of my sinful folly.
⁶I am bowed down and brought very
     low;
  all day long I go about mourning.
⁷My back is filled with searing pain;

a37 Or *there will be posterity* *b38* Or *posterity*

there is no health in my body.
[8] I am feeble and utterly crushed;
   I groan in anguish of heart.

[9] All my longings lie open before you,
   O Lord;
   my sighing is not hidden from you.
[10] My heart pounds, my strength fails me;
   even the light has gone from my
     eyes.
[11] My friends and companions avoid me
   because of my wounds;
   my neighbors stay far away.
[12] Those who seek my life set their traps,
   those who would harm me talk of
     my ruin;
   all day long they plot deception.

[13] I am like a deaf man, who cannot hear,
   like a mute, who cannot open his
     mouth;
[14] I have become like a man who does
   not hear,
   whose mouth can offer no reply.
[15] I wait for you, O LORD;
   you will answer, O Lord my God.
[16] For I said, "Do not let them gloat
   or exalt themselves over me when
     my foot slips."

[17] For I am about to fall,
   and my pain is ever with me.
[18] I confess my iniquity;
   I am troubled by my sin.
[19] Many are those who are my vigorous
   enemies;
   those who hate me without reason
     are numerous.
[20] Those who repay my good with evil
   slander me when I pursue what is
     good.

[21] O LORD, do not forsake me;
   be not far from me, O my God.
[22] Come quickly to help me,
   O Lord my Savior.

Psalm 39

For the director of music. For Jeduthun.
A psalm of David.

[1] I said, "I will watch my ways
   and keep my tongue from sin;
I will put a muzzle on my mouth
   as long as the wicked are in my
     presence."
[2] But when I was silent and still,
   not even saying anything good,

Tuesday

Temper, Temper

Read Psalm 39:1–3

Do you ever get so mad at someone you just have to yell? Me too. Sometimes, when someone really makes me angry, I go beyond yelling. I swear and tell that person exactly what I think of them.

You'd think it would make me feel better to get all that rage out. But it doesn't. I feel guilty for not controlling my temper, or for hurting the person's feelings, or for doing something I know I shouldn't have done.

Even though I know swearing and yelling at other people is wrong, I think the part I really need to work on is controlling my anger in the first place. God can help me do that. Instead of getting angry about things I really can't change, I can ask God to change *me*. I know God can help me be a calmer person. And when I'm not so angry, I probably won't swear as much.

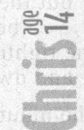
Chris, age 14

What about You?

❶ What really makes you angry?

❷ Think of 3 things you can do to calm down.

❸ Ask God to help you let go of anger.

Turn to page 654 for your next devotion.

my anguish increased.
[3] My heart grew hot within me,
   and as I meditated, the fire burned;
   then I spoke with my tongue:

[4] "Show me, O LORD, my life's end
   and the number of my days;
   let me know how fleeting is my life.
[5] You have made my days a mere
      handbreadth;
   the span of my years is as nothing
      before you.
   Each man's life is but a breath.
                                  Selah

[6] Man is a mere phantom as he goes to
      and fro:
   He bustles about, but only in vain;
   he heaps up wealth, not knowing
      who will get it.

[7] "But now, Lord, what do I look for?
   My hope is in you.
[8] Save me from all my transgressions;
   do not make me the scorn of fools.
[9] I was silent; I would not open my
      mouth,
   for you are the one who has done
      this.
[10] Remove your scourge from me;
   I am overcome by the blow of your
      hand.
[11] You rebuke and discipline men for
      their sin;
   you consume their wealth like a
      moth—
   each man is but a breath.   *Selah*

[12] "Hear my prayer, O LORD,
   listen to my cry for help;
   be not deaf to my weeping.
For I dwell with you as an alien,
   a stranger, as all my fathers were.
[13] Look away from me, that I may
      rejoice again
   before I depart and am no more."

Psalm 40

For the director of music.
Of David. A psalm.

[1] I waited patiently for the LORD;
   he turned to me and heard my cry.
[2] He lifted me out of the slimy pit,
   out of the mud and mire;
   he set my feet on a rock

and gave me a firm place to stand.
[3] He put a new song in my mouth,
   a hymn of praise to our God.
Many will see and fear
   and put their trust in the LORD.

Getting Slimed

Huh?

Psalm 40:2

Everybody gets slimed. Things happen that are neither fun nor your fault. Your parents split, your uncle dies, your house burns, your boyfriend or girlfriend dumps you. This verse reminds us that God rescues slimed (and slimy) people, wipes the goo from their shoes and gives them firm footing in him. Even when your outward life is in the mud, your inward life can be secure in God, the Rock.

---

[4] Blessed is the man
   who makes the LORD his trust,
   who does not look to the proud,
   to those who turn aside to false
      gods.[a]
[5] Many, O LORD my God,
   are the wonders you have done.
The things you planned for us
   no one can recount to you;
   were I to speak and tell of them,
   they would be too many to declare.

[6] Sacrifice and offering you did not
      desire,
   but my ears you have pierced[b,c];
   burnt offerings and sin offerings
   you did not require.
[7] Then I said, "Here I am, I have
      come—
   it is written about me in the scroll.[d]
[8] I desire to do your will, O my God;
   your law is within my heart."
[9] I proclaim righteousness in the great
      assembly;
   I do not seal my lips,
   as you know, O LORD.

a4 Or to falsehood   b6 Hebrew; Septuagint but a body you have prepared for me (see also Symmachus and Theodotion)   c6 Or opened   d7 Or come / with the scroll written for me

Pierced Ears

Huh?

Psalm 40:6
In Bible times, slaves often earned their freedom. But every so often, one who had a great relationship with his master would decide to serve him for life. As a sign of his devotion, he would have his master pierce his ear (see Exodus 21:6, page 96). In this psalm, David says God has pierced his ear. In other words, David is a fired-up, sold-out, God-follower forever. That's what God wants all of us to be. He wants loyal love, not just a little going-through-the-motions religion.

10 I do not hide your righteousness in
    my heart;
  I speak of your faithfulness and
    salvation.
  I do not conceal your love and your
    truth
    from the great assembly.

11 Do not withhold your mercy from me,
    O LORD;
  may your love and your truth
    always protect me.
12 For troubles without number surround
    me;
  my sins have overtaken me, and I
    cannot see.
  They are more than the hairs of my
    head,
  and my heart fails within me.

13 Be pleased, O LORD, to save me;
  O LORD, come quickly to help me.
14 May all who seek to take my life
  be put to shame and confusion;
  may all who desire my ruin
  be turned back in disgrace.
15 May those who say to me, "Aha!
    Aha!"
  be appalled at their own shame.
16 But may all who seek you
  rejoice and be glad in you;
  may those who love your salvation
    always say,
    "The LORD be exalted!"

17 Yet I am poor and needy;
  may the Lord think of me.
  You are my help and my deliverer;
  O my God, do not delay.

Psalm 41

For the director of music.
A psalm of David.

1 Blessed is he who has regard for the
    weak;
  the LORD delivers him in times of
    trouble.
2 The LORD will protect him and
    preserve his life;
  he will bless him in the land
  and not surrender him to the desire
    of his foes.
3 The LORD will sustain him on his
    sickbed
  and restore him from his bed of
    illness.

4 I said, "O LORD, have mercy on me;
  heal me, for I have sinned against
    you."
5 My enemies say of me in malice,
  "When will he die and his name
    perish?"
6 Whenever one comes to see me,
  he speaks falsely, while his heart
    gathers slander;
  then he goes out and spreads it
    abroad.

7 All my enemies whisper together
    against me;
  they imagine the worst for me,
    saying,
8 "A vile disease has beset him;
  he will never get up from the place
    where he lies."
9 Even my close friend, whom I trusted,
  he who shared my bread,
  has lifted up his heel against me.

10 But you, O LORD, have mercy on me;
  raise me up, that I may repay them.
11 I know that you are pleased with me,
  for my enemy does not triumph
    over me.
12 In my integrity you uphold me
  and set me in your presence forever.

13 Praise be to the LORD, the God of
    Israel,

from everlasting to everlasting.
Amen and Amen.

BOOK II
Psalms 42–72

Psalm 42[a]

For the director of music.
A *maskil*[b] of the Sons of Korah.

[1] As the deer pants for streams of water,
    so my soul pants for you, O God.
[2] My soul thirsts for God, for the living
        God.
    When can I go and meet with God?
[3] My tears have been my food
        day and night,
    while men say to me all day long,
        "Where is your God?"
[4] These things I remember
        as I pour out my soul:
    how I used to go with the multitude,
        leading the procession to the house
            of God,
    with shouts of joy and thanksgiving
        among the festive throng.

[5] Why are you downcast, O my soul?
        Why so disturbed within me?
    Put your hope in God,
        for I will yet praise him,
        my Savior and [6] my God.

My[c] soul is downcast within me;
        therefore I will remember you
    from the land of the Jordan,
        the heights of Hermon—from Mount
            Mizar.
[7] Deep calls to deep
        in the roar of your waterfalls;
    all your waves and breakers
        have swept over me.

[8] By day the LORD directs his love,
        at night his song is with me—
    a prayer to the God of my life.

[9] I say to God my Rock,
        "Why have you forgotten me?
    Why must I go about mourning,
        oppressed by the enemy?"
[10] My bones suffer mortal agony
        as my foes taunt me,
    saying to me all day long,
        "Where is your God?"

[11] Why are you downcast, O my soul?
        Why so disturbed within me?
    Put your hope in God,
        for I will yet praise him,
        my Savior and my God.

Psalm 43[a]

[1] Vindicate me, O God,
        and plead my cause against an
            ungodly nation;
    rescue me from deceitful and
        wicked men.
[2] You are God my stronghold.
        Why have you rejected me?
    Why must I go about mourning,
        oppressed by the enemy?
[3] Send forth your light and your truth,
        let them guide me;
    let them bring me to your holy
            mountain,
        to the place where you dwell.
[4] Then will I go to the altar of God,
        to God, my joy and my delight.
    I will praise you with the harp,
        O God, my God.

[5] Why are you downcast, O my soul?
        Why so disturbed within me?
    Put your hope in God,
        for I will yet praise him,
        my Savior and my God.

Psalm 44

For the director of music.
Of the Sons of Korah. A *maskil*.[b]

[1] We have heard with our ears, O God;
        our fathers have told us
    what you did in their days,
        in days long ago.
[2] With your hand you drove out the
            nations
        and planted our fathers;
    you crushed the peoples
        and made our fathers flourish.
[3] It was not by their sword that they
        won the land,

---

[a] In many Hebrew manuscripts Psalms 42 and 43
constitute one psalm.   [b] Title: Probably a literary or
musical term   [c] 5,6 A few Hebrew manuscripts,
Septuagint and Syriac; most Hebrew manuscripts
praise him for his saving help. / [6] O my God, my

nor did their arm bring them
  victory;
it was your right hand, your arm,
  and the light of your face, for you
  loved them.

⁴You are my King and my God,
  who decrees*a* victories for Jacob.
⁵Through you we push back our
  enemies;
  through your name we trample our
  foes.
⁶I do not trust in my bow,
  my sword does not bring me
  victory;
⁷but you give us victory over our
  enemies,
  you put our adversaries to shame.
⁸In God we make our boast all day
  long,
  and we will praise your name
  forever.   *Selah*

⁹But now you have rejected and
  humbled us;
  you no longer go out with our
  armies.

¹⁰You made us retreat before the
  enemy,
  and our adversaries have plundered
  us.
¹¹You gave us up to be devoured like
  sheep
  and have scattered us among the
  nations.
¹²You sold your people for a pittance,
  gaining nothing from their sale.

¹³You have made us a reproach to our
  neighbors,
  the scorn and derision of those
  around us.
¹⁴You have made us a byword among
  the nations;
  the peoples shake their heads at us.
¹⁵My disgrace is before me all day long,
  and my face is covered with shame
¹⁶at the taunts of those who reproach
  and revile me,
  because of the enemy, who is bent
  on revenge.

*a4 Septuagint, Aquila and Syriac; Hebrew King,
O God; / command*

Wednesday

Thirst-quencher

Read Psalm 42

Life isn't always easy, and sometimes we can really get discouraged. But
even in those times, we can be excited about God. This psalm helps me
remember how amazing God really is.

 When my dad died a few years ago, I needed comfort and hope. Nothing in the world could give it to me. The only time I felt any peace was when
I was singing or praying or reading God's Word. I was thirsty for comfort, and
only God could quench my thirst.

 Despite the things that go wrong in our lives, we must seek God. He is
our Rock, our Savior. He is all we need.

Jeff age 15

❶ Think about a time when you needed God's comfort. How did God
take care of you and help you feel better?

❷ Try to go all afternoon without drinking anything. How long can you
last without really craving something to drink? Once you do drink something, concentrate on how great it tastes and how much better you feel
after you've quenched your thirst.

❸ Talk to God. Tell him what's in your heart and ask him to fill you with his love.

Turn to page 659 for your next devotion.

¹⁷All this happened to us,
 though we had not forgotten you
 or been false to your covenant.
¹⁸Our hearts had not turned back;
 our feet had not strayed from your
 path.
¹⁹But you crushed us and made us a
 haunt for jackals
 and covered us over with deep
 darkness.

²⁰If we had forgotten the name of our
 God
 or spread out our hands to a foreign
 god,
²¹would not God have discovered it,
 since he knows the secrets of the
 heart?
²²Yet for your sake we face death all
 day long;
 we are considered as sheep to be
 slaughtered.

²³Awake, O Lord! Why do you sleep?
 Rouse yourself! Do not reject us
 forever.
²⁴Why do you hide your face
 and forget our misery and
 oppression?

²⁵We are brought down to the dust;
 our bodies cling to the ground.
²⁶Rise up and help us;
 redeem us because of your unfailing
 love.

Psalm 45

For the director of music. To the tune of "Lilies."
Of the Sons of Korah. A *maskil.*[a] A wedding song.

¹My heart is stirred by a noble theme
 as I recite my verses for the king;
 my tongue is the pen of a skillful
 writer.

²You are the most excellent of men
 and your lips have been anointed
 with grace,
 since God has blessed you forever.
³Gird your sword upon your side,
 O mighty one;
 clothe yourself with splendor and
 majesty.
⁴In your majesty ride forth victoriously
 in behalf of truth, humility and
 righteousness;

let your right hand display awesome
 deeds.
⁵Let your sharp arrows pierce the
 hearts of the king's enemies;
 let the nations fall beneath your
 feet.
⁶Your throne, O God, will last for ever
 and ever;
 a scepter of justice will be the
 scepter of your kingdom.
⁷You love righteousness and hate
 wickedness;
 therefore God, your God, has set
 you above your companions
 by anointing you with the oil of joy.
⁸All your robes are fragrant with myrrh
 and aloes and cassia;
 from palaces adorned with ivory
 the music of the strings makes you
 glad.
⁹Daughters of kings are among your
 honored women;
 at your right hand is the royal bride
 in gold of Ophir.

¹⁰Listen, O daughter, consider and give
 ear:
 Forget your people and your
 father's house.
¹¹The king is enthralled by your beauty;
 honor him, for he is your lord.
¹²The Daughter of Tyre will come with a
 gift,[b]
 men of wealth will seek your favor.

¹³All glorious is the princess within her
 chamber;
 her gown is interwoven with gold.
¹⁴In embroidered garments she is led to
 the king;
 her virgin companions follow her
 and are brought to you.
¹⁵They are led in with joy and gladness;
 they enter the palace of the king.

¹⁶Your sons will take the place of your
 fathers;
 you will make them princes
 throughout the land.
¹⁷I will perpetuate your memory
 through all generations;
 therefore the nations will praise you
 for ever and ever.

ᵃTitle: Probably a literary or musical term   ᵇ12 Or *A
Tyrian robe is among the gifts*

Psalm 46

For the director of music. Of the Sons of Korah. According to alamoth.[a] *A song.*

¹God is our refuge and strength,
   an ever-present help in trouble.
²Therefore we will not fear, though the
   earth give way
and the mountains fall into the
   heart of the sea,
³though its waters roar and foam
   and the mountains quake with their
   surging.   *Selah*

⁴There is a river whose streams make
   glad the city of God,
   the holy place where the Most High
   dwells.
⁵God is within her, she will not fall;
   God will help her at break of day.
⁶Nations are in uproar, kingdoms fall;
   he lifts his voice, the earth melts.

⁷The LORD Almighty is with us;
   the God of Jacob is our fortress.
                              Selah

⁸Come and see the works of the LORD,
   the desolations he has brought on
   the earth.
⁹He makes wars cease to the ends of
   the earth;
   he breaks the bow and shatters the
   spear,
   he burns the shields[b] with fire.
¹⁰"Be still, and know that I am God;
   I will be exalted among the
   nations,
   I will be exalted in the earth."

¹¹The LORD Almighty is with us;
   the God of Jacob is our fortress.
                              Selah

Psalm 47

*For the director of music.
Of the Sons of Korah. A psalm.*

¹Clap your hands, all you nations;
   shout to God with cries of joy.
²How awesome is the LORD Most High,
   the great King over all the earth!
³He subdued nations under us,
   peoples under our feet.
⁴He chose our inheritance for us,

the pride of Jacob, whom he loved.
                              Selah

⁵God has ascended amid shouts of joy,
   the LORD amid the sounding of
   trumpets.
⁶Sing praises to God, sing praises;
   sing praises to our King, sing
   praises.

⁷For God is the King of all the earth;
   sing to him a psalm[c] of praise.
⁸God reigns over the nations;
   God is seated on his holy throne.
⁹The nobles of the nations assemble
   as the people of the God of
   Abraham,
for the kings[d] of the earth belong to
   God;
   he is greatly exalted.

Psalm 48

A song. A psalm of the Sons of Korah.

¹Great is the LORD, and most worthy of
   praise,
   in the city of our God, his holy
   mountain.
²It is beautiful in its loftiness,
   the joy of the whole earth.
Like the utmost heights of Zaphon[e] is
   Mount Zion,
   the[f] city of the Great King.
³God is in her citadels;
   he has shown himself to be her
   fortress.

⁴When the kings joined forces,
   when they advanced together,
⁵they saw her and were astounded;
   they fled in terror.
⁶Trembling seized them there,
   pain like that of a woman in labor.
⁷You destroyed them like ships of
   Tarshish
   shattered by an east wind.

⁸As we have heard,
   so have we seen
in the city of the LORD Almighty,

---

[a] Title: Probably a musical term *[b]9 Or chariots*
[c]7 Or a maskil (probably a literary or musical term)
[d]9 Or shields *[e]2 Zaphon can refer to a sacred
mountain or the direction north.* *[f]2 Or earth, /
Mount Zion, on the northern side / of the*

in the city of our God:
  God makes her secure forever.

Selah

⁹Within your temple, O God,
  we meditate on your unfailing love.
¹⁰Like your name, O God,
    your praise reaches to the ends of
      the earth;
    your right hand is filled with
      righteousness.
¹¹Mount Zion rejoices,
    the villages of Judah are glad
    because of your judgments.

¹²Walk about Zion, go around her,
    count her towers,
¹³consider well her ramparts,
    view her citadels,
    that you may tell of them to the
      next generation.
¹⁴For this God is our God for ever and
      ever;
    he will be our guide even to the
      end.

Psalm 49

For the director of music.
Of the Sons of Korah. A psalm.

¹Hear this, all you peoples;
    listen, all who live in this world,
²both low and high,
    rich and poor alike:
³My mouth will speak words of
      wisdom;
    the utterance from my heart will
      give understanding.
⁴I will turn my ear to a proverb;
    with the harp I will expound my
      riddle:

⁵Why should I fear when evil days
      come,
    when wicked deceivers surround
      me—
⁶those who trust in their wealth
    and boast of their great riches?
⁷No man can redeem the life of
      another
    or give to God a ransom for him—
⁸the ransom for a life is costly,
    no payment is ever enough—
⁹that he should live on forever
    and not see decay.

¹⁰For all can see that wise men die;
    the foolish and the senseless alike
      perish
    and leave their wealth to others.
¹¹Their tombs will remain their houses*a*
      forever,
    their dwellings for endless
      generations,
    though they had*b* named lands after
      themselves.

¹²But man, despite his riches, does not
      endure;
    he is*c* like the beasts that perish.

¹³This is the fate of those who trust in
      themselves,
    and of their followers, who approve
      their sayings.   *Selah*
¹⁴Like sheep they are destined for the
      grave,*d*
    and death will feed on them.
  The upright will rule over them in the
      morning;
    their forms will decay in the
      grave,*d*
    far from their princely mansions.
¹⁵But God will redeem my life*e* from the
      grave;
    he will surely take me to himself.

Selah

¹⁶Do not be overawed when a man
      grows rich,
    when the splendor of his house
      increases;
¹⁷for he will take nothing with him
      when he dies,
    his splendor will not descend with
      him.
¹⁸Though while he lived he counted
      himself blessed—
    and men praise you when you
      prosper—
¹⁹he will join the generation of his
      fathers,
    who will never see the light of
      life.

²⁰A man who has riches without
      understanding
    is like the beasts that perish.

---

*a*11 Septuagint and Syriac; Hebrew *In their thoughts
their houses will remain*   *b*11 Or / *for they have*
*c*12 Hebrew; Septuagint and Syriac read verse 12
the same as verse 20.   *d*14 Hebrew *Sheol*; also in
verse 15   *e*15 Or *soul*

Psalm 50

A psalm of Asaph.

¹ The Mighty One, God, the LORD,
   speaks and summons the earth
   from the rising of the sun to the
      place where it sets.
² From Zion, perfect in beauty,
   God shines forth.
³ Our God comes and will not be silent;
   a fire devours before him,
   and around him a tempest rages.
⁴ He summons the heavens above,
   and the earth, that he may judge his
      people:
⁵ "Gather to me my consecrated ones,
   who made a covenant with me by
      sacrifice."
⁶ And the heavens proclaim his
      righteousness,
   for God himself is judge.   *Selah*

⁷ "Hear, O my people, and I will speak,
   O Israel, and I will testify against
      you:
   I am God, your God.
⁸ I do not rebuke you for your sacrifices
   or your burnt offerings, which are
      ever before me.
⁹ I have no need of a bull from your
      stall
   or of goats from your pens,
¹⁰ for every animal of the forest is mine,
   and the cattle on a thousand hills.
¹¹ I know every bird in the mountains,
   and the creatures of the field are
      mine.
¹² If I were hungry I would not tell you,
   for the world is mine, and all that is
      in it.
¹³ Do I eat the flesh of bulls
   or drink the blood of goats?
¹⁴ Sacrifice thank offerings to God,
   fulfill your vows to the Most High,
¹⁵ and call upon me in the day of
      trouble;
   I will deliver you, and you will
      honor me."

¹⁶ But to the wicked, God says:

   "What right have you to recite my
      laws
   or take my covenant on your lips?
¹⁷ You hate my instruction
   and cast my words behind you.
¹⁸ When you see a thief, you join with
      him;
   you throw in your lot with
      adulterers.
¹⁹ You use your mouth for evil
   and harness your tongue to deceit.
²⁰ You speak continually against your
      brother
   and slander your own mother's son.
²¹ These things you have done and I kept
      silent;
   you thought I was altogether[a] like
      you.
   But I will rebuke you
   and accuse you to your face.

²² "Consider this, you who forget God,
   or I will tear you to pieces, with
      none to rescue:
²³ He who sacrifices thank offerings
      honors me,
   and he prepares the way
   so that I may show him[b] the
      salvation of God."

Salvation Street

Psalm 50:23

There's a spiritual secret in this verse: Being grateful to God helps you feel closer to him. So when boulder-sized problems block your way, thank God anyway. Thank him for loving you. Thank him for being with you. Let him know that your confidence in him is bigger than your sadness. You'll steam-roll your problems on the path to Salvation Street. Before you know it, God will come to help you.

Psalm 51

*For the director of music. A psalm of David.
When the prophet Nathan came to him after David
had committed adultery with Bathsheba.*

¹ Have mercy on me, O God,
   according to your unfailing love;
   according to your great compassion

---

[a]21 Or *thought the 'I AM' was*   [b]23 Or *and to him
who considers his way / I will show*

blot out my transgressions.
² Wash away all my iniquity
and cleanse me from my sin.

³ For I know my transgressions,
and my sin is always before me.
⁴ Against you, you only, have I sinned
and done what is evil in your sight,
so that you are proved right when you
speak
and justified when you judge.
⁵ Surely I was sinful at birth,
sinful from the time my mother
conceived me.
⁶ Surely you desire truth in the inner
parts*ᵃ*;
you teach*ᵇ* me wisdom in the inmost
place.

⁷ Cleanse me with hyssop, and I will be
clean;

wash me, and I will be whiter than
snow.
⁸ Let me hear joy and gladness;
let the bones you have crushed
rejoice.
⁹ Hide your face from my sins
and blot out all my iniquity.

¹⁰ Create in me a pure heart, O God,
and renew a steadfast spirit within
me.
¹¹ Do not cast me from your presence
or take your Holy Spirit from me.
¹² Restore to me the joy of your
salvation
and grant me a willing spirit, to
sustain me.

*ᵃ6 The meaning of the Hebrew for this phrase is
uncertain.   ᵇ6 Or you desired . . . ; / you taught*

Thursday

The Best of Friends

Read Psalm 51

When I make a mistake, my first reaction is to cover it up. Once, when my brother and I were fighting, I went upstairs and told my mom it was my brother's fault, even though I knew I had something to do with it. She yelled at him and sent him to his room. Well, then I felt guilty. So I told my mom it wasn't all my brother's fault—I was partly to blame too.

When King David sinned against God, he could have ignored his conscience and pretended nothing was wrong. In fact, he did for a while. But God sent the prophet Nathan to tell David to confess his sins, and David finally owned up to his guilt. It's so much better to listen to God and confess what we've done wrong than to live with a guilty conscience.

After I talked to my mom about the situation with my brother, I knew what I had to do to make things right: Ask God for forgiveness and apologize to my brother. That's exactly what I did. And guess what? God forgave me, because he doesn't want sin coming between us. He wants me to be as close to him as a best friend.

Kristin age 12

What about You?

❶ Think about a time you tried to hide your sin from God. How did it feel? Why do you think God wants us to confess our sins to him?

❷ Imagine what it would be like trying to talk to a friend with a cement wall between you. Kind of hard to talk, huh? How is this like your relationship with God when sin comes between you?

❸ Ask the Holy Spirit to show you your sins. Thank God for forgiveness.

Turn to page 662 for your next devotion.

¹³Then I will teach transgressors your
    ways,
    and sinners will turn back to you.
¹⁴Save me from bloodguilt, O God,
    the God who saves me,
    and my tongue will sing of your
    righteousness.
¹⁵O Lord, open my lips,
    and my mouth will declare your
    praise.
¹⁶You do not delight in sacrifice, or I
    would bring it;
    you do not take pleasure in burnt
    offerings.
¹⁷The sacrifices of God are[a] a broken
    spirit;
    a broken and contrite heart,
    O God, you will not despise.

¹⁸In your good pleasure make Zion
    prosper;
    build up the walls of Jerusalem.
¹⁹Then there will be righteous sacrifices,
    whole burnt offerings to delight
    you;
    then bulls will be offered on your
    altar.

Psalm 52

For the director of music. A *maskil*[b] of David.
When Doeg the Edomite had gone to Saul and told
him: "David has gone to the house of Ahimelech."

¹Why do you boast of evil, you mighty
    man?
    Why do you boast all day long,
    you who are a disgrace in the eyes
    of God?
²Your tongue plots destruction;
    it is like a sharpened razor,
    you who practice deceit.
³You love evil rather than good,
    falsehood rather than speaking the
    truth.   *Selah*
⁴You love every harmful word,
    O you deceitful tongue!

⁵Surely God will bring you down to
    everlasting ruin:
    He will snatch you up and tear you
    from your tent;
    he will uproot you from the land of
    the living.   *Selah*
⁶The righteous will see and fear;
    they will laugh at him, saying,

⁷"Here now is the man
    who did not make God his
    stronghold
    but trusted in his great wealth
    and grew strong by destroying
    others!"
⁸But I am like an olive tree
    flourishing in the house of God;
    I trust in God's unfailing love
    for ever and ever.
⁹I will praise you forever for what you
    have done;
    in your name I will hope, for your
    name is good.
    I will praise you in the presence of
    your saints.

Psalm 53

For the director of music. According
to *mahalath*.[c] A *maskil*[b] of David.

¹The fool says in his heart,
    "There is no God."
    They are corrupt, and their ways are
    vile;
    there is no one who does good.

²God looks down from heaven
    on the sons of men
    to see if there are any who
    understand,
    any who seek God.
³Everyone has turned away,
    they have together become corrupt;
    there is no one who does good,
    not even one.

⁴Will the evildoers never learn—
    those who devour my people as
    men eat bread
    and who do not call on God?
⁵There they were, overwhelmed with
    dread,
    where there was nothing to dread.
    God scattered the bones of those who
    attacked you;
    you put them to shame, for God
    despised them.

⁶Oh, that salvation for Israel would
    come out of Zion!

---

a17 Or *My sacrifice, O God, is*   *b*Title: Probably a
literary or musical term   *c*Title: Probably a musical
term

When God restores the fortunes of
his people,
let Jacob rejoice and Israel be glad!

Psalm 54

For the director of music. With stringed instruments.
A *maskil*[a] of David. When the Ziphites had gone to
Saul and said, "Is not David hiding among us?"

¹ Save me, O God, by your name;
vindicate me by your might.
² Hear my prayer, O God;
listen to the words of my mouth.

³ Strangers are attacking me;
ruthless men seek my life—
men without regard for God.   *Selah*

⁴ Surely God is my help;
the Lord is the one who sustains
me.

⁵ Let evil recoil on those who slander
me;
in your faithfulness destroy them.

⁶ I will sacrifice a freewill offering to
you;
I will praise your name, O LORD,
for it is good.
⁷ For he has delivered me from all my
troubles,
and my eyes have looked in
triumph on my foes.

Psalm 55

For the director of music. With stringed
instruments. A *maskil*[a] of David.

¹ Listen to my prayer, O God,
do not ignore my plea;
²   hear me and answer me.
My thoughts trouble me and I am
distraught
³   at the voice of the enemy,
at the stares of the wicked;
for they bring down suffering upon
me
and revile me in their anger.

⁴ My heart is in anguish within me;
the terrors of death assail me.
⁵ Fear and trembling have beset me;
horror has overwhelmed me.
⁶ I said, "Oh, that I had the wings of a
dove!

I would fly away and be at rest—
⁷ I would flee far away
and stay in the desert;   *Selah*
⁸ I would hurry to my place of shelter,
far from the tempest and storm."

⁹ Confuse the wicked, O Lord, confound
their speech,
for I see violence and strife in the
city.
¹⁰ Day and night they prowl about on its
walls;
malice and abuse are within it.
¹¹ Destructive forces are at work in the
city;
threats and lies never leave its
streets.

¹² If an enemy were insulting me,
I could endure it;
if a foe were raising himself against
me,
I could hide from him.
¹³ But it is you, a man like myself,
my companion, my close friend,
¹⁴ with whom I once enjoyed sweet
fellowship
as we walked with the throng at the
house of God.

¹⁵ Let death take my enemies by
surprise;
let them go down alive to the
grave,[b]
for evil finds lodging among
them.

¹⁶ But I call to God,
and the LORD saves me.
¹⁷ Evening, morning and noon
I cry out in distress,
and he hears my voice.
¹⁸ He ransoms me unharmed
from the battle waged against me,
even though many oppose me.
¹⁹ God, who is enthroned forever,
will hear them and afflict them—
Selah
men who never change their ways
and have no fear of God.

²⁰ My companion attacks his friends;
he violates his covenant.
²¹ His speech is smooth as butter,
yet war is in his heart;

[a] Title: Probably a literary or musical term
[b] 15 Hebrew *Sheol*

his words are more soothing than oil,
    yet they are drawn swords.

²²Cast your cares on the LORD
    and he will sustain you;
    he will never let the righteous fall.
²³But you, O God, will bring down the
        wicked
    into the pit of corruption;
    bloodthirsty and deceitful men
        will not live out half their days.

But as for me, I trust in you.

Psalm 56

*For the director of music. To the tune of
"A Dove on Distant Oaks." Of David.
A* miktam.ᵃ *When the Philistines
had seized him in Gath.*

¹Be merciful to me, O God, for men
    hotly pursue me;

all day long they press their attack.
²My slanderers pursue me all day long;
    many are attacking me in their
        pride.

³When I am afraid,
    I will trust in you.
⁴In God, whose word I praise,
    in God I trust; I will not be afraid.
    What can mortal man do to me?

⁵All day long they twist my words;
    they are always plotting to harm
        me.
⁶They conspire, they lurk,
    they watch my steps,
    eager to take my life.

⁷On no account let them escape;
    in your anger, O God, bring down
        the nations.
⁸Record my lament;

ᵃTitle: Probably a literary or musical term

Friday

A Friend to the End

Read Psalm 55:12–16

Imagine you're walking down the hall at school. You spot some of your friends hanging around in front of their lockers. You walk over to say hi. But when you get there, they all walk away. There you are, alone and rejected. It's the worst feeling in the world.

Earlier this year, some of my friends turned against me for no reason. I was so hurt and confused. I didn't know what to do. They wouldn't talk to me about what was going on, and I felt so helpless. But the experience taught me that even though my friends might turn against me, God never will. Even when I felt more lonely than I ever had before, I knew I could trust God to listen to me and comfort me. And he did. When I felt like no one cared, God did. When I felt like I was all alone, God was there.

So when your friends let you down, remember that God is still there, ready to listen to you and help you get through hard times. He will be a friend to the end.

Jenna age 13

❶ Why does it hurt so much when friends reject you?

❷ Is there someone you've turned against? How can you repair your friendship with that person?

❸ When you feel rejected, ask God to comfort you and to show his love to you.

Turn to page 665 for your next devotion.

list my tears on your scroll[a]—
are they not in your record?

[9] Then my enemies will turn back
when I call for help.
By this I will know that God is for
me.
[10] In God, whose word I praise,
in the LORD, whose word I praise—
[11] in God I trust; I will not be afraid.
What can man do to me?

[12] I am under vows to you, O God;
I will present my thank offerings to
you.
[13] For you have delivered me[b] from
death
and my feet from stumbling,
that I may walk before God
in the light of life.[c]

Psalm 57

For the director of music. To the tune of
"Do Not Destroy." Of David. A *miktam*.[d]
When he had fled from Saul into the cave.

[1] Have mercy on me, O God, have
mercy on me,
for in you my soul takes refuge.
I will take refuge in the shadow of
your wings
until the disaster has passed.

[2] I cry out to God Most High,
to God, who fulfills his purpose for
me.
[3] He sends from heaven and saves me,
rebuking those who hotly pursue
me;   *Selah*
God sends his love and his
faithfulness.

[4] I am in the midst of lions;
I lie among ravenous beasts—
men whose teeth are spears and
arrows,
whose tongues are sharp swords.

[5] Be exalted, O God, above the
heavens;
let your glory be over all the earth.

[6] They spread a net for my feet—
I was bowed down in distress.
They dug a pit in my path—
but they have fallen into it
themselves.   *Selah*

[7] My heart is steadfast, O God,
my heart is steadfast;
I will sing and make music.
[8] Awake, my soul!
Awake, harp and lyre!
I will awaken the dawn.

[9] I will praise you, O Lord, among the
nations;
I will sing of you among the
peoples.
[10] For great is your love, reaching to the
heavens;
your faithfulness reaches to the
skies.

[11] Be exalted, O God, above the
heavens;
let your glory be over all the earth.

Psalm 58

For the director of music. To the tune of
"Do Not Destroy." Of David. A *miktam*.[d]

[1] Do you rulers indeed speak justly?
Do you judge uprightly among
men?
[2] No, in your heart you devise injustice,
and your hands mete out violence
on the earth.
[3] Even from birth the wicked go astray;
from the womb they are wayward
and speak lies.
[4] Their venom is like the venom of a
snake,
like that of a cobra that has stopped
its ears,
[5] that will not heed the tune of the
charmer,
however skillful the enchanter may
be.

[6] Break the teeth in their mouths,
O God;
tear out, O LORD, the fangs of the
lions!
[7] Let them vanish like water that flows
away;
when they draw the bow, let their
arrows be blunted.
[8] Like a slug melting away as it moves
along,

[a]8 Or / put my tears in your wineskin   [b]13 Or my
soul   [c]13 Or the land of the living   [d]Title: Probably
a literary or musical term

like a stillborn child, may they not
  see the sun.

⁹Before your pots can feel the heat of
  the thorns—
whether they be green or dry—the
  wicked will be swept away.ᵃ
¹⁰The righteous will be glad when they
  are avenged,
when they bathe their feet in the
  blood of the wicked.
¹¹Then men will say,
  "Surely the righteous still are
  rewarded;
surely there is a God who judges
  the earth."

Psalm 59

For the director of music. To the tune of
"Do Not Destroy." Of David. A *miktam*.ᵇ
When Saul had sent men to watch David's
house in order to kill him.

¹Deliver me from my enemies, O God;
  protect me from those who rise up
  against me.
²Deliver me from evildoers
  and save me from bloodthirsty men.

³See how they lie in wait for me!
  Fierce men conspire against me
for no offense or sin of mine,
  O LORD.
⁴I have done no wrong, yet they are
  ready to attack me.
Arise to help me; look on my
  plight!
⁵O LORD God Almighty, the God of
  Israel,
rouse yourself to punish all the
  nations;
show no mercy to wicked traitors.
     Selah

⁶They return at evening,
  snarling like dogs,
  and prowl about the city.
⁷See what they spew from their
  mouths—
they spew out swords from their
  lips,
  and they say, "Who can hear us?"
⁸But you, O LORD, laugh at them;
  you scoff at all those nations.

⁹O my Strength, I watch for you;

you, O God, are my fortress, ¹⁰my
  loving God.

God will go before me
  and will let me gloat over those
  who slander me.
¹¹But do not kill them, O Lord our
  shield,ᶜ
  or my people will forget.
In your might make them wander
  about,
  and bring them down.
¹²For the sins of their mouths,
  for the words of their lips,
  let them be caught in their pride.
For the curses and lies they utter,
¹³ consume them in wrath,
  consume them till they are no more.
Then it will be known to the ends of
  the earth
  that God rules over Jacob. *Selah*

¹⁴They return at evening,
  snarling like dogs,
  and prowl about the city.
¹⁵They wander about for food
  and howl if not satisfied.
¹⁶But I will sing of your strength,
  in the morning I will sing of your
  love;
for you are my fortress,
  my refuge in times of trouble.
¹⁷O my Strength, I sing praise to you;
  you, O God, are my fortress, my
  loving God.

Psalm 60

For the director of music. To the tune of "The Lily
of the Covenant." A *miktam*ᵇ of David. For teaching.
When he fought Aram Naharaimᵈ and Aram Zobah,ᵉ
and when Joab returned and struck down twelve
thousand Edomites in the Valley of Salt.

¹You have rejected us, O God, and
  burst forth upon us;
you have been angry—now restore
  us!
²You have shaken the land and torn it
  open;

ᵃ9 The meaning of the Hebrew for this verse is
uncertain. ᵇTitle: Probably a literary or musical
term ᶜ11 Or *sovereign* ᵈTitle: That is, Arameans of
Northwest Mesopotamia ᵉTitle: That is, Arameans
of central Syria

mend its fractures, for it is quaking.
³You have shown your people
    desperate times;
  you have given us wine that makes
    us stagger.

⁴But for those who fear you, you have
    raised a banner
  to be unfurled against the bow.

Selah

⁵Save us and help us with your right
    hand,
  that those you love may be
    delivered.
⁶God has spoken from his sanctuary:
  "In triumph I will parcel out
    Shechem
  and measure off the Valley of
    Succoth.
⁷Gilead is mine, and Manasseh is mine;

Week*end.*

Are You *Really* Sorry?

Read Isaiah 55:7 (page 861)

When you've been hurt there's nothing worse than an insincere apology. A "friend" mocks you with words that cut like razors. "Hey, don't be hurt. Sorry! I was just kidding!"—that's not exactly the apology you're looking for. The person spent plenty of energy cutting you down; why can't he put a little more effort into his "sorry"? A real apology is honest and heartfelt—that was the point of Kristin's devotion on Thursday.

Let's think about this topic a little more. We can't control how others apologize, but we can make sure our own "sorrys" are sincere so we can experience full forgiveness. Here's how:

- FACE IT. You have to face the fact that you really blew it, that it's your fault; that *you sinned*. Don't blame anyone else. Take full responsibility for your actions, the way David did in Psalm 51.
- FEEL IT. Stop and think about how you hurt the other person. Think about how you hurt God! Take a little time to feel the sadness you ought to feel before you actually say you're sorry.
- FIX IT. A real apology is not just a matter of words, but actions as well. Truly sorry people make amends. They pay for what was stolen, replace what was broken or try to repair the damage done to someone's reputation. A great Bible example is Zacchaeus in Luke 19 (page 1252).
- FORSAKE IT. It's not enough to merely confess; we must repent. To repent means to turn away from our sins and go a different direction. Unless that's our desire—even though we may fail again in the future—our "sorry" isn't all it should be.

What about You?

❶ How many times in the last week did you say a quick, casual "sorry"? Do you need to talk to some of these people and offer a real apology?

❷ For each person you've hurt this week, make a list of words that describe their feelings about what you did. Think about those feelings and "feel their pain" before you talk to them—God included.

❸ Tell God what you did wrong and how you feel about it. Then ask him to forgive you and give you the ability to make things right with the other people involved.

Turn to page 672 for your next devotion.

Ephraim is my helmet,
  Judah my scepter.
⁸Moab is my washbasin,
  upon Edom I toss my sandal;
  over Philistia I shout in triumph."

⁹Who will bring me to the fortified
    city?
  Who will lead me to Edom?
¹⁰Is it not you, O God, you who have
    rejected us
  and no longer go out with our
    armies?
¹¹Give us aid against the enemy,
  for the help of man is worthless.
¹²With God we will gain the victory,
  and he will trample down our
    enemies.

Psalm 61

For the director of music.
With stringed instruments. Of David.

¹Hear my cry, O God;
  listen to my prayer.

²From the ends of the earth I call to
    you,
  I call as my heart grows faint;
  lead me to the rock that is higher
    than I.
³For you have been my refuge,
  a strong tower against the foe.

⁴I long to dwell in your tent forever

---

and take refuge in the shelter of
    your wings.   *Selah*
⁵For you have heard my vows, O God;
  you have given me the heritage of
    those who fear your name.

⁶Increase the days of the king's life,
  his years for many generations.
⁷May he be enthroned in God's
    presence forever;
  appoint your love and faithfulness
    to protect him.

⁸Then will I ever sing praise to your
    name
  and fulfill my vows day after day.

Psalm 62

For the director of music.
For Jeduthun. A psalm of David.

¹My soul finds rest in God alone;
  my salvation comes from him.
²He alone is my rock and my salvation;
  he is my fortress, I will never be
    shaken.

³How long will you assault a man?
  Would all of you throw him down—
  this leaning wall, this tottering
    fence?
⁴They fully intend to topple him
    from his lofty place;
  they take delight in lies.
  With their mouths they bless,
    but in their hearts they curse. *Selah*

⁵Find rest, O my soul, in God alone;
  my hope comes from him.
⁶He alone is my rock and my salvation;
  he is my fortress, I will not be
    shaken.
⁷My salvation and my honor depend
    on God*ᵃ*;
  he is my mighty rock, my refuge.
⁸Trust in him at all times, O people;
  pour out your hearts to him,
  for God is our refuge.   *Selah*

⁹Lowborn men are but a breath,
  the highborn are but a lie;
  if weighed on a balance, they are
    nothing;
  together they are only a breath.

God's Wingspan

Psalm 61:4

God doesn't really have wings, but he has a huge span of care. He shelters us under his "wings" like a bird covers its chicks. This not only tells us of God's strength but also his tenderness. We might say that God is in touch with his "feminine side," portraying himself here as a mother hen. Jesus once wept over Jerusalem, saying he longed to gather its people like a hen gathers her chicks. Don't brush off God's affection or his protection. There's no safer place than under his "wings."

---

*ᵃ7 Or / God Most High is my salvation and my
honor*

¹⁰Do not trust in extortion
   or take pride in stolen goods;
though your riches increase,
   do not set your heart on them.

¹¹One thing God has spoken,
   two things have I heard:
that you, O God, are strong,
¹²   and that you, O Lord, are loving.
Surely you will reward each person
   according to what he has done.

Psalm 63

A psalm of David.
When he was in the Desert of Judah.

¹O God, you are my God,
   earnestly I seek you;
my soul thirsts for you,
   my body longs for you,
in a dry and weary land
   where there is no water.

²I have seen you in the sanctuary
   and beheld your power and your
      glory.
³Because your love is better than life,
   my lips will glorify you.
⁴I will praise you as long as I live,
   and in your name I will lift up my
      hands.
⁵My soul will be satisfied as with the
      richest of foods;
   with singing lips my mouth will
      praise you.

⁶On my bed I remember you;
   I think of you through the watches
      of the night.
⁷Because you are my help,
   I sing in the shadow of your wings.
⁸My soul clings to you;
   your right hand upholds me.

⁹They who seek my life will be
      destroyed;
   they will go down to the depths of
      the earth.
¹⁰They will be given over to the sword
   and become food for jackals.

¹¹But the king will rejoice in God;
   all who swear by God's name will
      praise him,
   while the mouths of liars will be
      silenced.

Psalm 64

For the director of music.
A psalm of David.

¹Hear me, O God, as I voice my
      complaint;
   protect my life from the threat of
      the enemy.
²Hide me from the conspiracy of the
      wicked,
   from that noisy crowd of evildoers.

³They sharpen their tongues like
      swords
   and aim their words like deadly
      arrows.
⁴They shoot from ambush at the
      innocent man;
   they shoot at him suddenly, without
      fear.

⁵They encourage each other in evil
      plans,
   they talk about hiding their snares;
   they say, "Who will see them*ᵃ*?"
⁶They plot injustice and say,
   "We have devised a perfect plan!"
Surely the mind and heart of man
   are cunning.

⁷But God will shoot them with arrows;
   suddenly they will be struck down.
⁸He will turn their own tongues against
      them
   and bring them to ruin;
   all who see them will shake their
      heads in scorn.

⁹All mankind will fear;
   they will proclaim the works of God
   and ponder what he has done.
¹⁰Let the righteous rejoice in the LORD
   and take refuge in him;
   let all the upright in heart praise
      him!

Psalm 65

For the director of music.
A psalm of David. A song.

¹Praise awaits*ᵇ* you, O God, in Zion;
   to you our vows will be fulfilled.
²O you who hear prayer,

ᵃ5 Or *us*   *ᵇ1* Or *befits*; the meaning of the Hebrew
for this word is uncertain.

to you all men will come.
³ When we were overwhelmed by sins,
  you forgave^a our transgressions.
⁴ Blessed are those you choose
    and bring near to live in your
      courts!
  We are filled with the good things of
      your house,
    of your holy temple.

⁵ You answer us with awesome deeds of
      righteousness,
    O God our Savior,
  the hope of all the ends of the earth
    and of the farthest seas,
⁶ who formed the mountains by your
      power,
    having armed yourself with
      strength,
⁷ who stilled the roaring of the seas,
    the roaring of their waves,
    and the turmoil of the nations.
⁸ Those living far away fear your
      wonders;
    where morning dawns and evening
      fades
    you call forth songs of joy.

⁹ You care for the land and water it;
    you enrich it abundantly.
  The streams of God are filled with
      water
    to provide the people with grain,
    for so you have ordained it.^b
¹⁰ You drench its furrows
    and level its ridges;
  you soften it with showers
    and bless its crops.
¹¹ You crown the year with your bounty,
    and your carts overflow with
      abundance.
¹² The grasslands of the desert overflow;
    the hills are clothed with gladness.
¹³ The meadows are covered with flocks
    and the valleys are mantled with
      grain;
    they shout for joy and sing.

Psalm 66

For the director of music.
A song. A psalm.

¹ Shout with joy to God, all the earth!
²   Sing the glory of his name;
    make his praise glorious!

³ Say to God, "How awesome are your
      deeds!
  So great is your power
    that your enemies cringe before
      you.
⁴ All the earth bows down to you;
    they sing praise to you,
    they sing praise to your name."
                                    Selah

⁵ Come and see what God has done,
    how awesome his works in man's
      behalf!
⁶ He turned the sea into dry land,
    they passed through the waters on
      foot—
    come, let us rejoice in him.
⁷ He rules forever by his power,
    his eyes watch the nations—
    let not the rebellious rise up against
      him.   *Selah*

⁸ Praise our God, O peoples,
    let the sound of his praise be heard;
⁹ he has preserved our lives
    and kept our feet from slipping.
¹⁰ For you, O God, tested us;
    you refined us like silver.
¹¹ You brought us into prison
    and laid burdens on our backs.
¹² You let men ride over our heads;
    we went through fire and water,
    but you brought us to a place of
      abundance.

¹³ I will come to your temple with burnt
      offerings
    and fulfill my vows to you—
¹⁴ vows my lips promised and my mouth
      spoke
    when I was in trouble.
¹⁵ I will sacrifice fat animals to you
    and an offering of rams;
  I will offer bulls and goats.   *Selah*

¹⁶ Come and listen, all you who fear
      God;
    let me tell you what he has done for
      me.
¹⁷ I cried out to him with my mouth;
    his praise was on my tongue.
¹⁸ If I had cherished sin in my heart,
    the Lord would not have listened;
¹⁹ but God has surely listened

^a3 Or *made atonement for* ^b9 Or *for that is how you*
prepare the land

and heard my voice in prayer.
²⁰Praise be to God,
who has not rejected my prayer
or withheld his love from me!

Psalm 67

*For the director of music.
With stringed instruments. A psalm. A song.*

¹May God be gracious to us and bless
us
and make his face shine upon us,
Selah

²that your ways may be known on
earth,
your salvation among all nations.

³May the peoples praise you, O God;
may all the peoples praise you.
⁴May the nations be glad and sing for
joy,
for you rule the peoples justly
and guide the nations of the earth.
Selah

⁵May the peoples praise you, O God;
may all the peoples praise you.

⁶Then the land will yield its harvest,
and God, our God, will bless us.
⁷God will bless us,
and all the ends of the earth will
fear him.

Psalm 68

*For the director of music. Of David.
A psalm. A song.*

¹May God arise, may his enemies be
scattered;
may his foes flee before him.
²As smoke is blown away by the wind,
may you blow them away;
as wax melts before the fire,
may the wicked perish before God.
³But may the righteous be glad
and rejoice before God;
may they be happy and joyful.

⁴Sing to God, sing praise to his name,
extol him who rides on the clouds^a—
his name is the LORD—
and rejoice before him.
⁵A father to the fatherless, a defender
of widows,

Repeat After Me
Huh?

Psalm 67:3, 5
The more the Bible repeats itself, the more it's trying to make a point. So when we read 4 times, "May all the peoples praise you," we know a major truth is being taught. It's this: Praising God is really important. God is not lifted as high as he should be until all people join in. So this is a missionary poem that goes with Jesus' command to make disciples of all nations in Matthew 28:19–20, page 1185.

is God in his holy dwelling.
⁶God sets the lonely in families,^b
he leads forth the prisoners with
singing;
but the rebellious live in a
sun-scorched land.

⁷When you went out before your
people, O God,
when you marched through the
wasteland,   *Selah*
⁸the earth shook,
the heavens poured down rain,
before God, the One of Sinai,
before God, the God of Israel.
⁹You gave abundant showers, O God;
you refreshed your weary
inheritance.
¹⁰Your people settled in it,
and from your bounty, O God, you
provided for the poor.

¹¹The Lord announced the word,
and great was the company of those
who proclaimed it:
¹²"Kings and armies flee in haste;
in the camps men divide the
plunder.
¹³Even while you sleep among the
campfires,^c
the wings of my dove are sheathed
with silver,
its feathers with shining gold."

^a4 Or / prepare the way for him who rides through the deserts   ^b6 Or the desolate in a homeland   ^c13 Or saddlebags

¹⁴When the Almighty[a] scattered the
  kings in the land,
  it was like snow fallen on Zalmon.

¹⁵The mountains of Bashan are majestic
    mountains;
  rugged are the mountains of
    Bashan.
¹⁶Why gaze in envy, O rugged
    mountains,
  at the mountain where God chooses
    to reign,
  where the LORD himself will dwell
    forever?
¹⁷The chariots of God are tens of
    thousands
  and thousands of thousands;
  the Lord has come from Sinai into
    his sanctuary.
¹⁸When you ascended on high,
  you led captives in your train;
  you received gifts from men,
even from[b] the rebellious—
  that you,[c] O LORD God, might dwell
    there.

¹⁹Praise be to the Lord, to God our
    Savior,
  who daily bears our burdens.   Selah
²⁰Our God is a God who saves;
  from the Sovereign LORD comes
    escape from death.

²¹Surely God will crush the heads of his
    enemies,
  the hairy crowns of those who go
    on in their sins.
²²The Lord says, "I will bring them from
    Bashan;
  I will bring them from the depths of
    the sea,
²³that you may plunge your feet in the
    blood of your foes,
  while the tongues of your dogs have
    their share."

²⁴Your procession has come into view,
    O God,
  the procession of my God and King
    into the sanctuary.
²⁵In front are the singers, after them the
    musicians;
  with them are the maidens playing
    tambourines.
²⁶Praise God in the great congregation;
  praise the LORD in the assembly of
    Israel.

²⁷There is the little tribe of Benjamin,
    leading them,
  there the great throng of Judah's
    princes,
  and there the princes of Zebulun
    and of Naphtali.
²⁸Summon your power, O God[d];
  show us your strength, O God, as
    you have done before.
²⁹Because of your temple at Jerusalem
  kings will bring you gifts.
³⁰Rebuke the beast among the reeds,
  the herd of bulls among the calves
    of the nations.
  Humbled, may it bring bars of silver.
  Scatter the nations who delight in
    war.
³¹Envoys will come from Egypt;
  Cush[e] will submit herself to God.

³²Sing to God, O kingdoms of the earth,
  sing praise to the Lord,   Selah
³³to him who rides the ancient skies
    above,
  who thunders with mighty voice.
³⁴Proclaim the power of God,
  whose majesty is over Israel,
  whose power is in the skies.
³⁵You are awesome, O God, in your
    sanctuary;
  the God of Israel gives power and
    strength to his people.

Praise be to God!

Psalm 69

For the director of music.
To the tune of "Lilies." Of David.

¹Save me, O God,
  for the waters have come up to my
    neck.
²I sink in the miry depths,
  where there is no foothold.
  I have come into the deep waters;
  the floods engulf me.
³I am worn out calling for help;
  my throat is parched.
  My eyes fail,

---

[a]14 Hebrew *Shaddai*   [b]18 Or *gifts for men, / even*
[c]18 Or *they*   [d]28 Many Hebrew manuscripts,
Septuagint and Syriac; most Hebrew manuscripts
Your God has summoned power for you   [e]31 That is,
the upper Nile region

looking for my God.
⁴Those who hate me without reason
outnumber the hairs of my head;
many are my enemies without cause,
those who seek to destroy me.
I am forced to restore
what I did not steal.

⁵You know my folly, O God;
my guilt is not hidden from you.

⁶May those who hope in you
not be disgraced because of me,
O Lord, the LORD Almighty;
may those who seek you
not be put to shame because of me,
O God of Israel.
⁷For I endure scorn for your sake,
and shame covers my face.
⁸I am a stranger to my brothers,
an alien to my own mother's sons;
⁹for zeal for your house consumes me,
and the insults of those who insult
you fall on me.
¹⁰When I weep and fast,
I must endure scorn;
¹¹when I put on sackcloth,
people make sport of me.
¹²Those who sit at the gate mock me,
and I am the song of the drunkards.

¹³But I pray to you, O LORD,
in the time of your favor;
in your great love, O God,
answer me with your sure salvation.
¹⁴Rescue me from the mire,
do not let me sink;
deliver me from those who hate me,
from the deep waters.
¹⁵Do not let the floodwaters engulf me
or the depths swallow me up
or the pit close its mouth over me.

¹⁶Answer me, O LORD, out of the
goodness of your love;
in your great mercy turn to me.
¹⁷Do not hide your face from your
servant;
answer me quickly, for I am in
trouble.
¹⁸Come near and rescue me;
redeem me because of my foes.

¹⁹You know how I am scorned,
disgraced and shamed;
all my enemies are before you.
²⁰Scorn has broken my heart
and has left me helpless;

I looked for sympathy, but there was
none,
for comforters, but I found none.
²¹They put gall in my food
and gave me vinegar for my thirst.

²²May the table set before them become
a snare;
may it become retribution andᵃ a
trap.
²³May their eyes be darkened so they
cannot see,
and their backs be bent forever.
²⁴Pour out your wrath on them;
let your fierce anger overtake them.
²⁵May their place be deserted;
let there be no one to dwell in their
tents.
²⁶For they persecute those you wound
and talk about the pain of those
you hurt.
²⁷Charge them with crime upon crime;
do not let them share in your
salvation.
²⁸May they be blotted out of the book
of life
and not be listed with the righteous.

²⁹I am in pain and distress;
may your salvation, O God, protect
me.

³⁰I will praise God's name in song
and glorify him with thanksgiving.
³¹This will please the LORD more than an
ox,
more than a bull with its horns and
hoofs.
³²The poor will see and be glad—
you who seek God, may your hearts
live!
³³The LORD hears the needy
and does not despise his captive
people.

³⁴Let heaven and earth praise him,
the seas and all that move in them,
³⁵for God will save Zion
and rebuild the cities of Judah.
Then people will settle there and
possess it;
³⁶ the children of his servants will
inherit it,
and those who love his name will
dwell there.

ᵃ22 Or snare / and their fellowship become

Psalm 70

*For the director of music.
Of David. A petition.*

¹Hasten, O God, to save me;
  O Lᴏʀᴅ, come quickly to help me.
²May those who seek my life
  be put to shame and confusion;
may all who desire my ruin
  be turned back in disgrace.
³May those who say to me, "Aha!
    Aha!"
  turn back because of their shame.
⁴But may all who seek you
  rejoice and be glad in you;
may those who love your salvation
    always say,
  "Let God be exalted!"

⁵Yet I am poor and needy;
  come quickly to me, O God.
You are my help and my deliverer;
  O Lᴏʀᴅ, do not delay.

Psalm 71

¹In you, O Lᴏʀᴅ, I have taken refuge;
  let me never be put to shame.
²Rescue me and deliver me in your
    righteousness;
  turn your ear to me and save me.
³Be my rock of refuge,
  to which I can always go;
give the command to save me,
  for you are my rock and my
    fortress.
⁴Deliver me, O my God, from the hand
    of the wicked,
  from the grasp of evil and cruel
    men.

⁵For you have been my hope,
    O Sovereign Lᴏʀᴅ,
  my confidence since my youth.
⁶From birth I have relied on you;
  you brought me forth from my
    mother's womb.
  I will ever praise you.

Monday

I Messed Up

Read Psalm 69

There's nothing worse than knowing you've messed up in a big way. You feel stupid, you feel guilty, you feel sick to your stomach. At least that's how I felt when I went out with a guy while I was going steady with someone else.

I don't know what I was thinking. I really cared about my boyfriend, but I liked this other guy too. And I felt horrible about it. I hurt him, I hurt the other guy and I hurt myself. I got myself into a huge mess and I didn't know how I would ever get out of it.

I wish I would have read this psalm then. It would have helped me to see that I could lean on God and he'd be there for me, even though I was in major trouble. God could have comforted me and given me the strength to try and make things right with my boyfriend.

The next time I mess up—and I'm sure there will be a next time—I'll know I can talk to God about it.

Cristina age 14

❶ Think about a time you were in big trouble. How did God help you get through?

❷ Take another look at Psalm 69, especially verses 1–5 and 13–18. How would you put those verses in your own words?

❸ Thank God for always being there to talk to.

Turn to page 674 for your next devotion.

⁷I have become like a portent to many,
   but you are my strong refuge.
⁸My mouth is filled with your praise,
   declaring your splendor all day
      long.

⁹Do not cast me away when I am old;
   do not forsake me when my
      strength is gone.
¹⁰For my enemies speak against me;
   those who wait to kill me conspire
      together.
¹¹They say, "God has forsaken him;
   pursue him and seize him,
      for no one will rescue him."
¹²Be not far from me, O God;
   come quickly, O my God, to help
      me.
¹³May my accusers perish in shame;
   may those who want to harm me
      be covered with scorn and disgrace.

¹⁴But as for me, I will always have
      hope;
   I will praise you more and more.
¹⁵My mouth will tell of your
      righteousness,
   of your salvation all day long,
      though I know not its measure.
¹⁶I will come and proclaim your mighty
      acts, O Sovereign LORD;
   I will proclaim your righteousness,
      yours alone.
¹⁷Since my youth, O God, you have
      taught me,
   and to this day I declare your
      marvelous deeds.
¹⁸Even when I am old and gray,
   do not forsake me, O God,
till I declare your power to the next
      generation,
   your might to all who are to come.

¹⁹Your righteousness reaches to the
      skies, O God,
   you who have done great things.
      Who, O God, is like you?
²⁰Though you have made me see
      troubles, many and bitter,
   you will restore my life again;
from the depths of the earth
   you will again bring me up.
²¹You will increase my honor
   and comfort me once again.

²²I will praise you with the harp
   for your faithfulness, O my God;

I will sing praise to you with the lyre,
   O Holy One of Israel.
²³My lips will shout for joy
   when I sing praise to you—
      I, whom you have redeemed.
²⁴My tongue will tell of your righteous
      acts
   all day long,
for those who wanted to harm me
   have been put to shame and
      confusion.

Psalm 72

Of Solomon.

¹Endow the king with your justice,
      O God,
   the royal son with your
      righteousness.
²He will[a] judge your people in
      righteousness,
   your afflicted ones with justice.
³The mountains will bring prosperity to
      the people,
   the hills the fruit of righteousness.
⁴He will defend the afflicted among the
      people
   and save the children of the needy;
      he will crush the oppressor.

⁵He will endure[b] as long as the sun,
   as long as the moon, through all
      generations.
⁶He will be like rain falling on a mown
      field,
   like showers watering the earth.
⁷In his days the righteous will flourish;
   prosperity will abound till the moon
      is no more.

⁸He will rule from sea to sea
   and from the River[c] to the ends of
      the earth.[d]
⁹The desert tribes will bow before him
   and his enemies will lick the dust.
¹⁰The kings of Tarshish and of distant
      shores
   will bring tribute to him;
the kings of Sheba and Seba
   will present him gifts.
¹¹All kings will bow down to him
   and all nations will serve him.

[a]2 Or *May he*; similarly in verses 3–11 and 17
[b]5 Septuagint; Hebrew *You will be feared*   [c]8 That
is, the Euphrates   [d]8 Or *the end of the land*

¹²For he will deliver the needy who cry
out,
   the afflicted who have no one to
help.
¹³He will take pity on the weak and the
needy
   and save the needy from death.
¹⁴He will rescue them from oppression
and violence,
   for precious is their blood in his
sight.

¹⁵Long may he live!
   May gold from Sheba be given him.
May people ever pray for him
   and bless him all day long.
¹⁶Let grain abound throughout the land;
   on the tops of the hills may it sway.
Let its fruit flourish like Lebanon;
   let it thrive like the grass of the
field.
¹⁷May his name endure forever;
   may it continue as long as the sun.

All nations will be blessed through
him,
   and they will call him blessed.

¹⁸Praise be to the LORD God, the God of
Israel,
   who alone does marvelous deeds.
¹⁹Praise be to his glorious name forever;
   may the whole earth be filled with
his glory.
     Amen and Amen.

²⁰This concludes the prayers of David
son of Jesse.

BOOK III
Psalms 73–89

Psalm 73

A psalm of Asaph.

¹Surely God is good to Israel,
   to those who are pure in heart.

²But as for me, my feet had almost
slipped;
   I had nearly lost my foothold.
³For I envied the arrogant

Tuesday

Words From the Wise

Read Psalm 71:17–18

A lot of people think the only thing older folks do well is boss others around and yell at them. Well, I think that too sometimes, but it really isn't true. What older people say is important.

   These verses show me that I should respect the wisdom of my elders. They've been around a while, so they've seen more of God and more of life than I have. They might even help me avoid making unnecessary mistakes if I listen carefully.

   And think about this: God has been around longer than anyone else. He never even had a beginning, and he'll never have an end! And when I've got gray hair, I know he'll still be teaching me and showing me new things.

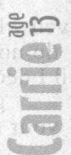
Carrie age 13

❶ Think of a time you had less respect for an older person than you should have. Why does God tell us to listen to our elders?

❷ Talk to a grandparent, great aunt or uncle, or an older person in your church. Ask them about some things God has taught them over the years and what he's teaching them now.

❸ Thank the Lord for the older people in your life.

Turn to page 679 for your next devotion.

Rare Pictures of God

Too bad that photography was invented way too late to catch God on film back in Bible times. But wait a minute. The Bible *does* have pictures of God. Not photos or drawings or paintings but *word* pictures.

These clear "self-portraits" of God show us who he is and what he's like: Father, King, Star of David, Bread of Life, Living Water. You've probably "seen" these pictures in your Bible—they're pretty popular. There are dozens and dozens of self-portraits in God's photo album (the Bible), including a few you may not have seen:

Lion: You may be surprised to learn that there's just one clear picture of Jesus the Lion in the entire Bible: Revelation 5:5, page 1555. In that scene, Jesus the Lion is the only One in the entire universe who's absolutely perfect. Perfectly ferocious, perfectly innocent. Our Lion is *not* tame. But he's good.

Rain: You probably don't think of God like rain. But it's one of his self-portraits, and you can see it for yourself in Psalm 72:6 (page 673). God the Rain pours himself on you—cleansing you, refreshing you, giving you what you need to grow. Don't hide in dry and dusty places. Go outside and play in the Rain!

Potter: OK, maybe you've seen this one, but it's still a great picture. And it's rare—only Isaiah, Jeremiah and Paul use it. God as the Potter is a Craftsman, working each of us into a unique, beautiful, useful creation. He didn't snap his fingers to make you. He worked at it—and he's proud of his work. See the Potter at work in Isaiah 64:8, page 870.

Hen: Hard to believe it, isn't it? But Jesus included this picture himself: You'll find it in Luke 13:34, page 1245. It's a great picture. If you approach a mother hen while she's supervising her fluffy little chicks, she'll throw out her wings, scoop in the kids and keep them covered till you go away. Of course, the hen can only guard the chicks if they're *willing* to be guarded. If they run out on their own, they may just get lost, gobbled up or trampled. And the same is true for you. God can protect you if you stick close to him. Wander off, and you're bound to get into trouble.

Eagle: It's easy to picture God as a great eagle soaring above the earth. But the eagle he uses as a self-portrait in the Bible isn't soaring above the problems—he's *solving* them. He guards his eaglets in the nest, and, if they fall out, he swoops down and saves them. Catch God, the Eagle, in action in Deuteronomy 32:10–11, page 238.

when I saw the prosperity of the
    wicked.
⁴They have no struggles;
    their bodies are healthy and strong.ᵃ
⁵They are free from the burdens
        common to man;
    they are not plagued by human ills.
⁶Therefore pride is their necklace;
    they clothe themselves with
        violence.
⁷From their callous hearts comes
        iniquityᵇ;
    the evil conceits of their minds
        know no limits.

⁸They scoff, and speak with malice;
    in their arrogance they threaten
        oppression.
⁹Their mouths lay claim to heaven,
    and their tongues take possession of
        the earth.
¹⁰Therefore their people turn to them
    and drink up waters in abundance.ᶜ
¹¹They say, "How can God know?

ᵃ4 With a different word division of the Hebrew;
Masoretic Text *struggles at their death; / their bodies
are healthy*   ᵇ7 Syriac (see also Septuagint); Hebrew
Their eyes bulge with fat   ᶜ10 The meaning of the
Hebrew for this verse is uncertain.

Does the Most High have
    knowledge?"
¹²This is what the wicked are like—
    always carefree, they increase in
        wealth.
¹³Surely in vain have I kept my heart
        pure;
    in vain have I washed my hands in
        innocence.

Are You Nearsighted?

Huh?

Psalm 73:13

Asaph is nearsighted. He knows it's harder to be good than bad. It's tougher to take a stand than to go with the flow. It's more difficult to say no than yes. And he wonders if it's worth it. Seeing only the nearsighted-ness of sin's pleasure, he almost can't see its far-off, long-term consequences. But a look through the lenses of time reveals the whole picture. In the end, sin leads to destruction and purity leads to paradise. Don't blow off the difference!

¹⁴All day long I have been plagued;
    I have been punished every
        morning.

¹⁵If I had said, "I will speak thus,"
    I would have betrayed your
        children.
¹⁶When I tried to understand all this,
    it was oppressive to me
¹⁷till I entered the sanctuary of God;
    then I understood their final
        destiny.

¹⁸Surely you place them on slippery
        ground;
    you cast them down to ruin.
¹⁹How suddenly are they destroyed,
    completely swept away by terrors!
²⁰As a dream when one awakes,
    so when you arise, O Lord,
    you will despise them as fantasies.

²¹When my heart was grieved
    and my spirit embittered,
²²I was senseless and ignorant;
    I was a brute beast before you.

²³Yet I am always with you;
    you hold me by my right hand.
²⁴You guide me with your counsel,
    and afterward you will take me into
        glory.
²⁵Whom have I in heaven but you?
    And earth has nothing I desire
        besides you.
²⁶My flesh and my heart may fail,
    but God is the strength of my heart
    and my portion forever.

²⁷Those who are far from you will
        perish;
    you destroy all who are unfaithful
        to you.
²⁸But as for me, it is good to be near
        God.
    I have made the Sovereign LORD my
        refuge;
    I will tell of all your deeds.

Psalm 74

A *maskil*[a] of Asaph.

¹Why have you rejected us forever,
        O God?
    Why does your anger smolder
        against the sheep of your
        pasture?
²Remember the people you purchased
        of old,
    the tribe of your inheritance, whom
        you redeemed—
    Mount Zion, where you dwelt.
³Turn your steps toward these
        everlasting ruins,
    all this destruction the enemy has
        brought on the sanctuary.

⁴Your foes roared in the place where
        you met with us;
    they set up their standards as signs.
⁵They behaved like men wielding axes
    to cut through a thicket of trees.
⁶They smashed all the carved paneling
    with their axes and hatchets.
⁷They burned your sanctuary to the
        ground;
    they defiled the dwelling place of
        your Name.
⁸They said in their hearts, "We will
        crush them completely!"

ᵃTitle: Probably a literary or musical term

They burned every place where God
  was worshiped in the land.
⁹We are given no miraculous signs;
  no prophets are left,
  and none of us knows how long
    this will be.

¹⁰How long will the enemy mock you,
    O God?
  Will the foe revile your name
    forever?
¹¹Why do you hold back your hand,
    your right hand?
  Take it from the folds of your
    garment and destroy them!

¹²But you, O God, are my king from of
    old;
  you bring salvation upon the earth.
¹³It was you who split open the sea by
    your power;
  you broke the heads of the monster
    in the waters.
¹⁴It was you who crushed the heads of
    Leviathan
  and gave him as food to the
    creatures of the desert.
¹⁵It was you who opened up springs and
    streams;
  you dried up the ever flowing
    rivers.
¹⁶The day is yours, and yours also the
    night;
  you established the sun and moon.
¹⁷It was you who set all the boundaries
    of the earth;
  you made both summer and winter.

¹⁸Remember how the enemy has
    mocked you, O LORD,
  how foolish people have reviled
    your name.
¹⁹Do not hand over the life of your dove
    to wild beasts;
  do not forget the lives of your
    afflicted people forever.
²⁰Have regard for your covenant,
  because haunts of violence fill the
    dark places of the land.
²¹Do not let the oppressed retreat in
    disgrace;
  may the poor and needy praise your
    name.

²²Rise up, O God, and defend your cause;
  remember how fools mock you all
    day long.

²³Do not ignore the clamor of your
    adversaries,
  the uproar of your enemies, which
    rises continually.

Psalm 75

For the director of music.
To the tune of "Do Not Destroy."
A psalm of Asaph. A song.

¹We give thanks to you, O God,
  we give thanks, for your Name is
    near;
  men tell of your wonderful deeds.

²You say, "I choose the appointed time;
  it is I who judge uprightly.
³When the earth and all its people
    quake,
  it is I who hold its pillars firm.
                                    Selah
⁴To the arrogant I say, 'Boast no more,'
  and to the wicked, 'Do not lift up
    your horns.
⁵Do not lift your horns against heaven;
  do not speak with outstretched
    neck.' "

⁶No one from the east or the west
  or from the desert can exalt a man.
⁷But it is God who judges:
  He brings one down, he exalts
    another.
⁸In the hand of the LORD is a cup
  full of foaming wine mixed with
    spices;
  he pours it out, and all the wicked of
    the earth
  drink it down to its very dregs.

⁹As for me, I will declare this forever;
  I will sing praise to the God of
    Jacob.
¹⁰I will cut off the horns of all the
    wicked,
  but the horns of the righteous will
    be lifted up.

Psalm 76

For the director of music.
With stringed instruments. A psalm
of Asaph. A song.

¹In Judah God is known;
  his name is great in Israel.

²His tent is in Salem,
  his dwelling place in Zion.
³There he broke the flashing arrows,
  the shields and the swords, the
      weapons of war. *Selah*

⁴You are resplendent with light,
  more majestic than mountains rich
      with game.
⁵Valiant men lie plundered,
  they sleep their last sleep;
 not one of the warriors
  can lift his hands.
⁶At your rebuke, O God of Jacob,
  both horse and chariot lie still.
⁷You alone are to be feared.
  Who can stand before you when
      you are angry?
⁸From heaven you pronounced
      judgment,
  and the land feared and was quiet—
⁹when you, O God, rose up to judge,
  to save all the afflicted of the land.
                                    Selah
¹⁰Surely your wrath against men brings
      you praise,
  and the survivors of your wrath are
      restrained.ᵃ

¹¹Make vows to the LORD your God and
      fulfill them;
  let all the neighboring lands
  bring gifts to the One to be feared.
¹²He breaks the spirit of rulers;
  he is feared by the kings of the
      earth.

Psalm 77

For the director of music. For Jeduthun.
Of Asaph. A psalm.

¹I cried out to God for help;
  I cried out to God to hear me.
²When I was in distress, I sought the
      Lord;
  at night I stretched out untiring
      hands
  and my soul refused to be
      comforted.

³I remembered you, O God, and I
      groaned;
  I mused, and my spirit grew faint.
                                    Selah
⁴You kept my eyes from closing;

  I was too troubled to speak.
⁵I thought about the former days,
  the years of long ago;
⁶I remembered my songs in the night.
  My heart mused and my spirit
      inquired:

⁷"Will the Lord reject forever?
  Will he never show his favor again?
⁸Has his unfailing love vanished
      forever?
  Has his promise failed for all time?
⁹Has God forgotten to be merciful?
  Has he in anger withheld his
      compassion?"   *Selah*

¹⁰Then I thought, "To this I will appeal:
  the years of the right hand of the
      Most High."
¹¹I will remember the deeds of the LORD;
  yes, I will remember your miracles
      of long ago.
¹²I will meditate on all your works
  and consider all your mighty deeds.

¹³Your ways, O God, are holy.
  What god is so great as our God?
¹⁴You are the God who performs
      miracles;
  you display your power among the
      peoples.
¹⁵With your mighty arm you redeemed
      your people,
  the descendants of Jacob and
      Joseph.   *Selah*

¹⁶The waters saw you, O God,
  the waters saw you and writhed;
  the very depths were convulsed.
¹⁷The clouds poured down water,
  the skies resounded with thunder;
  your arrows flashed back and forth.
¹⁸Your thunder was heard in the
      whirlwind,
  your lightning lit up the world;
  the earth trembled and quaked.
¹⁹Your path led through the sea,
  your way through the mighty
      waters,
  though your footprints were not
      seen.

²⁰You led your people like a flock
  by the hand of Moses and Aaron.

ᵃ10 Or *Surely the wrath of men brings you praise, /
and with the remainder of wrath you arm
yourself*

Psalm 78

A maskil[a] of Asaph.

[1] O my people, hear my teaching;
   listen to the words of my mouth.
[2] I will open my mouth in parables,
   I will utter hidden things, things
      from of old—
[3] what we have heard and known,
   what our fathers have told us.
[4] We will not hide them from their
      children;
   we will tell the next generation
the praiseworthy deeds of the LORD,
   his power, and the wonders he has
      done.
[5] He decreed statutes for Jacob
   and established the law in Israel,
which he commanded our
      forefathers
   to teach their children,
[6] so the next generation would know
      them,
   even the children yet to be born,

and they in turn would tell their
      children.
[7] Then they would put their trust in God
   and would not forget his deeds
   but would keep his commands.
[8] They would not be like their
      forefathers—
   a stubborn and rebellious
      generation,
whose hearts were not loyal to God,
   whose spirits were not faithful to him.

[9] The men of Ephraim, though armed
      with bows,
   turned back on the day of battle;
[10] they did not keep God's covenant
   and refused to live by his law.
[11] They forgot what he had done,
   the wonders he had shown them.
[12] He did miracles in the sight of their
      fathers
   in the land of Egypt, in the region
      of Zoan.

[a] Title: Probably a literary or musical term

Wednesday

Tall Tales?

Read Psalm 77:16–20

God is powerful! I take that for granted sometimes when I get too focused on myself. But when my family was caught in a dangerous rain storm not long ago, I had no choice but to admit that God is awesome. We were so scared, but God was in control the whole time.

In Psalm 77, David remembers how God's people suffered "storms" in the past. There were times when they didn't know where God was taking them. I'm sure they felt fearful and small too. But God took care of them, just like he took care of my family.

The more I see God lead our family safely through all kinds of situations, the more I learn to trust him. The more I trust him, the more I want to do what he says, and the more I see his faithfulness in my own life.

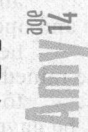
Amy, age 14

What about You?

❶ How has God been faithful to you over the past year? How has he taken care of your family?

❷ Pray for 3 different people or families in your church who have asked for a prayer as they face some terrible "storms." Ask God to comfort them and help them.

❸ Thank God for being faithful to you in the past, present and future.

Turn to page 691 for your next devotion.

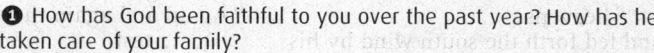

¹³He divided the sea and led them
  through;
    he made the water stand firm like a
    wall.
¹⁴He guided them with the cloud by day
    and with light from the fire all
    night.
¹⁵He split the rocks in the desert
    and gave them water as abundant
    as the seas;
¹⁶he brought streams out of a rocky
    crag
    and made water flow down like
    rivers.

¹⁷But they continued to sin against him,
    rebelling in the desert against the
    Most High.
¹⁸They willfully put God to the test
    by demanding the food they craved.
¹⁹They spoke against God, saying,
    "Can God spread a table in the
    desert?
²⁰When he struck the rock, water
    gushed out,
    and streams flowed abundantly.
  But can he also give us food?
  Can he supply meat for his people?"
²¹When the Lord heard them, he was
    very angry;
    his fire broke out against Jacob,
    and his wrath rose against Israel,
²²for they did not believe in God
    or trust in his deliverance.
²³Yet he gave a command to the skies
    above
    and opened the doors of the
    heavens;
²⁴he rained down manna for the people
    to eat,
    he gave them the grain of heaven.
²⁵Men ate the bread of angels;
    he sent them all the food they could
    eat.
²⁶He let loose the east wind from the
    heavens
    and led forth the south wind by his
    power.
²⁷He rained meat down on them like
    dust,
    flying birds like sand on the
    seashore.
²⁸He made them come down inside their
    camp,
    all around their tents.

²⁹They ate till they had more than
    enough,
    for he had given them what they
    craved.
³⁰But before they turned from the food
    they craved,
    even while it was still in their
    mouths,
³¹God's anger rose against them;
    he put to death the sturdiest among
    them,
    cutting down the young men of
    Israel.

³²In spite of all this, they kept on
    sinning;
    in spite of his wonders, they did not
    believe.
³³So he ended their days in futility
    and their years in terror.
³⁴Whenever God slew them, they would
    seek him;
    they eagerly turned to him again.
³⁵They remembered that God was their
    Rock,
    that God Most High was their
    Redeemer.
³⁶But then they would flatter him with
    their mouths,
    lying to him with their tongues;
³⁷their hearts were not loyal to him,
    they were not faithful to his
    covenant.
³⁸Yet he was merciful;
    he forgave their iniquities
    and did not destroy them.
  Time after time he restrained his anger
    and did not stir up his full wrath.
³⁹He remembered that they were but
    flesh,
    a passing breeze that does not
    return.

⁴⁰How often they rebelled against him
    in the desert
    and grieved him in the wasteland!
⁴¹Again and again they put God to the
    test;
    they vexed the Holy One of Israel.
⁴²They did not remember his power—
    the day he redeemed them from the
    oppressor,
⁴³the day he displayed his miraculous
    signs in Egypt,
    his wonders in the region of Zoan.
⁴⁴He turned their rivers to blood;

they could not drink from their
    streams.
⁴⁵He sent swarms of flies that devoured
    them,
    and frogs that devastated them.
⁴⁶He gave their crops to the grasshopper,
    their produce to the locust.
⁴⁷He destroyed their vines with hail
    and their sycamore-figs with sleet.
⁴⁸He gave over their cattle to the hail,
    their livestock to bolts of lightning.
⁴⁹He unleashed against them his hot
    anger,
    his wrath, indignation and
        hostility—
    a band of destroying angels.
⁵⁰He prepared a path for his anger;
    he did not spare them from death
    but gave them over to the plague.
⁵¹He struck down all the firstborn of
    Egypt,
    the firstfruits of manhood in the
        tents of Ham.
⁵²But he brought his people out like a
    flock;
    he led them like sheep through the
        desert.
⁵³He guided them safely, so they were
    unafraid;
    but the sea engulfed their enemies.
⁵⁴Thus he brought them to the border of
    his holy land,
    to the hill country his right hand
        had taken.
⁵⁵He drove out nations before them
    and allotted their lands to them as
        an inheritance;
    he settled the tribes of Israel in their
        homes.

⁵⁶But they put God to the test
    and rebelled against the Most High;
    they did not keep his statutes.
⁵⁷Like their fathers they were disloyal
    and faithless,
    as unreliable as a faulty bow.
⁵⁸They angered him with their high
    places;
    they aroused his jealousy with their
        idols.
⁵⁹When God heard them, he was very
    angry;
    he rejected Israel completely.
⁶⁰He abandoned the tabernacle of
    Shiloh,

the tent he had set up among men.
⁶¹He sent the ark of his might into
    captivity,
    his splendor into the hands of the
        enemy.
⁶²He gave his people over to the sword;
    he was very angry with his
        inheritance.
⁶³Fire consumed their young men,
    and their maidens had no wedding
        songs;
⁶⁴their priests were put to the sword,
    and their widows could not weep.

⁶⁵Then the Lord awoke as from sleep,
    as a man wakes from the stupor of
        wine.
⁶⁶He beat back his enemies;
    he put them to everlasting shame.
⁶⁷Then he rejected the tents of Joseph,
    he did not choose the tribe of
        Ephraim;
⁶⁸but he chose the tribe of Judah,
    Mount Zion, which he loved.
⁶⁹He built his sanctuary like the heights,
    like the earth that he established
        forever.
⁷⁰He chose David his servant
    and took him from the sheep pens;
⁷¹from tending the sheep he brought
    him
    to be the shepherd of his people
        Jacob,
    of Israel his inheritance.
⁷²And David shepherded them with
    integrity of heart;
    with skillful hands he led them.

Psalm 79

A psalm of Asaph.

¹O God, the nations have invaded your
    inheritance;
    they have defiled your holy temple,
    they have reduced Jerusalem to
        rubble.
²They have given the dead bodies of
    your servants
    as food to the birds of the air,
    the flesh of your saints to the beasts
        of the earth.
³They have poured out blood like
    water
    all around Jerusalem,

and there is no one to bury the dead.
⁴We are objects of reproach to our
    neighbors,
    of scorn and derision to those
      around us.

⁵How long, O LORD? Will you be angry
    forever?
    How long will your jealousy burn
      like fire?
⁶Pour out your wrath on the nations
    that do not acknowledge you,
  on the kingdoms
    that do not call on your name;
⁷for they have devoured Jacob
    and destroyed his homeland.
⁸Do not hold against us the sins of the
    fathers;
    may your mercy come quickly to
      meet us,
  for we are in desperate need.

⁹Help us, O God our Savior,
    for the glory of your name;
  deliver us and forgive our sins
    for your name's sake.

For God's Sake!

Psalm 79:9
We usually think God saves us just for our sake, because we're lost and doomed without him. That's true, but it's only part of the story. God didn't save us just for our sake; he saved us for his sake. Because he is God and deserves big-time glory, he saved us for his sake, to draw attention to his greatness and love.

¹⁰Why should the nations say,
    "Where is their God?"
  Before our eyes, make known among
    the nations
    that you avenge the outpoured
      blood of your servants.
¹¹May the groans of the prisoners come
    before you;
    by the strength of your arm
    preserve those condemned to die.

¹²Pay back into the laps of our
    neighbors seven times
    the reproach they have hurled at
      you, O Lord.
¹³Then we your people, the sheep of
    your pasture,
    will praise you forever;
  from generation to generation
    we will recount your praise.

Psalm 80

For the director of music.
To the tune of, "The Lilies of the Covenant."
Of Asaph. A psalm.

¹Hear us, O Shepherd of Israel,
    you who lead Joseph like a flock;
  you who sit enthroned between the
    cherubim, shine forth
²   before Ephraim, Benjamin and
      Manasseh.
  Awaken your might;
    come and save us.

³Restore us, O God;
    make your face shine upon us,
    that we may be saved.

⁴O LORD God Almighty,
    how long will your anger smolder
    against the prayers of your people?
⁵You have fed them with the bread of
    tears;
    you have made them drink tears by
      the bowlful.
⁶You have made us a source of
    contention to our neighbors,
  and our enemies mock us.

⁷Restore us, O God Almighty;
    make your face shine upon us,
    that we may be saved.

⁸You brought a vine out of Egypt;
    you drove out the nations and
      planted it.
⁹You cleared the ground for it,
    and it took root and filled the land.
¹⁰The mountains were covered with its
    shade,
    the mighty cedars with its branches.
¹¹It sent out its boughs to the Sea,ᵃ
    its shoots as far as the River.ᵇ

ᵃ*11* Probably the Mediterranean   ᵇ*11* That is, the
Euphrates

12 Why have you broken down its walls
　　so that all who pass by pick its
　　　grapes?
13 Boars from the forest ravage it
　　and the creatures of the field feed
　　　on it.
14 Return to us, O God Almighty!
　　Look down from heaven and see!
　　Watch over this vine,
15 　the root your right hand has
　　　planted,
　　the son[a] you have raised up for
　　　yourself.

16 Your vine is cut down, it is burned
　　with fire;
　　at your rebuke your people perish.
17 Let your hand rest on the man at your
　　right hand,
　　the son of man you have raised up
　　for yourself.
18 Then we will not turn away from
　　you;
　　revive us, and we will call on your
　　name.

19 Restore us, O LORD God Almighty;
　　make your face shine upon us,
　　that we may be saved.

Psalm 81

*For the director of music.
According to* gittith.[b] *Of Asaph.*

1 Sing for joy to God our strength;
　　shout aloud to the God of Jacob!
2 Begin the music, strike the
　　tambourine,
　　play the melodious harp and lyre.

3 Sound the ram's horn at the New
　　Moon,
　　and when the moon is full, on the
　　day of our Feast;
4 this is a decree for Israel,
　　an ordinance of the God of Jacob.
5 He established it as a statute for
　　Joseph
　　when he went out against Egypt,
　　where we heard a language we did
　　not understand.[c]

6 He says, "I removed the burden from
　　their shoulders;
　　their hands were set free from the
　　basket.

7 In your distress you called and I
　　rescued you,
　　I answered you out of a
　　thundercloud;
　　I tested you at the waters of
　　Meribah.　　　　　　　*Selah*

8 "Hear, O my people, and I will warn
　　you—
　　if you would but listen to me,
　　　O Israel!
9 You shall have no foreign god among
　　you;
　　you shall not bow down to an alien
　　god.
10 I am the LORD your God,
　　who brought you up out of Egypt.
　　Open wide your mouth and I will
　　fill it.

11 "But my people would not listen to
　　me;
　　Israel would not submit to me.
12 So I gave them over to their stubborn
　　hearts
　　to follow their own devices.

13 "If my people would but listen to me,
　　if Israel would follow my ways,
14 how quickly would I subdue their
　　enemies
　　and turn my hand against their
　　foes!
15 Those who hate the LORD would cringe
　　before him,
　　and their punishment would last
　　forever.
16 But you would be fed with the finest
　　of wheat;
　　with honey from the rock I would
　　satisfy you."

Psalm 82

A psalm of Asaph.

1 God presides in the great assembly;
　　he gives judgment among the
　　　"gods":

2 "How long will you[d] defend the unjust
　　and show partiality to the wicked?
　　　　　　　　　　　　Selah

---

[a]15 Or *branch*　　[b]Title: Probably a musical term
[c]5 Or / *and we heard a voice we had not known*
[d]2 The Hebrew is plural.

³Defend the cause of the weak and
fatherless;
   maintain the rights of the poor and
oppressed.
⁴Rescue the weak and needy;
   deliver them from the hand of the
wicked.

⁵"They know nothing, they understand
nothing.
They walk about in darkness;
   all the foundations of the earth are
shaken.

⁶"I said, 'You are "gods";
   you are all sons of the Most High.'
⁷But you will die like mere men;
   you will fall like every other ruler."

⁸Rise up, O God, judge the earth,
   for all the nations are your
inheritance.

Psalm 83

A song. A psalm of Asaph.

¹O God, do not keep silent;
   be not quiet, O God, be not still.
²See how your enemies are astir,
   how your foes rear their heads.
³With cunning they conspire against
your people;
   they plot against those you cherish.
⁴"Come," they say, "let us destroy them
as a nation,
   that the name of Israel be
remembered no more."

⁵With one mind they plot together;
   they form an alliance against you—
⁶the tents of Edom and the
Ishmaelites,
   of Moab and the Hagrites,
⁷Gebal,ᵃ Ammon and Amalek,
   Philistia, with the people of Tyre.
⁸Even Assyria has joined them
   to lend strength to the descendants
of Lot.   *Selah*

⁹Do to them as you did to Midian,
   as you did to Sisera and Jabin at
the river Kishon,
¹⁰who perished at Endor
   and became like refuse on the
ground.
¹¹Make their nobles like Oreb and Zeeb,

all their princes like Zebah and
Zalmunna,
¹²who said, "Let us take possession
   of the pasturelands of God."

¹³Make them like tumbleweed, O my
God,
   like chaff before the wind.
¹⁴As fire consumes the forest
   or a flame sets the mountains
ablaze,
¹⁵so pursue them with your tempest
   and terrify them with your storm.
¹⁶Cover their faces with shame
   so that men will seek your name,
O LORD.

¹⁷May they ever be ashamed and
dismayed;
   may they perish in disgrace.
¹⁸Let them know that you, whose name
is the LORD—
   that you alone are the Most High
over all the earth.

Psalm 84

For the director of music. According to gittith.ᵇ
Of the Sons of Korah. A psalm.

¹How lovely is your dwelling place,
   O LORD Almighty!
²My soul yearns, even faints,
   for the courts of the LORD;
my heart and my flesh cry out
   for the living God.

³Even the sparrow has found a home,
   and the swallow a nest for herself,
   where she may have her young—
a place near your altar,
   O LORD Almighty, my King and my
God.
⁴Blessed are those who dwell in your
house;
   they are ever praising you.   *Selah*

⁵Blessed are those whose strength is in
you,
   who have set their hearts on
pilgrimage.
⁶As they pass through the Valley of
Baca,
   they make it a place of springs;

ᵃ7 That is, Byblos   ᵇTitle: Probably a musical term

the autumn rains also cover it with
pools.ᵃ
⁷They go from strength to strength,
till each appears before God in Zion.

⁸Hear my prayer, O LORD God
Almighty;
listen to me, O God of Jacob.   *Selah*
⁹Look upon our shield,ᵇ O God;
look with favor on your anointed
one.

¹⁰Better is one day in your courts
than a thousand elsewhere;
I would rather be a doorkeeper in the
house of my God
than dwell in the tents of the
wicked.
¹¹For the LORD God is a sun and shield;
the LORD bestows favor and honor;
no good thing does he withhold
from those whose walk is blameless.

¹²O LORD Almighty,
blessed is the man who trusts in
you.

Psalm 85

For the director of music.
Of the Sons of Korah. A psalm.

¹You showed favor to your land,
O LORD;
you restored the fortunes of Jacob.
²You forgave the iniquity of your
people
and covered all their sins.   *Selah*
³You set aside all your wrath
and turned from your fierce anger.

⁴Restore us again, O God our Savior,
and put away your displeasure
toward us.
⁵Will you be angry with us forever?
Will you prolong your anger
through all generations?
⁶Will you not revive us again,
that your people may rejoice in
you?
⁷Show us your unfailing love, O LORD,
and grant us your salvation.

⁸I will listen to what God the LORD will
say;
he promises peace to his people, his
saints—

but let them not return to folly.
⁹Surely his salvation is near those who
fear him,
that his glory may dwell in our
land.

¹⁰Love and faithfulness meet together;
righteousness and peace kiss each
other.
¹¹Faithfulness springs forth from the
earth,
and righteousness looks down from
heaven.
¹²The LORD will indeed give what is
good,
and our land will yield its harvest.
¹³Righteousness goes before him
and prepares the way for his steps.

Psalm 86

A prayer of David.

¹Hear, O LORD, and answer me,
for I am poor and needy.
²Guard my life, for I am devoted to
you.
You are my God; save your servant
who trusts in you.
³Have mercy on me, O Lord,
for I call to you all day long.
⁴Bring joy to your servant,
for to you, O Lord,
I lift up my soul.

⁵You are forgiving and good, O Lord,
abounding in love to all who call to
you.
⁶Hear my prayer, O LORD;
listen to my cry for mercy.
⁷In the day of my trouble I will call to
you,
for you will answer me.

⁸Among the gods there is none like
you, O Lord;
no deeds can compare with yours.
⁹All the nations you have made
will come and worship before you,
O Lord;
they will bring glory to your name.
¹⁰For you are great and do marvelous
deeds;
you alone are God.

ᵃ6 Or *blessings*   ᵇ9 Or *sovereign*

Small "g" Gods

Huh?

Psalm 86:8–10

Our God is not one among many great gods. He has no competition. All small "g" gods are mere myths, frauds or things. They are either myths like Zeus and Apollo; frauds like Satan and demons; or things like money and popularity. Not one of them can stand even in the shadow of the greatness or glory of the real deal. We belong to God with a capital "G."

¹¹Teach me your way, O LORD,
and I will walk in your truth;
give me an undivided heart,
that I may fear your name.
¹²I will praise you, O Lord my God, with
all my heart;
I will glorify your name forever.
¹³For great is your love toward me;
you have delivered me from the
depths of the grave.ᵃ

¹⁴The arrogant are attacking me,
O God;
a band of ruthless men seeks my
life—
men without regard for you.
¹⁵But you, O Lord, are a compassionate
and gracious God,
slow to anger, abounding in love
and faithfulness.
¹⁶Turn to me and have mercy on me;
grant your strength to your servant
and save the son of your
maidservant.ᵇ
¹⁷Give me a sign of your goodness,
that my enemies may see it and be
put to shame,
for you, O LORD, have helped me
and comforted me.

Psalm 87

Of the Sons of Korah. A psalm. A song.

¹He has set his foundation on the holy
mountain;
²   the LORD loves the gates of Zion

more than all the dwellings of
Jacob.
³Glorious things are said of you,
O city of God: *Selah*
⁴"I will record Rahabᶜ and Babylon
among those who acknowledge
me—
Philistia too, and Tyre, along with
Cushᵈ—
and will say, 'Thisᵉ one was born in
Zion.' "

⁵Indeed, of Zion it will be said,
"This one and that one were born in
her,
and the Most High himself will
establish her."
⁶The LORD will write in the register of
the peoples:
"This one was born in Zion."   *Selah*
⁷As they make music they will sing,
"All my fountains are in you."

Psalm 88

A song. A psalm of the Sons of Korah.
For the director of music.
According to *mahalath leannoth*.ᶠ
A *maskil*ᵍ of Heman the Ezrahite.

¹O LORD, the God who saves me,
day and night I cry out before you.
²May my prayer come before you;
turn your ear to my cry.

³For my soul is full of trouble
and my life draws near the grave.ᵃ
⁴I am counted among those who go
down to the pit;
I am like a man without strength.
⁵I am set apart with the dead,
like the slain who lie in the grave,
whom you remember no more,
who are cut off from your care.

⁶You have put me in the lowest pit,
in the darkest depths.
⁷Your wrath lies heavily upon me;

ᵃ13,3 Hebrew *Sheol* ᵇ16 Or *save your faithful son*
ᶜ4 A poetic name for Egypt ᵈ4 That is, the upper
Nile region ᵉ4 Or *"O Rahab and Babylon, /
Philistia, Tyre and Cush, / I will record concerning
those who acknowledge me: / 'This* ᶠTitle: Possibly
a tune, "The Suffering of Affliction" ᵍTitle:
Probably a literary or musical term

you have overwhelmed me with all
   your waves.   *Selah*
⁸You have taken from me my closest
   friends
   and have made me repulsive to
   them.
I am confined and cannot escape;
⁹   my eyes are dim with grief.

I call to you, O Lᴏʀᴅ, every day;
   I spread out my hands to you.
¹⁰Do you show your wonders to the
   dead?
   Do those who are dead rise up and
   praise you?   *Selah*
¹¹Is your love declared in the grave,
   your faithfulness in Destruction*ᵃ*?
¹²Are your wonders known in the place
   of darkness,
   or your righteous deeds in the land
   of oblivion?

¹³But I cry to you for help, O Lᴏʀᴅ;
   in the morning my prayer comes
   before you.
¹⁴Why, O Lᴏʀᴅ, do you reject me
   and hide your face from me?

¹⁵From my youth I have been afflicted
   and close to death;
   I have suffered your terrors and am
   in despair.
¹⁶Your wrath has swept over me;
   your terrors have destroyed me.
¹⁷All day long they surround me like a
   flood;
   they have completely engulfed me.
¹⁸You have taken my companions and
   loved ones from me;
   the darkness is my closest friend.

Psalm 89

A *maskil*ᵇ of Ethan the Ezrahite.

¹I will sing of the Lᴏʀᴅ's great love
   forever;
   with my mouth I will make your
   faithfulness known through all
   generations.
²I will declare that your love stands
   firm forever,
   that you established your
   faithfulness in heaven itself.

³You said, "I have made a covenant
   with my chosen one,

I have sworn to David my servant,
⁴'I will establish your line forever
   and make your throne firm through
   all generations.' "   *Selah*

⁵The heavens praise your wonders,
   O Lᴏʀᴅ,
   your faithfulness too, in the
   assembly of the holy ones.
⁶For who in the skies above can
   compare with the Lᴏʀᴅ?
   Who is like the Lᴏʀᴅ among the
   heavenly beings?
⁷In the council of the holy ones God is
   greatly feared;
   he is more awesome than all who
   surround him.
⁸O Lᴏʀᴅ God Almighty, who is like
   you?
   You are mighty, O Lᴏʀᴅ, and your
   faithfulness surrounds you.

⁹You rule over the surging sea;
   when its waves mount up, you still
   them.
¹⁰You crushed Rahab like one of the
   slain;
   with your strong arm you scattered
   your enemies.
¹¹The heavens are yours, and yours also
   the earth;
   you founded the world and all that
   is in it.
¹²You created the north and the south;
   Tabor and Hermon sing for joy at
   your name.
¹³Your arm is endued with power;
   your hand is strong, your right
   hand exalted.

¹⁴Righteousness and justice are the
   foundation of your throne;
   love and faithfulness go before you.
¹⁵Blessed are those who have learned to
   acclaim you,
   who walk in the light of your
   presence, O Lᴏʀᴅ.
¹⁶They rejoice in your name all day
   long;
   they exult in your righteousness.
¹⁷For you are their glory and strength,
   and by your favor you exalt our
   horn.ᶜ

ᵃ11 Hebrew *Abaddon*   ᵇTitle: Probably a literary
or musical term   ᶜ*17 Horn* here symbolizes
strong one.

¹⁸ Indeed, our shield^a belongs to the
     LORD,
     our king to the Holy One of Israel.

¹⁹ Once you spoke in a vision,
     to your faithful people you said:
     "I have bestowed strength on a
       warrior;
     I have exalted a young man from
       among the people.
²⁰ I have found David my servant;
     with my sacred oil I have anointed
       him.
²¹ My hand will sustain him;
     surely my arm will strengthen him.
²² No enemy will subject him to tribute;
     no wicked man will oppress him.
²³ I will crush his foes before him
     and strike down his adversaries.
²⁴ My faithful love will be with him,
     and through my name his horn^b will
       be exalted.
²⁵ I will set his hand over the sea,
     his right hand over the rivers.
²⁶ He will call out to me, 'You are my
       Father,
     my God, the Rock my Savior.'
²⁷ I will also appoint him my firstborn,
     the most exalted of the kings of the
       earth.
²⁸ I will maintain my love to him forever,
     and my covenant with him will
       never fail.
²⁹ I will establish his line forever,
     his throne as long as the heavens
       endure.

³⁰ "If his sons forsake my law
     and do not follow my statutes,
³¹ if they violate my decrees
     and fail to keep my commands,
³² I will punish their sin with the rod,
     their iniquity with flogging;
³³ but I will not take my love from him,
     nor will I ever betray my
       faithfulness.
³⁴ I will not violate my covenant
     or alter what my lips have uttered.
³⁵ Once for all, I have sworn by my
       holiness—
     and I will not lie to David—
³⁶ that his line will continue forever
     and his throne endure before me
       like the sun;
³⁷ it will be established forever like the
       moon,

     the faithful witness in the sky."
                    Selah

³⁸ But you have rejected, you have
       spurned,
     you have been very angry with your
       anointed one.
³⁹ You have renounced the covenant
     with your servant
     and have defiled his crown in the
       dust.
⁴⁰ You have broken through all his walls
     and reduced his strongholds to
       ruins.
⁴¹ All who pass by have plundered him;
     he has become the scorn of his
       neighbors.
⁴² You have exalted the right hand of his
       foes;
     you have made all his enemies
       rejoice.
⁴³ You have turned back the edge of his
       sword
     and have not supported him in
       battle.
⁴⁴ You have put an end to his splendor
     and cast his throne to the ground.
⁴⁵ You have cut short the days of his
       youth;
     you have covered him with a
       mantle of shame.   *Selah*

⁴⁶ How long, O LORD? Will you hide
     yourself forever?
     How long will your wrath burn like
       fire?
⁴⁷ Remember how fleeting is my life.
     For what futility you have created
       all men!
⁴⁸ What man can live and not see death,
     or save himself from the power of
       the grave^c?   *Selah*
⁴⁹ O Lord, where is your former great
       love,
     which in your faithfulness you
       swore to David?
⁵⁰ Remember, Lord, how your servant
     has^d been mocked,
     how I bear in my heart the taunts of
       all the nations,
⁵¹ the taunts with which your enemies
     have mocked, O LORD,

---

^a18 Or *sovereign*   ^b24 *Horn* here symbolizes
strength.   ^c48 Hebrew *Sheol*   ^d50 Or *your servants
have*

with which they have mocked every
    step of your anointed one.

⁵²Praise be to the LORD forever!
    Amen and Amen.

BOOK IV
Psalms 90–106

Psalm 90

A prayer of Moses the man of God.

¹Lord, you have been our dwelling
    place
    throughout all generations.
²Before the mountains were born
    or you brought forth the earth and
      the world,
    from everlasting to everlasting you
      are God.

³You turn men back to dust,
    saying, "Return to dust, O sons of
      men."
⁴For a thousand years in your sight
    are like a day that has just gone by,
    or like a watch in the night.
⁵You sweep men away in the sleep of
      death;
    they are like the new grass of the
      morning—
⁶though in the morning it springs up
      new,
    by evening it is dry and withered.

⁷We are consumed by your anger
    and terrified by your indignation.
⁸You have set our iniquities before you,
    our secret sins in the light of your
      presence.
⁹All our days pass away under your
      wrath;
    we finish our years with a moan.
¹⁰The length of our days is seventy
      years—
    or eighty, if we have the strength;
    yet their span^a is but trouble and
      sorrow,
    for they quickly pass, and we fly
      away.
¹¹Who knows the power of your anger?
    For your wrath is as great as the
      fear that is due you.

¹²Teach us to number our days aright,
    that we may gain a heart of
      wisdom.

Life Is Short
Huh?

Psalm 90:12
Life may be short, but most people act as
if it's long. They spend their days like
they've got millions to waste. It takes a
heart of wisdom to see that life really is
short, that every day is important. So next
time you're tempted to veg in front of the
tube, pray this verse. Ask God not only to
help you count your days but to make your
days count.

¹³Relent, O LORD! How long will it be?
    Have compassion on your servants.
¹⁴Satisfy us in the morning with your
      unfailing love,
    that we may sing for joy and be
      glad all our days.
¹⁵Make us glad for as many days as you
      have afflicted us,
    for as many years as we have seen
      trouble.
¹⁶May your deeds be shown to your
      servants,
    your splendor to their children.

¹⁷May the favor^b of the Lord our God
      rest upon us;
    establish the work of our hands for
      us—
    yes, establish the work of our
      hands.

Psalm 91

¹He who dwells in the shelter of the
      Most High
    will rest in the shadow of the
      Almighty.^c
²I will say^d of the LORD, "He is my
      refuge and my fortress,
    my God, in whom I trust."

---

^a10 Or *yet the best of them*   ^b17 Or *beauty*
^c1 Hebrew *Shaddai*   ^d2 Or *He says*

³Surely he will save you from the
  fowler's snare
  and from the deadly pestilence.
⁴He will cover you with his feathers,
  and under his wings you will find
    refuge;
  his faithfulness will be your shield
    and rampart.
⁵You will not fear the terror of night,
  nor the arrow that flies by day,
⁶nor the pestilence that stalks in the
    darkness,
  nor the plague that destroys at
    midday.
⁷A thousand may fall at your side,
  ten thousand at your right hand,
  but it will not come near you.
⁸You will only observe with your eyes
  and see the punishment of the
    wicked.

⁹If you make the Most High your
    dwelling—
  even the LORD, who is my refuge—
¹⁰then no harm will befall you,
  no disaster will come near your
    tent.
¹¹For he will command his angels
    concerning you
  to guard you in all your ways;
¹²they will lift you up in their hands,
  so that you will not strike your foot
    against a stone.
¹³You will tread upon the lion and the
    cobra;
  you will trample the great lion and
    the serpent.

¹⁴"Because he loves me," says the LORD,
  "I will rescue him;
  I will protect him, for he
    acknowledges my name.
¹⁵He will call upon me, and I will
    answer him;
  I will be with him in trouble,
  I will deliver him and honor him.
¹⁶With long life will I satisfy him
  and show him my salvation."

Psalm 92

A psalm. A song. For the Sabbath day.

¹It is good to praise the LORD
  and make music to your name,
    O Most High,

²to proclaim your love in the morning
  and your faithfulness at night,
³to the music of the ten-stringed lyre
  and the melody of the harp.

⁴For you make me glad by your deeds,
    O LORD;
  I sing for joy at the works of your
    hands.
⁵How great are your works, O LORD,
  how profound your thoughts!
⁶The senseless man does not know,
  fools do not understand,
⁷that though the wicked spring up like
    grass
  and all evildoers flourish,
  they will be forever destroyed.

⁸But you, O LORD, are exalted forever.

⁹For surely your enemies, O LORD,
  surely your enemies will perish;
  all evildoers will be scattered.
¹⁰You have exalted my horn[a] like that of
    a wild ox;
  fine oils have been poured upon me.
¹¹My eyes have seen the defeat of my
    adversaries;
  my ears have heard the rout of my
    wicked foes.

¹²The righteous will flourish like a palm
    tree,
  they will grow like a cedar of
    Lebanon;
¹³planted in the house of the LORD,
  they will flourish in the courts of
    our God.
¹⁴They will still bear fruit in old age,
  they will stay fresh and green,
¹⁵proclaiming, "The LORD is upright;
  he is my Rock, and there is no
    wickedness in him."

Psalm 93

¹The LORD reigns, he is robed in
    majesty;
  the LORD is robed in majesty
  and is armed with strength.
  The world is firmly established;
  it cannot be moved.
²Your throne was established long ago;
  you are from all eternity.

---

[a]10 Horn here symbolizes strength.

³The seas have lifted up, O LORD,
    the seas have lifted up their voice;
    the seas have lifted up their
        pounding waves.
⁴Mightier than the thunder of the great
        waters,
    mightier than the breakers of the
        sea—
    the LORD on high is mighty.

⁵Your statutes stand firm;
    holiness adorns your house
    for endless days, O LORD.

Psalm 94

¹O LORD, the God who avenges,
    O God who avenges, shine forth.
²Rise up, O Judge of the earth;
    pay back to the proud what they
        deserve.
³How long will the wicked, O LORD,
    how long will the wicked be
        jubilant?

⁴They pour out arrogant words;
    all the evildoers are full of
        boasting.
⁵They crush your people, O LORD;
    they oppress your inheritance.
⁶They slay the widow and the alien;
    they murder the fatherless.
⁷They say, "The LORD does not see;
    the God of Jacob pays no heed."

⁸Take heed, you senseless ones among
        the people;
    you fools, when will you become
        wise?
⁹Does he who implanted the ear not
        hear?
    Does he who formed the eye not
        see?
¹⁰Does he who disciplines nations not
        punish?
    Does he who teaches man lack
        knowledge?
¹¹The LORD knows the thoughts of man;
    he knows that they are futile.

Thursday

In the Pilot's Seat

Read Psalm 91:1–4

My dad is a pilot. One day when he was flying a small plane something went wrong. He was coming in to land, but the landing gear didn't come down. He radioed the tower and they sent out emergency crews in case he crashed. All my dad could do was pray.

His only choice was to land without the landing gear, so he brought the plane in and skidded down the runway. He came to a stop and climbed out of the plane unhurt. I really believe God did just what these verses promise: God protected my dad and wrapped his "wings" around him like a shield.

A lot of scary things happen in the world. But as long as I know God is there, I feel more secure and peaceful. We can trust God to be our shelter and our shield. Just ask my dad.

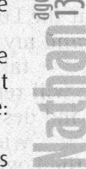

Nathan age 13

What about You?

❶ Trusting in God's protection doesn't mean nothing bad will ever happen to you. Think about what it really means to say that God is our shelter and our shield.

❷ You know how a winter coat keeps you warm even when it's freezing outside? Well, think of God in the same way. He protects us and shields us from bad-news stuff.

❸ Whenever you're facing hard times, remember that God is there, and, like that coat, he'll wrap you up in his love.

Turn to page 697 for your next devotion.

¹²Blessed is the man you discipline,
   O Lᴏʀᴅ,
   the man you teach from your law;
¹³you grant him relief from days of
     trouble,
   till a pit is dug for the wicked.
¹⁴For the Lᴏʀᴅ will not reject his people;
   he will never forsake his
     inheritance.
¹⁵Judgment will again be founded on
     righteousness,
   and all the upright in heart will
     follow it.

¹⁶Who will rise up for me against the
     wicked?
   Who will take a stand for me
     against evildoers?
¹⁷Unless the Lᴏʀᴅ had given me help,
   I would soon have dwelt in the
     silence of death.
¹⁸When I said, "My foot is slipping,"
   your love, O Lᴏʀᴅ, supported me.
¹⁹When anxiety was great within me,
   your consolation brought joy to my
     soul.

²⁰Can a corrupt throne be allied with
     you—
   one that brings on misery by its
     decrees?
²¹They band together against the
     righteous
   and condemn the innocent to death.
²²But the Lᴏʀᴅ has become my fortress,
   and my God the rock in whom I
     take refuge.
²³He will repay them for their sins
   and destroy them for their
     wickedness;
   the Lᴏʀᴅ our God will destroy them.

Psalm 95

¹Come, let us sing for joy to the Lᴏʀᴅ;
   let us shout aloud to the Rock of
     our salvation.
²Let us come before him with
     thanksgiving
   and extol him with music and
     song.
³For the Lᴏʀᴅ is the great God,
   the great King above all gods.
⁴In his hand are the depths of the
     earth,

and the mountain peaks belong to
     him.
⁵The sea is his, for he made it,
   and his hands formed the dry land.

⁶Come, let us bow down in worship,
   let us kneel before the Lᴏʀᴅ our
     Maker;
⁷for he is our God
   and we are the people of his
     pasture,
   the flock under his care.

Today, if you hear his voice,
⁸   do not harden your hearts as you
     did at Meribah,ᵃ
   as you did that day at Massahᵇ in
     the desert,
⁹where your fathers tested and tried
     me,
   though they had seen what I did.
¹⁰For forty years I was angry with that
     generation;
   I said, "They are a people whose
     hearts go astray,
   and they have not known my
     ways."
¹¹So I declared on oath in my anger,
   "They shall never enter my rest."

Psalm 96

¹Sing to the Lᴏʀᴅ a new song;
   sing to the Lᴏʀᴅ, all the earth.
²Sing to the Lᴏʀᴅ, praise his name;
   proclaim his salvation day after
     day.
³Declare his glory among the
     nations,
   his marvelous deeds among all
     peoples.

⁴For great is the Lᴏʀᴅ and most worthy
     of praise;
   he is to be feared above all gods.
⁵For all the gods of the nations are
     idols,
   but the Lᴏʀᴅ made the heavens.
⁶Splendor and majesty are before him;
   strength and glory are in his
     sanctuary.

⁷Ascribe to the Lᴏʀᴅ, O families of
     nations,

ᵃ8 Meribah means *quarreling.*   ᵇ8 Massah means
testing.

ascribe to the LORD glory and
strength.
⁸ Ascribe to the LORD the glory due his
name;
bring an offering and come into his
courts.
⁹ Worship the LORD in the splendor of
his*ᵃ holiness;
tremble before him, all the earth.

¹⁰ Say among the nations, "The LORD
reigns."
The world is firmly established, it
cannot be moved;
he will judge the peoples with
equity.
¹¹ Let the heavens rejoice, let the earth
be glad;
let the sea resound, and all that is
in it;
¹² let the fields be jubilant, and
everything in them.
Then all the trees of the forest will
sing for joy;
¹³ they will sing before the LORD, for
he comes,
he comes to judge the earth.
He will judge the world in
righteousness
and the peoples in his truth.

Psalm 97

¹ The LORD reigns, let the earth be glad;
let the distant shores rejoice.

² Clouds and thick darkness surround
him;
righteousness and justice are the
foundation of his throne.
³ Fire goes before him
and consumes his foes on every
side.
⁴ His lightning lights up the world;
the earth sees and trembles.
⁵ The mountains melt like wax before
the LORD,
before the Lord of all the earth.
⁶ The heavens proclaim his
righteousness,
and all the peoples see his glory.

⁷ All who worship images are put to
shame,
those who boast in idols—
worship him, all you gods!

⁸ Zion hears and rejoices
and the villages of Judah are glad
because of your judgments, O LORD.
⁹ For you, O LORD, are the Most High
over all the earth;
you are exalted far above all gods.

¹⁰ Let those who love the LORD hate evil,
for he guards the lives of his
faithful ones
and delivers them from the hand of
the wicked.
¹¹ Light is shed upon the righteous
and joy on the upright in heart.
¹² Rejoice in the LORD, you who are
righteous,
and praise his holy name.

Psalm 98

A psalm.

¹ Sing to the LORD a new song,
for he has done marvelous things;
his right hand and his holy arm
have worked salvation for him.
² The LORD has made his salvation
known
and revealed his righteousness to
the nations.
³ He has remembered his love
and his faithfulness to the house of
Israel;
all the ends of the earth have seen
the salvation of our God.

⁴ Shout for joy to the LORD, all the
earth,
burst into jubilant song with music;
⁵ make music to the LORD with the harp,
with the harp and the sound of
singing,
⁶ with trumpets and the blast of the
ram's horn—
shout for joy before the LORD, the
King.

⁷ Let the sea resound, and everything in
it,
the world, and all who live in it.
⁸ Let the rivers clap their hands,
let the mountains sing together for
joy;
⁹ let them sing before the LORD,

ᵃ9 Or *LORD with the splendor of*

for he comes to judge the earth.
He will judge the world in
    righteousness
and the peoples with equity.

Psalm 99

[1] The LORD reigns,
    let the nations tremble;
he sits enthroned between the
    cherubim,
    let the earth shake.
[2] Great is the LORD in Zion;
    he is exalted over all the nations.
[3] Let them praise your great and
    awesome name—
    he is holy.

[4] The King is mighty, he loves justice—
    you have established equity;
in Jacob you have done
    what is just and right.
[5] Exalt the LORD our God
    and worship at his footstool;
    he is holy.

[6] Moses and Aaron were among his
    priests,
    Samuel was among those who
    called on his name;
they called on the LORD
    and he answered them.
[7] He spoke to them from the pillar of
    cloud;
    they kept his statutes and the
    decrees he gave them.

[8] O LORD our God,
    you answered them;
you were to Israel[a] a forgiving God,
    though you punished their
    misdeeds.[b]
[9] Exalt the LORD our God
    and worship at his holy mountain,
    for the LORD our God is holy.

Psalm 100

A psalm. For giving thanks.

[1] Shout for joy to the LORD, all the
    earth.
[2]   Worship the LORD with gladness;
    come before him with joyful songs.
[3] Know that the LORD is God.
    It is he who made us, and we are his[c];

we are his people, the sheep of his
    pasture.
[4] Enter his gates with thanksgiving
    and his courts with praise;
    give thanks to him and praise his
    name.
[5] For the LORD is good and his love
    endures forever;
    his faithfulness continues through
    all generations.

Psalm 101

Of David. A psalm.

[1] I will sing of your love and justice;
    to you, O LORD, I will sing praise.
[2] I will be careful to lead a blameless
    life—
    when will you come to me?

I will walk in my house
    with blameless heart.
[3] I will set before my eyes
    no vile thing.

The deeds of faithless men I hate;
    they will not cling to me.
[4] Men of perverse heart shall be far
    from me;
    I will have nothing to do with evil.

[5] Whoever slanders his neighbor in
    secret,
    him will I put to silence;
whoever has haughty eyes and a
    proud heart,
    him will I not endure.

[6] My eyes will be on the faithful in the
    land,
    that they may dwell with me;
he whose walk is blameless
    will minister to me.

[7] No one who practices deceit
    will dwell in my house;
no one who speaks falsely
    will stand in my presence.

[8] Every morning I will put to silence
    all the wicked in the land;
    I will cut off every evildoer
    from the city of the LORD.

*a8 Hebrew them   b8 Or / an avenger of the wrongs
done to them   c3 Or and not we ourselves*

Psalm 102

*A prayer of an afflicted man.
When he is faint and pours out
his lament before the LORD.*

¹Hear my prayer, O LORD;
  let my cry for help come to you.
²Do not hide your face from me
  when I am in distress.
 Turn your ear to me;
  when I call, answer me quickly.

³For my days vanish like smoke;
  my bones burn like glowing embers.
⁴My heart is blighted and withered like
    grass;
  I forget to eat my food.
⁵Because of my loud groaning
  I am reduced to skin and bones.
⁶I am like a desert owl,
  like an owl among the ruins.
⁷I lie awake; I have become
  like a bird alone on a roof.
⁸All day long my enemies taunt me;
  those who rail against me use my
    name as a curse.
⁹For I eat ashes as my food
  and mingle my drink with tears
¹⁰because of your great wrath,
  for you have taken me up and
    thrown me aside.
¹¹My days are like the evening shadow;
  I wither away like grass.

¹²But you, O LORD, sit enthroned forever;
  your renown endures through all
    generations.
¹³You will arise and have compassion
    on Zion,
  for it is time to show favor to her;
  the appointed time has come.
¹⁴For her stones are dear to your
    servants;
  her very dust moves them to pity.
¹⁵The nations will fear the name of the
    LORD,
  all the kings of the earth will revere
    your glory.
¹⁶For the LORD will rebuild Zion
  and appear in his glory.
¹⁷He will respond to the prayer of the
    destitute;
  he will not despise their plea.

¹⁸Let this be written for a future
    generation,
that a people not yet created may
    praise the LORD:
¹⁹"The LORD looked down from his
    sanctuary on high,
  from heaven he viewed the earth,
²⁰to hear the groans of the prisoners
  and release those condemned to
    death."
²¹So the name of the LORD will be
    declared in Zion
  and his praise in Jerusalem
²²when the peoples and the kingdoms
  assemble to worship the LORD.

²³In the course of my life*a* he broke my
    strength;
  he cut short my days.
²⁴So I said:
 "Do not take me away, O my God,
    in the midst of my days;
  your years go on through all
    generations.
²⁵In the beginning you laid the
    foundations of the earth,
  and the heavens are the work of
    your hands.
²⁶They will perish, but you remain;
  they will all wear out like a
    garment.
 Like clothing you will change them
  and they will be discarded.
²⁷But you remain the same,
  and your years will never end.
²⁸The children of your servants will live
    in your presence;
  their descendants will be established
    before you."

Psalm 103

Of David.

¹Praise the LORD, O my soul;
  all my inmost being, praise his holy
    name.
²Praise the LORD, O my soul,
  and forget not all his benefits—
³who forgives all your sins
  and heals all your diseases,
⁴who redeems your life from the pit
  and crowns you with love and
    compassion,
⁵who satisfies your desires with good
    things

---

a23 Or *By his power*

so that your youth is renewed like
the eagle's.

⁶The LORD works righteousness
and justice for all the oppressed.

⁷He made known his ways to Moses,
his deeds to the people of Israel:
⁸The LORD is compassionate and
gracious,
slow to anger, abounding in love.
⁹He will not always accuse,
nor will he harbor his anger
forever;
¹⁰he does not treat us as our sins
deserve
or repay us according to our
iniquities.
¹¹For as high as the heavens are above
the earth,
so great is his love for those who
fear him;
¹²as far as the east is from the west,
so far has he removed our
transgressions from us.
¹³As a father has compassion on his
children,
so the LORD has compassion on
those who fear him;
¹⁴for he knows how we are formed,
he remembers that we are dust.
¹⁵As for man, his days are like grass,
he flourishes like a flower of the
field;
¹⁶the wind blows over it and it is
gone,
and its place remembers it no
more.
¹⁷But from everlasting to everlasting
the LORD's love is with those who
fear him,
and his righteousness with their
children's children—
¹⁸with those who keep his covenant
and remember to obey his precepts.

¹⁹The LORD has established his throne in
heaven,
and his kingdom rules over all.

²⁰Praise the LORD, you his angels,
you mighty ones who do his
bidding,
who obey his word.
²¹Praise the LORD, all his heavenly
hosts,
you his servants who do his will.

²²Praise the LORD, all his works
everywhere in his dominion.

Praise the LORD, O my soul.

Psalm 104

¹Praise the LORD, O my soul.

O LORD my God, you are very great;
you are clothed with splendor and
majesty.
²He wraps himself in light as with a
garment;
he stretches out the heavens like a
tent
³ and lays the beams of his upper
chambers on their waters.
He makes the clouds his chariot
and rides on the wings of the wind.
⁴He makes winds his messengers,ᵃ
flames of fire his servants.

⁵He set the earth on its foundations;
it can never be moved.
⁶You covered it with the deep as with a
garment;
the waters stood above the
mountains.
⁷But at your rebuke the waters fled,
at the sound of your thunder they
took to flight;
⁸they flowed over the mountains,
they went down into the valleys,
to the place you assigned for them.
⁹You set a boundary they cannot cross;
never again will they cover the
earth.

¹⁰He makes springs pour water into the
ravines;
it flows between the mountains.
¹¹They give water to all the beasts of
the field;
the wild donkeys quench their
thirst.
¹²The birds of the air nest by the waters;
they sing among the branches.
¹³He waters the mountains from his
upper chambers;
the earth is satisfied by the fruit of
his work.
¹⁴He makes grass grow for the cattle,
and plants for man to cultivate—
bringing forth food from the earth:

ᵃ4 Or *angels*

¹⁵wine that gladdens the heart of man,
  oil to make his face shine,
  and bread that sustains his heart.
¹⁶The trees of the LORD are well watered,
  the cedars of Lebanon that he
    planted.
¹⁷There the birds make their nests;
  the stork has its home in the pine
    trees.
¹⁸The high mountains belong to the
    wild goats;
  the crags are a refuge for the
    coneys.ᵃ

¹⁹The moon marks off the seasons,
  and the sun knows when to go
    down.
²⁰You bring darkness, it becomes night,
  and all the beasts of the forest
    prowl.
²¹The lions roar for their prey
  and seek their food from God.
²²The sun rises, and they steal away;
  they return and lie down in their
    dens.

²³Then man goes out to his work,
  to his labor until evening.

²⁴How many are your works, O LORD!
  In wisdom you made them all;
  the earth is full of your creatures.
²⁵There is the sea, vast and spacious,
  teeming with creatures beyond
    number—
  living things both large and small.
²⁶There the ships go to and fro,
  and the leviathan, which you
    formed to frolic there.

²⁷These all look to you
  to give them their food at the
    proper time.
²⁸When you give it to them,
  they gather it up;
  when you open your hand,
  they are satisfied with good things.
²⁹When you hide your face,
  they are terrified;
  when you take away their breath,

ᵃ18 That is, the hyrax or rock badger

Friday

Great Big Love

Read Psalm 103:11–12

One of my friends and I got into an argument a long time ago, and our friendship has never been the same since. We used to get along great, but now I get angry with him all the time. It seems like we fight over stuff that just doesn't matter. After reading this passage, I realize how many times God has forgiven me. And it reminds me that I need to be forgiving too.

I've always known that God forgives me. But I don't always think about what a huge and amazing thing forgiveness really is. I mean, God's love and forgiveness are pretty incredible. And if God can forgive us for the thousands of things we do wrong, it sure seems like we can learn to forgive other people.

❶ How do you feel when someone forgives you?

❷ Go for a walk someplace where there's sand or dirt you can write in with a stick. Write something you'd like to be forgiven for. Tell God you're sorry and ask him to forgive you. Now, use water or the stick to erase what you've written. What does this tell you about God's forgiveness?

❸ Thank God for his repeated forgiveness.

Turn to page 699 for your next devotion.

they die and return to the dust.
³⁰When you send your Spirit,
  they are created,
  and you renew the face of the earth.

³¹May the glory of the LORD endure
    forever;
  may the LORD rejoice in his works—
³²he who looks at the earth, and it
    trembles,
  who touches the mountains, and
    they smoke.

³³I will sing to the LORD all my life;
  I will sing praise to my God as long
    as I live.
³⁴May my meditation be pleasing to
    him,
  as I rejoice in the LORD.
³⁵But may sinners vanish from the earth
  and the wicked be no more.

Praise the LORD, O my soul.

Praise the LORD.^a

Psalm 105

¹Give thanks to the LORD, call on his
    name;
  make known among the nations
    what he has done.
²Sing to him, sing praise to him;
  tell of all his wonderful acts.
³Glory in his holy name;
  let the hearts of those who seek the
    LORD rejoice.
⁴Look to the LORD and his strength;
  seek his face always.

⁵Remember the wonders he has done,
  his miracles, and the judgments he
    pronounced,
⁶O descendants of Abraham his
    servant,
  O sons of Jacob, his chosen ones.
⁷He is the LORD our God;
  his judgments are in all the earth.

⁸He remembers his covenant forever,
  the word he commanded, for a
    thousand generations,
⁹the covenant he made with Abraham,
  the oath he swore to Isaac.
¹⁰He confirmed it to Jacob as a decree,
  to Israel as an everlasting covenant:
¹¹"To you I will give the land of Canaan
  as the portion you will inherit."

¹²When they were but few in number,
  few indeed, and strangers in it,
¹³they wandered from nation to nation,
  from one kingdom to another.
¹⁴He allowed no one to oppress them;
  for their sake he rebuked kings:
¹⁵"Do not touch my anointed ones;
  do my prophets no harm."

¹⁶He called down famine on the land
  and destroyed all their supplies of
    food;
¹⁷and he sent a man before them—
  Joseph, sold as a slave.
¹⁸They bruised his feet with shackles,
  his neck was put in irons,
¹⁹till what he foretold came to pass,
  till the word of the LORD proved him
    true.
²⁰The king sent and released him,
  the ruler of peoples set him free.
²¹He made him master of his household,
  ruler over all he possessed,
²²to instruct his princes as he pleased
  and teach his elders wisdom.

²³Then Israel entered Egypt;
  Jacob lived as an alien in the land
    of Ham.
²⁴The LORD made his people very
    fruitful;
  he made them too numerous for
    their foes,
²⁵whose hearts he turned to hate his
    people,
  to conspire against his servants.
²⁶He sent Moses his servant,
  and Aaron, whom he had chosen.
²⁷They performed his miraculous signs
    among them,
  his wonders in the land of Ham.
²⁸He sent darkness and made the land
    dark—
  for had they not rebelled against his
    words?
²⁹He turned their waters into blood,
  causing their fish to die.
³⁰Their land teemed with frogs,
  which went up into the bedrooms of
    their rulers.
³¹He spoke, and there came swarms of
    flies,
  and gnats throughout their country.

^a35 Hebrew *Hallelu Yah*; in the Septuagint this line
stands at the beginning of Psalm 105.

³²He turned their rain into hail,
   with lightning throughout their
      land;
³³he struck down their vines and fig
      trees
   and shattered the trees of their
      country.
³⁴He spoke, and the locusts came,
   grasshoppers without number;

³⁵they ate up every green thing in their
      land,
   ate up the produce of their soil.
³⁶Then he struck down all the firstborn
      in their land,
   the firstfruits of all their manhood.

³⁷He brought out Israel, laden with
      silver and gold,

Week end.

Two Kinds of Care Packages

Read 2 Corinthians 12:7–10 (page 1409)

This week you heard two stories of God's awesome power. He brought Amy and her family through a raging storm and enabled Nathan's father to safely land a plane without the landing gear. The Bible calls this *deliverance*. God delivers us from the storm and delivers us from death. When God works miracles to deliver us, it's easy to see how much he cares for us.

But *deliverance* is only one of God's care packages. The other is called *perseverance*. Perseverance is the power to hang in there, to keep going, to stick with it through tough times. And the power to persevere comes from God too—just as much as his miracle-working power does.

The passage for today describes the care package God sent Paul when he prayed for healing from his "thorn in the flesh" (some kind of illness he had). Three times Paul prayed for deliverance—he wanted to be healed. But each time God sent perseverance, the power to put up with the problem. Finally Paul accepted the gift of perseverance from God and was happy with it.

God usually sends perseverance packages, even though we usually pray for wonderful, gift-wrapped boxes of deliverance. In other words, God usually doesn't fix our problems with miracles. But he still cares about us. He still answers our prayers; he still helps us. But he helps us to endure.

Some people mistakenly think that if they pray with enough faith, God will always send a miracle. But he doesn't. Hey, do you think the apostle Paul lacked faith? No way. He just realized that God's help can come in 2 different packages.

What about You?

❶ Have you ever been frustrated with God for not fixing a problem, even though you prayed for help? Do you think you might have been looking for the wrong care package?

❷ Write a "perseverance plan" for the biggest problem in your life. If God were to give you the power to put up with this problem, what would you have the power to do? What attitudes and actions would you be able to take?

❸ You're still allowed to ask for miracles—for deliverance. But also ask God for perseverance and the ability to accept it if that's what he sends.

Turn to page 707 for your next devotion.

and from among their tribes no one
    faltered.
³⁸ Egypt was glad when they left,
    because dread of Israel had fallen
        on them.
³⁹ He spread out a cloud as a covering,
    and a fire to give light at night.
⁴⁰ They asked, and he brought them
        quail
    and satisfied them with the bread of
        heaven.
⁴¹ He opened the rock, and water gushed
        out;
    like a river it flowed in the desert.

⁴² For he remembered his holy promise
    given to his servant Abraham.
⁴³ He brought out his people with
        rejoicing,
    his chosen ones with shouts of joy;
⁴⁴ he gave them the lands of the nations,
    and they fell heir to what others
        had toiled for—
⁴⁵ that they might keep his precepts
    and observe his laws.

Praise the LORD.ᵃ

Psalm 106

¹ Praise the LORD.ᵇ

Give thanks to the LORD, for he is good;
    his love endures forever.
² Who can proclaim the mighty acts of
        the LORD
    or fully declare his praise?
³ Blessed are they who maintain justice,
    who constantly do what is right.
⁴ Remember me, O LORD, when you
        show favor to your people,
    come to my aid when you save
        them,
⁵ that I may enjoy the prosperity of
        your chosen ones,
    that I may share in the joy of your
        nation
    and join your inheritance in giving
        praise.

⁶ We have sinned, even as our fathers
        did;
    we have done wrong and acted
        wickedly.
⁷ When our fathers were in Egypt,
    they gave no thought to your
        miracles;

they did not remember your many
        kindnesses,
    and they rebelled by the sea, the
        Red Sea.ᶜ
⁸ Yet he saved them for his name's sake,
    to make his mighty power known.
⁹ He rebuked the Red Sea, and it dried
        up;
    he led them through the depths as
        through a desert.
¹⁰ He saved them from the hand of the
        foe;
    from the hand of the enemy he
        redeemed them.
¹¹ The waters covered their adversaries;
    not one of them survived.
¹² Then they believed his promises
    and sang his praise.

¹³ But they soon forgot what he had
        done
    and did not wait for his counsel.
¹⁴ In the desert they gave in to their
        craving;
    in the wasteland they put God to
        the test.
¹⁵ So he gave them what they asked for,
    but sent a wasting disease upon
        them.

¹⁶ In the camp they grew envious of
        Moses
    and of Aaron, who was consecrated
        to the LORD.
¹⁷ The earth opened up and swallowed
        Dathan;
    it buried the company of Abiram.
¹⁸ Fire blazed among their followers;
    a flame consumed the wicked.

¹⁹ At Horeb they made a calf
    and worshiped an idol cast from
        metal.
²⁰ They exchanged their Glory
    for an image of a bull, which eats
        grass.
²¹ They forgot the God who saved them,
    who had done great things in Egypt,
²² miracles in the land of Ham
    and awesome deeds by the Red Sea.
²³ So he said he would destroy them—
    had not Moses, his chosen one,
    stood in the breach before him

ᵃ45 Hebrew *Hallelu Yah*   ᵇ1 Hebrew *Hallelu Yah*;
also in verse 48   ᶜ7 Hebrew *Yam Suph*; that is, Sea
of Reeds; also in verses 9 and 22

to keep his wrath from destroying
   them.

²⁴Then they despised the pleasant land;
   they did not believe his promise.
²⁵They grumbled in their tents
   and did not obey the LORD.
²⁶So he swore to them with uplifted
   hand
   that he would make them fall in the
   desert,
²⁷make their descendants fall among the
   nations
   and scatter them throughout the
   lands.

²⁸They yoked themselves to the Baal of
   Peor
   and ate sacrifices offered to lifeless
   gods;
²⁹they provoked the LORD to anger by
   their wicked deeds,
   and a plague broke out among
   them.
³⁰But Phinehas stood up and
   intervened,
   and the plague was checked.
³¹This was credited to him as
   righteousness
   for endless generations to come.

³²By the waters of Meribah they
   angered the LORD,
   and trouble came to Moses because
   of them;
³³for they rebelled against the Spirit of
   God,
   and rash words came from Moses'
   lips.ᵃ

³⁴They did not destroy the peoples
   as the LORD had commanded them,
³⁵but they mingled with the nations
   and adopted their customs.
³⁶They worshiped their idols,
   which became a snare to them.
³⁷They sacrificed their sons
   and their daughters to demons.
³⁸They shed innocent blood,
   the blood of their sons and
   daughters,
   whom they sacrificed to the idols of
   Canaan,
   and the land was desecrated by
   their blood.
³⁹They defiled themselves by what they
   did;

by their deeds they prostituted
   themselves.

⁴⁰Therefore the LORD was angry with his
   people
   and abhorred his inheritance.
⁴¹He handed them over to the nations,
   and their foes ruled over them.
⁴²Their enemies oppressed them
   and subjected them to their power.
⁴³Many times he delivered them,
   but they were bent on rebellion
   and they wasted away in their sin.

⁴⁴But he took note of their distress
   when he heard their cry;
⁴⁵for their sake he remembered his
   covenant
   and out of his great love he
   relented.
⁴⁶He caused them to be pitied
   by all who held them captive.

⁴⁷Save us, O LORD our God,
   and gather us from the nations,
   that we may give thanks to your holy
   name
   and glory in your praise.

⁴⁸Praise be to the LORD, the God of
   Israel,
   from everlasting to everlasting.
   Let all the people say, "Amen!"

   Praise the LORD.

BOOK V
Psalms 107–150

Psalm 107

¹Give thanks to the LORD, for he is
   good;
   his love endures forever.
²Let the redeemed of the LORD say
   this—
   those he redeemed from the hand of
   the foe,
³those he gathered from the lands,
   from east and west, from north and
   south.ᵇ

⁴Some wandered in desert wastelands,

---

*ᵃ33 Or against his spirit, / and rash words came
from his lips   ᵇ3 Hebrew north and the sea*

finding no way to a city where they
could settle.
⁵They were hungry and thirsty,
and their lives ebbed away.
⁶Then they cried out to the LORD in
their trouble,
and he delivered them from their
distress.
⁷He led them by a straight way
to a city where they could settle.
⁸Let them give thanks to the LORD for
his unfailing love
and his wonderful deeds for men,
⁹for he satisfies the thirsty
and fills the hungry with good
things.

¹⁰Some sat in darkness and the deepest
gloom,
prisoners suffering in iron chains,
¹¹for they had rebelled against the
words of God
and despised the counsel of the
Most High.
¹²So he subjected them to bitter labor;
they stumbled, and there was no
one to help.
¹³Then they cried to the LORD in their
trouble,
and he saved them from their
distress.
¹⁴He brought them out of darkness and
the deepest gloom
and broke away their chains.
¹⁵Let them give thanks to the LORD for
his unfailing love
and his wonderful deeds for men,
¹⁶for he breaks down gates of bronze
and cuts through bars of iron.

¹⁷Some became fools through their
rebellious ways
and suffered affliction because of
their iniquities.
¹⁸They loathed all food
and drew near the gates of death.
¹⁹Then they cried to the LORD in their
trouble,
and he saved them from their
distress.
²⁰He sent forth his word and healed
them;
he rescued them from the grave.
²¹Let them give thanks to the LORD for
his unfailing love
and his wonderful deeds for men.

²²Let them sacrifice thank offerings
and tell of his works with songs of
joy.

²³Others went out on the sea in ships;
they were merchants on the mighty
waters.
²⁴They saw the works of the LORD,
his wonderful deeds in the deep.
²⁵For he spoke and stirred up a
tempest
that lifted high the waves.
²⁶They mounted up to the heavens and
went down to the depths;
in their peril their courage melted
away.
²⁷They reeled and staggered like
drunken men;
they were at their wits' end.
²⁸Then they cried out to the LORD in
their trouble,
and he brought them out of their
distress.
²⁹He stilled the storm to a whisper;
the waves of the sea were hushed.
³⁰They were glad when it grew calm,
and he guided them to their desired
haven.
³¹Let them give thanks to the LORD for
his unfailing love
and his wonderful deeds for men.
³²Let them exalt him in the assembly of
the people
and praise him in the council of the
elders.

³³He turned rivers into a desert,
flowing springs into thirsty
ground,
³⁴and fruitful land into a salt waste,
because of the wickedness of those
who lived there.
³⁵He turned the desert into pools of
water
and the parched ground into
flowing springs;
³⁶there he brought the hungry to live,
and they founded a city where they
could settle.
³⁷They sowed fields and planted
vineyards
that yielded a fruitful harvest;
³⁸he blessed them, and their numbers
greatly increased,
and he did not let their herds
diminish.

³⁹Then their numbers decreased, and
　　they were humbled
　　by oppression, calamity and
　　　sorrow;
⁴⁰he who pours contempt on nobles
　　made them wander in a trackless
　　　waste.
⁴¹But he lifted the needy out of their
　　affliction
　　and increased their families like
　　　flocks.
⁴²The upright see and rejoice,
　　but all the wicked shut their
　　　mouths.

⁴³Whoever is wise, let him heed these
　　things
　　and consider the great love of the
　　　LORD.

Psalm 108

A song. A psalm of David.

¹My heart is steadfast, O God;
　　I will sing and make music with all
　　my soul.
²Awake, harp and lyre!
　　I will awaken the dawn.
³I will praise you, O LORD, among the
　　nations;
　　I will sing of you among the
　　　peoples.
⁴For great is your love, higher than the
　　heavens;
　　your faithfulness reaches to the
　　　skies.
⁵Be exalted, O God, above the heavens,
　　and let your glory be over all the
　　　earth.

⁶Save us and help us with your right
　　hand,
　　that those you love may be
　　　delivered.
⁷God has spoken from his sanctuary:
　　"In triumph I will parcel out
　　　Shechem
　　and measure off the Valley of
　　　Succoth.
⁸Gilead is mine, Manasseh is mine;
　　Ephraim is my helmet,
　　Judah my scepter.
⁹Moab is my washbasin,
　　upon Edom I toss my sandal;
　　over Philistia I shout in triumph."

¹⁰Who will bring me to the fortified
　　city?
　　Who will lead me to Edom?
¹¹Is it not you, O God, you who have
　　rejected us
　　and no longer go out with our
　　　armies?
¹²Give us aid against the enemy,
　　for the help of man is worthless.
¹³With God we will gain the victory,
　　and he will trample down our
　　　enemies.

Psalm 109

For the director of music.
Of David. A psalm.

¹O God, whom I praise,
　　do not remain silent,
²for wicked and deceitful men
　　have opened their mouths against
　　　me;
　　they have spoken against me with
　　　lying tongues.
³With words of hatred they surround
　　me;
　　they attack me without cause.
⁴In return for my friendship they
　　accuse me,
　　but I am a man of prayer.
⁵They repay me evil for good,
　　and hatred for my friendship.

⁶Appoint*ᵃ* an evil man*ᵇ* to oppose him;
　　let an accuser*ᶜ* stand at his right
　　　hand.
⁷When he is tried, let him be found
　　guilty,
　　and may his prayers condemn him.
⁸May his days be few;
　　may another take his place of
　　　leadership.
⁹May his children be fatherless
　　and his wife a widow.
¹⁰May his children be wandering
　　beggars;
　　may they be driven*ᵈ* from their
　　　ruined homes.
¹¹May a creditor seize all he has;
　　may strangers plunder the fruits of
　　　his labor.

*ᵃ6 Or They say: "Appoint (with quotation marks at
the end of verse 19)　ᵇ6 Or the Evil One　ᶜ6 Or let
Satan　ᵈ10 Septuagint; Hebrew sought*

¹²May no one extend kindness to him
  or take pity on his fatherless
  children.
¹³May his descendants be cut off,
  their names blotted out from the
  next generation.
¹⁴May the iniquity of his fathers be
  remembered before the LORD;
  may the sin of his mother never be
  blotted out.
¹⁵May their sins always remain before
  the LORD,
  that he may cut off the memory of
  them from the earth.

¹⁶For he never thought of doing a
  kindness,
  but hounded to death the poor
  and the needy and the
  brokenhearted.
¹⁷He loved to pronounce a curse—
  may it[a] come on him;
  he found no pleasure in blessing—
  may it be[b] far from him.
¹⁸He wore cursing as his garment;
  it entered into his body like water,
  into his bones like oil.
¹⁹May it be like a cloak wrapped about
  him,
  like a belt tied forever around him.
²⁰May this be the LORD's payment to my
  accusers,
  to those who speak evil of me.

²¹But you, O Sovereign LORD,
  deal well with me for your name's
  sake;
  out of the goodness of your love,
  deliver me.
²²For I am poor and needy,
  and my heart is wounded within
  me.
²³I fade away like an evening shadow;
  I am shaken off like a locust.
²⁴My knees give way from fasting;
  my body is thin and gaunt.
²⁵I am an object of scorn to my
  accusers;
  when they see me, they shake their
  heads.

²⁶Help me, O LORD my God;
  save me in accordance with your
  love.
²⁷Let them know that it is your hand,
  that you, O LORD, have done it.

²⁸They may curse, but you will bless;
  when they attack they will be put to
  shame,
  but your servant will rejoice.
²⁹My accusers will be clothed with
  disgrace
  and wrapped in shame as in a
  cloak.

³⁰With my mouth I will greatly extol
  the LORD;
  in the great throng I will praise
  him.
³¹For he stands at the right hand of
  the needy one,
  to save his life from those who
  condemn him.

Psalm 110

Of David. A psalm.

¹The LORD says to my Lord:
  "Sit at my right hand
until I make your enemies
  a footstool for your feet."

²The LORD will extend your mighty
  scepter from Zion;
  you will rule in the midst of your
  enemies.
³Your troops will be willing
  on your day of battle.
Arrayed in holy majesty,
  from the womb of the dawn
  you will receive the dew of your
  youth.[c]

⁴The LORD has sworn
  and will not change his mind:
"You are a priest forever,
  in the order of Melchizedek."

⁵The Lord is at your right hand;
  he will crush kings on the day of
  his wrath.
⁶He will judge the nations, heaping up
  the dead
  and crushing the rulers of the whole
  earth.
⁷He will drink from a brook beside the
  way[d];
  therefore he will lift up his head.

*a 17 Or curse, / and it has   b 17 Or blessing, / and
it is   c 3 Or / your young men will come to you like
the dew   d 7 Or / The One who grants succession will
set him in authority*

Psalm 111[a]

¹Praise the LORD.[b]

I will extol the LORD with all my heart
in the council of the upright and in
the assembly.

²Great are the works of the LORD;
they are pondered by all who
delight in them.
³Glorious and majestic are his deeds,
and his righteousness endures
forever.
⁴He has caused his wonders to be
remembered;
the LORD is gracious and
compassionate.
⁵He provides food for those who fear
him;
he remembers his covenant forever.
⁶He has shown his people the power of
his works,
giving them the lands of other
nations.
⁷The works of his hands are faithful
and just;
all his precepts are trustworthy.
⁸They are steadfast for ever and ever,
done in faithfulness and
uprightness.
⁹He provided redemption for his
people;
he ordained his covenant forever—
holy and awesome is his name.

¹⁰The fear of the LORD is the beginning
of wisdom;
all who follow his precepts have
good understanding.
To him belongs eternal praise.

Psalm 112[a]

¹Praise the LORD.[b]

Blessed is the man who fears the LORD,
who finds great delight in his
commands.

²His children will be mighty in the
land;
the generation of the upright will be
blessed.
³Wealth and riches are in his house,
and his righteousness endures
forever.

⁴Even in darkness light dawns for the
upright,
for the gracious and compassionate
and righteous man.[c]
⁵Good will come to him who is
generous and lends freely,
who conducts his affairs with
justice.
⁶Surely he will never be shaken;
a righteous man will be remembered
forever.
⁷He will have no fear of bad news;
his heart is steadfast, trusting in the
LORD.
⁸His heart is secure, he will have no
fear;
in the end he will look in triumph
on his foes.
⁹He has scattered abroad his gifts to
the poor,
his righteousness endures forever;
his horn[d] will be lifted high in
honor.

¹⁰The wicked man will see and be
vexed,
he will gnash his teeth and waste
away;
the longings of the wicked will
come to nothing.

Psalm 113

¹Praise the LORD.[e]

Praise, O servants of the LORD,
praise the name of the LORD.
²Let the name of the LORD be praised,
both now and forevermore.
³From the rising of the sun to the place
where it sets,
the name of the LORD is to be
praised.

⁴The LORD is exalted over all the
nations,
his glory above the heavens.
⁵Who is like the LORD our God,
the One who sits enthroned on
high,

<hr>

*a This psalm is an acrostic poem, the lines of which
begin with the successive letters of the Hebrew
alphabet. b1 Hebrew Hallelu Yah c4 Or / for the
LORD is gracious and compassionate and righteous
d9 Horn here symbolizes dignity. e1 Hebrew Hallelu
Yah; also in verse 9*

⁶who stoops down to look
   on the heavens and the earth?

⁷He raises the poor from the dust
   and lifts the needy from the ash
    heap;
⁸he seats them with princes,
   with the princes of their people.
⁹He settles the barren woman in her
    home
   as a happy mother of children.

  Praise the LORD.

Psalm 114

¹When Israel came out of Egypt,
   the house of Jacob from a people of
    foreign tongue,
²Judah became God's sanctuary,
   Israel his dominion.

³The sea looked and fled,
   the Jordan turned back;
⁴the mountains skipped like rams,
   the hills like lambs.

⁵Why was it, O sea, that you fled,
   O Jordan, that you turned back,
⁶you mountains, that you skipped like
    rams,
   you hills, like lambs?

⁷Tremble, O earth, at the presence of
    the Lord,
   at the presence of the God of Jacob,
⁸who turned the rock into a pool,
   the hard rock into springs of water.

Psalm 115

¹Not to us, O LORD, not to us
   but to your name be the glory,
   because of your love and
    faithfulness.

²Why do the nations say,
   "Where is their God?"
³Our God is in heaven;
   he does whatever pleases him.
⁴But their idols are silver and gold,
   made by the hands of men.
⁵They have mouths, but cannot speak,
   eyes, but they cannot see;
⁶they have ears, but cannot hear,
   noses, but they cannot smell;
⁷they have hands, but cannot feel,
   feet, but they cannot walk;

nor can they utter a sound with
   their throats.
⁸Those who make them will be like
   them,
   and so will all who trust in them.

⁹O house of Israel, trust in the LORD—
   he is their help and shield.
¹⁰O house of Aaron, trust in the LORD—
   he is their help and shield.
¹¹You who fear him, trust in the LORD—
   he is their help and shield.

¹²The LORD remembers us and will bless
   us:
   He will bless the house of Israel,
   he will bless the house of Aaron,
¹³he will bless those who fear the LORD—
   small and great alike.

¹⁴May the LORD make you increase,
   both you and your children.
¹⁵May you be blessed by the LORD,
   the Maker of heaven and earth.

¹⁶The highest heavens belong to the
   LORD,
   but the earth he has given to man.
¹⁷It is not the dead who praise the LORD,
   those who go down to silence;
¹⁸it is we who extol the LORD,
   both now and forevermore.

  Praise the LORD.ᵃ

Psalm 116

¹I love the LORD, for he heard my
    voice;
   he heard my cry for mercy.
²Because he turned his ear to me,
   I will call on him as long as I live.

³The cords of death entangled me,
   the anguish of the graveᵇ came
    upon me;
   I was overcome by trouble and
    sorrow.
⁴Then I called on the name of the LORD:
   "O LORD, save me!"

⁵The LORD is gracious and righteous;
   our God is full of compassion.
⁶The LORD protects the simplehearted;
   when I was in great need, he saved
    me.

ᵃ18 Hebrew *Hallelu Yah*   ᵇ3 Hebrew *Sheol*

⁷Be at rest once more, O my soul,
　　for the LORD has been good to you.

⁸For you, O LORD, have delivered my
　　　　soul from death,
　　my eyes from tears,
　　my feet from stumbling,
⁹that I may walk before the LORD
　　in the land of the living.
¹⁰I believed; therefore[a] I said,
　　"I am greatly afflicted."
¹¹And in my dismay I said,
　　"All men are liars."

¹²How can I repay the LORD
　　for all his goodness to me?
¹³I will lift up the cup of salvation
　　and call on the name of the LORD.
¹⁴I will fulfill my vows to the LORD
　　in the presence of all his people.

¹⁵Precious in the sight of the LORD
　　is the death of his saints.
¹⁶O LORD, truly I am your servant;
　　I am your servant, the son of your
　　　　maidservant[b];
　　you have freed me from my chains.

¹⁷I will sacrifice a thank offering to you

and call on the name of the LORD.
¹⁸I will fulfill my vows to the LORD
　　in the presence of all his people,
¹⁹in the courts of the house of the
　　　　LORD—
　　in your midst, O Jerusalem.

　Praise the LORD.[c]

Psalm 117

¹Praise the LORD, all you nations;
　　extol him, all you peoples.
²For great is his love toward us,
　　and the faithfulness of the LORD
　　　　endures forever.

　Praise the LORD.[c]

Psalm 118

¹Give thanks to the LORD, for he is
　　　　good;
　　his love endures forever.

*[a]10 Or believed even when [b]16 Or servant, your
faithful son [c]19,2 Hebrew Hallelu Yah*

Monday

Wiping the Tears Away

Read Psalm 116

There are some times in our lives when we feel all alone. When a good
friend of mine died, I was filled with so much grief and sorrow that I thought
nobody could understand. I didn't even think God was listening. But Psalm
116:6 says, "The LORD protects the simplehearted; when I was in great need,
he saved me." As I read that, I realized that because God loves me, he will
take care of me in every situation. I can trust him.

　God *does* hear us when we're in pain. He was there when I cried out to
him about my friend, even though I couldn't hear his voice. He always
answers us, though the answers aren't always what we want them to be.

What about You?

❶ Think back on a time you couldn't "feel" God's presence in your life.
How did you start to sense his presence in your life again?

❷ Psalm 116 says the world is full of God's presence. We know that
God is all around us. How does that change how you feel about him?

❸ Ask God to heal your hurts. Thank him for being there, even when you're feeling pain.

Turn to page 712 for your next devotion.

2 Let Israel say:
 "His love endures forever."
3 Let the house of Aaron say:
 "His love endures forever."
4 Let those who fear the LORD say:
 "His love endures forever."

5 In my anguish I cried to the LORD,
 and he answered by setting me free.
6 The LORD is with me; I will not be
 afraid.
 What can man do to me?
7 The LORD is with me; he is my helper.
 I will look in triumph on my
 enemies.

8 It is better to take refuge in the LORD
 than to trust in man.
9 It is better to take refuge in the LORD
 than to trust in princes.

10 All the nations surrounded me,
 but in the name of the LORD I cut
 them off.
11 They surrounded me on every side,
 but in the name of the LORD I cut
 them off.
12 They swarmed around me like bees,
 but they died out as quickly as
 burning thorns;
 in the name of the LORD I cut them
 off.

13 I was pushed back and about to fall,
 but the LORD helped me.
14 The LORD is my strength and my song;
 he has become my salvation.

15 Shouts of joy and victory
 resound in the tents of the
 righteous:
 "The LORD's right hand has done
 mighty things!
16 The LORD's right hand is lifted high;
 the LORD's right hand has done
 mighty things!"

17 I will not die but live,
 and will proclaim what the LORD
 has done.
18 The LORD has chastened me severely,
 but he has not given me over to
 death.

19 Open for me the gates of
 righteousness;
 I will enter and give thanks to the
 LORD.

20 This is the gate of the LORD
 through which the righteous may
 enter.
21 I will give you thanks, for you
 answered me;
 you have become my salvation.

22 The stone the builders rejected
 has become the capstone;
23 the LORD has done this,
 and it is marvelous in our eyes.
24 This is the day the LORD has made;
 let us rejoice and be glad in it.

25 O LORD, save us;
 O LORD, grant us success.
26 Blessed is he who comes in the name
 of the LORD.
 From the house of the LORD we
 bless you.*a*
27 The LORD is God,
 and he has made his light shine
 upon us.
 With boughs in hand, join in the
 festal procession
 up*b* to the horns of the altar.

28 You are my God, and I will give you
 thanks;
 you are my God, and I will exalt
 you.

29 Give thanks to the LORD, for he is
 good;
 his love endures forever.

Psalm 119*c*

א Aleph

1 Blessed are they whose ways are
 blameless,
 who walk according to the law of
 the LORD.
2 Blessed are they who keep his statutes
 and seek him with all their heart.
3 They do nothing wrong;
 they walk in his ways.
4 You have laid down precepts
 that are to be fully obeyed.
5 Oh, that my ways were steadfast
 in obeying your decrees!
6 Then I would not be put to shame

a26 The Hebrew is plural. *b27* Or *Bind the festal
sacrifice with ropes / and take it* *c*This psalm is an
acrostic poem; the verses of each stanza begin with
the same letter of the Hebrew alphabet.

Monster Memory

Huh?

Psalm 119:1

This is the longest chapter in the Bible, and it's all about the Bible. In Hebrew, each of the first 8 verses starts with the first letter of the Hebrew alphabet, "aleph." Then the next 8 verses start with the second letter, and so on. Know why? Part of the reason was to help the average Joe Israel, who didn't have a Bible, memorize this long psalm! Imagine loading this puppy into your head's hard drive! OK, so maybe that's a bit extreme. But you can at least memorize a few famous verses, like 9, 11, 105 or 165.

when I consider all your commands.
⁷I will praise you with an upright heart
  as I learn your righteous laws.
⁸I will obey your decrees;
  do not utterly forsake me.

ב Beth

⁹How can a young man keep his way
    pure?
  By living according to your word.
¹⁰I seek you with all my heart;
  do not let me stray from your
    commands.
¹¹I have hidden your word in my heart
  that I might not sin against you.
¹²Praise be to you, O LORD;
  teach me your decrees.
¹³With my lips I recount
  all the laws that come from your
    mouth.
¹⁴I rejoice in following your statutes
  as one rejoices in great riches.
¹⁵I meditate on your precepts
  and consider your ways.
¹⁶I delight in your decrees;
  I will not neglect your word.

ג Gimel

¹⁷Do good to your servant, and I will
    live;
  I will obey your word.
¹⁸Open my eyes that I may see
  wonderful things in your law.

¹⁹I am a stranger on earth;
  do not hide your commands from
    me.
²⁰My soul is consumed with longing
  for your laws at all times.
²¹You rebuke the arrogant, who are
    cursed
  and who stray from your
    commands.
²²Remove from me scorn and contempt,
  for I keep your statutes.
²³Though rulers sit together and slander
    me,
  your servant will meditate on your
    decrees.
²⁴Your statutes are my delight;
  they are my counselors.

ד Daleth

²⁵I am laid low in the dust;
  preserve my life according to your
    word.
²⁶I recounted my ways and you
    answered me;
  teach me your decrees.
²⁷Let me understand the teaching of
    your precepts;
  then I will meditate on your
    wonders.
²⁸My soul is weary with sorrow;
  strengthen me according to your
    word.
²⁹Keep me from deceitful ways;
  be gracious to me through your law.
³⁰I have chosen the way of truth;
  I have set my heart on your laws.
³¹I hold fast to your statutes, O LORD;
  do not let me be put to shame.
³²I run in the path of your commands,
  for you have set my heart free.

ה He

³³Teach me, O LORD, to follow your
    decrees;
  then I will keep them to the end.
³⁴Give me understanding, and I will
    keep your law
  and obey it with all my heart.
³⁵Direct me in the path of your
    commands,
  for there I find delight.
³⁶Turn my heart toward your statutes
  and not toward selfish gain.
³⁷Turn my eyes away from worthless
    things;

preserve my life according to your
   word.[a]
38 Fulfill your promise to your servant,
   so that you may be feared.
39 Take away the disgrace I dread,
   for your laws are good.
40 How I long for your precepts!
   Preserve my life in your
   righteousness.

ℸ Waw

41 May your unfailing love come to me,
   O LORD,
   your salvation according to your
   promise;
42 then I will answer the one who taunts
   me,
   for I trust in your word.
43 Do not snatch the word of truth from
   my mouth,
   for I have put my hope in your
   laws.
44 I will always obey your law,
   for ever and ever.
45 I will walk about in freedom,
   for I have sought out your precepts.
46 I will speak of your statutes before
   kings
   and will not be put to shame,
47 for I delight in your commands
   because I love them.
48 I lift up my hands to[b] your commands,
   which I love,
   and I meditate on your decrees.

ℸ Zayin

49 Remember your word to your servant,
   for you have given me hope.
50 My comfort in my suffering is this:
   Your promise preserves my life.
51 The arrogant mock me without
   restraint,
   but I do not turn from your law.
52 I remember your ancient laws,
   O LORD,
   and I find comfort in them.
53 Indignation grips me because of the
   wicked,
   who have forsaken your law.
54 Your decrees are the theme of my
   song
   wherever I lodge.
55 In the night I remember your name,
   O LORD,
   and I will keep your law.

56 This has been my practice:
   I obey your precepts.

ח Heth

57 You are my portion, O LORD;
   I have promised to obey your
   words.
58 I have sought your face with all my
   heart;
   be gracious to me according to your
   promise.
59 I have considered my ways
   and have turned my steps to your
   statutes.
60 I will hasten and not delay
   to obey your commands.
61 Though the wicked bind me with
   ropes,
   I will not forget your law.
62 At midnight I rise to give you thanks
   for your righteous laws.
63 I am a friend to all who fear you,
   to all who follow your precepts.
64 The earth is filled with your love,
   O LORD;
   teach me your decrees.

ט Teth

65 Do good to your servant
   according to your word, O LORD.
66 Teach me knowledge and good
   judgment,
   for I believe in your commands.
67 Before I was afflicted I went astray,
   but now I obey your word.
68 You are good, and what you do is
   good;
   teach me your decrees.
69 Though the arrogant have smeared me
   with lies,
   I keep your precepts with all my
   heart.
70 Their hearts are callous and
   unfeeling,
   but I delight in your law.
71 It was good for me to be afflicted
   so that I might learn your decrees.
72 The law from your mouth is more
   precious to me
   than thousands of pieces of silver
   and gold.

a 37 Two manuscripts of the Masoretic Text and Dead
Sea Scrolls; most manuscripts of the Masoretic Text
life in your way   b 48 Or for

י Yodh

73 Your hands made me and formed me;
  give me understanding to learn
    your commands.
74 May those who fear you rejoice when
    they see me,
  for I have put my hope in your
    word.
75 I know, O LORD, that your laws are
    righteous,
  and in faithfulness you have
    afflicted me.
76 May your unfailing love be my
    comfort,
  according to your promise to your
    servant.
77 Let your compassion come to me that
    I may live,
  for your law is my delight.
78 May the arrogant be put to shame for
    wronging me without cause;
  but I will meditate on your precepts.
79 May those who fear you turn to me,
  those who understand your statutes.
80 May my heart be blameless toward
    your decrees,
  that I may not be put to shame.

כ Kaph

81 My soul faints with longing for your
    salvation,
  but I have put my hope in your
    word.
82 My eyes fail, looking for your
    promise;
  I say, "When will you comfort me?"
83 Though I am like a wineskin in the
    smoke,
  I do not forget your decrees.
84 How long must your servant wait?
  When will you punish my
    persecutors?
85 The arrogant dig pitfalls for me,
  contrary to your law.
86 All your commands are trustworthy;
  help me, for men persecute me
    without cause.
87 They almost wiped me from the earth,
  but I have not forsaken your
    precepts.
88 Preserve my life according to your
    love,
  and I will obey the statutes of your
    mouth.

ל Lamedh

89 Your word, O LORD, is eternal;
  it stands firm in the heavens.
90 Your faithfulness continues through
    all generations;
  you established the earth, and it
    endures.
91 Your laws endure to this day,
  for all things serve you.
92 If your law had not been my delight,
  I would have perished in my
    affliction.
93 I will never forget your precepts,
  for by them you have preserved my
    life.
94 Save me, for I am yours;
  I have sought out your precepts.
95 The wicked are waiting to destroy
    me,
  but I will ponder your statutes.
96 To all perfection I see a limit;
  but your commands are boundless.

מ Mem

97 Oh, how I love your law!
  I meditate on it all day long.
98 Your commands make me wiser than
    my enemies,
  for they are ever with me.
99 I have more insight than all my
    teachers,
  for I meditate on your statutes.
100 I have more understanding than the
    elders,
  for I obey your precepts.
101 I have kept my feet from every evil
    path
  so that I might obey your word.
102 I have not departed from your laws,
  for you yourself have taught me.
103 How sweet are your words to my
    taste,
  sweeter than honey to my mouth!
104 I gain understanding from your
    precepts;
  therefore I hate every wrong path.

נ Nun

105 Your word is a lamp to my feet
  and a light for my path.
106 I have taken an oath and
    confirmed it,
  that I will follow your righteous
    laws.

¹⁰⁷I have suffered much;
　　preserve my life, O Lord, according
　　　to your word.
¹⁰⁸Accept, O Lord, the willing praise of
　　my mouth,
　　and teach me your laws.
¹⁰⁹Though I constantly take my life in
　　my hands,
　　I will not forget your law.
¹¹⁰The wicked have set a snare for me,
　　but I have not strayed from your
　　　precepts.
¹¹¹Your statutes are my heritage forever;
　　they are the joy of my heart.
¹¹²My heart is set on keeping your
　　decrees
　　to the very end.

❏　Samekh

¹¹³I hate double-minded men,
　　but I love your law.
¹¹⁴You are my refuge and my shield;
　　I have put my hope in your word.
¹¹⁵Away from me, you evildoers,
　　that I may keep the commands of
　　　my God!
¹¹⁶Sustain me according to your
　　promise, and I will live;
　　do not let my hopes be dashed.

¹¹⁷Uphold me, and I will be delivered;
　　I will always have regard for your
　　　decrees.
¹¹⁸You reject all who stray from your
　　decrees,
　　for their deceitfulness is in vain.
¹¹⁹All the wicked of the earth you
　　discard like dross;
　　therefore I love your statutes.
¹²⁰My flesh trembles in fear of you;
　　I stand in awe of your laws.

ע　Ayin

¹²¹I have done what is righteous and
　　just;
　　do not leave me to my oppressors.
¹²²Ensure your servant's well-being;
　　let not the arrogant oppress me.
¹²³My eyes fail, looking for your
　　salvation,
　　looking for your righteous promise.
¹²⁴Deal with your servant according to
　　your love
　　and teach me your decrees.
¹²⁵I am your servant; give me
　　discernment
　　that I may understand your statutes.
¹²⁶It is time for you to act, O Lord;
　　your law is being broken.

Tuesday

God's Flashlight

Read Psalm 119:105

When I was in preschool, I was afraid of the dark. I thought that if there wasn't any light in a room, it wasn't safe to go in. I'm not so afraid of the dark now, of course, but I'm not crazy about it either. Walking in the dark can be dangerous.

Walking off the path God wants us to follow is dangerous too. But the Bible shows us the right path and helps us stay on it. It's kind of like having a flashlight at night. It helps you feel safe and keeps you out of trouble.

Julia age 13

What about You?

❶ Think of a time when you were struggling in some way. In what ways was the Bible "a light for [your] path"?

❷ Roam around your house in the dark. Think about why darkness can be so scary. Then turn on the lights. Makes quite a difference, huh?

❸ Thank God for giving us his Word to light our path.

Turn to page 718 for your next devotion.

¹²⁷Because I love your commands
    more than gold, more than pure
      gold,
¹²⁸and because I consider all your
    precepts right,
    I hate every wrong path.

ב Pe

¹²⁹Your statutes are wonderful;
    therefore I obey them.
¹³⁰The unfolding of your words gives
    light;
    it gives understanding to the simple.
¹³¹I open my mouth and pant,
    longing for your commands.
¹³²Turn to me and have mercy on me,
    as you always do to those who love
      your name.
¹³³Direct my footsteps according to your
    word;
    let no sin rule over me.
¹³⁴Redeem me from the oppression of
    men,
    that I may obey your precepts.
¹³⁵Make your face shine upon your
    servant
    and teach me your decrees.
¹³⁶Streams of tears flow from my eyes,
    for your law is not obeyed.

צ Tsadhe

¹³⁷Righteous are you, O LORD,
    and your laws are right.
¹³⁸The statutes you have laid down are
    righteous;
    they are fully trustworthy.
¹³⁹My zeal wears me out,
    for my enemies ignore your words.
¹⁴⁰Your promises have been thoroughly
    tested,
    and your servant loves them.
¹⁴¹Though I am lowly and despised,
    I do not forget your precepts.
¹⁴²Your righteousness is everlasting
    and your law is true.
¹⁴³Trouble and distress have come
    upon me,
    but your commands are my delight.
¹⁴⁴Your statutes are forever right;
    give me understanding that I may
      live.

ק Qoph

¹⁴⁵I call with all my heart; answer me,
    O LORD,

    and I will obey your decrees.
¹⁴⁶I call out to you; save me
    and I will keep your statutes.
¹⁴⁷I rise before dawn and cry for help;
    I have put my hope in your word.
¹⁴⁸My eyes stay open through the
      watches of the night,
    that I may meditate on your
      promises.
¹⁴⁹Hear my voice in accordance with
    your love;
    preserve my life, O LORD, according
      to your laws.
¹⁵⁰Those who devise wicked schemes are
    near,
    but they are far from your law.
¹⁵¹Yet you are near, O LORD,
    and all your commands are true.
¹⁵²Long ago I learned from your statutes
    that you established them to last
      forever.

ר Resh

¹⁵³Look upon my suffering and
    deliver me,
    for I have not forgotten your law.
¹⁵⁴Defend my cause and redeem me;
    preserve my life according to your
      promise.
¹⁵⁵Salvation is far from the wicked,
    for they do not seek out your
      decrees.
¹⁵⁶Your compassion is great, O LORD;
    preserve my life according to your
      laws.
¹⁵⁷Many are the foes who persecute me,
    but I have not turned from your
      statutes.
¹⁵⁸I look on the faithless with loathing,
    for they do not obey your word.
¹⁵⁹See how I love your precepts;
    preserve my life, O LORD, according
      to your love.
¹⁶⁰All your words are true;
    all your righteous laws are eternal.

ש Sin and Shin

¹⁶¹Rulers persecute me without cause,
    but my heart trembles at your word.
¹⁶²I rejoice in your promise
    like one who finds great spoil.
¹⁶³I hate and abhor falsehood
    but I love your law.
¹⁶⁴Seven times a day I praise you
    for your righteous laws.

¹⁶⁵Great peace have they who love your
   law,
   and nothing can make them
      stumble.
¹⁶⁶I wait for your salvation, O LORD,
   and I follow your commands.
¹⁶⁷I obey your statutes,
   for I love them greatly.
¹⁶⁸I obey your precepts and your
      statutes,
   for all my ways are known to you.

ת Taw

¹⁶⁹May my cry come before you,
      O LORD;
   give me understanding according to
      your word.
¹⁷⁰May my supplication come before
      you;
   deliver me according to your
      promise.
¹⁷¹May my lips overflow with praise,
   for you teach me your decrees.
¹⁷²May my tongue sing of your word,
   for all your commands are
      righteous.
¹⁷³May your hand be ready to help me,
   for I have chosen your precepts.
¹⁷⁴I long for your salvation, O LORD,
   and your law is my delight.
¹⁷⁵Let me live that I may praise you,
   and may your laws sustain me.
¹⁷⁶I have strayed like a lost sheep.
   Seek your servant,
      for I have not forgotten your
      commands.

Psalm 120

A song of ascents.

¹I call on the LORD in my distress,
   and he answers me.
²Save me, O LORD, from lying lips
   and from deceitful tongues.

³What will he do to you,
   and what more besides, O deceitful
      tongue?
⁴He will punish you with a warrior's
      sharp arrows,
   with burning coals of the broom
      tree.

Travelin' Tunes

Psalm 120

The next 15 psalms are known as "songs of ascent." They were sung by travelers as they ascended (walked up) the hills to Jerusalem for festivals. These folks didn't waste time singing about 99 bottles of soda pop. They used their travel time to get spiritually prepared to meet God. You can follow their pattern. Try jammin' to some Christian tunes on your way to church, so you show up ready to worship.

⁵Woe to me that I dwell in Meshech,
   that I live among the tents of
      Kedar!
⁶Too long have I lived
   among those who hate peace.
⁷I am a man of peace;
   but when I speak, they are for
      war.

Psalm 121

A song of ascents.

¹I lift up my eyes to the hills—
   where does my help come from?
²My help comes from the LORD,
   the Maker of heaven and earth.

³He will not let your foot slip—
   he who watches over you will not
      slumber;
⁴indeed, he who watches over Israel
   will neither slumber nor sleep.

⁵The LORD watches over you—
   the LORD is your shade at your right
      hand;
⁶the sun will not harm you by day,
   nor the moon by night.

⁷The LORD will keep you from all
      harm—
   he will watch over your life;
⁸the LORD will watch over your coming
      and going
   both now and forevermore.

Psalm 122

A song of ascents. Of David.

[1] I rejoiced with those who said to me,
    "Let us go to the house of the LORD."
[2] Our feet are standing
    in your gates, O Jerusalem.

[3] Jerusalem is built like a city
    that is closely compacted together.
[4] That is where the tribes go up,
    the tribes of the LORD,
  to praise the name of the LORD
    according to the statute given to
    Israel.
[5] There the thrones for judgment stand,
    the thrones of the house of David.

[6] Pray for the peace of Jerusalem:
    "May those who love you be secure.
[7] May there be peace within your walls
    and security within your citadels."
[8] For the sake of my brothers and
    friends,
    I will say, "Peace be within you."
[9] For the sake of the house of the LORD
    our God,
    I will seek your prosperity.

Psalm 123

A song of ascents.

[1] I lift up my eyes to you,
    to you whose throne is in heaven.
[2] As the eyes of slaves look to the hand
    of their master,
    as the eyes of a maid look to the
    hand of her mistress,
  so our eyes look to the LORD our God,
    till he shows us his mercy.

[3] Have mercy on us, O LORD, have
    mercy on us,
    for we have endured much
    contempt.
[4] We have endured much ridicule from
    the proud,
    much contempt from the arrogant.

Psalm 124

A song of ascents. Of David.

[1] If the LORD had not been on our side—
    let Israel say—
[2] if the LORD had not been on our side
    when men attacked us,
[3] when their anger flared against us,
    they would have swallowed us
    alive;
[4] the flood would have engulfed us,
    the torrent would have swept over
    us,
[5] the raging waters
    would have swept us away.

[6] Praise be to the LORD,
    who has not let us be torn by their
    teeth.
[7] We have escaped like a bird
    out of the fowler's snare;
  the snare has been broken,
    and we have escaped.
[8] Our help is in the name of the LORD,
    the Maker of heaven and earth.

Psalm 125

A song of ascents.

[1] Those who trust in the LORD are like
    Mount Zion,
    which cannot be shaken but
    endures forever.
[2] As the mountains surround Jerusalem,
    so the LORD surrounds his people
    both now and forevermore.

[3] The scepter of the wicked will not
    remain
    over the land allotted to the
    righteous,
  for then the righteous might use
    their hands to do evil.

[4] Do good, O LORD, to those who are
    good,
    to those who are upright in heart.
[5] But those who turn to crooked ways
    the LORD will banish with the
    evildoers.

Peace be upon Israel.

Psalm 126

A song of ascents.

[1] When the LORD brought back the
    captives to[a] Zion,

---

[a] 1 Or LORD restored the fortunes of

we were like men who dreamed.[a]
² Our mouths were filled with laughter,
    our tongues with songs of joy.
Then it was said among the nations,
    "The LORD has done great things for
    them."
³ The LORD has done great things for us,
    and we are filled with joy.

⁴ Restore our fortunes,[b] O LORD,
    like streams in the Negev.
⁵ Those who sow in tears
    will reap with songs of joy.
⁶ He who goes out weeping,
    carrying seed to sow,
will return with songs of joy,
    carrying sheaves with him.

Psalm 127

A song of ascents. Of Solomon.

¹ Unless the LORD builds the house,
    its builders labor in vain.
Unless the LORD watches over the
    city,
    the watchmen stand guard in vain.
² In vain you rise early
    and stay up late,
toiling for food to eat—
    for he grants sleep to[c] those he
    loves.

³ Sons are a heritage from the LORD,
    children a reward from him.
⁴ Like arrows in the hands of a warrior
    are sons born in one's youth.
⁵ Blessed is the man
    whose quiver is full of them.
They will not be put to shame
    when they contend with their
    enemies in the gate.

Psalm 128

A song of ascents.

¹ Blessed are all who fear the LORD,
    who walk in his ways.
² You will eat the fruit of your labor;
    blessings and prosperity will be
    yours.
³ Your wife will be like a fruitful vine
    within your house;
your sons will be like olive shoots
    around your table.

⁴ Thus is the man blessed
    who fears the LORD.

⁵ May the LORD bless you from Zion
    all the days of your life;
may you see the prosperity of
    Jerusalem,
⁶   and may you live to see your
    children's children.

Peace be upon Israel.

Psalm 129

A song of ascents.

¹ They have greatly oppressed me from
    my youth—
    let Israel say—
² they have greatly oppressed me from
    my youth,
    but they have not gained the
    victory over me.
³ Plowmen have plowed my back
    and made their furrows long.
⁴ But the LORD is righteous;
    he has cut me free from the cords of
    the wicked.

⁵ May all who hate Zion
    be turned back in shame.
⁶ May they be like grass on the roof,
    which withers before it can grow;
⁷ with it the reaper cannot fill his
    hands,
    nor the one who gathers fill his arms.
⁸ May those who pass by not say,
    "The blessing of the LORD be upon
    you;
    we bless you in the name of the
    LORD."

Psalm 130

A song of ascents.

¹ Out of the depths I cry to you, O LORD;
²   O Lord, hear my voice.
Let your ears be attentive
    to my cry for mercy.

³ If you, O LORD, kept a record of sins,
    O Lord, who could stand?

---

^a1 Or *men restored to health*   ^b4 Or *Bring back our
captives*   ^c2 Or *eat— / for while they sleep he
provides for*

⁴But with you there is forgiveness;
  therefore you are feared.

⁵I wait for the LORD, my soul waits,
  and in his word I put my hope.
⁶My soul waits for the Lord
  more than watchmen wait for the
    morning,
  more than watchmen wait for the
    morning.

⁷O Israel, put your hope in the LORD,
  for with the LORD is unfailing love
  and with him is full redemption.
⁸He himself will redeem Israel
  from all their sins.

Psalm 131

A song of ascents. Of David.

¹My heart is not proud, O LORD,
  my eyes are not haughty;
I do not concern myself with great
    matters
  or things too wonderful for me.
²But I have stilled and quieted my soul;
  like a weaned child with its mother,
  like a weaned child is my soul
    within me.

³O Israel, put your hope in the LORD
  both now and forevermore.

Psalm 132

A song of ascents.

¹O LORD, remember David
  and all the hardships he endured.

²He swore an oath to the LORD
  and made a vow to the Mighty One
    of Jacob:
³"I will not enter my house
  or go to my bed—
⁴I will allow no sleep to my eyes,
  no slumber to my eyelids,
⁵till I find a place for the LORD,
  a dwelling for the Mighty One of
    Jacob."

⁶We heard it in Ephrathah,
  we came upon it in the fields of
    Jaar[a]:[b]
⁷"Let us go to his dwelling place;
  let us worship at his footstool—

⁸arise, O LORD, and come to your
    resting place,
  you and the ark of your might.
⁹May your priests be clothed with
    righteousness;
  may your saints sing for joy."

¹⁰For the sake of David your servant,
  do not reject your anointed one.

¹¹The LORD swore an oath to David,
  a sure oath that he will not revoke:
"One of your own descendants
  I will place on your throne—
¹²if your sons keep my covenant
  and the statutes I teach them,
then their sons will sit
  on your throne for ever and ever."

¹³For the LORD has chosen Zion,
  he has desired it for his dwelling:
¹⁴"This is my resting place for ever and
    ever;
  here I will sit enthroned, for I have
    desired it—
¹⁵I will bless her with abundant
    provisions;
  her poor will I satisfy with food.
¹⁶I will clothe her priests with salvation,
  and her saints will ever sing for joy.

¹⁷"Here I will make a horn[c] grow for
    David
  and set up a lamp for my anointed
    one.
¹⁸I will clothe his enemies with shame,
  but the crown on his head will be
    resplendent."

Psalm 133

A song of ascents. Of David.

¹How good and pleasant it is
  when brothers live together in
    unity!
²It is like precious oil poured on the
    head,
  running down on the beard,
running down on Aaron's beard,
  down upon the collar of his robes.
³It is as if the dew of Hermon
  were falling on Mount Zion.

[a]6 That is, Kiriath Jearim   [b]6 Or *heard of it in
Ephrathah, / we found it in the fields of Jaar.* (And
no quotes around verses 7-9)   [c]17 *Horn* here
symbolizes strong one, that is, king.

For there the LORD bestows his
    blessing,
  even life forevermore.

Psalm 134

A song of ascents.

[1] Praise the LORD, all you servants of
    the LORD,
  who minister by night in the house
    of the LORD.
[2] Lift up your hands in the sanctuary
    and praise the LORD.

[3] May the LORD, the Maker of heaven
    and earth,
  bless you from Zion.

Psalm 135

[1] Praise the LORD.[a]

  Praise the name of the LORD;
    praise him, you servants of the
      LORD,
[2] you who minister in the house of the
    LORD,
  in the courts of the house of our
    God.

[3] Praise the LORD, for the LORD is good;
    sing praise to his name, for that is
      pleasant.
[4] For the LORD has chosen Jacob to be
    his own,
  Israel to be his treasured possession.

[a] 1 Hebrew *Hallelu Yah*; also in verses 3 and 21

Wednesday

Keep the Peace

Read Psalm 133

Sometimes I do some really stupid things that hurt my relationships with other people. Like the time I did something I shouldn't have and blamed it on my sister. I was scared my parents would yell at me. So when they asked about it, I lied and said I didn't have anything to do with it. Since I'm older, my parents believed me and got mad at my sister. As punishment, they wouldn't let her go to her friend's house. I felt a little bad, but to be honest, I was really thinking, *Hey, I didn't get into any trouble.*

  But a few days later my parents found out I was the one who did it and got *really* mad at me. They weren't all that angry about the original thing I did; they were upset with me for lying. My sister was mad at me too. And I started to realize that I'd messed up my relationships with 3 people I love, just to avoid getting into trouble. I felt terrible and tried to patch things up with my family.

  God wants us to get along with each other. Life is so much better when we live the way God wants us to and show each other love.

Catherine age 12

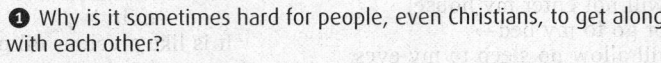

What about You?

❶ Why is it sometimes hard for people, even Christians, to get along with each other?

❷ Imagine what your family, your school or your church would be like if people got along all the time. Write down 3 things you can do to help strengthen your relationships with your family, your friends or your youth group.

❸ Ask God to help you be someone who makes your relationships better, not worse.

Turn to page 720 for your next devotion.

⁵I know that the LORD is great,
  that our Lord is greater than all
    gods.
⁶The LORD does whatever pleases him,
  in the heavens and on the earth,
  in the seas and all their depths.
⁷He makes clouds rise from the ends of
    the earth;
  he sends lightning with the rain
  and brings out the wind from his
    storehouses.

⁸He struck down the firstborn of Egypt,
  the firstborn of men and animals.
⁹He sent his signs and wonders into
    your midst, O Egypt,
  against Pharaoh and all his servants.
¹⁰He struck down many nations
  and killed mighty kings—
¹¹Sihon king of the Amorites,
  Og king of Bashan
  and all the kings of Canaan—
¹²and he gave their land as an
    inheritance,
  an inheritance to his people Israel.

¹³Your name, O LORD, endures forever,
  your renown, O LORD, through all
    generations.
¹⁴For the LORD will vindicate his people
  and have compassion on his
    servants.

¹⁵The idols of the nations are silver and
    gold,
  made by the hands of men.
¹⁶They have mouths, but cannot speak,
  eyes, but they cannot see;
¹⁷they have ears, but cannot hear,
  nor is there breath in their mouths.
¹⁸Those who make them will be like them,
  and so will all who trust in them.

¹⁹O house of Israel, praise the LORD;
  O house of Aaron, praise the LORD;
²⁰O house of Levi, praise the LORD;
  you who fear him, praise the LORD.
²¹Praise be to the LORD from Zion,
  to him who dwells in Jerusalem.

  Praise the LORD.

Psalm 136

¹Give thanks to the LORD, for he is
    good.
  His love endures forever.

²Give thanks to the God of gods.
  His love endures forever.
³Give thanks to the Lord of lords:
  His love endures forever.

⁴to him who alone does great wonders,
  His love endures forever.
⁵who by his understanding made the
    heavens,
  His love endures forever.
⁶who spread out the earth upon the
    waters,
  His love endures forever.
⁷who made the great lights—
  His love endures forever.
⁸the sun to govern the day,
  His love endures forever.
⁹the moon and stars to govern the
    night;
  His love endures forever.

¹⁰to him who struck down the firstborn
    of Egypt
  His love endures forever.
¹¹and brought Israel out from among
    them
  His love endures forever.
¹²with a mighty hand and outstretched
    arm;
  His love endures forever.
¹³to him who divided the Red Sea*ᵃ*
    asunder
  His love endures forever.
¹⁴and brought Israel through the midst
    of it,
  His love endures forever.
¹⁵but swept Pharaoh and his army into
    the Red Sea;
  His love endures forever.
¹⁶to him who led his people through the
    desert,
  His love endures forever.
¹⁷who struck down great kings,
  His love endures forever.
¹⁸and killed mighty kings—
  His love endures forever.
¹⁹Sihon king of the Amorites
  His love endures forever.
²⁰and Og king of Bashan—
  His love endures forever.
²¹and gave their land as an inheritance,
  His love endures forever.

ᵃ13 Hebrew *Yam Suph*; that is, Sea of Reeds; also in
verse 15

²² an inheritance to his servant Israel;
> *His love endures forever.*

²³ to the One who remembered us in our
low estate
> *His love endures forever.*

²⁴ and freed us from our enemies,
> *His love endures forever.*

²⁵ and who gives food to every creature.
> *His love endures forever.*

²⁶ Give thanks to the God of heaven.
> *His love endures forever.*

Psalm 137

¹ By the rivers of Babylon we sat and
wept
> when we remembered Zion.

² There on the poplars
> we hung our harps,

³ for there our captors asked us for
songs,

our tormentors demanded songs of
joy;
> they said, "Sing us one of the songs
of Zion!"

⁴ How can we sing the songs of the
L ORD
> while in a foreign land?

⁵ If I forget you, O Jerusalem,
> may my right hand forget its skill.

⁶ May my tongue cling to the roof of
my mouth
> if I do not remember you,
> if I do not consider Jerusalem
> my highest joy.

⁷ Remember, O L ORD, what the Edomites
did
> on the day Jerusalem fell.
> "Tear it down," they cried,
> "tear it down to its foundations!"

⁸ O Daughter of Babylon, doomed to
destruction,

Thursday

God's Forever-love

Read Psalm 136

God loves you no matter what. Even when you sin or turn away from him, he'll always forgive you if you confess that you've sinned and rebelled (See 1 John 1:9, page 1529.) God will never leave you.

You might not think of him this way, but God really should be your best friend. He's someone you can tell your innermost secrets, and he's someone you can be accountable to. He'll help you out of tough situations, like he helped the Israelites get away from Pharaoh. And he loves you more than anyone else will, ever. His love never goes away—it just seems to get bigger and bigger the more you know him.

❶ Think of things that seem to last a really, really long time, like the sun, jaw breakers, your least favorite class, whatever. Will any of these things last forever? How does it feel to know that God's love endures *forever*?

❷ Much of this psalm is like a time-line, with the Israelites remembering all that God had done for them in the past. Write your own "time-line psalm" with memories from your life, and make every other line *"His love endures forever."*

❸ Verse 1 says, "Give thanks to the L ORD, for he is good." When you pray today, thank the Lord for all the good things he has done for you.

Turn to page 722 for your next devotion.

happy is he who repays you
for what you have done to us—
⁹he who seizes your infants
and dashes them against the rocks.

Psalm 138

Of David.

¹I will praise you, O LORD, with all my
heart;
before the "gods" I will sing your
praise.
²I will bow down toward your holy
temple
and will praise your name
for your love and your faithfulness,
for you have exalted above all things
your name and your word.
³When I called, you answered me;
you made me bold and stouthearted.

⁴May all the kings of the earth praise
you, O LORD,
when they hear the words of your
mouth.
⁵May they sing of the ways of the
LORD,
for the glory of the LORD is great.

⁶Though the LORD is on high, he looks
upon the lowly,
but the proud he knows from afar.
⁷Though I walk in the midst of trouble,
you preserve my life;
you stretch out your hand against the
anger of my foes,
with your right hand you save me.
⁸The LORD will fulfill his purpose for
me;
your love, O LORD, endures forever—
do not abandon the works of your
hands.

Psalm 139

For the director of music.
Of David. A psalm.

¹O LORD, you have searched me
and you know me.
²You know when I sit and when I rise;
you perceive my thoughts from
afar.
³You discern my going out and my
lying down;

you are familiar with all my ways.
⁴Before a word is on my tongue
you know it completely, O LORD.

⁵You hem me in—behind and before;
you have laid your hand upon me.
⁶Such knowledge is too wonderful for
me,
too lofty for me to attain.

⁷Where can I go from your Spirit?
Where can I flee from your
presence?
⁸If I go up to the heavens, you are
there;
if I make my bed in the depths,ᵃ you
are there.
⁹If I rise on the wings of the dawn,
if I settle on the far side of the sea,
¹⁰even there your hand will guide me,
your right hand will hold me fast.
¹¹If I say, "Surely the darkness will hide
me
and the light become night around
me,"
¹²even the darkness will not be dark to
you;
the night will shine like the day,
for darkness is as light to you.

¹³For you created my inmost being;
you knit me together in my
mother's womb.
¹⁴I praise you because I am fearfully
and wonderfully made;
your works are wonderful,
I know that full well.
¹⁵My frame was not hidden from you
when I was made in the secret
place.
When I was woven together in the
depths of the earth,
¹⁶   your eyes saw my unformed body.
All the days ordained for me
were written in your book
before one of them came to be.

¹⁷How precious toᵇ me are your
thoughts, O God!
How vast is the sum of them!
¹⁸Were I to count them,
they would outnumber the grains of
sand.
When I awake,
I am still with you.

ᵃ8 Hebrew *Sheol*   ᵇ17 Or *concerning*

Not All Warm Fuzzies

Huh?

Psalm 139:23–24

Most of Psalm 139 speaks of the awesome benefits of God's closeness. It tells us there's no place where he isn't, no time when he's absent. God's closeness wraps us up in a blanket of security. But it's not all warm fuzzies. There's also the steel edge of God's holiness, which scrapes against our sinfulness. In that case, we need to invite God into the secret places of our hearts, so all our sins can be exposed, confessed and forgiven.

¹⁹ If only you would slay the wicked,
O God!
Away from me, you bloodthirsty
men!
²⁰ They speak of you with evil intent;
your adversaries misuse your name.

²¹ Do I not hate those who hate you,
O LORD,
and abhor those who rise up against
you?
²² I have nothing but hatred for them;
I count them my enemies.

²³ Search me, O God, and know my
heart;
test me and know my anxious
thoughts.
²⁴ See if there is any offensive way in
me,
and lead me in the way everlasting.

Psalm 140

For the director of music.
A psalm of David.

¹ Rescue me, O LORD, from evil men;
protect me from men of violence,
² who devise evil plans in their hearts
and stir up war every day.
³ They make their tongues as sharp as a
serpent's;

Friday

Handmade by God

Read Psalm 139:13–16

I've been really short all my life, and I'm not exactly built for sports. Sometimes I feel very self-conscious at school, especially around people who are super-athletic. I look at them and think, *Why did I have to be so small and weak?* Or when I'm around people who are really popular, I feel like I don't measure up.

Lucky for me, God doesn't judge me by how handsome or strong I am. He doesn't care how well I play sports or how popular I am. He loves me for who I am. And he's happy when he looks at my heart, because he sees a person who loves Jesus and is trying to do what's right.

So to anyone else who sometimes feels like a klutz or a nerd, I'd say, "God made you, and he loves you. Don't worry about who you aren't—praise God for who you are!"

Jonathan age 14

What about You?

❶ How do people at school judge who's "the best"? How do you think God judges who's "the best"?

❷ Write down 10 things you like about the way God made you.

❸ Praise God for creating you and loving you just the way you are.

Turn to page 726 for your next devotion.

the poison of vipers is on their lips.
Selah

⁴Keep me, O LORD, from the hands of
the wicked;
protect me from men of violence
who plan to trip my feet.
⁵Proud men have hidden a snare for
me;
they have spread out the cords of
their net
and have set traps for me along my
path.   *Selah*

⁶O LORD, I say to you, "You are my
God."
Hear, O LORD, my cry for mercy.
⁷O Sovereign LORD, my strong
deliverer,
who shields my head in the day of
battle—
⁸do not grant the wicked their desires,
O LORD;
do not let their plans succeed,
or they will become proud.   *Selah*

⁹Let the heads of those who surround
me
be covered with the trouble their
lips have caused.
¹⁰Let burning coals fall upon them;
may they be thrown into the fire,
into miry pits, never to rise.
¹¹Let slanderers not be established in
the land;
may disaster hunt down men of
violence.

¹²I know that the LORD secures justice
for the poor
and upholds the cause of the
needy.
¹³Surely the righteous will praise your
name
and the upright will live before you.

Psalm 141

A psalm of David.

¹O LORD, I call to you; come quickly to
me.
Hear my voice when I call to you.
²May my prayer be set before you like
incense;
may the lifting up of my hands be
like the evening sacrifice.

³Set a guard over my mouth, O LORD;
keep watch over the door of my
lips.
⁴Let not my heart be drawn to what is
evil,
to take part in wicked deeds
with men who are evildoers;
let me not eat of their delicacies.

⁵Let a righteous man*ᵃ* strike me—it is a
kindness;
let him rebuke me—it is oil on my
head.
My head will not refuse it.

Yet my prayer is ever against the
deeds of evildoers;
⁶   their rulers will be thrown down
from the cliffs,
and the wicked will learn that my
words were well spoken.
⁷They will say, "As one plows and
breaks up the earth,
so our bones have been scattered at
the mouth of the grave.*ᵇ*"

⁸But my eyes are fixed on you,
O Sovereign LORD;
in you I take refuge—do not give me
over to death.
⁹Keep me from the snares they have
laid for me,
from the traps set by evildoers.
¹⁰Let the wicked fall into their own nets,
while I pass by in safety.

Psalm 142

A *maskil*ᶜ of David.
When he was in the cave. A prayer.

¹I cry aloud to the LORD;
I lift up my voice to the LORD for
mercy.
²I pour out my complaint before him;
before him I tell my trouble.

³When my spirit grows faint within
me,
it is you who know my way.
In the path where I walk
men have hidden a snare for me.
⁴Look to my right and see;
no one is concerned for me.

ᵃ5 Or *Let the Righteous One*   ᵇ7 Hebrew *Sheol*
ᶜTitle: Probably a literary or musical term

I have no refuge;
  no one cares for my life.

[5] I cry to you, O LORD;
  I say, "You are my refuge,
    my portion in the land of the
      living."
[6] Listen to my cry,
  for I am in desperate need;
rescue me from those who pursue me,
  for they are too strong for me.
[7] Set me free from my prison,
  that I may praise your name.

Then the righteous will gather about
    me
  because of your goodness to me.

Psalm 143

A psalm of David.

[1] O LORD, hear my prayer,
  listen to my cry for mercy;
in your faithfulness and righteousness
  come to my relief.
[2] Do not bring your servant into
    judgment,
  for no one living is righteous before
    you.

[3] The enemy pursues me,
  he crushes me to the ground;
he makes me dwell in darkness
  like those long dead.
[4] So my spirit grows faint within me;
  my heart within me is dismayed.

[5] I remember the days of long ago;
  I meditate on all your works
  and consider what your hands have
    done.
[6] I spread out my hands to you;
  my soul thirsts for you like a
    parched land.   *Selah*

[7] Answer me quickly, O LORD;
  my spirit fails.
Do not hide your face from me
  or I will be like those who go down
    to the pit.
[8] Let the morning bring me word of
    your unfailing love,
  for I have put my trust in you.
Show me the way I should go,
  for to you I lift up my soul.
[9] Rescue me from my enemies, O LORD,

for I hide myself in you.
[10] Teach me to do your will,
  for you are my God;
may your good Spirit
  lead me on level ground.

[11] For your name's sake, O LORD,
  preserve my life;
in your righteousness, bring me out
  of trouble.
[12] In your unfailing love, silence my
    enemies;
  destroy all my foes,
  for I am your servant.

Psalm 144

Of David.

[1] Praise be to the LORD my Rock,
  who trains my hands for war,
  my fingers for battle.
[2] He is my loving God and my fortress,
  my stronghold and my deliverer,
my shield, in whom I take refuge,
  who subdues peoples[a] under me.

[3] O LORD, what is man that you care for
    him,
  the son of man that you think of
    him?
[4] Man is like a breath;
  his days are like a fleeting shadow.

[5] Part your heavens, O LORD, and come
    down;
  touch the mountains, so that they
    smoke.
[6] Send forth lightning and scatter the
    enemies;
  shoot your arrows and rout them.
[7] Reach down your hand from on high;
  deliver me and rescue me
from the mighty waters,
  from the hands of foreigners
[8] whose mouths are full of lies,
  whose right hands are deceitful.

[9] I will sing a new song to you, O God;
  on the ten-stringed lyre I will make
    music to you,
[10] to the One who gives victory to
    kings,

[a] 2 Many manuscripts of the Masoretic Text, Dead
Sea Scrolls, Aquila, Jerome and Syriac; most
manuscripts of the Masoretic Text *subdues my
people*

who delivers his servant David from
the deadly sword.
[11] Deliver me and rescue me
from the hands of foreigners
whose mouths are full of lies,
whose right hands are deceitful.

[12] Then our sons in their youth
will be like well-nurtured plants,
and our daughters will be like pillars
carved to adorn a palace.
[13] Our barns will be filled
with every kind of provision.
Our sheep will increase by
thousands,
by tens of thousands in our fields;
[14] our oxen will draw heavy loads.[a]
There will be no breaching of walls,
no going into captivity,
no cry of distress in our streets.

[15] Blessed are the people of whom this is
true;
blessed are the people whose God is
the LORD.

Psalm 145[b]

A psalm of praise. Of David.

[1] I will exalt you, my God the King;
I will praise your name for ever and
ever.
[2] Every day I will praise you
and extol your name for ever and
ever.

[3] Great is the LORD and most worthy of
praise;
his greatness no one can fathom.
[4] One generation will commend your
works to another;
they will tell of your mighty acts.
[5] They will speak of the glorious
splendor of your majesty,
and I will meditate on your
wonderful works.[c]
[6] They will tell of the power of your
awesome works,
and I will proclaim your great
deeds.
[7] They will celebrate your abundant
goodness
and joyfully sing of your
righteousness.

[8] The LORD is gracious and
compassionate,
slow to anger and rich in love.
[9] The LORD is good to all;
he has compassion on all he has
made.
[10] All you have made will praise you,
O LORD;
your saints will extol you.
[11] They will tell of the glory of your
kingdom
and speak of your might,
[12] so that all men may know of your
mighty acts
and the glorious splendor of your
kingdom.
[13] Your kingdom is an everlasting
kingdom,
and your dominion endures through
all generations.

The LORD is faithful to all his promises
and loving toward all he has made.[d]
[14] The LORD upholds all those who fall
and lifts up all who are bowed
down.
[15] The eyes of all look to you,
and you give them their food at the
proper time.
[16] You open your hand
and satisfy the desires of every
living thing.
[17] The LORD is righteous in all his ways
and loving toward all he has made.
[18] The LORD is near to all who call on
him,
to all who call on him in truth.
[19] He fulfills the desires of those who
fear him;
he hears their cry and saves them.
[20] The LORD watches over all who love
him,
but all the wicked he will destroy.

[21] My mouth will speak in praise of the
LORD.

a14 Or our chieftains will be firmly established
*b This psalm is an acrostic poem, the verses of which
(including verse 13b) begin with the successive
letters of the Hebrew alphabet.   c5 Dead Sea Scrolls
and Syriac (see also Septuagint); Masoretic Text On
the glorious splendor of your majesty / and on your
wonderful works I will meditate   d13 One
manuscript of the Masoretic Text, Dead Sea Scrolls
and Syriac (see also Septuagint); most manuscripts
of the Masoretic Text do not have the last two lines
of verse 13.*

Let every creature praise his holy
    name
for ever and ever.

Psalm 146

¹Praise the LORD.ᵃ

Praise the LORD, O my soul.
²   I will praise the LORD all my life;

I will sing praise to my God as long
    as I live.

³Do not put your trust in princes,
    in mortal men, who cannot save.
⁴When their spirit departs, they return
    to the ground;
  on that very day their plans come
    to nothing.

ᵃ1 Hebrew *Hallelu Yah*; also in verse 10

How Important Is the Bible?

Colossians 3:16–17 (page 1446)

On Tuesday, Julia called the Bible "God's Flashlight" because it shows us the path to take in life. You probably agree with that. Everybody needs a Bible.

But has that fact really sunk in? Do you look at reading your Bible as optional or essential? Colossians 3:16 challenges us to "let the word of Christ dwell in you richly." That means reading it and acting on it as much as possible.

Back in Psalm 119, the psalm that Julia wrote about, we find 3 verses that help us figure out whether the Bible is as important to us as it should be. Verse 72 says, "The law from your mouth is more precious to me than thousands of pieces of silver and gold." Could you say that? Is God's Word more important to you than money—even big stacks of it?

Verse 103 says, "How sweet are your words to my taste, sweeter than honey to my mouth!" If you had to choose between a quiet time and a gourmet meal, which would you pick? Is the Bible more important to you than food?

Verse 148 reads, "My eyes stay open through the watches of the night, that I may meditate on your promises." Is God's Word more important to you than sleep?

When our lives prove that the Bible holds more value to us than money, food or sleep, we know it is dwelling in us richly, changing our lives and lighting our path.

❶ When was the last time you made a sacrifice to get God's Word into your life?

❷ Try "fasting"—or skipping one meal this week—in order to have more time to read your Bible. Instead of snarfing down a burger, dig into a Bible. When you get hungry later, don't eat until mealtime. Tell God your stomach growls are your way of telling him that you're hungrier for his truth than for anything else.

❸ Ask God to help you to fall in love with his Word so that you'll read it not because you have to but because you want to!

Turn to page 734 for your next devotion.

⁵Blessed is he whose help is the God of
Jacob,
whose hope is in the LORD his God,
⁶the Maker of heaven and earth,
the sea, and everything in them—
the LORD, who remains faithful
forever.
⁷He upholds the cause of the oppressed
and gives food to the hungry.
The LORD sets prisoners free,
⁸ the LORD gives sight to the blind,
the LORD lifts up those who are bowed
down,
the LORD loves the righteous.
⁹The LORD watches over the alien
and sustains the fatherless and the
widow,
but he frustrates the ways of the
wicked.

¹⁰The LORD reigns forever,
your God, O Zion, for all generations.

Praise the LORD.

Psalm 147

¹Praise the LORD.ᵃ

How good it is to sing praises to our
God,
how pleasant and fitting to praise
him!

²The LORD builds up Jerusalem;
he gathers the exiles of Israel.
³He heals the brokenhearted
and binds up their wounds.

⁴He determines the number of the stars
and calls them each by name.
⁵Great is our Lord and mighty in
power;
his understanding has no limit.
⁶The LORD sustains the humble
but casts the wicked to the ground.

⁷Sing to the LORD with thanksgiving;
make music to our God on the harp.
⁸He covers the sky with clouds;
he supplies the earth with rain
and makes grass grow on the hills.
⁹He provides food for the cattle
and for the young ravens when they
call.

¹⁰His pleasure is not in the strength of
the horse,

nor his delight in the legs of a man;
¹¹the LORD delights in those who fear
him,
who put their hope in his unfailing
love.

¹²Extol the LORD, O Jerusalem;
praise your God, O Zion,
¹³for he strengthens the bars of your
gates
and blesses your people within you.
¹⁴He grants peace to your borders
and satisfies you with the finest of
wheat.

¹⁵He sends his command to the earth;
his word runs swiftly.
¹⁶He spreads the snow like wool
and scatters the frost like ashes.
¹⁷He hurls down his hail like pebbles.
Who can withstand his icy blast?
¹⁸He sends his word and melts them;
he stirs up his breezes, and the
waters flow.

¹⁹He has revealed his word to Jacob,
his laws and decrees to Israel.
²⁰He has done this for no other nation;
they do not know his laws.

Praise the LORD.

Psalm 148

¹Praise the LORD.ᵇ

Praise the LORD from the heavens,
praise him in the heights above.
²Praise him, all his angels,
praise him, all his heavenly hosts.
³Praise him, sun and moon,
praise him, all you shining stars.
⁴Praise him, you highest heavens
and you waters above the skies.
⁵Let them praise the name of the LORD,
for he commanded and they were
created.
⁶He set them in place for ever and
ever;
he gave a decree that will never
pass away.

⁷Praise the LORD from the earth,
you great sea creatures and all
ocean depths,

ᵃ1 Hebrew *Hallelu Yah*; also in verse 20   ᵇ1 Hebrew
Hallelu Yah; also in verse 14

8lightning and hail, snow and clouds,
    stormy winds that do his bidding,
9you mountains and all hills,
    fruit trees and all cedars,
10wild animals and all cattle,
    small creatures and flying birds,
11kings of the earth and all nations,
    you princes and all rulers on earth,
12young men and maidens,
    old men and children.

13Let them praise the name of the LORD,
    for his name alone is exalted;
    his splendor is above the earth and
        the heavens.
14He has raised up for his people a
        horn,*a*
    the praise of all his saints,
    of Israel, the people close to his
        heart.

    Praise the LORD.

Psalm 149

1Praise the LORD.*b*

Sing to the LORD a new song,
    his praise in the assembly of the
        saints.

2Let Israel rejoice in their Maker;
    let the people of Zion be glad in
        their King.
3Let them praise his name with
        dancing
    and make music to him with
        tambourine and harp.
4For the LORD takes delight in his
        people;
    he crowns the humble with
        salvation.
5Let the saints rejoice in this honor
    and sing for joy on their beds.

6May the praise of God be in their
        mouths
    and a double-edged sword in their
        hands,
7to inflict vengeance on the nations
    and punishment on the peoples,
8to bind their kings with fetters,
    their nobles with shackles of iron,

Rock On!

Huh?

Psalm 150:1–6

Psalms ends on a high note, with a call to wild, energetic praise. In addition to using the usual hymnbook and organ, we need to praise God in every way imaginable. This psalm, carefully chosen to close out the Worship Book of the Bible, calls for horn blasts, cymbal crashes and massive waves of sound.

9to carry out the sentence written
        against them.
    This is the glory of all his saints.

    Praise the LORD.

Psalm 150

1Praise the LORD.*c*

Praise God in his sanctuary;
    praise him in his mighty heavens.
2Praise him for his acts of power;
    praise him for his surpassing
        greatness.
3Praise him with the sounding of the
        trumpet,
    praise him with the harp and lyre,
4praise him with tambourine and
        dancing,
    praise him with the strings and
        flute,
5praise him with the clash of cymbals,
    praise him with resounding
        cymbals.

6Let everything that has breath praise
        the LORD.

    Praise the LORD.

a14 Horn here symbolizes strong one, that is, king.
b1 Hebrew *Hallelu Yah*; also in verse 9   *c1* Hebrew
Hallelu Yah; also in verse 6

Proverbs

 START

Almost everything you buy comes with instructions—you know, that piece of paper or that paragraph on the box you never read with all the important stuff on it? The instructions usually tell you how to put the thing together, how much to use or how you could get hurt if you don't follow the directions.

Well, if there were ever instructions for how to live right as a teenager (or any ager), they are in the book of Proverbs. Most of the book was written by the wisest, smartest man who ever lived: King Solomon.

Solomon loved God a ton, and people would come from all over just to hear what he had to say. He wrote about, well, just about everything like wisdom, power, sex, money, what to say, how to pipe down and how not to act like a fool!

The great thing about Proverbs is that it has lots of God's wisdom in a fun-sized package!

Cast OF Characters

Solomon
(SAHL-uh-mun)
Smart guy. Rich guy. Godly guy! He was king over God's people (the Israelites), and he always had something cool to say.

Wise Guys
Agur, King Lemuel, and others helped write this book. Like Solomon, these guys had a solid walk with God to go with their super-charged brains.

The Smart Guy
This is anyone who follows God's wise ways. Also known as the wise son, the righteous, the good man, the generous man, the prudent man, the faithful and a bunch more.

The Dumb Guy
This is anyone who follows the wrong way. Also known as the fool, the sluggard, the wicked man, the mocker, the hot-tempered man and so on.

What's Up with That?

Proverbs often uses opposites to help us understand what God wants us to do and not do. See if you can match up some of these positive and negative topics in Proverbs. Draw lines between the ones that match.

(You can look up these verses to help you: 3:33, 3:35, 11:2, 11:19, 12:22, 12:24, 14:8, 22:9)

Humility	**Righteous**
Death	**Wisdom**
Diligence	**Shame**
Lying	**Greed**
Generosity	**Life**
Honor	**Pride**
Foolishness	**Truth**
Wicked	**Laziness**

Snap shots

- Wise up *(chapter 1:1-7)*

- Father knows best *(chapters 1:8—9:18)*

- "But . . . but . . . but" *(chapters 10—15)*

- Live right *(chapters 16—21 and 22:16)*

- Other wise guys *(chapters 22:17—24:34)*

- Look what we found *(chapters 25—29)*

- Agur's 2 cents *(chapter 30)*

- What a woman! *(chapter 31)*

answers: humility and pride, death and life, diligence and laziness, lying and truth, generosity and greed, honor and shame, foolishness and wisdom, wicked and righteous

Prologue: Purpose and Theme

1 The proverbs of Solomon son of David, king of Israel:

² for attaining wisdom and discipline;
   for understanding words of insight;
³ for acquiring a disciplined and
      prudent life,
   doing what is right and just and
      fair;
⁴ for giving prudence to the simple,
   knowledge and discretion to the
      young—
⁵ let the wise listen and add to their
      learning,
   and let the discerning get
      guidance—
⁶ for understanding proverbs and
      parables,
   the sayings and riddles of the wise.

⁷ The fear of the LORD is the beginning
      of knowledge,
   but fools*a* despise wisdom and
      discipline.

Exhortations to Embrace Wisdom

Warning Against Enticement

⁸ Listen, my son, to your father's
      instruction
   and do not forsake your mother's
      teaching.
⁹ They will be a garland to grace your
      head
   and a chain to adorn your neck.

¹⁰ My son, if sinners entice you,
   do not give in to them.
¹¹ If they say, "Come along with us;
   let's lie in wait for someone's blood,
   let's waylay some harmless soul;
¹² let's swallow them alive, like the
      grave,*b*
   and whole, like those who go down
      to the pit;
¹³ we will get all sorts of valuable things
   and fill our houses with plunder;
¹⁴ throw in your lot with us,
   and we will share a common
      purse"—
¹⁵ my son, do not go along with them,
   do not set foot on their paths;
¹⁶ for their feet rush into sin,
   they are swift to shed blood.

¹⁷ How useless to spread a net
   in full view of all the birds!
¹⁸ These men lie in wait for their own
      blood;
   they waylay only themselves!
¹⁹ Such is the end of all who go after
      ill-gotten gain;
   it takes away the lives of those who
      get it.

Warning Against Rejecting Wisdom

²⁰ Wisdom calls aloud in the street,
   she raises her voice in the public
      squares;

The Wisdom Woman

Huh?

Proverbs 1:20

In Proverbs, wisdom is personified. In other words, it's treated as if it were a person. "She" speaks and teaches and helps those who listen to "her." Some people have taken this writing technique and made a whole belief system out of it. They say Wisdom is a goddess (a female god). That's goofy, to say the least. "Wisdom" is simply the smarts of God. The writer of Proverbs wants to get our attention so that we will pursue wisdom with a passion.

²¹ at the head of the noisy streets*c* she
      cries out,
   in the gateways of the city she
      makes her speech:

²² "How long will you simple ones*d* love
      your simple ways?
   How long will mockers delight in
      mockery
   and fools hate knowledge?
²³ If you had responded to my rebuke,
   I would have poured out my heart
      to you

---

a7 The Hebrew words rendered *fool* in Proverbs, and often elsewhere in the Old Testament, denote one who is morally deficient.   *b12* Hebrew *Sheol*   *c21* Hebrew; Septuagint / *on the tops of the walls*   *d22* The Hebrew word rendered *simple* in Proverbs generally denotes one without moral direction and inclined to evil.

and made my thoughts known to
   you.
²⁴But since you rejected me when I
   called
   and no one gave heed when I
   stretched out my hand,
²⁵since you ignored all my advice
   and would not accept my rebuke,
²⁶I in turn will laugh at your disaster;
   I will mock when calamity
   overtakes you—
²⁷when calamity overtakes you like a
   storm,
   when disaster sweeps over you like
   a whirlwind,
   when distress and trouble
   overwhelm you.

²⁸"Then they will call to me but I will
   not answer;
   they will look for me but will not
   find me.
²⁹Since they hated knowledge
   and did not choose to fear the LORD,
³⁰since they would not accept my
   advice
   and spurned my rebuke,
³¹they will eat the fruit of their ways
   and be filled with the fruit of their
   schemes.
³²For the waywardness of the simple
   will kill them,
   and the complacency of fools will
   destroy them;
³³but whoever listens to me will live in
   safety
   and be at ease, without fear of
   harm."

Moral Benefits of Wisdom

2 My son, if you accept my words
   and store up my commands within
   you,
²turning your ear to wisdom
   and applying your heart to
   understanding,
³and if you call out for insight
   and cry aloud for understanding,
⁴and if you look for it as for silver
   and search for it as for hidden
   treasure,
⁵then you will understand the fear of
   the LORD
   and find the knowledge of God.
⁶For the LORD gives wisdom,

and from his mouth come
   knowledge and understanding.
⁷He holds victory in store for the
   upright,
   he is a shield to those whose walk is
   blameless,
⁸for he guards the course of the just
   and protects the way of his faithful
   ones.

⁹Then you will understand what is
   right and just
   and fair—every good path.
¹⁰For wisdom will enter your heart,
   and knowledge will be pleasant to
   your soul.
¹¹Discretion will protect you,
   and understanding will guard you.
¹²Wisdom will save you from the ways
   of wicked men,
   from men whose words are
   perverse,
¹³who leave the straight paths
   to walk in dark ways,
¹⁴who delight in doing wrong
   and rejoice in the perverseness of
   evil,
¹⁵whose paths are crooked
   and who are devious in their ways.

¹⁶It will save you also from the
   adulteress,
   from the wayward wife with her
   seductive words,
¹⁷who has left the partner of her youth
   and ignored the covenant she made
   before God.^a
¹⁸For her house leads down to death
   and her paths to the spirits of the
   dead.
¹⁹None who go to her return
   or attain the paths of life.

²⁰Thus you will walk in the ways of
   good men
   and keep to the paths of the
   righteous.
²¹For the upright will live in the land,
   and the blameless will remain
   in it;
²²but the wicked will be cut off from the
   land,
   and the unfaithful will be torn
   from it.

^a17 Or *covenant of her God*

Your Own Words

Sometimes the best way to understand a Scripture passage is to put it in your own words. Write your own personal Proverbs 3:1–6. Use language you and your friends use every day. Use a dictionary if you don't know some of the Bible words.

1 My son, do not forget my teaching, but keep my commands in your heart, _____

_____

_____

_____

2 for they will prolong your life many years and bring you prosperity. _____

_____

_____

3 Let love and faithfulness never leave you; bind them around your neck, write them on the tablet of your heart. _____

_____

_____

4 Then you will win favor and a good name in the sight of God and man. _____

_____

_____

_____

5 Trust in the Lord with all your heart and lean not on your own understanding; _____

_____

_____

_____

6 in all your ways acknowledge him, and he will make your paths straight. _____

_____

_____

_____

Further Benefits of Wisdom

3 My son, do not forget my teaching,
but keep my commands in your
heart,

2 for they will prolong your life many
years
and bring you prosperity.

3 Let love and faithfulness never leave
you;
bind them around your neck,
write them on the tablet of your
heart.

4 Then you will win favor and a good
name
in the sight of God and man.

5 Trust in the Lord with all your heart
and lean not on your own
understanding;

6 in all your ways acknowledge him,
and he will make your paths
straight.[a]

7 Do not be wise in your own eyes;
fear the Lord and shun evil.

8 This will bring health to your body
and nourishment to your bones.

9 Honor the Lord with your wealth,
with the firstfruits of all your crops;

10 then your barns will be filled to
overflowing,
and your vats will brim over with
new wine.

11 My son, do not despise the Lord's
discipline
and do not resent his rebuke,

12 because the Lord disciplines those he
loves,
as a father[b] the son he delights in.

13 Blessed is the man who finds wisdom,
the man who gains understanding,

---

[a]6 Or *will direct your paths*   [b]12 Hebrew;
Septuagint / *and he punishes*

¹⁴for she is more profitable than silver
    and yields better returns than gold.
¹⁵She is more precious than rubies;
    nothing you desire can compare
        with her.
¹⁶Long life is in her right hand;
    in her left hand are riches and
        honor.
¹⁷Her ways are pleasant ways,
    and all her paths are peace.
¹⁸She is a tree of life to those who
        embrace her;
    those who lay hold of her will be
        blessed.

¹⁹By wisdom the LORD laid the earth's
        foundations,
    by understanding he set the
        heavens in place;
²⁰by his knowledge the deeps were
        divided,
    and the clouds let drop the dew.

²¹My son, preserve sound judgment and
        discernment,
    do not let them out of your sight;
²²they will be life for you,
    an ornament to grace your neck.
²³Then you will go on your way in
        safety,
    and your foot will not stumble;
²⁴when you lie down, you will not be
        afraid;
    when you lie down, your sleep will
        be sweet.
²⁵Have no fear of sudden disaster
    or of the ruin that overtakes the
        wicked,
²⁶for the LORD will be your confidence
    and will keep your foot from being
        snared.
²⁷Do not withhold good from those who
        deserve it,
    when it is in your power to act.

Monday

Good Enough for God

Read Proverbs 3:29–30

I've said some things in my life that I've regretted. One of the biggest things I regret saying involves a girl I hardly knew. When I was with a bunch of my friends at a slumber party, I started gossiping about this girl—talking about her behind her back and saying things about her that just weren't true. Eventually she found out, and I lost the chance to ever be her friend. I tried to make things right, but she never said another word to me.

    It was low of me to try to impress my friends by gossiping about an innocent person. Proverbs 3:29 says that I should not do any harm to the people around me. When I gossiped about this girl, I hurt her, and I hurt God too. God created each person in a special way. When we make fun of someone, it's like we're telling God, "That girl or guy isn't good enough for me." And how can we do that when that person is good enough for God?

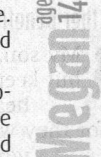

Megan age 14

❶ Think of a time you talked about someone behind his or her back. Why did you do it? How can you keep from doing it again?

❷ Name a person you find it easy to make fun of. Now, get a piece of paper and write down 5 qualities you admire in that person. The next time you see that girl or guy, focus on the things you like about him or her instead of the stuff you don't like.

❸ Thank God for loving you the way you are. Ask him to help you see what's special in others.

Turn to page 738 for your next devotion.

²⁸Do not say to your neighbor,
    "Come back later; I'll give it
        tomorrow"–
    when you now have it with you.

²⁹Do not plot harm against your
        neighbor,
    who lives trustfully near you.
³⁰Do not accuse a man for no reason–
    when he has done you no harm.
³¹Do not envy a violent man
    or choose any of his ways,
³²for the LORD detests a perverse man
    but takes the upright into his
        confidence.

³³The LORD's curse is on the house of
        the wicked,
    but he blesses the home of the
        righteous.
³⁴He mocks proud mockers
    but gives grace to the humble.
³⁵The wise inherit honor,
    but fools he holds up to shame.

Wisdom Is Supreme

4 Listen, my sons, to a father's
        instruction;
    pay attention and gain
        understanding.
²I give you sound learning,
    so do not forsake my teaching.
³When I was a boy in my father's
        house,
    still tender, and an only child of my
        mother,
⁴he taught me and said,
    "Lay hold of my words with all your
        heart;
    keep my commands and you will
        live.
⁵Get wisdom, get understanding;
    do not forget my words or swerve
        from them.
⁶Do not forsake wisdom, and she will
        protect you;
    love her, and she will watch over
        you.
⁷Wisdom is supreme; therefore get
        wisdom.
    Though it cost all you have,ᵃ get
        understanding.
⁸Esteem her, and she will exalt you;
    embrace her, and she will honor
        you.

⁹She will set a garland of grace on
        your head
    and present you with a crown of
        splendor."

¹⁰Listen, my son, accept what I say,
    and the years of your life will be
        many.
¹¹I guide you in the way of wisdom
    and lead you along straight paths.
¹²When you walk, your steps will not be
        hampered;
    when you run, you will not
        stumble.
¹³Hold on to instruction, do not let it
        go;
    guard it well, for it is your life.
¹⁴Do not set foot on the path of the
        wicked
    or walk in the way of evil men.
¹⁵Avoid it, do not travel on it;
    turn from it and go on your way.
¹⁶For they cannot sleep till they do evil;
    they are robbed of slumber till they
        make someone fall.
¹⁷They eat the bread of wickedness
    and drink the wine of violence.

¹⁸The path of the righteous is like the
        first gleam of dawn,
    shining ever brighter till the full
        light of day.
¹⁹But the way of the wicked is like deep
        darkness;
    they do not know what makes them
        stumble.

²⁰My son, pay attention to what I say;
    listen closely to my words.
²¹Do not let them out of your sight,
    keep them within your heart;
²²for they are life to those who find
        them
    and health to a man's whole body.
²³Above all else, guard your heart,
    for it is the wellspring of life.
²⁴Put away perversity from your mouth;
    keep corrupt talk far from your lips.
²⁵Let your eyes look straight ahead,
    fix your gaze directly before you.
²⁶Make levelᵇ paths for your feet
    and take only ways that are firm.
²⁷Do not swerve to the right or the left;
    keep your foot from evil.

ᵃ7 Or *Whatever else you get*   ᵇ26 Or *Consider the*

Warning Against Adultery

5 My son, pay attention to my wisdom,
listen well to my words of insight,
² that you may maintain discretion
and your lips may preserve
knowledge.
³ For the lips of an adulteress drip
honey,
and her speech is smoother than oil;
⁴ but in the end she is bitter as gall,
sharp as a double-edged sword.
⁵ Her feet go down to death;
her steps lead straight to the grave.ᵃ
⁶ She gives no thought to the way of
life;
her paths are crooked, but she
knows it not.

⁷ Now then, my sons, listen to me;
do not turn aside from what I say.
⁸ Keep to a path far from her,
do not go near the door of her
house,
⁹ lest you give your best strength to
others
and your years to one who is cruel,
¹⁰ lest strangers feast on your wealth
and your toil enrich another man's
house.
¹¹ At the end of your life you will groan,
when your flesh and body are spent.
¹² You will say, "How I hated discipline!
How my heart spurned correction!
¹³ I would not obey my teachers
or listen to my instructors.
¹⁴ I have come to the brink of utter ruin
in the midst of the whole assembly."

¹⁵ Drink water from your own cistern,
running water from your own well.
¹⁶ Should your springs overflow in the
streets,
your streams of water in the public
squares?
¹⁷ Let them be yours alone,
never to be shared with strangers.
¹⁸ May your fountain be blessed,
and may you rejoice in the wife of
your youth.
¹⁹ A loving doe, a graceful deer—
may her breasts satisfy you always,
may you ever be captivated by her
love.
²⁰ Why be captivated, my son, by an
adulteress?

Why embrace the bosom of another
man's wife?
²¹ For a man's ways are in full view of
the LORD,
and he examines all his paths.
²² The evil deeds of a wicked man
ensnare him;
the cords of his sin hold him fast.
²³ He will die for lack of discipline,
led astray by his own great folly.

Warnings Against Folly

6 My son, if you have put up security
for your neighbor,
if you have struck hands in pledge
for another,
² if you have been trapped by what you
said,
ensnared by the words of your
mouth,
³ then do this, my son, to free yourself,
since you have fallen into your
neighbor's hands:
Go and humble yourself;
press your plea with your neighbor!
⁴ Allow no sleep to your eyes,
no slumber to your eyelids.
⁵ Free yourself, like a gazelle from the
hand of the hunter,
like a bird from the snare of the
fowler.

⁶ Go to the ant, you sluggard;
consider its ways and be wise!
⁷ It has no commander,
no overseer or ruler,
⁸ yet it stores its provisions in summer
and gathers its food at harvest.

⁹ How long will you lie there, you
sluggard?
When will you get up from your
sleep?
¹⁰ A little sleep, a little slumber,
a little folding of the hands to rest—
¹¹ and poverty will come on you like a
bandit
and scarcity like an armed man.ᵇ

¹² A scoundrel and villain,
who goes about with a corrupt
mouth,
¹³   who winks with his eye,

ᵃ5 Hebrew *Sheol*   ᵇ11 Or *like a vagrant / and
scarcity like a beggar*

signals with his feet
and motions with his fingers,

14 who plots evil with deceit in his heart—
he always stirs up dissension.

15 Therefore disaster will overtake him in an instant;
he will suddenly be destroyed— without remedy.

16 There are six things the LORD hates,
seven that are detestable to him:

17 haughty eyes,
a lying tongue,
hands that shed innocent blood,

18 a heart that devises wicked schemes,
feet that are quick to rush into evil,

19 a false witness who pours out lies
and a man who stirs up dissension among brothers.

God's Hate List

Proverbs 6:16–19
Everybody has their pet peeves: fingernails on the chalkboard, "up" toilet seats, that kind of stuff. Some people even have things they can't stand: racism, pollution, animal extinction. Did you know God has a list of things he truly, massively hates? These things make his wrath erupt like a solar flare. Note that 2 of them have to do with lying. Uh oh.

Warning Against Adultery

20 My son, keep your father's commands
and do not forsake your mother's teaching.

21 Bind them upon your heart forever;
fasten them around your neck.

22 When you walk, they will guide you;
when you sleep, they will watch over you;
when you awake, they will speak to you.

23 For these commands are a lamp,
this teaching is a light,
and the corrections of discipline
are the way to life,

24 keeping you from the immoral woman,
from the smooth tongue of the wayward wife.

25 Do not lust in your heart after her beauty
or let her captivate you with her eyes,

26 for the prostitute reduces you to a loaf of bread,
and the adulteress preys upon your very life.

27 Can a man scoop fire into his lap
without his clothes being burned?

28 Can a man walk on hot coals
without his feet being scorched?

29 So is he who sleeps with another man's wife;
no one who touches her will go unpunished.

30 Men do not despise a thief if he steals
to satisfy his hunger when he is starving.

31 Yet if he is caught, he must pay sevenfold,
though it costs him all the wealth of his house.

32 But a man who commits adultery lacks judgment;
whoever does so destroys himself.

33 Blows and disgrace are his lot,
and his shame will never be wiped away;

34 for jealousy arouses a husband's fury,
and he will show no mercy when he takes revenge.

35 He will not accept any compensation;
he will refuse the bribe, however great it is.

Warning Against the Adulteress

7 My son, keep my words
and store up my commands within you.

2 Keep my commands and you will live;
guard my teachings as the apple of your eye.

3 Bind them on your fingers;
write them on the tablet of your heart.

4 Say to wisdom, "You are my sister,"
and call understanding your kinsman;

⁵they will keep you from the
    adulteress,
from the wayward wife with her
    seductive words.

⁶At the window of my house
    I looked out through the lattice.
⁷I saw among the simple,
    I noticed among the young men,
    a youth who lacked judgment.
⁸He was going down the street near her
    corner,
    walking along in the direction of
    her house
⁹at twilight, as the day was fading,
    as the dark of night set in.

¹⁰Then out came a woman to meet him,
    dressed like a prostitute and with
    crafty intent.
¹¹(She is loud and defiant,
    her feet never stay at home;
¹²now in the street, now in the squares,
    at every corner she lurks.)
¹³She took hold of him and kissed him
    and with a brazen face she said:

¹⁴"I have fellowship offerings ᵃ at home;
    today I fulfilled my vows.
¹⁵So I came out to meet you;
    I looked for you and have found
    you!
¹⁶I have covered my bed
    with colored linens from Egypt.
¹⁷I have perfumed my bed
    with myrrh, aloes and cinnamon.
¹⁸Come, let's drink deep of love till
    morning;
    let's enjoy ourselves with love!

ᵃ14 Traditionally *peace offerings*

Tuesday

Living on the Edge

Read Proverbs 6:27–29

Imagine looking through a store window at something you really want. But the store is closed. Would you break the window and steal it? Of course not!

    No one in their right mind would go for that! But it's kind of like that with sexual temptation. If you give in, you might be happy for a few minutes, or even a few days, but in the end there are real consequences. The guilt starts to set in. So does the regret.

    I never like to think about those. Satan does a good job of tricking us when it comes to sexual temptation. Often, he blinds us so we can't even see the danger. All of us need the wisdom of God and the voice of the Holy Spirit to help us avoid this dangerous trap.

    That's why these verses mean a lot to me. Basically they say that I can't play with fire for very long without getting burned. Sooner or later, the consequences of sin will catch up with me. When I think of it that way, it isn't hard to say no.

Robyn age 13

What about You?

❶ Have you ever been tempted to think or act in a way that you knew would be a sin? What did you do? What helped or could have helped you resist?

❷ Try to think of the characteristics of fire—what it's like, what it does, and so on. Reread the 3 verses for today. Why do you think the author of Proverbs compares sexual temptation with fire?

❸ Thank God for giving you the strength to resist temptation. Pray that the Holy Spirit will help you make wise decisions.

Turn to page 740 for your next devotion.

¹⁹"My husband is not at home;
  he has gone on a long journey.
²⁰He took his purse filled with money
  and will not be home till full
  moon."

²¹With persuasive words she led him
  astray;
  she seduced him with her smooth
  talk.
²²All at once he followed her
  like an ox going to the slaughter,
  like a deer^a stepping into a noose^b
²³ till an arrow pierces his liver,
  like a bird darting into a snare,
  little knowing it will cost him his
  life.

²⁴Now then, my sons, listen to me;
  pay attention to what I say.
²⁵Do not let your heart turn to her ways
  or stray into her paths.
²⁶Many are the victims she has brought
  down;
  her slain are a mighty throng.
²⁷Her house is a highway to the grave,^c
  leading down to the chambers of
  death.

Wisdom's Call

8 Does not wisdom call out?
  Does not understanding raise her
  voice?
²On the heights along the way,
  where the paths meet, she takes her
  stand;
³beside the gates leading into the city,
  at the entrances, she cries aloud:
⁴"To you, O men, I call out;
  I raise my voice to all mankind.
⁵You who are simple, gain prudence;
  you who are foolish, gain
  understanding.
⁶Listen, for I have worthy things to
  say;
  I open my lips to speak what is
  right.
⁷My mouth speaks what is true,
  for my lips detest wickedness.
⁸All the words of my mouth are just;
  none of them is crooked or
  perverse.
⁹To the discerning all of them are
  right;
  they are faultless to those who have
  knowledge.

¹⁰Choose my instruction instead of
  silver,
  knowledge rather than choice gold,
¹¹for wisdom is more precious than
  rubies,
  and nothing you desire can
  compare with her.

¹²"I, wisdom, dwell together with
  prudence;
  I possess knowledge and discretion.
¹³To fear the LORD is to hate evil;
  I hate pride and arrogance,
  evil behavior and perverse speech.
¹⁴Counsel and sound judgment are
  mine;
  I have understanding and power.
¹⁵By me kings reign
  and rulers make laws that are just;
¹⁶by me princes govern,
  and all nobles who rule on earth.^d
¹⁷I love those who love me,
  and those who seek me find me.
¹⁸With me are riches and honor,
  enduring wealth and prosperity.
¹⁹My fruit is better than fine gold;
  what I yield surpasses choice silver.
²⁰I walk in the way of righteousness,
  along the paths of justice,
²¹bestowing wealth on those who love
  me
  and making their treasuries full.

²²"The LORD brought me forth as the
  first of his works,^{e,f}
  before his deeds of old;
²³I was appointed^g from eternity,
  from the beginning, before the
  world began.
²⁴When there were no oceans, I was
  given birth,
  when there were no springs
  abounding with water;
²⁵before the mountains were settled in
  place,
  before the hills, I was given birth,
²⁶before he made the earth or its fields
  or any of the dust of the world.

^a22 Syriac (see also Septuagint); Hebrew *fool*
^b22 The meaning of the Hebrew for this line is
uncertain. ^c27 Hebrew *Sheol* ^d16 Many Hebrew
manuscripts and Septuagint; most Hebrew
manuscripts *and nobles—all righteous rulers* ^e22 Or
way; or *dominion* ^f22 Or *The LORD possessed me at
the beginning of his work*; or *The LORD brought me
forth at the beginning of his work* ^g23 Or *fashioned*

²⁷ I was there when he set the heavens
　　　in place,
　　when he marked out the horizon on
　　　　the face of the deep,
²⁸ when he established the clouds above
　　and fixed securely the fountains of
　　　　the deep,
²⁹ when he gave the sea its boundary
　　so the waters would not overstep
　　　　his command,
　and when he marked out the
　　　　foundations of the earth.
³⁰ 　Then I was the craftsman at his
　　　　side.
　I was filled with delight day after day,
　　rejoicing always in his presence,
³¹ rejoicing in his whole world
　　and delighting in mankind.

³² "Now then, my sons, listen to me;
　　blessed are those who keep my
　　　　ways.
³³ Listen to my instruction and be wise;
　　do not ignore it.

³⁴ Blessed is the man who listens to me,
　　watching daily at my doors,
　　waiting at my doorway.
³⁵ For whoever finds me finds life
　　and receives favor from the Lord.
³⁶ But whoever fails to find me harms
　　　　himself;
　　all who hate me love death."

Invitations of Wisdom and of Folly

9 Wisdom has built her house;
　　she has hewn out its seven
　　　　pillars.
² She has prepared her meat and mixed
　　　　her wine;
　　she has also set her table.
³ She has sent out her maids, and she
　　　　calls
　　from the highest point of the city.
⁴ "Let all who are simple come in here!"
　　she says to those who lack
　　　　judgment.
⁵ "Come, eat my food
　　and drink the wine I have mixed.

Wednesday

More Than Anything Else

Read Proverbs 8:10–11

It's easy to get hung up on worldly treasures. I mean, silver and gold and rubies are pretty valuable things. Most people my age aren't into jewels, but we've got our own treasures—CDs, video games and clothes, for instance. It's OK to have that stuff, but it's not what's truly valuable in life.

In today's passage, God says wisdom and instruction are worth more than anything else we could have. That's because those things actually help us live the right way. I know I don't look for wisdom and instruction enough. I should read my Bible more and pray when I'm wondering how to live everyday life. And I shouldn't look for answers in worldly treasures, because the answer isn't found there. When I talk to God, I know he's listening and he's got the right answers.

Adam age 13

What about You?

❶ What are your most valuable worldly treasures? Why do you think God's wisdom and instruction are worth so much more?

❷ Grab your most valuable possession. Now consider these questions: Has this worldly treasure made you a better person? Has it changed who you are? How does it help other people?

❸ Thank God for his good gifts to you. Thank him especially for wisdom and instruction.

Turn to page 742 for your next devotion.

⁶Leave your simple ways and you will
    live;
    walk in the way of understanding.

⁷"Whoever corrects a mocker invites
    insult;
    whoever rebukes a wicked man
      incurs abuse.
⁸Do not rebuke a mocker or he will
    hate you;
    rebuke a wise man and he will love
      you.
⁹Instruct a wise man and he will be
    wiser still;
    teach a righteous man and he will
      add to his learning.

¹⁰"The fear of the Lᴏʀᴅ is the beginning
    of wisdom,
    and knowledge of the Holy One is
      understanding.
¹¹For through me your days will be
    many,
    and years will be added to your life.
¹²If you are wise, your wisdom will
    reward you;
    if you are a mocker, you alone will
      suffer."

¹³The woman Folly is loud;
    she is undisciplined and without
      knowledge.
¹⁴She sits at the door of her house,
    on a seat at the highest point of the
      city,
¹⁵calling out to those who pass by,
    who go straight on their way.
¹⁶"Let all who are simple come in here!"
    she says to those who lack
      judgment.
¹⁷"Stolen water is sweet;
    food eaten in secret is delicious!"
¹⁸But little do they know that the dead
    are there,
    that her guests are in the depths of
      the grave.ᵃ

Proverbs of Solomon

10 The proverbs of Solomon:

A wise son brings joy to his father,
    but a foolish son grief to his
      mother.

²Ill-gotten treasures are of no value,
    but righteousness delivers from
      death.

³The Lᴏʀᴅ does not let the righteous go
    hungry
    but he thwarts the craving of the
      wicked.

⁴Lazy hands make a man poor,
    but diligent hands bring wealth.

⁵He who gathers crops in summer is a
    wise son,
    but he who sleeps during harvest is
      a disgraceful son.

⁶Blessings crown the head of the
    righteous,
    but violence overwhelms the mouth
      of the wicked.ᵇ

⁷The memory of the righteous will be a
    blessing,
    but the name of the wicked will rot.

⁸The wise in heart accept commands,
    but a chattering fool comes to ruin.

⁹The man of integrity walks securely,
    but he who takes crooked paths will
      be found out.

¹⁰He who winks maliciously causes
    grief,
    and a chattering fool comes to ruin.

¹¹The mouth of the righteous is a
    fountain of life,
    but violence overwhelms the mouth
      of the wicked.

¹²Hatred stirs up dissension,
    but love covers over all wrongs.

¹³Wisdom is found on the lips of the
    discerning,
    but a rod is for the back of him who
      lacks judgment.

¹⁴Wise men store up knowledge,
    but the mouth of a fool invites
      ruin.

¹⁵The wealth of the rich is their fortified
    city,
    but poverty is the ruin of the poor.

¹⁶The wages of the righteous bring them
    life,
    but the income of the wicked brings
      them punishment.

ᵃ18 Hebrew *Sheol* ᵇ6 Or *but the mouth of the*
wicked conceals violence; also in verse 11

¹⁷He who heeds discipline shows the
way to life,
but whoever ignores correction
leads others astray.

¹⁸He who conceals his hatred has lying
lips,
and whoever spreads slander is a
fool.

¹⁹When words are many, sin is not
absent,
but he who holds his tongue is wise.

²⁰The tongue of the righteous is choice
silver,
but the heart of the wicked is of
little value.

²¹The lips of the righteous nourish many,
but fools die for lack of judgment.

²²The blessing of the LORD brings
wealth,
and he adds no trouble to it.

²³A fool finds pleasure in evil conduct,
but a man of understanding delights
in wisdom.

²⁴What the wicked dreads will overtake
him;
what the righteous desire will be
granted.

²⁵When the storm has swept by, the
wicked are gone,
but the righteous stand firm
forever.

²⁶As vinegar to the teeth and smoke to
the eyes,
so is a sluggard to those who send
him.

²⁷The fear of the LORD adds length to
life,
but the years of the wicked are cut
short.

²⁸The prospect of the righteous is joy,
but the hopes of the wicked come to
nothing.

²⁹The way of the LORD is a refuge for
the righteous,
but it is the ruin of those who do
evil.

Thursday

Good Grief!

Read Proverbs 10:1

I've always thought sin was one of those things that was just between me and God. I mess up, I ask for forgiveness, God forgives me and I try not to mess up again. But this verse says my sins don't just affect me and God. They affect other people too. Especially my parents.

When I do something good, I know my parents are proud of me and happy for me. But I never really thought about how they must feel when I do something bad. It must hurt them when I disobey. And since my parents are Christians, I know they must be disappointed when I ignore God's commandments.

This verse has helped me grow closer to my parents. Now I see things from my parents' point of view too, instead of just my own.

❶ Think about a time your parents were upset with you. Why do you think your actions bothered them?

❷ Ask your parents how they feel when you do something wrong. The next time you're tempted to sin, think about what they said.

❸ Ask God to help you bring joy to your parents, not grief.

Turn to page 745 for your next devotion.

Slug Bug

Huh?

Proverbs 10:26

The sluggard is a repeating character in the book of Proverbs. This lazy couch-potato will do anything to avoid work. Sadly, his laziness not only affects him; it really annoys others. If you ever want to know how distasteful your laziness is to others (like your mom), go take a swig of vinegar from the bottle in the kitchen. Eeww!

³⁰ The righteous will never be uprooted,
    but the wicked will not remain in
      the land.

³¹ The mouth of the righteous brings
    forth wisdom,
    but a perverse tongue will be cut
      out.

³² The lips of the righteous know what is
    fitting,
    but the mouth of the wicked only
      what is perverse.

11 The LORD abhors dishonest scales,
    but accurate weights are his
      delight.

² When pride comes, then comes
    disgrace,
    but with humility comes wisdom.

³ The integrity of the upright guides
    them,
    but the unfaithful are destroyed by
      their duplicity.

⁴ Wealth is worthless in the day of
    wrath,
    but righteousness delivers from
      death.

⁵ The righteousness of the blameless
    makes a straight way for them,
    but the wicked are brought down by
      their own wickedness.

⁶ The righteousness of the upright
    delivers them,
    but the unfaithful are trapped by
      evil desires.

⁷ When a wicked man dies, his hope
    perishes;
    all he expected from his power
      comes to nothing.

⁸ The righteous man is rescued from
    trouble,
    and it comes on the wicked
      instead.

⁹ With his mouth the godless destroys
    his neighbor,
    but through knowledge the
      righteous escape.

¹⁰ When the righteous prosper, the city
    rejoices;
    when the wicked perish, there are
      shouts of joy.

¹¹ Through the blessing of the upright a
    city is exalted,
    but by the mouth of the wicked it is
      destroyed.

¹² A man who lacks judgment derides
    his neighbor,
    but a man of understanding holds
      his tongue.

¹³ A gossip betrays a confidence,
    but a trustworthy man keeps a
      secret.

¹⁴ For lack of guidance a nation falls,
    but many advisers make victory
      sure.

¹⁵ He who puts up security for another
    will surely suffer,
    but whoever refuses to strike hands
      in pledge is safe.

¹⁶ A kindhearted woman gains respect,
    but ruthless men gain only wealth.

¹⁷ A kind man benefits himself,
    but a cruel man brings trouble on
      himself.

¹⁸ The wicked man earns deceptive
    wages,
    but he who sows righteousness
      reaps a sure reward.

¹⁹ The truly righteous man attains life,
    but he who pursues evil goes to his
      death.

²⁰ The LORD detests men of perverse
    heart

but he delights in those whose ways
are blameless.

21 Be sure of this: The wicked will not go
unpunished,
but those who are righteous will go
free.

22 Like a gold ring in a pig's snout
is a beautiful woman who shows no
discretion.

23 The desire of the righteous ends only
in good,
but the hope of the wicked only in
wrath.

24 One man gives freely, yet gains even
more;
another withholds unduly, but
comes to poverty.

25 A generous man will prosper;
he who refreshes others will himself
be refreshed.

26 People curse the man who hoards
grain,
but blessing crowns him who is
willing to sell.

27 He who seeks good finds goodwill,
but evil comes to him who searches
for it.

28 Whoever trusts in his riches will fall,
but the righteous will thrive like a
green leaf.

29 He who brings trouble on his family
will inherit only wind,
and the fool will be servant to the
wise.

30 The fruit of the righteous is a tree of
life,
and he who wins souls is wise.

31 If the righteous receive their due on
earth,
how much more the ungodly and
the sinner!

12 Whoever loves discipline loves
knowledge,
but he who hates correction is
stupid.

2 A good man obtains favor from the
LORD,
but the LORD condemns a crafty man.

3 A man cannot be established through
wickedness,
but the righteous cannot be
uprooted.

4 A wife of noble character is her
husband's crown,
but a disgraceful wife is like decay
in his bones.

5 The plans of the righteous are just,
but the advice of the wicked is
deceitful.

6 The words of the wicked lie in wait for
blood,
but the speech of the upright
rescues them.

7 Wicked men are overthrown and are
no more,
but the house of the righteous
stands firm.

8 A man is praised according to his
wisdom,
but men with warped minds are
despised.

9 Better to be a nobody and yet have a
servant
than pretend to be somebody and
have no food.

10 A righteous man cares for the needs
of his animal,
but the kindest acts of the wicked
are cruel.

11 He who works his land will have
abundant food,
but he who chases fantasies lacks
judgment.

12 The wicked desire the plunder of evil
men,
but the root of the righteous
flourishes.

13 An evil man is trapped by his sinful
talk,
but a righteous man escapes
trouble.

14 From the fruit of his lips a man is
filled with good things
as surely as the work of his hands
rewards him.

15 The way of a fool seems right to him,
but a wise man listens to advice.

¹⁶ A fool shows his annoyance at once,
  but a prudent man overlooks an
    insult.

¹⁷ A truthful witness gives honest
    testimony,
  but a false witness tells lies.

¹⁸ Reckless words pierce like a sword,
  but the tongue of the wise brings
    healing.

¹⁹ Truthful lips endure forever,
  but a lying tongue lasts only a
    moment.

²⁰ There is deceit in the hearts of those
    who plot evil,
  but joy for those who promote peace.

²¹ No harm befalls the righteous,
  but the wicked have their fill of
    trouble.

²² The Lord detests lying lips,
  but he delights in men who are
    truthful.

²³ A prudent man keeps his knowledge
    to himself,
  but the heart of fools blurts out
    folly.

²⁴ Diligent hands will rule,
  but laziness ends in slave labor.

²⁵ An anxious heart weighs a man
    down,
  but a kind word cheers him up.

Friday

A Put-down

Read Proverbs 12:17–19

One of my friends used to brag about how great she was at sports. But the truth was that she really *wasn't* a very good athlete. Finally, my other friends and I decided we'd had enough of her boasting and exaggerating. So we told her what we really thought, and we weren't very nice about it.

Sure, we told the truth, but we didn't do it to be honest with her. We did it to put her in her place. She was crushed. Whenever we played any sports, she sort of hung back. She didn't enjoy herself anymore, and she thought everyone was laughing at her. Our words took away something that was fun for her and made her feel bad about herself. I didn't feel too good about myself, either.

We could have been a lot nicer about how we told her the truth. One of us could have said something to her in private, so she wouldn't have been embarrassed. We could have helped her feel good about some of her other great qualities instead of making fun of her weakness.

It's easy to put other people down. And when we say things without really thinking, we aren't following Jesus' command to love each other. We need to use our words to build each other up.

Cassy age 15

What about You?

❶ Have you ever been hurt by someone else's words? How did you feel?

❷ Think about a time you might have hurt someone with your words. Write a "script" of what happened. Now, rewrite the script so that your words build the person up instead of hurting them.

❸ Tell God about the times you've hurt people with your words and ask for his forgiveness.

Turn to page 748 for your next devotion.

26 A righteous man is cautious in
    friendship,[a]
  but the way of the wicked leads
    them astray.

27 The lazy man does not roast[b] his
    game,
  but the diligent man prizes his
    possessions.

28 In the way of righteousness there is
    life;
  along that path is immortality.

13

A wise son heeds his father's
    instruction,
  but a mocker does not listen to
    rebuke.

2 From the fruit of his lips a man enjoys
    good things,
  but the unfaithful have a craving
    for violence.

3 He who guards his lips guards his life,
  but he who speaks rashly will come
    to ruin.

4 The sluggard craves and gets nothing,
  but the desires of the diligent are
    fully satisfied.

5 The righteous hate what is false,
  but the wicked bring shame and
    disgrace.

6 Righteousness guards the man of
    integrity,
  but wickedness overthrows the
    sinner.

7 One man pretends to be rich, yet has
    nothing;
  another pretends to be poor, yet has
    great wealth.

8 A man's riches may ransom his life,
  but a poor man hears no threat.

9 The light of the righteous shines
    brightly,
  but the lamp of the wicked is
    snuffed out.

10 Pride only breeds quarrels,
  but wisdom is found in those who
    take advice.

11 Dishonest money dwindles away,
  but he who gathers money little by
    little makes it grow.

12 Hope deferred makes the heart sick,
  but a longing fulfilled is a tree of
    life.

13 He who scorns instruction will pay for
    it,
  but he who respects a command is
    rewarded.

14 The teaching of the wise is a fountain
    of life,
  turning a man from the snares of
    death.

15 Good understanding wins favor,
  but the way of the unfaithful is
    hard.[c]

16 Every prudent man acts out of
    knowledge,
  but a fool exposes his folly.

17 A wicked messenger falls into
    trouble,
  but a trustworthy envoy brings
    healing.

18 He who ignores discipline comes to
    poverty and shame,
  but whoever heeds correction is
    honored.

19 A longing fulfilled is sweet to the
    soul,
  but fools detest turning from evil.

20 He who walks with the wise grows
    wise,
  but a companion of fools suffers
    harm.

21 Misfortune pursues the sinner,
  but prosperity is the reward of the
    righteous.

22 A good man leaves an inheritance for
    his children's children,
  but a sinner's wealth is stored up
    for the righteous.

23 A poor man's field may produce
    abundant food,
  but injustice sweeps it away.

24 He who spares the rod hates his son,
  but he who loves him is careful to
    discipline him.

---

[a]26 Or *man is a guide to his neighbor* [b]27 The
meaning of the Hebrew for this word is uncertain.
[c]15 Or *unfaithful does not endure*

²⁵The righteous eat to their hearts'
content,
but the stomach of the wicked goes
hungry.

14 The wise woman builds her
house,
but with her own hands the foolish
one tears hers down.

²He whose walk is upright fears the
LORD,
but he whose ways are devious
despises him.

³A fool's talk brings a rod to his back,
but the lips of the wise protect
them.

⁴Where there are no oxen, the manger
is empty,
but from the strength of an ox
comes an abundant harvest.

⁵A truthful witness does not deceive,
but a false witness pours out lies.

⁶The mocker seeks wisdom and finds
none,
but knowledge comes easily to the
discerning.

⁷Stay away from a foolish man,
for you will not find knowledge on
his lips.

⁸The wisdom of the prudent is to give
thought to their ways,
but the folly of fools is deception.

⁹Fools mock at making amends for sin,
but goodwill is found among the
upright.

¹⁰Each heart knows its own bitterness,
and no one else can share its joy.

¹¹The house of the wicked will be
destroyed,
but the tent of the upright will
flourish.

¹²There is a way that seems right to a
man,
but in the end it leads to death.

¹³Even in laughter the heart may ache,
and joy may end in grief.

¹⁴The faithless will be fully repaid for
their ways,
and the good man rewarded for his.

¹⁵A simple man believes anything,
but a prudent man gives thought to
his steps.

¹⁶A wise man fears the LORD and shuns
evil,
but a fool is hotheaded and reckless.

¹⁷A quick-tempered man does foolish
things,
and a crafty man is hated.

¹⁸The simple inherit folly,
but the prudent are crowned with
knowledge.

¹⁹Evil men will bow down in the
presence of the good,
and the wicked at the gates of the
righteous.

²⁰The poor are shunned even by their
neighbors,
but the rich have many friends.

²¹He who despises his neighbor sins,
but blessed is he who is kind to the
needy.

²²Do not those who plot evil go astray?
But those who plan what is good
find[a] love and faithfulness.

²³All hard work brings a profit,
but mere talk leads only to poverty.

²⁴The wealth of the wise is their crown,
but the folly of fools yields folly.

²⁵A truthful witness saves lives,
but a false witness is deceitful.

²⁶He who fears the LORD has a secure
fortress,
and for his children it will be a
refuge.

²⁷The fear of the LORD is a fountain of
life,
turning a man from the snares of
death.

²⁸A large population is a king's glory,
but without subjects a prince is
ruined.

²⁹A patient man has great
understanding,
but a quick-tempered man displays
folly.

[a]22 Or *show*

³⁰ A heart at peace gives life to the body,
     but envy rots the bones.

³¹ He who oppresses the poor shows
       contempt for their Maker,
     but whoever is kind to the needy
       honors God.

³² When calamity comes, the wicked are
       brought down,
     but even in death the righteous
       have a refuge.

³³ Wisdom reposes in the heart of the
       discerning

and even among fools she lets
       herself be known.ᵃ

³⁴ Righteousness exalts a nation,
     but sin is a disgrace to any people.

³⁵ A king delights in a wise servant,
     but a shameful servant incurs his
       wrath.

15 A gentle answer turns away
       wrath,
     but a harsh word stirs up anger.

*ᵃ33 Hebrew; Septuagint and Syriac / but in the heart
of fools she is not known*

Week end.

Reaching Out

Read Luke 15:1–7 (page 1246)

Last Monday Megan admitted to hurting another girl by gossiping about her. It's cool that Megan was sensitive to what she had done and has changed her attitude. The truth is, we all need an attitude adjustment now and then when it comes to how we talk about other people.

One of the greatest personal criticisms ever made about Jesus was that he was a friend of tax collectors and sinners. Tax collecting was the lowest job a Jewish man could do, because he took money from his own Jewish people and turned it over to the Romans. The worst thing a woman could be was a "sinner," a polite way of saying "prostitute." So when people accused Jesus of being friends with tax collectors and sinners, they associated him with the rejects, the lowest of the low. And Jesus didn't mind! That's who he came to identify with. That's who he came to save!

As we read the Gospels, we find 3 stories of tax collectors and 3 stories of prostitutes. In each story these people are shown grace and mercy. But it is the rich, the popular and the successful who want nothing to do with Jesus.

If Jesus built his kingdom around the "lowlifes," why do we try to build our groups around the superstars? We need to try to reach everyone, but we must also remember that the "tax collectors and sinners"—those people society considers losers—often understand best their need for forgiveness. They usually respond most positively to our message about Jesus.

❶ Who in your school or neighborhood would most likely fit in with the kind of people Jesus hung out with?

❷ Next time you go to youth group, talk about what you all could do to reach out to a few of these people who need to know about Jesus.

❸ Ask God to give you creative ways to expand your social group so it includes even those nobody loves.

Turn to page 750 for your next devotion.

²The tongue of the wise commends
knowledge,
but the mouth of the fool gushes
folly.

³The eyes of the LORD are everywhere,
keeping watch on the wicked and
the good.

⁴The tongue that brings healing is a
tree of life,
but a deceitful tongue crushes the
spirit.

⁵A fool spurns his father's discipline,
but whoever heeds correction shows
prudence.

⁶The house of the righteous contains
great treasure,
but the income of the wicked brings
them trouble.

⁷The lips of the wise spread knowledge;
not so the hearts of fools.

⁸The LORD detests the sacrifice of the
wicked,
but the prayer of the upright pleases
him.

⁹The LORD detests the way of the
wicked
but he loves those who pursue
righteousness.

¹⁰Stern discipline awaits him who
leaves the path;
he who hates correction will die.

¹¹Death and Destruction^a lie open before
the LORD—
how much more the hearts of men!

¹²A mocker resents correction;
he will not consult the wise.

¹³A happy heart makes the face
cheerful,
but heartache crushes the spirit.

¹⁴The discerning heart seeks knowledge,
but the mouth of a fool feeds on
folly.

¹⁵All the days of the oppressed are
wretched,
but the cheerful heart has a
continual feast.

¹⁶Better a little with the fear of the LORD
than great wealth with turmoil.

¹⁷Better a meal of vegetables where
there is love
than a fattened calf with hatred.

¹⁸A hot-tempered man stirs up
dissension,
but a patient man calms a
quarrel.

¹⁹The way of the sluggard is blocked
with thorns,
but the path of the upright is a
highway.

²⁰A wise son brings joy to his father,
but a foolish man despises his
mother.

²¹Folly delights a man who lacks
judgment,
but a man of understanding keeps a
straight course.

²²Plans fail for lack of counsel,
but with many advisers they
succeed.

²³A man finds joy in giving an apt
reply—
and how good is a timely word!

²⁴The path of life leads upward for the
wise
to keep him from going down to the
grave.^b

²⁵The LORD tears down the proud man's
house
but he keeps the widow's
boundaries intact.

²⁶The LORD detests the thoughts of the
wicked,
but those of the pure are pleasing to
him.

²⁷A greedy man brings trouble to his
family,
but he who hates bribes will live.

²⁸The heart of the righteous weighs its
answers,
but the mouth of the wicked gushes
evil.

²⁹The LORD is far from the wicked
but he hears the prayer of the
righteous.

³⁰ A cheerful look brings joy to the
      heart,
   and good news gives health to the
      bones.
³¹ He who listens to a life-giving rebuke
   will be at home among the wise.
³² He who ignores discipline despises
      himself,
   but whoever heeds correction gains
      understanding.
³³ The fear of the LORD teaches a man
      wisdom,^a
   and humility comes before honor.

16 To man belong the plans of the
      heart,
   but from the LORD comes the reply
      of the tongue.
² All a man's ways seem innocent to
      him,

but motives are weighed by the
      LORD.
³ Commit to the LORD whatever
      you do,
   and your plans will succeed.
⁴ The LORD works out everything for his
      own ends—
   even the wicked for a day of
      disaster.
⁵ The LORD detests all the proud of
      heart.
   Be sure of this: They will not go
      unpunished.
⁶ Through love and faithfulness sin is
      atoned for;
   through the fear of the LORD a man
      avoids evil.

^a33 Or Wisdom teaches the fear of the LORD

Monday

Channel Surfing   **Read Proverbs 16:2**

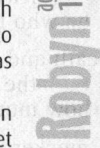

A lot of things that seem harmless to me might not be so harmless in God's
eyes. Take TV, for example. I usually don't think much about what I watch.
Of course, I know there's some bad stuff out there, and I should be more
careful. It's just so easy to watch whatever I want.

   Today's verse makes sense to me. When I turn on the TV, I *can* watch
anything and feel OK, as long as I don't think about it too much or check to
see what God says in the Bible. In other words, I can pretend I'm innocent as
long as I don't pay too much attention to what I'm doing.

   That's the wrong attitude. When I do that, I'm not looking at television
with the best motives. I'm just being lazy and watching whatever I can get
away with. And that's definitely not what God wants for me. He wants me to
do things that honor him and help me to grow as a Christian—not settle for
what seems "harmless."

❶ Think of a time you watched, read or did something that wasn't
exactly bad for you, but wasn't good either. How can this verse help
you make better choices so that won't happen again?

❷ Turn off the TV for 3 days. At the end of that time, ask yourself: *What
did I miss about TV? What did I learn about myself? About God?* Use what
you learn to help you decide what to watch in the future.

❸ Ask the Holy Spirit to help you make wise choices.

Turn to page 755 for your next devotion.

⁷When a man's ways are pleasing to
    the LORD,
  he makes even his enemies live at
    peace with him.

⁸Better a little with righteousness
  than much gain with injustice.

⁹In his heart a man plans his course,
  but the LORD determines his steps.

¹⁰The lips of a king speak as an oracle,
  and his mouth should not betray
    justice.

¹¹Honest scales and balances are from
    the LORD;
  all the weights in the bag are of his
    making.

¹²Kings detest wrongdoing,
  for a throne is established through
    righteousness.

¹³Kings take pleasure in honest lips;
  they value a man who speaks the
    truth.

¹⁴A king's wrath is a messenger of death,
  but a wise man will appease it.

¹⁵When a king's face brightens, it
    means life;
  his favor is like a rain cloud in
    spring.

¹⁶How much better to get wisdom than
    gold,
  to choose understanding rather than
    silver!

¹⁷The highway of the upright avoids
    evil;
  he who guards his way guards his
    life.

¹⁸Pride goes before destruction,
  a haughty spirit before a fall.

¹⁹Better to be lowly in spirit and among
    the oppressed
  than to share plunder with the
    proud.

²⁰Whoever gives heed to instruction
    prospers,
  and blessed is he who trusts in the
    LORD.

²¹The wise in heart are called discerning,
  and pleasant words promote
    instruction.ᵃ

²²Understanding is a fountain of life to
    those who have it,
  but folly brings punishment to fools.

²³A wise man's heart guides his mouth,
  and his lips promote instruction.ᵇ

²⁴Pleasant words are a honeycomb,
  sweet to the soul and healing to the
    bones.

²⁵There is a way that seems right to a
    man,
  but in the end it leads to death.

²⁶The laborer's appetite works for him;
  his hunger drives him on.

²⁷A scoundrel plots evil,
  and his speech is like a scorching
    fire.

²⁸A perverse man stirs up dissension,
  and a gossip separates close friends.

²⁹A violent man entices his neighbor
  and leads him down a path that is
    not good.

³⁰He who winks with his eye is plotting
    perversity;
  he who purses his lips is bent on
    evil.

³¹Gray hair is a crown of splendor;
  it is attained by a righteous life.

³²Better a patient man than a warrior,
  a man who controls his temper than
    one who takes a city.

Of Wimps and Warriors

Proverbs 16:32

We live in a world where power rules. If
you're big, mean and nasty enough you can
run the whole neighborhood. But warrior
violence can only make problems worse; it
can never solve them. Why do you think we
have more drugs, more gangs and more
senseless deaths every year? Patience and
self-control may look wimpy, but they're
far stronger.

ᵃ21 Or *words make a man persuasive*   ᵇ23 Or *mouth
/ and makes his lips persuasive*

³³The lot is cast into the lap,
  but its every decision is from the
    LORD.

17 Better a dry crust with peace and
  quiet
    than a house full of feasting,ᵃ with
      strife.

²A wise servant will rule over a
  disgraceful son,
    and will share the inheritance as
      one of the brothers.

³The crucible for silver and the furnace
  for gold,
    but the LORD tests the heart.

Refiner's Fire

Huh?

Proverbs 17:3
Just as fire purifies metal, trials purify people. That's the point of this proverb. God
allows pains and problems in our lives for
2 reasons. First, to bring our sins and
impurities to the surface, so they can be
skimmed away. Second, to refine our true
character, so we can become more like God.
Too bad growing has to hurt, but at least
our pain has a purpose.

⁴A wicked man listens to evil lips;
  a liar pays attention to a malicious
    tongue.

⁵He who mocks the poor shows
  contempt for their Maker;
    whoever gloats over disaster will
      not go unpunished.

⁶Children's children are a crown to the
  aged,
    and parents are the pride of their
      children.

⁷Arrogantᵇ lips are unsuited to a fool—
  how much worse lying lips to a ruler!

⁸A bribe is a charm to the one who
  gives it;
    wherever he turns, he succeeds.

⁹He who covers over an offense
  promotes love,

but whoever repeats the matter
  separates close friends.

¹⁰A rebuke impresses a man of
  discernment
    more than a hundred lashes a fool.

¹¹An evil man is bent only on rebellion;
  a merciless official will be sent
    against him.

¹²Better to meet a bear robbed of her
  cubs
    than a fool in his folly.

¹³If a man pays back evil for good,
  evil will never leave his house.

¹⁴Starting a quarrel is like breaching a
  dam;
    so drop the matter before a dispute
      breaks out.

¹⁵Acquitting the guilty and condemning
  the innocent—
    the LORD detests them both.

¹⁶Of what use is money in the hand of a
  fool,
    since he has no desire to get
      wisdom?

¹⁷A friend loves at all times,
  and a brother is born for adversity.

¹⁸A man lacking in judgment strikes
  hands in pledge
    and puts up security for his
      neighbor.

¹⁹He who loves a quarrel loves sin;
  he who builds a high gate invites
    destruction.

²⁰A man of perverse heart does not
  prosper;
    he whose tongue is deceitful falls
      into trouble.

²¹To have a fool for a son brings grief;
  there is no joy for the father of a
    fool.

²²A cheerful heart is good medicine,
  but a crushed spirit dries up the
    bones.

²³A wicked man accepts a bribe in
  secret
    to pervert the course of justice.

ᵃ1 Hebrew *sacrifices*   ᵇ7 Or *Eloquent*

24 A discerning man keeps wisdom in
        view,
    but a fool's eyes wander to the ends
        of the earth.

25 A foolish son brings grief to his father
    and bitterness to the one who bore
        him.

26 It is not good to punish an innocent
        man,
    or to flog officials for their
        integrity.

27 A man of knowledge uses words with
        restraint,
    and a man of understanding is
        even-tempered.

28 Even a fool is thought wise if he keeps
        silent,
    and discerning if he holds his
        tongue.

18 An unfriendly man pursues
        selfish ends;
    he defies all sound judgment.

2 A fool finds no pleasure in
        understanding
    but delights in airing his own
        opinions.

3 When wickedness comes, so does
        contempt,
    and with shame comes disgrace.

4 The words of a man's mouth are deep
        waters,
    but the fountain of wisdom is a
        bubbling brook.

5 It is not good to be partial to the wicked
    or to deprive the innocent of justice.

6 A fool's lips bring him strife,
    and his mouth invites a beating.

7 A fool's mouth is his undoing,
    and his lips are a snare to his soul.

8 The words of a gossip are like choice
        morsels;
    they go down to a man's inmost
        parts.

9 One who is slack in his work
    is brother to one who destroys.

10 The name of the LORD is a strong
        tower;
    the righteous run to it and are safe.

11 The wealth of the rich is their fortified
        city;
    they imagine it an unscalable wall.

12 Before his downfall a man's heart is
        proud,
    but humility comes before honor.

13 He who answers before listening—
    that is his folly and his shame.

14 A man's spirit sustains him in
        sickness,
    but a crushed spirit who can bear?

15 The heart of the discerning acquires
        knowledge;
    the ears of the wise seek it out.

16 A gift opens the way for the giver
    and ushers him into the presence of
        the great.

17 The first to present his case seems
        right,
    till another comes forward and
        questions him.

18 Casting the lot settles disputes
    and keeps strong opponents apart.

19 An offended brother is more
        unyielding than a fortified city,
    and disputes are like the barred
        gates of a citadel.

20 From the fruit of his mouth a man's
        stomach is filled;
    with the harvest from his lips he is
        satisfied.

21 The tongue has the power of life and
        death,
    and those who love it will eat its
        fruit.

22 He who finds a wife finds what is
        good
    and receives favor from the LORD.

23 A poor man pleads for mercy,
    but a rich man answers harshly.

24 A man of many companions may
        come to ruin,
    but there is a friend who sticks
        closer than a brother.

19 Better a poor man whose walk is
        blameless
    than a fool whose lips are
        perverse.

[2] It is not good to have zeal without
      knowledge,
    nor to be hasty and miss the way.

[3] A man's own folly ruins his life,
    yet his heart rages against the LORD.

[4] Wealth brings many friends,
    but a poor man's friend deserts him.

[5] A false witness will not go
      unpunished,
    and he who pours out lies will not
      go free.

[6] Many curry favor with a ruler,
    and everyone is the friend of a man
      who gives gifts.

[7] A poor man is shunned by all his
      relatives—
    how much more do his friends
      avoid him!
  Though he pursues them with pleading,
    they are nowhere to be found.[a]

[8] He who gets wisdom loves his own
      soul;
    he who cherishes understanding
      prospers.

[9] A false witness will not go
      unpunished,
    and he who pours out lies will
      perish.

[10] It is not fitting for a fool to live in
      luxury—
    how much worse for a slave to rule
      over princes!

[11] A man's wisdom gives him patience;
    it is to his glory to overlook an
      offense.

[12] A king's rage is like the roar of a lion,
    but his favor is like dew on the
      grass.

[13] A foolish son is his father's ruin,
    and a quarrelsome wife is like a
      constant dripping.

[14] Houses and wealth are inherited from
      parents,
    but a prudent wife is from the LORD.

[15] Laziness brings on deep sleep,
    and the shiftless man goes hungry.

[16] He who obeys instructions guards his
      life,

    but he who is contemptuous of his
      ways will die.

[17] He who is kind to the poor lends to
      the LORD,
    and he will reward him for what he
      has done.

[18] Discipline your son, for in that there
      is hope;
    do not be a willing party to his
      death.

[19] A hot-tempered man must pay the
      penalty;
    if you rescue him, you will have to
      do it again.

[20] Listen to advice and accept
      instruction,
    and in the end you will be wise.

[21] Many are the plans in a man's heart,
    but it is the LORD's purpose that
      prevails.

[22] What a man desires is unfailing love[b];
    better to be poor than a liar.

[23] The fear of the LORD leads to life:
    Then one rests content, untouched
      by trouble.

[24] The sluggard buries his hand in the
      dish;
    he will not even bring it back to his
      mouth!

[25] Flog a mocker, and the simple will
      learn prudence;
    rebuke a discerning man, and he
      will gain knowledge.

[26] He who robs his father and drives out
      his mother
    is a son who brings shame and
      disgrace.

[27] Stop listening to instruction, my son,
    and you will stray from the words
      of knowledge.

[28] A corrupt witness mocks at justice,
    and the mouth of the wicked gulps
      down evil.

[29] Penalties are prepared for mockers,
    and beatings for the backs of fools.

---

[a]7 The meaning of the Hebrew for this sentence is
uncertain.   [b]22 Or *A man's greed is his shame*

20 Wine is a mocker and beer a
       brawler;
  whoever is led astray by them is not
       wise.

² A king's wrath is like the roar of a
       lion;
  he who angers him forfeits his life.

³ It is to a man's honor to avoid strife,
  but every fool is quick to quarrel.

⁴ A sluggard does not plow in season;
  so at harvest time he looks but finds
       nothing.

⁵ The purposes of a man's heart are
       deep waters,
  but a man of understanding draws
       them out.

⁶ Many a man claims to have unfailing
       love,
  but a faithful man who can find?

⁷ The righteous man leads a blameless
       life;
  blessed are his children after him.

⁸ When a king sits on his throne to
       judge,
  he winnows out all evil with his eyes.

⁹ Who can say, "I have kept my heart
       pure;
  I am clean and without sin"?

¹⁰ Differing weights and differing
       measures—
  the LORD detests them both.

¹¹ Even a child is known by his actions,
  by whether his conduct is pure and
       right.

¹² Ears that hear and eyes that see—
  the LORD has made them both.

¹³ Do not love sleep or you will grow
       poor;
  stay awake and you will have food
       to spare.

¹⁴ "It's no good, it's no good!" says the
       buyer;
  then off he goes and boasts about
       his purchase.

Tuesday

Alcohol Abusers   **Read Proverbs 20:1**

My dad's best friend killed himself, and it had to do with drinking. So when
I hear people talking about how bad it is to drink too much beer and wine,
I know they're serious. This guy had started drinking a lot because he didn't
know how to handle his problems, but then he realized that his drinking
was the biggest problem of all. Now he's gone, and his family is stuck with
the problems.

   Drinking is a terrible thing to get started on because it can ruin your life.
Once you're into it, it's really hard to get out. God can help you stop drinking,
if you ask him, but some major damage might already be done. So don't
drink—it's not worth it!

Michael age 13

❶ Why do you think drinking is such a big temptation for so many
people?

❷ Have a serious talk with your parents about drinking. Find out what
they think about alcohol and why. If you want to, you can all write
and sign a "contract" where you promise to follow your parents' rules
about drinking.

❸ Ask God to help you and your friends resist the temptation of alcohol.

Turn to page 757 for your next devotion.

15 Gold there is, and rubies in
    abundance,
  but lips that speak knowledge are a
    rare jewel.

16 Take the garment of one who puts up
    security for a stranger;
  hold it in pledge if he does it for a
    wayward woman.

17 Food gained by fraud tastes sweet to a
    man,
  but he ends up with a mouth full of
    gravel.

18 Make plans by seeking advice;
  if you wage war, obtain guidance.

19 A gossip betrays a confidence;
  so avoid a man who talks too much.

20 If a man curses his father or mother,
  his lamp will be snuffed out in pitch
    darkness.

Rebels Beware!

Huh?

Proverbs 20:20
In a time when kids are suing, abusing and
even killing their parents, we need to hear
this verse. Cursing your parents means
"lights out" for you. And we're not talking
about going to bed with no dessert. We're
talking about having your spiritual life
extinguished. Poof. Hello hell. Listen closely
to the Fifth Commandment: Honor your
parents so things will go well with you.

21 An inheritance quickly gained at the
    beginning
  will not be blessed at the end.

22 Do not say, "I'll pay you back for this
    wrong!"
  Wait for the LORD, and he will
    deliver you.

23 The LORD detests differing weights,
  and dishonest scales do not please
    him.

24 A man's steps are directed by the LORD.
  How then can anyone understand
    his own way?

25 It is a trap for a man to dedicate
    something rashly
  and only later to consider his vows.

26 A wise king winnows out the wicked;
  he drives the threshing wheel over
    them.

27 The lamp of the LORD searches the
    spirit of a man[a];
  it searches out his inmost being.

28 Love and faithfulness keep a king
    safe;
  through love his throne is made
    secure.

29 The glory of young men is their
    strength,
  gray hair the splendor of the old.

30 Blows and wounds cleanse away evil,
  and beatings purge the inmost
    being.

21 The king's heart is in the hand of
    the LORD;
  he directs it like a watercourse
    wherever he pleases.

2 All a man's ways seem right to him,
  but the LORD weighs the heart.

3 To do what is right and just
  is more acceptable to the LORD than
    sacrifice.

4 Haughty eyes and a proud heart,
  the lamp of the wicked, are sin!

5 The plans of the diligent lead to profit
  as surely as haste leads to poverty.

6 A fortune made by a lying tongue
  is a fleeting vapor and a deadly
    snare.[b]

7 The violence of the wicked will drag
    them away,
  for they refuse to do what is right.

8 The way of the guilty is devious,
  but the conduct of the innocent is
    upright.

9 Better to live on a corner of the roof
  than share a house with a
    quarrelsome wife.

---

[a]27 Or *The spirit of man is the LORD's lamp*
[b]6 Some Hebrew manuscripts, Septuagint and
Vulgate; most Hebrew manuscripts *vapor for those
who seek death*

Doubts

We've all experienced doubts about God. We may wonder, *Is God real? Is he fair? Does he care? Is my life worth living? Will I ever be happy again?*

Having a case of the doubts doesn't mean you're a bad person. It just means you need something to boost your belief system. After all, being a Christian is all about believing what others don't. The Bible calls doubters "double-minded" (Psalm 119:113, page 712; James 1:8, page 1505). It's as if they have 2 minds, 2 heads. One head believes one thing, the other the opposite. One believes God is love; the other believes God is mean. One believes God can work a miracle; the other believes he'll never do it. That's being double-minded.

Most of the great "giants" of the faith were double-minded at least some of the time. Job was the greatest man of his day (Job 1:3, page 582), yet he doubted God's fairness. John the Baptist was the greatest of the prophets (Matthew 11:11, page 1155), yet he doubted that Jesus was the Messiah (Matthew 11:2). David was a man after God's own heart (1 Samuel 13:14, page 324), yet he expressed strong doubts about God's presence in many of his psalms (see Psalm 13, for example, page 628).

When you doubt, take heart. You're in good company. When Thomas doubted the resurrection, Jesus gave him proof (John 20:27, page 1301). When a doubting man asked for a miracle, Jesus helped him (Mark 9:17–27, page 1201). In fact, the Bible commands us to be merciful to those who doubt (Jude 22, page 1547).

So if you get the doubts, know that healing is available. Identify which strain of the doubting disease you have, then take the appropriate medicine. Here are three common symptoms:

1. "God's not fair!" Sometimes terrible tragedies cause us to doubt God's goodness or fairness. And, like Job, we complain about it. Loudly.

That's good; God can handle that. In fact, he would rather we express our doubts than ignore them. The best medicine in this case is prayer and patience. Just tell God how you feel and wait for him to remind you of his kindness and love.

"It's not true!" Do you ever wonder, *Is God real? Is the Bible true? Is Jesus the only way?* These doubts deal with factual matters, and even people like John the Baptist faced them. In Matthew 11 he doubted whether Jesus was really the Messiah, so Jesus gave him a dose of proof positive. He told John's friends to "Go back and report to John what you hear and see: The blind receive sight, the lame walk, those who have leprosy are cured, the deaf hear, the dead are raised, and the good news is preached to the poor." That's what we need sometimes too. If you doubt the basic truth of God or his Word, talk to your pastor or your parents. There are very good reasons why we believe.

"I'm not sure!" Sometimes we doubt our own faith. We wonder if we really belong to God or if we're really going to heaven. In this case, pop some promise pills. John 6:37 says Jesus will never drive away those who come to him. John 10:28 says no one can snatch God's people from his hand. Romans 8:38–39 says nothing can separate us from God's love. Thankfully, your salvation does not rest on the strength of your faith but on the power of God's promises. Take that medicine, and you'll start feeling much better!

eXtreme FAITH

Yes it's OK. In fact, as I write these words, I'm pretty angry with God myself. Recently I sat with one of my best friends as he heard the words, "We can't operate on your cancer. You need to prepare yourself for an early death." After trying to be strong for my friend and his family, I went outside and had a talk with God. I begged him to heal my friend. And I told him I had a lot of questions as to why my friend, who is such a wonderful person, has to die. I was angry.

That same evening in his hospital room, my friend asked me, "Do you ever doubt God?"

I told him, "Yes I do. And I have to doubt my doubts." "What do you mean?" he asked.

"To doubt doesn't mean you don't believe," I said. "It means there are times you just can't completely understand all there is to know about God."

I'm reminded of the Bible story where a man tells Jesus about his son's illness. The man says, "If you can do anything, take pity on us and help us." Jesus replies, "'If you can'? Everything is possible for him who believes." Then the man says, "I do believe; help me overcome my unbelief!" (Read the whole story in Mark 9:17–27, page 1201.)

My suggestion to you is to accept doubt and even anger as a part of your relationship with God. Because that's what the Christian faith really is: a relationship. You've probably already learned that the closer your relationship with someone is, the worse you feel when things aren't going the way you'd like.

A fight with your best friend is always tougher than a tiff with someone you hardly know. While doubt might make you feel like you're far away from God, it does not mean your relationship with God is over. Just look at "Doubting Thomas." Even though he was one of Jesus' disciples—one of Jesus' closest friends!—he still struggled with doubt. After Jesus rose from the dead, the other disciples told Thomas they had seen the Lord. Thomas said, "Unless I see the nail marks in his hands and put my finger where the nails were, and put my hand into his side, I will not believe it" (John 20:25).

A week later, all the disciples were together when Jesus showed up. He looked straight at Thomas and said, "Put your finger here; see my hands. Reach out your hand and put it into my side. Stop doubting and believe." I love Thomas's response: "My Lord and my God!" (see John 20:24–28, page 1301). So, even though we might have our doubts, we will eventually get to the point where we, too, can exclaim, "My Lord and my God!" It's normal for us, like Thomas, to doubt God at times. We doubt his will. We doubt his timing and we doubt his plan. Sometimes we even doubt his existence. But as we build a relationship with God, we can also rely on the fact that his Word is true and his existence in our lives is real.

God is most concerned about our relationship with him, and he wants us to do what we can to strengthen that relationship. When you have doubts, deal with them, talk to God about them and move beyond them toward a closer walk with your Creator and Savior.

— *Jim Burns, president of the National Institute of Youth Ministries and the author of the "Let's Talk" column in* Campus Life *magazine.*

¹⁰The wicked man craves evil;
his neighbor gets no mercy from him.

¹¹When a mocker is punished, the
simple gain wisdom;
when a wise man is instructed, he
gets knowledge.

¹²The Righteous One*ᵃ* takes note of the
house of the wicked
and brings the wicked to ruin.

¹³If a man shuts his ears to the cry of
the poor,
he too will cry out and not be
answered.

¹⁴A gift given in secret soothes anger,
and a bribe concealed in the cloak
pacifies great wrath.

¹⁵When justice is done, it brings joy to
the righteous
but terror to evildoers.

¹⁶A man who strays from the path of
understanding

comes to rest in the company of the
dead.

¹⁷He who loves pleasure will become
poor;
whoever loves wine and oil will
never be rich.

¹⁸The wicked become a ransom for the
righteous,
and the unfaithful for the upright.

¹⁹Better to live in a desert
than with a quarrelsome and
ill-tempered wife.

²⁰In the house of the wise are stores of
choice food and oil,
but a foolish man devours all he
has.

²¹He who pursues righteousness and
love
finds life, prosperity*ᵇ* and honor.

ᵃ12 Or The righteous man   *ᵇ21 Or righteousness*

Wednesday

Smelly Clothes

Read Proverbs 21:13

My youth group did a missions project in the inner city. I was excited about it at first, but when we actually got to the place we'd be working, I saw all these people with old, dirty clothes, smelling like they hadn't taken a shower in weeks. I couldn't help but be kind of grossed out.

But I knew it would be wrong to turn away and reject them because of their smelly clothes. So I forced myself to talk with some people. It didn't take long for me to realize they were real people who needed love. And when I showed them love, I found myself receiving love in return.

I went on the missions trip thinking I could make a difference in people's lives. And I believe I did make a difference. But the people I met made a difference in my life too. They taught me that God wants me to show love to other people, no matter who they are. He wants me to be thankful for what I have and use it to help people who don't have much. He wants me to reach out to all of his people, not just the ones with nice houses and clean clothes.

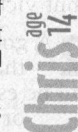
Chris, age 14

What about You?

❶ Why do we tend to resist helping poor people?

❷ List 5 ways you can help someone less fortunate than you. Choose one to do in the next 2 days.

❸ Ask God to help you reach out to the needy.

Turn to page 761 for your next devotion.

²²A wise man attacks the city of the
    mighty
  and pulls down the stronghold in
    which they trust.

²³He who guards his mouth and his
    tongue
  keeps himself from calamity.

²⁴The proud and arrogant man—
    "Mocker" is his name;
  he behaves with overweening pride.

²⁵The sluggard's craving will be the
    death of him,
  because his hands refuse to work.
²⁶All day long he craves for more,
  but the righteous give without
    sparing.

²⁷The sacrifice of the wicked is
    detestable—
  how much more so when brought
    with evil intent!

²⁸A false witness will perish,
  and whoever listens to him will be
    destroyed forever.ᵃ

²⁹A wicked man puts up a bold front,
  but an upright man gives thought to
    his ways.

³⁰There is no wisdom, no insight, no
    plan
  that can succeed against the LORD.

³¹The horse is made ready for the day of
    battle,
  but victory rests with the LORD.

22 A good name is more desirable
    than great riches;
  to be esteemed is better than silver
    or gold.

²Rich and poor have this in common:
  The LORD is the Maker of them all.

³A prudent man sees danger and takes
    refuge,
  but the simple keep going and
    suffer for it.

⁴Humility and the fear of the LORD
  bring wealth and honor and life.

⁵In the paths of the wicked lie thorns
    and snares,
  but he who guards his soul stays far
    from them.

⁶Trainᵇ a child in the way he should
    go,
  and when he is old he will not turn
    from it.

⁷The rich rule over the poor,
  and the borrower is servant to the
    lender.

⁸He who sows wickedness reaps
    trouble,
  and the rod of his fury will be
    destroyed.

⁹A generous man will himself be
    blessed,
  for he shares his food with the poor.

¹⁰Drive out the mocker, and out goes
    strife;
  quarrels and insults are ended.

¹¹He who loves a pure heart and whose
    speech is gracious
  will have the king for his friend.

¹²The eyes of the LORD keep watch over
    knowledge,
  but he frustrates the words of the
    unfaithful.

¹³The sluggard says, "There is a lion
    outside!"
  or, "I will be murdered in the
    streets!"

¹⁴The mouth of an adulteress is a deep
    pit;
  he who is under the LORD's wrath
    will fall into it.

¹⁵Folly is bound up in the heart of a
    child,
  but the rod of discipline will drive it
    far from him.

¹⁶He who oppresses the poor to increase
    his wealth
  and he who gives gifts to the rich—
    both come to poverty.

Sayings of the Wise

¹⁷Pay attention and listen to the sayings
    of the wise;
  apply your heart to what I teach,
¹⁸for it is pleasing when you keep them
    in your heart

ᵃ28 Or / but the words of an obedient man will
live on ᵇ6 Or Start

and have all of them ready on your
lips.

¹⁹ So that your trust may be in the LORD,
I teach you today, even you.

²⁰ Have I not written thirty*a* sayings for
you,
sayings of counsel and knowledge,

²¹ teaching you true and reliable words,
so that you can give sound answers
to him who sent you?

²² Do not exploit the poor because they
are poor
and do not crush the needy in
court,

²³ for the LORD will take up their case
and will plunder those who plunder
them.

²⁴ Do not make friends with a
hot-tempered man,
do not associate with one easily
angered,

²⁵ or you may learn his ways
and get yourself ensnared.

²⁶ Do not be a man who strikes hands in
pledge
or puts up security for debts;

²⁷ if you lack the means to pay,
your very bed will be snatched from
under you.

²⁸ Do not move an ancient boundary
stone
set up by your forefathers.

²⁹ Do you see a man skilled in his work?
He will serve before kings;
he will not serve before obscure
men.

23 When you sit to dine with a
ruler,
note well what*b* is before you,

² and put a knife to your throat
if you are given to gluttony.

³ Do not crave his delicacies,
for that food is deceptive.

⁴ Do not wear yourself out to get rich;
have the wisdom to show restraint.

⁵ Cast but a glance at riches, and they
are gone,
for they will surely sprout wings
and fly off to the sky like an eagle.

⁶ Do not eat the food of a stingy man,
do not crave his delicacies;

⁷ for he is the kind of man
who is always thinking about the
cost.*c*
"Eat and drink," he says to you,
but his heart is not with you.

⁸ You will vomit up the little you have
eaten
and will have wasted your
compliments.

⁹ Do not speak to a fool,
for he will scorn the wisdom of
your words.

¹⁰ Do not move an ancient boundary
stone
or encroach on the fields of the
fatherless,

¹¹ for their Defender is strong;
he will take up their case against
you.

¹² Apply your heart to instruction
and your ears to words of
knowledge.

¹³ Do not withhold discipline from a
child;
if you punish him with the rod, he
will not die.

¹⁴ Punish him with the rod
and save his soul from death.*d*

¹⁵ My son, if your heart is wise,
then my heart will be glad;

¹⁶ my inmost being will rejoice
when your lips speak what is right.

¹⁷ Do not let your heart envy sinners,
but always be zealous for the fear
of the LORD.

¹⁸ There is surely a future hope for you,
and your hope will not be cut off.

¹⁹ Listen, my son, and be wise,
and keep your heart on the right
path.

²⁰ Do not join those who drink too much
wine
or gorge themselves on meat,

²¹ for drunkards and gluttons become
poor,
and drowsiness clothes them in
rags.

---

a20 Or not formerly written; or not written excellent
b1 Or who   c7 Or for as he thinks within himself,
/ so he is; or for as he puts on a feast, / so he is
d14 Hebrew Sheol

²² Listen to your father, who gave you
 life,
 and do not despise your mother
 when she is old.
²³ Buy the truth and do not sell it;
 get wisdom, discipline and
 understanding.
²⁴ The father of a righteous man has
 great joy;
 he who has a wise son delights in
 him.
²⁵ May your father and mother be glad;
 may she who gave you birth rejoice!

²⁶ My son, give me your heart
 and let your eyes keep to my ways,
²⁷ for a prostitute is a deep pit
 and a wayward wife is a narrow
 well.
²⁸ Like a bandit she lies in wait,
 and multiplies the unfaithful among
 men.

²⁹ Who has woe? Who has sorrow?
 Who has strife? Who has
 complaints?
 Who has needless bruises? Who has
 bloodshot eyes?
³⁰ Those who linger over wine,
 who go to sample bowls of mixed
 wine.
³¹ Do not gaze at wine when it is red,
 when it sparkles in the cup,
 when it goes down smoothly!
³² In the end it bites like a snake
 and poisons like a viper.
³³ Your eyes will see strange sights
 and your mind imagine confusing
 things.
³⁴ You will be like one sleeping on the
 high seas,
 lying on top of the rigging.
³⁵ "They hit me," you will say, "but I'm
 not hurt!
 They beat me, but I don't feel it!
 When will I wake up
 so I can find another drink?"

24 Do not envy wicked men,
 do not desire their company;
² for their hearts plot violence,
 and their lips talk about making
 trouble.

³ By wisdom a house is built,
 and through understanding it is
 established;

⁴ through knowledge its rooms are filled
 with rare and beautiful treasures.

⁵ A wise man has great power,
 and a man of knowledge increases
 strength;
⁶ for waging war you need guidance,
 and for victory many advisers.

⁷ Wisdom is too high for a fool;
 in the assembly at the gate he has
 nothing to say.

⁸ He who plots evil
 will be known as a schemer.
⁹ The schemes of folly are sin,
 and men detest a mocker.

¹⁰ If you falter in times of trouble,
 how small is your strength!
¹¹ Rescue those being led away to death;
 hold back those staggering toward
 slaughter.
¹² If you say, "But we knew nothing
 about this,"
 does not he who weighs the heart
 perceive it?
 Does not he who guards your life
 know it?
 Will he not repay each person
 according to what he has done?

¹³ Eat honey, my son, for it is good;
 honey from the comb is sweet to
 your taste.
¹⁴ Know also that wisdom is sweet to
 your soul;
 if you find it, there is a future hope
 for you,
 and your hope will not be cut off.

¹⁵ Do not lie in wait like an outlaw
 against a righteous man's
 house,
 do not raid his dwelling place;
¹⁶ for though a righteous man falls seven
 times, he rises again,
 but the wicked are brought down by
 calamity.

¹⁷ Do not gloat when your enemy falls;
 when he stumbles, do not let your
 heart rejoice,
¹⁸ or the LORD will see and disapprove
 and turn his wrath away from him.

¹⁹ Do not fret because of evil men
 or be envious of the wicked,

²⁰ for the evil man has no future hope,
   and the lamp of the wicked will be
   snuffed out.

²¹ Fear the LORD and the king, my son,
   and do not join with the rebellious,
²² for those two will send sudden
   destruction upon them,
   and who knows what calamities
   they can bring?

Further Sayings of the Wise

²³ These also are sayings of the wise:

To show partiality in judging is not
   good:
²⁴ Whoever says to the guilty, "You are
   innocent"—
   peoples will curse him and nations
   denounce him.
²⁵ But it will go well with those who
   convict the guilty,
   and rich blessing will come upon
   them.

²⁶ An honest answer
   is like a kiss on the lips.

²⁷ Finish your outdoor work
   and get your fields ready;
   after that, build your house.

²⁸ Do not testify against your neighbor
   without cause,
   or use your lips to deceive.
²⁹ Do not say, "I'll do to him as he has
   done to me;
   I'll pay that man back for what he
   did."

³⁰ I went past the field of the sluggard,
   past the vineyard of the man who
   lacks judgment;
³¹ thorns had come up everywhere,
   the ground was covered with weeds,
   and the stone wall was in ruins.
³² I applied my heart to what I observed
   and learned a lesson from what I
   saw:
³³ A little sleep, a little slumber,

Thursday

Slippery Slope

Read Proverbs 24:30–34

Right now my grades are really bad. I knew they were going downhill, but I kept thinking, "They're not *that* bad." Well, now they are *that* bad and improving them is going to take a lot of work. It would have been easier if I'd put in a little extra effort when my grades first started slipping.

Grades aren't the only thing that can go downhill fast. When I push God aside or think other things are more important than praying or reading my Bible, it doesn't take long for my relationship with God to slip. I need to make God a priority in my life all the time.

These verses have a lot to say about keeping on top of the things that are important in my life. Leaving things for later—whether it's my homework or spending time with God—always leads to more work and trouble.

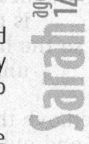
Sarah age 14

What about You?

❶ What are some things you avoid doing? What happens when you let those things slide?

❷ Make up a daily schedule and plan a time for the things you need to do every day, like quiet time, homework and chores. Stick with your schedule for the remainder of this week. How does it feel to stay on top of things?

❸ Make prayer part of your daily routine.

Turn to page 765 for your next devotion.

a little folding of the hands to rest—
³⁴ and poverty will come on you like a
     bandit
and scarcity like an armed man.^a

More Proverbs of Solomon

25 These are more proverbs of Solomon, copied by the men of Hezekiah king of Judah:

² It is the glory of God to conceal a
     matter;
     to search out a matter is the glory
       of kings.

God's Glory Versus Ours

Proverbs 25:2

There's a cool contrast in this verse. God's
greatness can be seen in all the mysteries
of the universe—even the ones we still
haven't figured out. A person's greatness
lies in the things he or she can discover.
Obviously God's glory is far greater. We
hardly know how the simplest atom works,
let alone how the universe was made or
what the spirit world is like—good reasons
to stay humble!

³ As the heavens are high and the earth
     is deep,
     so the hearts of kings are
       unsearchable.

⁴ Remove the dross from the silver,
     and out comes material for^b the
       silversmith;
⁵ remove the wicked from the king's
     presence,
     and his throne will be established
       through righteousness.

⁶ Do not exalt yourself in the king's
     presence,
     and do not claim a place among
       great men;
⁷ it is better for him to say to you,
     "Come up here,"
     than for him to humiliate you
       before a nobleman.

What you have seen with your eyes
⁸   do not bring^c hastily to court,
for what will you do in the end
     if your neighbor puts you to shame?

⁹ If you argue your case with a
     neighbor,
     do not betray another man's
       confidence,
¹⁰ or he who hears it may shame you
     and you will never lose your bad
       reputation.

¹¹ A word aptly spoken
     is like apples of gold in settings of
       silver.

¹² Like an earring of gold or an
     ornament of fine gold
     is a wise man's rebuke to a listening
       ear.

¹³ Like the coolness of snow at harvest
     time
     is a trustworthy messenger to those
       who send him;
     he refreshes the spirit of his
       masters.

¹⁴ Like clouds and wind without rain
     is a man who boasts of gifts he does
       not give.

¹⁵ Through patience a ruler can be
     persuaded,
     and a gentle tongue can break a
       bone.

¹⁶ If you find honey, eat just enough—
     too much of it, and you will vomit.
¹⁷ Seldom set foot in your neighbor's
     house—
     too much of you, and he will hate
       you.

¹⁸ Like a club or a sword or a sharp
     arrow
     is the man who gives false
       testimony against his neighbor.

¹⁹ Like a bad tooth or a lame foot
     is reliance on the unfaithful in
       times of trouble.

²⁰ Like one who takes away a garment
     on a cold day,

^a34 Or like a vagrant / and scarcity like a beggar
^b4 Or comes a vessel from   ^c7,8 Or nobleman / on
whom you had set your eyes. / ⁸Do not go

or like vinegar poured on soda,
is one who sings songs to a heavy
heart.

²¹ If your enemy is hungry, give him
food to eat;
if he is thirsty, give him water to
drink.
²² In doing this, you will heap burning
coals on his head,
and the LORD will reward you.

²³ As a north wind brings rain,
so a sly tongue brings angry looks.

²⁴ Better to live on a corner of the roof
than share a house with a
quarrelsome wife.

²⁵ Like cold water to a weary soul
is good news from a distant land.

²⁶ Like a muddied spring or a polluted
well
is a righteous man who gives way
to the wicked.

²⁷ It is not good to eat too much honey,
nor is it honorable to seek one's
own honor.

²⁸ Like a city whose walls are broken
down
is a man who lacks self-control.

26 Like snow in summer or rain in
harvest,
honor is not fitting for a fool.

² Like a fluttering sparrow or a darting
swallow,
an undeserved curse does not come
to rest.

³ A whip for the horse, a halter for the
donkey,
and a rod for the backs of fools!

⁴ Do not answer a fool according to his
folly,
or you will be like him yourself.

⁵ Answer a fool according to his folly,
or he will be wise in his own eyes.

⁶ Like cutting off one's feet or drinking
violence
is the sending of a message by the
hand of a fool.

⁷ Like a lame man's legs that hang limp
is a proverb in the mouth of a fool.

⁸ Like tying a stone in a sling
is the giving of honor to a fool.

⁹ Like a thornbush in a drunkard's hand
is a proverb in the mouth of a fool.

¹⁰ Like an archer who wounds at random
is he who hires a fool or any
passer-by.

¹¹ As a dog returns to its vomit,
so a fool repeats his folly.

¹² Do you see a man wise in his own
eyes?
There is more hope for a fool than
for him.

¹³ The sluggard says, "There is a lion in
the road,
a fierce lion roaming the streets!"

¹⁴ As a door turns on its hinges,
so a sluggard turns on his bed.

¹⁵ The sluggard buries his hand in the
dish;
he is too lazy to bring it back to his
mouth.

¹⁶ The sluggard is wiser in his own eyes
than seven men who answer
discreetly.

¹⁷ Like one who seizes a dog by the ears
is a passer-by who meddles in a
quarrel not his own.

¹⁸ Like a madman shooting
firebrands or deadly arrows
¹⁹ is a man who deceives his neighbor
and says, "I was only joking!"

²⁰ Without wood a fire goes out;
without gossip a quarrel dies down.

²¹ As charcoal to embers and as wood to
fire,
so is a quarrelsome man for
kindling strife.

²² The words of a gossip are like choice
morsels;
they go down to a man's inmost
parts.

²³ Like a coating of glaze*ᵃ* over
earthenware
are fervent lips with an evil heart.

ᵃ23 With a different word division of the Hebrew;
Masoretic Text *of silver dross*

²⁴A malicious man disguises himself
with his lips,
but in his heart he harbors deceit.
²⁵Though his speech is charming, do not
believe him,
for seven abominations fill his
heart.
²⁶His malice may be concealed by
deception,
but his wickedness will be exposed
in the assembly.

²⁷If a man digs a pit, he will fall into it;
if a man rolls a stone, it will roll
back on him.

²⁸A lying tongue hates those it hurts,
and a flattering mouth works ruin.

27

Do not boast about tomorrow,
for you do not know what a day
may bring forth.

²Let another praise you, and not your
own mouth;
someone else, and not your own
lips.

³Stone is heavy and sand a burden,
but provocation by a fool is heavier
than both.

⁴Anger is cruel and fury overwhelming,
but who can stand before jealousy?

⁵Better is open rebuke
than hidden love.

⁶Wounds from a friend can be trusted,
but an enemy multiplies kisses.

Love Gets in Your Face

Proverbs 27:5
Tolerance is a key value in the world these days. And it's fine when it comes to tolerating stuff like cultural differences. But too often tolerance means letting our friends do whatever they want. It means accepting their sin. In that case, Christians live by a different value: Love. Love gives us courage to get in a friend's face for his or her own good. Sometimes to confront is more loving than to tolerate.

⁷He who is full loathes honey,
but to the hungry even what is
bitter tastes sweet.

⁸Like a bird that strays from its nest
is a man who strays from his home.

⁹Perfume and incense bring joy to the
heart,
and the pleasantness of one's friend
springs from his earnest
counsel.

¹⁰Do not forsake your friend and the
friend of your father,
and do not go to your brother's
house when disaster strikes
you—
better a neighbor nearby than a
brother far away.

¹¹Be wise, my son, and bring joy to my
heart;
then I can answer anyone who
treats me with contempt.

¹²The prudent see danger and take refuge,
but the simple keep going and
suffer for it.

¹³Take the garment of one who puts up
security for a stranger;
hold it in pledge if he does it for a
wayward woman.

¹⁴If a man loudly blesses his neighbor
early in the morning,
it will be taken as a curse.

¹⁵A quarrelsome wife is like
a constant dripping on a rainy day;
¹⁶restraining her is like restraining the
wind
or grasping oil with the hand.

¹⁷As iron sharpens iron,
so one man sharpens another.

¹⁸He who tends a fig tree will eat its
fruit,
and he who looks after his master
will be honored.

¹⁹As water reflects a face,
so a man's heart reflects the man.

²⁰Death and Destruction[a] are never
satisfied,
and neither are the eyes of man.

[a]20 Hebrew *Sheol and Abaddon*

²¹The crucible for silver and the furnace
for gold,
but man is tested by the praise he
receives.

²²Though you grind a fool in a mortar,
grinding him like grain with a
pestle,
you will not remove his folly from
him.

²³Be sure you know the condition of
your flocks,
give careful attention to your herds;
²⁴for riches do not endure forever,
and a crown is not secure for all
generations.
²⁵When the hay is removed and new
growth appears
and the grass from the hills is
gathered in,
²⁶the lambs will provide you with
clothing,
and the goats with the price of a
field.
²⁷You will have plenty of goats' milk

to feed you and your family
and to nourish your servant girls.

28 The wicked man flees though no
one pursues,
but the righteous are as bold as a
lion.

²When a country is rebellious, it has
many rulers,
but a man of understanding and
knowledge maintains order.

³A ruler*ᵃ* who oppresses the poor
is like a driving rain that leaves no
crops.

⁴Those who forsake the law praise the
wicked,
but those who keep the law resist
them.

⁵Evil men do not understand justice,
but those who seek the LORD
understand it fully.

ᵃ3 Or A poor man

Fri day

The Buddy System

Read Proverbs 27:17

I have this friend who sometimes dresses, well, in a way that shows off her
body. I've never said anything to her about it, but after reading this verse,
I think I need to talk with her about my concern. I want her to start thinking
about honoring God by dressing in a less suggestive way.

One of the reasons God gives us Christian friends is so we can help each
other want to get stronger in our faith. We need to confront each other in a
loving way when we see stuff happening that shouldn't be happening. Being
corrected isn't a pleasant experience, but when our friends correct us, God's
using them to help *us* grow. And God can use us to help *them* grow too.

❶ How have your friends helped your faith grow? How have you
helped them?

❷ Think about something you want to do to get closer to God, like read
your Bible more often, get more involved in your youth group, or just be
more bold about your faith. Now, ask your best friend to help you do
that thing. Ask him or her to let you know when you've messed up and to encourage you when you're making progress.

❸ Thank God for friends who encourage you to grow closer to God.

Turn to page 769 for your next devotion.

⁶Better a poor man whose walk is
blameless
than a rich man whose ways are
perverse.

⁷He who keeps the law is a discerning
son,
but a companion of gluttons
disgraces his father.

⁸He who increases his wealth by
exorbitant interest
amasses it for another, who will be
kind to the poor.

⁹If anyone turns a deaf ear to the law,
even his prayers are detestable.

¹⁰He who leads the upright along an
evil path
will fall into his own trap,
but the blameless will receive a
good inheritance.

¹¹A rich man may be wise in his own
eyes,
but a poor man who has
discernment sees through him.

¹²When the righteous triumph, there is
great elation;
but when the wicked rise to power,
men go into hiding.

¹³He who conceals his sins does not
prosper,
but whoever confesses and
renounces them finds mercy.

¹⁴Blessed is the man who always fears
the LORD,
but he who hardens his heart falls
into trouble.

¹⁵Like a roaring lion or a charging bear
is a wicked man ruling over a
helpless people.

¹⁶A tyrannical ruler lacks judgment,
but he who hates ill-gotten gain
will enjoy a long life.

¹⁷A man tormented by the guilt of
murder
will be a fugitive till death;
let no one support him.

¹⁸He whose walk is blameless is kept
safe,
but he whose ways are perverse will
suddenly fall.

¹⁹He who works his land will have
abundant food,
but the one who chases fantasies
will have his fill of poverty.

²⁰A faithful man will be richly blessed,
but one eager to get rich will not go
unpunished.

²¹To show partiality is not good—
yet a man will do wrong for a piece
of bread.

²²A stingy man is eager to get rich
and is unaware that poverty awaits
him.

²³He who rebukes a man will in the end
gain more favor
than he who has a flattering
tongue.

²⁴He who robs his father or mother
and says, "It's not wrong"—
he is partner to him who destroys.

²⁵A greedy man stirs up dissension,
but he who trusts in the LORD will
prosper.

²⁶He who trusts in himself is a fool,
but he who walks in wisdom is kept
safe.

²⁷He who gives to the poor will lack
nothing,
but he who closes his eyes to them
receives many curses.

²⁸When the wicked rise to power, people
go into hiding;
but when the wicked perish, the
righteous thrive.

29 A man who remains stiff-necked
after many rebukes
will suddenly be destroyed—without
remedy.

²When the righteous thrive, the people
rejoice;
when the wicked rule, the people
groan.

³A man who loves wisdom brings joy
to his father,
but a companion of prostitutes
squanders his wealth.

⁴By justice a king gives a country
stability,

but one who is greedy for bribes
tears it down.

⁵Whoever flatters his neighbor
is spreading a net for his feet.

⁶An evil man is snared by his own sin,
but a righteous one can sing and be
glad.

⁷The righteous care about justice for
the poor,
but the wicked have no such concern.

⁸Mockers stir up a city,
but wise men turn away anger.

⁹If a wise man goes to court with a
fool,
the fool rages and scoffs, and there
is no peace.

¹⁰Bloodthirsty men hate a man of
integrity
and seek to kill the upright.

¹¹A fool gives full vent to his anger,
but a wise man keeps himself under
control.

¹²If a ruler listens to lies,
all his officials become wicked.

¹³The poor man and the oppressor have
this in common:
The Lord gives sight to the eyes of
both.

¹⁴If a king judges the poor with
fairness,
his throne will always be secure.

¹⁵The rod of correction imparts wisdom,
but a child left to himself disgraces
his mother.

¹⁶When the wicked thrive, so does sin,
but the righteous will see their
downfall.

¹⁷Discipline your son, and he will give
you peace;
he will bring delight to your soul.

¹⁸Where there is no revelation, the
people cast off restraint;
but blessed is he who keeps the law.

¹⁹A servant cannot be corrected by mere
words;
though he understands, he will not
respond.

Keep Me From Crashing!

Huh?

Proverbs 29:18
The Bible holds us together. It keeps our hearts from running wild and shows us how to turn our energies in the right direction. To ignore the Bible is to lose out on God's help. You might as well drive without brakes or skydive without a parachute.

²⁰Do you see a man who speaks in
haste?
There is more hope for a fool than
for him.

²¹If a man pampers his servant from
youth,
he will bring grief[a] in the end.

²²An angry man stirs up dissension,
and a hot-tempered one commits
many sins.

²³A man's pride brings him low,
but a man of lowly spirit gains
honor.

²⁴The accomplice of a thief is his own
enemy;
he is put under oath and dare not
testify.

²⁵Fear of man will prove to be a snare,
but whoever trusts in the Lord is
kept safe.

²⁶Many seek an audience with a ruler,
but it is from the Lord that man
gets justice.

²⁷The righteous detest the dishonest;
the wicked detest the upright.

Sayings of Agur

30 The sayings of Agur son of Jakeh—an oracle[b]:

This man declared to Ithiel,
to Ithiel and to Ucal:[c]

---

[a]21 The meaning of the Hebrew for this word is uncertain. [b]1 Or *Jakeh of Massa* [c]1 Masoretic Text; with a different word division of the Hebrew *declared, "I am weary, O God; / I am weary, O God, and faint.*

² "I am the most ignorant of men;
    I do not have a man's
        understanding.
³ I have not learned wisdom,
    nor have I knowledge of the Holy
        One.
⁴ Who has gone up to heaven and come
        down?
    Who has gathered up the wind in
        the hollow of his hands?
    Who has wrapped up the waters in his
        cloak?
    Who has established all the ends of
        the earth?
    What is his name, and the name of his
        son?
    Tell me if you know!

⁵ "Every word of God is flawless;
    he is a shield to those who take
        refuge in him.
⁶ Do not add to his words,
    or he will rebuke you and prove you
        a liar.

⁷ "Two things I ask of you, O LORD;
    do not refuse me before I die:
⁸ Keep falsehood and lies far from me;
    give me neither poverty nor riches,
    but give me only my daily bread.
⁹ Otherwise, I may have too much and
        disown you
    and say, 'Who is the LORD?'
    Or I may become poor and steal,
    and so dishonor the name of my
        God.

¹⁰ "Do not slander a servant to his
        master,
    or he will curse you, and you will
        pay for it.

¹¹ "There are those who curse their
        fathers
    and do not bless their mothers;
¹² those who are pure in their own eyes
    and yet are not cleansed of their
        filth;
¹³ those whose eyes are ever so haughty,
    whose glances are so disdainful;
¹⁴ those whose teeth are swords
    and whose jaws are set with knives
    to devour the poor from the earth,
        the needy from among mankind.

¹⁵ "The leech has two daughters.
    'Give! Give!' they cry.

"There are three things that are never
        satisfied,
    four that never say, 'Enough!':
¹⁶ the grave,ᵃ the barren womb,
    land, which is never satisfied with
        water,
    and fire, which never says,
        'Enough!'

¹⁷ "The eye that mocks a father,
    that scorns obedience to a mother,
    will be pecked out by the ravens of
        the valley,
    will be eaten by the vultures.

¹⁸ "There are three things that are too
        amazing for me,
    four that I do not understand:
¹⁹ the way of an eagle in the sky,
    the way of a snake on a rock,
    the way of a ship on the high seas,
    and the way of a man with a
        maiden.

²⁰ "This is the way of an adulteress:
    She eats and wipes her mouth
    and says, 'I've done nothing wrong.'

²¹ "Under three things the earth
        trembles,
    under four it cannot bear up:
²² a servant who becomes king,
    a fool who is full of food,
²³ an unloved woman who is married,
    and a maidservant who displaces
        her mistress.

²⁴ "Four things on earth are small,
    yet they are extremely wise:
²⁵ Ants are creatures of little strength,
    yet they store up their food in the
        summer;
²⁶ coneysᵇ are creatures of little power,
    yet they make their home in the
        crags;
²⁷ locusts have no king,
    yet they advance together in ranks;
²⁸ a lizard can be caught with the hand,
    yet it is found in kings' palaces.

²⁹ "There are three things that are stately
        in their stride,
    four that move with stately bearing:
³⁰ a lion, mighty among beasts,
    who retreats before nothing;

ᵃ16 Hebrew *Sheol*   ᵇ26 That is, the hyrax or rock
badger

³¹a strutting rooster, a he-goat,
  and a king with his army around
    him.ᵃ
³²"If you have played the fool and
    exalted yourself,
  or if you have planned evil,
  clap your hand over your mouth!
³³For as churning the milk produces
    butter,
  and as twisting the nose produces
    blood,
  so stirring up anger produces
    strife."

Sayings of King Lemuel

31 The sayings of King Lemuel—an
      oracleᵇ his mother taught him:

²"O my son, O son of my womb,
  O son of my vows,ᶜ
³do not spend your strength on
    women,
  your vigor on those who ruin kings.

ᵃ31 Or *king secure against revolt* ᵇ1 Or *of Lemuel
king of Massa, which* ᶜ2 Or / *the answer to my
prayers*

Weekend.

Gray Areas

Read 1 Corinthians 6:12–13 (page 1380)

This week 3 "gray areas" have come up—issues that are not clearly black or white, right or wrong. Television, alcohol, clothing styles—how do you know what to do in these areas? Of course, for kids alcohol is clearly out, since it's illegal. But what about the others?

There are 2 extremes to avoid. The first one is *license*—that's the party-on attitude that says, "Hey, if it's not illegal, it's fine." Christians get into all kinds of trouble if their standards aren't higher than this.

The other extreme is just as dangerous. It's called *legalism,* which is thinking that you have to obey a huge list of do's and don'ts in order to be close to God.

Between these 2 extremes is real *liberty*, the ability to enjoy what's good in life while avoiding what's bad. Based on today's reading, here are 4 questions to ask when you encounter a gray area:

(1) Will it please God? Avoid anything that God will eventually judge and destroy.

(2) Will it help me? Think about whether the activity is beneficial for your health and spiritual growth.

(3) Could it enslave me? If the activity is tempting, addicting or really time-consuming, watch out.

(4) Will it hurt someone else? How would it feel to be in their shoes?

Put your questionable activities to these tests, and you're likely to find your way through life's gray areas.

❶ What are the biggest gray areas you have to deal with (activities that the Bible doesn't specifically say are right or wrong)?

❷ Using the questions above, try to develop some guidelines to help make good decisions in these gray areas. Then talk to your parents or a youth group leader to get their opinions.

❸ Ask God to give you wisdom to live well in a gray world.

Turn to page 775 for your next devotion.

⁴"It is not for kings, O Lemuel—
  not for kings to drink wine,
  not for rulers to crave beer,
⁵lest they drink and forget what the
    law decrees,
  and deprive all the oppressed of
    their rights.
⁶Give beer to those who are perishing,
  wine to those who are in anguish;
⁷let them drink and forget their poverty
  and remember their misery no more.

⁸"Speak up for those who cannot speak
    for themselves,
  for the rights of all who are
    destitute.
⁹Speak up and judge fairly;
  defend the rights of the poor and
    needy."

Epilogue: The Wife of Noble Character

¹⁰ᵃA wife of noble character who can
    find?
  She is worth far more than rubies.
¹¹Her husband has full confidence in
    her
  and lacks nothing of value.
¹²She brings him good, not harm,
  all the days of her life.
¹³She selects wool and flax
  and works with eager hands.
¹⁴She is like the merchant ships,
  bringing her food from afar.
¹⁵She gets up while it is still dark;
  she provides food for her family
  and portions for her servant girls.
¹⁶She considers a field and buys it;
  out of her earnings she plants a
    vineyard.
¹⁷She sets about her work vigorously;
  her arms are strong for her tasks.
¹⁸She sees that her trading is profitable,
  and her lamp does not go out at
    night.
¹⁹In her hand she holds the distaff

and grasps the spindle with her
    fingers.
²⁰She opens her arms to the poor
  and extends her hands to the needy.
²¹When it snows, she has no fear for her
    household;
  for all of them are clothed in
    scarlet.
²²She makes coverings for her bed;
  she is clothed in fine linen and
    purple.
²³Her husband is respected at the city
    gate,
  where he takes his seat among the
    elders of the land.
²⁴She makes linen garments and sells
    them,
  and supplies the merchants with
    sashes.
²⁵She is clothed with strength and
    dignity;
  she can laugh at the days to come.
²⁶She speaks with wisdom,
  and faithful instruction is on her
    tongue.
²⁷She watches over the affairs of her
    household
  and does not eat the bread of
    idleness.
²⁸Her children arise and call her
    blessed;
  her husband also, and he praises
    her:
²⁹"Many women do noble things,
  but you surpass them all."
³⁰Charm is deceptive, and beauty is
    fleeting;
  but a woman who fears the LORD is
    to be praised.
³¹Give her the reward she has earned,
  and let her works bring her praise
    at the city gate.

ᵃ10 Verses 10-31 are an acrostic, each verse
beginning with a successive letter of the Hebrew
alphabet.

Ecclesiastes

START

Every day on the radio you can hear all kinds of angry and depressing songs about the meaninglessness of life. It seems like all you need is a tune and a 'tude and you can make millions—and still not be happy. The dark and depressing tone (often called angst) of a lot of music reminds us that money, pleasure and popularity are powerless to satisfy the soul. So what can we do?

That's the very question Ecclesiastes (ee-CLEE-zee-AS-tees) seeks to answer. The author was a guy who saw it all and did it all, but still wasn't happy. So he wrote all his frustrations down in his journal. Check it out and see how many of his 3,000-year-old themes you hear coming through in today's hit songs. This book sounds pretty familiar.

Even though he saw lots of bad stuff, he also saw the good stuff. Of course, this Bible writer did have some great thoughts. Since life is short and pretty senseless, he said you ought to do 3 things: Keep everything in balance, honor God and enjoy what you can. That's not the final word on what it means to be godly, but it's not a bad start. Especially if you've come down with a nasty case of teenage angst.

Cast OF Characters

The Teacher
The writer gives himself this title. He's Mr. I've-Done-It-All, so he's qualified to teach a few lessons. The Teacher also identifies himself in the very first verse as a son of David, king in Jerusalem. So he probably was Solomon, or someone else writing from Solomon's perspective.

The Listener
That's you! There are no other people in this book, leaving plenty of room for you to jump into its pages.

What's UP with That?

The Teacher sure felt like he was in a mess. Here are his

Top 10 Reasons for Hating His Miserable Life:

10 **There is nothing new under the sun (1:9)**
Everything is so The Same. Why can't somebody invent a new color or something?

9 **Smart people and not-so-smart people both die (2:15–20)**
And I don't want some slacker getting all my stuff!

8 **Stress, stress, stress, stress, stress, stress, stress, stress (2:22–23)**
I can't even get a decent night's sleep.

7 **I got things in my heart I can't understand (3:10–11)**
So if I was made for heaven, what am I doing on this stinking planet?

6 **You can't get away from wickedness (3:16)**
The bad guys are everywhere!

5 **The dead and the unborn have it better than I do (4:1–3)**
They don't have to put up with the crud I have to put up with.

4 **Everything is motivated by envy (4:4)**
I probably get invited to parties only because somebody wants to make somebody else jealous.

3 **The more money, the more trouble (5:10–17, 6:1–9)**
But, man I'd sure like to be rich— so what does that tell you about me?

2 **Lips flapping in the wind (6:11)**
The more you say, the less I want to hear, so pipe down!

1 **Meaningless! Meaningless! Everything is meaningless! (12:8)**
So why did I even write this book?

Snap shots

- Life makes no sense
  (chapter 1:1–11)

- Wisdom makes no sense
  (chapter 1:12–18)

- Pleasure makes no sense
  (chapter 2:1–26)

- Only God makes sense
  (chapter 3:1–22)

- Nothing else makes sense
  (chapters 4:1—6:12)

- Here's some advice
  (chapters 7:1—12:14)

The point of Ecclesiastes is that, even though God's people might feel depressed and bummed out, they should not give in to it. Instead they should learn to honor God and do right, regardless of the mess they're in. **GOOD ADVICE!**

Everything Is Meaningless

1 The words of the Teacher,[a] son of David, king in Jerusalem:

[2] "Meaningless! Meaningless!"
  says the Teacher.
"Utterly meaningless!
  Everything is meaningless."

[3] What does man gain from all his labor
  at which he toils under the sun?
[4] Generations come and generations go,
  but the earth remains forever.
[5] The sun rises and the sun sets,
  and hurries back to where it rises.
[6] The wind blows to the south
  and turns to the north;
round and round it goes,
  ever returning on its course.
[7] All streams flow into the sea,
  yet the sea is never full.
To the place the streams come from,
  there they return again.
[8] All things are wearisome,
  more than one can say.
The eye never has enough of seeing,
  nor the ear its fill of hearing.
[9] What has been will be again,
  what has been done will be done
    again;
  there is nothing new under the sun.
[10] Is there anything of which one can
    say,
  "Look! This is something new"?
It was here already, long ago;
  it was here before our time.
[11] There is no remembrance of men of
    old,
  and even those who are yet to
    come
will not be remembered
  by those who follow.

Wisdom Is Meaningless

[12] I, the Teacher, was king over Israel in Jerusalem. [13] I devoted myself to study and to explore by wisdom all that is done under heaven. What a heavy burden God has laid on men! [14] I have seen all the things that are done under the sun; all of them are meaningless, a chasing after the wind.

[15] What is twisted cannot be
    straightened;
  what is lacking cannot be counted.

Gone With the Wind

Huh?

Ecclesiastes 1:14
Chasing after the wind is dorky. You'll never catch it. Even if you caught it, you'd never know it because you can't see it. Anytime we go against what God wants, it's like we're chasing after the wind.

[16] I thought to myself, "Look, I have grown and increased in wisdom more than anyone who has ruled over Jerusalem before me; I have experienced much of wisdom and knowledge." [17] Then I applied myself to the understanding of wisdom, and also of madness and folly, but I learned that this, too, is a chasing after the wind.

[18] For with much wisdom comes much
    sorrow;
  the more knowledge, the more grief.

Pleasures Are Meaningless

2 I thought in my heart, "Come now, I will test you with pleasure to find out what is good." But that also proved to be meaningless. [2] "Laughter," I said, "is foolish. And what does pleasure accomplish?" [3] I tried cheering myself with wine, and embracing folly—my mind still guiding me with wisdom. I wanted to see what was worthwhile for men to do under heaven during the few days of their lives.

[4] I undertook great projects: I built houses for myself and planted vineyards. [5] I made gardens and parks and planted all kinds of fruit trees in them. [6] I made reservoirs to water groves of flourishing trees. [7] I bought male and female slaves and had other slaves who were born in my house. I also owned more herds and flocks than anyone in Jerusalem before me. [8] I amassed silver and gold for myself, and the treasure of kings and provinces. I acquired men and women singers, and a harem[b] as well—the

---

[a] 1 Or *leader of the assembly*; also in verses 2 and 12
[b] 8 The meaning of the Hebrew for this phrase is uncertain.

delights of the heart of man. ⁹I became greater by far than anyone in Jerusalem before me. In all this my wisdom stayed with me.

¹⁰I denied myself nothing my eyes
    desired;
  I refused my heart no pleasure.
My heart took delight in all my work,
    and this was the reward for all my
    labor.
¹¹Yet when I surveyed all that my hands
    had done
  and what I had toiled to achieve,
everything was meaningless, a
    chasing after the wind;
  nothing was gained under the sun.

Wisdom and Folly Are Meaningless

¹²Then I turned my thoughts to consider
    wisdom,
  and also madness and folly.
What more can the king's successor do
  than what has already been done?
¹³I saw that wisdom is better than folly,
  just as light is better than darkness.
¹⁴The wise man has eyes in his head,
  while the fool walks in the
    darkness;
but I came to realize
  that the same fate overtakes them
    both.

¹⁵Then I thought in my heart,

"The fate of the fool will overtake me
    also.
What then do I gain by being
    wise?"
I said in my heart,
  "This too is meaningless."
¹⁶For the wise man, like the fool, will
    not be long remembered;
  in days to come both will be
    forgotten.
Like the fool, the wise man too must
    die!

Toil Is Meaningless

¹⁷So I hated life, because the work that is done under the sun was grievous to me. All of it is meaningless, a chasing after the wind. ¹⁸I hated all the things I had toiled for under the sun, because I must leave them to the one who comes after me. ¹⁹And who knows whether he will be a wise man or a fool? Yet he will have control over all the work into which I have poured my effort and skill under the sun. This too is meaningless. ²⁰So my heart began to despair over all my toilsome labor under the sun. ²¹For a man may do his work with wisdom, knowledge and skill, and then he must leave all he owns to someone who has not worked for it. This too is meaningless and a great misfortune. ²²What does a man get for all the toil and anxious striving with which he labors under the sun? ²³All his days his work is pain and grief; even at night his mind does not rest. This too is meaningless.

²⁴A man can do nothing better than to eat and drink and find satisfaction in his work. This too, I see, is from the hand of God, ²⁵for without him, who can eat or find enjoyment? ²⁶To the man who pleases him, God gives wisdom, knowledge and happiness, but to the sinner he gives the task of gathering and storing up wealth to hand it over to the one who pleases God. This too is meaningless, a chasing after the wind.

A Time for Everything

3 There is a time for everything,
  and a season for every activity
    under heaven:

²   a time to be born and a time to die,
    a time to plant and a time to
      uproot,
³   a time to kill and a time to heal,
    a time to tear down and a time to
      build,
⁴   a time to weep and a time to laugh,
    a time to mourn and a time to
      dance,
⁵   a time to scatter stones and a time
      to gather them,
    a time to embrace and a time to
      refrain,
⁶   a time to search and a time to give
      up,
    a time to keep and a time to throw
      away,
⁷   a time to tear and a time to mend,
    a time to be silent and a time to
      speak,
⁸   a time to love and a time to hate,
    a time for war and a time for peace.

⁹What does the worker gain from his toil? ¹⁰I have seen the burden God has laid on men. ¹¹He has made everything beautiful in its time. He has also set eternity in the hearts of men; yet they cannot fathom what God has done from beginning to end. ¹²I know that there is nothing better for men than to be happy and do good while they live. ¹³That everyone may eat and drink, and find satisfaction in all his toil—this is the gift of God. ¹⁴I know that everything God does will endure forever; nothing can be added to it and nothing taken from it. God does it so that men will revere him.

¹⁵Whatever is has already been,
and what will be has been before;
and God will call the past to account.ᵃ

¹⁶And I saw something else under the sun:

In the place of judgment—wickedness was there,
in the place of justice—wickedness was there.

¹⁷I thought in my heart,

"God will bring to judgment
both the righteous and the wicked,
for there will be a time for every activity,
a time for every deed."

¹⁸I also thought, "As for men, God tests them so that they may see that they are like the animals. ¹⁹Man's fate is like that of the animals; the same fate awaits them both: As one dies, so dies the other. All have the same breathᵇ; man has no advantage over the animal. Everything is meaningless. ²⁰All go to the same place; all come from dust, and to dust all return. ²¹Who knows if the spirit of man rises upward and if the spirit of the animalᶜ goes down into the earth?"

²²So I saw that there is nothing better for a man than to enjoy his work,

ᵃ15 Or *God calls back the past*   ᵇ19 Or *spirit*
ᶜ21 Or *Who knows the spirit of man, which rises upward, or the spirit of the animal, which*

Mon day

A Lil' Bit of Everything

Read Ecclesiastes 3:1–11

God gives us work to do on earth. Most of the time, just knowing God doesn't automatically make the work easy. We'll have many difficulties. God will provide for our needs, though, and we need to accept the work he has for us—even if it's hard.

This is a great passage to remember when you're having a hard time. It reminds us that there is a time for everything. Life won't always be easy and perfect, but that doesn't mean God has lost control. He has special work cut out for each of us as Christians. He can see the whole picture, so he knows how the good and bad will fit together in the end. We just need to obey him, do his work and trust him *always!*

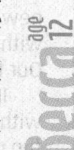

❶ Think of all the different things you do in a typical day. What would your life be like if you just did the same thing over and over again?

❷ Lie down flat on your lawn or your floor. Try to look around without lifting your head off the ground. How much can you see? Now stand up and look around. How much more can you see? What does this tell you about the way we see our lives versus the way God sees our lives?

❸ Thank God for being in control of everything that happens—good and bad.

Turn to page 776 for your next devotion.

because that is his lot. For who can bring him to see what will happen after him?

Oppression, Toil, Friendlessness

4 Again I looked and saw all the oppression that was taking place under the sun:

I saw the tears of the oppressed—
    and they have no comforter;
power was on the side of their
        oppressors—
    and they have no comforter.
² And I declared that the dead,
    who had already died,
are happier than the living,
    who are still alive.
³ But better than both
    is he who has not yet been,
who has not seen the evil
    that is done under the sun.

⁴ And I saw that all labor and all achievement spring from man's envy of his neighbor. This too is meaningless, a chasing after the wind.

⁵ The fool folds his hands
    and ruins himself.
⁶ Better one handful with tranquillity
    than two handfuls with toil
    and chasing after the wind.

⁷ Again I saw something meaningless under the sun:

⁸ There was a man all alone;
    he had neither son nor brother.
There was no end to his toil,
    yet his eyes were not content with
        his wealth.
"For whom am I toiling," he asked,
    "and why am I depriving myself of
        enjoyment?"

Tuesday

Dynamic Duo   **Read Ecclesiastes 4:9–12**

When I was in 4th grade, I didn't have a single friend in the world. Every day I would get picked on and teased because I wasn't very athletic or popular. Nobody stood up for me. Day after day I'd go to school feeling like a nobody.

Then 5th grade started, and there was a new girl in class. She was athletic, pretty and very talented. There was no way she'd ever be *my* friend— or so I thought. One day when the boys were picking on me (as usual), the new girl walked over and chased them off. She stuck around and hung out with me that day at recess, and we started hanging out together every day. Our friendship made me feel great. I wasn't lonely any more!

There's a lot of truth in what these verses say about friends. Working with a friend does help you get a lot more done, and you have a lot more fun doing it. Friends also help each other through hard times. And 2 people can definitely defend themselves against teasing and meanness a lot better than one person.

Life can be pretty tough without friends. So appreciate the friends you have, and reach out to people who need friends. It really can make a difference!

❶ What's the nicest thing a friend has ever done for you?

❷ Do something special for a close friend this week, like bringing them their favorite food or just saying, "Thanks for being there for me!"

❸ Pray for your friends, and thank God for them.

Turn to page 778 for your next devotion.

This too is meaningless—
  a miserable business!

⁹Two are better than one,
  because they have a good return for
    their work:
¹⁰If one falls down,
  his friend can help him up.
But pity the man who falls
  and has no one to help him up!
¹¹Also, if two lie down together, they
    will keep warm.
  But how can one keep warm
    alone?
¹²Though one may be overpowered,
  two can defend themselves.
A cord of three strands is not quickly
    broken.

Advancement Is Meaningless

¹³Better a poor but wise youth than an
old but foolish king who no longer
knows how to take warning. ¹⁴The youth
may have come from prison to the kingship, or he may have been born in poverty within his kingdom. ¹⁵I saw that all
who lived and walked under the sun followed the youth, the king's successor.
¹⁶There was no end to all the people who
were before them. But those who came
later were not pleased with the successor.
This too is meaningless, a chasing after
the wind.

Stand in Awe of God

5 Guard your steps when you go to the
house of God. Go near to listen rather than to offer the sacrifice of fools, who
do not know that they do wrong.

²Do not be quick with your mouth,
  do not be hasty in your heart
    to utter anything before God.
God is in heaven
  and you are on earth,
  so let your words be few.
³As a dream comes when there are
    many cares,
  so the speech of a fool when there
    are many words.

⁴When you make a vow to God, do not
delay in fulfilling it. He has no pleasure
in fools; fulfill your vow. ⁵It is better not
to vow than to make a vow and not ful-
fill it. ⁶Do not let your mouth lead you

into sin. And do not protest to the
temple messenger, "My vow was a mistake." Why should God be angry at what
you say and destroy the work of your
hands? ⁷Much dreaming and many
words are meaningless. Therefore stand
in awe of God.

Riches Are Meaningless

⁸If you see the poor oppressed in a dis-
trict, and justice and rights denied, do
not be surprised at such things; for one
official is eyed by a higher one, and over
them both are others higher still. ⁹The
increase from the land is taken by all; the
king himself profits from the fields.

¹⁰Whoever loves money never has
    money enough;
  whoever loves wealth is never
    satisfied with his income.
  This too is meaningless.

¹¹As goods increase,
  so do those who consume them.
And what benefit are they to the
    owner
  except to feast his eyes on them?

More Cash—Cure or Curse?

Ecclesiastes 5:12
Lots of folks think their problems would be
solved if they were rich. You could eat what
you want, wear what you want and buy
what you want. But cash can't cure all of
your worries. In fact, sometimes having
money keeps you tossing and turning at
night. Worrying about how to save it, how
to spend it, or living with the fear that you
will lose it can wear you out.

¹²The sleep of a laborer is sweet,
    whether he eats little or much,
  but the abundance of a rich man
    permits him no sleep.

¹³I have seen a grievous evil under the
sun:

  wealth hoarded to the harm of its
    owner,

¹⁴ or wealth lost through some
  misfortune,
so that when he has a son
  there is nothing left for him.
¹⁵Naked a man comes from his mother's
  womb,
  and as he comes, so he departs.
He takes nothing from his labor
  that he can carry in his hand.

¹⁶This too is a grievous evil:

As a man comes, so he departs,
  and what does he gain,
  since he toils for the wind?
¹⁷All his days he eats in darkness,
  with great frustration, affliction and
  anger.

¹⁸Then I realized that it is good and proper for a man to eat and drink, and to find satisfaction in his toilsome labor under the sun during the few days of life God has given him—for this is his lot. ¹⁹Moreover, when God gives any man wealth and possessions, and enables him to enjoy them, to accept his lot and be happy in his work—this is a gift of God. ²⁰He seldom reflects on the days of his life, because God keeps him occupied with gladness of heart.

6 I have seen another evil under the sun, and it weighs heavily on men: ²God gives a man wealth, possessions and honor, so that he lacks nothing his heart desires, but God does not enable him to enjoy them, and a stranger enjoys them instead. This is meaningless, a grievous evil.

³A man may have a hundred children and live many years; yet no matter how long he lives, if he cannot enjoy his prosperity and does not receive proper burial, I say that a stillborn child is better off than he. ⁴It comes without meaning, it departs in darkness, and in darkness its name is shrouded. ⁵Though it never saw the sun or knew anything, it has more rest than does that man— ⁶even if he lives a thousand years twice over but

---

Wednesday

More, More, More

Read Ecclesiastes 5:10–11

I love baseball cards. Whenever I make a little money, I go to the card shop and buy another pack to add to my collection. But then I look at the cards in that pack, and I wonder if I could get better ones if I just bought another pack or 2. Pretty soon I've bought several packs of cards, and I've spent all my money!

You'd think I would know better by now. It's not like I set out to waste all my money. I guess I trick myself by thinking that I'll be happy if I get the right cards or if I buy more of them. Lots of people try to make themselves happy with cars or clothes or other material possessions, but that just doesn't work. More stuff doesn't ever make us really happy. The only thing that will satisfy us is more of God.

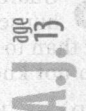

❶ What things make you happy? Why won't material things ever make you truly happy?

❷ The next time you really want to buy something, wait a week. Why? Waiting a week will keep you from buying on a whim. And it'll give you time to think about how God wants you to spend your money.

❸ Ask God to help you trust in him, not material things, for your happiness.

Turn to page 780 for your next devotion.

fails to enjoy his prosperity. Do not all go to the same place?

7 All man's efforts are for his mouth,
    yet his appetite is never satisfied.
8 What advantage has a wise man
    over a fool?
What does a poor man gain
    by knowing how to conduct himself
      before others?
9 Better what the eye sees
    than the roving of the appetite.
This too is meaningless,
    a chasing after the wind.

10 Whatever exists has already been
      named,
    and what man is has been known;
no man can contend
    with one who is stronger than he.
11 The more the words,
    the less the meaning,
    and how does that profit anyone?

12 For who knows what is good for a man in life, during the few and meaningless days he passes through like a shadow? Who can tell him what will happen under the sun after he is gone?

Wisdom

7 A good name is better than fine
      perfume,
    and the day of death better than the
      day of birth.
2 It is better to go to a house of
      mourning
    than to go to a house of feasting,
for death is the destiny of every man;
    the living should take this to heart.
3 Sorrow is better than laughter,
    because a sad face is good for the
      heart.
4 The heart of the wise is in the house
      of mourning,
    but the heart of fools is in the house
      of pleasure.
5 It is better to heed a wise man's
      rebuke
    than to listen to the song of fools.
6 Like the crackling of thorns under the
      pot,
    so is the laughter of fools.
    This too is meaningless.

7 Extortion turns a wise man into a fool,
    and a bribe corrupts the heart.

8 The end of a matter is better than its
      beginning,
    and patience is better than pride.
9 Do not be quickly provoked in your
      spirit,
    for anger resides in the lap of
      fools.
10 Do not say, "Why were the old days
      better than these?"
    For it is not wise to ask such
      questions.

11 Wisdom, like an inheritance, is a good
      thing
    and benefits those who see the
      sun.
12 Wisdom is a shelter
    as money is a shelter,
but the advantage of knowledge is
      this:
    that wisdom preserves the life of its
      possessor.

13 Consider what God has done:

Who can straighten
    what he has made crooked?
14 When times are good, be happy;
    but when times are bad, consider:
God has made the one
    as well as the other.
Therefore, a man cannot discover
    anything about his future.

15 In this meaningless life of mine I have seen both of these:

a righteous man perishing in his
      righteousness,
    and a wicked man living long in his
      wickedness.
16 Do not be overrighteous,
    neither be overwise—
    why destroy yourself?
17 Do not be overwicked,
    and do not be a fool—
    why die before your time?
18 It is good to grasp the one
    and not let go of the other.
The man who fears God will avoid
    all extremes.*a*
19 Wisdom makes one wise man more
      powerful
    than ten rulers in a city.

a 18 Or will follow them both

20 There is not a righteous man on earth
   who does what is right and never
     sins.

21 Do not pay attention to every word
     people say,
   or you may hear your servant
     cursing you—
22 for you know in your heart
   that many times you yourself have
     cursed others.

23 All this I tested by wisdom and I said,

"I am determined to be wise"—
   but this was beyond me.
24 Whatever wisdom may be,
   it is far off and most profound—
   who can discover it?
25 So I turned my mind to understand,
   to investigate and to search out
     wisdom and the scheme of
       things
   and to understand the stupidity of
     wickedness
   and the madness of folly.

26 I find more bitter than death
   the woman who is a snare,
     whose heart is a trap
     and whose hands are chains.
   The man who pleases God will escape
     her,
   but the sinner she will ensnare.

27 "Look," says the Teacher,[a] "this is
what I have discovered:

"Adding one thing to another to
     discover the scheme of
       things—
28   while I was still searching
     but not finding—
   I found one upright man among a
     thousand,
   but not one upright woman among
     them all.
29 This only have I found:
   God made mankind upright,
   but men have gone in search of
     many schemes."

8 Who is like the wise man?
   Who knows the explanation of
     things?

a27 Or leader of the assembly

Thursday

Dashed Dreams

Read Ecclesiastes 7:14

Right before 9th grade, everything was going great for me. I had tons of Christian friends, and I considered them my "brothers" and "sisters." After years of home schooling, I was all set to join my friends at a public high school. Four years of good times were right around the corner.

Then I found out my family was moving. One minute everything was awesome, and the next minute my dreams were all taken away.

But from that experience, I've learned that God doesn't always give us "Hollywood" lives. He guides us through trials and bad times too, so we can learn how to put our trust in him. God's the one with the perfect plan for our lives—not us.

age 14, Susanna

What about You?

❶ What's usually your first reaction when something doesn't go your way? Does that reaction help the situation or make it worse?

❷ Make a small sign that says "God's in control!" and put it someplace where you'll see it often.

❸ Thank God for being in control of your life.

Turn to page 783 for your next devotion.

Wisdom brightens a man's face
and changes its hard appearance.

Obey the King

[2] Obey the king's command, I say, because you took an oath before God. [3] Do not be in a hurry to leave the king's presence. Do not stand up for a bad cause, for he will do whatever he pleases. [4] Since a king's word is supreme, who can say to him, "What are you doing?"

[5] Whoever obeys his command will
come to no harm,
and the wise heart will know the
proper time and procedure.
[6] For there is a proper time and
procedure for every matter,
though a man's misery weighs
heavily upon him.

[7] Since no man knows the future,
who can tell him what is to come?
[8] No man has power over the wind to
contain it[a];
so no one has power over the day
of his death.
As no one is discharged in time of
war,
so wickedness will not release those
who practice it.

[9] All this I saw, as I applied my mind to everything done under the sun. There is a time when a man lords it over others to his own[b] hurt. [10] Then too, I saw the wicked buried—those who used to come and go from the holy place and receive praise[c] in the city where they did this. This too is meaningless. [11] When the sentence for a crime is not quickly carried out, the hearts of the people are filled with schemes to do wrong. [12] Although a wicked man commits a hundred crimes and still lives a long time, I know that it will go better with God-fearing men, who are reverent before God. [13] Yet because the wicked do not fear God, it will not go well with them, and their days will not lengthen like a shadow. [14] There is something else meaningless that occurs on earth: righteous men who get what the wicked deserve, and wicked men who get what the righteous deserve. This too, I say, is meaningless. [15] So I commend the enjoyment of life, because nothing is better for a man under the sun than to eat and drink and be glad. Then joy will accompany him in his work all the days of the life God has given him under the sun.

Sun Up, Down, All Around

Huh?

Ecclesiastes 8:15
You could probably trick a friend the next time it gets dark by asking her if the sun is still in the sky. She might say "no," but the correct answer is "yes." It's just shining in a different part of the world. Every minute of our day is spent under the sun. There's nothing you do that doesn't happen under the sun, and there is nothing you do that is not under the watchful eye of God. Just as the sun always shines, God always shines his light in your life.

[16] When I applied my mind to know wisdom and to observe man's labor on earth—his eyes not seeing sleep day or night— [17] then I saw all that God has done. No one can comprehend what goes on under the sun. Despite all his efforts to search it out, man cannot discover its meaning. Even if a wise man claims he knows, he cannot really comprehend it.

A Common Destiny for All

9 So I reflected on all this and concluded that the righteous and the wise and what they do are in God's hands, but no man knows whether love or hate awaits him. [2] All share a common destiny—the righteous and the wicked, the good and the bad,[d] the clean and the unclean, those who offer sacrifices and those who do not.

As it is with the good man,
so with the sinner;

---

[a]8 Or *over his spirit to retain it*   [b]9 Or *to their*
[c]10 Some Hebrew manuscripts and Septuagint (Aquila); most Hebrew manuscripts *and are forgotten*   [d]2 Septuagint (Aquila), Vulgate and Syriac; Hebrew does not have *and the bad.*

as it is with those who take oaths,
   so with those who are afraid to take
      them.

³This is the evil in everything that happens under the sun: The same destiny overtakes all. The hearts of men, moreover, are full of evil and there is madness in their hearts while they live, and afterward they join the dead. ⁴Anyone who is among the living has hope*ᵃ*—even a live dog is better off than a dead lion!

⁵For the living know that they will die,
   but the dead know nothing;
they have no further reward,
   and even the memory of them is
      forgotten.
⁶Their love, their hate
   and their jealousy have long since
      vanished;
never again will they have a part
   in anything that happens under the
      sun.

⁷Go, eat your food with gladness, and drink your wine with a joyful heart, for it is now that God favors what you do. ⁸Always be clothed in white, and always anoint your head with oil. ⁹Enjoy life with your wife, whom you love, all the days of this meaningless life that God has given you under the sun— all your meaningless days. For this is your lot in life and in your toilsome labor under the sun. ¹⁰Whatever your hand finds to do, do it with all your might, for in the grave,*ᵇ* where you are going, there is neither working nor planning nor knowledge nor wisdom.

¹¹I have seen something else under the sun:

The race is not to the swift
   or the battle to the strong,
nor does food come to the wise
   or wealth to the brilliant
   or favor to the learned;
but time and chance happen to them all.

¹²Moreover, no man knows when his hour will come:

As fish are caught in a cruel net,
   or birds are taken in a snare,
so men are trapped by evil times
   that fall unexpectedly upon them.

Wisdom Better Than Folly

¹³I also saw under the sun this example of wisdom that greatly impressed me: ¹⁴There was once a small city with only a few people in it. And a powerful king came against it, surrounded it and built huge siegeworks against it. ¹⁵Now there lived in that city a man poor but wise, and he saved the city by his wisdom. But nobody remembered that poor man. ¹⁶So I said, "Wisdom is better than strength." But the poor man's wisdom is despised, and his words are no longer heeded.

¹⁷The quiet words of the wise are more
      to be heeded
   than the shouts of a ruler of fools.
¹⁸Wisdom is better than weapons of
      war,
   but one sinner destroys much good.

10 As dead flies give perfume a bad
      smell,
   so a little folly outweighs wisdom
      and honor.
²The heart of the wise inclines to the
      right,
   but the heart of the fool to the left.
³Even as he walks along the road,
   the fool lacks sense
   and shows everyone how stupid he
      is.
⁴If a ruler's anger rises against you,
   do not leave your post;
   calmness can lay great errors to
      rest.
⁵There is an evil I have seen under the
      sun,
   the sort of error that arises from a
      ruler:
⁶Fools are put in many high positions,
   while the rich occupy the low ones.
⁷I have seen slaves on horseback,
   while princes go on foot like slaves.

⁸Whoever digs a pit may fall into it;
   whoever breaks through a wall may
      be bitten by a snake.
⁹Whoever quarries stones may be
      injured by them;
   whoever splits logs may be
      endangered by them.

*ᵃ4 Or What then is to be chosen? With all who live,
there is hope*   *ᵇ10 Hebrew Sheol*

¹⁰If the ax is dull
  and its edge unsharpened,
more strength is needed
  but skill will bring success.

¹¹If a snake bites before it is charmed,
  there is no profit for the charmer.

¹²Words from a wise man's mouth are
    gracious,
  but a fool is consumed by his own
    lips.
¹³At the beginning his words are folly;
  at the end they are wicked
    madness—
¹⁴ and the fool multiplies words.

No one knows what is coming—
  who can tell him what will happen
    after him?

¹⁵A fool's work wearies him;
  he does not know the way to town.

¹⁶Woe to you, O land whose king was a
    servant[a]
  and whose princes feast in the
    morning.
¹⁷Blessed are you, O land whose king is
    of noble birth
  and whose princes eat at a proper
    time—
  for strength and not for
    drunkenness.

¹⁸If a man is lazy, the rafters sag;
  if his hands are idle, the house
    leaks.

[a]16 Or *king is a child*

Friday

Making the Most of It

Read Ecclesiastes 10:1–15

When I became a Christian, I had some friends who weren't exactly helping me live my new faith. They still wanted me to be the old Chris. But I knew following God meant I had to be a new Chris, one who was living his life for Jesus.

I had to make some tough decisions. For a while I thought I could still hang around with my old friends and just stay away from anything that didn't fit with my faith. But that didn't work. I knew I needed friends who would build me up and encourage me to grow in my faith, not friends who were trying to drag me down with them. As hard as it was, I started to pull away from my old friends and look for other Christians who shared my values.

I thought it would be easy to find Christian friends at my church, but even there I had to look hard to find people who were serious about their faith. Eventually, I found a few people I really trusted—Christian friends who help me build a better relationship with God.

Yeah, it was hard to let go of my old friends. But my first loyalty is to God. If I'm really going to live for him, he has to be first in my life. I figure, I've got one life to live for Christ. I've got to make the most of it.

Chris, age 14

❶ Think about your closest friends. How do they help or hurt your Christian life?

❷ Write down some ways you can help your Christian friends grow in their faith.

❸ Ask God to help you live out your faith more, no matter who you're around.

Turn to page 785 for your next devotion.

Lifeguard Lingo

Huh?

Ecclesiastes 10:16
A lifeguard in Israel in the old days may have shouted, "Woe. There's a swift tide." Or, "Woe. Dangerous sharks out there." It sounds pretty lame today; but back then it would have made sense. Woe means "Watch out. Beware. Danger ahead." People knew they had better listen up anytime someone said, "Woe!"

¹⁹ A feast is made for laughter,
     and wine makes life merry,
     but money is the answer for
       everything.

²⁰ Do not revile the king even in your
       thoughts,
     or curse the rich in your bedroom,
     because a bird of the air may carry
       your words,
     and a bird on the wing may report
       what you say.

Bread Upon the Waters

11 Cast your bread upon the waters,
     for after many days you will find
       it again.
² Give portions to seven, yes to eight,
     for you do not know what disaster
       may come upon the land.

Soggy Slices

Huh?

Ecclesiastes 11:1
We use slang today; so did the writers of the Bible. Their slang made sense to them but sometimes seems kind of weird to us. Why would anyone want to throw bread into the ocean and then expect to find it again? In the days of King Solomon, throwing bread into the sea meant being adventurous and risking everything you had. God would honor that risk and take care of all your needs, including your food.

³ If clouds are full of water,
     they pour rain upon the earth.
Whether a tree falls to the south or to
       the north,
     in the place where it falls, there will
       it lie.
⁴ Whoever watches the wind will not
       plant;
     whoever looks at the clouds will not
       reap.

⁵ As you do not know the path of the
       wind,
     or how the body is formed*ᵃ* in a
       mother's womb,
so you cannot understand the work of
       God,
     the Maker of all things.

⁶ Sow your seed in the morning,
     and at evening let not your hands
       be idle,
for you do not know which will
       succeed,
     whether this or that,
     or whether both will do equally
       well.

Remember Your Creator While Young

⁷ Light is sweet,
     and it pleases the eyes to see the
       sun.
⁸ However many years a man may live,
     let him enjoy them all.
But let him remember the days of
       darkness,
     for they will be many.
     Everything to come is meaningless.

⁹ Be happy, young man, while you are
       young,
     and let your heart give you joy in
       the days of your youth.
Follow the ways of your heart
     and whatever your eyes see,
but know that for all these things
       God will bring you to judgment.
¹⁰ So then, banish anxiety from your
       heart
     and cast off the troubles of your
       body,
for youth and vigor are
       meaningless.

ᵃ 5 Or know how life (or the spirit) / enters the body being formed

12 Remember your Creator
in the days of your youth,
before the days of trouble come
and the years approach when you
will say,
"I find no pleasure in them"—
² before the sun and the light
and the moon and the stars grow
dark,
and the clouds return after the
rain;
³ when the keepers of the house
tremble,
and the strong men stoop,
when the grinders cease because they
are few,
and those looking through the
windows grow dim;
⁴ when the doors to the street are
closed
and the sound of grinding fades;

when men rise up at the sound of birds,
but all their songs grow faint;
⁵ when men are afraid of heights
and of dangers in the streets;
when the almond tree blossoms
and the grasshopper drags himself
along
and desire no longer is stirred.
Then man goes to his eternal home
and mourners go about the streets.

⁶ Remember him—before the silver cord
is severed,
or the golden bowl is broken;
before the pitcher is shattered at the
spring,
or the wheel broken at the well,
⁷ and the dust returns to the ground it
came from,
and the spirit returns to God who
gave it.

Week end.

Good Friends, Bad Friends

Read Proverbs 12:26 (page 746)

This week Stacy, Susanna and Chris each mentioned how important friend-ship is. Finding and keeping good friends is important now and always. Good friends are difficult to find and keep for _anyone_, regardless of their age.

What's a good friend? It's simple. A good friend is someone you can trust to tell you the truth, even when you don't want to hear it. A good friend likes you, likes being around you and is loyal to you. Jesus knew how to be a good friend. He called his disciples friends.

What is a bad friend? It's simple. A bad friend is a friend you can't trust. A bad friend is someone who doesn't respect what matters to you. A bad friend is someone who tries to get you to do things he or she knows you don't believe in. Here's the deal: It's better to have no friends than have friends who don't care what happens to you.

So keep looking for friends. But the writer of Proverbs warns you to be careful! Not all friendships are good for you. Uh . . . remember Judas?

What about You?

❶ Who is one of your good friends and why?

❷ Write a letter to this friend, telling him or her why you appreciate your friendship.

❸ Ask God to show you how to be a better friend.

Turn to page 790 for your next devotion.

Shattered and Snuffed

Huh?

Ecclesiastes 12:6

Before the days of electricity and light bulbs, some hanging lamps were made of candles hung by a silver cord and partly covered with a golden bowl. If even one link of the silver cord snapped, the beautiful bowl would drop and shatter into a zillion pieces. The candle would be snuffed out. Just like the lamp, life is fragile and can end in an instant. Try to appreciate every moment of every day.

[8] "Meaningless! Meaningless!" says the Teacher.[a]
"Everything is meaningless!"

The Conclusion of the Matter

[9] Not only was the Teacher wise, but also he imparted knowledge to the people. He pondered and searched out and set in order many proverbs. [10] The Teacher searched to find just the right words, and what he wrote was upright and true.

[11] The words of the wise are like goads, their collected sayings like firmly embedded nails—given by one Shepherd. [12] Be warned, my son, of anything in addition to them.

Of making many books there is no end, and much study wearies the body.

[13] Now all has been heard;
here is the conclusion of the matter:
Fear God and keep his commandments,
for this is the whole duty of man.
[14] For God will bring every deed into judgment,
including every hidden thing,
whether it is good or evil.

[a]8 Or *the leader of the assembly*; also in verses 9 and 10

❸ Ask God to show you how to be a better friend.

Turn to page 780 for your next devotion.

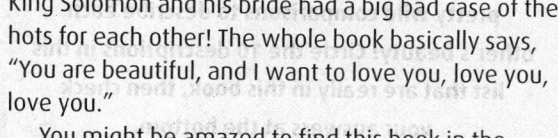

Song of Songs

START

King Solomon and his bride had a big bad case of the hots for each other! The whole book basically says, "You are beautiful, and I want to love you, love you, love you."

You might be amazed to find this book in the Bible—it sure is different from the other 65. But it's a fantastic, behind-the-scenes glimpse at the passionate love of 2 people about to get married.

This book has one mega huge lesson for you, it's this: Sex is good! God made it! When they're part of a marriage commitment, as God designed them, sex and love and desire and longings are gifts to be enjoyed. Bummer that our world has bought the "sex outside of marriage is fine" lie. What a way to wreck a great thing!

By the way, try not to giggle if you read this book during a church service!

CAST OF Characters

Solomon
(SAHL-uh-mun)
King David's son. Remember, he's the one who built the temple. In this book (written by none other than Solomon), Solomon's the bridegroom. His speaking parts are labeled "Lover."

The Young Woman
The bride—just about to marry the king. Her speaking parts are labeled "Beloved."

Friends of the Young Woman
This being a song-poem, these are kind of like the back-up singers. They're the female friends of the bride. Their speaking/singing parts are labeled "Friends."

Brothers of the Bride
They've got an itty-bitty part in chapter 8 and are also listed as "Friends."

What's UP with That?

Solomon and his love-muffin use some pretty wild comparisons to describe each other's beauty! Circle the 10 descriptions in this list that are really in this book, then check your answers at the bottom.

1. Your waist is like a pile of wheat.
2. Your teeth are as beautiful as mini-marshmallows.
3. Your hair is like squirt-cheese.
4. You smell like a home-cooked meal.
5. Your nose is like a tower.
6. Your teeth! Wow! You don't have any big gaping holes!
7. Your wrists are like, I don't know, nice wrists.
8. Your belly-button is like a wine glass.
9. Your breasts are, um, like two baby deer.
10. Your arms are like bendy-straws.
11. Your hair is like a bunch of goats.
12. Your tongue is like an eel.
13. Your cheeks are like huge spice racks.
14. Your lips are like red licorice.
15. Your eyes are like doves washed in milk.
16. Your neck is like a tower with a bunch of shields hanging on it.
17. Your forehead is like the State of Kansas.
18. You look like a tree.

answers: 1(7:2), 5(7:4), 6(4:2), 8(7:2), 9(4:5), 11(4:1), 13(5:13), 15(5:12), 16(4:4), 18(5:15)

Snap Shots

- I love you; let's get married *(chapters 1—3)*
- I love you; let me describe you *(chapter 4)*
- I love you, but I had a bad dream—then I described you *(chapter 5)*
- More describing *(chapters 6—7)*
- Some family stuff and some final lovey-dovey stuff *(chapter 8)*

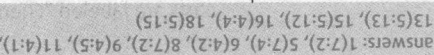

1 Solomon's Song of Songs.

Beloved[a]

[2] Let him kiss me with the kisses of his
    mouth—
  for your love is more delightful
    than wine.
[3] Pleasing is the fragrance of your
    perfumes;
  your name is like perfume poured
    out.
  No wonder the maidens love you!
[4] Take me away with you—let us hurry!
  Let the king bring me into his
    chambers.

Friends

  We rejoice and delight in you[b];
  we will praise your love more than
    wine.

Beloved

  How right they are to adore you!

[5] Dark am I, yet lovely,
  O daughters of Jerusalem,
  dark like the tents of Kedar,
  like the tent curtains of Solomon.[c]
[6] Do not stare at me because I am dark,
  because I am darkened by the sun.
  My mother's sons were angry with me
  and made me take care of the
    vineyards;
  my own vineyard I have neglected.
[7] Tell me, you whom I love, where you
    graze your flock
  and where you rest your sheep at
    midday.
  Why should I be like a veiled woman
  beside the flocks of your friends?

Friends

[8] If you do not know, most beautiful of
    women,
  follow the tracks of the sheep
  and graze your young goats
  by the tents of the shepherds.

Lover

[9] I liken you, my darling, to a mare
  harnessed to one of the chariots of
    Pharaoh.
[10] Your cheeks are beautiful with
    earrings,

  your neck with strings of jewels.
[11] We will make you earrings of gold,
  studded with silver.

Beloved

[12] While the king was at his table,
  my perfume spread its fragrance.
[13] My lover is to me a sachet of myrrh
  resting between my breasts.
[14] My lover is to me a cluster of henna
    blossoms
  from the vineyards of En Gedi.

Lover

[15] How beautiful you are, my darling!
  Oh, how beautiful!
  Your eyes are doves.

Beloved

[16] How handsome you are, my lover!
  Oh, how charming!
  And our bed is verdant.

Lover

[17] The beams of our house are cedars;
  our rafters are firs.

Beloved[d]

2 I am a rose[e] of Sharon,
  a lily of the valleys.

Lover

[2] Like a lily among thorns
  is my darling among the maidens.

Beloved

[3] Like an apple tree among the trees of
    the forest
  is my lover among the young men.
  I delight to sit in his shade,
  and his fruit is sweet to my taste.
[4] He has taken me to the banquet hall,
  and his banner over me is love.
[5] Strengthen me with raisins,
  refresh me with apples,
  for I am faint with love.
[6] His left arm is under my head,

[a] Primarily on the basis of the gender of the Hebrew
pronouns used, male and female speakers are
indicated in the margins by the captions *Lover* and
Beloved respectively. The words of others are marked
Friends. In some instances the divisions and their
captions are debatable.   [b] 4 The Hebrew is masculine
singular.   [c] Or *Salma*   [d] 1 Or *Lover*   [e] 1 Possibly a
member of the crocus family

Fly the Flag, Baby

Huh?

Song of Songs 2:4

A banner is a sign that's huge in size so everyone can see it. When Solomon's beloved says that the "banner" Solomon flies over her is love, imagine a gigantic flag waving in the air saying, "I love you, baby!" Like Solomon did for his beloved, God flies his flag of love over us.

and his right arm embraces me.
⁷Daughters of Jerusalem, I charge you
  by the gazelles and by the does of
  the field:

Do not arouse or awaken love
  until it so desires.

⁸Listen! My lover!
  Look! Here he comes,
leaping across the mountains,
  bounding over the hills.
⁹My lover is like a gazelle or a young
  stag.
Look! There he stands behind our
  wall,
gazing through the windows,
  peering through the lattice.
¹⁰My lover spoke and said to me,
  "Arise, my darling,
  my beautiful one, and come with
    me.
¹¹See! The winter is past;
  the rains are over and gone.
¹²Flowers appear on the earth;
  the season of singing has come,

Monday

The Right Time

Read Song of Songs 2:7

Recently this boy asked me to be his girlfriend. I told him no, because I think I'm too young to get into that kind of thing. And my mom doesn't want me to date until I'm 16 anyway. I knew it just wasn't the right time.

It's important to realize that love isn't something to play around with. This verse in Song of Songs makes that clear when it says, "Do not arouse or awaken love until it so desires." We shouldn't run into a dating relationship simply because everyone else thinks it's OK. God wants us to wait for the right person, not because he doesn't want us to have a good time but because he wants us to have the *best* time.

Because God cares about us so deeply, he wants us to save romantic love for a relationship he would be proud of. We don't know when or if that will happen, but we can trust God to take care of us in his way and in his time.

❶ Think about a time in your life when you had to wait a long time for something you were really excited about. When you finally had the experience, how did the waiting make it even better? Think of waiting for real love the same way.

❷ If you haven't already, talk to your parents about their rules for dating. Write them down, in the form of a contract, and then have everyone sign it. Keep it in a safe place in case you need to look at it later.

❸ Remember, God sees the big picture of your life. Ask him to help you be patient while you wait for him to bring true love into your life.

Turn to page 795 for your next devotion.

the cooing of doves
  is heard in our land.
¹³ The fig tree forms its early fruit;
  the blossoming vines spread their
    fragrance.
Arise, come, my darling;
  my beautiful one, come with me."

Lover

¹⁴ My dove in the clefts of the rock,
  in the hiding places on the
    mountainside,
show me your face,
  let me hear your voice;
for your voice is sweet,
  and your face is lovely.
¹⁵ Catch for us the foxes,
  the little foxes
that ruin the vineyards,
  our vineyards that are in bloom.

Beloved

¹⁶ My lover is mine and I am his;
  he browses among the lilies.
¹⁷ Until the day breaks
  and the shadows flee,
turn, my lover,
  and be like a gazelle
or like a young stag
  on the rugged hills.ᵃ

3 All night long on my bed
  I looked for the one my heart loves;
  I looked for him but did not find
    him.
² I will get up now and go about the
    city,
  through its streets and squares;
I will search for the one my heart
    loves.
  So I looked for him but did not find
    him.
³ The watchmen found me
  as they made their rounds in the
    city.
  "Have you seen the one my heart
    loves?"
⁴ Scarcely had I passed them
  when I found the one my heart
    loves.
I held him and would not let him go
  till I had brought him to my
    mother's house,
  to the room of the one who
    conceived me.

⁵ Daughters of Jerusalem, I charge you
  by the gazelles and by the does of
    the field:
Do not arouse or awaken love
  until it so desires.

⁶ Who is this coming up from the desert
  like a column of smoke,
perfumed with myrrh and incense
  made from all the spices of the
    merchant?
⁷ Look! It is Solomon's carriage,
  escorted by sixty warriors,
  the noblest of Israel,
⁸ all of them wearing the sword,
  all experienced in battle,
each with his sword at his side,
  prepared for the terrors of the night.
⁹ King Solomon made for himself the
    carriage;
  he made it of wood from Lebanon.
¹⁰ Its posts he made of silver,
  its base of gold.
Its seat was upholstered with purple,
  its interior lovingly inlaid
  byᵇ the daughters of Jerusalem.
¹¹ Come out, you daughters of Zion,
  and look at King Solomon wearing
    the crown,
  the crown with which his mother
    crowned him
on the day of his wedding,
  the day his heart rejoiced.

Lover

4 How beautiful you are, my darling!
  Oh, how beautiful!
  Your eyes behind your veil are doves.
Your hair is like a flock of goats
  descending from Mount Gilead.
² Your teeth are like a flock of sheep
    just shorn,
  coming up from the washing.
Each has its twin;
  not one of them is alone.
³ Your lips are like a scarlet ribbon;
  your mouth is lovely.
Your temples behind your veil
  are like the halves of a
    pomegranate.
⁴ Your neck is like the tower of David,
  built with eleganceᶜ;

ᵃ17 Or the hills of Bether   ᵇ10 Or its inlaid interior
a gift of love / from   ᶜ4 The meaning of the Hebrew
for this word is uncertain.

on it hang a thousand shields,
   all of them shields of warriors.
⁵ Your two breasts are like two
      fawns,
   like twin fawns of a gazelle
   that browse among the lilies.
⁶ Until the day breaks
   and the shadows flee,
I will go to the mountain of myrrh
   and to the hill of incense.
⁷ All beautiful you are, my darling;
   there is no flaw in you.

⁸ Come with me from Lebanon, my
      bride,
   come with me from Lebanon.
Descend from the crest of Amana,
   from the top of Senir, the summit of
      Hermon,
from the lions' dens

and the mountain haunts of the
      leopards.
⁹ You have stolen my heart, my sister,
      my bride;
   you have stolen my heart
with one glance of your eyes,
   with one jewel of your necklace.
¹⁰ How delightful is your love, my sister,
      my bride!
   How much more pleasing is your
      love than wine,
   and the fragrance of your perfume
      than any spice!
¹¹ Your lips drop sweetness as the
      honeycomb, my bride;
   milk and honey are under your
      tongue.
   The fragrance of your garments is
      like that of Lebanon.
¹² You are a garden locked up, my sister,
      my bride;
   you are a spring enclosed, a sealed
      fountain.
¹³ Your plants are an orchard of
      pomegranates
   with choice fruits,
   with henna and nard,
¹⁴   nard and saffron,
   calamus and cinnamon,
   with every kind of incense tree,
   with myrrh and aloes
   and all the finest spices.
¹⁵ You are*ᵃ* a garden fountain,
   a well of flowing water
   streaming down from Lebanon.

Beloved

¹⁶ Awake, north wind,
   and come, south wind!
Blow on my garden,
   that its fragrance may spread
      abroad.
Let my lover come into his garden
   and taste its choice fruits.

Lover

5 I have come into my garden, my
      sister, my bride;
   I have gathered my myrrh with my
      spice.
I have eaten my honeycomb and my
      honey;
   I have drunk my wine and my milk.

ᵃ *15* Or *I am* (spoken by the *Beloved*)

Friends

Eat, O friends, and drink;
　drink your fill, O lovers.

Beloved

[2] I slept but my heart was awake.
　Listen! My lover is knocking:
"Open to me, my sister, my darling,
　my dove, my flawless one.
My head is drenched with dew,
　my hair with the dampness of the
　　night."
[3] I have taken off my robe—
　must I put it on again?
I have washed my feet—
　must I soil them again?
[4] My lover thrust his hand through the
　　latch-opening;
　my heart began to pound for him.
[5] I arose to open for my lover,
　and my hands dripped with myrrh,
my fingers with flowing myrrh,
　on the handles of the lock.
[6] I opened for my lover,
　but my lover had left; he was
　　gone.
　My heart sank at his departure.[a]
I looked for him but did not find him.
I called him but he did not answer.
[7] The watchmen found me
　as they made their rounds in the
　　city.
They beat me, they bruised me;
　they took away my cloak,
　those watchmen of the walls!
[8] O daughters of Jerusalem, I charge
　　you—
　if you find my lover,
what will you tell him?
　Tell him I am faint with love.

Friends

[9] How is your beloved better than
　　others,
　most beautiful of women?
How is your beloved better than
　　others,
　that you charge us so?

Beloved

[10] My lover is radiant and ruddy,
　outstanding among ten thousand.
[11] His head is purest gold;
　his hair is wavy

and black as a raven.
[12] His eyes are like doves
　by the water streams,
washed in milk,
　mounted like jewels.
[13] His cheeks are like beds of spice
　yielding perfume.
His lips are like lilies
　dripping with myrrh.
[14] His arms are rods of gold
　set with chrysolite.
His body is like polished ivory
　decorated with sapphires.[b]
[15] His legs are pillars of marble
　set on bases of pure gold.
His appearance is like Lebanon,
　choice as its cedars.
[16] His mouth is sweetness itself;
　he is altogether lovely.
This is my lover, this my friend,
　O daughters of Jerusalem.

Friends

6 Where has your lover gone,
　most beautiful of women?
Which way did your lover turn,
　that we may look for him with you?

Beloved

[2] My lover has gone down to his garden,
　to the beds of spices,
to browse in the gardens
　and to gather lilies.
[3] I am my lover's and my lover is mine;
　he browses among the lilies.

Lover

[4] You are beautiful, my darling, as
　　Tirzah,
　lovely as Jerusalem,
　majestic as troops with banners.
[5] Turn your eyes from me;
　they overwhelm me.
Your hair is like a flock of goats
　descending from Gilead.
[6] Your teeth are like a flock of sheep
　coming up from the washing.
Each has its twin,
　not one of them is alone.
[7] Your temples behind your veil
　are like the halves of a
　　pomegranate.

---

[a] 6 Or *heart had gone out to him when he spoke*
[b] 14 Or *lapis lazuli*

[8] Sixty queens there may be,
    and eighty concubines,
    and virgins beyond number;
[9] but my dove, my perfect one, is
    unique,
    the only daughter of her mother,
    the favorite of the one who bore
    her.
The maidens saw her and called her
    blessed;
    the queens and concubines praised
    her.

Friends

[10] Who is this that appears like the
    dawn,
    fair as the moon, bright as the sun,
    majestic as the stars in procession?

Lover

[11] I went down to the grove of nut trees
    to look at the new growth in the
    valley,
    to see if the vines had budded
    or the pomegranates were in bloom.
[12] Before I realized it,
    my desire set me among the royal
    chariots of my people.[a]

Friends

[13] Come back, come back,
    O Shulammite;
    come back, come back, that we may
    gaze on you!

Lover

Why would you gaze on the
    Shulammite
    as on the dance of Mahanaim?

7 How beautiful your sandaled feet,
    O prince's daughter!
Your graceful legs are like jewels,
    the work of a craftsman's hands.
[2] Your navel is a rounded goblet
    that never lacks blended wine.
Your waist is a mound of wheat
    encircled by lilies.
[3] Your breasts are like two fawns,
    twins of a gazelle.
[4] Your neck is like an ivory tower.
Your eyes are the pools of Heshbon
    by the gate of Bath Rabbim.
Your nose is like the tower of Lebanon
    looking toward Damascus.

[5] Your head crowns you like Mount
    Carmel.
    Your hair is like royal tapestry;
    the king is held captive by its
    tresses.
[6] How beautiful you are and how
    pleasing,
    O love, with your delights!
[7] Your stature is like that of the palm,
    and your breasts like clusters of
    fruit.
[8] I said, "I will climb the palm tree;
    I will take hold of its fruit."
May your breasts be like the clusters
    of the vine,
    the fragrance of your breath like
    apples,
[9]   and your mouth like the best wine.

Beloved

May the wine go straight to my lover,
    flowing gently over lips and teeth.[b]
[10] I belong to my lover,
    and his desire is for me.
[11] Come, my lover, let us go to the
    countryside,
    let us spend the night in the
    villages.[c]
[12] Let us go early to the vineyards
    to see if the vines have budded,
    if their blossoms have opened,
    and if the pomegranates are in
    bloom—
    there I will give you my love.
[13] The mandrakes send out their
    fragrance,
    and at our door is every delicacy,
both new and old,
    that I have stored up for you, my
    lover.

8 If only you were to me like a
    brother,
    who was nursed at my mother's
    breasts!
Then, if I found you outside,
    I would kiss you,
    and no one would despise me.
[2] I would lead you
    and bring you to my mother's
    house—

---

[a] 12 Or *among the chariots of Amminadab; or
among the chariots of the people of the prince*
[b] 9 Septuagint, Aquila, Vulgate and Syriac; Hebrew
lips of sleepers   [c] 11 Or *henna bushes*

she who has taught me.
I would give you spiced wine to drink,
   the nectar of my pomegranates.
³His left arm is under my head
   and his right arm embraces me.
⁴Daughters of Jerusalem, I charge you:
   Do not arouse or awaken love
      until it so desires.

Friends

⁵Who is this coming up from the desert
   leaning on her lover?

Beloved

Under the apple tree I roused you;
   there your mother conceived you,
   there she who was in labor gave
      you birth.
⁶Place me like a seal over your heart,
   like a seal on your arm;
for love is as strong as death,
   its jealousy*ᵃ* unyielding as the
      grave.*ᵇ*
It burns like blazing fire,
   like a mighty flame.*ᶜ*
⁷Many waters cannot quench love;
   rivers cannot wash it away.
If one were to give
   all the wealth of his house for love,
   it*ᵈ* would be utterly scorned.

Forever Love

Huh?

Song of Songs 8:6

Have you ever heard of Romeo and Juliet? The major-bummer ending to their story is that they both died because they loved each other so much. This verse is kind of like that. The love between these 2 is really, *really* strong—even as strong as death. It's final. When 2 people truly love each other, that's it. It's a done deal. No one else can do anything about it.

Friends

⁸We have a young sister,
   and her breasts are not yet grown.
What shall we do for our sister
   for the day she is spoken for?
⁹If she is a wall,
   we will build towers of silver on her.
If she is a door,
   we will enclose her with panels of
      cedar.

ᵃ6 Or ardor   ᵇ6 Hebrew Sheol   ᶜ6 Or / like the very flame of the LORD   ᵈ7 Or he

Tuesday

True Love

Read Song of Songs 8:6–7

I suppose it's pretty normal for a junior high girl to think about love. These verses describe the kind of love I hope to find one day, because it's the real thing.

Sometimes I think love is taken so lightly. People talk about being in love with someone, then 2 weeks later, they're in love with someone else. But real love, the kind King Solomon and his beloved had, is a strong commitment. It's a solemn promise that lasts forever, not a few weeks. It's the kind of love God has for us. It can never die.

Stacey age 13

What about You?

❶ How is lasting love different from the "2-week" kind?

❷ Think of a married couple who really love each other. Watch them carefully and list some of the ways they show their love for each other.

❸ Ask God to help you wait patiently for real love.

Turn to page 800 for your next devotion.

Beloved

¹⁰I am a wall,
  and my breasts are like towers.
Thus I have become in his eyes
  like one bringing contentment.
¹¹Solomon had a vineyard in Baal
    Hamon;
  he let out his vineyard to tenants.
Each was to bring for its fruit
  a thousand shekels*ᵃ* of silver.
¹²But my own vineyard is mine to give;
  the thousand shekels are for you,
    O Solomon,
  and two hundred*ᵇ* are for those who
    tend its fruit.

Lover

¹³You who dwell in the gardens
  with friends in attendance,
  let me hear your voice!

Beloved

¹⁴Come away, my lover,
  and be like a gazelle
or like a young stag
  on the spice-laden
    mountains.

ᵃ11 That is, about 25 pounds (about 11.5 kilograms); also in verse 12   *ᵇ12* That is, about 5 pounds (about 2.3 kilograms)

Isaiah

START

Prophets were people chosen by God to speak for him. And Isaiah was a super-mega-prophet—one of the greatest prophets ever. If they had dictionaries in Jerusalem in 700 B.C. and you looked up the word *prophet*, it would talk about Isaiah!

Isaiah was God's megaphone to the people of Judah (remember, the country split in 2: Israel became the northern part, and Judah the southern part).

And while Isaiah did a lot of preaching about turning from sin, he also made some major prophetic predictions—even about Jesus Christ!

Even the structure of the book is prophetic in some ways: It has 66 chapters, just like the Bible has 66 books. The first section of 39 chapters starts with Israel's sin. The first 39 books of the Bible (the Old Testament) begin with Adam and Eve's sin. The last 27 chapters of Isaiah offer forgiveness and hope to everyone, just like the last 27 books of the Bible (the New Testament) offer Jesus Christ, our only source of forgiveness and hope, to the whole world. Isaiah wrote this hundreds of years before the New Testament books were even written. Cool, huh?

Cast OF Characters

Isaiah (eye-ZAY-uh)
God's prophet (spokesperson) to Judah for almost 60 years! He wrote this book and is the main character, besides God.

God
God plays a major role in this book. Since it's prophecy, these are words God gave Isaiah to say and write.

The People of Judah
They were the audience. Isaiah lived in Jerusalem and spoke, on God's behalf, to all the people of the country.

Jesus
Nope, his name never actually shows up in this book, but he's in here—all over the place! Isaiah prophesies about the coming Messiah: Jesus!

Uzziah, Jotham, Ahaz, Hezekiah and Manasseh
The 5 kings of Judah while Isaiah was God's prophet. A mixed bag: Uzziah started well but blew it, Jotham was OK, Ahaz didn't honor God, Hezekiah "did what was right" in God's eyes, but Manasseh "did evil in the eyes of the LORD." Seems like they couldn't get 2 good kings in a row!

(uz-ZY-uh, JOH-thum, AY-haz, hez-uh-KY-uh and muh-NASS-uh)

(SHEEahr-JAY-shub)

**Shear-Jashub and
Maher-Shalal-Hash-Baz**

(MAYher-SHAL-al-HASH-baz)

These 2 guys with long, crazy names are Isaiah's sons. The first one's name means "A remnant will return." The second one's name means "Quick to the plunder, swift to the spoil." Nice names, huh?

What's UP with That?

Jesus in the OT!

Jesus doesn't show up in a human body until the New Testament. But Isaiah's got a ton of prophecies about Jesus.

In the list below, pick out 10 real prophecies Isaiah made about Jesus—the things Isaiah predicted about Jesus (that were right on target!).

1. The Messiah will come from David's birth-line.

2. The son will be called: Wonderful Counselor, Mighty God, Everlasting Father, Prince of Peace.

3. Jesus' last name will be Christ.

4. A virgin will become pregnant and give birth to a son.

5. Someday there will be key chains, breath mints, posters and tons of other stuff about Jesus.

6. The Messiah will get disfigured (physically hurt).

7. The Son born to the virgin will be "Immanuel"—which means "God with us."

8. The Messiah will be a cornerstone, a strong foundation for those who believe.

9. The Messiah will have groovy, long hair.

10. Jesus will be taken away and judged.

11. The Messiah will hardly ever say, "Um."

12. Jesus will make kitchen cabinets before starting his public ministry.

13. A son will be given to you and me.

14. The Messiah will be called Fred.

15. The Messiah's blood will offer forgiveness.

16. The Messiah will be hated and rejected by many people.

Snap shots

- **Shape up!**
  (chapters 1—6)

- **The Savior to come**
  (chapters 7—12)

- **Other nations that will be toast**
  (chapters 13—23)

- **Judgment . . . and joy, part 1**
  (chapters 24—27)

- **Those poor unbelievers**
  (chapters 28—33)

- **Judgment . . . and joy, part 2**
  (chapters 34—35)

- **Let me tell ya 'bout Hezzy**
  (chapters 36—39)

- **Need comfort?**
  (chapters 40—48)

- **The Savior to come, part 2**
  (chapters 49—57)

- **A piece of peace**
  (chapters 58—66)

answers: 1(9:7), 2(9:6), 4(7:14), 6(53:5), 7(7:14), 8(28:16), 10(53:8), 13(9:6), 15(53:4–6), 16(53:8)

1 The vision concerning Judah and Jerusalem that Isaiah son of Amoz saw during the reigns of Uzziah, Jotham, Ahaz and Hezekiah, kings of Judah.

A Rebellious Nation

²Hear, O heavens! Listen, O earth!
　For the LORD has spoken:
"I reared children and brought them
　　up,
　but they have rebelled against me.
³The ox knows his master,
　the donkey his owner's manger,
but Israel does not know,
　my people do not understand."

⁴Ah, sinful nation,
　a people loaded with guilt,
a brood of evildoers,
　children given to corruption!
They have forsaken the LORD;
　they have spurned the Holy One of
　　Israel
　and turned their backs on him.

⁵Why should you be beaten anymore?
　Why do you persist in rebellion?
Your whole head is injured,
　your whole heart afflicted.
⁶From the sole of your foot to the top
　　of your head
　there is no soundness—
only wounds and welts
　and open sores,
not cleansed or bandaged
　or soothed with oil.

⁷Your country is desolate,
　your cities burned with fire;
your fields are being stripped by
　　foreigners
　right before you,
　laid waste as when overthrown by
　　strangers.
⁸The Daughter of Zion is left
　like a shelter in a vineyard,
like a hut in a field of melons,
　like a city under siege.
⁹Unless the LORD Almighty
　had left us some survivors,
we would have become like Sodom,
　we would have been like Gomorrah.

¹⁰Hear the word of the LORD,
　you rulers of Sodom;
listen to the law of our God,
　you people of Gomorrah!

Pass the Salt, Please

Huh?

Isaiah 1:9

Remember back in Genesis 19 when the cities of Sodom and Gomorrah were toasted for their totally constant sinning against God? Remember when Lot's wife looked back at the cities, and she turned into a pillar of salt? Well, Isaiah is trying to tell his people that they had become like the people of Sodom and Gomorrah—yep, super-duper sinners who kept rebelling against God. Talk about a terrible thing to be compared to!

¹¹"The multitude of your sacrifices—
　what are they to me?" says the
　　LORD.
"I have more than enough of burnt
　　offerings,
　of rams and the fat of fattened
　　animals;
I have no pleasure
　in the blood of bulls and lambs and
　　goats.
¹²When you come to appear before me,
　who has asked this of you,
　this trampling of my courts?
¹³Stop bringing meaningless offerings!
　Your incense is detestable to me.
New Moons, Sabbaths and
　　convocations—
　I cannot bear your evil assemblies.
¹⁴Your New Moon festivals and your
　　appointed feasts
　my soul hates.
They have become a burden to me;
　I am weary of bearing them.
¹⁵When you spread out your hands in
　　prayer,
　I will hide my eyes from you;
even if you offer many prayers,
　I will not listen.
Your hands are full of blood;
¹⁶　wash and make yourselves clean.
Take your evil deeds
　out of my sight!
Stop doing wrong,
¹⁷　learn to do right!

Seek justice,
    encourage the oppressed.[a]
Defend the cause of the fatherless,
    plead the case of the widow.

[18] "Come now, let us reason together,"
    says the LORD.
"Though your sins are like scarlet,
    they shall be as white as snow;
though they are red as crimson,
    they shall be like wool.
[19] If you are willing and obedient,
    you will eat the best from the land;
[20] but if you resist and rebel,
    you will be devoured by the sword."
            For the mouth of the LORD
                has spoken.

[21] See how the faithful city
    has become a harlot!
She once was full of justice;
    righteousness used to dwell in her—
    but now murderers!
[22] Your silver has become dross,
    your choice wine is diluted with
        water.

[23] Your rulers are rebels,
    companions of thieves;
they all love bribes
    and chase after gifts.
They do not defend the cause of the
        fatherless;
    the widow's case does not come
        before them.
[24] Therefore the Lord, the LORD Almighty,
    the Mighty One of Israel, declares:
"Ah, I will get relief from my foes
    and avenge myself on my enemies.
[25] I will turn my hand against you;
    I will thoroughly purge away your
        dross
    and remove all your impurities.
[26] I will restore your judges as in days of
        old,
    your counselors as at the beginning.
Afterward you will be called
    the City of Righteousness,
    the Faithful City."

[a]17 Or / rebuke the oppressor

Wednesday

The Big Clean-up
Read Isaiah 1:18

When I think of someone who's "dirty," I think of a garbage collector, or a little kid playing in mud, or maybe someone in a really poor country where people don't have showers. But inside, I'm as dirty as the dirtiest person on the planet. Or at least I would be if God hadn't cleaned me up.

My sins—the things that make me dirty inside—are all washed away because of my faith in Jesus Christ. I don't have to carry them anymore, because he carried them all with him to the cross.

This is one of my favorite verses in the whole Bible. It reminds me of everything Jesus did for me, and it reminds me to thank God for his forgiveness. My life would be a mess if I was stuck with my sins. But instead I'm free, clean, happy and forgiven.

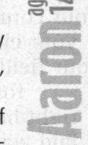
Aaron age 14

What about You?

❶ Imagine what life would be like if no one ever said "I forgive you." Why is forgiveness so important in your relationship with God?

❷ Imagine rolling in a mud pit. What a mess! Think of all that mud as sin. Then imagine washing up and realizing how good it feels to be clean.

❸ Thank God for his forgiveness.

Turn to page 806 for your next devotion.

27 Zion will be redeemed with justice,
    her penitent ones with
        righteousness.
28 But rebels and sinners will both be
        broken,
    and those who forsake the LORD will
        perish.

29 "You will be ashamed because of the
        sacred oaks
    in which you have delighted;
  you will be disgraced because of the
        gardens
    that you have chosen.
30 You will be like an oak with fading
        leaves,
    like a garden without water.
31 The mighty man will become tinder
    and his work a spark;
  both will burn together,
    with no one to quench the fire."

The Mountain of the LORD

2 This is what Isaiah son of Amoz saw
    concerning Judah and Jerusalem:

God's Messenger Man

Huh?

Isaiah 2:1

Isaiah was a prophet. It was his job to stay
in close contact with God, so he could deliver messages from God to the people. In
those days, prophets were pretty interesting. When the passage says this is what
Isaiah "saw," it doesn't mean he was sitting on his porch, checking out the action
one day. It means that this is a prophecy,
or message from God, to be delivered to
the people of Israel. This is kind of like
when we say someone had a vision.

---

2 In the last days

the mountain of the LORD's temple will
        be established
    as chief among the mountains;
  it will be raised above the hills,
    and all nations will stream to it.

3 Many peoples will come and say,

"Come, let us go up to the mountain
        of the LORD,
    to the house of the God of Jacob.
  He will teach us his ways,
    so that we may walk in his paths."
  The law will go out from Zion,
    the word of the LORD from
        Jerusalem.
4 He will judge between the nations
    and will settle disputes for many
        peoples.
  They will beat their swords into
        plowshares
    and their spears into pruning hooks.
  Nation will not take up sword against
        nation,
    nor will they train for war anymore.

5 Come, O house of Jacob,
    let us walk in the light of the LORD.

The Day of the LORD

6 You have abandoned your people,
    the house of Jacob.
  They are full of superstitions from the
        East;
    they practice divination like the
        Philistines
  and clasp hands with pagans.
7 Their land is full of silver and gold;
    there is no end to their treasures.
  Their land is full of horses;
    there is no end to their chariots.
8 Their land is full of idols;
    they bow down to the work of their
        hands,
    to what their fingers have made.
9 So man will be brought low
    and mankind humbled—
    do not forgive them.[a]

10 Go into the rocks,
    hide in the ground
  from dread of the LORD
    and the splendor of his majesty!
11 The eyes of the arrogant man will be
        humbled
    and the pride of men brought low;
  the LORD alone will be exalted in that
        day.

12 The LORD Almighty has a day in store
    for all the proud and lofty,
    for all that is exalted

---

a 9 Or not raise them up

(and they will be humbled),

¹³ for all the cedars of Lebanon, tall and
lofty,
and all the oaks of Bashan,

¹⁴ for all the towering mountains
and all the high hills,

¹⁵ for every lofty tower
and every fortified wall,

¹⁶ for every trading ship[a]
and every stately vessel.

¹⁷ The arrogance of man will be brought
low
and the pride of men humbled;
the LORD alone will be exalted in that
day,

¹⁸ and the idols will totally disappear.

¹⁹ Men will flee to caves in the rocks
and to holes in the ground
from dread of the LORD
and the splendor of his majesty,
when he rises to shake the earth.

²⁰ In that day men will throw away
to the rodents and bats
their idols of silver and idols of gold,
which they made to worship.

²¹ They will flee to caverns in the rocks
and to the overhanging crags
from dread of the LORD
and the splendor of his majesty,
when he rises to shake the earth.

²² Stop trusting in man,
who has but a breath in his nostrils.
Of what account is he?

Judgment on Jerusalem and Judah

3 See now, the Lord,
the LORD Almighty,
is about to take from Jerusalem and
Judah
both supply and support:
all supplies of food and all supplies of
water,

² the hero and warrior,
the judge and prophet,
the soothsayer and elder,

³ the captain of fifty and man of rank,
the counselor, skilled craftsman and
clever enchanter.

⁴ I will make boys their officials;
mere children will govern them.

⁵ People will oppress each other—
man against man, neighbor against
neighbor.

The young will rise up against the old,
the base against the honorable.

⁶ A man will seize one of his brothers
at his father's home, and say,
"You have a cloak, you be our leader;
take charge of this heap of ruins!"

⁷ But in that day he will cry out,
"I have no remedy.
I have no food or clothing in my house;
do not make me the leader of the
people."

⁸ Jerusalem staggers,
Judah is falling;
their words and deeds are against the
LORD,
defying his glorious presence.

⁹ The look on their faces testifies
against them;
they parade their sin like Sodom;
they do not hide it.
Woe to them!
They have brought disaster upon
themselves.

¹⁰ Tell the righteous it will be well with
them,
for they will enjoy the fruit of their
deeds.

¹¹ Woe to the wicked! Disaster is upon
them!
They will be paid back for what their
hands have done.

¹² Youths oppress my people,
women rule over them.
O my people, your guides lead you
astray;
they turn you from the path.

¹³ The LORD takes his place in court;
he rises to judge the people.

¹⁴ The LORD enters into judgment
against the elders and leaders of his
people:
"It is you who have ruined my
vineyard;
the plunder from the poor is in your
houses.

¹⁵ What do you mean by crushing my
people
and grinding the faces of the poor?"
declares the Lord,
the LORD Almighty.

─────

ᵃ16 Hebrew *every ship of Tarshish*

16 The LORD says,
   "The women of Zion are haughty,
walking along with outstretched
      necks,
   flirting with their eyes,
tripping along with mincing steps,
   with ornaments jingling on their
      ankles.
17 Therefore the Lord will bring sores on
      the heads of the women of
      Zion;
   the LORD will make their scalps
      bald."

18 In that day the Lord will snatch away
their finery: the bangles and headbands
and crescent necklaces, 19 the earrings
and bracelets and veils, 20 the headdresses
and ankle chains and sashes, the perfume
bottles and charms, 21 the signet rings and
nose rings, 22 the fine robes and the capes
and cloaks, the purses 23 and mirrors, and
the linen garments and tiaras and
shawls.

24 Instead of fragrance there will be a
      stench;
   instead of a sash, a rope;
instead of well-dressed hair, baldness;
   instead of fine clothing, sackcloth;
   instead of beauty, branding.
25 Your men will fall by the sword,
   your warriors in battle.
26 The gates of Zion will lament and
      mourn;
   destitute, she will sit on the ground.

4 In that day seven women
   will take hold of one man
and say, "We will eat our own food
   and provide our own clothes;
only let us be called by your name.
   Take away our disgrace!"

The Branch of the LORD

2 In that day the Branch of the LORD
will be beautiful and glorious, and the
fruit of the land will be the pride and
glory of the survivors in Israel. 3 Those
who are left in Zion, who remain in Jerusalem, will be called holy, all who are recorded among the living in Jerusalem.
4 The Lord will wash away the filth of the
women of Zion; he will cleanse the
bloodstains from Jerusalem by a spirit[a]
of judgment and a spirit[a] of fire. 5 Then
the LORD will create over all of Mount

Zion and over those who assemble there
a cloud of smoke by day and a glow of
flaming fire by night; over all the glory
will be a canopy. 6 It will be a shelter and
shade from the heat of the day, and a refuge and hiding place from the storm and
rain.

The Song of the Vineyard

5 I will sing for the one I love
   a song about his vineyard:
My loved one had a vineyard
   on a fertile hillside.
2 He dug it up and cleared it of
      stones
   and planted it with the choicest
      vines.
He built a watchtower in it
   and cut out a winepress as well.
Then he looked for a crop of good
      grapes,
   but it yielded only bad fruit.

3 "Now you dwellers in Jerusalem and
      men of Judah,
   judge between me and my
      vineyard.
4 What more could have been done for
      my vineyard
   than I have done for it?
When I looked for good grapes,
   why did it yield only bad?
5 Now I will tell you
   what I am going to do to my
      vineyard:
I will take away its hedge,
   and it will be destroyed;
I will break down its wall,
   and it will be trampled.
6 I will make it a wasteland,
   neither pruned nor cultivated,
   and briers and thorns will grow
      there.
I will command the clouds
   not to rain on it."

7 The vineyard of the LORD Almighty
   is the house of Israel,
and the men of Judah
   are the garden of his delight.
And he looked for justice, but saw
      bloodshed;
   for righteousness, but heard cries of
      distress.

a 4 Or the Spirit

Woes and Judgments

8 Woe to you who add house to house
and join field to field
till no space is left
and you live alone in the land.

9 The Lord Almighty has declared in my hearing:

"Surely the great houses will become
desolate,
the fine mansions left without
occupants.
10 A ten-acre[a] vineyard will produce
only a bath[b] of wine,
a homer[c] of seed only an ephah[d] of
grain."

11 Woe to those who rise early in the
morning
to run after their drinks,
who stay up late at night
till they are inflamed with wine.
12 They have harps and lyres at their
banquets,
tambourines and flutes and wine,
but they have no regard for the deeds
of the Lord,
no respect for the work of his
hands.
13 Therefore my people will go into exile
for lack of understanding;
their men of rank will die of hunger
and their masses will be parched
with thirst.
14 Therefore the grave[e] enlarges its
appetite
and opens its mouth without limit;
into it will descend their nobles and
masses
with all their brawlers and revelers.
15 So man will be brought low
and mankind humbled,
the eyes of the arrogant humbled.
16 But the Lord Almighty will be exalted
by his justice,
and the holy God will show himself
holy by his righteousness.
17 Then sheep will graze as in their own
pasture;
lambs will feed[f] among the ruins of
the rich.
18 Woe to those who draw sin along with
cords of deceit,
and wickedness as with cart ropes,

19 to those who say, "Let God hurry,
let him hasten his work
so we may see it.
Let it approach,
let the plan of the Holy One of
Israel come,
so we may know it."

20 Woe to those who call evil good
and good evil,
who put darkness for light
and light for darkness,
who put bitter for sweet
and sweet for bitter.

21 Woe to those who are wise in their
own eyes
and clever in their own sight.

22 Woe to those who are heroes at
drinking wine
and champions at mixing drinks,
23 who acquit the guilty for a bribe,
but deny justice to the innocent.
24 Therefore, as tongues of fire lick up
straw
and as dry grass sinks down in the
flames,
so their roots will decay
and their flowers blow away like
dust;
for they have rejected the law of the
Lord Almighty
and spurned the word of the Holy
One of Israel.
25 Therefore the Lord's anger burns
against his people;
his hand is raised and he strikes
them down.
The mountains shake,
and the dead bodies are like refuse
in the streets.

Yet for all this, his anger is not turned
away,
his hand is still upraised.

26 He lifts up a banner for the distant
nations,
he whistles for those at the ends of
the earth.

a 10 Hebrew *ten-yoke*, that is, the land plowed by 10 yoke of oxen in one day   b 10 That is, probably about 6 gallons (about 22 liters)   c 10 That is, probably about 6 bushels (about 220 liters)   d 10 That is, probably about 3/5 bushel (about 22 liters)   e 14 Hebrew *Sheol*   f 17 Septuagint; Hebrew / *strangers will eat*

Here they come,
  swiftly and speedily!
²⁷ Not one of them grows tired or
    stumbles,
  not one slumbers or sleeps;
  not a belt is loosened at the waist,
    not a sandal thong is broken.
²⁸ Their arrows are sharp,
  all their bows are strung;
  their horses' hoofs seem like flint,
    their chariot wheels like a
    whirlwind.
²⁹ Their roar is like that of the lion,
  they roar like young lions;
  they growl as they seize their prey
    and carry it off with no one to
    rescue.
³⁰ In that day they will roar over it
  like the roaring of the sea.
And if one looks at the land,
  he will see darkness and distress;
  even the light will be darkened by
    the clouds.

Isaiah's Commission

6 In the year that King Uzziah died, I
saw the Lord seated on a throne,
high and exalted, and the train of his
robe filled the temple. ²Above him were
seraphs, each with six wings: With two
wings they covered their faces, with two
they covered their feet, and with two they
were flying. ³And they were calling to
one another:

"Holy, holy, holy is the LORD
    Almighty;
  the whole earth is full of his glory."

⁴At the sound of their voices the door-
posts and thresholds shook and the temple was filled with smoke.
  ⁵"Woe to me!" I cried. "I am ruined!
For I am a man of unclean lips, and I live
among a people of unclean lips, and my
eyes have seen the King, the LORD Almighty."
  ⁶Then one of the seraphs flew to me
with a live coal in his hand, which he had
taken with tongs from the altar. ⁷With it
he touched my mouth and said, "See, this
has touched your lips; your guilt is taken
away and your sin atoned for."
  ⁸Then I heard the voice of the Lord
saying, "Whom shall I send? And who
will go for us?"

Correct Me If I'm Wrong

Isaiah 6:7
The word *atone* means "to correct" or
"make payment for." When it's used in the
Bible, it explains how God has corrected or
made payment for all the junk we've done
wrong. We call that "junk" sin. God corrects
our sin and clears it away. This is the reason
why Jesus died on the cross—to correct our
sins by paying the bill.

And I said, "Here am I. Send me!"
  ⁹He said, "Go and tell this people:

" 'Be ever hearing, but never
    understanding;
  be ever seeing, but never
    perceiving.'
¹⁰ Make the heart of this people
    calloused;
  make their ears dull
  and close their eyes.^a
Otherwise they might see with their
    eyes,
  hear with their ears,
  understand with their hearts,
and turn and be healed."

  ¹¹Then I said, "For how long, O Lord?"
And he answered:

"Until the cities lie ruined
    and without inhabitant,
until the houses are left deserted
    and the fields ruined and ravaged,
¹² until the LORD has sent everyone far
    away
  and the land is utterly forsaken.
¹³ And though a tenth remains in the
    land,
  it will again be laid waste.
But as the terebinth and oak
  leave stumps when they are cut
    down,
  so the holy seed will be the stump
    in the land."

^a9,10 Hebrew; Septuagint *'You will be ever hearing,
but never understanding; / you will be ever seeing,
but never perceiving.' / ¹⁰This people's heart has
become calloused; / they hardly hear with their ears,
/ and they have closed their eyes*

The Sign of Immanuel

7 When Ahaz son of Jotham, the son of Uzziah, was king of Judah, King Rezin of Aram and Pekah son of Remaliah king of Israel marched up to fight against Jerusalem, but they could not overpower it.

²Now the house of David was told, "Aram has allied itself with*ᵃ* Ephraim"; so the hearts of Ahaz and his people were shaken, as the trees of the forest are shaken by the wind.

³Then the LORD said to Isaiah, "Go out, you and your son Shear-Jashub,*ᵇ* to meet Ahaz at the end of the aqueduct of the Upper Pool, on the road to the Washerman's Field. ⁴Say to him, 'Be careful, keep calm and don't be afraid. Do not lose heart because of these two smoldering stubs of firewood—because of the fierce anger of Rezin and Aram and of the son of Remaliah. ⁵Aram, Ephraim and Remaliah's son have plotted your

ruin, saying, ⁶"Let us invade Judah; let us tear it apart and divide it among ourselves, and make the son of Tabeel king over it." ⁷Yet this is what the Sovereign LORD says:

" 'It will not take place,
   it will not happen,
⁸for the head of Aram is Damascus,
   and the head of Damascus is only
      Rezin.
Within sixty-five years
   Ephraim will be too shattered to be
      a people.
⁹The head of Ephraim is Samaria,
   and the head of Samaria is only
      Remaliah's son.
If you do not stand firm in your faith,
   you will not stand at all.' "

¹⁰Again the LORD spoke to Ahaz, ¹¹"Ask the LORD your God for a sign, whether in

---

ᵃ2 Or has set up camp in   *ᵇ3 Shear-Jashub means a remnant will return.*

Thursday

Send Me!

Read Isaiah 6:8

On the last night of our youth retreat, our youth pastor opened the mike up to us and invited us to talk about what God had done in our lives. We all just sat there. I finally went up, hoping God would have something to say through me. As I opened my mouth, I felt God giving me the words to say. I ignored my fears about talking in front of people and found out that I have a gift for sharing God's Word with others. Now I'm a regular speaker at my school's Fellowship of Christian Students.

That experience showed me that anyone willing to say, "Lord, send me" will be sent. Everyone has gifts. And God, the Creator and Ruler of the universe, uses the gifts of ordinary people to do his work. What a privilege!

Be open to God's plans for you and tell him you want to be called. And hang on tight, because when God starts using you, you move fast!

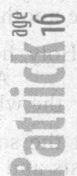
Patrick age 16

What about You?

❶ Why are we sometimes afraid to let God use us? How can you get over your fears and get ready to be used by God?

❷ Ask your youth leader how you can become more involved in your youth group and church. Maybe you can offer to lead a prayer group, help with the church nursery or bring cookies to your group meetings. Find a way to use your gifts.

❸ Tell God if you're ready to go wherever he leads you.

Turn to page 809 for your next devotion.

the deepest depths or in the highest heights."

[12]But Ahaz said, "I will not ask; I will not put the LORD to the test."

[13]Then Isaiah said, "Hear now, you house of David! Is it not enough to try the patience of men? Will you try the patience of my God also? [14]Therefore the Lord himself will give you[a] a sign: The virgin will be with child and will give birth to a son, and[b] will call him Immanuel.[c] [15]He will eat curds and honey when he knows enough to reject the wrong and choose the right. [16]But before the boy knows enough to reject the wrong and choose the right, the land of the two kings you dread will be laid waste. [17]The LORD will bring on you and on your people and on the house of your father a time unlike any since Ephraim broke away from Judah—he will bring the king of Assyria."

[18]In that day the LORD will whistle for flies from the distant streams of Egypt and for bees from the land of Assyria. [19]They will all come and settle in the steep ravines and in the crevices in the rocks, on all the thornbushes and at all the water holes. [20]In that day the Lord will use a razor hired from beyond the River[d]—the king of Assyria—to shave your head and the hair of your legs, and to take off your beards also. [21]In that day, a man will keep alive a young cow and two goats. [22]And because of the abundance of the milk they give, he will have curds to eat. All who remain in the land will eat curds and honey. [23]In that day, in every place where there were a thousand vines worth a thousand silver shekels,[e] there will be only briers and thorns. [24]Men will go there with bow and arrow, for the land will be covered with briers and thorns. [25]As for all the hills once cultivated by the hoe, you will no longer go there for fear of the briers and thorns; they will become places where cattle are turned loose and where sheep run.

Assyria, the LORD's Instrument

8 The LORD said to me, "Take a large scroll and write on it with an ordinary pen: Maher-Shalal-Hash-Baz.[f] [2]And I will call in Uriah the priest and Zechari-ah son of Jeberekiah as reliable witnesses for me."

[3]Then I went to the prophetess, and she conceived and gave birth to a son. And the LORD said to me, "Name him Maher-Shalal-Hash-Baz. [4]Before the boy knows how to say 'My father' or 'My mother,' the wealth of Damascus and the plunder of Samaria will be carried off by the king of Assyria."

[5]The LORD spoke to me again:

[6]"Because this people has rejected
    the gently flowing waters of
        Shiloah
and rejoices over Rezin
    and the son of Remaliah,
[7]therefore the Lord is about to bring
        against them
    the mighty floodwaters of the
        River[g]—
    the king of Assyria with all his
        pomp.
It will overflow all its channels,
    run over all its banks
[8]and sweep on into Judah, swirling
        over it,
    passing through it and reaching up
        to the neck.
Its outspread wings will cover the
        breadth of your land,
    O Immanuel[c]!"

[9]Raise the war cry,[h] you nations, and
        be shattered!
    Listen, all you distant lands.
Prepare for battle, and be shattered!
    Prepare for battle, and be shattered!
[10]Devise your strategy, but it will be
        thwarted;
    propose your plan, but it will not
        stand,
    for God is with us.[i]

Fear God

[11]The LORD spoke to me with his strong hand upon me, warning me not to follow the way of this people. He said:

---

[a]14 The Hebrew is plural.   [b]14 Masoretic Text; Dead Sea Scrolls *and he* or *and they*   [c]14,8 *Immanuel* means *God with us.*   [d]20 That is, the Euphrates   [e]23 That is, about 25 pounds (about 11.5 kilograms)   [f]1 *Maher-Shalal-Hash-Baz* means *quick to the plunder, swift to the spoil;* also in verse 3.   [g]7 That is, the Euphrates   [h]9 Or *Do your worst*   [i]10 Hebrew *Immanuel*

12 "Do not call conspiracy
   everything that these people call
      conspiracy[a];
do not fear what they fear,
   and do not dread it.
13 The LORD Almighty is the one you are
      to regard as holy,
   he is the one you are to fear,
   he is the one you are to dread,
14 and he will be a sanctuary;
   but for both houses of Israel he will
      be
a stone that causes men to stumble
   and a rock that makes them fall.
And for the people of Jerusalem he
      will be
a trap and a snare.
15 Many of them will stumble;
   they will fall and be broken,
   they will be snared and
      captured."

16 Bind up the testimony
   and seal up the law among my
      disciples.
17 I will wait for the LORD,
   who is hiding his face from the
      house of Jacob.
I will put my trust in him.

18 Here am I, and the children the LORD
has given me. We are signs and symbols
in Israel from the LORD Almighty, who
dwells on Mount Zion.

19 When men tell you to consult mediums and spiritists, who whisper and mutter, should not a people inquire of their
God? Why consult the dead on behalf of
the living? 20 To the law and to the testimony! If they do not speak according to
this word, they have no light of dawn.
21 Distressed and hungry, they will roam
through the land; when they are famished, they will become enraged and,
looking upward, will curse their king and
their God. 22 Then they will look toward
the earth and see only distress and darkness and fearful gloom, and they will be
thrust into utter darkness.

To Us a Child Is Born

9 Nevertheless, there will be no more
gloom for those who were in distress.
In the past he humbled the land of Zebulun and the land of Naphtali, but in the
future he will honor Galilee of the Gen-

tiles, by the way of the sea, along the
Jordan—

2 The people walking in darkness
   have seen a great light;
on those living in the land of the
      shadow of death[b]
   a light has dawned.
3 You have enlarged the nation
   and increased their joy;
they rejoice before you
   as people rejoice at the harvest,
as men rejoice
   when dividing the plunder.
4 For as in the day of Midian's defeat,
   you have shattered
the yoke that burdens them,
   the bar across their shoulders,
   the rod of their oppressor.
5 Every warrior's boot used in battle
   and every garment rolled in blood
will be destined for burning,
   will be fuel for the fire.
6 For to us a child is born,
   to us a son is given,
   and the government will be on his
      shoulders.
And he will be called
   Wonderful Counselor,[c] Mighty God,
   Everlasting Father, Prince of Peace.
7 Of the increase of his government and
      peace

Name-o-rama

Huh?

Isaiah 9:6
Many prophets in the Old Testament
(like Isaiah) said things that were about
Jesus. This is one of the most famous
prophecies about Jesus in the entire Old
Testament. In fact, we have songs that
are sung with these words. Look at all
the names used in reference to Jesus—
Wonderful Counselor, Mighty God, Everlasting Father, Prince of Peace. Talk about
a lot of names!

---

[a]12 Or *Do not call for a treaty / every time these
people call for a treaty*   [b]2 Or *land of darkness*
[c]6 Or *Wonderful, Counselor*

there will be no end.
He will reign on David's throne
and over his kingdom,
establishing and upholding it
with justice and righteousness
from that time on and forever.
The zeal of the LORD Almighty
will accomplish this.

The LORD's Anger Against Israel

⁸The Lord has sent a message against
Jacob;
it will fall on Israel.
⁹All the people will know it—
Ephraim and the inhabitants of
Samaria—
who say with pride
and arrogance of heart,
¹⁰"The bricks have fallen down,
but we will rebuild with dressed
stone;

the fig trees have been felled,
but we will replace them with
cedars."
¹¹But the LORD has strengthened Rezin's
foes against them
and has spurred their enemies on.
¹²Arameans from the east and
Philistines from the west
have devoured Israel with open
mouth.

Yet for all this, his anger is not turned
away,
his hand is still upraised.

¹³But the people have not returned to
him who struck them,
nor have they sought the LORD
Almighty.
¹⁴So the LORD will cut off from Israel
both head and tail,

Friday

What Child Is This?

Read Isaiah 9:2–7

If you ever think that maybe God's forgotten the world, this is the passage for you. Way back when the Old Testament was written, this prophet named Isaiah knew that people felt pretty hopeless. They had been through a lot of pain and suffering and thought it would never end.

But Isaiah promised them things would get better. He told the people about a baby who would save the world from sin. He told them that this baby would be the Son of God and that he would bring everlasting peace. It might have been hard for the people to believe Isaiah. Maybe they thought he was crazy for talking that way.

But we know Isaiah wasn't crazy. God *did* send his Son to live and die for us. When we accept Jesus as our Savior, we *will* have everlasting peace. We are God's children, and he will never leave us. That's a pretty amazing promise, and it's a promise we can count on.

Laura age 12

What about You?

❶ What are 2 things that make you feel hopeless? How can trusting God help you find hope?

❷ As you read through Isaiah, look for other prophecies about Jesus. Write down the things Isaiah says about Jesus on a piece of paper. When you finish, tuck the paper into the book of Matthew. The next time you read any of the Gospels, look for the ways Jesus fulfills Isaiah's prophecies.

❸ Thank God for keeping his promises and giving us hope for an incredible life with him.

Turn to page 816 for your next devotion.

both palm branch and reed in a
single day;
¹⁵ the elders and prominent men are the
head,
the prophets who teach lies are the
tail.
¹⁶ Those who guide this people mislead
them,
and those who are guided are led
astray.
¹⁷ Therefore the Lord will take no
pleasure in the young men,
nor will he pity the fatherless and
widows,
for everyone is ungodly and wicked,
every mouth speaks vileness.

Yet for all this, his anger is not turned
away,
his hand is still upraised.

¹⁸ Surely wickedness burns like a fire;
it consumes briers and thorns,
it sets the forest thickets ablaze,
so that it rolls upward in a column
of smoke.
¹⁹ By the wrath of the LORD Almighty
the land will be scorched
and the people will be fuel for the fire;
no one will spare his brother.
²⁰ On the right they will devour,
but still be hungry;
on the left they will eat,
but not be satisfied.
Each will feed on the flesh of his own
offspring ᵃ:
²¹   Manasseh will feed on Ephraim, and
Ephraim on Manasseh;
together they will turn against
Judah.

Yet for all this, his anger is not turned
away,
his hand is still upraised.

10 Woe to those who make unjust
laws,
to those who issue oppressive
decrees,
² to deprive the poor of their rights
and withhold justice from the
oppressed of my people,
making widows their prey
and robbing the fatherless.
³ What will you do on the day of
reckoning,

when disaster comes from afar?
To whom will you run for help?
Where will you leave your riches?
⁴ Nothing will remain but to cringe
among the captives
or fall among the slain.

Yet for all this, his anger is not turned
away,
his hand is still upraised.

God's Judgment on Assyria

⁵ "Woe to the Assyrian, the rod of my
anger,
in whose hand is the club of my
wrath!
⁶ I send him against a godless nation,
I dispatch him against a people who
anger me,
to seize loot and snatch plunder,
and to trample them down like mud
in the streets.
⁷ But this is not what he intends,
this is not what he has in mind;
his purpose is to destroy,
to put an end to many nations.
⁸ 'Are not my commanders all kings?'
he says.
⁹   'Has not Calno fared like
Carchemish?
Is not Hamath like Arpad,
and Samaria like Damascus?
¹⁰ As my hand seized the kingdoms of
the idols,
kingdoms whose images excelled
those of Jerusalem and
Samaria—
¹¹ shall I not deal with Jerusalem and
her images
as I dealt with Samaria and her
idols?' "

¹²When the Lord has finished all his
work against Mount Zion and Jerusalem,
he will say, "I will punish the king of Assyria for the willful pride of his heart and
the haughty look in his eyes. ¹³For he
says:

" 'By the strength of my hand I have
done this,
and by my wisdom, because I have
understanding.
I removed the boundaries of nations,
I plundered their treasures;

ᵃ20 Or arm

like a mighty one I subdued[a] their
    kings.
¹⁴ As one reaches into a nest,
    so my hand reached for the wealth
        of the nations;
as men gather abandoned eggs,
    so I gathered all the countries;
not one flapped a wing,
    or opened its mouth to chirp.' "

¹⁵ Does the ax raise itself above him
    who swings it,
    or the saw boast against him who
        uses it?
As if a rod were to wield him who
    lifts it up,
    or a club brandish him who is not
        wood!
¹⁶ Therefore, the Lord, the LORD
    Almighty,
    will send a wasting disease upon his
        sturdy warriors;
under his pomp a fire will be kindled
    like a blazing flame.
¹⁷ The Light of Israel will become a fire,
    their Holy One a flame;
in a single day it will burn and
        consume
    his thorns and his briers.
¹⁸ The splendor of his forests and fertile
    fields
    it will completely destroy,
    as when a sick man wastes away.
¹⁹ And the remaining trees of his forests
    will be so few
    that a child could write them down.

The Remnant of Israel

²⁰ In that day the remnant of Israel,
    the survivors of the house of
        Jacob,
will no longer rely on him
    who struck them down
but will truly rely on the LORD,
    the Holy One of Israel.
²¹ A remnant will return,[b] a remnant of
    Jacob
    will return to the Mighty God.
²² Though your people, O Israel, be like
    the sand by the sea,
    only a remnant will return.
Destruction has been decreed,
    overwhelming and righteous.
²³ The Lord, the LORD Almighty, will
    carry out

the destruction decreed upon the
    whole land.

²⁴ Therefore, this is what the Lord, the
LORD Almighty, says:

"O my people who live in Zion,
    do not be afraid of the Assyrians,
who beat you with a rod
    and lift up a club against you, as
        Egypt did.
²⁵ Very soon my anger against you will
    end
    and my wrath will be directed to
        their destruction."
²⁶ The LORD Almighty will lash them
    with a whip,
    as when he struck down Midian at
        the rock of Oreb;
and he will raise his staff over the
    waters,
    as he did in Egypt.
²⁷ In that day their burden will be lifted
    from your shoulders,
    their yoke from your neck;
the yoke will be broken
    because you have grown so fat.[c]

²⁸ They enter Aiath;
    they pass through Migron;
    they store supplies at Micmash.
²⁹ They go over the pass, and say,
    "We will camp overnight at Geba."
Ramah trembles;
    Gibeah of Saul flees.
³⁰ Cry out, O Daughter of Gallim!
    Listen, O Laishah!
    Poor Anathoth!
³¹ Madmenah is in flight;
    the people of Gebim take cover.
³² This day they will halt at Nob;
    they will shake their fist
at the mount of the Daughter of
    Zion,
    at the hill of Jerusalem.

³³ See, the Lord, the LORD Almighty,
    will lop off the boughs with great
        power.
The lofty trees will be felled,
    the tall ones will be brought low.
³⁴ He will cut down the forest thickets
    with an ax;

---

*a*13 Or / I subdued the mighty,   *b*21 Hebrew shear-
jashub; also in verse 22   *c*27 Hebrew; Septuagint
broken / from your shoulders

Lebanon will fall before the Mighty
One.

The Branch From Jesse

11 A shoot will come up from the
stump of Jesse;
from his roots a Branch will bear
fruit.
[2] The Spirit of the LORD will rest on
him—
the Spirit of wisdom and of
understanding,
the Spirit of counsel and of power,
the Spirit of knowledge and of the
fear of the LORD—
[3] and he will delight in the fear of the
LORD.

He will not judge by what he sees
with his eyes,
or decide by what he hears with his
ears;
[4] but with righteousness he will judge
the needy,
with justice he will give decisions
for the poor of the earth.
He will strike the earth with the rod of
his mouth;
with the breath of his lips he will
slay the wicked.
[5] Righteousness will be his belt
and faithfulness the sash around his
waist.

[6] The wolf will live with the lamb,
the leopard will lie down with the
goat,
the calf and the lion and the yearling[a]
together;
and a little child will lead them.
[7] The cow will feed with the bear,
their young will lie down together,
and the lion will eat straw like the
ox.
[8] The infant will play near the hole of
the cobra,
and the young child put his hand
into the viper's nest.
[9] They will neither harm nor destroy
on all my holy mountain,
for the earth will be full of the
knowledge of the LORD
as the waters cover the sea.

[10] In that day the Root of Jesse will
stand as a banner for the peoples; the
nations will rally to him, and his place of
rest will be glorious. [11] In that day the
Lord will reach out his hand a second
time to reclaim the remnant that is left of
his people from Assyria, from Lower
Egypt, from Upper Egypt,[b] from Cush,[c]
from Elam, from Babylonia,[d] from Hamath and from the islands of the sea.

[12] He will raise a banner for the nations
and gather the exiles of Israel;
he will assemble the scattered people
of Judah
from the four quarters of the earth.
[13] Ephraim's jealousy will vanish,
and Judah's enemies[e] will be cut
off;
Ephraim will not be jealous of
Judah,
nor Judah hostile toward Ephraim.
[14] They will swoop down on the slopes
of Philistia to the west;
together they will plunder the
people to the east.
They will lay hands on Edom and
Moab,
and the Ammonites will be subject
to them.
[15] The LORD will dry up
the gulf of the Egyptian sea;
with a scorching wind he will sweep
his hand
over the Euphrates River.[f]
He will break it up into seven streams
so that men can cross over in
sandals.
[16] There will be a highway for the
remnant of his people
that is left from Assyria,
as there was for Israel
when they came up from Egypt.

Songs of Praise

12 In that day you will say:

"I will praise you, O LORD.
Although you were angry with me,
your anger has turned away
and you have comforted me.
[2] Surely God is my salvation;
I will trust and not be afraid.

---

[a]6 Hebrew; Septuagint *lion will feed* [b]11 Hebrew
from Pathros [c]11 That is, the upper Nile region
[d]11 Hebrew *Shinar* [e]13 Or *hostility* [f]15 Hebrew
the River

The LORD, the LORD, is my strength
and my song;
he has become my salvation."
³With joy you will draw water
from the wells of salvation.

⁴In that day you will say:

"Give thanks to the LORD, call on his
name;
make known among the nations
what he has done,
and proclaim that his name is
exalted.
⁵Sing to the LORD, for he has done
glorious things;
let this be known to all the world.
⁶Shout aloud and sing for joy, people
of Zion,
for great is the Holy One of Israel
among you."

A Prophecy Against Babylon

13 An oracle concerning Babylon
that Isaiah son of Amoz saw:

²Raise a banner on a bare hilltop,
shout to them;
beckon to them
to enter the gates of the nobles.
³I have commanded my holy ones;
I have summoned my warriors to
carry out my wrath—
those who rejoice in my triumph.

⁴Listen, a noise on the mountains,
like that of a great multitude!
Listen, an uproar among the
kingdoms,
like nations massing together!
The LORD Almighty is mustering
an army for war.
⁵They come from faraway lands,
from the ends of the heavens—
the LORD and the weapons of his
wrath—
to destroy the whole country.

⁶Wail, for the day of the LORD is near;
it will come like destruction from
the Almighty.ᵃ
⁷Because of this, all hands will go limp,
every man's heart will melt.
⁸Terror will seize them,
pain and anguish will grip them;
they will writhe like a woman in
labor.

They will look aghast at each other,
their faces aflame.

⁹See, the day of the LORD is coming
—a cruel day, with wrath and fierce
anger—
to make the land desolate
and destroy the sinners within it.
¹⁰The stars of heaven and their
constellations
will not show their light.
The rising sun will be darkened
and the moon will not give its light.
¹¹I will punish the world for its evil,
the wicked for their sins.
I will put an end to the arrogance of
the haughty
and will humble the pride of the
ruthless.
¹²I will make man scarcer than pure
gold,
more rare than the gold of Ophir.
¹³Therefore I will make the heavens
tremble;
and the earth will shake from its
place
at the wrath of the LORD Almighty,
in the day of his burning anger.

¹⁴Like a hunted gazelle,
like sheep without a shepherd,
each will return to his own people,
each will flee to his native land.
¹⁵Whoever is captured will be thrust
through;
all who are caught will fall by the
sword.
¹⁶Their infants will be dashed to pieces
before their eyes;
their houses will be looted and their
wives ravished.

¹⁷See, I will stir up against them the
Medes,
who do not care for silver
and have no delight in gold.
¹⁸Their bows will strike down the young
men;
they will have no mercy on infants
nor will they look with compassion
on children.
¹⁹Babylon, the jewel of kingdoms,
the glory of the Babylonians'ᵇ pride,
will be overthrown by God

ᵃ6 Hebrew *Shaddai*   ᵇ19 Or *Chaldeans'*

like Sodom and Gomorrah.
²⁰ She will never be inhabited
   or lived in through all generations;
no Arab will pitch his tent there,
   no shepherd will rest his flocks
      there.
²¹ But desert creatures will lie there,
   jackals will fill her houses;
there the owls will dwell,
   and there the wild goats will leap
      about.
²² Hyenas will howl in her strongholds,
   jackals in her luxurious palaces.
Her time is at hand,
   and her days will not be prolonged.

14 The LORD will have compassion
      on Jacob;
   once again he will choose Israel
   and will settle them in their own
      land.
Aliens will join them
   and unite with the house of Jacob.
² Nations will take them
   and bring them to their own place.
And the house of Israel will possess
      the nations
   as menservants and maidservants in
      the LORD's land.
They will make captives of their
      captors
   and rule over their oppressors.

³ On the day the LORD gives you relief
from suffering and turmoil and cruel
bondage, ⁴ you will take up this taunt
against the king of Babylon:

How the oppressor has come to an
      end!
   How his fury*a* has ended!
⁵ The LORD has broken the rod of the
      wicked,
   the scepter of the rulers,
⁶ which in anger struck down peoples
   with unceasing blows,
and in fury subdued nations
   with relentless aggression.
⁷ All the lands are at rest and at peace;
   they break into singing.
⁸ Even the pine trees and the cedars of
      Lebanon
   exult over you and say,
"Now that you have been laid low,
   no woodsman comes to cut us
      down."

⁹ The grave*b* below is all astir
   to meet you at your coming;
it rouses the spirits of the departed to
      greet you—
   all those who were leaders in the
      world;
it makes them rise from their thrones—
   all those who were kings over the
      nations.
¹⁰ They will all respond,
   they will say to you,
"You also have become weak, as we
      are;
   you have become like us."
¹¹ All your pomp has been brought down
      to the grave,
   along with the noise of your harps;
maggots are spread out beneath you
   and worms cover you.

¹² How you have fallen from heaven,
   O morning star, son of the dawn!
You have been cast down to the earth,
   you who once laid low the nations!
¹³ You said in your heart,
   "I will ascend to heaven;
I will raise my throne
   above the stars of God;
I will sit enthroned on the mount of
      assembly,
   on the utmost heights of the sacred
      mountain.*c*
¹⁴ I will ascend above the tops of the
      clouds;
   I will make myself like the Most
      High."
¹⁵ But you are brought down to the
      grave,
   to the depths of the pit.

¹⁶ Those who see you stare at you,
   they ponder your fate:
"Is this the man who shook the earth
   and made kingdoms tremble,
¹⁷ the man who made the world a desert,
   who overthrew its cities
   and would not let his captives go
      home?"
¹⁸ All the kings of the nations lie in state,
   each in his own tomb.
¹⁹ But you are cast out of your tomb

---

a4 Dead Sea Scrolls, Septuagint and Syriac; the
meaning of the word in the Masoretic Text is
uncertain. *b9* Hebrew *Sheol*; also in verses 11
and 15 *c13* Or *the north*; Hebrew *Zaphon*

like a rejected branch;
you are covered with the slain,
   with those pierced by the sword,
   those who descend to the stones of
      the pit.
Like a corpse trampled underfoot,
²⁰ you will not join them in burial,
for you have destroyed your land
   and killed your people.

The offspring of the wicked
   will never be mentioned again.
²¹Prepare a place to slaughter his sons
   for the sins of their forefathers;
they are not to rise to inherit the land
   and cover the earth with their cities.

²²"I will rise up against them,"
   declares the LORD Almighty.
"I will cut off from Babylon her name
   and survivors,
   her offspring and descendants,"
            declares the LORD.
²³"I will turn her into a place for owls
   and into swampland;
I will sweep her with the broom of
    destruction,"
   declares the LORD Almighty.

A Prophecy Against Assyria

²⁴The LORD Almighty has sworn,

"Surely, as I have planned, so it will
    be,
and as I have purposed, so it will
    stand.
²⁵I will crush the Assyrian in my land;
   on my mountains I will trample him
    down.
His yoke will be taken from my
    people,
   and his burden removed from their
    shoulders."

²⁶This is the plan determined for the
    whole world;
   this is the hand stretched out over
    all nations.
²⁷For the LORD Almighty has purposed,
   and who can thwart him?
His hand is stretched out, and who
    can turn it back?

A Prophecy Against the Philistines

²⁸This oracle came in the year King
Ahaz died:

²⁹Do not rejoice, all you Philistines,
   that the rod that struck you is
    broken;
from the root of that snake will spring
    up a viper,
   its fruit will be a darting, venomous
    serpent.
³⁰The poorest of the poor will find
    pasture,
   and the needy will lie down in
    safety.
But your root I will destroy by
    famine;
   it will slay your survivors.

³¹Wail, O gate! Howl, O city!
   Melt away, all you Philistines!
A cloud of smoke comes from the
    north,
   and there is not a straggler in its
    ranks.
³²What answer shall be given
   to the envoys of that nation?
"The LORD has established Zion,
   and in her his afflicted people will
    find refuge."

A Prophecy Against Moab

15   An oracle concerning Moab:

Ar in Moab is ruined,
   destroyed in a night!
Kir in Moab is ruined,
   destroyed in a night!
²Dibon goes up to its temple,
   to its high places to weep;
Moab wails over Nebo and Medeba.
Every head is shaved
   and every beard cut off.
³In the streets they wear sackcloth;
   on the roofs and in the public
    squares
they all wail,
   prostrate with weeping.
⁴Heshbon and Elealeh cry out,
   their voices are heard all the way to
    Jahaz.
Therefore the armed men of Moab cry
    out,
   and their hearts are faint.

⁵My heart cries out over Moab;
   her fugitives flee as far as Zoar,
   as far as Eglath Shelishiyah.
They go up the way to Luhith,
   weeping as they go;

on the road to Horonaim
    they lament their destruction.
⁶The waters of Nimrim are dried up
    and the grass is withered;
the vegetation is gone
    and nothing green is left.
⁷So the wealth they have acquired and
       stored up
    they carry away over the Ravine of
       the Poplars.
⁸Their outcry echoes along the border
       of Moab;
    their wailing reaches as far as
       Eglaim,
    their lamentation as far as Beer Elim.
⁹Dimon's*ᵃ* waters are full of blood,
    but I will bring still more upon
       Dimon*ᵃ*—
a lion upon the fugitives of Moab
    and upon those who remain in the
       land.

16 Send lambs as tribute
    to the ruler of the land,
from Sela, across the desert,

to the mount of the Daughter of
       Zion.
²Like fluttering birds
    pushed from the nest,
so are the women of Moab
    at the fords of the Arnon.

³"Give us counsel,
    render a decision.
Make your shadow like night—
    at high noon.
Hide the fugitives,
    do not betray the refugees.
⁴Let the Moabite fugitives stay with
       you;
    be their shelter from the destroyer."

The oppressor will come to an end,
    and destruction will cease;
    the aggressor will vanish from the
       land.
⁵In love a throne will be established;
    in faithfulness a man will sit on it—

*ᵃ9 Masoretic Text; Dead Sea Scrolls, some
Septuagint manuscripts and Vulgate Dibon*

Week end.

Once a Sinner, Always a Sinner

Read Romans 7:15—8:4 (page 1360)

How do you stop struggling with sin? You don't. Aaron talked in Wednesday's devotion about getting clean from his sins because of Jesus Christ. Not being stuck with our sins is a very cool thing.

    The apostle Paul says that he had the desire to do good but sometimes couldn't make it happen. Can you relate? Whether you are 14 or 97, you struggle with sin. But the key word is *struggle*. Hopefully you'll always resist. Never give up *fighting* sin in your life.

    And here's the good news: No matter how many times you sin, no matter how many times you blow it, no matter how many times you fail, "There is now no condemnation for those who are in Christ Jesus." Jesus is more than willing to forgive you if you're willing to ask him to forgive you. That's why grace is amazing and why the love of Jesus is awesome.

What about You?

❶ Do you really believe God will forgive you no matter how many times you sin?

❷ Ask an adult you respect for some ideas on how to overcome a sin you are struggling with.

❸ Ask God to help you to keep from sinning in that area of your life.

Turn to page 824 for your next devotion.

one from the house[a] of David—
one who in judging seeks justice
    and speeds the cause of
        righteousness.

[6] We have heard of Moab's pride—
    her overweening pride and conceit,
her pride and her insolence—
    but her boasts are empty.
[7] Therefore the Moabites wail,
    they wail together for Moab.
Lament and grieve
    for the men[b] of Kir Hareseth.
[8] The fields of Heshbon wither,
    the vines of Sibmah also.
The rulers of the nations
    have trampled down the choicest
        vines,
which once reached Jazer
    and spread toward the desert.
Their shoots spread out
    and went as far as the sea.
[9] So I weep, as Jazer weeps,
    for the vines of Sibmah.
O Heshbon, O Elealeh,
    I drench you with tears!
The shouts of joy over your ripened
        fruit
    and over your harvests have been
        stilled.
[10] Joy and gladness are taken away from
        the orchards;
    no one sings or shouts in the
        vineyards;
no one treads out wine at the presses,
    for I have put an end to the
        shouting.
[11] My heart laments for Moab like a harp,
    my inmost being for Kir Hareseth.
[12] When Moab appears at her high place,
    she only wears herself out;
when she goes to her shrine to pray,
    it is to no avail.

[13] This is the word the LORD has already
spoken concerning Moab. [14] But now the
LORD says: "Within three years, as a servant bound by contract would count
them, Moab's splendor and all her many
people will be despised, and her survivors will be very few and feeble."

An Oracle Against Damascus

17 An oracle concerning Damascus:

"See, Damascus will no longer be a city

but will become a heap of ruins.
[2] The cities of Aroer will be deserted
    and left to flocks, which will lie
        down,
    with no one to make them afraid.
[3] The fortified city will disappear from
        Ephraim,
    and royal power from Damascus;
the remnant of Aram will be
    like the glory of the Israelites,"
            declares the LORD Almighty.

[4] "In that day the glory of Jacob will
        fade;
    the fat of his body will waste away.
[5] It will be as when a reaper gathers the
        standing grain
    and harvests the grain with his arm—
as when a man gleans heads of grain
    in the Valley of Rephaim.
[6] Yet some gleanings will remain,
    as when an olive tree is beaten,
leaving two or three olives on the
        topmost branches,
    four or five on the fruitful boughs,"
            declares the LORD,
                the God of Israel.

[7] In that day men will look to their
        Maker
    and turn their eyes to the Holy One
        of Israel.
[8] They will not look to the altars,
    the work of their hands,
and they will have no regard for the
        Asherah poles[c]
    and the incense altars their fingers
        have made.

[9] In that day their strong cities, which
they left because of the Israelites, will be
like places abandoned to thickets and
undergrowth. And all will be desolation.

[10] You have forgotten God your Savior;
    you have not remembered the Rock,
        your fortress.
Therefore, though you set out the
        finest plants
    and plant imported vines,
[11] though on the day you set them out,
    you make them grow,
and on the morning when you plant
        them, you bring them to bud,

---

[a] 5 Hebrew *tent*   [b] 7 Or "*raisin cakes*," a wordplay
[c] 8 That is, symbols of the goddess Asherah

yet the harvest will be as nothing
   in the day of disease and incurable
      pain.

¹²Oh, the raging of many nations—
   they rage like the raging sea!
Oh, the uproar of the peoples—
   they roar like the roaring of great
      waters!
¹³Although the peoples roar like the
      roar of surging waters,
   when he rebukes them they flee far
      away,
driven before the wind like chaff on
      the hills,
   like tumbleweed before a gale.
¹⁴In the evening, sudden terror!
   Before the morning, they are gone!
This is the portion of those who loot us,
   the lot of those who plunder us.

A Prophecy Against Cush

18 Woe to the land of whirring
         wings[a]
along the rivers of Cush,[b]
²which sends envoys by sea
   in papyrus boats over the water.

Go, swift messengers,
to a people tall and smooth-skinned,
to a people feared far and wide,
an aggressive nation of strange
      speech,
   whose land is divided by rivers.

³All you people of the world,
   you who live on the earth,
when a banner is raised on the
      mountains,
   you will see it,
and when a trumpet sounds,
   you will hear it.
⁴This is what the LORD says to me:
   "I will remain quiet and will look
      on from my dwelling place,
like shimmering heat in the sunshine,
   like a cloud of dew in the heat of
      harvest."
⁵For, before the harvest, when the
      blossom is gone
   and the flower becomes a ripening
      grape,
he will cut off the shoots with pruning
      knives,
   and cut down and take away the
      spreading branches.

⁶They will all be left to the mountain
      birds of prey
   and to the wild animals;
the birds will feed on them all
      summer,
   the wild animals all winter.

⁷At that time gifts will be brought to
the LORD Almighty

from a people tall and
      smooth-skinned,
   from a people feared far and wide,
an aggressive nation of strange
      speech,
   whose land is divided by rivers—

the gifts will be brought to Mount Zion,
the place of the Name of the LORD Almighty.

A Prophecy About Egypt

19 An oracle concerning Egypt:

See, the LORD rides on a swift cloud
   and is coming to Egypt.
The idols of Egypt tremble before him,
   and the hearts of the Egyptians melt
      within them.

²"I will stir up Egyptian against
      Egyptian—
   brother will fight against brother,
   neighbor against neighbor,
   city against city,
   kingdom against kingdom.
³The Egyptians will lose heart,
   and I will bring their plans to
      nothing;
they will consult the idols and the
      spirits of the dead,
   the mediums and the spiritists.
⁴I will hand the Egyptians over
   to the power of a cruel master,
and a fierce king will rule over them,"
   declares the Lord, the LORD
      Almighty.

⁵The waters of the river will dry up,
   and the riverbed will be parched
      and dry.
⁶The canals will stink;
   the streams of Egypt will dwindle
      and dry up.
The reeds and rushes will wither,

---

[a]1 Or *of locusts*   [b]1 That is, the upper Nile region

⁷also the plants along the Nile,
   at the mouth of the river.
Every sown field along the Nile
   will become parched, will blow
      away and be no more.
⁸The fishermen will groan and lament,
   all who cast hooks into the Nile;
those who throw nets on the water
   will pine away.
⁹Those who work with combed flax
      will despair,
   the weavers of fine linen will lose
      hope.
¹⁰The workers in cloth will be dejected,
   and all the wage earners will be
      sick at heart.

¹¹The officials of Zoan are nothing but
      fools;
   the wise counselors of Pharaoh give
      senseless advice.
How can you say to Pharaoh,
   "I am one of the wise men,
   a disciple of the ancient kings"?

¹²Where are your wise men now?
   Let them show you and make
      known
what the LORD Almighty
   has planned against Egypt.
¹³The officials of Zoan have become
      fools,
   the leaders of Memphisᵃ are
      deceived;
the cornerstones of her peoples
   have led Egypt astray.
¹⁴The LORD has poured into them
   a spirit of dizziness;
they make Egypt stagger in all that
      she does,
   as a drunkard staggers around in
      his vomit.
¹⁵There is nothing Egypt can do—
   head or tail, palm branch or reed.

¹⁶In that day the Egyptians will be like
women. They will shudder with fear at
the uplifted hand that the LORD Almighty
raises against them. ¹⁷And the land of
Judah will bring terror to the Egyptians;
everyone to whom Judah is mentioned
will be terrified, because of what the
LORD Almighty is planning against them.

¹⁸In that day five cities in Egypt will
speak the language of Canaan and swear
allegiance to the LORD Almighty. One of

them will be called the City of Destruction.ᵇ
¹⁹In that day there will be an altar to
the LORD in the heart of Egypt, and a
monument to the LORD at its border. ²⁰It
will be a sign and witness to the LORD
Almighty in the land of Egypt. When
they cry out to the LORD because of their
oppressors, he will send them a savior
and defender, and he will rescue them.
²¹So the LORD will make himself known
to the Egyptians, and in that day they
will acknowledge the LORD. They will
worship with sacrifices and grain offerings; they will make vows to the LORD
and keep them. ²²The LORD will strike
Egypt with a plague; he will strike them
and heal them. They will turn to the
LORD, and he will respond to their pleas
and heal them.
²³In that day there will be a highway
from Egypt to Assyria. The Assyrians
will go to Egypt and the Egyptians to
Assyria. The Egyptians and Assyrians
will worship together. ²⁴In that day Israel
will be the third, along with Egypt and
Assyria, a blessing on the earth. ²⁵The
LORD Almighty will bless them, saying,
"Blessed be Egypt my people, Assyria my
handiwork, and Israel my inheritance."

A Prophecy Against Egypt and Cush

20 In the year that the supreme commander, sent by Sargon king of
Assyria, came to Ashdod and attacked
and captured it— ²at that time the LORD
spoke through Isaiah son of Amoz. He
said to him, "Take off the sackcloth from
your body and the sandals from your
feet." And he did so, going around
stripped and barefoot.
³Then the LORD said, "Just as my servant Isaiah has gone stripped and barefoot for three years, as a sign and portent
against Egypt and Cush,ᶜ ⁴so the king of
Assyria will lead away stripped and
barefoot the Egyptian captives and Cushite exiles, young and old, with buttocks
bared—to Egypt's shame. ⁵Those who
trusted in Cush and boasted in Egypt will

ᵃ13 Hebrew *Noph* ᵇ18 Most manuscripts of the
Masoretic Text; some manuscripts of the Masoretic
Text, Dead Sea Scrolls and Vulgate *City of the Sun*
(that is, Heliopolis) ᶜ3 That is, the upper Nile
region; also in verse 5

Hot off the Press

You can't believe everything you hear. Sort through these fantastic front page headlines that might have appeared in *The Biblical Times* and pick out the ones that really happened (check the bottom of the page to see how you did):

a. Methusaleh, World's Oldest Man, Dead at Age 969

b. Common Criminal Appointed Vice-President

c. Egyptian Woman Births Baby With 4 Heads

d. Stripped Preacher Causes Stir

e. Sun Stands Still, No Sunset Occurs

f. Wealthy King Takes 700 Wives

g. Man Glows in the Dark After Lightning Strike, Witnesses Say

h. Preacher Outruns Horses, Eyes Kentucky Derby

i. Skillful Swimming Grandpa Found to Have Gills

j. Skeletons Come to Life, Form Huge Army

k. Religious Zealot Survives Lions' Den

l. Reluctant Prophet Survives Nightmare in Huge Fish's Stomach

For New Testament Tabloid Headlines, turn to Mark 7, page 1197.

answers: a) real; Genesis 5:27 b) real; Genesis 41:14-16, 33, 37-41 c) fake d) real; Isaiah 20:2-4 e) real; Joshua 10:13-14 f) real; 1 Kings 11:3 g) fake h) real; 1 Kings 18:46 i) fake j) real; Ezekiel 37:1-10 k) real; Daniel 6:16-23 l) real; Jonah 1:17—2:10

be afraid and put to shame. ⁶In that day the people who live on this coast will say, 'See what has happened to those we relied on, those we fled to for help and deliverance from the king of Assyria! How then can we escape?' "

A Prophecy Against Babylon

21 An oracle concerning the Desert by the Sea:

Like whirlwinds sweeping through the
    southland,
  an invader comes from the
    desert,
  from a land of terror.

²A dire vision has been shown to me:
  The traitor betrays, the looter takes
    loot.
Elam, attack! Media, lay siege!
  I will bring to an end all the
    groaning she caused.

³At this my body is racked with pain,
  pangs seize me, like those of a
    woman in labor;
I am staggered by what I hear,
  I am bewildered by what I see.
⁴My heart falters,
  fear makes me tremble;
the twilight I longed for
  has become a horror to me.

⁵They set the tables,
  they spread the rugs,
  they eat, they drink!
Get up, you officers,
  oil the shields!

⁶This is what the Lord says to me:

"Go, post a lookout
  and have him report what he sees.
⁷When he sees chariots
  with teams of horses,
riders on donkeys
  or riders on camels,
let him be alert,
  fully alert."

⁸And the lookout*ᵃ* shouted,

"Day after day, my lord, I stand on the
    watchtower;
  every night I stay at my post.
⁹Look, here comes a man in a chariot
  with a team of horses.
And he gives back the answer:
  'Babylon has fallen, has fallen!

ᵃ8 Dead Sea Scrolls and Syriac; Masoretic Text
A lion

All the images of its gods
   lie shattered on the ground!' "

[10] O my people, crushed on the threshing
    floor,
   I tell you what I have heard
from the LORD Almighty,
   from the God of Israel.

A Prophecy Against Edom

[11] An oracle concerning Dumah[a]:

Someone calls to me from Seir,
   "Watchman, what is left of the
    night?
   Watchman, what is left of the
    night?"
[12] The watchman replies,
   "Morning is coming, but also the
    night.
If you would ask, then ask;
   and come back yet again."

A Prophecy Against Arabia

[13] An oracle concerning Arabia:

You caravans of Dedanites,
   who camp in the thickets of
    Arabia,
[14]   bring water for the thirsty;
you who live in Tema,
   bring food for the fugitives.
[15] They flee from the sword,
   from the drawn sword,
from the bent bow
   and from the heat of battle.

[16] This is what the Lord says to me:
"Within one year, as a servant bound by
contract would count it, all the pomp of
Kedar will come to an end. [17] The survivors
of the bowmen, the warriors of Kedar,
will be few." The LORD, the God of
Israel, has spoken.

A Prophecy About Jerusalem

22 An oracle concerning the Valley
of Vision:

What troubles you now,
   that you have all gone up on the
    roofs,
[2] O town full of commotion,
   O city of tumult and revelry?
Your slain were not killed by the
    sword,

nor did they die in battle.
[3] All your leaders have fled together;
   they have been captured without
    using the bow.
All you who were caught were taken
    prisoner together,
   having fled while the enemy was
    still far away.
[4] Therefore I said, "Turn away from
    me;
   let me weep bitterly.
Do not try to console me
   over the destruction of my people."

[5] The Lord, the LORD Almighty, has a
    day
   of tumult and trampling and terror
   in the Valley of Vision,
a day of battering down walls
   and of crying out to the
    mountains.
[6] Elam takes up the quiver,
   with her charioteers and horses;
   Kir uncovers the shield.
[7] Your choicest valleys are full of
    chariots,
   and horsemen are posted at the city
    gates;
[8]   the defenses of Judah are stripped
    away.

And you looked in that day
   to the weapons in the Palace of the
    Forest;
[9] you saw that the City of David
   had many breaches in its
    defenses;
you stored up water
   in the Lower Pool.
[10] You counted the buildings in
    Jerusalem
   and tore down houses to strengthen
    the wall.
[11] You built a reservoir between the two
    walls
   for the water of the Old Pool,
but you did not look to the One who
    made it,
   or have regard for the One who
    planned it long ago.

[12] The Lord, the LORD Almighty,
   called you on that day

---

[a] 11 Dumah means silence or stillness, a wordplay on
Edom.

to weep and to wail,
to tear out your hair and put on
sackcloth.
¹³But see, there is joy and revelry,
slaughtering of cattle and killing of
sheep,
eating of meat and drinking of wine!
"Let us eat and drink," you say,
"for tomorrow we die!"

¹⁴The LORD Almighty has revealed this in my hearing: "Till your dying day this sin will not be atoned for," says the Lord, the LORD Almighty.

¹⁵This is what the Lord, the LORD Almighty, says:

"Go, say to this steward,
to Shebna, who is in charge of the
palace:
¹⁶What are you doing here and who
gave you permission
to cut out a grave for yourself here,
hewing your grave on the height
and chiseling your resting place in
the rock?

¹⁷"Beware, the LORD is about to take
firm hold of you
and hurl you away, O you mighty
man.
¹⁸He will roll you up tightly like a ball
and throw you into a large country.
There you will die
and there your splendid chariots
will remain—
you disgrace to your master's
house!
¹⁹I will depose you from your office,
and you will be ousted from your
position.

²⁰"In that day I will summon my servant, Eliakim son of Hilkiah. ²¹I will clothe him with your robe and fasten your sash around him and hand your authority over to him. He will be a father to those who live in Jerusalem and to the house of Judah. ²²I will place on his shoulder the key to the house of David; what he opens no one can shut, and what he shuts no one can open. ²³I will drive him like a peg into a firm place; he will be a seat[a] of honor for the house of his father. ²⁴All the glory of his family will hang on him: its offspring and off-shoots—all its lesser vessels, from the bowls to all the jars.

²⁵"In that day," declares the LORD Almighty, "the peg driven into the firm place will give way; it will be sheared off and will fall, and the load hanging on it will be cut down." The LORD has spoken.

A Prophecy About Tyre

23 An oracle concerning Tyre:

Wail, O ships of Tarshish!
For Tyre is destroyed
and left without house or harbor.
From the land of Cyprus[b]
word has come to them.

²Be silent, you people of the island
and you merchants of Sidon,
whom the seafarers have enriched.
³On the great waters
came the grain of the Shihor;
the harvest of the Nile[c] was the
revenue of Tyre,
and she became the marketplace of
the nations.

⁴Be ashamed, O Sidon, and you,
O fortress of the sea,
for the sea has spoken:
"I have neither been in labor nor
given birth;
I have neither reared sons nor
brought up daughters."
⁵When word comes to Egypt,
they will be in anguish at the report
from Tyre.

⁶Cross over to Tarshish;
wail, you people of the island.
⁷Is this your city of revelry,
the old, old city,
whose feet have taken her
to settle in far-off lands?
⁸Who planned this against Tyre,
the bestower of crowns,
whose merchants are princes,
whose traders are renowned in the
earth?
⁹The LORD Almighty planned it,
to bring low the pride of all glory

[a]23 Or throne   [b]1 Hebrew Kittim   [c]2,3 Masoretic Text; one Dead Sea Scroll Sidon, / who cross over the sea; / your envoys ³are on the great waters. / The grain of the Shihor, / the harvest of the Nile,

and to humble all who are
   renowned on the earth.
10 Till[a] your land as along the Nile,
   O Daughter of Tarshish,
   for you no longer have a harbor.
11 The LORD has stretched out his hand
      over the sea
   and made its kingdoms tremble.
He has given an order concerning
      Phoenicia[b]
   that her fortresses be destroyed.
12 He said, "No more of your reveling,
   O Virgin Daughter of Sidon, now
      crushed!

"Up, cross over to Cyprus[c];
   even there you will find no rest."
13 Look at the land of the Babylonians,[d]
   this people that is now of no
      account!
The Assyrians have made it
   a place for desert creatures;
they raised up their siege towers,
   they stripped its fortresses bare
   and turned it into a ruin.

14 Wail, you ships of Tarshish;
   your fortress is destroyed!

15 At that time Tyre will be forgotten
for seventy years, the span of a king's
life. But at the end of these seventy
years, it will happen to Tyre as in the
song of the prostitute:

16 "Take up a harp, walk through the
      city,
   O prostitute forgotten;
play the harp well, sing many a song,
   so that you will be remembered."

17 At the end of seventy years, the LORD
will deal with Tyre. She will return to her
hire as a prostitute and will ply her trade
with all the kingdoms on the face of the
earth. 18 Yet her profit and her earnings
will be set apart for the LORD; they will
not be stored up or hoarded. Her profits
will go to those who live before the LORD,
for abundant food and fine clothes.

The LORD's Devastation of the Earth

24 See, the LORD is going to lay
      waste the earth
   and devastate it;
he will ruin its face
   and scatter its inhabitants—

Nuke It!

Huh?

Isaiah 24:1
Isaiah is delivering a message to people
about their sins. He is showing them that
God is not a happy camper, and that his
judgment is just around the corner. God's
covenant (or promise) with Israel meant
that they were supposed to obey him. Since
they haven't done that, God rightfully
sends down his wrath.

---

2 it will be the same
   for priest as for people,
   for master as for servant,
   for mistress as for maid,
   for seller as for buyer,
   for borrower as for lender,
   for debtor as for creditor.
3 The earth will be completely laid
      waste
   and totally plundered.
                  The LORD has spoken
                        this word.

4 The earth dries up and withers,
   the world languishes and withers,
   the exalted of the earth languish.
5 The earth is defiled by its people;
   they have disobeyed the laws,
violated the statutes
   and broken the everlasting
      covenant.
6 Therefore a curse consumes the earth;
   its people must bear their guilt.
Therefore earth's inhabitants are
      burned up,
   and very few are left.
7 The new wine dries up and the vine
      withers;
   all the merrymakers groan.
8 The gaiety of the tambourines is
      stilled,
   the noise of the revelers has
      stopped,
   the joyful harp is silent.

---

a10 Dead Sea Scrolls and some Septuagint
manuscripts; Masoretic Text *Go through*
b11 Hebrew *Canaan*   c12 Hebrew *Kittim*
d13 Or *Chaldeans*

⁹No longer do they drink wine with a
song;
the beer is bitter to its drinkers.
¹⁰The ruined city lies desolate;
the entrance to every house is barred.
¹¹In the streets they cry out for wine;
all joy turns to gloom,
all gaiety is banished from the
earth.
¹²The city is left in ruins,
its gate is battered to pieces.
¹³So will it be on the earth
and among the nations,
as when an olive tree is beaten,
or as when gleanings are left after
the grape harvest.

¹⁴They raise their voices, they shout for
joy;
from the west they acclaim the
LORD's majesty.
¹⁵Therefore in the east give glory to the
LORD;
exalt the name of the LORD, the God
of Israel,
in the islands of the sea.

¹⁶From the ends of the earth we hear
singing:
"Glory to the Righteous One."

But I said, "I waste away, I waste away!
Woe to me!
The treacherous betray!
With treachery the treacherous
betray!"
¹⁷Terror and pit and snare await you,
O people of the earth.
¹⁸Whoever flees at the sound of terror
will fall into a pit;
whoever climbs out of the pit
will be caught in a snare.

The floodgates of the heavens are
opened,
the foundations of the earth shake.
¹⁹The earth is broken up,
the earth is split asunder,
the earth is thoroughly shaken.
²⁰The earth reels like a drunkard,
it sways like a hut in the wind;
so heavy upon it is the guilt of its
rebellion
that it falls—never to rise again.

Monday

Judgment Day

Read Isaiah 24:1–3

There are a lot of verses in the Bible that tell us about God's love. They're nice to read and make us feel good. But there are other parts of the Bible that aren't so nice to read. This is one of them.

Sometimes we forget just how powerful God is and how easy it would be for him to destroy everyone on the planet. This passage tells us that God will judge human beings one day. It won't matter if someone is rich or poor, strong or weak, a master or a servant. People who haven't given their lives to God will feel God's powerful judgment and wrath.

When I read these verses and hear what God will do to the earth one day, it makes me thankful that I've given my life to him. I know God's forgiven me and will have mercy on me when he judges the earth. I hope that's true for you too.

Tyler age 14

❶ What does this passage tell you about God?

❷ Read the rest of chapter 24, then read chapter 25. Draw a picture or write a poem about Isaiah's vision of heaven and earth.

❸ Thank God for his amazing gift of salvation.

Turn to page 826 for your next devotion.

²¹ In that day the LORD will punish
    the powers in the heavens above
    and the kings on the earth below.
²² They will be herded together
    like prisoners bound in a dungeon;
    they will be shut up in prison
    and be punished[a] after many days.
²³ The moon will be abashed, the sun
        ashamed;
    for the LORD Almighty will reign
    on Mount Zion and in Jerusalem,
    and before its elders, gloriously.

Praise to the LORD

25 O LORD, you are my God;
    I will exalt you and praise your
        name,
    for in perfect faithfulness
    you have done marvelous things,
        things planned long ago.
² You have made the city a heap of
        rubble,
    the fortified town a ruin,
    the foreigners' stronghold a city no
        more;
    it will never be rebuilt.
³ Therefore strong peoples will honor
        you;
    cities of ruthless nations will revere
        you.
⁴ You have been a refuge for the poor,
    a refuge for the needy in his
        distress,
    a shelter from the storm
    and a shade from the heat.
For the breath of the ruthless
    is like a storm driving against a wall
⁵   and like the heat of the desert.
You silence the uproar of foreigners;
    as heat is reduced by the shadow of
        a cloud,
    so the song of the ruthless is stilled.

⁶ On this mountain the LORD Almighty
        will prepare
    a feast of rich food for all peoples,
    a banquet of aged wine—
    the best of meats and the finest of
        wines.
⁷ On this mountain he will destroy
    the shroud that enfolds all peoples,
    the sheet that covers all nations;
⁸   he will swallow up death forever.
The Sovereign LORD will wipe away
        the tears

from all faces;
    he will remove the disgrace of his
        people
    from all the earth.
                    The LORD has spoken.

⁹ In that day they will say,

"Surely this is our God;
    we trusted in him, and he saved us.
This is the LORD, we trusted in him;
    let us rejoice and be glad in his
        salvation."

¹⁰ The hand of the LORD will rest on this
        mountain;
    but Moab will be trampled under
        him
    as straw is trampled down in the
        manure.
¹¹ They will spread out their hands in it,
    as a swimmer spreads out his hands
        to swim.
God will bring down their pride
    despite the cleverness[b] of their
        hands.
¹² He will bring down your high fortified
        walls
    and lay them low;
    he will bring them down to the
        ground,
    to the very dust.

A Song of Praise

26 In that day this song will be sung
    in the land of Judah:

We have a strong city;
    God makes salvation
    its walls and ramparts.
² Open the gates
    that the righteous nation may
        enter,
    the nation that keeps faith.
³ You will keep in perfect peace
    him whose mind is steadfast,
    because he trusts in you.
⁴ Trust in the LORD forever,
    for the LORD, the LORD, is the Rock
        eternal.
⁵ He humbles those who dwell on high,
    he lays the lofty city low;
    he levels it to the ground
    and casts it down to the dust.

---

a22 Or *released*   *b11* The meaning of the Hebrew for
this word is uncertain.

⁶Feet trample it down—
　　the feet of the oppressed,
　　the footsteps of the poor.

⁷The path of the righteous is level;
　　O upright One, you make the way of
　　　the righteous smooth.
⁸Yes, LORD, walking in the way of your
　　laws,ᵃ
　we wait for you;
　your name and renown
　　are the desire of our hearts.
⁹My soul yearns for you in the night;
　　in the morning my spirit longs for
　　　you.
　When your judgments come upon the
　　earth,
　　the people of the world learn
　　　righteousness.
¹⁰Though grace is shown to the wicked,
　　they do not learn righteousness;
　even in a land of uprightness they go
　　on doing evil
　　and regard not the majesty of the
　　　LORD.
¹¹O LORD, your hand is lifted high,
　　but they do not see it.
　Let them see your zeal for your people
　　and be put to shame;

let the fire reserved for your
　　enemies consume them.

¹²LORD, you establish peace for us;
　　all that we have accomplished you
　　　have done for us.
¹³O LORD, our God, other lords besides
　　you have ruled over us,
　but your name alone do we honor.
¹⁴They are now dead, they live no more;
　　those departed spirits do not rise.
　You punished them and brought them
　　to ruin;
　　you wiped out all memory of them.
¹⁵You have enlarged the nation, O LORD;
　　you have enlarged the nation.
　You have gained glory for yourself;
　　you have extended all the borders
　　　of the land.

¹⁶LORD, they came to you in their
　　distress;
　when you disciplined them,
　　they could barely whisper a prayer.ᵇ
¹⁷As a woman with child and about to
　　give birth
　writhes and cries out in her pain,

ᵃ8 Or judgments   ᵇ16 The meaning of the Hebrew for this clause is uncertain.

Tuesday

Give It Up

Read Isaiah 26:3–4

Every day I struggle with trusting God. I try to fix my problems by myself, which never works, and I end up worrying my head off!

　Then I remember to give all my problems to God. I feel so much better after that, because I know God's in control. I always wish I'd prayed and given all my worries to God in the first place.

　It is so much better to give all your worries to God. You don't have to worry about bugging him either, because he wants to hear your voice. He knows you, and he knows your future. Let him help.

Susanna age 14

❶ What are 3 things you worry about?

❷ Pick up something really heavy, like a backpack full of books, and carry it around for a few minutes. Think of it as the weight of your problems. Notice how good it feels to finally put it down—like the feeling you get when you give your problems to God.

❸ Give your worries to God in prayer.

Turn to page 831 for your next devotion.

so were we in your presence,
O LORD.
[18] We were with child, we writhed in
pain,
but we gave birth to wind.
We have not brought salvation to the
earth;
we have not given birth to people
of the world.

[19] But your dead will live;
their bodies will rise.
You who dwell in the dust,
wake up and shout for joy.
Your dew is like the dew of the
morning;
the earth will give birth to her dead.

[20] Go, my people, enter your rooms
and shut the doors behind you;
hide yourselves for a little while
until his wrath has passed by.
[21] See, the LORD is coming out of his
dwelling
to punish the people of the earth for
their sins.
The earth will disclose the blood shed
upon her;
she will conceal her slain no longer.

Deliverance of Israel

27 In that day,

the LORD will punish with his sword,
his fierce, great and powerful
sword,
Leviathan the gliding serpent,
Leviathan the coiling serpent;
he will slay the monster of the sea.

[2] In that day—

"Sing about a fruitful vineyard:
[3]   I, the LORD, watch over it;
I water it continually.
I guard it day and night
so that no one may harm it.
[4]   I am not angry.
If only there were briers and thorns
confronting me!
I would march against them in
battle;
I would set them all on fire.
[5] Or else let them come to me for
refuge;
let them make peace with me,
yes, let them make peace with me."

[6] In days to come Jacob will take root,
Israel will bud and blossom
and fill all the world with fruit.

[7] Has the LORD struck her
as he struck down those who struck
her?
Has she been killed
as those were killed who killed her?
[8] By warfare[a] and exile you contend
with her—
with his fierce blast he drives her out,
as on a day the east wind blows.
[9] By this, then, will Jacob's guilt be
atoned for,
and this will be the full fruitage of
the removal of his sin:
When he makes all the altar stones
to be like chalk stones crushed to
pieces,
no Asherah poles[b] or incense altars
will be left standing.
[10] The fortified city stands desolate,
an abandoned settlement, forsaken
like the desert;
there the calves graze,
there they lie down;
they strip its branches bare.
[11] When its twigs are dry, they are
broken off
and women come and make fires
with them.
For this is a people without
understanding;
so their Maker has no compassion
on them,
and their Creator shows them no
favor.

[12] In that day the LORD will thresh from
the flowing Euphrates[c] to the Wadi of
Egypt, and you, O Israelites, will be gathered up one by one. [13] And in that day a
great trumpet will sound. Those who
were perishing in Assyria and those who
were exiled in Egypt will come and worship the LORD on the holy mountain in
Jerusalem.

Woe to Ephraim

28 Woe to that wreath, the pride of
Ephraim's drunkards,

---

a8 See Septuagint; the meaning of the Hebrew for
this word is uncertain.   *b9* That is, symbols of the
goddess Asherah   *c12* Hebrew *River*

Sometimes You Gotta Hurl

The Bible is about real life. And in real life, people sometimes, um—how should we say this politely?—they sometimes hurl. You know, toss their cookies? Check out these verses—some of them are pretty gross! A couple of them are written out for you here; you'll have to look up the rest.

- ✗ Job 20:15
- ✗ Proverbs 23:8
- ✗ Proverbs 25:16
- ✗ Proverbs 26:11—"As a dog returns to its vomit, so a fool repeats his folly." (ick!)
- ✗ Isaiah 19:14
- ✗ Isaiah 28:8—"All the tables are covered with vomit and there is not a spot without filth." (yuck!)
- ✗ 2 Peter 2:22

to the fading flower, his glorious
    beauty,
set on the head of a fertile valley—
    to that city, the pride of those laid
      low by wine!
² See, the Lord has one who is powerful
    and strong.
    Like a hailstorm and a destructive
      wind,
like a driving rain and a flooding
    downpour,
he will throw it forcefully to the
    ground.
³ That wreath, the pride of Ephraim's
    drunkards,
    will be trampled underfoot.
⁴ That fading flower, his glorious
    beauty,
    set on the head of a fertile valley,
will be like a fig ripe before harvest—
    as soon as someone sees it and
      takes it in his hand,
    he swallows it.

⁵ In that day the LORD Almighty
    will be a glorious crown,
a beautiful wreath
    for the remnant of his people.
⁶ He will be a spirit of justice
    to him who sits in judgment,
a source of strength
    to those who turn back the battle at
      the gate.

⁷ And these also stagger from wine
    and reel from beer:
Priests and prophets stagger from beer
    and are befuddled with wine;
they reel from beer,
    they stagger when seeing visions,
    they stumble when rendering
      decisions.
⁸ All the tables are covered with vomit
    and there is not a spot without filth.

⁹ "Who is it he is trying to teach?
    To whom is he explaining his
      message?
To children weaned from their milk,
    to those just taken from the breast?
¹⁰ For it is:
    Do and do, do and do,
    rule on rule, rule on rule[a];
    a little here, a little there."

¹¹ Very well then, with foreign lips and
    strange tongues
God will speak to this people,
¹² to whom he said,
    "This is the resting place, let the
      weary rest";
and, "This is the place of repose"—
    but they would not listen.
¹³ So then, the word of the LORD to them
    will become:
    Do and do, do and do,
    rule on rule, rule on rule;
    a little here, a little there—
so that they will go and fall
    backward,
    be injured and snared and captured.

¹⁴ Therefore hear the word of the LORD,
    you scoffers
who rule this people in Jerusalem.
¹⁵ You boast, "We have entered into a
    covenant with death,

a 10 Hebrew / *sav lasav sav lasav / kav lakav kav lakav* (possibly meaningless sounds; perhaps a mimicking of the prophet's words); also in verse 13

with the grave[a] we have made an
agreement.
When an overwhelming scourge
sweeps by,
it cannot touch us,
for we have made a lie our refuge
and falsehood[b] our hiding place."

[16]So this is what the Sovereign LORD
says:

"See, I lay a stone in Zion,
a tested stone,
a precious cornerstone for a sure
foundation;
the one who trusts will never be
dismayed.
[17]I will make justice the measuring line
and righteousness the plumb line;
hail will sweep away your refuge, the
lie,
and water will overflow your hiding
place.
[18]Your covenant with death will be
annulled;
your agreement with the grave will
not stand.
When the overwhelming scourge
sweeps by,
you will be beaten down by it.
[19]As often as it comes it will carry you
away;
morning after morning, by day and
by night,
it will sweep through."

The understanding of this message
will bring sheer terror.
[20]The bed is too short to stretch out on,
the blanket too narrow to wrap
around you.
[21]The LORD will rise up as he did at
Mount Perazim,
he will rouse himself as in the
Valley of Gibeon—
to do his work, his strange work,
and perform his task, his alien task.
[22]Now stop your mocking,
or your chains will become
heavier;
the Lord, the LORD Almighty, has told
me
of the destruction decreed against
the whole land.

[23]Listen and hear my voice;
pay attention and hear what I say.

[24]When a farmer plows for planting,
does he plow continually?
Does he keep on breaking up and
harrowing the soil?
[25]When he has leveled the surface,
does he not sow caraway and
scatter cummin?
Does he not plant wheat in its place,[c]
barley in its plot,[c]
and spelt in its field?
[26]His God instructs him
and teaches him the right way.

[27]Caraway is not threshed with a sledge,
nor is a cartwheel rolled over
cummin;
caraway is beaten out with a rod,
and cummin with a stick.
[28]Grain must be ground to make bread;
so one does not go on threshing it
forever.
Though he drives the wheels of his
threshing cart over it,
his horses do not grind it.
[29]All this also comes from the LORD
Almighty,
wonderful in counsel and
magnificent in wisdom.

Woe to David's City

29 Woe to you, Ariel, Ariel,
the city where David settled!
Add year to year
and let your cycle of festivals go
on.
[2]Yet I will besiege Ariel;
she will mourn and lament,
she will be to me like an altar
hearth.[d]
[3]I will encamp against you all around;
I will encircle you with towers
and set up my siege works against
you.
[4]Brought low, you will speak from the
ground;
your speech will mumble out of the
dust.
Your voice will come ghostlike from
the earth;
out of the dust your speech will
whisper.

[a]15 Hebrew *Sheol*; also in verse 18   [b]15 Or *false
gods*   [c]25 The meaning of the Hebrew for this word
is uncertain.   [d]2 The Hebrew for *altar hearth*
sounds like the Hebrew for *Ariel*.

⁵But your many enemies will become
      like fine dust,
   the ruthless hordes like blown chaff.
Suddenly, in an instant,
⁶   the LORD Almighty will come
with thunder and earthquake and
      great noise,
   with windstorm and tempest and
      flames of a devouring fire.
⁷Then the hordes of all the nations that
      fight against Ariel,
   that attack her and her fortress and
      besiege her,
will be as it is with a dream,
   with a vision in the night—
⁸as when a hungry man dreams that he
      is eating,
   but he awakens, and his hunger
      remains;
as when a thirsty man dreams that he
      is drinking,
   but he awakens faint, with his thirst
      unquenched.
So will it be with the hordes of all the
      nations
   that fight against Mount Zion.

⁹Be stunned and amazed,
   blind yourselves and be sightless;
be drunk, but not from wine,
   stagger, but not from beer.
¹⁰The LORD has brought over you a deep
      sleep:
   He has sealed your eyes (the
      prophets);
   he has covered your heads (the seers).

¹¹For you this whole vision is nothing
but words sealed in a scroll. And if you
give the scroll to someone who can read,
and say to him, "Read this, please," he
will answer, "I can't; it is sealed." ¹²Or if
you give the scroll to someone who cannot read, and say, "Read this, please," he
will answer, "I don't know how to read."

¹³The Lord says:

"These people come near to me with
      their mouth
   and honor me with their lips,
   but their hearts are far from me.
Their worship of me
   is made up only of rules taught by
      men.ᵃ
¹⁴Therefore once more I will astound
      these people

with wonder upon wonder;
   the wisdom of the wise will perish,
   the intelligence of the intelligent
      will vanish."
¹⁵Woe to those who go to great depths
      to hide their plans from the LORD,
who do their work in darkness and
      think,
   "Who sees us? Who will know?"
¹⁶You turn things upside down,
   as if the potter were thought to be
      like the clay!
Shall what is formed say to him who
      formed it,
   "He did not make me"?
Can the pot say of the potter,
   "He knows nothing"?

¹⁷In a very short time, will not Lebanon
      be turned into a fertile field
   and the fertile field seem like a
      forest?
¹⁸In that day the deaf will hear the
      words of the scroll,
   and out of gloom and darkness
   the eyes of the blind will see.
¹⁹Once more the humble will rejoice in
      the LORD;
   the needy will rejoice in the Holy
      One of Israel.
²⁰The ruthless will vanish,
   the mockers will disappear,
   and all who have an eye for evil
      will be cut down—
²¹those who with a word make a man
      out to be guilty,
   who ensnare the defender in court
   and with false testimony deprive the
      innocent of justice.

²²Therefore this is what the LORD, who
redeemed Abraham, says to the house of
Jacob:

"No longer will Jacob be ashamed;
   no longer will their faces grow pale.
²³When they see among them their
      children,
   the work of my hands,
they will keep my name holy;
   they will acknowledge the holiness
      of the Holy One of Jacob,
   and will stand in awe of the God of
      Israel.

ᵃ13 Hebrew; Septuagint *They worship me in vain; /
their teachings are but rules taught by men*

²⁴Those who are wayward in spirit will
     gain understanding;
  those who complain will accept
     instruction."

Woe to the Obstinate Nation

30 "Woe to the obstinate children,"
     declares the LORD,
  "to those who carry out plans that are
     not mine,
  forming an alliance, but not by my
     Spirit,
  heaping sin upon sin;
²who go down to Egypt
  without consulting me;
  who look for help to Pharaoh's
     protection,
  to Egypt's shade for refuge.

³But Pharaoh's protection will be to
     your shame,
  Egypt's shade will bring you
     disgrace.
⁴Though they have officials in Zoan
  and their envoys have arrived in
     Hanes,
⁵everyone will be put to shame
  because of a people useless to them,
  who bring neither help nor advantage,
  but only shame and disgrace."

⁶An oracle concerning the animals of
the Negev:

Through a land of hardship and
     distress,
  of lions and lionesses,
  of adders and darting snakes,

Wednesday

My Way

Read Isaiah 30:1–3

I wanted to buy a bike. My parents told me to think about my decision and make sure that this was what I really wanted to do with my money. But I didn't want anybody to tell me what to do, so I just went out and bought a bike without really looking into what I wanted and how much I should pay. I made a bad decision because I was too stubborn to listen to my parents.

I'm not always so great about listening to God either. But deep down, I know God always knows what's best and that I should obey him. For every big decision we need to make, God has an answer. He wants us to live for him, to honor him and to love other people. If we do those things, we'll make good decisions. But if we just do whatever we want, we're asking for trouble.

That's what Isaiah was warning people about. I think most of us try to "carry out plans" that aren't God's. And every time we do, we're opening the door for big problems to come on in. If people—including me—would just realize that God's incredible wisdom can help us make good decisions, we could save ourselves a lot of trouble.

❶ Think about a time when you've stubbornly done what you wanted, even though you knew it wasn't smart. What was the result of acting stubborn?

❷ For one day, keep a record of all the decisions you have to make. At the end of the day, think about how you made those decisions. Did you talk with anyone about your decisions? How many of your decisions affected other people? How often did your faith affect your decisions?

❸ Ask God to help you follow his plans for your life.

Turn to page 842 for your next devotion.

the envoys carry their riches on
    donkeys' backs,
  their treasures on the humps of
    camels,
to that unprofitable nation,
7   to Egypt, whose help is utterly
    useless.
Therefore I call her
  Rahab the Do-Nothing.

"You ... You ... Do-Nothing!"

Huh?

Isaiah 30:7

Seems like a weird insult, doesn't it? Rahab
was a mythical sea monster, and the title
Do-Nothing literally means "to sit still." The
author uses this as a symbolic reference to
the Egyptians who were becoming friends
with the Israelites against God's wishes.
The Israelites were putting their trust in
Egypt instead of God. Whenever we put all
our hope and trust in somebody other than
God, we set ourselves up for failure.

8 Go now, write it on a tablet for them,
  inscribe it on a scroll,
that for the days to come
  it may be an everlasting witness.
9 These are rebellious people, deceitful
    children,
  children unwilling to listen to the
    LORD's instruction.
10 They say to the seers,
  "See no more visions!"
and to the prophets,
  "Give us no more visions of what is
    right!
Tell us pleasant things,
  prophesy illusions.
11 Leave this way,
  get off this path,
and stop confronting us
  with the Holy One of Israel!"

12 Therefore, this is what the Holy One
of Israel says:

"Because you have rejected this
    message,
  relied on oppression
  and depended on deceit,
13 this sin will become for you
  like a high wall, cracked and
    bulging,
  that collapses suddenly, in an
    instant.
14 It will break in pieces like pottery,
  shattered so mercilessly
that among its pieces not a fragment
    will be found
  for taking coals from a hearth
  or scooping water out of a
    cistern."

15 This is what the Sovereign LORD, the
Holy One of Israel, says:

"In repentance and rest is your
    salvation,
  in quietness and trust is your
    strength,
  but you would have none of it.
16 You said, 'No, we will flee on horses.'
  Therefore you will flee!
You said, 'We will ride off on swift
    horses.'
  Therefore your pursuers will be
    swift!
17 A thousand will flee
  at the threat of one;
at the threat of five
  you will all flee away,
till you are left
  like a flagstaff on a mountaintop,
  like a banner on a hill."

18 Yet the LORD longs to be gracious to
    you;
  he rises to show you compassion.
For the LORD is a God of justice.
  Blessed are all who wait for him!

19 O people of Zion, who live in Jerusalem, you will weep no more. How gracious he will be when you cry for help!
As soon as he hears, he will answer you.
20 Although the Lord gives you the bread
of adversity and the water of affliction,
your teachers will be hidden no more;
with your own eyes you will see them.
21 Whether you turn to the right or to the
left, your ears will hear a voice behind
you, saying, "This is the way; walk in it."
22 Then you will defile your idols overlaid
with silver and your images covered with
gold; you will throw them away like a
menstrual cloth and say to them, "Away
with you!"

²³He will also send you rain for the seed you sow in the ground, and the food that comes from the land will be rich and plentiful. In that day your cattle will graze in broad meadows. ²⁴The oxen and donkeys that work the soil will eat fodder and mash, spread out with fork and shovel. ²⁵In the day of great slaughter, when the towers fall, streams of water will flow on every high mountain and every lofty hill. ²⁶The moon will shine like the sun, and the sunlight will be seven times brighter, like the light of seven full days, when the LORD binds up the bruises of his people and heals the wounds he inflicted.

²⁷ See, the Name of the LORD comes from afar,
    with burning anger and dense
      clouds of smoke;
  his lips are full of wrath,
    and his tongue is a consuming fire.
²⁸ His breath is like a rushing torrent,
    rising up to the neck.
He shakes the nations in the sieve of
      destruction;
  he places in the jaws of the peoples
  a bit that leads them astray.
²⁹ And you will sing
    as on the night you celebrate a holy
      festival;
  your hearts will rejoice
    as when people go up with flutes
to the mountain of the LORD,
  to the Rock of Israel.
³⁰ The LORD will cause men to hear his
      majestic voice
  and will make them see his arm
      coming down
with raging anger and consuming fire,
  with cloudburst, thunderstorm and
      hail.
³¹ The voice of the LORD will shatter
    Assyria;
  with his scepter he will strike them
    down.
³² Every stroke the LORD lays on them
  with his punishing rod
will be to the music of tambourines
    and harps,
  as he fights them in battle with the
    blows of his arm.
³³ Topheth has long been prepared;
  it has been made ready for the king.

Its fire pit has been made deep and
    wide,
  with an abundance of fire and wood;
the breath of the LORD,
  like a stream of burning sulfur,
  sets it ablaze.

Woe to Those Who Rely on Egypt

31 Woe to those who go down to
    Egypt for help,
  who rely on horses,
who trust in the multitude of their
    chariots
  and in the great strength of their
    horsemen,
but do not look to the Holy One of
    Israel,
  or seek help from the LORD.
² Yet he too is wise and can bring
    disaster;
  he does not take back his words.
He will rise up against the house of
    the wicked,
  against those who help evildoers.
³ But the Egyptians are men and not
    God;
  their horses are flesh and not spirit.
When the LORD stretches out his hand,
  he who helps will stumble,
  he who is helped will fall;
  both will perish together.

⁴ This is what the LORD says to me:

"As a lion growls,
  a great lion over his prey—
and though a whole band of
    shepherds
  is called together against him,
he is not frightened by their shouts
  or disturbed by their clamor—
so the LORD Almighty will come down
  to do battle on Mount Zion and on
    its heights.
⁵ Like birds hovering overhead,
  the LORD Almighty will shield
    Jerusalem;
he will shield it and deliver it,
  he will 'pass over' it and will rescue
    it."

⁶Return to him you have so greatly revolted against, O Israelites. ⁷For in that day every one of you will reject the idols of silver and gold your sinful hands have made.

[8] "Assyria will fall by a sword that is
not of man;
a sword, not of mortals, will devour
them.
They will flee before the sword
and their young men will be put to
forced labor.
[9] Their stronghold will fall because of
terror;
at sight of the battle standard their
commanders will panic,"
declares the LORD,
whose fire is in Zion,
whose furnace is in Jerusalem.

The Kingdom of Righteousness

32 See, a king will reign in
righteousness
and rulers will rule with justice.
[2] Each man will be like a shelter from
the wind
and a refuge from the storm,
like streams of water in the desert
and the shadow of a great rock in a
thirsty land.

[3] Then the eyes of those who see will
no longer be closed,
and the ears of those who hear will
listen.
[4] The mind of the rash will know and
understand,
and the stammering tongue will be
fluent and clear.
[5] No longer will the fool be called noble
nor the scoundrel be highly respected.
[6] For the fool speaks folly,
his mind is busy with evil:
He practices ungodliness
and spreads error concerning the
LORD;
the hungry he leaves empty
and from the thirsty he withholds
water.
[7] The scoundrel's methods are wicked,
he makes up evil schemes
to destroy the poor with lies,
even when the plea of the needy is
just.
[8] But the noble man makes noble plans,
and by noble deeds he stands.

The Women of Jerusalem

[9] You women who are so complacent,
rise up and listen to me;

you daughters who feel secure,
hear what I have to say!
[10] In little more than a year
you who feel secure will tremble;
the grape harvest will fail,
and the harvest of fruit will not
come.
[11] Tremble, you complacent women;
shudder, you daughters who feel
secure!
Strip off your clothes,
put sackcloth around your waists.
[12] Beat your breasts for the pleasant
fields,
for the fruitful vines
[13] and for the land of my people,
a land overgrown with thorns and
briers—
yes, mourn for all houses of merriment
and for this city of revelry.
[14] The fortress will be abandoned,
the noisy city deserted;
citadel and watchtower will become a
wasteland forever,
the delight of donkeys, a pasture for
flocks,
[15] till the Spirit is poured upon us from
on high,
and the desert becomes a fertile
field,
and the fertile field seems like a
forest.
[16] Justice will dwell in the desert
and righteousness live in the fertile
field.
[17] The fruit of righteousness will be
peace;
the effect of righteousness will be
quietness and confidence
forever.
[18] My people will live in peaceful
dwelling places,
in secure homes,
in undisturbed places of rest.
[19] Though hail flattens the forest
and the city is leveled completely,
[20] how blessed you will be,
sowing your seed by every stream,
and letting your cattle and donkeys
range free.

Distress and Help

33 Woe to you, O destroyer,
you who have not been
destroyed!

Woe to you, O traitor,
  you who have not been betrayed!
When you stop destroying,
  you will be destroyed;
when you stop betraying,
  you will be betrayed.

²O LORD, be gracious to us;
  we long for you.
Be our strength every morning,
  our salvation in time of distress.
³At the thunder of your voice, the
    peoples flee;
  when you rise up, the nations
    scatter.
⁴Your plunder, O nations, is harvested
    as by young locusts;
  like a swarm of locusts men pounce
    on it.

⁵The LORD is exalted, for he dwells on
    high;
  he will fill Zion with justice and
    righteousness.
⁶He will be the sure foundation for
    your times,
  a rich store of salvation and
    wisdom and knowledge;
  the fear of the LORD is the key to
    this treasure.ᵃ

⁷Look, their brave men cry aloud in the
    streets;
  the envoys of peace weep
    bitterly.
⁸The highways are deserted,
  no travelers are on the roads.
The treaty is broken,
  its witnessesᵇ are despised,
  no one is respected.
⁹The land mournsᶜ and wastes away,
  Lebanon is ashamed and withers;
Sharon is like the Arabah,
  and Bashan and Carmel drop their
    leaves.

¹⁰"Now will I arise," says the LORD.
  "Now will I be exalted;
  now will I be lifted up.
¹¹You conceive chaff,
  you give birth to straw;
  your breath is a fire that consumes
    you.
¹²The peoples will be burned as if to
    lime;
  like cut thornbushes they will be set
    ablaze."

¹³You who are far away, hear what I
    have done;
  you who are near, acknowledge my
    power!
¹⁴The sinners in Zion are terrified;
  trembling grips the godless:
"Who of us can dwell with the
    consuming fire?
Who of us can dwell with
    everlasting burning?"
¹⁵He who walks righteously
  and speaks what is right,
who rejects gain from extortion
  and keeps his hand from accepting
    bribes,
who stops his ears against plots of
    murder
  and shuts his eyes against
    contemplating evil—
¹⁶this is the man who will dwell on the
    heights,
  whose refuge will be the mountain
    fortress.
His bread will be supplied,
  and water will not fail him.

¹⁷Your eyes will see the king in his
    beauty
  and view a land that stretches afar.
¹⁸In your thoughts you will ponder the
    former terror:
"Where is that chief officer?
Where is the one who took the
    revenue?
Where is the officer in charge of the
    towers?"
¹⁹You will see those arrogant people no
    more,
  those people of an obscure speech,
  with their strange,
    incomprehensible tongue.

²⁰Look upon Zion, the city of our
    festivals;
  your eyes will see Jerusalem,
a peaceful abode, a tent that will
    not be moved;
  its stakes will never be pulled up,
  nor any of its ropes broken.
²¹There the LORD will be our Mighty
    One.
  It will be like a place of broad rivers
    and streams.

ᵃ6 Or *is a treasure from him*   ᵇ8 Dead Sea Scrolls;
Masoretic Text / *the cities*   ᶜ9 Or *dries up*

No galley with oars will ride them,
  no mighty ship will sail them.
[22] For the LORD is our judge,
  the LORD is our lawgiver,
  the LORD is our king;
    it is he who will save us.

[23] Your rigging hangs loose:
  The mast is not held secure,
  the sail is not spread.
Then an abundance of spoils will be
    divided
  and even the lame will carry off
    plunder.
[24] No one living in Zion will say, "I am
    ill";
  and the sins of those who dwell
    there will be forgiven.

Judgment Against the Nations

34 Come near, you nations, and
    listen;
  pay attention, you peoples!
Let the earth hear, and all that is in it,
  the world, and all that comes out of
    it!
[2] The LORD is angry with all nations;
  his wrath is upon all their armies.
He will totally destroy[a] them,
  he will give them over to slaughter.
[3] Their slain will be thrown out,
  their dead bodies will send up a
    stench;
  the mountains will be soaked with
    their blood.
[4] All the stars of the heavens will be
    dissolved
  and the sky rolled up like a scroll;
all the starry host will fall
  like withered leaves from the vine,
  like shriveled figs from the fig tree.

[5] My sword has drunk its fill in the
    heavens;
  see, it descends in judgment on
    Edom,
  the people I have totally destroyed.
[6] The sword of the LORD is bathed in
    blood,
  it is covered with fat—
the blood of lambs and goats,
  fat from the kidneys of rams.
For the LORD has a sacrifice in Bozrah
  and a great slaughter in Edom.
[7] And the wild oxen will fall with them,
  the bull calves and the great bulls.

Their land will be drenched with
    blood,
  and the dust will be soaked with fat.

[8] For the LORD has a day of vengeance,
  a year of retribution, to uphold
    Zion's cause.
[9] Edom's streams will be turned into
    pitch,
  her dust into burning sulfur;
  her land will become blazing pitch!
[10] It will not be quenched night and day;
  its smoke will rise forever.
From generation to generation it will
    lie desolate;
  no one will ever pass through it
    again.
[11] The desert owl[b] and screech owl[b] will
    possess it;
  the great owl[b] and the raven will
    nest there.
God will stretch out over Edom
  the measuring line of chaos
  and the plumb line of desolation.
[12] Her nobles will have nothing there to
    be called a kingdom,
  all her princes will vanish away.
[13] Thorns will overrun her citadels,
  nettles and brambles her
    strongholds.
She will become a haunt for jackals,
  a home for owls.
[14] Desert creatures will meet with
    hyenas,
  and wild goats will bleat to each
    other;
  there the night creatures will also
    repose
  and find for themselves places of
    rest.
[15] The owl will nest there and lay eggs,
  she will hatch them, and care for
      her young under the shadow of
      her wings;
  there also the falcons will gather,
    each with its mate.

[16] Look in the scroll of the LORD and
read:

None of these will be missing,
  not one will lack her mate.

[a]2 The Hebrew term refers to the irrevocable giving
over of things or persons to the LORD, often by
totally destroying them; also in verse 5.   [b]11 The
precise identification of these birds is uncertain.

For it is his mouth that has given the
order,
and his Spirit will gather them
together.
¹⁷He allots their portions;
his hand distributes them by
measure.
They will possess it forever
and dwell there from generation to
generation.

Joy of the Redeemed

35 The desert and the parched land
will be glad;
the wilderness will rejoice and
blossom.
Like the crocus, ²it will burst into
bloom;
it will rejoice greatly and shout for
joy.
The glory of Lebanon will be given to
it,
the splendor of Carmel and Sharon;
they will see the glory of the LORD,
the splendor of our God.

³Strengthen the feeble hands,
steady the knees that give way;
⁴say to those with fearful hearts,
"Be strong, do not fear;
your God will come,
he will come with vengeance;
with divine retribution
he will come to save you."

⁵Then will the eyes of the blind be
opened
and the ears of the deaf unstopped.
⁶Then will the lame leap like a deer,
and the mute tongue shout for joy.
Water will gush forth in the wilderness
and streams in the desert.
⁷The burning sand will become a pool,
the thirsty ground bubbling springs.
In the haunts where jackals once lay,
grass and reeds and papyrus will
grow.

⁸And a highway will be there;
it will be called the Way of
Holiness.
The unclean will not journey on it;
it will be for those who walk in that
Way;
wicked fools will not go about on
it.^a

⁹No lion will be there,
nor will any ferocious beast get up
on it;
they will not be found there.
But only the redeemed will walk there,
¹⁰   and the ransomed of the LORD will
return.
They will enter Zion with singing;
everlasting joy will crown their
heads.
Gladness and joy will overtake them,
and sorrow and sighing will flee
away.

Sennacherib Threatens Jerusalem

36 In the fourteenth year of King
Hezekiah's reign, Sennacherib
king of Assyria attacked all the fortified
cities of Judah and captured them. ²Then
the king of Assyria sent his field commander with a large army from Lachish
to King Hezekiah at Jerusalem. When the
commander stopped at the aqueduct of
the Upper Pool, on the road to the
Washerman's Field, ³Eliakim son of Hilkiah the palace administrator, Shebna
the secretary, and Joah son of Asaph the
recorder went out to him.

⁴The field commander said to them,
"Tell Hezekiah,

" 'This is what the great king, the
king of Assyria, says: On what are
you basing this confidence of yours?
⁵You say you have strategy and mil-
itary strength—but you speak only
empty words. On whom are you depending, that you rebel against me?
⁶Look now, you are depending on
Egypt, that splintered reed of a staff,
which pierces a man's hand and
wounds him if he leans on it! Such is
Pharaoh king of Egypt to all who
depend on him. ⁷And if you say to
me, "We are depending on the LORD
our God"—isn't he the one whose
high places and altars Hezekiah removed, saying to Judah and Jerusalem, "You must worship before this
altar"?
⁸" 'Come now, make a bargain
with my master, the king of Assyria:
I will give you two thousand

^a8 Or / the simple will not stray from it

horses—if you can put riders on them! ⁹How then can you repulse one officer of the least of my master's officials, even though you are depending on Egypt for chariots and horsemen? ¹⁰Furthermore, have I come to attack and destroy this land without the LORD? The LORD himself told me to march against this country and destroy it.' "

¹¹Then Eliakim, Shebna and Joah said to the field commander, "Please speak to your servants in Aramaic, since we understand it. Don't speak to us in Hebrew in the hearing of the people on the wall."

¹²But the commander replied, "Was it only to your master and you that my master sent me to say these things, and not to the men sitting on the wall—who, like you, will have to eat their own filth and drink their own urine?"

¹³Then the commander stood and called out in Hebrew, "Hear the words of the great king, the king of Assyria! ¹⁴This is what the king says: Do not let Hezekiah deceive you. He cannot deliver you! ¹⁵Do not let Hezekiah persuade you to trust in the LORD when he says, 'The LORD will surely deliver us; this city will not be given into the hand of the king of Assyria.'

¹⁶"Do not listen to Hezekiah. This is what the king of Assyria says: Make peace with me and come out to me. Then every one of you will eat from his own vine and fig tree and drink water from his own cistern, ¹⁷until I come and take you to a land like your own—a land of grain and new wine, a land of bread and vineyards.

¹⁸"Do not let Hezekiah mislead you when he says, 'The LORD will deliver us.' Has the god of any nation ever delivered his land from the hand of the king of Assyria? ¹⁹Where are the gods of Hamath and Arpad? Where are the gods of Sepharvaim? Have they rescued Samaria from my hand? ²⁰Who of all the gods of these countries has been able to save his land from me? How then can the LORD deliver Jerusalem from my hand?"

²¹But the people remained silent and said nothing in reply, because the king had commanded, "Do not answer him."

²²Then Eliakim son of Hilkiah the palace administrator, Shebna the secretary, and Joah son of Asaph the recorder went to Hezekiah, with their clothes torn, and told him what the field commander had said.

Jerusalem's Deliverance Foretold

37 When King Hezekiah heard this, he tore his clothes and put on sackcloth and went into the temple of the LORD. ²He sent Eliakim the palace administrator, Shebna the secretary, and the leading priests, all wearing sackcloth, to the prophet Isaiah son of Amoz. ³They told him, "This is what Hezekiah says: This day is a day of distress and rebuke and disgrace, as when children come to the point of birth and there is no strength to deliver them. ⁴It may be that the LORD your God will hear the words of the field commander, whom his master, the king of Assyria, has sent to ridicule the living God, and that he will rebuke him for the words the LORD your God has heard. Therefore pray for the remnant that still survives."

⁵When King Hezekiah's officials came to Isaiah, ⁶Isaiah said to them, "Tell your master, 'This is what the LORD says: Do not be afraid of what you have heard—those words with which the underlings of the king of Assyria have blasphemed me. ⁷Listen! I am going to put a spirit in him so that when he hears a certain report, he will return to his own country, and there I will have him cut down with the sword.' "

⁸When the field commander heard that the king of Assyria had left Lachish, he withdrew and found the king fighting against Libnah.

⁹Now Sennacherib received a report that Tirhakah, the Cushite[a] king of Egypt, was marching out to fight against him. When he heard it, he sent messengers to Hezekiah with this word: ¹⁰"Say to Hezekiah king of Judah: Do not let the god you depend on deceive you when he says, 'Jerusalem will not be handed over to the king of Assyria.' ¹¹Surely you have heard what the kings of Assyria have done to all the countries, destroying

---

[a] 9 That is, from the upper Nile region

them completely. And will you be delivered? [12]Did the gods of the nations that were destroyed by my forefathers deliver them—the gods of Gozan, Haran, Rezeph and the people of Eden who were in Tel Assar? [13]Where is the king of Hamath, the king of Arpad, the king of the city of Sepharvaim, or of Hena or Ivvah?"

Hezekiah's Prayer

[14]Hezekiah received the letter from the messengers and read it. Then he went up to the temple of the LORD and spread it out before the LORD. [15]And Hezekiah prayed to the LORD: [16]"O LORD Almighty, God of Israel, enthroned between the cherubim, you alone are God over all the kingdoms of the earth. You have made heaven and earth. [17]Give ear, O LORD, and hear; open your eyes, O LORD, and see; listen to all the words Sennacherib has sent to insult the living God.

[18]"It is true, O LORD, that the Assyrian kings have laid waste all these peoples and their lands. [19]They have thrown their gods into the fire and destroyed them, for they were not gods but only wood and stone, fashioned by human hands. [20]Now, O LORD our God, deliver us from his hand, so that all kingdoms on earth may know that you alone, O LORD, are God.[a]"

Sennacherib's Fall

[21]Then Isaiah son of Amoz sent a message to Hezekiah: "This is what the LORD, the God of Israel, says: Because you have prayed to me concerning Sennacherib king of Assyria, [22]this is the word the LORD has spoken against him:

"The Virgin Daughter of Zion
  despises and mocks you.
The Daughter of Jerusalem
  tosses her head as you flee.
[23]Who is it you have insulted and
    blasphemed?
  Against whom have you raised your
    voice
and lifted your eyes in pride?
  Against the Holy One of Israel!
[24]By your messengers
  you have heaped insults on the
    Lord.
And you have said,
  'With my many chariots

I have ascended the heights of the
    mountains,
  the utmost heights of Lebanon.
I have cut down its tallest cedars,
  the choicest of its pines.
I have reached its remotest heights,
  the finest of its forests.
[25]I have dug wells in foreign lands[b]
  and drunk the water there.
With the soles of my feet
  I have dried up all the streams of
    Egypt.'

[26]"Have you not heard?
  Long ago I ordained it.
In days of old I planned it;
  now I have brought it to pass,
that you have turned fortified cities
  into piles of stone.
[27]Their people, drained of power,
  are dismayed and put to shame.
They are like plants in the field,
  like tender green shoots,
like grass sprouting on the roof,
  scorched[c] before it grows up.

[28]"But I know where you stay
  and when you come and go
  and how you rage against me.
[29]Because you rage against me
  and because your insolence has
    reached my ears,
I will put my hook in your nose
  and my bit in your mouth,
and I will make you return
  by the way you came.

[30]"This will be the sign for you, O Hezekiah:

"This year you will eat what grows by
    itself,
  and the second year what springs
    from that.
But in the third year sow and reap,
  plant vineyards and eat their fruit.
[31]Once more a remnant of the house of
    Judah
  will take root below and bear fruit
    above.

[a]20 Dead Sea Scrolls (see also 2 Kings 19:19); Masoretic Text *alone are the* LORD   [b]25 Dead Sea Scrolls (see also 2 Kings 19:24); Masoretic Text does not have *in foreign lands.*   [c]27 Some manuscripts of the Masoretic Text, Dead Sea Scrolls and some Septuagint manuscripts (see also 2 Kings 19:26); most manuscripts of the Masoretic Text *roof / and terraced fields*

³²For out of Jerusalem will come a
    remnant,
    and out of Mount Zion a band of
       survivors.
The zeal of the LORD Almighty
    will accomplish this.

³³"Therefore this is what the LORD says
concerning the king of Assyria:

"He will not enter this city
    or shoot an arrow here.
He will not come before it with shield
    or build a siege ramp against it.
³⁴By the way that he came he will
       return;
    he will not enter this city,"
                declares the LORD.
³⁵"I will defend this city and save it,
    for my sake and for the sake of
       David my servant!"

³⁶Then the angel of the LORD went out
and put to death a hundred and eighty-
five thousand men in the Assyrian camp.
When the people got up the next morn-
ing—there were all the dead bodies! ³⁷So
Sennacherib king of Assyria broke camp
and withdrew. He returned to Nineveh
and stayed there.

³⁸One day, while he was worshiping in
the temple of his god Nisroch, his sons
Adrammelech and Sharezer cut him
down with the sword, and they escaped
to the land of Ararat. And Esarhaddon
his son succeeded him as king.

Hezekiah's Illness

38 In those days Hezekiah became ill
and was at the point of death. The
prophet Isaiah son of Amoz went to him
and said, "This is what the LORD says: Put
your house in order, because you are going to die; you will not recover."
²Hezekiah turned his face to the wall
and prayed to the LORD, ³"Remember,
O LORD, how I have walked before you
faithfully and with wholehearted devotion and have done what is good in your
eyes." And Hezekiah wept bitterly.

⁴Then the word of the LORD came to
Isaiah: ⁵"Go and tell Hezekiah, 'This is
what the LORD, the God of your father
David, says: I have heard your prayer
and seen your tears; I will add fifteen
years to your life. ⁶And I will deliver you

and this city from the hand of the king of
Assyria. I will defend this city.

⁷" 'This is the LORD's sign to you that
the LORD will do what he has promised: ⁸I
will make the shadow cast by the sun go
back the ten steps it has gone down on
the stairway of Ahaz.' " So the sunlight
went back the ten steps it had gone
down.

⁹A writing of Hezekiah king of Judah
after his illness and recovery:

¹⁰I said, "In the prime of my life
    must I go through the gates of
       death^a
    and be robbed of the rest of my
       years?"
¹¹I said, "I will not again see the LORD,
    the LORD, in the land of the living;
no longer will I look on mankind,
    or be with those who now dwell in
       this world.^b
¹²Like a shepherd's tent my house
    has been pulled down and taken
       from me.
Like a weaver I have rolled up my life,
    and he has cut me off from the
       loom;
    day and night you made an end of
       me.
¹³I waited patiently till dawn,
    but like a lion he broke all my
       bones;
    day and night you made an end of
       me.
¹⁴I cried like a swift or thrush,
    I moaned like a mourning dove.
My eyes grew weak as I looked to the
       heavens.
    I am troubled; O Lord, come to my
       aid!"

¹⁵But what can I say?
    He has spoken to me, and he
       himself has done this.
I will walk humbly all my years
    because of this anguish of my soul.
¹⁶Lord, by such things men live;
    and my spirit finds life in them too.
You restored me to health
    and let me live.
¹⁷Surely it was for my benefit
    that I suffered such anguish.

---

^a10 Hebrew *Sheol*   ^b11 A few Hebrew manuscripts;
most Hebrew manuscripts *in the place of cessation*

In your love you kept me
from the pit of destruction;
you have put all my sins
behind your back.
[18] For the grave[a] cannot praise you,
death cannot sing your praise;
those who go down to the pit
cannot hope for your faithfulness.
[19] The living, the living—they praise
you,
as I am doing today;
fathers tell their children
about your faithfulness.

[20] The LORD will save me,
and we will sing with stringed
instruments
all the days of our lives
in the temple of the LORD.

[21] Isaiah had said, "Prepare a poultice of figs and apply it to the boil, and he will recover."

[22] Hezekiah had asked, "What will be the sign that I will go up to the temple of the LORD?"

Envoys From Babylon

39 At that time Merodach-Baladan son of Baladan king of Babylon sent Hezekiah letters and a gift, because he had heard of his illness and recovery. [2] Hezekiah received the envoys gladly and showed them what was in his storehouses—the silver, the gold, the spices, the fine oil, his entire armory and everything found among his treasures. There was nothing in his palace or in all his kingdom that Hezekiah did not show them.

[3] Then Isaiah the prophet went to King Hezekiah and asked, "What did those men say, and where did they come from?"

"From a distant land," Hezekiah replied. "They came to me from Babylon."

[4] The prophet asked, "What did they see in your palace?"

"They saw everything in my palace," Hezekiah said. "There is nothing among my treasures that I did not show them."

[5] Then Isaiah said to Hezekiah, "Hear the word of the LORD Almighty: [6] The time will surely come when everything in your palace, and all that your fathers have stored up until this day, will be carried off to Babylon. Nothing will be left, says the LORD. [7] And some of your descendants, your own flesh and blood who will be born to you, will be taken away, and they will become eunuchs in the palace of the king of Babylon."

[8] "The word of the LORD you have spoken is good," Hezekiah replied. For he thought, "There will be peace and security in my lifetime."

Comfort for God's People

40 Comfort, comfort my people,
says your God.
[2] Speak tenderly to Jerusalem,
and proclaim to her
that her hard service has been
completed,
that her sin has been paid for,
that she has received from the LORD's
hand
double for all her sins.

[3] A voice of one calling:
"In the desert prepare
the way for the LORD[b];
make straight in the wilderness
a highway for our God.[c]
[4] Every valley shall be raised up,
every mountain and hill made low;
the rough ground shall become
level,
the rugged places a plain.
[5] And the glory of the LORD will be
revealed,
and all mankind together will see it.
For the mouth of the LORD
has spoken."

[6] A voice says, "Cry out."
And I said, "What shall I cry?"

"All men are like grass,
and all their glory is like the flowers
of the field.
[7] The grass withers and the flowers fall,
because the breath of the LORD
blows on them.
Surely the people are grass.
[8] The grass withers and the flowers fall,
but the word of our God stands
forever."

[a]18 Hebrew *Sheol*   [b]3 Or *A voice of one calling in the desert: / "Prepare the way for the LORD*
[c]3 Hebrew; Septuagint *make straight the paths of our God*

⁹You who bring good tidings to Zion,
   go up on a high mountain.
You who bring good tidings to
      Jerusalem,ᵃ
   lift up your voice with a shout,
 lift it up, do not be afraid;
   say to the towns of Judah,
   "Here is your God!"
¹⁰See, the Sovereign LORD comes with
      power,
   and his arm rules for him.
   See, his reward is with him,
      and his recompense accompanies
      him.
¹¹He tends his flock like a shepherd:
   He gathers the lambs in his arms
 and carries them close to his heart;
   he gently leads those that have
      young.

¹²Who has measured the waters in the
      hollow of his hand,
   or with the breadth of his hand
      marked off the heavens?
Who has held the dust of the earth in
      a basket,
   or weighed the mountains on the
      scales

and the hills in a balance?
¹³Who has understood the mindᵇ of the
      LORD,
   or instructed him as his counselor?
¹⁴Whom did the LORD consult to
      enlighten him,
   and who taught him the right way?
Who was it that taught him
      knowledge
   or showed him the path of
      understanding?

¹⁵Surely the nations are like a drop in a
      bucket;
   they are regarded as dust on the
      scales;
   he weighs the islands as though
      they were fine dust.
¹⁶Lebanon is not sufficient for altar
      fires,
   nor its animals enough for burnt
      offerings.
¹⁷Before him all the nations are as
      nothing;

ᵃ9 Or *O Zion, bringer of good tidings, / go up on a
high mountain. / O Jerusalem, bringer of good
tidings*   ᵇ13 Or *Spirit*; or *spirit*

Thursday

Soaring Like Eagles

Read Isaiah 40:28–31

Isaiah says God never grows weary. So I know when I get tired of school, or all the other things I have to do, the first thing I need to do is ask for God's strength. God's happy to help me out in those situations, as long as I'm willing to let him lead my life.

   God loves to work in people's lives. He loves to see us victorious over sin, which gives him glory and honor. That's why he wants us to rely on his strength instead of our own. Those are the best times for us—the times we soar like eagles.

Tonia age 14

What about You?

❶ Think of a time you felt really worn out. How did God help you?

❷ Flip through some old magazines and look for things that represent strength or power: an athlete, a missile, a powerful political figure, a mountain . . . Then shut the magazines and, with a big, black marker write the word GOD across the covers to help you remember where *real* strength comes from.

❸ Ask God to help you trust in his strength.

Turn to page 847 for your next devotion.

they are regarded by him as
   worthless
and less than nothing.

¹⁸ To whom, then, will you compare
   God?
   What image will you compare him
     to?
¹⁹ As for an idol, a craftsman casts it,
   and a goldsmith overlays it with
     gold
   and fashions silver chains for it.
²⁰ A man too poor to present such an
     offering
   selects wood that will not rot.
He looks for a skilled craftsman
   to set up an idol that will not
     topple.

²¹ Do you not know?
   Have you not heard?
Has it not been told you from the
     beginning?
   Have you not understood since the
     earth was founded?
²² He sits enthroned above the circle of
     the earth,
   and its people are like grasshoppers.
He stretches out the heavens like a
     canopy,
   and spreads them out like a tent to
     live in.
²³ He brings princes to naught
   and reduces the rulers of this world
     to nothing.
²⁴ No sooner are they planted,
   no sooner are they sown,
   no sooner do they take root in the
     ground,
than he blows on them and they
     wither,
   and a whirlwind sweeps them away
     like chaff.

²⁵ "To whom will you compare me?
   Or who is my equal?" says the Holy
     One.
²⁶ Lift your eyes and look to the
     heavens:
   Who created all these?
He who brings out the starry host one
     by one,
   and calls them each by name.
Because of his great power and
     mighty strength,
   not one of them is missing.

²⁷ Why do you say, O Jacob,
   and complain, O Israel,
"My way is hidden from the LORD;
   my cause is disregarded by my
     God"?
²⁸ Do you not know?
   Have you not heard?
The LORD is the everlasting God,
   the Creator of the ends of the earth.
He will not grow tired or weary,
   and his understanding no one can
     fathom.
²⁹ He gives strength to the weary
   and increases the power of the
     weak.
³⁰ Even youths grow tired and weary,
   and young men stumble and fall;
³¹ but those who hope in the LORD
   will renew their strength.
They will soar on wings like eagles;
   they will run and not grow weary,
   they will walk and not be faint.

The Helper of Israel

41 "Be silent before me, you islands!
   Let the nations renew their
     strength!
Let them come forward and speak;
   let us meet together at the place of
     judgment.

² "Who has stirred up one from the east,
   calling him in righteousness to his
     service[a]?
He hands nations over to him
   and subdues kings before him.
He turns them to dust with his sword,
   to windblown chaff with his bow.
³ He pursues them and moves on
     unscathed,
   by a path his feet have not traveled
     before.
⁴ Who has done this and carried it
     through,
   calling forth the generations from
     the beginning?
I, the LORD—with the first of them
   and with the last—I am he."

⁵ The islands have seen it and fear;
   the ends of the earth tremble.
They approach and come forward;
⁶   each helps the other
   and says to his brother, "Be strong!"

a2 Or *| whom victory meets at every step*

7 The craftsman encourages the
    goldsmith,
  and he who smooths with the
    hammer
  spurs on him who strikes the anvil.
He says of the welding, "It is good."
  He nails down the idol so it will not
    topple.

8 "But you, O Israel, my servant,
  Jacob, whom I have chosen,
  you descendants of Abraham my
    friend,
9 I took you from the ends of the earth,
  from its farthest corners I called
    you.
I said, 'You are my servant';
  I have chosen you and have not
    rejected you.
10 So do not fear, for I am with you;
  do not be dismayed, for I am your
    God.
I will strengthen you and help you;
  I will uphold you with my righteous
    right hand.

11 "All who rage against you
  will surely be ashamed and
    disgraced;
those who oppose you
  will be as nothing and perish.
12 Though you search for your enemies,
  you will not find them.
Those who wage war against you
  will be as nothing at all.
13 For I am the LORD, your God,
  who takes hold of your right hand
and says to you, Do not fear;
  I will help you.
14 Do not be afraid, O worm Jacob,
  O little Israel,
for I myself will help you," declares
    the LORD,
  your Redeemer, the Holy One of
    Israel.
15 "See, I will make you into a threshing
    sledge,
  new and sharp, with many teeth.
You will thresh the mountains and
    crush them,
  and reduce the hills to chaff.
16 You will winnow them, the wind will
    pick them up,
  and a gale will blow them away.
But you will rejoice in the LORD
  and glory in the Holy One of Israel.

17 "The poor and needy search for water,
  but there is none;
  their tongues are parched with
    thirst.
But I the LORD will answer them;
  I, the God of Israel, will not forsake
    them.
18 I will make rivers flow on barren
    heights,
  and springs within the valleys.
I will turn the desert into pools of
    water,
  and the parched ground into springs.
19 I will put in the desert
  the cedar and the acacia, the myrtle
    and the olive.
I will set pines in the wasteland,
  the fir and the cypress together,
20 so that people may see and know,
  may consider and understand,
that the hand of the LORD has done
    this,
  that the Holy One of Israel has
    created it.

21 "Present your case," says the LORD.
  "Set forth your arguments," says
    Jacob's King.
22 "Bring in ⌊your idols⌋ to tell us
  what is going to happen.
Tell us what the former things were,
  so that we may consider them
  and know their final outcome.
Or declare to us the things to come,
23   tell us what the future holds,
  so we may know that you are gods.
Do something, whether good or bad,
  so that we will be dismayed and
    filled with fear.
24 But you are less than nothing
  and your works are utterly worthless;
  he who chooses you is detestable.

25 "I have stirred up one from the north,
    and he comes—
  one from the rising sun who calls
    on my name.
He treads on rulers as if they were
    mortar,
  as if he were a potter treading the
    clay.
26 Who told of this from the beginning,
    so we could know,
  or beforehand, so we could say, 'He
    was right'?
No one told of this,

no one foretold it,
no one heard any words from you.
²⁷I was the first to tell Zion, 'Look, here
they are!'
I gave to Jerusalem a messenger of
good tidings.
²⁸I look but there is no one—
no one among them to give counsel,
no one to give answer when I ask
them.
²⁹See, they are all false!
Their deeds amount to nothing;
their images are but wind and
confusion.

The Servant of the LORD

42 "Here is my servant, whom I
uphold,
my chosen one in whom I delight;
I will put my Spirit on him
and he will bring justice to the
nations.

Deja-vu

Huh?

Isaiah 42:1

Think you've heard this one before? Flip
in your Bible to Matthew 12:18–21 (page
1158). Check that out! Same stuff all over
again! Cool, huh? You see, a lot of Old
Testament Scripture makes sense when
applied to Jesus. Isaiah gives us a description of the Messiah. The Messiah
is Jesus!

---

²He will not shout or cry out,
or raise his voice in the streets.
³A bruised reed he will not break,
and a smoldering wick he will not
snuff out.
In faithfulness he will bring forth
justice;
⁴ he will not falter or be discouraged
till he establishes justice on earth.
In his law the islands will put their
hope."

⁵This is what God the LORD says—
he who created the heavens and
stretched them out,

who spread out the earth and all
that comes out of it,
who gives breath to its people,
and life to those who walk on it:
⁶"I, the LORD, have called you in
righteousness;
I will take hold of your hand.
I will keep you and will make you
to be a covenant for the people
and a light for the Gentiles,
⁷to open eyes that are blind,
to free captives from prison
and to release from the dungeon
those who sit in darkness.

⁸"I am the LORD; that is my name!
I will not give my glory to another
or my praise to idols.
⁹See, the former things have taken
place,
and new things I declare;
before they spring into being
I announce them to you."

Song of Praise to the LORD

¹⁰Sing to the LORD a new song,
his praise from the ends of the
earth,
you who go down to the sea, and all
that is in it,
you islands, and all who live in
them.
¹¹Let the desert and its towns raise their
voices;
let the settlements where Kedar
lives rejoice.
Let the people of Sela sing for joy;
let them shout from the
mountaintops.
¹²Let them give glory to the LORD
and proclaim his praise in the
islands.
¹³The LORD will march out like a mighty
man,
like a warrior he will stir up his zeal;
with a shout he will raise the battle
cry
and will triumph over his enemies.

¹⁴"For a long time I have kept silent,
I have been quiet and held myself
back.
But now, like a woman in childbirth,
I cry out, I gasp and pant.
¹⁵I will lay waste the mountains and
hills

and dry up all their vegetation;
I will turn rivers into islands
and dry up the pools.
¹⁶ I will lead the blind by ways they
have not known,
along unfamiliar paths I will guide
them;
I will turn the darkness into light
before them
and make the rough places smooth.
These are the things I will do;
I will not forsake them.
¹⁷ But those who trust in idols,
who say to images, 'You are our
gods,'
will be turned back in utter shame.

Israel Blind and Deaf

¹⁸ "Hear, you deaf;
look, you blind, and see!
¹⁹ Who is blind but my servant,
and deaf like the messenger I send?
Who is blind like the one committed
to me,
blind like the servant of the Lord?
²⁰ You have seen many things, but have
paid no attention;
your ears are open, but you hear
nothing."
²¹ It pleased the Lord
for the sake of his righteousness
to make his law great and glorious.
²² But this is a people plundered and
looted,
all of them trapped in pits
or hidden away in prisons.
They have become plunder,
with no one to rescue them;
they have been made loot,
with no one to say, "Send them
back."

²³ Which of you will listen to this
or pay close attention in time to
come?
²⁴ Who handed Jacob over to become
loot,
and Israel to the plunderers?
Was it not the Lord,
against whom we have sinned?
For they would not follow his ways;
they did not obey his law.
²⁵ So he poured out on them his burning
anger,
the violence of war.

It enveloped them in flames, yet they
did not understand;
it consumed them, but they did not
take it to heart.

Israel's Only Savior

43 But now, this is what the Lord
says—
he who created you, O Jacob,
he who formed you, O Israel:
"Fear not, for I have redeemed you;
I have summoned you by name;
you are mine.
² When you pass through the waters,
I will be with you;
and when you pass through the rivers,
they will not sweep over you.
When you walk through the fire,
you will not be burned;
the flames will not set you ablaze.
³ For I am the Lord, your God,
the Holy One of Israel, your Savior;
I give Egypt for your ransom,
Cush^a and Seba in your stead.
⁴ Since you are precious and honored in
my sight,
and because I love you,
I will give men in exchange for you,
and people in exchange for your
life.
⁵ Do not be afraid, for I am with you;
I will bring your children from the
east
and gather you from the west.
⁶ I will say to the north, 'Give them
up!'
and to the south, 'Do not hold them
back.'
Bring my sons from afar
and my daughters from the ends of
the earth—
⁷ everyone who is called by my name,
whom I created for my glory,
whom I formed and made."

⁸ Lead out those who have eyes but are
blind,
who have ears but are deaf.
⁹ All the nations gather together
and the peoples assemble.
Which of them foretold this
and proclaimed to us the former
things?

^a3 That is, the upper Nile region

Let them bring in their witnesses to
prove they were right,
so that others may hear and say, "It
is true."
¹⁰"You are my witnesses," declares the
LORD,
"and my servant whom I have
chosen,
so that you may know and believe me
and understand that I am he.
Before me no god was formed,
nor will there be one after me.
¹¹I, even I, am the LORD,
and apart from me there is no
savior.
¹²I have revealed and saved and
proclaimed—
I, and not some foreign god among
you.
You are my witnesses," declares the
LORD, "that I am God.
¹³ Yes, and from ancient days I am he.
No one can deliver out of my hand.
When I act, who can reverse it?"

God's Mercy and Israel's Unfaithfulness

¹⁴This is what the LORD says—
your Redeemer, the Holy One of
Israel:
"For your sake I will send to Babylon
and bring down as fugitives all the
Babylonians,ᵃ
in the ships in which they took
pride.
¹⁵I am the LORD, your Holy One,
Israel's Creator, your King."

¹⁶This is what the LORD says—
he who made a way through the
sea,
a path through the mighty waters,
¹⁷who drew out the chariots and horses,
the army and reinforcements
together,
and they lay there, never to rise again,
extinguished, snuffed out like a
wick:

ᵃ 14 Or *Chaldeans*

Friday

He Knows Your Name

Read Isaiah 43:1

This is a verse I'd like to share with my friends. It would show them how much they matter to God. God's not just some mighty ruler who looks down at earth and sees a bunch of nameless people running around. He knows each one of us by name.

God knows our troubles and our happiness. He calls out to us by name. He made each one of us special, and he wants to have a personal relationship with each of us.

When I think of God that way, I realize that he loves me and will never leave me. And best of all, I have God's promise that he called me to come to him so I can have eternal life.

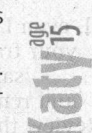

Katy, age 15

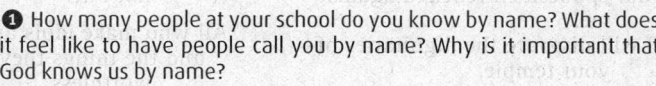
What about You?

❶ How many people at your school do you know by name? What does it feel like to have people call you by name? Why is it important that God knows us by name?

❷ Read Isaiah 43:1, replacing "O Jacob" and "O Israel" with your name. How does your understanding of this verse change when you think God is talking directly to you?

❸ Praise God for creating you and loving you.

Turn to page 859 for your next devotion.

¹⁸ "Forget the former things;
   do not dwell on the past.
¹⁹ See, I am doing a new thing!
   Now it springs up; do you not
      perceive it?
I am making a way in the desert
   and streams in the wasteland.
²⁰ The wild animals honor me,
   the jackals and the owls,
because I provide water in the desert
   and streams in the wasteland,
to give drink to my people, my
      chosen,
²¹   the people I formed for myself
   that they may proclaim my praise.

²² "Yet you have not called upon me,
      O Jacob,
   you have not wearied yourselves for
      me, O Israel.
²³ You have not brought me sheep for
      burnt offerings,
   nor honored me with your
      sacrifices.
I have not burdened you with grain
      offerings
   nor wearied you with demands for
      incense.
²⁴ You have not bought any fragrant
      calamus for me,
   or lavished on me the fat of your
      sacrifices.
But you have burdened me with your
      sins
   and wearied me with your offenses.

²⁵ "I, even I, am he who blots out
   your transgressions, for my own
      sake,
   and remembers your sins no more.
²⁶ Review the past for me,
   let us argue the matter together;
   state the case for your innocence.
²⁷ Your first father sinned;
   your spokesmen rebelled against
      me.
²⁸ So I will disgrace the dignitaries of
      your temple,
   and I will consign Jacob to
      destruction[a]
   and Israel to scorn.

Israel the Chosen

44 "But now listen, O Jacob, my
      servant,
   Israel, whom I have chosen.

²This is what the LORD says—
   he who made you, who formed you
      in the womb,
   and who will help you:
Do not be afraid, O Jacob, my servant,
   Jeshurun, whom I have chosen.
³ For I will pour water on the thirsty
      land,
   and streams on the dry ground;
I will pour out my Spirit on your
      offspring,
   and my blessing on your
      descendants.
⁴ They will spring up like grass in a
      meadow,
   like poplar trees by flowing streams.
⁵ One will say, 'I belong to the LORD';
   another will call himself by the
      name of Jacob;
still another will write on his hand,
   'The LORD's,'
   and will take the name Israel.

The LORD, Not Idols

⁶ "This is what the LORD says—
   Israel's King and Redeemer, the
      LORD Almighty:
I am the first and I am the last;
   apart from me there is no God.
⁷ Who then is like me? Let him
      proclaim it.
   Let him declare and lay out before
      me
what has happened since I established
   my ancient people,
   and what is yet to come—
   yes, let him foretell what will come.
⁸ Do not tremble, do not be afraid.
   Did I not proclaim this and foretell
      it long ago?
You are my witnesses. Is there any
   God besides me?
   No, there is no other Rock; I know
      not one."

⁹ All who make idols are nothing,
   and the things they treasure are
      worthless.
Those who would speak up for them
      are blind;
   they are ignorant, to their own
      shame.

---

a28 The Hebrew term refers to the irrevocable giving
over of things or persons to the LORD, often by
totally destroying them.

¹⁰Who shapes a god and casts an idol,
  which can profit him nothing?
¹¹He and his kind will be put to shame;
  craftsmen are nothing but men.
Let them all come together and take
    their stand;
  they will be brought down to terror
    and infamy.

¹²The blacksmith takes a tool
  and works with it in the coals;
he shapes an idol with hammers,
  he forges it with the might of his
    arm.
He gets hungry and loses his strength;
  he drinks no water and grows faint.
¹³The carpenter measures with a line
  and makes an outline with a
    marker;
he roughs it out with chisels
  and marks it with compasses.
He shapes it in the form of man,
  of man in all his glory,
  that it may dwell in a shrine.
¹⁴He cut down cedars,
  or perhaps took a cypress or oak.
He let it grow among the trees of the
    forest,
  or planted a pine, and the rain
    made it grow.
¹⁵It is man's fuel for burning;
  some of it he takes and warms
    himself,
  he kindles a fire and bakes bread.
But he also fashions a god and
    worships it;
  he makes an idol and bows down to
    it.
¹⁶Half of the wood he burns in the fire;
  over it he prepares his meal,
  he roasts his meat and eats his fill.
He also warms himself and says,
  "Ah! I am warm; I see the fire."
¹⁷From the rest he makes a god, his
    idol;
  he bows down to it and worships it.
He prays to it and says,
  "Save me; you are my god."
¹⁸They know nothing, they understand
    nothing;
  their eyes are plastered over so they
    cannot see,
  and their minds closed so they
    cannot understand.
¹⁹No one stops to think,

  no one has the knowledge or
    understanding to say,
"Half of it I used for fuel;
  I even baked bread over its coals,
  I roasted meat and I ate.
Shall I make a detestable thing from
    what is left?
  Shall I bow down to a block of
    wood?"
²⁰He feeds on ashes, a deluded heart
    misleads him;
  he cannot save himself, or say,
  "Is not this thing in my right hand a
    lie?"

²¹"Remember these things, O Jacob,
  for you are my servant, O Israel.
I have made you, you are my servant;
  O Israel, I will not forget you.
²²I have swept away your offenses like a
    cloud,
  your sins like the morning mist.
Return to me,
  for I have redeemed you."

²³Sing for joy, O heavens, for the Lord
    has done this;
  shout aloud, O earth beneath.
Burst into song, you mountains,
  you forests and all your trees,
for the Lord has redeemed Jacob,
  he displays his glory in Israel.

Jerusalem to Be Inhabited

²⁴"This is what the Lord says—
  your Redeemer, who formed you in
    the womb:

I am the Lord,
  who has made all things,
  who alone stretched out the heavens,
  who spread out the earth by myself,

²⁵who foils the signs of false prophets
  and makes fools of diviners,
who overthrows the learning of the
    wise
  and turns it into nonsense,
²⁶who carries out the words of his
    servants
  and fulfills the predictions of his
    messengers,

who says of Jerusalem, 'It shall be
    inhabited,'
  of the towns of Judah, 'They shall
    be built,'

and of their ruins, 'I will restore
    them,'
[27] who says to the watery deep, 'Be dry,
    and I will dry up your streams,'
[28] who says of Cyrus, 'He is my shepherd
    and will accomplish all that I
        please;
    he will say of Jerusalem, "Let it be
        rebuilt,"
    and of the temple, "Let its
        foundations be laid." '

45 "This is what the LORD says to
      his anointed,
    to Cyrus, whose right hand I take
      hold of
to subdue nations before him
    and to strip kings of their armor,
to open doors before him
    so that gates will not be shut:
[2] I will go before you
    and will level the mountains[a];
I will break down gates of bronze
    and cut through bars of iron.
[3] I will give you the treasures of
      darkness,
    riches stored in secret places,
so that you may know that I am the
      LORD,
    the God of Israel, who summons
      you by name.
[4] For the sake of Jacob my servant,
    of Israel my chosen,
I summon you by name
    and bestow on you a title of honor,
    though you do not acknowledge me.
[5] I am the LORD, and there is no other;
    apart from me there is no God.
I will strengthen you,
    though you have not acknowledged
      me,
[6] so that from the rising of the sun
    to the place of its setting
men may know there is none besides
      me.
    I am the LORD, and there is no other.
[7] I form the light and create darkness,
    I bring prosperity and create
      disaster;
    I, the LORD, do all these things.

[8] "You heavens above, rain down
      righteousness;
    let the clouds shower it down.
Let the earth open wide,

    let salvation spring up,
let righteousness grow with it;
    I, the LORD, have created it.

[9] "Woe to him who quarrels with his
      Maker,
    to him who is but a potsherd
      among the potsherds on the
      ground.
Does the clay say to the potter,
    'What are you making?'
Does your work say,
    'He has no hands'?
[10] Woe to him who says to his father,
    'What have you begotten?'
or to his mother,
    'What have you brought to birth?'

[11] "This is what the LORD says—
    the Holy One of Israel, and its
      Maker:
Concerning things to come,
    do you question me about my
      children,
    or give me orders about the work of
      my hands?
[12] It is I who made the earth
    and created mankind upon it.
My own hands stretched out the
      heavens;
    I marshaled their starry hosts.
[13] I will raise up Cyrus[b] in my
      righteousness:
    I will make all his ways straight.
He will rebuild my city
    and set my exiles free,
but not for a price or reward,
    says the LORD Almighty."

[14] This is what the LORD says:

"The products of Egypt and the
      merchandise of Cush,[c]
    and those tall Sabeans—
they will come over to you
    and will be yours;
they will trudge behind you,
    coming over to you in chains.
They will bow down before you
    and plead with you, saying,
'Surely God is with you, and there is
      no other;
    there is no other god.' "

---

[a]2 Dead Sea Scrolls and Septuagint; the meaning of
the word in the Masoretic Text is uncertain.
[b]13 Hebrew *him*   [c]14 That is, the upper Nile region

¹⁵Truly you are a God who hides
himself,
O God and Savior of Israel.
¹⁶All the makers of idols will be put to
shame and disgraced;
they will go off into disgrace
together.
¹⁷But Israel will be saved by the LORD
with an everlasting salvation;
you will never be put to shame or
disgraced,
to ages everlasting.

¹⁸For this is what the LORD says—
he who created the heavens,
he is God;
he who fashioned and made the earth,
he founded it;
he did not create it to be empty,
but formed it to be inhabited—
he says:
"I am the LORD,
and there is no other.
¹⁹I have not spoken in secret,
from somewhere in a land of
darkness;
I have not said to Jacob's
descendants,
'Seek me in vain.'
I, the LORD, speak the truth;
I declare what is right.

²⁰"Gather together and come;
assemble, you fugitives from the
nations.
Ignorant are those who carry about
idols of wood,
who pray to gods that cannot save.
²¹Declare what is to be, present it—
let them take counsel together.
Who foretold this long ago,
who declared it from the distant
past?
Was it not I, the LORD?
And there is no God apart from me,
a righteous God and a Savior;
there is none but me.

²²"Turn to me and be saved,
all you ends of the earth;
for I am God, and there is no other.
²³By myself I have sworn,
my mouth has uttered in all
integrity
a word that will not be revoked:
Before me every knee will bow;

by me every tongue will swear.
²⁴They will say of me, 'In the LORD
alone
are righteousness and strength.' "
All who have raged against him
will come to him and be put to
shame.
²⁵But in the LORD all the descendants of
Israel
will be found righteous and will
exult.

Gods of Babylon

46 Bel bows down, Nebo stoops
low;
their idols are borne by beasts of
burden.ᵃ
The images that are carried about are
burdensome,
a burden for the weary.
²They stoop and bow down together;
unable to rescue the burden,
they themselves go off into
captivity.

³"Listen to me, O house of Jacob,
all you who remain of the house of
Israel,
you whom I have upheld since you
were conceived,
and have carried since your birth.
⁴Even to your old age and gray hairs
I am he, I am he who will sustain
you.
I have made you and I will carry you;
I will sustain you and I will rescue
you.

⁵"To whom will you compare me or
count me equal?
To whom will you liken me that we
may be compared?
⁶Some pour out gold from their bags
and weigh out silver on the scales;
they hire a goldsmith to make it into a
god,
and they bow down and worship it.
⁷They lift it to their shoulders and
carry it;
they set it up in its place, and there
it stands.
From that spot it cannot move.
Though one cries out to it, it does not
answer;

ᵃ1 Or *are but beasts and cattle*

it cannot save him from his
    troubles.

[8] "Remember this, fix it in mind,
    take it to heart, you rebels.
[9] Remember the former things, those of
        long ago;
    I am God, and there is no other;
    I am God, and there is none like me.
[10] I make known the end from the
        beginning,
    from ancient times, what is still to
        come.
I say: My purpose will stand,
    and I will do all that I please.
[11] From the east I summon a bird of
        prey;
    from a far-off land, a man to fulfill
        my purpose.
What I have said, that will I bring
        about;
    what I have planned, that will I do.
[12] Listen to me, you stubborn-hearted,
    you who are far from righteousness.
[13] I am bringing my righteousness near,
    it is not far away;
    and my salvation will not be
        delayed.
I will grant salvation to Zion,
    my splendor to Israel.

The Fall of Babylon

47   "Go down, sit in the dust,
      Virgin Daughter of Babylon;
sit on the ground without a throne,
    Daughter of the Babylonians.[a]
No more will you be called
    tender or delicate.
[2] Take millstones and grind flour;
    take off your veil.
Lift up your skirts, bare your legs,
    and wade through the streams.
[3] Your nakedness will be exposed
    and your shame uncovered.
I will take vengeance;
    I will spare no one."

[4] Our Redeemer—the LORD Almighty is
      his name—
    is the Holy One of Israel.

[5] "Sit in silence, go into darkness,
    Daughter of the Babylonians;
no more will you be called
    queen of kingdoms.
[6] I was angry with my people

and desecrated my inheritance;
I gave them into your hand,
    and you showed them no mercy.
Even on the aged
    you laid a very heavy yoke.
[7] You said, 'I will continue forever—
    the eternal queen!'
But you did not consider these things
    or reflect on what might happen.

[8] "Now then, listen, you wanton
      creature,
    lounging in your security
and saying to yourself,
    'I am, and there is none besides me.
I will never be a widow
    or suffer the loss of children.'
[9] Both of these will overtake you
    in a moment, on a single day:
    loss of children and widowhood.
They will come upon you in full
      measure,
    in spite of your many sorceries
    and all your potent spells.
[10] You have trusted in your wickedness
    and have said, 'No one sees me.'
Your wisdom and knowledge mislead
      you
    when you say to yourself,
    'I am, and there is none besides me.'
[11] Disaster will come upon you,
    and you will not know how to
        conjure it away.
A calamity will fall upon you
    that you cannot ward off with a
        ransom;
    a catastrophe you cannot foresee
    will suddenly come upon you.

[12] "Keep on, then, with your magic spells
    and with your many sorceries,
    which you have labored at since
        childhood.
Perhaps you will succeed,
    perhaps you will cause terror.
[13] All the counsel you have received has
      only worn you out!
Let your astrologers come forward,
those stargazers who make predictions
      month by month,
    let them save you from what is
      coming upon you.
[14] Surely they are like stubble;
    the fire will burn them up.

---

a 1 Or Chaldeans; also in verse 5

They cannot even save themselves
  from the power of the flame.
Here are no coals to warm anyone;
  here is no fire to sit by.
¹⁵That is all they can do for you—
  these you have labored with
  and trafficked with since childhood.
Each of them goes on in his error;
  there is not one that can save you.

Stubborn Israel

48 "Listen to this, O house of Jacob,
  you who are called by the name
    of Israel
and come from the line of Judah,
you who take oaths in the name of the
    LORD
  and invoke the God of Israel—
  but not in truth or righteousness—
²you who call yourselves citizens of
    the holy city
  and rely on the God of Israel—
  the LORD Almighty is his name:
³I foretold the former things long ago,
  my mouth announced them and I
    made them known;
  then suddenly I acted, and they
    came to pass.
⁴For I knew how stubborn you were;
  the sinews of your neck were iron,
  your forehead was bronze.
⁵Therefore I told you these things long
    ago;
  before they happened I announced
    them to you
so that you could not say,
  'My idols did them;
  my wooden image and metal god
    ordained them.'
⁶You have heard these things; look at
    them all.
  Will you not admit them?

  "From now on I will tell you of new
    things,
  of hidden things unknown to you.
⁷They are created now, and not long
    ago;
  you have not heard of them before
    today.
So you cannot say,
  'Yes, I knew of them.'
⁸You have neither heard nor understood;
  from of old your ear has not been
    open.

Well do I know how treacherous you
    are;
  you were called a rebel from birth.
⁹For my own name's sake I delay my
    wrath;
  for the sake of my praise I hold it
    back from you,
  so as not to cut you off.
¹⁰See, I have refined you, though not as
    silver;
  I have tested you in the furnace of
    affliction.
¹¹For my own sake, for my own sake, I
    do this.
  How can I let myself be defamed?
  I will not yield my glory to another.

Israel Freed

¹²"Listen to me, O Jacob,
  Israel, whom I have called:
I am he;
  I am the first and I am the last.
¹³My own hand laid the foundations of
    the earth,
  and my right hand spread out the
    heavens;
when I summon them,
  they all stand up together.

¹⁴"Come together, all of you, and listen:
  Which of the idols has foretold
    these things?
The LORD's chosen ally
  will carry out his purpose against
    Babylon;
  his arm will be against the
    Babylonians.ᵃ
¹⁵I, even I, have spoken;
  yes, I have called him.
I will bring him,
  and he will succeed in his mission.

¹⁶"Come near me and listen to this:

"From the first announcement I have
    not spoken in secret;
  at the time it happens, I am there."

And now the Sovereign LORD has sent
    me,
  with his Spirit.

¹⁷This is what the LORD says—
  your Redeemer, the Holy One of
    Israel:

ᵃ14 Or *Chaldeans*; also in verse 20

"I am the LORD your God,
　　who teaches you what is best for
　　　you,
　　who directs you in the way you
　　　should go.

A Holy Gift Certificate

Huh?

Isaiah 48:17

Throughout the Bible you may see the word
Redeemer in reference to God. A redeemer
is someone who "buys back" something.
If you go to McDonald's and get some food
using a gift certificate, you have been the
"redeemer" of the gift certificate. You have
"bought back" something. Well, God is our
Redeemer because he has bought us back
through Jesus Christ. (We were lost because
of our sin.) He takes away our sin when we
ask forgiveness from him. He gives us a
holy gift certificate!

---

18 If only you had paid attention to my
　　commands,
　　your peace would have been like a
　　　river,
　　your righteousness like the waves of
　　　the sea.
19 Your descendants would have been
　　like the sand,
　　your children like its numberless
　　　grains;
　their name would never be cut off
　　nor destroyed from before me."

20 Leave Babylon,
　　flee from the Babylonians!
　Announce this with shouts of joy
　　and proclaim it.
　Send it out to the ends of the earth;
　　say, "The LORD has redeemed his
　　　servant Jacob."
21 They did not thirst when he led them
　　through the deserts;
　　he made water flow for them from
　　　the rock;
　he split the rock
　　and water gushed out.

22 "There is no peace," says the LORD,
　　"for the wicked."

The Servant of the LORD

49 Listen to me, you islands;
　　hear this, you distant nations:
Before I was born the LORD called me;
　　from my birth he has made mention
　　　of my name.
2 He made my mouth like a sharpened
　　sword,
　　in the shadow of his hand he hid
　　　me;
　he made me into a polished arrow
　　and concealed me in his quiver.
3 He said to me, "You are my servant,
　Israel, in whom I will display my
　　splendor."
4 But I said, "I have labored to no
　　purpose;
　I have spent my strength in vain
　　and for nothing.
Yet what is due me is in the LORD's
　　hand,
　　and my reward is with my God."

5 And now the LORD says—
　　he who formed me in the womb to
　　　be his servant
to bring Jacob back to him
　　and gather Israel to himself,
for I am honored in the eyes of the
　　LORD
　and my God has been my
　　strength—
6 he says:
"It is too small a thing for you to be
　　my servant
　to restore the tribes of Jacob
　　and bring back those of Israel I
　　　have kept.
I will also make you a light for the
　　Gentiles,
　that you may bring my salvation to
　　the ends of the earth."

7 This is what the LORD says—
　　the Redeemer and Holy One of
　　　Israel—
to him who was despised and
　　abhorred by the nation,
　to the servant of rulers:
"Kings will see you and rise up,
　　princes will see and bow down,
because of the LORD, who is
　　faithful,
　the Holy One of Israel, who has
　　chosen you."

Restoration of Israel

[8]This is what the LORD says:

"In the time of my favor I will answer
you,
    and in the day of salvation I will
    help you;
I will keep you and will make you
    to be a covenant for the people,
to restore the land
    and to reassign its desolate
    inheritances,
[9]to say to the captives, 'Come out,'
    and to those in darkness, 'Be free!'

"They will feed beside the roads
    and find pasture on every barren
    hill.
[10]They will neither hunger nor thirst,
    nor will the desert heat or the sun
    beat upon them.
He who has compassion on them will
    guide them
    and lead them beside springs of
    water.
[11]I will turn all my mountains into
    roads,
    and my highways will be raised up.
[12]See, they will come from afar—
    some from the north, some from the
    west,
    some from the region of Aswan.[a]"

[13]Shout for joy, O heavens;
    rejoice, O earth;
    burst into song, O mountains!
For the LORD comforts his people
    and will have compassion on his
    afflicted ones.

[14]But Zion said, "The LORD has forsaken
    me,
    the Lord has forgotten me."

[15]"Can a mother forget the baby at her
    breast
    and have no compassion on the
    child she has borne?
Though she may forget,
    I will not forget you!
[16]See, I have engraved you on the palms
    of my hands;
    your walls are ever before me.
[17]Your sons hasten back,
    and those who laid you waste
    depart from you.
[18]Lift up your eyes and look around;

all your sons gather and come to
you.
As surely as I live," declares the LORD,
    "you will wear them all as
    ornaments;
you will put them on, like a bride.

[19]"Though you were ruined and made
    desolate
    and your land laid waste,
now you will be too small for your
    people,
    and those who devoured you will be
    far away.
[20]The children born during your
    bereavement
will yet say in your hearing,
'This place is too small for us;
    give us more space to live in.'
[21]Then you will say in your heart,
    'Who bore me these?
I was bereaved and barren;
    I was exiled and rejected.
Who brought these up?
I was left all alone,
    but these—where have they come
    from?'"

[22]This is what the Sovereign LORD says:

"See, I will beckon to the Gentiles,
    I will lift up my banner to the
    peoples;
they will bring your sons in their arms
    and carry your daughters on their
    shoulders.
[23]Kings will be your foster fathers,
    and their queens your nursing
    mothers.
They will bow down before you with
    their faces to the ground;
    they will lick the dust at your feet.
Then you will know that I am the
    LORD;
    those who hope in me will not be
    disappointed."

[24]Can plunder be taken from warriors,
    or captives rescued from the fierce[b]?

[25]But this is what the LORD says:

"Yes, captives will be taken from
    warriors,

---

[a]12 Dead Sea Scrolls; Masoretic Text *Sinim*
[b]24 Dead Sea Scrolls, Vulgate and Syriac (see also
Septuagint and verse 25); Masoretic Text *righteous*

and plunder retrieved from the
    fierce;
I will contend with those who contend
    with you,
and your children I will save.
26 I will make your oppressors eat their
    own flesh;
    they will be drunk on their own
        blood, as with wine.
Then all mankind will know
    that I, the LORD, am your Savior,
    your Redeemer, the Mighty One of
        Jacob."

Israel's Sin and the Servant's Obedience

50 This is what the LORD says:

"Where is your mother's certificate of
    divorce
    with which I sent her away?
Or to which of my creditors
    did I sell you?
Because of your sins you were sold;
    because of your transgressions your
        mother was sent away.
2 When I came, why was there no one?
    When I called, why was there no
        one to answer?
Was my arm too short to ransom you?
    Do I lack the strength to rescue
        you?
By a mere rebuke I dry up the sea,
    I turn rivers into a desert;
their fish rot for lack of water
    and die of thirst.
3 I clothe the sky with darkness
    and make sackcloth its covering."

4 The Sovereign LORD has given me an
    instructed tongue,
    to know the word that sustains the
        weary.
He wakens me morning by morning,
    wakens my ear to listen like one
        being taught.
5 The Sovereign LORD has opened my
        ears,
    and I have not been rebellious;
    I have not drawn back.
6 I offered my back to those who beat me,
    my cheeks to those who pulled out
        my beard;
I did not hide my face
    from mocking and spitting.
7 Because the Sovereign LORD helps me,

I will not be disgraced.
Therefore have I set my face like flint,
    and I know I will not be put to
        shame.
8 He who vindicates me is near.
    Who then will bring charges against
        me?
    Let us face each other!
Who is my accuser?
    Let him confront me!
9 It is the Sovereign LORD who helps me.
    Who is he that will condemn me?
They will all wear out like a garment;
    the moths will eat them up.

10 Who among you fears the LORD
    and obeys the word of his servant?
Let him who walks in the dark,
    who has no light,
trust in the name of the LORD
    and rely on his God.
11 But now, all you who light fires
    and provide yourselves with
        flaming torches,
go, walk in the light of your fires
    and of the torches you have set
        ablaze.
This is what you shall receive from
        my hand:
    You will lie down in torment.

Everlasting Salvation for Zion

51 "Listen to me, you who pursue
        righteousness
    and who seek the LORD:
Look to the rock from which you were
        cut
    and to the quarry from which you
        were hewn;
2 look to Abraham, your father,
    and to Sarah, who gave you birth.
When I called him he was but one,
    and I blessed him and made him
        many.
3 The LORD will surely comfort Zion
    and will look with compassion on
        all her ruins;
he will make her deserts like Eden,
    her wastelands like the garden of
        the LORD.
Joy and gladness will be found in her,
    thanksgiving and the sound of
        singing.

4 "Listen to me, my people;
    hear me, my nation:

The law will go out from me;
  my justice will become a light to
    the nations.
⁵My righteousness draws near speedily,
  my salvation is on the way,
  and my arm will bring justice to the
    nations.
The islands will look to me
  and wait in hope for my arm.
⁶Lift up your eyes to the heavens,
  look at the earth beneath;
the heavens will vanish like smoke,
  the earth will wear out like a
    garment
  and its inhabitants die like flies.
But my salvation will last forever,
  my righteousness will never fail.

⁷"Hear me, you who know what is
    right,
  you people who have my law in
    your hearts:
Do not fear the reproach of men
  or be terrified by their insults.
⁸For the moth will eat them up like a
    garment;
  the worm will devour them like wool.
But my righteousness will last forever,
  my salvation through all
    generations."

⁹Awake, awake! Clothe yourself with
    strength,
  O arm of the LORD;
awake, as in days gone by,
  as in generations of old.
Was it not you who cut Rahab to
    pieces,
  who pierced that monster through?
¹⁰Was it not you who dried up the sea,
  the waters of the great deep,
who made a road in the depths of the
    sea
  so that the redeemed might cross
    over?
¹¹The ransomed of the LORD will return.
  They will enter Zion with singing;
  everlasting joy will crown their
    heads.
Gladness and joy will overtake them,
  and sorrow and sighing will flee
    away.

¹²"I, even I, am he who comforts you.
  Who are you that you fear mortal
    men,

the sons of men, who are but
    grass,
¹³that you forget the LORD your Maker,
  who stretched out the heavens
  and laid the foundations of the
    earth,
that you live in constant terror every
    day
  because of the wrath of the
    oppressor,
  who is bent on destruction?
For where is the wrath of the
    oppressor?
¹⁴ The cowering prisoners will soon be
    set free;
they will not die in their dungeon,
  nor will they lack bread.
¹⁵For I am the LORD your God,
  who churns up the sea so that its
    waves roar—
  the LORD Almighty is his name.
¹⁶I have put my words in your mouth
  and covered you with the shadow of
    my hand—
I who set the heavens in place,
  who laid the foundations of the
    earth,
  and who say to Zion, 'You are my
    people.' "

The Cup of the LORD's Wrath

¹⁷Awake, awake!
  Rise up, O Jerusalem,
you who have drunk from the hand of
    the LORD
  the cup of his wrath,
you who have drained to its dregs
  the goblet that makes men stagger.
¹⁸Of all the sons she bore
  there was none to guide her;
of all the sons she reared
  there was none to take her by the
    hand.
¹⁹These double calamities have come
    upon you—
  who can comfort you?—
ruin and destruction, famine and
    sword—
  who can*ᵃ* console you?
²⁰Your sons have fainted;
  they lie at the head of every street,
  like antelope caught in a net.

─────────────

ᵃ19 Dead Sea Scrolls, Septuagint, Vulgate and
Syriac; Masoretic Text / *how can I*

They are filled with the wrath of the
LORD
and the rebuke of your God.

²¹Therefore hear this, you afflicted one,
made drunk, but not with wine.
²²This is what your Sovereign LORD
says,
your God, who defends his people:
"See, I have taken out of your hand
the cup that made you stagger;
from that cup, the goblet of my wrath,
you will never drink again.
²³I will put it into the hands of your
tormentors,
who said to you,
'Fall prostrate that we may walk
over you.'
And you made your back like the
ground,
like a street to be walked over."

52 Awake, awake, O Zion,
clothe yourself with strength.
Put on your garments of splendor,
O Jerusalem, the holy city.
The uncircumcised and defiled
will not enter you again.
²Shake off your dust;
rise up, sit enthroned, O Jerusalem.
Free yourself from the chains on your
neck,
O captive Daughter of Zion.

³For this is what the LORD says:

"You were sold for nothing,
and without money you will be
redeemed."

⁴For this is what the Sovereign LORD
says:

"At first my people went down to
Egypt to live;
lately, Assyria has oppressed them.

⁵"And now what do I have here?" declares the LORD.

"For my people have been taken away
for nothing,
and those who rule them mock,ᵃ"
declares the LORD.
"And all day long
my name is constantly blasphemed.
⁶Therefore my people will know my
name;

therefore in that day they will know
that it is I who foretold it.
Yes, it is I."

⁷How beautiful on the mountains
are the feet of those who bring good
news,
who proclaim peace,
who bring good tidings,
who proclaim salvation,
who say to Zion,
"Your God reigns!"
⁸Listen! Your watchmen lift up their
voices;
together they shout for joy.
When the LORD returns to Zion,
they will see it with their own eyes.
⁹Burst into songs of joy together,
you ruins of Jerusalem,
for the LORD has comforted his people,
he has redeemed Jerusalem.
¹⁰The LORD will lay bare his holy arm
in the sight of all the nations,
and all the ends of the earth will see
the salvation of our God.

¹¹Depart, depart, go out from there!
Touch no unclean thing!
Come out from it and be pure,
you who carry the vessels of the
LORD.
¹²But you will not leave in haste
or go in flight;
for the LORD will go before you,
the God of Israel will be your rear
guard.

The Suffering and Glory of the Servant

¹³See, my servant will act wisely ᵇ;
he will be raised and lifted up and
highly exalted.
¹⁴Just as there were many who were
appalled at him ᶜ—
his appearance was so disfigured
beyond that of any man
and his form marred beyond human
likeness—
¹⁵so will he sprinkle many nations, ᵈ
and kings will shut their mouths
because of him.
For what they were not told, they will
see,

ᵃ5 Dead Sea Scrolls and Vulgate; Masoretic Text
wail   ᵇ13 Or *will prosper*   ᶜ14 Hebrew *you*
ᵈ15 Hebrew; Septuagint *so will many nations marvel
at him*

and what they have not heard, they
   will understand.

53 Who has believed our message
   and to whom has the arm of the
   LORD been revealed?
² He grew up before him like a tender
      shoot,
   and like a root out of dry ground.
He had no beauty or majesty to attract
      us to him,
   nothing in his appearance that we
      should desire him.
³ He was despised and rejected by men,
   a man of sorrows, and familiar with
      suffering.
Like one from whom men hide their
      faces

he was despised, and we esteemed
      him not.

⁴ Surely he took up our infirmities
   and carried our sorrows,
yet we considered him stricken by God,
   smitten by him, and afflicted.
⁵ But he was pierced for our
      transgressions,
   he was crushed for our iniquities;
the punishment that brought us peace
      was upon him,
   and by his wounds we are healed.
⁶ We all, like sheep, have gone astray,
   each of us has turned to his own
      way;
   and the LORD has laid on him
      the iniquity of us all.

Weekend

You Really Know Me

Read Isaiah 44:2 (page 848)

On Friday Katy reminded us that God knows our name, which is pretty
awesome. But here's something even more awesome—God knows how
you are "wired" because he *made* you!

He "who formed you" means that God made you a certain way. And
not just your body. Your personality, your talents and abilities, your likes
and dislikes—they're all from God.

When you like to do something, it's because you were made with
certain likes and dislikes. When you're good at something, you should be
grateful, not boastful (since you're good at it because of the strengths God
gave you). But here is the totally cool part: When you wonder what God
wants you to do with your life, you get to pay attention to the way you're
made. That means your future should include doing something you *like* to
do! Get it? God made you the way you are for a reason, a purpose.

Here are a few more things to think about: Your likes and dislikes will
change as you get older, so be patient. No matter how old you are, you may
not know what you like to do until you do it, which means you have to
take risks. One more thought: Whatever you do that's worthwhile takes
hard work.

❶ What do you like to do? Make a list. Does your list make you
happy or sad? Why?

❷ Take the time to write down some of your dreams for
your life.

❸ Ask God to give you the courage to follow your dreams. And, while
you're at it, thank him for forming you the way he did.

Turn to page 865 for your next devotion.

7 He was oppressed and afflicted,
    yet he did not open his mouth;
he was led like a lamb to the slaughter,
    and as a sheep before her shearers
        is silent,
    so he did not open his mouth.
8 By oppression[a] and judgment he was
        taken away.
    And who can speak of his
        descendants?
For he was cut off from the land of
        the living;
    for the transgression of my people
        he was stricken.[b]
9 He was assigned a grave with the
        wicked,
    and with the rich in his death,
though he had done no violence,
    nor was any deceit in his mouth.

10 Yet it was the LORD's will to crush him
        and cause him to suffer,
    and though the LORD makes[c] his life
        a guilt offering,
he will see his offspring and prolong
        his days,
    and the will of the LORD will prosper
        in his hand.
11 After the suffering of his soul,
    he will see the light of life[d] and be
        satisfied[e];
by his knowledge[f] my righteous
        servant will justify many,
    and he will bear their iniquities.
12 Therefore I will give him a portion
        among the great,[g]
    and he will divide the spoils with
        the strong,[h]
because he poured out his life unto
        death,
    and was numbered with the
        transgressors.
For he bore the sin of many,
    and made intercession for the
        transgressors.

The Future Glory of Zion

54 "Sing, O barren woman,
    you who never bore a child;
burst into song, shout for joy,
    you who were never in labor;
because more are the children of the
        desolate woman
    than of her who has a husband,"
                    says the LORD.

2 "Enlarge the place of your tent,
    stretch your tent curtains wide,
        do not hold back;
lengthen your cords,
    strengthen your stakes.
3 For you will spread out to the right
        and to the left;
    your descendants will dispossess
        nations
    and settle in their desolate cities.

4 "Do not be afraid; you will not suffer
        shame.
    Do not fear disgrace; you will not
        be humiliated.
You will forget the shame of your
        youth
    and remember no more the reproach
        of your widowhood.
5 For your Maker is your husband—
    the LORD Almighty is his name—
the Holy One of Israel is your
        Redeemer;
    he is called the God of all the earth.
6 The LORD will call you back
    as if you were a wife deserted and
        distressed in spirit—
a wife who married young,
    only to be rejected," says your God.
7 "For a brief moment I abandoned you,
    but with deep compassion I will
        bring you back.
8 In a surge of anger
    I hid my face from you for a
        moment,
but with everlasting kindness
    I will have compassion on you,"
    says the LORD your Redeemer.

9 "To me this is like the days of Noah,
    when I swore that the waters of
        Noah would never again cover
        the earth.
So now I have sworn not to be angry
        with you,
    never to rebuke you again.
10 Though the mountains be shaken

*a8 Or From arrest b8 Or away. / Yet who of his
generation considered / that he was cut off from the
land of the living / for the transgression of my
people, / to whom the blow was due? c10 Hebrew
though you make d11 Dead Sea Scrolls (see also
Septuagint); Masoretic Text does not have the light
of life. e11 Or (with Masoretic Text) 11He will see
the result of the suffering of his soul / and be
satisfied f11 Or by knowledge of him g12 Or
many h12 Or numerous*

and the hills be removed,
yet my unfailing love for you will not
be shaken
nor my covenant of peace be
removed,"
says the L ORD , who has compassion
on you.

¹¹"O afflicted city, lashed by storms and
not comforted,
I will build you with stones of
turquoise,*a*
your foundations with sapphires.*b*
¹²I will make your battlements of rubies,
your gates of sparkling jewels,
and all your walls of precious
stones.
¹³All your sons will be taught by the
L ORD ,
and great will be your children's
peace.
¹⁴In righteousness you will be
established:
Tyranny will be far from you;
you will have nothing to fear.
Terror will be far removed;
it will not come near you.
¹⁵If anyone does attack you, it will not
be my doing;
whoever attacks you will surrender
to you.

¹⁶"See, it is I who created the
blacksmith
who fans the coals into flame
and forges a weapon fit for its
work.
And it is I who have created the
destroyer to work havoc;
¹⁷   no weapon forged against you will
prevail,
and you will refute every tongue
that accuses you.
This is the heritage of the servants of
the L ORD ,
and this is their vindication from
me,"
declares the L ORD .

Invitation to the Thirsty

55 "Come, all you who are thirsty,
come to the waters;
and you who have no money,
come, buy and eat!
Come, buy wine and milk
without money and without cost.

²Why spend money on what is not
bread,
and your labor on what does not
satisfy?
Listen, listen to me, and eat what is
good,
and your soul will delight in the
richest of fare.
³Give ear and come to me;
hear me, that your soul may live.
I will make an everlasting covenant
with you,
my faithful love promised to David.
⁴See, I have made him a witness to the
peoples,
a leader and commander of the
peoples.
⁵Surely you will summon nations you
know not,
and nations that do not know you
will hasten to you,
because of the L ORD your God,
the Holy One of Israel,
for he has endowed you with
splendor."

⁶Seek the L ORD while he may be
found;
call on him while he is near.
⁷Let the wicked forsake his way
and the evil man his thoughts.
Let him turn to the L ORD , and he will
have mercy on him,
and to our God, for he will freely
pardon.

⁸"For my thoughts are not your
thoughts,
neither are your ways my ways,"
declares the L ORD .
⁹"As the heavens are higher than the
earth,
so are my ways higher than your
ways
and my thoughts than your
thoughts.
¹⁰As the rain and the snow
come down from heaven,
and do not return to it
without watering the earth
and making it bud and flourish,
so that it yields seed for the sower
and bread for the eater,

---

a 11 The meaning of the Hebrew for this word is
uncertain.   *b 11* Or *lapis lazuli*

[11] so is my word that goes out from my
　　　mouth:
　　It will not return to me empty,
　　but will accomplish what I desire
　　　and achieve the purpose for which I
　　　　sent it.
[12] You will go out in joy
　　　and be led forth in peace;
　　the mountains and hills
　　　will burst into song before you,
　　and all the trees of the field
　　　will clap their hands.
[13] Instead of the thornbush will grow the
　　　pine tree,
　　and instead of briers the myrtle will
　　　grow.
　　This will be for the LORD's renown,
　　　for an everlasting sign,
　　　which will not be destroyed."

Salvation for Others

56 This is what the LORD says:

"Maintain justice
　　and do what is right,
for my salvation is close at hand
　　and my righteousness will soon be
　　　revealed.
[2] Blessed is the man who does this,
　　the man who holds it fast,
who keeps the Sabbath without
　　desecrating it,
　　and keeps his hand from doing any
　　　evil."

[3] Let no foreigner who has bound
　　　himself to the LORD say,
　　"The LORD will surely exclude me
　　　from his people."
And let not any eunuch complain,
　　"I am only a dry tree."

[4] For this is what the LORD says:

"To the eunuchs who keep my
　　Sabbaths,
who choose what pleases me
　　and hold fast to my covenant—
[5] to them I will give within my temple
　　and its walls
a memorial and a name
　　better than sons and daughters;
I will give them an everlasting name
　　that will not be cut off.
[6] And foreigners who bind themselves
　　to the LORD

　to serve him,
to love the name of the LORD,
　and to worship him,
all who keep the Sabbath without
　desecrating it
　and who hold fast to my covenant—
[7] these I will bring to my holy mountain
　and give them joy in my house of
　　prayer.
Their burnt offerings and sacrifices
　will be accepted on my altar;
for my house will be called
　a house of prayer for all nations."
[8] The Sovereign LORD declares—
　he who gathers the exiles of Israel:
"I will gather still others to them
　besides those already gathered."

God's Accusation Against the Wicked

[9] Come, all you beasts of the field,
　come and devour, all you beasts of
　　the forest!
[10] Israel's watchmen are blind,
　they all lack knowledge;
they are all mute dogs,
　they cannot bark;
they lie around and dream,
　they love to sleep.
[11] They are dogs with mighty appetites;
　they never have enough.
They are shepherds who lack
　understanding;
they all turn to their own way,
　each seeks his own gain.
[12] "Come," each one cries, "let me get
　　wine!
Let us drink our fill of beer!
And tomorrow will be like today,
　or even far better."

57 The righteous perish,
　　and no one ponders it in his
　　　heart;
devout men are taken away,
　and no one understands
that the righteous are taken away
　to be spared from evil.
[2] Those who walk uprightly
　enter into peace;
　they find rest as they lie in death.

[3] "But you—come here, you sons of a
　　sorceress,
　you offspring of adulterers and
　　prostitutes!

⁴Whom are you mocking?
 At whom do you sneer
 and stick out your tongue?
Are you not a brood of rebels,
 the offspring of liars?
⁵You burn with lust among the oaks
 and under every spreading tree;
you sacrifice your children in the
 ravines
 and under the overhanging crags.
⁶The idols among the smooth stones of
 the ravines are your portion;
 they, they are your lot.
Yes, to them you have poured out
 drink offerings
 and offered grain offerings.
 In the light of these things, should I
 relent?
⁷You have made your bed on a high
 and lofty hill;
 there you went up to offer your
 sacrifices.
⁸Behind your doors and your doorposts
 you have put your pagan symbols.
Forsaking me, you uncovered your
 bed,
 you climbed into it and opened it
 wide;
you made a pact with those whose
 beds you love,
 and you looked on their nakedness.
⁹You went to Molech*ᵃ* with olive oil
 and increased your perfumes.
You sent your ambassadors*ᵇ* far away;
 you descended to the grave*ᶜ* itself!
¹⁰You were wearied by all your ways,
 but you would not say, 'It is
 hopeless.'
You found renewal of your strength,
 and so you did not faint.

¹¹"Whom have you so dreaded and
 feared
 that you have been false to me,
and have neither remembered me
 nor pondered this in your hearts?
Is it not because I have long been
 silent
 that you do not fear me?
¹²I will expose your righteousness and
 your works,
 and they will not benefit you.
¹³When you cry out for help,
 let your collection of idols save
 you!

The wind will carry all of them off,
 a mere breath will blow them away.
But the man who makes me his refuge
 will inherit the land
 and possess my holy mountain."

Comfort for the Contrite

¹⁴And it will be said:

"Build up, build up, prepare the road!
 Remove the obstacles out of the
 way of my people."
¹⁵For this is what the high and lofty
 One says—
 he who lives forever, whose name is
 holy:
"I live in a high and holy place,
 but also with him who is contrite
 and lowly in spirit,
to revive the spirit of the lowly
 and to revive the heart of the
 contrite.
¹⁶I will not accuse forever,
 nor will I always be angry,
for then the spirit of man would grow
 faint before me—
 the breath of man that I have
 created.
¹⁷I was enraged by his sinful greed;
 I punished him, and hid my face in
 anger,
 yet he kept on in his willful ways.
¹⁸I have seen his ways, but I will heal
 him;
 I will guide him and restore comfort
 to him,
¹⁹ creating praise on the lips of the
 mourners in Israel.
Peace, peace, to those far and near,"
 says the LORD. "And I will heal
 them."
²⁰But the wicked are like the tossing
 sea,
 which cannot rest,
 whose waves cast up mire and mud.
²¹"There is no peace," says my God, "for
 the wicked."

True Fasting

58 "Shout it aloud, do not hold
 back.
 Raise your voice like a trumpet.
 Declare to my people their rebellion

ᵃ9 Or to the king   ᵇ9 Or idols   ᶜ9 Hebrew Sheol

and to the house of Jacob their sins.
² For day after day they seek me out;
     they seem eager to know my ways,
as if they were a nation that does
         what is right
     and has not forsaken the commands
         of its God.
They ask me for just decisions
     and seem eager for God to come
         near them.
³ 'Why have we fasted,' they say,
     'and you have not seen it?
Why have we humbled ourselves,
     and you have not noticed?'

"Yet on the day of your fasting, you
         do as you please
     and exploit all your workers.
⁴ Your fasting ends in quarreling and
         strife,
     and in striking each other with
         wicked fists.
You cannot fast as you do today
     and expect your voice to be heard
         on high.
⁵ Is this the kind of fast I have chosen,
     only a day for a man to humble
         himself?
Is it only for bowing one's head like a
         reed
     and for lying on sackcloth and
         ashes?
Is that what you call a fast,
     a day acceptable to the LORD?

⁶ "Is not this the kind of fasting I have
         chosen:
to loose the chains of injustice
     and untie the cords of the yoke,
to set the oppressed free
     and break every yoke?
⁷ Is it not to share your food with the
         hungry
     and to provide the poor wanderer
         with shelter—
when you see the naked, to clothe him,
     and not to turn away from your
         own flesh and blood?
⁸ Then your light will break forth like
         the dawn,
     and your healing will quickly
         appear;
then your righteousness*ᵃ* will go
         before you,
     and the glory of the LORD will be
         your rear guard.

⁹ Then you will call, and the LORD will
         answer;
     you will cry for help, and he will
         say: Here am I.

"If you do away with the yoke of
         oppression,
     with the pointing finger and
         malicious talk,
¹⁰ and if you spend yourselves in behalf
         of the hungry
     and satisfy the needs of the
         oppressed,
then your light will rise in the
         darkness,
     and your night will become like the
         noonday.
¹¹ The LORD will guide you always;
     he will satisfy your needs in a
         sun-scorched land
     and will strengthen your frame.
You will be like a well-watered
         garden,
     like a spring whose waters never
         fail.
¹² Your people will rebuild the ancient
         ruins
     and will raise up the age-old
         foundations;
you will be called Repairer of Broken
         Walls,
     Restorer of Streets with Dwellings.

¹³ "If you keep your feet from breaking
         the Sabbath
     and from doing as you please on
         my holy day,
if you call the Sabbath a delight
     and the LORD's holy day honorable,
and if you honor it by not going your
         own way
     and not doing as you please or
         speaking idle words,
¹⁴ then you will find your joy in the LORD,
     and I will cause you to ride on the
         heights of the land
     and to feast on the inheritance of
         your father Jacob."
         The mouth of the LORD
         has spoken.

Sin, Confession and Redemption

59 Surely the arm of the LORD is not
         too short to save,

ᵃ8 Or your righteous One

nor his ear too dull to hear.
² But your iniquities have
separated
you from your God;
your sins have hidden his face from
you,
so that he will not hear.
³ For your hands are stained with
blood,
your fingers with guilt.
Your lips have spoken lies,
and your tongue mutters wicked
things.
⁴ No one calls for justice;
no one pleads his case with
integrity.
They rely on empty arguments and
speak lies;
they conceive trouble and give birth
to evil.
⁵ They hatch the eggs of vipers
and spin a spider's web.
Whoever eats their eggs will die,

and when one is broken, an adder is
hatched.
⁶ Their cobwebs are useless for clothing;
they cannot cover themselves with
what they make.
Their deeds are evil deeds,
and acts of violence are in their
hands.
⁷ Their feet rush into sin;
they are swift to shed innocent
blood.
Their thoughts are evil thoughts;
ruin and destruction mark their
ways.
⁸ The way of peace they do not know;
there is no justice in their paths.
They have turned them into crooked
roads;
no one who walks in them will
know peace.

⁹ So justice is far from us,
and righteousness does not reach us.

Monday

Life Raft

Read Isaiah 59:1

Sometimes life feels like a stormy sea. When that happens, it's nice to know that God is our life raft, rescuing us and keeping us safe.

As I read this verse it reminds me of when my grandpa had cancer. He was told he had only 4 to 6 weeks to live at first. He was such a godly man, and my whole family was sad about losing him. We prayed all the time and hoped God would heal him.

In the end, my grandpa lived for 2 more years—much longer than expected. And even though God didn't heal my grandpa and his death was still really hard on our family, at least God gave us more time with him.

God really does listen to our prayers. We can ask him anything, and he'll listen to us. And even if we don't feel close to God, this verse tells us he's still close to us, close enough to reach out and help us when we need him.

Katy age 15

What about You?

❶ Think about a time you felt far away from God. Looking back on it now, can you see how God was showing that he was still close to you?

❷ Ask a bunch of Christians you know—your parents, your friends, people in your youth group—to tell you about a time God answered their prayers.

❸ Thank God for hearing our prayers and reaching out to save us, no matter how far away from him we feel.

Turn to page 872 for your next devotion.

We look for light, but all is darkness;
  for brightness, but we walk in deep
    shadows.
¹⁰Like the blind we grope along the
    wall,
  feeling our way like men without
    eyes.
At midday we stumble as if it were
    twilight;
  among the strong, we are like the
    dead.
¹¹We all growl like bears;
  we moan mournfully like doves.
We look for justice, but find none;
  for deliverance, but it is far away.

¹²For our offenses are many in your
    sight,
  and our sins testify against us.
Our offenses are ever with us,
  and we acknowledge our iniquities:
¹³rebellion and treachery against the
    LORD,
  turning our backs on our God,
fomenting oppression and revolt,
  uttering lies our hearts have
    conceived.
¹⁴So justice is driven back,
  and righteousness stands at a
    distance;
truth has stumbled in the streets,
  honesty cannot enter.
¹⁵Truth is nowhere to be found,
  and whoever shuns evil becomes a
    prey.

The LORD looked and was displeased
  that there was no justice.
¹⁶He saw that there was no one,
  he was appalled that there was no
    one to intervene;
so his own arm worked salvation for
    him,
  and his own righteousness sustained
    him.
¹⁷He put on righteousness as his
    breastplate,
  and the helmet of salvation on his
    head;
he put on the garments of vengeance
  and wrapped himself in zeal as in a
    cloak.
¹⁸According to what they have done,
  so will he repay
wrath to his enemies
  and retribution to his foes;

he will repay the islands their due.
¹⁹From the west, men will fear the name
    of the LORD,
  and from the rising of the sun, they
    will revere his glory.
For he will come like a pent-up flood
  that the breath of the LORD drives
    along.ᵃ

²⁰"The Redeemer will come to Zion,
  to those in Jacob who repent of
    their sins,"
              declares the LORD.

²¹"As for me, this is my covenant with them," says the LORD. "My Spirit, who is on you, and my words that I have put in your mouth will not depart from your mouth, or from the mouths of your children, or from the mouths of their descendants from this time on and forever," says the LORD.

The Glory of Zion

60 "Arise, shine, for your light has
    come,
  and the glory of the LORD rises upon
    you.
²See, darkness covers the earth
  and thick darkness is over the
    peoples,
but the LORD rises upon you
  and his glory appears over you.
³Nations will come to your light,
  and kings to the brightness of your
    dawn.

⁴"Lift up your eyes and look about
    you:
  All assemble and come to you;
your sons come from afar,
  and your daughters are carried on
    the arm.
⁵Then you will look and be radiant,
  your heart will throb and swell with
    joy;
the wealth on the seas will be brought
    to you,
  to you the riches of the nations will
    come.
⁶Herds of camels will cover your land,
  young camels of Midian and Ephah.
And all from Sheba will come,

ᵃ19 Or *When the enemy comes in like a flood, / the Spirit of the LORD will put him to flight*

bearing gold and incense
and proclaiming the praise of the
LORD.
⁷ All Kedar's flocks will be gathered to
you,
the rams of Nebaioth will serve you;
they will be accepted as offerings on
my altar,
and I will adorn my glorious
temple.

⁸ "Who are these that fly along like
clouds,
like doves to their nests?
⁹ Surely the islands look to me;
in the lead are the ships of
Tarshish,ᵃ
bringing your sons from afar,
with their silver and gold,
to the honor of the LORD your God,
the Holy One of Israel,
for he has endowed you with
splendor.

¹⁰ "Foreigners will rebuild your walls,
and their kings will serve you.
Though in anger I struck you,
in favor I will show you
compassion.
¹¹ Your gates will always stand open,
they will never be shut, day or
night,
so that men may bring you the wealth
of the nations—
their kings led in triumphal
procession.
¹² For the nation or kingdom that will
not serve you will perish;
it will be utterly ruined.

¹³ "The glory of Lebanon will come to
you,
the pine, the fir and the cypress
together,
to adorn the place of my sanctuary;
and I will glorify the place of my
feet.
¹⁴ The sons of your oppressors will come
bowing before you;
all who despise you will bow down
at your feet
and will call you the City of the LORD,
Zion of the Holy One of Israel.

¹⁵ "Although you have been forsaken
and hated,

with no one traveling through,
I will make you the everlasting pride
and the joy of all generations.
¹⁶ You will drink the milk of nations
and be nursed at royal breasts.
Then you will know that I, the LORD,
am your Savior,
your Redeemer, the Mighty One of
Jacob.
¹⁷ Instead of bronze I will bring you
gold,
and silver in place of iron.
Instead of wood I will bring you
bronze,
and iron in place of stones.
I will make peace your governor
and righteousness your ruler.
¹⁸ No longer will violence be heard in
your land,
nor ruin or destruction within your
borders,
but you will call your walls Salvation
and your gates Praise.
¹⁹ The sun will no more be your light by
day,
nor will the brightness of the moon
shine on you,
for the LORD will be your everlasting
light,
and your God will be your glory.
²⁰ Your sun will never set again,
and your moon will wane no more;
the LORD will be your everlasting
light,
and your days of sorrow will end.
²¹ Then will all your people be righteous
and they will possess the land
forever.
They are the shoot I have planted,
the work of my hands,
for the display of my splendor.
²² The least of you will become a
thousand,
the smallest a mighty nation.
I am the LORD;
in its time I will do this swiftly."

The Year of the LORD's Favor

61 The Spirit of the Sovereign LORD
is on me,
because the LORD has anointed me
to preach good news to the poor.

ᵃ9 Or *the trading ships*

Double Duty

Huh?

Isaiah 61:1–2

This is a classic example of the Old Testament being quoted in the New Testament (see Luke 4:18–19, page 1224). Jesus used a lot of Old Testament Scripture to describe himself because the Jews knew the Old Testament Scripture so well. It was what they related to. Just like we tell stories of the past to explain to people who we are today, Jesus used the Scripture of the past to explain who he was to the people of his day.

He has sent me to bind up the
      brokenhearted,
  to proclaim freedom for the
      captives
  and release from darkness for the
      prisoners,[a]
² to proclaim the year of the LORD's
      favor
  and the day of vengeance of our
      God,
to comfort all who mourn,
³   and provide for those who grieve in
      Zion—
to bestow on them a crown of beauty
  instead of ashes,
the oil of gladness
  instead of mourning,
and a garment of praise
  instead of a spirit of despair.
They will be called oaks of
      righteousness,
  a planting of the LORD
  for the display of his splendor.

⁴ They will rebuild the ancient ruins
  and restore the places long
      devastated;
they will renew the ruined cities
  that have been devastated for
      generations.
⁵ Aliens will shepherd your flocks;
  foreigners will work your fields and
      vineyards.
⁶ And you will be called priests of the
      LORD,

you will be named ministers of our
      God.
You will feed on the wealth of
      nations,
  and in their riches you will boast.

⁷ Instead of their shame
  my people will receive a double
      portion,
and instead of disgrace
  they will rejoice in their
      inheritance;
and so they will inherit a double
      portion in their land,
  and everlasting joy will be theirs.

⁸ "For I, the LORD, love justice;
  I hate robbery and iniquity.
In my faithfulness I will reward them
  and make an everlasting covenant
      with them.
⁹ Their descendants will be known
      among the nations
  and their offspring among the
      peoples.
All who see them will acknowledge
  that they are a people the LORD has
      blessed."

¹⁰ I delight greatly in the LORD;
  my soul rejoices in my God.
For he has clothed me with garments
      of salvation
  and arrayed me in a robe of
      righteousness,
as a bridegroom adorns his head like a
      priest,
  and as a bride adorns herself with
      her jewels.
¹¹ For as the soil makes the sprout come
      up
  and a garden causes seeds to grow,
so the Sovereign LORD will make
      righteousness and praise
  spring up before all nations.

Zion's New Name

62 For Zion's sake I will not keep
      silent,
  for Jerusalem's sake I will not
      remain quiet,
till her righteousness shines out like
      the dawn,
  her salvation like a blazing torch.

---

[a] 1 Hebrew; Septuagint *the blind*

² The nations will see your
        righteousness,
    and all kings your glory;
you will be called by a new name
    that the mouth of the LORD will
        bestow.
³ You will be a crown of splendor in the
        LORD's hand,
    a royal diadem in the hand of your
        God.
⁴ No longer will they call you Deserted,
    or name your land Desolate.
But you will be called Hephzibah,ᵃ
    and your land Beulahᵇ;
for the LORD will take delight in you,
    and your land will be married.
⁵ As a young man marries a maiden,
    so will your sonsᶜ marry you;
as a bridegroom rejoices over his
        bride,
    so will your God rejoice over you.

⁶ I have posted watchmen on your
        walls, O Jerusalem;
    they will never be silent day or
        night.
You who call on the LORD,
    give yourselves no rest,
⁷ and give him no rest till he establishes
        Jerusalem
    and makes her the praise of the
        earth.

⁸ The LORD has sworn by his right hand
    and by his mighty arm:
"Never again will I give your grain
    as food for your enemies,
and never again will foreigners drink
        the new wine
    for which you have toiled;
⁹ but those who harvest it will eat it
    and praise the LORD,
and those who gather the grapes will
        drink it
    in the courts of my sanctuary."

¹⁰ Pass through, pass through the gates!
    Prepare the way for the people.
Build up, build up the highway!
    Remove the stones.
Raise a banner for the nations.

¹¹ The LORD has made proclamation
    to the ends of the earth:
"Say to the Daughter of Zion,
    'See, your Savior comes!
See, his reward is with him,

and his recompense accompanies
        him.' "
¹² They will be called the Holy People,
    the Redeemed of the LORD;
and you will be called Sought After,
    the City No Longer Deserted.

God's Day of Vengeance and Redemption

63 Who is this coming from Edom,
    from Bozrah, with his garments
        stained crimson?
Who is this, robed in splendor,
    striding forward in the greatness of
        his strength?

"It is I, speaking in righteousness,
    mighty to save."

² Why are your garments red,
    like those of one treading the
        winepress?

³ "I have trodden the winepress alone;
    from the nations no one was with
        me.
I trampled them in my anger
    and trod them down in my wrath;
their blood spattered my garments,
    and I stained all my clothing.
⁴ For the day of vengeance was in my
        heart,
    and the year of my redemption has
        come.
⁵ I looked, but there was no one to help,
    I was appalled that no one gave
        support;
so my own arm worked salvation for
        me,
    and my own wrath sustained me.
⁶ I trampled the nations in my anger;
    in my wrath I made them drunk
    and poured their blood on the
        ground."

Praise and Prayer

⁷ I will tell of the kindnesses of the
        LORD,
    the deeds for which he is to be
        praised,
    according to all the LORD has done
        for us—
yes, the many good things he has
        done
    for the house of Israel,

ᵃ4 *Hephzibah* means *my delight is in her.*   ᵇ4 *Beulah*
means *married.*   ᶜ5 Or *Builder*

according to his compassion and
    many kindnesses.
[8] He said, "Surely they are my people,
    sons who will not be false to me";
    and so he became their Savior.
[9] In all their distress he too was
      distressed,
    and the angel of his presence saved
      them.
In his love and mercy he redeemed
      them;
    he lifted them up and carried them
      all the days of old.
[10] Yet they rebelled
    and grieved his Holy Spirit.
So he turned and became their enemy
    and he himself fought against them.

[11] Then his people recalled[a] the days of
      old,
    the days of Moses and his people—
where is he who brought them
      through the sea,
    with the shepherd of his flock?
Where is he who set
    his Holy Spirit among them,
[12] who sent his glorious arm of power
    to be at Moses' right hand,
who divided the waters before them,
    to gain for himself everlasting
      renown,
[13] who led them through the depths?
Like a horse in open country,
    they did not stumble;
[14] like cattle that go down to the plain,
    they were given rest by the Spirit of
      the Lord.
This is how you guided your people
    to make for yourself a glorious name.

[15] Look down from heaven and see
    from your lofty throne, holy and
      glorious.
Where are your zeal and your might?
    Your tenderness and compassion are
      withheld from us.
[16] But you are our Father,
    though Abraham does not know us
    or Israel acknowledge us;
you, O Lord, are our Father,
    our Redeemer from of old is your
      name.
[17] Why, O Lord, do you make us wander
    from your ways
    and harden our hearts so we do not
      revere you?

Return for the sake of your servants,
    the tribes that are your inheritance.
[18] For a little while your people
    possessed your holy place,
    but now our enemies have trampled
      down your sanctuary.
[19] We are yours from of old;
    but you have not ruled over them,
    they have not been called by your
      name.[b]

64   Oh, that you would rend the
      heavens and come down,
    that the mountains would tremble
      before you!
[2] As when fire sets twigs ablaze
    and causes water to boil,
come down to make your name
      known to your enemies
    and cause the nations to quake
      before you!
[3] For when you did awesome things
      that we did not expect,
    you came down, and the mountains
      trembled before you.
[4] Since ancient times no one has heard,
    no ear has perceived,
no eye has seen any God besides you,
    who acts on behalf of those who
      wait for him.
[5] You come to the help of those who
      gladly do right,
    who remember your ways.
But when we continued to sin against
      them,
    you were angry.
    How then can we be saved?
[6] All of us have become like one who is
      unclean,
    and all our righteous acts are like
      filthy rags;
we all shrivel up like a leaf,
    and like the wind our sins sweep us
      away.
[7] No one calls on your name
    or strives to lay hold of you;
for you have hidden your face from us
    and made us waste away because of
      our sins.

[8] Yet, O Lord, you are our Father.
    We are the clay, you are the potter;

---

[a] 11 Or *But may he recall*   [b] 19 Or *We are like those
you have never ruled, / like those never called by
your name*

we are all the work of your hand.
⁹Do not be angry beyond measure,
    O Lᴏʀᴅ;
  do not remember our sins forever.
  Oh, look upon us, we pray,
    for we are all your people.
¹⁰Your sacred cities have become a
      desert;
    even Zion is a desert, Jerusalem a
      desolation.
¹¹Our holy and glorious temple, where
      our fathers praised you,
    has been burned with fire,
    and all that we treasured lies in ruins.
¹²After all this, O Lᴏʀᴅ, will you hold
      yourself back?
    Will you keep silent and punish us
      beyond measure?

Judgment and Salvation

65 "I revealed myself to those who
        did not ask for me;
    I was found by those who did not
      seek me.
  To a nation that did not call on my
      name,
    I said, 'Here am I, here am I.'
²All day long I have held out my hands
    to an obstinate people,
  who walk in ways not good,
    pursuing their own imaginations—
³a people who continually provoke me
    to my very face,
  offering sacrifices in gardens
    and burning incense on altars of
      brick;
⁴who sit among the graves
    and spend their nights keeping
      secret vigil;
  who eat the flesh of pigs,
    and whose pots hold broth of
      unclean meat;
⁵who say, 'Keep away; don't come near
      me,
    for I am too sacred for you!'
  Such people are smoke in my nostrils,
    a fire that keeps burning all day.

⁶"See, it stands written before me:
    I will not keep silent but will pay
      back in full;
  I will pay it back into their laps—
⁷both your sins and the sins of your
      fathers,"
    says the Lᴏʀᴅ.

"Because they burned sacrifices on the
      mountains
    and defied me on the hills,
  I will measure into their laps
    the full payment for their former
      deeds."

⁸This is what the Lᴏʀᴅ says:

"As when juice is still found in a
      cluster of grapes
    and men say, 'Don't destroy it,
      there is yet some good in it,'
  so will I do in behalf of my
      servants;
    I will not destroy them all.
⁹I will bring forth descendants from
      Jacob,
    and from Judah those who will
      possess my mountains;
  my chosen people will inherit them,
    and there will my servants live.
¹⁰Sharon will become a pasture for
      flocks,
    and the Valley of Achor a resting
      place for herds,
  for my people who seek me.

¹¹"But as for you who forsake the Lᴏʀᴅ
    and forget my holy mountain,
  who spread a table for Fortune
    and fill bowls of mixed wine for
      Destiny,
¹²I will destine you for the sword,
    and you will all bend down for the
      slaughter;
  for I called but you did not answer,
    I spoke but you did not listen.
  You did evil in my sight
    and chose what displeases me."

¹³Therefore this is what the Sovereign
Lᴏʀᴅ says:

"My servants will eat,
    but you will go hungry;
  my servants will drink,
    but you will go thirsty;
  my servants will rejoice,
    but you will be put to shame.
¹⁴My servants will sing
    out of the joy of their hearts,
  but you will cry out
    from anguish of heart
    and wail in brokenness of spirit.
¹⁵You will leave your name
    to my chosen ones as a curse;

the Sovereign LORD will put you to
    death,
  but to his servants he will give
    another name.
¹⁶Whoever invokes a blessing in the
    land
  will do so by the God of truth;
he who takes an oath in the land
  will swear by the God of truth.
For the past troubles will be forgotten
  and hidden from my eyes.

New Heavens and a New Earth

¹⁷"Behold, I will create
  new heavens and a new earth.
The former things will not be
    remembered,
  nor will they come to mind.
¹⁸But be glad and rejoice forever
  in what I will create,
for I will create Jerusalem to be a
    delight
  and its people a joy.
¹⁹I will rejoice over Jerusalem

  and take delight in my people;
the sound of weeping and of crying
  will be heard in it no more.

²⁰"Never again will there be in it
  an infant who lives but a few days,
  or an old man who does not live
    out his years;
he who dies at a hundred
  will be thought a mere youth;
he who fails to reach[a] a hundred
  will be considered accursed.
²¹They will build houses and dwell in
    them;
  they will plant vineyards and eat
    their fruit.
²²No longer will they build houses and
    others live in them,
  or plant and others eat.
For as the days of a tree,
  so will be the days of my people;
my chosen ones will long enjoy

a20 Or / the sinner who reaches

Tuesday

I'm Forgiven!
                   Read Isaiah 65:17

When I became a Christian on a church-organized backpacking trip, my
heart was immediately changed. Before the trip I had been going through
a really rough time, and the bad memories haunted me almost more than
I could handle. But the minute Jesus came into my heart, the pain of my
old life seemed so insignificant.

    God's forgiveness is complete—he treats us like we never sinned. His
forgiveness is the biggest reason I became a Christian. My old life was
weighing me down, and I couldn't break free on my own. God's love gave
me a new life.

    No matter what you've done, God will forget it all if you ask him for
forgiveness. You can't change what happened in the past, but you can find a
better future in him!

Amy age 14

What about You?

❶ How is being forgiven by God better than being forgiven by people?
Why do we need both?

❷ Draw a line down the middle of a piece of paper. On one side, write
words that describe life without God. On the other side, describe life
with God.

❸ Confess your sins to God and thank him for his forgiveness.

Turn to page 877 for your next devotion.

the works of their hands.
²³They will not toil in vain
or bear children doomed to
misfortune;
for they will be a people blessed by
the LORD,
they and their descendants with
them.
²⁴Before they call I will answer;
while they are still speaking I will
hear.
²⁵The wolf and the lamb will feed
together,
and the lion will eat straw like the ox,
but dust will be the serpent's food.
They will neither harm nor destroy
on all my holy mountain,"
says the LORD.

Judgment and Hope

66 This is what the LORD says:

"Heaven is my throne,
and the earth is my footstool.
Where is the house you will build for
me?
Where will my resting place be?
²Has not my hand made all these
things,
and so they came into being?"
declares the LORD.

"This is the one I esteem:
he who is humble and contrite in
spirit,
and trembles at my word.
³But whoever sacrifices a bull
is like one who kills a man,
and whoever offers a lamb,
like one who breaks a dog's neck;
whoever makes a grain offering
is like one who presents pig's blood,
and whoever burns memorial incense,
like one who worships an idol.
They have chosen their own ways,
and their souls delight in their
abominations;
⁴so I also will choose harsh treatment
for them
and will bring upon them what they
dread.
For when I called, no one answered,
when I spoke, no one listened.
They did evil in my sight
and chose what displeases me."

⁵Hear the word of the LORD,
you who tremble at his word:
"Your brothers who hate you,
and exclude you because of my
name, have said,
'Let the LORD be glorified,
that we may see your joy!'
Yet they will be put to shame.
⁶Hear that uproar from the city,
hear that noise from the temple!
It is the sound of the LORD
repaying his enemies all they
deserve.

⁷"Before she goes into labor,
she gives birth;
before the pains come upon her,
she delivers a son.
⁸Who has ever heard of such a thing?
Who has ever seen such things?
Can a country be born in a day
or a nation be brought forth in a
moment?
Yet no sooner is Zion in labor
than she gives birth to her children.
⁹Do I bring to the moment of birth
and not give delivery?" says the
LORD.
"Do I close up the womb
when I bring to delivery?" says
your God.
¹⁰"Rejoice with Jerusalem and be glad
for her,
all you who love her;
rejoice greatly with her,
all you who mourn over her.
¹¹For you will nurse and be satisfied
at her comforting breasts;
you will drink deeply
and delight in her overflowing
abundance."

¹²For this is what the LORD says:

"I will extend peace to her like a river,
and the wealth of nations like a
flooding stream;
you will nurse and be carried on her
arm
and dandled on her knees.
¹³As a mother comforts her child,
so will I comfort you;
and you will be comforted over
Jerusalem."

¹⁴When you see this, your heart will
rejoice

and you will flourish like grass;
the hand of the LORD will be made
known to his servants,
but his fury will be shown to his foes.
¹⁵ See, the LORD is coming with fire,
and his chariots are like a
whirlwind;
he will bring down his anger with
fury,
and his rebuke with flames of fire.
¹⁶ For with fire and with his sword
the LORD will execute judgment
upon all men,
and many will be those slain by the
LORD.

¹⁷"Those who consecrate and purify
themselves to go into the gardens, following the one in the midst of[a] those
who eat the flesh of pigs and rats and
other abominable things—they will meet
their end together," declares the LORD.

¹⁸"And I, because of their actions and
their imaginations, am about to come[b]
and gather all nations and tongues, and
they will come and see my glory.

¹⁹"I will set a sign among them, and I
will send some of those who survive to
the nations—to Tarshish, to the Libyans[c]
and Lydians (famous as archers), to Tubal and Greece, and to the distant islands

that have not heard of my fame or seen
my glory. They will proclaim my glory
among the nations. ²⁰And they will bring
all your brothers, from all the nations, to
my holy mountain in Jerusalem as an
offering to the LORD—on horses, in chariots and wagons, and on mules and camels," says the LORD. "They will bring
them, as the Israelites bring their grain
offerings, to the temple of the LORD in
ceremonially clean vessels. ²¹And I will
select some of them also to be priests and
Levites," says the LORD.

²²"As the new heavens and the new
earth that I make will endure before me,"
declares the LORD, "so will your name
and descendants endure. ²³From one New
Moon to another and from one Sabbath
to another, all mankind will come and
bow down before me," says the LORD.
²⁴"And they will go out and look upon
the dead bodies of those who rebelled
against me; their worm will not die, nor
will their fire be quenched, and they will
be loathsome to all mankind."

_____
[a]17 Or *gardens behind one of your temples, and*
[b]18 The meaning of the Hebrew for this clause is
uncertain.   [c]19 Some Septuagint manuscripts *Put*
(Libyans); Hebrew *Pul*

Jeremiah

START

Cast OF Characters

Jeremiah
(jer-uh-MY-yuh)
This priest-prophet saw it all . . . he *lived* it all—from the good ol' days of Josiah, through the bloody 3-year battle of Jerusalem, to being one of the few left behind in Judah after Nebuchadnezzar marched almost all the survivors away to Babylon.

Josiah (jo-SIGH-yuh)
This guy came to Judah's throne as an 8-year-old, and his 31-year reign was the last good thing Judah had going for it. He was killed in battle by the Egyptians. Jeremiah came on the scene while Josiah was king.

Jehoahaz
(jeh-HOE-uh-haz)
This son of Josiah lasted only 3 months as king before the Egyptian pharaoh invaded

So you thought only nice things happen to nice people?—that if you obeyed God, people would listen to you, respect and admire you, maybe even give you large sums of money?

Nah. At least not in Jeremiah's case. It was like being traded to a losing team, sitting on the bench for nearly the entire season (a losing season, at that) and then being sent in to play the final game in the last 2 minutes when your team's behind by a massive amount and doesn't have a whisper of a chance of winning. There's no hope. All that's left is bad news.

This was the kind of job God gave Jer. And his reward for obeying God in this ridiculously tough job? He was turned in to the authorities by his own family and thrown into prison. He felt like the world was against him. Jer didn't like it much of the time, and he let God know. But he never backed down, never stopped sharing what God wanted him to say. And in Jer's case—just like ours today—although God doesn't promise continual good times, he *does* promise his constant presence.

Jerusalem, dragged him off his throne, carted him to Egypt and, in his place, set up his brother . . .

Jehoiakim
(jeh-HOY-uh-kim)
He survived 11 years as Judah's king. This is the foolish guy (well, one of them) who imprisoned Jeremiah. He finally died after ticking off not only the Egyptians but the Babylonians too.

Zedekiah
(ze-dih-KIE-yuh)
Ruled 11 years before he too ticked off King Nebuchadnezzar, who came roaring back to Jerusalem—not merely to take some more captives, but to bulldoze the city with his thousands of soldier buds, then burn what remained. Not a pretty picture.

Nebuchadnezzar of Babylon
(neb-yoo-kad-NEZZ-ur)
The top dude of the ancient world at this time, head-quartered east of Judah in Babylon, also called Chaldea. Once Nebby took over a city or country, his word was law—and it didn't matter if you agreed with him.

Pharaoh of Egypt
As if having one enemy (Babylon) wasn't enough, there was Egypt too. Judah spent centuries being jerked around by these 2.

What's UP with That?
Object Lessons That Bite

Jeremiah explains God's plans for Judah in some really strange ways—strange to us, at least. Read about the object lesson in the Bible, then choose the explanation that most closely resembles the real thing.

1. Jer Can't Marry (chapter 16:1–4) to show that:
a. God thinks sex is bad.
b. Life is gonna get so bad that any child you'd have would die young anyway, so why bother?
c. Who can afford to get married? Just elope to Las Vegas—your folks won't talk to you for a year, but eventually they'll be glad you saved them all that money.

2. No Partying for Jer Either (chapter 16:8–13) because:
a. All parties were gonna end pretty soon, thanks to Nebuchadnezzar, the party-pooper.
b. Jer never could find a party that served that clam-garlic-anchovy dip that he just loved.
c. Before he became a prophet, he was a birthday clown, and he had bad memories of bratty kids pulling off his rubber nose and rainbow wig all the time.

3. The Yoke's on You! (chapter 27) Jer put an animal yoke on his own neck to show that:
a. The Babylonians were gonna kill all oxen and mules, so people would have to drag their own plows to till their fields.
b. Yokes on your neck are just messy, especially when the gooey yellow stuff drips onto your shirt . . . Oh, that's *yolk*.
c. Judah had to surrender to King Neb if they wanted to live.

4. Burial of Large Stones (chapter 43) showed that even in Egypt:
a. Jews who had escaped King Neb's massacre in Judah could still catch some rays and deepen their tans.
b. If you buried large stones, then dug them up a year later, you'd still have a bunch of large stones.
c. A remnant of unwilling-to-submit Jews could not escape the long (and mean) arm of King Neb.

Snap shots

This book goes in circles. It's not in order. Here's the one-minute version:

GOD—Jeremiah, tell my people to turn from their evil ways. Maybe they'll listen to you—and instead of disciplining them with disaster, I'll use plan B.

JER—*(to the people of Judah)* All right, listen up. God says you're all acting rude and selfish. Unless you turn to God, ask for forgiveness and stop this behavior, bad times are comin'.

JEWS—Hey, Jer! You are always sooo negative. Lighten up, will ya? *Us*, misbehaving? I mean, what are you, some kind of nut? Or a traitor? Yeah, he's a traitor—kill him!

answers: 1-b, 2-a, 3-c, 4-c

A BIG exception
to this doom and gloom is in chapters 30—33. God reminds his people there's always hope. He looks beyond the nightmare of war, death and being controlled by enemies. Chapter 31 is one of the most tender chapters in the entire Bible—a chapter of hope and joy and all-you-can-eat pizza for those who would someday return to the land and rebuild their homes.

1 The words of Jeremiah son of Hilkiah, one of the priests at Anathoth in the territory of Benjamin. ²The word of the LORD came to him in the thirteenth year of the reign of Josiah son of Amon king of Judah, ³and through the reign of Jehoiakim son of Josiah king of Judah, down to the fifth month of the eleventh year of Zedekiah son of Josiah king of Judah, when the people of Jerusalem went into exile.

The Call of Jeremiah

⁴The word of the LORD came to me, saying,

⁵ "Before I formed you in the womb I
knew*ᵃ* you,
before you were born I set you
apart;
I appointed you as a prophet to the
nations."

⁶"Ah, Sovereign LORD," I said, "I do not know how to speak; I am only a child."
⁷But the LORD said to me, "Do not say,

ᵃ5 Or chose

What's in a Name?

Huh?

Jeremiah 1:1

Unlike today, a few thousand years ago, parents chose names for their infant children not because of how it sounded but because of what it meant. There were a total of 10 guys in the Old Testament named Jeremiah. But surprisingly, we are still a little clueless about the meaning of the name Jeremiah. Most likely, it means "The Lord throws." God threw the prophet Jeremiah into a tough place to give a tough message. It seems his name fit him after all.

Wednesday

The Young and the Useful

Read Jeremiah 1:5–8

One of my brother's friends was at my house one day, and we started talking. I've known this guy for a while, and I knew he was into some bad stuff, like smoking. I also knew he wasn't a Christian. I really felt like I should talk to him about Jesus, but I was pretty nervous about it. But before we quit talking, God gave me the strength to tell this guy about Jesus and the glory of God. I don't know what my brother's friend thought, but I know God used me to at least tell him the truth.

I'm only 13 and can't do a lot of things, like drive or vote. But God can use me, even while I'm young. God put all of us on earth to tell other people about him—and you don't have to be an adult to do that! We are all important to God, and he can work through us, no matter how old or how young we are.

Bobby age 13

❶ What are some things you want to do for God when you get older? Do you really have to wait? Think about some ways God can work through you right *now*.

❷ Think of one thing you can do today to share God's love with another person. Get out there and go for it!

❸ Thank God for living in you and helping you share his love with others.

Turn to page 891 for your next devotion.

'I am only a child.' You must go to everyone I send you to and say whatever I command you. ⁸Do not be afraid of them, for I am with you and will rescue you," declares the LORD.

⁹Then the LORD reached out his hand and touched my mouth and said to me, "Now, I have put my words in your mouth. ¹⁰See, today I appoint you over nations and kingdoms to uproot and tear down, to destroy and overthrow, to build and to plant."

¹¹The word of the LORD came to me: "What do you see, Jeremiah?"

"I see the branch of an almond tree," I replied.

¹²The LORD said to me, "You have seen correctly, for I am watching[a] to see that my word is fulfilled."

¹³The word of the LORD came to me again: "What do you see?"

"I see a boiling pot, tilting away from the north," I answered.

¹⁴The LORD said to me, "From the north disaster will be poured out on all who live in the land. ¹⁵I am about to summon all the peoples of the northern kingdoms," declares the LORD.

"Their kings will come and set up
        their thrones
    in the entrance of the gates of
        Jerusalem;
they will come against all her
        surrounding walls
    and against all the towns of Judah.
¹⁶I will pronounce my judgments on my
        people
    because of their wickedness in
        forsaking me,
in burning incense to other gods
    and in worshiping what their hands
        have made.

¹⁷"Get yourself ready! Stand up and say to them whatever I command you. Do not be terrified by them, or I will terrify you before them. ¹⁸Today I have made you a fortified city, an iron pillar and a bronze wall to stand against the whole land—against the kings of Judah, its officials, its priests and the people of the land. ¹⁹They will fight against you but will not overcome you, for I am with you and will rescue you," declares the LORD.

Israel Forsakes God

2 The word of the LORD came to me: ²"Go and proclaim in the hearing of Jerusalem:

" 'I remember the devotion of your
        youth,
    how as a bride you loved me
and followed me through the desert,
    through a land not sown.
³Israel was holy to the LORD,
    the firstfruits of his harvest;
all who devoured her were held
        guilty,
    and disaster overtook them,' "
                declares the LORD.

⁴Hear the word of the LORD, O house of
        Jacob,
    all you clans of the house of Israel.

⁵This is what the LORD says:

"What fault did your fathers find in
        me,
    that they strayed so far from me?
They followed worthless idols
    and became worthless themselves.
⁶They did not ask, 'Where is the LORD,
    who brought us up out of Egypt
and led us through the barren
        wilderness,
    through a land of deserts and rifts,
a land of drought and darkness,[b]
    a land where no one travels and no
        one lives?'
⁷I brought you into a fertile land
    to eat its fruit and rich produce.
But you came and defiled my land
    and made my inheritance
        detestable.
⁸The priests did not ask,
    'Where is the LORD?'
Those who deal with the law did not
        know me;
    the leaders rebelled against me.
The prophets prophesied by Baal,
    following worthless idols.

⁹"Therefore I bring charges against you
        again,"
                declares the LORD.
"And I will bring charges against
    your children's children.

---

[a]12 The Hebrew for *watching* sounds like the Hebrew for *almond tree.*   [b]6 Or *and the shadow of death*

¹⁰ Cross over to the coasts of Kittim[a] and
　　look,
　send to Kedar[b] and observe closely;
　see if there has ever been anything
　　like this:
¹¹ Has a nation ever changed its gods?
　(Yet they are not gods at all.)
　But my people have exchanged their[c]
　　Glory
　for worthless idols.
¹² Be appalled at this, O heavens,
　and shudder with great horror,"
　　　　　　declares the LORD.
¹³ "My people have committed two sins:
　They have forsaken me,
　　the spring of living water,
　and have dug their own cisterns,
　　broken cisterns that cannot hold
　　　water.
¹⁴ Is Israel a servant, a slave by birth?
　Why then has he become plunder?
¹⁵ Lions have roared;
　　they have growled at him.
　They have laid waste his land;
　　his towns are burned and deserted.
¹⁶ Also, the men of Memphis[d] and
　　Tahpanhes
　have shaved the crown of your head.[e]
¹⁷ Have you not brought this on
　　yourselves
　by forsaking the LORD your God
　when he led you in the way?
¹⁸ Now why go to Egypt
　to drink water from the Shihor[f]?
　And why go to Assyria
　to drink water from the River[g]?
¹⁹ Your wickedness will punish you;
　　your backsliding will rebuke you.
　Consider then and realize
　　how evil and bitter it is for you
　when you forsake the LORD your God
　and have no awe of me,"
　　　　　　declares the Lord,
　　　　　　the LORD Almighty.

²⁰ "Long ago you broke off your yoke
　and tore off your bonds;
　　you said, 'I will not serve you!'
　Indeed, on every high hill
　and under every spreading tree
　you lay down as a prostitute.
²¹ I had planted you like a choice vine
　of sound and reliable stock.
　How then did you turn against me
　into a corrupt, wild vine?

²² Although you wash yourself with soda
　and use an abundance of soap,
　　the stain of your guilt is still before
　　　me,"
　　　　　declares the Sovereign LORD.
²³ "How can you say, 'I am not defiled;
　I have not run after the Baals'?
　See how you behaved in the valley;
　　consider what you have done.
　You are a swift she-camel
　　running here and there,
²⁴ a wild donkey accustomed to the
　　desert,
　sniffing the wind in her craving—
　　in her heat who can restrain her?
　Any males that pursue her need not
　　tire themselves;
　at mating time they will find her.
²⁵ Do not run until your feet are bare
　and your throat is dry.
　But you said, 'It's no use!
　I love foreign gods,
　and I must go after them.'

²⁶ "As a thief is disgraced when he is
　　caught,
　so the house of Israel is disgraced—
　they, their kings and their officials,
　　their priests and their prophets.
²⁷ They say to wood, 'You are my father,'
　and to stone, 'You gave me birth.'
　They have turned their backs to me
　　and not their faces;
　yet when they are in trouble, they say,
　　'Come and save us!'
²⁸ Where then are the gods you made for
　　yourselves?
　Let them come if they can save you
　　when you are in trouble!
　For you have as many gods
　　as you have towns, O Judah.

²⁹ "Why do you bring charges against
　　me?
　You have all rebelled against me,"
　　　　　　declares the LORD.
³⁰ "In vain I punished your people;
　　they did not respond to correction.
　Your sword has devoured your
　　prophets
　　like a ravening lion.

---

a 10 That is, Cyprus and western coastlands
b 10 The home of Bedouin tribes in the Syro-Arabian
desert　*c 11* Masoretic Text; an ancient Hebrew
scribal tradition *my*　*d 16* Hebrew *Noph*　*e 16* Or *have
cracked your skull*　*f 18* That is, a branch of the Nile
g 18 That is, the Euphrates

[31]"You of this generation, consider the word of the LORD:

"Have I been a desert to Israel
or a land of great darkness?
Why do my people say, 'We are free to
roam;
we will come to you no more'?
[32]Does a maiden forget her jewelry,
a bride her wedding ornaments?
Yet my people have forgotten me,
days without number.
[33]How skilled you are at pursuing
love!
Even the worst of women can learn
from your ways.
[34]On your clothes men find
the lifeblood of the innocent poor,
though you did not catch them
breaking in.
Yet in spite of all this
[35]   you say, 'I am innocent;
he is not angry with me.'
But I will pass judgment on you
because you say, 'I have not sinned.'
[36]Why do you go about so much,
changing your ways?
You will be disappointed by Egypt
as you were by Assyria.
[37]You will also leave that place
with your hands on your head,
for the LORD has rejected those you
trust;
you will not be helped by them.

3 "If a man divorces his wife
and she leaves him and marries
another man,
should he return to her again?
Would not the land be completely
defiled?
But you have lived as a prostitute
with many lovers—
would you now return to me?"
declares the LORD.
[2]"Look up to the barren heights and
see.
Is there any place where you have
not been ravished?
By the roadside you sat waiting for
lovers,
sat like a nomad[a] in the desert.
You have defiled the land
with your prostitution and
wickedness.

[3]Therefore the showers have been
withheld,
and no spring rains have fallen.
Yet you have the brazen look of a
prostitute;
you refuse to blush with shame.
[4]Have you not just called to me:
'My Father, my friend from my
youth,
[5]will you always be angry?
Will your wrath continue forever?'
This is how you talk,
but you do all the evil you can."

Unfaithful Israel

[6]During the reign of King Josiah, the LORD said to me, "Have you seen what faithless Israel has done? She has gone up on every high hill and under every spreading tree and has committed adultery there. [7]I thought that after she had done all this she would return to me but she did not, and her unfaithful sister Judah saw it. [8]I gave faithless Israel her certificate of divorce and sent her away because of all her adulteries. Yet I saw that her unfaithful sister Judah had no fear; she also went out and committed adultery. [9]Because Israel's immorality mattered so little to her, she defiled the land and committed adultery with stone and wood. [10]In spite of all this, her unfaithful sister Judah did not return to me with all her heart, but only in pretense," declares the LORD.

[11]The LORD said to me, "Faithless Israel is more righteous than unfaithful Judah. [12]Go, proclaim this message toward the north:

" 'Return, faithless Israel,' declares the
LORD,
'I will frown on you no longer,
for I am merciful,' declares the LORD,
'I will not be angry forever.
[13]Only acknowledge your guilt—
you have rebelled against the LORD
your God,
you have scattered your favors to
foreign gods
under every spreading tree,
and have not obeyed me,' "
declares the LORD.

a2 Or an Arab

¹⁴"Return, faithless people," declares the LORD, "for I am your husband. I will choose you—one from a town and two from a clan—and bring you to Zion. ¹⁵Then I will give you shepherds after my own heart, who will lead you with knowledge and understanding. ¹⁶In those days, when your numbers have increased greatly in the land," declares the LORD, "men will no longer say, 'The ark of the covenant of the LORD.' It will never enter their minds or be remembered; it will not be missed, nor will another one be made. ¹⁷At that time they will call Jerusalem The Throne of the LORD, and all nations will gather in Jerusalem to honor the name of the LORD. No longer will they follow the stubbornness of their evil hearts. ¹⁸In those days the house of Judah will join the house of Israel, and together they will come from a northern land to the land I gave your forefathers as an inheritance.

¹⁹"I myself said,

" 'How gladly would I treat you like sons
    and give you a desirable land,
    the most beautiful inheritance of any nation.'
I thought you would call me 'Father'
    and not turn away from following me.
²⁰But like a woman unfaithful to her husband,
    so you have been unfaithful to me, O house of Israel,"
        declares the LORD.

²¹A cry is heard on the barren heights,
    the weeping and pleading of the people of Israel,
because they have perverted their ways
    and have forgotten the LORD their God.

²²"Return, faithless people;
    I will cure you of backsliding."

"Yes, we will come to you,
    for you are the LORD our God.
²³Surely the idolatrous commotion on the hills
    and mountains is a deception;
surely in the LORD our God
    is the salvation of Israel.

²⁴From our youth shameful gods have consumed
    the fruits of our fathers' labor—
their flocks and herds,
    their sons and daughters.
²⁵Let us lie down in our shame,
    and let our disgrace cover us.
We have sinned against the LORD our God,
    both we and our fathers;
from our youth till this day
    we have not obeyed the LORD our God."

4 "If you will return, O Israel,
    return to me,"
        declares the LORD.
"If you put your detestable idols out of my sight
    and no longer go astray,
²and if in a truthful, just and righteous way
    you swear, 'As surely as the LORD lives,'
then the nations will be blessed by him
    and in him they will glory."

³This is what the LORD says to the men of Judah and to Jerusalem:

"Break up your unplowed ground
    and do not sow among thorns.
⁴Circumcise yourselves to the LORD,
    circumcise your hearts,
    you men of Judah and people of Jerusalem,
or my wrath will break out and burn like fire
    because of the evil you have done—
    burn with no one to quench it.

Disaster From the North

⁵"Announce in Judah and proclaim in Jerusalem and say:
    'Sound the trumpet throughout the land!'
Cry aloud and say:
    'Gather together!
    Let us flee to the fortified cities!'
⁶Raise the signal to go to Zion!
    Flee for safety without delay!
For I am bringing disaster from the north,
    even terrible destruction."

⁷A lion has come out of his lair;
    a destroyer of nations has set out.
He has left his place
    to lay waste your land.
Your towns will lie in ruins
    without inhabitant.
⁸So put on sackcloth,
    lament and wail,
for the fierce anger of the LORD
    has not turned away from us.

⁹"In that day," declares the LORD,
    "the king and the officials will lose
        heart,
the priests will be horrified,
    and the prophets will be appalled."

¹⁰Then I said, "Ah, Sovereign LORD,
how completely you have deceived this
people and Jerusalem by saying, 'You
will have peace,' when the sword is at our
throats."

¹¹At that time this people and Jerusalem will be told, "A scorching wind from
the barren heights in the desert blows toward my people, but not to winnow or
cleanse; ¹²a wind too strong for that
comes from me.ᵃ Now I pronounce my
judgments against them."

¹³Look! He advances like the clouds,
    his chariots come like a
        whirlwind,
his horses are swifter than eagles.
    Woe to us! We are ruined!
¹⁴O Jerusalem, wash the evil from your
        heart and be saved.
    How long will you harbor wicked
        thoughts?
¹⁵A voice is announcing from Dan,
    proclaiming disaster from the hills
        of Ephraim.
¹⁶"Tell this to the nations,
    proclaim it to Jerusalem:
'A besieging army is coming from a
        distant land,
    raising a war cry against the cities
        of Judah.
¹⁷They surround her like men guarding
        a field,
    because she has rebelled against
        me,'"
                declares the LORD.
¹⁸"Your own conduct and actions
    have brought this upon you.
This is your punishment.

How bitter it is!
    How it pierces to the heart!"
¹⁹Oh, my anguish, my anguish!
    I writhe in pain.
Oh, the agony of my heart!
    My heart pounds within me,
    I cannot keep silent.
For I have heard the sound of the
        trumpet;
    I have heard the battle cry.
²⁰Disaster follows disaster;
    the whole land lies in ruins.
In an instant my tents are destroyed,
    my shelter in a moment.
²¹How long must I see the battle
        standard
    and hear the sound of the trumpet?

²²"My people are fools;
    they do not know me.
They are senseless children;
    they have no understanding.
They are skilled in doing evil;
    they know not how to do good."

²³I looked at the earth,
    and it was formless and empty;
and at the heavens,
    and their light was gone.
²⁴I looked at the mountains,
    and they were quaking;
    all the hills were swaying.
²⁵I looked, and there were no people;
    every bird in the sky had flown
        away.
²⁶I looked, and the fruitful land was a
        desert;
    all its towns lay in ruins
    before the LORD, before his fierce
        anger.

²⁷This is what the LORD says:

"The whole land will be ruined,
    though I will not destroy it
        completely.
²⁸Therefore the earth will mourn
    and the heavens above grow dark,
because I have spoken and will not
        relent,
    I have decided and will not turn
        back."

²⁹At the sound of horsemen and archers
    every town takes to flight.

ᵃ12 Or comes at my command

Some go into the thickets;
 some climb up among the rocks.
All the towns are deserted;
 no one lives in them.

³⁰What are you doing, O devastated
  one?
 Why dress yourself in scarlet
 and put on jewels of gold?
Why shade your eyes with paint?
 You adorn yourself in vain.
Your lovers despise you;
 they seek your life.

³¹I hear a cry as of a woman in labor,
 a groan as of one bearing her first
  child—
the cry of the Daughter of Zion
 gasping for breath,
 stretching out her hands and saying,
"Alas! I am fainting;
 my life is given over to murderers."

Not One Is Upright

5 "Go up and down the streets of
  Jerusalem,
 look around and consider,
 search through her squares.
If you can find but one person
 who deals honestly and seeks the
  truth,
 I will forgive this city.
²Although they say, 'As surely as the
  LORD lives,'
 still they are swearing falsely."

³O LORD, do not your eyes look for
  truth?

You struck them, but they felt no
  pain;
 you crushed them, but they refused
  correction.
They made their faces harder than
  stone
 and refused to repent.
⁴I thought, "These are only the poor;
 they are foolish,
for they do not know the way of the
  LORD,
 the requirements of their God.
⁵So I will go to the leaders
 and speak to them;
surely they know the way of the LORD,
 the requirements of their God."
But with one accord they too had
  broken off the yoke
 and torn off the bonds.
⁶Therefore a lion from the forest will
  attack them,
 a wolf from the desert will ravage
  them,
a leopard will lie in wait near their
  towns
 to tear to pieces any who venture
  out,
for their rebellion is great
 and their backslidings many.

⁷"Why should I forgive you?
 Your children have forsaken me
 and sworn by gods that are not
  gods.
I supplied all their needs,
 yet they committed adultery
 and thronged to the houses of
  prostitutes.
⁸They are well-fed, lusty stallions,
 each neighing for another man's
  wife.
⁹Should I not punish them for this?"
 declares the LORD.
"Should I not avenge myself
 on such a nation as this?

¹⁰"Go through her vineyards and ravage
  them,
 but do not destroy them completely.
Strip off her branches,
 for these people do not belong to
  the LORD.
¹¹The house of Israel and the house of
  Judah
 have been utterly unfaithful to me,"
     declares the LORD.

¹²They have lied about the LORD;
    they said, "He will do nothing!
No harm will come to us;
    we will never see sword or famine.
¹³The prophets are but wind
    and the word is not in them;
    so let what they say be done to
      them."

¹⁴Therefore this is what the LORD God Almighty says:

"Because the people have spoken these
    words,
I will make my words in your
    mouth a fire
and these people the wood it
    consumes.
¹⁵O house of Israel," declares the LORD,
    "I am bringing a distant nation
      against you—
an ancient and enduring nation,
    a people whose language you do
      not know,
    whose speech you do not
      understand.
¹⁶Their quivers are like an open grave;
    all of them are mighty warriors.
¹⁷They will devour your harvests and
    food,
    devour your sons and daughters;
they will devour your flocks and
    herds,
    devour your vines and fig trees.
With the sword they will destroy
    the fortified cities in which you
      trust.

¹⁸"Yet even in those days," declares the LORD, "I will not destroy you completely. ¹⁹And when the people ask, 'Why has the LORD our God done all this to us?' you will tell them, 'As you have forsaken me and served foreign gods in your own land, so now you will serve foreigners in a land not your own.'

²⁰"Announce this to the house of Jacob
    and proclaim it in Judah:
²¹Hear this, you foolish and senseless
    people,
    who have eyes but do not see,
    who have ears but do not hear:
²²Should you not fear me?" declares the
    LORD.
    "Should you not tremble in my
      presence?

I made the sand a boundary for the sea,
    an everlasting barrier it cannot
      cross.
The waves may roll, but they cannot
    prevail;
    they may roar, but they cannot
      cross it.
²³But these people have stubborn and
    rebellious hearts;
    they have turned aside and gone
      away.
²⁴They do not say to themselves,
    'Let us fear the LORD our God,
who gives autumn and spring rains in
    season,
    who assures us of the regular weeks
      of harvest.'
²⁵Your wrongdoings have kept these
    away;
    your sins have deprived you of
      good.

²⁶"Among my people are wicked men
    who lie in wait like men who snare
      birds
    and like those who set traps to
      catch men.
²⁷Like cages full of birds,
    their houses are full of deceit;
they have become rich and powerful
²⁸   and have grown fat and sleek.
Their evil deeds have no limit;
    they do not plead the case of the
      fatherless to win it,
    they do not defend the rights of the
      poor.
²⁹Should I not punish them for this?"
    declares the LORD.
    "Should I not avenge myself
    on such a nation as this?

³⁰"A horrible and shocking thing
    has happened in the land:
³¹The prophets prophesy lies,
    the priests rule by their own
      authority,
and my people love it this way.
    But what will you do in the end?

Jerusalem Under Siege

6 "Flee for safety, people of
      Benjamin!
Flee from Jerusalem!
Sound the trumpet in Tekoa!
    Raise the signal over Beth
      Hakkerem!

Emotions

Back Stage Pass

Jennifer likes a guy at her school named Ryan. She talks and thinks about him constantly. Her friends think she's **psycho** because everything is always about Ryan, Ryan, Ryan! David gets angry and just about explodes. Sometimes he even breaks things! Amanda feels lonely all the time. She told a school counselor that she thinks no one would miss her if she died! And Brianna, well she's just all over the place. One minute she's totally excited about life, and the next minute she thinks everything stinks. No one ever has a clue what kind of mood Brianna's going to be in.

Ever feel like these people? Good! That means you're growing up! When you step into your teenage years, God gives your growing body the gift of **BIG EMOTIONS**. Really! You gain access to adult emotions that you've never felt before, and these emotions are turbo-charged! So when you feel love, it can knock you down! When you get mad, you feel like knocking someone else down. These grown-up emotions can take over and control you if you're not careful.

And these new emotions can make you feel like you're on a roller coaster. You wake up happy and excited; at school, someone makes fun of you and you feel lousy; then right before school gets out, a friend invites you over to her house—you're stoked! —till your mom says no. Then you get into a big argument with her and spend the rest of the night in your room feeling depressed. Whew! This kind of day can wear you out. Your emotions can make you feel awesome! Or they can make you feel stinkin' lousy!

So, what can you do? Here are some hints to help you get a grip on your emotions:

God understands your emotions. Not only did he *create* your emotions, he *has* them. He gets mad (Psalm 85:3, page 685), happy (1 Kings 3:10, page 387), even sad (Genesis 6:6, page 11). Jesus came to earth, lived a human life and knows what it's like to feel strong emotions.

Feelings can fool you. Feelings can be so intense that they can cause you to do things you know aren't right. Anger, depression and jealousy can hurt you and others. If you give them control, they can make life tough.

Act on faith, not on feelings. Jesus wants to help you control your emotions so they don't control you. Acting on faith is when you do what God wants you to do, in spite of your emotions. Don't worry—your feelings will follow. You might not feel love toward your little brother, but God says to love him (1 John 4:20, page 1533). The love feelings will probably show up later. If you wait for the love feeling, it might never show up! If you act on faith with your emotions, God can help you control all those up-and-down feelings.

eXtreme FAITH

"Sometimes when I pray, it doesn't seem like God is listening or doing anything. Why doesn't God answer all of my prayers?"

When I was 9 years old, my hero was a movie cowboy named "Hopalong Cassidy." I wanted to be a cowboy just like Hopalong when I grew up, and I begged my father to help make that possible. Then, when I was in high school, I started preparing for college. Wouldn't it have been weird if my dad had said, "College?!? What are you talking about? When you were 9, you said you wanted to be a cowboy! I spent all of our family's money to buy a ranch and a 100 cows. They're all waiting for you down in Texas!" I would have answered, "Dad, why did you do that? I was just a little kid when I said those things! You didn't really take me seriously, did you?" The good news is that my dad didn't give me what I thought I wanted when I was 9 years old. Why? Because he knew he could give me what I really wanted—and needed—when I got older.

I'm convinced God sometimes acts the same way my dad did. **Sometimes it might seem like God isn't answering our prayers, but he's really just refusing to give us what we think we want so he can later give us what we really need.** We have to remember that, in God's eyes, we're all pretty immature. We're all 9-year-olds who want to be cowboys. And God's too wise and loving to grant every prayer request from people who aren't spiritually "grown-up" enough to know what's really best for them.

A key to understanding what our prayers should be like comes from John 14:13–14, page 1293, where Jesus says we should pray "in his name." In Bible times, a person's name was an expression of what that person was all about. Often, a person's name also said what they did for a living. For instance, Mary Baker made donuts, Phil Carpenter built doghouses, Charles Farmer milked cows. You get the point.

So when Jesus says to pray in his name, he doesn't just mean we should mention the word "Jesus" here and there. He means that our prayers should fit in with what Jesus was all about—salvation, love and justice. In prayer, we should try to think like Jesus and to feel his emotions, to want the things he wants. That's what the apostle Paul meant when he said, "Your attitude should be the same as that of Christ Jesus" (Philippians 2:5).

We can't expect our prayers to be answered if they aren't in harmony with what God wants to do in us and through us. On the other hand, we shouldn't be afraid to pray prayers that are less than perfect.

Romans 8:26–27 (page 1361) says that none of us really knows how to pray perfectly. But this passage also says that even when our prayers aren't perfect, the Holy Spirit steps in for us before God. So when I finish praying, the Holy Spirit turns to the heavenly Father and says something like, "I know Tony's prayer was a little selfish. Maybe it even seemed a little immature to you. What Tony should have said was . . ." Then the Holy Spirit prays the prayer I should have prayed! I can't think of anything more comforting than that.

— Tony Campolo, sociology professor at Eastern College. Tony is a dynamic speaker and the author of several books for teens.

For disaster looms out of the north,
  even terrible destruction.
²I will destroy the Daughter of Zion,
  so beautiful and delicate.
³Shepherds with their flocks will come
    against her;
  they will pitch their tents around
    her,
  each tending his own portion."

⁴"Prepare for battle against her!
  Arise, let us attack at noon!
But, alas, the daylight is fading,
  and the shadows of evening grow
    long.
⁵So arise, let us attack at night
  and destroy her fortresses!"

⁶This is what the LORD Almighty says:

"Cut down the trees
  and build siege ramps against
    Jerusalem.
This city must be punished;
  it is filled with oppression.
⁷As a well pours out its water,
  so she pours out her wickedness.
Violence and destruction resound in
    her;
  her sickness and wounds are ever
    before me.
⁸Take warning, O Jerusalem,
  or I will turn away from you
and make your land desolate
  so no one can live in it."

⁹This is what the LORD Almighty says:

"Let them glean the remnant of Israel
  as thoroughly as a vine;
pass your hand over the branches
    again,
  like one gathering grapes."

¹⁰To whom can I speak and give
    warning?
  Who will listen to me?
Their ears are closed[a]
  so they cannot hear.
The word of the LORD is offensive to
    them;
  they find no pleasure in it.
¹¹But I am full of the wrath of the
    LORD,
  and I cannot hold it in.

"Pour it out on the children in the
    street

and on the young men gathered
    together;
both husband and wife will be caught
    in it,
  and the old, those weighed down
    with years.
¹²Their houses will be turned over to
    others,
  together with their fields and their
    wives,
when I stretch out my hand
  against those who live in the land,"
              declares the LORD.
¹³"From the least to the greatest,
  all are greedy for gain;
prophets and priests alike,
  all practice deceit.
¹⁴They dress the wound of my people
  as though it were not serious.
'Peace, peace,' they say,
  when there is no peace.
¹⁵Are they ashamed of their loathsome
    conduct?
  No, they have no shame at all;
  they do not even know how to
    blush.
So they will fall among the fallen;
  they will be brought down when I
    punish them,"
              says the LORD.

¹⁶This is what the LORD says:

"Stand at the crossroads and look;
  ask for the ancient paths,
ask where the good way is, and walk
    in it,
  and you will find rest for your
    souls.
  But you said, 'We will not walk in
    it.'
¹⁷I appointed watchmen over you and
    said,
  'Listen to the sound of the trumpet!'
  But you said, 'We will not listen.'
¹⁸Therefore hear, O nations;
  observe, O witnesses,
  what will happen to them.
¹⁹Hear, O earth:
I am bringing disaster on this people,
  the fruit of their schemes,
because they have not listened to my
    words
  and have rejected my law.

---

a 10 Hebrew *uncircumcised*

²⁰What do I care about incense from
  Sheba
    or sweet calamus from a distant
      land?
Your burnt offerings are not
    acceptable;
  your sacrifices do not please me."

²¹Therefore this is what the LORD says:

"I will put obstacles before this people.
  Fathers and sons alike will stumble
      over them;
  neighbors and friends will perish."

²²This is what the LORD says:

"Look, an army is coming
    from the land of the north;
a great nation is being stirred up
    from the ends of the earth.
²³They are armed with bow and spear;
    they are cruel and show no mercy.
They sound like the roaring sea
    as they ride on their horses;
they come like men in battle formation
    to attack you, O Daughter of Zion."

²⁴We have heard reports about them,
    and our hands hang limp.
Anguish has gripped us,
    pain like that of a woman in labor.
²⁵Do not go out to the fields
    or walk on the roads,
for the enemy has a sword,
    and there is terror on every side.
²⁶O my people, put on sackcloth
    and roll in ashes;
  mourn with bitter wailing
    as for an only son,
  for suddenly the destroyer
    will come upon us.

²⁷"I have made you a tester of metals
    and my people the ore,
that you may observe
    and test their ways.
²⁸They are all hardened rebels,
    going about to slander.
They are bronze and iron;
    they all act corruptly.
²⁹The bellows blow fiercely
    to burn away the lead with fire,
but the refining goes on in vain;
    the wicked are not purged out.
³⁰They are called rejected silver,
    because the LORD has rejected
      them."

False Religion Worthless

7 This is the word that came to Jeremiah from the LORD: ²"Stand at the gate of the LORD's house and there proclaim this message:

" 'Hear the word of the LORD, all you people of Judah who come through these gates to worship the LORD. ³This is what the LORD Almighty, the God of Israel, says: Reform your ways and your actions, and I will let you live in this place. ⁴Do not trust in deceptive words and say, "This is the temple of the LORD, the temple of the LORD, the temple of the LORD!" ⁵If you really change your ways and your actions and deal with each other justly, ⁶if you do not oppress the alien, the fatherless or the widow and do not shed innocent blood in this place, and if you do not follow other gods to your own harm, ⁷then I will let you live in this place, in the land I gave your forefathers for ever and ever. ⁸But look, you are trusting in deceptive words that are worthless.

⁹" 'Will you steal and murder, commit adultery and perjury,ᵃ burn incense to Baal and follow other gods you have not known, ¹⁰and then come and stand before me in this house, which bears my Name, and say, "We are safe"—safe to do all these detestable things? ¹¹Has this house, which bears my Name, become a den of robbers to you? But I have been watching! declares the LORD.

¹²" 'Go now to the place in Shiloh where I first made a dwelling for my Name, and see what I did to it because of the wickedness of my people Israel. ¹³While you were doing all these things, declares the LORD, I spoke to you again and again, but you did not listen; I called you, but you did not answer. ¹⁴Therefore, what I did to Shiloh I will now do to the house that bears my Name, the temple you trust in, the place I gave to you and your fathers. ¹⁵I will thrust you from my presence, just as I did all your brothers, the people of Ephraim.'

¹⁶"So do not pray for this people nor offer any plea or petition for them; do not plead with me, for I will not listen to

ᵃ9 Or *and swear by false gods*

you. ¹⁷Do you not see what they are doing in the towns of Judah and in the streets of Jerusalem? ¹⁸The children gather wood, the fathers light the fire, and the women knead the dough and make cakes of bread for the Queen of Heaven. They pour out drink offerings to other gods to provoke me to anger. ¹⁹But am I the one they are provoking? declares the Lord. Are they not rather harming themselves, to their own shame?

²⁰" 'Therefore this is what the Sovereign Lord says: My anger and my wrath will be poured out on this place, on man and beast, on the trees of the field and on the fruit of the ground, and it will burn and not be quenched.

²¹" 'This is what the Lord Almighty, the God of Israel, says: Go ahead, add your burnt offerings to your other sacrifices and eat the meat yourselves! ²²For when I brought your forefathers out of Egypt and spoke to them, I did not just give them commands about burnt offerings and sacrifices, ²³but I gave them this command: Obey me, and I will be your God and you will be my people. Walk in all the ways I command you, that it may go well with you. ²⁴But they did not listen or pay attention; instead, they followed the stubborn inclinations of their evil hearts. They went backward and not forward. ²⁵From the time your forefathers left Egypt until now, day after day, again and again I sent you my servants the prophets. ²⁶But they did not listen to me or pay attention. They were stiff-necked and did more evil than their forefathers.'

²⁷"When you tell them all this, they will not listen to you; when you call to them, they will not answer. ²⁸Therefore say to them, 'This is the nation that has not obeyed the Lord its God or responded to correction. Truth has perished; it has vanished from their lips. ²⁹Cut off your hair and throw it away; take up a lament on the barren heights, for the Lord has rejected and abandoned this generation that is under his wrath.

The Valley of Slaughter

³⁰" 'The people of Judah have done evil in my eyes, declares the Lord. They have set up their detestable idols in the house that bears my Name and have defiled it. ³¹They have built the high places of Topheth in the Valley of Ben Hinnom to burn their sons and daughters in the fire—something I did not command, nor did it enter my mind. ³²So beware, the days are coming, declares the Lord, when people will no longer call it Topheth or the Valley of Ben Hinnom, but the Valley of Slaughter, for they will bury the dead in Topheth until there is no more room. ³³Then the carcasses of this people will become food for the birds of the air and the beasts of the earth, and there will be no one to frighten them away. ³⁴I will bring an end to the sounds of joy and gladness and to the voices of bride and bridegroom in the towns of Judah and the streets of Jerusalem, for the land will become desolate.

8 " 'At that time, declares the Lord, the bones of the kings and officials of Judah, the bones of the priests and prophets, and the bones of the people of Jerusalem will be removed from their graves. ²They will be exposed to the sun and the moon and all the stars of the heavens, which they have loved and served and which they have followed and consulted and worshiped. They will not be gathered up or buried, but will be like refuse lying on the ground. ³Wherever I banish them, all the survivors of this evil nation will prefer death to life, declares the Lord Almighty.'

Sin and Punishment

⁴"Say to them, 'This is what the Lord says:

" 'When men fall down, do they not
    get up?
  When a man turns away, does he
    not return?
⁵Why then have these people turned
    away?
  Why does Jerusalem always turn
    away?
They cling to deceit;
  they refuse to return.
⁶I have listened attentively,
  but they do not say what is right.
No one repents of his wickedness,
  saying, "What have I done?"

Each pursues his own course
 like a horse charging into battle.
⁷Even the stork in the sky
 knows her appointed seasons,
and the dove, the swift and the thrush
 observe the time of their migration.
But my people do not know
 the requirements of the LORD.

⁸" 'How can you say, "We are wise,
 for we have the law of the LORD,"
when actually the lying pen of the
 scribes
 has handled it falsely?
⁹The wise will be put to shame;
 they will be dismayed and trapped.
Since they have rejected the word of
 the LORD,
 what kind of wisdom do they have?
¹⁰Therefore I will give their wives to
 other men
 and their fields to new owners.
From the least to the greatest,
 all are greedy for gain;
prophets and priests alike,
 all practice deceit.
¹¹They dress the wound of my people
 as though it were not serious.
"Peace, peace," they say,
 when there is no peace.
¹²Are they ashamed of their loathsome
 conduct?
 No, they have no shame at all;
 they do not even know how to
 blush.
So they will fall among the fallen;
 they will be brought down when
 they are punished,
 says the LORD.

¹³" 'I will take away their harvest,
 declares the LORD.
 There will be no grapes on the vine.
There will be no figs on the tree,
 and their leaves will wither.
What I have given them
 will be taken from them.^a' "

¹⁴"Why are we sitting here?
 Gather together!
Let us flee to the fortified cities
 and perish there!
For the LORD our God has doomed us
 to perish
 and given us poisoned water to
 drink,

because we have sinned against
 him.
¹⁵We hoped for peace
 but no good has come,
for a time of healing
 but there was only terror.
¹⁶The snorting of the enemy's horses
 is heard from Dan;
at the neighing of their stallions
 the whole land trembles.
They have come to devour
 the land and everything in it,
 the city and all who live there."

¹⁷"See, I will send venomous snakes
 among you,
 vipers that cannot be charmed,
 and they will bite you,"
 declares the LORD.

¹⁸O my Comforter^b in sorrow,
 my heart is faint within me.
¹⁹Listen to the cry of my people
 from a land far away:
"Is the LORD not in Zion?
 Is her King no longer there?"

"Why have they provoked me to anger
 with their images,
 with their worthless foreign idols?"

²⁰"The harvest is past,
 the summer has ended,
 and we are not saved."

²¹Since my people are crushed, I am
 crushed;
 I mourn, and horror grips me.
²²Is there no balm in Gilead?
 Is there no physician there?
Why then is there no healing
 for the wound of my people?

9 ¹Oh, that my head were a spring of
 water
 and my eyes a fountain of tears!
I would weep day and night
 for the slain of my people.
²Oh, that I had in the desert
 a lodging place for travelers,
so that I might leave my people
 and go away from them;
for they are all adulterers,
 a crowd of unfaithful people.

^a13 The meaning of the Hebrew for this sentence is
uncertain. ^b18 The meaning of the Hebrew for this
word is uncertain.

No Stink or Sting

Huh?

Jeremiah 8:22
Usually first-aid ointment either stinks or stings. But not the good stuff—the balm of Gilead. Balm is like an oil or lotion that oozes out of the fruit or stems of a tree. Gilead is a place to the south and east of the Sea of Galilee that was full of plants with healing power. Jeremiah knew that the balm of Gilead would heal lots of stuff, but maybe not the confusion and disobedience of Israel. Only God could heal this.

³"They make ready their tongue
　　like a bow, to shoot lies;
　it is not by truth
　　that they triumph*a* in the land.
They go from one sin to another;
　　they do not acknowledge me,"
　　　　　　　　declares the LORD.
⁴"Beware of your friends;
　　do not trust your brothers.
For every brother is a deceiver,*b*
　　and every friend a slanderer.
⁵Friend deceives friend,
　　and no one speaks the truth.
They have taught their tongues to lie;
　　they weary themselves with sinning.
⁶You*c* live in the midst of deception;
　　in their deceit they refuse to
　　　　acknowledge me,"
　　　　　　　　declares the LORD.

⁷Therefore this is what the LORD Almighty says:

"See, I will refine and test them,
　　for what else can I do
　　because of the sin of my people?
⁸Their tongue is a deadly arrow;
　　it speaks with deceit.
With his mouth each speaks cordially
　　to his neighbor,
　　but in his heart he sets a trap for
　　　　him.
⁹Should I not punish them for this?"
　　declares the LORD.
"Should I not avenge myself
　　on such a nation as this?"

¹⁰I will weep and wail for the
　　　　mountains
　　and take up a lament concerning
　　　　the desert pastures.
They are desolate and untraveled,
　　and the lowing of cattle is not
　　　　heard.
The birds of the air have fled
　　and the animals are gone.

¹¹"I will make Jerusalem a heap of ruins,
　　a haunt of jackals;
and I will lay waste the towns of
　　　　Judah
　　so no one can live there."

¹²What man is wise enough to understand this? Who has been instructed by the LORD and can explain it? Why has the land been ruined and laid waste like a desert that no one can cross?

¹³The LORD said, "It is because they have forsaken my law, which I set before them; they have not obeyed me or followed my law. ¹⁴Instead, they have followed the stubbornness of their hearts; they have followed the Baals, as their fathers taught them." ¹⁵Therefore, this is what the LORD Almighty, the God of Israel, says: "See, I will make this people eat bitter food and drink poisoned water. ¹⁶I will scatter them among nations that neither they nor their fathers have known, and I will pursue them with the sword until I have destroyed them."

¹⁷This is what the LORD Almighty says:

"Consider now! Call for the wailing
　　　　women to come;
　　send for the most skillful of them.
¹⁸Let them come quickly
　　and wail over us
till our eyes overflow with tears
　　and water streams from our eyelids.
¹⁹The sound of wailing is heard from
　　　　Zion:
'How ruined we are!
　　How great is our shame!
We must leave our land
　　because our houses are in ruins.'"

²⁰Now, O women, hear the word of the
　　　　LORD;

---

a3 Or *lies; / they are not valiant for truth*   *b4* Or *a deceiving Jacob*   *c6* That is, Jeremiah (the Hebrew is singular)

open your ears to the words of his
  mouth.
Teach your daughters how to wail;
  teach one another a lament.
²¹Death has climbed in through our
    windows
  and has entered our fortresses;
it has cut off the children from the
    streets
  and the young men from the public
    squares.

²²Say, "This is what the LORD declares:

" 'The dead bodies of men will lie
  like refuse on the open field,
like cut grain behind the reaper,
  with no one to gather them.' "

²³This is what the LORD says:

"Let not the wise man boast of his
    wisdom
  or the strong man boast of his
    strength
  or the rich man boast of his riches,
²⁴but let him who boasts boast about
    this:
  that he understands and knows me,
that I am the LORD, who exercises
    kindness,
  justice and righteousness on earth,
  for in these I delight,"
              declares the LORD.

²⁵"The days are coming," declares the
LORD, "when I will punish all who are
circumcised only in the flesh— ²⁶Egypt,
Judah, Edom, Ammon, Moab and all who
live in the desert in distant places.ᵃ For
all these nations are really uncircumcised, and even the whole house of Israel
is uncircumcised in heart."

God and Idols

10 Hear what the LORD says to you,
O house of Israel. ²This is what the
LORD says:

"Do not learn the ways of the nations
  or be terrified by signs in the sky,
  though the nations are terrified by
    them.
³For the customs of the peoples are
    worthless;
  they cut a tree out of the forest,
  and a craftsman shapes it with his
    chisel.

⁴They adorn it with silver and gold;
  they fasten it with hammer and
    nails
  so it will not totter.
⁵Like a scarecrow in a melon patch,
  their idols cannot speak;
they must be carried
  because they cannot walk.
Do not fear them;
  they can do no harm
  nor can they do any good."

⁶No one is like you, O LORD;
  you are great,
  and your name is mighty in power.
⁷Who should not revere you,
  O King of the nations?
  This is your due.
Among all the wise men of the
    nations
  and in all their kingdoms,
  there is no one like you.
⁸They are all senseless and foolish;
  they are taught by worthless
    wooden idols.
⁹Hammered silver is brought from
    Tarshish
  and gold from Uphaz.
What the craftsman and goldsmith
    have made
  is then dressed in blue and
    purple—
  all made by skilled workers.
¹⁰But the LORD is the true God;
  he is the living God, the eternal
    King.
When he is angry, the earth
    trembles;
  the nations cannot endure his
    wrath.

¹¹"Tell them this: 'These gods, who did
not make the heavens and the earth, will
perish from the earth and from under the
heavens.' "ᵇ

¹²But God made the earth by his power;
  he founded the world by his
    wisdom
  and stretched out the heavens by
    his understanding.
¹³When he thunders, the waters in the
    heavens roar;

ᵃ26 Or *desert and who clip the hair by their*
foreheads ᵇ11 The text of this verse is in Aramaic.

he makes clouds rise from the ends
　　of the earth.
He sends lightning with the rain
　　and brings out the wind from his
　　　storehouses.

¹⁴Everyone is senseless and without
　　knowledge;
　　every goldsmith is shamed by his
　　　idols.
His images are a fraud;
　　they have no breath in them.
¹⁵They are worthless, the objects of
　　mockery;
　　when their judgment comes, they
　　　will perish.
¹⁶He who is the Portion of Jacob is not
　　like these,
　　for he is the Maker of all things,
including Israel, the tribe of his
　　inheritance—
　　the LORD Almighty is his name.

Coming Destruction

¹⁷Gather up your belongings to leave
　　the land,
　　you who live under siege.
¹⁸For this is what the LORD says:
　　"At this time I will hurl out
　　　those who live in this land;
I will bring distress on them
　　so that they may be captured."

¹⁹Woe to me because of my injury!
　　My wound is incurable!
Yet I said to myself,
　　"This is my sickness, and I must
　　　endure it."
²⁰My tent is destroyed;
　　all its ropes are snapped.
My sons are gone from me and are no
　　more;
　　no one is left now to pitch my tent
　　　or to set up my shelter.
²¹The shepherds are senseless

Thursday

All You Need

Read Jeremiah 10:11–16

I love and trust God, but sometimes I don't feel like God is powerful enough
to know what's going on in my life. Those are the times when I let other
things take God's place as the most important part of my life. Even meaningless things like watching TV can take the place of spending time with
God. I guess this is because TV, friends and material things feel like they're
solving my problems *right now*, while God doesn't always act as fast as I
want him to.

But this passage says God is more powerful and more fulfilling than any of
the other things I try to put in his place. People all through history have had
idols. And that doesn't just mean gold statues. Idols can be clothes or sports or
anything we allow to take God's place. But God says those things, no matter
what they are, can never match his power, wisdom or understanding. And
he's right. When's the last time a TV show or a pair of new shoes really, truly,
changed your life the way God has?

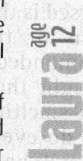
Laura, age 12

What about You?

❶ What are some of the idols you struggle with?

❷ Get one of your favorite possessions, like your bike or your CD player,
and take a really good look at it. What can that thing do? What *can't* it
do? Now think about how silly you'd feel if you prayed to that thing or
trusted it to take care of all your needs.

❸ Tell God you want him to be the most important part of your life.

Turn to page 900 for your next devotion.

and do not inquire of the LORD;
so they do not prosper
and all their flock is scattered.
[22] Listen! The report is coming—
a great commotion from the land of
the north!
It will make the towns of Judah
desolate,
a haunt of jackals.

Jeremiah's Prayer

[23] I know, O LORD, that a man's life is
not his own;
it is not for man to direct his steps.
[24] Correct me, LORD, but only with
justice—
not in your anger,
lest you reduce me to nothing.
[25] Pour out your wrath on the nations
that do not acknowledge you,
on the peoples who do not call on
your name.
For they have devoured Jacob;
they have devoured him completely
and destroyed his homeland.

The Covenant Is Broken

11 This is the word that came to Jeremiah from the LORD: [2]"Listen to the terms of this covenant and tell them to the people of Judah and to those who live in Jerusalem. [3]Tell them that this is what the LORD, the God of Israel, says: 'Cursed is the man who does not obey the terms of this covenant— [4]the terms I commanded your forefathers when I brought them out of Egypt, out of the iron-smelting furnace.' I said, 'Obey me and do everything I command you, and you will be my people, and I will be your God. [5]Then I will fulfill the oath I swore to your forefathers, to give them a land flowing with milk and honey'—the land you possess today."

I answered, "Amen, LORD."

[6]The LORD said to me, "Proclaim all these words in the towns of Judah and in the streets of Jerusalem: 'Listen to the terms of this covenant and follow them. [7]From the time I brought your forefathers up from Egypt until today, I warned them again and again, saying, "Obey me." [8]But they did not listen or pay attention; instead, they followed the stubbornness of their evil hearts. So I brought on them all the curses of the covenant I had commanded them to follow but that they did not keep.' "

[9]Then the LORD said to me, "There is a conspiracy among the people of Judah and those who live in Jerusalem. [10]They have returned to the sins of their forefathers, who refused to listen to my words. They have followed other gods to serve them. Both the house of Israel and the house of Judah have broken the covenant I made with their forefathers. [11]Therefore this is what the LORD says: 'I will bring on them a disaster they cannot escape. Although they cry out to me, I will not listen to them. [12]The towns of Judah and the people of Jerusalem will go and cry out to the gods to whom they burn incense, but they will not help them at all when disaster strikes. [13]You have as many gods as you have towns, O Judah; and the altars you have set up to burn incense to that shameful god Baal are as many as the streets of Jerusalem.'

[14]"Do not pray for this people nor offer any plea or petition for them, because I will not listen when they call to me in the time of their distress.

[15]"What is my beloved doing in my temple
as she works out her evil schemes with many?
Can consecrated meat avert your punishment?
When you engage in your wickedness, then you rejoice.[a]"

[16]The LORD called you a thriving olive tree
with fruit beautiful in form.
But with the roar of a mighty storm
he will set it on fire,
and its branches will be broken.

[17]The LORD Almighty, who planted you, has decreed disaster for you, because the house of Israel and the house of Judah have done evil and provoked me to anger by burning incense to Baal.

Plot Against Jeremiah

[18]Because the LORD revealed their plot to me, I knew it, for at that time he

a15 Or Could consecrated meat avert your punishment? / Then you would rejoice

showed me what they were doing. ¹⁹I had been like a gentle lamb led to the slaughter; I did not realize that they had plotted against me, saying,

"Let us destroy the tree and its fruit;
    let us cut him off from the land of
        the living,
    that his name be remembered no
        more."
²⁰But, O LORD Almighty, you who judge
        righteously
    and test the heart and mind,
    let me see your vengeance upon them,
        for to you I have committed my
            cause.

²¹"Therefore this is what the LORD says about the men of Anathoth who are seeking your life and saying, 'Do not prophesy in the name of the LORD or you will die by our hands'— ²²therefore this is what the LORD Almighty says: 'I will punish them. Their young men will die by the sword, their sons and daughters by famine. ²³Not even a remnant will be left to them, because I will bring disaster on the men of Anathoth in the year of their punishment.' "

Jeremiah's Complaint

12 You are always righteous, O LORD,
        when I bring a case before you.
    Yet I would speak with you about
            your justice:
    Why does the way of the wicked
            prosper?
    Why do all the faithless live at
            ease?
²You have planted them, and they have
        taken root;
    they grow and bear fruit.
    You are always on their lips
        but far from their hearts.
³Yet you know me, O LORD;
    you see me and test my thoughts
        about you.
    Drag them off like sheep to be
            butchered!
    Set them apart for the day of
            slaughter!
⁴How long will the land lie parched[a]
    and the grass in every field be
        withered?
    Because those who live in it are
        wicked,

the animals and birds have
        perished.
    Moreover, the people are saying,
    "He will not see what happens to
        us."

God's Answer

⁵"If you have raced with men on foot
    and they have worn you out,
    how can you compete with horses?
    If you stumble in safe country,[b]
    how will you manage in the thickets
        by[c] the Jordan?
⁶Your brothers, your own family—
    even they have betrayed you;
    they have raised a loud cry against
        you.
    Do not trust them,
        though they speak well of you.

⁷"I will forsake my house,
    abandon my inheritance;
    I will give the one I love
        into the hands of her enemies.
⁸My inheritance has become to me
    like a lion in the forest.
    She roars at me;
        therefore I hate her.
⁹Has not my inheritance become to me
    like a speckled bird of prey
    that other birds of prey surround
        and attack?
    Go and gather all the wild beasts;
        bring them to devour.
¹⁰Many shepherds will ruin my vineyard
    and trample down my field;
    they will turn my pleasant field
        into a desolate wasteland.
¹¹It will be made a wasteland,
    parched and desolate before me;
    the whole land will be laid waste
        because there is no one who cares.
¹²Over all the barren heights in the
            desert
    destroyers will swarm,
    for the sword of the LORD will devour
        from one end of the land to the
            other;
    no one will be safe.
¹³They will sow wheat but reap thorns;
    they will wear themselves out but
        gain nothing.

---

[a]4 Or *land mourn*   [b]5 Or *If you put your trust in a land of safety*   [c]5 Or *the flooding of*

So bear the shame of your harvest
    because of the LORD's fierce anger."

[14]This is what the LORD says: "As for all my wicked neighbors who seize the inheritance I gave my people Israel, I will uproot them from their lands and I will uproot the house of Judah from among them. [15]But after I uproot them, I will again have compassion and will bring each of them back to his own inheritance and his own country. [16]And if they learn well the ways of my people and swear by my name, saying, 'As surely as the LORD lives'—even as they once taught my people to swear by Baal—then they will be established among my people. [17]But if any nation does not listen, I will completely uproot and destroy it," declares the LORD.

A Linen Belt

13 This is what the LORD said to me: "Go and buy a linen belt and put it around your waist, but do not let it touch water." [2]So I bought a belt, as the LORD directed, and put it around my waist.

[3]Then the word of the LORD came to me a second time: [4]"Take the belt you bought and are wearing around your waist, and go now to Perath[a] and hide it there in a crevice in the rocks." [5]So I went and hid it at Perath, as the LORD told me.

[6]Many days later the LORD said to me, "Go now to Perath and get the belt I told you to hide there." [7]So I went to Perath and dug up the belt and took it from the place where I had hidden it, but now it was ruined and completely useless.

[8]Then the word of the LORD came to me: [9]"This is what the LORD says: 'In the same way I will ruin the pride of Judah and the great pride of Jerusalem. [10]These wicked people, who refuse to listen to my words, who follow the stubbornness of their hearts and go after other gods to serve and worship them, will be like this belt—completely useless! [11]For as a belt is bound around a man's waist, so I bound the whole house of Israel and the whole house of Judah to me,' declares the LORD, 'to be my people for my renown and praise and honor. But they have not listened.'

Wineskins

[12]"Say to them: 'This is what the LORD, the God of Israel, says: Every wineskin should be filled with wine.' And if they say to you, 'Don't we know that every wineskin should be filled with wine?' [13]then tell them, 'This is what the LORD says: I am going to fill with drunkenness all who live in this land, including the kings who sit on David's throne, the priests, the prophets and all those living in Jerusalem. [14]I will smash them one against the other, fathers and sons alike, declares the LORD. I will allow no pity or mercy or compassion to keep me from destroying them.'"

Threat of Captivity

[15]Hear and pay attention,
    do not be arrogant,
    for the LORD has spoken.
[16]Give glory to the LORD your God
    before he brings the darkness,
    before your feet stumble
        on the darkening hills.
You hope for light,
    but he will turn it to thick darkness
    and change it to deep gloom.
[17]But if you do not listen,
    I will weep in secret
    because of your pride;
my eyes will weep bitterly,
    overflowing with tears,
    because the LORD's flock will be
        taken captive.

Favorite Fabric

Huh?

Jeremiah 13:1-7

Linen, cotton, polyester, plastic . . . What's the difference? In Jeremiah's time it made a huge difference. The priests' clothes were made of linen because linen was supposed to be a pure and holy fabric. The fact that Jeremiah's linen belt got ruined meant that Israel's holiness had wasted away.

---

[a]4 Or possibly *the Euphrates*; also in verses 5-7

¹⁸Say to the king and to the queen mother,
"Come down from your thrones,
for your glorious crowns
    will fall from your heads."
¹⁹The cities in the Negev will be shut up,
    and there will be no one to open them.
All Judah will be carried into exile,
    carried completely away.

²⁰Lift up your eyes and see
    those who are coming from the north.
Where is the flock that was entrusted to you,
    the sheep of which you boasted?
²¹What will you say when ⌊the LORD⌋
    sets over you
those you cultivated as your special allies?
Will not pain grip you
    like that of a woman in labor?
²²And if you ask yourself,
    "Why has this happened to me?"—
it is because of your many sins
    that your skirts have been torn off
    and your body mistreated.
²³Can the Ethiopian^a change his skin
    or the leopard its spots?
Neither can you do good
    who are accustomed to doing evil.

²⁴"I will scatter you like chaff
    driven by the desert wind.
²⁵This is your lot,

^a23 Hebrew *Cushite* (probably a person from the upper Nile region)

the portion I have decreed for you,"
　　　　declares the LORD,
"because you have forgotten me
　and trusted in false gods.
26 I will pull up your skirts over your
　　face
　that your shame may be seen—
27 your adulteries and lustful neighings,
　your shameless prostitution!
I have seen your detestable acts
　on the hills and in the fields.
Woe to you, O Jerusalem!
　How long will you be unclean?"

Drought, Famine, Sword

14 This is the word of the LORD to Jeremiah concerning the drought:

2 "Judah mourns,
　her cities languish;
they wail for the land,
　and a cry goes up from Jerusalem.
3 The nobles send their servants for
　　water;
　they go to the cisterns
　but find no water.
They return with their jars unfilled;
　dismayed and despairing,
　they cover their heads.
4 The ground is cracked
　because there is no rain in the land;
the farmers are dismayed
　and cover their heads.
5 Even the doe in the field
　deserts her newborn fawn
　because there is no grass.
6 Wild donkeys stand on the barren
　　heights
　and pant like jackals;
their eyesight fails
　for lack of pasture."

7 Although our sins testify against us,
　O LORD, do something for the sake
　　of your name.
For our backsliding is great;
　we have sinned against you.
8 O Hope of Israel,
　its Savior in times of distress,
why are you like a stranger in the
　　land,
　like a traveler who stays only a
　　night?
9 Why are you like a man taken by
　　surprise,
　like a warrior powerless to save?

You are among us, O LORD,
　and we bear your name;
　do not forsake us!

10 This is what the LORD says about this
people:

"They greatly love to wander;
　they do not restrain their feet.
So the LORD does not accept them;
　he will now remember their
　　wickedness
　and punish them for their sins."

11 Then the LORD said to me, "Do not
pray for the well-being of this people.
12 Although they fast, I will not listen to
their cry; though they offer burnt offerings and grain offerings, I will not accept
them. Instead, I will destroy them with
the sword, famine and plague."

13 But I said, "Ah, Sovereign LORD, the
prophets keep telling them, 'You will not
see the sword or suffer famine. Indeed, I
will give you lasting peace in this
place.' "

14 Then the LORD said to me, "The
prophets are prophesying lies in my
name. I have not sent them or appointed
them or spoken to them. They are prophesying to you false visions, divinations,
idolatries[a] and the delusions of their own
minds. 15 Therefore, this is what the LORD
says about the prophets who are prophesying in my name: I did not send them,
yet they are saying, 'No sword or famine
will touch this land.' Those same prophets will perish by sword and famine.
16 And the people they are prophesying to
will be thrown out into the streets of Jerusalem because of the famine and
sword. There will be no one to bury them
or their wives, their sons or their daughters. I will pour out on them the calamity
they deserve.

17 "Speak this word to them:

" 'Let my eyes overflow with tears
　night and day without ceasing;
for my virgin daughter—my people—
　has suffered a grievous wound,
　a crushing blow.
18 If I go into the country,
　I see those slain by the sword;

---

a 14 Or *visions, worthless divinations*

if I go into the city,
  I see the ravages of famine.
Both prophet and priest
  have gone to a land they know
    not.' "

¹⁹ Have you rejected Judah
    completely?
  Do you despise Zion?
Why have you afflicted us
  so that we cannot be healed?
We hoped for peace
  but no good has come,
for a time of healing
  but there is only terror.
²⁰ O LORD, we acknowledge our
    wickedness
  and the guilt of our fathers;
  we have indeed sinned against
    you.
²¹ For the sake of your name do not
    despise us;
  do not dishonor your glorious
    throne.
Remember your covenant with us
  and do not break it.
²² Do any of the worthless idols of the
    nations bring rain?
  Do the skies themselves send down
    showers?
No, it is you, O LORD our God.
  Therefore our hope is in you,
  for you are the one who does all
    this.

15 Then the LORD said to me: "Even if
Moses and Samuel were to stand
before me, my heart would not go out to
this people. Send them away from my
presence! Let them go! ²And if they ask
you, 'Where shall we go?' tell them, 'This
is what the LORD says:

" 'Those destined for death, to death;
  those for the sword, to the sword;
  those for starvation, to starvation;
  those for captivity, to captivity.'

³ "I will send four kinds of destroyers
against them," declares the LORD, "the
sword to kill and the dogs to drag away
and the birds of the air and the beasts of
the earth to devour and destroy. ⁴I will
make them abhorrent to all the kingdoms
of the earth because of what Manasseh
son of Hezekiah king of Judah did in
Jerusalem.

⁵ "Who will have pity on you,
    O Jerusalem?
  Who will mourn for you?
  Who will stop to ask how you are?
⁶ You have rejected me," declares the
    LORD.
  "You keep on backsliding.
So I will lay hands on you and
    destroy you;
  I can no longer show compassion.
⁷ I will winnow them with a winnowing
    fork
  at the city gates of the land.
I will bring bereavement and
    destruction on my people,
  for they have not changed their
    ways.
⁸ I will make their widows more
    numerous
  than the sand of the sea.
At midday I will bring a destroyer
  against the mothers of their young
    men;
suddenly I will bring down on them
  anguish and terror.
⁹ The mother of seven will grow faint
  and breathe her last.
Her sun will set while it is still day;
  she will be disgraced and
    humiliated.
I will put the survivors to the sword
  before their enemies,"
                    declares the LORD.

¹⁰ Alas, my mother, that you gave me
    birth,
  a man with whom the whole land
    strives and contends!
I have neither lent nor borrowed,
  yet everyone curses me.

¹¹ The LORD said,

"Surely I will deliver you for a good
    purpose;
  surely I will make your enemies
    plead with you
  in times of disaster and times of
    distress.

¹² "Can a man break iron—
    iron from the north—or bronze?
¹³ Your wealth and your treasures
  I will give as plunder, without
    charge,
because of all your sins
  throughout your country.

[14]"I will enslave you to your enemies
    in[a] a land you do not know,
for my anger will kindle a fire
    that will burn against you."

[15]You understand, O LORD;
    remember me and care for me.
    Avenge me on my persecutors.
You are long-suffering—do not take
    me away;
    think of how I suffer reproach for
        your sake.
[16]When your words came, I ate them;
    they were my joy and my heart's
        delight,
for I bear your name,
    O LORD God Almighty.
[17]I never sat in the company of revelers,
    never made merry with them;
I sat alone because your hand was on
        me
    and you had filled me with
        indignation.
[18]Why is my pain unending
    and my wound grievous and
        incurable?
Will you be to me like a deceptive
        brook,
    like a spring that fails?

[19]Therefore this is what the LORD says:

"If you repent, I will restore you
    that you may serve me;
if you utter worthy, not worthless,
        words,
    you will be my spokesman.
Let this people turn to you,
    but you must not turn to them.
[20]I will make you a wall to this people,
    a fortified wall of bronze;
they will fight against you
    but will not overcome you,
for I am with you
    to rescue and save you,"
                  declares the LORD.
[21]"I will save you from the hands of the
        wicked
    and redeem you from the grasp of
        the cruel."

Day of Disaster

16 Then the word of the LORD came to me: [2]"You must not marry and have sons or daughters in this place." [3]For this is what the LORD says about the sons and daughters born in this land and about the women who are their mothers and the men who are their fathers: [4]"They will die of deadly diseases. They will not be mourned or buried but will be like refuse lying on the ground. They will perish by sword and famine, and their dead bodies will become food for the birds of the air and the beasts of the earth."

[5]For this is what the LORD says: "Do not enter a house where there is a funeral meal; do not go to mourn or show sympathy, because I have withdrawn my blessing, my love and my pity from this people," declares the LORD. [6]"Both high and low will die in this land. They will not be buried or mourned, and no one will cut himself or shave his head for them. [7]No one will offer food to comfort those who mourn for the dead—not even for a father or a mother—nor will anyone give them a drink to console them.

[8]"And do not enter a house where there is feasting and sit down to eat and drink. [9]For this is what the LORD Almighty, the God of Israel, says: Before your eyes and in your days I will bring an end to the sounds of joy and gladness and to the voices of bride and bridegroom in this place.

[10]"When you tell these people all this and they ask you, 'Why has the LORD decreed such a great disaster against us? What wrong have we done? What sin have we committed against the LORD our God?' [11]then say to them, 'It is because your fathers forsook me,' declares the LORD, 'and followed other gods and served and worshiped them. They forsook me and did not keep my law. [12]But you have behaved more wickedly than your fathers. See how each of you is following the stubbornness of his evil heart instead of obeying me. [13]So I will throw you out of this land into a land neither you nor your fathers have known, and there you will serve other gods day and night, for I will show you no favor.'

[14]"However, the days are coming," declares the LORD, "when men will no long-

---

[a]14 Some Hebrew manuscripts, Septuagint and Syriac (see also Jer. 17:4); most Hebrew manuscripts *I will cause your enemies to bring you / into*

er say, 'As surely as the LORD lives, who brought the Israelites up out of Egypt,' [15]but they will say, 'As surely as the LORD lives, who brought the Israelites up out of the land of the north and out of all the countries where he had banished them.' For I will restore them to the land I gave their forefathers.

[16]"But now I will send for many fishermen," declares the LORD, "and they will catch them. After that I will send for many hunters, and they will hunt them down on every mountain and hill and from the crevices of the rocks. [17]My eyes are on all their ways; they are not hidden from me, nor is their sin concealed from my eyes. [18]I will repay them double for their wickedness and their sin, because they have defiled my land with the lifeless forms of their vile images and have filled my inheritance with their detestable idols."

[19]O LORD, my strength and my fortress,
　my refuge in time of distress,
to you the nations will come
　from the ends of the earth and say,
"Our fathers possessed nothing but
　　false gods,
　worthless idols that did them no
　　good.
[20]Do men make their own gods?
　Yes, but they are not gods!"

[21]"Therefore I will teach them—
　this time I will teach them
　my power and might.
Then they will know
　that my name is the LORD.

17 "Judah's sin is engraved with an
　　iron tool,
　inscribed with a flint point,
on the tablets of their hearts
　and on the horns of their altars.
[2]Even their children remember
　their altars and Asherah poles[a]
beside the spreading trees
　and on the high hills.
[3]My mountain in the land
　and your[b] wealth and all your
　　treasures
I will give away as plunder,
　together with your high places,
　because of sin throughout your
　　country.

[4]Through your own fault you will lose
　the inheritance I gave you.
I will enslave you to your enemies
　in a land you do not know,
for you have kindled my anger,
　and it will burn forever."

[5]This is what the LORD says:

"Cursed is the one who trusts in man,
　who depends on flesh for his
　　strength
　and whose heart turns away from
　　the LORD.
[6]He will be like a bush in the
　　wastelands;
　he will not see prosperity when it
　　comes.
He will dwell in the parched places of
　　the desert,
　in a salt land where no one lives.

[7]"But blessed is the man who trusts in
　　the LORD,
　whose confidence is in him.
[8]He will be like a tree planted by the
　　water
　that sends out its roots by the
　　stream.
It does not fear when heat comes;
　its leaves are always green.
It has no worries in a year of drought
　and never fails to bear fruit."

[9]The heart is deceitful above all things
　and beyond cure.
　Who can understand it?

[10]"I the LORD search the heart
　and examine the mind,
to reward a man according to his
　　conduct,
　according to what his deeds
　　deserve."

[11]Like a partridge that hatches eggs it
　　did not lay
　is the man who gains riches by
　　unjust means.
When his life is half gone, they will
　　desert him,
　and in the end he will prove to be a
　　fool.

[12]A glorious throne, exalted from the
　　beginning,

---

[a]2 That is, symbols of the goddess Asherah　[b]2,3 Or
hills / [3]and the mountains of the land. / Your

is the place of our sanctuary.
¹³ O LORD, the hope of Israel,
all who forsake you will be put to
shame.
Those who turn away from you will
be written in the dust
because they have forsaken the
LORD,
the spring of living water.

¹⁴ Heal me, O LORD, and I will be
healed;
save me and I will be saved,
for you are the one I praise.
¹⁵ They keep saying to me,
"Where is the word of the LORD?
Let it now be fulfilled!"
¹⁶ I have not run away from being your
shepherd;
you know I have not desired the
day of despair.
What passes my lips is open before
you.
¹⁷ Do not be a terror to me;

you are my refuge in the day of
disaster.
¹⁸ Let my persecutors be put to shame,
but keep me from shame;
let them be terrified,
but keep me from terror.
Bring on them the day of disaster;
destroy them with double
destruction.

Keeping the Sabbath Holy

¹⁹ This is what the LORD said to me: "Go
and stand at the gate of the people,
through which the kings of Judah go in
and out; stand also at all the other gates
of Jerusalem. ²⁰ Say to them, 'Hear the
word of the LORD, O kings of Judah and
all people of Judah and everyone living
in Jerusalem who come through these
gates. ²¹ This is what the LORD says: Be
careful not to carry a load on the Sabbath day or bring it through the gates of
Jerusalem. ²² Do not bring a load out of

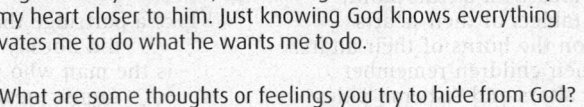

Everything About Me

Read Jeremiah 17:9–10

In one of my classes, I had to do a project with a partner. I was supposed to do half and my partner would do half. A few weeks after the project was assigned, my partner asked how my half was coming along. I said I was finished. But the truth was, I had hardly started. I never did do the work I'd promised to do on it, and we didn't get a very good grade.

I could lie to my partner for a while, but obviously the truth came out eventually. And that's kind of how it is with God. I can try to hide things from God, but he always knows the truth about me. He sees my heart, and he knows every thought and feeling I have.

I feel bad when I think about the sinful stuff God sees in my heart, but instead of pushing me away from God, that feeling makes me want to keep my mind and my heart closer to him. Just knowing God knows everything about me motivates me to do what he wants me to do.

Charissa age 13

❶ What are some thoughts or feelings you try to hide from God?

❷ Draw 2 large hearts on a piece of paper. Inside one heart, write down some of the things you try to hide from God. In the other, write down some of the things you want God to see in your heart. How can you empty out the heart full of "hidden" things?

❸ Ask God to help you have a pure heart.

Turn to page 903 for your next devotion.

your houses or do any work on the Sabbath, but keep the Sabbath day holy, as I commanded your forefathers. ²³Yet they did not listen or pay attention; they were stiff-necked and would not listen or respond to discipline. ²⁴But if you are careful to obey me, declares the LORD, and bring no load through the gates of this city on the Sabbath, but keep the Sabbath day holy by not doing any work on it, ²⁵then kings who sit on David's throne will come through the gates of this city with their officials. They and their officials will come riding in chariots and on horses, accompanied by the men of Judah and those living in Jerusalem, and this city will be inhabited forever. ²⁶People will come from the towns of Judah and the villages around Jerusalem, from the territory of Benjamin and the western foothills, from the hill country and the Negev, bringing burnt offerings and sacrifices, grain offerings, incense and thank offerings to the house of the LORD. ²⁷But if you do not obey me to keep the Sabbath day holy by not carrying any load as you come through the gates of Jerusalem on the Sabbath day, then I will kindle an unquenchable fire in the gates of Jerusalem that will consume her fortresses.' "

At the Potter's House

18 This is the word that came to Jeremiah from the LORD: ²"Go down to the potter's house, and there I will give you my message." ³So I went down to the potter's house, and I saw him working at the wheel. ⁴But the pot he was shaping from the clay was marred in his hands; so the potter formed it into another pot, shaping it as seemed best to him.

⁵Then the word of the LORD came to me: ⁶"O house of Israel, can I not do with you as this potter does?" declares the LORD. "Like clay in the hand of the potter, so are you in my hand, O house of Israel. ⁷If at any time I announce that a nation or kingdom is to be uprooted, torn down and destroyed, ⁸and if that nation I warned repents of its evil, then I will relent and not inflict on it the disaster I had planned. ⁹And if at another time I announce that a nation or kingdom is to be built up and planted, ¹⁰and if it does

evil in my sight and does not obey me, then I will reconsider the good I had intended to do for it.

Your Input, Please

Huh?

Jeremiah 18:7–10

God's going to do what he's going to do no matter what, right? Well, not quite. Lots of times God sets up "iffy" situations that allow us to have input into what's going to happen. If we tell God we're sorry, then he will forgive us and may save us from danger or from the punishment we deserve. Or else, like in this passage, if a nation does bad stuff, then God may let it be destroyed.

¹¹"Now therefore say to the people of Judah and those living in Jerusalem, 'This is what the LORD says: Look! I am preparing a disaster for you and devising a plan against you. So turn from your evil ways, each one of you, and reform your ways and your actions.' ¹²But they will reply, 'It's no use. We will continue with our own plans; each of us will follow the stubbornness of his evil heart.' "

¹³Therefore this is what the LORD says:

"Inquire among the nations:
　Who has ever heard anything like
　　this?
A most horrible thing has been done
　by Virgin Israel.
¹⁴Does the snow of Lebanon
　ever vanish from its rocky slopes?
Do its cool waters from distant
　　sources
　ever cease to flow?ᵃ
¹⁵Yet my people have forgotten me;
　they burn incense to worthless
　　idols,
which made them stumble in their
　　ways
　and in the ancient paths.
They made them walk in bypaths
　and on roads not built up.

ᵃ14 The meaning of the Hebrew for this sentence is uncertain.

¹⁶Their land will be laid waste,
    an object of lasting scorn;
all who pass by will be appalled
    and will shake their heads.
¹⁷Like a wind from the east,
    I will scatter them before their
        enemies;
I will show them my back and not my
        face
in the day of their disaster."

¹⁸They said, "Come, let's make plans against Jeremiah; for the teaching of the law by the priest will not be lost, nor will counsel from the wise, nor the word from the prophets. So come, let's attack him with our tongues and pay no attention to anything he says."

¹⁹Listen to me, O LORD;
    hear what my accusers are saying!
²⁰Should good be repaid with evil?
    Yet they have dug a pit for me.
Remember that I stood before you
    and spoke in their behalf
    to turn your wrath away from them.
²¹So give their children over to famine;
    hand them over to the power of the
        sword.
Let their wives be made childless and
        widows;
    let their men be put to death,
    their young men slain by the sword
        in battle.
²²Let a cry be heard from their houses
    when you suddenly bring invaders
        against them,
for they have dug a pit to capture me
    and have hidden snares for my feet.
²³But you know, O LORD,
    all their plots to kill me.
Do not forgive their crimes
    or blot out their sins from your
        sight.
Let them be overthrown before you;
    deal with them in the time of your
        anger.

19 This is what the LORD says: "Go and buy a clay jar from a potter. Take along some of the elders of the people and of the priests ²and go out to the Valley of Ben Hinnom, near the entrance of the Potsherd Gate. There proclaim the words I tell you, ³and say, 'Hear the word of the LORD, O kings of Judah and people of Jerusalem. This is what the LORD Almighty, the God of Israel, says: Listen! I am going to bring a disaster on this place that will make the ears of everyone who hears of it tingle. ⁴For they have forsaken me and made this a place of foreign gods; they have burned sacrifices in it to gods that neither they nor their fathers nor the kings of Judah ever knew, and they have filled this place with the blood of the innocent. ⁵They have built the high places of Baal to burn their sons in the fire as offerings to Baal—something I did not command or mention, nor did it enter my mind. ⁶So beware, the days are coming, declares the LORD, when people will no longer call this place Topheth or the Valley of Ben Hinnom, but the Valley of Slaughter.

⁷" 'In this place I will ruin^a the plans of Judah and Jerusalem. I will make them fall by the sword before their enemies, at the hands of those who seek their lives, and I will give their carcasses as food to the birds of the air and the beasts of the earth. ⁸I will devastate this city and make it an object of scorn; all who pass by will be appalled and will scoff because of all its wounds. ⁹I will make them eat the flesh of their sons and daughters, and they will eat one another's flesh during the stress of the siege imposed on them by the enemies who seek their lives.'

¹⁰"Then break the jar while those who go with you are watching, ¹¹and say to them, 'This is what the LORD Almighty says: I will smash this nation and this city just as this potter's jar is smashed and cannot be repaired. They will bury the dead in Topheth until there is no more room. ¹²This is what I will do to this place and to those who live here, declares the LORD. I will make this city like Topheth. ¹³The houses in Jerusalem and those of the kings of Judah will be defiled like this place, Topheth—all the houses where they burned incense on the roofs to all the starry hosts and poured out drink offerings to other gods.' "

¹⁴Jeremiah then returned from Topheth, where the LORD had sent him to prophesy, and stood in the court of the

---

^a7 The Hebrew for *ruin* sounds like the Hebrew for *jar* (see verses 1 and 10).

LORD's temple and said to all the people, ¹⁵"This is what the LORD Almighty, the God of Israel, says: 'Listen! I am going to bring on this city and the villages around it every disaster I pronounced against them, because they were stiff-necked and would not listen to my words.' "

Jeremiah and Pashhur

20 When the priest Pashhur son of Immer, the chief officer in the temple of the LORD, heard Jeremiah prophesying these things, ²he had Jeremiah the prophet beaten and put in the stocks at the Upper Gate of Benjamin at the LORD's temple. ³The next day, when Pashhur released him from the stocks, Jeremiah said to him, "The LORD's name for you is not Pashhur, but Magor-Missabib.ᵃ ⁴For this is what the LORD says: 'I will make you a terror to yourself and to all your friends; with your own eyes you will see them fall by the sword

of their enemies. I will hand all Judah over to the king of Babylon, who will carry them away to Babylon or put them to the sword. ⁵I will hand over to their enemies all the wealth of this city—all its products, all its valuables and all the treasures of the kings of Judah. They will take it away as plunder and carry it off to Babylon. ⁶And you, Pashhur, and all who live in your house will go into exile to Babylon. There you will die and be buried, you and all your friends to whom you have prophesied lies.' "

Jeremiah's Complaint

⁷O LORD, you deceivedᵇ me, and I was
        deceivedᵇ;
    you overpowered me and prevailed.
I am ridiculed all day long;
    everyone mocks me.

ᵃ3 *Magor-Missabib* means *terror on every side.*
ᵇ7 Or *persuaded*

Week end.

Careful What You Pray For

Read Mark 4:36–41 (page 1194)

Katy talked about being excited that God answered her prayer and gave her more time with her grandfather. She was glad to be convinced that God listens to our prayers. She feels closer to God now. That's good to know because closeness is what prayer is all about. We don't pray to get stuff; we pray to get closer to God.

Prayer is about recognizing God's presence in your life. And when you see it, you'll be glad (of course), but also a little nervous. Notice, in the passage you read today, that the disciples were *terrified!* Why? Because God answered their prayers—and it made them realize just how powerful God is!

So, be careful what you ask for—you just might get it!

What about You?

❶ Have you ever been afraid of God? When? Why?

❷ Make a list of what you are afraid of. Someone has said that our fears are kind of weird because they tell us what matters to us (like, if we're afraid of being ugly, we really want to be liked).

❸ Ask God to help you want *him*, more than stuff *from* him.

Turn to page 904 for your next devotion.

8 Whenever I speak, I cry out
  proclaiming violence and
    destruction.
So the word of the LORD has brought
  me
  insult and reproach all day long.
9 But if I say, "I will not mention him
  or speak any more in his name,"
his word is in my heart like a fire,
  a fire shut up in my bones.
I am weary of holding it in;
  indeed, I cannot.
10 I hear many whispering,
  "Terror on every side!
  Report him! Let's report him!"
All my friends
  are waiting for me to slip, saying,
"Perhaps he will be deceived;
  then we will prevail over him
  and take our revenge on him."

11 But the LORD is with me like a mighty
  warrior;
  so my persecutors will stumble and
    not prevail.
They will fail and be thoroughly
  disgraced;

their dishonor will never be
  forgotten.
12 O LORD Almighty, you who examine
  the righteous
  and probe the heart and mind,
let me see your vengeance upon them,
  for to you I have committed my
    cause.

13 Sing to the LORD!
  Give praise to the LORD!
He rescues the life of the needy
  from the hands of the wicked.

14 Cursed be the day I was born!
  May the day my mother bore me
    not be blessed!
15 Cursed be the man who brought my
  father the news,
  who made him very glad, saying,
"A child is born to you—a son!"
16 May that man be like the towns
  the LORD overthrew without pity.
May he hear wailing in the morning,
  a battle cry at noon.
17 For he did not kill me in the womb,
  with my mother as my grave,

Monday

What Would *You* Do?

Read Jeremiah 20:8–11

Like a lot of people, I sometimes wear stuff to school that shows I'm a Christian. It helps me think about the things I do and say. But deep inside, I'm scared someone will ask me what it means or make fun of me for wearing it. I have to admit, sometimes I'm embarrassed about my faith.

    When I read something like these verses in Jeremiah, it helps me remember that I'm not the first person to worry about what other people will think if I talk about my faith. These verses also help me remember that God gave me a job to do—to tell people about him. I could be the only Christian another person meets. I could be their only chance to find out about Jesus. If I keep quiet because I'm afraid that person will make fun of me, I'm not doing what God wants me to do.

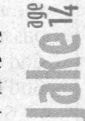

Jake age 14

❶ When have you been afraid to share your faith? What could have helped you feel more confident?

❷ Think of 3 things you could say to someone who asks why you're a Christian.

❸ Ask God to help you stand strong in your faith, even if others make fun of you.

Turn to page 914 for your next devotion.

her womb enlarged forever.
¹⁸Why did I ever come out of the
   womb
   to see trouble and sorrow
   and to end my days in shame?

God Rejects Zedekiah's Request

21 The word came to Jeremiah from the LORD when King Zedekiah sent to him Pashhur son of Malkijah and the priest Zephaniah son of Maaseiah. They said: ²"Inquire now of the LORD for us because Nebuchadnezzar^a king of Babylon is attacking us. Perhaps the LORD will perform wonders for us as in times past so that he will withdraw from us."

³But Jeremiah answered them, "Tell Zedekiah, ⁴"This is what the LORD, the God of Israel, says: I am about to turn against you the weapons of war that are in your hands, which you are using to fight the king of Babylon and the Babylonians^b who are outside the wall besieging you. And I will gather them inside this city. ⁵I myself will fight against you with an outstretched hand and a mighty arm in anger and fury and great wrath. ⁶I will strike down those who live in this city—both men and animals—and they will die of a terrible plague. ⁷After that, declares the LORD, I will hand over Zedekiah king of Judah, his officials and the people in this city who survive the plague, sword and famine, to Nebuchadnezzar king of Babylon and to their enemies who seek their lives. He will put them to the sword; he will show them no mercy or pity or compassion.'

⁸"Furthermore, tell the people, 'This is what the LORD says: See, I am setting before you the way of life and the way of death. ⁹Whoever stays in this city will die by the sword, famine or plague. But whoever goes out and surrenders to the Babylonians who are besieging you will live; he will escape with his life. ¹⁰I have determined to do this city harm and not good, declares the LORD. It will be given into the hands of the king of Babylon, and he will destroy it with fire.'

¹¹"Moreover, say to the royal house of Judah, 'Hear the word of the LORD; ¹²O house of David, this is what the LORD says:

" 'Administer justice every morning;
   rescue from the hand of his
      oppressor
   the one who has been robbed,
or my wrath will break out and burn
   like fire
because of the evil you have done—
   burn with no one to quench it.
¹³I am against you, Jerusalem,
   you who live above this valley
   on the rocky plateau,
                    declares the LORD—
you who say, "Who can come against
      us?
   Who can enter our refuge?"
¹⁴I will punish you as your deeds
      deserve,
                    declares the LORD.
I will kindle a fire in your forests
   that will consume everything
      around you.' "

Judgment Against Evil Kings

22 This is what the LORD says: "Go down to the palace of the king of Judah and proclaim this message there: ²'Hear the word of the LORD, O king of Judah, you who sit on David's throne—you, your officials and your people who come through these gates. ³This is what the LORD says: Do what is just and right. Rescue from the hand of his oppressor the one who has been robbed. Do no wrong or violence to the alien, the fatherless or the widow, and do not shed innocent blood in this place. ⁴For if you are careful to carry out these commands, then kings who sit on David's throne will come through the gates of this palace, riding in chariots and on horses, accompanied by their officials and their people. ⁵But if you do not obey these commands, declares the LORD, I swear by myself that this palace will become a ruin.' "

⁶For this is what the LORD says about the palace of the king of Judah:

"Though you are like Gilead to me,
   like the summit of Lebanon,
I will surely make you like a desert,
   like towns not inhabited.

^a2 Hebrew *Nebuchadrezzar*, of which *Nebuchadnezzar* is a variant; here and often in Jeremiah and Ezekiel   ^b4 Or *Chaldeans*; also in verse 9

⁷I will send destroyers against you,
  each man with his weapons,
and they will cut up your fine cedar
    beams
  and throw them into the fire.

⁸"People from many nations will pass
by this city and will ask one another,
'Why has the LORD done such a thing to
this great city?' ⁹And the answer will be:
'Because they have forsaken the covenant of the LORD their God and have
worshiped and served other gods.' "

¹⁰Do not weep for the dead ⌐king⌐ or
    mourn his loss;
  rather, weep bitterly for him who is
    exiled,
because he will never return
  nor see his native land again.

¹¹For this is what the LORD says about
Shallumᵃ son of Josiah, who succeeded
his father as king of Judah but has gone
from this place: "He will never return.
¹²He will die in the place where they have
led him captive; he will not see this land
again."

¹³"Woe to him who builds his palace by
    unrighteousness,
  his upper rooms by injustice,
making his countrymen work for
    nothing,
  not paying them for their labor.
¹⁴He says, 'I will build myself a great
    palace
  with spacious upper rooms.'
So he makes large windows in it,
  panels it with cedar
  and decorates it in red.

¹⁵"Does it make you a king
  to have more and more cedar?
Did not your father have food and
    drink?
He did what was right and just,
  so all went well with him.
¹⁶He defended the cause of the poor and
    needy,
  and so all went well.
Is that not what it means to know me?"
  declares the LORD.
¹⁷"But your eyes and your heart
  are set only on dishonest gain,
on shedding innocent blood
  and on oppression and extortion."

¹⁸Therefore this is what the LORD says
about Jehoiakim son of Josiah king of
Judah:

"They will not mourn for him:
  'Alas, my brother! Alas, my sister!'
They will not mourn for him:
  'Alas, my master! Alas, his
    splendor!'
¹⁹He will have the burial of a donkey—
  dragged away and thrown
  outside the gates of Jerusalem."

²⁰"Go up to Lebanon and cry out,
  let your voice be heard in Bashan,
cry out from Abarim,
  for all your allies are crushed.
²¹I warned you when you felt secure,
  but you said, 'I will not listen!'
This has been your way from your
    youth;
  you have not obeyed me.
²²The wind will drive all your shepherds
    away,
  and your allies will go into exile.
Then you will be ashamed and
    disgraced
  because of all your wickedness.
²³You who live in 'Lebanon,'ᵇ
  who are nestled in cedar buildings,
how you will groan when pangs come
    upon you,
  pain like that of a woman in labor!

²⁴"As surely as I live," declares the
LORD, "even if you, Jehoiachinᶜ son of
Jehoiakim king of Judah, were a signet
ring on my right hand, I would still pull
you off. ²⁵I will hand you over to those
who seek your life, those you fear—to
Nebuchadnezzar king of Babylon and to
the Babylonians.ᵈ ²⁶I will hurl you and
the mother who gave you birth into another country, where neither of you was
born, and there you both will die. ²⁷You
will never come back to the land you
long to return to."

²⁸Is this man Jehoiachin a despised,
    broken pot,
  an object no one wants?
Why will he and his children be
    hurled out,

ᵃ11 Also called Jehoahaz   ᵇ23 That is, the palace in
Jerusalem (see 1 Kings 7:2)   ᶜ24 Hebrew Coniah, a
variant of Jehoiachin; also in verse 28   ᵈ25 Or
Chaldeans

cast into a land they do not know?
²⁹O land, land, land,
  hear the word of the LORD!
³⁰This is what the LORD says:
  "Record this man as if childless,
    a man who will not prosper in his
      lifetime,
  for none of his offspring will
    prosper,
    none will sit on the throne of
      David
    or rule anymore in Judah."

The Righteous Branch

23 "Woe to the shepherds who are destroying and scattering the sheep of my pasture!" declares the LORD. ²Therefore this is what the LORD, the God of Israel, says to the shepherds who tend my people: "Because you have scattered my flock and driven them away and have not bestowed care on them, I will bestow punishment on you for the evil you have done," declares the LORD. ³"I myself will gather the remnant of my flock out of all the countries where I have driven them and will bring them back to their pasture, where they will be fruitful and increase in number. ⁴I will place shepherds over them who will tend them, and they will no longer be afraid or terrified, nor will any be missing," declares the LORD.

⁵"The days are coming," declares the
    LORD,
  "when I will raise up to David*ᵃ* a
    righteous Branch,
  a King who will reign wisely
    and do what is just and right in the
      land.
⁶In his days Judah will be saved
    and Israel will live in safety.
  This is the name by which he will be
    called:
    The LORD Our Righteousness.

⁷"So then, the days are coming," declares the LORD, "when people will no longer say, 'As surely as the LORD lives, who brought the Israelites up out of Egypt,' ⁸but they will say, 'As surely as the LORD lives, who brought the descendants of Israel up out of the land of the north and out of all the countries where he had banished them.' Then they will live in their own land."

Lying Prophets

⁹Concerning the prophets:

My heart is broken within me;
  all my bones tremble.
I am like a drunken man,
  like a man overcome by wine,
because of the LORD
  and his holy words.
¹⁰The land is full of adulterers;
  because of the curse*ᵇ* the land lies
    parched*ᶜ*
  and the pastures in the desert are
    withered.
The prophets follow an evil course
  and use their power unjustly.

¹¹"Both prophet and priest are godless;
  even in my temple I find their
    wickedness,"
              declares the LORD.
¹²"Therefore their path will become
    slippery;
  they will be banished to darkness
    and there they will fall.
I will bring disaster on them
  in the year they are punished,"
              declares the LORD.

¹³"Among the prophets of Samaria
  I saw this repulsive thing:
They prophesied by Baal
  and led my people Israel astray.
¹⁴And among the prophets of
    Jerusalem
  I have seen something horrible:
  They commit adultery and live a lie.
They strengthen the hands of
    evildoers,
  so that no one turns from his
    wickedness.
They are all like Sodom to me;
  the people of Jerusalem are like
    Gomorrah."

¹⁵Therefore, this is what the LORD Almighty says concerning the prophets:

"I will make them eat bitter food
  and drink poisoned water,
because from the prophets of
    Jerusalem
  ungodliness has spread throughout
    the land."

ᵃ5 Or up from David's line *ᵇ10 Or because of these things* *ᶜ10 Or land mourns*

¹⁶This is what the LORD Almighty says:

"Do not listen to what the prophets
    are prophesying to you;
they fill you with false hopes.
They speak visions from their own
    minds,
    not from the mouth of the LORD.
¹⁷They keep saying to those who despise
    me,
    'The LORD says: You will have
      peace.'
And to all who follow the
    stubbornness of their hearts
they say, 'No harm will come to
    you.'
¹⁸But which of them has stood in the
    council of the LORD
to see or to hear his word?
Who has listened and heard his
    word?
¹⁹See, the storm of the LORD
    will burst out in wrath,
a whirlwind swirling down
    on the heads of the wicked.
²⁰The anger of the LORD will not turn
    back
    until he fully accomplishes
    the purposes of his heart.
In days to come
    you will understand it clearly.
²¹I did not send these prophets,
    yet they have run with their
      message;
I did not speak to them,
    yet they have prophesied.
²²But if they had stood in my council,
    they would have proclaimed my
      words to my people
and would have turned them from
    their evil ways
    and from their evil deeds.

²³"Am I only a God nearby,"
              declares the LORD,
  "and not a God far away?
²⁴Can anyone hide in secret places
    so that I cannot see him?"
              declares the LORD.
  "Do not I fill heaven and earth?"
              declares the LORD.

²⁵"I have heard what the prophets say
who prophesy lies in my name. They say,
'I had a dream! I had a dream!' ²⁶How
long will this continue in the hearts of
these lying prophets, who prophesy the
delusions of their own minds? ²⁷They
think the dreams they tell one another
will make my people forget my name,
just as their fathers forgot my name
through Baal worship. ²⁸Let the prophet
who has a dream tell his dream, but let
the one who has my word speak it faithfully. For what has straw to do with
grain?" declares the LORD. ²⁹"Is not my
word like fire," declares the LORD, "and
like a hammer that breaks a rock in
pieces?

³⁰"Therefore," declares the LORD, "I am
against the prophets who steal from one
another words supposedly from me.
³¹Yes," declares the LORD, "I am against
the prophets who wag their own tongues
and yet declare, 'The LORD declares.' ³²In-
deed, I am against those who prophesy
false dreams," declares the LORD. "They
tell them and lead my people astray with
their reckless lies, yet I did not send or
appoint them. They do not benefit these
people in the least," declares the LORD.

False Oracles and False Prophets

³³"When these people, or a prophet or
a priest, ask you, 'What is the oracle[a] of
the LORD?' say to them, 'What oracle?[b] I
will forsake you, declares the LORD.' ³⁴If a
prophet or a priest or anyone else claims,
'This is the oracle of the LORD,' I will punish that man and his household. ³⁵This is
what each of you keeps on saying to his
friend or relative: 'What is the LORD's answer?' or 'What has the LORD spoken?'
³⁶But you must not mention 'the oracle of
the LORD' again, because every man's
own word becomes his oracle and so you
distort the words of the living God, the
LORD Almighty, our God. ³⁷This is what
you keep saying to a prophet: 'What is
the LORD's answer to you?' or 'What has
the LORD spoken?' ³⁸Although you claim,
'This is the oracle of the LORD,' this is
what the LORD says: You used the words,
'This is the oracle of the LORD,' even
though I told you that you must not
claim, 'This is the oracle of the LORD.'

---

[a]33 Or burden (see Septuagint and Vulgate)
[b]33 Hebrew; Septuagint and Vulgate 'You are the
burden. (The Hebrew for oracle and burden is the
same.)

³⁹Therefore, I will surely forget you and cast you out of my presence along with the city I gave to you and your fathers. ⁴⁰I will bring upon you everlasting disgrace—everlasting shame that will not be forgotten."

Two Baskets of Figs

24 After Jehoiachin*ᵃ* son of Jehoiakim king of Judah and the officials, the craftsmen and the artisans of Judah were carried into exile from Jerusalem to Babylon by Nebuchadnezzar king of Babylon, the LORD showed me two baskets of figs placed in front of the temple of the LORD. ²One basket had very good figs, like those that ripen early; the other basket had very poor figs, so bad they could not be eaten.

³Then the LORD asked me, "What do you see, Jeremiah?"

"Figs," I answered. "The good ones are very good, but the poor ones are so bad they cannot be eaten."

⁴Then the word of the LORD came to me: ⁵"This is what the LORD, the God of Israel, says: 'Like these good figs, I regard as good the exiles from Judah, whom I sent away from this place to the land of the Babylonians.*ᵇ* ⁶My eyes will watch over them for their good, and I will bring them back to this land. I will build them up and not tear them down; I will plant them and not uproot them. ⁷I will give them a heart to know me, that I am the LORD. They will be my people, and I will be their God, for they will return to me with all their heart.

⁸" 'But like the poor figs, which are so bad they cannot be eaten,' says the LORD, 'so will I deal with Zedekiah king of Judah, his officials and the survivors from Jerusalem, whether they remain in this land or live in Egypt. ⁹I will make them abhorrent and an offense to all the kingdoms of the earth, a reproach and a byword, an object of ridicule and cursing, wherever I banish them. ¹⁰I will send the sword, famine and plague against them until they are destroyed from the land I gave to them and their fathers.' "

Seventy Years of Captivity

25 The word came to Jeremiah concerning all the people of Judah in the fourth year of Jehoiakim son of Josiah king of Judah, which was the first year of Nebuchadnezzar king of Babylon. ²So Jeremiah the prophet said to all the people of Judah and to all those living in Jerusalem: ³For twenty-three years—from the thirteenth year of Josiah son of Amon king of Judah until this very day—the word of the LORD has come to me and I have spoken to you again and again, but you have not listened.

⁴And though the LORD has sent all his servants the prophets to you again and again, you have not listened or paid any attention. ⁵They said, "Turn now, each of you, from your evil ways and your evil practices, and you can stay in the land the LORD gave to you and your fathers for ever and ever. ⁶Do not follow other gods to serve and worship them; do not provoke me to anger with what your hands have made. Then I will not harm you."

⁷"But you did not listen to me," declares the LORD, "and you have provoked me with what your hands have made, and you have brought harm to yourselves."

⁸Therefore the LORD Almighty says this: "Because you have not listened to my words, ⁹I will summon all the peoples of the north and my servant Nebuchadnezzar king of Babylon," declares the LORD, "and I will bring them against this land and its inhabitants and against all the surrounding nations. I will completely destroy*ᶜ* them and make them an object of horror and scorn, and an everlasting ruin. ¹⁰I will banish from them the sounds of joy and gladness, the voices of bride and bridegroom, the sound of millstones and the light of the lamp. ¹¹This whole country will become a desolate wasteland, and these nations will serve the king of Babylon seventy years.

¹²"But when the seventy years are fulfilled, I will punish the king of Babylon and his nation, the land of the Babylonians,*ᵇ* for their guilt," declares the LORD, "and will make it desolate

---

ᵃ1 Hebrew *Jeconiah,* a variant of *Jehoiachin*
ᵇ5,12 Or *Chaldeans*   *ᶜ9* The Hebrew term refers to the irrevocable giving over of things or persons to the LORD, often by totally destroying them.

forever. ¹³I will bring upon that land all the things I have spoken against it, all that are written in this book and prophesied by Jeremiah against all the nations. ¹⁴They themselves will be enslaved by many nations and great kings; I will repay them according to their deeds and the work of their hands."

The Cup of God's Wrath

¹⁵This is what the LORD, the God of Israel, said to me: "Take from my hand this cup filled with the wine of my wrath and make all the nations to whom I send you drink it. ¹⁶When they drink it, they will stagger and go mad because of the sword I will send among them."

¹⁷So I took the cup from the LORD's hand and made all the nations to whom he sent me drink it: ¹⁸Jerusalem and the towns of Judah, its kings and officials, to make them a ruin and an object of horror and scorn and cursing, as they are today; ¹⁹Pharaoh king of Egypt, his attendants, his officials and all his people, ²⁰and all the foreign people there; all the kings of Uz; all the kings of the Philistines (those of Ashkelon, Gaza, Ekron, and the people left at Ashdod); ²¹Edom, Moab and Ammon; ²²all the kings of Tyre and Sidon; the kings of the coastlands across the sea; ²³Dedan, Tema, Buz and all who are in distant placesᵃ; ²⁴all the kings of Arabia and all the kings of the foreign people who live in the desert; ²⁵all the kings of Zimri, Elam and Media; ²⁶and all the kings of the north, near and far, one after the other—all the kingdoms on the face of the earth. And after all of them, the king of Sheshachᵇ will drink it too.

²⁷"Then tell them, 'This is what the LORD Almighty, the God of Israel, says: Drink, get drunk and vomit, and fall to rise no more because of the sword I will send among you.' ²⁸But if they refuse to take the cup from your hand and drink, tell them, 'This is what the LORD Almighty says: You must drink it! ²⁹See, I am beginning to bring disaster on the city that bears my Name, and will you indeed go unpunished? You will not go unpunished, for I am calling down a sword upon all who live on the earth, declares the LORD Almighty.'

³⁰"Now prophesy all these words against them and say to them:

" 'The LORD will roar from on high;
    he will thunder from his holy
      dwelling
    and roar mightily against his land.
He will shout like those who tread the
      grapes,
    shout against all who live on the
      earth.
³¹The tumult will resound to the ends of
      the earth,
    for the LORD will bring charges
      against the nations;
he will bring judgment on all
      mankind
    and put the wicked to the sword,' "
                        declares the LORD.

³²This is what the LORD Almighty says:

"Look! Disaster is spreading
    from nation to nation;
a mighty storm is rising
    from the ends of the earth."

³³At that time those slain by the LORD will be everywhere—from one end of the earth to the other. They will not be mourned or gathered up or buried, but will be like refuse lying on the ground.

³⁴Weep and wail, you shepherds;
    roll in the dust, you leaders of the
      flock.
For your time to be slaughtered has
      come;
    you will fall and be shattered like
      fine pottery.
³⁵The shepherds will have nowhere to
      flee,
    the leaders of the flock no place to
      escape.
³⁶Hear the cry of the shepherds,
    the wailing of the leaders of the
      flock,
    for the LORD is destroying their
      pasture.
³⁷The peaceful meadows will be laid
      waste
    because of the fierce anger of the
      LORD.
³⁸Like a lion he will leave his lair,

ᵃ23 Or *who clip the hair by their foreheads*
ᵇ26 *Sheshach* is a cryptogram for Babylon.

and their land will become desolate because of the sword[a] of the oppressor and because of the LORD's fierce anger.

Jeremiah Threatened With Death

26 Early in the reign of Jehoiakim son of Josiah king of Judah, this word came from the LORD: [2]"This is what the LORD says: Stand in the courtyard of the LORD's house and speak to all the people of the towns of Judah who come to worship in the house of the LORD. Tell them everything I command you; do not omit a word. [3]Perhaps they will listen and each will turn from his evil way. Then I will relent and not bring on them the disaster I was planning because of the evil they have done. [4]Say to them, 'This is what the LORD says: If you do not listen to me and follow my law, which I have set before you, [5]and if you do not listen to the words of my servants the prophets, whom I have sent to you again and again (though you have not listened), [6]then I will make this house like Shiloh and this city an object of cursing among all the nations of the earth.' "

[7]The priests, the prophets and all the people heard Jeremiah speak these words in the house of the LORD. [8]But as soon as Jeremiah finished telling all the people everything the LORD had commanded him to say, the priests, the prophets and all the people seized him and said, "You must die! [9]Why do you prophesy in the LORD's name that this house will be like Shiloh and this city will be desolate and deserted?" And all the people crowded around Jeremiah in the house of the LORD.

[10]When the officials of Judah heard about these things, they went up from the royal palace to the house of the LORD and took their places at the entrance of the New Gate of the LORD's house. [11]Then the priests and the prophets said to the officials and all the people, "This man should be sentenced to death because he has prophesied against this city. You have heard it with your own ears!"

[12]Then Jeremiah said to all the officials and all the people: "The LORD sent me to prophesy against this house and this city all the things you have heard. [13]Now re-form your ways and your actions and obey the LORD your God. Then the LORD will relent and not bring the disaster he has pronounced against you. [14]As for me, I am in your hands; do with me whatever you think is good and right. [15]Be assured, however, that if you put me to death, you will bring the guilt of innocent blood on yourselves and on this city and on those who live in it, for in truth the LORD has sent me to you to speak all these words in your hearing."

[16]Then the officials and all the people said to the priests and the prophets, "This man should not be sentenced to death! He has spoken to us in the name of the LORD our God."

[17]Some of the elders of the land stepped forward and said to the entire assembly of people, [18]"Micah of Moresheth prophesied in the days of Hezekiah king of Judah. He told all the people of Judah, 'This is what the LORD Almighty says:

> " 'Zion will be plowed like a field,
>   Jerusalem will become a heap of
>   rubble,
>   the temple hill a mound overgrown
>   with thickets.'[b]

[19]"Did Hezekiah king of Judah or anyone else in Judah put him to death? Did not Hezekiah fear the LORD and seek his favor? And did not the LORD relent, so that he did not bring the disaster he pronounced against them? We are about to bring a terrible disaster on ourselves!"

[20](Now Uriah son of Shemaiah from Kiriath Jearim was another man who prophesied in the name of the LORD; he prophesied the same things against this city and this land as Jeremiah did. [21]When King Jehoiakim and all his officers and officials heard his words, the king sought to put him to death. But Uriah heard of it and fled in fear to Egypt. [22]King Jehoiakim, however, sent Elnathan son of Acbor to Egypt, along with some other men. [23]They brought Uriah out of Egypt and took him to King Jehoiakim, who had him struck down with a

---

[a]38 *Some Hebrew manuscripts and Septuagint (see also Jer. 46:16 and 50:16); most Hebrew manuscripts* anger   [b]18 *Micah 3:12*

sword and his body thrown into the burial place of the common people.)

[24]Furthermore, Ahikam son of Shaphan supported Jeremiah, and so he was not handed over to the people to be put to death.

Judah to Serve Nebuchadnezzar

27 Early in the reign of Zedekiah[a] son of Josiah king of Judah, this word came to Jeremiah from the LORD: [2]This is what the LORD said to me: "Make a yoke out of straps and crossbars and put it on your neck. [3]Then send word to

What's a Yoke?

Huh?

Jeremiah 27:1–2

A dog looks pretty normal with a leash around his neck; but a person wearing a leash would look just plain weird. Yet that's exactly what God asked Jeremiah to do. Jeremiah wore a yoke, which is like a leash of wood and leather, around his neck out in public. Although Jeremiah, God's messenger, looked a little strange, God's message was clear: Because of the way the Israelites bucked God's plans for them, another nation was going to become their master.

the kings of Edom, Moab, Ammon, Tyre and Sidon through the envoys who have come to Jerusalem to Zedekiah king of Judah. [4]Give them a message for their masters and say, 'This is what the LORD Almighty, the God of Israel, says: "Tell this to your masters: [5]With my great power and outstretched arm I made the earth and its people and the animals that are on it, and I give it to anyone I please. [6]Now I will hand all your countries over to my servant Nebuchadnezzar king of Babylon; I will make even the wild animals subject to him. [7]All nations will serve him and his son and his grandson until the time for his land comes; then many nations and great kings will subjugate him.

[8]' "If, however, any nation or kingdom will not serve Nebuchadnezzar king

of Babylon or bow its neck under his yoke, I will punish that nation with the sword, famine and plague, declares the LORD, until I destroy it by his hand. [9]So do not listen to your prophets, your diviners, your interpreters of dreams, your mediums or your sorcerers who tell you, 'You will not serve the king of Babylon.' [10]They prophesy lies to you that will only serve to remove you far from your lands; I will banish you and you will perish. [11]But if any nation will bow its neck under the yoke of the king of Babylon and serve him, I will let that nation remain in its own land to till it and to live there, declares the LORD." ' "

[12]I gave the same message to Zedekiah king of Judah. I said, "Bow your neck under the yoke of the king of Babylon; serve him and his people, and you will live. [13]Why will you and your people die by the sword, famine and plague with which the LORD has threatened any nation that will not serve the king of Babylon? [14]Do not listen to the words of the prophets who say to you, 'You will not serve the king of Babylon,' for they are prophesying lies to you. [15]'I have not sent them,' declares the LORD. 'They are prophesying lies in my name. Therefore, I will banish you and you will perish, both you and the prophets who prophesy to you.' "

[16]Then I said to the priests and all these people, "This is what the LORD says: Do not listen to the prophets who say, 'Very soon now the articles from the LORD's house will be brought back from Babylon.' They are prophesying lies to you. [17]Do not listen to them. Serve the king of Babylon, and you will live. Why should this city become a ruin? [18]If they are prophets and have the word of the LORD, let them plead with the LORD Almighty that the furnishings remaining in the house of the LORD and in the palace of the king of Judah and in Jerusalem not be taken to Babylon. [19]For this is what the LORD Almighty says about the pillars, the Sea, the movable stands and the

---

[a]1 A few Hebrew manuscripts and Syriac (see also Jer. 27:3, 12 and 28:1); most Hebrew manuscripts *Jehoiakim* (Most Septuagint manuscripts do not have this verse.)

other furnishings that are left in this city, ²⁰which Nebuchadnezzar king of Babylon did not take away when he carried Jehoiachin[a] son of Jehoiakim king of Judah into exile from Jerusalem to Babylon, along with all the nobles of Judah and Jerusalem— ²¹yes, this is what the LORD Almighty, the God of Israel, says about the things that are left in the house of the LORD and in the palace of the king of Judah and in Jerusalem: ²²'They will be taken to Babylon and there they will remain until the day I come for them,' declares the LORD. 'Then I will bring them back and restore them to this place.' "

The False Prophet Hananiah

28 In the fifth month of that same year, the fourth year, early in the reign of Zedekiah king of Judah, the prophet Hananiah son of Azzur, who was from Gibeon, said to me in the house of the LORD in the presence of the priests and all the people: ²"This is what the LORD Almighty, the God of Israel, says: 'I will break the yoke of the king of Babylon. ³Within two years I will bring back to this place all the articles of the LORD's house that Nebuchadnezzar king of Babylon removed from here and took to Babylon. ⁴I will also bring back to this place Jehoiachin[a] son of Jehoiakim king of Judah and all the other exiles from Judah who went to Babylon,' declares the LORD, 'for I will break the yoke of the king of Babylon.' "

⁵Then the prophet Jeremiah replied to the prophet Hananiah before the priests and all the people who were standing in the house of the LORD. ⁶He said, "Amen! May the LORD do so! May the LORD fulfill the words you have prophesied by bringing the articles of the LORD's house and all the exiles back to this place from Babylon. ⁷Nevertheless, listen to what I have to say in your hearing and in the hearing of all the people: ⁸From early times the prophets who preceded you and me have prophesied war, disaster and plague against many countries and great kingdoms. ⁹But the prophet who prophesies peace will be recognized as one truly sent by the LORD only if his prediction comes true."

¹⁰Then the prophet Hananiah took the yoke off the neck of the prophet Jeremiah and broke it, ¹¹and he said before all the people, "This is what the LORD says: 'In the same way will I break the yoke of Nebuchadnezzar king of Babylon off the neck of all the nations within two years.' " At this, the prophet Jeremiah went on his way.

¹²Shortly after the prophet Hananiah had broken the yoke off the neck of the prophet Jeremiah, the word of the LORD came to Jeremiah: ¹³"Go and tell Hananiah, 'This is what the LORD says: You have broken a wooden yoke, but in its place you will get a yoke of iron. ¹⁴This is what the LORD Almighty, the God of Israel, says: I will put an iron yoke on the necks of all these nations to make them serve Nebuchadnezzar king of Babylon, and they will serve him. I will even give him control over the wild animals.' "

¹⁵Then the prophet Jeremiah said to Hananiah the prophet, "Listen, Hananiah! The LORD has not sent you, yet you have persuaded this nation to trust in lies. ¹⁶Therefore, this is what the LORD says: 'I am about to remove you from the face of the earth. This very year you are going to die, because you have preached rebellion against the LORD.' "

¹⁷In the seventh month of that same year, Hananiah the prophet died.

A Letter to the Exiles

29 This is the text of the letter that the prophet Jeremiah sent from Jerusalem to the surviving elders among the exiles and to the priests, the prophets and all the other people Nebuchadnezzar had carried into exile from Jerusalem to Babylon. ²(This was after King Jehoiachin[a] and the queen mother, the court officials and the leaders of Judah and Jerusalem, the craftsmen and the artisans had gone into exile from Jerusalem.) ³He entrusted the letter to Elasah son of Shaphan and to Gemariah son of Hilkiah, whom Zedekiah king of Judah sent to King Nebuchadnezzar in Babylon. It said:

⁴This is what the LORD Almighty, the God of Israel, says to all those I

---

[a]20,4,2 Hebrew *Jeconiah*, a variant of *Jehoiachin*

carried into exile from Jerusalem to Babylon: ⁵"Build houses and settle down; plant gardens and eat what they produce. ⁶Marry and have sons and daughters; find wives for your sons and give your daughters in marriage, so that they too may have sons and daughters. Increase in number there; do not decrease. ⁷Also, seek the peace and prosperity of the city to which I have carried you into exile. Pray to the LORD for it, because if it prospers, you too will prosper." ⁸Yes, this is what the LORD Almighty, the God of Israel, says: "Do not let the prophets and diviners among you deceive you. Do not listen to the dreams you encourage them to have. ⁹They are prophesying lies to you in my name. I have not sent them," declares the LORD.

¹⁰This is what the LORD says: "When seventy years are completed for Babylon, I will come to you and fulfill my gracious promise to bring you back to this place. ¹¹For I know the plans I have for you," declares the LORD, "plans to prosper you and not to harm you, plans to give you hope and a future. ¹²Then you will call upon me and come and pray to me, and I will listen to you. ¹³You

Tuesday

The Man With the Plan

Read Jeremiah 29:11

Recently, I went on a short-term missions trip with my youth group to England and Wales. I was really excited about it because I've thought about being a missionary after I finish college. I couldn't wait to start leading people to Jesus Christ!

On our first day there we started going to the homes of people around the town. But all day long we were met with slamming doors and negative comments. At the end of the day I was so discouraged. I thought this was what God wanted me to do for the rest of my life, but it was going so badly! I felt like such a failure.

But toward the end of that week, God led me to a man who desperately needed Jesus. I talked with him for 3 hours, and we had a wonderful conversation. By the time we finished, he decided he would look further into Christianity. If I had quit after that first day, I would never have had the chance to talk to this man.

This whole experience proved to me that I have to trust God with my life. He knows exactly what's in store for me, because he planned it all. I don't have to stress about where I'll go to college, what kind of job I'll have or even how I'll do in school next week. God has great plans for my life and will lead me wherever I need to go.

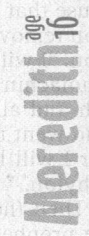

Meredith age 16

What about You?

❶ How do you feel when you think about your future? Why do you think you feel that way?

❷ Write out your testimony—the story of how Jesus has touched your life. To get started, focus on 2 or 3 times when you've really seen God take care of you. Whenever you feel stressed, read your testimony. Better yet, be ready to share it with a friend.

❸ Ask God to help you trust his plans for you.

Turn to page 931 for your next devotion.

will seek me and find me when you seek me with all your heart. [14]I will be found by you," declares the LORD, "and will bring you back from captivity.[a] I will gather you from all the nations and places where I have banished you," declares the LORD, "and will bring you back to the place from which I carried you into exile."

[15]You may say, "The LORD has raised up prophets for us in Babylon," [16]but this is what the LORD says about the king who sits on David's throne and all the people who remain in this city, your countrymen who did not go with you into exile— [17]yes, this is what the LORD Almighty says: "I will send the sword, famine and plague against them and I will make them like poor figs that are so bad they cannot be eaten. [18]I will pursue them with the sword, famine and plague and will make them abhorrent to all the kingdoms of the earth and an object of cursing and horror, of scorn and reproach, among all the nations where I drive them. [19]For they have not listened to my words," declares the LORD, "words that I sent to them again and again by my servants the prophets. And you exiles have not listened either," declares the LORD.

[20]Therefore, hear the word of the LORD, all you exiles whom I have sent away from Jerusalem to Babylon. [21]This is what the LORD Almighty, the God of Israel, says about Ahab son of Kolaiah and Zedekiah son of Maaseiah, who are prophesying lies to you in my name: "I will hand them over to Nebuchadnezzar king of Babylon, and he will put them to death before your very eyes. [22]Because of them, all the exiles from Judah who are in Babylon will use this curse: 'The LORD treat you like Zedekiah and Ahab, whom the king of Babylon burned in the fire.' [23]For they have done outrageous things in Israel; they have committed adultery with their neighbors' wives and in my name have spoken lies, which I did not tell them to do. I

know it and am a witness to it," declares the LORD.

Message to Shemaiah

[24]Tell Shemaiah the Nehelamite, [25]"This is what the LORD Almighty, the God of Israel, says: You sent letters in your own name to all the people in Jerusalem, to Zephaniah son of Maaseiah the priest, and to all the other priests. You said to Zephaniah, [26]'The LORD has appointed you priest in place of Jehoiada to be in charge of the house of the LORD; you should put any madman who acts like a prophet into the stocks and neckirons. [27]So why have you not reprimanded Jeremiah from Anathoth, who poses as a prophet among you? [28]He has sent this message to us in Babylon: It will be a long time. Therefore build houses and settle down; plant gardens and eat what they produce.' "

[29]Zephaniah the priest, however, read the letter to Jeremiah the prophet. [30]Then the word of the LORD came to Jeremiah: [31]"Send this message to all the exiles: 'This is what the LORD says about Shemaiah the Nehelamite: Because Shemaiah has prophesied to you, even though I did not send him, and has led you to believe a lie, [32]this is what the LORD says: I will surely punish Shemaiah the Nehelamite and his descendants. He will have no one left among this people, nor will he see the good things I will do for my people, declares the LORD, because he has preached rebellion against me.' "

Restoration of Israel

30 This is the word that came to Jeremiah from the LORD: [2]"This is what the LORD, the God of Israel, says: 'Write in a book all the words I have spoken to you. [3]The days are coming,' declares the LORD, 'when I will bring my people Israel and Judah back from captivity[b] and restore them to the land I gave their forefathers to possess,' says the LORD."

[4]These are the words the LORD spoke concerning Israel and Judah. [5]"This is what the LORD says:

---

[a]14 Or *will restore your fortunes*   [b]3 Or *will restore the fortunes of my people Israel and Judah*

¹⁷ So there is hope for your future,"
        declares the LORD.
    "Your children will return to their
        own land.

¹⁸ "I have surely heard Ephraim's
        moaning:
    'You disciplined me like an unruly
        calf,
    and I have been disciplined.
    Restore me, and I will return,
        because you are the LORD my God.

¹⁹ After I strayed,
    I repented;
    after I came to understand,
    I beat my breast.
    I was ashamed and humiliated
        because I bore the disgrace of my
        youth.'

²⁰ Is not Ephraim my dear son,
    the child in whom I delight?
    Though I often speak against him,
    I still remember him.
    Therefore my heart yearns for him;
    I have great compassion for him,"
        declares the LORD.

²¹ "Set up road signs;
    put up guideposts.
    Take note of the highway,
    the road that you take.
    Return, O Virgin Israel,
    return to your towns.

²² How long will you wander,
    O unfaithful daughter?
    The LORD will create a new thing on
        earth—
    a woman will surround[a] a man."

²³ This is what the LORD Almighty, the
God of Israel, says: "When I bring them
back from captivity,[b] the people in the
land of Judah and in its towns will once
again use these words: 'The LORD bless
you, O righteous dwelling, O sacred
mountain.' ²⁴ People will live together in
Judah and all its towns—farmers and
those who move about with their flocks.
²⁵ I will refresh the weary and satisfy the
faint."

²⁶ At this I awoke and looked around.
My sleep had been pleasant to me.

²⁷ "The days are coming," declares the
LORD, "when I will plant the house of Israel and the house of Judah with the offspring of men and of animals. ²⁸ Just as I

watched over them to uproot and tear
down, and to overthrow, destroy and
bring disaster, so I will watch over them
to build and to plant," declares the LORD.
²⁹ "In those days people will no longer
say,

    'The fathers have eaten sour grapes,
        and the children's teeth are set on
        edge.'

³⁰ Instead, everyone will die for his own
sin; whoever eats sour grapes—his own
teeth will be set on edge.

³¹ "The time is coming," declares the
        LORD,
    "when I will make a new covenant
    with the house of Israel
        and with the house of Judah.
³² It will not be like the covenant
    I made with their forefathers
    when I took them by the hand
        to lead them out of Egypt,
    because they broke my covenant,
        though I was a husband to[c] them,[d]"
        declares the LORD.
³³ "This is the covenant I will make with
        the house of Israel
    after that time," declares the LORD.
    "I will put my law in their minds
        and write it on their hearts.
    I will be their God,
        and they will be my people.
³⁴ No longer will a man teach his
        neighbor,
    or a man his brother, saying, 'Know
        the LORD,'
    because they will all know me,
        from the least of them to the
        greatest,"
        declares the LORD.
    "For I will forgive their wickedness
        and will remember their sins no
        more."

³⁵ This is what the LORD says,

    he who appoints the sun
        to shine by day,
    who decrees the moon and stars
        to shine by night,
    who stirs up the sea

─────────
a22 Or *will go about seeking* ; or *will protect*
b23 Or *I restore their fortunes*   *c32* Hebrew;
Septuagint and Syriac / *and I turned away from*
d32 Or *was their master*

so that its waves roar—
the LORD Almighty is his name:
³⁶"Only if these decrees vanish from my
sight,"
declares the LORD,
"will the descendants of Israel ever
cease
to be a nation before me."

³⁷This is what the LORD says:

"Only if the heavens above can be
measured
and the foundations of the earth
below be searched out
will I reject all the descendants of
Israel
because of all they have done,"
declares the LORD.

³⁸"The days are coming," declares the
LORD, "when this city will be rebuilt for
me from the Tower of Hananel to the
Corner Gate. ³⁹The measuring line will
stretch from there straight to the hill of
Gareb and then turn to Goah. ⁴⁰The
whole valley where dead bodies and
ashes are thrown, and all the terraces out
to the Kidron Valley on the east as far as
the corner of the Horse Gate, will be holy
to the LORD. The city will never again be
uprooted or demolished."

Jeremiah Buys a Field

32 This is the word that came to Jeremiah from the LORD in the tenth
year of Zedekiah king of Judah, which
was the eighteenth year of Nebuchadnezzar. ²The army of the king of Babylon
was then besieging Jerusalem, and Jeremiah the prophet was confined in the
courtyard of the guard in the royal palace of Judah.

³Now Zedekiah king of Judah had imprisoned him there, saying, "Why do you
prophesy as you do? You say, 'This is
what the LORD says: I am about to hand
this city over to the king of Babylon, and
he will capture it. ⁴Zedekiah king of Judah will not escape out of the hands of
the Babylonians^a but will certainly be
handed over to the king of Babylon, and
will speak with him face to face and see
him with his own eyes. ⁵He will take Zedekiah to Babylon, where he will remain
until I deal with him, declares the LORD.

If you fight against the Babylonians, you
will not succeed.' "

⁶Jeremiah said, "The word of the LORD
came to me: ⁷Hanamel son of Shallum
your uncle is going to come to you and
say, 'Buy my field at Anathoth, because
as nearest relative it is your right and
duty to buy it.'

⁸"Then, just as the LORD had said, my
cousin Hanamel came to me in the courtyard of the guard and said, 'Buy my field
at Anathoth in the territory of Benjamin.
Since it is your right to redeem it and
possess it, buy it for yourself.'

"I knew that this was the word of the
LORD; ⁹so I bought the field at Anathoth
from my cousin Hanamel and weighed
out for him seventeen shekels^b of silver.
¹⁰I signed and sealed the deed, had it witnessed, and weighed out the silver on the
scales. ¹¹I took the deed of purchase—the
sealed copy containing the terms and
conditions, as well as the unsealed
copy— ¹²and I gave this deed to Baruch
son of Neriah, the son of Mahseiah, in
the presence of my cousin Hanamel and
of the witnesses who had signed the deed
and of all the Jews sitting in the courtyard of the guard.

¹³"In their presence I gave Baruch
these instructions: ¹⁴This is what the
LORD Almighty, the God of Israel, says:
Take these documents, both the sealed
and unsealed copies of the deed of purchase, and put them in a clay jar so they
will last a long time. ¹⁵For this is what
the LORD Almighty, the God of Israel,
says: Houses, fields and vineyards will
again be bought in this land.'

¹⁶"After I had given the deed of purchase to Baruch son of Neriah, I prayed
to the LORD:

¹⁷"Ah, Sovereign LORD, you have
made the heavens and the earth by
your great power and outstretched
arm. Nothing is too hard for you.
¹⁸You show love to thousands but
bring the punishment for the fathers' sins into the laps of their children after them. O great and
powerful God, whose name is the

^a4 Or *Chaldeans*; also in verses 5, 24, 25, 28, 29
and 43   ^b9 That is, about 7 ounces (about 200
grams)

Jeremiah: [24]"Have you not noticed that these people are saying, 'The LORD has rejected the two kingdoms[a] he chose'? So they despise my people and no longer regard them as a nation. [25]This is what the LORD says: 'If I have not established my covenant with day and night and the fixed laws of heaven and earth, [26]then I will reject the descendants of Jacob and David my servant and will not choose one of his sons to rule over the descendants of Abraham, Isaac and Jacob. For I will restore their fortunes[b] and have compassion on them.'"

Warning to Zedekiah

34 While Nebuchadnezzar king of Babylon and all his army and all the kingdoms and peoples in the empire he ruled were fighting against Jerusalem and all its surrounding towns, this word came to Jeremiah from the LORD: [2]"This is what the LORD, the God of Israel, says: Go to Zedekiah king of Judah and tell him, 'This is what the LORD says: I am about to hand this city over to the king of Babylon, and he will burn it down. [3]You will not escape from his grasp but will surely be captured and handed over to him. You will see the king of Babylon with your own eyes, and he will speak with you face to face. And you will go to Babylon.

[4]" 'Yet hear the promise of the LORD, O Zedekiah king of Judah. This is what the LORD says concerning you: You will not die by the sword; [5]you will die peacefully. As people made a funeral fire in honor of your fathers, the former kings who preceded you, so they will make a fire in your honor and lament, "Alas, O master!" I myself make this promise, declares the LORD.' "

[6]Then Jeremiah the prophet told all this to Zedekiah king of Judah, in Jerusalem, [7]while the army of the king of Babylon was fighting against Jerusalem and the other cities of Judah that were still holding out—Lachish and Azekah. These were the only fortified cities left in Judah.

Freedom for Slaves

[8]The word came to Jeremiah from the LORD after King Zedekiah had made a covenant with all the people in Jerusalem to proclaim freedom for the slaves. [9]Everyone was to free his Hebrew slaves, both male and female; no one was to hold a fellow Jew in bondage. [10]So all the officials and people who entered into this covenant agreed that they would free their male and female slaves and no longer hold them in bondage. They agreed, and set them free. [11]But afterward they changed their minds and took back the slaves they had freed and enslaved them again.

[12]Then the word of the LORD came to Jeremiah: [13]"This is what the LORD, the God of Israel, says: I made a covenant with your forefathers when I brought them out of Egypt, out of the land of slavery. I said, [14]'Every seventh year each of you must free any fellow Hebrew who has sold himself to you. After he has served you six years, you must let him go free.'[c] Your fathers, however, did not listen to me or pay attention to me. [15]Recently you repented and did what is right in my sight: Each of you proclaimed freedom to his countrymen. You even made a covenant before me in the house that bears my Name. [16]But now you have turned around and profaned my name; each of you has taken back the male and female slaves you had set free to go where they wished. You have forced them to become your slaves again.

[17]"Therefore, this is what the LORD says: You have not obeyed me; you have not proclaimed freedom for your fellow countrymen. So I now proclaim 'freedom' for you, declares the LORD—'freedom' to fall by the sword, plague and famine. I will make you abhorrent to all the kingdoms of the earth. [18]The men who have violated my covenant and have not fulfilled the terms of the covenant they made before me, I will treat like the calf they cut in two and then walked between its pieces. [19]The leaders of Judah and Jerusalem, the court officials, the priests and all the people of the land who walked between the pieces of the calf, [20]I will hand over to their enemies who seek their lives. Their dead

bodies will become food for the birds of the air and the beasts of the earth.

²¹"I will hand Zedekiah king of Judah and his officials over to their enemies who seek their lives, to the army of the king of Babylon, which has withdrawn from you. ²²I am going to give the order, declares the LORD, and I will bring them back to this city. They will fight against it, take it and burn it down. And I will lay waste the towns of Judah so no one can live there."

The Recabites

35 This is the word that came to Jeremiah from the LORD during the reign of Jehoiakim son of Josiah king of Judah: ²"Go to the Recabite family and invite them to come to one of the side rooms of the house of the LORD and give them wine to drink."

³So I went to get Jaazaniah son of Jeremiah, the son of Habazziniah, and his brothers and all his sons—the whole family of the Recabites. ⁴I brought them into the house of the LORD, into the room of the sons of Hanan son of Igdaliah the man of God. It was next to the room of the officials, which was over that of Maaseiah son of Shallum the doorkeeper. ⁵Then I set bowls full of wine and some cups before the men of the Recabite family and said to them, "Drink some wine."

⁶But they replied, "We do not drink wine, because our forefather Jonadab son of Recab gave us this command: 'Neither you nor your descendants must ever drink wine. ⁷Also you must never build houses, sow seed or plant vineyards; you must never have any of these things, but must always live in tents. Then you will live a long time in the land where you are nomads.' ⁸We have obeyed everything our forefather Jonadab son of Recab commanded us. Neither we nor our wives nor our sons and daughters have ever drunk wine ⁹or built houses to live in or had vineyards, fields or crops. ¹⁰We have lived in tents and have fully obeyed everything our forefather Jonadab commanded us. ¹¹But when Nebuchadnezzar king of Babylon invaded this land, we said, 'Come, we must go to Jerusalem to escape the Babylonian^a and Ar-

amean armies.' So we have remained in Jerusalem."

¹²Then the word of the LORD came to Jeremiah, saying: ¹³"This is what the LORD Almighty, the God of Israel, says: Go and tell the men of Judah and the people of Jerusalem, 'Will you not learn a lesson and obey my words?' declares the LORD. ¹⁴Jonadab son of Recab ordered his sons not to drink wine and this command has been kept. To this day they do not drink wine, because they obey their forefather's command. But I have spoken to you again and again, yet you have not obeyed me. ¹⁵Again and again I sent all my servants the prophets to you. They said, "Each of you must turn from your wicked ways and reform your actions; do not follow other gods to serve them. Then you will live in the land I have given to you and your fathers." But you have not paid attention or listened to me. ¹⁶The descendants of Jonadab son of Recab have carried out the command their forefather gave them, but these people have not obeyed me.'

¹⁷"Therefore, this is what the LORD God Almighty, the God of Israel, says: 'Listen! I am going to bring on Judah and on everyone living in Jerusalem every disaster I pronounced against them. I spoke to them, but they did not listen; I called to them, but they did not answer.'"

¹⁸Then Jeremiah said to the family of the Recabites, "This is what the LORD Almighty, the God of Israel, says: 'You have obeyed the command of your forefather Jonadab and have followed all his instructions and have done everything he ordered.' ¹⁹Therefore, this is what the LORD Almighty, the God of Israel, says: 'Jonadab son of Recab will never fail to have a man to serve me.'"

Jehoiakim Burns Jeremiah's Scroll

36 In the fourth year of Jehoiakim son of Josiah king of Judah, this word came to Jeremiah from the LORD: ²"Take a scroll and write on it all the words I have spoken to you concerning Israel, Judah and all the other nations from the time I began speaking to you in the reign of Josiah till now. ³Perhaps

^a11 Or *Chaldean*

the people when he said, [2]"This is what the LORD says: 'Whoever stays in this city will die by the sword, famine or plague, but whoever goes over to the Babylonians[a] will live. He will escape with his life; he will live.' [3]And this is what the LORD says: 'This city will certainly be handed over to the army of the king of Babylon, who will capture it.'"

[4]Then the officials said to the king, "This man should be put to death. He is discouraging the soldiers who are left in this city, as well as all the people, by the things he is saying to them. This man is not seeking the good of these people but their ruin."

[5]"He is in your hands," King Zedekiah answered. "The king can do nothing to oppose you."

[6]So they took Jeremiah and put him into the cistern of Malkijah, the king's son, which was in the courtyard of the guard. They lowered Jeremiah by ropes into the cistern; it had no water in it, only mud, and Jeremiah sank down into the mud.

No Brotherly and Cisternly Love

Huh?

Jeremiah 38:6

Jeremiah's message really ticked off lots of people, including really important rulers. Guys who worked for King Zedekiah took Jeremiah and put him in a cistern. Cisterns were like bell-shaped pits in the ground used to store water. Jeremiah's cistern had no water, just some squishy mud. Zedekiah's helpers were trying to kill Jeremiah by starving him without actually murdering him with their own hands.

[7]But Ebed-Melech, a Cushite,[b] an official[c] in the royal palace, heard that they had put Jeremiah into the cistern. While the king was sitting in the Benjamin Gate, [8]Ebed-Melech went out of the palace and said to him, [9]"My lord the king, these men have acted wickedly in all they have done to Jeremiah the prophet. They have thrown him into a cistern, where he will starve to death when there is no longer any bread in the city."

[10]Then the king commanded Ebed-Melech the Cushite, "Take thirty men from here with you and lift Jeremiah the prophet out of the cistern before he dies."

[11]So Ebed-Melech took the men with him and went to a room under the treasury in the palace. He took some old rags and worn-out clothes from there and let them down with ropes to Jeremiah in the cistern. [12]Ebed-Melech the Cushite said to Jeremiah, "Put these old rags and worn-out clothes under your arms to pad the ropes." Jeremiah did so, [13]and they pulled him up with the ropes and lifted him out of the cistern. And Jeremiah remained in the courtyard of the guard.

Zedekiah Questions Jeremiah Again

[14]Then King Zedekiah sent for Jeremiah the prophet and had him brought to the third entrance to the temple of the LORD. "I am going to ask you something," the king said to Jeremiah. "Do not hide anything from me."

[15]Jeremiah said to Zedekiah, "If I give you an answer, will you not kill me? Even if I did give you counsel, you would not listen to me."

[16]But King Zedekiah swore this oath secretly to Jeremiah: "As surely as the LORD lives, who has given us breath, I will neither kill you nor hand you over to those who are seeking your life."

[17]Then Jeremiah said to Zedekiah, "This is what the LORD God Almighty, the God of Israel, says: 'If you surrender to the officers of the king of Babylon, your life will be spared and this city will not be burned down; you and your family will live. [18]But if you will not surrender to the officers of the king of Babylon, this city will be handed over to the Babylonians and they will burn it down; you yourself will not escape from their hands.'"

[19]King Zedekiah said to Jeremiah, "I am afraid of the Jews who have gone over to the Babylonians, for the Babylonians may hand me over to them and they will mistreat me."

[a]2 Or *Chaldeans*; also in verses 18, 19 and 23
[b]7 Probably from the upper Nile region   [c]7 Or *a eunuch*

²⁰"They will not hand you over," Jeremiah replied. "Obey the LORD by doing what I tell you. Then it will go well with you, and your life will be spared. ²¹But if you refuse to surrender, this is what the LORD has revealed to me: ²²All the women left in the palace of the king of Judah will be brought out to the officials of the king of Babylon. Those women will say to you:

" 'They misled you and overcame you—
    those trusted friends of yours.
Your feet are sunk in the mud;
    your friends have deserted you.'

²³"All your wives and children will be brought out to the Babylonians. You yourself will not escape from their hands but will be captured by the king of Babylon; and this city will*ᵃ* be burned down."

²⁴Then Zedekiah said to Jeremiah, "Do not let anyone know about this conversation, or you may die. ²⁵If the officials hear that I talked with you, and they come to you and say, 'Tell us what you said to the king and what the king said to you; do not hide it from us or we will kill you,' ²⁶then tell them, 'I was pleading with the king not to send me back to Jonathan's house to die there.' "

²⁷All the officials did come to Jeremiah and question him, and he told them everything the king had ordered him to say. So they said no more to him, for no one had heard his conversation with the king.

²⁸And Jeremiah remained in the courtyard of the guard until the day Jerusalem was captured.

The Fall of Jerusalem

39 This is how Jerusalem was taken: ¹In the ninth year of Zedekiah king of Judah, in the tenth month, Nebuchadnezzar king of Babylon marched against Jerusalem with his whole army and laid siege to it. ²And on the ninth day of the fourth month of Zedekiah's eleventh year, the city wall was broken through. ³Then all the officials of the king of Babylon came and took seats in the Middle Gate: Nergal-Sharezer of Samgar, Nebo-Sarsekim*ᵇ* a chief officer,

Nergal-Sharezer a high official and all the other officials of the king of Babylon. ⁴When Zedekiah king of Judah and all the soldiers saw them, they fled; they left the city at night by way of the king's garden, through the gate between the two walls, and headed toward the Arabah.*ᶜ*

⁵But the Babylonian*ᵈ* army pursued them and overtook Zedekiah in the plains of Jericho. They captured him and took him to Nebuchadnezzar king of Babylon at Riblah in the land of Hamath, where he pronounced sentence on him. ⁶There at Riblah the king of Babylon slaughtered the sons of Zedekiah before his eyes and also killed all the nobles of Judah. ⁷Then he put out Zedekiah's eyes and bound him with bronze shackles to take him to Babylon.

⁸The Babylonians*ᵉ* set fire to the royal palace and the houses of the people and broke down the walls of Jerusalem. ⁹Nebuzaradan commander of the imperial guard carried into exile to Babylon the people who remained in the city, along with those who had gone over to him, and the rest of the people. ¹⁰But Nebuzaradan the commander of the guard left behind in the land of Judah some of the poor people, who owned nothing; and at that time he gave them vineyards and fields.

¹¹Now Nebuchadnezzar king of Babylon had given these orders about Jeremiah through Nebuzaradan commander of the imperial guard: ¹²"Take him and look after him; don't harm him but do for him whatever he asks." ¹³So Nebuzaradan the commander of the guard, Nebushazban a chief officer, Nergal-Sharezer a high official and all the other officers of the king of Babylon ¹⁴sent and had Jeremiah taken out of the courtyard of the guard. They turned him over to Gedaliah son of Ahikam, the son of Shaphan, to take him back to his home. So he remained among his own people.

¹⁵While Jeremiah had been confined in the courtyard of the guard, the word of the LORD came to him: ¹⁶"Go and tell

---

ᵃ23 Or *and you will cause this city to*
ᵇ3 Or *Nergal-Sharezer, Samgar-Nebo, Sarsekim*
ᶜ4 Or *the Jordan Valley*   *ᵈ5* Or *Chaldean*
ᵉ8 Or *Chaldeans*

came to Jeremiah. [8]So he called together Johanan son of Kareah and all the army officers who were with him and all the people from the least to the greatest. [9]He said to them, "This is what the LORD, the God of Israel, to whom you sent me to present your petition, says: [10]'If you stay in this land, I will build you up and not tear you down; I will plant you and not uproot you, for I am grieved over the disaster I have inflicted on you. [11]Do not be afraid of the king of Babylon, whom you now fear. Do not be afraid of him, declares the LORD, for I am with you and will save you and deliver you from his hands. [12]I will show you compassion so that he will have compassion on you and restore you to your land.'

[13]"However, if you say, 'We will not stay in this land,' and so disobey the LORD your God, [14]and if you say, 'No, we will go and live in Egypt, where we will not see war or hear the trumpet or be hungry for bread,' [15]then hear the word of the LORD, O remnant of Judah. This is what the LORD Almighty, the God of Israel, says: 'If you are determined to go to Egypt and you do go to settle there, [16]then the sword you fear will overtake you there, and the famine you dread will follow you into Egypt, and there you will die. [17]Indeed, all who are determined to go to Egypt to settle there will die by the sword, famine and plague; not one of them will survive or escape the disaster I will bring on them.' [18]This is what the LORD Almighty, the God of Israel, says: 'As my anger and wrath have been poured out on those who lived in Jerusalem, so will my wrath be poured out on you when you go to Egypt. You will be an object of cursing and horror, of condemnation and reproach; you will never see this place again.'

[19]"O remnant of Judah, the LORD has told you, 'Do not go to Egypt.' Be sure of this: I warn you today [20]that you made a fatal mistake[a] when you sent me to the LORD your God and said, 'Pray to the LORD our God for us; tell us everything he says and we will do it.' [21]I have told you today, but you still have not obeyed the LORD your God in all he sent me to tell you. [22]So now, be sure of this: You will die by the sword, famine and plague

in the place where you want to go to settle."

43 When Jeremiah finished telling the people all the words of the LORD their God—everything the LORD had sent him to tell them— [2]Azariah son of Hoshaiah and Johanan son of Kareah and all the arrogant men said to Jeremiah, "You are lying! The LORD our God has not sent you to say, 'You must not go to Egypt to settle there.' [3]But Baruch son of Neriah is inciting you against us to hand us over to the Babylonians,[b] so they may kill us or carry us into exile to Babylon."

[4]So Johanan son of Kareah and all the army officers and all the people disobeyed the LORD's command to stay in the land of Judah. [5]Instead, Johanan son of Kareah and all the army officers led away all the remnant of Judah who had come back to live in the land of Judah from all the nations where they had been scattered. [6]They also led away all the men, women and children and the king's daughters whom Nebuzaradan commander of the imperial guard had left with Gedaliah son of Ahikam, the son of Shaphan, and Jeremiah the prophet and Baruch son of Neriah. [7]So they entered Egypt in disobedience to the LORD and went as far as Tahpanhes.

[8]In Tahpanhes the word of the LORD came to Jeremiah: [9]"While the Jews are watching, take some large stones with you and bury them in clay in the brick pavement at the entrance to Pharaoh's palace in Tahpanhes. [10]Then say to them, 'This is what the LORD Almighty, the God of Israel, says: I will send for my servant Nebuchadnezzar king of Babylon, and I will set his throne over these stones I have buried here; he will spread his royal canopy above them. [11]He will come and attack Egypt, bringing death to those destined for death, captivity to those destined for captivity, and the sword to those destined for the sword. [12]He[c] will set fire to the temples of the gods of Egypt; he will burn their temples and take their gods captive. As a shepherd wraps his garment around him, so will he wrap Egypt around himself and depart

[a]20 Or you erred in your hearts   [b]3 Or Chaldeans
[c]12 Or I

from there unscathed. [13]There in the temple of the sun[a] in Egypt he will demolish the sacred pillars and will burn down the temples of the gods of Egypt.' "

Disaster Because of Idolatry

44 This word came to Jeremiah concerning all the Jews living in Lower Egypt—in Migdol, Tahpanhes and Memphis[b]—and in Upper Egypt[c]: [2]"This is what the LORD Almighty, the God of Israel, says: You saw the great disaster I brought on Jerusalem and on all the towns of Judah. Today they lie deserted and in ruins [3]because of the evil they have done. They provoked me to anger by burning incense and by worshiping other gods that neither they nor you nor your fathers ever knew. [4]Again and again I sent my servants the prophets, who

said, 'Do not do this detestable thing that I hate!' [5]But they did not listen or pay attention; they did not turn from their wickedness or stop burning incense to other gods. [6]Therefore, my fierce anger was poured out; it raged against the towns of Judah and the streets of Jerusalem and made them the desolate ruins they are today.

[7]"Now this is what the LORD God Almighty, the God of Israel, says: Why bring such great disaster on yourselves by cutting off from Judah the men and women, the children and infants, and so leave yourselves without a remnant? [8]Why provoke me to anger with what your hands have made, burning incense

[a]13 Or in Heliopolis   [b]1 Hebrew Noph
[c]1 Hebrew in Pathros

Wednesday

Stand Your Ground

Read Jeremiah 43:1–3

Imagine a guy named Jeremy is walking down the hall at school when the fire alarm goes off. He knows that several other guys are in the bathroom smoking, so he runs in to warn them about the fire. "You need to get out of here!" Jeremy says. "This isn't a drill!"

"Yeah, right," says one of the guys, "you're just trying to get us in trouble with the principal." They refuse to leave the bathroom, no matter what Jeremy says to them.

This is kind of how the "arrogant men" in Jeremiah 43:2 responded to the prophet Jeremiah's warnings. They just wouldn't listen. But that didn't mean Jeremiah's message was false. He was right; they were wrong.

If you ever feel like no one will listen to you, even though you're telling the truth, think about Jeremiah. He got blasted every time he opened his mouth, but he kept speaking God's truth. Sometimes you just have to stand your ground.

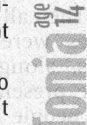

Tonia age 14

❶ Have you ever tried to tell somebody something important and that person just wouldn't listen? How did you feel?

❷ Imagine you've got a friend who doesn't believe in, say, gravity. Now, create an experiment that would demonstrate the law of gravity to your friend. Does the fact that gravity exists change just because your friend doesn't believe in it? Nope, and neither does God's truth.

❸ Ask God for the strength to keep telling his truth, even when people won't listen.

Turn to page 941 for your next devotion.

to other gods in Egypt, where you have come to live? You will destroy yourselves and make yourselves an object of cursing and reproach among all the nations on earth. ⁹Have you forgotten the wickedness committed by your fathers and by the kings and queens of Judah and the wickedness committed by you and your wives in the land of Judah and the streets of Jerusalem? ¹⁰To this day they have not humbled themselves or shown reverence, nor have they followed my law and the decrees I set before you and your fathers.

¹¹"Therefore, this is what the LORD Almighty, the God of Israel, says: I am determined to bring disaster on you and to destroy all Judah. ¹²I will take away the remnant of Judah who were determined to go to Egypt to settle there. They will all perish in Egypt; they will fall by the sword or die from famine. From the least to the greatest, they will die by sword or famine. They will become an object of cursing and horror, of condemnation and reproach. ¹³I will punish those who live in Egypt with the sword, famine and plague, as I punished Jerusalem. ¹⁴None of the remnant of Judah who have gone to live in Egypt will escape or survive to return to the land of Judah, to which they long to return and live; none will return except a few fugitives."

¹⁵Then all the men who knew that their wives were burning incense to other gods, along with all the women who were present—a large assembly—and all the people living in Lower and Upper Egypt,ᵃ said to Jeremiah, ¹⁶"We will not listen to the message you have spoken to us in the name of the LORD! ¹⁷We will certainly do everything we said we would: We will burn incense to the Queen of Heaven and will pour out drink offerings to her just as we and our fathers, our kings and our officials did in the towns of Judah and in the streets of Jerusalem. At that time we had plenty of food and were well off and suffered no harm. ¹⁸But ever since we stopped burning incense to the Queen of Heaven and pouring out drink offerings to her, we have had nothing and have been perishing by sword and famine."

¹⁹The women added, "When we burned incense to the Queen of Heaven and poured out drink offerings to her, did not our husbands know that we were making cakes like her image and pouring out drink offerings to her?"

²⁰Then Jeremiah said to all the people, both men and women, who were answering him, ²¹"Did not the LORD remember and think about the incense burned in the towns of Judah and the streets of Jerusalem by you and your fathers, your kings and your officials and the people of the land? ²²When the LORD could no longer endure your wicked actions and the detestable things you did, your land became an object of cursing and a desolate waste without inhabitants, as it is today. ²³Because you have burned incense and have sinned against the LORD and have not obeyed him or followed his law or his decrees or his stipulations, this disaster has come upon you, as you now see."

²⁴Then Jeremiah said to all the people, including the women, "Hear the word of the LORD, all you people of Judah in Egypt. ²⁵This is what the LORD Almighty, the God of Israel, says: You and your wives have shown by your actions what you promised when you said, 'We will certainly carry out the vows we made to burn incense and pour out drink offerings to the Queen of Heaven.'

"Go ahead then, do what you promised! Keep your vows! ²⁶But hear the word of the LORD, all Jews living in Egypt: 'I swear by my great name,' says the LORD, 'that no one from Judah living anywhere in Egypt will ever again invoke my name or swear, "As surely as the Sovereign LORD lives." ²⁷For I am watching over them for harm, not for good; the Jews in Egypt will perish by sword and famine until they are all destroyed. ²⁸Those who escape the sword and return to the land of Judah from Egypt will be very few. Then the whole remnant of Judah who came to live in Egypt will know whose word will stand—mine or theirs.

²⁹" 'This will be the sign to you that I will punish you in this place,' declares the LORD, 'so that you will know that my threats of harm against you will surely stand.' ³⁰This is what the LORD says: 'I am

ᵃ15 Hebrew *in Egypt and Pathros*

going to hand Pharaoh Hophra king of Egypt over to his enemies who seek his life, just as I handed Zedekiah king of Judah over to Nebuchadnezzar king of Babylon, the enemy who was seeking his life.' "

A Message to Baruch

45 This is what Jeremiah the prophet told Baruch son of Neriah in the fourth year of Jehoiakim son of Josiah king of Judah, after Baruch had written on a scroll the words Jeremiah was then dictating: ²"This is what the LORD, the God of Israel, says to you, Baruch: ³You said, 'Woe to me! The LORD has added sorrow to my pain; I am worn out with groaning and find no rest.' "

⁴The LORD said, "Say this to him: 'This is what the LORD says: I will overthrow what I have built and uproot what I have planted, throughout the land. ⁵Should you then seek great things for yourself? Seek them not. For I will bring disaster on all people, declares the LORD, but wherever you go I will let you escape with your life.' "

A Message About Egypt

46 This is the word of the LORD that came to Jeremiah the prophet concerning the nations:

²Concerning Egypt:

This is the message against the army of Pharaoh Neco king of Egypt, which was defeated at Carchemish on the Euphrates River by Nebuchadnezzar king of Babylon in the fourth year of Jehoiakim son of Josiah king of Judah:

³"Prepare your shields, both large and
  small,
  and march out for battle!
⁴Harness the horses,
  mount the steeds!
Take your positions
  with helmets on!
Polish your spears,
  put on your armor!
⁵What do I see?
  They are terrified,
they are retreating,
  their warriors are defeated.
They flee in haste

without looking back,
  and there is terror on every side,"
      declares the LORD.
⁶"The swift cannot flee
  nor the strong escape.
In the north by the River Euphrates
  they stumble and fall.

⁷"Who is this that rises like the Nile,
  like rivers of surging waters?
⁸Egypt rises like the Nile,
  like rivers of surging waters.
She says, 'I will rise and cover the
      earth;
  I will destroy cities and their
      people.'
⁹Charge, O horses!
  Drive furiously, O charioteers!
March on, O warriors—
  men of Cush[a] and Put who carry
      shields,
  men of Lydia who draw the bow.
¹⁰But that day belongs to the Lord, the
      LORD Almighty—
  a day of vengeance, for vengeance
      on his foes.
The sword will devour till it is
      satisfied,
  till it has quenched its thirst with
      blood.
For the Lord, the LORD Almighty, will
      offer sacrifice
  in the land of the north by the River
      Euphrates.

¹¹"Go up to Gilead and get balm,
  O Virgin Daughter of Egypt.
But you multiply remedies in vain;
  there is no healing for you.
¹²The nations will hear of your shame;
  your cries will fill the earth.
One warrior will stumble over
      another;
  both will fall down together."

¹³This is the message the LORD spoke to Jeremiah the prophet about the coming of Nebuchadnezzar king of Babylon to attack Egypt:

¹⁴"Announce this in Egypt, and
  proclaim it in Migdol;
  proclaim it also in Memphis[b] and
      Tahpanhes:

---

[a]9 That is, the upper Nile region   [b]14 Hebrew *Noph*;
also in verse 19

'Take your positions and get ready,
  for the sword devours those around
    you.'
¹⁵Why will your warriors be laid low?
  They cannot stand, for the LORD will
    push them down.
¹⁶They will stumble repeatedly;
  they will fall over each other.
They will say, 'Get up, let us go back
  to our own people and our native
    lands,
  away from the sword of the
    oppressor.'
¹⁷There they will exclaim,
  'Pharaoh king of Egypt is only a
    loud noise;
  he has missed his opportunity.'

¹⁸"As surely as I live," declares the King,
  whose name is the LORD Almighty,
"one will come who is like Tabor
    among the mountains,
  like Carmel by the sea.
¹⁹Pack your belongings for exile,
  you who live in Egypt,
for Memphis will be laid waste
  and lie in ruins without inhabitant.

²⁰"Egypt is a beautiful heifer,
  but a gadfly is coming
    against her from the north.
²¹The mercenaries in her ranks
  are like fattened calves.
They too will turn and flee together,
  they will not stand their ground,
for the day of disaster is coming upon
    them,
  the time for them to be punished.
²²Egypt will hiss like a fleeing serpent
  as the enemy advances in force;
they will come against her with axes,
  like men who cut down trees.
²³They will chop down her forest,"
                declares the LORD,
  "dense though it be.
They are more numerous than locusts,
  they cannot be counted.
²⁴The Daughter of Egypt will be put to
    shame,
  handed over to the people of the
    north."

²⁵The LORD Almighty, the God of Israel,
says: "I am about to bring punishment
on Amon god of Thebes,ᵃ on Pharaoh, on
Egypt and her gods and her kings, and on

those who rely on Pharaoh. ²⁶I will hand
them over to those who seek their lives,
to Nebuchadnezzar king of Babylon and
his officers. Later, however, Egypt will be
inhabited as in times past," declares the
LORD.

²⁷"Do not fear, O Jacob my servant;
  do not be dismayed, O Israel.
I will surely save you out of a distant
    place,
  your descendants from the land of
    their exile.
Jacob will again have peace and
    security,
  and no one will make him afraid.
²⁸Do not fear, O Jacob my servant,
  for I am with you," declares the
    LORD.
"Though I completely destroy all the
    nations
  among which I scatter you,
  I will not completely destroy you.
I will discipline you but only with
    justice;
  I will not let you go entirely
    unpunished."

A Message About the Philistines

47 This is the word of the LORD that
came to Jeremiah the prophet
concerning the Philistines before Pharaoh attacked Gaza:

²This is what the LORD says:

"See how the waters are rising in the
    north;
  they will become an overflowing
    torrent.
They will overflow the land and
    everything in it,
  the towns and those who live in
    them.
The people will cry out;
  all who dwell in the land will wail
³at the sound of the hoofs of galloping
    steeds,
  at the noise of enemy chariots
  and the rumble of their wheels.
Fathers will not turn to help their
    children;
  their hands will hang limp.
⁴For the day has come
  to destroy all the Philistines

ᵃ25 Hebrew No

and to cut off all survivors
who could help Tyre and Sidon.
The LORD is about to destroy the
Philistines,
the remnant from the coasts of
Caphtor.[a]
⁵Gaza will shave her head in
mourning;
Ashkelon will be silenced.
O remnant on the plain,
how long will you cut yourselves?

⁶" 'Ah, sword of the LORD,' you cry,
'how long till you rest?
Return to your scabbard;
cease and be still.'
⁷But how can it rest
when the LORD has commanded it,
when he has ordered it
to attack Ashkelon and the coast?"

A Message About Moab

48 Concerning Moab:

This is what the LORD Almighty, the
God of Israel, says:

"Woe to Nebo, for it will be ruined.
Kiriathaim will be disgraced and
captured;
the stronghold[b] will be disgraced
and shattered.
²Moab will be praised no more;
in Heshbon[c] men will plot her
downfall:
'Come, let us put an end to that
nation.'
You too, O Madmen,[d] will be
silenced;
the sword will pursue you.
³Listen to the cries from Horonaim,
cries of great havoc and
destruction.
⁴Moab will be broken;
her little ones will cry out.[e]
⁵They go up the way to Luhith,
weeping bitterly as they go;
on the road down to Horonaim
anguished cries over the destruction
are heard.
⁶Flee! Run for your lives;
become like a bush[f] in the desert.
⁷Since you trust in your deeds and
riches,
you too will be taken captive,
and Chemosh will go into exile,

together with his priests and
officials.
⁸The destroyer will come against every
town,
and not a town will escape.
The valley will be ruined
and the plateau destroyed,
because the LORD has spoken.
⁹Put salt on Moab,
for she will be laid waste[g];
her towns will become desolate,
with no one to live in them.

¹⁰"A curse on him who is lax in doing
the LORD's work!
A curse on him who keeps his
sword from bloodshed!

¹¹"Moab has been at rest from youth,
like wine left on its dregs,
not poured from one jar to another—
she has not gone into exile.
So she tastes as she did,
and her aroma is unchanged.
¹²But days are coming,"
declares the LORD,
"when I will send men who pour from
jars,
and they will pour her out;
they will empty her jars
and smash her jugs.
¹³Then Moab will be ashamed of
Chemosh,
as the house of Israel was ashamed
when they trusted in Bethel.

¹⁴"How can you say, 'We are warriors,
men valiant in battle'?
¹⁵Moab will be destroyed and her towns
invaded;
her finest young men will go down
in the slaughter,"
declares the King, whose name is
the LORD Almighty.
¹⁶"The fall of Moab is at hand;
her calamity will come quickly.
¹⁷Mourn for her, all who live around her,
all who know her fame;
say, 'How broken is the mighty
scepter,
how broken the glorious staff!'

---

a4 That is, Crete   *b1* Or / *Misgab*   *c2* The Hebrew for
Heshbon sounds like the Hebrew for *plot*.   *d2* The
name of the Moabite town Madmen sounds like the
Hebrew for *be silenced*.   *e4* Hebrew; Septuagint /
proclaim it to Zoar   *f6* Or *like Aroer*   *g9* Or *Give
wings to Moab*, / *for she will fly away*

¹⁸ "Come down from your glory
    and sit on the parched ground,
    O inhabitants of the Daughter of
      Dibon,
for he who destroys Moab
    will come up against you
    and ruin your fortified cities.
¹⁹ Stand by the road and watch,
    you who live in Aroer.
Ask the man fleeing and the woman
      escaping,
    ask them, 'What has happened?'
²⁰ Moab is disgraced, for she is
      shattered.
    Wail and cry out!
Announce by the Arnon
    that Moab is destroyed.
²¹ Judgment has come to the plateau—
    to Holon, Jahzah and Mephaath,
²²   to Dibon, Nebo and Beth
      Diblathaim,
²³   to Kiriathaim, Beth Gamul and Beth
      Meon,
²⁴   to Kerioth and Bozrah—
    to all the towns of Moab, far and
      near.
²⁵ Moab's horn*ᵃ* is cut off;
    her arm is broken,"
                declares the LORD.

²⁶ "Make her drunk,
    for she has defied the LORD.
Let Moab wallow in her vomit;
    let her be an object of ridicule.
²⁷ Was not Israel the object of your
      ridicule?
    Was she caught among thieves,
that you shake your head in scorn
    whenever you speak of her?
²⁸ Abandon your towns and dwell
      among the rocks,
    you who live in Moab.
Be like a dove that makes its nest
    at the mouth of a cave.

²⁹ "We have heard of Moab's pride—
    her overweening pride and conceit,
her pride and arrogance
    and the haughtiness of her heart.
³⁰ I know her insolence but it is futile,"
           declares the LORD,
    "and her boasts accomplish nothing.
³¹ Therefore I wail over Moab,
    for all Moab I cry out,
    I moan for the men of Kir Hareseth.
³² I weep for you, as Jazer weeps,

    O vines of Sibmah.
Your branches spread as far as the sea;
    they reached as far as the sea of
      Jazer.
The destroyer has fallen
    on your ripened fruit and grapes.
³³ Joy and gladness are gone
    from the orchards and fields of
      Moab.
I have stopped the flow of wine from
    the presses;
    no one treads them with shouts of
      joy.
Although there are shouts,
    they are not shouts of joy.

³⁴ "The sound of their cry rises
    from Heshbon to Elealeh and Jahaz,
from Zoar as far as Horonaim and
      Eglath Shelishiyah,
for even the waters of Nimrim are
      dried up.
³⁵ In Moab I will put an end
    to those who make offerings on the
      high places
    and burn incense to their gods,"
              declares the LORD.
³⁶ "So my heart laments for Moab like a
      flute;
    it laments like a flute for the men of
      Kir Hareseth.
The wealth they acquired is gone.
³⁷ Every head is shaved
    and every beard cut off;
every hand is slashed
    and every waist is covered with
      sackcloth.
³⁸ On all the roofs in Moab
    and in the public squares
there is nothing but mourning,
    for I have broken Moab
    like a jar that no one wants,"
              declares the LORD.
³⁹ "How shattered she is! How they wail!
    How Moab turns her back in shame!
Moab has become an object of
      ridicule,
    an object of horror to all those
      around her."

⁴⁰ This is what the LORD says:

"Look! An eagle is swooping down,
    spreading its wings over Moab.

ᵃ25 *Horn* here symbolizes strength.

⁴¹Kerioth*ᵃ* will be captured
  and the strongholds taken.
In that day the hearts of Moab's
    warriors
  will be like the heart of a woman in
    labor.
⁴²Moab will be destroyed as a nation
  because she defied the LORD.
⁴³Terror and pit and snare await you,
  O people of Moab,"
                    declares the LORD.
⁴⁴"Whoever flees from the terror
  will fall into a pit,
whoever climbs out of the pit
  will be caught in a snare;
for I will bring upon Moab
  the year of her punishment,"
                    declares the LORD.

⁴⁵"In the shadow of Heshbon
  the fugitives stand helpless,
for a fire has gone out from Heshbon,
  a blaze from the midst of Sihon;
it burns the foreheads of Moab,
  the skulls of the noisy boasters.
⁴⁶Woe to you, O Moab!
  The people of Chemosh are
    destroyed;
your sons are taken into exile
  and your daughters into captivity.

⁴⁷"Yet I will restore the fortunes of Moab
  in days to come,"
                    declares the LORD.

Here ends the judgment on Moab.

A Message About Ammon

49 Concerning the Ammonites:

This is what the LORD says:

"Has Israel no sons?
  Has she no heirs?
Why then has Molech*ᵇ* taken
    possession of Gad?
  Why do his people live in its towns?
²But the days are coming,"
    declares the LORD,
"when I will sound the battle cry
  against Rabbah of the Ammonites;
it will become a mound of ruins,
  and its surrounding villages will be
    set on fire.
Then Israel will drive out
  those who drove her out,"
                    says the LORD.

³"Wail, O Heshbon, for Ai is destroyed!
  Cry out, O inhabitants of Rabbah!
Put on sackcloth and mourn;
  rush here and there inside the
    walls,
for Molech will go into exile,
  together with his priests and
    officials.
⁴Why do you boast of your valleys,
  boast of your valleys so fruitful?
O unfaithful daughter,
  you trust in your riches and say,
  'Who will attack me?'
⁵I will bring terror on you
  from all those around you,"
                    declares the Lord,
                    the LORD Almighty.
"Every one of you will be driven away,
  and no one will gather the fugitives.

⁶"Yet afterward, I will restore the
    fortunes of the Ammonites,"
                    declares the LORD.

A Message About Edom

⁷Concerning Edom:

This is what the LORD Almighty says:

"Is there no longer wisdom in Teman?
  Has counsel perished from the
    prudent?
  Has their wisdom decayed?
⁸Turn and flee, hide in deep caves,
  you who live in Dedan,
for I will bring disaster on Esau
  at the time I punish him.
⁹If grape pickers came to you,
  would they not leave a few grapes?
If thieves came during the night,
  would they not steal only as much
    as they wanted?
¹⁰But I will strip Esau bare;
  I will uncover his hiding places,
  so that he cannot conceal himself.
His children, relatives and neighbors
    will perish,
  and he will be no more.
¹¹Leave your orphans; I will protect
    their lives.
  Your widows too can trust in me."

¹²This is what the LORD says: "If those
who do not deserve to drink the cup must

ᵃ41 Or *The cities*   *ᵇ1* Or *their king*; Hebrew *malcam*;
also in verse 3

drink it, why should you go unpunished? You will not go unpunished, but must drink it. ¹³I swear by myself," declares the LORD, "that Bozrah will become a ruin and an object of horror, of reproach and of cursing; and all its towns will be in ruins forever."

¹⁴I have heard a message from the LORD:
    An envoy was sent to the nations to say,
  "Assemble yourselves to attack it!
    Rise up for battle!"

¹⁵"Now I will make you small among the nations,
    despised among men.
¹⁶The terror you inspire
    and the pride of your heart have deceived you,
you who live in the clefts of the rocks,
    who occupy the heights of the hill.
Though you build your nest as high as the eagle's,
    from there I will bring you down,"
                declares the LORD.
¹⁷"Edom will become an object of horror;
    all who pass by will be appalled
    and will scoff because of all its wounds.
¹⁸As Sodom and Gomorrah were overthrown,
    along with their neighboring towns,"
                says the LORD,
"so no one will live there;
    no man will dwell in it.

¹⁹"Like a lion coming up from Jordan's thickets
    to a rich pastureland,
I will chase Edom from its land in an instant.
    Who is the chosen one I will appoint for this?
Who is like me and who can challenge me?
    And what shepherd can stand against me?"
²⁰Therefore, hear what the LORD has planned against Edom,
    what he has purposed against those who live in Teman:
The young of the flock will be dragged away;

    he will completely destroy their pasture because of them.
²¹At the sound of their fall the earth will tremble;
    their cry will resound to the Red Sea.ᵃ
²²Look! An eagle will soar and swoop down,
    spreading its wings over Bozrah.
In that day the hearts of Edom's warriors
    will be like the heart of a woman in labor.

A Message About Damascus

²³Concerning Damascus:

"Hamath and Arpad are dismayed,
    for they have heard bad news.
They are disheartened,
    troubled likeᵇ the restless sea.
²⁴Damascus has become feeble,
    she has turned to flee
    and panic has gripped her;
anguish and pain have seized her,
    pain like that of a woman in labor.
²⁵Why has the city of renown not been abandoned,
    the town in which I delight?
²⁶Surely, her young men will fall in the streets;
    all her soldiers will be silenced in that day,"
          declares the LORD Almighty.
²⁷"I will set fire to the walls of Damascus;
    it will consume the fortresses of Ben-Hadad."

A Message About Kedar and Hazor

²⁸Concerning Kedar and the kingdoms of Hazor, which Nebuchadnezzar king of Babylon attacked:

This is what the LORD says:

"Arise, and attack Kedar
    and destroy the people of the East.
²⁹Their tents and their flocks will be taken;
    their shelters will be carried off
    with all their goods and camels.
Men will shout to them,
    'Terror on every side!'

ᵃ21 Hebrew *Yam Suph*; that is, Sea of Reeds
ᵇ23 Hebrew *on* or *by*

30 "Flee quickly away!
    Stay in deep caves, you who live in
        Hazor,"
                            declares the LORD.
    "Nebuchadnezzar king of Babylon has
        plotted against you;
    he has devised a plan against you.

31 "Arise and attack a nation at ease,
    which lives in confidence,"
                            declares the LORD,
    "a nation that has neither gates nor
        bars;
    its people live alone.
32 Their camels will become plunder,
    and their large herds will be booty.
I will scatter to the winds those who
    are in distant places[a]
    and will bring disaster on them
        from every side,"
                            declares the LORD.
33 "Hazor will become a haunt of jackals,
    a desolate place forever.
No one will live there;
    no man will dwell in it."

A Message About Elam

34 This is the word of the LORD that
came to Jeremiah the prophet concerning Elam, early in the reign of Zedekiah
king of Judah:

35 This is what the LORD Almighty says:

    "See, I will break the bow of Elam,
        the mainstay of their might.
36 I will bring against Elam the four
        winds
    from the four quarters of the
        heavens;
I will scatter them to the four winds,
    and there will not be a nation
    where Elam's exiles do not go.
37 I will shatter Elam before their foes,
    before those who seek their lives;
I will bring disaster upon them,
    even my fierce anger,"
                            declares the LORD.
    "I will pursue them with the sword
        until I have made an end of them.
38 I will set my throne in Elam
    and destroy her king and officials,"
                            declares the LORD.

39 "Yet I will restore the fortunes of Elam
    in days to come,"
                            declares the LORD.

A Message About Babylon

50 This is the word the LORD spoke
through Jeremiah the prophet
concerning Babylon and the land of the
Babylonians[b]:

2 "Announce and proclaim among the
        nations,
    lift up a banner and proclaim it;
    keep nothing back, but say,
    'Babylon will be captured;
        Bel will be put to shame,
        Marduk filled with terror.
    Her images will be put to shame
        and her idols filled with terror.'
3 A nation from the north will attack
        her
    and lay waste her land.
No one will live in it;
    both men and animals will flee
        away.

North of North

Huh?

Jeremiah 50:3
Jeremiah talked plenty about the invading
army of the North. Up until now, that has
meant Babylon. But now Jeremiah is talking
about another nation of the North that will
beat up the Babylonians. He means Persia,
whose army attacked Babylon in 539 B.C.

4 "In those days, at that time,"
    declares the LORD,
    "the people of Israel and the people of
        Judah together
    will go in tears to seek the LORD
        their God.
5 They will ask the way to Zion
    and turn their faces toward it.
They will come and bind themselves
    to the LORD
    in an everlasting covenant
    that will not be forgotten.

6 "My people have been lost sheep;
    their shepherds have led them astray

a32 Or *who clip the hair by their foreheads*   b1 Or
Chaldeans; also in verses 8, 25, 35 and 45

and caused them to roam on the
   mountains.
They wandered over mountain and
   hill
   and forgot their own resting place.
⁷Whoever found them devoured them;
   their enemies said, 'We are not
      guilty,
for they sinned against the LORD, their
      true pasture,
   the LORD, the hope of their fathers.'

⁸"Flee out of Babylon;
   leave the land of the Babylonians,
   and be like the goats that lead the
      flock.
⁹For I will stir up and bring against
      Babylon
   an alliance of great nations from
      the land of the north.
They will take up their positions
      against her,
   and from the north she will be
      captured.
Their arrows will be like skilled
      warriors
   who do not return empty-handed.
¹⁰So Babylonia*ᵃ* will be plundered;
   all who plunder her will have their
      fill,"
               declares the LORD.

¹¹"Because you rejoice and are glad,
   you who pillage my inheritance,
because you frolic like a heifer
      threshing grain
   and neigh like stallions,
¹²your mother will be greatly ashamed;
   she who gave you birth will be
      disgraced.
She will be the least of the nations—
   a wilderness, a dry land, a desert.
¹³Because of the LORD's anger she will
      not be inhabited
   but will be completely desolate.
All who pass Babylon will be horrified
      and scoff
   because of all her wounds.

¹⁴"Take up your positions around
      Babylon,
   all you who draw the bow.
Shoot at her! Spare no arrows,
   for she has sinned against the LORD.
¹⁵Shout against her on every side!
   She surrenders, her towers fall,

her walls are torn down.
Since this is the vengeance of the
   LORD,
   take vengeance on her;
   do to her as she has done to others.
¹⁶Cut off from Babylon the sower,
   and the reaper with his sickle at
      harvest.
Because of the sword of the oppressor
   let everyone return to his own
      people,
   let everyone flee to his own land.

¹⁷"Israel is a scattered flock
   that lions have chased away.
The first to devour him
   was the king of Assyria;
the last to crush his bones
   was Nebuchadnezzar king of
      Babylon."

¹⁸Therefore this is what the LORD Almighty, the God of Israel, says:

"I will punish the king of Babylon and
      his land
   as I punished the king of Assyria.
¹⁹But I will bring Israel back to his own
      pasture
   and he will graze on Carmel and
      Bashan;
his appetite will be satisfied
   on the hills of Ephraim and Gilead.
²⁰In those days, at that time,"
   declares the LORD,
"search will be made for Israel's guilt,
   but there will be none,
and for the sins of Judah,
   but none will be found,
   for I will forgive the remnant I
      spare.

²¹"Attack the land of Merathaim
   and those who live in Pekod.
Pursue, kill and completely destroy*ᵇ*
      them,"
               declares the LORD.
"Do everything I have commanded
      you.
²²The noise of battle is in the land,
   the noise of great destruction!
²³How broken and shattered

ᵃ10 Or *Chaldea*   *ᵇ21* The Hebrew term refers to the
irrevocable giving over of things or persons to the
LORD, often by totally destroying them; also in
verse 26.

is the hammer of the whole earth!
How desolate is Babylon
 among the nations!
²⁴I set a trap for you, O Babylon,
 and you were caught before you
  knew it;
you were found and captured
 because you opposed the LORD.
²⁵The LORD has opened his arsenal
 and brought out the weapons of his
  wrath,
for the Sovereign LORD Almighty has
  work to do
 in the land of the Babylonians.
²⁶Come against her from afar.
 Break open her granaries;
 pile her up like heaps of grain.
Completely destroy her
 and leave her no remnant.

²⁷Kill all her young bulls;
 let them go down to the slaughter!
Woe to them! For their day has come,
 the time for them to be punished.
²⁸Listen to the fugitives and refugees
  from Babylon
declaring in Zion
how the LORD our God has taken
  vengeance,
 vengeance for his temple.

²⁹"Summon archers against Babylon,
 all those who draw the bow.
Encamp all around her;
 let no one escape.
Repay her for her deeds;
 do to her as she has done.
For she has defied the LORD,
 the Holy One of Israel.

Thursday

Forgive and Forget

Read Jeremiah 50:20

I used to feel really lonely and selfish when I sinned. I thought God would never forgive me. I especially felt that way when I committed the same sin more than once. I thought God would get tired of me doing the same wrong things all the time and would eventually stop forgiving me.

Wrong! When you read about all the bad stuff the people of Israel did and all the times they turned away from God or disobeyed him, you think, *Someday God is going to get these guys for good.* But this verse says just the opposite. It says one day God's going to search for Israel's guilt and not find a thing. After everything they did wrong, God will look at them as sinless.

Sin is a huge deal. But God's forgiveness and mercy are bigger than sin. That was true for Israel, and it's true for me too. Because I have Jesus in my heart, my sins are gone. I just need to confess my sins and ask God to forgive me. And one day, when I see God face to face, I believe he'll say to me what he said to Israel: "I searched for your sin and there is none."

Shawn, age 12

What about You?

❶ Do you feel forgiven? Why is it so hard for us to believe that God really forgives us?

❷ Find the dirtiest piece of clothing in your laundry basket. Put a safety pin on it. After it's been through the washer and dryer, check it out and notice how much cleaner it is.

❸ Write 1 John 1:9—"If we confess our sins, he is faithful and just and will forgive us our sins and purify us from all unrighteousness"—on a couple of sticky notes and place them where you can see them every day.

Turn to page 953 for your next devotion.

[30] Therefore, her young men will fall in
the streets;
all her soldiers will be silenced in
that day,"
declares the LORD.
[31] "See, I am against you, O arrogant
one,"
declares the Lord, the LORD
Almighty,
"for your day has come,
the time for you to be punished.
[32] The arrogant one will stumble and fall
and no one will help her up;
I will kindle a fire in her towns
that will consume all who are
around her."

[33] This is what the LORD Almighty says:

"The people of Israel are oppressed,
and the people of Judah as well.
All their captors hold them fast,
refusing to let them go.
[34] Yet their Redeemer is strong;
the LORD Almighty is his name.
He will vigorously defend their cause
so that he may bring rest to their
land,
but unrest to those who live in
Babylon.

[35] "A sword against the Babylonians!"
declares the LORD—
"against those who live in Babylon
and against her officials and wise
men!
[36] A sword against her false prophets!
They will become fools.
A sword against her warriors!
They will be filled with terror.
[37] A sword against her horses and
chariots
and all the foreigners in her ranks!
They will become women.
A sword against her treasures!
They will be plundered.
[38] A drought on[a] her waters!
They will dry up.
For it is a land of idols,
idols that will go mad with terror.

[39] "So desert creatures and hyenas will
live there,
and there the owl will dwell.
It will never again be inhabited
or lived in from generation to
generation.

[40] As God overthrew Sodom and
Gomorrah
along with their neighboring
towns,"
declares the LORD,
"so no one will live there;
no man will dwell in it.

[41] "Look! An army is coming from the
north;
a great nation and many kings
are being stirred up from the ends
of the earth.
[42] They are armed with bows and spears;
they are cruel and without mercy.
They sound like the roaring sea
as they ride on their horses;
they come like men in battle
formation
to attack you, O Daughter of
Babylon.
[43] The king of Babylon has heard reports
about them,
and his hands hang limp.
Anguish has gripped him,
pain like that of a woman in labor.
[44] Like a lion coming up from Jordan's
thickets
to a rich pastureland,
I will chase Babylon from its land in
an instant.
Who is the chosen one I will
appoint for this?
Who is like me and who can challenge
me?
And what shepherd can stand
against me?"
[45] Therefore, hear what the LORD has
planned against Babylon,
what he has purposed against the
land of the Babylonians:
The young of the flock will be
dragged away;
he will completely destroy their
pasture because of them.
[46] At the sound of Babylon's capture the
earth will tremble;
its cry will resound among the
nations.

51

This is what the LORD says:

"See, I will stir up the spirit of a
destroyer

[a] 38 Or A sword against

against Babylon and the people of
Leb Kamai.[a]
[2] I will send foreigners to Babylon
    to winnow her and to devastate her
        land;
they will oppose her on every side
    in the day of her disaster.
[3] Let not the archer string his bow,
    nor let him put on his armor.
Do not spare her young men;
    completely destroy[b] her army.
[4] They will fall down slain in Babylon,[c]
    fatally wounded in her streets.
[5] For Israel and Judah have not been
        forsaken
    by their God, the LORD Almighty,
though their land[d] is full of guilt
    before the Holy One of Israel.

[6] "Flee from Babylon!
    Run for your lives!
    Do not be destroyed because of her
        sins.
It is time for the LORD's vengeance;
    he will pay her what she deserves.
[7] Babylon was a gold cup in the LORD's
        hand;
    she made the whole earth drunk.
The nations drank her wine;
    therefore they have now gone mad.
[8] Babylon will suddenly fall and be
        broken.
    Wail over her!
Get balm for her pain;
    perhaps she can be healed.

[9] " 'We would have healed Babylon,
    but she cannot be healed;
let us leave her and each go to his
        own land,
    for her judgment reaches to the skies,
    it rises as high as the clouds.'

[10] " 'The LORD has vindicated us;
    come, let us tell in Zion
    what the LORD our God has done.'

[11] "Sharpen the arrows,
    take up the shields!
The LORD has stirred up the kings of
        the Medes,
    because his purpose is to destroy
        Babylon.
The LORD will take vengeance,
    vengeance for his temple.
[12] Lift up a banner against the walls of
        Babylon!

Reinforce the guard,
station the watchmen,
    prepare an ambush!
The LORD will carry out his purpose,
    his decree against the people of
        Babylon.
[13] You who live by many waters
    and are rich in treasures,
your end has come,
    the time for you to be cut off.
[14] The LORD Almighty has sworn by
        himself:
    I will surely fill you with men, as
        with a swarm of locusts,
    and they will shout in triumph over
        you.

[15] "He made the earth by his power;
    he founded the world by his
        wisdom
    and stretched out the heavens by
        his understanding.
[16] When he thunders, the waters in the
        heavens roar;
    he makes clouds rise from the ends
        of the earth.
He sends lightning with the rain
    and brings out the wind from his
        storehouses.

[17] "Every man is senseless and without
        knowledge;
    every goldsmith is shamed by his
        idols.
His images are a fraud;
    they have no breath in them.
[18] They are worthless, the objects of
        mockery;
    when their judgment comes, they
        will perish.
[19] He who is the Portion of Jacob is not
        like these,
    for he is the Maker of all things,
including the tribe of his inheritance—
    the LORD Almighty is his name.

[20] "You are my war club,
    my weapon for battle—
with you I shatter nations,
    with you I destroy kingdoms,
[21] with you I shatter horse and rider,

---

[a] 1 Leb Kamai is a cryptogram for Chaldea, that is,
Babylonia.   [b] 3 The Hebrew term refers to the
irrevocable giving over of things or persons to
the LORD, often by totally destroying them.
[c] 4 Or Chaldea   [d] 5 Or / and the land of the
Babylonians

with you I shatter chariot and
driver,
²²with you I shatter man and woman,
with you I shatter old man and
youth,
with you I shatter young man and
maiden,
²³with you I shatter shepherd and flock,
with you I shatter farmer and oxen,
with you I shatter governors and
officials.

²⁴"Before your eyes I will repay Babylon and all who live in Babylonia[a] for all the wrong they have done in Zion," declares the LORD.

²⁵"I am against you, O destroying
mountain,
you who destroy the whole earth,"
declares the LORD.
"I will stretch out my hand against
you,
roll you off the cliffs,
and make you a burned-out
mountain.
²⁶No rock will be taken from you for a
cornerstone,
nor any stone for a foundation,
for you will be desolate forever,"
declares the LORD.

²⁷"Lift up a banner in the land!
Blow the trumpet among the
nations!
Prepare the nations for battle against
her;
summon against her these
kingdoms:
Ararat, Minni and Ashkenaz.
Appoint a commander against her;
send up horses like a swarm of
locusts.
²⁸Prepare the nations for battle against
her—
the kings of the Medes,
their governors and all their officials,
and all the countries they rule.
²⁹The land trembles and writhes,
for the LORD's purposes against
Babylon stand—
to lay waste the land of Babylon
so that no one will live there.
³⁰Babylon's warriors have stopped
fighting;
they remain in their strongholds.

Their strength is exhausted;
they have become like women.
Her dwellings are set on fire;
the bars of her gates are broken.
³¹One courier follows another
and messenger follows messenger
to announce to the king of Babylon
that his entire city is captured,
³²the river crossings seized,
the marshes set on fire,
and the soldiers terrified."

³³This is what the LORD Almighty, the God of Israel, says:

"The Daughter of Babylon is like a
threshing floor
at the time it is trampled;
the time to harvest her will soon
come."

³⁴"Nebuchadnezzar king of Babylon has
devoured us,
he has thrown us into confusion,
he has made us an empty jar.
Like a serpent he has swallowed us
and filled his stomach with our
delicacies,
and then has spewed us out.
³⁵May the violence done to our flesh[b] be
upon Babylon,"
say the inhabitants of Zion.
"May our blood be on those who live
in Babylonia,"
says Jerusalem.

³⁶Therefore, this is what the LORD says:

"See, I will defend your cause
and avenge you;
I will dry up her sea
and make her springs dry.
³⁷Babylon will be a heap of ruins,
a haunt of jackals,
an object of horror and scorn,
a place where no one lives.
³⁸Her people all roar like young lions,
they growl like lion cubs.
³⁹But while they are aroused,
I will set out a feast for them
and make them drunk,
so that they shout with laughter—
then sleep forever and not awake,"
declares the LORD.

---

a24 Or *Chaldea*; also in verse 35
b35 Or *done to us and to our children*

⁴⁰"I will bring them down
  like lambs to the slaughter,
  like rams and goats.

⁴¹"How Sheshach*ᵃ* will be captured,
  the boast of the whole earth
    seized!
  What a horror Babylon will be
    among the nations!
⁴²The sea will rise over Babylon;
  its roaring waves will cover her.
⁴³Her towns will be desolate,
  a dry and desert land,
  a land where no one lives,
    through which no man travels.
⁴⁴I will punish Bel in Babylon
  and make him spew out what he
    has swallowed.
  The nations will no longer stream to
    him.
  And the wall of Babylon will fall.

⁴⁵"Come out of her, my people!
  Run for your lives!
  Run from the fierce anger of the
    LORD.
⁴⁶Do not lose heart or be afraid
  when rumors are heard in the land;
  one rumor comes this year, another
    the next,
  rumors of violence in the land
  and of ruler against ruler.
⁴⁷For the time will surely come
  when I will punish the idols of
    Babylon;
  her whole land will be disgraced
  and her slain will all lie fallen
    within her.
⁴⁸Then heaven and earth and all that is
    in them
  will shout for joy over Babylon,
  for out of the north
  destroyers will attack her,"
                declares the LORD.

⁴⁹"Babylon must fall because of Israel's
    slain,
  just as the slain in all the earth
  have fallen because of Babylon.
⁵⁰You who have escaped the sword,
  leave and do not linger!
  Remember the LORD in a distant land,
  and think on Jerusalem."

⁵¹"We are disgraced,
  for we have been insulted
  and shame covers our faces,

because foreigners have entered
  the holy places of the LORD's
    house."

⁵²"But days are coming," declares the
    LORD,
  "when I will punish her idols,
  and throughout her land
  the wounded will groan.
⁵³Even if Babylon reaches the sky
  and fortifies her lofty stronghold,
  I will send destroyers against her,"
                declares the LORD.

⁵⁴"The sound of a cry comes from
    Babylon,
  the sound of great destruction
  from the land of the Babylonians.*ᵇ*
⁵⁵The LORD will destroy Babylon;
  he will silence her noisy din.
  Waves of enemies will rage like great
    waters;
  the roar of their voices will resound.
⁵⁶A destroyer will come against
    Babylon;
  her warriors will be captured,
  and their bows will be broken.
  For the LORD is a God of retribution;
  he will repay in full.
⁵⁷I will make her officials and wise men
    drunk,
  her governors, officers and warriors
    as well;
  they will sleep forever and not awake,"
  declares the King, whose name is
    the LORD Almighty.

⁵⁸This is what the LORD Almighty says:

"Babylon's thick wall will be leveled
  and her high gates set on fire;
the peoples exhaust themselves for
    nothing,
  the nations' labor is only fuel for
    the flames."

⁵⁹This is the message Jeremiah gave to
the staff officer Seraiah son of Neriah,
the son of Mahseiah, when he went to
Babylon with Zedekiah king of Judah in
the fourth year of his reign. ⁶⁰Jeremiah
had written on a scroll about all the disasters that would come upon Babylon—
all that had been recorded concerning
Babylon. ⁶¹He said to Seraiah, "When

ᵃ41 Sheshach is a cryptogram for Babylon.
ᵇ54 Or Chaldeans

you get to Babylon, see that you read all these words aloud. [62]Then say, 'O LORD, you have said you will destroy this place, so that neither man nor animal will live in it; it will be desolate forever.' [63]When you finish reading this scroll, tie a stone to it and throw it into the Euphrates. [64]Then say, 'So will Babylon sink to rise no more because of the disaster I will bring upon her. And her people will fall.'"

The words of Jeremiah end here.

The Fall of Jerusalem

52 Zedekiah was twenty-one years old when he became king, and he reigned in Jerusalem eleven years. His mother's name was Hamutal daughter of Jeremiah; she was from Libnah. [2]He did evil in the eyes of the LORD, just as Jehoiakim had done. [3]It was because of the LORD's anger that all this happened to Jerusalem and Judah, and in the end he thrust them from his presence.

Now Zedekiah rebelled against the king of Babylon.

[4]So in the ninth year of Zedekiah's reign, on the tenth day of the tenth month, Nebuchadnezzar king of Babylon marched against Jerusalem with his whole army. They camped outside the city and built siege works all around it. [5]The city was kept under siege until the eleventh year of King Zedekiah.

[6]By the ninth day of the fourth month the famine in the city had become so severe that there was no food for the people to eat. [7]Then the city wall was broken through, and the whole army fled. They left the city at night through the gate between the two walls near the king's garden, though the Babylonians[a] were surrounding the city. They fled toward the Arabah,[b] [8]but the Babylonian[c] army pursued King Zedekiah and overtook him in the plains of Jericho. All his soldiers were separated from him and scattered, [9]and he was captured.

He was taken to the king of Babylon at Riblah in the land of Hamath, where he pronounced sentence on him. [10]There at Riblah the king of Babylon slaughtered the sons of Zedekiah before his eyes; he also killed all the officials of Judah.

[11]Then he put out Zedekiah's eyes, bound him with bronze shackles and took him to Babylon, where he put him in prison till the day of his death.

[12]On the tenth day of the fifth month, in the nineteenth year of Nebuchadnezzar king of Babylon, Nebuzaradan commander of the imperial guard, who served the king of Babylon, came to Jerusalem. [13]He set fire to the temple of the LORD, the royal palace and all the houses of Jerusalem. Every important building he burned down. [14]The whole Babylonian army under the commander of the imperial guard broke down all the walls around Jerusalem. [15]Nebuzaradan the commander of the guard carried into exile some of the poorest people and those who remained in the city, along with the rest of the craftsmen[d] and those who had gone over to the king of Babylon. [16]But Nebuzaradan left behind the rest of the poorest people of the land to work the vineyards and fields.

[17]The Babylonians broke up the bronze pillars, the movable stands and the bronze Sea that were at the temple of the LORD and they carried all the bronze to Babylon. [18]They also took away the pots, shovels, wick trimmers, sprinkling bowls, dishes and all the bronze articles used in the temple service. [19]The commander of the imperial guard took away the basins, censers, sprinkling bowls, pots, lampstands, dishes and bowls used for drink offerings—all that were made of pure gold or silver.

[20]The bronze from the two pillars, the Sea and the twelve bronze bulls under it, and the movable stands, which King Solomon had made for the temple of the LORD, was more than could be weighed. [21]Each of the pillars was eighteen cubits high and twelve cubits in circumference[e]; each was four fingers thick, and hollow. [22]The bronze capital on top of the one pillar was five cubits[f] high and was decorated with a network and pomegranates of bronze all around. The other

pillar, with its pomegranates, was similar. ²³There were ninety-six pomegranates on the sides; the total number of pomegranates above the surrounding network was a hundred.

²⁴The commander of the guard took as prisoners Seraiah the chief priest, Zephaniah the priest next in rank and the three doorkeepers. ²⁵Of those still in the city, he took the officer in charge of the fighting men, and seven royal advisers. He also took the secretary who was chief officer in charge of conscripting the people of the land and sixty of his men who were found in the city. ²⁶Nebuzaradan the commander took them all and brought them to the king of Babylon at Riblah. ²⁷There at Riblah, in the land of Hamath, the king had them executed.

So Judah went into captivity, away from her land. ²⁸This is the number of the people Nebuchadnezzar carried into exile:

in the seventh year, 3,023 Jews;

²⁹in Nebuchadnezzar's eighteenth year,

832 people from Jerusalem;

³⁰in his twenty-third year,

745 Jews taken into exile by Nebuzaradan the commander of the imperial guard.

There were 4,600 people in all.

Jehoiachin Released

³¹In the thirty-seventh year of the exile of Jehoiachin king of Judah, in the year Evil-Merodach^a became king of Babylon, he released Jehoiachin king of Judah and freed him from prison on the twenty-fifth day of the twelfth month. ³²He spoke kindly to him and gave him a seat of honor higher than those of the other kings who were with him in Babylon. ³³So Jehoiachin put aside his prison clothes and for the rest of his life ate regularly at the king's table. ³⁴Day by day the king of Babylon gave Jehoiachin a regular allowance as long as he lived, till the day of his death.

---

a31 Also called *Amel-Marduk*

Lamentations

START

Except for a few German submarines surfacing at night off the New Jersey coastline during World War II, no foreign enemy has touched the shores of the United States since the War of 1812, when the British—still ticked about losing their American colonies—invaded this country and burned the U.S. capital.

Such a doomsday picture hardly seems possible today. Americans can't really imagine waking up, dressing, eating a bowl of Cap'n Crunch and walking out the door to school—only to see enemy tanks in the streets and enemy troops stationed in front of every house. (Unless you're at the movies!)

Jeremiah the prophet-preacher saw worse: He somehow lived through the bloodiest street-fighting in the history of Jerusalem up to that time. Then, although the Babylonians dragged away all the Jewish survivors except the old and the poor, Jer was permitted to stay. So there weren't many Jews left to hear Jer sing the blues.

In fact, Lamentations is the bluesiest, saddest book in the Bible. The book is actually 5 funeral poems—a.k.a. dirges—so get ready for lots of sadness, weeping and tears.

Cast OF Characters

Jeremiah
(jer-uh-MY-yuh)
Although the writer of this book never reveals who he is, most scholars agree that the writer was probably Jeremiah. And there's a big clue in 2 Chronicles 35:25, that ol' Jer was known for his cry-fests.

Jerusalem
(jeh-ROO-suh-lum)
(also known as Zion)

Yeah, well, this is a city, but it's still a character: Jerusalem has always been like a sweetheart to Jews. Maybe that's why this city has always been called a "she" (check out 1:17: "Zion stretches out her hands, but there is no one to comfort her" or chapter 2:1: "How the Lord has covered the Daughter of Zion with the cloud of his anger!").

What's UP with That?

Do you know what an acrostic is?
You know, like in a Mother's Day card—

M is for the meals you cook for me
O is for outstanding love I always see
M is for the money you loan to me—

Put them all together, and they spell MOM!

Well, each chapter in Lamentations (except the last chapter) is an acrostic poem—in Hebrew, anyway, which is the language these poems were written in. If Jer had written these blues in English, the first few verses of Lamentations might read like this:

Absolutely deserted lies the city,
    once so full of people!
Bitterly she weeps at night,
    tears are upon her cheeks.
Cruel affliction and harsh labor first,
    then exile . . .
Deserted are all roads to Zion,
    for no one comes to her anymore.

PRETTY COOL, HUH?

Snap shots

Jer talks about pretty much the same things in all 5 chapters of this Bible book. He recalls:

- The Babylonian siege
- The famine and starvation
- The eventual Babylonian break-in through the city walls
- The burning of the city and the temple
- The massacre of the Jewish defenders

1 [a] How deserted lies the city,
　　once so full of people!
How like a widow is she,
　　who once was great among the
　　　　nations!
She who was queen among the
　　provinces
　　has now become a slave.

[2] Bitterly she weeps at night,
　　tears are upon her cheeks.
Among all her lovers
　　there is none to comfort her.
All her friends have betrayed her;
　　they have become her enemies.

[3] After affliction and harsh labor,
　　Judah has gone into exile.
She dwells among the nations;
　　she finds no resting place.
All who pursue her have overtaken her
　　in the midst of her distress.

[4] The roads to Zion mourn,
　　for no one comes to her appointed
　　　　feasts.
All her gateways are desolate,
　　her priests groan,
her maidens grieve,
　　and she is in bitter anguish.

[5] Her foes have become her masters;
　　her enemies are at ease.
The LORD has brought her grief
　　because of her many sins.
Her children have gone into exile,
　　captive before the foe.

[6] All the splendor has departed
　　from the Daughter of Zion.
Her princes are like deer
　　that find no pasture;
in weakness they have fled
　　before the pursuer.

[7] In the days of her affliction and
　　　　wandering
　　Jerusalem remembers all the
　　　　treasures
　　that were hers in days of old.
When her people fell into enemy
　　　　hands,
　　there was no one to help her.
Her enemies looked at her
　　and laughed at her destruction.

[8] Jerusalem has sinned greatly
　　and so has become unclean.

All who honored her despise her,
　　for they have seen her nakedness;
she herself groans
　　and turns away.

[9] Her filthiness clung to her skirts;
　　she did not consider her future.
Her fall was astounding;
　　there was none to comfort her.
"Look, O LORD, on my affliction,
　　for the enemy has triumphed."

[10] The enemy laid hands
　　on all her treasures;
she saw pagan nations
　　enter her sanctuary—
those you had forbidden
　　to enter your assembly.

[11] All her people groan
　　as they search for bread;
they barter their treasures for food
　　to keep themselves alive.
"Look, O LORD, and consider,
　　for I am despised."

[12] "Is it nothing to you, all you who pass
　　　　by?
Look around and see.
Is any suffering like my suffering
　　that was inflicted on me,
that the LORD brought on me
　　in the day of his fierce anger?

[13] "From on high he sent fire,
　　sent it down into my bones.
He spread a net for my feet
　　and turned me back.
He made me desolate,
　　faint all the day long.

[14] "My sins have been bound into a
　　　　yoke [b];
　　by his hands they were woven
　　　　together.
They have come upon my neck
　　and the Lord has sapped my
　　　　strength.
He has handed me over
　　to those I cannot withstand.

[15] "The Lord has rejected
　　all the warriors in my midst;
he has summoned an army against me

---

[a] This chapter is an acrostic poem, the verses of
which begin with the successive letters of the
Hebrew alphabet.   [b] 14 Most Hebrew manuscripts;
Septuagint *He kept watch over my sins*

to*a* crush my young men.
In his winepress the Lord has trampled
the Virgin Daughter of Judah.

¹⁶ "This is why I weep
and my eyes overflow with tears.
No one is near to comfort me,
no one to restore my spirit.
My children are destitute
because the enemy has prevailed."

¹⁷ Zion stretches out her hands,
but there is no one to comfort her.
The LORD has decreed for Jacob
that his neighbors become his foes;
Jerusalem has become
an unclean thing among them.

¹⁸ "The LORD is righteous,
yet I rebelled against his command.
Listen, all you peoples;
look upon my suffering.
My young men and maidens
have gone into exile.

¹⁹ "I called to my allies
but they betrayed me.
My priests and my elders
perished in the city
while they searched for food
to keep themselves alive.

²⁰ "See, O LORD, how distressed I am!
I am in torment within,
and in my heart I am disturbed,
for I have been most rebellious.
Outside, the sword bereaves;
inside, there is only death.

²¹ "People have heard my groaning,
but there is no one to comfort me.
All my enemies have heard of my
distress;
they rejoice at what you have done.
May you bring the day you have
announced
so they may become like me.

²² "Let all their wickedness come before
you;
deal with them
as you have dealt with me
because of all my sins.
My groans are many
and my heart is faint."

2 *b* How the Lord has covered the
Daughter of Zion

with the cloud of his anger*c*!
He has hurled down the splendor of
Israel
from heaven to earth;
he has not remembered his footstool
in the day of his anger.

² Without pity the Lord has swallowed up
all the dwellings of Jacob;
in his wrath he has torn down
the strongholds of the Daughter of
Judah.
He has brought her kingdom and its
princes
down to the ground in dishonor.

³ In fierce anger he has cut off
every horn*d* of Israel.
He has withdrawn his right hand
at the approach of the enemy.
He has burned in Jacob like a flaming
fire
that consumes everything around it.

⁴ Like an enemy he has strung his bow;
his right hand is ready.
Like a foe he has slain
all who were pleasing to the eye;
he has poured out his wrath like fire
on the tent of the Daughter of Zion.

⁵ The Lord is like an enemy;
he has swallowed up Israel.
He has swallowed up all her palaces
and destroyed her strongholds.
He has multiplied mourning and
lamentation
for the Daughter of Judah.

⁶ He has laid waste his dwelling like a
garden;
he has destroyed his place of
meeting.
The LORD has made Zion forget
her appointed feasts and her
Sabbaths;
in his fierce anger he has spurned
both king and priest.

⁷ The Lord has rejected his altar
and abandoned his sanctuary.

---

a15 Or *has set a time for me / when he will*   *b*This
chapter is an acrostic poem, the verses of which
begin with the successive letters of the Hebrew
alphabet.   *c1* Or *How the Lord in his anger / has
treated the Daughter of Zion with contempt*   *d3* Or /
all the strength; or *every king*; *horn* here symbolizes
strength.

He has handed over to the enemy
the walls of her palaces;
they have raised a shout in the house
of the LORD
as on the day of an appointed feast.

⁸The LORD determined to tear down
the wall around the Daughter of
Zion.
He stretched out a measuring line
and did not withhold his hand from
destroying.
He made ramparts and walls lament;
together they wasted away.

⁹Her gates have sunk into the ground;
their bars he has broken and
destroyed.
Her king and her princes are exiled
among the nations,
the law is no more,
and her prophets no longer find
visions from the LORD.

¹⁰The elders of the Daughter of Zion
sit on the ground in silence;
they have sprinkled dust on their
heads
and put on sackcloth.
The young women of Jerusalem
have bowed their heads to the
ground.

¹¹My eyes fail from weeping,
I am in torment within,
my heart is poured out on the ground
because my people are destroyed,
because children and infants faint
in the streets of the city.

¹²They say to their mothers,
"Where is bread and wine?"
as they faint like wounded men
in the streets of the city,
as their lives ebb away
in their mothers' arms.

¹³What can I say for you?
With what can I compare you,
O Daughter of Jerusalem?
To what can I liken you,
that I may comfort you,
O Virgin Daughter of Zion?
Your wound is as deep as the sea.
Who can heal you?

¹⁴The visions of your prophets
were false and worthless;

they did not expose your sin
to ward off your captivity.
The oracles they gave you
were false and misleading.

¹⁵All who pass your way
clap their hands at you;
they scoff and shake their heads
at the Daughter of Jerusalem:
"Is this the city that was called
the perfection of beauty,
the joy of the whole earth?"

¹⁶All your enemies open their mouths
wide against you;
they scoff and gnash their teeth
and say, "We have swallowed her
up.
This is the day we have waited for;
we have lived to see it."

¹⁷The LORD has done what he planned;
he has fulfilled his word,
which he decreed long ago.
He has overthrown you without pity,
he has let the enemy gloat over
you,
he has exalted the horn*ᵃ* of your foes.

¹⁸The hearts of the people
cry out to the Lord.
O wall of the Daughter of Zion,
let your tears flow like a river
day and night;
give yourself no relief,
your eyes no rest.

¹⁹Arise, cry out in the night,
as the watches of the night begin;
pour out your heart like water
in the presence of the Lord.
Lift up your hands to him
for the lives of your children,
who faint from hunger
at the head of every street.

²⁰"Look, O LORD, and consider:
Whom have you ever treated like
this?
Should women eat their offspring,
the children they have cared for?
Should priest and prophet be killed
in the sanctuary of the Lord?

²¹"Young and old lie together
in the dust of the streets;

ᵃ*17 Horn* here symbolizes strength.

my young men and maidens
  have fallen by the sword.
You have slain them in the day of
    your anger;
  you have slaughtered them without
    pity.

22 "As you summon to a feast day,
  so you summoned against me
    terrors on every side.
In the day of the LORD's anger
  no one escaped or survived;
those I cared for and reared,
  my enemy has destroyed."

3 [a] I am the man who has seen
    affliction
  by the rod of his wrath.
2 He has driven me away and made me
    walk
  in darkness rather than light;
3 indeed, he has turned his hand against
    me
  again and again, all day long.

4 He has made my skin and my flesh
  grow old

and has broken my bones.
5 He has besieged me and surrounded
    me
  with bitterness and hardship.
6 He has made me dwell in darkness
  like those long dead.

7 He has walled me in so I cannot
    escape;
  he has weighed me down with
    chains.
8 Even when I call out or cry for help,
  he shuts out my prayer.
9 He has barred my way with blocks of
    stone;
  he has made my paths crooked.

10 Like a bear lying in wait,
  like a lion in hiding,
11 he dragged me from the path and
    mangled me
  and left me without help.
12 He drew his bow

[a] This chapter is an acrostic poem; the verses of each
stanza begin with the successive letters of the
Hebrew alphabet, and the verses within each stanza
begin with the same letter.

Friday

His Love Never Fails

Read Lamentations 3:16–24

Sometimes people can be really mean. They can pick on you, make fun of you, and give you such a hard time you don't even want to get out of bed in the morning. They can make you feel like you're all alone.

But God says we're not alone. God sees us walking in the halls at school. He knows when people are hurting us. And he understands how it feels, because people have hurt him too. God loves us and knows when we've been hurt. That's why we can always trust God to be there. He can comfort us like no one else can. And he never, ever fails.

When people pick on you, remember that you have value because you are the Lord's child. And that's something no one can ever change.

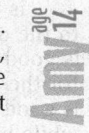

❶ Think about a time when you've been hurt. How did you find comfort?

❷ Find a small stone you can keep in your backpack or pocket during the day. When you feel hurt or alone, use the stone to remind yourself that Jesus is your rock and will always be with you.

❸ Start each day by asking God to be with you and to help you through hard times.

Turn to page 957 for your next devotion.

and made me the target for his arrows.

¹³He pierced my heart
with arrows from his quiver.
¹⁴I became the laughingstock of all my people;
they mock me in song all day long.
¹⁵He has filled me with bitter herbs
and sated me with gall.

¹⁶He has broken my teeth with gravel;
he has trampled me in the dust.
¹⁷I have been deprived of peace;
I have forgotten what prosperity is.
¹⁸So I say, "My splendor is gone
and all that I had hoped from the LORD."

¹⁹I remember my affliction and my wandering,
the bitterness and the gall.
²⁰I well remember them,
and my soul is downcast within me.
²¹Yet this I call to mind
and therefore I have hope:

²²Because of the LORD's great love we are not consumed,
for his compassions never fail.
²³They are new every morning;
great is your faithfulness.
²⁴I say to myself, "The LORD is my portion;
therefore I will wait for him."

²⁵The LORD is good to those whose hope is in him,
to the one who seeks him;
²⁶it is good to wait quietly
for the salvation of the LORD.
²⁷It is good for a man to bear the yoke
while he is young.

²⁸Let him sit alone in silence,
for the LORD has laid it on him.
²⁹Let him bury his face in the dust—
there may yet be hope.
³⁰Let him offer his cheek to one who would strike him,
and let him be filled with disgrace.

³¹For men are not cast off
by the Lord forever.
³²Though he brings grief, he will show compassion,
so great is his unfailing love.

³³For he does not willingly bring affliction
or grief to the children of men.

Life Stinks, but Here's Hope!

Lamentations 3:21–33
Look what we have here! In the middle of all this depressing stuff, the author has a super-incredible point to make—that God loves us a ton! Even when we sin big-time and feel like nobody could ever like us if they knew what we've done, God has a love for us that never stops. He will never leave us, and he will always love us—even when we mess up.

³⁴To crush underfoot
all prisoners in the land,
³⁵to deny a man his rights
before the Most High,
³⁶to deprive a man of justice—
would not the Lord see such things?

³⁷Who can speak and have it happen
if the Lord has not decreed it?
³⁸Is it not from the mouth of the Most High
that both calamities and good things come?
³⁹Why should any living man complain
when punished for his sins?

⁴⁰Let us examine our ways and test them,
and let us return to the LORD.
⁴¹Let us lift up our hearts and our hands
to God in heaven, and say:
⁴²"We have sinned and rebelled
and you have not forgiven.

⁴³"You have covered yourself with anger and pursued us;
you have slain without pity.
⁴⁴You have covered yourself with a cloud
so that no prayer can get through.
⁴⁵You have made us scum and refuse among the nations.

46 "All our enemies have opened their
  mouths
    wide against us.
47 We have suffered terror and pitfalls,
    ruin and destruction."
48 Streams of tears flow from my eyes
    because my people are destroyed.

49 My eyes will flow unceasingly,
    without relief,
50 until the LORD looks down
    from heaven and sees.
51 What I see brings grief to my soul
    because of all the women of my
      city.

52 Those who were my enemies without
      cause
    hunted me like a bird.
53 They tried to end my life in a pit
    and threw stones at me;
54 the waters closed over my head,
    and I thought I was about to be cut
      off.

55 I called on your name, O LORD,
    from the depths of the pit.
56 You heard my plea: "Do not close
      your ears
    to my cry for relief."
57 You came near when I called you,
    and you said, "Do not fear."

58 O Lord, you took up my case;
    you redeemed my life.
59 You have seen, O LORD, the wrong
      done to me.
    Uphold my cause!
60 You have seen the depth of their
      vengeance,
    all their plots against me.

61 O LORD, you have heard their insults,
    all their plots against me—
62 what my enemies whisper and
      mutter
    against me all day long.
63 Look at them! Sitting or standing,
    they mock me in their songs.

64 Pay them back what they deserve,
      O LORD,
    for what their hands have done.
65 Put a veil over their hearts,
    and may your curse be on them!
66 Pursue them in anger and destroy
      them
    from under the heavens of the LORD.

4 [a] How the gold has lost its luster,
    the fine gold become dull!
The sacred gems are scattered
    at the head of every street.

2 How the precious sons of Zion,
    once worth their weight in gold,
are now considered as pots of clay,
    the work of a potter's hands!

3 Even jackals offer their breasts
    to nurse their young,
but my people have become heartless
    like ostriches in the desert.

4 Because of thirst the infant's tongue
    sticks to the roof of its mouth;
the children beg for bread,
    but no one gives it to them.

5 Those who once ate delicacies
    are destitute in the streets.
Those nurtured in purple
    now lie on ash heaps.

6 The punishment of my people
    is greater than that of Sodom,
which was overthrown in a moment
    without a hand turned to help her.

7 Their princes were brighter than snow
    and whiter than milk,
their bodies more ruddy than rubies,
    their appearance like sapphires.[b]

8 But now they are blacker than soot;
    they are not recognized in the
      streets.
Their skin has shriveled on their
      bones;
    it has become as dry as a stick.

9 Those killed by the sword are better
      off
    than those who die of famine;
racked with hunger, they waste away
    for lack of food from the field.

10 With their own hands compassionate
      women
    have cooked their own children,
who became their food
    when my people were destroyed.

11 The LORD has given full vent to his
    wrath;

---

[a] This chapter is an acrostic poem, the verses of
which begin with the successive letters of the
Hebrew alphabet.   [b] 7 Or *lapis lazuli*

he has poured out his fierce anger.
He kindled a fire in Zion
   that consumed her foundations.

[12] The kings of the earth did not believe,
   nor did any of the world's people,
that enemies and foes could enter
   the gates of Jerusalem.

[13] But it happened because of the sins of
   her prophets
   and the iniquities of her priests,
who shed within her
   the blood of the righteous.

[14] Now they grope through the streets
   like men who are blind.
They are so defiled with blood
   that no one dares to touch their
   garments.

[15] "Go away! You are unclean!" men cry
   to them.
   "Away! Away! Don't touch us!"
When they flee and wander about,
   people among the nations say,
   "They can stay here no longer."

[16] The LORD himself has scattered them;
   he no longer watches over them.
The priests are shown no honor,
   the elders no favor.

[17] Moreover, our eyes failed,
   looking in vain for help;
from our towers we watched
   for a nation that could not save us.

[18] Men stalked us at every step,
   so we could not walk in our streets.
Our end was near, our days were
   numbered,
   for our end had come.

[19] Our pursuers were swifter
   than eagles in the sky;
they chased us over the mountains
   and lay in wait for us in the
   desert.

[20] The LORD's anointed, our very life
   breath,
   was caught in their traps.
We thought that under his shadow
   we would live among the nations.

[21] Rejoice and be glad, O Daughter of
   Edom,
   you who live in the land of Uz.
But to you also the cup will be passed;

you will be drunk and stripped
   naked.

[22] O Daughter of Zion, your punishment
   will end;
   he will not prolong your exile.
But, O Daughter of Edom, he will
   punish your sin
   and expose your wickedness.

5 Remember, O LORD, what has
   happened to us;
   look, and see our disgrace.
[2] Our inheritance has been turned over
   to aliens,
   our homes to foreigners.
[3] We have become orphans and
   fatherless,
   our mothers like widows.
[4] We must buy the water we drink;
   our wood can be had only at a
   price.
[5] Those who pursue us are at our heels;
   we are weary and find no rest.
[6] We submitted to Egypt and Assyria
   to get enough bread.
[7] Our fathers sinned and are no more,
   and we bear their punishment.
[8] Slaves rule over us,
   and there is none to free us from
   their hands.
[9] We get our bread at the risk of our
   lives
   because of the sword in the desert.
[10] Our skin is hot as an oven,
   feverish from hunger.
[11] Women have been ravished in Zion,
   and virgins in the towns of Judah.
[12] Princes have been hung up by their
   hands;
   elders are shown no respect.
[13] Young men toil at the millstones;
   boys stagger under loads of wood.
[14] The elders are gone from the city
   gate;
   the young men have stopped their
   music.
[15] Joy is gone from our hearts;
   our dancing has turned to
   mourning.
[16] The crown has fallen from our head.
   Woe to us, for we have sinned!
[17] Because of this our hearts are faint,
   because of these things our eyes
   grow dim

¹⁸ for Mount Zion, which lies desolate,
with jackals prowling over it.

¹⁹ You, O Lord, reign forever;
your throne endures from
generation to generation.
²⁰ Why do you always forget us?

Why do you forsake us so long?
²¹ Restore us to yourself, O Lord, that we
may return;
renew our days as of old
²² unless you have utterly rejected us
and are angry with us beyond
measure.

Week end.

Been There, Done That

Read John 1:14 (page 1267)

Amy's comments in Friday's devotional were painfully true. People, including kids and teenagers, can be really mean. Amy reminded us of another important truth—we're never alone. Jesus is always with us, even in tough times. And Jesus really does *understand* what it's like to go through tough times—because *he* was alone, *he* was picked on and made fun of, *he* had tons of tough times too.

In the passage you read today, John says that Jesus not only came down from heaven but that he also *moved in* right here on Planet Earth! That's right, Jesus decided to hang out with ordinary people. And, as Philippians 2:6–11 says, he *gave up* the glory and privileges of being God. His 33 years on earth allowed him to experience what it's like to be human, to be rejected, to be hurt, to be abandoned.

It's so cool to follow Jesus because he's not some distant, head-in-the-clouds God. Nope. You're following a genuine, in-your-life God who wants to know you and (this is the amazing part) wants to know what you *experience*. When you cry, Jesus can feel deep inside what it is like to have tears, because he cried real tears himself. When you're lonely, Jesus feels that too—he lived through loneliness himself. Jesus is way more than someone who loves us with a detached kind of love . . . he is a God who is with us and understands what we experience and feel. He's been there too.

❶ When was the last time you felt really alone? How did God help you through it?

❷ The next time you feel lonely or down, take time to read Matthew 26:36—27:56, page 1180. Remember, Jesus knows how you feel.

❸ Thank God for understanding what you feel every day.

Turn to page 960 for your next devotion.

Ezekiel

START

Sometimes it took a major jolt to get the attention of the people of Judah. More conventional methods just didn't seem to cut it. In those days King Nebuchadnezzar (neb-you-kad-NEZZ-ur) of Babylon was the landlord of most of the known world, including Judah. Ol' Nebby told Judah's king* to behave, or else. The Jewish king didn't, so Nebby invaded, posing this rather blunt question to the king: "So what part of 'do what I say or I'll kill you' don't you understand?" Then he slit the king's throat.

The murdered king's son became the new king, and—being just as sassy as his dad—lasted all of 3 months before Nebuchadnezzar invaded Judah again. This time he didn't kill the Jewish king but instead dragged him back to Babylon as a war trophy. All the Jewish leaders, law makers, builders, surviving soldiers and a bunch of other VIPs went along with the Jewish king. The only ones Neb left alive in Judah were the old and the poor.

Among the Jewish captives who were forced to set up housekeeping in Babylon was the priest Ezekiel. God told him—and he told his fellow captives—that King Nebuchadnezzar wasn't through with Judah yet. Unless its people stopped worshiping idols, God would send Nebby right back to Judah and *really* waste it this time.

*Jehoiakim (jeh-HOY-uh-kim; read about him in 2 Kings 23:36—24:7, page 451)

Cast OF Characters

Ezekiel

A priest who lived among other Jewish people in Babylon and prophesied about the current idol worship and coming destruction in his hometown of Jerusalem 700 miles away.

(ee-ZEEK-ee-ell)

What's UP with That?

Where Did That Come From?

Oddball Object Lessons.
"Shave your head with a sharp sword, then weigh your hairs" (chapter 5), "Dig a hole in a wall" (chapter 12), "Lie down on your left side . . . okay, now switch to your right side" (chapter 4).

Could It Be . . . Satan?—the devil chapter (28).
Sure, Ezekiel was preaching about the king of Tyre—apparently a proud, arrogant monarch. But a lot of Bible readers over the years claim that you don't have to be a brain surgeon or a Bible scholar to see that verses 11–17 sure sound like the devil.

Baaa—the sheep chapter (34).
Here and there in the Bible you catch glimpses of how God is our gentle, protective Shepherd. But nowhere except here in Ezekiel will you find such a loving, lengthy development of the God-is-our-Shepherd-and-we're-his-sheep idea.

Rising Bones—the skeleton chapter (37).
In a vision Ezekiel looked into a valley full of dry, lifeless, human bones, and he watched as they joined themselves into upright skeletons, then grew connecting tendons and muscles, then grew a covering of flesh—and finally were filled with the breath of God and became living people once again. The meaning? God would take the defeated, exiled, lifeless nation of Judah, "resurrect" it back to its own land, and breathe his spirit into the restored bodies. God would settle the Jews again in their own land.

Some Temple!—the blueprint chapters (40–43).
As if it weren't exciting enough for Jews to imagine being back in their own land, here was a detailed plan of God's holy temple.

Snap shots

- Idolatry (Idol worship) causes Judah's brutal destruction *(chapters 1—24)*

- Nebuchadnezzar trashes surrounding nations along with Judah *(chapters 25—32)*

- God eventually rescues his scattered Jews again and restores them to the land *(chapters 33—39)*

- A vision of something new *(chapters 40—48)*

The Living Creatures and the Glory of the LORD

1 In the[a] thirtieth year, in the fourth month on the fifth day, while I was among the exiles by the Kebar River, the heavens were opened and I saw visions of God.

[2]On the fifth of the month—it was the fifth year of the exile of King Jehoiachin— [3]the word of the LORD came to Ezekiel the priest, the son of Buzi,[b] by the Kebar River in the land of the Babylonians.[c] There the hand of the LORD was upon him.

[4]I looked, and I saw a windstorm coming out of the north—an immense cloud with flashing lightning and surrounded by brilliant light. The center of the fire looked like glowing metal, [5]and in the fire was what looked like four living creatures. In appearance their form was that of a man, [6]but each of them had four faces and four wings. [7]Their legs were straight; their feet were like those of a calf and gleamed like burnished bronze. [8]Under their wings on their four sides they had the hands of a man. All four of them had faces and wings, [9]and their wings touched one another. Each one went straight ahead; they did not turn as they moved.

[10]Their faces looked like this: Each of the four had the face of a man, and on the right side each had the face of a lion, and on the left the face of an ox; each also had the face of an eagle. [11]Such were their faces. Their wings were spread out upward; each had two wings, one touching the wing of another creature on either side, and two wings covering its body. [12]Each one went straight ahead. Wherever the spirit would go, they would go, without turning as they went. [13]The appearance of the living creatures was like burning coals of fire or like torches. Fire moved back and forth among the creatures; it was bright, and lightning flashed out of it. [14]The creatures sped back and forth like flashes of lightning.

[15]As I looked at the living creatures, I saw a wheel on the ground beside each creature with its four faces. [16]This was the appearance and structure of the wheels: They sparkled like chrysolite,

---

[a]1 Or *my*   [b]3 Or *Ezekiel son of Buzi the priest*   [c]3 Or *Chaldeans*

Monday

Amazing God!

Read Ezekiel 1:25–28

All I could think after I read this passage was, "God is amazing, and all the stuff he does is amazing!" God is full of light, fire, love, compassion and forgiveness. If he can be full of all those things, I know he's huge.

The great thing about God is that he's not too big to remember us. Sure, he can do whatever he wants. But that shouldn't be scary, because what he *wants* is to have a relationship with us. That means he's not going to use all that power and glory to get us. He's going to use it to love us! Now *that's* amazing.

Drew age 13

❶ Why did Ezekiel fall flat on his face when he saw the glory of God? What does Ezekiel's reaction say about God and his greatness?

❷ What images come into your head when you think about this passage? Get a sheet of paper and either jot down your thoughts or draw a picture about these verses.

❸ Thank God for his power and glory. Thank him for remembering you.

Turn to page 980 for your next devotion.

and all four looked alike. Each appeared to be made like a wheel intersecting a wheel. ¹⁷As they moved, they would go in any one of the four directions the creatures faced; the wheels did not turn about*a* as the creatures went. ¹⁸Their rims were high and awesome, and all four rims were full of eyes all around.

¹⁹When the living creatures moved, the wheels beside them moved; and when the living creatures rose from the ground, the wheels also rose. ²⁰Wherever the spirit would go, they would go, and the wheels would rise along with them, because the spirit of the living creatures was in the wheels. ²¹When the creatures moved, they also moved; when the creatures stood still, they also stood still; and when the creatures rose from the ground, the wheels rose along with them, because the spirit of the living creatures was in the wheels.

²²Spread out above the heads of the living creatures was what looked like an expanse, sparkling like ice, and awesome. ²³Under the expanse their wings were stretched out one toward the other, and each had two wings covering its body. ²⁴When the creatures moved, I heard the sound of their wings, like the roar of rushing waters, like the voice of the Almighty,*b* like the tumult of an army. When they stood still, they lowered their wings.

²⁵Then there came a voice from above the expanse over their heads as they stood with lowered wings. ²⁶Above the expanse over their heads was what looked like a throne of sapphire,*c* and high above on the throne was a figure like that of a man. ²⁷I saw that from what appeared to be his waist up he looked like glowing metal, as if full of fire, and that from there down he looked like fire; and brilliant light surrounded him. ²⁸Like the appearance of a rainbow in the clouds on a rainy day, so was the radiance around him.

This was the appearance of the likeness of the glory of the LORD. When I saw it, I fell facedown, and I heard the voice of one speaking.

Ezekiel's Call

2 He said to me, "Son of man, stand up on your feet and I will speak to you."

²As he spoke, the Spirit came into me and raised me to my feet, and I heard him speaking to me.

³He said: "Son of man, I am sending you to the Israelites, to a rebellious nation that has rebelled against me; they and their fathers have been in revolt against me to this very day. ⁴The people to whom I am sending you are obstinate and stubborn. Say to them, 'This is what the Sovereign LORD says.' ⁵And whether they listen or fail to listen—for they are a rebellious house—they will know that a prophet has been among them. ⁶And you, son of man, do not be afraid of them or their words. Do not be afraid, though briers and thorns are all around you and you live among scorpions. Do not be afraid of what they say or terrified by them, though they are a rebellious house. ⁷You must speak my words to them, whether they listen or fail to listen, for they are rebellious. ⁸But you, son of man, listen to what I say to you. Do not rebel like that rebellious house; open your mouth and eat what I give you."

⁹Then I looked, and I saw a hand stretched out to me. In it was a scroll, ¹⁰which he unrolled before me. On both sides of it were written words of lament and mourning and woe.

3 And he said to me, "Son of man, eat what is before you, eat this scroll; then go and speak to the house of Israel." ²So I opened my mouth, and he gave me the scroll to eat.

³Then he said to me, "Son of man, eat this scroll I am giving you and fill your stomach with it." So I ate it, and it tasted as sweet as honey in my mouth.

⁴He then said to me: "Son of man, go now to the house of Israel and speak my words to them. ⁵You are not being sent to a people of obscure speech and difficult language, but to the house of Israel— ⁶not to many peoples of obscure speech and difficult language, whose words you cannot understand. Surely if I had sent you to them, they would have listened to you. ⁷But the house of Israel is not willing to listen to you because they are not willing to listen to me, for the whole

a17 Or aside   b24 Hebrew Shaddai   c26 Or lapis lazuli

It's Gonna Go Platinum!

Here's your chance. You're a music industry big-wig. You've landed one of the top acts in early human history—the lo-fi, hip-hop alterna-pop band "Living Creature." It's your job to promote their new #1 single, "Swing Low, Four Wheel Freak." As part of the promotion for this hit, you'll need to design the cover for their latest CD: *It's Not Called the Old Testament Yet*. Below is the cover of the CD. Read Ezekiel, chapter 1, then design a cover based on what you imagine.

It's Not Called the Old Testament Yet

Featuring the hit single
"Swing Low, Four Wheel Freak"

house of Israel is hardened and obstinate. ⁸But I will make you as unyielding and hardened as they are. ⁹I will make your forehead like the hardest stone, harder than flint. Do not be afraid of them or terrified by them, though they are a rebellious house."

¹⁰And he said to me, "Son of man, listen carefully and take to heart all the words I speak to you. ¹¹Go now to your countrymen in exile and speak to them. Say to them, 'This is what the Sovereign LORD says,' whether they listen or fail to listen."

¹²Then the Spirit lifted me up, and I heard behind me a loud rumbling sound—May the glory of the LORD be praised in his dwelling place!— ¹³the sound of the wings of the living creatures brushing against each other and the sound of the wheels beside them, a loud rumbling sound. ¹⁴The Spirit then lifted me up and took me away, and I went in bitterness and in the anger of my spirit, with the strong hand of the LORD upon me. ¹⁵I came to the exiles who lived at Tel Abib near the Kebar River. And there, where they were living, I sat among them for seven days—overwhelmed.

Warning to Israel

¹⁶At the end of seven days the word of the LORD came to me: ¹⁷"Son of man, I

have made you a watchman for the house of Israel; so hear the word I speak and give them warning from me. [18]When I say to a wicked man, 'You will surely die,' and you do not warn him or speak out to dissuade him from his evil ways in order to save his life, that wicked man will die for[a] his sin, and I will hold you accountable for his blood. [19]But if you do warn the wicked man and he does not turn from his wickedness or from his evil ways, he will die for his sin; but you will have saved yourself.

[20]"Again, when a righteous man turns from his righteousness and does evil, and I put a stumbling block before him, he will die. Since you did not warn him, he will die for his sin. The righteous things he did will not be remembered, and I will hold you accountable for his blood. [21]But if you do warn the righteous man not to sin and he does not sin, he will surely live because he took warning, and you will have saved yourself."

[22]The hand of the LORD was upon me there, and he said to me, "Get up and go out to the plain, and there I will speak to you." [23]So I got up and went out to the plain. And the glory of the LORD was standing there, like the glory I had seen by the Kebar River, and I fell facedown. [24]Then the Spirit came into me and raised me to my feet. He spoke to me and said: "Go, shut yourself inside your house. [25]And you, son of man, they will tie with ropes; you will be bound so that you cannot go out among the people. [26]I will make your tongue stick to the roof of your mouth so that you will be silent and unable to rebuke them, though they are a rebellious house. [27]But when I speak to you, I will open your mouth and you shall say to them, 'This is what the Sovereign LORD says.' Whoever will listen let him listen, and whoever will refuse let him refuse; for they are a rebellious house.

Siege of Jerusalem Symbolized

4 "Now, son of man, take a clay tablet, put it in front of you and draw the city of Jerusalem on it. [2]Then lay siege to it: Erect siege works against it, build a ramp up to it, set up camps against it and put battering rams around it. [3]Then take

an iron pan, place it as an iron wall between you and the city and turn your face toward it. It will be under siege, and you shall besiege it. This will be a sign to the house of Israel.

[4]"Then lie on your left side and put the sin of the house of Israel upon yourself.[b] You are to bear their sin for the number of days you lie on your side. [5]I have assigned you the same number of days as the years of their sin. So for 390 days you will bear the sin of the house of Israel.

[6]"After you have finished this, lie down again, this time on your right side, and bear the sin of the house of Judah. I have assigned you 40 days, a day for each year. [7]Turn your face toward the siege of Jerusalem and with bared arm prophesy against her. [8]I will tie you up with ropes so that you cannot turn from one side to the other until you have finished the days of your siege.

[9]"Take wheat and barley, beans and lentils, millet and spelt; put them in a storage jar and use them to make bread for yourself. You are to eat it during the 390 days you lie on your side. [10]Weigh out twenty shekels[c] of food to eat each day and eat it at set times. [11]Also measure out a sixth of a hin[d] of water and drink it at set times. [12]Eat the food as you would a barley cake; bake it in the sight of the people, using human excrement for fuel." [13]The LORD said, "In this way the people of Israel will eat defiled food among the nations where I will drive them."

[14]Then I said, "Not so, Sovereign LORD! I have never defiled myself. From my youth until now I have never eaten anything found dead or torn by wild animals. No unclean meat has ever entered my mouth."

[15]"Very well," he said, "I will let you bake your bread over cow manure instead of human excrement."

[16]He then said to me: "Son of man, I will cut off the supply of food in Jerusalem. The people will eat rationed food in anxiety and drink rationed water in

---

[a]18 Or in; also in verses 19 and 20   [b]4 Or your side
[c]10 That is, about 8 ounces (about 0.2 kilogram)
[d]11 That is, about 2/3 quart (about 0.6 liter)

despair, ¹⁷for food and water will be scarce. They will be appalled at the sight of each other and will waste away because of[a] their sin.

5 "Now, son of man, take a sharp sword and use it as a barber's razor to shave your head and your beard. Then take a set of scales and divide up the hair. ²When the days of your siege come to an end, burn a third of the hair with fire inside the city. Take a third and strike it with the sword all around the city. And scatter a third to the wind. For I will pursue them with drawn sword. ³But take a few strands of hair and tuck them away in the folds of your garment. ⁴Again, take a few of these and throw them into the fire and burn them up. A fire will spread from there to the whole house of Israel.

⁵"This is what the Sovereign LORD says: This is Jerusalem, which I have set in the center of the nations, with countries all around her. ⁶Yet in her wickedness she has rebelled against my laws

Jerusalem, Front and Center!

Huh?

Ezekiel 5:5

Jerusalem was the center of the life of Israel. Because God had such a special relationship with the people of Jerusalem, he gave them "most favored city" status. However, this also meant he gave them more responsibility than the other cities. In Ezekiel, God is talking about how wicked Jerusalem had been. Since Jerusalem was God's favored city, you can guess how displeased he was with its behavior.

and decrees more than the nations and countries around her. She has rejected my laws and has not followed my decrees.

⁷"Therefore this is what the Sovereign LORD says: You have been more unruly than the nations around you and have not followed my decrees or kept my laws. You have not even[b] conformed to the standards of the nations around you.

⁸"Therefore this is what the Sovereign LORD says: I myself am against you, Jerusalem, and I will inflict punishment on you in the sight of the nations. ⁹Because of all your detestable idols, I will do to you what I have never done before and will never do again. ¹⁰Therefore in your midst fathers will eat their children, and children will eat their fathers. I will inflict punishment on you and will scatter all your survivors to the winds. ¹¹Therefore as surely as I live, declares the Sovereign LORD, because you have defiled my sanctuary with all your vile images and detestable practices, I myself will withdraw my favor; I will not look on you with pity or spare you. ¹²A third of your people will die of the plague or perish by famine inside you; a third will fall by the sword outside your walls; and a third I will scatter to the winds and pursue with drawn sword.

¹³"Then my anger will cease and my wrath against them will subside, and I will be avenged. And when I have spent my wrath upon them, they will know that I the LORD have spoken in my zeal.

¹⁴"I will make you a ruin and a reproach among the nations around you, in the sight of all who pass by. ¹⁵You will be a reproach and a taunt, a warning and an object of horror to the nations around you when I inflict punishment on you in anger and in wrath and with stinging rebuke. I the LORD have spoken. ¹⁶When I shoot at you with my deadly and destructive arrows of famine, I will shoot to destroy you. I will bring more and more famine upon you and cut off your supply of food. ¹⁷I will send famine and wild beasts against you, and they will leave you childless. Plague and bloodshed will sweep through you, and I will bring the sword against you. I the LORD have spoken."

A Prophecy Against the Mountains of Israel

6 The word of the LORD came to me: ²"Son of man, set your face against the mountains of Israel; prophesy against them ³and say: 'O mountains of Israel, hear the word of the Sovereign

[a]17 Or *away in*   [b]7 Most Hebrew manuscripts; some Hebrew manuscripts and Syriac *You have*

LORD. This is what the Sovereign LORD says to the mountains and hills, to the ravines and valleys: I am about to bring a sword against you, and I will destroy your high places. [4]Your altars will be demolished and your incense altars will be smashed; and I will slay your people in front of your idols. [5]I will lay the dead bodies of the Israelites in front of their idols, and I will scatter your bones around your altars. [6]Wherever you live, the towns will be laid waste and the high places demolished, so that your altars will be laid waste and devastated, your idols smashed and ruined, your incense altars broken down, and what you have made wiped out. [7]Your people will fall slain among you, and you will know that I am the LORD.

[8]" 'But I will spare some, for some of you will escape the sword when you are scattered among the lands and nations. [9]Then in the nations where they have been carried captive, those who escape will remember me—how I have been grieved by their adulterous hearts, which have turned away from me, and by their eyes, which have lusted after their idols. They will loathe themselves for the evil they have done and for all their detestable practices. [10]And they will know that I am the LORD; I did not threaten in vain to bring this calamity on them.

[11]" 'This is what the Sovereign LORD says: Strike your hands together and stamp your feet and cry out "Alas!" because of all the wicked and detestable practices of the house of Israel, for they will fall by the sword, famine and plague. [12]He that is far away will die of the plague, and he that is near will fall by the sword, and he that survives and is spared will die of famine. So will I spend my wrath upon them. [13]And they will know that I am the LORD, when their people lie slain among their idols around their altars, on every high hill and on all the mountaintops, under every spreading tree and every leafy oak—places where they offered fragrant incense to all their idols. [14]And I will stretch out my hand against them and make the land a desolate waste from the desert to Diblah[a]—wherever they live. Then they will know that I am the LORD.' "

The End Has Come

7 The word of the LORD came to me: [2]"Son of man, this is what the Sovereign LORD says to the land of Israel: The end! The end has come upon the four

Flesh and Bones

Huh?

Ezekiel 7:1–2

If you counted, you would find Ezekiel uses the term "Son of man" 93 times. He's going overboard to show how human he is compared with how holy and divine God is. But you might remember that the same term is used to refer to Jesus in the New Testament. In fact, Jesus uses the phrase to talk about himself. The phrase means something different when applied to Jesus. Since he was God too, the term "Son of man" means that, even though he was born of humans, Jesus was also the Son of God. Jesus is totally human and totally God.

corners of the land. [3]The end is now upon you and I will unleash my anger against you. I will judge you according to your conduct and repay you for all your detestable practices. [4]I will not look on you with pity or spare you; I will surely repay you for your conduct and the detestable practices among you. Then you will know that I am the LORD.

[5]"This is what the Sovereign LORD says: Disaster! An unheard-of[b] disaster is coming. [6]The end has come! The end has come! It has roused itself against you. It has come! [7]Doom has come upon you—you who dwell in the land. The time has come, the day is near; there is panic, not joy, upon the mountains. [8]I am about to pour out my wrath on you and spend my anger against you; I will judge you according to your conduct and repay you for all your detestable practices. [9]I will not look on you with pity or spare you; I will repay you in accordance with your conduct and the detestable practices

[a]14 Most Hebrew manuscripts; a few Hebrew manuscripts *Riblah*   [b]5 Most Hebrew manuscripts; some Hebrew manuscripts and Syriac *Disaster after*

among you. Then you will know that it is I the LORD who strikes the blow.

¹⁰"The day is here! It has come! Doom has burst forth, the rod has budded, arrogance has blossomed! ¹¹Violence has grown into*a* a rod to punish wickedness; none of the people will be left, none of that crowd—no wealth, nothing of value. ¹²The time has come, the day has arrived. Let not the buyer rejoice nor the seller grieve, for wrath is upon the whole crowd. ¹³The seller will not recover the land he has sold as long as both of them live, for the vision concerning the whole crowd will not be reversed. Because of their sins, not one of them will preserve his life. ¹⁴Though they blow the trumpet and get everything ready, no one will go into battle, for my wrath is upon the whole crowd.

¹⁵"Outside is the sword, inside are plague and famine; those in the country will die by the sword, and those in the city will be devoured by famine and plague. ¹⁶All who survive and escape will be in the mountains, moaning like doves of the valleys, each because of his sins. ¹⁷Every hand will go limp, and every knee will become as weak as water. ¹⁸They will put on sackcloth and be clothed with terror. Their faces will be covered with shame and their heads will be shaved. ¹⁹They will throw their silver into the streets, and their gold will be an unclean thing. Their silver and gold will not be able to save them in the day of the LORD's wrath. They will not satisfy their hunger or fill their stomachs with it, for it has made them stumble into sin. ²⁰They were proud of their beautiful jewelry and used it to make their detestable idols and vile images. Therefore I will turn these into an unclean thing for them. ²¹I will hand it all over as plunder to foreigners and as loot to the wicked of the earth, and they will defile it. ²²I will turn my face away from them, and they will desecrate my treasured place; robbers will enter it and desecrate it.

²³"Prepare chains, because the land is full of bloodshed and the city is full of violence. ²⁴I will bring the most wicked of the nations to take possession of their houses; I will put an end to the pride of the mighty, and their sanctuaries will be

desecrated. ²⁵When terror comes, they will seek peace, but there will be none. ²⁶Calamity upon calamity will come, and rumor upon rumor. They will try to get a vision from the prophet; the teaching of the law by the priest will be lost, as will the counsel of the elders. ²⁷The king will mourn, the prince will be clothed with despair, and the hands of the people of the land will tremble. I will deal with them according to their conduct, and by their own standards I will judge them. Then they will know that I am the LORD."

Idolatry in the Temple

8 In the sixth year, in the sixth month on the fifth day, while I was sitting in my house and the elders of Judah were sitting before me, the hand of the Sovereign LORD came upon me there. ²I looked, and I saw a figure like that of a man.*b* From what appeared to be his waist down he was like fire, and from there up his appearance was as bright as glowing metal. ³He stretched out what looked like a hand and took me by the hair of my head. The Spirit lifted me up between earth and heaven and in visions of God he took me to Jerusalem, to the entrance to the north gate of the inner court, where the idol that provokes to jealousy stood. ⁴And there before me was the glory of the God of Israel, as in the vision I had seen in the plain.

⁵Then he said to me, "Son of man, look toward the north." So I looked, and in the entrance north of the gate of the altar I saw this idol of jealousy.

⁶And he said to me, "Son of man, do you see what they are doing—the utterly detestable things the house of Israel is doing here, things that will drive me far from my sanctuary? But you will see things that are even more detestable."

⁷Then he brought me to the entrance to the court. I looked, and I saw a hole in the wall. ⁸He said to me, "Son of man, now dig into the wall." So I dug into the wall and saw a doorway there.

⁹And he said to me, "Go in and see the wicked and detestable things they are doing here." ¹⁰So I went in and looked,

a11 Or *The violent one has become* *b2* Or *saw a fiery figure*

and I saw portrayed all over the walls all kinds of crawling things and detestable animals and all the idols of the house of Israel. [11]In front of them stood seventy elders of the house of Israel, and Jaazaniah son of Shaphan was standing among them. Each had a censer in his hand, and a fragrant cloud of incense was rising.

[12]He said to me, "Son of man, have you seen what the elders of the house of Israel are doing in the darkness, each at the shrine of his own idol? They say, 'The LORD does not see us; the LORD has forsaken the land.' " [13]Again, he said, "You will see them doing things that are even more detestable."

[14]Then he brought me to the entrance to the north gate of the house of the LORD, and I saw women sitting there, mourning for Tammuz. [15]He said to me, "Do you see this, son of man? You will see things that are even more detestable than this."

[16]He then brought me into the inner court of the house of the LORD, and there at the entrance to the temple, between the portico and the altar, were about twenty-five men. With their backs toward the temple of the LORD and their faces toward the east, they were bowing down to the sun in the east.

[17]He said to me, "Have you seen this, son of man? Is it a trivial matter for the house of Judah to do the detestable things they are doing here? Must they also fill the land with violence and continually provoke me to anger? Look at them putting the branch to their nose! [18]Therefore I will deal with them in anger; I will not look on them with pity or spare them. Although they shout in my ears, I will not listen to them."

Idolaters Killed

9 Then I heard him call out in a loud voice, "Bring the guards of the city here, each with a weapon in his hand." [2]And I saw six men coming from the direction of the upper gate, which faces north, each with a deadly weapon in his hand. With them was a man clothed in linen who had a writing kit at his side. They came in and stood beside the bronze altar.

[3]Now the glory of the God of Israel went up from above the cherubim, where it had been, and moved to the threshold of the temple. Then the LORD called to the man clothed in linen who had the writing kit at his side [4]and said to him, "Go throughout the city of Jerusalem and put a mark on the foreheads of those who grieve and lament over all the detestable things that are done in it."

[5]As I listened, he said to the others, "Follow him through the city and kill, without showing pity or compassion. [6]Slaughter old men, young men and maidens, women and children, but do not touch anyone who has the mark. Begin at my sanctuary." So they began with the elders who were in front of the temple.

[7]Then he said to them, "Defile the temple and fill the courts with the slain. Go!" So they went out and began killing throughout the city. [8]While they were killing and I was left alone, I fell facedown, crying out, "Ah, Sovereign LORD! Are you going to destroy the entire remnant of Israel in this outpouring of your wrath on Jerusalem?"

[9]He answered me, "The sin of the house of Israel and Judah is exceedingly great; the land is full of bloodshed and the city is full of injustice. They say, 'The LORD has forsaken the land; the LORD does not see.' [10]So I will not look on them with pity or spare them, but I will bring down on their own heads what they have done."

[11]Then the man in linen with the writing kit at his side brought back word, saying, "I have done as you commanded."

The Glory Departs From the Temple

10 I looked, and I saw the likeness of a throne of sapphire[a] above the expanse that was over the heads of the cherubim. [2]The LORD said to the man clothed in linen, "Go in among the wheels beneath the cherubim. Fill your hands with burning coals from among the cherubim and scatter them over the city." And as I watched, he went in.

[3]Now the cherubim were standing on

---

[a] 1 Or *lapis lazuli*

the south side of the temple when the man went in, and a cloud filled the inner court. [4]Then the glory of the LORD rose from above the cherubim and moved to the threshold of the temple. The cloud filled the temple, and the court was full of the radiance of the glory of the LORD. [5]The sound of the wings of the cherubim could be heard as far away as the outer court, like the voice of God Almighty[a] when he speaks.

[6]When the LORD commanded the man in linen, "Take fire from among the wheels, from among the cherubim," the man went in and stood beside a wheel. [7]Then one of the cherubim reached out his hand to the fire that was among them. He took up some of it and put it into the hands of the man in linen, who took it and went out. [8](Under the wings of the cherubim could be seen what looked like the hands of a man.)

[9]I looked, and I saw beside the cherubim four wheels, one beside each of the cherubim; the wheels sparkled like chrysolite. [10]As for their appearance, the four of them looked alike; each was like a wheel intersecting a wheel. [11]As they moved, they would go in any one of the four directions the cherubim faced; the wheels did not turn about[b] as the cherubim went. The cherubim went in whatever direction the head faced, without turning as they went. [12]Their entire bodies, including their backs, their hands and their wings, were completely full of eyes, as were their four wheels. [13]I heard the wheels being called "the whirling wheels." [14]Each of the cherubim had four faces: One face was that of a cherub, the second the face of a man, the third the face of a lion, and the fourth the face of an eagle.

[15]Then the cherubim rose upward. These were the living creatures I had seen by the Kebar River. [16]When the cherubim moved, the wheels beside them moved; and when the cherubim spread their wings to rise from the ground, the wheels did not leave their side. [17]When the cherubim stood still, they also stood still; and when the cherubim rose, they rose with them, because the spirit of the living creatures was in them.

[18]Then the glory of the LORD departed from over the threshold of the temple and stopped above the cherubim. [19]While I watched, the cherubim spread their wings and rose from the ground, and as they went, the wheels went with them. They stopped at the entrance to the east gate of the LORD's house, and the glory of the God of Israel was above them.

[20]These were the living creatures I had seen beneath the God of Israel by the Kebar River, and I realized that they were cherubim. [21]Each had four faces and four wings, and under their wings was what looked like the hands of a man. [22]Their faces had the same appearance as those I had seen by the Kebar River. Each one went straight ahead.

Judgment on Israel's Leaders

11 Then the Spirit lifted me up and brought me to the gate of the house of the LORD that faces east. There at the entrance to the gate were twenty-five men, and I saw among them Jaazaniah son of Azzur and Pelatiah son of Benaiah, leaders of the people. [2]The LORD said to me, "Son of man, these are the men who are plotting evil and giving wicked advice in this city. [3]They say, 'Will it not soon be time to build houses?[c] This city is a cooking pot, and we are the meat.' [4]Therefore prophesy against them; prophesy, son of man."

[5]Then the Spirit of the LORD came upon me, and he told me to say: "This is what the LORD says: That is what you are saying, O house of Israel, but I know what is going through your mind. [6]You have killed many people in this city and filled its streets with the dead.

[7]"Therefore this is what the Sovereign LORD says: The bodies you have thrown there are the meat and this city is the pot, but I will drive you out of it. [8]You fear the sword, and the sword is what I will bring against you, declares the Sovereign LORD. [9]I will drive you out of the city and hand you over to foreigners and inflict punishment on you. [10]You will fall by the sword, and I will execute judgment on you at the borders of Israel. Then you will know that I am the LORD. [11]This city

---

[a]5 Hebrew *El-Shaddai*   [b]11 Or *aside*   [c]3 Or *This is not the time to build houses.*

will not be a pot for you, nor will you be the meat in it; I will execute judgment on you at the borders of Israel. [12]And you will know that I am the LORD, for you have not followed my decrees or kept my laws but have conformed to the standards of the nations around you."

[13]Now as I was prophesying, Pelatiah son of Benaiah died. Then I fell facedown and cried out in a loud voice, "Ah, Sovereign LORD! Will you completely destroy the remnant of Israel?"

[14]The word of the LORD came to me: [15]"Son of man, your brothers—your brothers who are your blood relatives[a] and the whole house of Israel—are those of whom the people of Jerusalem have said, 'They are[b] far away from the LORD; this land was given to us as our possession.'

Promised Return of Israel

[16]"Therefore say: 'This is what the Sovereign LORD says: Although I sent them far away among the nations and scattered them among the countries, yet for a little while I have been a sanctuary for them in the countries where they have gone.'

[17]"Therefore say: 'This is what the Sovereign LORD says: I will gather you from the nations and bring you back from the countries where you have been scattered, and I will give you back the land of Israel again.'

[18]"They will return to it and remove all its vile images and detestable idols. [19]I will give them an undivided heart and put a new spirit in them; I will remove from them their heart of stone and give them a heart of flesh. [20]Then they will follow my decrees and be careful to keep my laws. They will be my people, and I will be their God. [21]But as for those whose hearts are devoted to their vile images and detestable idols, I will bring down on their own heads what they have done, declares the Sovereign LORD."

[22]Then the cherubim, with the wheels beside them, spread their wings, and the glory of the God of Israel was above them. [23]The glory of the LORD went up from within the city and stopped above the mountain east of it. [24]The Spirit lifted me up and brought me to the exiles in Babylonia[c] in the vision given by the Spirit of God.

Then the vision I had seen went up from me, [25]and I told the exiles everything the LORD had shown me.

The Exile Symbolized

12 The word of the LORD came to me: [2]"Son of man, you are living among a rebellious people. They have eyes to see but do not see and ears to hear but do not hear, for they are a rebellious people.

[3]"Therefore, son of man, pack your belongings for exile and in the daytime, as they watch, set out and go from where you are to another place. Perhaps they will understand, though they are a rebellious house. [4]During the daytime, while they watch, bring out your belongings packed for exile. Then in the evening, while they are watching, go out like those who go into exile. [5]While they watch, dig through the wall and take your belongings out through it. [6]Put them on your shoulder as they are watching and carry them out at dusk. Cover your face so that you cannot see the land, for I have made you a sign to the house of Israel."

[7]So I did as I was commanded. During the day I brought out my things packed for exile. Then in the evening I dug through the wall with my hands. I took my belongings out at dusk, carrying them on my shoulders while they watched.

[8]In the morning the word of the LORD came to me: [9]"Son of man, did not that rebellious house of Israel ask you, 'What are you doing?'

[10]"Say to them, 'This is what the Sovereign LORD says: This oracle concerns the prince in Jerusalem and the whole house of Israel who are there.' [11]Say to them, 'I am a sign to you.'

"As I have done, so it will be done to them. They will go into exile as captives.

[12]"The prince among them will put his things on his shoulder at dusk and leave, and a hole will be dug in the wall for him

---

[a]15 Or *are in exile with you* (see Septuagint and Syriac)   [b]15 Or *those to whom the people of Jerusalem have said, 'Stay*   [c]24 Or *Chaldea*

to go through. He will cover his face so that he cannot see the land. ¹³I will spread my net for him, and he will be caught in my snare; I will bring him to Babylonia, the land of the Chaldeans, but he will not see it, and there he will die. ¹⁴I will scatter to the winds all those around him—his staff and all his troops—and I will pursue them with drawn sword.

¹⁵"They will know that I am the LORD, when I disperse them among the nations and scatter them through the countries. ¹⁶But I will spare a few of them from the sword, famine and plague, so that in the nations where they go they may acknowledge all their detestable practices. Then they will know that I am the LORD."

¹⁷The word of the LORD came to me: ¹⁸"Son of man, tremble as you eat your food, and shudder in fear as you drink your water. ¹⁹Say to the people of the land: 'This is what the Sovereign LORD says about those living in Jerusalem and in the land of Israel: They will eat their food in anxiety and drink their water in despair, for their land will be stripped of everything in it because of the violence of all who live there. ²⁰The inhabited towns will be laid waste and the land will be desolate. Then you will know that I am the LORD.'"

²¹The word of the LORD came to me: ²²"Son of man, what is this proverb you have in the land of Israel: 'The days go by and every vision comes to nothing'? ²³Say to them, 'This is what the Sovereign LORD says: I am going to put an end to this proverb, and they will no longer quote it in Israel.' Say to them, 'The days are near when every vision will be fulfilled. ²⁴For there will be no more false visions or flattering divinations among the people of Israel. ²⁵But I the LORD will speak what I will, and it shall be fulfilled without delay. For in your days, you rebellious house, I will fulfill whatever I say, declares the Sovereign LORD.'"

²⁶The word of the LORD came to me: ²⁷"Son of man, the house of Israel is saying, 'The vision he sees is for many years from now, and he prophesies about the distant future.'

²⁸"Therefore say to them, 'This is what the Sovereign LORD says: None of my words will be delayed any longer; what-

ever I say will be fulfilled, declares the Sovereign LORD.' "

False Prophets Condemned

13 The word of the LORD came to me: ²"Son of man, prophesy against the prophets of Israel who are now prophesying. Say to those who prophesy out of their own imagination: 'Hear the word of the LORD! ³This is what the Sovereign LORD says: Woe to the foolish[a]

Wanna-be Prophets

Huh?

Ezekiel 13:2
A false prophet is someone who says they have a message from God when they don't. Basically, they are wanna-be prophets. We might call someone a false prophet today who says that God hates people who drink Pepsi and will destroy them all. Since we know that God loves everyone regardless of what kind of soda they drink, we can tell that this person is a false prophet. The best way to know if someone is a prophet wanna-be or the real deal is to see if their message agrees with what the Bible says.

---

prophets who follow their own spirit and have seen nothing! ⁴Your prophets, O Israel, are like jackals among ruins. ⁵You have not gone up to the breaks in the wall to repair it for the house of Israel so that it will stand firm in the battle on the day of the LORD. ⁶Their visions are false and their divinations a lie. They say, "The LORD declares," when the LORD has not sent them; yet they expect their words to be fulfilled. ⁷Have you not seen false visions and uttered lying divinations when you say, "The LORD declares," though I have not spoken?

⁸" 'Therefore this is what the Sovereign LORD says: Because of your false words and lying visions, I am against you, declares the Sovereign LORD. ⁹My hand will be against the prophets who see false visions and utter lying divinations. They

---

a 3 Or wicked

will not belong to the council of my people or be listed in the records of the house of Israel, nor will they enter the land of Israel. Then you will know that I am the Sovereign LORD.

¹⁰" 'Because they lead my people astray, saying, "Peace," when there is no peace, and because, when a flimsy wall is built, they cover it with whitewash, ¹¹therefore tell those who cover it with whitewash that it is going to fall. Rain will come in torrents, and I will send hailstones hurtling down, and violent winds will burst forth. ¹²When the wall collapses, will people not ask you, "Where is the whitewash you covered it with?"

¹³" 'Therefore this is what the Sovereign LORD says: In my wrath I will unleash a violent wind, and in my anger hailstones and torrents of rain will fall with destructive fury. ¹⁴I will tear down the wall you have covered with whitewash and will level it to the ground so that its foundation will be laid bare. When it*a* falls, you will be destroyed in it; and you will know that I am the LORD. ¹⁵So I will spend my wrath against the wall and against those who covered it with whitewash. I will say to you, "The wall is gone and so are those who whitewashed it, ¹⁶those prophets of Israel who prophesied to Jerusalem and saw visions of peace for her when there was no peace, declares the Sovereign LORD." '

¹⁷"Now, son of man, set your face against the daughters of your people who prophesy out of their own imagination. Prophesy against them ¹⁸and say, 'This is what the Sovereign LORD says: Woe to the women who sew magic charms on all their wrists and make veils of various lengths for their heads in order to ensnare people. Will you ensnare the lives of my people but preserve your own? ¹⁹You have profaned me among my people for a few handfuls of barley and scraps of bread. By lying to my people, who listen to lies, you have killed those who should not have died and have spared those who should not live.

²⁰" 'Therefore this is what the Sovereign LORD says: I am against your magic charms with which you ensnare people like birds and I will tear them from your arms; I will set free the people that you ensnare like birds. ²¹I will tear off your veils and save my people from your hands, and they will no longer fall prey to your power. Then you will know that I am the LORD. ²²Because you disheartened the righteous with your lies, when I had brought them no grief, and because you encouraged the wicked not to turn from their evil ways and so save their lives, ²³therefore you will no longer see false visions or practice divination. I will save my people from your hands. And then you will know that I am the LORD.' "

Idolaters Condemned

14 Some of the elders of Israel came to me and sat down in front of me. ²Then the word of the LORD came to me: ³"Son of man, these men have set up idols in their hearts and put wicked stumbling blocks before their faces. Should I let them inquire of me at all? ⁴Therefore speak to them and tell them, 'This is what the Sovereign LORD says: When any Israelite sets up idols in his heart and puts a wicked stumbling block before his face and then goes to a prophet, I the LORD will answer him myself in keeping with his great idolatry. ⁵I will do this to recapture the hearts of the people of Israel, who have all deserted me for their idols.'

⁶"Therefore say to the house of Israel, 'This is what the Sovereign LORD says: Repent! Turn from your idols and renounce all your detestable practices!

⁷" 'When any Israelite or any alien living in Israel separates himself from me and sets up idols in his heart and puts a wicked stumbling block before his face and then goes to a prophet to inquire of me, I the LORD will answer him myself. ⁸I will set my face against that man and make him an example and a byword. I will cut him off from my people. Then you will know that I am the LORD.

⁹" 'And if the prophet is enticed to utter a prophecy, I the LORD have enticed that prophet, and I will stretch out my hand against him and destroy him from among my people Israel. ¹⁰They will bear their guilt—the prophet will be as guilty

---

a14 Or the city

as the one who consults him. [11]Then the people of Israel will no longer stray from me, nor will they defile themselves anymore with all their sins. They will be my people, and I will be their God, declares the Sovereign LORD.' "

Judgment Inescapable

[12]The word of the LORD came to me: [13]"Son of man, if a country sins against me by being unfaithful and I stretch out my hand against it to cut off its food supply and send famine upon it and kill its men and their animals, [14]even if these three men—Noah, Daniel[a] and Job—were in it, they could save only themselves by their righteousness, declares the Sovereign LORD.

[15]"Or if I send wild beasts through that country and they leave it childless and it becomes desolate so that no one can pass through it because of the beasts, [16]as surely as I live, declares the Sovereign LORD, even if these three men were in it, they could not save their own sons or daughters. They alone would be saved, but the land would be desolate.

[17]"Or if I bring a sword against that country and say, 'Let the sword pass throughout the land,' and I kill its men and their animals, [18]as surely as I live, declares the Sovereign LORD, even if these three men were in it, they could not save their own sons or daughters. They alone would be saved.

[19]"Or if I send a plague into that land and pour out my wrath upon it through bloodshed, killing its men and their animals, [20]as surely as I live, declares the Sovereign LORD, even if Noah, Daniel and Job were in it, they could save neither son nor daughter. They would save only themselves by their righteousness.

[21]"For this is what the Sovereign LORD says: How much worse will it be when I send against Jerusalem my four dreadful judgments—sword and famine and wild beasts and plague—to kill its men and their animals! [22]Yet there will be some survivors—sons and daughters who will be brought out of it. They will come to you, and when you see their conduct and their actions, you will be consoled regarding the disaster I have brought upon Jerusalem—every disaster I have brought upon it. [23]You will be consoled when you see their conduct and their actions, for you will know that I have done nothing in it without cause, declares the Sovereign LORD."

Jerusalem, A Useless Vine

15 The word of the LORD came to me: [2]"Son of man, how is the wood of a vine better than that of a branch on any of the trees in the forest? [3]Is wood ever taken from it to make anything useful? Do they make pegs from it to hang things on? [4]And after it is thrown on the fire as fuel and the fire burns both ends and chars the middle, is it then useful for anything? [5]If it was not useful for anything when it was whole, how much less can it be made into something useful when the fire has burned it and it is charred?

[6]"Therefore this is what the Sovereign LORD says: As I have given the wood of the vine among the trees of the forest as fuel for the fire, so will I treat the people living in Jerusalem. [7]I will set my face against them. Although they have come out of the fire, the fire will yet consume them. And when I set my face against them, you will know that I am the LORD. [8]I will make the land desolate because they have been unfaithful, declares the Sovereign LORD."

An Allegory of Unfaithful Jerusalem

16 The word of the LORD came to me: [2]"Son of man, confront Jerusalem with her detestable practices [3]and say, 'This is what the Sovereign LORD says to Jerusalem: Your ancestry and birth were in the land of the Canaanites; your father was an Amorite and your mother a Hittite. [4]On the day you were born your cord was not cut, nor were you washed with water to make you clean, nor were you rubbed with salt or wrapped in cloths. [5]No one looked on you with pity or had compassion enough to do any of these things for you. Rather, you were thrown out into the open field, for on the day you were born you were despised.

---

[a]14 Or Danel; the Hebrew spelling may suggest a person other than the prophet Daniel; also in verse 20.

⁶" 'Then I passed by and saw you kicking about in your blood, and as you lay there in your blood I said to you, "Live!"ᵃ ⁷I made you grow like a plant of the field. You grew up and developed and became the most beautiful of jewels.ᵇ Your breasts were formed and your hair grew, you who were naked and bare.

⁸" 'Later I passed by, and when I looked at you and saw that you were old enough for love, I spread the corner of my garment over you and covered your nakedness. I gave you my solemn oath and entered into a covenant with you, declares the Sovereign LORD, and you became mine.

⁹" 'I bathedᶜ you with water and washed the blood from you and put ointments on you. ¹⁰I clothed you with an embroidered dress and put leather sandals on you. I dressed you in fine linen and covered you with costly garments. ¹¹I adorned you with jewelry: I put bracelets on your arms and a necklace around your neck, ¹²and I put a ring on your nose, earrings on your ears and a beautiful crown on your head. ¹³So you were adorned with gold and silver; your clothes were of fine linen and costly fabric and embroidered cloth. Your food was fine flour, honey and olive oil. You became very beautiful and rose to be a queen. ¹⁴And your fame spread among the nations on account of your beauty, because the splendor I had given you made your beauty perfect, declares the Sovereign LORD.

¹⁵" 'But you trusted in your beauty and used your fame to become a prostitute. You lavished your favors on anyone who passed by and your beauty became his.ᵈ ¹⁶You took some of your garments to make gaudy high places, where you carried on your prostitution. Such things should not happen, nor should they ever occur. ¹⁷You also took the fine jewelry I gave you, the jewelry made of my gold and silver, and you made for yourself male idols and engaged in prostitution with them. ¹⁸And you took your embroidered clothes to put on them, and you offered my oil and incense before them. ¹⁹Also the food I provided for you—the fine flour, olive oil and honey I gave you to eat—you offered as fragrant incense

before them. That is what happened, declares the Sovereign LORD.

²⁰" 'And you took your sons and daughters whom you bore to me and sacrificed them as food to the idols. Was your prostitution not enough? ²¹You slaughtered my children and sacrificed themᵉ to the idols. ²²In all your detestable practices and your prostitution you did not remember the days of your youth, when you were naked and bare, kicking about in your blood.

²³" 'Woe! Woe to you, declares the Sovereign LORD. In addition to all your other wickedness, ²⁴you built a mound for yourself and made a lofty shrine in every public square. ²⁵At the head of every street you built your lofty shrines and degraded your beauty, offering your body with increasing promiscuity to anyone who passed by. ²⁶You engaged in prostitution with the Egyptians, your lustful neighbors, and provoked me to anger with your increasing promiscuity. ²⁷So I stretched out my hand against you and reduced your territory; I gave you over to the greed of your enemies, the daughters of the Philistines, who were shocked by your lewd conduct. ²⁸You engaged in prostitution with the Assyrians too, because you were insatiable; and even after that, you still were not satisfied. ²⁹Then you increased your promiscuity to include Babylonia,ᶠ a land of merchants, but even with this you were not satisfied.

³⁰" 'How weak-willed you are, declares the Sovereign LORD, when you do all these things, acting like a brazen prostitute! ³¹When you built your mounds at the head of every street and made your lofty shrines in every public square, you were unlike a prostitute, because you scorned payment.

³²" 'You adulterous wife! You prefer strangers to your own husband! ³³Every prostitute receives a fee, but you give

---

ᵃ6 A few Hebrew manuscripts, Septuagint and Syriac; most Hebrew manuscripts *"Live!" And as you lay there in your blood I said to you, "Live!"* ᵇ7 Or *became mature* ᶜ9 Or *I had bathed* ᵈ15 Most Hebrew manuscripts; one Hebrew manuscript (see some Septuagint manuscripts) *by. Such a thing should not happen* ᵉ21 Or *and made them pass through the fire* ᶠ29 Or *Chaldea*

gifts to all your lovers, bribing them to come to you from everywhere for your illicit favors. [34]So in your prostitution you are the opposite of others; no one runs after you for your favors. You are the very opposite, for you give payment and none is given to you.

[35]" 'Therefore, you prostitute, hear the word of the LORD! [36]This is what the Sovereign LORD says: Because you poured out your wealth[a] and exposed your nakedness in your promiscuity with your lovers, and because of all your detestable idols, and because you gave them your children's blood, [37]therefore I am going to gather all your lovers, with whom you found pleasure, those you loved as well as those you hated. I will gather them against you from all around and will strip you in front of them, and they will see all your nakedness. [38]I will sentence you to the punishment of women who commit adultery and who shed blood; I will bring upon you the blood vengeance of my wrath and jealous anger. [39]Then I will hand you over to your lovers, and they will tear down your mounds and destroy your lofty shrines. They will strip you of your clothes and take your fine jewelry and leave you naked and bare. [40]They will bring a mob against you, who will stone you and hack you to pieces with their swords. [41]They will burn down your houses and inflict punishment on you in the sight of many women. I will put a stop to your prostitution, and you will no longer pay your lovers. [42]Then my wrath against you will subside and my jealous anger will turn away from you; I will be calm and no longer angry.

[43]" 'Because you did not remember the days of your youth but enraged me with all these things, I will surely bring down on your head what you have done, declares the Sovereign LORD. Did you not add lewdness to all your other detestable practices?

[44]" 'Everyone who quotes proverbs will quote this proverb about you: "Like mother, like daughter." [45]You are a true daughter of your mother, who despised her husband and her children; and you are a true sister of your sisters, who despised their husbands and their children. Your mother was a Hittite and your fa-

ther an Amorite. [46]Your older sister was Samaria, who lived to the north of you with her daughters; and your younger sister, who lived to the south of you with her daughters, was Sodom. [47]You not only walked in their ways and copied their detestable practices, but in all your ways you soon became more depraved than they. [48]As surely as I live, declares the Sovereign LORD, your sister Sodom and her daughters never did what you and your daughters have done.

[49]" 'Now this was the sin of your sister Sodom: She and her daughters were arrogant, overfed and unconcerned; they did not help the poor and needy. [50]They were haughty and did detestable things before me. Therefore I did away with them as you have seen. [51]Samaria did not commit half the sins you did. You have done more detestable things than they, and have made your sisters seem righteous by all these things you have done. [52]Bear your disgrace, for you have furnished some justification for your sisters. Because your sins were more vile than theirs, they appear more righteous than you. So then, be ashamed and bear your disgrace, for you have made your sisters appear righteous.

[53]" 'However, I will restore the fortunes of Sodom and her daughters and of Samaria and her daughters, and your fortunes along with them, [54]so that you may bear your disgrace and be ashamed of all you have done in giving them comfort. [55]And your sisters, Sodom with her daughters and Samaria with her daughters, will return to what they were before; and you and your daughters will return to what you were before. [56]You would not even mention your sister Sodom in the day of your pride, [57]before your wickedness was uncovered. Even so, you are now scorned by the daughters of Edom[b] and all her neighbors and the daughters of the Philistines—all those around you who despise you. [58]You will bear the consequences of your lewdness and your detestable practices, declares the LORD.

---

[a]36 Or *lust*   [b]57 Many Hebrew manuscripts and Syriac; most Hebrew manuscripts, Septuagint and Vulgate *Aram*

⁵⁹" 'This is what the Sovereign LORD says: I will deal with you as you deserve, because you have despised my oath by breaking the covenant. ⁶⁰Yet I will remember the covenant I made with you in the days of your youth, and I will establish an everlasting covenant with you. ⁶¹Then you will remember your ways and be ashamed when you receive your sisters, both those who are older than you and those who are younger. I will give them to you as daughters, but not on the basis of my covenant with you. ⁶²So I will establish my covenant with you, and you will know that I am the LORD. ⁶³Then, when I make atonement for you for all you have done, you will remember and be ashamed and never again open your mouth because of your humiliation, declares the Sovereign LORD.' "

Two Eagles and a Vine

17 The word of the LORD came to me: ²"Son of man, set forth an allegory and tell the house of Israel a parable. ³Say to them, 'This is what the Sovereign LORD says: A great eagle with powerful wings, long feathers and full plumage of varied colors came to Lebanon. Taking hold of the top of a cedar, ⁴he broke off its topmost shoot and carried it away to a land of merchants, where he planted it in a city of traders.

⁵" 'He took some of the seed of your land and put it in fertile soil. He planted it like a willow by abundant water, ⁶and it sprouted and became a low, spreading vine. Its branches turned toward him, but its roots remained under it. So it became a vine and produced branches and put out leafy boughs.

⁷" 'But there was another great eagle with powerful wings and full plumage. The vine now sent out its roots toward him from the plot where it was planted and stretched out its branches to him for water. ⁸It had been planted in good soil by abundant water so that it would produce branches, bear fruit and become a splendid vine.'

⁹"Say to them, 'This is what the Sovereign LORD says: Will it thrive? Will it not be uprooted and stripped of its fruit so that it withers? All its new growth will wither. It will not take a strong arm or many people to pull it up by the roots. ¹⁰Even if it is transplanted, will it thrive? Will it not wither completely when the east wind strikes it—wither away in the plot where it grew?' "

¹¹Then the word of the LORD came to me: ¹²"Say to this rebellious house, 'Do you not know what these things mean?' Say to them: 'The king of Babylon went to Jerusalem and carried off her king and her nobles, bringing them back with him to Babylon. ¹³Then he took a member of the royal family and made a treaty with him, putting him under oath. He also carried away the leading men of the land, ¹⁴so that the kingdom would be brought low, unable to rise again, surviving only by keeping his treaty. ¹⁵But the king rebelled against him by sending his envoys to Egypt to get horses and a large army. Will he succeed? Will he who does such things escape? Will he break the treaty and yet escape?

¹⁶" 'As surely as I live, declares the Sovereign LORD, he shall die in Babylon, in the land of the king who put him on the throne, whose oath he despised and whose treaty he broke. ¹⁷Pharaoh with his mighty army and great horde will be of no help to him in war, when ramps are built and siege works erected to destroy many lives. ¹⁸He despised the oath by breaking the covenant. Because he had given his hand in pledge and yet did all these things, he shall not escape.

¹⁹" 'Therefore this is what the Sovereign LORD says: As surely as I live, I will bring down on his head my oath that he despised and my covenant that he broke. ²⁰I will spread my net for him, and he will be caught in my snare. I will bring him to Babylon and execute judgment upon him there because he was unfaithful to me. ²¹All his fleeing troops will fall by the sword, and the survivors will be scattered to the winds. Then you will know that I the LORD have spoken.

²²" 'This is what the Sovereign LORD says: I myself will take a shoot from the very top of a cedar and plant it; I will break off a tender sprig from its topmost shoots and plant it on a high and lofty mountain. ²³On the mountain heights of Israel I will plant it; it will produce branches and bear fruit and become a

splendid cedar. Birds of every kind will nest in it; they will find shelter in the shade of its branches. ²⁴All the trees of the field will know that I the LORD bring down the tall tree and make the low tree grow tall. I dry up the green tree and make the dry tree flourish.

" 'I the LORD have spoken, and I will do it.' "

The Soul Who Sins Will Die

18 The word of the LORD came to me: ²"What do you people mean by quoting this proverb about the land of Israel:

" 'The fathers eat sour grapes,
   and the children's teeth are set on
     edge'?

³"As surely as I live, declares the Sovereign LORD, you will no longer quote this proverb in Israel. ⁴For every living soul belongs to me, the father as well as the son—both alike belong to me. The soul who sins is the one who will die.

⁵"Suppose there is a righteous man
   who does what is just and right.
⁶He does not eat at the mountain
   shrines
   or look to the idols of the house of
     Israel.
He does not defile his neighbor's wife
   or lie with a woman during her
     period.
⁷He does not oppress anyone,
   but returns what he took in pledge
     for a loan.
He does not commit robbery
   but gives his food to the hungry
   and provides clothing for the
     naked.
⁸He does not lend at usury
   or take excessive interest.^a
He withholds his hand from doing
   wrong
   and judges fairly between man and
     man.
⁹He follows my decrees
   and faithfully keeps my laws.
That man is righteous;
   he will surely live,
     declares the Sovereign LORD.

¹⁰"Suppose he has a violent son, who sheds blood or does any of these other things^b ¹¹(though the father has done none of them):

"He eats at the mountain shrines.
He defiles his neighbor's wife.
¹²He oppresses the poor and needy.
He commits robbery.
He does not return what he took in
   pledge.
He looks to the idols.
He does detestable things.
¹³He lends at usury and takes excessive
   interest.

Will such a man live? He will not! Because he has done all these detestable things, he will surely be put to death and his blood will be on his own head.

¹⁴"But suppose this son has a son who sees all the sins his father commits, and though he sees them, he does not do such things:

¹⁵"He does not eat at the mountain
   shrines
   or look to the idols of the house of
     Israel.
He does not defile his neighbor's wife.
¹⁶He does not oppress anyone
   or require a pledge for a loan.
He does not commit robbery
   but gives his food to the hungry
   and provides clothing for the naked.
¹⁷He withholds his hand from sin^c
   and takes no usury or excessive
     interest.
He keeps my laws and follows my
   decrees.

He will not die for his father's sin; he will surely live. ¹⁸But his father will die for his own sin, because he practiced extortion, robbed his brother and did what was wrong among his people.

¹⁹"Yet you ask, 'Why does the son not share the guilt of his father?' Since the son has done what is just and right and has been careful to keep all my decrees, he will surely live. ²⁰The soul who sins is the one who will die. The son will not share the guilt of the father, nor will the father share the guilt of the son. The righteousness of the righteous man will

---

^a8 Or *take interest*; similarly in verses 13 and 17
^b10 Or *things to a brother*   ^c17 Septuagint (see also verse 8); Hebrew *from the poor*

be credited to him, and the wickedness of the wicked will be charged against him.

²¹"But if a wicked man turns away from all the sins he has committed and keeps all my decrees and does what is just and right, he will surely live; he will not die. ²²None of the offenses he has committed will be remembered against him. Because of the righteous things he has done, he will live. ²³Do I take any

Scum Lover

Huh?

Ezekiel 18:23

Sometimes wicked or cruel people are called the "scum of the earth." The truth is, God loves these people as much as he loves Christians. Of course, God would rather have people turn from their wicked ways than continue to sin. In this passage, God shows his compassionate heart. He wants people to freely enjoy his love. Even when you read about people being destroyed in the Old Testament, remember that God would prefer that they turn from their sins and come to know his love.

pleasure in the death of the wicked? declares the Sovereign LORD. Rather, am I not pleased when they turn from their ways and live?

²⁴"But if a righteous man turns from his righteousness and commits sin and does the same detestable things the wicked man does, will he live? None of the righteous things he has done will be remembered. Because of the unfaithfulness he is guilty of and because of the sins he has committed, he will die. ²⁵"Yet you say, 'The way of the Lord is not just.' Hear, O house of Israel: Is my way unjust? Is it not your ways that are unjust? ²⁶If a righteous man turns from his righteousness and commits sin, he will die for it; because of the sin he has committed he will die. ²⁷But if a wicked man turns away from the wickedness he has committed and does what is just and right, he will save his life. ²⁸Because he considers all the offenses he has commit-

ted and turns away from them, he will surely live; he will not die. ²⁹Yet the house of Israel says, 'The way of the Lord is not just.' Are my ways unjust, O house of Israel? Is it not your ways that are unjust?

³⁰"Therefore, O house of Israel, I will judge you, each one according to his ways, declares the Sovereign LORD. Repent! Turn away from all your offenses; then sin will not be your downfall. ³¹Rid yourselves of all the offenses you have committed, and get a new heart and a new spirit. Why will you die, O house of Israel? ³²For I take no pleasure in the death of anyone, declares the Sovereign LORD. Repent and live!

A Lament for Israel's Princes

19 "Take up a lament concerning the princes of Israel ²and say:

" 'What a lioness was your mother
    among the lions!
She lay down among the young lions
    and reared her cubs.
³ She brought up one of her cubs,
    and he became a strong lion.
He learned to tear the prey
    and he devoured men.
⁴ The nations heard about him,
    and he was trapped in their pit.
They led him with hooks
    to the land of Egypt.

⁵ " 'When she saw her hope unfulfilled,
    her expectation gone,
she took another of her cubs
    and made him a strong lion.
⁶ He prowled among the lions,
    for he was now a strong lion.
He learned to tear the prey
    and he devoured men.
⁷ He broke down[a] their strongholds
    and devastated their towns.
The land and all who were in it
    were terrified by his roaring.
⁸ Then the nations came against him,
    those from regions round about.
They spread their net for him,
    and he was trapped in their pit.
⁹ With hooks they pulled him into a cage
    and brought him to the king of
        Babylon.

[a]7 Targum (see Septuagint); Hebrew He knew

They put him in prison,
  so his roar was heard no longer
  on the mountains of Israel.

¹⁰" 'Your mother was like a vine in your
      vineyard*
  planted by the water;
it was fruitful and full of branches
  because of abundant water.
¹¹Its branches were strong,
  fit for a ruler's scepter.
It towered high
  above the thick foliage,
conspicuous for its height
  and for its many branches.
¹²But it was uprooted in fury
  and thrown to the ground.
The east wind made it shrivel,
  it was stripped of its fruit;
its strong branches withered
  and fire consumed them.
¹³Now it is planted in the desert,
  in a dry and thirsty land.
¹⁴Fire spread from one of its main*
      branches
  and consumed its fruit.
No strong branch is left on it
  fit for a ruler's scepter.'

This is a lament and is to be used as a lament."

Rebellious Israel

20 In the seventh year, in the fifth month on the tenth day, some of the elders of Israel came to inquire of the LORD, and they sat down in front of me.

²Then the word of the LORD came to me: ³"Son of man, speak to the elders of Israel and say to them, 'This is what the Sovereign LORD says: Have you come to inquire of me? As surely as I live, I will not let you inquire of me, declares the Sovereign LORD.'

⁴"Will you judge them? Will you judge them, son of man? Then confront them with the detestable practices of their fathers ⁵and say to them: 'This is what the Sovereign LORD says: On the day I chose Israel, I swore with uplifted hand to the descendants of the house of Jacob and revealed myself to them in Egypt. With uplifted hand I said to them, "I am the LORD your God." ⁶On that day I swore to them that I would bring them out of Egypt into a land I had searched out for them, a land flowing with milk and honey, the most beautiful of all lands. ⁷And I said to them, "Each of you, get rid of the vile images you have set your eyes on, and do not defile yourselves with the idols of Egypt. I am the LORD your God."

⁸" 'But they rebelled against me and would not listen to me; they did not get rid of the vile images they had set their eyes on, nor did they forsake the idols of Egypt. So I said I would pour out my wrath on them and spend my anger against them in Egypt. ⁹But for the sake of my name I did what would keep it from being profaned in the eyes of the nations they lived among and in whose sight I had revealed myself to the Israelites by bringing them out of Egypt. ¹⁰Therefore I led them out of Egypt and brought them into the desert. ¹¹I gave them my decrees and made known to them my laws, for the man who obeys them will live by them. ¹²Also I gave them my Sabbaths as a sign between us, so they would know that I the LORD made them holy.

¹³" 'Yet the people of Israel rebelled against me in the desert. They did not follow my decrees but rejected my laws—although the man who obeys them will live by them—and they utterly desecrated my Sabbaths. So I said I would pour out my wrath on them and destroy them in the desert. ¹⁴But for the sake of my name I did what would keep it from being profaned in the eyes of the nations in whose sight I had brought them out. ¹⁵Also with uplifted hand I swore to them in the desert that I would not bring them into the land I had given them—a land flowing with milk and honey, most beautiful of all lands— ¹⁶because they rejected my laws and did not follow my decrees and desecrated my Sabbaths. For their hearts were devoted to their idols. ¹⁷Yet I looked on them with pity and did not destroy them or put an end to them in the desert. ¹⁸I said to their children in the desert, "Do not follow the statutes of your fathers or keep their laws or defile yourselves with their idols. ¹⁹I am the LORD your God; follow my decrees and be careful to keep

---

a 10 Two Hebrew manuscripts; most Hebrew manuscripts *your blood*   *b 14* Or *from under its*

my laws. ²⁰Keep my Sabbaths holy, that they may be a sign between us. Then you will know that I am the LORD your God."

²¹" 'But the children rebelled against me: They did not follow my decrees, they were not careful to keep my laws—although the man who obeys them will live by them—and they desecrated my Sabbaths. So I said I would pour out my wrath on them and spend my anger against them in the desert. ²²But I withheld my hand, and for the sake of my name I did what would keep it from being profaned in the eyes of the nations in whose sight I had brought them out. ²³Also with uplifted hand I swore to them in the desert that I would disperse them among the nations and scatter them through the countries, ²⁴because they had not obeyed my laws but had rejected my decrees and desecrated my Sabbaths, and their eyes lusted after their fathers' idols. ²⁵I also gave them over to statutes that were not good and laws they could not live by; ²⁶I let them become defiled through their gifts—the sacrifice of every firstborn*a*—that I might fill them with horror so they would know that I am the LORD.'

²⁷"Therefore, son of man, speak to the people of Israel and say to them, 'This is what the Sovereign LORD says: In this also your fathers blasphemed me by forsaking me: ²⁸When I brought them into the land I had sworn to give them and they saw any high hill or any leafy tree, there they offered their sacrifices, made offerings that provoked me to anger, presented their fragrant incense and poured out their drink offerings. ²⁹Then I said to them: What is this high place you go to?' " (It is called Bamah*b* to this day.)

Judgment and Restoration

³⁰"Therefore say to the house of Israel: 'This is what the Sovereign LORD says: Will you defile yourselves the way your fathers did and lust after their vile images? ³¹When you offer your gifts—the sacrifice of your sons in*c* the fire—you continue to defile yourselves with all your idols to this day. Am I to let you inquire of me, O house of Israel? As surely as I live, declares the Sovereign LORD, I will not let you inquire of me.

³²" 'You say, "We want to be like the nations, like the peoples of the world, who serve wood and stone." But what you have in mind will never happen. ³³As surely as I live, declares the Sovereign LORD, I will rule over you with a mighty hand and an outstretched arm and with outpoured wrath. ³⁴I will bring you from the nations and gather you from the countries where you have been scattered—with a mighty hand and an outstretched arm and with outpoured wrath. ³⁵I will bring you into the desert of the nations and there, face to face, I will execute judgment upon you. ³⁶As I judged your fathers in the desert of the land of Egypt, so I will judge you, declares the Sovereign LORD. ³⁷I will take note of you as you pass under my rod, and I will bring you into the bond of the covenant. ³⁸I will purge you of those who revolt and rebel against me. Although I will bring them out of the land where they are living, yet they will not enter the land of Israel. Then you will know that I am the LORD.

³⁹" 'As for you, O house of Israel, this is what the Sovereign LORD says: Go and serve your idols, every one of you! But afterward you will surely listen to me and no longer profane my holy name with your gifts and idols. ⁴⁰For on my holy mountain, the high mountain of Israel, declares the Sovereign LORD, there in the land the entire house of Israel will serve me, and there I will accept them. There I will require your offerings and your choice gifts,*d* along with all your holy sacrifices. ⁴¹I will accept you as fragrant incense when I bring you out from the nations and gather you from the countries where you have been scattered, and I will show myself holy among you in the sight of the nations. ⁴²Then you will know that I am the LORD, when I bring you into the land of Israel, the land I had sworn with uplifted hand to give to your fathers. ⁴³There you will remember your conduct and all the actions by which you have defiled yourselves, and

---

a26 Or *—making every firstborn pass through the fire*   *b29 Bamah* means *high place.*   *c31* Or *—making your sons pass through*   *d40* Or *and the gifts of your firstfruits*

you will loathe yourselves for all the evil you have done. ⁴⁴You will know that I am the LORD, when I deal with you for my name's sake and not according to your evil ways and your corrupt practices, O house of Israel, declares the Sovereign LORD.' "

Prophecy Against the South

⁴⁵The word of the LORD came to me: ⁴⁶"Son of man, set your face toward the south; preach against the south and prophesy against the forest of the southland. ⁴⁷Say to the southern forest: 'Hear the word of the LORD. This is what the Sovereign LORD says: I am about to set fire to you, and it will consume all your trees, both green and dry. The blazing flame will not be quenched, and every face from south to north will be scorched by it. ⁴⁸Everyone will see that I the LORD have kindled it; it will not be quenched.' "

⁴⁹Then I said, "Ah, Sovereign LORD! They are saying of me, 'Isn't he just telling parables?' "

Babylon, God's Sword of Judgment

21 The word of the LORD came to me: ²"Son of man, set your face against Jerusalem and preach against the sanctuary. Prophesy against the land of Israel ³and say to her: 'This is what the LORD says: I am against you. I will draw my sword from its scabbard and cut off from you both the righteous and the wicked. ⁴Because I am going to cut off the righteous and the wicked, my sword will be unsheathed against everyone from south to north. ⁵Then all people will know that I the LORD have drawn my sword from its scabbard; it will not return again.'

⁶"Therefore groan, son of man! Groan before them with broken heart and bitter grief. ⁷And when they ask you, 'Why are you groaning?' you shall say, 'Because of

---

Tuesday

Under Pressure

Read Ezekiel 20:32

I guess we all do it sooner or later. We give in to the pressure to be like everyone else. Maybe we tell a lie or drink a beer or 2. Maybe we just hide our faith so other people won't think we're too "religious." Even if we don't give in permanently, we all let peer pressure get to us sometimes. I know I do.

There are times when I change myself so other people will like me. I start thinking some of my friends have cooler lives than I do, so I start acting like them. But whenever I change myself like that, I never end up happier. I just end up feeling like a fake.

Maybe that's because I know the real me is someone who wants to follow God, even when it's not the cool thing to do. The truth is, God loves me for who I am on the inside. All that stuff that the world thinks makes a person cool doesn't really matter to God. And in the end, he's the only one I really need to please.

Chris age 14

❶ Think about the last time you gave in to peer pressure. How did you feel afterward?

❷ What are some of the ways your friends tempt you? Write down specific ways you can resist those temptations.

❸ Ask God to help you follow him when you're tempted to follow the crowd.

Turn to page 997 for your next devotion.

the news that is coming. Every heart will melt and every hand go limp; every spirit will become faint and every knee become as weak as water.' It is coming! It will surely take place, declares the Sovereign LORD."

[8]The word of the LORD came to me: [9]"Son of man, prophesy and say, 'This is what the Lord says:

" 'A sword, a sword,
    sharpened and polished—
[10]sharpened for the slaughter,
    polished to flash like lightning!

" 'Shall we rejoice in the scepter of my son Judah? The sword despises every such stick.

[11]" 'The sword is appointed to be polished,
    to be grasped with the hand;
  it is sharpened and polished,
    made ready for the hand of the slayer.
[12]Cry out and wail, son of man,
    for it is against my people;
  it is against all the princes of Israel.
They are thrown to the sword
    along with my people.
Therefore beat your breast.

[13]" 'Testing will surely come. And what if the scepter of Judah, which the sword despises, does not continue? declares the Sovereign LORD.'

[14]"So then, son of man, prophesy
    and strike your hands together.
Let the sword strike twice,
    even three times.
  It is a sword for slaughter—
    a sword for great slaughter,
    closing in on them from every side.
[15]So that hearts may melt
    and the fallen be many,
  I have stationed the sword for slaughter[a]
    at all their gates.
Oh! It is made to flash like lightning,
    it is grasped for slaughter.
[16]O sword, slash to the right,
    then to the left,
    wherever your blade is turned.
[17]I too will strike my hands together,
    and my wrath will subside.
I the LORD have spoken."

[18]The word of the LORD came to me: [19]"Son of man, mark out two roads for the sword of the king of Babylon to take, both starting from the same country. Make a signpost where the road branches off to the city. [20]Mark out one road for the sword to come against Rabbah of the Ammonites and another against Judah and fortified Jerusalem. [21]For the king of Babylon will stop at the fork in the road, at the junction of the two roads, to seek an omen: He will cast lots with arrows, he will consult his idols, he will examine the liver. [22]Into his right hand will come the lot for Jerusalem, where he is to set up battering rams, to give the command to slaughter, to sound the battle cry, to set battering rams against the gates, to build a ramp and to erect siege works. [23]It will seem like a false omen to those who have sworn allegiance to him, but he will remind them of their guilt and take them captive.

[24]"Therefore this is what the Sovereign LORD says: 'Because you people have brought to mind your guilt by your open rebellion, revealing your sins in all that you do—because you have done this, you will be taken captive.

[25]" 'O profane and wicked prince of Israel, whose day has come, whose time of punishment has reached its climax, [26]this is what the Sovereign LORD says: Take off the turban, remove the crown. It will not be as it was: The lowly will be exalted and the exalted will be brought low. [27]A ruin! A ruin! I will make it a ruin! It will not be restored until he comes to whom it rightfully belongs; to him I will give it.'

[28]"And you, son of man, prophesy and say, 'This is what the Sovereign LORD says about the Ammonites and their insults:

" 'A sword, a sword,
    drawn for the slaughter,
  polished to consume
    and to flash like lightning!
[29]Despite false visions concerning you
    and lying divinations about you,
  it will be laid on the necks
    of the wicked who are to be slain,
  whose day has come,

---

[a]15 Septuagint; the meaning of the Hebrew for this word is uncertain.

whose time of punishment has
    reached its climax.
30 Return the sword to its scabbard.
    In the place where you were
        created,
    in the land of your ancestry,
        I will judge you.
31 I will pour out my wrath upon you
        and breathe out my fiery anger
            against you;
    I will hand you over to brutal men,
        men skilled in destruction.
32 You will be fuel for the fire,
        your blood will be shed in your
            land,
    you will be remembered no more;
        for I the LORD have spoken.' "

Jerusalem's Sins

22 The word of the LORD came to me:
2 "Son of man, will you judge her?
Will you judge this city of bloodshed?
Then confront her with all her detestable
practices 3 and say: 'This is what the Sovereign LORD says: O city that brings on
herself doom by shedding blood in her
midst and defiles herself by making
idols, 4 you have become guilty because
of the blood you have shed and have become defiled by the idols you have made.
You have brought your days to a close,
and the end of your years has come.
Therefore I will make you an object of
scorn to the nations and a laughingstock
to all the countries. 5 Those who are near
and those who are far away will mock
you, O infamous city, full of turmoil.

6 " 'See how each of the princes of Israel who are in you uses his power to shed
blood. 7 In you they have treated father
and mother with contempt; in you they
have oppressed the alien and mistreated
the fatherless and the widow. 8 You have
despised my holy things and desecrated
my Sabbaths. 9 In you are slanderous men
bent on shedding blood; in you are those
who eat at the mountain shrines and
commit lewd acts. 10 In you are those who
dishonor their fathers' bed; in you are
those who violate women during their
period, when they are ceremonially unclean. 11 In you one man commits a detestable offense with his neighbor's wife,
another shamefully defiles his daughter-
in-law, and another violates his sister,

his own father's daughter. 12 In you men
accept bribes to shed blood; you take
usury and excessive interest[a] and make
unjust gain from your neighbors by extortion. And you have forgotten me, declares the Sovereign LORD.

13 " 'I will surely strike my hands together at the unjust gain you have made
and at the blood you have shed in your
midst. 14 Will your courage endure or
your hands be strong in the day I deal
with you? I the LORD have spoken, and I
will do it. 15 I will disperse you among the
nations and scatter you through the
countries; and I will put an end to your
uncleanness. 16 When you have been
defiled[b] in the eyes of the nations, you
will know that I am the LORD.' "

17 Then the word of the LORD came to
me: 18 "Son of man, the house of Israel
has become dross to me; all of them are
the copper, tin, iron and lead left inside a
furnace. They are but the dross of silver.
19 Therefore this is what the Sovereign
LORD says: 'Because you have all become
dross, I will gather you into Jerusalem.
20 As men gather silver, copper, iron, lead
and tin into a furnace to melt it with a fiery blast, so will I gather you in my anger and my wrath and put you inside the
city and melt you. 21 I will gather you and
I will blow on you with my fiery wrath,
and you will be melted inside her. 22 As
silver is melted in a furnace, so you will
be melted inside her, and you will know
that I the LORD have poured out my wrath
upon you.' "

23 Again the word of the LORD came to
me: 24 "Son of man, say to the land, 'You
are a land that has had no rain or
showers[c] in the day of wrath.' 25 There is a
conspiracy of her princes[d] within her like
a roaring lion tearing its prey; they devour people, take treasures and precious
things and make many widows within
her. 26 Her priests do violence to my law
and profane my holy things; they do not
distinguish between the holy and the
common; they teach that there is no difference between the unclean and the

---

a 12 Or usury and interest   b 16 Or When I have
allotted you your inheritance   c 24 Septuagint;
Hebrew has not been cleansed or rained on
d 25 Septuagint; Hebrew prophets

clean; and they shut their eyes to the keeping of my Sabbaths, so that I am profaned among them. ²⁷Her officials within her are like wolves tearing their prey; they shed blood and kill people to make unjust gain. ²⁸Her prophets whitewash these deeds for them by false visions and lying divinations. They say, 'This is what the Sovereign LORD says'— when the LORD has not spoken. ²⁹The people of the land practice extortion and commit robbery; they oppress the poor and needy and mistreat the alien, denying them justice.

³⁰"I looked for a man among them who would build up the wall and stand before me in the gap on behalf of the land so I would not have to destroy it, but I found none. ³¹So I will pour out my wrath on them and consume them with my fiery anger, bringing down on their own heads all they have done, declares the Sovereign LORD."

Two Adulterous Sisters

23 The word of the LORD came to me: ²"Son of man, there were two women, daughters of the same mother. ³They became prostitutes in Egypt, engaging in prostitution from their youth. In that land their breasts were fondled and their virgin bosoms caressed. ⁴The older was named Oholah, and her sister was Oholibah. They were mine and gave birth to sons and daughters. Oholah is Samaria, and Oholibah is Jerusalem.

⁵"Oholah engaged in prostitution while she was still mine; and she lusted after her lovers, the Assyrians—warriors ⁶clothed in blue, governors and commanders, all of them handsome young men, and mounted horsemen. ⁷She gave herself as a prostitute to all the elite of the Assyrians and defiled herself with all the idols of everyone she lusted after. ⁸She did not give up the prostitution she began in Egypt, when during her youth men slept with her, caressed her virgin bosom and poured out their lust upon her.

⁹"Therefore I handed her over to her lovers, the Assyrians, for whom she lusted. ¹⁰They stripped her naked, took away her sons and daughters and killed her with the sword. She became a byword among women, and punishment was inflicted on her.

¹¹"Her sister Oholibah saw this, yet in her lust and prostitution she was more depraved than her sister. ¹²She too lusted after the Assyrians—governors and commanders, warriors in full dress, mounted horsemen, all handsome young men. ¹³I saw that she too defiled herself; both of them went the same way.

¹⁴"But she carried her prostitution still further. She saw men portrayed on a wall, figures of Chaldeans[a] portrayed in red, ¹⁵with belts around their waists and flowing turbans on their heads; all of them looked like Babylonian chariot officers, natives of Chaldea.[b] ¹⁶As soon as she saw them, she lusted after them and sent messengers to them in Chaldea. ¹⁷Then the Babylonians came to her, to the bed of love, and in their lust they defiled her. After she had been defiled by them, she turned away from them in disgust. ¹⁸When she carried on her prostitution openly and exposed her nakedness, I turned away from her in disgust, just as I had turned away from her sister. ¹⁹Yet she became more and more promiscuous as she recalled the days of her youth, when she was a prostitute in Egypt. ²⁰There she lusted after her lovers, whose genitals were like those of donkeys and whose emission was like that of horses. ²¹So you longed for the lewdness of your youth, when in Egypt your bosom was caressed and your young breasts fondled.[c]

²²"Therefore, Oholibah, this is what the Sovereign LORD says: I will stir up your lovers against you, those you turned away from in disgust, and I will bring them against you from every side— ²³the Babylonians and all the Chaldeans, the men of Pekod and Shoa and Koa, and all the Assyrians with them, handsome young men, all of them governors and commanders, chariot officers and men of high rank, all mounted on horses. ²⁴They will come against you with weapons,[d] chariots and wagons and with a throng

---

a14 Or *Babylonians*   *b15* Or *Babylonia*; also in verse 16   *c21* Syriac (see also verse 3); Hebrew *caressed because of your young breasts*   *d24* The meaning of the Hebrew for this word is uncertain.

of people; they will take up positions against you on every side with large and small shields and with helmets. I will turn you over to them for punishment, and they will punish you according to their standards. [25]I will direct my jealous anger against you, and they will deal with you in fury. They will cut off your noses and your ears, and those of you who are left will fall by the sword. They will take away your sons and daughters, and those of you who are left will be consumed by fire. [26]They will also strip you of your clothes and take your fine jewelry. [27]So I will put a stop to the lewdness and prostitution you began in Egypt. You will not look on these things with longing or remember Egypt anymore.

[28]"For this is what the Sovereign LORD says: I am about to hand you over to those you hate, to those you turned away from in disgust. [29]They will deal with you in hatred and take away everything you have worked for. They will leave you naked and bare, and the shame of your prostitution will be exposed. Your lewdness and promiscuity [30]have brought this upon you, because you lusted after the nations and defiled yourself with their idols. [31]You have gone the way of your sister; so I will put her cup into your hand.

[32]"This is what the Sovereign LORD says:

"You will drink your sister's cup,
　a cup large and deep;
it will bring scorn and derision,
　for it holds so much.
[33]You will be filled with drunkenness
　　and sorrow,
　the cup of ruin and desolation,
　　the cup of your sister Samaria.
[34]You will drink it and drain it dry;
　you will dash it to pieces
　and tear your breasts.

I have spoken, declares the Sovereign LORD.

[35]"Therefore this is what the Sovereign LORD says: Since you have forgotten me and thrust me behind your back, you must bear the consequences of your lewdness and prostitution."

[36]The LORD said to me: "Son of man, will you judge Oholah and Oholibah? Then confront them with their detestable practices, [37]for they have committed adultery and blood is on their hands. They committed adultery with their idols; they even sacrificed their children, whom they bore to me,[a] as food for them. [38]They have also done this to me: At that same time they defiled my sanctuary and desecrated my Sabbaths. [39]On the very day they sacrificed their children to their idols, they entered my sanctuary and desecrated it. That is what they did in my house.

[40]"They even sent messengers for men who came from far away, and when they arrived you bathed yourself for them, painted your eyes and put on your jewelry. [41]You sat on an elegant couch, with a table spread before it on which you had placed the incense and oil that belonged to me.

[42]"The noise of a carefree crowd was around her; Sabeans[b] were brought from the desert along with men from the rabble, and they put bracelets on the arms of the woman and her sister and beautiful crowns on their heads. [43]Then I said about the one worn out by adultery, 'Now let them use her as a prostitute, for that is all she is.' [44]And they slept with her. As men sleep with a prostitute, so they slept with those lewd women, Oholah and Oholibah. [45]But righteous men will sentence them to the punishment of women who commit adultery and shed blood, because they are adulterous and blood is on their hands.

[46]"This is what the Sovereign LORD says: Bring a mob against them and give them over to terror and plunder. [47]The mob will stone them and cut them down with their swords; they will kill their sons and daughters and burn down their houses.

[48]"So I will put an end to lewdness in the land, that all women may take warning and not imitate you. [49]You will suffer the penalty for your lewdness and bear the consequences of your sins of idolatry. Then you will know that I am the Sovereign LORD."

---

[a]37 Or *even made the children they bore to me pass through the fire*　　[b]42 Or *drunkards*

The Cooking Pot

24 In the ninth year, in the tenth month on the tenth day, the word of the LORD came to me: ²"Son of man, record this date, this very date, because the king of Babylon has laid siege to Jerusalem this very day. ³Tell this rebellious house a parable and say to them: 'This is what the Sovereign LORD says:

" 'Put on the cooking pot; put it on
  and pour water into it.
⁴Put into it the pieces of meat,
  all the choice pieces—the leg and
    the shoulder.
Fill it with the best of these bones;
⁵ take the pick of the flock.
Pile wood beneath it for the bones;
  bring it to a boil
  and cook the bones in it.

⁶" 'For this is what the Sovereign LORD says:

" 'Woe to the city of bloodshed,
  to the pot now encrusted,
  whose deposit will not go away!
Empty it piece by piece
  without casting lots for them.

⁷" 'For the blood she shed is in her
    midst:
She poured it on the bare rock;
she did not pour it on the ground,
  where the dust would cover it.
⁸To stir up wrath and take revenge
  I put her blood on the bare rock,
  so that it would not be covered.

⁹" 'Therefore this is what the Sovereign LORD says:

" 'Woe to the city of bloodshed!
  I, too, will pile the wood high.
¹⁰So heap on the wood
  and kindle the fire.
Cook the meat well,
  mixing in the spices;
  and let the bones be charred.
¹¹Then set the empty pot on the
    coals
  till it becomes hot and its copper
    glows
so its impurities may be melted
  and its deposit burned away.
¹²It has frustrated all efforts;

its heavy deposit has not been
    removed,
  not even by fire.

¹³" 'Now your impurity is lewdness. Because I tried to cleanse you but you would not be cleansed from your impurity, you will not be clean again until my wrath against you has subsided.

¹⁴" 'I the LORD have spoken. The time has come for me to act. I will not hold back; I will not have pity, nor will I relent. You will be judged according to your conduct and your actions, declares the Sovereign LORD.' "

Ezekiel's Wife Dies

¹⁵The word of the LORD came to me: ¹⁶"Son of man, with one blow I am about to take away from you the delight of your eyes. Yet do not lament or weep or shed any tears. ¹⁷Groan quietly; do

Hang On, Zeke

Huh?

Ezekiel 24:16

God wasn't being cruel when he told Ezekiel not to mourn for his wife's death. Some people read this and think that God is a big meanie who thinks we shouldn't be sad when bad things happen. Not true! Instead, Ezekiel's wife is a symbol of Jerusalem. Just as Ezekiel's wife was the "delight" of his eyes, so Jerusalem was the "delight" of Israel's eyes. Jerusalem was about to fall to another conqueror, and God didn't want Israel to mourn publicly for it. So he had Ezekiel demonstrate what he wanted the Israelites to do.

not mourn for the dead. Keep your turban fastened and your sandals on your feet; do not cover the lower part of your face or eat the customary food of mourners."

¹⁸So I spoke to the people in the morning, and in the evening my wife died. The next morning I did as I had been commanded.

¹⁹Then the people asked me, "Won't

you tell us what these things have to do with us?"

²⁰So I said to them, "The word of the LORD came to me: ²¹Say to the house of Israel, 'This is what the Sovereign LORD says: I am about to desecrate my sanctuary—the stronghold in which you take pride, the delight of your eyes, the object of your affection. The sons and daughters you left behind will fall by the sword. ²²And you will do as I have done. You will not cover the lower part of your face or eat the customary food of mourners. ²³You will keep your turbans on your heads and your sandals on your feet. You will not mourn or weep but will waste away because of^a your sins and groan among yourselves. ²⁴Ezekiel will be a sign to you; you will do just as he has done. When this happens, you will know that I am the Sovereign LORD.'

²⁵"And you, son of man, on the day I take away their stronghold, their joy and glory, the delight of their eyes, their heart's desire, and their sons and daughters as well— ²⁶on that day a fugitive will come to tell you the news. ²⁷At that time your mouth will be opened; you will speak with him and will no longer be silent. So you will be a sign to them, and they will know that I am the LORD."

A Prophecy Against Ammon

25 The word of the LORD came to me: ²"Son of man, set your face against the Ammonites and prophesy against them. ³Say to them, 'Hear the word of the Sovereign LORD. This is what the Sovereign LORD says: Because you said "Aha!" over my sanctuary when it was desecrated and over the land of Israel when it was laid waste and over the people of Judah when they went into exile, ⁴therefore I am going to give you to the people of the East as a possession. They will set up their camps and pitch their tents among you; they will eat your fruit and drink your milk. ⁵I will turn Rabbah into a pasture for camels and Ammon into a resting place for sheep. Then you will know that I am the LORD. ⁶For this is what the Sovereign LORD says: Because you have clapped your hands and stamped your feet, rejoicing with all the malice of your heart against

the land of Israel, ⁷therefore I will stretch out my hand against you and give you as plunder to the nations. I will cut you off from the nations and exterminate you from the countries. I will destroy you, and you will know that I am the LORD.' "

A Prophecy Against Moab

⁸"This is what the Sovereign LORD says: 'Because Moab and Seir said, "Look, the house of Judah has become like all the other nations," ⁹therefore I will expose the flank of Moab, beginning at its frontier towns—Beth Jeshimoth, Baal Meon and Kiriathaim—the glory of that land. ¹⁰I will give Moab along with the Ammonites to the people of the East as a possession, so that the Ammonites will not be remembered among the nations; ¹¹and I will inflict punishment on Moab. Then they will know that I am the LORD.' "

A Prophecy Against Edom

¹²"This is what the Sovereign LORD says: 'Because Edom took revenge on the house of Judah and became very guilty by doing so, ¹³therefore this is what the Sovereign LORD says: I will stretch out my hand against Edom and kill its men and their animals. I will lay it waste, and from Teman to Dedan they will fall by the sword. ¹⁴I will take vengeance on Edom by the hand of my people Israel, and they will deal with Edom in accordance with my anger and my wrath; they will know my vengeance, declares the Sovereign LORD.' "

A Prophecy Against Philistia

¹⁵"This is what the Sovereign LORD says: 'Because the Philistines acted in vengeance and took revenge with malice in their hearts, and with ancient hostility sought to destroy Judah, ¹⁶therefore this is what the Sovereign LORD says: I am about to stretch out my hand against the Philistines, and I will cut off the Kerethites and destroy those remaining along the coast. ¹⁷I will carry out great vengeance on them and punish them in my wrath. Then they will know that I am the LORD, when I take vengeance on them.' "

^a23 Or away in

A Prophecy Against Tyre

26 In the eleventh year, on the first day of the month, the word of the LORD came to me: ²"Son of man, because Tyre has said of Jerusalem, 'Aha! The gate to the nations is broken, and its doors have swung open to me; now that she lies in ruins I will prosper,' ³therefore this is what the Sovereign LORD says: I am against you, O Tyre, and I will bring many nations against you, like the sea casting up its waves. ⁴They will destroy the walls of Tyre and pull down her towers; I will scrape away her rubble and make her a bare rock. ⁵Out in the sea she will become a place to spread fishnets, for I have spoken, declares the Sovereign LORD. She will become plunder for the nations, ⁶and her settlements on the mainland will be ravaged by the sword. Then they will know that I am the LORD.

⁷"For this is what the Sovereign LORD says: From the north I am going to bring against Tyre Nebuchadnezzar[a] king of Babylon, king of kings, with horses and chariots, with horsemen and a great army. ⁸He will ravage your settlements on the mainland with the sword; he will set up siege works against you, build a ramp up to your walls and raise his shields against you. ⁹He will direct the blows of his battering rams against your walls and demolish your towers with his weapons. ¹⁰His horses will be so many that they will cover you with dust. Your walls will tremble at the noise of the war horses, wagons and chariots when he enters your gates as men enter a city whose walls have been broken through. ¹¹The hoofs of his horses will trample all your streets; he will kill your people with the sword, and your strong pillars will fall to the ground. ¹²They will plunder your wealth and loot your merchandise; they will break down your walls and demolish your fine houses and throw your stones, timber and rubble into the sea. ¹³I will put an end to your noisy songs, and the music of your harps will be heard no more. ¹⁴I will make you a bare rock, and you will become a place to spread fishnets. You will never be rebuilt, for I the LORD have spoken, declares the Sovereign LORD.

¹⁵"This is what the Sovereign LORD says to Tyre: Will not the coastlands tremble at the sound of your fall, when the wounded groan and the slaughter takes place in you? ¹⁶Then all the princes of the coast will step down from their thrones and lay aside their robes and take off their embroidered garments. Clothed with terror, they will sit on the ground, trembling every moment, appalled at you. ¹⁷Then they will take up a lament concerning you and say to you:

" 'How you are destroyed, O city of
      renown,
   peopled by men of the sea!
You were a power on the seas,
   you and your citizens;
you put your terror
   on all who lived there.
¹⁸Now the coastlands tremble
   on the day of your fall;
the islands in the sea
   are terrified at your collapse.'

¹⁹"This is what the Sovereign LORD says: When I make you a desolate city, like cities no longer inhabited, and when I bring the ocean depths over you and its vast waters cover you, ²⁰then I will bring you down with those who go down to the pit, to the people of long ago. I will make you dwell in the earth below, as in ancient ruins, with those who go down to the pit, and you will not return or take your place[b] in the land of the living. ²¹I will bring you to a horrible end and you will be no more. You will be sought, but you will never again be found, declares the Sovereign LORD."

A Lament for Tyre

27 The word of the LORD came to me: ²"Son of man, take up a lament concerning Tyre. ³Say to Tyre, situated at the gateway to the sea, merchant of peoples on many coasts, 'This is what the Sovereign LORD says:

" 'You say, O Tyre,
   "I am perfect in beauty."
⁴Your domain was on the high seas;

---

[a]7 Hebrew *Nebuchadrezzar,* of which *Nebuchadnezzar* is a variant; here and often in Ezekiel and Jeremiah   [b]20 Septuagint; Hebrew *return, and I will give glory*

your builders brought your beauty
    to perfection.
⁵They made all your timbers
    of pine trees from Senir*ᵃ*;
they took a cedar from Lebanon
    to make a mast for you.
⁶Of oaks from Bashan
    they made your oars;
of cypress wood*ᵇ* from the coasts of
      Cyprus*ᶜ*
they made your deck, inlaid with
      ivory.
⁷Fine embroidered linen from Egypt
    was your sail
    and served as your banner;
your awnings were of blue and
      purple
    from the coasts of Elishah.
⁸Men of Sidon and Arvad were your
      oarsmen;
    your skilled men, O Tyre, were
      aboard as your seamen.
⁹Veteran craftsmen of Gebal*ᵈ* were on
      board
    as shipwrights to caulk your seams.
All the ships of the sea and their
      sailors
    came alongside to trade for your
      wares.

¹⁰" 'Men of Persia, Lydia and Put
    served as soldiers in your army.
They hung their shields and helmets
      on your walls,
    bringing you splendor.
¹¹Men of Arvad and Helech
    manned your walls on every side;
men of Gammad
    were in your towers.
They hung their shields around your
      walls;
    they brought your beauty to
      perfection.

¹²" 'Tarshish did business with you because of your great wealth of goods; they
exchanged silver, iron, tin and lead for
your merchandise.

¹³" 'Greece, Tubal and Meshech traded
with you; they exchanged slaves and articles of bronze for your wares.

¹⁴" 'Men of Beth Togarmah exchanged
work horses, war horses and mules for
your merchandise.

¹⁵" 'The men of Rhodes*ᵉ* traded with
you, and many coastlands were your

customers; they paid you with ivory
tusks and ebony.

¹⁶" 'Aram*ᶠ* did business with you because of your many products; they
exchanged turquoise, purple fabric, embroidered work, fine linen, coral and rubies for your merchandise.

¹⁷" 'Judah and Israel traded with you;
they exchanged wheat from Minnith and
confections,*ᵍ* honey, oil and balm for
your wares.

¹⁸" 'Damascus, because of your many
products and great wealth of goods, did
business with you in wine from Helbon
and wool from Zahar.

¹⁹" 'Danites and Greeks from Uzal
bought your merchandise; they exchanged wrought iron, cassia and calamus for your wares.

²⁰" 'Dedan traded in saddle blankets
with you.

²¹" 'Arabia and all the princes of Kedar
were your customers; they did business
with you in lambs, rams and goats.

²²" 'The merchants of Sheba and Raamah traded with you; for your merchandise they exchanged the finest of all
kinds of spices and precious stones, and
gold.

²³" 'Haran, Canneh and Eden and merchants of Sheba, Asshur and Kilmad
traded with you. ²⁴In your marketplace
they traded with you beautiful garments,
blue fabric, embroidered work and multi-
colored rugs with cords twisted and
tightly knotted.

²⁵" 'The ships of Tarshish serve
    as carriers for your wares.
You are filled with heavy cargo
    in the heart of the sea.
²⁶Your oarsmen take you
    out to the high seas.
But the east wind will break you to
      pieces
    in the heart of the sea.
²⁷Your wealth, merchandise and wares,
    your mariners, seamen and
      shipwrights,

ᵃ5 That is, Hermon   *ᵇ6* Targum; the Masoretic Text
has a different division of the consonants.
ᶜ6 Hebrew *Kittim*   *ᵈ9* That is, Byblos
ᵉ15 Septuagint; Hebrew *Dedan*   *ᶠ16* Most Hebrew
manuscripts; some Hebrew manuscripts and Syriac
Edom   *ᵍ17* The meaning of the Hebrew for this word
is uncertain.

your merchants and all your soldiers,
  and everyone else on board
will sink into the heart of the sea
  on the day of your shipwreck.
²⁸The shorelands will quake
  when your seamen cry out.
²⁹All who handle the oars
  will abandon their ships;
the mariners and all the seamen
  will stand on the shore.
³⁰They will raise their voice
  and cry bitterly over you;
they will sprinkle dust on their heads
  and roll in ashes.
³¹They will shave their heads because of
    you
  and will put on sackcloth.
They will weep over you with anguish
    of soul
  and with bitter mourning.
³²As they wail and mourn over you,
  they will take up a lament
    concerning you:
  "Who was ever silenced like Tyre,
    surrounded by the sea?"
³³When your merchandise went out on
    the seas,
  you satisfied many nations;
with your great wealth and your wares
  you enriched the kings of the earth.
³⁴Now you are shattered by the sea
  in the depths of the waters;
your wares and all your company
  have gone down with you.
³⁵All who live in the coastlands
  are appalled at you;
their kings shudder with horror
  and their faces are distorted with
    fear.
³⁶The merchants among the nations hiss
    at you;
  you have come to a horrible end
    and will be no more.' "

A Prophecy Against the King of Tyre

28 The word of the LORD came to me:
²"Son of man, say to the ruler of
Tyre, 'This is what the Sovereign LORD
says:

" 'In the pride of your heart
  you say, "I am a god;
I sit on the throne of a god
  in the heart of the seas."
But you are a man and not a god,

though you think you are as wise as
    a god.
³Are you wiser than Daniel^a?
  Is no secret hidden from you?
⁴By your wisdom and understanding
  you have gained wealth for yourself
and amassed gold and silver
  in your treasuries.
⁵By your great skill in trading
  you have increased your wealth,
and because of your wealth
  your heart has grown proud.

⁶" 'Therefore this is what the Sovereign
LORD says:

" 'Because you think you are wise,
  as wise as a god,
⁷I am going to bring foreigners against
    you,
  the most ruthless of nations;
they will draw their swords against
    your beauty and wisdom
  and pierce your shining splendor.
⁸They will bring you down to the pit,
  and you will die a violent death
    in the heart of the seas.
⁹Will you then say, "I am a god,"
  in the presence of those who kill
    you?
You will be but a man, not a god,
  in the hands of those who slay you.
¹⁰You will die the death of the
    uncircumcised
  at the hands of foreigners.

I have spoken, declares the Sovereign
LORD.' "

¹¹The word of the LORD came to me:
¹²"Son of man, take up a lament concern-
ing the king of Tyre and say to him: 'This
is what the Sovereign LORD says:

" 'You were the model of perfection,
  full of wisdom and perfect in
    beauty.
¹³You were in Eden,
  the garden of God;
every precious stone adorned you:
  ruby, topaz and emerald,
  chrysolite, onyx and jasper,
  sapphire,^b turquoise and beryl.^c

---

^a3 Or *Danel*; the Hebrew spelling may suggest a
person other than the prophet Daniel.   ^b13 Or *lapis
lazuli*   ^c13 The precise identification of some of
these precious stones is uncertain.

Your settings and mountings*a* were
　　made of gold;
　　on the day you were created they
　　　were prepared.
¹⁴You were anointed as a guardian
　　cherub,
　　for so I ordained you.
　You were on the holy mount of God;
　　you walked among the fiery stones.
¹⁵You were blameless in your ways
　　from the day you were created
　　till wickedness was found in you.
¹⁶Through your widespread trade
　　you were filled with violence,
　　and you sinned.
　So I drove you in disgrace from the
　　mount of God,
　　and I expelled you, O guardian
　　cherub,
　　from among the fiery stones.
¹⁷Your heart became proud
　　on account of your beauty,
　　and you corrupted your wisdom
　　because of your splendor.
　So I threw you to the earth;
　　I made a spectacle of you before
　　　kings.
¹⁸By your many sins and dishonest
　　trade
　　you have desecrated your
　　　sanctuaries.
　So I made a fire come out from you,
　　and it consumed you,
　　and I reduced you to ashes on the
　　　ground
　　in the sight of all who were
　　　watching.
¹⁹All the nations who knew you
　　are appalled at you;
　　you have come to a horrible end
　　and will be no more.’ ”

A Prophecy Against Sidon

²⁰The word of the LORD came to me:
²¹“Son of man, set your face against Sidon; prophesy against her ²²and say:
‘This is what the Sovereign LORD says:

　“ ‘I am against you, O Sidon,
　　and I will gain glory within you.
　They will know that I am the LORD,
　　when I inflict punishment on her
　　and show myself holy within her.
²³I will send a plague upon her
　　and make blood flow in her streets.

The slain will fall within her,
　　with the sword against her on every
　　　side.
　Then they will know that I am the
　　LORD.

²⁴“ ‘No longer will the people of Israel
have malicious neighbors who are painful briers and sharp thorns. Then they
will know that I am the Sovereign LORD.

²⁵“ ‘This is what the Sovereign LORD
says: When I gather the people of Israel
from the nations where they have been
scattered, I will show myself holy among
them in the sight of the nations. Then
they will live in their own land, which I
gave to my servant Jacob. ²⁶They will
live there in safety and will build houses
and plant vineyards; they will live in
safety when I inflict punishment on all
their neighbors who maligned them.
Then they will know that I am the LORD
their God.’ ”

A Prophecy Against Egypt

29 In the tenth year, in the tenth
month on the twelfth day, the
word of the LORD came to me: ²“Son of
man, set your face against Pharaoh king
of Egypt and prophesy against him and
against all Egypt. ³Speak to him and say:
‘This is what the Sovereign LORD says:

　“ ‘I am against you, Pharaoh king of
　　Egypt,
　　you great monster lying among
　　　your streams.
　You say, “The Nile is mine;
　　I made it for myself.”
⁴But I will put hooks in your jaws
　　and make the fish of your streams
　　　stick to your scales.
　I will pull you out from among your
　　streams,
　　with all the fish sticking to your
　　　scales.
⁵I will leave you in the desert,
　　you and all the fish of your streams.
　You will fall on the open field
　　and not be gathered or picked up.
　I will give you as food
　　to the beasts of the earth and the
　　　birds of the air.

*a13 The meaning of the Hebrew for this phrase is
uncertain.*

⁶Then all who live in Egypt will know that I am the LORD.

" 'You have been a staff of reed for the house of Israel. ⁷When they grasped you with their hands, you splintered and you tore open their shoulders; when they leaned on you, you broke and their backs were wrenched.ᵃ

⁸" 'Therefore this is what the Sovereign LORD says: I will bring a sword against you and kill your men and their animals. ⁹Egypt will become a desolate wasteland. Then they will know that I am the LORD.

" 'Because you said, "The Nile is mine; I made it," ¹⁰therefore I am against you and against your streams, and I will make the land of Egypt a ruin and a desolate waste from Migdol to Aswan, as far as the border of Cush.ᵇ ¹¹No foot of man or animal will pass through it; no one will live there for forty years. ¹²I will make the land of Egypt desolate among devastated lands, and her cities will lie desolate forty years among ruined cities. And I will disperse the Egyptians among the nations and scatter them through the countries.

¹³" 'Yet this is what the Sovereign LORD says: At the end of forty years I will gather the Egyptians from the nations where they were scattered. ¹⁴I will bring them back from captivity and return them to Upper Egypt,ᶜ the land of their ancestry. There they will be a lowly kingdom. ¹⁵It will be the lowliest of kingdoms and will never again exalt itself above the other nations. I will make it so weak that it will never again rule over the nations. ¹⁶Egypt will no longer be a source of confidence for the people of Israel but will be a reminder of their sin in turning to her for help. Then they will know that I am the Sovereign LORD.' "

¹⁷In the twenty-seventh year, in the first month on the first day, the word of the LORD came to me: ¹⁸"Son of man, Nebuchadnezzar king of Babylon drove his army in a hard campaign against Tyre; every head was rubbed bare and every shoulder made raw. Yet he and his army got no reward from the campaign he led against Tyre. ¹⁹Therefore this is what the Sovereign LORD says: I am going to give Egypt to Nebuchadnezzar king of Babylon, and he will carry off its wealth. He will loot and plunder the land as pay for his army. ²⁰I have given him Egypt as a reward for his efforts because he and his army did it for me, declares the Sovereign LORD. ²¹"On that day I will make a hornᵈ grow for the house of Israel, and I will open your mouth among them. Then they will know that I am the LORD."

A Lament for Egypt

30 The word of the LORD came to me: ²"Son of man, prophesy and say: 'This is what the Sovereign LORD says:

" 'Wail and say,
  "Alas for that day!"
³For the day is near,
  the day of the LORD is near—
a day of clouds,
  a time of doom for the nations.
⁴A sword will come against Egypt,
  and anguish will come upon Cush.ᵉ
When the slain fall in Egypt,
  her wealth will be carried away
  and her foundations torn down.

⁵Cush and Put, Lydia and all Arabia, Libyaᶠ and the people of the covenant land will fall by the sword along with Egypt.

⁶" 'This is what the LORD says:

" 'The allies of Egypt will fall
  and her proud strength will fail.
From Migdol to Aswan
  they will fall by the sword within her,
      declares the Sovereign LORD.
⁷" 'They will be desolate
  among desolate lands,
and their cities will lie
  among ruined cities.
⁸Then they will know that I am the LORD,
  when I set fire to Egypt
  and all her helpers are crushed.

⁹" 'On that day messengers will go out from me in ships to frighten Cush out of

---

ᵃ7 Syriac (see also Septuagint and Vulgate); Hebrew *and you caused their backs to stand*   ᵇ10 That is, the upper Nile region   ᶜ14 Hebrew *to Pathros*   ᵈ21 Horn here symbolizes strength.   ᵉ4 That is, the upper Nile region; also in verses 5 and 9   ᶠ5 Hebrew *Cub*

her complacency. Anguish will take hold of them on the day of Egypt's doom, for it is sure to come.

[10]" 'This is what the Sovereign LORD says:

" 'I will put an end to the hordes of Egypt
        by the hand of Nebuchadnezzar
            king of Babylon.
[11]He and his army—the most ruthless of nations—
        will be brought in to destroy the land.
    They will draw their swords against Egypt
        and fill the land with the slain.
[12]I will dry up the streams of the Nile
        and sell the land to evil men;
    by the hand of foreigners
        I will lay waste the land and
            everything in it.

I the LORD have spoken.

[13]" 'This is what the Sovereign LORD says:

" 'I will destroy the idols
        and put an end to the images in
            Memphis.[a]
    No longer will there be a prince in Egypt,
        and I will spread fear throughout
            the land.
[14]I will lay waste Upper Egypt,[b]
        set fire to Zoan
        and inflict punishment on Thebes.[c]
[15]I will pour out my wrath on
            Pelusium,[d]
        the stronghold of Egypt,
        and cut off the hordes of Thebes.
[16]I will set fire to Egypt;
        Pelusium will writhe in agony.
    Thebes will be taken by storm;
        Memphis will be in constant
            distress.
[17]The young men of Heliopolis[e] and
            Bubastis[f]
        will fall by the sword,
        and the cities themselves will go
            into captivity.
[18]Dark will be the day at Tahpanhes
        when I break the yoke of Egypt;
        there her proud strength will come
            to an end.

She will be covered with clouds,
        and her villages will go into
            captivity.
[19]So I will inflict punishment on Egypt,
        and they will know that I am the
            LORD.' "

[20]In the eleventh year, in the first month on the seventh day, the word of the LORD came to me: [21]"Son of man, I have broken the arm of Pharaoh king of Egypt. It has not been bound up for healing or put in a splint so as to become strong enough to hold a sword. [22]Therefore this is what the Sovereign LORD says: I am against Pharaoh king of Egypt. I will break both his arms, the good arm as well as the broken one, and make the sword fall from his hand. [23]I will disperse the Egyptians among the nations and scatter them through the countries. [24]I will strengthen the arms of the king of Babylon and put my sword in his hand, but I will break the arms of Pharaoh, and he will groan before him like a mortally wounded man. [25]I will strengthen the arms of the king of Babylon, but the arms of Pharaoh will fall limp. Then they will know that I am the LORD, when I put my sword into the hand of the king of Babylon and he brandishes it against Egypt. [26]I will disperse the Egyptians among the nations and scatter them through the countries. Then they will know that I am the LORD."

A Cedar in Lebanon

31 In the eleventh year, in the third month on the first day, the word of the LORD came to me: [2]"Son of man, say to Pharaoh king of Egypt and to his hordes:

" 'Who can be compared with you in
            majesty?
[3]Consider Assyria, once a cedar in
            Lebanon,
    with beautiful branches
        overshadowing the forest;
    it towered on high,
        its top above the thick foliage.
[4]The waters nourished it,

---

[a]13 Hebrew *Noph*; also in verse 16   [b]14 Hebrew
waste Pathros   [c]14 Hebrew *No*; also in verses 15
and 16   [d]15 Hebrew *Sin*; also in verse 16
[e]17 Hebrew *Awen* (or *On*)   [f]17 Hebrew *Pi Beseth*

deep springs made it grow tall;
their streams flowed
all around its base
and sent their channels
to all the trees of the field.
⁵So it towered higher
than all the trees of the field;
its boughs increased
and its branches grew long,
spreading because of abundant
waters.
⁶All the birds of the air
nested in its boughs,
all the beasts of the field
gave birth under its branches;
all the great nations
lived in its shade.
⁷It was majestic in beauty,
with its spreading boughs,
for its roots went down
to abundant waters.
⁸The cedars in the garden of God
could not rival it,
nor could the pine trees
equal its boughs,
nor could the plane trees
compare with its branches—
no tree in the garden of God
could match its beauty.
⁹I made it beautiful
with abundant branches,
the envy of all the trees of Eden
in the garden of God.

¹⁰" 'Therefore this is what the Sovereign LORD says: Because it towered on high, lifting its top above the thick foliage, and because it was proud of its height, ¹¹I handed it over to the ruler of the nations, for him to deal with according to its wickedness. I cast it aside, ¹²and the most ruthless of foreign nations cut it down and left it. Its boughs fell on the mountains and in all the valleys; its branches lay broken in all the ravines of the land. All the nations of the earth came out from under its shade and left it. ¹³All the birds of the air settled on the fallen tree, and all the beasts of the field were among its branches. ¹⁴Therefore no other trees by the waters are ever to tower proudly on high, lifting their tops above the thick foliage. No other trees so well-watered are ever to reach such a height; they are all destined for death,

for the earth below, among mortal men, with those who go down to the pit.

¹⁵" 'This is what the Sovereign LORD says: On the day it was brought down to the grave*ᵃ* I covered the deep springs with mourning for it; I held back its streams, and its abundant waters were restrained. Because of it I clothed Lebanon with gloom, and all the trees of the field withered away. ¹⁶I made the nations tremble at the sound of its fall when I brought it down to the grave with those who go down to the pit. Then all the trees of Eden, the choicest and best of Lebanon, all the trees that were well-watered, were consoled in the earth below. ¹⁷Those who lived in its shade, its allies among the nations, had also gone down to the grave with it, joining those killed by the sword.

¹⁸" 'Which of the trees of Eden can be compared with you in splendor and majesty? Yet you, too, will be brought down with the trees of Eden to the earth below; you will lie among the uncircumcised, with those killed by the sword.

" 'This is Pharaoh and all his hordes, declares the Sovereign LORD.' "

A Lament for Pharaoh

32 In the twelfth year, in the twelfth month on the first day, the word of the LORD came to me: ²"Son of man, take up a lament concerning Pharaoh king of Egypt and say to him:

" 'You are like a lion among the
nations;
you are like a monster in the seas
thrashing about in your streams,
churning the water with your feet
and muddying the streams.

³" 'This is what the Sovereign LORD says:

" 'With a great throng of people
I will cast my net over you,
and they will haul you up in my
net.
⁴I will throw you on the land
and hurl you on the open field.
I will let all the birds of the air settle
on you

---

*ᵃ15 Hebrew *Sheol*; also in verses 16 and 17*

and all the beasts of the earth gorge
  themselves on you.
⁵I will spread your flesh on the
    mountains
  and fill the valleys with your
    remains.
⁶I will drench the land with your
    flowing blood
  all the way to the mountains,
  and the ravines will be filled with
    your flesh.
⁷When I snuff you out, I will cover the
    heavens
  and darken their stars;
 I will cover the sun with a cloud,
  and the moon will not give its light.
⁸All the shining lights in the heavens
  I will darken over you;
  I will bring darkness over your
    land,
        declares the Sovereign LORD.
⁹I will trouble the hearts of many
    peoples
  when I bring about your destruction
    among the nations,
  amongᵃ lands you have not known.
¹⁰I will cause many peoples to be
    appalled at you,
  and their kings will shudder with
    horror because of you
  when I brandish my sword before
    them.
 On the day of your downfall
  each of them will tremble
  every moment for his life.

¹¹" 'For this is what the Sovereign LORD
says:

 " 'The sword of the king of Babylon
    will come against you.
¹²I will cause your hordes to fall
  by the swords of mighty men—
  the most ruthless of all nations.
 They will shatter the pride of Egypt,
  and all her hordes will be
    overthrown.
¹³I will destroy all her cattle
  from beside abundant waters
 no longer to be stirred by the foot of
    man
  or muddied by the hoofs of cattle.
¹⁴Then I will let her waters settle
  and make her streams flow like oil,
        declares the Sovereign LORD.
¹⁵When I make Egypt desolate

and strip the land of everything in
    it,
 when I strike down all who live there,
  then they will know that I am the
    LORD.'

¹⁶"This is the lament they will chant
for her. The daughters of the nations will
chant it; for Egypt and all her hordes
they will chant it, declares the Sovereign
LORD."

¹⁷In the twelfth year, on the fifteenth
day of the month, the word of the LORD
came to me: ¹⁸"Son of man, wail for the
hordes of Egypt and consign to the earth
below both her and the daughters of
mighty nations, with those who go down
to the pit. ¹⁹Say to them, 'Are you more
favored than others? Go down and be
laid among the uncircumcised.' ²⁰They
will fall among those killed by the sword.
The sword is drawn; let her be dragged
off with all her hordes. ²¹From within the
graveᵇ the mighty leaders will say of
Egypt and her allies, 'They have come
down and they lie with the uncircumcised, with those killed by the sword.'

²²"Assyria is there with her whole
army; she is surrounded by the graves of
all her slain, all who have fallen by the
sword. ²³Their graves are in the depths of
the pit and her army lies around her
grave. All who had spread terror in the
land of the living are slain, fallen by the
sword.

²⁴"Elam is there, with all her hordes
around her grave. All of them are slain,
fallen by the sword. All who had spread
terror in the land of the living went down
uncircumcised to the earth below. They
bear their shame with those who go
down to the pit. ²⁵A bed is made for her
among the slain, with all her hordes
around her grave. All of them are uncircumcised, killed by the sword. Because
their terror had spread in the land of the
living, they bear their shame with those
who go down to the pit; they are laid
among the slain.

²⁶"Meshech and Tubal are there, with
all their hordes around their graves. All

ᵃ9 Hebrew; Septuagint *bring you into captivity
among the nations,* / to   ᵇ21 Hebrew *Sheol*; also in
verse 27

of them are uncircumcised, killed by the sword because they spread their terror in the land of the living. ²⁷Do they not lie with the other uncircumcised warriors who have fallen, who went down to the grave with their weapons of war, whose swords were placed under their heads? The punishment for their sins rested on their bones, though the terror of these warriors had stalked through the land of the living.

²⁸"You too, O Pharaoh, will be broken and will lie among the uncircumcised, with those killed by the sword.

²⁹"Edom is there, her kings and all her princes; despite their power, they are laid with those killed by the sword. They lie with the uncircumcised, with those who go down to the pit.

³⁰"All the princes of the north and all the Sidonians are there; they went down with the slain in disgrace despite the terror caused by their power. They lie uncircumcised with those killed by the sword and bear their shame with those who go down to the pit.

³¹"Pharaoh—he and all his army—will see them and he will be consoled for all his hordes that were killed by the sword, declares the Sovereign Lord. ³²Although I had him spread terror in the land of the living, Pharaoh and all his hordes will be laid among the uncircumcised, with those killed by the sword, declares the Sovereign Lord."

Ezekiel a Watchman

33 The word of the Lord came to me: ²"Son of man, speak to your countrymen and say to them: 'When I bring the sword against a land, and the people of the land choose one of their men and make him their watchman, ³and he sees the sword coming against the land and blows the trumpet to warn the people, ⁴then if anyone hears the trumpet but does not take warning and the sword comes and takes his life, his blood will be on his own head. ⁵Since he heard the sound of the trumpet but did not take warning, his blood will be on his own head. If he had taken warning, he would have saved himself. ⁶But if the watchman sees the sword coming and does not blow the trumpet to warn the people and the

sword comes and takes the life of one of them, that man will be taken away because of his sin, but I will hold the watchman accountable for his blood.'

⁷"Son of man, I have made you a watchman for the house of Israel; so hear the word I speak and give them warning from me. ⁸When I say to the wicked, 'O wicked man, you will surely die,' and you do not speak out to dissuade him from his ways, that wicked man will die for[a] his sin, and I will hold you accountable for his blood. ⁹But if you do warn the wicked man to turn from his ways and he does not do so, he will die for his sin, but you will have saved yourself.

¹⁰"Son of man, say to the house of Israel, 'This is what you are saying: "Our offenses and sins weigh us down, and we are wasting away because of[b] them. How then can we live?"' ¹¹Say to them, 'As surely as I live, declares the Sovereign Lord, I take no pleasure in the death of the wicked, but rather that they turn from their ways and live. Turn! Turn from your evil ways! Why will you die, O house of Israel?'

¹²"Therefore, son of man, say to your countrymen, 'The righteousness of the righteous man will not save him when he disobeys, and the wickedness of the wicked man will not cause him to fall when he turns from it. The righteous man, if he sins, will not be allowed to live because of his former righteousness.' ¹³If I tell the righteous man that he will surely live, but then he trusts in his righteousness and does evil, none of the righteous things he has done will be remembered; he will die for the evil he has done. ¹⁴And if I say to the wicked man, 'You will surely die,' but he then turns away from his sin and does what is just and right— ¹⁵if he gives back what he took in pledge for a loan, returns what he has stolen, follows the decrees that give life, and does no evil, he will surely live; he will not die. ¹⁶None of the sins he has committed will be remembered against him. He has done what is just and right; he will surely live.

¹⁷"Yet your countrymen say, 'The way of the Lord is not just.' But it is their way

<hr>

ᵃ8 Or *in*; also in verse 9   ᵇ10 Or *away in*

that is not just. [18]If a righteous man turns from his righteousness and does evil, he will die for it. [19]And if a wicked man turns away from his wickedness and does what is just and right, he will live by doing so. [20]Yet, O house of Israel, you say, 'The way of the Lord is not just.' But I will judge each of you according to his own ways."

Jerusalem's Fall Explained

[21]In the twelfth year of our exile, in the tenth month on the fifth day, a man who had escaped from Jerusalem came to me and said, "The city has fallen!" [22]Now the evening before the man arrived, the hand of the LORD was upon me, and he opened my mouth before the man came to me in the morning. So my mouth was opened and I was no longer silent.

[23]Then the word of the LORD came to me: [24]"Son of man, the people living in those ruins in the land of Israel are saying, 'Abraham was only one man, yet he possessed the land. But we are many; surely the land has been given to us as our possession.' [25]Therefore say to them, 'This is what the Sovereign LORD says: Since you eat meat with the blood still in it and look to your idols and shed blood, should you then possess the land? [26]You rely on your sword, you do detestable things, and each of you defiles his neighbor's wife. Should you then possess the land?'

[27]"Say this to them: 'This is what the Sovereign LORD says: As surely as I live, those who are left in the ruins will fall by the sword, those out in the country I will give to the wild animals to be devoured, and those in strongholds and caves will die of a plague. [28]I will make the land a desolate waste, and her proud strength will come to an end, and the mountains of Israel will become desolate so that no one will cross them. [29]Then they will know that I am the LORD, when I have made the land a desolate waste because of all the detestable things they have done.'

[30]"As for you, son of man, your countrymen are talking together about you by the walls and at the doors of the houses, saying to each other, 'Come and hear the message that has come from the LORD.'

[31]My people come to you, as they usually do, and sit before you to listen to your words, but they do not put them into practice. With their mouths they express devotion, but their hearts are greedy for unjust gain. [32]Indeed, to them you are nothing more than one who sings love songs with a beautiful voice and plays an instrument well, for they hear your words but do not put them into practice.

[33]"When all this comes true—and it surely will—then they will know that a prophet has been among them."

Shepherds and Sheep

34 The word of the LORD came to me: [2]"Son of man, prophesy against the shepherds of Israel; prophesy and say to them: 'This is what the Sovereign LORD says: Woe to the shepherds of Israel who only take care of themselves! Should not shepherds take care of the flock? [3]You eat the curds, clothe yourselves with the wool and slaughter the choice animals, but you do not take care of the flock. [4]You have not strengthened the weak or healed the sick or bound up the injured. You have not brought back the strays or searched for the lost. You have ruled them harshly and brutally. [5]So they were scattered because there was no shepherd, and when they were scattered they became food for all the wild animals. [6]My sheep wandered over all the mountains and on every high hill. They were scattered over the whole earth, and no one searched or looked for them.

[7]" 'Therefore, you shepherds, hear the word of the LORD: [8]As surely as I live, declares the Sovereign LORD, because my flock lacks a shepherd and so has been plundered and has become food for all the wild animals, and because my shepherds did not search for my flock but cared for themselves rather than for my flock, [9]therefore, O shepherds, hear the word of the LORD: [10]This is what the Sovereign LORD says: I am against the shepherds and will hold them accountable for my flock. I will remove them from tending the flock so that the shepherds can no longer feed themselves. I will rescue my flock from their mouths, and it will no longer be food for them.

[11]" 'For this is what the Sovereign LORD

says: I myself will search for my sheep and look after them. ¹²As a shepherd looks after his scattered flock when he is with them, so will I look after my sheep. I will rescue them from all the places where they were scattered on a day of clouds and darkness. ¹³I will bring them out from the nations and gather them from the countries, and I will bring them into their own land. I will pasture them on the mountains of Israel, in the ravines and in all the settlements in the land. ¹⁴I will tend them in a good pasture, and the mountain heights of Israel will be their grazing land. There they will lie down in good grazing land, and there they will feed in a rich pasture on the mountains of Israel. ¹⁵I myself will tend my sheep and have them lie down, declares the Sovereign LORD. ¹⁶I will search for the lost and bring back the strays. I will bind up the injured and strengthen the weak, but the sleek and the strong I will destroy. I will shepherd the flock with justice.

¹⁷" 'As for you, my flock, this is what the Sovereign LORD says: I will judge between one sheep and another, and between rams and goats. ¹⁸Is it not enough for you to feed on the good pasture? Must you also trample the rest of your pasture with your feet? Is it not enough for you to drink clear water? Must you also muddy the rest with your feet? ¹⁹Must my flock feed on what you have trampled and drink what you have muddied with your feet?

²⁰" 'Therefore this is what the Sovereign LORD says to them: See, I myself will judge between the fat sheep and the lean sheep. ²¹Because you shove with flank and shoulder, butting all the weak sheep with your horns until you have driven them away, ²²I will save my flock, and they will no longer be plundered. I will judge between one sheep and another. ²³I will place over them one shepherd, my servant David, and he will tend them; he will tend them and be their shepherd. ²⁴I the LORD will be their God, and my servant David will be prince among them. I the LORD have spoken.

Wednesday

Rejects

Read Ezekiel 34:16

Sometimes I wear Christian T-shirts, and every time I do, it seems like someone makes fun of me. I know I'm doing the right thing by being bold about my faith, but it's still hard to be teased.

I get a lot of comfort from verses like this one. This verse tells me that God will reward people who choose him instead of money or popularity. It really is better for me to follow God and get teased for it than to reject God so I can try and fit in.

I know God is always looking out for me, even when other people reject me. And that's a pretty good feeling.

Matt age 13

❶ Have you ever been teased about your faith? What happened? What did you do?

❷ What do people talk about, wear or do that makes them look "cool"? Ask your parents what was "cool" when they were your age. Why do you think our ideas about what's "cool" change so quickly?

❸ Thank God for caring about you, even when it seems like the world is rejecting you.

Turn to page 998 for your next devotion.

²⁵" 'I will make a covenant of peace with them and rid the land of wild beasts so that they may live in the desert and sleep in the forests in safety. ²⁶I will bless them and the places surrounding my hill.ᵃ I will send down showers in season; there will be showers of blessing. ²⁷The trees of the field will yield their fruit and the ground will yield its crops; the people will be secure in their land. They will know that I am the LORD, when I break the bars of their yoke and rescue them from the hands of those who enslaved them. ²⁸They will no longer be plundered by the nations, nor will wild animals devour them. They will live in safety, and no one will make them afraid. ²⁹I will provide for them a land renowned for its crops, and they will no longer be victims of famine in the land or bear the scorn of the nations. ³⁰Then they will know that I, the LORD their God, am with them and that they, the house of Israel, are my people, declares the Sovereign LORD.

³¹You my sheep, the sheep of my pasture, are people, and I am your God, declares the Sovereign LORD.' "

A Prophecy Against Edom

35 The word of the LORD came to me: ²"Son of man, set your face against Mount Seir; prophesy against it ³and say: 'This is what the Sovereign LORD says: I am against you, Mount Seir, and I will stretch out my hand against you and make you a desolate waste. ⁴I will turn your towns into ruins and you will be desolate. Then you will know that I am the LORD.

⁵" 'Because you harbored an ancient hostility and delivered the Israelites over to the sword at the time of their calamity, the time their punishment reached its climax, ⁶therefore as surely as I live, declares the Sovereign LORD, I will give you

ᵃ26 Or I will make them and the places surrounding my hill a blessing

---

Thursday

Sin Comes Creepin' In

Read Ezekiel 35:6

Do you ever think about hating something? Sometimes I think I hate my brothers, school and occasionally homework. But instead of hating this kind of stuff, God wants us to hate the things he hates, like sin, evil and violence.

We live in a pretty violent world. Sometimes I feel kind of violent myself, like when I want to punch my brothers. But if we hate something that's wrong, like violence, then we won't be so tempted to give in to it. We need to hate violent TV shows, movies and music as much as God does.

Think about it: If you hate something, you don't want to have anything to do with it. You want to stay as far away from it as possible. But if you don't hate it, you're more vulnerable to it and a lot more likely to let it creep into your life.

Kelsey age 13

What about You?

❶ What are some things the Bible says God hates? What are some things you hate? Are there differences between those things?

❷ Look through today's newspaper. Find a story that tells about something bad in the world or your community. Pray that God would bring peace, hope and healing to that situation.

❸ Ask God to help you resist violence.

Turn to page 1011 for your next devotion.

over to bloodshed and it will pursue you. Since you did not hate bloodshed, bloodshed will pursue you. ⁷I will make Mount Seir a desolate waste and cut off from it all who come and go. ⁸I will fill your mountains with the slain; those killed by the sword will fall on your hills and in your valleys and in all your ravines. ⁹I will make you desolate forever; your towns will not be inhabited. Then you will know that I am the LORD.

¹⁰" 'Because you have said, "These two nations and countries will be ours and we will take possession of them," even though I the LORD was there, ¹¹therefore as surely as I live, declares the Sovereign LORD, I will treat you in accordance with the anger and jealousy you showed in your hatred of them and I will make myself known among them when I judge you. ¹²Then you will know that I the LORD have heard all the contemptible things you have said against the mountains of Israel. You said, "They have been laid waste and have been given over to us to devour." ¹³You boasted against me and spoke against me without restraint, and I heard it. ¹⁴This is what the Sovereign LORD says: While the whole earth rejoices, I will make you desolate. ¹⁵Because you rejoiced when the inheritance of the house of Israel became desolate, that is how I will treat you. You will be desolate, O Mount Seir, you and all of Edom. Then they will know that I am the LORD.' "

A Prophecy to the Mountains of Israel

36 "Son of man, prophesy to the mountains of Israel and say, 'O mountains of Israel, hear the word of the LORD. ²This is what the Sovereign LORD says: The enemy said of you, "Aha! The ancient heights have become our possession." ' ³Therefore prophesy and say, 'This is what the Sovereign LORD says: Because they ravaged and hounded you from every side so that you became the possession of the rest of the nations and the object of people's malicious talk and slander, ⁴therefore, O mountains of Israel, hear the word of the Sovereign LORD: This is what the Sovereign LORD says to the mountains and hills, to the ravines and valleys, to the desolate ruins

and the deserted towns that have been plundered and ridiculed by the rest of the nations around you— ⁵this is what the Sovereign LORD says: In my burning zeal I have spoken against the rest of the nations, and against all Edom, for with glee and with malice in their hearts they made my land their own possession so that they might plunder its pastureland.' ⁶Therefore prophesy concerning the land of Israel and say to the mountains and hills, to the ravines and valleys: 'This is what the Sovereign LORD says: I speak in my jealous wrath because you have suffered the scorn of the nations. ⁷Therefore this is what the Sovereign LORD says: I swear with uplifted hand that the nations around you will also suffer scorn.

⁸" 'But you, O mountains of Israel, will produce branches and fruit for my people Israel, for they will soon come home. ⁹I am concerned for you and will look on you with favor; you will be plowed and sown, ¹⁰and I will multiply the number of people upon you, even the whole house of Israel. The towns will be inhabited and the ruins rebuilt. ¹¹I will increase the number of men and animals upon you, and they will be fruitful and become numerous. I will settle people on you as in the past and will make you prosper more than before. Then you will know that I am the LORD. ¹²I will cause people, my people Israel, to walk upon you. They will possess you, and you will be their inheritance; you will never again deprive them of their children.

¹³" 'This is what the Sovereign LORD says: Because people say to you, "You devour men and deprive your nation of its children," ¹⁴therefore you will no longer devour men or make your nation childless, declares the Sovereign LORD. ¹⁵No longer will I make you hear the taunts of the nations, and no longer will you suffer the scorn of the peoples or cause your nation to fall, declares the Sovereign LORD.' "

¹⁶Again the word of the LORD came to me: ¹⁷"Son of man, when the people of Israel were living in their own land, they defiled it by their conduct and their actions. Their conduct was like a woman's monthly uncleanness in my sight. ¹⁸So I poured out my wrath on them because

they had shed blood in the land and because they had defiled it with their idols. [19]I dispersed them among the nations, and they were scattered through the countries; I judged them according to their conduct and their actions. [20]And wherever they went among the nations they profaned my holy name, for it was said of them, 'These are the LORD's people, and yet they had to leave his land.' [21]I had concern for my holy name, which the house of Israel profaned among the nations where they had gone.

[22]"Therefore say to the house of Israel, 'This is what the Sovereign LORD says: It is not for your sake, O house of Israel, that I am going to do these things, but for the sake of my holy name, which you have profaned among the nations where you have gone. [23]I will show the holiness of my great name, which has been profaned among the nations, the name you have profaned among them. Then the nations will know that I am the LORD, declares the Sovereign LORD, when I show myself holy through you before their eyes.

[24]" 'For I will take you out of the nations; I will gather you from all the countries and bring you back into your own land. [25]I will sprinkle clean water on you, and you will be clean; I will cleanse you from all your impurities and from all your idols. [26]I will give you a new heart and put a new spirit in you; I will remove from you your heart of stone and give you a heart of flesh. [27]And I will put my Spirit in you and move you to follow my decrees and be careful to keep my laws. [28]You will live in the land I gave your forefathers; you will be my people, and I will be your God. [29]I will save you from all your uncleanness. I will call for the grain and make it plentiful and will not bring famine upon you. [30]I will increase the fruit of the trees and the crops of the field, so that you will no longer suffer disgrace among the nations because of famine. [31]Then you will remember your evil ways and wicked deeds, and you will loathe yourselves for your sins and detestable practices. [32]I want you to know that I am not doing this for your sake, declares the Sovereign LORD. Be ashamed and disgraced for your conduct, O house of Israel!

[33]" 'This is what the Sovereign LORD says: On the day I cleanse you from all your sins, I will resettle your towns, and the ruins will be rebuilt. [34]The desolate land will be cultivated instead of lying desolate in the sight of all who pass through it. [35]They will say, "This land that was laid waste has become like the garden of Eden; the cities that were lying in ruins, desolate and destroyed, are now fortified and inhabited." [36]Then the nations around you that remain will know that I the LORD have rebuilt what was destroyed and have replanted what was desolate. I the LORD have spoken, and I will do it.'

[37]"This is what the Sovereign LORD says: Once again I will yield to the plea of the house of Israel and do this for them: I will make their people as numerous as sheep, [38]as numerous as the flocks for offerings at Jerusalem during her appointed feasts. So will the ruined cities be filled with flocks of people. Then they will know that I am the LORD."

The Valley of Dry Bones

37 The hand of the LORD was upon me, and he brought me out by the Spirit of the LORD and set me in the middle of a valley; it was full of bones. [2]He led me back and forth among them, and I saw a great many bones on the floor of the valley, bones that were very dry. [3]He asked me, "Son of man, can these bones live?"

I said, "O Sovereign LORD, you alone know."

[4]Then he said to me, "Prophesy to these bones and say to them, 'Dry bones, hear the word of the LORD! [5]This is what the Sovereign LORD says to these bones: I will make breath[a] enter you, and you will come to life. [6]I will attach tendons to you and make flesh come upon you and cover you with skin; I will put breath in you, and you will come to life. Then you will know that I am the LORD.' "

[7]So I prophesied as I was commanded. And as I was prophesying, there was a noise, a rattling sound, and the bones came together, bone to bone. [8]I looked,

---

[a]5 The Hebrew for this word can also mean *wind* or *spirit* (see verses 6-14).

and tendons and flesh appeared on them and skin covered them, but there was no breath in them.

[9]Then he said to me, "Prophesy to the breath; prophesy, son of man, and say to it, 'This is what the Sovereign LORD says: Come from the four winds, O breath, and breathe into these slain, that they may live.' " [10]So I prophesied as he commanded me, and breath entered them; they came to life and stood up on their feet—a vast army.

[11]Then he said to me: "Son of man, these bones are the whole house of Israel. They say, 'Our bones are dried up and our hope is gone; we are cut off.' [12]Therefore prophesy and say to them: 'This is what the Sovereign LORD says: O my people, I am going to open your graves and bring you up from them; I will bring you back to the land of Israel. [13]Then you, my people, will know that I am the LORD, when I open your graves and bring you up from them. [14]I will put my Spirit in you and you will live, and I will settle you in your own land. Then you will know that I the LORD have spoken, and I have done it, declares the LORD.' "

One Nation Under One King

[15]The word of the LORD came to me: [16]"Son of man, take a stick of wood and write on it, 'Belonging to Judah and the Israelites associated with him.' Then take another stick of wood, and write on it, 'Ephraim's stick, belonging to Joseph and all the house of Israel associated with him.' [17]Join them together into one stick so that they will become one in your hand.

[18]"When your countrymen ask you, 'Won't you tell us what you mean by this?' [19]say to them, 'This is what the Sovereign LORD says: I am going to take the stick of Joseph—which is in Ephraim's hand—and of the Israelite tribes associated with him, and join it to Judah's stick, making it a single stick of wood, and they will become one in my hand.' [20]Hold before their eyes the sticks you have written on [21]and say to them, 'This is what the Sovereign LORD says: I will take the Israelites out of the nations where they have gone. I will gather them from all around and bring them back

into their own land. [22]I will make them one nation in the land, on the mountains of Israel. There will be one king over all of them and they will never again be two nations or be divided into two kingdoms. [23]They will no longer defile themselves with their idols and vile images or with any of their offenses, for I will save them from all their sinful backsliding,[a] and I will cleanse them. They will be my people, and I will be their God.

[24]" 'My servant David will be king over them, and they will all have one shepherd. They will follow my laws and be careful to keep my decrees. [25]They will live in the land I gave to my servant Jacob, the land where your fathers lived. They and their children and their children's children will live there forever, and David my servant will be their prince forever. [26]I will make a covenant of peace with them; it will be an everlasting covenant. I will establish them and increase their numbers, and I will put my sanctuary among them forever. [27]My dwelling place will be with them; I will be their God, and they will be my people. [28]Then the nations will know that I the LORD make Israel holy, when my sanctuary is among them forever.' "

A Prophecy Against Gog

38 The word of the LORD came to me: [2]"Son of man, set your face against Gog, of the land of Magog, the chief prince of[b] Meshech and Tubal; prophesy against him [3]and say: 'This is what the Sovereign LORD says: I am against you, O Gog, chief prince of[c] Meshech and Tubal. [4]I will turn you around, put hooks in your jaws and bring you out with your whole army—your horses, your horsemen fully armed, and a great horde with large and small shields, all of them brandishing their swords. [5]Persia, Cush[d] and Put will be with them, all with shields and helmets, [6]also Gomer with all its troops, and Beth Togarmah from the far north with all its troops—the many nations with you.

---

a23 Many Hebrew manuscripts (see also Septuagint); most Hebrew manuscripts *all their dwelling places where they sinned*   *b2* Or *the prince of Rosh,*   *c3* Or *Gog, prince of Rosh,*   *d5* That is, the upper Nile region

[7]" 'Get ready; be prepared, you and all the hordes gathered about you, and take command of them. [8]After many days you will be called to arms. In future years you will invade a land that has recovered from war, whose people were gathered from many nations to the mountains of Israel, which had long been desolate. They had been brought out from the nations, and now all of them live in safety. [9]You and all your troops and the many nations with you will go up, advancing like a storm; you will be like a cloud covering the land.

[10]" 'This is what the Sovereign LORD says: On that day thoughts will come into your mind and you will devise an evil scheme. [11]You will say, "I will invade a land of unwalled villages; I will attack a peaceful and unsuspecting people—all of them living without walls and without gates and bars. [12]I will plunder and loot and turn my hand against the resettled ruins and the people gathered from the nations, rich in livestock and goods, living at the center of the land." [13]Sheba and Dedan and the merchants of Tarshish and all her villages[a] will say to you, "Have you come to plunder? Have you gathered your hordes to loot, to carry off silver and gold, to take away livestock and goods and to seize much plunder?" '

[14]"Therefore, son of man, prophesy and say to Gog: 'This is what the Sovereign LORD says: In that day, when my people Israel are living in safety, will you not take notice of it? [15]You will come from your place in the far north, you and many nations with you, all of them riding on horses, a great horde, a mighty army. [16]You will advance against my people Israel like a cloud that covers the land. In days to come, O Gog, I will bring you against my land, so that the nations may know me when I show myself holy through you before their eyes.

[17]" 'This is what the Sovereign LORD says: Are you not the one I spoke of in former days by my servants the prophets of Israel? At that time they prophesied for years that I would bring you against them. [18]This is what will happen in that day: When Gog attacks the land of Israel, my hot anger will be aroused, declares the Sovereign LORD. [19]In my zeal and fiery wrath I declare that at that time there shall be a great earthquake in the land of Israel. [20]The fish of the sea, the birds of the air, the beasts of the field, every creature that moves along the ground, and all the people on the face of the earth will tremble at my presence. The mountains will be overturned, the cliffs will crumble and every wall will fall to the ground. [21]I will summon a sword against Gog on all my mountains, declares the Sovereign LORD. Every man's sword will be against his brother. [22]I will execute judgment upon him with plague and bloodshed; I will pour down torrents of rain, hailstones and burning sulfur on him and on his troops and on the many nations with him. [23]And so I will show my greatness and my holiness, and I will make myself known in the sight of many nations. Then they will know that I am the LORD.'

39 "Son of man, prophesy against Gog and say: 'This is what the Sovereign LORD says: I am against you, O Gog, chief prince of[b] Meshech and Tubal. [2]I will turn you around and drag you along. I will bring you from the far north and send you against the mountains of Israel. [3]Then I will strike your bow from your left hand and make your arrows drop from your right hand. [4]On the mountains of Israel you will fall, you and all your troops and the nations with you. I will give you as food to all kinds of carrion birds and to the wild animals. [5]You will fall in the open field, for I have spoken, declares the Sovereign LORD. [6]I will send fire on Magog and on those who live in safety in the coastlands, and they will know that I am the LORD.

[7]" 'I will make known my holy name among my people Israel. I will no longer let my holy name be profaned, and the nations will know that I the LORD am the Holy One in Israel. [8]It is coming! It will surely take place, declares the Sovereign LORD. This is the day I have spoken of.

[9]" 'Then those who live in the towns of Israel will go out and use the weapons for fuel and burn them up—the small and large shields, the bows and arrows, the war clubs and spears. For seven years

---

[a] 13 Or *her strong lions* [b] 1 Or *Gog, prince of Rosh,*

they will use them for fuel. ¹⁰They will not need to gather wood from the fields or cut it from the forests, because they will use the weapons for fuel. And they will plunder those who plundered them and loot those who looted them, declares the Sovereign LORD.

¹¹" 'On that day I will give Gog a burial place in Israel, in the valley of those who travel east toward*ᵃ* the Sea.*ᵇ* It will block the way of travelers, because Gog and all his hordes will be buried there. So it will be called the Valley of Hamon Gog.*ᶜ*

¹²" 'For seven months the house of Israel will be burying them in order to cleanse the land. ¹³All the people of the land will bury them, and the day I am glorified will be a memorable day for them, declares the Sovereign LORD.

¹⁴" 'Men will be regularly employed to cleanse the land. Some will go throughout the land and, in addition to them, others will bury those that remain on the ground. At the end of the seven months they will begin their search. ¹⁵As they go through the land and one of them sees a human bone, he will set up a marker beside it until the gravediggers have buried it in the Valley of Hamon Gog. ¹⁶(Also a town called Hamonah*ᵈ* will be there.) And so they will cleanse the land.'

¹⁷"Son of man, this is what the Sovereign LORD says: Call out to every kind of bird and all the wild animals: 'Assemble and come together from all around to the sacrifice I am preparing for you, the great sacrifice on the mountains of Israel. There you will eat flesh and drink blood. ¹⁸You will eat the flesh of mighty men and drink the blood of the princes of the earth as if they were rams and lambs, goats and bulls—all of them fattened animals from Bashan. ¹⁹At the sacrifice I am preparing for you, you will eat fat till you are glutted and drink blood till you are drunk. ²⁰At my table you will eat your fill of horses and riders, mighty men and soldiers of every kind,' declares the Sovereign LORD.

²¹"I will display my glory among the nations, and all the nations will see the punishment I inflict and the hand I lay upon them. ²²From that day forward the house of Israel will know that I am the LORD their God. ²³And the nations will know that the people of Israel went into exile for their sin, because they were unfaithful to me. So I hid my face from them and handed them over to their enemies, and they all fell by the sword. ²⁴I dealt with them according to their uncleanness and their offenses, and I hid my face from them.

²⁵"Therefore this is what the Sovereign LORD says: I will now bring Jacob back from captivity*ᵉ* and will have compassion on all the people of Israel, and I will be zealous for my holy name. ²⁶They will forget their shame and all the unfaithfulness they showed toward me when they lived in safety in their land with no one to make them afraid. ²⁷When I have brought them back from the nations and have gathered them from the countries of their enemies, I will show myself holy through them in the sight of many nations. ²⁸Then they will know that I am the LORD their God, for though I sent them into exile among the nations, I will gather them to their own land, not leaving any behind. ²⁹I will no longer hide my face from them, for I will pour out my Spirit on the house of Israel, declares the Sovereign LORD."

The New Temple Area

40 In the twenty-fifth year of our exile, at the beginning of the year, on the tenth of the month, in the fourteenth year after the fall of the city—on that very day the hand of the LORD was upon me and he took me there. ²In visions of God he took me to the land of Israel and set me on a very high mountain, on whose south side were some buildings that looked like a city. ³He took me there, and I saw a man whose appearance was like bronze; he was standing in the gateway with a linen cord and a measuring rod in his hand. ⁴The man said to me, "Son of man, look with your eyes and hear with your ears and pay attention to everything I am going to show you, for that is why you have been brought here. Tell the house of Israel everything you see."

ᵃ11 Or of   ᵇ11 That is, the Dead Sea   ᶜ11 Hamon Gog means hordes of Gog.   ᵈ16 Hamonah means horde.   ᵉ25 Or now restore the fortunes of Jacob

The East Gate to the Outer Court

⁵I saw a wall completely surrounding the temple area. The length of the measuring rod in the man's hand was six long cubits, each of which was a cubit*a* and a handbreadth.*b* He measured the wall; it was one measuring rod thick and one rod high.

⁶Then he went to the gate facing east. He climbed its steps and measured the threshold of the gate; it was one rod deep.*c* ⁷The alcoves for the guards were one rod long and one rod wide, and the projecting walls between the alcoves were five cubits thick. And the threshold of the gate next to the portico facing the temple was one rod deep.

⁸Then he measured the portico of the gateway; ⁹it*d* was eight cubits deep and its jambs were two cubits thick. The portico of the gateway faced the temple.

¹⁰Inside the east gate were three alcoves on each side; the three had the same measurements, and the faces of the projecting walls on each side had the same measurements. ¹¹Then he measured the width of the entrance to the gateway; it was ten cubits and its length was thirteen cubits. ¹²In front of each alcove was a wall one cubit high, and the alcoves were six cubits square. ¹³Then he measured the gateway from the top of the rear wall of one alcove to the top of the opposite one; the distance was twenty-five cubits from one parapet opening to the opposite one. ¹⁴He measured along the faces of the projecting walls all around the inside of the gateway—sixty cubits. The measurement was up to the portico*e* facing the courtyard.*f* ¹⁵The distance from the entrance of the gateway to the far end of its portico was fifty cubits. ¹⁶The alcoves and the projecting walls inside the gateway were surmounted by narrow parapet openings all around, as was the portico; the openings all around faced inward. The faces of the projecting walls were decorated with palm trees.

The Outer Court

¹⁷Then he brought me into the outer court. There I saw some rooms and a pavement that had been constructed all around the court; there were thirty rooms along the pavement. ¹⁸It abutted the sides of the gateways and was as wide as they were long; this was the lower pavement. ¹⁹Then he measured the distance from the inside of the lower gateway to the outside of the inner court; it was a hundred cubits on the east side as well as on the north.

The North Gate

²⁰Then he measured the length and width of the gate facing north, leading into the outer court. ²¹Its alcoves—three on each side—its projecting walls and its portico had the same measurements as those of the first gateway. It was fifty cubits long and twenty-five cubits wide. ²²Its openings, its portico and its palm tree decorations had the same measurements as those of the gate facing east. Seven steps led up to it, with its portico opposite them. ²³There was a gate to the inner court facing the north gate, just as there was on the east. He measured from one gate to the opposite one; it was a hundred cubits.

The South Gate

²⁴Then he led me to the south side and I saw a gate facing south. He measured

---

---

a5 The common cubit was about 1 1/2 feet (about 0.5 meter). *b5* That is, about 3 inches (about 8 centimeters) *c6* Septuagint; Hebrew *deep, the first threshold, one rod deep* *d8,9* Many Hebrew manuscripts, Septuagint, Vulgate and Syriac; most Hebrew manuscripts *gateway facing the temple; it was one rod deep. 9Then he measured the portico of the gateway; it* *e14* Septuagint; Hebrew *projecting wall* *f14* The meaning of the Hebrew for this verse is uncertain.

its jambs and its portico, and they had the same measurements as the others. ²⁵The gateway and its portico had narrow openings all around, like the openings of the others. It was fifty cubits long and twenty-five cubits wide. ²⁶Seven steps led up to it, with its portico opposite them; it had palm tree decorations on the faces of the projecting walls on each side. ²⁷The inner court also had a gate facing south, and he measured from this gate to the outer gate on the south side; it was a hundred cubits.

Gates to the Inner Court

²⁸Then he brought me into the inner court through the south gate, and he measured the south gate; it had the same measurements as the others. ²⁹Its alcoves, its projecting walls and its portico had the same measurements as the others. The gateway and its portico had openings all around. It was fifty cubits long and twenty-five cubits wide. ³⁰(The porticoes of the gateways around the inner court were twenty-five cubits wide and five cubits deep.) ³¹Its portico faced the outer court; palm trees decorated its jambs, and eight steps led up to it.

³²Then he brought me to the inner court on the east side, and he measured the gateway; it had the same measurements as the others. ³³Its alcoves, its projecting walls and its portico had the same measurements as the others. The gateway and its portico had openings all around. It was fifty cubits long and twenty-five cubits wide. ³⁴Its portico faced the outer court; palm trees decorated the jambs on either side, and eight steps led up to it.

³⁵Then he brought me to the north gate and measured it. It had the same measurements as the others, ³⁶as did its alcoves, its projecting walls and its portico, and it had openings all around. It was fifty cubits long and twenty-five cubits wide. ³⁷Its portico[a] faced the outer court; palm trees decorated the jambs on either side, and eight steps led up to it.

The Rooms for Preparing Sacrifices

³⁸A room with a doorway was by the portico in each of the inner gateways, where the burnt offerings were washed. ³⁹In the portico of the gateway were two tables on each side, on which the burnt offerings, sin offerings and guilt offerings were slaughtered. ⁴⁰By the outside wall of the portico of the gateway, near the steps at the entrance to the north gateway were two tables, and on the other side of the steps were two tables. ⁴¹So there were four tables on one side of the gateway and four on the other—eight tables in all—on which the sacrifices were slaughtered. ⁴²There were also four tables of dressed stone for the burnt offerings, each a cubit and a half long, a cubit and a half wide and a cubit high. On them were placed the utensils for slaughtering the burnt offerings and the other sacrifices. ⁴³And double-pronged hooks, each a handbreadth long, were attached to the wall all around. The tables were for the flesh of the offerings.

Rooms for the Priests

⁴⁴Outside the inner gate, within the inner court, were two rooms, one[b] at the side of the north gate and facing south, and another at the side of the south[c] gate and facing north. ⁴⁵He said to me, "The room facing south is for the priests who have charge of the temple, ⁴⁶and the room facing north is for the priests who have charge of the altar. These are the sons of Zadok, who are the only Levites who may draw near to the LORD to minister before him."

⁴⁷Then he measured the court: It was square—a hundred cubits long and a hundred cubits wide. And the altar was in front of the temple.

The Temple

⁴⁸He brought me to the portico of the temple and measured the jambs of the portico; they were five cubits wide on either side. The width of the entrance was fourteen cubits and its projecting walls were[d] three cubits wide on either side. ⁴⁹The portico was twenty cubits wide, and twelve[e] cubits from front to back. It was reached by a flight of stairs,[f] and

---

[a]37 Septuagint (see also verses 31 and 34); Hebrew *jambs*   [b]44 Septuagint; Hebrew *were rooms for singers, which were*   [c]44 Septuagint; Hebrew *east*   [d]48 Septuagint; Hebrew *entrance was*   [e]49 Septuagint; Hebrew *eleven*   [f]49 Hebrew; Septuagint *Ten steps led up to it*

there were pillars on each side of the jambs.

41

Then the man brought me to the outer sanctuary and measured the jambs; the width of the jambs was six cubits[a] on each side.[b] [2]The entrance was ten cubits wide, and the projecting walls on each side of it were five cubits wide. He also measured the outer sanctuary; it was forty cubits long and twenty cubits wide.

[3]Then he went into the inner sanctuary and measured the jambs of the entrance; each was two cubits wide. The entrance was six cubits wide, and the projecting walls on each side of it were seven cubits wide. [4]And he measured the length of the inner sanctuary; it was twenty cubits, and its width was twenty cubits across the end of the outer sanctuary. He said to me, "This is the Most Holy Place."

[5]Then he measured the wall of the temple; it was six cubits thick, and each side room around the temple was four cubits wide. [6]The side rooms were on three levels, one above another, thirty on each level. There were ledges all around the wall of the temple to serve as supports for the side rooms, so that the supports were not inserted into the wall of the temple. [7]The side rooms all around the temple were wider at each successive level. The structure surrounding the temple was built in ascending stages, so that the rooms widened as one went upward. A stairway went up from the lowest floor to the top floor through the middle floor.

[8]I saw that the temple had a raised base all around it, forming the foundation of the side rooms. It was the length of the rod, six long cubits. [9]The outer wall of the side rooms was five cubits thick. The open area between the side rooms of the temple [10]and the priests' rooms was twenty cubits wide all around the temple. [11]There were entrances to the side rooms from the open area, one on the north and another on the south; and the base adjoining the open area was five cubits wide all around.

[12]The building facing the temple courtyard on the west side was seventy cubits wide. The wall of the building was five cubits thick all around, and its length was ninety cubits.

[13]Then he measured the temple; it was a hundred cubits long, and the temple courtyard and the building with its walls were also a hundred cubits long. [14]The width of the temple courtyard on the east, including the front of the temple, was a hundred cubits.

[15]Then he measured the length of the building facing the courtyard at the rear of the temple, including its galleries on each side; it was a hundred cubits.

The outer sanctuary, the inner sanctuary and the portico facing the court, [16]as well as the thresholds and the narrow windows and galleries around the three of them—everything beyond and including the threshold was covered with wood. The floor, the wall up to the windows, and the windows were covered. [17]In the space above the outside of the entrance to the inner sanctuary and on the walls at regular intervals all around the inner and outer sanctuary [18]were carved cherubim and palm trees. Palm trees alternated with cherubim. Each cherub had two faces: [19]the face of a man toward the palm tree on one side and the face of a lion toward the palm tree on the other. They were carved all around the whole temple. [20]From the floor to the area above the entrance, cherubim and palm trees were carved on the wall of the outer sanctuary.

[21]The outer sanctuary had a rectangular doorframe, and the one at the front of the Most Holy Place was similar. [22]There was a wooden altar three cubits high and two cubits square[c]; its corners, its base[d] and its sides were of wood. The man said to me, "This is the table that is before the LORD." [23]Both the outer sanctuary and the Most Holy Place had double doors. [24]Each door had two leaves—two hinged leaves for each door. [25]And on the doors of the outer sanctuary were carved cherubim and palm trees like those carved on the walls, and there was a wooden overhang on the front of the portico. [26]On the sidewalls of the portico were narrow windows with palm trees carved on each

---

[a]1 The common cubit was about 1 1/2 feet (about 0.5 meter).   [b]1 One Hebrew manuscript and Septuagint; most Hebrew manuscripts *side, the width of the tent*   [c]22 Septuagint; Hebrew *long* [d]22 Septuagint; Hebrew *length*

side. The side rooms of the temple also had overhangs.

Rooms for the Priests

42 Then the man led me northward into the outer court and brought me to the rooms opposite the temple courtyard and opposite the outer wall on the north side. ²The building whose door faced north was a hundred cubits*a* long and fifty cubits wide. ³Both in the section twenty cubits from the inner court and in the section opposite the pavement of the outer court, gallery faced gallery at the three levels. ⁴In front of the rooms was an inner passageway ten cubits wide and a hundred cubits*b* long. Their doors were on the north. ⁵Now the upper rooms were narrower, for the galleries took more space from them than from the rooms on the lower and middle floors of the building. ⁶The rooms on the third floor had no pillars, as the courts had; so they were smaller in floor space than those on the lower and middle floors. ⁷There was an outer wall parallel to the rooms and the outer court; it extended in front of the rooms for fifty cubits. ⁸While the row of rooms on the side next to the outer court was fifty cubits long, the row on the side nearest the sanctuary was a hundred cubits long. ⁹The lower rooms had an entrance on the east side as one enters them from the outer court.

¹⁰On the south side*c* along the length of the wall of the outer court, adjoining the temple courtyard and opposite the outer wall, were rooms ¹¹with a passageway in front of them. These were like the rooms on the north; they had the same length and width, with similar exits and dimensions. Similar to the doorways on the north ¹²were the doorways of the rooms on the south. There was a doorway at the beginning of the passageway that was parallel to the corresponding wall extending eastward, by which one enters the rooms.

¹³Then he said to me, "The north and south rooms facing the temple courtyard are the priests' rooms, where the priests who approach the Lord will eat the most holy offerings. There they will put the most holy offerings—the grain offerings, the sin offerings and the guilt offerings—

for the place is holy. ¹⁴Once the priests enter the holy precincts, they are not to go into the outer court until they leave behind the garments in which they minister, for these are holy. They are to put on other clothes before they go near the places that are for the people."

¹⁵When he had finished measuring what was inside the temple area, he led me out by the east gate and measured the area all around: ¹⁶He measured the east side with the measuring rod; it was five hundred cubits.*d* ¹⁷He measured the north side; it was five hundred cubits*e* by the measuring rod. ¹⁸He measured the south side; it was five hundred cubits by the measuring rod. ¹⁹Then he turned to the west side and measured; it was five hundred cubits by the measuring rod. ²⁰So he measured the area on all four sides. It had a wall around it, five hundred cubits long and five hundred cubits wide, to separate the holy from the common.

The Glory Returns to the Temple

43 Then the man brought me to the gate facing east, ²and I saw the glory of the God of Israel coming from the east. His voice was like the roar of rushing waters, and the land was radiant with his glory. ³The vision I saw was like the vision I had seen when he*f* came to destroy the city and like the visions I had seen by the Kebar River, and I fell facedown. ⁴The glory of the Lord entered the temple through the gate facing east. ⁵Then the Spirit lifted me up and brought me into the inner court, and the glory of the Lord filled the temple.

⁶While the man was standing beside me, I heard someone speaking to me from inside the temple. ⁷He said: "Son of man, this is the place of my throne and the place for the soles of my feet. This is where I will live among the Israelites forever. The house of Israel will never again defile my holy name—neither they nor

---

a2 The common cubit was about 1 1/2 feet (about 0.5 meter).   *b4* Septuagint and Syriac; Hebrew *and one cubit*   *c10* Septuagint; Hebrew *Eastward*   *d16* See Septuagint of verse 17; Hebrew *rods*; also in verses 18 and 19.   *e17* Septuagint; Hebrew *rods*   *f3* Some Hebrew manuscripts and Vulgate; most Hebrew manuscripts *I*

their kings—by their prostitution[a] and the lifeless idols[b] of their kings at their high places. [8]When they placed their threshold next to my threshold and their doorposts beside my doorposts, with only a wall between me and them, they defiled my holy name by their detestable practices. So I destroyed them in my anger. [9]Now let them put away from me their prostitution and the lifeless idols of their kings, and I will live among them forever.

[10]"Son of man, describe the temple to the people of Israel, that they may be ashamed of their sins. Let them consider the plan, [11]and if they are ashamed of all they have done, make known to them the design of the temple—its arrangement, its exits and entrances—its whole design and all its regulations[c] and laws. Write these down before them so that they may be faithful to its design and follow all its regulations.

[12]"This is the law of the temple: All the surrounding area on top of the mountain will be most holy. Such is the law of the temple.

The Altar

[13]"These are the measurements of the altar in long cubits, that cubit being a cubit[d] and a handbreadth[e]: Its gutter is a cubit deep and a cubit wide, with a rim of one span[f] around the edge. And this is the height of the altar: [14]From the gutter on the ground up to the lower ledge it is two cubits high and a cubit wide, and from the smaller ledge up to the larger ledge it is four cubits high and a cubit wide. [15]The altar hearth is four cubits high, and four horns project upward from the hearth. [16]The altar hearth is square, twelve cubits long and twelve cubits wide. [17]The upper ledge also is square, fourteen cubits long and fourteen cubits wide, with a rim of half a cubit and a gutter of a cubit all around. The steps of the altar face east."

[18]Then he said to me, "Son of man, this is what the Sovereign LORD says: These will be the regulations for sacrificing burnt offerings and sprinkling blood upon the altar when it is built: [19]You are to give a young bull as a sin offering to the priests, who are Levites, of the family of Zadok, who come near to minister before me, declares the Sovereign LORD. [20]You are to take some of its blood and put it on the four horns of the altar and on the four corners of the upper ledge and all around the rim, and so purify the altar and make atonement for it. [21]You are to take the bull for the sin offering and burn it in the designated part of the temple area outside the sanctuary.

[22]"On the second day you are to offer a male goat without defect for a sin offering, and the altar is to be purified as it was purified with the bull. [23]When you have finished purifying it, you are to offer a young bull and a ram from the flock, both without defect. [24]You are to offer them before the LORD, and the priests are to sprinkle salt on them and sacrifice them as a burnt offering to the LORD.

[25]"For seven days you are to provide a male goat daily for a sin offering; you are also to provide a young bull and a ram from the flock, both without defect. [26]For seven days they are to make atonement for the altar and cleanse it; thus they will dedicate it. [27]At the end of these days, from the eighth day on, the priests are to present your burnt offerings and fellowship offerings[g] on the altar. Then I will accept you, declares the Sovereign LORD."

The Prince, the Levites, the Priests

44 Then the man brought me back to the outer gate of the sanctuary, the one facing east, and it was shut. [2]The LORD said to me, "This gate is to remain shut. It must not be opened; no one may enter through it. It is to remain shut because the LORD, the God of Israel, has entered through it. [3]The prince himself is the only one who may sit inside the gateway to eat in the presence of the LORD. He is to enter by way of the portico of the gateway and go out the same way."

---

[a]7 Or *their spiritual adultery*; also in verse 9
[b]7 Or *the corpses*; also in verse 9   [c]11 Some Hebrew manuscripts and Septuagint; most Hebrew manuscripts *regulations and its whole design*
[d]13 The common cubit was about 1 1/2 feet (about 0.5 meter).   [e]13 That is, about 3 inches (about 8 centimeters)   [f]13 That is, about 9 inches (about 22 centimeters)   [g]27 Traditionally *peace offerings*

⁴Then the man brought me by way of the north gate to the front of the temple. I looked and saw the glory of the LORD filling the temple of the LORD, and I fell facedown.

⁵The LORD said to me, "Son of man, look carefully, listen closely and give attention to everything I tell you concerning all the regulations regarding the temple of the LORD. Give attention to the entrance of the temple and all the exits of the sanctuary. ⁶Say to the rebellious house of Israel, 'This is what the Sovereign LORD says: Enough of your detestable practices, O house of Israel! ⁷In addition to all your other detestable practices, you brought foreigners uncircumcised in heart and flesh into my sanctuary, desecrating my temple while you offered me food, fat and blood, and you broke my covenant. ⁸Instead of carrying out your duty in regard to my holy things, you put others in charge of my sanctuary. ⁹This is what the Sovereign LORD says: No foreigner uncircumcised in heart and flesh is to enter my sanctuary, not even the foreigners who live among the Israelites.

¹⁰'The Levites who went far from me when Israel went astray and who wandered from me after their idols must bear the consequences of their sin. ¹¹They may serve in my sanctuary, having charge of the gates of the temple and serving in it; they may slaughter the burnt offerings and sacrifices for the people and stand before the people and serve them. ¹²But because they served them in the presence of their idols and made the house of Israel fall into sin, therefore I have sworn with uplifted hand that they must bear the consequences of their sin, declares the Sovereign LORD. ¹³They are not to come near to serve me as priests or come near any of my holy things or my most holy offerings; they must bear the shame of their detestable practices. ¹⁴Yet I will put them in charge of the duties of the temple and all the work that is to be done in it.

¹⁵'But the priests, who are Levites and descendants of Zadok and who faithfully carried out the duties of my sanctuary when the Israelites went astray from me, are to come near to minister before me; they are to stand before me to offer sacrifices of fat and blood, declares the Sovereign LORD. ¹⁶They alone are to enter my sanctuary; they alone are to come near my table to minister before me and perform my service.

¹⁷'When they enter the gates of the inner court, they are to wear linen clothes; they must not wear any woolen garment while ministering at the gates of the inner court or inside the temple. ¹⁸They are to wear linen turbans on their heads and linen undergarments around their waists. They must not wear anything that makes them perspire. ¹⁹When they go out into the outer court where the people are, they are to take off the clothes they have been ministering in and are to leave them in the sacred rooms, and put on other clothes, so that they do not consecrate the people by means of their garments.

²⁰'They must not shave their heads or let their hair grow long, but they are to keep the hair of their heads trimmed. ²¹No priest is to drink wine when he enters the inner court. ²²They must not marry widows or divorced women; they may marry only virgins of Israelite descent or widows of priests. ²³They are to teach my people the difference between the holy and the common and show them how to distinguish between the unclean and the clean.

²⁴'In any dispute, the priests are to serve as judges and decide it according to my ordinances. They are to keep my laws and my decrees for all my appointed feasts, and they are to keep my Sabbaths holy.

²⁵'A priest must not defile himself by going near a dead person; however, if the dead person was his father or mother, son or daughter, brother or unmarried sister, then he may defile himself. ²⁶After he is cleansed, he must wait seven days. ²⁷On the day he goes into the inner court of the sanctuary to minister in the sanctuary, he is to offer a sin offering for himself, declares the Sovereign LORD.

²⁸'I am to be the only inheritance the priests have. You are to give them no possession in Israel; I will be their possession. ²⁹They will eat the grain offerings, the sin offerings and the guilt

offerings; and everything in Israel devoted[a] to the LORD will belong to them. [30]The best of all the firstfruits and of all your special gifts will belong to the priests. You are to give them the first portion of your ground meal so that a blessing may rest on your household. [31]The priests must not eat anything, bird or animal, found dead or torn by wild animals.

Division of the Land

45 " 'When you allot the land as an inheritance, you are to present to the LORD a portion of the land as a sacred district, 25,000 cubits long and 20,000[b] cubits wide; the entire area will be holy. [2]Of this, a section 500 cubits square is to be for the sanctuary, with 50 cubits around it for open land. [3]In the sacred district, measure off a section 25,000 cubits[c] long and 10,000 cubits[d] wide. In it will be the sanctuary, the Most Holy Place. [4]It will be the sacred portion of the land for the priests, who minister in the sanctuary and who draw near to minister before the LORD. It will be a place for their houses as well as a holy place for the sanctuary. [5]An area 25,000 cubits long and 10,000 cubits wide will belong to the Levites, who serve in the temple, as their possession for towns to live in.[e]

[6]" 'You are to give the city as its property an area 5,000 cubits wide and 25,000 cubits long, adjoining the sacred portion; it will belong to the whole house of Israel.

[7]" 'The prince will have the land bordering each side of the area formed by the sacred district and the property of the city. It will extend westward from the west side and eastward from the east side, running lengthwise from the western to the eastern border parallel to one of the tribal portions. [8]This land will be his possession in Israel. And my princes will no longer oppress my people but will allow the house of Israel to possess the land according to their tribes.

[9]" 'This is what the Sovereign LORD says: You have gone far enough, O princes of Israel! Give up your violence and oppression and do what is just and right. Stop dispossessing my people, declares the Sovereign LORD. [10]You are to

use accurate scales, an accurate ephah[f] and an accurate bath.[g] [11]The ephah and the bath are to be the same size, the bath containing a tenth of a homer[h] and the ephah a tenth of a homer; the homer is to be the standard measure for both. [12]The shekel[i] is to consist of twenty gerahs. Twenty shekels plus twenty-five shekels plus fifteen shekels equal one mina.[j]

Offerings and Holy Days

[13]" 'This is the special gift you are to offer: a sixth of an ephah from each homer of wheat and a sixth of an ephah from each homer of barley. [14]The prescribed portion of oil, measured by the bath, is a tenth of a bath from each cor (which consists of ten baths or one homer, for ten baths are equivalent to a homer). [15]Also one sheep is to be taken from every flock of two hundred from the well-watered pastures of Israel. These will be used for the grain offerings, burnt offerings and fellowship offerings[k] to make atonement for the people, declares the Sovereign LORD. [16]All the people of the land will participate in this special gift for the use of the prince in Israel. [17]It will be the duty of the prince to provide the burnt offerings, grain offerings and drink offerings at the festivals, the New Moons and the Sabbaths—at all the appointed feasts of the house of Israel. He will provide the sin offerings, grain offerings, burnt offerings and fellowship offerings to make atonement for the house of Israel.

[18]" 'This is what the Sovereign LORD says: In the first month on the first day you are to take a young bull without defect and purify the sanctuary. [19]The priest is to take some of the blood of the sin offering and put it on the doorposts of the

---

[a]29 The Hebrew term refers to the irrevocable giving over of things or persons to the LORD.
[b]1 Septuagint (see also verses 3 and 5 and 48:9); Hebrew *10,000*   [c]3 That is, about 7 miles (about 12 kilometers)   [d]3 That is, about 3 miles (about 5 kilometers)   [e]5 Septuagint; Hebrew *temple; they will have as their possession 20 rooms*   [f]10 An ephah was a dry measure.   [g]10 A bath was a liquid measure.   [h]11 A homer was a dry measure.   [i]12 A shekel weighed about 2/5 ounce (about 11.5 grams).   [j]12 That is, 60 shekels; the common mina was 50 shekels.   [k]15 Traditionally *peace offerings*; also in verse 17

temple, on the four corners of the upper ledge of the altar and on the gateposts of the inner court. ²⁰You are to do the same on the seventh day of the month for anyone who sins unintentionally or through ignorance; so you are to make atonement for the temple.

²¹" 'In the first month on the fourteenth day you are to observe the Passover, a feast lasting seven days, during which you shall eat bread made without yeast. ²²On that day the prince is to provide a bull as a sin offering for himself and for all the people of the land. ²³Every day during the seven days of the Feast he is to provide seven bulls and seven rams without defect as a burnt offering to the LORD, and a male goat for a sin offering. ²⁴He is to provide as a grain offering an ephah for each bull and an ephah for each ram, along with a hin*ᵃ* of oil for each ephah.

²⁵" 'During the seven days of the Feast,

which begins in the seventh month on the fifteenth day, he is to make the same provision for sin offerings, burnt offerings, grain offerings and oil.

46 " 'This is what the Sovereign LORD says: The gate of the inner court facing east is to be shut on the six working days, but on the Sabbath day and on the day of the New Moon it is to be opened. ²The prince is to enter from the outside through the portico of the gateway and stand by the gatepost. The priests are to sacrifice his burnt offering and his fellowship offerings.*ᵇ* He is to worship at the threshold of the gateway and then go out, but the gate will not be shut until evening. ³On the Sabbaths and New Moons the people of the land are to worship in the presence of the LORD at

ᵃ24 That is, probably about 4 quarts (about 4 liters); *ᵇ2 Traditionally* peace offerings; *also in verse 12*

Fri day

Getting Even

Read Ezekiel 45:9

Sometimes when I'm jealous of someone or angry at something they've said or done, I find myself thinking about ways to get even. I rarely end up going through with my plans for revenge, but I know that even my *desire* to hurt someone is against God's commands.

So many people I know think it's a sign of strength when they fight with someone or deliberately hurt someone's feelings. But I think it's more impressive when someone is able to just walk away from someone who's trying to pick a fight. God tells us to be merciful with other people, even when we're tempted to hurt them. It takes a lot of strength to do that.

God knows we're tempted to hurt other people or take advantage of them in the name of "revenge." But God would much rather have us leave our problems in his hands.

I know the next time someone hurts me, I'll be tempted to hurt them back. But I have to remember, that's not how God wants us to handle our struggles.

Emile age 14

What about You?

❶ How do you respond when someone hurts your feelings?

❷ Think about someone you may have taken advantage of or hurt. How can you make things right with that person?

❸ Ask God to help you resist taking revenge on people who hurt you.

Turn to page 1015 for your next devotion.

the entrance to that gateway. ⁴The burnt offering the prince brings to the LORD on the Sabbath day is to be six male lambs and a ram, all without defect. ⁵The grain offering given with the ram is to be an ephah,ᵃ and the grain offering with the lambs is to be as much as he pleases, along with a hinᵇ of oil for each ephah. ⁶On the day of the New Moon he is to offer a young bull, six lambs and a ram, all without defect. ⁷He is to provide as a grain offering one ephah with the bull, one ephah with the ram, and with the lambs as much as he wants to give, along with a hin of oil with each ephah. ⁸When the prince enters, he is to go in through the portico of the gateway, and he is to come out the same way.

⁹" 'When the people of the land come before the LORD at the appointed feasts, whoever enters by the north gate to worship is to go out the south gate; and whoever enters by the south gate is to go out the north gate. No one is to return through the gate by which he entered, but each is to go out the opposite gate. ¹⁰The prince is to be among them, going in when they go in and going out when they go out.

¹¹" 'At the festivals and the appointed feasts, the grain offering is to be an ephah with a bull, an ephah with a ram, and with the lambs as much as one pleases, along with a hin of oil for each ephah. ¹²When the prince provides a freewill offering to the LORD—whether a burnt offering or fellowship offerings—the gate facing east is to be opened for him. He shall offer his burnt offering or his fellowship offerings as he does on the Sabbath day. Then he shall go out, and after he has gone out, the gate will be shut.

¹³" 'Every day you are to provide a year-old lamb without defect for a burnt offering to the LORD; morning by morning you shall provide it. ¹⁴You are also to provide with it morning by morning a grain offering, consisting of a sixth of an ephah with a third of a hin of oil to moisten the flour. The presenting of this grain offering to the LORD is a lasting ordinance. ¹⁵So the lamb and the grain offering and the oil shall be provided morning by morning for a regular burnt offering.

¹⁶" 'This is what the Sovereign LORD says: If the prince makes a gift from his inheritance to one of his sons, it will also belong to his descendants; it is to be their property by inheritance. ¹⁷If, however, he makes a gift from his inheritance to one of his servants, the servant may keep it until the year of freedom; then it will revert to the prince. His inheritance belongs to his sons only; it is theirs. ¹⁸The prince must not take any of the inheritance of the people, driving them off their property. He is to give his sons their inheritance out of his own property, so that none of my people will be separated from his property.' "

¹⁹Then the man brought me through the entrance at the side of the gate to the sacred rooms facing north, which belonged to the priests, and showed me a place at the western end. ²⁰He said to me, "This is the place where the priests will cook the guilt offering and the sin offering and bake the grain offering, to avoid bringing them into the outer court and consecrating the people."

²¹He then brought me to the outer court and led me around to its four corners, and I saw in each corner another court. ²²In the four corners of the outer court were enclosedᶜ courts, forty cubits long and thirty cubits wide; each of the courts in the four corners was the same size. ²³Around the inside of each of the four courts was a ledge of stone, with places for fire built all around under the ledge. ²⁴He said to me, "These are the kitchens where those who minister at the temple will cook the sacrifices of the people."

The River From the Temple

47 The man brought me back to the entrance of the temple, and I saw water coming out from under the threshold of the temple toward the east (for the temple faced east). The water was coming down from under the south side of the temple, south of the altar. ²He then brought me out through the north gate

---

ᵃ5 That is, probably about 3/5 bushel (about 22 liters)   ᵇ5 That is, probably about 4 quarts (about 4 liters)   ᶜ22 The meaning of the Hebrew for this word is uncertain.

Making Your Faith Your Own

Back Stage Pass

You may wonder, *How can I not make my faith my own? I mean, if it's mine then it's not anyone else's, right?* Er . . . sort of. Faith comes from a whole lot of places—the Bible (Romans 10:17, page 1364; John 20:31, page 1301), your parents (Deuteronomy 6:6–7, page 210) and other people (2 Corinthians 3:2–3, page 1401). The people around you have influenced your faith (the stuff you believe about God and life). When you were a little kid, if Mom and Dad believed in God, you probably believed in God. If Mom and Dad didn't believe, then you probably didn't. Here's the cool part. As you get older, which is what you are doing right this second, you begin to check out your faith and see if it really is yours.

And you know what else? You start figuring out what your faith is just by living your everyday life! That's because faith is not only *what* you believe, but also *how* you live. You probably don't remember the first time you sat down on a chair and were kind of wondering if it would hold you up. Now you just sit; but every time you sit on a chair you are exercising faith. Sitting in a lot of chairs, for example, is what has taught you to have faith in chairs.

Remember when you may have thought Santa delivered the presents at Christmas? And then how one day you began to think about this Santa stuff, putting one and one together and suddenly realized they didn't add up to two? Like, how does Santa get to so many places in the world so fast? How can Santa deliver all the presents in one night? How come your older brother never tells Santa what he wants? One day you realize Santa's bogus, so you don't leave out cookies and milk for Santa anymore. What you thought about Santa changed because getting older caused you to think differently, and now you act differently.

So here you are, growing up, believing in God, the God your parents hopefully told you about, the God your youth worker tells you about, and now you are beginning to wonder who this God really is and how true is this God. In other words, you are beginning the process of making faith your own.

COOL. So how do you make faith your own?

First. Discover what faith is by learning from your mistakes. Look at the disciples (Peter on the water, little kids coming to Jesus). They constantly made mistakes; but in the process they learned what their faith was and what it wasn't.

Second. Do nothing. Yeah, faith sometimes comes when we just stop doing stuff and think about life. Thinking is a great way to figure out faith and life.

Third. Watch others. It's amazing what we can learn about faith when we watch others who have faith.

Fourth. Courage. It's a fancy word that means doing what you know you should. Take a risk! Share your faith with your friends, stand up for what you believe! Think about David's courage when he stepped out in faith to fight the giant Goliath in 1 Samuel 17, page 330.

Fifth. Talk about it. Really. The more you talk about your faith, the more it becomes your own, a part of you—in other words, your faith (see Romans 1:16–17, page 1351).

eXtreme FAITH

OK, I know it's probably gonna be a long time before you're a mom or dad, but just imagine it for a moment . . . You've got a son named Chad. You've hidden a treasure chest full of Chad's favorite stuff in the backyard, and you tell him to go find it. He's excited, but he's got a ton of questions like, "How will I know where to find it?" and "Where do I start?" You hand him a map and tell him you've marked out the path to the treasure.

Chad grabs the map and heads toward the swings. You gently guide him toward the old oak tree. Then Chad notices the sandbox and starts heading for it; you lovingly turn him toward the old oak tree again. Then Chad stops and tosses a Frisbee to his dog, and then he heads for the garden. Again, you gently turn him toward the old oak tree. As a loving parent, you're constantly guiding Chad toward the treasure, because you want to make sure he finds it.

It works the same way spiritually. God, your heavenly Father, has an incredible plan for your life, and he's given you a wonderful map—the Bible, the guide for your path (see Psalm 119:105, page 711). But you have to read it, learn it and apply it to your life. If you do this and still end up taking take a wrong turn, God will gently turn you around and guide you in the right direction. You see, God wants you to fulfill his plan for your life even more than you can imagine (see Philippians 2:13, page 1437).

It's God's responsibility to make sure we "get" his plan; it's our responsibility to communicate with him often. But communicating with God means more than just talking to him. We've got to listen too. Sometimes we're so busy talking to God that we forget to listen for his voice.

God uses other ways to show us his will. He also works through our thoughts, our interests, our spiritual leaders (pastor, youth minister, parents, church school teacher) and our gifts. God has given you specific gifts and abilities to use for his glory. So use 'em! If you're a real "people-person," for example, God's will for you probably includes working with people.

When seeking God's will for your life, it's important to remember that "God's will" doesn't simply mean what your career will be, whom you'll marry and where you'll live. Those things are only parts of his will. His plan for you includes the things going on in your life right now, at this very moment. So instead of asking God what he wants you to do 5 years from now, ask him, "Lord, help me to be all you want me to be. What is your will for me today?"

— Susie Shellenberger, editor of Brio, Focus on the Family's monthly magazine for teen girls. Susie has written 22 books and is a national youth speaker who loves Honeycomb cereal.

and led me around the outside to the outer gate facing east, and the water was flowing from the south side.

³As the man went eastward with a measuring line in his hand, he measured off a thousand cubits[a] and then led me through water that was ankle-deep. ⁴He measured off another thousand cubits and led me through water that was knee-deep. He measured off another thousand and led me through water that was up to the waist. ⁵He measured off another thousand, but now it was a river that I could not cross, because the water had risen and was deep enough to swim in—a river that no one could cross. ⁶He asked me, "Son of man, do you see this?"

Then he led me back to the bank of the river. ⁷When I arrived there, I saw a great number of trees on each side of the river. ⁸He said to me, "This water flows toward the eastern region and goes down into the Arabah,[b] where it enters the Sea.[c] When it empties into the Sea,[c] the water there becomes fresh. ⁹Swarms of living creatures will live wherever the river flows. There will be large numbers of fish, because this water flows there and makes the salt water fresh; so where the river flows everything will live. ¹⁰Fishermen will stand along the shore; from En Gedi to En Eglaim there will be places for spreading nets. The fish will be of many kinds—like the fish of the Great Sea.[d] ¹¹But the swamps and marshes will not become fresh; they will be left for salt. ¹²Fruit trees of all kinds will grow on both banks of the river. Their leaves will not wither, nor will their fruit fail. Every month they will bear, because the water from the sanctuary flows to them. Their fruit will serve for food and their leaves for healing."

The Boundaries of the Land

¹³This is what the Sovereign LORD says: "These are the boundaries by which you are to divide the land for an inheritance among the twelve tribes of Israel, with two portions for Joseph. ¹⁴You are to divide it equally among them. Because I swore with uplifted hand to give it to your forefathers, this land will become your inheritance.

¹⁵"This is to be the boundary of the land:

"On the north side it will run from the Great Sea by the Hethlon road past Lebo[e] Hamath to Zedad, ¹⁶Berothah[f] and Sibraim (which lies on the border between Damascus and Hamath), as far as Hazer Hatticon, which is on the border of Hauran. ¹⁷The boundary will extend from the sea to Hazar Enan,[g] along the northern border of Damascus, with the border of Hamath to the north. This will be the north boundary. ¹⁸"On the east side the boundary will run between Hauran and Damascus, along the Jordan between Gilead and the land of Israel, to the eastern sea and as far as Tamar.[h] This will be the east boundary. ¹⁹"On the south side it will run from Tamar as far as the waters of Meribah Kadesh, then along the Wadi of Egypt to the Great Sea. This will be the south boundary. ²⁰"On the west side, the Great Sea will be the boundary to a point opposite Lebo[i] Hamath. This will be the west boundary.

²¹"You are to distribute this land among yourselves according to the tribes of Israel. ²²You are to allot it as an inheritance for yourselves and for the aliens who have settled among you and who have children. You are to consider them as native-born Israelites; along with you they are to be allotted an inheritance among the tribes of Israel. ²³In whatever tribe the alien settles, there you are to give him his inheritance," declares the Sovereign LORD.

The Division of the Land

48 "These are the tribes, listed by name: At the northern frontier, Dan will have one portion; it will follow

---

[a]3 That is, about 1,500 feet (about 450 meters)
[b]8 Or the Jordan Valley   [c]8 That is, the Dead Sea
[d]10 That is, the Mediterranean; also in verses 15, 19 and 20   [e]15 Or past the entrance to   [f]15,16 See Septuagint and Ezekiel 48:1; Hebrew road to go into Zedad, ¹⁶Hamath, Berothah   [g]17 Hebrew Enon, a variant of Enan   [h]18 Septuagint and Syriac; Hebrew Israel. You will measure to the eastern sea   [i]20 Or opposite the entrance to

the Hethlon road to Lebo[a] Hamath; Hazar Enan and the northern border of Damascus next to Hamath will be part of its border from the east side to the west side.

²"Asher will have one portion; it will border the territory of Dan from east to west.

³"Naphtali will have one portion; it will border the territory of Asher from east to west.

⁴"Manasseh will have one portion; it will border the territory of Naphtali from east to west.

⁵"Ephraim will have one portion; it will border the territory of Manasseh from east to west.

⁶"Reuben will have one portion; it will border the territory of Ephraim from east to west.

⁷"Judah will have one portion; it will border the territory of Reuben from east to west.

⁸"Bordering the territory of Judah from east to west will be the portion you are to present as a special gift. It will be 25,000 cubits[b] wide, and its length from east to west will equal one of the tribal portions; the sanctuary will be in the center of it.

⁹"The special portion you are to offer to the LORD will be 25,000 cubits long and 10,000 cubits[c] wide. ¹⁰This will be the sacred portion for the priests. It will be 25,000 cubits long on the north side, 10,000 cubits wide on the west side, 10,000 cubits wide on the east side and 25,000 cubits long on the south side. In the center of it will be the sanctuary of the LORD. ¹¹This will be for the consecrated priests, the Zadokites, who were faithful in serving me and did not go astray as the Levites did when the Israelites went astray. ¹²It will be a special gift to them from the sacred portion of the land, a most holy portion, bordering the territory of the Levites.

¹³"Alongside the territory of the priests, the Levites will have an allotment 25,000 cubits long and 10,000 cubits wide. Its total length will be 25,000 cubits and its width 10,000 cubits. ¹⁴They must not sell or exchange any of it. This is the best of the land and must not pass into other hands, because it is holy to the LORD.

¹⁵"The remaining area, 5,000 cubits wide and 25,000 cubits long, will be for the common use of the city, for houses and for pastureland. The city will be in the center of it ¹⁶and will have these measurements: the north side 4,500 cubits, the south side 4,500 cubits, the east side 4,500 cubits, and the west side 4,500 cubits. ¹⁷The pastureland for the city will be 250 cubits on the north, 250 cubits on the south, 250 cubits on the east, and 250 cubits on the west. ¹⁸What remains of the area, bordering on the sacred portion and running the length of it, will be 10,000 cubits on the east side and 10,000 cubits on the west side. Its produce will supply food for the workers of the city. ¹⁹The workers from the city who farm it will come from all the tribes of Israel. ²⁰The entire portion will be a square, 25,000 cubits on each side. As a special gift you will set aside the sacred portion, along with the property of the city.

²¹"What remains on both sides of the area formed by the sacred portion and the city property will belong to the prince. It will extend eastward from the 25,000 cubits of the sacred portion to the eastern border, and westward from the 25,000 cubits to the western border. Both these areas running the length of the tribal portions will belong to the prince, and the sacred portion with the temple sanctuary will be in the center of them. ²²So the property of the Levites and the property of the city will lie in the center of the area that belongs to the prince. The area belonging to the prince will lie between the border of Judah and the border of Benjamin.

²³"As for the rest of the tribes: Benjamin will have one portion; it will extend from the east side to the west side.

²⁴"Simeon will have one portion; it will border the territory of Benjamin from east to west.

²⁵"Issachar will have one portion; it will border the territory of Simeon from east to west.

²⁶"Zebulun will have one portion; it

---

[a]1 Or *to the entrance to*   [b]8 That is, about 7 miles (about 12 kilometers)   [c]9 That is, about 3 miles (about 5 kilometers)

will border the territory of Issachar from east to west.

²⁷"Gad will have one portion; it will border the territory of Zebulun from east to west.

²⁸"The southern boundary of Gad will run south from Tamar to the waters of Meribah Kadesh, then along the Wadi of Egypt to the Great Sea.ᵃ

²⁹"This is the land you are to allot as an inheritance to the tribes of Israel, and these will be their portions," declares the Sovereign LORD.

The Gates of the City

³⁰"These will be the exits of the city: Beginning on the north side, which is 4,500 cubits long, ³¹the gates of the city will be named after the tribes of Israel. The three gates on the north side will be the gate of Reuben, the gate of Judah and the gate of Levi.

³²"On the east side, which is 4,500 cubits long, will be three gates: the gate of

ᵃ*28* That is, the Mediterranean

Weekend.

I'm So Mad I Could Scream!

Read Matthew 26:47–54 (page 1180)

When Emile talked about her anger in Friday's devotional, all of us could relate. We know what it's like to be wronged. We know how it feels when we find out someone has spread vicious rumors about us or dissed us to all our friends.

Anger is real. We all experience it. Because anger is such a strong emotion, it's easy to act on it with some kind of physical response. It happens all the time.

But Emile pointed out that there's a better way. Trouble is, the better way is not always the easy way. Sometimes doing what's right is much harder than doing what's not right. That's why the Bible is so great. It gives us examples that we can relate to. It shows us how others reacted at tense moments when violence would have seemed like the right response.

Take Jesus, for instance. He was betrayed by his friend and disiple, and he was being arrested for something he didn't do. Peter was ready to fight, but Jesus stopped him. What Jesus said was shocking. He said something like, "Hey, I could wipe these guys out with a whole truckload of angels, but I'm not going to fight these people. I am going to trust in the power of God instead of the power of violence." Wow! Jesus resisted using violence, and he can help us do the same.

What about You?

❶ What are 2 bad habits that you have when you get angry? Commit yourself to not behave this way the next time you feel angry.

❷ Think about the last time you responded to someone in anger (your parents? brother? sister? friend at school?). If you haven't apologized, why not think about how you might start the process of making up?

❸ Ask God to help you find healthy ways of dealing with your anger.

Turn to page 1020 for your next devotion.

Joseph, the gate of Benjamin and the gate of Dan.

³³"On the south side, which measures 4,500 cubits, will be three gates: the gate of Simeon, the gate of Issachar and the

gate of Zebulun.

³⁴"On the west side, which is 4,500 cubits long, will be three gates: the gate of Gad, the gate of Asher and the gate of Naphtali.

³⁵"The distance all around will be 18,000 cubits.

"And the name of the city from that time on will be:

THE LORD IS THERE."

Daniel

START

A young guy named Daniel and his buddies (and a bunch of other Israelites) are captured and taken from their homes and families in Judah and forced to live in Babylon under the rule of King Nebuchadnezzar. Daniel and the guys have to make a choice. Will they say to themselves, "Poor us! We're prisoners in this foreign country! God must not love us anymore!" Or will they stick out their tongues at the Babylonians and refuse to cooperate at all, which probably would earn them a death sentence?

Well, they find a place between the 2 extremes by relying completely on God. Sure, they participate in the educational programs of the king, but they don't eat the food they are given because they know it isn't good for them. And Daniel interprets many dreams for 4 of the kings who reign while he's in Babylon, but he doesn't spare the gory details or just tell them what they want to hear.

You may be thinking, *Big deal! So they don't eat food and tell the truth. I could do that!* But these guys are even more daring! They refuse to bow down to King Nebuchadnezzar's statue. And Daniel continues to pray to God 3 times a day, rather than to King Darius, as the law commanded. Their disobedience brings with it some pretty tough punishments, like being thrown into a super hot furnace or into a den of hungry lions for a sleepover. As a result of their bonus-sized faith and courage, God uses these guys to teach some kings (and us) a thing or 2 about living out our faith when things don't go our way.

Cast OF Characters

Daniel (DAN-yul)

This young man courageously lives out his faith and trusts God even after he's captured and held prisoner by the Babylonians. Daniel continues to trust God during his 69 years away from home, and God uses Daniel over and over again in the lives of Babylonians and the other away-from-home Israelites.

Shadrach (SHAD-rack), Meshach (ME-shack) and Abednego (a-BED-nee-go)

These are Daniel's buds. These guys never forget their own God and refuse to bow down and worship old Neb's statue of gold. Their refusal earns them "hot time" in a furnace, but God is faithful to protect them from the flames!

King Nebuchadnezzar (NEB-you-kad-NEZZ-ur)

This meany king loves to conquer other lands and take the strongest, smartest, most talented and beautiful people back to his own country. Then he tries to use Babylonian names, education and training to get the captives to serve and even worship him.

King Belshazzar
(BELL-shaz-ur)

He doesn't learn from Nebby's mistakes. So during one of the king's rowdy parties, God uses a message written by some mysterious fingers to get his attention. None of the staff can tell the king what the words mean, so Daniel is brought in to interpret the message of doom.

King Darius
(DARE-ee-us)

Darius is basically a good king who makes the huge mistake of listening to some of his jealous advisors. These whiners don't like how quickly Daniel's rising in the ranks. So they ask the king to sign a law that says the people can only pray to the king for the next 30 days. But the king makes things right again, and the underlings' evil scheme backfires in a big way!

What's UP with That?

Tabloids use really wacked-out and untrue headlines about celebrities, aliens, religious figures and natural disasters in order to sell the trash they call "news" to gullible folks every day. And the writers make millions doing it! Which headlines could have announced something that really appeared in the book of Daniel?

1. Daniel Gains 100 Pounds on King Nebby's Grass Diet
2. King Throws Down Some Funky-Fresh Names on Babylonian Kids
3. Daniel Delivers Bad News to Bad King and Gets a Promotion!
4. Shadrach, Meshach and Abednego Ordered to Wash Pigeon Paste From King's Statue
5. Flame On! Foreign Guys to Meet the Giant Toaster
6. Daniel Predicts Winner of Gladiator Games
7. King Nebby Snaps Out of It, Worships Israel's God and Returns to the Throne
8. King Belshazzar Choked to Death by Invisible Hands
9. King Darius Creates a New Dance Craze: the Darius Jiggle
10. Here Kitty, Kitty: Loser Accusers Meet the Lion King

Don't believe everything you see or hear in this world. Make sure you know God's Word, maintain a tight relationship with God through regular prayer and are always prepared to take a stand for him—even in the face of persecution, hatred, fire or a den of hungry lions!

Snap shots

- An Israelite by any other name . . . *(chapter 1:1–7)*
- Pass the spinach and Evian, please! *(chapter 1:8–16)*
- Top of the class *(chapter 1:17–21)*
- Sweet dreams! *(chapter 2)*
- Don't forget the s'mores! *(chapter 3)*
- Not-so-sweet dreams *(chapter 4)*
- The writing's on the wall *(chapter 5)*
- The jaws of life *(chapter 6)*
- Visions of things to come *(chapters 7—12)*

answers: 2(1:7), 3(2:36-48), 5(3:19-27), 7(4:34-37), 10(6:24)

Daniel's Training in Babylon

1 In the third year of the reign of Jehoiakim king of Judah, Nebuchadnezzar king of Babylon came to Jerusalem and besieged it. [2]And the Lord delivered Jehoiakim king of Judah into his hand, along with some of the articles from the temple of God. These he carried off to the temple of his god in Babylonia[a] and put in the treasure house of his god.

[3]Then the king ordered Ashpenaz, chief of his court officials, to bring in some of the Israelites from the royal family and the nobility— [4]young men without any physical defect, handsome, showing aptitude for every kind of learning, well informed, quick to understand, and qualified to serve in the king's palace. He was to teach them the language and literature of the Babylonians.[b] [5]The king assigned them a daily amount of food and wine from the king's table. They were to be trained for three years, and after that they were to enter the king's service.

[6]Among these were some from Judah: Daniel, Hananiah, Mishael and Azariah. [7]The chief official gave them new names: to Daniel, the name Belteshazzar; to Hananiah, Shadrach; to Mishael, Meshach; and to Azariah, Abednego.

[8]But Daniel resolved not to defile himself with the royal food and wine, and he asked the chief official for permission not to defile himself this way. [9]Now God had caused the official to show favor and sympathy to Daniel, [10]but the official told Daniel, "I am afraid of my lord the king, who has assigned your[c] food and drink. Why should he see you looking worse than the other young men your age? The king would then have my head because of you."

[11]Daniel then said to the guard whom the chief official had appointed over Daniel, Hananiah, Mishael and Azariah, [12]"Please test your servants for ten days: Give us nothing but vegetables to eat and water to drink. [13]Then compare our appearance with that of the young men who eat the royal food, and treat your servants in accordance with what you see." [14]So he agreed to this and tested them for ten days.

[15]At the end of the ten days they looked healthier and better nourished than any of the young men who ate the royal food. [16]So the guard took away their choice food and the wine they were to drink and gave them vegetables instead.

[17]To these four young men God gave knowledge and understanding of all kinds of literature and learning. And Daniel could understand visions and dreams of all kinds.

[18]At the end of the time set by the king to bring them in, the chief official presented them to Nebuchadnezzar. [19]The king talked with them, and he found none equal to Daniel, Hananiah, Mishael and Azariah; so they entered the king's service. [20]In every matter of wisdom and understanding about which the king questioned them, he found them ten times better than all the magicians and enchanters in his whole kingdom.

[21]And Daniel remained there until the first year of King Cyrus.

Nebuchadnezzar's Dream

2 In the second year of his reign, Nebuchadnezzar had dreams; his mind was troubled and he could not sleep. [2]So the king summoned the magicians, enchanters, sorcerers and astrologers[d] to tell him what he had dreamed. When they came in and stood before the king, [3]he said to them, "I have had a dream that troubles me and I want to know what it means.[e]"

[4]Then the astrologers answered the king in Aramaic,[f] "O king, live forever! Tell your servants the dream, and we will interpret it."

[5]The king replied to the astrologers, "This is what I have firmly decided: If you do not tell me what my dream was and interpret it, I will have you cut into pieces and your houses turned into piles of rubble. [6]But if you tell me the dream and explain it, you will receive from me gifts and rewards and great honor. So tell me the dream and interpret it for me."

---

a2 Hebrew *Shinar*　*b4* Or *Chaldeans*　*c10* The Hebrew for *your* and *you* in this verse is plural.
d2 Or *Chaldeans*; also in verses 4, 5 and 10
e3 Or *was*　*f4* The text from here through chapter 7 is in Aramaic.

⁷Once more they replied, "Let the king tell his servants the dream, and we will interpret it."

⁸Then the king answered, "I am certain that you are trying to gain time, because you realize that this is what I have firmly decided: ⁹If you do not tell me the dream, there is just one penalty for you. You have conspired to tell me misleading and wicked things, hoping the situation will change. So then, tell me the dream, and I will know that you can interpret it for me."

¹⁰The astrologers answered the king, "There is not a man on earth who can do what the king asks! No king, however great and mighty, has ever asked such a thing of any magician or enchanter or astrologer. ¹¹What the king asks is too difficult. No one can reveal it to the king except the gods, and they do not live among men."

¹²This made the king so angry and furious that he ordered the execution of all the wise men of Babylon. ¹³So the decree was issued to put the wise men to death, and men were sent to look for Daniel and his friends to put them to death.

¹⁴When Arioch, the commander of the king's guard, had gone out to put to death the wise men of Babylon, Daniel spoke to him with wisdom and tact. ¹⁵He asked the king's officer, "Why did the king issue such a harsh decree?" Arioch then explained the matter to Daniel. ¹⁶At this, Daniel went in to the king and asked for time, so that he might interpret the dream for him.

¹⁷Then Daniel returned to his house and explained the matter to his friends Hananiah, Mishael and Azariah. ¹⁸He urged them to plead for mercy from the God of heaven concerning this mystery, so that he and his friends might not be executed with the rest of the wise men of Babylon. ¹⁹During the night the mystery

Monday

Just a Little Respect

Read Daniel 2:14

I sure wish I'd thought about this verse a few weeks ago when we got a new leader in our youth group. The first time I met him, I said something pretty lame. Ever since that first meeting, he's thought of me as a trouble-maker. He always thinks I'm up to something, even when I'm not. And he's a little tougher on me than he is on other kids. I guess I deserve it.

I have a hard time showing respect to people in authority, and it's caused me a lot of problems. I have teachers who have never liked me because I was rude when I first met them. I wish I could take back all those bad first impressions, because once people make up their minds about you, it's pretty tough to change their opinions. I've learned the hard way that when you're disrespectful, you pay the price.

God wants us to respect the people who are above us, like parents, teachers and youth leaders. When we respect those people, we show respect for God too.

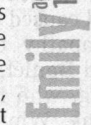
Emily age 14

❶ How does it feel when someone doesn't respect you? How do you think your parents or teachers feel when people don't respect them?

❷ Think about some ways you can show respect to authority figures. For the next week, practice being a respectful person.

❸ Ask God to help you show others respect.

Turn to page 1023 for your next devotion.

was revealed to Daniel in a vision. Then Daniel praised the God of heaven ²⁰and said:

"Praise be to the name of God for ever
and ever;
wisdom and power are his.
²¹He changes times and seasons;
he sets up kings and deposes them.
He gives wisdom to the wise
and knowledge to the discerning.
²²He reveals deep and hidden things;
he knows what lies in darkness,
and light dwells with him.
²³I thank and praise you, O God of my
fathers:
You have given me wisdom and
power,
you have made known to me what we
asked of you,
you have made known to us the
dream of the king."

Daniel Interprets the Dream

²⁴Then Daniel went to Arioch, whom the king had appointed to execute the wise men of Babylon, and said to him, "Do not execute the wise men of Babylon. Take me to the king, and I will interpret his dream for him."

²⁵Arioch took Daniel to the king at once and said, "I have found a man among the exiles from Judah who can tell the king what his dream means."

²⁶The king asked Daniel (also called Belteshazzar), "Are you able to tell me what I saw in my dream and interpret it?"

²⁷Daniel replied, "No wise man, enchanter, magician or diviner can explain to the king the mystery he has asked about, ²⁸but there is a God in heaven who reveals mysteries. He has shown King Nebuchadnezzar what will happen in days to come. Your dream and the visions that passed through your mind as you lay on your bed are these:

²⁹"As you were lying there, O king, your mind turned to things to come, and the revealer of mysteries showed you what is going to happen. ³⁰As for me, this mystery has been revealed to me, not because I have greater wisdom than other living men, but so that you, O king, may know the interpretation and that you

may understand what went through your mind.

³¹"You looked, O king, and there before you stood a large statue—an enormous, dazzling statue, awesome in appearance. ³²The head of the statue was made of pure gold, its chest and arms of silver, its belly and thighs of bronze, ³³its legs of iron, its feet partly of iron and partly of baked clay. ³⁴While you were watching, a rock was cut out, but not by human hands. It struck the statue on its feet of iron and clay and smashed them. ³⁵Then the iron, the clay, the bronze, the silver and the gold were broken to pieces at the same time and became like chaff on a threshing floor in the summer. The wind swept them away without leaving a trace. But the rock that struck the statue became a huge mountain and filled the whole earth.

³⁶"This was the dream, and now we will interpret it to the king. ³⁷You, O king, are the king of kings. The God of heaven has given you dominion and power and might and glory; ³⁸in your hands he has placed mankind and the beasts of the field and the birds of the air. Wherever they live, he has made you ruler over them all. You are that head of gold.

³⁹"After you, another kingdom will rise, inferior to yours. Next, a third kingdom, one of bronze, will rule over the whole earth. ⁴⁰Finally, there will be a fourth kingdom, strong as iron—for iron breaks and smashes everything—and as iron breaks things to pieces, so it will crush and break all the others. ⁴¹Just as you saw that the feet and toes were partly of baked clay and partly of iron, so this will be a divided kingdom; yet it will have some of the strength of iron in it, even as you saw iron mixed with clay. ⁴²As the toes were partly iron and partly clay, so this kingdom will be partly strong and partly brittle. ⁴³And just as you saw the iron mixed with baked clay, so the people will be a mixture and will not remain united, any more than iron mixes with clay.

⁴⁴"In the time of those kings, the God of heaven will set up a kingdom that will never be destroyed, nor will it be left to another people. It will crush all those

kingdoms and bring them to an end, but it will itself endure forever. [45]This is the meaning of the vision of the rock cut out of a mountain, but not by human hands—a rock that broke the iron, the bronze, the clay, the silver and the gold to pieces.

"The great God has shown the king what will take place in the future. The dream is true and the interpretation is trustworthy."

[46]Then King Nebuchadnezzar fell prostrate before Daniel and paid him honor and ordered that an offering and incense be presented to him. [47]The king said to Daniel, "Surely your God is the God of gods and the Lord of kings and a revealer of mysteries, for you were able to reveal this mystery."

[48]Then the king placed Daniel in a high position and lavished many gifts on him. He made him ruler over the entire province of Babylon and placed him in charge of all its wise men. [49]Moreover, at Daniel's request the king appointed Shadrach, Meshach and Abednego administrators over the province of Babylon, while Daniel himself remained at the royal court.

The Image of Gold and the Fiery Furnace

3 King Nebuchadnezzar made an image of gold, ninety feet high and nine feet[a] wide, and set it up on the plain of Dura in the province of Babylon. [2]He then summoned the satraps, prefects, governors, advisers, treasurers, judges, magistrates and all the other provincial officials to come to the dedication of the image he had set up. [3]So the satraps, prefects, governors, advisers, treasurers, judges, magistrates and all the other provincial officials assembled for the dedication of the image that King Nebuchadnezzar had set up, and they stood before it.

[4]Then the herald loudly proclaimed, "This is what you are commanded to do, O peoples, nations and men of every language: [5]As soon as you hear the sound of the horn, flute, zither, lyre, harp, pipes and all kinds of music, you must fall down and worship the image of gold that King Nebuchadnezzar has set up. [6]Whoever does not fall down and worship will

immediately be thrown into a blazing furnace."

[7]Therefore, as soon as they heard the sound of the horn, flute, zither, lyre, harp and all kinds of music, all the peoples, nations and men of every language fell down and worshiped the image of gold that King Nebuchadnezzar had set up.

[8]At this time some astrologers[b] came forward and denounced the Jews. [9]They said to King Nebuchadnezzar, "O king, live forever! [10]You have issued a decree, O king, that everyone who hears the sound of the horn, flute, zither, lyre, harp, pipes and all kinds of music must fall down and worship the image of gold, [11]and that whoever does not fall down and worship will be thrown into a blazing furnace. [12]But there are some Jews whom you have set over the affairs of the province of Babylon—Shadrach, Meshach and Abednego—who pay no attention to you, O king. They neither serve your gods nor worship the image of gold you have set up."

[13]Furious with rage, Nebuchadnezzar summoned Shadrach, Meshach and Abednego. So these men were brought before the king, [14]and Nebuchadnezzar said to them, "Is it true, Shadrach, Meshach and Abednego, that you do not serve my gods or worship the image of gold I have set up? [15]Now when you hear the sound of the horn, flute, zither, lyre, harp, pipes and all kinds of music, if you are ready to fall down and worship the image I made, very good. But if you do not worship it, you will be thrown immediately into a blazing furnace. Then what god will be able to rescue you from my hand?"

[16]Shadrach, Meshach and Abednego replied to the king, "O Nebuchadnezzar, we do not need to defend ourselves before you in this matter. [17]If we are thrown into the blazing furnace, the God we serve is able to save us from it, and he will rescue us from your hand, O king. [18]But even if he does not, we want you to know, O king, that we will not serve your gods or worship the image of gold you have set up."

---

[a]1 Aramaic *sixty cubits high and six cubits wide* (about 27 meters high and 2.7 meters wide)
[b]8 Or *Chaldeans*

¹⁹Then Nebuchadnezzar was furious with Shadrach, Meshach and Abednego, and his attitude toward them changed. He ordered the furnace heated seven times hotter than usual ²⁰and commanded some of the strongest soldiers in his army to tie up Shadrach, Meshach and Abednego and throw them into the blazing furnace. ²¹So these men, wearing their robes, trousers, turbans and other clothes, were bound and thrown into the blazing furnace. ²²The king's command was so urgent and the furnace so hot that the flames of the fire killed the soldiers who took up Shadrach, Meshach and Abednego, ²³and these three men, firmly tied, fell into the blazing furnace.

²⁴Then King Nebuchadnezzar leaped to his feet in amazement and asked his advisers, "Weren't there three men that we tied up and threw into the fire?"

They replied, "Certainly, O king."

²⁵He said, "Look! I see four men walking around in the fire, unbound and unharmed, and the fourth looks like a son of the gods."

²⁶Nebuchadnezzar then approached the opening of the blazing furnace and shouted, "Shadrach, Meshach and Abednego, servants of the Most High God, come out! Come here!"

So Shadrach, Meshach and Abednego came out of the fire, ²⁷and the satraps, prefects, governors and royal advisers crowded around them. They saw that the fire had not harmed their bodies, nor was a hair of their heads singed; their robes were not scorched, and there was no smell of fire on them.

²⁸Then Nebuchadnezzar said, "Praise be to the God of Shadrach, Meshach and Abednego, who has sent his angel and rescued his servants! They trusted in him and defied the king's command and were willing to give up their lives rather than serve or worship any god except their

Tuesday

Hey, Obey

Read Daniel 3:16–18

It was a big deal when Shadrach, Meshach and Abednego obeyed God instead of the king. Their lives were on the line! I have trouble being obedient even with the smallest things. Like a few days ago, my mom told me not to eat anything when I got home from school so I wouldn't ruin my dinner. Well, she wasn't around when I came home, so I ate a few things. When dinner rolled around, I wasn't hungry at all. It seemed like no big deal when I disobeyed, but I felt guilty later.

Many times it is easier to disobey than to obey. It would have been much easier for Shadrach, Meshach and Abednego. Think about it: obey God, go to the fiery furnace; disobey God, stay alive. I mean, they didn't know whether they would live or die if they obeyed God. But they obeyed anyway, because it was the right thing to do. I'm not facing any fiery furnaces, but I do have to choose every day whether to obey God or not. This passage encourages me to make the right move.

 Adam, age 13

 What about You?

❶ When was the last time you disobeyed God? Why did you do it? How can you avoid disobeying again?

❷ Decide right now that you will do the next 5 things your parents ask you to do—with no complaining.

❸ Ask God to help you obey joyfully!

Turn to page 1028 for your next devotion.

own God. [29]Therefore I decree that the people of any nation or language who say anything against the God of Shadrach, Meshach and Abednego be cut into pieces and their houses be turned into piles of rubble, for no other god can save in this way."

[30]Then the king promoted Shadrach, Meshach and Abednego in the province of Babylon.

Nebuchadnezzar's Dream of a Tree

4 King Nebuchadnezzar,

To the peoples, nations and men of every language, who live in all the world:

May you prosper greatly!

[2]It is my pleasure to tell you about the miraculous signs and wonders that the Most High God has performed for me.

[3]How great are his signs,
    how mighty his wonders!
His kingdom is an eternal
        kingdom;
    his dominion endures from
        generation to generation.

[4]I, Nebuchadnezzar, was at home in my palace, contented and prosperous. [5]I had a dream that made me afraid. As I was lying in my bed, the images and visions that passed through my mind terrified me. [6]So I commanded that all the wise men of Babylon be brought before me to interpret the dream for me. [7]When the magicians, enchanters, astrologers[a] and diviners came, I told them the dream, but they could not interpret it for me. [8]Finally, Daniel came into my presence and I told him the dream. (He is called Belteshazzar, after the name of my god, and the spirit of the holy gods is in him.)

[9]I said, "Belteshazzar, chief of the magicians, I know that the spirit of the holy gods is in you, and no mystery is too difficult for you. Here is my dream; interpret it for me. [10]These are the visions I saw while lying in my bed: I looked, and there before me stood a tree in the middle of the land. Its height was enormous. [11]The tree grew large and strong and its top touched the sky; it was visible to the ends of the earth. [12]Its leaves were beautiful, its fruit abundant, and on it was food for all. Under it the beasts of the field found shelter, and the birds of the air lived in its branches; from it every creature was fed.

[13]"In the visions I saw while lying in my bed, I looked, and there before me was a messenger,[b] a holy one, coming down from heaven. [14]He called in a loud voice: 'Cut down the tree and trim off its branches; strip off its leaves and scatter its fruit. Let the animals flee from under it and the birds from its branches. [15]But let the stump and its roots, bound with iron and bronze, remain in the ground, in the grass of the field.

" 'Let him be drenched with the dew of heaven, and let him live with the animals among the plants of the earth. [16]Let his mind be changed from that of a man and let him be given the mind of an animal, till seven times[c] pass by for him.

[17]" 'The decision is announced by messengers, the holy ones declare the verdict, so that the living may know that the Most High is sovereign over the kingdoms of men and gives them to anyone he wishes and sets over them the lowliest of men.'

[18]"This is the dream that I, King Nebuchadnezzar, had. Now, Belteshazzar, tell me what it means, for none of the wise men in my kingdom can interpret it for me. But you can, because the spirit of the holy gods is in you."

Daniel Interprets the Dream

[19]Then Daniel (also called Belteshazzar) was greatly perplexed for a time, and his thoughts terrified him. So the king said, "Belteshazzar, do not let the dream or its meaning alarm you."

[a]7 Or *Chaldeans*   [b]13 Or *watchman*; also in verses 17 and 23   [c]16 Or *years*; also in verses 23, 25 and 32

Belteshazzar answered, "My lord, if only the dream applied to your enemies and its meaning to your adversaries! [20]The tree you saw, which grew large and strong, with its top touching the sky, visible to the whole earth, [21]with beautiful leaves and abundant fruit, providing food for all, giving shelter to the beasts of the field, and having nesting places in its branches for the birds of the air— [22]you, O king, are that tree! You have become great and strong; your greatness has grown until it reaches the sky, and your dominion extends to distant parts of the earth.

[23]"You, O king, saw a messenger, a holy one, coming down from heaven and saying, 'Cut down the tree and destroy it, but leave the stump, bound with iron and bronze, in the grass of the field, while its roots remain in the ground. Let him be drenched with the dew of heaven; let him live like the wild animals, until seven times pass by for him.'

[24]"This is the interpretation, O king, and this is the decree the Most High has issued against my lord the king: [25]You will be driven away from people and will live with the wild animals; you will eat grass like cattle and be drenched with the dew of heaven. Seven times will pass by for you until you acknowledge that the Most High is sovereign over the kingdoms of men and gives them to anyone he wishes. [26]The command to leave the stump of the tree with its roots means that your kingdom will be restored to you when you acknowledge that Heaven rules. [27]Therefore, O king, be pleased to accept my advice: Renounce your sins by doing what is right, and your wickedness by being kind to the oppressed. It may be that then your prosperity will continue."

The Dream Is Fulfilled

[28]All this happened to King Nebuchadnezzar. [29]Twelve months later, as the king was walking on the roof of the royal palace of Babylon, [30]he said, "Is not this the great Babylon I have built as the royal residence, by my mighty power and for the glory of my majesty?"

[31]The words were still on his lips when a voice came from heaven, "This is what is decreed for you, King Nebuchadnezzar: Your royal authority has been taken from you. [32]You will be driven away from people and will live with the wild animals; you will eat grass like cattle. Seven times will pass by for you until you acknowledge that the Most High is sovereign over the kingdoms of men and gives them to anyone he wishes."

God Is . . .

Huh?

Daniel 4:17, 25, 32

Ultimate. Awesome. Incredible. Chief Ruler. Head of everything. Highest Authority. No comparison. Is that an accurate description of God? Well, it's a start: There's so much more to say. But that's a tiny taste of what the word "sovereign" means. God is totally and completely *in charge*.

[33]Immediately what had been said about Nebuchadnezzar was fulfilled. He was driven away from people and ate grass like cattle. His body was drenched with the dew of heaven until his hair grew like the feathers of an eagle and his nails like the claws of a bird.

[34]At the end of that time, I, Nebuchadnezzar, raised my eyes toward heaven, and my sanity was restored. Then I praised the Most High; I honored and glorified him who lives forever.

His dominion is an eternal dominion;
   his kingdom endures from
      generation to generation.
[35]All the peoples of the earth
   are regarded as nothing.
He does as he pleases
   with the powers of heaven

and the peoples of the earth.
No one can hold back his hand
    or say to him: "What have you
        done?"

[36]At the same time that my sanity was restored, my honor and splendor were returned to me for the glory of my kingdom. My advisers and nobles sought me out, and I was restored to my throne and became even greater than before. [37]Now I, Nebuchadnezzar, praise and exalt and glorify the King of heaven, because everything he does is right and all his ways are just. And those who walk in pride he is able to humble.

The Writing on the Wall

5 King Belshazzar gave a great banquet for a thousand of his nobles and drank wine with them. [2]While Belshazzar was drinking his wine, he gave orders to bring in the gold and silver goblets that Nebuchadnezzar his father[a] had taken from the temple in Jerusalem, so that the king and his nobles, his wives and his concubines might drink from them. [3]So they brought in the gold goblets that had been taken from the temple of God in Jerusalem, and the king and his nobles, his wives and his concubines drank from them. [4]As they drank the wine, they praised the gods of gold and silver, of bronze, iron, wood and stone.

[5]Suddenly the fingers of a human hand appeared and wrote on the plaster of the wall, near the lampstand in the royal palace. The king watched the hand as it wrote. [6]His face turned pale and he was so frightened that his knees knocked together and his legs gave way.

[7]The king called out for the enchanters, astrologers[b] and diviners to be brought and said to these wise men of Babylon, "Whoever reads this writing and tells me what it means will be clothed in purple and have a gold chain placed around his neck, and he will be made the third highest ruler in the kingdom."

[8]Then all the king's wise men came in, but they could not read the writing or tell the king what it meant. [9]So King Bel-

shazzar became even more terrified and his face grew more pale. His nobles were baffled.

[10]The queen,[c] hearing the voices of the king and his nobles, came into the banquet hall. "O king, live forever!" she said. "Don't be alarmed! Don't look so pale! [11]There is a man in your kingdom who has the spirit of the holy gods in him. In the time of your father he was found to have insight and intelligence and wisdom like that of the gods. King Nebuchadnezzar your father—your father the king, I say—appointed him chief of the magicians, enchanters, astrologers and diviners. [12]This man Daniel, whom the king called Belteshazzar, was found to have a keen mind and knowledge and understanding, and also the ability to interpret dreams, explain riddles and solve difficult problems. Call for Daniel, and he will tell you what the writing means."

[13]So Daniel was brought before the king, and the king said to him, "Are you Daniel, one of the exiles my father the king brought from Judah? [14]I have heard that the spirit of the gods is in you and that you have insight, intelligence and outstanding wisdom. [15]The wise men and enchanters were brought before me to read this writing and tell me what it means, but they could not explain it. [16]Now I have heard that you are able to give interpretations and to solve difficult problems. If you can read this writing and tell me what it means, you will be clothed in purple and have a gold chain placed around your neck, and you will be made the third highest ruler in the kingdom."

[17]Then Daniel answered the king, "You may keep your gifts for yourself and give your rewards to someone else. Nevertheless, I will read the writing for the king and tell him what it means.

[18]"O king, the Most High God gave your father Nebuchadnezzar sovereignty and greatness and glory and splendor. [19]Because of the high position he gave him, all the peoples and nations and men

---

[a]2 Or *ancestor*; or *predecessor*; also in verses 11, 13 and 18   [b]7 Or *Chaldeans*; also in verse 11   [c]10 Or *queen mother*

of every language dreaded and feared him. Those the king wanted to put to death, he put to death; those he wanted to spare, he spared; those he wanted to promote, he promoted; and those he wanted to humble, he humbled. [20]But when his heart became arrogant and hardened with pride, he was deposed from his royal throne and stripped of his glory. [21]He was driven away from people and given the mind of an animal; he lived with the wild donkeys and ate grass like cattle; and his body was drenched with the dew of heaven, until he acknowledged that the Most High God is sovereign over the kingdoms of men and sets over them anyone he wishes.

[22]"But you his son,[a] O Belshazzar, have not humbled yourself, though you knew all this. [23]Instead, you have set yourself up against the Lord of heaven. You had the goblets from his temple brought to you, and you and your nobles, your wives and your concubines drank wine from them. You praised the gods of silver and gold, of bronze, iron, wood and stone, which cannot see or hear or understand. But you did not honor the God who holds in his hand your life and all your ways. [24]Therefore he sent the hand that wrote the inscription.

[25]"This is the inscription that was written:

MENE, MENE, TEKEL, PARSIN[b]

[26]"This is what these words mean:

Mene[c]: God has numbered the days of your reign and brought it to an end.
[27]*Tekel*[d]: You have been weighed on the scales and found wanting.
[28]*Peres*[e]: Your kingdom is divided and given to the Medes and Persians."

[29]Then at Belshazzar's command, Daniel was clothed in purple, a gold chain was placed around his neck, and he was proclaimed the third highest ruler in the kingdom. [30]That very night Belshazzar, king of the Babylonians,[f] was slain, [31]and Darius the Mede took over the kingdom, at the age of sixty-two.

Daniel in the Den of Lions

6 It pleased Darius to appoint 120 satraps to rule throughout the kingdom, [2]with three administrators over them, one of whom was Daniel. The satraps were made accountable to them so that the king might not suffer loss. [3]Now Daniel so distinguished himself among the administrators and the satraps by his exceptional qualities that the king planned to set him over the whole kingdom. [4]At this, the administrators and the satraps tried to find grounds for charges against Daniel in his conduct of government affairs, but they were unable to do so. They could find no corruption in him, because he was trustworthy and neither corrupt nor negligent. [5]Finally these men said, "We will never find any basis for charges against this man Daniel unless it has something to do with the law of his God."

[6]So the administrators and the satraps went as a group to the king and said: "O King Darius, live forever! [7]The royal administrators, prefects, satraps, advisers and governors have all agreed that the king should issue an edict and enforce the decree that anyone who prays to any god or man during the next thirty days, except to you, O king, shall be thrown into the lions' den. [8]Now, O king, issue the decree and put it in writing so that it cannot be altered—in accordance with the laws of the Medes and Persians, which cannot be repealed." [9]So King Darius put the decree in writing.

[10]Now when Daniel learned that the decree had been published, he went home to his upstairs room where the windows opened toward Jerusalem. Three times a day he got down on his knees and prayed, giving thanks to his God, just as he had done before. [11]Then these men went as a group and found Daniel praying and asking God for help. [12]So they went to the king and spoke to him about his royal decree: "Did you not publish a

---

[a]22 Or *descendant*; or *successor*   [b]25 Aramaic
UPARSIN (that is, *AND PARSIN*)   [c]26 *Mene* can
mean *numbered* or *mina* (a unit of money).
[d]27 *Tekel* can mean *weighed* or *shekel.*   [e]28 *Peres*
(the singular of *Parsin*) can mean *divided* or *Persia*
or *a half mina* or *a half shekel.*   [f]30 Or *Chaldeans*

decree that during the next thirty days anyone who prays to any god or man except to you, O king, would be thrown into the lions' den?"

The king answered, "The decree stands—in accordance with the laws of the Medes and Persians, which cannot be repealed."

[13]Then they said to the king, "Daniel, who is one of the exiles from Judah, pays no attention to you, O king, or to the decree you put in writing. He still prays three times a day." [14]When the king heard this, he was greatly distressed; he was determined to rescue Daniel and made every effort until sundown to save him.

[15]Then the men went as a group to the king and said to him, "Remember, O king, that according to the law of the Medes and Persians no decree or edict that the king issues can be changed."

[16]So the king gave the order, and they brought Daniel and threw him into the lions' den. The king said to Daniel, "May your God, whom you serve continually, rescue you!"

[17]A stone was brought and placed over the mouth of the den, and the king sealed it with his own signet ring and with the rings of his nobles, so that Daniel's situation might not be changed. [18]Then the king returned to his palace and spent the night without eating and without any entertainment being brought to him. And he could not sleep.

[19]At the first light of dawn, the king got up and hurried to the lions' den. [20]When he came near the den, he called to Daniel in an anguished voice, "Daniel, servant of the living God, has your God, whom you serve continually, been able to rescue you from the lions?"

[21]Daniel answered, "O king, live forever! [22]My God sent his angel, and he shut the mouths of the lions. They have not hurt me, because I was found innocent in his sight. Nor have I ever done any wrong before you, O king."

[23]The king was overjoyed and gave orders to lift Daniel out of the den. And when Daniel was lifted from the den, no wound was found on him, because he had trusted in his God.

Wednesday

On My Sleeve

Read Daniel 6:10–13

A few weeks ago, I wore a Christian T-shirt to school, and I was surprised at how many people noticed. All day, people came up to me and asked about the message on my shirt. They wanted to know what it meant and why I was wearing it. It was amazing how many people I talked with about God that day, just because of a T-shirt.

I believe God put us on this earth so we can share the good news about Jesus. We shouldn't hide our relationship with Jesus—we should be proud of it. We have something other people need, and we are the ones who can tell them about it. When we stand up for our beliefs, it shows other people our faith is real. It shows them that *God* is real in our lives and can be real in their lives too.

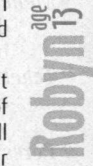
Robyn age 13

❶ What are some ways you can stand up for your faith at school?

❷ Wear a cross or a Christian T-shirt to school. How do people respond? How can you use these items to show your faith to others?

❸ Read this passage again. Ask God to give you faith like Daniel's.

Turn to page 1041 for your next devotion.

²⁴At the king's command, the men who had falsely accused Daniel were brought in and thrown into the lions' den, along with their wives and children. And before they reached the floor of the den, the lions overpowered them and crushed all their bones.

²⁵Then King Darius wrote to all the peoples, nations and men of every language throughout the land:

"May you prosper greatly!

²⁶"I issue a decree that in every part of my kingdom people must fear and reverence the God of Daniel.

"For he is the living God
      and he endures forever;
his kingdom will not be destroyed,
      his dominion will never end.

God's Turf

Huh?

Daniel 6:26

Be honest. Do you act a little nicer when you're at church? You know, a bit more patient, loving, kind—that kind of stuff? Do you act that way at school? What about at home? Many of us are guilty of playing the church game because we think God lives at church. Guess what? His dominion—or his authority and control—is everywhere! That means we ought to live for him wherever we are.

---

²⁷He rescues and he saves;
      he performs signs and wonders
      in the heavens and on the earth.
He has rescued Daniel
      from the power of the lions."

²⁸So Daniel prospered during the reign of Darius and the reign of Cyrus[a] the Persian.

Daniel's Dream of Four Beasts

7 In the first year of Belshazzar king of Babylon, Daniel had a dream, and visions passed through his mind as he was lying on his bed. He wrote down the substance of his dream.

Pass Play

Huh?

Daniel 7:1

Have you ever passed a note in class? When you take it from one person and give it to another, you're a messenger. That's what Daniel was doing! God gave Daniel dreams and visions so he could pass info on to the people. God had stuff he wanted people to know, so he used Daniel as his messenger. Maybe he will use you as a messenger too.

---

²Daniel said: "In my vision at night I looked, and there before me were the four winds of heaven churning up the great sea. ³Four great beasts, each different from the others, came up out of the sea.

⁴"The first was like a lion, and it had the wings of an eagle. I watched until its wings were torn off and it was lifted from the ground so that it stood on two feet like a man, and the heart of a man was given to it.

⁵"And there before me was a second beast, which looked like a bear. It was raised up on one of its sides, and it had three ribs in its mouth between its teeth. It was told, 'Get up and eat your fill of flesh!'

⁶"After that, I looked, and there before me was another beast, one that looked like a leopard. And on its back it had four wings like those of a bird. This beast had four heads, and it was given authority to rule.

⁷"After that, in my vision at night I looked, and there before me was a fourth beast—terrifying and frightening and very powerful. It had large iron teeth; it crushed and devoured its victims and trampled underfoot whatever was left. It was different from all the former beasts, and it had ten horns.

⁸"While I was thinking about the horns, there before me was another horn, a little one, which came up among them; and three of the first horns were

---

*a*28 Or *Darius, that is, the reign of Cyrus*

uprooted before it. This horn had eyes like the eyes of a man and a mouth that spoke boastfully.

⁹"As I looked,

"thrones were set in place,
    and the Ancient of Days took his seat.
His clothing was as white as snow;
    the hair of his head was white like wool.
His throne was flaming with fire,
    and its wheels were all ablaze.
¹⁰A river of fire was flowing,
    coming out from before him.
Thousands upon thousands attended him;
    ten thousand times ten thousand stood before him.
The court was seated,
    and the books were opened.

¹¹"Then I continued to watch because of the boastful words the horn was speaking. I kept looking until the beast was slain and its body destroyed and thrown into the blazing fire. ¹²(The other beasts had been stripped of their authority, but were allowed to live for a period of time.)

¹³"In my vision at night I looked, and there before me was one like a son of man, coming with the clouds of heaven. He approached the Ancient of Days and was led into his presence. ¹⁴He was given authority, glory and sovereign power; all peoples, nations and men of every language worshiped him. His dominion is an everlasting dominion that will not pass away, and his kingdom is one that will never be destroyed.

The Interpretation of the Dream

¹⁵"I, Daniel, was troubled in spirit, and the visions that passed through my mind disturbed me. ¹⁶I approached one of those standing there and asked him the true meaning of all this.

"So he told me and gave me the interpretation of these things: ¹⁷'The four great beasts are four kingdoms that will rise from the earth. ¹⁸But the saints of the Most High will receive the kingdom and will possess it forever—yes, for ever and ever.'

¹⁹"Then I wanted to know the true meaning of the fourth beast, which was different from all the others and most terrifying, with its iron teeth and bronze claws—the beast that crushed and devoured its victims and trampled underfoot whatever was left. ²⁰I also wanted to know about the ten horns on its head and about the other horn that came up, before which three of them fell—the horn that looked more imposing than the others and that had eyes and a mouth that spoke boastfully. ²¹As I watched, this horn was waging war against the saints and defeating them, ²²until the Ancient of Days came and pronounced judgment in favor of the saints of the Most High, and the time came when they possessed the kingdom.

²³"He gave me this explanation: 'The fourth beast is a fourth kingdom that will appear on earth. It will be different from all the other kingdoms and will devour the whole earth, trampling it down and crushing it. ²⁴The ten horns are ten kings who will come from this kingdom. After them another king will arise, different from the earlier ones; he will subdue three kings. ²⁵He will speak against the Most High and oppress his saints and try to change the set times and the laws. The saints will be handed over to him for a time, times and half a time.ᵃ

²⁶" 'But the court will sit, and his power will be taken away and completely destroyed forever. ²⁷Then the sovereignty, power and greatness of the kingdoms under the whole heaven will be handed over to the saints, the people of the Most High. His kingdom will be an everlasting kingdom, and all rulers will worship and obey him.'

²⁸"This is the end of the matter. I, Daniel, was deeply troubled by my thoughts, and my face turned pale, but I kept the matter to myself."

Daniel's Vision of a Ram and a Goat

8 In the third year of King Belshazzar's reign, I, Daniel, had a vision, after the one that had already appeared to me. ²In my vision I saw myself in the citadel of Susa in the province of Elam; in

ᵃ25 Or *for a year, two years and half a year*

the vision I was beside the Ulai Canal. [3]I looked up, and there before me was a ram with two horns, standing beside the canal, and the horns were long. One of the horns was longer than the other but grew up later. [4]I watched the ram as he charged toward the west and the north and the south. No animal could stand against him, and none could rescue from his power. He did as he pleased and became great.

[5]As I was thinking about this, suddenly a goat with a prominent horn between his eyes came from the west, crossing the whole earth without touching the ground. [6]He came toward the two-horned ram I had seen standing beside the canal and charged at him in great rage. [7]I saw him attack the ram furiously, striking the ram and shattering his two horns. The ram was powerless to stand against him; the goat knocked him to the ground and trampled on him, and none could rescue the ram from his power. [8]The goat became very great, but at the height of his power his large horn was broken off, and in its place four prominent horns grew up toward the four winds of heaven.

[9]Out of one of them came another horn, which started small but grew in power to the south and to the east and toward the Beautiful Land. [10]It grew until it reached the host of the heavens, and it threw some of the starry host down to the earth and trampled on them. [11]It set itself up to be as great as the Prince of the host; it took away the daily sacrifice from him, and the place of his sanctuary was brought low. [12]Because of rebellion, the host of the saints[a] and the daily sacrifice were given over to it. It prospered in everything it did, and truth was thrown to the ground.

[13]Then I heard a holy one speaking, and another holy one said to him, "How long will it take for the vision to be fulfilled—the vision concerning the daily sacrifice, the rebellion that causes desolation, and the surrender of the sanctuary and of the host that will be trampled underfoot?"

[14]He said to me, "It will take 2,300 evenings and mornings; then the sanctuary will be reconsecrated."

The Interpretation of the Vision

[15]While I, Daniel, was watching the vision and trying to understand it, there before me stood one who looked like a man. [16]And I heard a man's voice from the Ulai calling, "Gabriel, tell this man the meaning of the vision."

[17]As he came near the place where I was standing, I was terrified and fell prostrate. "Son of man," he said to me, "understand that the vision concerns the time of the end."

[18]While he was speaking to me, I was in a deep sleep, with my face to the ground. Then he touched me and raised me to my feet.

[19]He said: "I am going to tell you what will happen later in the time of wrath, because the vision concerns the appointed time of the end.[b] [20]The two-horned ram that you saw represents the kings of Media and Persia. [21]The shaggy goat is the king of Greece, and the large horn between his eyes is the first king. [22]The four horns that replaced the one that was broken off represent four kingdoms that will emerge from his nation but will not have the same power.

[23]"In the latter part of their reign, when rebels have become completely wicked, a stern-faced king, a master of intrigue, will arise. [24]He will become very strong, but not by his own power. He will cause astounding devastation and will succeed in whatever he does. He will destroy the mighty men and the holy people. [25]He will cause deceit to prosper, and he will consider himself superior. When they feel secure, he will destroy many and take his stand against the Prince of princes. Yet he will be destroyed, but not by human power.

[26]"The vision of the evenings and mornings that has been given you is true, but seal up the vision, for it concerns the distant future."

[27]I, Daniel, was exhausted and lay ill for several days. Then I got up and went about the king's business. I was appalled by the vision; it was beyond understanding.

---

[a]12 Or *rebellion, the armies*   [b]19 Or *because the end will be at the appointed time*

Daniel's Prayer

9 In the first year of Darius son of Xerxes[a] (a Mede by descent), who was made ruler over the Babylonian[b] kingdom— [2]in the first year of his reign, I, Daniel, understood from the Scriptures, according to the word of the LORD given to Jeremiah the prophet, that the desolation of Jerusalem would last seventy years. [3]So I turned to the Lord God and pleaded with him in prayer and petition, in fasting, and in sackcloth and ashes.

[4]I prayed to the LORD my God and confessed:

"O Lord, the great and awesome God, who keeps his covenant of love with all who love him and obey his commands, [5]we have sinned and done wrong. We have been wicked and have rebelled; we have turned away from your commands and laws. [6]We have not listened to your servants the prophets, who spoke in your name to our kings, our princes and our fathers, and to all the people of the land.

[7]"Lord, you are righteous, but this day we are covered with shame—the men of Judah and people of Jerusalem and all Israel, both near and far, in all the countries where you have scattered us because of our unfaithfulness to you. [8]O LORD, we and our kings, our princes and our fathers are covered with shame because we have sinned against you. [9]The Lord our God is merciful and forgiving, even though we have rebelled against him; [10]we have not obeyed the LORD our God or kept the laws he gave us through his servants the prophets. [11]All Israel has transgressed your law and turned away, refusing to obey you.

"Therefore the curses and sworn judgments written in the Law of Moses, the servant of God, have been poured out on us, because we have sinned against you. [12]You have fulfilled the words spoken against us and against our rulers by bringing upon us great disaster. Under the whole heaven nothing has ever been done like what has been done to Je-rusalem. [13]Just as it is written in the Law of Moses, all this disaster has come upon us, yet we have not sought the favor of the LORD our God by turning from our sins and giving attention to your truth. [14]The LORD did not hesitate to bring the disaster upon us, for the LORD our God is righteous in everything he does; yet we have not obeyed him.

[15]"Now, O Lord our God, who brought your people out of Egypt with a mighty hand and who made for yourself a name that endures to this day, we have sinned, we have done wrong. [16]O Lord, in keeping with all your righteous acts, turn away your anger and your wrath from Jerusalem, your city, your holy hill. Our sins and the iniquities of our fathers have made Jerusalem and your people an object of scorn to all those around us.

[17]"Now, our God, hear the prayers and petitions of your servant. For your sake, O Lord, look with favor on your desolate sanctuary. [18]Give ear, O God, and hear; open your eyes and see the desolation of the city that bears your Name. We do not make requests of you because we are righteous, but because of your great mercy. [19]O Lord, listen! O Lord, forgive! O Lord, hear and act! For your sake, O my God, do not delay, because your city and your people bear your Name."

The Seventy "Sevens"

[20]While I was speaking and praying, confessing my sin and the sin of my people Israel and making my request to the LORD my God for his holy hill— [21]while I was still in prayer, Gabriel, the man I had seen in the earlier vision, came to me in swift flight about the time of the evening sacrifice. [22]He instructed me and said to me, "Daniel, I have now come to give you insight and understanding. [23]As soon as you began to pray, an answer was given, which I have come to tell you, for you are highly esteemed. Therefore,

---

[a]1 Hebrew *Ahasuerus*   [b]1 Or *Chaldean*

Angel Sightings

As ruler of the entire universe, God's got a big job. That's not a problem for our big God—he can do anything and everything, all at once, anytime he wants. But sometimes he uses special servants and soldiers to do some of this important work. The Bible calls these godly workers *angels*. There are a bunch of them:

Michael

Job Description: Michael is a warrior and protector of Israel. That's not an easy job, since Satan's gang works overtime in their attempts to stomp out Israel and their protector. Michael is one of the chief princes, and he has a habit of flying to rescue people who get stuck fighting demons. He's also known as the *archangel*—the top angel.

Sightings: One of Michael's rescue missions occurs when an unnamed angel is sent to deliver an important message to Daniel but gets sideswiped by a demon. Michael swoops in to save the day (Daniel 10:13, 21; 12:1). This great angel also fights Satan the dragon . . . and wins again (Revelation 12:7, page 1559).

Gabriel

Job Description: Gabriel's big job is birth announcements, although he does some dream explaining on the side. His favorite line is "Do not be afraid." But it doesn't always work—some people freak out anyway.

Sightings: Gabe shows up in one of Daniel's prophetic visions . . . and scares him so badly that Daniel calls in sick for days afterward (Daniel 8:16–27, 9:20–27). In another surprise visit, he pops in on Zechariah, the soon-to-be father of John the Baptist, and pretty much has to peel him off the ceiling (Luke 1:11, page 1217). Mary, the soon-to-be mother of Jesus, is more startled by the message than the messenger: Gabriel tells her she's going to be the mother of the world's Savior (Luke 1:28, page 1218).

Messengers

Job Description: These angels show up all over the Bible. Like Gabriel, they deliver urgent messages from God.

Sightings: Balaam gets a visit from one of these angels, but his donkey sees the messenger first . . . and starts to talk! (Numbers 22:1–35, page 182). Gideon's messenger has to keep making return visits till Gideon gets the story straight (Judges 6:11, page 281). When Philip needs directions—bingo—a messenger appears to steer him down the right path (Acts 8:26, page 1319). When some shepherds spot a certain suspiciously shiny star, an entire *mob* of messenger angels explain it as the world's best baby announcement (Luke 2:9, page 1220). Years later, when Jesus has been resurrected from the tomb, a thoughtful messenger sticks around to tell the troubled Marys why the body is gone (Matthew 28:2, page 1184).

Enforcers

Job Description: These angels handle some of the unpleasant work, like wiping out God's enemies and punishing people for their evil deeds.

Sightings: Two of these guys show up at Lot's house in the wicked city of Sodom, hustle the Lot family out of town, then toast the town—literally (Genesis 19:1–26, page 26). In King Hezekiah's day, God sends a lone angelic enforcer to destroy the entire Assyrian army. And when Herod decides to play God, another enforcer gives him a fatal case of worms (Acts 12:23, page 1325).

Bodyguards

Job Description: To protect God's children. They're often referred to as guardian angels.

Sightings: Although we don't get to see these angels at work in the Bible, God's Word tells us that they exist. Jesus says that children have them (Matthew 18:10, page 1166), and the writer of Hebrews tells us that *all* angels act as servants to help us (Hebrews 1:14, page 1488).

consider the message and understand the vision:

[24]"Seventy 'sevens'[a] are decreed for your people and your holy city to finish[b] transgression, to put an end to sin, to atone for wickedness, to bring in everlasting righteousness, to seal up vision and prophecy and to anoint the most holy.[c]

[25]"Know and understand this: From the issuing of the decree[d] to restore and rebuild Jerusalem until the Anointed One,[e] the ruler, comes, there will be seven 'sevens,' and sixty-two 'sevens.' It will be rebuilt with streets and a trench, but in times of trouble. [26]After the sixty-two 'sevens,' the Anointed One will be cut off and will have nothing.[f] The people of the ruler who will come will destroy the city and the sanctuary. The end will come like a flood: War will continue until the end, and desolations have been decreed. [27]He will confirm a covenant with many for one 'seven.'[g] In the middle of the 'seven'[g] he will put an end to sacrifice and offering. And on a wing of the temple he will set up an abomination that causes desolation, until the end that is decreed is poured out on him.[h]"[i]

Daniel's Vision of a Man

10 In the third year of Cyrus king of Persia, a revelation was given to Daniel (who was called Belteshazzar). Its message was true and it concerned a great war.[j] The understanding of the message came to him in a vision.

[2]At that time I, Daniel, mourned for three weeks. [3]I ate no choice food; no meat or wine touched my lips; and I used no lotions at all until the three weeks were over.

[4]On the twenty-fourth day of the first month, as I was standing on the bank of the great river, the Tigris, [5]I looked up and there before me was a man dressed in linen, with a belt of the finest gold around his waist. [6]His body was like chrysolite, his face like lightning, his eyes like flaming torches, his arms and legs like the gleam of burnished bronze, and his voice like the sound of a multitude.

[7]I, Daniel, was the only one who saw the vision; the men with me did not see it, but such terror overwhelmed them that they fled and hid themselves. [8]So I was left alone, gazing at this great vision; I had no strength left, my face turned deathly pale and I was helpless. [9]Then I heard him speaking, and as I listened to him, I fell into a deep sleep, my face to the ground.

[10]A hand touched me and set me trembling on my hands and knees. [11]He said, "Daniel, you who are highly esteemed, consider carefully the words I am about to speak to you, and stand up, for I have now been sent to you." And when he said this to me, I stood up trembling.

[12]Then he continued, "Do not be afraid, Daniel. Since the first day that you set your mind to gain understanding and to humble yourself before your God, your words were heard, and I have come in response to them. [13]But the prince of the Persian kingdom resisted me twenty-one days. Then Michael, one of the chief princes, came to help me, because I was detained there with the king of Persia. [14]Now I have come to explain to you what will happen to your people in the future, for the vision concerns a time yet to come."

[15]While he was saying this to me, I bowed with my face toward the ground and was speechless. [16]Then one who looked like a man[k] touched my lips, and I opened my mouth and began to speak. I said to the one standing before me, "I am overcome with anguish because of the vision, my lord, and I am helpless. [17]How can I, your servant, talk with you, my lord? My strength is gone and I can hardly breathe."

[18]Again the one who looked like a man touched me and gave me strength. [19]"Do not be afraid, O man highly esteemed,"

---

[a]24 Or 'weeks'; also in verses 25 and 26   [b]24 Or restrain   [c]24 Or Most Holy Place; or most holy One   [d]25 Or word   [e]25 Or an anointed one; also in verse 26   [f]26 Or off and will have no one; or off, but not for himself   [g]27 Or 'week'   [h]27 Or it   [i]27 Or And one who causes desolation will come upon the pinnacle of the abominable temple, until the end that is decreed is poured out on the desolated city,   [j]1 Or true and burdensome   [k]16 Most manuscripts of the Masoretic Text; one manuscript of the Masoretic Text, Dead Sea Scrolls and Septuagint Then something that looked like a man's hand

he said. "Peace! Be strong now; be strong."

When he spoke to me, I was strengthened and said, "Speak, my lord, since you have given me strength."

²⁰So he said, "Do you know why I have come to you? Soon I will return to fight against the prince of Persia, and when I go, the prince of Greece will come; ²¹but first I will tell you what is written in the Book of Truth. (No one supports me against them except Michael, your prince. ¹And in the first year of Darius the Mede, I took my stand to support and protect him.)

The Kings of the South and the North

²"Now then, I tell you the truth: Three more kings will appear in Persia, and then a fourth, who will be far richer than all the others. When he has gained power by his wealth, he will stir up everyone against the kingdom of Greece. ³Then a mighty king will appear, who will rule with great power and do as he pleases. ⁴After he has appeared, his empire will be broken up and parceled out toward the four winds of heaven. It will not go to his descendants, nor will it have the power he exercised, because his empire will be uprooted and given to others.

⁵"The king of the South will become strong, but one of his commanders will become even stronger than he and will rule his own kingdom with great power. ⁶After some years, they will become allies. The daughter of the king of the South will go to the king of the North to make an alliance, but she will not retain her power, and he and his power[a] will not last. In those days she will be handed over, together with her royal escort and her father[b] and the one who supported her. ⁷"One from her family line will arise to take her place. He will attack the forces of the king of the North and enter his fortress; he will fight against them and be victorious. ⁸He will also seize their gods, their metal images and their valuable articles of silver and gold and carry them off to Egypt. For some years he will leave the king of the North alone. ⁹Then the king of the North will invade the realm of the king of the South but will retreat to his own country. ¹⁰His sons will

prepare for war and assemble a great army, which will sweep on like an irresistible flood and carry the battle as far as his fortress.

¹¹"Then the king of the South will march out in a rage and fight against the king of the North, who will raise a large army, but it will be defeated. ¹²When the army is carried off, the king of the South will be filled with pride and will slaughter many thousands, yet he will not remain triumphant. ¹³For the king of the North will muster another army, larger than the first; and after several years, he will advance with a huge army fully equipped.

¹⁴"In those times many will rise against the king of the South. The violent men among your own people will rebel in fulfillment of the vision, but without success. ¹⁵Then the king of the North will come and build up siege ramps and will capture a fortified city. The forces of the South will be powerless to resist; even their best troops will not have the strength to stand. ¹⁶The invader will do as he pleases; no one will be able to stand against him. He will establish himself in the Beautiful Land and will have the power to destroy it. ¹⁷He will determine to come with the might of his entire kingdom and will make an alliance with the king of the South. And he will give him a daughter in marriage in order to overthrow the kingdom, but his plans[c] will not succeed or help him. ¹⁸Then he will turn his attention to the coastlands and will take many of them, but a commander will put an end to his insolence and will turn his insolence back upon him. ¹⁹After this, he will turn back toward the fortresses of his own country but will stumble and fall, to be seen no more.

²⁰"His successor will send out a tax collector to maintain the royal splendor. In a few years, however, he will be destroyed, yet not in anger or in battle.

²¹"He will be succeeded by a contemptible person who has not been given the honor of royalty. He will invade the kingdom when its people feel secure, and he will seize it through intrigue. ²²Then

---

a6 Or *offspring* *b6* Or *child* (see Vulgate and Syriac) *c17* Or *but she*

an overwhelming army will be swept away before him; both it and a prince of the covenant will be destroyed. ²³After coming to an agreement with him, he will act deceitfully, and with only a few people he will rise to power. ²⁴When the richest provinces feel secure, he will invade them and will achieve what neither his fathers nor his forefathers did. He will distribute plunder, loot and wealth among his followers. He will plot the overthrow of fortresses—but only for a time.

²⁵"With a large army he will stir up his strength and courage against the king of the South. The king of the South will wage war with a large and very powerful army, but he will not be able to stand because of the plots devised against him. ²⁶Those who eat from the king's provisions will try to destroy him; his army will be swept away, and many will fall in battle. ²⁷The two kings, with their hearts bent on evil, will sit at the same table and lie to each other, but to no avail, because an end will still come at the appointed time. ²⁸The king of the North will return to his own country with great wealth, but his heart will be set against the holy covenant. He will take action against it and then return to his own country.

²⁹"At the appointed time he will invade the South again, but this time the outcome will be different from what it was before. ³⁰Ships of the western coastlands*a* will oppose him, and he will lose heart. Then he will turn back and vent his fury against the holy covenant. He will return and show favor to those who forsake the holy covenant.

³¹"His armed forces will rise up to desecrate the temple fortress and will abolish the daily sacrifice. Then they will set up the abomination that causes desolation. ³²With flattery he will corrupt those who have violated the covenant, but the people who know their God will firmly resist him.

³³"Those who are wise will instruct many, though for a time they will fall by the sword or be burned or captured or plundered. ³⁴When they fall, they will receive a little help, and many who are not sincere will join them. ³⁵Some of the wise will stumble, so that they may be refined, purified and made spotless until the time of the end, for it will still come at the appointed time.

The King Who Exalts Himself

³⁶"The king will do as he pleases. He will exalt and magnify himself above every god and will say unheard-of things against the God of gods. He will be successful until the time of wrath is completed, for what has been determined must take place. ³⁷He will show no regard for the gods of his fathers or for the one desired by women, nor will he regard any god, but will exalt himself above them all. ³⁸Instead of them, he will honor a god of fortresses; a god unknown to his fathers he will honor with gold and silver, with precious stones and costly gifts. ³⁹He will attack the mightiest fortresses with the help of a foreign god and will greatly honor those who acknowledge him. He will make them rulers over many people and will distribute the land at a price.*b*

⁴⁰"At the time of the end the king of the South will engage him in battle, and the king of the North will storm out against him with chariots and cavalry and a great fleet of ships. He will invade many countries and sweep through them like a flood. ⁴¹He will also invade the Beautiful Land. Many countries will fall, but Edom, Moab and the leaders of Ammon will be delivered from his hand. ⁴²He will extend his power over many countries; Egypt will not escape. ⁴³He will gain control of the treasures of gold and silver and all the riches of Egypt, with the Libyans and Nubians in submission. ⁴⁴But reports from the east and the north will alarm him, and he will set out in a great rage to destroy and annihilate many. ⁴⁵He will pitch his royal tents between the seas at*c* the beautiful holy mountain. Yet he will come to his end, and no one will help him.

The End Times

12 "At that time Michael, the great prince who protects your people,

---

a30 Hebrew *of Kittim*   *b39* Or *land for a reward*   *c45* Or *the sea and*

will arise. There will be a time of distress such as has not happened from the beginning of nations until then. But at that time your people—everyone whose name is found written in the book—will be delivered. [2]Multitudes who sleep in the dust of the earth will awake: some to everlasting life, others to shame and everlasting contempt. [3]Those who are wise[a] will shine like the brightness of the heavens, and those who lead many to righteousness, like the stars for ever and ever. [4]But you, Daniel, close up and seal the words of the scroll until the time of the end. Many will go here and there to increase knowledge."

[5]Then I, Daniel, looked, and there before me stood two others, one on this bank of the river and one on the opposite bank. [6]One of them said to the man clothed in linen, who was above the waters of the river, "How long will it be before these astonishing things are fulfilled?"

[7]The man clothed in linen, who was above the waters of the river, lifted his right hand and his left hand toward heaven, and I heard him swear by him who lives forever, saying, "It will be for a time, times and half a time.[b] When the power of the holy people has been finally broken, all these things will be completed."

[8]I heard, but I did not understand. So I asked, "My lord, what will the outcome of all this be?"

[9]He replied, "Go your way, Daniel, because the words are closed up and sealed until the time of the end. [10]Many will be purified, made spotless and refined, but the wicked will continue to be wicked. None of the wicked will understand, but those who are wise will understand.

[11]"From the time that the daily sacrifice is abolished and the abomination that causes desolation is set up, there will be 1,290 days. [12]Blessed is the one who waits for and reaches the end of the 1,335 days.

[13]"As for you, go your way till the end. You will rest, and then at the end of the days you will rise to receive your allotted inheritance."

---

[a]3 Or *who impart wisdom*   [b]7 Or *a year, two years and half a year*

Hosea

START

"Marry a what? You've got to be kidding, God!" That's what Hosea must have said when God asked him to marry a prostitute.

Have you ever had a teacher use an "object lesson"—where she shows you something as an illustration to help you understand something else? Well, that's exactly what God did. He made Hosea's whole life a total object lesson, and in it Hosea represents God who loves his people even though they turn away from him. Gomer (yup, that was actually Hosea's wife's name!) illustrated the people of Israel. They were acting like prostitutes because they kept running away from God to sins and idols.

Hosea was a prophet (spokesperson) of God to Israel (the northern kingdom) about the same time that Isaiah was a prophet to Judah (the southern kingdom). Hosea kept loving Gomer even though she kept loving other men. And God keeps on loving us—even when we love other people or stuff more than him.

CAST OF Characters

Hosea
(ho-ZAY-uh)
The author of the book.
A prophet of God to Israel.
The loving husband of
a prostitute. His name
means "salvation."

Gomer (GO-mur)
A name you'll probably
want to avoid when naming
your daughter someday!
Gomer's a prostitute,
Hosea's wife and a mother
of 3.

People of Israel
(IZ-ray-el)
If you've read some of
the earlier books in the
Old Testament, you've
learned that Israel
used to be bigger.
The country split in 2, and
the northern part kept the
name (the southern part
became Judah). Israel was,
at this point, totally wicked.

God
God does a lot of the talking
in this story—through
Hosea. And the whole thing
is a love story—a story of
God's love for his people.

What's UP with That?

Teenage Idols

God was frustrated with the Israelites because they were worshiping idols and letting other people and things replace him in their affections. We do this all the time too! From the list below, circle the things that can become "idols" or distractions. Then look at the list again and put a star by one or two you struggle with.

popularity
jocks
grades
babes
string cheese
friends
wrestlers
Spam
movie stars
hunks
cheerleaders
music
cliques
gang wannabes
partying

druggies
playing an instrument
geeks
getting attention
preps
shopping/buying stuff
models
clipping your toenails
weight lifters
clothes
beef jerky
hobbies
money
computer stuff
other:_____

Snap shots

- Hosea and Gomer, sittin' in a tree . . . (chapter 1)

- Israel's sleeping around (chapter 2)

- Bring 'er back; love 'er more (chapter 3)

- Missing the target (chapters 4—10)

- But I love you; I want you back (chapters 11—12)

- I am just a tad ticked, however (chapter 13)

- But I want to forgive you (chapter 14)

1

The word of the LORD that came to Hosea son of Beeri during the reigns of Uzziah, Jotham, Ahaz and Hezekiah, kings of Judah, and during the reign of Jeroboam son of Jehoash[a] king of Israel:

Hosea's Wife and Children

[2]When the LORD began to speak through Hosea, the LORD said to him, "Go, take to yourself an adulterous wife and children of unfaithfulness, because the land is guilty of the vilest adultery in departing from the LORD." [3]So he married Gomer daughter of Diblaim, and she conceived and bore him a son.

[4]Then the LORD said to Hosea, "Call him Jezreel, because I will soon punish the house of Jehu for the massacre at Jezreel, and I will put an end to the kingdom of Israel. [5]In that day I will break Israel's bow in the Valley of Jezreel."

[6]Gomer conceived again and gave birth to a daughter. Then the LORD said to Hosea, "Call her Lo-Ruhamah,[b] for I will no longer show love to the house of Israel, that I should at all forgive them. [7]Yet I will show love to the house of Judah; and I will save them—not by bow, sword or battle, or by horses and horsemen, but by the LORD their God."

[8]After she had weaned Lo-Ruhamah, Gomer had another son. [9]Then the LORD said, "Call him Lo-Ammi,[c] for you are not my people, and I am not your God.

[10]"Yet the Israelites will be like the sand on the seashore, which cannot be measured or counted. In the place where it was said to them, 'You are not my people,' they will be called 'sons of the living God.' [11]The people of Judah and the people of Israel will be reunited, and they will appoint one leader and will come up out of the land, for great will be the day of Jezreel.

2

"Say of your brothers, 'My people,' and of your sisters, 'My loved one.'

Israel Punished and Restored

[2]"Rebuke your mother, rebuke her,
  for she is not my wife,
  and I am not her husband.
Let her remove the adulterous look
    from her face
  and the unfaithfulness from
    between her breasts.
[3]Otherwise I will strip her naked
  and make her as bare as on the day
    she was born;
I will make her like a desert,
  turn her into a parched land,
  and slay her with thirst.
[4]I will not show my love to her
    children,
  because they are the children of
    adultery.
[5]Their mother has been unfaithful
  and has conceived them in disgrace.
She said, 'I will go after my lovers,
  who give me my food and my
    water,
  my wool and my linen, my oil and
    my drink.'
[6]Therefore I will block her path with
    thornbushes;
  I will wall her in so that she cannot
    find her way.
[7]She will chase after her lovers but not
    catch them;
  she will look for them but not find
    them.
Then she will say,
  'I will go back to my husband as at
    first,
  for then I was better off than now.'
[8]She has not acknowledged that I was
    the one

Lame Names

Hosea 1:6, 9

The names "Jezreel," "Lo-Ruhamah," and "Lo-Ammi" sound pretty odd. They also have pretty harsh meanings. With each of Hosea and Gomer's 3 children, the names got worse. Jezreel means "God scatters" since Israel's sin would cause their eventual military disaster. Lo-Ruhamah and Lo-Ammi mean "not loved" and "not my people," since Israel's sin was blocking their special relationship with God. The bad names meant bad news for the Israelites.

who gave her the grain, the new
wine and oil,
who lavished on her the silver and
gold—
which they used for Baal.

⁹"Therefore I will take away my grain
when it ripens,
and my new wine when it is ready.
I will take back my wool and my
linen,
intended to cover her nakedness.
¹⁰So now I will expose her lewdness
before the eyes of her lovers;
no one will take her out of my
hands.
¹¹I will stop all her celebrations:
her yearly festivals, her New
Moons,
her Sabbath days—all her appointed
feasts.
¹²I will ruin her vines and her fig trees,
which she said were her pay from
her lovers;
I will make them a thicket,
and wild animals will devour
them.
¹³I will punish her for the days

she burned incense to the Baals;
she decked herself with rings and
jewelry,
and went after her lovers,
but me she forgot,"

declares the LORD.

¹⁴"Therefore I am now going to allure
her;
I will lead her into the desert
and speak tenderly to her.
¹⁵There I will give her back her
vineyards,
and will make the Valley of Achor*ᵃ*
a door of hope.
There she will sing*ᵇ* as in the days of
her youth,
as in the day she came up out of
Egypt.

¹⁶"In that day," declares the LORD,
"you will call me 'my husband';
you will no longer call me 'my
master.*ᶜ*'
¹⁷I will remove the names of the Baals
from her lips;

ᵃ15 Achor means *trouble.* *ᵇ15 Or respond*
ᶜ16 Hebrew baal

Thursday

Even When It Hurts

Read Hosea 3:1

I think one of the hardest parts of being a Christian is showing love to people who hurt you. For instance, if a friend talks about me behind my back, my first reaction is to get angry at her and never want to speak with her again.

But then I think about how often I hurt God. No matter how much I mess up, God still loves me unconditionally. He forgives me and forgets about my sins. His love for me never changes. I'm supposed to show others the same kind of love I get from God—even to friends who talk about me.

Jamie age 14

What about You?

❶ Why is it so hard to show love to people who don't love us back? Why should we show them love anyway?

❷ Think of someone you've fought with in the past. How can you patch things up?

❸ Ask God to help you be a loving person, even when others don't show you love in return.

Turn to page 1045 for your next devotion.

Bowing to the . . . Cake?!?

Hosea 3:1 People worshiped all kinds of odd idols in the Bible—even raisin cakes! Can you say weird? Other oddball idols:

✗ a golden baby cow (Exodus 32:1–6)

✗ a wooden pole (1 Kings 15:13)

✗ a bronze snake (2 Kings 18:4)

no longer will their names be
     invoked.
¹⁸ In that day I will make a covenant for
     them
     with the beasts of the field and the
       birds of the air
     and the creatures that move along
       the ground.
Bow and sword and battle
     I will abolish from the land,
     so that all may lie down in safety.
¹⁹ I will betroth you to me forever;
     I will betroth you in[a] righteousness
       and justice,
     in[b] love and compassion.
²⁰ I will betroth you in faithfulness,
     and you will acknowledge the LORD.

²¹ "In that day I will respond,"
     declares the LORD—
"I will respond to the skies,
     and they will respond to the earth;
²² and the earth will respond to the
       grain,
     the new wine and oil,
     and they will respond to Jezreel.[c]
²³ I will plant her for myself in the
       land;
     I will show my love to the one I
       called 'Not my loved one.'[d]
I will say to those called 'Not my
       people,'[e] 'You are my
       people';
     and they will say, 'You are my
       God.' "

Hosea's Reconciliation With His Wife

3 The LORD said to me, "Go, show your love to your wife again, though she is loved by another and is an adulteress. Love her as the LORD loves the Israelites, though they turn to other gods and love the sacred raisin cakes."

² So I bought her for fifteen shekels[f] of silver and about a homer and a lethek[g] of barley. ³ Then I told her, "You are to live

Buy Her Back

Hosea 3:2
When someone really blew it in Hosea's time and town, he or she became a slave. Because Gomer blew it big-time, she became a slave. She was for sale. The only way Hosea could get her back was to buy her back. I guess when you think about it, that's what God has done for all of us, through Jesus Christ.

with[h] me many days; you must not be a prostitute or be intimate with any man, and I will live with[h] you."

⁴ For the Israelites will live many days without king or prince, without sacrifice or sacred stones, without ephod or idol. ⁵ Afterward the Israelites will return and seek the LORD their God and David their king. They will come trembling to the LORD and to his blessings in the last days.

The Charge Against Israel

4 Hear the word of the LORD, you
     Israelites,
because the LORD has a charge to
       bring
     against you who live in the land:
"There is no faithfulness, no love,
     no acknowledgment of God in the
       land.
² There is only cursing,[i] lying and
       murder,

^a*19* Or *with*; also in verse 20   ^b*19* Or *with*
^c*22 Jezreel* means *God plants*.   ^d*23* Hebrew *Lo-Ruhamah*   ^e*23* Hebrew *Lo-Ammi*   ^f*2* That is, about 6 ounces (about 170 grams)   ^g*2* That is, probably about 10 bushels (about 330 liters)   ^h*3* Or *wait for* ⁱ*2* That is, to pronounce a curse upon

stealing and adultery;
　they break all bounds,
　　and bloodshed follows bloodshed.
[3]Because of this the land mourns,[a]
　and all who live in it waste away;
the beasts of the field and the birds of
　　the air
　and the fish of the sea are dying.

[4]"But let no man bring a charge,
　let no man accuse another,
for your people are like those
　who bring charges against a priest.
[5]You stumble day and night,
　and the prophets stumble with you.
So I will destroy your mother—
[6]　my people are destroyed from lack
　　of knowledge.

"Because you have rejected
　　knowledge,
　I also reject you as my priests;
because you have ignored the law of
　　your God,
　I also will ignore your children.
[7]The more the priests increased,
　the more they sinned against me;
they exchanged[b] their[c] Glory for
　　something disgraceful.
[8]They feed on the sins of my people
　and relish their wickedness.
[9]And it will be: Like people, like priests.
　I will punish both of them for their
　　ways
　and repay them for their deeds.

[10]"They will eat but not have enough;
　they will engage in prostitution but
　　not increase,
because they have deserted the LORD
　to give themselves [11]to prostitution,
to old wine and new,
　which take away the understanding
　　[12]of my people.
They consult a wooden idol
　and are answered by a stick of
　　wood.
A spirit of prostitution leads them
　　astray;
　they are unfaithful to their God.
[13]They sacrifice on the mountaintops
　and burn offerings on the hills,
under oak, poplar and terebinth,
　where the shade is pleasant.
Therefore your daughters turn to
　　prostitution

and your daughters-in-law to
　　adultery.

[14]"I will not punish your daughters
　when they turn to prostitution,
nor your daughters-in-law
　when they commit adultery,
because the men themselves consort
　　with harlots
　and sacrifice with shrine
　　prostitutes—
a people without understanding will
　　come to ruin!

[15]"Though you commit adultery,
　　O Israel,
　let not Judah become guilty.

"Do not go to Gilgal;
　do not go up to Beth Aven.[d]
　And do not swear, 'As surely as the
　　LORD lives!'
[16]The Israelites are stubborn,
　like a stubborn heifer.
How then can the LORD pasture them
　like lambs in a meadow?
[17]Ephraim is joined to idols;
　leave him alone!
[18]Even when their drinks are gone,
　they continue their prostitution;
　their rulers dearly love shameful
　　ways.
[19]A whirlwind will sweep them away,
　and their sacrifices will bring them
　　shame.

Judgment Against Israel

5 "Hear this, you priests!
　Pay attention, you Israelites!
Listen, O royal house!
　This judgment is against you:
You have been a snare at Mizpah,
　a net spread out on Tabor.
[2]The rebels are deep in slaughter.
　I will discipline all of them.
[3]I know all about Ephraim;
　Israel is not hidden from me.
Ephraim, you have now turned to
　　prostitution;
　Israel is corrupt.

---

[a]3 Or *dries up*　　[b]7 Syriac and an ancient Hebrew
scribal tradition; Masoretic Text *I will exchange*
[c]7 Masoretic Text; an ancient Hebrew scribal
tradition *my*　　[d]15 *Beth Aven* means *house of
wickedness* (a name for Bethel, which means *house
of God*).

⁴"Their deeds do not permit them
  to return to their God.
A spirit of prostitution is in their
    heart;
  they do not acknowledge the LORD.
⁵Israel's arrogance testifies against
    them;
  the Israelites, even Ephraim,
    stumble in their sin;
  Judah also stumbles with them.
⁶When they go with their flocks and
    herds
  to seek the LORD,
they will not find him;
  he has withdrawn himself from
    them.
⁷They are unfaithful to the LORD;
  they give birth to illegitimate
    children.
Now their New Moon festivals
  will devour them and their fields.

⁸"Sound the trumpet in Gibeah,
  the horn in Ramah.
Raise the battle cry in Beth Aven*a*;
  lead on, O Benjamin.
⁹Ephraim will be laid waste
  on the day of reckoning.
Among the tribes of Israel
  I proclaim what is certain.
¹⁰Judah's leaders are like those
  who move boundary stones.
I will pour out my wrath on them
  like a flood of water.
¹¹Ephraim is oppressed,
  trampled in judgment,
  intent on pursuing idols.*b*
¹²I am like a moth to Ephraim,
  like rot to the people of Judah.

¹³"When Ephraim saw his sickness,
  and Judah his sores,
then Ephraim turned to Assyria,
  and sent to the great king for
    help.
But he is not able to cure you,
  not able to heal your sores.
¹⁴For I will be like a lion to Ephraim,
  like a great lion to Judah.
I will tear them to pieces and go
    away;
  I will carry them off, with no one to
    rescue them.
¹⁵Then I will go back to my place
  until they admit their guilt.
And they will seek my face;

in their misery they will earnestly
    seek me."

Israel Unrepentant

6 "Come, let us return to the LORD.
  He has torn us to pieces
  but he will heal us;
he has injured us
  but he will bind up our wounds.
²After two days he will revive us;
  on the third day he will restore us,
  that we may live in his presence.
³Let us acknowledge the LORD;
  let us press on to acknowledge him.
As surely as the sun rises,
  he will appear;
he will come to us like the winter rains,
  like the spring rains that water the
    earth."

⁴"What can I do with you, Ephraim?
  What can I do with you, Judah?
Your love is like the morning mist,
  like the early dew that disappears.
⁵Therefore I cut you in pieces with my
    prophets,
  I killed you with the words of my
    mouth;
  my judgments flashed like lightning
    upon you.
⁶For I desire mercy, not sacrifice,
  and acknowledgment of God rather
    than burnt offerings.
⁷Like Adam,*c* they have broken the
    covenant—
  they were unfaithful to me there.
⁸Gilead is a city of wicked men,
  stained with footprints of blood.
⁹As marauders lie in ambush for a man,
  so do bands of priests;
they murder on the road to Shechem,
  committing shameful crimes.
¹⁰I have seen a horrible thing
  in the house of Israel.
There Ephraim is given to prostitution
  and Israel is defiled.

¹¹"Also for you, Judah,
  a harvest is appointed.

"Whenever I would restore the
    fortunes of my people,

---

a8 Beth Aven means *house of wickedness* (a name for
Bethel, which means *house of God*) *b11* The
meaning of the Hebrew for this word is uncertain.
c7 Or *As at Adam*; or *Like men*

7 ¹whenever I would heal Israel,
the sins of Ephraim are exposed
and the crimes of Samaria revealed.
They practice deceit,
thieves break into houses,
bandits rob in the streets;
²but they do not realize
that I remember all their evil deeds.
Their sins engulf them;
they are always before me.

³"They delight the king with their
wickedness,
the princes with their lies.
⁴They are all adulterers,
burning like an oven
whose fire the baker need not stir
from the kneading of the dough till
it rises.
⁵On the day of the festival of our king
the princes become inflamed with
wine,
and he joins hands with the
mockers.
⁶Their hearts are like an oven;
they approach him with intrigue.
Their passion smolders all night;

in the morning it blazes like a
flaming fire.
⁷All of them are hot as an oven;
they devour their rulers.
All their kings fall,
and none of them calls on me.

⁸"Ephraim mixes with the nations;
Ephraim is a flat cake not turned
over.
⁹Foreigners sap his strength,
but he does not realize it.
His hair is sprinkled with gray,
but he does not notice.
¹⁰Israel's arrogance testifies against him,
but despite all this
he does not return to the LORD his God
or search for him.

¹¹"Ephraim is like a dove,
easily deceived and senseless—
now calling to Egypt,
now turning to Assyria.
¹²When they go, I will throw my net
over them;
I will pull them down like birds of
the air.

Friday

Attitude Counts!

Read Hosea 6:6

Sometimes being a Christian seems like it's all rules and no fun. We can get caught up in worrying about everything we do and everything we say.

But this verse says that following the rules isn't always the same as following God. Being a Christian isn't just about our actions; it's about our attitude. Sure, we need to live by the Ten Commandments and ask for forgiveness when we sin. But the most important thing to God is what's going on in our hearts.

We can try to live perfect lives, but unless we truly love God with our whole hearts, we're not really following God. God wants us to live completely for him, not for ourselves. He wants us to follow his commandments because we love and honor him, not just because we're supposed to.

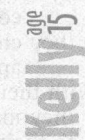

❶ What are some things you do to try to please God? Do you do them out of love or because you think you should?

❷ What are some ways you can show your faith to others?

❸ Pray that God will show you ways to follow him with your heart, to walk your talk.

Turn to page 1050 for your next devotion.

When I hear them flocking together,
  I will catch them.
¹³Woe to them,
  because they have strayed from me!
Destruction to them,
  because they have rebelled against
    me!
I long to redeem them
  but they speak lies against me.
¹⁴They do not cry out to me from their
    hearts
  but wail upon their beds.
They gather together*ᵃ* for grain and
    new wine
  but turn away from me.
¹⁵I trained them and strengthened them,
  but they plot evil against me.
¹⁶They do not turn to the Most High;
  they are like a faulty bow.
Their leaders will fall by the sword
  because of their insolent words.
For this they will be ridiculed
  in the land of Egypt.

Israel to Reap the Whirlwind

8 "Put the trumpet to your lips!
An eagle is over the house of the
    LORD
because the people have broken my
    covenant
  and rebelled against my law.
²Israel cries out to me,
  'O our God, we acknowledge you!'
³But Israel has rejected what is good;
  an enemy will pursue him.
⁴They set up kings without my
    consent;
  they choose princes without my
    approval.
With their silver and gold
  they make idols for themselves
  to their own destruction.
⁵Throw out your calf-idol, O Samaria!
  My anger burns against them.
How long will they be incapable of
    purity?
⁶   They are from Israel!
This calf—a craftsman has made it;
  it is not God.
It will be broken in pieces,
  that calf of Samaria.

⁷"They sow the wind
  and reap the whirlwind.
The stalk has no head;

Moo Worship

Huh?

Hosea 8:5

It's one thing to like your pets, but it's pretty strange to worship them. Yet throughout Israel's history, people have worshiped lots of animals. King Jeroboam set up all sorts of golden cows that Israel was supposed to bow down and worship. One problem, though, was that the cows were idols, and God hates idols. Why not take an inventory of your life to make sure you aren't doing the idol-worship thing?

---

  it will produce no flour.
Were it to yield grain,
  foreigners would swallow it up.
⁸Israel is swallowed up;
  now she is among the nations
  like a worthless thing.
⁹For they have gone up to Assyria
  like a wild donkey wandering alone.
  Ephraim has sold herself to lovers.
¹⁰Although they have sold themselves
    among the nations,
  I will now gather them together.
They will begin to waste away
  under the oppression of the mighty
    king.

¹¹"Though Ephraim built many altars
  for sin offerings,
  these have become altars for
    sinning.
¹²I wrote for them the many things of
    my law,
  but they regarded them as
    something alien.
¹³They offer sacrifices given to me
  and they eat the meat,
  but the LORD is not pleased with
    them.
Now he will remember their
    wickedness
  and punish their sins:
  They will return to Egypt.
¹⁴Israel has forgotten his Maker
  and built palaces;

ᵃ14 Most Hebrew manuscripts; some Hebrew manuscripts and Septuagint They slash themselves

Judah has fortified many towns.
But I will send fire upon their cities
    that will consume their fortresses."

Punishment for Israel

9 Do not rejoice, O Israel;
    do not be jubilant like the other
        nations.
For you have been unfaithful to your
        God;
    you love the wages of a prostitute
    at every threshing floor.
[2] Threshing floors and winepresses will
        not feed the people;
    the new wine will fail them.
[3] They will not remain in the LORD's land;
    Ephraim will return to Egypt
    and eat unclean[a] food in Assyria.
[4] They will not pour out wine offerings
        to the LORD,
    nor will their sacrifices please him.
Such sacrifices will be to them like the
        bread of mourners;
    all who eat them will be unclean.
This food will be for themselves;
    it will not come into the temple of
        the LORD.

[5] What will you do on the day of your
        appointed feasts,
    on the festival days of the LORD?
[6] Even if they escape from destruction,
    Egypt will gather them,
    and Memphis will bury them.
Their treasures of silver will be taken
        over by briers,
    and thorns will overrun their tents.
[7] The days of punishment are coming,
    the days of reckoning are at hand.
    Let Israel know this.
Because your sins are so many
    and your hostility so great,
the prophet is considered a fool,
    the inspired man a maniac.
[8] The prophet, along with my God,
    is the watchman over Ephraim,[b]
yet snares await him on all his paths,
    and hostility in the house of his God.
[9] They have sunk deep into corruption,
    as in the days of Gibeah.
God will remember their wickedness
    and punish them for their sins.

[10] "When I found Israel,
    it was like finding grapes in the
        desert;

when I saw your fathers,
    it was like seeing the early fruit on
        the fig tree.
But when they came to Baal Peor,
    they consecrated themselves to that
        shameful idol
and became as vile as the thing
    they loved.
[11] Ephraim's glory will fly away like a
        bird—
    no birth, no pregnancy, no
        conception.
[12] Even if they rear children,
    I will bereave them of every one.
Woe to them
    when I turn away from them!
[13] I have seen Ephraim, like Tyre,
    planted in a pleasant place.
But Ephraim will bring out
    their children to the slayer."

[14] Give them, O LORD—
    what will you give them?
Give them wombs that miscarry
    and breasts that are dry.

[15] "Because of all their wickedness in
        Gilgal,
    I hated them there.
Because of their sinful deeds,
    I will drive them out of my house.
I will no longer love them;
    all their leaders are rebellious.
[16] Ephraim is blighted,
    their root is withered,
    they yield no fruit.
Even if they bear children,
    I will slay their cherished
        offspring."

[17] My God will reject them
    because they have not obeyed him;
    they will be wanderers among the
        nations.

10 Israel was a spreading vine;
    he brought forth fruit for himself.
As his fruit increased,
    he built more altars;
as his land prospered,
    he adorned his sacred stones.
[2] Their heart is deceitful,
    and now they must bear their guilt.

a3 That is, ceremonially unclean   b8 Or The prophet
is the watchman over Ephraim, / the people of
my God

The LORD will demolish their altars
and destroy their sacred stones.
³ Then they will say, "We have no king
because we did not revere the LORD.
But even if we had a king,
what could he do for us?"
⁴ They make many promises,
take false oaths
and make agreements;
therefore lawsuits spring up
like poisonous weeds in a plowed
field.
⁵ The people who live in Samaria fear
for the calf-idol of Beth Aven.ᵃ
Its people will mourn over it,
and so will its idolatrous priests,
those who had rejoiced over its
splendor,
because it is taken from them into
exile.
⁶ It will be carried to Assyria
as tribute for the great king.
Ephraim will be disgraced;
Israel will be ashamed of its
wooden idols.ᵇ
⁷ Samaria and its king will float away
like a twig on the surface of the
waters.
⁸ The high places of wickednessᶜ will be
destroyed—
it is the sin of Israel.
Thorns and thistles will grow up
and cover their altars.
Then they will say to the mountains,
"Cover us!"
and to the hills, "Fall on us!"

⁹ "Since the days of Gibeah, you have
sinned, O Israel,
and there you have remained.ᵈ
Did not war overtake
the evildoers in Gibeah?
¹⁰ When I please, I will punish them;
nations will be gathered against
them
to put them in bonds for their
double sin.
¹¹ Ephraim is a trained heifer
that loves to thresh;
so I will put a yoke
on her fair neck.
I will drive Ephraim,
Judah must plow,
and Jacob must break up the
ground.

¹² Sow for yourselves righteousness,
reap the fruit of unfailing love,
and break up your unplowed ground;
for it is time to seek the LORD,
until he comes
and showers righteousness on you.
¹³ But you have planted wickedness,
you have reaped evil,
you have eaten the fruit of
deception.
Because you have depended on your
own strength
and on your many warriors,
¹⁴ the roar of battle will rise against
your people,
so that all your fortresses will be
devastated—
as Shalman devastated Beth Arbel on
the day of battle,
when mothers were dashed to the
ground with their children.
¹⁵ Thus will it happen to you, O Bethel,
because your wickedness is great.
When that day dawns,
the king of Israel will be completely
destroyed.

God's Love for Israel

11 "When Israel was a child, I loved
him,
and out of Egypt I called my son.
² But the more Iᵉ called Israel,
the further they went from me.ᶠ
They sacrificed to the Baals
and they burned incense to images.
³ It was I who taught Ephraim to walk,
taking them by the arms;
but they did not realize
it was I who healed them.
⁴ I led them with cords of human
kindness,
with ties of love;
I lifted the yoke from their neck
and bent down to feed them.

⁵ "Will they not return to Egypt
and will not Assyria rule over them
because they refuse to repent?
⁶ Swords will flash in their cities,

ᵃ5 Beth Aven means *house of wickedness* (a name for
Bethel, which means *house of God*). ᵇ6 Or *its
counsel* ᶜ8 Hebrew *aven*, a reference to Beth Aven
(a derogatory name for Bethel) ᵈ9 Or *there a stand
was taken* ᵉ2 Some Septuagint manuscripts;
Hebrew *they* ᶠ2 Septuagint; Hebrew *them*

will destroy the bars of their gates
and put an end to their plans.
7 My people are determined to turn
    from me.
Even if they call to the Most High,
he will by no means exalt them.

8 "How can I give you up, Ephraim?
How can I hand you over, Israel?
How can I treat you like Admah?
How can I make you like Zeboiim?
My heart is changed within me;
    all my compassion is aroused.
9 I will not carry out my fierce anger,
    nor will I turn and devastate
        Ephraim.
For I am God, and not man—
    the Holy One among you.
I will not come in wrath.ᵃ
10 They will follow the LORD;
    he will roar like a lion.
When he roars,
    his children will come trembling
        from the west.
11 They will come trembling
    like birds from Egypt,
    like doves from Assyria.
I will settle them in their homes,"
    declares the LORD.

Israel's Sin

12 Ephraim has surrounded me with lies,
    the house of Israel with deceit.
And Judah is unruly against God,
    even against the faithful Holy One.

12 ¹Ephraim feeds on the wind;
    he pursues the east wind all day
    and multiplies lies and violence.
He makes a treaty with Assyria
    and sends olive oil to Egypt.
2 The LORD has a charge to bring
        against Judah;
    he will punish Jacobᵇ according to
        his ways
    and repay him according to his
        deeds.
3 In the womb he grasped his brother's
        heel;
    as a man he struggled with God.
4 He struggled with the angel and
        overcame him;
    he wept and begged for his favor.
He found him at Bethel
    and talked with him there—
5 the LORD God Almighty,

the LORD is his name of renown!
6 But you must return to your God;
    maintain love and justice,
    and wait for your God always.

7 The merchant uses dishonest scales;
    he loves to defraud.
8 Ephraim boasts,
    "I am very rich; I have become
        wealthy.
With all my wealth they will not find
        in me
    any iniquity or sin."

9 "I am the LORD your God,
    who brought you out ofᶜ Egypt;
I will make you live in tents again,
    as in the days of your appointed
        feasts.
10 I spoke to the prophets,
    gave them many visions
    and told parables through them."

11 Is Gilead wicked?
    Its people are worthless!
Do they sacrifice bulls in Gilgal?
    Their altars will be like piles of
        stones
    on a plowed field.
12 Jacob fled to the country of Aramᵈ;
    Israel served to get a wife,
    and to pay for her he tended sheep.
13 The LORD used a prophet to bring
        Israel up from Egypt,
    by a prophet he cared for him.
14 But Ephraim has bitterly provoked
        him to anger;
    his Lord will leave upon him the
        guilt of his bloodshed
    and will repay him for his
        contempt.

The LORD's Anger Against Israel

13 When Ephraim spoke, men
        trembled;
    he was exalted in Israel.
But he became guilty of Baal
        worship and died.
2 Now they sin more and more;
    they make idols for themselves from
        their silver,
    cleverly fashioned images,

ᵃ9 Or *come against any city*   ᵇ2 *Jacob* means *he
grasps the heel* (figuratively, *he deceives*).   ᶜ9 Or
God / ever since you were in   ᵈ12 That is, Northwest
Mesopotamia

all of them the work of craftsmen.
It is said of these people,
  "They offer human sacrifice
    and kiss*ᵃ* the calf-idols."
³Therefore they will be like the
    morning mist,
  like the early dew that disappears,
  like chaff swirling from a threshing
    floor,
  like smoke escaping through a
    window.

⁴"But I am the LORD your God,
  who brought you out of*ᵇ* Egypt.
You shall acknowledge no God but
    me,
  no Savior except me.

⁵I cared for you in the desert,
  in the land of burning heat.
⁶When I fed them, they were satisfied;
  when they were satisfied, they
    became proud;
  then they forgot me.
⁷So I will come upon them like a lion,
  like a leopard I will lurk by the
    path.
⁸Like a bear robbed of her cubs,
  I will attack them and rip them
    open.
Like a lion I will devour them;
  a wild animal will tear them apart.

*ᵃ2 Or "Men who sacrifice / kiss ᵇ4 Or God /
ever since you were in*

Week end.

Big Bibles?

Read Matthew 23:27–28 (page 1174)

Kelly was right on when she said that attitude is more important than
actions (that was earlier this week—did you read it?). You can do all the
right things but still have a bad attitude, and the right things won't mean
anything. The apostle Paul even said in 1 Corinthians 13 that you can die
for God, but if you don't have love, it's worthless.

Jesus makes it very clear that the main way people can recognize his
followers is by their really huge Bibles. No, wait, that's not it—it's by, um,
their church attendance. Oh—that's not it either. Oh yeah, the truth is, Jesus
says people can recognize his followers by their love for each other.

What Jesus wants are disciples who love one another, not necessarily
disciples who live perfect lives. That's why the gospel is called "Good News."
Jesus knows all about our behavior and our actions. But, just as much, he
knows our hearts—he knows what we're thinking and why we do what we
do. So cheer up! Maybe your actions aren't always what you want them to
be, but if you love Jesus and care deeply about him, he knows about it, and
your love for him and others is what matters most.

❶ What is your attitude toward God at this very moment? How
about your attitude toward other Christians? Would people be
able to tell that you're a Christ-follower by the way you show
your love for others?

❷ Pretend Jesus is writing you a letter right now. What would
he say to you about what's going on in your heart?

❸ Ask God to help you have a better attitude toward him and other
Christians.

Turn to page 1057 for your next devotion.

[9] "You are destroyed, O Israel,
    because you are against me, against
        your helper.
[10] Where is your king, that he may save
        you?
    Where are your rulers in all your
        towns,
  of whom you said,
    'Give me a king and princes'?
[11] So in my anger I gave you a king,
    and in my wrath I took him away.
[12] The guilt of Ephraim is stored up,
    his sins are kept on record.
[13] Pains as of a woman in childbirth
        come to him,
    but he is a child without wisdom;
  when the time arrives,
    he does not come to the opening of
        the womb.
[14] "I will ransom them from the power of
        the grave[a];
    I will redeem them from death.
  Where, O death, are your plagues?
    Where, O grave,[a] is your
        destruction?

  "I will have no compassion,
[15]   even though he thrives among his
        brothers.
  An east wind from the LORD will
        come,
    blowing in from the desert;
  his spring will fail
    and his well dry up.
  His storehouse will be plundered
    of all its treasures.
[16] The people of Samaria must bear their
        guilt,
    because they have rebelled against
        their God.
  They will fall by the sword;
    their little ones will be dashed to
        the ground,
    their pregnant women ripped open."

Repentance to Bring Blessing

14 Return, O Israel, to the LORD
        your God.

Your sins have been your downfall!
[2] Take words with you
    and return to the LORD.
  Say to him:
    "Forgive all our sins
  and receive us graciously,
    that we may offer the fruit of our
        lips.[b]
[3] Assyria cannot save us;
    we will not mount war-horses.
  We will never again say 'Our gods'
    to what our own hands have made,
    for in you the fatherless find
        compassion."

[4] "I will heal their waywardness
    and love them freely,
    for my anger has turned away from
        them.
[5] I will be like the dew to Israel;
    he will blossom like a lily.
  Like a cedar of Lebanon
    he will send down his roots;
[6]   his young shoots will grow.
  His splendor will be like an olive
        tree,
    his fragrance like a cedar of
        Lebanon.
[7] Men will dwell again in his shade.
  He will flourish like the grain.
  He will blossom like a vine,
    and his fame will be like the wine
        from Lebanon.
[8] O Ephraim, what more have I[c] to do
        with idols?
    I will answer him and care for him.
  I am like a green pine tree;
    your fruitfulness comes from me."

[9] Who is wise? He will realize these
        things.
  Who is discerning? He will
        understand them.
  The ways of the LORD are right;
    the righteous walk in them,
    but the rebellious stumble in them.

---

*a14 Hebrew Sheol   b2 Or offer our lips as sacrifices
of bulls   c8 Or What more has Ephraim*

Joel

START

Meet the preacher-prophet Joel. Joel has one thing on his mind: grasshoppers (a.k.a. locusts). Clouds of them, thick enough to blacken the sun. The kind of disaster that you just sit and watch happen because you can't do anything about it anyway.

It's not like the movie *Starship Troopers* where a giant insect grabs you with 2 of its 6 legs and proceeds to suck out all your body fluids. Watching grasshoppers devour your crops is like watching your death warrant being signed—it doesn't kill you right then. But you know that without crops you won't eat, and within months your family will gradually die from starvation.

But Joel looks beyond a mere grasshopper disaster to a totally worse disaster—one that will end the world as we know it: the day of the Lord. Apocalypse. Armageddon. Disaster movies have been made of this kind of stuff—final judgment on a nation, whether by terrorists, asteroids or aliens. This is the kind of destruction that Joel's really talking about.

Cast OF Characters

Joel
A preacher-prophet with a thing about grasshoppers. That's about all we know about him. He was probably from Judah, the southern kingdom, but even that's a guess.

Grasshoppers
Code name: locusts.

(Low-custs)

What's UP with That?

These preacher-prophets were a mixed bunch.
Getting them together in one room would've
been like sitting down for a burger with
the president of a huge bank, an auto
mechanic from the south side of Philadelphia,
your state governor and a hired hand
from a Wyoming ranch.
Take a look at the really different kinds of
people these preacher-prophets were:

Ezekiel —a priest (to the Jews, priests
were way up there)

Zephaniah —a member of the royal
family (actually, the
great-great-grandson
of King Hezekiah of Judah)

Joel —just some guy

Amos —a sheep herder

Snap shots

- Not just grass-hoppers, but fire and drought too
  (*chapters 1:1—2:17*)

- The good days of healing to come
  (*chapters 2:18—3:21*)

As SOMEONE once said,
there ain't NOBODY that God can't use.

1 The word of the LORD that came to Joel son of Pethuel.

An Invasion of Locusts

² Hear this, you elders;
    listen, all who live in the land.
Has anything like this ever happened
    in your days
    or in the days of your forefathers?
³ Tell it to your children,
    and let your children tell it to their
        children,
    and their children to the next
        generation.
⁴ What the locust swarm has left
    the great locusts have eaten;
what the great locusts have left
    the young locusts have eaten;
what the young locusts have left
    other locusts*a* have eaten.

⁵ Wake up, you drunkards, and weep!
    Wail, all you drinkers of wine;
wail because of the new wine,
    for it has been snatched from your
        lips.
⁶ A nation has invaded my land,
    powerful and without number;
it has the teeth of a lion,
    the fangs of a lioness.
⁷ It has laid waste my vines
    and ruined my fig trees.
It has stripped off their bark
    and thrown it away,
    leaving their branches white.

⁸ Mourn like a virgin*b* in sackcloth
    grieving for the husband*c* of her
        youth.
⁹ Grain offerings and drink offerings
    are cut off from the house of the
        LORD.
The priests are in mourning,
    those who minister before the LORD.
¹⁰ The fields are ruined,
    the ground is dried up*d*;
the grain is destroyed,
    the new wine is dried up,
    the oil fails.
¹¹ Despair, you farmers,
    wail, you vine growers;
grieve for the wheat and the barley,
    because the harvest of the field is
        destroyed.
¹² The vine is dried up

and the fig tree is withered;
the pomegranate, the palm and the
    apple tree—
    all the trees of the field—are dried
    up.
Surely the joy of mankind
    is withered away.

A Call to Repentance

¹³ Put on sackcloth, O priests, and mourn;
    wail, you who minister before the
        altar.
Come, spend the night in sackcloth,
    you who minister before my God;
for the grain offerings and drink
        offerings
    are withheld from the house of your
        God.
¹⁴ Declare a holy fast;
    call a sacred assembly.
Summon the elders
    and all who live in the land
to the house of the LORD your God,
    and cry out to the LORD.

¹⁵ Alas for that day!
    For the day of the LORD is near;
    it will come like destruction from
        the Almighty.*e*

¹⁶ Has not the food been cut off
    before our very eyes—
joy and gladness
    from the house of our God?
¹⁷ The seeds are shriveled
    beneath the clods.*f*
The storehouses are in ruins,
    the granaries have been broken
        down,
    for the grain has dried up.
¹⁸ How the cattle moan!
    The herds mill about
because they have no pasture;
    even the flocks of sheep are
        suffering.

¹⁹ To you, O LORD, I call,
    for fire has devoured the open
        pastures
    and flames have burned up all the
        trees of the field.

---

a4 The precise meaning of the four Hebrew words
used here for locusts is uncertain.   *b8* Or *young
woman*   *c8* Or *betrothed*   *d10* Or *ground mourns*
e15 Hebrew *Shaddai*   *f17* The meaning of the
Hebrew for this word is uncertain.

²⁰Even the wild animals pant for you;
  the streams of water have dried up
  and fire has devoured the open
    pastures.

An Army of Locusts

2 Blow the trumpet in Zion;
  sound the alarm on my holy hill.
Let all who live in the land tremble,
  for the day of the LORD is coming.
It is close at hand—
²   a day of darkness and gloom,
  a day of clouds and blackness.
Like dawn spreading across the
    mountains
  a large and mighty army comes,
such as never was of old
  nor ever will be in ages to come.

³Before them fire devours,
  behind them a flame blazes.
Before them the land is like the
    garden of Eden,
  behind them, a desert waste—
  nothing escapes them.
⁴They have the appearance of horses;
  they gallop along like cavalry.
⁵With a noise like that of chariots
  they leap over the mountaintops,
like a crackling fire consuming
    stubble,
  like a mighty army drawn up for
    battle.

⁶At the sight of them, nations are in
    anguish;
  every face turns pale.
⁷They charge like warriors;
  they scale walls like soldiers.
They all march in line,
  not swerving from their course.
⁸They do not jostle each other;
  each marches straight ahead.
They plunge through defenses
  without breaking ranks.
⁹They rush upon the city;
  they run along the wall.
They climb into the houses;
  like thieves they enter through the
    windows.

¹⁰Before them the earth shakes,
  the sky trembles,
the sun and moon are darkened,
  and the stars no longer shine.
¹¹The LORD thunders
at the head of his army;
his forces are beyond number,
  and mighty are those who obey his
    command.
The day of the LORD is great;
  it is dreadful.
Who can endure it?

Rend Your Heart

¹²"Even now," declares the LORD,
  "return to me with all your heart,
  with fasting and weeping and
    mourning."

¹³Rend your heart
  and not your garments.
Return to the LORD your God,
  for he is gracious and
    compassionate,
  slow to anger and abounding in
    love,
  and he relents from sending
    calamity.
¹⁴Who knows? He may turn and have
    pity
  and leave behind a blessing—
grain offerings and drink offerings
  for the LORD your God.

¹⁵Blow the trumpet in Zion,
  declare a holy fast,
  call a sacred assembly.
¹⁶Gather the people,
  consecrate the assembly;
bring together the elders,
  gather the children,
  those nursing at the breast.
Let the bridegroom leave his room
  and the bride her chamber.
¹⁷Let the priests, who minister before
    the LORD,
  weep between the temple porch and
    the altar.
Let them say, "Spare your people,
    O LORD.
Do not make your inheritance an
    object of scorn,
  a byword among the nations.
Why should they say among the
    peoples,
  'Where is their God?' "

The LORD's Answer

¹⁸Then the LORD will be jealous for his
    land
  and take pity on his people.

¹⁹The LORD will reply[a] to them:

"I am sending you grain, new wine
and oil,
enough to satisfy you fully;
never again will I make you
an object of scorn to the nations.

²⁰"I will drive the northern army far
from you,
pushing it into a parched and
barren land,
with its front columns going into the
eastern sea[b]
and those in the rear into the
western sea.[c]
And its stench will go up;
its smell will rise."

Surely he has done great things.[d]
²¹   Be not afraid, O land;
be glad and rejoice.
Surely the LORD has done great things.
²²   Be not afraid, O wild animals,
for the open pastures are becoming
green.
The trees are bearing their fruit;
the fig tree and the vine yield their
riches.
²³Be glad, O people of Zion,
rejoice in the LORD your God,
for he has given you
the autumn rains in righteousness.[e]
He sends you abundant showers,
both autumn and spring rains, as
before.
²⁴The threshing floors will be filled with
grain;
the vats will overflow with new
wine and oil.

²⁵"I will repay you for the years the
locusts have eaten—
the great locust and the young
locust,
the other locusts and the locust
swarm[f]—
my great army that I sent among you.
²⁶You will have plenty to eat, until you
are full,
and you will praise the name of the
LORD your God,
who has worked wonders for you;
never again will my people be
shamed.
²⁷Then you will know that I am in
Israel,

that I am the LORD your God,
and that there is no other;
never again will my people be
shamed.

The Day of the LORD

²⁸"And afterward,
I will pour out my Spirit on all
people.
Your sons and daughters will
prophesy,
your old men will dream dreams,
your young men will see visions.
²⁹Even on my servants, both men and
women,
I will pour out my Spirit in those
days.
³⁰I will show wonders in the heavens
and on the earth,
blood and fire and billows of
smoke.
³¹The sun will be turned to darkness
and the moon to blood
before the coming of the great and
dreadful day of the LORD.
³²And everyone who calls

---

[a] 18,19 Or LORD was jealous . . . / and took pity . . .
/ ¹⁹The LORD replied   [b] 20 That is, the Dead Sea
[c] 20 That is, the Mediterranean   [d] 20 Or rise. / Surely
it has done great things."   [e] 23 Or / the teacher for
righteousness: [f] 25 The precise meaning of the four
Hebrew words used here for locusts is uncertain.

on the name of the LORD will be
saved;
for on Mount Zion and in Jerusalem
there will be deliverance,
as the LORD has said,
among the survivors
whom the LORD calls.

The Nations Judged

3 "In those days and at that time,
when I restore the fortunes of
Judah and Jerusalem,
²I will gather all nations
and bring them down to the Valley
of Jehoshaphat.ᵃ
There I will enter into judgment
against them
concerning my inheritance, my
people Israel,
for they scattered my people among
the nations
and divided up my land.
³They cast lots for my people

and traded boys for prostitutes;
they sold girls for wine
that they might drink.

⁴"Now what have you against me,
O Tyre and Sidon and all you regions of
Philistia? Are you repaying me for something I have done? If you are paying me
back, I will swiftly and speedily return
on your own heads what you have done.
⁵For you took my silver and my gold and
carried off my finest treasures to your
temples. ⁶You sold the people of Judah
and Jerusalem to the Greeks, that you
might send them far from their homeland.

⁷"See, I am going to rouse them out of
the places to which you sold them, and I
will return on your own heads what you
have done. ⁸I will sell your sons and
daughters to the people of Judah, and

ᵃ2 *Jehoshaphat* means *the LORD judges*; also in
verse 12.

Monday

Anyone, Anywhere

Read Joel 2:28–29

My parents are missionaries, and we knew someone in Zambia, Africa, whose parents weren't rich enough to send their son to school past 7th grade. But even though he didn't finish school, he read everything he could get his hands on. Now he's the pastor of a growing church. I always knew about his situation, but I never thought less of him for it because he was always striving to do what he thought the Lord wanted him to do.

God is so powerful that his Spirit can work through anyone—whether it's a man who didn't finish school or a child who can barely speak. Obviously God won't work through everyone the same way. Some people talk in front of big groups, and some people just tell one other person about God's love. Some people are leaders and some are followers. But everyone can make a difference.

 Christy age 13

 What about You?

❶ Who's the oldest person in your church? Who's the youngest? How are each of these people important to your church and to God?

❷ Try to think of the things that need to be done at your church each week, from preaching the sermon to sweeping the floor. Isn't it great that God created so many different people to do so many different things? Send a note to one of these people thanking them for their ministry.

❸ Tell God you're willing to serve him, even while you're young.

Turn to page 1065 for your next devotion.

they will sell them to the Sabeans, a nation far away." The LORD has spoken.

9 Proclaim this among the nations:
    Prepare for war!
Rouse the warriors!
    Let all the fighting men draw near
        and attack.
10 Beat your plowshares into swords
        and your pruning hooks into
            spears.
    Let the weakling say,
        "I am strong!"
11 Come quickly, all you nations from
        every side,
    and assemble there.

    Bring down your warriors, O LORD!

12 "Let the nations be roused;
    let them advance into the Valley of
        Jehoshaphat,
    for there I will sit
        to judge all the nations on every
            side.
13 Swing the sickle,
    for the harvest is ripe.
Come, trample the grapes,
    for the winepress is full
        and the vats overflow—
    so great is their wickedness!"

14 Multitudes, multitudes
    in the valley of decision!
For the day of the LORD is near
    in the valley of decision.
15 The sun and moon will be darkened,
    and the stars no longer shine.
16 The LORD will roar from Zion
    and thunder from Jerusalem;

the earth and the sky will tremble.
But the LORD will be a refuge for his
        people,
    a stronghold for the people of
        Israel.

Blessings for God's People

17 "Then you will know that I, the LORD
        your God,
    dwell in Zion, my holy hill.
Jerusalem will be holy;
    never again will foreigners invade
        her.

18 "In that day the mountains will drip
        new wine,
    and the hills will flow with milk;
    all the ravines of Judah will run
        with water.
A fountain will flow out of the LORD's
        house
    and will water the valley of
        acacias.ᵃ
19 But Egypt will be desolate,
    Edom a desert waste,
because of violence done to the people
        of Judah,
    in whose land they shed innocent
        blood.
20 Judah will be inhabited forever
    and Jerusalem through all
        generations.
21 Their bloodguilt, which I have not
        pardoned,
    I will pardon."

    The LORD dwells in Zion!

ᵃ18 Or Valley of Shittim

Amos

START

We find out a lot about this book from the first verse:

(1) Amos was a shepherd (not a priest like Jeremiah, or royalty like Zephaniah, two other prophets with Bible books named after them).

(2) Amos preached to Israel (that's the northern kingdom; Judah was the southern one). Think civil war—a nation that tore itself in half, fought with each other now and then, but generally kept an uneasy peace across the border from each other.

(3) Amos preached and prophesied during the rule of an Israelite king named Uzziah (also known as Azariah). This tells us that Israel was only 60-some years away from being invaded and trashed by the army of Assyria (where Iraq is now), which promptly shipped away and scattered the survivors. Judgment was just around the corner for Israel.

Beyond the first verse in this book, you'll see that Amos doesn't slam Israel for its typical Big Sin—idolatry—but rather for "trampling on the poor . . . depriving the poor of justice . . . taking bribes . . . oppressing the righteous." You get the picture of a nation's well-to-do citizens "feasting, lounging and dining," to use Amos's words; meanwhile, outside the doors of their fanciest department stores, health clubs and $50-a-plate restaurants were the poor—those the wealthy not only ignored, but actually kept down.

CAST OF Characters

Amos
(A-mus)
A preacher-prophet, like Jeremiah and Zephaniah and the rest. Except Amos was a shepherd. Probably smelled of sheep, too—peee-ewe!

Israel (IZ-ray-el)
The nation that Amos preached his warnings to.

Amaziah (am-uh-ZY-uh)
This guy was a priest with an itty-bitty part in Amos's drama (7:10–17). Amaziah basically gets in Amos's face and tells him to butt out, to take his doom-and-gloom prophecies out of Israel and go back home to his sheep.

What's UP with That?

Hook 'Em Up!

The Assyrians—the army that invaded, burned and massacred Israel—had a reputation as ruthless warriors and brutal terrorists. Here's a mild example of their cruelty: The people they *didn't* kill would be taken to another part of their empire. But they didn't just tie them up and force them to walk hundreds of miles. They actually put hooks through the mouths of the captives—and *then* pulled them along for hundreds of miles (which is what chapter 4:2 is talking about).

Moo

It wasn't just the men who were mean to the poor. The women were too. They ignored the needy and did all they could to keep them out of the way—and keep themselves well furnished with café mochas and new BMWs.

"You cows!" Amos called the women. Amazing what prophets can get away with. You can see why prophets weren't often on the favorite-people-to-invite-to-a-party list.

Snap shots

- Israel says, "Go get 'em, God! Dust our enemies! Death to them!" (*chapters 1:1—2:5*)

- "Whaddya mean, you're gonna judge *us,* too?" (*chapters 3—6*)

- Grasshoppers, fire and a plumb line (*chapters 7:1—9:10*)

- And now for the good news . . . (*chapter 9:11-15*)

1 The words of Amos, one of the shepherds of Tekoa—what he saw concerning Israel two years before the earthquake, when Uzziah was king of Judah and Jeroboam son of Jehoash[a] was king of Israel.

²He said:

"The LORD roars from Zion
    and thunders from Jerusalem;
the pastures of the shepherds dry up,[b]
    and the top of Carmel withers."

Judgment on Israel's Neighbors

³This is what the LORD says:

"For three sins of Damascus,
    even for four, I will not turn back
    my wrath.
Because she threshed Gilead
    with sledges having iron teeth,

Crispy Critters

Huh?

Amos 1:3

Just picture God up in heaven counting sins on his fingers. Lying to your friend, 1. Being mean to your brother, 2. Cheating, 3. Gossip, 4. If this picture of God was true, we'd all be crispy critters (i.e., toast). The real truth is that the "three and four" sins in Amos 1:3 don't mean God waits until we reach a "magic sin line" and then blasts us. It's Bible poetry's way of describing lots and lots of sins.

⁴I will send fire upon the house of
        Hazael
    that will consume the fortresses of
        Ben-Hadad.
⁵I will break down the gate of
        Damascus;
    I will destroy the king who is in[c] the
        Valley of Aven[d]
and the one who holds the scepter in
        Beth Eden.
    The people of Aram will go into
        exile to Kir,"
                    says the LORD.

⁶This is what the LORD says:

"For three sins of Gaza,
    even for four, I will not turn back
    my wrath.
Because she took captive whole
        communities
    and sold them to Edom,
⁷I will send fire upon the walls of Gaza
    that will consume her fortresses.
⁸I will destroy the king[e] of Ashdod
    and the one who holds the scepter
        in Ashkelon.
I will turn my hand against Ekron,
    till the last of the Philistines is
        dead,"
                says the Sovereign LORD.

⁹This is what the LORD says:

"For three sins of Tyre,
    even for four, I will not turn back
    my wrath.
Because she sold whole communities
        of captives to Edom,
    disregarding a treaty of
        brotherhood,
¹⁰I will send fire upon the walls of
        Tyre
    that will consume her fortresses."

¹¹This is what the LORD says:

"For three sins of Edom,
    even for four, I will not turn back
    my wrath.
Because he pursued his brother with a
        sword,
    stifling all compassion,[f]
because his anger raged continually
    and his fury flamed unchecked,
¹²I will send fire upon Teman
    that will consume the fortresses of
        Bozrah."

¹³This is what the LORD says:

"For three sins of Ammon,
    even for four, I will not turn back
    my wrath.
Because he ripped open the pregnant
        women of Gilead
    in order to extend his borders,
¹⁴I will set fire to the walls of Rabbah
    that will consume her fortresses
amid war cries on the day of battle,

---

a1 Hebrew *Joash,* a variant of *Jehoash*   *b2* Or
shepherds mourn   *c5* Or *the inhabitants of*   *d5 Aven*
means *wickedness.*   *e8* Or *inhabitants*   *f11* Or *sword*
/ and destroyed his allies

Yearbook Entries

Genesis Junior High yearbook:
Oldest surviving graduate: Methuselah
(Genesis 5:27, page 11)

Nazirite Academy yearbook:
Worst haircut: Samson
(Judges 16:19, page 295)

Moabite West Middle School yearbook:
Coolest couple: Ruth and Boaz
(Ruth 2, page 305)

Gath East Junior High yearbook:
Captain, MVP, basketball team: Goliath
(1 Samuel 17:4, page 330)

Jerusalem Middle School yearbook:
Most likely to succeed: David
(1 Samuel 18:14, page 333)

Jerusalem Academy yearbook:
Brainiest: Solomon
(1 Kings 4:29, page 390)

Tishbe Junior High yearbook:
Captain, Cross-country Team: Elijah
(1 Kings 18:46, page 413)

Susa South Middle School yearbook:
9th Grade Class Homecoming Queen: Esther
(Esther 2:17, page 572)

Tekoa Middle School yearbook:
President, Future Farmers of America: Amos
(Amos 1:1)

Jordan Academy yearbook:
Worst dressed: John the Baptist
(Mark 1:6, page 1188)

Thyatira Middle School yearbook:
Sewing Club President: Lydia
(Acts 16:14, page 1331)

amid violent winds on a stormy
    day.
[15] Her king[a] will go into exile,
    he and his officials together,"
                says the LORD.

2 This is what the LORD says:

"For three sins of Moab,
    even for four, I will not turn back
      my wrath.
Because he burned, as if to lime,
    the bones of Edom's king,
[2] I will send fire upon Moab
    that will consume the fortresses of
      Kerioth.[b]
Moab will go down in great tumult
    amid war cries and the blast of the
      trumpet.
[3] I will destroy her ruler
    and kill all her officials with him,"
                says the LORD.

[4] This is what the LORD says:

"For three sins of Judah,
    even for four, I will not turn back
      my wrath.
Because they have rejected the law of
      the LORD
    and have not kept his decrees,

because they have been led astray by
    false gods,[c]
the gods[d] their ancestors followed,
[5] I will send fire upon Judah
    that will consume the fortresses of
      Jerusalem."

Judgment on Israel

[6] This is what the LORD says:

"For three sins of Israel,
    even for four, I will not turn back
      my wrath.
They sell the righteous for silver,
    and the needy for a pair of sandals.
[7] They trample on the heads of the poor
    as upon the dust of the ground
    and deny justice to the oppressed.
Father and son use the same girl
    and so profane my holy name.
[8] They lie down beside every altar
    on garments taken in pledge.
In the house of their god
    they drink wine taken as fines.

[9] "I destroyed the Amorite before them,
    though he was tall as the cedars

---

[a] 15 Or / Molech; Hebrew malcam   [b] 2 Or of her cities
[c] 4 Or by lies   [d] 4 Or lies

and strong as the oaks.
I destroyed his fruit above
and his roots below.

10 "I brought you up out of Egypt,
and I led you forty years in the
desert
to give you the land of the
Amorites.
11 I also raised up prophets from among
your sons
and Nazirites from among your
young men.
Is this not true, people of Israel?"
declares the LORD.
12 "But you made the Nazirites drink
wine
and commanded the prophets not to
prophesy.

13 "Now then, I will crush you
as a cart crushes when loaded with
grain.
14 The swift will not escape,
the strong will not muster their
strength,
and the warrior will not save his
life.
15 The archer will not stand his ground,
the fleet-footed soldier will not get
away,
and the horseman will not save his
life.
16 Even the bravest warriors
will flee naked on that day,"
declares the LORD.

Witnesses Summoned Against Israel

3 Hear this word the LORD has spoken
against you, O people of Israel—
against the whole family I brought up
out of Egypt:

2 "You only have I chosen
of all the families of the earth;
therefore I will punish you
for all your sins."

3 Do two walk together
unless they have agreed to do so?
4 Does a lion roar in the thicket
when he has no prey?
Does he growl in his den
when he has caught nothing?
5 Does a bird fall into a trap on the
ground
where no snare has been set?

Does a trap spring up from the earth
when there is nothing to catch?
6 When a trumpet sounds in a city,
do not the people tremble?
When disaster comes to a city,
has not the LORD caused it?
7 Surely the Sovereign LORD does
nothing
without revealing his plan
to his servants the prophets.

8 The lion has roared—
who will not fear?
The Sovereign LORD has spoken—
who can but prophesy?

9 Proclaim to the fortresses of Ashdod
and to the fortresses of Egypt:
"Assemble yourselves on the
mountains of Samaria;
see the great unrest within her
and the oppression among her
people."
10 "They do not know how to do right,"
declares the LORD,
"who hoard plunder and loot in
their fortresses."

11 Therefore this is what the Sovereign
LORD says:

"An enemy will overrun the land;
he will pull down your strongholds
and plunder your fortresses."

12 This is what the LORD says:

"As a shepherd saves from the lion's
mouth
only two leg bones or a piece of an
ear,
so will the Israelites be saved,
those who sit in Samaria
on the edge of their beds
and in Damascus on their
couches.*"

13 "Hear this and testify against the
house of Jacob," declares the Lord, the
LORD God Almighty.

14 "On the day I punish Israel for her sins,
I will destroy the altars of Bethel;
the horns of the altar will be cut off
and fall to the ground.

a 12 The meaning of the Hebrew for this line is
uncertain.

¹⁵I will tear down the winter house
    along with the summer house;
the houses adorned with ivory will be
    destroyed
    and the mansions will be
      demolished,"
               declares the LORD.

Israel Has Not Returned to God

4 Hear this word, you cows of
      Bashan on Mount Samaria,
you women who oppress the poor
    and crush the needy
and say to your husbands, "Bring us
    some drinks!"
²The Sovereign LORD has sworn by his
    holiness:
"The time will surely come
when you will be taken away with
    hooks,
    the last of you with fishhooks.
³You will each go straight out
    through breaks in the wall,
    and you will be cast out toward
      Harmon,ᵃ"
              declares the LORD.

⁴"Go to Bethel and sin;
    go to Gilgal and sin yet more.
Bring your sacrifices every morning,
    your tithes every three years.ᵇ
⁵Burn leavened bread as a thank
    offering
and brag about your freewill
    offerings—
boast about them, you Israelites,
    for this is what you love to do,"
       declares the Sovereign LORD.

⁶"I gave you empty stomachsᶜ in every
    city
and lack of bread in every town,
    yet you have not returned to me,"
          declares the LORD.

⁷"I also withheld rain from you
    when the harvest was still three
      months away.
I sent rain on one town,
    but withheld it from another.
One field had rain;
    another had none and dried up.
⁸People staggered from town to town
    for water
but did not get enough to drink,
    yet you have not returned to me,"
          declares the LORD.

⁹"Many times I struck your gardens
    and vineyards,
    I struck them with blight and
      mildew.
Locusts devoured your fig and olive
    trees,
    yet you have not returned to me,"
          declares the LORD.

¹⁰"I sent plagues among you
    as I did to Egypt.
I killed your young men with the
    sword,
    along with your captured horses.
I filled your nostrils with the stench of
    your camps,
    yet you have not returned to me,"
          declares the LORD.

¹¹"I overthrew some of you
    as Iᵈ overthrew Sodom and
      Gomorrah.
You were like a burning stick snatched
    from the fire,
    yet you have not returned to me,"
          declares the LORD.

¹²"Therefore this is what I will do to
    you, Israel,
    and because I will do this to you,
      prepare to meet your God, O Israel."

¹³He who forms the mountains,
    creates the wind,
    and reveals his thoughts to man,
he who turns dawn to darkness,
    and treads the high places of the
      earth—
    the LORD God Almighty is his name.

A Lament and Call to Repentance

5 Hear this word, O house of Israel,
    this lament I take up concerning
you:

²"Fallen is Virgin Israel,
    never to rise again,
deserted in her own land,
    with no one to lift her up."

³This is what the Sovereign LORD says:

"The city that marches out a thousand
    strong for Israel

ᵃ3 Masoretic Text; with a different word division of
the Hebrew (see Septuagint) *out, O mountain of
oppression*   ᵇ4 Or *tithes on the third day*
ᶜ6 Hebrew *you cleanness of teeth*   ᵈ11 Hebrew *God*

will have only a hundred left;
the town that marches out a hundred
strong
will have only ten left."

[4] This is what the LORD says to the
house of Israel:

"Seek me and live;
[5]   do not seek Bethel,
do not go to Gilgal,
   do not journey to Beersheba.
For Gilgal will surely go into exile,
   and Bethel will be reduced to
      nothing.[a]"
[6] Seek the LORD and live,
   or he will sweep through the house
      of Joseph like a fire;
it will devour,
   and Bethel will have no one to
      quench it.

[7] You who turn justice into bitterness
   and cast righteousness to the
      ground

[8] (he who made the Pleiades and Orion,
   who turns blackness into dawn
   and darkens day into night,
who calls for the waters of the sea
   and pours them out over the face of
      the land—
   the LORD is his name—
[9] he flashes destruction on the
      stronghold
   and brings the fortified city to ruin),
[10] you hate the one who reproves in
      court
   and despise him who tells the truth.

[11] You trample on the poor
   and force him to give you grain.
Therefore, though you have built
      stone mansions,
   you will not live in them;
though you have planted lush
      vineyards,

[a] 5 Or *grief*; or *wickedness*; Hebrew *aven*, a reference
to Beth Aven (a derogatory name for Bethel)

Tuesday

Should I Stay or Go?

Read Amos 5:14–15

Is it just me, or is junior high one temptation after another? Like the party I
was invited to a while ago. The person having the party invited 12 guys
and girls, enough to make 6 couples. And even though the person said it
wasn't going to be a make-out party and that their parents would be
around, I still knew there'd be a lot of temptation to pair off with some girl
and make out. That's why I decided not to go.

I don't know what would have happened if I'd been at that party. Maybe
everything would have been fine and I would've just had fun with my
friends. But since I wasn't sure, I stayed away.

If you ask me, God's a no-nonsense God. He's pretty clear about how he
wants us to live. He wants us to seek good and stay away from evil, period. It's
not always easy, but it's what's right.

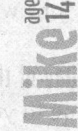

Mike age 14

❶ Think about a time you had to choose between following God and
giving in to temptation. What did you do? How did you make your decision?

❷ Characters in movies and on TV are tempted all the time. Think about
temptation as you watch TV this week. How do characters make their
decisions? What can you learn from their mistakes?

❸ Ask God to help you resist evil and choose good.

Turn to page 1068 for your next devotion.

you will not drink their wine.
[12] For I know how many are your
offenses
and how great your sins.

You oppress the righteous and take
bribes
and you deprive the poor of justice
in the courts.
[13] Therefore the prudent man keeps quiet
in such times,
for the times are evil.

[14] Seek good, not evil,
that you may live.
Then the LORD God Almighty will be
with you,
just as you say he is.
[15] Hate evil, love good;
maintain justice in the courts.
Perhaps the LORD God Almighty will
have mercy
on the remnant of Joseph.

[16] Therefore this is what the Lord, the
LORD God Almighty, says:

"There will be wailing in all the
streets
and cries of anguish in every public
square.
The farmers will be summoned to
weep
and the mourners to wail.
[17] There will be wailing in all the
vineyards,
for I will pass through your midst,"
says the LORD.

The Day of the LORD

[18] Woe to you who long
for the day of the LORD!
Why do you long for the day of the
LORD?
That day will be darkness, not
light.
[19] It will be as though a man fled from a
lion
only to meet a bear,
as though he entered his house
and rested his hand on the
wall
only to have a snake bite him.
[20] Will not the day of the LORD be
darkness, not light—
pitch-dark, without a ray of
brightness?

[21] "I hate, I despise your religious
feasts;
I cannot stand your assemblies.
[22] Even though you bring me burnt
offerings and grain offerings,
I will not accept them.
Though you bring choice fellowship
offerings,[a]
I will have no regard for them.
[23] Away with the noise of your songs!
I will not listen to the music of your
harps.
[24] But let justice roll on like a river,
righteousness like a never-failing
stream!

[25] "Did you bring me sacrifices and
offerings
forty years in the desert, O house of
Israel?
[26] You have lifted up the shrine of your
king,
the pedestal of your idols,
the star of your god[b]—
which you made for yourselves.
[27] Therefore I will send you into exile
beyond Damascus,"
says the LORD, whose name is God
Almighty.

Woe to the Complacent

6 Woe to you who are complacent in
Zion,
and to you who feel secure on
Mount Samaria,
you notable men of the foremost
nation,
to whom the people of Israel come!
[2] Go to Calneh and look at it;
go from there to great Hamath,
and then go down to Gath in
Philistia.
Are they better off than your two
kingdoms?
Is their land larger than yours?
[3] You put off the evil day
and bring near a reign of terror.
[4] You lie on beds inlaid with ivory
and lounge on your couches.
You dine on choice lambs
and fattened calves.

---

[a]22 Traditionally *peace offerings*   [b]26 Or *lifted up
Sakkuth your king / and Kaiwan your idols, / your
star-gods*; Septuagint *lifted up the shrine of Molech /
and the star of your god Rephan, / their idols*

⁵You strum away on your harps like
    David
    and improvise on musical
        instruments.
⁶You drink wine by the bowlful
    and use the finest lotions,
    but you do not grieve over the ruin
        of Joseph.
⁷Therefore you will be among the first
        to go into exile;
    your feasting and lounging will
        end.

The Lord Abhors the Pride of Israel

⁸The Sovereign LORD has sworn by
himself—the LORD God Almighty declares:

"I abhor the pride of Jacob
    and detest his fortresses;
I will deliver up the city
    and everything in it."

⁹If ten men are left in one house, they
too will die. ¹⁰And if a relative who is to
burn the bodies comes to carry them out
of the house and asks anyone still hiding
there, "Is anyone with you?" and he says,
"No," then he will say, "Hush! We must
not mention the name of the LORD."

¹¹For the LORD has given the command,
    and he will smash the great house
        into pieces
    and the small house into bits.

¹²Do horses run on the rocky crags?
    Does one plow there with oxen?
But you have turned justice into
        poison
    and the fruit of righteousness into
        bitterness—
¹³you who rejoice in the conquest of Lo
        Debar*ᵃ*
    and say, "Did we not take Karnaim*ᵇ*
        by our own strength?"

¹⁴For the LORD God Almighty declares,
    "I will stir up a nation against you,
        O house of Israel,
that will oppress you all the way
    from Lebo*ᶜ* Hamath to the valley of
        the Arabah."

Locusts, Fire and a Plumb Line

7 This is what the Sovereign LORD
showed me: He was preparing

swarms of locusts after the king's share
had been harvested and just as the second crop was coming up. ²When they
had stripped the land clean, I cried out,
"Sovereign LORD, forgive! How can Jacob
survive? He is so small!"

³So the LORD relented.

"This will not happen," the LORD said.

⁴This is what the Sovereign LORD
showed me: The Sovereign LORD was
calling for judgment by fire; it dried up
the great deep and devoured the land.
⁵Then I cried out, "Sovereign LORD, I beg
you, stop! How can Jacob survive? He is
so small!"

⁶So the LORD relented.

"This will not happen either," the Sovereign LORD said.

⁷This is what he showed me: The Lord
was standing by a wall that had been
built true to plumb, with a plumb line in
his hand. ⁸And the LORD asked me, "What
do you see, Amos?"

Plumb Line

Huh?

Amos 7:7

You're hired by a construction company,
and your first job is to test a wall to see if
it is straight. All your boss gives you to test
it with is a string and small metal ball. You
don't know it, but you've got all you need
to test whether it's straight because you've
got a plumb line in your hand. You tie the
metal ball to the end of the string and hang
it from the top of the wall. If it hangs
straight, you've got yourself a straight wall.
If the line doesn't hang straight, well, you
give 'em the bad news.

"A plumb line," I replied.

Then the Lord said, "Look, I am setting
a plumb line among my people Israel; I
will spare them no longer.

⁹"The high places of Isaac will be
        destroyed

ᵃ13 Lo Debar means *nothing.* *ᵇ13 Karnaim* means
horns; horn here symbolizes strength. *ᶜ14 Or from
the entrance to*

and the sanctuaries of Israel will be
   ruined;
with my sword I will rise against
   the house of Jeroboam."

Amos and Amaziah

¹⁰Then Amaziah the priest of Bethel
sent a message to Jeroboam king of Israel: "Amos is raising a conspiracy against
you in the very heart of Israel. The land
cannot bear all his words. ¹¹For this is
what Amos is saying:

" 'Jeroboam will die by the sword,
   and Israel will surely go into exile,
     away from their native land.' "

¹²Then Amaziah said to Amos, "Get
out, you seer! Go back to the land of Judah. Earn your bread there and do your
prophesying there. ¹³Don't prophesy
anymore at Bethel, because this is the
king's sanctuary and the temple of the
kingdom."

¹⁴Amos answered Amaziah, "I was neither a prophet nor a prophet's son, but I
was a shepherd, and I also took care of
sycamore-fig trees. ¹⁵But the LORD took
me from tending the flock and said to
me, 'Go, prophesy to my people Israel.'
¹⁶Now then, hear the word of the LORD.
You say,

" 'Do not prophesy against Israel,
   and stop preaching against the
     house of Isaac.'

¹⁷"Therefore this is what the LORD says:

" 'Your wife will become a prostitute
   in the city,
   and your sons and daughters will
     fall by the sword.
Your land will be measured and
   divided up,
   and you yourself will die in a
     pagan*a* country.

---

a17 Hebrew *an unclean*

Wednesday

Just a Regular Guy

Read Amos 7:14–15

I think about the future sometimes, and I wonder what God wants me to do.
I guess I won't know all the details till I get older, but I do know this: God
definitely has a plan for me, and he can use me.

   Amos, the guy in these verses, was just a regular guy—a shepherd who
also took care of trees. He didn't have any special training or a lot of money,
but God made him a prophet.

   It really doesn't matter if you're flipping burgers at a fast-food joint or just
hanging around, wondering what your future will be like. God has plans for all
of us, no matter how ordinary we think we are.

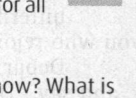

❶ What are some ways you think God can use you right now? What is
one way you have seen God use your life already?

❷ Get a sheet of paper and divide it in half. On one half, write down
everything about you that's ordinary—you ride the bus, you watch TV,
you eat bread, you get the idea. On the other side, write down everything about you that's unique—you can sing "Amazing Grace" in Spanish, you've
got 5 turtles, you run marathons. Think about ways God can use all these things
about you to make a difference in the world.

❸ Thank God for using "ordinary" people like you to share his love.

Turn to page 1074 for your next devotion.

And Israel will certainly go into exile,
  away from their native land.' "

A Basket of Ripe Fruit

8 This is what the Sovereign LORD
  showed me: a basket of ripe fruit.
²"What do you see, Amos?" he asked.

"A basket of ripe fruit," I answered.

Then the LORD said to me, "The time is
ripe for my people Israel; I will spare
them no longer.

³"In that day," declares the Sovereign
LORD, "the songs in the temple will turn
to wailing.ᵃ Many, many bodies—flung
everywhere! Silence!"

⁴Hear this, you who trample the needy
  and do away with the poor of the
    land,

⁵saying,

"When will the New Moon be over
  that we may sell grain,
and the Sabbath be ended
  that we may market wheat?"—
skimping the measure,
  boosting the price
  and cheating with dishonest scales,
⁶buying the poor with silver
  and the needy for a pair of sandals,
  selling even the sweepings with the
    wheat.

⁷The LORD has sworn by the Pride of
Jacob: "I will never forget anything they
have done.

⁸"Will not the land tremble for this,
  and all who live in it mourn?
The whole land will rise like the Nile;
  it will be stirred up and then sink
    like the river of Egypt.

⁹"In that day," declares the Sovereign
LORD,

"I will make the sun go down at noon
  and darken the earth in broad
    daylight.
¹⁰I will turn your religious feasts into
    mourning
  and all your singing into weeping.
I will make all of you wear sackcloth
  and shave your heads.
I will make that time like mourning
    for an only son
  and the end of it like a bitter day.

¹¹"The days are coming," declares the
    Sovereign LORD,
  "when I will send a famine through
    the land—
not a famine of food or a thirst for
    water,
  but a famine of hearing the words
    of the LORD.
¹²Men will stagger from sea to sea
  and wander from north to east,
searching for the word of the LORD,
  but they will not find it.

¹³"In that day

"the lovely young women and strong
    young men
  will faint because of thirst.
¹⁴They who swear by the shameᵇ of
    Samaria,
  or say, 'As surely as your god lives,
    O Dan,'
  or, 'As surely as the godᶜ of
    Beersheba lives'—
they will fall,
  never to rise again."

Israel to Be Destroyed

9 I saw the Lord standing by the altar,
  and he said:

"Strike the tops of the pillars
  so that the thresholds shake.
Bring them down on the heads of all
    the people;
  those who are left I will kill with
    the sword.
Not one will get away,
  none will escape.
²Though they dig down to the depths
    of the grave,ᵈ
  from there my hand will take them.
Though they climb up to the
    heavens,
  from there I will bring them down.
³Though they hide themselves on the
    top of Carmel,
  there I will hunt them down and
    seize them.
Though they hide from me at the
    bottom of the sea,
  there I will command the serpent to
    bite them.

ᵃ3 Or "the temple singers will wail   ᵇ14 Or by
Ashima; or by the idol   ᶜ14 Or power   ᵈ2 Hebrew to
Sheol

⁴Though they are driven into exile by
  their enemies,
  there I will command the sword to
    slay them.
I will fix my eyes upon them
  for evil and not for good."

⁵The Lord, the LORD Almighty,
  he who touches the earth and it
    melts,
  and all who live in it mourn—
the whole land rises like the Nile,
  then sinks like the river of Egypt—
⁶he who builds his lofty palace*ᵃ* in the
    heavens
  and sets its foundation*ᵇ* on the
    earth,
who calls for the waters of the sea
  and pours them out over the face of
    the land—
  the LORD is his name.

⁷"Are not you Israelites
  the same to me as the Cushites*ᶜ*?"
    declares the LORD.
"Did I not bring Israel up from
    Egypt,
  the Philistines from Caphtor*ᵈ*
and the Arameans from Kir?

⁸"Surely the eyes of the Sovereign LORD
  are on the sinful kingdom.
I will destroy it
  from the face of the earth—
yet I will not totally destroy
  the house of Jacob,"
    declares the LORD.
⁹"For I will give the command,
  and I will shake the house of Israel
    among all the nations
as grain is shaken in a sieve,
  and not a pebble will reach the
    ground.
¹⁰All the sinners among my people
  will die by the sword,
  all those who say,

'Disaster will not overtake or meet
    us.'

Israel's Restoration

¹¹"In that day I will restore
    David's fallen tent.
I will repair its broken places,
    restore its ruins,
  and build it as it used to be,
¹²so that they may possess the remnant
    of Edom
  and all the nations that bear my
    name,*ᵉ*"
      declares the LORD, who will
        do these things.

¹³"The days are coming," declares the
LORD,

"when the reaper will be overtaken by
    the plowman
  and the planter by the one treading
    grapes.
New wine will drip from the
    mountains
  and flow from all the hills.
¹⁴I will bring back my exiled*ᶠ* people
    Israel;
  they will rebuild the ruined cities
    and live in them.
They will plant vineyards and drink
    their wine;
  they will make gardens and eat
    their fruit.
¹⁵I will plant Israel in their own land,
  never again to be uprooted
  from the land I have given them,"
      says the LORD your God.

---

*ᵃ6 The meaning of the Hebrew for this phrase is
uncertain.   ᵇ6 The meaning of the Hebrew for this
word is uncertain.   ᶜ7 That is, people from the
upper Nile region   ᵈ7 That is, Crete   ᵉ12 Hebrew;
Septuagint* so that the remnant of men / and all the
nations that bear my name may seek *the Lord*.
ᶠ14 Or will restore the fortunes of my

Obadiah

START

CAST OF Characters

Obadiah
(oh-buh-DYE-yuh)

Absolutely nothing is known of this prophet—well, except that he is, uh, a prophet. And that his name's Obadiah. But that's it.

Edom (EEE-dum)

The nation started by Esau that was next door to brother Jacob's nation of Israel. When Judah (a part of Israel) was attacked by Babylon, Edom betrayed its "brother" and joined the Babylonian army in ripping Judah apart.

The book of Obadiah is the next-to-the-last episode in an ugly story of family betrayal. If you remember the book of Genesis, you'll remember the Esau incident—Esau, twin brother to Jacob. Remember how Esau was so hungry he traded his birthright for a bowl of soup? Well, Jacob went on to inherit almost everything from his father, and he started the nation of Israel. Esau settled nearby and started the nation of Edom—a nation that never quite forgot or forgave Jacob for ripping off its status of God's favored nation.

So off and on for a thousand years or so, Edom picks and pokes at its brother-nation Israel, often ganging up with other enemies of Israel and generally making Israel's hard times even harder. (Meanwhile, God was telling Israel, "Don't hate the Edomites—they're family, after all. Maybe not *nice* family, but still family.")

The long-standing cold war becomes brutally hot when King Nebuchadnezzar and his Babylonian army swarm into Israel to squash it once and for all. Next-door neighbor Edom sees its chance to *really* avenge itself on its brother-nation. Not only do the Edomites not defend their brother-nation Israel (Judah) against Babylon, they actually join Babylon in stealing everything from Judah.

God doesn't think this is a cool way for brothers—or brother-nations—to treat each other. So Edom gets hit with God's vengeance, *hard*. Like we said, this is the next-to-the-last story in Edom's life as a nation. Its *last* episode shows that the destruction Obadiah prophesies in this book actually comes true, and Edom is extinguished forever.

What's UP with That?

Remember toward the end of
"Indiana Jones and the Last Crusade"

when Indy, his dad and their 2 friends arrive on horseback at the temple carved right into the red-rock cliff, where inside Indy faced and passed his 3 tests? The inside scenes were filmed on a sound-stage, of course. But what you see in the outside shot of that red, rock-cut temple is just one "building" in the real rock-cut city of Petra—a city in what used to be the kingdom of Edom.

This city called Petra (or, in Hebrew, *Sela*) was the Chicago of Edom—a muscular, centrally located city where several caravan routes inter-sected. Kind of like where a bunch of freeways intersect right near the Chicago airport.

Yet despite its studly defenses (how do you smash down a mountain to get to your enemy inside it?), God had the last word (he always does). It's not like Edom wasn't warned or anything. Read Obadiah verse 3: "The pride of your heart has deceived you, you who live in the clefts of the rocks and make your home on the heights." Within a few hundred years, this ancient tough city was emptied out by invaders. You won't find anything there now but wind, lizards and tourists.

Snap shots

Hey, it's a short book—only a single chapter with 21 verses. Obadiah always comes back to these 2 ideas:

- **The reasons why God would destroy Edom** *(verses 10 and 14)*

- **What that destruction's going to be like** *(verses 6 and 18)*

¹The vision of Obadiah.

This is what the Sovereign LORD says about Edom—

We have heard a message from the
   LORD:
  An envoy was sent to the nations to
    say,
"Rise, and let us go against her for
    battle"—

²"See, I will make you small among the
   nations;
  you will be utterly despised.
³The pride of your heart has deceived
   you,
  you who live in the clefts of the
    rocks^a
  and make your home on the
    heights,
you who say to yourself,
  'Who can bring me down to the
    ground?'
⁴Though you soar like the eagle
  and make your nest among the stars,
  from there I will bring you down,"
           declares the LORD.

⁵"If thieves came to you,
  if robbers in the night—
Oh, what a disaster awaits you—
  would they not steal only as much
    as they wanted?
If grape pickers came to you,
  would they not leave a few
    grapes?
⁶But how Esau will be ransacked,
  his hidden treasures pillaged!
⁷All your allies will force you to the
   border;
  your friends will deceive and
    overpower you;
those who eat your bread will set a
   trap for you,^b
  but you will not detect it.

⁸"In that day," declares the LORD,
  "will I not destroy the wise men of
    Edom,
  men of understanding in the
    mountains of Esau?
⁹Your warriors, O Teman, will be
   terrified,
  and everyone in Esau's mountains
  will be cut down in the slaughter.

¹⁰Because of the violence against your
   brother Jacob,
  you will be covered with shame;
  you will be destroyed forever.
¹¹On the day you stood aloof
  while strangers carried off his
    wealth
and foreigners entered his gates
  and cast lots for Jerusalem,
  you were like one of them.
¹²You should not look down on your
   brother
  in the day of his misfortune,
nor rejoice over the people of Judah
  in the day of their destruction,
nor boast so much
  in the day of their trouble.
¹³You should not march through the
   gates of my people
  in the day of their disaster,
nor look down on them in their
   calamity
  in the day of their disaster,
nor seize their wealth
  in the day of their disaster.
¹⁴You should not wait at the
   crossroads
  to cut down their fugitives,
nor hand over their survivors
  in the day of their trouble.

¹⁵"The day of the LORD is near
  for all nations.
As you have done, it will be done to
   you;
  your deeds will return upon your
    own head.
¹⁶Just as you drank on my holy hill,
  so all the nations will drink
    continually;
they will drink and drink
  and be as if they had never been.
¹⁷But on Mount Zion will be
   deliverance;
  it will be holy,
and the house of Jacob
  will possess its inheritance.
¹⁸The house of Jacob will be a fire
  and the house of Joseph a flame;
the house of Esau will be stubble,
  and they will set it on fire and
    consume it.
There will be no survivors

---

^a3 Or *of Sela* ^b7 The meaning of the Hebrew for
this clause is uncertain.

from the house of Esau."
The LORD has spoken.

Drink Up

Huh?

Obadiah 16

The people were going to have to drink bitter stuff that was worse than rotten milk or sour orange juice (or the two combined)! It was God's judgment that they were going to drink, which is a fancy, poetic way of saying that they were going to have to experience the consequences for their sin. And that never tastes good.

---

¹⁹ People from the Negev will occupy
the mountains of Esau,
and people from the foothills will
possess
the land of the Philistines.
They will occupy the fields of Ephraim
and Samaria,
and Benjamin will possess Gilead.
²⁰ This company of Israelite exiles who
are in Canaan
will possess the land as far as
Zarephath;
the exiles from Jerusalem who are in
Sepharad
will possess the towns of the Negev.
²¹ Deliverers will go up on^a Mount
Zion
to govern the mountains of Esau.
And the kingdom will be the LORD's.

a 21 Or from

Thursday

An Enemy in Need

Read Obadiah 12

If there's someone you don't like very much, it's pretty easy to wish that something bad would happen to them. And if something bad does happen to them, it's pretty easy to think they deserved it—or at least not feel bad for them or not offer them any help.

But God doesn't want us to do that. God wants us to help other people when they're having a hard time, even if it's someone we don't like.

This is a verse that reminds me not to rejoice when other people are hurting. It reminds me to be kind to people who are suffering. God always comforts me when something bad happens to me, and he wants me to do the same thing for others.

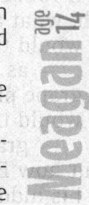

Meagan age 14

What about You?

❶ Think about a time you were secretly happy when something bad happened to a person you don't like. How would you have felt if you were that other person?

❷ Go to a shoe store and find a cheap pair of shoes. These are your "Other Guy's Shoes" (OGS). Keep them in your locker or your closet. Whenever you stop caring about another person's troubles, take a look at your OGS and think about what it's like to be in the other guy's shoes.

❸ Ask God to help you reach out to people who are embarrassed or hurting, no matter who they are.

Turn to page 1077 for your next devotion.

Jonah

START

Cast OF Characters

Jonah (JOE-nuh)

A prophet with a big job and a lot to learn about God's mercy. Jonah is afraid of what the Assyrians might do to him when he warns them about God's plan to destroy them. But he's also worried that they will change their ways and God will forgive them!

God

The book of Jonah shows us over and over again that our God is a God of second chances. From the ship full of sailors to the sinful Assyrians to his own prophet Jonah, God proves that he doesn't

Think about some of the meanest kids at your school. Can you picture them picking on someone because that person is younger, smaller or just plain different?

One day you're sitting in the school cafeteria, eating your lunch, minding your own business, when suddenly you sense God telling you to walk over to the table where those bullies always sit. So you do, and once you're standing in front of them you realize God wants you to warn these guys that, if they don't shape up, the principal is going to expel them from school. What would you do?

Jonah is faced with a similar problem. God tells him to go to a city called Nineveh and warn the Assyrians that they'd better change their ways—or else! Well, Jonah freaks out and tries to run away—not only from the assignment God has given him but also from God.

You know what? God isn't through with Jonah yet. In fact, all God needed was a storm, a really big fish, a vine, a worm and some hot air to teach Jonah a few little lessons about God's great love and mercy for all people—even a table full of mean and nasty bullies.

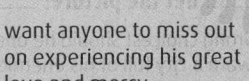

want anyone to miss out on experiencing his great love and mercy.

Sailors (Yo ho ho)

These guys worship other gods, but they still try to spare Jonah's life, even

after they know he is the cause of the storm threatening to drown them all! In the end, and in spite of Jonah's mistake, their lives are greatly changed—and not just because the storm disappeared!

Assyrians
(uh-SEER-ee-unz)

The Bible calls them an evil race of people and identifies them as one of Israel's greatest enemies at the time. About 120,000 of them live in Assyria's capital city, Nineveh (NIN-uh-vuh). Deep down Jonah is hoping he has a front row seat when God flattens this city full of sinners.

What's UP with That?

Jonah had some tough choices to make.

He kept finding himself in "should I do this or that?" situations. And the problem was, the right thing almost always seemed way more difficult, way more risky and much less fun!

When we read the book of Jonah, we're pretty quick to frown at Jonah and think badly of him (after all, he did make a bunch of wrong choices). But, hey now, be honest: What would you have done?! Put yourself in these Jonah-like situations. Circle the option you would choose in column one or column two for each pair. Would you rather:

Make a speech in front of your entire school about how cool God is.	Take an all-expenses-paid cruise to some tropical location.
Confess to your science teacher and principal that you were the one who cheated on the final exam.	Keep your mouth shut so everyone in your class has to write a 10-page, not-for-credit paper on the importance of recycling.
Find out that a kid who always calls you mean names is coming to your youth group retreat.	Find out that a kid who always calls you mean names fell and broke his leg.

Snap shots

- **See ya!**
  (chapter 1:1–7)
- **Thanks for nothin'**
  (chapter 1:8–17)
- **On second thought . . .**
  (chapter 2)
- **Do the right thing**
  (chapter 3)
- **How embarrassing!**
  (chapter 4:1–5)
- **God cares about all people (even whiny prophets!)**
  (chapter 4:6–10)

Get the picture?

You bet, Jonah made some wrong choices! Should he obey God or take a cruise on the Mediterranean Sea? Should he warn a city full of his enemies that God was going to destroy them or pretend he didn't hear God's instructions and let them all die? Should he let the sailors throw him overboard so the storm would stop or lie and catch a few more hours of sleep below deck? Well, if you're thinking to yourself, "Duh! The right choices seem pretty obvious," take a look at your own answers (if you answered honestly!).

Jonah flees from the LORD

1 The word of the LORD came to Jonah son of Amittai: ²"Go to the great city of Nineveh and preach against it, because its wickedness has come up before me."

³But Jonah ran away from the LORD and headed for Tarshish. He went down to Joppa, where he found a ship bound for that port. After paying the fare, he went aboard and sailed for Tarshish to flee from the LORD.

⁴Then the LORD sent a great wind on the sea, and such a violent storm arose that the ship threatened to break up. ⁵All the sailors were afraid and each cried out to his own god. And they threw the cargo into the sea to lighten the ship.

But Jonah had gone below deck, where he lay down and fell into a deep sleep. ⁶The captain went to him and said, "How can you sleep? Get up and call on your god! Maybe he will take notice of us, and we will not perish."

⁷Then the sailors said to each other, "Come, let us cast lots to find out who is responsible for this calamity." They cast lots and the lot fell on Jonah.

⁸So they asked him, "Tell us, who is responsible for making all this trouble for us? What do you do? Where do you come from? What is your country? From what people are you?"

⁹He answered, "I am a Hebrew and I worship the LORD, the God of heaven, who made the sea and the land."

¹⁰This terrified them and they asked, "What have you done?" (They knew he was running away from the LORD, because he had already told them so.)

¹¹The sea was getting rougher and rougher. So they asked him, "What should we do to you to make the sea calm down for us?"

¹²"Pick me up and throw me into the sea," he replied, "and it will become calm. I know that it is my fault that this great storm has come upon you."

Friday

My Fault

Read Jonah 1:12

This summer I looked at some things on the Internet that I shouldn't have. My parents knew someone had been looking at these bad sites and when they asked me about it, I blamed my brother. He got punished and I didn't. But after a few days, I started to feel really bad about getting him in trouble. So I told my parents the truth and apologized to my brother.

It would have been pretty easy for me to just keep my mouth shut and let my brother take my punishment, just like it would have been pretty easy for Jonah to be quiet about causing the storm that might have drowned his shipmates. But that's not right.

God wants us to take responsibility for the things we do wrong. When we admit our mistakes, God can help us keep from making the same mistakes later on.

Tim, age 13

What about You?

❶ Why is it so tempting to blame others when we mess up? Why is it better to take responsibility for our own mistakes?

❷ Next time you get into an argument with someone, try being the first one to say, "I'm sorry." How does your apology affect the other person? How does it affect you?

❸ Ask God to help you learn from your mistakes.

Turn to page 1080 for your next devotion.

¹³Instead, the men did their best to row back to land. But they could not, for the sea grew even wilder than before. ¹⁴Then they cried to the LORD, "O LORD, please do not let us die for taking this man's life. Do not hold us accountable for killing an innocent man, for you, O LORD, have done as you pleased." ¹⁵Then they took Jonah and threw him overboard, and the raging sea grew calm. ¹⁶At this the men greatly feared the LORD, and they offered a sacrifice to the LORD and made vows to him.

¹⁷But the LORD provided a great fish to swallow Jonah, and Jonah was inside the fish three days and three nights.

Here Comes That Scary Music

Huh?

Jonah 1:17
When you're watching a scary movie, and you start to hear that freaky music get louder, you know there's a scary scene ahead. That's called foreshadowing, because it gives you some hints about what's coming up. Jonah's 3 days inside the fish are sometimes thought to foreshadow the 3 days that Jesus stayed inside the tomb.

Jonah's Prayer

2 From inside the fish Jonah prayed to the LORD his God. ²He said:

"In my distress I called to the LORD,
    and he answered me.
From the depths of the grave[a] I called
        for help,
    and you listened to my cry.
³You hurled me into the deep,
    into the very heart of the seas,
    and the currents swirled about me;
all your waves and breakers
    swept over me.
⁴I said, 'I have been banished
    from your sight;
yet I will look again
    toward your holy temple.'
⁵The engulfing waters threatened me,[b]
    the deep surrounded me;

seaweed was wrapped around my
        head.
⁶To the roots of the mountains I sank
        down;
    the earth beneath barred me in
        forever.
But you brought my life up from the
        pit,
    O LORD my God.

⁷"When my life was ebbing away,
    I remembered you, LORD,
and my prayer rose to you,
    to your holy temple.

⁸"Those who cling to worthless idols
    forfeit the grace that could be
        theirs.
⁹But I, with a song of thanksgiving,
    will sacrifice to you.
What I have vowed I will make good.
    Salvation comes from the LORD."

¹⁰And the LORD commanded the fish, and it vomited Jonah onto dry land.

Jonah Goes to Nineveh

3 Then the word of the LORD came to Jonah a second time: ²"Go to the great city of Nineveh and proclaim to it the message I give you."

³Jonah obeyed the word of the LORD and went to Nineveh. Now Nineveh was a very important city—a visit required three days. ⁴On the first day, Jonah started into the city. He proclaimed: "Forty more days and Nineveh will be overturned." ⁵The Ninevites believed God. They declared a fast, and all of them, from the greatest to the least, put on sackcloth.

⁶When the news reached the king of Nineveh, he rose from his throne, took off his royal robes, covered himself with sackcloth and sat down in the dust. ⁷Then he issued a proclamation in Nineveh:

"By the decree of the king and his nobles:

    Do not let any man or beast, herd or flock, taste anything; do not let them eat or drink. ⁸But let man and beast be covered with sackcloth. Let everyone call urgently on God. Let them give up their evil ways and

---

ᵃ2 Hebrew *Sheol*   *ᵇ5* Or *waters were at my throat*

Saggy and Baggy

Huh?

Jonah 3:5–8

Saggy and baggy clothes have been popular for thousands of years, including way back in Nineveh. The king wanted every person and animal to be covered with baggy sacks as a traditional way of saying "I'm sorry" to God.

their violence. ⁹Who knows? God may yet relent and with compassion turn from his fierce anger so that we will not perish."

¹⁰When God saw what they did and how they turned from their evil ways, he had compassion and did not bring upon them the destruction he had threatened.

Jonah's Anger at the LORD's Compassion

4 But Jonah was greatly displeased and became angry. ²He prayed to the LORD, "O LORD, is this not what I said when I was still at home? That is why I was so quick to flee to Tarshish. I knew that you are a gracious and compassionate God, slow to anger and abounding in love, a God who relents from sending calamity. ³Now, O LORD, take away my life, for it is better for me to die than to live."

⁴But the LORD replied, "Have you any right to be angry?"

⁵Jonah went out and sat down at a place east of the city. There he made himself a shelter, sat in its shade and waited to see what would happen to the city. ⁶Then the LORD God provided a vine and made it grow up over Jonah to give shade for his head to ease his discomfort, and Jonah was very happy about the vine. ⁷But at dawn the next day God provided a worm, which chewed the vine so that it withered. ⁸When the sun rose, God provided a scorching east wind, and the sun blazed on Jonah's head so that he grew faint. He wanted to die, and said, "It

Who Am I?

Try this with a friend. Read the first clue and pause to see if he or she has an answer. If not, read the second clue, and so on. If your friend still doesn't have a guess after the fourth clue, or if you want to check your answer, look up the verses given at the bottom.

Round 1

Clue 1 — Jesus hung out at my house.
Clue 2 — I had big bucks!
Clue 3 — I was always picked last for basketball.
Clue 4 — I climbed a tree to see Jesus.
(Luke 19:1–10)

Round 2

Clue 1 — I was Vice President of Egypt.
Clue 2 — I was thrown in the slammer for nothin'!
Clue 3 — My brothers put me on sale.
Clue 4 — I had a coat of many colors.
(Genesis 37—45)

Round 3

Clue 1 — I babysat sheep.
Clue 2 — I wrote a lot of hit music.
Clue 3 — I became head honcho in Israel.
Clue 4 — I beat up a big guy with a rock.
(1 Samuel 17)

Round 4

Clue 1 — God asked me to go right, I went left.
Clue 2 — I preached to a city I hated.
Clue 3 — I got tossed into the sea.
Clue 4 — I was dinner for a fish!
(Jonah 1—4)

would be better for me to die than to live."

⁹But God said to Jonah, "Do you have a right to be angry about the vine?"

"I do," he said. "I am angry enough to die."

¹⁰But the LORD said, "You have been

concerned about this vine, though you did not tend it or make it grow. It sprang up overnight and died overnight. ¹¹But Nineveh has more than a hundred and twenty thousand people who cannot tell their right hand from their left, and many cattle as well. Should I not be concerned about that great city?"

Week end.

Ordinary People
Mark 12:41–43 (page 1208)

Wednesday, Ruslan (cool name, huh?) commented on how ordinary Amos was—he was just a shepherd who liked trees. Why would God want to use a guy like that? According to the world's standards, this guy was not on anyone's VIP list.

Luckily God doesn't have that same value system. He looks at the inside of people to see what's in their hearts. Turns out that good looks and money and power often become distractions. Those who think they are somebodies often ignore their own desperate need for God.

But people like Amos or the poor widow—people who have fewer distractions—tend to be more quickly drawn to God. And God is drawn to them. So the next time you're wondering if you're too young for God or too irresponsible to be a disciple, remember the people God worked through. They were often inconsistent, young, ordinary people just like you. Cool.

What about You?

❶ What are the distractions in your life that keep you from having a closer relationship with God?

❷ Make a list of the people who have made a difference in your life. Next to their name list the qualities in them that influenced you.

❸ Tell God how thankful you are for the way he made you. Ask him to give you confidence that you can make a difference in the world and then to show you how.

Turn to page 1087 for your next devotion.

Micah

START

Imagine you're in the rowdiest class in your school. (You may not need to imagine this.) The behavior is getting worse and worse; in fact, things are basically out of control. No matter what the teacher says, no one listens.

Micah lived with a rowdy bunch. They ignored God's rules and did the opposite—lying, cheating, stealing and murdering. His job was to try to get them to listen to God and change the way they were acting. Check out how often Micah says something like, "Listen up!" He tells them how they're blowing it and about God's punishment for people who live that way.

The best part of the book is when Micah tells the people that God is planning to send Jesus someday. He tells how Jesus will forgive people for the wrong they are doing and to make things right between them and God.

Cast OF Characters

Micah (MIKE-uh)
Another prophet—God's mouthpiece—speaking on God's behalf to get the attention of a group of people who were really behaving badly.

Jotham (rhymes with Gotham)
Ahaz (rhymes with "they has")
and Hezekiah
(heh-zeh-KYE-uh)

These were the 3 kings who ruled while Micah was speaking for God. In those days they didn't have calendars like we do. So saying who was king was an easy way to know when things happened.

Jesus
Although Micah didn't actually use the name Jesus, whenever he talked about the coming "ruler" he was predicting things about Jesus and how he would save people from their sins.

What's UP with That?

Special Effects

Imagine making a movie with the predictions from the book of Micah. Which of the following special effects would you need to produce so you could tell the whole story?

A melt a mountain

B have someone jump from one plane to another

C create a giant rocky landslide to fill up a valley

D strip the skin off people's bodies

E change a man into a dog

F sink a really huge ship

G organize a nude parade

H turn a city into a heap of rubble

I land a group of aliens in a parking lot

J explode carved idols and large stones

K fly a guy with tights and a cape over a city

Snap Shots

● Bad news is . . . you guys are really blowing it *(chapters 1—3)*

● Good news is . . . I have a plan to forgive you *(chapters 4—5)*

● Bad news is . . . I have to punish you first *(chapter 6)*

● Good news is . . . the story will have a happy ending *(chapter 7)*

answers: a (1:4), c (1:6), d (3:2), g (1:11), h (3:12), j (5:13)

1

The word of the LORD that came to Micah of Moresheth during the reigns of Jotham, Ahaz and Hezekiah, kings of Judah—the vision he saw concerning Samaria and Jerusalem.

² Hear, O peoples, all of you,
    listen, O earth and all who are in it,
that the Sovereign LORD may witness
        against you,
    the Lord from his holy temple.

Judgment Against Samaria and Jerusalem

³ Look! The LORD is coming from his
        dwelling place;
    he comes down and treads the high
        places of the earth.
⁴ The mountains melt beneath him
    and the valleys split apart,
like wax before the fire,
    like water rushing down a slope.
⁵ All this is because of Jacob's
        transgression,
    because of the sins of the house of
        Israel.
What is Jacob's transgression?
    Is it not Samaria?
What is Judah's high place?
    Is it not Jerusalem?

⁶ "Therefore I will make Samaria a heap
        of rubble,
    a place for planting vineyards.
I will pour her stones into the valley
    and lay bare her foundations.
⁷ All her idols will be broken to pieces;
    all her temple gifts will be burned
        with fire;
    I will destroy all her images.
Since she gathered her gifts from the
        wages of prostitutes,
    as the wages of prostitutes they will
        again be used."

Weeping and Mourning

⁸ Because of this I will weep and wail;
    I will go about barefoot and naked.
I will howl like a jackal
    and moan like an owl.
⁹ For her wound is incurable;
    it has come to Judah.
It^a has reached the very gate of my
        people,
    even to Jerusalem itself.
¹⁰ Tell it not in Gath^b;
    weep not at all.^c

In Beth Ophrah^d
    roll in the dust.
¹¹ Pass on in nakedness and shame,
    you who live in Shaphir.^e
Those who live in Zaanan^f
    will not come out.
Beth Ezel is in mourning;
    its protection is taken from you.
¹² Those who live in Maroth^g writhe in
        pain,
    waiting for relief,
because disaster has come from the
        LORD,
    even to the gate of Jerusalem.
¹³ You who live in Lachish,^h
    harness the team to the chariot.
You were the beginning of sin
    to the Daughter of Zion,
for the transgressions of Israel
    were found in you.
¹⁴ Therefore you will give parting gifts
    to Moresheth Gath.
The town of Aczib^i will prove
        deceptive
    to the kings of Israel.
¹⁵ I will bring a conqueror against you
    who live in Mareshah.^j
He who is the glory of Israel
    will come to Adullam.
¹⁶ Shave your heads in mourning
    for the children in whom you
        delight;
make yourselves as bald as the
        vulture,
    for they will go from you into exile.

Man's Plans and God's

2

Woe to those who plan iniquity,
    to those who plot evil on their beds!
At morning's light they carry it out
    because it is in their power to do it.
² They covet fields and seize them,
    and houses, and take them.
They defraud a man of his home,
    a fellowman of his inheritance.

---

^a9 Or *He*   ^b10 *Gath* sounds like the Hebrew for *tell.*
^c10 Hebrew; Septuagint may suggest *not in Acco.*
The Hebrew for *in Acco* sounds like the Hebrew for
weep.   ^d10 *Beth Ophrah* means *house of dust.*
^e11 *Shaphir* means *pleasant.*   ^f11 *Zaanan* sounds
like the Hebrew for *come out.*   ^g12 *Maroth* sounds
like the Hebrew for *bitter.*   ^h13 *Lachish* sounds like
the Hebrew for *team.*   ^i14 *Aczib* means *deception.*
^j15 *Mareshah* sounds like the Hebrew for
conqueror.

³Therefore, the LORD says:

"I am planning disaster against this
people,
from which you cannot save
yourselves.
You will no longer walk proudly,
for it will be a time of calamity.
⁴In that day men will ridicule you;
they will taunt you with this
mournful song:
'We are utterly ruined;
my people's possession is divided up.
He takes it from me!
He assigns our fields to traitors.' "

⁵Therefore you will have no one in the
assembly of the LORD
to divide the land by lot.

False Prophets

⁶"Do not prophesy," their prophets say.
"Do not prophesy about these
things;
disgrace will not overtake us."
⁷Should it be said, O house of Jacob:
"Is the Spirit of the LORD angry?
Does he do such things?"

"Do not my words do good
to him whose ways are upright?
⁸Lately my people have risen up
like an enemy.
You strip off the rich robe
from those who pass by without a
care,
like men returning from battle.
⁹You drive the women of my people
from their pleasant homes.
You take away my blessing
from their children forever.
¹⁰Get up, go away!
For this is not your resting place,
because it is defiled,
it is ruined, beyond all remedy.
¹¹If a liar and deceiver comes and says,
'I will prophesy for you plenty of
wine and beer,'
he would be just the prophet for
this people!

Deliverance Promised

¹²"I will surely gather all of you,
O Jacob;
I will surely bring together the
remnant of Israel.

I will bring them together like sheep
in a pen,
like a flock in its pasture;
the place will throng with people.
¹³One who breaks open the way will go
up before them;
they will break through the gate
and go out.
Their king will pass through before
them,
the LORD at their head."

Leaders and Prophets Rebuked

3 Then I said,

"Listen, you leaders of Jacob,
you rulers of the house of Israel.
Should you not know justice,
²   you who hate good and love evil;
who tear the skin from my people
and the flesh from their bones;
³who eat my people's flesh,
strip off their skin
and break their bones in pieces;
who chop them up like meat for the
pan,
like flesh for the pot?"

⁴Then they will cry out to the LORD,
but he will not answer them.
At that time he will hide his face from
them
because of the evil they have done.

⁵This is what the LORD says:

"As for the prophets
who lead my people astray,
if one feeds them,
they proclaim 'peace';
if he does not,
they prepare to wage war against
him.
⁶Therefore night will come over you,
without visions,
and darkness, without divination.
The sun will set for the prophets,
and the day will go dark for them.
⁷The seers will be ashamed
and the diviners disgraced.
They will all cover their faces
because there is no answer from
God."

⁸But as for me, I am filled with power,
with the Spirit of the LORD,
and with justice and might,

to declare to Jacob his transgression,
  to Israel his sin.
⁹Hear this, you leaders of the house of
    Jacob,
  you rulers of the house of Israel,
who despise justice
  and distort all that is right;
¹⁰who build Zion with bloodshed,
  and Jerusalem with wickedness.
¹¹Her leaders judge for a bribe,
  her priests teach for a price,
  and her prophets tell fortunes for
    money.
Yet they lean upon the LORD and say,
  "Is not the LORD among us?
  No disaster will come upon us."
¹²Therefore because of you,
  Zion will be plowed like a field,
Jerusalem will become a heap of
    rubble,
  the temple hill a mound overgrown
    with thickets.

The Mountain of the LORD

4 In the last days

the mountain of the LORD's temple will
    be established
  as chief among the mountains;
it will be raised above the hills,
  and peoples will stream to it.

²Many nations will come and say,

"Come, let us go up to the mountain
    of the LORD,
  to the house of the God of Jacob.
He will teach us his ways,
  so that we may walk in his paths."
The law will go out from Zion,
  the word of the LORD from
    Jerusalem.
³He will judge between many peoples
  and will settle disputes for strong
    nations far and wide.
They will beat their swords into
    plowshares
  and their spears into pruning hooks.
Nation will not take up sword against
    nation,
  nor will they train for war anymore.
⁴Every man will sit under his own vine
  and under his own fig tree,
and no one will make them afraid,
  for the LORD Almighty has spoken.
⁵All the nations may walk

in the name of their gods;
  we will walk in the name of the LORD
  our God for ever and ever.

The LORD's Plan

⁶"In that day," declares the LORD,

"I will gather the lame;
  I will assemble the exiles
  and those I have brought to grief.
⁷I will make the lame a remnant,
  those driven away a strong nation.
The LORD will rule over them in Mount
    Zion
  from that day and forever.
⁸As for you, O watchtower of the flock,
  O stronghold*ᵃ* of the Daughter of
    Zion,
the former dominion will be restored
    to you;
  kingship will come to the Daughter
    of Jerusalem."

⁹Why do you now cry aloud—
  have you no king?
Has your counselor perished,
  that pain seizes you like that of a
    woman in labor?
¹⁰Writhe in agony, O Daughter of Zion,
  like a woman in labor,
for now you must leave the city
  to camp in the open field.
You will go to Babylon;
  there you will be rescued.
There the LORD will redeem you
  out of the hand of your enemies.

¹¹But now many nations
  are gathered against you.
They say, "Let her be defiled,
  let our eyes gloat over Zion!"
¹²But they do not know
  the thoughts of the LORD;
they do not understand his plan,
  he who gathers them like sheaves to
    the threshing floor.

¹³"Rise and thresh, O Daughter of Zion,
  for I will give you horns of iron;
I will give you hoofs of bronze
  and you will break to pieces many
    nations."

You will devote their ill-gotten gains
  to the LORD,

ᵃ8 Or *hill*

their wealth to the Lord of all the
earth.

A Promised Ruler From Bethlehem

5 Marshal your troops, O city of
troops,[a]
for a siege is laid against us.
They will strike Israel's ruler
on the cheek with a rod.

2 "But you, Bethlehem Ephrathah,
though you are small among the
clans[b] of Judah,
out of you will come for me
one who will be ruler over Israel,
whose origins[c] are from of old,
from ancient times.[d]"

Down to the Last Detail

Huh?

Micah 5:2
Here it is, 700 years before Jesus was born,
and God already has Jesus' birthplace picked
out. To get Mary and Joseph to Bethlehem
at the exact time of Jesus' birth meant that
a lot of details had to be worked out. God
has a perfect plan for your life too; you can
count on him to work out every detail.

3 Therefore Israel will be abandoned
until the time when she who is in
labor gives birth
and the rest of his brothers return
to join the Israelites.

4 He will stand and shepherd his flock
in the strength of the LORD,
in the majesty of the name of the
LORD his God.
And they will live securely, for then
his greatness
will reach to the ends of the earth.
5 And he will be their peace.

Deliverance and Destruction

When the Assyrian invades our land
and marches through our
fortresses,
we will raise against him seven
shepherds,

even eight leaders of men.
6 They will rule[e] the land of Assyria
with the sword,
the land of Nimrod with drawn
sword.[f]
He will deliver us from the
Assyrian
when he invades our land
and marches into our borders.

7 The remnant of Jacob will be
in the midst of many peoples
like dew from the LORD,
like showers on the grass,
which do not wait for man
or linger for mankind.
8 The remnant of Jacob will be among
the nations,
in the midst of many peoples,
like a lion among the beasts of the
forest,
like a young lion among flocks of
sheep,
which mauls and mangles as it goes,
and no one can rescue.
9 Your hand will be lifted up in triumph
over your enemies,
and all your foes will be
destroyed.

10 "In that day," declares the LORD,

"I will destroy your horses from
among you
and demolish your chariots.
11 I will destroy the cities of your land
and tear down all your
strongholds.
12 I will destroy your witchcraft
and you will no longer cast spells.
13 I will destroy your carved images
and your sacred stones from among
you;
you will no longer bow down
to the work of your hands.
14 I will uproot from among you your
Asherah poles[g]
and demolish your cities.
15 I will take vengeance in anger and
wrath
upon the nations that have not
obeyed me."

[a]1 Or *Strengthen your walls, O walled city*   [b]2 Or
rulers   [c]2 Hebrew *going out*   [d]2 Or *from days of
eternity*   [e]6 Or *crush*   [f]6 Or *Nimrod in its gates*
[g]14 That is, symbols of the goddess Asherah

The Lord's Case Against Israel

6 Listen to what the Lord says:

"Stand up, plead your case before the
mountains;
let the hills hear what you have to
say.
² Hear, O mountains, the Lord's
accusation;
listen, you everlasting foundations
of the earth.
For the Lord has a case against his
people;
he is lodging a charge against
Israel.

³ "My people, what have I done to you?
How have I burdened you? Answer
me.
⁴ I brought you up out of Egypt

and redeemed you from the land of
slavery.
I sent Moses to lead you,
also Aaron and Miriam.
⁵ My people, remember
what Balak king of Moab counseled
and what Balaam son of Beor
answered.
Remember your journey from Shittim
to Gilgal,
that you may know the righteous
acts of the Lord."

⁶ With what shall I come before the
Lord
and bow down before the exalted
God?
Shall I come before him with burnt
offerings,
with calves a year old?

Mon~~day~~

What God Really Wants

Read Micah 6:6–8

I feel really encouraged when I read this passage. It tells me that God
doesn't expect us to be perfect. What matters to God is that we are really
living for him.

To me the key point of this passage is that it says we should walk
humbly with God. If we really surrender ourselves to God and his will, we
can be the people God wants us to be. We will be just and merciful. And,
most important, we will be obeying God.

The only way I can learn about God's will for my life is by spending time
with him every day. Sometimes I feel too busy to read the Bible or pray, but
that's where humility comes in. Pride makes me think that I can make
decisions all alone, or that I know more than God does about what's best
for me. But when I humble myself before God, I know that nothing else in
my life is as important as God, and I can't do anything without him. The
more time I spend with God, the more I want to live my life for him.

It's good to know that God doesn't expect perfection from me, because
I'm definitely not perfect. All God asks is that I live for him. And I'm really trying to.

Jeff age 15

What about You?

❶ What do you think it means to act justly? To love mercy? To walk
humbly with God? How can you do those things?

❷ Commit yourself to spend one afternoon a month to help neighbors
and friends with some need they are facing.

❸ Ask God to show you ways you can act justly, mercifully and humbly.

Turn to page 1089 for your next devotion.

⁷Will the LORD be pleased with
    thousands of rams,
  with ten thousand rivers of oil?
Shall I offer my firstborn for my
    transgression,
  the fruit of my body for the sin of
    my soul?
⁸He has showed you, O man, what is
    good.
  And what does the LORD require of
    you?
To act justly and to love mercy
  and to walk humbly with your God.

Calves & Rams & Lambs, Oh My!

Micah 6:6–8

How do you figure out what makes God
happy? Before Jesus was born, people used
to offer gifts to God as a way to be forgiven
from their sins. The kinds of things they offered to him included calves, lambs, rams
and bottles of oil. Micah says that the way
to get God's attention is not to come with
all kinds of gifts but to please him with how
they live their lives.

Israel's Guilt and Punishment

⁹Listen! The LORD is calling to the city—
  and to fear your name is wisdom—
  "Heed the rod and the One who
    appointed it.ᵃ
¹⁰Am I still to forget, O wicked house,
  your ill-gotten treasures
  and the short ephah,ᵇ which is
    accursed?
¹¹Shall I acquit a man with dishonest
    scales,
  with a bag of false weights?
¹²Her rich men are violent;
  her people are liars
  and their tongues speak deceitfully.
¹³Therefore, I have begun to destroy
    you,
  to ruin you because of your sins.
¹⁴You will eat but not be satisfied;
  your stomach will still be empty.ᶜ
You will store up but save nothing,
  because what you save I will give to
    the sword.

¹⁵You will plant but not harvest;
  you will press olives but not use the
    oil on yourselves,
  you will crush grapes but not drink
    the wine.
¹⁶You have observed the statutes of
    Omri
  and all the practices of Ahab's
    house,
  and you have followed their
    traditions.
Therefore I will give you over to ruin
  and your people to derision;
  you will bear the scorn of the
    nations.ᵈ"

Israel's Misery

7 What misery is mine!
I am like one who gathers summer
    fruit
  at the gleaning of the vineyard;
there is no cluster of grapes to eat,
  none of the early figs that I crave.
²The godly have been swept from the
    land;
  not one upright man remains.
All men lie in wait to shed blood;
  each hunts his brother with a net.
³Both hands are skilled in doing evil;
  the ruler demands gifts,
  the judge accepts bribes,
  the powerful dictate what they
    desire—
  they all conspire together.
⁴The best of them is like a brier,
  the most upright worse than a thorn
    hedge.
The day of your watchmen has come,
  the day God visits you.
Now is the time of their confusion.
⁵Do not trust a neighbor;
  put no confidence in a friend.
Even with her who lies in your
    embrace
  be careful of your words.
⁶For a son dishonors his father,
  a daughter rises up against her
    mother,
  a daughter-in-law against her mother-
    in-law—

ᵃ9 The meaning of the Hebrew for this line is
uncertain.   ᵇ10 An ephah was a dry measure.
ᶜ14 The meaning of the Hebrew for this word is
uncertain.   ᵈ16 Septuagint; Hebrew *scorn due my
people*

a man's enemies are the members of
his own household.

⁷But as for me, I watch in hope for the
LORD,
I wait for God my Savior;
my God will hear me.

Israel Will Rise

⁸Do not gloat over me, my enemy!
Though I have fallen, I will rise.
Though I sit in darkness,
the LORD will be my light.
⁹Because I have sinned against him,
I will bear the LORD's wrath,
until he pleads my case
and establishes my right.
He will bring me out into the light;
I will see his righteousness.
¹⁰Then my enemy will see it
and will be covered with shame,
she who said to me,

"Where is the LORD your God?"
My eyes will see her downfall;
even now she will be trampled
underfoot
like mire in the streets.

¹¹The day for building your walls will
come,
the day for extending your
boundaries.
¹²In that day people will come to you
from Assyria and the cities of Egypt,
even from Egypt to the Euphrates
and from sea to sea
and from mountain to mountain.
¹³The earth will become desolate
because of its inhabitants,
as the result of their deeds.

Prayer and Praise

¹⁴Shepherd your people with your staff,
the flock of your inheritance,

Tuesday

Off a Cliff

Read Micah 7:18–19

This passage helps me remember that God is a God of mercy. He will always forgive me for any sin I commit. This passage comforts me when I sin, because I know God won't hold a grudge against me. He always has compassion on me when I ask for forgiveness. When I read these verses in Micah, I get a mental picture of God pushing my sins off a cliff where they'll never be seen again. What a great God!

God doesn't want anyone to sin, but he knows we will. He provided a way for us to have complete forgiveness through his Son Jesus. And he not only gives us a way out, he's also excited about forgiving us. The Bible says he *delights* in showing us mercy.

If you're like me and you sometimes wonder if God can really forgive you, remember that God will *always* forgive us when we are sincerely sorry for what we've done and believe that Jesus took our sins away when he died on the cross and rose from the dead.

Merry age 13

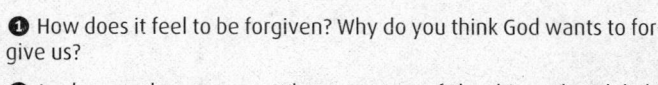

What about You?

❶ How does it feel to be forgiven? Why do you think God wants to forgive us?

❷ Look around your room. What are some of the things that delight you—you know, that really make you happy? Next time you ask for forgiveness, think of that feeling of delight; it's just a tiny glimpse of the delight God feels when he shows mercy toward you.

❸ Thank God for his never-ending forgiveness.

Turn to page 1093 for your next devotion.

which lives by itself in a forest,
in fertile pasturelands.[a]
Let them feed in Bashan and Gilead
as in days long ago.

[15] "As in the days when you came out of Egypt,
I will show them my wonders."

[16] Nations will see and be ashamed,
deprived of all their power.
They will lay their hands on their mouths
and their ears will become deaf.
[17] They will lick dust like a snake,
like creatures that crawl on the ground.
They will come trembling out of their dens;
they will turn in fear to the Lord our God

and will be afraid of you.
[18] Who is a God like you,
who pardons sin and forgives the transgression
of the remnant of his inheritance?
You do not stay angry forever
but delight to show mercy.
[19] You will again have compassion on us;
you will tread our sins underfoot
and hurl all our iniquities into the depths of the sea.
[20] You will be true to Jacob,
and show mercy to Abraham,
as you pledged on oath to our fathers
in days long ago.

*a*14 Or *in the middle of Carmel*

Nahum

START

The only thing worse than a bully is a bully who never gets caught. He thinks he's so cool, picking on people younger or smaller than himself. It seems like the more he gets away with, the meaner he becomes.

When the prophet Nahum was speaking for God, the nation of Assyria with its huge capital city of Nineveh was the bully nation in that part of the world. Its people were cruel and heartless, destroying lives wherever they went. God had put up with this bully city long enough. He had already sent Jonah to warn these people, and for a little while they had improved. But now they were back to their mean old ways. It was time for God to even the score.

Nahum predicts that Nineveh will be destroyed forever. Look on any map. You won't find Nineveh, because God followed through on his promise. And just a few years after Nahum spoke, Nineveh was bully history.

Cast OF Characters

Nahum (NAY-hum)
We don't know much about Nahum, except that his name means "comfort," which he certainly wasn't for the Assyrians.

The Assyrians
(uh-SEAR-ee-uns)
A nation that was bad to the bone. Their leaders were cruel and their armies were bloodthirsty. They had been especially mean to God's people.

What's UP with That?

Nahum (with God's help) predicted that Nineveh would soon be destroyed.

The people must have laughed because:

- the walls around the city were up to 100 feet tall.

- those walls were so wide that 4 chariots could drive side by side on top of them.

- the city was surrounded by a moat 100 feet wide and 60 feet deep—no word on crocodiles.

- the palaces were guarded by the best trained and equipped soldiers of that day.

- tall towers around the whole city allowed lookouts to see for miles.

Snap shots

- Here comes the judge (chapter 1)

- Guilty on all counts (chapters 2:1—3:4)

- It's all over except for the crying (chapter 3:5–19)

INCREDIBLY the city was flooded and

burned in a series of disasters soon after Nahum made his prediction. Archaeologists finally found the buried leftovers of the city in 1845 and proved that all the things God said would happen to this proud, evil city did, in fact, happen.

1 An oracle concerning Nineveh. The book of the vision of Nahum the Elkoshite.

The Lord's Anger Against Nineveh

²The Lord is a jealous and avenging
 God;
  the Lord takes vengeance and is
   filled with wrath.
The Lord takes vengeance on his
  foes
 and maintains his wrath against his
  enemies.
³The Lord is slow to anger and great in
  power;
  the Lord will not leave the guilty
   unpunished.
His way is in the whirlwind and the
  storm,
 and clouds are the dust of his feet.

⁴He rebukes the sea and dries it up;
  he makes all the rivers run dry.
Bashan and Carmel wither
  and the blossoms of Lebanon fade.
⁵The mountains quake before him
  and the hills melt away.
The earth trembles at his presence,
  the world and all who live in it.
⁶Who can withstand his
    indignation?
  Who can endure his fierce anger?
His wrath is poured out like fire;
  the rocks are shattered before him.

⁷The Lord is good,
  a refuge in times of trouble.
He cares for those who trust in him,
⁸ but with an overwhelming flood
he will make an end of Nineveh;
  he will pursue his foes into
   darkness.

Wednesday

Why, God?

Read Nahum 1:7–8

I'm old enough to know that bad things happen to good people. But when I found out my grandfather had cancer, I couldn't understand what God was doing. My grandfather had lived a good life, and he had never smoked or done harmful things to his body. Now he goes to the doctor all the time for radiation treatment, and he feels so sick sometimes he can hardly move.

In the verses for today, Nahum explains that God is just, no matter what we think about him. Everything is in his hands, and nothing gets by him. That's hard for me to handle at times, because my grandfather's cancer doesn't seem fair. It seems like bad things should happen to bad people, and good things to good people. If I didn't know better, I would want to blame God for my grandfather's sickness. But my grandfather himself doesn't do that. He hasn't given up, and he's stayed strong. More than that, he's put his trust in God to take care of him. That helps me to see that even in hard situations we can't explain, God is always with us.

 Colleen age 14

 **What about You?**

❶ How do today's verses help you make sense out of situations you don't understand?

❷ Pick up a major newspaper. Look through the articles and reports on the front page, thinking about the people involved. So many bad things happen every day! Why is it important to trust that God is just, no matter what?

❸ Thank God for caring about you. Ask him to watch over those you love.

Turn to page 1099 for your next devotion.

[9] Whatever they plot against the LORD
he[a] will bring to an end;
trouble will not come a second time.
[10] They will be entangled among thorns
and drunk from their wine;
they will be consumed like dry
stubble.[b]
[11] From you, O Nineveh, has one come
forth
who plots evil against the LORD
and counsels wickedness.

[12] This is what the LORD says:

"Although they have allies and are
numerous,
they will be cut off and pass away.
Although I have afflicted you,
O Judah,
I will afflict you no more.
[13] Now I will break their yoke from your
neck
and tear your shackles away."

[14] The LORD has given a command
concerning you, Nineveh:
"You will have no descendants to
bear your name.
I will destroy the carved images and
cast idols
that are in the temple of your gods.
I will prepare your grave,
for you are vile."

[15] Look, there on the mountains,
the feet of one who brings good
news,
who proclaims peace!
Celebrate your festivals, O Judah,
and fulfill your vows.
No more will the wicked invade you;
they will be completely destroyed.

Nineveh to Fall

2 An attacker advances against you,
Nineveh.
Guard the fortress,
watch the road,
brace yourselves,
marshal all your strength!

[2] The LORD will restore the splendor of
Jacob
like the splendor of Israel,
though destroyers have laid them
waste
and have ruined their vines.

[3] The shields of his soldiers are red;
the warriors are clad in scarlet.
The metal on the chariots flashes
on the day they are made ready;
the spears of pine are brandished.[c]
[4] The chariots storm through the streets,
rushing back and forth through the
squares.
They look like flaming torches;
they dart about like lightning.

[5] He summons his picked troops,
yet they stumble on their way.
They dash to the city wall;
the protective shield is put in place.
[6] The river gates are thrown open
and the palace collapses.

I Told You So

Huh?

Nahum 2:6
Nineveh stood on the banks of the mighty
Tigris River, and the city walls were thick
and high. People must have been amazed
when a few years after Micah predicted the
details, a flood poured through the city and
opened it up to attack from enemy armies.
It happened just like God said it would.

[7] It is decreed[d] that the city
be exiled and carried away.
Its slave girls moan like doves
and beat upon their breasts.
[8] Nineveh is like a pool,
and its water is draining away.
"Stop! Stop!" they cry,
but no one turns back.
[9] Plunder the silver!
Plunder the gold!
The supply is endless,
the wealth from all its treasures!
[10] She is pillaged, plundered, stripped!
Hearts melt, knees give way,
bodies tremble, every face grows
pale.

[a]9 Or *What do you foes plot against the LORD? / He*
[b]10 The meaning of the Hebrew for this verse is
uncertain.   [c]3 Hebrew; Septuagint and Syriac / *the
horsemen rush to and fro*   [d]7 The meaning of the
Hebrew for this word is uncertain.

¹¹Where now is the lions' den,
    the place where they fed their
        young,
where the lion and lioness went,
    and the cubs, with nothing to fear?
¹²The lion killed enough for his cubs
    and strangled the prey for his mate,
filling his lairs with the kill
    and his dens with the prey.

¹³"I am against you,"
    declares the LORD Almighty.
"I will burn up your chariots in
        smoke,
    and the sword will devour your
        young lions.
I will leave you no prey on the
        earth.
The voices of your messengers
    will no longer be heard."

Woe to Nineveh

3 Woe to the city of blood,
    full of lies,
full of plunder,
    never without victims!
²The crack of whips,
    the clatter of wheels,
galloping horses
    and jolting chariots!
³Charging cavalry,
    flashing swords
    and glittering spears!
Many casualties,
    piles of dead,
bodies without number,
    people stumbling over the corpses—
⁴all because of the wanton lust of a
        harlot,
    alluring, the mistress of sorceries,
who enslaved nations by her
        prostitution
    and peoples by her witchcraft.

⁵"I am against you," declares the LORD
        Almighty.
    "I will lift your skirts over your
        face.
I will show the nations your
        nakedness
    and the kingdoms your shame.
⁶I will pelt you with filth,
    I will treat you with contempt
    and make you a spectacle.
⁷All who see you will flee from you
    and say,

'Nineveh is in ruins—who will
        mourn for her?'
    Where can I find anyone to comfort
        you?"

⁸Are you better than Thebes,^a
    situated on the Nile,
    with water around her?
The river was her defense,
    the waters her wall.
⁹Cush^b and Egypt were her boundless
        strength;
    Put and Libya were among her
        allies.
¹⁰Yet she was taken captive
    and went into exile.
Her infants were dashed to pieces
    at the head of every street.
Lots were cast for her nobles,
    and all her great men were put in
        chains.
¹¹You too will become drunk;
    you will go into hiding
    and seek refuge from the enemy.

¹²All your fortresses are like fig trees
    with their first ripe fruit;
when they are shaken,
    the figs fall into the mouth of the
        eater.
¹³Look at your troops—
    they are all women!
The gates of your land
    are wide open to your enemies;
    fire has consumed their bars.

¹⁴Draw water for the siege,
    strengthen your defenses!
Work the clay,
    tread the mortar,
    repair the brickwork!
¹⁵There the fire will devour you;
    the sword will cut you down
and, like grasshoppers, consume
        you.
Multiply like grasshoppers,
    multiply like locusts!
¹⁶You have increased the number of
        your merchants
    till they are more than the stars of
        the sky,
but like locusts they strip the land
    and then fly away.

^a8 Hebrew *No Amon* ^b9 That is, the upper Nile
region

¹⁷Your guards are like locusts,
   your officials like swarms of
      locusts
   that settle in the walls on a cold
      day—
but when the sun appears they fly
      away,
   and no one knows where.

¹⁸O king of Assyria, your shepherds*a*
      slumber;
   your nobles lie down to rest.

Your people are scattered on the
      mountains
   with no one to gather them.
¹⁹Nothing can heal your wound;
   your injury is fatal.
Everyone who hears the news about
      you
   claps his hands at your fall,
for who has not felt
   your endless cruelty?

a18 Or rulers

Habakkuk

START

Do you ever feel like your parents and teachers only notice when you blow it? No matter how hard you try to be good, they just don't see it. You feel like you're getting punished all the time, and—even worse—the people who couldn't care less about how they live seem to get away with everything!

Habakkuk felt that way. He saw good people suffering and evil people succeeding. Instead of getting angry, Habakkuk asks God if he would mind explaining this.

God isn't uncomfortable with Habakkuk's tough questions. In fact, God answers those questions in a way that helps Habakkuk trust him more deeply than ever.

Cast OF Characters

Habakkuk
(Huh-BACK-uk)
He wrote the book. And he's honest enough with God to ask some really tough questions. No one knows for sure what his name means, but it may mean "to hold on," which is what he does—even when he doesn't completely understand what God is doing.

(Bab-uh-LO-nee-uns)

Babylonians
The people who lived in Babylonia. Just have a look at how they're described in chapter 1. These are not nice people!

God
He gets about half the lines in this little question-and-answer drama. Isn't it great to know that God can handle our doubts and confusion?

What's UP with That?

Do you ever have questions for God?
Don't be afraid to talk to him about things
you don't understand.

Take a few minutes to finish some of these
sentence prayers with your own words.

Dear God,
why do my friends . . . ?

Dear God, something I wish
I could understand
about my family is . . . .

Dear God, I know you created
me the way I am,
but when I look in the mirror . . . .

Dear God, how long will you
keep letting _____
get away with . . . ?

Dear God, I want to trust you
even when I don't fully understand what you're doing.

Snap shots

● Habakkuk: "Will you
let your people get
away with this?"
(chapter 1:1-4)

● God: "Don't worry—
the Babylonians will
kick their patooties"
(chapter 1:5-11)

● Habakkuk: "Speaking
of the Babylonians . . .
what about them?"
(chapter 1:12-17)

● God: "Don't worry—
they'll lose big-time in
the end" *(chapter 2)*

● Habakkuk:
"Thanks. That helps
me understand"
(chapter 3)

1 The oracle that Habakkuk the prophet received.

Habakkuk's Complaint

² How long, O LORD, must I call for
    help,
  but you do not listen?
 Or cry out to you, "Violence!"
  but you do not save?
³ Why do you make me look at
    injustice?
  Why do you tolerate wrong?
 Destruction and violence are before me;
  there is strife, and conflict abounds.
⁴ Therefore the law is paralyzed,
  and justice never prevails.
 The wicked hem in the righteous,
  so that justice is perverted.

The LORD's Answer

⁵ "Look at the nations and watch—
  and be utterly amazed.
 For I am going to do something in
    your days

 that you would not believe,
  even if you were told.
⁶ I am raising up the Babylonians,ᵃ
  that ruthless and impetuous people,
 who sweep across the whole earth
  to seize dwelling places not their
    own.
⁷ They are a feared and dreaded people;
  they are a law to themselves
  and promote their own honor.
⁸ Their horses are swifter than leopards,
  fiercer than wolves at dusk.
 Their cavalry gallops headlong;
  their horsemen come from afar.
 They fly like a vulture swooping to
    devour;
⁹ they all come bent on violence.
 Their hordesᵇ advance like a desert
    wind
  and gather prisoners like sand.
¹⁰ They deride kings

ᵃ6 Or *Chaldeans* ᵇ9 The meaning of the Hebrew for
this word is uncertain.

Thursday

Tough Situations
Read Habakkuk 1:13

So many bad things happen to Christians all over the world, and it seems
like God keeps silent. Sometimes at church we hear about countries where
Christians get thrown in jail just because they're Christians. And then we
hear about people in our own church who have trouble with mean neighbors or become crime victims. Even in my own life there have been times
when I've asked God, "Why is this happening to me?"

 But even though these bad situations are really hard, they have a purpose. My pastor says they're a test of our faithfulness and trust. God allows
these tests so we'll see how much we need to cling to Jesus. God knows that
our faith won't get very deep if our lives are always easy. So the things that
make us ask God what he's doing actually bring us closer to him. It's a hard
way to learn a lesson, but it's all part of God's perfect plan.

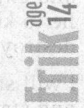
Erik 14

❶ What are some times you've asked God, "Why me?" How did he answer you?

❷ Talk to an elderly person in your extended family or in your church
about some of the hard times they've lived through. As they tell their
stories, ask what they learned from each experience.

❸ Ask God to help you trust him, even when life is hard.

Turn to page 1102 for your next devotion.

and scoff at rulers.
They laugh at all fortified cities;
   they build earthen ramps and
     capture them.
[11] Then they sweep past like the wind
   and go on—
   guilty men, whose own strength is
     their god."

Habakkuk's Second Complaint

[12] O LORD, are you not from everlasting?
   My God, my Holy One, we will not
     die.
O LORD, you have appointed them to
     execute judgment;
   O Rock, you have ordained them to
     punish.
[13] Your eyes are too pure to look on evil;
   you cannot tolerate wrong.
Why then do you tolerate the
     treacherous?
   Why are you silent while the wicked
     swallow up those more righteous
     than themselves?
[14] You have made men like fish in the
     sea,
   like sea creatures that have no ruler.
[15] The wicked foe pulls all of them up
     with hooks,
   he catches them in his net,
he gathers them up in his dragnet;
   and so he rejoices and is glad.
[16] Therefore he sacrifices to his net
   and burns incense to his dragnet,
for by his net he lives in luxury
   and enjoys the choicest food.
[17] Is he to keep on emptying his net,
   destroying nations without mercy?

2 I will stand at my watch
   and station myself on the ramparts;
I will look to see what he will say to
     me,
   and what answer I am to give to
     this complaint.[a]

The LORD's Answer

[2] Then the LORD replied:

"Write down the revelation
   and make it plain on tablets
   so that a herald[b] may run with it.
[3] For the revelation awaits an appointed
     time;
   it speaks of the end
   and will not prove false.

Though it linger, wait for it;
   it[c] will certainly come and will not
     delay.

[4] "See, he is puffed up;
   his desires are not upright—
   but the righteous will live by his
     faith[d]—
[5] indeed, wine betrays him;
   he is arrogant and never at rest.
Because he is as greedy as the grave[e]
   and like death is never satisfied,
he gathers to himself all the nations
   and takes captive all the peoples.

[6] "Will not all of them taunt him with
ridicule and scorn, saying,

" 'Woe to him who piles up stolen
     goods
   and makes himself wealthy by
     extortion!
   How long must this go on?'
[7] Will not your debtors[f] suddenly arise?
   Will they not wake up and make
     you tremble?
   Then you will become their victim.
[8] Because you have plundered many
     nations,
   the peoples who are left will
     plunder you.
For you have shed man's blood;
   you have destroyed lands and cities
     and everyone in them.

[9] "Woe to him who builds his realm by
     unjust gain
   to set his nest on high,
   to escape the clutches of ruin!
[10] You have plotted the ruin of many
     peoples,
   shaming your own house and
     forfeiting your life.
[11] The stones of the wall will cry out,
   and the beams of the woodwork
     will echo it.

[12] "Woe to him who builds a city with
     bloodshed
   and establishes a town by crime!
[13] Has not the LORD Almighty
     determined

---

[a]1 Or *and what to answer when I am rebuked*   [b]2 Or
so that whoever reads it   [c]3 Or *Though he linger,
wait for him; / he*   [d]4 Or *faithfulness*   [e]5 Hebrew
Sheol   [f]7 Or *creditors*

that the people's labor is only fuel
  for the fire,
that the nations exhaust themselves
  for nothing?
¹⁴For the earth will be filled with the
    knowledge of the glory of the
    LORD,
  as the waters cover the sea.

¹⁵"Woe to him who gives drink to his
    neighbors,
  pouring it from the wineskin till
    they are drunk,
  so that he can gaze on their naked
    bodies.
¹⁶You will be filled with shame instead
    of glory.
  Now it is your turn! Drink and be
    exposed*!
The cup from the LORD's right hand is
    coming around to you,
  and disgrace will cover your glory.
¹⁷The violence you have done to
    Lebanon will overwhelm you,
  and your destruction of animals will
    terrify you.
For you have shed man's blood;
  you have destroyed lands and cities
    and everyone in them.

¹⁸"Of what value is an idol, since a man
    has carved it?
  Or an image that teaches lies?
For he who makes it trusts in his own
    creation;
  he makes idols that cannot speak.
¹⁹Woe to him who says to wood, 'Come
    to life!'

Or to lifeless stone, 'Wake up!'
Can it give guidance?
  It is covered with gold and silver;
    there is no breath in it.
²⁰But the LORD is in his holy temple;
  let all the earth be silent before
    him."

Habakkuk's Prayer

3 A prayer of Habakkuk the prophet.
  On *shigionoth.*ᵇ

²LORD, I have heard of your fame;
  I stand in awe of your deeds,
    O LORD.
Renew them in our day,
  in our time make them known;
  in wrath remember mercy.

³God came from Teman,
  the Holy One from Mount Paran.
                    *Selah*ᶜ
His glory covered the heavens
  and his praise filled the earth.
⁴His splendor was like the sunrise;
  rays flashed from his hand,
  where his power was hidden.
⁵Plague went before him;
  pestilence followed his steps.
⁶He stood, and shook the earth;
  he looked, and made the nations
    tremble.
The ancient mountains crumbled
  and the age-old hills collapsed.
  His ways are eternal.
⁷I saw the tents of Cushan in distress,
  the dwellings of Midian in anguish.

⁸Were you angry with the rivers,
    O LORD?
  Was your wrath against the
    streams?
Did you rage against the sea
  when you rode with your horses
  and your victorious chariots?
⁹You uncovered your bow,
  you called for many arrows.   *Selah*
You split the earth with rivers;
¹⁰   the mountains saw you and
    writhed.
Torrents of water swept by;

Wooden Ears

Habakkuk 2:18

Can a carved piece of wood or chiseled rock
answer your prayers? Will the ears you
carve actually hear you, or the eyes you
paint onto a face actually see you? Not a
chance. God created the trees and rocks
that these phony gods are made of. He,
and no one or nothing else, will hear your
prayers.

ᵃ*16* Masoretic Text; Dead Sea Scrolls, Aquila,
Vulgate and Syriac (see also Septuagint) *and stagger*
ᵇ*1* Probably a literary or musical term   ᶜ*3* A word of
uncertain meaning; possibly a musical term; also in
verses 9 and 13

the deep roared
and lifted its waves on high.

¹¹ Sun and moon stood still in the
heavens
at the glint of your flying arrows,
at the lightning of your flashing
spear.
¹² In wrath you strode through the
earth
and in anger you threshed the
nations.
¹³ You came out to deliver your
people,
to save your anointed one.
You crushed the leader of the land of
wickedness,
you stripped him from head to foot.
Selah
¹⁴ With his own spear you pierced his
head
when his warriors stormed out to
scatter us,
gloating as though about to devour
the wretched who were in hiding.

¹⁵ You trampled the sea with your
horses,
churning the great waters.

¹⁶ I heard and my heart pounded,
my lips quivered at the
sound;
decay crept into my bones,
and my legs trembled.

Whatever Happens

Habakkuk 3:17–18
It's not good enough to worship God only
when things are going well. There's no
doubt that it's easier, but Habakkuk says
that he will trust God even when things are
tough. Whatever happens, he says, God is
trustworthy. No grapes, no sheep—no
problem.

Friday

Those Bad Days

Read Habakkuk 3:17–19

My life hasn't been easy. One of my parents died, and I have had a lot of bad
days since then. People try to help me feel better, but it doesn't always
work. Sometimes I feel completely alone, with no one to talk to. But even in
those bad times, I know God is there for me.

I guess it's normal to get down sometimes. And it's normal to feel like
your life is a big mess, especially when something awful happens. That's
why God wants us to know we can count on him even when it seems like
the whole world is against us.

No matter how down we feel, no matter how bad life seems, God is there.
He has seen me through some really tough times, and I know he will do the
same for anyone who asks for his help.

Brian age 14

❶ Think about a time you felt like nothing was going right. How did you
feel about God during this time?

❷ Write down some things that are really good about your life. The
next time you feel down, take a look at that list and thank God for
those good things.

❸ Ask God to help you find joy in him, even in tough times.

Turn to page 1107 for your next devotion.

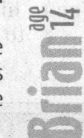

Yet I will wait patiently for the day of
calamity
to come on the nation invading us.
¹⁷Though the fig tree does not bud
and there are no grapes on the
vines,
though the olive crop fails
and the fields produce no food,
though there are no sheep in the pen
and no cattle in the stalls,

¹⁸yet I will rejoice in the LORD,
I will be joyful in God my Savior.

¹⁹The Sovereign LORD is my strength;
he makes my feet like the feet of a
deer,
he enables me to go on the
heights.

For the director of music. On my
stringed instruments.

Zephaniah

START

Here's what the nation of Judah was like before Zephaniah showed up on the scene: The times were good. Businesspeople were making good money, then putting their earnings into new houses, so there was a lot of construction going on. Homeowners built bigger vineyards and farms too, creating jobs for just about everybody.

Meanwhile, they believed in God, sure. But they didn't believe they should get bent out of shape over whether God actually *did* anything anymore. (They were pretty sure he didn't.) But that's not quite the whole story either.

In the middle of their cash bonanza and their who-cares attitude about God, these same folks sacrificed their children to Molech, the fire god. Ritual prostitution as an act of worship was common, as was the worship of sun, moon, planets and stars. City officials were filling their pockets with bribes. Not pretty. Downright evil, in fact.

Enter Zeph. "You're dead meat," he says for openers to the lunchtime crowd in the middle of the mall. "The day of the Lord is just around the corner, and you're the targets."

Believe it or not, something clicked. Thanks in part to Zeph's preaching, the young king of Judah (Josiah) triggered a spiritual and moral turnaround, something the people of Judah hadn't seen in a generation. (Read more about that one in 2 Kings 22—23.)

CAST OF Characters

Zephaniah

Yeah, well, he kind of has the book to himself. Zeph was—get this—the great-great grandson of King Hezekiah of Judah. Kind of like a direct descendant of Abraham Lincoln popping up one day on "Good Morning, America." Hey, Jason Lincoln, a new celebrity!—but one with big bad news for his country.

(zeh-fuh-NIE-uh)

What's UP with That?

Toasty Nations

Several nations are mentioned in Zeph's book.
Match the city with its description.

1. Their land will be reduced to sheep pens.

2. This place will become a place of weeds and salt pits.

3. The concrete skateboard park in this city will be jackhammered to pieces.

4. Here comes the sword!

5. Screech owls will live in the ruins of its cities.

6. God will take great delight in this city's people and will quiet them with his love.

7. Merchants in this city will be wiped out.

A. Cush

B. Philistia

C. Brainerd, Minnesota

D. Jerusalem

E. Assyria

F. Moab & Ammon

G. none of the above

answers: 1-b, 2-f, 3-g, 4-a, 5-e, 6-d

Snap shots

- Judah is toast! (chapter 1 and chapter 2:1–3)

- And you neighboring nations of Judah, you're next! (chapter 2:4–15)

- Yes, Jerusalem is bad— but better days are coming (chapter 3)

1

The word of the LORD that came to Zephaniah son of Cushi, the son of Gedaliah, the son of Amariah, the son of Hezekiah, during the reign of Josiah son of Amon king of Judah:

Warning of Coming Destruction

² "I will sweep away everything
  from the face of the earth,"
                    declares the LORD.
³ "I will sweep away both men and
    animals;
  I will sweep away the birds of the
    air
  and the fish of the sea.
The wicked will have only heaps of
    rubble*a*
  when I cut off man from the face of
    the earth,"
                    declares the LORD.

Against Judah

⁴ "I will stretch out my hand against
    Judah
  and against all who live in
    Jerusalem.
I will cut off from this place every
    remnant of Baal,
  the names of the pagan and the
    idolatrous priests—
⁵ those who bow down on the roofs
  to worship the starry host,
  those who bow down and swear by
    the LORD
  and who also swear by Molech,*b*
⁶ those who turn back from following
    the LORD
  and neither seek the LORD nor
    inquire of him.

⁷ Be silent before the Sovereign
    LORD,
  for the day of the LORD is near.
The LORD has prepared a sacrifice;
  he has consecrated those he has
    invited.
⁸ On the day of the LORD's sacrifice
  I will punish the princes
  and the king's sons
and all those clad
  in foreign clothes.
⁹ On that day I will punish
  all who avoid stepping on the
    threshold,*c*
who fill the temple of their gods
  with violence and deceit.

¹⁰ "On that day," declares the LORD,
  "a cry will go up from the Fish
    Gate,
  wailing from the New Quarter,
  and a loud crash from the hills.
¹¹ Wail, you who live in the market
    district*d*;
  all your merchants will be wiped
    out,
  all who trade with*e* silver will be
    ruined.
¹² At that time I will search Jerusalem
    with lamps
  and punish those who are
    complacent,
  who are like wine left on its dregs,
who think, 'The LORD will do nothing,
  either good or bad.'
¹³ Their wealth will be plundered,
  their houses demolished.
They will build houses
  but not live in them;
they will plant vineyards
  but not drink the wine.

The Great Day of the LORD

¹⁴ "The great day of the LORD is near—
  near and coming quickly.
Listen! The cry on the day of the LORD
  will be bitter,
  the shouting of the warrior there.
¹⁵ That day will be a day of wrath,
  a day of distress and anguish,
a day of trouble and ruin,
  a day of darkness and gloom,
  a day of clouds and blackness,
¹⁶ a day of trumpet and battle cry
  against the fortified cities
  and against the corner towers.
¹⁷ I will bring distress on the people
  and they will walk like blind men,
  because they have sinned against
    the LORD.
Their blood will be poured out like
    dust
  and their entrails like filth.
¹⁸ Neither their silver nor their gold
  will be able to save them
  on the day of the LORD's wrath.
In the fire of his jealousy
  the whole world will be consumed,

---

a3 The meaning of the Hebrew for this line is
uncertain. *b5* Hebrew *Malcam,* that is, Milcom
c9 See 1 Samuel 5:5. *d11* Or *the Mortar* *e11* Or *in*

for he will make a sudden end
  of all who live in the earth."

2 Gather together, gather together,
  O shameful nation,
² before the appointed time arrives
  and that day sweeps on like
    chaff,
before the fierce anger of the LORD
    comes upon you,
before the day of the LORD's wrath
    comes upon you.
³ Seek the LORD, all you humble of the
    land,
  you who do what he commands.
Seek righteousness, seek humility;
  perhaps you will be sheltered
  on the day of the LORD's anger.

Against Philistia

⁴ Gaza will be abandoned
  and Ashkelon left in ruins.
At midday Ashdod will be emptied
  and Ekron uprooted.
⁵ Woe to you who live by the sea,
  O Kerethite people;
the word of the LORD is against you,
  O Canaan, land of the Philistines.

"I will destroy you,
  and none will be left."

⁶ The land by the sea, where the
  Kerethites[a] dwell,

ᵃ6 The meaning of the Hebrew for this word is uncertain.

Week end.

Is He There?

Read Job 23:1–10 (page 601)

On Wednesday, Thursday and Friday of this week, Colleen, Erik and Brian basically raised the same question: "Where *is* God when we need him?" It's a question you might ask in lots of different ways. *Why doesn't God show up when I'm hurting? Why doesn't God rescue me from trouble or help me get rid of my pain? If God is always with me then why do I feel lonely?*

Job admits that if he could find God, he knows God would be sympathetic to his plight. The trouble is he can't find him. Colleen, Erik, Brian, and all of us are in good company when we ask these questions.

Now here's the good/weird part. Colleen says, "I would want to blame God for my grandfather's sickness. But my grandfather himself doesn't do that." Erik says, " . . . the things that make us ask God what he's doing actually bring us closer to him." And Brian says, "No matter how down we feel, no matter how bad life seems, God is there." They're all saying the same thing Job ended up saying: "I don't know *where* God is or *what God is doing.* All I know is that *God is!*" It's important for us to remember, when we don't "feel" like God is close by that he's still in control. Our faith in him, in his existence, in his goodness, can give us strength to carry on.

❶ Think of a time you experienced God giving you strength even when you didn't "feel" like he was there.

❷ Try this. Sit down in your room alone. Stay silent for a few minutes. Think of God being present in the room with you. Take a piece of paper and begin writing what you think God is saying to you right now. See what happens.

❸ Ask God to help you notice his presence in your life.

Turn to page 1109 for your next devotion.

will be a place for shepherds and
sheep pens.
⁷ It will belong to the remnant of the
house of Judah;
there they will find pasture.
In the evening they will lie down
in the houses of Ashkelon.
The LORD their God will care for them;
he will restore their fortunes.ᵃ

Against Moab and Ammon

⁸ "I have heard the insults of Moab
and the taunts of the Ammonites,
who insulted my people
and made threats against their land.
⁹ Therefore, as surely as I live,"
declares the LORD Almighty, the God
of Israel,
"surely Moab will become like Sodom,
the Ammonites like Gomorrah—
a place of weeds and salt pits,
a wasteland forever.
The remnant of my people will
plunder them;
the survivors of my nation will
inherit their land."

¹⁰ This is what they will get in return for
their pride,
for insulting and mocking the
people of the LORD Almighty.
¹¹ The LORD will be awesome to them
when he destroys all the gods of the
land.
The nations on every shore will
worship him,
every one in its own land.

Against Cush

¹² "You too, O Cushites,ᵇ
will be slain by my sword."

Against Assyria

¹³ He will stretch out his hand against
the north
and destroy Assyria,
leaving Nineveh utterly desolate
and dry as the desert.
¹⁴ Flocks and herds will lie down there,
creatures of every kind.
The desert owl and the screech owl
will roost on her columns.
Their calls will echo through the
windows,
rubble will be in the doorways,

the beams of cedar will be exposed.
¹⁵ This is the carefree city
that lived in safety.
She said to herself,
"I am, and there is none besides me."
What a ruin she has become,
a lair for wild beasts!
All who pass by her scoff
and shake their fists.

The Future of Jerusalem

3 Woe to the city of oppressors,
rebellious and defiled!
² She obeys no one,
she accepts no correction.
She does not trust in the LORD,
she does not draw near to her God.
³ Her officials are roaring lions,
her rulers are evening wolves,
who leave nothing for the morning.
⁴ Her prophets are arrogant;
they are treacherous men.
Her priests profane the sanctuary
and do violence to the law.
⁵ The LORD within her is righteous;
he does no wrong.
Morning by morning he dispenses his
justice,
and every new day he does not fail,
yet the unrighteous know no shame.

⁶ "I have cut off nations;
their strongholds are demolished.
I have left their streets deserted,

ᵃ7 Or *will bring back their captives*   ᵇ12 That is,
people from the upper Nile region

with no one passing through.
Their cities are destroyed;
  no one will be left—no one at all.
⁷I said to the city,
  'Surely you will fear me
  and accept correction!'
Then her dwelling would not be cut
    off,
  nor all my punishments come upon
    her.
But they were still eager
  to act corruptly in all they did.
⁸Therefore wait for me," declares the
    LORD,
  "for the day I will stand up to
    testify.ᵃ
I have decided to assemble the
    nations,
  to gather the kingdoms
and to pour out my wrath on them—
  all my fierce anger.
The whole world will be consumed
  by the fire of my jealous anger.

⁹"Then will I purify the lips of the
    peoples,

that all of them may call on the
    name of the LORD
  and serve him shoulder to shoulder.
¹⁰From beyond the rivers of Cushᵇ
  my worshipers, my scattered people,
  will bring me offerings.
¹¹On that day you will not be put to
    shame
  for all the wrongs you have done to
    me,
because I will remove from this city
  those who rejoice in their pride.
Never again will you be haughty
  on my holy hill.
¹²But I will leave within you
  the meek and humble,
  who trust in the name of the LORD.
¹³The remnant of Israel will do no
    wrong;
  they will speak no lies,
  nor will deceit be found in their
    mouths.

ᵃ8 Septuagint and Syriac; Hebrew *will rise up to plunder*   ᵇ10 That is, the upper Nile region

Monday

The Best Love

Read Zephaniah 3:17

Remember when you were little and you did something wrong? You were probably terrified your parents would find out because you knew you'd get in trouble. Sometimes I think of God that way. I'm afraid to tell him about my sins and ask forgiveness because I'm scared of the punishment I'll get.

But no matter what I do, God is ready to forgive me if I'm truly sorry. He wants me to come to him with all my problems and sins because he loves me so much. I can tell him everything and he'll forgive and comfort me.

God's love is so much greater than we can even understand. His love is deep and pure. It's the best love we will ever experience. And he doesn't just love us, he *delights* in us. He rejoices over us. He's excited about having a relationship with us. And he wants us to love him too.

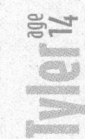
Tyler age 14

What about You?

❶ Have you ever wanted to hide from God? What happened when you finally confessed to God?

❷ Make a list of the ways God shows his love to you.

❸ Confess your sins to God. Be honest and open with God as you ask for forgiveness.

Turn to page 1114 for your next devotion.

They will eat and lie down
 and no one will make them afraid."

¹⁴Sing, O Daughter of Zion;
 shout aloud, O Israel!
Be glad and rejoice with all your
 heart,
 O Daughter of Jerusalem!
¹⁵The LORD has taken away your
 punishment,
 he has turned back your enemy.
The LORD, the King of Israel, is with
 you;
 never again will you fear any harm.
¹⁶On that day they will say to
 Jerusalem,
 "Do not fear, O Zion;
 do not let your hands hang limp.
¹⁷The LORD your God is with you,
 he is mighty to save.
He will take great delight in you,
 he will quiet you with his love,
 he will rejoice over you with
 singing."

¹⁸"The sorrows for the appointed feasts
 I will remove from you;
 they are a burden and a reproach to
 you.ᵃ
¹⁹At that time I will deal
 with all who oppressed you;
I will rescue the lame
 and gather those who have been
 scattered.
I will give them praise and honor
 in every land where they were put
 to shame.
²⁰At that time I will gather you;
 at that time I will bring you home.
I will give you honor and praise
 among all the peoples of the earth
when I restore your fortunesᵇ
 before your very eyes,"
 says the LORD.

ᵃ18 Or "I will gather you who mourn for the
appointed feasts; / your reproach is a burden to
you ᵇ20 Or I bring back your captives

Haggai

START

As you read this book, you can almost hear Haggai the preacher letting the Jews have it: "C'mon, guys—what gives? God brings you back, on schedule, to this bombed-out shell of a city—back here to Jerusalem—and you start building houses, remodeling rooms, adding redwood decks, wallpapering. Meanwhile, you let God's house, the temple, just sit there in ruins.

"And you wonder why it's been getting tough here lately? You wonder why the little you *do* scrape together anymore—whether it's crops, building materials or the cash you try to save for a second chariot—God simply blows away?

"HEL-LO. Anybody see a connection here?"

They did, thanks to leaders who listened to Haggai and took God's words seriously. They coughed up the money and materials needed and began work on *God's* house for a change. Their luck changed too.

Cast OF Characters

Haggai (HAG-eye)
This prophet was among the 50,000 or so Jews who, after 70 years of living "as strangers in a strange land" in Babylon, were permitted to return and start all over in their home nation of Judah and its holy city of Jerusalem.

Zerubbabel
(zuh-RUB-uh-bull)

The appointed governor of Judah—who just happened to be the grandson of the former king of Judah (the guy who was king way back before Nebuchadnezzar invaded Babylon). He's got no speaking part in this book, but what a really cool name!

Joshua (JAH-shoo-uh)
OK, so he doesn't have a speaking part either. But when you were the *high priest* of the One True Living God, you got mentioned, whether you had any part of the action or not.

What's UP with That?

5 Basic Uses for a Ring

Check the correct use for the ring Haggai talks about toward the end of his book of prophecies. The answer's at the bottom of the page.

☐ **❶ Ring:** Symbolizes a promise of one person to another, usually in the general direction of marriage.

☐ **❷ Ring:** Going steady. You just want one girlfriend or boyfriend all to yourself for a least a month of dates. A ring just might do that for you.

☐ **❸ Ring:** Secret decoding device found in occasional boxes of sugary cereal.

☐ **❹ Ring:** A legal and binding representation of the ring's owner (usually royalty). Like in the old days, a king would use his ring like a stamp. It was called a "signet ring" because it was used to sign documents, contracts, treaties, money orders. The king would ink the flat part of the ring and press the imprint onto the paper. There. When people in the next town saw the stamp of the king's ring, they knew this was no forgery but that the king really signed this.

☐ **❺ Ring:** A ring is what you insert in a bull's nose so you can lead it where you want without him resisting. (Hey, the inside of your nose is, like, *tender*. No bull's gonna resist for long.)

Snap Shots

- "All right already," say the Jews *(chapter 1)*

- "Hey, what about *my* house?" says God *(chapter 2:1–9)*

- And now for an object lesson . . . *(chapter 2:10–19)*

- "God will take good care of you," says Haggai *(chapter 2:20–23)*

Here's the kicker: God says that *we're* his signet rings. We're the little instruments he uses to make his impression visible to others. COOL!

answer: if you guessed Basic Ring Use number four, you are correct.

A Call to Build the House of the LORD

1 In the second year of King Darius, on the first day of the sixth month, the word of the LORD came through the prophet Haggai to Zerubbabel son of Shealtiel, governor of Judah, and to Joshua[a] son of Jehozadak, the high priest:

²This is what the LORD Almighty says: "These people say, 'The time has not yet come for the LORD's house to be built.'"

³Then the word of the LORD came through the prophet Haggai: ⁴"Is it a time

God's Shack

Haggai 1:3

There was something majorly wrong with the picture Haggai saw. God's house was trashed. Obviously no one had been paying much attention to it, because they were too busy making sure that their own houses were perfect. There was no place for the people to worship God. Haggai wanted the people to rebuild the temple and stop thinking just about themselves.

for you yourselves to be living in your paneled houses, while this house remains a ruin?"

⁵Now this is what the LORD Almighty says: "Give careful thought to your ways. ⁶You have planted much, but have harvested little. You eat, but never have enough. You drink, but never have your fill. You put on clothes, but are not warm. You earn wages, only to put them in a purse with holes in it."

⁷This is what the LORD Almighty says: "Give careful thought to your ways. ⁸Go up into the mountains and bring down timber and build the house, so that I may take pleasure in it and be honored," says the LORD. ⁹"You expected much, but see, it turned out to be little. What you brought home, I blew away. Why?" declares the LORD Almighty. "Because of my house, which remains a ruin, while each of you is busy with his own house.

¹⁰Therefore, because of you the heavens have withheld their dew and the earth its crops. ¹¹I called for a drought on the fields and the mountains, on the grain, the new wine, the oil and whatever the ground produces, on men and cattle, and on the labor of your hands."

¹²Then Zerubbabel son of Shealtiel, Joshua son of Jehozadak, the high priest, and the whole remnant of the people obeyed the voice of the LORD their God and the message of the prophet Haggai, because the LORD their God had sent him. And the people feared the LORD.

¹³Then Haggai, the LORD's messenger, gave this message of the LORD to the people: "I am with you," declares the LORD. ¹⁴So the LORD stirred up the spirit of Zerubbabel son of Shealtiel, governor of Judah, and the spirit of Joshua son of Jehozadak, the high priest, and the spirit of the whole remnant of the people. They came and began to work on the house of the LORD Almighty, their God, ¹⁵on the twenty-fourth day of the sixth month in the second year of King Darius.

The Promised Glory of the New House

2 On the twenty-first day of the seventh month, the word of the LORD came through the prophet Haggai: ²"Speak to Zerubbabel son of Shealtiel, governor of Judah, to Joshua son of Jehozadak, the high priest, and to the remnant of the people. Ask them, ³'Who of you is left who saw this house in its former glory? How does it look to you now? Does it not seem to you like nothing? ⁴But now be strong, O Zerubbabel,' declares the LORD. 'Be strong, O Joshua son of Jehozadak, the high priest. Be strong, all you people of the land,' declares the LORD, 'and work. For I am with you,' declares the LORD Almighty. ⁵'This is what I covenanted with you when you came out of Egypt. And my Spirit remains among you. Do not fear.'

⁶"This is what the LORD Almighty says: 'In a little while I will once more shake the heavens and the earth, the sea and the dry land. ⁷I will shake all nations,

---

ᵃ1 A variant of *Jeshua*; here and elsewhere in Haggai

and the desired of all nations will come, and I will fill this house with glory,' says the LORD Almighty. ⁸'The silver is mine and the gold is mine,' declares the LORD Almighty. ⁹'The glory of this present house will be greater than the glory of the former house,' says the LORD Almighty. 'And in this place I will grant peace,' declares the LORD Almighty."

Blessings for a Defiled People

¹⁰On the twenty-fourth day of the ninth month, in the second year of Darius, the word of the LORD came to the prophet Haggai: ¹¹"This is what the LORD Almighty says: 'Ask the priests what the law says: ¹²If a person carries consecrated meat in the fold of his garment, and that fold touches some bread or stew, some wine, oil or other food, does it become consecrated?' "

The priests answered, "No."

¹³Then Haggai said, "If a person defiled by contact with a dead body touches one of these things, does it become defiled?"

"Yes," the priests replied, "it becomes defiled."

¹⁴Then Haggai said, " 'So it is with this people and this nation in my sight,' declares the LORD. 'Whatever they do and whatever they offer there is defiled.

¹⁵" 'Now give careful thought to this from this day on*ᵃ*—consider how things were before one stone was laid on another in the LORD's temple. ¹⁶When anyone came to a heap of twenty measures, there were only ten. When anyone went to a wine vat to draw fifty measures, there were only twenty. ¹⁷I struck all the work of your hands with blight, mildew and

ᵃ15 Or to the days past

Tuesday

Who Do I Belong To?

Read Haggai 2:23

My 6th grade class was really small. There were only 5 girls in the whole class, and our friendships were changing weekly. I often felt like the "odd one out." When the other girls chose their friends, it seemed like they never chose me.

I would have felt a lot better if I had remembered that even when nobody else paid much attention to me, God still thought I was worthwhile. Today's verse says God looked at Zerubbabel like a signet ring. That's a ring with the owner's initials on it. A signet ring shows who it belongs to. And that's how God thinks of us. He chose us, marked us with his name and wants us to show the world who we belong to by the way we live. Just like a person's initials are on a signet ring, God's name is written all over us.

Knowing how important I am to God reminds me of his eternal plan and my place in it. It's awesome!

Kate, age 13

What about You?

❶ Think of something you own that you'd never want to lose, like an antique necklace that belonged to your grandmother or a stack of rare baseball cards your dad gave you. Why is this possession so important to you? How much more do you think God values you?

❷ Try to count all the things in your room that have your name written on them.

❸ Thank God for loving you and calling you by name.

Turn to page 1122 for your next devotion.

hail, yet you did not turn to me,' declares the LORD. ¹⁸'From this day on, from this twenty-fourth day of the ninth month, give careful thought to the day when the foundation of the LORD's temple was laid. Give careful thought: ¹⁹Is there yet any seed left in the barn? Until now, the vine and the fig tree, the pomegranate and the olive tree have not borne fruit.

" 'From this day on I will bless you.' "

Zerubbabel the LORD's Signet Ring

²⁰The word of the LORD came to Haggai a second time on the twenty-fourth day of the month: ²¹"Tell Zerubbabel governor of Judah that I will shake the heavens and the earth. ²²I will overturn royal thrones and shatter the power of the foreign kingdoms. I will overthrow chariots and their drivers; horses and their riders will fall, each by the sword of his brother.

²³" 'On that day,' declares the LORD Almighty, 'I will take you, my servant Zerubbabel son of Shealtiel,' declares the LORD, 'and I will make you like my signet ring, for I have chosen you,' declares the LORD Almighty."

Zechariah

START

CAST OF Characters

Zechariah
(zeck-uh-RYE-uh)
God assigns his prophet Zech the job of encouraging the returned castaways by talking about all the good times that are just around the corner. It is also Zech's job to *warn* the Jews that, unless they clean up their act, these good times may not come after all.

Angel (AIN-jell)
An angel talks with Zechariah. No, don't think of a humanoid wearing white and waving wings of feathers. The Hebrew word for *angel* simply means "messenger"; it says nothing about wings or feathers.

Joshua (JAH-shoe-uh)
You're introduced to him in chapter 3. He is the high priest at the time. (No, this Joshua isn't the one who captured Jericho with the falling-wall strategy.) The squeaky clean transformation that Joshua gets symbolizes the transformation that Judah would receive from God in the future.

What do you know about the Great Depression of the 1930s? Probably not much, apart from maybe a one-week unit in U.S. history, or—if you ask—what a grandparent tells you. Tough times, back then. When money simply lost its value and people lost their jobs, most children got used to one change of clothes per year and an orange for Christmas.

When this book was written, a new generation of Jews need to be reminded about what *their* grandparents and great-grandparents went through, why this Jerusalem—a land they had never seen—is really their home, and why it is so important. They have just moved *back* to Jerusalem 70 years after the Jewish massacre and deportation—when a Babylonian army bulldozed and burned the city, killed the citizens and dragged survivors back to Babylon.

Enter Zechariah. Zech and his bud Haggai are among those who return, and the job God gives them is to preach and prophesy—to warn and encourage the men and women who are clearing away the 70-year-old rubble. Though Zechariah uses a lot of bizarre symbols to get his point across to the Jews—colored horses, flying scrolls, myrtle trees, a woman in a basket—the point itself is pretty simple: You've come home! Finally, a rest! Time to rebuild, especially the temple! God has made your fasts into feasts! Peace is just around the corner!

Zerubbabel
(zuh-RUB-uh-bull)
This governor of Judah seems to be doing a pretty decent job of keeping the work of rebuilding going, and encouraging the people to trust in God.

What's UP with That?

Joshua, Jesus—How Symbolic!

There's some juicy symbolism that even Zechariah didn't completely understand. We can see it a little more clearly because we live 2,500 years after he lived and know some stuff that's happened since then.

What's wild is that when Zechariah was writing about his bud, the high priest Joshua, he was probably thinking of, well, his bud the high priest Joshua. Period. But we know something that Zechariah didn't know—500 years later another "Joshua" showed up on the scene: Jesus Christ. *Joshua* (Hebrew) and *Jesus* (Greek) are actually the same name—like William and Bill.

So look how right-on Zechariah was about Jesus (the Christ), when he thought he was only writing about Joshua (his bud the high priest):

Snap shots

- Good times are in store for you!
  (chapters 1—8)
  — weird visions galore
  (chapters 1—6)
  — words of promise
  (chapters 6—8)
- Let me tell you about a really strange vision
  (chapters 9—11)
- Oh, yeah, one more weird vision
  (chapters 12—14)

Zechariah Sez About Josh	Connection With Jesus
Another name for Joshua was "The Branch" (Zechariah 6:12) . . .	a common name for the King-who-was-to-come, whom we know as Jesus Christ (see John 15:5). Isaiah talked about this (Isaiah 4:2), and so did Jeremiah (Jeremiah 23:5).
Zechariah told everyone that God wanted Joshua (the priest) to sit on a throne, which would make him a priest-king—the duties of 2 men in one.	Exactly like Jesus Christ—a priest (the book of Hebrews makes this clear) as well as a king.
Zechariah wrote that the Jews should shout in happiness because "your king comes to you . . . gentle and riding on a donkey" (Zechariah 9:9). Remind you of anything?	Maybe how Jesus entered Jerusalem—on a donkey—6 days before his death? (see Matthew 21:1–11 and John 12:14–16)
Then there's the vision Zechariah had about getting paid the paltry sum of 30 pieces of silver—and then throwing the money to the potter.	This is exactly the same amount of money the chief priests paid Judas to turn Jesus over to them so they could kill him. But within hours Judas got to feeling real guilty, so he came back and threw the 30 pieces of silver back at the chief priests who used the money to buy what they called "the *potter's* field" as a burial place for foreigners (Matthew 27:3–10, emphasis added).
The Lord told Zechariah that the day would come when Judah would look on the one they had pierced and would mourn for him as for a son (Zechariah 12:10).	Hey, guess what son was pierced and was mourned for, at least by a handful of people? You're right. Jesus, at his crucifixion!

A Call to Return to the LORD

1 In the eighth month of the second year of Darius, the word of the LORD came to the prophet Zechariah son of Berekiah, the son of Iddo:

²"The LORD was very angry with your forefathers. ³Therefore tell the people: This is what the LORD Almighty says: 'Return to me,' declares the LORD Almighty, 'and I will return to you,' says the LORD Almighty. ⁴Do not be like your forefathers, to whom the earlier prophets proclaimed: This is what the LORD Almighty says: 'Turn from your evil ways and your evil practices.' But they would not listen or pay attention to me, declares the LORD. ⁵Where are your forefathers now? And the prophets, do they live forever? ⁶But did not my words and my decrees, which I commanded my servants the prophets, overtake your forefathers?

"Then they repented and said, 'The LORD Almighty has done to us what our ways and practices deserve, just as he determined to do.' "

The Man Among the Myrtle Trees

⁷On the twenty-fourth day of the eleventh month, the month of Shebat, in the second year of Darius, the word of the LORD came to the prophet Zechariah son of Berekiah, the son of Iddo.

⁸During the night I had a vision—and there before me was a man riding a red horse! He was standing among the myrtle trees in a ravine. Behind him were red, brown and white horses.

⁹I asked, "What are these, my lord?"

The angel who was talking with me answered, "I will show you what they are."

¹⁰Then the man standing among the myrtle trees explained, "They are the ones the LORD has sent to go throughout the earth."

¹¹And they reported to the angel of the LORD, who was standing among the myrtle trees, "We have gone throughout the earth and found the whole world at rest and in peace."

¹²Then the angel of the LORD said, "LORD Almighty, how long will you withhold mercy from Jerusalem and from the towns of Judah, which you have been angry with these seventy years?" ¹³So the LORD spoke kind and comforting words to the angel who talked with me.

¹⁴Then the angel who was speaking to me said, "Proclaim this word: This is what the LORD Almighty says: 'I am very jealous for Jerusalem and Zion, ¹⁵but I am very angry with the nations that feel secure. I was only a little angry, but they added to the calamity.'

¹⁶"Therefore, this is what the LORD says: 'I will return to Jerusalem with mercy, and there my house will be rebuilt. And the measuring line will be stretched out over Jerusalem,' declares the LORD Almighty.

¹⁷"Proclaim further: This is what the LORD Almighty says: 'My towns will again overflow with prosperity, and the LORD will again comfort Zion and choose Jerusalem.' "

The Horn Section

Huh?

Zechariah 1:18-21

God often used interesting pictures to show prophets what was happening and what would happen in the future. In this passage Zechariah talks about seeing the 4 horns that scattered God's people. He's probably talking about Assyria, Egypt, Babylonia and Persia—the enemy nations that had been hassling God's people for years.

Four Horns and Four Craftsmen

¹⁸Then I looked up—and there before me were four horns! ¹⁹I asked the angel who was speaking to me, "What are these?"

He answered me, "These are the horns that scattered Judah, Israel and Jerusalem."

²⁰Then the LORD showed me four craftsmen. ²¹I asked, "What are these coming to do?"

He answered, "These are the horns that scattered Judah so that no one could raise his head, but the craftsmen have come to terrify them and throw down these horns of the nations who lifted up their horns against the land of Judah to scatter its people."

A Man With a Measuring Line

2 Then I looked up—and there before me was a man with a measuring line in his hand! ²I asked, "Where are you going?"

He answered me, "To measure Jerusalem, to find out how wide and how long it is."

³Then the angel who was speaking to me left, and another angel came to meet him ⁴and said to him: "Run, tell that young man, 'Jerusalem will be a city without walls because of the great number of men and livestock in it. ⁵And I myself will be a wall of fire around it,' declares the LORD, 'and I will be its glory within.'

⁶"Come! Come! Flee from the land of the north," declares the LORD, "for I have scattered you to the four winds of heaven," declares the LORD.

⁷"Come, O Zion! Escape, you who live in the Daughter of Babylon!" ⁸For this is what the LORD Almighty says: "After he has honored me and has sent me against the nations that have plundered you—for whoever touches you touches the apple of his eye— ⁹I will surely raise my hand against them so that their slaves will plunder them.ᵃ Then you will know that the LORD Almighty has sent me.

¹⁰"Shout and be glad, O Daughter of Zion. For I am coming, and I will live among you," declares the LORD. ¹¹"Many nations will be joined with the LORD in that day and will become my people. I will live among you and you will know that the LORD Almighty has sent me to you. ¹²The LORD will inherit Judah as his portion in the holy land and will again choose Jerusalem. ¹³Be still before the LORD, all mankind, because he has roused himself from his holy dwelling."

Clean Garments for the High Priest

3 Then he showed me Joshuaᵇ the high priest standing before the angel of the LORD, and Satanᶜ standing at his right side to accuse him. ²The LORD said to Satan, "The LORD rebuke you, Satan! The LORD, who has chosen Jerusalem, rebuke

you! Is not this man a burning stick snatched from the fire?"

³Now Joshua was dressed in filthy clothes as he stood before the angel. ⁴The angel said to those who were standing before him, "Take off his filthy clothes."

Then he said to Joshua, "See, I have taken away your sin, and I will put rich garments on you."

⁵Then I said, "Put a clean turban on his head." So they put a clean turban on his head and clothed him, while the angel of the LORD stood by.

⁶The angel of the LORD gave this charge to Joshua: ⁷"This is what the LORD Almighty says: 'If you will walk in my ways and keep my requirements, then you will govern my house and have charge of my courts, and I will give you a place among these standing here.

⁸"'Listen, O high priest Joshua and your associates seated before you, who are men symbolic of things to come: I am going to bring my servant, the Branch. ⁹See, the stone I have set in front of Joshua! There are seven eyesᵈ on that one stone, and I will engrave an inscription on it,' says the LORD Almighty, 'and I will remove the sin of this land in a single day.

¹⁰"'In that day each of you will invite his neighbor to sit under his vine and fig tree,' declares the LORD Almighty."

The Gold Lampstand and the Two Olive Trees

4 Then the angel who talked with me returned and wakened me, as a man is wakened from his sleep. ²He asked me, "What do you see?"

I answered, "I see a solid gold lampstand with a bowl at the top and seven lights on it, with seven channels to the lights. ³Also there are two olive trees by it, one on the right of the bowl and the other on its left."

⁴I asked the angel who talked with me, "What are these, my lord?"

⁵He answered, "Do you not know what these are?"

"No, my lord," I replied.

⁶So he said to me, "This is the word of

ᵃ8,9 Or says after . . . eye: ⁹"I . . . plunder them." ᵇ1 A variant of Jeshua; here and elsewhere in Zechariah ᶜ1 Satan means accuser. ᵈ9 Or facets

the Lord to Zerubbabel: 'Not by might nor by power, but by my Spirit,' says the Lord Almighty.

⁷"What*ᵃ* are you, O mighty mountain? Before Zerubbabel you will become level ground. Then he will bring out the capstone to shouts of 'God bless it! God bless it!' "

⁸Then the word of the Lord came to me: ⁹"The hands of Zerubbabel have laid the foundation of this temple; his hands will also complete it. Then you will know that the Lord Almighty has sent me to you.

¹⁰"Who despises the day of small things? Men will rejoice when they see the plumb line in the hand of Zerubbabel.

"(These seven are the eyes of the Lord, which range throughout the earth.)"

¹¹Then I asked the angel, "What are these two olive trees on the right and the left of the lampstand?"

¹²Again I asked him, "What are these two olive branches beside the two gold pipes that pour out golden oil?"

¹³He replied, "Do you not know what these are?"

"No, my lord," I said.

¹⁴So he said, "These are the two who are anointed toᵇ serve the Lord of all the earth."

The Flying Scroll

5 I looked again—and there before me was a flying scroll!

²He asked me, "What do you see?"

I answered, "I see a flying scroll, thirty feet long and fifteen feet wide.ᶜ"

³And he said to me, "This is the curse that is going out over the whole land; for according to what it says on one side, every thief will be banished, and according to what it says on the other, everyone who swears falsely will be banished. ⁴The Lord Almighty declares, 'I will send it out, and it will enter the house of the thief and the house of him who swears falsely by my name. It will remain in his house and destroy it, both its timbers and its stones.' "

The Woman in a Basket

⁵Then the angel who was speaking to me came forward and said to me, "Look

up and see what this is that is appearing."

⁶I asked, "What is it?"

He replied, "It is a measuring basket.ᵈ" And he added, "This is the iniquityᵉ of the people throughout the land."

⁷Then the cover of lead was raised, and there in the basket sat a woman! ⁸He said, "This is wickedness," and he pushed her back into the basket and pushed the lead cover down over its mouth.

⁹Then I looked up—and there before me were two women, with the wind in their wings! They had wings like those of a stork, and they lifted up the basket between heaven and earth.

¹⁰"Where are they taking the basket?" I asked the angel who was speaking to me.

¹¹He replied, "To the country of Babyloniaᶠ to build a house for it. When it is ready, the basket will be set there in its place."

Four Chariots

6 I looked up again—and there before me were four chariots coming out from between two mountains—mountains of bronze! ²The first chariot had red horses, the second black, ³the third white, and the fourth dappled—all of them powerful. ⁴I asked the angel who was speaking to me, "What are these, my lord?"

⁵The angel answered me, "These are the four spiritsᵍ of heaven, going out from standing in the presence of the Lord of the whole world. ⁶The one with the black horses is going toward the north country, the one with the white horses toward the west,ʰ and the one with the dappled horses toward the south."

⁷When the powerful horses went out, they were straining to go throughout the earth. And he said, "Go throughout the earth!" So they went throughout the earth.

⁸Then he called to me, "Look, those going toward the north country have given my Spiritⁱ rest in the land of the north."

ᵃ7 Or *Who*   ᵇ14 Or *two who bring oil and*
ᶜ2 Hebrew *twenty cubits long and ten cubits wide* (about 9 meters long and 4.5 meters wide)
ᵈ6 Hebrew *an ephah*; also in verses 7-11   ᵉ6 Or *appearance*   ᶠ11 Hebrew *Shinar*   ᵍ5 Or *winds*
ʰ6 Or *horses after them*   ⁱ8 Or *spirit*

A Crown for Joshua

⁹The word of the LORD came to me: ¹⁰"Take silver and gold from the exiles Heldai, Tobijah and Jedaiah, who have arrived from Babylon. Go the same day to the house of Josiah son of Zephaniah. ¹¹Take the silver and gold and make a crown, and set it on the head of the high priest, Joshua son of Jehozadak. ¹²Tell him this is what the LORD Almighty says: 'Here is the man whose name is the Branch, and he will branch out from his place and build the temple of the LORD. ¹³It is he who will build the temple of the LORD, and he will be clothed with majesty and will sit and rule on his throne. And he will be a priest on his throne. And there will be harmony between the two.' ¹⁴The crown will be given to Heldai,*a* Tobijah, Jedaiah and Hen*b* son of Zephaniah as a memorial in the temple of the LORD. ¹⁵Those who are far away will come and help to build the temple of the LORD, and you will know that the LORD Almighty has sent me to you. This will happen if you diligently obey the LORD your God."

Justice and Mercy, Not Fasting

7 In the fourth year of King Darius, the word of the LORD came to Zechariah on the fourth day of the ninth month, the month of Kislev. ²The people of Bethel had sent Sharezer and Regem-Melech, together with their men, to entreat the LORD ³by asking the priests of the house of the LORD Almighty and the prophets, "Should I mourn and fast in the fifth month, as I have done for so many years?"

⁴Then the word of the LORD Almighty came to me: ⁵"Ask all the people of the land and the priests, 'When you fasted and mourned in the fifth and seventh months for the past seventy years, was it really for me that you fasted? ⁶And when you were eating and drinking, were you not just feasting for yourselves? ⁷Are these not the words the LORD proclaimed through the earlier prophets when Jerusalem and its surrounding towns were at rest and prosperous, and the Negev and the western foothills were settled?'"

⁸And the word of the LORD came again to Zechariah: ⁹"This is what the LORD Almighty says: 'Administer true justice; show mercy and compassion to one another. ¹⁰Do not oppress the widow or the fatherless, the alien or the poor. In your hearts do not think evil of each other.'

¹¹"But they refused to pay attention; stubbornly they turned their backs and stopped up their ears. ¹²They made their hearts as hard as flint and would not listen to the law or to the words that the LORD Almighty had sent by his Spirit through the earlier prophets. So the LORD Almighty was very angry.

¹³" 'When I called, they did not listen; so when they called, I would not listen,' says the LORD Almighty. ¹⁴'I scattered them with a whirlwind among all the nations, where they were strangers. The land was left so desolate behind them that no one could come or go. This is how they made the pleasant land desolate.' "

The Lord Promises to Bless Jerusalem

8 Again the word of the LORD Almighty came to me. ²This is what the LORD Almighty says: "I am very jealous for Zion; I am burning with jealousy for her."

³This is what the LORD says: "I will return to Zion and dwell in Jerusalem. Then Jerusalem will be called the City of Truth, and the mountain of the LORD Almighty will be called the Holy Mountain."

⁴This is what the LORD Almighty says: "Once again men and women of ripe old age will sit in the streets of Jerusalem, each with cane in hand because of his age. ⁵The city streets will be filled with boys and girls playing there."

⁶This is what the LORD Almighty says: "It may seem marvelous to the remnant of this people at that time, but will it seem marvelous to me?" declares the LORD Almighty.

⁷This is what the LORD Almighty says: "I will save my people from the countries of the east and the west. ⁸I will bring them back to live in Jerusalem; they will

---

*a*14 Syriac; Hebrew *Helem*   *b*14 Or *and the gracious one, the*

be my people, and I will be faithful and righteous to them as their God."

⁹This is what the LORD Almighty says: "You who now hear these words spoken by the prophets who were there when the foundation was laid for the house of the LORD Almighty, let your hands be strong so that the temple may be built. ¹⁰Before that time there were no wages for man or beast. No one could go about his business safely because of his enemy, for I had turned every man against his neighbor. ¹¹But now I will not deal with the remnant of this people as I did in the past," declares the LORD Almighty.

¹²"The seed will grow well, the vine will yield its fruit, the ground will produce its crops, and the heavens will drop their dew. I will give all these things as an inheritance to the remnant of this people. ¹³As you have been an object of cursing among the nations, O Judah and Israel, so will I save you, and you will be a blessing. Do not be afraid, but let your hands be strong."

¹⁴This is what the LORD Almighty says: "Just as I had determined to bring disaster upon you and showed no pity when your fathers angered me," says the LORD Almighty, ¹⁵"so now I have determined to do good again to Jerusalem and Judah. Do not be afraid. ¹⁶These are the things you are to do: Speak the truth to each other, and render true and sound judgment in your courts; ¹⁷do not plot evil against your neighbor, and do not love to swear falsely. I hate all this," declares the LORD.

¹⁸Again the word of the LORD Almighty came to me. ¹⁹This is what the LORD Almighty says: "The fasts of the fourth, fifth, seventh and tenth months will become joyful and glad occasions and happy festivals for Judah. Therefore love truth and peace."

Wednesday

True Cool

Read Zechariah 7:8–10

Marissa, age 14

I look around my school and I see a lot of lonely people. There's one guy in particular who is always sitting by himself. I know I need to reach out to him and to the other lonely kids I see.

The hard part is that I want to look cool. I want other kids to like me and think I'm a nice, normal person, not someone who hangs out with loners. So how do I look cool and still be a friend to this guy who's always alone?

I probably can't. The truth is, sometimes doing what God wants me to do isn't cool, at least not here on earth. But God's got a different idea of what's cool. To him, it's cool when we reach out to people who are lonely and hurting. It's cool when we do what's right instead of what will impress other people. It's cool when people know that the Lord is first in our lives.

So when I see that guy sitting alone at lunch or in the hall after school, I can walk up to him knowing I have nothing to lose because God is with me. And that's *really* cool.

What about You?

❶ Have you ever had to choose between looking cool and doing what's right? What did you do?

❷ What is one way you can reach out to a person who is lonely or needs a friend? When can you do this?

❸ Ask God to help you show compassion and love to people who are hurting.

Turn to page 1123 for your next devotion.

²⁰This is what the LORD Almighty says: "Many peoples and the inhabitants of many cities will yet come, ²¹and the inhabitants of one city will go to another and say, 'Let us go at once to entreat the LORD and seek the LORD Almighty. I myself am going.' ²²And many peoples and powerful nations will come to Jerusalem to seek the LORD Almighty and to entreat him."

²³This is what the LORD Almighty says: "In those days ten men from all languages and nations will take firm hold of one Jew by the hem of his robe and say, 'Let us go with you, because we have heard that God is with you.' "

Judgment on Israel's Enemies

An Oracle

9 The word of the LORD is against the land of Hadrach
and will rest upon Damascus—
for the eyes of men and all the tribes of Israel
are on the LORD—^a
² and upon Hamath too, which borders on it,
and upon Tyre and Sidon, though they are very skillful.

^a1 Or *Damascus. / For the eye of the LORD is on all mankind, / as well as on the tribes of Israel,*

Thursday

The Words You Choose

Read Zechariah 8:16–17

You wouldn't believe the number of kids at my school who lie, swear and say awful things to each other. When you walk down the hall, you can always hear people swearing and can see them getting into fights. It really bugs me!

One time, some kids came up to the boy whose locker is next to mine and started shouting at him, swearing at him and shoving him. They threatened to really hurt him. Finally I said, "Hey guys, cut it out!" They just laughed at me and kept swearing and yelling. But before long, they stopped and walked away.

Whenever we hear people swearing or see them acting mean, we should not be afraid to tell them to stop. Most people, even if they're not Christians, know it's not right to abuse or swear at people. When we confront them, they might think, *You know, maybe it's not so cool to talk this way.* Sure, they might laugh at us, but we'll still be letting them know that not everyone appreciates violence or bad language.

But most of all, Christians need to be good examples of using our words to build other people up. We need to try to be kind and fair in the things we say. That's something no one can argue with.

Laura age 12

What about You?

❶ Why do you think so many people are comfortable with lying, swearing and saying mean things about others?

❷ Next time you're at school, spend the morning listening for all the ways people use their words to hurt others. In the afternoon, listen to the ways people use words to build each other up. Which do you hear more often: hurtful words or helpful words?

❸ Ask God to help you use words that heal instead of hurt.

Turn to page 1132 for your next devotion.

³Tyre has built herself a stronghold;
  she has heaped up silver like dust,
  and gold like the dirt of the streets.
⁴But the Lord will take away her
    possessions
  and destroy her power on the sea,
  and she will be consumed by fire.
⁵Ashkelon will see it and fear;
  Gaza will writhe in agony,
  and Ekron too, for her hope will
    wither.
 Gaza will lose her king
  and Ashkelon will be deserted.
⁶Foreigners will occupy Ashdod,
  and I will cut off the pride of the
    Philistines.
⁷I will take the blood from their
    mouths,
  the forbidden food from between
    their teeth.
 Those who are left will belong to our
    God
  and become leaders in Judah,
  and Ekron will be like the Jebusites.
⁸But I will defend my house
  against marauding forces.
 Never again will an oppressor overrun
    my people,
  for now I am keeping watch.

The Coming of Zion's King

⁹Rejoice greatly, O Daughter of Zion!
  Shout, Daughter of Jerusalem!
 See, your king^a comes to you,
  righteous and having salvation,
  gentle and riding on a donkey,
  on a colt, the foal of a donkey.
¹⁰I will take away the chariots from
    Ephraim
  and the war-horses from Jerusalem,
  and the battle bow will be broken.
 He will proclaim peace to the nations.
  His rule will extend from sea to sea
  and from the River^b to the ends of
    the earth.^c
¹¹As for you, because of the blood of
    my covenant with you,
  I will free your prisoners from the
    waterless pit.
¹²Return to your fortress, O prisoners of
    hope;
  even now I announce that I will
    restore twice as much to you.
¹³I will bend Judah as I bend my bow
  and fill it with Ephraim.

 I will rouse your sons, O Zion,
  against your sons, O Greece,
  and make you like a warrior's
    sword.

The LORD Will Appear

¹⁴Then the LORD will appear over them;
  his arrow will flash like lightning.
 The Sovereign LORD will sound the
    trumpet;
  he will march in the storms of the
    south,
¹⁵ and the LORD Almighty will shield
    them.
 They will destroy
  and overcome with slingstones.
 They will drink and roar as with wine;
  they will be full like a bowl
  used for sprinkling^d the corners of
    the altar.
¹⁶The LORD their God will save them on
    that day
  as the flock of his people.
 They will sparkle in his land
  like jewels in a crown.
¹⁷How attractive and beautiful they will
    be!
  Grain will make the young men
    thrive,
  and new wine the young women.

The LORD Will Care for Judah

10 Ask the LORD for rain in the
    springtime;
  it is the LORD who makes the storm
    clouds.
 He gives showers of rain to men,
  and plants of the field to everyone.
²The idols speak deceit,
  diviners see visions that lie;
 they tell dreams that are false,
  they give comfort in vain.
 Therefore the people wander like
    sheep
  oppressed for lack of a shepherd.

³"My anger burns against the
    shepherds,
  and I will punish the leaders;
 for the LORD Almighty will care
  for his flock, the house of Judah,
  and make them like a proud horse
    in battle.

---

^a9 Or *King* ^b10 That is, the Euphrates ^c10 Or *the end of the land* ^d15 Or *bowl, / like*

⁴From Judah will come the cornerstone,
    from him the tent peg,
    from him the battle bow,
    from him every ruler.
⁵Together they*ᵃ* will be like mighty
    men
    trampling the muddy streets in
      battle.
Because the LORD is with them,
    they will fight and overthrow the
      horsemen.

⁶"I will strengthen the house of Judah
    and save the house of Joseph.
I will restore them
    because I have compassion on them.
They will be as though
    I had not rejected them,
for I am the LORD their God
    and I will answer them.
⁷The Ephraimites will become like
      mighty men,
    and their hearts will be glad as with
      wine.
Their children will see it and be joyful;
    their hearts will rejoice in the LORD.
⁸I will signal for them
    and gather them in.
Surely I will redeem them;
    they will be as numerous as before.
⁹Though I scatter them among the
      peoples,
    yet in distant lands they will
      remember me.
They and their children will survive,
    and they will return.
¹⁰I will bring them back from Egypt
    and gather them from Assyria.
I will bring them to Gilead and
      Lebanon,
    and there will not be room enough
      for them.
¹¹They will pass through the sea of
      trouble;
    the surging sea will be subdued
    and all the depths of the Nile will
      dry up.
Assyria's pride will be brought down
    and Egypt's scepter will pass away.
¹²I will strengthen them in the LORD
    and in his name they will walk,"
           declares the LORD.

11 Open your doors, O Lebanon,
    so that fire may devour your
      cedars!

²Wail, O pine tree, for the cedar has
      fallen;
    the stately trees are ruined!
Wail, oaks of Bashan;
    the dense forest has been cut
      down!
³Listen to the wail of the shepherds;
    their rich pastures are destroyed!
Listen to the roar of the lions;
    the lush thicket of the Jordan is
      ruined!

Two Shepherds

⁴This is what the LORD my God says: "Pasture the flock marked for slaughter. ⁵Their buyers slaughter them and go unpunished. Those who sell them say, 'Praise the LORD, I am rich!' Their own shepherds do not spare them. ⁶For I will no longer have pity on the people of the land," declares the LORD. "I will hand everyone over to his neighbor and his king. They will oppress the land, and I will not rescue them from their hands."

⁷So I pastured the flock marked for slaughter, particularly the oppressed of the flock. Then I took two staffs and called one Favor and the other Union, and I pastured the flock. ⁸In one month I got rid of the three shepherds.

The flock detested me, and I grew weary of them ⁹and said, "I will not be your shepherd. Let the dying die, and the perishing perish. Let those who are left eat one another's flesh."

¹⁰Then I took my staff called Favor and broke it, revoking the covenant I had made with all the nations. ¹¹It was revoked on that day, and so the afflicted of the flock who were watching me knew it was the word of the LORD.

¹²I told them, "If you think it best, give me my pay; but if not, keep it." So they paid me thirty pieces of silver.

¹³And the LORD said to me, "Throw it to the potter"—the handsome price at which they priced me! So I took the thirty pieces of silver and threw them into the house of the LORD to the potter.

¹⁴Then I broke my second staff called Union, breaking the brotherhood between Judah and Israel.

¹⁵Then the LORD said to me, "Take

ᵃ4,5 Or ruler, all of them together. / ⁵They

again the equipment of a foolish shepherd. ¹⁶For I am going to raise up a shepherd over the land who will not care for the lost, or seek the young, or heal the injured, or feed the healthy, but will eat the meat of the choice sheep, tearing off their hoofs.

¹⁷ "Woe to the worthless shepherd,
who deserts the flock!
May the sword strike his arm and his
right eye!
May his arm be completely
withered,
his right eye totally blinded!"

Jerusalem's Enemies to Be Destroyed

An Oracle

12 This is the word of the LORD concerning Israel. The LORD, who stretches out the heavens, who lays the foundation of the earth, and who forms the spirit of man within him, declares: ²"I am going to make Jerusalem a cup that sends all the surrounding peoples reeling. Judah will be besieged as well as Jerusalem. ³On that day, when all the nations of the earth are gathered against her, I will make Jerusalem an immovable rock for all the nations. All who try to move it will injure themselves. ⁴On that day I will strike every horse with panic and its rider with madness," declares the LORD. "I will keep a watchful eye over the house of Judah, but I will blind all the horses of the nations. ⁵Then the leaders of Judah will say in their hearts, 'The people of Jerusalem are strong, because the LORD Almighty is their God.'

⁶"On that day I will make the leaders of Judah like a firepot in a woodpile, like a flaming torch among sheaves. They will consume right and left all the surrounding peoples, but Jerusalem will remain intact in her place.

⁷"The LORD will save the dwellings of Judah first, so that the honor of the house of David and of Jerusalem's inhabitants may not be greater than that of Judah. ⁸On that day the LORD will shield those who live in Jerusalem, so that the feeblest among them will be like David, and the house of David will be like God, like the Angel of the LORD going before them. ⁹On that day I will set out to de-stroy all the nations that attack Jerusalem.

Mourning for the One They Pierced

¹⁰"And I will pour out on the house of David and the inhabitants of Jerusalem a spirit*a* of grace and supplication. They will look on*b* me, the one they have pierced, and they will mourn for him as one mourns for an only child, and grieve bitterly for him as one grieves for a firstborn son. ¹¹On that day the weeping in

A Few More Clues

Huh?

Zechariah 12:10
The world was sitting on the edge of its seat, waiting for the Messiah to come. Even though it was still hundreds of years before Jesus would be born, Zechariah gives us a few more clues about this mystery Savior who was coming. In this verse he tells us that Jesus will be pierced (the nails and the spear did it) and that he would be a firstborn son.

Jerusalem will be great, like the weeping of Hadad Rimmon in the plain of Megiddo. ¹²The land will mourn, each clan by itself, with their wives by themselves: the clan of the house of David and their wives, the clan of the house of Nathan and their wives, ¹³the clan of the house of Levi and their wives, the clan of Shimei and their wives, ¹⁴and all the rest of the clans and their wives.

Cleansing From Sin

13 "On that day a fountain will be opened to the house of David and the inhabitants of Jerusalem, to cleanse them from sin and impurity.

²"On that day, I will banish the names of the idols from the land, and they will be remembered no more," declares the LORD Almighty. "I will remove both the prophets and the spirit of impurity from the land. ³And if anyone still prophesies,

a 10 Or *the Spirit*   *b 10* Or *to*

Have You Ever Wondered . . .

Did Adam and Eve have belly buttons?
As the original "Mom and Dad" of our human race, Adam and Eve would not have had an umbilical cord attached to them at birth. There would have been no functional need for a belly button, but we really don't know for sure.

Did Jesus use a toothbrush?
Jesus didn't use a nylon bristle brush like the one you've got in your bathroom, but he did clean his teeth. People in Jesus' time would chew on a root or pick their teeth clean with a stiff quill after a meal. The Romans manufactured their own brass and silver toothpicks.

Were there bacteria in the Garden of Eden?
Yes! There was a full working ecosystem at that time. Bacteria eat away at fruit. If they did not exist, how would fruit age? Can you imagine the pile of fruit that would've been found underneath trees if bacteria hadn't done their job? Bacteria didn't make people sick, but they were a part of God's complete and perfect creation.

Did King David take showers?
Under the rule of David and Solomon (about 1000 B.C.), complex water works were constructed throughout Palestine, made from glazed pottery pipes slotted together, much like today's pipes. King David probably took a lot of baths, because Moses' law was clear that bodily cleanliness was part of moral purity.

Did Caesar invent the salad?
No.

his father and mother, to whom he was born, will say to him, 'You must die, because you have told lies in the LORD's name.' When he prophesies, his own parents will stab him.

⁴"On that day every prophet will be ashamed of his prophetic vision. He will not put on a prophet's garment of hair in order to deceive. ⁵He will say, 'I am not a prophet. I am a farmer; the land has been my livelihood since my youth.'ᵃ' ⁶If someone asks him, 'What are these wounds on your bodyᵇ?' he will answer, 'The wounds I was given at the house of my friends.'

The Shepherd Struck, the Sheep Scattered

⁷"Awake, O sword, against my
            shepherd,
    against the man who is close to
            me!"
    declares the LORD Almighty.
"Strike the shepherd,
    and the sheep will be scattered,
    and I will turn my hand against the
            little ones.
⁸In the whole land," declares the
    LORD,

"two-thirds will be struck down and
            perish;
    yet one-third will be left in it.
⁹This third I will bring into the fire;
    I will refine them like silver
    and test them like gold.
They will call on my name
    and I will answer them;
I will say, 'They are my people,'
    and they will say, 'The LORD is our
            God.' "

The LORD Comes and Reigns

14 A day of the LORD is coming when your plunder will be divided among you.

²I will gather all the nations to Jerusalem to fight against it; the city will be captured, the houses ransacked, and the women raped. Half of the city will go into exile, but the rest of the people will not be taken from the city. ³Then the LORD will go out and fight against those nations, as he fights in the day of battle. ⁴On that day his feet will

---

ᵃ5 Or *farmer; a man sold me in my youth*   ᵇ6 Or *wounds between your hands*

stand on the Mount of Olives, east of Jerusalem, and the Mount of Olives will be split in two from east to west, forming a great valley, with half of the mountain moving north and half moving south. [5]You will flee by my mountain valley, for it will extend to Azel. You will flee as you fled from the earthquake[a] in the days of Uzziah king of Judah. Then the LORD my God will come, and all the holy ones with him.

[6]On that day there will be no light, no cold or frost. [7]It will be a unique day, without daytime or nighttime—a day known to the LORD. When evening comes, there will be light.

[8]On that day living water will flow out from Jerusalem, half to the eastern sea[b] and half to the western sea,[c] in summer and in winter.

[9]The LORD will be king over the whole earth. On that day there will be one LORD, and his name the only name.

[10]The whole land, from Geba to Rimmon, south of Jerusalem, will become like the Arabah. But Jerusalem will be raised up and remain in its place, from the Benjamin Gate to the site of the First Gate, to the Corner Gate, and from the Tower of Hananel to the royal winepresses. [11]It will be inhabited; never again will it be destroyed. Jerusalem will be secure.

[12]This is the plague with which the LORD will strike all the nations that fought against Jerusalem: Their flesh will rot while they are still standing on their feet, their eyes will rot in their sockets, and their tongues will rot in their mouths. [13]On that day men will be stricken by the LORD with great panic. Each man will seize the hand of another, and they will attack each other. [14]Judah too will fight at Jerusalem. The wealth of all the surrounding nations will be collected—great quantities of gold and silver and clothing. [15]A similar plague will strike the horses and mules, the camels and donkeys, and all the animals in those camps.

[16]Then the survivors from all the nations that have attacked Jerusalem will go up year after year to worship the King, the LORD Almighty, and to celebrate the Feast of Tabernacles. [17]If any of the peoples of the earth do not go up to Jerusalem to worship the King, the LORD Almighty, they will have no rain. [18]If the Egyptian people do not go up and take part, they will have no rain. The LORD[d] will bring on them the plague he inflicts on the nations that do not go up to celebrate the Feast of Tabernacles. [19]This will be the punishment of Egypt and the punishment of all the nations that do not go up to celebrate the Feast of Tabernacles.

[20]On that day HOLY TO THE LORD will be inscribed on the bells of the horses, and the cooking pots in the LORD's house will be like the sacred bowls in front of the altar. [21]Every pot in Jerusalem and Judah will be holy to the LORD Almighty, and all who come to sacrifice will take some of the pots and cook in them. And on that day there will no longer be a Canaanite[e] in the house of the LORD Almighty.

---

[a]5 Or [5]My mountain valley will be blocked and will extend to Azel. It will be blocked as it was blocked because of the earthquake   [b]8 That is, the Dead Sea   [c]8 That is, the Mediterranean   [d]18 Or part, then the LORD   [e]21 Or merchant

Malachi

START

Cast OF Characters

Malachi (MAL-uh-kie)
God's mouthpiece, a prophet-preacher.

God
Through Malachi, the Lord Almighty (that's what Malachi usually calls God in his book) starts off gently—"I have loved you"—but quickly dips into all the ways that Judah has ignored and rejected him.

Judah
Its common people as well as its priests, are now back in their homeland after nearly 100 years of forced time in Babylon. This book is kind of a list of their sins.

Malachi is probably the last of the Old Testament prophets. He has some pretty strong words for the Jews who have returned from Babylon to the ruins of his homeland. There in Judah (that's the name of the Jews' homeland) they rebuild and settle down to life as their grandparents once knew it. The problem is that they also settle back into their old ways—not only ho-hum, boring worship, but total spiritual badness. Just like old times.

God has 7 big problems with the people he loves, the people he wants the best for. The first 4 involve the *priests* in particular, who . . .

1. Sacrifice second-rate animals to God (1:8).
2. Mess up people's lives with their wrong teaching (2:8).
3. Treat people unfairly in religious and legal matters (2:9).
4. Make evil look good, and good look evil (2:17).

Meanwhile, the regular people are no better behaved than the priests. They . . .

5. Break their marriage promises with frequent divorces (2:14).
6. Rob God by not giving God what is rightfully his (3:9–10).
7. Forget everything God has done for them (3:14).

Despite the people of Judah starting down the same careless road that had leads to their ruin and capture a century earlier, God makes it clear early in this prophecy that their disobedience will not change who he is. He insists, "My name will be great" (Malachi 1:5,11,14).

(JOO-duh)

What's UP with That?

The final (and very brief) chapter in Malachi ends with a curious reference to Elijah, a prophet-preacher who had ticked off unrighteous and sinful kings of Israel nearly 4 centuries earlier. (You can read about his weirdly exciting life from 1 Kings 17—2 Kings 2, off and on in those chapters.) What God, through Malachi, said about Elijah was this: "See, I will send you the prophet Elijah before that great and dreadful day of the LORD comes."

For the next 400 years the Jews were waiting for, they're not quite sure what—some kind of second Elijah, whatever that meant.

Play **Where's Elijah?** and you'll find out who this mysterious Elijah, The Sequel is; and you'll find out the gory details of a beheading, a sleepy prayer meeting that suddenly lightened up and more neat stuff.

Below, read what several people said about Elijah. Try to figure who's talking by skimming the chapter in the Bible that's listed. (If you *still* need answers, you'll find them below.)

Snap shots

- The 7 Grrrs of God and a mini-revival (*chapters 1—3*)

- Here's what's gonna happen someday (says God)—and most of you are gonna like it (*chapter 4*)

Elijah, the Sequel

1. "Whaddaya mean, who am I? Just a minute—you actually think *I'm* the *Christ*? No way. I'm not even Elijah. I'm really just a voice from way outside the city limits, way out where people have gotta really *want* to hear me before they take the trouble to come out." **Who said this?** (answer is in John 1)

2. "So you really wanna hear the truth? Okay, here it is. Swallow it if you can—my cousin is the Elijah that the prophets said would come. **Who was the cousin?** (answer is in Malachi 4 and Matthew 11)

3. "He was a pain in the neck, so I gave *him* a pain in the neck—cut off his head actually. Decapitation. Really, it's a pretty humane way to die. That's what my executioner says, at least. But now . . . something's funny . . . everybody's talking about this miracle worker out in the suburbs. Has this the guy I axed come back to life? Or is he that Elijah dude the Jews keep looking for? Like, what's goin' on here, anyway?" **Who said this?** (answer is in Mark 6 or Luke 9)

4. "So, who are people saying I am?"

   "Well, some say you're John the Baptizer. Some say you're Elijah. Others say you're Jeremiah. It seems everyone has a theory."

   "But how 'bout you? Who do *you* say I am?"

   What two people are having this conversation?
   (answer is in Matthew 16, Mark 8, or Luke 9)

answers: 1-John the Baptizer. 2-John the Baptizer. 3-King Herod. 4-Jesus and Peter.

An oracle: The word of the LORD to Israel through Malachi.[a]

Jacob Loved, Esau Hated

[2]"I have loved you," says the LORD.

"But you ask, 'How have you loved us?'

"Was not Esau Jacob's brother?" the LORD says. "Yet I have loved Jacob, [3]but Esau I have hated, and I have turned his mountains into a wasteland and left his inheritance to the desert jackals."

[4]Edom may say, "Though we have been crushed, we will rebuild the ruins."

But this is what the LORD Almighty says: "They may build, but I will demolish. They will be called the Wicked Land, a people always under the wrath of the LORD. [5]You will see it with your own eyes and say, 'Great is the LORD—even beyond the borders of Israel!'

Blemished Sacrifices

[6]"A son honors his father, and a servant his master. If I am a father, where is the honor due me? If I am a master, where is the respect due me?" says the LORD Almighty. "It is you, O priests, who show contempt for my name.

"But you ask, 'How have we shown contempt for your name?'

[7]"You place defiled food on my altar.

"But you ask, 'How have we defiled you?'

"By saying that the LORD's table is contemptible. [8]When you bring blind animals for sacrifice, is that not wrong? When you sacrifice crippled or diseased animals, is that not wrong? Try offering them to your governor! Would he be pleased with you? Would he accept you?" says the LORD Almighty.

[9]"Now implore God to be gracious to us. With such offerings from your hands, will he accept you?"—says the LORD Almighty.

[10]"Oh, that one of you would shut the temple doors, so that you would not light useless fires on my altar! I am not pleased with you," says the LORD Almighty, "and I will accept no offering from your hands. [11]My name will be great among the nations, from the rising to the setting of the sun. In every place incense and pure offerings will be brought to my name, because my name will be great among the nations," says the LORD Almighty.

[12]"But you profane it by saying of the Lord's table, 'It is defiled,' and of its food, 'It is contemptible.' [13]And you say, 'What a burden!' and you sniff at it contemptuously," says the LORD Almighty.

"When you bring injured, crippled or diseased animals and offer them as sacrifices, should I accept them from your hands?" says the LORD. [14]"Cursed is the cheat who has an acceptable male in his flock and vows to give it, but then sacrifices a blemished animal to the Lord. For I am a great king," says the LORD Almighty, "and my name is to be feared among the nations.

Thanks, but No Thanks

Huh?

Malachi 1:10–14
It might sound like God is really picky about the gifts we give him, but think about it. You wouldn't consider giving your best friend a broken game or a book with pages torn out of it as a birthday present, would you? These people were giving God beat-up sheep and blind goats. He was about to give them his only Son. No wonder he wasn't impressed.

Admonition for the Priests

"And now this admonition is for you, O priests. [2]If you do not listen, and if you do not set your heart to honor my name," says the LORD Almighty, "I will send a curse upon you, and I will curse your blessings. Yes, I have already cursed them, because you have not set your heart to honor me.

[3]"Because of you I will rebuke[b] your descendants[c]; I will spread on your faces the offal from your festival sacrifices, and you will be carried off with it. [4]And you will know that I have sent you this admonition so that my covenant with

[a]1 *Malachi* means *my messenger.*   [b]3 Or *cut off* (see Septuagint)   [c]3 Or *will blight your grain*

Levi may continue," says the LORD Almighty. [5]"My covenant was with him, a covenant of life and peace, and I gave them to him; this called for reverence and he revered me and stood in awe of my name. [6]True instruction was in his mouth and nothing false was found on his lips. He walked with me in peace and uprightness, and turned many from sin.

[7]"For the lips of a priest ought to preserve knowledge, and from his mouth men should seek instruction—because he is the messenger of the LORD Almighty. [8]But you have turned from the way and by your teaching have caused many to stumble; you have violated the covenant with Levi," says the LORD Almighty. [9]"So I have caused you to be despised and humiliated before all the people, because you have not followed my ways but have shown partiality in matters of the law."

Judah Unfaithful

[10]Have we not all one Father[a]? Did not one God create us? Why do we profane the covenant of our fathers by breaking faith with one another?

[11]Judah has broken faith. A detestable thing has been committed in Israel and in Jerusalem: Judah has desecrated the sanctuary the LORD loves, by marrying the daughter of a foreign god. [12]As for the man who does this, whoever he may be, may the LORD cut him off from the tents of Jacob[b]—even though he brings offerings to the LORD Almighty.

[13]Another thing you do: You flood the LORD's altar with tears. You weep and wail because he no longer pays attention to your offerings or accepts them with pleasure from your hands. [14]You ask, "Why?" It is because the LORD is acting as the witness between you and the wife of your youth, because you have broken faith with her, though she is your partner, the wife of your marriage covenant.

a 10 Or father   b 12 Or [12]*May the LORD cut off from the tents of Jacob anyone who gives testimony in behalf of the man who does this*

Friday

Your Best Shot

Read Malachi 1:14

I think it's pretty common for people my age to kind of slack off when it comes to God. I know I don't always make God my top priority. Take Sunday mornings, for example. I have one hour set aside during the week when I can go to church with my family, worship God and spend time with other Christians. But almost every week I'm late for church. And when I'm late, I cheat God out of my time and attention.

We can all make excuses about why we cheat God out of our time, our talents or whatever. But really, there's no excuse. God is so good to us and deserves our very best. Even if no one is looking, even if there are no immediate rewards for giving God our best, that's what we need to do.

When we cheat God out of our best, we're really cheating ourselves out of the best possible relationship with him.

Nikki age 15

❶ What are some ways you cheat God out of your best? What changes would you need to make to really give God your very best?

❷ Make a list of your "bests": your best talent, best possession, best personality trait . . . you get the idea. How can God use these things?

❸ Ask God to help you give him your very best.

Turn to page 1134 for your next devotion.

One-minute History

The Bible covers a lot of history. See if you can put some of that history in order, starting with what happens in the book of Exodus. (We left out all the stuff that happens in Genesis, which covers a giant time line all by itself.) Match each historical summary to the approximate years in the time line by drawing a line between them.

Time Line

1. 1440–1400 B.C.

2. 1400–1050 B.C.

3. 1050–930 B.C.

4. 930–600 B.C.

5. 600–530 B.C.

6. 530–4 B.C.

7. 4 B.C.–30 A.D.

8. 30–100 A.D.

What Happened

a. *Good News:* Jesus' followers sit down and write the New Testament, traveling around the Mediterranean to preach and start churches.

b. *Starting Over:* The Jewish people rebuild Jerusalem and their temple. Then we don't hear much from them till a certain Someone shows up.

c. *Lost on the Way:* The Israelites make a big escape from Egypt, head for the Promised Land, but get sidetracked by their own disobedience.

d. *God Arrives:* Jesus shows up to extend our own time line into eternity.

e. *Home Away From Home:* The people of Judah spend 70 years slaving for Babylon and Persia before they're allowed to go back home.

f. *From Bad to Worse:* The Israelite nation has a fight and gets divorced. The northern kingdom, Israel, gets stomped by the Assyrians. The southern kingdom of Judah eventually gets carted off to Babylon.

g. *This Land Is Our Land:* The Israelite people take over the promised land and set up a nation with God as their King.

h. *We Three Kings:* Israel gets in a royal mood, appoints a king named Saul, then another named David, then one more named Solomon.

answer: 1-c, 2-g, 3-h, 4-f, 5-e, 6-b, 7-d, 8-a

¹⁵Has not the LORD made them one? In flesh and spirit they are his. And why one? Because he was seeking godly offspring.ᵃ So guard yourself in your spirit, and do not break faith with the wife of your youth.

¹⁶"I hate divorce," says the LORD God of Israel, "and I hate a man's covering himselfᵇ with violence as well as with his garment," says the LORD Almighty.

So guard yourself in your spirit, and do not break faith.

The Day of Judgment

¹⁷You have wearied the LORD with your words.

"How have we wearied him?" you ask.

By saying, "All who do evil are good in the eyes of the LORD, and he is pleased with them" or "Where is the God of justice?"

ᵃ15 Or ¹⁵But the one who is our father did not do this, not as long as life remained in him. And what was he seeking? An offspring from God ᵇ16 Or his wife

3 "See, I will send my messenger, who will prepare the way before me. Then suddenly the Lord you are seeking will come to his temple; the messenger of the covenant, whom you desire, will come," says the LORD Almighty.

²But who can endure the day of his coming? Who can stand when he appears? For he will be like a refiner's fire or a launderer's soap. ³He will sit as a refiner and purifier of silver; he will purify the Levites and refine them like gold and silver. Then the LORD will have men who will bring offerings in righteousness, ⁴and the offerings of Judah and Jerusalem will be acceptable to the LORD, as in days gone by, as in former years.

⁵"So I will come near to you for judgment. I will be quick to testify against sorcerers, adulterers and perjurers, against those who defraud laborers of their wages, who oppress the widows and the fatherless, and deprive aliens of justice, but do not fear me," says the LORD Almighty.

Robbing God

⁶"I the LORD do not change. So you, O descendants of Jacob, are not destroyed. ⁷Ever since the time of your forefathers you have turned away from my decrees and have not kept them. Return to me, and I will return to you," says the LORD Almighty.

"But you ask, 'How are we to return?'

⁸"Will a man rob God? Yet you rob me.

"But you ask, 'How do we rob you?'

"In tithes and offerings. ⁹You are under a curse—the whole nation of you—because you are robbing me. ¹⁰Bring the whole tithe into the storehouse, that there may be food in my house. Test me

---

Weekend.

Written All Over Us

Read Romans 1:6 (page 1351)

What a great statement by Kate in Tuesday's devotion: "God's name is written all over us." That's a pretty radical statement. And it's important to understand what it means—*and what it doesn't mean.*

It doesn't mean God makes us into religious zombies who walk around like robots and say "Hallelujah" all the time. And it doesn't mean we live perfect lives. No. God's name is written all over us in *the way we are made*— our gifts, our personalities, our strengths and weaknesses, our likes and dislikes, our desire to know God better. All those things come from God, all of them draw us closer. Everything about us is *at home* when we are with God. When we give ourselves to God, we are *coming home to God!* Since we *belong* to God, we never feel really whole or full or completed until we come back *to where we belong.* It is like we are the missing piece in a huge puzzle, and when we fit our unique shape into God's puzzle, the puzzle is complete.

What about You?

❶ Think back to the time you first asked Jesus to come into your life. How did you feel? Write down how you felt.

❷ Take some time to write down what you think Kate meant by saying that "God's name is written all over us." Carry what you write inside your school notebook and look at it each day this week.

❸ Then pray, "God, help me to see you in me every day this week. Help me to show others your name written all over me."

Turn to page 1141 for your next devotion.

in this," says the LORD Almighty, "and see if I will not throw open the floodgates of heaven and pour out so much blessing that you will not have room enough for it. ¹¹I will prevent pests from devouring your crops, and the vines in your fields will not cast their fruit," says the LORD Almighty. ¹²"Then all the nations will call you blessed, for yours will be a delightful land," says the LORD Almighty.

¹³"You have said harsh things against me," says the LORD.

"Yet you ask, 'What have we said against you?'

¹⁴"You have said, 'It is futile to serve God. What did we gain by carrying out his requirements and going about like mourners before the LORD Almighty? ¹⁵But now we call the arrogant blessed. Certainly the evildoers prosper, and even those who challenge God escape.' "

¹⁶Then those who feared the LORD talked with each other, and the LORD listened and heard. A scroll of remembrance was written in his presence concerning those who feared the LORD and honored his name.

¹⁷"They will be mine," says the LORD Almighty, "in the day when I make up my treasured possession.ᵃ I will spare them, just as in compassion a man spares his son who serves him. ¹⁸And you will

again see the distinction between the righteous and the wicked, between those who serve God and those who do not.

The Day of the LORD

4 "Surely the day is coming; it will burn like a furnace. All the arrogant and every evildoer will be stubble, and that day that is coming will set them on fire," says the LORD Almighty. "Not a root or a branch will be left to them. ²But for you who revere my name, the sun of righteousness will rise with healing in its wings. And you will go out and leap like calves released from the stall. ³Then you will trample down the wicked; they will be ashes under the soles of your feet on the day when I do these things," says the LORD Almighty.

⁴"Remember the law of my servant Moses, the decrees and laws I gave him at Horeb for all Israel.

⁵"See, I will send you the prophet Elijah before that great and dreadful day of the LORD comes. ⁶He will turn the hearts of the fathers to their children, and the hearts of the children to their fathers; or else I will come and strike the land with a curse."

ᵃ17 Or Almighty, "my treasured possession, in the day when I act

New
Testament

Matthew

START

Was Matthew a slime ball? That's what everyone would've thought in Bible times because he was a tax collector. Tax collectors were known to be bad news because they often cheated people. Even when they didn't, they represented the long arm of the government and often took money from "the little people."

When Jesus walked up to Matthew (also called Levi) in his little tax-collecting booth and said, "Leave everything and follow me," it was a pretty big request. Tax collecting was a cushy job—it paid big bucks and was an easy way of life (except for the part that nobody could stand them!). Matthew knew that if he left his tax office, he could never come back. But there was something about this Jesus guy . . .

So Matthew left. And followed. He became one of the 12 disciples who followed Jesus everywhere. About 30 years after Jesus' death, Matthew put his old record-keeping skills to use again and wrote this summary of Jesus' life and teaching.

Cast OF Characters

Matthew
One of the 12 disciples, and the author of this book.

Jesus
This is the true story of his life—recorded by a guy who was good with details.

The Jews
While Jesus came to offer free salvation to everyone, Jews and non-Jews, Matthew wrote mostly to the Jews. They were the ones already looking for a Messiah; and Matthew wanted to show them that Jesus was the answer to their search.

Mary and Joseph
Jesus' mother and step-father (God was Jesus' real Father). Mary was still a virgin when God placed Jesus in her womb.

John the Baptist
John was Jesus' cousin. He was also a guy God used to announce Jesus' arrival. He wasn't called "the Baptist" because of a church name or something like that but because he baptized people, including Jesus. Oh, and he ate weird stuff too.

The 12 Disciples
(diss-SY-pulls)
Matthew was one of them. These guys spent a few years with Jesus—saw everything he did, heard everything he said. Then they became key leaders in the early Christian movement (see the book of Acts).

What's Up with That?

Story Time

Jesus uses some cool stories in his teachings. They're called parables (PAIR-uh-bulls). They're kind of like verbal pictures. Jesus used them for a few reasons: to illustrate what he was teaching, to make people think, to confuse some of the religious leaders. Try to pick some of his stories out of this list:

1 One Seed, Two Seed, Red Seed, Blue Seed

2 I Love My Pearl!

3 The Kitten Drank Too Much Milk

4 Who's That Guy With the Goatee?

5 Servants Who Slaughter!

6 Of Smelly Armpits and Bad Breath

7 Smart Bridesmaids, Not So Smart Bridesmaids

8 Who's in the Net?

9 Marching Orders for Marge

10 Work 12 Hours, Get 5 Bucks; Work 1 Hour, Get 5 Bucks

11 That's Not Nougat!

12 The Weird Wedding Party

Snap Shots

- A babe is born *(chapters 1:1—2:23)*

- Jesus starts doing his thing *(chapters 3:1—4:11)*

- Jesus rocks the world *(chapters 4:12—25:46)*

- A plot, a beating, a murder *(chapters 26:1—27:66)*

- A miracle *(chapter 28:1–20)*

answers: 1(13:3-9), 2(13:45-46), 5(21:33-41), 7(25:1-13), 8(13:47-50), 10(20:1-16), 12(22:1-14)

The Genealogy of Jesus

1 A record of the genealogy of Jesus Christ the son of David, the son of Abraham:

² Abraham was the father of Isaac,
Isaac the father of Jacob,
Jacob the father of Judah and his brothers,
³ Judah the father of Perez and Zerah, whose mother was Tamar,
Perez the father of Hezron,
Hezron the father of Ram,
⁴ Ram the father of Amminadab,
Amminadab the father of Nahshon,
Nahshon the father of Salmon,
⁵ Salmon the father of Boaz, whose mother was Rahab,
Boaz the father of Obed, whose mother was Ruth,
Obed the father of Jesse,
⁶ and Jesse the father of King David.

David was the father of Solomon, whose mother had been Uriah's wife,
⁷ Solomon the father of Rehoboam,
Rehoboam the father of Abijah,
Abijah the father of Asa,
⁸ Asa the father of Jehoshaphat,
Jehoshaphat the father of Jehoram,
Jehoram the father of Uzziah,
⁹ Uzziah the father of Jotham,
Jotham the father of Ahaz,
Ahaz the father of Hezekiah,
¹⁰ Hezekiah the father of Manasseh,
Manasseh the father of Amon,
Amon the father of Josiah,
¹¹ and Josiah the father of Jeconiah^a and his brothers at the time of the exile to Babylon.

¹² After the exile to Babylon:
Jeconiah was the father of Shealtiel,
Shealtiel the father of Zerubbabel,
¹³ Zerubbabel the father of Abiud,
Abiud the father of Eliakim,
Eliakim the father of Azor,
¹⁴ Azor the father of Zadok,
Zadok the father of Akim,
Akim the father of Eliud,
¹⁵ Eliud the father of Eleazar,

Eleazar the father of Matthan,
Matthan the father of Jacob,
¹⁶ and Jacob the father of Joseph, the husband of Mary, of whom was born Jesus, who is called Christ.

¹⁷ Thus there were fourteen generations in all from Abraham to David, fourteen from David to the exile to Babylon, and fourteen from the exile to the Christ.^b

The Birth of Jesus Christ

¹⁸ This is how the birth of Jesus Christ came about: His mother Mary was pledged to be married to Joseph, but before they came together, she was found to be with child through the Holy Spirit. ¹⁹ Because Joseph her husband was a righteous man and did not want to expose her to public disgrace, he had in mind to divorce her quietly.

²⁰ But after he had considered this, an angel of the Lord appeared to him in a dream and said, "Joseph son of David, do not be afraid to take Mary home as your wife, because what is conceived in her is from the Holy Spirit. ²¹ She will give birth to a son, and you are to give him the name Jesus,^c because he will save his people from their sins."

---

^a11 That is, Jehoiachin; also in verse 12   ^b17 Or *Messiah*. "The Christ" (Greek) and "the Messiah" (Hebrew) both mean "the Anointed One."   ^c21 *Jesus* is the Greek form of *Joshua*, which means *the LORD saves.*

Nice Roots

Huh?

Matthew 1:1
Who's your great-great-great-grandfather? Don't know? The Bible has a record of Jesus' human family tree. We can see all the folks who are related to Jesus all the way back to Abraham. This connects him with the past as a relative of Israel's greatest kings and leaders. Kings don't just burst onto the scene; they have to belong to a royal bloodline. Matthew sets the stage with Jesus' roots.

Guys and Girls

Back Stage Pass

At age 16, most kids feel it's their God-given right to buckle up, start the engine and cruise the planet. It's instinctive. From somewhere deep within, they discover the drive to drive. But just because they feel it doesn't mean they automatically get to do it. Adults are quick to remind kids that driving is a privilege, not a right. It takes time and training before a person can safely operate a car. So you begin with driver's education class and a learner's permit. Later you take written and physical exams, followed by a test of your driving skills. If you pass everything—and can afford insurance—you get to *drive*.

Now, no matter how eager you feel, you have to admit that the system makes sense. Driving is an awesome and useful skill, but it's also complicated and dangerous. Lives are at stake. You have to prove yourself capable of handling the responsibility. The same is true of sex. At about age 12 (sometimes younger for girls) God sends a wild thing called "puberty" your way. It's the beginnings of the "sex drive" he builds into every human body. Girls who made you gag in 4th grade make you goggle in 7th grade. Guys who once had cooties now look like cuties. Happens to everyone.

But just because you begin to feel a sex drive doesn't mean you're ready to have sex. It means you are ready to learn about sex. There are so many lessons to learn that this driver's ed phase lasts a long time. (Ugh!) But sometime later in life you'll probably get your license. It's called a marriage license. In order to prepare, you'll need to learn to:

Control your body. First Thessalonians 4:3–8 (page 1454) tells us that God wants us to learn to control our bodies in holy and honorable ways. We're not sensual sex machines.

We're God's holy people. And "holy" ought to describe us sexually as well as spiritually.

Live like family. Galatians 3:26–28 (page 1419) tells us that all Christians are God's children. We're all brothers and sisters. That means the girl you like is first and foremost your sister in Christ. She's also a princess, a daughter of the King (yeah, God's the King). Learn to treat her accordingly. And that awesome hunk of a guy? He's your brother in Christ!

Think purely. Ephesians 5:3–4 (page 1429) warns us to guard against every hint of sexual impurity, including obscene talk and crude jokes. In the perverted world we live in, this is hard to do! But begin training your mind and mouth now. The power and purity of your sex life depend on it.

Love appropriately. You need to learn to love without having sex before you can "make love" by having sex. First Corinthians 13 (page 1389) is the greatest description of love in the Bible. Work on developing the qualities it describes, especially in verses 4–7. When you can put your name into this passage in place of the word *love*—"Heather is patient, Heather is kind. She does not envy, she does not boast . . ." —then you'll really understand love and be ready to share it with the person you marry.

FAITH

"I know the Bible is God's Word, but times and customs have changed since it was written. Should I take every word for real?"

The world has changed a lot since the Bible was written. But that doesn't create as much of a problem as you might think.

First, we have to understand some things about literature and language. The Bible is God's Word, spoken through the lips and pens of human beings. Even when God himself spoke out loud, people who heard him wrote the words down as they remembered them. Because God chose to speak through people (see Hebrews 1:1-2, page 1488), he also chose the words that would mean the most to those who heard him, just like we do today. If we want to say that something moved very fast, we might say it moved "like a rocket." If you'd said that in Jesus' day, nobody would have had a clue what you were talking about, so you might have said "like a flying arrow" instead—something they'd understand.

All of literature includes "figures of speech" that are meant to make something clearer. They aren't to be taken literally. For example, the Bible speaks of the "four corners of the earth" (Revelation 7:1). This doesn't mean the earth really has 4 corners. It means "to all of the extremes" or "as far as you can go." In another example, Jesus called Peter a "rock" (Matthew 16:18). He obviously didn't confuse Peter with a boulder; he was saying that Peter was solid and dependable.

If you were reading a book for school, your teacher would ask you to read it carefully, look up the words you didn't understand and learn some facts about its author and the time it was written. We have to approach the Bible in much the same way—as serious students. That's why our pastors study for many years, even learning the ancient languages in which the Bible was originally written. Pastors want to make sure they get it right so their sermons can be clear and accurate.

When we don't understand something in the Bible, we should ask our parents or our church leaders to explain it to us. That'll help keep us from doing something foolish because we thought we understood what a certain passage meant. For example, the Bible says that if our hand or foot causes us to sin, we should cut it off, and if our eye causes us to sin, we should pluck it out (see Mark 9:43-47, page 1202). Obviously, God doesn't want us all to grab big knives and trim off our toes. The verse is just meant to show us how serious sin is, and how we can hurt others by our actions. It's telling us to get serious about getting rid of the sin in our lives.

So, the Bible is God speaking clearly and without confusion.

— Jay Kesler, president of Taylor University and a former contributing editor to Campus Life magazine. Jay has also written several books for teens.

²²All this took place to fulfill what the Lord had said through the prophet: ²³"The virgin will be with child and will give birth to a son, and they will call him Immanuel"*ᵃ*—which means, "God with us."

²⁴When Joseph woke up, he did what the angel of the Lord had commanded him and took Mary home as his wife. ²⁵But he had no union with her until she gave birth to a son. And he gave him the name Jesus.

The Visit of the Magi

2 After Jesus was born in Bethlehem in Judea, during the time of King Herod, Magi*ᵇ* from the east came to Jerusalem ²and asked, "Where is the one who has been born king of the Jews? We saw his star in the east*ᶜ* and have come to worship him."

³When King Herod heard this he was disturbed, and all Jerusalem with him. ⁴When he had called together all the peo-ple's chief priests and teachers of the law, he asked them where the Christ*ᵈ* was to be born. ⁵"In Bethlehem in Judea," they replied, "for this is what the prophet has written:

⁶" 'But you, Bethlehem, in the land of Judah,
        are by no means least among the rulers of Judah;
for out of you will come a ruler
    who will be the shepherd of my people Israel.'*ᵉ*"

⁷Then Herod called the Magi secretly and found out from them the exact time the star had appeared. ⁸He sent them to Bethlehem and said, "Go and make a careful search for the child. As soon as you find him, report to me, so that I too may go and worship him."

⁹After they had heard the king, they

ᵃ23 Isaiah 7:14   *ᵇ1* Traditionally *Wise Men*
ᶜ2 Or *star when it rose*   *ᵈ4* Or *Messiah*   *ᵉ6* Micah 5:2

Mon day

Jesus' Relatives

Read Matthew 1:1–17

When I first read these verses, I didn't see how they could possibly mean much of anything for me personally. It's just a list of names! But then I re-membered who some of these people were, and I started to get the idea.

All the people on this list are Jesus' relatives, so you'd think they'd be pretty good people. But some of them weren't very good at all. Remember Jacob and Esau? Jacob totally tricked his brother and stole his birthright—but Jacob's on the list. Tamar was thought to be a prostitute, and Rahab actually was one. David killed Uriah in order to take his wife Bathsheba. All these people are related to Jesus!

I guess this proves that God really can use anyone to bring about his plan. So if you ever feel that you are worthless or good-for-nothing, this passage can help you realize that God has a special plan for everyone—including you.

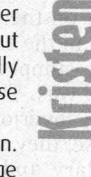
Kristen age 13

What about You?

❶ Why do you think God allowed such "imperfect" people to be a part of Jesus' family tree?

❷ With your parents' help, write out your own family tree. Ask about the people whose names you see. What can you learn from their good and bad examples?

❸ Thank God that he knows exactly how everyone fits into his plan.

Turn to page 1144 for your next devotion.

What's in a Name?

Matthew 1:21 *Melchizedek* means "king of righteousness." He's the cool king and high priest of ancient Jerusalem. Centuries later, Israel's kings are descendants of Judah, but the *priests* must be descendants of Judah's brother Levi—a different branch on the family tree. So when people ask how *King* Jesus of Judah can also be a priest, the Christians point to old Mel and say, "Mel was a king *and* priest before Judah and Levi were even born. *And so was Jesus!*" So there (Genesis 14:18–20; Psalm 110:4; Hebrews 5:4–10).

Abraham means "father of many." Abram's wife is 90 years old, so when God adds a syllable to his name and tells him he's going to become the father of many nations, old Abe falls on the floor laughing. But God isn't joking, and now all Jews and Arabs can count Abraham as their forefather. God picks good names (Genesis 17:1–22).

Sarah means "princess." God gives her that name when she's 90, right before she's about to have her first child! It's a great name because she becomes the very great-great- etc. grandmother of all Jews (Genesis 17:15).

Israel means "he who struggles with God." God gives Jacob that name after they wrestle! And since all Jews are descended from this God-wrestler, Israel became the name of the nation too (Genesis 32:28).

Peter means "rock." It's the name Jesus gives to Simon, a guy no one would ever think to nickname Rocky. No one except Jesus, that is. But Jesus sees more in Simon than meets the eye, and the disciple eventually lives up to his new name (Matthew 16:18).

Boanerges means "Sons of Thunder." That's what Jesus calls James and John. Apparently they had a lot of spirit! (Mark 3:17).

....Best Name Ever

Jesus means "The Lord saves." It's a great name! Every time we say it, we're declaring, "Hey! God is salvation!" So to use his name as a curse is not only wrong, it's stupid! When people use the name of Jesus as a curse word, they obviously don't know what they're *really* saying. Jesus came to earth to tell us, "God is our salvation!" His own death and resurrection made that salvation possible. And in case we forget, he puts this great message right within his name (Matthew 1:21).

went on their way, and the star they had seen in the east[a] went ahead of them until it stopped over the place where the child was. ¹⁰When they saw the star, they were overjoyed. ¹¹On coming to the house, they saw the child with his mother Mary, and they bowed down and worshiped him. Then they opened their treasures and presented him with gifts of gold and of incense and of myrrh. ¹²And having been warned in a dream not to go back to Herod, they returned to their country by another route.

The Escape to Egypt

¹³When they had gone, an angel of the Lord appeared to Joseph in a dream. "Get up," he said, "take the child and his mother and escape to Egypt. Stay there until I tell you, for Herod is going to search for the child to kill him."

¹⁴So he got up, took the child and his mother during the night and left for Egypt, ¹⁵where he stayed until the death of Herod. And so was fulfilled what the Lord had said through the prophet: "Out of Egypt I called my son."[b]

¹⁶When Herod realized that he had been outwitted by the Magi, he was furious, and he gave orders to kill all the boys in Bethlehem and its vicinity who were two years old and under, in accordance with the time he had learned from the Magi. ¹⁷Then what was said through the prophet Jeremiah was fulfilled:

¹⁸"A voice is heard in Ramah,

a9 Or seen when it rose   *b15 Hosea 11:1*

weeping and great mourning,
Rachel weeping for her children
   and refusing to be comforted,
because they are no more."[a]

The Return to Nazareth

¹⁹After Herod died, an angel of the Lord appeared in a dream to Joseph in Egypt ²⁰and said, "Get up, take the child and his mother and go to the land of Israel, for those who were trying to take the child's life are dead."

²¹So he got up, took the child and his mother and went to the land of Israel. ²²But when he heard that Archelaus was reigning in Judea in place of his father Herod, he was afraid to go there. Having been warned in a dream, he withdrew to the district of Galilee, ²³and he went and lived in a town called Nazareth. So was fulfilled what was said through the prophets: "He will be called a Nazarene."

John the Baptist Prepares the Way

3 In those days John the Baptist came, preaching in the Desert of Judea ²and saying, "Repent, for the kingdom of heaven is near." ³This is he who was spoken of through the prophet Isaiah:

"A voice of one calling in the desert,
'Prepare the way for the Lord,
   make straight paths for him.' "[b]

⁴John's clothes were made of camel's hair, and he had a leather belt around his waist. His food was locusts and wild honey. ⁵People went out to him from Je-

rusalem and all Judea and the whole region of the Jordan. ⁶Confessing their sins, they were baptized by him in the Jordan River.

⁷But when he saw many of the Pharisees and Sadducees coming to where he was baptizing, he said to them: "You brood of vipers! Who warned you to flee from the coming wrath? ⁸Produce fruit in keeping with repentance. ⁹And do not think you can say to yourselves, 'We have Abraham as our father.' I tell you that out of these stones God can raise up children for Abraham. ¹⁰The ax is already at the root of the trees, and every tree that does not produce good fruit will be cut down and thrown into the fire.

¹¹"I baptize you with[c] water for repentance. But after me will come one who is more powerful than I, whose sandals I am not fit to carry. He will baptize you with the Holy Spirit and with fire. ¹²His winnowing fork is in his hand, and he will clear his threshing floor, gathering

---

[a]18 Jer. 31:15   [b]3 Isaiah 40:3   [c]11 Or *in*

his wheat into the barn and burning up the chaff with unquenchable fire."

The Baptism of Jesus

¹³Then Jesus came from Galilee to the Jordan to be baptized by John. ¹⁴But John tried to deter him, saying, "I need to be baptized by you, and do you come to me?"

¹⁵Jesus replied, "Let it be so now; it is proper for us to do this to fulfill all righteousness." Then John consented.

¹⁶As soon as Jesus was baptized, he went up out of the water. At that moment heaven was opened, and he saw the Spirit of God descending like a dove and lighting on him. ¹⁷And a voice from heaven said, "This is my Son, whom I love; with him I am well pleased."

The Temptation of Jesus

4 Then Jesus was led by the Spirit into the desert to be tempted by the devil.

²After fasting forty days and forty nights, he was hungry. ³The tempter came to him and said, "If you are the Son of God, tell these stones to become bread."

⁴Jesus answered, "It is written: 'Man does not live on bread alone, but on every word that comes from the mouth of God.'ᵃ"

⁵Then the devil took him to the holy city and had him stand on the highest point of the temple. ⁶"If you are the Son of God," he said, "throw yourself down. For it is written:

" 'He will command his angels
     concerning you,
   and they will lift you up in their
     hands,
so that you will not strike your foot
     against a stone.'ᵇ"

ᵃ4 Deut. 8:3 ᵇ6 Psalm 91:11,12

Tuesday

Breakin' the Rules

Read Matthew 4:1–10

One of my friends wanted me to stay over at his house one night when his parents weren't home. I knew my parents wouldn't approve, but I did it anyway. The next day, we were both in big trouble with our parents for having a sleepover without their permission.

I'm faced with temptation every day. There's always someone asking me to go out and do something I shouldn't. It's tempting to break my parents' rules. Most of the time, I can stand up to temptation. But every once in a while, I give in.

It helps to know that Jesus faced temptation too. He knows how it feels to resist the temptation to do something we shouldn't. He also knows that rules are there for a reason.

God loves us and doesn't want us to get hurt or in trouble. If I can remember that the next time I face temptation, I'll be more likely to follow God and do the right thing.

Justin age 14

What about You?

❶ What are some things that really tempt you? What would happen if you gave in to those temptations? How would you feel?

❷ Pick one of your temptations. What would you say to someone who asks you to give in to this temptation? Practice so that saying no to temptation becomes a habit.

❸ Ask God to give you the strength to resist temptation.

Turn to page 1146 for your next devotion.

[7]Jesus answered him, "It is also written: 'Do not put the Lord your God to the test.'[a]"

[8]Again, the devil took him to a very high mountain and showed him all the kingdoms of the world and their splendor. [9]"All this I will give you," he said, "if you will bow down and worship me."

[10]Jesus said to him, "Away from me, Satan! For it is written: 'Worship the Lord your God, and serve him only.'[b]"

[11]Then the devil left him, and angels came and attended him.

Jesus Begins to Preach

[12]When Jesus heard that John had been put in prison, he returned to Galilee. [13]Leaving Nazareth, he went and lived in Capernaum, which was by the lake in the area of Zebulun and Naphtali— [14]to fulfill what was said through the prophet Isaiah:

[15]"Land of Zebulun and land of
       Naphtali,
   the way to the sea, along the
       Jordan,
   Galilee of the Gentiles—
[16]the people living in darkness
   have seen a great light;
on those living in the land of the
       shadow of death
   a light has dawned."[c]

[17]From that time on Jesus began to preach, "Repent, for the kingdom of heaven is near."

The Calling of the First Disciples

[18]As Jesus was walking beside the Sea of Galilee, he saw two brothers, Simon called Peter and his brother Andrew. They were casting a net into the lake, for they were fishermen. [19]"Come, follow me," Jesus said, "and I will make you fishers of men." [20]At once they left their nets and followed him.

[21]Going on from there, he saw two other brothers, James son of Zebedee and his brother John. They were in a boat with their father Zebedee, preparing their nets. Jesus called them, [22]and immediately they left the boat and their father and followed him.

Jesus Heals the Sick

[23]Jesus went throughout Galilee, teaching in their synagogues, preaching the good news of the kingdom, and healing every disease and sickness among the people. [24]News about him spread all

Super-good News

Huh?

Matthew 4:23

Jesus is the good news. His arrival on earth, death on the cross and resurrection from death are the best news we could ever receive. This news means that if you believe in Jesus and give your life to him, you are forgiven of all your sin. You've started a relationship with God and will live with him in heaven for eternity. *Talk about good news!*

over Syria, and people brought to him all who were ill with various diseases, those suffering severe pain, the demon-possessed, those having seizures, and the paralyzed, and he healed them. [25]Large crowds from Galilee, the Decapolis,[d] Jerusalem, Judea and the region across the Jordan followed him.

The Beatitudes

5 Now when he saw the crowds, he went up on a mountainside and sat down. His disciples came to him, [2]and he began to teach them, saying:

[3]"Blessed are the poor in spirit,
   for theirs is the kingdom of
       heaven.
[4]Blessed are those who mourn,
   for they will be comforted.
[5]Blessed are the meek,
   for they will inherit the earth.
[6]Blessed are those who hunger and
       thirst for righteousness,
   for they will be filled.
[7]Blessed are the merciful,
   for they will be shown mercy.

[a]7 Deut. 6:16   [b]10 Deut. 6:13   [c]16 Isaiah 9:1,2
[d]25 That is, the Ten Cities

⁸Blessed are the pure in heart,
    for they will see God.
⁹Blessed are the peacemakers,
    for they will be called sons of God.
¹⁰Blessed are those who are persecuted
    because of righteousness,
    for theirs is the kingdom of heaven.

¹¹"Blessed are you when people insult you, persecute you and falsely say all kinds of evil against you because of me. ¹²Rejoice and be glad, because great is your reward in heaven, for in the same way they persecuted the prophets who were before you.

Salt and Light

¹³"You are the salt of the earth. But if the salt loses its saltiness, how can it be made salty again? It is no longer good for anything, except to be thrown out and trampled by men.

¹⁴"You are the light of the world. A city on a hill cannot be hidden. ¹⁵Neither do people light a lamp and put it under a bowl. Instead they put it on its stand, and it gives light to everyone in the house. ¹⁶In the same way, let your light shine before men, that they may see your good deeds and praise your Father in heaven.

The Fulfillment of the Law

¹⁷"Do not think that I have come to abolish the Law or the Prophets; I have not come to abolish them but to fulfill them. ¹⁸I tell you the truth, until heaven and earth disappear, not the smallest letter, not the least stroke of a pen, will by any means disappear from the Law until everything is accomplished. ¹⁹Anyone who breaks one of the least of these commandments and teaches others to do the same will be called least in the kingdom of heaven, but whoever practices and teaches these commands will be called great in the kingdom of heaven. ²⁰For I tell you that unless your righteousness surpasses that of the Pharisees and the teachers of the law, you will certainly not enter the kingdom of heaven.

Wednesday

No Worries

Read Matthew 5:11

I once memorized the Beatitudes (Matthew 5:3–12), but I never noticed what this particular one was saying. If I had, I would have saved myself a lot of grief. See, I've always felt that if I dressed and acted the way God wanted me to, people at school wouldn't accept me. But if I tried to please the people at school, I knew God wouldn't be happy with me. I didn't know what to do, so I spent a lot of time worrying.

Instead of worrying, I should have spent that time thinking about God. He's the One who makes right judgments; he'll never make fun of me for doing the right thing. I need to be concerned with what he thinks of me, not what anybody else thinks.

❶ Have you ever been insulted because of your beliefs? What happened, and how did you react?

❷ Blow up a balloon as big as you can. Start squeezing it until it pops. Ask yourself: How am I like the balloon? What or who is putting pressure on your life to make you fit in? What can you do to be sure the pressure doesn't make you pop?

❸ Ask God to help you stand your ground when people give you a hard time.

Turn to page 1149 for your next devotion.

Murder

[21]"You have heard that it was said to the people long ago, 'Do not murder,[a] and anyone who murders will be subject to judgment.' [22]But I tell you that anyone who is angry with his brother[b] will be subject to judgment. Again, anyone who says to his brother, 'Raca,'[c] is answerable to the Sanhedrin. But anyone who says, 'You fool!' will be in danger of the fire of hell.

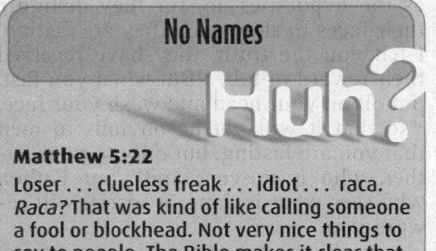

No Names

Huh?

Matthew 5:22

Loser . . . clueless freak . . . idiot . . . raca. *Raca?* That was kind of like calling someone a fool or blockhead. Not very nice things to say to people. The Bible makes it clear that name-calling is a no-no! That other person is made in God's image, just like you. So when you call him or her a name, you're really criticizing God.

[23]"Therefore, if you are offering your gift at the altar and there remember that your brother has something against you, [24]leave your gift there in front of the altar. First go and be reconciled to your brother; then come and offer your gift.

[25]"Settle matters quickly with your adversary who is taking you to court. Do it while you are still with him on the way, or he may hand you over to the judge, and the judge may hand you over to the officer, and you may be thrown into prison. [26]I tell you the truth, you will not get out until you have paid the last penny.[d]

Adultery

[27]"You have heard that it was said, 'Do not commit adultery.'[e] [28]But I tell you that anyone who looks at a woman lustfully has already committed adultery with her in his heart. [29]If your right eye causes you to sin, gouge it out and throw it away. It is better for you to lose one part of your body than for your whole body to be thrown into hell. [30]And if your right hand causes you to sin, cut it off and throw it away. It is better for you to lose one part of your body than for your whole body to go into hell.

Divorce

[31]"It has been said, 'Anyone who divorces his wife must give her a certificate of divorce.'[f] [32]But I tell you that anyone who divorces his wife, except for marital unfaithfulness, causes her to become an adulteress, and anyone who marries the divorced woman commits adultery.

Oaths

[33]"Again, you have heard that it was said to the people long ago, 'Do not break your oath, but keep the oaths you have made to the Lord.' [34]But I tell you, Do not swear at all: either by heaven, for it is God's throne; [35]or by the earth, for it is his footstool; or by Jerusalem, for it is the city of the Great King. [36]And do not swear by your head, for you cannot make even one hair white or black. [37]Simply let your 'Yes' be 'Yes,' and your 'No,' 'No'; anything beyond this comes from the evil one.

An Eye for an Eye

[38]"You have heard that it was said, 'Eye for eye, and tooth for tooth.'[g] [39]But I tell you, Do not resist an evil person. If someone strikes you on the right cheek, turn to him the other also. [40]And if someone wants to sue you and take your tunic, let him have your cloak as well. [41]If someone forces you to go one mile, go with him two miles. [42]Give to the one who asks you, and do not turn away from the one who wants to borrow from you.

Love for Enemies

[43]"You have heard that it was said, 'Love your neighbor[h] and hate your enemy.' [44]But I tell you: Love your enemies[i] and pray for those who persecute you,

---

[a]21 Exodus 20:13   [b]22 Some manuscripts *brother without cause*   [c]22 An Aramaic term of contempt   [d]26 Greek *kodrantes*   [e]27 Exodus 20:14   [f]31 Deut. 24:1   [g]38 Exodus 21:24; Lev. 24:20; Deut. 19:21   [h]43 Lev. 19:18   [i]44 Some late manuscripts *enemies, bless those who curse you, do good to those who hate you*

[45]that you may be sons of your Father in heaven. He causes his sun to rise on the evil and the good, and sends rain on the righteous and the unrighteous. [46]If you love those who love you, what reward will you get? Are not even the tax collectors doing that? [47]And if you greet only your brothers, what are you doing more than others? Do not even pagans do that? [48]Be perfect, therefore, as your heavenly Father is perfect.

Giving to the Needy

6 "Be careful not to do your 'acts of righteousness' before men, to be seen by them. If you do, you will have no reward from your Father in heaven.

[2]"So when you give to the needy, do not announce it with trumpets, as the hypocrites do in the synagogues and on the streets, to be honored by men. I tell you the truth, they have received their reward in full. [3]But when you give to the needy, do not let your left hand know what your right hand is doing, [4]so that your giving may be in secret. Then your Father, who sees what is done in secret, will reward you.

Prayer

[5]"And when you pray, do not be like the hypocrites, for they love to pray standing in the synagogues and on the street corners to be seen by men. I tell you the truth, they have received their reward in full. [6]But when you pray, go into your room, close the door and pray to your Father, who is unseen. Then your Father, who sees what is done in secret, will reward you. [7]And when you pray, do not keep on babbling like pagans, for they think they will be heard because of their many words. [8]Do not be like them, for your Father knows what you need before you ask him.

[9]"This, then, is how you should pray:

" 'Our Father in heaven,
hallowed be your name,
[10]your kingdom come,
your will be done
on earth as it is in heaven.
[11]Give us today our daily bread.
[12]Forgive us our debts,
as we also have forgiven our
debtors.
[13]And lead us not into temptation,
but deliver us from the evil one.[a]'

[14]For if you forgive men when they sin against you, your heavenly Father will also forgive you. [15]But if you do not forgive men their sins, your Father will not forgive your sins.

Fasting

[16]"When you fast, do not look somber as the hypocrites do, for they disfigure their faces to show men they are fasting. I tell you the truth, they have received their reward in full. [17]But when you fast, put oil on your head and wash your face, [18]so that it will not be obvious to men that you are fasting, but only to your Father, who is unseen; and your Father, who sees what is done in secret, will reward you.

Treasures in Heaven

[19]"Do not store up for yourselves treasures on earth, where moth and rust destroy, and where thieves break in and steal. [20]But store up for yourselves treasures in heaven, where moth and rust do not destroy, and where thieves do not break in and steal. [21]For where your treasure is, there your heart will be also.

[22]"The eye is the lamp of the body. If your eyes are good, your whole body will be full of light. [23]But if your eyes are bad, your whole body will be full of darkness. If then the light within you is darkness, how great is that darkness!

[24]"No one can serve two masters. Either he will hate the one and love the other, or he will be devoted to the one and despise the other. You cannot serve both God and Money.

Do Not Worry

[25]"Therefore I tell you, do not worry about your life, what you will eat or drink; or about your body, what you will wear. Is not life more important than food, and the body more important than clothes? [26]Look at the birds of the air;

---

a13 Or from evil; some late manuscripts *one, / for yours is the kingdom and the power and the glory forever. Amen.*

they do not sow or reap or store away in barns, and yet your heavenly Father feeds them. Are you not much more valuable than they? ²⁷Who of you by worrying can add a single hour to his life*?

²⁸"And why do you worry about clothes? See how the lilies of the field grow. They do not labor or spin. ²⁹Yet I tell you that not even Solomon in all his splendor was dressed like one of these. ³⁰If that is how God clothes the grass of the field, which is here today and tomorrow is thrown into the fire, will he not much more clothe you, O you of little faith? ³¹So do not worry, saying, 'What shall we eat?' or 'What shall we drink?' or 'What shall we wear?' ³²For the pagans run after all these things, and your heavenly Father knows that you need them. ³³But seek first his kingdom and

his righteousness, and all these things will be given to you as well. ³⁴Therefore do not worry about tomorrow, for tomorrow will worry about itself. Each day has enough trouble of its own.

Judging Others

7 "Do not judge, or you too will be judged. ²For in the same way you judge others, you will be judged, and with the measure you use, it will be measured to you.

³"Why do you look at the speck of sawdust in your brother's eye and pay no attention to the plank in your own eye? ⁴How can you say to your brother, 'Let me take the speck out of your eye,' when all the time there is a plank in your own eye? ⁵You hypocrite, first take the plank

*27 Or *single cubit to his height*

Thursday

Stress Test

Read Matthew 6:25-34

I tend to get pretty stressed out about tests. But this passage tells me not to get so worried about stuff like school. That doesn't mean I should give up studying and just wait for God to help me pass my tests. It just means that as long as God is first in my life, I can be confident that he'll give me everything I need.

I like the way the passage talks about God caring for even the smallest animals. If he looks after them, I know he'll look after me, because God loves me even more than the animals. He'll always take care of me. And when I look at my life, I know that's true. I have friends, a family who cares about me, a place to live, food to eat and clothes to wear.

Seeing the way God takes care of the big things in my life, I know I can trust him to take care of the little things too. So I don't have to stress out about anything, including tests!

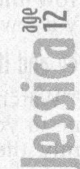
Jessica age 12

❶ What are some things that stress you out? How can God help you deal with those things?

❷ Write down all the things you're worried about. Now, put on a piece of clothing (like a hat, a sweater, extra socks) for each of those worries. How many "worries" can you wear before you feel totally weighed down? Now take off all those extra clothes. How does it feel to shed all those "worries"?

❸ Ask God to help you give your worries to him.

Turn to page 1154 for your next devotion.

out of your own eye, and then you will see clearly to remove the speck from your brother's eye.

⁶"Do not give dogs what is sacred; do not throw your pearls to pigs. If you do, they may trample them under their feet, and then turn and tear you to pieces.

Ask, Seek, Knock

⁷"Ask and it will be given to you; seek and you will find; knock and the door will be opened to you. ⁸For everyone who asks receives; he who seeks finds; and to him who knocks, the door will be opened.

⁹"Which of you, if his son asks for bread, will give him a stone? ¹⁰Or if he asks for a fish, will give him a snake? ¹¹If you, then, though you are evil, know how to give good gifts to your children, how much more will your Father in heaven give good gifts to those who ask him! ¹²So in everything, do to others what you would have them do to you, for this sums up the Law and the Prophets.

The Narrow and Wide Gates

¹³"Enter through the narrow gate. For wide is the gate and broad is the road that leads to destruction, and many enter through it. ¹⁴But small is the gate and narrow the road that leads to life, and only a few find it.

A Tree and Its Fruit

¹⁵"Watch out for false prophets. They come to you in sheep's clothing, but inwardly they are ferocious wolves. ¹⁶By their fruit you will recognize them. Do people pick grapes from thornbushes, or figs from thistles? ¹⁷Likewise every good tree bears good fruit, but a bad tree bears bad fruit. ¹⁸A good tree cannot bear bad fruit, and a bad tree cannot bear good fruit. ¹⁹Every tree that does not bear good fruit is cut down and thrown into the fire. ²⁰Thus, by their fruit you will recognize them.

²¹"Not everyone who says to me, 'Lord, Lord,' will enter the kingdom of heaven, but only he who does the will of my Father who is in heaven. ²²Many will say to me on that day, 'Lord, Lord, did we not prophesy in your name, and in your name drive out demons and perform many miracles?' ²³Then I will tell them plainly, 'I never knew you. Away from me, you evildoers!'

The Wise and Foolish Builders

²⁴"Therefore everyone who hears these words of mine and puts them into practice is like a wise man who built his house on the rock. ²⁵The rain came down, the streams rose, and the winds blew and beat against that house; yet it did not fall, because it had its foundation on the rock. ²⁶But everyone who hears these words of mine and does not put them into practice is like a foolish man who built his house on sand. ²⁷The rain came down, the streams rose, and the winds blew and beat against that house, and it fell with a great crash."

²⁸When Jesus had finished saying these things, the crowds were amazed at his teaching, ²⁹because he taught as one who had authority, and not as their teachers of the law.

The Man With Leprosy

8 When he came down from the mountainside, large crowds followed him. ²A man with leprosy[a] came and knelt before him and said, "Lord, if you are willing, you can make me clean."

³Jesus reached out his hand and touched the man. "I am willing," he said. "Be clean!" Immediately he was cured[b] of his leprosy. ⁴Then Jesus said to him, "See that you don't tell anyone. But go, show yourself to the priest and offer the gift Moses commanded, as a testimony to them."

The Faith of the Centurion

⁵When Jesus had entered Capernaum, a centurion came to him, asking for help. ⁶"Lord," he said, "my servant lies at home paralyzed and in terrible suffering."

⁷Jesus said to him, "I will go and heal him."

⁸The centurion replied, "Lord, I do not deserve to have you come under my roof. But just say the word, and my servant will be healed. ⁹For I myself am a man

---

[a]2 The Greek word was used for various diseases affecting the skin—not necessarily leprosy. [b]3 Greek *made clean*

under authority, with soldiers under me. I tell this one, 'Go,' and he goes; and that one, 'Come,' and he comes. I say to my servant, 'Do this,' and he does it."

¹⁰When Jesus heard this, he was astonished and said to those following him, "I tell you the truth, I have not found anyone in Israel with such great faith. ¹¹I say to you that many will come from the east and the west, and will take their places at the feast with Abraham, Isaac and Jacob in the kingdom of heaven. ¹²But the subjects of the kingdom will be thrown outside, into the darkness, where there will be weeping and gnashing of teeth."

¹³Then Jesus said to the centurion, "Go! It will be done just as you believed it would." And his servant was healed at that very hour.

Jesus Heals Many

¹⁴When Jesus came into Peter's house, he saw Peter's mother-in-law lying in bed with a fever. ¹⁵He touched her hand and the fever left her, and she got up and began to wait on him.

¹⁶When evening came, many who were demon-possessed were brought to him, and he drove out the spirits with a word and healed all the sick. ¹⁷This was to fulfill what was spoken through the prophet Isaiah:

"He took up our infirmities
    and carried our diseases."ᵃ

The Cost of Following Jesus

¹⁸When Jesus saw the crowd around him, he gave orders to cross to the other side of the lake. ¹⁹Then a teacher of the law came to him and said, "Teacher, I will follow you wherever you go."

²⁰Jesus replied, "Foxes have holes and birds of the air have nests, but the Son of Man has no place to lay his head."

²¹Another disciple said to him, "Lord, first let me go and bury my father."

²²But Jesus told him, "Follow me, and let the dead bury their own dead."

Jesus Calms the Storm

²³Then he got into the boat and his disciples followed him. ²⁴Without warning, a furious storm came up on the lake, so that the waves swept over the boat. But Jesus was sleeping. ²⁵The disciples went and woke him, saying, "Lord, save us! We're going to drown!"

²⁶He replied, "You of little faith, why are you so afraid?" Then he got up and rebuked the winds and the waves, and it was completely calm.

²⁷The men were amazed and asked, "What kind of man is this? Even the winds and the waves obey him!"

The Healing of Two Demon-possessed Men

²⁸When he arrived at the other side in the region of the Gadarenes,ᵇ two demon-possessed men coming from the tombs met him. They were so violent that no one could pass that way. ²⁹"What do you want with us, Son of God?" they shouted. "Have you come here to torture us before the appointed time?"

³⁰Some distance from them a large herd of pigs was feeding. ³¹The demons begged Jesus, "If you drive us out, send us into the herd of pigs."

³²He said to them, "Go!" So they came out and went into the pigs, and the whole herd rushed down the steep bank into the lake and died in the water. ³³Those tending the pigs ran off, went into the town and reported all this, including what had happened to the demon-possessed men. ³⁴Then the whole town went out to meet Jesus. And when they saw him, they pleaded with him to leave their region.

Jesus Heals a Paralytic

9 Jesus stepped into a boat, crossed over and came to his own town. ²Some men brought to him a paralytic, lying on a mat. When Jesus saw their faith, he said to the paralytic, "Take heart, son; your sins are forgiven."

³At this, some of the teachers of the law said to themselves, "This fellow is blaspheming!"

⁴Knowing their thoughts, Jesus said, "Why do you entertain evil thoughts in your hearts? ⁵Which is easier: to say, 'Your sins are forgiven,' or to say, 'Get up and walk'? ⁶But so that you may know that the Son of Man has authority on earth to forgive sins . . . ." Then he said to

ᵃ17 Isaiah 53:4 ᵇ28 Some manuscripts *Gergesenes*; others *Gerasenes*

You Ain't God

Huh?

Matthew 9:3

What if you went to your family and friends and announced, "I am God, and your sins are forgiven"? People would think you were nuts. To claim abilities that only belong to God is stupid. Only God knows hearts, and only God can forgive sins. So it makes sense that anyone who didn't recognize Jesus as the Son of God would consider his words of forgiveness blasphemy (mocking God or speaking untruth about him). It might surprise you to know that in Jesus' day blasphemy was illegal and punishable by death.

the paralytic, "Get up, take your mat and go home." [7]And the man got up and went home. [8]When the crowd saw this, they were filled with awe; and they praised God, who had given such authority to men.

The Calling of Matthew

[9]As Jesus went on from there, he saw a man named Matthew sitting at the tax collector's booth. "Follow me," he told him, and Matthew got up and followed him.

[10]While Jesus was having dinner at Matthew's house, many tax collectors and "sinners" came and ate with him and his disciples. [11]When the Pharisees saw this, they asked his disciples, "Why does your teacher eat with tax collectors and 'sinners'?"

[12]On hearing this, Jesus said, "It is not the healthy who need a doctor, but the sick. [13]But go and learn what this means: 'I desire mercy, not sacrifice.'[a] For I have not come to call the righteous, but sinners."

Jesus Questioned About Fasting

[14]Then John's disciples came and asked him, "How is it that we and the Pharisees fast, but your disciples do not fast?"

[15]Jesus answered, "How can the guests of the bridegroom mourn while he is

with them? The time will come when the bridegroom will be taken from them; then they will fast.

[16]"No one sews a patch of unshrunk cloth on an old garment, for the patch will pull away from the garment, making the tear worse. [17]Neither do men pour new wine into old wineskins. If they do, the skins will burst, the wine will run out and the wineskins will be ruined. No, they pour new wine into new wineskins, and both are preserved."

A Dead Girl and a Sick Woman

[18]While he was saying this, a ruler came and knelt before him and said, "My daughter has just died. But come and put your hand on her, and she will live." [19]Jesus got up and went with him, and so did his disciples.

[20]Just then a woman who had been subject to bleeding for twelve years came up behind him and touched the edge of his cloak. [21]She said to herself, "If I only touch his cloak, I will be healed."

[22]Jesus turned and saw her. "Take heart, daughter," he said, "your faith has healed you." And the woman was healed from that moment.

[23]When Jesus entered the ruler's house and saw the flute players and the noisy crowd, [24]he said, "Go away. The girl is not dead but asleep." But they laughed at him. [25]After the crowd had been put outside, he went in and took the girl by the hand, and she got up. [26]News of this spread through all that region.

Jesus Heals the Blind and Mute

[27]As Jesus went on from there, two blind men followed him, calling out, "Have mercy on us, Son of David!"

[28]When he had gone indoors, the blind men came to him, and he asked them, "Do you believe that I am able to do this?"

"Yes, Lord," they replied.

[29]Then he touched their eyes and said, "According to your faith will it be done to you"; [30]and their sight was restored. Jesus warned them sternly, "See that no one knows about this." [31]But they went out and spread the news about him all over that region.

[a]13 Hosea 6:6

A Dozen Guys

Matthew 10:1 When Jesus chose his 12 disciples, he didn't pick from some local honor roll or a Hebrew *Who's Who* list. He picked ordinary people. Which means he wound up with a dozen guys who occasionally did some pretty dumb stuff. Here are a few of the disciples' sillier moments:

Fishing Tips: Peter is an expert fisherman, but this time he's having no luck at all. When Jesus, the *inventor* of fish, shows up and makes a suggestion, Pete politely tells him that he already tried that. But he does as Jesus says anyway, and the net comes back so full that it almost sinks the boat. Pete and his net-tossing buddies give up fishing and follow Jesus (Luke 5:1–11).

Wake-up Call: The disciples are on a boating trip when a big storm blows in. Jesus is taking a nap. They freak out and scream, "Master, Master, we're going to drown!" Jesus wakes up, tells the storm to stop, then asks the stunned disciples what happened to their faith. Why should they doubt that the guy who could fish better than anyone, cure leprosy, make a lame person walk and turn dead people into live ones could make the wind and waves obey him? (Luke 8:22–25).

Big Picnic: During a big outdoor revival meeting, the disciples tell Jesus to wrap it up so the crowd can go to dinner. Jesus says,

"You feed them." The disciples look in their small picnic basket: five loaves of bread, two skinny fish. They look at the crowd: over 5,000 people. Then they say, "No way!" The thing is, Jesus had just given them the power to cure diseases and chase out demons. But they still can't muster the faith to put on a picnic (Luke 9:10–17).

Me First: After all Jesus had done for sick people, dead people and other folks running in last place in this life, you'd think the disciples would have figured out his game rules. They didn't. So when they get into a verbal fight about which of them will get to be first in heaven, Jesus ends the argument by holding up a little kid: *The people in last place in this life will be first in the next one* (Luke 9:46–48).

No Touching: After that last lesson, the disciples now know what Jesus thinks of kids, right? Wrong. When some parents start crowding in on Jesus, holding up their babies so Jesus will touch them, the disciples start acting like secret service agents and push the people away. Jesus tells them to let the little children come to him, then repeats his "Who's First" lesson (Luke 18:15–17).

---

³²While they were going out, a man who was demon-possessed and could not talk was brought to Jesus. ³³And when the demon was driven out, the man who had been mute spoke. The crowd was amazed and said, "Nothing like this has ever been seen in Israel."

³⁴But the Pharisees said, "It is by the prince of demons that he drives out demons."

The Workers Are Few

³⁵Jesus went through all the towns and villages, teaching in their synagogues, preaching the good news of the kingdom and healing every disease and sickness. ³⁶When he saw the crowds, he had compassion on them, because they were harassed and helpless, like sheep without a

shepherd. ³⁷Then he said to his disciples, "The harvest is plentiful but the workers are few. ³⁸Ask the Lord of the harvest, therefore, to send out workers into his harvest field."

Jesus Sends Out the Twelve

10 He called his twelve disciples to him and gave them authority to drive out evil*ᵃ* spirits and to heal every disease and sickness.

²These are the names of the twelve apostles: first, Simon (who is called Peter) and his brother Andrew; James son of Zebedee, and his brother John; ³Philip and Bartholomew; Thomas and Matthew the tax collector; James son of Alphaeus,

ᵃ1 Greek unclean

and Thaddaeus; ⁴Simon the Zealot and Judas Iscariot, who betrayed him.

⁵These twelve Jesus sent out with the following instructions: "Do not go among the Gentiles or enter any town of the Samaritans. ⁶Go rather to the lost sheep of Israel. ⁷As you go, preach this message: 'The kingdom of heaven is near.' ⁸Heal the sick, raise the dead, cleanse those who have leprosy,ᵃ drive out demons. Freely you have received, freely give. ⁹Do not take along any gold or silver or copper in your belts; ¹⁰take no bag for the journey, or extra tunic, or sandals or a staff; for the worker is worth his keep.

¹¹"Whatever town or village you enter, search for some worthy person there and stay at his house until you leave. ¹²As you enter the home, give it your greeting. ¹³If the home is deserving, let your peace rest on it; if it is not, let your peace return to you. ¹⁴If anyone will not welcome you or listen to your words, shake the dust off your feet when you leave that home or town. ¹⁵I tell you the truth, it will be more bearable for Sodom and Gomorrah on the day of judgment than for that town. ¹⁶I am sending you out like sheep among wolves. Therefore be as shrewd as snakes and as innocent as doves.

¹⁷"Be on your guard against men; they will hand you over to the local councils and flog you in their synagogues. ¹⁸On my account you will be brought before governors and kings as witnesses to them and to the Gentiles. ¹⁹But when they arrest you, do not worry about what to say or how to say it. At that time you will be given what to say, ²⁰for it will not be you speaking, but the Spirit of your Father speaking through you.

²¹"Brother will betray brother to death, and a father his child; children will rebel against their parents and have them put to death. ²²All men will hate you because of me, but he who stands firm to the end will be saved. ²³When you are persecuted in one place, flee to another. I tell you the truth, you will not finish going

---

ᵃ8 The Greek word was used for various diseases affecting the skin—not necessarily leprosy.

Friday

Safe With God

Read Matthew 10:29–37

When I was about 6 or 7, I'd get really concerned about the wild animals near my house, especially during bad storms. It seemed like they had no one to take care of them. But this verse about the sparrows always helped me feel better, because it reminded me that God cares for them—and he cares for me even more.

God, the greatest Being in the universe, pays attention to little creatures like sparrows and 7-year-old girls. So no matter how stormy it gets outside or in my own life, I can take comfort in knowing God cares. Nothing is too big or scary for him.

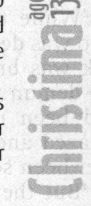
christina, age 13

What about You?

❶ Think of something that's very important to you. How do you take care of it? What are some similar ways God takes care of you?

❷ Walk around your house and notice all the things that keep you safe: locks on the doors, storm windows, maybe even a security system. How is God's protection even better than all of these things?

❸ Thank God for caring about you and protecting you.

Turn to page 1156 for your next devotion.

through the cities of Israel before the Son of Man comes.

²⁴"A student is not above his teacher, nor a servant above his master. ²⁵It is enough for the student to be like his teacher, and the servant like his master. If the head of the house has been called Beelzebub,ᵃ how much more the members of his household!

²⁶"So do not be afraid of them. There is nothing concealed that will not be disclosed, or hidden that will not be made known. ²⁷What I tell you in the dark, speak in the daylight; what is whispered in your ear, proclaim from the roofs. ²⁸Do not be afraid of those who kill the body but cannot kill the soul. Rather, be afraid of the One who can destroy both soul and body in hell. ²⁹Are not two sparrows sold for a pennyᵇ? Yet not one of them will fall to the ground apart from the will of your Father. ³⁰And even the very hairs of your head are all numbered. ³¹So don't be afraid; you are worth more than many sparrows.

³²"Whoever acknowledges me before men, I will also acknowledge him before my Father in heaven. ³³But whoever disowns me before men, I will disown him before my Father in heaven.

³⁴"Do not suppose that I have come to bring peace to the earth. I did not come to bring peace, but a sword. ³⁵For I have come to turn

" 'a man against his father,
   a daughter against her mother,
a daughter-in-law against her mother-
   in-law—
³⁶   a man's enemies will be the
     members of his own
     household.'ᶜ

³⁷"Anyone who loves his father or mother more than me is not worthy of me; anyone who loves his son or daughter more than me is not worthy of me; ³⁸and anyone who does not take his cross and follow me is not worthy of me. ³⁹Whoever finds his life will lose it, and whoever loses his life for my sake will find it.

⁴⁰"He who receives you receives me, and he who receives me receives the one who sent me. ⁴¹Anyone who receives a prophet because he is a prophet will re-

ceive a prophet's reward, and anyone who receives a righteous man because he is a righteous man will receive a righteous man's reward. ⁴²And if anyone gives even a cup of cold water to one of these little ones because he is my disciple, I tell you the truth, he will certainly not lose his reward."

Jesus and John the Baptist

11 After Jesus had finished instructing his twelve disciples, he went on from there to teach and preach in the towns of Galilee.ᵈ

²When John heard in prison what Christ was doing, he sent his disciples ³to ask him, "Are you the one who was to come, or should we expect someone else?"

⁴Jesus replied, "Go back and report to John what you hear and see: ⁵The blind receive sight, the lame walk, those who have leprosyᵉ are cured, the deaf hear, the dead are raised, and the good news is preached to the poor. ⁶Blessed is the man who does not fall away on account of me."

⁷As John's disciples were leaving, Jesus began to speak to the crowd about John: "What did you go out into the desert to see? A reed swayed by the wind? ⁸If not, what did you go out to see? A man dressed in fine clothes? No, those who wear fine clothes are in kings' palaces. ⁹Then what did you go out to see? A prophet? Yes, I tell you, and more than a prophet. ¹⁰This is the one about whom it is written:

" 'I will send my messenger ahead of
   you,
  who will prepare your way before
   you.'ᶠ

¹¹I tell you the truth: Among those born of women there has not risen anyone greater than John the Baptist; yet he who is least in the kingdom of heaven is greater than he. ¹²From the days of John the Baptist until now, the kingdom of heaven has been forcefully advancing,

---

ᵃ25 Greek *Beezeboul* or *Beelzeboul*   ᵇ29 Greek *an assarion*   ᶜ36 Micah 7:6   ᵈ1 Greek *in their towns* ᵉ5 The Greek word was used for various diseases affecting the skin—not necessarily leprosy. ᶠ10 Mal. 3:1

and forceful men lay hold of it. ¹³For all the Prophets and the Law prophesied until John. ¹⁴And if you are willing to accept it, he is the Elijah who was to come. ¹⁵He who has ears, let him hear.

¹⁶"To what can I compare this generation? They are like children sitting in the marketplaces and calling out to others:

¹⁷ " 'We played the flute for you,
    and you did not dance;
   we sang a dirge,
    and you did not mourn.'

¹⁸For John came neither eating nor drinking, and they say, 'He has a demon.' ¹⁹The Son of Man came eating and drinking, and they say, 'Here is a glutton and a drunkard, a friend of tax collectors and "sinners." ' But wisdom is proved right by her actions."

Woe on Unrepentant Cities

²⁰Then Jesus began to denounce the cities in which most of his miracles had been performed, because they did not re-

---

Week end.

Family Stuff

Read Mark 3:21 (page 1191)

Kristen's Monday devotion reminded us that even Jesus' family life wasn't perfect. That's good news for us, because it helps us realize that life isn't perfect in anyone's family.

Families have different ways of acting. Some of those ways are healthy, some aren't. In the passage you read today, Jesus' family thought he was crazy, and they wanted to protect him and force him to rest. (Since he was 30, he figured he could decide for himself.)

Some families have mothers or fathers who can't stand to have anything out of place in the house. Some are just the opposite. Every family has certain "rules" (behaviors that are considered acceptable or unacceptable) like: we don't cry when we're hurt, we can't express our anger, or only certain family members do certain household chores. The different things that make your family unique will affect you for the rest of your life (in good and bad ways).

One of the hard parts of growing up is figuring out which of your family's habits are healthy and which are not. So pay attention. Watch how your family responds to different situations. And, when you see stuff you don't really like or agree with, remember that Jesus had family problems too!

What about You?

❶ Every family has an unwritten set of "do's and don'ts." What are some of the things that are expected of you, and what are some of the things that are not allowed in your home?

❷ Ask your mom and dad what their own parents were like when they were growing up. What were the family rules?

❸ Ask God to help you see the good things going on in your family. And ask him to help you with the not-so-good things.

Turn to page 1157 for your next devotion.

pent. ²¹"Woe to you, Korazin! Woe to you, Bethsaida! If the miracles that were performed in you had been performed in Tyre and Sidon, they would have repented long ago in sackcloth and ashes. ²²But I tell you, it will be more bearable for Tyre and Sidon on the day of judgment than for you. ²³And you, Capernaum, will you be lifted up to the skies? No, you will go down to the depths.ᵃ If the miracles that were performed in you had been performed in Sodom, it would have remained to this day. ²⁴But I tell you that it will be more bearable for Sodom on the day of judgment than for you."

Rest for the Weary

²⁵At that time Jesus said, "I praise you, Father, Lord of heaven and earth, because you have hidden these things from the wise and learned, and revealed them

to little children. ²⁶Yes, Father, for this was your good pleasure.

²⁷"All things have been committed to me by my Father. No one knows the Son except the Father, and no one knows the Father except the Son and those to whom the Son chooses to reveal him.

²⁸"Come to me, all you who are weary and burdened, and I will give you rest. ²⁹Take my yoke upon you and learn from me, for I am gentle and humble in heart, and you will find rest for your souls. ³⁰For my yoke is easy and my burden is light."

Lord of the Sabbath

12 At that time Jesus went through the grainfields on the Sabbath. His disciples were hungry and began to pick

ᵃ23 Greek *Hades*

Mon day

A Tough Assignment
Read Matthew 11:28–30

A little while ago, my family decided to leave our big suburban church and move 30 miles away to start a sister church in a tough neighborhood in Chicago. I had to leave my friends, my school and the only home I had ever known. I didn't want to go.

But I saw how at peace my parents were about the move and how sure they were God wanted us in Chicago. I wanted to share their peace and confidence, so I asked God to help me. I told him I wanted to do his will, but it was going to be really hard on me and I needed supernatural strength.

God gave me even more than I asked for. He completely changed my attitude about moving. I actually wanted to move. Can you believe it? He gave me supportive friends and showed me in many different ways that going to Chicago was what he wanted for me. When I let God take control of my life, the plan that seemed totally "out there" turned into the plan I knew was best for me.

Susanna age 14

What about You?

❶ Why do you think God sometimes wants us to do things that are difficult for us?

❷ Ask a Christian adult, like your parents or your youth leader, about a time in their life when they had to give something up to follow God's plan. Ask them what they learned from the experience.

❸ Thank God for his perfect plan.

Turn to page 1161 for your next devotion.

some heads of grain and eat them. ²When the Pharisees saw this, they said to him, "Look! Your disciples are doing what is unlawful on the Sabbath."

³He answered, "Haven't you read what David did when he and his companions were hungry? ⁴He entered the house of God, and he and his companions ate the consecrated bread—which was not lawful for them to do, but only for the priests. ⁵Or haven't you read in the Law that on the Sabbath the priests in the temple desecrate the day and yet are innocent? ⁶I tell you that one*ᵃ* greater than the temple is here. ⁷If you had known what these words mean, 'I desire mercy, not sacrifice,'ᵇ you would not have condemned the innocent. ⁸For the Son of Man is Lord of the Sabbath."

⁹Going on from that place, he went into their synagogue, ¹⁰and a man with a shriveled hand was there. Looking for a reason to accuse Jesus, they asked him, "Is it lawful to heal on the Sabbath?"

¹¹He said to them, "If any of you has a sheep and it falls into a pit on the Sabbath, will you not take hold of it and lift it out? ¹²How much more valuable is a man than a sheep! Therefore it is lawful to do good on the Sabbath."

¹³Then he said to the man, "Stretch out your hand." So he stretched it out and it was completely restored, just as sound as the other. ¹⁴But the Pharisees went out and plotted how they might kill Jesus.

God's Chosen Servant

¹⁵Aware of this, Jesus withdrew from that place. Many followed him, and he healed all their sick, ¹⁶warning them not to tell who he was. ¹⁷This was to fulfill what was spoken through the prophet Isaiah:

¹⁸ "Here is my servant whom I have chosen,
      the one I love, in whom I delight;
    I will put my Spirit on him,
      and he will proclaim justice to the nations.
¹⁹He will not quarrel or cry out;
      no one will hear his voice in the streets.
²⁰A bruised reed he will not break,
      and a smoldering wick he will not snuff out,
    till he leads justice to victory.
²¹   In his name the nations will put their hope."ᶜ

Jesus and Beelzebub

²²Then they brought him a demon-possessed man who was blind and mute, and Jesus healed him, so that he could both talk and see. ²³All the people were astonished and said, "Could this be the Son of David?"

²⁴But when the Pharisees heard this, they said, "It is only by Beelzebub,ᵈ the prince of demons, that this fellow drives out demons."

²⁵Jesus knew their thoughts and said to them, "Every kingdom divided against itself will be ruined, and every city or household divided against itself will not stand. ²⁶If Satan drives out Satan, he is divided against himself. How then can his kingdom stand? ²⁷And if I drive out demons by Beelzebub, by whom do your people drive them out? So then, they will be your judges. ²⁸But if I drive out demons by the Spirit of God, then the kingdom of God has come upon you.

²⁹"Or again, how can anyone enter a strong man's house and carry off his possessions unless he first ties up the strong man? Then he can rob his house.

³⁰"He who is not with me is against me, and he who does not gather with me scatters. ³¹And so I tell you, every sin and blasphemy will be forgiven men, but the blasphemy against the Spirit will not be forgiven. ³²Anyone who speaks a word against the Son of Man will be forgiven, but anyone who speaks against the Holy Spirit will not be forgiven, either in this age or in the age to come.

³³"Make a tree good and its fruit will be good, or make a tree bad and its fruit will be bad, for a tree is recognized by its fruit. ³⁴You brood of vipers, how can you who are evil say anything good? For out of the overflow of the heart the mouth speaks. ³⁵The good man brings good things out of the good stored up in him,

---

ᵃ6 Or *something*; also in verses 41 and 42
ᵇ7 Hosea 6:6   ᶜ21 Isaiah 42:1-4   ᵈ24 Greek
Beezeboul or *Beelzeboul*; also in verse 27

and the evil man brings evil things out of the evil stored up in him. ³⁶But I tell you that men will have to give account on the day of judgment for every careless word they have spoken. ³⁷For by your words you will be acquitted, and by your words you will be condemned."

The Sign of Jonah

³⁸Then some of the Pharisees and teachers of the law said to him, "Teacher, we want to see a miraculous sign from you."

³⁹He answered, "A wicked and adulterous generation asks for a miraculous sign! But none will be given it except the sign of the prophet Jonah. ⁴⁰For as Jonah was three days and three nights in the belly of a huge fish, so the Son of Man will be three days and three nights in the heart of the earth. ⁴¹The men of Nineveh will stand up at the judgment with this generation and condemn it; for they repented at the preaching of Jonah, and now one*a* greater than Jonah is here. ⁴²The Queen of the South will rise at the judgment with this generation and condemn it; for she came from the ends of the earth to listen to Solomon's wisdom, and now one greater than Solomon is here.

⁴³"When an evil*b* spirit comes out of a man, it goes through arid places seeking rest and does not find it. ⁴⁴Then it says, 'I will return to the house I left.' When it arrives, it finds the house unoccupied, swept clean and put in order. ⁴⁵Then it goes and takes with it seven other spirits more wicked than itself, and they go in and live there. And the final condition of that man is worse than the first. That is how it will be with this wicked generation."

Jesus' Mother and Brothers

⁴⁶While Jesus was still talking to the crowd, his mother and brothers stood outside, wanting to speak to him. ⁴⁷Someone told him, "Your mother and brothers are standing outside, wanting to speak to you."*c*

⁴⁸He replied to him, "Who is my mother, and who are my brothers?" ⁴⁹Pointing to his disciples, he said, "Here are my mother and my brothers. ⁵⁰For whoever does the will of my Father in heaven is my brother and sister and mother."

The Parable of the Sower

13 That same day Jesus went out of the house and sat by the lake. ²Such large crowds gathered around him that he got into a boat and sat in it, while all the people stood on the shore. ³Then he told them many things in parables, saying: "A farmer went out to sow his seed. ⁴As he was scattering the seed,

some fell along the path, and the birds came and ate it up. ⁵Some fell on rocky places, where it did not have much soil. It sprang up quickly, because the soil was shallow. ⁶But when the sun came up, the plants were scorched, and they withered because they had no root. ⁷Other seed fell among thorns, which grew up and choked the plants. ⁸Still other seed fell on good soil, where it produced a crop—a hundred, sixty or thirty times what was sown. ⁹He who has ears, let him hear."

¹⁰The disciples came to him and asked, "Why do you speak to the people in parables?"

¹¹He replied, "The knowledge of the secrets of the kingdom of heaven has been

---

a41 Or *something*; also in verse 42 *b43* Greek *unclean* *c47* Some manuscripts do not have verse 47.

given to you, but not to them. ¹²Whoever has will be given more, and he will have an abundance. Whoever does not have, even what he has will be taken from him. ¹³This is why I speak to them in parables:

"Though seeing, they do not see;
  though hearing, they do not hear or
    understand.

¹⁴In them is fulfilled the prophecy of Isaiah:

" 'You will be ever hearing but never
    understanding;
  you will be ever seeing but never
    perceiving.
¹⁵For this people's heart has become
    calloused;
  they hardly hear with their ears,
  and they have closed their eyes.
Otherwise they might see with their
    eyes,
  hear with their ears,
  understand with their hearts
and turn, and I would heal them.'ᵃ

¹⁶But blessed are your eyes because they see, and your ears because they hear. ¹⁷For I tell you the truth, many prophets and righteous men longed to see what you see but did not see it, and to hear what you hear but did not hear it.

¹⁸"Listen then to what the parable of the sower means: ¹⁹When anyone hears the message about the kingdom and does not understand it, the evil one comes and snatches away what was sown in his heart. This is the seed sown along the path. ²⁰The one who received the seed that fell on rocky places is the man who hears the word and at once receives it with joy. ²¹But since he has no root, he lasts only a short time. When trouble or persecution comes because of the word, he quickly falls away. ²²The one who received the seed that fell among the thorns is the man who hears the word, but the worries of this life and the deceitfulness of wealth choke it, making it unfruitful. ²³But the one who received the seed that fell on good soil is the man who hears the word and understands it. He produces a crop, yielding a hundred, sixty or thirty times what was sown."

The Parable of the Weeds

²⁴Jesus told them another parable: "The kingdom of heaven is like a man who sowed good seed in his field. ²⁵But while everyone was sleeping, his enemy came and sowed weeds among the wheat, and went away. ²⁶When the wheat sprouted and formed heads, then the weeds also appeared.

²⁷"The owner's servants came to him and said, 'Sir, didn't you sow good seed in your field? Where then did the weeds come from?'

²⁸" 'An enemy did this,' he replied.

"The servants asked him, 'Do you want us to go and pull them up?'

²⁹" 'No,' he answered, 'because while you are pulling the weeds, you may root up the wheat with them. ³⁰Let both grow together until the harvest. At that time I will tell the harvesters: First collect the weeds and tie them in bundles to be burned; then gather the wheat and bring it into my barn.' "

The Parables of the Mustard Seed and the Yeast

³¹He told them another parable: "The kingdom of heaven is like a mustard seed, which a man took and planted in his field. ³²Though it is the smallest of all your seeds, yet when it grows, it is the largest of garden plants and becomes a tree, so that the birds of the air come and perch in its branches."

³³He told them still another parable: "The kingdom of heaven is like yeast that a woman took and mixed into a large amountᵇ of flour until it worked all through the dough."

³⁴Jesus spoke all these things to the crowd in parables; he did not say anything to them without using a parable. ³⁵So was fulfilled what was spoken through the prophet:

"I will open my mouth in
    parables,
  I will utter things hidden since the
    creation of the world."ᶜ

ᵃ15 Isaiah 6:9,10   ᵇ33 Greek *three satas* (probably about 1/2 bushel or 22 liters)   ᶜ35 Psalm 78:2

The Parable of the Weeds Explained

³⁶Then he left the crowd and went into the house. His disciples came to him and said, "Explain to us the parable of the weeds in the field."

³⁷He answered, "The one who sowed the good seed is the Son of Man. ³⁸The field is the world, and the good seed stands for the sons of the kingdom. The weeds are the sons of the evil one, ³⁹and the enemy who sows them is the devil. The harvest is the end of the age, and the harvesters are angels.

⁴⁰"As the weeds are pulled up and burned in the fire, so it will be at the end of the age. ⁴¹The Son of Man will send out his angels, and they will weed out of his kingdom everything that causes sin and all who do evil. ⁴²They will throw them into the fiery furnace, where there will be weeping and gnashing of teeth. ⁴³Then the righteous will shine like the sun in the kingdom of their Father. He who has ears, let him hear.

The Parables of the Hidden Treasure and the Pearl

⁴⁴"The kingdom of heaven is like treasure hidden in a field. When a man found it, he hid it again, and then in his joy went and sold all he had and bought that field.

⁴⁵"Again, the kingdom of heaven is like a merchant looking for fine pearls. ⁴⁶When he found one of great value, he went away and sold everything he had and bought it.

The Parable of the Net

⁴⁷"Once again, the kingdom of heaven is like a net that was let down into the lake and caught all kinds of fish. ⁴⁸When it was full, the fishermen pulled it up on the shore. Then they sat down and collected the good fish in baskets, but threw the bad away. ⁴⁹This is how it will be at the end of the age. The angels will come and separate the wicked from the righteous ⁵⁰and throw them into the fiery

Tuesday

Small Wonders

Read Matthew 13:31-33

This passage could have helped me when I was at camp. I was so afraid to speak out about God in front of people who didn't share my beliefs. I was scared I would say something wrong, because I'm young and there's lots I don't know yet. But if I would have spoken up, the Holy Spirit would have helped me to say the right thing. God doesn't expect us to do great things on our own. We'd fail every time without his help!

After camp, I sort of made a pact with myself to be brave and stand up for God in the future. Even in situations where I feel small or unwanted, I should go ahead and try to make a difference. God doesn't just use adults or people with all the answers—he uses anyone who asks for his help and isn't afraid to speak up. That means I can do something for God, whether or not I think I can. God thinks I can, and that's what really counts.

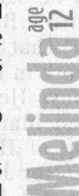

Melinda age 12

What about You?

❶ When was a time you felt afraid to speak up for God? What could have helped you feel more confident in that situation?

❷ Think about how beautiful flowers come from tiny seeds. Then think about how God uses the smallest things to accomplish something great.

❸ Thank God for being so awesome that he can use anyone to do his work.

Turn to page 1167 for your next devotion.

furnace, where there will be weeping and gnashing of teeth.

⁵¹"Have you understood all these things?" Jesus asked.

"Yes," they replied.

⁵²He said to them, "Therefore every teacher of the law who has been instructed about the kingdom of heaven is like the owner of a house who brings out of his storeroom new treasures as well as old."

A Prophet Without Honor

⁵³When Jesus had finished these parables, he moved on from there. ⁵⁴Coming to his hometown, he began teaching the people in their synagogue, and they were amazed. "Where did this man get this wisdom and these miraculous powers?" they asked. ⁵⁵"Isn't this the carpenter's son? Isn't his mother's name Mary, and aren't his brothers James, Joseph, Simon and Judas? ⁵⁶Aren't all his sisters with us? Where then did this man get all these things?" ⁵⁷And they took offense at him.

But Jesus said to them, "Only in his hometown and in his own house is a prophet without honor."

⁵⁸And he did not do many miracles there because of their lack of faith.

John the Baptist Beheaded

14 At that time Herod the tetrarch heard the reports about Jesus, ²and he said to his attendants, "This is John the Baptist; he has risen from the dead! That is why miraculous powers are at work in him."

³Now Herod had arrested John and bound him and put him in prison because of Herodias, his brother Philip's wife, ⁴for John had been saying to him: "It is not lawful for you to have her." ⁵Herod wanted to kill John, but he was afraid of the people, because they considered him a prophet.

⁶On Herod's birthday the daughter of Herodias danced for them and pleased Herod so much ⁷that he promised with an oath to give her whatever she asked. ⁸Prompted by her mother, she said, "Give me here on a platter the head of John the Baptist." ⁹The king was distressed, but because of his oaths and his dinner guests, he ordered that her request be granted ¹⁰and had John beheaded in the prison. ¹¹His head was brought in on a platter and given to the girl, who carried it to her mother. ¹²John's disciples came and took his body and buried it. Then they went and told Jesus.

Jesus Feeds the Five Thousand

¹³When Jesus heard what had happened, he withdrew by boat privately to a solitary place. Hearing of this, the crowds followed him on foot from the towns. ¹⁴When Jesus landed and saw a large crowd, he had compassion on them and healed their sick.

¹⁵As evening approached, the disciples came to him and said, "This is a remote place, and it's already getting late. Send the crowds away, so they can go to the villages and buy themselves some food."

¹⁶Jesus replied, "They do not need to go away. You give them something to eat."

¹⁷"We have here only five loaves of bread and two fish," they answered.

¹⁸"Bring them here to me," he said. ¹⁹And he directed the people to sit down on the grass. Taking the five loaves and the two fish and looking up to heaven, he gave thanks and broke the loaves. Then he gave them to the disciples, and the disciples gave them to the people. ²⁰They all ate and were satisfied, and the disciples picked up twelve basketfuls of broken pieces that were left over. ²¹The number of those who ate was about five thousand men, besides women and children.

Jesus Walks on the Water

²²Immediately Jesus made the disciples get into the boat and go on ahead of him to the other side, while he dismissed the crowd. ²³After he had dismissed them, he went up on a mountainside by himself to pray. When evening came, he was there alone, ²⁴but the boat was already a considerable distance*a* from land, buffeted by the waves because the wind was against it.

²⁵During the fourth watch of the night Jesus went out to them, walking on the lake. ²⁶When the disciples saw him walk-

a24 Greek *many stadia*

ing on the lake, they were terrified. "It's a ghost," they said, and cried out in fear.

²⁷But Jesus immediately said to them: "Take courage! It is I. Don't be afraid."

²⁸"Lord, if it's you," Peter replied, "tell me to come to you on the water."

²⁹"Come," he said.

Then Peter got down out of the boat, walked on the water and came toward Jesus. ³⁰But when he saw the wind, he was afraid and, beginning to sink, cried out, "Lord, save me!"

³¹Immediately Jesus reached out his hand and caught him. "You of little faith," he said, "why did you doubt?"

³²And when they climbed into the boat, the wind died down. ³³Then those who were in the boat worshiped him, saying, "Truly you are the Son of God."

Title, Please

Matthew 14:33
The president of the United States, your doctor and your school principal all have titles that let you know something about who they are and what they do. Jesus was often called "Son of God" and "Son of David." These titles represent his relationship to God, as well as his earthly royal bloodline. They show that people recognized him as the Messiah, God's chosen Savior of the world.

³⁴When they had crossed over, they landed at Gennesaret. ³⁵And when the men of that place recognized Jesus, they sent word to all the surrounding country. People brought all their sick to him ³⁶and begged him to let the sick just touch the edge of his cloak, and all who touched him were healed.

Clean and Unclean

15 Then some Pharisees and teachers of the law came to Jesus from Jerusalem and asked, ²"Why do your disciples break the tradition of the elders? They don't wash their hands before they eat!"

³Jesus replied, "And why do you break the command of God for the sake of your tradition? ⁴For God said, 'Honor your father and mother'ᵃ and 'Anyone who curses his father or mother must be put to death.'ᵇ ⁵But you say that if a man says to his father or mother, 'Whatever help you might otherwise have received from me is a gift devoted to God,' ⁶he is not to 'honor his father'ᶜ with it. Thus you nullify the word of God for the sake of your tradition. ⁷You hypocrites! Isaiah was right when he prophesied about you:

⁸"'These people honor me with their lips,
　but their hearts are far from me.
⁹They worship me in vain;
　their teachings are but rules taught by men.'ᵈ"

¹⁰Jesus called the crowd to him and said, "Listen and understand. ¹¹What goes into a man's mouth does not make him 'unclean,' but what comes out of his mouth, that is what makes him 'unclean.' "

¹²Then the disciples came to him and asked, "Do you know that the Pharisees were offended when they heard this?"

¹³He replied, "Every plant that my heavenly Father has not planted will be pulled up by the roots. ¹⁴Leave them; they are blind guides.ᵉ If a blind man leads a blind man, both will fall into a pit."

¹⁵Peter said, "Explain the parable to us."

¹⁶"Are you still so dull?" Jesus asked them. ¹⁷"Don't you see that whatever enters the mouth goes into the stomach and then out of the body? ¹⁸But the things that come out of the mouth come from the heart, and these make a man 'unclean.' ¹⁹For out of the heart come evil thoughts, murder, adultery, sexual immorality, theft, false testimony, slander. ²⁰These are what make a man 'unclean'; but eating with unwashed hands does not make him 'unclean.' "

ᵃ4 Exodus 20:12; Deut. 5:16　ᵇ4 Exodus 21:17; Lev. 20:9　ᶜ6 Some manuscripts *father or his mother*　ᵈ9 Isaiah 29:13　ᵉ14 Some manuscripts *guides of the blind*

The Faith of the Canaanite Woman

²¹Leaving that place, Jesus withdrew to the region of Tyre and Sidon. ²²A Canaanite woman from that vicinity came to him, crying out, "Lord, Son of David, have mercy on me! My daughter is suffering terribly from demon-possession."

²³Jesus did not answer a word. So his disciples came to him and urged him, "Send her away, for she keeps crying out after us."

²⁴He answered, "I was sent only to the lost sheep of Israel."

²⁵The woman came and knelt before him. "Lord, help me!" she said.

²⁶He replied, "It is not right to take the children's bread and toss it to their dogs."

²⁷"Yes, Lord," she said, "but even the dogs eat the crumbs that fall from their masters' table."

²⁸Then Jesus answered, "Woman, you have great faith! Your request is granted." And her daughter was healed from that very hour.

Jesus Feeds the Four Thousand

²⁹Jesus left there and went along the Sea of Galilee. Then he went up on a mountainside and sat down. ³⁰Great crowds came to him, bringing the lame, the blind, the crippled, the mute and many others, and laid them at his feet; and he healed them. ³¹The people were amazed when they saw the mute speaking, the crippled made well, the lame walking and the blind seeing. And they praised the God of Israel.

³²Jesus called his disciples to him and said, "I have compassion for these people; they have already been with me three days and have nothing to eat. I do not want to send them away hungry, or they may collapse on the way."

³³His disciples answered, "Where could we get enough bread in this remote place to feed such a crowd?"

³⁴"How many loaves do you have?" Jesus asked.

"Seven," they replied, "and a few small fish."

³⁵He told the crowd to sit down on the ground. ³⁶Then he took the seven loaves and the fish, and when he had given thanks, he broke them and gave them to the disciples, and they in turn to the people. ³⁷They all ate and were satisfied. Afterward the disciples picked up seven basketfuls of broken pieces that were left over. ³⁸The number of those who ate was four thousand, besides women and children. ³⁹After Jesus had sent the crowd away, he got into the boat and went to the vicinity of Magadan.

The Demand for a Sign

16 The Pharisees and Sadducees came to Jesus and tested him by asking him to show them a sign from heaven.

²He replied,[a] "When evening comes, you say, 'It will be fair weather, for the sky is red,' ³and in the morning, 'Today it will be stormy, for the sky is red and overcast.' You know how to interpret the appearance of the sky, but you cannot interpret the signs of the times. ⁴A wicked and adulterous generation looks for a miraculous sign, but none will be given it except the sign of Jonah." Jesus then left them and went away.

The Yeast of the Pharisees and Sadducees

⁵When they went across the lake, the disciples forgot to take bread. ⁶"Be careful," Jesus said to them. "Be on your guard against the yeast of the Pharisees and Sadducees."

⁷They discussed this among themselves and said, "It is because we didn't bring any bread."

⁸Aware of their discussion, Jesus asked, "You of little faith, why are you talking among yourselves about having no bread? ⁹Do you still not understand? Don't you remember the five loaves for the five thousand, and how many basketfuls you gathered? ¹⁰Or the seven loaves for the four thousand, and how many basketfuls you gathered? ¹¹How is it you don't understand that I was not talking to you about bread? But be on your guard against the yeast of the Pharisees and Sadducees." ¹²Then they understood that he was not telling them to guard against the yeast used in bread, but

---

[a]2 Some early manuscripts do not have the rest of verse 2 and all of verse 3.

against the teaching of the Pharisees and Sadducees.

Peter's Confession of Christ

¹³When Jesus came to the region of Caesarea Philippi, he asked his disciples, "Who do people say the Son of Man is?" ¹⁴They replied, "Some say John the Baptist; others say Elijah; and still others, Jeremiah or one of the prophets."

¹⁵"But what about you?" he asked. "Who do you say I am?"

¹⁶Simon Peter answered, "You are the Christ,ᵃ the Son of the living God."

¹⁷Jesus replied, "Blessed are you, Simon son of Jonah, for this was not revealed to you by man, but by my Father in heaven. ¹⁸And I tell you that you are Peter,ᵇ and on this rock I will build my church, and the gates of Hadesᶜ will not overcome it.ᵈ ¹⁹I will give you the keys of the kingdom of heaven; whatever you bind on earth will beᵉ bound in heaven, and whatever you loose on earth will beᵉ loosed in heaven." ²⁰Then he warned his disciples not to tell anyone that he was the Christ.

Jesus Predicts His Death

²¹From that time on Jesus began to explain to his disciples that he must go to Jerusalem and suffer many things at the hands of the elders, chief priests and teachers of the law, and that he must be killed and on the third day be raised to life.

²²Peter took him aside and began to rebuke him. "Never, Lord!" he said. "This shall never happen to you!"

²³Jesus turned and said to Peter, "Get behind me, Satan! You are a stumbling block to me; you do not have in mind the things of God, but the things of men."

²⁴Then Jesus said to his disciples, "If anyone would come after me, he must deny himself and take up his cross and follow me. ²⁵For whoever wants to save his lifeᶠ will lose it, but whoever loses his life for me will find it. ²⁶What good will it be for a man if he gains the whole world, yet forfeits his soul? Or what can a man give in exchange for his soul? ²⁷For the Son of Man is going to come in his Father's glory with his angels, and then he will reward each person according to

what he has done. ²⁸I tell you the truth, some who are standing here will not taste death before they see the Son of Man coming in his kingdom."

The Transfiguration

17 After six days Jesus took with him Peter, James and John the brother of James, and led them up a high mountain by themselves. ²There he was transfigured before them. His face shone like the sun, and his clothes became as white as the light. ³Just then there appeared before them Moses and Elijah, talking with Jesus.

⁴Peter said to Jesus, "Lord, it is good for us to be here. If you wish, I will put up three shelters—one for you, one for Moses and one for Elijah."

⁵While he was still speaking, a bright cloud enveloped them, and a voice from the cloud said, "This is my Son, whom I love; with him I am well pleased. Listen to him!"

⁶When the disciples heard this, they fell facedown to the ground, terrified. ⁷But Jesus came and touched them. "Get up," he said. "Don't be afraid." ⁸When they looked up, they saw no one except Jesus.

⁹As they were coming down the mountain, Jesus instructed them, "Don't tell anyone what you have seen, until the Son of Man has been raised from the dead."

¹⁰The disciples asked him, "Why then do the teachers of the law say that Elijah must come first?"

¹¹Jesus replied, "To be sure, Elijah comes and will restore all things. ¹²But I tell you, Elijah has already come, and they did not recognize him, but have done to him everything they wished. In the same way the Son of Man is going to suffer at their hands." ¹³Then the disciples understood that he was talking to them about John the Baptist.

The Healing of a Boy With a Demon

¹⁴When they came to the crowd, a man approached Jesus and knelt before him.

ᵃ16 Or *Messiah*; also in verse 20   ᵇ18 *Peter* means *rock.*   ᶜ18 Or *hell*   ᵈ18 Or *not prove stronger than it*   ᵉ19 Or *have been*   ᶠ25 The Greek word means either *life* or *soul*; also in verse 26.

¹⁵"Lord, have mercy on my son," he said. "He has seizures and is suffering greatly. He often falls into the fire or into the water. ¹⁶I brought him to your disciples, but they could not heal him."

¹⁷"O unbelieving and perverse generation," Jesus replied, "how long shall I stay with you? How long shall I put up with you? Bring the boy here to me." ¹⁸Jesus rebuked the demon, and it came out of the boy, and he was healed from that moment.

¹⁹Then the disciples came to Jesus in private and asked, "Why couldn't we drive it out?"

²⁰He replied, "Because you have so little faith. I tell you the truth, if you have faith as small as a mustard seed, you can say to this mountain, 'Move from here to there' and it will move. Nothing will be impossible for you.ᵃ"

²²When they came together in Galilee, he said to them, "The Son of Man is going to be betrayed into the hands of men. ²³They will kill him, and on the third day he will be raised to life." And the disciples were filled with grief.

The Temple Tax

²⁴After Jesus and his disciples arrived in Capernaum, the collectors of the two-drachma tax came to Peter and asked, "Doesn't your teacher pay the temple taxᵇ?"

²⁵"Yes, he does," he replied.

When Peter came into the house, Jesus was the first to speak. "What do you think, Simon?" he asked. "From whom do the kings of the earth collect duty and taxes—from their own sons or from others?"

²⁶"From others," Peter answered.

"Then the sons are exempt," Jesus said to him. ²⁷"But so that we may not offend them, go to the lake and throw out your line. Take the first fish you catch; open its mouth and you will find a four-drachma coin. Take it and give it to them for my tax and yours."

The Greatest in the Kingdom of Heaven

18 At that time the disciples came to Jesus and asked, "Who is the greatest in the kingdom of heaven?"

²He called a little child and had him stand among them. ³And he said: "I tell you the truth, unless you change and become like little children, you will never enter the kingdom of heaven. ⁴Therefore, whoever humbles himself like this child is the greatest in the kingdom of heaven.

I Don't Wanna Grow Up!

Huh?

Matthew 18:3

Children have a cool sense of trust. Have you ever noticed this? Life seems simpler for them. Most kids rely completely on parents or other adults for their care. They don't worry about life too much. Someone else provides their food, clothing, home, spending money—everything! Well, God wants us to come to him with this same trust. We can rely on him! We don't need to worry; he will care for us. Take a lesson from little children.

⁵"And whoever welcomes a little child like this in my name welcomes me. ⁶But if anyone causes one of these little ones who believe in me to sin, it would be better for him to have a large millstone hung around his neck and to be drowned in the depths of the sea.

⁷"Woe to the world because of the things that cause people to sin! Such things must come, but woe to the man through whom they come! ⁸If your hand or your foot causes you to sin, cut it off and throw it away. It is better for you to enter life maimed or crippled than to have two hands or two feet and be thrown into eternal fire. ⁹And if your eye causes you to sin, gouge it out and throw it away. It is better for you to enter life with one eye than to have two eyes and be thrown into the fire of hell.

The Parable of the Lost Sheep

¹⁰"See that you do not look down on one of these little ones. For I tell you that

---

ᵃ20 Some manuscripts you. ²¹But this kind does not go out except by prayer and fasting. ᵇ24 Greek the two drachmas

their angels in heaven always see the face of my Father in heaven.*

¹²"What do you think? If a man owns a hundred sheep, and one of them wanders away, will he not leave the ninety-nine on the hills and go to look for the one that wandered off? ¹³And if he finds it, I tell you the truth, he is happier about that one sheep than about the ninety-nine that did not wander off. ¹⁴In the same way your Father in heaven is not willing that any of these little ones should be lost.

A Brother Who Sins Against You

¹⁵"If your brother sins against you,ᵇ go and show him his fault, just between the two of you. If he listens to you, you have won your brother over. ¹⁶But if he will not listen, take one or two others along, so that 'every matter may be established by the testimony of two or three witnesses.'ᶜ ¹⁷If he refuses to listen to them, tell it to the church; and if he refuses to listen even to the church, treat

him as you would a pagan or a tax collector.

¹⁸"I tell you the truth, whatever you bind on earth will beᵈ bound in heaven, and whatever you loose on earth will beᵈ loosed in heaven.

¹⁹"Again, I tell you that if two of you on earth agree about anything you ask for, it will be done for you by my Father in heaven. ²⁰For where two or three come together in my name, there am I with them."

The Parable of the Unmerciful Servant

²¹Then Peter came to Jesus and asked, "Lord, how many times shall I forgive my brother when he sins against me? Up to seven times?"

²²Jesus answered, "I tell you, not seven times, but seventy-seven times.ᵉ

---

*10 Some manuscripts *heaven.* ¹¹*The Son of Man came to save what was lost.* ᵇ15 Some manuscripts do not have *against you.* ᶜ16 Deut. 19:15 ᵈ18 Or *have been* ᵉ22 Or *seventy times seven*

Wednesday

Think Small

Read Matthew 18:1–5

Sometimes I get so caught up in myself, like the time not too long ago that I canceled plans with my dad to hang out with my friends. Dad was really looking forward to going to a movie with me, but I didn't even think about his feelings. I just thought about what I wanted to do. I never would have done that 5 years ago. But it seems like the older I get, the more selfish and stuck-up I become, especially toward my family.

Small children rarely seem to push away the people they love. In this way, Jesus was kind of like a child, because he always accepted other people and thought of them first. And I think this is part of what Jesus meant when he said Christians should become like little children. We need to stop thinking we're so important and think about how important other people are instead.

Carolyn age 13

What about You?

❶ What are some other characteristics of children that you think Christians should try to imitate?

❷ Ask your parents to tell you some of their favorite memories of you as a child. What are some ways you wish you could be more like you were back then?

❸ Ask God to help you be humble like a little child.

Turn to page 1173 for your next devotion.

²³"Therefore, the kingdom of heaven is like a king who wanted to settle accounts with his servants. ²⁴As he began the settlement, a man who owed him ten thousand talents*a* was brought to him. ²⁵Since he was not able to pay, the master ordered that he and his wife and his children and all that he had be sold to repay the debt.

²⁶"The servant fell on his knees before him. 'Be patient with me,' he begged, 'and I will pay back everything.' ²⁷The servant's master took pity on him, canceled the debt and let him go.

²⁸"But when that servant went out, he found one of his fellow servants who owed him a hundred denarii.*b* He grabbed him and began to choke him. 'Pay back what you owe me!' he demanded.

²⁹"His fellow servant fell to his knees and begged him, 'Be patient with me, and I will pay you back.'

³⁰"But he refused. Instead, he went off and had the man thrown into prison until he could pay the debt. ³¹When the other servants saw what had happened, they were greatly distressed and went and told their master everything that had happened.

³²"Then the master called the servant in. 'You wicked servant,' he said, 'I canceled all that debt of yours because you begged me to. ³³Shouldn't you have had mercy on your fellow servant just as I had on you?' ³⁴In anger his master turned him over to the jailers to be tortured, until he should pay back all he owed.

³⁵"This is how my heavenly Father will treat each of you unless you forgive your brother from your heart."

Divorce

19 When Jesus had finished saying these things, he left Galilee and went into the region of Judea to the other side of the Jordan. ²Large crowds followed him, and he healed them there.

³Some Pharisees came to him to test him. They asked, "Is it lawful for a man to divorce his wife for any and every reason?"

⁴"Haven't you read," he replied, "that at the beginning the Creator 'made them male and female,'*c* ⁵and said, 'For this reason a man will leave his father and mother and be united to his wife, and the two will become one flesh'*d*? ⁶So they are no longer two, but one. Therefore what God has joined together, let man not separate."

⁷"Why then," they asked, "did Moses command that a man give his wife a certificate of divorce and send her away?"

⁸Jesus replied, "Moses permitted you to divorce your wives because your hearts were hard. But it was not this way from the beginning. ⁹I tell you that anyone who divorces his wife, except for marital unfaithfulness, and marries another woman commits adultery."

¹⁰The disciples said to him, "If this is the situation between a husband and wife, it is better not to marry."

¹¹Jesus replied, "Not everyone can accept this word, but only those to whom it has been given. ¹²For some are eunuchs because they were born that way; others were made that way by men; and others have renounced marriage*e* because of the kingdom of heaven. The one who can accept this should accept it."

The Little Children and Jesus

¹³Then little children were brought to Jesus for him to place his hands on them and pray for them. But the disciples rebuked those who brought them.

¹⁴Jesus said, "Let the little children come to me, and do not hinder them, for the kingdom of heaven belongs to such as these." ¹⁵When he had placed his hands on them, he went on from there.

The Rich Young Man

¹⁶Now a man came up to Jesus and asked, "Teacher, what good thing must I do to get eternal life?"

¹⁷"Why do you ask me about what is good?" Jesus replied. "There is only One who is good. If you want to enter life, obey the commandments."

¹⁸"Which ones?" the man inquired.

Jesus replied, " 'Do not murder, do not commit adultery, do not steal, do not give false testimony, ¹⁹honor your father

---

a24 That is, millions of dollars   *b28* That is, a few dollars   *c4* Gen. 1:27   *d5* Gen. 2:24   *e12* Or *have made themselves eunuchs*

and mother,'*a* and 'love your neighbor as yourself.'*b*"

²⁰"All these I have kept," the young man said. "What do I still lack?"

²¹Jesus answered, "If you want to be perfect, go, sell your possessions and give to the poor, and you will have treasure in heaven. Then come, follow me."

²²When the young man heard this, he went away sad, because he had great wealth.

²³Then Jesus said to his disciples, "I tell you the truth, it is hard for a rich man to enter the kingdom of heaven. ²⁴Again I tell you, it is easier for a camel to go through the eye of a needle than for a rich man to enter the kingdom of God."

More, More, MORE!

Huh?

Matthew 19:24

What would you give up to get 50 million dollars? Your family and friends? Money is important in life. But it causes pain and grief for so many people (rich and poor and in-between). Money will never satisfy your needs in life—only Jesus will. The Bible warns us about the love of money over and over again. Love God, love people, but be sure you never fall in love with money.

²⁵When the disciples heard this, they were greatly astonished and asked, "Who then can be saved?"

²⁶Jesus looked at them and said, "With man this is impossible, but with God all things are possible."

²⁷Peter answered him, "We have left everything to follow you! What then will there be for us?"

²⁸Jesus said to them, "I tell you the truth, at the renewal of all things, when the Son of Man sits on his glorious throne, you who have followed me will also sit on twelve thrones, judging the twelve tribes of Israel. ²⁹And everyone who has left houses or brothers or sisters or father or mother*c* or children or fields for my sake will receive a hundred times as much and will inherit eternal life.

³⁰But many who are first will be last, and many who are last will be first.

The Parable of the Workers in the Vineyard

20 "For the kingdom of heaven is like a landowner who went out early in the morning to hire men to work in his vineyard. ²He agreed to pay them a denarius for the day and sent them into his vineyard.

³"About the third hour he went out and saw others standing in the marketplace doing nothing. ⁴He told them, 'You also go and work in my vineyard, and I will pay you whatever is right.' ⁵So they went.

"He went out again about the sixth hour and the ninth hour and did the same thing. ⁶About the eleventh hour he went out and found still others standing around. He asked them, 'Why have you been standing here all day long doing nothing?'

⁷" 'Because no one has hired us,' they answered.

"He said to them, 'You also go and work in my vineyard.'

⁸"When evening came, the owner of the vineyard said to his foreman, 'Call the workers and pay them their wages, beginning with the last ones hired and going on to the first.'

⁹"The workers who were hired about the eleventh hour came and each received a denarius. ¹⁰So when those came who were hired first, they expected to receive more. But each one of them also received a denarius. ¹¹When they received it, they began to grumble against the landowner. ¹²'These men who were hired last worked only one hour,' they said, 'and you have made them equal to us who have borne the burden of the work and the heat of the day.'

¹³"But he answered one of them, 'Friend, I am not being unfair to you. Didn't you agree to work for a denarius? ¹⁴Take your pay and go. I want to give the man who was hired last the same as I gave you. ¹⁵Don't I have the right to do what I want with my own money? Or are you envious because I am generous?'

a19 Exodus 20:12-16; Deut. 5:16-20   *b19* Lev. 19:18
c29 Some manuscripts *mother or wife*

¹⁶"So the last will be first, and the first will be last."

Jesus Again Predicts His Death

¹⁷Now as Jesus was going up to Jerusalem, he took the twelve disciples aside and said to them, ¹⁸"We are going up to Jerusalem, and the Son of Man will be betrayed to the chief priests and the teachers of the law. They will condemn him to death ¹⁹and will turn him over to the Gentiles to be mocked and flogged and crucified. On the third day he will be raised to life!"

A Mother's Request

²⁰Then the mother of Zebedee's sons came to Jesus with her sons and, kneeling down, asked a favor of him.

²¹"What is it you want?" he asked.

She said, "Grant that one of these two sons of mine may sit at your right and the other at your left in your kingdom."

²²"You don't know what you are asking," Jesus said to them. "Can you drink the cup I am going to drink?"

"We can," they answered.

²³Jesus said to them, "You will indeed drink from my cup, but to sit at my right or left is not for me to grant. These places belong to those for whom they have been prepared by my Father."

²⁴When the ten heard about this, they were indignant with the two brothers. ²⁵Jesus called them together and said, "You know that the rulers of the Gentiles lord it over them, and their high officials exercise authority over them. ²⁶Not so with you. Instead, whoever wants to become great among you must be your servant, ²⁷and whoever wants to be first must be your slave— ²⁸just as the Son of Man did not come to be served, but to serve, and to give his life as a ransom for many."

Two Blind Men Receive Sight

²⁹As Jesus and his disciples were leaving Jericho, a large crowd followed him. ³⁰Two blind men were sitting by the roadside, and when they heard that Jesus was going by, they shouted, "Lord, Son of David, have mercy on us!"

³¹The crowd rebuked them and told them to be quiet, but they shouted all the louder, "Lord, Son of David, have mercy on us!"

³²Jesus stopped and called them. "What do you want me to do for you?" he asked.

³³"Lord," they answered, "we want our sight."

³⁴Jesus had compassion on them and touched their eyes. Immediately they received their sight and followed him.

The Triumphal Entry

21 As they approached Jerusalem and came to Bethphage on the Mount of Olives, Jesus sent two disciples, ²saying to them, "Go to the village ahead of you, and at once you will find a donkey tied there, with her colt by her. Untie them and bring them to me. ³If anyone says anything to you, tell him that the Lord needs them, and he will send them right away."

⁴This took place to fulfill what was spoken through the prophet:

⁵"Say to the Daughter of Zion,
  'See, your king comes to you,
gentle and riding on a donkey,
  on a colt, the foal of a donkey.' "ᵃ

⁶The disciples went and did as Jesus had instructed them. ⁷They brought the donkey and the colt, placed their cloaks on them, and Jesus sat on them. ⁸A very large crowd spread their cloaks on the road, while others cut branches from the trees and spread them on the road. ⁹The crowds that went ahead of him and those that followed shouted,

"Hosannaᵇ to the Son of David!"

"Blessed is he who comes in the name of the Lord!"ᶜ

"Hosannaᵇ in the highest!"

¹⁰When Jesus entered Jerusalem, the whole city was stirred and asked, "Who is this?"

¹¹The crowds answered, "This is Jesus, the prophet from Nazareth in Galilee."

ᵃ5 Zech. 9:9   ᵇ9 A Hebrew expression meaning "Save!" which became an exclamation of praise; also in verse 15   ᶜ9 Psalm 118:26

Jesus at the Temple

¹²Jesus entered the temple area and drove out all who were buying and selling there. He overturned the tables of the money changers and the benches of those selling doves. ¹³"It is written," he said to them, " 'My house will be called a house of prayer,'ᵃ but you are making it a 'den of robbers.'ᵇ"

¹⁴The blind and the lame came to him at the temple, and he healed them. ¹⁵But when the chief priests and the teachers of the law saw the wonderful things he did and the children shouting in the temple area, "Hosanna to the Son of David," they were indignant.

¹⁶"Do you hear what these children are saying?" they asked him.

"Yes," replied Jesus, "have you never read,

" 'From the lips of children and
       infants
    you have ordained praise'ᶜ?"

¹⁷And he left them and went out of the city to Bethany, where he spent the night.

The Fig Tree Withers

¹⁸Early in the morning, as he was on his way back to the city, he was hungry. ¹⁹Seeing a fig tree by the road, he went up to it but found nothing on it except leaves. Then he said to it, "May you never bear fruit again!" Immediately the tree withered.

²⁰When the disciples saw this, they were amazed. "How did the fig tree wither so quickly?" they asked.

²¹Jesus replied, "I tell you the truth, if you have faith and do not doubt, not only can you do what was done to the fig tree, but also you can say to this mountain, 'Go, throw yourself into the sea,' and it will be done. ²²If you believe, you will receive whatever you ask for in prayer."

The Authority of Jesus Questioned

²³Jesus entered the temple courts, and, while he was teaching, the chief priests and the elders of the people came to him. "By what authority are you doing these things?" they asked. "And who gave you this authority?"

²⁴Jesus replied, "I will also ask you one question. If you answer me, I will tell you by what authority I am doing these things. ²⁵John's baptism—where did it come from? Was it from heaven, or from men?"

They discussed it among themselves and said, "If we say, 'From heaven,' he will ask, 'Then why didn't you believe him?' ²⁶But if we say, 'From men'—we are afraid of the people, for they all hold that John was a prophet."

²⁷So they answered Jesus, "We don't know."

Then he said, "Neither will I tell you by what authority I am doing these things.

The Parable of the Two Sons

²⁸"What do you think? There was a man who had two sons. He went to the first and said, 'Son, go and work today in the vineyard.'

²⁹" 'I will not,' he answered, but later he changed his mind and went.

³⁰"Then the father went to the other son and said the same thing. He answered, 'I will, sir,' but he did not go.

³¹"Which of the two did what his father wanted?"

"The first," they answered.

Jesus said to them, "I tell you the truth, the tax collectors and the prostitutes are entering the kingdom of God ahead of you. ³²For John came to you to show you the way of righteousness, and you did not believe him, but the tax collectors and the prostitutes did. And even after you saw this, you did not repent and believe him.

The Parable of the Tenants

³³"Listen to another parable: There was a landowner who planted a vineyard. He put a wall around it, dug a winepress in it and built a watchtower. Then he rented the vineyard to some farmers and went away on a journey. ³⁴When the harvest time approached, he sent his servants to the tenants to collect his fruit.

³⁵"The tenants seized his servants; they beat one, killed another, and stoned a third. ³⁶Then he sent other servants to them, more than the first time, and the

ᵃ13 Isaiah 56:7   ᵇ13 Jer. 7:11   ᶜ16 Psalm 8:2

tenants treated them the same way. ³⁷Last of all, he sent his son to them. 'They will respect my son,' he said.

³⁸"But when the tenants saw the son, they said to each other, 'This is the heir. Come, let's kill him and take his inheritance.' ³⁹So they took him and threw him out of the vineyard and killed him.

⁴⁰"Therefore, when the owner of the vineyard comes, what will he do to those tenants?"

⁴¹"He will bring those wretches to a wretched end," they replied, "and he will rent the vineyard to other tenants, who will give him his share of the crop at harvest time."

⁴²Jesus said to them, "Have you never read in the Scriptures:

" 'The stone the builders rejected
　　has become the capstone*a*;
　the Lord has done this,
　　and it is marvelous in our eyes'*b*?

⁴³"Therefore I tell you that the kingdom of God will be taken away from you and given to a people who will produce its fruit. ⁴⁴He who falls on this stone will be broken to pieces, but he on whom it falls will be crushed."*c*

⁴⁵When the chief priests and the Pharisees heard Jesus' parables, they knew he was talking about them. ⁴⁶They looked for a way to arrest him, but they were afraid of the crowd because the people held that he was a prophet.

The Parable of the Wedding Banquet

22 Jesus spoke to them again in parables, saying: ²"The kingdom of heaven is like a king who prepared a wedding banquet for his son. ³He sent his servants to those who had been invited to the banquet to tell them to come, but they refused to come.

⁴"Then he sent some more servants and said, 'Tell those who have been invited that I have prepared my dinner: My oxen and fattened cattle have been butchered, and everything is ready. Come to the wedding banquet.'

⁵"But they paid no attention and went off—one to his field, another to his business. ⁶The rest seized his servants, mistreated them and killed them. ⁷The king was enraged. He sent his army and de-

stroyed those murderers and burned their city.

⁸"Then he said to his servants, 'The wedding banquet is ready, but those I invited did not deserve to come. ⁹Go to the street corners and invite to the banquet anyone you find.' ¹⁰So the servants went out into the streets and gathered all the people they could find, both good and bad, and the wedding hall was filled with guests.

¹¹"But when the king came in to see the guests, he noticed a man there who was not wearing wedding clothes. ¹²'Friend,' he asked, 'how did you get in here without wedding clothes?' The man was speechless.

¹³"Then the king told the attendants, 'Tie him hand and foot, and throw him outside, into the darkness, where there will be weeping and gnashing of teeth.'

¹⁴"For many are invited, but few are chosen."

Paying Taxes to Caesar

¹⁵Then the Pharisees went out and laid plans to trap him in his words. ¹⁶They sent their disciples to him along with the Herodians. "Teacher," they said, "we know you are a man of integrity and that you teach the way of God in accordance with the truth. You aren't swayed by men, because you pay no attention to who they are. ¹⁷Tell us then, what is your opinion? Is it right to pay taxes to Caesar or not?"

¹⁸But Jesus, knowing their evil intent, said, "You hypocrites, why are you trying to trap me? ¹⁹Show me the coin used for paying the tax." They brought him a denarius, ²⁰and he asked them, "Whose portrait is this? And whose inscription?"

²¹"Caesar's," they replied.

Then he said to them, "Give to Caesar what is Caesar's, and to God what is God's."

²²When they heard this, they were amazed. So they left him and went away.

Marriage at the Resurrection

²³That same day the Sadducees, who say there is no resurrection, came to him

---

*a*42 Or *cornerstone*　*b*42 Psalm 118:22,23　*c*44 Some manuscripts do not have verse 44.

with a question. ²⁴"Teacher," they said, "Moses told us that if a man dies without having children, his brother must marry the widow and have children for him. ²⁵Now there were seven brothers among us. The first one married and died, and since he had no children, he left his wife to his brother. ²⁶The same thing happened to the second and third brother, right on down to the seventh. ²⁷Finally, the woman died. ²⁸Now then, at the resurrection, whose wife will she be of the seven, since all of them were married to her?"

²⁹Jesus replied, "You are in error because you do not know the Scriptures or the power of God. ³⁰At the resurrection people will neither marry nor be given in marriage; they will be like the angels in heaven. ³¹But about the resurrection of the dead—have you not read what God said to you, ³²'I am the God of Abraham, the God of Isaac, and the God of Jacob'ᵃ? He is not the God of the dead but of the living."

³³When the crowds heard this, they were astonished at his teaching.

The Greatest Commandment

³⁴Hearing that Jesus had silenced the Sadducees, the Pharisees got together. ³⁵One of them, an expert in the law, tested him with this question: ³⁶"Teacher, which is the greatest commandment in the Law?"

³⁷Jesus replied: " 'Love the Lord your God with all your heart and with all your soul and with all your mind.'ᵇ ³⁸This is the first and greatest commandment. ³⁹And the second is like it: 'Love your neighbor as yourself.'ᶜ ⁴⁰All the Law and the Prophets hang on these two commandments."

Whose Son Is the Christ?

⁴¹While the Pharisees were gathered together, Jesus asked them, ⁴²"What do

ᵃ32 Exodus 3:6   *ᵇ37* Deut. 6:5   *ᶜ39* Lev. 19:18

Thursday

Top Priority

Read Matthew 22:34–40

There was a time I wasn't as close to God as I should have been. I started focusing on material possessions, and I found myself making those things more important than God.

This passage shows me that God wants to be my top priority. He wants me to realize he's the most important part of my life. Without him, the rest of my life is pretty meaningless. He needs to be my motivation in everything I do.

The earthly things in my life won't last, but God's love lasts forever. His love needs to influence my thoughts, actions and words. God's love is real and, in the end, it's the only thing that really matters.

Natalie age 14

What about You?

❶ What are some of the ways you let God know he's your top priority?

❷ Write "God" in large letters on a couple of note cards. Tape the cards where you'll see them every day, like on your mirror or in your locker. Every time you see one of the cards, ask yourself if you're putting God first in your life.

❸ Tell God you want him to be first in your life. Then ask him to help you make it happen.

Turn to page 1178 for your next devotion.

you think about the Christ[a]? Whose son is he?"

"The son of David," they replied.

[43]He said to them, "How is it then that David, speaking by the Spirit, calls him 'Lord'? For he says,

[44]" 'The Lord said to my Lord:
"Sit at my right hand
until I put your enemies
under your feet." '[b]

[45]If then David calls him 'Lord,' how can he be his son?" [46]No one could say a word in reply, and from that day on no one dared to ask him any more questions.

Seven Woes

23 Then Jesus said to the crowds and to his disciples: [2]"The teachers of the law and the Pharisees sit in Moses' seat. [3]So you must obey them and do everything they tell you. But do not do what they do, for they do not practice what they preach. [4]They tie up heavy loads and put them on men's shoulders, but they themselves are not willing to lift a finger to move them.

[5]"Everything they do is done for men to see: They make their phylacteries[c] wide and the tassels on their garments long; [6]they love the place of honor at banquets and the most important seats in the synagogues; [7]they love to be greeted in the marketplaces and to have men call them 'Rabbi.'

[8]"But you are not to be called 'Rabbi,' for you have only one Master and you are all brothers. [9]And do not call anyone on earth 'father,' for you have one Father, and he is in heaven. [10]Nor are you to be called 'teacher,' for you have one Teacher, the Christ.[a] [11]The greatest among you will be your servant. [12]For whoever exalts himself will be humbled, and whoever humbles himself will be exalted.

[13]"Woe to you, teachers of the law and Pharisees, you hypocrites! You shut the kingdom of heaven in men's faces. You yourselves do not enter, nor will you let those enter who are trying to.[d]

[15]"Woe to you, teachers of the law and Pharisees, you hypocrites! You travel over land and sea to win a single convert, and when he becomes one, you make him twice as much a son of hell as you are.

[16]"Woe to you, blind guides! You say, 'If anyone swears by the temple, it means nothing; but if anyone swears by the gold of the temple, he is bound by his oath.' [17]You blind fools! Which is greater: the gold, or the temple that makes the gold sacred? [18]You also say, 'If anyone swears by the altar, it means nothing; but if anyone swears by the gift on it, he is bound by his oath.' [19]You blind men! Which is greater: the gift, or the altar that makes the gift sacred? [20]Therefore, he who swears by the altar swears by it and by everything on it. [21]And he who swears by the temple swears by it and by the one who dwells in it. [22]And he who swears by heaven swears by God's throne and by the one who sits on it.

[23]"Woe to you, teachers of the law and Pharisees, you hypocrites! You give a tenth of your spices—mint, dill and cummin. But you have neglected the more important matters of the law—justice, mercy and faithfulness. You should have practiced the latter, without neglecting the former. [24]You blind guides! You strain out a gnat but swallow a camel.

[25]"Woe to you, teachers of the law and Pharisees, you hypocrites! You clean the outside of the cup and dish, but inside they are full of greed and self-indulgence. [26]Blind Pharisee! First clean the inside of the cup and dish, and then the outside also will be clean.

[27]"Woe to you, teachers of the law and Pharisees, you hypocrites! You are like whitewashed tombs, which look beautiful on the outside but on the inside are full of dead men's bones and everything unclean. [28]In the same way, on the outside you appear to people as righteous but on the inside you are full of hypocrisy and wickedness.

[29]"Woe to you, teachers of the law and Pharisees, you hypocrites! You build tombs for the prophets and decorate the

---

a42,10 Or *Messiah* *b44* Psalm 110:1 *c5* That is, boxes containing Scripture verses, worn on forehead and arm *d13* Some manuscripts *to.* *14Woe to you, teachers of the law and Pharisees, you hypocrites! You devour widows' houses and for a show make lengthy prayers. Therefore you will be punished more severely.*

Nice Suit! What's That Smell?

Huh?

Matthew 23:27

Have you ever cleaned your room by just pushing everything under the bed—the dirty socks, the leftover box of pepperoni pizza and the half-eaten bowl of Cap'n Crunch? Can you imagine the smell after a week? (Maybe you don't have to imagine.) Jesus is talking about something like that: looks nice on the outside, but something's rotten on the inside. Jesus cares about your insides (not your guts, but your inner thoughts, desires, hopes, fears and joys). Who you are has very little to do with what you look like. Get real with Jesus and let him work on your inner-stuff— the real you.

graves of the righteous. [30]And you say, 'If we had lived in the days of our forefathers, we would not have taken part with them in shedding the blood of the prophets.' [31]So you testify against yourselves that you are the descendants of those who murdered the prophets. [32]Fill up, then, the measure of the sin of your forefathers!

[33]"You snakes! You brood of vipers! How will you escape being condemned to hell? [34]Therefore I am sending you prophets and wise men and teachers. Some of them you will kill and crucify; others you will flog in your synagogues and pursue from town to town. [35]And so upon you will come all the righteous blood that has been shed on earth, from the blood of righteous Abel to the blood of Zechariah son of Berekiah, whom you murdered between the temple and the altar. [36]I tell you the truth, all this will come upon this generation.

[37]"O Jerusalem, Jerusalem, you who kill the prophets and stone those sent to you, how often I have longed to gather your children together, as a hen gathers her chicks under her wings, but you were not willing. [38]Look, your house is left to you desolate. [39]For I tell you, you will not see me again until you say,

'Blessed is he who comes in the name of the Lord.'[a]"

Signs of the End of the Age

24 Jesus left the temple and was walking away when his disciples came up to him to call his attention to its buildings. [2]"Do you see all these things?" he asked. "I tell you the truth, not one stone here will be left on another; every one will be thrown down."

[3]As Jesus was sitting on the Mount of Olives, the disciples came to him privately. "Tell us," they said, "when will this happen, and what will be the sign of your coming and of the end of the age?"

[4]Jesus answered: "Watch out that no one deceives you. [5]For many will come in my name, claiming, 'I am the Christ,[b]' and will deceive many. [6]You will hear of wars and rumors of wars, but see to it that you are not alarmed. Such things must happen, but the end is still to come. [7]Nation will rise against nation, and kingdom against kingdom. There will be famines and earthquakes in various places. [8]All these are the beginning of birth pains.

[9]"Then you will be handed over to be persecuted and put to death, and you will be hated by all nations because of me. [10]At that time many will turn away from the faith and will betray and hate each other, [11]and many false prophets will appear and deceive many people. [12]Because of the increase of wickedness, the love of most will grow cold, [13]but he who stands firm to the end will be saved. [14]And this gospel of the kingdom will be preached in the whole world as a testimony to all nations, and then the end will come.

[15]"So when you see standing in the holy place 'the abomination that causes desolation,'[c] spoken of through the prophet Daniel—let the reader understand— [16]then let those who are in Judea flee to the mountains. [17]Let no one on the roof of his house go down to take anything out of the house. [18]Let no one in the field go back to get his cloak. [19]How dreadful it will be in those days for pregnant women and nursing mothers! [20]Pray

---

[a]39 Psalm 118:26   [b]5 Or *Messiah*; also in verse 23
[c]15 Daniel 9:27; 11:31; 12:11

that your flight will not take place in winter or on the Sabbath. [21]For then there will be great distress, unequaled from the beginning of the world until now—and never to be equaled again. [22]If those days had not been cut short, no one would survive, but for the sake of the elect those days will be shortened. [23]At that time if anyone says to you, 'Look, here is the Christ!' or, 'There he is!' do not believe it. [24]For false Christs and false prophets will appear and perform great signs and miracles to deceive even the elect—if that were possible. [25]See, I have told you ahead of time.

[26]"So if anyone tells you, 'There he is, out in the desert,' do not go out; or, 'Here he is, in the inner rooms,' do not believe it. [27]For as lightning that comes from the east is visible even in the west, so will be the coming of the Son of Man. [28]Wherever there is a carcass, there the vultures will gather.

[29]"Immediately after the distress of those days

" 'the sun will be darkened,
   and the moon will not give its light;
the stars will fall from the sky,
   and the heavenly bodies will be
      shaken.'[a]

[30]"At that time the sign of the Son of Man will appear in the sky, and all the nations of the earth will mourn. They will see the Son of Man coming on the clouds of the sky, with power and great glory. [31]And he will send his angels with a loud trumpet call, and they will gather his elect from the four winds, from one end of the heavens to the other.

[32]"Now learn this lesson from the fig tree: As soon as its twigs get tender and its leaves come out, you know that summer is near. [33]Even so, when you see all these things, you know that it[b] is near, right at the door. [34]I tell you the truth, this generation[c] will certainly not pass away until all these things have happened. [35]Heaven and earth will pass away, but my words will never pass away.

The Day and Hour Unknown

[36]"No one knows about that day or hour, not even the angels in heaven, nor

the Son,[d] but only the Father. [37]As it was in the days of Noah, so it will be at the coming of the Son of Man. [38]For in the days before the flood, people were eating and drinking, marrying and giving in marriage, up to the day Noah entered the ark; [39]and they knew nothing about what would happen until the flood came and took them all away. That is how it will be at the coming of the Son of Man. [40]Two men will be in the field; one will be taken and the other left. [41]Two women will be grinding with a hand mill; one will be taken and the other left.

[42]"Therefore keep watch, because you do not know on what day your Lord will come. [43]But understand this: If the owner of the house had known at what time of night the thief was coming, he would have kept watch and would not have let his house be broken into. [44]So you also must be ready, because the Son of Man will come at an hour when you do not expect him.

[45]"Who then is the faithful and wise servant, whom the master has put in charge of the servants in his household to give them their food at the proper time? [46]It will be good for that servant whose master finds him doing so when he returns. [47]I tell you the truth, he will put him in charge of all his possessions. [48]But suppose that servant is wicked and says to himself, 'My master is staying away a long time,' [49]and he then begins to beat his fellow servants and to eat and drink with drunkards. [50]The master of that servant will come on a day when he does not expect him and at an hour he is not aware of. [51]He will cut him to pieces and assign him a place with the hypocrites, where there will be weeping and gnashing of teeth.

The Parable of the Ten Virgins

25 "At that time the kingdom of heaven will be like ten virgins who took their lamps and went out to meet the bridegroom. [2]Five of them were foolish and five were wise. [3]The foolish ones took their lamps but did not take any oil with them. [4]The wise, however,

---

[a]29 Isaiah 13:10; 34:4   [b]33 Or he   [c]34 Or race
[d]36 Some manuscripts do not have *nor the Son.*

took oil in jars along with their lamps. ⁵The bridegroom was a long time in coming, and they all became drowsy and fell asleep.

⁶"At midnight the cry rang out: 'Here's the bridegroom! Come out to meet him!'

⁷"Then all the virgins woke up and trimmed their lamps. ⁸The foolish ones said to the wise, 'Give us some of your oil; our lamps are going out.'

⁹" 'No,' they replied, 'there may not be enough for both us and you. Instead, go to those who sell oil and buy some for yourselves.'

¹⁰"But while they were on their way to buy the oil, the bridegroom arrived. The virgins who were ready went in with him to the wedding banquet. And the door was shut.

¹¹"Later the others also came. 'Sir! Sir!' they said. 'Open the door for us!'

¹²"But he replied, 'I tell you the truth, I don't know you.'

¹³"Therefore keep watch, because you do not know the day or the hour.

The Parable of the Talents

¹⁴"Again, it will be like a man going on a journey, who called his servants and entrusted his property to them. ¹⁵To one he gave five talents*a* of money, to another two talents, and to another one talent, each according to his ability. Then he went on his journey. ¹⁶The man who had received the five talents went at once and put his money to work and gained five more. ¹⁷So also, the one with the two talents gained two more. ¹⁸But the man who had received the one talent went off, dug a hole in the ground and hid his master's money.

¹⁹"After a long time the master of those servants returned and settled accounts with them. ²⁰The man who had received the five talents brought the other five. 'Master,' he said, 'you entrusted me with five talents. See, I have gained five more.'

²¹"His master replied, 'Well done, good and faithful servant! You have been faithful with a few things; I will put you in charge of many things. Come and share your master's happiness!'

²²"The man with the two talents also came. 'Master,' he said, 'you entrusted me

with two talents; see, I have gained two more.'

²³"His master replied, 'Well done, good and faithful servant! You have been faithful with a few things; I will put you in charge of many things. Come and share your master's happiness!'

²⁴"Then the man who had received the one talent came. 'Master,' he said, 'I knew that you are a hard man, harvesting where you have not sown and gathering where you have not scattered seed. ²⁵So I was afraid and went out and hid your talent in the ground. See, here is what belongs to you.'

²⁶"His master replied, 'You wicked, lazy servant! So you knew that I harvest where I have not sown and gather where I have not scattered seed? ²⁷Well then, you should have put my money on deposit with the bankers, so that when I returned I would have received it back with interest.

²⁸" 'Take the talent from him and give it to the one who has the ten talents. ²⁹For everyone who has will be given more, and he will have an abundance. Whoever does not have, even what he has will be taken from him. ³⁰And throw that worthless servant outside, into the darkness, where there will be weeping and gnashing of teeth.'

The Sheep and the Goats

³¹"When the Son of Man comes in his glory, and all the angels with him, he will sit on his throne in heavenly glory. ³²All the nations will be gathered before him, and he will separate the people one from another as a shepherd separates the sheep from the goats. ³³He will put the sheep on his right and the goats on his left.

³⁴"Then the King will say to those on his right, 'Come, you who are blessed by my Father; take your inheritance, the kingdom prepared for you since the creation of the world. ³⁵For I was hungry and you gave me something to eat, I was thirsty and you gave me something to drink, I was a stranger and you invited me in, ³⁶I needed clothes and you

---

a15 A talent was worth more than a thousand dollars.

clothed me, I was sick and you looked after me, I was in prison and you came to visit me.'

37"Then the righteous will answer him, 'Lord, when did we see you hungry and feed you, or thirsty and give you something to drink? 38When did we see you a stranger and invite you in, or needing clothes and clothe you? 39When did we see you sick or in prison and go to visit you?'

40"The King will reply, 'I tell you the truth, whatever you did for one of the least of these brothers of mine, you did for me.'

41"Then he will say to those on his left, 'Depart from me, you who are cursed, into the eternal fire prepared for the devil and his angels. 42For I was hungry and you gave me nothing to eat, I was thirsty and you gave me nothing to drink, 43I was a stranger and you did not invite me in, I needed clothes and you did not

clothe me, I was sick and in prison and you did not look after me.'

44"They also will answer, 'Lord, when did we see you hungry or thirsty or a stranger or needing clothes or sick or in prison, and did not help you?'

45"He will reply, 'I tell you the truth, whatever you did not do for one of the least of these, you did not do for me.'

46"Then they will go away to eternal punishment, but the righteous to eternal life."

The Plot Against Jesus

26 When Jesus had finished saying all these things, he said to his disciples, 2"As you know, the Passover is two days away—and the Son of Man will be handed over to be crucified."

3Then the chief priests and the elders of the people assembled in the palace of the high priest, whose name was Caiaphas, 4and they plotted to arrest Jesus in

---

Friday

Serving Others

Read Matthew 25:34-40

If you think about it, there are a lot of opportunities for teenagers to serve others. My dad and I sometimes go serve the homeless with a local inner-city ministry. I try to stand up for kids at my school who are being picked on. And I show I care by visiting my grandma and the other people at the nursing home where she lives.

There are all kinds of people around us who need help. Jesus tells us to serve them as if we were serving him. Most of us have been given so much, and we need to share it with others. God has given me gifts like kindness, joy, time, energy and wisdom. I can easily use those gifts to help other people.

The greatest gift God has given me is eternal life with him in heaven. When I serve others, it's my way of saying, "Thank you."

Ashley age 12

What about You?

❶ What are some of the gifts God has given you? How can you use those gifts to serve others?

❷ Think about the people in your school. Whom would you consider "the least of these"? Write down 5 ways you could serve some of those people. When Monday comes, try out some of these ways on them.

❸ Ask God to help you find ways to serve other people.

Turn to page 1181 for your next devotion.

some sly way and kill him. [5]"But not during the Feast," they said, "or there may be a riot among the people."

Jesus Anointed at Bethany

[6]While Jesus was in Bethany in the home of a man known as Simon the Leper, [7]a woman came to him with an alabaster jar of very expensive perfume, which she poured on his head as he was reclining at the table.

[8]When the disciples saw this, they were indignant. "Why this waste?" they asked. [9]"This perfume could have been sold at a high price and the money given to the poor."

[10]Aware of this, Jesus said to them, "Why are you bothering this woman? She has done a beautiful thing to me. [11]The poor you will always have with you, but you will not always have me. [12]When she poured this perfume on my body, she did it to prepare me for burial. [13]I tell you the truth, wherever this gospel is preached throughout the world, what she has done will also be told, in memory of her."

Judas Agrees to Betray Jesus

[14]Then one of the Twelve—the one called Judas Iscariot—went to the chief priests [15]and asked, "What are you willing to give me if I hand him over to you?" So they counted out for him thirty silver coins. [16]From then on Judas watched for an opportunity to hand him over.

The Lord's Supper

[17]On the first day of the Feast of Unleavened Bread, the disciples came to Jesus and asked, "Where do you want us to make preparations for you to eat the Passover?"

[18]He replied, "Go into the city to a certain man and tell him, 'The Teacher says: My appointed time is near. I am going to celebrate the Passover with my disciples at your house.'" [19]So the disciples did as Jesus had directed them and prepared the Passover.

[20]When evening came, Jesus was reclining at the table with the Twelve.

Remember When . . . ?

Huh?

Matthew 26:18

We celebrate birthdays, anniversaries, Christmas, Easter, Veteran's Day, Presidents' Day, and a whole bunch of other days to remember special moments in our lives and history. Passover is a celebration for Jews that helps them remember when God really took care of them and got them out of slavery in Egypt. We need to look back and celebrate what God's done in each of our lives too. Not only does this honor God, but your faith in him will grow as a result.

---

[21]And while they were eating, he said, "I tell you the truth, one of you will betray me."

[22]They were very sad and began to say to him one after the other, "Surely not I, Lord?"

[23]Jesus replied, "The one who has dipped his hand into the bowl with me will betray me. [24]The Son of Man will go just as it is written about him. But woe to that man who betrays the Son of Man! It would be better for him if he had not been born."

[25]Then Judas, the one who would betray him, said, "Surely not I, Rabbi?"

Jesus answered, "Yes, it is you."[a]

[26]While they were eating, Jesus took bread, gave thanks and broke it, and gave it to his disciples, saying, "Take and eat; this is my body."

[27]Then he took the cup, gave thanks and offered it to them, saying, "Drink from it, all of you. [28]This is my blood of the[b] covenant, which is poured out for many for the forgiveness of sins. [29]I tell you, I will not drink of this fruit of the vine from now on until that day when I drink it anew with you in my Father's kingdom."

[30]When they had sung a hymn, they went out to the Mount of Olives.

[a]25 Or *"You yourself have said it"*   [b]28 Some manuscripts *the new*

Jesus Predicts Peter's Denial

³¹Then Jesus told them, "This very night you will all fall away on account of me, for it is written:

" 'I will strike the shepherd,
    and the sheep of the flock will be
        scattered.'ᵃ

³²But after I have risen, I will go ahead of you into Galilee."

³³Peter replied, "Even if all fall away on account of you, I never will."

³⁴"I tell you the truth," Jesus answered, "this very night, before the rooster crows, you will disown me three times."

³⁵But Peter declared, "Even if I have to die with you, I will never disown you." And all the other disciples said the same.

Gethsemane

³⁶Then Jesus went with his disciples to a place called Gethsemane, and he said to them, "Sit here while I go over there and pray." ³⁷He took Peter and the two sons of Zebedee along with him, and he began to be sorrowful and troubled. ³⁸Then he said to them, "My soul is overwhelmed with sorrow to the point of death. Stay here and keep watch with me."

³⁹Going a little farther, he fell with his face to the ground and prayed, "My Father, if it is possible, may this cup be taken from me. Yet not as I will, but as you will."

⁴⁰Then he returned to his disciples and found them sleeping. "Could you men not keep watch with me for one hour?" he asked Peter. ⁴¹"Watch and pray so that you will not fall into temptation. The spirit is willing, but the body is weak."

⁴²He went away a second time and prayed, "My Father, if it is not possible for this cup to be taken away unless I drink it, may your will be done."

⁴³When he came back, he again found them sleeping, because their eyes were heavy. ⁴⁴So he left them and went away once more and prayed the third time, saying the same thing.

⁴⁵Then he returned to the disciples and said to them, "Are you still sleeping and resting? Look, the hour is near, and the Son of Man is betrayed into the hands of sinners. ⁴⁶Rise, let us go! Here comes my betrayer!"

Jesus Arrested

⁴⁷While he was still speaking, Judas, one of the Twelve, arrived. With him was a large crowd armed with swords and clubs, sent from the chief priests and the elders of the people. ⁴⁸Now the betrayer had arranged a signal with them: "The one I kiss is the man; arrest him." ⁴⁹Going at once to Jesus, Judas said, "Greetings, Rabbi!" and kissed him.

⁵⁰Jesus replied, "Friend, do what you came for."ᵇ

Then the men stepped forward, seized Jesus and arrested him. ⁵¹With that, one of Jesus' companions reached for his sword, drew it out and struck the servant of the high priest, cutting off his ear.

⁵²"Put your sword back in its place," Jesus said to him, "for all who draw the sword will die by the sword. ⁵³Do you think I cannot call on my Father, and he will at once put at my disposal more than twelve legions of angels? ⁵⁴But how then would the Scriptures be fulfilled that say it must happen in this way?"

⁵⁵At that time Jesus said to the crowd, "Am I leading a rebellion, that you have come out with swords and clubs to capture me? Every day I sat in the temple courts teaching, and you did not arrest me. ⁵⁶But this has all taken place that the writings of the prophets might be fulfilled." Then all the disciples deserted him and fled.

Before the Sanhedrin

⁵⁷Those who had arrested Jesus took him to Caiaphas, the high priest, where the teachers of the law and the elders had assembled. ⁵⁸But Peter followed him at a distance, right up to the courtyard of the high priest. He entered and sat down with the guards to see the outcome.

⁵⁹The chief priests and the whole Sanhedrin were looking for false evidence against Jesus so that they could put him to death. ⁶⁰But they did not find any, though many false witnesses came forward.

Finally two came forward ⁶¹and de-

ᵃ31 Zech. 13:7   ᵇ50 Or "Friend, why have you come?"

clared, "This fellow said, 'I am able to destroy the temple of God and rebuild it in three days.'"

⁶²Then the high priest stood up and said to Jesus, "Are you not going to answer? What is this testimony that these men are bringing against you?" ⁶³But Jesus remained silent.

The high priest said to him, "I charge you under oath by the living God: Tell us if you are the Christ,ᵃ the Son of God."

⁶⁴"Yes, it is as you say," Jesus replied. "But I say to all of you: In the future you will see the Son of Man sitting at the right hand of the Mighty One and coming on the clouds of heaven."

⁶⁵Then the high priest tore his clothes and said, "He has spoken blasphemy! Why do we need any more witnesses?

Look, now you have heard the blasphemy. ⁶⁶What do you think?"

"He is worthy of death," they answered.

⁶⁷Then they spit in his face and struck him with their fists. Others slapped him ⁶⁸and said, "Prophesy to us, Christ. Who hit you?"

Peter Disowns Jesus

⁶⁹Now Peter was sitting out in the courtyard, and a servant girl came to him. "You also were with Jesus of Galilee," she said.

⁷⁰But he denied it before them all. "I don't know what you're talking about," he said.

ᵃ63 Or *Messiah*; also in verse 68

Week end.

Seize the Day

Read James 4:14 (page 1511)

Wednesday's devotional really makes you think. Carolyn admitted that she missed a great moment with her dad because she chose to do something else. Wow! It's pretty easy to relate to what Carolyn is talking about, isn't it?

It seems like there will be tons of time left in life to do all those things you know you should do: spend time with your parents, read the Bible, learn important stuff, whatever. And it's really easy to choose to sleep in, watch TV, play video games, cruise the Net or chat online and skip the "important" stuff. Not that there's anything wrong with sleeping in or going online. It's just that all of a sudden you'll be 18 and find even more reasons to ignore those "important things."

So, just like James said in the passage you read today—take advantage of life now. Don't wait until you're older. Develop relationships with your parents, spend time with God and get going with those things you're tempted to push off until you're older. You won't regret it.

❶ Think about one area in your life that causes you to waste time. What can you do to decrease the wasted time in your life?

❷ Decide you're going to take one night a week and spend time with your parents. No phone calls, no CD player, no Internet. If your parents are busy doing things, see if you can tag along with them.

❸ Ask God to give you the courage to not waste time. Ask God to help you spend more time with him.

Turn to page 1184 for your next devotion.

⁷¹Then he went out to the gateway, where another girl saw him and said to the people there, "This fellow was with Jesus of Nazareth."

⁷²He denied it again, with an oath: "I don't know the man!"

⁷³After a little while, those standing there went up to Peter and said, "Surely you are one of them, for your accent gives you away."

⁷⁴Then he began to call down curses on himself and he swore to them, "I don't know the man!"

Immediately a rooster crowed. ⁷⁵Then Peter remembered the word Jesus had spoken: "Before the rooster crows, you will disown me three times." And he went outside and wept bitterly.

Judas Hangs Himself

27 Early in the morning, all the chief priests and the elders of the people came to the decision to put Jesus to death. ²They bound him, led him away and handed him over to Pilate, the governor.

³When Judas, who had betrayed him, saw that Jesus was condemned, he was seized with remorse and returned the thirty silver coins to the chief priests and the elders. ⁴"I have sinned," he said, "for I have betrayed innocent blood."

"What is that to us?" they replied. "That's your responsibility."

⁵So Judas threw the money into the temple and left. Then he went away and hanged himself.

⁶The chief priests picked up the coins and said, "It is against the law to put this into the treasury, since it is blood money." ⁷So they decided to use the money to buy the potter's field as a burial place for foreigners. ⁸That is why it has been called the Field of Blood to this day. ⁹Then what was spoken by Jeremiah the prophet was fulfilled: "They took the thirty silver coins, the price set on him by the people of Israel, ¹⁰and they used them to buy the potter's field, as the Lord commanded me."[a]

Jesus Before Pilate

¹¹Meanwhile Jesus stood before the governor, and the governor asked him, "Are you the king of the Jews?"

"Yes, it is as you say," Jesus replied.

¹²When he was accused by the chief priests and the elders, he gave no answer. ¹³Then Pilate asked him, "Don't you hear the testimony they are bringing against you?" ¹⁴But Jesus made no reply, not even to a single charge—to the great amazement of the governor.

¹⁵Now it was the governor's custom at the Feast to release a prisoner chosen by the crowd. ¹⁶At that time they had a notorious prisoner, called Barabbas. ¹⁷So when the crowd had gathered, Pilate asked them, "Which one do you want me to release to you: Barabbas, or Jesus who is called Christ?" ¹⁸For he knew it was out of envy that they had handed Jesus over to him.

¹⁹While Pilate was sitting on the judge's seat, his wife sent him this message: "Don't have anything to do with that innocent man, for I have suffered a great deal today in a dream because of him."

²⁰But the chief priests and the elders persuaded the crowd to ask for Barabbas and to have Jesus executed.

²¹"Which of the two do you want me to release to you?" asked the governor.

"Barabbas," they answered.

²²"What shall I do, then, with Jesus who is called Christ?" Pilate asked.

They all answered, "Crucify him!"

²³"Why? What crime has he committed?" asked Pilate.

But they shouted all the louder, "Crucify him!"

²⁴When Pilate saw that he was getting nowhere, but that instead an uproar was starting, he took water and washed his hands in front of the crowd. "I am innocent of this man's blood," he said. "It is your responsibility!"

²⁵All the people answered, "Let his blood be on us and on our children!"

²⁶Then he released Barabbas to them. But he had Jesus flogged, and handed him over to be crucified.

The Soldiers Mock Jesus

²⁷Then the governor's soldiers took Jesus into the Praetorium and gathered the whole company of soldiers around

---

a 10 See Zech. 11:12,13; Jer. 19:1-13; 32:6-9.

him. [28]They stripped him and put a scarlet robe on him, [29]and then twisted together a crown of thorns and set it on his head. They put a staff in his right hand and knelt in front of him and mocked him. "Hail, king of the Jews!" they said. [30]They spit on him, and took the staff and struck him on the head again and again. [31]After they had mocked him, they took off the robe and put his own clothes on him. Then they led him away to crucify him.

The Crucifixion

[32]As they were going out, they met a man from Cyrene, named Simon, and they forced him to carry the cross. [33]They came to a place called Golgotha (which means The Place of the Skull). [34]There they offered Jesus wine to drink, mixed with gall; but after tasting it, he refused to drink it. [35]When they had crucified him, they divided up his clothes by casting lots.[a] [36]And sitting down, they kept watch over him there. [37]Above his head they placed the written charge against him: THIS IS JESUS, THE KING OF THE JEWS. [38]Two robbers were crucified with him, one on his right and one on his left. [39]Those who passed by hurled insults at him, shaking their heads [40]and saying, "You who are going to destroy the temple and build it in three days, save yourself! Come down from the cross, if you are the Son of God!"

[41]In the same way the chief priests, the teachers of the law and the elders mocked him. [42]"He saved others," they said, "but he can't save himself! He's the King of Israel! Let him come down now from the cross, and we will believe in him. [43]He trusts in God. Let God rescue him now if he wants him, for he said, 'I am the Son of God.'" [44]In the same way the robbers who were crucified with him also heaped insults on him.

The Death of Jesus

[45]From the sixth hour until the ninth hour darkness came over all the land. [46]About the ninth hour Jesus cried out in a loud voice, *"Eloi, Eloi,[b] lama sabachthani?"*—which means, "My God, my God, why have you forsaken me?"[c]

[47]When some of those standing there heard this, they said, "He's calling Elijah."

[48]Immediately one of them ran and got a sponge. He filled it with wine vinegar, put it on a stick, and offered it to Jesus to drink. [49]The rest said, "Now leave him alone. Let's see if Elijah comes to save him."

[50]And when Jesus had cried out again in a loud voice, he gave up his spirit.

[51]At that moment the curtain of the temple was torn in two from top to bottom. The earth shook and the rocks split. [52]The tombs broke open and the bodies of many holy people who had died were raised to life. [53]They came out of the tombs, and after Jesus' resurrection they went into the holy city and appeared to many people.

[54]When the centurion and those with him who were guarding Jesus saw the earthquake and all that had happened, they were terrified, and exclaimed, "Surely he was the Son[d] of God!"

[55]Many women were there, watching from a distance. They had followed Jesus from Galilee to care for his needs. [56]Among them were Mary Magdalene, Mary the mother of James and Joses, and the mother of Zebedee's sons.

The Burial of Jesus

[57]As evening approached, there came a rich man from Arimathea, named Joseph, who had himself become a disciple of Jesus. [58]Going to Pilate, he asked for Jesus' body, and Pilate ordered that it be given to him. [59]Joseph took the body, wrapped it in a clean linen cloth, [60]and placed it in his own new tomb that he had cut out of the rock. He rolled a big stone in front of the entrance to the tomb and went away. [61]Mary Magdalene and the other Mary were sitting there opposite the tomb.

The Guard at the Tomb

[62]The next day, the one after Preparation Day, the chief priests and the Pharisees went to Pilate. [63]"Sir," they said, "we

---

[a]35 A few late manuscripts *lots that the word spoken by the prophet might be fulfilled: "They divided my garments among themselves and cast lots for my clothing"* (Psalm 22:18)   [b]46 Some manuscripts *Eli, Eli*   [c]46 Psalm 22:1   [d]54 Or *a son*

remember that while he was still alive that deceiver said, 'After three days I will rise again.' [64]So give the order for the tomb to be made secure until the third day. Otherwise, his disciples may come and steal the body and tell the people that he has been raised from the dead. This last deception will be worse than the first."

[65]"Take a guard," Pilate answered. "Go, make the tomb as secure as you know how." [66]So they went and made the tomb secure by putting a seal on the stone and posting the guard.

The Resurrection

28 After the Sabbath, at dawn on the first day of the week, Mary Magdalene and the other Mary went to look at the tomb.

[2]There was a violent earthquake, for an angel of the Lord came down from heaven and, going to the tomb, rolled back the stone and sat on it. [3]His appearance was like lightning, and his clothes were white as snow. [4]The guards were so afraid of him that they shook and became like dead men.

[5]The angel said to the women, "Do not be afraid, for I know that you are looking for Jesus, who was crucified. [6]He is not here; he has risen, just as he said. Come and see the place where he lay. [7]Then go quickly and tell his disciples: 'He has risen from the dead and is going ahead of you into Galilee. There you will see him.' Now I have told you."

[8]So the women hurried away from the tomb, afraid yet filled with joy, and ran to tell his disciples. [9]Suddenly Jesus met them. "Greetings," he said. They came to him, clasped his feet and worshiped him. [10]Then Jesus said to them, "Do not be afraid. Go and tell my brothers to go to Galilee; there they will see me."

Monday

"Everyone" Means Everyone

Read Matthew 28:19–20

I knew a girl named Brittany, and I really didn't like her. She was so mean to my friends and to me! I thought, *Why should I invite her to church?—I don't like being around her.*

Then I read this passage about making disciples of all nations. God wants everyone, even Brittany, to hear his amazing news. But I still didn't want to be the one to tell her.

Verse 20 changed my mind. God says he'll be with me always. However scary it might be to talk to Brittany about my faith, God will be there, helping me.

It's awesome how God gives us this huge responsibility. This is the Great Commission, after all! But when he gives us this command, he gives us a promise, too: We'll never have to witness alone.

What about You?

❶ What seems more difficult to you—witnessing to people in another country or witnessing to people you already know? What's tough about each kind of witnessing?

❷ Think of one person you know who isn't a Christian and invite him or her to church or a youth group activity this week.

❸ Ask God to give you courage to share the gospel.

Turn to page 1190 for your next devotion.

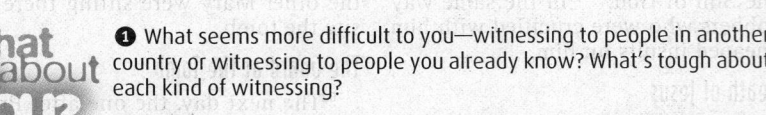

The Guards' Report

[11]While the women were on their way, some of the guards went into the city and reported to the chief priests everything that had happened. [12]When the chief priests had met with the elders and devised a plan, they gave the soldiers a large sum of money, [13]telling them, "You are to say, 'His disciples came during the night and stole him away while we were asleep.' [14]If this report gets to the governor, we will satisfy him and keep you out of trouble." [15]So the soldiers took the money and did as they were instructed. And this story has been widely circulated among the Jews to this very day.

The Great Commission

[16]Then the eleven disciples went to Galilee, to the mountain where Jesus had told them to go. [17]When they saw him, they worshiped him; but some doubted. [18]Then Jesus came to them and said, "All authority in heaven and on earth has been given to me. [19]Therefore go and make disciples of all nations, baptizing them in[a] the name of the Father and of the Son and of the Holy Spirit, [20]and teaching them to obey everything I have commanded you. And surely I am with you always, to the very end of the age."

[a]19 Or *into*; see Acts 8:16; 19:5; Romans 6:3; 1 Cor. 1:13; 10:2 and Gal. 3:27.

Be a Tutor

Matthew 28:19

If you get a bad grade in a class, maybe you need a tutor. A tutor can work with you and help you improve your grade. The tutor "disciples" you in that subject. One of Jesus' last instructions to his followers was to go out and make disciples. Making disciples means helping people learn how to be more like Jesus. And you know what? In order to be good teachers, we have to be good learners.

Mark

START

Mark's Gospel reads like an in-your-face action flick. Taking quick cuts from one scene to the next, Mark's camera never rests long in any one place or on any one person. Not only is Mark's version of the Good News big on plot and short on talk, it's just plain short. This book is the briefest of the 4 Gospels—it's the Cliffs Notes version!

Mark moves you around farther and faster in the first 20 verses of his Gospel than you get in the first 3 chapters of either Matthew or Luke. First, Mark pitches you a no-nonsense, just-the-facts-ma'am introduction to John the Baptist and his baptism of Jesus. Then it's off to the desert where Satan tempted Jesus. Then you're back in town where Jesus is recruiting his first disciples.

Why did Mark write Mark this way? Because he knew who he was writing to—the Romans. Everyone knew the Romans were big on action. While the Greeks were sitting around discussing ideas, the Romans conquered the known world and took in afternoon gladiator matches at the Coliseum. The Romans could really get into Mark's version of Jesus' life. Now here was a man of action!

Cast OF Characters

Mark

A.k.a. John Mark, probably a good Roman kid (Marcus is a good Roman name). This is the same young guy who was the reason for the split-up between former friends Paul and Barnabas (see Acts 15:36–40, page 1330, for this hot disagreement that didn't end up swell). Many Bible scholars think this could be Mark himself with the cameo appearance in his own book (chapter 14:51). And, no, he wasn't one of the 12 disciples.

Jesus

Here he is, the God-man. You don't get any info about Jesus' birth from Mark like you do from Matthew and Luke. You just read about Jesus as an adult. He preaches, performs miracles and encounters both great popularity and deadly opposition.

(diss-SY-pulls)

The 12 Disciples

Jesus had lots more than a dozen disciples, but he appointed these 12 in particular to travel with him and share in his work and witness in a special way.

Pharisees

(FAIR-uh-seez) Also called "teachers of the law." These guys spent their time asking Jesus trick questions in public, trying their best to humiliate him and ruin his credibility in front of everyone. (They never did accomplish this, thanks to Jesus. He had a way of always turning the question back on the Pharisees that showed everyone how petty and jealous they were.) They also accuse Jesus of breaking various traditions of theirs. (Well, yeah, Jesus did break the Pharisees' traditions—but those traditions were not part of God's law, which Jesus never broke.) And they look for ways to arrest and kill Jesus (which they eventually accomplish).

What's UP with That?

Sometimes we come across puzzling passages from the Bible. Take Mark 8:34 for instance. Jesus says, "If anyone would come after me, he must . . . take up his cross and follow me." Does this mean we all have to carry crosses? No. Jesus used this powerful image to illustrate the price of following him. Back in Bible times, the Romans required a criminal to carry his own cross to the place of execution. Jesus was warning his people that they would endure pain and hardship if they put him first in their life. But they would get a great reward—eternal life!

Whenever you stumble over a puzzling passage, just remember this **No-Jive, King-Size Guide:**

GUIDE 1 What seems to you like a bizarre Bible verse was perfectly natural to the people the verse was originally written to. After all, the Bible is an ancient book, written to people long ago. Browse your youth leader's bookshelf for a good Bible dictionary or commentary that'll help answer some of your questions.

GUIDE 2 The Bible will usually explain its weird parts in other, unweird parts. So look for those unweird, clear, plain parts. Youth leaders are good at this; so is software or books called concordances (big lists of where in the Bible to find the word you want).

GUIDE 3 Christian tradition is very helpful in interpreting weird passages. Find out what Christians over the last several hundred years have thought about your "weird" verse (ask your pastor or youth leader). Christian tradition isn't perfect, just helpful.

GUIDE 4 Use your common sense (which isn't perfect either, but is still helpful).

GUIDE 5 Remember that the simplest explanation is often the most likely one. God didn't give you the Bible to confuse you but to help you. And if you're still confused by a weird verse in the Bible, don't worry about it. Flip to another chapter that you do understand. The Bible is like life—some parts will make sense to you only as you keep on living, experiencing life and learning to trust God.

Snap Shots

Sorry, there's nothing even resembling an outline in this book. It's just a wild ride through a swirl of accusations, miracles, exorcisms, stories, murder plots, hope, despair, belief, frustration, jealousy, politics, death by execution and a final death-to-life episode that is unlike any other! It has the power to change our destiny.

John the Baptist Prepares the Way

1 The beginning of the gospel about Jesus Christ, the Son of God.[a]

[2] It is written in Isaiah the prophet:

"I will send my messenger ahead
    of you,
  who will prepare your way"[b]—
[3] "a voice of one calling in the desert,
'Prepare the way for the Lord,
  make straight paths for him.' "[c]

[4] And so John came, baptizing in the desert region and preaching a baptism of repentance for the forgiveness of sins. [5] The whole Judean countryside and all the people of Jerusalem went out to him. Confessing their sins, they were baptized by him in the Jordan River. [6] John wore clothing made of camel's hair, with a leather belt around his waist, and he ate locusts and wild honey. [7] And this was his message: "After me will come one more powerful than I, the thongs of whose sandals I am not worthy to stoop down and untie. [8] I baptize you with[d] water, but he will baptize you with the Holy Spirit."

The Baptism and Temptation of Jesus

[9] At that time Jesus came from Nazareth in Galilee and was baptized by John in the Jordan. [10] As Jesus was coming up out of the water, he saw heaven being torn open and the Spirit descending on him like a dove. [11] And a voice came from heaven: "You are my Son, whom I love; with you I am well pleased."

[12] At once the Spirit sent him out into the desert, [13] and he was in the desert forty days, being tempted by Satan. He was with the wild animals, and angels attended him.

The Calling of the First Disciples

[14] After John was put in prison, Jesus went into Galilee, proclaiming the good news of God. [15] "The time has come," he said. "The kingdom of God is near. Repent and believe the good news!"

[16] As Jesus walked beside the Sea of Galilee, he saw Simon and his brother Andrew casting a net into the lake, for they were fishermen. [17] "Come, follow me," Jesus said, "and I will make you fishers of men." [18] At once they left their nets and followed him.

[19] When he had gone a little farther, he saw James son of Zebedee and his brother John in a boat, preparing their nets. [20] Without delay he called them, and they left their father Zebedee in the boat with the hired men and followed him.

Jesus Drives Out an Evil Spirit

[21] They went to Capernaum, and when the Sabbath came, Jesus went into the synagogue and began to teach. [22] The people were amazed at his teaching, because he taught them as one who had authority, not as the teachers of the law. [23] Just then a man in their synagogue who was possessed by an evil[e] spirit cried out, [24] "What do you want with us, Jesus of Nazareth? Have you come to destroy us? I know who you are—the Holy One of God!"

[25] "Be quiet!" said Jesus sternly. "Come out of him!" [26] The evil spirit shook the man violently and came out of him with a shriek.

[27] The people were all so amazed that

That's a Big Birthday Cake

Huh?

Mark 1:14–15

The phrase "kingdom of God" is used a lot in the New Testament. Here in Mark it's a big theme. There were a bunch of people who thought Jesus would begin a political kingdom and rule the earth. But in the parables of this book Jesus describes God's kingdom in spiritual ways. In one sense, because of Jesus, the "kingdom of God" is already here. In another sense, it isn't quite all here. Think about your birthdays. You've already had a few of them, so in a sense they are already here. But, you haven't had all of them, and you look forward to each one that comes. That's a lot like the kingdom of God. It's had a few birthdays, but nowhere near all of them.

---

[a] 1 Some manuscripts do not have *the Son of God.*
[b] 2 Mal. 3:1   [c] 3 Isaiah 40:3   [d] 8 Or *in*   [e] 23 Greek *unclean*; also in verses 26 and 27

they asked each other, "What is this? A new teaching—and with authority! He even gives orders to evil spirits and they obey him." ²⁸News about him spread quickly over the whole region of Galilee.

Jesus Heals Many

²⁹As soon as they left the synagogue, they went with James and John to the home of Simon and Andrew. ³⁰Simon's mother-in-law was in bed with a fever, and they told Jesus about her. ³¹So he went to her, took her hand and helped her up. The fever left her and she began to wait on them.

³²That evening after sunset the people brought to Jesus all the sick and demon-possessed. ³³The whole town gathered at the door, ³⁴and Jesus healed many who had various diseases. He also drove out many demons, but he would not let the demons speak because they knew who he was.

Jesus Prays in a Solitary Place

³⁵Very early in the morning, while it was still dark, Jesus got up, left the house and went off to a solitary place, where he prayed. ³⁶Simon and his companions went to look for him, ³⁷and when they found him, they exclaimed: "Everyone is looking for you!"

³⁸Jesus replied, "Let us go somewhere else—to the nearby villages—so I can preach there also. That is why I have come." ³⁹So he traveled throughout Galilee, preaching in their synagogues and driving out demons.

A Man With Leprosy

⁴⁰A man with leprosy*ᵃ* came to him and begged him on his knees, "If you are willing, you can make me clean."

⁴¹Filled with compassion, Jesus reached out his hand and touched the man. "I am willing," he said. "Be clean!" ⁴²Immediately the leprosy left him and he was cured.

⁴³Jesus sent him away at once with a strong warning: ⁴⁴"See that you don't tell this to anyone. But go, show yourself to the priest and offer the sacrifices that Moses commanded for your cleansing, as a testimony to them." ⁴⁵Instead he went

out and began to talk freely, spreading the news. As a result, Jesus could no longer enter a town openly but stayed outside in lonely places. Yet the people still came to him from everywhere.

Jesus Heals a Paralytic

2 A few days later, when Jesus again entered Capernaum, the people heard that he had come home. ²So many gathered that there was no room left, not even outside the door, and he preached the word to them. ³Some men came, bringing to him a paralytic, carried by four of them. ⁴Since they could not get him to Jesus because of the crowd, they made an opening in the roof above Jesus and, after digging through it, lowered the mat the paralyzed man was lying on. ⁵When Jesus saw their faith, he said to the paralytic, "Son, your sins are forgiven."

⁶Now some teachers of the law were sitting there, thinking to themselves, ⁷"Why does this fellow talk like that? He's blaspheming! Who can forgive sins but God alone?"

⁸Immediately Jesus knew in his spirit that this was what they were thinking in their hearts, and he said to them, "Why are you thinking these things? ⁹Which is easier: to say to the paralytic, 'Your sins are forgiven,' or to say, 'Get up, take your mat and walk'? ¹⁰But that you may know that the Son of Man has authority on earth to forgive sins . . ." He said to the paralytic, ¹¹"I tell you, get up, take your mat and go home." ¹²He got up, took his mat and walked out in full view of them all. This amazed everyone and they praised God, saying, "We have never seen anything like this!"

The Calling of Levi

¹³Once again Jesus went out beside the lake. A large crowd came to him, and he began to teach them. ¹⁴As he walked along, he saw Levi son of Alphaeus sitting at the tax collector's booth. "Follow me," Jesus told him, and Levi got up and followed him.

¹⁵While Jesus was having dinner at

ᵃ40 The Greek word was used for various diseases affecting the skin—not necessarily leprosy.

Levi's house, many tax collectors and "sinners" were eating with him and his disciples, for there were many who followed him. [16]When the teachers of the law who were Pharisees saw him eating with the "sinners" and tax collectors, they asked his disciples: "Why does he eat with tax collectors and 'sinners'?"

[17]On hearing this, Jesus said to them, "It is not the healthy who need a doctor, but the sick. I have not come to call the righteous, but sinners."

Jesus Questioned About Fasting

[18]Now John's disciples and the Pharisees were fasting. Some people came and asked Jesus, "How is it that John's disciples and the disciples of the Pharisees are fasting, but yours are not?"

[19]Jesus answered, "How can the guests of the bridegroom fast while he is with them? They cannot, so long as they have him with them. [20]But the time will come when the bridegroom will be taken from them, and on that day they will fast.

[21]"No one sews a patch of unshrunk cloth on an old garment. If he does, the new piece will pull away from the old, making the tear worse. [22]And no one pours new wine into old wineskins. If he does, the wine will burst the skins, and both the wine and the wineskins will be ruined. No, he pours new wine into new wineskins."

Lord of the Sabbath

[23]One Sabbath Jesus was going through the grainfields, and as his disciples walked along, they began to pick some heads of grain. [24]The Pharisees said

---

Tuesday

Get Away From It All
Read Mark 1:35

Sometimes a person just has to be alone. Like when my dog—my long-time friend—died. I went up to my room that night and cried and prayed. I didn't have to worry about anyone seeing how upset I was or thinking I was silly to cry so hard about a dog. It was just me and God up there, and he cared about how I felt.

When people pray in public, they don't necessarily pray about the same stuff they would pray about in private. I mean, I've actually heard someone pray out loud to get a strike in bowling! I really hope that person prays in private too, because there are a lot more important things to pray for than a strike. I like to pray with others, but there is also something great about praying to God one on one.

Jesus is our example in everything, and while the Bible tells us he prayed in front of people a lot, it also tells us he made a special effort to spend time alone with God. And if that time was a big deal to Jesus, it should be a big deal to everyone.

Viannah age 13

❶ Why do you think Jesus liked to have time alone with his Father?

❷ Take some time out of your day today—even if it's just 5 minutes—to be alone with God. Talk to him about what's going on in your life. Try to spend time with God every day this week.

❸ Ask God to help you remember to pray.

Turn to page 1193 for your next devotion.

to him, "Look, why are they doing what is unlawful on the Sabbath?"

²⁵He answered, "Have you never read what David did when he and his companions were hungry and in need? ²⁶In the days of Abiathar the high priest, he entered the house of God and ate the consecrated bread, which is lawful only for priests to eat. And he also gave some to his companions."

²⁷Then he said to them, "The Sabbath was made for man, not man for the Sabbath. ²⁸So the Son of Man is Lord even of the Sabbath."

Nap Time

Mark 2:23–27

The Sabbath, or day of rest, was really important to people in Israel. You weren't supposed to do anything that day—work in the field, wash your camel, rake your sand—nothing. For many people, observing the Sabbath had turned into a way to judge who was holy and who wasn't. The same people who wanted to judge others by the do's and don'ts of the Sabbath tried to judge Jesus. But he would have none of that. The point was to love God and serve others.

3 Another time he went into the synagogue, and a man with a shriveled hand was there. ²Some of them were looking for a reason to accuse Jesus, so they watched him closely to see if he would heal him on the Sabbath. ³Jesus said to the man with the shriveled hand, "Stand up in front of everyone."

⁴Then Jesus asked them, "Which is lawful on the Sabbath: to do good or to do evil, to save life or to kill?" But they remained silent.

⁵He looked around at them in anger and, deeply distressed at their stubborn hearts, said to the man, "Stretch out your hand." He stretched it out, and his hand was completely restored. ⁶Then the

Pharisees went out and began to plot with the Herodians how they might kill Jesus.

Crowds Follow Jesus

⁷Jesus withdrew with his disciples to the lake, and a large crowd from Galilee followed. ⁸When they heard all he was doing, many people came to him from Judea, Jerusalem, Idumea, and the regions across the Jordan and around Tyre and Sidon. ⁹Because of the crowd he told his disciples to have a small boat ready for him, to keep the people from crowding him. ¹⁰For he had healed many, so that those with diseases were pushing forward to touch him. ¹¹Whenever the evil*a* spirits saw him, they fell down before him and cried out, "You are the Son of God." ¹²But he gave them strict orders not to tell who he was.

The Appointing of the Twelve Apostles

¹³Jesus went up on a mountainside and called to him those he wanted, and they came to him. ¹⁴He appointed twelve—designating them apostles*b*—that they might be with him and that he might send them out to preach ¹⁵and to have authority to drive out demons. ¹⁶These are the twelve he appointed: Simon (to whom he gave the name Peter); ¹⁷James son of Zebedee and his brother John (to them he gave the name Boanerges, which means Sons of Thunder); ¹⁸Andrew, Philip, Bartholomew, Matthew, Thomas, James son of Alphaeus, Thaddaeus, Simon the Zealot ¹⁹and Judas Iscariot, who betrayed him.

Jesus and Beelzebub

²⁰Then Jesus entered a house, and again a crowd gathered, so that he and his disciples were not even able to eat. ²¹When his family heard about this, they went to take charge of him, for they said, "He is out of his mind."

²²And the teachers of the law who came down from Jerusalem said, "He is possessed by Beelzebub*c*! By the prince of demons he is driving out demons."

---

*a*11 Greek *unclean*; also in verse 30   *b*14 Some manuscripts do not have *designating them apostles*.
*c*22 Greek *Beezeboul* or *Beelzeboul*

Hey, Bub

Huh?

Mark 3:22

Here's one of those names you won't want to use when it comes to naming your children someday! Beelzebub (Bee-EL-zuh-bub) is another name for Satan. In this passage, the people who were calling Jesus a fake said he was from Beelzebub. The truth is, they were just trying to find any way they could to diss him. They couldn't stand him, and they figured this was a good way to turn the people against him. Boy, were they wrong!

²³So Jesus called them and spoke to them in parables: "How can Satan drive out Satan? ²⁴If a kingdom is divided against itself, that kingdom cannot stand. ²⁵If a house is divided against itself, that house cannot stand. ²⁶And if Satan opposes himself and is divided, he cannot stand; his end has come. ²⁷In fact, no one can enter a strong man's house and carry off his possessions unless he first ties up the strong man. Then he can rob his house. ²⁸I tell you the truth, all the sins and blasphemies of men will be forgiven them. ²⁹But whoever blasphemes against the Holy Spirit will never be forgiven; he is guilty of an eternal sin."

³⁰He said this because they were saying, "He has an evil spirit."

Jesus' Mother and Brothers

³¹Then Jesus' mother and brothers arrived. Standing outside, they sent someone in to call him. ³²A crowd was sitting around him, and they told him, "Your mother and brothers are outside looking for you."

³³"Who are my mother and my brothers?" he asked.

³⁴Then he looked at those seated in a circle around him and said, "Here are my mother and my brothers! ³⁵Whoever does God's will is my brother and sister and mother."

The Parable of the Sower

4 Again Jesus began to teach by the lake. The crowd that gathered around him was so large that he got into a boat and sat in it out on the lake, while all the people were along the shore at the water's edge. ²He taught them many things by parables, and in his teaching said: ³"Listen! A farmer went out to sow his seed. ⁴As he was scattering the seed, some fell along the path, and the birds came and ate it up. ⁵Some fell on rocky places, where it did not have much soil. It sprang up quickly, because the soil was shallow. ⁶But when the sun came up, the plants were scorched, and they withered because they had no root. ⁷Other seed fell among thorns, which grew up and choked the plants, so that they did not bear grain. ⁸Still other seed fell on good soil. It came up, grew and produced a crop, multiplying thirty, sixty, or even a hundred times."

⁹Then Jesus said, "He who has ears to hear, let him hear."

¹⁰When he was alone, the Twelve and the others around him asked him about the parables. ¹¹He told them, "The secret of the kingdom of God has been given to you. But to those on the outside everything is said in parables ¹²so that,

" 'they may be ever seeing but never
        perceiving,
    and ever hearing but never
        understanding;
otherwise they might turn and be
        forgiven!'ᵃ

¹³Then Jesus said to them, "Don't you understand this parable? How then will you understand any parable? ¹⁴The farmer sows the word. ¹⁵Some people are like seed along the path, where the word is sown. As soon as they hear it, Satan comes and takes away the word that was sown in them. ¹⁶Others, like seed sown on rocky places, hear the word and at once receive it with joy. ¹⁷But since they have no root, they last only a short time. When trouble or persecution comes because of the word, they quickly fall away. ¹⁸Still others, like seed sown

ᵃ12 Isaiah 6:9,10

among thorns, hear the word; ¹⁹but the worries of this life, the deceitfulness of wealth and the desires for other things come in and choke the word, making it unfruitful. ²⁰Others, like seed sown on good soil, hear the word, accept it, and produce a crop—thirty, sixty or even a hundred times what was sown."

A Lamp on a Stand

²¹He said to them, "Do you bring in a lamp to put it under a bowl or a bed? Instead, don't you put it on its stand? ²²For whatever is hidden is meant to be disclosed, and whatever is concealed is meant to be brought out into the open. ²³If anyone has ears to hear, let him hear."

²⁴"Consider carefully what you hear," he continued. "With the measure you use, it will be measured to you—and even more. ²⁵Whoever has will be given more;

whoever does not have, even what he has will be taken from him."

The Parable of the Growing Seed

²⁶He also said, "This is what the kingdom of God is like. A man scatters seed on the ground. ²⁷Night and day, whether he sleeps or gets up, the seed sprouts and grows, though he does not know how. ²⁸All by itself the soil produces grain—first the stalk, then the head, then the full kernel in the head. ²⁹As soon as the grain is ripe, he puts the sickle to it, because the harvest has come."

The Parable of the Mustard Seed

³⁰Again he said, "What shall we say the kingdom of God is like, or what parable shall we use to describe it? ³¹It is like a mustard seed, which is the smallest seed you plant in the ground. ³²Yet when planted, it grows and becomes the largest

Wednesday

Heart Conditions

Read Mark 4:1–9

When the disciples first heard this parable, they didn't get it. What does a gardening lesson have to do with following God? It starts to make sense when you think of the different kinds of soil as different kinds of hearts. Some people's hearts aren't ready to accept Jesus. Their hearts are the bad soil. But some people's hearts *are* ready, and these hearts are the good soil.

Jesus is always ready to come into people's hearts, even the worst people in the world. All they have to do is invite him in, and they become like the good soil. A love for God and for other people grows in that good soil, and those people can become strong Christians.

I used to think my heart was bad soil because I'd sinned so many times. I asked myself, *Would Jesus really want to come live in my heart?* But I found out that I could be good soil too, if I just believed in Jesus and asked for his forgiveness. I'm a growing Christian now!

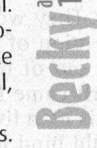

Becky age 13

❶ Even good soil isn't perfect. What are some times in your life when you've "withered" or struggled because your faith wasn't deep enough? How can you make your heart an even better place for faith to grow?

❷ Imagine that you are pulling weeds from your yard or garden. As you pull those weeds, think about some "weeds" in your own heart that need to be pulled out.

❸ Ask God to help you plant the "seeds" of his Word in other people's hearts.

Turn to page 1200 for your next devotion.

of all garden plants, with such big branches that the birds of the air can perch in its shade."

³³With many similar parables Jesus spoke the word to them, as much as they could understand. ³⁴He did not say anything to them without using a parable. But when he was alone with his own disciples, he explained everything.

Jesus Calms the Storm

³⁵That day when evening came, he said to his disciples, "Let us go over to the other side." ³⁶Leaving the crowd behind, they took him along, just as he was, in the boat. There were also other boats with him. ³⁷A furious squall came up, and the waves broke over the boat, so that it was nearly swamped. ³⁸Jesus was in the stern, sleeping on a cushion. The disciples woke him and said to him, "Teacher, don't you care if we drown?"

³⁹He got up, rebuked the wind and said to the waves, "Quiet! Be still!" Then the wind died down and it was completely calm.

⁴⁰He said to his disciples, "Why are you so afraid? Do you still have no faith?"

⁴¹They were terrified and asked each other, "Who is this? Even the wind and the waves obey him!"

The Healing of a Demon-possessed Man

5 They went across the lake to the region of the Gerasenes.ᵃ ²When Jesus got out of the boat, a man with an evilᵇ spirit came from the tombs to meet him. ³This man lived in the tombs, and no one could bind him any more, not even with a chain. ⁴For he had often been chained hand and foot, but he tore the chains apart and broke the irons on his feet. No one was strong enough to subdue him. ⁵Night and day among the tombs and in the hills he would cry out and cut himself with stones.

⁶When he saw Jesus from a distance, he ran and fell on his knees in front of him. ⁷He shouted at the top of his voice, "What do you want with me, Jesus, Son of the Most High God? Swear to God that you won't torture me!" ⁸For Jesus had said to him, "Come out of this man, you evil spirit!"

⁹Then Jesus asked him, "What is your name?"

"My name is Legion," he replied, "for we are many." ¹⁰And he begged Jesus again and again not to send them out of the area.

¹¹A large herd of pigs was feeding on the nearby hillside. ¹²The demons begged Jesus, "Send us among the pigs; allow us to go into them." ¹³He gave them permission, and the evil spirits came out and went into the pigs. The herd, about two thousand in number, rushed down the steep bank into the lake and were drowned.

¹⁴Those tending the pigs ran off and reported this in the town and countryside, and the people went out to see what had happened. ¹⁵When they came to Jesus, they saw the man who had been possessed by the legion of demons, sitting there, dressed and in his right mind; and they were afraid. ¹⁶Those who had seen it told the people what had happened to the demon-possessed man—and told about the pigs as well. ¹⁷Then the people began to plead with Jesus to leave their region.

¹⁸As Jesus was getting into the boat, the man who had been demon-possessed begged to go with him. ¹⁹Jesus did not let him, but said, "Go home to your family and tell them how much the Lord has done for you, and how he has had mercy on you." ²⁰So the man went away and began to tell in the Decapolisᶜ how much Jesus had done for him. And all the people were amazed.

A Dead Girl and a Sick Woman

²¹When Jesus had again crossed over by boat to the other side of the lake, a large crowd gathered around him while he was by the lake. ²²Then one of the synagogue rulers, named Jairus, came there. Seeing Jesus, he fell at his feet ²³and pleaded earnestly with him, "My little daughter is dying. Please come and put your hands on her so that she will be healed and live." ²⁴So Jesus went with him.

ᵃ1 Some manuscripts *Gadarenes*; other manuscripts *Gergesenes*   ᵇ2 Greek *unclean*; also in verses 8 and 13   ᶜ20 That is, the Ten Cities

A large crowd followed and pressed around him. ²⁵And a woman was there who had been subject to bleeding for twelve years. ²⁶She had suffered a great deal under the care of many doctors and had spent all she had, yet instead of getting better she grew worse. ²⁷When she heard about Jesus, she came up behind him in the crowd and touched his cloak, ²⁸because she thought, "If I just touch his clothes, I will be healed." ²⁹Immediately her bleeding stopped and she felt in her body that she was freed from her suffering.

³⁰At once Jesus realized that power had gone out from him. He turned around in the crowd and asked, "Who touched my clothes?"

³¹"You see the people crowding against you," his disciples answered, "and yet you can ask, 'Who touched me?' "

³²But Jesus kept looking around to see who had done it. ³³Then the woman, knowing what had happened to her, came and fell at his feet and, trembling with fear, told him the whole truth. ³⁴He said to her, "Daughter, your faith has healed you. Go in peace and be freed from your suffering."

³⁵While Jesus was still speaking, some men came from the house of Jairus, the synagogue ruler. "Your daughter is dead," they said. "Why bother the teacher any more?"

³⁶Ignoring what they said, Jesus told the synagogue ruler, "Don't be afraid; just believe."

³⁷He did not let anyone follow him except Peter, James and John the brother of James. ³⁸When they came to the home of the synagogue ruler, Jesus saw a commotion, with people crying and wailing loudly. ³⁹He went in and said to them, "Why all this commotion and wailing? The child is not dead but asleep." ⁴⁰But they laughed at him.

After he put them all out, he took the child's father and mother and the disciples who were with him, and went in where the child was. ⁴¹He took her by the hand and said to her, *"Talitha koum!"* (which means, "Little girl, I say to you, get up!"). ⁴²Immediately the girl stood up and walked around (she was twelve years old). At this they were completely astonished. ⁴³He gave strict orders not to let anyone know about this, and told them to give her something to eat.

A Prophet Without Honor

6 Jesus left there and went to his hometown, accompanied by his disciples. ²When the Sabbath came, he began to teach in the synagogue, and many who heard him were amazed.

"Where did this man get these things?" they asked. "What's this wisdom that has been given him, that he even does miracles! ³Isn't this the carpenter? Isn't this Mary's son and the brother of James, Joseph,ᵃ Judas and Simon? Aren't his sisters here with us?" And they took offense at him.

⁴Jesus said to them, "Only in his hometown, among his relatives and in his own house is a prophet without honor." ⁵He could not do any miracles there, except lay his hands on a few sick people and heal them. ⁶And he was amazed at their lack of faith.

Jesus Sends Out the Twelve

Then Jesus went around teaching from village to village. ⁷Calling the Twelve to him, he sent them out two by two and gave them authority over evilᵇ spirits.

⁸These were his instructions: "Take nothing for the journey except a staff— no bread, no bag, no money in your belts. ⁹Wear sandals but not an extra tunic. ¹⁰Whenever you enter a house, stay there until you leave that town. ¹¹And if any place will not welcome you or listen to you, shake the dust off your feet when you leave, as a testimony against them."

¹²They went out and preached that people should repent. ¹³They drove out many demons and anointed many sick people with oil and healed them.

John the Baptist Beheaded

¹⁴King Herod heard about this, for Jesus' name had become well known. Some were saying,ᶜ "John the Baptist has

---

ᵃ3 Greek *Joses*, a variant of *Joseph*　ᵇ7 Greek *unclean*　ᶜ14 Some early manuscripts *He was saying*

been raised from the dead, and that is why miraculous powers are at work in him."

[15]Others said, "He is Elijah."

And still others claimed, "He is a prophet, like one of the prophets of long ago."

[16]But when Herod heard this, he said, "John, the man I beheaded, has been raised from the dead!"

[17]For Herod himself had given orders to have John arrested, and he had him bound and put in prison. He did this because of Herodias, his brother Philip's wife, whom he had married. [18]For John had been saying to Herod, "It is not lawful for you to have your brother's wife." [19]So Herodias nursed a grudge against John and wanted to kill him. But she was not able to, [20]because Herod feared John and protected him, knowing him to be a righteous and holy man. When Herod heard John, he was greatly puzzled[a]; yet he liked to listen to him.

[21]Finally the opportune time came. On his birthday Herod gave a banquet for his high officials and military commanders and the leading men of Galilee. [22]When the daughter of Herodias came in and danced, she pleased Herod and his dinner guests.

The king said to the girl, "Ask me for anything you want, and I'll give it to you." [23]And he promised her with an oath, "Whatever you ask I will give you, up to half my kingdom."

[24]She went out and said to her mother, "What shall I ask for?"

"The head of John the Baptist," she answered.

[25]At once the girl hurried in to the king with the request: "I want you to give me right now the head of John the Baptist on a platter."

[26]The king was greatly distressed, but because of his oaths and his dinner guests, he did not want to refuse her. [27]So he immediately sent an executioner with orders to bring John's head. The man went, beheaded John in the prison, [28]and brought back his head on a platter. He presented it to the girl, and she gave it to her mother. [29]On hearing of this, John's disciples came and took his body and laid it in a tomb.

Jesus Feeds the Five Thousand

[30]The apostles gathered around Jesus and reported to him all they had done and taught. [31]Then, because so many people were coming and going that they did not even have a chance to eat, he said to them, "Come with me by yourselves to a quiet place and get some rest."

[32]So they went away by themselves in a boat to a solitary place. [33]But many who saw them leaving recognized them and ran on foot from all the towns and got there ahead of them. [34]When Jesus landed and saw a large crowd, he had compassion on them, because they were like sheep without a shepherd. So he began teaching them many things.

[35]By this time it was late in the day, so his disciples came to him. "This is a remote place," they said, "and it's already very late. [36]Send the people away so they can go to the surrounding countryside and villages and buy themselves something to eat."

[37]But he answered, "You give them something to eat."

They said to him, "That would take eight months of a man's wages[b]! Are we to go and spend that much on bread and give it to them to eat?"

[38]"How many loaves do you have?" he asked. "Go and see."

When they found out, they said, "Five—and two fish."

[39]Then Jesus directed them to have all the people sit down in groups on the green grass. [40]So they sat down in groups of hundreds and fifties. [41]Taking the five loaves and the two fish and looking up to heaven, he gave thanks and broke the loaves. Then he gave them to his disciples to set before the people. He also divided the two fish among them all. [42]They all ate and were satisfied, [43]and the disciples picked up twelve basketfuls of broken pieces of bread and fish. [44]The number of the men who had eaten was five thousand.

Jesus Walks on the Water

[45]Immediately Jesus made his disciples get into the boat and go on ahead of him

---

[a]20 Some early manuscripts *he did many things*
[b]37 Greek *take two hundred denarii*

to Bethsaida, while he dismissed the crowd. ⁴⁶After leaving them, he went up on a mountainside to pray.

⁴⁷When evening came, the boat was in the middle of the lake, and he was alone on land. ⁴⁸He saw the disciples straining at the oars, because the wind was against them. About the fourth watch of the night he went out to them, walking on the lake. He was about to pass by them, ⁴⁹but when they saw him walking on the lake, they thought he was a ghost. They cried out, ⁵⁰because they all saw him and were terrified.

Immediately he spoke to them and said, "Take courage! It is I. Don't be afraid." ⁵¹Then he climbed into the boat with them, and the wind died down. They were completely amazed, ⁵²for they had not understood about the loaves; their hearts were hardened.

⁵³When they had crossed over, they landed at Gennesaret and anchored there. ⁵⁴As soon as they got out of the boat, people recognized Jesus. ⁵⁵They ran throughout that whole region and carried the sick on mats to wherever they heard he was. ⁵⁶And wherever he went—into villages, towns or countryside—they placed the sick in the marketplaces. They begged him to let them touch even the edge of his cloak, and all who touched him were healed.

Clean and Unclean

7 The Pharisees and some of the teachers of the law who had come from Jerusalem gathered around Jesus and ²saw some of his disciples eating food with hands that were "unclean," that is, unwashed. ³(The Pharisees and all the Jews do not eat unless they give their hands a ceremonial washing, holding to the tradition of the elders. ⁴When they come from the marketplace they do not eat unless they wash. And they observe many other traditions, such as the washing of cups, pitchers and kettles.ᵃ)

⁵So the Pharisees and teachers of the law asked Jesus, "Why don't your disciples live according to the tradition of the elders instead of eating their food with 'unclean' hands?"

⁶He replied, "Isaiah was right when he

prophesied about you hypocrites; as it is written:

" 'These people honor me with their
          lips,
     but their hearts are far from me.
⁷They worship me in vain;
     their teachings are but rules taught
          by men.'ᵇ

ᵃ4 Some early manuscripts *pitchers, kettles and dining couches*   ᵇ6,7 Isaiah 29:13

8You have let go of the commands of God and are holding on to the traditions of men."

9And he said to them: "You have a fine way of setting aside the commands of God in order to observe*a* your own traditions! 10For Moses said, 'Honor your father and your mother,'*b* and, 'Anyone who curses his father or mother must be put to death.'*c* 11But you say that if a man says to his father or mother: 'Whatever help you might otherwise have received from me is Corban' (that is, a gift devoted to God), 12then you no longer let him do anything for his father or mother. 13Thus you nullify the word of God by your tradition that you have handed down. And you do many things like that."

14Again Jesus called the crowd to him and said, "Listen to me, everyone, and understand this. 15Nothing outside a man can make him 'unclean' by going into him. Rather, it is what comes out of a man that makes him 'unclean.'*d*"

17After he had left the crowd and entered the house, his disciples asked him about this parable. 18"Are you so dull?" he asked. "Don't you see that nothing that enters a man from the outside can make him 'unclean'? 19For it doesn't go into his heart but into his stomach, and then out of his body." (In saying this, Jesus declared all foods "clean.")

20He went on: "What comes out of a man is what makes him 'unclean.' 21For from within, out of men's hearts, come evil thoughts, sexual immorality, theft, murder, adultery, 22greed, malice, deceit, lewdness, envy, slander, arrogance and folly. 23All these evils come from inside and make a man 'unclean.'"

The Faith of a Syrophoenician Woman

24Jesus left that place and went to the vicinity of Tyre.*e* He entered a house and did not want anyone to know it; yet he could not keep his presence secret. 25In fact, as soon as she heard about him, a woman whose little daughter was possessed by an evil*f* spirit came and fell at his feet. 26The woman was a Greek, born in Syrian Phoenicia. She begged Jesus to drive the demon out of her daughter.

27"First let the children eat all they want," he told her, "for it is not right to take the children's bread and toss it to their dogs."

28"Yes, Lord," she replied, "but even the dogs under the table eat the children's crumbs."

29Then he told her, "For such a reply, you may go; the demon has left your daughter."

30She went home and found her child lying on the bed, and the demon gone.

The Healing of a Deaf and Mute Man

31Then Jesus left the vicinity of Tyre and went through Sidon, down to the Sea of Galilee and into the region of the Decapolis.*g* 32There some people brought to him a man who was deaf and could hardly talk, and they begged him to place his hand on the man.

33After he took him aside, away from the crowd, Jesus put his fingers into the man's ears. Then he spit and touched the man's tongue. 34He looked up to heaven and with a deep sigh said to him, *"Ephphatha!"* (which means, "Be opened!"). 35At this, the man's ears were opened, his tongue was loosened and he began to speak plainly.

36Jesus commanded them not to tell anyone. But the more he did so, the more they kept talking about it. 37People were overwhelmed with amazement. "He has done everything well," they said. "He even makes the deaf hear and the mute speak."

Jesus Feeds the Four Thousand

8 During those days another large crowd gathered. Since they had nothing to eat, Jesus called his disciples to him and said, 2"I have compassion for these people; they have already been with me three days and have nothing to eat. 3If I send them home hungry, they will collapse on the way, because some of them have come a long distance."

4His disciples answered, "But where in this remote place can anyone get enough bread to feed them?"

a9 Some manuscripts *set up* *b10* Exodus 20:12; Deut. 5:16 *c10* Exodus 21:17; Lev. 20:9 *d15* Some early manuscripts *'unclean.' 16If anyone has ears to hear, let him hear.* *e24* Many early manuscripts *Tyre and Sidon* *f25* Greek *unclean* *g31* That is, the Ten Cities

[5]"How many loaves do you have?" Jesus asked.

"Seven," they replied.

[6]He told the crowd to sit down on the ground. When he had taken the seven loaves and given thanks, he broke them and gave them to his disciples to set before the people, and they did so. [7]They had a few small fish as well; he gave thanks for them also and told the disciples to distribute them. [8]The people ate and were satisfied. Afterward the disciples picked up seven basketfuls of broken pieces that were left over. [9]About four thousand men were present. And having sent them away, [10]he got into the boat with his disciples and went to the region of Dalmanutha.

[11]The Pharisees came and began to question Jesus. To test him, they asked him for a sign from heaven. [12]He sighed deeply and said, "Why does this generation ask for a miraculous sign? I tell you the truth, no sign will be given to it." [13]Then he left them, got back into the boat and crossed to the other side.

The Yeast of the Pharisees and Herod

[14]The disciples had forgotten to bring bread, except for one loaf they had with them in the boat. [15]"Be careful," Jesus warned them. "Watch out for the yeast of the Pharisees and that of Herod."

[16]They discussed this with one another and said, "It is because we have no bread."

[17]Aware of their discussion, Jesus asked them: "Why are you talking about having no bread? Do you still not see or understand? Are your hearts hardened? [18]Do you have eyes but fail to see, and ears but fail to hear? And don't you remember? [19]When I broke the five loaves for the five thousand, how many basketfuls of pieces did you pick up?"

"Twelve," they replied.

[20]"And when I broke the seven loaves for the four thousand, how many basketfuls of pieces did you pick up?"

They answered, "Seven."

[21]He said to them, "Do you still not understand?"

The Healing of a Blind Man at Bethsaida

[22]They came to Bethsaida, and some people brought a blind man and begged Jesus to touch him. [23]He took the blind man by the hand and led him outside the village. When he had spit on the man's eyes and put his hands on him, Jesus asked, "Do you see anything?"

[24]He looked up and said, "I see people; they look like trees walking around."

[25]Once more Jesus put his hands on the man's eyes. Then his eyes were opened, his sight was restored, and he saw everything clearly. [26]Jesus sent him home, saying, "Don't go into the village.[a]"

Peter's Confession of Christ

[27]Jesus and his disciples went on to the villages around Caesarea Philippi. On the way he asked them, "Who do people say I am?"

[28]They replied, "Some say John the Baptist; others say Elijah; and still others, one of the prophets."

[29]"But what about you?" he asked. "Who do you say I am?"

Peter answered, "You are the Christ.[b]"

[30]Jesus warned them not to tell anyone about him.

Jesus Predicts His Death

[31]He then began to teach them that the Son of Man must suffer many things and be rejected by the elders, chief priests and teachers of the law, and that he must be killed and after three days rise again. [32]He spoke plainly about this, and Peter took him aside and began to rebuke him.

[33]But when Jesus turned and looked at his disciples, he rebuked Peter. "Get behind me, Satan!" he said. "You do not have in mind the things of God, but the things of men."

[34]Then he called the crowd to him along with his disciples and said: "If anyone would come after me, he must deny himself and take up his cross and follow me. [35]For whoever wants to save his life[c] will lose it, but whoever loses his life for me and for the gospel will save it. [36]What good is it for a man to gain the whole world, yet forfeit his soul? [37]Or what can a man give in exchange for

[a]26 Some manuscripts *Don't go and tell anyone in the village*   [b]29 Or *Messiah*. "The Christ" (Greek) and "the Messiah" (Hebrew) both mean "the Anointed One."   [c]35 The Greek word means either *life* or *soul*; also in verse 36.

his soul? ³⁸If anyone is ashamed of me and my words in this adulterous and sinful generation, the Son of Man will be ashamed of him when he comes in his Father's glory with the holy angels."

9 And he said to them, "I tell you the truth, some who are standing here will not taste death before they see the kingdom of God come with power."

The Transfiguration

²After six days Jesus took Peter, James and John with him and led them up a high mountain, where they were all alone. There he was transfigured before them. ³His clothes became dazzling white, whiter than anyone in the world could bleach them. ⁴And there appeared before them Elijah and Moses, who were talking with Jesus.

⁵Peter said to Jesus, "Rabbi, it is good for us to be here. Let us put up three shelters—one for you, one for Moses and one for Elijah." ⁶(He did not know what to say, they were so frightened.)

⁷Then a cloud appeared and enveloped them, and a voice came from the cloud: "This is my Son, whom I love. Listen to him!"

⁸Suddenly, when they looked around, they no longer saw anyone with them except Jesus.

⁹As they were coming down the mountain, Jesus gave them orders not to tell anyone what they had seen until the Son of Man had risen from the dead. ¹⁰They kept the matter to themselves, discussing what "rising from the dead" meant.

¹¹And they asked him, "Why do the teachers of the law say that Elijah must come first?"

¹²Jesus replied, "To be sure, Elijah does come first, and restores all things. Why then is it written that the Son of Man

---

Thursday

Say What?

Read Mark 8:27–29

One night at a sleepover, 2 of my non-Christian friends were asking me and another Christian friend about our religion. They were really curious—and really confused—about Jesus. I'd always figured that people basically knew who he was and what he came to earth to do. But my friends sure didn't.

It took me and my Christian friend a long time to explain that Jesus was the Son of God and he came to earth to die for our sins. I guess that's a pretty weird thing to think about for someone who doesn't have Jesus in her heart. I didn't think I did a very good job explaining it, but somehow God used that conversation. Both of my friends are Christians now.

We don't have to be great speakers to tell people about Jesus, but it doesn't hurt to be prepared. Since that sleepover, I've thought a lot about what I'd say to someone else who asked me about Jesus. I'll be more ready next time.

Amy age 14

❶ Imagine that you've never been to church or Sunday school. Why would it be hard to understand: a.) Jesus, b.) God and c.) the Bible?

❷ Write a paragraph about who Jesus is and what he came to do. Keep this sheet in your Bible so you'll have a place to turn to when someone asks you questions about what you believe. You can also turn to page 1582 and check out the Plan of Salvation.

❸ Ask God to help you know what to say when you share your faith.

Turn to page 1203 for your next devotion.

What Are YOU Doing Here?

Huh?

Mark 9:4

Elijah and Moses show up with Jesus in this passage for important reasons. Moses was a symbol of God's promise with Israel. Elijah was a symbol of the fact that God had brought Israel back home. Having them stand with Jesus on the mountain was meant to show how the story of Jesus is tied to the story of the people of Israel. Jesus is the One who fulfills the promise God made with the Jews. And Jesus is the One who completes the project of restoring God's people. This passage is a way to show that Jesus is both the reason for the story of Israel and the completion of the story, all in one.

must suffer much and be rejected? ¹³But I tell you, Elijah has come, and they have done to him everything they wished, just as it is written about him."

The Healing of a Boy With an Evil Spirit

¹⁴When they came to the other disciples, they saw a large crowd around them and the teachers of the law arguing with them. ¹⁵As soon as all the people saw Jesus, they were overwhelmed with wonder and ran to greet him.

¹⁶"What are you arguing with them about?" he asked.

¹⁷A man in the crowd answered, "Teacher, I brought you my son, who is possessed by a spirit that has robbed him of speech. ¹⁸Whenever it seizes him, it throws him to the ground. He foams at the mouth, gnashes his teeth and becomes rigid. I asked your disciples to drive out the spirit, but they could not."

¹⁹"O unbelieving generation," Jesus replied, "how long shall I stay with you? How long shall I put up with you? Bring the boy to me."

²⁰So they brought him. When the spirit saw Jesus, it immediately threw the boy into a convulsion. He fell to the ground and rolled around, foaming at the mouth.

²¹Jesus asked the boy's father, "How long has he been like this?"

"From childhood," he answered. ²²"It has often thrown him into fire or water to kill him. But if you can do anything, take pity on us and help us."

²³" 'If you can'?" said Jesus. "Everything is possible for him who believes."

²⁴Immediately the boy's father exclaimed, "I do believe; help me overcome my unbelief!"

²⁵When Jesus saw that a crowd was running to the scene, he rebuked the evil*ᵃ* spirit. "You deaf and mute spirit," he said, "I command you, come out of him and never enter him again."

²⁶The spirit shrieked, convulsed him violently and came out. The boy looked so much like a corpse that many said, "He's dead." ²⁷But Jesus took him by the hand and lifted him to his feet, and he stood up.

²⁸After Jesus had gone indoors, his disciples asked him privately, "Why couldn't we drive it out?"

²⁹He replied, "This kind can come out only by prayer.*ᵇ*

³⁰They left that place and passed through Galilee. Jesus did not want anyone to know where they were, ³¹because he was teaching his disciples. He said to them, "The Son of Man is going to be betrayed into the hands of men. They will kill him, and after three days he will rise." ³²But they did not understand what he meant and were afraid to ask him about it.

Who Is the Greatest?

³³They came to Capernaum. When he was in the house, he asked them, "What were you arguing about on the road?" ³⁴But they kept quiet because on the way they had argued about who was the greatest.

³⁵Sitting down, Jesus called the Twelve and said, "If anyone wants to be first, he must be the very last, and the servant of all."

³⁶He took a little child and had him stand among them. Taking him in his arms, he said to them, ³⁷"Whoever welcomes one of these little children in my name welcomes me; and whoever

ᵃ25 Greek *unclean*   *ᵇ29* Some manuscripts *prayer and fasting*

welcomes me does not welcome me but the one who sent me."

Whoever Is Not Against Us Is for Us

38"Teacher," said John, "we saw a man driving out demons in your name and we told him to stop, because he was not one of us."

39"Do not stop him," Jesus said. "No one who does a miracle in my name can in the next moment say anything bad about me, 40for whoever is not against us is for us. 41I tell you the truth, anyone who gives you a cup of water in my name because you belong to Christ will certainly not lose his reward.

Causing to Sin

42"And if anyone causes one of these little ones who believe in me to sin, it would be better for him to be thrown into the sea with a large millstone tied around his neck. 43If your hand causes you to sin, cut it off. It is better for you to enter life maimed than with two hands to go into hell, where the fire never goes out.a 45And if your foot causes you to sin, cut it off. It is better for you to enter life crippled than to have two feet and be thrown into hell.b 47And if your eye causes you to sin, pluck it out. It is better for you to enter the kingdom of God with one eye than to have two eyes and be thrown into hell, 48where

" 'their worm does not die,
    and the fire is not quenched.'c

49Everyone will be salted with fire. 50"Salt is good, but if it loses its saltiness, how can you make it salty again? Have salt in yourselves, and be at peace with each other."

Divorce

10 Jesus then left that place and went into the region of Judea and across the Jordan. Again crowds of people came to him, and as was his custom, he taught them.

2Some Pharisees came and tested him by asking, "Is it lawful for a man to divorce his wife?"

3"What did Moses command you?" he replied.

4They said, "Moses permitted a man to write a certificate of divorce and send her away."

5"It was because your hearts were hard that Moses wrote you this law," Jesus replied. 6"But at the beginning of creation God 'made them male and female.'d 7'For this reason a man will leave his father and mother and be united to his wife,e 8and the two will become one flesh.'f So they are no longer two, but one. 9Therefore what God has joined together, let man not separate."

10When they were in the house again, the disciples asked Jesus about this. 11He answered, "Anyone who divorces his wife and marries another woman commits adultery against her. 12And if she divorces her husband and marries another man, she commits adultery."

The Little Children and Jesus

13People were bringing little children to Jesus to have him touch them, but the disciples rebuked them. 14When Jesus saw this, he was indignant. He said to them, "Let the little children come to me, and do not hinder them, for the kingdom of God belongs to such as these. 15I tell you the truth, anyone who will not receive the kingdom of God like a little child will never enter it." 16And he took the children in his arms, put his hands on them and blessed them.

The Rich Young Man

17As Jesus started on his way, a man ran up to him and fell on his knees before him. "Good teacher," he asked, "what must I do to inherit eternal life?"

18"Why do you call me good?" Jesus answered. "No one is good—except God alone. 19You know the commandments: 'Do not murder, do not commit adultery, do not steal, do not give false testimony, do not defraud, honor your father and mother.'g"

20"Teacher," he declared, "all these I have kept since I was a boy."

---

a43 Some manuscripts out, 44where / " 'their worm does not die, / and the fire is not quenched.'
b45 Some manuscripts hell, 46where / " 'their worm does not die, / and the fire is not quenched.'
c48 Isaiah 66:24 d6 Gen. 1:27 e7 Some early manuscripts do not have and be united to his wife.
f8 Gen. 2:24 g19 Exodus 20:12-16; Deut. 5:16-20

²¹Jesus looked at him and loved him. "One thing you lack," he said. "Go, sell everything you have and give to the poor, and you will have treasure in heaven. Then come, follow me."

²²At this the man's face fell. He went away sad, because he had great wealth.

²³Jesus looked around and said to his disciples, "How hard it is for the rich to enter the kingdom of God!"

²⁴The disciples were amazed at his words. But Jesus said again, "Children, how hard it is*ᵃ* to enter the kingdom of God! ²⁵It is easier for a camel to go through the eye of a needle than for a rich man to enter the kingdom of God."

²⁶The disciples were even more amazed, and said to each other, "Who then can be saved?"

²⁷Jesus looked at them and said, "With man this is impossible, but not with God; all things are possible with God."

²⁸Peter said to him, "We have left everything to follow you!"

²⁹"I tell you the truth," Jesus replied, "no one who has left home or brothers or sisters or mother or father or children or fields for me and the gospel ³⁰will fail to receive a hundred times as much in this present age (homes, brothers, sisters, mothers, children and fields—and with them, persecutions) and in the age to come, eternal life. ³¹But many who are first will be last, and the last first."

Jesus Again Predicts His Death

³²They were on their way up to Jerusalem, with Jesus leading the way, and the disciples were astonished, while those who followed were afraid. Again he took the Twelve aside and told them what was going to happen to him. ³³"We are going up to Jerusalem," he said, "and the Son of Man will be betrayed to the chief priests and teachers of the law. They will condemn him to death and will hand him over to the Gentiles, ³⁴who will mock him

ᵃ24 Some manuscripts is for those who trust in riches

Friday

Give a Little, Get a Lot

Read Mark 10:17–22

I've never had so much money or material stuff that I got distracted from God, but I used to have 2 friends who were really bad influences on me. I finally decided that even though I liked hanging out with those guys, I needed to give them up as friends because they were dragging me down. It was definitely a tough choice to make, but it made me feel much, much better inside. It helped me focus on the person who should be most important to me: Jesus.

Sometimes following God will mean giving up things that seem important. But Jesus has promised that any time we give up something for him, we'll get a reward that's way better than whatever we gave up. In my case, I gave up bad friends to get a better relationship with Jesus. Even though it was a hard decision, I know I did the right thing.

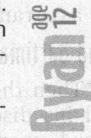
Ryan age 12

What about You?

❶ What have you had to give up to follow Jesus?

❷ Look around your room for some things you could give away, like clothes and games that are still in good condition. Give these items to your church, secondhand store or a local charity.

❸ Ask God to show you what you need to give up in your life.

Turn to page 1207 for your next devotion.

and spit on him, flog him and kill him. Three days later he will rise."

The Request of James and John

[35]Then James and John, the sons of Zebedee, came to him. "Teacher," they said, "we want you to do for us whatever we ask."

[36]"What do you want me to do for you?" he asked.

[37]They replied, "Let one of us sit at your right and the other at your left in your glory."

[38]"You don't know what you are asking," Jesus said. "Can you drink the cup I drink or be baptized with the baptism I am baptized with?"

[39]"We can," they answered.

Jesus said to them, "You will drink the cup I drink and be baptized with the baptism I am baptized with, [40]but to sit at my right or left is not for me to grant. These places belong to those for whom they have been prepared."

[41]When the ten heard about this, they became indignant with James and John. [42]Jesus called them together and said, "You know that those who are regarded as rulers of the Gentiles lord it over them, and their high officials exercise authority over them. [43]Not so with you. Instead, whoever wants to become great among you must be your servant, [44]and whoever wants to be first must be slave of all. [45]For even the Son of Man did not come to be served, but to serve, and to give his life as a ransom for many."

Blind Bartimaeus Receives His Sight

[46]Then they came to Jericho. As Jesus and his disciples, together with a large crowd, were leaving the city, a blind man, Bartimaeus (that is, the Son of Timaeus), was sitting by the roadside begging. [47]When he heard that it was Jesus of Nazareth, he began to shout, "Jesus, Son of David, have mercy on me!"

[48]Many rebuked him and told him to be quiet, but he shouted all the more, "Son of David, have mercy on me!"

[49]Jesus stopped and said, "Call him."

So they called to the blind man, "Cheer up! On your feet! He's calling you." [50]Throwing his cloak aside, he jumped to his feet and came to Jesus.

[51]"What do you want me to do for you?" Jesus asked him.

The blind man said, "Rabbi, I want to see."

[52]"Go," said Jesus, "your faith has healed you." Immediately he received his sight and followed Jesus along the road.

The Triumphal Entry

11 As they approached Jerusalem and came to Bethphage and Bethany at the Mount of Olives, Jesus sent two of his disciples, [2]saying to them, "Go to the village ahead of you, and just as you enter it, you will find a colt tied there, which no one has ever ridden. Untie it and bring it here. [3]If anyone asks you, 'Why are you doing this?' tell him, 'The Lord needs it and will send it back here shortly.' "

[4]They went and found a colt outside in the street, tied at a doorway. As they untied it, [5]some people standing there asked, "What are you doing, untying that colt?" [6]They answered as Jesus had told them to, and the people let them go. [7]When they brought the colt to Jesus and threw their cloaks over it, he sat on it. [8]Many people spread their cloaks on the road, while others spread branches they had cut in the fields. [9]Those who went ahead and those who followed shouted,

"Hosanna![a]"

"Blessed is he who comes in the name of the Lord!"[b]

[10]"Blessed is the coming kingdom of our father David!"

"Hosanna in the highest!"

[11]Jesus entered Jerusalem and went to the temple. He looked around at everything, but since it was already late, he went out to Bethany with the Twelve.

Jesus Clears the Temple

[12]The next day as they were leaving Bethany, Jesus was hungry. [13]Seeing in the distance a fig tree in leaf, he went to find out if it had any fruit. When he reached it, he found nothing but leaves,

---

[a]9 A Hebrew expression meaning "Save!" which became an exclamation of praise; also in verse 10
[b]9 Psalm 118:25,26

because it was not the season for figs. [14]Then he said to the tree, "May no one ever eat fruit from you again." And his disciples heard him say it.

[15]On reaching Jerusalem, Jesus entered the temple area and began driving out those who were buying and selling there. He overturned the tables of the money changers and the benches of those selling doves, [16]and would not allow anyone to carry merchandise through the temple courts. [17]And as he taught them, he said, "Is it not written:

" 'My house will be called
a house of prayer for all nations'[a]?

But you have made it 'a den of robbers.'[b]"

[18]The chief priests and the teachers of the law heard this and began looking for a way to kill him, for they feared him, because the whole crowd was amazed at his teaching.

[19]When evening came, they[c] went out of the city.

The Withered Fig Tree

[20]In the morning, as they went along, they saw the fig tree withered from the roots. [21]Peter remembered and said to Jesus, "Rabbi, look! The fig tree you cursed has withered!"

[22]"Have[d] faith in God," Jesus answered. [23]"I tell you the truth, if anyone says to this mountain, 'Go, throw yourself into the sea,' and does not doubt in his heart but believes that what he says

will happen, it will be done for him. [24]Therefore I tell you, whatever you ask for in prayer, believe that you have received it, and it will be yours. [25]And when you stand praying, if you hold anything against anyone, forgive him, so that your Father in heaven may forgive you your sins.[e]"

The Authority of Jesus Questioned

[27]They arrived again in Jerusalem, and while Jesus was walking in the temple courts, the chief priests, the teachers of the law and the elders came to him. [28]"By what authority are you doing these things?" they asked. "And who gave you authority to do this?"

[29]Jesus replied, "I will ask you one question. Answer me, and I will tell you by what authority I am doing these things. [30]John's baptism—was it from heaven, or from men? Tell me!"

[31]They discussed it among themselves and said, "If we say, 'From heaven,' he will ask, 'Then why didn't you believe him?' [32]But if we say, 'From men'. . ." (They feared the people, for everyone held that John really was a prophet.)

[33]So they answered Jesus, "We don't know."

Jesus said, "Neither will I tell you by what authority I am doing these things."

The Parable of the Tenants

12 He then began to speak to them in parables: "A man planted a vineyard. He put a wall around it, dug a pit for the winepress and built a watchtower. Then he rented the vineyard to some farmers and went away on a journey. [2]At harvest time he sent a servant to the tenants to collect from them some of the fruit of the vineyard. [3]But they seized him, beat him and sent him away empty-handed. [4]Then he sent another servant to them; they struck this man on the head and treated him shamefully. [5]He sent still another, and that one they killed. He sent many others; some of them they beat, others they killed.

---

[a]17 Isaiah 56:7   [b]17 Jer. 7:11   [c]19 Some early manuscripts *he*   [d]22 Some early manuscripts *If you have*   [e]25 Some manuscripts *sins.* [26]*But if you do not forgive, neither will your Father who is in heaven forgive your sins.*

⁶"He had one left to send, a son, whom he loved. He sent him last of all, saying, 'They will respect my son.'

⁷"But the tenants said to one another, 'This is the heir. Come, let's kill him, and the inheritance will be ours.' ⁸So they took him and killed him, and threw him out of the vineyard.

⁹"What then will the owner of the vineyard do? He will come and kill those tenants and give the vineyard to others. ¹⁰Haven't you read this scripture:

" 'The stone the builders rejected
    has become the capstone*a*;
¹¹the Lord has done this,
    and it is marvelous in our eyes'*b*?"

¹²Then they looked for a way to arrest him because they knew he had spoken the parable against them. But they were afraid of the crowd; so they left him and went away.

Paying Taxes to Caesar

¹³Later they sent some of the Pharisees and Herodians to Jesus to catch him in his words. ¹⁴They came to him and said, "Teacher, we know you are a man of integrity. You aren't swayed by men, because you pay no attention to who they are; but you teach the way of God in accordance with the truth. Is it right to pay taxes to Caesar or not? ¹⁵Should we pay or shouldn't we?"

But Jesus knew their hypocrisy. "Why are you trying to trap me?" he asked. "Bring me a denarius and let me look at it." ¹⁶They brought the coin, and he asked them, "Whose portrait is this? And whose inscription?"

"Caesar's," they replied.

¹⁷Then Jesus said to them, "Give to Caesar what is Caesar's and to God what is God's."

And they were amazed at him.

Marriage at the Resurrection

¹⁸Then the Sadducees, who say there is no resurrection, came to him with a question. ¹⁹"Teacher," they said, "Moses wrote for us that if a man's brother dies and leaves a wife but no children, the man must marry the widow and have children for his brother. ²⁰Now there

Oh No, Not the Salad Guy

Mark 12:17
Caesar (SEE-zer) was a guy from Rome with a big job. He was the politician in charge, kind of like the president. He had a huge influence over everything that happened in the land of Israel, because Rome controlled Israel.

were seven brothers. The first one married and died without leaving any children. ²¹The second one married the widow, but he also died, leaving no child. It was the same with the third. ²²In fact, none of the seven left any children. Last of all, the woman died too. ²³At the resurrection*c* whose wife will she be, since the seven were married to her?"

²⁴Jesus replied, "Are you not in error because you do not know the Scriptures or the power of God? ²⁵When the dead rise, they will neither marry nor be given in marriage; they will be like the angels in heaven. ²⁶Now about the dead rising—have you not read in the book of Moses, in the account of the bush, how God said to him, 'I am the God of Abraham, the God of Isaac, and the God of Jacob'*d*? ²⁷He is not the God of the dead, but of the living. You are badly mistaken!"

The Greatest Commandment

²⁸One of the teachers of the law came and heard them debating. Noticing that Jesus had given them a good answer, he asked him, "Of all the commandments, which is the most important?"

²⁹"The most important one," answered Jesus, "is this: 'Hear, O Israel, the Lord our God, the Lord is one.*e* ³⁰Love the Lord your God with all your heart and with all your soul and with all your mind and with all your strength.'*f* ³¹The second is

---

*a*10 Or *cornerstone*   *b*11 Psalm 118:22,23
*c*23 Some manuscripts *resurrection, when men rise from the dead,*   *d*26 Exodus 3:6   *e*29 Or *the Lord our God is one Lord*   *f*30 Deut. 6:4,5

this: 'Love your neighbor as yourself.'[a] There is no commandment greater than these."

[32]"Well said, teacher," the man replied. "You are right in saying that God is one and there is no other but him. [33]To love him with all your heart, with all your understanding and with all your strength, and to love your neighbor as yourself is more important than all burnt offerings and sacrifices."

[34]When Jesus saw that he had answered wisely, he said to him, "You are not far from the kingdom of God." And from then on no one dared ask him any more questions.

Whose Son Is the Christ?

[35]While Jesus was teaching in the temple courts, he asked, "How is it that the teachers of the law say that the Christ[b] is the son of David? [36]David himself, speaking by the Holy Spirit, declared:

" 'The Lord said to my Lord:
　"Sit at my right hand
until I put your enemies
　　under your feet." '[c]

[37]David himself calls him 'Lord.' How then can he be his son?"

[a]31 Lev. 19:18　　[b]35 Or *Messiah*　　[c]36 Psalm 110:1

Week end.

Dare to Ask
Read Luke 2:52 (page 1221)

In Thursday's devotion, Amy mentions how she tried to answer some questions her friends were asking her about Jesus. Do you ever have questions too? Do you ever wonder if this Christian stuff is worth it? Do you wonder if it's real?

It's OK to ask those questions. In fact (ready for this?), it's really good to ask those questions! This time of your life (junior high, middle school, young teen—whatever you want to call it) is all about change. Your body will change more during these years than at any other time other than when you were a little tiny baby. And that's not all: Your emotions are changing (have you noticed?); your brain is changing (you can think in new and different ways); and your faith is changing. Or, at least, your faith *should* be changing. Most Christian kids wander into their teen years with a faith (belief in God and God-stuff) that's pretty close to what their parents believe. But now you're beginning to form your own beliefs about everything, God included.

So go on, ask those tough questions. Ask your parents. Ask your youth leader. Ask your pastor. And definitely ask God. He, and his people, will help you understand and develop your own personal faith. That's a good thing!

❶ What are some of your biggest questions about God, the Bible and Christianity?

❷ Choose one question (you can choose more later) and talk about it with your parents, your youth leader or some other Christian adult.

❸ Ask God your question. Pray that he'll give you wisdom and understanding.

Turn to page 1209 for your next devotion.

The large crowd listened to him with delight.

[38] As he taught, Jesus said, "Watch out for the teachers of the law. They like to walk around in flowing robes and be greeted in the marketplaces, [39] and have the most important seats in the synagogues and the places of honor at banquets. [40] They devour widows' houses and for a show make lengthy prayers. Such men will be punished most severely."

The Widow's Offering

[41] Jesus sat down opposite the place where the offerings were put and watched the crowd putting their money into the temple treasury. Many rich people threw in large amounts. [42] But a poor widow came and put in two very small copper coins,[a] worth only a fraction of a penny.[b]

[43] Calling his disciples to him, Jesus said, "I tell you the truth, this poor widow has put more into the treasury than all the others. [44] They all gave out of their wealth; but she, out of her poverty, put in everything—all she had to live on."

Signs of the End of the Age

13 As he was leaving the temple, one of his disciples said to him, "Look, Teacher! What massive stones! What magnificent buildings!"

[2] "Do you see all these great buildings?" replied Jesus. "Not one stone here will be left on another; every one will be thrown down."

[3] As Jesus was sitting on the Mount of Olives opposite the temple, Peter, James, John and Andrew asked him privately, [4] "Tell us, when will these things happen? And what will be the sign that they are all about to be fulfilled?"

[5] Jesus said to them: "Watch out that no one deceives you. [6] Many will come in my name, claiming, 'I am he,' and will deceive many. [7] When you hear of wars and rumors of wars, do not be alarmed. Such things must happen, but the end is still to come. [8] Nation will rise against nation, and kingdom against kingdom. There will be earthquakes in various places, and famines. These are the beginning of birth pains.

[9] "You must be on your guard. You will be handed over to the local councils and flogged in the synagogues. On account of me you will stand before governors and kings as witnesses to them. [10] And the gospel must first be preached to all nations. [11] Whenever you are arrested and brought to trial, do not worry beforehand about what to say. Just say whatever is given you at the time, for it is not you speaking, but the Holy Spirit.

[12] "Brother will betray brother to death, and a father his child. Children will rebel against their parents and have them put to death. [13] All men will hate you because of me, but he who stands firm to the end will be saved.

[14] "When you see 'the abomination that causes desolation'[c] standing where it[d] does not belong—let the reader understand—then let those who are in Judea flee to the mountains. [15] Let no one on the roof of his house go down or enter the house to take anything out. [16] Let no one in the field go back to get his cloak. [17] How dreadful it will be in those days for pregnant women and nursing mothers! [18] Pray that this will not take place in winter, [19] because those will be days of distress unequaled from the beginning, when God created the world, until now—and never to be equaled again. [20] If the Lord had not cut short those days, no one would survive. But for the sake of the elect, whom he has chosen, he has shortened them. [21] At that time if anyone says to you, 'Look, here is the Christ[e]!' or, 'Look, there he is!' do not believe it. [22] For false Christs and false prophets will appear and perform signs and miracles to deceive the elect—if that were possible. [23] So be on your guard; I have told you everything ahead of time.

[24] "But in those days, following that distress,

" 'the sun will be darkened,
    and the moon will not give its light;
[25] the stars will fall from the sky,
    and the heavenly bodies will be
        shaken.'[f]

[26] "At that time men will see the Son of Man coming in clouds with great power

---

[a]42 Greek *two lepta*   [b]42 Greek *kodrantes*
[c]14 Daniel 9:27; 11:31; 12:11   [d]14 Or *he*; also in
verse 29   [e]21 Or *Messiah*   [f]25 Isaiah 13:10; 34:4

and glory. ²⁷And he will send his angels and gather his elect from the four winds, from the ends of the earth to the ends of the heavens.

²⁸"Now learn this lesson from the fig tree: As soon as its twigs get tender and its leaves come out, you know that summer is near. ²⁹Even so, when you see these things happening, you know that it is near, right at the door. ³⁰I tell you the truth, this generation*ᵃ* will certainly not pass away until all these things have happened. ³¹Heaven and earth will pass away, but my words will never pass away.

The Day and Hour Unknown

³²"No one knows about that day or hour, not even the angels in heaven, nor the Son, but only the Father. ³³Be on guard! Be alert*ᵇ*! You do not know when that time will come. ³⁴It's like a man going away: He leaves his house and puts his servants in charge, each with his as-

signed task, and tells the one at the door to keep watch.

³⁵"Therefore keep watch because you do not know when the owner of the house will come back—whether in the evening, or at midnight, or when the rooster crows, or at dawn. ³⁶If he comes suddenly, do not let him find you sleeping. ³⁷What I say to you, I say to everyone: 'Watch!' "

Jesus Anointed at Bethany

14 Now the Passover and the Feast of Unleavened Bread were only two days away, and the chief priests and the teachers of the law were looking for some sly way to arrest Jesus and kill him. ²"But not during the Feast," they said, "or the people may riot."

³While he was in Bethany, reclining at the table in the home of a man known as

---

ᵃ30 Or *race*   *ᵇ33* Some manuscripts *alert and pray*

Monday

Following God

Read Mark 13:32–37

I think today's verses would be scary to non-Christians, because the passage warns us to be ready when Jesus comes back to earth. If you don't believe in Jesus, you're sure not ready! And the thing is, we don't know when he's coming back. Some of my friends live like he's never going to return. They do whatever they want and not what God wants. I'd say they're spiritually asleep.

Well, I'm trying to wake them up! But when I tell them that they're living in a way that displeases God, they usually say that it's OK for now—they'll become Christians later, after they've lived it up for a while. Today's passage reminds me of why that excuse isn't good enough: We don't know how much time we've been given on this earth, so we've got to make each day count. And if we're doing that, we can look forward to Jesus' return with joy, not fear.

Jonathan age 13

What about You?

❶ If you knew that Jesus was going to return next week, what things would you change about your life?

❷ Imagine that you're waiting for a very important phone call. You can hardly wait to answer the phone . . . but when is it going to ring? How is this anticipation kind of like waiting for Jesus to return?

❸ Ask God to help you live for him from now on.

Turn to page 1213 for your next devotion.

Simon the Leper, a woman came with an alabaster jar of very expensive perfume, made of pure nard. She broke the jar and poured the perfume on his head.

⁴Some of those present were saying indignantly to one another, "Why this waste of perfume? ⁵It could have been sold for more than a year's wages[a] and the money given to the poor." And they rebuked her harshly.

⁶"Leave her alone," said Jesus. "Why are you bothering her? She has done a beautiful thing to me. ⁷The poor you will always have with you, and you can help them any time you want. But you will not always have me. ⁸She did what she could. She poured perfume on my body beforehand to prepare for my burial. ⁹I tell you the truth, wherever the gospel is preached throughout the world, what she has done will also be told, in memory of her."

¹⁰Then Judas Iscariot, one of the Twelve, went to the chief priests to betray Jesus to them. ¹¹They were delighted to hear this and promised to give him money. So he watched for an opportunity to hand him over.

The Lord's Supper

¹²On the first day of the Feast of Unleavened Bread, when it was customary to sacrifice the Passover lamb, Jesus' disciples asked him, "Where do you want us to go and make preparations for you to eat the Passover?"

¹³So he sent two of his disciples, telling them, "Go into the city, and a man carrying a jar of water will meet you. Follow him. ¹⁴Say to the owner of the house he enters, 'The Teacher asks: Where is my guest room, where I may eat the Passover with my disciples?' ¹⁵He will show you a large upper room, furnished and ready. Make preparations for us there."

¹⁶The disciples left, went into the city and found things just as Jesus had told them. So they prepared the Passover.

¹⁷When evening came, Jesus arrived with the Twelve. ¹⁸While they were reclining at the table eating, he said, "I tell you the truth, one of you will betray me—one who is eating with me."

¹⁹They were saddened, and one by one they said to him, "Surely not I?"

White or Whole Wheat?

Mark 14:12–16

The Feast of Unleavened Bread was a Jewish celebration that lasted for 7 days after the Passover meal. Jews eat the Passover meal in remembrance of when the angel of death "passed over" their homes in Egypt, not killing their firstborn sons (read about it in Exodus 12, page 83). For these big feasts and celebrations, lots of people would come to Jerusalem. The Last Supper (the first communion) took place on the first day of the Feast of Unleavened Bread.

²⁰"It is one of the Twelve," he replied, "one who dips bread into the bowl with me. ²¹The Son of Man will go just as it is written about him. But woe to that man who betrays the Son of Man! It would be better for him if he had not been born."

²²While they were eating, Jesus took bread, gave thanks and broke it, and gave it to his disciples, saying, "Take it; this is my body."

²³Then he took the cup, gave thanks and offered it to them, and they all drank from it.

²⁴"This is my blood of the[b] covenant, which is poured out for many," he said to them. ²⁵"I tell you the truth, I will not drink again of the fruit of the vine until that day when I drink it anew in the kingdom of God."

²⁶When they had sung a hymn, they went out to the Mount of Olives.

Jesus Predicts Peter's Denial

²⁷"You will all fall away," Jesus told them, "for it is written:

" 'I will strike the shepherd,
    and the sheep will be scattered.'[c]

²⁸But after I have risen, I will go ahead of you into Galilee."

²⁹Peter declared, "Even if all fall away, I will not."

³⁰"I tell you the truth," Jesus answered,

---

[a]5 Greek *than three hundred denarii*   [b]24 Some manuscripts *the new*   [c]27 Zech. 13:7

"today—yes, tonight—before the rooster crows twice[a] you yourself will disown me three times."

³¹But Peter insisted emphatically, "Even if I have to die with you, I will never disown you." And all the others said the same.

Gethsemane

³²They went to a place called Gethsemane, and Jesus said to his disciples, "Sit here while I pray." ³³He took Peter, James and John along with him, and he began to be deeply distressed and troubled. ³⁴"My soul is overwhelmed with sorrow to the point of death," he said to them. "Stay here and keep watch."

³⁵Going a little farther, he fell to the ground and prayed that if possible the hour might pass from him. ³⁶"Abba,[b] Father," he said, "everything is possible for you. Take this cup from me. Yet not what I will, but what you will."

³⁷Then he returned to his disciples and found them sleeping. "Simon," he said to Peter, "are you asleep? Could you not keep watch for one hour? ³⁸Watch and pray so that you will not fall into temptation. The spirit is willing, but the body is weak."

³⁹Once more he went away and prayed the same thing. ⁴⁰When he came back, he again found them sleeping, because their eyes were heavy. They did not know what to say to him.

⁴¹Returning the third time, he said to them, "Are you still sleeping and resting? Enough! The hour has come. Look, the Son of Man is betrayed into the hands of sinners. ⁴²Rise! Let us go! Here comes my betrayer!"

Jesus Arrested

⁴³Just as he was speaking, Judas, one of the Twelve, appeared. With him was a crowd armed with swords and clubs, sent from the chief priests, the teachers of the law, and the elders.

⁴⁴Now the betrayer had arranged a signal with them: "The one I kiss is the man; arrest him and lead him away under guard." ⁴⁵Going at once to Jesus, Judas said, "Rabbi!" and kissed him. ⁴⁶The men seized Jesus and arrested him. ⁴⁷Then one of those standing near drew his sword

and struck the servant of the high priest, cutting off his ear.

⁴⁸"Am I leading a rebellion," said Jesus, "that you have come out with swords and clubs to capture me? ⁴⁹Every day I was with you, teaching in the temple courts, and you did not arrest me. But the Scriptures must be fulfilled." ⁵⁰Then everyone deserted him and fled.

⁵¹A young man, wearing nothing but a linen garment, was following Jesus. When they seized him, ⁵²he fled naked, leaving his garment behind.

Before the Sanhedrin

⁵³They took Jesus to the high priest, and all the chief priests, elders and teachers of the law came together. ⁵⁴Peter followed him at a distance, right into the courtyard of the high priest. There he sat with the guards and warmed himself at the fire.

⁵⁵The chief priests and the whole Sanhedrin were looking for evidence against Jesus so that they could put him to death, but they did not find any. ⁵⁶Many testified falsely against him, but their statements did not agree.

⁵⁷Then some stood up and gave this false testimony against him: ⁵⁸"We heard him say, 'I will destroy this man-made temple and in three days will build another, not made by man.'" ⁵⁹Yet even then their testimony did not agree.

⁶⁰Then the high priest stood up before them and asked Jesus, "Are you not going to answer? What is this testimony that these men are bringing against you?" ⁶¹But Jesus remained silent and gave no answer.

Again the high priest asked him, "Are you the Christ,[c] the Son of the Blessed One?"

⁶²"I am," said Jesus. "And you will see the Son of Man sitting at the right hand of the Mighty One and coming on the clouds of heaven."

⁶³The high priest tore his clothes. "Why do we need any more witnesses?" he asked. ⁶⁴"You have heard the blasphemy. What do you think?"

They all condemned him as worthy of

---

[a]30 Some early manuscripts do not have *twice*.
[b]36 Aramaic for *Father*   [c]61 Or *Messiah*

death. ⁶⁵Then some began to spit at him; they blindfolded him, struck him with their fists, and said, "Prophesy!" And the guards took him and beat him.

Peter Disowns Jesus

⁶⁶While Peter was below in the courtyard, one of the servant girls of the high priest came by. ⁶⁷When she saw Peter warming himself, she looked closely at him.

"You also were with that Nazarene, Jesus," she said.

⁶⁸But he denied it. "I don't know or understand what you're talking about," he said, and went out into the entryway.ᵃ

⁶⁹When the servant girl saw him there, she said again to those standing around, "This fellow is one of them." ⁷⁰Again he denied it.

After a little while, those standing near said to Peter, "Surely you are one of them, for you are a Galilean."

⁷¹He began to call down curses on himself, and he swore to them, "I don't know this man you're talking about."

⁷²Immediately the rooster crowed the second time.ᵇ Then Peter remembered the word Jesus had spoken to him: "Before the rooster crows twiceᶜ you will disown me three times." And he broke down and wept.

Jesus Before Pilate

15 Very early in the morning, the chief priests, with the elders, the teachers of the law and the whole Sanhedrin, reached a decision. They bound Jesus, led him away and handed him over to Pilate.

²"Are you the king of the Jews?" asked Pilate.

"Yes, it is as you say," Jesus replied.

³The chief priests accused him of many things. ⁴So again Pilate asked him, "Aren't you going to answer? See how many things they are accusing you of."

⁵But Jesus still made no reply, and Pilate was amazed.

⁶Now it was the custom at the Feast to release a prisoner whom the people requested. ⁷A man called Barabbas was in prison with the insurrectionists who had committed murder in the uprising. ⁸The

crowd came up and asked Pilate to do for them what he usually did.

⁹"Do you want me to release to you the king of the Jews?" asked Pilate, ¹⁰knowing it was out of envy that the chief priests had handed Jesus over to him. ¹¹But the chief priests stirred up the crowd to have Pilate release Barabbas instead.

¹²"What shall I do, then, with the one you call the king of the Jews?" Pilate asked them.

¹³"Crucify him!" they shouted.

¹⁴"Why? What crime has he committed?" asked Pilate.

But they shouted all the louder, "Crucify him!"

¹⁵Wanting to satisfy the crowd, Pilate released Barabbas to them. He had Jesus flogged, and handed him over to be crucified.

The Soldiers Mock Jesus

¹⁶The soldiers led Jesus away into the palace (that is, the Praetorium) and called together the whole company of soldiers. ¹⁷They put a purple robe on him, then twisted together a crown of thorns and set it on him. ¹⁸And they began to call out to him, "Hail, king of the Jews!" ¹⁹Again and again they struck him on the head with a staff and spit on him. Falling on their knees, they paid homage to him. ²⁰And when they had mocked him, they took off the purple robe and put his own clothes on him. Then they led him out to crucify him.

The Crucifixion

²¹A certain man from Cyrene, Simon, the father of Alexander and Rufus, was passing by on his way in from the country, and they forced him to carry the cross. ²²They brought Jesus to the place called Golgotha (which means The Place of the Skull). ²³Then they offered him wine mixed with myrrh, but he did not take it. ²⁴And they crucified him. Dividing up his clothes, they cast lots to see what each would get.

²⁵It was the third hour when they cru-

ᵃ68 Some early manuscripts *entryway and the rooster crowed* ᵇ72 Some early manuscripts do not have *the second time.* ᶜ72 Some early manuscripts do not have *twice.*

cified him. [26]The written notice of the charge against him read: THE KING OF THE JEWS. [27]They crucified two robbers with him, one on his right and one on his left.[a] [29]Those who passed by hurled insults at him, shaking their heads and saying, "So! You who are going to destroy the temple and build it in three days, [30]come down from the cross and save yourself!"

[31]In the same way the chief priests and the teachers of the law mocked him among themselves. "He saved others," they said, "but he can't save himself! [32]Let this Christ,[b] this King of Israel, come down now from the cross, that we may see and believe." Those crucified with him also heaped insults on him.

The Death of Jesus

[33]At the sixth hour darkness came over the whole land until the ninth hour. [34]And at the ninth hour Jesus cried out in a loud voice, *"Eloi, Eloi, lama sabach-*

thani?"—which means, "My God, my God, why have you forsaken me?"[c]

[35]When some of those standing near heard this, they said, "Listen, he's calling Elijah."

[36]One man ran, filled a sponge with wine vinegar, put it on a stick, and offered it to Jesus to drink. "Now leave him alone. Let's see if Elijah comes to take him down," he said.

[37]With a loud cry, Jesus breathed his last.

[38]The curtain of the temple was torn in two from top to bottom. [39]And when the centurion, who stood there in front of Jesus, heard his cry and[d] saw how he died, he said, "Surely this man was the Son[e] of God!"

[40]Some women were watching from a

[a]27 Some manuscripts left, [28]and the scripture was fulfilled which says, "He was counted with the lawless ones" (Isaiah 53:12)   [b]32 Or Messiah   [c]34 Psalm 22:1   [d]39 Some manuscripts do not have heard his cry and   [e]39 Or a son

Tuesday

Been There, Done That

Read Mark 15:16–20

When I was younger, I got teased a lot. People called me names and made fun of me. Even though I'm older now, it still hurts to think about being teased by my classmates.

Now I know I can turn to Jesus when other people make fun of me or give me a hard time, because Jesus was teased too. He didn't do anything wrong, but people laughed at him, spit on him, hit him and mocked him. So when people are mean to me, Jesus knows how I feel. I know he cries with me and feels the same pain I feel. I know he cares about me and loves me.

Jesus was teased and mocked. He was put to death like a criminal so we could be saved. God's Son experienced pain because he loves us. And Jesus is ready to listen to us when we hurt. I think that's amazing.

Gabe, age 13

What about You?

❶ Think about a time you were teased. How did you feel? Now think about a time you teased someone else. How do you think your words affected that person?

❷ The next time you're really hurting, put a chair next to your bed and imagine Jesus sitting in that chair listening to you. Tell him how you feel.

❸ Tell God about times when other people's words have hurt you. Ask him to comfort you and help you forgive those people.

Turn to page 1217 for your next devotion.

distance. Among them were Mary Magdalene, Mary the mother of James the younger and of Joses, and Salome. ⁴¹In Galilee these women had followed him and cared for his needs. Many other women who had come up with him to Jerusalem were also there.

The Burial of Jesus

⁴²It was Preparation Day (that is, the day before the Sabbath). So as evening approached, ⁴³Joseph of Arimathea, a prominent member of the Council, who was himself waiting for the kingdom of God, went boldly to Pilate and asked for Jesus' body. ⁴⁴Pilate was surprised to hear that he was already dead. Summoning the centurion, he asked him if Jesus had already died. ⁴⁵When he learned from the centurion that it was so, he gave the body to Joseph. ⁴⁶So Joseph bought some linen cloth, took down the body, wrapped it in the linen, and placed it in a tomb cut out of rock. Then he rolled a stone against the entrance of the tomb. ⁴⁷Mary Magdalene and Mary the mother of Joses saw where he was laid.

The Resurrection

16 When the Sabbath was over, Mary Magdalene, Mary the mother of James, and Salome bought spices so that they might go to anoint Jesus' body. ²Very early on the first day of the week, just after sunrise, they were on their way to the tomb ³and they asked each other, "Who will roll the stone away from the entrance of the tomb?"

⁴But when they looked up, they saw that the stone, which was very large, had been rolled away. ⁵As they entered the tomb, they saw a young man dressed in a white robe sitting on the right side, and they were alarmed.

⁶"Don't be alarmed," he said. "You are looking for Jesus the Nazarene, who was crucified. He has risen! He is not here. See the place where they laid him. ⁷But go, tell his disciples and Peter, 'He is going ahead of you into Galilee. There you will see him, just as he told you.' "

⁸Trembling and bewildered, the women went out and fled from the tomb. They said nothing to anyone, because they were afraid.

[The earliest manuscripts and some other ancient witnesses do not have Mark 16:9-20.]

⁹When Jesus rose early on the first day of the week, he appeared first to Mary Magdalene, out of whom he had driven seven demons. ¹⁰She went and told those who had been with him and who were mourning and weeping. ¹¹When they heard that Jesus was alive and that she had seen him, they did not believe it.

¹²Afterward Jesus appeared in a different form to two of them while they were walking in the country. ¹³These returned and reported it to the rest; but they did not believe them either.

¹⁴Later Jesus appeared to the Eleven as they were eating; he rebuked them for their lack of faith and their stubborn refusal to believe those who had seen him after he had risen.

¹⁵He said to them, "Go into all the world and preach the good news to all creation. ¹⁶Whoever believes and is baptized will be saved, but whoever does not believe will be condemned. ¹⁷And these signs will accompany those who believe: In my name they will drive out demons; they will speak in new tongues; ¹⁸they will pick up snakes with their hands; and when they drink deadly poison, it will not hurt them at all; they will place their hands on sick people, and they will get well."

¹⁹After the Lord Jesus had spoken to them, he was taken up into heaven and he sat at the right hand of God. ²⁰Then the disciples went out and preached everywhere, and the Lord worked with them and confirmed his word by the signs that accompanied it.

Luke

START

Dr. Luke, physician and historian, writes this "Good News" about Jesus, the Great Physician. No doubt Luke found his heart beating in sync with Christ's. Both love health and wholeness. Both ooze compassion. Both care about the hurting and helpless.

So Luke emphasizes the humanness of Jesus. While being fully God, Jesus still had a body that required food, needed rest and felt pain. Luke shines his light on this side of Jesus' life, reminding us that Jesus knows what it means to be human. He also shows the Lord's care for people who are hurting, from shunned leprosy sufferers to unpopular tax collectors.

Women also play a big role in this story. Though most people of that time regarded them as second-class citizens, Jesus treats them with dignity and respect. In fact, he even counts on them to help support his work financially. That was way ahead of the times!

Some call the Gospel of Luke the most beautiful book ever written. But it's not a flowery poem; it's the warm, human story of a God who cares enough to touch us and heal us. We constantly see Jesus teaching truths and working miracles, right where people live—often right in their own homes. This Great Physician makes house calls!

Cast OF Characters

Luke
Yup, he wrote it. He wasn't one of the 12 disciples, but he hung out with some of them.

Theophilus (thee-AH-fill-us)
Luke addresses the story to this guy, but make no mistake about it: It's for you and me too.

Jesus
He's the Great Physician. The world is his ER.

Mary
We learn more about Jesus' mom in this Gospel than in any other.

The Prodigal Son
Famous pig-feeder comes clean in Luke 15.

The Disciples (diss-SY-pulls)
They're the interns who followed the Head Doc and learned how to help people who were hurting.

Zacchaeus (za-KEE-us)
Little tree-climbing crook finds new life in Luke 19.

The Good Samaritan
Hated foreigner from the "wrong side of the tracks" becomes model of kindness in Luke 10.

What's UP with That?

Dr. Luke shows that Jesus has the cure for whatever needs fixing in your life. As you read, find out who would have come to Jesus complaining of the following symptoms. Then see what he did to help.

1. "Jesus, I'm on fire! Check it and see. I got a fever of 103, minimum." (Luke 4:38 and following)

2. "Lord, my foot fell asleep and it won't wake up! Please, can you help me?" (Luke 5:12–13)

3. "I lay around on this thing all day. My friends call me Matt. But if you fix me I'll change my name to Walker." (Luke 5:17–26)

4. "Yeah, I know my hand looks funny. I've been teased about it all my life. Can you do something about it?" (Luke 6:6–10)

5. "Doc, it feels like the Devil's buzzing in my brain. It's making me crazy." (Luke 8:26–39)

6. "Um, excuse me, I, um, don't mean to bother you, Sir. I'll just, um, touch your coat for just a sec." (Luke 8:42–48)

7. "Doctor, please . . . My little girl's not doin' too good. She's lookin' a little blue in the face." (Luke 8:40–56)

8. "The whole busload of us is starving and there's not one full lunch box among us. We've got the tummy-grumblies bad!" (Luke 9:10–17)

9. "Hey, who do I look like, Vinny Van Gogh? It's like I just lost half my hearing." (Luke 22:47–51)

Snap Shots

- It's a boy!—Jesus breaks onto the scene (chapters 1:1—4:13)

- Let's get to work!—Jesus begins his ministry in Galilee (chapters 4:14—9:50)

- Road trip!—Jesus heads south to Jerusalem (chapters 9:51—19:27)

- The end is near!—Jesus has one week to live (chapters 19:28—23:56)

- He's baa-aack!—Jesus rises from the dead (chapter 24:1–53)

Answers: 1-Simon Peter's mom, 2-Man with leprosy, 3-Paralyzed man, 4-Man with a withered hand, 5-The Gerasene demon-possessed man, 6-The bleeding woman, 7-Jairus, 8-Crowd of 5,000, 9-The high priest's servant

Introduction

1 Many have undertaken to draw up an account of the things that have been fulfilled*a* among us, ²just as they were handed down to us by those who from the first were eyewitnesses and servants of the word. ³Therefore, since I myself have carefully investigated everything from the beginning, it seemed good also to me to write an orderly account for you, most excellent Theophilus, ⁴so that you may know the certainty of the things you have been taught.

The Birth of John the Baptist Foretold

⁵In the time of Herod king of Judea there was a priest named Zechariah, who belonged to the priestly division of Abijah; his wife Elizabeth was also a descendant of Aaron. ⁶Both of them were upright in the sight of God, observing all the Lord's commandments and regulations blamelessly. ⁷But they had no chil-

dren, because Elizabeth was barren; and they were both well along in years.

⁸Once when Zechariah's division was on duty and he was serving as priest before God, ⁹he was chosen by lot, according to the custom of the priesthood, to go into the temple of the Lord and burn incense. ¹⁰And when the time for the burning of incense came, all the assembled worshipers were praying outside.

¹¹Then an angel of the Lord appeared to him, standing at the right side of the altar of incense. ¹²When Zechariah saw him, he was startled and was gripped with fear. ¹³But the angel said to him: "Do not be afraid, Zechariah; your prayer has been heard. Your wife Elizabeth will bear you a son, and you are to give him the name John. ¹⁴He will be a joy and delight to you, and many will rejoice because of his birth, ¹⁵for he will be great in

---

*a*1 Or *been surely believed*

Wednesday

Just Say Yes

Read Luke 1:26–38

Can you imagine being Mary? She was just a young girl, probably not much older than I am, when an angel showed up to tell her she was going to have a baby. That would be a big deal for anybody, but especially for a young girl who was still a virgin. But Mary didn't say, "Forget it. I'm way too young. Pick someone else." She humbly told the angel she would do whatever God wanted her to do.

God will probably never ask me to do something as important as the job he gave Mary, but God still wants me to be willing to serve him. For instance, I love drawing. Even though I think God has been telling me for a long time to use my skills to glorify him, I've resisted. But after reading about Mary's willingness to serve God, I know I need to be more willing to serve him any way I can.

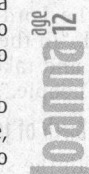
Joanna age 12

What about You?

❶ How can you be more open to letting God use your gifts to share his love with others?

❷ Being an unwed, pregnant teenager couldn't have been easy for Mary. Write down some ways you think Mary's life changed after saying yes to God. Now write down some ways *your* life might change if you really let God use you.

❸ Ask God to help you find ways to serve him.

Turn to page 1222 for your next devotion.

the sight of the Lord. He is never to take wine or other fermented drink, and he will be filled with the Holy Spirit even from birth.[a] [16]Many of the people of Israel will he bring back to the Lord their God. [17]And he will go on before the Lord, in the spirit and power of Elijah, to turn the hearts of the fathers to their children and the disobedient to the wisdom of the righteous—to make ready a people prepared for the Lord."

[18]Zechariah asked the angel, "How can I be sure of this? I am an old man and my wife is well along in years."

[19]The angel answered, "I am Gabriel. I stand in the presence of God, and I have been sent to speak to you and to tell you this good news. [20]And now you will be silent and not able to speak until the day this happens, because you did not believe my words, which will come true at their proper time."

[21]Meanwhile, the people were waiting for Zechariah and wondering why he stayed so long in the temple. [22]When he came out, he could not speak to them. They realized he had seen a vision in the temple, for he kept making signs to them but remained unable to speak.

[23]When his time of service was completed, he returned home. [24]After this his wife Elizabeth became pregnant and for five months remained in seclusion. [25]"The Lord has done this for me," she said. "In these days he has shown his favor and taken away my disgrace among the people."

The Birth of Jesus Foretold

[26]In the sixth month, God sent the angel Gabriel to Nazareth, a town in Galilee, [27]to a virgin pledged to be married to a man named Joseph, a descendant of David. The virgin's name was Mary. [28]The angel went to her and said, "Greetings, you who are highly favored! The Lord is with you."

[29]Mary was greatly troubled at his words and wondered what kind of greeting this might be. [30]But the angel said to her, "Do not be afraid, Mary, you have found favor with God. [31]You will be with child and give birth to a son, and you are to give him the name Jesus. [32]He will be great and will be called the Son of the

Most High. The Lord God will give him the throne of his father David, [33]and he will reign over the house of Jacob forever; his kingdom will never end."

[34]"How will this be," Mary asked the angel, "since I am a virgin?"

[35]The angel answered, "The Holy Spirit will come upon you, and the power of the Most High will overshadow you. So the holy one to be born will be called[b] the Son of God. [36]Even Elizabeth your relative is going to have a child in her old age, and she who was said to be barren is in her sixth month. [37]For nothing is impossible with God."

[38]"I am the Lord's servant," Mary answered. "May it be to me as you have said." Then the angel left her.

Touched by Angels

Luke 1:26–38 If you want to find angels in the Bible, just take a look at the story of Jesus' birth. The angel Gabriel told Mary that she would give birth to the baby Jesus (Luke 1:31). Angels told Joseph, Mary's fiancé, what he could expect (Matthew 1:20–21; 2:13, 19–20). And tons of angels filled the sky when Jesus was born (Luke 2:8–15). Angels also appeared in the New Testament to:

✗ roll away the stone at Jesus' grave (Matthew 28:2)

✗ tell Philip where he should go next (Acts 8:26)

✗ help Peter escape from prison (Acts 12:5–19)

Mary Visits Elizabeth

[39]At that time Mary got ready and hurried to a town in the hill country of Judea, [40]where she entered Zechariah's

---

[a]15 Or *from his mother's womb*   [b]35 Or *So the child to be born will be called holy,*

home and greeted Elizabeth. ⁴¹When Elizabeth heard Mary's greeting, the baby leaped in her womb, and Elizabeth was filled with the Holy Spirit. ⁴²In a loud voice she exclaimed: "Blessed are you among women, and blessed is the child you will bear! ⁴³But why am I so favored, that the mother of my Lord should come to me? ⁴⁴As soon as the sound of your greeting reached my ears, the baby in my womb leaped for joy. ⁴⁵Blessed is she who has believed that what the Lord has said to her will be accomplished!"

Mary's Song

⁴⁶And Mary said:

"My soul glorifies the Lord
⁴⁷   and my spirit rejoices in God my
          Savior,
⁴⁸for he has been mindful
     of the humble state of his servant.
From now on all generations will call
          me blessed,
⁴⁹   for the Mighty One has done great
          things for me—
     holy is his name.
⁵⁰His mercy extends to those who fear
          him,
     from generation to generation.
⁵¹He has performed mighty deeds with
          his arm;
     he has scattered those who are
          proud in their inmost thoughts.
⁵²He has brought down rulers from their
          thrones
     but has lifted up the humble.

⁵³He has filled the hungry with good
          things
     but has sent the rich away empty.
⁵⁴He has helped his servant Israel,
     remembering to be merciful
⁵⁵to Abraham and his descendants
          forever,
     even as he said to our fathers."

⁵⁶Mary stayed with Elizabeth for about three months and then returned home.

The Birth of John the Baptist

⁵⁷When it was time for Elizabeth to have her baby, she gave birth to a son. ⁵⁸Her neighbors and relatives heard that the Lord had shown her great mercy, and they shared her joy.

⁵⁹On the eighth day they came to circumcise the child, and they were going to name him after his father Zechariah, ⁶⁰but his mother spoke up and said, "No! He is to be called John."

⁶¹They said to her, "There is no one among your relatives who has that name."

⁶²Then they made signs to his father, to find out what he would like to name the child. ⁶³He asked for a writing tablet, and to everyone's astonishment he wrote, "His name is John." ⁶⁴Immediately his mouth was opened and his tongue was loosed, and he began to speak, praising God. ⁶⁵The neighbors were all filled with awe, and throughout the hill country of Judea people were talking about all these things. ⁶⁶Everyone who heard this wondered about it, asking, "What then is this child going to be?" For the Lord's hand was with him.

Zechariah's Song

⁶⁷His father Zechariah was filled with the Holy Spirit and prophesied:

⁶⁸"Praise be to the Lord, the God of
          Israel,
     because he has come and has
          redeemed his people.
⁶⁹He has raised up a horn*a* of salvation
          for us
     in the house of his servant David
⁷⁰(as he said through his holy prophets
          of long ago),

a 69 Horn here symbolizes strength.

Fill Me Up!

Luke 1:53

"Filled" the hungry? Sent the rich away empty? Huh? Remember when that girl or guy you have been wanting to notice you noticed you? Or when you opened that present and got exactly what you wanted? Or the last night of camp and you felt like you could touch God? That is what "filled" means. "Filled" means inside you feel like you just can't feel any better.

[71] salvation from our enemies
and from the hand of all who
hate us—
[72] to show mercy to our fathers
and to remember his holy
covenant,
[73] the oath he swore to our father
Abraham:
[74] to rescue us from the hand of our
enemies,
and to enable us to serve him
without fear
[75] in holiness and righteousness before
him all our days.

[76] And you, my child, will be called a
prophet of the Most High;
for you will go on before the Lord
to prepare the way for him,
[77] to give his people the knowledge of
salvation
through the forgiveness of their
sins,
[78] because of the tender mercy of our
God,
by which the rising sun will come
to us from heaven
[79] to shine on those living in darkness
and in the shadow of death,
to guide our feet into the path of
peace."

[80] And the child grew and became
strong in spirit; and he lived in the desert
until he appeared publicly to Israel.

The Birth of Jesus

2 In those days Caesar Augustus issued
a decree that a census should be
taken of the entire Roman world.
[2] (This was the first census that took place
while Quirinius was governor of Syria.)
[3] And everyone went to his own town to
register.
[4] So Joseph also went up from the town
of Nazareth in Galilee to Judea, to Bethlehem the town of David, because he belonged to the house and line of David.
[5] He went there to register with Mary,
who was pledged to be married to him
and was expecting a child. [6] While they
were there, the time came for the baby
to be born, [7] and she gave birth to her
firstborn, a son. She wrapped him in
cloths and placed him in a manger, because there was no room for them in
the inn.

The Shepherds and the Angels

[8] And there were shepherds living out
in the fields nearby, keeping watch over
their flocks at night. [9] An angel of the
Lord appeared to them, and the glory of
the Lord shone around them, and they
were terrified. [10] But the angel said to
them, "Do not be afraid. I bring you good
news of great joy that will be for all the
people. [11] Today in the town of David a
Savior has been born to you; he is Christ[a]
the Lord. [12] This will be a sign to you: You
will find a baby wrapped in cloths and
lying in a manger."

[13] Suddenly a great company of the
heavenly host appeared with the angel,
praising God and saying,

[14] "Glory to God in the highest,
and on earth peace to men on
whom his favor rests."

[15] When the angels had left them and
gone into heaven, the shepherds said to
one another, "Let's go to Bethlehem and
see this thing that has happened, which
the Lord has told us about."

[16] So they hurried off and found Mary
and Joseph, and the baby, who was lying
in the manger. [17] When they had seen
him, they spread the word concerning
what had been told them about this
child, [18] and all who heard it were amazed
at what the shepherds said to them. [19] But
Mary treasured up all these things and
pondered them in her heart. [20] The shepherds returned, glorifying and praising
God for all the things they had heard and
seen, which were just as they had been
told.

Jesus Presented in the Temple

[21] On the eighth day, when it was time
to circumcise him, he was named Jesus,
the name the angel had given him before
he had been conceived.

[22] When the time of their purification
according to the Law of Moses had been
completed, Joseph and Mary took him to

---

[a] 11 Or *Messiah.* "The Christ" (Greek) and "the
Messiah" (Hebrew) both mean "the Anointed One";
also in verse 26.

Jerusalem to present him to the Lord ²³(as it is written in the Law of the Lord, "Every firstborn male is to be consecrated to the Lord"[a]), ²⁴and to offer a sacrifice in keeping with what is said in the Law of the Lord: "a pair of doves or two young pigeons."[b]

²⁵Now there was a man in Jerusalem called Simeon, who was righteous and devout. He was waiting for the consolation of Israel, and the Holy Spirit was upon him. ²⁶It had been revealed to him by the Holy Spirit that he would not die before he had seen the Lord's Christ. ²⁷Moved by the Spirit, he went into the temple courts. When the parents brought in the child Jesus to do for him what the custom of the Law required, ²⁸Simeon took him in his arms and praised God, saying:

²⁹"Sovereign Lord, as you have
        promised,
    you now dismiss[c] your servant in
        peace.
³⁰For my eyes have seen your salvation,
³¹   which you have prepared in the
        sight of all people,
³²a light for revelation to the Gentiles
        and for glory to your people Israel."

³³The child's father and mother marveled at what was said about him. ³⁴Then Simeon blessed them and said to Mary, his mother: "This child is destined to cause the falling and rising of many in Israel, and to be a sign that will be spoken against, ³⁵so that the thoughts of many hearts will be revealed. And a sword will pierce your own soul too."

³⁶There was also a prophetess, Anna, the daughter of Phanuel, of the tribe of Asher. She was very old; she had lived with her husband seven years after her marriage, ³⁷and then was a widow until she was eighty-four.[d] She never left the temple but worshiped night and day, fasting and praying. ³⁸Coming up to them at that very moment, she gave thanks to God and spoke about the child to all who were looking forward to the redemption of Jerusalem.

³⁹When Joseph and Mary had done everything required by the Law of the Lord, they returned to Galilee to their own town of Nazareth. ⁴⁰And the child grew and became strong; he was filled with wisdom, and the grace of God was upon him.

The Boy Jesus at the Temple

⁴¹Every year his parents went to Jerusalem for the Feast of the Passover. ⁴²When he was twelve years old, they went up to the Feast, according to the custom. ⁴³After the Feast was over, while his parents were returning home, the boy Jesus stayed behind in Jerusalem, but they were unaware of it. ⁴⁴Thinking he was in their company, they traveled on for a day. Then they began looking for him among their relatives and friends. ⁴⁵When they did not find him, they went back to Jerusalem to look for him. ⁴⁶After three days they found him in the temple courts, sitting among the teachers, listening to them and asking them questions. ⁴⁷Everyone who heard him was amazed at his understanding and his answers. ⁴⁸When his parents saw him, they were astonished. His mother said to him, "Son, why have you treated us like this? Your father and I have been anxiously searching for you."

⁴⁹"Why were you searching for me?" he asked. "Didn't you know I had to be in my Father's house?" ⁵⁰But they did not understand what he was saying to them. ⁵¹Then he went down to Nazareth with them and was obedient to them. But his mother treasured all these things in her heart. ⁵²And Jesus grew in wisdom and stature, and in favor with God and men.

John the Baptist Prepares the Way

3 In the fifteenth year of the reign of Tiberius Caesar—when Pontius Pilate was governor of Judea, Herod tetrarch of Galilee, his brother Philip tetrarch of Iturea and Traconitis, and Lysanias tetrarch of Abilene— ²during the high priesthood of Annas and Caiaphas, the word of God came to John son of Zechariah in the desert. ³He went into all the country around the Jordan, preaching a baptism of repentance for the forgiveness of sins.

*a23 Exodus 13:2,12 *b24 Lev. 12:8 *c29 Or promised, / now dismiss *d37 Or widow for eighty-four years

[4]As is written in the book of the words of Isaiah the prophet:

> "A voice of one calling in the desert,
> 'Prepare the way for the Lord,
>   make straight paths for him.
> [5]Every valley shall be filled in,
>   every mountain and hill made low.
> The crooked roads shall become
>   straight,
>   the rough ways smooth.
> [6]And all mankind will see God's
>   salvation.'"[a]

[7]John said to the crowds coming out to be baptized by him, "You brood of vipers! Who warned you to flee from the coming wrath? [8]Produce fruit in keeping with repentance. And do not begin to say to yourselves, 'We have Abraham as our father.' For I tell you that out of these stones God can raise up children for Abraham. [9]The ax is already at the root of the trees, and every tree that does not produce good fruit will be cut down and thrown into the fire."

[10]"What should we do then?" the crowd asked.

[11]John answered, "The man with two tunics should share with him who has none, and the one who has food should do the same."

[12]Tax collectors also came to be baptized. "Teacher," they asked, "what should we do?"

[13]"Don't collect any more than you are required to," he told them.

[14]Then some soldiers asked him, "And what should we do?"

He replied, "Don't extort money and don't accuse people falsely—be content with your pay."

[15]The people were waiting expectantly and were all wondering in their hearts if John might possibly be the Christ.[b]

---

[a]6 Isaiah 40:3-5   [b]15 Or *Messiah*

Thursday

Gotta Grow

Read Luke 2:51–52

I remember when all I wanted was to be bigger and stronger. I thought, *If I could just bench press a little more, I'd be happy.* But I realized later that there will always be someone bigger and stronger than me. And even if my muscles got huge, physical strength doesn't last forever.

What *does* last forever is spiritual strength. We all need to grow closer to God every day. If we're not moving closer to God, we're moving farther away. So we have to do everything we can to help our faith grow, like read the Bible and pray every day.

And if we ever think we've got our faith all figured out, we just need to look at Jesus to know that we all need to work at exercising our faith. Even though he was the Son of God, Jesus prayed constantly. He was always seeking God's will.

If we want to have a relationship with God, we have to put some work into it, no matter how strong we think our faith is.

Ben age 16

What about You?

❶ What are 2 things you do that help you feel closer to God?

❷ Do 10 push-ups in a row. As you do them, think about how your spiritual strength compares to your physical strength.

❸ Ask God to help you grow stronger in your faith.

Turn to page 1225 for your next devotion.

[16]John answered them all, "I baptize you with[a] water. But one more powerful than I will come, the thongs of whose sandals I am not worthy to untie. He will baptize you with the Holy Spirit and with fire. [17]His winnowing fork is in his hand to clear his threshing floor and to gather the wheat into his barn, but he will burn up the chaff with unquenchable fire." [18]And with many other words John exhorted the people and preached the good news to them.

[19]But when John rebuked Herod the tetrarch because of Herodias, his brother's wife, and all the other evil things he had done, [20]Herod added this to them all: He locked John up in prison.

The Baptism and Genealogy of Jesus

[21]When all the people were being baptized, Jesus was baptized too. And as he was praying, heaven was opened [22]and the Holy Spirit descended on him in bodily form like a dove. And a voice came from heaven: "You are my Son, whom I love; with you I am well pleased."

[23]Now Jesus himself was about thirty years old when he began his ministry. He was the son, so it was thought, of Joseph,

the son of Heli, [24]the son of Matthat,
the son of Levi, the son of Melki,
the son of Jannai, the son of Joseph,
[25]the son of Mattathias, the son of Amos,
the son of Nahum, the son of Esli,
the son of Naggai, [26]the son of Maath,
the son of Mattathias, the son of Semein,
the son of Josech, the son of Joda,
[27]the son of Joanan, the son of Rhesa,
the son of Zerubbabel, the son of Shealtiel,
the son of Neri, [28]the son of Melki,
the son of Addi, the son of Cosam,
the son of Elmadam, the son of Er,
[29]the son of Joshua, the son of Eliezer,
the son of Jorim, the son of Matthat,
the son of Levi, [30]the son of Simeon,
the son of Judah, the son of Joseph,
the son of Jonam, the son of Eliakim,

[31]the son of Melea, the son of Menna,
the son of Mattatha, the son of Nathan,
the son of David, [32]the son of Jesse,
the son of Obed, the son of Boaz,
the son of Salmon,[b] the son of Nahshon,
[33]the son of Amminadab, the son of Ram,[c]
the son of Hezron, the son of Perez,
the son of Judah, [34]the son of Jacob,
the son of Isaac, the son of Abraham,
the son of Terah, the son of Nahor,
[35]the son of Serug, the son of Reu,
the son of Peleg, the son of Eber,
the son of Shelah, [36]the son of Cainan,
the son of Arphaxad, the son of Shem,
the son of Noah, the son of Lamech,
[37]the son of Methuselah, the son of Enoch,
the son of Jared, the son of Mahalalel,
the son of Kenan, [38]the son of Enosh,
the son of Seth, the son of Adam,
the son of God.

The Temptation of Jesus

4 Jesus, full of the Holy Spirit, returned from the Jordan and was led by the Spirit in the desert, [2]where for forty days he was tempted by the devil. He ate nothing during those days, and at the end of them he was hungry.

[3]The devil said to him, "If you are the Son of God, tell this stone to become bread."

[4]Jesus answered, "It is written: 'Man does not live on bread alone.'[d]"

[5]The devil led him up to a high place and showed him in an instant all the kingdoms of the world. [6]And he said to him, "I will give you all their authority and splendor, for it has been given to me, and I can give it to anyone I want to. [7]So if you worship me, it will all be yours."

[8]Jesus answered, "It is written: 'Worship

---

[a]16 Or *in*   [b]32 Some early manuscripts *Sala*
[c]33 Some manuscripts *Amminadab, the son of Admin, the son of Arni*; other manuscripts vary widely.   [d]4 Deut. 8:3

the Lord your God and serve him only.'ᵃ"

⁹The devil led him to Jerusalem and had him stand on the highest point of the temple. "If you are the Son of God," he said, "throw yourself down from here. ¹⁰For it is written:

" 'He will command his angels
 concerning you
 to guard you carefully;
¹¹ they will lift you up in their hands,
 so that you will not strike your foot
 against a stone.'ᵇ"

¹²Jesus answered, "It says: 'Do not put the Lord your God to the test.'ᶜ"

¹³When the devil had finished all this tempting, he left him until an opportune time.

Jesus Rejected at Nazareth

¹⁴Jesus returned to Galilee in the power of the Spirit, and news about him spread through the whole countryside. ¹⁵He taught in their synagogues, and everyone praised him.

¹⁶He went to Nazareth, where he had been brought up, and on the Sabbath day he went into the synagogue, as was his custom. And he stood up to read. ¹⁷The scroll of the prophet Isaiah was handed to him. Unrolling it, he found the place where it is written:

¹⁸ "The Spirit of the Lord is on me,
 because he has anointed me
 to preach good news to the poor.
He has sent me to proclaim freedom
 for the prisoners
 and recovery of sight for the blind,
to release the oppressed,
¹⁹ to proclaim the year of the Lord's
 favor."ᵈ

²⁰Then he rolled up the scroll, gave it back to the attendant and sat down. The eyes of everyone in the synagogue were fastened on him, ²¹and he began by saying to them, "Today this scripture is fulfilled in your hearing."

²²All spoke well of him and were amazed at the gracious words that came from his lips. "Isn't this Joseph's son?" they asked.

²³Jesus said to them, "Surely you will quote this proverb to me: 'Physician, heal yourself! Do here in your hometown what we have heard that you did in Capernaum.' "

²⁴"I tell you the truth," he continued, "no prophet is accepted in his hometown. ²⁵I assure you that there were many widows in Israel in Elijah's time, when the sky was shut for three and a half years and there was a severe famine throughout the land. ²⁶Yet Elijah was not sent to any of them, but to a widow in Zarephath in the region of Sidon. ²⁷And there were many in Israel with leprosyᵉ in the time of Elisha the prophet, yet not one of them was cleansed—only Naaman the Syrian."

²⁸All the people in the synagogue were furious when they heard this. ²⁹They got up, drove him out of the town, and took him to the brow of the hill on which the town was built, in order to throw him down the cliff. ³⁰But he walked right through the crowd and went on his way.

Jesus Drives Out an Evil Spirit

³¹Then he went down to Capernaum, a town in Galilee, and on the Sabbath began to teach the people. ³²They were amazed at his teaching, because his message had authority.

³³In the synagogue there was a man possessed by a demon, an evilᶠ spirit. He cried out at the top of his voice, ³⁴"Ha! What do you want with us, Jesus of Nazareth? Have you come to destroy us? I know who you are—the Holy One of God!"

³⁵"Be quiet!" Jesus said sternly. "Come out of him!" Then the demon threw the man down before them all and came out without injuring him.

³⁶All the people were amazed and said to each other, "What is this teaching? With authority and power he gives orders to evil spirits and they come out!" ³⁷And the news about him spread throughout the surrounding area.

Jesus Heals Many

³⁸Jesus left the synagogue and went to the home of Simon. Now Simon's

---

ᵃ8 Deut. 6:13   ᵇ11 Psalm 91:11,12   ᶜ12 Deut. 6:16   ᵈ19 Isaiah 61:1,2   ᵉ27 The Greek word was used for various diseases affecting the skin—not necessarily leprosy.   ᶠ33 Greek *unclean*; also in verse 36

mother-in-law was suffering from a high fever, and they asked Jesus to help her. ³⁹So he bent over her and rebuked the fever, and it left her. She got up at once and began to wait on them.

⁴⁰When the sun was setting, the people brought to Jesus all who had various kinds of sickness, and laying his hands on each one, he healed them. ⁴¹Moreover, demons came out of many people, shouting, "You are the Son of God!" But he rebuked them and would not allow them to speak, because they knew he was the Christ.[a]

⁴²At daybreak Jesus went out to a solitary place. The people were looking for him and when they came to where he was, they tried to keep him from leaving them. ⁴³But he said, "I must preach the good news of the kingdom of God to the other towns also, because that is why I was sent." ⁴⁴And he kept on preaching in the synagogues of Judea.[b]

The Calling of the First Disciples

5 One day as Jesus was standing by the Lake of Gennesaret,[c] with the people crowding around him and listening to the word of God, ²he saw at the water's edge two boats, left there by the fishermen, who were washing their nets. ³He got into one of the boats, the one belonging to Simon, and asked him to put out a little from shore. Then he sat down and taught the people from the boat.

⁴When he had finished speaking, he said to Simon, "Put out into deep water, and let down[d] the nets for a catch."

⁵Simon answered, "Master, we've worked hard all night and haven't caught anything. But because you say so, I will let down the nets."

[a]41 Or *Messiah*   [b]44 Or *the land of the Jews*; some manuscripts *Galilee*   [c]1 That is, Sea of Galilee   [d]4 The Greek verb is plural.

Friday

Popular and Unpopular Alike

Read Luke 4:14–21

It's pretty easy to be nice to our friends and to the popular people we *wish* were our friends. It's a lot harder to be nice to the ones who are slow or mean or don't play sports or don't wear the "right" clothes. If someone doesn't have any friends, you don't exactly want to volunteer to be the first one.

Jesus didn't have this problem. He talked to wealthy and popular people, but he paid special attention to the poor and unpopular. When many of the people of that day were ignoring these people, Jesus encouraged the poor by saying, "Hey! Know what? The Lord's favor is on *you!*"

Because I'm a Christian, Jesus calls me to be friendly to people who have no friends. The only way I can reach out is to stay close to God, so that he can show me what to do next. If Jesus reached out to the unpopular, shouldn't I?

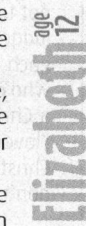
Elizabeth age 12

What about You?

❶ Think about a time when you've felt like you had no friends. What was it like?

❷ At lunch, look for someone who's eating alone and invite them to your table.

❸ Thank God for reaching out to everyone, and ask him to help you do the same thing.

Turn to page 1226 for your next devotion.

⁶When they had done so, they caught such a large number of fish that their nets began to break. ⁷So they signaled their partners in the other boat to come and help them, and they came and filled both boats so full that they began to sink.

⁸When Simon Peter saw this, he fell at Jesus' knees and said, "Go away from me, Lord; I am a sinful man!" ⁹For he and all his companions were astonished at the catch of fish they had taken, ¹⁰and so were James and John, the sons of Zebedee, Simon's partners.

Then Jesus said to Simon, "Don't be afraid; from now on you will catch men." ¹¹So they pulled their boats up on shore, left everything and followed him.

The Man With Leprosy

¹²While Jesus was in one of the towns, a man came along who was covered with leprosy.ᵃ When he saw Jesus, he fell with his face to the ground and begged him, "Lord, if you are willing, you can make me clean."

ᵃ12 The Greek word was used for various diseases affecting the skin—not necessarily leprosy.

Weekend.

Who You Judge

Read 1 Corinthians 5:12 (page 1380)

It seems that this week's devotions had a lot to do with acceptance—how other people accept us and how we accept other people. You might be able to relate to Gabe, who was teased and made fun of when he was younger. All of us can relate to what Elizabeth said about wanting to be popular!

As Christ-followers, it's important that we think about how we accept (or don't accept) other kids. You know what it means to judge someone, right? (Just like a judge in a court might pronounce someone "guilty" or "not guilty.")

Well, it's easy to judge Christians and non-Christians by the same set of standards. But the Bible says we shouldn't do this: Paul tells us that we are not to judge those outside of the church (non-Christians), while we should judge those inside the church. In other words, as Christians we are to hold each other accountable for living and loving like Jesus would. Your friends who don't know Jesus probably don't have the same standards you have as a Christian (they don't have a reason to!). But those friends need to be "loved into a relationship with Jesus," not "judged into one." If you see non-Christians this way, it makes it easier to love and accept them, even if you don't love and accept some of their behavior.

❶ How can you show love for a non-Christian and at the same time disagree with the wrong things they might be doing?

❷ Go to a trusted Christian friend or adult and ask, "What's an area in my life that I could improve?" (for example, a hot temper, a negative attitude, having trouble accepting others, etc.). And then ask, "Will you help me to improve in this area?"

❸ Ask God to give you the strength to improve a weak area in your life. Ask him to help you to love non-Christians the way he would love them.

Turn to page 1229 for your next devotion.

¹³Jesus reached out his hand and touched the man. "I am willing," he said. "Be clean!" And immediately the leprosy left him.

¹⁴Then Jesus ordered him, "Don't tell anyone, but go, show yourself to the priest and offer the sacrifices that Moses commanded for your cleansing, as a testimony to them."

¹⁵Yet the news about him spread all the more, so that crowds of people came to hear him and to be healed of their sicknesses. ¹⁶But Jesus often withdrew to lonely places and prayed.

Jesus Heals a Paralytic

¹⁷One day as he was teaching, Pharisees and teachers of the law, who had come from every village of Galilee and from Judea and Jerusalem, were sitting there. And the power of the Lord was present for him to heal the sick. ¹⁸Some men came carrying a paralytic on a mat and tried to take him into the house to lay him before Jesus. ¹⁹When they could not find a way to do this because of the crowd, they went up on the roof and lowered him on his mat through the tiles into the middle of the crowd, right in front of Jesus.

²⁰When Jesus saw their faith, he said, "Friend, your sins are forgiven."

²¹The Pharisees and the teachers of the law began thinking to themselves, "Who is this fellow who speaks blasphemy? Who can forgive sins but God alone?"

²²Jesus knew what they were thinking and asked, "Why are you thinking these things in your hearts? ²³Which is easier: to say, 'Your sins are forgiven,' or to say, 'Get up and walk'? ²⁴But that you may know that the Son of Man has authority on earth to forgive sins . . ." He said to the paralyzed man, "I tell you, get up, take your mat and go home." ²⁵Immediately he stood up in front of them, took what he had been lying on and went home praising God. ²⁶Everyone was amazed and gave praise to God. They were filled with awe and said, "We have seen remarkable things today."

The Calling of Levi

²⁷After this, Jesus went out and saw a tax collector by the name of Levi sitting at his tax booth. "Follow me," Jesus said to him, ²⁸and Levi got up, left everything and followed him.

Chuck the Money

Huh?

Luke 5:27–28

Tax collectors were not exactly well liked. They collected taxes for the bad guys, the Roman government. But they were very wealthy and powerful. Tax collectors had it made, if you didn't mind being a traitor. Here's what's so weird about this story. Jesus walks by, says "Follow me!" and Matthew (also known as Levi) does follow! What's going on? Here's a guy who's loaded with money and all the stuff that comes with being rich, and he chucks it all to follow Jesus. Hmmmm. No doubt about it—following Jesus is better than lots of money and a cool car!

²⁹Then Levi held a great banquet for Jesus at his house, and a large crowd of tax collectors and others were eating with them. ³⁰But the Pharisees and the teachers of the law who belonged to their sect complained to his disciples, "Why do you eat and drink with tax collectors and 'sinners'?"

³¹Jesus answered them, "It is not the healthy who need a doctor, but the sick. ³²I have not come to call the righteous, but sinners to repentance."

Jesus Questioned About Fasting

³³They said to him, "John's disciples often fast and pray, and so do the disciples of the Pharisees, but yours go on eating and drinking."

³⁴Jesus answered, "Can you make the guests of the bridegroom fast while he is with them? ³⁵But the time will come when the bridegroom will be taken from them; in those days they will fast."

³⁶He told them this parable: "No one tears a patch from a new garment and sews it on an old one. If he does, he will have torn the new garment, and the patch from the new will not match the old. ³⁷And no one pours new wine into

old wineskins. If he does, the new wine will burst the skins, the wine will run out and the wineskins will be ruined. ³⁸No, new wine must be poured into new wineskins. ³⁹And no one after drinking old wine wants the new, for he says, 'The old is better.'"

Lord of the Sabbath

6 One Sabbath Jesus was going through the grainfields, and his disciples began to pick some heads of grain, rub them in their hands and eat the kernels. ²Some of the Pharisees asked, "Why are you doing what is unlawful on the Sabbath?"

³Jesus answered them, "Have you never read what David did when he and his companions were hungry? ⁴He entered the house of God, and taking the consecrated bread, he ate what is lawful only for priests to eat. And he also gave some to his companions." ⁵Then Jesus said to them, "The Son of Man is Lord of the Sabbath."

⁶On another Sabbath he went into the synagogue and was teaching, and a man was there whose right hand was shriveled. ⁷The Pharisees and the teachers of the law were looking for a reason to accuse Jesus, so they watched him closely to see if he would heal on the Sabbath. ⁸But Jesus knew what they were thinking and said to the man with the shriveled hand, "Get up and stand in front of everyone." So he got up and stood there.

⁹Then Jesus said to them, "I ask you, which is lawful on the Sabbath: to do good or to do evil, to save life or to destroy it?"

¹⁰He looked around at them all, and then said to the man, "Stretch out your hand." He did so, and his hand was completely restored. ¹¹But they were furious and began to discuss with one another what they might do to Jesus.

The Twelve Apostles

¹²One of those days Jesus went out to a mountainside to pray, and spent the night praying to God. ¹³When morning came, he called his disciples to him and chose twelve of them, whom he also designated apostles: ¹⁴Simon (whom he named Peter), his brother Andrew, James, John, Philip, Bartholomew, ¹⁵Matthew, Thomas,

James son of Alphaeus, Simon who was called the Zealot, ¹⁶Judas son of James, and Judas Iscariot, who became a traitor.

Blessings and Woes

¹⁷He went down with them and stood on a level place. A large crowd of his disciples was there and a great number of people from all over Judea, from Jerusalem, and from the coast of Tyre and Sidon, ¹⁸who had come to hear him and to be healed of their diseases. Those troubled by evilᵃ spirits were cured, ¹⁹and the people all tried to touch him, because power was coming from him and healing them all.

²⁰Looking at his disciples, he said:

"Blessed are you who are poor,
    for yours is the kingdom of God.
²¹Blessed are you who hunger now,
    for you will be satisfied.
Blessed are you who weep now,
    for you will laugh.
²²Blessed are you when men hate you,
    when they exclude you and insult
        you
    and reject your name as evil,
        because of the Son of Man.

²³"Rejoice in that day and leap for joy, because great is your reward in heaven. For that is how their fathers treated the prophets.

²⁴"But woe to you who are rich,
    for you have already received your
        comfort.
²⁵Woe to you who are well fed now,
    for you will go hungry.
Woe to you who laugh now,
    for you will mourn and weep.
²⁶Woe to you when all men speak well
        of you,
    for that is how their fathers treated
        the false prophets.

Love for Enemies

²⁷"But I tell you who hear me: Love your enemies, do good to those who hate you, ²⁸bless those who curse you, pray for those who mistreat you. ²⁹If someone strikes you on one cheek, turn to him the other also. If someone takes your cloak,

---

ᵃ18 Greek *unclean*

do not stop him from taking your tunic. ³⁰Give to everyone who asks you, and if anyone takes what belongs to you, do not demand it back. ³¹Do to others as you would have them do to you.

³²"If you love those who love you, what credit is that to you? Even 'sinners' love those who love them. ³³And if you do good to those who are good to you, what credit is that to you? Even 'sinners' do that. ³⁴And if you lend to those from whom you expect repayment, what credit is that to you? Even 'sinners' lend to 'sinners,' expecting to be repaid in full. ³⁵But love your enemies, do good to them, and lend to them without expecting to get anything back. Then your reward will be great, and you will be sons of the Most High, because he is kind to the ungrateful and wicked. ³⁶Be merciful, just as your Father is merciful.

Judging Others

³⁷"Do not judge, and you will not be judged. Do not condemn, and you will not be condemned. Forgive, and you will be forgiven. ³⁸Give, and it will be given to you. A good measure, pressed down, shaken together and running over, will be poured into your lap. For with the measure you use, it will be measured to you."

³⁹He also told them this parable: "Can a blind man lead a blind man? Will they not both fall into a pit? ⁴⁰A student is not above his teacher, but everyone who is fully trained will be like his teacher.

⁴¹"Why do you look at the speck of sawdust in your brother's eye and pay no attention to the plank in your own eye? ⁴²How can you say to your brother, 'Brother, let me take the speck out of your eye,' when you yourself fail to see the plank in your own eye? You hypocrite, first take the plank out of your eye, and then you will see clearly to remove the speck from your brother's eye.

A Tree and Its Fruit

⁴³"No good tree bears bad fruit, nor does a bad tree bear good fruit. ⁴⁴Each tree is recognized by its own fruit. People do not pick figs from thornbushes, or

Monday

Picking at Specks

Read Luke 6:37–42

I'm pretty good at picking "specks" out of my brother's eye. Just the other day, I told my brother not to do something. Then later that day I found myself doing the same thing! That wasn't a very smooth move on my part.

I'd be in big trouble if God judged me for all the bad things I do. But instead of judging me—which he definitely has the right to do, since he's God—he gives me grace, because I know and believe in Jesus. He forgives my sins, no matter how bad I mess up. And he calls me his very own child. Because God's been so merciful to me, I have no excuse for judging my brother. . . or anyone else.

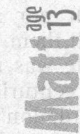

Matt age 13

❶ Why is it easy to judge other people for their sins? Why does Jesus tell us not to judge?

❷ Get a bar of soap and use it to write the word "forgiven," on your mirror. When you look at yourself in that mirror, remember that's how God sees you—as forgiven. And he sees other Christians the same way.

❸ Thank God for giving you his grace.

Turn to page 1231 for your next devotion.

grapes from briers. ⁴⁵The good man brings good things out of the good stored up in his heart, and the evil man brings evil things out of the evil stored up in his heart. For out of the overflow of his heart his mouth speaks.

The Wise and Foolish Builders

⁴⁶"Why do you call me, 'Lord, Lord,' and do not do what I say? ⁴⁷I will show you what he is like who comes to me and hears my words and puts them into practice. ⁴⁸He is like a man building a house, who dug down deep and laid the foundation on rock. When a flood came, the torrent struck that house but could not shake it, because it was well built. ⁴⁹But the one who hears my words and does not put them into practice is like a man who built a house on the ground without a foundation. The moment the torrent struck that house, it collapsed and its destruction was complete."

The Faith of the Centurion

7 When Jesus had finished saying all this in the hearing of the people, he entered Capernaum. ²There a centurion's servant, whom his master valued highly, was sick and about to die. ³The centurion heard of Jesus and sent some elders of the Jews to him, asking him to come and heal his servant. ⁴When they came to Jesus, they pleaded earnestly with him, "This man deserves to have you do this, ⁵because he loves our nation and has built our synagogue." ⁶So Jesus went with them.

He was not far from the house when the centurion sent friends to say to him: "Lord, don't trouble yourself, for I do not deserve to have you come under my roof. ⁷That is why I did not even consider myself worthy to come to you. But say the word, and my servant will be healed. ⁸For I myself am a man under authority, with soldiers under me. I tell this one, 'Go,' and he goes; and that one, 'Come,' and he comes. I say to my servant, 'Do this,' and he does it."

⁹When Jesus heard this, he was amazed at him, and turning to the crowd following him, he said, "I tell you, I have not found such great faith even in Israel." ¹⁰Then the men who had been sent returned to the house and found the servant well.

Jesus Raises a Widow's Son

¹¹Soon afterward, Jesus went to a town called Nain, and his disciples and a large crowd went along with him. ¹²As he approached the town gate, a dead person was being carried out—the only son of his mother, and she was a widow. And a large crowd from the town was with her. ¹³When the Lord saw her, his heart went out to her and he said, "Don't cry."

¹⁴Then he went up and touched the coffin, and those carrying it stood still. He said, "Young man, I say to you, get up!" ¹⁵The dead man sat up and began to talk, and Jesus gave him back to his mother.

¹⁶They were all filled with awe and praised God. "A great prophet has appeared among us," they said. "God has come to help his people." ¹⁷This news about Jesus spread throughout Judea[a] and the surrounding country.

Jesus and John the Baptist

¹⁸John's disciples told him about all these things. Calling two of them, ¹⁹he sent them to the Lord to ask, "Are you the one who was to come, or should we expect someone else?"

²⁰When the men came to Jesus, they said, "John the Baptist sent us to you to ask, 'Are you the one who was to come, or should we expect someone else?' "

²¹At that very time Jesus cured many who had diseases, sicknesses and evil spirits, and gave sight to many who were blind. ²²So he replied to the messengers, "Go back and report to John what you have seen and heard: The blind receive sight, the lame walk, those who have leprosy[b] are cured, the deaf hear, the dead are raised, and the good news is preached to the poor. ²³Blessed is the man who does not fall away on account of me."

²⁴After John's messengers left, Jesus began to speak to the crowd about John: "What did you go out into the desert to see? A reed swayed by the wind? ²⁵If not, what did you go out to see? A man dressed in fine clothes? No, those who

[a]17 Or *the land of the Jews*   [b]22 The Greek word was used for various diseases affecting the skin—not necessarily leprosy.

wear expensive clothes and indulge in luxury are in palaces. ²⁶But what did you go out to see? A prophet? Yes, I tell you, and more than a prophet. ²⁷This is the one about whom it is written:

" 'I will send my messenger ahead of you,
who will prepare your way before you.'ᵃ

²⁸I tell you, among those born of women there is no one greater than John; yet the one who is least in the kingdom of God is greater than he."

²⁹(All the people, even the tax collectors, when they heard Jesus' words, acknowledged that God's way was right, because they had been baptized by John. ³⁰But the Pharisees and experts in the law rejected God's purpose for themselves, because they had not been baptized by John.)

³¹"To what, then, can I compare the

people of this generation? What are they like? ³²They are like children sitting in the marketplace and calling out to each other:

" 'We played the flute for you,
and you did not dance;
we sang a dirge,
and you did not cry.'

³³For John the Baptist came neither eating bread nor drinking wine, and you say, 'He has a demon.' ³⁴The Son of Man came eating and drinking, and you say, 'Here is a glutton and a drunkard, a friend of tax collectors and "sinners." ' ³⁵But wisdom is proved right by all her children."

Jesus Anointed by a Sinful Woman

³⁶Now one of the Pharisees invited Jesus to have dinner with him, so he

ᵃ27 Mal. 3:1

Tuesday

Gotta Have Faith
Read Luke 7:1–10

Reading about the centurion's faith reminds me of writing this devotion. At first, I didn't want to do it because I didn't think I had anything to say. But I asked God to help me think about these verses and help me understand them. When I worked on the devotion the next day, I really felt like I knew what to write. I never could have done it without God's help.

I guess that's kind of what's going on in these verses. The centurion's servant was sick. And even though the centurion had all kinds of power and authority, he couldn't do anything to help his servant. So he needed to trust in the only One who could: Jesus.

God is always there to help us in hard times. We just need to trust him and have faith that he will give us everything we need.

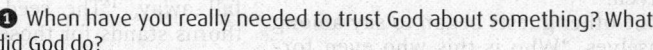

What about You?

❶ When have you really needed to trust God about something? What did God do?

❷ Get 3 or 4 of your good friends and do a "trust fall." Stand about 3 feet away from your friends and turn your back to them. Now, count to 3 and let yourself fall backward into your friends' arms (no goofy stuff allowed—this takes serious trust). How does it feel to really have faith in someone else? How can you have that kind of faith in God?

❸ Ask God to give you more faith in his power.

Turn to page 1233 for your next devotion.

went to the Pharisee's house and reclined at the table. [37]When a woman who had lived a sinful life in that town learned that Jesus was eating at the Pharisee's house, she brought an alabaster jar of perfume, [38]and as she stood behind him at his feet weeping, she began to wet his feet with her tears. Then she wiped them with her hair, kissed them and poured perfume on them.

[39]When the Pharisee who had invited him saw this, he said to himself, "If this man were a prophet, he would know who is touching him and what kind of woman she is—that she is a sinner."

[40]Jesus answered him, "Simon, I have something to tell you."

"Tell me, teacher," he said.

[41]"Two men owed money to a certain moneylender. One owed him five hundred denarii,[a] and the other fifty. [42]Neither of them had the money to pay him back, so he canceled the debts of both. Now which of them will love him more?"

[43]Simon replied, "I suppose the one who had the bigger debt canceled."

"You have judged correctly," Jesus said.

[44]Then he turned toward the woman and said to Simon, "Do you see this woman? I came into your house. You did not give me any water for my feet, but she wet my feet with her tears and wiped them with her hair. [45]You did not give me a kiss, but this woman, from the time I entered, has not stopped kissing my feet. [46]You did not put oil on my head, but she has poured perfume on my feet. [47]Therefore, I tell you, her many sins have been forgiven—for she loved much. But he who has been forgiven little loves little."

[48]Then Jesus said to her, "Your sins are forgiven."

[49]The other guests began to say among themselves, "Who is this who even forgives sins?"

[50]Jesus said to the woman, "Your faith has saved you; go in peace."

The Parable of the Sower

8 After this, Jesus traveled about from one town and village to another, proclaiming the good news of the kingdom of God. The Twelve were with him, [2]and also some women who had been

cured of evil spirits and diseases: Mary (called Magdalene) from whom seven demons had come out; [3]Joanna the wife of Cuza, the manager of Herod's household; Susanna; and many others. These women were helping to support them out of their own means.

[4]While a large crowd was gathering and people were coming to Jesus from town after town, he told this parable: [5]"A farmer went out to sow his seed. As he was scattering the seed, some fell along the path; it was trampled on, and the birds of the air ate it up. [6]Some fell on rock, and when it came up, the plants withered because they had no moisture. [7]Other seed fell among thorns, which grew up with it and choked the plants. [8]Still other seed fell on good soil. It came up and yielded a crop, a hundred times more than was sown."

When he said this, he called out, "He who has ears to hear, let him hear."

[9]His disciples asked him what this parable meant. [10]He said, "The knowledge of the secrets of the kingdom of God has been given to you, but to others I speak in parables, so that,

" 'though seeing, they may not see;
  though hearing, they may not
      understand.'[b]

[11]"This is the meaning of the parable: The seed is the word of God. [12]Those along the path are the ones who hear, and then the devil comes and takes away the word from their hearts, so that they may not believe and be saved. [13]Those on the rock are the ones who receive the word with joy when they hear it, but they have no root. They believe for a while, but in the time of testing they fall away. [14]The seed that fell among thorns stands for those who hear, but as they go on their way they are choked by life's worries, riches and pleasures, and they do not mature. [15]But the seed on good soil stands for those with a noble and good heart, who hear the word, retain it, and by persevering produce a crop.

---

[a]41 A denarius was a coin worth about a day's wages.
[b]10 Isaiah 6:9

A Lamp on a Stand

¹⁶"No one lights a lamp and hides it in a jar or puts it under a bed. Instead, he puts it on a stand, so that those who come in can see the light. ¹⁷For there is nothing hidden that will not be disclosed, and nothing concealed that will not be known or brought out into the open. ¹⁸Therefore consider carefully how you listen. Whoever has will be given more; whoever does not have, even what he thinks he has will be taken from him."

Jesus' Mother and Brothers

¹⁹Now Jesus' mother and brothers came to see him, but they were not able to get near him because of the crowd. ²⁰Someone told him, "Your mother and brothers are standing outside, wanting to see you."

²¹He replied, "My mother and brothers are those who hear God's word and put it into practice."

Jesus Calms the Storm

²²One day Jesus said to his disciples, "Let's go over to the other side of the lake." So they got into a boat and set out. ²³As they sailed, he fell asleep. A squall came down on the lake, so that the boat was being swamped, and they were in great danger.

²⁴The disciples went and woke him, saying, "Master, Master, we're going to drown!"

He got up and rebuked the wind and the raging waters; the storm subsided, and all was calm. ²⁵"Where is your faith?" he asked his disciples.

In fear and amazement they asked one another, "Who is this? He commands even the winds and the water, and they obey him."

The Healing of a Demon-possessed Man

²⁶They sailed to the region of the Gerasenes,ᵃ which is across the lake from Galilee. ²⁷When Jesus stepped ashore, he was met by a demon-possessed man from the town. For a long time this man had not worn clothes or lived in a

ᵃ26 Some manuscripts *Gadarenes*; other manuscripts *Gergesenes*; also in verse 37

Wednesday

God Did It

Read Luke 8:26–36

God does a lot of good things in our lives. Take the time I broke my arm, for example. I should have landed on my left arm, but I kind of flipped over and ended up landing on my right arm. So it was my right arm that broke, not my left. Since I'm left-handed, that was about the best thing that could have happened. I really think God sort of helped turn me over as I fell, so I wouldn't break my left arm. I told many people about what a wonderful thing God did.

God's not just sitting up in heaven, ignoring the world. He does great things for us all the time, and we need to tell other people. When God helps us, he's showing us how much he cares for us. And when we tell other people about the good things God's done, they'll see that he cares too.

❶ What great things has God done for you this week? This month? Have you told anyone about God's goodness?

❷ The next time you talk with a friend, tell them 1 or 2 ways you've experienced God's goodness recently.

❸ Thank God for all the ways he's blessed you.

Turn to page 1238 for your next devotion.

house, but had lived in the tombs. [28]When he saw Jesus, he cried out and fell at his feet, shouting at the top of his voice, "What do you want with me, Jesus, Son of the Most High God? I beg you, don't torture me!" [29]For Jesus had commanded the evil[a] spirit to come out of the man. Many times it had seized him, and though he was chained hand and foot and kept under guard, he had broken his chains and had been driven by the demon into solitary places.

[30]Jesus asked him, "What is your name?"

"Legion," he replied, because many demons had gone into him. [31]And they begged him repeatedly not to order them to go into the Abyss.

[32]A large herd of pigs was feeding there on the hillside. The demons begged Jesus to let them go into them, and he gave them permission. [33]When the demons came out of the man, they went into the pigs, and the herd rushed down the steep bank into the lake and was drowned.

[34]When those tending the pigs saw what had happened, they ran off and reported this in the town and countryside, [35]and the people went out to see what had happened. When they came to Jesus, they found the man from whom the demons had gone out, sitting at Jesus' feet, dressed and in his right mind; and they were afraid. [36]Those who had seen it told the people how the demon-possessed man had been cured. [37]Then all the people of the region of the Gerasenes asked Jesus to leave them, because they were overcome with fear. So he got into the boat and left.

[38]The man from whom the demons had gone out begged to go with him, but Jesus sent him away, saying, [39]"Return home and tell how much God has done for you." So the man went away and told all over town how much Jesus had done for him.

A Dead Girl and a Sick Woman

[40]Now when Jesus returned, a crowd welcomed him, for they were all expecting him. [41]Then a man named Jairus, a ruler of the synagogue, came and fell at Jesus' feet, pleading with him to come to his house [42]because his only daughter, a girl of about twelve, was dying.

As Jesus was on his way, the crowds almost crushed him. [43]And a woman was there who had been subject to bleeding for twelve years,[b] but no one could heal her. [44]She came up behind him and touched the edge of his cloak, and immediately her bleeding stopped.

[45]"Who touched me?" Jesus asked.

When they all denied it, Peter said, "Master, the people are crowding and pressing against you."

Huh? What?

Huh?

Luke 8:45

Talk about duh! Peter, one of the disciples, had no idea what Jesus is talking about. This is cool because how many times have you read the Bible and said to yourself, "Uh . . . what does that mean?" So if the disciples didn't get it and you don't get it, maybe you can be a disciple even when you don't get it every time.

[46]But Jesus said, "Someone touched me; I know that power has gone out from me."

[47]Then the woman, seeing that she could not go unnoticed, came trembling and fell at his feet. In the presence of all the people, she told why she had touched him and how she had been instantly healed. [48]Then he said to her, "Daughter, your faith has healed you. Go in peace."

[49]While Jesus was still speaking, someone came from the house of Jairus, the synagogue ruler. "Your daughter is dead," he said. "Don't bother the teacher any more."

[50]Hearing this, Jesus said to Jairus, "Don't be afraid; just believe, and she will be healed."

[51]When he arrived at the house of Jai-

[a]29 Greek *unclean* [b]43 Many manuscripts *years, and she had spent all she had on doctors*

rus, he did not let anyone go in with him except Peter, John and James, and the child's father and mother. [52]Meanwhile, all the people were wailing and mourning for her. "Stop wailing," Jesus said. "She is not dead but asleep."

[53]They laughed at him, knowing that she was dead. [54]But he took her by the hand and said, "My child, get up!" [55]Her spirit returned, and at once she stood up. Then Jesus told them to give her something to eat. [56]Her parents were astonished, but he ordered them not to tell anyone what had happened.

Jesus Sends Out the Twelve

9 When Jesus had called the Twelve together, he gave them power and authority to drive out all demons and to cure diseases, [2]and he sent them out to preach the kingdom of God and to heal the sick. [3]He told them: "Take nothing for the journey—no staff, no bag, no bread, no money, no extra tunic. [4]Whatever house you enter, stay there until you leave that town. [5]If people do not welcome you, shake the dust off your feet when you leave their town, as a testimony against them." [6]So they set out and went from village to village, preaching the gospel and healing people everywhere.

[7]Now Herod the tetrarch heard about all that was going on. And he was perplexed, because some were saying that John had been raised from the dead, [8]others that Elijah had appeared, and still others that one of the prophets of long ago had come back to life. [9]But Herod said, "I beheaded John. Who, then, is this I hear such things about?" And he tried to see him.

Jesus Feeds the Five Thousand

[10]When the apostles returned, they reported to Jesus what they had done. Then he took them with him and they withdrew by themselves to a town called Bethsaida, [11]but the crowds learned about it and followed him. He welcomed them and spoke to them about the kingdom of God, and healed those who needed healing.

[12]Late in the afternoon the Twelve came to him and said, "Send the crowd away so they can go to the surrounding villages and countryside and find food and lodging, because we are in a remote place here."

[13]He replied, "You give them something to eat."

They answered, "We have only five loaves of bread and two fish—unless we go and buy food for all this crowd." [14](About five thousand men were there.)

But he said to his disciples, "Have them sit down in groups of about fifty each." [15]The disciples did so, and everybody sat down. [16]Taking the five loaves and the two fish and looking up to heaven, he gave thanks and broke them. Then he gave them to the disciples to set before the people. [17]They all ate and were satisfied, and the disciples picked up twelve basketfuls of broken pieces that were left over.

Peter's Confession of Christ

[18]Once when Jesus was praying in private and his disciples were with him, he asked them, "Who do the crowds say I am?"

[19]They replied, "Some say John the Baptist; others say Elijah; and still others, that one of the prophets of long ago has come back to life."

[20]"But what about you?" he asked. "Who do you say I am?"

Peter answered, "The Christ[a] of God."

[21]Jesus strictly warned them not to tell this to anyone. [22]And he said, "The Son of Man must suffer many things and be rejected by the elders, chief priests and teachers of the law, and he must be killed and on the third day be raised to life."

[23]Then he said to them all: "If anyone would come after me, he must deny himself and take up his cross daily and follow me. [24]For whoever wants to save his life will lose it, but whoever loses his life for me will save it. [25]What good is it for a man to gain the whole world, and yet lose or forfeit his very self? [26]If anyone is ashamed of me and my words, the Son of Man will be ashamed of him when he

a20 Or Messiah

comes in his glory and in the glory of the Father and of the holy angels. ²⁷I tell you the truth, some who are standing here will not taste death before they see the kingdom of God."

The Transfiguration

²⁸About eight days after Jesus said this, he took Peter, John and James with him and went up onto a mountain to pray. ²⁹As he was praying, the appearance of his face changed, and his clothes became as bright as a flash of lightning. ³⁰Two men, Moses and Elijah, ³¹appeared in glorious splendor, talking with Jesus. They spoke about his departure, which he was about to bring to fulfillment at Jerusalem. ³²Peter and his companions were very sleepy, but when they became fully awake, they saw his glory and the two men standing with him. ³³As the men were leaving Jesus, Peter said to him, "Master, it is good for us to be here. Let us put up three shelters—one for you, one for Moses and one for Elijah." (He did not know what he was saying.)

³⁴While he was speaking, a cloud appeared and enveloped them, and they were afraid as they entered the cloud. ³⁵A voice came from the cloud, saying, "This is my Son, whom I have chosen; listen to him." ³⁶When the voice had spoken, they found that Jesus was alone. The disciples kept this to themselves, and told no one at that time what they had seen.

The Healing of a Boy With an Evil Spirit

³⁷The next day, when they came down from the mountain, a large crowd met him. ³⁸A man in the crowd called out, "Teacher, I beg you to look at my son, for he is my only child. ³⁹A spirit seizes him and he suddenly screams; it throws him into convulsions so that he foams at the mouth. It scarcely ever leaves him and is destroying him. ⁴⁰I begged your disciples to drive it out, but they could not."

⁴¹"O unbelieving and perverse generation," Jesus replied, "how long shall I stay with you and put up with you? Bring your son here."

⁴²Even while the boy was coming, the demon threw him to the ground in a convulsion. But Jesus rebuked the evil*ᵃ* spirit, healed the boy and gave him back to his father. ⁴³And they were all amazed at the greatness of God.

While everyone was marveling at all that Jesus did, he said to his disciples, ⁴⁴"Listen carefully to what I am about to tell you: The Son of Man is going to be betrayed into the hands of men." ⁴⁵But they did not understand what this meant. It was hidden from them, so that they did not grasp it, and they were afraid to ask him about it.

Who Will Be the Greatest?

⁴⁶An argument started among the disciples as to which of them would be the greatest. ⁴⁷Jesus, knowing their thoughts, took a little child and had him stand beside him. ⁴⁸Then he said to them, "Whoever welcomes this little child in my name welcomes me; and whoever welcomes me welcomes the one who sent me. For he who is least among you all— he is the greatest."

⁴⁹"Master," said John, "we saw a man driving out demons in your name and we tried to stop him, because he is not one of us."

⁵⁰"Do not stop him," Jesus said, "for whoever is not against you is for you."

Samaritan Opposition

⁵¹As the time approached for him to be taken up to heaven, Jesus resolutely set out for Jerusalem. ⁵²And he sent messengers on ahead, who went into a Samaritan village to get things ready for him; ⁵³but the people there did not welcome him, because he was heading for Jerusalem. ⁵⁴When the disciples James and John saw this, they asked, "Lord, do you want us to call fire down from heaven to destroy them*ᵇ*?" ⁵⁵But Jesus turned and rebuked them, ⁵⁶and*ᶜ* they went to another village.

ᵃ42 Greek *unclean* *ᵇ54* Some manuscripts *them, even as Elijah did* *ᶜ55,56* Some manuscripts *them. And he said, "You do not know what kind of spirit you are of, for the Son of Man did not come to destroy men's lives, but to save them."* *⁵⁶And*

The Cost of Following Jesus

⁵⁷As they were walking along the road, a man said to him, "I will follow you wherever you go."

⁵⁸Jesus replied, "Foxes have holes and birds of the air have nests, but the Son of Man has no place to lay his head."

⁵⁹He said to another man, "Follow me." But the man replied, "Lord, first let me go and bury my father."

⁶⁰Jesus said to him, "Let the dead bury their own dead, but you go and proclaim the kingdom of God."

⁶¹Still another said, "I will follow you, Lord; but first let me go back and say good-by to my family."

⁶²Jesus replied, "No one who puts his hand to the plow and looks back is fit for service in the kingdom of God."

Jesus Sends Out the Seventy-two

10 After this the Lord appointed seventy-two*ᵃ* others and sent them two by two ahead of him to every town and place where he was about to go. ²He told them, "The harvest is plentiful, but the workers are few. Ask the Lord of the harvest, therefore, to send out workers into his harvest field. ³Go! I am sending you out like lambs among wolves. ⁴Do not take a purse or bag or sandals; and do not greet anyone on the road.

⁵"When you enter a house, first say, 'Peace to this house.' ⁶If a man of peace is there, your peace will rest on him; if not, it will return to you. ⁷Stay in that house, eating and drinking whatever they give you, for the worker deserves his wages. Do not move around from house to house.

⁸"When you enter a town and are welcomed, eat what is set before you. ⁹Heal the sick who are there and tell them, 'The kingdom of God is near you.' ¹⁰But when you enter a town and are not welcomed, go into its streets and say, ¹¹'Even the dust of your town that sticks to our feet we wipe off against you. Yet be sure of this: The kingdom of God is near.' ¹²I tell you, it will be more bearable on that day for Sodom than for that town.

¹³"Woe to you, Korazin! Woe to you, Bethsaida! For if the miracles that were performed in you had been performed in Tyre and Sidon, they would have repented long ago, sitting in sackcloth and ashes. ¹⁴But it will be more bearable for Tyre and Sidon at the judgment than for you. ¹⁵And you, Capernaum, will you be lifted up to the skies? No, you will go down to the depths.*ᵇ*

¹⁶"He who listens to you listens to me; he who rejects you rejects me; but he who rejects me rejects him who sent me."

¹⁷The seventy-two returned with joy and said, "Lord, even the demons submit to us in your name."

¹⁸He replied, "I saw Satan fall like lightning from heaven. ¹⁹I have given you authority to trample on snakes and scorpions and to overcome all the power of the enemy; nothing will harm you. ²⁰However, do not rejoice that the spirits submit to you, but rejoice that your names are written in heaven."

²¹At that time Jesus, full of joy through the Holy Spirit, said, "I praise you, Father, Lord of heaven and earth, because you have hidden these things from the wise and learned, and revealed them to little children. Yes, Father, for this was your good pleasure.

²²"All things have been committed to me by my Father. No one knows who the Son is except the Father, and no one knows who the Father is except the Son and those to whom the Son chooses to reveal him."

²³Then he turned to his disciples and said privately, "Blessed are the eyes that see what you see. ²⁴For I tell you that many prophets and kings wanted to see what you see but did not see it, and to hear what you hear but did not hear it."

The Parable of the Good Samaritan

²⁵On one occasion an expert in the law stood up to test Jesus. "Teacher," he asked, "what must I do to inherit eternal life?"

²⁶"What is written in the Law?" he replied. "How do you read it?"

²⁷He answered: " 'Love the Lord your God with all your heart and with all your soul and with all your strength and with

all your mind'*a*; and, 'Love your neighbor as yourself.'*b*"

²⁸"You have answered correctly," Jesus replied. "Do this and you will live."

²⁹But he wanted to justify himself, so he asked Jesus, "And who is my neighbor?"

³⁰In reply Jesus said: "A man was going down from Jerusalem to Jericho, when he fell into the hands of robbers. They stripped him of his clothes, beat him and went away, leaving him half dead. ³¹A priest happened to be going down the same road, and when he saw the man, he passed by on the other side. ³²So too, a Levite, when he came to the place and saw him, passed by on the other side. ³³But a Samaritan, as he traveled, came where the man was; and when he saw him, he took pity on him. ³⁴He went to him and bandaged his wounds, pouring on oil and wine. Then he put the man on his own donkey, took him to an inn and took care of him. ³⁵The next day he took out two silver coins*c* and gave them

to the innkeeper. 'Look after him,' he said, 'and when I return, I will reimburse you for any extra expense you may have.'

³⁶"Which of these three do you think was a neighbor to the man who fell into the hands of robbers?"

³⁷The expert in the law replied, "The one who had mercy on him."

Jesus told him, "Go and do likewise."

At the Home of Martha and Mary

³⁸As Jesus and his disciples were on their way, he came to a village where a woman named Martha opened her home to him. ³⁹She had a sister called Mary, who sat at the Lord's feet listening to what he said. ⁴⁰But Martha was distracted by all the preparations that had to be made. She came to him and asked, "Lord, don't you care that my sister has left me to do the work by myself? Tell her to help me!"

a27 Deut. 6:5   *b27* Lev. 19:18   *c35* Greek *two denarii*

Thurs day

First Things First

Read Luke 10:38–42

Sometimes when my sister and I are supposed to do the dishes, she'll make some lame excuse to get out of it. I get so mad when she does that! I worry about whether or not she's doing her fair share of the work. So when I first looked at these verses, I totally agreed with Martha.

But really, this passage isn't about doing dishes or cooking or any other chores. It's about remembering what's really important in life, and that's spending time with Jesus. I might worry that my sister doesn't spend enough time in the kitchen, but I *know* I don't spend enough time reading my Bible or praying. So I guess until I get my own priorities in order I really can't complain too much about my sister's. Maybe if I keep spending more time with Jesus, I won't get so mad at little things like doing the dishes.

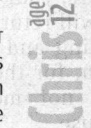

❶ How do you think Martha felt after Jesus spoke to her? Why did Jesus say what he did? What did he want Martha to understand?

❷ Make a list of things that distract you from God. What can you do to eliminate these distractions—or at least stay focused on God despite them?

❸ Ask God to help you focus on what's really important in life.

Turn to page 1240 for your next devotion.

⁴¹"Martha, Martha," the Lord answered, "you are worried and upset about many things, ⁴²but only one thing is needed.ᵃ Mary has chosen what is better, and it will not be taken away from her."

Jesus' Teaching on Prayer

11 One day Jesus was praying in a certain place. When he finished, one of his disciples said to him, "Lord, teach us to pray, just as John taught his disciples."

²He said to them, "When you pray, say:

" 'Father,ᵇ
hallowed be your name,
your kingdom come.ᶜ
³Give us each day our daily bread.
⁴Forgive us our sins,
for we also forgive everyone who
sins against us.ᵈ
And lead us not into temptation.ᵉ' "

⁵Then he said to them, "Suppose one of you has a friend, and he goes to him at midnight and says, 'Friend, lend me three loaves of bread, ⁶because a friend of mine on a journey has come to me, and I have nothing to set before him.'

⁷"Then the one inside answers, 'Don't bother me. The door is already locked, and my children are with me in bed. I can't get up and give you anything.' ⁸I tell you, though he will not get up and give him the bread because he is his friend, yet because of the man's boldness,ᶠ he will get up and give him as much as he needs.

⁹"So I say to you: Ask and it will be given to you; seek and you will find; knock and the door will be opened to you. ¹⁰For everyone who asks receives; he who seeks finds; and to him who knocks, the door will be opened.

¹¹"Which of you fathers, if your son asks forᵍ a fish, will give him a snake instead? ¹²Or if he asks for an egg, will give him a scorpion? ¹³If you then, though you are evil, know how to give good gifts to your children, how much more will your Father in heaven give the Holy Spirit to those who ask him!"

Jesus and Beelzebub

¹⁴Jesus was driving out a demon that was mute. When the demon left, the man who had been mute spoke, and the crowd was amazed. ¹⁵But some of them said, "By Beelzebub,ʰ the prince of demons, he is driving out demons." ¹⁶Others tested him by asking for a sign from heaven.

¹⁷Jesus knew their thoughts and said to them: "Any kingdom divided against itself will be ruined, and a house divided against itself will fall. ¹⁸If Satan is divided against himself, how can his kingdom stand? I say this because you claim that I drive out demons by Beelzebub. ¹⁹Now if I drive out demons by Beelzebub, by whom do your followers drive them out? So then, they will be your judges. ²⁰But if I drive out demons by the finger of God, then the kingdom of God has come to you.

²¹"When a strong man, fully armed, guards his own house, his possessions are safe. ²²But when someone stronger attacks and overpowers him, he takes away the armor in which the man trusted and divides up the spoils.

²³"He who is not with me is against me, and he who does not gather with me, scatters.

²⁴"When an evilⁱ spirit comes out of a man, it goes through arid places seeking rest and does not find it. Then it says, 'I will return to the house I left.' ²⁵When it arrives, it finds the house swept clean and put in order. ²⁶Then it goes and takes seven other spirits more wicked than itself, and they go in and live there. And the final condition of that man is worse than the first."

²⁷As Jesus was saying these things, a woman in the crowd called out, "Blessed is the mother who gave you birth and nursed you."

²⁸He replied, "Blessed rather are those who hear the word of God and obey it."

The Sign of Jonah

²⁹As the crowds increased, Jesus said, "This is a wicked generation. It asks for a

---

ᵃ42 Some manuscripts *but few things are needed—or only one*   ᵇ2 Some manuscripts *Our Father in heaven*   ᶜ2 Some manuscripts *come. May your will be done on earth as it is in heaven.*   ᵈ4 Greek *everyone who is indebted to us*   ᵉ4 Some manuscripts *temptation but deliver us from the evil one*   ᶠ8 Or *persistence*   ᵍ11 Some manuscripts *for bread, will give him a stone; or if he asks for*   ʰ15 Greek *Beezeboul* or *Beelzeboul*; also in verses 18 and 19   ⁱ24 Greek *unclean*

miraculous sign, but none will be given it except the sign of Jonah. ³⁰For as Jonah was a sign to the Ninevites, so also will the Son of Man be to this generation. ³¹The Queen of the South will rise at the judgment with the men of this generation and condemn them; for she came from the ends of the earth to listen to Solomon's wisdom, and now one*a* greater than Solomon is here. ³²The men of Nineveh will stand up at the judgment with this generation and condemn it; for they repented at the preaching of Jonah, and now one greater than Jonah is here.

The Lamp of the Body

³³"No one lights a lamp and puts it in a place where it will be hidden, or under a bowl. Instead he puts it on its stand, so that those who come in may see the light. ³⁴Your eye is the lamp of your body. When your eyes are good, your whole body also is full of light. But when they are bad, your body also is full of darkness. ³⁵See to it, then, that the light within you is not darkness. ³⁶Therefore, if your whole body is full of light, and no part of it dark, it will be completely lighted, as when the light of a lamp shines on you."

Six Woes

³⁷When Jesus had finished speaking, a Pharisee invited him to eat with him; so he went in and reclined at the table. ³⁸But the Pharisee, noticing that Jesus did not first wash before the meal, was surprised.

³⁹Then the Lord said to him, "Now then, you Pharisees clean the outside of the cup and dish, but inside you are full of greed and wickedness. ⁴⁰You foolish people! Did not the one who made the outside make the inside also? ⁴¹But give what is inside ˌthe dish˅*b* to the poor, and everything will be clean for you.

⁴²"Woe to you Pharisees, because you give God a tenth of your mint, rue and all other kinds of garden herbs, but you neglect justice and the love of God. You should have practiced the latter without leaving the former undone.

a31 Or something; also in verse 32   b41 Or what you have

Friday

Leave the Light On

Read Luke 11:33–36

I haven't always filled my mind with the greatest things. Sometimes I watch movies or TV shows I probably shouldn't. And there's so much more junk out there in magazines, on the Internet and on the radio that just isn't good for people who want to grow closer to God.

I need to be more careful about what I see and hear. Every day I have to make decisions about the kind of stuff I let into my life. And this passage can help me make decisions that fill me with light, not darkness.

Jesus is a shining light, and his love allows me to shine too. I don't want to let the darkness of the world block out God's light in me.

❶ Think of some things you read, watch or listen to that you know aren't good for you. How can you get rid of those things?

❷ The next time you feel tempted to watch something you shouldn't, call up a friend and shoot hoops or go to the mall instead.

❸ Ask God to help you get rid of the things that bring spiritual darkness into your life.

Turn to page 1244 for your next devotion.

⁴³"Woe to you Pharisees, because you love the most important seats in the synagogues and greetings in the marketplaces.

⁴⁴"Woe to you, because you are like unmarked graves, which men walk over without knowing it."

⁴⁵One of the experts in the law answered him, "Teacher, when you say these things, you insult us also."

⁴⁶Jesus replied, "And you experts in the law, woe to you, because you load people down with burdens they can hardly carry, and you yourselves will not lift one finger to help them.

⁴⁷"Woe to you, because you build tombs for the prophets, and it was your forefathers who killed them. ⁴⁸So you testify that you approve of what your forefathers did; they killed the prophets, and you build their tombs. ⁴⁹Because of this, God in his wisdom said, 'I will send them prophets and apostles, some of whom they will kill and others they will persecute.' ⁵⁰Therefore this generation will be held responsible for the blood of all the prophets that has been shed since the beginning of the world, ⁵¹from the blood of Abel to the blood of Zechariah, who was killed between the altar and the sanctuary. Yes, I tell you, this generation will be held responsible for it all.

⁵²"Woe to you experts in the law, because you have taken away the key to knowledge. You yourselves have not entered, and you have hindered those who were entering."

⁵³When Jesus left there, the Pharisees and the teachers of the law began to oppose him fiercely and to besiege him with questions, ⁵⁴waiting to catch him in something he might say.

Warnings and Encouragements

12 Meanwhile, when a crowd of many thousands had gathered, so that they were trampling on one another, Jesus began to speak first to his disciples, saying: "Be on your guard against the yeast of the Pharisees, which is hypocrisy. ²There is nothing concealed that will not be disclosed, or hidden that will not be made known. ³What you have said in the dark will be heard in the daylight, and what you have whispered in the ear

in the inner rooms will be proclaimed from the roofs.

⁴"I tell you, my friends, do not be afraid of those who kill the body and after that can do no more. ⁵But I will show you whom you should fear: Fear him who, after the killing of the body, has power to throw you into hell. Yes, I tell you, fear him. ⁶Are not five sparrows sold for two pennies[a]? Yet not one of them is forgotten by God. ⁷Indeed, the very hairs of your head are all numbered. Don't be afraid; you are worth more than many sparrows.

⁸"I tell you, whoever acknowledges me before men, the Son of Man will also acknowledge him before the angels of God. ⁹But he who disowns me before men will be disowned before the angels of God. ¹⁰And everyone who speaks a word against the Son of Man will be forgiven, but anyone who blasphemes against the Holy Spirit will not be forgiven.

¹¹"When you are brought before synagogues, rulers and authorities, do not worry about how you will defend yourselves or what you will say, ¹²for the Holy Spirit will teach you at that time what you should say."

The Parable of the Rich Fool

¹³Someone in the crowd said to him, "Teacher, tell my brother to divide the inheritance with me."

¹⁴Jesus replied, "Man, who appointed me a judge or an arbiter between you?" ¹⁵Then he said to them, "Watch out! Be on your guard against all kinds of greed; a man's life does not consist in the abundance of his possessions."

¹⁶And he told them this parable: "The ground of a certain rich man produced a good crop. ¹⁷He thought to himself, 'What shall I do? I have no place to store my crops.'

¹⁸"Then he said, 'This is what I'll do. I will tear down my barns and build bigger ones, and there I will store all my grain and my goods. ¹⁹And I'll say to myself, "You have plenty of good things laid up for many years. Take life easy; eat, drink and be merry." '

²⁰"But God said to him, 'You fool! This

---

[a] 6 Greek *two assaria*

very night your life will be demanded from you. Then who will get what you have prepared for yourself?'

²¹"This is how it will be with anyone who stores up things for himself but is not rich toward God."

Do Not Worry

²²Then Jesus said to his disciples: "Therefore I tell you, do not worry about your life, what you will eat; or about your body, what you will wear. ²³Life is more than food, and the body more than clothes. ²⁴Consider the ravens: They do not sow or reap, they have no storeroom or barn; yet God feeds them. And how much more valuable you are than birds! ²⁵Who of you by worrying can add a single hour to his life*? ²⁶Since you cannot do this very little thing, why do you worry about the rest?

²⁷"Consider how the lilies grow. They do not labor or spin. Yet I tell you, not even Solomon in all his splendor was dressed like one of these. ²⁸If that is how God clothes the grass of the field, which is here today, and tomorrow is thrown into the fire, how much more will he clothe you, O you of little faith! ²⁹And do not set your heart on what you will eat or drink; do not worry about it. ³⁰For the pagan world runs after all such things, and your Father knows that you need them. ³¹But seek his kingdom, and these things will be given to you as well.

³²"Do not be afraid, little flock, for your Father has been pleased to give you the kingdom. ³³Sell your possessions and give to the poor. Provide purses for yourselves that will not wear out, a treasure in heaven that will not be exhausted, where no thief comes near and no moth destroys. ³⁴For where your treasure is, there your heart will be also.

Watchfulness

³⁵"Be dressed ready for service and keep your lamps burning, ³⁶like men waiting for their master to return from a wedding banquet, so that when he comes and knocks they can immediately open the door for him. ³⁷It will be good for those servants whose master finds them watching when he comes. I tell you the truth, he will dress himself to serve, will

It's Not About Stuff

Luke 12:34

Wow! How many times does Jesus have to say this? He is telling his disciples, "Hey, guys, I really am telling you the truth. Life is not about getting a bunch of stuff. Life is about following me, loving me, seeking after me! You don't need to worry about the small stuff like everyone else worries about—a great-looking body, cars, boyfriends and girlfriends. I'm looking out for you—seriously."

have them recline at the table and will come and wait on them. ³⁸It will be good for those servants whose master finds them ready, even if he comes in the second or third watch of the night. ³⁹But understand this: If the owner of the house had known at what hour the thief was coming, he would not have let his house be broken into. ⁴⁰You also must be ready, because the Son of Man will come at an hour when you do not expect him."

⁴¹Peter asked, "Lord, are you telling this parable to us, or to everyone?"

⁴²The Lord answered, "Who then is the faithful and wise manager, whom the master puts in charge of his servants to give them their food allowance at the proper time? ⁴³It will be good for that servant whom the master finds doing so when he returns. ⁴⁴I tell you the truth, he will put him in charge of all his possessions. ⁴⁵But suppose the servant says to himself, 'My master is taking a long time in coming,' and he then begins to beat the menservants and maidservants and to eat and drink and get drunk. ⁴⁶The master of that servant will come on a day when he does not expect him and at an hour he is not aware of. He will cut him to pieces and assign him a place with the unbelievers.

⁴⁷"That servant who knows his master's will and does not get ready or does not do what his master wants will

25 Or single cubit to his height

be beaten with many blows. [48]But the one who does not know and does things deserving punishment will be beaten with few blows. From everyone who has been given much, much will be demanded; and from the one who has been entrusted with much, much more will be asked.

Not Peace but Division

[49]"I have come to bring fire on the earth, and how I wish it were already kindled! [50]But I have a baptism to undergo, and how distressed I am until it is completed! [51]Do you think I came to bring peace on earth? No, I tell you, but division. [52]From now on there will be five in one family divided against each other, three against two and two against three. [53]They will be divided, father against son and son against father, mother against daughter and daughter against mother, mother-in-law against daughter-in-law and daughter-in-law against mother-in-law."

Interpreting the Times

[54]He said to the crowd: "When you see a cloud rising in the west, immediately you say, 'It's going to rain,' and it does. [55]And when the south wind blows, you say, 'It's going to be hot,' and it is. [56]Hypocrites! You know how to interpret the appearance of the earth and the sky. How is it that you don't know how to interpret this present time?

[57]"Why don't you judge for yourselves what is right? [58]As you are going with your adversary to the magistrate, try hard to be reconciled to him on the way, or he may drag you off to the judge, and the judge turn you over to the officer, and the officer throw you into prison. [59]I tell you, you will not get out until you have paid the last penny.[a]"

Repent or Perish

13 Now there were some present at that time who told Jesus about the Galileans whose blood Pilate had mixed with their sacrifices. [2]Jesus answered, "Do you think that these Galileans were worse sinners than all the other Galileans because they suffered this way? [3]I tell you, no! But unless you repent, you too

will all perish. [4]Or those eighteen who died when the tower in Siloam fell on them—do you think they were more guilty than all the others living in Jerusalem? [5]I tell you, no! But unless you repent, you too will all perish."

[6]Then he told this parable: "A man had a fig tree, planted in his vineyard, and he went to look for fruit on it, but did not find any. [7]So he said to the man who took care of the vineyard, 'For three years now I've been coming to look for fruit on this fig tree and haven't found any. Cut it down! Why should it use up the soil?'

[8]" 'Sir,' the man replied, 'leave it alone for one more year, and I'll dig around it and fertilize it. [9]If it bears fruit next year, fine! If not, then cut it down.'"

A Crippled Woman Healed on the Sabbath

[10]On a Sabbath Jesus was teaching in one of the synagogues, [11]and a woman was there who had been crippled by a spirit for eighteen years. She was bent over and could not straighten up at all. [12]When Jesus saw her, he called her forward and said to her, "Woman, you are set free from your infirmity." [13]Then he put his hands on her, and immediately she straightened up and praised God.

[14]Indignant because Jesus had healed on the Sabbath, the synagogue ruler said to the people, "There are six days for work. So come and be healed on those days, not on the Sabbath."

[15]The Lord answered him, "You hypocrites! Doesn't each of you on the Sabbath untie his ox or donkey from the stall and lead it out to give it water? [16]Then should not this woman, a daughter of Abraham, whom Satan has kept bound for eighteen long years, be set free on the Sabbath day from what bound her?"

[17]When he said this, all his opponents were humiliated, but the people were delighted with all the wonderful things he was doing.

The Parables of the Mustard Seed and the Yeast

[18]Then Jesus asked, "What is the kingdom of God like? What shall I compare it

a 59 Greek *lepton*

to? ¹⁹It is like a mustard seed, which a man took and planted in his garden. It grew and became a tree, and the birds of the air perched in its branches."

²⁰Again he asked, "What shall I compare the kingdom of God to? ²¹It is like yeast that a woman took and mixed into a large amount^a of flour until it worked all through the dough."

The Narrow Door

²²Then Jesus went through the towns and villages, teaching as he made his way to Jerusalem. ²³Someone asked him, "Lord, are only a few people going to be saved?"

He said to them, ²⁴"Make every effort to enter through the narrow door, because many, I tell you, will try to enter and will not be able to. ²⁵Once the owner

of the house gets up and closes the door, you will stand outside knocking and pleading, 'Sir, open the door for us.'

"But he will answer, 'I don't know you or where you come from.'

²⁶Then you will say, 'We ate and drank with you, and you taught in our streets.'

²⁷"But he will reply, 'I don't know you or where you come from. Away from me, all you evildoers!'

²⁸"There will be weeping there, and gnashing of teeth, when you see Abraham, Isaac and Jacob and all the prophets in the kingdom of God, but you yourselves thrown out. ²⁹People will come from east and west and north and

^a21 Greek three satas (probably about 1/2 bushel or 22 liters)

Week end.

A Soft Heart
Read 2 Samuel 12:7–13 (page 361)

Way back on Monday, Matt talked about being judgmental. That attitude is a reflection of the "condition of your heart." Is it "soft" (ready to be used by God, quick to respond to sin) or "hard" (ignoring sin, living for yourself)? All your actions and attitudes say something about who you are and what your heart is like. But nothing reveals the condition of your heart more clearly than how you respond when someone (another person or the Holy Spirit) points out sin in your life.

When David got caught for doing some pretty rotten things, the condition of his heart quickly became known. David had two choices: 1) deny everything, curse Nathan and walk away, or 2) admit that he was wrong and ask for forgiveness. David chose the second option. You may want to read Psalm 51 (page 658) to see how David's heart was softened. David was sorry for the wrong that he had done, and he recognized that he had sinned against God. Why? Because he had a "soft" heart.

❶ What's the condition of your heart—or how do you respond—when God shows you something wrong you've done?

❷ Ask your parents about a time when you were little and did something wrong. How did you respond to their correction? Did you learn anything from that situation?

❸ Ask God to help reveal the condition of your heart when you do something wrong. Ask him to make your heart soft. Thank him for helping you see yourself as you really are.

Turn to page 1247 for your next devotion.

south, and will take their places at the feast in the kingdom of God. [30]Indeed there are those who are last who will be first, and first who will be last."

Jesus' Sorrow for Jerusalem

[31]At that time some Pharisees came to Jesus and said to him, "Leave this place and go somewhere else. Herod wants to kill you."

[32]He replied, "Go tell that fox, 'I will drive out demons and heal people today and tomorrow, and on the third day I will reach my goal.' [33]In any case, I must keep going today and tomorrow and the next day—for surely no prophet can die outside Jerusalem!

[34]"O Jerusalem, Jerusalem, you who kill the prophets and stone those sent to you, how often I have longed to gather your children together, as a hen gathers her chicks under her wings, but you were not willing! [35]Look, your house is left to you desolate. I tell you, you will not see me again until you say, 'Blessed is he who comes in the name of the Lord.'[a]

Jesus at a Pharisee's House

14 One Sabbath, when Jesus went to eat in the house of a prominent Pharisee, he was being carefully watched. [2]There in front of him was a man suffering from dropsy. [3]Jesus asked the Pharisees and experts in the law, "Is it lawful to heal on the Sabbath or not?" [4]But they remained silent. So taking hold of the man, he healed him and sent him away.

[5]Then he asked them, "If one of you has a son[b] or an ox that falls into a well on the Sabbath day, will you not immediately pull him out?" [6]And they had nothing to say.

[7]When he noticed how the guests picked the places of honor at the table, he told them this parable: [8]"When someone invites you to a wedding feast, do not take the place of honor, for a person more distinguished than you may have been invited. [9]If so, the host who invited both of you will come and say to you, 'Give this man your seat.' Then, humiliated, you will have to take the least important place. [10]But when you are invited, take the lowest place, so that when your host comes, he will say to you, 'Friend, move up to a better place.' Then you will be honored in the presence of all your fellow guests. [11]For everyone who exalts himself will be humbled, and he who humbles himself will be exalted."

[12]Then Jesus said to his host, "When you give a luncheon or dinner, do not invite your friends, your brothers or relatives, or your rich neighbors; if you do, they may invite you back and so you will be repaid. [13]But when you give a banquet, invite the poor, the crippled, the lame, the blind, [14]and you will be blessed. Although they cannot repay you, you will be repaid at the resurrection of the righteous."

The Parable of the Great Banquet

[15]When one of those at the table with him heard this, he said to Jesus, "Blessed is the man who will eat at the feast in the kingdom of God."

[16]Jesus replied: "A certain man was preparing a great banquet and invited many guests. [17]At the time of the banquet he sent his servant to tell those who had been invited, 'Come, for everything is now ready.'

[18]"But they all alike began to make excuses. The first said, 'I have just bought a field, and I must go and see it. Please excuse me.'

[19]"Another said, 'I have just bought five yoke of oxen, and I'm on my way to try them out. Please excuse me.'

[20]"Still another said, 'I just got married, so I can't come.'

[21]"The servant came back and reported this to his master. Then the owner of the house became angry and ordered his servant, 'Go out quickly into the streets and alleys of the town and bring in the poor, the crippled, the blind and the lame.'

[22]"'Sir,' the servant said, 'what you ordered has been done, but there is still room.'

[23]"Then the master told his servant, 'Go out to the roads and country lanes and make them come in, so that my house will be full. [24]I tell you, not one of those men who were invited will get a taste of my banquet.'"

---

*a*35 Psalm 118:26   *b*5 Some manuscripts *donkey*

Stinky Stories

The Bible is full of all kinds of stories: lovey-dovey romances, tough-guy fights, cool acts of courage and even . . . some stinky stories! Can you match up the references with the stinky descriptions?

Column 1

1. Dead fish all over the place
2. Huge piles of rotting, dead frogs
3. Dead flies in the perfume
4. Baking food over human excrement
5. Camping in a fish gut
6. Eatin pig food

Column 2

a. Exodus 8:13 14
b. Jonah 2:1
c. Ezekiel 4:12
d. Ecclesiastes 10:1
e. Exodus 7:18
f. Luke 15:16

answers: 1(e), 2(a), 3(d), 4(c), 5(b), 6(f)

The Cost of Being a Disciple

²⁵Large crowds were traveling with Jesus, and turning to them he said: ²⁶"If anyone comes to me and does not hate his father and mother, his wife and children, his brothers and sisters—yes, even his own life—he cannot be my disciple. ²⁷And anyone who does not carry his cross and follow me cannot be my disciple.

²⁸"Suppose one of you wants to build a tower. Will he not first sit down and estimate the cost to see if he has enough money to complete it? ²⁹For if he lays the foundation and is not able to finish it, everyone who sees it will ridicule him, ³⁰saying, 'This fellow began to build and was not able to finish.'

³¹"Or suppose a king is about to go to war against another king. Will he not first sit down and consider whether he is able with ten thousand men to oppose the one coming against him with twenty thousand? ³²If he is not able, he will send a delegation while the other is still a long way off and will ask for terms of peace. ³³In the same way, any of you who does not give up everything he has cannot be my disciple.

³⁴"Salt is good, but if it loses its saltiness, how can it be made salty again? ³⁵It is fit neither for the soil nor for the manure pile; it is thrown out.

"He who has ears to hear, let him hear."

The Parable of the Lost Sheep

15 Now the tax collectors and "sinners" were all gathering around to hear him. ²But the Pharisees and the teachers of the law muttered, "This man welcomes sinners and eats with them."

³Then Jesus told them this parable: ⁴"Suppose one of you has a hundred sheep and loses one of them. Does he not leave the ninety-nine in the open country and go after the lost sheep until he finds it? ⁵And when he finds it, he joyfully puts it on his shoulders ⁶and goes home. Then he calls his friends and neighbors together and says, 'Rejoice with me; I have found my lost sheep.' ⁷I tell you that in the same way there will be more rejoicing in heaven over one sinner who repents than over ninety-nine righteous persons who do not need to repent.

The Parable of the Lost Coin

⁸"Or suppose a woman has ten silver coins^a and loses one. Does she not light a lamp, sweep the house and search care-

^a8 Greek *ten drachmas,* each worth about a day's wages

fully until she finds it? ⁹And when she finds it, she calls her friends and neighbors together and says, 'Rejoice with me; I have found my lost coin.' ¹⁰In the same way, I tell you, there is rejoicing in the presence of the angels of God over one sinner who repents."

The Parable of the Lost Son

¹¹Jesus continued: "There was a man who had two sons. ¹²The younger one said to his father, 'Father, give me my share of the estate.' So he divided his property between them.

¹³"Not long after that, the younger son got together all he had, set off for a distant country and there squandered his wealth in wild living. ¹⁴After he had spent everything, there was a severe famine in that whole country, and he began to be in need. ¹⁵So he went and hired himself out to a citizen of that country, who sent him to his fields to feed pigs. ¹⁶He longed to fill his stomach with the pods that the pigs were eating, but no one gave him anything.

¹⁷"When he came to his senses, he said, 'How many of my father's hired men have food to spare, and here I am starving to death! ¹⁸I will set out and go back to my father and say to him: Father, I have sinned against heaven and against you. ¹⁹I am no longer worthy to be called your son; make me like one of your hired men.' ²⁰So he got up and went to his father.

"But while he was still a long way off, his father saw him and was filled

---

Monday

Lost and Found

Read Luke 15:3–7

I think there's a time in everyone's life when they feel far away from God. Bad things happen, or you just start to feel like God doesn't care about you. I know I've felt that way sometimes. But for me, something always happens that lets me know God hasn't forgotten me. Maybe I read a verse in the Bible that really helps me feel better. Or maybe God sends me a friend who helps me get through a difficult time in my life. God won't forget you either. God loves us and he'll never leave us.

When we feel lost, it's because we've moved away from God, not the other way around. It's just like the sheep in this passage. The shepherd leads the whole flock together, but sometimes a few of the sheep wander off. Then the shepherd goes out to find the lost sheep, just like God goes out to get us when we move away from him.

God cares about each one of us. He'll never leave us behind or give up on us. He'll never forget us, because each of us matters to him. And when he finds us again, no one is happier than God.

Megan, age 14

What about You?

❶ Think about a time you felt separated from God. How did God seek you out and bring you back?

❷ Look at a map of your state. Now find where you live by following the expressways, highways and main roads. It's easy to find your way because you know your surroundings. But what if you didn't? Think of the Bible as a map that God gives us. It helps you know where to go—even if you've never been there before.

❸ Thank God for always looking for you, even when you wander away from him.

Turn to page 1250 for your next devotion.

with compassion for him; he ran to his son, threw his arms around him and kissed him.

²¹"The son said to him, 'Father, I have sinned against heaven and against you. I am no longer worthy to be called your son.ᵃ'

²²"But the father said to his servants, 'Quick! Bring the best robe and put it on him. Put a ring on his finger and sandals on his feet. ²³Bring the fattened calf and kill it. Let's have a feast and celebrate. ²⁴For this son of mine was dead and is alive again; he was lost and is found.' So they began to celebrate.

²⁵"Meanwhile, the older son was in the field. When he came near the house, he heard music and dancing. ²⁶So he called one of the servants and asked him what was going on. ²⁷'Your brother has come,' he replied, 'and your father has killed the fattened calf because he has him back safe and sound.'

²⁸"The older brother became angry and refused to go in. So his father went out and pleaded with him. ²⁹But he answered his father, 'Look! All these years I've been slaving for you and never disobeyed your orders. Yet you never gave me even a young goat so I could celebrate with my friends. ³⁰But when this son of yours who has squandered your property with prostitutes comes home, you kill the fattened calf for him!'

³¹" 'My son,' the father said, 'you are always with me, and everything I have is yours. ³²But we had to celebrate and be glad, because this brother of yours was dead and is alive again; he was lost and is found.' "

The Parable of the Shrewd Manager

16 Jesus told his disciples: "There was a rich man whose manager was accused of wasting his possessions. ²So he called him in and asked him, 'What is this I hear about you? Give an account of your management, because you cannot be manager any longer.'

³"The manager said to himself, 'What shall I do now? My master is taking away my job. I'm not strong enough to dig, and I'm ashamed to beg— ⁴I know what I'll do so that, when I lose my job here, people will welcome me into their houses.'

⁵"So he called in each one of his master's debtors. He asked the first, 'How much do you owe my master?'

⁶" 'Eight hundred gallonsᵇ of olive oil,' he replied.

"The manager told him, 'Take your bill, sit down quickly, and make it four hundred.'

⁷"Then he asked the second, 'And how much do you owe?'

" 'A thousand bushelsᶜ of wheat,' he replied.

"He told him, 'Take your bill and make it eight hundred.'

⁸"The master commended the dishonest manager because he had acted shrewdly. For the people of this world are more shrewd in dealing with their own kind than are the people of the light. ⁹I tell you, use worldly wealth to gain friends for yourselves, so that when it is gone, you will be welcomed into eternal dwellings.

¹⁰"Whoever can be trusted with very little can also be trusted with much, and whoever is dishonest with very little will also be dishonest with much. ¹¹So if you have not been trustworthy in handling worldly wealth, who will trust you with true riches? ¹²And if you have not been trustworthy with someone else's property, who will give you property of your own?

¹³"No servant can serve two masters. Either he will hate the one and love the other, or he will be devoted to the one and despise the other. You cannot serve both God and Money."

¹⁴The Pharisees, who loved money, heard all this and were sneering at Jesus. ¹⁵He said to them, "You are the ones who justify yourselves in the eyes of men, but God knows your hearts. What is highly valued among men is detestable in God's sight.

Additional Teachings

¹⁶"The Law and the Prophets were proclaimed until John. Since that time, the good news of the kingdom of God is being preached, and everyone is forcing his

---

ᵃ21 Some early manuscripts *son. Make me like one of your hired men.*   ᵇ6 Greek *one hundred batous* (probably about 3 kiloliters)   ᶜ7 Greek *one hundred korous* (probably about 35 kiloliters)

way into it. [17]It is easier for heaven and earth to disappear than for the least stroke of a pen to drop out of the Law.

[18]"Anyone who divorces his wife and marries another woman commits adultery, and the man who marries a divorced woman commits adultery.

The Rich Man and Lazarus

[19]"There was a rich man who was dressed in purple and fine linen and lived in luxury every day. [20]At his gate was laid a beggar named Lazarus, covered with sores [21]and longing to eat what fell from the rich man's table. Even the dogs came and licked his sores.

[22]"The time came when the beggar died and the angels carried him to Abraham's side. The rich man also died and was buried. [23]In hell,[a] where he was in torment, he looked up and saw Abraham far away, with Lazarus by his side. [24]So he called to him, 'Father Abraham, have pity on me and send Lazarus to dip the tip of his finger in water and cool my tongue, because I am in agony in this fire.'

[25]"But Abraham replied, 'Son, remember that in your lifetime you received your good things, while Lazarus received bad things, but now he is comforted here and you are in agony. [26]And besides all this, between us and you a great chasm has been fixed, so that those who want to go from here to you cannot, nor can anyone cross over from there to us.'

[27]"He answered, 'Then I beg you, father, send Lazarus to my father's house, [28]for I have five brothers. Let him warn them, so that they will not also come to this place of torment.'

[29]"Abraham replied, 'They have Moses and the Prophets; let them listen to them.'

[30]" 'No, father Abraham,' he said, 'but if someone from the dead goes to them, they will repent.'

[31]"He said to him, 'If they do not listen to Moses and the Prophets, they will not be convinced even if someone rises from the dead.' "

Sin, Faith, Duty

17 Jesus said to his disciples: "Things that cause people to sin are bound

to come, but woe to that person through whom they come. [2]It would be better for him to be thrown into the sea with a millstone tied around his neck than for him to cause one of these little ones to sin. [3]So watch yourselves.

"If your brother sins, rebuke him, and if he repents, forgive him. [4]If he sins against you seven times in a day, and seven times comes back to you and says, 'I repent,' forgive him."

[5]The apostles said to the Lord, "Increase our faith!"

[6]He replied, "If you have faith as small as a mustard seed, you can say to this mulberry tree, 'Be uprooted and planted in the sea,' and it will obey you.

[7]"Suppose one of you had a servant plowing or looking after the sheep. Would he say to the servant when he comes in from the field, 'Come along now and sit down to eat'? [8]Would he not rather say, 'Prepare my supper, get yourself ready and wait on me while I eat and drink; after that you may eat and drink'? [9]Would he thank the servant because he did what he was told to do? [10]So you also, when you have done everything you were told to do, should say, 'We are unworthy servants; we have only done our duty.' "

Ten Healed of Leprosy

[11]Now on his way to Jerusalem, Jesus traveled along the border between Samaria and Galilee. [12]As he was going into a village, ten men who had leprosy[b] met him. They stood at a distance [13]and called out in a loud voice, "Jesus, Master, have pity on us!"

[14]When he saw them, he said, "Go, show yourselves to the priests." And as they went, they were cleansed.

[15]One of them, when he saw he was healed, came back, praising God in a loud voice. [16]He threw himself at Jesus' feet and thanked him—and he was a Samaritan.

[17]Jesus asked, "Were not all ten cleansed? Where are the other nine? [18]Was no one found to return and give

---

[a]23 Greek *Hades*   [b]12 The Greek word was used for various diseases affecting the skin—not necessarily leprosy.

praise to God except this foreigner?" [19]Then he said to him, "Rise and go; your faith has made you well."

The Coming of the Kingdom of God

[20]Once, having been asked by the Pharisees when the kingdom of God would come, Jesus replied, "The kingdom of God does not come with your careful observation, [21]nor will people say, 'Here it is,' or 'There it is,' because the kingdom of God is within[a] you."

[22]Then he said to his disciples, "The time is coming when you will long to see one of the days of the Son of Man, but you will not see it. [23]Men will tell you, 'There he is!' or 'Here he is!' Do not go running off after them. [24]For the Son of Man in his day[b] will be like the lightning, which flashes and lights up the sky from one end to the other. [25]But first he must suffer many things and be rejected by this generation.

[26]"Just as it was in the days of Noah, so also will it be in the days of the Son of Man. [27]People were eating, drinking, marrying and being given in marriage up to the day Noah entered the ark. Then the flood came and destroyed them all.

[28]"It was the same in the days of Lot. People were eating and drinking, buying and selling, planting and building. [29]But the day Lot left Sodom, fire and sulfur rained down from heaven and destroyed them all.

[30]"It will be just like this on the day the Son of Man is revealed. [31]On that day no one who is on the roof of his house, with his goods inside, should go down to get them. Likewise, no one in the field should go back for anything. [32]Remember Lot's wife! [33]Whoever tries to keep his life will lose it, and whoever loses his life will preserve it. [34]I tell you, on that night two people will be in one

[a]21 Or *among*   [b]24 Some manuscripts do not have *in his day.*

Tuesday

Just Say "Thanks!"

Read Luke 17:11–19

Last year I went to Mexico on a short-term missions trip with my youth group. I really didn't like the housing conditions or the food we ate, and I complained a lot. But reading the story of the 10 lepers tells me that I need to always be thankful to God.

In the story, the only person who came back to thank Jesus was a Samaritan, a hated foreigner. He must have been nervous about talking to Jesus. He could have made excuses for not saying thank you. But he didn't. I was a foreigner when I was in Mexico. I was out of my comfort zone, and I didn't like it. But I should have been thankful that I had any housing and food at all. And I should have been thankful that God gave me the opportunity to serve other people and tell them about Jesus.

God has done so many things for me. I want to do a better job of thanking him and praising him, no matter what happens.

Jesse age 14

❶ What are some of the things you're thankful for? When was the last time you really told God how grateful you are for all he's done for you?

❷ Keep a "thanksgiving" journal for one week. Each night before you go to bed make a list of the things you're thankful for.

❸ Before you go to bed tonight, thank God for the things you wrote in your journal.

Turn to page 1253 for your next devotion.

bed; one will be taken and the other left. ³⁵Two women will be grinding grain together; one will be taken and the other left.ᵃˮ

³⁷"Where, Lord?" they asked.

He replied, "Where there is a dead body, there the vultures will gather."

The Parable of the Persistent Widow

18 Then Jesus told his disciples a parable to show them that they should always pray and not give up. ²He said: "In a certain town there was a judge who neither feared God nor cared about men. ³And there was a widow in that town who kept coming to him with the plea, 'Grant me justice against my adversary.'

⁴"For some time he refused. But finally he said to himself, 'Even though I don't fear God or care about men, ⁵yet because this widow keeps bothering me, I will see that she gets justice, so that she won't eventually wear me out with her coming!' "

⁶And the Lord said, "Listen to what the unjust judge says. ⁷And will not God bring about justice for his chosen ones, who cry out to him day and night? Will he keep putting them off? ⁸I tell you, he will see that they get justice, and quickly. However, when the Son of Man comes, will he find faith on the earth?"

The Parable of the Pharisee and the Tax Collector

⁹To some who were confident of their own righteousness and looked down on everybody else, Jesus told this parable: ¹⁰"Two men went up to the temple to pray, one a Pharisee and the other a tax collector. ¹¹The Pharisee stood up and prayed aboutᵇ himself: 'God, I thank you that I am not like other men—robbers, evildoers, adulterers—or even like this tax collector. ¹²I fast twice a week and give a tenth of all I get.'

¹³"But the tax collector stood at a distance. He would not even look up to heaven, but beat his breast and said, 'God, have mercy on me, a sinner.'

¹⁴"I tell you that this man, rather than the other, went home justified before God. For everyone who exalts himself will be humbled, and he who humbles himself will be exalted."

The Little Children and Jesus

¹⁵People were also bringing babies to Jesus to have him touch them. When the disciples saw this, they rebuked them. ¹⁶But Jesus called the children to him and said, "Let the little children come to me, and do not hinder them, for the kingdom of God belongs to such as these. ¹⁷I tell you the truth, anyone who will not receive the kingdom of God like a little child will never enter it."

The Rich Ruler

¹⁸A certain ruler asked him, "Good teacher, what must I do to inherit eternal life?"

¹⁹"Why do you call me good?" Jesus answered. "No one is good—except God alone. ²⁰You know the commandments: 'Do not commit adultery, do not murder, do not steal, do not give false testimony, honor your father and mother.'ᶜ "

²¹"All these I have kept since I was a boy," he said.

²²When Jesus heard this, he said to him, "You still lack one thing. Sell everything you have and give to the poor, and you will have treasure in heaven. Then come, follow me."

²³When he heard this, he became very sad, because he was a man of great wealth. ²⁴Jesus looked at him and said, "How hard it is for the rich to enter the kingdom of God! ²⁵Indeed, it is easier for a camel to go through the eye of a needle than for a rich man to enter the kingdom of God."

²⁶Those who heard this asked, "Who then can be saved?"

²⁷Jesus replied, "What is impossible with men is possible with God."

²⁸Peter said to him, "We have left all we had to follow you!"

²⁹"I tell you the truth," Jesus said to them, "no one who has left home or wife or brothers or parents or children for the sake of the kingdom of God ³⁰will fail to receive many times as much in this age and, in the age to come, eternal life."

ᵃ35 Some manuscripts *left.* ³⁶*Two men will be in the field; one will be taken and the other left.*   ᵇ11 Or *to*   ᶜ20 Exodus 20:12-16; Deut. 5:16-20

Jesus Again Predicts His Death

³¹Jesus took the Twelve aside and told them, "We are going up to Jerusalem, and everything that is written by the prophets about the Son of Man will be fulfilled. ³²He will be handed over to the Gentiles. They will mock him, insult him, spit on him, flog him and kill him. ³³On the third day he will rise again."

³⁴The disciples did not understand any of this. Its meaning was hidden from them, and they did not know what he was talking about.

A Blind Beggar Receives His Sight

³⁵As Jesus approached Jericho, a blind man was sitting by the roadside begging. ³⁶When he heard the crowd going by, he asked what was happening. ³⁷They told him, "Jesus of Nazareth is passing by."

³⁸He called out, "Jesus, Son of David, have mercy on me!"

³⁹Those who led the way rebuked him and told him to be quiet, but he shouted all the more, "Son of David, have mercy on me!"

⁴⁰Jesus stopped and ordered the man to be brought to him. When he came near, Jesus asked him, ⁴¹"What do you want me to do for you?"

"Lord, I want to see," he replied.

⁴²Jesus said to him, "Receive your sight; your faith has healed you." ⁴³Immediately he received his sight and followed Jesus, praising God. When all the people saw it, they also praised God.

Zacchaeus the Tax Collector

19 Jesus entered Jericho and was passing through. ²A man was there by the name of Zacchaeus; he was a chief tax collector and was wealthy. ³He wanted to see who Jesus was, but being a short man he could not, because of the crowd. ⁴So he ran ahead and climbed a sycamore-fig tree to see him, since Jesus was coming that way.

⁵When Jesus reached the spot, he looked up and said to him, "Zacchaeus, come down immediately. I must stay at your house today." ⁶So he came down at once and welcomed him gladly.

⁷All the people saw this and began to mutter, "He has gone to be the guest of a 'sinner.'"

⁸But Zacchaeus stood up and said to the Lord, "Look, Lord! Here and now I give half of my possessions to the poor, and if I have cheated anybody out of anything, I will pay back four times the amount."

⁹Jesus said to him, "Today salvation has come to this house, because this man, too, is a son of Abraham. ¹⁰For the Son of Man came to seek and to save what was lost."

The Parable of the Ten Minas

¹¹While they were listening to this, he went on to tell them a parable, because he was near Jerusalem and the people thought that the kingdom of God was going to appear at once. ¹²He said: "A man of noble birth went to a distant country to have himself appointed king and then to return. ¹³So he called ten of his servants and gave them ten minas.ª 'Put this money to work,' he said, 'until I come back.'

¹⁴"But his subjects hated him and sent a delegation after him to say, 'We don't want this man to be our king.'

¹⁵"He was made king, however, and returned home. Then he sent for the servants to whom he had given the money, in order to find out what they had gained with it.

¹⁶"The first one came and said, 'Sir, your mina has earned ten more.'

¹⁷"'Well done, my good servant!' his master replied. 'Because you have been trustworthy in a very small matter, take charge of ten cities.'

¹⁸"The second came and said, 'Sir, your mina has earned five more.'

¹⁹"His master answered, 'You take charge of five cities.'

²⁰"Then another servant came and said, 'Sir, here is your mina; I have kept it laid away in a piece of cloth. ²¹I was afraid of you, because you are a hard man. You take out what you did not put in and reap what you did not sow.'

²²"His master replied, 'I will judge you by your own words, you wicked servant! You knew, did you, that I am a hard man,

---

ª13 A mina was about three months' wages.

taking out what I did not put in, and reaping what I did not sow? ²³Why then didn't you put my money on deposit, so that when I came back, I could have collected it with interest?'

²⁴"Then he said to those standing by, 'Take his mina away from him and give it to the one who has ten minas.'

²⁵" 'Sir,' they said, 'he already has ten!'

²⁶"He replied, 'I tell you that to everyone who has, more will be given, but as for the one who has nothing, even what he has will be taken away. ²⁷But those enemies of mine who did not want me to be king over them—bring them here and kill them in front of me.'"

The Triumphal Entry

²⁸After Jesus had said this, he went on ahead, going up to Jerusalem. ²⁹As he approached Bethphage and Bethany at the hill called the Mount of Olives, he sent two of his disciples, saying to them, ³⁰"Go to the village ahead of you, and as you enter it, you will find a colt tied there, which no one has ever ridden. Untie it and bring it here. ³¹If anyone asks you, 'Why are you untying it?' tell him, 'The Lord needs it.'"

³²Those who were sent ahead went and found it just as he had told them. ³³As they were untying the colt, its owners asked them, "Why are you untying the colt?"

³⁴They replied, "The Lord needs it."

³⁵They brought it to Jesus, threw their cloaks on the colt and put Jesus on it. ³⁶As he went along, people spread their cloaks on the road.

³⁷When he came near the place where the road goes down the Mount of Olives, the whole crowd of disciples began joyfully to praise God in loud voices for all the miracles they had seen:

³⁸"Blessed is the king who comes in the name of the Lord!"ᵃ

ᵃ*38* Psalm 118:26

Wednesday

A Big Change for a Little Guy

Read Luke 19:1-10

This passage helped me when I got in a fight with my sister. I was upset with her because she wouldn't listen to me. So I hit her. Naturally, she started to cry. That's when I realized what I'd done and how mean I was to her. I went to my room and wrote her a note to apologize. I gave it to her, and thankfully she forgave me.

It's pretty easy to ignore our mistakes and pretend nothing happened. But when we hurt someone or cause a problem, we need to do what we can to fix it. Zacchaeus had never been a great guy, but he figured out what he'd done wrong and what he needed to do to make it right. His heart was changed, and—right then and there—Zacchaeus was saved.

Kelli age 13

What about You?

❶ Imagine that Zacchaeus recognized his sins but never made an attempt to pay back the people he'd cheated. What kind of example would he have been? Why was it so important for Zacchaeus to act on his new faith?

❷ Write a note to someone you've hurt. Tell them what you did wrong, apologize and ask for their forgiveness. Then really work at changing whatever it was that caused the problem, like anger, jealousy, pride or whatever.

❸ Ask God to help you fix the sin in your life.

Turn to page 1256 for your next devotion.

"Peace in heaven and glory in the highest!"

[39]Some of the Pharisees in the crowd said to Jesus, "Teacher, rebuke your disciples!"

[40]"I tell you," he replied, "if they keep quiet, the stones will cry out."

[41]As he approached Jerusalem and saw the city, he wept over it [42]and said, "If you, even you, had only known on this day what would bring you peace—but now it is hidden from your eyes. [43]The days will come upon you when your enemies will build an embankment against you and encircle you and hem you in on every side. [44]They will dash you to the ground, you and the children within your walls. They will not leave one stone on another, because you did not recognize the time of God's coming to you."

Jesus at the Temple

[45]Then he entered the temple area and began driving out those who were selling. [46]"It is written," he said to them, " 'My house will be a house of prayer'[a]; but you have made it 'a den of robbers.'[b]"

[47]Every day he was teaching at the temple. But the chief priests, the teachers of the law and the leaders among the people were trying to kill him. [48]Yet they could not find any way to do it, because all the people hung on his words.

The Authority of Jesus Questioned

20 One day as he was teaching the people in the temple courts and preaching the gospel, the chief priests and the teachers of the law, together with the elders, came up to him. [2]"Tell us by what authority you are doing these things," they said. "Who gave you this authority?"

[3]He replied, "I will also ask you a question. Tell me, [4]John's baptism—was it from heaven, or from men?"

[5]They discussed it among themselves and said, "If we say, 'From heaven,' he will ask, 'Why didn't you believe him?' [6]But if we say, 'From men,' all the people will stone us, because they are persuaded that John was a prophet."

[7]So they answered, "We don't know where it was from."

[8]Jesus said, "Neither will I tell you by what authority I am doing these things."

The Parable of the Tenants

[9]He went on to tell the people this parable: "A man planted a vineyard, rented it to some farmers and went away for a long time. [10]At harvest time he sent a servant to the tenants so they would give him some of the fruit of the vineyard. But the tenants beat him and sent him away empty-handed. [11]He sent another servant, but that one also they beat and treated shamefully and sent away empty-handed. [12]He sent still a third, and they wounded him and threw him out.

[13]"Then the owner of the vineyard said, 'What shall I do? I will send my son, whom I love; perhaps they will respect him.'

[14]"But when the tenants saw him, they talked the matter over. 'This is the heir,' they said. 'Let's kill him, and the inheritance will be ours.' [15]So they threw him out of the vineyard and killed him.

"What then will the owner of the vineyard do to them? [16]He will come and kill those tenants and give the vineyard to others."

When the people heard this, they said, "May this never be!"

[17]Jesus looked directly at them and asked, "Then what is the meaning of that which is written:

" 'The stone the builders rejected
   has become the capstone[c],[d]'?

[18]Everyone who falls on that stone will be broken to pieces, but he on whom it falls will be crushed."

[19]The teachers of the law and the chief priests looked for a way to arrest him immediately, because they knew he had spoken this parable against them. But they were afraid of the people.

Paying Taxes to Caesar

[20]Keeping a close watch on him, they sent spies, who pretended to be honest. They hoped to catch Jesus in something he said so that they might hand him over

---

[a]46 Isaiah 56:7   [b]46 Jer. 7:11   [c]17 Or cornerstone
[d]17 Psalm 118:22

to the power and authority of the governor. [21]So the spies questioned him: "Teacher, we know that you speak and teach what is right, and that you do not show partiality but teach the way of God in accordance with the truth. [22]Is it right for us to pay taxes to Caesar or not?"

[23]He saw through their duplicity and said to them, [24]"Show me a denarius. Whose portrait and inscription are on it?"

[25]"Caesar's," they replied.

He said to them, "Then give to Caesar what is Caesar's, and to God what is God's."

[26]They were unable to trap him in what he had said there in public. And astonished by his answer, they became silent.

The Resurrection and Marriage

[27]Some of the Sadducees, who say there is no resurrection, came to Jesus with a question. [28]"Teacher," they said, "Moses wrote for us that if a man's brother dies and leaves a wife but no children, the man must marry the widow and have children for his brother. [29]Now there were seven brothers. The first one married a woman and died childless. [30]The second [31]and then the third married her, and in the same way the seven died, leaving no children. [32]Finally, the woman died too. [33]Now then, at the resurrection whose wife will she be, since the seven were married to her?"

[34]Jesus replied, "The people of this age marry and are given in marriage. [35]But those who are considered worthy of taking part in that age and in the resurrection from the dead will neither marry nor be given in marriage, [36]and they can no longer die; for they are like the angels. They are God's children, since they are children of the resurrection. [37]But in the account of the bush, even Moses showed that the dead rise, for he calls the Lord 'the God of Abraham, and the God of Isaac, and the God of Jacob.'[a] [38]He is not the God of the dead, but of the living, for to him all are alive."

[39]Some of the teachers of the law responded, "Well said, teacher!" [40]And no one dared to ask him any more questions.

Whose Son Is the Christ?

[41]Then Jesus said to them, "How is it that they say the Christ[b] is the Son of David? [42]David himself declares in the Book of Psalms:

" 'The Lord said to my Lord:
"Sit at my right hand
[43]until I make your enemies
a footstool for your feet." '[c]

[44]David calls him 'Lord.' How then can he be his son?"

[45]While all the people were listening, Jesus said to his disciples, [46]"Beware of the teachers of the law. They like to walk around in flowing robes and love to be greeted in the marketplaces and have the most important seats in the synagogues and the places of honor at banquets. [47]They devour widows' houses and for a show make lengthy prayers. Such men will be punished most severely."

The Widow's Offering

21 As he looked up, Jesus saw the rich putting their gifts into the temple treasury. [2]He also saw a poor widow put in two very small copper coins.[d] [3]"I tell you the truth," he said, "this poor widow has put in more than all the others. [4]All these people gave their gifts out of their wealth; but she out of her poverty put in all she had to live on."

Signs of the End of the Age

[5]Some of his disciples were remarking about how the temple was adorned with beautiful stones and with gifts dedicated to God. But Jesus said, [6]"As for what you see here, the time will come when not one stone will be left on another; every one of them will be thrown down."

[7]"Teacher," they asked, "when will these things happen? And what will be the sign that they are about to take place?"

[8]He replied: "Watch out that you are not deceived. For many will come in my name, claiming, 'I am he,' and, 'The time is near.' Do not follow them. [9]When you hear of wars and revolutions, do not be

---

[a]37 Exodus 3:6   [b]41 Or *Messiah*   [c]43 Psalm 110:1
[d]2 Greek *two lepta*

frightened. These things must happen first, but the end will not come right away."

¹⁰Then he said to them: "Nation will rise against nation, and kingdom against kingdom. ¹¹There will be great earthquakes, famines and pestilences in various places, and fearful events and great signs from heaven.

¹²"But before all this, they will lay hands on you and persecute you. They will deliver you to synagogues and prisons, and you will be brought before kings and governors, and all on account of my name. ¹³This will result in your being witnesses to them. ¹⁴But make up your mind not to worry beforehand how you will defend yourselves. ¹⁵For I will give you words and wisdom that none of your adversaries will be able to resist or contradict. ¹⁶You will be betrayed even by parents, brothers, relatives and friends, and they will put some of you to death. ¹⁷All men will hate you because of me. ¹⁸But not a hair of your head will

perish. ¹⁹By standing firm you will gain life.

²⁰"When you see Jerusalem being surrounded by armies, you will know that its desolation is near. ²¹Then let those who are in Judea flee to the mountains, let those in the city get out, and let those in the country not enter the city. ²²For this is the time of punishment in fulfillment of all that has been written. ²³How dreadful it will be in those days for pregnant women and nursing mothers! There will be great distress in the land and wrath against this people. ²⁴They will fall by the sword and will be taken as prisoners to all the nations. Jerusalem will be trampled on by the Gentiles until the times of the Gentiles are fulfilled.

²⁵"There will be signs in the sun, moon and stars. On the earth, nations will be in anguish and perplexity at the roaring and tossing of the sea. ²⁶Men will faint from terror, apprehensive of what is coming on the world, for the heavenly bodies will be shaken. ²⁷At that time they

---

Thursday

Giving What You've Got

Read Luke 21:1–4

When I was about 6, I had a stuffed animal I really loved. My mom heard about an orphanage where the kids had very few toys, so she asked me to share some of mine. I didn't want to include my favorite stuffed animal, but my mom told me that it could make some little boy or girl very happy. It was hard, but I gave away my favorite animal.

I know that's not quite the same as giving God everything you have, but when you're 6, your toys mean a lot to you—at least, mine did. But it didn't take long for me to realize I had plenty of other things in my life that made me happy.

God has given me so much. I need to always give back as much as I can, whether it's my time, my effort—or my stuffed animals.

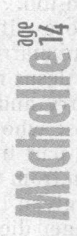

Michelle age 14

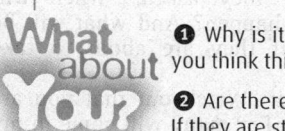

❶ Why is it hard to give away things that mean a lot to you? Why do you think this kind of giving is important to God?

❷ Are there any toys that are down in your basement collecting dust? If they are still in halfway decent condition, think about donating them to a local charity.

❸ Ask God to help you share the gifts he's given you.

Turn to page 1259 for your next devotion.

will see the Son of Man coming in a cloud with power and great glory. ²⁸When these things begin to take place, stand up and lift up your heads, because your redemption is drawing near."

²⁹He told them this parable: "Look at the fig tree and all the trees. ³⁰When they sprout leaves, you can see for yourselves and know that summer is near. ³¹Even so, when you see these things happening, you know that the kingdom of God is near.

³²"I tell you the truth, this generation*ᵃ* will certainly not pass away until all these things have happened. ³³Heaven and earth will pass away, but my words will never pass away.

³⁴"Be careful, or your hearts will be weighed down with dissipation, drunkenness and the anxieties of life, and that day will close on you unexpectedly like a trap. ³⁵For it will come upon all those who live on the face of the whole earth. ³⁶Be always on the watch, and pray that you may be able to escape all that is about to happen, and that you may be able to stand before the Son of Man."

³⁷Each day Jesus was teaching at the temple, and each evening he went out to spend the night on the hill called the Mount of Olives, ³⁸and all the people came early in the morning to hear him at the temple.

Judas Agrees to Betray Jesus

22 Now the Feast of Unleavened Bread, called the Passover, was approaching, ²and the chief priests and the teachers of the law were looking for some way to get rid of Jesus, for they were afraid of the people. ³Then Satan entered Judas, called Iscariot, one of the Twelve. ⁴And Judas went to the chief priests and the officers of the temple guard and discussed with them how he might betray Jesus. ⁵They were delighted and agreed to give him money. ⁶He consented, and watched for an opportunity to hand Jesus over to them when no crowd was present.

The Last Supper

⁷Then came the day of Unleavened Bread on which the Passover lamb had to be sacrificed. ⁸Jesus sent Peter and John,

saying, "Go and make preparations for us to eat the Passover."

⁹"Where do you want us to prepare for it?" they asked.

¹⁰He replied, "As you enter the city, a man carrying a jar of water will meet you. Follow him to the house that he enters, ¹¹and say to the owner of the house, 'The Teacher asks: Where is the guest room, where I may eat the Passover with my disciples?' ¹²He will show you a large upper room, all furnished. Make preparations there."

¹³They left and found things just as Jesus had told them. So they prepared the Passover.

¹⁴When the hour came, Jesus and his apostles reclined at the table. ¹⁵And he said to them, "I have eagerly desired to eat this Passover with you before I suffer. ¹⁶For I tell you, I will not eat it again until it finds fulfillment in the kingdom of God."

¹⁷After taking the cup, he gave thanks and said, "Take this and divide it among you. ¹⁸For I tell you I will not drink again of the fruit of the vine until the kingdom of God comes."

¹⁹And he took bread, gave thanks and broke it, and gave it to them, saying, "This is my body given for you; do this in remembrance of me."

²⁰In the same way, after the supper he took the cup, saying, "This cup is the new covenant in my blood, which is poured out for you. ²¹But the hand of him who is going to betray me is with mine on the table. ²²The Son of Man will go as it has been decreed, but woe to that man who betrays him." ²³They began to question among themselves which of them it might be who would do this.

²⁴Also a dispute arose among them as to which of them was considered to be greatest. ²⁵Jesus said to them, "The kings of the Gentiles lord it over them; and those who exercise authority over them call themselves Benefactors. ²⁶But you are not to be like that. Instead, the greatest among you should be like the youngest, and the one who rules like the one who serves. ²⁷For who is greater, the one who is at the table or the one who

ᵃ32 Or race

serves? Is it not the one who is at the table? But I am among you as one who serves. ²⁸You are those who have stood by me in my trials. ²⁹And I confer on you a kingdom, just as my Father conferred one on me, ³⁰so that you may eat and drink at my table in my kingdom and sit on thrones, judging the twelve tribes of Israel.

³¹"Simon, Simon, Satan has asked to sift you*ᵃ* as wheat. ³²But I have prayed for you, Simon, that your faith may not fail. And when you have turned back, strengthen your brothers."

³³But he replied, "Lord, I am ready to go with you to prison and to death."

³⁴Jesus answered, "I tell you, Peter, before the rooster crows today, you will deny three times that you know me."

³⁵Then Jesus asked them, "When I sent you without purse, bag or sandals, did you lack anything?"

"Nothing," they answered.

³⁶He said to them, "But now if you have a purse, take it, and also a bag; and if you don't have a sword, sell your cloak and buy one. ³⁷It is written: 'And he was numbered with the transgressors'ᵇ; and I tell you that this must be fulfilled in me. Yes, what is written about me is reaching its fulfillment."

³⁸The disciples said, "See, Lord, here are two swords."

"That is enough," he replied.

Jesus Prays on the Mount of Olives

³⁹Jesus went out as usual to the Mount of Olives, and his disciples followed him. ⁴⁰On reaching the place, he said to them, "Pray that you will not fall into temptation." ⁴¹He withdrew about a stone's throw beyond them, knelt down and prayed, ⁴²"Father, if you are willing, take this cup from me; yet not my will, but yours be done." ⁴³An angel from heaven appeared to him and strengthened him. ⁴⁴And being in anguish, he prayed more earnestly, and his sweat was like drops of blood falling to the ground.ᶜ

⁴⁵When he rose from prayer and went back to the disciples, he found them asleep, exhausted from sorrow. ⁴⁶"Why are you sleeping?" he asked them. "Get up and pray so that you will not fall into temptation."

Jesus Arrested

⁴⁷While he was still speaking a crowd came up, and the man who was called Judas, one of the Twelve, was leading them. He approached Jesus to kiss him, ⁴⁸but Jesus asked him, "Judas, are you betraying the Son of Man with a kiss?"

⁴⁹When Jesus' followers saw what was going to happen, they said, "Lord, should we strike with our swords?" ⁵⁰And one of them struck the servant of the high priest, cutting off his right ear.

⁵¹But Jesus answered, "No more of this!" And he touched the man's ear and healed him.

⁵²Then Jesus said to the chief priests, the officers of the temple guard, and the elders, who had come for him, "Am I leading a rebellion, that you have come with swords and clubs? ⁵³Every day I was with you in the temple courts, and you did not lay a hand on me. But this is your hour—when darkness reigns."

Peter Disowns Jesus

⁵⁴Then seizing him, they led him away and took him into the house of the high priest. Peter followed at a distance. ⁵⁵But when they had kindled a fire in the middle of the courtyard and had sat down together, Peter sat down with them. ⁵⁶A servant girl saw him seated there in the firelight. She looked closely at him and said, "This man was with him."

⁵⁷But he denied it. "Woman, I don't know him," he said.

⁵⁸A little later someone else saw him and said, "You also are one of them."

"Man, I am not!" Peter replied.

⁵⁹About an hour later another asserted, "Certainly this fellow was with him, for he is a Galilean."

⁶⁰Peter replied, "Man, I don't know what you're talking about!" Just as he was speaking, the rooster crowed. ⁶¹The Lord turned and looked straight at Peter. Then Peter remembered the word the Lord had spoken to him: "Before the rooster crows today, you will disown me three times." ⁶²And he went outside and wept bitterly.

ᵃ31 The Greek is plural.   *ᵇ37* Isaiah 53:12
ᶜ44 Some early manuscripts do not have verses 43 and 44.

The Guards Mock Jesus

⁶³The men who were guarding Jesus began mocking and beating him. ⁶⁴They blindfolded him and demanded, "Prophesy! Who hit you?" ⁶⁵And they said many other insulting things to him.

Jesus Before Pilate and Herod

⁶⁶At daybreak the council of the elders of the people, both the chief priests and teachers of the law, met together, and Jesus was led before them. ⁶⁷"If you are the Christ,ᵃ" they said, "tell us."

Jesus answered, "If I tell you, you will not believe me, ⁶⁸and if I asked you, you would not answer. ⁶⁹But from now on, the Son of Man will be seated at the right hand of the mighty God."

⁷⁰They all asked, "Are you then the Son of God?"

He replied, "You are right in saying I am."

⁷¹Then they said, "Why do we need any more testimony? We have heard it from his own lips."

23 Then the whole assembly rose and led him off to Pilate. ²And they began to accuse him, saying, "We have found this man subverting our nation. He opposes payment of taxes to Caesar and claims to be Christ,ᵇ a king."

³So Pilate asked Jesus, "Are you the king of the Jews?"

ᵃ67 Or *Messiah*   ᵇ2 Or *Messiah*; also in verses 35 and 39

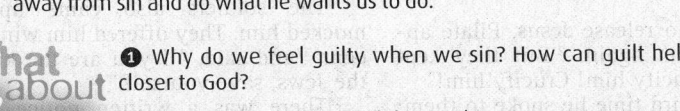

Only Human

Read Luke 22:56-62

Whenever I sin, I start feeling really bad about myself. I feel like if I could just get closer to God, I could get rid of sin for good. But when I read about Peter and the way he messed up, I realize that no matter how close we are to God, we're all still sinners.

Peter spent a lot of time with Jesus. He was one of Jesus' closest friends. He even promised Jesus he'd stick with him no matter how tough things got. But when someone put Peter to the test and accused him of being one of Jesus' friends, Peter acted like he'd never heard of Jesus. Peter broke his promise.

We all break promises to Jesus. We give in to peer pressure and act like we're not Christians. Sometimes we're ashamed of knowing Jesus, just like Peter was. We sin for the same reason Peter sinned: We're human.

But God created us. He knows everything we do even before we do it. So we don't have to try to hide from God when we do something wrong. We can tell him anything and confess all our sins. We can ask him to help us turn away from sin and do what he wants us to do.

❶ Why do we feel guilty when we sin? How can guilt help us grow closer to God?

❷ Write about a time you did something you regret. Now, rewrite the story so that you resist sin and follow God instead. How does the rest of the story change?

❸ Tell God about your sins. Be totally honest. Tell him you're sorry and ask for his forgiveness. Ask God to help you follow him.

Turn to page 1262 for your next devotion.

"Yes, it is as you say," Jesus replied.

[4]Then Pilate announced to the chief priests and the crowd, "I find no basis for a charge against this man."

[5]But they insisted, "He stirs up the people all over Judea[a] by his teaching. He started in Galilee and has come all the way here."

[6]On hearing this, Pilate asked if the man was a Galilean. [7]When he learned that Jesus was under Herod's jurisdiction, he sent him to Herod, who was also in Jerusalem at that time.

[8]When Herod saw Jesus, he was greatly pleased, because for a long time he had been wanting to see him. From what he had heard about him, he hoped to see him perform some miracle. [9]He plied him with many questions, but Jesus gave him no answer. [10]The chief priests and the teachers of the law were standing there, vehemently accusing him. [11]Then Herod and his soldiers ridiculed and mocked him. Dressing him in an elegant robe, they sent him back to Pilate. [12]That day Herod and Pilate became friends—before this they had been enemies.

[13]Pilate called together the chief priests, the rulers and the people, [14]and said to them, "You brought me this man as one who was inciting the people to rebellion. I have examined him in your presence and have found no basis for your charges against him. [15]Neither has Herod, for he sent him back to us; as you can see, he has done nothing to deserve death. [16]Therefore, I will punish him and then release him.[b]"

[18]With one voice they cried out, "Away with this man! Release Barabbas to us!" [19](Barabbas had been thrown into prison for an insurrection in the city, and for murder.)

[20]Wanting to release Jesus, Pilate appealed to them again. [21]But they kept shouting, "Crucify him! Crucify him!"

[22]For the third time he spoke to them: "Why? What crime has this man committed? I have found in him no grounds for the death penalty. Therefore I will have him punished and then release him."

[23]But with loud shouts they insistently demanded that he be crucified, and their shouts prevailed. [24]So Pilate decided to grant their demand. [25]He released the man who had been thrown into prison for insurrection and murder, the one they asked for, and surrendered Jesus to their will.

The Crucifixion

[26]As they led him away, they seized Simon from Cyrene, who was on his way in from the country, and put the cross on him and made him carry it behind Jesus. [27]A large number of people followed him, including women who mourned and wailed for him. [28]Jesus turned and said to them, "Daughters of Jerusalem, do not weep for me; weep for yourselves and for your children. [29]For the time will come when you will say, 'Blessed are the barren women, the wombs that never bore and the breasts that never nursed!' [30]Then

" 'they will say to the mountains, "Fall on us!"
and to the hills, "Cover us!" '[c]

[31]For if men do these things when the tree is green, what will happen when it is dry?"

[32]Two other men, both criminals, were also led out with him to be executed. [33]When they came to the place called the Skull, there they crucified him, along with the criminals—one on his right, the other on his left. [34]Jesus said, "Father, forgive them, for they do not know what they are doing."[d] And they divided up his clothes by casting lots.

[35]The people stood watching, and the rulers even sneered at him. They said, "He saved others; let him save himself if he is the Christ of God, the Chosen One."

[36]The soldiers also came up and mocked him. They offered him wine vinegar [37]and said, "If you are the king of the Jews, save yourself."

[38]There was a written notice above him, which read: THIS IS THE KING OF THE JEWS.

[39]One of the criminals who hung there

---

[a]5 Or over the land of the Jews   [b]16 Some manuscripts him." [17]Now he was obliged to release one man to them at the Feast.   [c]30 Hosea 10:8
[d]34 Some early manuscripts do not have this sentence.

hurled insults at him: "Aren't you the Christ? Save yourself and us!"

⁴⁰But the other criminal rebuked him. "Don't you fear God," he said, "since you are under the same sentence? ⁴¹We are punished justly, for we are getting what our deeds deserve. But this man has done nothing wrong."

⁴²Then he said, "Jesus, remember me when you come into your kingdom.ᵃ"

⁴³Jesus answered him, "I tell you the truth, today you will be with me in paradise."

Jesus' Death

⁴⁴It was now about the sixth hour, and darkness came over the whole land until the ninth hour, ⁴⁵for the sun stopped shining. And the curtain of the temple was torn in two. ⁴⁶Jesus called out with a loud voice, "Father, into your hands I commit my spirit." When he had said this, he breathed his last.

⁴⁷The centurion, seeing what had happened, praised God and said, "Surely this was a righteous man." ⁴⁸When all the

Death Watch

Huh?

Luke 23:47

Did you notice how the Roman centurion was impressed with Jesus? Think about this guy. He had no interest in religion or God or Jesus, for that matter. And helping put Jesus to death didn't bother him until . . . until he saw the way Jesus lived as he died. Then the centurion took notice of Jesus. He believed in Jesus by watching what Jesus did. Are people watching how you live?

people who had gathered to witness this sight saw what took place, they beat their breasts and went away. ⁴⁹But all those who knew him, including the women who had followed him from Galilee, stood at a distance, watching these things.

Jesus' Burial

⁵⁰Now there was a man named Joseph, a member of the Council, a good and upright man, ⁵¹who had not consented to their decision and action. He came from the Judean town of Arimathea and he was waiting for the kingdom of God. ⁵²Going to Pilate, he asked for Jesus' body. ⁵³Then he took it down, wrapped it in linen cloth and placed it in a tomb cut in the rock, one in which no one had yet been laid. ⁵⁴It was Preparation Day, and the Sabbath was about to begin.

⁵⁵The women who had come with Jesus from Galilee followed Joseph and saw the tomb and how his body was laid in it. ⁵⁶Then they went home and prepared spices and perfumes. But they rested on the Sabbath in obedience to the commandment.

The Resurrection

24 On the first day of the week, very early in the morning, the women took the spices they had prepared and went to the tomb. ²They found the stone rolled away from the tomb, ³but when they entered, they did not find the body of the Lord Jesus. ⁴While they were wondering about this, suddenly two men in clothes that gleamed like lightning stood beside them. ⁵In their fright the women bowed down with their faces to the ground, but the men said to them, "Why do you look for the living among the dead? ⁶He is not here; he has risen! Remember how he told you, while he was still with you in Galilee: ⁷'The Son of Man must be delivered into the hands of sinful men, be crucified and on the third day be raised again.' " ⁸Then they remembered his words.

⁹When they came back from the tomb, they told all these things to the Eleven and to all the others. ¹⁰It was Mary Magdalene, Joanna, Mary the mother of James, and the others with them who told this to the apostles. ¹¹But they did not believe the women, because their words seemed to them like nonsense. ¹²Peter, however, got up and ran to the tomb. Bending over, he saw the strips of

ᵃ42 Some manuscripts *come with your kingly power*

linen lying by themselves, and he went away, wondering to himself what had happened.

On the Road to Emmaus

¹³Now that same day two of them were going to a village called Emmaus, about seven miles*ª* from Jerusalem. ¹⁴They were talking with each other about everything that had happened. ¹⁵As they talked and discussed these things with each other, Jesus himself came up and walked along with them; ¹⁶but they were kept from recognizing him.

¹⁷He asked them, "What are you discussing together as you walk along?"

They stood still, their faces downcast. ¹⁸One of them, named Cleopas, asked him, "Are you only a visitor to Jerusalem and do not know the things that have happened there in these days?"

¹⁹"What things?" he asked.

"About Jesus of Nazareth," they replied. "He was a prophet, powerful in word and deed before God and all the people. ²⁰The chief priests and our rulers handed him over to be sentenced to death, and they crucified him; ²¹but we had hoped that he was the one who was going to redeem Israel. And what is more, it is the third day since all this took place. ²²In addition, some of our women amazed us. They went to the tomb early this morning ²³but didn't find his body. They came and told us that they had seen a vision of angels, who said he was alive. ²⁴Then some of our companions went to the tomb and found it just as the women had said, but him they did not see."

²⁵He said to them, "How foolish you

ª13 Greek sixty stadia *(about 11 kilometers)*

Week end.

Thanks

Read Psalm 100 (page 694)

Even if your life's pretty tough, you still have a lot to be thankful for. A bunch of reasons to be thankful were mentioned in this week's devos: Monday—God's love and protection; Tuesday—God's provision for us; Wednesday and Friday—forgiveness from God and others; and Thursday—being able to share with others and again, God's provision for us (and for stuffed animals!).

When you read Psalm 100, it's totally obvious that the writer is joyful and thankful! Look at verse 4. It mentions giving thanks twice; and it mentions the word *praise* twice! Sometimes the word *praise* can sound like a real "churchy" word, and you might wonder what it means to praise God. The writers of this week's devotions make it simple: We praise God by giving thanks to him and telling him how much we appreciate all the things he's done for us! More importantly we thank and praise him simply for who he is: our super-loving, perfect Dad!

❶ How would you explain "giving praise to God"?

❷ The book of Psalms is filled with great praise songs and songs of thanks. Remember the list of things you have to be thankful for that you started on Tuesday? Try to write a little poem to God using that list. (Who knows, it might make a great psalm or song of praise.)

❸ Praise God for all that he has done for you and for simply being God!

Turn to page 1268 for your next devotion.

are, and how slow of heart to believe all that the prophets have spoken! ²⁶Did not the Christ*ᵃ* have to suffer these things and then enter his glory?" ²⁷And beginning with Moses and all the Prophets, he explained to them what was said in all the Scriptures concerning himself.

²⁸As they approached the village to which they were going, Jesus acted as if he were going farther. ²⁹But they urged him strongly, "Stay with us, for it is nearly evening; the day is almost over." So he went in to stay with them.

³⁰When he was at the table with them, he took bread, gave thanks, broke it and began to give it to them. ³¹Then their eyes were opened and they recognized him, and he disappeared from their sight. ³²They asked each other, "Were not our hearts burning within us while he talked with us on the road and opened the Scriptures to us?"

³³They got up and returned at once to Jerusalem. There they found the Eleven and those with them, assembled together ³⁴and saying, "It is true! The Lord has risen and has appeared to Simon." ³⁵Then the two told what had happened on the way, and how Jesus was recognized by them when he broke the bread.

Jesus Appears to the Disciples

³⁶While they were still talking about this, Jesus himself stood among them and said to them, "Peace be with you."

³⁷They were startled and frightened, thinking they saw a ghost. ³⁸He said to them, "Why are you troubled, and why do doubts rise in your minds? ³⁹Look at my hands and my feet. It is I myself! Touch me and see; a ghost does not have flesh and bones, as you see I have."

⁴⁰When he had said this, he showed them his hands and feet. ⁴¹And while they still did not believe it because of joy and amazement, he asked them, "Do you have anything here to eat?" ⁴²They gave him a piece of broiled fish, ⁴³and he took it and ate it in their presence.

⁴⁴He said to them, "This is what I told you while I was still with you: Everything must be fulfilled that is written about me in the Law of Moses, the Prophets and the Psalms."

⁴⁵Then he opened their minds so they could understand the Scriptures. ⁴⁶He told them, "This is what is written: The Christ will suffer and rise from the dead on the third day, ⁴⁷and repentance and forgiveness of sins will be preached in his name to all nations, beginning at Jerusalem. ⁴⁸You are witnesses of these things. ⁴⁹I am going to send you what my Father has promised; but stay in the city until you have been clothed with power from on high."

The Ascension

⁵⁰When he had led them out to the vicinity of Bethany, he lifted up his hands and blessed them. ⁵¹While he was blessing them, he left them and was taken up into heaven. ⁵²Then they worshiped him and returned to Jerusalem with great joy. ⁵³And they stayed continually at the temple, praising God.

ᵃ26 Or Messiah; also in verse 46

Luke Wordsearch

Herod (1:5)
Zechariah (1:5)
Elizabeth (1:5)
John (1:13)
Gabriel (1:19)
Joseph (1:27)
Mary (1:27)
Jesus (1:31)
Simeon (2:25)
Anna (2:36)
Pontius Pilate (3:1)
Annas (3:2)
Caiaphas (3:2)
Isaiah (3:4)

Possessed man (4:33)
Peter (6:14)
James (5:10)
Leper (5:12)
Pharisees (5:17)
Paralytic (5:18)
Levi (5:27)
Philip (6:14)
Bartholomew (6:14)
Alphaeus's James (6:15)
Matthew (6:15)
Thomas (6:15)
Judas of James (6:16)
Judas Iscariot (6:16)

Centurion (7:3)
Mary Magdalene (8:2)
Jairus (8:41)
Moses (9:30)
Elijah (9:30)
Martha (10:38)
Crowd (12:1)
Zacchaeus (19:2)
Caesar (20:22)
Sadducees (20:27)
Barabbas (23:18)
Simon from Cyrene (23:26)
Criminal (23:40)
Joanna (24:10)

```
N P D A F R E M S X H W J I Z U S O L M A R T H A
H E R O D C B P A P K T T R Y P Z L R N X H Q C N
O P Q A S E Y I H R A G N O O G E L Y O T F U J N
J O Z K S J I R P S Z S F W H D C Z K I P I D X A
U S G B O V K Z A R E I Q D M J H A C O J E S U S
D S U R R J P N I M J N P Y E H A K W G T Z L U P
A E Z J C Y N U A Y S I M O N F R O M C Y R E N E
S S O Q R A B J C H R S H F K Q I X N A M I G Z N
I S F P O N T I U S P I L A T E A E P H I L I P F
S E W J W A G N U D K X A B N O H E L M I P O N U
C D P T D E P C D R A A G P Q W I C R I M I N A L
A M O U S L R I T J O S E P H N Y T Z A J R S M T
R A L F C Q X D P I G L O Z M Z H X R P E A F O Q
I N J Q A P B A N E K D G F M K O Y U P S D H R I
O L S U E A H C C A Z E C I J L M D E S E S S O P
T P A X S L C E N T U R I O N A P L B I P Q K A H
L F D P A E I U P J O H N A G L M U H T H S R Z A
Q E D W R I S Z B X P S O D U S P E T E R A J P R
K M U I R Q A D A U A I A C J E C H S J L M A U I
I A C B H L I N F B X L O F E S J O Z Y T O I M S
Y W E H T T A M B R E S I M E O N C T Z L H R L E
H T E Z Y L H A K N R T X F A M F I Q W U T U A E
P U S H E B R L E N O L H X K E C Y Z B I P S L S
Z X J V Q A B B A R T H O L O M E W T P L O T A E
L E I R B A G Y A L P H A E U S S J A M E S F H Z
```

Can you solve this puzzle? See if you can
find the names listed above. They're all in
the book of Luke (the chapter and verse
are next to each name).

John

START

This is the last of the 4 Jesus Gospels. In a very important way, it's different from the first 3. All 4 of the men who recorded the story of Jesus' life wanted the story to be accurate. John was no exception: After all, most of the stories he tells are stories he was actually there to see! But he had another reason for writing this book.

John didn't just want us to know *about* Jesus and the things he did. He wanted us to *know* Jesus, his very special friend. John often refers to himself as "the disciple whom Jesus loved." Imagine having that kind of a close friendship with Jesus.

The events John chose to describe help us know who Jesus is. They show us Jesus' kindness, gentleness, love and care. We also see his sadness, anger, steadfastness and joy. It's kind of an insider's behind-the-scenes look at Jesus.

When you get down to it though, John really had us in mind when he wrote the story. Right near the end of the book, in chapter 20:31, John says he wrote it so you would "believe that Jesus is the Christ, the Son of God, and that by believing you may have life in his name." Pay attention as you read John's book . . . It'll introduce you to someone who could change your life.

Cast of Characters

Jesus
He's God, you know. He does some very cool stuff and says some very cool things in this story of his life.

John the Baptist
Wild and woolly, this guy looks like he hasn't showered in years, but God chooses him to announce Jesus' arrival.

John
Jesus picks 12 close friends; out of those 12, Peter, James and John are the closest to Jesus. John is called "the beloved disciple."

The Other Disciples
That strange mix of men who walk and talk with Jesus and know him better than anyone else. John is one of them.

A Wild Collection of People
A party crowd at a wedding, a spoiled rich kid, prostitutes and street people, politicians and preachers, little kids and grown-ups. Jesus loves them all, including the soldiers who end up nailing him to the cross.

What's UP with That?

A lot of people get nicknames that tell us something about them. **Rusty** has red hair, **Stretch** is tall, **Moose** plays football and **Einstein** rocks in math class. Jesus has a ton of names in this story of his life.

See if you can identify the nicknames John uses to describe something about Jesus.

A The Word

B The Wind Beneath My Wings

C The Light

D The Big Cheese

E A Spring of Water

F The Good Shepherd

G A Closet to Hide In

H The Bread of Life

I The Man

J The Starship Enterprise

K A King

L The Book

M The Way and the Truth and the Life

N The Eternal-Life-inator

Snap shots

- God in sandals *(chapter 1:1–18)*

- Get ready, get set . . . *(chapter 1:19–51)*

- Teaching, healing and hangin' out with the people *(chapters 2—11)*

- Famous last words *(chapters 12—17)*

- The worst *and* the best days in history *(chapters 18—19)*

- Guess what? I'm back *(chapters 20—21)*

answers: a (1:1), c (8:12), e (4:14), f (10:11), h (6:48), i (9:9), k (18:37), m (14:6)

The Word Became Flesh

1 In the beginning was the Word, and the Word was with God, and the Word was God. ²He was with God in the beginning.

Word Up

John 1:1

When Jews were reading and came across "Word" with a capital W, they knew it meant one thing: the Savior. So why didn't John just say Savior? John was writing not just to Jews, but also to the Gentiles, who were pretty much everybody else. When the Gentiles saw "Word" with a capital W, they thought it meant a big idea that controls a bunch of stuff. So John was showing everyone that Savior = Jesus, the One with the ultimate authority—involved in creation, sustaining, redeeming. Goes to show that John was pretty clever.

³Through him all things were made; without him nothing was made that has been made. ⁴In him was life, and that life was the light of men. ⁵The light shines in the darkness, but the darkness has not understood*ᵃ* it.

⁶There came a man who was sent from God; his name was John. ⁷He came as a witness to testify concerning that light, so that through him all men might believe. ⁸He himself was not the light; he came only as a witness to the light. ⁹The true light that gives light to every man was coming into the world.*ᵇ*

¹⁰He was in the world, and though the world was made through him, the world did not recognize him. ¹¹He came to that which was his own, but his own did not receive him. ¹²Yet to all who received him, to those who believed in his name, he gave the right to become children of God— ¹³children born not of natural descent,*ᶜ* nor of human decision or a husband's will, but born of God.

¹⁴The Word became flesh and made his dwelling among us. We have seen his glory, the glory of the One and Only,*ᵈ* who came from the Father, full of grace and truth.

¹⁵John testifies concerning him. He cries out, saying, "This was he of whom I said, 'He who comes after me has surpassed me because he was before me.'" ¹⁶From the fullness of his grace we have all received one blessing after another. ¹⁷For the law was given through Moses; grace and truth came through Jesus Christ. ¹⁸No one has ever seen God, but God the One and Only,*ᵈ,ᵉ* who is at the Father's side, has made him known.

John the Baptist Denies Being the Christ

¹⁹Now this was John's testimony when the Jews of Jerusalem sent priests and Levites to ask him who he was. ²⁰He did not fail to confess, but confessed freely, "I am not the Christ.*ᶠ*"

²¹They asked him, "Then who are you? Are you Elijah?"

He said, "I am not."

"Are you the Prophet?"

He answered, "No."

²²Finally they said, "Who are you? Give us an answer to take back to those who sent us. What do you say about yourself?"

²³John replied in the words of Isaiah the prophet, "I am the voice of one calling in the desert, 'Make straight the way for the Lord.'"*ᵍ*

²⁴Now some Pharisees who had been sent ²⁵questioned him, "Why then do you baptize if you are not the Christ, nor Elijah, nor the Prophet?"

²⁶"I baptize with*ʰ* water," John replied, "but among you stands one you do not know. ²⁷He is the one who comes after me, the thongs of whose sandals I am not worthy to untie."

²⁸This all happened at Bethany on the other side of the Jordan, where John was baptizing.

ᵃ5 Or *darkness, and the darkness has not overcome* *ᵇ9* Or *This was the true light that gives light to every man who comes into the world* *ᶜ13* Greek of *bloods* *ᵈ14,18* Or *the Only Begotten* *ᵉ18* Some manuscripts *but the only* (or *only begotten*) *Son* *ᶠ20* Or *Messiah*. "The Christ" (Greek) and "the Messiah" (Hebrew) both mean "the Anointed One"; also in verse 25. *ᵍ23* Isaiah 40:3 *ʰ26* Or *in*; also in verses 31 and 33

Jesus the Lamb of God

²⁹The next day John saw Jesus coming toward him and said, "Look, the Lamb of God, who takes away the sin of the world! ³⁰This is the one I meant when I said, 'A man who comes after me has surpassed me because he was before me.' ³¹I myself did not know him, but the reason I came baptizing with water was that he might be revealed to Israel."

³²Then John gave this testimony: "I saw the Spirit come down from heaven as a dove and remain on him. ³³I would not have known him, except that the one who sent me to baptize with water told me, 'The man on whom you see the Spirit come down and remain is he who will baptize with the Holy Spirit.' ³⁴I have seen and I testify that this is the Son of God."

Jesus' First Disciples

³⁵The next day John was there again with two of his disciples. ³⁶When he saw Jesus passing by, he said, "Look, the Lamb of God!"

³⁷When the two disciples heard him say this, they followed Jesus. ³⁸Turning around, Jesus saw them following and asked, "What do you want?"

They said, "Rabbi" (which means Teacher), "where are you staying?"

³⁹"Come," he replied, "and you will see."

So they went and saw where he was staying, and spent that day with him. It was about the tenth hour.

⁴⁰Andrew, Simon Peter's brother, was one of the two who heard what John had said and who had followed Jesus. ⁴¹The first thing Andrew did was to find his brother Simon and tell him, "We have found the Messiah" (that is, the Christ). ⁴²And he brought him to Jesus.

Jesus looked at him and said, "You are Simon son of John. You will be called Cephas" (which, when translated, is Peter*ᵃ*).

ᵃ42 Both *Cephas* (Aramaic) and *Peter* (Greek) mean *rock*.

Monday

Play Your Part

Read John 1:19–28

A few years ago, my friend's parents got divorced. There wasn't anything I could do about it, and I felt pretty helpless. But my friend really needed someone to talk to about how she felt, and I was able to be that person. I felt like God used me to help her get through a really difficult time.

But sometimes I feel pretty useless—like I don't really have a place in the world. That's what this passage is about. John the Baptist kind of lived in Jesus' shadow. Maybe he felt like he didn't have much to offer. But John knew God gave him a special job to do anyway: to help people prepare for Jesus to arrive. God really does have a purpose for everyone. God used me in my friend's life. I wonder how he'll use me again.

Emily age 13

What about You?

❶ How has God used you in someone else's life? How has God used other people in your life?

❷ Think of a tough situation one of your friends is facing. Then make 2 lists: one of things you can do to help, the other of things only *God* can do. Make a plan to do all you can to help your friend.

❸ Ask God to use you in the lives of others.

Turn to page 1270 for your next devotion.

Jesus Calls Philip and Nathanael

[43]The next day Jesus decided to leave for Galilee. Finding Philip, he said to him, "Follow me."

[44]Philip, like Andrew and Peter, was from the town of Bethsaida. [45]Philip found Nathanael and told him, "We have found the one Moses wrote about in the Law, and about whom the prophets also wrote—Jesus of Nazareth, the son of Joseph."

[46]"Nazareth! Can anything good come from there?" Nathanael asked.

"Come and see," said Philip.

[47]When Jesus saw Nathanael approaching, he said of him, "Here is a true Israelite, in whom there is nothing false."

[48]"How do you know me?" Nathanael asked.

Jesus answered, "I saw you while you were still under the fig tree before Philip called you."

[49]Then Nathanael declared, "Rabbi, you are the Son of God; you are the King of Israel."

[50]Jesus said, "You believe[a] because I told you I saw you under the fig tree. You shall see greater things than that." [51]He then added, "I tell you[b] the truth, you[b] shall see heaven open, and the angels of God ascending and descending on the Son of Man."

Jesus Changes Water to Wine

2 On the third day a wedding took place at Cana in Galilee. Jesus' mother was there, [2]and Jesus and his disciples had also been invited to the wedding. [3]When the wine was gone, Jesus' mother said to him, "They have no more wine."

[4]"Dear woman, why do you involve me?" Jesus replied. "My time has not yet come."

[5]His mother said to the servants, "Do whatever he tells you."

[6]Nearby stood six stone water jars, the kind used by the Jews for ceremonial washing, each holding from twenty to thirty gallons.[c]

[7]Jesus said to the servants, "Fill the jars with water"; so they filled them to the brim.

[8]Then he told them, "Now draw some out and take it to the master of the banquet."

They did so, [9]and the master of the banquet tasted the water that had been turned into wine. He did not realize where it had come from, though the servants who had drawn the water knew. Then he called the bridegroom aside [10]and said, "Everyone brings out the choice wine first and then the cheaper wine after the guests have had too much to drink; but you have saved the best till now."

[11]This, the first of his miraculous signs, Jesus performed at Cana in Galilee. He thus revealed his glory, and his disciples put their faith in him.

Jesus Clears the Temple

[12]After this he went down to Capernaum with his mother and brothers and his disciples. There they stayed for a few days.

[13]When it was almost time for the Jewish Passover, Jesus went up to Jerusalem. [14]In the temple courts he found men selling cattle, sheep and doves, and others sitting at tables exchanging money. [15]So

Flea Market

Huh?

John 2:14

Most churches today would say no animals allowed. But in Jesus' day, the temple not only allowed animals, they needed them—noises, smells and all. Money was being exchanged and animals were being sold for sacrificing. Jesus was ticked, though, because the part of the temple where Gentiles could come to pray had become a flea market.

he made a whip out of cords, and drove all from the temple area, both sheep and cattle; he scattered the coins of the money changers and overturned their tables.

[a]50 Or *Do you believe . . . ?*   [b]51 The Greek is plural.
[c]6 Greek *two to three metretes* (probably about 75 to 115 liters)

¹⁶To those who sold doves he said, "Get these out of here! How dare you turn my Father's house into a market!"

¹⁷His disciples remembered that it is written: "Zeal for your house will consume me."ᵃ

¹⁸Then the Jews demanded of him, "What miraculous sign can you show us to prove your authority to do all this?"

¹⁹Jesus answered them, "Destroy this temple, and I will raise it again in three days."

²⁰The Jews replied, "It has taken forty-six years to build this temple, and you are going to raise it in three days?" ²¹But the temple he had spoken of was his body. ²²After he was raised from the dead, his disciples recalled what he had said. Then they believed the Scripture and the words that Jesus had spoken.

²³Now while he was in Jerusalem at the Passover Feast, many people saw the miraculous signs he was doing and believed in his name.ᵇ ²⁴But Jesus would not entrust himself to them, for he knew all

men. ²⁵He did not need man's testimony about man, for he knew what was in a man.

Jesus Teaches Nicodemus

3 Now there was a man of the Pharisees named Nicodemus, a member of the Jewish ruling council. ²He came to Jesus at night and said, "Rabbi, we know you are a teacher who has come from God. For no one could perform the miraculous signs you are doing if God were not with him."

³In reply Jesus declared, "I tell you the truth, no one can see the kingdom of God unless he is born again.ᶜ"

⁴"How can a man be born when he is old?" Nicodemus asked. "Surely he cannot enter a second time into his mother's womb to be born!"

⁵Jesus answered, "I tell you the truth, no one can enter the kingdom of God

---

ᵃ17 Psalm 69:9　ᵇ23 Or and believed in him　ᶜ3 Or born from above; also in verse 7

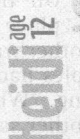

Tuesday

"Positively" Furious

Read John 2:13–17

This story is kind of confusing. It looks like Jesus lost his temper and went ballistic all of a sudden. I mean, if I did that, I'd get into big trouble! The difference here is that Jesus was angry for a really good reason. The people he chased out of the temple were messing with God and turning a holy place into a very unholy place. No wonder Jesus got so mad!

There are some things in life worth getting mad about, like abuse and murder and people who say terrible things about God. But there are lots of things that *aren't* worth getting mad about, like your brother sneaking one of your CDs or your parents asking you to do something you don't want to do. The key is to ask yourself, "Would Jesus get mad about this?" If he would, ask him how you should respond. But if he wouldn't, ask him to help you get over it before you do something you'll regret.

What about You?

❶ When is anger a good thing? When is it a bad thing?

❷ Make a list of things that make you angry, then look at each one carefully and ask, *Is this really worth getting upset about? What should I do the next time I'm feeling angry about this?*

❸ Ask God to help you decide what's a big deal and what isn't.

Turn to page 1273 for your next devotion.

unless he is born of water and the Spirit. [6]Flesh gives birth to flesh, but the Spirit[a] gives birth to spirit. [7]You should not be surprised at my saying, 'You[b] must be born again.' [8]The wind blows wherever it pleases. You hear its sound, but you cannot tell where it comes from or where it is going. So it is with everyone born of the Spirit."

[9]"How can this be?" Nicodemus asked.

[10]"You are Israel's teacher," said Jesus, "and do you not understand these things? [11]I tell you the truth, we speak of what we know, and we testify to what we have seen, but still you people do not accept our testimony. [12]I have spoken to you of earthly things and you do not believe; how then will you believe if I speak of heavenly things? [13]No one has ever gone into heaven except the one who came from heaven—the Son of Man.[c] [14]Just as Moses lifted up the snake in the desert, so the Son of Man must be lifted up, [15]that everyone who believes in him may have eternal life.[d]

[16]"For God so loved the world that he gave his one and only Son,[e] that whoever believes in him shall not perish but have eternal life. [17]For God did not send his Son into the world to condemn the world, but to save the world through him. [18]Whoever believes in him is not condemned, but whoever does not believe stands condemned already because he has not believed in the name of God's one and only Son.[f] [19]This is the verdict: Light has come into the world, but men loved darkness instead of light because their deeds were evil. [20]Everyone who does evil hates the light, and will not come into the light for fear that his deeds will be exposed. [21]But whoever lives by the truth comes into the light, so that it may be seen plainly that what he has done has been done through God."[g]

John the Baptist's Testimony About Jesus

[22]After this, Jesus and his disciples went out into the Judean countryside, where he spent some time with them, and baptized. [23]Now John also was baptizing at Aenon near Salim, because there was plenty of water, and people were constantly coming to be baptized. [24](This was before John was put in prison.) [25]An argument developed between some of John's disciples and a certain Jew[h] over the matter of ceremonial washing. [26]They came to John and said to him, "Rabbi, that man who was with you on the other side of the Jordan—the one you testified about—well, he is baptizing, and everyone is going to him."

[27]To this John replied, "A man can receive only what is given him from heaven. [28]You yourselves can testify that I said, 'I am not the Christ[i] but am sent ahead of him.' [29]The bride belongs to the bridegroom. The friend who attends the bridegroom waits and listens for him, and is full of joy when he hears the bridegroom's voice. That joy is mine, and it is now complete. [30]He must become greater; I must become less.

[31]"The one who comes from above is above all; the one who is from the earth belongs to the earth, and speaks as one from the earth. The one who comes from heaven is above all. [32]He testifies to what he has seen and heard, but no one accepts his testimony. [33]The man who has accepted it has certified that God is truthful. [34]For the one whom God has sent speaks the words of God, for God[j] gives the Spirit without limit. [35]The Father loves the Son and has placed everything in his hands. [36]Whoever believes in the Son has eternal life, but whoever rejects the Son will not see life, for God's wrath remains on him."[k]

Jesus Talks With a Samaritan Woman

4 The Pharisees heard that Jesus was gaining and baptizing more disciples than John, [2]although in fact it was not Jesus who baptized, but his disciples. [3]When the Lord learned of this, he left Judea and went back once more to Galilee.

[4]Now he had to go through Samaria. [5]So he came to a town in Samaria called Sychar, near the plot of ground Jacob

[a]6 Or but spirit [b]7 The Greek is plural. [c]13 Some manuscripts Man, who is in heaven [d]15 Or believes may have eternal life in him [e]16 Or his only begotten Son [f]18 Or God's only begotten Son [g]21 Some interpreters end the quotation after verse 15. [h]25 Some manuscripts and certain Jews [i]28 Or Messiah [j]34 Greek he [k]36 Some interpreters end the quotation after verse 30.

had given to his son Joseph. ⁶Jacob's well was there, and Jesus, tired as he was from the journey, sat down by the well. It was about the sixth hour.

⁷When a Samaritan woman came to draw water, Jesus said to her, "Will you give me a drink?" ⁸(His disciples had gone into the town to buy food.)

⁹The Samaritan woman said to him, "You are a Jew and I am a Samaritan woman. How can you ask me for a drink?" (For Jews do not associate with Samaritans.ᵃ)

Bust the Wall

Huh?

John 4:9

Ask any Jew from Bible times and they would've told you the same thing: Samaritans were scum. Lowlifes. The Jews thought that even a glass could not be used if it had belonged to a Samaritan. And yet Jesus punched a hole in this dividing wall of hatred when he asked a Samaritan woman for a drink. He was willing to go against what everyone thought to help a woman in need, regardless of where she came from. He let her give him a drink, and then he gave her living water for eternity.

¹⁰Jesus answered her, "If you knew the gift of God and who it is that asks you for a drink, you would have asked him and he would have given you living water."

¹¹"Sir," the woman said, "you have nothing to draw with and the well is deep. Where can you get this living water? ¹²Are you greater than our father Jacob, who gave us the well and drank from it himself, as did also his sons and his flocks and herds?"

¹³Jesus answered, "Everyone who drinks this water will be thirsty again, ¹⁴but whoever drinks the water I give him will never thirst. Indeed, the water I give him will become in him a spring of water welling up to eternal life."

¹⁵The woman said to him, "Sir, give me this water so that I won't get thirsty and have to keep coming here to draw water."

¹⁶He told her, "Go, call your husband and come back."

¹⁷"I have no husband," she replied.

Jesus said to her, "You are right when you say you have no husband. ¹⁸The fact is, you have had five husbands, and the man you now have is not your husband. What you have just said is quite true."

¹⁹"Sir," the woman said, "I can see that you are a prophet. ²⁰Our fathers worshiped on this mountain, but you Jews claim that the place where we must worship is in Jerusalem."

²¹Jesus declared, "Believe me, woman, a time is coming when you will worship the Father neither on this mountain nor in Jerusalem. ²²You Samaritans worship what you do not know; we worship what we do know, for salvation is from the Jews. ²³Yet a time is coming and has now come when the true worshipers will worship the Father in spirit and truth, for they are the kind of worshipers the Father seeks. ²⁴God is spirit, and his worshipers must worship in spirit and in truth."

²⁵The woman said, "I know that Messiah" (called Christ) "is coming. When he comes, he will explain everything to us."

²⁶Then Jesus declared, "I who speak to you am he."

The Disciples Rejoin Jesus

²⁷Just then his disciples returned and were surprised to find him talking with a woman. But no one asked, "What do you want?" or "Why are you talking with her?"

²⁸Then, leaving her water jar, the woman went back to the town and said to the people, ²⁹"Come, see a man who told me everything I ever did. Could this be the Christᵇ?" ³⁰They came out of the town and made their way toward him.

³¹Meanwhile his disciples urged him, "Rabbi, eat something."

³²But he said to them, "I have food to eat that you know nothing about."

³³Then his disciples said to each other, "Could someone have brought him food?"

ᵃ9 Or *do not use dishes Samaritans have used*
ᵇ29 Or *Messiah*

³⁴"My food," said Jesus, "is to do the will of him who sent me and to finish his work. ³⁵Do you not say, 'Four months more and then the harvest'? I tell you, open your eyes and look at the fields! They are ripe for harvest. ³⁶Even now the reaper draws his wages, even now he harvests the crop for eternal life, so that the sower and the reaper may be glad together. ³⁷Thus the saying 'One sows and another reaps' is true. ³⁸I sent you to reap what you have not worked for. Others have done the hard work, and you have reaped the benefits of their labor."

Many Samaritans Believe

³⁹Many of the Samaritans from that town believed in him because of the woman's testimony, "He told me everything I ever did." ⁴⁰So when the Samaritans came to him, they urged him to stay with them, and he stayed two days. ⁴¹And because of his words many more became believers.

⁴²They said to the woman, "We no longer believe just because of what you said; now we have heard for ourselves, and we know that this man really is the Savior of the world."

Jesus Heals the Official's Son

⁴³After the two days he left for Galilee. ⁴⁴(Now Jesus himself had pointed out that a prophet has no honor in his own country.) ⁴⁵When he arrived in Galilee, the Galileans welcomed him. They had seen all that he had done in Jerusalem at the Passover Feast, for they also had been there.

⁴⁶Once more he visited Cana in Galilee, where he had turned the water into wine. And there was a certain royal official whose son lay sick at Capernaum. ⁴⁷When this man heard that Jesus had arrived in Galilee from Judea, he went to him and begged him to come and heal his son, who was close to death.

⁴⁸"Unless you people see miraculous

Wednesday

Prejudices

Read John 4:7–10

In Alaska, where I live, many of the Native Americans I know have problems with drugs and alcohol, and they get into trouble at school. Whites and Native Americans often form separate cliques because of bad feelings between the 2 groups. I find myself almost expecting *all* of them to be troublemakers, even though I know that's not true.

When I'm struggling with my prejudices, I can look at the great example of Jesus. Jesus reached out to someone who was different from him. He didn't allow racial differences to keep him from being kind to another person. He showed God's love to the Samaritan woman, even though he could have been ridiculed or hurt for talking to her. He took a stand against racism, and I need to do the same.

God commands us to love others as we love ourselves. Treating people like they are inferior to us is the exact opposite of God's commandment. If we want to obey God, we have to reach out to people, no matter what race or culture they come from.

Emile age 14

❶ What are some examples of racism at your school or where you live?

❷ Why do you think people get caught up in racism?

❸ Ask God to help you take a stand against racism.

Turn to page 1277 for your next devotion.

signs and wonders," Jesus told him, "you will never believe."

⁴⁹The royal official said, "Sir, come down before my child dies."

⁵⁰Jesus replied, "You may go. Your son will live."

The man took Jesus at his word and departed. ⁵¹While he was still on the way, his servants met him with the news that his boy was living. ⁵²When he inquired as to the time when his son got better, they said to him, "The fever left him yesterday at the seventh hour."

⁵³Then the father realized that this was the exact time at which Jesus had said to him, "Your son will live." So he and all his household believed.

⁵⁴This was the second miraculous sign that Jesus performed, having come from Judea to Galilee.

The Healing at the Pool

5 Some time later, Jesus went up to Jerusalem for a feast of the Jews. ²Now there is in Jerusalem near the Sheep Gate a pool, which in Aramaic is called Bethesda*ᵃ* and which is surrounded by five covered colonnades. ³Here a great number of disabled people used to lie—the blind, the lame, the paralyzed.*ᵇ* ⁵One who was there had been an invalid for thirty-eight years. ⁶When Jesus saw him lying there and learned that he had been in this condition for a long time, he asked him, "Do you want to get well?"

⁷"Sir," the invalid replied, "I have no one to help me into the pool when the water is stirred. While I am trying to get in, someone else goes down ahead of me."

⁸Then Jesus said to him, "Get up! Pick up your mat and walk." ⁹At once the man was cured; he picked up his mat and walked.

The day on which this took place was a Sabbath, ¹⁰and so the Jews said to the man who had been healed, "It is the Sabbath; the law forbids you to carry your mat."

¹¹But he replied, "The man who made me well said to me, 'Pick up your mat and walk.' "

¹²So they asked him, "Who is this fellow who told you to pick it up and walk?"

¹³The man who was healed had no idea who it was, for Jesus had slipped away into the crowd that was there.

¹⁴Later Jesus found him at the temple and said to him, "See, you are well again. Stop sinning or something worse may happen to you." ¹⁵The man went away and told the Jews that it was Jesus who had made him well.

Life Through the Son

¹⁶So, because Jesus was doing these things on the Sabbath, the Jews persecuted him. ¹⁷Jesus said to them, "My Father is always at his work to this very day, and I, too, am working." ¹⁸For this reason the Jews tried all the harder to kill him; not only was he breaking the Sabbath, but he was even calling God his own Father, making himself equal with God.

¹⁹Jesus gave them this answer: "I tell you the truth, the Son can do nothing by himself; he can do only what he sees his Father doing, because whatever the Father does the Son also does. ²⁰For the Father loves the Son and shows him all he does. Yes, to your amazement he will show him even greater things than these. ²¹For just as the Father raises the dead

---

A Silly Question?

Huh?

John 5:6

What kind of silly question is Jesus asking? "Do you want to get well?" Of course the answer would be yes—or would it? The question was important because the man had not asked Jesus for help. Jesus wanted to make sure the guy wanted to get better before he healed him.

ᵃ2 Some manuscripts *Bethzatha*; other manuscripts *Bethsaida* *ᵇ3* Some less important manuscripts *paralyzed—and they waited for the moving of the waters. ⁴From time to time an angel of the Lord would come down and stir up the waters. The first one into the pool after each such disturbance would be cured of whatever disease he had.*

and gives them life, even so the Son gives life to whom he is pleased to give it. ²²Moreover, the Father judges no one, but has entrusted all judgment to the Son, ²³that all may honor the Son just as they honor the Father. He who does not honor the Son does not honor the Father, who sent him.

²⁴"I tell you the truth, whoever hears my word and believes him who sent me has eternal life and will not be condemned; he has crossed over from death to life. ²⁵I tell you the truth, a time is coming and has now come when the dead will hear the voice of the Son of God and those who hear will live. ²⁶For as the Father has life in himself, so he has granted the Son to have life in himself. ²⁷And he has given him authority to judge because he is the Son of Man.

²⁸"Do not be amazed at this, for a time is coming when all who are in their graves will hear his voice ²⁹and come out—those who have done good will rise to live, and those who have done evil will rise to be condemned. ³⁰By myself I can do nothing; I judge only as I hear, and my judgment is just, for I seek not to please myself but him who sent me.

Testimonies About Jesus

³¹"If I testify about myself, my testimony is not valid. ³²There is another who testifies in my favor, and I know that his testimony about me is valid.

³³"You have sent to John and he has testified to the truth. ³⁴Not that I accept human testimony; but I mention it that you may be saved. ³⁵John was a lamp that burned and gave light, and you chose for a time to enjoy his light.

³⁶"I have testimony weightier than that of John. For the very work that the Father has given me to finish, and which I am doing, testifies that the Father has sent me. ³⁷And the Father who sent me has himself testified concerning me. You have never heard his voice nor seen his form, ³⁸nor does his word dwell in you, for you do not believe the one he sent. ³⁹You diligently study ᵃ the Scriptures because you think that by them you possess eternal life. These are the Scriptures that testify about me, ⁴⁰yet you refuse to come to me to have life.

⁴¹"I do not accept praise from men, ⁴²but I know you. I know that you do not have the love of God in your hearts. ⁴³I have come in my Father's name, and you do not accept me; but if someone else comes in his own name, you will accept him. ⁴⁴How can you believe if you accept praise from one another, yet make no effort to obtain the praise that comes from the only God ᵇ?

⁴⁵"But do not think I will accuse you before the Father. Your accuser is Moses, on whom your hopes are set. ⁴⁶If you believed Moses, you would believe me, for he wrote about me. ⁴⁷But since you do not believe what he wrote, how are you going to believe what I say?"

Jesus Feeds the Five Thousand

6 Some time after this, Jesus crossed to the far shore of the Sea of Galilee (that is, the Sea of Tiberias), ²and a great crowd of people followed him because they saw the miraculous signs he had performed on the sick. ³Then Jesus went up on a mountainside and sat down with his disciples. ⁴The Jewish Passover Feast was near.

⁵When Jesus looked up and saw a great crowd coming toward him, he said to Philip, "Where shall we buy bread for these people to eat?" ⁶He asked this only to test him, for he already had in mind what he was going to do.

⁷Philip answered him, "Eight months' wages ᶜ would not buy enough bread for each one to have a bite!"

⁸Another of his disciples, Andrew, Simon Peter's brother, spoke up, ⁹"Here is a boy with five small barley loaves and two small fish, but how far will they go among so many?"

¹⁰Jesus said, "Have the people sit down." There was plenty of grass in that place, and the men sat down, about five thousand of them. ¹¹Jesus then took the loaves, gave thanks, and distributed to those who were seated as much as they wanted. He did the same with the fish.

¹²When they had all had enough to eat, he said to his disciples, "Gather the

---

ᵃ39 Or *Study diligently* (the imperative) ᵇ44 Some early manuscripts *the Only One* ᶜ7 Greek *two hundred denarii*

pieces that are left over. Let nothing be wasted." ¹³So they gathered them and filled twelve baskets with the pieces of the five barley loaves left over by those who had eaten.

¹⁴After the people saw the miraculous sign that Jesus did, they began to say, "Surely this is the Prophet who is to come into the world." ¹⁵Jesus, knowing that they intended to come and make him king by force, withdrew again to a mountain by himself.

Jesus Walks on the Water

¹⁶When evening came, his disciples went down to the lake, ¹⁷where they got into a boat and set off across the lake for Capernaum. By now it was dark, and Jesus had not yet joined them. ¹⁸A strong wind was blowing and the waters grew rough. ¹⁹When they had rowed three or three and a half miles,ᵃ they saw Jesus approaching the boat, walking on the water; and they were terrified. ²⁰But he said to them, "It is I; don't be afraid." ²¹Then they were willing to take him into the boat, and immediately the boat reached the shore where they were heading.

²²The next day the crowd that had stayed on the opposite shore of the lake realized that only one boat had been there, and that Jesus had not entered it with his disciples, but that they had gone away alone. ²³Then some boats from Tiberias landed near the place where the people had eaten the bread after the Lord had given thanks. ²⁴Once the crowd realized that neither Jesus nor his disciples were there, they got into the boats and went to Capernaum in search of Jesus.

Jesus the Bread of Life

²⁵When they found him on the other side of the lake, they asked him, "Rabbi, when did you get here?"

²⁶Jesus answered, "I tell you the truth, you are looking for me, not because you saw miraculous signs but because you ate the loaves and had your fill. ²⁷Do not work for food that spoils, but for food that endures to eternal life, which the Son of Man will give you. On him God the Father has placed his seal of approval."

²⁸Then they asked him, "What must we do to do the works God requires?"

²⁹Jesus answered, "The work of God is this: to believe in the one he has sent."

³⁰So they asked him, "What miraculous sign then will you give that we may see it and believe you? What will you do? ³¹Our forefathers ate the manna in the desert; as it is written: 'He gave them bread from heaven to eat.'ᵇ"

³²Jesus said to them, "I tell you the truth, it is not Moses who has given you the bread from heaven, but it is my Father who gives you the true bread from heaven. ³³For the bread of God is he who comes down from heaven and gives life to the world."

³⁴"Sir," they said, "from now on give us this bread."

³⁵Then Jesus declared, "I am the bread of life. He who comes to me will never go hungry, and he who believes in me will never be thirsty. ³⁶But as I told you, you have seen me and still you do not believe. ³⁷All that the Father gives me will come to me, and whoever comes to me I will never drive away. ³⁸For I have come down from heaven not to do my will but to do the will of him who sent me. ³⁹And this is the will of him who sent me, that I shall lose none of all that he has given me, but raise them up at the last day. ⁴⁰For my Father's will is that everyone who looks to the Son and believes in him shall have eternal life, and I will raise him up at the last day."

⁴¹At this the Jews began to grumble about him because he said, "I am the bread that came down from heaven." ⁴²They said, "Is this not Jesus, the son of Joseph, whose father and mother we know? How can he now say, 'I came down from heaven'?"

⁴³"Stop grumbling among yourselves," Jesus answered. ⁴⁴"No one can come to me unless the Father who sent me draws him, and I will raise him up at the last day. ⁴⁵It is written in the Prophets: 'They will all be taught by God.'ᶜ Everyone who listens to the Father and learns from him comes to me. ⁴⁶No one has seen the Fa-

---

ᵃ*19* Greek *rowed twenty-five or thirty stadia* (about 5 or 6 kilometers)   ᵇ*31* Exodus 16:4; Neh. 9:15; Psalm 78:24,25   ᶜ*45* Isaiah 54:13

ther except the one who is from God; only he has seen the Father. [47]I tell you the truth, he who believes has everlasting life. [48]I am the bread of life. [49]Your forefathers ate the manna in the desert, yet they died. [50]But here is the bread that comes down from heaven, which a man may eat and not die. [51]I am the living bread that came down from heaven. If anyone eats of this bread, he will live forever. This bread is my flesh, which I will give for the life of the world."

[52]Then the Jews began to argue sharply among themselves, "How can this man give us his flesh to eat?"

[53]Jesus said to them, "I tell you the truth, unless you eat the flesh of the Son of Man and drink his blood, you have no life in you. [54]Whoever eats my flesh and drinks my blood has eternal life, and I will raise him up at the last day. [55]For my flesh is real food and my blood is real drink. [56]Whoever eats my flesh and drinks my blood remains in me, and I in

him. [57]Just as the living Father sent me and I live because of the Father, so the one who feeds on me will live because of me. [58]This is the bread that came down from heaven. Your forefathers ate manna and died, but he who feeds on this bread will live forever." [59]He said this while teaching in the synagogue in Capernaum.

Many Disciples Desert Jesus

[60]On hearing it, many of his disciples said, "This is a hard teaching. Who can accept it?"

[61]Aware that his disciples were grumbling about this, Jesus said to them, "Does this offend you? [62]What if you see the Son of Man ascend to where he was before! [63]The Spirit gives life; the flesh counts for nothing. The words I have spoken to you are spirit[a] and they are life. [64]Yet there are some of you who do

[a]63 Or *Spirit*

Thursday

Turning From God

Read John 6:60–69

It takes commitment and strength to follow God. The world pressures us to ignore our commitment to God. And sometimes we give in to the pressure and let our commitment slide. There was a time when I turned away from God. I thought I'd finally be able to do what I wanted instead of being "trapped" by all God's rules. But I ended up really unhappy and feeling horrible.

Finally, a good friend asked me why I had turned from God. When I thought about it, I realized I really didn't know why. There was no reason for me to live apart from God. Nothing I had experienced was better than the life I had with God.

Yes, it's challenging to be a Christian. But I know there's nothing out in the world that's better than my relationship with God. There's nothing better than the joy I have when I'm growing in my faith and trying to live for him.

❶ When have you felt like living a Christian life is just too hard? What makes being a Christian so challenging?

❷ Write down 2 things you can do as you grow as a Christian in the next month.

❸ Spend some time thanking God for the ways he's helped you grow in your faith.

Turn to page 1280 for your next devotion.

not believe." For Jesus had known from the beginning which of them did not believe and who would betray him. ⁶⁵He went on to say, "This is why I told you that no one can come to me unless the Father has enabled him."

⁶⁶From this time many of his disciples turned back and no longer followed him.

⁶⁷"You do not want to leave too, do you?" Jesus asked the Twelve.

⁶⁸Simon Peter answered him, "Lord, to whom shall we go? You have the words of eternal life. ⁶⁹We believe and know that you are the Holy One of God."

⁷⁰Then Jesus replied, "Have I not chosen you, the Twelve? Yet one of you is a devil!" ⁷¹(He meant Judas, the son of Simon Iscariot, who, though one of the Twelve, was later to betray him.)

Jesus Goes to the Feast of Tabernacles

7 After this, Jesus went around in Galilee, purposely staying away from Judea because the Jews there were waiting to take his life. ²But when the Jewish Feast of Tabernacles was near, ³Jesus' brothers said to him, "You ought to leave here and go to Judea, so that your disciples may see the miracles you do. ⁴No one who wants to become a public figure acts in secret. Since you are doing these things, show yourself to the world." ⁵For even his own brothers did not believe in him.

⁶Therefore Jesus told them, "The right time for me has not yet come; for you any time is right. ⁷The world cannot hate you, but it hates me because I testify that what it does is evil. ⁸You go to the Feast. I am not yet* going up to this Feast, because for me the right time has not yet come." ⁹Having said this, he stayed in Galilee.

¹⁰However, after his brothers had left for the Feast, he went also, not publicly, but in secret. ¹¹Now at the Feast the Jews were watching for him and asking, "Where is that man?"

¹²Among the crowds there was widespread whispering about him. Some said, "He is a good man."

Others replied, "No, he deceives the people." ¹³But no one would say anything publicly about him for fear of the Jews.

Jesus Teaches at the Feast

¹⁴Not until halfway through the Feast did Jesus go up to the temple courts and begin to teach. ¹⁵The Jews were amazed and asked, "How did this man get such learning without having studied?"

¹⁶Jesus answered, "My teaching is not my own. It comes from him who sent me. ¹⁷If anyone chooses to do God's will, he will find out whether my teaching comes from God or whether I speak on my own. ¹⁸He who speaks on his own does so to gain honor for himself, but he who works for the honor of the one who sent him is a man of truth; there is nothing false about him. ¹⁹Has not Moses given you the law? Yet not one of you keeps the law. Why are you trying to kill me?"

²⁰"You are demon-possessed," the crowd answered. "Who is trying to kill you?"

²¹Jesus said to them, "I did one miracle, and you are all astonished. ²²Yet, because Moses gave you circumcision (though actually it did not come from Moses, but from the patriarchs), you circumcise a child on the Sabbath. ²³Now if a child can be circumcised on the Sabbath so that the law of Moses may not be broken, why are you angry with me for healing the whole man on the Sabbath? ²⁴Stop judging by mere appearances, and make a right judgment."

Is Jesus the Christ?

²⁵At that point some of the people of Jerusalem began to ask, "Isn't this the man they are trying to kill? ²⁶Here he is, speaking publicly, and they are not saying a word to him. Have the authorities really concluded that he is the Christ*? ²⁷But we know where this man is from; when the Christ comes, no one will know where he is from."

²⁸Then Jesus, still teaching in the temple courts, cried out, "Yes, you know me, and you know where I am from. I am not here on my own, but he who sent me is true. You do not know him, ²⁹but I know him because I am from him and he sent me."

³⁰At this they tried to seize him, but no

---

*a 8 Some early manuscripts do not have *yet*.
*b 26 Or *Messiah*; also in verses 27, 31, 41 and 42

one laid a hand on him, because his time had not yet come. ³¹Still, many in the crowd put their faith in him. They said, "When the Christ comes, will he do more miraculous signs than this man?"

³²The Pharisees heard the crowd whispering such things about him. Then the chief priests and the Pharisees sent temple guards to arrest him.

³³Jesus said, "I am with you for only a short time, and then I go to the one who sent me. ³⁴You will look for me, but you will not find me; and where I am, you cannot come."

³⁵The Jews said to one another, "Where does this man intend to go that we cannot find him? Will he go where our people live scattered among the Greeks, and teach the Greeks? ³⁶What did he mean when he said, 'You will look for me, but you will not find me,' and 'Where I am, you cannot come'?"

³⁷On the last and greatest day of the Feast, Jesus stood and said in a loud voice, "If anyone is thirsty, let him come to me and drink. ³⁸Whoever believes in me, as[a] the Scripture has said, streams of living water will flow from within him."

Two-thirds Water

Huh?

John 7:38

Touch your elbow. Now your knee. They seem pretty solid, don't they? Surprise, surprise. Your body is actually two-thirds water. So why would we need any more water inside us? Is Jesus trying to turn us into jellyfish? When Jesus says "streams of living water," he means the Holy Spirit. Just like our physical bodies need water to live, our spiritual souls need the Holy Spirit.

³⁹By this he meant the Spirit, whom those who believed in him were later to receive. Up to that time the Spirit had not been given, since Jesus had not yet been glorified.

⁴⁰On hearing his words, some of the people said, "Surely this man is the Prophet."

⁴¹Others said, "He is the Christ."

Still others asked, "How can the Christ come from Galilee? ⁴²Does not the Scripture say that the Christ will come from David's family[b] and from Bethlehem, the town where David lived?" ⁴³Thus the people were divided because of Jesus. ⁴⁴Some wanted to seize him, but no one laid a hand on him.

Unbelief of the Jewish Leaders

⁴⁵Finally the temple guards went back to the chief priests and Pharisees, who asked them, "Why didn't you bring him in?"

⁴⁶"No one ever spoke the way this man does," the guards declared.

⁴⁷"You mean he has deceived you also?" the Pharisees retorted. ⁴⁸"Has any of the rulers or of the Pharisees believed in him? ⁴⁹No! But this mob that knows nothing of the law—there is a curse on them."

⁵⁰Nicodemus, who had gone to Jesus earlier and who was one of their own number, asked, ⁵¹"Does our law condemn anyone without first hearing him to find out what he is doing?"

⁵²They replied, "Are you from Galilee, too? Look into it, and you will find that a prophet[c] does not come out of Galilee."

[The earliest manuscripts and many other ancient witnesses do not have John 7:53-8:11.]

⁵³Then each went to his own home.

8 But Jesus went to the Mount of Olives. ²At dawn he appeared again in the temple courts, where all the people gathered around him, and he sat down to teach them. ³The teachers of the law and the Pharisees brought in a woman caught in adultery. They made her stand before the group ⁴and said to Jesus, "Teacher, this woman was caught in the act of adultery. ⁵In the Law Moses commanded us to stone such women. Now what do you say?" ⁶They were using this

a37,38 Or | If anyone is thirsty, let him come to me. / And let him drink, 38who believes in me. / As *b42 Greek seed* *c52 Two early manuscripts the Prophet*

question as a trap, in order to have a basis for accusing him.

But Jesus bent down and started to write on the ground with his finger. ⁷When they kept on questioning him, he straightened up and said to them, "If any one of you is without sin, let him be the first to throw a stone at her." ⁸Again he stooped down and wrote on the ground.

⁹At this, those who heard began to go away one at a time, the older ones first, until only Jesus was left, with the woman still standing there. ¹⁰Jesus straightened up and asked her, "Woman, where are they? Has no one condemned you?"

¹¹"No one, sir," she said.

"Then neither do I condemn you," Jesus declared. "Go now and leave your life of sin."

The Validity of Jesus' Testimony

¹²When Jesus spoke again to the people, he said, "I am the light of the world. Whoever follows me will never walk in darkness, but will have the light of life." ¹³The Pharisees challenged him, "Here you are, appearing as your own witness; your testimony is not valid."

¹⁴Jesus answered, "Even if I testify on my own behalf, my testimony is valid, for I know where I came from and where I am going. But you have no idea where I come from or where I am going. ¹⁵You judge by human standards; I pass judgment on no one. ¹⁶But if I do judge, my decisions are right, because I am not alone. I stand with the Father, who sent me. ¹⁷In your own Law it is written that the testimony of two men is valid. ¹⁸I am one who testifies for myself; my other witness is the Father, who sent me."

Friday

Leaving Sin Behind   **Read John 8:3–11**

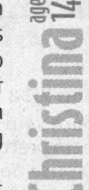

This passage means a lot to me. I can relate to the woman accused of adultery because I've also had sexual sin in my life. But because Jesus forgave this woman, I know he forgives me too.

Forgiveness is a wonderful gift from our loving, caring God. But there's a lot more to being forgiven than just having my sins washed away. Jesus says something very important to the woman in this passage. He tells her to "leave [her] life of sin." She's forgiven, but she also needs to change her life. Jesus' words remind me that I need to keep living for him, even when I've sinned. I shouldn't keep sinning just because God will keep forgiving me. I need to try not to sin.

It's not easy, and I know I'll always be a sinner. But I also know God wants me to do my best to stay away from sin. God knows I only hurt myself and others when I do things he's told me not to do. He wants me to learn from my mistakes and leave my life of sin behind.

❶ Think of one sin you really struggle with. How does that sin affect you? How does it affect other people? How does it affect your relationship with God?

❷ When you're ready to get rid of this sin, write a letter to God. Tell him you're sorry and ask him to forgive you. Tell him you need his help to change. Thank him for his forgiveness.

❸ Read your letter out loud as a prayer to God.

Turn to page 1283 for your next devotion.

¹⁹Then they asked him, "Where is your father?"

"You do not know me or my Father," Jesus replied. "If you knew me, you would know my Father also." ²⁰He spoke these words while teaching in the temple area near the place where the offerings were put. Yet no one seized him, because his time had not yet come.

²¹Once more Jesus said to them, "I am going away, and you will look for me, and you will die in your sin. Where I go, you cannot come."

²²This made the Jews ask, "Will he kill himself? Is that why he says, 'Where I go, you cannot come'?"

²³But he continued, "You are from below; I am from above. You are of this world; I am not of this world. ²⁴I told you that you would die in your sins; if you do not believe that I am the one I claim to be,ᵃ you will indeed die in your sins."

²⁵"Who are you?" they asked.

"Just what I have been claiming all along," Jesus replied. ²⁶"I have much to say in judgment of you. But he who sent me is reliable, and what I have heard from him I tell the world."

²⁷They did not understand that he was telling them about his Father. ²⁸So Jesus said, "When you have lifted up the Son of Man, then you will know that I am the one I claim to be and that I do nothing on my own but speak just what the Father has taught me. ²⁹The one who sent me is with me; he has not left me alone, for I always do what pleases him." ³⁰Even as he spoke, many put their faith in him.

The Children of Abraham

³¹To the Jews who had believed him, Jesus said, "If you hold to my teaching, you are really my disciples. ³²Then you will know the truth, and the truth will set you free."

³³They answered him, "We are Abraham's descendantsᵇ and have never been slaves of anyone. How can you say that we shall be set free?"

³⁴Jesus replied, "I tell you the truth, everyone who sins is a slave to sin. ³⁵Now a slave has no permanent place in the family, but a son belongs to it forever. ³⁶So if the Son sets you free, you will be free indeed. ³⁷I know you are Abraham's descendants. Yet you are ready to kill me, because you have no room for my word. ³⁸I am telling you what I have seen in the Father's presence, and you do what you have heard from your father.ᶜ"

³⁹"Abraham is our father," they answered.

"If you were Abraham's children," said Jesus, "then you wouldᵈ do the things Abraham did. ⁴⁰As it is, you are determined to kill me, a man who has told you the truth that I heard from God. Abraham did not do such things. ⁴¹You are doing the things your own father does."

"We are not illegitimate children," they protested. "The only Father we have is God himself."

The Children of the Devil

⁴²Jesus said to them, "If God were your Father, you would love me, for I came from God and now am here. I have not come on my own; but he sent me. ⁴³Why is my language not clear to you? Because you are unable to hear what I say. ⁴⁴You belong to your father, the devil, and you want to carry out your father's desire. He was a murderer from the beginning, not holding to the truth, for there is no truth in him. When he lies, he speaks his native language, for he is a liar and the father of lies. ⁴⁵Yet because I tell the truth, you do not believe me! ⁴⁶Can any of you prove me guilty of sin? If I am telling the truth, why don't you believe me? ⁴⁷He who belongs to God hears what God says. The reason you do not hear is that you do not belong to God."

The Claims of Jesus About Himself

⁴⁸The Jews answered him, "Aren't we right in saying that you are a Samaritan and demon-possessed?"

⁴⁹"I am not possessed by a demon," said Jesus, "but I honor my Father and you dishonor me. ⁵⁰I am not seeking glory for myself; but there is one who seeks it, and he is the judge. ⁵¹I tell you the

---

ᵃ24 Or *I am he*; also in verse 28   ᵇ33 Greek *seed*; also in verse 37   ᶜ38 Or *presence. Therefore do what you have heard from the Father.*   ᵈ39 Some early manuscripts *"If you are Abraham's children," said Jesus, "then*

truth, if anyone keeps my word, he will never see death."

⁵²At this the Jews exclaimed, "Now we know that you are demon-possessed! Abraham died and so did the prophets, yet you say that if anyone keeps your word, he will never taste death. ⁵³Are you greater than our father Abraham? He died, and so did the prophets. Who do you think you are?"

⁵⁴Jesus replied, "If I glorify myself, my glory means nothing. My Father, whom you claim as your God, is the one who glorifies me. ⁵⁵Though you do not know him, I know him. If I said I did not, I would be a liar like you, but I do know him and keep his word. ⁵⁶Your father Abraham rejoiced at the thought of seeing my day; he saw it and was glad."

⁵⁷"You are not yet fifty years old," the Jews said to him, "and you have seen Abraham!"

⁵⁸"I tell you the truth," Jesus answered, "before Abraham was born, I am!" ⁵⁹At this, they picked up stones to stone him, but Jesus hid himself, slipping away from the temple grounds.

The Oldest Guy Around

Huh?

John 8:58–59

Who is the oldest person you know? No matter whom you came up with, Jesus is way older. He's been around since way before the world was created. He was in heaven when Adam and Eve, Abraham, Moses and David were alive. If Jesus were just a human, um . . . he'd be dead. But because he's God, he's still just as big and strong as ever.

Jesus Heals a Man Born Blind

9 As he went along, he saw a man blind from birth. ²His disciples asked him, "Rabbi, who sinned, this man or his parents, that he was born blind?"

³"Neither this man nor his parents sinned," said Jesus, "but this happened so that the work of God might be displayed in his life. ⁴As long as it is day, we

must do the work of him who sent me. Night is coming, when no one can work. ⁵While I am in the world, I am the light of the world."

⁶Having said this, he spit on the ground, made some mud with the saliva, and put it on the man's eyes. ⁷"Go," he told him, "wash in the Pool of Siloam" (this word means Sent). So the man went and washed, and came home seeing.

⁸His neighbors and those who had formerly seen him begging asked, "Isn't this the same man who used to sit and beg?" ⁹Some claimed that he was.

Others said, "No, he only looks like him."

But he himself insisted, "I am the man."

¹⁰"How then were your eyes opened?" they demanded.

¹¹He replied, "The man they call Jesus made some mud and put it on my eyes. He told me to go to Siloam and wash. So I went and washed, and then I could see."

¹²"Where is this man?" they asked him.

"I don't know," he said.

The Pharisees Investigate the Healing

¹³They brought to the Pharisees the man who had been blind. ¹⁴Now the day on which Jesus had made the mud and opened the man's eyes was a Sabbath. ¹⁵Therefore the Pharisees also asked him how he had received his sight. "He put mud on my eyes," the man replied, "and I washed, and now I see."

¹⁶Some of the Pharisees said, "This man is not from God, for he does not keep the Sabbath."

But others asked, "How can a sinner do such miraculous signs?" So they were divided.

¹⁷Finally they turned again to the blind man, "What have you to say about him? It was your eyes he opened."

The man replied, "He is a prophet."

¹⁸The Jews still did not believe that he had been blind and had received his sight until they sent for the man's parents. ¹⁹"Is this your son?" they asked. "Is this the one you say was born blind? How is it that now he can see?"

²⁰"We know he is our son," the parents answered, "and we know he was born

blind. ²¹But how he can see now, or who opened his eyes, we don't know. Ask him. He is of age; he will speak for himself." ²²His parents said this because they were afraid of the Jews, for already the Jews had decided that anyone who acknowledged that Jesus was the Christ^a

would be put out of the synagogue. ²³That was why his parents said, "He is of age; ask him."

²⁴A second time they summoned the man who had been blind. "Give glory to

^a 22 Or *Messiah*

Week end.

Follow, Follow

Read John 8:48–59

In Friday's devotional, Christina said that Jesus' words helped her remember that she needed to "keep living for him." Living for him means following him and trying to do what he does (like loving people and stuff like that). But sometimes it's hard to know what he would do!

Even when he was on earth, hardly anybody could figure Jesus out—not his family, not his disciples, not the religious leaders, not his friends and not his enemies. There are examples all over the Gospels (the 4 Jesus-stories) where people either misunderstood his teaching or didn't get it at all, questioned his actions and just basically missed the point. His actions were so different, his claims so outrageous, his words so strange and his talk about God so "way out" that people were confused at best and totally ticked off at worst. Everywhere Jesus went he shattered people's ideas of what he *should* do and how he was *supposed* to act. In the verses you read today, he so offended the people around him that they tried to kill him by throwing rocks at him.

It's important to remember (and Jesus says this in these verses) that Jesus Christ was not "sort of" God or somehow a second-level God or a good man with godly qualities. His statement here is pretty much the same as what God said to Moses in Exodus 3:14–15: "I AM WHO I AM. This is what you are to say to the Israelites: 'I AM has sent me to you.' " So Jesus was telling everybody that he was God. Again, just when everyone thought they had Jesus figured out, many found out they were wrong.

But the fact that Jesus is God, not just a good man, is exactly why we should live for him and try to be like him. He's the King!

What about You?

❶ How would your friends who don't go to a church describe Jesus? Do they think you're crazy to live for him? (Do they even know you're living for him?)

❷ On the left side of a note card or piece of paper, make a short list of a few words that say why you want to live for Jesus (like "he's my friend," "he cares," "he's powerful"). On the right side, make a list of what you lose out on by *not* living for him (like "on my own," "lonely inside"). As you look at these 2 lists, which sounds more "nuts"—to live for Jesus or not to? Keep this list in a place where you can pull it out when you feel like you're "nuts" for being his disciple.

❸ Ask God to give you confidence to follow him during the coming week.

Turn to page 1285 for your next devotion.

God,[a]" they said. "We know this man is a sinner."

[25]He replied, "Whether he is a sinner or not, I don't know. One thing I do know. I was blind but now I see!"

[26]Then they asked him, "What did he do to you? How did he open your eyes?"

[27]He answered, "I have told you already and you did not listen. Why do you want to hear it again? Do you want to become his disciples, too?"

[28]Then they hurled insults at him and said, "You are this fellow's disciple! We are disciples of Moses! [29]We know that God spoke to Moses, but as for this fellow, we don't even know where he comes from."

[30]The man answered, "Now that is remarkable! You don't know where he comes from, yet he opened my eyes. [31]We know that God does not listen to sinners. He listens to the godly man who does his will. [32]Nobody has ever heard of opening the eyes of a man born blind. [33]If this man were not from God, he could do nothing."

[34]To this they replied, "You were steeped in sin at birth; how dare you lecture us!" And they threw him out.

Spiritual Blindness

[35]Jesus heard that they had thrown him out, and when he found him, he said, "Do you believe in the Son of Man?"

[36]"Who is he, sir?" the man asked. "Tell me so that I may believe in him."

[37]Jesus said, "You have now seen him; in fact, he is the one speaking with you."

[38]Then the man said, "Lord, I believe," and he worshiped him.

[39]Jesus said, "For judgment I have come into this world, so that the blind will see and those who see will become blind."

[40]Some Pharisees who were with him heard him say this and asked, "What? Are we blind too?"

[41]Jesus said, "If you were blind, you would not be guilty of sin; but now that you claim you can see, your guilt remains.

The Shepherd and His Flock

10 "I tell you the truth, the man who does not enter the sheep pen by the gate, but climbs in by some other way, is a thief and a robber. [2]The man who enters by the gate is the shepherd of his sheep. [3]The watchman opens the gate for him, and the sheep listen to his voice. He calls his own sheep by name and leads them out. [4]When he has brought out all his own, he goes on ahead of them, and his sheep follow him because they know his voice. [5]But they will never follow a stranger; in fact, they will run away from him because they do not recognize a stranger's voice." [6]Jesus used this figure of speech, but they did not understand what he was telling them.

[7]Therefore Jesus said again, "I tell you the truth, I am the gate for the sheep. [8]All who ever came before me were thieves and robbers, but the sheep did not listen to them. [9]I am the gate; whoever enters through me will be saved.[b] He will come in and go out, and find pasture. [10]The thief comes only to steal and kill and destroy; I have come that they may have life, and have it to the full.

[11]"I am the good shepherd. The good shepherd lays down his life for the sheep. [12]The hired hand is not the shepherd who owns the sheep. So when he sees the wolf coming, he abandons the sheep and runs away. Then the wolf attacks the flock and scatters it. [13]The man runs away because he is a hired hand and cares nothing for the sheep.

[14]"I am the good shepherd; I know my sheep and my sheep know me— [15]just as the Father knows me and I know the Father—and I lay down my life for the sheep. [16]I have other sheep that are not of this sheep pen. I must bring them also. They too will listen to my voice, and there shall be one flock and one shepherd. [17]The reason my Father loves me is that I lay down my life—only to take it up again. [18]No one takes it from me, but I lay it down of my own accord. I have authority to lay it down and authority to take it up again. This command I received from my Father."

[19]At these words the Jews were again divided. [20]Many of them said, "He is de-

---

[a]24 A solemn charge to tell the truth (see Joshua 7:19)   [b]9 Or *kept safe*

mon-possessed and raving mad. Why listen to him?"

²¹But others said, "These are not the sayings of a man possessed by a demon. Can a demon open the eyes of the blind?"

The Unbelief of the Jews

²²Then came the Feast of Dedication*a* at Jerusalem. It was winter, ²³and Jesus was in the temple area walking in Solomon's Colonnade. ²⁴The Jews gathered around him, saying, "How long will you keep us in suspense? If you are the Christ,*b* tell us plainly."

²⁵Jesus answered, "I did tell you, but you do not believe. The miracles I do in my Father's name speak for me, ²⁶but you do not believe because you are not my sheep. ²⁷My sheep listen to my voice; I know them, and they follow me. ²⁸I give them eternal life, and they shall never perish; no one can snatch them out of my hand. ²⁹My Father, who has given them to me, is greater than all*c*; no one

can snatch them out of my Father's hand. ³⁰I and the Father are one."

³¹Again the Jews picked up stones to stone him, ³²but Jesus said to them, "I have shown you many great miracles from the Father. For which of these do you stone me?"

³³"We are not stoning you for any of these," replied the Jews, "but for blasphemy, because you, a mere man, claim to be God."

³⁴Jesus answered them, "Is it not written in your Law, 'I have said you are gods'*d*? ³⁵If he called them 'gods,' to whom the word of God came—and the Scripture cannot be broken— ³⁶what about the one whom the Father set apart as his very own and sent into the world? Why then do you accuse me of blasphemy because I said, 'I am God's Son'? ³⁷Do

a22 That is, Hanukkah b24 Or Messiah c29 Many early manuscripts What my Father has given me is greater than all d34 Psalm 82:6

Mon day

God's No Party Pooper!

Read John 10:10

I used to think that being a Christian was about the most boring thing in the world. It seemed like it was a bunch of do's and don'ts. I thought God didn't want me to have any fun.

But when I see all the problems sin causes in people's lives, I realize there's a reason God wants us to live life his way. God wants us to stay away from the stuff that *seems* fun but really only gets us into trouble, like sex outside of marriage and drugs and drinking. God's way is so much better.

When we follow God, we avoid problems like drunk driving, an unwanted pregnancy, sexual diseases and drug overdoses. Instead, we get to live free from those things and enjoy life to the fullest.

Shannon age 13

What about You?

❶ Think about someone you know who's really caught up in sin. Does that person seem happy to you? If so, do you think that happiness will last? Why do you think God warns us to stay away from things that the world says are "fun"?

❷ Think of 3 things that help you enjoy life to the fullest as a Christian. Try to do at least 1 of those things this week.

❸ Tell God how great it is to have him in your life.

Turn to page 1291 for your next devotion.

not believe me unless I do what my Father does. [38]But if I do it, even though you do not believe me, believe the miracles, that you may know and understand that the Father is in me, and I in the Father." [39]Again they tried to seize him, but he escaped their grasp.

[40]Then Jesus went back across the Jordan to the place where John had been baptizing in the early days. Here he stayed [41]and many people came to him. They said, "Though John never performed a miraculous sign, all that John said about this man was true." [42]And in that place many believed in Jesus.

The Death of Lazarus

11 Now a man named Lazarus was sick. He was from Bethany, the village of Mary and her sister Martha. [2]This Mary, whose brother Lazarus now lay sick, was the same one who poured perfume on the Lord and wiped his feet with her hair. [3]So the sisters sent word to Jesus, "Lord, the one you love is sick."

[4]When he heard this, Jesus said, "This sickness will not end in death. No, it is for God's glory so that God's Son may be glorified through it." [5]Jesus loved Martha and her sister and Lazarus. [6]Yet when he heard that Lazarus was sick, he stayed where he was two more days.

[7]Then he said to his disciples, "Let us go back to Judea."

[8]"But Rabbi," they said, "a short while ago the Jews tried to stone you, and yet you are going back there?"

[9]Jesus answered, "Are there not twelve hours of daylight? A man who walks by day will not stumble, for he sees by this world's light. [10]It is when he walks by night that he stumbles, for he has no light."

[11]After he had said this, he went on to tell them, "Our friend Lazarus has fallen asleep; but I am going there to wake him up."

[12]His disciples replied, "Lord, if he sleeps, he will get better." [13]Jesus had been speaking of his death, but his disciples thought he meant natural sleep.

[14]So then he told them plainly, "Lazarus is dead, [15]and for your sake I am glad I was not there, so that you may believe. But let us go to him."

[16]Then Thomas (called Didymus) said to the rest of the disciples, "Let us also go, that we may die with him."

Jesus Comforts the Sisters

[17]On his arrival, Jesus found that Lazarus had already been in the tomb for four days. [18]Bethany was less than two miles[a] from Jerusalem, [19]and many Jews had come to Martha and Mary to comfort them in the loss of their brother. [20]When Martha heard that Jesus was coming, she went out to meet him, but Mary stayed at home.

[21]"Lord," Martha said to Jesus, "if you had been here, my brother would not have died. [22]But I know that even now God will give you whatever you ask."

[23]Jesus said to her, "Your brother will rise again."

[24]Martha answered, "I know he will rise again in the resurrection at the last day."

[25]Jesus said to her, "I am the resurrection and the life. He who believes in me will live, even though he dies; [26]and whoever lives and believes in me will never die. Do you believe this?"

[27]"Yes, Lord," she told him, "I believe that you are the Christ,[b] the Son of God, who was to come into the world."

[28]And after she had said this, she went back and called her sister Mary aside. "The Teacher is here," she said, "and is asking for you." [29]When Mary heard this, she got up quickly and went to him. [30]Now Jesus had not yet entered the village, but was still at the place where Martha had met him. [31]When the Jews who had been with Mary in the house, comforting her, noticed how quickly she got up and went out, they followed her, supposing she was going to the tomb to mourn there.

[32]When Mary reached the place where Jesus was and saw him, she fell at his feet and said, "Lord, if you had been here, my brother would not have died."

[33]When Jesus saw her weeping, and the Jews who had come along with her also weeping, he was deeply moved in spirit and troubled. [34]"Where have you laid him?" he asked.

---

[a]18 Greek *fifteen stadia* (about 3 kilometers)
[b]27 Or *Messiah*

Interesting Facts About Jesus

Jesus was a human being, like you and me. Here are some interesting, rare, unique ways of thinking about who Jesus is. These may even help you think about who Jesus is to you personally.

Was Jesus born on December 25?
Jesus probably wasn't born on December 25. The early church didn't think it was important to note the exact day when Jesus was born. But we do have a general idea. The Gospel of Luke states that the shepherds received the announcement of Jesus Christ's birth while watching their sheep by night (see Luke 2:8, page 1220). Shepherds guarded their flocks day and night only at lambing time, in the spring. During winter months, animals were kept in corrals at night, and there was no need to tend to them.

Jesus spoke 3 languages.
Jesus grew up in a culturally diverse area where the common language was Aramaic. Since he was a Jew, he had to know how to read Hebrew in order to read Scripture. He is also quoted as speaking Greek.

Jesus liked a party.
Jesus tells 3 stories in Luke 15: the lost sheep, the lost coin, the lost son. All of them end in a giant celebration.

Jesus' teenage years are a secret.
Ever wondered what Jesus was like as a teenager? Well, so does everybody else. Nothing was ever recorded in the Bible. The last reference we see about Jesus before he was an adult was when he disappeared for 3 days and stressed his parents out. Jesus' teenage years are described in one sentence in Luke 2:52, page 1221.

Jesus participated in sports.
The sports Jesus may have participated in include hiking (look at the distances he traveled on foot) and sailing (check out Matthew 8:24–27, page 1151). And he probably liked fishing (for people, as well as fish; see Luke 5:10, page 1226).

Jesus grew up just outside of a major city.
Just 3 miles away from where Jesus grew up was a city called Sepphoris. Sepphoris was known as the jewel of the Galilee. It was one of the capital cities of Galilee and was the first capital of Herod's son. This was a pretty happening place at the time. It had Greek theaters (the people went to plays), plumbing, a full-working aqueduct system (that's what got water to the city) and Roman baths.

Jesus hung out with a wild bunch of friends.
Jesus spent time with people other than the disciples, you know. Some of them had pretty wild reputations. A good example is when Jesus had dinner with a guy who was a social outcast (Luke 19:5–10, page 1252).

The shortest verse is about Jesus.
Did you ever wonder what's the shortest verse in the entire Bible? It's "Jesus wept" (John 11:35).

"Come and see, Lord," they replied.

³⁵Jesus wept.

³⁶Then the Jews said, "See how he loved him!"

³⁷But some of them said, "Could not he who opened the eyes of the blind man have kept this man from dying?"

Jesus Raises Lazarus From the Dead

³⁸Jesus, once more deeply moved, came to the tomb. It was a cave with a stone laid across the entrance. ³⁹"Take away the stone," he said.

"But, Lord," said Martha, the sister of the dead man, "by this time there is a bad odor, for he has been there four days."

⁴⁰Then Jesus said, "Did I not tell you that if you believed, you would see the glory of God?"

⁴¹So they took away the stone. Then Jesus looked up and said, "Father, I thank you that you have heard me. ⁴²I knew that you always hear me, but I said this for the benefit of the people standing here, that they may believe that you sent me."

[43]When he had said this, Jesus called in a loud voice, "Lazarus, come out!" [44]The dead man came out, his hands and feet wrapped with strips of linen, and a cloth around his face.

Jesus said to them, "Take off the grave clothes and let him go."

The Plot to Kill Jesus

[45]Therefore many of the Jews who had come to visit Mary, and had seen what Jesus did, put their faith in him. [46]But some of them went to the Pharisees and told them what Jesus had done. [47]Then the chief priests and the Pharisees called a meeting of the Sanhedrin.

"What are we accomplishing?" they asked. "Here is this man performing many miraculous signs. [48]If we let him go on like this, everyone will believe in him, and then the Romans will come and take away both our place[a] and our nation."

[49]Then one of them, named Caiaphas, who was high priest that year, spoke up, "You know nothing at all! [50]You do not realize that it is better for you that one man die for the people than that the whole nation perish."

Order in the Court

Huh?

John 11:47–50
The Jews had this big fancy name for their Supreme Court: the Sanhedrin. Not just anybody could be in the Sanhedrin. You had to be a chief priest, elder or a guy who taught the law (sorry, no women allowed on this court). As long as the Romans were in control, the 71 members of the Sanhedrin could make all sorts of important decisions, except for the decision to kill someone (only the Roman government could pass a death sentence). The Sanhedrin was never quite sure what to do about Jesus. They wanted him dead, but they didn't have the authority to kill him.

[51]He did not say this on his own, but as high priest that year he prophesied that Jesus would die for the Jewish nation,

[52]and not only for that nation but also for the scattered children of God, to bring them together and make them one. [53]So from that day on they plotted to take his life.

[54]Therefore Jesus no longer moved about publicly among the Jews. Instead he withdrew to a region near the desert, to a village called Ephraim, where he stayed with his disciples.

[55]When it was almost time for the Jewish Passover, many went up from the country to Jerusalem for their ceremonial cleansing before the Passover. [56]They kept looking for Jesus, and as they stood in the temple area they asked one another, "What do you think? Isn't he coming to the Feast at all?" [57]But the chief priests and Pharisees had given orders that if anyone found out where Jesus was, he should report it so that they might arrest him.

Jesus Anointed at Bethany

12 Six days before the Passover, Jesus arrived at Bethany, where Lazarus lived, whom Jesus had raised from the dead. [2]Here a dinner was given in Jesus' honor. Martha served, while Lazarus was among those reclining at the table with him. [3]Then Mary took about a pint[b] of pure nard, an expensive perfume; she poured it on Jesus' feet and wiped his feet with her hair. And the house was filled with the fragrance of the perfume.

[4]But one of his disciples, Judas Iscariot, who was later to betray him, objected, [5]"Why wasn't this perfume sold and the money given to the poor? It was worth a year's wages.[c]" [6]He did not say this because he cared about the poor but because he was a thief; as keeper of the money bag, he used to help himself to what was put into it.

[7]"Leave her alone," Jesus replied. "It was intended, that she should save this perfume for the day of my burial. [8]You will always have the poor among you, but you will not always have me."

[9]Meanwhile a large crowd of Jews found out that Jesus was there and came,

---

[a]48 Or *temple*   [b]3 Greek *a litra* (probably about 0.5 liter)   [c]5 Greek *three hundred denarii*

not only because of him but also to see Lazarus, whom he had raised from the dead. ¹⁰So the chief priests made plans to kill Lazarus as well, ¹¹for on account of him many of the Jews were going over to Jesus and putting their faith in him.

The Triumphal Entry

¹²The next day the great crowd that had come for the Feast heard that Jesus was on his way to Jerusalem. ¹³They took palm branches and went out to meet him, shouting,

"Hosanna!ᵃ"

"Blessed is he who comes in the name of the Lord!"ᵇ

"Blessed is the King of Israel!"

The Wave
Huh?

John 12:13
Usually when we wave at someone, we're saying "Hi" or "Goodbye." But in Jesus' day, people waved palm branches at those they considered heroes. It was like rolling out the red carpet to honor a famous celebrity.

¹⁴Jesus found a young donkey and sat upon it, as it is written,

¹⁵"Do not be afraid, O Daughter of Zion; see, your king is coming, seated on a donkey's colt."ᶜ

¹⁶At first his disciples did not understand all this. Only after Jesus was glorified did they realize that these things had been written about him and that they had done these things to him.

¹⁷Now the crowd that was with him when he called Lazarus from the tomb and raised him from the dead continued to spread the word. ¹⁸Many people, because they had heard that he had given this miraculous sign, went out to meet him. ¹⁹So the Pharisees said to one another, "See, this is getting us nowhere. Look how the whole world has gone after him!"

Jesus Predicts His Death

²⁰Now there were some Greeks among those who went up to worship at the Feast. ²¹They came to Philip, who was from Bethsaida in Galilee, with a request. "Sir," they said, "we would like to see Jesus." ²²Philip went to tell Andrew; Andrew and Philip in turn told Jesus.

²³Jesus replied, "The hour has come for the Son of Man to be glorified. ²⁴I tell you the truth, unless a kernel of wheat falls to the ground and dies, it remains only a single seed. But if it dies, it produces many seeds. ²⁵The man who loves his life will lose it, while the man who hates his life in this world will keep it for eternal life. ²⁶Whoever serves me must follow me; and where I am, my servant also will be. My Father will honor the one who serves me.

²⁷"Now my heart is troubled, and what shall I say? 'Father, save me from this hour'? No, it was for this very reason I came to this hour. ²⁸Father, glorify your name!"

Then a voice came from heaven, "I have glorified it, and will glorify it again." ²⁹The crowd that was there and heard it said it had thundered; others said an angel had spoken to him.

³⁰Jesus said, "This voice was for your benefit, not mine. ³¹Now is the time for judgment on this world; now the prince of this world will be driven out. ³²But I, when I am lifted up from the earth, will draw all men to myself." ³³He said this to show the kind of death he was going to die.

³⁴The crowd spoke up, "We have heard from the Law that the Christᵈ will remain forever, so how can you say, 'The Son of Man must be lifted up'? Who is this 'Son of Man'?"

³⁵Then Jesus told them, "You are going to have the light just a little while longer. Walk while you have the light, before darkness overtakes you. The man who walks in the dark does not know where he is going. ³⁶Put your trust in the light while you have it, so that you may become sons of light." When he had

ᵃ*13* A Hebrew expression meaning "Save!" which became an exclamation of praise   ᵇ*13* Psalm 118:25,26   ᶜ*15* Zech. 9:9   ᵈ*34* Or *Messiah*

finished speaking, Jesus left and hid himself from them.

The Jews Continue in Their Unbelief

[37]Even after Jesus had done all these miraculous signs in their presence, they still would not believe in him. [38]This was to fulfill the word of Isaiah the prophet:

"Lord, who has believed our message
    and to whom has the arm of the
        Lord been revealed?"[a]

[39]For this reason they could not believe, because, as Isaiah says elsewhere:

[40]"He has blinded their eyes
    and deadened their hearts,
so they can neither see with their
      eyes,
    nor understand with their hearts,
nor turn—and I would heal them."[b]

[41]Isaiah said this because he saw Jesus' glory and spoke about him.

[42]Yet at the same time many even among the leaders believed in him. But because of the Pharisees they would not confess their faith for fear they would be put out of the synagogue; [43]for they loved praise from men more than praise from God.

[44]Then Jesus cried out, "When a man believes in me, he does not believe in me only, but in the one who sent me. [45]When he looks at me, he sees the one who sent me. [46]I have come into the world as a light, so that no one who believes in me should stay in darkness.

[47]"As for the person who hears my words but does not keep them, I do not judge him. For I did not come to judge the world, but to save it. [48]There is a judge for the one who rejects me and does not accept my words; that very word which I spoke will condemn him at the last day. [49]For I did not speak of my own accord, but the Father who sent me commanded me what to say and how to say it. [50]I know that his command leads to eternal life. So whatever I say is just what the Father has told me to say."

Jesus Washes His Disciples' Feet

13 It was just before the Passover Feast. Jesus knew that the time had come for him to leave this world and go to the Father. Having loved his own who were in the world, he now showed them the full extent of his love.[c]

[2]The evening meal was being served, and the devil had already prompted Judas Iscariot, son of Simon, to betray Jesus. [3]Jesus knew that the Father had put all things under his power, and that he had come from God and was returning to God; [4]so he got up from the meal, took off his outer clothing, and wrapped a towel around his waist. [5]After that, he poured water into a basin and began to wash his disciples' feet, drying them with the towel that was wrapped around him.

Stinky Feet

Huh?

John 13:5

If 12 of your friends walked around in dirt for several days, didn't shower and then took off their shoes, their feet would stink something awful. Usually servants did lowly tasks such as washing feet, but Jesus wanted to make a point. Serving means volunteering to do the job no one else wants to do (even if you have to plug your nose as you do it!).

[6]He came to Simon Peter, who said to him, "Lord, are you going to wash my feet?"

[7]Jesus replied, "You do not realize now what I am doing, but later you will understand."

[8]"No," said Peter, "you shall never wash my feet."

Jesus answered, "Unless I wash you, you have no part with me."

[9]"Then, Lord," Simon Peter replied, "not just my feet but my hands and my head as well!"

[10]Jesus answered, "A person who has had a bath needs only to wash his feet; his whole body is clean. And you are clean, though not every one of you."

---

[a]38 Isaiah 53:1   [b]40 Isaiah 6:10   [c]1 Or he loved them to the last

¹¹For he knew who was going to betray him, and that was why he said not every one was clean.

¹²When he had finished washing their feet, he put on his clothes and returned to his place. "Do you understand what I have done for you?" he asked them. ¹³"You call me 'Teacher' and 'Lord,' and rightly so, for that is what I am. ¹⁴Now that I, your Lord and Teacher, have washed your feet, you also should wash one another's feet. ¹⁵I have set you an example that you should do as I have done for you. ¹⁶I tell you the truth, no servant is greater than his master, nor is a messenger greater than the one who sent him. ¹⁷Now that you know these things, you will be blessed if you do them.

Jesus Predicts His Betrayal

¹⁸"I am not referring to all of you; I know those I have chosen. But this is to fulfill the scripture: 'He who shares my bread has lifted up his heel against me.'ᵃ

¹⁹"I am telling you now before it happens, so that when it does happen you will believe that I am He. ²⁰I tell you the truth, whoever accepts anyone I send accepts me; and whoever accepts me accepts the one who sent me."

²¹After he had said this, Jesus was troubled in spirit and testified, "I tell you the truth, one of you is going to betray me."

²²His disciples stared at one another, at a loss to know which of them he meant. ²³One of them, the disciple whom Jesus loved, was reclining next to him. ²⁴Simon Peter motioned to this disciple and said, "Ask him which one he means."

²⁵Leaning back against Jesus, he asked him, "Lord, who is it?"

²⁶Jesus answered, "It is the one to

ᵃ18 Psalm 41:9

Tuesday

His Love in Us
Read John 13:34–35

One of my friends wasn't a Christian, but she knew I was. I didn't know it, but she was really watching me to see what this whole Christianity thing was all about. One day, she told me she'd been paying attention to the way I treated people. She said one of my best traits was that I never hated anyone; or at least never acted like I did.

From that day on, she began to talk to me more about my faith. She was hesitant to become a Christian herself, but she always had a lot of questions for me. Finally, right before Christmas, she gave her life to the Lord!

I feel fortunate that God used me as an example of the love Christians have for other people. Whenever we show our love to our friends and family, we show people that our relationship with Jesus Christ is based on love. And there's not a person in the world who doesn't need love.

God tells us to love others so that they'll see *his* love in us. When we show God's love to people, powerful things can happen. Just ask my friend!

Mindy, age 14

What about You?

❶ What are some of the ways other Christians have shown you God's love?

❷ Think of a person at your school who could use a dose of God's love. What can you do to show love to this person?

❸ Ask God to help you show his love to others.

Turn to page 1292 for your next devotion.

whom I will give this piece of bread when I have dipped it in the dish." Then, dipping the piece of bread, he gave it to Judas Iscariot, son of Simon. ²⁷As soon as Judas took the bread, Satan entered into him.

"What you are about to do, do quickly," Jesus told him, ²⁸but no one at the meal understood why Jesus said this to him. ²⁹Since Judas had charge of the money, some thought Jesus was telling him to buy what was needed for the Feast, or to give something to the poor. ³⁰As soon as Judas had taken the bread, he went out. And it was night.

Jesus Predicts Peter's Denial

³¹When he was gone, Jesus said, "Now is the Son of Man glorified and God is glorified in him. ³²If God is glorified in him,ᵃ God will glorify the Son in himself, and will glorify him at once.

³³"My children, I will be with you only a little longer. You will look for me, and just as I told the Jews, so I tell you now: Where I am going, you cannot come.

³⁴"A new command I give you: Love one another. As I have loved you, so you must love one another. ³⁵By this all men will know that you are my disciples, if you love one another."

³⁶Simon Peter asked him, "Lord, where are you going?"

Jesus replied, "Where I am going, you cannot follow now, but you will follow later."

³⁷Peter asked, "Lord, why can't I follow you now? I will lay down my life for you."

³⁸Then Jesus answered, "Will you really lay down your life for me? I tell you the truth, before the rooster crows, you will disown me three times!

Jesus Comforts His Disciples

14 "Do not let your hearts be troubled. Trust in Godᵇ; trust also in me. ²In my Father's house are many rooms; if it were not so, I would have

ᵃ32 Many early manuscripts do not have *If God is glorified in him.*   ᵇ1 Or *You trust in God*

Wednesday

It's the Truth!

Read John 14:6

Last Friday night, I went on a hayride with my friend's youth group. We played games, ate sloppy joes and made s'mores over a campfire. It was an outreach night, so there were lots of non-Christians there. During the hayride, my friend and I tried to talk to some kids who weren't Christians. It was hard trying to talk to them about God. I didn't know what to say. I wish I had thought of telling them this verse.

This verse tells us that the only way to know God is through Jesus. We have to trust in him alone. That means doing good things or going to church won't make you a Christian. If anyone tells you that they will, they don't know what they're talking about.

Jesus said, "I am the truth." So when Jesus tells us he's the only way, we'd better believe him.

Malachi age 12

❶ Have you ever tried to earn favor with God? Why doesn't that work?

❷ Memorize John 14:6. The next time you get a chance to witness to a friend, share this verse with him or her.

❸ Thank Jesus for showing you the way to God.

Turn to page 1295 for your next devotion.

told you. I am going there to prepare a place for you. ³And if I go and prepare a place for you, I will come back and take you to be with me that you also may be where I am. ⁴You know the way to the place where I am going."

Jesus the Way to the Father

⁵Thomas said to him, "Lord, we don't know where you are going, so how can we know the way?"

⁶Jesus answered, "I am the way and the truth and the life. No one comes to the Father except through me. ⁷If you really knew me, you would know*a* my Father as well. From now on, you do know him and have seen him."

⁸Philip said, "Lord, show us the Father and that will be enough for us."

⁹Jesus answered: "Don't you know me, Philip, even after I have been among you such a long time? Anyone who has seen me has seen the Father. How can you say, 'Show us the Father'? ¹⁰Don't you believe that I am in the Father, and that the Father is in me? The words I say to you are not just my own. Rather, it is the Father, living in me, who is doing his work. ¹¹Believe me when I say that I am in the Father and the Father is in me; or at least believe on the evidence of the miracles themselves. ¹²I tell you the truth, anyone who has faith in me will do what I have been doing. He will do even greater things than these, because I am going to the Father. ¹³And I will do whatever you ask in my name, so that the Son may bring glory to the Father. ¹⁴You may ask me for anything in my name, and I will do it.

Jesus Promises the Holy Spirit

¹⁵"If you love me, you will obey what I command. ¹⁶And I will ask the Father, and he will give you another Counselor to be with you forever— ¹⁷the Spirit of truth. The world cannot accept him, because it neither sees him nor knows him. But you know him, for he lives with you and will be*b* in you. ¹⁸I will not leave you as orphans; I will come to you. ¹⁹Before long, the world will not see me anymore, but you will see me. Because I live, you also will live. ²⁰On that day you will realize that I am in my Father, and you are in

Always on Call

Huh?

John 14:16–17
When you've got big problems, you need some good counsel—maybe from a parent, teacher or friend. Yet they can't be there all the time. After all, they have their own lives, jobs, families and friends. But there is a Counselor who is always on call. He's the Holy Spirit, and his pure wisdom is available 24 hours a day, 7 days a week.

me, and I am in you. ²¹Whoever has my commands and obeys them, he is the one who loves me. He who loves me will be loved by my Father, and I too will love him and show myself to him."

²²Then Judas (not Judas Iscariot) said, "But, Lord, why do you intend to show yourself to us and not to the world?"

²³Jesus replied, "If anyone loves me, he will obey my teaching. My Father will love him, and we will come to him and make our home with him. ²⁴He who does not love me will not obey my teaching. These words you hear are not my own; they belong to the Father who sent me.

²⁵"All this I have spoken while still with you. ²⁶But the Counselor, the Holy Spirit, whom the Father will send in my name, will teach you all things and will remind you of everything I have said to you. ²⁷Peace I leave with you; my peace I give you. I do not give to you as the world gives. Do not let your hearts be troubled and do not be afraid.

²⁸"You heard me say, 'I am going away and I am coming back to you.' If you loved me, you would be glad that I am going to the Father, for the Father is greater than I. ²⁹I have told you now before it happens, so that when it does happen you will believe. ³⁰I will not speak with you much longer, for the prince of this world is coming. He has no hold on me, ³¹but the world must learn that I love

a7 Some early manuscripts If you really have known me, you will know   b17 Some early manuscripts and is

the Father and that I do exactly what my Father has commanded me.

"Come now; let us leave.

The Vine and the Branches

15 "I am the true vine, and my Father is the gardener. [2]He cuts off every branch in me that bears no fruit, while every branch that does bear fruit he prunes[a] so that it will be even more fruitful. [3]You are already clean because of the word I have spoken to you. [4]Remain in me, and I will remain in you. No branch can bear fruit by itself; it must remain in the vine. Neither can you bear fruit unless you remain in me.

[5]"I am the vine; you are the branches. If a man remains in me and I in him, he will bear much fruit; apart from me you can do nothing. [6]If anyone does not remain in me, he is like a branch that is thrown away and withers; such branches are picked up, thrown into the fire and burned. [7]If you remain in me and my words remain in you, ask whatever you wish, and it will be given you. [8]This is to my Father's glory, that you bear much fruit, showing yourselves to be my disciples.

[9]"As the Father has loved me, so have I loved you. Now remain in my love. [10]If you obey my commands, you will remain in my love, just as I have obeyed my Father's commands and remain in his love. [11]I have told you this so that my joy may be in you and that your joy may be complete. [12]My command is this: Love each other as I have loved you. [13]Greater love has no one than this, that he lay down his life for his friends. [14]You are my friends if you do what I command. [15]I no longer call you servants, because a servant does not know his master's business. Instead, I have called you friends, for everything that I learned from my Father I have made known to you. [16]You did not choose me, but I chose you and appointed you to go and bear fruit—fruit that will last. Then the Father will give you whatever you ask in my name. [17]This is my command: Love each other.

The World Hates the Disciples

[18]"If the world hates you, keep in mind that it hated me first. [19]If you belonged to the world, it would love you as its own. As it is, you do not belong to the world, but I have chosen you out of the world. That is why the world hates you. [20]Remember the words I spoke to you: 'No servant is greater than his master.'[b] If they persecuted me, they will persecute you also. If they obeyed my teaching, they will obey yours also. [21]They will treat you this way because of my name, for they do not know the One who sent me. [22]If I had not come and spoken to them, they would not be guilty of sin. Now, however, they have no excuse for their sin. [23]He who hates me hates my Father as well. [24]If I had not done among them what no one else did, they would not be guilty of sin. But now they have seen these miracles, and yet they have hated both me and my Father. [25]But this is to fulfill what is written in their Law: 'They hated me without reason.'[c]

[26]"When the Counselor comes, whom I will send to you from the Father, the Spirit of truth who goes out from the Father, he will testify about me. [27]And you also must testify, for you have been with me from the beginning.

16 "All this I have told you so that you will not go astray. [2]They will put you out of the synagogue; in fact, a time is coming when anyone who kills you will think he is offering a service to God. [3]They will do such things because they have not known the Father or me. [4]I have told you this, so that when the time comes you will remember that I warned you. I did not tell you this at first because I was with you.

The Work of the Holy Spirit

[5]"Now I am going to him who sent me, yet none of you asks me, 'Where are you going?' [6]Because I have said these things, you are filled with grief. [7]But I tell you the truth: It is for your good that I am going away. Unless I go away, the Counselor will not come to you; but if I go, I will send him to you. [8]When he comes, he will convict the world of guilt[d] in regard to sin and righteousness and

---

[a]2 The Greek for *prunes* also means *cleans*.
[b]20 John 13:16   [c]25 Psalms 35:19; 69:4   [d]8 Or *will expose the guilt of the world*

judgment: ⁹in regard to sin, because men do not believe in me; ¹⁰in regard to righteousness, because I am going to the Father, where you can see me no longer; ¹¹and in regard to judgment, because the prince of this world now stands condemned.

¹²"I have much more to say to you, more than you can now bear. ¹³But when he, the Spirit of truth, comes, he will guide you into all truth. He will not speak on his own; he will speak only what he hears, and he will tell you what is yet to come. ¹⁴He will bring glory to me by taking from what is mine and making it known to you. ¹⁵All that belongs to the Father is mine. That is why I said the Spirit will take from what is mine and make it known to you.

¹⁶"In a little while you will see me no more, and then after a little while you will see me."

The Disciples' Grief Will Turn to Joy

¹⁷Some of his disciples said to one another, "What does he mean by saying, 'In a little while you will see me no more, and then after a little while you will see me,' and 'Because I am going to the Father'?" ¹⁸They kept asking, "What does he mean by 'a little while'? We don't understand what he is saying."

¹⁹Jesus saw that they wanted to ask him about this, so he said to them, "Are you asking one another what I meant when I said, 'In a little while you will see me no more, and then after a little while you will see me'? ²⁰I tell you the truth, you will weep and mourn while the world rejoices. You will grieve, but your grief will turn to joy. ²¹A woman giving birth to a child has pain because her time has come; but when her baby is born she forgets the anguish because of her joy that a child is born into the world. ²²So with you: Now is your time of grief, but I will see you again and you will rejoice, and no one will take away your joy. ²³In that day you will no longer ask me anything. I tell you the truth, my Father will give you whatever you ask in my name. ²⁴Until now you have not asked for anything in my name. Ask and you will receive, and your joy will be complete.

²⁵"Though I have been speaking figuratively, a time is coming when I will no

Thursday

A Holy Guide

Read John 16:5–15

I don't think the disciples had a clue what Jesus was talking about when he said he was sending them the Spirit. All they knew was that Jesus was going away. They were sad for themselves and their problems, because they thought Jesus was leaving them alone.

The disciples forgot that Jesus always keeps his promises. He promised them a Counselor who would always be with them in times of need. That's exactly what he gave them. And when we commit our lives to God, the Holy Spirit is there for us too.

We don't have to be sad because Jesus is in heaven and is no longer here on earth with us. The Holy Spirit will guide us the rest of the way.

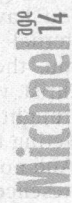Michael age 14

❶ What does a counselor do? How is the Holy Spirit like a counselor?

❷ Ask your parents or your youth leader how they've seen the Holy Spirit's guidance in their lives.

❸ Thank God for sending the Holy Spirit to be with you always.

Turn to page 1301 for your next devotion.

longer use this kind of language but will tell you plainly about my Father. ²⁶In that day you will ask in my name. I am not saying that I will ask the Father on your behalf. ²⁷No, the Father himself loves you because you have loved me and have believed that I came from God. ²⁸I came from the Father and entered the world; now I am leaving the world and going back to the Father.”

²⁹Then Jesus’ disciples said, “Now you are speaking clearly and without figures of speech. ³⁰Now we can see that you know all things and that you do not even need to have anyone ask you questions. This makes us believe that you came from God.”

³¹“You believe at last!”ᵃ Jesus answered. ³²“But a time is coming, and has come, when you will be scattered, each to his own home. You will leave me all alone. Yet I am not alone, for my Father is with me.

³³“I have told you these things, so that in me you may have peace. In this world you will have trouble. But take heart! I have overcome the world.”

Jesus Prays for Himself

17 After Jesus said this, he looked toward heaven and prayed:

“Father, the time has come. Glorify your Son, that your Son may glorify you. ²For you granted him authority over all people that he might give eternal life to all those you have given him. ³Now this is eternal life: that they may know you, the only true God, and Jesus Christ, whom you have sent. ⁴I have brought you glory on earth by completing the work you gave me to do. ⁵And now, Father, glorify me in your presence with the glory I had with you before the world began.

Jesus Prays for His Disciples

⁶“I have revealed youᵇ to those whom you gave me out of the world. They were yours; you gave them to me and they have obeyed your word. ⁷Now they know that everything you have given me comes from you. ⁸For I gave them the words you gave me and they accepted them. They knew with certainty that I came from you, and they believed that you sent me. ⁹I pray for them. I am not praying for the world, but for those you have given me, for they are yours. ¹⁰All I have is yours, and all you have is mine. And glory has come to me through them. ¹¹I will remain in the world no longer, but they are still in the world, and I am coming to you. Holy Father, protect them by the power of your name—the name you gave me—so that they may be one as we are one. ¹²While I was with them, I protected them and kept them safe by that name you gave me. None has been lost except the one doomed to destruction so that Scripture would be fulfilled.

¹³“I am coming to you now, but I say these things while I am still in the world, so that they may have the full measure of my joy within them. ¹⁴I have given them your word and the world has hated them, for they are not of the world any more than I am of the world. ¹⁵My prayer is not that you take them out of the world but that you protect them from the evil one. ¹⁶They are not of the world, even as I am not of it. ¹⁷Sanctifyᶜ them by the truth; your word is truth. ¹⁸As you sent me into the world, I have sent them into the world. ¹⁹For them I sanctify myself, that they too may be truly sanctified.

Jesus Prays for All Believers

²⁰“My prayer is not for them alone. I pray also for those who will believe in me through their message, ²¹that all of them may be one, Father, just as you are in me and I am in you. May they also be in us so that the world may believe that you have sent me. ²²I have given them the glory that you gave me, that they may be one as we are one: ²³I in them and you in me. May they be

---

ᵃ31 Or “Do you now believe?” ᵇ6 Greek your name; also in verse 26 ᶜ17 Greek hagiazo (set apart for sacred use or make holy); also in verse 19

brought to complete unity to let the world know that you sent me and have loved them even as you have loved me.

²⁴"Father, I want those you have given me to be with me where I am, and to see my glory, the glory you have given me because you loved me before the creation of the world. ²⁵"Righteous Father, though the world does not know you, I know you, and they know that you have sent me. ²⁶I have made you known to them, and will continue to make you known in order that the love you have for me may be in them and that I myself may be in them."

Jesus Arrested

18 When he had finished praying, Jesus left with his disciples and crossed the Kidron Valley. On the other side there was an olive grove, and he and his disciples went into it.

²Now Judas, who betrayed him, knew the place, because Jesus had often met there with his disciples. ³So Judas came to the grove, guiding a detachment of soldiers and some officials from the chief priests and Pharisees. They were carrying torches, lanterns and weapons.

⁴Jesus, knowing all that was going to happen to him, went out and asked them, "Who is it you want?"

⁵"Jesus of Nazareth," they replied.

"I am he," Jesus said. (And Judas the traitor was standing there with them.) ⁶When Jesus said, "I am he," they drew back and fell to the ground.

⁷Again he asked them, "Who is it you want?"

And they said, "Jesus of Nazareth."

⁸"I told you that I am he," Jesus answered. "If you are looking for me, then let these men go." ⁹This happened so that the words he had spoken would be fulfilled: "I have not lost one of those you gave me."[a]

¹⁰Then Simon Peter, who had a sword, drew it and struck the high priest's servant, cutting off his right ear. (The servant's name was Malchus.)

¹¹Jesus commanded Peter, "Put your sword away! Shall I not drink the cup the Father has given me?"

Jesus Taken to Annas

¹²Then the detachment of soldiers with its commander and the Jewish officials arrested Jesus. They bound him ¹³and brought him first to Annas, who was the father-in-law of Caiaphas, the high priest that year. ¹⁴Caiaphas was the one who had advised the Jews that it would be good if one man died for the people.

Peter's First Denial

¹⁵Simon Peter and another disciple were following Jesus. Because this disciple was known to the high priest, he went with Jesus into the high priest's courtyard, ¹⁶but Peter had to wait outside at the door. The other disciple, who was known to the high priest, came back, spoke to the girl on duty there and brought Peter in.

¹⁷"You are not one of his disciples, are you?" the girl at the door asked Peter.

He replied, "I am not."

¹⁸It was cold, and the servants and officials stood around a fire they had made to keep warm. Peter also was standing with them, warming himself.

The High Priest Questions Jesus

¹⁹Meanwhile, the high priest questioned Jesus about his disciples and his teaching.

²⁰"I have spoken openly to the world," Jesus replied. "I always taught in synagogues or at the temple, where all the Jews come together. I said nothing in secret. ²¹Why question me? Ask those who heard me. Surely they know what I said."

²²When Jesus said this, one of the officials nearby struck him in the face. "Is this the way you answer the high priest?" he demanded.

²³"If I said something wrong," Jesus replied, "testify as to what is wrong. But if I spoke the truth, why did you strike me?" ²⁴Then Annas sent him, still bound, to Caiaphas the high priest.[b]

Peter's Second and Third Denials

²⁵As Simon Peter stood warming himself, he was asked, "You are not one of his disciples, are you?"

[a]9 John 6:39   [b]24 Or (Now Annas had sent him, still bound, to Caiaphas the high priest.)

He denied it, saying, "I am not."

²⁶One of the high priest's servants, a relative of the man whose ear Peter had cut off, challenged him, "Didn't I see you with him in the olive grove?" ²⁷Again Peter denied it, and at that moment a rooster began to crow.

Jesus Before Pilate

²⁸Then the Jews led Jesus from Caiaphas to the palace of the Roman governor. By now it was early morning, and to avoid ceremonial uncleanness the Jews did not enter the palace; they wanted to be able to eat the Passover. ²⁹So Pilate came out to them and asked, "What charges are you bringing against this man?"

³⁰"If he were not a criminal," they replied, "we would not have handed him over to you."

³¹Pilate said, "Take him yourselves and judge him by your own law."

"But we have no right to execute anyone," the Jews objected. ³²This happened so that the words Jesus had spoken indicating the kind of death he was going to die would be fulfilled.

³³Pilate then went back inside the palace, summoned Jesus and asked him, "Are you the king of the Jews?"

³⁴"Is that your own idea," Jesus asked, "or did others talk to you about me?"

³⁵"Am I a Jew?" Pilate replied. "It was your people and your chief priests who handed you over to me. What is it you have done?"

³⁶Jesus said, "My kingdom is not of this world. If it were, my servants would fight to prevent my arrest by the Jews. But now my kingdom is from another place."

³⁷"You are a king, then!" said Pilate.

Jesus answered, "You are right in saying I am a king. In fact, for this reason I was born, and for this I came into the world, to testify to the truth. Everyone on the side of truth listens to me."

³⁸"What is truth?" Pilate asked. With this he went out again to the Jews and said, "I find no basis for a charge against him. ³⁹But it is your custom for me to release to you one prisoner at the time of the Passover. Do you want me to release 'the king of the Jews'?"

⁴⁰They shouted back, "No, not him! Give us Barabbas!" Now Barabbas had taken part in a rebellion.

Jesus Sentenced to Be Crucified

19 Then Pilate took Jesus and had him flogged. ²The soldiers twisted together a crown of thorns and put it on his head. They clothed him in a purple robe ³and went up to him again and again, saying, "Hail, king of the Jews!" And they struck him in the face.

⁴Once more Pilate came out and said to the Jews, "Look, I am bringing him out to you to let you know that I find no basis for a charge against him." ⁵When Jesus came out wearing the crown of thorns and the purple robe, Pilate said to them, "Here is the man!"

⁶As soon as the chief priests and their officials saw him, they shouted, "Crucify! Crucify!"

But Pilate answered, "You take him and crucify him. As for me, I find no basis for a charge against him."

⁷The Jews insisted, "We have a law, and according to that law he must die, because he claimed to be the Son of God."

⁸When Pilate heard this, he was even more afraid, ⁹and he went back inside the palace. "Where do you come from?" he asked Jesus, but Jesus gave him no answer. ¹⁰"Do you refuse to speak to me?" Pilate said. "Don't you realize I have power either to free you or to crucify you?"

¹¹Jesus answered, "You would have no power over me if it were not given to you from above. Therefore the one who handed me over to you is guilty of a greater sin."

¹²From then on, Pilate tried to set Jesus free, but the Jews kept shouting, "If you let this man go, you are no friend of Caesar. Anyone who claims to be a king opposes Caesar."

¹³When Pilate heard this, he brought Jesus out and sat down on the judge's seat at a place known as the Stone Pavement (which in Aramaic is Gabbatha). ¹⁴It was the day of Preparation of Passover Week, about the sixth hour.

"Here is your king," Pilate said to the Jews.

¹⁵But they shouted, "Take him away! Take him away! Crucify him!"

"Shall I crucify your king?" Pilate asked.

"We have no king but Caesar," the chief priests answered.

¹⁶Finally Pilate handed him over to them to be crucified.

The Crucifixion

So the soldiers took charge of Jesus. ¹⁷Carrying his own cross, he went out to the place of the Skull (which in Aramaic is called Golgotha). ¹⁸Here they crucified him, and with him two others—one on each side and Jesus in the middle.

The Last Load

John 19:17

As if the beating, crown of thorns, purple robe and mocking crowd weren't enough, Jesus had one last load to carry—his own cross. In those days crosses were shaped like a T, Y, X or I. No matter what the shape, they were super heavy. Jesus was so weak that the cross beam could have crushed him. But he kept walking, plodding and stumbling along. Never forget, he did not carry this load for himself; he carried it for us.

¹⁹Pilate had a notice prepared and fastened to the cross. It read: JESUS OF NAZARETH, THE KING OF THE JEWS. ²⁰Many of the Jews read this sign, for the place where Jesus was crucified was near the city, and the sign was written in Aramaic, Latin and Greek. ²¹The chief priests of the Jews protested to Pilate, "Do not write 'The King of the Jews,' but that this man claimed to be king of the Jews."

²²Pilate answered, "What I have written, I have written."

²³When the soldiers crucified Jesus, they took his clothes, dividing them into four shares, one for each of them, with the undergarment remaining. This garment was seamless, woven in one piece from top to bottom.

²⁴"Let's not tear it," they said to one another. "Let's decide by lot who will get it."

This happened that the scripture might be fulfilled which said,

"They divided my garments among them
and cast lots for my clothing."ᵃ

So this is what the soldiers did.

²⁵Near the cross of Jesus stood his mother, his mother's sister, Mary the wife of Clopas, and Mary Magdalene. ²⁶When Jesus saw his mother there, and the disciple whom he loved standing nearby, he said to his mother, "Dear woman, here is your son," ²⁷and to the disciple, "Here is your mother." From that time on, this disciple took her into his home.

The Death of Jesus

²⁸Later, knowing that all was now completed, and so that the Scripture would be fulfilled, Jesus said, "I am thirsty." ²⁹A jar of wine vinegar was there, so they soaked a sponge in it, put the sponge on a stalk of the hyssop plant, and lifted it to Jesus' lips. ³⁰When he had received the drink, Jesus said, "It is finished." With that, he bowed his head and gave up his spirit.

³¹Now it was the day of Preparation, and the next day was to be a special Sabbath. Because the Jews did not want the bodies left on the crosses during the Sabbath, they asked Pilate to have the legs broken and the bodies taken down. ³²The soldiers therefore came and broke the legs of the first man who had been crucified with Jesus, and then those of the other. ³³But when they came to Jesus and found that he was already dead, they did not break his legs. ³⁴Instead, one of the soldiers pierced Jesus' side with a spear, bringing a sudden flow of blood and water. ³⁵The man who saw it has given testimony, and his testimony is true. He knows that he tells the truth, and he testifies so that you also may believe. ³⁶These things happened so that the scripture would be fulfilled: "Not one of his bones will be broken,"ᵇ ³⁷and, as an-

ᵃ24 Psalm 22:18   ᵇ36 Exodus 12:46; Num. 9:12; Psalm 34:20

True Prophecy

Huh?

John 19:32–36

Generation after generation of Jews had passed down all sorts of prophecies (or messages) from God about what the Savior would be like. The Bible predicted stuff about how he would be born, how he would live and how he would die. Jesus matched 100% of them, even down to what would happen to him after he died. Most dead people on crosses had their legs broken to make sure they were dead. Jesus was different. He was pierced with a spear. This fulfilled 2 prophecies at once.

other scripture says, "They will look on the one they have pierced."[a]

The Burial of Jesus

³⁸Later, Joseph of Arimathea asked Pilate for the body of Jesus. Now Joseph was a disciple of Jesus, but secretly because he feared the Jews. With Pilate's permission, he came and took the body away. ³⁹He was accompanied by Nicodemus, the man who earlier had visited Jesus at night. Nicodemus brought a mixture of myrrh and aloes, about seventy-five pounds.[b] ⁴⁰Taking Jesus' body, the two of them wrapped it, with the spices, in strips of linen. This was in accordance with Jewish burial customs. ⁴¹At the place where Jesus was crucified, there was a garden, and in the garden a new tomb, in which no one had ever been laid. ⁴²Because it was the Jewish day of Preparation and since the tomb was nearby, they laid Jesus there.

The Empty Tomb

20 Early on the first day of the week, while it was still dark, Mary Magdalene went to the tomb and saw that the stone had been removed from the entrance. ²So she came running to Simon Peter and the other disciple, the one Jesus loved, and said, "They have taken the Lord out of the tomb, and we don't know where they have put him!"

³So Peter and the other disciple started for the tomb. ⁴Both were running, but the other disciple outran Peter and reached the tomb first. ⁵He bent over and looked in at the strips of linen lying there but did not go in. ⁶Then Simon Peter, who was behind him, arrived and went into the tomb. He saw the strips of linen lying there, ⁷as well as the burial cloth that had been around Jesus' head. The cloth was folded up by itself, separate from the linen. ⁸Finally the other disciple, who had reached the tomb first, also went inside. He saw and believed. ⁹(They still did not understand from Scripture that Jesus had to rise from the dead.)

Jesus Appears to Mary Magdalene

¹⁰Then the disciples went back to their homes, ¹¹but Mary stood outside the tomb crying. As she wept, she bent over to look into the tomb ¹²and saw two angels in white, seated where Jesus' body had been, one at the head and the other at the foot.

¹³They asked her, "Woman, why are you crying?"

"They have taken my Lord away," she said, "and I don't know where they have put him." ¹⁴At this, she turned around and saw Jesus standing there, but she did not realize that it was Jesus.

¹⁵"Woman," he said, "why are you crying? Who is it you are looking for?"

Thinking he was the gardener, she said, "Sir, if you have carried him away, tell me where you have put him, and I will get him."

¹⁶Jesus said to her, "Mary."

She turned toward him and cried out in Aramaic, "Rabboni!" (which means Teacher).

¹⁷Jesus said, "Do not hold on to me, for I have not yet returned to the Father. Go instead to my brothers and tell them, 'I am returning to my Father and your Father, to my God and your God.'"

¹⁸Mary Magdalene went to the disciples with the news: "I have seen the Lord!" And she told them that he had said these things to her.

---

[a]37 Zech. 12:10   [b]39 Greek *a hundred litrai* (about 34 kilograms)

Jesus Appears to His Disciples

¹⁹On the evening of that first day of the week, when the disciples were together, with the doors locked for fear of the Jews, Jesus came and stood among them and said, "Peace be with you!" ²⁰After he said this, he showed them his hands and side. The disciples were overjoyed when they saw the Lord.

²¹Again Jesus said, "Peace be with you! As the Father has sent me, I am sending you." ²²And with that he breathed on them and said, "Receive the Holy Spirit. ²³If you forgive anyone his sins, they are forgiven; if you do not forgive them, they are not forgiven."

Jesus Appears to Thomas

²⁴Now Thomas (called Didymus), one of the Twelve, was not with the disciples when Jesus came. ²⁵So the other disciples told him, "We have seen the Lord!"

But he said to them, "Unless I see the nail marks in his hands and put my finger where the nails were, and put my hand into his side, I will not believe it."

²⁶A week later his disciples were in the house again, and Thomas was with them. Though the doors were locked, Jesus came and stood among them and said, "Peace be with you!" ²⁷Then he said to Thomas, "Put your finger here; see my hands. Reach out your hand and put it into my side. Stop doubting and believe."

²⁸Thomas said to him, "My Lord and my God!"

²⁹Then Jesus told him, "Because you have seen me, you have believed; blessed are those who have not seen and yet have believed."

³⁰Jesus did many other miraculous signs in the presence of his disciples, which are not recorded in this book. ³¹But these are written that you may*ᵃ*

ᵃ31 Some manuscripts may continue to

Friday

No Doubt About It

Read John 20:24–29

I was walking home with one of my unsaved friends. We started talking about what she calls "religion and stuff." I asked her if she believed God existed. She said no, because she doesn't believe in things she can't see.

I started trying to think of something she couldn't see but believed in anyway. She believed in gravity, obviously, and molecules and TV signals and satellites. "But those things are different," she argued. Well, they *are* different, but it got her thinking. I invited her to a youth group activity scheduled for the next day. She has started coming to youth group with me sometimes, but she hasn't accepted Jesus as her Savior yet.

It's not always easy to believe in things we can't see. That's why Jesus says, "Blessed are those who have not seen and yet have believed." I guess that means us, because we haven't seen Jesus the way Thomas did. We will, though, in heaven—no doubt about it!

Stacy age 15

❶ What are some things you believe in that you've never seen?

❷ We can't see wind or electricity, but we know both exist and that they can be *very* powerful. How could these examples be a bridge to discussing your faith with a non-Christian friend?

❸ Thank God for working in your life.

Turn to page 1302 for your next devotion.

believe that Jesus is the Christ, the Son of God, and that by believing you may have life in his name.

Jesus and the Miraculous Catch of Fish

21 Afterward Jesus appeared again to his disciples, by the Sea of Tiberias.ᵃ It happened this way: ²Simon Peter, Thomas (called Didymus), Nathanael from Cana in Galilee, the sons of Zebedee, and two other disciples were together. ³"I'm going out to fish," Simon Peter told them, and they said, "We'll go with you." So they went out and got into the boat, but that night they caught nothing.

⁴Early in the morning, Jesus stood on the shore, but the disciples did not realize that it was Jesus.

⁵He called out to them, "Friends, haven't you any fish?"

"No," they answered.

⁶He said, "Throw your net on the right side of the boat and you will find some."

ᵃ1 That is, Sea of Galilee

Week end.

More Than Enough

Read John 21:5–11

When Shannon wrote that God is no party pooper (Monday's devotional), she said that God wants us to "live life to the fullest!"

It's kind of like this: Your mom says she's got dinner ready for you, but when you get to the table there are 2 lousy, cold french fries on the plate—that's it! Your mom wouldn't do that, right? But that's how we often think God's going to treat us.

Even if you believe that God's way is the best way, you might think about God like that fictional mom—sure, he *knows* we need stuff, but we treat him as if he's only willing to toss us an occasional french fry. It's almost as if we think God made us, came to die for us but then took a nap for 2,000 years.

But God isn't like that. Jesus didn't just give the disciples 2 little guppies (in the passage you're supposed to read for today). He knew the disciples had been up all night doing what they usually did—trying to fish but, in this instance, never really catching anything. Here comes Jesus, and—Wham!—they catch so many fish they have to sit on the beach and count 'em! 153 FISH!! He wants to give you the same—not necessarily lots of "stuff" but other kinds of good things.

❶ Think about it—on a 1 (low) to 10 (high) scale, how much do you think God wants to do for you? Do you believe that, as he did for the disciples, he wants to give you far more than you could ever need? Or is he somehow holding out on you for one reason or another?

❷ When's a time that God surprised you—when he gave you more than you asked for?

❸ This weekend ask God to show you how much he wants to give you; then spend the week looking for him to come through.

Turn to page 1306 for your next devotion.

When they did, they were unable to haul the net in because of the large number of fish.

⁷Then the disciple whom Jesus loved said to Peter, "It is the Lord!" As soon as Simon Peter heard him say, "It is the Lord," he wrapped his outer garment around him (for he had taken it off) and jumped into the water. ⁸The other disciples followed in the boat, towing the net full of fish, for they were not far from shore, about a hundred yards.ᵃ ⁹When they landed, they saw a fire of burning coals there with fish on it, and some bread.

¹⁰Jesus said to them, "Bring some of the fish you have just caught."

¹¹Simon Peter climbed aboard and dragged the net ashore. It was full of large fish, 153, but even with so many the net was not torn. ¹²Jesus said to them, "Come and have breakfast." None of the disciples dared ask him, "Who are you?" They knew it was the Lord. ¹³Jesus came, took the bread and gave it to them, and did the same with the fish. ¹⁴This was now the third time Jesus appeared to his disciples after he was raised from the dead.

Jesus Reinstates Peter

¹⁵When they had finished eating, Jesus said to Simon Peter, "Simon son of John, do you truly love me more than these?"

"Yes, Lord," he said, "you know that I love you."

Jesus said, "Feed my lambs."

¹⁶Again Jesus said, "Simon son of John, do you truly love me?"

He answered, "Yes, Lord, you know that I love you."

Jesus said, "Take care of my sheep."

¹⁷The third time he said to him, "Simon son of John, do you love me?"

Peter was hurt because Jesus asked him the third time, "Do you love me?" He said, "Lord, you know all things; you know that I love you."

Jesus said, "Feed my sheep. ¹⁸I tell you the truth, when you were younger you dressed yourself and went where you wanted; but when you are old you will stretch out your hands, and someone else will dress you and lead you where you do not want to go." ¹⁹Jesus said this to indicate the kind of death by which Peter would glorify God. Then he said to him, "Follow me!"

²⁰Peter turned and saw that the disciple whom Jesus loved was following them. (This was the one who had leaned back against Jesus at the supper and had said, "Lord, who is going to betray you?") ²¹When Peter saw him, he asked, "Lord, what about him?"

²²Jesus answered, "If I want him to remain alive until I return, what is that to you? You must follow me." ²³Because of this, the rumor spread among the brothers that this disciple would not die. But Jesus did not say that he would not die; he only said, "If I want him to remain alive until I return, what is that to you?"

²⁴This is the disciple who testifies to these things and who wrote them down. We know that his testimony is true.

²⁵Jesus did many other things as well. If every one of them were written down, I suppose that even the whole world would not have room for the books that would be written.

ᵃ8 Greek *about two hundred cubits* (about 90 meters)

Acts

START

Imagine that you and a couple hundred kids from your school are sitting in the gym. A teacher has just finished explaining a little trick he stumbled on to that makes each of you able to wiggle your ears. And now you all have been asked to get the news about his discovery out to the world. You can't drive and you have no access to TV, radio, newspapers, magazines or the Internet. What do you do?

This is kind of like the job a few hundred early Christians had—except their news was much more important. Their news was about Jesus.

Matthew, Mark, Luke and John—the first 4 books of the New Testament—tell the story of Jesus. And most of the rest of the New Testament is made up of letters that were written to different churches and groups of believers. The book of Acts is the bridge between those two sections—without it, much of the New Testament would be really confusing.

Luke, a medical doctor, records the spread of the Jesus-news and the beginning of the church (at least the really important stuff).

Cast OF Characters

Luke
He wrote the book of Acts as well as the book of Luke. He wasn't one of the 12 disciples, but he was an early convert and traveled with Paul.

Jesus
He makes his grand exit in the first chapter.

The Holy Spirit
The third member of the Trinity (God in 3 persons, or "Godhead") makes his first appearance. With Jesus gone from the earth, the Holy Spirit is sent to be God in us.

Peter
One of the 12 disciples and a major mover and shaker for getting the Jesus-news out. He becomes the main man of the early church.

John
Another one of the 12, he's majorly active at preaching and starting churches.

Paul
Wow! What a story! Paul is a total enemy of Christians—even killing them. Then he has a meeting with Jesus that changes his life. He starts more churches than anyone else and goes on to write lots of the books in the New Testament.

Stephen
He gets killed for believing in Jesus.

(BAR-nuh-bus)

Timothy, James, Philip, Barnabas, Silas, (SIGH-less)
Lydia and a bunch of other people.
(LID-ee-uh)

Hey, this is a true story, and there are a whole lotta people mentioned!

What's UP with That?

My World

Right before Jesus is taken up to heaven, he tells the disciples that they will be his witnesses and will tell the Jesus-news "in Jerusalem and in all Judea and Samaria, and to the ends of the earth"— these were Jesus' very last words on earth.

For those hearing this, Jerusalem was where they were; Judea was the surrounding area; Samaria was the neighboring area; and the ends of the earth were, well, the rest of the then-known world.

The Holy Spirit whom Jesus promised to these believers has been given to you too (if you believe in Jesus Christ)! So that means Jesus is saying the same thing to you—bonus!

In the spaces below, personalize this passage as if Jesus were saying it to you today:

Snap shots

- **Baby church**
  (chapters 1—2)

- **First church of Jerusalem**
  (chapters 3—5)

- **Nearby churches**
  (chapters 6—12)

- **Churches further away**
  (chapters 13:1—21:17)

- **Even further**
  (chapters 21:18—28)

But you will receive power when the Holy Spirit comes upon you; and you will be my witnesses in

_____
(my "Jerusalem"),

and in all _____
(my "Judea")

and _____
(my "Samaria"),

and to _____
(the ends of my earth!)

Jesus Taken Up Into Heaven

1 In my former book, Theophilus, I wrote about all that Jesus began to do and to teach ²until the day he was taken up to heaven, after giving instructions through the Holy Spirit to the apostles he had chosen. ³After his suffering, he showed himself to these men and gave many convincing proofs that he was alive. He appeared to them over a period of forty days and spoke about the kingdom of God. ⁴On one occasion, while he was eating with them, he gave them this command: "Do not leave Jerusalem, but wait for the gift my Father promised, which you have heard me speak about. ⁵For John baptized with*ᵃ* water, but in a few days you will be baptized with the Holy Spirit."

⁶So when they met together, they asked him, "Lord, are you at this time going to restore the kingdom to Israel?"

⁷He said to them: "It is not for you to know the times or dates the Father has set by his own authority. ⁸But you will receive power when the Holy Spirit comes on you; and you will be my witnesses in Jerusalem, and in all Judea and Samaria, and to the ends of the earth."

⁹After he said this, he was taken up before their very eyes, and a cloud hid him from their sight.

¹⁰They were looking intently up into the sky as he was going, when suddenly two men dressed in white stood beside them. ¹¹"Men of Galilee," they said, "why do you stand here looking into the sky? This same Jesus, who has been taken from you into heaven, will come back in the same way you have seen him go into heaven."

Matthias Chosen to Replace Judas

¹²Then they returned to Jerusalem from the hill called the Mount of Olives, a Sabbath day's walk*ᵇ* from the city.

ᵃ5 Or in   *ᵇ12 That is, about 3/4 mile (about 1,100 meters)*

Monday

Gotta Have Guts

Read Acts 1:8

Have you ever had an experience at youth group where you get all excited about telling your friends about Jesus? But then by the time you're at school the next day, you can't even open your mouth! It's a lot easier for me to talk about faith with my Christian friends at youth group than it is with the people at school who think church is for losers.

I'm never going to get up the courage to witness to people if I have to do it alone. That's why I need to remember that I'm *not* alone. I have the Holy Spirit with me to help me know what to say—and to have the guts to say it.

When we have the Holy Spirit, we have the power of God to do amazing things. We can't just waste all that power. We need to use it to spread the good news of the gospel everywhere, starting with our own schools.

Elizabeth age 12

What about You?

❶ What was one time that you were afraid to do something, but God gave you the courage and power to do it?

❷ Sit down with your youth leader or some of your Christian friends and think of some ways you can be a witness at school.

❸ Thank God for the power he's given you in the Holy Spirit, and ask him to help you use it.

Turn to page 1310 for your next devotion.

[13]When they arrived, they went upstairs to the room where they were staying. Those present were Peter, John, James and Andrew; Philip and Thomas, Bartholomew and Matthew; James son of Alphaeus and Simon the Zealot, and Judas son of James. [14]They all joined together constantly in prayer, along with the women and Mary the mother of Jesus, and with his brothers.

[15]In those days Peter stood up among the believers[a] (a group numbering about a hundred and twenty) [16]and said, "Brothers, the Scripture had to be fulfilled which the Holy Spirit spoke long ago through the mouth of David concerning Judas, who served as guide for those who arrested Jesus— [17]he was one of our number and shared in this ministry."

[18](With the reward he got for his wickedness, Judas bought a field; there he fell headlong, his body burst open and all his intestines spilled out. [19]Everyone in Jerusalem heard about this, so they called that field in their language Akeldama, that is, Field of Blood.)

[20]"For," said Peter, "it is written in the book of Psalms,

" 'May his place be deserted;
    let there be no one to dwell in it,'[b]

and,

" 'May another take his place of
    leadership.'[c]

[21]Therefore it is necessary to choose one of the men who have been with us the whole time the Lord Jesus went in and out among us, [22]beginning from John's baptism to the time when Jesus was taken up from us. For one of these must become a witness with us of his resurrection."

[23]So they proposed two men: Joseph called Barsabbas (also known as Justus) and Matthias. [24]Then they prayed, "Lord, you know everyone's heart. Show us which of these two you have chosen [25]to take over this apostolic ministry, which Judas left to go where he belongs." [26]Then they cast lots, and the lot fell to Matthias; so he was added to the eleven apostles.

The Holy Spirit Comes at Pentecost

2 When the day of Pentecost came, they were all together in one place.

Let's Celebrate

Huh?

Acts 2:1

The Day of Pentecost is a holiday—no school! The Jews celebrated it 50 days after Passover (another holiday). It was a time to thank God for the newly grown grain. While everyone was together for the holiday, the Holy Spirit came to earth to live in all Christians. The Spirit brought guidance, comfort and direction. This same Spirit who came 2,000 years ago is still with us today. Now that's worth celebrating!

[2]Suddenly a sound like the blowing of a violent wind came from heaven and filled the whole house where they were sitting. [3]They saw what seemed to be tongues of fire that separated and came to rest on each of them. [4]All of them were filled with the Holy Spirit and began to speak in other tongues[d] as the Spirit enabled them.

[5]Now there were staying in Jerusalem God-fearing Jews from every nation under heaven. [6]When they heard this sound, a crowd came together in bewilderment, because each one heard them speaking in his own language. [7]Utterly amazed, they asked: "Are not all these men who are speaking Galileans? [8]Then how is it that each of us hears them in his own native language? [9]Parthians, Medes and Elamites; residents of Mesopotamia, Judea and Cappadocia, Pontus and Asia, [10]Phrygia and Pamphylia, Egypt and the parts of Libya near Cyrene; visitors from Rome [11](both Jews and converts to Judaism); Cretans and Arabs—we hear them

[a]15 Greek *brothers* [b]20 Psalm 69:25 [c]20 Psalm 109:8 [d]4 Or *languages*; also in verse 11

Spectacular Entrances

In the Bible, God usually sent angels or prophets to deliver his messages. But every once in a while, the message is so important he delivers it personally. When God himself shows up, you know it's a big occasion. Here are some of God's big entrances—including a few Jesus made while he was hanging around on earth, and one yet to come.

Occasion	Entrance	See for Yourself
Invention of clothing	Out for a garden stroll, God busts Adam and Eve	*Genesis 3:6–13, 21*
Abram gets longer name	God introduces himself, gives Abram a syllable (and a son to start the Israelite nation!)	*Genesis 17:1–7*
Ultimate wrestling match	God wrestles with Jacob, renames his opponent "Israel" (the nation gets its name!)	*Genesis 32:24–30*
Moses gets a promotion	God speaks from flaming shrubbery (Israel gets a hero)	*Exodus 3:1–10*
Israelites meet the One in Charge	Fireworks, earthquake . . . and a trumpet	*Exodus 19:16–19*
Big birthday	God's best entrance turns out something like *your* first appearance	*Luke 2:6–7*
Water walking	Jesus walks in on the waves	*Matthew 14:22–33*
Visit from Dad	God speaks from cloud to ID his one and only Son	*Luke 9:28–36*
Defeat of death	Mary confronts gardener at empty tomb . . . but he's no gardener	*John 20:10–18*
Defeat of locked door	Disciples hide out in a locked room; Jesus enters anyway	*John 20:26*
Invention of church	Holy Spirit rocks the room in flames; disciples start preaching	*Acts 2:1–13*
Saul gets a new job	Troublemaker sees the light, changes his ways	*Acts 9:1–6*
Final entrance	The Hero comes again, riding a white horse	*Revelation 19:11–16*

declaring the wonders of God in our own tongues!" ¹²Amazed and perplexed, they asked one another, "What does this mean?"

¹³Some, however, made fun of them and said, "They have had too much wine."[a]

Peter Addresses the Crowd

¹⁴Then Peter stood up with the Eleven, raised his voice and addressed the crowd: "Fellow Jews and all of you who live in Jerusalem, let me explain this to you; lis-

[a] 13 Or *sweet wine*

ten carefully to what I say. [15]These men are not drunk, as you suppose. It's only nine in the morning! [16]No, this is what was spoken by the prophet Joel:

[17]" 'In the last days, God says,
  I will pour out my Spirit on all
    people.
  Your sons and daughters will
    prophesy,
    your young men will see visions,
    your old men will dream dreams.
[18]Even on my servants, both men and
    women,
  I will pour out my Spirit in those
    days,
    and they will prophesy.
[19]I will show wonders in the heaven
    above
    and signs on the earth below,
    blood and fire and billows of
      smoke.
[20]The sun will be turned to darkness
    and the moon to blood
    before the coming of the great and
      glorious day of the Lord.
[21]And everyone who calls
    on the name of the Lord will be
      saved.'[a]

[22]"Men of Israel, listen to this: Jesus of Nazareth was a man accredited by God to you by miracles, wonders and signs, which God did among you through him, as you yourselves know. [23]This man was handed over to you by God's set purpose and foreknowledge; and you, with the help of wicked men,[b] put him to death by nailing him to the cross. [24]But God raised him from the dead, freeing him from the agony of death, because it was impossible for death to keep its hold on him. [25]David said about him:

" 'I saw the Lord always before me.
    Because he is at my right hand,
    I will not be shaken.
[26]Therefore my heart is glad and my
    tongue rejoices;
    my body also will live in hope,
[27]because you will not abandon me to
    the grave,
    nor will you let your Holy One see
      decay.
[28]You have made known to me the
    paths of life;

you will fill me with joy in your
    presence.'[c]

[29]"Brothers, I can tell you confidently that the patriarch David died and was buried, and his tomb is here to this day. [30]But he was a prophet and knew that God had promised him on oath that he would place one of his descendants on his throne. [31]Seeing what was ahead, he spoke of the resurrection of the Christ,[d] that he was not abandoned to the grave, nor did his body see decay. [32]God has raised this Jesus to life, and we are all witnesses of the fact. [33]Exalted to the right hand of God, he has received from the Father the promised Holy Spirit and has poured out what you now see and hear. [34]For David did not ascend to heaven, and yet he said,

" 'The Lord said to my Lord:
    "Sit at my right hand
[35]until I make your enemies
    a footstool for your feet." '[e]

[36]"Therefore let all Israel be assured of this: God has made this Jesus, whom you crucified, both Lord and Christ."

[37]When the people heard this, they were cut to the heart and said to Peter and the other apostles, "Brothers, what shall we do?"

[38]Peter replied, "Repent and be baptized, every one of you, in the name of Jesus Christ for the forgiveness of your sins. And you will receive the gift of the Holy Spirit. [39]The promise is for you and your children and for all who are far off—for all whom the Lord our God will call."

[40]With many other words he warned them; and he pleaded with them, "Save yourselves from this corrupt generation." [41]Those who accepted his message were baptized, and about three thousand were added to their number that day.

The Fellowship of the Believers

[42]They devoted themselves to the apostles' teaching and to the fellowship,

---

[a]21 Joel 2:28-32   [b]23 Or *of those not having the law* (that is, Gentiles)   [c]28 Psalm 16:8-11   [d]31 Or *Messiah.* "The Christ" (Greek) and "the Messiah" (Hebrew) both mean "the Anointed One"; also in verse 36.   [e]35 Psalm 110:1

to the breaking of bread and to prayer. [43]Everyone was filled with awe, and many wonders and miraculous signs were done by the apostles. [44]All the believers were together and had everything in common. [45]Selling their possessions and goods, they gave to anyone as he had need. [46]Every day they continued to meet together in the temple courts. They broke bread in their homes and ate together with glad and sincere hearts, [47]praising God and enjoying the favor of all the people. And the Lord added to their number daily those who were being saved.

Peter Heals the Crippled Beggar

3 One day Peter and John were going up to the temple at the time of prayer—at three in the afternoon. [2]Now a man crippled from birth was being carried to the temple gate called Beautiful, where he was put every day to beg from those going into the temple courts. [3]When he saw Peter and John about to enter, he asked them for money. [4]Peter looked straight at him, as did John. Then Peter said, "Look at us!" [5]So the man gave them his attention, expecting to get something from them.

[6]Then Peter said, "Silver or gold I do not have, but what I have I give you. In the name of Jesus Christ of Nazareth, walk." [7]Taking him by the right hand, he helped him up, and instantly the man's feet and ankles became strong. [8]He jumped to his feet and began to walk. Then he went with them into the temple

---

Tuesday

A Good Place to Be

Read Acts 2:42

There are lots of times I really don't feel like going to church. But a few weeks ago, something happened that showed me how important church really is.

I had been in an argument with some of my friends for a few days. Well, I went to church the next Sunday morning and the sermon was on the importance of loving each other and being kind to each other. I realized that my friends and I weren't being very kind by arguing and being mad at each other. So after church that day we got together, talked about the situation and fixed our friendship. That might not have happened if it hadn't been for that sermon.

Even though church can seem kind of boring sometimes, it's our chance to be with other Christians, to learn more about God and to worship him and get fired up about sharing the good news of Jesus Christ to others. That's the stuff that helps our faith grow. And if we really pay attention, we might even learn something.

Luke, age 12

What about You?

❶ What do you like about your church? What don't you like? How can God use you in your church?

❷ Write today's passage on a piece of paper and take it with you to worship this week. During the service, watch for the things this passage talks about—teaching, fellowship, the breaking of bread (communion) and prayer. Why are those things important to the service? Ask your pastor why your church does things the way they do.

❸ Thank God for giving you a place where you can grow in your faith.

Turn to page 1313 for your next devotion.

courts, walking and jumping, and praising God. [9]When all the people saw him walking and praising God, [10]they recognized him as the same man who used to sit begging at the temple gate called Beautiful, and they were filled with wonder and amazement at what had happened to him.

Peter Speaks to the Onlookers

[11]While the beggar held on to Peter and John, all the people were astonished and came running to them in the place called Solomon's Colonnade. [12]When Peter saw this, he said to them: "Men of Israel, why does this surprise you? Why do you stare at us as if by our own power or godliness we had made this man walk? [13]The God of Abraham, Isaac and Jacob, the God of our fathers, has glorified his servant Jesus. You handed him over to be killed, and you disowned him before Pilate, though he had decided to let him go. [14]You disowned the Holy and Righteous One and asked that a murderer be released to you. [15]You killed the author of life, but God raised him from the dead. We are witnesses of this. [16]By faith in the name of Jesus, this man whom you see and know was made strong. It is Jesus' name and the faith that comes through him that has given this complete healing to him, as you can all see.

[17]"Now, brothers, I know that you acted in ignorance, as did your leaders. [18]But this is how God fulfilled what he had foretold through all the prophets, saying that his Christ[a] would suffer. [19]Repent, then, and turn to God, so that your sins may be wiped out, that times of refreshing may come from the Lord, [20]and that he may send the Christ, who has been appointed for you—even Jesus. [21]He must remain in heaven until the time comes for God to restore everything, as he promised long ago through his holy prophets. [22]For Moses said, 'The Lord your God will raise up for you a prophet like me from among your own people; you must listen to everything he tells you. [23]Anyone who does not listen to him will be completely cut off from among his people.'[b]

[24]"Indeed, all the prophets from Samuel on, as many as have spoken, have foretold these days. [25]And you are heirs of the prophets and of the covenant God made with your fathers. He said to Abraham, 'Through your offspring all peoples on earth will be blessed.'[c] [26]When God raised up his servant, he sent him first to you to bless you by turning each of you from your wicked ways."

Peter and John Before the Sanhedrin

4 The priests and the captain of the temple guard and the Sadducees came up to Peter and John while they were speaking to the people. [2]They were greatly disturbed because the apostles were teaching the people and proclaiming in Jesus the resurrection of the dead. [3]They seized Peter and John, and because it was evening, they put them in jail until the next day. [4]But many who heard the message believed, and the number of men grew to about five thousand.

[5]The next day the rulers, elders and teachers of the law met in Jerusalem. [6]Annas the high priest was there, and so were Caiaphas, John, Alexander and the other men of the high priest's family. [7]They had Peter and John brought before them and began to question them: "By what power or what name did you do this?"

[8]Then Peter, filled with the Holy Spirit, said to them: "Rulers and elders of the people! [9]If we are being called to account today for an act of kindness shown to a cripple and are asked how he was healed, [10]then know this, you and all the people of Israel: It is by the name of Jesus Christ of Nazareth, whom you crucified but whom God raised from the dead, that this man stands before you healed. [11]He is

" 'the stone you builders rejected,
    which has become the capstone.'[d][e]

[12]Salvation is found in no one else, for there is no other name under heaven given to men by which we must be saved."

[13]When they saw the courage of Peter and John and realized that they were unschooled, ordinary men, they were astonished and they took note that these

---

[a]18 Or *Messiah*; also in verse 20   [b]23 Deut.
18:15,18,19   [c]25 Gen. 22:18; 26:4   [d]11 Or
cornerstone   [e]11 Psalm 118:22

Make the Cut

Huh?

Acts 4:11–12

Imagine you're a coach and you find out that a player you once cut from your team is now, a couple years later, the best player in the entire league—at a different school. Peter tells the people that they made a much more serious mistake with Jesus. The Jesus they had rejected had become the Savior of the world. Ouch!

men had been with Jesus. [14]But since they could see the man who had been healed standing there with them, there was nothing they could say. [15]So they ordered them to withdraw from the Sanhedrin and then conferred together. [16]"What are we going to do with these men?" they asked. "Everybody living in Jerusalem knows they have done an outstanding miracle, and we cannot deny it. [17]But to stop this thing from spreading any further among the people, we must warn these men to speak no longer to anyone in this name."

[18]Then they called them in again and commanded them not to speak or teach at all in the name of Jesus. [19]But Peter and John replied, "Judge for yourselves whether it is right in God's sight to obey you rather than God. [20]For we cannot help speaking about what we have seen and heard."

[21]After further threats they let them go. They could not decide how to punish them, because all the people were praising God for what had happened. [22]For the man who was miraculously healed was over forty years old.

The Believers' Prayer

[23]On their release, Peter and John went back to their own people and reported all that the chief priests and elders had said to them. [24]When they heard this, they raised their voices together in prayer to God. "Sovereign Lord," they said, "you made the heaven and the earth and the sea, and everything in them. [25]You spoke

by the Holy Spirit through the mouth of your servant, our father David:

" 'Why do the nations rage
and the peoples plot in vain?
[26]The kings of the earth take their stand
and the rulers gather together
against the Lord
and against his Anointed One.[a],[b]

[27]Indeed Herod and Pontius Pilate met together with the Gentiles and the people[c] of Israel in this city to conspire against your holy servant Jesus, whom you anointed. [28]They did what your power and will had decided beforehand should happen. [29]Now, Lord, consider their threats and enable your servants to speak your word with great boldness. [30]Stretch out your hand to heal and perform miraculous signs and wonders through the name of your holy servant Jesus."

[31]After they prayed, the place where they were meeting was shaken. And they were all filled with the Holy Spirit and spoke the word of God boldly.

The Believers Share Their Possessions

[32]All the believers were one in heart and mind. No one claimed that any of his possessions was his own, but they shared everything they had. [33]With great power the apostles continued to testify to the resurrection of the Lord Jesus, and much grace was upon them all. [34]There were no needy persons among them. For from time to time those who owned lands or houses sold them, brought the money from the sales [35]and put it at the apostles' feet, and it was distributed to anyone as he had need.

[36]Joseph, a Levite from Cyprus, whom the apostles called Barnabas (which means Son of Encouragement), [37]sold a field he owned and brought the money and put it at the apostles' feet.

Ananias and Sapphira

5 Now a man named Ananias, together with his wife Sapphira, also sold a piece of property. [2]With his wife's full knowledge he kept back part of the mon-

---

[a]26 That is, Christ or Messiah   [b]26 Psalm 2:1,2
[c]27 The Greek is plural.

ey for himself, but brought the rest and put it at the apostles' feet.

³Then Peter said, "Ananias, how is it that Satan has so filled your heart that you have lied to the Holy Spirit and have kept for yourself some of the money you received for the land? ⁴Didn't it belong to you before it was sold? And after it was sold, wasn't the money at your disposal? What made you think of doing such a thing? You have not lied to men but to God."

⁵When Ananias heard this, he fell down and died. And great fear seized all who heard what had happened. ⁶Then the young men came forward, wrapped up his body, and carried him out and buried him.

⁷About three hours later his wife came in, not knowing what had happened. ⁸Peter asked her, "Tell me, is this the price you and Ananias got for the land?"

"Yes," she said, "that is the price."

⁹Peter said to her, "How could you agree to test the Spirit of the Lord? Look! The feet of the men who buried your husband are at the door, and they will carry you out also."

¹⁰At that moment she fell down at his feet and died. Then the young men came in and, finding her dead, carried her out and buried her beside her husband. ¹¹Great fear seized the whole church and all who heard about these events.

The Apostles Heal Many

¹²The apostles performed many miraculous signs and wonders among the people. And all the believers used to meet together in Solomon's Colonnade. ¹³No one else dared join them, even though they were highly regarded by the people. ¹⁴Nevertheless, more and more men and women believed in the Lord and

Wednesday

Wrestling With a Lie

Read Acts 4:32—5:11

I started wrestling this year, and so far I think it's a great sport—except for the part about "cutting weight." Wrestlers compete in different weight classes, with a maximum weight for each one. If you get too heavy for one class, you get bumped up into the next one, where you have to face bigger guys. So some guys will do almost anything to lose a few pounds and keep from getting bumped up. I was one of those guys.

For 2 weeks before a big meet, I starved myself. My friends saw what I was doing and tried to get me to stop, but I lied to them and said nothing was wrong. When they didn't believe my lies, I got angry with them and wouldn't talk to them. I was mean to them when they were only trying to help.

The problem with lying is that it hurts everyone. When you lie, you hurt yourself emotionally and, like me, sometimes physically too. You hurt the people who love you, because they can't get close to you when you won't tell them the truth. Worst of all, you hurt God because lying is sinning.

Being honest isn't always easy, but it's always better than telling a lie.

David age 14

What about You?

❶ Have you ever thought to yourself, "It's only a little lie"? How can "little lies" cause "big problems"?

❷ Have you hurt someone with a lie you told?

❸ Ask God to help you tell the truth, even when it isn't easy.

Turn to page 1318 for your next devotion.

were added to their number. [15]As a result, people brought the sick into the streets and laid them on beds and mats so that at least Peter's shadow might fall on some of them as he passed by. [16]Crowds gathered also from the towns around Jerusalem, bringing their sick and those tormented by evil[a] spirits, and all of them were healed.

The Apostles Persecuted

[17]Then the high priest and all his associates, who were members of the party of the Sadducees, were filled with jealousy. [18]They arrested the apostles and put them in the public jail. [19]But during the night an angel of the Lord opened the doors of the jail and brought them out. [20]"Go, stand in the temple courts," he said, "and tell the people the full message of this new life."

[21]At daybreak they entered the temple courts, as they had been told, and began to teach the people.

When the high priest and his associates arrived, they called together the Sanhedrin—the full assembly of the elders of Israel—and sent to the jail for the apostles. [22]But on arriving at the jail, the officers did not find them there. So they went back and reported, [23]"We found the jail securely locked, with the guards standing at the doors; but when we opened them, we found no one inside." [24]On hearing this report, the captain of the temple guard and the chief priests were puzzled, wondering what would come of this.

[25]Then someone came and said, "Look! The men you put in jail are standing in the temple courts teaching the people." [26]At that, the captain went with his officers and brought the apostles. They did not use force, because they feared that the people would stone them.

[27]Having brought the apostles, they made them appear before the Sanhedrin to be questioned by the high priest. [28]"We gave you strict orders not to teach in this name," he said. "Yet you have filled Jerusalem with your teaching and are determined to make us guilty of this man's blood."

[29]Peter and the other apostles replied: "We must obey God rather than men!

[30]The God of our fathers raised Jesus from the dead—whom you had killed by hanging him on a tree. [31]God exalted him to his own right hand as Prince and Savior that he might give repentance and forgiveness of sins to Israel. [32]We are witnesses of these things, and so is the Holy Spirit, whom God has given to those who obey him."

[33]When they heard this, they were furious and wanted to put them to death. [34]But a Pharisee named Gamaliel, a teacher of the law, who was honored by all the people, stood up in the Sanhedrin and ordered that the men be put outside for a little while. [35]Then he addressed them: "Men of Israel, consider carefully what you intend to do to these men. [36]Some time ago Theudas appeared, claiming to be somebody, and about four hundred men rallied to him. He was killed, all his followers were dispersed, and it all came to nothing. [37]After him, Judas the Galilean appeared in the days of the census and led a band of people in revolt. He too was killed, and all his followers were scattered. [38]Therefore, in the present case I advise you: Leave these men alone! Let them go! For if their purpose or activity is of human origin, it will fail. [39]But if it is from God, you will not be able to stop these men; you will only find yourselves fighting against God."

[40]His speech persuaded them. They called the apostles in and had them flogged. Then they ordered them not to speak in the name of Jesus, and let them go.

[41]The apostles left the Sanhedrin, rejoicing because they had been counted worthy of suffering disgrace for the Name. [42]Day after day, in the temple courts and from house to house, they never stopped teaching and proclaiming the good news that Jesus is the Christ.[b]

The Choosing of the Seven

6 In those days when the number of disciples was increasing, the Grecian Jews among them complained against the Hebraic Jews because their widows were being overlooked in the daily

[a]16 Greek *unclean*   [b]42 Or *Messiah*

distribution of food. ²So the Twelve gathered all the disciples together and said, "It would not be right for us to neglect the ministry of the word of God in order to wait on tables. ³Brothers, choose seven men from among you who are known to be full of the Spirit and wisdom. We will turn this responsibility over to them ⁴and will give our attention to prayer and the ministry of the word."

⁵This proposal pleased the whole group. They chose Stephen, a man full of faith and of the Holy Spirit; also Philip, Procorus, Nicanor, Timon, Parmenas, and Nicolas from Antioch, a convert to Judaism. ⁶They presented these men to the apostles, who prayed and laid their hands on them.

⁷So the word of God spread. The number of disciples in Jerusalem increased rapidly, and a large number of priests became obedient to the faith.

Stephen Seized

⁸Now Stephen, a man full of God's grace and power, did great wonders and miraculous signs among the people. ⁹Opposition arose, however, from members of the Synagogue of the Freedmen (as it was called)—Jews of Cyrene and Alexandria as well as the provinces of Cilicia and Asia. These men began to argue with Stephen, ¹⁰but they could not stand up against his wisdom or the Spirit by whom he spoke.

¹¹Then they secretly persuaded some men to say, "We have heard Stephen speak words of blasphemy against Moses and against God."

¹²So they stirred up the people and the elders and the teachers of the law. They seized Stephen and brought him before the Sanhedrin. ¹³They produced false witnesses, who testified, "This fellow never stops speaking against this holy place and against the law. ¹⁴For we have heard him say that this Jesus of Nazareth will destroy this place and change the customs Moses handed down to us."

¹⁵All who were sitting in the Sanhedrin looked intently at Stephen, and they saw that his face was like the face of an angel.

Stephen's Speech to the Sanhedrin

7 Then the high priest asked him, "Are these charges true?"

²To this he replied: "Brothers and fathers, listen to me! The God of glory appeared to our father Abraham while he was still in Mesopotamia, before he lived in Haran. ³'Leave your country and your people,' God said, 'and go to the land I will show you.'ᵃ

⁴"So he left the land of the Chaldeans and settled in Haran. After the death of his father, God sent him to this land where you are now living. ⁵He gave him no inheritance here, not even a foot of ground. But God promised him that he and his descendants after him would possess the land, even though at that time Abraham had no child. ⁶God spoke to him in this way: 'Your descendants will be strangers in a country not their own, and they will be enslaved and mistreated four hundred years. ⁷But I will punish the nation they serve as slaves,' God said, 'and afterward they will come out of that country and worship me in this place.'ᵇ ⁸Then he gave Abraham the covenant of circumcision. And Abraham became the father of Isaac and circumcised him eight days after his birth. Later Isaac became the father of Jacob, and Jacob became the father of the twelve patriarchs.

⁹"Because the patriarchs were jealous of Joseph, they sold him as a slave into Egypt. But God was with him ¹⁰and rescued him from all his troubles. He gave Joseph wisdom and enabled him to gain the goodwill of Pharaoh king of Egypt; so he made him ruler over Egypt and all his palace.

¹¹"Then a famine struck all Egypt and Canaan, bringing great suffering, and our fathers could not find food. ¹²When Jacob heard that there was grain in Egypt, he sent our fathers on their first visit. ¹³On their second visit, Joseph told his brothers who he was, and Pharaoh learned about Joseph's family. ¹⁴After this, Joseph sent for his father Jacob and his whole family, seventy-five in all. ¹⁵Then Jacob went down to Egypt, where

---

ᵃ3 Gen. 12:1   *ᵇ7* Gen. 15:13,14

he and our fathers died. ¹⁶Their bodies were brought back to Shechem and placed in the tomb that Abraham had bought from the sons of Hamor at Shechem for a certain sum of money.

¹⁷"As the time drew near for God to fulfill his promise to Abraham, the number of our people in Egypt greatly increased. ¹⁸Then another king, who knew nothing about Joseph, became ruler of Egypt. ¹⁹He dealt treacherously with our people and oppressed our forefathers by forcing them to throw out their newborn babies so that they would die.

²⁰"At that time Moses was born, and he was no ordinary child.ᵃ For three months he was cared for in his father's house. ²¹When he was placed outside, Pharaoh's daughter took him and brought him up as her own son. ²²Moses was educated in all the wisdom of the Egyptians and was powerful in speech and action.

²³"When Moses was forty years old, he decided to visit his fellow Israelites. ²⁴He saw one of them being mistreated by an Egyptian, so he went to his defense and avenged him by killing the Egyptian. ²⁵Moses thought that his own people would realize that God was using him to rescue them, but they did not. ²⁶The next day Moses came upon two Israelites who were fighting. He tried to reconcile them by saying, 'Men, you are brothers; why do you want to hurt each other?'

²⁷"But the man who was mistreating the other pushed Moses aside and said, 'Who made you ruler and judge over us? ²⁸Do you want to kill me as you killed the Egyptian yesterday?'ᵇ ²⁹When Moses heard this, he fled to Midian, where he settled as a foreigner and had two sons.

³⁰"After forty years had passed, an angel appeared to Moses in the flames of a burning bush in the desert near Mount Sinai. ³¹When he saw this, he was amazed at the sight. As he went over to look more closely, he heard the Lord's voice: ³²'I am the God of your fathers, the God of Abraham, Isaac and Jacob.'ᶜ Moses trembled with fear and did not dare to look.

³³"Then the Lord said to him, 'Take off your sandals; the place where you are standing is holy ground. ³⁴I have indeed seen the oppression of my people in Egypt. I have heard their groaning and have come down to set them free. Now come, I will send you back to Egypt.'ᵈ

³⁵"This is the same Moses whom they had rejected with the words, 'Who made you ruler and judge?' He was sent to be their ruler and deliverer by God himself, through the angel who appeared to him in the bush. ³⁶He led them out of Egypt and did wonders and miraculous signs in Egypt, at the Red Seaᵉ and for forty years in the desert.

³⁷"This is that Moses who told the Israelites, 'God will send you a prophet like me from your own people.'ᶠ ³⁸He was in the assembly in the desert, with the angel who spoke to him on Mount Sinai, and with our fathers; and he received living words to pass on to us.

³⁹"But our fathers refused to obey him. Instead, they rejected him and in their hearts turned back to Egypt. ⁴⁰They told Aaron, 'Make us gods who will go before us. As for this fellow Moses who led us out of Egypt—we don't know what has happened to him!'ᵍ ⁴¹That was the time they made an idol in the form of a calf. They brought sacrifices to it and held a celebration in honor of what their hands had made. ⁴²But God turned away and gave them over to the worship of the heavenly bodies. This agrees with what is written in the book of the prophets:

" 'Did you bring me sacrifices and
      offerings
   forty years in the desert, O house of
      Israel?
⁴³You have lifted up the shrine of
      Molech
   and the star of your god Rephan,
   the idols you made to worship.
Therefore I will send you into exile'ʰ
      beyond Babylon.

⁴⁴"Our forefathers had the tabernacle of the Testimony with them in the desert. It had been made as God directed Moses, according to the pattern he had seen. ⁴⁵Having received the tabernacle, our fathers under Joshua brought it with them

---

ᵃ20 Or *was fair in the sight of God* ᵇ28 Exodus 2:14 ᶜ32 Exodus 3:6 ᵈ34 Exodus 3:5,7,8,10 ᵉ36 That is, Sea of Reeds ᶠ37 Deut. 18:15 ᵍ40 Exodus 32:1 ʰ43 Amos 5:25-27

when they took the land from the nations God drove out before them. It remained in the land until the time of David, ⁴⁶who enjoyed God's favor and asked that he might provide a dwelling place for the God of Jacob.ᵃ ⁴⁷But it was Solomon who built the house for him.

⁴⁸"However, the Most High does not live in houses made by men. As the prophet says:

⁴⁹" 'Heaven is my throne,
    and the earth is my footstool.
What kind of house will you build for
        me?
                        says the Lord.
    Or where will my resting place be?
⁵⁰Has not my hand made all these
        things?'ᵇ

⁵¹"You stiff-necked people, with uncircumcised hearts and ears! You are just like your fathers: You always resist the Holy Spirit! ⁵²Was there ever a prophet your fathers did not persecute? They even killed those who predicted the coming of the Righteous One. And now you have betrayed and murdered him— ⁵³you who have received the law that was put into effect through angels but have not obeyed it."

The Stoning of Stephen

⁵⁴When they heard this, they were furious and gnashed their teeth at him. ⁵⁵But Stephen, full of the Holy Spirit, looked up to heaven and saw the glory of God, and Jesus standing at the right hand of God. ⁵⁶"Look," he said, "I see heaven open and the Son of Man standing at the right hand of God."

⁵⁷At this they covered their ears and, yelling at the top of their voices, they all rushed at him, ⁵⁸dragged him out of the city and began to stone him. Meanwhile, the witnesses laid their clothes at the feet of a young man named Saul. ⁵⁹While they were stoning him, Stephen prayed, "Lord Jesus, receive my spirit." ⁶⁰Then he fell on his knees and cried out, "Lord, do not hold this sin against them." When he had said this, he fell asleep.

8 And Saul was there, giving approval to his death.

The Church Persecuted and Scattered

On that day a great persecution broke out against the church at Jerusalem, and all except the apostles were scattered throughout Judea and Samaria. ²Godly men buried Stephen and mourned deeply for him. ³But Saul began to destroy the church. Going from house to house, he dragged off men and women and put them in prison.

Diehard Dudes

Huh?

Acts 8:1

Tons of people got cut off from their families when they became Christ-followers. You'd think this rejection, persecution and even torture would have snuffed out Christianity like a candle. But instead, the people who got kicked out of their homes kept talking about Jesus while they were moving to their new cities! Because of their excitement and witness, *lots* of people joined them—and Christianity grew.

Philip in Samaria

⁴Those who had been scattered preached the word wherever they went. ⁵Philip went down to a city in Samaria and proclaimed the Christᶜ there. ⁶When the crowds heard Philip and saw the miraculous signs he did, they all paid close attention to what he said. ⁷With shrieks, evilᵈ spirits came out of many, and many paralytics and cripples were healed. ⁸So there was great joy in that city.

Simon the Sorcerer

⁹Now for some time a man named Simon had practiced sorcery in the city and amazed all the people of Samaria. He boasted that he was someone great, ¹⁰and all the people, both high and low, gave him their attention and exclaimed, "This man is the divine power known as the Great Power." ¹¹They followed him

---

ᵃ46 Some early manuscripts *the house of Jacob*
ᵇ50 Isaiah 66:1,2   ᶜ5 Or *Messiah*   ᵈ7 Greek *unclean*

because he had amazed them for a long time with his magic. ¹²But when they believed Philip as he preached the good news of the kingdom of God and the name of Jesus Christ, they were baptized, both men and women. ¹³Simon himself believed and was baptized. And he followed Philip everywhere, astonished by the great signs and miracles he saw.

¹⁴When the apostles in Jerusalem heard that Samaria had accepted the word of God, they sent Peter and John to them. ¹⁵When they arrived, they prayed for them that they might receive the Holy Spirit, ¹⁶because the Holy Spirit had not yet come upon any of them; they had simply been baptized into[a] the name of the Lord Jesus. ¹⁷Then Peter and John placed their hands on them, and they received the Holy Spirit.

¹⁸When Simon saw that the Spirit was given at the laying on of the apostles' hands, he offered them money ¹⁹and said,

"Give me also this ability so that everyone on whom I lay my hands may receive the Holy Spirit."

²⁰Peter answered: "May your money perish with you, because you thought you could buy the gift of God with money! ²¹You have no part or share in this ministry, because your heart is not right before God. ²²Repent of this wickedness and pray to the Lord. Perhaps he will forgive you for having such a thought in your heart. ²³For I see that you are full of bitterness and captive to sin."

²⁴Then Simon answered, "Pray to the Lord for me so that nothing you have said may happen to me."

²⁵When they had testified and proclaimed the word of the Lord, Peter and John returned to Jerusalem, preaching the gospel in many Samaritan villages.

[a] 16 Or in

Thursday

Fakey Faith

Read Acts 8:9–23

I see a lot of people at my school wearing Christian T-shirts and jewelry. Then I see them do all kinds of stuff I know Jesus would never do, like make fun of people or swear or gossip. That really bothers me, because on the outside they look like great Christians. But inside they're just like everyone else.

It's pretty easy to pretend you're a great Christian. You just have to throw on a cross necklace, lead a few youth group discussions and show up at church every week. Those things are great if they're backed up with real faith. But sometimes people just do that kind of stuff to impress other people.

Being a Christian isn't about putting on a show. It's about loving God with your whole heart. Anyone can act like a Christian on the outside, but unless you're right with God on the inside, none of those things matter.

What about You?

❶ What are some ways people pretend they're great Christians? How do you think God feels about that kind of fake faith?

❷ Write down several things that make a person a "genuine Christian." What is one change you can make in your life that will make your own faith more real and genuine?

❸ Ask God to help you keep your faith real.

Turn to page 1322 for your next devotion.

Philip and the Ethiopian

²⁶Now an angel of the Lord said to Philip, "Go south to the road—the desert road—that goes down from Jerusalem to Gaza." ²⁷So he started out, and on his way he met an Ethiopian[a] eunuch, an important official in charge of all the treasury of Candace, queen of the Ethiopians. This man had gone to Jerusalem to worship, ²⁸and on his way home was sitting in his chariot reading the book of Isaiah the prophet. ²⁹The Spirit told Philip, "Go to that chariot and stay near it."

³⁰Then Philip ran up to the chariot and heard the man reading Isaiah the prophet. "Do you understand what you are reading?" Philip asked.

³¹"How can I," he said, "unless someone explains it to me?" So he invited Philip to come up and sit with him.

³²The eunuch was reading this passage of Scripture:

"He was led like a sheep to the
        slaughter,
    and as a lamb before the shearer is
        silent,
    so he did not open his mouth.
³³ In his humiliation he was deprived of
        justice.
    Who can speak of his descendants?
    For his life was taken from the
        earth."[b]

³⁴The eunuch asked Philip, "Tell me, please, who is the prophet talking about, himself or someone else?" ³⁵Then Philip began with that very passage of Scripture and told him the good news about Jesus.

³⁶As they traveled along the road, they came to some water and the eunuch said, "Look, here is water. Why shouldn't I be baptized?"[c] ³⁸And he gave orders to stop the chariot. Then both Philip and the eunuch went down into the water and Philip baptized him. ³⁹When they came up out of the water, the Spirit of the Lord suddenly took Philip away, and the eunuch did not see him again, but went on his way rejoicing. ⁴⁰Philip, however, appeared at Azotus and traveled about, preaching the gospel in all the towns until he reached Caesarea.

Saul's Conversion

9 Meanwhile, Saul was still breathing out murderous threats against the Lord's disciples. He went to the high priest ²and asked him for letters to the synagogues in Damascus, so that if he found any there who belonged to the Way, whether men or women, he might take them as prisoners to Jerusalem. ³As he neared Damascus on his journey, suddenly a light from heaven flashed around him. ⁴He fell to the ground and heard a voice say to him, "Saul, Saul, why do you persecute me?"

Way Cool

Huh?

Acts 9:2
Do you belong to "the Way"? You do if you're a Christian. People used the term "the Way" to refer to Christianity back in the first century. It comes from John 14:6, where Jesus said he is "the way." The way to what? Jesus is the only way to God. No way. Yes way! Way cool!

⁵"Who are you, Lord?" Saul asked.

"I am Jesus, whom you are persecuting," he replied. ⁶"Now get up and go into the city, and you will be told what you must do."

⁷The men traveling with Saul stood there speechless; they heard the sound but did not see anyone. ⁸Saul got up from the ground, but when he opened his eyes he could see nothing. So they led him by the hand into Damascus. ⁹For three days he was blind, and did not eat or drink anything.

¹⁰In Damascus there was a disciple named Ananias. The Lord called to him in a vision, "Ananias!"

"Yes, Lord," he answered.

¹¹The Lord told him, "Go to the house

---

[a] 27 That is, from the upper Nile region   [b] 33 Isaiah 53:7,8   [c] 36 Some late manuscripts *baptized?"*
³⁷Philip said, "If you believe with all your heart, you may." The eunuch answered, "I believe that Jesus Christ is the Son of God."

holy angel told him to have you come to his house so that he could hear what you have to say." ²³Then Peter invited the men into the house to be his guests.

Peter at Cornelius's House

The next day Peter started out with them, and some of the brothers from Joppa went along. ²⁴The following day he arrived in Caesarea. Cornelius was expecting them and had called together his relatives and close friends. ²⁵As Peter entered the house, Cornelius met him and fell at his feet in reverence. ²⁶But Peter made him get up. "Stand up," he said, "I am only a man myself."

²⁷Talking with him, Peter went inside and found a large gathering of people. ²⁸He said to them: "You are well aware that it is against our law for a Jew to associate with a Gentile or visit him. But God has shown me that I should not call any man impure or unclean. ²⁹So when I was sent for, I came without raising any objection. May I ask why you sent for me?"

³⁰Cornelius answered: "Four days ago I was in my house praying at this hour, at three in the afternoon. Suddenly a man in shining clothes stood before me ³¹and said, 'Cornelius, God has heard your prayer and remembered your gifts to the poor. ³²Send to Joppa for Simon who is called Peter. He is a guest in the home of Simon the tanner, who lives by the sea.' ³³So I sent for you immediately, and it was good of you to come. Now we are all here in the presence of God to listen to everything the Lord has commanded you to tell us."

³⁴Then Peter began to speak: "I now realize how true it is that God does not show favoritism ³⁵but accepts men from every nation who fear him and do what is right. ³⁶You know the message God sent to the people of Israel, telling the good news of peace through Jesus Christ, who is Lord of all. ³⁷You know what has

---

Friday

No Favorites

Read Acts 10:34–35

I'm embarrassed to admit it, but there have been times when I've been tempted to distance myself from people because they were "different" or didn't fit in.

But this passage tells us that God doesn't play favorites. He loves all people equally, no matter what race they are, how smart they are or how much money they have. Since we're supposed to be like Jesus, we shouldn't show favorites either. We need to share God's love with all people, even people who are different from us.

God wants all people to know him, not just a select few. He judges us all the same and offers salvation to all of us. If God, who knows us best, can look past our differences, we should too.

Ryan·age 14

What about You?

❶ What kind of people do you sometimes look down on or exclude? How do you think God views those people?

❷ Choose a culture that's different from your own and read more about it. Ask your parents to help you make a typical meal from that culture or find some music that comes from that culture. What do you think your life would be like if you'd been born into that culture?

❸ Thank God for creating all kinds of people.

Turn to page 1329 for your next devotion.

happened throughout Judea, beginning in Galilee after the baptism that John preached— [38]how God anointed Jesus of Nazareth with the Holy Spirit and power, and how he went around doing good and healing all who were under the power of the devil, because God was with him.

[39]"We are witnesses of everything he did in the country of the Jews and in Jerusalem. They killed him by hanging him on a tree, [40]but God raised him from the dead on the third day and caused him to be seen. [41]He was not seen by all the people, but by witnesses whom God had already chosen—by us who ate and drank with him after he rose from the dead. [42]He commanded us to preach to the people and to testify that he is the one whom God appointed as judge of the living and the dead. [43]All the prophets testify about him that everyone who believes in him receives forgiveness of sins through his name."

[44]While Peter was still speaking these words, the Holy Spirit came on all who heard the message. [45]The circumcised believers who had come with Peter were astonished that the gift of the Holy Spirit had been poured out even on the Gentiles. [46]For they heard them speaking in tongues[a] and praising God.

Then Peter said, [47]"Can anyone keep these people from being baptized with water? They have received the Holy Spirit just as we have." [48]So he ordered that they be baptized in the name of Jesus Christ. Then they asked Peter to stay with them for a few days.

Peter Explains His Actions

11 The apostles and the brothers throughout Judea heard that the Gentiles also had received the word of God. [2]So when Peter went up to Jerusalem, the circumcised believers criticized him [3]and said, "You went into the house of uncircumcised men and ate with them."

[4]Peter began and explained everything to them precisely as it had happened: [5]"I was in the city of Joppa praying, and in a trance I saw a vision. I saw something like a large sheet being let down from heaven by its four corners, and it came down to where I was. [6]I looked into it and

saw four-footed animals of the earth, wild beasts, reptiles, and birds of the air. [7]Then I heard a voice telling me, 'Get up, Peter. Kill and eat.'

[8]"I replied, 'Surely not, Lord! Nothing impure or unclean has ever entered my mouth.'

[9]"The voice spoke from heaven a second time, 'Do not call anything impure that God has made clean.' [10]This happened three times, and then it was all pulled up to heaven again.

[11]"Right then three men who had been sent to me from Caesarea stopped at the house where I was staying. [12]The Spirit told me to have no hesitation about going with them. These six brothers also went with me, and we entered the man's house. [13]He told us how he had seen an angel appear in his house and say, 'Send to Joppa for Simon who is called Peter. [14]He will bring you a message through which you and all your household will be saved.'

[15]"As I began to speak, the Holy Spirit came on them as he had come on us at the beginning. [16]Then I remembered what the Lord had said: 'John baptized with[b] water, but you will be baptized with the Holy Spirit.' [17]So if God gave them the same gift as he gave us, who believed in the Lord Jesus Christ, who was I to think that I could oppose God?"

[18]When they heard this, they had no further objections and praised God, saying, "So then, God has granted even the Gentiles repentance unto life."

The Church in Antioch

[19]Now those who had been scattered by the persecution in connection with Stephen traveled as far as Phoenicia, Cyprus and Antioch, telling the message only to Jews. [20]Some of them, however, men from Cyprus and Cyrene, went to Antioch and began to speak to Greeks also, telling them the good news about the Lord Jesus. [21]The Lord's hand was with them, and a great number of people believed and turned to the Lord.

[22]News of this reached the ears of the church at Jerusalem, and they sent Barnabas to Antioch. [23]When he arrived and

[a]46 Or *other languages*   [b]16 Or *in*

What a Way to Go!

Acts 12:23 Herod, one of the cruelest kings in the Bible, beheaded James, arrested Peter and agreed with the people's claim that he was a god. But Herod got it when it was his turn to die: He was eaten by worms! That's not the only bizarre death in the Bible. Check out these yuck-o ways to die:

✗ swallowed by the earth (Numbers 16:23–34)

✗ bombarded with giant hailstones (Joshua 10:11)

✗ a tent peg driven through the head (Judges 4:18–21)

✗ stabbed and beheaded (2 Samuel 4:5–8)

✗ trampled by horses and eaten by dogs (2 Kings 9:30–37)

✗ falling down, bursting open, guts spilling out (Acts 1:18)

saw the evidence of the grace of God, he was glad and encouraged them all to remain true to the Lord with all their hearts. ²⁴He was a good man, full of the Holy Spirit and faith, and a great number of people were brought to the Lord.

²⁵Then Barnabas went to Tarsus to look for Saul, ²⁶and when he found him, he brought him to Antioch. So for a whole year Barnabas and Saul met with the church and taught great numbers of people. The disciples were called Christians first at Antioch.

²⁷During this time some prophets came down from Jerusalem to Antioch. ²⁸One of them, named Agabus, stood up and through the Spirit predicted that a severe famine would spread over the entire Roman world. (This happened during the reign of Claudius.) ²⁹The disciples, each according to his ability, decided to provide help for the brothers living in Judea.

³⁰This they did, sending their gift to the elders by Barnabas and Saul.

Peter's Miraculous Escape From Prison

12 It was about this time that King Herod arrested some who belonged to the church, intending to persecute them. ²He had James, the brother of John, put to death with the sword. ³When he saw that this pleased the Jews, he proceeded to seize Peter also. This happened during the Feast of Unleavened Bread. ⁴After arresting him, he put him in prison, handing him over to be guarded by four squads of four soldiers each. Herod intended to bring him out for public trial after the Passover.

⁵So Peter was kept in prison, but the church was earnestly praying to God for him.

⁶The night before Herod was to bring him to trial, Peter was sleeping between two soldiers, bound with two chains, and sentries stood guard at the entrance. ⁷Suddenly an angel of the Lord appeared and a light shone in the cell. He struck Peter on the side and woke him up. "Quick, get up!" he said, and the chains fell off Peter's wrists.

⁸Then the angel said to him, "Put on your clothes and sandals." And Peter did so. "Wrap your cloak around you and follow me," the angel told him. ⁹Peter followed him out of the prison, but he had no idea that what the angel was doing was really happening; he thought he was seeing a vision. ¹⁰They passed the first and second guards and came to the iron gate leading to the city. It opened for them by itself, and they went through it. When they had walked the length of one street, suddenly the angel left him.

¹¹Then Peter came to himself and said, "Now I know without a doubt that the Lord sent his angel and rescued me from Herod's clutches and from everything the Jewish people were anticipating."

¹²When this had dawned on him, he went to the house of Mary the mother of John, also called Mark, where many people had gathered and were praying. ¹³Peter knocked at the outer entrance, and a servant girl named Rhoda came to answer the door. ¹⁴When she recognized Peter's voice, she was so overjoyed she

ran back without opening it and exclaimed, "Peter is at the door!"

[15]"You're out of your mind," they told her. When she kept insisting that it was so, they said, "It must be his angel."

[16]But Peter kept on knocking, and when they opened the door and saw him, they were astonished. [17]Peter motioned with his hand for them to be quiet and described how the Lord had brought him out of prison. "Tell James and the brothers about this," he said, and then he left for another place.

[18]In the morning, there was no small commotion among the soldiers as to what had become of Peter. [19]After Herod had a thorough search made for him and did not find him, he cross-examined the guards and ordered that they be executed.

Herod's Death

Then Herod went from Judea to Caesarea and stayed there a while. [20]He had been quarreling with the people of Tyre and Sidon; they now joined together and sought an audience with him. Having secured the support of Blastus, a trusted personal servant of the king, they asked for peace, because they depended on the king's country for their food supply.

[21]On the appointed day Herod, wearing his royal robes, sat on his throne and delivered a public address to the people. [22]They shouted, "This is the voice of a god, not of a man." [23]Immediately, because Herod did not give praise to God, an angel of the Lord struck him down, and he was eaten by worms and died.

[24]But the word of God continued to increase and spread.

[25]When Barnabas and Saul had finished their mission, they returned from[a] Jerusalem, taking with them John, also called Mark.

Barnabas and Saul Sent Off

13 In the church at Antioch there were prophets and teachers: Barnabas, Simeon called Niger, Lucius of Cyrene, Manaen (who had been brought up with Herod the tetrarch) and Saul. [2]While they were worshiping the Lord and fasting, the Holy Spirit said, "Set apart for me Barnabas and Saul for the work to which I have called them." [3]So

after they had fasted and prayed, they placed their hands on them and sent them off.

Fast Food

Huh?

Acts 13:2–3
A fast is when you choose not to eat food (or not watch TV, not talk on the phone or something like that) for a certain period of time. All through the Bible fasting is practiced and taught. Here's why you should try it: Maybe you have some serious stuff to talk to God about, or you want to spend extra time with God. Fasting for a little while helps you stay focused on God instead of on a Twinkie or the latest TV show.

On Cyprus

[4]The two of them, sent on their way by the Holy Spirit, went down to Seleucia and sailed from there to Cyprus. [5]When they arrived at Salamis, they proclaimed the word of God in the Jewish synagogues. John was with them as their helper.

[6]They traveled through the whole island until they came to Paphos. There they met a Jewish sorcerer and false prophet named Bar-Jesus, [7]who was an attendant of the proconsul, Sergius Paulus. The proconsul, an intelligent man, sent for Barnabas and Saul because he wanted to hear the word of God. [8]But Elymas the sorcerer (for that is what his name means) opposed them and tried to turn the proconsul from the faith. [9]Then Saul, who was also called Paul, filled with the Holy Spirit, looked straight at Elymas and said, [10]"You are a child of the devil and an enemy of everything that is right! You are full of all kinds of deceit and trickery. Will you never stop perverting the right ways of the Lord? [11]Now the hand of the Lord is against you. You are going to be blind, and for a time you will be unable to see the light of the sun."

[a]25 Some manuscripts to

Immediately mist and darkness came over him, and he groped about, seeking someone to lead him by the hand. [12]When the proconsul saw what had happened, he believed, for he was amazed at the teaching about the Lord.

In Pisidian Antioch

[13]From Paphos, Paul and his companions sailed to Perga in Pamphylia, where John left them to return to Jerusalem. [14]From Perga they went on to Pisidian Antioch. On the Sabbath they entered the synagogue and sat down. [15]After the reading from the Law and the Prophets, the synagogue rulers sent word to them, saying, "Brothers, if you have a message of encouragement for the people, please speak."

[16]Standing up, Paul motioned with his hand and said: "Men of Israel and you Gentiles who worship God, listen to me! [17]The God of the people of Israel chose our fathers; he made the people prosper during their stay in Egypt, with mighty power he led them out of that country, [18]he endured their conduct[a] for about forty years in the desert, [19]he overthrew seven nations in Canaan and gave their land to his people as their inheritance. [20]All this took about 450 years.

"After this, God gave them judges until the time of Samuel the prophet. [21]Then the people asked for a king, and he gave them Saul son of Kish, of the tribe of Benjamin, who ruled forty years. [22]After removing Saul, he made David their king. He testified concerning him: 'I have found David son of Jesse a man after my own heart; he will do everything I want him to do.'

[23]"From this man's descendants God has brought to Israel the Savior Jesus, as he promised. [24]Before the coming of Jesus, John preached repentance and baptism to all the people of Israel. [25]As John was completing his work, he said: 'Who do you think I am? I am not that one. No, but he is coming after me, whose sandals I am not worthy to untie.'

[26]"Brothers, children of Abraham, and you God-fearing Gentiles, it is to us that this message of salvation has been sent. [27]The people of Jerusalem and their rulers did not recognize Jesus, yet in condemning him they fulfilled the words of the prophets that are read every Sabbath. [28]Though they found no proper ground for a death sentence, they asked Pilate to have him executed. [29]When they had carried out all that was written about him, they took him down from the tree and laid him in a tomb. [30]But God raised him from the dead, [31]and for many days he was seen by those who had traveled with him from Galilee to Jerusalem. They are now his witnesses to our people.

[32]"We tell you the good news: What God promised our fathers [33]he has fulfilled for us, their children, by raising up Jesus. As it is written in the second Psalm:

> " 'You are my Son;
> today I have become your Father.'[b][c]

[34]The fact that God raised him from the dead, never to decay, is stated in these words:

> " 'I will give you the holy and sure
> blessings promised to David.'[d]

[35]So it is stated elsewhere:

> " 'You will not let your Holy One see
> decay.'[e]

[36]"For when David had served God's purpose in his own generation, he fell asleep; he was buried with his fathers and his body decayed. [37]But the one whom God raised from the dead did not see decay.

[38]"Therefore, my brothers, I want you to know that through Jesus the forgiveness of sins is proclaimed to you. [39]Through him everyone who believes is justified from everything you could not be justified from by the law of Moses. [40]Take care that what the prophets have said does not happen to you:

[41]" 'Look, you scoffers,
> wonder and perish,
> for I am going to do something in
> your days
> that you would never believe,
> even if someone told you.'[f]"

[a]18 Some manuscripts *and cared for them*
[b]33 Or *have begotten you*   [c]33 Psalm 2:7
[d]34 Isaiah 55:3   [e]35 Psalm 16:10   [f]41 Hab. 1:5

⁴²As Paul and Barnabas were leaving the synagogue, the people invited them to speak further about these things on the next Sabbath. ⁴³When the congregation was dismissed, many of the Jews and devout converts to Judaism followed Paul and Barnabas, who talked with them and urged them to continue in the grace of God.

⁴⁴On the next Sabbath almost the whole city gathered to hear the word of the Lord. ⁴⁵When the Jews saw the crowds, they were filled with jealousy and talked abusively against what Paul was saying.

⁴⁶Then Paul and Barnabas answered them boldly: "We had to speak the word of God to you first. Since you reject it and do not consider yourselves worthy of eternal life, we now turn to the Gentiles. ⁴⁷For this is what the Lord has commanded us:

" 'I have made you*ᵃ* a light for the
        Gentiles,
    that you*ᵃ* may bring salvation to
        the ends of the earth.'*ᵇ*"

⁴⁸When the Gentiles heard this, they were glad and honored the word of the Lord; and all who were appointed for eternal life believed.

⁴⁹The word of the Lord spread through the whole region. ⁵⁰But the Jews incited the God-fearing women of high standing and the leading men of the city. They stirred up persecution against Paul and Barnabas, and expelled them from their region. ⁵¹So they shook the dust from their feet in protest against them and went to Iconium. ⁵²And the disciples were filled with joy and with the Holy Spirit.

In Iconium

14 At Iconium Paul and Barnabas went as usual into the Jewish synagogue. There they spoke so effectively that a great number of Jews and Gentiles believed. ²But the Jews who refused to believe stirred up the Gentiles and poisoned their minds against the brothers. ³So Paul and Barnabas spent considerable time there, speaking boldly for the Lord, who confirmed the message of his grace by enabling them to do miraculous signs and wonders. ⁴The people of the city were divided; some sided with the Jews, others with the apostles. ⁵There was a plot afoot among the Gentiles and Jews, together with their leaders, to mistreat them and stone them. ⁶But they found out about it and fled to the Lycaonian cities of Lystra and Derbe and to the surrounding country, ⁷where they continued to preach the good news.

In Lystra and Derbe

⁸In Lystra there sat a man crippled in his feet, who was lame from birth and had never walked. ⁹He listened to Paul as he was speaking. Paul looked directly at him, saw that he had faith to be healed ¹⁰and called out, "Stand up on your feet!" At that, the man jumped up and began to walk.

¹¹When the crowd saw what Paul had done, they shouted in the Lycaonian language, "The gods have come down to us in human form!" ¹²Barnabas they called Zeus, and Paul they called Hermes because he was the chief speaker. ¹³The priest of Zeus, whose temple was just outside the city, brought bulls and wreaths to the city gates because he and the crowd wanted to offer sacrifices to them.

¹⁴But when the apostles Barnabas and Paul heard of this, they tore their clothes and rushed out into the crowd, shouting: ¹⁵"Men, why are you doing this? We too are only men, human like you. We are bringing you good news, telling you to turn from these worthless things to the living God, who made heaven and earth and sea and everything in them. ¹⁶In the past, he let all nations go their own way. ¹⁷Yet he has not left himself without testimony: He has shown kindness by giving you rain from heaven and crops in their seasons; he provides you with plenty of food and fills your hearts with joy." ¹⁸Even with these words, they had difficulty keeping the crowd from sacrificing to them.

¹⁹Then some Jews came from Antioch and Iconium and won the crowd over. They stoned Paul and dragged him outside the city, thinking he was dead. ²⁰But

---

ᵃ47 The Greek is singular.   *ᵇ47* Isaiah 49:6

after the disciples had gathered around him, he got up and went back into the city. The next day he and Barnabas left for Derbe.

The Return to Antioch in Syria

²¹They preached the good news in that city and won a large number of disciples. Then they returned to Lystra, Iconium and Antioch, ²²strengthening the disciples and encouraging them to remain true to the faith. "We must go through many hardships to enter the kingdom of God," they said. ²³Paul and Barnabas appointed elders*a* for them in each church and, with prayer and fasting, committed them to the Lord, in whom they had put their trust. ²⁴After going through Pisidia, they came into Pamphylia, ²⁵and when they had preached the word in Perga, they went down to Attalia.

²⁶From Attalia they sailed back to Antioch, where they had been committed to the grace of God for the work they had now completed. ²⁷On arriving there, they gathered the church together and reported all that God had done through them and how he had opened the door of faith to the Gentiles. ²⁸And they stayed there a long time with the disciples.

The Council at Jerusalem

15 Some men came down from Judea to Antioch and were teaching the brothers: "Unless you are circumcised, according to the custom taught by Mo-

ses, you cannot be saved." ²This brought Paul and Barnabas into sharp dispute and debate with them. So Paul and Barnabas were appointed, along with some other believers, to go up to Jerusalem to see the apostles and elders about this question. ³The church sent them on their way, and as they traveled through Phoenicia and Samaria, they told how the Gentiles had been converted. This news made all the brothers very glad. ⁴When they came to Jerusalem, they were welcomed by the church and the apostles and elders, to whom they reported everything God had done through them.

⁵Then some of the believers who belonged to the party of the Pharisees stood up and said, "The Gentiles must be circumcised and required to obey the law of Moses."

⁶The apostles and elders met to consider this question. ⁷After much discussion, Peter got up and addressed them: "Brothers, you know that some time ago God made a choice among you that the Gentiles might hear from my lips the message of the gospel and believe. ⁸God, who knows the heart, showed that he accepted them by giving the Holy Spirit to them, just as he did to us. ⁹He made no distinction between us and them, for he purified their hearts by faith. ¹⁰Now then, why do you try to test God by putting on the necks of the disciples a yoke that neither we nor our fathers have been able to bear? ¹¹No! We believe it is through the grace of our Lord Jesus that we are saved, just as they are."

¹²The whole assembly became silent as they listened to Barnabas and Paul telling about the miraculous signs and wonders God had done among the Gentiles through them. ¹³When they finished, James spoke up: "Brothers, listen to me. ¹⁴Simon*b* has described to us how God at first showed his concern by taking from the Gentiles a people for himself. ¹⁵The words of the prophets are in agreement with this, as it is written:

¹⁶ " 'After this I will return
         and rebuild David's fallen tent.

Painful Extra Credit

Acts 15:1

Have you ever had a teacher who made you do a ton of extra credit just to get a good grade? That's what's happening here. The Jews were incorrectly saying that if any non-Jew wanted to be saved, they'd have to do some extra credit. And the extra credit was—ouch!—circumcision (a really painful surgery performed on a, um, sensitive area for guys). Of course, to be saved all you need to do is believe in Jesus.

---

*a*23 Or *Barnabas ordained elders*; or *Barnabas had elders elected*   *b*14 Greek *Simeon*, a variant of *Simon*; that is, Peter

Its ruins I will rebuild,
　and I will restore it,
[17] that the remnant of men may seek the
　　　Lord,
　and all the Gentiles who bear my
　　　name,
says the Lord, who does these things'[a]
[18]　that have been known for ages.[b]

[19]"It is my judgment, therefore, that we should not make it difficult for the Gentiles who are turning to God. [20]Instead we should write to them, telling them to abstain from food polluted by idols, from

[a]17 Amos 9:11,12　[b]17,18 Some manuscripts things'– / [18]known to the Lord for ages is his work

Week end.

Loving Disagreement

Read Acts 15:36–41

Thursday Lauren talked about those who *pretend* to be "great Christians." Her devotional reminded us not to "put on a show" but to love God with our whole hearts. But what happens when there are disagreements between people who really love God? Some people think you can't be a "real" Christian and still have disagreements. The Bible shows us differently.

Acts 15 shows us that from the very beginning, the disciples had disagreements (and even fights) with each other. But it's *how* they handled those disagreements that really mattered. In Acts 15 there were 2 ways disciples of Jesus handled disagreements:

1) In the first 21 verses (verses we didn't ask you to read), the disciples had a big meeting to argue over who could be a Christian and what being a Christian meant. You can bet there were strong feelings in that crowd! But they figured it out *together*, with the help of the Holy Spirit.

2) And then in the verses we *did* ask you to read, Paul and Barnabas had such a heated disagreement that they went separate directions—but God still used both of them in big ways.

Both of these examples are good reminders that Christians need to try to get along and work together. God tells us to love each other (and, as Luke said on Tuesday, "to be with other Christians"), even when it's hard. That's the most important thing to remember when you struggle with other Christians. It's OK to disagree; but never forget to love!

❶ Do you think that 2 people who love Jesus can "agree to disagree" and stay close, even in a conflict?

❷ Think of a person you are having a struggle with right now. Would it be better for you to go to that person one-on-one and try to come to an agreement or to get a few friends or an adult to help the 2 of you work things out? Whichever one you think is best, go for it this week.

❸ Ask God to help you love a Christian you don't like or agree with.

Turn to page 1331 for your next devotion.

sexual immorality, from the meat of strangled animals and from blood. [21]For Moses has been preached in every city from the earliest times and is read in the synagogues on every Sabbath."

The Council's Letter to Gentile Believers

[22]Then the apostles and elders, with the whole church, decided to choose some of their own men and send them to Antioch with Paul and Barnabas. They chose Judas (called Barsabbas) and Silas, two men who were leaders among the brothers. [23]With them they sent the following letter:

The apostles and elders, your brothers,

To the Gentile believers in Antioch, Syria and Cilicia:

Greetings.

[24]We have heard that some went out from us without our authorization and disturbed you, troubling your minds by what they said. [25]So we all agreed to choose some men and send them to you with our dear friends Barnabas and Paul— [26]men who have risked their lives for the name of our Lord Jesus Christ. [27]Therefore we are sending Judas and Silas to confirm by word of mouth what we are writing. [28]It seemed good to the Holy Spirit and to us not to burden you with anything beyond the following requirements: [29]You are to abstain from food sacrificed to idols, from blood, from the meat of strangled animals and from sexual immorality. You will do well to avoid these things.

Farewell.

[30]The men were sent off and went down to Antioch, where they gathered the church together and delivered the letter. [31]The people read it and were glad for its encouraging message. [32]Judas and Silas, who themselves were prophets, said much to encourage and strengthen the brothers. [33]After spending some time there, they were sent off by the brothers with the blessing of peace to return to those who had sent them.[a] [35]But Paul and Barnabas remained in Antioch, where they and many others taught and preached the word of the Lord.

Disagreement Between Paul and Barnabas

[36]Some time later Paul said to Barnabas, "Let us go back and visit the brothers in all the towns where we preached the word of the Lord and see how they are doing." [37]Barnabas wanted to take John, also called Mark, with them, [38]but Paul did not think it wise to take him, because he had deserted them in Pamphylia and had not continued with them in the work. [39]They had such a sharp disagreement that they parted company. Barnabas took Mark and sailed for Cyprus, [40]but Paul chose Silas and left, commended by the brothers to the grace of the Lord. [41]He went through Syria and Cilicia, strengthening the churches.

Timothy Joins Paul and Silas

16 He came to Derbe and then to Lystra, where a disciple named Timothy lived, whose mother was a Jewess and a believer, but whose father was a Greek. [2]The brothers at Lystra and Iconium spoke well of him. [3]Paul wanted to take him along on the journey, so he circumcised him because of the Jews who lived in that area, for they all knew that his father was a Greek. [4]As they traveled from town to town, they delivered the decisions reached by the apostles and elders in Jerusalem for the people to obey. [5]So the churches were strengthened in the faith and grew daily in numbers.

Paul's Vision of the Man of Macedonia

[6]Paul and his companions traveled throughout the region of Phrygia and Galatia, having been kept by the Holy Spirit from preaching the word in the province of Asia. [7]When they came to the border of Mysia, they tried to enter Bithynia, but the Spirit of Jesus would not allow them to. [8]So they passed by Mysia and went down to Troas. [9]During the night Paul had a vision of a man of Macedonia standing and begging him, "Come

---

[a]33 Some manuscripts *them,* [34]*but Silas decided to remain there*

over to Macedonia and help us." ¹⁰After Paul had seen the vision, we got ready at once to leave for Macedonia, concluding that God had called us to preach the gospel to them.

Lydia's Conversion in Philippi

¹¹From Troas we put out to sea and sailed straight for Samothrace, and the next day on to Neapolis. ¹²From there we traveled to Philippi, a Roman colony and the leading city of that district of Macedonia. And we stayed there several days.

¹³On the Sabbath we went outside the city gate to the river, where we expected to find a place of prayer. We sat down and began to speak to the women who had gathered there. ¹⁴One of those listening was a woman named Lydia, a dealer in purple cloth from the city of Thyatira, who was a worshiper of God. The Lord opened her heart to respond to Paul's message. ¹⁵When she and the members of her household were baptized, she invited us to her home. "If you consider me a believer in the Lord," she said, "come and stay at my house." And she persuaded us.

Paul and Silas in Prison

¹⁶Once when we were going to the place of prayer, we were met by a slave girl who had a spirit by which she predicted the future. She earned a great deal of money for her owners by fortune-telling. ¹⁷This girl followed Paul and the rest of us, shouting, "These men are servants of the Most High God, who are telling you the way to be saved." ¹⁸She kept this up for many days. Finally Paul became so troubled that he turned around and said to the spirit, "In the name of Jesus Christ I command you to come out of her!" At that moment the spirit left her.

Monday

Praise? Now?

Read Acts 16:22–25

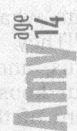

I was at a Christian ska concert with a bunch of my friends. They were all praising God, singing along and dancing to the music. But I was having a hard time enjoying myself because I felt like nothing was going right in my life. My 17-year-old sister thought she might be pregnant, my family was fighting constantly, and one of my good friends was flirting with the guy I really liked. I wanted to jump up and down like everybody else at the concert, but I hardly had the energy to stand up. I couldn't stop thinking about everything that was going wrong.

But as the concert went on, I realized I had to give up my problems to God. I couldn't handle everything by myself. Actually, I couldn't handle any of it by myself. Trusting God was the only way I was going to survive. So I said a little prayer and thanked God for being in control of my life.

It wasn't like God instantly solved all my problems or anything, but when I gave them to him, I felt like I could start praising him again. Soon I was dancing and singing with everyone else at the concert. God had wanted me to give him control of my situation all along. I'm so glad I did.

Amy, age 14

❶ When is it toughest for you to praise God?

❷ Imagine you were the prison guard in charge of Paul and Silas. Write down what you saw, heard and felt when they started singing.

❸ Say a prayer of praise to God.

Turn to page 1337 for your next devotion.

[19]When the owners of the slave girl realized that their hope of making money was gone, they seized Paul and Silas and dragged them into the marketplace to face the authorities. [20]They brought them before the magistrates and said, "These men are Jews, and are throwing our city into an uproar [21]by advocating customs unlawful for us Romans to accept or practice."

[22]The crowd joined in the attack against Paul and Silas, and the magistrates ordered them to be stripped and beaten. [23]After they had been severely flogged, they were thrown into prison, and the jailer was commanded to guard them carefully. [24]Upon receiving such orders, he put them in the inner cell and fastened their feet in the stocks.

[25]About midnight Paul and Silas were praying and singing hymns to God, and the other prisoners were listening to them. [26]Suddenly there was such a violent earthquake that the foundations of the prison were shaken. At once all the prison doors flew open, and everybody's chains came loose. [27]The jailer woke up, and when he saw the prison doors open, he drew his sword and was about to kill himself because he thought the prisoners had escaped. [28]But Paul shouted, "Don't harm yourself! We are all here!"

[29]The jailer called for lights, rushed in and fell trembling before Paul and Silas. [30]He then brought them out and asked, "Sirs, what must I do to be saved?"

[31]They replied, "Believe in the Lord Jesus, and you will be saved—you and your household." [32]Then they spoke the word of the Lord to him and to all the others in his house. [33]At that hour of the night the jailer took them and washed their wounds; then immediately he and all his family were baptized. [34]The jailer brought them into his house and set a meal before them; he was filled with joy because he had come to believe in God— he and his whole family.

[35]When it was daylight, the magistrates sent their officers to the jailer with the order: "Release those men." [36]The jailer told Paul, "The magistrates have ordered that you and Silas be released. Now you can leave. Go in peace."

[37]But Paul said to the officers: "They beat us publicly without a trial, even though we are Roman citizens, and threw us into prison. And now do they want to get rid of us quietly? No! Let them come themselves and escort us out."

[38]The officers reported this to the magistrates, and when they heard that Paul and Silas were Roman citizens, they were alarmed. [39]They came to appease them and escorted them from the prison, requesting them to leave the city. [40]After Paul and Silas came out of the prison, they went to Lydia's house, where they met with the brothers and encouraged them. Then they left.

In Thessalonica

17 When they had passed through Amphipolis and Apollonia, they came to Thessalonica, where there was a Jewish synagogue. [2]As his custom was, Paul went into the synagogue, and on three Sabbath days he reasoned with them from the Scriptures, [3]explaining and proving that the Christ[a] had to suffer and rise from the dead. "This Jesus I am proclaiming to you is the Christ,[a]" he said. [4]Some of the Jews were persuaded and joined Paul and Silas, as did a large number of God-fearing Greeks and not a few prominent women.

[5]But the Jews were jealous; so they rounded up some bad characters from the marketplace, formed a mob and started a riot in the city. They rushed to Jason's house in search of Paul and Silas in order to bring them out to the crowd.[b] [6]But when they did not find them, they dragged Jason and some other brothers before the city officials, shouting: "These men who have caused trouble all over the world have now come here, [7]and Jason has welcomed them into his house. They are all defying Caesar's decrees, saying that there is another king, one called Jesus." [8]When they heard this, the crowd and the city officials were thrown into turmoil. [9]Then they made Jason and the others post bond and let them go.

In Berea

[10]As soon as it was night, the brothers sent Paul and Silas away to Berea. On ar-

[a]3 Or *Messiah*   [b]5 Or *the assembly of the people*

Back Stage Pass

Do you ever feel like you can't wait to grow up? Here you are: You're not a kid anymore, but you're not an adult either. It's like you're stuck in the middle of life and can't get out soon enough.

Yeah, it's true, the goal of life is to get more mature and wise and "adult." But when it comes to faith, Jesus tells us to move in the other direction. Check out what he says: "I tell you the truth, unless you change and become like little children, you will never enter the kingdom of heaven" (Matthew 18:3, page 1166).

Did you get that? If heaven were a ride at the amusement park, there would be a sign out front that reads, THOSE WHO ACT TOO MATURE MAY NOT TAKE THIS RIDE. According to Jesus, there's something about a childlike attitude that's essential to admission into heaven.

But wait a minute. Does Jesus mean that we should return to our preschools, Play-doh and Pampers? Not likely (although the Play-doh part sounds fun). No, Jesus is talking about something else. He's not telling us to be childish—we've already been there. He's telling us to become childlike.

What are little kids like? For one thing, they're *trusting*. They trust that their parents love them, know what's best for them and will always be there for them. Many grown-ups (and kids who try to act grown-up) are cynical—they don't trust their lives to others. They figure they know what's best for themselves. And too often they figure wrong.

For another thing, children are *innocent*. (That's not to say they're always

innocent—kids can do some pretty nasty stuff. Little brothers and sisters are especially talented in this area.) But most little kids try to please their parents, and when they do something wrong, they often regret it, say sorry and move on.

Maybe this is the childlike spirit Jesus is talking about. He wants us to be trusting—to believe that our Father in heaven loves us, knows what's best for us and will always be there for us. Jesus wants us to cherish innocence—to do things that are pleasing to the Father. When we fail, he wants us to seek forgiveness and do better next time. Maybe he wants us to act like children in other ways too—children who are quick to love, quick to forgive, quick to laugh and thrilled with the simple things in life.

So, before you leap into this world's great big race to grow up, just stop for a moment. Turn around. Look back. Ask yourself, "Are there any childlike qualities I'm leaving behind?" God gave you some traits he meant you to keep for a lifetime. And some of these traits are exactly what you need to live forever.

FAITH

"Does God really send people to hell?"

If I got pulled over for driving 50 mph in a 35 mph zone, would it be the policeman's fault that I got a ticket? Of course not. I knew the rules, and I chose to ignore them. The ticket is just the result of my own behavior. It's pretty much the same thing with hell, though with much more serious consequences. When a person goes to hell, that person has done what a speeder has done—made a choice to ignore laws—except in this instance, God's laws.

Some of God's laws, like the law of gravity, can't be ignored. If you jump up, you have no choice but to come back down. But God has other laws that we can choose to obey or disobey. These laws, which concern our relationships with others and with God, are summarized in the Ten Commandments. Jesus said that we do our best at obeying these laws when we love God and our neighbors as much as we love ourselves (see Matthew 22:34–40, page 1173). Like the law of gravity, these laws will never change. But unlike the law of gravity, these laws don't "force" us to react in a specific way. We can choose how we will respond.

But even if we choose to obey God's laws, we really can't obey them on our own. We need God's help. And as Christians, we have that kind of help from the Holy Spirit, who gives us the power to obey God's laws.

There's an important Bible verse that clarifies this whole issue of heaven and hell: "For the wages of sin is death, but the gift of God is eternal life in Christ Jesus our Lord" (Romans 6:23). The first part of that verse tells us the consequence of sin: death. Specifically, eternal death in hell.

But as scary as that is, the second part of the verse—the gift of eternal life—is what Christians call the "good news." As Christians, we don't have to suffer the consequence of going to hell, because Jesus paid the price for our sins by dying on the cross and rising from the dead. All we have to do is believe it. That's the basic message of John 3:16: "For God so loved the world that he gave his one and only Son, that whoever believes in him shall not perish but have eternal life."

God desires to have a real relationship with all people. Whoever believes that Jesus Christ is their Savior will spend forever with God. That's the best news we could ever get.

—Buster Soaries, a popular youth speaker and the pastor of First Baptist Church of Lincoln Gardens in Somerset, New Jersey. He is also the host of the popular "Straight Up!" video series, which tackles the issues teens deal with every day.

riving there, they went to the Jewish synagogue. [11]Now the Bereans were of more noble character than the Thessalonians, for they received the message with great eagerness and examined the Scriptures every day to see if what Paul said was true. [12]Many of the Jews believed, as did also a number of prominent Greek women and many Greek men.

[13]When the Jews in Thessalonica learned that Paul was preaching the word of God at Berea, they went there too, agitating the crowds and stirring them up. [14]The brothers immediately sent Paul to the coast, but Silas and Timothy stayed at Berea. [15]The men who escorted Paul brought him to Athens and then left with instructions for Silas and Timothy to join him as soon as possible.

In Athens

[16]While Paul was waiting for them in Athens, he was greatly distressed to see that the city was full of idols. [17]So he reasoned in the synagogue with the Jews and the God-fearing Greeks, as well as in the marketplace day by day with those who happened to be there. [18]A group of Epicurean and Stoic philosophers began to dispute with him. Some of them asked, "What is this babbler trying to say?" Others remarked, "He seems to be advocating foreign gods." They said this because Paul was preaching the good news about Jesus and the resurrection. [19]Then they took him and brought him to a meeting of the Areopagus, where they said to him, "May we know what this new teaching is that you are presenting? [20]You are bringing some strange ideas to our ears, and we want to know what they mean." [21](All the Athenians and the foreigners who lived there spent their time doing nothing but talking about and listening to the latest ideas.)

[22]Paul then stood up in the meeting of the Areopagus and said: "Men of Athens! I see that in every way you are very religious. [23]For as I walked around and looked carefully at your objects of worship, I even found an altar with this inscription: TO AN UNKNOWN GOD. Now what you worship as something unknown I am going to proclaim to you.

[24]"The God who made the world and everything in it is the Lord of heaven and earth and does not live in temples built by hands. [25]And he is not served by human hands, as if he needed anything, because he himself gives all men life and breath and everything else. [26]From one man he made every nation of men, that they should inhabit the whole earth; and he determined the times set for them and the exact places where they should live. [27]God did this so that men would seek him and perhaps reach out for him and find him, though he is not far from each one of us. [28]'For in him we live and move and have our being.' As some of your own poets have said, 'We are his offspring.'

[29]"Therefore since we are God's offspring, we should not think that the divine being is like gold or silver or stone—an image made by man's design and skill. [30]In the past God overlooked such ignorance, but now he commands all people everywhere to repent. [31]For he has set a day when he will judge the world with justice by the man he has appointed. He has given proof of this to all men by raising him from the dead."

[32]When they heard about the resurrection of the dead, some of them sneered, but others said, "We want to hear you again on this subject." [33]At that, Paul left the Council. [34]A few men became followers of Paul and believed. Among them was Dionysius, a member of the

Is It an Act?

Huh?

Acts 17:22-23

Have you ever known someone who's religious but isn't a Christian? Someone who goes through the motions—goes to church, prays, reads the Bible, all that stuff—but doesn't really have Jesus in his or her heart? Doing Christian stuff doesn't make someone a Christian, just like going to a fast-food place doesn't turn you into a hamburger or a taco! Paul is saying the same thing. The only way to be a Christian is to invite Jesus Christ to come into your heart and take away your sins.

Areopagus, also a woman named Dama-ris, and a number of others.

In Corinth

18 After this, Paul left Athens and went to Corinth. [2]There he met a Jew named Aquila, a native of Pontus, who had recently come from Italy with his wife Priscilla, because Claudius had ordered all the Jews to leave Rome. Paul went to see them, [3]and because he was a tentmaker as they were, he stayed and worked with them. [4]Every Sabbath he reasoned in the synagogue, trying to per-suade Jews and Greeks.

[5]When Silas and Timothy came from Macedonia, Paul devoted himself exclu-sively to preaching, testifying to the Jews that Jesus was the Christ.[a] [6]But when the Jews opposed Paul and became abusive, he shook out his clothes in pro-test and said to them, "Your blood be on your own heads! I am clear of my re-sponsibility. From now on I will go to the Gentiles."

[7]Then Paul left the synagogue and went next door to the house of Titius Justus, a worshiper of God. [8]Crispus, the synagogue ruler, and his entire house-hold believed in the Lord; and many of the Corinthians who heard him believed and were baptized.

[9]One night the Lord spoke to Paul in a vision: "Do not be afraid; keep on speak-ing, do not be silent. [10]For I am with you, and no one is going to attack and harm you, because I have many people in this city." [11]So Paul stayed for a year and a half, teaching them the word of God.

[12]While Gallio was proconsul of Acha-ia, the Jews made a united attack on Paul and brought him into court. [13]"This man," they charged, "is persuading the people to worship God in ways contrary to the law."

[14]Just as Paul was about to speak, Gal-lio said to the Jews, "If you Jews were making a complaint about some misde-meanor or serious crime, it would be rea-sonable for me to listen to you. [15]But since it involves questions about words and names and your own law—settle the matter yourselves. I will not be a judge of such things." [16]So he had them ejected from the court. [17]Then they all turned on Sosthenes the synagogue ruler and beat him in front of the court. But Gallio showed no concern whatever.

Priscilla, Aquila and Apollos

[18]Paul stayed on in Corinth for some time. Then he left the brothers and sailed for Syria, accompanied by Priscilla and Aquila. Before he sailed, he had his hair cut off at Cenchrea because of a vow he had taken. [19]They arrived at Ephesus, where Paul left Priscilla and Aquila. He himself went into the synagogue and reasoned with the Jews. [20]When they asked him to spend more time with them, he declined. [21]But as he left, he promised, "I will come back if it is God's will." Then he set sail from Ephesus. [22]When he landed at Caesarea, he went up and greeted the church and then went down to Antioch.

[23]After spending some time in Antioch, Paul set out from there and traveled from place to place throughout the region of Galatia and Phrygia, strengthening all the disciples.

[24]Meanwhile a Jew named Apollos, a native of Alexandria, came to Ephesus. He was a learned man, with a thorough knowledge of the Scriptures. [25]He had been instructed in the way of the Lord, and he spoke with great fervor[b] and taught about Jesus accurately, though he knew only the baptism of John. [26]He be-gan to speak boldly in the synagogue. When Priscilla and Aquila heard him, they invited him to their home and ex-plained to him the way of God more ad-equately.

[27]When Apollos wanted to go to Acha-ia, the brothers encouraged him and wrote to the disciples there to welcome him. On arriving, he was a great help to those who by grace had believed. [28]For he vigorously refuted the Jews in public debate, proving from the Scriptures that Jesus was the Christ.

Paul in Ephesus

19 While Apollos was at Corinth, Paul took the road through the interior and arrived at Ephesus. There he found

---

[a]5 Or *Messiah;* also in verse 28   [b]25 Or *with fervor in the Spirit*

some disciples [2]and asked them, "Did you receive the Holy Spirit when[a] you believed?"

They answered, "No, we have not even heard that there is a Holy Spirit."

[3]So Paul asked, "Then what baptism did you receive?"

"John's baptism," they replied.

[4]Paul said, "John's baptism was a baptism of repentance. He told the people to believe in the one coming after him, that is, in Jesus." [5]On hearing this, they were baptized into[b] the name of the Lord Jesus. [6]When Paul placed his hands on them, the Holy Spirit came on them, and they spoke in tongues[c] and prophesied. [7]There were about twelve men in all.

[8]Paul entered the synagogue and spoke boldly there for three months, arguing persuasively about the kingdom of God. [9]But some of them became obstinate; they refused to believe and publicly maligned the Way. So Paul left them. He took the disciples with him and had discussions daily in the lecture hall of Tyrannus. [10]This went on for two years, so that all the Jews and Greeks who lived in the province of Asia heard the word of the Lord.

[11]God did extraordinary miracles through Paul, [12]so that even handkerchiefs and aprons that had touched him were taken to the sick, and their illnesses were cured and the evil spirits left them.

[13]Some Jews who went around driving out evil spirits tried to invoke the name of the Lord Jesus over those who were demon-possessed. They would say, "In the name of Jesus, whom Paul preaches, I command you to come out." [14]Seven sons of Sceva, a Jewish chief priest, were doing this. [15]One day the evil spirit answered them, "Jesus I know, and I know about Paul, but who are you?" [16]Then the man who had the evil spirit jumped on them and overpowered them all. He gave them such a beating that they ran out of the house naked and bleeding.

[17]When this became known to the Jews and Greeks living in Ephesus, they were all seized with fear, and the name of the Lord Jesus was held in high honor. [18]Many of those who believed now came and openly confessed their evil deeds. [19]A number who had practiced sorcery brought their scrolls together and burned them publicly. When they calculated the value of the scrolls, the total came to fifty thousand drachmas.[d] [20]In this way the word of the Lord spread widely and grew in power.

[21]After all this had happened, Paul decided to go to Jerusalem, passing through Macedonia and Achaia. "After I have been there," he said, "I must visit Rome also." [22]He sent two of his helpers, Timothy and Erastus, to Macedonia, while he stayed in the province of Asia a little longer.

The Riot in Ephesus

[23]About that time there arose a great disturbance about the Way. [24]A silversmith named Demetrius, who made silver shrines of Artemis, brought in no little business for the craftsmen. [25]He called them together, along with the workmen in related trades, and said: "Men, you know we receive a good income from this business. [26]And you see and hear how this fellow Paul has convinced and led astray large numbers of people here in Ephesus and in practically the whole province of Asia. He says that man-made gods are no gods at all. [27]There is danger not only that our trade will lose its good name, but also that the temple of the great goddess Artemis will be discredited, and the goddess herself, who is worshiped throughout the province of Asia and the world, will be robbed of her divine majesty."

[28]When they heard this, they were furious and began shouting: "Great is Artemis of the Ephesians!" [29]Soon the whole city was in an uproar. The people seized Gaius and Aristarchus, Paul's traveling companions from Macedonia, and rushed as one man into the theater. [30]Paul wanted to appear before the crowd, but the disciples would not let him. [31]Even some of the officials of the province, friends of Paul, sent him a message begging him not to venture into the theater.

[32]The assembly was in confusion:

---

[a]2 Or *after*   [b]5 Or *in*   [c]6 Or *other languages*
[d]19 A drachma was a silver coin worth about a day's wages.

Some were shouting one thing, some another. Most of the people did not even know why they were there. [33]The Jews pushed Alexander to the front, and some of the crowd shouted instructions to him. He motioned for silence in order to make a defense before the people. [34]But when they realized he was a Jew, they all shouted in unison for about two hours: "Great is Artemis of the Ephesians!"

[35]The city clerk quieted the crowd and said: "Men of Ephesus, doesn't all the world know that the city of Ephesus is the guardian of the temple of the great Artemis and of her image, which fell from heaven? [36]Therefore, since these facts are undeniable, you ought to be quiet and not do anything rash. [37]You have brought these men here, though they have neither robbed temples nor blasphemed our goddess. [38]If, then, Demetrius and his fellow craftsmen have a grievance against anybody, the courts are open and there are proconsuls. They can press charges. [39]If there is anything further you want to bring up, it must be settled in a legal assembly. [40]As it is, we are in danger of being charged with rioting because of today's events. In that case we would not be able to account for this commotion, since there is no reason for it." [41]After he had said this, he dismissed the assembly.

Through Macedonia and Greece

20 When the uproar had ended, Paul sent for the disciples and, after encouraging them, said good-by and set out for Macedonia. [2]He traveled through that area, speaking many words of encouragement to the people, and finally arrived in Greece, [3]where he stayed three months. Because the Jews made a plot against him just as he was about to sail for Syria, he decided to go back through Macedonia. [4]He was accompanied by Sopater son of Pyrrhus from Berea, Aristarchus and Secundus from Thessalonica, Gaius from Derbe, Timothy also, and Tychicus and Trophimus from the province of Asia. [5]These men went on ahead and waited for us at Troas. [6]But we sailed from Philippi after the Feast of Unleavened Bread, and five days later joined the others at Troas, where we stayed seven days.

Eutychus Raised From the Dead at Troas

[7]On the first day of the week we came together to break bread. Paul spoke to the people and, because he intended to leave the next day, kept on talking until midnight. [8]There were many lamps in the upstairs room where we were meeting. [9]Seated in a window was a young man named Eutychus, who was sinking into a deep sleep as Paul talked on and on. When he was sound asleep, he fell to the ground from the third story and was picked up dead. [10]Paul went down, threw himself on the young man and put his arms around him. "Don't be alarmed," he said. "He's alive!" [11]Then he went upstairs again and broke bread and ate. After talking until daylight, he left. [12]The people took the young man home alive and were greatly comforted.

Paul's Farewell to the Ephesian Elders

[13]We went on ahead to the ship and sailed for Assos, where we were going to take Paul aboard. He had made this arrangement because he was going there on foot. [14]When he met us at Assos, we took him aboard and went on to Mitylene. [15]The next day we set sail from there and arrived off Kios. The day after that we crossed over to Samos, and on the following day arrived at Miletus. [16]Paul had decided to sail past Ephesus to avoid spending time in the province of Asia, for he was in a hurry to reach Jerusalem, if possible, by the day of Pentecost.

[17]From Miletus, Paul sent to Ephesus for the elders of the church. [18]When they arrived, he said to them: "You know how I lived the whole time I was with you, from the first day I came into the province of Asia. [19]I served the Lord with great humility and with tears, although I was severely tested by the plots of the Jews. [20]You know that I have not hesitated to preach anything that would be helpful to you but have taught you publicly and from house to house. [21]I have declared to both Jews and Greeks that they must turn to God in repentance and have faith in our Lord Jesus.

[22]"And now, compelled by the Spirit, I

am going to Jerusalem, not knowing what will happen to me there. ²³I only know that in every city the Holy Spirit warns me that prison and hardships are facing me. ²⁴However, I consider my life worth nothing to me, if only I may finish the race and complete the task the Lord Jesus has given me—the task of testifying to the gospel of God's grace.

²⁵"Now I know that none of you among whom I have gone about preaching the kingdom will ever see me again. ²⁶Therefore, I declare to you today that I am innocent of the blood of all men. ²⁷For I have not hesitated to proclaim to you the whole will of God. ²⁸Keep watch over yourselves and all the flock of which the Holy Spirit has made you overseers.ᵃ Be shepherds of the church of God,ᵇ which he bought with his own blood. ²⁹I know that after I leave, savage wolves will come in among you and will not spare the flock. ³⁰Even from your own number men will arise and distort the truth in order to draw away disciples after them. ³¹So be on your guard! Re-

member that for three years I never stopped warning each of you night and day with tears.

³²"Now I commit you to God and to the word of his grace, which can build you up and give you an inheritance among all those who are sanctified. ³³I have not coveted anyone's silver or gold or clothing. ³⁴You yourselves know that these hands of mine have supplied my own needs and the needs of my companions. ³⁵In everything I did, I showed you that by this kind of hard work we must help the weak, remembering the words the Lord Jesus himself said: 'It is more blessed to give than to receive.' "

³⁶When he had said this, he knelt down with all of them and prayed. ³⁷They all wept as they embraced him and kissed him. ³⁸What grieved them most was his statement that they would never see his face again. Then they accompanied him to the ship.

ᵃ28 Traditionally *bishops*   ᵇ28 Many manuscripts *of the Lord*

Tuesday

The Unknown Future

Read Acts 20:22–24

My family moved when I was 8 years old, so I remember what it was like not knowing what you'd find in a new place. I didn't know what kind of church we would join or what my new school would be like. I wondered if anyone would even notice the new girl who didn't have any friends.

Even though some people didn't notice me at first, I always knew God remembered me. He helped me see that popularity wasn't really very important, as long as he was my best friend. I was lonely at times, but I was never really alone.

Moving taught me that I can't always know what's ahead in my life. But whatever it is, God will be there.

Cindy age 13

❶ Why do we sometimes wish we knew what would happen in the future? Why do you think God only lets us see one step at a time?

❷ Paul's big challenge was going to Jerusalem, but yours will probably be different. Rewrite these verses in a personal way, describing how God will be with you in a difficult situation.

❸ Thank God for his promise to always be your friend.

Turn to page 1344 for your next devotion.

Sancti-what?

Huh?

Acts 20:32

Ever voted in a school election? Everyone gets all psyched, and they have banners and buttons all over the place. Well, the winners are "set apart" to do a special job. One person is the president, one person is the treasurer, and so on. When you become a Christian, you are set apart ("sanctified") to become more and more like Jesus Christ. That means God works on you and changes you. Pretty cool, huh?

On to Jerusalem

21 After we had torn ourselves away from them, we put out to sea and sailed straight to Cos. The next day we went to Rhodes and from there to Patara. ²We found a ship crossing over to Phoenicia, went on board and set sail. ³After sighting Cyprus and passing to the south of it, we sailed on to Syria. We landed at Tyre, where our ship was to unload its cargo. ⁴Finding the disciples there, we stayed with them seven days. Through the Spirit they urged Paul not to go on to Jerusalem. ⁵But when our time was up, we left and continued on our way. All the disciples and their wives and children accompanied us out of the city, and there on the beach we knelt to pray. ⁶After saying good-by to each other, we went aboard the ship, and they returned home.

⁷We continued our voyage from Tyre and landed at Ptolemais, where we greeted the brothers and stayed with them for a day. ⁸Leaving the next day, we reached Caesarea and stayed at the house of Philip the evangelist, one of the Seven. ⁹He had four unmarried daughters who prophesied.

¹⁰After we had been there a number of days, a prophet named Agabus came down from Judea. ¹¹Coming over to us, he took Paul's belt, tied his own hands and feet with it and said, "The Holy Spirit says, 'In this way the Jews of Jerusalem will bind the owner of this belt and will hand him over to the Gentiles.'"

¹²When we heard this, we and the people there pleaded with Paul not to go up to Jerusalem. ¹³Then Paul answered, "Why are you weeping and breaking my heart? I am ready not only to be bound, but also to die in Jerusalem for the name of the Lord Jesus." ¹⁴When he would not be dissuaded, we gave up and said, "The Lord's will be done."

¹⁵After this, we got ready and went up to Jerusalem. ¹⁶Some of the disciples from Caesarea accompanied us and brought us to the home of Mnason, where we were to stay. He was a man from Cyprus and one of the early disciples.

Paul's Arrival at Jerusalem

¹⁷When we arrived at Jerusalem, the brothers received us warmly. ¹⁸The next day Paul and the rest of us went to see James, and all the elders were present. ¹⁹Paul greeted them and reported in detail what God had done among the Gentiles through his ministry.

²⁰When they heard this, they praised God. Then they said to Paul: "You see, brother, how many thousands of Jews have believed, and all of them are zealous for the law. ²¹They have been informed that you teach all the Jews who live among the Gentiles to turn away from Moses, telling them not to circumcise their children or live according to our customs. ²²What shall we do? They will certainly hear that you have come, ²³so do what we tell you. There are four men with us who have made a vow. ²⁴Take these men, join in their purification rites and pay their expenses, so that they can have their heads shaved. Then everybody will know there is no truth in these reports about you, but that you yourself are living in obedience to the law. ²⁵As for the Gentile believers, we have written to them our decision that they should abstain from food sacrificed to idols, from blood, from the meat of strangled animals and from sexual immorality."

²⁶The next day Paul took the men and purified himself along with them. Then he went to the temple to give notice of the date when the days of purification would end and the offering would be made for each of them.

Paul Arrested

²⁷When the seven days were nearly over, some Jews from the province of Asia saw Paul at the temple. They stirred up the whole crowd and seized him, ²⁸shouting, "Men of Israel, help us! This is the man who teaches all men everywhere against our people and our law and this place. And besides, he has brought Greeks into the temple area and defiled this holy place." ²⁹(They had previously seen Trophimus the Ephesian in the city with Paul and assumed that Paul had brought him into the temple area.)

³⁰The whole city was aroused, and the people came running from all directions. Seizing Paul, they dragged him from the temple, and immediately the gates were shut. ³¹While they were trying to kill him, news reached the commander of the Roman troops that the whole city of Jerusalem was in an uproar. ³²He at once took some officers and soldiers and ran down to the crowd. When the rioters saw the commander and his soldiers, they stopped beating Paul.

³³The commander came up and arrested him and ordered him to be bound with two chains. Then he asked who he was and what he had done. ³⁴Some in the crowd shouted one thing and some another, and since the commander could not get at the truth because of the uproar, he ordered that Paul be taken into the barracks. ³⁵When Paul reached the steps, the violence of the mob was so great he had to be carried by the soldiers. ³⁶The crowd that followed kept shouting, "Away with him!"

Paul Speaks to the Crowd

³⁷As the soldiers were about to take Paul into the barracks, he asked the commander, "May I say something to you?"

"Do you speak Greek?" he replied. ³⁸"Aren't you the Egyptian who started a revolt and led four thousand terrorists out into the desert some time ago?"

³⁹Paul answered, "I am a Jew, from Tarsus in Cilicia, a citizen of no ordinary city. Please let me speak to the people."

⁴⁰Having received the commander's permission, Paul stood on the steps and motioned to the crowd. When they were all silent, he said to them in Aramaic[a]:

22 ¹"Brothers and fathers, listen now to my defense."

²When they heard him speak to them in Aramaic, they became very quiet.

Then Paul said: ³"I am a Jew, born in Tarsus of Cilicia, but brought up in this city. Under Gamaliel I was thoroughly trained in the law of our fathers and was just as zealous for God as any of you are today. ⁴I persecuted the followers of this Way to their death, arresting both men and women and throwing them into prison, ⁵as also the high priest and all the Council can testify. I even obtained letters from them to their brothers in Damascus, and went there to bring these people as prisoners to Jerusalem to be punished.

⁶"About noon as I came near Damascus, suddenly a bright light from heaven flashed around me. ⁷I fell to the ground and heard a voice say to me, 'Saul! Saul! Why do you persecute me?'

⁸" 'Who are you, Lord?' I asked.

" 'I am Jesus of Nazareth, whom you are persecuting,' he replied. ⁹My companions saw the light, but they did not understand the voice of him who was speaking to me.

¹⁰" 'What shall I do, Lord?' I asked.

" 'Get up,' the Lord said, 'and go into Damascus. There you will be told all that you have been assigned to do.' ¹¹My companions led me by the hand into Damascus, because the brilliance of the light had blinded me.

¹²"A man named Ananias came to see me. He was a devout observer of the law and highly respected by all the Jews living there. ¹³He stood beside me and said, 'Brother Saul, receive your sight!' And at that very moment I was able to see him.

¹⁴"Then he said: 'The God of our fathers has chosen you to know his will and to see the Righteous One and to hear words from his mouth. ¹⁵You will be his witness to all men of what you have seen and heard. ¹⁶And now what are you waiting for? Get up, be baptized and wash your sins away, calling on his name.'

¹⁷"When I returned to Jerusalem and

---

[a]40 Or possibly *Hebrew*; also in 22:2

was praying at the temple, I fell into a trance [18]and saw the Lord speaking. 'Quick!' he said to me. 'Leave Jerusalem immediately, because they will not accept your testimony about me.'

[19]" 'Lord,' I replied, 'these men know that I went from one synagogue to another to imprison and beat those who believe in you. [20]And when the blood of your martyr[a] Stephen was shed, I stood there giving my approval and guarding the clothes of those who were killing him.'

[21]"Then the Lord said to me, 'Go; I will send you far away to the Gentiles.' "

Paul the Roman Citizen

[22]The crowd listened to Paul until he said this. Then they raised their voices and shouted, "Rid the earth of him! He's not fit to live!"

[23]As they were shouting and throwing off their cloaks and flinging dust into the air, [24]the commander ordered Paul to be taken into the barracks. He directed that he be flogged and questioned in order to find out why the people were shouting at him like this. [25]As they stretched him out to flog him, Paul said to the centurion standing there, "Is it legal for you to flog a Roman citizen who hasn't even been found guilty?"

[26]When the centurion heard this, he went to the commander and reported it. "What are you going to do?" he asked. "This man is a Roman citizen."

[27]The commander went to Paul and asked, "Tell me, are you a Roman citizen?"

"Yes, I am," he answered.

[28]Then the commander said, "I had to pay a big price for my citizenship."

"But I was born a citizen," Paul replied.

[29]Those who were about to question him withdrew immediately. The commander himself was alarmed when he realized that he had put Paul, a Roman citizen, in chains.

Before the Sanhedrin

[30]The next day, since the commander wanted to find out exactly why Paul was being accused by the Jews, he released him and ordered the chief priests and all the Sanhedrin to assemble. Then he brought Paul and had him stand before them.

23 Paul looked straight at the Sanhedrin and said, "My brothers, I have fulfilled my duty to God in all good conscience to this day." [2]At this the high priest Ananias ordered those standing near Paul to strike him on the mouth. [3]Then Paul said to him, "God will strike you, you whitewashed wall! You sit there to judge me according to the law, yet you yourself violate the law by commanding that I be struck!"

[4]Those who were standing near Paul said, "You dare to insult God's high priest?"

[5]Paul replied, "Brothers, I did not realize that he was the high priest; for it is written: 'Do not speak evil about the ruler of your people.'[b]"

[6]Then Paul, knowing that some of them were Sadducees and the others Pharisees, called out in the Sanhedrin, "My brothers, I am a Pharisee, the son of a Pharisee. I stand on trial because of my hope in the resurrection of the dead." [7]When he said this, a dispute broke out between the Pharisees and the Sadducees, and the assembly was divided. [8](The Sadducees say that there is no resurrection, and that there are neither angels nor spirits, but the Pharisees acknowledge them all.)

[9]There was a great uproar, and some of the teachers of the law who were Pharisees stood up and argued vigorously. "We find nothing wrong with this man," they said. "What if a spirit or an angel has spoken to him?" [10]The dispute became so violent that the commander was afraid Paul would be torn to pieces by them. He ordered the troops to go down and take him away from them by force and bring him into the barracks.

[11]The following night the Lord stood near Paul and said, "Take courage! As you have testified about me in Jerusalem, so you must also testify in Rome."

The Plot to Kill Paul

[12]The next morning the Jews formed a conspiracy and bound themselves with an oath not to eat or drink until they had

---

[a]20 Or *witness*   [b]5 Exodus 22:28

killed Paul. ¹³More than forty men were involved in this plot. ¹⁴They went to the chief priests and elders and said, "We have taken a solemn oath not to eat anything until we have killed Paul. ¹⁵Now then, you and the Sanhedrin petition the commander to bring him before you on the pretext of wanting more accurate information about his case. We are ready to kill him before he gets here."

¹⁶But when the son of Paul's sister heard of this plot, he went into the barracks and told Paul.

¹⁷Then Paul called one of the centurions and said, "Take this young man to the commander; he has something to tell him." ¹⁸So he took him to the commander.

The centurion said, "Paul, the prisoner, sent for me and asked me to bring this young man to you because he has something to tell you."

¹⁹The commander took the young man by the hand, drew him aside and asked, "What is it you want to tell me?"

²⁰He said: "The Jews have agreed to ask you to bring Paul before the Sanhedrin tomorrow on the pretext of wanting more accurate information about him. ²¹Don't give in to them, because more than forty of them are waiting in ambush for him. They have taken an oath not to eat or drink until they have killed him. They are ready now, waiting for your consent to their request."

²²The commander dismissed the young man and cautioned him, "Don't tell anyone that you have reported this to me."

Paul Transferred to Caesarea

²³Then he called two of his centurions and ordered them, "Get ready a detachment of two hundred soldiers, seventy horsemen and two hundred spearmen*a* to go to Caesarea at nine tonight. ²⁴Provide mounts for Paul so that he may be taken safely to Governor Felix."

²⁵He wrote a letter as follows:

²⁶Claudius Lysias,

To His Excellency, Governor Felix:

Greetings.

²⁷This man was seized by the Jews and they were about to kill him, but I came with my troops and rescued him, for I had learned that he is a Roman citizen. ²⁸I wanted to know why they were accusing him, so I brought him to their Sanhedrin. ²⁹I found that the accusation had to do with questions about their law, but there was no charge against him that deserved death or imprisonment. ³⁰When I was informed of a plot to be carried out against the man, I sent him to you at once. I also ordered his accusers to present to you their case against him.

³¹So the soldiers, carrying out their orders, took Paul with them during the night and brought him as far as Antipatris. ³²The next day they let the cavalry go on with him, while they returned to the barracks. ³³When the cavalry arrived in Caesarea, they delivered the letter to the governor and handed Paul over to him. ³⁴The governor read the letter and asked what province he was from. Learning that he was from Cilicia, ³⁵he said, "I will hear your case when your accusers get here." Then he ordered that Paul be kept under guard in Herod's palace.

The Trial Before Felix

24 Five days later the high priest Ananias went down to Caesarea with some of the elders and a lawyer named Tertullus, and they brought their charges against Paul before the governor. ²When Paul was called in, Tertullus presented his case before Felix: "We have enjoyed a long period of peace under you, and your foresight has brought about reforms in this nation. ³Everywhere and in every way, most excellent Felix, we acknowledge this with profound gratitude. ⁴But in order not to weary you further, I would request that you be kind enough to hear us briefly.

⁵"We have found this man to be a troublemaker, stirring up riots among the Jews all over the world. He is a ringleader of the Nazarene sect ⁶and even tried to desecrate the temple; so we seized him.

---

a23 The meaning of the Greek for this word is uncertain.

[8]By[a] examining him yourself you will be able to learn the truth about all these charges we are bringing against him."

[9]The Jews joined in the accusation, asserting that these things were true.

[10]When the governor motioned for him to speak, Paul replied: "I know that for a number of years you have been a judge over this nation; so I gladly make my defense. [11]You can easily verify that no more than twelve days ago I went up to Jerusalem to worship. [12]My accusers did not find me arguing with anyone at the temple, or stirring up a crowd in the synagogues or anywhere else in the city. [13]And they cannot prove to you the charges they are now making against me. [14]However, I admit that I worship the God of our fathers as a follower of the Way, which they call a sect. I believe everything that agrees with the Law and that is written in the Prophets, [15]and I have the same hope in God as these men, that there will be a resurrection of both the righteous and the wicked. [16]So I strive always to keep my conscience clear before God and man.

[17]"After an absence of several years, I came to Jerusalem to bring my people gifts for the poor and to present offerings. [18]I was ceremonially clean when they found me in the temple courts doing this. There was no crowd with me, nor was I involved in any disturbance. [19]But there are some Jews from the province of Asia, who ought to be here before you and bring charges if they have anything against me. [20]Or these who are here should state what crime they found in me when I stood before the Sanhedrin— [21]unless it was this one thing I shouted as I stood in their presence: 'It is concerning the resurrection of the dead that I am on trial before you today.' "

[22]Then Felix, who was well acquainted with the Way, adjourned the proceedings. "When Lysias the commander comes," he said, "I will decide your case." [23]He ordered the centurion to keep Paul under guard but to give him some freedom and permit his friends to take care of his needs.

[24]Several days later Felix came with his wife Drusilla, who was a Jewess. He sent for Paul and listened to him as he spoke about faith in Christ Jesus. [25]As Paul discoursed on righteousness, self-control and the judgment to come, Felix was afraid and said, "That's enough for now! You may leave. When I find it convenient, I will send for you." [26]At the same time he was hoping that Paul would offer him a bribe, so he sent for him frequently and talked with him.

[27]When two years had passed, Felix was succeeded by Porcius Festus, but because Felix wanted to grant a favor to the Jews, he left Paul in prison.

The Trial Before Festus

25 Three days after arriving in the province, Festus went up from Caesarea to Jerusalem, [2]where the chief priests and Jewish leaders appeared before him and presented the charges against Paul. [3]They urgently requested Festus, as a favor to them, to have Paul transferred to Jerusalem, for they were preparing an ambush to kill him along the way. [4]Festus answered, "Paul is being held at Caesarea, and I myself am going there soon. [5]Let some of your leaders come with me and press charges against the man there, if he has done anything wrong."

[6]After spending eight or ten days with them, he went down to Caesarea, and the next day he convened the court and ordered that Paul be brought before him. [7]When Paul appeared, the Jews who had come down from Jerusalem stood around him, bringing many serious charges against him, which they could not prove.

[8]Then Paul made his defense: "I have done nothing wrong against the law of the Jews or against the temple or against Caesar."

[9]Festus, wishing to do the Jews a favor, said to Paul, "Are you willing to go up to Jerusalem and stand trial before me there on these charges?"

[10]Paul answered: "I am now standing before Caesar's court, where I ought to be tried. I have not done any wrong to the Jews, as you yourself know very well.

[a]6-8 Some manuscripts *him and wanted to judge him according to our law.* [7]*But the commander, Lysias, came and with the use of much force snatched him from our hands* [8]*and ordered his accusers to come before you. By*

¹¹If, however, I am guilty of doing anything deserving death, I do not refuse to die. But if the charges brought against me by these Jews are not true, no one has the right to hand me over to them. I appeal to Caesar!"

¹²After Festus had conferred with his council, he declared: "You have appealed to Caesar. To Caesar you will go!"

Festus Consults King Agrippa

¹³A few days later King Agrippa and Bernice arrived at Caesarea to pay their respects to Festus. ¹⁴Since they were spending many days there, Festus discussed Paul's case with the king. He said: "There is a man here whom Felix left as a prisoner. ¹⁵When I went to Jerusalem, the chief priests and elders of the Jews brought charges against him and asked that he be condemned.

¹⁶"I told them that it is not the Roman custom to hand over any man before he has faced his accusers and has had an opportunity to defend himself against their charges. ¹⁷When they came here with me, I did not delay the case, but convened the court the next day and ordered the man to be brought in. ¹⁸When his accusers got up to speak, they did not charge him with any of the crimes I had expected. ¹⁹Instead, they had some points of dispute with him about their own religion and about a dead man named Jesus who Paul claimed was alive. ²⁰I was at a loss how to investigate such matters; so I asked if he would be willing to go to Jerusalem and stand trial there on these charges. ²¹When Paul made his appeal to be held over for the Emperor's decision, I ordered him held until I could send him to Caesar."

²²Then Agrippa said to Festus, "I would like to hear this man myself."

He replied, "Tomorrow you will hear him."

Paul Before Agrippa

²³The next day Agrippa and Bernice came with great pomp and entered the audience room with the high ranking officers and the leading men of the city. At the command of Festus, Paul was brought in. ²⁴Festus said: "King Agrippa, and all who are present with us, you see this man! The whole Jewish community has petitioned me about him in Jerusalem and here in Caesarea, shouting that he ought not to live any longer. ²⁵I found he had done nothing deserving of death, but because he made his appeal to the Emperor I decided to send him to Rome. ²⁶But I have nothing definite to write to His Majesty about him. Therefore I have brought him before all of you, and especially before you, King Agrippa, so that as a result of this investigation I may have something to write. ²⁷For I think it is unreasonable to send on a prisoner without specifying the charges against him."

26 Then Agrippa said to Paul, "You have permission to speak for yourself."

So Paul motioned with his hand and began his defense: ²"King Agrippa, I consider myself fortunate to stand before you today as I make my defense against all the accusations of the Jews, ³and especially so because you are well acquainted with all the Jewish customs and controversies. Therefore, I beg you to listen to me patiently.

⁴"The Jews all know the way I have lived ever since I was a child, from the beginning of my life in my own country, and also in Jerusalem. ⁵They have known me for a long time and can testify, if they are willing, that according to the strictest sect of our religion, I lived as a Pharisee. ⁶And now it is because of my hope in what God has promised our fathers that I am on trial today. ⁷This is the promise our twelve tribes are hoping to see fulfilled as they earnestly serve God day and night. O king, it is because of this hope that the Jews are accusing me. ⁸Why should any of you consider it incredible that God raises the dead?

⁹"I too was convinced that I ought to do all that was possible to oppose the name of Jesus of Nazareth. ¹⁰And that is just what I did in Jerusalem. On the authority of the chief priests I put many of the saints in prison, and when they were put to death, I cast my vote against them. ¹¹Many a time I went from one synagogue to another to have them punished, and I tried to force them to blaspheme. In my obsession against them, I even went to foreign cities to persecute them.

¹²"On one of these journeys I was going to Damascus with the authority and commission of the chief priests. ¹³About noon, O king, as I was on the road, I saw a light from heaven, brighter than the sun, blazing around me and my companions. ¹⁴We all fell to the ground, and I heard a voice saying to me in Aramaic,ᵃ 'Saul, Saul, why do you persecute me? It is hard for you to kick against the goads.'

¹⁵"Then I asked, 'Who are you, Lord?'

" 'I am Jesus, whom you are persecuting,' the Lord replied. ¹⁶'Now get up and stand on your feet. I have appeared to you to appoint you as a servant and as a witness of what you have seen of me and what I will show you. ¹⁷I will rescue you from your own people and from the Gentiles. I am sending you to them ¹⁸to open their eyes and turn them from darkness to light, and from the power of Satan to God, so that they may receive forgiveness of sins and a place among those who are sanctified by faith in me.'

¹⁹"So then, King Agrippa, I was not disobedient to the vision from heaven. ²⁰First to those in Damascus, then to those in Jerusalem and in all Judea, and to the Gentiles also, I preached that they should repent and turn to God and prove their repentance by their deeds. ²¹That is why the Jews seized me in the temple courts and tried to kill me. ²²But I have had God's help to this very day, and so I stand here and testify to small and great alike. I am saying nothing beyond what the prophets and Moses said would happen— ²³that the Christᵇ would suffer and, as the first to rise from the dead, would proclaim light to his own people and to the Gentiles."

²⁴At this point Festus interrupted Paul's defense. "You are out of your mind, Paul!" he shouted. "Your great learning is driving you insane."

²⁵"I am not insane, most excellent Festus," Paul replied. "What I am saying is true and reasonable. ²⁶The king is familiar with these things, and I can speak

ᵃ14 Or Hebrew   ᵇ23 Or Messiah

Wednesday

Switcheroo

Read Acts 26:9–18

If I meet someone who isn't living a Christian life, that doesn't mean they'll always be that way. God loves everyone, even his enemies, and he can turn people's lives completely around. He totally changed Saul. Saul's life changed so much that God even gave him a new name—Paul.

I also need to learn to love the people I don't like. Instead of looking down on them or getting mad, I should pray for them. Maybe someone seems like a bad person to me, but he or she wouldn't always be that way if they got to know God. And if I can help them do that, I'll feel great about myself because I helped change someone's life.

Melinda   age 12

❶ Who are your enemies? What can you do to help them know more about God?

❷ Find some of your baby pictures. See how much you've changed? Now, if people can change that much physically, think about how much they can change spiritually.

❸ Pray for people you don't like, that God would come into their lives and change them.

Turn to page 1347 for your next devotion.

freely to him. I am convinced that none of this has escaped his notice, because it was not done in a corner. ²⁷King Agrippa, do you believe the prophets? I know you do."

²⁸Then Agrippa said to Paul, "Do you think that in such a short time you can persuade me to be a Christian?"

²⁹Paul replied, "Short time or long—I pray God that not only you but all who are listening to me today may become what I am, except for these chains."

³⁰The king rose, and with him the governor and Bernice and those sitting with them. ³¹They left the room, and while talking with one another, they said, "This man is not doing anything that deserves death or imprisonment."

³²Agrippa said to Festus, "This man could have been set free if he had not appealed to Caesar."

Paul Sails for Rome

27 When it was decided that we would sail for Italy, Paul and some other prisoners were handed over to a centurion named Julius, who belonged to the Imperial Regiment. ²We boarded a ship from Adramyttium about to sail for ports along the coast of the province of Asia, and we put out to sea. Aristarchus, a Macedonian from Thessalonica, was with us.

³The next day we landed at Sidon; and Julius, in kindness to Paul, allowed him to go to his friends so they might provide for his needs. ⁴From there we put out to sea again and passed to the lee of Cyprus because the winds were against us. ⁵When we had sailed across the open sea off the coast of Cilicia and Pamphylia, we landed at Myra in Lycia. ⁶There the centurion found an Alexandrian ship sailing for Italy and put us on board. ⁷We made slow headway for many days and had difficulty arriving off Cnidus. When the wind did not allow us to hold our course, we sailed to the lee of Crete, opposite Salmone. ⁸We moved along the coast with difficulty and came to a place called Fair Havens, near the town of Lasea.

⁹Much time had been lost, and sailing had already become dangerous because by now it was after the Fast.ᵃ So Paul warned them, ¹⁰"Men, I can see that our voyage is going to be disastrous and bring great loss to ship and cargo, and to our own lives also." ¹¹But the centurion, instead of listening to what Paul said, followed the advice of the pilot and of the owner of the ship. ¹²Since the harbor was unsuitable to winter in, the majority decided that we should sail on, hoping to reach Phoenix and winter there. This was a harbor in Crete, facing both southwest and northwest.

The Storm

¹³When a gentle south wind began to blow, they thought they had obtained what they wanted; so they weighed anchor and sailed along the shore of Crete. ¹⁴Before very long, a wind of hurricane force, called the "northeaster," swept down from the island. ¹⁵The ship was caught by the storm and could not head into the wind; so we gave way to it and were driven along. ¹⁶As we passed to the lee of a small island called Cauda, we were hardly able to make the lifeboat secure. ¹⁷When the men had hoisted it aboard, they passed ropes under the ship itself to hold it together. Fearing that they would run aground on the sandbars of Syrtis, they lowered the sea anchor and let the ship be driven along. ¹⁸We took such a violent battering from the storm that the next day they began to throw the cargo overboard. ¹⁹On the third day, they threw the ship's tackle overboard with their own hands. ²⁰When neither sun nor stars appeared for many days and the storm continued raging, we finally gave up all hope of being saved.

²¹After the men had gone a long time without food, Paul stood up before them and said: "Men, you should have taken my advice not to sail from Crete; then you would have spared yourselves this damage and loss. ²²But now I urge you to keep up your courage, because not one of you will be lost; only the ship will be destroyed. ²³Last night an angel of the God whose I am and whom I serve stood beside me ²⁴and said, 'Do not be afraid, Paul. You must stand trial before Caesar;

ᵃ9 That is, the Day of Atonement (Yom Kippur)

what your views are, for we know that people everywhere are talking against this sect."

²³They arranged to meet Paul on a certain day, and came in even larger numbers to the place where he was staying. From morning till evening he explained and declared to them the kingdom of God and tried to convince them about Jesus from the Law of Moses and from the Prophets. ²⁴Some were convinced by what he said, but others would not believe. ²⁵They disagreed among themselves and began to leave after Paul had made this final statement: "The Holy Spirit spoke the truth to your forefathers when he said through Isaiah the prophet:

²⁶" 'Go to this people and say,
"You will be ever hearing but never
        understanding;
    you will be ever seeing but never
        perceiving."

²⁷For this people's heart has become
        calloused;
    they hardly hear with their ears,
    and they have closed their eyes.
Otherwise they might see with their
        eyes,
    hear with their ears,
    understand with their hearts
    and turn, and I would heal them.'ᵃ

²⁸"Therefore I want you to know that God's salvation has been sent to the Gentiles, and they will listen!"ᵇ

³⁰For two whole years Paul stayed there in his own rented house and welcomed all who came to see him. ³¹Boldly and without hindrance he preached the kingdom of God and taught about the Lord Jesus Christ.

ᵃ27 Isaiah 6:9,10   ᵇ28 Some manuscripts listen!"
²⁹After he said this, the Jews left, arguing vigorously among themselves.

Back to the Basics

Read Acts 27:33-44

In the story of Paul and the shipwreck, the other people on the boat were so scared and anxious they didn't eat for 14 days. And when the ship was getting closer and closer to land, they did everything they could to save the boat. But Paul stopped them in the middle of all their panic and made them eat. He knew that without food, they would die, no matter what happened to the boat. When their boat did crash, the people on board had enough strength to swim to shore.

God has always taken care of the basic needs in my life. I've never had to sleep in the cold or go hungry. I've never been without water to drink or medicine to help me get well. Since I don't have to worry about the basics, I have the energy to do something more with my life, like help other people.

I think God wants us to be like Paul and pay attention to other people's physical needs, as well as their spiritual needs. If someone is cold or hungry or sick, the best way we can show them God's love is to make sure they have food and shelter. That's what Paul did, and that's what we need to do too.

❶ What are some ways God has taken care of your physical needs? How do those things help your spiritual life?

❷ Ask your parents or your pastor to help you find a soup kitchen or homeless shelter where you can volunteer. Hey, you could even bring some friends or your whole youth group along.

❸ Ask God to help you reach out to people in need.

Turn to page 1352 for your next devotion.

Romans

START

If you combined the business muscle of New York City with the political leadership of Washington, D.C., you'd have something like ancient Rome. It was the center of its world, with the "biggest and best" of everything. In the middle of this, a little group of new Christians swelled into a large Christian church. Paul's letter to these Christians reads like a lawyer's argument. On trial is the human race, and Paul proves that we're all pretty useless when it comes to living right with others and with God, but that the death and resurrection of Jesus changes all that.

Paul wanted to make sure that Christians in this busy, smart capital city started off on the right foot spiritually. Paul may have sensed some darker days coming. Christianity was already getting blamed for stuff it had nothing to do with. And soon Christians would be persecuted in ways they couldn't imagine: imprisonment, needing to worship secretly in caves beneath the streets of Rome, group killings, being forced to "fight" hungry lions for the entertainment of the entire city. Paul himself would eventually be executed in Rome because of his faith.

With this just around the corner, Roman Christians really needed to hear how "neither death nor life, neither angels nor demons . . . nor anything else in all creation, will be able to separate us from the love of God" (Romans 8:38–39).

Cast OF Characters

Paul

The writer of this and a bunch of other letters in the New Testament. He earned a lot of Frequent Sailor miles; he traveled a ton, taking the Good News of Jesus Christ all around the western half of the Mediterranean.

Law

Not a person, but still a major player. When Paul writes about the law in this letter, he usually meant what we call the Ten Commandments (check out Exodus 20:1–17, page 94) plus the hundreds of specifics that spell out exactly how to obey the Big Ten. God gave people the law to demonstrate how hopeless we are at following rules: we always break 'em. That's why Paul makes a big deal about . . .

Faith

Also a major player in this letter. Having faith means believing that Jesus was God, that he died and lived again, and that this new life of his points to a new life for us too.

Jesus Christ

The only Sacrifice for our sin that will put us right with God, whether we're Jewish, Roman, Nebraskan or Indonesian.

What's UP with That?

What's a Fish Got to Do With It?

Ever see that fish thing on someone's car? Ever wonder what it means? Here's the story. In Rome's catacombs—underground chambers where early Christians buried their dead and occasionally met together during the worst persecution—you can see the earliest drawings of a fish as a Christian symbol. Why a *fish*? Why not a boat? Or a sandal? Take a look at these possible explanations for choosing a fish. Pick the ones you think are real, then check your answers at the bottom (c'mon, don't cheat!):

A Jesus recruited fishermen as disciples by saying they'd be catching people, not fish, from then on.

B It was fashionable for Roman Christians to have little carved-wood fish stuck on the back of their chariots.

C The first recorded meal of Jesus after his resurrection was fish.

D One of Jesus' more memorable miracles was feeding a few thousand people with a handful of fish.

E The Palestinian waiter at the Last Supper was named Shif, which is *fish* spelled backwards, kind of.

So the early Christians played this little game—kind of a secret code, actually, that came in handy when they wanted to keep a low profile around the mean Roman soldiers. They'd draw a fish ("C'mon, officer, all I did was draw a fish—no law against that, is there?"), but the entire Christian community knew what that innocent-looking little fish sketch *really* meant: Jesus Christ, God's Son, Savior.

That's what you oughta think when you see a fish, whether it's chrome on the back of a pick-up or deep-fried in your Fish Burger Supreme.

Snap shots

- **What a bunch of goof-ups we are** (chapter 1)

- **The law shows us what sinners we are** (chapters 2:1—3:20)

- **The answer is grace!** (chapters 3:21—5:21)

- **Thanks to Jesus, we're dead to sin and alive to God!** (chapters 6—8)

- **How all this affects Jews** (chapters 9—11)

- **Tips for getting along with others** (chapters 12:1—15:22)

- **Personal plans and greetings to friends in Rome** (chapter 15:23 and following)

answers: a (Matthew 4:18-20), c (Luke 24:36-43), and d (Matthew 15:32-38) are correct. b and e probably are not. But you never know . . .

1 Paul, a servant of Christ Jesus, called to be an apostle and set apart for the gospel of God— ²the gospel he promised beforehand through his prophets in the Holy Scriptures ³regarding his Son, who as to his human nature was a descendant of David, ⁴and who through the Spirit*ᵃ* of holiness was declared with power to be the Son of God*ᵇ* by his resurrection from the dead: Jesus Christ our Lord. ⁵Through him and for his name's sake, we received grace and apostleship to call people from among all the Gentiles to the obedience that comes from faith. ⁶And you also are among those who are called to belong to Jesus Christ.

⁷To all in Rome who are loved by God and called to be saints:

Grace and peace to you from God our Father and from the Lord Jesus Christ.

Paul's Longing to Visit Rome

⁸First, I thank my God through Jesus Christ for all of you, because your faith is being reported all over the world. ⁹God, whom I serve with my whole heart in preaching the gospel of his Son, is my witness how constantly I remember you ¹⁰in my prayers at all times; and I pray that now at last by God's will the way may be opened for me to come to you.

¹¹I long to see you so that I may impart to you some spiritual gift to make you strong— ¹²that is, that you and I may be mutually encouraged by each other's faith. ¹³I do not want you to be unaware, brothers, that I planned many times to come to you (but have been prevented from doing so until now) in order that I might have a harvest among you, just as I have had among the other Gentiles.

¹⁴I am obligated both to Greeks and non-Greeks, both to the wise and the foolish. ¹⁵That is why I am so eager to preach the gospel also to you who are at Rome.

¹⁶I am not ashamed of the gospel, because it is the power of God for the salvation of everyone who believes: first for the Jew, then for the Gentile. ¹⁷For in the gospel a righteousness from God is revealed, a righteousness that is by faith from first to last,*ᶜ* just as it is written: "The righteous will live by faith."*ᵈ*

God's Wrath Against Mankind

¹⁸The wrath of God is being revealed from heaven against all the godlessness and wickedness of men who suppress the truth by their wickedness, ¹⁹since what may be known about God is plain to them, because God has made it plain to them. ²⁰For since the creation of the world God's invisible qualities—his eternal power and divine nature—have been clearly seen, being understood from what has been made, so that men are without excuse.

²¹For although they knew God, they neither glorified him as God nor gave thanks to him, but their thinking became futile and their foolish hearts were darkened. ²²Although they claimed to be wise, they became fools ²³and exchanged the glory of the immortal God for images made to look like mortal man and birds and animals and reptiles.

²⁴Therefore God gave them over in the sinful desires of their hearts to sexual impurity for the degrading of their bodies with one another. ²⁵They exchanged the truth of God for a lie, and worshiped and served created things rather than the Creator—who is forever praised. Amen.

²⁶Because of this, God gave them over to shameful lusts. Even their women exchanged natural relations for unnatural ones. ²⁷In the same way the men also abandoned natural relations with women and were inflamed with lust for one another. Men committed indecent acts with other men, and received in themselves the due penalty for their perversion.

²⁸Furthermore, since they did not think it worthwhile to retain the knowledge of God, he gave them over to a depraved mind, to do what ought not to be done. ²⁹They have become filled with every kind of wickedness, evil, greed and depravity. They are full of envy, murder, strife, deceit and malice. They are gossips, ³⁰slanderers, God-haters, insolent, arrogant and boastful; they invent ways of doing evil; they disobey their parents; ³¹they are senseless, faithless, heartless, ruthless. ³²Although they know God's

---

ᵃ4 Or who as to his spirit   ᵇ4 Or was appointed to be the Son of God with power   ᶜ17 Or is from faith to faith   ᵈ17 Hab. 2:4

righteous decree that those who do such things deserve death, they not only continue to do these very things but also approve of those who practice them.

God's Righteous Judgment

2 You, therefore, have no excuse, you who pass judgment on someone else, for at whatever point you judge the other, you are condemning yourself, because you who pass judgment do the same things. ²Now we know that God's judgment against those who do such things is based on truth. ³So when you, a mere man, pass judgment on them and yet do the same things, do you think you will escape God's judgment? ⁴Or do you show contempt for the riches of his kindness, tolerance and patience, not realizing that God's kindness leads you toward repentance?

⁵But because of your stubbornness and your unrepentant heart, you are storing

No "Ho Ho Ho"

Romans 2:4

Just like the people in Rome, some of your friends probably think of God as a jolly Santa Claus "Ho Ho Ho"ing and giving out brightly wrapped presents to good little boys and girls. This kind of God would never punish people. But the real God is not a softy. His kindness has a sharp purpose: to give people a chance to make a U-turn away from their sin and back to him.

up wrath against yourself for the day of God's wrath, when his righteous judgment will be revealed. ⁶God "will give to each person according to what he has

Fri day

Share the Excitement

Read Romans 1:16

When I first became a Christian, I was afraid to tell some of my non-Christian friends. I didn't know what they would think, and I was scared they might make fun of me.

But I've learned that I need to be excited about my faith. If I say I'm a Christian, I'm saying I believe what the Bible says and that I want to give my life to God. That's a serious commitment. So if I believe in the gospel enough to base my whole life on it, I should believe in it enough to share it with other people.

If somebody gave you a really cool present for your birthday, you'd tell other people about it, right? Well, the salvation God gave us through Jesus is the greatest gift ever. And we need to be excited about sharing it with our friends so they can have the same great gift we've been given.

Andy age 12

❶ Think about a time you were embarrassed to tell people about your faith. What could you have said or done differently?

❷ The next time you get a gift or buy something you really love, try not to tell anyone about it for 2 days. What's it like to keep a secret about something you're excited about? How can you feel that same excitement about sharing your faith?

❸ Ask God to help you be bold about your faith.

Turn to page 1354 for your next devotion.

done."[a] [7]To those who by persistence in doing good seek glory, honor and immortality, he will give eternal life. [8]But for those who are self-seeking and who reject the truth and follow evil, there will be wrath and anger. [9]There will be trouble and distress for every human being who does evil: first for the Jew, then for the Gentile; [10]but glory, honor and peace for everyone who does good: first for the Jew, then for the Gentile. [11]For God does not show favoritism.

[12]All who sin apart from the law will also perish apart from the law, and all who sin under the law will be judged by the law. [13]For it is not those who hear the law who are righteous in God's sight, but it is those who obey the law who will be declared righteous. [14](Indeed, when Gentiles, who do not have the law, do by nature things required by the law, they are a law for themselves, even though they do not have the law, [15]since they show that the requirements of the law are written on their hearts, their consciences also bearing witness, and their thoughts now accusing, now even defending them.) [16]This will take place on the day when God will judge men's secrets through Jesus Christ, as my gospel declares.

The Jews and the Law

[17]Now you, if you call yourself a Jew; if you rely on the law and brag about your relationship to God; [18]if you know his will and approve of what is superior because you are instructed by the law; [19]if you are convinced that you are a guide for the blind, a light for those who are in the dark, [20]an instructor of the foolish, a teacher of infants, because you have in the law the embodiment of knowledge and truth— [21]you, then, who teach others, do you not teach yourself? You who preach against stealing, do you steal? [22]You who say that people should not commit adultery, do you commit adultery? You who abhor idols, do you rob temples? [23]You who brag about the law, do you dishonor God by breaking the law? [24]As it is written: "God's name is blasphemed among the Gentiles because of you."[b]

[25]Circumcision has value if you observe the law, but if you break the law, you have become as though you had not been circumcised. [26]If those who are not circumcised keep the law's requirements, will they not be regarded as though they were circumcised? [27]The one who is not circumcised physically and yet obeys the law will condemn you who, even though you have the[c] written code and circumcision, are a lawbreaker.

[28]A man is not a Jew if he is only one outwardly, nor is circumcision merely outward and physical. [29]No, a man is a Jew if he is one inwardly; and circumcision is circumcision of the heart, by the Spirit, not by the written code. Such a man's praise is not from men, but from God.

Heart Surgery?

Huh?

Romans 2:28–29

Before you get worrying that circumcision of the heart means God's going to plunge a big old knife into your heart and cut it to pieces, stop and think a little more. Circumcision was a sign of devotion to God. A circumcised heart is one that is totally and completely devoted to God. More than the outward and physical circumcision that the Jews have been doing since Abraham, God wants a pure heart.

God's Faithfulness

3 What advantage, then, is there in being a Jew, or what value is there in circumcision? [2]Much in every way! First of all, they have been entrusted with the very words of God.

[3]What if some did not have faith? Will their lack of faith nullify God's faithfulness? [4]Not at all! Let God be true, and every man a liar. As it is written:

"So that you may be proved right
    when you speak
and prevail when you judge."[d]

[a]6 Psalm 62:12; Prov. 24:12   [b]24 Isaiah 52:5; Ezek. 36:22   [c]27 Or *who, by means of a*
[d]4 Psalm 51:4

⁵But if our unrighteousness brings out God's righteousness more clearly, what shall we say? That God is unjust in bringing his wrath on us? (I am using a human argument.) ⁶Certainly not! If that were so, how could God judge the world? ⁷Someone might argue, "If my falsehood enhances God's truthfulness and so increases his glory, why am I still condemned as a sinner?" ⁸Why not say—as we are being slanderously reported as saying and as some claim that we say— "Let us do evil that good may result"? Their condemnation is deserved.

No One Is Righteous

⁹What shall we conclude then? Are we any better*a*? Not at all! We have already made the charge that Jews and Gentiles alike are all under sin. ¹⁰As it is written:

"There is no one righteous, not even one;
¹¹ there is no one who understands,
no one who seeks God.
¹² All have turned away,
they have together become worthless;
there is no one who does good,
not even one."*b*
¹³ "Their throats are open graves;
their tongues practice deceit."*c*
"The poison of vipers is on their lips."*d*
¹⁴ "Their mouths are full of cursing
and bitterness."*e*
¹⁵ "Their feet are swift to shed blood;
¹⁶ ruin and misery mark their ways,
¹⁷ and the way of peace they do not know."*f*
¹⁸ "There is no fear of God before their eyes."*g*

¹⁹Now we know that whatever the law says, it says to those who are under the

a9 Or *worse*   *b12* Psalms 14:1-3; 53:1-3; Eccles. 7:20   *c13* Psalm 5:9   *d13* Psalm 140:3   *e14* Psalm 10:7   *f17* Isaiah 59:7,8   *g18* Psalm 36:1

Weekend.

How Do You Look at Others?

Read Luke 23:26–34 (page 1260)

Isn't it amazing how God looks at people with loving eyes? On Wednesday Melinda talked about how God can turn lives completely around and how we need to be careful not to look down on people. It's easy to get mad at people who sin, but God calls us to love sinners and only be mad at the sin. (That's good for us, since we're all sinners!)

Think about what Jesus said, right before he was crucified: "Father, forgive them, for they do not know what they are doing." Even when he was in extreme pain and suffering greatly, Jesus looked on people with compassion and love. No doubt he was mad about their sin, but he still loved them—he even *died* for them.

How do you look at others? Do you judge people by how they act and make decisions about them based on their behavior? Allow God to use you to love people. God knows how to balance love and judgment. We don't—so stick to loving instead of judging.

❶ Is there someone you don't get along with because of something they did?

❷ Talk with a friend. Tell them how you are trying to change the way you view sin in others. It will help you think it through.

❸ Ask God, "How do you do it? Teach me to love others like you do."

Turn to page 1355 for your next devotion.

law, so that every mouth may be silenced and the whole world held accountable to God. [20]Therefore no one will be declared righteous in his sight by observing the law; rather, through the law we become conscious of sin.

Righteousness Through Faith

[21]But now a righteousness from God, apart from law, has been made known, to which the Law and the Prophets testify. [22]This righteousness from God comes through faith in Jesus Christ to all who believe. There is no difference, [23]for all have sinned and fall short of the glory of God, [24]and are justified freely by his grace through the redemption that came by Christ Jesus. [25]God presented him as a sacrifice of atonement,[a] through faith in his blood. He did this to demonstrate his justice, because in his forbearance he had left the sins committed beforehand

[a]25 Or *as the one who would turn aside his wrath, taking away sin*

Mirror Mirror

Romans 3:20

Stumbling past the bathroom mirror when you first get up can be a jolt. Your eyes are half closed and you have massive bedhead. The mirror has told you the truth about how you really look. In the same way, God's law, or commandments, reflects the big-time sinners we are. When we see our sin, we're going to want to get cleaned up.

Monday

A Bunch of Sinners

Read Romans 3:22–24

This is one of those passages I want to share with every new Christian I meet. A lot of people think you can earn salvation. But the truth is, no matter how much you pray, how many times you go to church, how often you read the Bible or how many good deeds you do, the only thing that will matter on judgment day is whether or not you have accepted Jesus Christ into your heart.

God knew we were all sinners and that we would suffer because of our sins. But he loved us so much that he sent Jesus to suffer for us. God did what was needed to save us. Jesus' death and resurrection took care of our sins. We didn't have anything to do with it. But we do have to accept this truth. We do that by trusting in Jesus our Savior.

All that other stuff, like going to church and reading the Bible, is important, because it helps us grow in our faith. But we can't earn salvation by trying to be the very best Christian in the world. All we have to do is accept what God did for us.

Kent age 13

What about You?

❶ Why is it impossible to "earn" God's love? How can it be possible that we get it anyway?

❷ Ask your parents or another adult you're close to why they love you. Do their reasons have anything to do with how good you are or how well you do things? How is God's love like that?

❸ Thank God for his incredible gift of salvation.

Turn to page 1357 for your next devotion.

unpunished— [26]he did it to demonstrate his justice at the present time, so as to be just and the one who justifies those who have faith in Jesus.

[27]Where, then, is boasting? It is excluded. On what principle? On that of observing the law? No, but on that of faith. [28]For we maintain that a man is justified by faith apart from observing the law. [29]Is God the God of Jews only? Is he not the God of Gentiles too? Yes, of Gentiles too, [30]since there is only one God, who will justify the circumcised by faith and the uncircumcised through that same faith. [31]Do we, then, nullify the law by this faith? Not at all! Rather, we uphold the law.

Abraham Justified by Faith

4 What then shall we say that Abraham, our forefather, discovered in this matter? [2]If, in fact, Abraham was justified by works, he had something to boast about—but not before God. [3]What does the Scripture say? "Abraham believed God, and it was credited to him as righteousness."[a]

[4]Now when a man works, his wages are not credited to him as a gift, but as an obligation. [5]However, to the man who does not work but trusts God who justifies the wicked, his faith is credited as righteousness. [6]David says the same thing when he speaks of the blessedness of the man to whom God credits righteousness apart from works:

[7]"Blessed are they
    whose transgressions are
        forgiven,
    whose sins are covered.
[8]Blessed is the man
    whose sin the Lord will never count
        against him."[b]

[9]Is this blessedness only for the circumcised, or also for the uncircumcised? We have been saying that Abraham's faith was credited to him as righteousness. [10]Under what circumstances was it credited? Was it after he was circumcised, or before? It was not after, but before! [11]And he received the sign of circumcision, a seal of the righteousness that he had by faith while he was still uncircumcised. So then, he is the father of all who believe but have not been circumcised, in order that righteousness might be credited to them. [12]And he is also the father of the circumcised who not only are circumcised but who also walk in the footsteps of the faith that our father Abraham had before he was circumcised.

[13]It was not through law that Abraham and his offspring received the promise that he would be heir of the world, but through the righteousness that comes by faith. [14]For if those who live by law are heirs, faith has no value and the promise is worthless, [15]because law brings wrath. And where there is no law there is no transgression.

[16]Therefore, the promise comes by faith, so that it may be by grace and may be guaranteed to all Abraham's offspring—not only to those who are of the law but also to those who are of the faith of Abraham. He is the father of us all. [17]As it is written: "I have made you a father of many nations."[c] He is our father in the sight of God, in whom he believed—the God who gives life to the dead and calls things that are not as though they were.

[18]Against all hope, Abraham in hope believed and so became the father of many nations, just as it had been said to him, "So shall your offspring be."[d] [19]Without weakening in his faith, he faced the fact that his body was as good as dead—since he was about a hundred years old—and that Sarah's womb was also dead. [20]Yet he did not waver through unbelief regarding the promise of God, but was strengthened in his faith and gave glory to God, [21]being fully persuaded that God had power to do what he had promised. [22]This is why "it was credited to him as righteousness." [23]The words "it was credited to him" were written not for him alone, [24]but also for us, to whom God will credit righteousness—for us who believe in him who raised Jesus our Lord from the dead. [25]He was delivered over to death for our sins and was raised to life for our justification.

---

[a]3 Gen. 15:6; also in verse 22 [b]8 Psalm 32:1,2
[c]17 Gen. 17:5 [d]18 Gen. 15:5

Justified

Romans 4:25

When you do something dumb, wouldn't it be cool if you could rewind the tape of your life so that it never happened? When God justifies us, it's just as if our sin never happened. It's gone. Vanished. Good thing we don't have to work for justification because no amount of work would ever outweigh our mound of sin. Being justified is a gift from God that we get when we believe in Jesus.

Peace and Joy

5 Therefore, since we have been justified through faith, we[a] have peace with God through our Lord Jesus Christ, [2]through whom we have gained access by faith into this grace in which we now stand. And we[a] rejoice in the hope of the glory of God. [3]Not only so, but we[a] also rejoice in our sufferings, because we know that suffering produces perseverance; [4]perseverance, character; and character, hope. [5]And hope does not disappoint us, because God has poured out his love into our hearts by the Holy Spirit, whom he has given us.

[6]You see, at just the right time, when we were still powerless, Christ died for the ungodly. [7]Very rarely will anyone die for a righteous man, though for a good man someone might possibly dare to die. [8]But God demonstrates his own love for us in this: While we were still sinners, Christ died for us.

[9]Since we have now been justified by his blood, how much more shall we be saved from God's wrath through him! [10]For if, when we were God's enemies, we were reconciled to him through the death

[a] 1,2,3 Or let us

Tuesday

He Loved You First

Read Romans 5:6-8

One time when I was telling a friend about Jesus, she didn't understand what I was saying. She kept thinking that she had to be good first, and then maybe God would love her. But I showed her these verses in Romans, and she started to understand that God already loved her—enough to send Jesus to die for her. My friend was amazed that anyone would love her that much.

God's love amazes me too. Romans 5:7 talks about how unusual it is that anyone would die for someone else. But Jesus died for us, before we knew him or cared about him at all. The truth is, Jesus even died for murderers and the worst of criminals. No one else would have done that. Only Jesus. Knowing that Jesus loves me so much has helped me love him too. I'm going to keep telling my friends about Jesus' love, because I don't want them to miss out!

Amy age 13

❶ How would you tell a non-Christian friend about Jesus' love?

❷ Look through the newspaper or watch the TV news until you find a story about someone who did something really bad. Then think about how amazing it is that Jesus died for this person too.

❸ Praise God for his amazing love!

Turn to page 1362 for your next devotion.

Second Chances

The Bible is filled with stories of people who took God's blessing, messed it up and then got another chance to do it right. God is big on second chances!

First Chance	Oops!	Second Chance	That's Better!
Moses is saved from drowning (Exodus 2:5–10),	but grows up and murders someone (Exodus 2:12).	God calls him to rescue the Israelites (Exodus 3:4–12),	and he does it! (the rest of Exodus).
Gideon gets a message from God to save the Israelites from their enemies (Judges 6:14),	but he doesn't quite believe it (Judges 6:15–19).	God gives him proof after proof until he believes (Judges 6:20–40),	and Gideon does what he's told and wins the war! (Judges 7:19–25).
David gets picked to be king of Israel (1 Samuel 16:12),	and has an affair (2 Samuel 11:2–27).	God forgives him, lets him keep the king job (2 Samuel 12:13),	and David serves God better! (the rest of 2 Samuel).
Saul gets a great education and knows the Bible as well as anyone (Philippians 3:4–6),	but he uses his religious position to torment the Christians (Acts 9:1–2).	God tells him to knock it off (Acts 9:3–9),	and Saul gets a new name, then tells the world about Jesus! (the rest of Acts).
Everybody! God gives each of us a hint of who he is and how we're supposed to behave (Romans 1:18–20),	but we still act selfishly and pretend that God doesn't count. We're sinners (Romans 3:10–12).	God gives us another chance, sending Jesus to die for our sins (Romans 5:8),	and the next move is up to us. We can accept his payment and live forever with him! (John 5:24).

of his Son, how much more, having been reconciled, shall we be saved through his life! ¹¹Not only is this so, but we also rejoice in God through our Lord Jesus Christ, through whom we have now received reconciliation.

Death Through Adam, Life Through Christ

¹²Therefore, just as sin entered the world through one man, and death through sin, and in this way death came to all men, because all sinned— ¹³for before the law was given, sin was in the world. But sin is not taken into account when there is no law. ¹⁴Nevertheless, death reigned from the time of Adam to the time of Moses, even over those who did not sin by breaking a command, as did Adam, who was a pattern of the one to come.

¹⁵But the gift is not like the trespass. For if the many died by the trespass of the one man, how much more did God's grace and the gift that came by the grace of the one man, Jesus Christ, overflow to the many! ¹⁶Again, the gift of God is not like the result of one man's sin: The judgment followed one sin and brought

condemnation, but the gift followed many trespasses and brought justification. [17]For if, by the trespass of the one man, death reigned through that one man, how much more will those who receive God's abundant provision of grace and of the gift of righteousness reign in life through the one man, Jesus Christ.

[18]Consequently, just as the result of one trespass was condemnation for all men, so also the result of one act of righteousness was justification that brings life for all men. [19]For just as through the disobedience of the one man the many were made sinners, so also through the obedience of the one man the many will be made righteous.

[20]The law was added so that the trespass might increase. But where sin increased, grace increased all the more, [21]so that, just as sin reigned in death, so also grace might reign through righteousness to bring eternal life through Jesus Christ our Lord.

Dead to Sin, Alive in Christ

6 What shall we say, then? Shall we go on sinning so that grace may increase? [2]By no means! We died to sin; how can we live in it any longer? [3]Or don't you know that all of us who were baptized into Christ Jesus were baptized into his death? [4]We were therefore buried with him through baptism into death in order that, just as Christ was raised from the dead through the glory of the Father, we too may live a new life.

[5]If we have been united with him like this in his death, we will certainly also be united with him in his resurrection. [6]For we know that our old self was crucified with him so that the body of sin might be done away with,[a] that we should no longer be slaves to sin— [7]because anyone who has died has been freed from sin.

[8]Now if we died with Christ, we believe that we will also live with him. [9]For we know that since Christ was raised from the dead, he cannot die again; death no longer has mastery over him. [10]The death he died, he died to sin once for all; but the life he lives, he lives to God.

[11]In the same way, count yourselves dead to sin but alive to God in Christ Jesus. [12]Therefore do not let sin reign in your mortal body so that you obey its evil desires. [13]Do not offer the parts of your body to sin, as instruments of wickedness, but rather offer yourselves to God, as those who have been brought from death to life; and offer the parts of your body to him as instruments of righteousness. [14]For sin shall not be your master, because you are not under law, but under grace.

Slaves to Righteousness

[15]What then? Shall we sin because we are not under law but under grace? By no means! [16]Don't you know that when you offer yourselves to someone to obey him as slaves, you are slaves to the one whom you obey—whether you are slaves to sin, which leads to death, or to obedience, which leads to righteousness? [17]But thanks be to God that, though you used to be slaves to sin, you wholeheartedly obeyed the form of teaching to which you were entrusted. [18]You have been set free from sin and have become slaves to righteousness.

[19]I put this in human terms because you are weak in your natural selves. Just as you used to offer the parts of your body in slavery to impurity and to everincreasing wickedness, so now offer them in slavery to righteousness leading to holiness. [20]When you were slaves to sin, you were free from the control of righteousness. [21]What benefit did you reap at that time from the things you are now ashamed of? Those things result in death! [22]But now that you have been set free from sin and have become slaves to God, the benefit you reap leads to holiness, and the result is eternal life. [23]For the wages of sin is death, but the gift of God is eternal life in[b] Christ Jesus our Lord.

An Illustration From Marriage

7 Do you not know, brothers—for I am speaking to men who know the law—that the law has authority over a man only as long as he lives? [2]For example, by law a married woman is bound to her husband as long as he is alive, but if her

a6 Or be rendered powerless   b23 Or through

husband dies, she is released from the law of marriage. ³So then, if she marries another man while her husband is still alive, she is called an adulteress. But if her husband dies, she is released from that law and is not an adulteress, even though she marries another man.

⁴So, my brothers, you also died to the law through the body of Christ, that you might belong to another, to him who was raised from the dead, in order that we might bear fruit to God. ⁵For when we were controlled by the sinful nature,[a] the sinful passions aroused by the law were at work in our bodies, so that we bore fruit for death. ⁶But now, by dying to what once bound us, we have been released from the law so that we serve in the new way of the Spirit, and not in the old way of the written code.

Struggling With Sin

⁷What shall we say, then? Is the law sin? Certainly not! Indeed I would not have known what sin was except through the law. For I would not have known what coveting really was if the law had not said, "Do not covet."[b] ⁸But sin, seizing the opportunity afforded by the commandment, produced in me every kind of covetous desire. For apart from law, sin is dead. ⁹Once I was alive apart from law; but when the commandment came, sin sprang to life and I died. ¹⁰I found that the very commandment that was intended to bring life actually brought death. ¹¹For sin, seizing the opportunity afforded by the commandment, deceived me, and through the commandment put me to death. ¹²So then, the law is holy, and the commandment is holy, righteous and good.

¹³Did that which is good, then, become death to me? By no means! But in order that sin might be recognized as sin, it produced death in me through what was good, so that through the commandment sin might become utterly sinful. ¹⁴We know that the law is spiritual; but I am unspiritual, sold as a slave to sin. ¹⁵I do not understand what I do. For what I want to do I do not do, but what I hate I do. ¹⁶And if I do what I do not want to do, I agree that the law is good. ¹⁷As it is, it is no longer I myself who do it,

but it is sin living in me. ¹⁸I know that nothing good lives in me, that is, in my sinful nature.[c] For I have the desire to do what is good, but I cannot carry it out. ¹⁹For what I do is not the good I want to do; no, the evil I do not want to do—this I keep on doing. ²⁰Now if I do what I do not want to do, it is no longer I who do it, but it is sin living in me that does it.

²¹So I find this law at work: When I want to do good, evil is right there with me. ²²For in my inner being I delight in God's law; ²³but I see another law at work in the members of my body, waging war against the law of my mind and making me a prisoner of the law of sin at work within my members. ²⁴What a wretched man I am! Who will rescue me from this body of death? ²⁵Thanks be to God—through Jesus Christ our Lord!

So then, I myself in my mind am a slave to God's law, but in the sinful nature a slave to the law of sin.

Tug of War

Huh?

Romans 7:22–25

You've got a tug-of-war going on inside you right now. You want God's side to win, but your sin and your desire to do your own thing is pulling you the other way. Just when you're ready to let go of the rope, Jesus walks onto God's side, grabs on to the rope and starts pulling with you. Now you have the power to pull harder and beat sin.

Life Through the Spirit

8 Therefore, there is now no condemnation for those who are in Christ Jesus,[d] ²because through Christ Jesus the law of the Spirit of life set me free from the law of sin and death. ³For what the law was powerless to do in that it was

---

[a]5 Or *the flesh*; also in verse 25   [b]7 Exodus 20:17; Deut. 5:21   [c]18 Or *my flesh*   [d]1 Some later manuscripts *Jesus, who do not live according to the sinful nature but according to the Spirit,*

weakened by the sinful nature,[a] God did by sending his own Son in the likeness of sinful man to be a sin offering.[b] And so he condemned sin in sinful man,[c] [4]in order that the righteous requirements of the law might be fully met in us, who do not live according to the sinful nature but according to the Spirit.

[5]Those who live according to the sinful nature have their minds set on what that nature desires; but those who live in accordance with the Spirit have their minds set on what the Spirit desires. [6]The mind of sinful man[d] is death, but the mind controlled by the Spirit is life and peace; [7]the sinful mind[e] is hostile to God. It does not submit to God's law, nor can it do so. [8]Those controlled by the sinful nature cannot please God.

[9]You, however, are controlled not by the sinful nature but by the Spirit, if the Spirit of God lives in you. And if anyone does not have the Spirit of Christ, he does not belong to Christ. [10]But if Christ is in you, your body is dead because of sin, yet your spirit is alive because of righteousness. [11]And if the Spirit of him who raised Jesus from the dead is living in you, he who raised Christ from the dead will also give life to your mortal bodies through his Spirit, who lives in you.

[12]Therefore, brothers, we have an obligation—but it is not to the sinful nature, to live according to it. [13]For if you live according to the sinful nature, you will die; but if by the Spirit you put to death the misdeeds of the body, you will live, [14]because those who are led by the Spirit of God are sons of God. [15]For you did not receive a spirit that makes you a slave again to fear, but you received the Spirit of sonship.[f] And by him we cry, "Abba,[g] Father." [16]The Spirit himself testifies with our spirit that we are God's children. [17]Now if we are children, then we are heirs—heirs of God and co-heirs with Christ, if indeed we share in his sufferings in order that we may also share in his glory.

Future Glory

[18]I consider that our present sufferings are not worth comparing with the glory that will be revealed in us. [19]The creation waits in eager expectation for the sons of

God to be revealed. [20]For the creation was subjected to frustration, not by its own choice, but by the will of the one who subjected it, in hope [21]that[h] the creation itself will be liberated from its bondage to decay and brought into the glorious freedom of the children of God.

[22]We know that the whole creation has been groaning as in the pains of childbirth right up to the present time. [23]Not only so, but we ourselves, who have the firstfruits of the Spirit, groan inwardly as we wait eagerly for our adoption as sons, the redemption of our bodies. [24]For in this hope we were saved. But hope that is seen is no hope at all. Who hopes for what he already has? [25]But if we hope for what we do not yet have, we wait for it patiently.

[26]In the same way, the Spirit helps us in our weakness. We do not know what we ought to pray for, but the Spirit himself intercedes for us with groans that words cannot express. [27]And he who searches our hearts knows the mind of the Spirit, because the Spirit intercedes for the saints in accordance with God's will.

More Than Conquerors

[28]And we know that in all things God works for the good of those who love him,[i] who[j] have been called according to his purpose. [29]For those God foreknew he also predestined to be conformed to the likeness of his Son, that he might be the firstborn among many brothers. [30]And those he predestined, he also called; those he called, he also justified; those he justified, he also glorified.

[31]What, then, shall we say in response to this? If God is for us, who can be against us? [32]He who did not spare his own Son, but gave him up for us all—how will he not also, along with him, graciously give us all things? [33]Who will bring any charge against those whom

---

[a]3 Or the flesh; also in verses 4, 5, 8, 9, 12 and 13
[b]3 Or man, for sin   [c]3 Or in the flesh   [d]6 Or mind set on the flesh   [e]7 Or the mind set on the flesh
[f]15 Or adoption   [g]15 Aramaic for Father
[h]20,21 Or subjected it in hope. [21]For   [i]28 Some manuscripts And we know that all things work together for good to those who love God   [j]28 Or works together with those who love him to bring about what is good—with those who

God has chosen? It is God who justifies. ³⁴Who is he that condemns? Christ Jesus, who died—more than that, who was raised to life—is at the right hand of God and is also interceding for us. ³⁵Who shall separate us from the love of Christ? Shall trouble or hardship or persecution or famine or nakedness or danger or sword? ³⁶As it is written:

> "For your sake we face death all day
>   long;
>   we are considered as sheep to be
>   slaughtered."ᵃ

³⁷No, in all these things we are more than conquerors through him who loved us. ³⁸For I am convinced that neither death nor life, neither angels nor demons,ᵇ neither the present nor the future, nor any powers, ³⁹neither height nor depth, nor anything else in all creation, will be able to separate us from the love of God that is in Christ Jesus our Lord.

God's Sovereign Choice

9 I speak the truth in Christ—I am not lying, my conscience confirms it in the Holy Spirit— ²I have great sorrow and unceasing anguish in my heart. ³For I could wish that I myself were cursed and cut off from Christ for the sake of my brothers, those of my own race, ⁴the people of Israel. Theirs is the adoption as sons; theirs the divine glory, the covenants, the receiving of the law, the temple worship and the promises. ⁵Theirs are the patriarchs, and from them is traced the human ancestry of Christ, who is God over all, forever praised!ᶜ Amen.

⁶It is not as though God's word had failed. For not all who are descended from Israel are Israel. ⁷Nor because they are his descendants are they all Abraham's children. On the contrary, "It is through Isaac that your offspring will be reckoned."ᵈ ⁸In other words, it is not the natural children who are God's children, but it is the children of the promise who are regarded as Abraham's offspring. ⁹For this was how the promise was stated: "At the appointed time I will return, and Sarah will have a son."ᵉ

ᵃ36 Psalm 44:22   ᵇ38 Or nor heavenly rulers   ᶜ5 Or Christ, who is over all. God be forever praised! Or Christ. God who is over all be forever praised! ᵈ7 Gen. 21:12   ᵉ9 Gen. 18:10,14

Wednesday

Love, Always

Read Romans 8:35–39

I recently went through a month when I got really depressed. Even when I was with my friends, I felt like no one cared about me. I could barely get out of bed in the morning.

Somehow I had forgotten the truth of these verses. I needed someone to remind me, "Don't think that no one cares about you, because God does!" God still loved me, and nothing was going to change that.

God must really care for us if there isn't anything that can separate us from his love. Knowing that I can always turn to him keeps me going during hard situations. He is even there when things in my life are fun and easy. He is there with me through the worst of times and the best of times.

Sarah age 14

What about You?

❶ How do you feel when you know you're loved?

❷ Think of someone you know who's hurting and needs a little love. What is one thing you can do to encourage this person this week?

❸ Thank God for his constant love.

Turn to page 1366 for your next devotion.

¹⁰Not only that, but Rebekah's children had one and the same father, our father Isaac. ¹¹Yet, before the twins were born or had done anything good or bad—in order that God's purpose in election might stand: ¹²not by works but by him who calls—she was told, "The older will serve the younger."ᵃ ¹³Just as it is written: "Jacob I loved, but Esau I hated."ᵇ

¹⁴What then shall we say? Is God unjust? Not at all! ¹⁵For he says to Moses,

"I will have mercy on whom I have
     mercy,
and I will have compassion on
     whom I have compassion."ᶜ

¹⁶It does not, therefore, depend on man's desire or effort, but on God's mercy. ¹⁷For the Scripture says to Pharaoh: "I raised you up for this very purpose, that I might display my power in you and that my name might be proclaimed in all the earth."ᵈ ¹⁸Therefore God has mercy on whom he wants to have mercy, and he hardens whom he wants to harden.

¹⁹One of you will say to me: "Then why does God still blame us? For who resists his will?" ²⁰But who are you, O man, to talk back to God? "Shall what is formed say to him who formed it, 'Why did you make me like this?' "ᵉ ²¹Does not the potter have the right to make out of the same lump of clay some pottery for noble purposes and some for common use?

²²What if God, choosing to show his wrath and make his power known, bore with great patience the objects of his wrath—prepared for destruction? ²³What if he did this to make the riches of his glory known to the objects of his mercy, whom he prepared in advance for glory— ²⁴even us, whom he also called, not only from the Jews but also from the Gentiles? ²⁵As he says in Hosea:

"I will call them 'my people' who are
     not my people;
and I will call her 'my loved one'
     who is not my loved one,"ᶠ

²⁶and,

"It will happen that in the very place
     where it was said to them,
'You are not my people,'

they will be called 'sons of the living
     God.' "ᵍ

²⁷Isaiah cries out concerning Israel:

"Though the number of the Israelites
     be like the sand by the sea,
     only the remnant will be saved.
²⁸For the Lord will carry out
     his sentence on earth with speed
          and finality."ʰ

²⁹It is just as Isaiah said previously:

"Unless the Lord Almighty
     had left us descendants,
we would have become like Sodom,
     we would have been like
          Gomorrah."ⁱ

Israel's Unbelief

³⁰What then shall we say? That the Gentiles, who did not pursue righteousness, have obtained it, a righteousness that is by faith; ³¹but Israel, who pursued a law of righteousness, has not attained it. ³²Why not? Because they pursued it not by faith but as if it were by works. They stumbled over the "stumbling stone." ³³As it is written:

"See, I lay in Zion a stone that causes
     men to stumble

God's Grinning

Huh?

Romans 9:32
You get an allowance because you do your chores. You get a good grade in your math class because you study. But getting salvation is different. You don't work for it. The Jews kept blowing it because they thought doing good stuff, even if they had a lousy attitude, would make God smile upon them. Instead, God grins at the attitude of those who believe in Jesus with their hearts first, before they serve with their hands. When a heart is sold out for Jesus, the hands will follow.

ᵃ12 Gen. 25:23   ᵇ13 Mal. 1:2,3   ᶜ15 Exodus 33:19
ᵈ17 Exodus 9:16   ᵉ20 Isaiah 29:16; 45:9
ᶠ25 Hosea 2:23   ᵍ26 Hosea 1:10
ʰ28 Isaiah 10:22,23   ⁱ29 Isaiah 1:9

and a rock that makes them fall,
and the one who trusts in him will
    never be put to shame."[a]

10 Brothers, my heart's desire and prayer to God for the Israelites is that they may be saved. [2]For I can testify about them that they are zealous for God, but their zeal is not based on knowledge. [3]Since they did not know the righteousness that comes from God and sought to establish their own, they did not submit to God's righteousness. [4]Christ is the end of the law so that there may be righteousness for everyone who believes.

[5]Moses describes in this way the righteousness that is by the law: "The man who does these things will live by them."[b] [6]But the righteousness that is by faith says: "Do not say in your heart, 'Who will ascend into heaven?'[c]" (that is, to bring Christ down) [7]"or 'Who will descend into the deep?'[d]" (that is, to bring Christ up from the dead). [8]But what does it say? "The word is near you; it is in your mouth and in your heart,"[e] that is, the word of faith we are proclaiming: [9]That if you confess with your mouth, "Jesus is Lord," and believe in your heart that God raised him from the dead, you will be saved. [10]For it is with your heart that you believe and are justified, and it is with your mouth that you confess and are saved. [11]As the Scripture says, "Anyone who trusts in him will never be put to shame."[f] [12]For there is no difference between Jew and Gentile—the same Lord is Lord of all and richly blesses all who call on him, [13]for, "Everyone who calls on the name of the Lord will be saved."[g]

[14]How, then, can they call on the one they have not believed in? And how can they believe in the one of whom they have not heard? And how can they hear without someone preaching to them? [15]And how can they preach unless they are sent? As it is written, "How beautiful are the feet of those who bring good news!"[h]

[16]But not all the Israelites accepted the good news. For Isaiah says, "Lord, who has believed our message?"[i] [17]Consequently, faith comes from hearing the message, and the message is heard through the word of Christ. [18]But I ask: Did they not hear? Of course they did:

"Their voice has gone out into all the
    earth,
their words to the ends of the
    world."[j]

[19]Again I ask: Did Israel not understand? First, Moses says,

"I will make you envious by those
    who are not a nation;
I will make you angry by a nation
    that has no understanding."[k]

[20]And Isaiah boldly says,

"I was found by those who did not
    seek me;
I revealed myself to those who did
    not ask for me."[l]

[21]But concerning Israel he says,

"All day long I have held out my
    hands
to a disobedient and obstinate
    people."[m]

The Remnant of Israel

11 I ask then: Did God reject his people? By no means! I am an Israelite myself, a descendant of Abraham, from the tribe of Benjamin. [2]God did not reject his people, whom he foreknew. Don't you know what the Scripture says in the passage about Elijah—how he appealed to God against Israel: [3]"Lord, they have killed your prophets and torn down your altars; I am the only one left, and they are trying to kill me"[n]? [4]And what was God's answer to him? "I have reserved for myself seven thousand who have not bowed the knee to Baal."[o] [5]So too, at the present time there is a remnant chosen by grace. [6]And if by grace, then it is no longer by works; if it were, grace would no longer be grace.[p]

[7]What then? What Israel sought so earnestly it did not obtain, but the elect did. The others were hardened, [8]as it is written:

[a]33 Isaiah 8:14; 28:16   [b]5 Lev. 18:5
[c]6 Deut. 30:12   [d]7 Deut. 30:13   [e]8 Deut. 30:14
[f]11 Isaiah 28:16   [g]13 Joel 2:32   [h]15 Isaiah 52:7
[i]16 Isaiah 53:1   [j]18 Psalm 19:4   [k]19 Deut. 32:21
[l]20 Isaiah 65:1   [m]21 Isaiah 65:2   [n]3 1 Kings 19:10,14
[o]4 1 Kings 19:18   [p]6 Some manuscripts *by grace.
But if by works, then it is no longer grace; if it were,
work would no longer be work.*

"God gave them a spirit of stupor,
    eyes so that they could not see
    and ears so that they could not hear,
to this very day."[a]

[9]And David says:

"May their table become a snare and a
    trap,
    a stumbling block and a retribution
    for them.
[10]May their eyes be darkened so they
    cannot see,
    and their backs be bent forever."[b]

Ingrafted Branches

[11]Again I ask: Did they stumble so as to fall beyond recovery? Not at all! Rather, because of their transgression, salvation has come to the Gentiles to make Israel envious. [12]But if their transgression means riches for the world, and their loss means riches for the Gentiles, how much greater riches will their fullness bring!

[13]I am talking to you Gentiles. Inasmuch as I am the apostle to the Gentiles, I make much of my ministry [14]in the hope that I may somehow arouse my own people to envy and save some of them. [15]For if their rejection is the reconciliation of the world, what will their acceptance be but life from the dead? [16]If the part of the dough offered as firstfruits is holy, then the whole batch is holy; if the root is holy, so are the branches.

[17]If some of the branches have been broken off, and you, though a wild olive shoot, have been grafted in among the others and now share in the nourishing sap from the olive root, [18]do not boast over those branches. If you do, consider this: You do not support the root, but the root supports you. [19]You will say then, "Branches were broken off so that I could be grafted in." [20]Granted. But they were broken off because of unbelief, and you stand by faith. Do not be arrogant, but be afraid. [21]For if God did not spare the natural branches, he will not spare you either.

[22]Consider therefore the kindness and sternness of God: sternness to those who fell, but kindness to you, provided that you continue in his kindness. Otherwise, you also will be cut off. [23]And if they do not persist in unbelief, they will be grafted in, for God is able to graft them in again. [24]After all, if you were cut out of an olive tree that is wild by nature, and contrary to nature were grafted into a cultivated olive tree, how much more readily will these, the natural branches, be grafted into their own olive tree!

All Israel Will Be Saved

[25]I do not want you to be ignorant of this mystery, brothers, so that you may not be conceited: Israel has experienced a hardening in part until the full number of the Gentiles has come in. [26]And so all Israel will be saved, as it is written:

"The deliverer will come from Zion;
    he will turn godlessness away from
    Jacob.
[27]And this is[c] my covenant with them
    when I take away their sins."[d]

[28]As far as the gospel is concerned, they are enemies on your account; but as far as election is concerned, they are loved on account of the patriarchs, [29]for God's gifts and his call are irrevocable. [30]Just as you who were at one time disobedient to God have now received mercy as a result of their disobedience, [31]so they too have now become disobedient in order that they too may now[e] receive mercy as a result of God's mercy to you.

[a]8 Deut. 29:4; Isaiah 29:10   [b]10 Psalm 69:22,23
[c]27 Or *will be*   [d]27 Isaiah 59:20,21; 27:9;
Jer. 31:33,34   [e]31 Some manuscripts do not have *now*.

³²For God has bound all men over to disobedience so that he may have mercy on them all.

Doxology

³³Oh, the depth of the riches of the
wisdom and*ᵃ* knowledge of
God!
How unsearchable his judgments,
and his paths beyond tracing out!
³⁴"Who has known the mind of the
Lord?
Or who has been his counselor?"*ᵇ*
³⁵"Who has ever given to God,
that God should repay him?"*ᶜ*
³⁶For from him and through him and to
him are all things.
To him be the glory forever! Amen.

Living Sacrifices

12 Therefore, I urge you, brothers, in
view of God's mercy, to offer your bodies as living sacrifices, holy and pleasing to God—this is your spiritual*ᵈ* act of worship. ²Do not conform any longer to the pattern of this world, but be transformed by the renewing of your mind. Then you will be able to test and approve what God's will is—his good, pleasing and perfect will.

³For by the grace given me I say to every one of you: Do not think of yourself more highly than you ought, but rather think of yourself with sober judgment, in accordance with the measure of faith God has given you. ⁴Just as each of us has one body with many members, and these members do not all have the same function, ⁵so in Christ we who are many form one body, and each member belongs to all the others. ⁶We have different

ᵃ33 Or *riches and the wisdom and the*
ᵇ34 Isaiah 40:13   *ᶜ35* Job 41:11   *ᵈ1* Or *reasonable*

Thursday

Perfectly Willing

Read Romans 12:1–2

I learned a lot about giving myself to God and living for him when I went on a missions trip to a very poor part of the United States with my youth group. The work was hard and we were a long way from home. If I had been doing it all for myself, I would have just given up. But I knew I was working for God, and he was there with me during the whole trip. He helped me through the hard times, and he helped me make some great new friends.

Living to please God isn't always easy. Sometimes following him means looking uncool in front of other people. Sometimes it means giving up what *I* want and doing what *he* wants instead. But it's worth it because I know God's will is perfect—why would I want to do anything else?

Lisa age 13

What about You?

❶ Think of a time in your life when you had to choose between what you wanted and what God wanted. Which did you choose? Would you make the same choice today?

❷ Write out an "equation" for the good life according to the world: $1 million + 5 cars + whatever = the good life. Write out another equation for the good life according to God. How can you focus on the things in God's "formula" for success?

❸ Tell God you're willing to live your life for him; ask him to guide you in the way he wants you to go. If you find it difficult to pray this, ask God to change your heart.

Turn to page 1368 for your next devotion.

gifts, according to the grace given us. If a man's gift is prophesying, let him use it in proportion to his*a* faith. *7*If it is serving, let him serve; if it is teaching, let him teach; *8*if it is encouraging, let him encourage; if it is contributing to the needs of others, let him give generously; if it is leadership, let him govern diligently; if it is showing mercy, let him do it cheerfully.

Love

*9*Love must be sincere. Hate what is evil; cling to what is good. *10*Be devoted to one another in brotherly love. Honor one another above yourselves. *11*Never be lacking in zeal, but keep your spiritual fervor, serving the Lord. *12*Be joyful in hope, patient in affliction, faithful in prayer. *13*Share with God's people who are in need. Practice hospitality.

*14*Bless those who persecute you; bless and do not curse. *15*Rejoice with those who rejoice; mourn with those who mourn. *16*Live in harmony with one another. Do not be proud, but be willing to associate with people of low position.*b* Do not be conceited.

*17*Do not repay anyone evil for evil. Be careful to do what is right in the eyes of everybody. *18*If it is possible, as far as it depends on you, live at peace with everyone. *19*Do not take revenge, my friends, but leave room for God's wrath, for it is written: "It is mine to avenge; I will repay,"*c* says the Lord. *20*On the contrary:

"If your enemy is hungry, feed him;
   if he is thirsty, give him something
     to drink.
In doing this, you will heap burning
    coals on his head."*d*

*21*Do not be overcome by evil, but overcome evil with good.

Submission to the Authorities

13 Everyone must submit himself to the governing authorities, for there is no authority except that which God has established. The authorities that exist have been established by God. *2*Consequently, he who rebels against the authority is rebelling against what God has instituted, and those who do so will bring judgment on themselves. *3*For rulers hold no terror for those who do right, but for those who do wrong. Do you want to be free from fear of the one in authority? Then do what is right and he will commend you. *4*For he is God's servant to do you good. But if you do wrong, be afraid, for he does not bear the sword for nothing. He is God's servant, an agent of wrath to bring punishment on the wrongdoer. *5*Therefore, it is necessary to submit to the authorities, not only because of possible punishment but also because of conscience.

*6*This is also why you pay taxes, for the authorities are God's servants, who give their full time to governing. *7*Give everyone what you owe him: If you owe taxes, pay taxes; if revenue, then revenue; if respect, then respect; if honor, then honor.

Love, for the Day Is Near

*8*Let no debt remain outstanding, except the continuing debt to love one another, for he who loves his fellowman has fulfilled the law. *9*The commandments, "Do not commit adultery," "Do not murder," "Do not steal," "Do not covet,"*e* and whatever other commandment there may be, are summed up in this one rule: "Love your neighbor as yourself."*f* *10*Love does no harm to its neighbor. Therefore love is the fulfillment of the law.

*11*And do this, understanding the present time. The hour has come for you to wake up from your slumber, because our salvation is nearer now than when we first believed. *12*The night is nearly over; the day is almost here. So let us put aside the deeds of darkness and put on the armor of light. *13*Let us behave decently, as in the daytime, not in orgies and drunkenness, not in sexual immorality and debauchery, not in dissension and jealousy. *14*Rather, clothe yourselves with the Lord Jesus Christ, and do not think about how to gratify the desires of the sinful nature.*g*

---

a6 Or in agreement with the   *b16 Or willing to do menial work*   *c19 Deut. 32:35*   *d20 Prov. 25:21,22*   *e9 Exodus 20:13-15,17; Deut. 5:17-19,21*   *f9 Lev. 19:18*   *g14 Or the flesh*

The Weak and the Strong

14 Accept him whose faith is weak, without passing judgment on disputable matters. ²One man's faith allows him to eat everything, but another man, whose faith is weak, eats only vegetables. ³The man who eats everything must not look down on him who does not, and the man who does not eat everything must not condemn the man who does, for God has accepted him. ⁴Who are you to judge someone else's servant? To his own master he stands or falls. And he will stand, for the Lord is able to make him stand.

⁵One man considers one day more sacred than another; another man considers every day alike. Each one should be fully convinced in his own mind. ⁶He who regards one day as special, does so to the Lord. He who eats meat, eats to the Lord, for he gives thanks to God; and he who abstains, does so to the Lord and gives thanks to God. ⁷For none of us lives to himself alone and none of us dies to himself alone. ⁸If we live, we live to the Lord; and if we die, we die to the Lord. So, whether we live or die, we belong to the Lord.

⁹For this very reason, Christ died and returned to life so that he might be the Lord of both the dead and the living. ¹⁰You, then, why do you judge your brother? Or why do you look down on

---

Friday

Stumbling Block

Read Romans 14:13

I was on a retreat and met this guy who really bothered me. I saw him hanging around with all the girls and pegged him as a big flirt. I told my friends what I thought of him and pretty soon he had a reputation that he probably didn't deserve. None of the girls wanted to talk to him, and neither did the guys. He really didn't make many friends during the retreat.

Afterward, I realized I'd really messed up. I'd labeled this guy and gotten other people to think the same way I did. I judged him and encouraged other people to judge him too. Because of me, he didn't get the chance to make some great new Christian friends. He didn't get to leave the retreat feeling charged up about his faith. Instead, he probably left thinking there were a lot of judgmental, unfriendly people there.

Even if he was flirty, it wasn't my place to turn everyone against him. Instead, maybe some of us could have helped him. We could have talked with him about it or prayed with him. We could have shown him that Christians help each other grow.

Whenever we judge people, we become stumbling blocks for them. If we don't show them love and kindness, we can't show them Jesus.

❶ Think about times you've been a stumbling block to someone else's faith. What changes could you make in your life to keep from being a stumbling block?

❷ Ask a friend how you can help him or her grow closer to God. Do what your friend asks for the next month and see how God works through you.

❸ Pray that you will be a good example of living for God.

Turn to page 1370 for your next devotion.

your brother? For we will all stand before God's judgment seat. [11]It is written:

" 'As surely as I live,' says the Lord,
'every knee will bow before me;
    every tongue will confess to God.' "[a]

[12]So then, each of us will give an account of himself to God.

[13]Therefore let us stop passing judgment on one another. Instead, make up your mind not to put any stumbling block or obstacle in your brother's way. [14]As one who is in the Lord Jesus, I am fully convinced that no food[b] is unclean in itself. But if anyone regards something as unclean, then for him it is unclean. [15]If your brother is distressed because of what you eat, you are no longer acting in love. Do not by your eating destroy your brother for whom Christ died. [16]Do not allow what you consider good to be spoken of as evil. [17]For the kingdom of God is not a matter of eating and drinking, but of righteousness, peace and joy in the Holy Spirit, [18]because anyone who serves Christ in this way is pleasing to God and approved by men.

[19]Let us therefore make every effort to do what leads to peace and to mutual edification. [20]Do not destroy the work of God for the sake of food. All food is clean, but it is wrong for a man to eat anything that causes someone else to stumble. [21]It is better not to eat meat or drink wine or to do anything else that will cause your brother to fall.

[22]So whatever you believe about these things keep between yourself and God. Blessed is the man who does not condemn himself by what he approves. [23]But the man who has doubts is condemned if he eats, because his eating is not from faith; and everything that does not come from faith is sin.

15 We who are strong ought to bear with the failings of the weak and not to please ourselves. [2]Each of us should please his neighbor for his good, to build him up. [3]For even Christ did not please himself but, as it is written: "The insults of those who insult you have fallen on me."[c] [4]For everything that was written in the past was written to teach us, so that through endurance and the encouragement of the Scriptures we might have hope.

[5]May the God who gives endurance and encouragement give you a spirit of unity among yourselves as you follow Christ Jesus, [6]so that with one heart and mouth you may glorify the God and Father of our Lord Jesus Christ.

[7]Accept one another, then, just as Christ accepted you, in order to bring praise to God. [8]For I tell you that Christ has become a servant of the Jews[d] on behalf of God's truth, to confirm the promises made to the patriarchs [9]so that the Gentiles may glorify God for his mercy, as it is written:

"Therefore I will praise you among the
    Gentiles;
    I will sing hymns to your name."[e]

[10]Again, it says,

"Rejoice, O Gentiles, with his
    people."[f]

[11]And again,

"Praise the Lord, all you Gentiles,
    and sing praises to him, all you
    peoples."[g]

[12]And again, Isaiah says,

"The Root of Jesse will spring up,
    one who will arise to rule over the
        nations;
    the Gentiles will hope in him."[h]

[13]May the God of hope fill you with all joy and peace as you trust in him, so that you may overflow with hope by the power of the Holy Spirit.

Paul the Minister to the Gentiles

[14]I myself am convinced, my brothers, that you yourselves are full of goodness, complete in knowledge and competent to instruct one another. [15]I have written you quite boldly on some points, as if to remind you of them again, because of the grace God gave me [16]to be a minister of Christ Jesus to the Gentiles with the priestly duty of proclaiming the gospel of God, so that the Gentiles might become

---

[a]11 Isaiah 45:23   [b]14 Or *that nothing*
[c]3 Psalm 69:9   [d]8 Greek *circumcision*
[e]9 2 Samuel 22:50; Psalm 18:49   [f]10 Deut. 32:43
[g]11 Psalm 117:1   [h]12 Isaiah 11:10

an offering acceptable to God, sanctified by the Holy Spirit.

[17]Therefore I glory in Christ Jesus in my service to God. [18]I will not venture to speak of anything except what Christ has accomplished through me in leading the Gentiles to obey God by what I have said and done-- [19]by the power of signs and miracles, through the power of the Spirit. So from Jerusalem all the way around to Illyricum, I have fully proclaimed the gospel of Christ. [20]It has always been my ambition to preach the gospel where Christ was not known, so that I would not be building on someone else's foundation. [21]Rather, as it is written:

"Those who were not told about him
        will see,
    and those who have not heard will
        understand."[a]

[22]This is why I have often been hindered from coming to you.

Paul's Plan to Visit Rome

[23]But now that there is no more place for me to work in these regions, and since I have been longing for many years to see you, [24]I plan to do so when I go to Spain. I hope to visit you while passing through and to have you assist me on my journey there, after I have enjoyed your company for a while. [25]Now, however, I am on my way to Jerusalem in the service of the saints there. [26]For Macedonia and Achaia were pleased to make a contribution for the poor among the saints in Jerusalem. [27]They were pleased to do it, and indeed they owe it to them. For if

[a]21 Isaiah 52:15

Weekend.

What the Law Can't Do

Read 1 Timothy 1:6–11 (page 1464)

On Monday Kent got it right. No matter what activity you do—pray, go to church, read your Bible—these things won't get you to heaven. It's not what you do; it's what Jesus did for you.

When a builder constructs a wall, he uses a level to make sure the wall is straight. If it's crooked, he doesn't use the level to repair the wall. The level only exposes the problem on the outside. Instead, he uses his saw and hammer to repair the studs inside. If he didn't repair from the inside first, no matter how hard he pushed on the outside, the wall would always go back to its original crooked state.

Pushing on the outside of the wall is like trying to fix your guilty behavior on your own. Just like the level, God's law reveals the problem of sin but doesn't repair the problem. The repair is found in Jesus. He, in sacrificing himself, nailed your guilt and sin onto the cross.

You have to be repaired from the inside by Jesus. This happens when you put your faith in him every day.

What about You?

❶ Have God's laws (you know, his rules) ever frustrated you? Which one has frustrated you the most?

❷ Looking back, have you ever allowed Jesus to come into your life? When was it? If you haven't, talk with your parents or pastor about this once-and-for-all commitment.

❸ Ask God to help you. Pray that he'll continue to repair you from the inside.

Turn to page 1376 for your next devotion.

the Gentiles have shared in the Jews' spiritual blessings, they owe it to the Jews to share with them their material blessings. [28]So after I have completed this task and have made sure that they have received this fruit, I will go to Spain and visit you on the way. [29]I know that when I come to you, I will come in the full measure of the blessing of Christ.

[30]I urge you, brothers, by our Lord Jesus Christ and by the love of the Spirit, to join me in my struggle by praying to God for me. [31]Pray that I may be rescued from the unbelievers in Judea and that my service in Jerusalem may be acceptable to the saints there, [32]so that by God's will I may come to you with joy and together with you be refreshed. [33]The God of peace be with you all. Amen.

Personal Greetings

16 I commend to you our sister Phoebe, a servant[a] of the church in Cenchrea. [2]I ask you to receive her in the Lord in a way worthy of the saints and to give her any help she may need from you, for she has been a great help to many people, including me.

[3]Greet Priscilla[b] and Aquila, my fellow workers in Christ Jesus. [4]They risked their lives for me. Not only I but all the churches of the Gentiles are grateful to them.

[5]Greet also the church that meets at their house.

Greet my dear friend Epenetus, who was the first convert to Christ in the province of Asia.

[6]Greet Mary, who worked very hard for you.

[7]Greet Andronicus and Junias, my relatives who have been in prison with me. They are outstanding among the apostles, and they were in Christ before I was.

[8]Greet Ampliatus, whom I love in the Lord.

[9]Greet Urbanus, our fellow worker in Christ, and my dear friend Stachys.

[10]Greet Apelles, tested and approved in Christ.

Greet those who belong to the household of Aristobulus.

[11]Greet Herodion, my relative.

Greet those in the household of Narcissus who are in the Lord.

[12]Greet Tryphena and Tryphosa, those women who work hard in the Lord.

Greet my dear friend Persis, another woman who has worked very hard in the Lord.

[13]Greet Rufus, chosen in the Lord, and his mother, who has been a mother to me, too.

[14]Greet Asyncritus, Phlegon, Hermes, Patrobas, Hermas and the brothers with them.

[15]Greet Philologus, Julia, Nereus and his sister, and Olympas and all the saints with them.

[16]Greet one another with a holy kiss.

All the churches of Christ send greetings.

Smooching Saints

Huh?

Romans 16:16

If you tried to kiss someone next to you in church, your mom would probably give you the "sit down and behave yourself" look. Yet Paul encouraged people to greet each other with a holy kiss. We know from a second century historian named Justin Martyr that a simple kiss was a regular part of the worship services back then. Like a handshake or hug today, a kiss was a sign of friendship. It's probably best not to try this out on your neighbor in church this week though.

[17]I urge you, brothers, to watch out for those who cause divisions and put obstacles in your way that are contrary to the teaching you have learned. Keep away from them. [18]For such people are not serving our Lord Christ, but their own appetites. By smooth talk and flattery they deceive the minds of naive people. [19]Everyone has heard about your obedience, so I am full of joy over you; but I want you to be wise about what is good, and innocent about what is evil.

---

[a]1 Or *deaconess*   [b]3 Greek *Prisca*, a variant of *Priscilla*

[20]The God of peace will soon crush Satan under your feet.

The grace of our Lord Jesus be with you.

[21]Timothy, my fellow worker, sends his greetings to you, as do Lucius, Jason and Sosipater, my relatives.

[22]I, Tertius, who wrote down this letter, greet you in the Lord.

[23]Gaius, whose hospitality I and the whole church here enjoy, sends you his greetings.

Erastus, who is the city's director of public works, and our brother Quartus send you their greetings.[a]

[25]Now to him who is able to establish you by my gospel and the proclamation of Jesus Christ, according to the revelation of the mystery hidden for long ages past, [26]but now revealed and made known through the prophetic writings by the command of the eternal God, so that all nations might believe and obey him— [27]to the only wise God be glory forever through Jesus Christ! Amen.

---

[a]23 Some manuscripts *their greetings.* [24]*May the grace of our Lord Jesus Christ be with all of you. Amen.*

1 Corinthians

START

Ever get a bad report card—one with a D or even worse? That's what happened to the church at Corinth. Paul was the founder and teacher of this church for a year-and-a-half, but then left to start other churches. He heard that the church was not doing well. In fact, they were flunking Christianity 101. They were acting just like all the other people in their busy city. And the people in their city had a totally sleazy reputation. They were caught up in all kinds of garbage—arguing, getting drunk on communion wine and sleeping around. Paul wasn't happy about any of this, and he let them know it.

But Paul didn't just scold the church and move on. He gave them lots of solid advice for cleaning up their act. He told them how to relate to each other as Christians. He told them how to hang on to God, even when they were tempted. And in one of the most famous chapters in the Bible (chapter 13), he wrote down the qualities of real love—the kind of love the church at Corinth (and all of us) need to show each other.

CAST OF Characters

Paul
He was a Jewish leader who was a Christian's biggest enemy until he became one. He started traveling around, telling people about Jesus. He was kind of the first missionary, taking the Good News to people from a culture completely different from his own.

Believers From Chloe's Household
Some solid Christians in Corinth who were sick of the wimpy faith of others in the church and told Paul what was going on.

The Church at Corinth, the Corinthians
(CORE-inth)
(Core-INTH-ee-uns)
All the Christians who lived in the city of Corinth. Some were real followers of Jesus, some were flakes; others were beginners, and many weren't getting along very well.

Timothy
One of Paul's most trusted buds. He was like the son Paul never had, and Paul was the spiritual dad Timothy needed. If Paul couldn't visit one of the churches, he would often send Timothy.

What's UP with That?

Chapter 13 talks about LOVE!

The Christians in Corinth had trouble loving each other, so Paul describes true love. From the list below, circle the love-descriptions that you think Paul used. When you're done, check your answers in chapter 13.

LOVE . . .

always protects

is not rude

is kind

stinks!

keeps no record of wrongs

is all we need

is fun

is patient

killed the dinosaurs

can do anything

is for wimps

is like a hamster

is not easily angered

feels great

never fails

makes good cookies

does not boast

smells good

always hopes

always flushes

is not self-seeking

can fool you

wears ruby slippers

always trusts

is groovy, baby

1 Paul, called to be an apostle of Christ Jesus by the will of God, and our brother Sosthenes,

²To the church of God in Corinth, to those sanctified in Christ Jesus and called to be holy, together with all those everywhere who call on the name of our Lord Jesus Christ—their Lord and ours:

³Grace and peace to you from God our Father and the Lord Jesus Christ.

What a Gift!

Huh?

1 Corinthians 1:3

Imagine being convicted of murder and being sentenced to death. While on death row you receive word that you are free to go because someone else took your place. Wow! You were given a gift of grace. It was a gift you didn't deserve, since you *did* murder someone (remember, you're imagining). God shows this grace to us. We deserve to die and go to hell because of our sins. But the good news is that God's Son, Jesus, died in our place and gave us the gift of eternal life with God, if we accept it.

Thanksgiving

⁴I always thank God for you because of his grace given you in Christ Jesus. ⁵For in him you have been enriched in every way—in all your speaking and in all your knowledge— ⁶because our testimony about Christ was confirmed in you. ⁷Therefore you do not lack any spiritual gift as you eagerly wait for our Lord Jesus Christ to be revealed. ⁸He will keep you strong to the end, so that you will be blameless on the day of our Lord Jesus Christ. ⁹God, who has called you into fellowship with his Son Jesus Christ our Lord, is faithful.

Divisions in the Church

¹⁰I appeal to you, brothers, in the name of our Lord Jesus Christ, that all of you agree with one another so that there may be no divisions among you and that you

may be perfectly united in mind and thought. ¹¹My brothers, some from Chloe's household have informed me that there are quarrels among you. ¹²What I mean is this: One of you says, "I follow Paul"; another, "I follow Apollos"; another, "I follow Cephas*a*"; still another, "I follow Christ."

¹³Is Christ divided? Was Paul crucified for you? Were you baptized into*b* the name of Paul? ¹⁴I am thankful that I did not baptize any of you except Crispus and Gaius, ¹⁵so no one can say that you were baptized into my name. ¹⁶(Yes, I also baptized the household of Stephanas; beyond that, I don't remember if I baptized anyone else.) ¹⁷For Christ did not send me to baptize, but to preach the gospel—not with words of human wisdom, lest the cross of Christ be emptied of its power.

Christ the Wisdom and Power of God

¹⁸For the message of the cross is foolishness to those who are perishing, but to us who are being saved it is the power of God. ¹⁹For it is written:

"I will destroy the wisdom of the wise;
  the intelligence of the intelligent I
    will frustrate."*c*

²⁰Where is the wise man? Where is the scholar? Where is the philosopher of this age? Has not God made foolish the wisdom of the world? ²¹For since in the wisdom of God the world through its wisdom did not know him, God was pleased through the foolishness of what was preached to save those who believe. ²²Jews demand miraculous signs and Greeks look for wisdom, ²³but we preach Christ crucified: a stumbling block to Jews and foolishness to Gentiles, ²⁴but to those whom God has called, both Jews and Greeks, Christ the power of God and the wisdom of God. ²⁵For the foolishness of God is wiser than man's wisdom, and the weakness of God is stronger than man's strength.

²⁶Brothers, think of what you were when you were called. Not many of you were wise by human standards; not many were influential; not many were of

---

a12 That is, Peter   *b13* Or *in*; also in verse 15
c19 Isaiah 29:14

Truth Blocker

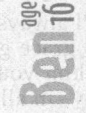

1 Corinthians 1:23

Stumbling blocks are things that get in the way—they are roadblocks to truth. Most Jews weren't able to see the truth about Jesus. They had their own ideas about what the Messiah was going to be like. When Jesus didn't match those ideas, they weren't able to accept the truth about him. Their false ideas blocked them from seeing the truth.

noble birth. ²⁷But God chose the foolish things of the world to shame the wise;

God chose the weak things of the world to shame the strong. ²⁸He chose the lowly things of this world and the despised things—and the things that are not—to nullify the things that are, ²⁹so that no one may boast before him. ³⁰It is because of him that you are in Christ Jesus, who has become for us wisdom from God— that is, our righteousness, holiness and redemption. ³¹Therefore, as it is written: "Let him who boasts boast in the Lord."ᵃ

2 When I came to you, brothers, I did not come with eloquence or superior wisdom as I proclaimed to you the testimony about God.ᵇ ²For I resolved to know nothing while I was with you except Jesus Christ and him crucified. ³I

ᵃ31 Jer. 9:24 ᵇ1 Some manuscripts *as I proclaimed to you God's mystery*

Monday

Get It Together

Read 1 Corinthians 1:10

Recently I was talking to a non-Christian friend, and a Christian friend overheard me and started answering all my non-Christian friend's questions before I could. I got frustrated that this other Christian was "interrupting" me. But then I realized that God could work through my Christian friend as much as he could work through me. The important thing was that my non-Christian friend was learning about Jesus. It didn't really matter who was doing the talking.

God likes it when his children are at peace with each other. He is glorified when we work together to build his kingdom. All Christians have the same mission: to lead people to Jesus. We might have different personalities or different ways of saying things, but we shouldn't let that keep us from working together to share Jesus Christ with others.

When we work with other Christians and focus on Jesus, we can build better relationships with each other. And when we do that, we also build a better relationship with God, because God can reveal himself to us through other people. It's hard enough being a Christian in our society. We need each other if we want to change the world for Jesus.

Ben age 16

❶ Think about a Christian group you hang out with, like your youth group. What are some of the things that keep your group from working together all the time?

❷ Talk to your youth leader about this passage. Ask your leader to help you plan an activity that can help your group become more unified.

❸ Thank God for your brothers and sisters in Christ.

Turn to page 1378 for your next devotion.

came to you in weakness and fear, and with much trembling. [4]My message and my preaching were not with wise and persuasive words, but with a demonstration of the Spirit's power, [5]so that your faith might not rest on men's wisdom, but on God's power.

Wisdom from the Spirit

[6]We do, however, speak a message of wisdom among the mature, but not the wisdom of this age or of the rulers of this age, who are coming to nothing. [7]No, we speak of God's secret wisdom, a wisdom that has been hidden and that God destined for our glory before time began. [8]None of the rulers of this age understood it, for if they had, they would not have crucified the Lord of glory. [9]However, as it is written:

"No eye has seen,
    no ear has heard,
  no mind has conceived
      what God has prepared for those
          who love him"[a]—

[10]but God has revealed it to us by his Spirit.

Hide and Seek
Huh?

1 Corinthians 2:7

God's secret wisdom? A hidden wisdom? Here's the deal: In Old Testament times, the people only had hints of God's great plan. It was kind of like a secret. But with Jesus, God's plan and his wisdom are right out in the open for everyone to see!

The Spirit searches all things, even the deep things of God. [11]For who among men knows the thoughts of a man except the man's spirit within him? In the same way no one knows the thoughts of God except the Spirit of God. [12]We have not received the spirit of the world but the Spirit who is from God, that we may understand what God has freely given us. [13]This is what we speak, not in words taught us by human wisdom but in words taught by the Spirit, expressing spiritual truths in spiritual words.[b] [14]The man without the Spirit does not accept the things that come from the Spirit of God, for they are foolishness to him, and he cannot understand them, because they are spiritually discerned. [15]The spiritual man makes judgments about all things, but he himself is not subject to any man's judgment:

[16]"For who has known the mind of the
    Lord
  that he may instruct him?"[c]

But we have the mind of Christ.

A Big Bonus
Huh?

1 Corinthians 2:16

Drinking milk is good for your body because there's calcium in it that makes your bones stronger. The calcium becomes part of you and helps you grow. When Jesus comes into your life, you get a big bonus—the Holy Spirit. The Holy Spirit helps make you a stronger Christian. He helps you and encourages you to follow God's way.

On Divisions in the Church

3 Brothers, I could not address you as spiritual but as worldly—mere infants in Christ. [2]I gave you milk, not solid food, for you were not yet ready for it. Indeed, you are still not ready. [3]You are still worldly. For since there is jealousy and quarreling among you, are you not worldly? Are you not acting like mere men? [4]For when one says, "I follow Paul," and another, "I follow Apollos," are you not mere men?

[5]What, after all, is Apollos? And what is Paul? Only servants, through whom you came to believe—as the Lord has assigned to each his task. [6]I planted the seed, Apollos watered it, but God made it grow. [7]So neither he who plants nor he who waters is anything, but only God,

[a]9 Isaiah 64:4   [b]13 Or Spirit, interpreting spiritual truths to spiritual men   [c]16 Isaiah 40:13

who makes things grow. ⁸The man who plants and the man who waters have one purpose, and each will be rewarded according to his own labor. ⁹For we are God's fellow workers; you are God's field, God's building.

¹⁰By the grace God has given me, I laid a foundation as an expert builder, and someone else is building on it. But each one should be careful how he builds. ¹¹For no one can lay any foundation other than the one already laid, which is Jesus Christ. ¹²If any man builds on this foundation using gold, silver, costly stones, wood, hay or straw, ¹³his work will be shown for what it is, because the Day will bring it to light. It will be revealed with fire, and the fire will test the quality of each man's work. ¹⁴If what he has built survives, he will receive his reward. ¹⁵If it is burned up, he will suffer loss; he himself will be saved, but only as one escaping through the flames.

¹⁶Don't you know that you yourselves are God's temple and that God's Spirit lives in you? ¹⁷If anyone destroys God's temple, God will destroy him; for God's temple is sacred, and you are that temple.

¹⁸Do not deceive yourselves. If any one of you thinks he is wise by the standards of this age, he should become a "fool" so that he may become wise. ¹⁹For the wisdom of this world is foolishness in God's sight. As it is written: "He catches the wise in their craftiness"ᵃ; ²⁰and again, "The Lord knows that the thoughts of the

Who's the Fool?

Huh?

1 Corinthians 3:18–19
A lot of people think Christians are pretty stupid. They think we're fools for what we believe. This verse turns it around! Once you become a "fool" (as those accusers say), you see the real truth and become wise. And those who think they are so wise will find out that they're the real fools.

ᵃ*19* Job 5:13

Tuesday

Rock-solid Faith

Read 1 Corinthians 3:10–15

At the beginning of 7th grade, I had bad grades and started getting into trouble. Things that should have been important to me just didn't seem to matter. I wasn't paying attention to the kind of life I was living.

God wants me to do better than that. After all, he's given me a great foundation in Jesus, who is as solid as a rock. My job is to build on his example, making sure my choices are pure and holy. And when I'm not sure what to choose, I can ask God for help and know that his answer is true.

If I want my faith to be strong, I need to get serious about it every day.

Tommy age 12

What about You?

❶ What are some big decisions in your life right now? How can you make sure you're choosing wisely?

❷ Think of one "weak spot" in your faith. Keep a journal of how you do in that area every day for a week. Then set a specific goal to do better the next week.

❸ Ask God to help you make wise decisions.

Turn to page 1381 for your next devotion.

wise are futile."[a] [21]So then, no more boasting about men! All things are yours, [22]whether Paul or Apollos or Cephas[b] or the world or life or death or the present or the future—all are yours, [23]and you are of Christ, and Christ is of God.

Apostles of Christ

4 So then, men ought to regard us as servants of Christ and as those entrusted with the secret things of God. [2]Now it is required that those who have been given a trust must prove faithful. [3]I care very little if I am judged by you or by any human court; indeed, I do not even judge myself. [4]My conscience is clear, but that does not make me innocent. It is the Lord who judges me. [5]Therefore judge nothing before the appointed time; wait till the Lord comes. He will bring to light what is hidden in darkness and will expose the motives of men's hearts. At that time each will receive his praise from God.

[6]Now, brothers, I have applied these things to myself and Apollos for your benefit, so that you may learn from us the meaning of the saying, "Do not go beyond what is written." Then you will not take pride in one man over against another. [7]For who makes you different from anyone else? What do you have that you did not receive? And if you did receive it, why do you boast as though you did not?

[8]Already you have all you want! Already you have become rich! You have become kings—and that without us! How I wish that you really had become kings so that we might be kings with you! [9]For it seems to me that God has put us apostles on display at the end of the procession, like men condemned to die in the arena. We have been made a spectacle to the whole universe, to angels as well as to men. [10]We are fools for Christ, but you are so wise in Christ! We are weak, but you are strong! You are honored, we are dishonored! [11]To this very hour we go hungry and thirsty, we are in rags, we are brutally treated, we are homeless. [12]We work hard with our own hands. When we are cursed, we bless; when we are persecuted, we endure it; [13]when we are slandered, we answer kindly. Up to th... ment we have become the scum of ... earth, the refuse of the world.

[14]I am not writing this to shame you, but to warn you, as my dear children. [15]Even though you have ten thousand guardians in Christ, you do not have many fathers, for in Christ Jesus I became your father through the gospel. [16]Therefore I urge you to imitate me. [17]For this reason I am sending to you Timothy, my son whom I love, who is faithful in the Lord. He will remind you of my way of life in Christ Jesus, which agrees with what I teach everywhere in every church.

[18]Some of you have become arrogant, as if I were not coming to you. [19]But I will come to you very soon, if the Lord is willing, and then I will find out not only how these arrogant people are talking, but what power they have. [20]For the kingdom of God is not a matter of talk but of power. [21]What do you prefer? Shall I come to you with a whip, or in love and with a gentle spirit?

Expel the Immoral Brother!

5 It is actually reported that there is sexual immorality among you, and of a kind that does not occur even among pagans: A man has his father's wife. [2]And you are proud! Shouldn't you rather have been filled with grief and have put out of your fellowship the man who did this? [3]Even though I am not physically present, I am with you in spirit. And I have already passed judgment on the one who did this, just as if I were present. [4]When you are assembled in the name of our Lord Jesus and I am with you in spirit, and the power of our Lord Jesus is present, [5]hand this man over to Satan, so that the sinful nature[c] may be destroyed and his spirit saved on the day of the Lord.

[6]Your boasting is not good. Don't you know that a little yeast works through the whole batch of dough? [7]Get rid of the old yeast that you may be a new batch without yeast—as you really are. For Christ, our Passover lamb, has been sac-

[a]20 Psalm 94:11   [b]22 That is, Peter   [c]5 Or *that his body*; or *that the flesh*

...us keep the Festi-... yeast, the yeast of ...ness, but with bread ... bread of sincerity and ... but to want you, as in... ...en you in my letter not to associate with sexually immoral people— [10]not at all meaning the people of this world who are immoral, or the greedy and swindlers, or idolaters. In that case you would have to leave this world. [11]But now I am writing you that you must not associate with anyone who calls himself a brother but is sexually immoral or greedy, an idolater or a slanderer, a drunkard or a swindler. With such a man do not even eat.

[12]What business is it of mine to judge those outside the church? Are you not to judge those inside? [13]God will judge those outside. "Expel the wicked man from among you."[a]

Lawsuits Among Believers

6 If any of you has a dispute with an-other, dare he take it before the un-godly for judgment instead of before the saints? [2]Do you not know that the saints will judge the world? And if you are to judge the world, are you not competent to judge trivial cases? [3]Do you not know that we will judge angels? How much more the things of this life! [4]Therefore, if you have disputes about such matters, appoint as judges even men of little ac-count in the church![b] [5]I say this to shame you. Is it possible that there is nobody among you wise enough to judge a dis-pute between believers? [6]But instead, one brother goes to law against another—and this in front of unbelievers!

[7]The very fact that you have lawsuits among you means you have been com-pletely defeated already. Why not rather be wronged? Why not rather be cheated? [8]Instead, you yourselves cheat and do wrong, and you do this to your brothers.

[9]Do you not know that the wicked will not inherit the kingdom of God? Do not be deceived: Neither the sexually immor-al nor idolaters nor adulterers nor male prostitutes nor homosexual offenders [10]nor thieves nor the greedy nor drunk-ards nor slanderers nor swindlers will in-herit the kingdom of God. [11]And that is

what some of you were. But you were washed, you were sanctified, you were justified in the name of the Lord Jesus Christ and by the Spirit of our God.

Let's Party!

Huh?

1 Corinthians 6:11

When you get ready for a party, you take a shower, put on your deodorant (hopefully!) and get dressed. Now you're ready to go! Heaven's going to be a party. Wanna go? Jesus has to get you ready. His blood, from his death on the cross, makes you clean (washed), he makes you pure (sanctified), and he dresses you with his *own* rightness (justified). The party is waiting . . . will you be ready to go?

Sexual Immorality

[12]"Everything is permissible for me"— but not everything is beneficial. "Every-thing is permissible for me"—but I will not be mastered by anything. [13]"Food for the stomach and the stomach for food"— but God will destroy them both. The body is not meant for sexual immorality, but for the Lord, and the Lord for the body. [14]By his power God raised the Lord from the dead, and he will raise us also. [15]Do you not know that your bodies are members of Christ himself? Shall I then take the members of Christ and unite them with a prostitute? Never! [16]Do you not know that he who unites himself with a prostitute is one with her in body? For it is said, "The two will become one flesh."[c] [17]But he who unites himself with the Lord is one with him in spirit.

[18]Flee from sexual immorality. All oth-er sins a man commits are outside his body, but he who sins sexually sins against his own body. [19]Do you not know that your body is a temple of the Holy Spirit, who is in you, whom you have re-ceived from God? You are not your own;

[a]13 Deut. 17:7; 19:19; 21:21; 22:21,24; 24:7 [b]4 Or matters, do you appoint as judges men of little account in the church? [c]16 Gen. 2:24

²⁰you were bought at a price. Therefore honor God with your body.

Marriage

7 Now for the matters you wrote about: It is good for a man not to marry.ᵃ ²But since there is so much immorality, each man should have his own wife, and each woman her own husband. ³The husband should fulfill his marital duty to his wife, and likewise the wife to her husband. ⁴The wife's body does not belong to her alone but also to her husband. In the same way, the husband's body does not belong to him alone but also to his wife. ⁵Do not deprive each other except by mutual consent and for a time, so that you may devote yourselves to prayer. Then come together again so that Satan will not tempt you because of your lack of self-control. ⁶I say this as a concession, not as a command. ⁷I wish that all men were as I am. But each man

has his own gift from God; one has this gift, another has that.

⁸Now to the unmarried and the widows I say: It is good for them to stay unmarried, as I am. ⁹But if they cannot control themselves, they should marry, for it is better to marry than to burn with passion.

¹⁰To the married I give this command (not I, but the Lord): A wife must not separate from her husband. ¹¹But if she does, she must remain unmarried or else be reconciled to her husband. And a husband must not divorce his wife.

¹²To the rest I say this (I, not the Lord): If any brother has a wife who is not a believer and she is willing to live with him, he must not divorce her. ¹³And if a woman has a husband who is not a believer and he is willing to live with her, she must not divorce him. ¹⁴For the unbeliev-

---

ᵃ1 Or "It is good for a man not to have sexual relations with a woman."

Wednesday

It's Everywhere!

Read 1 Corinthians 6:18-20

Sex is everywhere. And wow is it ever a big temptation for teenagers like me. If you believed everything you saw on TV or in movies, you'd think everyone in the world is sleeping around, and you'd get the impression that this lifestyle is the greatest thing in the world. But the truth is, God's got better plans for his gift of sex.

You wouldn't know it from watching movies, but God created sex to be something special to share with the person you marry, the person you give your whole life to. Sex outside of marriage causes serious problems and pulls us away from God. That's why God wants us to stay away from sexual immorality. He wants us to keep our minds on him, not on sex.

God has every right to ask us to obey him. After all, he paid for our salvation with the blood of his Son. Our lives and our bodies belong to God.

Jon age 14

What about You?

❶ What sexual sins do you struggle with? How can you avoid being tempted to give in to those sins?

❷ Find a small wooden or clay bead and a cord you can make into a necklace or a bracelet. Think of it as your "flee" bead. Whenever you are tempted by sexual sin, use your bead as a reminder to get away from that temptation—fast!

❸ Ask God to help you be strong and resist sexual temptation.

Turn to page 1384 for your next devotion.

ing husband has been sanctified through his wife, and the unbelieving wife has been sanctified through her believing husband. Otherwise your children would be unclean, but as it is, they are holy.

[15]But if the unbeliever leaves, let him do so. A believing man or woman is not bound in such circumstances; God has called us to live in peace. [16]How do you know, wife, whether you will save your husband? Or, how do you know, husband, whether you will save your wife?

[17]Nevertheless, each one should retain the place in life that the Lord assigned to him and to which God has called him. This is the rule I lay down in all the churches. [18]Was a man already circumcised when he was called? He should not become uncircumcised. Was a man uncircumcised when he was called? He should not be circumcised. [19]Circumcision is nothing and uncircumcision is nothing. Keeping God's commands is what counts. [20]Each one should remain in the situation which he was in when God called him. [21]Were you a slave when you were called? Don't let it trouble you—although if you can gain your freedom, do so. [22]For he who was a slave when he was called by the Lord is the Lord's freedman; similarly, he who was a free man when he was called is Christ's slave. [23]You were bought at a price; do not become slaves of men. [24]Brothers, each man, as responsible to God, should remain in the situation God called him to.

[25]Now about virgins: I have no command from the Lord, but I give a judgment as one who by the Lord's mercy is trustworthy. [26]Because of the present crisis, I think that it is good for you to remain as you are. [27]Are you married? Do not seek a divorce. Are you unmarried? Do not look for a wife. [28]But if you do marry, you have not sinned; and if a virgin marries, she has not sinned. But those who marry will face many troubles in this life, and I want to spare you this.

[29]What I mean, brothers, is that the time is short. From now on those who have wives should live as if they had none; [30]those who mourn, as if they did not; those who are happy, as if they were not; those who buy something, as if it were not theirs to keep; [31]those who use

the things of the world, as if not engrossed in them. For this world in its present form is passing away.

[32]I would like you to be free from concern. An unmarried man is concerned about the Lord's affairs—how he can please the Lord. [33]But a married man is concerned about the affairs of this world—how he can please his wife— [34]and his interests are divided. An unmarried woman or virgin is concerned about the Lord's affairs: Her aim is to be devoted to the Lord in both body and spirit. But a married woman is concerned about the affairs of this world—how she can please her husband. [35]I am saying this for your own good, not to restrict you, but that you may live in a right way in undivided devotion to the Lord.

[36]If anyone thinks he is acting improperly toward the virgin he is engaged to, and if she is getting along in years and he feels he ought to marry, he should do as he wants. He is not sinning. They should get married. [37]But the man who has settled the matter in his own mind, who is under no compulsion but has control over his own will, and who has made up his mind not to marry the virgin—this man also does the right thing. [38]So then, he who marries the virgin does right, but he who does not marry her does even better.[a]

[39]A woman is bound to her husband as long as he lives. But if her husband dies, she is free to marry anyone she wishes, but he must belong to the Lord. [40]In my judgment, she is happier if she stays as she is—and I think that I too have the Spirit of God.

Food Sacrificed to Idols

8 Now about food sacrificed to idols: We know that we all possess knowledge.[b] Knowledge puffs up, but love

---

[a]36-38 Or [36]If anyone thinks he is not treating his daughter properly, and if she is getting along in years, and he feels she ought to marry, he should do as he wants. He is not sinning. He should let her get married. [37]But the man who has settled the matter in his own mind, who is under no compulsion but has control over his own will, and who has made up his mind to keep the virgin unmarried—this man also does the right thing. [38]So then, he who gives his virgin in marriage does right, but he who does not give her in marriage does even better. [b]1 Or "We all possess knowledge," as you say

builds up. [2]The man who thinks he knows something does not yet know as he ought to know. [3]But the man who loves God is known by God.

[4]So then, about eating food sacrificed to idols: We know that an idol is nothing at all in the world and that there is no God but one. [5]For even if there are so-called gods, whether in heaven or on earth (as indeed there are many "gods" and many "lords"), [6]yet for us there is but one God, the Father, from whom all things came and for whom we live; and there is but one Lord, Jesus Christ, through whom all things came and through whom we live.

[7]But not everyone knows this. Some people are still so accustomed to idols that when they eat such food they think of it as having been sacrificed to an idol, and since their conscience is weak, it is defiled. [8]But food does not bring us near to God; we are no worse if we do not eat, and no better if we do.

[9]Be careful, however, that the exercise of your freedom does not become a stumbling block to the weak. [10]For if anyone with a weak conscience sees you who have this knowledge eating in an idol's temple, won't he be emboldened to eat what has been sacrificed to idols? [11]So this weak brother, for whom Christ died, is destroyed by your knowledge. [12]When you sin against your brothers in this way and wound their weak conscience, you sin against Christ. [13]Therefore, if what I eat causes my brother to fall into sin, I will never eat meat again, so that I will not cause him to fall.

The Rights of an Apostle

9 Am I not free? Am I not an apostle? Have I not seen Jesus our Lord? Are you not the result of my work in the Lord? [2]Even though I may not be an apostle to others, surely I am to you! For you are the seal of my apostleship in the Lord.

[3]This is my defense to those who sit in judgment on me. [4]Don't we have the right to food and drink? [5]Don't we have the right to take a believing wife along with us, as do the other apostles and the Lord's brothers and Cephas[a]? [6]Or is it only I and Barnabas who must work for a living?

[7]Who serves as a soldier at his own expense? Who plants a vineyard and does not eat of its grapes? Who tends a flock and does not drink of the milk? [8]Do I say this merely from a human point of view? Doesn't the Law say the same thing? [9]For it is written in the Law of Moses: "Do not muzzle an ox while it is treading out the grain."[b] Is it about oxen that God is concerned? [10]Surely he says this for us, doesn't he? Yes, this was written for us, because when the plowman plows and the thresher threshes, they ought to do so in the hope of sharing in the harvest. [11]If we have sown spiritual seed among you, is it too much if we reap a material harvest from you? [12]If others have this right of support from you, shouldn't we have it all the more?

But we did not use this right. On the contrary, we put up with anything rather than hinder the gospel of Christ. [13]Don't you know that those who work in the temple get their food from the temple, and those who serve at the altar share in what is offered on the altar? [14]In the same way, the Lord has commanded that those who preach the gospel should receive their living from the gospel.

[15]But I have not used any of these rights. And I am not writing this in the hope that you will do such things for me. I would rather die than have anyone deprive me of this boast. [16]Yet when I preach the gospel, I cannot boast, for I am compelled to preach. Woe to me if I do not preach the gospel! [17]If I preach voluntarily, I have a reward; if not voluntarily, I am simply discharging the trust committed to me. [18]What then is my reward? Just this: that in preaching the gospel I may offer it free of charge, and so not make use of my rights in preaching it.

[19]Though I am free and belong to no man, I make myself a slave to everyone, to win as many as possible. [20]To the Jews I became like a Jew, to win the Jews. To those under the law I became like one under the law (though I myself am not under the law), so as to win those under the law. [21]To those not having the law I became like one not having the law

[a]5 That is, Peter   [b]9 Deut. 25:4

(though I am not free from God's law but am under Christ's law), so as to win those not having the law. ²²To the weak I became weak, to win the weak. I have become all things to all men so that by all possible means I might save some. ²³I do all this for the sake of the gospel, that I may share in its blessings.

²⁴Do you not know that in a race all the runners run, but only one gets the prize? Run in such a way as to get the prize. ²⁵Everyone who competes in the games goes into strict training. They do it to get a crown that will not last; but we do it to get a crown that will last forever. ²⁶Therefore I do not run like a man running aimlessly; I do not fight like a man beating the air. ²⁷No, I beat my body and make it my slave so that after I have preached to others, I myself will not be disqualified for the prize.

Warnings From Israel's History

10 For I do not want you to be ignorant of the fact, brothers, that our forefathers were all under the cloud and that they all passed through the sea. ²They were all baptized into Moses in the cloud and in the sea. ³They all ate the same spiritual food ⁴and drank the same spiritual drink; for they drank from the spiritual rock that accompanied them, and that rock was Christ. ⁵Nevertheless, God was not pleased with most of them; their bodies were scattered over the desert.

⁶Now these things occurred as examples*a* to keep us from setting our hearts on evil things as they did. ⁷Do not be idolaters, as some of them were; as it is written: "The people sat down to eat and drink and got up to indulge in pagan revelry."*b* ⁸We should not commit sexual immorality, as some of them did—and in one day twenty-three thousand of them died. ⁹We should not test the Lord, as some of them did—and were killed by snakes. ¹⁰And do not grumble, as some of

a6 Or types; also in verse 11   *b7 Exodus 32:6*

Thursday

High Priority
Read 1 Corinthians 9:24–25

I can't believe how busy I am! When I started 9th grade, I got involved with all kinds of extracurricular activities. With all of those, plus the increased homework load, I thought I'd never find time for everything—and I didn't. The first thing that slipped was my relationship with God. I'd skip my Bible reading time or forget to pray, and, before I knew it, God had dropped down on my list of priorities.

These verses help me remember that I need to find time for God, even though it's not always easy to do that. God is waiting for me at life's finish line, and I need to keep my focus on him, no matter how busy my life gets. When my schedule gets crazy and my calendar gets full, I need to make sure my relationship with God stays on top.

Marissa age 14

❶ What are some time-wasters you could get rid of?

❷ Write down some of your favorite verses on note cards. Stick a card in your locker, in your backpack and in some of your textbooks. Whenever you see them, take a quick moment to think about God and about his love for you.

❸ Ask God to help you manage your time wisely.

Turn to page 1385 for your next devotion.

them did—and were killed by the destroying angel. [11]These things happened to them as examples and were written down as warnings for us, on whom the fulfillment of the ages has come. [12]So, if you think you are standing firm, be careful that you don't fall! [13]No temptation has seized you except what is common to man. And God is faithful; he will not let you be tempted beyond what you can bear. But when you are tempted, he will also provide a way out so that you can stand up under it.

Idol Feasts and the Lord's Supper

[14]Therefore, my dear friends, flee from idolatry. [15]I speak to sensible people; judge for yourselves what I say. [16]Is not the cup of thanksgiving for which we give thanks a participation in the blood of Christ? And is not the bread that we break a participation in the body of

Parts of the Whole

1 Corinthians 10:17

All of us Christians are good at different things, and God uses each of us in special ways. Together we make up a pretty good thing. It's like your body. All the parts do different things, and together they make up a whole working, living, breathing you. Christians need to work together the same way. All the different things we do should work together and bring honor to God.

Christ? [17]Because there is one loaf, we, who are many, are one body, for we all partake of the one loaf.

[18]Consider the people of Israel: Do not those who eat the sacrifices participate in

Friday

A Way Out

Read 1 Corinthians 10:13

Ever since the Garden of Eden, people have faced temptation. For Adam and Eve, it was the forbidden fruit. For me, it could be drugs or sex or cheating or lying. Each of these things is a test of my faith, and I have to rely on God to keep from falling.

Fortunately, God makes 2 important promises for me to remember when I'm being tempted. First, he'll make sure the temptation is never more than I can bear. It might be more than I can handle by myself, but it can't possibly be more than God can handle. He's always there for me to lean on.

Second, God promises to give me a way out of the temptation. He'll show me the way if I ask. He's already given me a lot of advice in the Bible. Memorizing his Word helps me to know the right thing to do. Without God, I wouldn't have a chance against temptation. With God, I know I can stand strong.

Sarah age 14

❶ What are some ways God helps you escape temptation?

❷ Memorize 1 Corinthians 10:13 and repeat it to yourself when you feel tempted.

❸ Talk to God about the temptations you feel; ask him to help you resist them.

Turn to page 1387 for your next devotion.

the altar? [19]Do I mean then that a sacrifice offered to an idol is anything, or that an idol is anything? [20]No, but the sacrifices of pagans are offered to demons, not to God, and I do not want you to be participants with demons. [21]You cannot drink the cup of the Lord and the cup of demons too; you cannot have a part in both the Lord's table and the table of demons. [22]Are we trying to arouse the Lord's jealousy? Are we stronger than he?

The Believer's Freedom

[23]"Everything is permissible"—but not everything is beneficial. "Everything is permissible"—but not everything is constructive. [24]Nobody should seek his own good, but the good of others.

[25]Eat anything sold in the meat market without raising questions of conscience, [26]for, "The earth is the Lord's, and everything in it."[a]

[27]If some unbeliever invites you to a meal and you want to go, eat whatever is put before you without raising questions of conscience. [28]But if anyone says to you, "This has been offered in sacrifice," then do not eat it, both for the sake of the man who told you and for conscience' sake[b]— [29]the other man's conscience, I mean, not yours. For why should my freedom be judged by another's conscience? [30]If I take part in the meal with thankfulness, why am I denounced because of something I thank God for?

[31]So whether you eat or drink or whatever you do, do it all for the glory of God. [32]Do not cause anyone to stumble, whether Jews, Greeks or the church of God— [33]even as I try to please everybody in every way. For I am not seeking my own good but the good of many, so that they may be saved. [1]Follow my example, as I follow the example of Christ.

Propriety in Worship

[2]I praise you for remembering me in everything and for holding to the teachings,[c] just as I passed them on to you.

[3]Now I want you to realize that the head of every man is Christ, and the head of the woman is man, and the head of Christ is God. [4]Every man who prays or prophesies with his head covered dishonors his head. [5]And every woman who prays or prophesies with her head uncovered dishonors her head—it is just as though her head were shaved. [6]If a woman does not cover her head, she should have her hair cut off; and if it is a disgrace for a woman to have her hair cut or shaved off, she should cover her head. [7]A man ought not to cover his head,[d] since he is the image and glory of God; but the woman is the glory of man. [8]For man did not come from woman, but woman from man; [9]neither was man created for woman, but woman for man. [10]For this reason, and because of the angels, the woman ought to have a sign of authority on her head.

[11]In the Lord, however, woman is not independent of man, nor is man independent of woman. [12]For as woman came from man, so also man is born of woman. But everything comes from God. [13]Judge for yourselves: Is it proper for a woman to pray to God with her head uncovered? [14]Does not the very nature of things teach you that if a man has long hair, it is a disgrace to him, [15]but that if a woman has long hair, it is her glory? For long hair is given to her as a covering. [16]If anyone wants to be contentious about this, we have no other practice—nor do the churches of God.

The Lord's Supper

[17]In the following directives I have no praise for you, for your meetings do more harm than good. [18]In the first place, I hear that when you come together as a church, there are divisions among you, and to some extent I believe it. [19]No doubt there have to be differences among you to show which of you have God's approval. [20]When you come together, it is

---

a26 Psalm 24:1   *b28* Some manuscripts *conscience' sake, for "the earth is the Lord's and everything in it"*   *c2* Or *traditions*   *d4-7* Or *4Every man who prays or prophesies with long hair dishonors his head. 5And every woman who prays or prophesies with no covering of hair on her head dishonors her head—she is just like one of the "shorn women." 6If a woman has no covering, let her be for now with short hair, but since it is a disgrace for a woman to have her hair shorn or shaved, she should grow it again. 7A man ought not to have long hair*

not the Lord's Supper you eat, ²¹for as you eat, each of you goes ahead without waiting for anybody else. One remains hungry, another gets drunk. ²²Don't you have homes to eat and drink in? Or do you despise the church of God and humiliate those who have nothing? What shall I say to you? Shall I praise you for this? Certainly not!

²³For I received from the Lord what I also passed on to you: The Lord Jesus, on the night he was betrayed, took bread, ²⁴and when he had given thanks, he broke it and said, "This is my body, which is for you; do this in remembrance of me." ²⁵In the same way, after supper he took the cup, saying, "This cup is the new covenant in my blood; do this, whenever you drink it, in remembrance of me." ²⁶For whenever you eat this bread and drink this cup, you proclaim the Lord's death until he comes.

²⁷Therefore, whoever eats the bread or drinks the cup of the Lord in an unworthy manner will be guilty of sinning against the body and blood of the Lord. ²⁸A man ought to examine himself before he eats of the bread and drinks of the cup. ²⁹For anyone who eats and drinks without recognizing the body of the Lord eats and drinks judgment on himself. ³⁰That is why many among you are weak and sick, and a number of you have fallen asleep. ³¹But if we judged ourselves,

---

Week end.

Put Your Fruit-hat Away

Read 1 Corinthians 11:6–10

Don't get all worked up after you read this passage. You might think it's about women being second-class citizens in the church—but you'd be wrong! There are lots of people who misunderstand what this passage is about.

Here's the deal: Paul was writing about some women who were being a distraction in worship services. This would be like a woman sitting in your church wearing a 4-foot-tall hat with all kinds of fruit stuck all over it. That would definitely take away your focus from God. No one would even be looking at the pastor! God desires all of our attention, so that we can fully worship him.

Sometimes sitting in church isn't the most exciting thing in the world; but remember, the message is not always aimed just at you. What if God is trying to get a major message to the person next to you, but that person is too distracted by the disruption you and your friends are causing? On Tuesday, when Tommy talked about following God, he made it clear that he wasn't paying attention to what God wanted. Sure, God wants you to worship, and he wants to say stuff to you in church. But he also wants to say stuff to the people sitting around you—so don't be a distraction!

What about You?

❶ Have you ever noticed someone being a distraction during the service? What did he or she do?

❷ Look back at the last month and think about how you acted in worship. Is there anyone you sit next to that you probably shouldn't?

❸ Begin your worship time with a prayer to God asking him to help you get the most out of your worship time.

Turn to page 1389 for your next devotion.

we would not come under judgment.
[32]When we are judged by the Lord, we
are being disciplined so that we will not
be condemned with the world.

[33]So then, my brothers, when you
come together to eat, wait for each other.
[34]If anyone is hungry, he should eat at
home, so that when you meet together it
may not result in judgment.

And when I come I will give further directions.

Spiritual Gifts

12 Now about spiritual gifts, brothers,
I do not want you to be ignorant.

Your Gifts

Huh?

1 Corinthians 12:1

Don't you just love opening presents? The
excitement of not knowing what's inside
and the joy of seeing what you got is
awesome. Well, God has given each of us
special talents and abilities as gifts. Finding
out what they are is like tearing back the
wrapping paper—you see a little bit, then
a little more, until you see the whole gift.
So start rippin' that paper and explore the
gifts God has given you.

---

[2]You know that when you were pagans,
somehow or other you were influenced
and led astray to mute idols. [3]Therefore I
tell you that no one who is speaking by
the Spirit of God says, "Jesus be cursed,"
and no one can say, "Jesus is Lord," except by the Holy Spirit.

[4]There are different kinds of gifts, but
the same Spirit. [5]There are different kinds
of service, but the same Lord. [6]There are
different kinds of working, but the same
God works all of them in all men.

[7]Now to each one the manifestation of
the Spirit is given for the common good.
[8]To one there is given through the
Spirit the message of wisdom, to another
the message of knowledge by means of
the same Spirit, [9]to another faith by the
same Spirit, to another gifts of healing
by that one Spirit, [10]to another miracu-

lous powers, to another prophecy, to another distinguishing between spirits, to
another speaking in different kinds of
tongues,[a] and to still another the interpretation of tongues.[a] [11]All these are the
work of one and the same Spirit, and he
gives them to each one, just as he determines.

One Body, Many Parts

[12]The body is a unit, though it is made
up of many parts; and though all its parts
are many, they form one body. So it is
with Christ. [13]For we were all baptized
by[b] one Spirit into one body—whether
Jews or Greeks, slave or free—and we
were all given the one Spirit to drink.

[14]Now the body is not made up of one
part but of many. [15]If the foot should say,
"Because I am not a hand, I do not belong to the body," it would not for that
reason cease to be part of the body. [16]And
if the ear should say, "Because I am not
an eye, I do not belong to the body," it
would not for that reason cease to be
part of the body. [17]If the whole body were
an eye, where would the sense of hearing
be? If the whole body were an ear, where
would the sense of smell be? [18]But in fact
God has arranged the parts in the body,
every one of them, just as he wanted
them to be. [19]If they were all one part,
where would the body be? [20]As it is, there
are many parts, but one body.

[21]The eye cannot say to the hand, "I
don't need you!" And the head cannot
say to the feet, "I don't need you!" [22]On
the contrary, those parts of the body that
seem to be weaker are indispensable,
[23]and the parts that we think are less
honorable we treat with special honor.
And the parts that are unpresentable are
treated with special modesty, [24]while our
presentable parts need no special treatment. But God has combined the members of the body and has given greater
honor to the parts that lacked it, [25]so that
there should be no division in the body,
but that its parts should have equal concern for each other. [26]If one part suffers,
every part suffers with it; if one part is
honored, every part rejoices with it.

[27]Now you are the body of Christ, and

[a]10 Or languages; also in verse 28   [b]13 Or with; or in

each one of you is a part of it. ²⁸And in the church God has appointed first of all apostles, second prophets, third teachers, then workers of miracles, also those having gifts of healing, those able to help others, those with gifts of administration, and those speaking in different kinds of tongues. ²⁹Are all apostles? Are all prophets? Are all teachers? Do all work miracles? ³⁰Do all have gifts of healing? Do all speak in tongues*ᵃ*? Do all interpret? ³¹But eagerly desire*ᵇ* the greater gifts.

Love

And now I will show you the most excellent way.

13 If I speak in the tongues*ᶜ* of men and of angels, but have not love, I am only a resounding gong or a clanging cymbal. ²If I have the gift of prophecy and can fathom all mysteries and all knowledge, and if I have a faith that can move mountains, but have not love, I am

nothing. ³If I give all I possess to the poor and surrender my body to the flames,*ᵈ* but have not love, I gain nothing.

⁴Love is patient, love is kind. It does not envy, it does not boast, it is not proud. ⁵It is not rude, it is not self-seeking, it is not easily angered, it keeps no record of wrongs. ⁶Love does not delight in evil but rejoices with the truth. ⁷It always protects, always trusts, always hopes, always perseveres.

⁸Love never fails. But where there are prophecies, they will cease; where there are tongues, they will be stilled; where there is knowledge, it will pass away. ⁹For we know in part and we prophesy in part, ¹⁰but when perfection comes, the imperfect disappears. ¹¹When I was a child, I talked like a child, I thought like a

ᵃ30 Or other languages   ᵇ31 Or But you are eagerly desiring   ᶜ1 Or languages   ᵈ3 Some early manuscripts body that I may boast

---

Monday

God's Bod

Read 1 Corinthians 12:12–27

There's a kid I know from church who gets picked on a lot at school because he's a little weird. You know how it is: If someone is "different," they're going to get picked on. Well, one day, I saw some people picking on this kid, and I wondered why no one was doing anything about it. Finally, I told the other people to leave him alone. After that, I got teased too. But I don't regret sticking up for this kid. He might be different, but he deserves care and respect as much as anyone else.

Danielle age 12

Christians are all part of the body of Christ. So we need to remember that God made all of us different for a reason. Just like no part of your body is more important than the other parts, no person is more important than other people. In God's eyes, every person he created is special and has a purpose. It doesn't matter what color you are or how much money you have—in God's eyes, you matter.

What about You?

❶ Who are some of the people our society tells us are "important"? Who are the people God thinks are "important"?

❷ Try not using one of your arms for a few hours. What things are harder to do with only one arm? What does this exercise teach you about today's passage?

❸ Praise God for creating all kinds of people.

Turn to page 1390 for your next devotion.

child, I reasoned like a child. When I became a man, I put childish ways behind me. ¹²Now we see but a poor reflection as in a mirror; then we shall see face to face. Now I know in part; then I shall know fully, even as I am fully known.

¹³And now these three remain: faith, hope and love. But the greatest of these is love.

Gifts of Prophecy and Tongues

14 Follow the way of love and eagerly desire spiritual gifts, especially the gift of prophecy. ²For anyone who speaks in a tongue*a* does not speak to men but to God. Indeed, no one understands him; he utters mysteries with his spirit.*b* ³But everyone who prophesies speaks to men for their strengthening, encouragement and comfort. ⁴He who speaks in a tongue edifies himself, but he who prophe-

sies edifies the church. ⁵I would like every one of you to speak in tongues,*c* but I would rather have you prophesy. He who prophesies is greater than one who speaks in tongues,*c* unless he interprets, so that the church may be edified.

⁶Now, brothers, if I come to you and speak in tongues, what good will I be to you, unless I bring you some revelation or knowledge or prophecy or word of instruction? ⁷Even in the case of lifeless things that make sounds, such as the flute or harp, how will anyone know what tune is being played unless there is a distinction in the notes? ⁸Again, if the trumpet does not sound a clear call, who will get ready for battle? ⁹So it is with

*a*2 Or *another language*; also in verses 4, 13, 14, 19, 26 and 27　*b*2 Or *by the Spirit*　*c*5 Or *other languages*; also in verses 6, 18, 22, 23 and 39

Tuesday

You Call That Love?

Read 1 Corinthians 13:4–8

I was dating this guy named Keith, and he seemed like a totally great guy— a strong Christian involved in church and youth group. Then one night on a retreat we were all playing a night game where we hid in the woods while people looked for us with flashlights. I hid with Keith, and my friend Katie and her boyfriend hid with us.

We'd only been hiding a few minutes when Katie started making out with her boyfriend. Suddenly, Keith wanted to get real friendly with me too. Well, I got out of there in a hurry. I didn't want anything to do with that kind of stuff!

Keith's kind of "love" was about self-seeking pleasures. He wanted to see what he could get out of our dating relationship. But that's not the way God wants it to be. God wants us to think about what we can put into a relationship to build the other person up.

God wants us to love the way he loves, with patience, kindness and respect. Knowing about God's perfect love makes me want to be more like him in my relationships too.

Stacy, age 15

❶ What are some false definitions of "love"?

❷ Write down all the qualities of love mentioned in 1 Corinthians 13:4–8 (patient, kind, and so on); then write a way you could show each quality to people you love.

❸ Praise God for his perfect love.

Turn to page 1392 for your next devotion.

you. Unless you speak intelligible words with your tongue, how will anyone know what you are saying? You will just be speaking into the air. [10]Undoubtedly there are all sorts of languages in the world, yet none of them is without meaning. [11]If then I do not grasp the meaning of what someone is saying, I am a foreigner to the speaker, and he is a foreigner to me. [12]So it is with you. Since you are eager to have spiritual gifts, try to excel in gifts that build up the church.

[13]For this reason anyone who speaks in a tongue should pray that he may interpret what he says. [14]For if I pray in a tongue, my spirit prays, but my mind is unfruitful. [15]So what shall I do? I will pray with my spirit, but I will also pray with my mind; I will sing with my spirit, but I will also sing with my mind. [16]If you are praising God with your spirit, how can one who finds himself among those who do not understand[a] say "Amen" to your thanksgiving, since he does not know what you are saying? [17]You may be giving thanks well enough, but the other man is not edified.

[18]I thank God that I speak in tongues more than all of you. [19]But in the church I would rather speak five intelligible words to instruct others than ten thousand words in a tongue.

[20]Brothers, stop thinking like children. In regard to evil be infants, but in your thinking be adults. [21]In the Law it is written:

"Through men of strange tongues
    and through the lips of foreigners
I will speak to this people,
    but even then they will not listen
        to me,"[b]
says the Lord.

[22]Tongues, then, are a sign, not for believers but for unbelievers; prophecy, however, is for believers, not for unbelievers. [23]So if the whole church comes together and everyone speaks in tongues, and some who do not understand[c] or some unbelievers come in, will they not say that you are out of your mind? [24]But if an unbeliever or someone who does not understand[d] comes in while everybody is prophesying, he will be con-

vinced by all that he is a sinner and will be judged by all, [25]and the secrets of his heart will be laid bare. So he will fall down and worship God, exclaiming, "God is really among you!"

Orderly Worship

[26]What then shall we say, brothers? When you come together, everyone has a hymn, or a word of instruction, a revelation, a tongue or an interpretation. All of these must be done for the strengthening of the church. [27]If anyone speaks in a tongue, two—or at the most three—should speak, one at a time, and someone must interpret. [28]If there is no interpreter, the speaker should keep quiet in the church and speak to himself and God.

[29]Two or three prophets should speak, and the others should weigh carefully what is said. [30]And if a revelation comes to someone who is sitting down, the first speaker should stop. [31]For you can all prophesy in turn so that everyone may be instructed and encouraged. [32]The spirits of prophets are subject to the control of prophets. [33]For God is not a God of disorder but of peace.

As in all the congregations of the saints, [34]women should remain silent in the churches. They are not allowed to speak, but must be in submission, as the Law says. [35]If they want to inquire about something, they should ask their own husbands at home; for it is disgraceful for a woman to speak in the church.

[36]Did the word of God originate with you? Or are you the only people it has reached? [37]If anybody thinks he is a prophet or spiritually gifted, let him acknowledge that what I am writing to you is the Lord's command. [38]If he ignores this, he himself will be ignored.[e]

[39]Therefore, my brothers, be eager to prophesy, and do not forbid speaking in tongues. [40]But everything should be done in a fitting and orderly way.

The Resurrection of Christ

15 Now, brothers, I want to remind you of the gospel I preached to

---

[a]16 Or *among the inquirers*   [b]21 Isaiah 28:11,12
[c]23 Or *some inquirers*   [d]24 Or *or some inquirer*
[e]38 Some manuscripts *If he is ignorant of this, let him be ignorant*

you, which you received and on which you have taken your stand. ²By this gospel you are saved, if you hold firmly to the word I preached to you. Otherwise, you have believed in vain.

³For what I received I passed on to you as of first importance *ᵃ*: that Christ died for our sins according to the Scriptures, ⁴that he was buried, that he was raised on the third day according to the Scriptures, ⁵and that he appeared to Peter,*ᵇ* and then to the Twelve. ⁶After that, he appeared to more than five hundred of the brothers at the same time, most of whom are still living, though some have fallen asleep. ⁷Then he appeared to James, then to all the apostles, ⁸and last of all he appeared to me also, as to one abnormally born.

⁹For I am the least of the apostles and do not even deserve to be called an apostle, because I persecuted the church of God. ¹⁰But by the grace of God I am what I am, and his grace to me was not without effect. No, I worked harder than all of them—yet not I, but the grace of God that was with me. ¹¹Whether, then, it was I or they, this is what we preach, and this is what you believed.

The Resurrection of the Dead

¹²But if it is preached that Christ has been raised from the dead, how can some of you say that there is no resurrection of the dead? ¹³If there is no resurrection of the dead, then not even Christ has been raised. ¹⁴And if Christ has not been raised, our preaching is useless and so is your faith. ¹⁵More than that, we are then found to be false witnesses about God, for we have testified about God that he raised Christ from the dead. But he did not raise him if in fact the dead are not raised. ¹⁶For if the dead are not raised, then Christ has not been raised either. ¹⁷And if Christ has not been raised, your faith is futile; you are still in your sins. ¹⁸Then those also who have fallen asleep in Christ are lost. ¹⁹If only for this life we have hope in Christ, we are to be pitied more than all men.

ᵃ3 Or you at the first　*ᵇ5 Greek Cephas*

Wednesday

He's Alive!

Read 1 Corinthians 15:14–17

Some people don't believe the resurrection happened. But think about this: If Jesus didn't come back to life, our Christian faith would be useless. There wouldn't be any Easter. In fact, we would have nothing true to live for!

When Jesus died for us, all of our sins were forgiven. If he hadn't died, we'd still be stuck in our sins. And if he hadn't risen, it would be like sin won the battle—like death was stronger than God. That's not the kind of God we have!

Because Jesus rose, we can have faith in a *living* God, not a dead guy who's still in a tomb. Jesus' resurrection gives me something to live for. He took the punishment for my sins, and now I can spend eternity with him in heaven.

Meg age 14

❶ Why is Jesus' resurrection the most important miracle in the Bible?

❷ Imagine you were one of the people who saw Jesus after he came back to life. Write a letter to a friend describing what it was like to see him.

❸ Praise God for his awesome power over death!

Turn to page 1394 for your next devotion.

²⁰But Christ has indeed been raised from the dead, the firstfruits of those who have fallen asleep. ²¹For since death came through a man, the resurrection of the dead comes also through a man. ²²For as in Adam all die, so in Christ all will be

Homeward Bound

Huh?

1 Corinthians 15:20–22

Jesus is coming back. When he does, the bodies of those who were Christians and have already died are going to rise from the grave. Nice thought, huh? Will there be dead bodies flying all over the place? We don't know exactly how, but Jesus tells us that it *will* happen. He was the first resurrected, never to die again . . . and others will follow. They're going home—for good.

made alive. ²³But each in his own turn: Christ, the firstfruits; then, when he comes, those who belong to him. ²⁴Then the end will come, when he hands over the kingdom to God the Father after he has destroyed all dominion, authority and power. ²⁵For he must reign until he has put all his enemies under his feet. ²⁶The last enemy to be destroyed is death. ²⁷For he "has put everything under his feet."ᵃ Now when it says that "everything" has been put under him, it is clear that this does not include God himself, who put everything under Christ. ²⁸When he has done this, then the Son himself will be made subject to him who put everything under him, so that God may be all in all.

²⁹Now if there is no resurrection, what will those do who are baptized for the dead? If the dead are not raised at all, why are people baptized for them? ³⁰And as for us, why do we endanger ourselves every hour? ³¹I die every day—I mean that, brothers—just as surely as I glory over you in Christ Jesus our Lord. ³²If I fought wild beasts in Ephesus for merely human reasons, what have I gained? If the dead are not raised,

"Let us eat and drink,
    for tomorrow we die."ᵇ

³³Do not be misled: "Bad company corrupts good character." ³⁴Come back to your senses as you ought, and stop sinning; for there are some who are ignorant of God—I say this to your shame.

The Resurrection Body

³⁵But someone may ask, "How are the dead raised? With what kind of body will they come?" ³⁶How foolish! What you sow does not come to life unless it dies. ³⁷When you sow, you do not plant the body that will be, but just a seed, perhaps of wheat or of something else. ³⁸But God gives it a body as he has determined, and to each kind of seed he gives its own body. ³⁹All flesh is not the same: Men have one kind of flesh, animals have another, birds another and fish another. ⁴⁰There are also heavenly bodies and there are earthly bodies; but the splendor of the heavenly bodies is one kind, and the splendor of the earthly bodies is another. ⁴¹The sun has one kind of splendor, the moon another and the stars another; and star differs from star in splendor.

⁴²So will it be with the resurrection of the dead. The body that is sown is perishable, it is raised imperishable; ⁴³it is sown in dishonor, it is raised in glory; it is sown in weakness, it is raised in power; ⁴⁴it is sown a natural body, it is raised a spiritual body.

If there is a natural body, there is also a spiritual body. ⁴⁵So it is written: "The first man Adam became a living being"ᶜ; the last Adam, a life-giving spirit. ⁴⁶The spiritual did not come first, but the natural, and after that the spiritual. ⁴⁷The first man was of the dust of the earth, the second man from heaven. ⁴⁸As was the earthly man, so are those who are of the earth; and as is the man from heaven, so also are those who are of heaven. ⁴⁹And just as we have borne the likeness of the earthly man, so shall weᵈ bear the likeness of the man from heaven.

⁵⁰I declare to you, brothers, that flesh and blood cannot inherit the kingdom of

ᵃ27 Psalm 8:6   ᵇ32 Isaiah 22:13   ᶜ45 Gen. 2:7
ᵈ49 Some early manuscripts so let us

God, nor does the perishable inherit the imperishable. [51]Listen, I tell you a mystery: We will not all sleep, but we will all be changed— [52]in a flash, in the twinkling of an eye, at the last trumpet. For the trumpet will sound, the dead will be raised imperishable, and we will be changed. [53]For the perishable must clothe itself with the imperishable, and the mortal with immortality. [54]When the perishable has been clothed with the imperishable, and the mortal with immortality, then the saying that is written will come true: "Death has been swallowed up in victory."[a]

[55]"Where, O death, is your victory?
    Where, O death, is your sting?"[b]

[56]The sting of death is sin, and the power of sin is the law. [57]But thanks be to God! He gives us the victory through our Lord Jesus Christ.

[58]Therefore, my dear brothers, stand firm. Let nothing move you. Always give yourselves fully to the work of the Lord, because you know that your labor in the Lord is not in vain.

The Collection for God's People

16 Now about the collection for God's people: Do what I told the Galatian churches to do. [2]On the first day of every week, each one of you should set aside a sum of money in keeping with his income, saving it up, so that when I come no collections will have to be made. [3]Then, when I arrive, I will give letters of introduction to the men you approve and send them with your gift to Jerusalem. [4]If it seems advisable for me to go also, they will accompany me.

Personal Requests

[5]After I go through Macedonia, I will come to you—for I will be going through

_____
[a]54 Isaiah 25:8 [b]55 Hosea 13:14

Thursday

Peer Pressure

Read 1 Corinthians 15:33

Some of my friends and I used to hang around with a couple of girls who were always getting into trouble. It didn't take us long to realize we didn't want to be associated with them. We knew they would only be a bad influence on us. They didn't respect anyone, including themselves.

The people you hang out with affect the things you do. They also affect the way other people see you. So if you're with a group of people who have a bad attitude, you might just start to share their attitude. It's like being with someone who's got a cold. If you hang around with that person long enough, eventually you're probably going to catch a cold too.

My 3 best friends are strong Christians. They're the kind of friends who help me grow closer to God. And they're the best kind of friends to have.

Emily age 14

What about You?

❶ Do your friends help or hurt your faith? How can you find some friends who will encourage you to grow in your faith?

❷ Once a week, meet with 1 or 2 other Christian friends. Talk about things you're struggling with and find ways to encourage each other during the week.

❸ Ask God to help you find strong Christian friends, and ask him to help you be that type of friend too.

Turn to page 1398 for your next devotion.

Macedonia. [6]Perhaps I will stay with you awhile, or even spend the winter, so that you can help me on my journey, wherever I go. [7]I do not want to see you now and make only a passing visit; I hope to spend some time with you, if the Lord permits. [8]But I will stay on at Ephesus until Pentecost, [9]because a great door for effective work has opened to me, and there are many who oppose me.

[10]If Timothy comes, see to it that he has nothing to fear while he is with you, for he is carrying on the work of the Lord, just as I am. [11]No one, then, should refuse to accept him. Send him on his way in peace so that he may return to me. I am expecting him along with the brothers.

[12]Now about our brother Apollos: I strongly urged him to go to you with the brothers. He was quite unwilling to go now, but he will go when he has the opportunity.

[13]Be on your guard; stand firm in the faith; be men of courage; be strong. [14]Do everything in love.

[15]You know that the household of Stephanas were the first converts in Achaia, and they have devoted themselves to the service of the saints. I urge you, brothers, [16]to submit to such as these and to everyone who joins in the work, and labors at it. [17]I was glad when Stephanas, Fortunatus and Achaicus arrived, because they have supplied what was lacking from you. [18]For they refreshed my spirit and yours also. Such men deserve recognition.

Final Greetings

[19]The churches in the province of Asia send you greetings. Aquila and Priscilla[a] greet you warmly in the Lord, and so does the church that meets at their house. [20]All the brothers here send you greetings. Greet one another with a holy kiss.

[21]I, Paul, write this greeting in my own hand.

[22]If anyone does not love the Lord—a curse be on him. Come, O Lord[b]!

[23]The grace of the Lord Jesus be with you.

[24]My love to all of you in Christ Jesus. Amen.[c]

[a]19 Greek *Prisca*, a variant of *Priscilla*   [b]22 In Aramaic the expression *Come, O Lord* is *Marana tha*.   [c]24 Some manuscripts do not have *Amen*.

2 Corinthians

START

Ever have someone spread rumors about you or someone you know? That's exactly what was happening in the church at Corinth. As if they hadn't learned their lesson after Paul's first letter (1 Corinthians), a few people had been talking trash about Paul, the founder of their church. They were saying he wasn't good enough to be an apostle, that he thought he was better than everyone else and that he was a big wimp!

As you might guess, Paul was pretty frustrated about this. So he sent one of his most trusted buddies, Titus, to straighten out the trouble-makers. Titus rocked—he got the job done! Most of the people admitted they were wrong (although some kept talking about Paul behind his back). Paul was thrilled about their response. He wrote this letter to thank them for their turnaround. Paul also reminds the few who are still talking about him that God has put him in charge and they'd better learn to deal with it.

CAST OF Characters

Paul
The guy who wrote this book. He wanted everyone in the world to know about Jesus, so he went all over the place telling people. He started a bunch of the early churches, including this one in Corinth.

(CORE-inth)

The Church in Corinth, Corinthians
(Core-INTH-ee-uns)
The people who got this letter from Paul. Many of the Jesus-followers in the city of Corinth had been mad and upset at Paul, but most were sorry and wanted to make up with their spiritual leader.

Titus (TITE-us)
One of Paul's right hand men. Paul sent Titus to Corinth to take care of the church and deal with some problems, including attacks on Paul's reputation.

False Apostles (a.k.a. false brothers)
The few people who didn't think Paul was an apostle (God's man) and were leading the church at Corinth down the wrong path. A lot of people followed them at first, but then realized they were wrong and Paul was right.

What's UP with That?

You can often tell how important a book's subject is by how much it is mentioned.

Here are some words used in the book of 2 Corinthians. Order them from 1 to 8, beginning with the one you think is used most, then second most, and so on. The 8th one isn't even in the book! Oh, and by the way, it's an open book quiz.

_____ Comfort

_____ Heart(s)

_____ Ministry

_____ Sky Diving

_____ Christ('s)

_____ Boast(ing)

_____ Titus

_____ Apostle(s)

Snap shots

- It ain't been easy (chapter 1:1–11)

- Plan B (chapters 1:12—2:13)

- Ministry ins and outs (chapters 2:13—6:10)

- Get things right (chapters 6:11—7:16)

- Sweet cash (chapters 8—9)

- I'm not a wimp! (chapter 10)

- I'm the real deal! (chapters 11:1—12:13)

- Ready or not, here I come (chapter 12:14 to the end)

answers: #1 = Christ (59 times), #2 = Boast (28 times), #3 = Heart (17 times), #4 = Titus (10 times), #5 = Comfort (5 times), #6 = Ministry (8 times), #7 = Apostle (6 times), #8 = Sky Diving (0 times, duh!)

1 Paul, an apostle of Christ Jesus by the will of God, and Timothy our brother,

To the church of God in Corinth, together with all the saints throughout Achaia:

²Grace and peace to you from God our Father and the Lord Jesus Christ.

The God of All Comfort

³Praise be to the God and Father of our Lord Jesus Christ, the Father of compassion and the God of all comfort, ⁴who comforts us in all our troubles, so that we can comfort those in any trouble with the comfort we ourselves have received from God. ⁵For just as the sufferings of Christ flow over into our lives, so also through Christ our comfort overflows. ⁶If we are distressed, it is for your comfort and salvation; if we are comforted, it is for your comfort, which produces in you patient endurance of the same sufferings we suffer. ⁷And our hope for you is firm, because we know that just as you share

in our sufferings, so also you share in our comfort.

⁸We do not want you to be uninformed, brothers, about the hardships we suffered in the province of Asia. We were under great pressure, far beyond our ability to endure, so that we despaired even of life. ⁹Indeed, in our hearts we felt the sentence of death. But this happened that we might not rely on ourselves but on God, who raises the dead. ¹⁰He has delivered us from such a deadly peril, and he will deliver us. On him we have set our hope that he will continue to deliver us, ¹¹as you help us by your prayers. Then many will give thanks on our*a* behalf for the gracious favor granted us in answer to the prayers of many.

Paul's Change of Plans

¹²Now this is our boast: Our conscience testifies that we have conducted ourselves in the world, and especially in our

---

a 11 Many manuscripts *your*

Friday

My Comforter

Read 2 Corinthians 1:3–7

My mom is really sick right now. She's been in the hospital a lot, and the doctors ran a bunch of tests. I guess it's something about a tumor. But my parents won't even tell me how bad it is, which makes me worry even more. The only comfort I have right now is knowing God is in control.

Some people look for comfort in worldly things, but that's just a waste of time. The Bible tells me where to find comfort. If I go to Jesus Christ, he'll give me as much love and support as I could ever possibly need. Jesus gives us comfort to help us, but also so we can pass it on. Maybe some day one of my friends will have the same problems I do, and I'll be able to give comfort.

I might not understand why all this is happening to me. But I do know where to find comfort, no matter how bad it gets.

Cassy, age 15

What about You?

❶ What are some ways God uses other people to comfort you?

❷ Do you know anyone who might need comforting? Think of something you can do this week to share Christ's love with that person.

❸ Thank God for the ways he comforts you, and ask him to help you comfort others.

Turn to page 1400 for your next devotion.

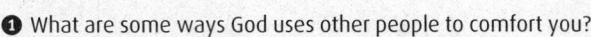

relations with you, in the holiness and sincerity that are from God. We have done so not according to worldly wisdom but according to God's grace. [13]For we do not write you anything you cannot read or understand. And I hope that, [14]as you have understood us in part, you will come to understand fully that you can boast of us just as we will boast of you in the day of the Lord Jesus.

[15]Because I was confident of this, I planned to visit you first so that you might benefit twice. [16]I planned to visit you on my way to Macedonia and to come back to you from Macedonia, and then to have you send me on my way to Judea. [17]When I planned this, did I do it lightly? Or do I make my plans in a worldly manner so that in the same breath I say, "Yes, yes" and "No, no"?

Change of Plans

Huh?

2 Corinthians 1:15–16

Paul had to change his travel plans and, boy, were some people in Corinth frustrated! Originally he was going to visit the Corinthians twice—before he went to Macedonia and after. But now he planned to pay them one long visit instead. Paul's enemies in Corinth began to claim that he was a liar who couldn't be trusted. In 2 Corinthians Paul takes time to explain that they could trust him and the Christ that he had described to them.

[18]But as surely as God is faithful, our message to you is not "Yes" and "No." [19]For the Son of God, Jesus Christ, who was preached among you by me and Silas[a] and Timothy, was not "Yes" and "No," but in him it has always been "Yes." [20]For no matter how many promises God has made, they are "Yes" in Christ. And so through him the "Amen" is spoken by us to the glory of God. [21]Now it is God who makes both us and you stand firm in Christ. He anointed us, [22]set his seal of ownership on us, and put his Spirit in our hearts as a deposit, guaranteeing what is to come.

[23]I call God as my witness that it was in order to spare you that I did not return to Corinth. [24]Not that we lord it over your faith, but we work with you for your joy, because it is by faith you stand firm. [2] [1]So I made up my mind that I would not make another painful visit to you. [2]For if I grieve you, who is left to make me glad but you whom I have grieved? [3]I wrote as I did so that when I came I should not be distressed by those who ought to make me rejoice. I had confidence in all of you, that you would all share my joy. [4]For I wrote you out of great distress and anguish of heart and with many tears, not to grieve you but to let you know the depth of my love for you.

Forgiveness for the Sinner

[5]If anyone has caused grief, he has not so much grieved me as he has grieved all of you, to some extent—not to put it too severely. [6]The punishment inflicted on him by the majority is sufficient for him. [7]Now instead, you ought to forgive and comfort him, so that he will not be overwhelmed by excessive sorrow. [8]I urge you, therefore, to reaffirm your love for him. [9]The reason I wrote you was to see if you would stand the test and be obedient in everything. [10]If you forgive anyone, I also forgive him. And what I have forgiven—if there was anything to forgive—I have forgiven in the sight of Christ for your sake, [11]in order that Satan might not

Who's the Mystery Man?

Huh?

2 Corinthians 2:5–11

Paul writes about a specific person who had obviously done something wrong in Corinth and had been disciplined by the church. Paul never tells us his name and never tells us what he did. But Paul does tell us the best way to respond once someone has admitted they were wrong: Paul urges the Corinthian church to forgive and accept him and welcome him back.

[a]19 Greek *Silvanus*, a variant of *Silas*

outwit us. For we are not unaware of his schemes.

Ministers of the New Covenant

[12]Now when I went to Troas to preach the gospel of Christ and found that the Lord had opened a door for me, [13]I still had no peace of mind, because I did not find my brother Titus there. So I said good-by to them and went on to Macedonia.

[14]But thanks be to God, who always leads us in triumphal procession in Christ and through us spreads everywhere the fragrance of the knowledge of him. [15]For we are to God the aroma of Christ among those who are being saved and those who are perishing. [16]To the one we are the smell of death; to the other, the fragrance of life. And who is equal to such a task? [17]Unlike so many, we do not peddle the word of God for profit. On the

Weekend.

Big-time Dead
Read Luke 23:44–49 (page 1261)

Meg is one smart 14-year-old. Check out what she wrote in Wednesday's devotion. She knows that if the resurrection didn't really happen, we're wasting our time putting our faith in Jesus. Jesus was seen by lots of people after he rose from the dead—in fact, over 500! So many people saw him that, if you believe the Bible, you cannot question whether Jesus was alive after the crucifixion. But much like some people say Jesus never rose from the dead, others say he never even died. An example of this is the Koran (the Muslim bible), which says that Jesus only pretended to be dead.

Here's what you need to understand to know that Jesus really died:
1. Jesus survived a Roman scourging. A scourging meant being beaten with a 3-lash whip with pieces of bone and glass stuck on the ends. This ripped open the skin and exposed muscles.
2. A crown of thorns was pushed into his head.
3. Jesus had nails driven through his wrists, which damaged major arteries.
4. Jesus was stabbed in the side with a spear by a Roman soldier who was trained to know just where to stick it. This would have been enough to kill him all by itself!
5. Finally Jesus said, "Father, into your hands I commit my spirit." Then he hung his head down, breathed his last breath . . . and died.

Jesus really died (and rose again)! There are too many recorded facts to ignore. Point out these facts to skeptics and maybe they'll begin to think more about whether or not God exists. Then they will need to face the big question: If Jesus said he was going to die and then be raised, and it really happened, what else did he say that I need to know?

❶ What would you say to a person who claims they believe Jesus lived and died but doesn't believe he rose again?

❷ Take time to memorize John 3:16 (page 1271). It'll help you tell others about Jesus.

❸ Pray that God will prepare that person's heart for what you will share with them.

Turn to page 1402 for your next devotion.

contrary, in Christ we speak before God with sincerity, like men sent from God.

3 Are we beginning to commend ourselves again? Or do we need, like some people, letters of recommendation to you or from you? ²You yourselves are our letter, written on our hearts, known and read by everybody. ³You show that you are a letter from Christ, the result of our ministry, written not with ink but with the Spirit of the living God, not on tablets of stone but on tablets of human hearts.

⁴Such confidence as this is ours through Christ before God. ⁵Not that we are competent in ourselves to claim anything for ourselves, but our competence comes from God. ⁶He has made us competent as ministers of a new covenant—not of the letter but of the Spirit; for the letter kills, but the Spirit gives life.

The Glory of the New Covenant

⁷Now if the ministry that brought death, which was engraved in letters on stone, came with glory, so that the Israelites could not look steadily at the face of Moses because of its glory, fading though it was, ⁸will not the ministry of the Spirit be even more glorious? ⁹If the ministry that condemns men is glorious, how much more glorious is the ministry that brings righteousness! ¹⁰For what was glorious has no glory now in comparison with the surpassing glory. ¹¹And if what was fading away came with glory, how much greater is the glory of that which lasts!

¹²Therefore, since we have such a hope, we are very bold. ¹³We are not like Moses, who would put a veil over his face to keep the Israelites from gazing at it while the radiance was fading away. ¹⁴But their minds were made dull, for to this day the same veil remains when the old covenant is read. It has not been removed, because only in Christ is it taken away. ¹⁵Even to this day when Moses is read, a veil covers their hearts. ¹⁶But whenever anyone turns to the Lord, the veil is taken away. ¹⁷Now the Lord is the Spirit, and where the Spirit of the Lord is, there is freedom. ¹⁸And we, who with unveiled faces all reflect[a] the Lord's glory, are being transformed into his like-

ness with ever-increasing glory, which comes from the Lord, who is the Spirit.

Treasures in Jars of Clay

4 Therefore, since through God's mercy we have this ministry, we do not lose heart. ²Rather, we have renounced secret and shameful ways; we do not use deception, nor do we distort the word of God. On the contrary, by setting forth the truth plainly we commend ourselves to every man's conscience in the sight of God. ³And even if our gospel is veiled, it is veiled to those who are perishing. ⁴The god of this age has blinded the minds of unbelievers, so that they cannot see the light of the gospel of the glory of Christ, who is the image of God. ⁵For we do not preach ourselves, but Jesus Christ as Lord, and ourselves as your servants for Jesus' sake. ⁶For God, who said, "Let light shine out of darkness,"[b] made his light shine in our hearts to give us the light of the knowledge of the glory of God in the face of Christ.

⁷But we have this treasure in jars of clay to show that this all-surpassing power is from God and not from us. ⁸We are hard pressed on every side, but not crushed; perplexed, but not in despair; ⁹persecuted, but not abandoned; struck

---

No More Veils

Huh?

2 Corinthians 3:13–16

The "old covenant," or the Old Testament, was very important to the Israelites back in Paul's time; it's still important to all of us today. But the Bible doesn't stop at Malachi, the last book of the Old Testament. Jesus has come, and he has brought a "new covenant" that we read about in the New Testament. Paul describes the folks who still don't understand the importance of the new covenant as wearing a veil over their faces (they can't see clearly). Only through Jesus Christ is the veil ripped away. Then the new covenant makes sense.

---

a 18 Or *contemplate*　*b 6* Gen. 1:3

down, but not destroyed. ¹⁰We always carry around in our body the death of Jesus, so that the life of Jesus may also be revealed in our body. ¹¹For we who are alive are always being given over to death for Jesus' sake, so that his life may be revealed in our mortal body. ¹²So then, death is at work in us, but life is at work in you.

¹³It is written: "I believed; therefore I have spoken."ᵃ With that same spirit of faith we also believe and therefore speak, ¹⁴because we know that the one who raised the Lord Jesus from the dead will also raise us with Jesus and present us with you in his presence. ¹⁵All this is for your benefit, so that the grace that is reaching more and more people may cause thanksgiving to overflow to the glory of God.

¹⁶Therefore we do not lose heart. Though outwardly we are wasting away, yet inwardly we are being renewed day by day. ¹⁷For our light and momentary troubles are achieving for us an eternal glory that far outweighs them all. ¹⁸So we fix our eyes not on what is seen, but on what is unseen. For what is seen is temporary, but what is unseen is eternal.

Our Heavenly Dwelling

5 Now we know that if the earthly tent we live in is destroyed, we have a building from God, an eternal house in heaven, not built by human hands. ²Meanwhile we groan, longing to be clothed with our heavenly dwelling, ³because when we are clothed, we will not be found naked. ⁴For while we are in this tent, we groan and are burdened, because we do not wish to be unclothed but to be clothed with our heavenly dwelling, so that what is mortal may be swallowed up by life. ⁵Now it is God who has

ᵃ13 Psalm 116:10

Monday

Jars of Clay

Read 2 Corinthians 4:7

I like to think I'm good at things. But one time I tried to lead a Bible study at my school, and I wasn't very good at it. I think I was trying to impress people with how much I knew, instead of just leading the discussion. These verses help me remember that it's God who's great, not me. I'm just his servant.

It's an amazing honor that God chooses us to tell others about him. He's so powerful that he can pick all kinds of ways to tell people about himself. But he chooses to use us—people who sin, who mess up, who struggle to follow God. God wants us to serve him and share his love with everyone we meet. We are just ordinary, imperfect people, but God can do amazing things through us.

That's really encouraging to me. I know that God is in me and working through me all the time.

Katy age 15

What about You?

❶ Why do you think God chooses ordinary people to spread his love? How do you feel about carrying the "treasure" of the gospel?

❷ Dig around in your basement for a little clay pot or bowl. Put it where you'll see it every day. Whenever you look at it, remember that God chose *you* to spread his message of love.

❸ Thank God for the great honor of serving him and sharing him with the world.

Turn to page 1403 for your next devotion.

made us for this very purpose and has given us the Spirit as a deposit, guaranteeing what is to come.

⁶Therefore we are always confident and know that as long as we are at home in the body we are away from the Lord. ⁷We live by faith, not by sight. ⁸We are confident, I say, and would prefer to be away from the body and at home with the Lord. ⁹So we make it our goal to please him, whether we are at home in the body or away from it. ¹⁰For we must all appear before the judgment seat of Christ, that each one may receive what is due him for the things done while in the body, whether good or bad.

The Ministry of Reconciliation

¹¹Since, then, we know what it is to fear the Lord, we try to persuade men. What we are is plain to God, and I hope it is also plain to your conscience. ¹²We are not trying to commend ourselves to you again, but are giving you an opportunity to take pride in us, so that you can an-

swer those who take pride in what is seen rather than in what is in the heart. ¹³If we are out of our mind, it is for the sake of God; if we are in our right mind, it is for you. ¹⁴For Christ's love compels us, because we are convinced that one died for all, and therefore all died. ¹⁵And he died for all, that those who live should no longer live for themselves but for him who died for them and was raised again.

¹⁶So from now on we regard no one from a worldly point of view. Though we once regarded Christ in this way, we do so no longer. ¹⁷Therefore, if anyone is in Christ, he is a new creation; the old has gone, the new has come! ¹⁸All this is from God, who reconciled us to himself through Christ and gave us the ministry of reconciliation: ¹⁹that God was reconciling the world to himself in Christ, not counting men's sins against them. And he has committed to us the message of reconciliation. ²⁰We are therefore Christ's ambassadors, as though God were making his appeal through us. We

---

Tuesday

New and Improved

Read 2 Corinthians 5:17

Until a few years ago, I didn't know what being a Christian really meant. I would show up at church and go through the motions, but I didn't really understand what God wanted from me. Then I started getting more serious about my faith and learning more about God and how much he loves me. I read my Bible more. I prayed more. I got baptized. And I started to see the Lord in a new light. Now I strive to be more like him every day.

I think it's really awesome how God can turn someone's life around. When we accept Jesus as our Savior, we become totally different people than we were before. The old junk is gone, and we have the chance to start all over again.

Experiencing a new life in Jesus Christ has given me the confidence to trust God with everything. If he can change my heart, I know he can do anything.

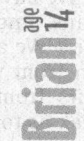
Brian age 14

What about You?

❶ What were you like before you became a Christian? How are you different now?

❷ Make a change in your life. Rearrange your room or eat something different for lunch. How does it feel to try something new?

❸ Praise God for the new life he's given you in Christ.

Turn to page 1405 for your next devotion.

implore you on Christ's behalf: Be reconciled to God. [21] God made him who had no sin to be sin[a] for us, so that in him we might become the righteousness of God.

6 As God's fellow workers we urge you not to receive God's grace in vain. [2] For he says,

> "In the time of my favor I heard you,
> and in the day of salvation I helped
> you."[b]

I tell you, now is the time of God's favor, now is the day of salvation.

Paul's Hardships

[3] We put no stumbling block in anyone's path, so that our ministry will not be discredited. [4] Rather, as servants of God we commend ourselves in every way: in great endurance; in troubles, hardships and distresses; [5] in beatings, imprisonments and riots; in hard work, sleepless nights and hunger; [6] in purity, understanding, patience and kindness; in the Holy Spirit and in sincere love; [7] in truthful speech and in the power of God; with weapons of righteousness in the right hand and in the left; [8] through glory and dishonor, bad report and good report; genuine, yet regarded as impostors; [9] known, yet regarded as unknown; dying, and yet we live on; beaten, and yet not killed; [10] sorrowful, yet always rejoicing; poor, yet making many rich; having nothing, and yet possessing everything.

[11] We have spoken freely to you, Corinthians, and opened wide our hearts to you. [12] We are not withholding our affection from you, but you are withholding yours from us. [13] As a fair exchange—I speak as to my children—open wide your hearts also.

Do Not Be Yoked With Unbelievers

[14] Do not be yoked together with unbelievers. For what do righteousness and wickedness have in common? Or what fellowship can light have with darkness? [15] What harmony is there between Christ and Belial[c]? What does a believer have in common with an unbeliever? [16] What agreement is there between the temple of God and idols? For we are the temple of the living God. As God has said: "I will live with them and walk among them,

Tied Together

Huh?

2 Corinthians 6:14

When you hear "yoke" you probably think of an egg "yolk." Well, in this verse Paul is talking about the kind of yoke that farmers use to tie together cows and then steer them in the same direction. Paul warns Christians to beware of being too closely tied to someone who is going to steer you in a wrong direction and away from God!

and I will be their God, and they will be my people."[d]

[17] "Therefore come out from them
　and be separate,
　　　　　says the Lord.
Touch no unclean thing,
　and I will receive you."[e]
[18] "I will be a Father to you,
　and you will be my sons and
　　daughters,
　　　　　says the Lord Almighty."[f]

7 Since we have these promises, dear friends, let us purify ourselves from everything that contaminates body and spirit, perfecting holiness out of reverence for God.

Paul's Joy

[2] Make room for us in your hearts. We have wronged no one, we have corrupted no one, we have exploited no one. [3] I do not say this to condemn you; I have said before that you have such a place in our hearts that we would live or die with you. [4] I have great confidence in you; I take great pride in you. I am greatly encouraged; in all our troubles my joy knows no bounds.

[5] For when we came into Macedonia, this body of ours had no rest, but we were harassed at every turn—conflicts on the outside, fears within. [6] But God, who

---

[a] 21 Or *be a sin offering*　[b] 2 Isaiah 49:8　[c] 15 Greek *Beliar*, a variant of *Belial*　[d] 16 Lev. 26:12; Jer. 32:38; Ezek. 37:27　[e] 17 Isaiah 52:11; Ezek. 20:34,41　[f] 18 2 Samuel 7:14; 7:8

comforts the downcast, comforted us by the coming of Titus, [7]and not only by his coming but also by the comfort you had given him. He told us about your longing for me, your deep sorrow, your ardent concern for me, so that my joy was greater than ever.

[8]Even if I caused you sorrow by my letter, I do not regret it. Though I did regret it—I see that my letter hurt you, but only for a little while— [9]yet now I am happy, not because you were made sorry, but because your sorrow led you to repentance. For you became sorrowful as God intended and so were not harmed in any way by us. [10]Godly sorrow brings repentance that leads to salvation and leaves no regret, but worldly sorrow brings death. [11]See what this godly sorrow has produced in you: what earnestness, what eagerness to clear yourselves, what indignation, what alarm, what longing, what concern, what readiness to see justice done. At every point you have proved yourselves to be innocent in this matter. [12]So even though I wrote to you, it was not on account of the one who did the wrong or of the injured party, but rather that before God you could see for yourselves how devoted to us you are. [13]By all this we are encouraged.

In addition to our own encouragement, we were especially delighted to see how happy Titus was, because his spirit has been refreshed by all of you. [14]I had boasted to him about you, and you have not embarrassed me. But just as everything we said to you was true, so our boasting about you to Titus has proved to be true as well. [15]And his affection for you is all the greater when he remembers that you were all obedient, receiving him with fear and trembling. [16]I am glad I can have complete confidence in you.

Generosity Encouraged

8 And now, brothers, we want you to know about the grace that God has given the Macedonian churches. [2]Out of the most severe trial, their overflowing joy and their extreme poverty welled up in rich generosity. [3]For I testify that they gave as much as they were able, and even beyond their ability. Entirely on

---

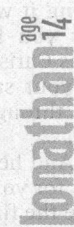

Wednesday

The Friendship Factor

Read 2 Corinthians 7:5–7

Everybody has bad days—when they're stressed out about a decision, when someone cuts them down or when they just don't feel very good. On my bad days, I've found that turning to a friend goes a long way. It means a lot to me when someone notices that I'm down in the dumps and cheers me up. It helps me know that my friend cares for me.

Someone once told me God speaks to us in our struggles but shouts to us in our tragedies. He's always there, but he wants to make extra sure we *know* he's there when we hurt. One of the ways he shows us is by sending help, and one of the ways he sends help is through our friends.

So if you have something that's bugging you, or if you feel horrible or sad about something, talk to God about it, then share it with a friend. You'll feel a lot better when you know you're not alone.

Jonathan age 14

❶ Think of a time you cheered up a friend. Was it easy? Was it worth it?

❷ Give someone a note or a word of encouragement this week.

❸ Thank God for his gift of friends.

Turn to page 1407 for your next devotion.

their own, [4]they urgently pleaded with us for the privilege of sharing in this service to the saints. [5]And they did not do as we expected, but they gave themselves first to the Lord and then to us in keeping with God's will. [6]So we urged Titus, since he had earlier made a beginning, to bring also to completion this act of grace on

A Complete Collection

Huh?

2 Corinthians 8:6

More than a year before this was written, Titus started collecting money from the Corinthians to give to the poor Christians in Jerusalem. Because of all the division and accusations in the Corinthian church, no one had given any money in a while. Paul sent Titus back to the Corinthians to give people a chance to give some more money and make the collection full and complete. (If you read 2 Corinthians 9:12-13, you'll see that the Corinthians responded big-time.)

your part. [7]But just as you excel in everything—in faith, in speech, in knowledge, in complete earnestness and in your love for us[a]—see that you also excel in this grace of giving.

[8]I am not commanding you, but I want to test the sincerity of your love by comparing it with the earnestness of others. [9]For you know the grace of our Lord Jesus Christ, that though he was rich, yet for your sakes he became poor, so that you through his poverty might become rich.

[10]And here is my advice about what is best for you in this matter: Last year you were the first not only to give but also to have the desire to do so. [11]Now finish the work, so that your eager willingness to do it may be matched by your completion of it, according to your means. [12]For if the willingness is there, the gift is acceptable according to what one has, not according to what he does not have.

[13]Our desire is not that others might be relieved while you are hard pressed, but that there might be equality. [14]At the present time your plenty will supply what they need, so that in turn their plenty will supply what you need. Then there will be equality, [15]as it is written: "He who gathered much did not have too much, and he who gathered little did not have too little."[b]

Titus Sent to Corinth

[16]I thank God, who put into the heart of Titus the same concern I have for you. [17]For Titus not only welcomed our appeal, but he is coming to you with much enthusiasm and on his own initiative. [18]And we are sending along with him the brother who is praised by all the churches for his service to the gospel. [19]What is more, he was chosen by the churches to accompany us as we carry the offering, which we administer in order to honor the Lord himself and to show our eagerness to help. [20]We want to avoid any criticism of the way we administer this liberal gift. [21]For we are taking pains to do what is right, not only in the eyes of the Lord but also in the eyes of men.

[22]In addition, we are sending with them our brother who has often proved to us in many ways that he is zealous, and now even more so because of his great confidence in you. [23]As for Titus, he is my partner and fellow worker among you; as for our brothers, they are representatives of the churches and an honor to Christ. [24]Therefore show these men the proof of your love and the reason for our pride in you, so that the churches can see it.

9 There is no need for me to write to you about this service to the saints. [2]For I know your eagerness to help, and I have been boasting about it to the Macedonians, telling them that since last year you in Achaia were ready to give; and your enthusiasm has stirred most of them to action. [3]But I am sending the brothers in order that our boasting about you in this matter should not prove hollow, but that you may be ready, as I said you would be. [4]For if any Macedonians come with me and find you unprepared, we—

[a]7 Some manuscripts in our love for you
[b]15 Exodus 16:18

not to say anything about you—would be ashamed of having been so confident. [5]So I thought it necessary to urge the brothers to visit you in advance and finish the arrangements for the generous gift you had promised. Then it will be ready as a generous gift, not as one grudgingly given.

Sowing Generously

[6]Remember this: Whoever sows sparingly will also reap sparingly, and whoever sows generously will also reap generously. [7]Each man should give what he has decided in his heart to give, not reluctantly or under compulsion, for God loves a cheerful giver. [8]And God is able to make all grace abound to you, so that in all things at all times, having all that you need, you will abound in every good work. [9]As it is written:

"He has scattered abroad his gifts to the poor;
his righteousness endures forever."[a]

[10]Now he who supplies seed to the sower and bread for food will also supply and increase your store of seed and will enlarge the harvest of your righteousness. [11]You will be made rich in every way so that you can be generous on every occasion, and through us your generosity will result in thanksgiving to God.

[12]This service that you perform is not only supplying the needs of God's people but is also overflowing in many expressions of thanks to God. [13]Because of the service by which you have proved yourselves, men will praise God for the obedience that accompanies your confession of the gospel of Christ, and for your generosity in sharing with them and with everyone else. [14]And in their prayers for you their hearts will go out to you, because of the surpassing grace God has given you. [15]Thanks be to God for his indescribable gift!

[a]9 Psalm 112:9

Thursday

Give It Away!

Read 2 Corinthians 9:6–7

After our outreach events, our youth leader asks each of us to make a phone call to 2 of the new people who came to the event, whether we know them or not.

Some weeks I'm not too thrilled about spending my time and energy calling total strangers. But these verses remind me that people who give a lot are the ones who really make a difference. And when I think about it, it's true—when I give up some of my time to call someone, that person's a lot more likely to come back to youth group. So I give up 5 minutes, but I get the great feeling that I've done something good for someone else.

What I need to work on is having a positive attitude every time I call someone. Being a cheerful giver means serving others, not because you have to, but because you want to. And that's the kind of giving God really loves.

Meg, age 14

❶ A lot of people give money to the church as an offering. But an offering doesn't have to be just money. What else can you give to your church or youth group?

❷ Ask someone in your family what you can do to help them today.

❸ Ask God to help you be a more cheerful giver.

Turn to page 1410 for your next devotion.

Paul's Defense of His Ministry

10 By the meekness and gentleness of Christ, I appeal to you—I, Paul, who am "timid" when face to face with you, but "bold" when away! [2]I beg you that when I come I may not have to be as bold as I expect to be toward some people who think that we live by the standards of this world. [3]For though we live in the world, we do not wage war as the world does. [4]The weapons we fight with are not the weapons of the world. On the contrary, they have divine power to demolish strongholds. [5]We demolish arguments and every pretension that sets itself up against the knowledge of God, and we take captive every thought to make it obedient to Christ. [6]And we will be ready to punish every act of disobedience, once your obedience is complete.

[7]You are looking only on the surface of things.[a] If anyone is confident that he belongs to Christ, he should consider again that we belong to Christ just as much as he. [8]For even if I boast somewhat freely about the authority the Lord gave us for building you up rather than pulling you down, I will not be ashamed of it. [9]I do not want to seem to be trying to frighten you with my letters. [10]For some say, "His letters are weighty and forceful, but in person he is unimpressive and his speaking amounts to nothing." [11]Such people should realize that what we are in our letters when we are absent, we will be in our actions when we are present.

[12]We do not dare to classify or compare ourselves with some who commend themselves. When they measure themselves by themselves and compare themselves with themselves, they are not wise. [13]We, however, will not boast beyond proper limits, but will confine our boasting to the field God has assigned to us, a field that reaches even to you. [14]We are not going too far in our boasting, as would be the case if we had not come to you, for we did get as far as you with the gospel of Christ. [15]Neither do we go beyond our limits by boasting of work done by others.[b] Our hope is that, as your faith continues to grow, our area of activity among you will greatly expand, [16]so that we can preach the gospel in the regions beyond you. For we do not want to boast about work already done in another man's territory. [17]But, "Let him who boasts boast in the Lord."[c] [18]For it is not the one who commends himself who is approved, but the one whom the Lord commends.

Paul and the False Apostles

11 I hope you will put up with a little of my foolishness; but you are already doing that. [2]I am jealous for you with a godly jealousy. I promised you to one husband, to Christ, so that I might present you as a pure virgin to him. [3]But I am afraid that just as Eve was deceived by the serpent's cunning, your minds may somehow be led astray from your sincere and pure devotion to Christ. [4]For if someone comes to you and preaches a Jesus other than the Jesus we preached, or if you receive a different spirit from the one you received, or a different gospel from the one you accepted, you put up with it easily enough. [5]But I do not think I am in the least inferior to those "super-apostles." [6]I may not be a trained speaker, but I do have knowledge. We

Corinthian "Supermen"

Huh?

2 Corinthians 11:5

Look! Up in the air—is it a bird or a plane? No, it's the Corinthian supermen. Well, not exactly. When Paul refers to people as "super-apostles," he's being sarcastic. Instead of being super great, these teachers were super lame. They bragged about themselves and how holy they were. Paul makes it clear that this is not what any Christian is supposed to do.

---

a7 Or Look at the obvious facts   *b13–15 Or* [13]*We, however, will not boast about things that cannot be measured, but we will boast according to the standard of measurement that the God of measure has assigned us—a measurement that relates even to you.* [14] *. . .* [15]*Neither do we boast about things that cannot be measured in regard to the work done by others.*   *c17 Jer. 9:24*

have made this perfectly clear to you in every way.

⁷Was it a sin for me to lower myself in order to elevate you by preaching the gospel of God to you free of charge? ⁸I robbed other churches by receiving support from them so as to serve you. ⁹And when I was with you and needed something, I was not a burden to anyone, for the brothers who came from Macedonia supplied what I needed. I have kept myself from being a burden to you in any way, and will continue to do so. ¹⁰As surely as the truth of Christ is in me, nobody in the regions of Achaia will stop this boasting of mine. ¹¹Why? Because I do not love you? God knows I do! ¹²And I will keep on doing what I am doing in order to cut the ground from under those who want an opportunity to be considered equal with us in the things they boast about.

¹³For such men are false apostles, deceitful workmen, masquerading as apostles of Christ. ¹⁴And no wonder, for Satan himself masquerades as an angel of light. ¹⁵It is not surprising, then, if his servants masquerade as servants of righteousness. Their end will be what their actions deserve.

Paul Boasts About His Sufferings

¹⁶I repeat: Let no one take me for a fool. But if you do, then receive me just as you would a fool, so that I may do a little boasting. ¹⁷In this self-confident boasting I am not talking as the Lord would, but as a fool. ¹⁸Since many are boasting in the way the world does, I too will boast. ¹⁹You gladly put up with fools since you are so wise! ²⁰In fact, you even put up with anyone who enslaves you or exploits you or takes advantage of you or pushes himself forward or slaps you in the face. ²¹To my shame I admit that we were too weak for that!

What anyone else dares to boast about—I am speaking as a fool—I also dare to boast about. ²²Are they Hebrews? So am I. Are they Israelites? So am I. Are they Abraham's descendants? So am I. ²³Are they servants of Christ? (I am out of my mind to talk like this.) I am more. I have worked much harder, been in prison more frequently, been flogged more se-

verely, and been exposed to death again and again. ²⁴Five times I received from the Jews the forty lashes minus one. ²⁵Three times I was beaten with rods, once I was stoned, three times I was shipwrecked, I spent a night and a day in the open sea, ²⁶I have been constantly on the move. I have been in danger from rivers, in danger from bandits, in danger from my own countrymen, in danger from Gentiles; in danger in the city, in danger in the country, in danger at sea; and in danger from false brothers. ²⁷I have labored and toiled and have often gone without sleep; I have known hunger and thirst and have often gone without food; I have been cold and naked. ²⁸Besides everything else, I face daily the pressure of my concern for all the churches. ²⁹Who is weak, and I do not feel weak? Who is led into sin, and I do not inwardly burn?

³⁰If I must boast, I will boast of the things that show my weakness. ³¹The God and Father of the Lord Jesus, who is to be praised forever, knows that I am not lying. ³²In Damascus the governor under King Aretas had the city of the Damascenes guarded in order to arrest me. ³³But I was lowered in a basket from a window in the wall and slipped through his hands.

Paul's Vision and His Thorn

12 I must go on boasting. Although there is nothing to be gained, I will go on to visions and revelations from the Lord. ²I know a man in Christ who fourteen years ago was caught up to the third heaven. Whether it was in the body or out of the body I do not know—God knows. ³And I know that this man—whether in the body or apart from the body I do not know, but God knows—⁴was caught up to paradise. He heard inexpressible things, things that man is not permitted to tell. ⁵I will boast about a man like that, but I will not boast about myself, except about my weaknesses. ⁶Even if I should choose to boast, I would not be a fool, because I would be speaking the truth. But I refrain, so no one will think more of me than is warranted by what I do or say.

⁷To keep me from becoming conceited

because of these surpassingly great revelations, there was given me a thorn in my flesh, a messenger of Satan, to torment me. ⁸Three times I pleaded with the Lord to take it away from me. ⁹But he said to me, "My grace is sufficient for you, for my power is made perfect in weakness." Therefore I will boast all the more gladly about my weaknesses, so that Christ's power may rest on me. ¹⁰That is why, for Christ's sake, I delight in weaknesses, in insults, in hardships, in persecutions, in difficulties. For when I am weak, then I am strong.

Paul's Concern for the Corinthians

¹¹I have made a fool of myself, but you drove me to it. I ought to have been commended by you, for I am not in the least inferior to the "super-apostles," even though I am nothing. ¹²The things that mark an apostle—signs, wonders and miracles—were done among you with great perseverance. ¹³How were you infe-

Funny Paul

Huh?

2 Corinthians 12:14–18
What does Paul mean when he writes, "I caught you by trickery"? Has our friend Paul become our sneaky enemy? Not at all. Paul is being sarcastic in repeating the charges that were being made against him by the false teachers in Corinth. They claimed he pocketed some of the money he was collecting for believers in Jerusalem. Paul makes it clear that he never tricked anybody and that everything he did, he did for their good.

Friday

God's Strength
Read 2 Corinthians 12:9–10

I learned a lesson about weakness when I was hit by a bus on my way home from school. I was in the hospital for a month and in a body cast for 6 weeks. I couldn't do anything by myself. Even after the cast came off, it was a long time before I could move around without help. I had to depend on my family and friends for everything.

As I got better, it was clear to me that the people who stood by me when I was hurt were the people who really loved me and cared about me.

The same thing is true when I'm spiritually weak. This is a time in my life when I'm going through so many changes and struggles. My weaknesses as a Christian seem to be magnified right now.

But our God is a great God. He can use my struggles to show me how much he cares for me. When things are going my way, I sometimes forget to lean on God. But when I see how God is there for me during my hard times, it gives me a passion for him and a desire to draw closer to him, even when life's good.

Mike age 14

What about You?

❶ Think about a time you really needed to lean on God. How did God work in your life?

❷ Write about a time you felt God gave you the strength to do something. Read this story the next time you lose confidence.

❸ Ask God to use you, even when you're struggling.

Turn to page 1411 for your next devotion.

rior to the other churches, except that I was never a burden to you? Forgive me this wrong!

¹⁴Now I am ready to visit you for the third time, and I will not be a burden to you, because what I want is not your possessions but you. After all, children should not have to save up for their parents, but parents for their children. ¹⁵So I will very gladly spend for you everything I have and expend myself as well. If I love you more, will you love me less? ¹⁶Be that as it may, I have not been a burden to you. Yet, crafty fellow that I am, I caught you by trickery! ¹⁷Did I exploit you through any of the men I sent you? ¹⁸I urged Titus to go to you and I sent our brother with him. Ti-

tus did not exploit you, did he? Did we not act in the same spirit and follow the same course?

¹⁹Have you been thinking all along that we have been defending ourselves to you? We have been speaking in the sight of God as those in Christ; and everything we do, dear friends, is for your strengthening. ²⁰For I am afraid that when I come I may not find you as I want you to be, and you may not find me as you want me to be. I fear that there may be quarreling, jealousy, outbursts of anger, factions, slander, gossip, arrogance and disorder. ²¹I am afraid that when I come again my God will humble me before you, and I will be grieved over many who have sinned earlier and have not repented of

Weekend.

Mike and Job

Read Job 23:10 (page 601)

After reading Friday's devotion from Mike, you really have to respect him. Wow! Hit by a bus! Unbelievable! Mike responded to his tragedy by talking about how great God is in the midst of pain. How could something like this happen to a good guy like him?

If you've ever asked yourself a question like this, you're not alone. People have been wondering why bad things happen to good people for, like, forever. The Bible gives an example of someone who went through horrendous suffering too. Job's world came crashing down on him. His servants were slaughtered, his sheep were toast and his family was killed.

The Bible doesn't always give a clear answer to the question of why people are hurting. But one thing is clear in the story of Job; God didn't cause the pain. God used Job's pain (and Mike's pain) to bring about huge spiritual growth in their lives! Evil brings suffering; God uses it! In the midst of pain God shows us that there are better things beyond the misery.

When you're facing suffering, respond like Mike and Job did, and call out to God for strength. God will respond!

❶ How did you respond the last time you went through pain?

❷ People are suffering all around you in places like hospitals and nursing homes, and many are asking themselves this tough question. If Mike's story has touched your heart, go find someone like Mike and support him or her in the midst of their pain.

❸ If you are suffering, go to God and tell him your pain. He's always there for you.

Turn to page 1415 for your next devotion.

the impurity, sexual sin and debauchery in which they have indulged.

Final Warnings

13 This will be my third visit to you. "Every matter must be established by the testimony of two or three witnesses."[a] [2]I already gave you a warning when I was with you the second time. I now repeat it while absent: On my return I will not spare those who sinned earlier or any of the others, [3]since you are demanding proof that Christ is speaking through me. He is not weak in dealing with you, but is powerful among you. [4]For to be sure, he was crucified in weakness, yet he lives by God's power. Likewise, we are weak in him, yet by God's power we will live with him to serve you.

[5]Examine yourselves to see whether you are in the faith; test yourselves. Do you not realize that Christ Jesus is in you—unless, of course, you fail the test? [6]And I trust that you will discover that we have not failed the test. [7]Now we pray to God that you will not do anything

wrong. Not that people will see that we have stood the test but that you will do what is right even though we may seem to have failed. [8]For we cannot do anything against the truth, but only for the truth. [9]We are glad whenever we are weak but you are strong; and our prayer is for your perfection. [10]This is why I write these things when I am absent, that when I come I may not have to be harsh in my use of authority—the authority the Lord gave me for building you up, not for tearing you down.

Final Greetings

[11]Finally, brothers, good-by. Aim for perfection, listen to my appeal, be of one mind, live in peace. And the God of love and peace will be with you.

[12]Greet one another with a holy kiss. [13]All the saints send their greetings.

[14]May the grace of the Lord Jesus Christ, and the love of God, and the fellowship of the Holy Spirit be with you all.

1 Deut. 19:15

Galatians

START

Paul was totally ticked! He was fightin' mad! Sometime earlier he'd traveled to the cities of Galatia (a region kind of like a state or big county) and preached the Good News of Jesus Christ. Churches had been started in all those cities—churches with Jewish Christians and non-Jewish (Gentile) Christians—and they believed they were saved by God's grace alone.

A bunch of Jewish Christians were preaching that the non-Jewish Christians had to follow Jewish law to be saved (more specifically, that the men had to be circumcised). Paul's not just mad because false teaching is in the air. He's ticked because the Galatian Christians are believing it!

So Paul writes this letter to all the churches in Galatia to say, "Listen up! It's God's grace alone that saves you. You can't earn your own salvation."

There are certainly Christians today who need to hear this same strong message!

Cast OF Characters

Paul
Used to be a persecutor of Christians, until Jesus got ahold of him. Now he's an apostle, a missionary (especially to Gentiles) and a church planter.

Christians in Derbe (DER-bee), Lystra and Iconium (eye-CONE-ee-um)
(LIE-struh)
These people are the audience—the churches of Galatia.

False Teachers
Paul doesn't hold back against these people who are teaching that good deeds earn salvation.

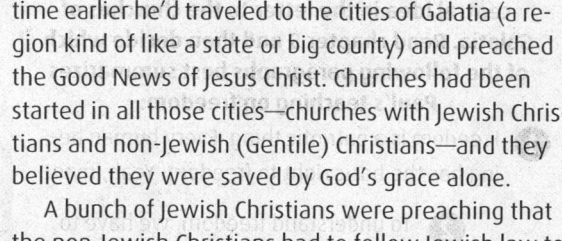

What's UP with That?

Free to Be . . .

Paul makes a big deal out of freedom. It's a central idea in the letter to the churches of Galatia. Read chapter 5 and then decide which of the following paragraphs best summarizes Paul's teaching on freedom:

1. Freedom is a patriotic thing. Every human being has the basic right to freedom. Yeah, man!

2. To understand freedom, we have to look at the parts of the word—"free" and "dom" (or "dumb"). So, freedom is really being free to be dumb.

3. Before Jesus, people tried to be right with God by following the detailed rules of religious law. Of course no one was perfect—just as none of us is today. Jesus gives us freedom because he offers us salvation based on his grace, not based on our goodness.

4. The Jewish people were tied to the law—hundreds of rules that said do this or don't do that. But now we have freedom, man! That means it doesn't really matter how you live, as long as you experience your freedom. Go ahead and sin! You know God will forgive you.

5. Freedom has its limits. Because of Jesus, we are free to choose right or wrong (although people were probably free to do that *before* Jesus too). Anyway, your choices and your behavior still make a difference as to whether or not you'll get to go to heaven. So, you know, don't get carried away with this freedom stuff!

Snap shots

- Hola! *(chapter 1:1–9)*

- Here's who I am *(chapters 1:10—2:21)*

- The gospel rocks! *(chapters 3—4)*

- And here's how it works *(chapters 5:1—6:15)*

- Adios! *(chapter 6:16–18)*

answer: paragraph 3

FREEDOM!

1 Paul, an apostle—sent not from men nor by man, but by Jesus Christ and God the Father, who raised him from the dead— ²and all the brothers with me,

To the churches in Galatia:

³Grace and peace to you from God our Father and the Lord Jesus Christ, ⁴who gave himself for our sins to rescue us from the present evil age, according to the will of our God and Father, ⁵to whom be glory for ever and ever. Amen.

No Other Gospel

⁶I am astonished that you are so quickly deserting the one who called you by the grace of Christ and are turning to a different gospel— ⁷which is really no gospel at all. Evidently some people are throwing you into confusion and are trying to pervert the gospel of Christ. ⁸But even if we or an angel from heaven should preach a gospel other than the one we preached to you, let him be eter-

nally condemned! ⁹As we have already said, so now I say again: If anybody is preaching to you a gospel other than what you accepted, let him be eternally condemned!

¹⁰Am I now trying to win the approval of men, or of God? Or am I trying to please men? If I were still trying to please men, I would not be a servant of Christ.

Sound the Alarm!

Huh?

Galatians 1:6
The word *gospel* means "Good News." Paul begins this letter with a bit of a punch—he's "astonished" that the good news of Jesus is being twisted and ignored. And to Paul, that's a subject that deserves alarms and red flags. How right he was!

Monday

People Pleasers

Read Galatians 1:10

The other day, my friends and I were sitting at the lunch table, just talking and joking around. I said something kind of sarcastic about one of my friends because I thought the other people would think it was funny. But I ended up hurting my friend's feelings instead.

There are a lot of things we do to try to impress other people or make them like us. Some people start smoking because other people will think it's cool. Some people swear or gossip or make fun of other people to seem funny or smart. But those things don't please God. Every day we have to decide if we want to follow the crowd or obey God. We can't always do both.

In the long run, it's much better for us to obey God. He loves us and gives us eternal life. Obeying him is our way of saying, "Thanks!"

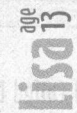 Lisa age 13

 **What about You?**

❶ What are 3 ways you try to please other people? Why is it so tempting to please people instead of God?

❷ For one day concentrate more on pleasing God than on pleasing people. How does it affect the decisions you make and the things you say?

❸ Ask God to help you obey him, even when it's not the popular thing to do.

Turn to page 1418 for your next devotion.

Looks Like, Sounds Like, but Isn't

When a friend at school tells you she's a Christian, and you know she's a Mormon, it's tough to know what to say. All of the groups below have some significant belief that makes them not-quite-Christian. See if you can match each group with one of their opposite-of-what-the-Bible-says beliefs.

Column 1

1. There is not one God—everyone is an immortal spirit with power over his or her own universe.

2. God the Father was once a man, had a wife, and Jesus was created as a spirit-child who is now a separate god.

3. God is everything and everyone, an impersonal force; Jesus is not God but a guru.

4. God is one person, Jehovah; Jesus is not God—he was a heavenly being, a created being, before coming to earth.

5. Jesus saved us spiritually through his death on the cross. Sun Myung Moon is the leader of this Church and believes he is the messiah who will accomplish physical salvation.

6. Death and sickness don't exist. God is all that exists; and heaven and hell are just a state of mind.

Column 2

a. Mormonism

b. Jehovah's Witnesses

c. Unification Church

d. Christian Science

e. Scientology

f. New Age

Look in the Book!
Remember, if someone says something about God that goes against what's in the Bible, it's wrong! Before you believe anything: *Look in the Book*. When told about Jesus, the Bereans looked in the book. And they got this good stuff said about them: "Now the Bereans were of more noble character than the Thessalonians, for they received the message with great eagerness and examined the Scriptures every day to see if what Paul said was true" (Acts 17:11).

Answers: 1(e), 2(a), 3(f), 4(b), 5(c), 6(d)

Paul Called by God

[11] I want you to know, brothers, that the gospel I preached is not something that man made up. [12] I did not receive it from any man, nor was I taught it; rather, I received it by revelation from Jesus Christ.

[13] For you have heard of my previous way of life in Judaism, how intensely I persecuted the church of God and tried to destroy it. [14] I was advancing in Judaism beyond many Jews of my own age and was extremely zealous for the traditions of my fathers. [15] But when God, who set me apart from birth[a] and called me by his grace, was pleased [16] to reveal his Son in me so that I might preach him among the Gentiles, I did not consult any man, [17] nor did I go up to Jerusalem to see those who were apostles before I was, but I went immediately into Arabia and later returned to Damascus.

[18] Then after three years, I went up to Jerusalem to get acquainted with Peter[b] and stayed with him fifteen days. [19] I saw none of the other apostles—only James, the Lord's brother. [20] I assure you before God that what I am writing you is no lie. [21] Later I went to Syria and Cilicia. [22] I was personally unknown to the churches of Judea that are in Christ. [23] They only

[a]15 Or *from my mother's womb*   [b]18 Greek *Cephas*

heard the report: "The man who formerly persecuted us is now preaching the faith he once tried to destroy." [24]And they praised God because of me.

Paul Accepted by the Apostles

2 Fourteen years later I went up again to Jerusalem, this time with Barnabas. I took Titus along also. [2]I went in response to a revelation and set before them the gospel that I preach among the Gentiles. But I did this privately to those who seemed to be leaders, for fear that I was running or had run my race in vain. [3]Yet not even Titus, who was with me, was compelled to be circumcised, even though he was a Greek. [4]This matter arose because some false brothers had infiltrated our ranks to spy on the freedom we have in Christ Jesus and to make us slaves. [5]We did not give in to them for a moment, so that the truth of the gospel might remain with you.

[6]As for those who seemed to be important—whatever they were makes no difference to me; God does not judge by external appearance—those men added nothing to my message. [7]On the contrary, they saw that I had been entrusted with the task of preaching the gospel to the Gentiles,[a] just as Peter had been to the Jews.[b] [8]For God, who was at work in the ministry of Peter as an apostle to the Jews, was also at work in my ministry as an apostle to the Gentiles. [9]James, Peter[c] and John, those reputed to be pillars, gave me and Barnabas the right hand of fellowship when they recognized the grace given to me. They agreed that we should go to the Gentiles, and they to the Jews. [10]All they asked was that we should continue to remember the poor, the very thing I was eager to do.

Paul Opposes Peter

[11]When Peter came to Antioch, I opposed him to his face, because he was clearly in the wrong. [12]Before certain men came from James, he used to eat with the Gentiles. But when they arrived, he began to draw back and separate himself from the Gentiles because he was afraid of those who belonged to the circumcision group. [13]The other Jews joined him in his hypocrisy, so that by their hypocrisy even Barnabas was led astray.

[14]When I saw that they were not acting in line with the truth of the gospel, I said to Peter in front of them all, "You are a Jew, yet you live like a Gentile and not like a Jew. How is it, then, that you force Gentiles to follow Jewish customs?

[15]"We who are Jews by birth and not 'Gentile sinners' [16]know that a man is not justified by observing the law, but by faith in Jesus Christ. So we, too, have put our faith in Christ Jesus that we may be justified by faith in Christ and not by observing the law, because by observing the law no one will be justified.

[17]"If, while we seek to be justified in Christ, it becomes evident that we ourselves are sinners, does that mean that Christ promotes sin? Absolutely not! [18]If I rebuild what I destroyed, I prove that I am a lawbreaker. [19]For through the law I died to the law so that I might live for God. [20]I have been crucified with Christ and I no longer live, but Christ lives in me. The life I live in the body, I live by faith in the Son of God, who loved me and gave himself for me. [21]I do not set

Hands off the Steering Wheel

Huh?

Galatians 2:20

Once you're a Christian, the big question for your daily life becomes this: Who's driving? Who's in control? Who's choosing the direction? Is it you, or is it Jesus? Jesus wants control of your whole life—he wants to steer. And there's absolutely no question about it: He'll guide your life *way* better than you ever could. So . . . daily, moment-by-moment, give him the control. Let him steer.

aside the grace of God, for if righteousness could be gained through the law, Christ died for nothing!"[d]

---

[a]7 Greek *uncircumcised*   [b]7 Greek *circumcised*; also in verses 8 and 9   [c]9 Greek *Cephas*; also in verses 11 and 14   [d]21 Some interpreters end the quotation after verse 14.

Faith or Observance of the Law

3 You foolish Galatians! Who has bewitched you? Before your very eyes Jesus Christ was clearly portrayed as crucified. ²I would like to learn just one thing from you: Did you receive the Spirit by observing the law, or by believing what you heard? ³Are you so foolish? After beginning with the Spirit, are you now trying to attain your goal by human effort? ⁴Have you suffered so much for nothing—if it really was for nothing? ⁵Does God give you his Spirit and work miracles among you because you observe the law, or because you believe what you heard?

⁶Consider Abraham: "He believed God, and it was credited to him as righteousness."ᵃ ⁷Understand, then, that those who believe are children of Abraham. ⁸The Scripture foresaw that God would justify the Gentiles by faith, and announced the gospel in advance to Abraham: "All nations will be blessed through you."ᵇ ⁹So those who have faith are blessed along with Abraham, the man of faith.

¹⁰All who rely on observing the law are under a curse, for it is written: "Cursed is everyone who does not continue to do everything written in the Book of the Law."ᶜ ¹¹Clearly no one is justified before God by the law, because, "The righteous will live by faith."ᵈ ¹²The law is not based on faith; on the contrary, "The man who does these things will live by them."ᵉ ¹³Christ redeemed us from the curse of the law by becoming a curse for us, for it is written: "Cursed is everyone who is hung on a tree."ᶠ ¹⁴He redeemed us in order that the blessing given to Abraham might come to the Gentiles through Christ Jesus, so that by faith we might receive the promise of the Spirit.

ᵃ6 Gen. 15:6   ᵇ8 Gen. 12:3; 18:18; 22:18
ᶜ10 Deut. 27:26   ᵈ11 Hab. 2:4   ᵉ12 Lev. 18:5
ᶠ13 Deut. 21:23

Tuesday

We Are Equal

Read Galatians 3:28–29

Some people in my school are looked down on. They don't have many friends, and it's easy to make fun of them. I have to admit, I've been part of the crowd that's doing the "looking down." But that's just not the way God wants things to be.

God doesn't care what color people are or how popular they are or what they look like. God cares about what's going on inside a person's heart. I shouldn't judge people by how they look. God wants me to treat all people the same and to accept, and even love, them for who they are.

Knowing God cares about people no matter what they look like or which group they belong to makes me feel better about myself too. I'm so glad we have a God who looks beyond the barriers the world puts up between people. Everyone who follows Jesus is equal in God's eyes.

Lindsey age 12

❶ Who are some of the people you don't like because they're "different"?

❷ Next time you're tempted to make fun of people or judge them, imagine that you're seeing them the way Jesus sees them.

❸ Ask God to help you look at people's hearts, not just their outward appearances.

Turn to page 1421 for your next devotion.

The Law and the Promise

[15]Brothers, let me take an example from everyday life. Just as no one can set aside or add to a human covenant that has been duly established, so it is in this case. [16]The promises were spoken to Abraham and to his seed. The Scripture does not say "and to seeds," meaning many people, but "and to your seed,"[a] meaning one person, who is Christ. [17]What I mean is this: The law, introduced 430 years later, does not set aside the covenant previously established by God and thus do away with the promise. [18]For if the inheritance depends on the law, then it no longer depends on a promise; but God in his grace gave it to Abraham through a promise.

[19]What, then, was the purpose of the law? It was added because of transgressions until the Seed to whom the promise referred had come. The law was put into effect through angels by a mediator. [20]A mediator, however, does not represent just one party; but God is one.

[21]Is the law, therefore, opposed to the promises of God? Absolutely not! For if a law had been given that could impart life, then righteousness would certainly have come by the law. [22]But the Scripture declares that the whole world is a prisoner of sin, so that what was promised, being given through faith in Jesus Christ, might be given to those who believe.

[23]Before this faith came, we were held prisoners by the law, locked up until faith should be revealed. [24]So the law was put in charge to lead us to Christ[b] that we might be justified by faith. [25]Now that faith has come, we are no longer under the supervision of the law.

Sons of God

[26]You are all sons of God through faith in Christ Jesus, [27]for all of you who were baptized into Christ have clothed yourselves with Christ. [28]There is neither Jew nor Greek, slave nor free, male nor female, for you are all one in Christ Jesus. [29]If you belong to Christ, then you are Abraham's seed, and heirs according to the promise.

4 What I am saying is that as long as the heir is a child, he is no different from a slave, although he owns the whole estate. [2]He is subject to guardians and trustees until the time set by his father. [3]So also, when we were children, we were in slavery under the basic principles of the world. [4]But when the time had fully come, God sent his Son, born of a woman, born under law, [5]to redeem those under law, that we might receive the full rights of sons. [6]Because you are sons, God sent the Spirit of his Son into our hearts, the Spirit who calls out, "Abba,[c] Father." [7]So you are no longer a slave, but a son; and since you are a son, God has made you also an heir.

Paul's Concern for the Galatians

[8]Formerly, when you did not know God, you were slaves to those who by nature are not gods. [9]But now that you know God—or rather are known by God—how is it that you are turning back to those weak and miserable principles? Do you wish to be enslaved by them all over again? [10]You are observing special days and months and seasons and years! [11]I fear for you, that somehow I have wasted my efforts on you.

[12]I plead with you, brothers, become like me, for I became like you. You have done me no wrong. [13]As you know, it was because of an illness that I first preached the gospel to you. [14]Even though my illness was a trial to you, you did not treat me with contempt or scorn. Instead, you welcomed me as if I were an angel of God, as if I were Christ Jesus himself. [15]What has happened to all your joy? I can testify that, if you could have done so, you would have torn out your eyes and given them to me. [16]Have I now become your enemy by telling you the truth?

[17]Those people are zealous to win you over, but for no good. What they want is to alienate you ⌊from us⌋, so that you may be zealous for them. [18]It is fine to be zealous, provided the purpose is good, and to be so always and not just when I am with you. [19]My dear children, for whom I am again in the pains of childbirth until Christ is formed in you, [20]how

---

[a]16 Gen. 12:7; 13:15; 24:7   [b]24 Or *charge until Christ came*   [c]6 Aramaic for *Father*

I wish I could be with you now and change my tone, because I am perplexed about you!

Hagar and Sarah

²¹Tell me, you who want to be under the law, are you not aware of what the law says? ²²For it is written that Abraham had two sons, one by the slave woman and the other by the free woman. ²³His son by the slave woman was born in the ordinary way; but his son by the free woman was born as the result of a promise.

²⁴These things may be taken figuratively, for the women represent two covenants. One covenant is from Mount Sinai and bears children who are to be slaves: This is Hagar. ²⁵Now Hagar stands for Mount Sinai in Arabia and corresponds to the present city of Jerusalem, because she is in slavery with her children. ²⁶But the Jerusalem that is above is free, and she is our mother. ²⁷For it is written:

"Be glad, O barren woman,
    who bears no children;
break forth and cry aloud,
    you who have no labor pains;
because more are the children of the
        desolate woman
    than of her who has a husband."ᵃ

²⁸Now you, brothers, like Isaac, are children of promise. ²⁹At that time the son born in the ordinary way persecuted the son born by the power of the Spirit. It is the same now. ³⁰But what does the Scripture say? "Get rid of the slave woman and her son, for the slave woman's son will never share in the inheritance with the free woman's son."ᵇ ³¹Therefore, brothers, we are not children of the slave woman, but of the free woman.

Freedom in Christ

5 It is for freedom that Christ has set us free. Stand firm, then, and do not let yourselves be burdened again by a yoke of slavery.

²Mark my words! I, Paul, tell you that if you let yourselves be circumcised, Christ will be of no value to you at all. ³Again I declare to every man who lets himself be circumcised that he is obligat-

You're Free

Huh?

Galatians 5:1

Have you ever made fun of a friend but then felt really bad and tried to make up for it by complimenting her? It's hard; it feels hollow; it feels fake. It's difficult to do good things when you're still feeling guilty about bad things. God has forgiven us for every bad thing we've ever done, not so that we can turn around and continue to sin, but so that we're free to love others and have a relationship with him.

ed to obey the whole law. ⁴You who are trying to be justified by law have been alienated from Christ; you have fallen away from grace. ⁵But by faith we eagerly await through the Spirit the righteousness for which we hope. ⁶For in Christ Jesus neither circumcision nor uncircumcision has any value. The only thing that counts is faith expressing itself through love.

⁷You were running a good race. Who cut in on you and kept you from obeying the truth? ⁸That kind of persuasion does not come from the one who calls you. ⁹"A little yeast works through the whole batch of dough." ¹⁰I am confident in the Lord that you will take no other view. The one who is throwing you into confusion will pay the penalty, whoever he may be. ¹¹Brothers, if I am still preaching circumcision, why am I still being persecuted? In that case the offense of the cross has been abolished. ¹²As for those agitators, I wish they would go the whole way and emasculate themselves!

¹³You, my brothers, were called to be free. But do not use your freedom to indulge the sinful natureᶜ; rather, serve one another in love. ¹⁴The entire law is summed up in a single command: "Love your neighbor as yourself."ᵈ ¹⁵If you keep on biting and devouring each other, watch out or you will be destroyed by each other.

ᵃ27 Isaiah 54:1   ᵇ30 Gen. 21:10   ᶜ13 Or the flesh; also in verses 16, 17, 19 and 24   ᵈ14 Lev. 19:18

Life by the Spirit

[16]So I say, live by the Spirit, and you will not gratify the desires of the sinful nature. [17]For the sinful nature desires what is contrary to the Spirit, and the Spirit what is contrary to the sinful nature. They are in conflict with each other, so that you do not do what you want. [18]But if you are led by the Spirit, you are not under law.

[19]The acts of the sinful nature are obvious: sexual immorality, impurity and debauchery; [20]idolatry and witchcraft; hatred, discord, jealousy, fits of rage, selfish ambition, dissensions, factions [21]and envy; drunkenness, orgies, and the like. I warn you, as I did before, that those who live like this will not inherit the kingdom of God.

[22]But the fruit of the Spirit is love, joy, peace, patience, kindness, goodness, faithfulness, [23]gentleness and self-control. Against such things there is no law. [24]Those who belong to Christ Jesus have crucified the sinful nature with its passions and desires. [25]Since we live by the Spirit, let us keep in step with the Spirit. [26]Let us not become conceited, provoking and envying each other.

Doing Good to All

6 Brothers, if someone is caught in a sin, you who are spiritual should restore him gently. But watch yourself, or you also may be tempted. [2]Carry each other's burdens, and in this way you will fulfill the law of Christ. [3]If anyone thinks he is something when he is nothing, he deceives himself. [4]Each one should test his own actions. Then he can take pride in himself, without comparing himself to somebody else, [5]for each one should carry his own load.

[6]Anyone who receives instruction in the word must share all good things with his instructor.

[7]Do not be deceived: God cannot be mocked. A man reaps what he sows. [8]The one who sows to please his sinful nature, from that nature[a] will reap destruction; the one who sows to please the Spirit, from the Spirit will reap eternal life. [9]Let us not become weary in doing good, for at the proper time we will reap a harvest if we do not give up. [10]Therefore, as we have opportunity, let us do good to all people, especially to

[a]8 Or *his flesh, from the flesh*

Wednesday

Fabulous Fruit

Read Galatians 5:22–23

There are lots of times when I don't really act like a Christian—like when my brother is making me mad. At those times, I need to think about this passage and try to let the Holy Spirit guide me to do the right thing.

That's what the fruit of the Spirit is all about. These qualities are the signs that God is in control of our lives. If I want to share my faith with others or just stay out of trouble, I need to look at this list of traits and I'll know how to live. The passage says we can't go wrong when we let the Holy Spirit lead us.

Gus age 14

What about You?

❶ What would you think of a person who had all the traits listed in today's passage? Which of these traits do you look for in a friend?

❷ Imagine that you're walking through a vegetable garden or an orchard. How do you know what kinds of plants or trees you're looking at? What kinds of "fruit" do people see when they look at you?

❸ Ask the Holy Spirit to help you grow great spiritual fruit.

Turn to page 1426 for your next devotion.

those who belong to the family of believers.

Not Circumcision but a New Creation

¹¹See what large letters I use as I write to you with my own hand!

¹²Those who want to make a good impression outwardly are trying to compel you to be circumcised. The only reason they do this is to avoid being persecuted for the cross of Christ. ¹³Not even those who are circumcised obey the law, yet they want you to be circumcised that they may boast about your flesh. ¹⁴May I

never boast except in the cross of our Lord Jesus Christ, through which[a] the world has been crucified to me, and I to the world. ¹⁵Neither circumcision nor uncircumcision means anything; what counts is a new creation. ¹⁶Peace and mercy to all who follow this rule, even to the Israel of God.

¹⁷Finally, let no one cause me trouble, for I bear on my body the marks of Jesus.

¹⁸The grace of our Lord Jesus Christ be with your spirit, brothers. Amen.

[a] 14 Or *whom*

Ephesians

START

Wannabes. They've got all the right clothes, the hair, the stuff. Maybe they even know the right words—but they're fakes. It takes a lot of hard work to get good at something like skating, snowboarding, skiing or rounding up cattle. That could be why so many people just buy the costume. They want to pretend that they're someone they're not.

Being a true believer is hard work too. It's got to go a lot deeper than the size of your Bible, the cross around your neck or the words you say.

Paul wants his good friends in the city of Ephesus to understand the connection between what they know about God and how they live out their everyday lives. He starts out his letter by reminding them how awesome God is. Then he tells them that if their faith in Jesus doesn't change the way they treat others, it's just not real.

CAST OF Characters

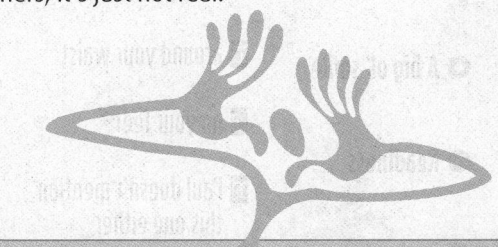

Paul

Locked up in a Roman jail (because of his faith in God), Paul was thinking of his friends in the church at Ephesus. He spent 3 years with them as their pastor/teacher, so he really wants to see them grow in their faith.

(Ee-FEE-zhuns)

The Church at Ephesus, (EFF-uh-sus) the Ephesians

These believers were some of Paul's favorite people. They lived in a city where most of the people weren't really interested in church, so they needed some extra encouragement to live out their faith.

What's UP with That?

Near the end of his letter, Paul tells his friends to get dressed for war. If you're thinking army boots, machine guns and bulletproof vests, you've got the wrong idea. As Paul says, this is a different kind of battle. It's a spiritual battle with the forces of darkness! Match each piece of "armor" with the place Paul says it should be worn.

① Truth

② Groovy-ness

③ Righteousness

④ A big ol' smile

⑤ Readiness

⑥ Faith

⑦ Salvation

⑧ The Word of God

Ⓐ as a sword

Ⓑ as a helmet

Ⓒ Paul doesn't mention this one

Ⓓ around your waist

Ⓔ on your feet

Ⓕ Paul doesn't mention this one either

Ⓖ as a shield

Ⓗ on your chest

Snap shots

- Hi, how are ya?
  (chapter 1:1–2)

- The bonuses of being born again
  (chapters 1:3—3:21)

- Can't we all just get along?
  (chapter 4:1–16)

- Life's little instructions
  (chapters 4:17—5:20)

- Home improvement
  (chapters 5:21—6:9)

- This means war
  (chapter 6:10–20)

- Buh-bye
  (chapter 6:21–24)

answers: 1-d, 2-c, 3-h, 4-f, 5-e, 6-g, 7-b, 8-a

1 Paul, an apostle of Christ Jesus by the will of God,

To the saints in Ephesus,[a] the faithful[b] in Christ Jesus:

[2]Grace and peace to you from God our Father and the Lord Jesus Christ.

Spiritual Blessings in Christ

[3]Praise be to the God and Father of our Lord Jesus Christ, who has blessed us in the heavenly realms with every spiritual blessing in Christ. [4]For he chose us in him before the creation of the world to be holy and blameless in his sight. In love [5]he[c] predestined us to be adopted as his sons through Jesus Christ, in accordance with his pleasure and will— [6]to the praise of his glorious grace, which he has freely given us in the One he loves. [7]In him we have redemption through his blood, the forgiveness of sins, in accordance with the riches of God's grace [8]that he lavished on us with all wisdom and understanding. [9]And he[d] made known to us the mystery of his will according to his good pleasure, which he purposed in Christ, [10]to be put into effect when the times will have reached their fulfillment—to bring all things in heaven and on earth together under one head, even Christ.

[11]In him we were also chosen,[e] having been predestined according to the plan of him who works out everything in conformity with the purpose of his will, [12]in order that we, who were the first to hope in Christ, might be for the praise of his glory. [13]And you also were included in Christ when you heard the word of truth, the gospel of your salvation. Having believed, you were marked in him with a seal, the promised Holy Spirit, [14]who is a deposit guaranteeing our inheritance until the redemption of those who are God's possession—to the praise of his glory.

Thanksgiving and Prayer

[15]For this reason, ever since I heard about your faith in the Lord Jesus and your love for all the saints, [16]I have not stopped giving thanks for you, remembering you in my prayers. [17]I keep asking that the God of our Lord Jesus Christ, the glorious Father, may give you the Spirit[f]

of wisdom and revelation, so that you may know him better. [18]I pray also that the eyes of your heart may be enlightened in order that you may know the hope to which he has called you, the riches of his glorious inheritance in the saints, [19]and his incomparably great power for us who believe. That power is like the working of his mighty strength, [20]which he exerted in Christ when he raised him from the dead and seated him at his right hand in the heavenly realms, [21]far above all rule and authority, power and dominion, and every title that can be given, not only in the present age but also in the one to come. [22]And God placed all things under his feet and appointed him to be head over everything for the church, [23]which is his body, the fullness of him who fills everything in every way.

Made Alive in Christ

2 As for you, you were dead in your transgressions and sins, [2]in which you used to live when you followed the ways of this world and of the ruler of the kingdom of the air, the spirit who is now at work in those who are disobedient. [3]All of us also lived among them at one time, gratifying the cravings of our sinful nature[g] and following its desires and thoughts. Like the rest, we were by nature objects of wrath. [4]But because of his great love for us, God, who is rich in mercy, [5]made us alive with Christ even when we were dead in transgressions—it is by grace you have been saved. [6]And God raised us up with Christ and seated us with him in the heavenly realms in Christ Jesus, [7]in order that in the coming ages he might show the incomparable riches of his grace, expressed in his kindness to us in Christ Jesus. [8]For it is by grace you have been saved, through faith—and this not from yourselves, it is the gift of God— [9]not by works, so that no one can boast. [10]For we are God's workmanship, created in Christ Jesus to

[a]1 Some early manuscripts do not have in Ephesus.
[b]1 Or believers who are   [c]4,5 Or sight in love. [5]He
[d]8,9 Or us. With all wisdom and understanding,
[9]he   [e]11 Or were made heirs   [f]17 Or a spirit   [g]3 Or our flesh

It's Who Ya Know

Huh?

Ephesians 2:8–9

Working hard at being a good Christian isn't how you get into heaven. That's why Paul uses the word *works*, which means "rule keeping" or "doing good." Simply put, it's not what you do, but who you know (that "who" would be Jesus, by the way). Verse 10 says that doing good works is a "no duh" response for us if we believe in Christ Jesus.

do good works, which God prepared in advance for us to do.

One in Christ

[11]Therefore, remember that formerly you who are Gentiles by birth and called "uncircumcised" by those who call them-selves "the circumcision" (that done in the body by the hands of men)— [12]remember that at that time you were separate from Christ, excluded from citizenship in Israel and foreigners to the covenants of the promise, without hope and without God in the world. [13]But now in Christ Jesus you who once were far away have been brought near through the blood of Christ.

[14]For he himself is our peace, who has made the two one and has destroyed the barrier, the dividing wall of hostility, [15]by abolishing in his flesh the law with its commandments and regulations. His purpose was to create in himself one new man out of the two, thus making peace, [16]and in this one body to reconcile both of them to God through the cross, by which he put to death their hostility. [17]He came and preached peace to you who were far away and peace to those who were near. [18]For through him we both have access to the Father by one Spirit.

Thursday

For Me, for Free

Read Ephesians 2:8–9

I think I understood these verses the best when I first asked Jesus into my heart. I remember thinking it was the most amazing thing in the world that God loved me so much. It was almost unimaginable. God wanted to forgive every single sin of mine. God wanted to give me salvation, just because I asked. I didn't have to do anything except ask for forgiveness and invite him into my heart.

Now that I've been a Christian for a while, I think it's easy to forget just how amazing God's grace really is. Sometimes we take credit for things God has done. We brag about how strong our faith is. But it's God who makes us strong, not anything we do to make ourselves strong.

When I remember how powerfully I felt God's grace when I first became a Christian, I can't help but want to be an example of his love. He loves me so much and gave me such a wonderful gift; it only seems right for me to live my life for him.

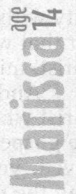

Marissa, age 14

❶ What does grace mean to you? How has God shown you his grace?

❷ Think of someone who has hurt your feelings. How can you show grace to this person?

❸ Thank God for his amazing gift of grace.

Turn to page 1428 for your next devotion.

Can't We All Just Get Along?

Huh?

Ephesians 2:11–13

How many kinds of true Christians are there? Just one! At this time, Jews did not like the Gentiles (non-Jews). In fact, Jews often rudely referred to Gentiles as "dogs." What counts for us Christians now is that we are all Christ-followers. It doesn't matter what color we are, how smart we are or how much money we have. Instead of focusing on our differences, we are called to unite through Jesus Christ.

[19]Consequently, you are no longer foreigners and aliens, but fellow citizens with God's people and members of God's household, [20]built on the foundation of the apostles and prophets, with Christ Jesus himself as the chief cornerstone. [21]In him the whole building is joined together and rises to become a holy temple in the Lord. [22]And in him you too are being built together to become a dwelling in which God lives by his Spirit.

Paul the Preacher to the Gentiles

3 For this reason I, Paul, the prisoner of Christ Jesus for the sake of you Gentiles—

[2]Surely you have heard about the administration of God's grace that was given to me for you, [3]that is, the mystery made known to me by revelation, as I have already written briefly. [4]In reading this, then, you will be able to understand my insight into the mystery of Christ, [5]which was not made known to men in other generations as it has now been revealed by the Spirit to God's holy apostles and prophets. [6]This mystery is that through the gospel the Gentiles are heirs together with Israel, members together of one body, and sharers together in the promise in Christ Jesus.

[7]I became a servant of this gospel by the gift of God's grace given me through the working of his power. [8]Although I am less than the least of all God's people, this grace was given me: to preach to the Gentiles the unsearchable riches of Christ, [9]and to make plain to everyone the administration of this mystery, which for ages past was kept hidden in God, who created all things. [10]His intent was that now, through the church, the manifold wisdom of God should be made known to the rulers and authorities in the heavenly realms, [11]according to his eternal purpose which he accomplished in Christ Jesus our Lord. [12]In him and through faith in him we may approach God with freedom and confidence. [13]I ask you, therefore, not to be discouraged because of my sufferings for you, which are your glory.

A Prayer for the Ephesians

[14]For this reason I kneel before the Father, [15]from whom his whole family[a] in heaven and on earth derives its name. [16]I pray that out of his glorious riches he may strengthen you with power through his Spirit in your inner being, [17]so that Christ may dwell in your hearts through faith. And I pray that you, being rooted and established in love, [18]may have power, together with all the saints, to grasp how wide and long and high and deep is the love of Christ, [19]and to know this love that surpasses knowledge—that you may be filled to the measure of all the fullness of God.

[20]Now to him who is able to do immeasurably more than all we ask or imagine, according to his power that is at work within us, [21]to him be glory in the church and in Christ Jesus throughout all generations, for ever and ever! Amen.

Unity in the Body of Christ

4 As a prisoner for the Lord, then, I urge you to live a life worthy of the calling you have received. [2]Be completely humble and gentle; be patient, bearing with one another in love. [3]Make every effort to keep the unity of the Spirit through the bond of peace. [4]There is one body and one Spirit— just as you were called to one hope when you were called— [5]one Lord, one faith, one baptism; [6]one God and Father of all, who is over all and through all and in all.

[a]15 Or *whom all fatherhood*

[7]But to each one of us grace has been given as Christ apportioned it. [8]This is why it[a] says:

"When he ascended on high,
   he led captives in his train
   and gave gifts to men."[b]

[9](What does "he ascended" mean except that he also descended to the lower, earthly regions[c]? [10]He who descended is the very one who ascended higher than all the heavens, in order to fill the whole universe.) [11]It was he who gave some to be apostles, some to be prophets, some to be evangelists, and some to be pastors and teachers, [12]to prepare God's people for works of service, so that the body of Christ may be built up [13]until we all reach unity in the faith and in the knowledge of the Son of God and become mature, attaining to the whole measure of the fullness of Christ.

[14]Then we will no longer be infants, tossed back and forth by the waves, and blown here and there by every wind of teaching and by the cunning and craftiness of men in their deceitful scheming.

[15]Instead, speaking the truth in love, we will in all things grow up into him who is the Head, that is, Christ. [16]From him the whole body, joined and held together by every supporting ligament, grows and builds itself up in love, as each part does its work.

Living as Children of Light

[17]So I tell you this, and insist on it in the Lord, that you must no longer live as the Gentiles do, in the futility of their thinking. [18]They are darkened in their understanding and separated from the life of God because of the ignorance that is in them due to the hardening of their hearts. [19]Having lost all sensitivity, they have given themselves over to sensuality so as to indulge in every kind of impurity, with a continual lust for more.

[20]You, however, did not come to know Christ that way. [21]Surely you heard of him and were taught in him in accordance with the truth that is in Jesus.

[a]8 Or God [b]8 Psalm 68:18 [c]9 Or the depths of the earth

Friday

Growin' God's Way

Read Ephesians 4:15–16

I was trying to decide if I should play the piano for the kindergarten class during the second hour of church. I wanted to help out, but I wanted to hear the sermon too. I finally decided to switch off—kindergarten class one Sunday, and the sermon the next Sunday.

I need to follow Christ's example and serve people in order to mature in my faith. But I also need to get together with other Christians to worship and praise God, because this strengthens my faith too. Both of these things are part of being in the body of Christ.

By serving in church and worshiping God with other Christians, I'll be a stronger Christian. Christ is the head of the Christian body, and I need to grow so I can be more like him.

Kate, age 12

❶ What are 2 or 3 signs that a person is growing into a mature Christian?

❷ Ask your pastor or youth leader how you might be able to help out during church or at youth group meetings.

❸ Ask God to show you ways to serve in your church.

Turn to page 1430 for your next devotion.

²²You were taught, with regard to your former way of life, to put off your old self, which is being corrupted by its deceitful desires; ²³to be made new in the attitude of your minds; ²⁴and to put on the new self, created to be like God in true righteousness and holiness.

²⁵Therefore each of you must put off falsehood and speak truthfully to his neighbor, for we are all members of one body. ²⁶"In your anger do not sin"ᵃ: Do not let the sun go down while you are still angry, ²⁷and do not give the devil a foothold. ²⁸He who has been stealing must steal no longer, but must work, doing something useful with his own hands, that he may have something to share with those in need.

²⁹Do not let any unwholesome talk come out of your mouths, but only what is helpful for building others up according to their needs, that it may benefit those who listen. ³⁰And do not grieve the

Ninja Mouth

Huh?

Ephesians 4:29

Is your mouth dangerous to others? Do the words you speak leave others beat up on the inside? This Scripture is about more than just swearing. Unwholesome talk can be a lot of things: being mean to your little sister, gossiping about people or just spreading a lousy attitude. The last part of this passage helps us know what is important: building others up and saying only what helps people.

Holy Spirit of God, with whom you were sealed for the day of redemption. ³¹Get rid of all bitterness, rage and anger, brawling and slander, along with every form of malice. ³²Be kind and compassionate to one another, forgiving each other, just as in Christ God forgave you.

5 Be imitators of God, therefore, as dearly loved children ²and live a life of love, just as Christ loved us and gave himself up for us as a fragrant offering and sacrifice to God.

³But among you there must not be even a hint of sexual immorality, or of any kind of impurity, or of greed, because these are improper for God's holy people. ⁴Nor should there be obscenity, foolish talk or coarse joking, which are out of place, but rather thanksgiving. ⁵For of this you can be sure: No immoral, impure or greedy person—such a man is an idolater—has any inheritance in the kingdom of Christ and of God.ᵇ ⁶Let no one deceive you with empty words, for because of such things God's wrath comes on those who are disobedient. ⁷Therefore do not be partners with them.

⁸For you were once darkness, but now you are light in the Lord. Live as children of light ⁹(for the fruit of the light consists in all goodness, righteousness and truth) ¹⁰and find out what pleases the Lord. ¹¹Have nothing to do with the fruitless deeds of darkness, but rather expose them. ¹²For it is shameful even to mention what the disobedient do in secret. ¹³But everything exposed by the light becomes visible, ¹⁴for it is light that makes everything visible. This is why it is said:

"Wake up, O sleeper,
　rise from the dead,
　and Christ will shine on you."

¹⁵Be very careful, then, how you live—not as unwise but as wise, ¹⁶making the most of every opportunity, because the days are evil. ¹⁷Therefore do not be foolish, but understand what the Lord's will is. ¹⁸Do not get drunk on wine, which leads to debauchery. Instead, be filled with the Spirit. ¹⁹Speak to one another with psalms, hymns and spiritual songs. Sing and make music in your heart to the Lord, ²⁰always giving thanks to God the Father for everything, in the name of our Lord Jesus Christ.

²¹Submit to one another out of reverence for Christ.

Wives and Husbands

²²Wives, submit to your husbands as to the Lord. ²³For the husband is the head of the wife as Christ is the head of the church, his body, of which he is the Savior. ²⁴Now as the church submits to

---

ᵃ26 Psalm 4:4　ᵇ5 Or *kingdom of the Christ and God*

Christ, so also wives should submit to their husbands in everything.

²⁵Husbands, love your wives, just as Christ loved the church and gave himself up for her ²⁶to make her holy, cleansing*a* her by the washing with water through the word, ²⁷and to present her to himself as a radiant church, without stain or wrinkle or any other blemish, but holy and blameless. ²⁸In this same way, husbands ought to love their wives as their own bodies. He who loves his wife loves himself. ²⁹After all, no one ever hated his own body, but he feeds and cares for it, just as Christ does the church— ³⁰for we are members of his body. ³¹"For this reason a man will leave his father and mother and be united to his wife, and the two will become one flesh."*b* ³²This is a profound mystery—but I am talking about Christ and the church. ³³However,

each one of you also must love his wife as he loves himself, and the wife must respect her husband.

Children and Parents

6 Children, obey your parents in the Lord, for this is right. ²"Honor your father and mother"—which is the first commandment with a promise— ³"that it may go well with you and that you may enjoy long life on the earth."*c*

⁴Fathers, do not exasperate your children; instead, bring them up in the training and instruction of the Lord.

Slaves and Masters

⁵Slaves, obey your earthly masters with respect and fear, and with sincerity of heart, just as you would obey Christ.

a26 Or having cleansed   b31 Gen. 2:24   c3 Deut. 5:16

Weekend.

The World's Scariest Prayer
Read Proverbs 29:23 (page 767)

What is the world's scariest prayer? How about, "Lord, make me humble." Is this prayer going to mean that you're in for some major embarrassing moments, like walking around with a piece of food on your face or forgetting your locker combination? Probably not (at least not because of your prayer!).

Don't be afraid to ask God for humility, even though it might seem unnatural. On Monday, Lisa referred to all the things we try to do to impress other people or to make them like us. On Tuesday, when Lindsey was talking about loving others, she pointed out that we shouldn't judge other people. She said we should treat all people the same and love them for who they are. This is impossible if you are always worried about what others are thinking of you. Being a Christian is about being a humble servant, not being too full of pride. So . . . do you have the guts to pray this prayer? It's a scary one. Go for it; pray the tough prayer. Ask God to remove your pride, and he will bless you with a humble spirit.

What about You?

❶ Think of a time when you stole the conversation and talked about yourself the whole time.

❷ Try to go through a day putting all your effort into drawing attention to others and to God.

❸ Pray the tough prayer and ask God to remove your pride and bless you with a humble spirit.

Turn to page 1431 for your next devotion.

⁶Obey them not only to win their favor when their eye is on you, but like slaves of Christ, doing the will of God from your heart. ⁷Serve wholeheartedly, as if you were serving the Lord, not men, ⁸because you know that the Lord will reward everyone for whatever good he does, whether he is slave or free.

⁹And masters, treat your slaves in the same way. Do not threaten them, since you know that he who is both their Master and yours is in heaven, and there is no favoritism with him.

The Armor of God

¹⁰Finally, be strong in the Lord and in his mighty power. ¹¹Put on the full armor of God so that you can take your stand against the devil's schemes. ¹²For our struggle is not against flesh and blood, but against the rulers, against the authorities, against the powers of this dark world and against the spiritual forces of evil in the heavenly realms. ¹³Therefore put on the full armor of God, so that

Dressed for Battle

Huh?

Ephesians 6:11–17
No one was tougher than a Roman soldier. At the time Paul wrote this, these Roman soldiers had conquered the world! Paul calls us as Christians to be prepared for battle against sin, just as soldiers are ready for war against a dangerous opponent. All of this armor is for defense. Christians are only given one offensive weapon: "the sword of the Spirit, which is the word of God." How well are you trained to use this weapon?

when the day of evil comes, you may be able to stand your ground, and after you have done everything, to stand. ¹⁴Stand firm then, with the belt of truth buckled around your waist, with the breastplate of righteousness in place, ¹⁵and

Monday

Ready for Battle

Read Ephesians 6:10–18

We need armor to fight the battle over good and evil. The devil is just way too powerful for us to fight on our own. But God wants to protect us, so he gives us enough armor to be ready for anything.

The part of the armor that I really noticed in this passage is the helmet of salvation, because it's the part that protects your head. I think your head, or actually your mind, is one of the first places the devil attacks. He can tempt you to doubt your faith or be afraid of all kinds of things you don't really need to fear. But with the helmet of salvation, you're protected. And when you know you're protected, you can have peace—even in the middle of the battle.

Susan age 12

What about You?

❶ Look at the pieces of God's armor: truth, righteousness, readiness, faith, salvation and the Word of God. Which of these areas are you strongest in? Which one might be a weak spot?

❷ If you're not sure what armor looked like, find out by looking in an encyclopedia or an illustrated Bible. Why is this picture of armor such a good way to think about God's protection?

❸ Thank God for his protection.

Turn to page 1436 for your next devotion.

with your feet fitted with the readiness that comes from the gospel of peace. [16]In addition to all this, take up the shield of faith, with which you can extinguish all the flaming arrows of the evil one. [17]Take the helmet of salvation and the sword of the Spirit, which is the word of God. [18]And pray in the Spirit on all occasions with all kinds of prayers and requests. With this in mind, be alert and always keep on praying for all the saints.

[19]Pray also for me, that whenever I open my mouth, words may be given me so that I will fearlessly make known the mystery of the gospel, [20]for which I am an ambassador in chains. Pray that I may declare it fearlessly, as I should.

Final Greetings

[21]Tychicus, the dear brother and faithful servant in the Lord, will tell you everything, so that you also may know how I am and what I am doing. [22]I am sending him to you for this very purpose, that you may know how we are, and that he may encourage you.

[23]Peace to the brothers, and love with faith from God the Father and the Lord Jesus Christ. [24]Grace to all who love our Lord Jesus Christ with an undying love.

Philippians

START

If ever there's a reason for feeling bummed, it's being cooped up in your house for a week with no place to go. Imagine being stuck there for 2 years!

Paul, the author of this book, was restricted to his house and guarded by Roman soldiers for 2 whole years. Did it put him in a rotten mood? Nope! In fact, this is one of his most upbeat letters. Instead of complaining and feeling miserable, Paul used his time to write his friends to encourage them. He realized there was nothing he could do to change his situation, so he decided to make the best of it. Is there a lesson to learn here?

Cast OF Characters

Paul

As a traveling missionary, Paul had visited the city of Philippi. He writes to say thanks to them for their help and to encourage them to be joyful.

(FILL-ih-pie)

The Church of Philippi, the Philippians

They were Roman citizens living in a wealthy city, and they got together and sent Paul a care package when they found out he was under house arrest.

(Fih-LIP-ee-uhns)

(You-OH-dee-ah)

Euodia and Syntyche

(SIN-tih-kee)

A couple of arguing women in the church. Paul knew that it was about time for them to learn to get along.

What's Up with That?

Match That Name

When you go to summer camp or on a vacation, you often meet people along the way. You might have an old address or autograph book where you've kept the names and addresses of people you've bumped into in various places. It seems that wherever Paul went he developed friendships with people he met. We don't know if he kept track of all these friends in an address book or not, but in this letter he mentions several people specifically. Match the names of the people with the description in the second column.

❶ Timothy

❷ Hercules

❸ Epaphroditus

❹ Euodia

❺ Macaroni

❻ Syntyche

❼ Brutus

❽ Caesar

Ⓐ Not mentioned—not even once

Ⓑ Couldn't seem to get along with Euodia

Ⓒ Had Paul's friends in his household

Ⓓ Uh-uh, not mentioned

Ⓔ A fellow soldier, like a brother

Ⓕ Couldn't seem to get along with Syntyche

Ⓖ Won't find this name in this letter

Ⓗ Like a son to Paul

Snap Shots

- Hey there, hi there, ho there (chapter 1:1–2)

- You guys rock! (chapter 1:3–11)

- I'm doing great. Honest, I am. Really. (chapter 1:12–26)

- Attitude check (chapters 1:27—2:18)

- My good buddies (chapter 2:19–30)

- Important lessons I've learned (chapter 3)

- Straight from the heart (chapter 4)

answers: 1-h, 2-a, 3-e, 4-f, 5-g, 6-b, 7-d, 8-c

1 Paul and Timothy, servants of Christ Jesus,

To all the saints in Christ Jesus at Philippi, together with the overseers[a] and deacons:

[2]Grace and peace to you from God our Father and the Lord Jesus Christ.

Thanksgiving and Prayer

[3]I thank my God every time I remember you. [4]In all my prayers for all of you, I always pray with joy [5]because of your partnership in the gospel from the first day until now, [6]being confident of this, that he who began a good work in you will carry it on to completion until the day of Christ Jesus.

[7]It is right for me to feel this way about all of you, since I have you in my heart; for whether I am in chains or defending and confirming the gospel, all of you share in God's grace with me. [8]God can testify how I long for all of you with the affection of Christ Jesus.

All Tied Up

Huh?

Philippians 1:7

When Paul wrote about being in chains, he wasn't just talking in symbols; he really meant it. Since he was writing to the Philippians while he was under house arrest in Rome, Paul was literally tied up in chains. But even though Paul was under arrest, he still wrote letters to churches and shared the message about Jesus with anyone who came to visit him.

[9]And this is my prayer: that your love may abound more and more in knowledge and depth of insight, [10]so that you may be able to discern what is best and may be pure and blameless until the day of Christ, [11]filled with the fruit of righteousness that comes through Jesus Christ—to the glory and praise of God.

Paul's Chains Advance the Gospel

[12]Now I want you to know, brothers, that what has happened to me has really served to advance the gospel. [13]As a result, it has become clear throughout the whole palace guard[b] and to everyone else that I am in chains for Christ. [14]Because of my chains, most of the brothers in the Lord have been encouraged to speak the word of God more courageously and fearlessly.

[15]It is true that some preach Christ out of envy and rivalry, but others out of goodwill. [16]The latter do so in love, knowing that I am put here for the defense of the gospel. [17]The former preach Christ out of selfish ambition, not sincerely, supposing that they can stir up trouble for me while I am in chains.[c] [18]But what does it matter? The important thing is that in every way, whether from false motives or true, Christ is preached. And because of this I rejoice.

Yes, and I will continue to rejoice, [19]for I know that through your prayers and the help given by the Spirit of Jesus Christ, what has happened to me will turn out for my deliverance.[d] [20]I eagerly expect and hope that I will in no way be ashamed, but will have sufficient courage so that now as always Christ will be exalted in my body, whether by life or by death. [21]For to me, to live is Christ and to die is gain. [22]If I am to go on living in the body, this will mean fruitful labor for me. Yet what shall I choose? I do not know! [23]I am torn between the two: I desire to depart and be with Christ, which is better by far; [24]but it is more necessary for you that I remain in the body. [25]Convinced of this, I know that I will remain, and I will continue with all of you for your progress and joy in the faith, [26]so that through my being with you again your joy in Christ Jesus will overflow on account of me.

[27]Whatever happens, conduct yourselves in a manner worthy of the gospel of Christ. Then, whether I come and see you or only hear about you in my absence, I will know that you stand firm in one spirit, contending as one man for the faith of the gospel [28]without being frightened in any way by those who

[a]1 Traditionally *bishops*   [b]13 Or *whole palace*
[c]16,17 Some late manuscripts have verses 16 and 17 in reverse order.   [d]19 Or *salvation*

oppose you. This is a sign to them that they will be destroyed, but that you will be saved—and that by God. ²⁹For it has been granted to you on behalf of Christ not only to believe on him, but also to suffer for him, ³⁰since you are going through the same struggle you saw I had, and now hear that I still have.

Imitating Christ's Humility

2 If you have any encouragement from being united with Christ, if any comfort from his love, if any fellowship with the Spirit, if any tenderness and compassion, ²then make my joy complete by being like-minded, having the same love, being one in spirit and purpose. ³Do nothing out of selfish ambition or vain conceit, but in humility consider others better than yourselves. ⁴Each of you should look not only to your own interests, but also to the interests of others.

⁵Your attitude should be the same as that of Christ Jesus:

⁶Who, being in very nature*ᵃ* God,
   did not consider equality with God
      something to be grasped,
⁷but made himself nothing,
   taking the very nature*ᵇ* of a servant,
   being made in human likeness.
⁸And being found in appearance as a man,
   he humbled himself
   and became obedient to death—
      even death on a cross!
⁹Therefore God exalted him to the highest place
   and gave him the name that is
      above every name,
¹⁰that at the name of Jesus every knee
   should bow,

ᵃ6 Or in the form of   ᵇ7 Or the form

Tuesday

Me First!

Read Philippians 2:3–5

I don't know about you, but I have a tendency to think the whole world revolves around me. Sometimes this attitude gets me in a lot of trouble.

Once I was feeling really jealous of my best friend. I don't even remember what it was about, but I was so mad I sent her a note that said, "I hate you!" Afterward I felt really bad for making her so sad, but I was too proud to ask her to forgive me. We're still best friends, and she never brings up the subject, but sometimes I really wish I would have apologized.

Jesus didn't have to live with this kind of guilt because he never treated anyone badly. Even though he was the Son of God, he wasn't too proud to wash his friends' dirty feet. I'm just a human, but I still need to try to be humble and act like Jesus did toward other people. The least I can do is think about other people before I do something that might hurt them. I wish I'd thought about my friend's feelings before I sent that note. Maybe it's not too late to say something after all.

Viannah age 13

What about You?

❶ What would the world be like if people put the needs of others first? What problems would disappear? What great things might happen?

❷ Think of one person you know who is really good at putting others first. What can you do to be more like this person?

❸ Ask God to help you be humble.

Turn to page 1437 for your next devotion.

in heaven and on earth and under
the earth,
[11] and every tongue confess that Jesus
Christ is Lord,
to the glory of God the Father.

Shining as Stars

[12]Therefore, my dear friends, as you
have always obeyed—not only in my
presence, but now much more in my absence—continue to work out your salvation with fear and trembling, [13]for it is
God who works in you to will and to act
according to his good purpose.

[14]Do everything without complaining
or arguing, [15]so that you may become
blameless and pure, children of God
without fault in a crooked and depraved
generation, in which you shine like stars
in the universe [16]as you hold out[a]
the word of life—in order that I may boast on
the day of Christ that I did not run or labor for nothing. [17]But even if I am being

poured out like a drink offering on the
sacrifice and service coming from your
faith, I am glad and rejoice with all of
you. [18]So you too should be glad and rejoice with me.

Timothy and Epaphroditus

[19]I hope in the Lord Jesus to send
Timothy to you soon, that I also may be
cheered when I receive news about you.
[20]I have no one else like him, who takes a
genuine interest in your welfare. [21]For
everyone looks out for his own interests,
not those of Jesus Christ. [22]But you know
that Timothy has proved himself, because as a son with his father he has
served with me in the work of the gospel.
[23]I hope, therefore, to send him as soon
as I see how things go with me. [24]And I
am confident in the Lord that I myself
will come soon.

[a]16 Or *hold on to*

Wednesday

Don't Be a Downer

Read Philippians 2:14

When I was little, I always got toys for Christmas. Whatever I got, my mom
told me to say thank you and at least *pretend* I liked it. She explained that
it would hurt people's feelings if I complained about a gift or just ignored it.
Now that I'm older and I've heard people make fun of gifts I've given them,
I can totally see what Mom was saying. It really hurts when someone
doesn't appreciate what you've given them!

It's the same with life. All of life is a gift from God. Every time we complain about something, we're telling God we don't appreciate what he's
done for us. We're hurting his feelings. Besides, when we complain, we're
not very fun to be around. We bring ourselves down, and we bring everybody else down too.

Reading this verse reminds me that complaining makes me miserable,
but being grateful makes me a happier, more Christlike person. It's pretty
obvious which option's the way to go.

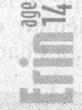

❶ What kind of stuff do you complain about? Why?

❷ Ask someone like your best friend or your parents to give you a
secret signal when you start whining or complaining. When you realize
you're doing it, try to stop right away.

❸ Thank God for all he's given you today.

Turn to page 1439 for your next devotion.

²⁵But I think it is necessary to send back to you Epaphroditus, my brother, fellow worker and fellow soldier, who is also your messenger, whom you sent to take care of my needs. ²⁶For he longs for all of you and is distressed because you heard he was ill. ²⁷Indeed he was ill, and almost died. But God had mercy on him, and not on him only but also on me, to spare me sorrow upon sorrow. ²⁸Therefore I am all the more eager to send him, so that when you see him again you may be glad and I may have less anxiety. ²⁹Welcome him in the Lord with great joy, and honor men like him, ³⁰because he almost died for the work of Christ, risking his life to make up for the help you could not give me.

No Confidence in the Flesh

3 Finally, my brothers, rejoice in the Lord! It is no trouble for me to write the same things to you again, and it is a safeguard for you.

²Watch out for those dogs, those men who do evil, those mutilators of the flesh. ³For it is we who are the circumcision, we who worship by the Spirit of God, who glory in Christ Jesus, and who put no confidence in the flesh— ⁴though I myself have reasons for such confidence.

If anyone else thinks he has reasons to put confidence in the flesh, I have more: ⁵circumcised on the eighth day, of the people of Israel, of the tribe of Benjamin, a Hebrew of Hebrews; in regard to the law, a Pharisee; ⁶as for zeal, persecuting

the church; as for legalistic righteousness, faultless.

⁷But whatever was to my profit I now consider loss for the sake of Christ. ⁸What is more, I consider everything a loss compared to the surpassing greatness of knowing Christ Jesus my Lord, for whose sake I have lost all things. I consider them rubbish, that I may gain Christ ⁹and be found in him, not having a righteousness of my own that comes from the law, but that which is through faith in Christ—the righteousness that comes from God and is by faith. ¹⁰I want to know Christ and the power of his resurrection and the fellowship of sharing in his sufferings, becoming like him in his death, ¹¹and so, somehow, to attain to the resurrection from the dead.

Pressing on Toward the Goal

¹²Not that I have already obtained all this, or have already been made perfect, but I press on to take hold of that for which Christ Jesus took hold of me. ¹³Brothers, I do not consider myself yet to have taken hold of it. But one thing I do: Forgetting what is behind and straining toward what is ahead, ¹⁴I press on toward the goal to win the prize for which God has called me heavenward in Christ Jesus.

¹⁵All of us who are mature should take such a view of things. And if on some point you think differently, that too God will make clear to you. ¹⁶Only let us live up to what we have already attained.

¹⁷Join with others in following my example, brothers, and take note of those who live according to the pattern we gave you. ¹⁸For, as I have often told you before and now say again even with tears, many live as enemies of the cross of Christ. ¹⁹Their destiny is destruction, their god is their stomach, and their glory is in their shame. Their mind is on earthly things. ²⁰But our citizenship is in heaven. And we eagerly await a Savior from there, the Lord Jesus Christ, ²¹who, by the power that enables him to bring everything under his control, will transform our lowly bodies so that they will be like his glorious body.

4 Therefore, my brothers, you whom I love and long for, my joy and

Jewish to the Core

Huh?

Philippians 3:4–6

When Paul rattles off his background, he isn't trying to brag. Instead, he's just showing how Jewish he is. He's Jewish to the core, educated by the best Jewish teachers and given the best Jewish jobs. And yet Jesus made such a huge change in his life that being 100% Jewish doesn't matter as much as following Jesus 100%.

crown, that is how you should stand firm in the Lord, dear friends!

Exhortations

²I plead with Euodia and I plead with Syntyche to agree with each other in the Lord. ³Yes, and I ask you, loyal yoke-fellow,ᵃ help these women who have contended at my side in the cause of the gospel, along with Clement and the rest of my fellow workers, whose names are in the book of life.

⁴Rejoice in the Lord always. I will say it again: Rejoice! ⁵Let your gentleness be evident to all. The Lord is near. ⁶Do not be anxious about anything, but in everything, by prayer and petition, with thanksgiving, present your requests to God. ⁷And the peace of God, which transcends all understanding, will guard your hearts and your minds in Christ Jesus.

⁸Finally, brothers, whatever is true, whatever is noble, whatever is right, whatever is pure, whatever is lovely, whatever is admirable—if anything is excel-

lent or praiseworthy—think about such things. ⁹Whatever you have learned or received or heard from me, or seen in

ᵃ3 Or *loyal Syzygus*

me—put it into practice. And the God of peace will be with you.

Thanks for Their Gifts

[10]I rejoice greatly in the Lord that at last you have renewed your concern for me. Indeed, you have been concerned, but you had no opportunity to show it. [11]I am not saying this because I am in need, for I have learned to be content whatever the circumstances. [12]I know what it is to be in need, and I know what it is to have plenty. I have learned the secret of being content in any and every situation, whether well fed or hungry, whether living in plenty or in want. [13]I can do everything through him who gives me strength.

[14]Yet it was good of you to share in my troubles. [15]Moreover, as you Philippians know, in the early days of your acquaintance with the gospel, when I set out from Macedonia, not one church shared with me in the matter of giving and receiving, except you only; [16]for even when I was in Thessalonica, you sent me aid again and again when I was in need. [17]Not that I am looking for a gift, but I am looking for what may be credited to your account. [18]I have received full payment and even more; I am amply supplied, now that I have received from Epaphroditus the gifts you sent. They are a fragrant offering, an acceptable sacrifice, pleasing to God. [19]And my God will meet all your needs according to his glorious riches in Christ Jesus.

[20]To our God and Father be glory for ever and ever. Amen.

Final Greetings

[21]Greet all the saints in Christ Jesus. The brothers who are with me send greetings. [22]All the saints send you greetings, especially those who belong to Caesar's household.

[23]The grace of the Lord Jesus Christ be with your spirit. Amen.[a]

[a]23 Some manuscripts do not have Amen.

Colossians

START

Have you ever written a letter home from camp? Did you gush? You know . . . Just like a drinking fountain that squirts out too much water, sometimes we gush about love, homesickness or a strong craving for a Quarter Pounder with Cheese. In his letter to the Colossians, Paul gushes in a major way!

It's kind of like a letter home from camp. Paul started the church in the city of Colosse (*Colossians* is the name for the people in the city of *Colosse*—just like people from Chicago are called Chicagoans and people from Los Angeles are called Angelinos). The people in Colosse had been really open to Paul, and he quickly became very close friends with those who joined the church there. Then he left and went to start other churches. While Paul was gone, he missed the people in Colosse.

In his letter, Paul gushes about 2 things: He gushes about his love for the people in the church, and he gushes about the perfect, amazing, powerful, totally awesome person and work of Jesus Christ. Paul just can't contain himself. Like that drinking fountain that massively soaks your face, Paul drenches the Colossians with his devotion to them and his joy in Jesus.

Cast OF Characters

Paul
Paul had been a major Christian killer. Then Jesus met him on a road, scaled over his eyes a bit (only temporarily), and the next thing you know, Paul was this radical Christian. Paul started most of the earliest churches, including the one receiving this letter.

(Co-LAH-suh)

The Church of Colosse, Colossians
(Co-LAH-shuns)
The people of this church received one of Paul's nicest letters. Sure, it has some instructions in it too. But for the most part, it's a love letter. They must have been an amazing church!

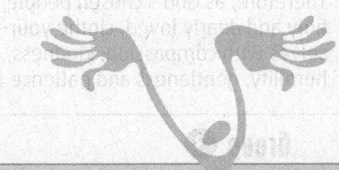

The Greeting Gang
There's a bunch of other people (men and women) mentioned at the end of the letter. They're all people who knew Paul was writing a letter to the Colossians and said, "Ooh, Paul, make sure you say 'hi' to everyone there for me!"

What's UP with That?

There are some really cool verses in this book. A few of them are listed below. See if you can figure out which version of each verse is the real one. Try to guess first; then look at the clues at the bottom to check your answer.

Group 1

And whatever you do, whether in word or deed, do it all in the name of the Lord Jesus, giving thanks to God the Father through him.

And whatever you do, make sure you don't get caught.

And whatever you do, don't say bad things about others, and make sure you go to church a lot.

Group 2

Therefore, as God's chosen people, holy and dearly loved, clothe yourselves with all cotton natural fabrics.

Therefore, as God's chosen people, holy and dearly loved, clothe yourselves with some good spiritual stuff, but wear some real clothes too.

Therefore, as God's chosen people, holy and dearly loved, clothe yourselves with compassion, kindness, humility, gentleness and patience.

Group 3

Set your minds on things that will help you get a really high paying job someday.

Set your minds on things above, not on earthly things.

Set your minds on a shelf.

clues: 3:17, 3:12, 3:1-2

Snap Shots

- You're the coolest people in the world!
  (chapter 1:1-14)

- Jesus is 3 words— Lord of everything
  (chapter 1:15-23)

- I'm working hard 'cause I love you
  (chapters 1:24—2:5)

- Jesus isn't just a bunch of rules
  (chapter 2:6-23)

- You're not you, you're new!
  (chapters 3:1—4:6)

- Howdy doody
  (chapter 4:7-18)

1 Paul, an apostle of Christ Jesus by the will of God, and Timothy our brother,

²To the holy and faithful*ᵃ* brothers in Christ at Colosse:

Grace and peace to you from God our Father.*ᵇ*

Thanksgiving and Prayer

³We always thank God, the Father of our Lord Jesus Christ, when we pray for you, ⁴because we have heard of your faith in Christ Jesus and of the love you have for all the saints— ⁵the faith and love that spring from the hope that is stored up for you in heaven and that you have already heard about in the word of truth, the gospel ⁶that has come to you. All over the world this gospel is bearing fruit and growing, just as it has been doing among you since the day you heard it and understood God's grace in all its truth. ⁷You learned it from Epaphras, our dear fellow servant, who is a faithful minister of Christ on our*ᶜ* behalf, ⁸and who also told us of your love in the Spirit.

⁹For this reason, since the day we heard about you, we have not stopped praying for you and asking God to fill you with the knowledge of his will through all spiritual wisdom and understanding. ¹⁰And we pray this in order that you may live a life worthy of the Lord and may please him in every way: bearing fruit in every good work, growing in the knowledge of God, ¹¹being strengthened with all power according to his glorious might so that you may have great endurance and patience, and joyfully ¹²giving thanks to the Father, who has qualified you*ᵈ* to share in the inheritance of the saints in the kingdom of light. ¹³For he has rescued us from the dominion of darkness and brought us into the kingdom of the Son he loves, ¹⁴in whom we have redemption,*ᵉ* the forgiveness of sins.

The Supremacy of Christ

¹⁵He is the image of the invisible God, the firstborn over all creation. ¹⁶For by him all things were created: things in heaven and on earth, visible and invis-

ible, whether thrones or powers or rulers or authorities; all things were created by him and for him. ¹⁷He is before all things, and in him all things hold together. ¹⁸And he is the head of the body, the church; he is the beginning and the firstborn from among the dead, so that in everything he might have the supremacy. ¹⁹For God was pleased to have all his fullness dwell in him, ²⁰and through him to reconcile to himself all things, whether things on earth or things in heaven, by making peace through his blood, shed on the cross.

²¹Once you were alienated from God and were enemies in your minds because of*ᶠ* your evil behavior. ²²But now he has reconciled you by Christ's physical body through death to present you holy in his sight, without blemish and free from accusation— ²³if you continue in your faith,

All Spiffed Up

Huh?

Colossians 1:22

To *reconcile* means "to put something back together and make it right." (If you were to reconcile a headless Barbie doll, you'd glue her head back on.) Our relationship with God was broken because of our sin. But God has reconciled us to himself. Through Jesus Christ our relationship with God is right and good and glued back together. When Jesus hung on the cross and died in our place, he reconciled us to God.

established and firm, not moved from the hope held out in the gospel. This is the gospel that you heard and that has been proclaimed to every creature under heaven, and of which I, Paul, have become a servant.

ᵃ2 Or believing   ᵇ2 Some manuscripts Father and the Lord Jesus Christ   ᶜ7 Some manuscripts your   ᵈ12 Some manuscripts us   ᵉ14 A few late manuscripts redemption through his blood   ᶠ21 Or minds, as shown by

Paul's Labor for the Church

²⁴Now I rejoice in what was suffered for you, and I fill up in my flesh what is still lacking in regard to Christ's afflictions, for the sake of his body, which is the church. ²⁵I have become its servant by the commission God gave me to present to you the word of God in its fullness— ²⁶the mystery that has been kept hidden for ages and generations, but is now disclosed to the saints. ²⁷To them God has chosen to make known among the Gentiles the glorious riches of this mystery, which is Christ in you, the hope of glory.

²⁸We proclaim him, admonishing and teaching everyone with all wisdom, so that we may present everyone perfect in Christ. ²⁹To this end I labor, struggling with all his energy, which so powerfully works in me.

2 I want you to know how much I am struggling for you and for those at Laodicea, and for all who have not met me personally. ²My purpose is that they may be encouraged in heart and united in love, so that they may have the full riches of complete understanding, in order that they may know the mystery of God, namely, Christ, ³in whom are hidden all the treasures of wisdom and knowledge. ⁴I tell you this so that no one may deceive you by fine-sounding arguments. ⁵For though I am absent from you in body, I am present with you in spirit and delight to see how orderly you are and how firm your faith in Christ is.

Freedom From Human Regulations Through Life With Christ

⁶So then, just as you received Christ Jesus as Lord, continue to live in him, ⁷rooted and built up in him, strengthened in the faith as you were taught, and overflowing with thankfulness.

⁸See to it that no one takes you captive

Fri day

Anything Goes?

Read Colossians 2:8

In this verse, Paul is talking to a crowd of people who have been influenced by old traditions and teachers who don't follow Jesus. But Paul says that God's truth is the only message that matters.

In today's world a lot of people follow the popular path. This path tells them to put themselves first. It says "truth" is something that changes and anything is acceptable. Take dating, for example. For a lot of teens, dating is about getting something. People think, "What's in it for me?" But God tells us that love is *not* about pleasing ourselves; it's about giving to others, sharing with them and respecting their purity in Christ.

God's Word tells us to love others, which is the opposite of putting ourselves first. It tells us that God's Word is the ultimate truth and it never, ever changes. And God's Word tells us that Jesus Christ is the only way to salvation. That's God's message—the only message people need to follow.

Tonia age 14

What about You?

❶ Why is it so easy to listen to the messages society gives us?

❷ Next time you watch TV, pay extra attention to the commercials. What do they say you have to do to be happy? Who do they tell you to be? How is that different from what God wants you to be?

❸ Ask God to help you follow *his* plans for your life, not society's.

Turn to page 1447 for your next devotion.

Hall of Wacky Religions

Our world is filled with weird religions dedicated to goofy gods and disgusting deities. It was the same back in Bible times. Some of the worst and weirdest:

Hocus Pocus! Sorcerers, psychics, magicians, enchanters, witches—the Bible has all of them. They counted on trickery or demonic powers to lure customers and influence events. God is not impressed (Exodus 22:18, page 97).

Cults! There were tons of them—each dedicated to a goofy god or goddess. Some of Israel's neighbors believed in the goddess Asherah, who cranked out 70 gods herself. Many of the Jews were obsessed with her, setting up hilltop shrines made of "sacred" stones and poles. Every time a good king came along, he had to go from hill to hill, knocking down all the shrines. One of Asherah's sons was Baal, another hokey hoax that seduced many Jews. Elijah makes a joke of Baal in 1 Kings 18, page 411.

Knuckleheads! One of the most popular fads during New Testament times was Gnosticism (forget the "G"; it's said like NAH-stih-sizz-um), a convenient little philosophy that says "spirit good, body bad." For some Gnostics, this meant that their bodies had to be beaten into submission. Others took the philosophy the other way, getting drunk and letting their bodies do whatever without worrying about corrupting their permanently "sweet spirits." Does Gnosticism work? The Bible says gno. See Colossians 2:20–23 and 1 John 3:4–10, page 1531.

Spiritual Stews! In the New Testament, some folks tried to cook up a faith with one part freedom in Christ and one part bondage to old Jewish rules. But you can't use both ingredients. Choose one or the other. Choose Christ. And while you're at it, read Colossians 2:6–17.

through hollow and deceptive philosophy, which depends on human tradition and the basic principles of this world rather than on Christ.

⁹For in Christ all the fullness of the Deity lives in bodily form, ¹⁰and you have been given fullness in Christ, who is the head over every power and authority. ¹¹In him you were also circumcised, in the putting off of the sinful nature,ᵃ not with a circumcision done by the hands of men but with the circumcision done by Christ, ¹²having been buried with him in baptism and raised with him through your faith in the power of God, who raised him from the dead.

¹³When you were dead in your sins and in the uncircumcision of your sinful nature,ᵇ God made youᶜ alive with Christ. He forgave us all our sins, ¹⁴having canceled the written code, with its regulations, that was against us and that stood opposed to us; he took it away, nailing it to the cross. ¹⁵And having disarmed the powers and authorities, he made a public

spectacle of them, triumphing over them by the cross.ᵈ

¹⁶Therefore do not let anyone judge you by what you eat or drink, or with regard to a religious festival, a New Moon celebration or a Sabbath day. ¹⁷These are a shadow of the things that were to come; the reality, however, is found in Christ. ¹⁸Do not let anyone who delights in false humility and the worship of angels disqualify you for the prize. Such a person goes into great detail about what he has seen, and his unspiritual mind puffs him up with idle notions. ¹⁹He has lost connection with the Head, from whom the whole body, supported and held together by its ligaments and sinews, grows as God causes it to grow.

²⁰Since you died with Christ to the basic principles of this world, why, as though you still belonged to it, do you submit to its rules: ²¹"Do not handle! Do

ᵃ11 Or *the flesh* ᵇ13 Or *your flesh* ᶜ13 Some manuscripts *us* ᵈ15 Or *them in him*

Rule #473

Huh?

Colossians 2:20–23

There are lots of rules in churches. Almost all of them are created by us—not by God. Paul points out in these verses that rules that try to make us look like we're living for God are a waste of time. God cares about us *really* living for him, not just looking like we are.

not taste! Do not touch!"? ²²These are all destined to perish with use, because they are based on human commands and teachings. ²³Such regulations indeed have an appearance of wisdom, with their self-imposed worship, their false humility and their harsh treatment of the body, but they lack any value in restraining sensual indulgence.

Rules for Holy Living

3 Since, then, you have been raised with Christ, set your hearts on things above, where Christ is seated at the right hand of God. ²Set your minds on things above, not on earthly things. ³For you died, and your life is now hidden with Christ in God. ⁴When Christ, who is your[a] life, appears, then you also will appear with him in glory.

⁵Put to death, therefore, whatever belongs to your earthly nature: sexual immorality, impurity, lust, evil desires and greed, which is idolatry. ⁶Because of these, the wrath of God is coming.[b] ⁷You used to walk in these ways, in the life you once lived. ⁸But now you must rid yourselves of all such things as these: anger, rage, malice, slander, and filthy language from your lips. ⁹Do not lie to each other, since you have taken off your old self with its practices ¹⁰and have put on the new self, which is being renewed in knowledge in the image of its Creator. ¹¹Here there is no Greek or Jew, circumcised or uncircumcised, barbarian, Scythian, slave or free, but Christ is all, and is in all.

¹²Therefore, as God's chosen people, holy and dearly loved, clothe yourselves with compassion, kindness, humility, gentleness and patience. ¹³Bear with each other and forgive whatever grievances you may have against one another. Forgive as the Lord forgave you. ¹⁴And over all these virtues put on love, which binds them all together in perfect unity.

¹⁵Let the peace of Christ rule in your hearts, since as members of one body you were called to peace. And be thankful. ¹⁶Let the word of Christ dwell in you richly as you teach and admonish one another with all wisdom, and as you sing psalms, hymns and spiritual songs with gratitude in your hearts to God. ¹⁷And whatever you do, whether in word or deed, do it all in the name of the Lord Jesus, giving thanks to God the Father through him.

Rules for Christian Households

¹⁸Wives, submit to your husbands, as is fitting in the Lord.

¹⁹Husbands, love your wives and do not be harsh with them.

Legos of Love

Huh?

Colossians 3:18–22

Every relationship has "rules" for how we live, communicate and act. This is true in our families too. But the Lego bricks that make up our rules are not made of plastic; they're made of love. Wives are to submit out of love, not out of weakness. Husbands are to love as God loves (that's pretty huge love). Children are to obey out of love. And parents are supposed to be careful that they don't make their kids bitter forever. These "love Legos" are much stronger than plastic! Our job is to invest time and energy putting them together.

---

²⁰Children, obey your parents in everything, for this pleases the Lord.

²¹Fathers, do not embitter your children, or they will become discouraged.

²²Slaves, obey your earthly masters in everything; and do it, not only when their eye is on you and to win their favor, but with sincerity of heart and reverence for the Lord. ²³Whatever you do, work at it with all your heart, as working for the Lord, not for men, ²⁴since you know that you will receive an inheritance from the Lord as a reward. It is the Lord Christ you are serving. ²⁵Anyone who does wrong will be repaid for his wrong, and there is no favoritism.

4 Masters, provide your slaves with what is right and fair, because you know that you also have a Master in heaven.

Further Instructions

²Devote yourselves to prayer, being watchful and thankful. ³And pray for us, too, that God may open a door for our message, so that we may proclaim the mystery of Christ, for which I am in chains. ⁴Pray that I may proclaim it clearly, as I should. ⁵Be wise in the way you act toward outsiders; make the most of every opportunity. ⁶Let your conversa-

Weekend.

Mashed Potato Ice Cream

Read Mark 12:30 (page 1206)

Isn't it amazing how awesome food can look on TV and in magazines? Even baby food and dog food can look tasty! Well, what you see is not always what you it is:

- When you see someone licking an ice cream cone on TV or in the movies (are you ready for this?), they're really licking mashed potatoes (real ice cream would melt)!
- How about that beautiful whipped cream on top of the pie? It almost looks like shaving cream. Probably because it is!

Plain and simple, what you see on TV does not always match reality when it comes to food commercials, sales pitches, even sexual stuff. So next time you're watching that sexy movie or looking at those suggestive magazines, realize it is not reality. (And ask yourself why you're looking at this kind of stuff in the first place!)

Jesus warned us that watching and looking at that kind of stuff is really dangerous: "I tell you that anyone who looks at a woman lustfully has already committed adultery with her in his heart" (Matthew 5:28).

When you find yourself drawn to shows or magazines you know aren't good for you, ask for God's strength to help you resist the temptation. Thursday, Karen was right on when she said, "When I keep my thoughts on God, my actions follow right along."

What about You?

❶ What are some things on TV that are "too good to be true"?

❷ Can you think of a TV show or magazine that you like but that probably isn't good for you? Which one? Try to give it up for one week, then maybe try another week.

❸ Ask God to help you focus on him when you face temptations.

Turn to page 1448 for your next devotion.

tion be always full of grace, seasoned with salt, so that you may know how to answer everyone.

Final Greetings

[7]Tychicus will tell you all the news about me. He is a dear brother, a faithful minister and fellow servant in the Lord. [8]I am sending him to you for the express purpose that you may know about our[a] circumstances and that he may encourage your hearts. [9]He is coming with Onesimus, our faithful and dear brother, who is one of you. They will tell you everything that is happening here.

[10]My fellow prisoner Aristarchus sends you his greetings, as does Mark, the

cousin of Barnabas. (You have received instructions about him; if he comes to you, welcome him.) [11]Jesus, who is called Justus, also sends greetings. These are the only Jews among my fellow workers for the kingdom of God, and they have proved a comfort to me. [12]Epaphras, who is one of you and a servant of Christ Jesus, sends greetings. He is always wrestling in prayer for you, that you may stand firm in all the will of God, mature and fully assured. [13]I vouch for him that he is working hard for you and for those at Laodicea and Hierapolis. [14]Our dear friend Luke, the doctor, and Demas send greetings. [15]Give my greetings to the

[a]8 Some manuscripts *that he may know about your*

Monday

Obey My Parents?   **Read Colossians 3:20**

One night I really wanted to go to a youth group meeting with a friend, but my family had some stuff we needed to do, so my mom said no. I snuck out of the house and went anyway. Halfway through the youth pastor's talk, my mom showed up. Boy, was she steamed!

Now I thought going to that meeting was definitely something God wanted me to do. But the fact is, I went against God's will that night by disobeying my mom. As a result, I lost my mom's trust.

God knew what he was doing when he put my family together. He gave me my parents so there would be someone to help me grow into an adult. Obviously, God wants our parents to follow and obey him. But he also wants them to instruct us and guide us in the way we should live our lives. That's *their* responsibility. As long as the things our parents ask us to do don't go against God's commands, we need to lovingly obey them. That's *our* responsibility.

God gave us the Ten Commandments, and one of them is to honor our parents. By willingly obeying Mom and Dad, we're obeying God.

Meredith age 14

What about You?

❶ What are some things that really bug you about your parents? What things do you appreciate about them?

❷ Think of 4 ways to show respect to your parents. For the next month, do one of those things each week.

❸ Ask God to help you learn to respect and obey your parents.

Turn to page 1453 for your next devotion.

brothers at Laodicea, and to Nympha and the church in her house.

¹⁶After this letter has been read to you, see that it is also read in the church of the Laodiceans and that you in turn read the letter from Laodicea.

¹⁷Tell Archippus: "See to it that you complete the work you have received in the Lord."

¹⁸I, Paul, write this greeting in my own hand. Remember my chains. Grace be with you.

1 Thessalonians

START

Paul was on a roll. He was hopping from city to city, traveling by ship, by foot and any other way he could get around. He was so pumped about telling people that Jesus was the Messiah that he couldn't contain his excitement.

In many cities Paul couldn't stay around long enough to make sure that the new believers understood everything about their faith. The city of Thessalonica was one of many cities where Paul stopped to preach and people became Christ-followers. After Paul moved on, he realized they still had tons of questions—especially about Jesus coming back someday. This letter is Paul's way of answering a bunch of those questions.

CAST OF Characters

Paul

As a traveling missionary, Paul made a quick stop in the city of Thessalonica. He hadn't been able to stay there as long as he would have liked. But he really cared about the Christians there.

(Thess-uh-low-NIGH-kuh)

The Church at Thessalonica, the Thessalonians (Thess-uh-LOW-nee-uns)

This group of believers began meeting in a Jewish church building when Paul came to town. It was a mixed group of Jewish believers and those from other backgrounds.

Timothy

A close friend of Paul, he probably delivered this letter to the church. He also told Paul how well these people were doing in their walk with God.

What's UP with That?

Parent-talk

Have you noticed all the one-liners that parents collect to help their kids succeed in life?

It's like they all go to some kind of parent school to learn these lines—"If all your friends jumped off a bridge, would you?". . . blah blah blah. Paul is like a spiritual parent to these new Christians, and he has some great one-liners for them. Some of the things on the list below are things Papa Paul says to his "kids" in Thessalonica. See if you can find the real instructions in the list below. If you need some help, look in the book—most are in the last half of the letter.

A Brush your teeth after every meal

B You guys are awesome

C Don't mess around with sex

D Keep your room neat and tidy

E Mind your own business

F Be sure to call home if you're planning to be late

G Happy, happy, joy, joy

H No dating until you're 35

I Don't be like everybody else

J Steer clear of every kind of evil

K Eat plenty of broccoli and lima beans

L Go to the bathroom before leaving on a long trip

M Pucker up to say hi in church

answers: b (1:2), c (4:3), e (4:11), g (5:16), i (5:6), j (5:22), m (5:26)

Snap shots

- Thanks for being awesome friends *(chapter 1:1–3)*

- Remember our great times together *(chapters 1:4—2:16)*

- I've been a little worried about you *(chapters 2:17—3:5)*

- Tim says you're doing great! *(chapter 3:6–13)*

- Keep your standards high *(chapter 4:1–12)*

- He's coming back—here's how it'll be *(chapters 4:13—5:11)*

- P.S., P.P.S. and, oh yeah, P.P.P.S. *(chapter 5:12–28)*

1

Paul, Silas[a] and Timothy,

To the church of the Thessalonians in God the Father and the Lord Jesus Christ:

Grace and peace to you.[b]

Thanksgiving for the Thessalonians' Faith

[2] We always thank God for all of you, mentioning you in our prayers. [3] We continually remember before our God and Father your work produced by faith, your labor prompted by love, and your endurance inspired by hope in our Lord Jesus Christ.

The Little Church That Could

Huh?

1 Thessalonians 1:3

Paul worked hard to start a bunch of churches, including this one in Thessalonica. With so many of these baby churches having major problems, Paul was always hoping that they would stay on track. So when he heard about the Thessalonian church, how they were hanging tough and standing firm, it made him feel awesome, and his faith was strengthened.

[4] For we know, brothers loved by God, that he has chosen you, [5] because our gospel came to you not simply with words, but also with power, with the Holy Spirit and with deep conviction. You know how we lived among you for your sake. [6] You became imitators of us and of the Lord; in spite of severe suffering, you welcomed the message with the joy given by the Holy Spirit. [7] And so you became a model to all the believers in Macedonia and Achaia. [8] The Lord's message rang out from you not only in Macedonia and Achaia—your faith in God has become known everywhere. Therefore we do not need to say anything about it, [9] for they themselves report what kind of reception you gave us. They tell how you turned to God from idols to serve the living and true God, [10] and to wait for his Son from heaven, whom he

raised from the dead—Jesus, who rescues us from the coming wrath.

Paul's Ministry in Thessalonica

2

You know, brothers, that our visit to you was not a failure. [2] We had previously suffered and been insulted in Philippi, as you know, but with the help of our God we dared to tell you his gospel in spite of strong opposition. [3] For the appeal we make does not spring from error or impure motives, nor are we trying to trick you. [4] On the contrary, we speak as men approved by God to be entrusted with the gospel. We are not trying to please men but God, who tests our hearts. [5] You know we never used flattery, nor did we put on a mask to cover up greed—God is our witness. [6] We were not looking for praise from men, not from you or anyone else.

As apostles of Christ we could have been a burden to you, [7] but we were gentle among you, like a mother caring for her little children. [8] We loved you so much that we were delighted to share with you not only the gospel of God but our lives as well, because you had become so dear to us. [9] Surely you remember, brothers, our toil and hardship; we worked night and day in order not to be a burden to anyone while we preached the gospel of God to you.

[10] You are witnesses, and so is God, of how holy, righteous and blameless we were among you who believed. [11] For you know that we dealt with each of you as a father deals with his own children, [12] encouraging, comforting and urging you to live lives worthy of God, who calls you into his kingdom and glory.

[13] And we also thank God continually because, when you received the word of God, which you heard from us, you accepted it not as the word of men, but as it actually is, the word of God, which is at work in you who believe. [14] For you, brothers, became imitators of God's churches in Judea, which are in Christ Jesus: You suffered from your own countrymen the same things those churches

---

[a]1 Greek *Silvanus*, a variant of *Silas*   [b]1 Some early manuscripts *you from God our Father and the Lord Jesus Christ*

suffered from the Jews, [15]who killed the Lord Jesus and the prophets and also drove us out. They displease God and are hostile to all men [16]in their effort to keep us from speaking to the Gentiles so that they may be saved. In this way they always heap up their sins to the limit. The wrath of God has come upon them at last.[a]

Paul's Longing to See the Thessalonians

[17]But, brothers, when we were torn away from you for a short time (in person, not in thought), out of our intense longing we made every effort to see you. [18]For we wanted to come to you—certainly I, Paul, did, again and again—but Satan stopped us. [19]For what is our hope, our joy, or the crown in which we will glory in the presence of our Lord Jesus when he comes? Is it not you? [20]Indeed, you are our glory and joy.

3 So when we could stand it no longer, we thought it best to be left by ourselves in Athens. [2]We sent Timothy, who is our brother and God's fellow worker[b] in spreading the gospel of Christ, to strengthen and encourage you in your faith, [3]so that no one would be unsettled by these trials. You know quite well that we were destined for them. [4]In fact, when we were with you, we kept telling you that we would be persecuted. And it turned out that way, as you well know. [5]For this reason, when I could stand it no longer, I sent to find out about your faith. I was afraid that in some way the tempter might have tempted you and our efforts might have been useless.

[a]16 Or them fully   [b]2 Some manuscripts brother and fellow worker; other manuscripts brother and God's servant

---

Tuesday

We Can Be Heroes

Read 1 Thessalonians 1:6–7

There is a guy in my youth group who is a really strong Christian. He's a great leader who lives his life for God. Lots of people, including me, look up to him. Whenever I see him do something that shows his love for God, I think, "That's so cool! I want to be like that." I've learned a lot from him, and now I know God better than I used to.

It's great to have a role model, someone who *shows* you how to live out your faith. That's what my friend does for me, so now I'm trying to do the same thing for other people. I really try to show how important my faith is by how I live and what I say. Now I have the courage to talk to my best friend about God, because I want her to see that my faith really means something. She's not a Christian yet, but I hope she will be soon!

God wants everyone to know him. So if you can be a role model to someone else, do it. And if you need a role model to help live out your faith more, find one. Having someone to look up to made a big difference for me.

Rebecca, age 13

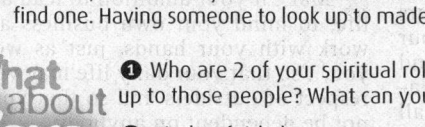

What about You?

❶ Who are 2 of your spiritual role models or heroes? Why do you look up to those people? What can you learn from them?

❷ Find a faith hero—someone in your family, your church, your school—whose faith you really admire. Ask that person to help you live out your faith more.

❸ Ask God to help you find a great Christian role model.

Turn to page 1455 for your next devotion.

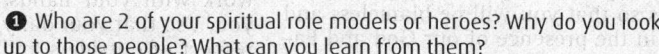

Timothy's Encouraging Report

[6]But Timothy has just now come to us from you and has brought good news about your faith and love. He has told us that you always have pleasant memories of us and that you long to see us, just as we also long to see you. [7]Therefore, brothers, in all our distress and persecution we were encouraged about you because of your faith. [8]For now we really live, since you are standing firm in the Lord. [9]How can we thank God enough for

Surf's Up

Huh?

1 Thessalonians 3:8
Waves crash day after day after day against a pier, and yet it stays standing. The foundation of that pier had been built deep beneath the surface to give it strength. As Christians, we face the pounding crash of "waves" when we go through hard times in life and persecution for our beliefs. Spending time in the Bible, praying and developing a strong faith help us build a deep foundation (just like the pier) so we can stand strong in the Lord.

you in return for all the joy we have in the presence of our God because of you? [10]Night and day we pray most earnestly that we may see you again and supply what is lacking in your faith.

[11]Now may our God and Father himself and our Lord Jesus clear the way for us to come to you. [12]May the Lord make your love increase and overflow for each other and for everyone else, just as ours does for you. [13]May he strengthen your hearts so that you will be blameless and holy in the presence of our God and Father when our Lord Jesus comes with all his holy ones.

Living to Please God

4 Finally, brothers, we instructed you how to live in order to please God, as in fact you are living. Now we ask you and urge you in the Lord Jesus to do this

more and more. [2]For you know what instructions we gave you by the authority of the Lord Jesus.

[3]It is God's will that you should be sanctified: that you should avoid sexual immorality; [4]that each of you should

You've Got a Purpose

Huh?

1 Thessalonians 4:3–4
Would you paint a white house with a dirty paintbrush? Clean dishes with an oily rag? Of course not! To "sanctify" means to set something aside for a special or sacred purpose. God loves you so much that he wants to set you apart from sin in order to do his special work—loving people.

learn to control his own body[a] in a way that is holy and honorable, [5]not in passionate lust like the heathen, who do not know God; [6]and that in this matter no one should wrong his brother or take advantage of him. The Lord will punish men for all such sins, as we have already told you and warned you. [7]For God did not call us to be impure, but to live a holy life. [8]Therefore, he who rejects this instruction does not reject man but God, who gives you his Holy Spirit.

[9]Now about brotherly love we do not need to write to you, for you yourselves have been taught by God to love each other. [10]And in fact, you do love all the brothers throughout Macedonia. Yet we urge you, brothers, to do so more and more.

[11]Make it your ambition to lead a quiet life, to mind your own business and to work with your hands, just as we told you, [12]so that your daily life may win the respect of outsiders and so that you will not be dependent on anybody.

The Coming of the Lord

[13]Brothers, we do not want you to be ignorant about those who fall asleep, or

[a]4 Or *learn to live with his own wife*; or *learn to acquire a wife*

to grieve like the rest of men, who have no hope. ¹⁴We believe that Jesus died and rose again and so we believe that God will bring with Jesus those who have fallen asleep in him. ¹⁵According to the Lord's own word, we tell you that we who are still alive, who are left till the coming of the Lord, will certainly not precede those who have fallen asleep. ¹⁶For the Lord himself will come down from heaven, with a loud command, with the voice of the archangel and with the trumpet call of God, and the dead in Christ will rise first. ¹⁷After that, we who are still alive and are left will be caught up together with them in the clouds to meet the Lord in the air. And so we will be with the Lord forever. ¹⁸Therefore encourage each other with these words.

5 Now, brothers, about times and dates we do not need to write to you, ²for you know very well that the day of the Lord will come like a thief in the night. ³While people are saying, "Peace and safety," destruction will come on them suddenly, as labor pains on a pregnant woman, and they will not escape.

⁴But you, brothers, are not in darkness so that this day should surprise you like a thief. ⁵You are all sons of the light and sons of the day. We do not belong to the night or to the darkness. ⁶So then, let us not be like others, who are asleep, but let us be alert and self-controlled. ⁷For those who sleep, sleep at night, and those who get drunk, get drunk at night. ⁸But since we belong to the day, let us be self-controlled, putting on faith and love as a breastplate, and the hope of salvation as a helmet. ⁹For God did not appoint us to suffer wrath but to receive salvation through our Lord Jesus Christ. ¹⁰He died for us so that, whether we are awake or asleep, we may live together with him. ¹¹Therefore encourage one another and build each other up, just as in fact you are doing.

Final Instructions

¹²Now we ask you, brothers, to respect those who work hard among you, who are over you in the Lord and who admonish you. ¹³Hold them in the highest regard in love because of their work. Live in peace with each other. ¹⁴And we urge

---

Wednesday

God's Purity Plan

Read 1 Thessalonians 4:3–7

"Avoid sexual immorality" might sound like an outdated rule, but think about it. God has always wanted us to follow his commands and save sex for marriage. But what have people done? They've dragged his plan through the mud and messed up their lives big-time.

    God gives us rules about sex because he cares for us. He knows all about the unexpected pregnancies and broken hearts and other problems that happen when people don't stay sexually pure. Following God's guidelines might be tough sometimes, but not following them can get us in situations that are a whole lot tougher!

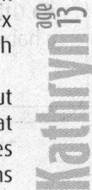

Kathryn age 13

What about You?

❶ Think about popular TV shows, movies and songs. What do these things say about sexuality?

❷ Ask your youth leader about the "True Love Waits" program, and find out how your group might be able to get involved.

❸ Pray for the strength to stay sexually pure.

Turn to page 1456 for your next devotion.

you, brothers, warn those who are idle, encourage the timid, help the weak, be patient with everyone. [15]Make sure that nobody pays back wrong for wrong, but always try to be kind to each other and to everyone else.

[16]Be joyful always; [17]pray continually; [18]give thanks in all circumstances, for this is God's will for you in Christ Jesus.

[19]Do not put out the Spirit's fire; [20]do not treat prophecies with contempt. [21]Test everything. Hold on to the good. [22]Avoid every kind of evil.

[23]May God himself, the God of peace, sanctify you through and through. May your whole spirit, soul and body be kept blameless at the coming of our Lord Jesus Christ. [24]The one who calls you is faithful and he will do it.

[25]Brothers, pray for us. [26]Greet all the brothers with a holy kiss. [27]I charge you before the Lord to have this letter read to all the brothers.

[28]The grace of our Lord Jesus Christ be with you.

Thursday

Joy Ride

Read 1 Thessalonians 5:16–18

When bad things happen to me, my first reaction is not to be joyful. I don't feel like giving thanks when I'm hurt by a good friend or when I fight with my parents or get a bad grade on a test. I'm more likely to wonder, *What is God doing?* I feel like saying, "That's it! If God really loved me, this wouldn't be happening!"

But then I look at all the ways God *has* blessed me. God gives me great, amazing gifts all the time, and I hardly ever remember to say "Thank you." If I paid more attention to praising God and less attention to my problems, I'd be a much more joyful person.

Christ age 14

❶ Think back to a time when something bad happened to you. What were your prayers like then?

❷ Start a list of the ways God has been good to you. Whenever you think of another reason to be thankful, add it to the list.

❸ Offer God a prayer of pure thanksgiving, with no requests in it. Try to make this a habit.

Turn to page 1460 for your next devotion.

2 Thessalonians

START

Cross your fingers, squeeze that lucky coin, watch for a falling star and make sure you blow out all the candles with one giant puff. People have tried to invent all kinds of ways to make sure that the things they hope for will happen.

But understand this: Believing in Jesus gives us a hope that isn't based on silly superstitions. The Christians in Thessalonica needed something to hope for. People were persecuting them, and their lives were not easy because of it. Paul wanted to remind them that it was worth hanging on to their faith even when times were tough. Why? Jesus is coming back someday.

Cast OF Characters

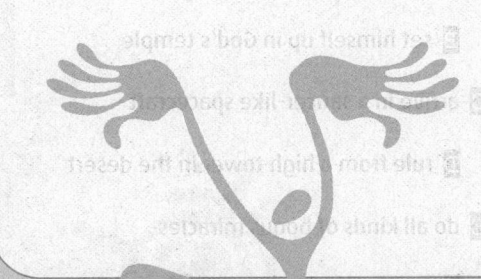

Paul

He already sent a letter to these fine folks. That first letter answered a lot of their questions. Now they had more questions, and, being the patient teacher he was, Paul takes the time to answer these as well.

(Thess-uh-low-NIGH-kuh)

(Thess-uh-LOW-nee-uns)

The Church at Thessalonica, the Thessalonians

These believers were suffering because of their faith. It must have been tough to hang on when things weren't going very well. But Paul gives them hope by telling them that Jesus will come back for them someday.

What's  Up with That?

The Bad Guy Wears Black

In old Western movies you could always tell who the bad guy was by the color of his hat: Bad guys wore black hats, and good guys wore white. In his second letter to the Thessalonians, Paul talks about an enemy of Jesus who will show up at the end of the world, just before Jesus returns. He'll be tough to recognize, so Paul describes him. Which of the following descriptions of this bad guy are true according to the 2 Thessalonians? He will:

A tell us he's God

B set himself up in God's temple

C arrive in a saucer-like spacecraft

D rule from a high tower in the desert

E do all kinds of bogus miracles

F get toasted in the end

G have secret powers

H have an army uniformed in white

I be everywhere at the same time

J trick people into believing him

Snap shots

- You grow, baby! *(chapter 1)*

- Tae kwon do's a comin' *(chapter 2:1–12)*

- Hang in there *(chapter 2:13–17)*

- No goofing off *(chapter 3:1–15)*

- Yours truly *(chapter 3:16–18)*

answers: a (2:4), b (2:4), e (2:9), f (2:8), g (2:7), j (2:9)

1 Paul, Silas[a] and Timothy,

To the church of the Thessalonians in God our Father and the Lord Jesus Christ:

²Grace and peace to you from God the Father and the Lord Jesus Christ.

Thanksgiving and Prayer

³We ought always to thank God for you, brothers, and rightly so, because your faith is growing more and more, and the love every one of you has for each other is increasing. ⁴Therefore, among God's churches we boast about your perseverance and faith in all the persecutions and trials you are enduring.

⁵All this is evidence that God's judgment is right, and as a result you will be counted worthy of the kingdom of God, for which you are suffering. ⁶God is just: He will pay back trouble to those who trouble you ⁷and give relief to you who

The Best Judge
Huh?

2 Thessalonians 1:6
Often justice has to be left in the hands of someone who has ultimate power and control, like a judge. We have to have faith that God knows what's going on and that he'll do what's right, delivering fair judgment in the end.

are troubled, and to us as well. This will happen when the Lord Jesus is revealed from heaven in blazing fire with his powerful angels. ⁸He will punish those who do not know God and do not obey the gospel of our Lord Jesus. ⁹They will be punished with everlasting destruction and shut out from the presence of the Lord and from the majesty of his power ¹⁰on the day he comes to be glorified in his holy people and to be marveled at among all those who have believed. This includes you, because you believed our testimony to you.

¹¹With this in mind, we constantly pray for you, that our God may count you worthy of his calling, and that by his power he may fulfill every good purpose of yours and every act prompted by your faith. ¹²We pray this so that the name of our Lord Jesus may be glorified in you, and you in him, according to the grace of our God and the Lord Jesus Christ.[b]

The Man of Lawlessness

2 Concerning the coming of our Lord Jesus Christ and our being gathered to him, we ask you, brothers, ²not to become easily unsettled or alarmed by some prophecy, report or letter supposed to have come from us, saying that the day of the Lord has already come. ³Don't let anyone deceive you in any way, for that day will not come until the rebellion occurs and the man of lawlessness[c] is revealed, the man doomed to destruction. ⁴He will oppose and will exalt himself over everything that is called God or is worshiped, so that he sets himself up in God's temple, proclaiming himself to be God.

⁵Don't you remember that when I was with you I used to tell you these things? ⁶And now you know what is holding him back, so that he may be revealed at the proper time. ⁷For the secret power of lawlessness is already at work; but the one who now holds it back will continue to do so till he is taken out of the way. ⁸And then the lawless one will be revealed, whom the Lord Jesus will overthrow with the breath of his mouth and destroy by the splendor of his coming. ⁹The coming of the lawless one will be in accordance with the work of Satan displayed in all kinds of counterfeit miracles, signs and wonders, ¹⁰and in every sort of evil that deceives those who are perishing. They perish because they refused to love the truth and so be saved. ¹¹For this reason God sends them a powerful delusion so that they will believe the lie ¹²and so that all will be condemned who have not believed the truth but have delighted in wickedness.

Stand Firm

¹³But we ought always to thank God for you, brothers loved by the Lord,

---

[a]1 Greek *Silvanus*, a variant of *Silas*   [b]12 Or *God and Lord, Jesus Christ*   [c]3 Some manuscripts *sin*

because from the beginning God chose you[a] to be saved through the sanctifying work of the Spirit and through belief in the truth. [14]He called you to this through our gospel, that you might share in the glory of our Lord Jesus Christ. [15]So then, brothers, stand firm and hold to the teachings[b] we passed on to you, whether by word of mouth or by letter.

[16]May our Lord Jesus Christ himself and God our Father, who loved us and by his grace gave us eternal encouragement and good hope, [17]encourage your hearts and strengthen you in every good deed and word.

Request for Prayer

3 Finally, brothers, pray for us that the message of the Lord may spread rapidly and be honored, just as it was with you. [2]And pray that we may be delivered from wicked and evil men, for not everyone has faith. [3]But the Lord is faithful, and he will strengthen and protect you from the evil one. [4]We have confidence in the Lord that you are doing and will continue to do the things we command.

[5]May the Lord direct your hearts into God's love and Christ's perseverance.

Warning Against Idleness

[6]In the name of the Lord Jesus Christ, we command you, brothers, to keep away from every brother who is idle and does not live according to the teaching[c] you received from us. [7]For you yourselves know how you ought to follow our example. We were not idle when we were with you, [8]nor did we eat anyone's food without paying for it. On the contrary, we worked night and day, laboring and toiling so that we would not be a burden to any of you. [9]We did this, not because we do not have the right to such help, but in order to make ourselves a model for you to follow. [10]For even when we were with you, we gave you this rule: "If a man will not work, he shall not eat."

[11]We hear that some among you are idle. They are not busy; they are busy-

---

[a]13 Some manuscripts *because God chose you as his firstfruits*   [b]15 Or *traditions*   [c]6 Or *tradition*

Friday

Prayer Power

Read 2 Thessalonians 1:11–12

Praying for my friends is really important to me. Every night I pray for my Christian and non-Christian friends on a list I call my "Circle of Concern." And I know my Christian friends are praying for me too.

One semester I prayed especially for my friend Heather because she hadn't been to church in a while, and I hardly ever saw her at school. I asked God to give me more opportunities to see her. The next semester, I had the same lunch period as Heather, and we ate together every day. Soon she started coming to church again, and the next thing I knew, she was telling me how she was witnessing to some of our non-Christian friends.

Praying for your friends can strengthen your relationship with them and your relationship with God. You can really see the difference prayer makes!

Stacy age 15

What about You?

❶ How does praying for others help you grow deeper as a Christian?

❷ Make your own list of 5 friends and pray for them every day this week.

❸ Thank God for your friends.

Turn to page 1461 for your next devotion.

down and earn the bread they eat. ¹³And as for you, brothers, never tire of doing what is right.

¹⁴If anyone does not obey our instruction in this letter, take special note of him. Do not associate with him, in order that he may feel ashamed. ¹⁵Yet do not regard him as an enemy, but warn him as a brother.

Final Greetings

¹⁶Now may the Lord of peace himself give you peace at all times and in every way. The Lord be with all of you.

¹⁷I, Paul, write this greeting in my own hand, which is the distinguishing mark in all my letters. This is how I write.

¹⁸The grace of our Lord Jesus Christ be with you all.

Advice About Advice

Huh?

2 Thessalonians 3:6
Would you call some students who are close to flunking and ask them for help with your homework? God tells us to avoid getting advice from someone who doesn't know him, and doesn't know the truth. God wants us to be truth-tellers. People ought to see God's wisdom in us and come seeking good advice from someone who knows God.

bodies. ¹²Such people we command and urge in the Lord Jesus Christ to settle

---

Weekend.

How to Impress God

Read 1 Samuel 15:22 (page 328)

How would you feel if you gave someone money to buy you a pepperoni pizza, and they came back with an anchovy and squid pizza? And then they told you, "I know what you asked for, but this is better." We do that all the time to God! He asks for our obedience, but we decide we've got a better plan. Remember Meredith's story on Monday? That's exactly what she did. Meredith can tell what she did wrong now that she's looking back.

God's instructions are simple to understand, and it's our responsibility to know them and obey them. Saul ignored God's instructions and rationalized away those he thought were "no big deal." Then the prophet Samuel called him on it. Saul paid a pretty hefty price for his lame excuses. Even after he pleaded for forgiveness, God removed him from power. He lost his job as king of Israel.

❶ Name one of God's instructions that you have a hard time obeying.

❷ Try writing a letter to God, telling him your plan for obeying him in that tough situation. This will make it easier for you to remember your plan when the time comes.

❸ Pray, "Lord, help me to see when I am not following your instructions. And help me not to pretend that I know what's best for me better than you do."

Turn to page 1465 for your next devotion.

1 Timothy

START

Imagine this: The pastor of your church is really into missions. He thinks you're a pretty sharp kid and takes you on a couple of his mission trips where you learn a ton. Then you find out that one of the churches the two of you "planted" is having some problems. So your pastor sends you there to be their leader!

That's Timothy's story! Paul put him in charge of the church at Ephesus (the same church for whom Paul wrote the book of Ephesians). And to make it even more tough, Timothy was kind of shy!

Paul writes this letter, 1 Timothy, to give Timothy some instructions, because Paul has become Tim's spiritual "father." Paul writes this letter to encourage his "son."

It's a kickin' book for teenage readers because the main point is: Don't wait until you're old to be a leader.

Cast OF Characters

Timothy
(TIM-uh-thee)

Young Timothy was appointed by Paul to lead the church in Ephesus. He'd become a Christian on Paul's first missionary journey and traveled with Paul on his second and third missionary trips.

Paul

Tim's spiritual dad. Paul, of course, started tons of churches in the 30 years after Jesus' death and resurrection.

The Church of Ephesus
(EFF-uh-sus)

Paul and Timothy had started this church a few years back. But now there were some false teachers in the church leading people away from the truth. In fact, there were all kinds of problems in this church.

What's UP with That

You're Not Too Young

One of the coolest verses in the whole Bible for teenagers is here in 1 Timothy. Pick it out from this list, then find it in your Bible and circle it!

1 "Don't let anyone look down on you because you're short, but set an example for the taller people by the way you can get through small openings quickly."

2 "Don't let anyone look down on you because you are young, but set an example for the believers in speech, in life, in love, in faith and in purity."

3 "Don't let anyone look down on you because you are young, but look really bored and mention stuff like wrinkles and gray hair. Oh, and play your music really loud too!"

4 "Don't let anyone look down on you because you are young, but set an example for all the believers by singing loudly in church, wearing a snappy tie or dress to church, and saying 'hallelujah' after every sentence."

5 "Don't let anyone look down on you because you are young. Just say, 'Hey, I'm a lot older than little kids!'"

answer: #2 (1 Timothy 4:12)

Snap shots

- Hey, dude! *(chapter 1)*

- When in church . . . *(chapter 2)*

- The stuff of real leaders *(chapter 3)*

- Liar, liar, pants on fire *(chapter 4)*

- Listen up, boy *(chapter 5)*

- Money, and other last thoughts *(chapter 6)*

1 Paul, an apostle of Christ Jesus by the command of God our Savior and of Christ Jesus our hope,

[2]To Timothy my true son in the faith:

Grace, mercy and peace from God the Father and Christ Jesus our Lord.

Warning Against False Teachers of the Law

[3]As I urged you when I went into Macedonia, stay there in Ephesus so that you may command certain men not to teach false doctrines any longer [4]nor to devote

The Pepperoni Doctrine

Huh?

1 Timothy 1:3, 10

Doctrines are pretty serious. But to explain what they are, let's use this off-the-wall, made-up example: "I'm convinced and live my life by my belief that pizza with pepperoni is the only pizza that deserves to be called pizza." That's a doctrine. It's a conviction, a belief, that we can defend (OK, so it's a stupid doctrine). When it comes to the Bible and following Jesus, doctrines are those beliefs you hold, based on the Word of God, that affect the way you live.

themselves to myths and endless genealogies. These promote controversies rather than God's work—which is by faith. [5]The goal of this command is love, which comes from a pure heart and a good conscience and a sincere faith. [6]Some have wandered away from these and turned to meaningless talk. [7]They want to be teachers of the law, but they do not know what they are talking about or what they so confidently affirm.

[8]We know that the law is good if one uses it properly. [9]We also know that law[a] is made not for the righteous but for lawbreakers and rebels, the ungodly and sinful, the unholy and irreligious; for those who kill their fathers or mothers, for murderers, [10]for adulterers and perverts, for slave traders and liars and perjurers—and for whatever else is contrary to the

sound doctrine [11]that conforms to the glorious gospel of the blessed God, which he entrusted to me.

The Lord's Grace to Paul

[12]I thank Christ Jesus our Lord, who has given me strength, that he considered me faithful, appointing me to his service. [13]Even though I was once a blasphemer and a persecutor and a violent man, I was shown mercy because I acted in ignorance and unbelief. [14]The grace of our Lord was poured out on me abundantly, along with the faith and love that are in Christ Jesus.

[15]Here is a trustworthy saying that deserves full acceptance: Christ Jesus came into the world to save sinners—of whom I am the worst. [16]But for that very reason I was shown mercy so that in me, the worst of sinners, Christ Jesus might display his unlimited patience as an example for those who would believe on him and receive eternal life. [17]Now to the King eternal, immortal, invisible, the only God, be honor and glory for ever and ever. Amen.

[18]Timothy, my son, I give you this instruction in keeping with the prophecies once made about you, so that by following them you may fight the good fight, [19]holding on to faith and a good conscience. Some have rejected these and so have shipwrecked their faith. [20]Among them are Hymenaeus and Alexander, whom I have handed over to Satan to be taught not to blaspheme.

Instructions on Worship

2 I urge, then, first of all, that requests, prayers, intercession and thanksgiving be made for everyone— [2]for kings and all those in authority, that we may live peaceful and quiet lives in all godliness and holiness. [3]This is good, and pleases God our Savior, [4]who wants all men to be saved and to come to a knowledge of the truth. [5]For there is one God and one mediator between God and men, the man Christ Jesus, [6]who gave himself as a ransom for all men—the testimony given in its proper time. [7]And for this purpose I was appointed a herald and an

[a]9 Or that the law

apostle—I am telling the truth, I am not lying—and a teacher of the true faith to the Gentiles.

[8]I want men everywhere to lift up holy hands in prayer, without anger or disputing.

[9]I also want women to dress modestly, with decency and propriety, not with braided hair or gold or pearls or expensive clothes, [10]but with good deeds, appropriate for women who profess to worship God.

[11]A woman should learn in quietness and full submission. [12]I do not permit a woman to teach or to have authority over a man; she must be silent. [13]For Adam was formed first, then Eve. [14]And Adam was not the one deceived; it was the woman who was deceived and became a sinner. [15]But women[a] will be saved[b] through childbearing—if they continue in faith, love and holiness with propriety.

Overseers and Deacons

3 Here is a trustworthy saying: If anyone sets his heart on being an overseer,[c] he desires a noble task. [2]Now the overseer must be above reproach, the husband of but one wife, temperate, self-controlled, respectable, hospitable, able to teach, [3]not given to drunkenness, not violent but gentle, not quarrelsome, not a lover of money. [4]He must manage his own family well and see that his children obey him with proper respect. [5](If anyone does not know how to manage his own family, how can he take care of God's church?) [6]He must not be a recent convert, or he may become conceited and fall under the same judgment as the devil. [7]He must also have a good reputation with outsiders, so that he will not fall into disgrace and into the devil's trap.

[8]Deacons, likewise, are to be men worthy of respect, sincere, not indulging in much wine, and not pursuing dishonest gain. [9]They must keep hold of the deep truths of the faith with a clear conscience. [10]They must first be tested; and

---

[a]15 Greek *she*　[b]15 Or *restored*　[c]1 Traditionally *bishop*; also in verse 2

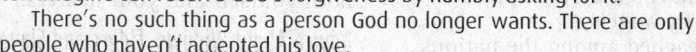

Monday

Unlimited Love

Read 1 Timothy 1:15–17

My mom works with a group that goes to local prisons to share about God. One time I got to go with them. While I was there, I heard one of the prisoners say he thought of himself as "someone God no longer wanted." Then a member of my mom's group read him 1 Timothy 1:15–16, sharing God's mercy to the worst of sinners. The prisoner gave his life to Jesus that day.

No matter how much or how badly people have sinned, God's love can still reach them. Even drug dealers. Even murderers. The worst person you can imagine can receive God's forgiveness by humbly asking for it.

There's no such thing as a person God no longer wants. There are only people who haven't accepted his love.

Brian age 14

What about You?

❶ Think of a troublemaker you know. Imagine God looking right into that person's face and saying, "I forgive you." Imagine doing the same thing yourself.

❷ Write today's verses down, or memorize them. You never know when they might be exactly what someone needs to hear.

❸ Thank God for forgiving you, and ask him to help you forgive others.

Turn to page 1467 for your next devotion.

then if there is nothing against them, let them serve as deacons.

[11]In the same way, their wives[a] are to be women worthy of respect, not malicious talkers but temperate and trustworthy in everything.

[12]A deacon must be the husband of but one wife and must manage his children and his household well. [13]Those who have served well gain an excellent standing and great assurance in their faith in Christ Jesus.

Character Contest

Huh?

1 Timothy 3:1–13
You've played follow-the-leader. If the person leading does a good job, it's fun, right? In the same way, overseers, elders and deacons are the people who lead the church. So how do you become a church leader? Well, it's not supposed to be a popularity contest. Paul says it's a character contest. Those who follow close to Jesus are to be the leaders.

[14]Although I hope to come to you soon, I am writing you these instructions so that, [15]if I am delayed, you will know how people ought to conduct themselves in God's household, which is the church of the living God, the pillar and foundation of the truth. [16]Beyond all question, the mystery of godliness is great:

He[b] appeared in a body,[c]
    was vindicated by the Spirit,
was seen by angels,
    was preached among the nations,
was believed on in the world,
    was taken up in glory.

Instructions to Timothy

4 The Spirit clearly says that in later times some will abandon the faith and follow deceiving spirits and things taught by demons. [2]Such teachings come through hypocritical liars, whose consciences have been seared as with a hot iron. [3]They forbid people to marry and order them to abstain from certain foods, which God created to be received with thanksgiving by those who believe and who know the truth. [4]For everything God created is good, and nothing is to be rejected if it is received with thanksgiving, [5]because it is consecrated by the word of God and prayer.

[6]If you point these things out to the brothers, you will be a good minister of Christ Jesus, brought up in the truths of the faith and of the good teaching that you have followed. [7]Have nothing to do with godless myths and old wives' tales; rather, train yourself to be godly. [8]For physical training is of some value, but godliness has value for all things, holding promise for both the present life and the life to come.

[9]This is a trustworthy saying that deserves full acceptance [10](and for this we labor and strive), that we have put our hope in the living God, who is the Savior of all men, and especially of those who believe.

[11]Command and teach these things. [12]Don't let anyone look down on you because you are young, but set an example for the believers in speech, in life, in love, in faith and in purity. [13]Until I come, devote yourself to the public reading of Scripture, to preaching and to teaching. [14]Do not neglect your gift, which was given you through a prophetic message when the body of elders laid their hands on you.

[15]Be diligent in these matters; give yourself wholly to them, so that everyone may see your progress. [16]Watch your life and doctrine closely. Persevere in them, because if you do, you will save both yourself and your hearers.

Advice About Widows, Elders and Slaves

5 Do not rebuke an older man harshly, but exhort him as if he were your father. Treat younger men as brothers, [2]older women as mothers, and younger women as sisters, with absolute purity.

[3]Give proper recognition to those widows who are really in need. [4]But if a widow has children or grandchildren,

---

[a]11 Or *way, deaconesses*   [b]16 Some manuscripts *God*
[c]16 Or *in the flesh*

these should learn first of all to put their religion into practice by caring for their own family and so repaying their parents and grandparents, for this is pleasing to God. ⁵The widow who is really in need and left all alone puts her hope in God and continues night and day to pray and to ask God for help. ⁶But the widow who lives for pleasure is dead even while she lives. ⁷Give the people these instructions, too, so that no one may be open to blame. ⁸If anyone does not provide for his relatives, and especially for his immediate family, he has denied the faith and is worse than an unbeliever.

⁹No widow may be put on the list of widows unless she is over sixty, has been faithful to her husband,ᵃ ¹⁰and is well known for her good deeds, such as bringing up children, showing hospitality, washing the feet of the saints, helping those in trouble and devoting herself to all kinds of good deeds.

¹¹As for younger widows, do not put them on such a list. For when their sen-sual desires overcome their dedication to Christ, they want to marry. ¹²Thus they bring judgment on themselves, because they have broken their first pledge. ¹³Besides, they get into the habit of being idle and going about from house to house. And not only do they become idlers, but also gossips and busybodies, saying things they ought not to. ¹⁴So I counsel younger widows to marry, to have children, to manage their homes and to give the enemy no opportunity for slander. ¹⁵Some have in fact already turned away to follow Satan.

¹⁶If any woman who is a believer has widows in her family, she should help them and not let the church be burdened with them, so that the church can help those widows who are really in need.

¹⁷The elders who direct the affairs of the church well are worthy of double honor, especially those whose work is preaching and teaching. ¹⁸For the Scrip-

---

ᵃ9 Or *has had but one husband*

Tuesday

No Fear

Read 1 Timothy 4:12

When my friend and I volunteered to help organize "See You at the Pole"—a once-a-year event when people gather at the flagpole before school and pray—we were really excited. But when it came to asking some teachers to come and pray with us, we started to get nervous. Talking to teachers can be kind of scary. They could have said no or asked us all kinds of questions we couldn't answer.

We decided to go for it anyway, and we got a great group of students and teachers to meet us at the flagpole to pray. We saw how God gives young people the courage and the strength to stand up for what they believe. God wants us all to be examples, like Jesus was our example. When we're following him, God will give us the courage we need.

Elizabeth age 12

❶ What do you think is the worst thing that could happen when you stand up for your faith at school? What's the best thing?

❷ Wear a T-shirt with a Christian message on it to school this week, or maybe put your Bible in your backpack and read it on your lunch break. Be prepared to answer the questions people might ask.

❸ Thank God for giving you courage as you serve him.

Turn to page 1468 for your next devotion.

ture says, "Do not muzzle the ox while it is treading out the grain,"[a] and "The worker deserves his wages."[b] ¹⁹Do not entertain an accusation against an elder unless it is brought by two or three witnesses. ²⁰Those who sin are to be rebuked publicly, so that the others may take warning.

²¹I charge you, in the sight of God and Christ Jesus and the elect angels, to keep these instructions without partiality, and to do nothing out of favoritism.

²²Do not be hasty in the laying on of hands, and do not share in the sins of others. Keep yourself pure.

²³Stop drinking only water, and use a little wine because of your stomach and your frequent illnesses.

²⁴The sins of some men are obvious, reaching the place of judgment ahead of them; the sins of others trail behind them. ²⁵In the same way, good deeds are obvious, and even those that are not cannot be hidden.

6 All who are under the yoke of slavery should consider their masters worthy of full respect, so that God's name and our teaching may not be slandered. ²Those who have believing masters are not to show less respect for them because they are brothers. Instead, they are to serve them even better, because those who benefit from their service are believers, and dear to them. These are the things you are to teach and urge on them.

Love of Money

³If anyone teaches false doctrines and does not agree to the sound instruction of our Lord Jesus Christ and to godly teaching, ⁴he is conceited and understands nothing. He has an unhealthy interest in controversies and quarrels about words that result in envy, strife, malicious talk, evil suspicions ⁵and constant friction between men of corrupt mind, who have been robbed of the truth and who think that godliness is a means to financial gain.

⁶But godliness with contentment is great gain. ⁷For we brought nothing into

[a]18 Deut. 25:4 [b]18 Luke 10:7

Wednesday

Gotta Have It?

Read 1 Timothy 6:6–10

We get a lot of mail-order catalogs for clothes and other things at my house, and I love to look through them. Sometimes I think, *Oh, I'd like this*, or, *If I earned some money, I could get that*. But then I remember that I should be content with what I have. When I think about it, I really have more than I need already.

Most people want to have the latest, coolest things. But these won't last, and they sure don't bring us any closer to God. Focusing on what I don't have makes me forget to thank God for what I do have—a home, a family who loves me, food to eat, good friends. God wants us to be content with what we have. He has given us so much more than we could ever find in a catalog.

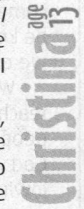
Christina age 13

What about You?

❶ Why do you think we want material things?

❷ Go through your room and find something you thought you couldn't live without. How did you feel when you got that thing? How do you feel about it now?

❸ Ask God to help you be content with what you have.

Turn to page 1472 for your next devotion.

the world, and we can take nothing out of it. [8]But if we have food and clothing, we will be content with that. [9]People who want to get rich fall into temptation and a trap and into many foolish and harmful desires that plunge men into ruin and destruction. [10]For the love of money is a root of all kinds of evil. Some people, eager for money, have wandered from the faith and pierced themselves with many griefs.

Paul's Charge to Timothy

[11]But you, man of God, flee from all this, and pursue righteousness, godliness, faith, love, endurance and gentleness. [12]Fight the good fight of the faith. Take hold of the eternal life to which you

Mirror, Mirror on the Wall

Huh?

1 Timothy 6:3–6, 11
Godliness is behaving so much like God that it shows. Think of your life as a big mirror that God can look into and see his own reflection. The people around you will be able to see this God-reflection also. The more you act like Jesus, the more godly your reflection will be.

were called when you made your good confession in the presence of many witnesses. [13]In the sight of God, who gives life to everything, and of Christ Jesus, who while testifying before Pontius Pilate made the good confession, I charge you [14]to keep this command without spot or blame until the appearing of our Lord Jesus Christ, [15]which God will bring about in his own time—God, the blessed and only Ruler, the King of kings and Lord of lords, [16]who alone is immortal and who lives in unapproachable light, whom no one has seen or can see. To him be honor and might forever. Amen.

[17]Command those who are rich in this present world not to be arrogant nor to put their hope in wealth, which is so uncertain, but to put their hope in God, who richly provides us with everything for our enjoyment. [18]Command them to do good, to be rich in good deeds, and to be generous and willing to share. [19]In this way they will lay up treasure for themselves as a firm foundation for the coming age, so that they may take hold of the life that is truly life.

[20]Timothy, guard what has been entrusted to your care. Turn away from godless chatter and the opposing ideas of what is falsely called knowledge, [21]which some have professed and in so doing have wandered from the faith.

Grace be with you.

2 Timothy

START

Let's say you're 25 years old, and your uncle is about to die. He's leaving his company for you to run, and he's written you a letter from the hospital, telling you what he considers to be the most important advice he can leave you.

Paul wasn't Timothy's uncle—he was more like an adopted father—and he wasn't leaving Tim his company. He was entrusting Tim with the spiritual leadership of a church and the ongoing work of spreading the Jesus-news. And Paul wasn't dying in a hospital—he was in a Roman prison, sentenced to die because he preached about Jesus. That makes this book a big deal.

Paul wrote most of the New Testament, and these are his last recorded words. (History tells us he was executed shortly after writing this.) So this second letter to Timothy shows us the things that Paul thought were really, really important to say one last time.

CAST
OF
Characters

Paul
Missionary. Church-starter.
Prisoner. About to die.
Author of this letter.

Timothy
(TIM-uh-thee)
Young church leader.
Spiritual "son" of Paul.

What's  with That?

You Be Paul

In Paul's final letter he chose to highlight some issues that were really important in his eyes. What if you were Paul? Write a short note to Timothy, or at least jot down the main points. What are some of the most important things for young Christians, especially leaders, to understand?

Snap shots

- You da man, Tim *(chapter 1)*
- Don't forget what I taught ya *(chapter 2)*
- It's tough sometimes *(chapter 3)*
- Bye-bye *(chapter 4)*

Dear Timothy,

_____

_____

_____

_____

_____

_____

_____

_____

_____

_____

_____

_____

_____

_____

Love,

_____

1 Paul, an apostle of Christ Jesus by the will of God, according to the promise of life that is in Christ Jesus,

²To Timothy, my dear son:

Grace, mercy and peace from God the Father and Christ Jesus our Lord.

Encouragement to Be Faithful

³I thank God, whom I serve, as my forefathers did, with a clear conscience, as night and day I constantly remember you in my prayers. ⁴Recalling your tears, I long to see you, so that I may be filled with joy. ⁵I have been reminded of your sincere faith, which first lived in your grandmother Lois and in your mother Eunice and, I am persuaded, now lives in you also. ⁶For this reason I remind you to fan into flame the gift of God, which is in you through the laying on of my hands. ⁷For God did not give us a spirit of timidity, but a spirit of power, of love and of self-discipline.

⁸So do not be ashamed to testify about our Lord, or ashamed of me his prisoner. But join with me in suffering for the gospel, by the power of God, ⁹who has saved us and called us to a holy life—not because of anything we have done but because of his own purpose and grace. This grace was given us in Christ Jesus before the beginning of time, ¹⁰but it has now been revealed through the appearing of our Savior, Christ Jesus, who has destroyed death and has brought life and immortality to light through the gospel. ¹¹And of this gospel I was appointed a herald and an apostle and a teacher. ¹²That is why I am suffering as I am. Yet I am not ashamed, because I know whom I have believed, and am convinced that he is able to guard what I have entrusted to him for that day.

¹³What you heard from me, keep as the pattern of sound teaching, with faith and love in Christ Jesus. ¹⁴Guard the good deposit that was entrusted to you—guard it with the help of the Holy Spirit who lives in us.

¹⁵You know that everyone in the province of Asia has deserted me, including Phygelus and Hermogenes.

¹⁶May the Lord show mercy to the household of Onesiphorus, because he often refreshed me and was not ashamed

---

Thursday

Within Reach

Read 2 Timothy 1:7–8

Some of my friends and I wanted to start a Bible study at our school. I was scared to do it because I knew we'd get teased. But we started the group anyway. Sure enough, we got teased. People called us names and made fun of us. But I'm willing to put up with it because the Bible study is an important part of my life.

I think our whole purpose as Christians is to share the gospel with others. God's love is an incredible thing, and we can't be afraid to tell people about it. We have to stand up and show our faith to others.

Jamie age 14

What about You?

❶ Have you ever hidden your faith to avoid being teased? How did you feel about hiding your faith?

❷ Start a prayer group, a Bible study or a Christian fellowship group at your school, and ask your youth leader to help you get started. Or, if there's already a Christian group at school, consider joining it.

❸ Pray that God will help you be bold about your faith.

Turn to page 1474 for your next devotion.

of my chains. ¹⁷On the contrary, when he was in Rome, he searched hard for me until he found me. ¹⁸May the Lord grant that he will find mercy from the Lord on that day! You know very well in how many ways he helped me in Ephesus.

2 You then, my son, be strong in the grace that is in Christ Jesus. ²And the things you have heard me say in the presence of many witnesses entrust to reliable men who will also be qualified to teach others. ³Endure hardship with us like a good soldier of Christ Jesus. ⁴No one serving as a soldier gets involved in civilian affairs—he wants to please his commanding officer. ⁵Similarly, if anyone competes as an athlete, he does not receive the victor's crown unless he competes according to the rules. ⁶The hardworking farmer should be the first to receive a share of the crops. ⁷Reflect on what I am saying, for the Lord will give you insight into all this.

⁸Remember Jesus Christ, raised from the dead, descended from David. This is my gospel, ⁹for which I am suffering even to the point of being chained like a criminal. But God's word is not chained. ¹⁰Therefore I endure everything for the sake of the elect, that they too may obtain the salvation that is in Christ Jesus, with eternal glory.

¹¹Here is a trustworthy saying:

If we died with him,
   we will also live with him;
¹²if we endure,
   we will also reign with him.
If we disown him,
   he will also disown us;
¹³if we are faithless,
   he will remain faithful,
   for he cannot disown himself.

A Workman Approved by God

¹⁴Keep reminding them of these things. Warn them before God against quarreling about words; it is of no value, and only ruins those who listen. ¹⁵Do your best to present yourself to God as one approved, a workman who does not need to be ashamed and who correctly handles the word of truth. ¹⁶Avoid godless chatter, because those who indulge in it will become more and more ungodly. ¹⁷Their

teaching will spread like gangrene. Among them are Hymenaeus and Philetus, ¹⁸who have wandered away from the truth. They say that the resurrection has already taken place, and they destroy the faith of some. ¹⁹Nevertheless, God's solid foundation stands firm, sealed with this inscription: "The Lord knows those who are his,"ᵃ and, "Everyone who confesses the name of the Lord must turn away from wickedness."

²⁰In a large house there are articles not only of gold and silver, but also of wood and clay; some are for noble purposes and some for ignoble. ²¹If a man cleanses himself from the latter, he will be an instrument for noble purposes, made holy, useful to the Master and prepared to do any good work.

²²Flee the evil desires of youth, and pursue righteousness, faith, love and peace, along with those who call on the Lord out of a pure heart. ²³Don't have

A Perfect Score

Huh?

2 Timothy 2:22

Righteousness means to be right before God. Imagine having to take a test and the only way to pass is to get a perfect score. Only one person has ever passed the test, and he will take the test in your place! You get his right answers, his righteousness. When you become a Christian, Jesus takes your life-test for you and you pass with his right answers: his righteousness. So, to live righteously is to let Jesus' "answers" show in your life.

anything to do with foolish and stupid arguments, because you know they produce quarrels. ²⁴And the Lord's servant must not quarrel; instead, he must be kind to everyone, able to teach, not resentful. ²⁵Those who oppose him he must gently instruct, in the hope that God will grant them repentance leading them to a knowledge of the truth, ²⁶and that they

ᵃ19 Num. 16:5 (see Septuagint)

will come to their senses and escape from the trap of the devil, who has taken them captive to do his will.

Godlessness in the Last Days

3 But mark this: There will be terrible times in the last days. ²People will be lovers of themselves, lovers of money, boastful, proud, abusive, disobedient to their parents, ungrateful, unholy, ³without love, unforgiving, slanderous, without self-control, brutal, not lovers of the good, ⁴treacherous, rash, conceited, lovers of pleasure rather than lovers of God— ⁵having a form of godliness but denying its power. Have nothing to do with them.

⁶They are the kind who worm their way into homes and gain control over weak-willed women, who are loaded down with sins and are swayed by all kinds of evil desires, ⁷always learning but never able to acknowledge the truth.

⁸Just as Jannes and Jambres opposed Moses, so also these men oppose the truth—men of depraved minds, who, as far as the faith is concerned, are rejected. ⁹But they will not get very far because, as in the case of those men, their folly will be clear to everyone.

Paul's Charge to Timothy

¹⁰You, however, know all about my teaching, my way of life, my purpose, faith, patience, love, endurance, ¹¹persecutions, sufferings—what kinds of things happened to me in Antioch, Iconium and Lystra, the persecutions I endured. Yet the Lord rescued me from all of them. ¹²In fact, everyone who wants to live a godly life in Christ Jesus will be persecuted, ¹³while evil men and impostors will go from bad to worse, deceiving and being deceived. ¹⁴But as for you, continue in what you have learned and have become convinced of, because you

---

Friday

Truce!

Read 2 Timothy 2:22–24

I don't know what gets into me sometimes, but I start the stupidest arguments with my parents and my brother. These spats aren't even about anything important—I want to watch a different TV show or have toast instead of cereal, and all of a sudden we're fighting! I've even lost privileges at home because of these dumb arguments. I always feel foolish afterward, but for some reason I keep picking these silly fights.

These verses make it clear that arguing is foolish and wrong. God doesn't want us tearing each other down with our words. He wants us to have pure hearts and to live in peace with each other—especially in our families, because those are the people we have to live with every day.

It's good for me to think about how God wants me to live. Arguing doesn't do anybody any good, and it puts up a wall between me and God. But if I want to be close to God, I need to start by speaking kind words instead of mean ones.

Kate age 13

What about You?

❶ Who are 2 people you tend to argue with? How can you make your conversations more positive?

❷ Over the weekend, write a nice note to each person in your family. Place the notes someplace where they'll be sure to find them.

❸ Ask God to help you use your words to build people up.

Turn to page 1476 for your next devotion.

know those from whom you learned it, [15]and how from infancy you have known the holy Scriptures, which are able to make you wise for salvation through faith in Christ Jesus. [16]All Scripture is God-breathed and is useful for teaching, rebuking, correcting and training in righteousness, [17]so that the man of God may be thoroughly equipped for every good work.

It's Go Time

Huh?

2 Timothy 4:7

Did you know it's OK to get into fights? That doesn't mean we beat up people, but we act like a well-trained boxer. A good boxer knows his opponent, is in shape, keeps his guard up and never gives in. Sounds hard! Being a Christian is kind of the same. We have to fight hard against our enemy (the devil) to make God-pleasing decisions. It's not physical fighting, but spiritual fighting to keep our relationship with God close and strong.

News Breath

Huh?

2 Timothy 3:16

"All Scripture is God-breathed." This is a poetic way of saying that God chose some cool people to help and inspired them to write *his* words. It's almost like the writers are TV newscasters and God is the producer and head writer of the news. And since God wrote the Bible, it has the power to teach, correct and prepare us for every area of life.

4 In the presence of God and of Christ Jesus, who will judge the living and the dead, and in view of his appearing and his kingdom, I give you this charge: [2]Preach the Word; be prepared in season and out of season; correct, rebuke and encourage—with great patience and careful instruction. [3]For the time will come when men will not put up with sound doctrine. Instead, to suit their own desires, they will gather around them a great number of teachers to say what their itching ears want to hear. [4]They will turn their ears away from the truth and turn aside to myths. [5]But you, keep your head in all situations, endure hardship, do the work of an evangelist, discharge all the duties of your ministry.

[6]For I am already being poured out like a drink offering, and the time has come for my departure. [7]I have fought the good fight, I have finished the race, I have kept the faith. [8]Now there is in store for me the crown of righteousness, which the Lord, the righteous Judge, will award to me on that day—and not only to me, but also to all who have longed for his appearing.

Personal Remarks

[9]Do your best to come to me quickly, [10]for Demas, because he loved this world, has deserted me and has gone to Thessalonica. Crescens has gone to Galatia, and Titus to Dalmatia. [11]Only Luke is with me. Get Mark and bring him with you, because he is helpful to me in my ministry. [12]I sent Tychicus to Ephesus. [13]When you come, bring the cloak that I left with Carpus at Troas, and my scrolls, especially the parchments.

[14]Alexander the metalworker did me a great deal of harm. The Lord will repay him for what he has done. [15]You too should be on your guard against him, because he strongly opposed our message.

[16]At my first defense, no one came to my support, but everyone deserted me. May it not be held against them. [17]But the Lord stood at my side and gave me strength, so that through me the message might be fully proclaimed and all the Gentiles might hear it. And I was delivered from the lion's mouth. [18]The Lord will rescue me from every evil attack and will bring me safely to his heavenly kingdom. To him be glory for ever and ever. Amen.

Final Greetings

¹⁹Greet Priscilla*ᵃ* and Aquila and the household of Onesiphorus. ²⁰Erastus stayed in Corinth, and I left Trophimus sick in Miletus. ²¹Do your best to get here before winter. Eubulus greets you, and so do Pudens, Linus, Claudia and all the brothers.

²²The Lord be with your spirit. Grace be with you.

ᵃ19 Greek Prisca, a variant of Priscilla

Week end.

You Want Me to Do What?!

Read Hosea 1:1–3 (page 1040)

Ever tried writing with your opposite hand? Kind of awkward, eh? You know it would be much easier to write with the hand you're used to. Well, sometimes obeying God's will feels like writing with your opposite hand. It doesn't come naturally.

Brian and Elizabeth on Monday and Tuesday both share about being a part of activities that don't come naturally. Sharing your love for Jesus Christ with prisoners or organizing prayer at your school can make you stand out and feel uncomfortable. But God calls us to obey; he has a history of asking his people to demonstrate extraordinary obedience while facing extraordinary situations. Whether you're a prophet like Hosea or a teenager facing difficult problems, God calls you to obey. Remember God's perspective. He not only sees the present situation but he also sees the outcome.

Think of it this way: God has the view from the road map and can see every turn. Our perspective, on the other hand, is limited to what we can see at that moment. So, if God asks you to do something strange, how will you respond?

❶ When was a time that you felt God called you to do something that seemed strange?

❷ When's the last time you asked God for instructions? (How can you obey if you don't know what the instructions are?)

❸ Pray to God and ask him what your instructions are. What's his message to you?

Turn to page 1479 for your next devotion.

Titus

START

Paul was probably in a Roman prison when he wrote this letter to his young friend Titus. Paul starts out basically saying, "I left you in Crete to straighten out what was left unfinished."

There is a lot for Titus to finish. The first chore on his to-do list is to select reliable church leaders (Paul calls them *elders*). Then it's on to silencing some wanna-be church leaders whose "teachings" are actually lies and slander that are confusing Christians who live there. What makes these lies especially dangerous is that they sound religious—strict rules and churchy-sounding controversies that Paul says have absolutely *nothing* to do with Jesus or real spirituality.

The third chore on Titus's to-do list (see chapter 2:1–10) is to teach 5 groups in the church how to live with and behave toward each other: older men, older women, younger women, younger men and slaves.

Cast OF Characters

Paul
The Christian-killer-turned-Christ-lover, the apostle (*apostle* means "one who is sent"), the missionary (possibly the first Christian to take the gospel to Europe) and, to Titus, a friend and partner.

(TIE-tuss)

Titus
One of the younger men Paul selected, mentored and took with him on many of his trips (Timothy and Luke are others). Paul assigned Titus to oversee and lead the Christians on the big Mediterranean island of Crete, just south of Greece. That's where Titus was when Paul wrote this letter to him.

What's UP with That?

So You Wanna Be a Church Leader?

Decide which of the following requirements for church leaders in Crete are Paul's actual guidelines, which ones are bogus, and which ones you might want to talk to your youth leader about because you're not sure. (Hey, you're not alone—Bible scholars can't even agree on some of these.) Check your answers by looking at chapter 1:5–9.

Snap shots

- Hi there!
  (chapter 1:1–4)

- Guidelines galore
  (chapters 1:5—3:2)

- An encouragement and a warning
  (chapter 3:3–11)

- Bye for now!
  (chapter 3:12–15)

Yup, this is what Paul wrote to Titus.
Are you kidding? This is bogus!
Hmmm . . . not sure about this one.
Maybe, maybe not.

☐	☐		Must welcome people into their homes.
☐	☐	☐	Must welcome hungry friends of their teenage children into their homes.
☐	☐	☐	Must not go ballistic.
☐	☐	☐	Must not react to people who blow them off.
☐	☐	☐	Must not get upset about the messy bedrooms of their children.
☐	☐	☐	Must not be difficult to live with or work with.
☐	☐	☐	Must be married.
☐	☐	☐	Can have 2 wives.
☐	☐	☐	Must have 2 wives.
☐	☐	☐	Must never have been divorced.
☐	☐	☐	Must not get drunk on alcohol.
☐	☐	☐	Must not drink alcohol.
☐	☐	☐	Must not drink; must just eat.
☐	☐	☐	Must get in the faces of teachers who teach wrong stuff.
☐	☐	☐	Must have children who are perfect.
☐	☐	☐	Must have children who aren't wild.
☐	☐	☐	Must have children.
☐	☐	☐	Must be a child.

1 Paul, a servant of God and an apostle of Jesus Christ for the faith of God's elect and the knowledge of the truth that leads to godliness— [2]a faith and knowledge resting on the hope of eternal life, which God, who does not lie, promised before the beginning of time, [3]and at his appointed season he brought his word to light through the preaching entrusted to me by the command of God our Savior,

[4]To Titus, my true son in our common faith:

Grace and peace from God the Father and Christ Jesus our Savior.

Titus's Task on Crete

[5]The reason I left you in Crete was that you might straighten out what was left unfinished and appoint[a] elders in every town, as I directed you. [6]An elder must be blameless, the husband of but one wife, a man whose children believe and are not open to the charge of being wild and disobedient. [7]Since an overseer[b] is entrusted with God's work, he must be blameless—not overbearing, not quick-tempered, not given to drunkenness, not violent, not pursuing dishonest gain. [8]Rather he must be hospitable, one who loves what is good, who is self-controlled, upright, holy and disciplined. [9]He must hold firmly to the trustworthy message as it has been taught, so that he can encourage others by sound doctrine and refute those who oppose it.

[10]For there are many rebellious people, mere talkers and deceivers, especially those of the circumcision group. [11]They must be silenced, because they are ruining whole households by teaching things they ought not to teach—and that for the sake of dishonest gain. [12]Even one of their own prophets has said, "Cretans are always liars, evil brutes, lazy gluttons." [13]This testimony is true. Therefore, rebuke them sharply, so that they will be sound in the faith [14]and will pay no attention to Jewish myths or to the commands of those who reject the truth. [15]To the pure, all things are pure, but to those who are corrupted and do not believe,

---

[a]5 Or *ordain*　　[b]7 Traditionally *bishop*

Monday

Less Than Meets the Eye

Read Titus 1:15–16

I go to a Christian school, so most people claim to be Christians. But the reality is that most people don't live out this claim. Some people say one thing and do another. People who say one thing and do another are called hypocrites, and the Bible says to watch out for them. They'll make you think they're following God, but their actions don't back it up.

But before I start calling people hypocrites, I need to take a good look at my own life. I know I don't always live out what I say I believe either. Sure, I believe the Bible, but sometimes I don't do what it says. I don't want to be a hypocrite. I need to rely on God and stick close to him.

Laura age 13

What about You?

❶ Think about a time you said one thing and did another. Why did you do it? How can you keep from doing it again?

❷ This week when you see someone acting like a hypocrite, pray for that person . . . and pray for you! Ask God to help you both resist being hypocrites.

❸ Ask God to help you be the "real thing" in your Christian life.

Turn to page 1481 for your next devotion.

nothing is pure. In fact, both their minds and consciences are corrupted. ¹⁶They claim to know God, but by their actions they deny him. They are detestable, disobedient and unfit for doing anything good.

What Must Be Taught to Various Groups

2 You must teach what is in accord with sound doctrine. ²Teach the older men to be temperate, worthy of respect,

Teach It, Baby!

Titus 2:1

Almost everyone has thoughts and opinions about God. But lots of their thoughts and opinions are wrong. Paul tells Titus to "teach sound doctrine." Doctrine is a fancy word for "beliefs." Since lots of people believe funky stuff, Paul is saying "only teach the absolute truth about God."

self-controlled, and sound in faith, in love and in endurance.

³Likewise, teach the older women to be reverent in the way they live, not to be slanderers or addicted to much wine, but to teach what is good. ⁴Then they can train the younger women to love their husbands and children, ⁵to be self-controlled and pure, to be busy at home, to be kind, and to be subject to their husbands, so that no one will malign the word of God.

⁶Similarly, encourage the young men to be self-controlled. ⁷In everything set them an example by doing what is good. In your teaching show integrity, seriousness ⁸and soundness of speech that cannot be condemned, so that those who oppose you may be ashamed because they have nothing bad to say about us.

⁹Teach slaves to be subject to their masters in everything, to try to please them, not to talk back to them, ¹⁰and not to steal from them, but to show that they can be fully trusted, so that in every way

they will make the teaching about God our Savior attractive.

¹¹For the grace of God that brings salvation has appeared to all men. ¹²It teaches us to say "No" to ungodliness and worldly passions, and to live self-controlled, upright and godly lives in this present age, ¹³while we wait for the blessed hope—the glorious appearing of our great God and Savior, Jesus Christ, ¹⁴who gave himself for us to redeem us from all wickedness and to purify for himself a people that are his very own, eager to do what is good.

¹⁵These, then, are the things you should teach. Encourage and rebuke with all authority. Do not let anyone despise you.

Doing What Is Good

3 Remind the people to be subject to rulers and authorities, to be obedient, to be ready to do whatever is good, ²to slander no one, to be peaceable and considerate, and to show true humility toward all men.

³At one time we too were foolish, disobedient, deceived and enslaved by all kinds of passions and pleasures. We lived in malice and envy, being hated and hating one another. ⁴But when the kindness and love of God our Savior appeared, ⁵he saved us, not because of righteous things we had done, but because of his mercy. He saved us through the washing of rebirth and renewal by the Holy Spirit,

Squeaky Clean

Titus 3:5

Being a Christian is cool. Paul says we get "washed and renewed" by the Holy Spirit. Big deal? It sure is! When we become Christians, we get a brand new start. Yep, God washes *all* that garbage out of our lives. But wait—there's more! "Renewed" means we've got a fresh supply of God's power to live for Christ. Cleaned up and powered—that rocks!

⁶whom he poured out on us generously through Jesus Christ our Savior, ⁷so that, having been justified by his grace, we might become heirs having the hope of eternal life. ⁸This is a trustworthy saying. And I want you to stress these things, so that those who have trusted in God may be careful to devote themselves to doing what is good. These things are excellent and profitable for everyone.

⁹But avoid foolish controversies and genealogies and arguments and quarrels about the law, because these are unprofitable and useless. ¹⁰Warn a divisive person once, and then warn him a second time. After that, have nothing to do with him. ¹¹You may be sure that such a man is warped and sinful; he is self-condemned.

Final Remarks

¹²As soon as I send Artemas or Tychicus to you, do your best to come to me at Nicopolis, because I have decided to winter there. ¹³Do everything you can to help Zenas the lawyer and Apollos on their way and see that they have everything they need. ¹⁴Our people must learn to devote themselves to doing what is good, in order that they may provide for daily necessities and not live unproductive lives.

¹⁵Everyone with me sends you greetings. Greet those who love us in the faith.

Grace be with you all.

Tuesday

A Good Plan

Read Titus 3:1–2

I'm basically a nice person, and I treat most other people with respect and patience. But I don't treat my sister that way. I say mean things to her and try to get back at her when she has hurt me first. I know it's wrong to treat her that way, and this passage reminds me of *why* it's wrong.

God wants us to be people who love others, people who are kind and peace-loving and respectful. I know I can be that way because I treat people outside my family that way every day. This isn't a hard passage to understand, but it can be a hard passage to live out. But with God's help, I think I can be nicer to my sister, even when she's not so nice to me.

❶ Everyone has a hard time being nice to certain people. Who is one person you have a tough time being kind to? How can you change that?

❷ Think of that one person who really bugs you. For the rest of this week, show that person kindness and consideration. It might only take a compliment or a smile to show him or her your friendly side.

❸ Ask God to help you live out this passage.

Turn to page 1484 for your next devotion.

Philemon

START

Have you ever been tempted to read someone else's mail? Here's your chance! Philemon is a private letter Paul wrote to solve a problem. Take a look and see how Paul calls 2 fellow believers to live by God's ways rather than following what most people were doing.

CAST OF Characters

Paul
The author of this quick-reading, 468-word letter—the guy whose mail you're reading!

Philemon
(figh-LEE-mun)
The guy on the other end with the mailbox—the letter receiver. He's a slave owner who would normally have punished Onesimus, but is asked instead to forgive and relate to Onesimus as a new Christian brother.

Onesimus
(oh-NESS-eh-muss)
He's the run-away slave whose life hangs in the balance.

What's UP with That?

How well do you know the book of Philemon? Take this quiz and see.

Onesimus was:
1. Founder of Taco Bell
2. Pharaoh's pet 200-pound mastiff (that's a kind of dog, in case you didn't know)
3. A runaway slave

Where did Paul and Onesimus become close friends?
1. At summer camp
2. In prison
3. Onesimus was with Paul when Paul was blinded and came to know Jesus

True or false.
Paul says, "Cut this slave some slack. I'm comin' to your house for a sleepover" (see verse 22).

answers: Aw, come on! You can find the answers!

Snap shots

You don't need a snap-shot here—it might be longer than the letter!

Good Names, Great Owners

Barnabas means "son of encouragement." Good choice—Barny sells his possessions to help fund the apostles, and he gives up his day job to help his missionary friend Paul (Acts 4:36-37, page 1312).

Hannah means "grace." It's not a reference to her table manners. Hannah can't have kids, but when she prays for a kid anyway, God gives her baby Sam. So it's God's grace that makes Hannah special (1 Samuel 2:2-21, page 313).

Rebekah means "noose." Wait a minute! That's a good name? Well, in Rebekah's case it is. Becky's beauty was captivating—it captures Isaac's eye and throws a rope around his heart. They get married and have kids, including Jacob, the forefather of all Jews (Genesis 24:15-16, 61-67, page 31).

Onesimus means "useful." You might think he's true to his name because he was a slave. Well . . . maybe. But here's something more important: he was "useful" in helping Paul spread the Good News of Jesus Christ to others. They got to know each other in jail; they probably spent their days talking back and forth between bars. These talks changed Onesimus' life because it was there that he became a Christian (Philemon).

¹Paul, a prisoner of Christ Jesus, and Timothy our brother,

To Philemon our dear friend and fellow worker, ²to Apphia our sister, to Archippus our fellow soldier and to the church that meets in your home:

³Grace to you and peace from God our Father and the Lord Jesus Christ.

Thanksgiving and Prayer

⁴I always thank my God as I remember you in my prayers, ⁵because I hear about your faith in the Lord Jesus and your love for all the saints. ⁶I pray that you may be active in sharing your faith, so that you will have a full understanding of every good thing we have in Christ. ⁷Your love has given me great joy and encouragement, because you, brother, have refreshed the hearts of the saints.

Paul's Plea for Onesimus

⁸Therefore, although in Christ I could be bold and order you to do what you ought to do, ⁹yet I appeal to you on the

Busted!

Huh?

Philemon 9
Basically, the politicians and Jewish leaders didn't like the fact that Paul was always talking about Jesus. So they busted him. Because of that, Paul called himself a "prisoner of Christ." Imagine getting put in jail because you love Jesus! But Paul was still able to serve God because he wrote letters (like this one to Philemon) from his jail cell in Rome.

basis of love. I then, as Paul—an old man and now also a prisoner of Christ Jesus— ¹⁰I appeal to you for my son Onesimus,ᵃ who became my son while I was in chains. ¹¹Formerly he was useless to you, but now he has become useful both to you and to me.

¹²I am sending him—who is my very heart—back to you. ¹³I would have liked to keep him with me so that he could take your place in helping me while I am in chains for the gospel. ¹⁴But I did not want to do anything without your consent, so that any favor you do will be spontaneous and not forced. ¹⁵Perhaps the reason he was separated from you for a little while was that you might have him back for good— ¹⁶no longer as a slave, but better than a slave, as a dear brother. He is very dear to me but even dearer to you, both as a man and as a brother in the Lord.

¹⁷So if you consider me a partner, welcome him as you would welcome me. ¹⁸If he has done you any wrong or owes you anything, charge it to me. ¹⁹I, Paul, am writing this with my own hand. I will pay it back—not to mention that you owe me your very self. ²⁰I do wish, brother, that I may have some benefit from you in the Lord; refresh my heart in Christ. ²¹Confi-

ᵃ10 *Onesimus* means *useful*.

Wednesday

Everything I Do . . .

Read Philemon 5

This verse gave me a reality check. Even though I really try to live like a Christian and don't have a *bad* reputation, this verse did make me think about how others see my faith. I realized I need to pay more attention to the reputation I'm building.

Most people's reputations are based on how tough they are, or on how popular or smart or rich they are. But as a Christian, I want my reputation to be based on my faith in Jesus. I want to set an example of someone who loves God and lives to serve him. I want the people at my school to say, "Yep, Jessi's definitely a Christian."

To make that happen, I need to think about the decisions I make. I need to ask myself, *Will this choice show people I'm living a godly life? Will it change the way they view me? Will it affect the way they view God?* If I want people to know God, I need to show them God in everything I do.

What about You?

❶ What kind of reputation do you have at school? How did you earn that reputation? Are you happy to have that rep?

❷ When you walk down the hall at school tomorrow, spend some time observing people around you. How are they acting? What are they saying? How are they dressed? Now think about this: What does this little exercise tell you about the way people gain a reputation?

❸ Ask God to help you be a great example of his love and grace.

Turn to page 1490 for your next devotion.

dent of your obedience, I write to you, knowing that you will do even more than I ask.

²²And one thing more: Prepare a guest room for me, because I hope to be restored to you in answer to your prayers.

²³Epaphras, my fellow prisoner in Christ Jesus, sends you greetings. ²⁴And so do Mark, Aristarchus, Demas and Luke, my fellow workers.

²⁵The grace of the Lord Jesus Christ be with your spirit.

Hebrews

The writer of this letter (no one knows for sure who it was) had the job of trying to persuade Jews that the new faith Jesus Christ brought to the world was better than traditional Jewish faith. That's like trying to teach your teacher. After all, didn't God himself give the Jews the law? Didn't God require his priests to regularly sacrifice animals to cover the sins of the Jews? And wasn't Jesus himself a Jew? How could *anything* be better than that system?

Well, yeah, the writer says. God *is* the creator and giver of the law. It's not that the law or all the rules God laid down for his priests and people are wrong or ever were wrong—just the opposite; they were good then, and they're good now. It's just that Jesus Christ is *better*—in fact, his presence on earth is the best thing his Father cooked up for making the world's people right with God.

You can tell that this letter is written to people who had grown up in Judaism, who were very familiar with the Torah (the Jewish term for the Bible's first 5 books), with the stories of Abraham and Moses, with the high priests and sacrifices and basic Jewish history. The writer is often quoting passages from the Old Testament, just to remind his Jewish readers that even the Old Testament writers knew it wasn't the end of the line . . . There was something—Someone, actually—better than the law just around the corner.

That corner was turned at Golgotha, "The Place of the Skull" (see Mark 15:22), where Jesus died on the cross. At this execution site a Jewish sacrifice was made that so totally satisfied God that no more sacrifices are needed. Jesus did it all, and he did it right. Just for us.

Cast OF Characters

Jesus
The most important Jewish guy ever. In fact, the most important guy ever. The most caring high priest you'll ever find. The perfect and final Sacrifice.

The Law
The Ten Commandments, plus the hundreds of little, specific instructions that explain to the Jews how to obey the Big Ten. The writer of this letter was not saying that the law was bad—but just that God sent Jesus to be an improvement on the law.

Melchizedek
(mel-KIZZ-uh-deck)
This guy is a mystery. The Bible speaks about Mel being "without father or mother, without genealogy, without beginning of days or end of life." He's no Jew, yet he's a priest of God—and a king too, of what would later be known as Jerusalem.

What's UP with That?

Perfect Heroes?

Some say Hebrews chapter 11 is a kind of Hall of Fame for believers in God. Just look at the kind of guys and gals listed here—Noah, Abraham, Isaac, Jacob, Joseph, Moses, Rahab, Gideon, Samson, David. All of them saints, men and women who always obeyed God and—

Wait a minute. Isn't this the same Noah who got drunk on homemade wine within months of God bailing him out of a watery mess?

Is this the same Abraham who was so afraid of getting hurt that twice he lied to kings and told them his wife was his sister?

Jacob, who lied to his blind father in order to get his brother Esau's inheritance?

Rahab, who walked the street corners in Jericho as a working prostitute?

Samson, whose appetite for women, food and revenge usually drowned out God's voice to him?

You get the picture. Even heroes of faith are flawed, weak, scared, rough around the edges. Just like you. Just like all of us.

You see, being faithful does *not* mean being perfect. If perfection was required, no one would measure up. These people were called faithful because, even when they fell into sin, they got up and followed God's ways again. That takes a lot of faith.

Snap shots

- Jesus is better than angels or Moses (chapters 1–10)

- Even before Jesus came, living by faith was the only way to please God (chapter 11)

- Like a good parent, God disciplines us in love (chapter 12)

- Closing commands (chapter 13)

- Plus a bonus!—the writer interrupts himself several times with pointers, warnings and encouragement:
  —Pay attention! (chapter 2:1–4)
  —Don't give in to unbelief! (chapter 3:7–19)
  —Don't fall away! (chapters 5:11—6:12)
  —Hang on! (chapter 10:19–39)
  —Don't miss the grace of God! (chapter 12:14–17)

The Son Superior to Angels

1 In the past God spoke to our forefathers through the prophets at many times and in various ways, [2]but in these last days he has spoken to us by his Son, whom he appointed heir of all things, and through whom he made the universe. [3]The Son is the radiance of God's glory and the exact representation of his being, sustaining all things by his powerful word. After he had provided purification for sins, he sat down at the right hand of the Majesty in heaven. [4]So he became as much superior to the angels as the name he has inherited is superior to theirs.

[5]For to which of the angels did God ever say,

"You are my Son;
today I have become your
Father[a]"[b]?

Or again,

"I will be his Father,
and he will be my Son"[c]?

[6]And again, when God brings his first-born into the world, he says,

"Let all God's angels worship him."[d]

[7]In speaking of the angels he says,

"He makes his angels winds,
his servants flames of fire."[e]

[8]But about the Son he says,

"Your throne, O God, will last for ever
and ever,
and righteousness will be the
scepter of your kingdom.
[9]You have loved righteousness and
hated wickedness;
therefore God, your God, has set
you above your companions
by anointing you with the oil of
joy."[f]

[10]He also says,

"In the beginning, O Lord, you laid
the foundations of the earth,
and the heavens are the work of
your hands.
[11]They will perish, but you remain;
they will all wear out like a
garment.

[12]You will roll them up like a robe;
like a garment they will be changed.
But you remain the same,
and your years will never end."[g]

[13]To which of the angels did God ever say,

"Sit at my right hand
until I make your enemies
a footstool for your feet"[h]?

[14]Are not all angels ministering spirits sent to serve those who will inherit salvation?

Warning to Pay Attention

2 We must pay more careful attention, therefore, to what we have heard, so that we do not drift away. [2]For if the message spoken by angels was binding, and every violation and disobedience received its just punishment, [3]how shall we escape if we ignore such a great salvation? This salvation, which was first announced by the Lord, was confirmed to us by those who heard him. [4]God also testified to it by signs, wonders and various miracles, and gifts of the Holy Spirit distributed according to his will.

Jesus Made Like His Brothers

[5]It is not to angels that he has subjected the world to come, about which we are speaking. [6]But there is a place where someone has testified:

"What is man that you are mindful of
him,
the son of man that you care for
him?
[7]You made him a little[i] lower than the
angels;
you crowned him with glory and
honor
[8]   and put everything under his feet."[j]

In putting everything under him, God left nothing that is not subject to him. Yet at present we do not see everything subject to him. [9]But we see Jesus, who

---

[a]5 Or *have begotten you*   [b]5 Psalm 2:7
[c]5 2 Samuel 7:14; 1 Chron. 17:13   [d]6 Deut. 32:43
(see Dead Sea Scrolls and Septuagint)
[e]7 Psalm 104:4   [f]9 Psalm 45:6,7
[g]12 Psalm 102:25-27   [h]13 Psalm 110:1
[i]7 Or *him for a little while*; also in verse 9
[j]8 Psalm 8:4-6

was made a little lower than the angels, now crowned with glory and honor because he suffered death, so that by the grace of God he might taste death for everyone.

[10]In bringing many sons to glory, it was fitting that God, for whom and through whom everything exists, should make the author of their salvation perfect through suffering. [11]Both the one who makes men holy and those who are made holy are of the same family. So Jesus is not ashamed to call them brothers. [12]He says,

> "I will declare your name to my
>   brothers;
>   in the presence of the congregation
>   I will sing your praises."[a]

[13]And again,

> "I will put my trust in him."[b]

And again he says,

> "Here am I, and the children God has
>   given me."[c]

[14]Since the children have flesh and blood, he too shared in their humanity so that by his death he might destroy him who holds the power of death—that is, the devil— [15]and free those who all their lives were held in slavery by their fear of death. [16]For surely it is not angels he helps, but Abraham's descendants. [17]For

Give Me Some Skin

Hebrews 2:14–15
Was Jesus a man or was he God? Actually, he's both. Pretty trippy, huh? These verses mention the "humanity" of Jesus. That's another way of saying God put on skin. Why did he do that? To destroy the devil so that nothing gets in the way of us knowing God. What a great example of how much Jesus loves us!

this reason he had to be made like his brothers in every way, in order that he might become a merciful and faithful

high priest in service to God, and that he might make atonement for[d] the sins of the people. [18]Because he himself suffered when he was tempted, he is able to help those who are being tempted.

Jesus Greater Than Moses

3 Therefore, holy brothers, who share in the heavenly calling, fix your thoughts on Jesus, the apostle and high priest whom we confess. [2]He was faithful to the one who appointed him, just as Moses was faithful in all God's house. [3]Jesus has been found worthy of greater honor than Moses, just as the builder of a house has greater honor than the house itself. [4]For every house is built by someone, but God is the builder of everything. [5]Moses was faithful as a servant in all God's house, testifying to what would be said in the future. [6]But Christ is faithful as a son over God's house. And we are his house, if we hold on to our courage and the hope of which we boast.

Warning Against Unbelief

[7]So, as the Holy Spirit says:

> "Today, if you hear his voice,
> [8] do not harden your hearts
> as you did in the rebellion,
>   during the time of testing in the
>   desert,
> [9]where your fathers tested and tried me
>   and for forty years saw what I did.
> [10]That is why I was angry with that
>   generation,
>   and I said, 'Their hearts are always
>   going astray,
>   and they have not known my ways.'
> [11]So I declared on oath in my anger,
>   'They shall never enter my rest.' "[e]

[12]See to it, brothers, that none of you has a sinful, unbelieving heart that turns away from the living God. [13]But encourage one another daily, as long as it is called Today, so that none of you may be hardened by sin's deceitfulness. [14]We have come to share in Christ if we hold firmly till the end the confidence we had at first. [15]As has just been said:

[a]12 Psalm 22:22   [b]13 Isaiah 8:17   [c]13 Isaiah 8:18
[d]17 Or *and that he might turn aside God's wrath, taking away*   [e]11 Psalm 95:7-11

"Today, if you hear his voice,
  do not harden your hearts
  as you did in the rebellion."[a]

[16]Who were they who heard and rebelled? Were they not all those Moses led out of Egypt? [17]And with whom was he angry for forty years? Was it not with those who sinned, whose bodies fell in the desert? [18]And to whom did God swear that they would never enter his rest if not to those who disobeyed[b]? [19]So we see that they were not able to enter, because of their unbelief.

A Sabbath-Rest for the People of God

4 Therefore, since the promise of entering his rest still stands, let us be careful that none of you be found to have fallen short of it. [2]For we also have had the gospel preached to us, just as they did; but the message they heard was of no value to them, because those who heard did not combine it with faith.[c] [3]Now we who have believed enter that rest, just as God has said,

"So I declared on oath in my anger,
  'They shall never enter my rest.'"[d]

And yet his work has been finished since the creation of the world. [4]For somewhere he has spoken about the seventh day in these words: "And on the seventh day God rested from all his work."[e] [5]And again in the passage above he says, "They shall never enter my rest."

[6]It still remains that some will enter that rest, and those who formerly had the gospel preached to them did not go in, because of their disobedience. [7]Therefore God again set a certain day, calling it Today, when a long time later he spoke through David, as was said before:

"Today, if you hear his voice,
  do not harden your hearts."[a]

[8]For if Joshua had given them rest, God would not have spoken later about an-

---

[a]15,7 Psalm 95:7,8   [b]18 Or *disbelieved*   [c]2 Many manuscripts *because they did not share in the faith of those who obeyed*   [d]3 Psalm 95:11; also in verse 5   [e]4 Gen. 2:2

Thursday

When I'm Tempted

Read Hebrews 2:18

A bunch of my friends were going to a movie I knew I shouldn't see. They begged me to go with them. I knew it was wrong for me to see the movie, but I went anyway.

Instead of just giving in to my friends, I should have asked Jesus to help me resist temptation. I know he would have given me the strength to do the right thing and say no to the movie.

Sometimes I forget that Jesus was a real live human being who experienced a lot of the same things I experience, like temptation. Because of that, I know I can look to him for help and guidance when I'm facing a difficult situation.

Ashley age 14

What about You?

❶ What do you do when you feel tempted? What are some things that can help you resist temptation?

❷ Ask a Christian friend to be your "bad-idea buddy"—a friend who will help you say no to something you know is a "bad idea."

❸ Thank God for understanding the power of temptation. Ask him to help you say no to things that tempt you.

Turn to page 1491 for your next devotion.

other day. ⁹There remains, then, a Sabbath-rest for the people of God; ¹⁰for anyone who enters God's rest also rests from his own work, just as God did from his. ¹¹Let us, therefore, make every effort to enter that rest, so that no one will fall by following their example of disobedience.

¹²For the word of God is living and active. Sharper than any double-edged sword, it penetrates even to dividing soul and spirit, joints and marrow; it judges the thoughts and attitudes of the heart. ¹³Nothing in all creation is hidden from God's sight. Everything is uncovered and laid bare before the eyes of him to whom we must give account.

Jesus the Great High Priest

¹⁴Therefore, since we have a great high priest who has gone through the heavens,ᵃ Jesus the Son of God, let us hold firmly to the faith we profess. ¹⁵For we do not have a high priest who is unable to sympathize with our weak-

nesses, but we have one who has been tempted in every way, just as we are—yet was without sin. ¹⁶Let us then approach the throne of grace with confidence, so

ᵃ14 Or gone into heaven

He's Been There

Hebrews 4:14–16

Any type of junk you face or think about is the same stuff Jesus went through. The situation might look different, but the basic issues of temptation, hurt, frustration, disappointment, sadness—all that—Jesus faced them all. And the Bible says he made it through all this junk. So now he wants to use his experience, and the fact that he's God, to help us!

Friday

My Friend the King

Read Hebrews 4:16

Have you ever had to go to the principal's office? Pretty scary, huh? But what if the principal of your school was your best friend? Then going to see the principal wouldn't be scary at all.

That's how it is when God, the King of Creation, is our best friend. He's not like Henry VIII or some other historical king who might cut off your head just for walking into the room. God is glad to see us when we come to him in prayer. He is a loving, caring King who wants to help his people, and he promises he'll listen and give us grace. We can go to God with an attitude of hope, not fear. We can be confident that he hears our prayers and answers them. We never have to be afraid or ashamed to talk to our best friend, the King.

Robyn age 13

What about You?

❶ Why do you think God wants you to talk to him? Why are we sometimes afraid to talk to God?

❷ Write an honest letter to God, telling him stuff you might not even tell your best friend. Seal it in an envelope, then put the letter in a shoe box and label the box: "Letters to the King." Write a new letter to put in the box whenever you're feeling anxious about talking to God.

❸ Thank God for being a King we can talk to without fear.

Turn to page 1494 for your next devotion.

that we may receive mercy and find grace to help us in our time of need.

5 Every high priest is selected from among men and is appointed to represent them in matters related to God, to offer gifts and sacrifices for sins. ²He is able to deal gently with those who are ignorant and are going astray, since he himself is subject to weakness. ³This is why he has to offer sacrifices for his own sins, as well as for the sins of the people.

⁴No one takes this honor upon himself; he must be called by God, just as Aaron was. ⁵So Christ also did not take upon himself the glory of becoming a high priest. But God said to him,

"You are my Son;
 today I have become your Father."*a"b*

⁶And he says in another place,

"You are a priest forever,
 in the order of Melchizedek."*c*

⁷During the days of Jesus' life on earth, he offered up prayers and petitions with loud cries and tears to the one who could save him from death, and he was heard because of his reverent submission. ⁸Although he was a son, he learned obedience from what he suffered ⁹and, once made perfect, he became the source of eternal salvation for all who obey him ¹⁰and was designated by God to be high priest in the order of Melchizedek.

Warning Against Falling Away

¹¹We have much to say about this, but it is hard to explain because you are slow to learn. ¹²In fact, though by this time you ought to be teachers, you need someone to teach you the elementary truths of God's word all over again. You need milk, not solid food! ¹³Anyone who lives on milk, being still an infant, is not acquainted with the teaching about righteousness. ¹⁴But solid food is for the mature, who by constant use have trained themselves to distinguish good from evil.

6 Therefore let us leave the elementary teachings about Christ and go on to maturity, not laying again the foundation of repentance from acts that lead to death,*d* and of faith in God, ²instruction about baptisms, the laying on of hands, the resurrection of the dead, and eternal

judgment. ³And God permitting, we will do so.

⁴It is impossible for those who have once been enlightened, who have tasted the heavenly gift, who have shared in the Holy Spirit, ⁵who have tasted the goodness of the word of God and the powers of the coming age, ⁶if they fall away, to be brought back to repentance, because*e* to their loss they are crucifying the Son of God all over again and subjecting him to public disgrace.

⁷Land that drinks in the rain often falling on it and that produces a crop useful to those for whom it is farmed receives the blessing of God. ⁸But land that produces thorns and thistles is worthless and is in danger of being cursed. In the end it will be burned.

⁹Even though we speak like this, dear friends, we are confident of better things in your case—things that accompany salvation. ¹⁰God is not unjust; he will not forget your work and the love you have shown him as you have helped his people and continue to help them. ¹¹We want each of you to show this same diligence to the very end, in order to make your hope sure. ¹²We do not want you to become lazy, but to imitate those who through faith and patience inherit what has been promised.

The Certainty of God's Promise

¹³When God made his promise to Abraham, since there was no one greater for him to swear by, he swore by himself, ¹⁴saying, "I will surely bless you and give you many descendants."*f* ¹⁵And so after waiting patiently, Abraham received what was promised.

¹⁶Men swear by someone greater than themselves, and the oath confirms what is said and puts an end to all argument. ¹⁷Because God wanted to make the unchanging nature of his purpose very clear to the heirs of what was promised, he confirmed it with an oath. ¹⁸God did this so that, by two unchangeable things in which it is impossible for God to lie, we who have fled to take hold of the hope offered to us may be greatly en-

---

*a 5 Or have begotten you   b 5 Psalm 2:7
c 6 Psalm 110:4   d 1 Or from useless rituals
e 6 Or repentance while   f 14 Gen. 22:17*

couraged. [19]We have this hope as an anchor for the soul, firm and secure. It enters the inner sanctuary behind the curtain, [20]where Jesus, who went before us, has entered on our behalf. He has become a high priest forever, in the order of Melchizedek.

Melchizedek the Priest

7 This Melchizedek was king of Salem and priest of God Most High. He met Abraham returning from the defeat of the kings and blessed him, [2]and Abraham gave him a tenth of everything. First, his name means "king of righteousness"; then also, "king of Salem" means "king of peace." [3]Without father or mother, without genealogy, without beginning of days or end of life, like the Son of God he remains a priest forever.

[4]Just think how great he was: Even the patriarch Abraham gave him a tenth of the plunder! [5]Now the law requires the descendants of Levi who become priests to collect a tenth from the people—that is, their brothers—even though their brothers are descended from Abraham. [6]This man, however, did not trace his descent from Levi, yet he collected a tenth from Abraham and blessed him who had the promises. [7]And without doubt the lesser person is blessed by the greater. [8]In the one case, the tenth is collected by men who die; but in the other case, by him who is declared to be living. [9]One might even say that Levi, who collects the tenth, paid the tenth through Abraham, [10]because when Melchizedek met Abraham, Levi was still in the body of his ancestor.

Jesus Like Melchizedek

[11]If perfection could have been attained through the Levitical priesthood (for on the basis of it the law was given to the people), why was there still need for another priest to come—one in the order of Melchizedek, not in the order of Aaron? [12]For when there is a change of the priesthood, there must also be a change of the law. [13]He of whom these things are said belonged to a different tribe, and no one from that tribe has ever served at the altar. [14]For it is clear that our Lord descended from Judah, and in regard to that tribe Moses said nothing

about priests. [15]And what we have said is even more clear if another priest like Melchizedek appears, [16]one who has become a priest not on the basis of a regulation as to his ancestry but on the basis of the power of an indestructible life. [17]For it is declared:

"You are a priest forever,
in the order of Melchizedek."[a]

[18]The former regulation is set aside because it was weak and useless [19](for the law made nothing perfect), and a better hope is introduced, by which we draw near to God.

[20]And it was not without an oath! Others became priests without any oath, [21]but he became a priest with an oath when God said to him:

"The Lord has sworn
and will not change his mind:
'You are a priest forever.'"[a]

[22]Because of this oath, Jesus has become the guarantee of a better covenant.

[23]Now there have been many of those priests, since death prevented them from continuing in office; [24]but because Jesus lives forever, he has a permanent priesthood. [25]Therefore he is able to save completely[b] those who come to God through him, because he always lives to intercede for them.

[26]Such a high priest meets our need—one who is holy, blameless, pure, set apart from sinners, exalted above the heavens. [27]Unlike the other high priests, he does not need to offer sacrifices day after day, first for his own sins, and then for the sins of the people. He sacrificed for their sins once for all when he offered himself. [28]For the law appoints as high priests men who are weak; but the oath, which came after the law, appointed the Son, who has been made perfect forever.

The High Priest of a New Covenant

8 The point of what we are saying is this: We do have such a high priest, who sat down at the right hand of the throne of the Majesty in heaven, [2]and who serves in the sanctuary, the true tabernacle set up by the Lord, not by man.

[a]17,21 Psalm 110:4   [b]25 Or forever

³Every high priest is appointed to offer both gifts and sacrifices, and so it was necessary for this one also to have something to offer. ⁴If he were on earth, he would not be a priest, for there are already men who offer the gifts prescribed by the law. ⁵They serve at a sanctuary that is a copy and shadow of what is in heaven. This is why Moses was warned when he was about to build the tabernacle: "See to it that you make everything according to the pattern shown you on the mountain."ᵃ ⁶But the ministry Jesus has received is as superior to theirs as the covenant of which he is mediator is superior to the old one, and it is founded on better promises.

⁷For if there had been nothing wrong with that first covenant, no place would have been sought for another. ⁸But

God found fault with the people and saidᵇ:

"The time is coming, declares the Lord,
    when I will make a new covenant
with the house of Israel
    and with the house of Judah.
⁹It will not be like the covenant
    I made with their forefathers
when I took them by the hand
    to lead them out of Egypt,
because they did not remain faithful
      to my covenant,
    and I turned away from them,
           declares the Lord.
¹⁰This is the covenant I will make with
    the house of Israel

ᵃ5 Exodus 25:40   ᵇ8 Some manuscripts may be translated *fault and said to the people.*

Week end.

Obedience Party

Read Matthew 7:24–29 (page 1150)

Have you ever owned a dog? Dogs are great fun, but training them when they're puppies can be frustrating (not as frustrating as training your goldfish, but still pretty tough). You go over and over what you want the dog to do—but he still just barks and yips and does the opposite.

Then one day the cute little thing *gets* it. He obeys! And you're ready to throw a party. God throws a party too when his children finally get it and start to obey. Our devotions this week from Laura and Jessi encouraged us to live the way God wants us to; that's called obedience.

Jesus said in Matthew 7:24 that the person who hears his words and puts them into practice is like a man who builds his house on rock and not sand. That's the key: putting what we hear into *practice*. When we live like Jesus Christ wants us to live, then we're obeying God. And when we live Christlike lives, God sends the party invitations out all over heaven.

❶ What is one area of your life that you've been the most disobedient to God?

❷ Think of one word that describes how you can be obedient to God in this area. Then take a piece of paper and write it in big letters with a marker and tape it to your alarm clock so you'll see it first thing every day.

❸ Ask God to give you the strength to live the way he wants you to live. Pray that the very next time you need to obey God, you'll have the courage to do it.

Turn to page 1497 for your next devotion.

after that time, declares the Lord.
I will put my laws in their minds
 and write them on their hearts.
I will be their God,
 and they will be my people.
[11] No longer will a man teach his
 neighbor,
 or a man his brother, saying, 'Know
 the Lord,'
because they will all know me,
 from the least of them to the
 greatest.
[12] For I will forgive their wickedness
 and will remember their sins no
 more."[a]

[13] By calling this covenant "new," he
has made the first one obsolete; and
what is obsolete and aging will soon disappear.

You Promise?

Hebrews 8:7–13

Do you keep promises? Let's say your friend asks you, "Do you promise to keep this secret?" If you say yes, you need to keep the secret—or your promise doesn't mean anything. In this chapter, the writer of Hebrews is talking about the new covenant (or new promise). It describes awesome things God promises to us (see verses 10–12). But the very best part of all is that God absolutely, positively always keeps his promises.

Worship in the Earthly Tabernacle

9 Now the first covenant had regulations for worship and also an earthly
sanctuary. [2] A tabernacle was set up. In
its first room were the lampstand, the table and the consecrated bread; this was
called the Holy Place. [3] Behind the second
curtain was a room called the Most Holy
Place, [4] which had the golden altar of incense and the gold-covered ark of the
covenant. This ark contained the gold jar
of manna, Aaron's staff that had budded,
and the stone tablets of the covenant.
[5] Above the ark were the cherubim of the

Glory, overshadowing the atonement
cover.[b] But we cannot discuss these
things in detail now.

[6] When everything had been arranged
like this, the priests entered regularly
into the outer room to carry on their
ministry. [7] But only the high priest entered the inner room, and that only once
a year, and never without blood, which
he offered for himself and for the sins the
people had committed in ignorance. [8] The
Holy Spirit was showing by this that the
way into the Most Holy Place had not yet
been disclosed as long as the first tabernacle was still standing. [9] This is an illustration for the present time, indicating
that the gifts and sacrifices being offered
were not able to clear the conscience of
the worshiper. [10] They are only a matter of
food and drink and various ceremonial
washings—external regulations applying
until the time of the new order.

The Blood of Christ

[11] When Christ came as high priest of
the good things that are already here,[c] he
went through the greater and more perfect tabernacle that is not man-made,
that is to say, not a part of this creation.
[12] He did not enter by means of the blood
of goats and calves; but he entered the
Most Holy Place once for all by his own
blood, having obtained eternal redemption. [13] The blood of goats and bulls and
the ashes of a heifer sprinkled on those
who are ceremonially unclean sanctify
them so that they are outwardly clean.
[14] How much more, then, will the blood of
Christ, who through the eternal Spirit offered himself unblemished to God,
cleanse our consciences from acts that
lead to death,[d] so that we may serve the
living God!

[15] For this reason Christ is the mediator
of a new covenant, that those who are
called may receive the promised eternal
inheritance—now that he has died as a
ransom to set them free from the sins
committed under the first covenant.
[16] In the case of a will,[e] it is necessary

---

[a]12 Jer. 31:31-34   [b]5 Traditionally *the mercy seat*
[c]11 Some early manuscripts *are to come*   [d]14 Or
from useless rituals   [e]16 Same Greek word as
covenant; also in verse 17

to prove the death of the one who made it, [17]because a will is in force only when somebody has died; it never takes effect while the one who made it is living. [18]This is why even the first covenant was not put into effect without blood. [19]When Moses had proclaimed every commandment of the law to all the people, he took the blood of calves, together with water, scarlet wool and branches of hyssop, and sprinkled the scroll and all the people. [20]He said, "This is the blood of the covenant, which God has commanded you to keep."[a] [21]In the same way, he sprinkled with the blood both the tabernacle and everything used in its ceremonies. [22]In fact, the law requires that nearly everything be cleansed with blood, and without the shedding of blood there is no forgiveness.

Blood Bank

Huh?

Hebrews 9:22

You probably haven't thought about this much, but your blood is important. Good blood means life. Bad blood, or not enough blood, means certain death. This passage talks about the role blood plays in forgiveness. The Bible often talks about the importance of Jesus' death by mentioning his blood. In one way, it's poetic language. But in a very real way, it was Jesus' act of love for us, his blood poured out, that offers us life. There's no other way for us to get forgiveness other than to accept Jesus' spilled blood as payment for our sin.

[23]It was necessary, then, for the copies of the heavenly things to be purified with these sacrifices, but the heavenly things themselves with better sacrifices than these. [24]For Christ did not enter a manmade sanctuary that was only a copy of the true one; he entered heaven itself, now to appear for us in God's presence. [25]Nor did he enter heaven to offer himself again and again, the way the high priest enters the Most Holy Place every year with blood that is not his own.

[26]Then Christ would have had to suffer many times since the creation of the world. But now he has appeared once for all at the end of the ages to do away with sin by the sacrifice of himself. [27]Just as man is destined to die once, and after that to face judgment, [28]so Christ was sacrificed once to take away the sins of many people; and he will appear a second time, not to bear sin, but to bring salvation to those who are waiting for him.

Christ's Sacrifice Once for All

10 The law is only a shadow of the good things that are coming—not the realities themselves. For this reason it can never, by the same sacrifices repeated endlessly year after year, make perfect those who draw near to worship. [2]If it could, would they not have stopped being offered? For the worshipers would have been cleansed once for all, and would no longer have felt guilty for their sins. [3]But those sacrifices are an annual reminder of sins, [4]because it is impossible for the blood of bulls and goats to take away sins.

[5]Therefore, when Christ came into the world, he said:

"Sacrifice and offering you did not
        desire,
    but a body you prepared for me;
[6] with burnt offerings and sin offerings
        you were not pleased.
[7] Then I said, 'Here I am—it is written
        about me in the scroll—
    I have come to do your will,
        O God.' "[b]

[8]First he said, "Sacrifices and offerings, burnt offerings and sin offerings you did not desire, nor were you pleased with them" (although the law required them to be made). [9]Then he said, "Here I am, I have come to do your will." He sets aside the first to establish the second. [10]And by that will, we have been made holy through the sacrifice of the body of Jesus Christ once for all.

[11]Day after day every priest stands and performs his religious duties; again and again he offers the same sacrifices,

[a]20 Exodus 24:8   [b]7 Psalm 40:6-8 (see Septuagint)

which can never take away sins. ¹²But when this priest had offered for all time one sacrifice for sins, he sat down at the right hand of God. ¹³Since that time he waits for his enemies to be made his footstool, ¹⁴because by one sacrifice he has made perfect forever those who are being made holy.

¹⁵The Holy Spirit also testifies to us about this. First he says:

¹⁶ "This is the covenant I will make with them
    after that time, says the Lord.
 I will put my laws in their hearts,
    and I will write them on their
        minds."ᵃ

¹⁷Then he adds:

 "Their sins and lawless acts
    I will remember no more."ᵇ

¹⁸And where these have been forgiven, there is no longer any sacrifice for sin.

A Call to Persevere

¹⁹Therefore, brothers, since we have confidence to enter the Most Holy Place by the blood of Jesus, ²⁰by a new and living way opened for us through the curtain, that is, his body, ²¹and since we have a great priest over the house of God, ²²let us draw near to God with a sincere heart in full assurance of faith, having our hearts sprinkled to cleanse us from a guilty conscience and having our bodies washed with pure water. ²³Let us hold unswervingly to the hope we profess, for he who promised is faithful. ²⁴And let us consider how we may spur one another on toward love and good deeds. ²⁵Let us not give up meeting together, as some are in the habit of doing, but let us encourage one another—and all the more as you see the Day approaching.

ᵃ16 Jer. 31:33   ᵇ17 Jer. 31:34

Monday

The Buddy System

Read Hebrews 10:24–25

One of my friends from church was going through a rough time. She felt like her parents didn't care about her. She thought they paid more attention to her brother and ignored her. I couldn't do much to help her relationship with her parents, but I knew she could use some encouragement. So I tried to listen to her when she needed to talk and help her see that things were probably going to get better.

I think it's really important for people to have Christian friends. My youth group is so special to me because we support each other and encourage each other to grow in our faith. Each person in the group is an important part of the other people's lives. We need each other.

We all need Christian fellowship, whether we're helping a friend through a hard time or going through one ourselves. We just can't make it without the fellowship we find in church and the support of Christian friends.

Jessica, age 12

❶ How have your Christian friends supported you in the past? How have they helped you grow in your faith?

❷ Write a note or call 1 or 2 of your Christian friends and thank them for helping you get closer to God.

❸ Ask God to help you be an encouraging friend.

Turn to page 1499 for your next devotion.

²⁶If we deliberately keep on sinning after we have received the knowledge of the truth, no sacrifice for sins is left, ²⁷but only a fearful expectation of judgment and of raging fire that will consume the enemies of God. ²⁸Anyone who rejected the law of Moses died without mercy on the testimony of two or three witnesses. ²⁹How much more severely do you think a man deserves to be punished who has trampled the Son of God under foot, who has treated as an unholy thing the blood of the covenant that sanctified him, and who has insulted the Spirit of grace? ³⁰For we know him who said, "It is mine to avenge; I will repay,"ᵃ and again, "The Lord will judge his people."ᵇ ³¹It is a dreadful thing to fall into the hands of the living God.

³²Remember those earlier days after you had received the light, when you stood your ground in a great contest in the face of suffering. ³³Sometimes you were publicly exposed to insult and persecution; at other times you stood side by side with those who were so treated. ³⁴You sympathized with those in prison and joyfully accepted the confiscation of your property, because you knew that you yourselves had better and lasting possessions.

³⁵So do not throw away your confidence; it will be richly rewarded. ³⁶You need to persevere so that when you have done the will of God, you will receive what he has promised. ³⁷For in just a very little while,

"He who is coming will come and will not delay.
³⁸ But my righteous oneᶜ will live by faith.
And if he shrinks back,
I will not be pleased with him."ᵈ

³⁹But we are not of those who shrink back and are destroyed, but of those who believe and are saved.

By Faith

11 Now faith is being sure of what we hope for and certain of what we do not see. ²This is what the ancients were commended for.

³By faith we understand that the universe was formed at God's command, so that what is seen was not made out of what was visible.

⁴By faith Abel offered God a better sacrifice than Cain did. By faith he was commended as a righteous man, when God spoke well of his offerings. And by faith he still speaks, even though he is dead.

⁵By faith Enoch was taken from this life, so that he did not experience death; he could not be found, because God had taken him away. For before he was taken, he was commended as one who pleased God. ⁶And without faith it is impossible to please God, because anyone who comes to him must believe that he exists and that he rewards those who earnestly seek him.

⁷By faith Noah, when warned about things not yet seen, in holy fear built an ark to save his family. By his faith he condemned the world and became heir of the righteousness that comes by faith.

⁸By faith Abraham, when called to go to a place he would later receive as his inheritance, obeyed and went, even though he did not know where he was going. ⁹By faith he made his home in the promised land like a stranger in a foreign country; he lived in tents, as did Isaac and Jacob, who were heirs with him of the same promise. ¹⁰For he was looking forward to the city with foundations, whose architect and builder is God.

¹¹By faith Abraham, even though he was past age—and Sarah herself was barren—was enabled to become a father because heᵉ considered him faithful who had made the promise. ¹²And so from this one man, and he as good as dead, came descendants as numerous as the stars in the sky and as countless as the sand on the seashore.

¹³All these people were still living by faith when they died. They did not receive the things promised; they only saw them and welcomed them from a distance. And they admitted that they were aliens and strangers on earth. ¹⁴People who say such things show that they are

---

ᵃ30 Deut. 32:35 ᵇ30 Deut. 32:36; Psalm 135:14
ᶜ38 One early manuscript *But the righteous*
ᵈ38 Hab. 2:3,4 ᵉ11 Or *By faith even Sarah, who was past age, was enabled to bear children because she*

looking for a country of their own. ¹⁵If they had been thinking of the country they had left, they would have had opportunity to return. ¹⁶Instead, they were longing for a better country—a heavenly one. Therefore God is not ashamed to be called their God, for he has prepared a city for them.

¹⁷By faith Abraham, when God tested him, offered Isaac as a sacrifice. He who had received the promises was about to sacrifice his one and only son, ¹⁸even though God had said to him, "It is through Isaac that your offspring*ᵃ* will be reckoned."*ᵇ* ¹⁹Abraham reasoned that God could raise the dead, and figuratively speaking, he did receive Isaac back from death.

²⁰By faith Isaac blessed Jacob and Esau in regard to their future.

²¹By faith Jacob, when he was dying, blessed each of Joseph's sons, and worshiped as he leaned on the top of his staff.

²²By faith Joseph, when his end was near, spoke about the exodus of the Israelites from Egypt and gave instructions about his bones.

²³By faith Moses' parents hid him for three months after he was born, because they saw he was no ordinary child, and they were not afraid of the king's edict.

²⁴By faith Moses, when he had grown up, refused to be known as the son of Pharaoh's daughter. ²⁵He chose to be mistreated along with the people of God rather than to enjoy the pleasures of sin for a short time. ²⁶He regarded disgrace for the sake of Christ as of greater value than the treasures of Egypt, because he was looking ahead to his reward. ²⁷By faith he left Egypt, not fearing the king's anger; he persevered because he saw him who is invisible. ²⁸By faith he kept the Passover and the sprinkling of blood, so

ᵃ18 Greek *seed*   *ᵇ18* Gen. 21:12

Tuesday

His Time, Not Mine

Read Hebrews 11:1

About 4 years ago, my family joined a new, larger church. I didn't know anyone at first, and I asked God to provide new friends for me. God did provide some great friends eventually, but I can't say he came through exactly the way I asked him to. It took me almost 2 years to start making solid friendships.

Part of faith is being "certain of what we do not see." For the longest time, I didn't see God working. But now that I have many good, Christian friends, I can look back and see he was there, helping me all along.

Sometimes it's hard to trust God and have the patience to wait for him. When I feel like God isn't listening, that's when I need to take verses like this one seriously. If I have faith in God's plan for me, he will see my faith and work everything out in his time.

Mike *age 14*

What about You?

❶ Why does God sometimes make us wait for answers to our prayers?

❷ Think about some Bible characters who had to wait a long time before God answered their prayers—Abram (Genesis 12:1–3), Joseph (Genesis 40:23—41:13), Job (the whole book) and others. What can you learn from their stories?

❸ Ask God to help you have faith even when you can't see him working in your life.

Turn to page 1505 for your next devotion.

Attention Sports Fans!

There's nothing like sports to teach you how to handle life's struggles. Sports help you learn how to push yourself in order to be more than you ever thought possible. The Word of God uses many analogies from sports. Listed below are a few Bible passages that involve some type of sports activity. Take the "Sports Challenge" and try to match the verses to the different sports.

Column 1

1. Marathon running
2. Archery
3. Training to win 1st Prize
4. Boxing
5. Wrestling

Column 2

a. Genesis 32:24–26
b. 1 Samuel 20:18–23
c. 1 Corinthians 9:24
d. 1 Corinthians 9:26
e. Hebrews 12:1–2

answer: 1(e), 2(b), 3(c), 4(d), 5(a)

---

that the destroyer of the firstborn would not touch the firstborn of Israel.

²⁹By faith the people passed through the Red Sea*a* as on dry land; but when the Egyptians tried to do so, they were drowned.

³⁰By faith the walls of Jericho fell, after the people had marched around them for seven days.

³¹By faith the prostitute Rahab, because she welcomed the spies, was not killed with those who were disobedient.*b*

³²And what more shall I say? I do not have time to tell about Gideon, Barak, Samson, Jephthah, David, Samuel and the prophets, ³³who through faith conquered kingdoms, administered justice, and gained what was promised; who shut the mouths of lions, ³⁴quenched the fury of the flames, and escaped the edge of the sword; whose weakness was turned to strength; and who became powerful in battle and routed foreign armies. ³⁵Women received back their dead, raised to life again. Others were tortured and refused to be released, so that they might gain a better resurrection. ³⁶Some faced jeers and flogging, while still others were chained and put in prison. ³⁷They were

stoned*c*; they were sawed in two; they were put to death by the sword. They went about in sheepskins and goatskins, destitute, persecuted and mistreated— ³⁸the world was not worthy of them. They wandered in deserts and mountains, and in caves and holes in the ground.

³⁹These were all commended for their faith, yet none of them received what had been promised. ⁴⁰God had planned something better for us so that only together with us would they be made perfect.

God Disciplines His Sons

12 Therefore, since we are surrounded by such a great cloud of witnesses, let us throw off everything that hinders and the sin that so easily entangles, and let us run with perseverance the race marked out for us. ²Let us fix our eyes on Jesus, the author and perfecter of our faith, who for the joy set before him endured the cross, scorning its shame, and

---

a 29 That is, Sea of Reeds   *b* 31 Or *unbelieving*
c 37 Some early manuscripts *stoned; they were put to the test;*

sat down at the right hand of the throne of God. [3]Consider him who endured such opposition from sinful men, so that you will not grow weary and lose heart.

[4]In your struggle against sin, you have not yet resisted to the point of shedding your blood. [5]And you have forgotten that word of encouragement that addresses you as sons:

"My son, do not make light of the
    Lord's discipline,
and do not lose heart when he
    rebukes you,
[6]because the Lord disciplines those he
    loves,
and he punishes everyone he
    accepts as a son."[a]

[7]Endure hardship as discipline; God is treating you as sons. For what son is not disciplined by his father? [8]If you are not disciplined (and everyone undergoes discipline), then you are illegitimate children and not true sons. [9]Moreover, we have all had human fathers who disciplined us and we respected them for it. How much more should we submit to the Father of our spirits and live! [10]Our fathers disciplined us for a little while as they thought best; but God disciplines us for our good, that we may share in his holiness. [11]No discipline seems pleasant at the time, but painful. Later on, however, it produces a harvest of righteousness and peace for those who have been trained by it.

[12]Therefore, strengthen your feeble arms and weak knees. [13]"Make level paths for your feet,"[b] so that the lame may not be disabled, but rather healed.

Warning Against Refusing God

[14]Make every effort to live in peace with all men and to be holy; without holiness no one will see the Lord. [15]See to it that no one misses the grace of God and that no bitter root grows up to cause trouble and defile many. [16]See that no one is sexually immoral, or is godless like Esau, who for a single meal sold his inheritance rights as the oldest son. [17]Afterward, as you know, when he wanted to inherit this blessing, he was rejected. He could bring about no change of mind, though he sought the blessing with tears.

[18]You have not come to a mountain that can be touched and that is burning with fire; to darkness, gloom and storm; [19]to a trumpet blast or to such a voice speaking words that those who heard it begged that no further word be spoken to them, [20]because they could not bear what was commanded: "If even an animal touches the mountain, it must be stoned."[c] [21]The sight was so terrifying that Moses said, "I am trembling with fear."[d]

Hands Off!

Huh?

Hebrews 12:18–21

What happens if you stare at the sun? Eye toasties! That's because it's so bright and powerful. This passage reminds us about a story from Exodus 19. The mountain was special because God was there, physically. God is way more powerful than the sun (he created the sun!), and anyone who touched the mountain died (even worse than eye toasties). These verses remind us of how awesome God is and that we should obey him.

[22]But you have come to Mount Zion, to the heavenly Jerusalem, the city of the living God. You have come to thousands upon thousands of angels in joyful assembly, [23]to the church of the firstborn, whose names are written in heaven. You have come to God, the judge of all men, to the spirits of righteous men made perfect, [24]to Jesus the mediator of a new covenant, and to the sprinkled blood that speaks a better word than the blood of Abel.

[25]See to it that you do not refuse him who speaks. If they did not escape when they refused him who warned them on earth, how much less will we, if we turn away from him who warns us from heaven? [26]At that time his voice shook the earth, but now he has promised, "Once more I will shake not only the earth but

[a]6 Prov. 3:11,12   [b]13 Prov. 4:26
[c]20 Exodus 19:12,13   [d]21 Deut. 9:19

also the heavens."[a] [27]The words "once more" indicate the removing of what can be shaken—that is, created things—so that what cannot be shaken may remain.

[28]Therefore, since we are receiving a kingdom that cannot be shaken, let us be thankful, and so worship God acceptably with reverence and awe, [29]for our "God is a consuming fire."[b]

Concluding Exhortations

13 Keep on loving each other as brothers. [2]Do not forget to entertain strangers, for by so doing some people have entertained angels without knowing it. [3]Remember those in prison as if you were their fellow prisoners, and those who are mistreated as if you yourselves were suffering.

[4]Marriage should be honored by all, and the marriage bed kept pure, for God will judge the adulterer and all the sexually immoral. [5]Keep your lives free from the love of money and be content with what you have, because God has said,

"Never will I leave you;
    never will I forsake you."[c]

[6]So we say with confidence,

"The Lord is my helper; I will not be afraid.
    What can man do to me?"[d]

[7]Remember your leaders, who spoke the word of God to you. Consider the outcome of their way of life and imitate their faith. [8]Jesus Christ is the same yesterday and today and forever.

[9]Do not be carried away by all kinds of strange teachings. It is good for our hearts to be strengthened by grace, not by ceremonial foods, which are of no value to those who eat them. [10]We have an altar from which those who minister at the tabernacle have no right to eat.

[11]The high priest carries the blood of animals into the Most Holy Place as a sin offering, but the bodies are burned out-side the camp. [12]And so Jesus also suffered outside the city gate to make the people holy through his own blood. [13]Let us, then, go to him outside the camp, bearing the disgrace he bore. [14]For here we do not have an enduring city, but we are looking for the city that is to come.

[15]Through Jesus, therefore, let us continually offer to God a sacrifice of praise—the fruit of lips that confess his name. [16]And do not forget to do good and to share with others, for with such sacrifices God is pleased.

[17]Obey your leaders and submit to their authority. They keep watch over you as men who must give an account. Obey them so that their work will be a joy, not a burden, for that would be of no advantage to you.

[18]Pray for us. We are sure that we have a clear conscience and desire to live honorably in every way. [19]I particularly urge you to pray so that I may be restored to you soon.

[20]May the God of peace, who through the blood of the eternal covenant brought back from the dead our Lord Jesus, that great Shepherd of the sheep, [21]equip you with everything good for doing his will, and may he work in us what is pleasing to him, through Jesus Christ, to whom be glory for ever and ever. Amen.

[22]Brothers, I urge you to bear with my word of exhortation, for I have written you only a short letter.

[23]I want you to know that our brother Timothy has been released. If he arrives soon, I will come with him to see you.

[24]Greet all your leaders and all God's people. Those from Italy send you their greetings.

[25]Grace be with you all.

[a]26 Haggai 2:6   [b]29 Deut. 4:24   [c]5 Deut. 31:6
[d]6 Psalm 118:6,7

James

START

"Don't just talk about it"
— that's what was on James's mind.

Have you ever had a class where you were supposed to do a project—and it seems you could find time to do everything else but work on that project? You know what I mean. You'd rather go to the dentist, mow the lawn, change the kitty litter, do just about anything rather than complete that project. And then it gets worse. You're sitting in discussion groups in class talking about. . . oh no. . . the project! You've read the assignment, but you haven't done a single thing about the project.

If you've ever been in a jam like this, then you'll be able to relate to the original readers of the book of James. James is the teacher who gets fired up at students who don't complete their assignment. He is not an eloquent writer like Paul. But James wants to be sure that we put our faith into practice—that we're ready to live what we believe.

Cast
OF
Characters

James
He's like a construction foreman. He tells you, "This is how to do it, and this is the ONLY way to do it." No excuses! No whining!

Twelve Tribes
They're the construction workers. In other words, they're the believers in the early church.

What's Up with That?

The main point of this book is simple:
Don't just talk about it, do it. Here's your chance
to figure out what "it" is. Look at the verses
below and write out what . . .

1 Chapter 1:5
are you supposed to do?

2 Chapter 1:22
are you supposed to do?

3 Chapter 2:1
are you NOT supposed to do?

4 Chapter 2:14-16
are you supposed to do?

5 Chapter 3:9
is supposed to come out of your mouth?

6 Chapter 4:7
are you supposed to do?

7 Chapter 4:16
are you NOT supposed to do?

8 Chapter 5:13-20
are you supposed to do?

Now if you can't figure out the answers, turn your Bible
upside down and presto! You'll find 'em.

If you got them all right, give yourself a star.

8-Pray
7-Don't boast or brag
6-Resist the devil
5-Praise
4-Take care of others' physical needs.
3-Don't play favorites.
2-Don't just listen to the Word, do what it says.
1-Ask for wisdom

Snap Shots

- Trials and temptations make you tough and buff *(chapter 1:2-18)*

- Don't just talk about it, DO IT! *(chapter 1:19-27)*

- No favorites *(chapter 2:1-13)*

- Tough talk about living like you believe in God *(chapter 2:14-25)*

- Watch your words *(chapter 3:1-12)*

- People will know you're smart by the choices you make *(chapter 3:13-18)*

- Recognize God's the boss and you're not *(chapter 4:1-17)*

- A gory description of what can happen to the rich *(chapter 5:1-6)*

- Hang in there — you can make it *(chapter 5:7-12)*

- Wise words about prayer *(chapter 5:13-20)*

1 James, a servant of God and of the Lord Jesus Christ,

To the twelve tribes scattered among the nations:

Greetings.

Trials and Temptations

²Consider it pure joy, my brothers, whenever you face trials of many kinds, ³because you know that the testing of your faith develops perseverance. ⁴Perseverance must finish its work so that you may be mature and complete, not lacking anything. ⁵If any of you lacks wisdom, he should ask God, who gives generously to all without finding fault, and it will be given to him. ⁶But when he asks, he must believe and not doubt, because he who doubts is like a wave of the sea, blown and tossed by the wind. ⁷That man should not think he will receive anything from the Lord; ⁸he is a double-minded man, unstable in all he does.

⁹The brother in humble circumstances ought to take pride in his high position.

Keep Going!

Huh?

James 1:3–4

To have perseverance means to keep going, even when it's hard. Someone playing a video game would have perseverance if he or she kept playing and didn't give up, even after he or she got stuck at a certain place in the game. In our relationship with God, James encourages us to keep going when times are difficult because it develops perseverance. Remember that people with perseverance make it to the end.

¹⁰But the one who is rich should take pride in his low position, because he will pass away like a wild flower. ¹¹For the sun rises with scorching heat and withers the plant; its blossom falls and its beauty

Wednesday

Worth the Trouble

Read James 1:2–4

When I was 7, my family lived in the suburbs of Detroit. I thought everything about my life was perfect. But then one day my dad announced we were moving to California. Because I had everything I wanted right there in Detroit, I didn't want to move. When we moved though, we found a much better church, I went to a good school and my life actually improved considerably.

God puts us through trials for a reason. He doesn't do things to hurt us—only to help us grow and develop. He knows that we really grow when we're in tough situations, because those are the times we need to work extra hard to be close to God. Trials help us mature, so we should view them with joy. They really are some of our best opportunities to become strong Christians.

Matt age 13

What about You?

❶ Taking tests, getting a tetanus shot, exercising . . . what are some other things that seem painful at first but you know are good for you?

❷ Offer to do something that you usually hate doing, like studying your least favorite subject in school or helping out your little brother or sister.

❸ Thank God for knowing what's best for you.

Turn to page 1507 for your next devotion.

is destroyed. In the same way, the rich man will fade away even while he goes about his business.

[12]Blessed is the man who perseveres under trial, because when he has stood the test, he will receive the crown of life that God has promised to those who love him.

[13]When tempted, no one should say, "God is tempting me." For God cannot be tempted by evil, nor does he tempt anyone; [14]but each one is tempted when, by his own evil desire, he is dragged away and enticed. [15]Then, after desire has conceived, it gives birth to sin; and sin, when it is full-grown, gives birth to death.

[16]Don't be deceived, my dear brothers. [17]Every good and perfect gift is from above, coming down from the Father of the heavenly lights, who does not change like shifting shadows. [18]He chose to give us birth through the word of truth, that we might be a kind of firstfruits of all he created.

Orange Ya Glad?

Huh?

James 1:18
Firstfruits means just what it sounds like. The first fruit picked by a farmer in Israel was to be given to God. The firstfruit was special because it was set apart from the rest; it belonged to God. When we hear God's Word of Truth (the Bible) and become Christians, we are like first fruit. We belong to God and are set apart for him.

Listening and Doing

[19]My dear brothers, take note of this: Everyone should be quick to listen, slow to speak and slow to become angry, [20]for man's anger does not bring about the righteous life that God desires. [21]Therefore, get rid of all moral filth and the evil that is so prevalent and humbly accept the word planted in you, which can save you.

[22]Do not merely listen to the word, and so deceive yourselves. Do what it says. [23]Anyone who listens to the word but does not do what it says is like a man who looks at his face in a mirror [24]and, after looking at himself, goes away and immediately forgets what he looks like. [25]But the man who looks intently into the perfect law that gives freedom, and continues to do this, not forgetting what he has heard, but doing it—he will be blessed in what he does.

[26]If anyone considers himself religious and yet does not keep a tight rein on his tongue, he deceives himself and his religion is worthless. [27]Religion that God our Father accepts as pure and faultless is this: to look after orphans and widows in their distress and to keep oneself from being polluted by the world.

Favoritism Forbidden

2 My brothers, as believers in our glorious Lord Jesus Christ, don't show favoritism. [2]Suppose a man comes into your meeting wearing a gold ring and fine clothes, and a poor man in shabby clothes also comes in. [3]If you show special attention to the man wearing fine clothes and say, "Here's a good seat for you," but say to the poor man, "You stand there" or "Sit on the floor by my feet," [4]have you not discriminated among yourselves and become judges with evil thoughts?

[5]Listen, my dear brothers: Has not God chosen those who are poor in the eyes of the world to be rich in faith and to inherit the kingdom he promised those who love him? [6]But you have insulted the poor. Is it not the rich who are exploiting you? Are they not the ones who are dragging you into court? [7]Are they not the ones who are slandering the noble name of him to whom you belong?

[8]If you really keep the royal law found in Scripture, "Love your neighbor as yourself," [a] you are doing right. [9]But if you show favoritism, you sin and are convicted by the law as lawbreakers. [10]For whoever keeps the whole law and yet stumbles at just one point is guilty of breaking all of it. [11]For he who said, "Do not commit adultery," [b] also said, "Do not

[a]8 Lev. 19:18   [b]11 Exodus 20:14; Deut. 5:18

murder."[a] If you do not commit adultery but do commit murder, you have become a lawbreaker.

¹²Speak and act as those who are going to be judged by the law that gives freedom, ¹³because judgment without mercy will be shown to anyone who has not been merciful. Mercy triumphs over judgment!

Faith and Deeds

¹⁴What good is it, my brothers, if a man claims to have faith but has no deeds? Can such faith save him? ¹⁵Suppose a brother or sister is without clothes and daily food. ¹⁶If one of you says to him, "Go, I wish you well; keep warm and well fed," but does nothing about his physical needs, what good is it? ¹⁷In the same way, faith by itself, if it is not accompanied by action, is dead.

¹⁸But someone will say, "You have faith; I have deeds."

Show me your faith without deeds, and I will show you my faith by what I do. ¹⁹You believe that there is one God. Good! Even the demons believe that—and shudder.

²⁰You foolish man, do you want evidence that faith without deeds is useless[b]? ²¹Was not our ancestor Abraham considered righteous for what he did when he offered his son Isaac on the

[a]11 Exodus 20:13; Deut. 5:17   [b]20 Some early manuscripts *dead*

Thursday

Don't Just Sit There . . .   Read James 2:14–17

I changed schools right before 8th grade, and when classes started at my new school, I wanted to make a good impression. I went out of my way to be nice to people and help them if I could. Other students went out of their way to be nice to me too, which really helped me feel welcome. Now I have lots of good friends.

It makes a big difference when you put actions with your feelings. I could have just hoped that the students at my new school would like me, but I bet I would have spent a lot of lonely weeks waiting around for people to notice me. I needed to get out there and *do* something to show people I wanted to be their friend.

Being friendly was something I did mostly for myself, but the things I do for God are even more important. In these verses, James talks about the deeds that come from faith, like taking care of people who need clothes and food. Just like it wasn't enough for me to hope people would like me, it's not enough to hope poor people will get everything they need. My church has some programs to help people out, and I've done little things like bringing in clothes and toys to give away. It makes me happy to know I'm helping other people. And I know it makes God happy too.

Amy age 13

❶ Why do "actions speak louder than words"?

❷ At the beginning of the day, put 10 pennies in your right pocket. Each time you do something good for someone else, transfer one penny to your left pocket. At the end of the day, count how many "good deeds" you have in your left pocket. Try this several days in a row.

❸ Ask God to show you ways to act out your faith.

Turn to page 1509 for your next devotion.

Nicknames

God loves to give people nicknames. He might even have one for you! Draw a line and connect these Bible characters' real names (column 1) with their nicknames (column 2). Watch out: there might be some fake ones.

Column 1

1. James (Mark 3:17)
2. Joseph (Acts 4:36)
3. Simon (Matthew 4:18)
4. Jacob (Genesis 32:28)
5. Gideon (Judges 6:12)
6. David (Acts 13:22)
7. Jebariah (Hosea 15:3)
8. Abraham (James 2:23)

Column 2

a. Peter (Rock)
b. One who snores loudly
c. "God's friend"
d. "a man after my own heart"
e. One of the "Sons of Thunder"
f. "mighty warrior"
g. Israel (God overcomes)
h. Barnabas (Encourager)

If you were to add your name to the list, what do you think God's nickname for you would be?

answers: 1 (e), 2 (h), 3 (a), 4 (g), 5 (f), 6 (d), 7 (b—fake alert!), 8 (c)

altar? ²²You see that his faith and his actions were working together, and his faith was made complete by what he did. ²³And the scripture was fulfilled that says, "Abraham believed God, and it was credited to him as righteousness,"[a] and he was called God's friend. ²⁴You see that a person is justified by what he does and not by faith alone.

²⁵In the same way, was not even Rahab the prostitute considered righteous for what she did when she gave lodging to the spies and sent them off in a different direction? ²⁶As the body without the spirit is dead, so faith without deeds is dead.

Taming the Tongue

3 Not many of you should presume to be teachers, my brothers, because you know that we who teach will be judged more strictly. ²We all stumble in many ways. If anyone is never at fault in what he says, he is a perfect man, able to keep his whole body in check.

³When we put bits into the mouths of horses to make them obey us, we can turn the whole animal. ⁴Or take ships as an example. Although they are so large and are driven by strong winds, they are steered by a very small rudder wherever the pilot wants to go. ⁵Likewise the tongue is a small part of the body, but it makes great boasts. Consider what a great forest is set on fire by a small spark. ⁶The tongue also is a fire, a world of evil among the parts of the body. It corrupts the whole person, sets the whole course of his life on fire, and is itself set on fire by hell.

⁷All kinds of animals, birds, reptiles and creatures of the sea are being tamed and have been tamed by man, ⁸but no man can tame the tongue. It is a restless evil, full of deadly poison.

⁹With the tongue we praise our Lord and Father, and with it we curse men, who have been made in God's likeness. ¹⁰Out of the same mouth come praise and cursing. My brothers, this should not be.

[a]23 Gen. 15:6

¹¹Can both fresh water and salt*ᵃ* water flow from the same spring? ¹²My brothers, can a fig tree bear olives, or a grapevine bear figs? Neither can a salt spring produce fresh water.

Two Kinds of Wisdom

¹³Who is wise and understanding among you? Let him show it by his good life, by deeds done in the humility that comes from wisdom. ¹⁴But if you harbor bitter envy and selfish ambition in your hearts, do not boast about it or deny the truth. ¹⁵Such "wisdom" does not come down from heaven but is earthly, unspiritual, of the devil. ¹⁶For where you have envy and selfish ambition, there you find disorder and every evil practice.

¹⁷But the wisdom that comes from heaven is first of all pure; then peace-loving, considerate, submissive, full of mercy and good fruit, impartial and sincere. ¹⁸Peacemakers who sow in peace raise a harvest of righteousness.

Submit Yourselves to God

4 What causes fights and quarrels among you? Don't they come from your desires that battle within you? ²You want something but don't get it. You kill and covet, but you cannot have what you want. You quarrel and fight. You do not have, because you do not ask God. ³When you ask, you do not receive, be-

ᵃ11 Greek *bitter* (see also verse 14)

It's Show Time!

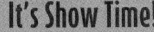

James 3:13

Deeds are what you do, the actions of your body, and the choices you make. James is saying that your actions should show everyone that God lives in you. Your deeds are like a big screen that shows movies from your heart. If Jesus lives in your heart, he should be showing up in what you do.

Tongue in Check

Read James 3:3–10

When I'm mad at somebody, it's tempting to use my words to hurt them or get even. But I can keep myself from saying something mean if I remember that God didn't give me a tongue to cut other people down. He gave me a tongue so I could praise him and speak encouraging words to others.

Words are just so easy to throw around. Before you know it, you can really hurt someone's feelings without even meaning to. So it's good to look at these verses and remember that words have power. They need to be handled carefully and in a way that pleases God.

What about You?

❶ James uses a lot of word pictures, or "metaphors," in this passage—like a horse's bit and a ship. What are the other metaphors? What's the common idea in all of them?

❷ Get yourself a little jar. Every time you say something God wouldn't be proud of, drop a nickel in the jar. Makes you think, doesn't it? At the end of every week, put whatever money you've collected into the offering plate at church.

❸ Ask God to help you watch your words.

Turn to page 1510 for your next devotion.

cause you ask with wrong motives, that you may spend what you get on your pleasures.

⁴You adulterous people, don't you know that friendship with the world is hatred toward God? Anyone who chooses to be a friend of the world becomes an enemy of God. ⁵Or do you think Scripture says without reason that the spirit he caused to live in us envies intensely?ᵃ ⁶But he gives us more grace. That is why Scripture says:

"God opposes the proud
but gives grace to the humble."ᵇ

⁷Submit yourselves, then, to God. Resist the devil, and he will flee from you. ⁸Come near to God and he will come near to you. Wash your hands, you sinners, and purify your hearts, you double-minded. ⁹Grieve, mourn and wail. Change your laughter to mourning and your joy to gloom. ¹⁰Humble yourselves before the Lord, and he will lift you up.

¹¹Brothers, do not slander one another. Anyone who speaks against his brother

ᵃ5 Or that God jealously longs for the spirit that he made to live in us; or that the Spirit he caused to live in us longs jealously   ᵇ6 Prov. 3:34

Weekend.

Owls and Old Folks

Read 2 Chronicles 1:7–13 (page 497)

Wisdom is a word usually associated with a) people who've lived a long time; or b) owls, though nobody actually knows why owls would be wise, except that maybe since they sleep in the daytime they never watch brain-draining soap operas. It's not a word usually tied to teenagers (or 12-year-olds either!); but from the Bible's perspective, it should be. That's because wisdom comes from God, not from reading a million books or living a long life. Those things may bring knowledge. But wisdom—understanding how to apply knowledge—comes from the Creator.

Several years ago a church was thinking about constructing a new building and had a meeting to discuss it. A thousand people were there to argue and debate whether this was a wise move. A 14-year-old asked to speak at the microphone—much to the surprise of the adults—and (wouldn't you know it?) his eloquent words about building for the future swung the vote to put up the new building. His words rang true with wisdom, because he was in tune with God.

Solomon was tuned in. He didn't want a lot of stuff; he just wanted to be wise. God granted the request.

It doesn't matter how old you are; the Bible says you too can be wise and understanding. The test of your wisdom isn't age—it's your heart.

❶ Do you desire wisdom? Why or why not?

❷ Do you know a person who seems to make really wise decisions? What makes that person different? How do they show their wisdom? The next time you see this person, take a minute to ask him or her how he or she seeks godly wisdom and understanding.

❸ Pray that God will make you a source of wisdom for others. Ask him to help you to be humble and unselfish as he uses you.

Turn to page 1514 for your next devotion.

or judges him speaks against the law and judges it. When you judge the law, you are not keeping it, but sitting in judgment on it. [12]There is only one Lawgiver and Judge, the one who is able to save and destroy. But you—who are you to judge your neighbor?

Boasting About Tomorrow

[13]Now listen, you who say, "Today or tomorrow we will go to this or that city, spend a year there, carry on business and make money." [14]Why, you do not even know what will happen tomorrow. What is your life? You are a mist that appears for a little while and then vanishes. [15]Instead, you ought to say, "If it is the Lord's will, we will live and do this or that." [16]As it is, you boast and brag. All such boasting is evil. [17]Anyone, then, who knows the good he ought to do and doesn't do it, sins.

Warning to Rich Oppressors

5 Now listen, you rich people, weep and wail because of the misery that is coming upon you. [2]Your wealth has rotted, and moths have eaten your clothes. [3]Your gold and silver are corroded. Their corrosion will testify against you and eat your flesh like fire. You have hoarded wealth in the last days. [4]Look! The wages you failed to pay the workmen who mowed your fields are crying out against you. The cries of the harvesters have reached the ears of the Lord Almighty. [5]You have lived on earth in luxury and self-indulgence. You have fattened yourselves in the day of slaughter.[a] [6]You have condemned and murdered innocent men, who were not opposing you.

Patience in Suffering

[7]Be patient, then, brothers, until the Lord's coming. See how the farmer waits for the land to yield its valuable crop and how patient he is for the autumn and spring rains. [8]You too, be patient and stand firm, because the Lord's coming is near. [9]Don't grumble against each other, brothers, or you will be judged. The Judge is standing at the door!

[10]Brothers, as an example of patience in the face of suffering, take the prophets who spoke in the name of the Lord. [11]As you know, we consider blessed those who have persevered. You have heard of Job's perseverance and have seen what the Lord finally brought about. The Lord is full of compassion and mercy.

[12]Above all, my brothers, do not swear—not by heaven or by earth or by anything else. Let your "Yes" be yes, and your "No," no, or you will be condemned.

The Prayer of Faith

[13]Is any one of you in trouble? He should pray. Is anyone happy? Let him sing songs of praise. [14]Is any one of you sick? He should call the elders of the church to pray over him and anoint him with oil in the name of the Lord. [15]And the prayer offered in faith will make the sick person well; the Lord will raise him up. If he has sinned, he will be forgiven.

Active Faith

Huh?

James 5:15
Faith is a one-word way to say that you believe in Jesus and trust in him. James also says that the test of real faith is the way you act. So all the things you do, think and say about your relationship with God can be summed up and called your "faith."

[16]Therefore confess your sins to each other and pray for each other so that you may be healed. The prayer of a righteous man is powerful and effective.

[17]Elijah was a man just like us. He prayed earnestly that it would not rain, and it did not rain on the land for three and a half years. [18]Again he prayed, and the heavens gave rain, and the earth produced its crops.

[19]My brothers, if one of you should wander from the truth and someone should bring him back, [20]remember this: Whoever turns a sinner from the error of his way will save him from death and cover over a multitude of sins.

[a]5 Or *yourselves as in a day of feasting*

1 Peter

START

"What's God want from me?" Have you ever asked that question? It's a great question—one you should be asking all the time. Peter gives you a bunch of answers to that question.

This is your mission, should you choose to accept it (are you ready for this?): Praise God, put your hope in him, be self-controlled, obedient, holy, submissive and respectful. Don't pound on someone when they pound on you. Suffer for God, treat your friends (and one day, your spouse!) as you would treat Christ himself. *And* live in peace with everyone, be compassionate, sympathetic and love everyone. Sound easy? Yeah, right!

The truth is, being a Christian can be really tough. In fact, there's a 0% chance that you'll pull it off all by yourself. (That's where the Holy Spirit giving you God's power comes in.) But this list that Peter presents gives you a good idea of some of the things that will mark you as a Christ-follower. And it all starts with giving God the credit (sometimes the Bible calls this "giving God glory") for *everything*.

Cast OF Characters

Peter

He's the guy who wrote this book. Remember him? He was the loudmouth disciple who followed Jesus around for 3 years. He also said he didn't know Jesus when it came to crunch time at the cross. But here he is writing as the leader of the early church. Jesus once called him "the Rock." It was through Peter that God began the church. This is his letter to everybody on how to live like Jesus lived.

Silas

(SIGH-lus)

A friend of Peter who loved Jesus and helped write this great letter.

Mark

Another buddy of Peter who wrote "The Gospel according to Mark."

What's UP with That?

Peter talks a ton about what it means to "suffer" for Jesus Christ. From the following list, circle the suffering situations that Peter wrote about (c'mon, don't look at the upside-down answers at the bottom until you're done!):

1. Never buy another CD.

2. When someone calls you a name, don't call 'em one back.

3. Take your Bible to class, even though people might think you're a freak.

4. Only shop at stores that your parents choose.

5. Do the right thing, even when it costs you big-time.

6. Obey God even when stuff doesn't seem to make sense.

7. Choose to never, ever use the TV remote again.

answers: 2, 5, 6

Snap Shots

- Give it up for God why don't ya? *(chapter 1)*

- The bad stuff gets you every time *(chapter 2:1–12)*

- Be cool to the folks in charge *(chapter 2:13–25)*

- That husband-wife thang *(chapter 3:1–7)*

- So whose team are you playing on? *(chapter 3:8–22)*

- Don't be surprised by suffering *(chapter 4)*

- Some final thoughts for church dudes and teens *(chapter 5)*

1 Peter, an apostle of Jesus Christ,

To God's elect, strangers in the world, scattered throughout Pontus, Galatia, Cappadocia, Asia and Bithynia, ²who have been chosen according to the foreknowledge of God the Father, through the sanctifying work of the Spirit, for obedience to Jesus Christ and sprinkling by his blood:

Grace and peace be yours in abundance.

Praise to God for a Living Hope

³Praise be to the God and Father of our Lord Jesus Christ! In his great mercy he has given us new birth into a living hope through the resurrection of Jesus Christ from the dead, ⁴and into an inheritance that can never perish, spoil or fade—kept in heaven for you, ⁵who through faith are shielded by God's power until the coming of the salvation that is ready to be revealed in the last time. ⁶In this you greatly rejoice, though now for a little while you may have had to suffer grief in all kinds of trials. ⁷These have come so that your faith—of greater worth than gold, which perishes even though refined by fire—may be proved genuine and may result in praise, glory and honor when Jesus Christ is revealed. ⁸Though you have not seen him, you love him; and even though you do not see him now, you believe in him and are filled with an inexpressible and glorious joy, ⁹for you are receiving the goal of your faith, the salvation of your souls.

¹⁰Concerning this salvation, the prophets, who spoke of the grace that was to come to you, searched intently and with the greatest care, ¹¹trying to find out the time and circumstances to which the Spirit of Christ in them was pointing when he predicted the sufferings of Christ and the glories that would follow. ¹²It was revealed to them that they were

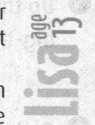

Monday

Out of Control?

Read 1 Peter 1:13–16

When I have a ton of homework, I often get really stressed out and discouraged. It takes all the self-control I have to sit down and actually do my work.

Some of my friends struggle with self-control too. They might give in to temptation and do things they shouldn't, or they might get mad at another person and lose their temper. All of us need to practice self-control and not give in to "evil desires."

Jesus was a great example of how we are supposed to live. He was calm and forgiving. He did the things he needed to do, even when he might have wanted to do something else. Like when he was 12 and he had to leave the temple and go home with his parents (see Luke 2:41–52, page 1221). Jesus always made good decisions. When we work at having self-control, we can be more like Jesus.

Lisa, age 13

What about You?

❶ What are 2 ways you can increase your self-control?

❷ Write a little note to yourself. Remind yourself how great it feels when you make a wise decision and follow God. Keep the note in your backpack or your locker. Read it when you feel out of "self" control.

❸ Ask God to help you live for him and not for the world.

Turn to page 1516 for your next devotion.

not serving themselves but you, when they spoke of the things that have now been told you by those who have preached the gospel to you by the Holy Spirit sent from heaven. Even angels long to look into these things.

Be Holy

[13]Therefore, prepare your minds for action; be self-controlled; set your hope fully on the grace to be given you when Jesus Christ is revealed. [14]As obedient children, do not conform to the evil desires you had when you lived in ignorance. [15]But just as he who called you is holy, so be holy in all you do; [16]for it is written: "Be holy, because I am holy."[a]

[17]Since you call on a Father who judges each man's work impartially, live your lives as strangers here in reverent fear. [18]For you know that it was not with perishable things such as silver or gold that you were redeemed from the empty way of life handed down to you from your forefathers, [19]but with the precious blood of Christ, a lamb without blemish or defect. [20]He was chosen before the creation of the world, but was revealed in these last times for your sake. [21]Through him you believe in God, who raised him from the dead and glorified him, and so your faith and hope are in God.

[22]Now that you have purified yourselves by obeying the truth so that you have sincere love for your brothers, love one another deeply, from the heart.[b] [23]For you have been born again, not of perishable seed, but of imperishable, through the living and enduring word of God. [24]For,

"All men are like grass,
    and all their glory is like the flowers
        of the field;
the grass withers and the flowers fall,
[25] but the word of the Lord stands
        forever."[c]

And this is the word that was preached to you.

2 Therefore, rid yourselves of all malice and all deceit, hypocrisy, envy, and slander of every kind. [2]Like newborn babies, crave pure spiritual milk, so that by it you may grow up in your salvation,

[3]now that you have tasted that the Lord is good.

The Living Stone and a Chosen People

[4]As you come to him, the living Stone—rejected by men but chosen by God and precious to him— [5]you also, like living stones, are being built into a spiritual house to be a holy priesthood, offering spiritual sacrifices acceptable to God through Jesus Christ. [6]For in Scripture it says:

"See, I lay a stone in Zion,
    a chosen and precious cornerstone,
and the one who trusts in him
    will never be put to shame."[d]

[7]Now to you who believe, this stone is precious. But to those who do not believe,

"The stone the builders rejected
    has become the capstone,[e]"[f]

[8]and,

"A stone that causes men to stumble
    and a rock that makes them fall."[g]

They stumble because they disobey the message—which is also what they were destined for.

[9]But you are a chosen people, a royal priesthood, a holy nation, a people

A Living Temple

Huh?

1 Peter 2:4–8

During Old Testament times, God's presence lived in the temple—a building. But now God lives in a new kind of building, one built with "living stones"—you and me! The first and most important stone in any building is the cornerstone. It helps hold the whole place up. Jesus is the living cornerstone, and we're the rest of the "stones." God lives in us—isn't that cool?

[a]16 Lev. 11:44,45; 19:2; 20:7 [b]22 Some early manuscripts *from a pure heart* [c]25 Isaiah 40:6-8 [d]6 Isaiah 28:16 [e]7 Or *cornerstone* [f]7 Psalm 118:22 [g]8 Isaiah 8:14

belonging to God, that you may declare the praises of him who called you out of darkness into his wonderful light. ¹⁰Once you were not a people, but now you are the people of God; once you had not received mercy, but now you have received mercy.

¹¹Dear friends, I urge you, as aliens and strangers in the world, to abstain from sinful desires, which war against your soul. ¹²Live such good lives among the pagans that, though they accuse you of doing wrong, they may see your good deeds and glorify God on the day he visits us.

Submission to Rulers and Masters

¹³Submit yourselves for the Lord's sake to every authority instituted among men: whether to the king, as the supreme authority, ¹⁴or to governors, who are sent by him to punish those who do wrong and to commend those who do right. ¹⁵For it is God's will that by doing good you should silence the ignorant talk of foolish men. ¹⁶Live as free men, but do not use your freedom as a cover-up for evil; live as servants of God. ¹⁷Show proper respect to everyone: Love the

brotherhood of believers, fear God, honor the king.

¹⁸Slaves, submit yourselves to your masters with all respect, not only to those who are good and considerate, but also to those who are harsh. ¹⁹For it is commendable if a man bears up under the pain of unjust suffering because he is conscious of God. ²⁰But how is it to your credit if you receive a beating for doing wrong and endure it? But if you suffer for doing good and you endure it, this is commendable before God. ²¹To this you were called, because Christ suffered for you, leaving you an example, that you should follow in his steps.

²²"He committed no sin,
    and no deceit was found in his
        mouth."ᵃ

²³When they hurled their insults at him, he did not retaliate; when he suffered, he made no threats. Instead, he entrusted himself to him who judges justly. ²⁴He himself bore our sins in his body on the tree, so that we might die to sins and live for righteousness; by his wounds you have been healed. ²⁵For you were like

ᵃ22 Isaiah 53:9

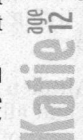

You're Special!

Read 1 Peter 2:9–10

I remember when I was having a really bad day. I got 2 test grades back that weren't too hot. My friends were being mean to me, and my mom and I got into a fight! I remember thinking that no one really liked me.

Eventually I stopped feeling sorry for myself long enough to realize that I was so wrong—God still liked me. He cares about me! He loves me! Ever since that day, I know God has a place for me in his heart. Since God says I'm "chosen," "royal" and "holy," it's hard to mope around. It's easier to praise God!

❶ The next time you have a bad day, remember this: In God's eyes, you're amazing!

❷ Look up the words "chosen," "royal" and "holy" in the dictionary. That's how God describes you! Doesn't that feel good?

❸ Thank God for loving you as his own child.

Turn to page 1518 for your next devotion.

sheep going astray, but now you have returned to the Shepherd and Overseer of your souls.

Wives and Husbands

3 Wives, in the same way be submissive to your husbands so that, if any of them do not believe the word, they may be won over without words by the behavior of their wives, ²when they see the purity and reverence of your lives. ³Your beauty should not come from outward adornment, such as braided hair and the wearing of gold jewelry and fine clothes. ⁴Instead, it should be that of your inner self, the unfading beauty of a gentle and quiet spirit, which is of great worth in God's sight. ⁵For this is the way the holy women of the past who put their hope in God used to make themselves beautiful. They were submissive to their own husbands, ⁶like Sarah, who obeyed Abraham and called him her master. You are her daughters if you do what is right and do not give way to fear.

⁷Husbands, in the same way be considerate as you live with your wives, and treat them with respect as the weaker partner and as heirs with you of the gracious gift of life, so that nothing will hinder your prayers.

Suffering for Doing Good

⁸Finally, all of you, live in harmony with one another; be sympathetic, love as brothers, be compassionate and humble. ⁹Do not repay evil with evil or insult with insult, but with blessing, because to this you were called so that you may inherit a blessing. ¹⁰For,

"Whoever would love life
    and see good days
must keep his tongue from evil
    and his lips from deceitful speech.
¹¹He must turn from evil and do good;
    he must seek peace and pursue it.
¹²For the eyes of the Lord are on the righteous
    and his ears are attentive to their prayer,
but the face of the Lord is against those who do evil."ᵃ

¹³Who is going to harm you if you are eager to do good? ¹⁴But even if you should suffer for what is right, you are blessed. "Do not fear what they fearᵇ; do not be frightened."ᶜ ¹⁵But in your hearts

> ## Good Suffering?
>
> # Huh?
>
> **1 Peter 3:14**
> Ever had someone treat you bad because you're a Jesus follower? That's "good suffering." Peter tells us not to be surprised when this happens; we should be glad and hold on to our faith in God through those hard times. If we do this, our relationship with him will get super-strong.

set apart Christ as Lord. Always be prepared to give an answer to everyone who asks you to give the reason for the hope that you have. But do this with gentleness and respect, ¹⁶keeping a clear conscience, so that those who speak maliciously against your good behavior in Christ may be ashamed of their slander. ¹⁷It is better, if it is God's will, to suffer for doing good than for doing evil. ¹⁸For Christ died for sins once for all, the righteous for the unrighteous, to bring you to God. He was put to death in the body but made alive by the Spirit, ¹⁹through whomᵈ also he went and preached to the spirits in prison ²⁰who disobeyed long ago when God waited patiently in the days of Noah while the ark was being built. In it only a few people, eight in all, were saved through water, ²¹and this water symbolizes baptism that now saves you also—not the removal of dirt from the body but the pledgeᵉ of a good conscience toward God. It saves you by the resurrection of Jesus Christ, ²²who has gone into heaven and is at God's right hand—with angels, authorities and powers in submission to him.

Living for God

4 Therefore, since Christ suffered in his body, arm yourselves also with

---

ᵃ12 Psalm 34:12-16   ᵇ14 Or *not fear their threats*
ᶜ14 Isaiah 8:12   ᵈ18,19 Or *alive in the spirit,*
¹⁹*through which*   ᵉ21 Or *response*

the same attitude, because he who has suffered in his body is done with sin. ²As a result, he does not live the rest of his earthly life for evil human desires, but rather for the will of God. ³For you have spent enough time in the past doing what pagans choose to do—living in debauchery, lust, drunkenness, orgies, carousing and detestable idolatry. ⁴They think it strange that you do not plunge with them into the same flood of dissipation, and they heap abuse on you. ⁵But they will have to give account to him who is ready to judge the living and the dead. ⁶For this is the reason the gospel was preached even to those who are now dead, so that they might be judged according to men in regard to the body, but live according to God in regard to the spirit.

⁷The end of all things is near. Therefore be clear minded and self-controlled so that you can pray. ⁸Above all, love each other deeply, because love covers over a multitude of sins. ⁹Offer hospitality to one another without grumbling. ¹⁰Each one should use whatever gift he has received to serve others, faithfully administering God's grace in its various forms. ¹¹If anyone speaks, he should do it as one speaking the very words of God. If anyone serves, he should do it with the strength God provides, so that in all things God may be praised through Jesus Christ. To him be the glory and the power for ever and ever. Amen.

Suffering for Being a Christian

¹²Dear friends, do not be surprised at the painful trial you are suffering, as though something strange were happening to you. ¹³But rejoice that you participate in the sufferings of Christ, so that you may be overjoyed when his glory is revealed. ¹⁴If you are insulted because of the name of Christ, you are blessed, for the Spirit of glory and of God rests on you. ¹⁵If you suffer, it should not be as a

---

Wednesday

Speak Up

Read 1 Peter 3:15

I know a lot of people who don't go to church and probably don't know Jesus. Some people at my school follow other religions, like Buddhism and Islam. I really worry about all of these people. I know that if they don't have a relationship with God before they die, they won't go to heaven.

Sometimes I get down because some of my friends won't come to the Lord. Even when I try to talk to them about God, it seems like they don't want to listen. That's when I pray and ask God for the confidence to keep trying anyway.

But I have seen changes in some of my friends. One person I've shared with has accepted Jesus into her heart, and another one is almost there. I wish I could see all of my friends make those decisions, but I can't make people change. Only God can. All I can do is stick with it and be the best friend I can be.

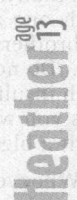

Heather age 13

❶ What kinds of questions might your friends have about God? How would you answer them?

❷ Think of one person you know who isn't a Christian. How can you share your faith with him or her this week?

❸ Ask God to give you confidence to talk about your faith.

Turn to page 1519 for your next devotion.

The Good Stuff

1 Peter 4:11–14

Glory is the good stuff you get when you do a good job. At the Olympics—when the winners stand on that platform, get their medals and everyone cheers—they're receiving a bunch of glory. As Christians, we get to share in all the glory, or good stuff, of God because of what Jesus did for us—he won the battle against sin!

murderer or thief or any other kind of criminal, or even as a meddler. ¹⁶However, if you suffer as a Christian, do not be ashamed, but praise God that you bear that name. ¹⁷For it is time for judgment to begin with the family of God; and if it begins with us, what will the outcome be for those who do not obey the gospel of God? ¹⁸And,

> "If it is hard for the righteous to be
>   saved,
>   what will become of the ungodly
>   and the sinner?"ᵃ

¹⁹So then, those who suffer according to God's will should commit themselves to their faithful Creator and continue to do good.

To Elders and Young Men

5 To the elders among you, I appeal as a fellow elder, a witness of Christ's sufferings and one who also will share in the glory to be revealed: ²Be shepherds of God's flock that is under your care, serving as overseers—not because you must,

ᵃ18 Prov. 11:31

Thursday

Stay Strong

Read 1 Peter 5:8–9

Imagine you're walking down the hallways at school on a Friday afternoon. A lot of students are talking about weekend parties, how they're going to get drunk or high. You stop to talk to some people, and the next thing you know, you're invited to their party. Everybody's looking at you. Will you say yes or no?

Temptation is all around us—it fills the air. The devil wants us to fall, but we can defeat him by standing strong with Christ Jesus. God knows when we're being tempted. He'll always help us if we ask him for strength and guidance.

We can help each other fight temptation too. When one person resists the pressure, it's easier for others to resist. God gives us power to help other people to be strong. And when it comes to temptation, we need all the help we can get.

Amy age 14

What about You?

❶ What are some of the toughest temptations you face? What can you do to avoid these situations?

❷ Set up an "emergency hotline" with your youth leader or a trusted friend. When you face a really tough temptation, you'll have someone to call who can help you to stay strong.

❸ Ask God to help you say "no" to temptation.

Turn to page 1523 for your next devotion.

but because you are willing, as God wants you to be; not greedy for money, but eager to serve; ³not lording it over those entrusted to you, but being examples to the flock. ⁴And when the Chief Shepherd appears, you will receive the crown of glory that will never fade away.

⁵Young men, in the same way be submissive to those who are older. All of you, clothe yourselves with humility toward one another, because,

> "God opposes the proud
> but gives grace to the humble."ᵃ

⁶Humble yourselves, therefore, under God's mighty hand, that he may lift you up in due time. ⁷Cast all your anxiety on him because he cares for you.

⁸Be self-controlled and alert. Your enemy the devil prowls around like a roaring lion looking for someone to devour. ⁹Resist him, standing firm in the faith, because you know that your brothers throughout the world are undergoing the same kind of sufferings.

¹⁰And the God of all grace, who called you to his eternal glory in Christ, after you have suffered a little while, will himself restore you and make you strong, firm and steadfast. ¹¹To him be the power for ever and ever. Amen.

Final Greetings

¹²With the help of Silas,ᵇ whom I regard as a faithful brother, I have written to you briefly, encouraging you and testifying that this is the true grace of God. Stand fast in it.

¹³She who is in Babylon, chosen together with you, sends you her greetings, and so does my son Mark. ¹⁴Greet one another with a kiss of love.

Peace to all of you who are in Christ.

ᵃ5 Prov. 3:34   ᵇ12 Greek *Silvanus*, a variant of *Silas*

2 Peter

START

You're the star basketball player on your team, and it's the championship game. Your team is behind by one point with a minute left, and your coach calls time-out. Everything's looking good until your coach tells you to try a ridiculous play. In fact, this play is so strange that it goes completely against everything you know about basketball—it's more like a figure-skating routine. Not knowing what else to do, you go out and try the strange play only to lose the game and look like a total idiot in the process.

Can you imagine having a coach like that? With everything on the line, the coach changes the entire way you play for no apparent reason. Well, Peter had to deal with some stuff like that in this letter. Not only were there some bad "coaches" (teachers) in the church, but some were getting the "players" (Jesus-followers) to do the exact opposite of what God wanted them to do.

This book was Peter's way of warning those "players" to watch out. The warnings are good for us too. They can help us to live as Jesus lived.

Cast OF Characters

Peter

Yeah, this is the same guy who wrote the last book. He knew Jesus very well after hanging out with him for 2 or 3 years. Even though he messed up a lot as he learned how to live for Jesus, Peter still turned out to be a great teacher with some pretty cool things to say.

We

Uh . . . what? Well, just in case you miss it, the word "we" appears in chapter 1, talking about a bunch of folks who heard voices from heaven. These were the disciples who saw Jesus on the mountain with Elijah and Moses.

Noah (NO-uh), Lot (laht), Balaam (BAY-lum)

Remember these guys from the book of Genesis? They don't really show up here, but Peter uses them as examples in his writing. Kind of like photo illustrations.

What's UP with That?

Ancient Times Tabloid Newspaper

Which tabloid newspaper headlines could have been real (according to 2 Peter)?

1 Heavenly Bodies Seen Melting as Heaven Blazes On

2 Jesus, "The Robbing Revelator," Comes Back and Steals the Show

3 God Spares Floating Zoo Cruise Director

4 Donkey Arrested for Verbal Harassment of Misguided Owner

5 Man Says He Can Surf Standing Up Without Board

6 Disciple Thrown in Prison After World Wrestling Federation Impersonation of Roman Soldier

7 Dogs Seen Spewing Chunks and Checking Them Out Later

Snap shots

- Did God call you collect? *(chapter 1:1–11)*

- I was *there*, baby *(chapter 1:12–20)*

- Ooh, bad coach! *(chapter 2)*

- Heee's coming baaaaack! *(chapter 3)*

answers: 1 (3:10), 2 (1:16; 3:10), 3 (2:5), 4 (2:16), 7 (2:22)

1

Simon Peter, a servant and apostle of Jesus Christ,

To those who through the righteousness of our God and Savior Jesus Christ have received a faith as precious as ours:

²Grace and peace be yours in abundance through the knowledge of God and of Jesus our Lord.

Making One's Calling and Election Sure

³His divine power has given us everything we need for life and godliness through our knowledge of him who called us by his own glory and goodness. ⁴Through these he has given us his very great and precious promises, so that through them you may participate in the divine nature and escape the corruption in the world caused by evil desires.

⁵For this very reason, make every effort to add to your faith goodness; and to goodness, knowledge; ⁶and to knowledge, self-control; and to self-control, perseverance; and to perseverance, godliness; ⁷and to godliness, brotherly kindness; and to brotherly kindness, love. ⁸For if you possess these qualities in increasing measure, they will keep you from being ineffective and unproductive in your knowledge of our Lord Jesus Christ. ⁹But if anyone does not have them, he is nearsighted and blind, and has forgotten that he has been cleansed from his past sins.

¹⁰Therefore, my brothers, be all the more eager to make your calling and election sure. For if you do these things, you will never fall, ¹¹and you will receive a rich welcome into the eternal kingdom of our Lord and Savior Jesus Christ.

Friday

Skyscrapers

Read 2 Peter 1:5–9

Growing in our faith is like building a skyscraper. You have to start small. The foundation is faith. Then goodness, knowledge and self-control are added. You finish with godliness, kindness, perseverance and love. It's a process done in stages, not all at once.

At recess one day in grammar school I saw a girl who was sad. I went over to her, and, although I didn't know quite what to say, I tried my best to cheer her up. But kindness wasn't enough—it took perseverance to do it! That's how we become more like Christ. We use the qualities we do have, like kindness, to build the ones we don't, like perseverance. Pretty soon, I'll have a skyscraper on display!

Matt age 13

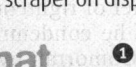
What about You?

❶ Why is it sometimes difficult to grow in your faith? How does this passage encourage you?

❷ Draw a skyscraper. Write the word "faith" at the foundation of your building. Divide your skyscraper into 7 floors. Label each floor with the qualities from 2 Peter 1:5–7—goodness, knowledge, self-control, perseverance, godliness, kindness and love. Tape your skyscraper someplace where you'll see it often. Let it remind you of the wonderful qualities God is building within you.

❸ Ask God to help you add Christlike qualities to your life. Thank him for giving you the strength to do it.

Turn to page 1526 for your next devotion.

The Results Are in

Huh?

2 Peter 1:10

If you run for president and enough people choose you, you'll win the election! In the same way, as Christians, God chooses us—and we win! We don't just win an election to be "The President"; we are elected to be part of God's very own family.

Prophecy of Scripture

¹²So I will always remind you of these things, even though you know them and are firmly established in the truth you now have. ¹³I think it is right to refresh your memory as long as I live in the tent of this body, ¹⁴because I know that I will soon put it aside, as our Lord Jesus Christ has made clear to me. ¹⁵And I will make every effort to see that after my departure you will always be able to remember these things.

¹⁶We did not follow cleverly invented stories when we told you about the power and coming of our Lord Jesus Christ, but we were eyewitnesses of his majesty. ¹⁷For he received honor and glory from God the Father when the voice came to him from the Majestic Glory, saying, "This is my Son, whom I love; with him I am well pleased."ᵃ ¹⁸We ourselves heard this voice that came from heaven when we were with him on the sacred mountain.

¹⁹And we have the word of the prophets made more certain, and you will do well to pay attention to it, as to a light shining in a dark place, until the day dawns and the morning star rises in your hearts. ²⁰Above all, you must understand that no prophecy of Scripture came about by the prophet's own interpretation. ²¹For prophecy never had its origin in the will of man, but men spoke from God as they were carried along by the Holy Spirit.

False Teachers and Their Destruction

2 But there were also false prophets among the people, just as there will be false teachers among you. They will secretly introduce destructive heresies, even denying the sovereign Lord who bought them—bringing swift destruction on themselves. ²Many will follow their

False Prophet Alert!

2 Peter 2:1

A true prophet is someone God uses to speak his words to others. Peter warns about false prophets or teachers—those who claim to speak for God but don't. How can you spot a false prophet? Look in the Bible! If someone teaches something about God that isn't in the Bible—Sorry! Wrong answer! False prophet alert! These false prophets are still running around today: New Age self-help programs, cults, the Psychic Friends Network. Yep, false, false, and false!

shameful ways and will bring the way of truth into disrepute. ³In their greed these teachers will exploit you with stories they have made up. Their condemnation has long been hanging over them, and their destruction has not been sleeping.

⁴For if God did not spare angels when they sinned, but sent them to hell,ᵇ putting them into gloomy dungeonsᶜ to be held for judgment; ⁵if he did not spare the ancient world when he brought the flood on its ungodly people, but protected Noah, a preacher of righteousness, and seven others; ⁶if he condemned the cities of Sodom and Gomorrah by burning them to ashes, and made them an example of what is going to happen to the ungodly; ⁷and if he rescued Lot, a righteous man, who was distressed by the filthy lives of lawless men ⁸(for that righteous man, living among them day after day, was tormented in his righteous soul by the lawless deeds he saw and heard)— ⁹if this is so, then the Lord knows how to

ᵃ17 Matt. 17:5; Mark 9:7; Luke 9:35   ᵇ4 Greek *Tartarus*   ᶜ4 Some manuscripts *into chains of darkness*

FAITH

"Why do I have to go to church? Can't I just worship God my own way, on my own?"

First, you need to ask yourself, **WHAT IS CHURCH?** We tend to think of the "First Church of . . ." or "United Church of . . ." But church is more than just a building; it's a group of believers getting together to worship God, grow spiritually, and prepare for taking the message of salvation to the world.

If you and a group of Christian friends meet regularly for prayer and encouragement before school, guess what? You're having church! But just meeting with your friends during the week isn't enough. An actual local church has much more to offer.

The biggest reason we need to go to church is to be like Jesus (see Ephesians 5:1, page 1429). He went to church regularly (check out Luke 4:16, page 1224). He knew how important it was for God's people to meet together to learn about God and grow in their faith.

Church also helps with another important part of the Christian life—**ACCOUNTABILITY.** You might know people who used to seem like strong Christians, but now they're into doing their own thing. What happened? They probably had no accountability—no other Christians to help keep them on track in their faith. If we're not involved in the church, we may very well lose that, and we become sort of "Lone Ranger" Christians. But God never meant for us to walk alone. Although there are times we have to stand alone, God wants us to grow and be challenged by a other believers in church (see Hebrews 10:25, page 1497).

But just going to church isn't enough. God wants each of us to plug into **MINSTRY.** That means we can't just sit near the back every Sunday and leave as soon as the pastor says "Amen." We need to be involved—teaching a class, helping out in the nursery, whatever. This helps us discover and develop the gifts God has given us (see 1 Corinthians 12:8–10, page 1388). This also helps us grow as Christians.

Other reasons to go to church include encouraging others to grow in their faith and hearing older Christians talk about how they've faced many of life's challenges. I love to hear from these people in my church. It's cool to see what God is still doing in their lives or how he helped them through tough times. We need to share that wisdom.

So, as you can see, there are all kinds of good reasons to plug into a local church. Just think of all the great things you'd miss if you didn't!

— Susie Shellenberger, editor of Brio, Focus on the Family's monthly magazine for teen girls. Susie has written 22 books and is a national youth speaker who loves Honeycomb cereal.

eXtreme FAITH

"It seems like a lot of religions are 'good.' But Christians say Jesus is the only way. Is that true?"

Great question. The answer completely depends on Jesus Christ . . . and who he really is.

Historical documents outside of the Bible give us solid evidence that there really was a man, Jesus of Nazareth, who lived on Planet Earth some 2,000 years ago. We know he was a real person. But here's the question: Was he the Savior of the world?

The Bible is clear that Jesus claimed to be the only way to God. He said such things as "I and the Father are one" (John 10:30, page 1285); "I am the way and the truth and the life; no one comes to the Father except through me" (John 14:6); and "Anyone who has seen me has seen the Father" (John 14:9).

Knowing that Jesus made those claims about himself, you only have 2 options: Either Jesus was who he said he was—the Son of God—or else he was nuts. You have to decide which of those options you're going to believe. After I studied the evidence, including Jesus' resurrection from the dead, I decided that Jesus was exactly who he said he was—the Son of God, Savior of the world.

Other religions can look pretty good on the surface. Like Christianity, many other religions talk about love and harmony, and they encourage people to do nice things. But while these religions might offer a good set of rules to live by, they can't give anyone a relationship with God. The only way God offers us a RELATIONSHIP with him is through Jesus: "There is one God and one mediator between God and men, the man Christ Jesus, who gave himself as a ransom for all" (1 Timothy 2:5, page 1464).

If I were you, I'd do 2 things:

First, ask God to make himself real to you. Ask him to bring people into your life who can help point you to the truth. Don't demand a "sign" or try to understand everything about God all at once—just ask for God's help as you search.

Second, commit yourself to reading through the New Testament. That's the best way to examine the evidence for Jesus. Then your decision will come back to this question: Do I accept that Jesus is, in fact, the Son of God, the Savior of the world?

— Jim Burns, president of the National Institute of Youth Ministries and the author of the "Let's Talk" column in Campus Life magazine.

rescue godly men from trials and to hold the unrighteous for the day of judgment, while continuing their punishment.[a] [10]This is especially true of those who follow the corrupt desire of the sinful nature[b] and despise authority.

Bold and arrogant, these men are not afraid to slander celestial beings; [11]yet even angels, although they are stronger and more powerful, do not bring slanderous accusations against such beings in the presence of the Lord. [12]But these men blaspheme in matters they do not understand. They are like brute beasts, creatures of instinct, born only to be caught and destroyed, and like beasts they too will perish.

[13]They will be paid back with harm for the harm they have done. Their idea of pleasure is to carouse in broad daylight. They are blots and blemishes, reveling in their pleasures while they feast with you.[c] [14]With eyes full of adultery, they never stop sinning; they seduce the unstable; they are experts in greed—an accursed brood! [15]They have left the straight way and wandered off to follow the way of Balaam son of Beor, who loved the wages of wickedness. [16]But he was rebuked for his wrongdoing by a donkey—a beast without speech—who spoke with a man's voice and restrained the prophet's madness.

[17]These men are springs without water and mists driven by a storm. Blackest darkness is reserved for them. [18]For they mouth empty, boastful words and, by appealing to the lustful desires of sinful human nature, they entice people who are just escaping from those who live in error. [19]They promise them freedom, while they themselves are slaves of depravity—for a man is a slave to whatever has mastered him. [20]If they have escaped the corruption of the world by knowing our Lord and Savior Jesus Christ and are again entangled in it and overcome, they are worse off at the end than they were at the beginning. [21]It would have been better for them not to have known the way of righteousness, than to have known it and then to turn their backs on the sacred command that was passed on to them. [22]Of them the proverbs are true: "A dog returns to its vomit,"[d] and, "A sow

that is washed goes back to her wallowing in the mud."

The Day of the Lord

3 Dear friends, this is now my second letter to you. I have written both of them as reminders to stimulate you to wholesome thinking. [2]I want you to recall the words spoken in the past by the holy prophets and the command given by our Lord and Savior through your apostles.

[3]First of all, you must understand that in the last days scoffers will come, scoffing and following their own evil desires. [4]They will say, "Where is this 'coming' he promised? Ever since our fathers died, everything goes on as it has since the beginning of creation." [5]But they deliberately forget that long ago by God's word the heavens existed and the earth was formed out of water and by water. [6]By these waters also the world of that time was deluged and destroyed. [7]By the same word the present heavens and earth are reserved for fire, being kept for the day of judgment and destruction of ungodly men.

[8]But do not forget this one thing, dear friends: With the Lord a day is like a thousand years, and a thousand years are like a day. [9]The Lord is not slow in keeping his promise, as some understand slowness. He is patient with you, not wanting anyone to perish, but everyone to come to repentance.

[10]But the day of the Lord will come like a thief. The heavens will disappear with a roar; the elements will be destroyed by fire, and the earth and everything in it will be laid bare.[e]

[11]Since everything will be destroyed in this way, what kind of people ought you to be? You ought to live holy and godly lives [12]as you look forward to the day of God and speed its coming.[f] That day will bring about the destruction of the heavens by fire, and the elements will melt in the heat. [13]But in keeping with his promise we are looking forward to a new

heaven and a new earth, the home of righteousness.

[14]So then, dear friends, since you are looking forward to this, make every effort to be found spotless, blameless and at peace with him. [15]Bear in mind that our Lord's patience means salvation, just as our dear brother Paul also wrote you with the wisdom that God gave him. [16]He writes the same way in all his letters, speaking in them of these matters. His letters contain some things that are hard to understand, which ignorant and unstable people distort, as they do the other Scriptures, to their own destruction.

[17]Therefore, dear friends, since you already know this, be on your guard so that you may not be carried away by the error of lawless men and fall from your secure position. [18]But grow in the grace and knowledge of our Lord and Savior Jesus Christ. To him be glory both now and forever! Amen.

Weekend.

Us Versus Them

Read Colossians 4:2–6 (page 1447)

Sharing our faith usually begins as an act of love. We realize that people are lost and hopeless without Jesus, so we share the gospel with them. That's what Heather reminded us about on Wednesday.

But what starts out as compassion can quickly become a contest. Instead of one sinner reaching out to another, our witnessing becomes one gladiator battling with another. We argue that God is real, the Bible is true and Jesus is the only way. Our friend argues that we're crazy. Soon it's "us versus them," and we find ourselves more interested in winning the argument than in helping our friend get to know Jesus.

The only competition in witnessing is between us and the devil. The only war we wage is spiritual, as we ask God to open doors for our message and give us courage to speak. But when it comes to witnessing to our friends, we must never fight with them.

Check out Colossians 4:5–6. Here are 3 words that describe the right approach to reaching your friends:

- **Wise.** We need to be wise in our actions, so we don't turn people off to Jesus but rather draw them to him.
- **Winsome.** To be winsome means to be upbeat and positive in our attitude, so that we're "full of grace."
- **Wholesome.** Our words should be "seasoned with salt," or tasty and good. Crude talk can kill our credibility and take the focus off our message.

What about You?

❶ When your witnessing breaks down, which of the 3 Ws—wise actions, winsome attitudes or wholesome language—did you forget to use?

❷ Use a 3 x 5 card to help keep you on track in your witnessing. Put 3 names of non-Christian friends on your card. Then pray "3-by-5"—3 names, 5 minutes a day—for their eternal salvation.

❸ Ask God to help you avoid an "us versus them" attitude in your witnessing. Then do your battle in prayer, asking God to give you opportunities to tell others about him.

Turn to page 1529 for your next devotion.

1 John

START

Cast OF Characters

John
One of the few writers of New Testament books who was a member of Jesus' inner circle—one of the 12. (Matthew and Peter were the only other ones.) Also he was the only New Testament writer to write a Gospel, a letter (actually 3 letters) and a vision (the book of Revelation).

Liars
These are people that John warns his readers about. They make claims like:

"I don't sin." But John says they're just lying to themselves (1:8).

"Of course I know Christ." But John says they're lying,

"All you need is love" is John's point in this letter. But hold it—first you gotta know what he means by *love*. It's not warm fuzzies. It's not holding hands, a walk on the beach, a mushy kiss. It's not even a close friendship.

To John, love isn't what you feel, it's what you do. Do you say you love God? Then obey his commands. Do you say you love people? Then show your love with actions. The bottom line is this: What you *say* you believe isn't nearly as important as what you *do*. Your behavior matters more than your words.

If you think that John is too hard-nosed, notice the tenderness of this apostle. At least 14 times in this short book he addresses his readers as "dear children" or "dear friends." And at the end of the letter, he sums up his purpose for writing—not to make Christians' lives more difficult than they already are, but to convince them that God always hears their prayers, and they don't have to worry about losing the new life that God gave them. That's very encouraging stuff.

because they don't obey Christ (2:4).

"Jesus wasn't really the Christ—he wasn't really God." But John says that whoever says that is actually against God (2:22).

"It's okay if I keep on sinning." But John says that

whoever says this doesn't really know God at all (3:6).

"I love God." But John says that if people say this *and* keep on hating other Christians, they're liars and don't really love God at all (4:20).

What's UP with That ?

Let's play a quick game of word association. Under the words below, write the first 5 words that come to your mind. Don't think about it—just write! Okay, go:

Light

_____

_____

_____

_____

_____

Dark

_____

_____

_____

_____

_____

Snap shots

- I talked with Jesus, listened to him teach, touched him and ate with him!
  (chapter 1:1–4)

- Prove your love for God by loving others
  (the rest of the letter).

Time's up!

Now look over your 2 lists. Did you write "Jesus" or "God" under the word "light?" How about in the "Dark" column—did you include words like "sin," "devil," or "antichrist?"

In the book of 1 John, John used all of those words as he described how to live and how not to live as children of God. He urges all who read his letter (this means YOU) to "walk in the light" (1:7). But how do we do that? For starters, read 1 John. As you're reading, make yourself 2 new lists. Label one "Light Do's" and the other "Dark Don'ts," then write down the things that John says the children of God (again, this means YOU) do and don't do.

This will help you get started—DO read 1 John . . . .

The Word of Life

1 That which was from the beginning, which we have heard, which we have seen with our eyes, which we have looked at and our hands have touched— this we proclaim concerning the Word of life. ²The life appeared; we have seen it and testify to it, and we proclaim to you the eternal life, which was with the Father and has appeared to us. ³We proclaim to you what we have seen and heard, so that you also may have fellowship with us. And our fellowship is with the Father and with his Son, Jesus Christ. ⁴We write this to make our*ᵃ* joy complete.

Walking in the Light

⁵This is the message we have heard from him and declare to you: God is light; in him there is no darkness at all. ⁶If we claim to have fellowship with him yet walk in the darkness, we lie and do not live by the truth. ⁷But if we walk in the light, as he is in the light, we have fellowship with one another, and the

True Confessions

1 John 1:9
To confess means more than just admitting you blew it. It actually means agreeing with God about what you've done and how wrong it is. Next time you confess something to God, try starting with the words, "Dear God, I agree with what you've said about . . . "

blood of Jesus, his Son, purifies us from all*ᵇ* sin.

⁸If we claim to be without sin, we deceive ourselves and the truth is not in us. ⁹If we confess our sins, he is faithful and just and will forgive us our sins and purify us from all unrighteousness. ¹⁰If we

ᵃ4 Some manuscripts *your* *ᵇ7* Or *every*

Monday

Forgiven!
Read 1 John 1:8–10

Every one of us sins, so it's a good thing God is forgiving. Like the time I wanted to pierce my ears. My mom told me I couldn't, but I disobeyed her and did it myself. Not only did my ears hurt really bad, but my mom got mad and lost her trust in me. That day, I realized what I'd done was wrong. I apologized to my mom, and I asked God to forgive me. Then I felt a lot better. I was still punished for disobeying my mom, but it felt good to be honest about my sin and ask for forgiveness.

When we sin, we can confess our sins to God and know that he'll forgive us. The Bible says God will show us mercy and make us pure again.

Sarah age 12

❶ What sins do you need to confess? How would it feel to be honest about your sins?

❷ Before you go to bed tonight, kneel down and take the time to really confess your sins to God. Be as specific as you can. Ask God to forgive you for the ways you've sinned today. Everybody sins . . . every single day. Don't be afraid to admit your sins. God will forgive you if you bring them to him and tell him you're sorry.

❸ Thank God for being so forgiving and loving.

Turn to page 1531 for your next devotion.

claim we have not sinned, we make him out to be a liar and his word has no place in our lives.

2 My dear children, I write this to you so that you will not sin. But if anybody does sin, we have one who speaks to the Father in our defense—Jesus Christ, the Righteous One. ²He is the atoning sacrifice for our sins, and not only for ours but also for[a] the sins of the whole world.

³We know that we have come to know him if we obey his commands. ⁴The man who says, "I know him," but does not do what he commands is a liar, and the truth is not in him. ⁵But if anyone obeys his word, God's love[b] is truly made complete in him. This is how we know we are in him: ⁶Whoever claims to live in him must walk as Jesus did.

⁷Dear friends, I am not writing you a new command but an old one, which you have had since the beginning. This old command is the message you have heard. ⁸Yet I am writing you a new command; its truth is seen in him and you, because the darkness is passing and the true light is already shining.

⁹Anyone who claims to be in the light but hates his brother is still in the darkness. ¹⁰Whoever loves his brother lives in

Disconnect Hate

Huh?

1 John 2:9
Being a believer in Jesus has to make a difference in the way you treat people. If it doesn't, something's not connecting between your faith and your actions. Feelings of anger, hatred and revenge are a sign that something is wrong inside. It's not good to say you hate someone—even as a joke.

the light, and there is nothing in him[c] to make him stumble. ¹¹But whoever hates his brother is in the darkness and walks around in the darkness; he does not know where he is going; because the darkness has blinded him.

¹²I write to you, dear children,
  because your sins have been
    forgiven on account of his
      name.
¹³I write to you, fathers,
  because you have known him who
    is from the beginning.
I write to you, young men,
  because you have overcome the evil
    one.
I write to you, dear children,
  because you have known the Father.
¹⁴I write to you, fathers,
  because you have known him who
    is from the beginning.
I write to you, young men,
  because you are strong,
  and the word of God lives in you,
  and you have overcome the evil
    one.

Do Not Love the World

¹⁵Do not love the world or anything in the world. If anyone loves the world, the love of the Father is not in him. ¹⁶For everything in the world—the cravings of sinful man, the lust of his eyes and the boasting of what he has and does—comes not from the Father but from the world. ¹⁷The world and its desires pass away, but the man who does the will of God lives forever.

Warning Against Antichrists

¹⁸Dear children, this is the last hour; and as you have heard that the antichrist is coming, even now many antichrists have come. This is how we know it is the last hour. ¹⁹They went out from us, but they did not really belong to us. For if they had belonged to us, they would have remained with us; but their going showed that none of them belonged to us.

²⁰But you have an anointing from the Holy One, and all of you know the truth.[d] ²¹I do not write to you because you do not know the truth, but because you do know it and because no lie comes from the truth. ²²Who is the liar? It is the man

[a]2 Or *He is the one who turns aside God's wrath, taking away our sins, and not only ours but also* [b]5 Or *word, love for God* [c]10 Or it [d]20 Some manuscripts *and you know all things*

who denies that Jesus is the Christ. Such a man is the antichrist—he denies the Father and the Son. ²³No one who denies the Son has the Father; whoever acknowledges the Son has the Father also.

²⁴See that what you have heard from the beginning remains in you. If it does, you also will remain in the Son and in the Father. ²⁵And this is what he promised us—even eternal life.

²⁶I am writing these things to you about those who are trying to lead you astray. ²⁷As for you, the anointing you received from him remains in you, and you do not need anyone to teach you. But as his anointing teaches you about all things and as that anointing is real, not counterfeit—just as it has taught you, remain in him.

Children of God

²⁸And now, dear children, continue in him, so that when he appears we may be confident and unashamed before him at his coming.

²⁹If you know that he is righteous, you know that everyone who does what is right has been born of him.

3 How great is the love the Father has lavished on us, that we should be called children of God! And that is what we are! The reason the world does not know us is that it did not know him. ²Dear friends, now we are children of God, and what we will be has not yet been made known. But we know that when he appears,ᵃ we shall be like him, for we shall see him as he is. ³Everyone who has this hope in him purifies himself, just as he is pure.

⁴Everyone who sins breaks the law; in fact, sin is lawlessness. ⁵But you know that he appeared so that he might take away our sins. And in him is no sin. ⁶No one who lives in him keeps on sinning. No one who continues to sin has either seen him or known him.

⁷Dear children, do not let anyone lead you astray. He who does what is right is righteous, just as he is righteous. ⁸He who does what is sinful is of the devil, because the devil has been sinning from the beginning. The reason the Son of God appeared was to destroy the devil's work. ⁹No one who is born of God will continue to sin, because God's seed remains in him; he cannot go on sinning, because he has been born of God. ¹⁰This is how

ᵃ2 Or *when it is made known*

Tuesday

Amazing Love

Read 1 John 3:1

Whenever I feel insignificant or unloved, I have to remember how God has declared his love for me. He never forgets who I am, because I'm his child. He never ignores me. He loves me more than anyone else ever could.

One of the most amazing things about God's love is that it's infinite—it never ends. And it isn't like I have to work really hard and be perfect to get this love, because he already loves me more than I can imagine.

The more I learn about God's love for me, the more I want to love him and show his love to others. His love is a model for me every day.

Stacey age 13

❶ What does it mean to be a child of God?

❷ List 10 ways God has shown his love for you lately.

❸ Thank God for his love and ask him to help you show that love to others.

Turn to page 1533 for your next devotion.

we know who the children of God are and who the children of the devil are: Anyone who does not do what is right is not a child of God; nor is anyone who does not love his brother.

Love One Another

¹¹This is the message you heard from the beginning: We should love one another. ¹²Do not be like Cain, who belonged to the evil one and murdered his brother. And why did he murder him? Because his own actions were evil and his brother's were righteous. ¹³Do not be surprised, my brothers, if the world hates you. ¹⁴We know that we have passed from death to life, because we love our brothers. Anyone who does not love remains in death. ¹⁵Anyone who hates his brother is a murderer, and you know that no murderer has eternal life in him.

¹⁶This is how we know what love is: Jesus Christ laid down his life for us. And we ought to lay down our lives for our brothers. ¹⁷If anyone has material possessions and sees his brother in need but has no pity on him, how can the love of God be in him? ¹⁸Dear children, let us not love with words or tongue but with actions and in truth. ¹⁹This then is how we know that we belong to the truth, and how we set our hearts at rest in his presence ²⁰whenever our hearts condemn us. For God is greater than our hearts, and he knows everything.

²¹Dear friends, if our hearts do not condemn us, we have confidence before God ²²and receive from him anything we ask, because we obey his commands and do what pleases him. ²³And this is his command: to believe in the name of his Son, Jesus Christ, and to love one another as he commanded us. ²⁴Those who obey his commands live in him, and he in them. And this is how we know that he lives in us: We know it by the Spirit he gave us.

Test the Spirits

4 Dear friends, do not believe every spirit, but test the spirits to see whether they are from God, because many false prophets have gone out into the world. ²This is how you can recognize the Spirit of God: Every spirit that

---

The Real Deal

Huh?

1 John 4:1–3
It seems as though new religions are popping up all over the place. "Find the true meaning of life." "The secrets of the universe explained." "You can be your own god." You've heard lines like this on TV commercials and seen them in magazines. John tells his friends to test new ideas with a simple clue he gives them in verses 2 and 3: Don't believe everything you hear. But if people acknowledge Jesus and that he came to earth in the flesh, they are part of God's family.

---

acknowledges that Jesus Christ has come in the flesh is from God, ³but every spirit that does not acknowledge Jesus is not from God. This is the spirit of the antichrist, which you have heard is coming and even now is already in the world.

⁴You, dear children, are from God and have overcome them, because the one who is in you is greater than the one who is in the world. ⁵They are from the world and therefore speak from the viewpoint of the world, and the world listens to them. ⁶We are from God, and whoever knows God listens to us; but whoever is not from God does not listen to us. This is how we recognize the Spirit^a of truth and the spirit of falsehood.

God's Love and Ours

⁷Dear friends, let us love one another, for love comes from God. Everyone who loves has been born of God and knows God. ⁸Whoever does not love does not know God, because God is love. ⁹This is how God showed his love among us: He sent his one and only Son^b into the world that we might live through him. ¹⁰This is love: not that we loved God, but that he loved us and sent his Son as an atoning sacrifice for^c our sins. ¹¹Dear friends, since God so loved us, we also ought to

---

^a6 Or *spirit*   ^b9 Or *his only begotten Son*   ^c10 Or *as the one who would turn aside his wrath, taking away*

love one another. ¹²No one has ever seen God; but if we love one another, God lives in us and his love is made complete in us.

¹³We know that we live in him and he in us, because he has given us of his Spirit. ¹⁴And we have seen and testify that the Father has sent his Son to be the Savior of the world. ¹⁵If anyone acknowledges that Jesus is the Son of God, God lives in him and he in God. ¹⁶And so we know and rely on the love God has for us.

God is love. Whoever lives in love lives in God, and God in him. ¹⁷In this way, love is made complete among us so that we will have confidence on the day of judgment, because in this world we are like him. ¹⁸There is no fear in love. But perfect love drives out fear, because fear has to do with punishment. The one who fears is not made perfect in love.

¹⁹We love because he first loved us. ²⁰If anyone says, "I love God," yet hates his brother, he is a liar. For anyone who does not love his brother, whom he has seen, cannot love God, whom he has not seen. ²¹And he has given us this command: Whoever loves God must also love his brother.

Faith in the Son of God

5 Everyone who believes that Jesus is the Christ is born of God, and everyone who loves the father loves his child as well. ²This is how we know that we love the children of God: by loving God and carrying out his commands. ³This is love for God: to obey his commands. And his commands are not burdensome,

---

Wednesday

Fearless

Read 1 John 4:18

My basketball team was playing in a championship game. I was so nervous and scared before the game that I felt sick to my stomach. I managed not to throw up, but I did have a really bad cramp that hurt when I ran. And I was so psyched out that I made all kinds of mental mistakes during the game. I played terrible.

That game taught me something: Don't let fear take over your life. I guess there's always something to be afraid of. But God wants us to trust him to take care of us. In my basketball game, my fear just made things worse. If I had prayed and trusted God to help me play my best, I probably would have felt and played better.

God wants the best for us. So we don't need to be afraid of the future. God is in control, and he'll make everything turn out OK in the end. Knowing this truth can help me conquer my fears before my fears conquer me.

Amy age 13

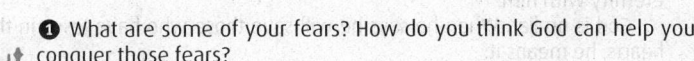

❶ What are some of your fears? How do you think God can help you conquer those fears?

❷ Get the VeggieTales video "Where is God When I'm Scared?" (You can probably borrow it from your church.) Yeah, it's for little kids, but you'll laugh too. Anyway, watch it, then memorize the song, "God is Bigger Than the Boogeyman." The next time you're scared or nervous, sing the song to yourself. Not only will it remind you that God's in control, it's so silly, you just might forget why you're afraid.

❸ Thank God for taking care of all your fears.

Turn to page 1534 for your next devotion.

⁴for everyone born of God overcomes the world. This is the victory that has overcome the world, even our faith. ⁵Who is it that overcomes the world? Only he who believes that Jesus is the Son of God.

⁶This is the one who came by water and blood—Jesus Christ. He did not come by water only, but by water and blood. And it is the Spirit who testifies, because the Spirit is the truth. ⁷For there are three that testify: ⁸the*a* Spirit, the water and the blood; and the three are in agreement. ⁹We accept man's testimony, but God's testimony is greater because it is the testimony of God, which he has given about his Son. ¹⁰Anyone who believes in the Son of God has this testimony in his heart. Anyone who does not believe God has made him out to be a liar, because he has not believed the testimony God has given about his Son. ¹¹And this is the tes-

timony: God has given us eternal life, and this life is in his Son. ¹²He who has the Son has life; he who does not have the Son of God does not have life.

Concluding Remarks

¹³I write these things to you who believe in the name of the Son of God so that you may know that you have eternal life. ¹⁴This is the confidence we have in approaching God: that if we ask anything according to his will, he hears us. ¹⁵And if we know that he hears us—whatever we ask—we know that we have what we asked of him.

¹⁶If anyone sees his brother commit a

a7,8 Late manuscripts of the Vulgate *testify in heaven: the Father, the Word and the Holy Spirit, and these three are one.* ⁸*And there are three that testify on earth: the* (not found in any Greek manuscript before the sixteenth century)

Thursday

Check It Out

Read 1 John 5:11–14

A few years ago I really started to doubt my salvation. I wondered how I could *know* there was a God, how I could be sure I was *really* forgiven. I wondered if I'd really go to heaven. To help me deal with all my questions, my dad showed me these verses. They helped me understand that we can always trust in God's promise to save us.

Sure, it can be hard to believe in something we can't see. But whenever I start to doubt that my salvation is real, I think about checks. That's right, checks. When I babysit for someone and they pay me with a check, I know I've been paid. They haven't given me actual money; they've given me a promise of money. And I *know* I'll see that money eventually. That's kind of how salvation works. I won't actually experience eternal life for a long time. But I trust God's promise that he has saved me and I *will* spend eternity with him.

God is no liar. When he says he will save those who have Jesus in their hearts, he means it.

Emily age 14

❶ Have you ever had doubts about God? What did you do about those doubts?

❷ The next time you have questions about God, think of yourself as an investigative reporter. Dig through the Bible, talk to other Christians, and pray about your questions until you have answers.

❸ Thank God for keeping his promises, even when you have doubts.

Turn to page 1538 for your next devotion.

Simple Stuff

Huh?

1 John 5:12

You can't "sort of" be a Christian. It's not something you ease into over a few years. Fading in and out isn't an option. John says it very clearly—either you are or you aren't. Either you believe in God's Son or you don't. If you do, you've got eternal life. If you don't, you don't. It's as simple as that.

sin that does not lead to death, he should pray and God will give him life. I refer to those whose sin does not lead to death. There is a sin that leads to death. I am not saying that he should pray about that. [17]All wrongdoing is sin, and there is sin that does not lead to death.

[18]We know that anyone born of God does not continue to sin; the one who was born of God keeps him safe, and the evil one cannot harm him. [19]We know that we are children of God, and that the whole world is under the control of the evil one. [20]We know also that the Son of God has come and has given us understanding, so that we may know him who is true. And we are in him who is true—even in his Son Jesus Christ. He is the true God and eternal life.

[21]Dear children, keep yourselves from idols.

2 John

"Knock knock."

"Who's there?"

"A traveling teacher."

"A traveling teacher who?"

"Hey, whaddaya think this is, a joke or something? Really, I'm a traveling teacher with the good news of Jesus of Nazareth. May I come in and teach the church that meets in your home?"

This sort of thing happened a lot the first century or 2 after Jesus left the earth. The only problem was that, just like these days, not all Bible teachers were worth listening to. Some of these traveling teachers were good. Some were misinformed but willing to be corrected. Some were really stuck-up, teaching only to get attention. Others had weird ideas about Jesus that were simply dead wrong. So how was a church to know the difference between a reliable teacher and a smooth-talking deceiver?

John comes to the rescue. He fires off a quick note with this message: "When the traveling teachers come knocking, make sure they believe Jesus was 100% man as well as 100% God. If they don't believe that, don't even open the door."

CAST OF Characters

John
When John wrote this letter, he was probably the only living apostle of the original 12. He tried to steer churches away from wrong teaching and toward love and obedience.

The Chosen Lady
This was either a real lady or a reference to a local church. (Kind of like calling a boat a "she." "Cool boat, but will she float?")

Her Children
Again, this was either the lady's kids or a reference to the folks in the church.

What's UP with That?

Give 'Em the Boot!

"Welcome to 'Kick the Liar,' the new show that allows you to get a running start before giving a swift kick to the liar of the day! Here's how we play: You'll hear comments from 2 people claiming to be Christians. When you think one of them is lying, strap on our specially-designed size 44 kicker and 'give 'em the boot!' (Crowd noise here). That's right, according to 2 John this is the only way to deal with those liars!"

Huh? Is that for real?

Yes, and no. John warns us to be careful with who we let teach the Bible. It's never OK to let someone who claims to be a Christian tell lies about Jesus. So should you "give 'em the boot"? Probably not. A lot of times people get confused and just need you or a friend to help them understand the truth. But when they're totally out-of-line you have a responsibility to . . . well, read 2 John and find out!

Snap shots

- "How's it goin'?" (verses 1–3)

- "You guys rock!" (verse 4)

- "Watch out for those losers" (verses 5–11)

- "See ya soon?" (verses 12–13)

A lot of times people get *CONFUSED* and just need you or a friend to help them understand.

¹The elder,

To the chosen lady and her children, whom I love in the truth—and not I only, but also all who know the truth— ²because of the truth, which lives in us and will be with us forever:

³Grace, mercy and peace from God the Father and from Jesus Christ, the Father's Son, will be with us in truth and love.

⁴It has given me great joy to find some of your children walking in the truth, just as the Father commanded us. ⁵And now, dear lady, I am not writing you a new command but one we have had from the beginning. I ask that we love one another. ⁶And this is love: that we walk in obedience to his commands. As you have heard from the beginning, his command is that you walk in love.

⁷Many deceivers, who do not acknowledge Jesus Christ as coming in the flesh, have gone out into the world. Any such

---

Slumber Party

Huh?

2 John 10

Traveling preachers and teachers needed a place to stay when they got to town. Motel 6 hadn't been invented yet, so John knew that people from churches often invited these folks into their homes. All he's saying here is to be careful not to invite in one of the false teachers.

---

person is the deceiver and the antichrist. ⁸Watch out that you do not lose what you have worked for, but that you may be rewarded fully. ⁹Anyone who runs ahead and does not continue in the teaching of Christ does not have God; whoever continues in the teaching has both the Father and the Son. ¹⁰If anyone comes to you and does not bring this teaching, do

---

Fri day

Wholehearted Love
Read 2 John 6

I grew up in a Christian family, and I heard about Jesus from the time I was a baby. I'd go to church every week. I'd sing "I love Jesus" in praise songs. If you'd asked me, I would have said, "Sure, I love Jesus." But the truth is, I wasn't doing a very good job of following God the other 6 days of the week.

We shouldn't say we love Jesus and then turn around and do things that displease him. He wants us to obey him because we love him. And he wants us to show love to others. God's commands are there to help us live the way he wants us to live. When we obey his commands, we are showing God we trust him and love him with our whole hearts.

Jesse age 14

What about You?

❶ What are some ways you show God you love him? What are some ways you show God's love to other people?

❷ Think of one way you can obey God today. Maybe it's by showing your parents or teachers more respect, not cursing, or taking more time to talk to God. Whatever you decide to do, do it because you love God.

❸ Think of one area in your life where you have been trying to obey God and have done a good job. Ask God to help you keep following him.

Turn to page 1542 for your next devotion.

not take him into your house or welcome him. ¹¹Anyone who welcomes him shares in his wicked work.

¹²I have much to write to you, but I do not want to use paper and ink. Instead, I hope to visit you and talk with you face to face, so that our joy may be complete.

¹³The children of your chosen sister send their greetings.

not take him into your house or welcome ... you and talk with you face
him. ¹¹Anyone who welcomes him ... to ... our joy may be complete.
in his wicked work. ... ...

¹³I have much to write to you, but I do ... 14 ... men of your chosen sister
not want to use paper and ink. Instead, I ... send their greetings.

3 John

START

"Thanks, Gaius. You're awesome!"

When was the last time you wrote a thank-you note? You know, writing a card to Aunt Lois and thanking her for the new CD. (Don't worry, you can exchange it!) It's so important to thank others, even if it's for stuff you don't like, because it shows you appreciate the other person. John is doing that— thanking his friend Gaius for the kindness he showed to traveling Bible teachers.

But in his note, John also points out why he's so thankful. Because creeps like Diotrephes don't know the meaning of kindness! John lays into Dio and can't wait to deal with him face to face. Read about why he's so hot and then you'll see why he's glad his buddy Gaius came through for him.

Cast OF Characters

The Elder
This is John, one of Jesus' 12 apostles.

Gaius (GAY-us)
This letter (3rd John) is addressed to him. He was a leader in his church and a friend of John.

Diotrephes
(die-AH-truh-feez)

This guy was a real loser. Why? Diotrephes had to be first, he gossiped, he bad-mouthed others, he refused to welcome visiting Christians, and he wanted others to think and act like he did! Know anyone like him?

(duh-ME-tree-us)

Demetrius
This guy is happenin'! He's got a great reputation and John agrees with all the positive stuff being said.

What's UP with That?

John's letter shows that he's psyched about one person and ticked about another. Who's who? And which characteristics are true? Which person do you want to be like?

Person #1

A called a "dear friend"

B called a "friend of deer"

C a faithful brother

D full of love

E cooks great nachos

F full of hot air

Person #2

A shoots spit balls

B kicks people out

C eats raw eggs

D gossips

E loves to be first

Snap shots

- "Wa 'sup, G?" *(verses 1–2)*

- John gives props to his boy, Gaius *(verses 3–8)*

- Smooth-talkin' D gets busted! *(verses 9–10)*

- John tells G to "keep it straight" *(verse 11)*

- Demetrius is "all that!" *(verse 12)*

- "Hope to see ya soon" *(verses 13–14)*

answers: person #1 is Gaius (verses 2, 5, 11); c (verse 3, 5); d (verse 6).
person #2 is Diotrephes; b (verse 10); d (verse 10); e (verse 9).

¹The elder,

To my dear friend Gaius, whom I love in the truth.

²Dear friend, I pray that you may enjoy good health and that all may go well with you, even as your soul is getting along well. ³It gave me great joy to have some brothers come and tell about your faithfulness to the truth and how you continue to walk in the truth. ⁴I have no greater joy than to hear that my children are walking in the truth.

⁵Dear friend, you are faithful in what you are doing for the brothers, even though they are strangers to you. ⁶They have told the church about your love. You will do well to send them on their way in a manner worthy of God. ⁷It was for the sake of the Name that they went

---

Lookin' Out for #1

Huh?

3 John 9
Diotrephes wanted power. He pushed people around by saying mean things and telling them they could or couldn't come to church anymore. Sometimes people who are given leadership of a group can't handle it. It goes to their heads, and they abuse those around them. If you are a natural leader, ask God to help you to stay humble.

Weekend.

Prove It

Read 1 John 2:3–6 (page 1530)

There are a lot of different ways to play the classic basketball game "Horse." The basic rules say that when one player makes a shot and the next one misses, a letter is given. But if you play "Prove It" no letter is given right away. Instead, the player who misses has a choice. Either he can try the shot again, or he can make the first player make the shot a second time. In this way no letters are given until you "prove" a second time that they are truly deserved.

Assurance of your salvation works much the same way. Once you sincerely trust Jesus, you're saved. But your life needs to show it.

Notice that 1 John 2:3 says *we know* that we have come to know him if we obey his commands. In other words, obedience proves our salvation to ourselves. But on the other hand, to say we're saved without living like it is to lie to ourselves. It's like the old challenge: "You can talk the talk, but can you walk the walk?" Anyone who wants to know for sure that he or she is a Christian must prove it by walking, or living, as Jesus did.

❶ On a scale of 1 to 10, how sure are you of your salvation? If you headed into eternity today, would you be confident that you would go to heaven?

❷ Make a simple list of the evidence for your own salvation. How has God changed your life? How has your faith made a difference to you? What do you do as a result of what you believe?

❸ Ask God to strengthen your desire to obey him completely. Rededicate yourself to walking as Jesus did.

Turn to page 1547 for your next devotion.

out, receiving no help from the pagans. [8]We ought therefore to show hospitality to such men so that we may work together for the truth.

[9]I wrote to the church, but Diotrephes, who loves to be first, will have nothing to do with us. [10]So if I come, I will call attention to what he is doing, gossiping maliciously about us. Not satisfied with that, he refuses to welcome the brothers. He also stops those who want to do so and puts them out of the church.

[11]Dear friend, do not imitate what is evil but what is good. Anyone who does what is good is from God. Anyone who does what is evil has not seen God. [12]Demetrius is well spoken of by everyone— and even by the truth itself. We also speak well of him, and you know that our testimony is true.

[13]I have much to write you, but I do not want to do so with pen and ink. [14]I hope to see you soon, and we will talk face to face.

Peace to you. The friends here send their greetings. Greet the friends there by name.

Jude

START

After a New Testament full of good news—that God came to earth as a human, that he died voluntarily to save us from our sin, that his resurrection means we'll be resurrected too, that we can love and be loved by an extended family called the church—after all this, Jude drops a dark warning.

The warning is this: You've gotta look out for bogus Christians who aren't really Christians at all. These phonies say Jesus wasn't actually God. They say the forgiving grace of God means you can keep sinning—hey, God will always forgive you, right?

Jude doesn't hold out much hope for them. He says they're like clouds without rain or dead trees (see verse 12). They're spiritually dead. Doomed to "blackest darkness."

Yet to his readers Jude speaks tenderly. Dear friends, he says, keep praying, keep yourselves in God's love, be merciful to those who doubt. Most important, remember what you've been taught.

CAST OF Characters

Jude
The writer of this little letter (for more about him, see "What's Up With That?" on the next page). Jude packs a lot of Old Testament names into just 25 verses:

Sodom (SAH-dum) and Gomorrah (guh-MORE-ruh)
Ancient cities that "gave themselves up to sexual immorality and perversion." (Read Genesis 19, page 26, for the whole twisted story.)

Michael the archangel (ARK-ain-jell)
One of the generals of God's spirit troops. Michael is also mentioned in Daniel (12:1, page 1036) and in Revelation (12:7, page 1559).

Cain (cane)
Guilty of jealousy, then murder . . . of his brother! (Read the complete episode—a short one—in Genesis 4, page 9.)

Balaam (BAY-lum)
Hired by Israel's enemy to curse Israel. Agreed to do it, but Balaam could never quite get the words out. Having a shouting match with his donkey made him feel like a total idiot! (Get the whole story in Numbers 22, page 182.)

Korah (CORE-ruh)
Arrogant and rebellious. One of those "Nobody can tell *me* what to do" types. (Read about him and his earth-splitting end in Numbers 16, page 176.)

Enoch (EE-knock)
The father of Methuselah and great-grandfather of Noah. Curious circumstances surrounded his departure from this life (see Genesis 5:21–23, page 11). Jude quotes Enoch to prove that what he's talking about is nothing new—judgment will come to those who ignore God.

What's UP with That?

Jesus & Bros., Inc.

We know that Jude and his brother James (the James who wrote the letter on page 1505) are brothers of Jesus himself—younger sons of Mary and Joseph. And these aren't the only siblings Jesus grew up with, either—there were Simon and Joseph too, plus some sisters (see Matthew 13:53–57, page 1162).

The sad thing is that Jesus' brothers treated him exactly like any bunch of guys would treat a brother who said and did the radical things Jesus did—healing people, forgiving their sins, out-reasoning the religious leaders who were twice his age, claiming to be the Son of God. His brothers said "No way"—they didn't believe him (read John 7:1–5, page 1278). Can you imagine what it was like growing up in the same house with a *perfect* brother and how hard it was for Joseph and Mary *not* to favor Jesus above their other kids?

But here's the miracle: At least 2 of these skeptical brothers not only became believers in their brother but even church leaders! It probably helped that, after the resurrected Jesus appeared to hundreds of his disciples who believed in him, he risked popping in on someone who didn't—his brother James (1 Corinthians 15:3–8, page 1392). Next thing we know, this brother is the leader of the big church in Jerusalem (Acts 15:13 and 21:17–18, page 1328).

Later on, the Lord's brothers James and Jude write letters that are short but powerful, bold and in-your-face. Not surprising, the writers being related to Jesus and all.

CAN YOU IMAGINE WHAT IT WAS LIKE GROWING UP WITH A *PERFECT* BROTHER?

Snap shots

- A sorry description of ungodly people who love to ruin the faith of others (verses 1–16)

- How to avoid being fooled and save others from being fooled (verses 17–23)

- An upbeat, encouraging blessing for his readers (verses 24–25)

[1]Jude, a servant of Jesus Christ and a brother of James,

To those who have been called, who are loved by God the Father and kept by[a] Jesus Christ:

[2]Mercy, peace and love be yours in abundance.

The Sin and Doom of Godless Men

[3]Dear friends, although I was very eager to write to you about the salvation we share, I felt I had to write and urge you to contend for the faith that was once for all entrusted to the saints. [4]For certain men whose condemnation was written about[b] long ago have secretly slipped in among you. They are godless men, who change the grace of our God into a license for immorality and deny Jesus Christ our only Sovereign and Lord.

[5]Though you already know all this, I want to remind you that the Lord[c] delivered his people out of Egypt, but later destroyed those who did not believe. [6]And the angels who did not keep their positions of authority but abandoned their own home—these he has kept in darkness, bound with everlasting chains for judgment on the great Day. [7]In a similar way, Sodom and Gomorrah and the surrounding towns gave themselves up to sexual immorality and perversion. They serve as an example of those who suffer the punishment of eternal fire.

[8]In the very same way, these dreamers pollute their own bodies, reject authority and slander celestial beings. [9]But even the archangel Michael, when he was disputing with the devil about the body of Moses, did not dare to bring a slanderous accusation against him, but said, "The Lord rebuke you!" [10]Yet these men speak abusively against whatever they do not understand; and what things they do understand by instinct, like unreasoning animals—these are the very things that destroy them.

[11]Woe to them! They have taken the way of Cain; they have rushed for profit into Balaam's error; they have been destroyed in Korah's rebellion.

[12]These men are blemishes at your love feasts, eating with you without the slightest qualm—shepherds who feed only themselves. They are clouds without rain, blown along by the wind; autumn trees, without fruit and uprooted—twice dead. [13]They are wild waves of the sea, foaming up their shame; wandering stars, for whom blackest darkness has been reserved forever.

[14]Enoch, the seventh from Adam, prophesied about these men: "See, the Lord is coming with thousands upon thousands of his holy ones [15]to judge everyone, and to convict all the ungodly of all the ungodly acts they have done in the ungodly way, and of all the harsh words ungodly sinners have spoken against him." [16]These men are grumblers and faultfinders; they follow their own evil desires; they boast about themselves and flatter others for their own advantage.

A Call to Persevere

[17]But, dear friends, remember what the apostles of our Lord Jesus Christ foretold. [18]They said to you, "In the last times there will be scoffers who will follow their own ungodly desires." [19]These are the men who divide you, who follow mere natural instincts and do not have the Spirit.

[20]But you, dear friends, build yourselves up in your most holy faith and

Three Strikes

Huh?

Jude 11

Jude points to 3 Old Testament guys who blew it in different ways. If we're honest, we have to admit that each of these things could be a problem for us today too. Cain (Genesis 4, page 9) was jealous and hateful, Korah (Numbers 16, page 176) was proud and uncooperative, and Balaam (Numbers 22, page 182) was greedy and selfish. Are any of these things problems for you?

---

[a]1 Or for; or in   [b]4 Or men who were marked out for condemnation   [c]5 Some early manuscripts Jesus

pray in the Holy Spirit. ²¹Keep yourselves in God's love as you wait for the mercy of our Lord Jesus Christ to bring you to eternal life.

²²Be merciful to those who doubt; ²³snatch others from the fire and save them; to others show mercy, mixed with fear—hating even the clothing stained by corrupted flesh.

Doxology

²⁴To him who is able to keep you from falling and to present you before his glorious presence without fault and with great joy— ²⁵to the only God our Savior be glory, majesty, power and authority, through Jesus Christ our Lord, before all ages, now and forevermore! Amen.

Monday

Never Give Up

Read Jude 22–23

I had a friend who used to say some really bad things about Jesus. He'd make fun of Christians and laugh at God. He'd make me so angry, I'd want to hit him!

But these verses remind me that a person who makes fun of God or has doubts about God needs to know the truth. When I got angry at my friend about his feelings toward God, I wasn't helping him get to know God; I was just making the situation worse.

I wish I had tried to tell my friend the truth about God instead of getting angry at him. I should have talked to him about his feelings. After all, Jesus had mercy on people who laughed at him. God still loves people who doubt him. God never gives up on anyone, and neither should I.

Justin, age 13

What about You?

❶ How can doubts about God actually work to deepen your faith?

❷ Do you know someone who has doubts about God? Ask that person to talk to you about those doubts. Then ask your pastor or youth leader to help you find some answers for your friend.

❸ Ask God to make you more patient with people who have doubts about him.

Turn to page 1551 for your next devotion.

Revelation

START

Cast OF Characters

Jesus

He's the Lamb of God and Conquering Hero. The book reveals him first and foremost, then reveals his plan for the end of the world.

Satan

Portrayed as a serpent or dragon, Satan attacks God and his people.

The Beast

The figure of the antichrist who, controlled by Satan, tries to get everyone to worship him.

The Woman

A symbolic image for God's people, attacked and persecuted by "her" enemies (chapter 12).

Remember your first roller coaster ride? You wondered if you could handle the speed, the shaking, the twists and turns of this awesome ride. Even its name was scary: the Corkscrew, Tidal Wave, the Colossus, the Blue Streak.

You didn't know everything that would happen on your first roller coaster ride, but the view before you gave you a feel for it . . . and issued a challenge to ride. That is exactly what the Book of Revelation does.

The end of history will be a wild ride in which the power of Satan is met and overcome by the power of God. Revelation, with its weird and frightening images, doesn't tell us exactly how everything will happen. But it gives us a feel for what the end of history will be like. And it challenges us to have faith, courage and loyalty to God, even if we're not alive at that time.

As you read, remember that this book is filled with symbolic numbers and images that no one can fully understand. So don't worry too much about the details. Just take in all the sights and sounds, and let it give you an impression of the wild ride yet to come.

The Prostitute

A picture of all those involved in worship to anyone or anything other than God (chapter 17).

The Earth-dwellers

This refers to unbelievers—not to Christians (who are called "citizens of heaven"). In other words, Christians will receive protection from the judgments poured out on the earth.

The Great Multitude

A crowd of 144,000 faithful people (a symbolic number indicating a lot) still live on earth at the end of history. They are protected from God's wrath. A huge number of Christians no one can count has already arrived in heaven. These are God's people who have already died, from all times and places (chapter 7).

What's UP with That?

Revelation is bursting with symbolism. Here's a guide to help you understand some of the symbols.

Numbers

6 The famous "666" is the number of the Beast, which many people think is a symbol of imperfection or falling short. God is a perfect 7. Everything else is 6.

7 It's everywhere in this book: 7 churches, lampstands, seals, trumpets, bowls. This is the number of God's perfection and wholeness.

12 This number shows complete representation, like on a committee or council. There were 12 tribes in Israel and 12 apostles of Jesus Christ. And there will be a complete representation of God's people on earth

at the end, who are completely protected by God.

42 Many scholars understand the final period of history to be 7 years in length. Half of that would be 42 months, or 1,260 days. Apparently some big things will happen to help us distinguish 2 separate phases to the end of history (see Revelation 11:2-3).

1,000 A thousand shows great size and vastness. Like 12 x 12 x 1,000 of God's people we see in chapter 7, or the 1,000 year reign of Christ in chapter 20, or the thousands used to show the size of God's Holy City in chapter 21.

Images

Lampstands. These represent churches, which shine the light of God's truth in a dark world (chapter 1).

Seals. Wax stamps that hold closed the scroll of God's judgment. As each seal is broken, an event takes place, bringing the world closer to the time when God pours out his judgment (chapter 6).

The Four Horsemen. The horse was the main weapon of war in Bible times. The four horsemen show a steady increase of war and violence on the earth.

Trumpets. These announce some of God's judgments (chapter 8).

Locusts. A symbol of destruction. We don't know exactly what these "locusts" are, but they have supernatural, evil power (chapter 9).

Dragon, Beast, and Prophet. These are the unholy trinity, Satan's false "godhead" he tries to pull over on the world. Terms like "dragon" and "beast" obviously speak of ugly, evil power (chapters 12—13).

Bowls. These are used to quickly pour out the punishment God's enemies deserve (chapter 16).

Babylon. The source of false religion. The original Tower of Babel, way back in Genesis 11, was humanity's first attempt to worship something other than God. So Babylon has represented idolatry and false worship ever since.

The New Jerusalem. The place of true worship. If Babylon is the city of idolatry, then the new Jerusalem is the City of God. We get to live there someday!

Snap shots

- "Welcome, roller coaster riders, I'm in charge here" *(the revelation of Jesus, chapter 1)*

- Instructions for your safety and comfort *(the letters to the churches, chapters 2—3)*

- Climbing the first big hill *(the view in heaven, chapters 4—5)*

- The big dive downward *(the judgments of God, chapters 6—10, 15—16)*

- Twists and turns *(the battle of Good and Evil, chapters 11—14)*

- The Corkscrew *(the defeat of false religion, chapters 17—18)*

- Back to the terminal *(the return of Jesus, chapters 19—20)*

- "Let's do it again!" *(the new heaven and new earth, chapters 21—22)*

Prologue

1 The revelation of Jesus Christ, which God gave him to show his servants what must soon take place. He made it known by sending his angel to his servant John, [2]who testifies to everything he saw—that is, the word of God and the testimony of Jesus Christ. [3]Blessed is the one who reads the words of this prophecy, and blessed are those who hear it and take to heart what is written in it, because the time is near.

Greetings and Doxology

[4]John,

To the seven churches in the province of Asia:

Grace and peace to you from him who is, and who was, and who is to come, and from the seven spirits[a] before his throne, [5]and from Jesus Christ, who is the faithful witness, the firstborn from the dead, and the ruler of the kings of the earth.

To him who loves us and has freed us from our sins by his blood, [6]and has made us to be a kingdom and priests to serve his God and Father—to him be glory and power for ever and ever! Amen.

[7]Look, he is coming with the clouds,
and every eye will see him,
even those who pierced him;
and all the peoples of the earth will
mourn because of him.
So shall it be! Amen.

[8]"I am the Alpha and the Omega," says the Lord God, "who is, and who was, and who is to come, the Almighty."

One Like a Son of Man

[9]I, John, your brother and companion in the suffering and kingdom and patient endurance that are ours in Jesus, was on the island of Patmos because of the word of God and the testimony of Jesus. [10]On the Lord's Day I was in the Spirit, and I heard behind me a loud voice like a trumpet, [11]which said: "Write on a scroll what you see and send it to the seven churches: to Ephesus, Smyrna, Pergamum, Thyatira, Sardis, Philadelphia and Laodicea."

As Easy as A, B, Z

Huh?

Revelation 1:8
In the Greek language (which is the language people spoke where this part of the Bible was written), the first letter of the alphabet was "alpha" and the last letter was "omega." Jesus is saying that he is the beginning and the end. In English he might have said, "I am the A and the Z." This was especially important because this book deals with end-of-the-world stuff, and Jesus wanted us to understand that he will still be in charge.

[12]I turned around to see the voice that was speaking to me. And when I turned I saw seven golden lampstands, [13]and among the lampstands was someone "like a son of man,"[b] dressed in a robe reaching down to his feet and with a golden sash around his chest. [14]His head and hair were white like wool, as white as snow, and his eyes were like blazing fire. [15]His feet were like bronze glowing in a furnace, and his voice was like the sound of rushing waters. [16]In his right hand he held seven stars, and out of his mouth came a sharp double-edged sword. His face was like the sun shining in all its brilliance.

[17]When I saw him, I fell at his feet as though dead. Then he placed his right hand on me and said: "Do not be afraid. I am the First and the Last. [18]I am the Living One; I was dead, and behold I am alive for ever and ever! And I hold the keys of death and Hades.

[19]"Write, therefore, what you have seen, what is now and what will take place later. [20]The mystery of the seven stars that you saw in my right hand and of the seven golden lampstands is this: The seven stars are the angels[c] of the seven churches, and the seven lampstands are the seven churches.

[a]4 Or *the sevenfold Spirit*   [b]13 Daniel 7:13
[c]20 Or *messengers*

To the Church in Ephesus

2 "To the angel[a] of the church in Ephesus write:

These are the words of him who holds the seven stars in his right hand and walks among the seven golden lampstands: [2]I know your deeds, your hard work and your perseverance. I know that you cannot tolerate wicked men, that you have tested those who claim to be apostles but are not, and have found them false. [3]You have persevered and have endured hardships for my name, and have not grown weary.

[4]Yet I hold this against you: You have forsaken your first love. [5]Remember the height from which you have fallen! Repent and do the things you did at first. If you do not repent, I will come to you and remove your lampstand from its place. [6]But you have this in your favor: You hate the practices of the Nicolaitans, which I also hate.

[7]He who has an ear, let him hear what the Spirit says to the churches. To him who overcomes, I will give the right to eat from the tree of life, which is in the paradise of God.

To the Church in Smyrna

[8]"To the angel of the church in Smyrna write:

These are the words of him who is the First and the Last, who died and came to life again. [9]I know your afflictions and your poverty—yet you are rich! I know the slander of those who say they are Jews and are not, but are a synagogue of Satan. [10]Do not be afraid of what you are about to suffer. I tell you, the devil will put some of you in prison to test you, and you will suffer persecution for ten days. Be faithful, even to the point of death, and I will give you the crown of life.

a1 Or *messenger*; also in verses 8, 12 and 18

Tuesday

Super Power

Read Revelation 1:17–18

When I accepted Jesus as my Savior, my itty-bitty existence exploded into true life. The everlasting Creator of the universe placed his hand on me, and I woke up from the sleep of death. Since the day I first realized Jesus hung on a cross for me, I'm constantly learning more about his amazing love and power.

God has so much more power in the fingernail of his pinky finger than I have in my whole body. He used his great power to form the world. He used that power to conquer death through Jesus' resurrection. And he used that power to reach out to insignificant little me.

The God who can do absolutely anything chooses to love *me*. I can't think of a better feeling.

❶ What are some things that only God can do?

❷ Write "God shows his power by . . ." at the top of a piece of paper, and finish the sentence with as many phrases or pictures as you can think of.

❸ Praise God for his power through a song or a prayer.

Turn to page 1553 for your next devotion.

[11]He who has an ear, let him hear what the Spirit says to the churches. He who overcomes will not be hurt at all by the second death.

To the Church in Pergamum

[12]"To the angel of the church in Pergamum write:

These are the words of him who has the sharp, double-edged sword. [13]I know where you live—where Satan has his throne. Yet you remain true to my name. You did not renounce your faith in me, even in the days of Antipas, my faithful witness, who was put to death in your city—where Satan lives.

[14]Nevertheless, I have a few things against you: You have people there who hold to the teaching of Balaam, who taught Balak to entice the Israelites to sin by eating food sacrificed to idols and by committing sexual immorality. [15]Likewise you also have those who hold to the teaching of the Nicolaitans. [16]Repent therefore! Otherwise, I will soon come to you and will fight against them with the sword of my mouth.

[17]He who has an ear, let him hear what the Spirit says to the churches. To him who overcomes, I will give some of the hidden manna. I will also give him a white stone with a new name written on it, known only to him who receives it.

To the Church in Thyatira

[18]"To the angel of the church in Thyatira write:

These are the words of the Son of God, whose eyes are like blazing fire and whose feet are like burnished bronze. [19]I know your deeds, your love and faith, your service and perseverance, and that you are now doing more than you did at first.

[20]Nevertheless, I have this against you: You tolerate that woman Jezebel, who calls herself a prophetess. By her teaching she misleads my servants into sexual immorality and the eating of food sacrificed to idols. [21]I have given her time to repent of her immorality, but she is unwilling. [22]So I will cast her on a bed of suffering, and I will make those who commit adultery with her suffer intensely, unless they repent of her ways. [23]I will strike her children dead. Then all the churches will know that I am he who searches hearts and minds, and I will repay each of you according to your deeds. [24]Now I say to the rest of you in Thyatira, to you who do not hold to her teaching and have not learned Satan's so-called deep secrets (I will not impose any other burden on you): [25]Only hold on to what you have until I come.

[26]To him who overcomes and does my will to the end, I will give authority over the nations—

[27]'He will rule them with an iron scepter;
    he will dash them to pieces
    like pottery'[a]—

just as I have received authority from my Father. [28]I will also give him the morning star. [29]He who has an ear, let him hear what the Spirit says to the churches.

To the Church in Sardis

3 "To the angel[b] of the church in Sardis write:

These are the words of him who holds the seven spirits[c] of God and the seven stars. I know your deeds; you have a reputation of being alive, but you are dead. [2]Wake up! Strengthen what remains and is about to die, for I have not found your deeds complete in the sight of my God. [3]Remember, therefore, what you have received and heard; obey it, and repent. But if you do not wake up, I will come like a thief, and you will not know at what time I will come to you.

[4]Yet you have a few people in Sardis who have not soiled their clothes. They will walk with me,

dressed in white, for they are worthy. ⁵He who overcomes will, like them, be dressed in white. I will never blot out his name from the book of life, but will acknowledge his name before my Father and his angels. ⁶He who has an ear, let him hear what the Spirit says to the churches.

To the Church in Philadelphia

⁷"To the angel of the church in Philadelphia write:

These are the words of him who is holy and true, who holds the key of David. What he opens no one can shut, and what he shuts no one can open. ⁸I know your deeds. See, I have placed before you an open door that no one can shut. I know that you have little strength, yet you have kept my word and have not denied my name. ⁹I will make those who are of the synagogue of Satan, who claim to be Jews though they are not, but are liars—I will make them come and fall down at your feet and acknowledge that I have loved you. ¹⁰Since you have kept my command to endure patiently, I will also keep you from the hour of trial that is going to come upon the whole world to test those who live on the earth.

¹¹I am coming soon. Hold on to what you have, so that no one will take your crown. ¹²Him who overcomes I will make a pillar in the temple of my God. Never again will he leave it. I will write on him the name of my God and the name of the city of my God, the new Jerusalem, which is coming down out of heaven from my God; and I will also write on him my new name. ¹³He

Wednesday

Staying Close

Read Revelation 3:15–16

At the beginning of this school year, I didn't know where my relationship with God was going. Some days I felt like I was sinning way too much, but other days I felt like I was walking right next to God. It really bothered me to have such an "iffy" feeling about my faith.

God has promised never to leave me. Unfortunately, that doesn't mean I'll always be as close to him as I should be. I have to make a daily choice whether to keep growing with God or to do my own thing and let my faith sort of slide.

I made a decision to fight the "iffy" feeling and get back on track with God. Once I did, I found out he was there all along, waiting for me to get serious. Even now, I know that sometimes I'll still wander further away from God than I should. But I've started this journey of living for God, and I'm determined to stick with it.

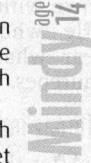
Mindy age 14

What about You?

❶ Have you ever felt "iffy" about your faith? What did you do about it?

❷ Rate yourself 1-5 in each of these areas: prayer life, reading the Bible, obedience to parents and other authorities, loving others, telling others about Jesus. Which one is weakest for you? How can you strengthen that area?

❸ Ask God to help you stay serious about your walk with him.

Turn to page 1563 for your next devotion.

who has an ear, let him hear what the Spirit says to the churches.

To the Church in Laodicea

[14]"To the angel of the church in Laodicea write:

These are the words of the Amen, the faithful and true witness, the ruler of God's creation. [15]I know your deeds, that you are neither cold nor hot. I wish you were either one or the other! [16]So, because you are lukewarm—neither hot nor cold—I am about to spit you out of my mouth. [17]You say, 'I am rich; I have acquired wealth and do not need a thing.' But you do not realize that you are wretched, pitiful, poor, blind and naked. [18]I counsel you to buy from me gold refined in the fire, so you can become rich; and white clothes to wear, so you can cover your shameful nakedness; and salve to put on your eyes, so you can see.

[19]Those whom I love I rebuke and discipline. So be earnest, and repent. [20]Here I am! I stand at the door and knock. If anyone hears my voice and opens the door, I will come in and eat with him, and he with me.

[21]To him who overcomes, I will give the right to sit with me on my throne, just as I overcame and sat down with my Father on his throne. [22]He who has an ear, let him hear what the Spirit says to the churches."

The Throne in Heaven

4 After this I looked, and there before me was a door standing open in heaven. And the voice I had first heard speaking to me like a trumpet said, "Come up here, and I will show you what must take place after this." [2]At once I was in the Spirit, and there before me was a throne in heaven with someone sitting on it. [3]And the one who sat there had the appearance of jasper and carnelian. A rainbow, resembling an emerald, encircled the throne. [4]Surrounding the throne were twenty-four other thrones, and seated on them were twenty-four elders. They were dressed in white and had

crowns of gold on their heads. [5]From the throne came flashes of lightning, rumblings and peals of thunder. Before the throne, seven lamps were blazing. These are the seven spirits[a] of God. [6]Also before the throne there was what looked like a sea of glass, clear as crystal.

In the center, around the throne, were four living creatures, and they were covered with eyes, in front and in back. [7]The

Now *That's* Some Worship Band Huh?

Revelation 4:6–8
This book is filled with wild pictures of bizarre creatures—like something from a special effects museum. The 4 mentioned here are covered with eyes and wings. We can hardly even imagine all that God has created as part of heaven, but we do know one thing. The creatures around God's throne have just one job. They are there to worship him. Hey, isn't that what he created us to do too?

first living creature was like a lion, the second was like an ox, the third had a face like a man, the fourth was like a flying eagle. [8]Each of the four living creatures had six wings and was covered with eyes all around, even under his wings. Day and night they never stop saying:

"Holy, holy, holy
is the Lord God Almighty,
who was, and is, and is to come."

[9]Whenever the living creatures give glory, honor and thanks to him who sits on the throne and who lives for ever and ever, [10]the twenty-four elders fall down before him who sits on the throne, and worship him who lives for ever and ever. They lay their crowns before the throne and say:

[11] "You are worthy, our Lord and God,
    to receive glory and honor and
        power,

---

[a]5 Or *the sevenfold Spirit*

for you created all things,
  and by your will they were created
  and have their being."

The Scroll and the Lamb

5 Then I saw in the right hand of him who sat on the throne a scroll with writing on both sides and sealed with seven seals. [2]And I saw a mighty angel proclaiming in a loud voice, "Who is worthy to break the seals and open the scroll?" [3]But no one in heaven or on earth or under the earth could open the scroll or even look inside it. [4]I wept and wept because no one was found who was worthy to open the scroll or look inside. [5]Then one of the elders said to me, "Do not weep! See, the Lion of the tribe of Judah, the Root of David, has triumphed. He is able to open the scroll and its seven seals."

[6]Then I saw a Lamb, looking as if it had been slain, standing in the center of the throne, encircled by the four living creatures and the elders. He had seven horns and seven eyes, which are the seven spirits[a] of God sent out into all the earth. [7]He came and took the scroll from the right hand of him who sat on the throne. [8]And when he had taken it, the four living creatures and the twenty-four elders fell down before the Lamb. Each one had a harp and they were holding golden bowls full of incense, which are the prayers of the saints. [9]And they sang a new song:

"You are worthy to take the scroll
    and to open its seals,
because you were slain,
    and with your blood you purchased
      men for God
  from every tribe and language and
      people and nation.
[10]You have made them to be a kingdom
      and priests to serve our God,
  and they will reign on the
      earth."

[11]Then I looked and heard the voice of many angels, numbering thousands upon thousands, and ten thousand times ten thousand. They encircled the throne and the living creatures and the elders. [12]In a loud voice they sang:

"Worthy is the Lamb, who was slain,
to receive power and wealth and
    wisdom and strength
and honor and glory and praise!"

[13]Then I heard every creature in heaven and on earth and under the earth and on the sea, and all that is in them, singing:

"To him who sits on the throne and to
    the Lamb
be praise and honor and glory and
    power,
    for ever and ever!"

[14]The four living creatures said, "Amen," and the elders fell down and worshiped.

The Seals

6 I watched as the Lamb opened the first of the seven seals. Then I heard one of the four living creatures say in a voice like thunder, "Come!" [2]I looked, and there before me was a white horse! Its rider held a bow, and he was given a crown, and he rode out as a conqueror bent on conquest.

[3]When the Lamb opened the second seal, I heard the second living creature say, "Come!" [4]Then another horse came out, a fiery red one. Its rider was given power to take peace from the earth and to make men slay each other. To him was given a large sword.

[5]When the Lamb opened the third seal, I heard the third living creature say, "Come!" I looked, and there before me was a black horse! Its rider was holding a pair of scales in his hand. [6]Then I heard what sounded like a voice among the four living creatures, saying, "A quart[b] of wheat for a day's wages,[c] and three quarts of barley for a day's wages,[c] and do not damage the oil and the wine!"

[7]When the Lamb opened the fourth seal, I heard the voice of the fourth living creature say, "Come!" [8]I looked, and there before me was a pale horse! Its rider was named Death, and Hades was following close behind him. They were given power over a fourth of the earth to kill by sword, famine and plague, and by the wild beasts of the earth.

[a]6 Or *the sevenfold Spirit*   [b]6 Greek *a choinix* (probably about a liter)   [c]6 Greek *a denarius*

[9]When he opened the fifth seal, I saw under the altar the souls of those who had been slain because of the word of God and the testimony they had maintained. [10]They called out in a loud voice, "How long, Sovereign Lord, holy and true, until you judge the inhabitants of the earth and avenge our blood?" [11]Then each of them was given a white robe, and they were told to wait a little longer, until the number of their fellow servants and brothers who were to be killed as they had been was completed.

[12]I watched as he opened the sixth seal. There was a great earthquake. The sun turned black like sackcloth made of goat hair, the whole moon turned blood red, [13]and the stars in the sky fell to earth, as late figs drop from a fig tree when shaken by a strong wind. [14]The sky receded like a scroll, rolling up, and every mountain and island was removed from its place.

[15]Then the kings of the earth, the princes, the generals, the rich, the mighty, and every slave and every free man hid in caves and among the rocks of the mountains. [16]They called to the mountains and the rocks, "Fall on us and hide us from the face of him who sits on the throne and from the wrath of the Lamb! [17]For the great day of their wrath has come, and who can stand?"

144,000 Sealed

7 After this I saw four angels standing at the four corners of the earth, holding back the four winds of the earth to prevent any wind from blowing on the land or on the sea or on any tree. [2]Then I saw another angel coming up from the east, having the seal of the living God. He called out in a loud voice to the four angels who had been given power to harm the land and the sea: [3]"Do not harm the land or the sea or the trees until we put a seal on the foreheads of the servants of our God." [4]Then I heard the number of those who were sealed: 144,000 from all the tribes of Israel.

[5]From the tribe of Judah 12,000
  were sealed,
from the tribe of Reuben 12,000,
from the tribe of Gad 12,000,

[6]from the tribe of Asher 12,000,
  from the tribe of Naphtali 12,000,
  from the tribe of Manasseh 12,000,
[7]from the tribe of Simeon 12,000,
  from the tribe of Levi 12,000,
  from the tribe of Issachar 12,000,
[8]from the tribe of Zebulun 12,000,
  from the tribe of Joseph 12,000,
  from the tribe of Benjamin 12,000.

The Great Multitude in White Robes

[9]After this I looked and there before me was a great multitude that no one could count, from every nation, tribe, people and language, standing before the throne and in front of the Lamb. They were wearing white robes and were holding palm branches in their hands. [10]And they cried out in a loud voice:

"Salvation belongs to our God,
  who sits on the throne,
  and to the Lamb."

[11]All the angels were standing around the throne and around the elders and the four living creatures. They fell down on their faces before the throne and worshiped God, [12]saying:

"Amen!
Praise and glory
and wisdom and thanks and honor
and power and strength
be to our God for ever and ever.
Amen!"

[13]Then one of the elders asked me, "These in white robes—who are they, and where did they come from?"

[14]I answered, "Sir, you know."

And he said, "These are they who have come out of the great tribulation; they have washed their robes and made them white in the blood of the Lamb. [15]Therefore,

"they are before the throne of God
  and serve him day and night in his
    temple;
and he who sits on the throne will
    spread his tent over them.
[16]Never again will they hunger;
  never again will they thirst.
The sun will not beat upon them,
  nor any scorching heat.
[17]For the Lamb at the center of the
    throne will be their shepherd;

he will lead them to springs of
  living water.
And God will wipe away every tear
  from their eyes."

No More Sadness

Huh?

Revelation 7:14–17
The people John saw in this part of his
vision had suffered terribly. They had been
through the worst experiences humanly
possible. But now Jesus wanted to reward
them for enduring their pain. John sees a
place in heaven where they can finally
relax and enjoy being with the Lamb—
Jesus. There will be no more sadness for
them.

The Seventh Seal and the Golden Censer

8 When he opened the seventh seal,
there was silence in heaven for
about half an hour.

²And I saw the seven angels who stand
before God, and to them were given
seven trumpets.

³Another angel, who had a golden censer, came and stood at the altar. He was
given much incense to offer, with the
prayers of all the saints, on the golden
altar before the throne. ⁴The smoke of
the incense, together with the prayers of
the saints, went up before God from the
angel's hand. ⁵Then the angel took the
censer, filled it with fire from the altar,
and hurled it on the earth; and there
came peals of thunder, rumblings,
flashes of lightning and an earthquake.

The Trumpets

⁶Then the seven angels who had the
seven trumpets prepared to sound them.

⁷The first angel sounded his trumpet,
and there came hail and fire mixed with
blood, and it was hurled down upon the
earth. A third of the earth was burned up,
a third of the trees were burned up, and
all the green grass was burned up.

⁸The second angel sounded his trumpet, and something like a huge mountain, all ablaze, was thrown into the sea.

A third of the sea turned into blood, ⁹a
third of the living creatures in the sea
died, and a third of the ships were destroyed.

¹⁰The third angel sounded his trumpet,
and a great star, blazing like a torch, fell
from the sky on a third of the rivers and
on the springs of water— ¹¹the name of
the star is Wormwood.ᵃ A third of the
waters turned bitter, and many people
died from the waters that had become
bitter.

¹²The fourth angel sounded his trumpet, and a third of the sun was struck, a
third of the moon, and a third of the
stars, so that a third of them turned dark.
A third of the day was without light, and
also a third of the night.

¹³As I watched, I heard an eagle that
was flying in midair call out in a loud
voice: "Woe! Woe! Woe to the inhabitants of the earth, because of the trumpet
blasts about to be sounded by the other
three angels!"

9 The fifth angel sounded his trumpet,
and I saw a star that had fallen from
the sky to the earth. The star was given
the key to the shaft of the Abyss. ²When
he opened the Abyss, smoke rose from it
like the smoke from a gigantic furnace.
The sun and sky were darkened by the
smoke from the Abyss. ³And out of the
smoke locusts came down upon the earth
and were given power like that of scorpions of the earth. ⁴They were told not to
harm the grass of the earth or any plant
or tree, but only those people who did
not have the seal of God on their foreheads. ⁵They were not given power to kill
them, but only to torture them for five
months. And the agony they suffered
was like that of the sting of a scorpion
when it strikes a man. ⁶During those days
men will seek death, but will not find it;
they will long to die, but death will elude
them.

⁷The locusts looked like horses prepared for battle. On their heads they
wore something like crowns of gold, and
their faces resembled human faces.
⁸Their hair was like women's hair, and
their teeth were like lions' teeth. ⁹They
had breastplates like breastplates of iron,

ᵃ11 That is, Bitterness

and the sound of their wings was like the thundering of many horses and chariots rushing into battle. [10]They had tails and stings like scorpions, and in their tails they had power to torment people for five months. [11]They had as king over them the angel of the Abyss, whose name in Hebrew is Abaddon, and in Greek, Apollyon.[a]

[12]The first woe is past; two other woes are yet to come.

[13]The sixth angel sounded his trumpet, and I heard a voice coming from the horns[b] of the golden altar that is before God. [14]It said to the sixth angel who had the trumpet, "Release the four angels who are bound at the great river Euphrates." [15]And the four angels who had been kept ready for this very hour and day and month and year were released to kill a third of mankind. [16]The number of the mounted troops was two hundred million. I heard their number.

[17]The horses and riders I saw in my vision looked like this: Their breastplates were fiery red, dark blue, and yellow as sulfur. The heads of the horses resembled the heads of lions, and out of their mouths came fire, smoke and sulfur. [18]A third of mankind was killed by the three plagues of fire, smoke and sulfur that came out of their mouths. [19]The power of the horses was in their mouths and in their tails; for their tails were like snakes, having heads with which they inflict injury.

[20]The rest of mankind that were not killed by these plagues still did not repent of the work of their hands; they did not stop worshiping demons, and idols of gold, silver, bronze, stone and wood—idols that cannot see or hear or walk. [21]Nor did they repent of their murders, their magic arts, their sexual immorality or their thefts.

The Angel and the Little Scroll

10 Then I saw another mighty angel coming down from heaven. He was robed in a cloud, with a rainbow above his head; his face was like the sun, and his legs were like fiery pillars. [2]He was holding a little scroll, which lay open in his hand. He planted his right foot on the sea and his left foot on the

land, [3]and he gave a loud shout like the roar of a lion. When he shouted, the voices of the seven thunders spoke. [4]And when the seven thunders spoke, I was about to write; but I heard a voice from heaven say, "Seal up what the seven thunders have said and do not write it down."

[5]Then the angel I had seen standing on the sea and on the land raised his right hand to heaven. [6]And he swore by him who lives for ever and ever, who created the heavens and all that is in them, the earth and all that is in it, and the sea and all that is in it, and said, "There will be no more delay! [7]But in the days when the seventh angel is about to sound his trumpet, the mystery of God will be accomplished, just as he announced to his servants the prophets."

[8]Then the voice that I had heard from heaven spoke to me once more: "Go, take the scroll that lies open in the hand of the angel who is standing on the sea and on the land."

[9]So I went to the angel and asked him to give me the little scroll. He said to me, "Take it and eat it. It will turn your stomach sour, but in your mouth it will be as sweet as honey." [10]I took the little scroll from the angel's hand and ate it. It tasted as sweet as honey in my mouth, but when I had eaten it, my stomach turned sour. [11]Then I was told, "You must prophesy again about many peoples, nations, languages and kings."

The Two Witnesses

11 I was given a reed like a measuring rod and was told, "Go and measure the temple of God and the altar, and count the worshipers there. [2]But exclude the outer court; do not measure it, because it has been given to the Gentiles. They will trample on the holy city for 42 months. [3]And I will give power to my two witnesses, and they will prophesy for 1,260 days, clothed in sackcloth." [4]These are the two olive trees and the two lampstands that stand before the Lord of the earth. [5]If anyone tries to harm them, fire comes from their mouths and devours their enemies. This is how anyone

[a]11 *Abaddon* and *Apollyon* mean *Destroyer.*
[b]13 That is, projections

who wants to harm them must die. ⁶These men have power to shut up the sky so that it will not rain during the time they are prophesying; and they have power to turn the waters into blood and to strike the earth with every kind of plague as often as they want.

⁷Now when they have finished their testimony, the beast that comes up from the Abyss will attack them, and overpower and kill them. ⁸Their bodies will lie in the street of the great city, which is figuratively called Sodom and Egypt, where also their Lord was crucified. ⁹For three and a half days men from every people, tribe, language and nation will gaze on their bodies and refuse them burial. ¹⁰The inhabitants of the earth will gloat over them and will celebrate by sending each other gifts, because these two prophets had tormented those who live on the earth.

¹¹But after the three and a half days a breath of life from God entered them, and they stood on their feet, and terror struck those who saw them. ¹²Then they heard a loud voice from heaven saying to them, "Come up here." And they went up to heaven in a cloud, while their enemies looked on.

¹³At that very hour there was a severe earthquake and a tenth of the city collapsed. Seven thousand people were killed in the earthquake, and the survivors were terrified and gave glory to the God of heaven.

¹⁴The second woe has passed; the third woe is coming soon.

The Seventh Trumpet

¹⁵The seventh angel sounded his trumpet, and there were loud voices in heaven, which said:

> "The kingdom of the world has
>   become the kingdom of our
>   Lord and of his Christ,
> and he will reign for ever and ever."

¹⁶And the twenty-four elders, who were seated on their thrones before God, fell on their faces and worshiped God, ¹⁷saying:

> "We give thanks to you, Lord God
>   Almighty,

> the One who is and who was,
> because you have taken your great
>   power
> and have begun to reign.
> ¹⁸The nations were angry;
> and your wrath has come.
> The time has come for judging the dead,
> and for rewarding your servants the
>   prophets
> and your saints and those who
>   reverence your name,
> both small and great—
> and for destroying those who destroy
>   the earth."

¹⁹Then God's temple in heaven was opened, and within his temple was seen the ark of his covenant. And there came flashes of lightning, rumblings, peals of thunder, an earthquake and a great hailstorm.

The Woman and the Dragon

12 A great and wondrous sign appeared in heaven: a woman clothed with the sun, with the moon under her feet and a crown of twelve stars on her head. ²She was pregnant and cried out in pain as she was about to give birth. ³Then another sign appeared in heaven: an enormous red dragon with seven heads and ten horns and seven crowns on his heads. ⁴His tail swept a third of the stars out of the sky and flung them to the earth. The dragon stood in front of the woman who was about to give birth, so that he might devour her child the moment it was born. ⁵She gave birth to a son, a male child, who will rule all the nations with an iron scepter. And her child was snatched up to God and to his throne. ⁶The woman fled into the desert to a place prepared for her by God, where she might be taken care of for 1,260 days.

⁷And there was war in heaven. Michael and his angels fought against the dragon, and the dragon and his angels fought back. ⁸But he was not strong enough, and they lost their place in heaven. ⁹The great dragon was hurled down—that ancient serpent called the devil, or Satan, who leads the whole world astray. He was hurled to the earth, and his angels with him.

Satan's Final Chapter

Huh?

Revelation 12:7–9
The battle between good and evil will finally be over. Satan has been messing up the lives of people all over the world with his evil plans, and God finally puts an end to it. Michael and the good angels go head to head with the Dragon (Satan) and the evil angels. When we feel discouraged by Satan's temptations, it's great to know the end of the story.

¹⁰Then I heard a loud voice in heaven say:

"Now have come the salvation and the
      power and the kingdom of our
      God,
   and the authority of his Christ.
For the accuser of our brothers,
   who accuses them before our God
      day and night,
   has been hurled down.
¹¹They overcame him
   by the blood of the Lamb
   and by the word of their testimony;
they did not love their lives so much
   as to shrink from death.
¹²Therefore rejoice, you heavens
   and you who dwell in them!
But woe to the earth and the sea,
   because the devil has gone down to
      you!
He is filled with fury,
   because he knows that his time is
      short."

¹³When the dragon saw that he had been hurled to the earth, he pursued the woman who had given birth to the male child. ¹⁴The woman was given the two wings of a great eagle, so that she might fly to the place prepared for her in the desert, where she would be taken care of for a time, times and half a time, out of the serpent's reach. ¹⁵Then from his mouth the serpent spewed water like a river, to overtake the woman and sweep her away with the torrent. ¹⁶But the earth helped the woman by opening its mouth and swallowing the river that the dragon had spewed out of his mouth. ¹⁷Then the dragon was enraged at the woman and went off to make war against the rest of her offspring—those who obey God's commandments and hold to the testimony of Jesus. **13** ¹And the dragon*ᵃ* stood on the shore of the sea.

The Beast out of the Sea

And I saw a beast coming out of the sea. He had ten horns and seven heads, with ten crowns on his horns, and on each head a blasphemous name. ²The beast I saw resembled a leopard, but had feet like those of a bear and a mouth like that of a lion. The dragon gave the beast his power and his throne and great authority. ³One of the heads of the beast seemed to have had a fatal wound, but the fatal wound had been healed. The whole world was astonished and followed the beast. ⁴Men worshiped the dragon because he had given authority to the beast, and they also worshiped the beast and asked, "Who is like the beast? Who can make war against him?"

⁵The beast was given a mouth to utter proud words and blasphemies and to exercise his authority for forty-two months. ⁶He opened his mouth to blaspheme God, and to slander his name and his dwelling place and those who live in heaven. ⁷He was given power to make war against the saints and to conquer them. And he was given authority over every tribe, people, language and nation. ⁸All inhabitants of the earth will worship the beast—all whose names have not been written in the book of life belonging to the Lamb that was slain from the creation of the world.*ᵇ*

⁹He who has an ear, let him hear.

¹⁰If anyone is to go into captivity,
   into captivity he will go.
If anyone is to be killed*ᶜ* with the
      sword,
   with the sword he will be killed.

This calls for patient endurance and faithfulness on the part of the saints.

ᵃ1 Some late manuscripts *And I* *ᵇ8* Or *written from the creation of the world in the book of life belonging to the Lamb that was slain* *ᶜ10* Some manuscripts *anyone kills*

The Satan Gang

Satan and his demonic buddies are serious bad news. Their criminal records are covered in the Bible from beginning to end. Their rap sheets:

Satan
A.k.a.: Serpent, Accuser, Crafty One, Deceiver, Beelzebub, Belial, The Prince of Demons, The Enemy, The Dragon, The devil
Description: A wicked angel, Satan gets kicked out of heaven for going against God; he becomes the gang leader to other angels who joined him in the attempted mutiny. He seeks to destroy all humans by separating them from God forever. He's Enemy #1.
Offenses: Treason, fraud, deceit, slander, assault, battery, murder
Record: (the entire Bible)
Sentence: Eternal torment in the lake of fire

Antichrist
A.k.a.: The Beast out of the Sea
Description: An evil being who works for Satan. He has a mouthful of lies and a bag full of tricks to deceive people in the final days of the world before Jesus returns. He's the tattoo specialist who makes it mandatory for everyone to wear "666" as a pledge of their loyalty to him.
Offenses: Deceit, fraud, murder

Record: 2 Thessalonians 2:3–10, page 1459; 1 John 2:22, 4:3, page 1530; Revelation 13—17, 16:13, 19:20, 20:10
Sentence: Eternal torment in the lake of fire

The False Prophet
A.k.a.: The Beast out of the Earth
Description: The Antichrist's campaign manager, appointed by Satan to get people to worship their beastly candidate. He enforces the evil worship and does a lot of the antichrist's dirty work.
Offenses: Corruption, deceit, conspiracy
Record: Revelation 13, 16:13, 19:20, 20:10
Sentence: Eternal torment in the lake of fire

Demons
A.k.a.: unclean spirits, Satan's army
Description: Known to be slick and crafty like their boss Satan, these wicked soldiers are among the pack of angels that rebel against God and get thrown out of heaven. Their business is evil. Their ambition is to make the lives of God's children miserable.
Offenses: Fraud, deceit, soul-kidnapping
Record: (throughout the New Testament)
Sentence: Eternal torment in the lake of fire

The Beast out of the Earth

¹¹Then I saw another beast, coming out of the earth. He had two horns like a lamb, but he spoke like a dragon. ¹²He exercised all the authority of the first beast on his behalf, and made the earth and its inhabitants worship the first beast, whose fatal wound had been healed. ¹³And he performed great and miraculous signs, even causing fire to come down from heaven to earth in full view of men. ¹⁴Because of the signs he was given power to do on behalf of the first beast, he deceived the inhabitants of the earth. He ordered them to set up an image in honor of the beast who was wounded by the sword and yet lived. ¹⁵He was given power to give breath to the image of the first beast, so that it could speak and cause all who refused to worship the image to be killed. ¹⁶He also forced everyone, small and great, rich and poor, free and slave, to receive a mark on his right hand or on his forehead, ¹⁷so that no one could buy or sell unless he had the mark, which is the name of the beast or the number of his name.

¹⁸This calls for wisdom. If anyone has insight, let him calculate the number of the beast, for it is man's number. His number is 666.

The Lamb and the 144,000

14 Then I looked, and there before me was the Lamb, standing on Mount Zion, and with him 144,000 who had his name and his Father's name written on their foreheads. [2]And I heard a sound from heaven like the roar of rushing waters and like a loud peal of thunder. The sound I heard was like that of harpists playing their harps. [3]And they sang a new song before the throne and before the four living creatures and the elders. No one could learn the song except the 144,000 who had been redeemed from the earth. [4]These are those who did not defile themselves with women, for they kept themselves pure. They follow the Lamb wherever he goes. They were purchased from among men and offered as firstfruits to God and the Lamb. [5]No lie was found in their mouths; they are blameless.

The Three Angels

[6]Then I saw another angel flying in midair, and he had the eternal gospel to proclaim to those who live on the earth— to every nation, tribe, language and people. [7]He said in a loud voice, "Fear God and give him glory, because the hour of his judgment has come. Worship him who made the heavens, the earth, the sea and the springs of water."

[8]A second angel followed and said, "Fallen! Fallen is Babylon the Great, which made all the nations drink the maddening wine of her adulteries."

[9]A third angel followed them and said in a loud voice: "If anyone worships the beast and his image and receives his mark on the forehead or on the hand, [10]he, too, will drink of the wine of God's fury, which has been poured full strength into the cup of his wrath. He will be tormented with burning sulfur in the presence of the holy angels and of the Lamb. [11]And the smoke of their torment rises for ever and ever. There is no rest day or night for those who worship the beast and his image, or for anyone who receives the mark of his name." [12]This calls for patient endurance on the part of the saints who obey God's commandments and remain faithful to Jesus.

[13]Then I heard a voice from heaven say, "Write: Blessed are the dead who die in the Lord from now on."

"Yes," says the Spirit, "they will rest from their labor, for their deeds will follow them."

The Harvest of the Earth

[14]I looked, and there before me was a white cloud, and seated on the cloud was one "like a son of man"[a] with a crown of gold on his head and a sharp sickle in his hand. [15]Then another angel came out of the temple and called in a loud voice to him who was sitting on the cloud, "Take your sickle and reap, because the time to reap has come, for the harvest of the earth is ripe." [16]So he who was seated on the cloud swung his sickle over the earth, and the earth was harvested.

[17]Another angel came out of the temple in heaven, and he too had a sharp sickle. [18]Still another angel, who had charge of the fire, came from the altar and called in a loud voice to him who had the sharp sickle, "Take your sharp sickle and gather the clusters of grapes from the earth's vine, because its grapes are ripe." [19]The angel swung his sickle on the earth, gathered its grapes and threw them into the great winepress of God's wrath. [20]They were trampled in the winepress outside the city, and blood flowed out of the press, rising as high as the horses' bridles for a distance of 1,600 stadia.[b]

Seven Angels With Seven Plagues

15 I saw in heaven another great and marvelous sign: seven angels with the seven last plagues—last, because with them God's wrath is completed. [2]And I saw what looked like a sea of glass mixed with fire and, standing beside the sea, those who had been victorious over the beast and his image and over the number of his name. They held harps given them by God [3]and sang the song of Moses the servant of God and the song of the Lamb:

"Great and marvelous are your deeds,
  Lord God Almighty.
Just and true are your ways,
  King of the ages.
[4]Who will not fear you, O Lord,
  and bring glory to your name?
For you alone are holy.

---

[a]14 Daniel 7:13   [b]20 That is, about 180 miles (about 300 kilometers)

All nations will come
and worship before you,
for your righteous acts have been
revealed."

[5] After this I looked and in heaven the temple, that is, the tabernacle of the Testimony, was opened. [6] Out of the temple came the seven angels with the seven plagues. They were dressed in clean, shining linen and wore golden sashes around their chests. [7] Then one of the four living creatures gave to the seven angels seven golden bowls filled with the wrath of God, who lives for ever and ever. [8] And the temple was filled with smoke from the glory of God and from his power, and no one could enter the temple until the seven plagues of the seven angels were completed.

The Seven Bowls of God's Wrath

16 Then I heard a loud voice from the temple saying to the seven angels, "Go, pour out the seven bowls of God's wrath on the earth."

[2] The first angel went and poured out his bowl on the land, and ugly and painful sores broke out on the people who had the mark of the beast and worshiped his image.

[3] The second angel poured out his bowl on the sea, and it turned into blood like that of a dead man, and every living thing in the sea died.

[4] The third angel poured out his bowl on the rivers and springs of water, and they became blood. [5] Then I heard the angel in charge of the waters say:

"You are just in these judgments,
you who are and who were, the
Holy One,
because you have so judged;
[6] for they have shed the blood of your
saints and prophets,
and you have given them blood to
drink as they deserve."

[7] And I heard the altar respond:

"Yes, Lord God Almighty,
true and just are your judgments."

[8] The fourth angel poured out his bowl on the sun, and the sun was given power to scorch people with fire. [9] They were seared by the intense heat and they

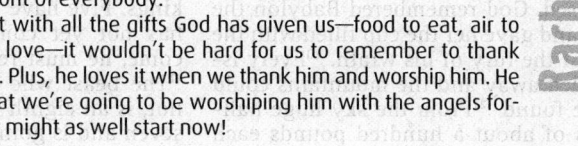

Thursday

Hey, Thanks!

Read Revelation 15:3–4

How often do you take God for granted? I know I do it all the time. When I went to Colorado to go skiing, I saw the Rocky Mountains for the first time. I could have been thinking, *Wow! These are so beautiful, and God made them! He's awesome!* Instead, I was worrying about falling off my skis and looking stupid in front of everybody.

You'd think that with all the gifts God has given us—food to eat, air to breathe, people to love—it wouldn't be hard for us to remember to thank him once in a while. Plus, he loves it when we thank him and worship him. He loves it so much that we're going to be worshiping him with the angels forever in heaven. We might as well start now!

Rachel age 12

What about You?

❶ Why do you think it's so easy to take God for granted?

❷ Think of 10 ways God shows his love, mercy and forgiveness toward you and people you know.

❸ Pray the words of Revelation 15:3–4.

Turn to page 1568 for your next devotion.

cursed the name of God, who had control over these plagues, but they refused to repent and glorify him.

[10]The fifth angel poured out his bowl on the throne of the beast, and his kingdom was plunged into darkness. Men gnawed their tongues in agony [11]and cursed the God of heaven because of their pains and their sores, but they refused to repent of what they had done.

[12]The sixth angel poured out his bowl on the great river Euphrates, and its water was dried up to prepare the way for the kings from the East. [13]Then I saw three evil[a] spirits that looked like frogs; they came out of the mouth of the dragon, out of the mouth of the beast and out of the mouth of the false prophet. [14]They are spirits of demons performing miraculous signs, and they go out to the kings of the whole world, to gather them for the battle on the great day of God Almighty.

[15]"Behold, I come like a thief! Blessed is he who stays awake and keeps his clothes with him, so that he may not go naked and be shamefully exposed."

[16]Then they gathered the kings together to the place that in Hebrew is called Armageddon.

[17]The seventh angel poured out his bowl into the air, and out of the temple came a loud voice from the throne, saying, "It is done!" [18]Then there came flashes of lightning, rumblings, peals of thunder and a severe earthquake. No earthquake like it has ever occurred since man has been on earth, so tremendous was the quake. [19]The great city split into three parts, and the cities of the nations collapsed. God remembered Babylon the Great and gave her the cup filled with the wine of the fury of his wrath. [20]Every island fled away and the mountains could not be found. [21]From the sky huge hailstones of about a hundred pounds each fell upon men. And they cursed God on account of the plague of hail, because the plague was so terrible.

The Woman on the Beast

17 One of the seven angels who had the seven bowls came and said to me, "Come, I will show you the punishment of the great prostitute, who sits on many waters. [2]With her the kings of the earth committed adultery and the inhabitants of the earth were intoxicated with the wine of her adulteries."

[3]Then the angel carried me away in the Spirit into a desert. There I saw a woman sitting on a scarlet beast that was covered with blasphemous names and had seven heads and ten horns. [4]The woman was dressed in purple and scarlet, and was glittering with gold, precious stones and pearls. She held a golden cup in her hand, filled with abominable things and the filth of her adulteries. [5]This title was written on her forehead:

MYSTERY
BABYLON THE GREAT
THE MOTHER OF PROSTITUTES
AND OF THE ABOMINATIONS OF THE EARTH.

[6]I saw that the woman was drunk with the blood of the saints, the blood of those who bore testimony to Jesus.

When I saw her, I was greatly astonished. [7]Then the angel said to me: "Why are you astonished? I will explain to you the mystery of the woman and of the beast she rides, which has the seven heads and ten horns. [8]The beast, which you saw, once was, now is not, and will come up out of the Abyss and go to his destruction. The inhabitants of the earth whose names have not been written in the book of life from the creation of the world will be astonished when they see the beast, because he once was, now is not, and yet will come.

[9]"This calls for a mind with wisdom. The seven heads are seven hills on which the woman sits. [10]They are also seven kings. Five have fallen, one is, the other has not yet come; but when he does come, he must remain for a little while. [11]The beast who once was, and now is not, is an eighth king. He belongs to the seven and is going to his destruction.

[12]"The ten horns you saw are ten kings who have not yet received a kingdom, but who for one hour will receive authority as kings along with the beast. [13]They have one purpose and will give their power and authority to the beast. [14]They will make war against the Lamb,

[a]13 Greek unclean

but the Lamb will overcome them because he is Lord of lords and King of kings—and with him will be his called, chosen and faithful followers."

¹⁵Then the angel said to me, "The waters you saw, where the prostitute sits, are peoples, multitudes, nations and languages. ¹⁶The beast and the ten horns you saw will hate the prostitute. They will bring her to ruin and leave her naked; they will eat her flesh and burn her with fire. ¹⁷For God has put it into their hearts to accomplish his purpose by agreeing to give the beast their power to rule, until God's words are fulfilled. ¹⁸The woman you saw is the great city that rules over the kings of the earth."

The Fall of Babylon

18 After this I saw another angel coming down from heaven. He had great authority, and the earth was illuminated by his splendor. ²With a mighty voice he shouted:

> "Fallen! Fallen is Babylon the Great!
>   She has become a home for demons
> and a haunt for every evil*ᵃ* spirit,
>   a haunt for every unclean and
>   detestable bird.
> ³For all the nations have drunk
>   the maddening wine of her
>   adulteries.
> The kings of the earth committed
>   adultery with her,
>   and the merchants of the earth grew
>   rich from her excessive
>   luxuries."

⁴Then I heard another voice from heaven say:

> "Come out of her, my people,
>   so that you will not share in her
>   sins,
>   so that you will not receive any of
>   her plagues;
> ⁵for her sins are piled up to heaven,
>   and God has remembered her
>   crimes.
> ⁶Give back to her as she has given;
>   pay her back double for what she
>   has done.
>   Mix her a double portion from her
>   own cup.
> ⁷Give her as much torture and grief

as the glory and luxury she gave
   herself.
In her heart she boasts,
   'I sit as queen; I am not a widow,
   and I will never mourn.'
⁸Therefore in one day her plagues will
     overtake her:
   death, mourning and famine.
She will be consumed by fire,
   for mighty is the Lord God who
     judges her.

⁹"When the kings of the earth who committed adultery with her and shared her luxury see the smoke of her burning, they will weep and mourn over her. ¹⁰Terrified at her torment, they will stand far off and cry:

> " 'Woe! Woe, O great city,
>   O Babylon, city of power!
> In one hour your doom has come!'

¹¹"The merchants of the earth will weep and mourn over her because no one buys their cargoes any more— ¹²cargoes of gold, silver, precious stones and pearls; fine linen, purple, silk and scarlet cloth; every sort of citron wood, and articles of every kind made of ivory, costly wood, bronze, iron and marble; ¹³cargoes of cinnamon and spice, of incense, myrrh and frankincense, of wine and olive oil, of fine flour and wheat; cattle and sheep; horses and carriages; and bodies and souls of men.

¹⁴"They will say, 'The fruit you longed for is gone from you. All your riches and splendor have vanished, never to be recovered.' ¹⁵The merchants who sold these things and gained their wealth from her will stand far off, terrified at her torment. They will weep and mourn ¹⁶and cry out:

> " 'Woe! Woe, O great city,
>   dressed in fine linen, purple and
>   scarlet,
>   and glittering with gold, precious
>   stones and pearls!
> ¹⁷In one hour such great wealth has
>   been brought to ruin!'

"Every sea captain, and all who travel by ship, the sailors, and all who earn their living from the sea, will stand far

---

*ᵃ*2 Greek *unclean*

off. [18]When they see the smoke of her burning, they will exclaim, 'Was there ever a city like this great city?' [19]They will throw dust on their heads, and with weeping and mourning cry out:

" 'Woe! Woe, O great city,
  where all who had ships on the sea
    became rich through her wealth!
In one hour she has been brought to
    ruin!
[20]Rejoice over her, O heaven!
  Rejoice, saints and apostles and
    prophets!
God has judged her for the way she
    treated you.' "

[21]Then a mighty angel picked up a boulder the size of a large millstone and threw it into the sea, and said:

"With such violence
  the great city of Babylon will be
    thrown down,
  never to be found again.
[22]The music of harpists and musicians,
    flute players and trumpeters,
  will never be heard in you again.
No workman of any trade
  will ever be found in you again.
The sound of a millstone
  will never be heard in you again.
[23]The light of a lamp
  will never shine in you again.
The voice of bridegroom and bride
  will never be heard in you again.
Your merchants were the world's great
    men.
  By your magic spell all the nations
    were led astray.
[24]In her was found the blood of
    prophets and of the saints,
  and of all who have been killed on
    the earth."

Hallelujah!

19 After this I heard what sounded like the roar of a great multitude in heaven shouting:

"Hallelujah!
Salvation and glory and power belong
  to our God,
[2] for true and just are his judgments.
He has condemned the great prostitute
  who corrupted the earth by her
    adulteries.

He has avenged on her the blood of
  his servants."

[3]And again they shouted:

"Hallelujah!
The smoke from her goes up for ever
  and ever."

[4]The twenty-four elders and the four living creatures fell down and worshiped God, who was seated on the throne. And they cried:

"Amen, Hallelujah!"

[5]Then a voice came from the throne, saying:

"Praise our God,
  all you his servants,
you who fear him,
  both small and great!"

[6]Then I heard what sounded like a great multitude, like the roar of rushing waters and like loud peals of thunder, shouting:

"Hallelujah!
  For our Lord God Almighty reigns.
[7]Let us rejoice and be glad
  and give him glory!
For the wedding of the Lamb has
    come,
  and his bride has made herself
    ready.
[8]Fine linen, bright and clean,
  was given her to wear."
(Fine linen stands for the righteous acts of the saints.)

[9]Then the angel said to me, "Write: 'Blessed are those who are invited to the wedding supper of the Lamb!' " And he added, "These are the true words of God."

[10]At this I fell at his feet to worship him. But he said to me, "Do not do it! I am a fellow servant with you and with your brothers who hold to the testimony of Jesus. Worship God! For the testimony of Jesus is the spirit of prophecy."

The Rider on the White Horse

[11]I saw heaven standing open and there before me was a white horse, whose rider is called Faithful and True. With justice he judges and makes war. [12]His eyes are like blazing fire, and on his head

are many crowns. He has a name written on him that no one knows but himself. ¹³He is dressed in a robe dipped in blood, and his name is the Word of God. ¹⁴The armies of heaven were following him, riding on white horses and dressed in fine linen, white and clean. ¹⁵Out of

I Hardly Recognized You

Huh?

Revelation 19:11–15

Think of the Jesus you got to know in the stories of his years on earth. He was a simple carpenter, walking where he went, hanging out with poor people and, in the end, nailed to an ugly cross. Look at him now. He's back where he came from—in heaven and in charge. The One on the white horse with fire in his eyes and crowns on his head—that's your friend Jesus. He promises he's coming to take you to heaven someday soon. Can you think of anything more awesome?

his mouth comes a sharp sword with which to strike down the nations. "He will rule them with an iron scepter."ᵃ He treads the winepress of the fury of the wrath of God Almighty. ¹⁶On his robe and on his thigh he has this name written:

KING OF KINGS AND LORD OF LORDS.

¹⁷And I saw an angel standing in the sun, who cried in a loud voice to all the birds flying in midair, "Come, gather together for the great supper of God, ¹⁸so that you may eat the flesh of kings, generals, and mighty men, of horses and their riders, and the flesh of all people, free and slave, small and great."

¹⁹Then I saw the beast and the kings of the earth and their armies gathered together to make war against the rider on the horse and his army. ²⁰But the beast was captured, and with him the false prophet who had performed the miraculous signs on his behalf. With these signs he had deluded those who had received the mark of the beast and worshiped his

image. The two of them were thrown alive into the fiery lake of burning sulfur. ²¹The rest of them were killed with the sword that came out of the mouth of the rider on the horse, and all the birds gorged themselves on their flesh.

The Thousand Years

20 And I saw an angel coming down out of heaven, having the key to the Abyss and holding in his hand a great chain. ²He seized the dragon, that ancient serpent, who is the devil, or Satan, and bound him for a thousand years. ³He threw him into the Abyss, and locked and sealed it over him, to keep him from deceiving the nations anymore until the thousand years were ended. After that, he must be set free for a short time.

⁴I saw thrones on which were seated those who had been given authority to judge. And I saw the souls of those who had been beheaded because of their testimony for Jesus and because of the word of God. They had not worshiped the beast or his image and had not received his mark on their foreheads or their hands. They came to life and reigned with Christ a thousand years. ⁵(The rest of the dead did not come to life until the thousand years were ended.) This is the first resurrection. ⁶Blessed and holy are those who have part in the first resurrection. The second death has no power over them, but they will be priests of God and of Christ and will reign with him for a thousand years.

Satan's Doom

⁷When the thousand years are over, Satan will be released from his prison ⁸and will go out to deceive the nations in the four corners of the earth—Gog and Magog—to gather them for battle. In number they are like the sand on the seashore. ⁹They marched across the breadth of the earth and surrounded the camp of God's people, the city he loves. But fire came down from heaven and devoured them. ¹⁰And the devil, who deceived them, was thrown into the lake of burning sulfur, where the beast and the false prophet had been thrown. They will be

ᵃ15 Psalm 2:9

tormented day and night for ever and ever.

The Dead Are Judged

¹¹Then I saw a great white throne and him who was seated on it. Earth and sky fled from his presence, and there was no place for them. ¹²And I saw the dead, great and small, standing before the throne, and books were opened. Another book was opened, which is the book of life. The dead were judged according to what they had done as recorded in the books. ¹³The sea gave up the dead that were in it, and death and Hades gave up the dead that were in them, and each person was judged according to what he had done. ¹⁴Then death and Hades were thrown into the lake of fire. The lake of fire is the second death. ¹⁵If anyone's name was not found written in the book of life, he was thrown into the lake of fire.

The New Jerusalem

21 Then I saw a new heaven and a new earth, for the first heaven and the first earth had passed away, and there was no longer any sea. ²I saw the Holy City, the new Jerusalem, coming down out of heaven from God, prepared as a bride beautifully dressed for her husband. ³And I heard a loud voice from the throne saying, "Now the dwelling of God is with men, and he will live with them. They will be his people, and God himself will be with them and be their God. ⁴He will wipe every tear from their eyes. There will be no more death or mourning or crying or pain, for the old order of things has passed away."

⁵He who was seated on the throne said, "I am making everything new!" Then he said, "Write this down, for these words are trustworthy and true."

⁶He said to me: "It is done. I am the Alpha and the Omega, the Beginning and

---

Friday

No More Tears
Read Revelation 21:4

When my uncle died, I kept asking God why it happened. But I realized that my uncle was going to the perfect place: heaven. This verse reminds me that I should be crying tears of joy for my uncle, who is now free from pain and sadness. My uncle is living with God in a perfect place.

I don't think about heaven very often. But this verse makes it sound like a pretty amazing place. There will be no more tears or death or any of the other things that make life hard for us on earth. Nothing bad will ever happen to us there. Now, when something bad happens to me or to someone I love, I can think about heaven and remember that my life here is only part of God's plan for me. I can look forward to a happy, perfect life with God that will last forever.

Anna age 13

❶ What do you think heaven will be like? How can your thoughts about heaven help you right now?

❷ As you read through the rest of Revelation, make a list of the things that make heaven such a perfect place. Once you're done, draw a picture, write a poem or compose a song that describes heaven the way it is portrayed in the book of Revelation.

❸ Thank God for creating such a perfect place for you.

Turn to page 1570 for your next devotion.

the End. To him who is thirsty I will give to drink without cost from the spring of the water of life. [7]He who overcomes will inherit all this, and I will be his God and he will be my son. [8]But the cowardly, the unbelieving, the vile, the murderers, the sexually immoral, those who practice magic arts, the idolaters and all liars—their place will be in the fiery lake of burning sulfur. This is the second death."

[9]One of the seven angels who had the seven bowls full of the seven last plagues came and said to me, "Come, I will show you the bride, the wife of the Lamb." [10]And he carried me away in the Spirit to a mountain great and high, and showed me the Holy City, Jerusalem, coming down out of heaven from God. [11]It shone with the glory of God, and its brilliance was like that of a very precious jewel, like a jasper, clear as crystal. [12]It had a great, high wall with twelve gates, and with twelve angels at the gates. On the gates were written the names of the twelve tribes of Israel. [13]There were three gates on the east, three on the north, three on the south and three on the west. [14]The wall of the city had twelve foundations, and on them were the names of the twelve apostles of the Lamb.

[15]The angel who talked with me had a measuring rod of gold to measure the city, its gates and its walls. [16]The city was laid out like a square, as long as it was wide. He measured the city with the rod and found it to be 12,000 stadia[a] in length, and as wide and high as it is long. [17]He measured its wall and it was 144 cubits[b] thick,[c] by man's measurement, which the angel was using. [18]The wall was made of jasper, and the city of pure gold, as pure as glass. [19]The foundations of the city walls were decorated with every kind of precious stone. The first foundation was jasper, the second sapphire, the third chalcedony, the fourth emerald, [20]the fifth sardonyx, the sixth carnelian, the seventh chrysolite, the eighth beryl, the ninth topaz, the tenth chrysoprase, the eleventh jacinth, and the twelfth amethyst.[d] [21]The twelve gates were twelve pearls, each gate made of a single pearl. The great street of the city was of pure gold, like transparent glass.

[22]I did not see a temple in the city, because the Lord God Almighty and the Lamb are its temple. [23]The city does not need the sun or the moon to shine on it, for the glory of God gives it light, and the Lamb is its lamp. [24]The nations will walk by its light, and the kings of the earth will bring their splendor into it. [25]On no day will its gates ever be shut, for there will be no night there. [26]The glory and honor of the nations will be brought into it. [27]Nothing impure will ever enter it, nor will anyone who does what is shameful or deceitful, but only those whose names are written in the Lamb's book of life.

The River of Life

22 Then the angel showed me the river of the water of life, as clear as crystal, flowing from the throne of God and of the Lamb [2]down the middle of the great street of the city. On each side of the river stood the tree of life, bearing twelve crops of fruit, yielding its fruit every month. And the leaves of the tree are for the healing of the nations. [3]No longer will there be any curse. The throne of God and of the Lamb will be in the city, and his servants will serve him. [4]They will see his face, and his name will be on their foreheads. [5]There will be no more night. They will not need the light of a lamp or the light of the sun, for the Lord God will give them light. And they will reign for ever and ever.

[6]The angel said to me, "These words are trustworthy and true. The Lord, the God of the spirits of the prophets, sent his angel to show his servants the things that must soon take place."

Jesus Is Coming

[7]"Behold, I am coming soon! Blessed is he who keeps the words of the prophecy in this book."

[8]I, John, am the one who heard and saw these things. And when I had heard and seen them, I fell down to worship at the feet of the angel who had been show-

---

[a]16 That is, about 1,400 miles (about 2,200 kilometers)   [b]17 That is, about 200 feet (about 65 meters)   [c]17 Or high   [d]20 The precise identification of some of these precious stones is uncertain.

ing them to me. ⁹But he said to me, "Do not do it! I am a fellow servant with you and with your brothers the prophets and of all who keep the words of this book. Worship God!"

¹⁰Then he told me, "Do not seal up the words of the prophecy of this book, because the time is near. ¹¹Let him who does wrong continue to do wrong; let him who is vile continue to be vile; let him who does right continue to do right; and let him who is holy continue to be holy."

¹²"Behold, I am coming soon! My reward is with me, and I will give to everyone according to what he has done. ¹³I am the Alpha and the Omega, the First and the Last, the Beginning and the End.

¹⁴"Blessed are those who wash their robes, that they may have the right to the tree of life and may go through the gates into the city. ¹⁵Outside are the dogs, those who practice magic arts, the sexually immoral, the murderers, the idolaters and everyone who loves and practices falsehood.

¹⁶"I, Jesus, have sent my angel to give you*a* this testimony for the churches. I am the Root and the Offspring of David, and the bright Morning Star."

¹⁷The Spirit and the bride say, "Come!" And let him who hears say, "Come!"

a16 The Greek is plural.

Week end.

A World Full of Christians

Read Revelation 7:9–12 (page 1556)

On Thursday Rachel asked us to read a song of praise from Revelation 15. The lyrics mention "all nations" worshiping God. That reminds us that God's kingdom is not single-colored. It's made up of all kinds of people.

Revelation 7 makes the same point. In this vision of heaven we see "a great multitude" from every "nation, tribe, people and language." Do you realize what that means?

Many of us live in places dominated by one race or another. And when we think of heaven, we probably imagine a bunch of people just like us. But heaven is completely integrated.

Christians from all over the world will be united in heaven. How cool! The God who created an infinite variety of beetles, birds and butterflies has also called a wide variety of believers to populate his heaven. And that's good news. After all, how boring heaven would be if everyone looked the same.

When you think about it, life would be pretty boring on *earth* if we were all the same too.

What about You?

❶ Do you have any friends who are a different race then you? Does it matter what's on the outside compared to what's on the inside?

❷ Next time you're in a store, make a point to notice people from other ethnic groups. The world is full of all kinds of races. Heaven will be too!

❸ Pray for good race relations in your community and for opportunities to be around people who are different from you.

Turn to page 5 for your next devotion.

Whoever is thirsty, let him come; and whoever wishes, let him take the free gift of the water of life.

[18]I warn everyone who hears the words of the prophecy of this book: If anyone adds anything to them, God will add to him the plagues described in this book. [19]And if anyone takes words away from this book of prophecy, God will take away from him his share in the tree of life and in the holy city, which are described in this book.

[20]He who testifies to these things says, "Yes, I am coming soon."

Amen. Come, Lord Jesus.

[21]The grace of the Lord Jesus be with God's people. Amen.

Weights & Measures

	BIBLICAL UNIT	APPROXIMATE AMERICAN EQUIVALENT	APPROXIMATE METRIC EQUIVALENT
WEIGHTS	talent (60 minas)	75 pounds	34 kilograms
	mina (50 shekels)	1 1/4 pounds	0.6 kilogram
	shekel (2 bekas)	2/5 ounce	11.5 grams
	pim (2/3 shekel)	1/3 ounce	7.6 grams
	beka (10 gerahs)	1/5 ounce	5.5 grams
	gerah	1/50 ounce	0.6 gram
LENGTH	cubit	18 inches	0.5 meter
	span	9 inches	23 centimeters
	handbreadth	3 inches	8 centimeters
CAPACITY			
Dry Measure	cor [homer] (10 ephahs)	6 bushels	220 liters
	lethek (5 ephahs)	3 bushels	110 liters
	ephah (10 omers)	3/5 bushel	22 liters
	seah (1/3 ephah)	7 quarts	7.3 liters
	omer (1/10 ephah)	2 quarts	2 liters
	cab (1/18 ephah)	1 quart	1 liter
Liquid Measure	bath (1 ephah)	6 gallons	22 liters
	hin (1/6 bath)	4 quarts	4 liters
	log (1/72 bath)	1/3 quart	0.3 liter

The figures of the table are calculated on the basis of a shekel equaling 11.5 grams, a cubit equaling 18 inches and an ephah equaling 22 liters. The quart referred to is either a dry quart (slightly larger than a liter) or a liquid quart (slightly smaller than a liter), whichever is applicable. The ton referred to in the footnotes is the American ton of 2,000 pounds.

This table is based upon the best available information, but it is not intended to be mathematically precise; like the measurement equivalents in the footnotes, it merely gives approximate amounts and distances. Weights and measures differed somewhat at various times and places in the ancient world. There is uncertainty particularly about the ephah and the bath; further discoveries may shed more light on these units of capacity.

Study Helps

Study Helps

Subject Index

Plan of Salvation

Reading Plans

Here's What I Think

Subject Index

This subject index will help you find just where you need to look to find information about a particular topic. Look through the list, and you'll probably find something you want to look up and read.

God's Plan for You

Thank you, Lord, for loving me.
Thank you for your forgiveness.
Thank you for a new beginning!   Amen.

In the pages of this Bible you'll find God's words of love, written specifically for you. You'll also find God's great plan for your life here on earth, and for eternity.

God loves you and wants to have a relationship with you. That's the basis of his plan for your life. John 3:16 (page 1271) says, "For God so loved the world that he gave his one and only Son, that whoever believes in him shall not perish but have eternal life."

In the pages of this Bible you'll find God's words of love, written specifically for you. You'll also find God's great plan for your life here on earth, and for eternity.

God loves you and wants to have a relationship with you. That's the basis of his plan for your life. John 3:16 (page 1271) says, "For God so loved the world that he gave his one and only Son, that whoever believes in him shall not perish but have eternal life."

God's love is available to you today if you open your heart to receive it. Take a moment to **WRITE** your name into the spaces provided below to see how much God loves you:

"For God so loved _____ that he gave his one and only Son, that if _____ believes in him _____ shall not perish but have eternal life."

If you'd like to invite Jesus Christ into your life or if you'd like to renew your relationship with him, **SAY** the following prayer:

> Jesus, I want you to live in my heart and lead my life. I need you to show me how to develop a deep and meaningful relationship with you.
>
> I know I have done things that are wrong in your eyes, and I'm sorry. Help me to do the things that bring joy to your heart and help me to stop doing the things that break your heart.
>
> Give me your wisdom so I can know what is right and wrong. When I read the Bible, send your Holy Spirit to teach me. Help me to learn to talk with you every day through prayer. I want to be in a living relationship with you; help me to grow more close to you every day.

Now take a moment to **READ** these promises that God has made to you:

"If we confess our sins, [God] is faithful and just and will forgive us our sins and purify us from all unrighteousness" (1 John 1:9, page 1529).

"For I am convinced that neither death nor life, neither angels nor demons, neither the present nor the future, nor any powers, neither height nor depth, nor anything else in all creation, will be able to separate us from the love of god that is in Christ jesus our Lord" (Romans 8:38–39, page 1362).

"I give them eternal life, and they shall never perish; no one can snatch them out of my hand" (Jesus, speaking in John 10:28, page 1285).

That's God's plan for your life. He wants to help you direct your thoughts, actions and activities in a way that pleases him.

Reading Plans

God's Word is his personal message of love to you today. The best way to grow as a Christian and get to know God in a more personal way is to spend time in his Word. Here are 3 ways for you to read through the Bible.

1 If you are reading the Bible for the first time:
  • Begin by reading the Gospel of Mark or the Gospel of John in the New Testament.
  • After reading 1 of these gospels, read the book of Acts or the book of Romans.
  • After reading Acts or Romans, pick an Old Testament book like Genesis or perhaps Psalms.

2 If you want to read through the entire Bible in 1 year:
  • Read 3 chapters each day, Monday through Saturday, and 5 chapters on Sunday.

3 If you want to read through the entire Bible in 2 years:
  • Read 2 chapters each day, Sunday through Saturday.

The following chart covers every book and chapter of the Bible. To keep track of what you have read, mark off each chapter as you complete it.

GENESIS ☐1 ☐2 ☐3 ☐4 ☐5 ☐6
☐7 ☐8 ☐9 ☐10 ☐11 ☐12 ☐13 ☐14
☐15 ☐16 ☐17 ☐18 ☐19 ☐20 ☐21 ☐22
☐23 ☐24 ☐25 ☐26 ☐27 ☐28 ☐29 ☐30
☐31 ☐32 ☐33 ☐34 ☐35 ☐36 ☐37 ☐38
☐39 ☐40 ☐41 ☐42 ☐43 ☐44 ☐45 ☐46
☐47 ☐48 ☐49 ☐50

EXODUS ☐1 ☐2 ☐3 ☐4 ☐5 ☐6
☐7 ☐8 ☐9 ☐10 ☐11 ☐12 ☐13 ☐14
☐15 ☐16 ☐17 ☐18 ☐19 ☐20 ☐21 ☐22
☐23 ☐24 ☐25 ☐26 ☐27 ☐28 ☐29 ☐30
☐31 ☐32 ☐33 ☐34 ☐35 ☐36 ☐37 ☐38
☐39 ☐40

LEVITICUS ☐1 ☐2 ☐3 ☐4 ☐5 ☐6
☐7 ☐8 ☐9 ☐10 ☐11 ☐12 ☐13 ☐14
☐15 ☐16 ☐17 ☐18 ☐19 ☐20 ☐21 ☐22
☐23 ☐24 ☐25 ☐26 ☐27

NUMBERS ☐1 ☐2 ☐3 ☐4 ☐5 ☐6
☐7 ☐8 ☐9 ☐10 ☐11 ☐12 ☐13 ☐14
☐15 ☐16 ☐17 ☐18 ☐19 ☐20 ☐21 ☐22
☐23 ☐24 ☐25 ☐26 ☐27 ☐28 ☐29 ☐30
☐31 ☐32 ☐33 ☐34 ☐35 ☐36

DEUTERONOMY ☐1 ☐2 ☐3 ☐4 ☐5
☐6 ☐7 ☐8 ☐9 ☐10 ☐11 ☐12 ☐13

☐14 ☐15 ☐16 ☐17 ☐18 ☐19 ☐20 ☐21
☐22 ☐23 ☐24 ☐25 ☐26 ☐27 ☐28 ☐29
☐30 ☐31 ☐32 ☐33 ☐34

JOSHUA ☐1 ☐2 ☐3 ☐4 ☐5 ☐6
☐7 ☐8 ☐9 ☐10 ☐11 ☐12 ☐13 ☐14
☐15 ☐16 ☐17 ☐18 ☐19 ☐20 ☐21 ☐22
☐23 ☐24

JUDGES ☐1 ☐2 ☐3 ☐4 ☐5 ☐6
☐7 ☐8 ☐9 ☐10 ☐11 ☐12 ☐13 ☐14
☐15 ☐16 ☐17 ☐18 ☐19 ☐20 ☐21

RUTH ☐1 ☐2 ☐3 ☐4

1 SAMUEL ☐1 ☐2 ☐3 ☐4 ☐5 ☐6
☐7 ☐8 ☐9 ☐10 ☐11 ☐12 ☐13 ☐14
☐15 ☐16 ☐17 ☐18 ☐19 ☐20 ☐21 ☐22
☐23 ☐24 ☐25 ☐26 ☐27 ☐28 ☐29 ☐30
☐31

2 SAMUEL ☐1 ☐2 ☐3 ☐4 ☐5 ☐6
☐7 ☐8 ☐9 ☐10 ☐11 ☐12 ☐13 ☐14
☐15 ☐16 ☐17 ☐18 ☐19 ☐20 ☐21 ☐22
☐23 ☐24

1 KINGS ☐1 ☐2 ☐3 ☐4 ☐5 ☐6
☐7 ☐8 ☐9 ☐10 ☐11 ☐12 ☐13 ☐14
☐15 ☐16 ☐17 ☐18 ☐19 ☐20 ☐21 ☐22

2 KINGS ☐1 ☐2 ☐3 ☐4 ☐5 ☐6
☐7 ☐8 ☐9 ☐10 ☐11 ☐12 ☐13 ☐14
☐15 ☐16 ☐17 ☐18 ☐19 ☐20 ☐21 ☐22
☐23 ☐24 ☐25

1 CHRONICLES ☐1 ☐2 ☐3 ☐4 ☐5
☐6 ☐7 ☐8 ☐9 ☐10 ☐11 ☐12 ☐13
☐14 ☐15 ☐16 ☐17 ☐18 ☐19 ☐20 ☐21
☐22 ☐23 ☐24 ☐25 ☐26 ☐27 ☐28 ☐29

2 CHRONICLES ☐1 ☐2 ☐3 ☐4 ☐5
☐6 ☐7 ☐8 ☐9 ☐10 ☐11 ☐12 ☐13
☐14 ☐15 ☐16 ☐17 ☐18 ☐19 ☐20 ☐21
☐22 ☐23 ☐24 ☐25 ☐26 ☐27 ☐28 ☐29
☐30 ☐31 ☐32 ☐33 ☐34 ☐35 ☐36

EZRA ☐1 ☐2 ☐3 ☐4 ☐5 ☐6
☐7 ☐8 ☐9 ☐10

NEHEMIAH ☐1 ☐2 ☐3 ☐4 ☐5 ☐6
☐7 ☐8 ☐9 ☐10 ☐11 ☐12 ☐13

ESTHER ☐1 ☐2 ☐3 ☐4 ☐5 ☐6
☐7 ☐8 ☐9 ☐10

JOB ☐1 ☐2 ☐3 ☐4 ☐5 ☐6 ☐7
☐8 ☐9 ☐10 ☐11 ☐12 ☐13 ☐14 ☐15
☐16 ☐17 ☐18 ☐19 ☐20 ☐21 ☐22 ☐23
☐24 ☐25 ☐26 ☐27 ☐28 ☐29 ☐30 ☐31
☐32 ☐33 ☐34 ☐35 ☐36 ☐37 ☐38 ☐39
☐40 ☐41 ☐42

PSALMS ☐1 ☐2 ☐3 ☐4 ☐5
☐6 ☐7 ☐8 ☐9 ☐10 ☐11 ☐12
☐13 ☐14 ☐15 ☐16 ☐17 ☐18 ☐19
☐20 ☐21 ☐22 ☐23 ☐24 ☐25 ☐26
☐27 ☐28 ☐29 ☐30 ☐31 ☐32 ☐33
☐34 ☐35 ☐36 ☐37 ☐38 ☐39 ☐40
☐41 ☐42 ☐43 ☐44 ☐45 ☐46 ☐47
☐48 ☐49 ☐50 ☐51 ☐52 ☐53 ☐54
☐55 ☐56 ☐57 ☐58 ☐59 ☐60 ☐61
☐62 ☐63 ☐64 ☐65 ☐66 ☐67 ☐68
☐69 ☐70 ☐71 ☐72 ☐73 ☐74 ☐75
☐76 ☐77 ☐78 ☐79 ☐80 ☐81 ☐82
☐83 ☐84 ☐85 ☐86 ☐87 ☐88 ☐89
☐90 ☐91 ☐92 ☐93 ☐94 ☐95 ☐96
☐97 ☐98 ☐99 ☐100 ☐101 ☐102 ☐103
☐104 ☐105 ☐106 ☐107 ☐108 ☐109 ☐110
☐111 ☐112 ☐113 ☐114 ☐115 ☐116 ☐117
☐118 ☐119 ☐120 ☐121 ☐122 ☐123 ☐124
☐125 ☐126 ☐127 ☐128 ☐129 ☐130 ☐131
☐132 ☐133 ☐134 ☐135 ☐136 ☐137 ☐138
☐139 ☐140 ☐141 ☐142 ☐143 ☐144 ☐145
☐146 ☐147 ☐148 ☐149 ☐150

PROVERBS ☐1 ☐2 ☐3 ☐4 ☐5 ☐6
☐7 ☐8 ☐9 ☐10 ☐11 ☐12 ☐13 ☐14
☐15 ☐16 ☐17 ☐18 ☐19 ☐20 ☐21 ☐22
☐23 ☐24 ☐25 ☐26 ☐27 ☐28 ☐29 ☐30
☐31

ECCLESIASTES ☐1 ☐2 ☐3 ☐4 ☐5
☐6 ☐7 ☐8 ☐9 ☐10 ☐11 ☐12

SONG OF SONGS ☐1 ☐2 ☐3 ☐4 ☐5
☐6 ☐7 ☐8

ISAIAH ☐1 ☐2 ☐3 ☐4 ☐5 ☐6
☐7 ☐8 ☐9 ☐10 ☐11 ☐12 ☐13 ☐14
☐15 ☐16 ☐17 ☐18 ☐19 ☐20 ☐21 ☐22
☐23 ☐24 ☐25 ☐26 ☐27 ☐28 ☐29 ☐30
☐31 ☐32 ☐33 ☐34 ☐35 ☐36 ☐37 ☐38
☐39 ☐40 ☐41 ☐42 ☐43 ☐44 ☐45 ☐46
☐47 ☐48 ☐49 ☐50 ☐51 ☐52 ☐53 ☐54
☐55 ☐56 ☐57 ☐58 ☐59 ☐60 ☐61 ☐62
☐63 ☐64 ☐65 ☐66

JEREMIAH ☐1 ☐2 ☐3 ☐4 ☐5 ☐6
☐7 ☐8 ☐9 ☐10 ☐11 ☐12 ☐13 ☐14
☐15 ☐16 ☐17 ☐18 ☐19 ☐20 ☐21 ☐22
☐23 ☐24 ☐25 ☐26 ☐27 ☐28 ☐29 ☐30
☐31 ☐32 ☐33 ☐34 ☐35 ☐36 ☐37 ☐38
☐39 ☐40 ☐41 ☐42 ☐43 ☐44 ☐45 ☐46
☐47 ☐48 ☐49 ☐50 ☐51 ☐52

LAMENTATIONS ☐1 ☐2 ☐3 ☐4 ☐5

EZEKIEL ☐1 ☐2 ☐3 ☐4 ☐5 ☐6
☐7 ☐8 ☐9 ☐10 ☐11 ☐12 ☐13 ☐14
☐15 ☐16 ☐17 ☐18 ☐19 ☐20 ☐21 ☐22
☐23 ☐24 ☐25 ☐26 ☐27 ☐28 ☐29 ☐30
☐31 ☐32 ☐33 ☐34 ☐35 ☐36 ☐37 ☐38
☐39 ☐40 ☐41 ☐42 ☐43 ☐44 ☐45 ☐46
☐47 ☐48

DANIEL ☐1 ☐2 ☐3 ☐4 ☐5 ☐6
☐7 ☐8 ☐9 ☐10 ☐11 ☐12

HOSEA ☐1 ☐2 ☐3 ☐4 ☐5 ☐6
☐7 ☐8 ☐9 ☐10 ☐11 ☐12 ☐13 ☐14

JOEL ☐1 ☐2 ☐3

AMOS ☐1 ☐2 ☐3 ☐4 ☐5 ☐6 ☐7 ☐8 ☐9

OBADIAH ☐OBADIAH

JONAH ☐1 ☐2 ☐3 ☐4

MICAH ☐1 ☐2 ☐3 ☐4 ☐5 ☐6 ☐7

NAHUM ☐1 ☐2 ☐3

HABAKKUK ☐1 ☐2 ☐3

ZEPHANIAH ☐1 ☐2 ☐3

HAGGAI ☐1 ☐2

ZECHARIAH ☐1 ☐2 ☐3 ☐4 ☐5 ☐6 ☐7 ☐8 ☐9 ☐10 ☐11 ☐12 ☐13 ☐14

MALACHI ☐1 ☐2 ☐3 ☐4

MATTHEW ☐1 ☐2 ☐3 ☐4 ☐5 ☐6 ☐7 ☐8 ☐9 ☐10 ☐11 ☐12 ☐13 ☐14 ☐15 ☐16 ☐17 ☐18 ☐19 ☐20 ☐21 ☐22 ☐23 ☐24 ☐25 ☐26 ☐27 ☐28

MARK ☐1 ☐2 ☐3 ☐4 ☐5 ☐6 ☐7 ☐8 ☐9 ☐10 ☐11 ☐12 ☐13 ☐14 ☐15 ☐16

LUKE ☐1 ☐2 ☐3 ☐4 ☐5 ☐6 ☐7 ☐8 ☐9 ☐10 ☐11 ☐12 ☐13 ☐14 ☐15 ☐16 ☐17 ☐18 ☐19 ☐20 ☐21 ☐22 ☐23 ☐24

JOHN ☐1 ☐2 ☐3 ☐4 ☐5 ☐6 ☐7 ☐8 ☐9 ☐10 ☐11 ☐12 ☐13 ☐14 ☐15 ☐16 ☐17 ☐18 ☐19 ☐20 ☐21

ACTS ☐1 ☐2 ☐3 ☐4 ☐5 ☐6 ☐7 ☐8 ☐9 ☐10 ☐11 ☐12 ☐13 ☐14 ☐15 ☐16 ☐17 ☐18 ☐19 ☐20 ☐21 ☐22 ☐23 ☐24 ☐25 ☐26 ☐27 ☐28

ROMANS ☐1 ☐2 ☐3 ☐4 ☐5 ☐6 ☐7 ☐8 ☐9 ☐10 ☐11 ☐12 ☐13 ☐14 ☐15 ☐16

1 CORINTHIANS ☐1 ☐2 ☐3 ☐4 ☐5 ☐6 ☐7 ☐8 ☐9 ☐10 ☐11 ☐12 ☐13 ☐14 ☐15 ☐16

2 CORINTHIANS ☐1 ☐2 ☐3 ☐4 ☐5 ☐6 ☐7 ☐8 ☐9 ☐10 ☐11 ☐12 ☐13

GALATIANS ☐1 ☐2 ☐3 ☐4 ☐5 ☐6

EPHESIANS ☐1 ☐2 ☐3 ☐4 ☐5 ☐6

PHILIPPIANS ☐1 ☐2 ☐3 ☐4

COLOSSIANS ☐1 ☐2 ☐3 ☐4

1 THESSALONIANS ☐1 ☐2 ☐3 ☐4 ☐5

2 THESSALONIANS ☐1 ☐2 ☐3

1 TIMOTHY ☐1 ☐2 ☐3 ☐4 ☐5 ☐6

2 TIMOTHY ☐1 ☐2 ☐3 ☐4

TITUS ☐1 ☐2 ☐3

PHILEMON ☐PHILEMON

HEBREWS ☐1 ☐2 ☐3 ☐4 ☐5 ☐6 ☐7 ☐8 ☐9 ☐10 ☐11 ☐12 ☐13

JAMES ☐1 ☐2 ☐3 ☐4 ☐5

1 PETER ☐1 ☐2 ☐3 ☐4 ☐5

2 PETER ☐1 ☐2 ☐3

1 JOHN ☐1 ☐2 ☐3 ☐4 ☐5

2 JOHN ☐2 JOHN

3 JOHN ☐3 JOHN

JUDE ☐JUDE

REVELATION ☐1 ☐2 ☐3 ☐4 ☐5 ☐6 ☐7 ☐8 ☐9 ☐10 ☐11 ☐12 ☐13 ☐14 ☐15 ☐16 ☐17 ☐18 ☐19 ☐20 ☐21 ☐22

Here's what I think . . .

The NIV Teen Devotional Bible

Project Management and Editorial: Catherine DeVries

Editorial Assistance: Dirk Buursma, Kevin and Sherry Harney,
Donna Huisjen, Kris Johnson, Ryan Knutzen

Production Management: Mark Luce

Interior Design: Sharon Wright, Belmont, MI

Cover Design: Cindy Davis

Tip-in Design: Chris Tobias, Grandville, MI

Typesetting: The Livingstone Corporation, Carol Stream, IL

Interior Proofreading: Peachtree Editorial and
Proofreading Service, Peachtree City, GA

Guarantee

*Zondervan Publishing House guarantees leather Bibles
unconditionally against manufacturing defects for a lifetime and
hardcover, softcover and Leather-Look™ Bibles for four years. This
guarantee does not apply to normal wear. Contact Zondervan
Customer Service, 800-727-1309, for replacement instructions.*

Care

*We suggest loosening the binding of your new Bible by
gently pressing on a small section of pages at a time from the
center. To ensure against breakage of the spine, it is best
not to bend the cover backward around the spine or to carry
study notes, church bulletins, pens, etc., inside the cover.
Because a felt-tipped marker will "bleed" through the pages,
we recommend use of a ball-point pen or pencil to
underline favorite passages. Your Bible should not be
exposed to excessive heat, cold, or humidity.*